T4-AHH-879

MIGRATION FROM THE RUSSIAN EMPIRE

Lists of Passengers Arriving at U.S. Ports

Lists of Passengers Arriving at
U.S. Ports

Volume 4

January 1888 – May 1889

Edited by
Ira A. Glazier
Director, Temple-Balch Center for Immigration Research

Genealogical Publishing Co., Inc.
Baltimore, Maryland

Library of Congress Catalogue Card Number 95-75722
International Standard Book Number, Volume 4: 0-8063-1540-7
Made in the United States of America

INTRODUCTION

This work contains data on passengers of Russian nationality who emigrated to the United States from Russian territories between 1875 and 1910. The information was extracted from the original ship manifests held at the Temple-Balch Center for Immigration Research in Philadelphia. From the year 1820, these manifests, or passenger lists, were filed by all vessels entering U.S. ports from abroad.

In this work, passenger lists are arranged in chronological order by date of arrival. The records of passengers of Russian nationality—Poles, Finns, and Russians—are given here in their entirety, while records of non-Russian nationals are excluded.

Information in the passenger lists regarding nationality changed several times during the nineteenth century. Until 1882 passenger lists gave the name of the country to which the passengers *belonged*. This was interpreted to mean either country of citizenship, country of last residence, or country of birth. Beginning in 1882, however, immigrants were required to name their *native country*, citizenship, or country of birth. From 1898 to 1934 passenger lists recorded aliens according to race, religion, or people, in addition to country of origin.

Passenger lists make possible a detailed reconstruction of population movements from the major sender countries by including information on the age, sex, occupation, nationality, residence, and intended destination of each passenger. This information enables the researcher to distinguish between U.S. citizens returning to their country of origin, persons traveling to destinations outside the United States, and immigrants. Manifests record deaths during the voyage, but information on mortality is not presented here. The lists also give the name of the ship, the port of embarkation, and the date of arrival in the U.S. port.

Historical Background and Causes of Russian Migration in the Nineteenth Century

The United States was the primary destination for Russian overseas migration between 1871 and 1910. Over 2.3 million migrants from Russia arrived between 1871 and 1910: approximately 600,000 between 1871 and 1898 and 1.7 million between 1899 and 1910 (Table 1). Almost all came from the western part of Russia. Several nationalities and ethnic groups, Slav and non-Slav, were represented—Poles, Byelorussians, Great Russians, Ukrainians, Jews, Finns, Lithuanians, Latvians, Estonians, and Germans[1]. Ethnic Russians migrated in far greater numbers than indigenous Russians. Of the 1.7 million emigrants who arrived in the U.S. between 1899 and 1910, 43 percent were Jews, 27 percent Poles, 9 percent Lithuanians, 8 percent Finns, 5 percent Germans, and 4 percent Russians (Tables 2 and 3).

Many factors contributed to migration from the Russian Empire at the end of the nineteenth century. The most important was the transition from a pre-industrial to a modern industrial State. This led to disruption of traditional agriculture and the demise of the small-scale, family economy. The transition started with the abolition of serfdom in the 1860s, the beginning of railroad construction, and government-financed industrial development. It led to mass overseas migration, first of Jews, Poles, Finns, and Germans, and later also of Russians.

The transition overlapped with a land tenure system that led to land scarcity and unemployment because of the persistence of the large *latifundia,* a worldwide agrarian depression, widening income differentials that led to pauperization of the rural population, and legal discrimination against ethnic and religious minorities.

In the last quarter of the nineteenth century, the Russian Empire underwent a demographic transition that had dramatic effects on the region. The population of the Polish lands doubled in the nineteenth century. New industries in Warsaw and Łódź, which were centers of Russian industrial development in the late nineteenth century, could not absorb this surplus population. Three million Poles migrated to other countries from Prussian, Austrian, and Russian Poland by World War I. The heaviest migration was from agricultural provinces in the north—Suwałki, Płock, and Łomzȧ. Over 600,000 Poles migrated from Congress Poland (Russian Poland) to the U.S. between 1871 and 1914, 80 percent of them after 1900.

The population of Finland grew to 2.6 million between 1850 and 1900 as the rural population doubled in size. Finns migrated in the eighteenth century to Stockholm, other parts of Scandinavia, and St. Petersburg. In the 1870s, after a succession of poor harvests and a shift from arable farming to dairy farming, they began migrating to the U.S. Finnish migration grew rapidly between 1880 and 1893. The migration spread from north to south, rising to over a quarter of a million people between 1894 and 1914.

In Russian Baltic territories, Lithuanians migrated from Kovno, Suwałki and Vilna; Latvians from Courland, Livonia, and Vitebsk; and Estonians from the Russian provinces of Estonia. Estonians moved to underpopulated areas in Russia; Lithuanians to Latvia, St. Petersburg, Moscow, and Odessa, and also to England and Scotland.

In the northwestern region of Russia (Byelorussia), Russians migrated to the west from Vilna, Grodno, Minsk, and Mohilev—territories formerly under Polish-Lithuanian rule. In the South (Ukraine), migration was from Volhynia, Podolia, and Kiev, at first as seasonal migrants to European countries, and later to England, Argentina, Brazil, and North America. Over 90 percent of those who migrated overseas went to the United States as laborers, agricultural workers, and domestic servants.

In the late nineteenth century, overseas migration of Russians was relatively limited; it became a mass migration only between 1907 and 1914. Most Russian migration prior to 1907 was internal to industrial cities and settlements in the east, to farms in southern Russia, and to western Siberia.

Between 1875 and 1880 some 25,000 Russian Germans migrated to the U.S. These were Volga Germans, whose ancestors—from Hesse, Baden, Wuerttemburg, Alsace, and the Palatinate—had been invited in the second half of the eighteenth century by Catherine the Great to establish agricultural colonies in Russia. Many settled in the lower Volga and Black Sea regions. They were attracted by the promise of exemption from military service and religious toleration, which they had enjoyed for 150 years. When their status was changed in the 1870s they migrated to the U.S.[2] Many were Mennonites who went first to Mexico and afterwards to the U.S. The migration of Volga Germans to the U.S. slowed in the 1880s but revived in the 1890s during a period of poor harvests and hard times in Russia. Additional incentives to migrate came from the Russification policy of the government and pressure to convert to the Russian Orthodox Church. Over a quarter of a million Volga Germans migrated by the early twentieth century to Kansas, Minnesota, the Dakota Territories, and Nebraska.

The largest number of migrants from the Russian Empire were Poles and Russian Jews. The Jewish population in the Empire increased from 1.5 million to over 5.2 million by the end of the nineteenth century. About 1.5 million Jews emigrated to the United States between 1880 and 1914, while half a million went to South America, Canada, South Africa, Western Europe, and Palestine.

Jewish emigration originated in the 25 provinces of the Pale of Settlement. There were 4.9 million Jews living in the Pale, which extended from the Baltic to the Black Sea and consisted of Lithuania, Byelorussia, the southwestern provinces (Ukraine), and parts of Poland. The Pale had four main regions: ten Polish provinces (Suwałki, Siedlce, Łublin, Łomzȧ, Płock, Warsaw, Łódź, Kalisz, Radom, and Kielce), with 27 percent of the Jewish population; six provinces in northwest Russia (Kovno, Vilna, Grodno, Minsk, Mohilev, and Vitebsk), with 29 percent; five provinces in southwest Russia (Volhynia, Podolia, Kiev, Poltava, and Chernigov), with 29 percent; and four provinces in southern Russia (Bessarabia, Kherson, Tauria, and Ekaterinoslav), with 14 percent of the Jewish population.

The Polish provinces Suwałki, Łomzȧ, and Płock, together with the provinces of the northwest region, had the highest population density and were therefore the poorest in the Pale.

In addition to the general factors mentioned previously that contributed to migration from the Russian Empire, there were specific factors that affected the migration of Russian Jews. Emigration was heavily influenced by the role of the State in Russia. Jews had migrated to Poland in the Middle Ages and had been Russian subjects since the late eighteenth century. After 1835, however, they were allowed to settle only in the Pale. The prohibition against Jews buying land in Russia began with the Polish insurrection in 1864 and the May Laws of 1882. Jews were excluded from rural localities and also prohibited from settling in some cities in the Pale. These restrictions were sufficient to keep the majority of Russian Jews in non-agricultural activities.

Under Alexander II concessions were made to Jewish merchants, who could live outside the Pale, and Jews were given limited opportunities for social mobility. Under Alexander III and Nicholas II, however, there was a reactionary transformation of government policies concerning Jews.

Mass migration of Russian Jews began under Alexander III in 1881. There were two major waves: the first was between 1882 and 1892, the second between 1898 and 1906. Fluctuations in annual migration to the U.S. after 1880 reflected changing political and economic conditions in Russia. The May Laws of May 3, 1882 were promulgated as a result of a series of anti-Jewish pogroms and massacres in the Ukraine and Bessarabia in 1881. They prohibited further settlement of Jews in rural districts and prohibited Jews from buying or renting lands outside the cities and incorporated towns (*miestechkos*). A mass exodus followed the May Laws of 1882.

Another exodus occurred in 1887 when the government revived anti-Jewish policies with educational restrictions and expulsions. New migration peaks occurred in 1891 and 1892, following restrictions on residence and the wholesale expulsions of some 20,000 Jews from Moscow. Thousands of families of Jewish artisans and merchants were forced to leave Moscow and other interior cities to seek new homes in the cities of the Pale. In 1892 emigration was given official legal toleration by the State, but emigrants were forced to renounce their right to return.

A second, larger wave of migration began in 1898 and continued to 1906. It coincided with the start of a new period of economic depression, revolutionary terrorism, and anti-Jewish propaganda. Pogroms broke out throughout the Pale—starting with the massacres in Nikolaev (1902), Kischinev (1903), and Gomel (1904)—and spread in 1905 and 1906 into the Polish provinces of Bialystok and Siedlce. Almost half a million Russian Jews fled to the U.S. during the period of the Russo-Japanese War, the abortive revolution of 1905, and the anti-Jewish massacres in the Pale. By the outbreak of war in 1914, another 300,000 had followed.

Emigration was not legally regulated in Russia until 1892. Emigrants were thus at the mercy of shipping agents and speculators. After the May pogroms of 1881, many Jews who left Odessa for the U.S. traveled by way of Hamburg. There was direct rail communication to Bremen and Hamburg from the German border. Starting in 1888 there was also service from Libau, a Baltic port. However, direct embarkation from Russia was not feasible for most emigrants because of the high cost of passports. After 1898, Russian emigrants crossed the Russian German border at Eydtkuhnen, Prostken, and Tilsit, then traveled by rail to Hamburg and Bremen to board ships for America. About 70 percent of the migration from the Russian Empire between 1890 and 1910 went by way of Hamburg and Bremen[3].

Origins, Destinations, and Personal Characteristics of Migrants from the Russian Empire

Overseas migration of Poles from Russia began in the 1870s, accelerated during the 1890s, and continued until World War I. Migration from Congress (Russian) Poland reached its high point between 1895 and 1913 with over 450,000 emigrants to the U.S. The U.S. was the most important overseas destination, although Poles also migrated to Canada, Argentina, and Brazil.

The population of Russian Poland grew from 5 to 10 million between 1815 and 1910. Population increased more rapidly than urbanization, and agricultural production lagged because of excessive fragmentation of farms. Villages became overpopulated because peasants were unable to migrate to cities. In the early years of Polish migration, the main objective of the migrants was to save money to buy land. In later years migrants left in search of work, and the migrant population was more evenly distributed between peasants and workers. By the early twentieth century Polish peasants were buying land with immigrant remittances from the U.S.[4]

In addition to overseas migration, however, there was a massive seasonal movement of agricultural laborers from Congress Poland to the large Junker estates in eastern Germany and into the mines and metallurgical industries of Silesia. This internal east-west flow grew out of the increasing demand for labor created by Germany's industrial revolution.

Polish migrants to the U.S. came from low-wage agrarian districts on the Prussian border. Over two-thirds of the villagers were landless farmhands or owners of "dwarf" farms. About 12 to 15 percent were urban workers. Female migrants were largely servants. Poles migrated for the most part as singles. The proportion of females and children to adult males was low. Suwalki provided the heaviest overseas emigration between 1890 and 1904. Poles showed a high rate of return; about 30 percent of the migrants returned to Poland.

Russian overseas migration was similar in structure to Polish migration but was more of a temporary labor migration. It started later and reached a critical mass only between 1907 and 1914. Russians lived in close proximity to Lithuanians, Poles, and Jews. Overseas migrants originated in Byelorussia and the Ukraine. Vilna and Volhynia were major centers of Russian migration. Some 18,000 Russians emigrated from Vilna to the U.S. between 1908 and 1910. Immigrant remittances from Russians and

Lithuanians in the U.S. were one of the most important sources of income in the region. Overseas migration from the province of Minsk led to a shortage of agricultural labor and rising agricultural wages in 1910[5].

Russian migration intensified in 1907 with government repression of strikes of farmers and farm workers in western and southern Russia. The Stolypin agrarian reforms freed peasants from legal and economic obligations to the *mir* and started a wave of migration both internal to eastern Russia and overseas to the U.S.

Russian migrants were predominantly farm laborers, landless peasants, and small farmers who left parents and families at home. Forty percent were illiterate and one-third returned to Russia.

There were marked differences in migration patterns among Russian Jews in the Pale based on population densities, age, sex, and occupational background. Russian census data for 1897 suggest that the early wave of immigration to the U.S. was probably from Lithuania and Byelorussia. There was more poverty and overcrowding in the northwestern region where Jews constituted almost three-fifths of the urban population, hence a greater propensity to migrate. The northwest also had a larger share of Jews in handicrafts and manufacturing than in trade or commerce and a lower ratio of males in the prime migrating age group than in the south and southwest[6]. In the less-crowded southern and southwestern regions there were fewer restrictions on Jews and more employment opportunities as a result of industrial growth.

As with most other groups, the propensity to migrate among Russian Jews was higher among males than females, among people in prime working ages than the very young or very old, and among the lower income groups more vulnerable to dislocation in the transition to industrialization and modernization. Those who were oppressed by legal restrictions and persecution were also more likely to emigrate.[7]

Jews migrating from the interior regions of Russia into the Pale were economically stronger than those who had originally settled there. Older settlers were forced out and thus the first to migrate to the U.S. Economic conditions in the south were better. Jews began to migrate from the south and southwest only after the pogroms of the pre-World War I decade, which were concentrated there.

The exile of Jews from rural areas to the cities and towns of the Pale, and the limitations on their mobility, had long-term economic effects. Jews were excluded from employment in government and higher education.

Government-sponsored discriminatory policies deprived them of economic opportunities to enter new regions, markets, and areas of employment, which forced massive emigration abroad.

Russian Jewish immigrants were more urban, more married, and had a higher ratio of females to males than most other immigrant groups. A quarter were children under fourteen years of age. The high proportion of women and children indicates a movement of families.

Chain migration played an important role in Jewish immigration. Personal ties to family and friends in the community of origin were very important. Russian Jews left extended families at home and migrated to families of orientation (father, mother, sister, brother) and procreation (wife, husband, son, daughter)—that is to nuclear family networks already in the U.S.[8]

Russian Jewish immigration had a high proportion of skilled workers. Small craftsmen and skilled workers made up over two-thirds of the occupations of migrants, but they accounted for less than two-fifths of the census population. Small shopkeepers and peddlers accounted for 5 percent of migrant occupations, but were nearly one-third of the census population[9]. The large number of skilled laborers and artisans among immigrants reflected the overcrowded conditions of these trades, particularly in the northwest region of the Pale.

Because of discriminatory policies of the State, Jews did not benefit from the industrialization of Russia at the end of the nineteenth century. To relieve poverty and unemployment, Jewish workers had to move from petty trades and commerce into higher productivity sectors in industry and handicrafts.

The majority of Jewish immigrants were skilled workers. Almost half were garment workers—tailors, dressmakers, seamstresses, etc. Carpenters, cabinet makers, woodworkers, shoemakers, clerks, painters, glaziers, butchers, bakers, watch makers, metal workers, and machinists made up about 30 percent of the skilled workers. Farmers and unskilled laborers, on the other hand, accounted for only 25 percent of the labor force.

Large-scale migration of artisans to western Europe and to the U.S. made room for Jews to move from rural to urban areas and from commerce into industry and handicrafts. Interregional migration to southern Russia and the Polish districts from the densely populated northwest made possible the shift from unskilled to skilled occupations. Thus, while Jews were moving interregionally from north to south and from rural areas to towns in Russia, they were also moving overseas to commercial and manufacturing centers in the northeastern United States. The majority went to New York, Philadelphia, and Massachusetts. But others settled in New Jersey, Connecticut, Illinois, Ohio, and Maryland. The high concentration of Russian Jews in skilled crafts and trades explains to a large degree the occupational and urban distribution of Jewish immigrants in the U.S[10].

Conclusion

Historians and genealogists in the field of immigration research have relied on aggregate level data to examine the development, extent, and character of population movements. With information available in these volumes, researchers will be able to go beyond gross statistical profiles to study these movements at the level of microhistory—to follow individuals and families from their place of origin to their destination and to focus on personal circumstances. This will enable scholars to assess the push-and-pull factors that contributed to the migration phenomenon and to give a more human dimension to the mass movement.

The editor would like to take this opportunity to express his deep appreciation to Mr. Robert I. Silverman, The Lucius N. Littauer Foundation and the Jewish Genealogical Society of Greater Washington for their contributions to the project. Without their support these volumes would not have been possible.

Ira A. Glazier

Director, Temple-Balch Institute
Center for Immigration Research

FOOTNOTES

1. V.V. Oblensky (Osinskyii), *Mezhdunarodnye i Mezhdukontinental 'nye migratsii dovoennoj Rossi i CCCR* (Moscow, 1928), 22–23.

2. N.L. Tudorianu, *Ocherki Rossiskoi Trudovoi Emigratsii Perioda Imperializma* (Kishinev, 1986), 124–25.

3. Ibid., 124–25, 138.

4. K. Groniowski, "Emigration from Poland to America," *Emigration from Northern Central and Southern Europe* (Cracow, 1981), 151–64.

5. R. Melville, "Permanent Emigration and Temporary Transnational Migration: Jewish, Polish and Russian Emigration From Tsarist Russia, 1861–1914," *Overseas Migration From East-Central and Southeastern Europe 1880–1940,* edited by J. Puskas (Budapest, 1990), 139–42.

6. S. Kuznets, "Immigration of Russian Jews to the United States: Background and Structure," *Perspectives in American History,* 9 (1975), 62–79.

7. Ibid., 93–112.

8. I.A. Glazier and R.J. Kleiner, "Analisi comparate degli emigranti dell 'Europa meridionale e orientale attraverso le liste passeggeri delle navi statunitensi," *Altreitalie,* 7 (1992), 115–25.

9. Oblensky, op. cit., 25.

10. A. Kahan, *Essays in Jewish Social and Economic History,* edited by R. Weiss (Chicago, 1986), 101–17.

Table 1

Emigration from the Russian Empire to the U.S. 1871–1910

Gross Immigration

Year	Russian Empire (1)	Poland (2)	Russian Hebrews (3)	Russian Hebrews to N.Y. (4)	Russian Hebrews as % of Russian Empire (5)=(3)/(1)
1871	673	535	121	—	18.0
1872	1018	1647	266	—	26.1
1873	1634	3338	497	—	30.4
1874	4073	1795	587	—	14.4
1875	7997	984	898	1796	11.2
1876	4775	925	570	1140	11.9
1877	6599	533	713	1426	10.8
1878	3048	547	360	719	11.8
1879	4453	489	494	988	11.1
1880	5014	2177	4165	4332	83.1
1881	5041	5614	5218	7949	—
1882	16918	4672	13249	9955	78.3
1883	9909	2011	7542	5269	76.1
1884	12689	4536	10248	11753	80.8
1885	17158	3085	12939	12095	75.4
1886	17800	3939	13646	12874	76.7
1887	30766	6128	23381	21404	76.0

Year	Russian Empire (1)	Poland (2)	Russian Hebrews (3)	Russian Hebrews to N.Y. (4)	Russian Hebrews as % of Russian Empire (5)=(3)/(1)
1888	33487	5826	25195	18784	75.2
1889	33916	4922	25265	17209	74.5
1890	35598	11073	28252	19557	79.4
1891	47426	24797	40662	39587	85.7
1892	82511	40536	69959	55996	84.8
1893	43310	16374	35246	20741	81.4
1894	39278	1941	28079	16731	71.5
1895	35907	709	25348	14152	70.6
1896	51445	691	36219	17617	70.4
1897	25816	4165	19325	11106	74.9
1898	29828	4726	22302	11581	74.8
1899	60982	*	24275	*	39.8
1900	90787	*	37011	*	40.8
1901	85257	*	37660	*	44.2
1902	107347	*	37846	*	35.2
1903	136093	*	47609	*	35.0
1904	145141	*	77544	*	53.4
1905	184897	*	92388	*	50.0
1906	215665	*	125234	*	58.1
1907	258943	*	114932	*	44.4
1908	156711	*	71922	*	45.9

1909	120460	*	39150	*	32.5
1910	186792	*	59824	*	32.0
Total	2357162	158715	1216141	334761	

* n.d.

Columns 1 and 2 are from the *Reports of the Immigration Commission*, vol. III (*Statistical Review of Immigration, 1819–1910*), 61st Cong., 3rd sess., S. Doc. 756 (Washington, D.C., 1911), Table 9, Pt. 2, Arno Press 1970. These data are compiled from official returns of the Bureau of Statistics, U.S. Treasury Department.

Column 2: Poland, a country without a State, was partitioned by the Austro-Hungarian, German, and Russian Empires for the third time in 1795. Between 1820 and 1898 Poland was recognized as an independent country only by American statisticians. From 1899 to 1919 Polish statistics are combined with the migration statistics of the countries to which she belonged.

Column 3: Annual series have been calculated from Columns 1 and 2 following S. Kuznets, "Immigration of Russian Jews to the United States: Background and Structure," *Perspectives in American History*, 9 (1975): 40–41. Immigration of Jews from the Russian Empire has been estimated at 70 percent of total immigration and from Poland at 43 percent of total immigration. The proportion of immigrants from Poland is based on the ratios of foreign born from Russian Poland in the U.S. Census of 1890. (*Statistical Review of Immigration*, Table 9, p.416). No allowance has been made for immigration from Canada. For 1899–1910, official data on race is from the *Statistical Review of Immigration.*

There are no official statistics on Jewish immigration between 1875 and 1898. S. Joseph has constructed a series from partial returns collected by the Hebrew immigrant aid societies of New York, Philadelphia, and Baltimore between 1886 and 1898 and has extrapolated his estimates back to 1881–1885. The statistical series on Russian Jewish arrivals in the *Evreiskaia Entsiklopedia,* vol. 3, "Amerika" (St. Petersburg, 1907) assumes mistakenly that migration from Russia consisted only of Russian Jews.

Column 4 is derived from ships' passenger lists: 1875–1879 arrivals include all U.S. ports; 1880–1898 is only for New York arrivals. Between 1875 and 1879 Russian Jewish arrivals are estimated at 20 percent of the combined totals of Columns 1 and 2. From 1881 to 1886 Russian Empire arrivals are deflated by a factor of 0.70 and Polish arrivals by 0.43. The anomaly of larger numbers to New York in 1880, 1881, and 1884 (Column 4) than to all U.S. ports (Column 3) results from New York being on a calendar year (January–December) rather than a fiscal year basis (July–June). From 1887 to 1898 data are from S. Joseph, *Jewish Immigration to United States*, Table V[1], 161. Official data on race after 1899 is reported in *Statistical Review of Immigration.*

Table 2

Immigration to the U.S. from the Russian Empire and Finland (by race or people and country of last permanent residence)

1899–1910

Year	Finnish	German	Jewish	Lithuanian	Polish	Russian
1899	6048	5383	24275	6838	15517	1657
1900	12515	5349	37011	10297	22500	1165
1901	9966	5643	37660	8805	21475	655
1902	13854	8452	37846	9975	33859	1536
1903	18776	10485	47689	14420	39548	3565
1904	10077	7128	77544	12707	32577	3907
1905	16671	6722	92388	17649	47224	3278
1906	13461	10279	125234	13697	46204	5282
1907	14311	13480	114932	24811	73122	16085
1908	6303	10009	71978	13270	37947	16324
1909	11202	7781	39150	14595	37770	9099
1910	14999	10016	59824	21676	63635	14768
Total	148183	100727	765531	168740	471378	77321

Source: *Reports of the Immigration Commission*, vol. III (*Statistical Review of Immigration 1819–1910)*, 61st Cong., 3rd sess., S. Doc. 756 (Washington, D.C., 1911), Table 14, p. 62.

Table 3

Immigration to the U.S. from the Russian Empire
(by race, people, and country of last permanent residence)
1899–1910
(percent)

Year	Finnish (1)	German (2)	Jewish (3)	Lithuanian (4)	Polish (5)	Russian (6)
1899	9.9	8.8	39.8	11.2	25.4	2.7
1900	13.8	5.9	40.8	11.3	24.8	1.3
1901	11.7	1.6	44.2	10.0	25.2	0.8
1902	12.9	8.0	35.3	9.3	31.5	1.4
1903	13.8	7.7	35.0	10.6	29.1	2.6
1904	7.0	5.0	53.9	8.8	22.6	2.7
1905	9.0	3.6	50.0	9.5	25.5	1.8
1906	6.2	4.8	58.1	6.4	21.4	2.4
1907	5.5	5.2	44.4	9.6	28.2	6.2
1908	4.0	6.4	45.9	8.5	24.2	10.4
1909	9.3	6.5	32.5	12.1	31.4	7.6
1910	8.0	5.4	32.1	11.6	34.1	2.9

Source: Calculated from *Reports of the Immigration Commission*, vol. III (*Statistical Review of Immigration 1819–1910*), 61st Cong., 3rd sess., S. Doc. 756 (Washington, D.C., 1911), Table 14, p.62.

BIBLIOGRAPHY

Dinnerstein, L. "East European Jewish Migration to the United States 1880–1914." *Les Migrations Internationale De La Fin Du XVIII Siecle a Nos Jours* (1980).

Evreisksaia Entsiklopedia. 16 vols. St. Petersburg, 1915.

Ferenczi, I., and W. Willcox. *International Migrations*. 2 vols. New York, 1931.

Glazier, I.A., and R.J. Kleiner. "Analisi comparate degli emigranti dell'Europa meridionale e orientale attraverso le liste passeggeri delle navi statunitensi." *Altreitalie*, 7 (1992).

Groniowski, K. "Emigration from Poland to America." *Emigration from Northern, Central and Southern Europe*. Cracow, 1981.

Joseph, S. *Immigration to the United States 1881–1910*. New York, 1914.

Just, M. *Ost und sudosteuropaische Amerika-wanderung 1881–1914*. Stuttgart, 1988.

Kahan, A. *Essays in Jewish Social and Economic History*. Edited by R. Weiss. Chicago, 1986.

Kuznets, S. "Immigration of Russian Jews to the United States: Background and Structure." *Perspectives in American History*, 9 (1975).

Melville, R. "Permanent Emigration and Temporary Transnational Migration: Jewish, Polish and Russian Emigration From Tsarist Russia, 1861–1914." *Overseas Migration From East-Central and Southeastern Europe 1880–1940*. Edited by J. Puskas. Budapest, 1990.

Oblensky (Osinskyii), V.V. *Mezhdunarodnye i Mezhdukontinental 'nye migratsii dovoennoj Rossi i CCCR*. Moscow, 1928.

________. "Emigration from and Immigration into Russia." *International Migrations*. Vol. 2. Edited by W. Willcox. New York, 1931.

Recueil De Materiaux Sur La Situation Economique Des Israelistes De Russie. 2 vols. Paris, 1906.

Reports of the Immigration Commission, vol. III. *(Statistical Review of Immigration, 1819-1910; Distribution of Immigrants 1850–1900)*. 61st Cong., 3rd sess., S. Doc., 756. Washington, D.C.: Government Printing Office, 1911.

Ritterband, P., B. Kosmin, and J. Scheckner. "Counting Jewish Populations: Methods and Problems." *American Jewish Year Book* 88 (1988).

Rubinow, I.M. "Economic Conditions of the Jews in Russia." *Bulletin of the Bureau of Labor* 72. Washington, D.C.: Department of Commerce and Labor, 1907.

Sarna, J. "The Myth of No Return: Jewish Return Migration to Eastern Europe 1881–1914." *Labor Migration in the Atlantic Economies*. Edited by D. Hoerder. Westport, Conn., 1985.

Stampfer, S. "The Geographic Background of East European Jewish Migration." *Migration Across Time and Nations*. Edited by I.A. Glazier and L. De Rosa. New York, 1986, 220–30.

Tudorianu, N.L. *Ocherki Rossiskoi Trudovoi Emigratsii Perioda Imperializma*. Kishinev, 1986.

Virtanen, Keijo. *Settlement or Return: Finnish Emigrants (1860–1930) in the International Overseas Return Migration Movement*. Turku, Finland: Migration Institute, 1979.

Wischnitzer, M. *To Dwell in Safety: The Story of Jewish Migration since 1800*. Philadelphia, 1948.

KEY *

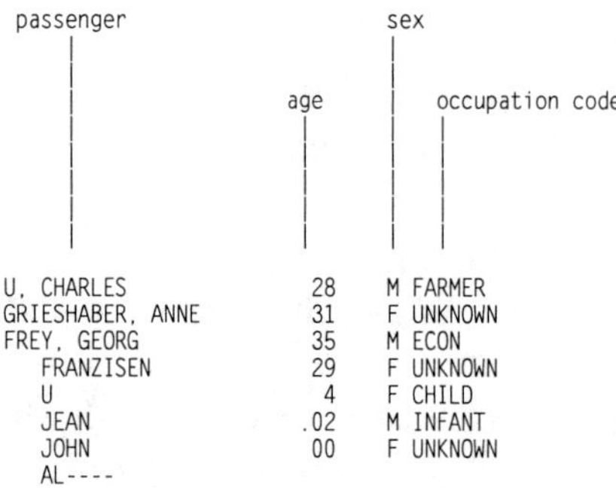

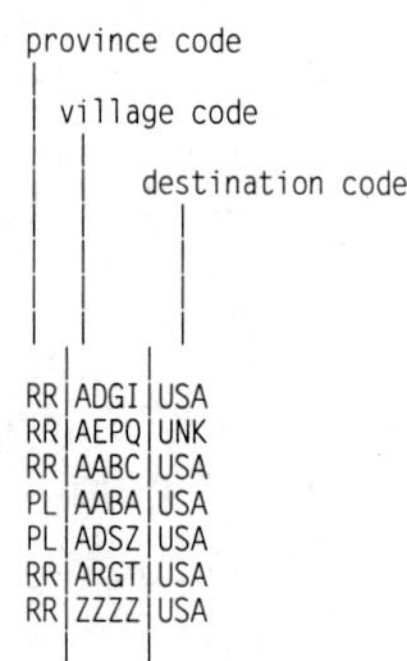

passenger	age	sex	occupation code	province code	village code	destination code
U, CHARLES	28	M	FARMER	RR	ADGI	USA
GRIESHABER, ANNE	31	F	UNKNOWN	RR	AEPQ	UNK
FREY, GEORG	35	M	ECON	RR	AABC	USA
FRANZISEN	29	F	UNKNOWN	PL	AABA	USA
U	4	F	CHILD	PL	ADSZ	USA
JEAN	.02	M	INFANT	RR	ARGT	USA
JOHN	00	F	UNKNOWN	RR	ZZZZ	USA
AL----						

.02 - two month old infant
00 unknown age

UNK - unknown destination
ZZZZ - unknown village
UN - unknown province

--- letters illegible
U unknown last name
U unknown first name

* Information in the above fields is as it appears in the document. For this reason, information on the provinces and villages can often be the same. Information on occupation may also include data on personal status.

LIST OF PROVINCE (OR COUNTRY) CODES

RR RUSSIA
FN FINLAND
PL POLAND

LIST OF OCCUPATIONS WITH CODES

ABSR	AMBASSADOR
ACCT	ACCOUNTANT
ACHTT	ARCHITECT
ACROBAT	ACROBAT
ADJ	ADJUSTER
ADLR	ANTIQUE DEALER
ADV	ADVOCATE
AGNT	AGENT
AGNTTH	THEATRICAL AGENT
AGRC	AGRICULTURIST
AGRT	AGRICULTURALIST
AGT	RETIRED
AHR	AUTHOR
AMR	ARMOURER
ANT	AERONAUT
APDST	APPRENTICE
APTC	APOTHECARY
AR	ACTOR
ART	ARTIST
ASST	ASSISTANT
ASTR	ASTRONOMER
ATH	ATHLETE
ATR	ACTUARY
ATSN	ARTISAN
ATTEND	ATTENDANT
ATTNY	ATTORNEY
AUC	AUCTIONEER
AXMKR	AX MAKER
AY	ARMY
AY-LT	ARMY OFFICER
B	BROTHER
BALR	BAILER
BAR	BARRISTER
BARRELMKR	BARRELMAKER
BAT	BATTER
BBR	BARBER
BCHR	BUTCHER
BCK	BACKER
BCKM	BRICK MAKER
BCKMKR	BUCKLE MAKER
BDM	BIRD MAN
BDMKR	BEAD MAKER
BDS	BIRD SELLER
BGR	BAGGER
BILLPOSTER	BILL POSTER
BKBNDR	BOOKBINDER
BKLYR	BRICKLAYER
BKMKR	BRICK MAKER
BKMN	BOOK DEALER
BKMR	BOOKMAKER
BKPR	BOOKKEEPER
BKR	BAKER
BKRB	BREAD BAKER
BKRC	CAKE BAKER
BKSL	BOOKSELLER
BL	BLEACHER
BLDMKR	BLADE MAKER
BLDR	BUILDER
BLKGMKR	BLACKING MAKER
BLKMKR	BLOCK MAKER
BLKSMH	BLACKSMITH
BLMKR	BOWL MAKER
BLMN	BELLMAN
BLR	BOILER MAKER
BMKR	BROOM MAKER
BND	BINDER
BNKR	BANKER
BOAT	BOATMAN
BOMKR	BONNET MAKER
BOO	BOOKER
BOTT	BOTANIST
BR	BARKER
BRCMKR	BRACE MAKER
BRDE	BRIDE
BRDKP	BOARDINGHOUSE KEEPER
BRF	BRASS FOUNDER
BRFHR	BRASS FINISHER
BRG	BURGESS
BRK	BARKEEPER
BRKR	BROKER
BRKSTR	BRICK SETTER
BRM	BRUSH MAKER
BRN	BARON
BRR	BREWER
BRRGM	BARGEMAN
BRSMKR	BRUSH MAKER
BRWKR	BRASS WORKER
BRZ	BRAZIER
BSCKMR	BISCUIT MAKER
BSKM	BASKETMAKER
BSP	BISHOP
BST	BLASTER
BTBLK	BOOTBLACK
BTC	BOOT CLOSER
BTDR	BARTENDER
BTH	BATHER
BTL	BUTLER
BTLMKR	BOTTLE MAKER
BTM	BIT MAKER
BTMK	BOATMAKER
BTMKR	BOOTMAKER
BTNM	BUTTON MAKER
BXMR	BOX MAKER
BY	BOY
BYR	BUYER
C	COUSIN
CABL	CABLER
CADR	CARDER
CAGT	COMMERCIAL AGENT
CAND	CANDIDATE
CAR	CARRIER
CASEMAKER	CASE MAKER
CBDR	CABDRIVER
CBLDR	CARRIAGE BUILDER/MAKER
CBLR	COBBLER
CBMKR	CLOG AND BUTTON MAKER
CBTMKR	CABINET MAKER
CCHBLDR	COACH BUILDER
CCHMKR	COACH MAKER
CCHMN	COACHMAN
CCHPNTR	COACHPAINTER
CCMCHT	COMMERCIAL MERCHANT
CDN	COMEDIAN
CDR	CAR DRIVER
CDTR	CORD CUTTER
CDW	CORD WINDER
CDWN	CORDWAINER
CFEKPP	COFFEEHOUSE KEEPER
CFNMK	COFFIN MAKER
CGR	CHARGER
CGRMKR	CIGAR MAKER
CGRTW	CIGAR TWISTER
CH	CHILD
CHAIR	CHAIR MAKER
CHAR	CHARWOMAN
CHASE	CHAISE MAKER
CHBRMD	CHAMBER MAID
CHD	CHEESE DEALER
CHFRMN	CHIEF FOREMAN
CHIMKR	CHINAMAKER
CHMAK	CHEESE MAKER
CHMGR	CHEESE MANAGER
CHMKR	CLOTH MAKER
CHMKRR	CHEST MAKER
CHMMTR	CHEMICAL MANUFACTURER
CHND	CHANDLER
CHND	CHILD MAID
CHR	CHASER
CHRMKR	CHAIRMAKER
CHSWP	CHIMNEY SWEEPER
CHTMR	COACH TRIMMER
CHWKR	CLOTH WORKER
CK	COOK
CKCTR	CORK CUTTER

LIST OF OCCUPATIONS WITH CODES

CKM	COOK MAID
CKR	CHECKER
CL	CLERK
CLCMKR	COUCH LACE MAKER
CLDRS	CLOTH DRESSER
CLGMKR	CLOGMAKER
CLGYMN	CLERGYMAN
CLK	CLICKER
CLKMKR	CLOCK MAKER
CLLMN	CELLAR MAN
CLLR	COLLECTOR
CLMKR	COLOR MAKER
CLMNFTR	CLOTH MANUFACTURER
CLNT	COLONISATOR
CLR	COLLIER
CLRMKR	COLLAR MAKER
CLSH	CLOTH SHEARER
CLWN	CLOWN
CMAGT	COMMISSION AGENT
CMDR	COMMODORE
CMMR	COMMERCE MAN
CMMSR	COMMISSIONER
CMN	COALMAN
CMP	COMPOSER
CMPR	COMPOSITOR
CMST	CHEMIST
CNDL	CANDLE MAKER
CNF	CONFECTIONER
COL	COLONEL
COMP	COMPANION
CON	CONDUCTOR
COUM	COUCHMAN
COUMKR	COUCH MAKER
CPMKR	CAP MAKER
CPR	COOPER
CPRMNR	COPPER MINER
CPRSMH	COPPERSMITH
CPSPNGMKR	CAPSPRING MAKER
CPT	CAPTAIN
CPTLT	CAPITALIST
CPTR	CARPENTER
CPYR	COPIER
CRBLDR	CAR BUILDER
CRDMKR	CARD MAKER
CRMN	CAR MAN
CRNDLR	CORN DEALER
CRPM	CARPET MAKER
CRR	COURIER
CRT	CARTER
CRTMK	CART MAKER
CRTMN	CARTMAN
CRTR	CROFTER
CSHR	CASHIER
CSL	CONSUL
CSLR	COUNSELOR
CSTR	CASTER
CTHR	CLOTHIER
CTL	CUTLER
CTLDLR	CATTLE DEALER
CTLDR	CATTLE DRIVER
CTLMN	CATTLE ATTENDANT
CTM	CATTLE MAN
CTMKR	CRATE MAKER
CTNPTR	COTTON PRINTER
CTNSP	COTTON SPINNER
CTR	CUTTER
CTRMN	MOUNTAIN CUTTER
CTRV	COMMERCIAL TRAVELLER
CTTR	CONTRACTOR
CTW	CARTWRIGHT
CTYM	COUNTRY MAN
CULT	CULTIVATOR
CUR	CURRIER
CURE	CURER
CVER	CIVIL ENGINEER
CVMKR	COVER MAKER
CVR	CARVER
CVR-GLDR	CARVER AND GILDER
D	DAUGHTER
DARY	DAIRYMAN
DCT	DECORATOR
DETECTIVE	DETECTIVE
DFTMN	DRAFTSMAN
DGR	DIGGER
DIACTR	DIAMOND SETTER
DIP	DIPLOMAT
DIR	DIVER
DISP	DISPATCHER
DLR	DEALER
DMS	DOMESTIC
DNC	DANCING MASTER/TEACHER
DPR	DRAPER
DPRASST	DRAPER ASSISTANT
DR	DOCTOR
DRG	DRUGGIST
DRKP	DOORKEEPER
DRMR	DRUMMER
DRS	DRESSER
DRSMKR	DRESSMAKER
DRV	DROVER
DRVR	DRIVER
DSGR	DESIGNER
DSTLR	LIQUOR MAKER
DT	DENTIST
DTR	DIRECTOR
DYR	DYER
ECON	ECONOMIST
ED	EDITOR
EGR	ENGRAVER
ELN	ELECTRICIAN
EMBD	EMBROIDERER
EMBL	EMBELLISHER
EMBS	EMBOSSER
EMPL	EMPLOYEE
ENGD	ENGINE DRIVER
ENGMN	ENGINEMAN
ENGR	ENGINEER
ENMKR	ENGINE MAKER
ENMLR	ENAMELLER
EQ	EQUESTRIAN
EXCV	EXCAVATOR
F	STEPDAUGHTER
FA	FATHER
FAB	FABRICANT
FCTR	FILE CUTTER
FDR	FOUNDER
FDRS	FUR DRESSER
FEFNDR	IRON FOUNDER
FELMO	FELLMONGER
FFMR	FRUIT GROWER
FGR	FIGURIST
FHAD	FARM HAND
FID	FIDDLER
FIL	FILER
FINA	FINANCE AGENT
FLABR	FARM LABORER
FLC	FLOCK MAKER
FLINTMAKER	FLINT MAKER
FLMLR	FLOUR MILLER
FLSH	FLESHER
FLSMH	FILE SMITH
FLST	FLORIST
FLUMR	FLUTE MAKER
FLWMKR	FLOWER MAKER
FLWSLR	FLOWER SELLER
FLXNR	FLAXENER
FMGR	FISH MERCHANT
FMR	FARMER
FMR-MECH	FARMER AND MECHANIC
FMSTWD	FARM STEWARD
FNR	FANNER
FORMN	FOREMAN
FRD	FRUIT DEALER,SELLER
FRDYR	FUR DYER

LIST OF OCCUPATIONS WITH CODES

FRG	FORGEMAN
FRMKR	FRAME MAKER
FRMN	FIREMAN
FRNGMR	FRINGE MAKER
FRR	FARRIER
FRWKR	FRAME WORKER
FSHMN	FISHERMAN
FSR	FORESTER
FSVNT	FARM SERVANT
FT	FACTOR
FTMN	FOOTMAN
FTR	FITTER
FUL	FULLER
FUNSHR	FURNISHER
FUR	FURRIER
FURNM	FURNITURE MAKER
FWKR	FACTORY WORKER
FY	FOYER
FYMN	FOUNDRYMAN
G	STEPSON
GALVANIZER	GALVANIZER
GAMB	GAMBLER
GCR	GROCER
GCRCL	GROCERY CLERK
GDBT	GOLDBEATER
GDMRMK	GAS METER MAKER
GDNR	GARDENER,GROWER
GDR	GRINDER
GDSM	GOLDSMITH
GDWK	GOLDWORKER
GEN	GENERAL
GENT	GENTLEMAN
GEOL	GEOLOGIST
GEOM	GEOMETER
GKPR	GAMESKEEPER
GL	GIRL
GLABR	GOLD LABORER
GLDR	GILDER
GLMK	GLOVE MAKER
GLSBR	GLASS BLOWER
GLSCTR	GLASS CUTTER
GLSGDR	GLASS GRINDER
GLSL	GLASS SELLER
GLSMKR	GLASS MAKER
GLSR	GLASSER
GLSSTR	GLASS STAINER
GLVR	GLOVER
GM	GROOM
GNGMKR	GINGER MAKER
GNMKR	GUN MAKER
GNR	GRAINER
GRL	GIRDLER
GRN-GCR	GREEN GROCER
GRVMKR	GROVE MAKER
GSF	GASFITTER
GSMH	GUNSMITH
GSMN	GAS MAN
GSW	GAS WORKER
GTFTR	GRATE FITTER
GUL	GUILDER
GUNNR	US NAVY GUNNER
GVNS	GOVERNESS
GVR	GRAVER
GVTS	GOVERNMENT SERVICES
GYMN	GYMNAST
GYP	GYPSER
GZR	GLAZIER
H	HUSBAND
HAMF	HAT MANUFACTURER
HARB	HARBOR MASTER
HBRDSR	HABERDASHER
HD	HERD
HDWMR	HARDWARE MERCHANT
HJNR	HOUSE JOINER
HKR	HACKER
HMRMN	HAMMER MAN
HNTR	HUNTER
HP	HELPER
HPNTR	HOUSE PAINTER
HRCTR	HAIRCUTTER
HRDRS	HAIRDRESSER
HRHRCR	HORSE-HAIR CURLER
HRNSNR	HORN SHINER
HRPR	HARPER
HRSB	HARNESS MAKER
HRSDLR	HORSE DEALER
HRSKPR	HORSE KEEPER
HRSM	HARNESS MAKER
HRSMN	HORSEMAN
HS	HOSIER
HSKPR	HOUSEKEEPER
HSMD	HOUSE MAID
HSPTR	HOUSE CARPENTER
HSTLR	HOSTLER
HSW	HOUSE WORKER
HSWF	HOUSEWIFE
HSWR	HOUSEWRIGHT
HTDRS	HATDRESSER
HTL	HOSTLER
HTLKPR	HOTEL KEEPER
HTLMGR	HOTEL MANAGER
HTR	HATTER
HTTR	HAT TRIMMER
HUSB	HUSBAND
HWK	HAWKER
IMKR	INSTRUMENT MAKER
IMPLIT	IMPRINTER, LITHOGRAPHER
IND	INDEPENDENT
INDT	INDUSTRIALIST
INF	INFANT
INKP	INNKEEPER
INMKR	IRON MAKER
INMNGR	IRON MONGER
INS	INSURANCE BROKER
INSTR	INSTITUTOR
INSTRU	INSTRUCTOR
INT-B	FAMILY-GOING TO BROTHER
INT-FA	INTENDING TO GO TO FAMILY
INT-H	FAMILY-GOING TO HUSBAND
INT-S	FAMILY-GOING TO SON
INTP	INTERPRETER
INWKR	IRON WORKER
IPTR	IMPORTER
IRDR	IRON DRESSER
IRGR	IRON GROVER
IRN	IRONER
IRNMLDR	IRON MOULDER
IRNT	IRON TURNER
IRSMH	IRON SMITH
ISP	INSPECTOR
JAP	JAPANNER
JCK	JOCKEY
JDG	JUDGE
JLR	JAILER
JNLST	JOURNALIST
JNR	JOINER
JNTR	JANITOR
JRNM	JOURNEYMAN
JRNW	JOURNEYWOMAN
JRT	JURIST
JUG	JUGGLER
JUR	JURIST
JWLR	JEWELLER
KEMK	KEY MAKER
KMNFTR	KNIFE MANUFACTURER
KNGR	KNIFE GRINDER
KNR	KEENER
KNSMH	KNIFESMITH
KNTR	KNITTER
KPR	KEEPER
KTM	KETTLE MAKER
L	IN LAW
LABR	LABORER
LAD	LAUNDRY WORKER

LIST OF OCCUPATIONS WITH CODES

LANDMAN	LANDMAN
LCMKR	LACE MAKER
LCT	LECTOR
LDGHKPR	LODGINGHOUSE KEEPER
LDMA	LADY'S MAID
LDOWR	LAND OWNER
LDPR	LINEN DRAPER
LDY	LADY
LEDLR	LEATHER DEALER
LFNDR	LETTER FOUNDER
LITGR	LITHOGRAPHER
LKMKR	LOCKMAKER
LKSH	LOCKSMITH
LLD	LANDLORD
LMBRM	LUMBERMAN
LMKR	LOOM MAKER
LMNFTR	LEATHER MANUFACTURER
LMP	LUMPER
LNG	LINGUIST
LNM	LINEN WORKER
LNWVR	LINEN WEAVER
LPLTR	LAMP LIGHTER
LPMKR	LAMP MAKER
LPR	LAPPER
LQT	LIQUORIST
LRCTR	LEATHER CUTTER
LRDR	LARD RENDERER
LRDRS	LEATHER DRESSER
LSORT	LETTER SORTER
LSPNR	LACE SPINNER
LSTDNT	LAW STUDENT
LT	LIEUTENANT
LTRCRR	LETTER CARRIER
LTRMN	LITERARY MAN
LWYR	LAWYER
M	MOTHER
MA	MATRON
MACH	MACHINIST
MACHMKR	MACHINE MAKER
MAGISTRAT	MAGISTRATE
MAR	MARRIER
MARMSN	MARBLE MASON
MARN	MARINE
MARWKR	MARBLE WORKER
MAT	MATTRESS MAKER
MCHR	MARBLE CUTTER
MCHT	MERCHANT
MCHT-CL	MERCHANT AND CLERK
MCTR	MARBLE CUTTER
MD	PHYSICIAN
MDW	MIDWIFE
ME	MEALER
MECH	MECHANIC
MED	MEDICAL WORKER
METLGT	METALLURGIST
MGR	MANAGER
MILT	MILITARY
MKDLR	MILK DEALER
MKMD	MILKMAID
MKMN	MILKMAN
MKR	MAKER
MLBLDR	MILL BUILDER
MLCCHR	MOLE CATCHER
MLDR	MOLDER
MLHND	MILL HAND
MLKPR	MULE KEEPER
MLNR	MILLINER
MLR	MILLER BAKER
MLSTR	MALTSTER
MLW	MILL WORKER
MLWR	MILLWRIGHT
MMRNR	MASTER MARINER
MNFTR	MANUFACTURER
MNLG	MINERALOGIST
MNR	MINER
MNRES	MINING ENGINEER
MNSTR	MINISTER
MNTL	MANTLE MAKER
MNTR	MOUNTER
MOD	MODELER
MODIST	MODIST
MODMKR	MODEL MAKER
MON	MONK
MPOL	MARBLE POLISHER
MRCR	MERCER
MRMKR	MIRROR MAKER
MRNR	MARINER
MSMK	MASON MAKER
MSN	MASON
MSNY	MISSIONARY
MSR	MEASURER
MST	MASTER
MSTMKR	MILLSTONE MAKER
MSVNT	MANSERVANT
MTE	MATE
MTH	MATCHMAKER
MTLDLR	METAL DEALER
MTMKR	MANTEAU MAKER
MTMLDR	METAL MOLDER
MTWKR	METAL WORKER
MUSDIR	MUSICAL DIRECTOR
MUSMR	MASTER OF MUSIC
MUSN	MUSICIAN
MUSTCHR	MUSIC TEACHER
MYR	MAYOR
N	NIECE/NEPHEW
NDM	NEEDLE MANUFACTURER
NDMKR	NEEDLEMAKER
NLR	NAILER
NLRM	NAIL MAKER
NLSMH	NAILSMITH
NN	NONE
NOTPUB	NOTARY PUBLIC
NRS	NURSE
NRSN	NIGHT NURSE
NRSYMN	NURSERYMAN
NTRL	NATURALIST
NVGT	NAVIGATOR
NVOF	NAVAL OFFICER
NVYLT	NAVY LIEUTENANT
NWP	NEWSPAPER
OFF	OFFICER
OGNBDR	ORGAN BUILDER
OGNMK	ORGAN MAKER
OGNST	ORGANIST
OLM	OILMAN
OLMKR	OIL MAKER
OLREF	OIL REFINER
OP	OPERATIVE
OPSGR	OPERA SINGER
OPTC	OPTICIAN
OST	OSTLER
OVRSR	OVERSEER
PASM	PASTRY MAKER
PAST	POST ASSISTANT
PBL	PUBLICAN
PCR	PIECER
PDLR	PEDDLER
PEN	PENSIONER
PFNL	PROFESSIONAL
PH	PHOTOGRAPHER
PHD	DOCTOR OF PHILOSOPHY
PHLG	PHILOLOGIST
PHRS	PHARMACIST
PHS	PHILOSOPHER
PIMK	PIPE MAKER
PINST	PIANIST
PK	PACKER
PKBCHR	PORK CUTTER
PLGM	PLOUGHMAN
PLH	PLOW HOLDER
PLMN	POLICEMAN
PLN	PLANER
PLNTR	PLANTER

LIST OF OCCUPATIONS WITH CODES

PLR	PLAITER
PLSTR	PLASTERER
PLT	POLITICIAN
PLTR	POULTERER
PLTWKR	PLATE WORKER
PLTYR	PLATE LAYER
PMBR	PLUMBER
PMKR	PIANO MAKER
PMM	PORTMANTEAU MAKER
PMNFTR	PIANO MANUFACTURER
PNM	PIN MAKER
PNR	POINTER
PNTR	PAINTER
PORKMAN	PORK MAN
POST	POST OFFICER
POT	PILOT
POUT	UNKNOWN
PPHGR	PAPER HANGER
PPMFR	PAPER MANUFACTURER
PPMKR	PAPER MAKER
PPNTMKR	PRINT MAKER
PPNTR	PORTRAIT PAINTER
PPR	PIPER
PPTR	PROPRIETOR
PRCH	PREACHER
PREST	PRIEST
PRF	PERFUMER
PRNTR	PRINTER
PROF	PROFESSOR
PROF-MUS	PROFESSOR OF MUSIC
PRS	PRESSMAN
PRSR	PRESSER
PRTR	PORTER
PRWKR	PRINT WORKER
PSMK	PASTE MAKER
PSN	PARSON
PSNT	PEASANT
PSP	LAPIDARY
PSR	PURSER
PSSR	PROPRIETOR
PST	PASTER
PSTR	PASTOR
PT	POTTER
PTLON	POSTILION
PTMKR	PATTERN MAKER
PTNR	PIANO TUNER
PTR	PUTTER
PTYM	POTTERY MAKER
PUB	PUBLISHER
PUD	PUDDLER
PUMK	PUMP MAKER
PURMKR	PURSE MAKER
PVMT	PROVISION MERCHANT
PVR	PAVER
PVTM	PRIVATE MAN
PVTR	PRIVATIER
PVTW	PRIVATE WOMAN
PWT	PEWTERER
QA	QUAY WORKER
QRYMN	QUARRYMAN
R	RELATIVE
RAB	RABBI
RBM	RIBBON MAKER
RCR	RANCHER
RDMKR	ROAD MAKER
RE	RELIGIOUS
RE-MERCY	SISTER OF MERCY
REAGT	REAL ESTATE AGENT
REF	REFINER
REST	RESTAURANT
RFMK	ROOF MAKER
RGM	RAGMAN
RKCTR	ROCK CUTTER
RKMKR	RAKE MAKER
RMKR	RULE MAKER
RNGR	RANGER
RPR	ROPE MAKER
RPTR	REPORTER
RR	RENTER
RRCL	RAILWAY CLERK
RROFF	RAILWAY OFFICER
RRWKR	RAILWAY WORKER
RST	RESTORER
RTR	RENTIER
RVR	RIVETER
RZMKR	RAZOR MAKER
S	SON
S-FRM	SON OF FARMER
SALT	SALTER
SCH	SCHOLAR
SCHM	SCHOOL MASTER
SCHMS	SCHOOL MISTRESS
SCM	SCALE MAKER
SCMKR	SCREW MAKER
SCP	SCULPTOR
SCR	SCOURER
SCRBLR	SCRIBBLER
SCRV	SCRIVENER
SDLMKR	SADDLE MAKER
SDLR	SADDLER
SDM	SEEDMAN
SDWM	SODA WATER MAKER
SDYR	SILK DYER
SEALMAKER	SEAL MAKER
SEC	SECRETARY
SEMN	SEAMAN
SGL	SINGLE
SGN	SURGEON
SGNMKR	SIGN MAKER
SHAGNT	SHIP AGENT
SHCHND	SHIP CHANDLER
SHDL	SHEEP JOBBER
SHFM	SHEPHERD
SHGLR	SHINGLER
SHIBRO	SHIP BROKER
SHMK	SHOEMAKER
SHMST	SHIP MASTER
SHNR	SHINER
SHPAST	SHOP ASSISTANT
SHPC	SHIP'S CARPENTER
SHPKR	SHOPKEEPER
SHPMKR	SHIP MAKER
SHPMN	SHOPMAN
SHPNTR	SHIP PAINTER
SHPO	SHIP OWNER
SHPR	SHIPPER
SHPWRT	SHIPWRIGHT
SHR	SHEARER
SHSM	SHIPSMITH
SHUMK	SHUTTLE MAKER
SHV	SHAVER
SHW	SHOWMAN
SI	SISTER
SING	SINGER
SJNR	SHIP JOINER
SKDR	SKIN DRESSER
SKR	SKINNER
SLD	SOLDIER
SLKDRS	SILK DRESSER
SLKP	SALOON KEEPER
SLL	SELLER
SLMK	SALESPERSON
SLMKR	SAIL MAKER
SLPL	SILVER PLATER
SLPMK	SLIPPER MAKER
SLR	SAILOR
SLSMH	SILVERSMITH
SLSMN	SALESMAN
SLT	SLATER
SMH	SMITH
SML	SMELTER
SMNFTR	SILK MANUFACTURER
SMSTS	SEAMSTRESS
SP	SPINSTER

LIST OF OCCUPATIONS WITH CODES

SPB	SOAP BOILER
SPDLR	SOAP DEALER
SPM	SOAP MAKER
SPMKR	SPADE MAKER
SPMNFTR	SOAP MANUFACTURER
SPNMK	SPOON MAKER
SPNMSTR	SPINNING MASTER
SPNR	SPINNER
SPNTR	SIGN PAINTER
SPRTMN	SPORTSMAN
SRTMKR	SHIRT MAKER
SSPNR	SILK SPINNER
STAMKR	STAMP MAKER
STB	STONE BREAKER
STBLR	STABLER
STCL	STORE CLERK
STCLR	STREET CLEANER
STCTR	STONE CUTTER
STDNT	STUDENT
STDR	STAGE DRIVER
STGKPR	STAGE KEEPER
STK	STOKER
STKB	STOCK BROKER
STKPR	STOREKEEPER
STKR	STOCK RAISER
STKW	STOCKING WEAVER
STLMN	STABLEMAN
STLR	STONE LAYER
STMAKR	STICK MAKER
STMKR	STEEL MAKER
STMN	STATESMAN
STMSN	STONE MASON
STNER	STATIONER
STNG	STENOGRAPHER
STNR	STONER
STPLH	STONE POLISHER
STRK	STRIKER
STRW	SILK THROWSTER
STRY	STATUARY
STVMKR	STOVE MANUFACTURER
STW	SILK TWISTER
STWD	STEWARD
STWPR	STRAW PRESSER
STWS	STEWARDESS
STWVR	STEAM WEAVER
SUGB	SUGAR BAKER
SUGBBLR	SUGAR BOILER
SUGF	SUGAR REFINER
SUGM	SUGAR MAKER
SVNT	SERVANT
SVYR	SURVEYOR
SWMKR	SAW MAKER
SWP	SWEEPER
SWR	SAWYER
SWVR	SILK WEAVER
SXT	SEXTON
TAPMKR	TAPESTRY MAKER
TBCL	TOBACCO LABORER
TBCMNFTR	TOBACCO MANUFACTURER
TBCNST	TOBACCONIST
TBKR	TABLE MAKER
TBMR	TUBE MAKER
TCH	TECHNICIAN
TCHR	TEACHER
TCHRL	TEACHER OF LANGUAGES
TDR	TRADER
TECH	TECHNICIAN
TELG	TELEGRAPHER
TER	TEAMSTER
TERM	TERRACE MAKER
TGC	TELEGRAPH CLERK
THEO	THEOLOGIAN
THPROF	THEOLOGY PROFESSOR
THR	THATCHER
TIL	TILLER
TILM	TILE MAKER
TIR	TINNER
TIREMN	TIRE DEALER
TKMKR	TRUNK MAKER
TKR	TINKER
TLKPR	TOLL KEEPER
TLR	TAILOR
TLRW	WAISTCOAT MAKER
TMKR	THREAD MAKER
TNG	TECHNOLOGIST
TNM	TINMAN
TNMICH	TIN MAN,IRON WORKER,COPPER SMITH
TNMK	TIN MAKER
TNR	TANNER
TNSTH	TINSMITH
TPCTR	TYPE CUTTER
TPGPH	TYPOGRAPHER
TPMK	TAPE MAKER
TPS	TYPESETTER
TR	TILER
TRANSLATOR	TRANSLATOR
TRDM	MAN OF TRADE
TRDSMN	TRADESMAN
TRMM	TRIMMING MAKER
TRMR	TRIMMER
TRNR	TRAINER
TRSR	TREASURER
TRVLR	TRAVELLER
TSLMK	TASSEL MAKER
TT	TOURIST
TU	TURNER
TUT	TUTOR
TVN	TAVERNER
TYMN	TOYMAN
U	UNCLE
UMKR	UMBRELLA MAKER
UNDTKR	UNDERTAKER
UPHST	UPHOLSTERER
VAL	VALET
VAR	VARNISHER
VET	VETERINARIAN
VINM	VINEGAR MAKER
VIOL	VIOLINIST
VLNTR	VOLUNTEER
VLT	VELVET WORKER
VND	VENDER
VNDRS	VINE-DRESSER
VNT	VINTNER
VSGN	VETERINARIAN SURGEON
W	WIFE
W-FMR	WIFE OF FARMER
W-SHMK	WIFE OF SHOEMAKER
WCHMKR	WATCHMAKER
WDCDR	WOOD CORDER
WDCTR	WOOD CUTTER
WDCV	WOOD CARVER
WDMCHT	WOOD MERCHANT
WDMN	WOOD MAN
WDRNGR	WOOD RANGER
WDTU	WOOD TURNER
WET	WATERMAN
WGGM	WAGON MAKER
WGHR	WEIGHER
WGNR	WAGONER
WGR	WINE GROWER
WGT	WRIGHT
WHLR	WHEELER
WHR	WHEELWRIGHT
WI	WIDOW/WIDOWER
WI-FMR	WIDOW/WIDOWER-FARMER
WIDLR	WIRE DEALER
WIDR	WIRE DRAWER
WIWKR	WIRE WORKER
WIWVR	WIRE WEAVER
WLCR	WALL CLEANER
WLD	WELDER
WLDPR	WOOL DRAPER
WLS	WOOL SPINNER
WLSR	WOOL SORTER

LIST OF OCCUPATIONS WITH CODES

WLST	WOOL STAPLER
WLWRK	WOOL WORKER
WMCHT	WINE MERCHANT
WMN	WATCHMAN
WO	WOMAN
WPMKR	WHIP MAKER
WPRTR	WINE PORTER
WRHSMN	WAREHOUSE MAN
WRMKR	WIRE MAKER
WRT	WRITER
WSHR	WASHER
WSMH	WHITESMITH
WTR	WAITER
WTRPR	WATERPROOF MAKER
WTRS	WAITRESS
WVR	WEAVER
WWSH	WHITE WASHER
WXM	WAX MAKER
Y	GRANDPARENT
ZWKR	ZINC WORKER

LIST OF VILLAGE CODES

****	BORN-AT-SEA
AADE	ALTONA
AADQ	AMSTERDAM
AAEC	ANTWERP
AAER	ARNSTEIN
AAHU	BASEL
AAJV	BERGA
AAJX	BERGEN
AAKH	BERLIN
AAMJ	BILLIGHEIM
AAQH	BOSTON
AARR	BREMEN
AAXF	CASSEL
AAXL	CHICAGO
AAYK	COPENHAGEN
AAYZ	CULM
AAZF	DAHLEN
AAZQ	DANZIG
ABBX	DOBRA
ABHT	ELBERFELD
ABIJ	ALSACE
ABPN	FREUDENTHAL
ABPS	FRIEDENSDORF
ABQB	FRIEDRICHSTADT
ABUT	GNESEN
ABVE	GOERLITZ
ACBD	HAMBERG
ACBF	HAMBURG
ACBR	HANNOVER
ACDS	HAVRE
ACDU	HECHINGEN
ACNZ	JOHANNISTHAL
ACON	KALISCH
ACOV	KANDEL
ACSD	KOENIGSBERG
ACSX	KONITZ
ACTC	KRAKAU
ACTQ	KROTOSCHIN
ACWP	LAUFFEN
ACXZ	LEMBERG
ACZG	LICHTENTHAL
ADAT	LISSA
ADAX	LIVERPOOL
ADBQ	LONDON
ADCR	LUEBECK
ADDQ	MAGDEBURG
ADED	MANCHESTER
ADGO	MEMEL
ADIJ	MINDEN
ADIM	MIROSLAW
ADJJ	MOLLEN
ADNB	NEUDORF
ADNI	NEUENKIRCHEN
ADOI	NEUSTADT
ADQU	NORDEL
ADWH	OSTELSHEIM
ADXW	PARIS
ADYN	PETERSBERG
ADZU	POLZIN
AEAB	POSEN
AEAP	PRUSSIA
AEFL	RIGA
AEGC	RODEN
AEGT	ROHRBACH
AEHV	ROTHENBERG
AEIY	RUSSDORF
AEMA	SCHLAWE
AEQH	SEDLETZ
AEQQ	SEIDEL
AERS	SILESIA
AESF	SMOLENSK
AESM	SOLINGEN
AETS	SPEYER
AETV	SPIEKA
AETZ	SPRINGFELD
AEUW	STADELHOFEN
AEWM	STETTIN
AEWS	STOCKHOLM
AEXK	STRASSBURG
AFAJ	TORGAU
AFDK	VEGESACK
AFQV	WORMS
AFTM	AUSTRIA
AFTP	BELFAST
AFTS	BOHEMIA
AFVG	ODESSA
AFVH	OXFORD
AFWJ	WARSAW
AFZD	POLAND
AGAL	WUERTEMBERG
AGDD	WIELITZ
AGDU	CZERSK
AGFI	LIBAU
AGHK	NUSSDORF
AGQK	POPOWO
AGQX	RUNOWO
AGRA	SCHADOW
AGRH	SITTARD
AGRT	WILNA
AGUZ	GOTHENBURG
AGVP	LANDER
AHCJ	BURGEN
AHDV	TEREK
AHLP	ROGOWO
AHNX	BARDISCHEW
AHNY	BARDISCHEW
AHOA	BELAK
AHOC	COSSE-LE-VIVIEN
AHOJ	KICHINEV
AHOK	KIEV
AHOO	MOSCOW
AHPZ	SMOLK
AHQC	ST PETERSBURG
AHQD	ST PETERSBURG
AHQE	SZERENCA
AHQF	URSK
AHQH	ST PETERSBURG
AHQO	DOBEROW
AHQP	ELISAVETGRAD
AHQQ	GOTTIN
AHQR	KIRSANOV
AHQU	GRODNO
AHRF	NERCHINSK
AHRK	POLTAWA
AHRM	SIBERIA
AHRS	TEREK
AHRW	ZUDOWKA
AHRY	ASKUTO
AHRZ	AUGUSTOWO
AHSA	BECKLOROWA
AHSB	BERDIANSK
AHSC	BOLESLAWA
AHSD	DEKOV
AHSE	DERSCHUMISCHOK
AHSF	DOMBRA
AHSG	DRUSCHKOPOL
AHSH	DUBNO
AHSI	DULUTH
AHSJ	FARIOW
AHSK	GALJEWO
AHSL	GEORGENBURG
AHSM	GIKULA
AHSN	GLOGOW
AHSO	GORDISCHZE
AHSP	GRAJEWO
AHSQ	GRINSCHOK
AHSR	HABODKE
AHSS	HAGDEN
AHST	IANOWA
AHSU	JABLONOWA
AHSV	JULIANOWO
AHSW	KALWARY
AHSX	KAMENETZ
AHSY	KAROCZIN
AHSZ	KEDAN
AHTA	KELM
AHTB	KOBRIN
AHTC	KOJDONOWO
AHTD	KOLO
AHTE	KORONOW
AHTF	KOWNO
AHTG	KRASNOPOL
AHTH	KURTSCHOW
AHTI	LANGENOW
AHTJ	LESCHOW
AHTK	LIPNO
AHTL	LIPSK
AHTM	LITTOWA
AHTN	LODZ
AHTO	LOMZA
AHTP	LOSDEY
AHTQ	LUDWINOWO
AHTR	MARIANPOL
AHTS	MERETZ
AHTT	MEROKNOW
AHTU	MINSK
AHTV	MISCHINETZ
AHTW	MLAWA
AHTX	MOHILEW
AHTY	OPALEWO
AHTZ	OZEROV
AHUA	PAJURA
AHUB	PAPESCHKY
AHUC	PASKOVE-GUSKI
AHUD	PIEWICK
AHUE	PINSK
AHUF	PLOCK
AHUG	PLONSK
AHUH	PLOTZ
AHUI	PLOTZK
AHUJ	POLOTZK
AHUK	RADISCHKOWITZ
AHUL	REPIN
AHUM	RETOWA
AHUN	ROSKOW
AHUO	ROWNO
AHUP	SACKY
AHUQ	SALUNDSK
AHUR	SARATOV
AHUS	SERY
AHUT	SIERPE
AHUU	SIMNO
AHUV	SLABODKA
AHUW	SMITZKOWO
AHUX	SNOWSK
AHUY	SOKOLOW
AHUZ	STANIN
AHVA	TAUROGGEN
AHVB	TERECZEWO
AHVC	WARANKOW
AHVD	WARTA
AHVE	WEMPIELSK
AHVF	WERNEWITZ
AHVG	WIDERNIK
AHVH	WIERZOW
AHVI	WIESNEWSK
AHVJ	WILCOWICK
AHVK	WILKEWISK
AHVL	WILKOMIR
AHVM	WISCHNOVE
AHVN	WISS
AHVO	WIZAN
AHVP	WODZLAWEK
AHVQ	WOLOSIN
AHVR	ZANOWO
AHVS	ZEMPLIN
AHVT	ZIPLISCHOK
AHVU	BIALYSTOCK
AHVV	BIELSK
AHVW	BOLTA
AHVX	BREST LITOVSK

LIST OF VILLAGE CODES

AHVY	CHERNIGOV
AHVZ	CHMELNIK
AHWA	DIMABURG
AHWB	DOLZY
AHWC	DOMBROWNO
AHWD	DRAZGOWO
AHWE	DUNABURG
AHWF	ELIZABETHGRAD
AHWG	GRISCHKEBUDE
AHWH	GUDELI
AHWI	GUMBIN
AHWJ	ILGE
AHWK	JESNE
AHWL	KALICH
AHWM	KALWARY
AHWN	KAMENETZ
AHWO	KELLEM
AHWP	KIBARTI
AHWQ	KISHINEV
AHWR	KOLA
AHWS	KOLACZY
AHWT	KORZUN
AHWU	KOWEL
AHWV	KOWIN
AHWW	KOZLOW
AHWX	KRAKINOF
AHWY	KREMENCZUG
AHWZ	KROTINGEN
AHXA	KRUIM
AHXB	LAHTI
AHXC	LANDEROW
AHXD	LASZICE
AHXE	LERCY
AHXF	LESCHANOWA
AHXG	LESNOV
AHXH	LIBAU
AHXI	LIDE
AHXJ	LINKOW
AHXK	MAHOWA
AHXL	MARIANPOL
AHXM	MESBICH
AHXN	MULOW
AHXO	NAROWOSK
AHXP	NAWARODOWZ
AHXQ	NEWOGRODNE
AHXR	NICZIN
AHXS	OSCMANIE
AHXT	OSINOWKA
AHXU	PANIEWA
AHXV	PILLWESCHKOW
AHXW	PILWISCHKY
AHXX	PODOLSK
AHXY	PORSCHA
AHXZ	PRASNITZ
AHYA	PRETZKOW
AHYB	PRZEMYSL
AHYC	REPIN
AHYD	RITTOWO
AHYE	ROMANOWO
AHYF	ROSSIN
AHYG	ROTNITZA
AHYH	SANDOWDZ
AHYI	SCHARKOW
AHYJ	SCHUEBIN
AHYK	SELTZ
AHYL	SHERWINSK
AHYM	SLUZEWO
AHYN	SMOALK
AHYO	SPOLSKI
AHYP	STRALZEWO
AHYQ	STUSTZIN
AHYR	SUCHOWOLA
AHYS	SYDA
AHYT	TELEPOWA
AHYU	WALKOMIR
AHYV	WALKOWICH
AHYW	WALOCZIN
AHYX	WASSERY
AHYY	WEICHE
AHYZ	WISAN
AHZA	WISHEGRAD
AHZB	WLADOWA
AHZC	ZICHAWOWA
AHZD	DOBREZYN
AHZE	FRISCHEK
AHZF	GRUTA
AHZG	LAPINECZ
AHZH	OSTROLENKA
AHZI	PLUMGIAN
AHZJ	PONIEWESH
AHZK	OLSIN
AHZL	RATZKE
AHZM	RIPPIN
AHZN	ROSZAN
AHZO	RUTZEWITZ
AHZP	SCHAULEN
AHZQ	SKUDVILL
AHZR	STAWISCHE
AHZS	SUWALKEN
AHZT	WAMPIELSKI
AHZU	WLADISLAWO
AIAA	ABO
AIAB	ACKERMANN
AIAC	ALBANY
AIAD	ALEXANDRIA
AIAE	ALEXANDROWO
AIAF	ALINKEN
AIAG	ALT DARBER
AIAH	ARACHOW
AIAI	ARAU
AIAJ	ARCUGOWO
AIAK	ARMAGH
AIAL	AVGUSTOWO
AIAM	BABROWNIK
AIAN	BADEN
AIAO	BALBIRISCH
AIAP	BALTIMORE
AIAQ	BALZER
AIAR	BANSK
AIAS	BAR
AIAT	BARANOW
AIAU	BARDAUCKER
AIAV	BASLOW
AIAW	BAUZEN
AIAX	BELS
AIAY	BERGDORF
AIAZ	BERN
AIBA	BERTA
AIBB	BIALOZERKOW
AIBC	BINSFELD
AIBD	BITSCHENWALDE
AIBE	BLAWA
AIBF	BLIWIEZKI
AIBG	BLUMENTHAL
AIBH	BOBROWNIK
AIBI	BOBRUISK
AIBJ	BOEBLINGEN
AIBK	BOLOCHOW
AIBL	BORODINO
AIBM	BRADFORD
AIBN	BRESLAU
AIBO	BREST
AIBP	BRODY
AIBQ	BUDA
AIBR	BUFFALO
AIBS	BULAKOW
AIBT	BURG
AIBU	BYALISTOCK
AIBV	CARLSRUHE
AIBW	CERES
AIBX	CERNOWIZ
AIBY	CHARKOW
AIBZ	CHICAGO ILLINOIS
AICA	CHODROW
AICB	CHRISTIANSEN
AICC	COBRIN
AICD	CONNELVILLE
AICE	COPENGAGEN
AICF	COURLAND
AICG	CREFELD
AICH	CZARNA
AICI	CZERNIGOW
AICJ	DAHLENBURG
AICK	DAKOTA
AICL	DENISON-OH
AICM	DIRSCHAU
AICN	DNIEPR
AICO	DOBRIZYN
AICP	DOCHONOWO
AICQ	DOEBELN
AICR	DOLBERG
AICS	DOMBROWICE
AICT	DOMBROWKA
AICU	DOMBROWKI
AICV	DOMBRWICE
AICW	DOMZE
AICX	DONINOW
AICY	DORGUSCH
AICZ	DUBIN
AIDA	DUBUQUE
AIDB	DULSK
AIDC	EILENBERG
AIDD	FILIPOWO
AIDE	FINLAND
AIDF	FRANKENBERG
AIDG	FRIEDENTHAL
AIDH	GALATZ
AIDI	GARSDEN
AIDJ	GERMANY
AIDK	GERSON
AIDL	GLASGOW
AIDM	GOLDINGEN
AIDN	GOLLUB
AIDO	GRATNA
AIDP	GREIFFENBERG
AIDQ	GUMBINNEN
AIDR	HAGENAU
AIDS	HANGO
AIDT	HARODOK
AIDU	HARTHAUSEN
AIDV	HASTEDT
AIDW	HAVINCK
AIDX	HAZELTON
AIDY	HEIDE
AIDZ	HEIDENHEIM
AIEA	HELIGOLAND
AIEB	HERNE
AIEC	HILDESHEIM
AIED	HOERDE
AIEE	HOFFNUNGSTHAL
AIEF	HULL
AIEG	HUNGARY
AIEH	IACOBSTADT
AIEI	IGGELHEIM
AIEJ	ILENBURG
AIEK	JACOBSTADT
AIEL	JAEGERSDORF
AIEM	JANISCHECK
AIEN	JANOW
AIEO	JANOWA
AIEP	JANOWE
AIEQ	JANOWO
AIER	JARLY
AIES	JAROSLAW
AIET	JASSY
AIEU	JELOWKA
AIEV	JESCHKOWITZ
AIEW	JOGUSTOWO
AIEX	KALVARY
AIEY	KALWARIEN
AIEZ	KAMENITZ

LIST OF VILLAGE CODES

AIFA	KAMINCK
AIFB	KAMINETZ
AIFC	KAMNITZ
AIFD	KANSAS
AIFE	KATNO
AIFF	KAZAN
AIFG	KE-RIN
AIFH	KEDANE
AIFI	KEIDAN
AIFJ	KEIDANY
AIFK	KENTUCKY
AIFL	KERTCH
AIFM	KHERSON
AIFN	KIBARTY
AIFO	KIKOL
AIFP	KIMSCHIN
AIFQ	KINZEN
AIFR	KISCHINEW
AIFS	KLETZKOW
AIFT	KLINGENBERG
AIFU	KOBILNIK
AIFV	KOBISK
AIFW	KOBISZEK
AIFX	KOBYLE
AIFY	KOHRIN
AIFZ	KOLISCH
AIGA	KOMIN
AIGB	KONOPACZ
AIGC	KOPIS
AIGD	KORNO
AIGE	KORVINSK-
AIGF	KOSELITZ
AIGG	KOTYN
AIGH	KOVNO
AIGI	KOWENSKI
AIGJ	KRASNAPOL
AIGK	KREMENTSCHUK
AIGL	KREUZBURG
AIGM	KRIM
AIGN	KROMSK
AIGO	KRUNKI
AIGP	KUPIN
AIGQ	KUTNO
AIGR	LABOMA
AIGS	LABYISCHKA
AIGT	LACHOWOLA
AIGU	LACKOW
AIGV	LAMOWO
AIGW	LAPOSISCHKI
AIGX	LARNE
AIGY	LAUTBACH
AIGZ	LAUTERBACH
AIHA	LEEDS
AIHB	LIDA
AIHC	LIEBENTHAL
AIHD	LIEFLAND
AIHE	LIMANIA
AIHF	LIPETSK
AIHG	LIPNA
AIHH	LIPTO
AIHI	LITOMIR
AIHJ	LITOWJAN
AIHK	LIVERPOOOL
AIHL	LIVONIA
AIHM	LOMSA
AIHN	LONZE
AIHO	LOUISVILLE
AIHP	LOWICZ
AIHQ	LOZDEY
AIHR	LUBLIN
AIHS	LUBOW
AIHT	LUDOMIR
AIHU	LUXEMBURG
AIHV	LYDIA
AIHW	MAKOVICE
AIHX	MAKOWA
AIHY	MALMO
AIHZ	MANOWO
AIIA	MARCZUKINIS
AIIB	MARKOWO
AIIC	MASSACHUSETTS
AIID	MATTENDORF
AIIE	MCKEES PORT
AIIF	MERITZ
AIIG	MESERITZ
AIIH	METZ
AIII	MIDDLEBORO
AIIJ	MINNESOTA
AIIK	MIRGOROD
AIIL	MISSOURI
AIIM	MITAN
AIIN	MITAU
AIIO	MOGILEW
AIIP	MOLIVO
AIIQ	MONTREAL
AIIR	MOSCHIN
AIIS	MULNO
AIIT	NASCHELSK
AIIU	NESWIN
AIIV	NEUMARK
AIIW	NEUWEDEL
AIIX	NEW YORK
AIIY	NIEDERWEIMAR
AIIZ	NIESZAWA
AIJA	NORDSTRAND
AIJB	NORGA
AIJC	NORKA
AIJD	ODERBERG
AIJE	OHIO
AIJF	OLDENBURG
AIJG	OSMANY
AIJH	OSTERMARK
AIJI	OSTRIN
AIJJ	OSTROW
AIJK	OSTROWO
AIJL	PADOL
AIJM	PADOLSK
AIJN	PENNSYLVANIA
AIJO	PEST
AIJP	PETROWICZ
AIJQ	PHILIPOW
AIJR	PITTSBURGH
AIJS	PLOCH
AIJT	PLOCKA
AIJU	PLOTSH
AIJV	PLOTSK
AIJW	PLUNGIAN
AIJX	PODLESKI
AIJY	POLANGEN
AIJZ	POLANO
AIKA	POSWEL
AIKB	PRENY
AIKC	PROSKOROW
AIKD	PRUZANY
AIKE	PRYSLAZ
AIKF	PSKOW
AIKG	RADOM
AIKH	RADOMIR
AIKI	RADZIWILOW
AIKJ	RAGUSA
AIKK	RAKOW
AIKL	REINN
AIKM	REUTLINGEN
AIKN	REVAL
AIKO	RIDTYSTOCH
AIKP	ROCK
AIKQ	RODISKOWITZ
AIKR	ROGGENHAUSEN
AIKS	ROSEN
AIKT	ROSOW
AIKU	ROSSIANI
AIKV	ROSSIANY
AIKW	ROTTERDAM
AIKX	ROWEL
AIKY	RUBIN
AIKZ	RUPIN
AILA	RUSSIA
AILB	RYPIM
AILC	RYPYN
AILD	RZESZOW
AILE	SAARBRUECKEN
AILF	SABROW
AILG	SALZBURG
AILH	SAMARA
AILI	SAMBOR
AILJ	SARATOW
AILK	SAROS
AILL	SASLOW
AILM	SAWEL
AILN	SCHADOWO
AILO	SCHUBIN
AILP	SCHUKI
AILQ	SCHWETZ
AILR	SEINI
AILS	SERCI
AILT	SEVASTOPOL
AILU	SHENANDOAH
AILV	SIEDLCE
AILW	SLAVATKE
AILX	SLOBODA
AILY	SLOMIN
AILZ	SLONIM
AIMA	SLONIN
AIMB	SLUTZK
AIMC	SMARGON
AIMD	SMARGOW
AIME	SOKOLOWO
AIMF	SOMZE
AIMG	SOROKI
AIMH	STADZINE
AIMI	STANFORD
AIMJ	STANISLAV
AIMK	STUTTGART
AIML	SULZBACH
AIMM	SYRACUSE
AIMN	TALSEN
AIMO	TAPACZKI
AIMP	TARNOW
AIMQ	TARUTINO
AIMR	TELSCH
AIMS	TELSCHEN
AIMT	TEPLIK
AIMU	TIFLIS
AIMV	TIKACZYN
AIMW	TIKOCZYN
AIMX	TILSIT
AIMY	TINKOWITZ
AIMZ	TOBOLSK
AINA	TOPOLSK
AINB	TORGOWITZ
AINC	TRAB
AIND	TRIPOLIA
AINE	TULA
AINF	TUREK
AING	TWER
AINH	UMAN
AINI	USA
AINJ	VENETIA
AINK	VIENNA
AINL	VILKOVO
AINM	VILNA
AINN	WALK
AINO	WASA
AINP	WEIMAR
AINQ	WELMA
AINR	WERBALLEN
AINS	WIBORG
AINT	WIDNES
AINU	WIES DOBROY
AINV	WIES TROMBIN
AINW	WIESNIEWO

LIST OF VILLAGE CODES

AINX	WIGODA
AINY	WILKOWO
AINZ	WIRBALLEN
AIOA	WISKOWO
AIOB	WISSENBACH
AIOC	WITKOWO
AIOD	WITOWO
AIOE	WITTENBERG
AIOF	WOLIN
AIOG	WOLINSK
AIOH	WOLINSKI
AIOI	WOLOCZIN
AIOJ	WOLYN
AIOK	WORNO
AIOL	ZAGROWO
AIOM	ZAKREWO
AION	ZASLAW
AIOO	ZITOMIR
AIOP	ZWENIGOROD
ZZZZ	UNKNOWN

LIST OF DESTINATION CODES

ABG	ALTENBURG
ACC	APPLE CREEK
ADA	ADAMS
ADD	ADDISON
ADR	ADRIAN
AGT	ARGENTINA
AIO	ALBION
AKR	AKRON
AL	ALABAMA
ALB	ALBANY
ALE	ALLEGHENY
ALI	ALLIANCE
ALL	ALLENTOWN
ALP	ALPENA
ALT	ALTOONA
ALX	ALEXANDRIA
AMS	AMSTERDAM
ANN	ANN ARBOR
ANT	ATLANTIC
AOA	AURORA
APP	APPLETON
AR	ARKANSAS
ARM	ARMSTRONG
ASH	ASHLAND
AST	ASTORIA
ATC	ATCHISON
ATK	ATKINSON
ATL	ATLANTA
ATO	ALTON
ATR	AUSTRALIA
ATT	ATTICA
AUB	AUBURN
AUG	AUGUSTA
AUS	AUSTRIA
AZ	ARIZONA
BAA	BATAVIA
BAD	BADEN
BAL	BALTIMORE
BAR	BARCELONA
BAT	BATTLE CREEK
BAV	BAVARIA
BAW	BALDWIN
BCK	BECKUM
BEA	BEACONSFIELD
BED	BEDFORD
BEE	BELLE PLAINE
BEL	BELLEVILLE
BEM	BERMUDA
BEN	BENSENVILLE
BER	BEREA
BET	BETHLEHEM
BEV	BELLEVUE
BGL	BURLINGTON
BGM	BELGIUM
BIL	BILBAO
BIS	BLUE ISLAND
BKL	BUNKER HILL
BLO	BLOOMINGTON
BLV	BELLVILLE
BMG	BIRMINGHAM
BNG	BRANDENBURG
BO	BOSTON
BOI	BOLIVIA
BOL	BOLLINGTON
BON	BOONEVILLE
BOO	BLOOMFIELD
BRA	BRAZIL
BRC	BRANCH
BRD	BRIDGEPORT
BRE	BREMEN
BRH	BRENHAM
BRI	BRISTOL
BRL	BERLIN
BRN	BRANDON
BRO	BROOKLYN
BRT	BRITISH COLUMBIA
BTL	BUTLER
BUE	BUENOS AYRES
BUF	BUFFALO
BUR	BURTON
CA	CENTRAL AMERICA
CAA	CANAAN
CAB	CANBY
CAC	CANON CITY
CAE	CALEDONIA
CAI	CAIRO
CAL	CALIFORNIA
CAM	CAMBRIDGE
CAN	CANADA
CAO	CAROLINA
CAR	CAMERON
CAS	CASSELTON
CAT	CANTON
CBA	CUBA
CDE	CAMDEN
CEA	CEDAR FALLS
CEB	CEDARBURG
CED	CEDAR RAPIDS
CEG	CEDAR GROVE
CEN	CENTRALIA
CER	CANTERBURY
CGD	CAPE GIRARDEAU
CH	CHICAGO
CHA	CHARLES CITY
CHE	CHESTER
CHI	CHILTON
CHL	CHILE
CHN	CHINA
CHO	CHEROKEE TOWN
CHR	CHARLESTON
CIA	CHRISTIAN
CIN	CINCINNATI
CLA	CLARENDON
CLE	CLEVELAND
CLF	CLEARFIELD
CLI	CLINTON
CLN	CLINTONVILLE
CLR	CLARKSVILLE
CME	CAMETA
CNN	CANNON
CO	COLORADO
COA	CORONA
COC	COLCHESTER
COD	COLD WATER
COE	CONNELLSVILLE
COI	CORNING
COL	COLUMBIA
CON	CONCORD
COO	COLON
COR	CONCORDIA
COS	COSTA RICA
COT	CORINTH
COU	COLUMBUS
COV	COVINGTON
CPO	CITYPOINT
CRC	COSTA RICA
CRE	CIRCLEVILLE
CRK	CROOKSTON
CRM	CARMEL
CRO	CROWN POINT
CRS	CHARLESTOWN
CT	CONNECTICUT
CUM	CUMBERLAND
CUR	CURACAO
CVL	CHARLESVILLE
DAD	DAVID CITY
DAK	DAKOTA
DAN	DANVILLE
DAV	DAVENPORT
DBQ	DUBUQUE
DE	DELAWARE
DEE	DUNDEE
DEL	DELANO
DER	DERBY
DES	DESPLAINES
DET	DETROIT
DIX	DIXON
DKK	DUNKIRK
DMK	DENMARK
DOR	DORCHESTER
DRE	DRESDEN
DUB	DUBLIN
DYE	DYERSVILLE
DYT	DAYTON
EAU	EAU CLAIRE
EB	ELIZABETH
EBT	ELIZABETHTOWN
EDG	EDGARTOWN
EDI	EDINA
EI	EAST INDIES
ELD	ELDORADO
ELG	ELGIN
ELK	ELK RIVER
ELL	ELLWOOD
ELP	EL PASO
ELY	ELYRIA
EMA	ELMIRA
EME	EMERSON
EMP	EMPORIA
EN	ENGLAND
ERE	ERIE
ESC	ESCANABA
EVA	EVANSVILLE
EXC	EXCELSIOR
FAI	FAIRFIELD
FAL	FALMOUTH
FAS	FALLS CITY
FDE	FREDONIA
FDG	FORT DODGE
FKL	FRANKLIN GROVE
FL	FLORIDA
FOE	FOREST
FOR	FORDHAM
FOT	FORT ATKINSON
FR	FRANCE
FRA	FRANKFORT
FRE	FREMONT
FRK	FRANKLIN
FRO	FERNANDO
FRP	FREEPORT
FRS	FRESNO
FRY	FRYEBURG
FTL	FORT LANDING
FTM	FORT MADISON
FTP	FORT PLAIN
FUL	FULTON
FWY	FORT WAYNE
GA	GEORGIA
GAI	GALICIA
GAL	GALVESTON
GAP	GALLIPOLIS
GBY	GREEN BAY
GEN	GENOA
GES	GREEN ISLAND
GFD	GREENFIELD
GHV	GRAND HAVEN
GIR	GIRARD
GLA	GALENA
GLO	GLOUCESTER
GR	GERMANY
GRA	GRAFTON
GRE	GREENWICH
GRL	GREEN LEE
GRN	GRAND RAPIDS
GRS	GREENSBURG
GRT	GREAT BRITAIN
GTR	GERMANTOWN
GUA	GUAYAQUIL
GUD	GUADELOUPE
GUE	GUATEMALA
GUT	GUTTENBERG

LIST OF DESTINATION CODES

GVE	GREENVILLE
HAA	HARLAN
HAI	HARRISON
HAK	HACKENSACK
HAL	HALIFAX
HAM	HAMBURG
HAN	HENDERSON
HAR	HARRISBURG
HAS	HASTINGS
HAT	HAMILTON
HAV	HAVRE
HAZ	HAZELTON
HBI	HANNIBAL
HBK	HOBOKEN
HDT	HERMANNSTADT
HEL	HELENA
HES	HESSE
HFT	HATFIELD
HIG	HIGHLAND
HII	HIGGINSVILLE
HIN	HINSDALE
HLU	HONOLULU
HMN	HARMON
HMR	HOMER
HMY	HARMONY
HOA	HOWARD CITY
HOD	HONDURAS
HOG	HONG KONG
HOL	HOLLAND
HOM	HOMESTEAD
HON	HUNGARY
HOU	HOUSTON
HOW	HOWARD
HRL	HARLEM
HRW	HAVERSTRAW
HTD	HARTFORD
HTI	HAITI
HTO	HAMPTON
HTT	HUNTINGTON
HUD	HUDSON
HUM	HUMBOLDT
HUR	HURON
HVA	HAVANA
HVR	HANNOVER
IA	IOWA
ICE	ICELAND
ID	IDAHO
IL	ILLINOIS
IN	INDIANA
INA	INDIA
IND	INDIANAPOLIS
INE	INDEPENDENCE
IRE	IRELAND
IVH	IVANHOE
JAE	JASPER
JAI	JAMAICA
JAK	JACKSONVILLE
JAM	JAMESTOWN
JAP	JAPAN
JAS	JASONVILLE
JDA	JORDAN
JEF	JEFFERSON
JER	JERSEY
JKS	JACKSON
JOH	JOHNSTON
JON	JOHNSTOWN
JRV	JERSEYVILLE
JSB	JAMESBURG
JUN	JUNCTION CITY
KAL	KALAMAZOO
KAN	KANKAKEE
KAS	KANSAS CITY
KEL	KELLOGG
KEN	KENSINGTON
KEO	KENOSHA
KEW	KEWANEE
KIN	KINGSTON
KNX	KNOXVILLE
KS	KANSAS
KY	KENTUCKY
LA	LOUISIANA
LAA	LACKAWANNA
LAB	LABRADOR
LAC	LA CROSSE
LAI	LANSING
LAM	LA MARZE
LAN	LANCASTER
LAS	LA SALLE
LAW	LAWRENCE
LEA	LEAVENWORTH
LEB	LEBANON
LEM	LEMONT
LER	LE MARS
LEX	LEXINGTON
LGH	LONGHILL
LIB	LIBERTY
LIM	LIMA
LIP	LIVERPOOL
LIS	LONG ISLAND
LIT	LITTLE FALLS
LIV	LIVINGSTON
LOB	LOUISBURG
LOG	LOGANSPORT
LON	LONDON
LOR	LORRAINE
LOS	LOS ANGELES
LOU	LOUISVILLE
LOW	LOWELL
LPE	LA PORTE
LPR	LA PRAIRIE
LRT	LITTLE ROCK
LUX	LUXEMBURG
LWG	LAWRENCEBURG
LYE	LAFAYETTE
LYO	LYON
MA	MASSACHUSETTS
MAA	MAYAGUEZ
MAD	MADELIA
MAE	MANISTEE
MAG	MARENGO
MAH	MARSHFIELD
MAI	MASSILLON
MAN	MANCHESTER
MAR	MARION
MAS	MANSFIELD
MAT	MATAMOROS
MAY	MARYSVILLE
MCK	MC KEESPORT
MCL	MT. CARMEL
MD	MARYLAND
ME	MAINE
MEA	MEADVILLE
MEC	MECKLENBURG
MEL	MELLEN
MEN	MENDOTA
MEO	MENOMINEE
MER	MERIDIAN
MET	METROPOLIS
MI	MICHIGAN
MID	MIDDLETOWN
MIL	MILWAUKEE
MIN	MINNEAPOLIS
MIQ	MIQUELON
MIT	MITCHELL
MLL	MARSCHALLTOWN
MN	MINNESOTA
MO	MISSOURI
MOB	MOBILE
MOI	MONTICELLO
MOL	MOLINE
MON	MONTCLAIR
MOO	MONROEVILLE
MOR	MORRILTON
MOT	MONTGOMERY
MPS	MEMPHIS
MRE	MONROE
MRL	MONTREAL
MRQ	MARQUETTE
MRR	MORRIS
MS	MISSISSIPPI
MSN	MADISON
MT	MONTANA
MTA	MANITOBA
MTC	MT. CARROLL
MTO	MILTON
MTR	MONTROSE
MTS	MARTINSBURG
MTV	MT. VERNON
MUC	MUSCATINE
MUS	MUSKEGON
MVL	MELVILLE
MX	MEXICO
NAN	NANCY
NAS	NASHVILLE
NAT	NANTICOKE
NAU	NAUVOO
NBG	NEWBURG
NBH	NEWBURGH
NBR	NEW BERLIN
NC	NORTH CAROLINA
NCY	NEW CITY
ND	NORTH DAKOTA
NDF	NEW BEDFORD
NE	NEBRASKA
NEB	NEBRASKA CITY
NEF	NEWFOUNDLAND
NEH	NEW HAMPTON
NEL	NELSONVILLE
NEW	NEW LEXINGTON
NEZ	NATCHEZ
NFA	NIAGARA FALLS
NFF	NEW BUFFALO
NFK	NORFOLK
NFL	NEW BRAUNFELS
NGD	NEW GRANADA
NH	NEW HAMPSHIRE
NHB	NEW HAMBURG
NJ	NEW JERSEY
NLB	NEW ALBANY
NLO	NEW LONDON
NM	NEW MEXICO
NME	NEW BREMEN
NO	NEW ORLEANS
NOL	NEW HOLSTEIN
NOO	NORWOOD
NOR	NORTHWOOD
NOT	NOTRE DAME
NOV	NOVA SCOTIA
NOW	NORWALK
NPO	NAPOLEON
NPT	NEWPORT
NRD	NEW MADRID
NRW	NORWICH
NSS	NASSAU
NST	NEW AMSTERDAM
NUE	NEUSTADT
NUL	NEW ULM
NUV	NEUVILLE
NV	NEVADA
NVE	NEW HAVEN
NW	NEWARK
NWK	NEW BRUNSWICK
NWY	NORWAY
NY	NEW YORK
NZL	NEW ZEALAND
OAK	OAK HARBOR
ODE	ODESSA
OH	OHIO
OIL	OIL CITY
OLD	OLDENBURG
OLY	OLNY

LIST OF DESTINATION CODES

OMA	OMAHA
ONE	ONEIDA
OR	OREGON
ORA	ORANGE CITY
ORG	ORANGE
ORO	OROVILLE
OSC	OSCEOLA
OSH	OSHKOSH
OSS	OSSINING
OSW	OSWEGO
OTT	OTTAWA
OWS	OWENS
OXF	OXFORD
PA	PENNSYLVANIA
PAL	PALMYRA
PAN	PANAMA
PAR	PARIS
PAT	PATERSON
PE	PERU
PEE	PETERBOROUGH
PEM	PEMBROKE
PEO	PEORIA
PER	PERTH AMBOY
PET	PETERSBURG
PHI	PHILADELPHIA
PIT	PITTSBURGH
PJV	PORT JERVIS
PKE	POUGHKEEPSIE
PLA	PLATTSMOUTH
PLR	PALMER
PLT	PLATTEVILLE
PLY	PLYMOUTH
PMT	PYRMONT
POE	POTTER
POM	POMERANIA
POR	PORTUGAL
POS	POTTSTOWN
POT	POTTSVILLE
PRI	PRINCETON
PRU	PRUSSIA
PSN	PATTERSON
PTL	PORTLAND
PTS	PORTSMOUTH
PTT	PITTSFIELD
PTW	PORT WASHINGTON
PUE	PUERTO RICO
PUR	PORT HURON
PVD	PROVIDENCE
PVX	PHOENIXVILLE
QBC	QUEBEC
QUI	QUINCY
RAC	RACINE
RAD	RADOM
RAY	RAYMOND
RBI	RUBICON
RCI	ROCK ISLAND
RDE	RIO DE JANEIRO
RDG	READING
RDT	RONDOUT
REP	REPUBLIC
REY	REYNOLDSVILLE
RI	RHODE ISLAND
RIC	RICHMOND
RIP	RIPON
RKV	ROCKVILLE
RME	ROME
ROC	ROCHESTER
ROK	ROCKAWAY
ROS	ROSEVILLE
RSS	RUSSIA
RUS	RUSH
SAA	SAARLOUIS
SAC	ST. CLAIR
SAD	SANDWICH
SAE	SALEM
SAG	SAGINAW
SAI	SALINAS
SAJ	SAN JOSE
SAL	SALISBURY
SAM	SALAMANCA
SAN	SANDUSKY
SAO	SANTO DOMINGO
SAR	SARATOGA
SAS	SAN SALVADOR
SAT	SAN ANTONIO
SAU	SAUK RAPIDS
SAV	SAVANNAH
SAX	SAXONY
SBG	SHEBOYGAN
SC	SOUTH CAROLINA
SCH	SCHENECTADY
SCR	SCRANTON
SCT	SCOTLAND
SCU	SCHULENBURG
SDH	SANDWICH ISLAND
SED	SEDGWICK
SEG	SEGUIN
SFC	SAN FRANCISCO
SFE	SANTA FE
SGN	SOUTHINGTON
SHA	SHANGHAI
SHE	SHEBOYGAN FALLS
SHH	SOUTHAMPTON
SHL	SHELDON
SHM	SHAMOKIN
SHN	SHENANDOAH
SHR	SHERBORNE
SID	SIDNEY
SIO	SIOUX CITY
SIS	STATEN ISLAND
SLG	STERLING
SOT	SOUTH AMERICA
SOU	SOUTH BEND
SP	ST. PAUL
SPA	SPARTA
SPI	SPAIN
SPP	ST. PIERRE
SPR	SPRINGFIELD
SRB	SHARPSBURG
SRE	SACRAMENTO
SRY	ST. MARY
SSB	STRASBOURG
STA	ST. LAURENT
STC	ST. CHARLES
STE	STERLING
STF	STRATFORD
STG	ST. PIERRE MIQUELON
STI	STILLWATER
STJ	ST. JOSEPH
STL	ST. LOUIS
STO	ST. CLOUD
STP	ST. PETER
STR	STREATOR
STU	STURGIS
STV	STEVENS POINT
STW	STONEWALL
STZ	SCHWEIDNITZ
SVT	ST. VINCENT
SW	SWITZERLAND
SWD	SWEDEN
SY	SYRACUSE
SYL	SCHUYLER
TAH	TAHITI
TAY	TARRYTOWN
TFF	TIFFIN
THO	THOMASTON
THT	TERRE HAUTE
THU	THURINGIA
TKY	TURKEY
TN	TENNESSEE
TOL	TOLEDO
TOP	TOPEKA
TOR	TORONTO
TRA	TRAVERSE CITY
TRE	TRENTON
TRI	TRINIDAD
TRN	TURNER
TRY	TROY
TWD	TONAWANDA
TX	TEXAS
UNK	UNKNOWN
UON	UNION
UPC	UPPER CANADA
URB	URBANA
USA	UNITED STATES
USY	UPPER SANDUSKY
UT	UTICA
VA	VIRGINIA
VAC	VERACRUZ
VAN	VAN WERT
VCK	VICKSBURG
VLP	VALPARAISO
VMT	VERMONT
VUL	VULCAN
VZU	VENEZUELA
WAB	WABASH
WAC	WASECA
WAE	WATERTOWN
WAL	WALNUT
WAR	WARSAW
WAS	WASHINGTON
WAT	WATERLOO
WBK	WESTBROOK
WDC	WASHINGTON D.C.
WDV	WOODVILLE
WEB	WEBSTER
WEF	WESTFIELD
WEI	WELLINGTON
WES	WESTERLY
WET	WEST NEWTON
WFD	WATERFORD
WGT	WILLINGTON
WHE	WHEELING
WI	WISCONSIN
WIK	WILKES BARRE
WIL	WILLIAMSBURG
WIM	WILMINGTON
WIN	WINDSOR
WIO	WINONA
WIT	WILMINGTON
WOD	WOODLAND
WOH	WOODHAVEN
WOO	WOODSTOCK
WOS	WOOSTER
WPA	WESTPHALIA
WPT	WEST POINT
WRR	WATERBURY
WRT	WUERTEMBERG
WTM	WESTMINSTER
WTP	WESTPORT
WV	WEST VIRGINIA
WY	WYOMING
WYA	WYANDOTTE
WYC	WYCKOFF
YAN	YANKTON
YOK	YOKOHAMA
YOR	YORKVILLE
YOU	YOUNGSTOWN
ZAN	ZANESVILLE
***	DIED ON BOARD

MIGRATION FROM THE RUSSIAN EMPIRE

Lists of Passengers Arriving at U.S. Ports

PASSENGER	AGE	SEX	OCCUPATION	PRV VIL DES

SHIP: NEVADA

FROM: LIVERPOOL AND QUEENSTOWN
TO: NEW YORK
ARRIVED: 01 JANUARY 1888

PASSENGER	AGE	SEX	OCCUPATION	PRV VIL DES
WELENSKY, ISAAC	30	M	LABR	PLACBFUSA
ULITZKI, MOSES	45	M	SHMK	PLACBFUSA
FINKELSTEIN, DANL.	00	M	INF	PLACBFUSA
GATGEUS, HEINRICH	40	M	MCHT	PLACBFUSA
KOWALSKI, HIRSCH	28	M	LABR	PLACBFUSA
PINKOWSKY, WOLF	26	M	LABR	PLACBFUSA
LIPKIEVITZ, MOJK.	55	M	LABR	PLACBFUSA
SCHWARZ, ESTER	18	M	SP	PLACBFUSA
PINKOWSKY, SISAL	24	M	SP	PLACBFUSA
LEVIN, LEA	46	F	W	PLACBFUSA
SORAK	9	M	CHILD	PLACBFUSA
SCHIMEN	7	M	CHILD	PLACBFUSA
JUWIE	4	F	CHILD	PLACBFUSA
SCHEINT	00	M	INF	PLACBFUSA
RACHAEL	00	F	INF	PLACBFUSA
LALINTZKI, DWORE	27	F	SP	PLACBFUSA
SCHMUKLER, CHAIE	20	F	SP	PLACBFUSA
WILENSKI, PESCHE	16	F	SP	PLACBFUSA
RADMSKIE, RIORKE	18	F	SP	PLACBFUSA
FINKESSKIN, RACHEL	20	F	SP	PLACBFUSA
JAKOBSON, ANNA	30	F	SP	PLACBFUSA

SHIP: WAESLAND

FROM: ANTWERP
TO: NEW YORK
ARRIVED: 02 JANUARY 1888

PASSENGER	AGE	SEX	OCCUPATION	PRV VIL DES
GOLDMAN, ISAAC	20	M	LABR	RRZZZZNY
ROBIN, ISAAC	20	M	LABR	RRZZZZNY
KOTTOWICZ, H-SICH	50	M	HWK	RRZZZZNY
BRAWKER, SCHERI	36	M	SHMK	RRZZZZNY
PARIS, HIRSCH	21	M	LABR	RRZZZZNY
KURZOH, KAYDUM	21	M	LABR	RRZZZZNY
SCHREIBER, ISRAEL	22	M	LABR	RRZZZZNY
SCHWARZ, MOSES	51	M	LABR	RRZZZZNY

SHIP: LAKE ONTARIO

FROM: DANZIG
TO: BOSTON
ARRIVED: G UNKNOWN

PASSENGER	AGE	SEX	OCCUPATION	PRV VIL DES
SOLOMON, AB.	20	M	TLR	PLZZZZPHI
PINZUG, ITZIG	24	M	MECH	RRZZZZNY
STOLER, SELIG	22	M	MECH	RRZZZZUNK
GRASBROWSKY, KOS.	28	M	LABR	RRZZZZNY
STOUMAKER, ISRAEL	22	M	MECH	RRZZZZNY

SHIP: HERMANN

FROM: BREMEN
TO: BALTIMORE
ARRIVED: 03 JANUARY 1888

PASSENGER	AGE	SEX	OCCUPATION	PRV VIL DES
SCHMISSMANN, CHANNE	30	F	UNKNOWN	RRAEABUSA
FRIEDE	11	F	CH	RRAEABUSA
FEIGE	9	F	CHILD	RRAEABUSA
ESTER	8	F	CHILD	RRAEABUSA
BERL	6	F	CHILD	RRAEABUSA
JOSEF	3	M	CHILD	RRAEABUSA
CHAJEM	2	M	CHILD	RRAEABUSA
JANKEL	.07	M	INFANT	RRAEABUSA
BLEIWEISS, MEIER	22	M	PDLR	RRAEABUSA
CHALLUM, ELKAN	40	M	PDLR	RRAEABUSA
SANATA, ROSALIE	22	F	UNKNOWN	RRAHOOUSA
LUDWIKA	3	F	CHILD	RRAHOOUSA
WRINA, LAIZER	20	M	PDLR	RRAICNUSA
BLASKIEWICZ, JOSEF	22	M	UNKNOWN	RRAFWJUSA
PUNIATEWSKY, MARIA	27	F	UNKNOWN	RRAFWJUSA
WLADISLAW	4	M	CHILD	RRAFWJUSA
ANTON	3	M	CHILD	RRAFWJUSA
ALEXANDER	.11	M	INFANT	RRAFWJUSA
HAKERMANN, MICHLE	45	M	LABR	RRAFWJUSA
ELYAS	10	M	CH	RRAFWJUSA
HERMANN	7	M	CHILD	RRAFWJUSA
LEISER	3	M	CHILD	RRAFWJUSA
MIREL	.11	M	INFANT	RRAFWJUSA
SCHAPIRE, BORECH	16	M	UNKNOWN	RRAFWJUSA
LEWNSOHN, LEIB	30	M	DLR	RRAFWJUSA
RUDKOWSKA, MARIE	31	F	UNKNOWN	RRAESFUSA
ANTONIE	9	F	CHILD	RRAESFUSA
JOHANN	7	M	CHILD	RRAESFUSA
FRANZISKA	.01	F	INFANT	RRAESFUSA
MARNOWSKA, HELENE	22	F	UNKNOWN	RRAFVGUSA
SCHMOLINSKI, ANTON	19	M	UNKNOWN	RRAFVGUSA
SCHNEIDER, PETER	34	M	LABR	RRAFVGUSA
WEINER, MALI	22	F	UNKNOWN	RRAFVGUSA
SCHPARBER, SCHANZE	24	M	LABR	RRAFVGUSA
SCHNEIDERMANN, JANKE	40	M	LABR	RRAAZQUSA
SOREK	24	M	LABR	RRAFVGUSA
BERNSTEIN, ABRAHAM	26	M	PDLR	RRZZZZUSA
KOTLAR, TUEBEL	26	M	PDLR	RRZZZZUSA
LORSCHE	26	F	W	RRZZZZUSA
ROZA	2	F	CHILD	RRZZZZUSA
BEILE	.05	F	INFANT	RRZZZZUSA
SCHNEIDERMANN, JUDES	38	M	PDLR	RRAFVGUSA
NACHMANN	18	M	PDLR	RRAFVGUSA
ABRAHAM	16	M	UNKNOWN	RRAFVGUSA
FEIGE	11	F	CH	RRAFVGUSA
MALKE	9	F	CHILD	RRAFVGUSA
PESCHE	3	F	CHILD	RRAFVGUSA
SCHIE	2	F	CHILD	RRAFVGUSA
ESTHER	1	F	CHILD	RRAFVGUSA
TRELLER, ABRAHAM	23	M	PDLR	RRAFVGUSA
RUCHEL	20	F	W	RRAFVGUSA
SCHULEM	.11	M	INFANT	RRAFVGUSA
RABINAWIK, MOSES	50	M	PDLR	RRAFVGUSA
GELL, ETTE	22	F	UNKNOWN	RRAFVGUSA
HENDELMANN, JACOB	50	M	PDLR	RRAFVGUSA
ROSENBLATT, CHAJE	50	F	UNKNOWN	RRAIFLUSA
MOSES	.11	M	INFANT	RRAIFLUSA
LANSEROWITSCH, HAWWE	30	F	UNKNOWN	RRAIFLUSA
LOZEROWETSCH, JOSEF	9	F	CHILD	RRAIFLUSA
NESSER	6	M	CHILD	RRAIFLUSA
SACK, ABRAHAM	19	M	UNKNOWN	RRAIFLUSA
CHIPINSKI, JOSEF	16	M	UNKNOWN	RRAIFLUSA
SWERZENSKA, WERONIKA	20	F	UNKNOWN	RRAFWJUSA
PIKOWSKY, MARIAN	28	M	LABR	RRAFWJUSA
GAWENSKI, ALEXANDER	30	M	LABR	RRAFWJUSA
MICHALINA	26	F	W	RRAFWJUSA
CAROLINE	4	F	CHILD	RRAFWJUSA
VERONIKA	.11	F	INFANT	RRAFWJUSA

PASSENGER	AGE	SEX	OCCUPATION	PRV	VIL	DES
WISCHEWSKI, WLDISLAW	27	M	LABR	RR	AFWJ	USA
KOLLITA, WINCENTY	20	M	LABR	RR	AFWJ	USA
KOCZKINSKI, JOSEF	23	M	LABR	RR	AFWJ	USA

SHIP: POLARIA

FROM: HAMBURG
TO: NEW YORK
ARRIVED: 03 JANUARY 1888

PASSENGER	AGE	SEX	OCCUPATION	PRV	VIL	DES
KRIMWONOGA, JENTE	18	F	SGL	RR	ZZZZ	NY
LEWIN, HIRSCH	40	M	DLR	RR	ZZZZ	NY
BALTZER, PAUL	24	M	MCHT	RR	ZZZZ	NY
CHMILEWSKA, JOS.	56	M	FARMER	RR	ZZZZ	NY
THOMAS	20	M	FARMER	RR	ZZZZ	NY
HILLA, ANNA	20	F	SGL	RR	ZZZZ	UNK
SERKOWSKA, MICHALINE	25	F	WO	RR	ZZZZ	NY
STANISLAW	4	M	CHILD	RR	ZZZZ	NY
ANTON	.11	M	INFANT	RR	ZZZZ	NY
GOLDBERG, HIRSCH	15	M	LABR	RR	ZZZZ	NY
MOSES	9	M	CHILD	RR	ZZZZ	NY
PLASKOW, FILIMANN	30	M	LABR	RR	ZZZZ	NY
SERAPHINE	24	F	W	RR	ZZZZ	NY
BICK, SCHMUL	19	M	LABR	RR	ZZZZ	NY
FRANKEL, JACOB	21	M	LABR	RR	ZZZZ	NY
ISAC	20	M	LABR	RR	ZZZZ	NY
ADAMZAK, LONAS	25	M	LABR	RR	ZZZZ	NY
ROSENSTEIN, DAVID	18	M	MCHT	RR	ZZZZ	NY
OCHILSKA, CACILIE	18	F	SGL	RR	ZZZZ	NY
MARIE	9	F	CHILD	RR	ZZZZ	NY
SCHECHANARKI, WLADISLAW	23	F	CH	RR	ZZZZ	NY
RADGIP, IVO	30	M	LABR	RR	ZZZZ	NY
MANDELBAUM, SALI	16	F	SGL	RR	ZZZZ	NY
EISEN, AMALIA	19	F	SGL	RR	ZZZZ	NY
ZYGLA, FRANZ	36	M	LABR	RR	ZZZZ	NY
SEIDEL, ROBERT	26	M	MCHT	RR	ZZZZ	NY
TASMANN, ABRAHAM	27	M	MCHT	RR	ZZZZ	PIT
BOBMANN, MARKUS	43	M	LABR	RR	ZZZZ	PIT

SHIP: ITALIA

FROM: LIVERPOOL
TO: NEW YORK
ARRIVED: 05 JANUARY 1888

PASSENGER	AGE	SEX	OCCUPATION	PRV	VIL	DES
KING, RICHARD	34	M	TLR	RR	ADBQ	ROC
ANNA	30	F	W	RR	ADBQ	ROC
ROSE	16	F	SP	RR	ADBQ	ROC
LOUIS	11	M	CH	RR	ADBQ	ROC
POLLIP	9	M	CHILD	RR	ADBQ	ROC
HARVIS	5	M	CHILD	RR	ADBQ	ROC
ABRAHAM	4	M	CHILD	RR	ADBQ	ROC
LEAH	.03	F	INFANT	RR	ADBQ	ROC
SIMON	26	M	TLR	RR	ADBQ	KS
LEAH	24	F	W	RR	ADBQ	KS
WOOLF, ABRAH	3	M	CHILD	RR	ADBQ	KS
JOSEPH	.11	M	INFANT	RR	ADBQ	KS
GORDON, MORRIS	20	M	TLR	RR	ADBQ	KS
HILSTEIN, JA-	18	M	LABR	RR	ACBF	NY
BASE	18	F	SP	RR	ACBF	NY
NESE	16	F	SP	RR	ACBF	NY
RACHEN, MICK	14	M	LABR	RR	ACBF	NY
MALLERD, ABRAHAM	30	M	LABR	RR	ADBQ	NY
SILBERBERG, S-I-	35	M	LABR	RR	ACBF	NY
--GO	32	F	W	RR	ACBF	NY

PASSENGER	AGE	SEX	OCCUPATION	PRV	VIL	DES
KIN-OKWE, SICHIEL	20	M	LABR	RR	ACBF	NY
MOLIACKY, KALMAN	24	M	LABR	RR	ACBF	PHI
KAHAN, HESSON	30	M	LABR	RR	ACBF	PHI
SCHWASKY, MOSES	20	M	LABR	RR	ACBF	PHI
LEWIS, NOCH	45	M	LABR	RR	ACBF	PHI
GLASER, LAB	14	M	LABR	RR	ACBF	NY
KRO--, CHONE	19	F	SP	RR	ACBF	NY
RACHMAL, ANCAIL	24	M	LABR	RR	ACBF	NY
B-BY, MARICE	14	F	SP	RR	ACBF	NY
-APIDO, MI-WAL	33	M	LABR	RR	ACBF	NY
CHASONEA, MOSCHI	22	M	LABR	RR	ACBF	NY
SCHILWEISKY, ANDREAS	22	M	LABR	RR	ACBF	NY
ROSALIE	20	F	SP	RR	ACBF	NY
PIESER, ESTAR	24	F	W	RR	ACBF	NY
CHANI	5	F	CHILD	RR	ACBF	NY
HERMAN	.11	M	INFANT	RR	ACBF	NY
PAULON, JANKY	25	M	LABR	RR	ACBF	NY
KAPLAN, ABRAHAM	20	M	LABR	RR	ACBF	NY
L-WIN, DAVID	20	M	LABR	RR	ACBF	NY
BERGMANN, HIRSCH	24	M	LABR	RR	ACBF	NY
FRIEDBERG, BE-	24	M	LABR	RR	ACBF	NY
ROSENFIELD, BAR-S	24	M	LABR	RR	ACBF	PHI
CHARI---, ROSA	19	F	SP	RR	ACBF	NY
DAN-YGER, DEBORAH	28	F	SP	RR	ACBF	NY
BLOCK, FANNY	20	F	SP	RR	ACBF	NY
HERMANN, NORRIS	20	M	LABR	RR	ACBF	NY
SOMAN, MOSES	18	M	LABR	RR	ACBF	NY
SPIROD, GITTEL	28	F	W	RR	ACBF	NY
MAROWITZ, DWORE	20	F	SP	RR	ACBF	NY
GOLDSTEID, JACOB	22	M	LABR	RR	ACBF	NY
KERINSKI, ABRAHAM	20	M	LABR	RR	ACBF	NY
SCH-NIE-ELSKY, BONIS	20	M	LABR	RR	ACBF	NY
PETAK, HERSCH	24	M	LABR	RR	ACBF	NY
ESCILI	20	M	LABR	RR	ACBF	NY
SCHUNERTA-TY, JANKEL	31	M	LABR	RR	ACBF	NY
SILBERGLICK, SA--EL	33	M	LABR	RR	ACBF	NY
NODSOWIT-, JURGIS	20	M	LABR	RR	ACBF	NY
KURTWESKY, MIKAS	18	M	LABR	RR	ACBF	NY
-ENCON-AS, SIMPAN	24	M	LABR	RR	ACBF	PHI
MASA-MSKI, JAKOF	23	M	LABR	RR	ACBF	PHI
JENTOWSKY, JOSEPH	24	M	LABR	RR	ACBF	NY
DWORSKI, L-T-	20	M	LABR	RR	ACBF	NY
SCHWALLOWSKY, JANKEL	22	M	LABR	RR	ACBF	NY

SHIP: CIRCASSIAN

FROM: LIVERPOOL
TO: BALTIMORE
ARRIVED: 06 JANUARY 1888

PASSENGER	AGE	SEX	OCCUPATION	PRV	VIL	DES
GOLDFEIN, LOUIS	18	M	LABR	PL	ZZZZ	CH
MIKLIS, JOSEPH	56	M	LABR	PL	ZZZZ	CH
ANTON	28	M	AGRC	PL	ZZZZ	CH
KURITSCHKIN, CHAWE	19	M	AGRC	RR	ZZZZ	CH
JOSSELSON, ARON	24	M	LABR	RR	ZZZZ	BAL
NACKMANN, NOCHEN	30	M	LABR	RR	ZZZZ	BAL
ILZKOWSKI, SCHOLEM	24	M	RRWKR	PL	ZZZZ	IL
LISEN	16	M	RRWKR	PL	ZZZZ	IL
ROSINSKA, MARIANNA	27	F	DMS	PL	ZZZZ	IL
PERSDOTTER, INGEBORG	22	F	DMS	FN	ZZZZ	MN
LILSTRONG, MATTI	22	M	UNKNOWN	FN	ZZZZ	MN
STERN, WOLF	25	M	TLR	RR	ZZZZ	PIT
KOLASGYNSKA, ANNA	19	F	DMS	PL	ZZZZ	OH
ROSALIE	22	F	DMS	PL	ZZZZ	OH

SHIP: CITY OF RICHMOND

FROM: LIVERPOOL AND QUEENSTOWN
TO: NEW YORK
ARRIVED: 06 JANUARY 1888

PASSENGER	AGE	SEX	OCCUPATION	PRV VIL DES
JAFFE, JUDEL	20	M	WCHMKR	PLACBFNY
FUNK, FRED.	27	M	LABR	PLACBFMI
FRIEDMAN, REMAT	24	M	LABR	PLACBFNY
KLEEN, MALKA	26	F	W	PLACBFNY
KUSHNER, FISHEL	37	M	LABR	PLACBFNY
GLUCKEBERG, ITTE	27	F	W	PLACBFNY
BERL	10	M	CH	PLACBFNY
SELENNI	7	F	CHILD	PLACBFNY
IDES	3	F	CHILD	PLACBFNY
DOLUNTZ, JOSEPH	33	M	LABR	PLACBFNY
ROSENBERG, OTTO	28	M	LABR	PLACBFNY
REST, KUWI	59	M	PDLR	PLACBFNY
FRIEDMAN, MOSES	18	M	TLR	PLACBFNY
HERONSOHGN, FRIEDE	40	F	W	PLACBFPHI
NEUMANN, JOSEFA	18	F	SVNT	PLACBFNY
COHN, ITSCHEL	11	F	CH	PLACBFNY
BERKOWITZ, SPRINO	50	F	W	PLACBFNY
KOPPEL	16	M	LABR	PLACBFNY
SHEFER	10	M	CH	PLACBFNY
IRUNIC	10	M	CH	PLACBFNY
STINGATZ, MOSCHE	27	M	TLR	PLACBFNY
ADLERSTEIN, SOLOMON	27	M	BLKSMH	PLACBFNY
SILBERSTEIN, MALKA	49	F	W	PLACBFNY
JANKEL	19	M	TLR	PLACBFNY
JOT.	12	M	TLR	PLACBFNY
ABRAM	10	M	CH	PLACBFNY
CHAWE	8	M	CHILD	PLACBFNY
ROSE	6	F	CHILD	PLACBFNY
LEKIS, ANTON	29	M	LABR	PLACBFNY
SCHAPIRE, MINDEL	20	M	TLR	PLACBFNY
BRAEMSTEIN, JAN	20	M	TLR	PLACBFNY
SCHMUKLER, LEIBS	33	M	SMH	PLACBFNY
GRUNER, CHANE	17	F	SVNT	PLACBFNY
PRIMAK, SCHURK	30	F	W	PLACBFPHI
FLUDES	11	M	CH	PLACBFPHI
JOSSEL	9	M	CHILD	PLACBFPHI
CHAJE	8	M	CHILD	PLACBFPHI
HERSCH	6	M	CHILD	PLACBFPHI
TAYBE	.11	F	INFANT	PLACBFPHI
SURE	.01	F	INFANT	PLACBFPHI
KLEN, ISAAC	3	M	CHILD	PLACBFPHI

SHIP: ELBE

FROM: BREMEN
TO: NEW YORK
ARRIVED: 09 JANUARY 1888

PASSENGER	AGE	SEX	OCCUPATION	PRV VIL DES
DOGOLS, MAMORT	24	M	LABR	RRZZZZUSA
CARL	18	M	LABR	RRZZZZUSA
SCHANKER, CHAG	64	M	LABR	RRZZZZUSA
KOPP, BENZIGOR	43	M	LABR	RRZZZZUNK
MOSES	16	M	LABR	RRZZZZUNK
SCHULZ, EDUARD	24	M	BKLYR	RRZZZZWI
GAPOWETZ, MENEL	27	M	FARMER	RRZZZZOH
WOJTKIEWIEZ, ANTON	29	M	LABR	RRZZZZBAL
SCHWARZMANN, ABRAH.	17	M	LABR	RRZZZZBAL
ABRAH.	17	M	LABR	RRZZZZBAL
JECHIEL	39	M	LABR	RRZZZZBAL
TRAUGOTT, IVAN	17	M	LABR	RRZZZZBAL
IFISTZUKOF, ULAS	24	M	LABR	RRZZZZNY
WIERKA	22	F	UNKNOWN	RRZZZZNY
LARS	.04	M	INFANT	RRZZZZNY
SPRING, FRANZ	52	M	LABR	RRZZZZDAK
CHRIST.	49	F	UNKNOWN	RRZZZZDAK
PHILIPP	21	M	FARMER	RRZZZZDAK
EVELINE	18	F	UNKNOWN	RRZZZZDAK
FRANZ	16	M	FARMER	RRZZZZDAK
JACOB	24	M	FARMER	RRZZZZDAK
CATH.	23	F	UNKNOWN	RRZZZZDAK
PETER	2	F	CHILD	RRZZZZDAK
MARIE	.10	F	INFANT	RRZZZZDAK
KRUCHELSKA, MARIA	24	F	W	RRZZZZDAK
ANTON	9	M	CHILD	RRZZZZDAK
SCHER, ITA	32	F	W	RRZZZZOH
MINNA	32	F	W	RRZZZZOH
ALEXANDER	6	M	CHILD	RRZZZZOH
SARAH	.09	F	INFANT	RRZZZZOH
FANIANSKY, MARIE	40	F	W	RRZZZZBAL
SAHRAH	11	F	UNKNOWN	RRZZZZBAL
ABRAH.	8	M	CHILD	RRZZZZBAL
MARIE	8	F	CHILD	RRZZZZBAL
JONTIF	5	M	CHILD	RRZZZZBAL
KUPER, CHANNE	25	F	SVNT	RRZZZZNY

SHIP: MARSALA

FROM: HAMBURG
TO: NEW YORK
ARRIVED: 10 JANUARY 1888

PASSENGER	AGE	SEX	OCCUPATION	PRV VIL DES
KRYSKY, HIRSCH	17	M	MCHT	RRZZZZNY
INNEWITZ, KRIST	23	M	LABR	RRZZZZNY
KNITTER, AUGUST	45	M	LABR	RRZZZZNY
AUGUST	17	M	LABR	RRZZZZNY
JANER, ABE	21	M	LABR	RRZZZZCH
STANOWITCZ, LOUIS	17	M	LABR	RRZZZZNY
SCHULIK, MOTEI	23	M	LABR	RRZZZZNY
KESSLER, SAMUEL	30	M	LABR	RRZZZZNY
GOEBEL, PETER	37	M	FARMER	RRZZZZNY
BRYNOWSKY, JOHN	20	M	LABR	RRZZZZNY
ULEWICZ, VINCENTTI	27	M	LABR	RRZZZZNY
RABUNOWITZ, MAX	20	M	TLR	RRZZZZNY
KRINANOYO, ISRAEL	19	M	LABR	RRZZZZNY
KOCH, MOSES	30	M	UNKNOWN	RRZZZZNY
KOLONTEI, WALDEMAR	19	M	LABR	RRZZZZNY
BENDER, CAROLINE	24	F	WO	RRZZZZNY
WILH.	.11	M	INFANT	RRZZZZNY
KOZLOWSKA, ANNA	30	F	WO	RRZZZZNY
ANTONIA	8	F	CHILD	RRZZZZNY
JOS.	6	M	CHILD	RRZZZZNY
ANDRAS	.11	M	INFANT	RRZZZZNY
RIKA, MYKOLAY	28	M	LABR	RRZZZZNY
ROTTMAN, LORAH	22	F	SGL	RRZZZZNY
PRUGER, WOLT.	21	M	LABR	RRZZZZNY
DAVID, MARCUS	26	M	LABR	RRZZZZCH
BEHRMAN, MARCUS	26	M	MCHT	RRZZZZCH
MITTELSBACH, LUEBKE	22	M	TLR	RRZZZZCH
HERZFELD, CARL	44	M	CK	RRZZZZCH
EUG.	21	F	W	RRZZZZCH
GRUGEWSKY, MOSES	25	M	LABR	RRZZZZCH
STURMANN, LACINO	33	M	LABR	RRZZZZCH
KAPLAN, FANNY	24	F	SGL	RRZZZZCH
HOROWITZ, JULIE	42	F	WO	RRZZZZCH
SEIKITES, ADOLF	29	M	DLR	RRZZZZCH
LEWINSKY, MOSES	26	M	LABR	RRZZZZCH
PASTNELKA, BLUME	40	F	WO	RRZZZZCH
BENIE	16	F	CH	RRZZZZCH
SCHMERL	8	F	CHILD	RRZZZZCH
ZEREL	6	F	CHILD	RRZZZZCH
ALIOSBERG, ISRAEL	32	M	LABR	RRZZZZCH
HALPERN, MOSES	35	M	LABR	RRZZZZCH
WITSCHICZ, JOS	22	M	LABR	RRZZZZCH

PASSENGER	AGE	SEX	OCCUPATION	PVRIVL	DES
LEWIN, CHAIM	25	M	LABR	RRZZZZ	CH
ZIRLSTEIN, BASCHE	23	F	WO	RRZZZZ	CH
LEIB	.09	M	INFANT	RRZZZZ	CH

SHIP: WYOMING

FROM: LIVERPOOL AND QUEENSTOWN
TO: NEW YORK
ARRIVED: 11 JANUARY 1888

PASSENGER	AGE	SEX	OCCUPATION	PVRIVL	DES
RIWKIND, JUDEL	25	F	SP	RRZZZZ	USA
NEIGENOLATT, S.	20	M	LABR	RRZZZZ	USA
WOLANSTOCK, MARTHA	23	F	SP	RRZZZZ	USA
LUSERTHORICK, J.	18	M	LABR	RRZZZZ	USA
SKOLNIK, C.M.	26	M	LABR	RRZZZZ	USA
HERDIMAN, ZANTA	20	M	LABR	RRZZZZ	USA
WORGARYER, P.	14	M	LABR	RRZZZZ	USA
SAFIUS, MARY	20	F	SP	RRZZZZ	USA
SCHSCHURANZ, MARTA	22	F	SP	RRZZZZ	USA
ANDERSON, MARIA	25	F	SP	RRZZZZ	USA
ALAKANGUS, ALEKSI	29	F	SP	RRZZZZ	USA
TELNOLIN, G.	18	M	LABR	RRZZZZ	USA
SWOLA, AUGUST	35	M	LABR	RRZZZZ	USA
NIKOLA, J.	18	M	LABR	RRZZZZ	USA
NICASELA, E.	18	M	ENGR	RRZZZZ	USA
ALAKUHGAS, K.	39	M	ENGR	RRZZZZ	USA
SURASKI, L.	22	M	ENGR	RRZZZZ	USA
HERMAN, C.	26	F	W	RRZZZZ	USA
LEIBESCH	8	F	CHILD	RRZZZZ	USA
SENTO	7	M	CHILD	RRZZZZ	USA
KALL	3	M	CHILD	RRZZZZ	USA
WOLF	00	M	INF	RRZZZZ	USA

SHIP: BOTHNIA

FROM: LIVERPOOL AND QUEENSTOWN
TO: NEW YORK
ARRIVED: 12 JANUARY 1888

PASSENGER	AGE	SEX	OCCUPATION	PVRIVL	DES
MARG---, H	40	M	LABR	RRZZZZ	USA
ZATZKUWUZ, MICH	20	M	LABR	RRZZZZ	USA
ISAKOW, JOSE-	26	M	LABR	RRZZZZ	USA
KO-IN, SCHOPSEL	23	M	LABR	RRZZZZ	USA
PARMET, ABRAHAM	18	M	LABR	RRZZZZ	USA
FRA-BLAN, MORITZ	28	M	LABR	RRZZZZ	USA
HUL--N, WE-L	24	M	PDLR	RRZZZZ	USA
LA-OWITZKI, JAK	29	M	TLR	RRZZZZ	USA
MARKUS	22	M	TLR	RRZZZZ	USA
WESBERG, SALI	40	F	MA	RRZZZZ	USA
TONI	15	F	SP	RRZZZZ	USA
LEVIG	10	M	CH	RRZZZZ	USA
SAM	7	M	CHILD	RRZZZZ	USA
GELLMANN, SUSCHE	24	M	MLR	RRZZZZ	USA
LEA	20	F	W	RRZZZZ	USA
PROPP, ANNA	20	F	SP	RRZZZZ	USA
SCHWERG, KREMIE	29	F	W	RRZZZZ	USA
MASCHE	3	F	CHILD	RRZZZZ	USA
-HASE	1	F	CHILD	RRZZZZ	USA
SI-BERMAN, DEBORAH	22	F	SP	RRZZZZ	USA

SHIP: WERRA

FROM: BREMEN AND SOUTHAMPTON
TO: NEW YORK
ARRIVED: 16 JANUARY 1888

PASSENGER	AGE	SEX	OCCUPATION	PVRIVL	DES
BERLIN, ISRAEL	36	M	FARMER	RRAILA	USA
WALKONIMONA, ANNA	30	F	NN	RRZZZZ	USA
POCINKONIS, JOSEF	30	M	LABR	RRZZZZ	USA
SLOWIEMSKI, MOSES	26	M	LABR	RRAHQU	USA
ELISABETH	20	F	W	RRAHQU	USA
PIKMAS, FRANZ	43	M	LABR	RRAHQU	USA
SLAVITZKI, ANZEI	27	M	LABR	RRAHQU	USA
KOWSAN, IGNATZ	19	M	LABR	RRAHQU	USA
COHEN, SAIMAN	20	M	LABR	RRAHQU	USA
MACIEJIMAS, MARCIN	40	M	LABR	RRAHQU	USA
CHARES, CUNE	30	M	LABR	RRAHQU	USA
STERN, SELIG	20	M	PNTR	RRAINM	USA

SHIP: OHIO

FROM: LIVERPOOL AND QUEENSTOWN
TO: NEW YORK
ARRIVED: 16 JANUARY 1888

PASSENGER	AGE	SEX	OCCUPATION	PVRIVL	DES
CHRYANS, J.	20	M	LABR	RRZZZZ	NY
FEINSTEIN, EMMA	7	F	CHILD	RRZZZZ	NY
FRIGIN, F.DWORCE	26	F	W	RRZZZZ	NY
PECHE	5	F	CHILD	RRZZZZ	NY
S.	.07	M	INFANT	RRZZZZ	NY
FELDSTEIN, J.	11	M	CH	RRZZZZ	NY
DORE	26	F	W	RRZZZZ	NY
R.	23	M	LABR	RRZZZZ	NY
GACH, D.	20	M	LABR	RRZZZZ	NY
GURLASKI, CHAIN	40	F	W	RRZZZZ	MA
SORE	15	F	SP	RRZZZZ	MA
ABR.	5	M	CHILD	RRZZZZ	MA
JOSEROWITZ, O.	24	M	LABR	RRZZZZ	PA
KRUGLIG, S.	21	M	LABR	RRZZZZ	PA
LISS, R.	59	M	LABR	PLZZZZ	NY
MERKEWITZ, M.	21	M	LABR	RRZZZZ	PA
MARTON, JOSE	18	M	LABR	RRZZZZ	NY
MUKWIKI, MARIUS	45	F	W	RRZZZZ	NY
A.	10	M	CH	RRZZZZ	NY
B.	3	M	CHILD	RRZZZZ	NY
ROSHBERG, F.	17	M	LABR	RRZZZZ	MA
RLADANSKY, A.S.	17	M	LABR	RRZZZZ	NY
RUSZKOWSKY, B.	18	M	LABR	RRZZZZ	NY
C.	17	M	LABR	RRZZZZ	NY
ROKOWSKY, F.	36	M	LABR	RRZZZZ	NY
ROSENTHAL, J.	22	M	LABR	RRZZZZ	NY
SAPICKS, BEILE	29	F	W	RRZZZZ	NY
L.	7	M	CHILD	RRZZZZ	NY
B.	3	M	CHILD	RRZZZZ	NY
TEWELWITZ, A.	16	M	LABR	RRZZZZ	NY
TLATYK, A.	38	M	LABR	RRZZZZ	NY
WEINER, K.	30	M	LABR	RRZZZZ	MA

SHIP: LAKE SUPERIOR

FROM: HAMBURG AND STETTIN
TO: BOSTON
ARRIVED: UNKNOWN

PASSENGER	AGE	SEX	OCCUPATION	PRV VIL DES
LEVY, BERNARD	25	M	BKBNDR	RRZZZZBO
FREYDLEY, SCHAUL	21	M	TLR	RRZZZZNY
SOLOMON, RIEVE	23	F	W	RRZZZZNY
ESTER	1	F	CHILD	RRZZZZNY
MARCOVITCH, MEYER	30	M	TLR	RRZZZZPHI
HELD, BARNET	23	M	TLR	RRZZZZBO
GOTY, JACOB	20	M	TLR	RRZZZZBO
MOZYCKE, ABRAHAM	30	M	BKBNDR	RRZZZZBO
GISIMDIS, ELIAS	35	M	TLR	RRZZZZNY
VEICHMAN, JUMAN	18	M	TLR	RRZZZZNY
WEIRYAR, ABR.	23	M	MECH	RRZZZZBO
LUCIE	20	F	W	RRZZZZBO
SEWEL, MOSCHEL	23	M	BKLYR	RRZZZZBO

SHIP: WESTERLAND

FROM: ANTWERP
TO: NEW YORK
ARRIVED: 19 JANUARY 1888

PASSENGER	AGE	SEX	OCCUPATION	PRV VIL DES
DENNES, KALMAN	24	M	LABR	RRZZZZNY
FEKAIUS, J.	32	M	FARMER	RRZZZZNY
SONEBERG, FRD.	26	M	SHMK	RRZZZZNY
ORLENCHL, HCH.	22	M	LABR	PLZZZZNY
OPKE, HENRY	24	M	LABR	PLZZZZNY
TIBORSE, GUSTAV	24	M	LABR	RRZZZZNY
MARIA	4	F	CHILD	RRZZZZNY
PARKER, U	30	F	UNKNOWN	RRZZZZNY

SHIP: SARMATIAN

FROM: LIVERPOOL
TO: BALTIMORE
ARRIVED: 20 JANUARY 1888

PASSENGER	AGE	SEX	OCCUPATION	PRV VIL DES
STRASBRONG, MARIA	50	F	W	RRZZZZMI
JACOB	25	M	MNR	RRZZZZMI
EMILIA	15	F	DMS	RRZZZZMI
---NKESKI, JACOB	22	M	MNR	RRZZZZMI
KAURMEN, JOHAN	23	M	MNR	RRZZZZMI
JAEKINEN, M.	23	M	MNR	RRZZZZMI
LOYD, JOHAN	27	M	MNR	RRZZZZMI
JOKINEN, MATZ	28	M	MNR	RRZZZZMI
KARLSON, JOHAN	28	M	MNR	RRZZZZMI
ERICKSON, SYLVESTER	34	M	MNR	RRZZZZMI
LORGA, MATZ	30	M	MNR	RRZZZZMI
MELLNER, CHANE	17	M	MNR	RRZZZZMI
KERSCH, WOLFSOHN	23	M	MNR	RRZZZZMI
MESSKOWSKY, T.	52	F	W	RRZZZZMI
PESCHE	11	F	CH	RRZZZZMI
SILBERMAN, LEIB	25	M	FLABR	PLZZZZBAL
DANIEL, ANNA	40	F	W	PLZZZZIL
KARL	4	M	CHILD	PLZZZZIL
EMIL	.06	M	INFANT	PLZZZZIL
MAJEWSKI, FRANCES	28	M	LABR	PLZZZZIL

SHIP: CITY OF BERLIN

FROM: LIVERPOOL AND QUEENSTOWN
TO: NEW YORK
ARRIVED: 23 JANUARY 1888

PASSENGER	AGE	SEX	OCCUPATION	PRV VIL DES
DISSERIT, HANNA	2	F	CHILD	RRZZZZNY
SRAGOWITSCH, HIRSCH	45	M	PH	RRACBFNY
JOSEF	17	M	CMST	RRACBFNY
MORISCH	11	F	CH	RRACBFNY
SALOREITZIK, ALEXANDER	19	M	PH	RRZZZZNY
MIRSKI, LEIB	25	M	SHMK	RRZZZZNY
SAENELSOHN, LINA	23	F	W	RRAIGHNY
ROSENBERG, SELIG	23	M	UNKNOWN	RRZZZZUNK
KIRSTALKER, JACOB	25	M	PVTR	RRZZZZNY
GOLDSTEIN, ETTEL	18	F	FARMER	RRZZZZUNK
FORKLER, EDMUND	27	M	UNKNOWN	RRZZZZUNK
DICK, FELIX	52	M	UNKNOWN	RRAHZSUNK
HAREMAZA, PELAGIA	20	F	W	PLZZZZBUF
CARL	00	M	INF	PLZZZZBUF
HAREUSZD, JOSEFA	35	F	W	PLZZZZBUF
DESSEREIT, LUDWIG	32	M	WHR	RRZZZZNY
CAROLINE	30	F	W	RRZZZZNY
EZLI, JOKES	17	F	SVNT	RRZZZZNY
FREIDLAUDER, BASSE	20	F	W	RRZZZZNY
MOLUKOU, ANDREI	20	M	BBR	RRZZZZBAL
SALOMON, JANKEL	20	M	UNKNOWN	RRZZZZNY
CHAGEH, HENDE	18	M	UNKNOWN	RRAGRTNY
BUSKIN, SELIG	20	M	PNTR	RRAGRTNY
LEA	20	F	SVNT	RRAGRTNY
SELLE	9	M	CHILD	RRAGRTNY
SCHULEM	8	M	CHILD	RRAGRTNY

SHIP: SLAVONIA

FROM: STETTIN
TO: NEW YORK
ARRIVED: 23 JANUARY 1888

PASSENGER	AGE	SEX	OCCUPATION	PRV VIL DES
SODROWSKI, MICHAEL	22	M	LABR	RRZZZZUSA
CHO-NOWSKI, FRANZ	24	M	LABR	RRAICOUSA
-OSILEWITSCH, MOSES	23	M	LKSH	RRAFVGUSA
LINTEND--LE, SCHE--SEL	23	M	TLR	RRAHXHUSA
KUNTZMANN, ABRAHAM	23	M	TLR	RRZZZZUSA
KANTEROWITZ, DAVID	35	M	LABR	RRZZZZUSA
CHO-NOWSKI, PETER	38	M	LABR	RRZZZZUSA

SHIP: EMS

FROM: BREMEN AND SOUTHAMPTON
TO: NEW YORK
ARRIVED: 23 JANUARY 1888

PASSENGER	AGE	SEX	OCCUPATION	PRV VIL DES
LIPPSTEIN, HERMANN	33	M	MCHT	RRAHQDUSA
ASAMEIT, AMALIE	23	F	UNKNOWN	RRAHOOUSA
REVERT, FRITZ	23	M	LABR	RRAHOOUSA
MANKOWSKI, JOSEF	26	M	LABR	RRAHOOUSA
NOWAKOWSKA, ANNIELA	22	F	UNKNOWN	RRAHOOUSA
JURNOWSKY, THOMAS	31	M	LABR	RRAHQDUSA
WILKOWSKY, IPOLIT	27	M	LABR	RRAHQDUSA
WASCHLEWSKY, ANDRIS	25	M	LABR	RRAHQDUSA
LIPMANOWITSCH, MICH.	35	M	LABR	RRAHQDUSA
KARLINSKY, PHILIPP	23	M	LABR	RRAHOOUSA

PASSENGER	AGE	SEX	OCCUPATION	PRIV	DES

SHIP: PAVONIA

FROM: BELIZE, LIVINGSTON AND VERA CRUZ
TO: BOSTON
ARRIVED: UNKNOWN

PASSENGER	AGE	SEX	OCCUPATION	PRIV	DES
LKATZ, ARON	28	M	LABR	RRZZZZ	NY
HUBARK, SPRINCE	19	F	SP	RRZZZZ	NY
LAYND, ISAAC	21	M	LABR	RRZZZZ	PA
VOLSKY, JANKEL	25	M	LABR	RRZZZZ	BO
WLOSCHANSKY, RUBEN	45	M	LABR	RRZZZZ	BO
MOSES	19	M	LABR	RRZZZZ	BO
ZABELL	14	M	LABR	RRZZZZ	BO
HAASE, HERMAN	21	M	LABR	RRZZZZ	NY
LIETZNER, KAPEL	26	M	LABR	RRZZZZ	NY
ROHRITS, NOPL	47	M	LABR	RRZZZZ	NY
SARAH	38	F	W	RRZZZZ	NY
EITCHISKY, HIRSCH	27	M	LABR	RRZZZZ	NY
BUNNUSKY, LEIB	20	M	LABR	RRZZZZ	NY
EIDEL	19	F	SP	RRZZZZ	NY
MOTOWSKY, BEILE	16	F	SP	RRZZZZ	NY
HALPERIN, SALOME	11	M	CH	RRZZZZ	NY
BUSCHEL, CHIEL	23	M	LABR	RRZZZZ	NY
WEITZMANN, ABRAH	27	M	GDNR	RRZZZZ	NY
CHAUTZIN, KOPEL	17	M	LABR	RRZZZZ	NY
SCHWARZ, ALTER	35	M	LABR	RRZZZZ	NY
RAHEL	40	F	W	RRZZZZ	NY
WELNER, LEA	28	F	MA	RRZZZZ	NY
INETA	6	F	CHILD	RRZZZZ	NY
CHENNA	2	F	CHILD	RRZZZZ	NY
SARA	.11	F	INFANT	RRZZZZ	NY
ORELOWITZ, FERGE	28	M	MA	RRZZZZ	NY
REIVE	.07	M	INFANT	RRZZZZ	NY
GORDON, BASCHE	22	F	MA	RRZZZZ	NY
NOCHEM	.10	M	INFANT	RRZZZZ	NY
GREESBORD, KALMAR	16	M	LABR	RRZZZZ	NY
STILLMANN, BARUCH	30	M	LABR	RRZZZZ	NY
KOSJOL, ALEXANDER	38	M	LABR	RRZZZZ	NY
NOTCK, LEA	20	F	MA	RRZZZZ	NY
BRZYSKI, FRANCISEK	26	M	LABR	RRZZZZ	NY
VICTORIA	21	F	W	RRZZZZ	NY
BINE, JENTE	21	F	MA	RRZZZZ	NY
MOSES	.11	M	INFANT	RRZZZZ	NY
SEEDMANN, SESTE	11	M	CH	RRZZZZ	NY
MELZER, ISRAEL	18	M	LABR	RRZZZZ	NY
SELDE	16	F	W	RRZZZZ	NY
STRASCHAN, HIRSCH	26	M	LABR	RRZZZZ	BO
WERNICK, MEYER	29	M	LABR	RRZZZZ	PA
RAVUSCHKOW, ABRAH	26	M	LABR	RRZZZZ	NY
MILSCHEN, ISAAC	39	M	LABR	RRZZZZ	NY
SIMSON, BARUCH	30	M	LABR	RRZZZZ	NY
LAPPIN, MICK	45	M	LABR	RRZZZZ	NY
KARPAS, ABRAHAM	38	M	LABR	RRZZZZ	BO
LIDIN, ELIAS	36	M	LABR	RRZZZZ	NY
KRIM, KIWE	19	M	LABR	RRZZZZ	NY
KROWITZ, ABRAH	34	M	LABR	RRZZZZ	NY
PROCZYTZKY, SALOMS	28	M	LABR	RRZZZZ	NY
HIRSCH, RUBEN	22	M	LABR	RRZZZZ	BO
ARENKTAM, JULIUS	18	M	CL	RRZZZZ	BO
KLATZKI, ABRAH	00	M	LABR	RRZZZZ	BO
LUERGBAUM, LEA	34	F	MA	RRZZZZ	NY
CHASEL	11	M	CH	RRZZZZ	NY
HIRSCH	7	M	CHILD	RRZZZZ	NY
MOSES	3	M	CHILD	RRZZZZ	NY
CHAIM	.11	M	INFANT	RRZZZZ	NY

SHIP: SERVIA

FROM: LIVERPOOL AND QUEENSTOWN
TO: NEW YORK
ARRIVED: 25 JANUARY 1888

PASSENGER	AGE	SEX	OCCUPATION	PRIV	DES
BUTKOWSKY, MARIA	16	F	SP	RRZZZZ	NY
WILKIN, ELIAS	27	M	PDLR	RRZZZZ	NY
FIEN, SCHIFFRE	25	F	W	RRZZZZ	NY
ISRAELOWITZ, MICHL.	21	M	CGRMKR	RRZZZZ	NY
HOSZKIEWIEZ, MORRIS	21	M	TLR	RRZZZZ	NY
BRODE, HEUTZ	46	M	MCHT	RRZZZZ	NY
LEA	45	F	W	RRZZZZ	NY
REIZL	11	F	CH	RRZZZZ	NY
EPRASIN	10	M	CH	RRZZZZ	NY
ESTER	5	F	CHILD	RRZZZZ	NY
SIMEHE	3	M	CHILD	RRZZZZ	NY
KOSLOWSKY, ISAAC	25	M	TLR	RRZZZZ	NY
JENTE	20	F	W	RRZZZZ	NY
PFEIFFER, ALFRED	29	M	MCHT	RRZZZZ	CAL

SHIP: EIDER

FROM: BREMERHAVEN AND SOUTHAMPTON
TO: NEW YORK
ARRIVED: 25 JANUARY 1888

PASSENGER	AGE	SEX	OCCUPATION	PRIV	DES
LITWA-TIS, KA-EMIR	30	M	FARMER	RRZZZZ	USA
KOMIS	8	M	CHILD	RRZZZZ	USA
GUMPERT, LANDOLF	40	M	LABR	RRZZZZ	USA
GRZIBOWSKY, ANARZI	23	M	LABR	RRZZZZ	USA

SHIP: RUGIA

FROM: HAMBURG
TO: NEW YORK
ARRIVED: 25 JANUARY 1888

PASSENGER	AGE	SEX	OCCUPATION	PRIV	DES
KALISKE, ABRAHAM	31	M	TLR	RRZZZZ	USA
LIPSCHUETZ, ROSA	50	F	W	RRZZZZ	USA
MATHL	18	F	SGL	RRZZZZ	USA
BRZOZA, PHIL.	38	M	DLR	RRZZZZ	USA
NIEWCZYK, PAULINE	28	F	W	RRZZZZ	USA
MINNA	6	F	CHILD	RRZZZZ	USA
CARL	4	M	CHILD	RRZZZZ	USA
JOH.	.11	M	INFANT	RRZZZZ	USA
REINERT, MASCHE	18	F	SGL	RRZZZZ	USA
DELSON, REBECCA	19	F	SGL	RRZZZZ	USA
DWORE	17	F	SGL	RRZZZZ	USA
GLUECKMANN, ESTHER	45	F	W	RRZZZZ	USA
MOTEL	9	F	CHILD	RRZZZZ	USA
LIPE	8	F	CHILD	RRZZZZ	USA
MACHBI, SAMUEL	35	M	LABR	RRZZZZ	USA
CHAIM	9	M	CHILD	RRZZZZ	USA
MARDACZEWITZ, JOS.	18	M	LABR	RRZZZZ	USA
OLDAKOWSKI, JOS.	16	M	LABR	RRZZZZ	USA
LEWANDOWSKI, VAD.	23	M	LABR	RRZZZZ	USA
LORENZ, FRANZ	25	M	LABR	RRZZZZ	USA
ZABLONSKI, FRANZ	24	M	LABR	RRZZZZ	USA
KOSCHINSKY, LUDW.	30	M	LABR	RRZZZZ	USA
KOSCHELATZKI, IGNATZ	23	M	LABR	RRZZZZ	USA
MATHEASZ, WOYCECH	33	M	LABR	RRZZZZ	USA
ZENSKI, JOS.	25	M	LABR	RRZZZZ	USA
GOSINSKI, MARIAM	23	M	LABR	RRZZZZ	USA

PASSENGER	AGE	SEX	OCCUPATION	PRV VIL DES
BALITZKI, FRANZ	47	M	LABR	RRZZZZUSA
SCHLEIFKOWSKI, JOS.	18	M	LABR	RRZZZZUSA
ZIPLICOWSKI, MOSES	18	M	LABR	RRZZZZUSA
HABURA, WASYL	19	M	LABR	RRZZZZUSA
DALLAK, JATZKO	43	M	LABR	RRZZZZUSA
NATHALIE	9	F	CHILD	RRZZZZUSA
RABINOWITZ, NOACHIM	46	F	SGL	RRZZZZUSA
DAVID	26	M	SGL	RRZZZZUSA
PESCHE	19	F	SGL	RRZZZZUSA
JOSEPH	19	M	DLR	RRZZZZUSA
ABRAMSKI, S.	55	M	LABR	RRZZZZUSA
CZINSZINSKA, MARIANNE	26	F	SGL	RRZZZZUSA
CHIAIKIM, SAMUEL	53	M	FARMER	RRZZZZUSA
MOSES	17	M	APTC	RRZZZZUSA
LIPSCHUETZ, ROSA	50	F	W	RRZZZZUSA

SHIP: DEVONIA

FROM: GLASGOW
TO: NEW YORK
ARRIVED: 26 JANUARY 1888

PASSENGER	AGE	SEX	OCCUPATION	PRV VIL DES
BOBELLUS, ANTONIUS	22	M	LABR	RRZZZZUSA
MISCHISKAIS, JOS	23	M	LABR	RRZZZZUSA
ORENT, ANTONIO	24	M	LABR	RRZZZZUSA
LINDE, BUNE	45	F	UNKNOWN	RRABQBUSA
MOTEL	11	M	UNKNOWN	RRABQBUSA
ITZIG	6	M	CHILD	RRABQBUSA
GRUBNBERG, DAVID	26	M	LABR	RRAHTUUSA
GRAMBO, PIOL	30	M	LABR	RRAGRTUSA
NADEL, RAFAEL	26	M	BCHR	RRAGRTUSA
WASCHINKOWITZ, ISRAEL	22	M	LABR	RRZZZZUSA
HOFFMANN, MAJE	18	F	SVNT	RRAHTUUSA
ROSENTHAL, SARAH	20	F	SVNT	RRZZZZUSA

SHIP: AMERICA

FROM: BREMEN
TO: BALTIMORE
ARRIVED: 26 JANUARY 1888

PASSENGER	AGE	SEX	OCCUPATION	PRV VIL DES
KOLOKEWSKI, CONSTANTIN	29	M	FARMER	RRZZZZUSA
MOMEWSKI, STEPHAN	33	M	FARMER	RRZZZZUSA
WYTKOWSKY, STANISL.	40	M	FARMER	RRZZZZUSA
MICHELMANN, MEINE	20	M	FARMER	RRZZZZUSA
ZUCKER, PESE	19	M	FARMER	RRZZZZUSA
MUELLER, MINNA	13	F	CH	RRZZZZUSA
HOFF, ISAANE	16	F	SVNT	RRZZZZUSA
ROSANOWSKY, LEONHARD	36	M	SHMK	RRZZZZUSA
JOSEFA	23	F	W	RRZZZZUSA
POLOGIA	3	F	CHILD	RRZZZZUSA
JOSEFA	.11	F	INFANT	RRZZZZUSA
KODROWSKI, AUGUST	30	M	FARMER	RRZZZZUSA
CLARA	20	F	W	RRZZZZUSA
BERNHARD	2	M	CHILD	RRZZZZUSA

SHIP: PENNLAND

FROM: ANTWERP
TO: NEW YORK
ARRIVED: 27 JANUARY 1888

PASSENGER	AGE	SEX	OCCUPATION	PRV VIL DES
SARKOWSKY, SARAH	50	F	NN	PLZZZZNY
SCHONE	17	F	NN	PLZZZZNY
LEVI	15	M	NN	PLZZZZNY
RIBANOWSKY, GILDA	50	F	NN	PLZZZZPHI

SHIP: ST. OF PENNSYLVANIA

FROM: GLASGOW AND LARNE
TO: NEW YORK
ARRIVED: 28 JANUARY 1888

PASSENGER	AGE	SEX	OCCUPATION	PRV VIL DES
ALEXANDROWICZ, PERCY	23	M	MCHT	RRZZZZUSA
BRINBERG, JACOB	33	M	MCHT	RRAIDHUSA
CHANNE	30	F	UNKNOWN	RRAIDHUSA
MARGARETHE	3	F	CHILD	RRAIDHUSA
HEINRICH	2	M	CHILD	RRAIDHUSA
TANE	.06	F	INFANT	RRAIDHUSA
DOBOWA, CLARA	22	F	MNR	RRAIDHUSA
JACOB	2	M	CHILD	RRAIDHUSA
SIMON	.07	M	INFANT	RRAIDHUSA
FEID, ANNA	19	F	SVNT	RRAIDHUSA
FELDMANN, MANKUS	35	F	MCHT	RRAIDHUSA
FEINBERG, ARON	30	M	MCHT	RRAIDHUSA
FRANK, MORITZ	23	M	MCHT	RRAIDHUSA
GEDINSKI, TATIANA	22	F	SVNT	RRAINYUSA
FELBERMAN, HERMAN	3	M	CHILD	RRAIDHUSA
MARIA	1	F	CHILD	RRAIDHUSA
HARKAVE, GITEL	17	F	SVNT	RRZZZZUSA
JAFFE, ABEL	35	M	TLR	RRZZZZUSA
KATZ, GOLDA	30	F	W	RRZZZZUSA
JOSSEL	2	M	CHILD	RRZZZZUSA
HIRSCH	1	F	CHILD	RRZZZZUSA
KANSKY, PETER	30	M	CPTR	RRZZZZUSA
LUSTY, SALY	18	F	SVNT	RRZZZZUSA
MARSHROCK, SCHEINDEL	16	M	SVNT	RRZZZZUSA
MULLER, ISSER	30	M	TNM	RRZZZZUSA
MISKA, JOHN	22	M	LABR	RRZZZZUSA
MOLIWICZKY, MENDEL	25	M	MCHT	RRZZZZUSA
PORLEWSKY, JUDEL	27	M	MCHT	RRZZZZUSA
SCHNEIDER, DINKE	22	F	W	RRZZZZUSA

SHIP: AUSTRALIA

FROM: HAMBURG
TO: NEW YORK
ARRIVED: 28 JANUARY 1888

PASSENGER	AGE	SEX	OCCUPATION	PRV VIL DES
CARICKI, ANTON	20	M	LABR	RRZZZZNY
SMOKOWSKI, GRANIKI	18	F	FLWMKR	RRZZZZNY
KULSKI, ELIAS	16	M	CGRMKR	RRZZZZNY
CINRER, MICHAL	24	M	LABR	RRZZZZNY
ZAKLOWSKI, ANTON	44	M	LABR	RRZZZZNY
KRAWICZ, LANKO	17	M	LABR	RRZZZZNY
MAWSCHOWITZ, SORACH	20	M	LABR	RRZZZZNY
JAGEWSKI, JOS.	27	M	LABR	RRZZZZNY
STEFAN, ANDR.	38	M	LABR	RRZZZZNY
ROSDAN, ABRAHAM	17	M	DLR	RRZZZZUNK
MISCHER, SANOS	43	M	LABR	RRZZZZUNK

PASSENGER	AGE	SEX	OCCUPATION	PRVIL	DES
EISENBERG, ARON	18	M	TLR	RRZZZZ	UNK
HOCHBERG, BACCE	55	F	WO	RRZZZZ	UNK
JENNY	18	F	D	RRZZZZ	UNK
ELIAS	9	M	CHILD	RRZZZZ	UNK
RUD.	8	M	CHILD	RRZZZZ	UNK
WANZIKOWSKY, ADAM	21	M	LABR	RRZZZZ	UNK
KREIT, BERIL	30	M	TNM	RRZZZZ	UNK
SCHAECHTMANN, JANKEL	20	M	TLR	RRZZZZ	UNK
HARTBROD, BASCHE	21	F	SVNT	RRZZZZ	DET
GRUNDLER, HERM.	32	M	LKSH	RRZZZZ	NY
WILH.	30	F	W	RRZZZZ	NY
MARG.	4	F	CHILD	RRZZZZ	NY
RICH.	.11	M	INFANT	RRZZZZ	NY
BRENDA, BEHR.	22	M	MCHT	RRZZZZ	NY
WERBSA, MOSES	22	M	DLR	RRZZZZ	NY
ZYNOSKI, ADAM	38	M	MSN	RRZZZZ	CH

SHIP: SAALE

FROM: BREMEN
TO: NEW YORK
ARRIVED: 30 JANUARY 1888

PASSENGER	AGE	SEX	OCCUPATION	PRVIL	DES
REIMBERG, REGINA	40	F	UNKNOWN	RRZZZZ	USA
SCHMIDT, GEROG	28	M	DR	RRZZZZ	USA
SCHULHERR, SIGM.	17	M	CL	RRZZZZ	USA
LINDHEIMER, MATHDE.	16	F	UNKNOWN	RRZZZZ	USA
SUESSKIND, JACOB	37	M	MCHT	RRZZZZ	USA
REINKE, JOSEF	23	M	FARMER	RRZZZZ	USA
LIMBURGER, JUL.	24	M	MCHT	RRZZZZ	USA
SCHNIEB, ALFRED	20	M	MCHT	RRZZZZ	USA
SOMMER, MAX	18	M	CL	RRZZZZ	USA
THOMAS, EMIL	21	M	BCHR	RRZZZZ	USA
EPPINGER, MAX	19	M	JNR	RRZZZZ	USA
JACOB	16	M	TLR	RRZZZZ	USA
FUERTH, KARL	20	M	SMH	RRZZZZ	USA
THOMAS, ERNST	25	M	CPTR	RRZZZZ	USA
SCHLUETER, HEINR.	24	M	PNTR	RRZZZZ	USA
STECKER, ANNA	14	F	UNKNOWN	RRZZZZ	USA
GERCKEN, ANNA	17	F	UNKNOWN	RRZZZZ	USA
BOHLMANN, SOPHIE	45	F	UNKNOWN	RRZZZZ	USA
GOEKE, AUG.	16	M	BKR	RRZZZZ	USA
FEIST, MARIANE	40	F	UNKNOWN	RRZZZZ	USA
SCHLUETER, MARIE	18	F	UNKNOWN	RRZZZZ	USA
TIEDEMANN, CARL	16	M	BKLYR	RRZZZZ	USA
ILCHMAN, WILH.	31	M	BKLYR	RRZZZZ	USA
MARTHA	3	F	CHILD	RRZZZZ	USA
GERTRUDE	.11	F	INFANT	RRZZZZ	USA
DERRA, MARIA	18	F	UNKNOWN	RRZZZZ	USA
DIEHL, PETER	26	M	LABR	RRZZZZ	USA
ZITSCH, MARIE	22	F	UNKNOWN	RRZZZZ	USA
REICHERT, BARBA.	20	F	UNKNOWN	RRZZZZ	USA
THIERSTEIN, ADELHDE.	30	F	UNKNOWN	RRZZZZ	USA
BERGER, CARL	23	M	SMH	RRZZZZ	USA
POELTE, JOSEF	35	M	SHMK	RRZZZZ	USA
BRAUN, JOSEF	38	M	SHMK	RRZZZZ	USA
MACKIEWICZ, LIEZER	33	M	LABR	RRZZZZ	USA
JUDELAWSKY, HIRSCH	18	M	LABR	RRZZZZ	USA
BEDNARSKY, JOS.	28	M	LABR	RRZZZZ	USA
NANNDTKOWA, FRANZKA.	26	F	W	RRZZZZ	USA
JULIAN	3	M	CHILD	RRZZZZ	USA
KURPYESKA, AGATA	22	F	W	RRZZZZ	USA
FRANZ	37	M	LABR	RRZZZZ	USA
VERONICA	.11	F	INFANT	RRZZZZ	USA
PANGONIS, FELIX	23	M	LABR	RRZZZZ	USA
LAUSTATZKUS, ANTON	25	F	UNKNOWN	RRZZZZ	USA
SUBRYS, JOSEF	28	M	LABR	RRZZZZ	USA
WRONA, SCHLAMA	21	F	UNKNOWN	RRZZZZ	USA
RIRCHENHORN, RUCHLA	19	F	UNKNOWN	RRZZZZ	USA
ZEITLIN, ZIWGE	39	M	LABR	RRZZZZ	USA

PASSENGER	AGE	SEX	OCCUPATION	PRVIL	DES
LUBA	18	F	UNKNOWN	RRZZZZ	USA
NEMETZKI, HENACH	38	M	LABR	RRZZZZ	USA

SHIP: GERMANIC

FROM: LIVERPOOL AND QUEENSTOWN
TO: NEW YORK
ARRIVED: 30 JANUARY 1888

PASSENGER	AGE	SEX	OCCUPATION	PRVIL	DES
HALEWSKI, EFRIAM	58	M	LABR	PLZZZZ	USA
LECI	20	M	LABR	PLZZZZ	USA
FREEDEL	11	M	CH	PLZZZZ	USA
IHESSER, ITZEK	11	M	CH	PLZZZZ	USA
GOTTEMANN, ABRAM	29	M	LABR	PLZZZZ	USA
HELEPINA, MIBE	27	M	LABR	PLZZZZ	USA
GELEZYNSKI, ISAAK	28	M	LABR	PLZZZZ	USA
FENER, NOAH	23	M	LABR	PLZZZZ	USA
LEWFKOWITZ, SCHEWE	18	F	LABR	PLZZZZ	USA
FRANKELDSEN, HINDA	58	F	W	PLZZZZ	USA
MELWICKI, JULIA	43	F	W	PLZZZZ	USA
VOGEL, CHA	21	M	LABR	PLZZZZ	USA
KOSSACH, RAFALEL	40	M	LABR	PLZZZZ	USA
CHANNE	40	F	W	PLZZZZ	USA
LIPE	21	M	LABR	PLZZZZ	USA
KUSCH	8	M	CHILD	PLZZZZ	USA
LOLE	3	M	CHILD	PLZZZZ	USA
BARACHE	1	F	CHILD	PLZZZZ	USA

SHIP: GALLIA

FROM: LIVERPOOL AND QUEENSTOWN
TO: NEW YORK
ARRIVED: 01 FEBRUARY 1888

PASSENGER	AGE	SEX	OCCUPATION	PRVIL	DES
HELNI, WILLIAM	33	M	CPTR	FNZZZZ	SFC
MARKEL, DAVID	22	M	TLR	FNACBF	USA
SALOMON, MARCUS	19	M	LABR	FNACBF	USA
PEKER, SELIG	18	M	LABR	FNACBF	USA
LUBOWSKY, ABRAH	19	M	LABR	FNACBF	USA
NADEL, SIMON	23	M	TLR	FNACBF	USA
WEISS, JANKEL	20	M	TLR	FNACBF	USA
NASCHKOWITZ, LEIZER	32	M	LABR	FNACBF	USA
SLABOTZKI, SAM	17	M	LABR	FNACBF	USA
SILBERBERG, JACOB	22	M	TLR	FNACBF	USA
GRODZINSKI, PAUL	17	M	LABR	FNAIJO	USA
SCHULMANN, SAM	18	M	LABR	FNAIJO	USA
BOJARSKI, JASEL	17	M	LABR	FNACBF	USA
GEUNBERG, JOSEPH	29	M	TLR	FNACBF	USA
TRUBATZ, SCHALEM	25	M	LABR	FNACBF	USA
MELZER, HIRSCH	29	M	LABR	FNACBF	USA
SCHMALSAL, SCHMULKE	20	M	TLR	FNACBF	USA
STANISLAUSKI, ISRAEL	28	M	LABR	FNACBF	USA
GERBER, ABRAHAM	18	M	LABR	FNACBF	USA
LUBOWITZ, MOSES	20	M	LABR	FNACBF	USA
ESCHELBAUM, ALBER	22	M	LABR	FNACBF	USA
CHASMANN, ARAN	35	M	LABR	FNACBF	USA
NOLL, MOSES	35	M	LABR	FNACBF	USA
GALDBERG, LEIB	38	M	LABR	FNACBF	USA
ITZKOWITZ, SALOMON	23	M	LABR	FNACBF	USA
EPSTEIN, MORDECHA	24	M	LABR	FNACBF	USA
SCHUSTER, SCHEU	24	M	SHMK	FNACBF	USA
KORBE, REBECCA	48	F	MA	FNACBF	USA
CHANE	20	F	SVNT	FNACBF	USA
PELTER, RAHEL	24	F	SVNT	FNACBF	USA
WATTEL, RIEVE	20	F	MA	FNACBF	USA

PASSENGER	AGE	SEX	OCCUPATION	PRV VIL DES
FEUSTER, MARIAN	17	F	SVNT	FNACBFUSA
LEWIN, ARON	36	M	LABR	FNACBFUSA
RIGNIKOWSKI, ALTER	11	M	CH	FNACBFUSA
MOSES	10	M	CH	FNACBFUSA
CERIL	4	F	CHILD	FNACBFUSA
GOMONDSKI, TAUBE	23	F	MA	FNACBFUSA
SAMUEL	1	M	CHILD	FNACBFUSA
ORAN, SUSCHE	22	M	LABR	FNACBFUSA
GITEL	22	F	W	FNACBFUSA
MAZEPA, KASTKA	25	F	MA	FNACBFUSA
WAGNER, ROSE	35	F	MA	FNACBFUSA
MOSES	9	M	CHILD	FNACBFUSA
FIGE	6	M	CHILD	FNACBFUSA
MARKUS	3	F	CHILD	FNACBFUSA
GERSON	2	M	CHILD	FNACBFUSA

SHIP: LAKE HURON

FROM: GALWAY AND LONDON
TO: BOSTON
ARRIVED: UNKNOWN H

PASSENGER	AGE	SEX	OCCUPATION	PRV VIL DES
LASCHKIN, JOHN	20	M	FARMER	RRZZZZBUF
SUMBERG, ABRAHAM	26	M	TLR	RRZZZZNY
POSNAK, PAUL	23	M	BTMKR	RRZZZZPHI
RABBINOWITZ, HARRIS	35	M	TLR	RRZZZZKS
U, LAZARUS	34	M	APTC	RRZZZZNY
TAYLOR, JACOB	23	M	APTC	RRZZZZNY
LUCAS, MAX	35	M	PRCH	RRZZZZNY
BELINKES, WLADUK	24	M	LABR	RRZZZZNY
BUNEMOURTZ, MOSSEN	21	M	LABR	RRZZZZNY
URBANOWITZ, JOHAN	21	M	CPTR	RRZZZZNY
TEREVITCH, ANTON	46	M	CPTR	RRZZZZNY
TOMAPOLSKI, TERWASCH	20	M	TLR	RRZZZZNY
BOAZEWSKI, MENDEL	20	M	CPMKR	RRZZZZNY
FRANZKOWITZ, ANTON	25	M	LABR	RRZZZZNY
ADAMOWITZ, JOSEF	33	M	LABR	RRZZZZNY
GABELAIS, ASSIS	23	M	LABR	RRZZZZNY
LISIS, PETRIS	30	M	SMH	RRZZZZNY
MADEIKE, JOHAN	29	M	TLR	RRZZZZNY

SHIP: GERMANIC

FROM: LIVERPOOL AND QUEENSTOWN
TO: NEW YORK
ARRIVED: 02 FEBRUARY 1888

PASSENGER	AGE	SEX	OCCUPATION	PRV VIL DES
BUKOWITZ, ABRAHAM	26	M	LABR	RRZZZZUSA
GRAGINSKI, LEIH	43	M	LABR	RRZZZZUSA

SHIP: BOHEMIA

FROM: HAMBURG AND HAVRE
TO: NEW YORK
ARRIVED: 02 FEBRUARY 1888

PASSENGER	AGE	SEX	OCCUPATION	PRV VIL DES
STENELINSKA, JAN	26	M	LABR	RRZZZZUSA
DIMANDSTEIN, HETTEL	21	F	W	RRAHXLUSA
DAVID	.11	M	INFANT	RRAHXLUSA
ADAMSKI, MACZIC	32	M	LABR	RRZZZZUSA

PASSENGER	AGE	SEX	OCCUPATION	PRV VIL DES
BIELITZKI, MARIELL	41	M	LABR	RRZZZZUSA
ROMAN	35	M	LABR	RRZZZZUSA
URBANSKI, JOS.	38	M	LABR	RRZZZZUSA
SALEGA, WLADISLAW	28	M	LABR	RRZZZZUSA
MORGAN, PETER	26	M	LABR	RRAHZSUSA
EISENBERG, JANKEL	40	M	DLR	RRZZZZUSA
SPINAK, MOTTLE	17	F	SGL	RRZZZZUSA
BRAUN, ROBT	23	M	STDNT	RRAIKNUSA
PRUSSOT, WILH.	49	M	LABR	RRAIGHUSA
ANNA	34	F	W	RRAIGHUSA
BORANIC, AMBROSIAS	25	M	LABR	RRAIGHUSA
WITTE, JOH	27	M	LABR	RRAIGHUSA
JAKSLIS, PETER	27	M	LABR	RRAIGHUSA
BELSKY, LUDWIG	25	M	LABR	RRAIGHUSA
RUNKUS, LEON	23	M	LABR	RRAIGHUSA
BUNULUS, KAS	28	M	LABR	RRAIGHUSA
WANAZOS, ALMO	28	M	LABR	RRAIGHUSA
BURAKUS, DANIEL	23	M	LABR	RRAIGHUSA
BOGIS, ANDRAS	27	M	LABR	RRAHZSUSA
POLANKOSKI, STANISL	28	M	LABR	RRZZZZUSA
RUCZKOWSKI, JAN	44	M	LABR	RRZZZZUSA
CICZKIWICZ, VINCENT	26	M	LABR	RRAHZSUSA
GRUBART, TAUBE	20	F	SGL	RRZZZZUSA
JANORSIK, ISTWAN	24	M	LABR	RRZZZZUSA
SARTANOWICZ, JAN	19	M	LABR	RRZZZZUSA
ISROLUK, LEIB	36	M	TLR	RRZZZZUSA
WOINKO, NICODEM	20	M	LABR	RRAHZSUSA
HORNE, HEDWIG	17	F	SGL	RRAFVGUSA
LEIB	9	F	CHILD	RRAFVGUSA
CHAIN	7	F	CHILD	RRAFVGUSA
EFROIM	5	M	CHILD	RRAFVGUSA
KUCHARSKI, RIVKE	45	F	WO	RRAFVGUSA
ABR.	3	F	CHILD	RRAFVGUSA
KASARNOWSKY, STANISL	33	M	MCHT	RRAHOOUSA

SHIP: ETRURIA

FROM: LIVERPOOL
TO: NEW YORK
ARRIVED: 02 FEBRUARY 1888

PASSENGER	AGE	SEX	OCCUPATION	PRV VIL DES
BAND, REBECCA	11	F	CH	RRADAXUSA
BOROTKIN, MARCUS	23	M	LABR	RRADAXUSA
BETT, ROSA	25	F	MA	RRADAXUSA
BOGIN, DAUL	18	M	PDLR	RRADAXUSA
DWORSKE, ROSA	18	F	SP	RRADAXUSA
U, LEA	11	F	CH	RRADAXUSA
DAVEDOWITSCH, JANKEL	24	M	LABR	RRADAXUSA
JENKEL, MOSES	24	M	UNKNOWN	RRADAXUSA
MOTTLES, CHAIN	26	M	UNKNOWN	RRADAXUSA
EMMER, LEA	22	F	SP	RRADAXUSA
EIDLESTEIN, ARON	23	M	CPRSMH	RRADAXUSA
TEODOROWESZ, KASIMIR	25	M	LABR	RRADAXUSA
GASCHKAVSKY, MEYER	21	M	LKSH	RRADAXUSA
GODPAN, DALOMO	56	M	LABR	RRADAXUSA
HARAWITZ, MOSES	22	M	CL	RRADAXUSA
HAMM, GOŁDE	18	F	SP	RRADAXUSA
JUGRLAWRIEZ, KACIMIR	29	M	LABR	RRADAXUSA
KUPRITZ, MOSES	21	M	UNKNOWN	RRADAXUSA
KALLMANN, SAMUEL	32	M	UNKNOWN	RRADAXUSA
KLATZKO, DAVID	25	M	CGRMKR	RRADAXUSA
KUPER, LEISER	20	M	PNTR	RRADAXUSA
KAHAN, ABRAHAM	37	M	LABR	RRADAXUSA
LUCHFEL, MOSES	48	M	MCHT	RRADAXUSA
LUFESK-, SIMECH	22	M	UNKNOWN	RRADAXUSA
LEIBOWI, FEIWISCH	32	M	GDSM	RRADAXUSA
POLLENOWSKI, DEHAGE	33	M	UNKNOWN	RRADAXUSA
CHAIN	00	M	UNKNOWN	RRADAXUSA
POLACK, JACOB	00	M	LABR	RRADAXUSA
U, ABRAHAM	44	M	PNTR	RRADAXUSA

PASSENGER	AGE	SEX	OCCUPATION	PRIVL	DES
STAVISKER, LASCHA	42	M	LABR	RRADAX	USA
BENDEROW, MENDEL	22	M	UNKNOWN	RRADAX	USA
STREIN, CHAI	16	F	SP	RRADAX	USA
SLOT, MICHEL	24	M	LABR	RRADAX	USA
STRONGIN, ELIZA	27	M	TLR	RRADAX	USA
ISRAEL	6	M	CHILD	RRADAX	USA
NECHANE	11	M	CH	RRADAX	USA
BILET, ANTON	22	M	LABR	RRADAX	USA
BIDONIS, JOSEPH	35	M	LABR	RRADAX	USA
WOYLACKE, GELADYE	28	M	CGRMKR	RRADAX	USA

SHIP: CALIFORNIA

FROM: HAMBURG
TO: NEW YORK
ARRIVED: 03 FEBRUARY 1888

PASSENGER	AGE	SEX	OCCUPATION	PRIVL	DES
ANDRULEITZ, AUGUSTIN	21	M	LABR	RRZZZZ	NY
JETKO, KARL	16	M	LABR	RRZZZZ	NY
AMALIA	9	F	CHILD	RRZZZZ	NY
KORENKEWITZ, HELENE	24	F	UNKNOWN	RRZZZZ	NY
BALUTA, ANDRE	17	M	LABR	RRZZZZ	NY
ULUSZEK, JOH.	30	M	LABR	RRZZZZ	NY
WICZNIEWSKY, JOS.	24	M	LABR	RRZZZZ	NY
ALEKO--Y, HEUMANN	31	M	LKSH	RRZZZZ	NY
TOBJES, SIMON	22	M	JNR	RRZZZZ	NY
DORFMANN, LEIB	19	M	DLR	RRZZZZ	NY
MALENOWITZ, SCHLOMER	26	M	JNR	RRZZZZ	NY
KRUK, SARA	50	F	UNKNOWN	RRZZZZ	NY
SINKEWITZ, JOS.	18	M	LABR	RRZZZZ	NY
NAMIOTKI, JOS.	22	M	LABR	RRZZZZ	NY
SOCHODA, DANIEL	18	M	DLR	RRZZZZ	NY
SWIRSKY, ABR.	20	M	LABR	RRZZZZ	NY
BENSEL, BERTHA	42	F	UNKNOWN	RRZZZZ	NY
GABRIEL	15	M	UNKNOWN	RRZZZZ	NY
ISIDOR	9	M	CHILD	RRZZZZ	NY
SARA	8	F	CHILD	RRZZZZ	NY
CARIUS	7	M	CHILD	RRZZZZ	NY
LISA	6	F	CHILD	RRZZZZ	NY
ARNHOLD	4	M	CHILD	RRZZZZ	NY
ELISA	.11	F	INFANT	RRZZZZ	NY
KUFERT, GUSTE	32	F	W	RRZZZZ	NY
MAREUS	8	M	CHILD	RRZZZZ	NY
LANG, LEONARD	22	M	MCHT	RRZZZZ	NY
MARDER, CHASKEL	25	M	MCHT	RRZZZZ	NY

SHIP: AMALFI

FROM: HAMBURG
TO: NEW YORK
ARRIVED: 03 FEBRUARY 1888

PASSENGER	AGE	SEX	OCCUPATION	PRIVL	DES
LAVATA, LEON	31	M	LABR	RRZZZZ	USA
ZIMINOWSKI, SARAH	9	F	CHILD	RRZZZZ	USA
SCHEINE	8	M	CHILD	RRZZZZ	USA
ROMANOV, ISAAC	9	M	CHILD	RRZZZZ	USA
LEISER	8	F	CHILD	RRZZZZ	USA
ZARANSKI, ANTONIA	17	F	SGL	RRZZZZ	USA
GORECKE, MARY	.03	F	INFANT	RRZZZZ	USA
BRANDT, FRIEDRICH	21	M	TLR	RRZZZZ	USA
LEIFER, SCHAYRRE	31	M	UNKNOWN	RRZZZZ	USA
DISKIN, MOITSCHE	55	M	GDNR	RRZZZZ	USA
KISCHNAWCKE, ALEXANDER	00	M	LABR	RRZZZZ	USA
BUSDZINSKI, MIHAL	26	F	W	RRZZZZ	USA
CATHA	26	F	D	RRZZZZ	USA

PASSENGER	AGE	SEX	OCCUPATION	PRIVL	DES
MARIANE	2	F	CHILD	RRZZZZ	USA
JOH.	.11	M	INFANT	RRZZZZ	USA
SCHREIDMANN, ANNA	26	F	WO	RRZZZZ	USA
PAULINE	3	F	CHILD	RRZZZZ	USA
PALE	.11	M	INFANT	RRZZZZ	USA
LEWIN, DAVID	26	M	DLR	RRZZZZ	USA
WODKOWSKI, CASIMIR	18	M	LABR	RRZZZZ	USA
MAKOWSKI, JOSEF	20	M	LABR	RRZZZZ	USA
STRGZAK, LEIB	36	M	LABR	RRZZZZ	USA
POTRABINK, SOMON	35	M	DLR	RRZZZZ	USA
MAGITZ, LEON	17	M	MCHT	RRZZZZ	USA

SHIP: POLYNESIAN

FROM: LIVERPOOL
TO: BALTIMORE
ARRIVED: 03 FEBRUARY 1888

PASSENGER	AGE	SEX	OCCUPATION	PRIVL	DES
CHODZEK, GITTEL	20	F	DMS	RRZZZZ	BAL
MISSEWITZ, JAN	24	M	BLKSMH	RRZZZZ	BAL
FODELIO, RASSIMIR	24	M	LABR	RRZZZZ	BAL
SCHEBLINSKY, FRANZ	23	M	FARMER	RRZZZZ	BAL
LUCHONSKY, PIETRO	20	M	FARMER	RRZZZZ	BAL
DOMNIOFSKY, JOSEF	20	M	BLKSMH	RRZZZZ	PIT
CLAFF, SAMUEL	17	M	SHMK	RRZZZZ	BAL
WONSAL, BENJAMIN	30	M	SHMK	RRZZZZ	BAL
RIMAWSKI, HERSCH	22	M	TLR	RRZZZZ	BAL
PELUTIO, JOSEF	26	M	FARMER	RRZZZZ	BAL

SHIP: CEPHALONIA

FROM: LIVERPOOL
TO: BOSTON
ARRIVED: UR UNKNOWN AND

PASSENGER	AGE	SEX	OCCUPATION	PRIVL	DES
SLIPRAN, JACOB	21	M	LABR	RRZZZZ	USA
KLEPPER, JOSEPH	32	M	LABR	RRZZZZ	USA
KURAON, JULIUS	24	M	PPMKR	RRZZZZ	USA
KROMM, BEELE	18	F	SVNT	RRZZZZ	USA
ISCHITZETRIGKI, REBECCA	22	F	MA	RRZZZZ	USA
SCHMURSKY, ELIAS	58	M	SHMK	RRZZZZ	USA
ROSA	32	F	W	RRZZZZ	USA
ANNA	15	F	SP	RRZZZZ	USA
ALEXANDER	10	M	CH	RRZZZZ	USA
WILENSKY, CHANE	30	F	MA	RRZZZZ	USA
MAX	8	M	CHILD	RRZZZZ	USA
EPHRAIM	2	M	CHILD	RRZZZZ	USA
HOFFMAN, MARDECHAI	20	M	LABR	RRZZZZ	USA
FEEGE	16	F	SVNT	RRZZZZ	USA
MATTSON, MATTS	16	M	LABR	FNZZZZ	USA
JYCZKA, MICHAEL	31	M	LABR	PLZZZZ	USA

SHIP: ZAANDAM

FROM: AMSTERDAM
TO: NEW YORK
ARRIVED: 06 FEBRUARY 1888

PASSENGER	AGE	SEX	OCCUPATION	PRIVL	DES
KAPLAN, JOSSEL	22	M	PHRS	RRZZZZ	USA

PASSENGER	AGE	SEX	OCCUPATION	PRVIL	DES

SHIP: RHAETIA

FROM: HAMBURG AND HAVRE
TO: NEW YORK
ARRIVED: 06 FEBRUARY 1888

PASSENGER	AGE	SEX	OCCUPATION	PRVIL	DES
GOLDBERG, CHANNE	28	M	LABR	RRZZZZ	USA
LEIFER, EFRAIM	25	M	LABR	RRZZZZ	USA
SCHMEISSER, SCHMUEL	36	M	LABR	RRZZZZ	USA
PINKIEWIECZ, ANTON	23	M	LABR	RRZZZZ	USA
OKINKIEWICZ, ANNA	30	F	SGL	RRZZZZ	USA
KRICZONIS, IGNATZ	19	M	LABR	RRZZZZ	USA
ANTON	18	M	LABR	RRZZZZ	USA
NIEWALLIS, VINCENT	26	M	LABR	RRZZZZ	USA
CZERNICS, IVAN	41	M	LABR	RRZZZZ	USA
MURANSKY, MARIAN	25	M	LABR	RRZZZZ	USA
WADLANSKY, CONSTANTIN	27	M	LABR	RRZZZZ	USA
DEUTSCHENDORFF, JACOB	22	M	LABR	RRZZZZ	USA
RINKIEWICZ, GEORG	35	M	LABR	RRZZZZ	USA
BRAUN, ABRAH.	47	M	LABR	RRZZZZ	USA
HORNS, SCHACHET	44	F	WO	RRZZZZ	USA
RIEFKE	20	F	CH	RRZZZZ	USA
ELKE	14	M	CH	RRZZZZ	USA
VETSCHE	9	M	CHILD	RRZZZZ	USA
REDLER, MARCUS	23	M	BBR	RRZZZZ	USA
ROSALIE	19	F	W	RRZZZZ	USA
LEWIN, JOISCHEN	23	M	DLR	RRZZZZ	USA
KOPELOWITZ, HIRSCH	29	M	DLR	RRZZZZ	USA
LEVITAS, MEYER	22	M	MUSN	RRZZZZ	USA
KANEGIS, THOMAS	40	M	LABR	RRZZZZ	USA
GOLONBEMSKY, VINCENT	26	M	LABR	RRZZZZ	USA
BROSOVER, SCHMUL	19	M	LABR	RRZZZZ	USA
DWORE	20	M	LABR	RRZZZZ	USA
EPSTEIN, MINDEL	25	F	WO	RRZZZZ	USA
DWORE	.11	M	INFANT	RRZZZZ	USA
GRUSKEWITZ, ANTON	22	M	LABR	RRZZZZ	USA
SELNAK, MAYE	21	M	LABR	RRZZZZ	USA
WOLOKINES, KASTETIN	28	M	LABR	RRZZZZ	USA
KLIFRANES, PETRI	18	M	LABR	RRZZZZ	USA
AMSCHE, ALEXANDER	24	M	LABR	RRZZZZ	USA
LIKOWSKY, JUSCO	22	M	LABR	RRZZZZ	USA
FILLANES, KASTELIN	24	M	LABR	RRZZZZ	USA
WEIKSCHNER, BOLTRE	9	M	CHILD	RRZZZZ	USA

SHIP: ELBE

FROM: BREMEN
TO: NEW YORK
ARRIVED: 06 FEBRUARY 1888

PASSENGER	AGE	SEX	OCCUPATION	PRVIL	DES
ROESSNEK, OTTO	38	M	TT	RRZZZZ	USA
BRUEGGEMANN, PETER	34	M	TT	RRAICG	USA
LEIPUNER, LEIB	24	M	LABR	RRAIL	NY
JANROWSKY, MARCIN	18	M	FARMER	RRAIL	NY
SCHLOSSER, MARTIN	24	M	LABR	RRAIL	NY
KARLIN, CHAJE	20	M	FARMER	RRAIL	NY
ARON	11	M	FARMER	RRAIL	NY
BROZIN, AUG.	26	M	FARMER	RRAIL	NY
STARGENSKY, JAN	26	M	FARMER	RRAIL	NY
MORRIS, AUG.	23	M	FARMER	RRAIL	NY
KARASCH, FELIX	36	M	FARMER	RRAIL	NY
LEWICZKA, ANNIELA	20	F	UNKNOWN	RRAIL	USA
SCHLOSSER, HENRIETTE	24	F	UNKNOWN	RRAIL	USA
WOTKEN, JACOB	36	M	LABR	RRAIL	USA
SOPHIE	33	F	W	RRAIL	USA
ANNA	16	F	CH	RRAIL	USA
MICH.	7	M	CHILD	RRAIL	USA
HILLE	5	M	CHILD	RRAIL	USA
DAVID	4	M	CHILD	RRAIL	USA
SIGAL, MARKUS	28	M	BLKSMH	RRAIL	USA
MALKE	65	F	UNKNOWN	RRAIL	USA
KARASCH, MICHAL	31	M	LABR	RRZZZZ	USA
MARYANA	24	F	W	RRZZZZ	USA
BUBLIK, DAVID	23	M	FARMER	RRZZZZ	USA
CHAJE	23	F	W	RRZZZZ	USA

SHIP: AURANIA

FROM: LIVERPOOL AND QUEENSTOWN
TO: NEW YORK
ARRIVED: 06 FEBRUARY 1888

PASSENGER	AGE	SEX	OCCUPATION	PRVIL	DES
KOMUCA, JOHN	40	M	LABR	FNZZZZ	NY
KAREKKA, MATT	40	M	LABR	FNZZZZ	NY
GELBERT, SAMUEL	37	M	TLR	PLZZZZ	NY
BERKOWITZ, LEIB	22	M	LABR	RRZZZZ	NY
BEILE	22	F	SP	RRZZZZ	NY
BABIN, JANCHON	19	M	SHMK	RRZZZZ	NY
MASUR, ABAND	30	M	TLR	RRZZZZ	NY
CHRIFITZ, SANDER	44	M	CPTR	RRZZZZ	NY
GRUSSER, ISAAC	20	M	HTR	RRZZZZ	NY
LINZNER, JOSEF	19	M	LABR	RRZZZZ	NY
APRLZIN, MOSES	28	M	BKBNDR	RRZZZZ	NY
KASDIN, BERL	24	M	TLR	RRZZZZ	NY
PRRESS, SALOMON	30	M	TLR	RRZZZZ	NY
CHINGIN, MOSES	25	M	TLR	RRZZZZ	NY
SCHENKMANN, HIRSCH	45	M	BRR	RRZZZZ	NY
LIPI	11	M	CH	RRZZZZ	NY
MULLER, SAMUEL	18	M	PNTR	RRZZZZ	NY
BECKER, ABRAH.	23	M	SHMK	RRZZZZ	NY
SCHEFFMANN, JACOB	19	M	GDBT	RRZZZZ	NY
SCHLESTAK, MACHMANN	52	M	LABR	RRZZZZ	CT
ABRAHAM	21	M	LABR	RRZZZZ	CT
SCHNEIDER, CHAIM	30	M	TLR	RRZZZZ	PHI
KIRSCH, MOSES	56	M	MACH	RRZZZZ	NY
GUNNHAUS, WOLF	17	M	SHMK	RRZZZZ	NY
SCHNEIDERMANN, MOSES	30	M	TLR	RRZZZZ	PHI

SHIP: ARABIC

FROM: LIVERPOOL
TO: NEW YORK
ARRIVED: 07 FEBRUARY 1888

PASSENGER	AGE	SEX	OCCUPATION	PRVIL	DES
BLYINSKY, MICHAEL	33	M	LABR	RRACBF	USA
MIHILINPH, KARL	34	M	LABR	RRACBF	USA
MELHORN, AUG	27	M	LABR	RRACBF	USA

SHIP: LAHN

FROM: BREMEN AND SOUTHAMPTON
TO: NEW YORK
ARRIVED: 09 FEBRUARY 1888

PASSENGER	AGE	SEX	OCCUPATION	PRVIL	DES
REIHMANN, MARIE	19	F	UNKNOWN	RRAFWJ	USA
MALCZEWSKY, BRONISL.	30	M	PROF	RRAFWJ	USA
OLGA	24	F	W	RRAFWJ	USA
BRISK, ELIAS	26	M	CPMKR	RRAHTF	USA
TOBIAS	8	M	CHILD	RRAHTF	USA

PASSENGER	AGE	SEX	OCCUPATION	PRIVL	DES
WELT, AUGUST	36	M	LKSH	RRAHUH	USA
WISGODISKY, ABRAHAM	50	M	TLR	RRAHTF	USA
DEMONT, BONIFACIUS	28	M	STDNT	RRZZZZ	USA
SKULSKI, LEINB	18	M	TLR	RRAHZS	USA
HALPERIN, ICKO	20	M	LABR	RRAIOF	USA

SHIP: VANCOUVER

FROM: LIVERPOOL
TO: BALTIMORE
ARRIVED: 09 FEBRUARY 1888

PASSENGER	AGE	SEX	OCCUPATION	PRIVL	DES
VESWINCKI, LEWIN	19	M	LABR	RRZZZZ	CIN
ABEAMOWITZ, B.	26	M	TLR	RRZZZZ	BAL
BLUMINTAL, HB.	20	M	BKLYR	RRZZZZ	BAL
MEHR, JOSE	21	F	SVNT	RRZZZZ	CH
LIPXHITZ, B.	26	M	BLDR	RRZZZZ	CH
RAKOUSKI, K.	24	M	LABR	PLZZZZ	BAL
SASLOUKA, F.	28	M	LABR	PLZZZZ	BAL
GOOSETROUSKI, V.	22	M	SDLR	PLZZZZ	BAL
SAIKA, JAS	28	M	LABR	PLZZZZ	BAL
POWECHOWSKI, P.	32	M	CBTMKR	PLZZZZ	BAL
SCHAUFRANOWICH, B.	25	M	LABR	RRZZZZ	USA

SHIP: RHEIN

FROM: BREMEN
TO: BALTIMORE
ARRIVED: 09 FEBRUARY 1888

PASSENGER	AGE	SEX	OCCUPATION	PRIVL	DES
SEGEL, RACHEL	20	F	UNKNOWN	RRZZZZ	USA
BULKWIN, ZOZIA	27	F	UNKNOWN	RRZZZZ	USA
NOVEIKA, STEPHAN	49	M	LABR	RRZZZZ	USA
WITTMANN, JOSEF	50	M	FARMER	RRZZZZ	USA
CATHARINA	52	F	W	RRZZZZ	USA
CLEMENS	28	M	FARMER	RRZZZZ	USA
MAGDALENE	30	F	W	RRZZZZ	USA
JOHANNE	15	F	UNKNOWN	RRZZZZ	USA
ANNA	20	F	UNKNOWN	RRZZZZ	USA
NILL, JOHANNES	38	M	LABR	RRZZZZ	USA
ABRAMOWITZ, MARY	18	F	UNKNOWN	RRZZZZ	USA
SALOMON, JOSEL	17	M	UNKNOWN	RRZZZZ	USA
SMENTKOWSKI, WLADISL	33	M	LABR	RRZZZZ	USA
BIESIADA, VALERIE	21	F	UNKNOWN	RRZZZZ	USA
HARINSKA, MARYANA	59	F	UNKNOWN	RRZZZZ	USA
JAN	23	M	LABR	RRZZZZ	USA
KOSOBUCKI, JAN	36	M	LABR	RRZZZZ	USA
SIWE, ESTER	24	M	UNKNOWN	RRZZZZ	USA
OSIAS	1	M	CHILD	RRZZZZ	USA
HINDE	.03	M	INFANT	RRZZZZ	USA
KOPLENOWSKY, RAPHAEL	26	M	LABR	RRZZZZ	USA

SHIP: STATE OF NEVADA

FROM: GLASGOW AND LARNE
TO: NEW YORK
ARRIVED: 10 FEBRUARY 1888

PASSENGER	AGE	SEX	OCCUPATION	PRIVL	DES
HUBERSTEIN, HIRSCH	27	M	TLR	RRZZZZ	USA
ETTEL	20	F	W	RRZZZZ	USA
RIEMAN, ISRAEL	35	M	TLR	RRZZZZ	USA
LAUZAUSKI, ISAAC	40	M	TLR	RRZZZZ	USA
LEIB	9	M	CHILD	RRZZZZ	USA
KOPALOW, ITZIG	27	M	TLR	RRZZZZ	USA
NOWESELSKY, ISRAEL	24	M	TLR	RRZZZZ	USA
STALL, LEIB	19	M	TLR	RRZZZZ	USA
PELTER, LEIB	22	M	TLR	RRZZZZ	USA
PRADAU, BENJAMIN	20	M	TLR	RRZZZZ	USA
LEGALLOWITZ, MORDCHE	22	M	TLR	RRZZZZ	USA
SEGALL, JANKEL	22	M	PDLR	RRZZZZ	USA
MOSCHEINK, JOSSEL	21	M	PDLR	RRZZZZ	USA
NEIBEITZKY, NACHEM	22	M	PDLR	RRZZZZ	USA
FELDSTEIN, MORIS	21	M	PDLR	RRZZZZ	USA
GESCHMISKY, ITZIG	22	M	PDLR	RRZZZZ	USA
RACHELSKY, HERSCH	27	M	PDLR	RRZZZZ	USA
KAUTRINOWITZ, SIMON	28	M	PDLR	RRZZZZ	USA
BOJERD, LEIB	37	M	PDLR	RRZZZZ	USA
DOHUSKY, DAVID	37	M	PDLR	RRZZZZ	USA
LIBERTSCH, MOSES	18	M	PDLR	RRZZZZ	USA
FRIEDKIN, LEON	51	M	PDLR	RRZZZZ	USA
AUSCHER, SUESSEL	17	M	LABR	RRZZZZ	USA
LUTALL, ABBE	15	M	LABR	RRZZZZ	USA
MISCHELOWITZ, JOSSEL	24	M	LABR	RRZZZZ	USA
WASLONSKY, ANTON	38	M	LABR	RRZZZZ	USA
SALZMAN, SAMUEL	50	M	TNM	RRZZZZ	USA
GRUSSMANN, ABRAHAM	18	M	BTMKR	RRZZZZ	USA
SCHKOLNIK, JACOB	35	M	BTMKR	RRZZZZ	USA
ABRAHAM	9	M	CHILD	RRZZZZ	USA
FRIEDLAND, ISRAEL	42	M	BTMKR	RRZZZZ	USA
ITZIG	10	M	CH	RRZZZZ	USA
HELPERN, HEUSCH	30	M	SMH	RRZZZZ	USA
RABINOWITZ, MICHAEL	24	M	DRG	RRZZZZ	USA
DOLGON, MASCHKE	18	F	SP	RRZZZZ	USA
SALESNIK, CHAJE	20	F	SP	RRZZZZ	USA
PERSKY, CHAJE	26	F	W	RRZZZZ	USA
RUBIN	2	M	CHILD	RRZZZZ	USA
CHAIE	.06	F	INFANT	RRZZZZ	USA

SHIP: WAESLAND

FROM: ANTWERP
TO: NEW YORK
ARRIVED: 11 FEBRUARY 1888

PASSENGER	AGE	SEX	OCCUPATION	PRIVL	DES
IMBRUCK, WILH.	20	M	SVNT	RRZZZZ	MN
LASORSKY, CHAN	19	F	SVNT	RRZZZZ	CH
SCHIFKE	28	F	UNKNOWN	RRZZZZ	CH
JANCKE	00	M	INF	RRZZZZ	CH
WEBER, BRUNO	15	M	UNKNOWN	RRZZZZ	OH
SCHMITZ, HCH	30	M	GLSR	RRZZZZ	USA
LINA	30	F	CPR	RRZZZZ	USA
BAIERN, JACOB	19	M	SMH	RRZZZZ	USA
ENGEL, LUDWIG	24	M	GDSM	RRZZZZ	NY
SIEGEL, CHRISTIAN	23	M	SMH	RRZZZZ	NY
PAULE, GOTTLIEB	59	M	GDNR	RRZZZZ	STL
LIPPOLD, CHR	24	M	LABR	RRZZZZ	NY
HAULISCH, JOH.	31	M	WVR	RRZZZZ	NY
MULLER, JOHANN	44	M	CPR	RRZZZZ	NY
MESTEL, JOSEF	24	M	LKSH	RRZZZZ	NY
SCHAHL, JOH.	23	M	LABR	RRZZZZ	NY
WEIMER, FRITZ	21	M	MSN	RRZZZZ	NY
SCHAUF, ADAM	23	M	BRR	RRZZZZ	NY
STAAB, WENDELIN	35	M	LABR	RRZZZZ	NY
DETTERBECK, FRANZ	23	M	CPR	RRZZZZ	NY
FORSTNER, SEBASTIAN	23	M	LABR	RRZZZZ	NY
ZIMMERMANN, ANNA	40	F	LABR	RRZZZZ	NY
SCHOMBS, LILLIE	18	F	UNKNOWN	RRZZZZ	NY
HOLZSCHUH, PANKRATZ	18	M	LABR	RRZZZZ	NY
GUNTHER, MARG	24	F	LABR	RRZZZZ	NY
HESS, ANDREAS	25	M	BTMKR	RRZZZZ	NY

PASSENGER	AGE	SEX	OCCUPATION	PRIV	VIL	DES
HERER, ALOIS	21	M	BKR	RR	ZZZZ	NY
NEUMER, PETER	50	M	BBR	RR	ZZZZ	NY
STEINBAUER, JACOB	36	M	BTMKR	RR	ZZZZ	NY
JUNG, LOUIS	17	M	UNKNOWN	RR	ZZZZ	NY
SCHARF, BARB	18	F	SVNT	RR	ZZZZ	NY
HEINRICH, GEO	18	M	BKR	RR	ZZZZ	NY
GRUBER, ADAM	17	M	LABR	RR	ZZZZ	NY
KASSEWITZ, JONAS	24	M	MCHT	RR	ZZZZ	NY
MILINSKI, MOWACHE	36	M	LABR	RR	ZZZZ	MI
BIALYTOTZ, SCHMUL	20	M	LABR	RR	ZZZZ	MI
STONEK, RUGELA	18	F	SVNT	RR	ZZZZ	MI
WELUTA, FRANZ	38	M	LABR	RR	ZZZZ	MI
TELLNER, LEIB	26	M	TLR	RR	ZZZZ	MI
SCHIFFMAN, JOSEF	21	M	LABR	RR	ZZZZ	MI

SHIP: LAHN

FROM: BREMEN AND SOUTHAMPTON
TO: NEW YORK
ARRIVED: 11 FEBRUARY 1888

PASSENGER	AGE	SEX	OCCUPATION	PRIV	VIL	DES
RECIKOWSKI, MATJICK	23	M	LABR	RR	ZZZZ	USA
NIEMCZYK, CHARLOTTE	21	F	NN	RR	ZZZZ	USA
ZAWADZKI, AUG.	20	M	LABR	RR	ZZZZ	USA
SILBERMANN, BROCHE	35	F	W	RR	ZZZZ	USA
CHAIM	9	M	CHILD	RR	ZZZZ	USA
ROCHEL	7	M	CHILD	RR	ZZZZ	USA
DAVID	5	M	CHILD	RR	ZZZZ	USA
GERSON	3	M	CHILD	RR	ZZZZ	USA
OSIAS	2	M	CHILD	RR	ZZZZ	USA
WENGER, CHAIM	26	M	PDLR	RR	ZZZZ	USA
KAINSCHEFSKY, ISAAC	28	M	PDLR	RR	ZZZZ	USA
KROSCHINSKY, CHRANE	20	M	PDLR	RR	ZZZZ	USA
ROEDEL, JACOB	41	M	JNR	RR	ZZZZ	USA

SHIP: ADRIATIC

FROM: LIVERPOOL AND QUEENSTOWN
TO: NEW YORK
ARRIVED: 11 FEBRUARY 1888

PASSENGER	AGE	SEX	OCCUPATION	PRIV	VIL	DES
WARGOWITZ, JANOS	19	M	LABR	RR	ACBF	USA
SCHEFFLER, POJE	36	F	W	RR	ACBF	USA
MARIN	1	F	CHILD	RR	ACBF	USA
BRAUN, MISCH	25	M	LABR	RR	ACBF	USA
SCHEFFLER, OSIAS	16	M	LABR	RR	ACBF	USA
BLITZ, S.DAVID	23	M	LABR	RR	ACBF	USA
MARK, CHAMI	19	M	LABR	RR	ACBF	USA
FINIBLUT, JUDA	18	M	LABR	RR	ACBF	USA
GOLDSTEIN, CHAIM-R.	11	M	CH	RR	ACBF	USA
PRAETZKO, MARIE	20	F	SVNT	RR	ACBF	USA
NOVAK, ANNA	24	F	SVNT	RR	ACBF	USA
KLIEN, SAMUEL	30	M	LABR	RR	ACBF	USA
CZAKO, BARBARA	30	F	SVNT	RR	ACBF	USA
ZOFEN, KALOMEN	26	M	LABR	RR	ACBF	USA
SCHMITMANN, MEIER	22	M	LABR	RR	ACBF	USA
OSCHEROWITZ, SCHLOME	24	M	LABR	RR	ACBF	USA
MASE, FEIGE	19	F	SVNT	RR	ACBF	USA
LEWANDOWSKY, JOHAN	28	M	LABR	RR	ACBF	USA
SCHMIDT, LUDWIG	22	M	LABR	RR	ACBF	USA
KUSCHIN, LASAR	23	M	LABR	RR	ACBF	USA
SONJE	20	F	W	RR	ACBF	USA
BASOLEK, MOSCHE	17	F	SP	RR	ACBF	USA
ROCHINSKI, HENOCK	25	M	LABR	RR	ACBF	USA
BEER, SCHAFE	30	M	LABR	RR	ACBF	USA
SCHNIEDER, FRIED.	33	F	W	RR	ACBF	USA
ARON	10	M	CH	RR	ACBF	USA
CHAJE	2	F	CHILD	RR	ACBF	USA
LIEW, SALY	22	F	W	RR	ACBF	USA
HENINE	1	F	CHILD	RR	ACBF	USA
JONAH, CHANE-L.	18	F	SVNT	RR	ACBF	USA
OLSINER, CHAIM	10	M	CH	RR	ACBF	USA
KAUFMANN, MOSES	10	M	CH	RR	ACBF	USA
SCHUR, NOCHEN	18	M	LABR	RR	ACBF	USA
PERUMINSKI, ITZKE	18	M	LABR	RR	ACBF	USA
GATTERER, BATISTE.	26	F	SVNT	RR	ACBF	USA
PIETRO	24	M	LABR	RR	ACBF	USA
SCHWARTZ, HERMAN	16	M	LABR	RR	ACBF	USA
KATZ, JOSEPH-L.	17	M	LABR	RR	ACBF	USA
GELBERT, MORITZ	38	M	LABR	RR	ACBF	USA

SHIP: CATALONIA

FROM: LIVERPOOL
TO: BOSTON
ARRIVED: UNKNOWN

PASSENGER	AGE	SEX	OCCUPATION	PRIV	VIL	DES
BAGARI, AUG.	19	M	LABR	FN	ZZZZ	USA
PENOLN, JAFET	23	M	LABR	FN	ZZZZ	USA
HAUTATORFA, JOH.	28	M	LABR	FN	ZZZZ	USA
U, JOH.	24	M	LABR	FN	ZZZZ	USA
MYERCKOSKI, JOH.	19	M	LABR	FN	ZZZZ	USA
SURELA, ISAK	28	M	LABR	FN	ZZZZ	USA
PAGRIOGA, AND.	25	M	LABR	FN	ZZZZ	USA
MATTILDA, ALEX	28	M	LABR	FN	ZZZZ	USA
FORSUAS, MATTS	24	M	LABR	FN	ZZZZ	USA
ANDERSON, NILS	21	M	LABR	FN	ZZZZ	USA
KALLIS, KARL	35	M	LABR	FN	ZZZZ	USA
LESKELA, AND.	36	M	LABR	FN	ZZZZ	USA
MATTILA, JOH.	32	M	LABR	FN	ZZZZ	USA
TILLIKA, JOH.	00	M	LABR	FN	ZZZZ	USA
SELTOLA, JOH.	34	M	LABR	FN	ZZZZ	USA
IKKALEGEROI, HENR.	33	M	LABR	FN	ZZZZ	USA
HENRIKSON, DAVID	42	M	LABR	FN	ZZZZ	USA
TANOLA, ISAK	26	M	LABR	FN	ZZZZ	USA
WINTER, FELIX	26	M	LABR	FN	ZZZZ	USA
LEFFANAU, JOH.	44	M	LABR	FN	ZZZZ	USA
PARKIOLA, MATTS	42	M	LABR	FN	ZZZZ	USA
PERSKA, HERMAN	32	M	LABR	FN	ZZZZ	USA
HAUTATORGRE, GUST.	23	M	LABR	FN	ZZZZ	USA
HANIKOMEN, EITH	31	M	LABR	FN	ZZZZ	USA
SAARELA, AND.	26	M	LABR	FN	ZZZZ	USA
POLISAK, NESSA	38	F	W	RR	ZZZZ	USA
LEME	15	F	SVNT	RR	ZZZZ	USA
CHANE	11	F	CH	RR	ZZZZ	USA
ROSA	8	F	CHILD	RR	ZZZZ	USA
NOA	5	M	CHILD	RR	ZZZZ	USA
GOLDE	3	F	CHILD	RR	ZZZZ	USA
LIKEL	.11	F	INFANT	RR	ZZZZ	USA

SHIP: POLYNESIA

FROM: HAMBURG
TO: NEW YORK
ARRIVED: 13 FEBRUARY 1888

PASSENGER	AGE	SEX	OCCUPATION	PRIV	VIL	DES
ALSMANN, SARA	18	F	SGL	RR	ZZZZ	NY
VILLINS, ALEXANDRA	33	F	WO	RR	ZZZZ	NY
MAXMILIAN	9	M	CHILD	RR	ZZZZ	NY
STEFAN	8	M	CHILD	RR	ZZZZ	NY

PASSENGER	AGE	SEX	OCCUPATION	PRV VIL DES
LEONHARD	4	M	CHILD	RRZZZZNY
JULIAN	.06	M	INFANT	RRZZZZNY
DRUSDOWSKA, BOCHELLA	22	F	WO	RRZZZZNY
MICHALIA	.03	F	INFANT	RRZZZZNY
LEONA	8	F	CHILD	RRZZZZNY
LEWIN, HINDE	23	F	WO	RRZZZZNY
HESPE	.11	F	INFANT	RRZZZZNY
PACZKOWSKI, JOSEF	39	M	LABR	RRZZZZNY
KRAWISNIWICZ, TEOFEL	40	M	LABR	RRZZZZNY
KRAKOWSKYE, MIKAS	27	M	LABR	RRZZZZNY
NIWULES, JOH.	27	M	LABR	RRZZZZNY
KUBISKI, JERZI	22	M	LABR	RRZZZZNY
MURGE, DOMINICK	28	M	LABR	RRZZZZNY
LANDA, VINCENDI	26	M	LABR	RRZZZZNY
GERSTON, SIDER	36	M	LABR	RRZZZZNY
KERGAILIS, JOHN.	43	M	LABR	RRZZZZNY
PETTKY, JOSEF	37	M	LABR	RRZZZZNY
PASZULIS, JOSUS	22	M	LABR	RRZZZZNY
PACZINKA, VINCENTI	26	M	LABR	RRZZZZNY
LIPSCHETZ, HIRSCH	25	M	MCHT	RRZZZZNY
SCHNITTMAN, ARON	28	M	TLR	RRZZZZNY
SLATHIN, ISAAK	46	M	TLR	RRZZZZNY
GIBULUSK, ANTON	24	M	TLR	RRZZZZNY
NEUMANN, JOSEF	40	M	LABR	RRZZZZNY
WENZEL, SCHLIMEN	38	M	DLR	RRZZZZNY
PAGAWIS, ANTON	27	M	LABR	RRZZZZNY
MAKSZRAITIS, ANTON	9	M	CHILD	RRZZZZNY
JAN	9	M	CHILD	RRZZZZNY
CZERNALIS, VINCENT	24	M	LABR	RRZZZZNY
GELINSKI, CASISS	22	M	LABR	RRZZZZNY
SAWATZKI, JURAS	26	M	LABR	RRZZZZNY
CERDETZKI, THOMAS	24	M	LABR	RRZZZZNY
FILUYENET, ABR.	21	M	LABR	RRZZZZNY
SZAMAS, HERTZ	25	M	TLR	RRZZZZNY
SATANOWSKYE, JOSEF	21	M	TLR	RRZZZZNY

SHIP: MORAVIA

FROM: HAMBURG AND HAVRE
TO: NEW YORK
ARRIVED: 13 FEBRUARY 1888

PASSENGER	AGE	SEX	OCCUPATION	PRV VIL DES
GEORGIEWICZ, ANTON	20	M	LABR	RRAHUGUSA
NEIBERGER, DAVID	22	M	CL	RRAHUGUSA
SAMSENOWICZ, BENEDICTA	22	F	SGL	RRZZZZUSA
STANISLAWA	19	F	SGL	RRZZZZUSA
ROSENBERG, GRONOM	26	M	LABR	RRZZZZUSA
ZACHOROWICZ, LEPKE	26	M	TLR	RRZZZZUSA
TOPOROWSKI, HIRSCH	33	M	TLR	RRZZZZUSA
LANDAU, LEISER	20	M	LABR	RRAIKXUSA
PERLMANN, NOCHEM	60	M	MCHT	RRAIKXUSA
MALKE	50	F	W	RRZZZZUSA
RAHEL	9	F	CHILD	RRZZZZUSA
PAMERANCICZ, SALMON	23	M	DLR	RRZZZZUSA
PLOTNIK, MOSES	25	M	DLR	RRZZZZUSA
STREICHER, CHAIM	26	M	DLR	RRZZZZUSA
SZAKSON, SCHIE	42	M	DLR	RRZZZZUSA
BORENBAUM, SCHAWEL	36	M	DLR	RRAHTBUSA
GREENBERG, JANKEL	35	M	DLR	RRAHTBUSA
ROTHSCHILD, JUDEL	9	M	CHILD	RRAHTBUSA
ORMLAND, FISCHEL	29	M	DLR	RRAHTBUSA
WEINSTEIN, DAVID	27	M	DLR	RRAHTBUSA
SILBERMANN, SCHIE	28	M	DLR	RRZZZZUSA
CHEJE	25	F	W	RRZZZZUSA
ABRAH	.09	M	INFANT	RRZZZZUSA
PESCHE	20	F	SGL	RRZZZZUSA
CHEIKE	18	F	SGL	RRZZZZUSA
GAUCE, NACHAMANN	26	M	DLR	RRAIJWUSA
BOMBRES, JOH.	50	M	LABR	RRAINYUSA
CATH	40	F	W	RRAINYUSA
MICH	9	M	CHILD	RRAINYUSA
MARIANE	4	F	CHILD	RRAINYUSA
PELAGIA	3	F	CHILD	RRAINYUSA
RADZIEWICZ, CASIMIR	19	M	LABR	RRZZZZUSA
SZIMZEK, CONSTANTIN	19	M	LABR	RRZZZZUSA
STANISL	22	M	LABR	RRZZZZUSA
ZOELLNER, ANTON	26	M	LABR	RRAHUFUSA
RUCZYNSKI, THOMAS	27	M	LABR	RRAHUFUSA
NASS, MICHAL	35	M	LABR	RRAHUFUSA
SEIKOWSKI, PAWEL	20	M	LABR	RRZZZZUSA
KASCHEL, AUGUST	21	M	TLR	RRAIFNUSA
LOTTERMOSER, AUGUST	22	M	TLR	RRAINZUSA
KLEINSCHMIDT, JULS	19	M	SMH	RRZZZZUSA
SEMMELSEN, WILH.	23	M	LABR	RRZZZZUSA
JOH	39	M	LABR	RRZZZZUSA
ISECKSOHN, SAMEL	25	M	LABR	RRZZZZUSA
LOMMI, ALEX	25	M	LABR	RRZZZZUSA
TUSKOLO, ALEX	28	M	LABR	RRZZZZUSA
JACOBSEN, VALERIUS	23	M	LABR	RRZZZZUSA
FRAUTTE, SAMUEL	25	M	LABR	RRZZZZUSA
PAHOKORPI, ISAK	49	M	LABR	RRZZZZUSA
WAARA, JOH.	35	M	LABR	RRZZZZUSA
ONTERO, MATS	25	M	LABR	RRZZZZUSA
PUKKILA, HERM.	47	M	LABR	RRZZZZUSA
THOMAS	36	M	LABR	RRZZZZUSA
KASKI, VALENTIN	22	M	LABR	RRZZZZUSA
JOH	26	M	LABR	RRZZZZUSA
ALPHOLUMIA, ANDRERS	25	M	LABR	RRZZZZUSA
LUOKKALA, JOH	47	M	LABR	RRZZZZUSA
LEKTINEN, NESTOR	28	M	LABR	RRAIJHUSA
STEIG, JOH	26	M	LABR	RRZZZZUSA
JACOB	18	M	LABR	RRZZZZUSA
KECK, CARL	25	F	WO	RRAIAEUSA
HELENKA	.11	F	INFANT	RRAIAEUSA
SVABA, BRONYE	26	F	WO	RRAIAEUSA
WLADISLAV	.11	M	INFANT	RRAIAEUSA
RUSKOWSKI, JAN	29	M	LABR	RRAIAEUSA
KAPLAN, MORDCHE	52	M	DLR	RRZZZZUSA
CHASCHE	19	M	DLR	RRZZZZUSA
ETTEL	9	M	CHILD	RRZZZZUSA
KASSMANN, MERE	24	F	WO	RRZZZZUSA
CHAJE	.11	F	INFANT	RRZZZZUSA
WEINTRAUB, MOSES	23	M	TLR	RRZZZZUSA
SAKOW, JOSSEL	22	M	DLR	RRAHTUUSA
MUELLER, RUBEN	29	M	DLR	RRZZZZUSA
HODE	26	F	W	RRZZZZUSA
LEIB	.09	F	INFANT	RRZZZZUSA
LIEBE	20	F	WO	RRZZZZUSA
SORE	.09	F	INFANT	RRZZZZUSA
FRIEDMANN, TAUBE	18	F	SGL	RRZZZZUSA
WEISCHESKI, CHAIM	31	M	TLR	RRAHZSUSA
WEINSTOCK, OSCHER	35	M	TNM	RRAHQUUSA
SUSKA, TYMKO	25	M	LABR	PLZZZZUSA
EHRLLICH, MOSES	17	M	LABR	PLZZZZUSA
TUS, DYMIKO	24	M	LABR	PLZZZZUSA
KOWAL, IWAN	16	M	LABR	PLZZZZUSA
SIERAK, MICHAEL	16	M	LABR	PLZZZZUSA
SKAMBER, MARIA	21	F	SGL	PLZZZZUSA
KONOVAL, TYTUS	32	M	LABR	PLZZZZUSA
KORNAJ, DENNIAN	24	M	LABR	PLZZZZUSA
MISLOCKY, SYLVESTER	25	M	LABR	PLZZZZUSA
WAWERCZAK, JOHANN	24	M	LABR	PLZZZZUSA
MYTRYK, MIKOLAJ	29	M	LABR	PLZZZZUSA
SWANYSZYK, STEFAN	29	M	LABR	PLZZZZUSA
DOBRZANSKI, ADAM	28	M	LABR	PLZZZZUSA
IYWANICZ, ILMAS	26	M	LABR	PLZZZZUSA
PAWELKO, MIHAL	33	M	LABR	PLZZZZUSA
ANDRAS, KOLAR	35	M	LABR	PLZZZZUSA
DRUTOVICZ, JOSEF	27	M	LABR	PLZZZZUSA
LIPTAK, JOSEF	29	M	LABR	PLZZZZUSA
BUKAIS, JOSEF	17	M	LABR	PLZZZZUSA

SHIP: ETRURIA

FROM: LIVERPOOL
TO: NEW YORK
ARRIVED: 13 FEBRUARY 1888

PASSENGER	AGE	SEX	OCCUPATION	PRV VIL DES
ZISEWSKY, IVAN	34	M	LABR	PLADAXNY
DROWITZ, THOS.ALEXAN.	30	M	LABR	PLADAXNY
FEIWINS, BARNS	40	M	LABR	PLADAXNY
STARINSKY, SIMON	31	M	LABR	PLADAXNY
WACHANSKY, LEA	25	F	SP	PLADAXNY
ISRAEL	23	M	BCHR	PLADAXNY
CHAGE	24	F	SP	PLADAXNY
RUBEN	21	M	TLR	PLADAXNY
SISSIE	11	F	CH	PLADAXNY
ZIMBALL, SAMUEL	26	M	BCHR	PLADAXNY
HANTATORPA, AND.	20	M	FARMER	PLADAXNY
LAPPI, JOHAN	20	M	LABR	PLADAXNY
BARTINK, FRANZ	16	M	LABR	PLADAXNY
MELSGA, GYNRI	20	M	LABR	PLADAXNY
ZI--, JACOB	50	M	MCHT	PLADAXNY

SHIP: WYOMING

FROM: LIVERPOOL AND QUEENSTOWN
TO: NEW YORK
ARRIVED: 14 FEBRUARY 1888

PASSENGER	AGE	SEX	OCCUPATION	PRV VIL DES
WISKIELISKI, J	14	M	LABR	PLZZZZUSA
GEUSCHIKA, L	20	M	LABR	PLZZZZUSA
KEROINSKIN, MORITZ	24	M	LABR	PLZZZZUSA
SPEIGEL, C	17	M	LABR	PLZZZZUSA
MALKOWSKY, T	4	M	CHILD	PLZZZZUSA
BIANOSKIN, C	00	F	INF	PLZZZZUSA
FRIEDMAN, I	7	M	CHILD	PLZZZZUSA
REWKE	5	F	CHILD	PLZZZZUSA
ISAAC	3	M	CHILD	PLZZZZUSA
CHAIM	00	M	INF	PLZZZZUSA
PAULSON, R	30	M	LABR	PLZZZZUSA
LEINSIS, M.	25	M	LABR	PLZZZZUSA
BARTEVCK, SARAH	55	F	SP	PLZZZZUSA
FRIEDMAN, B	40	F	W	PLZZZZUSA
GITTEL	19	M	FARMER	PLZZZZUSA
DEBORA	8	F	CHILD	PLZZZZUSA
MICH	7	M	CHILD	PLZZZZUSA
MENDELSOHN, G	20	M	LABR	PLZZZZUSA
KOHN, KIFKE	20	F	SP	PLZZZZUSA
MALKOWSKA, H	26	F	W	PLZZZZUSA
KAPEL	00	F	INF	PLZZZZUSA
BERNSOHN, J	23	M	LABR	PLZZZZUSA
TARINKA, APO	24	M	UNKNOWN	RRZZZZUSA
KLEMSTI, K.	31	M	LABR	RRZZZZUSA
WITTSBUERG, H	29	M	LABR	RRZZZZUSA
HANTONEUS, A	20	M	LABR	RRZZZZUSA
HEIKKILN, JOHAN	35	M	LABR	RRZZZZUSA
WILLGAUEN, C	26	M	LABR	RRZZZZUSA
JOHANSON, J	31	M	LABR	RRZZZZUSA
ANTILLEN, J	29	M	LABR	RRZZZZUSA
OLLIPATTI, J	56	M	LABR	RRZZZZUSA
BAUM, J	32	M	LABR	RRZZZZUSA
LANG, VICTOR	35	M	LABR	RRZZZZUSA
AMMOLI, L	24	M	FARMER	RRZZZZUSA
HANAUKEREN, J	25	M	FARMER	RRZZZZUSA
LASILA, M	40	M	FARMER	RRZZZZUSA
SARNIG, JACOB	37	M	FARMER	RRZZZZUSA
JAFT, J	24	M	FARMER	RRZZZZUSA
BOUSTIN, MICH	53	M	FARMER	RRZZZZUSA
IVENDHOHN, W	24	M	FARMER	RRZZZZUSA
HUMMEL, ANDRIAS	36	M	LABR	RRZZZZUSA
OIJA, J	35	M	LABR	RRZZZZUSA
PETKENEN, L	17	M	LABR	RRZZZZUSA

SHIP: WERRA

FROM: BREMEN AND SOUTHAMPTON
TO: NEW YORK
ARRIVED: 15 FEBRUARY 1888

PASSENGER	AGE	SEX	OCCUPATION	PRV VIL DES
LAPOWSKY, LUDWIG	30	M	MCHT	RRZZZZUSA
DRZEWICKA, KATERYNA	24	F	W	RRZZZZUSA
STANISLAUS	.01	M	INFANT	RRZZZZUSA
CATHARYNA	24	F	W	RRZZZZUSA
CATHARZYNA	.09	F	INFANT	RRZZZZUSA
STACHOWSKI, MATEUS	24	M	LABR	RRZZZZUSA
JALDOWSKI, STANISLAUS	26	M	LABR	RRZZZZUSA
DRZEWSKI, MATEUS	29	M	LABR	RRZZZZUSA
CHALUKI, WOJEICH	64	M	LABR	RRZZZZUSA
POTOCKI, CONSTANT	27	M	LABR	RRZZZZUSA
BLOCK, MICHAEL	46	M	LABR	RRZZZZUSA
KRANOCZYNSKI, JOSEF	24	M	LABR	RRZZZZUSA
MELLER, ADAM	26	M	LABR	RRZZZZUSA
WOJCIECK	25	M	LABR	RRZZZZUSA
BEIGOROWICZ, JAN	30	M	LABR	RRZZZZUSA
SULECKI, ANTON	39	M	UNKNOWN	RRZZZZUSA
GURIN, SCHLAMER	40	M	FARMER	RRZZZZUSA

SHIP: ITALY

FROM: LIVERPOOL
TO: NEW YORK
ARRIVED: 16 FEBRUARY 1888

PASSENGER	AGE	SEX	OCCUPATION	PRV VIL DES
ALKER, DAVID	24	M	CGRMKR	RRADAXPHI
REINARD, KADESCH	30	M	LABR	RRZZZZBAL
KANKOWSKY, SIMON	23	M	UNKNOWN	RRADBQBRO
SMITH, JOSEPH	32	M	UNKNOWN	RRADBQBRO
MITCHELE, GEORGE	24	M	UNKNOWN	RRADBQBRO
PHELLIPZ, JON	30	M	UNKNOWN	RRADBQBRO
SOLOMON, JOSEPH	20	M	UNKNOWN	RRADAXNY
BERTIE	30	F	W	RRADAXNY
WOLF	6	M	CHILD	RRADAXNY
MOSES	4	M	CHILD	RRADAXNY
GETLY	.11	F	INFANT	RRADAXNY
MAX	5	M	CHILD	RRADAXNY
ROSSENSTEIN, J.	22	M	TLR	RRADBQNY
CALZMON, PHILIP	23	M	CGRMKR	RRADBQUNK
HIMMINSKY, AHOLE	31	M	LABR	RRACBFUNK
SCHEFLEBOWITZ, ANNA	55	F	W	RRACBFUNK
ROSA	11	F	CH	RRACBFUNK
SAKOLER, JOSEF	36	M	LABR	RRACBFUNK
HEUDELMANN, DAVID	23	M	LABR	RRACBFUNK
KALEG, JOSEF	44	M	LABR	RRACBFUNK
HICKBE, B.	20	M	LABR	RRACBFUNK
NORBOYOROD, ITSIK	40	M	LABR	RRACBFUNK
ATEMBURG, HERTY	48	M	LABR	RRACBFUNK
ZUMERMANN, BASCH	48	F	SP	RRACBFUNK
SAELIS, BEHER	34	M	SMH	RRACBFPHI
CHAEI	33	F	W	RRACBFPHI
AXELBRAUD, HERSCH	25	M	SMH	RRACBFPHI
SACLIS, MOSES	10	M	CH	RRACBFPHI
CHAIE	8	F	CHILD	RRACBFPHI
JINTI	6	M	CHILD	RRACBFPHI
JONNE	4	M	CHILD	RRACBFPHI
BRODER	1	F	CHILD	RRACBFPHI

PASSENGER	AGE	SEX	OCCUPATION	PRV VIL DES
NEYER	.09	F	INFANT	RRACBFPHI
IBINCHOWITZ, JUSTEL	22	F	W	RRACBFNY
JUSTEL	22	F	W	RRACBFNY
CATHER	2	F	CHILD	RRACBFNY
MALESEWITZ, ABRAH.	35	M	LABR	RRACBFNY
SUKOLSKY, SEIB	11	M	CH	RRACBFNY
KOHN, LELI	35	F	W	RRACBFNY
LEIB	8	M	CHILD	RRACBFNY
MERKA	3	F	CHILD	RRACBFNY
SAM, ABRAHAM	32	M	SHMK	RRACBFNY
RUBIN, RIDCHI	16	M	LABR	RRACBFNY
STOLOKEN, ISRAEL	20	M	LABR	RRACBFNY
SOCLENOWITZ, JACOB	56	M	LABR	RRACBFNY
KENOTIN, ABR.	20	M	LABR	RRACBFNY
JETSER, ABR.	38	M	LABR	RRACBFNY
SAFT, RIMA	17	F	SP	RRACBFNY
MOSOK, CHANE	18	F	SP	RRACBFNY
SCLUMBEWISKY, U	26	F	W	RRACBFNY
MARIE	4	F	CHILD	RRACBFNY
JUDELSMAN, MOS.	38	M	LABR	RRACBFNY
GRIM, AFR.	19	M	LABR	RRACBFNY
SALMONOWITZ, SCHEM	44	M	LABR	RRACBFNY
JANNERBAUM, BER.	24	M	LABR	RRACBFNY
EFROSIN	34	M	LABR	RRACBFNY
GUIDER, STEFAN	18	M	LABR	RRACBFNY
RACH, GUSFA	24	M	LABR	RRACBFNY
SEGARD, MARK	20	M	LABR	RRADBQBAL

SHIP: SARGENT

FROM: LIVERPOOL AND QUEENSTOWN
TO: NEW YORK
ARRIVED: 18 FEBRUARY 1888

PASSENGER	AGE	SEX	OCCUPATION	PRV VIL DES
DOBKIS, FRANZ	30	M	FARMER	RRZZZZNY
DAHL, L.	41	M	LABR	RRZZZZMI
FRIN, H.	25	M	LABR	PLZZZZNY
FREINSTEIN, HODRE	51	F	W	PLZZZZNY
P.	9	F	CHILD	PLZZZZNY
H.	6	M	CHILD	PLZZZZNY
GROSSFIELD, H.	21	M	CH	PLZZZZNY
SELIG, GRABLER	24	M	CH	PLZZZZNY
CHAWE	25	F	W	PLZZZZNY
GOTTLIEB, C.	20	M	LABR	PLZZZZNY
HEIPKILA, J.E.	29	M	LABR	RRZZZZMI
KLEIN, H.	32	M	LABR	PLZZZZNY
HERM.	36	F	W	PLZZZZNY
KOPINSKA, ANNA	18	F	SP	PLZZZZNY
KOPPER, ARON	20	M	LABR	PLZZZZNY
KONTONY, A.	17	M	LABR	PLZZZZOH
LAILOLA, J.	31	M	LABR	RRZZZZMI
LINGVIST, OTTO	21	M	LABR	RRZZZZUSA
LAINS, G.	24	M	LABR	RRZZZZNY
MAKKILD, J.	31	M	LABR	RRZZZZMI
V.	26	M	LABR	RRZZZZMI
MIEMELA, Z.	30	M	LABR	RRZZZZMI
PERLONA, J.	19	M	LABR	RRZZZZMI
PELB-AKI, VICTOR	28	M	LABR	RRZZZZMI
RAUBMOGA, H.	42	M	LABR	RRZZZZMI
TEITEL, S.	34	M	FARMER	RRZZZZMI
WASBRGA, FRANZ	30	M	LABR	RRZZZZNY
YNTSKOWIE, APOLINA	26	F	W	PLZZZZNY
F.	2	M	CHILD	PLZZZZNY
S.	4	M	CHILD	PLZZZZNY
SAGOSKI, MOSSE	38	M	FARMER	RRZZZZNY

SHIP: LESSING

FROM: HAMBURG AND HAVRE
TO: NEW YORK
ARRIVED: 18 FEBRUARY 1888

PASSENGER	AGE	SEX	OCCUPATION	PRV VIL DES
ZAZAZISKI, CHEIM	40	M	LABR	RRZZZZUSA
ULROCH, DOROTHEA	46	F	WO	RRAEFLUSA
HUGO	14	M	S	RRAEFLUSA
JASWANSKY, SALOMON	14	M	LABR	RRAIGHUSA
HAGEN, ANNA	34	F	WO	RRAEFLUSA
JOHS.	13	M	S	RRAEFLUSA
GEGELEWICZ, ANTON	44	M	LABR	RRAHZSUSA
GEROLTOWSKY, JOS	28	M	LABR	RRAHZSUSA
ROMEIKO, JAN	25	M	LABR	RRAHZSUSA
STRANKANTZKY, MICHAEL	25	M	LABR	RRAHZSUSA
MOSCHECKO, MICHAEL	42	M	LABR	RRAHZSUSA
BARTSCHES, JERSY	20	M	LABR	RRAHZSUSA
RADJUNIS, FRANT	33	M	LABR	RRAIGHUSA
MARRIES, FRANZ	18	M	LABR	RRAIGHUSA
SZIKS, ANTON	24	M	LABR	RRAIGHUSA
KRUSCHAS, JANOS	25	M	LABR	RRAIGHUSA
RUSCHLANK, CASIMIR	23	M	LABR	RRAIGHUSA
WONSKI, ANDRZEI	24	M	LABR	RRAFWJUSA
MILWITZ, MICHAEL	45	M	LABR	RRAFWJUSA
HOPPNER, JEA	28	F	WO	RRAHUVUSA
BENZION	7	M	CHILD	RRAHUVUSA
ASNE	5	F	CHILD	RRAHUVUSA
RUBIN, DAVID	26	M	LABR	RRZZZZUSA
MICHAEL, MORRIS	28	M	TLR	RRAHTWUSA
FRIEDLANDER, ERNESTINE	22	F	WO	RRAHRZUSA
WOLF	00	M	INF	RRAHRZUSA
SCHWARZ, SARA	40	F	WO	RRAIGHUSA
PLEN, SAMUEL	29	M	DLR	RRAIGHUSA
GITE	21	F	W	RRAIGHUSA
LIEBE	.11	F	INFANT	RRAIGHUSA
SCHWARZ, DAVID	19	M	MCHT	RRAIGAUSA
LEWINSOHN, LEIB	27	M	LABR	RRAHWQUSA
RAHEL	25	F	W	RRAHWQUSA
SOBEL	9	M	CHILD	RRAHWQUSA
BERKMANN, MOSES	17	M	DLR	RRAIGHUSA
WRZESZUNSKA, SUSANA	18	F	SGL	RRAIAEUSA
CATHARINE	9	F	CHILD	RRAIAEUSA
KRENTZBERG, ALBERT	26	M	MCHT	RRAEFLUSA
SCHERESCHEWSKI, ISAAC	32	M	DLR	RRAIFNUSA
LUCHMANN, WOLF	14	M	LABR	RRAIGHUSA
ESAAC	9	M	CHILD	RRAIGHUSA
KOWALSKI, MARIANNE	20	F	SGL	RRZZZZUSA
WRZESCZENSKI, ADAM	26	M	LABR	RRZZZZUSA
JOSEFA	24	F	W	RRZZZZUSA
BEIKER, HERSCH	27	M	DLR	RRZZZZUSA
HITELMANN, ROSA	26	F	SGL	RRZZZZUSA
BINSTOCK, ISAAC	26	M	TLR	RRZZZZUSA
ZWICK, JACOB	26	M	MCHT	RRZZZZUSA
BANKOVER, PEISACH	28	M	MCHT	RRZZZZUSA
PARTICIES, MOSES	38	M	MCHT	RRAIFRUSA
DRAGELIS, JANOS	22	M	LABR	RRZZZZUSA
GRAMPITZ, GOTTL.	48	M	LABR	RRAHZSUSA
TOPOLENSKY, JACOB	34	M	LABR	RRAHZSUSA
CZIBONSKI, JAN	26	M	MCHT	RRAHZSUSA
CHUTKEWICZ, ANDR.	25	M	MCHT	RRAHZSUSA
KRUSCHANSKI, JOS.	24	M	MCHT	RRAHZSUSA
BUSKOWSKI, JOSEF	23	M	MCHT	RRAHZSUSA
BSUSCHKI, ANTON	47	M	MCHT	RRAHZSUSA
SCHMILEWSKI, FRANZ	25	M	MCHT	RRAHZSUSA
GANSCHAUTZKI, MICHAEL	24	M	MCHT	RRAHZSUSA
RAPUSTA, FRANZ	24	M	MCHT	RRAHZSUSA
SEITSCHOS, ANTON	22	M	MCHT	RRAHZSUSA
GUTFRANZKI, JACOB	36	M	MCHT	RRAHZSUSA
BRUSCHINTZKI, JOSEF	25	M	MCHT	RRAHZSUSA
BUSALEWSKI, MARCIN	32	M	MCHT	RRAHZSUSA
GAHSCHAUTZKI, JOSEF	22	M	MCHT	RRAHZSUSA
MATKOWSKI, JOS.	32	M	MCHT	RRAHZSUSA
JANKEL, JOSSE	40	M	MCHT	RRAHWKUSA

PASSENGER	AGE	SEX	OCCUPATION	PRI VIL	DES
PUPKO, ALBR.	30	M	LABR	RRAIHB	USA
KELBAN, ABR.	46	M	LABR	RRAHXI	USA
ARON	9	M	CHILD	RRAHXI	USA
MULSCHASKY, HERSCH	51	M	LABR	RRAHXI	USA
JESSUNSKY, MUSCHEN	24	M	LABR	RRAHXI	USA
JURKAUSKI, MOSES	17	M	LABR	RRAHXI	USA
WISINAKOWSKY, ARON	18	M	LABR	RRAHXI	USA
LEWINSKY, MERCL	20	F	SGL	RRAHXI	USA
BERKOVIC, BER.	36	M	LABR	RRAHXI	USA
SCESKAL, KARL	33	M	LABR	RRAHXI	USA
MONES, JOSEF	28	M	LABR	RRAHXI	USA
KIRSCHBAUM, JOSEF	26	M	LABR	RRAHXI	USA
SINK, JOHN.	22	M	MCHT	RRAEFL	USA
SAAKOFF, GREGOR	32	M	MCHT	RRAHWF	USA

SHIP: EMS

FROM: BREMEN AND SOUTHAMPTON
TO: NEW YORK
ARRIVED: 18 FEBRUARY 1888

PASSENGER	AGE	SEX	OCCUPATION	PRI VIL	DES
HAZENBEIN, ANNA	43	F	UNKNOWN	RRAHQD	NY

SHIP: TAORMINA

FROM: HAMBURG
TO: NEW YORK
ARRIVED: 20 FEBRUARY 1888

PASSENGER	AGE	SEX	OCCUPATION	PRI VIL	DES
SCHUMACHER, WOLF	35	M	SHMK	RRZZZZ	NY
KOWALIZYK, JACOB	27	M	LABR	RRZZZZ	NY
URSULA	23	F	W	RRZZZZ	NY
PATULSKA, JOSEFA	43	F	WO	RRZZZZ	NY
ANDR	16	M	CH	RRZZZZ	NY
STEPHAN	9	M	CHILD	RRZZZZ	NY
BRENNING, FRANZ	17	M	LABR	RRZZZZ	NY
----KERT, U	20	M	LABR	RRZZZZ	NY
SCHULZ, OSKAR	33	M	LABR	RRZZZZ	NY
NOVAK, DANIEL	35	M	MCHT	RRZZZZ	NY
CHRISTIANSEN, LORENZ	24	M	UNKNOWN	RRZZZZ	NY
MAASDORF, U	23	F	SGL	RRZZZZ	NY
SCHREIBER, FERD	64	M	LABR	RRZZZZ	CH
LUISE	57	F	W	RRZZZZ	CH
GUSTAV	16	M	CH	RRZZZZ	CH
WILHELM	15	M	CH	RRZZZZ	CH
ULKUS, FERDINAND	21	M	LABR	RRZZZZ	NY
WALINEWSKY, JOS	18	M	LABR	RRZZZZ	NY
LISKOWSKY, ALEX	27	M	LABR	RRZZZZ	NY
LANKOWSKY, MATH	27	M	LABR	RRZZZZ	NY
ADAM	25	M	LABR	RRZZZZ	NY
DILE-SKY, LUDW	19	M	LABR	RRZZZZ	NY
LUBA, JOS	35	M	JNR	RRZZZZ	NY
S--ISCHEWSKY, SIMON	33	M	LABR	RRZZZZ	NY
---YNSKY, U	22	M	LABR	RRZZZZ	NY
DONEBROWSKY, MATH	23	M	LABR	RRZZZZ	NY
S--ANOWICZ, JERSY	24	M	LABR	RRZZZZ	NY
BERENDT, D--MIK	24	M	LABR	RRZZZZ	NY
MILEWSKY, MICHAEL	31	M	LABR	RRZZZZ	NY
BUDCZEWICZ, JAN	21	M	LABR	RRZZZZ	NY
RAUDEN-, JOS	26	M	LABR	RRZZZZ	NY
STRAGAN-ZKY, JULIAN	24	M	LABR	RRZZZZ	NY
PETROWSKA, ANNA	20	F	SGL	RRZZZZ	NY
KWIASKOWSKY, SCHERER	19	M	LKSH	RRZZZZ	NY
PRETSCHANSKY, ALTE	30	F	WO	RRZZZZ	NY
NATHALIA	.08	F	INFANT	RRZZZZ	NY
BECKER, SALMEN	22	M	DLR	RRZZZZ	NY
KUSCZINSKY, FRANS	24	M	LABR	RRZZZZ	NY
GORALSKY, FRANZ	22	M	LABR	RRZZZZ	NY
SPIBULAWSKY, ANDR	28	M	LABR	RRZZZZ	NY
WACHLEWICZ, PA-E	24	M	LABR	RRZZZZ	NY
SAWE-KA, VINCENT	36	M	LABR	RRZZZZ	NY
MAR--K--WICZ, JOS	26	M	LABR	RRZZZZ	NY
CASIMIR	25	M	LABR	RRZZZZ	NY
LIMANOWSKY, JACOB	31	M	TLR	RRZZZZ	NY
RIFKE	30	F	W	RRZZZZ	NY
WOLF	6	M	CHILD	RRZZZZ	NY
PEIGE	3	F	CHILD	RRZZZZ	NY
BEILE	.11	F	INFANT	RRZZZZ	NY
HIRSCHBERG, SARA	24	F	SGL	RRZZZZ	NY
DRU-SEL, BERTHA	25	F	SGL	RRZZZZ	NY
--UMASCHIN, ABR	32	M	LABR	RRZZZZ	NY
CZIBOWSKY, THOMAS	48	M	LABR	RRZZZZ	NY
MILIAN, VICTOR	27	M	LABR	RRZZZZ	NY
PALLASCH, FRANZ	23	M	LABR	RRZZZZ	NY
KO-HAN, FRANK	26	M	LABR	RRZZZZ	NY
KOSLOWSKY, JOSEF	26	M	LABR	RRZZZZ	NY
GELBER, EISIG	18	M	LABR	RRZZZZ	NY
P-NKO, MARIA	16	F	SGL	RRZZZZ	NY
RUBINSTEIN, ISRAEL	58	M	LABR	RRZZZZ	NY
ISAAK	18	M	CH	RRZZZZ	NY
ESTHER	15	F	CH	RRZZZZ	NY
GETTEL	9	F	CHILD	RRZZZZ	NY
BELICKY, MENDEL	22	M	LABR	RRZZZZ	NY
SARA	20	F	W	RRZZZZ	NY
REGORDECKI, ARON	17	M	LABR	RRZZZZ	NY
GOLDBERG, DAVID	22	M	LABR	RRZZZZ	NY
U	19	F	W	RRZZZZ	NY
HAMBERG, ELIAS	42	M	LABR	RRZZZZ	NY
S-RZELBA, SCHLOME	26	M	LABR	RRZZZZ	NY
KRAJCIK, MOSES	26	M	LABR	RRZZZZ	NY
-NDOW, MICHAEL	26	M	LABR	RRZZZZ	JON
RAB-OWITZ, ARON	46	M	TLR	RRZZZZ	JON
R-FKE	35	F	W	RRZZZZ	JON
CHANNE	15	F	CH	RRZZZZ	JON
FAU-E	8	F	CHILD	RRZZZZ	JON
DAVID	8	M	CHILD	RRZZZZ	JON
CHEIM	4	M	CHILD	RRZZZZ	JON
MEYER	2	M	CHILD	RRZZZZ	JON
LEISER	.11	M	INFANT	RRZZZZ	JON

SHIP: SERVIA

FROM: LIVERPOOL AND QUEENSTOWN
TO: NEW YORK
ARRIVED: 20 FEBRUARY 1888

PASSENGER	AGE	SEX	OCCUPATION	PRI VIL	DES
CREMENER, NE---E	40	F	W	RRZZZZ	NY
ROXE	18	F	SP	RRZZZZ	NY
IDA	12	F	SP	RRZZZZ	NY
OCEF	10	M	CH	RRZZZZ	NY
ZAXAF	8	M	CHILD	RRZZZZ	NY
DYANKA	3	F	CHILD	RRZZZZ	NY
DORDA-	.11	F	INFANT	RRZZZZ	NY
STEIN, PINCAS	20	M	LABR	RRZZZZ	NY
SCHMUL, NACH-ME	37	M	LABR	RRZZZZ	NY
SIMON, BENKO	65	M	TCHR	RRZZZZ	UNK
CHAGE	20	F	SP	RRZZZZ	UNK
KRAVITZ, ARON	43	M	TLR	RRZZZZ	NY
LEISER, MENDEL	53	M	BKR	RRZZZZ	NY
ABRAH	11	M	CH	RRZZZZ	NY
TAWSU-CKO, ABRAH	30	M	JNR	RRZZZZ	NY
WEISSMANN, MOSES	20	M	LABR	RRZZZZ	NY
RUBENSTEIN, JOS	28	M	TLR	RRZZZZ	NY
STERN, ISAAC	11	M	CH	RRZZZZ	NY
KAPLAN, LEIB	50	M	CL	RRZZZZ	PA

PASSENGER	AGE	SEX	OCCUPATION	PV RI VL	DES
EISENBERG, HERSCHEL	11	M	CH	RRZZZZ	PA
R-GNUEZ, JOHAN	23	M	LABR	RRZZZZ	PA
ALEXANDER	22	M	LABR	RRZZZZ	PA
SCHA-EWITZ, MOSES	30	M	BCHR	RRZZZZ	PA
BERKOWITZ, SCHIE	43	M	TLR	RRZZZZ	NY
BERKE	11	M	CH	RRZZZZ	NY
CZERNISK, MATIAS	21	M	LABR	RRZZZZ	NY
FEI-BERG, MARK	57	M	MCHT	RRZZZZ	MA
LEGASCHINSKY, MICHL	37	M	LABR	RRZZZZ	NY
KURTEWITZ, CONSTANTIN	14	M	LABR	RRZZZZ	NY
WLADISLAW	11	M	CH	RRZZZZ	NY
SKALSKI, FRANZ	39	M	LABR	RRZZZZ	NY
SAPERIA, ETTA	24	F	W	RRZZZZ	MA
ELLEN	19	F	SP	RRZZZZ	MA
MARRIS, HANNAH	21	F	SP	RRZZZZ	MA

SHIP: ISLAND

FROM: CHRISTIANA, CHRISTIANSAND AND COPENHAGEN
TO: NEW YORK
ARRIVED: 20 FEBRUARY 1888

PASSENGER	AGE	SEX	OCCUPATION	PV RI VL	DES
STARKASSNAES, U	14	M	LABR	FNZZZZ	USA
GREFNE, JOHAN	23	M	LABR	FNZZZZ	USA
CEDERLOEF, HINRIK	27	M	LABR	FNZZZZ	USA
LOFGUIST, FRANS	23	M	LABR	FNZZZZ	USA
KULLNABBE, JOHAN	28	M	LABR	FNZZZZ	USA
NYGAARD, ALEX	24	M	LABR	FNZZZZ	USA
FI-PUS, MATS	40	M	LABR	FNZZZZ	USA
FISKARS, MATS	36	M	LABR	FNZZZZ	USA
SOEDERMAN, ALFRED	30	M	LABR	FNZZZZ	USA
-UND, JOHAN	21	M	LABR	FNZZZZ	USA
CRONHOLM, AND	39	M	LABR	FNZZZZ	USA
TARPS, JOHN	26	M	LABR	FNZZZZ	USA
BRAMMAS, CARL	23	M	LABR	FNZZZZ	USA
CEDERBERG, AUG	32	M	LABR	FNZZZZ	USA
VILH	26	M	LABR	FNZZZZ	USA
-ROOKS, BRITA	41	F	SGL	FNZZZZ	USA

SHIP: EIDER

FROM: BREMEN AND SOUTHAMPTON
TO: NEW YORK
ARRIVED: 21 FEBRUARY 1888

PASSENGER	AGE	SEX	OCCUPATION	PV RI VL	DES
KRASCHEWSKI, APPOLLIN	29	M	NN	RRZZZZ	USA
KOHN, MICHLE	59	M	MCHT	RRZZZZ	USA
PEPENDICK, ERNST	30	M	FARMER	RRZZZZ	USA
BERLINGHAUS, PETER	35	M	FARMER	RRZZZZ	USA
HOLZ, GERH.	32	M	FARMER	RRZZZZ	USA
WOLF, JOSEF	27	M	FARMER	RRZZZZ	USA
FRIETWISCH, JOSEF	18	M	FARMER	RRZZZZ	USA

SHIP: ANCHORIA

FROM: GLASGOW AND MOVILLE
TO: NEW YORK
ARRIVED: 21 FEBRUARY 1888

PASSENGER	AGE	SEX	OCCUPATION	PV RI VL	DES
MENDELOWITZ, GALE	31	M	TLR	RRAIGH	USA
ROIKE	10	M	CH	RRAIGH	USA
JOSEEL	7	M	CHILD	RRAIGH	USA
MENDEL	17	M	TLR	RRAIGH	USA
KAPEL, ETTE	30	F	W	RRAIGH	USA
MALKE	9	F	CHILD	RRAIGH	USA
ABRAM	6	M	CHILD	RRAIGH	USA
MINE	4	F	CHILD	RRAIGH	USA
GURIAN, CHAIM	46	M	TLR	RRAIGH	USA
WOLF	14	M	TLR	RRAIGH	USA
MERI	19	F	SVNT	RRAIGH	USA
KAPLAN, ABEL	40	M	MLR	RRAHTU	USA
SCHMUL	14	M	MLR	RRAHTU	USA
BER	10	M	CH	RRAHTU	USA
CAHN, JACOB	30	M	TLR	RRAIGH	USA
EDELMAN, ABRAM	42	M	JNR	RRAGRT	USA
CHAIE	14	F	SVNT	RRAGRT	USA
GERSERNI, LEIB	18	M	CGRMKR	RRAGRT	USA
FEIGE	18	F	SVNT	RRAIGH	USA
DEVINSKI, FEIGE	34	F	W	RRAIGH	USA
SARA	7	F	CHILD	RRAIGH	USA
SCHULZ, LEIB	22	M	TLR	RRAIGH	USA
MORDCH	11	M	CH	RRAIGH	USA
PIK, SOLOMON	50	M	LABR	RRAHTU	USA
RUWEL	30	M	LABR	RRAIGH	USA
MARUR, FEIGE	21	F	SVNT	RRAIGH	USA
SCHONI	18	F	SVNT	RRAIGH	USA
PARTNEI, BENGIE	38	M	TLR	RRAHOK	USA
PIEK, MICHAEL	16	M	TLR	RRAHTU	USA
GOLDSTEIN, ADOLF	21	M	TLR	RRZZZZ	USA
CHASCHURIM, JACOB	34	M	TLR	RRAHTU	USA
JOCKELMAN, JACOB	21	M	TLR	RRAHTU	USA
SCHUSTER, JOSEF	16	M	TLR	RRAHTU	USA
ARONOWITZ, JOSSEL	18	M	TLR	RRAHTU	USA
WILITZKY, ARON	38	M	TLR	RRAHTU	USA
SCHWITZKY, BERKY	28	M	TLR	RRAHTU	USA
SALOMON, BERKY	28	M	TLR	RRAHTU	USA
KARTAW, SAM	26	M	TLR	RRAHTU	USA
GELPER, CHAIM	15	M	TLR	RRAHTU	USA
EPELBAUM, ISAK	34	M	TLR	RRAHQU	USA
ALBUT, SENDER	38	M	TLR	RRAHQU	USA
STEINBERG, LEISER	28	M	TLR	RRAHQU	USA
WORSPER, SAUL	20	M	TLR	RRAHQU	USA
EBRAN, INOCK	40	M	TLR	RRAHQU	USA
PUSNAK, SAM	26	M	BLKSMH	RRAHTU	USA
FRAENKEL, MOS	18	M	SHMK	RRAHTU	USA
SCHAPIRA, MORDCHE	45	M	DLR	RRAHTU	USA
PULKE, GRAU	21	M	SLMK	RRAHTU	USA
HALPERSWITZ, MORD	36	M	GZR	RRAGRT	USA
ROEDANSKI, MOSES	20	M	SHMK	RRAGRT	USA
LEWIN, VIGDOR	36	M	PDLR	RRAGRT	USA
MALZO, MITROFAN	20	M	LABR	RRAGRT	USA
EHRLICK, JOSSEL	19	M	SHMK	RRAICF	USA
MOSKWITZ, ITZIG	30	M	JNR	RRAIDH	USA
DISKIN, DAVID	42	M	CPR	RRZZZZ	USA
SCHWARZ, MOSES	17	M	SMH	RRAIGH	USA
MATZKEWITZ, JOSEFA	50	F	MA	RRAIGH	USA
ROSINSKI, SORA	21	F	SVNT	RRAHZS	USA

SHIP: GOTHIA

FROM: SWINEMUNDE
TO: NEW YORK
ARRIVED: 21 FEBRUARY 1888

PASSENGER	AGE	SEX	OCCUPATION	PRV VIL DES
WISCZNEWSKA, KATARZYNA	23	F	W	RRZZZZUSA
JOSEPH	3	M	CHILD	RRZZZZUSA
WISZNEWSKA, JOHANN	1	M	CHILD	RRZZZZUSA
FINK, ADOLF	18	M	MLR	RRZZZZUSA
KMIETEK, MAGDALENA	23	F	SGL	PLZZZZUSA
THIESSEN, PETER	23	M	LABR	RRZZZZUSA
GUNTHER, JOHANN	26	M	LABR	RRZZZZUSA
REGINA	26	F	W	RRZZZZUSA
SUSANNE	1	F	CHILD	RRZZZZUSA
REGINA	.05	F	INFANT	RRZZZZUSA

SHIP: HERMANN

FROM: BREMEN
TO: BALTIMORE
ARRIVED: 22 FEBRUARY 1888

PASSENGER	AGE	SEX	OCCUPATION	PRV VIL DES
COHEN, GITEL	30	F	UNKNOWN	RRZZZZUSA
RUCHEL	8	F	CHILD	RRZZZZUSA
ROSENBLATT, ISRAEL	35	M	UNKNOWN	RRZZZZUSA
KOVETZKY, KOPPEL	24	M	PDLR	RRZZZZUSA
INSCHIENEWICZ, LUDWIGA	19	F	UNKNOWN	RRAINZUSA
JONIEFA	.01	F	INFANT	RRAINZUSA
SIEMMSKA, REGINA	20	F	UNKNOWN	RRAINZUSA
BABRUN, LEIB	50	M	PDLR	RRAIJJUSA
RACHEL	45	F	W	RRAIJJUSA
SAMUEL	1	M	CHILD	RRAIJJUSA
NATHAN	8	M	CHILD	RRAIJJUSA
BERTERUMOWITZ, IWAN	25	M	PDLR	RRZZZZUSA
VOLOTZKA, VINCENT	25	M	PDLR	RRZZZZUSA

SHIP: ENGLAND

FROM: LIVERPOOL
TO: NEW YORK
ARRIVED: 23 FEBRUARY 1888

PASSENGER	AGE	SEX	OCCUPATION	PRV VIL DES
GONVEMOS, LEOPOLD	26	M	LABR	RRZZZZLA
LOEBENWERTH, JOSEPH	26	M	LABR	RRZZZZNY
ROSENTHAL, MORRIS	21	M	LABR	RRZZZZNY
MARGOLIS, AARON	40	M	LABR	RRZZZZSTL
FRIEDLAND, LEIB.	25	M	LABR	RRZZZZNY
RISKIND, JACOB	45	M	LABR	RRZZZZNY
KOPELWEN, HIRSCH	22	M	LABR	RRZZZZNY
BRAIMSSEN, LEIB	18	M	LABR	RRZZZZNY
KISBRICK, KASIMER	30	M	LABR	RRZZZZNY
JOSEPH, CHAINE	26	M	LABR	RRZZZZNY
MASEITIS, JOSEPH	40	M	LABR	RRZZZZNY
ROMANANKIS, VINE	21	M	LABR	RRZZZZNY
RUSKAN, VINCENT	42	M	LABR	RRZZZZNY
KLIMBERT, LAZAR	26	M	LABR	RRZZZZCH
WIGOROWITSCH, DAVID	28	M	LABR	RRZZZZNY
NACH, LEIB	16	M	LABR	RRZZZZNY
GORDON, JOSEL	24	M	LABR	RRZZZZNY
BLANKIFELD, LAZAR	19	M	LABR	RRZZZZNY
ZERKES, ISRAEL	23	M	LABR	RRZZZZNY
MARGOLIS, JACOB	19	M	LABR	RRZZZZNY
SOUNTAG, ABRAHAM	27	M	LABR	RRZZZZNY
KRUKOW, ANGEVEL	20	M	LABR	RRZZZZNY
POSKOWIC, ISAK	17	M	LABR	RRZZZZNY
HALFERN, ABRAHAM	34	M	LABR	RRZZZZNY
STEINILLA, VINC.	27	M	LABR	RRZZZZNY
SAMBOWITZ, PAUL	22	M	LABR	RRZZZZNY
LAKOLOW, SCHLEGER	30	M	LABR	RRZZZZNY
GANONEKCH, SAMUEL	22	M	LABR	RRZZZZNY
KAHN, THEODOR	16	M	LABR	RRZZZZNY
FEINSKIN, BER.	22	M	LABR	RRZZZZPHI
KALIN, ISAK	45	M	LABR	RRZZZZNY
CHAREST, BERKE	22	M	LABR	RRZZZZNY
LUNSKY, ABRAHAM	22	M	LABR	RRZZZZNY
SCHULESKIL, MAIZIA	21	M	LABR	RRZZZZNY
BLACHER, RAFAEL	23	M	LABR	RRZZZZNY
BENDELSTEIN, MOSES	36	M	LABR	RRZZZZNY
GOSEZEWSKY, JOS.	27	M	LABR	RRZZZZNY
POLEGIS, ISRAEL	30	M	LABR	RRZZZZNY
CHODESCH, MORDCHE	26	M	LABR	RRZZZZNY
TAMISCHWESKY, JACOB	20	M	LABR	RRZZZZNY
ORLOW, OMELKO	20	M	LABR	RRZZZZNY
TERMOLEIAW, SCHIDOR	21	M	LABR	RRZZZZNY
ATHOV, HEIKKI	33	M	LABR	RRZZZZNY
LAPISTA, JULIAN	30	M	LABR	FNZZZZNY
LEPISTA, NATTI	18	M	LABR	FNZZZZNY
LISSALA, AUGUST	26	M	LABR	FNZZZZNY
WIKKI, KRISTIAN	26	M	LABR	FNZZZZNY
TELEVERAS, DOMINIC	30	M	LABR	FNZZZZNY
AIKAN, VICTOR	18	M	LABR	FNZZZZNY
SUANALA, JULIAN	22	M	LABR	FNZZZZNY
WAERN, KRISTIAN	18	M	LABR	FNZZZZNY
WERTANEN, ALEX	24	M	LABR	FNZZZZNY
SOERN, ALEX	20	M	LABR	FNZZZZNY
WESTANEN, DAVID	24	M	LABR	FNZZZZNY
TAKOLA, JULIAN	32	M	LABR	FNZZZZNY
APOKKA, ERKI	24	M	LABR	FNZZZZNY
WANNUAKI, KANE	36	M	LABR	FNZZZZNY
SOLOMOWITZ, BENJ.	58	M	LABR	RRZZZZNY
JENNY	19	F	SP	RRZZZZNY
POLISKY, HOLDE	40	F	W	RRZZZZNY
LAIZ	16	F	SP	RRZZZZNY
BEISER	11	M	CH	RRZZZZNY
JACK	9	M	CHILD	RRZZZZNY
ALLI	7	M	CHILD	RRZZZZNY
JACOBSON, WOLF	22	M	LABR	RRZZZZNY
SLAVICH	24	F	SP	RRZZZZNY
BERCHWAIN, SCHALEIE	30	M	LABR	RRZZZZNY
JENTE	30	F	W	RRZZZZNY
HINE	18	F	SVNT	RRZZZZNY
OKRUST, ESTHER	18	F	SVNT	RRZZZZNY
MOGULIKI, ELIZTH.	20	F	SVNT	RRZZZZNY
BUSEZANSKY, RACHEL	41	F	W	RRZZZZNY
CHAIE	15	F	SP	RRZZZZNY
MINA	11	F	CH	RRZZZZNY
MODSCHE	9	M	CHILD	RRZZZZNY
BOSCHE	3	F	CHILD	RRZZZZNY
ESTHER	21	F	SVNT	RRZZZZNY
ELKE	.09	F	INFANT	RRZZZZNY
SCHLEIZERBACH, MODSCHE	48	M	LABR	RRZZZZNY
CHAIE	48	F	W	RRZZZZNY
SCHEINE	16	F	SP	RRZZZZNY
SAMUEL	9	M	CHILD	RRZZZZNY
SCHOLEM	8	M	CHILD	RRZZZZNY
WILKOWISCHKY, SALOMON	18	M	LABR	RRZZZZNY
EISENSCHMIDT, SELE	18	F	SVNT	RRZZZZNY
GERSCHEWORWITZ, LINA	20	F	SVNT	RRZZZZPHI
KOSLOWSKY, TAUBE	20	F	W	RRZZZZNY
MICHLE	1	M	CHILD	RRZZZZNY
HADOWSKY, EIZERNE	16	F	SVNT	RRZZZZNY
KATTOVSITEZ, MERE	18	F	SVNT	RRZZZZNY
KETTLER, CHASE	17	F	SVNT	RRZZZZNY
TOPER, MALKE	37	F	W	RRZZZZNY
CHANE	20	F	SP	RRZZZZNY
BEILE	17	F	SP	RRZZZZNY
NACHAME	10	M	CH	RRZZZZNY
NOCHEM	7	F	CHILD	RRZZZZNY

PASSENGER	AGE	SEX	OCCUPATION	PRIV	VIL	DES
ABRAHAM	.11	F	INFANT	RR	ZZZZ	NY
FILOT, NOCHEN	11	F	CH	RR	ZZZZ	NY
BRAMER, NOCHEM	46	F	W	RR	ZZZZ	NY
FIEGE	10	F	CH	RR	ZZZZ	NY
NICHEUMAS	9	M	CHILD	RR	ZZZZ	NY
MILZER, JANKEL	11	F	CH	RR	ZZZZ	NY

SHIP: RHYNLAND

FROM: ANTWERP
TO: NEW YORK
ARRIVED: 23 FEBRUARY 1888

PASSENGER	AGE	SEX	OCCUPATION	PRIV	VIL	DES
SANDROWSKY, M	17	M	WCHMKR	RR	ADBQ	PHI
SEELARS, B	28	F	WCHMKR	RR	ADBQ	PHI
U	28	F	UNKNOWN	RR	ADBQ	PHI
HARRI	2	M	CHILD	RR	ADBQ	PHI
MISHNOWSKY, B	19	F	UNKNOWN	RR	ADBQ	PHI

SHIP: STATE OF INDIANA

FROM: GLASGOW AND LARNE
TO: NEW YORK
ARRIVED: 23 FEBRUARY 1888

PASSENGER	AGE	SEX	OCCUPATION	PRIV	VIL	DES
LASKOWSKI, MATHIAS	29	M	LABR	RR	ZZZZ	USA
PIECIK, JOHAN	32	M	LABR	RR	ZZZZ	USA
JAKOBKOWSKY, ISRAEL	34	M	LABR	RR	ZZZZ	USA
PERSCHOWITZ, JACOB	26	M	LABR	RR	ZZZZ	USA
JAFFE, MOSES	19	M	FARMER	RR	ZZZZ	USA
DIANOWSKI, MARIE	23	M	PDLR	RR	ZZZZ	USA
ELIZABETH	28	F	W	RR	ZZZZ	USA
SCHACHNOWITZ, CHAECHE	30	F	W	RR	ZZZZ	USA
JOSEPGH	2	M	CHILD	RR	ZZZZ	USA
DUNSCHE	1	F	CHILD	RR	ZZZZ	USA
SAWDER, CAULIE	22	F	DMS	RR	ZZZZ	USA
POLANSKE, DORE	18	F	DMS	RR	ZZZZ	USA

SHIP: SAALE

FROM: BREMEN AND SOUTHAMPTON
TO: NEW YORK
ARRIVED: 24 FEBRUARY 1888

PASSENGER	AGE	SEX	OCCUPATION	PRIV	VIL	DES
MEYERSKI, STANISL	29	M	LABR	RR	ZZZZ	USA
WALTUKO, JOHN	20	M	LABR	RR	ZZZZ	USA
BRENNER, EMILIE	15	F	UNKNOWN	RR	ZZZZ	USA
MIKOTOJESCH, PETRO	28	M	LABR	RR	ZZZZ	USA
MAKOWSKI, VOISTADT	60	M	LABR	RR	ZZZZ	USA
SOWIENSKI, JOSEF	33	M	LABR	RR	ZZZZ	USA
KOMOSCHINSKI, JOH..	29	M	LABR	RR	ZZZZ	USA

SHIP: CITY OF BERLIN

FROM: LIVERPOOL
TO: NEW YORK
ARRIVED: 24 FEBRUARY 1888

PASSENGER	AGE	SEX	OCCUPATION	PRIV	VIL	DES
MARHILLA, MARIA	25	F	SVNT	RR	AINO	NY
DULNEA, LUCINA	25	F	SVNT	RR	AINO	NY
HANSON, JACOB	23	M	LABR	RR	AINO	CO
HAMANSON, ANDRAS	23	M	LABR	RR	AINO	CO
ERICKSON, ANDRAS	25	M	LABR	RR	AINO	CO
HERMANSON, JOHAN	20	M	LABR	RR	AINO	NY
ANDERSON, ANDRAS	18	M	LABR	RR	AINO	CO
ALADALA, ERICK	43	M	LABR	RR	AINO	NY
AGALLS, H.	30	M	LABR	RR	AINO	NY
AEKONGERS, U	44	M	LABR	RR	AINO	NY
ISALLES, JACOB	45	M	LABR	RR	AINO	NY
LOUISSELLA, INO	18	M	LABR	RR	AINO	CO
SILLYGURST, ERIC	50	M	LABR	RR	AINO	CO
SOLLA, JOHAN	34	M	LABR	RR	AINO	NY
ADD, JOHAN	23	M	LABR	RR	AINO	MI
ULIKA	24	F	W	RR	AINO	MI
LUMOLA, H.	20	M	LABR	RR	AINO	CO
LOMOLA, J.	43	M	LABR	RR	AINO	NY
WEIKALO, J.	18	M	LABR	RR	AINO	NY
STOFFER, MATT	27	M	LABR	RR	AINO	NY

SHIP: GELLERT

FROM: HAMBURG AND HAVRE
TO: NEW YORK
ARRIVED: 25 FEBRUARY 1888

PASSENGER	AGE	SEX	OCCUPATION	PRIV	VIL	DES
GROSS, RADMIDLE	18	M	PNTR	RR	ZZZZ	USA
FISCHMANN, ESTHER	23	F	WO	RR	AHZH	USA
DAVID	5	M	CHILD	RR	AHZH	USA
RACHEL	.11	F	INFANT	RR	AHZH	USA
DUBLICKI, MORDCHE	24	M	LABR	RR	AFVG	USA
MORDCHE	9	M	CHILD	RR	AFVG	USA
DONCCZYNSKI, JANKEL	47	M	LABR	RR	AFVG	USA
FINKELSTEIN, ISRAEL	18	M	LABR	RR	AFVG	USA
SIMON, KANKEL	23	M	JNR	RR	ACBF	USA
NOREZKY, ARON	20	M	DLR	RR	AIHN	USA
OPPENHEIM, JISSLE	30	F	W	RR	AIHN	USA
MOSES	6	M	CHILD	RR	AIHN	USA
DWORE	4	M	CHILD	RR	AIHN	USA
CHAJE	.06	M	INFANT	RR	AIHN	USA
WICHEWSKY, ABRAM	34	M	LABR	RR	AHTD	USA
MAZULEVSITZ, STANISLAUS	32	M	LABR	RR	ZZZZ	USA
BERGMANN, ISAAC	26	M	DLR	RR	ZZZZ	USA
PERL	22	M	W	RR	ZZZZ	USA
CHAIE	9	F	CHILD	RR	ZZZZ	USA
WOLF	.06	M	INFANT	RR	ZZZZ	USA
TOUCHANSKY, MOSES	36	M	LABR	RR	ZZZZ	USA
JAWIDZIK, JANS	21	M	LABR	RR	ZZZZ	USA
RAFALSKI, IGNATZ	26	M	LABR	RR	ZZZZ	USA
NAWADSHI, STEFAN	29	M	LABR	RR	ZZZZ	USA
HENE, JACOB	33	M	LABR	RR	ZZZZ	USA
JABLONSKI, MAXIMILIAN	22	M	LABR	RR	ZZZZ	USA
GRABOWSKY, WOYCECH	29	M	LABR	RR	ZZZZ	USA
JABLONSKY, FRANZ	35	M	LABR	RR	ZZZZ	USA
SWOBONAS, JOSEF	29	M	LABR	RR	ZZZZ	USA
MARIE	23	F	W	RR	ZZZZ	USA
PAULIKONIS, FRANZ	29	M	LABR	RR	ZZZZ	USA
FROMM, ALBERT	25	M	LABR	RR	ZZZZ	USA
SIGAL, MALI	20	F	SGL	RR	AIGU	USA
EWET, JOH.	24	M	LABR	RR	ZZZZ	USA
KOZIN, SCHLOME	25	M	LABR	RR	ZZZZ	USA
MARGULIS, MASCHE	9	M	CHILD	RR	ZZZZ	USA

PASSENGER	AGE	SEX	OCCUPATION	PRV	VIL	DES
SCHOLEM, MENDEL	30	M	LABR	RR	AHTU	USA
RUBIN, JOS.	32	M	LABR	RR	AHTU	USA
SCHUSTER, SCHOLEM	19	M	LABR	RR	AHTU	USA
MINEWITZKI, HIRSCH	29	M	LABR	RR	AHTU	USA
POSENGZEK, CHAIM	30	M	LABR	RR	AHTU	USA
LIDSHI, JOSSEL	34	M	LABR	RR	AHTU	USA
ELTERMANN, SCHMUL	29	M	LABR	RR	AIBO	USA
PALEI, SCHOLEM	9	M	CHILD	RR	AIBO	USA
STREBENIK, CHAIM	30	M	LABR	RR	AIBO	USA
JASGUR, ULRICH	37	M	LABR	RR	AIBO	USA
ADLAWANKEN, ABRAM	28	M	LABR	RR	AHTU	USA
GLISINSKI, ITZKO	29	M	LABR	RR	AHTU	USA
HASS, FERDINAND	31	M	LABR	RR	AHTU	USA
BURGOW, IWAN	28	M	LABR	RR	AHTU	USA
MARKOWITZ, ALEX	24	M	LKSH	RR	AHTU	USA
NYKOZINSKI, JAN	24	M	SHMK	RR	AHTU	USA
ZEGLINSKI, ANTON	32	M	SHMK	RR	AHTU	USA
KLEMENT, JAN	22	M	LABR	RR	ZZZZ	USA
BECKER, ABRAM	22	M	LABR	RR	ZZZZ	USA
STEIN, MEIER	21	M	LABR	RR	ZZZZ	USA
SZAGOWITZ, SCHEEL	24	M	LABR	RR	ZZZZ	USA
LUNGIN, SCHMUL	28	M	LABR	RR	ZZZZ	USA
GITTEL	25	F	W	RR	ZZZZ	USA
KAHNOWSKI, MASCHE	32	F	WO	RR	ZZZZ	USA
RUBINSTEIN, KAPEL	21	M	TLR	RR	ZZZZ	USA
SCHAPIRO, MORDUCH	21	M	TLR	RR	ZZZZ	USA
SACHERER, ISAAC	55	M	LABR	RR	ZZZZ	USA
JANKEL	22	M	LABR	RR	ZZZZ	USA
ABRAHAM	18	M	LABR	RR	ZZZZ	USA
BLUMENTAL, SCHLOME	21	M	LABR	RR	ZZZZ	USA
NATHANSON, DAVID	22	M	LABR	RR	AHTF	USA
OKIN, JERKO	24	M	LABR	RR	AHTF	USA
LEWIN, ORE	25	M	LABR	RR	AHTF	USA
KURATZ, CONRAD	28	M	LABR	RR	AHTF	USA
SEROW, ISRAEL	54	M	LABR	RR	AHTF	USA
EICHNER, ANTONIA	21	F	LABR	RR	AHTF	USA
GIOVANNI	20	F	W	RR	AHTF	USA
ALMA	.01	F	INFANT	RR	AHTF	USA
KAULOROWICZ, ARON	23	M	LABR	RR	AHTU	USA
BERNSTEIN, CHAIM	23	M	SLR	RR	AHTU	USA
NOWITZKI, KLEMENTY	58	M	LABR	RR	AHTU	USA
SUTIN, RACHMEL	36	M	LABR	RR	AHTU	USA
ARIC	9	M	CHILD	RR	AHTU	USA
ISRAEL	35	M	LABR	RR	AHTU	USA
FRIEDLAENDER, JOSSEL	30	M	LABR	RR	AHTU	USA
PLATZKI, ABRAM	15	M	LABR	RR	AHTU	USA
JUST, EMIL	27	M	LABR	RR	AHTU	USA
KAPLAN, DEBORAH	23	F	SGL	RR	AHTU	USA
WIRPEL, SARAH	28	F	W	RR	AHTF	USA
EISEGH	4	M	CHILD	RR	ZZZZ	USA
JECHESKEL	3	M	CHILD	RR	ZZZZ	USA
ARON	.11	M	INFANT	RR	ZZZZ	USA
NECHEMIE	.04	M	INFANT	RR	ZZZZ	USA
BUSSEL, PESCHE	23	F	SGL	RR	AHTU	USA
RABINOWITZ, SAMUEL	30	M	LABR	RR	ZZZZ	USA

SHIP: UMBRIA

FROM: LIVERPOOL
TO: NEW YORK
ARRIVED: 27 FEBRUARY 1888

PASSENGER	AGE	SEX	OCCUPATION	PRV	VIL	DES
AUMANN, WILLIAM	32	M	FARMER	RR	AERS	USA
ANACKEL, BOMES	31	M	LABR	RR	AERS	USA
HETIN, MUDIES	18	M	LABR	RR	AIKG	USA
BESCHINSKY, FRANZ	32	M	LABR	RR	AHOO	USA
BANCHOWITZ, JACOB	35	M	LABR	RR	AHOO	USA
SOLOMON	17	M	LABR	RR	ZZZZ	USA
BELOCH, MORDICEA	25	M	LABR	RR	AIFM	USA
CZZCHOWSKY, RUDOLF	27	M	LABR	RR	AIFM	USA
CHAUES, OTTOMAN	19	M	LABR	RR	ZZZZ	USA
CHINSLINSKY, HAIDEL	26	M	MA	RR	ACBF	USA
JANE	4	F	CHILD	RR	ACBF	USA
SEIWA	.03	M	INFANT	RR	ACBF	USA
TOMA	.11	M	INFANT	RR	ACBF	USA
JACOB	.11	M	INFANT	RR	ACBF	USA
KATZ, SOM	59	M	TLR	RR	ACBF	USA
DANKO, MIHALY	20	M	TLR	RR	AIHL	USA
DAUESCHEWSKI, MENACHAM	24	M	LABR	RR	AIHL	USA
DALINSKY, HIRSCH	44	M	LABR	RR	AIFM	USA
EFRIN, LEIB	18	M	LABR	RR	AHOO	USA
ELIASKOWITZ, MAMOW	24	M	DR	RR	AHOO	USA
FIDLER, FISCHEL	45	M	FARMER	RR	AILT	USA
FRICO, FIEDE	19	M	LABR	RR	ACBF	USA
FRIEDRICH, ANTONIA	18	M	LABR	RR	ACBF	USA
GUROLIEWICZ, ANTONIA	18	M	LABR	RR	ACBF	USA
MOSES	20	M	TLR	RR	ACBF	USA
GRUMBER, CHANE	23	M	TLR	RR	ACBF	USA
GERSCHAY, JULIUS	25	M	LABR	RR	AIKG	USA
GARLEET, THOMME	13	F	SVNT	RR	AIKG	USA
HERMANSON, MICH	31	M	LABR	RR	AIKG	USA
HOPSCHEIM, NISCHON	19	M	LABR	RR	AIKG	USA
HADZY, GABRIEL	16	M	LABR	RR	AIKG	USA
KASLAWSKY, KUSCHIEL	19	M	LABR	RR	AIKG	USA
KOSLOWSKY, HITZO	27	M	TLR	RR	ZZZZ	USA
KETZKY, DAVID	15	M	LABR	RR	AHOO	USA
MOSES	17	M	LABR	RR	AHOO	USA
KUOMKISA, NESSIS	28	M	LABR	RR	AHOO	USA
KIRKER, OTTOMON	31	M	LABR	RR	ZZZZ	USA
KUMITZ, NACHIEM	39	M	LABR	RR	AIHE	USA
LIFSCHITZ, GALLAL	16	M	LABR	RR	AIHE	USA
LOW, MOSES	36	M	LABR	RR	AIHE	USA
MAKOWSKY, ANTON	20	M	LABR	RR	AHOO	USA
MAJEWSKY, TAIE	30	M	LABR	RR	AHOO	USA
MICHALSKY, JOSEF	23	M	LABR	RR	AHOO	USA
MUGERDESCH, HOTSCHE	30	M	LABR	RR	ZZZZ	USA
OLSA, SCHAIS	30	M	LABR	RR	ZZZZ	USA
OPATOWSKY, MOSES	27	M	JWLR	RR	ACBF	USA
PET, BARSCHI	28	M	LABR	RR	ACBF	USA
ELIAS	7	M	CHILD	RR	ACBF	USA
PERLMUTTER, LEON	22	M	LABR	RR	ACBF	USA
ROKOCZI, JACOB	27	M	LABR	RR	AHOO	USA
RABINOWITZ, KIWAI	20	M	LABR	RR	AHOO	USA
ROTHENBERG, ALEXANDER	19	M	PDLR	RR	ACBF	USA
AMMTA	22	F	SVNT	RR	ACBF	USA
SUSSELL	20	M	SVNT	RR	ACBF	USA
SUSMAN, SAMUEL	25	M	JWLR	RR	AFVG	USA
SPITZER, JACOB	19	M	JNR	RR	AFVG	USA
SCHUNFELD, JOSSEL	30	M	LABR	RR	ACBF	USA
STOMPKOWSKI, VALUCH	27	M	LABR	RR	ACBF	USA
SATINSKY, STANISLAUS	37	M	LABR	RR	AIFM	USA
STERZKY, CREDZYK	31	M	LABR	RR	AIFM	USA
SUBITZKY, LEIB	36	M	GCR	RR	AIFM	USA
KUNE	16	M	LABR	RR	AIFM	USA
ELIAS	9	M	CHILD	RR	AIFM	USA
ISAAC	9	M	CHILD	RR	AIFM	USA
SALMANN, ABRAHAM	18	M	LABR	RR	AIFM	USA
SCHSUEN, ABRAHAM	24	M	LABR	RR	ZZZZ	USA
SCHOCHAT, ISRAEL	24	M	LABR	RR	ZZZZ	USA
TOPOLESKI, JOSEF	27	M	LABR	RR	AHOO	USA
VAGIMJAM, KEBINK	30	M	LABR	RR	AHOO	USA
UHELSCHINSKY, JOSEF	27	M	LABR	RR	AHOO	USA
ZAMESZDA, PETIE	20	M	LABR	RR	AHOO	USA
LIKIMK, ISAAC	27	M	LABR	RR	AIFL	USA
LI, LI	22	M	SVNT	RR	ADBQ	USA
U, FERDENAND	38	M	MCHT	RR	ZZZZ	USA
LIDIE	24	F	W	RR	ZZZZ	USA

PASSENGER	AGE	SEX	OCCUPATION	PRIV	DES

SHIP: POLARIA

FROM: HAMBURG
TO: NEW YORK
ARRIVED: 27 FEBRUARY 1888

PASSENGER	AGE	SEX	OCCUPATION	PRIV	DES
TOMASCHKEIT, JANOS	15	M	LABR	RRZZZZ	NY
BLANK, MARIA	27	F	WO	RRZZZZ	NY
EMILIE	.11	F	INFANT	RRZZZZ	NY
KASPEROWICZ, FRANZ	26	M	LABR	RRZZZZ	NY
BUDKOWITZ, JANOS	26	M	LABR	RRZZZZ	NY
GRABOWSKI, CASIMIR	30	M	LABR	RRZZZZ	NY
ROSLEIN, H	47	M	LABR	RRZZZZ	NY
GREIPER, SCHAP	38	M	LABR	RRZZZZ	NY
KANTOROWICZ, LEMKO	47	M	HTR	RRZZZZ	CH
LINA	48	F	W	RRZZZZ	NY
JOSSEL	18	M	S	RRZZZZ	NY
SANDSER, WOLF	45	M	GDNR	RRZZZZ	SY
GLUDMANOWITZ, RIWKE	23	F	WO	RRZZZZ	NY
CHANNE	7	F	CHILD	RRZZZZ	NY
RAPHAEL	.09	M	INFANT	RRZZZZ	NY
MOSCHEWSKY, MENASCHE	29	M	LABR	RRZZZZ	NY
HOLJAK, LEISER	30	M	TLR	RRZZZZ	NY
RUBIN, HIRSCH	50	M	MCHT	RRZZZZ	NY
SKROBISZUARK, CATH	23	F	SGL	RRZZZZ	NY
FINKELSTEIN, ESTHER	43	F	WO	RRZZZZ	NY
SANDEL	9	M	CHILD	RRZZZZ	NY
LEISER	7	M	CHILD	RRZZZZ	NY
CHAWE	4	F	CHILD	RRZZZZ	NY
MOSES	.11	M	INFANT	RRZZZZ	NY
LUTZ, JOSEF	28	M	LABR	RRZZZZ	PHI
ELENA	30	F	W	RRZZZZ	PHI
PLUNGE, CASINIA	28	M	LABR	RRZZZZ	PHI
LAMOTOWITSCH, CASSIMIR	24	M	LABR	RRZZZZ	PHI
KOMITES, JUSTIN	27	M	LABR	RRZZZZ	PHI
VALENCWIC, CASIMIR	22	M	LABR	RRZZZZ	PHI
NOVOROWSKY, JOS	32	M	LABR	RRZZZZ	PHI
URBAN, ESIP	20	M	LABR	RRZZZZ	PHI
IWANOWSKI, IWAN	26	M	LABR	RRZZZZ	PHI
OSTROWSKY, STANISL	20	M	LABR	RRZZZZ	PHI
WOSILEWSKI, NIESDAU	20	M	LABR	RRZZZZ	PHI
KERNSIC, IVAN	33	M	LABR	RRZZZZ	PHI
SAZEWITSCH, SEAS	54	M	LABR	RRZZZZ	PHI
SABISKY, PAWEL	28	M	LABR	RRZZZZ	PHI

SHIP: FULDA

FROM: BREMEN AND SOUTHAMPTON
TO: NEW YORK
ARRIVED: 28 FEBRUARY 1888

PASSENGER	AGE	SEX	OCCUPATION	PRIV	DES
WAJOSCHOWSKI, MATEUS	20	M	LABR	RRZZZZ	USA
IGNATZ	32	M	LABR	RRZZZZ	USA
BULLE, ADAM	18	M	LABR	RRZZZZ	USA
CHOVALSKY, ANTON	23	M	LABR	RRZZZZ	USA
WLADISLAUS	19	M	LABR	RRZZZZ	USA
THIEL, JOHANN	41	M	LABR	RRZZZZ	USA
AGATHE	34	F	UNKNOWN	RRZZZZ	USA
JACOB	7	M	CHILD	RRZZZZ	USA
CAROLINE	4	F	CHILD	RRZZZZ	USA
PETER	.11	M	INFANT	RRZZZZ	USA
SAUER, JOHANN	35	M	LABR	RRZZZZ	USA
ANNA	35	F	UNKNOWN	RRZZZZ	USA
ANNA	6	F	CHILD	RRZZZZ	USA
ANNA	8	F	CHILD	RRZZZZ	USA
MARIA	2	F	CHILD	RRZZZZ	USA
ANNA	.11	F	INFANT	RRZZZZ	USA
KATZENTOUER, ANTON	39	M	LABR	RRZZZZ	USA
MARIA	39	F	UNKNOWN	RRZZZZ	USA
ANNA	15	F	UNKNOWN	RRZZZZ	USA
PIUS	8	M	CHILD	RRZZZZ	USA
LEO	7	M	CHILD	RRZZZZ	USA
SAMUEL	4	M	CHILD	RRZZZZ	USA
MARIA	.04	F	INFANT	RRZZZZ	USA
STECKLEIN, ANNA	24	F	INF	RRZZZZ	USA
MARIA	.03	F	INFANT	RRZZZZ	USA
SPORNER, AUGUST	31	M	FARMER	RRZZZZ	USA
HEINZ, PETER	31	M	CPTR	RRZZZZ	USA
GLADE, FRIEDR	32	M	TLR	RRZZZZ	USA
KOSSAKOWSKI, JOSEF	41	M	LABR	RRZZZZ	USA
WISNIEWSKI, JOSEF	21	M	LABR	RRZZZZ	USA
GRAEF, MICHAL	38	M	FARMER	RRZZZZ	USA
BOLCH, HANNES	28	M	FARMER	RRZZZZ	USA
GAERBER, ANTON	27	M	FARMER	RRZZZZ	USA
SOPHIE	26	F	UNKNOWN	RRZZZZ	USA
MARGARETHA	5	F	CHILD	RRZZZZ	USA
LEWIN, SIMON	41	M	LABR	RRZZZZ	USA
DAVID	8	M	CHILD	RRZZZZ	USA
LEIB	8	M	CHILD	RRZZZZ	USA
ABRAMOWITZ, S	22	M	FARMER	RRZZZZ	USA
RESKA, AUGUST	50	M	MCHT	RRZZZZ	USA

SHIP: WISCONSIN

FROM: LIVERPOOL AND QUEENSTOWN
TO: NEW YORK
ARRIVED: 29 FEBRUARY 1888

PASSENGER	AGE	SEX	OCCUPATION	PRIV	DES
KJERSTROM, GUSTAF	40	M	FARMER	RRAIDE	USA
NYBONDE, ERIK	29	M	FARMER	RRAIDE	USA
STROM, JOHAN	31	M	FARMER	RRAIDE	USA
-JELLSTR, CARL	21	M	FARMER	RRAIDE	USA
KJAL, JOHANNES	21	F	SP	RRAIDE	USA
PELLAS, VICTOR	19	M	LABR	RRAIDE	USA
NYBONDE, JOHAN	20	M	LABR	RRAIDE	USA
BACK, GUSTAF	19	M	LABR	RRAIDE	USA
DAHL, ERIK	20	M	MSN	RRAIDE	USA
MAMMAS, OGRE	18	M	JNR	RRAIDE	USA
ROODD, JOHAN	46	M	FARMER	RRAIDE	USA
WOLPE, SANDER	18	M	FARMER	RRAIDE	USA
BACK, JOHANNA	27	F	SP	RRAIDE	USA
STOLPE, CARL	19	M	JNR	RRAIDE	USA
DAHL, ABRAHAM	23	M	MSN	RRAIDE	USA
HALBECK, HERMAN	33	M	FARMER	RRAIDE	USA
JOHNSON, MICKEL	38	M	FARMER	RRAIDE	USA
W-ORI, JACOB	35	M	FARMER	RRAIDE	USA
KNUTTI, MATTI	26	M	FARMER	RRAIDE	USA
YAMMELIN, MIKKO	30	M	FARMER	FNZZZZ	USA
MAMMI, MIKKO	30	M	FARMER	FNZZZZ	USA
SALMINA, MATTO	33	M	LABR	FNZZZZ	USA
PUKKA, MIKKO	28	M	MNR	FNZZZZ	USA
PROTUSCOWITZ, HERSCH	23	M	GZR	RRZZZZ	USA
NE-SER, GERSON	23	M	GZR	RRZZZZ	USA
RAGOWITZ, JAN-E	21	F	W	RRZZZZ	USA
MICKEL	3	M	CHILD	RRZZZZ	USA
CHAMMOVITZ, ABRM	19	M	FARMER	RRZZZZ	USA
ESTER	19	F	W	RRZZZZ	USA
GOLOMBEK, SAML	40	M	FARMER	RRZZZZ	USA
SARA	56	F	W	RRZZZZ	USA
JENKON, MOSES	33	M	PNTR	RRZZZZ	USA
SMARGONSKI, CHANE	35	F	SP	RRZZZZ	USA
K-R, FRADE	24	F	SP	RRZZZZ	USA
KURZ, RAPHAEL	23	F	SP	RRZZZZ	USA
ROPEKE, WILHELM	32	M	PMBR	RRZZZZ	USA
MARGARETHA	29	F	W	RRZZZZ	USA
ZURATHOWSKY, ANTON	44	M	FARMER	RRZZZZ	USA
SOOBODA, LEONARD	18	M	FARMER	RRZZZZ	USA
ROSENFELD, HILLE	36	F	SP	RRZZZZ	USA
WASSERSTEIN, ISAAC	25	M	PMBR	RRZZZZ	USA

PASSENGER	AGE	SEX	OCCUPATION	PRV VIL DES
ARONWICZ, ABRAH	38	M	MSN	RRZZZZUSA
KARPULO, ABRAH	17	M	TLR	RRZZZZUSA
SEGAL, NENDAL	28	M	TKR	RRZZZZUSA
GARMAZE, SEKE	20	M	PNTR	RRZZZZUSA
BERLIN, SOCHE	19	M	PNTR	RRZZZZUSA
RASCHEWSKI, ICHEME	20	F	SP	RRZZZZUSA
EUROTHOWSKI, ANTON	59	M	FARMER	RRZZZZUSA
RAKOS, JOHN	22	M	MECH	PLZZZZUSA
RATHOWSKY, L	29	M	GZR	RRZZZZUSA
LEPARTO, ISAAC	25	M	FARMER	RRZZZZUSA

SHIP: REPUBLIC

FROM: LIVERPOOL AND QUEENSTOWN
TO: NEW YORK
ARRIVED: 03 MARCH 1888

PASSENGER	AGE	SEX	OCCUPATION	PRV VIL DES
KOLTO-GORSKI, NIKE	25	M	MNR	PLZZZZUSA
OLTANAI, BELA.	00	F	SVNT	PLZZZZUSA
MARKS, -ECKEL	16	M	LABR	PLZZZZUSA
SCHARF, RETTE	38	F	W	PLZZZZUSA
JOSEF	11	M	CH	PLZZZZUSA
SELBEIM, JENKIN-A.	19	M	LABR	PLZZZZUSA
BECKRI, DOMS.	00	M	LABR	PLZZZZUSA
OHNGRIST, CARL-J.	15	M	LABR	PLZZZZUSA
RESSICH, LEIN	46	M	LABR	PLZZZZUSA
VDOWYEK, MOSEK	30	M	LABR	PLZZZZUSA
HAIGO	18	F	W	PLZZZZUSA
JAHASZ, U	15	F	SP	PLZZZZUSA
LANHER, SARA	17	F	SP	PLZZZZUSA
TRAUENHAAR, GERSON	41	M	LABR	PLZZZZUSA
ORLANSKI, NUTE	18	M	LABR	PLZZZZUSA
REICH, NAFLATE	33	M	LABR	PLZZZZUSA
BECHER, SAL.	23	M	LABR	PLZZZZUSA
DRILLICH, LEON	15	M	LABR	PLZZZZUSA
TANNERLING, EL.	28	M	LABR	PLZZZZUSA
GOLDE	18	F	SVNT	PLZZZZUSA
REICH, LEIB	21	M	LABR	PLZZZZUSA
BEMER, JACOB	19	M	LABR	PLZZZZUSA
GRELL, NACHMANN	28	M	LABR	PLZZZZUSA
EREDLICH, ABRAHAM	19	M	LABR	PLZZZZUSA
MOHRKOF, OSIAS	25	M	LABR	PLZZZZUSA
GRUNTHAL, GITTEL	17	F	SP	PLZZZZUSA
SCHEER, BEREL	28	M	LABR	PLZZZZUSA
RIFKE	18	F	SVNT	PLZZZZUSA
SCHULUM	11	M	CH	PLZZZZUSA
POSTOR, SARA	28	F	W	PLZZZZUSA
SAMUEL	9	M	CHILD	PLZZZZUSA
SOLOMON	7	M	CHILD	PLZZZZUSA
CHAWE	8	F	CHILD	PLZZZZUSA
LEIB	3	M	CHILD	PLZZZZUSA
BERGER, ZIPPE	30	F	W	PLZZZZUSA
JOSEPH	11	M	CH	PLZZZZUSA
MOSES	9	M	CHILD	PLZZZZUSA
MALKE	5	F	CHILD	PLZZZZUSA
ZIWGI	1	F	CHILD	PLZZZZUSA
UDWIN, GOLDE	35	F	W	PLZZZZUSA
MARKIN	10	M	CH	PLZZZZUSA
BELE	9	F	CHILD	PLZZZZUSA
HOPPET	4	M	CHILD	PLZZZZUSA
JOSEPH	3	M	CHILD	PLZZZZUSA
LEBHIN	2	F	CHILD	PLZZZZUSA
JACOB	1	M	CHILD	PLZZZZUSA
LEONSHIE, BEILE	21	F	SVNT	PLZZZZUSA
KLEIN, HERM.	22	M	LABR	PLZZZZUSA
FALKSTEIN, LEA	21	F	SVNT	PLZZZZUSA
REBECCA	17	F	SVNT	PLZZZZUSA
BILFER, JOS.	26	M	LABR	PLZZZZUSA
GROVOWSKY, FRANZIS-CHEC	31	M	LABR	PLZZZZUSA
SOCHOSKI, TRONG	42	M	LABR	PLZZZZUSA

PASSENGER	AGE	SEX	OCCUPATION	PRV VIL DES
SERCHOSKI, MAX	39	M	LABR	PLZZZZUSA
MORAWSKI, SILS.	36	M	LABR	PLZZZZUSA
NOWOKOWSKI, JOSEF	20	M	LABR	PLZZZZUSA
SEWANDOWIKA, MANUEL	00	M	LABR	PLZZZZUSA

SHIP: CITY OF CHESTER

FROM: LIVERPOOL
TO: NEW YORK
ARRIVED: 03 MARCH 1888

PASSENGER	AGE	SEX	OCCUPATION	PRV VIL DES
NENDELMANN, KATMANN	26	M	TLR	PLAGRTNY
WIRS--KOWSKI, FLISCH	30	M	BLKSMH	PLAGRTNY
SCHWARTZ, HANZ	40	M	BLKSMH	PLAGRTNY
KRAVITZ, SAMUEL	46	M	TLR	PLAGRTNY
FRIEDMANN, FERENZ	36	M	TLR	PLAGRTNY
HAMM, ARON	9	M	CHILD	PLAFWJNY
SCH--BILES, JURGES	30	M	LABR	PLAFWJNY
BIAL-STRICK-, SCHAPSEL	44	M	GDSM	PLAFWJNY
BAL----, LEISER	22	M	LABR	PLAFWJNY
WOHMANN, SALMANN	25	M	UNKNOWN	PLAFWJNY
GOTTLIEB, ABRAHAM	24	M	JNR	PLAFWJNY
JAFFE, JACOB	38	M	TNR	PLAIHFNY
WID----, VINCENT	23	M	LABR	PLAIHFNY
MULLER, MARTINAS	25	M	LABR	PLAIHFDET
S-TZ, DAVID	20	M	TNR	PLAIBONY
MILEWSKI, LUDWIG	23	M	LABR	PLAGRTNY
STAAS, M--CHE	32	M	CL	RRZZZZNY
SCHWARZ, ELIE	36	M	CL	RRZZZZNY
LIND, DAVID	19	M	CL	RRZZZZNY
DAMBROWSKI, ANG	25	M	LABR	RRAFWJNY
DAMMIS, JOSEPH	58	M	LABR	RRZZZZNY
KINZER, CHAIM	32	M	TLR	RRZZZZNY
ZESING, K--ST	41	M	LABR	RRZZZZIL
CHAIT--, CHAIM	33	M	CL	RRZZZZNY
SCHL---, DAVID	24	M	LABR	RRZZZZNY
SCHLAPIN, SCHIGE	30	M	TLR	RRAHTUNY
FORTGANG, HIRSCH	19	M	SHMK	RRAHTUNY
FRIEDMANN, ELIAS	30	M	JNR	RRAHTUNY
LENNIN, CR--SN	29	M	TLR	RRAHTUNY
FRIEDBERG, MIKSO	20	M	LABR	RRAHTUNY
GOLDBLATT, SONDE	28	M	TLR	RRZZZZNY
STZKOWSKI, MANDEL	26	M	SHMK	RRZZZZNY
LEBART--, MOSES	30	M	FARMER	RRZZZZNY
SEBARSKI, MICHAEL	34	M	LABR	RRZZZZPA
GEREWSKI, JOSEF	28	M	LABR	RRZZZZNY
CRESLER, MORITZ	24	M	CPTR	RRZZZZNY
PISZCREK, AND	25	M	LABR	RRZZZZUNK
STW-ERY, ANT	28	M	LABR	RRZZZZUNK
ZINMANN, KASIMIR	22	M	LABR	RRZZZZNY
GERSEWSKI, JOH	25	M	LABR	RRZZZZNY
KIPET-L, JOHANN	26	M	LABR	RRZZZZNY
SCHULEWSKI, MICHAEL	18	M	LABR	RRACSDNY
LINDEN, SAMUEL	29	M	CL	RRZZZZNY
KASSEN-A, STANISLAW	24	M	LABR	RRZZZZNY
AN-ELEIAN, LUDWIG	22	M	LABR	RRZZZZNY
STRO-NZ, ANDRE-	32	M	LABR	RRACTCNY
KAMINSKY, MENDE	25	M	SHMK	RRACTCNY
S-KOLOWSKY, STAN	44	M	JNR	RRACTCPHI
RASKINSKY, JACK	23	M	JNR	RRACTCNY
SCHEWILANTZ, MANSCHE	18	M	TLR	RRAHTUNY
CHWOLOWSKY, -ALE	22	M	JNR	RRZZZZNY
BARANANSKY, LOUIS	35	M	LABR	RRZZZZNY
RA--AWOPKI, RU-EN	40	M	JNR	RRZZZZNY
PI-O, ADAM	43	M	LABR	RRZZZZPA
-NDBERG, LOISE-	22	M	TLR	RRZZZZNY
LAJAN, POLAK	17	M	SHMK	RRZZZZNY
APPELBAUMM, MOSES	20	M	CL	RRAIDOPA
MINZ, -OSEN	32	M	CL	RRAGRTNY
KOPA-CWIZ, NARLAW	19	M	TLR	RRAGRTNY

PASSENGER	AGE	SEX	OCCUPATION	PRV VIL DES
KA-EZAK, MARIA	25	F	TLR	RRZZZZNY
STR-KA, HAL-PA	18	F	SVNT	RRZZZZNY
SCHAP--, CHAM	20	F	SVNT	RRAIBONY
SI-HAPI--, ZINTE	18	F	SVNT	RRAFWJNY
PISKORSKY, SIHINE	22	F	SVNT	RRAFWJNY
SWIADUSCHT, SEMME	19	F	TLR	RRZZZZNY
ROCHE	11	F	CH	RRZZZZNY
RESOWSKY, HIRSCH	40	M	JNR	RRZZZZNY
SARA	10	F	CH	RRZZZZNY
PACANTEK, FRANZ	49	M	LABR	RRZZZZNY
KA-TO	45	F	W	RRZZZZNY
JANKISKKOWSKI, IGRETO	26	M	BLKSMH	RRAFWJPA
WISBERG, FRANC	25	M	BLKSMH	RRAFWJUNK
SUTTERZ, VERONIKA	28	F	W	RRAFWJUNK
ANNA	3	F	CHILD	RRAFWJUNK
KLARA	.11	F	INFANT	RRAFWJUNK
ANDRASNO, FANNY	26	F	W	RRZZZZNY
BELA	3	F	CHILD	RRZZZZNY
RWZA	.09	F	INFANT	RRZZZZNY
ABRAMOWITZ, LIEBRE	38	F	W	RRZZZZPA
JANKE	16	F	CH	RRZZZZPA
RIWE	4	F	CHILD	RRZZZZPA
KLEINMANN, MOSES	32	M	TLR	RRZZZZPA
SIFFRE	25	F	W	RRZZZZPA
FRED	5	M	CHILD	RRZZZZPA
DAVID	2	M	CHILD	RRZZZZPA
DW---	.10	F	INFANT	RRZZZZPA
LEW, SIMM	26	M	TLR	RRAFWJBO
RACHEL	21	F	W	RRAFWJBO
DAVID	44	M	LABR	RRAFWJBO
MARIA	14	F	CH	RRAFWJBO
ANN	6	F	CHILD	RRAFWJBO
FIRGE	8	F	CHILD	RRAFWJBO
CHAIE	4	F	CHILD	RRAFWJBO
JACOB	.08	M	INFANT	RRAFWJBO
TR-MPETER, -ESTER	30	F	W	RRAFWJNY
FR-DEL	8	F	CHILD	RRAFWJNY
RI--KA	3	F	CHILD	RRAFWJNY
MODEKA	00	F	INF	RRAFWJNY
KABLER, STATE	28	F	W	RRAFWJPA
LEN	6	M	CHILD	RRAFWJPA
MOSES	2	M	CHILD	RRAFWJPA
HERSCHEL	00	M	INF	RRAFWJPA
KOWITZ, ABA	30	M	CL	RRZZZZNE
GILA	24	F	W	RRZZZZNE
NACHANNE	3	M	CHILD	RRZZZZNE
SCHL--MME	2	M	CHILD	RRZZZZNE
ELISE	00	F	INF	RRZZZZNE

SHIP: STATE OF ALABAMA

FROM: GLASGOW AND LARNE
TO: NEW YORK
ARRIVED: 03 MARCH 1888

PASSENGER	AGE	SEX	OCCUPATION	PRV VIL DES
ALPER, NACHUM	19	M	MCHT	RRZZZZUSA
BROCZINSKI, ANTONI	22	M	LABR	RRZZZZUSA
BERSON, DAVIR	40	M	TLR	RRZZZZUSA
BEMER, MINNA	50	F	MRNR	RRZZZZUSA
ROSALINA	19	F	SVNT	RRZZZZUSA
BIALYSTOKY, CHAIM	24	M	TLR	RRZZZZUSA
ELISCHEWSKY, SALLY	18	F	SVNT	RRAHQUUSA
ELLE, ESAAC	38	M	TLR	RRAHTUUSA
GOLDIN, JANCKEL	36	M	TLR	RRZZZZUSA
GRAN, SIMON	44	M	TLR	RRZZZZUSA
GRUNBLATT, RACHEL	19	F	SVNT	RRAHVUUSA
JAMOWITZ, SNOGS	23	M	LABR	RRAHVUUSA
JADONSKY, LEWY	17	M	TLR	RRZZZZUSA
FEFFRIEN, RACHMID	29	M	TLR	RRZZZZUSA
MITEKROWITS, JOSEF	20	M	LABR	RRAHVUUSA
MILLER, ESTHER	19	F	SVNT	RRZZZZUSA
MARINK, MALE	33	F	MAR	RRZZZZUSA
HILNE	6	M	CHILD	RRZZZZUSA
HANNI	4	F	CHILD	RRZZZZUSA
ROSI	2	F	CHILD	RRZZZZUSA
ESTHER	.09	F	INFANT	RRZZZZUSA
NACMINOWIEZ, SCHMUL	43	M	TLR	RRAIMBUSA
PANISCHEWITZ, JOSEF	25	M	LABR	RRZZZZUSA
PETRUKANIS, MATOR.	23	M	LABR	RRZZZZUSA
BORTSACHNIK, JADOB	33	M	MCHT	RRAHQUUSA
PALSSTER, MOSES	24	M	MCHT	RRAFWJUSA
SHINZE	24	F	MAR	RRAFWJUSA
PINS, WOLF	21	M	TLR	RRZZZZUSA
SCHER, LEIB	38	M	TLR	RRAHZPUSA
SELMON	26	M	TLR	RRZZZZUSA
SCHULTZ, RAFAEL	23	M	TLR	RRZZZZUSA
SCHERESCHEWSKY, SELDE	18	F	SVNT	RRAHQUUSA
STATEGNE, ABR.	18	M	MCHT	RRZZZZUSA
SCHMUBINSKY, ISAAC	28	M	MCHT	RRZZZZUSA
ELTE	19	F	MAR	RRZZZZUSA
STUPIAN, MOSES	26	M	TLR	RRZZZZUSA
SANNERD, SHLOME	18	F	SVNT	RRZZZZUSA
SCHAF, ABR.	35	M	TLR	RRZZZZUSA
IKLANDER, KARL	40	M	CLKMKR	RRZZZZUSA
SCHEPS, BEREL	44	M	TLR	RRZZZZUSA
WALINSCH, MATHIAS	25	M	LABR	RRZZZZUSA
WIMSTEIN, JOSSEL	30	M	MCHT	RRAHTUUSA
WOLF, BENZIEN	40	M	JNR	RRAHTUUSA

SHIP: SORRENTO

FROM: HAMBURG
TO: NEW YORK
ARRIVED: 05 MARCH 1888

PASSENGER	AGE	SEX	OCCUPATION	PRV VIL DES
BLISCHAT, FRIEDR.	28	M	JNR	RRZZZZNY
EMILIE	29	F	W	RRZZZZNY
JULIANA	.11	F	INFANT	RRZZZZNY
MEYER, FRITZ	27	M	FARMER	RRZZZZNY
RZCBSZINSKI, FRANZ	41	M	LABR	RRZZZZNY
DOLITZKI, IGNATZ	24	M	LABR	RRZZZZNY
SZIEWITZ, STANISL.	25	M	LABR	RRZZZZNY
ROCHWALSKI, RAFAEL	35	M	TLR	RRZZZZNY
RATOWSKY, HESTER	35	F	W	RRZZZZNY
MARIE	5	F	CHILD	RRZZZZNY
ELIE	4	F	CHILD	RRZZZZNY
BORKY	15	F	SGL	RRZZZZNY
BEER, ISAAC	19	M	LABR	RRZZZZNY
RATOWSKY, MINNA	2	F	CHILD	RRZZZZNY
MINKOWSKY, ABRAH.	23	M	DLR	RRZZZZNY
JALURSKY, MARTIN	48	M	LABR	RRZZZZNY
LAPINSKY, ADAM	00	M	UNKNOWN	RRZZZZNY
KOTSCHEFSKY, JAN	25	M	LLD	RRZZZZNY
NOJIK, JACOB	23	M	LABR	RRZZZZNY
ZINGER, MALKE	30	F	WO	RRZZZZNY
MENKA	.11	F	INFANT	RRZZZZNY
KONSTANTINEWSKI, GERSCH	40	M	LABR	RRZZZZNY
HARMLAND, ISRAEL	18	M	LABR	RRZZZZNY
COHN, ISAAC	29	M	LABR	RRZZZZNY
SCHIFFRE	19	F	UNKNOWN	RRZZZZNY
LINKOWSKI, IGNATZ	28	M	LABR	RRZZZZNY
GORETZKI, STANISLAUS	24	M	LABR	RRZZZZNY
KWASINEWSKI, W.	45	M	LABR	RRZZZZNY
ROSENBEROF, AUGUST	18	M	LABR	RRZZZZNY
RICKOWSKY, PIETER	30	M	LABR	RRZZZZNY
KLINKOWSKI, W.	28	M	LABR	RRZZZZNY
HARBARDT, WILH.	27	M	LABR	RRZZZZNY
KOLWATZKI, PAWEL	50	M	LABR	RRZZZZNY
LUKEWSKA, ANTECK	34	M	LABR	RRZZZZNY
JOS.	31	M	LABR	RRZZZZNY

PASSENGER	AGE	SEX	OCCUPATION	PRV VIL DES
JULIA	23	F	W	RRZZZZNY
CATHINKA	3	F	CHILD	RRZZZZNY
COLPATZKI, I.	27	M	LABR	RRZZZZNY
TZACHOWSKY, JOS.	45	M	LABR	RRZZZZNY
SOFI	20	F	SGL	RRZZZZNY
GUSZINSKI, MARIAN	30	M	LABR	RRZZZZNY
SZERLPWSKY, JOS.	26	M	LABR	RRZZZZNY
KALAKOWSKI, ISAAC	36	M	DLR	RRZZZZNY
RABINOWITZ, ZEMACH	19	M	DLR	RRZZZZNY
MILLER, BENJAMIN	18	M	DLR	RRZZZZNY
THALER, JACOB	27	M	DLR	RRZZZZNY

SHIP: RUGIA

FROM: HAMBURG AND HAVRE
TO: NEW YORK
ARRIVED: 05 MARCH 1888

PASSENGER	AGE	SEX	OCCUPATION	PRV VIL DES
KOMITAT, JOSEF	29	M	UNKNOWN	RRZZZZUSA
GRIVNIK, FRAN.	27	M	UNKNOWN	RRZZZZUSA
BRISCHKOWITZ, MIHAL	31	M	UNKNOWN	RRZZZZUSA
MARIANNA	34	F	W	RRZZZZUSA
WLADISLAW	.11	M	INFANT	RRZZZZUSA
ZUGALSKA, FRANZISKA	21	F	SGL	RRZZZZUSA
BIERNATZKY, STANISLAUS	25	M	UNKNOWN	RRZZZZUSA
GURSKI, ANTON	22	M	MSN	RRZZZZUSA
AENKIEWICZ, ALEXANDER	28	M	LABR	RRZZZZUSA
QIUT, ANIE	22	F	WO	RRZZZZUSA
HIRSCH	.11	M	INFANT	RRZZZZUSA
PAUSNER, TAUBE	22	F	WO	RRZZZZUSA
BARUCH	3	M	CHILD	RRZZZZUSA
SISEL	.11	F	INFANT	RRZZZZUSA
LEWIN, LINE	19	F	UNKNOWN	RRZZZZUSA
RESITZ, LIEBE	26	F	UNKNOWN	RRZZZZUSA
JACUBOSKA, ULIANA	24	F	UNKNOWN	RRZZZZUSA
BERNHARDI, JOH.	19	M	FARMER	RRZZZZUSA
CZARNOWSKI, FRANZ	28	M	FARMER	RRZZZZUSA
GLOWATZKI, JOS.	33	M	FARMER	RRZZZZUSA
RUKOWSKI, JOS.	29	M	FARMER	RRZZZZUSA
KLESCHINSKI, LEON	31	M	FARMER	RRZZZZUSA
GOLUBIEWSKY, MAREIN	24	M	FARMER	RRZZZZUSA
LUKASCHEWSKY, FRANZ	19	M	FARMER	RRZZZZUSA
LASZEREK, WLADISL.	20	M	FARMER	RRZZZZUSA
ZINDETZKI, LUDW.	23	M	FARMER	RRZZZZUSA
GURSKI, IGNATZ	19	M	FARMER	RRZZZZUSA
OSTROWSKI, ALEX	33	M	FARMER	RRZZZZUSA
PURKOWSKI, FAUDSS	31	M	FARMER	RRZZZZUSA
LOHMIELEWSKI, JOS.	18	M	FARMER	RRZZZZUSA
SCHUTZKOWSKI, IGNATZ	24	F	SGL	RRZZZZUSA
POBOLINSKI, CHAIE	20	F	SGL	RRZZZZUSA
GARBORSKI, ESTER	20	F	SGL	RRZZZZUSA
ZUSKER, GITTEL	49	F	WO	RRZZZZUSA
SCHMIEGELSKY, RAINE	30	F	WO	RRZZZZUSA
HIRSCH	10	M	CH	RRZZZZUSA
REISEL	8	M	CHILD	RRZZZZUSA
BER.	6	M	CHILD	RRZZZZUSA
KOHLIE, CIWIE	22	F	WO	RRZZZZUSA
EISIK	.11	F	INFANT	RRZZZZUSA
GOMANN, SIMON	31	M	MCHT	RRZZZZUSA
PERREI, HENRIETTE	30	F	WO	RRZZZZUSA
JACOB	26	M	LABR	RRZZZZUSA
WOLFF, FRIEDR.	33	M	LABR	RRZZZZUSA
ZANDER, DOROTHEA	17	F	SGL	RRZZZZUSA
DINGFELD, MATHER	32	M	LABR	RRZZZZUSA
DRIEDERMANN, JANKEL	40	M	LABR	RRZZZZUSA
BARAN, SCHAJE	44	M	LABR	RRZZZZUSA
EILWIRTH, JENTE	30	F	WO	RRZZZZUSA
BELE	5	F	CHILD	RRZZZZUSA
SCHENDEL	3	F	CHILD	RRZZZZUSA
WIENCKOSKA, FRANZISKA	20	F	WO	RRZZZZUSA
FRANZISKA	.10	F	INFANT	RRZZZZUSA
DRAGEWSCZEWSKI, FRANZ	24	M	LABR	RRZZZZUSA
ARIES, CHANNE	50	F	WO	RRZZZZUSA
MALKE	20	F	D	RRZZZZUSA
DRIEKERMANN, SZEMACH	16	M	LABR	RRZZZZUSA
SZUFE	9	M	CHILD	RRZZZZUSA
LATWAK, WILF	36	M	DLR	RRZZZZUSA
MUEHLSTEIN, HERMANN	27	M	TNM	RRZZZZUSA
EPPSTEIN, BARNHD.	19	M	APTC	RRZZZZUSA
LIPPSCHUETZ, ISAAC	21	M	LABR	RRZZZZUSA
CHAIE	21	F	W	RRZZZZUSA
WEISS, MICHAEL	22	M	LABR	RRZZZZUSA
MANTEL, JACOB	23	M	LABR	RRZZZZUSA
KANOWROSKI, JAN.	30	M	LABR	RRZZZZUSA
WIERZBIELOW, KASEMIR	29	M	LABR	RRZZZZUSA
MILUNAS, JANOS	22	M	LABR	RRZZZZUSA
SCHMIEGELSKI, MAYER	4	M	CHILD	RRZZZZUSA
GLEICHENHAUS, CHANNE	30	F	WO	RRZZZZUSA
MICHEL	9	M	CHILD	RRZZZZUSA
FROME	5	F	CHILD	RRZZZZUSA
CHANNE	8	F	CHILD	RRZZZZUSA
CHOMKE	4	F	CHILD	RRZZZZUSA
WEISS, FRIEDR.	18	M	UNKNOWN	RRZZZZUSA
ZOBST, AUGUST	22	M	LABR	RRZZZZUSA
FLITNIK, ADAM	20	M	LABR	RRZZZZUSA
WEISS, ERNST	20	M	LABR	RRZZZZUSA
WEGENER, AUGUST	20	M	LABR	RRZZZZUSA
NESKE, FERD.	24	M	LABR	RRZZZZUSA
WURZAL, JAN	25	M	LABR	RRZZZZUSA
BARSEFSKY, JOS.	25	M	LABR	RRZZZZUSA
JELINSKY, ANT.	24	M	LABR	RRZZZZUSA
GRZINDA, JAN	36	M	LABR	RRZZZZUSA
RAUBIN, MARTIN	28	M	LABR	RRZZZZUSA
PUVINSKI, STANISL.	30	M	LABR	RRZZZZUSA
KILIANOWSKI, MARIAN	28	M	LABR	RRZZZZUSA
KAMINSKI, THOMAS	26	M	LABR	RRZZZZUSA
CHOSINSKI, CASEMIR	26	M	LABR	RRZZZZUSA
KENDZIERSKI, JAN	28	M	LABR	RRZZZZUSA
KOSZITTLOWSKI, JACOB	29	M	LABR	RRZZZZUSA
HUEBNER, HEINR.	48	M	LABR	RRZZZZUSA
NEWOLOFF, HILLEL	18	M	LABR	RRZZZZUSA
RADJUS, PAUL	25	M	LABR	RRZZZZUSA
MATEWUS, STATUS	22	M	LABR	RRZZZZUSA
MAREINKEWICZ, MIHAL	26	M	LABR	RRZZZZUSA
SVENS, CARL	30	M	UNKNOWN	RRZZZZUSA
SALORSEN, ERIK	27	M	UNKNOWN	RRZZZZUSA
NIVALA, HENRIC	45	M	UNKNOWN	RRZZZZUSA
KAROSLE, MATTI	27	M	UNKNOWN	RRZZZZUSA
JOKITALPA, HENRIC	37	M	UNKNOWN	RRZZZZUSA
PETEJO, MATS	36	M	UNKNOWN	RRZZZZUSA
ERKILA, THOMAS	25	M	UNKNOWN	RRZZZZUSA
KANKOUEN, MATS	41	M	UNKNOWN	RRZZZZUSA
PYSAYS, ANDERS	26	M	UNKNOWN	RRZZZZUSA
STORGARD, HERMAN	43	M	LABR	RRZZZZUSA
NAS, JOH.	30	M	LABR	RRZZZZUSA
LONNBAECK, AUGUST	26	M	LABR	RRZZZZUSA
KUELL, REINHOLD	28	M	LABR	RRZZZZUSA
GRAUHOLM, ISAAC	29	M	LABR	RRZZZZUSA
SMED, JANOS	20	M	LABR	RRZZZZUSA
STAF, JOH.	30	M	LABR	RRZZZZUSA
HERM.	19	M	LABR	RRZZZZUSA
ISAAC	30	M	LABR	RRZZZZUSA
SKOM, KARL	27	M	LABR	RRZZZZUSA
SJOVIK, MICHEL	24	M	LABR	RRZZZZUSA
JOH.	24	M	LABR	RRZZZZUSA
STOLPE, JONAS	40	M	LABR	RRZZZZUSA
JOKITULPA, JOH.	37	M	LABR	RRZZZZUSA
HEIKOFA, SIMON	47	M	LABR	RRZZZZUSA
RICHSMOEKI, ISAAC	18	M	LABR	RRZZZZUSA
SUNTARLO, JOH.	26	M	LABR	RRZZZZUSA
MALOKIASON, KARL	22	M	LABR	RRZZZZUSA
ZEKNLAM, STANISLAUS	25	M	LABR	RRZZZZUSA
WARSCHEWSKY, ZIRE	22	F	SGL	RRZZZZUSA
MAXIMOWSTZ, JAN.	32	M	LABR	RRZZZZUSA
RUSCHKOWSKY, ANTON	27	M	LABR	RRZZZZUSA

PASSENGER	AGE	SEX	OCCUPATION	PRV	VIL	DES
WERSCHBITZKI, MATWEI	26	M	LABR	RR	ZZZZ	USA
FARWIEN, GUSTAV	32	M	PNTR	RR	ZZZZ	USA
FERVOKUSKI, MICHEL	27	M	LABR	RR	ZZZZ	USA
LEWARTOWICZ, MINDEL	30	M	LABR	RR	ZZZZ	USA
LOWENTHAL, MOSES	35	M	TCHR	RR	ZZZZ	USA
SLAVINSKI, JOS.	30	M	LABR	RR	ZZZZ	USA
SAWATZKI, FRANZ	27	M	LABR	RR	ZZZZ	USA
WASZKIEWICZ, FRANZ	23	M	LABR	RR	ZZZZ	USA
WASCKKEWICZ, VETAL	27	M	LABR	RR	ZZZZ	USA
GOLOSCHEFSKI, JOS.	23	M	LABR	RR	ZZZZ	USA
ANDRALIS, MARCIN	27	M	LABR	RR	ZZZZ	USA
ZENDER, CASIMIR	30	M	LABR	RR	ZZZZ	USA

SHIP: AURANIA

FROM: LIVERPOOL AND QUEENSTOWN
TO: NEW YORK
ARRIVED: 05 MARCH 1888

PASSENGER	AGE	SEX	OCCUPATION	PRV	VIL	DES
A--ET, HIBLET	40	M	LABR	RR	ZZZZ	NY
POTWIKA, J-A	19	M	CL	RR	ZZZZ	NE
ABRAMSOHR, LE--	49	M	FARMER	RR	ZZZZ	NY
SILBERSTEIN, JOSEF	24	M	LABR	RR	ZZZZ	NY
BERNENSTOCK, ADOLPH	25	M	LABR	RR	ZZZZ	NY
-LAK, DAME	28	M	LABR	RR	ZZZZ	NY
MASLO, JACOB	30	M	CPTR	RR	ZZZZ	NY
PENAKER, ASCHER	35	M	LABR	RR	ZZZZ	NY
DEMFROWSKY, ABRAH	25	M	LABR	RR	ZZZZ	NY
KAVATERITZK, TUDEL	25	M	LABR	RR	ZZZZ	NY
BAROW, ABRAHAM	22	M	LABR	RR	ZZZZ	NY
LISCH, MONDER-AR	27	M	LABR	RR	ZZZZ	NY
PO-ETOWSKY, ISAAC	42	M	LABR	RR	ZZZZ	NY
ALTER	15	M	CH	RR	ZZZZ	NY
SCHWANN, DAVID	59	M	LABR	RR	ZZZZ	NY
MOSKOWITZ, ISAAC	21	M	LABR	RR	ZZZZ	NY
LAZARAWIZ, ISRAEL	23	M	SHMK	RR	ZZZZ	NY
RUSMANN, ELIAS	20	M	LABR	RR	ZZZZ	NY
DUBOCHEWITZ, MARTIN	32	M	FSHMN	RR	ZZZZ	PA
LUCKMANN, ALBERT	35	M	LABR	RR	ZZZZ	NY
POTT, ISAAC	30	M	LABR	RR	ZZZZ	NY
BOBROWSKY, H--NDI	28	F	MA	PL	ZZZZ	NY
SARAH	15	F	SP	PL	ZZZZ	NY
MOSES	9	M	CHILD	PL	ZZZZ	NY
CHANN-	5	M	CHILD	PL	ZZZZ	NY
SCHEME	.10	F	INFANT	PL	ZZZZ	NY
LEN, HERMANN	24	M	LABR	PL	ZZZZ	NY
--TKO	23	F	W	PL	ZZZZ	NY
MACHLAS, CHA-E	27	M	LABR	PL	ZZZZ	NY
AUGUSTOWSKY, THEOD	40	M	LABR	PL	ZZZZ	NY
IGNAS	9	M	CHILD	PL	ZZZZ	NY
ADOLPH	6	M	CHILD	PL	ZZZZ	NY
-AME	3	F	CHILD	PL	ZZZZ	NY
SCHAPIRO, ZIRE	22	M	LABR	PL	ZZZZ	NY
WERNER, SARA	49	F	MA	PL	ZZZZ	NY
CHA-O	16	M	LABR	PL	ZZZZ	NY
GERSON	6	M	CHILD	PL	ZZZZ	NY
BURCH-	3	F	CHILD	PL	ZZZZ	NY
ABRAH	.11	M	INFANT	PL	ZZZZ	NY

SHIP: TRAVE

FROM: BREMEN
TO: NEW YORK
ARRIVED: 07 MARCH 1888

PASSENGER	AGE	SEX	OCCUPATION	PRV	VIL	DES
WOTOSKA, VICTORIA	20	F	UNKNOWN	RR	ZZZZ	USA
STURMATH, KARL	43	M	LABR	RR	ZZZZ	USA
BORKAZ, KOSTIK	23	M	LABR	RR	ZZZZ	USA
POLUKOITIS, MICH.	31	M	LABR	RR	ZZZZ	USA
HESS, ALBERT	27	M	LABR	RR	ZZZZ	USA
SCHNEIDEREIT, MICH.	25	M	LABR	RR	ZZZZ	USA
STEPUNDIS, JOS.	21	M	LABR	RR	ZZZZ	USA
MIKULEITIS, JURGIS	34	M	LABR	RR	ZZZZ	USA
SCHNEIDEREIT, JONS	18	M	LABR	RR	ZZZZ	USA
JANKUS, JONS	27	M	LABR	RR	ZZZZ	USA
RENKELIS, JONS	22	M	LABR	RR	ZZZZ	USA
EDRULATIS, JURGIS	23	M	LABR	RR	ZZZZ	USA
GRAWENATIS, JONS	28	M	LABR	RR	ZZZZ	USA
GRUINAS, WINZAS	23	M	LABR	RR	ZZZZ	USA
MASKOLATIS, SYDOR	23	M	LABR	RR	ZZZZ	USA
MIKKULAITIS, JONS	28	M	LABR	RR	ZZZZ	USA
MASCHKEWICZ, WAWCZYNCKA	30	M	LABR	RR	ZZZZ	USA
CIENCZYNSKI, WOJCIECH	31	M	LABR	RR	ZZZZ	USA
MANEMED, GUSTAV	22	M	LABR	RR	ZZZZ	USA
BRAUN, CARL	41	M	LABR	RR	ZZZZ	USA
JANISCHEWSKI, JOSEF	37	M	LABR	RR	ZZZZ	USA
GOLDENBERG, JUDEL	24	M	MCHT	RR	ZZZZ	USA
REPIPORT, LEB.	51	M	LABR	RR	ZZZZ	USA

SHIP: CIRCASSIA

FROM: GLASGOW AND MOVILLE
TO: NEW YORK
ARRIVED: 08 MARCH 1888

PASSENGER	AGE	SEX	OCCUPATION	PRV	VIL	DES
BLECHER, MOSES	21	M	TLR	RR	ZZZZ	USA
KUPTEROWITZ, S.	30	M	CPRSMH	RR	ZZZZ	USA
KUEGENSKI, WOL.	31	M	DLR	RR	ZZZZ	USA
WOJRACK, AND.	27	M	DLR	RR	ZZZZ	USA
SLUSMAN, MORDUCH-S.	34	M	TLR	RR	ZZZZ	USA
GRANAT, MOSES	30	M	TLR	RR	ZZZZ	USA
KALATSTEIN, MOSES	28	M	DLR	RR	ZZZZ	USA
TURGEL, ITZ	20	M	TNSTH	RR	ZZZZ	USA
STREIEHB, MOSEL	25	M	TLR	RR	ZZZZ	USA
KLOTZKY, WOLFF	27	M	DLR	RR	ZZZZ	USA
MERLIN, HIRSCH	22	M	DLR	RR	ZZZZ	USA
TENNEBAUM, CHONE	33	M	BKBNDR	RR	ZZZZ	USA
SCHMGUSK, BURGET	48	M	TLR	RR	ZZZZ	USA
SCHULMAN, MOSCHE	46	M	DLR	RR	ZZZZ	USA
KALUTZIK, LEISLOR	46	M	TLR	RR	ZZZZ	USA
CHAJATIN, DAVID	26	M	TLR	RR	ZZZZ	USA
KISCHINSKI, THEO	30	M	TLR	RR	ZZZZ	USA
GOLLIN, ALTER	16	M	CL	RR	ZZZZ	USA
LAPIDES, ISRAEL	36	M	JNR	RR	ZZZZ	USA
SUNIN, BEREL	33	M	SHMK	RR	ZZZZ	USA
SLATTKIND, MOSCHE	40	M	TLR	RR	ZZZZ	USA
DOENERSTEIN, HIRSCH	40	M	JNR	RR	ZZZZ	USA
KOSZIOK, ABRAHAM	47	M	TLR	RR	ZZZZ	USA
RUBERMANN, SAM.	42	M	FARMER	RR	ZZZZ	USA
TOURIAN, SAM	30	M	TLR	RR	ZZZZ	USA
TURETZIKI, EISIK	21	M	TLR	RR	ZZZZ	USA
ROSEN, HIRSCH	19	M	TLR	RR	ZZZZ	USA
GINBURG, KRAUNE	20	M	CGRMKR	RR	ZZZZ	USA
PERGAMERST, KASRIEL	26	M	JNR	RR	ZZZZ	USA
LIPMANN, ABR.M.	24	M	JNR	RR	ZZZZ	USA
JAZEROSKI, WASON	36	M	LABR	RR	ZZZZ	USA
SLOTEGORE, ISAK	34	M	TLR	RR	ZZZZ	USA
ZARKOWSKY, MATTEUS	24	M	LABR	RR	ZZZZ	USA

PASSENGER	AGE	SEX	OCCUPATION	PRVL	VIL	DES
PALLI, LEISER	40	M	TLR	RR	ZZZZ	USA
BUTKEWIETZ, LUDWIG	26	M	TLR	RR	ZZZZ	USA
LAPIDES, BEN	27	M	JNR	RR	ZZZZ	USA
SCHETLER, JUDEL	39	M	DLR	RR	ZZZZ	USA
GERELWITZ, MAZER	29	M	LABR	RR	ZZZZ	USA
KAUTEROWITZ, ISRAEL	48	M	TLR	RR	ZZZZ	USA
LUKENITZKI, MENDEL	38	M	DLR	RR	ZZZZ	USA
KURATINEL, SCH.	32	M	DLR	RR	ZZZZ	USA
WEITZIG, NOACH	51	M	TLR	RR	ZZZZ	USA
LUDLOWINSKI, JOSEF	42	M	LABR	RR	ZZZZ	USA
ROBONOWITZ, BORUCK	19	M	CGRMKR	RR	ZZZZ	USA
BEHRMAN, MOSSEN	18	M	DLR	RR	ZZZZ	USA
BUNSTEIN, LEISER	26	M	TLR	RR	ZZZZ	USA
KAPLAN, SIMON	28	M	SHMK	RR	ZZZZ	USA
GUTSOHN, SIMCHE	29	M	LABR	RR	ZZZZ	USA
MEYER	26	M	LABR	RR	ZZZZ	USA
ZOROWITSCH, JACOB	28	M	BKBNDR	RR	ZZZZ	USA
PIKUS, SCHLOME	21	M	MLR	RR	ZZZZ	USA
LEWIN, NAFTALIE	20	M	SHMK	RR	ZZZZ	USA
KUPERSCHMIDT, ABR.	40	M	TNSTH	RR	ZZZZ	USA
BUNIN, WILGOR	30	M	DLR	RR	ZZZZ	USA
KAPLAN, ABR.	21	M	LABR	RR	ZZZZ	USA
BLOCHER, ITZCHOK	45	M	LABR	RR	ZZZZ	USA
SIFSCHITZ, B.K.	33	M	TLR	RR	ZZZZ	USA
EUKOWSKI, CHAPIN	16	M	LABR	RR	ZZZZ	USA
BLOSTEIN, ARON	35	M	TCHR	RR	ZZZZ	USA
KOPELMAN, LEIB	19	M	LABR	RR	ZZZZ	USA
PORTON, MORDACH	32	M	SDLR	RR	ZZZZ	USA
SALOMON, MOSES	20	M	LABR	RR	ZZZZ	USA
MOSES	20	M	LABR	RR	ZZZZ	USA
BOSWINSKI, MEIER	30	M	SHMK	RR	ZZZZ	USA
PIKUS, ABR.	45	M	TLR	RR	ZZZZ	USA
KOMSIZKI, BEREL	48	M	LABR	RR	ZZZZ	USA
SCHLOMINSKI, ABR.	63	M	TLR	RR	ZZZZ	USA
KANTOR, RACHMIL	23	M	SHMK	RR	ZZZZ	USA
ZIRELSOHN, CHONE	35	M	WCHMKR	RR	ZZZZ	USA
SCHLOME	20	F	W	RR	ZZZZ	USA
SAM.	20	M	LABR	RR	ZZZZ	USA
MOSES	10	M	CH	RR	ZZZZ	USA
ISAK	6	M	CHILD	RR	ZZZZ	USA
REBECCA	3	F	CHILD	RR	ZZZZ	USA
EPPBAUM, GITTEL	36	F	W	RR	ZZZZ	USA
DWORE	10	F	CH	RR	ZZZZ	USA
JACOB	9	M	CHILD	RR	ZZZZ	USA
CHASE	7	F	CHILD	RR	ZZZZ	USA
ESTER	3	F	CHILD	RR	ZZZZ	USA
SUKOWITZKI, CHLOME	10	F	CH	RR	ZZZZ	USA
PFLANNENBAUM, CIDEK	35	M	SMH	RR	ZZZZ	USA
SORE	30	F	W	RR	ZZZZ	USA
ABRAHAM	3	M	CHILD	RR	ZZZZ	USA
ABRAMOWITZ, BERK	27	M	SMH	RR	ZZZZ	USA
CHENE	23	F	W	RR	ZZZZ	USA
JENE	1	F	CHILD	RR	ZZZZ	USA
EPSTEIN, ABR	25	M	TLR	RR	ZZZZ	USA
ASNE	20	F	W	RR	ZZZZ	USA
TROZKI, SCHMIEL	53	M	LABR	RR	ZZZZ	USA
RACHEL	40	F	W	RR	ZZZZ	USA
SORRE-E.	30	F	W	RR	ZZZZ	USA
MOCHEN	9	M	CHILD	RR	ZZZZ	USA
MOSES	7	M	CHILD	RR	ZZZZ	USA
BEREBEIZK, CHANE	40	F	W	RR	ZZZZ	USA
DINA	12	F	CH	RR	ZZZZ	USA
DAVID	7	M	CHILD	RR	ZZZZ	USA
LEA	3	F	CHILD	RR	ZZZZ	USA
REBECCA	.11	F	INFANT	RR	ZZZZ	USA
HAMMER, MARIA	20	F	HP	RR	ZZZZ	USA
IDA	13	F	HP	RR	ZZZZ	USA
MOTTEL	14	F	HP	RR	ZZZZ	USA
DAJON, ETTEL	55	F	HP	RR	ZZZZ	USA
NECHAME	18	F	HP	RR	ZZZZ	USA
KROETMALNITZE, DOBE	25	F	W	RR	ZZZZ	USA
SCHLOME	.10	F	INFANT	RR	ZZZZ	USA
WIMSCHKA, MENDEL	50	M	FARMER	RR	ZZZZ	USA
METHA	14	F	CH	RR	ZZZZ	USA
MORDECKE	9	F	CHILD	RR	ZZZZ	USA
SCHABNIS, RUBEN	40	M	SHMK	RR	ZZZZ	USA
FREIDE	16	F	HP	RR	ZZZZ	USA
BERNSTEIN, DORA	19	F	HP	RR	ZZZZ	USA
SCHAPIRO, FEIGE	17	F	HP	RR	ZZZZ	USA
LISCHANSKY, RIVA	20	F	HP	RR	ZZZZ	USA
DOMIGALA, JOSEFA	18	F	HP	RR	ZZZZ	USA

SHIP: ELBE

FROM: BREMEN
TO: NEW YORK
ARRIVED: 08 MARCH 1888

PASSENGER	AGE	SEX	OCCUPATION	PRVL	VIL	DES
RATKOWSKY, ANT.	26	M	LABR	RR	AIL	ANY
KWAS, FRANZ	18	M	LABR	RR	AIL	ANY
BOBROWSKY, JOH.	27	M	LABR	RR	AIL	ANY
NAWICKI, KAZIMIR	25	M	LABR	RR	AIL	ANY
BARANKO, JANEK	29	M	LABR	RR	AIL	ANY
MORANKO, JAN.	22	M	LABR	RR	AIL	ANY
MARZOFKE, FRANZ	29	M	LABR	RR	AIL	ANY
KOSLOFSKY, ALBERT	28	M	LABR	RR	AIL	ANY
MORANKO, ALBERT	22	M	LABR	RR	AIL	ANY
SADOWSKY, ANTONY	24	M	LABR	RR	AIL	ANY
MORAWKO, ANDRAS	30	M	LABR	RR	AIL	ANY
BARBIER, ISAAC	28	M	BBR	RR	AIL	ANY
LEBOWITZ, KOPAL	19	M	DLR	RR	AIL	ANY
WEISSMANN, GDALJE	19	M	DLR	RR	AIL	ANY
STEINER, JACOB	44	M	DLR	RR	AIL	ANY
SCHNEIDER, RASCHKE	28	F	UNKNOWN	RR	AIL	ANY
SCHEINE	6	F	CHILD	RR	AIL	ANY
ARON	4	M	CHILD	RR	AIL	ANY
DAVID	3	M	CHILD	RR	AIL	ANY
ZALKE, LIBE	34	M	UNKNOWN	RR	AIL	ANY
LEIB	14	M	UNKNOWN	RR	AIL	ANY
MAIER	9	M	CHILD	RR	AIL	ANY
RIEKE	6	F	CHILD	RR	AIL	ANY
JOEL	.09	M	INFANT	RR	AIL	ANY
COHN, SARAH	26	F	UNKNOWN	RR	AIL	AUNK
RIEWE	4	F	CHILD	RR	AIL	AUNK
VAPER, DAROLINA	18	F	UNKNOWN	RR	AIL	AUNK
NUCHEM	3	M	CHILD	RR	AIL	AUNK

SHIP: ST. OF PENNSYLVANIA

FROM: GLASGOW AND LARNE
TO: NEW YORK
ARRIVED: 08 MARCH 1888

PASSENGER	AGE	SEX	OCCUPATION	PRVL	VIL	DES
ANDREILANIS, MATEJ	24	M	LABR	RR	ZZZZ	USA
BERSON, BEREL	30	M	JNR	RR	ZZZZ	USA
DATZKAFSKY, EPHRAIM	45	M	TLR	RR	ZZZZ	USA
MANY	43	F	W	RR	ZZZZ	USA
SIREL	17	F	SVNT	RR	ZZZZ	USA
MENDEL	14	M	CH	RR	ZZZZ	USA
RIWE	7	F	CHILD	RR	ZZZZ	USA
LEA	5	F	CHILD	RR	ZZZZ	USA
FRUME	3	F	CHILD	RR	ZZZZ	USA
EPSTEIN, DORA	22	F	NN	RR	ZZZZ	USA
FELDMANN, SARAH	38	F	W	RR	ZZZZ	USA
HANNE	17	F	SVNT	RR	ZZZZ	USA
IDA	11	F	CH	RR	ZZZZ	USA
BRINO	7	M	CHILD	RR	ZZZZ	USA
RULING	8	M	CHILD	RR	ZZZZ	USA
JOSEF	5	M	CHILD	RR	ZZZZ	USA
DAVID	2	M	CHILD	RR	ZZZZ	USA

PASSENGER	AGE	SEX	OCCUPATION	PRV VIL DES
FRIEDMANN, CHANNE	19	F	SVNT	RRZZZZUSA
GENS, CHAWE	30	F	W	RRZZZZUSA
ISRAEL	9	M	CHILD	RRZZZZUSA
BASIE	8	F	CHILD	RRZZZZUSA
NISSEN	6	M	CHILD	RRZZZZUSA
LEA	3	F	CHILD	RRZZZZUSA
ESTER	2	F	CHILD	RRZZZZUSA
GEDAJA	.11	F	INFANT	RRZZZZUSA
JACKOWITZ, JOSEL	11	M	CH	RRZZZZUSA
GHICK, SELIG	27	M	TLR	RRZZZZUSA
JAFFE, JENTE	35	F	W	RRZZZZUSA
MOSES	16	M	LABR	RRZZZZUSA
THEODOR	10	M	CH	RRZZZZUSA
JACHWES	9	F	CHILD	RRZZZZUSA
ISAAC	7	M	CHILD	RRZZZZUSA
HIRSCH	6	M	CHILD	RRZZZZUSA
JUDELMAN, HIRSCH	24	M	MLR	RRZZZZUSA
KANTOROWITZ, ILZCHOK	11	M	CH	RRZZZZUSA
MARKEWITZ, ANTON	22	M	PDLR	RRZZZZUSA
MEIROWITZ, DAVID	21	M	PDLR	RRZZZZUSA
TAUBE, M.	16	F	SVNT	RRZZZZUSA
MENDELOWITZ, ABRAHAM	30	M	BCHR	RRZZZZUSA
ETTE	30	F	W	RRZZZZUSA
JANKEL	1	M	CHILD	RRZZZZUSA
REWKE	.03	F	INFANT	RRZZZZUSA
NEU, FANNY	19	F	SVNT	RRZZZZUSA
NOSIK, ISAAC	21	M	PDLR	RRZZZZUSA
PECKEI, HZSCHOK	30	M	SMH	RRZZZZUSA
RADISCHENSKY, WIZENTE	22	M	LABR	RRZZZZUSA
SELANIS, SIMON	18	M	LABR	RRZZZZUSA
RATZKOWSKY, ABRAHAM	18	M	TLR	RRZZZZUSA
SCHEYMAN, CHATZEL	51	M	DLR	RRZZZZUSA
DAVID	8	M	CHILD	RRZZZZUSA
DAVID	8	M	CHILD	RRZZZZUSA
SALNITZKY, GERSCH	26	M	TLR	RRZZZZUSA
SALMITZKY, GERSCH	26	M	TLR	RRZZZZUSA
SARITZKY, CHAIE	26	F	W	RRZZZZUSA
MENDEL	6	M	CHILD	RRZZZZUSA
SINKEWITZ, ANTON	28	M	LABR	RRZZZZUSA
SZUZRICK, SUSSKIND	55	M	TLR	RRZZZZUSA
TARBOWSKY, BORRIS	17	M	LABR	RRZZZZUSA
TUWALEWIS, MATEJ	15	M	LABR	RRZZZZUSA
LEGANIS, MARTIN	23	M	LABR	RRZZZZUSA
WOLBONIK, MARRIS	39	M	MCHT	RRZZZZUSA
SUESSKIND, LOUIS	20	M	BKPR	RRZZZZUSA

SHIP: LAHN

FROM: BREMEN AND SOUTHAMPTON
TO: NEW YORK
ARRIVED: 10 MARCH 1888

PASSENGER	AGE	SEX	OCCUPATION	PRV VIL DES
PRATKIEWICZ, ADOLF	32	M	LABR	RRAHZSUSA
PILIBAS, KAZIMIR	23	M	LABR	RRAHZSUSA
NAWROCKI, VINCENT	26	M	LABR	RRAHZSUSA
HUCIANSKA, PETRUCHA	23	M	LABR	RRAHZSUSA
SMANTEK, JOSEF	24	M	LABR	RRAEABUSA
KROSCHOMOWITZ, FELIX	27	M	LABR	RRAHZSUSA
ESSNER, FRIEDR	34	M	LABR	RRAHZSUSA
BONDRE, LOEW	22	M	LABR	RRAHZSUSA
DIDCZUM, MATTHIAS	48	M	LABR	RRAHZSUSA
MARINICZ, TEODOR	18	M	LABR	RRAHZSUSA
GRIBAWSKY, OLICZ	24	M	LABR	RRAHZSUSA
IGNACZIK, TEODOR	26	M	LABR	RRAHZSUSA
SOSNIF, WASILI	26	M	LABR	RRAHZSUSA
BRUNSKI, VALENT	45	M	LABR	RRAHZSUSA
KAROLISKI, ANT	34	M	BKLYR	RRAHZSUSA
JULIANE	47	F	W	RRAHZSUSA
LUDWIG	7	M	CHILD	RRAHZSUSA
MARIA	3	F	CHILD	RRAHZSUSA

PASSENGER	AGE	SEX	OCCUPATION	PRV VIL DES
MARTHA	.05	F	INFANT	RRAHZSUSA
PITZENKA, SALWESTRA	24	M	LABR	RRAHZSUSA
NRKAVITZ, KASIS	23	M	LABR	RRAHZSUSA
KALBUCKY, WINZES	25	M	LABR	RRAHZSUSA
GLISIN, MAIKIL	24	M	LABR	RRAHZSUSA
ABERBUCH, BEHR	32	M	BKLYR	RRAHZSUSA
TRUNKIN, TEWEL	23	M	CGRMKR	RRAHZSUSA
WOZELAK, MARYAN	40	M	LABR	RRAHUFUSA
BOJERSKI, JULIAN	20	M	LABR	RRAHUFUSA
BENGOWSKY, JAN	24	M	LABR	RRAHUFUSA
GAGUSKE, AUG	34	M	LABR	RRAHZSUSA
RINKO, JAN	35	M	LABR	RRAHZSUSA
KLIMAK, MARTIN	23	M	LABR	RRAHZSUSA
KULICH, JACOB	23	M	LABR	RRAHZSUSA
STREIGITZ, DOMINIK	20	M	LABR	RRAHZSUSA
STANKOWICZ, BARTHOL	23	M	LABR	RRAHZSUSA
JANKOWSKY, JOSEF	27	M	LABR	RRAHZSUSA
KUSARA, WOJCIECH	21	M	LABR	RRZZZZUSA
WIESENEWSKI, ANT	25	M	LABR	RRZZZZUSA
SANTOWSKI, JAN	23	M	LABR	RRZZZZUSA
SKUNKOSKA, ANT	22	M	LABR	RRZZZZUSA
KAESMARASIK, JUL	23	M	LABR	RRZZZZUSA
RINKO, MARTIN	27	M	LABR	RRAHZSUSA
ABRAMOWSKY, JULIAN	26	M	LABR	RRAHZSUSA
ROSACHSKY, JAN	29	M	LABR	RRAHZSUSA
AHSMANN, LUDWIG	27	M	LABR	RRAHZSUSA
GRADZISCKY, KLEMENS	27	M	LABR	RRAHZSUSA
SCHASLEY, ANTON	23	M	LABR	RRAHZSUSA
KARDEL, JOSEF	26	M	LABR	RRAHZSUSA
SCHINKOWICH, MARTIN	23	M	LABR	RRAHZSUSA
SOSTAK, FRANZOS	25	M	LABR	RRAHZSUSA

SHIP: CITY OF CHICAGO

FROM: LIVERPOOL AND QUEENSTOWN
TO: NEW YORK
ARRIVED: 10 MARCH 1888

PASSENGER	AGE	SEX	OCCUPATION	PRV VIL DES
WAZANEL, ALBERT	24	M	LABR	PLZZZZMA
MEDUS, RUDOLPH	18	M	LABR	PLZZZZMA
WAGANSOWIK, MARTIN	25	M	LABR	PLZZZZMA
LUDKE, F	55	M	SMH	RRZZZZCAN

SHIP: AMERICA

FROM: BREMEN
TO: BALTIMORE
ARRIVED: 10 MARCH 1888

PASSENGER	AGE	SEX	OCCUPATION	PRV VIL DES
WISNIEWSKY, ANTON	30	M	FARMER	RRZZZZUSA
KOZL---K, STANISL	20	M	FARMER	RRZZZZUSA
ELLERRN, MARCUS	26	M	FARMER	RRZZZZUSA
MILKEREIT, ADAM	28	M	FARMER	RRZZZZUSA
BERSBERODTSKY, ADAM	30	M	FARMER	RRZZZZUSA
REPSTEIN, FRIEDR	31	M	FARMER	RRZZZZUSA
HASE, CARL	24	M	FARMER	RRZZZZUSA
WISNIEWSKI, MICHAEL	24	M	FARMER	RRZZZZUSA
HEISE, JULIUS	22	M	FARMER	RRZZZZUSA
RENN, MICHAEL	40	M	FARMER	RRZZZZUSA
WALENTINNOW, PALITAS	27	M	FARMER	RRZZZZUSA
MUNSCHINSKI, JAN	21	M	FARMER	RRZZZZUSA
KOETSCHIGEWSKI, JOSEPH	21	M	FARMER	RRZZZZUSA
STANKEWICZ, VALENTY	21	M	FARMER	RRZZZZUSA
CONNTER, LEMES	19	M	FARMER	RRZZZZUSA
SESSHINA, SALMEN	36	M	FARMER	RRZZZZUSA

PASSENGER	AGE	SEX	OCCUPATION	PRIV	VIL	DES
KRAEMER, EDUARD	28	M	FARMER	RR	ZZZZ	USA
GELINNSKI, WOJCECH	26	M	FARMER	RR	ZZZZ	USA
KEIRPIK, JOSEF	29	M	FARMER	RR	ZZZZ	USA
MALACHOWSKI, MICHAEL	32	M	FARMER	RR	ZZZZ	USA
LISENSKY, FRANZ	29	M	FARMER	RR	ZZZZ	USA
JUSERYK, PETER	23	M	FARMER	RR	ZZZZ	USA
PELCH, JOSEF	23	M	FARMER	RR	ZZZZ	USA
MASCHINSKI, JOSEF	18	M	FARMER	RR	ZZZZ	USA
MAERTENS, JOHANN	23	F	SVNT	RR	ZZZZ	USA
MARIA	26	F	SVNT	RR	ZZZZ	USA
BAEHNCKE, WILH	21	F	SVNT	RR	ZZZZ	USA
KAEBINOWITZ, BEBELE	44	F	SVNT	RR	ZZZZ	USA
KABINOWITZ, ROSALIA	45	F	W	RR	ZZZZ	USA
MALACHOWSKA, AGNES	24	F	W	RR	ZZZZ	USA
MARIANNA	.11	F	INFANT	RR	ZZZZ	USA
AUGUSTYAK, MARIANNA	26	F	W	RR	ZZZZ	USA
ROSALIA	3	F	CHILD	RR	ZZZZ	USA
VICTORIA	2	F	CHILD	RR	ZZZZ	USA
STANISLAUS	.09	M	INFANT	RR	ZZZZ	USA
SAWOBIZ, ELIJAS	29	F	W	RR	ZZZZ	USA
MINNA	9	F	CHILD	RR	ZZZZ	USA
ROSA	6	F	CHILD	RR	ZZZZ	USA
KREISA	3	F	CHILD	RR	ZZZZ	USA
GREISS, CZERNA	25	F	W	RR	ZZZZ	USA
SURE	6	F	CHILD	RR	ZZZZ	USA
ABE	17	F	SVNT	RR	ZZZZ	USA
RITZMANN, CHASE	39	F	W	RR	ZZZZ	USA
CHASE	11	F	CH	RR	ZZZZ	USA
HODE	9	F	CHILD	RR	ZZZZ	USA
ZUSCHINSKI, ANNA	29	F	W	RR	ZZZZ	USA

SHIP: ETRURIA

FROM: LIVERPOOL AND QUEENSTOWN
TO: NEW YORK
ARRIVED: 12 MARCH 1888

PASSENGER	AGE	SEX	OCCUPATION	PRIV	VIL	DES
LICHTERMAN, ABRAH	28	M	LABR	RR	ZZZZ	NY
LEESEROWITSCH, MESER	24	M	LABR	RR	ZZZZ	NY
KARDAN, JOSEL	36	M	LABR	RR	ZZZZ	NY
MOSES	27	M	LABR	RR	ZZZZ	NY
OLIK, JACOB	28	M	LABR	RR	ZZZZ	NY
HAROWITZ, JOSEF	10	M	BY	RR	ZZZZ	NY
MAHLE, KUND	21	M	LABR	RR	ZZZZ	IA
SMOLINSKI, MARTA	23	F	SP	RR	ZZZZ	NY

SHIP: EDAM

FROM: AMSTERDAM
TO: NEW YORK
ARRIVED: 13 MARCH 1888

PASSENGER	AGE	SEX	OCCUPATION	PRIV	VIL	DES
KAPLAN, CHAIM	36	M	TLR	RR	ZZZZ	NY
DANIELEWITZ, NICOLA	49	M	LABR	RR	ZZZZ	NY
PARAY, ANDRAS	44	M	LABR	RR	ZZZZ	NY
PAL, NYLATRA	27	M	LABR	RR	ZZZZ	NY
ISTVAN, GERGELY	15	M	LABR	RR	ZZZZ	NY
VARGA, JANOS	20	M	LABR	RR	ZZZZ	NY
PUPENITZ, KAREL	20	M	LABR	RR	ZZZZ	NY
REGINA	34	F	LABR	RR	ZZZZ	NY
KANKEWITZ, MARTIN	44	M	LABR	RR	ZZZZ	NY
NATHALIE	23	F	LABR	RR	ZZZZ	NY
JOSEFA	.06	F	INFANT	RR	ZZZZ	NY
PLITNIK, DOMINIK	21	M	INF	RR	ZZZZ	NY
IWANOWSKI, ANTON	18	M	INF	RR	ZZZZ	NY
PETRUSCHKEWITZ, PETER	26	M	INF	RR	ZZZZ	NY
WILKIN, PETER	28	M	INF	RR	ZZZZ	NY
PARKEWITZ, MATHIAS	22	M	INF	RR	ZZZZ	NY
MAKNIS, FELIX	25	M	INF	RR	ZZZZ	NY
POTUSCHKANIS, MICH.	25	M	INF	RR	ZZZZ	NY
KIREL, KAREL	24	M	INF	RR	ZZZZ	NY
MUROWSKI, IGNATZ	24	M	INF	RR	ZZZZ	NY
KREUTZMAN, JOS.	26	M	INF	RR	ZZZZ	NY
SEGLENSKI, STANISL.	26	M	INF	RR	ZZZZ	NY
KUSCHANOWSKI, VAVR.	24	M	INF	RR	ZZZZ	NY
GEWENSKI, JOS.	27	M	INF	RR	ZZZZ	NY
LEGRIN, PIETRO	24	M	INF	RR	ZZZZ	NY
SPUND, EPHR.	33	M	TLR	RR	ZZZZ	NY
SKRUP, JUDES	23	M	LABR	RR	ZZZZ	NY
WILKOWSKI, MARTIN	29	M	LABR	RR	ZZZZ	NY
PACKOWSKY, AND.	29	M	LABR	RR	ZZZZ	NY
LESEWITZ, VIN.	27	M	LABR	RR	ZZZZ	NY
PILETZKY, JOS.	41	M	LABR	RR	ZZZZ	NY
ALEXINIS, BALAMIEL	32	M	LABR	RR	ZZZZ	NY
LEHIS, JOS.	19	M	LABR	RR	ZZZZ	NY
BUDWIS, FRANS	24	M	LABR	RR	ZZZZ	NY

SHIP: BOHEMIA

FROM: HAMBURG AND HAVRE
TO: NEW YORK
ARRIVED: 13 MARCH 1888

PASSENGER	AGE	SEX	OCCUPATION	PRIV	VIL	DES
WOLPERT, GITTEL	21	F	UNKNOWN	RR	AIGH	NY
PACZURKOWSKI, IGNACI	30	M	LABR	RR	ZZZZ	NY
POPLANSKI, CASIMIR	25	M	LABR	RR	ZZZZ	NY
MURAWSKI, JOHN	25	M	LABR	RR	ZZZZ	NY
JANKOWSKI, JAN	23	M	UNKNOWN	RR	AHUL	NY
RUCINSKY, JOSEF	23	M	UNKNOWN	RR	AHUL	NY
KULINOWSKI, JAN	22	M	UNKNOWN	RR	AHUL	NY
PACZKOWSKI, VALENTY	22	M	UNKNOWN	RR	AHUL	NY
KRONDZIEZEWSKI, SIMON	21	M	UNKNOWN	RR	AHUL	NY
TRAZYKOWSKA, MARIE	23	F	SGL	RR	AHUL	NY
DROSDOWSKI, STEFAN	22	M	LABR	RR	AHUL	NY
PRZYTOKIEWICZ, ANTON	24	M	UNKNOWN	RR	ZZZZ	NY
SPIEGEL, A.S.	28	M	LABR	RR	AIAE	NY
GUSTA	23	F	UNKNOWN	RR	AIAE	NY
ZARINZANSKY, SCHEINE	28	F	WO	RR	ZZZZ	NY
RIWKE	4	M	CHILD	RR	ZZZZ	NY
CHAIM	3	M	CHILD	RR	ZZZZ	NY
STOLER, ROCHEL	17	F	SGL	RR	ZZZZ	NY
MELLER, SARA	25	F	WO	RR	ZZZZ	NY
MALKE	9	F	CHILD	RR	ZZZZ	NY
ABE	6	M	CHILD	RR	ZZZZ	NY
CHANE	3	F	CHILD	RR	ZZZZ	NY
SOHORRMANN, ABR.	23	M	LABR	RR	ZZZZ	NY
FEGL.	20	F	W	RR	ZZZZ	NY
FISCHBACH, CHAPIN	24	M	LABR	RR	AHWN	NY
CHMIELEWSKI, WOYCICH	45	M	UNKNOWN	RR	ZZZZ	NY
MOSZCZINSKI, FRANZ	20	M	LABR	RR	ZZZZ	NY
SLAVIENSKI, WLADISLAV	21	M	LABR	RR	ZZZZ	NY
TORBICKI, ADOLF	27	M	SMH	RR	ZZZZ	NY
KALINOWSKY, ADAM	27	M	LABR	RR	AHZS	NY
MALACHOWSKI, JAN	26	M	LABR	RR	AHZS	NY
ANTON	28	M	LABR	RR	AHZS	NY
OKUNTZKI, JOSEF	21	M	LABR	RR	AHZS	NY
SUBIETZKI, JAN	25	M	LABR	RR	AHZS	NY
WIEZNIEWSKI, STANISL.	28	M	LABR	RR	AHZS	NY
STAWITSKI, ANTON	21	M	UNKNOWN	RR	AHUF	NY
DANIELEWSICZ, JOSEF	23	M	UNKNOWN	RR	AHZS	NY
BISKIS, VINCENT	25	M	UNKNOWN	RR	AHZS	NY
CHMIELEWSKY, ANTON	22	M	UNKNOWN	RR	AHZS	NY
CZINKIEWIEZ, CASES	32	M	UNKNOWN	RR	AHZS	NY
CZANNOWSKY, ANTON	29	M	UNKNOWN	RR	AHZS	NY
DRZEWIEKI, JOH.	29	M	UNKNOWN	RR	AHZS	NY

PASSENGER	AGE	SEX	OCCUPATION	PRIV	DES
WISCHNIEWSKY, JAN	27	M	LABR	RRZZZZ	PA
RIPCZINSKI, MATHIAS	29	M	LABR	RRZZZZ	PA
STRUCZINSKI, JAN	26	M	LABR	RRZZZZ	PA
GRSESKEWIEZ, MARION	26	M	LABR	RRZZZZ	PA
ANTON	27	M	LABR	RRZZZZ	PA
CZAMINSKI, FRANZ	34	M	LABR	RRAIJT	NY
KUNDRAD, SIMON	17	M	LABR	RRZZZZ	NY
BULAKER, LEOPOLD	32	M	LABR	RRAHXL	NY
CHRISTINE	22	F	W	RRAHXL	NY
EMILIE	5	F	CHILD	RRAHXL	NY
HIESINSKI, MARTIN	34	M	LABR	RRAHZS	NY
KOZLANZKIS, JANOS	43	M	LABR	RRAHZS	NY
URBAN, ANTON	26	M	LABR	RRAHZS	NY
MISCHKEWIEZ, JOSUS	22	M	LABR	RRAHZS	NY
SMUSEWSKI, ANDR.	28	M	LABR	RRAIJT	NY
ZOBERZKI, MATH.	27	M	LABR	RRAIJT	NY
KONSLANTZKIS, CASES	30	M	LABR	RRAHZS	NY
CZIKINSKI, ANDR.	30	M	LABR	RRAHZS	NY
LEMANDOWIEZ, PETER	22	M	LABR	RRAHZS	NY
MRUZULIS, JOSUS	23	M	LABR	RRAHZS	NY
SINKOWSKY, JAN	22	M	LABR	RRZZZZ	NY
KUSZMIERIK, JAN	35	M	LABR	RRZZZZ	IL
GURAS, JOSUS	20	M	UNKNOWN	RRAHZS	OH
BRUNSAS, JOS.	22	M	UNKNOWN	RRAHZS	OH
PETER	20	M	UNKNOWN	RRAHZS	OH
FRIEDLAND, ITTE	27	F	WO	RRZZZZ	NE
EMMI	7	F	CHILD	RRZZZZ	NE
MERI	5	F	CHILD	RRZZZZ	NE
FRIEDMANN, ITZOCH	27	M	LABR	RRAIBW	IL
ROCHEL	27	F	W	RRAIBW	IL
HANNY	.11	F	INFANT	RRAIBW	IL
BLOOMBERG, MEYER	19	M	SHMK	RRAIMN	IL
JOHANNE	18	F	W	RRAIMN	IL
GRUENHAUS, NOCHIM	27	M	UNKNOWN	RRAHWJ	IL
MELZER, MOSES	20	M	UNKNOWN	RRZZZZ	IL
KOPOLOWITZ, LIPE	20	F	SGL	RRZZZZ	IL
KULINZKI, LEA	22	F	SGL	RRAFVG	IL
FISCHMANN, HANNY	21	F	UNKNOWN	RRAIHT	IL
MOSES	21	M	UNKNOWN	RRAIHT	IL
KROSCHENSKI, BALIE	29	F	SGL	RRZZZZ	IL
WOLOSCHINSKI, MASCHE	35	F	WO	RRZZZZ	IL
SALOMON	7	M	CHILD	RRZZZZ	IL
RACHEL	5	F	CHILD	RRZZZZ	IL
CHAIM	.11	M	INFANT	RRZZZZ	IL
JAWORSKA, ANNA	33	F	WO	RRZZZZ	IA
ROMAN	9	M	CHILD	RRZZZZ	IA
WLADISLAV	.11	M	INFANT	RRZZZZ	IA
PRUSKI, ALEXANDER	21	M	LABR	RRZZZZ	IL
EVENZIAK, BASCHE	24	F	WO	RRAHTU	NE
LEA	.11	F	INFANT	RRAHTU	NE
CHAJSIEL, SCHMUL	40	M	TLR	RRZZZZ	NE
LEOIN, PINKUS	35	M	UNKNOWN	RRAHTU	NE
JESNER, RACHEL	40	F	WO	RRADOI	NE
BREINE	18	F	CH	RRADOI	NE
CHAIME	8	F	CHILD	RRADOI	NE
RECHAME	6	F	CHILD	RRADOI	NE
ZORIZANSKI, CHAJE	9	F	CHILD	RRZZZZ	NY
SORGEL, LUDWIG	40	M	LABR	RRAHLP	IL
PACZKOSKA, MARIANNA	43	F	WO	RRAICO	OH
WIELGUSKI, FRANK	25	M	LABR	RRZZZZ	NE
OSCHINSKI, SCHMUL	16	M	DLR	RRAHSL	NE
BERYT, THEODOR	24	M	LABR	RRZZZZ	PA
STRYJOWA, STEFAN	24	M	LABR	RRZZZZ	PHI
CZARNY, JACOB	24	M	LABR	RRZZZZ	PHI
SOKOLOWSKI, JOSEF	27	M	LABR	RRZZZZ	PHI
RUTKOWSKI, CONSTANTIN	35	M	SMH	RRAHUI	NE
CHMIEJEWSKI, LEOPOLD	37	M	LABR	RRAHUI	NE
DANIES, STANISL.	27	M	SHMK	RRAHUI	NE
BAIER, MICH.	26	M	MLR	RRAHUI	NE
DEDOSCHINDSKI, WLAD.	22	M	LABR	RRAHUI	NE
ROSALSKI, ANTON	33	M	JNR	RRAHUI	NE
GRABOWSKI, MICH.	30	M	WHR	RRAHUI	NE
SZIBIANSKI, FRANZ	36	M	SHMK	RRAHUI	IL
KROSCHINSKI, IGNATZ	27	M	LABR	RRAHUI	IL
GROBINSKI, PETER	30	M	LABR	RRAHUI	IL
KALINOWSKI, ANTON	27	M	LABR	RRAHUI	IL
GOLAU, FRANZ	27	M	LABR	RRAHUI	IL
RUPINSKI, ANTON	40	M	SMH	RRAHUI	OH
FUGALSKI, CASIMIR	27	M	LABR	RRAHUI	OH
POJAWSKI, JAN	20	M	LABR	RRAHUI	OH
CZOCH, ANTON	40	M	LABR	RRAHUI	OH
ZIEGELSKI, JACOB	25	M	LABR	RRAHUI	OH
PAWLOWSKI, MICHL.	29	M	LABR	RRAHUI	OH
PTECHENSAPOLSKI, BOLESL	22	M	JNR	RRAHUI	OH
SOHWENDETZKI, KARL	23	M	LABR	RRAHUI	NE
ENGELQUIST, JOHN	19	M	FARMER	RRADOI	NY
GUSS, ERIK	19	M	FARMER	RRZZZZ	NY
SVARTBAK, JOSEF	25	M	FARMER	RRADOI	NY
STORLAHLS, ERIK	24	M	FARMER	RRZZZZ	NY
INGRES, JOH.	30	M	FARMER	RRZZZZ	NY
HOLM, JOS.	23	M	FARMER	RRZZZZ	NY
KAMB, JOH.	26	M	FARMER	RRADOI	NY
NYGAARD, JOH.	27	M	FARMER	RRZZZZ	IL
MAHYS, GABR.	23	M	FARMER	RRADOI	IL
ERLAND, HENRIK	20	M	FARMER	RRZZZZ	IL
CARL	40	M	FARMER	RRZZZZ	IL
HANNUS, GABR.	35	M	FARMER	RRADOI	IL
MORIS, CARL	26	M	FARMER	RRADOI	IL
KAMB, GABRES	18	M	FARMER	RRADOI	IL
ERLAND, CARL	27	M	FARMER	RRZZZZ	IL
MARS, HENRIK	28	M	FARMER	RRAAJV	IL
OLTERHOLM, CARL	18	M	FARMER	RRZZZZ	IL
MAAHRS, MATH.	31	M	FARMER	RRZZZZ	NE
JUNTH, JOH.	45	M	FARMER	RRZZZZ	IL
CARL	56	M	FARMER	RRADOI	IL
STORLOHLS, CARL	33	M	FARMER	RRZZZZ	IL
HUNKS, JOS.	35	M	FARMER	RRZZZZ	IL
ROOS, JOH.	27	M	FARMER	RRADOI	IL
ERLAND, JOH.	29	M	FARMER	RRZZZZ	IL
HEINDS, EMANUEL	35	M	FARMER	RRZZZZ	IA
MATHLIN, CARL	19	M	FARMER	RRZZZZ	IA
INGRES, BERNH.	30	M	FARMER	RRZZZZ	IA
HAKUS, KAPA	23	F	SGL	RRZZZZ	IA
STAH, ERIK	38	M	FARMER	RRZZZZ	IA
MATHLIN, ANDERS	48	M	FARMER	RRZZZZ	IA
MARTEN	17	M	FARMER	RRZZZZ	IA
IMAUS, ANDERS	30	M	FARMER	RRZZZZ	IA
CUPRANSKI, JAN	37	M	LABR	RRZZZZ	NY
POLAKOWSKI, MARTIN	26	M	LABR	RRZZZZ	NY
KURMASS, THOMAS	26	M	LABR	RRZZZZ	NY
VULSCHESKY, JAS.	40	M	LABR	RRZZZZ	NY
BERLMANN, JAN.	28	M	LABR	RRZZZZ	NY
GOLDBERG, MENDEL	28	M	DLR	RRAIBO	NE
KLEIN, MARKUS	9	M	CHILD	RRAIBO	NE
LEOPOLD	9	M	CHILD	RRAIBO	NE
HERM.	8	M	CHILD	RRAIBO	NE
DEICZ, HENE	23	F	WO	RRAIBO	NE
LEA	.11	F	INFANT	RRAIBO	NE
MARK, HARRY	16	M	LABR	RRZZZZ	CLE
JAFFE, SARAH	18	F	SGL	RRZZZZ	MD
SATZ, ABR.	26	M	LABR	RRZZZZ	NY
FANNY	22	F	W	RRZZZZ	NY
JOACHIM	3	M	CHILD	RRZZZZ	NY
LEIB	.11	M	INFANT	RRZZZZ	NY
SELIKOWITZ, PESCHE	20	F	SGL	RRZZZZ	NY
BUCHMANN, BER.	34	M	DLR	RRZZZZ	CH
KALMANOWICZ, HIRSCH	27	M	LABR	RRZZZZ	IL
KONAT, LUDWIG	26	M	LABR	RRZZZZ	IL
BRZOZOWSKY, ANTON	23	M	LABR	RRZZZZ	IL
CILOKOWSKI, JULIAN	26	M	LABR	RRAIOM	IL
SENDEROVICZ, MOSES	19	M	LABR	RRAFVG	NE
ACHSELROD, DAVID	31	M	LABR	RRAIOO	PHI
BEREZOWSKI, ETEL	25	F	SGL	RRAHVZ	PHI
ELSOHN, SELIG	22	M	LABR	RRAHVZ	MD
LEW, EFROIM	19	M	LABR	RRAHTU	MD
DANIEL	17	M	LABR	RRAHTU	MD
BERESOWSKY, BERL.	27	M	LABR	RRZZZZ	NY
SAJE	23	F	W	RRZZZZ	NY
DAVID	2	M	CHILD	RRZZZZ	UNK
DWORE	.09	M	INFANT	RRZZZZ	NY

PASSENGER	AGE	SEX	OCCUPATION	PRV IL	DES
KATZENELLSOHN, ISAAC	25	M	LABR	RRAHVZ	IA
HANNA	24	F	W	RRAHVZ	IA
MORIS	9	M	CHILD	RRAHVZ	IA
FENNY	7	F	CHILD	RRAHVZ	IA
ROCHLL	5	F	CHILD	RRAHVZ	IA
GOLDSTEIN, TEER	20	M	MCHT	RRZZZZ	NY
DOMBOWSKI, MARIAN	53	M	LABR	RRAHUI	IL
WEICHERT, FRANZ	21	M	SHMK	RRAHUI	IL
GRAMAS, JOSEPH	23	M	LABR	RRAIGH	IL
BRASEITUS, ADAM	29	M	LABR	RRAIGH	IL
SCHAPIRO, SALOMON	43	M	MCHT	RRAIMC	IL
CHAJE	35	F	W	RRAIMC	IL
SAMUEL	19	M	CH	RRAIMC	IL
LEON	15	M	CH	RRAIMC	IL
ISRAEL	8	M	CHILD	RRAIMC	IL
CHAJE	7	F	CHILD	RRAIMC	IL
FRANKFURT, LEON	28	M	MCHT	RRAIMC	NY
KATZ, MOSES	25	M	LABR	RRAIIP	NY
KORENFELD, MENDEL	19	M	DLR	RRAIBO	NE
JUROWSKI, LEOB	22	M	UNKNOWN	RRAIOO	NY
ANDROWSKY, FRDRK.	34	M	LABR	RRAHWU	IL
FANNY	36	F	W	RRAHWU	IL
SCHMUEL, LEW.	45	M	MCHT	RRZZZZ	CLE
LORE, CHAJE	8	F	CHILD	RRZZZZ	CLE
KLEINER, DAVID	30	M	LABR	RRZZZZ	IL

SHIP: ALASKA

FROM: LIVERPOOL AND QUEENSTOWN
TO: NEW YORK
ARRIVED: 14 MARCH 1888

PASSENGER	AGE	SEX	OCCUPATION	PRV IL	DES
PERLMANN, MARIASCH	24	F	SP	RRADAX	USA
RABINOWITZ, CHANE	21	F	SP	RRADAX	USA
LEA	10	F	CH	RRADAX	USA
BERGER, LEA	18	F	SP	RRADAX	USA
LICHTERMANN, ABRAHAM	17	M	LABR	RRADAX	USA
JOSSEL	16	F	CH	RRADAX	USA
MOSES	15	M	LABR	RRADAX	USA
GITTEL	11	F	CH	RRADAX	USA
WEISS, SCHEMI	17	F	SP	RRADAX	USA
SALOMON, TH	44	M	LABR	RRADAX	USA
MALACZ, OTTELA	20	F	SP	RRADAX	USA
CERUL, WOJCOCH	25	M	LABR	RRADAX	USA
FELLMAN, SCHEINE	32	F	MA	RRADAX	USA
SCHLOME	11	M	CH	RRADAX	USA
CLARE	9	F	CHILD	RRADAX	USA
BARLE	7	M	CHILD	RRADAX	USA
ESTER	4	F	CHILD	RRADAX	USA
SIMON	2	M	CHILD	RRADAX	USA
GLUCKLMAN, PHILIPP	26	M	LABR	RRADAX	USA
POMMERANSKY, PEREL	21	M	LABR	RRADAX	USA
SCHEFF, CLARE	20	F	SP	RRADAX	USA
LAPIDUS, HEINE	26	F	MA	RRADAX	USA
MAX	8	M	CHILD	RRADAX	USA
STADIN, DOROTHEA	20	F	SP	RRADAX	USA
MENSKEWITZ, LADISL	24	M	LABR	RRADAX	USA
GELLER, ISAC	25	M	LABR	RRADAX	USA
BASCHET, CHAIE	40	F	MA	RRADAX	USA
MIER	11	M	CH	RRADAX	USA
MOSES	6	M	CHILD	RRADAX	USA
CIPE	.11	M	INFANT	RRADAX	USA
ABRAM	25	M	LABR	RRADAX	USA
SCHEME	23	F	W	RRADAX	USA
CHAIM	2	M	CHILD	RRADAX	USA
WASSERMANN, MORRIS	30	M	LABR	RRADAX	USA

SHIP: KANSAS

FROM: LIVERPOOL
TO: BOSTON
ARRIVED: IZ UNKNOWN , LI

PASSENGER	AGE	SEX	OCCUPATION	PRV IL	DES
ROZE, ANNA	24	F	SP	RRZZZZ	PHI
FELDHULER, PAUL	21	M	CH	RRZZZZ	NY
WEINER, RUBIN	25	M	CH	RRZZZZ	MA
ROZE, ABRAHAM	25	M	LABR	RRZZZZ	PHI
LAMP, MICHAEL	37	M	LABR	RRZZZZ	PHI
SARACHON, HIRST	25	M	LABR	PLZZZZ	MA
RADNER, TOBIA	22	M	LABR	RRZZZZ	NY
GONEIEROWSKY, DAVID	22	M	LABR	RRZZZZ	NY
KAUFONENARD, ABRAHAM	50	M	LABR	RRZZZZ	MA

SHIP: MARSALA

FROM: HAMBURG
TO: NEW YORK
ARRIVED: 15 MARCH 1888

PASSENGER	AGE	SEX	OCCUPATION	PRV IL	DES
BEREGIN, VICTOR	35	M	LABR	RRZZZZ	NY
MARIA	25	F	W	RRZZZZ	NY
MAKSYM	45	M	LABR	RRZZZZ	NY
SASANNA, MUKSIAR	32	F	WO	RRZZZZ	NY
ZANI-	5	M	CHILD	RRZZZZ	NY
KARABIN, JOS	24	M	LABR	RRZZZZ	NY
KOWALCZYK, MICHAL	38	M	LABR	RRZZZZ	NY
KULAZAK, MICHAEL	22	M	LABR	RRZZZZ	NY
PORTULA, ANT	24	M	LABR	RRZZZZ	NY
LUDWIGA	24	F	W	RRZZZZ	NY
PETNU-, NICOLAI	28	M	LABR	RRZZZZ	NY
HOFFMAN, JOSEF	27	M	LABR	RRZZZZ	NY
PIONTKOWSKY, ANTON	27	M	LABR	RRZZZZ	NY
KASPNEWICZ, JAN	35	M	LABR	RRZZZZ	NY
WISNIEWSKY, JOS	24	M	LABR	RRZZZZ	NY
PI-TROWSKI, CASIMIR	27	M	LABR	RRZZZZ	NY
ADAM	23	M	LABR	RRZZZZ	NY
SCHOENHAUSEN, ROSA	20	F	W	RRZZZZ	NY
HILTUEMEN, JOH	32	M	PVTM	FNZZZZ	NY
LYPSIMAA, ANDERS	39	M	LABR	FNZZZZ	NY
HENDRIK	18	M	LABR	FNZZZZ	NY
KAIVIST-, THOMAS	25	M	LABR	FNZZZZ	NY
-EINTON, EFRAIM	27	M	LABR	FNZZZZ	NY
RANTABA, ELIAS	35	M	LABR	FNZZZZ	NY
LAICHEL, JOH	34	M	LABR	FNZZZZ	NY
PANIKOS, JOH	32	M	LABR	FNZZZZ	NY
SUNTALA, JOH	30	M	LABR	FNZZZZ	NY
MATY, JACOB	17	M	LABR	FNZZZZ	NY
HAASE, CARL	21	M	LABR	FNZZZZ	NY
HAKOLA, SALOMON	20	M	LABR	FNZZZZ	NY
WIHAMAKI, ERLAND	23	M	LABR	FNZZZZ	NY
LYPSIMMA, JOH	44	M	LABR	FNZZZZ	NY
SAGEWSKY, KAS	19	M	LABR	RRZZZZ	NY
GEBERT, VINCT	28	M	LABR	RRZZZZ	NY
LIPINTSKI, IGNATZ	28	M	LABR	RRZZZZ	NY
GOLDFARL, SIMON	47	M	DLR	RRZZZZ	NY
NOSSEN	21	M	DLR	RRZZZZ	NY
CISICOWSKI, MACIEY	56	M	LABR	RRZZZZ	NY
STEPHAN	22	M	LABR	RRZZZZ	NY
ANTON	18	M	LABR	RRZZZZ	NY
MIKULSKI, JAN	37	M	SMH	RRZZZZ	NY
L-ICKLER, MENDEL	30	M	TLR	RRZZZZ	NY
HUNAY, JOS	43	M	LABR	RRZZZZ	NY
ISTR	36	M	LABR	RRZZZZ	NY
DICK, CHARLES	25	M	GDSM	RRZZZZ	NY
SCHAKOWITZ, FRANCK	21	M	LABR	RRZZZZ	NY
GREGOROWI-TZ, MICHAL	23	M	LABR	RRZZZZ	NY

PASSENGER	AGE	SEX	OCCUPATION	PRIV	DES
ORLANSKI, MASCHE	25	M	DLR	RRZZZZ	NY
LEGAD, ARON	25	M	DLR	RRZZZZ	NY
ANTOHOLSKI, LAISER	18	M	DLR	RRZZZZ	NY
ANZELEWSKY, CHANE	20	M	DLR	RRZZZZ	NY
GOTTLIEB	45	M	DLR	RRZZZZ	NY
POLSTEIN, MEYER	30	M	LABR	RRZZZZ	NY
WEINSTEIN, SAMA	20	F	SGL	RRZZZZ	NY
JAMUSCHIK, IVAN	40	M	DLR	RRZZZZ	NY
FUNT, JOS	23	M	DLR	RRZZZZ	NY
SASKIND, FEIME	24	F	SGL	RRZZZZ	NY
SIMON	35	M	DLR	RRZZZZ	NY
GOLDBERG, WOLF	37	M	DLR	RRZZZZ	NY
ANNA	26	F	W	RRZZZZ	NY
LEVY	.09	M	INFANT	RRZZZZ	NY
JERUSALINSKY, ITSCHCE	23	M	SHMK	RRZZZZ	NY
PEZTKA, JACOB	35	M	FARMER	RRZZZZ	NY
MARIANNE	34	F	W	RRZZZZ	NY
JOSEFA	8	F	CHILD	RRZZZZ	NY
JOH	5	M	CHILD	RRZZZZ	NY
MIRSKE, JAN	32	M	LABR	RRZZZZ	NY
MAGDA	32	F	UNKNOWN	RRZZZZ	NY
MIRSKA, APOLLONIA	18	F	SGL	RRZZZZ	NY
KROBNITZKI, HIRSCH	21	M	LABR	RRZZZZ	NY
BREINE	20	F	W	RRZZZZ	NY
BIRSTEIN, ALEXANDER	23	M	JNR	RRZZZZ	NY
KAMINSKI, JOH	24	M	LABR	RRZZZZ	NY
BUSKOWSZKI, SALOMON	30	M	DLR	RRZZZZ	NY
POMASZOWSKI, NATHALIA	17	F	SGL	RRZZZZ	NY
PLEKO, VINCENTI	21	M	LABR	RRZZZZ	NY
ZASPASMK, JAN	27	M	SHMK	RRZZZZ	NY
TEWS, JOS	23	M	LABR	RRZZZZ	NY
LABOSZ, JOS	28	M	LABR	RRZZZZ	NY
KOROPOSAK, ANTON	19	M	LABR	RRZZZZ	NY
LIWSCHUETZ, JOS	39	M	LABR	RRZZZZ	NY
CHARASCH, MENDEL	36	M	DLR	RRZZZZ	NY
EPSTEIN, BARUCH	27	M	DLR	RRZZZZ	NY
WISNEWSKI, FRANZ	19	M	LABR	RRZZZZ	NY
WEISER, MIREL	34	F	WO	RRZZZZ	NY
ANNA	10	F	CH	RRZZZZ	NY
SIMON	9	M	CHILD	RRZZZZ	NY
ABRAHAM	3	M	CHILD	RRZZZZ	NY

SHIP: WERRA

FROM: BREMEN AND SOUTHAMPTON
TO: NEW YORK
ARRIVED: 15 MARCH 1888

PASSENGER	AGE	SEX	OCCUPATION	PRIV	DES
SAWYCKI, WOCIECH	23	M	LABR	RRZZZZ	USA
BEINHOLZ, JACOB	18	M	LABR	RRZZZZ	USA
REINHOLTZ, MICHAEL	22	M	LABR	RRZZZZ	USA
OZIEMKIWIECZ, PIOTR.	48	M	LABR	RRZZZZ	USA
JOSEF	18	M	LABR	RRZZZZ	USA
GRZENDA, JAN	27	M	LABR	RRZZZZ	USA
WROBLEWSKY, KAZWIN	28	M	LABR	RRZZZZ	USA
SOWOL, JOH.	38	M	LABR	RRZZZZ	USA
DRUCHOWITZ, ANTONI	35	F	NN	RRZZZZ	USA
ZDANIA, ANTONI	22	F	NN	RRZZZZ	USA
GLOWACKI, MICHAEL	27	M	LABR	RRZZZZ	USA
GRABKOWSKY, KONSTANZ	25	M	LABR	RRZZZZ	USA
ROSINSKI, JAN	22	M	LABR	RRZZZZ	USA
KRUCEWSKI, FRANZISEK	25	M	LABR	RRZZZZ	USA
POLITOWSKI, MIHAL	35	M	LABR	RRZZZZ	USA
SOLKOWSKA, PAULIN	30	F	W	RRZZZZ	USA
PALOSINA	9	F	CHILD	RRZZZZ	USA
FRANZ	7	M	CHILD	RRZZZZ	USA
WLADISLAUS	8	M	CHILD	RRZZZZ	USA
WLADISLAUS	6	M	CHILD	RRZZZZ	USA
JULIANA	.11	F	INFANT	RRZZZZ	USA
GOLDSTEIN, JOSEPH	38	M	FARMER	RRAFZD	USA
FILINSKY, JOHN	31	M	FARMER	RRAFZD	USA
JETZKOFSKY, ANTONI	31	F	NN	RRAFZD	USA
MICHAEL	36	M	LABR	RRAFZD	USA
SEIDEL, JOSEF	29	M	LABR	RRAFZD	USA
SZASZTA, JOSEF	26	M	LABR	RRAFZD	USA
FERENZ, MATHEUS	38	M	LABR	RRAFZD	USA
LUBARCEK, MARCIEN	23	M	LABR	RRAFZD	USA
FRANZ	30	M	LABR	RRAFZD	USA
NANOVITZ, JOSEF	30	M	LABR	RRZZZZ	USA
URBANSVITZ, ANTONI	25	F	NN	RRZZZZ	USA
BRONEBERG, MIHAL	23	M	LABR	RRZZZZ	USA
KRABCZOK, ERZBETTHA	33	F	NN	RRZZZZ	USA
ANDRUSKOWICZ, ANDRZY	30	M	LABR	RRZZZZ	USA
JESENSKI, ANTONIE	34	F	NN	RRZZZZ	USA
SVECZENSKY, JAN	28	M	LABR	RRZZZZ	USA
BARANOVSKY, JAN	24	M	LABR	RRZZZZ	USA
SOBOLEVSKY, OJOSEF	26	M	LABR	RRZZZZ	USA
BUTANOVIC, OJOSEF	18	M	LABR	RRZZZZ	USA

SHIP: THE QUEEN

FROM: LIVERPOOL
TO: NEW YORK
ARRIVED: 15 MARCH 1888

PASSENGER	AGE	SEX	OCCUPATION	PRIV	DES
OPENHEIM, B.	24	M	LABR	RRZZZZ	NY
GOLDBERG, SOLOMON	50	M	LABR	RRADBQ	BAL
MARY	48	F	W	RRADBQ	BAL
YETTA	20	F	SP	RRADBQ	BAL
BETSY	18	F	SP	RRADBQ	BAL
JANIE	15	F	SP	RRADBQ	BAL
LEIDHUDE, M.	27	M	LABR	RRZZZZ	BAL
SCHAMES, MORRIS	29	M	LABR	RRZZZZ	BAL
GOLDBERG, ELIAS	29	M	LABR	RRZZZZ	CH
BLACHER, LESER	29	M	LABR	RRZZZZ	CH
BEINENSTOCK, LEIB	30	M	LABR	RRZZZZ	BO
GOLDMAN, B.	26	M	LABR	RRZZZZ	BO
ODETMAN, M.	23	M	LABR	RRADBQ	BO
TEIN, LEIB	19	M	LABR	RRADBQ	BO
CEMENSKI, MARAST	29	M	LABR	RRZZZZ	NY
SOKOLOWSKI, INO	27	M	LABR	RRADED	NY
RENZINKOWITZ, R.	20	F	SP	RRZZZZ	NY
LEVIN, DWORE	50	F	W	RRZZZZ	NY
RACHEL	10	F	CH	RRZZZZ	NY
MARKIN, SCHOS	11	F	CH	RRZZZZ	NY
BLAN, CHAR.	13	M	LABR	RRZZZZ	NY
LEWSON, SCH.	40	F	W	RRZZZZ	NY
MACH.	9	F	CHILD	RRZZZZ	NY
GAAKOWITZ, SARA	18	F	SP	RRZZZZ	NY
MUHBRAD, SCHEINTZ	20	F	W	RRZZZZ	NY
MOSES	1	M	CHILD	RRZZZZ	NY
ZEFF, NOVS	18	M	LABR	RRZZZZ	PIT
THILL-N. SCH.	22	M	LABR	RRZZZZ	PIT
VARHANE, MOSES	43	M	LABR	RRZZZZ	NY
SARA	42	F	W	RRZZZZ	NY
VANHANE, JAN	18	F	SP	RRZZZZ	NY
KRAUM, CHAN	20	F	SP	RRZZZZ	NY
BEILE	15	F	SP	RRZZZZ	NY
ANSELSWITZ, RIN	26	F	W	RRZZZZ	NY
NORD	4	F	CHILD	RRZZZZ	NY
SARI	1	F	CHILD	RRZZZZ	NY
POTSCHER, RIV.	18	F	SP	RRZZZZ	NY
ZAKEWITZ, JOSEF	22	M	LABR	RRZZZZ	STL
POPENSKY, F.	22	M	LABR	RRZZZZ	STL
MASCHLEWITZ, JOS.	26	M	LABR	RRZZZZ	STL
JORDGEWITZ, K.	28	M	LABR	RRZZZZ	STL
MOSES, MATHIAS	21	M	LABR	RRZZZZ	STL
POSNER, MOSES	18	M	LABR	RRZZZZ	NY
BASEWITZ, V.	25	M	LABR	RRZZZZ	NY
REWITZ, MATH.	29	M	LABR	RRZZZZ	NY

PASSENGER	AGE	SEX	OCCUPATION	PRV VIL DES
SABANIS, STANISH	25	M	LABR	RRZZZZNY
ANTON	25	M	LABR	RRZZZZNY
STAVINSKY, ADOLF	22	M	LABR	RRZZZZNY
RASHSCHKEWITZ, WAI	22	M	LABR	RRZZZZNY
DABISCHINSKY, W.	27	M	LABR	RRZZZZCH
BARCHEWITZ, XAX	29	M	LABR	RRZZZZCH
WINIK, MEYN	42	M	LABR	RRZZZZPHI
SURGALOWITZ, D.	18	M	LABR	RRZZZZPHI
JORK	27	F	SP	RRZZZZPHI
ADELSOHN, A.	29	M	LABR	RRZZZZPHI
KARGAN, SAML.	38	M	LABR	RRZZZZNY
HURWITZ, HAST.	39	M	LABR	RRZZZZNY
LEVIN, MEYER	30	M	LABR	RRZZZZNY
SUMSKY, R.	20	F	SP	RRZZZZNY
AGASABIV, TIK.	26	M	LABR	RRZZZZNY
SAMAGRAN, DON.	21	F	SP	RRZZZZNY
RESCHO, MICH.	70	M	LABR	RRZZZZNY
KAPINO, ANTON	17	M	LABR	RRZZZZNY
LUKIA, ANDRE	21	M	LABR	RRZZZZNY
CESZWINAK, J.	17	M	LABR	RRZZZZNY
CRZEMAZETH, J.	25	M	LABR	RRZZZZNY
JUSKO, JANOS	18	M	LABR	RRZZZZNY
PRONSS, ABE	22	M	LABR	RRZZZZNY
SAYOPIAN, K.	27	M	LABR	RRZZZZNY
RADON, CHAISE	21	F	SP	RRZZZZNY
BRANDWEIN, L.	17	F	SP	RRZZZZNY
FECHTER, ZENE	20	F	SP	RRZZZZNY
SCHAPIRO, R.	52	F	SP	RRZZZZNY
JADELEWITZ, B.	20	M	LABR	RRZZZZNY
JOSELOWITZ, K.	22	M	LABR	RRZZZZNY
WEISSMAN, MEYER	37	M	LABR	RRZZZZNY
SARI	28	F	W	RRZZZZNY
STECHER, MALKE	50	M	LABR	RRZZZZNY
SEGALL, B.	45	F	W	RRZZZZPIT
HINDE	22	F	SP	RRZZZZPIT
BERTHA	20	F	SP	RRZZZZPIT
OS.	18	F	SP	RRZZZZPIT
LEE, ROCHE	16	F	SP	RRZZZZNY
RAMINSKY, L.	48	M	LABR	RRZZZZTOR
SOBOSINSKY, SIMON	26	F	SP	RRZZZZTOR
KAFFANSKY, MARWIO	27	F	SP	RRZZZZTOR
GOGELEWITZ, JAN	46	F	SP	RRZZZZTOR
TREDVILL, PAUL	31	M	LABR	RRZZZZNY
LEVENSKY, ANTON	33	M	LABR	RRZZZZNY
PIZIKOLSKY, MARIA	25	F	SP	RRZZZZNY
HEZEMASKY, WHADISH	46	M	LABR	RRZZZZNY
MATULINEWITZ, A.	23	M	LABR	RRZZZZNY
DOBREWOLSKY, ALEX	44	M	LABR	RRZZZZNY
KESELENSKY, W.	22	M	LABR	RRZZZZNY
DWONSKY, F.	30	M	LABR	RRZZZZNY
JULIA	25	F	W	RRZZZZNY
JAN	3	F	CHILD	RRZZZZNY
FRIEDBERG, N.	29	M	LABR	RRZZZZNY
KOLOWDIRE, L.	23	M	LABR	RRZZZZNY
SEBNARTZMAN, N.	18	M	LABR	RRZZZZNY
HOLSTEIN, FELIX	24	M	LABR	RRZZZZNY
RUDERMAN, L.	42	M	LABR	RRZZZZNY
BUBINS, MAR.	23	M	LABR	RRZZZZBO
PLOTTHEWSKY, W.	27	M	LABR	RRZZZZBO
KUPTA, ANTON	30	M	LABR	RRZZZZNY
JUKAIT, AUG.	23	M	LABR	RRZZZZNY
WANDUSKY, L.	25	M	LABR	RRZZZZNY
LEES, JAC.	25	M	LABR	RRZZZZBO
SESCELIA, S.	23	M	LABR	RRZZZZBO
GINALKOWSKY, A.	32	M	LABR	RRZZZZNY
ULINSKY, A.	32	M	LABR	RRZZZZNY
DOMROWSKY, AL.	27	M	LABR	RRZZZZNY
JEMER, ANT.	25	M	LABR	RRZZZZNY
WISNEWSKY, JOH.	19	M	LABR	RRZZZZNY
DONBROWSKY, THO.	22	M	LABR	RRZZZZNY
STACHIOWSKY, M.	29	M	LABR	RRZZZZUNK
DUGOWITZ, Z.	30	M	LABR	RRZZZZNY
SCHASLALSKY, W.	29	M	LABR	RRZZZZNY
GABRONSKY, M.	40	M	LABR	RRZZZZNY
HENFINAN, LOUIS	17	M	LABR	RRZZZZNY
GOLDENBERG, S.	23	M	LABR	RRZZZZCH
ELANE	18	F	W	RRZZZZCH
WROMIKOW, WOLF	44	M	LABR	RRZZZZCH
WENDEL, WOLF	27	M	LABR	RRZZZZCH
LASCIKO, MAT.	26	M	LABR	RRZZZZNY
MARZINKEWITZ, P.	27	M	LABR	RRZZZZNY
JURGELOUR, A.	24	M	LABR	RRZZZZNY
BALUVITZ, A.	17	M	LABR	RRZZZZNY
KOTZWITZKY, Z.	22	M	LABR	RRZZZZNY
AUSCHER, AUG.	26	M	LABR	RRZZZZNY
KASCHULSWIS, A.	32	M	LABR	RRZZZZNY
WOLATKEWITZ, A.	27	M	LABR	RRZZZZBAL
SWIKOWSKY, M.	24	M	LABR	RRZZZZBAL
OKONSKY, JOSEF	23	M	LABR	RRZZZZNY
KORNGSFEST, BENG.	27	M	LABR	RRZZZZNY
LEFUKOW, ELIE	10	F	CH	RRZZZZNY
SEYBALOWITZ, M.	29	M	LABR	RRZZZZNY
JUCHT, HODE	19	F	SP	RRZZZZNY
SCHUMKAV, JUDEL	38	M	LABR	RRZZZZNY
CHAISE	31	F	W	RRZZZZNY
DWORE	13	F	SP	RRZZZZNY
SARAH	11	F	CH	RRZZZZNY
RACHEL	10	F	CH	RRZZZZNY
MOSES	8	M	CHILD	RRZZZZNY
BERLO	5	M	CHILD	RRZZZZNY
ARON	3	M	CHILD	RRZZZZNY
MICH	1	F	CHILD	RRZZZZNY
REICHSTEIN, J.	32	M	LABR	RRZZZZNY
ELENBERG, ISRAEL	44	M	LABR	RRZZZZSTL
ZIMMERMANN, P.	48	F	W	RRZZZZSTL
CHAIE	28	F	SP	RRZZZZSTL
BELA	11	F	CH	RRZZZZSTL
SELINE	3	F	CHILD	RRZZZZSTL
JUDE	1	M	CHILD	RRZZZZSTL
RATZ, KATH.	15	M	LABR	RRZZZZNY
ROSENBERG, S.	18	M	LABR	RRZZZZCH
BERGER, JACOB	20	M	LABR	RRZZZZNY
RAPPEPORT, L.	26	M	LABR	RRZZZZNY
ENGELMAN, G.	24	M	LABR	RRZZZZNY
KOWALTSKY, J.	42	M	LABR	RRZZZZNY
GELSCHEVSKY, F.	23	M	LABR	RRZZZZNY
LWUBOWITZ, A.	29	M	LABR	RRZZZZBAL
VICK, GOTTHEL	36	M	LABR	RRZZZZBAL
ROHN, HENRIK	26	M	LABR	RRZZZZJER
GURSKY, STAN.	28	M	LABR	RRZZZZNY
KRAIEWSKY, JOS.	26	M	LABR	RRZZZZNY
HELENA	24	F	W	RRZZZZNY
JOS.	1	M	CHILD	RRZZZZNY
PLIFFERLING, H.	22	M	LABR	RRZZZZNY
GRAGUWSKY, F.	21	M	LABR	RRZZZZNY
BECHNAROWITZ, K.	28	M	LABR	RRZZZZNY
SCHWARTZ, BERG.	36	M	LABR	RRZZZZNY
HORN, CHAINE	22	M	LABR	RRZZZZNY
KELA	19	F	W	RRZZZZNY
SCHECH, ISRAEL	11	M	CH	RRZZZZNY
BORASCH, ROSA	16	F	SP	RRZZZZNY

SHIP: STATE OF GEORGIA

FROM: GLASGOW AND LARNE
TO: NEW YORK
ARRIVED: 15 MARCH 1888

PASSENGER	AGE	SEX	OCCUPATION	PRV VIL DES
STRAUCH, JOSEF	24	M	LABR	RRZZZZUSA
MAYER, TOBIAS	50	M	LABR	RRZZZZUSA
-AEABY, JULIUS	16	M	LABR	RRZZZZUSA
RESCHEWITSKY, FELIX	36	M	LABR	RRZZZZUSA
LISEWITZ, FRANZIZESK	28	M	LABR	RRZZZZUSA
ADAMOWITZ, PETRO	25	M	LABR	RRZZZZUSA
TASCHMANN, PESACH	27	M	LABR	RRZZZZUSA

PASSENGER	AGE	SEX	OCCUPATION	PRV	VIL	DES
GULLBERG, JOHANN	23	M	LABR	RR	ZZZZ	USA
BOILIUSKY, BEILE	14	M	LABR	RR	ZZZZ	USA
GRENEWITZ, ADAM	26	M	LABR	RR	ZZZZ	USA
NORTOFT, JOSEF	24	M	LABR	RR	ZZZZ	USA
SISKUTZ, IVAN	27	M	LABR	RR	ZZZZ	USA
GRENEWITZ, -URIE	31	M	LABR	RR	ZZZZ	USA
KANNESKY, FRANZ	32	M	LABR	RR	ZZZZ	USA
KASCHU-A, FRANZ	25	M	LABR	RR	ZZZZ	USA
SASTA-, KASIMIR	27	M	LABR	RR	ZZZZ	USA
SARMATIS, JACOB	22	M	LABR	RR	ZZZZ	USA
GOLDSTEIN, -UDEL	24	M	LABR	RR	ZZZZ	USA
SCHEINDEL	22	F	W	RR	ZZZZ	USA
CHAIME	.09	F	INFANT	RR	ZZZZ	USA
WROBLEWSKY, MARTIN	33	M	LABR	RR	ZZZZ	USA
-AIDIUZIG, ADOF	34	M	LABR	RR	ZZZZ	USA
CHA--OWSKY, JOHAN	26	M	LABR	RR	ZZZZ	USA
PODBELSKI, BALTAS	23	M	LABR	RR	ZZZZ	USA
KANAT, JOHAN	36	M	LABR	RR	ZZZZ	USA
OLSCHEWSKY, FRANZ	23	M	LABR	RR	ZZZZ	USA
WEIN, HIRSCH	52	M	SPDLR	RR	ZZZZ	USA
DRESCHSEL, CHRISTIAN	22	M	BKR	RR	ZZZZ	USA
WIGDEROWITZ, JANKEL	21	M	PDLR	RR	ZZZZ	USA
SCHRADER, BENJAMIN	19	M	PDLR	RR	ZZZZ	USA
LANDLER, SALOMON	20	M	PDLR	RR	ZZZZ	USA
KIRSCHUER, GERSHIN	20	M	PDLR	RR	ZZZZ	USA
WILSTEIN, SCHI-EN	22	M	PDLR	RR	ZZZZ	USA
WEISS, --UEL	20	M	PDLR	RR	ZZZZ	USA
NEYER, NAPHTALI	27	M	PDLR	RR	ZZZZ	USA
SCHUSTER, NOTA	42	M	PDLR	RR	ZZZZ	USA
KOLLAT, RUDOLF	21	M	PDLR	RR	ZZZZ	USA
GOLDSHMIDT, CHAIM	18	M	PDLR	RR	ZZZZ	USA
HIMMELSTEIN, CHAIM	24	M	PDLR	RR	ZZZZ	USA
HURWITZ, MOSES	24	M	PDLR	RR	ZZZZ	USA
NECKRITZ, MOSES	45	M	PDLR	RR	ZZZZ	USA
PER---NTHER, ABRAHAM	17	M	PDLR	RR	ZZZZ	USA
ESTER	15	F	SP	RR	ZZZZ	USA
KARP, CHASHEL	44	M	PDLR	RR	ZZZZ	USA
SARAH	44	F	W	RR	ZZZZ	USA
BERL	10	M	BY	RR	ZZZZ	USA
HUSAR, ANNA	24	F	SP	RR	ZZZZ	USA
KRACKON, GOLDE	19	F	SP	RR	ZZZZ	USA
WOLSCHINSKY, ZIVIE	16	F	SP	RR	ZZZZ	USA
MASE, SULE	19	F	SP	RR	ZZZZ	USA
SU--ER, DAVORA	18	F	SP	RR	ZZZZ	USA
NAUMMER, CHAJE	17	F	SP	RR	ZZZZ	USA
-KTAWARSKY, ETTEL	17	F	SP	RR	ZZZZ	USA
RASOWSKY, -OLDE	18	F	SP	RR	ZZZZ	USA
MASAR, ANNA	25	F	SP	RR	ZZZZ	USA
KASCHA, BISCHAWETZKA	22	F	SP	RR	ZZZZ	USA
LEWGOWO, MARIA	31	F	SP	RR	ZZZZ	USA
LEWOSHA	25	F	SP	RR	ZZZZ	USA
LEWASHIK, ANNA	23	F	SP	RR	ZZZZ	USA
SCHUMAN, FREIDE	30	F	SP	RR	ZZZZ	USA
ABRAHAM	6	M	CHILD	RR	ZZZZ	USA
AUGUST, REBECCA	43	F	W	RR	ZZZZ	USA
MORTIZ	10	M	BY	RR	ZZZZ	USA
NAFTELOWITZ, MERE	50	F	W	RR	ZZZZ	USA
SARAH	25	F	W	RR	ZZZZ	USA
CHANE	11	F	CH	RR	ZZZZ	USA
S-RINGE	2	F	CHILD	RR	ZZZZ	USA
ROCHEL	1	F	CHILD	RR	ZZZZ	USA
RADULSKY, ITTE	30	F	W	RR	ZZZZ	USA
MORDCHE	9	F	CHILD	RR	ZZZZ	USA
ETTEL	6	F	CHILD	RR	ZZZZ	USA
LEIB	2	F	CHILD	RR	ZZZZ	USA
POLOWITCH, BEILE	50	F	W	RR	ZZZZ	USA
LEIB	10	F	CH	RR	ZZZZ	USA

SHIP: SLAVONIA

FROM: STETTIN
TO: NEW YORK
ARRIVED: 16 MARCH 1888

PASSENGER	AGE	SEX	OCCUPATION	PRV	VIL	DES
MASZCYNSKA, MARIA	60	F	WI	RR	AHXZ	USA
ADAM	26	M	LABR	RR	AHXZ	USA
WOLF, GOTTLIEBE	60	F	WO	RR	ZZZZ	USA
PERLEWICZ, KASIMIR	21	M	LABR	RR	AHZS	USA
ARMPRESS, SHODES	19	M	LABR	RR	AGRT	USA
LIBNITZKI, HIRSCH	42	M	UNKNOWN	RR	AHXI	USA
KOTLARSKI, BARUCH	29	M	PNTR	RR	AHXI	USA
JUSCHKOWSKI, ELIAS	44	M	TLR	RR	ZZZZ	USA
SOLEZKY, PIETRO	24	M	LABR	RR	ZZZZ	USA
BLAKA, ANDREI	23	M	LABR	RR	ZZZZ	USA
SOLEZKY, MICHAEL	23	M	LABR	RR	ZZZZ	USA
MAZALIS, ANTON	50	M	LABR	RR	ZZZZ	USA
BONEWITZ, KASIMIR	25	M	LABR	RR	ZZZZ	USA
WILKISCH, KASIMIR	26	M	LABR	RR	ZZZZ	USA
GUDONIS, ANTON	30	M	LABR	RR	AICY	USA
BUKEWICZ, MAGDALENA	40	F	WO	RR	ZZZZ	USA
ANNA	13	F	CH	RR	ZZZZ	USA
JAN	10	M	CH	RR	ZZZZ	USA
MARIA	2	F	CHILD	RR	ZZZZ	USA
KUPSTACZ, JOHANN	28	M	LABR	RR	ZZZZ	USA
WILSGA, MATIE	22	M	LABR	RR	ZZZZ	USA
ANUSKIEWICZ, MATHAUS	27	M	LABR	RR	ZZZZ	USA
BRZEZINSKI, VOICHECH	25	M	LABR	RR	AHXZ	USA
EIDOFFSKY, FRANZ	33	M	LABR	RR	ZZZZ	USA
VINCENZ	38	M	LABR	RR	ZZZZ	USA
LEWANDOWSKY, STANISLAUS	27	M	LABR	RR	ZZZZ	USA
SZINSKY, MARIAN	23	M	LABR	RR	ZZZZ	USA

SHIP: SARDINIAN

FROM: HALIFAX AND LIVERPOOL
TO: BALTIMORE
ARRIVED: 17 MARCH 1888

PASSENGER	AGE	SEX	OCCUPATION	PRV	VIL	DES
CHASKEL, RAFAEL	19	M	BLKSMH	PL	ZZZZ	PA
RACHEMNA	17	F	W	PL	ZZZZ	PA
HINDE, COHN	17	F	NN	PL	ZZZZ	BAL
FEIGE	10	F	CH	PL	ZZZZ	BAL
BASCHE	40	F	W	PL	ZZZZ	BAL
NOSKI	6	M	CHILD	PL	ZZZZ	BAL
ISSER	4	M	CHILD	PL	ZZZZ	BAL
CHAJE	21	F	NN	PL	ZZZZ	BAL
SUCKENNAU, MARKEL	20	M	LABR	RR	ZZZZ	NE
SERAK, MIKE	19	M	LABR	PL	ZZZZ	UNK
ANNE	16	F	NN	PL	ZZZZ	UNK
BERKS, LAVENSON	26	M	LABR	PL	ZZZZ	PA
KARPOWSKI, VALENTINE	35	M	LABR	PL	ZZZZ	OH
KATONNIO	27	F	W	PL	ZZZZ	OH
MERIVIO, ALTE	30	F	W	PL	ZZZZ	BAL
EISIG	10	M	CH	PL	ZZZZ	BAL
MOSES	6	M	CHILD	PL	ZZZZ	BAL
MINA	.06	F	INFANT	PL	ZZZZ	BAL
MARIAN, KARPOWSKI	22	M	LABR	PL	ZZZZ	BAL
ITZIG, WEINER	20	M	LABR	PL	ZZZZ	BAL
GOLDBERG, PINKUS	22	M	MLR	PL	ZZZZ	BAL
TURBICKY, ESTHER	44	F	W	PL	ZZZZ	BAL
LEIB	22	M	LABR	PL	ZZZZ	BAL
SARAH	20	F	NN	PL	ZZZZ	BAL
MALKE	17	M	LABR	PL	ZZZZ	BAL
SAM.	11	F	CH	PL	ZZZZ	BAL
MICHEL	10	M	CH	PL	ZZZZ	BAL
TURBECKY, CHAN.	9	M	CHILD	PL	ZZZZ	BAL
HIRSCH	8	M	CHILD	PL	ZZZZ	BAL

PASSENGER	AGE	SEX	OCCUPATION	PRV VIL DES
GOELVICINI, HARNI	26	M	LABR	RRZZZZBAL
SILBERBERG, MIAL	22	M	LABR	RRZZZZBAL
BERKIWITZ, MARIE	28	F	W	PLZZZZBAL
RISCH	5	M	CHILD	PLZZZZBAL
SCHOLEM	4	M	CHILD	PLZZZZBAL
LIEBE	2	F	CHILD	PLZZZZBAL
EIDE	.08	F	INFANT	PLZZZZBAL
OKINSKI, JOHAN	34	M	LABR	PLZZZZBAL
WISNIEWSKI, IGNAZ	20	M	LABR	PLZZZZBAL
AESZYNSKI, JOHAN	30	M	LABR	PLZZZZBAL
DAMBROWSKI, JOHAN	27	M	LABR	PLZZZZBAL

SHIP: CATALONIA

FROM: LIVERPOOL AND QUEENSTOWN
TO: BOSTON
ARRIVED: GS UNKNOWN ON A

PASSENGER	AGE	SEX	OCCUPATION	PRV VIL DES
KAUPPI, JOHA	38	M	LABR	FNZZZZUSA
MAUTILA, TUOMAS	25	M	LABR	FNZZZZUSA
RINKI, JASOKO	25	M	LABR	FNZZZZUSA
BURKI, KARLE	24	M	LABR	FNZZZZUSA
WALTA, JASOKO	21	M	LABR	FNZZZZUSA
HUVVARI, HERMAN	23	M	LABR	FNZZZZUSA
TARKKO, THOMAS	25	M	LABR	FNZZZZUSA
LAITENON, MIKKO	32	M	LABR	FNZZZZUSA
HAKELS, JASOKO	27	M	LABR	FNZZZZUSA
KAUFFI, JOH	40	M	LABR	FNZZZZUSA
SAMMELSHU, LOUIS	59	M	LABR	FNZZZZUSA
MICHELE	58	F	W	FNZZZZUSA
MASI, HERSCH	20	M	LABR	FNZZZZUSA
STECHER, DAVID	16	M	LABR	FNZZZZUSA
FEIGENBAMM, HERSCH	29	M	LABR	RRZZZZUSA
DEBORAH	28	F	W	RRZZZZUSA
DAVID	3	M	CHILD	RRZZZZUSA
MOSES	.11	M	INFANT	RRZZZZUSA
FAST, CHANE	18	F	SVNT	RRZZZZUSA
SINGER, GOLDE	20	F	SVNT	RRZZZZUSA
KAPLAN, JENNY	18	F	SVNT	RRZZZZUSA
ROSENRGWEIG, L	27	M	LABR	RRZZZZUSA
SURE	22	F	W	RRZZZZUSA
MOSES	2	M	CHILD	RRZZZZUSA
MERI	.07	F	INFANT	RRZZZZUSA
ZIPERSKI, LEISER	35	M	LABR	RRZZZZUSA
ISRAEL	17	M	LABR	RRZZZZUSA
FEDER, MORDECLAI	31	M	LABR	RRZZZZUSA
WEIMANN, BERESCH	22	M	LABR	RRZZZZUSA
GOLDMANN, ABRAHAM	30	M	LABR	RRZZZZUSA
KAIGER, FEIRREL	32	M	LABR	RRZZZZUSA
ALISIUS, OSIP	50	M	LABR	RRZZZZUSA

SHIP: SERVIA

FROM: LIVERPOOL AND QUEENSTOWN
TO: NEW YORK
ARRIVED: 19 MARCH 1888

PASSENGER	AGE	SEX	OCCUPATION	PRV VIL DES
GEETHEN, HERMAN	17	M	LABR	RRADAXNY
GOLDBERG, JANKEL	42	M	LABR	RRADAXNY
JABACKER, HIRSCH	35	M	LABR	RRADAXPA
SCHULMAN, EISIK	35	M	LABR	RRADAXNY
EPSTEIN, SOLOMON	40	M	LABR	RRADAXNY
HUTNER, JOSEF	38	M	LABR	RRADAXNY
STERNGUT, ELIAS	24	M	LABR	RRADAXNY
DURKOWSKY, JAKOB	30	M	LABR	RRADAXNY
STOL-, JOHAN	19	M	LABR	RRADAXNY
RAPANA, HEDWICK	50	M	LABR	RRADAXNY
ANALA, JOHAN	50	M	LABR	RRADAXNY
JACOBSON, JEREMIAS	44	M	LABR	RRADAXNY
HENRICKSON, ANDREAS	19	M	LABR	RRADAXNY
RASAKA, MICHAEL	25	M	LABR	RRADAXNY
BUKI, OLO-	38	M	LABR	RRADAXNY
BETELA, AU--	36	M	LABR	RRADAXNY
JOGELA, GUSTAV	19	M	LABR	RRADAXNY
JOHANSON, WILH	23	M	LABR	RRADAXNY
JACOBSON, JOHAN	28	M	LABR	RRADAXNY
JOHANSON, JOHAN	47	M	LABR	RRADAXNY
MIKA	26	M	LABR	RRADAXNY
SCHLAUPPE, JEAN	41	M	LABR	RRADAXNY
BROMISCH, JOHAN	30	M	LABR	RRADAXPA
LUNKURN, JOH	34	M	LABR	RRADAXPA
BERKOWITCH, WOLFF	23	M	TLR	RRADAXMA
MENMARK, LEA	18	F	SP	RRADAXNY
SPECTER, ESTHER	50	F	W	RRADAXNY
SENDER	11	M	CH	RRADAXNY
CHAZKE-	9	M	CHILD	RRADAXNY
REISEL	7	F	CHILD	RRADAXNY
CHANE	3	F	CHILD	RRADAXNY
GOOBMSUSOWA, URTTE	30	F	W	RRADAXNY
GUILDE	11	F	CH	RRADAXNY
SOLOM-	9	M	CHILD	RRADAXNY
SURA	7	F	CHILD	RRADAXNY
MOSES	3	M	CHILD	RRADAXNY
FISZBEIN, SYLME	34	F	W	RRADAXNY
BUSKE	9	F	CHILD	RRADAXNY
MOSES	7	M	CHILD	RRADAXNY
FEI--	3	F	CHILD	RRADAXNY
INDEL	.09	M	INFANT	RRADAXNY
RENTOWITZ, BEREL	27	M	TLR	RRADAXNY
MENN---	22	F	W	RRADAXNY
BRAUNSTEIN, MARIE	26	F	W	RRADAXNY
JACOB	.11	M	INFANT	RRADAXNY
SIMONSKY, ISTRA--	19	F	W	RRADAXNY
JANKO	.10	M	INFANT	RRADAXNY
WIANKOOPIE, INSOP---	35	M	LABR	RRADAXNY
GRETE	35	F	W	RRADAXNY

SHIP: RHAETIA

FROM: HAMBURG AND HAVRE
TO: NEW YORK
ARRIVED: 19 MARCH 1888

PASSENGER	AGE	SEX	OCCUPATION	PRV VIL DES
ZURAWO, JANOS	20	M	LABR	RRZZZZUSA
STEFAN	33	M	LABR	RRZZZZUSA
KUCZ, JOSEF	27	M	LABR	RRZZZZUSA
WALESAK, WASKO	24	M	FARMER	RRZZZZUSA
SCHUCHMANN, CIPPE	32	F	UNKNOWN	RRZZZZUSA
JOSEF	9	F	CHILD	RRZZZZUSA
TESCHE	8	F	CHILD	RRZZZZUSA
MICHEL	7	M	CHILD	RRZZZZUSA
SAMUEL	4	M	CHILD	RRZZZZUSA
ISRAEL	.11	M	INFANT	RRZZZZUSA
LEGOL, JUDEL	28	M	UNKNOWN	RRZZZZUSA
MISKIEL, VICTOR	20	M	LABR	RRZZZZUSA
NAMOSKA, VICTOR	18	M	LABR	RRZZZZUSA
JILZ, ROSALIE	27	F	SGL	RRZZZZUSA
GURSKI, JAN	45	M	LABR	RRZZZZUSA
PATSCHKOWSKY, JAN	57	M	FARMER	RRZZZZUSA
PERKUNTZKI, MATHAUS	42	M	FARMER	RRZZZZUSA
WEINIKOWICZ, CASIS	21	M	UNKNOWN	RRZZZZUSA
SCHIPLIS, JURAS	25	M	UNKNOWN	RRZZZZUSA
WEINANTZKA, GUTONAS	26	M	UNKNOWN	RRZZZZUSA
MARIE	24	F	UNKNOWN	RRZZZZUSA
JONAS	.03	M	INFANT	RRZZZZUSA

PASSENGER	AGE	SEX	OCCUPATION	PRVIL	DES
DABITZKAS, JONAS	25	M	LABR	RRZZZZ	USA
SCHEPRETSKI, DA---	21	M	LABR	RRZZZZ	USA
---KUS, U	23	M	LABR	RRZZZZ	USA
KASCHANTZKI, BENEDICT	22	M	LABR	RRZZZZ	USA
PANLUKONITS, HASSIS	22	M	LABR	RRZZZZ	USA
RUSSATZKIS, BALTUS	41	M	LABR	RRZZZZ	USA
SCHANZEWICZ, FRANZ	24	M	LABR	RRZZZZ	USA
KUSZINICKI, FRANZISZEK	24	M	LABR	RRZZZZ	USA
NORSAWICH, CASIMIR	42	M	LABR	RRZZZZ	USA
ANUZEWICZ, CASIMIR	38	M	UNKNOWN	RRZZZZ	USA
DOMEINSKI, FRANZIZEK	20	M	UNKNOWN	RRZZZZ	USA
MAKAKAZEWICZ, FRANZ	28	M	UNKNOWN	RRZZZZ	USA
SCHANZEWICZ, JOSEF	25	M	UNKNOWN	RRZZZZ	USA
DORSCHEWICZ, FRANZ	31	M	UNKNOWN	RRZZZZ	USA
SZYLOWSKI, MOSES	28	M	UNKNOWN	RRZZZZ	USA
WEISSMER, JOH	24	M	UNKNOWN	RRZZZZ	USA
WESSEL, WADISL	27	M	UNKNOWN	RRZZZZ	USA
FRANZISKA	24	F	W	RRZZZZ	USA
WILLENZIEK, NATHAN	60	M	LABR	RRZZZZ	USA
TAMARE	57	F	W	RRZZZZ	USA
RIVKE	19	F	W	RRZZZZ	USA
FISCHER, DWORE	27	F	SGL	RRZZZZ	USA
LEWIN, ESTHER	30	F	WO	RRZZZZ	USA
ABRAH	7	M	CHILD	RRZZZZ	USA
SCHEINE	.11	F	INFANT	RRZZZZ	USA
BABEKUHL, HELENE	17	F	SGL	RRZZZZ	USA
WINDGRAD, MOSES	34	M	LABR	RRZZZZ	USA
BINE	34	F	W	RRZZZZ	USA
ESTHER	15	F	CH	RRZZZZ	USA
LEIB	9	M	CHILD	RRZZZZ	USA
BALZSINCIWNA, TEKLA	21	F	SGL	RRZZZZ	USA
SCHAPIRA, PESCHE	26	F	WO	RRZZZZ	USA
ROCHEL	9	F	CHILD	RRZZZZ	USA
MORDCHE	6	M	CHILD	RRZZZZ	USA
ZIPE	.11	F	INFANT	RRZZZZ	USA
KOHEN, ABRAHAM	57	M	MCHT	RRZZZZ	USA
WESSELOWSKY, ANTONY	31	M	LABR	RRZZZZ	USA
WRUBLEWSKY, JAN	38	M	LABR	RRZZZZ	USA
STOLIKOWSKY, JAN	25	M	LABR	RRZZZZ	USA
DUSCHINSKI, BENEDICT	34	M	LABR	RRZZZZ	USA
MORDSCHOWITZ, BERL	35	M	FUR	RRZZZZ	USA
GUTTMANN, CAROL	18	F	SGL	RRZZZZ	USA
TIRSBIR, JULS	29	M	LKSH	RRZZZZ	USA
SALOWIZIK, ISRAEL	19	M	CL	RRZZZZ	USA
FILENDA, ADAM	32	M	LABR	RRZZZZ	USA
KOLOCZA, JAN	30	M	LABR	RRZZZZ	USA
JAN	22	M	LABR	RRZZZZ	USA
KORALCZKY, TOMAS	30	M	LABR	RRZZZZ	USA
WARKOVSKY, JULIAN	23	M	LABR	RRZZZZ	USA
KEISZELOWSKY, ADAM	22	M	LABR	RRZZZZ	USA
MOSTENSZKY, JAN	31	M	LABR	RRZZZZ	USA
CHOJNOWSKY, CASIMIR	25	M	LABR	RRZZZZ	USA
PHILIPORITS, JOSEF	25	M	LABR	RRZZZZ	USA
SZAVAL, JOSEF	25	M	LABR	RRZZZZ	USA
LEPSKI, ALEXANDRE	28	M	LKSH	RRZZZZ	USA
LEWIN, LEA	26	F	WO	RRZZZZ	USA
GREGOR	9	M	CHILD	RRZZZZ	USA
SIMON	7	M	CHILD	RRZZZZ	USA
ELIAS	5	M	CHILD	RRZZZZ	USA
RABINOWITZ, FEIGE	26	F	WO	RRZZZZ	USA
ROSA	4	F	CHILD	RRZZZZ	USA
SAMUEL	2	M	CHILD	RRZZZZ	USA
REBECKA	.09	F	INFANT	RRZZZZ	USA
PASSEMANICZ, DWEIZE	23	F	SGL	RRZZZZ	USA
JARKOWSKY, ANTON	38	M	LABR	RRZZZZ	USA
KOLOSCHINSKY, IGNATZ	20	M	LABR	RRZZZZ	USA
ROSS, STANISL	25	M	LABR	RRZZZZ	USA
BRIECK, JOSEF	38	M	LABR	RRZZZZ	USA
BERMANN, SARA	23	F	WO	RRZZZZ	USA
ABRAH	.11	M	INFANT	RRZZZZ	USA
SALOMONSOHN, MALKE	20	F	SGL	RRZZZZ	USA
LEBENDIGES, GITTEL	37	F	WO	RRZZZZ	USA
ITKE	17	F	CH	RRZZZZ	USA
SCHIMEN	9	M	CHILD	RRZZZZ	USA
LEIB	7	M	CHILD	RRZZZZ	USA
BARUCH	5	M	CHILD	RRZZZZ	USA
SARAH	20	F	SGL	RRZZZZ	USA
BASCHENE	16	F	SGL	RRZZZZ	USA
ABRAH	9	M	CHILD	RRZZZZ	USA
CLAUSEN, PETER	25	M	FARMER	RRZZZZ	USA
STEINHAMMER, JACOB	45	M	FARMER	RRZZZZ	USA
WITTMACK, AUGUST	9	M	CHILD	RRZZZZ	USA
PETERSEN, JACOB	18	M	FARMER	RRZZZZ	USA

SHIP: CITY OF RICHMOND

FROM: LIVERPOOL
TO: NEW YORK
ARRIVED: 19 MARCH 1888

PASSENGER	AGE	SEX	OCCUPATION	PRVIL	DES
SKUTER, PETER	27	M	LABR	RRACBF	PHI
KRULUS, Z----US	28	M	LABR	RRACBF	PHI
OPPENHEIM, BENJ	44	M	PNTR	RRACBF	PHI
CHA--	44	F	W	RRACBF	PHI
NESCHE	7	F	CHILD	RRACBF	PHI
HERMANN, MUSCHKE	39	F	W	RRACBF	PHI
--ORE	7	F	CHILD	RRACBF	PHI
MOSCHE	4	F	CHILD	RRACBF	PHI
KREMER, SORE	20	M	LABR	RRACBF	PHI
STERN, ADOLF	20	M	LABR	RRACBF	PHI
BETTY	19	F	W	RRACBF	PHI
SRUKOWSKA, AND--RIKA	22	F	SVNT	RRACBF	OH
SW--RINSKA, JOSEFA	21	F	SVNT	RRACBF	OH
ETSERTOWSKI, ANTONE	24	M	LABR	RRACBF	NY
NAWAKOWSKI, JOHANN	23	M	LABR	RRACBF	NY
-IESMANN, JOHANN	23	M	LABR	RRACBF	NY
-OISER, SARE	20	F	W	RRACBF	NY
RUIE	.11	F	INFANT	RRACBF	NY
HORN, O-SER	29	M	TLR	RRAFWJ	NY
STEINER, NACHMAN	26	M	TLR	RRACBF	NY
SOFMACHER, SZ-JE	27	M	TLR	RRACBF	NY
HOROWITZ, HERSCH	22	M	CGRMKR	RRACBF	PA
CACHTMANN, GERSON	27	M	TLR	RRACBF	PHI
GACHTMANN, ISAK	33	M	TLR	RRACBF	PHI
MIGDALSKA, AGNES	60	F	W	RRACBF	OH
EVA	23	F	SVNT	RRACBF	OH
MOTILENSKI, JOSEF	25	M	LABR	RRACBF	NY
KLOSWOWSKI, FRANZ	25	M	LABR	RRACBF	NY
STANIZANSKI, STANISLAUS	22	M	LABR	RRACBF	NY
KAPUCZYNSKI, ANTON	32	M	LABR	RRACBF	NY
RATSCHKOWSKI, ETTEL	20	M	LABR	RRACBF	NY
GORDON, SIMES	29	M	PDLR	RRACBF	NY
SKYZYPZAK, AGNISKA	33	F	W	RRACBF	NY
STANISLAUS	.11	F	INFANT	RRACBF	NY
-ILAK, ANDRAS	10	M	CH	RRACBF	OH
JANOS	8	M	CHILD	RRACBF	OH
SPOR-HOLZ, FREDERICK	15	M	LABR	RRACBF	MN
BISELBERG, -EMME	18	F	SVNT	RRACBF	NY
RYBSKI, JOSEPH	19	M	TLR	RRACBF	PA
-ILAK, ANNA	17	F	SVNT	RRACBF	OH
SADERBERG, ERIK	19	M	SEMN	RRACBF	NY
JARABSON, MATTS	35	M	LABR	RRACBF	CH
BACKMAN, ERIKS	33	M	LABR	RRACBF	CH

SHIP: ALLER

FROM: BREMEN AND SOUTHAMPTON
TO: NEW YORK
ARRIVED: 19 MARCH 1888

PASSENGER	AGE	SEX	OCCUPATION	PRIV VIL DES
SCHAPIRO, HIRSCH	24	M	GDNR	RRZZZZUSA
BINACHEWSKY, VALENT	35	M	FARMER	RRZZZZUSA
ROBICZ, WERNER	34	M	FARMER	RRZZZZUSA
MAGEROWITZ, ANTON	36	M	FARMER	RRZZZZUSA
GABRISCHEFSKY, JOS	32	M	FARMER	RRZZZZUSA
FARWONFSKY, MARIAN	30	M	FARMER	RRZZZZUSA

SHIP: ETHIOPIA

FROM: GLASGOW AND MOVILLE
TO: NEW YORK
ARRIVED: 20 MARCH 1888

PASSENGER	AGE	SEX	OCCUPATION	PRIV VIL DES
KAMARUS, JAKOB	46	M	LKSH	RRZZZZUSA
KIHNIK, MORDSCHE	40	M	DLR	RRZZZZUSA
SCHAKOWSKY, MEUR	36	M	SMH	RRZZZZUSA
SHAKOWITZ, VINZENTZ	25	M	LABR	RRZZZZUSA
FRANTISCHEK	33	M	LABR	RRZZZZUSA
JOSCHULOWITZ, STANISLAW	70	M	LABR	RRZZZZUSA
ZELMEKY, FRANZ	36	M	LABR	RRZZZZUSA
SANDLER, ITZIG	30	M	BCHR	RRZZZZUSA
SUKOTOSKI, E.	38	F	UNKNOWN	RRZZZZUSA
RAMUS	10	M	CH	RRZZZZUSA
HERSCH	8	M	CHILD	RRZZZZUSA
NIC-LAMA	4	F	CHILD	RRZZZZUSA
SCHMIL	1	M	CHILD	RRZZZZUSA
CAKOWSKY, HOTTLIEB	28	M	MSN	RRZZZZUSA
KARALUS, KAZYS	18	M	LABR	RRZZZZUSA
MAT---TZ, BARTOLOMUS	34	M	LABR	RRZZZZUSA
ZUPPIN, CHAINE	33	F	UNKNOWN	RRZZZZUSA
MERI	14	F	UNKNOWN	RRZZZZUSA
MASCHA	9	F	CHILD	RRZZZZUSA
NICHAME-	7	F	CHILD	RRZZZZUSA
ABRAHAM	1	M	CHILD	RRZZZZUSA
SAWITZKI, JEAN	75	M	LABR	RRZZZZUSA
SCHMIDT, KATE	70	F	W	RRZZZZUSA
HUMBERG, HENE	78	F	W	RRZZZZUSA
FEIGO	8	F	CHILD	RRZZZZUSA
SLAMM, DOBO	60	F	UNKNOWN	RRZZZZUSA
DRASNUS, CHANE	42	F	UNKNOWN	RRZZZZUSA
IWGE	78	F	UNKNOWN	RRZZZZUSA
HIRSCH	11	M	UNKNOWN	RRZZZZUSA
SALMON	9	M	CHILD	RRZZZZUSA
CHANZIG	7	M	CHILD	RRZZZZUSA
JANNKEL	3	M	CHILD	RRZZZZUSA
LEIB	1	M	CHILD	RRZZZZUSA
SGOLDBERG, SCHLOME	39	M	DLR	RRZZZZUSA
BANMAN, SCHLOME	11	U	DLR	RRZZZZUSA
LANDMAN, SCHEME	18	F	UNKNOWN	RRZZZZUSA
BARS, JANKEL	28	M	UNKNOWN	RRZZZZUSA
SCHAWELSOHN, GOTTLIEB	15	M	LABR	RRZZZZUSA
KLEWANSKY, CHANE	26	F	UNKNOWN	RRZZZZUSA
ALFER	8	M	CHILD	RRZZZZUSA
CHAJE	5	F	CHILD	RRZZZZUSA
FEIGE	1	F	CHILD	RRZZZZUSA
ROSENBAUM, MERZ--	70	F	UNKNOWN	RRZZZZUSA
SELIG	6	F	CHILD	RRZZZZUSA
GOTTFRUD, MAX	17	M	LABR	RRZZZZUSA
HOFSCHOWITZ, RUSCHE	18	M	HTR	RRZZZZUSA
HEIPERN, BASCHE	44	M	UNKNOWN	RRZZZZUSA
NOWIEL	11	M	UNKNOWN	RRZZZZUSA
DWEDE	8	M	CHILD	RRZZZZUSA
KOHN, JOSSEL	18	M	TLR	RRZZZZUSA
LIPSCHITSCH, ELIE	22	M	JNR	RRZZZZUSA
JEREL	52	F	UNKNOWN	RRZZZZUSA
LEISER	9	M	CHILD	RRZZZZUSA
JOSSEL	8	M	CHILD	RRZZZZUSA
SARTAWSKI, SCHAJE	42	M	BCHR	RRZZZZUSA
ELKE	18	M	UNKNOWN	RRZZZZUSA
SCHERKOWSKI, DAVID	42	M	UNKNOWN	RRZZZZUSA
SCHUDMAN, WOLF	43	M	MACH	RRZZZZUSA
GLUMAN, LEIB	26	M	PNTR	RRZZZZUSA
ROSA	20	F	UNKNOWN	RRZZZZUSA
SUNKEN, MICHEL	70	M	LKSH	RRZZZZUSA
MELZEN, ESRAL	22	M	TLR	RRZZZZUSA
LADEZKI, JOSEB	24	M	TLR	RRZZZZUSA
CHRET, ISRAEL	23	M	MSN	RRZZZZUSA
ISAK	19	M	MSN	RRZZZZUSA
CHUT, THERESSA	19	F	W	RRZZZZUSA
OSCHMANEK, FANNE	18	F	TLR	RRZZZZUSA
ROGORKE, JOSEL	49	M	UNKNOWN	RRZZZZUSA
TUZOWITZ, SMUL	35	M	BCHR	RRZZZZUSA
PERL---, ISAK	20	M	PNTR	RRZZZZUSA

SHIP: EIDER

FROM: BREMEN AND SOUTHAMPTON
TO: NEW YORK
ARRIVED: 22 MARCH 1888

PASSENGER	AGE	SEX	OCCUPATION	PRIV VIL DES
ZERWINSCKKI, JAC.	32	M	MNR	RRZZZZUSA
KENDRIORSKI, FRANZ	26	M	MNR	RRZZZZUSA
U, MARIE	15	F	NN	RRZZZZUSA
SCHMIDT, THERESIA	20	F	NN	RRZZZZUSA
SCHNAEBEL, HEINR.	31	M	BLKSMH	RRZZZZUSA
LEIPINGER, JOSF	21	F	NN	RRZZZZUSA
GADOMOKI, FR.	28	M	LABR	RRZZZZUSA
BRUDER, FR.	24	M	LABR	RRZZZZUSA
SACHS, THEOD.	25	M	LABR	RRZZZZUSA
AMALIE	25	F	W	RRZZZZUSA
BIEBELT, LEOPOLD	22	M	LABR	RRZZZZUSA
SCHMIDT, WILH.	29	M	LABR	RRZZZZUSA
AULL, GEORG	39	M	LABR	RRZZZZUSA
OPITZ, FRANZ	24	M	LABR	RRZZZZUSA
MENSING, JOHANN	16	M	LABR	RRZZZZUSA
VONIDAMOSCZ, VOLERG	30	M	LABR	RRZZZZUSA
SIRCINSKI, JOSEF	28	M	LABR	RRZZZZUSA
BRANSKI, ALEX	22	M	LABR	RRZZZZUSA
SAWOKI, ALEX	36	M	LABR	RRZZZZUSA
STASIEWSKI, LUDW.	35	M	LABR	RRZZZZUSA
BOLEWSKI, JAN	22	M	LABR	RRZZZZUSA
TRAZANOWSKI, IGN.	30	M	LABR	RRZZZZUSA
TABLOWSKI, CONSTANZ	27	M	LABR	RRZZZZUSA
JOSEF	22	M	LABR	RRZZZZUSA
CICHOCKI, ARNOLD	28	M	LABR	RRZZZZUSA
KONOPNICKI, ROCH.	18	M	LABR	RRZZZZUSA
ULCOWSKI, MARGAN.	38	M	LABR	RRZZZZUSA
NICUTHONIZ, VINCENTE	30	M	LABR	RRZZZZUSA
RONOPOCKI, SOFIA	19	F	NN	RRZZZZUSA
KANTORSKA, FLORENTINA	23	F	NN	RRZZZZUSA
LUCKOSKI, AUGUST	22	M	LABR	RRZZZZUSA
MOELAN, JACOB	24	M	LABR	RRZZZZUSA
WARDIN, JAN	37	M	LABR	RRZZZZUSA
ROTTER, ADOLF	24	M	LABR	RRZZZZUSA
CZENOINSKY, JAN	20	M	LABR	RRZZZZUSA
WIBOSKY, SATM.	32	M	LABR	RRZZZZUSA
SCOWIONSKY, ROZMIR	28	M	LABR	RRZZZZUSA
VITZIKOWSKY, RAZMIR	26	M	UNKNOWN	RRZZZZUSA
REISITZKY, STANISL.	24	M	UNKNOWN	RRZZZZUSA
KOSTEZKY, LEON	29	M	UNKNOWN	RRZZZZUSA
PITLEWSKY, JAN	29	M	UNKNOWN	RRZZZZUSA
CHILINSKY, STEFANIA	23	F	NN	RRZZZZUSA
STANISLAUS	20	M	LABR	RRZZZZUSA

PASSENGER	AGE	SEX	OCCUPATION	PRIVL	DES
DOMBROWSKI, WAZLAN	40	M	LABR	RRZZZZ	USA
TOMAS, KAROAL	40	F	LABR	RRZZZZ	USA
HAWASZINSKA, BRUNISLAW	.11	M	INFANT	RRZZZZ	USA
WEINBERG, S.MENDEL	25	M	MNR	RRZZZZ	USA
NECHE	23	F	W	RRZZZZ	USA
ORLOWSKY, JOHN	28	M	FARMER	RRZZZZ	USA
SOERENSEN, MICH.	21	M	FARMER	RRZZZZ	USA
MAJOROS, HANS	32	M	LABR	RRZZZZ	USA
SCHNEIDER, CERENCY	17	M	NN	RRZZZZ	USA
PETER, JOHANNE	25	F	LABR	RRZZZZ	USA
FORSSELLE, JOSEF	32	M	LABR	RRZZZZ	USA
PINKOWSKI, JACOB	25	M	LABR	RRZZZZ	USA
JOSEFA	22	F	W	RRZZZZ	USA
ANDREAS	11	M	CH	RRZZZZ	USA

SHIP: SPAIN

FROM: LIVERPOOL
TO: NEW YORK
ARRIVED: 22 MARCH 1888

PASSENGER	AGE	SEX	OCCUPATION	PRIVL	DES
-ELDMAN, HERSCH	30	M	LABR	RRAFWJ	USA
SAROKA, ANTON	20	M	LABR	RRAFWJ	USA
INDECK, HERSCH	30	M	LABR	RRAFWJ	USA
LABENSKY, H-AH	22	M	LABR	RRAFWJ	USA
RIMISA, IVAN	25	M	LABR	RRAFWJ	USA
SHAWINSKY, S	40	M	LABR	RRAFWJ	USA
WINBERG, A	41	M	LABR	RRAFWJ	USA
SISSELMAN, SCHAIE	35	M	LABR	RRAFWJ	USA
ESKING, MEYER	34	M	LABR	RRAFWJ	USA
RUPLEWITZ, IVAN	25	M	LABR	RRAFWJ	USA
-ARTHERT, MOBL	20	M	LABR	RRAFWJ	USA
SILVERWAN, CHAIN	20	M	LABR	RRAFWJ	USA
SCHAMEWSKI, ANTON	26	M	LABR	RRAFWJ	USA
SADGAGETZ, SCHAZE	37	M	LABR	RRAFWJ	USA
WONGROWSKY, M	21	M	LABR	RRAFWJ	USA
LIFSDITZ, ABR	22	M	LABR	RRAFWJ	USA
--RIN, KASPAR	19	M	LABR	RRAFWJ	USA
SADLEWSKI, PAUL	19	M	LABR	RRAFWJ	USA
DOORAKOWSKI, JOHAN	25	M	LABR	RRAFWJ	USA
SAKOWITZ, ANTON	29	M	LABR	RRAFWJ	USA
GRESKEVITZ, WOGE	25	M	LABR	RRAFWJ	USA
MAKULMSKY, MARIAN	25	M	LABR	RRAFWJ	USA
LAMSKY, SIMON	24	M	LABR	RRAFWJ	USA
ULEWITZ, OSYS	29	M	LABR	RRAFWJ	USA
ZABORSKY, WINC	30	M	LABR	RRAFWJ	USA
WALOUSO, WIKA	40	M	LABR	RRAFWJ	USA
RUPLEWITZ, ZOJNAZ	40	M	LABR	RRAFWJ	USA
MALE-ZKY, N	45	M	LABR	RRAFWJ	USA
PENZINSKY, J	41	M	LABR	RRAFWJ	USA
RUTZOWSKI, S	26	M	LABR	RRAFWJ	USA
MALACHOWSKY, THOM	21	M	LABR	RRAFWJ	USA
KASPARIAN, AGOL	38	M	LABR	RRAFWJ	USA
SAWICHE, ANTON	18	M	LABR	RRAFWJ	USA
MA-BALSKY, M	46	M	LABR	RRAFWJ	USA
KASCHKEL, S	30	M	LABR	RRAILG	USA
MAZULIS, L	31	M	LABR	RRAILG	USA
BORKONSKY, WLAD	26	M	LABR	RRAILG	USA
KULANCZIK, Z	45	M	LABR	RRAILG	USA
BOZALSKI, ABE	41	M	LABR	RRAILG	USA
HAIDLIS, -URES	23	M	LABR	RRAILG	USA
ENDE, SAM	28	M	LABR	RRAILG	USA
KANTEROVIN, JOS	27	M	LABR	RRAILG	USA
AVADZUZ, W	32	M	LABR	RRAILG	USA
SCHUNDE---E, A	18	M	LABR	RRAILG	USA
OBRENSKY, J	24	M	LABR	RRAILG	USA
ZORJACHOROSKY, CONST	27	M	LABR	RRAILG	USA
ROSCHEN, LEIL	35	M	LABR	RRAILG	USA
ROSSMAN, LIZZIE	28	M	LABR	RRAILG	USA
GIBACH, W	27	M	LABR	RRAILG	USA
KORSCHEWSKY, A	25	M	LABR	RRAILG	USA
FRIEDMAN, CHAIN	26	M	LABR	RRAILG	USA
SPIRO, BEN	25	M	LABR	RRAILG	USA
RUBIN, J	20	M	LABR	RRAILG	USA
ANDERSON, W	37	F	W	RRAILG	USA
HAREN	39	M	LABR	RRAILG	USA
NARDIN, ERIK	73	M	LABR	RRAILG	USA
KAREN	60	F	W	RRAILG	USA
KAHN, H	30	F	W	RRAILG	USA
ABR	6	M	CHILD	RRAILG	USA
JOS	3	M	CHILD	RRAILG	USA
SISSEL	.09	M	INFANT	RRAILG	USA
HELMANN, S	36	M	LABR	RRAILG	USA
F	32	F	W	RRAILG	USA
-ACKEL, NA--O	18	F	SVNT	RRACTC	USA
WINZZEL, J	18	F	SVNT	RRACTC	USA
HOFFMAN, PERCHE	21	F	SVNT	RRACTC	USA
FRIEDRICH, RACHEL	24	F	SVNT	RRACTC	USA
POLLACK, ESSE	30	F	W	RRACTC	USA
SARE	7	F	CHILD	RRACTC	USA
CHAIN	2	M	CHILD	RRACTC	USA
FREIDE	.09	M	INFANT	RRACTC	USA
FRIEDLAND, C	27	F	W	RRACTC	USA
A	4	M	CHILD	RRACTC	USA
BLUMBERG, ANNA	22	F	SVNT	RRACTC	USA
KANICK, A	20	F	SVNT	RRACTC	USA
KON-Z, N	27	M	LABR	RRACTC	USA
LEISSE	22	F	W	RRACTC	USA
BAUMGARTEN, ED	20	F	SVNT	RRACTC	USA
KIRCHBAME, CHA-ESE	30	F	W	RRACTC	USA
CHAME	7	M	CHILD	RRACTC	USA
J	4	M	CHILD	RRACTC	USA
KAHN, BASCHE	37	F	W	RRACTC	USA
CHAIN	10	M	CH	RRACTC	USA
N	6	F	CHILD	RRACTC	USA
H	.07	M	INFANT	RRACTC	USA

SHIP: ARABIC

FROM: LIVERPOOL
TO: NEW YORK
ARRIVED: 22 MARCH 1888

PASSENGER	AGE	SEX	OCCUPATION	PRIVL	DES
DRUCKER, PERT.	25	M	LABR	RRZZZZ	USA
GALONSKY, FEIGI	40	M	LABR	RRZZZZ	USA
JANKEL	11	M	CH	RRZZZZ	USA
ISAK	4	M	CHILD	RRZZZZ	USA
MENDELSOHN, SCHINDEL	42	M	LABR	RRZZZZ	USA
CARL	17	M	LABR	RRZZZZ	USA
KOPPEL	11	M	CH	RRZZZZ	USA
CHOJE	8	M	CHILD	RRZZZZ	USA
ISRAEL	7	M	CHILD	RRZZZZ	USA
ROSENBLUM, JENKEL	46	M	LABR	RRZZZZ	USA
SPITZEN, CHASKEL	30	M	LABR	RRZZZZ	USA
ANNA	22	F	W	RRZZZZ	USA
CHAIMOWITZ, MAX	17	M	LABR	RRZZZZ	USA
HEYMANN, WOLF	18	M	LABR	RRZZZZ	USA
SCHNEIDER, BETTY	32	F	W	RRZZZZ	USA
ISIDOR	3	M	CHILD	RRZZZZ	USA
ROSA	00	F	INF	RRZZZZ	USA
F.	00	F	INF	RRZZZZ	USA
DEWOS, RECKEL	15	F	SP	RRZZZZ	USA
KEULLIS, BERL	32	M	LABR	RRZZZZ	USA
DOBNUGH, CONSTANTINE	25	M	LABR	RRZZZZ	USA
U, SELIG	22	M	LABR	RRZZZZ	USA
HAFTER, H.	26	F	W	RRZZZZ	USA
SAMUEL	00	M	INF	RRZZZZ	USA
HOLLANDER, MOSES	30	M	LABR	RRZZZZ	USA
SPITZER, MOSES	19	M	LABR	RRZZZZ	USA
SPIELBERGER, SAMUEL	47	M	LABR	RRZZZZ	USA

PASSENGER	AGE	SEX	OCCUPATION	PRIVL	DES
ETTEL	15	M	LABR	RRZZZZ	USA
KARPINOWITZ, HIRSCH	26	M	LABR	RRZZZZ	USA
SCHEFER, METE	18	M	LABR	RRZZZZ	USA
FURSTENBONEN, BENJORI	25	M	LABR	RRZZZZ	USA
MOZER	24	M	LABR	RRZZZZ	USA
HALTZEL, SOLOMON	20	M	LABR	RRZZZZ	USA
DEAMONT, SEIEWELL	44	M	LABR	RRZZZZ	USA
KRAUSE, ALONS	27	M	LABR	RRZZZZ	USA
BAUMANN, GITTEL	17	M	LABR	RRZZZZ	USA
SCHWARZ, TAUBE	20	M	LABR	RRZZZZ	USA
REWKE	16	M	LABR	RRZZZZ	USA
POLAZEK, LEA	17	M	LABR	RRZZZZ	USA

SHIP: WYOMING

FROM: LIVERPOOL AND QUEENSTOWN
TO: NEW YORK
ARRIVED: 22 MARCH 1888

PASSENGER	AGE	SEX	OCCUPATION	PRIVL	DES
ZILIKOWI-, CHA--	40	F	W	PLZZZZ	USA
CHAIK	8	M	CHILD	PLZZZZ	USA
KATZ, RACHEL	20	F	SP	PLZZZZ	USA
ROCKEL	21	F	SP	PLZZZZ	USA
KIRCHANSKI, A.	20	M	LABR	PLZZZZ	USA
SCHWARTZ, ROSI	21	F	SP	PLZZZZ	USA
GUSTI	16	M	FARMER	PLZZZZ	USA
RODIRSKIE, SIMON	30	M	FARMER	PLZZZZ	USA
POCHARSKI, ADAM	8	M	CHILD	PLZZZZ	USA
EVA	5	F	CHILD	PLZZZZ	USA
LANUTZIKY, R.	37	M	LABR	PLZZZZ	USA
SCHIFKO, AUGT.	21	M	LABR	PLZZZZ	USA
CARL	36	M	LABR	PLZZZZ	USA
SCHANLINSKY, J.	29	M	LABR	PLZZZZ	USA
KIMM, R.	25	M	LABR	PLZZZZ	USA
SARA	8	F	CHILD	PLZZZZ	USA
ABRAM	5	M	CHILD	PLZZZZ	USA
LIEBEMAN, H.	28	M	MSN	PLZZZZ	USA
BEIGELFELD, ALTEI	28	M	MSN	PLZZZZ	USA
SIDERSKI, LEIB	8	F	CHILD	PLZZZZ	USA
SIEBNIK, ESTIR	24	F	W	RRZZZZ	USA
CHANE	00	M	INF	RRZZZZ	USA
RISACH	00	F	INF	RRZZZZ	USA
MARGOLIES, GITEL	8	F	CHILD	RRZZZZ	USA
FINKELMAN, J.	14	M	LABR	RRZZZZ	USA
CHANE	8	M	CHILD	RRZZZZ	USA
THOELIN, ESTIR	27	F	W	RRZZZZ	USA
ISAAC	20	M	LABR	RRZZZZ	USA
KEILS	8	F	CHILD	RRZZZZ	USA
JOSSEL	7	M	CHILD	RRZZZZ	USA
FRIEDS	3	M	CHILD	RRZZZZ	USA
WILENEZCK, JOSSEL	26	M	LABR	RRZZZZ	USA
ARAMOWITZ, BEILE	28	F	W	RRZZZZ	USA
MALKO	7	F	CHILD	RRZZZZ	USA
MOSES	00	M	INF	RRZZZZ	USA
GRIMBERG, MALKO	46	M	LABR	PLZZZZ	USA
S.	29	M	LABR	PLZZZZ	USA
GROSSMAN, HINDR.	21	M	LABR	PLZZZZ	USA
ORING, L.	25	M	LABR	PLZZZZ	USA
SIEGLIN, MOSES	40	M	LABR	PLZZZZ	USA
VERLINSCO, J.	23	M	LABR	PLZZZZ	USA

SHIP: SAALE

FROM: BREMEN AND SOUTHAMPTON
TO: NEW YORK
ARRIVED: 24 MARCH 1888

PASSENGER	AGE	SEX	OCCUPATION	PRIVL	DES
NAWICKI, JACOB	27	M	LABR	RRZZZZ	USA
LICHOWITZ, CLAIM	23	M	LABR	RRZZZZ	USA
HASENBEIN, ANT.	25	M	LABR	RRZZZZ	USA
ELISE	21	F	W	RRZZZZ	USA
ALBRECHT, JACOB	43	M	FARMER	RRZZZZ	USA
FISSENEWERT, LUDW.	46	M	FARMER	RRZZZZ	USA
REITZ, ANNA	22	F	UNKNOWN	RRZZZZ	USA
HOFMANN, PHIL.	28	M	TLR	RRZZZZ	USA
FRUCHT, GERTRUD	21	F	UNKNOWN	RRZZZZ	USA
BOLD, MICH.	31	M	SMH	RRZZZZ	USA
MICHEL, JOH.	21	M	SMH	RRZZZZ	USA
HEUSSMANN, JOH.	35	M	FARMER	RRZZZZ	USA
DOROTHEA	33	F	W	RRZZZZ	USA
WILH.	9	M	CHILD	RRZZZZ	USA
DORA	4	F	CHILD	RRZZZZ	USA
JOH.	3	M	CHILD	RRZZZZ	USA
SOPHIE	2	F	CHILD	RRZZZZ	USA
MARIE	.06	F	INFANT	RRZZZZ	USA
FRITZ	35	M	FARMER	RRZZZZ	USA
HOCKMANN, JOH.	27	M	BKR	RRZZZZ	USA
MEYER, HEINR.	18	M	LABR	RRZZZZ	USA
AHRENS, FRIEDA	10	F	CH	RRZZZZ	USA
BODER, BARBA.	18	F	UNKNOWN	RRZZZZ	USA
MATHES, MARIE	18	F	UNKNOWN	RRZZZZ	USA
WERFELMANN, ADELE	18	F	UNKNOWN	RRZZZZ	USA
BOENTJE, AUG.	25	M	SMH	RRZZZZ	USA
KRETZMER, FINGER	49	M	SMH	RRZZZZ	USA
EGGERT, KONZTANTIN	22	M	JNR	RRZZZZ	USA
WATNKE, HIRN.	17	M	JNR	RRZZZZ	USA
ULIILAKER, BARBA.	26	F	UNKNOWN	RRZZZZ	USA
HUETTNER, JUL.	38	M	CPTR	RRZZZZ	USA
SCHOBERT, JOH.	24	M	SHMK	RRZZZZ	USA
SCHALLER, MARGA.	25	F	UNKNOWN	RRZZZZ	USA
MUELLER, HEINR.	24	M	SHMK	RRZZZZ	USA
FIECZAK, WAWRACZ	45	M	LABR	RRZZZZ	USA
STAFFLER, KARL	30	M	TLR	RRZZZZ	USA
PAWLACZYK, MART.	41	M	TLR	RRZZZZ	USA
KROL, ANDRAS	27	M	TLR	RRZZZZ	USA
PERKOWSKI, ADALB.	24	M	JNR	RRZZZZ	USA
BRACISZEWSKI, ANDR.	27	M	JNR	RRZZZZ	USA
ZEUGNER, AUG.	22	M	JNR	RRZZZZ	USA
SIMON, JUL.	18	M	TLR	RRZZZZ	USA
WILL, ADAM	18	M	TLR	RRZZZZ	USA
CASPER, GERH.	26	M	SHMK	RRZZZZ	USA
HELMS, GERH.	29	M	SHMK	RRZZZZ	USA
OELTJENBRUNS, JOH.	28	M	SHMK	RRZZZZ	USA
JANSSEN, ELMT.	27	M	SMH	RRZZZZ	USA
REUTER, HEINR.	24	M	TCHR	RRZZZZ	USA
WOLFF, SIGMD.	24	M	FARMER	RRZZZZ	USA
AMALIE	22	F	W	RRZZZZ	USA
SIEGMANN, HEINR.	46	M	FARMER	RRZZZZ	USA
MARIE	44	F	W	RRZZZZ	USA
SOPHIE	11	F	UNKNOWN	RRZZZZ	USA
WILH.	9	M	CHILD	RRZZZZ	USA
KRATZ, HEINR.	23	M	MLR	RRZZZZ	USA
JAEGER, CARL	23	M	TLR	RRZZZZ	USA
HERDEN, ANNA	24	F	UNKNOWN	RRZZZZ	USA
GELLRICH, PAULE.	23	F	UNKNOWN	RRZZZZ	USA
RICHTER, AD.	15	M	SHMK	RRZZZZ	USA
DINTER, MARTHA	18	F	UNKNOWN	RRZZZZ	USA
NEUMANN, ERNST	29	M	CPTR	RRZZZZ	USA
SIEMER, DIEDR.	27	M	BCHR	RRZZZZ	USA
DOELL, JOHS.	32	M	JNR	RRZZZZ	USA
SCHMIDT, MATHA.	22	F	UNKNOWN	RRZZZZ	USA
MOOS, CAROLE.	18	F	UNKNOWN	RRZZZZ	USA
ERNSTING, HEINR.	22	M	SMH	RRZZZZ	USA
MUELLER, PHIL.	27	M	SMH	RRZZZZ	USA
BAR, MEYER	28	M	MLR	RRZZZZ	USA

PASSENGER	AGE	SEX	OCCUPATION	PRIV	VIL	DES
CROPECTA, MENDEL	29	M	BKLYR	RR	ZZZ	ZUSA
BORTH, HERM.	23	M	BBR	RR	ZZZ	ZUSA
NIEDERMEYER, GEORG	17	M	LABR	RR	ZZZ	ZUSA
STRAUCH, HEINR.	27	M	JNR	RR	ZZZ	ZUSA
ROSALIE	22	F	W	RR	ZZZ	ZUSA
TUERKE, GUST.	24	M	LABR	RR	ZZZ	ZUSA
HILGART, WILH.	22	M	LABR	RR	ZZZ	ZUSA
VOGE, JOS.	26	M	LABR	RR	ZZZ	ZUSA
LIEBE, JOHE.	22	F	W	RR	ZZZ	ZUSA
JOSEF	.11	M	INFANT	RR	ZZZ	ZUSA
VOGE, BARBA.	27	F	UNKNOWN	RR	ZZZ	ZUSA
SAALFELD, SOPHIE	22	F	W	RR	ZZZ	ZUSA
JOH.	.11	M	INFANT	RR	ZZZ	ZUSA
RITTERHOF, JOHE.	23	F	UNKNOWN	RR	ZZZ	ZUSA
KLOSTERMANN, LOUISE	26	F	UNKNOWN	RR	ZZZ	ZUSA
BOENING, JOHE.	24	F	UNKNOWN	RR	ZZZ	ZUSA
SCHROEDER, ALB.	28	M	TLR	RR	ZZZ	ZUSA
METTA	19	F	UNKNOWN	RR	ZZZ	ZUSA
BRAND, CHRIST.	17	M	SMH	RR	ZZZ	ZUSA
GEHRKEN, META	22	F	UNKNOWN	RR	ZZZ	ZUSA
HAMMELMANN, PHIL.	30	M	SLR	RR	ZZZ	ZUSA
KLINKEL, ELISAB.	20	F	UNKNOWN	RR	ZZZ	ZUSA
MARIE	18	F	UNKNOWN	RR	ZZZ	ZUSA
VORBACH, GEORG	18	M	TLR	RR	ZZZ	ZUSA
WILTS, WILH.	18	M	TLR	RR	ZZZ	ZUSA
FICHTENMEYER, CHRISTE.	18	F	UNKNOWN	RR	ZZZ	ZUSA
VALENTIN	11	M	UNKNOWN	RR	ZZZ	ZUSA
STURM, JACOB	20	M	CPTR	RR	ZZZ	ZUSA
BOSSONG, ADOLF	23	M	CPTR	RR	ZZZ	ZUSA
WEIMER, ANNA	20	F	UNKNOWN	RR	ZZZ	ZUSA
BABETTE	18	F	UNKNOWN	RR	ZZZ	ZUSA
KRAFTHOEFER, LOUIS	22	M	CPTR	RR	ZZZ	ZUSA
BECK, HELENA	15	F	UNKNOWN	RR	ZZZ	ZUSA
BOESE, JACOB	16	M	BCHR	RR	ZZZ	ZUSA
STRIEDER, KARL	18	M	BCHR	RR	ZZZ	ZUSA
NOLL, HELENA	22	F	UNKNOWN	RR	ZZZ	ZUSA
KATHA.	20	F	UNKNOWN	RR	ZZZ	ZUSA
KLEIN, HENRIETTE	15	F	UNKNOWN	RR	ZZZ	ZUSA
STEBER, HENRY	20	M	SMH	RR	ZZZ	ZUSA
HELWIG	16	M	UNKNOWN	RR	ZZZ	ZUSA
HERGUTH, JOHN	22	M	TCHR	RR	ZZZ	ZUSA
ULLMANN, ABRAH.	16	M	SHMK	RR	ZZZ	ZUSA
LUTZ, ELISAB.	23	F	UNKNOWN	RR	ZZZ	ZUSA
MARSCHALL, AMALIE	18	F	UNKNOWN	RR	ZZZ	ZUSA
HERMANN, JOH.	21	M	BKR	RR	ZZZ	ZUSA
HALEMEIER, ILSABEIN	23	M	BKR	RR	ZZZ	ZUSA
JOH.	2	M	CHILD	RR	ZZZ	ZUSA
MAX, FRIEDR.	14	M	LABR	RR	ZZZ	ZUSA
BIKKER, HEINR.	24	M	LABR	RR	ZZZ	ZUSA
MEIER, AUG.	14	M	LABR	RR	ZZZ	ZUSA
TOLLE, CHRIST.	48	M	FARMER	RR	ZZZ	ZUSA
MINNA	46	F	W	RR	ZZZ	ZUSA
CHRIST.	24	M	LABR	RR	ZZZ	ZUSA
CHRISTE.	22	F	UNKNOWN	RR	ZZZ	ZUSA
LOUIS	16	M	LABR	RR	ZZZ	ZUSA
MINNA	14	F	UNKNOWN	RR	ZZZ	ZUSA
LINA	11	F	UNKNOWN	RR	ZZZ	ZUSA
DUERGELOH, FRITZ	31	M	CPTR	RR	ZZZ	ZUSA
AUGUSTE.	28	F	W	RR	ZZZ	ZUSA
AUGUSTE.	4	F	CHILD	RR	ZZZ	ZUSA
SOPHIE	2	F	CHILD	RR	ZZZ	ZUSA
HASSE, HERM.	19	M	CPTR	RR	ZZZ	ZUSA
KARL	15	M	TLR	RR	ZZZ	ZUSA
ARNING, JAS.	25	M	TLR	RR	ZZZ	ZUSA
DARLIG, HEINR.	24	M	BCHR	RR	ZZZ	ZUSA
GIESELING, CHRISTE.	18	F	UNKNOWN	RR	ZZZ	ZUSA
BAST, EUGELBERT	41	M	FARMER	RR	ZZZ	ZUSA
ANNA	34	F	W	RR	ZZZ	ZUSA
ANT.	9	M	CHILD	RR	ZZZ	ZUSA
PETER	7	M	CHILD	RR	ZZZ	ZUSA
JOH.	6	M	CHILD	RR	ZZZ	ZUSA
ELISAB.	4	F	CHILD	RR	ZZZ	ZUSA
GERTRUD	2	F	CHILD	RR	ZZZ	ZUSA
JOSEF	.03	M	INFANT	RR	ZZZ	ZUSA
SCHUSTER, NIKOL.	43	M	FARMER	RR	ZZZ	ZUSA

PASSENGER	AGE	SEX	OCCUPATION	PRIV	VIL	DES
LOBENMEIER, JOS.	24	M	BKR	RR	ZZZ	ZUSA
KUCHLER, FRANZ	17	M	TLR	RR	ZZZ	ZUSA
SCHWARZFISCHER, LOUIS	16	M	TLR	RR	ZZZ	ZUSA
JOH.	18	M	TLR	RR	ZZZ	ZUSA
REIL, GEORG	18	M	SMH	RR	ZZZ	ZUSA
REITINGER, MICH.	23	M	SMH	RR	ZZZ	ZUSA
SCHMIDBAUSER, KATHI.	17	F	UNKNOWN	RR	ZZZ	ZUSA
MEINDL, FRANZCA.	22	F	UNKNOWN	RR	ZZZ	ZUSA
HAFENSTEINER, ANNA	22	F	UNKNOWN	RR	ZZZ	ZUSA
NOEGERL, GEORG	16	M	CPTR	RR	ZZZ	ZUSA
FUSCHS, ELISE	25	F	UNKNOWN	RR	ZZZ	ZUSA
FRIEDR.	18	M	CPTR	RR	ZZZ	ZUSA
ANNA	53	F	UNKNOWN	RR	ZZZ	ZUSA
GROSS, FRANZ	16	M	CPTR	RR	ZZZ	ZUSA
BURGYNSKA, KAROLE.	23	F	UNKNOWN	RR	ZZZ	ZUSA
GENOVEFA	2	F	CHILD	RR	ZZZ	ZUSA
SAWICKI, JACENTY	36	M	LABR	RR	ZZZ	ZUSA
MILLER, FRIEDR.	26	M	LABR	RR	ZZZ	ZUSA
SCHALKOSKA, HENRY	40	M	LABR	RR	ZZZ	ZUSA
JANKE, KARL	40	M	LABR	RR	ZZZ	ZUSA
MILLER, JOH.	30	M	LABR	RR	ZZZ	ZUSA
ZOLURWSKY, FRANTIS	20	M	LABR	RR	ZZZ	ZUSA
KORNACKY, FRANTIS	23	M	LABR	RR	ZZZ	ZUSA
ZWOLKOWSKY, JAN	40	M	LABR	RR	ZZZ	ZUSA
DARMSFALSKY, MATH.	28	M	LABR	RR	ZZZ	ZUSA
LITWIANSKY, JULIAN	24	M	LABR	RR	ZZZ	ZUSA
RADLECKY, IGNATZ	22	M	LABR	RR	ZZZ	ZUSA
ILGAL, JOSEL	20	M	LABR	RR	ZZZ	ZUSA
KORNOCKY, THEOPIL	19	M	LABR	RR	ZZZ	ZUSA
URIAN, RAPHAEL	54	M	LABR	RR	ZZZ	ZUSA
SZAFANOWSKA, JOS.	37	M	LABR	RR	ZZZ	ZUSA
LESWIEWSKY, ADAM	21	M	LABR	RR	ZZZ	ZUSA
MAKOWITZ, KASMIR	21	M	LABR	RR	ZZZ	ZUSA
SCHIRST, LOUIS	30	M	LABR	RR	ZZZ	ZUSA
SCHORE	50	F	W	RR	ZZZ	ZUSA
ESTER	50	M	LABR	RR	ZZZ	ZUSA
RENONIE	15	F	UNKNOWN	RR	ZZZ	ZUSA
CHANE	18	M	LABR	RR	ZZZ	ZUSA
GITEL	.02	M	INFANT	RR	ZZZ	ZUSA
LOSNOWSKY, JAN	17	M	LABR	RR	ZZZ	ZUSA
SCHINA, AUGSTE.	20	F	UNKNOWN	RR	ZZZ	ZUSA
STAWICKY, JAN	40	M	LABR	RR	ZZZ	ZUSA
MARTISCHES, JAN	23	M	LABR	RR	ZZZ	ZUSA
RUSCHEVITZ, JOS.	23	M	LABR	RR	ZZZ	ZUSA
BLOCK, ED.	40	M	LABR	RR	ZZZ	ZUSA
GUTOWSKI, FRIEDR.	43	M	LABR	RR	ZZZ	ZUSA
ZUWAL, CHRIST	30	M	LABR	RR	ZZZ	ZUSA
WALTER, PAUL	18	M	LABR	RR	ZZZ	ZUSA
KURZ, HEINR.	30	M	LABR	RR	ZZZ	ZUSA

SHIP: BOTHNIA

FROM: LIVERPOOL AND QUEENSTOWN
TO: NEW YORK
ARRIVED: 24 MARCH 1888

PASSENGER	AGE	SEX	OCCUPATION	PRIV	VIL	DES
WELINSKY, TISACH	24	F	SP	RR	ZZZ	ZUSA
DAUCHER, JOSEPH	24	M	MNR	RR	ZZZ	ZUSA
MORISNIE	20	F	W	RR	ZZZ	ZUSA
DAUKSCHOR, VINCENTZ	19	F	LABR	RR	ZZZ	ZUSA
KLEMEROV, MOSES	23	F	LABR	RR	ZZZ	ZUSA
KITAI, BENGAL	18	F	LABR	RR	ZZZ	ZUSA
PODMOS, BENGO	25	F	LABR	RR	ZZZ	ZUSA
BELLRCHT, RUDOLPH	26	F	TLR	RR	ZZZ	ZUSA
JORGENSEN, JOHAN	18	M	LABR	RR	ZZZ	ZUSA
NIELSEN, NIEL	21	M	LABR	RR	ZZZ	ZUSA
JENSEN, ANNA	18	F	SP	RR	ZZZ	ZUSA
SORENSEN, ALWINE	23	F	SP	RR	ZZZ	ZUSA
LARSEN, LARS	17	F	LABR	RR	ZZZ	ZUSA
MATT	17	F	LABR	RR	ZZZ	ZUSA

PASSENGER	AGE	SEX	OCCUPATION	PRV VIL DES
F---, ALEXANDER	35	F	SP	RRZZZZUSA

SHIP: STATE OF NEVADA

FROM: GLASGOW AND LARNE
TO: NEW YORK
ARRIVED: 24 MARCH 1888

PASSENGER	AGE	SEX	OCCUPATION	PRV VIL DES
FANTOWSKY, JOSEF	26	M	LABR	RRZZZZUSA
LEURTZKY, ABRAM	24	M	LABR	RRZZZZUSA
STANKOWSKY, JESUS	25	M	LABR	RRZZZZUSA
ZIKUS, FRANCISEK	28	M	LABR	RRZZZZUSA
THEKLA	18	F	W	RRZZZZUSA
ANTONIO	.09	F	INFANT	RRZZZZUSA
ZABOTNA, MARYANNA	50	F	W	RRZZZZUSA
ANNE	10	F	CH	RRZZZZUSA
KANTER, ISSAC	14	M	MCHT	RRZZZZUSA
FREIDEN, ABRAHAM	16	M	MCHT	RRZZZZUSA
FELDMANN, ITZIG	35	M	LABR	RRZZZZUSA
STEINHACKER, WOLF	52	M	FARMER	RRZZZZUSA
GRENHAUS, SHIE	24	M	MCHT	RRZZZZUSA
WASCHLIKOWSKY, SARE	37	M	SHMK	RRZZZZUSA
DUNBER, ITZIG	30	M	CGRMKR	RRZZZZUSA
BASSIN, MUENDEL	18	M	MCHT	RRZZZZUSA
RADKUNSKY, JAVEL	27	M	CPTR	RRZZZZUSA
INKELSTEIN, LOUIS	42	M	MCHT	RRZZZZUSA
CHLEBINSKY, HIRSCH	34	M	SHMK	RRZZZZUSA
BIALYSHOCKI, NORCHE	26	M	MCHT	RRZZZZUSA
BARKIN, SALOMON	23	M	CPTR	RRZZZZUSA
COHN, ISCHOR	16	M	MCHT	RRZZZZUSA
SCHUMLOWITZ, JOSEL	26	M	MCHT	RRZZZZUSA
KANTROWITZ, ISAAC	40	M	MCHT	RRZZZZUSA
WAFWAOS, ROLF	36	M	CGRMKR	RRZZZZUSA
SCHIRELSOHN, ISAAC	18	M	MCHT	RRZZZZUSA
SALAMANSKY, JANKEL	45	M	MCHT	RRZZZZUSA
ABRAHAM	18	M	MCHT	RRZZZZUSA
CHATZKEL	15	M	MCHT	RRZZZZUSA
SERKE	9	M	CHILD	RRZZZZUSA
KRUSBERG, H	23	M	MCHT	RRZZZZUSA
APRIN, ISRAEL	17	M	MCHT	RRZZZZUSA
HUREWITZ, JANKEL	17	M	TLR	RRZZZZUSA
GILLMANN	29	M	MCHT	RRZZZZUSA
ABRASCHIN, LEIB	25	M	TLR	RRZZZZUSA
AVASCHE	18	F	W	RRZZZZUSA
ABRAHAMOWITZ, FEIGE	48	F	W	RRZZZZUSA
ORENSTEIN, ZIREL	36	F	W	RRZZZZUSA
CHODOSCH, FREIDE	40	M	TLR	RRZZZZUSA
THERESE	22	F	SP	RRZZZZUSA
MARAIS	17	M	UNKNOWN	RRZZZZUSA
DAVID	8	M	CHILD	RRZZZZUSA
FERSCHWASCHSOHN, RIWOKE	26	F	W	RRZZZZUSA
FERSWASCHSOHN, ABRAHAM	5	M	CHILD	RRZZZZUSA
FISCHEL	2	M	CHILD	RRZZZZUSA
BAKOSCHTOWSKY, HENE	30	F	W	RRZZZZUSA
ROANE	8	F	CHILD	RRZZZZUSA
MOSCHE	6	M	CHILD	RRZZZZUSA
JERUSALEM	4	M	CHILD	RRZZZZUSA
KNOPER, MOSEL	28	F	W	RRZZZZUSA
SARA	3	F	CHILD	RRZZZZUSA
CHAVE	2	F	CHILD	RRZZZZUSA
IDA	1	F	CHILD	RRZZZZUSA
GRIN, CHAI	35	M	W	RRZZZZUSA
POBBE	18	F	UNKNOWN	RRZZZZUSA
ETHEL	50	F	UNKNOWN	RRZZZZUSA
ITSAK	5	M	CHILD	RRZZZZUSA
MESSAM	1	M	CHILD	RRZZZZUSA
EHRLICH, CHANE	20	F	UNKNOWN	RRZZZZUSA
UTZER, BELA	45	F	UNKNOWN	RRZZZZUSA
ELIE	1	F	CHILD	RRZZZZUSA
BLECHMANN, BRONE	34	F	W	RRZZZZUSA
LEVY	11	M	CH	RRZZZZUSA
BERTH	10	M	CH	RRZZZZUSA
NATHAN	7	M	CHILD	RRZZZZUSA
ISRAEL	5	M	CHILD	RRZZZZUSA
MOSES	1	M	CHILD	RRZZZZUSA
SALAME, BEILE	35	F	W	RRZZZZUSA
REWE	11	M	CH	RRZZZZUSA
KOCHIE	9	M	CHILD	RRZZZZUSA
SARE	7	F	CHILD	RRZZZZUSA
U	3	F	CHILD	RRZZZZUSA
FLANUM, FENWIL	37	M	MCHT	RRZZZZUSA
ROSE	26	F	W	RRZZZZUSA
HEEAK, LEIB	59	M	MCHT	RRZZZZUSA
TAUBE	49	F	W	RRZZZZUSA
FANNY	19	F	SP	RRZZZZUSA
SINAI, SCHEINE	42	F	UNKNOWN	RRZZZZUSA
BEALOBZETH, MORASCHE	11	F	CH	RRZZZZUSA
KOPPEL, REBECA	22	F	SP	RRZZZZUSA
ITSAC, NIKOLAI	32	M	MCHT	PLZZZZUSA
DAVIS, ERIK	17	M	TLR	PLZZZZUSA
SKHAI, BENJAMIN	20	M	TLR	PLZZZZUSA
SCHMALOWSKY, ---ER	00	M	TLR	PLZZZZUSA
HAFBEL, JOSEL	30	M	MCHT	PLZZZZUSA
ELIAS	20	M	MCHT	PLZZZZUSA
PROHOVELIS, MORACHE	16	M	MCHT	PLZZZZUSA
JOSSELMEIG, MARCUS	17	M	MCHT	PLZZZZUSA
JAKOBINKSOHN, MEYER	34	M	CPTR	PLZZZZUSA
POLAK, BENJAMIN	35	M	TLR	PLZZZZUSA
SCHIFFES, SARAH	22	F	W	PLZZZZUSA
JANSSEN, HENRIK	50	M	CPTR	FNZZZZUSA
NYMAN, MATS	40	M	CPTR	FNZZZZUSA
HENRIKSON, CHRISTIAN	33	M	CPTR	FNZZZZUSA
FREDERIKSSEN, MATS	39	M	CPTR	FNZZZZUSA
ASPLUND, KARL	29	M	CPTR	FNZZZZUSA

SHIP: KRONPRINZ FRIDERICK

FROM: BREMEN
TO: BALTIMORE
ARRIVED: 25 MARCH 1888

PASSENGER	AGE	SEX	OCCUPATION	PRV VIL DES
PYKOWSLOOSKY, RUZA	36	F	UNKNOWN	RRZZZZBAL
ANDR	10	M	CH	RRZZZZBAL
JOSEF	7	M	CHILD	RRZZZZBAL
FRANCISCA	4	F	CHILD	RRZZZZBAL
ANNA	.09	F	INFANT	RRZZZZBAL
ORAGLY, ALRICH	32	M	LABR	RRZZZZBAL
ROSENBLUM, BUSE	30	F	UNKNOWN	RRZZZZBAL
SOPHIE	.11	F	INFANT	RRZZZZBAL
VENAR, SARA	45	F	UNKNOWN	RRZZZZBAL
U	45	F	UNKNOWN	RRZZZZBAL
MICHAEL	20	M	LABR	RRZZZZBAL
SCHNEIDER, SIMON	24	M	LABR	RRZZZZBAL
STUTZIN, ESTER	22	F	UNKNOWN	RRZZZZBAL
DIMOND, ABEL	24	M	JNR	RRZZZZBAL
SCHWED, ADOLF	33	M	FARMER	RRZZZZBAL
MARIE	26	F	UNKNOWN	RRZZZZBAL
FRITZ	7	M	CHILD	RRZZZZBAL
LENE	5	F	CHILD	RRZZZZBAL
MARIA	3	F	CHILD	RRZZZZBAL
ANNA	.07	F	INFANT	RRZZZZBAL
PASKY, Z	20	F	UNKNOWN	RRZZZZBAL
KKIMDECIAK, M	24	M	LABR	RRZZZZBAL
SCHMIDT, S	38	M	LABR	RRZZZZBAL
JOSEFA	27	F	UNKNOWN	RRZZZZBAL
CASMIR	7	M	CHILD	RRZZZZBAL
MARIE	.11	F	INFANT	RRZZZZBAL
FUIHSLUBER, EDIDUES	28	M	LABR	RRZZZZBAL
WECKER, JOH	31	M	LABR	RRZZZZBAL
SCHWALIN, WILH	25	M	LABR	RRZZZZBAL

PASSENGER	AGE	SEX	OCCUPATION	PRVIL	DES
RINGELT, CAROLINE	55	F	UNKNOWN	RRZZZZ	BAL
AUGUST	31	M	LABR	RRZZZZ	BAL
WILHELM	10	M	CH	RRZZZZ	BAL
STORBACH, FR	52	M	LABR	RRZZZZ	BAL
CAROL	52	F	UNKNOWN	RRZZZZ	BAL
PAULINE	9	F	CHILD	RRZZZZ	BAL
EMMA	8	F	CHILD	RRZZZZ	BAL
MARIA	7	F	CHILD	RRZZZZ	BAL
AUG	5	M	CHILD	RRZZZZ	BAL
HEIDEN, H	42	M	MLR	RRZZZZ	BAL
WILH	43	F	UNKNOWN	RRZZZZ	BAL
AUG	10	M	CH	RRZZZZ	BAL
VOIGT, WILH	25	M	MCHT	RRZZZZ	BAL
SONNEMANN, EMILIA	20	F	UNKNOWN	RRZZZZ	BAL
ROHDE, JOH	30	M	FARMER	RRZZZZ	BAL
AUG	25	F	UNKNOWN	RRZZZZ	BAL
RIGGE, MARIE	19	F	UNKNOWN	RRZZZZ	BAL
MATH	7	F	CHILD	RRZZZZ	BAL
DEMSEN, JOSEF	28	M	LABR	RRZZZZ	BAL
WILIMOWIETZ, W	26	M	LABR	RRZZZZ	BAL
DOBLINKA, VICTORIA	26	F	UNKNOWN	RRZZZZ	BAL
KAZIMIR	30	M	LABR	RRZZZZ	BAL
LENZ, JULIUS	32	M	LABR	RRZZZZ	BAL
AUGUSTE	30	F	UNKNOWN	RRZZZZ	BAL
WILH	9	M	CHILD	RRZZZZ	BAL
EMILIE	8	F	CHILD	RRZZZZ	BAL
FRZ	.06	M	INFANT	RRZZZZ	BAL
DAKIN, KON	45	M	LABR	RRZZZZ	BAL
BUTTLER, CH	23	M	LABR	RRZZZZ	BAL
HIRKMANN, JOSEF	20	M	LABR	RRZZZZ	BAL
KOROSZASZ, ALEX	25	M	LABR	RRZZZZ	BAL
HADOWSKA, HANNA	25	F	UNKNOWN	RRZZZZ	BAL
JOFFE, HARY	16	M	LABR	RRZZZZ	BAL
BARSKI, ROSEL	18	F	UNKNOWN	RRZZZZ	BAL
ASCHAKEN, ANTON	27	M	LABR	RRZZZZ	BAL
BARAMOSKY, AUG	33	M	LABR	RRZZZZ	BAL
SOKOLOWSKY, JOSEF	33	M	LABR	RRZZZZ	BAL
GRUTOWSKY, JAN	25	M	LABR	RRZZZZ	BAL
HILMAN, STANISL	23	M	LABR	RRZZZZ	BAL
BARSKY, C	28	M	LABR	RRZZZZ	PA
RAZOWSKI, HERM	23	M	LABR	RRZZZZ	BAL
ZUSMANOWITZ, C	24	F	UNKNOWN	RRZZZZ	BAL
FRANALEWITZ, JULIUS	28	M	LABR	RRZZZZ	OH
JERSCHKE, FRZ	24	M	LABR	RRZZZZ	WI
DEGNER, WILH	61	M	LABR	RRZZZZ	WI
WILH	18	M	LABR	RRZZZZ	WI
RAROLL, ANNA	18	F	UNKNOWN	RRZZZZ	BAL
SCH	10	F	CH	RRZZZZ	BAL
WOISHACK, JOSEF	25	M	LABR	RRZZZZ	BAL
SCHABASAWITZ, ALIA	16	F	UNKNOWN	RRZZZZ	BAL
SUGALSKI, JOSEF	28	M	LABR	RRZZZZ	BAL
JAN	22	M	LABR	RRZZZZ	BAL
LAUSEROWITZ, NEAH	18	M	LABR	RRZZZZ	BAL
LAUSEROWICZ, JOH	20	M	LABR	RRZZZZ	PA
PEKARTZ, JAN	22	M	LABR	RRZZZZ	PA
KANNISCHI, A	26	M	LABR	RRZZZZ	BAL
WISNISENSKI, W	25	M	LABR	RRZZZZ	BAL
SZILLENSKI, ADAM	24	M	LABR	RRZZZZ	BAL
HARAPOWSKI, FRZ	20	M	LABR	RRZZZZ	MI
JACKIEWIZ, ANDR	22	M	LABR	RRZZZZ	MI
HOWACKI, FRZ	34	M	LABR	RRZZZZ	BAL
HOWALEWSKI, JAN	25	M	LABR	RRZZZZ	BAL
PAWLONSKY, JOSEF	34	M	LABR	RRZZZZ	BAL
ROSAL	30	F	UNKNOWN	RRZZZZ	BAL

SHIP: OHIO

FROM: LIVERPOOL
TO: NEW YORK
ARRIVED: 26 MARCH 1888

PASSENGER	AGE	SEX	OCCUPATION	PRVIL	DES
ASSOTHEKER, MUMIE	19	F	SP	PLZZZZ	NY
ZUKOWSKI, MORCY	27	F	W	PLZZZZ	NY
BORROWIER, ADVIE	21	F	SP	PLZZZZ	NY
GURMINSKA, A	30	M	LABR	PLZZZZ	NY
GLUSARYKO, J	25	M	LABR	PLZZZZ	NY
JOSWIAK, V	19	M	LABR	PLZZZZ	NY
JANIK, S	47	M	LABR	PLZZZZ	NY
CATHARINA	42	F	W	PLZZZZ	NY
M	21	F	SP	PLZZZZ	NY
S	11	M	CH	PLZZZZ	NY
H	4	M	CHILD	PLZZZZ	NY
U	.11	M	INFANT	PLZZZZ	NY
M	.01	M	INFANT	PLZZZZ	NY
KASPIKA, F	34	M	LABR	PLZZZZ	NY
JOSEFA	33	F	W	PLZZZZ	NY
M	4	M	CHILD	PLZZZZ	NY
T	3	M	CHILD	PLZZZZ	NY
M	.04	M	INFANT	PLZZZZ	NY
M	9	M	CHILD	PLZZZZ	NY
KAMINSKY, W	28	M	LABR	PLZZZZ	NY
KACHNOSKI, T	36	M	FARMER	PLZZZZ	NY
MOCH, V	26	M	LABR	PLZZZZ	NY
JOSEFA	19	F	W	PLZZZZ	NY
P	26	M	LABR	PLZZZZ	NY
NOWAK, K	24	M	LABR	PLZZZZ	NY
PERSSON, J	44	M	LABR	PLZZZZ	NY
ELNA	27	F	W	PLZZZZ	NY
A	2	M	CHILD	PLZZZZ	NY
PRZESSIORRA, ELIGA	23	F	W	PLZZZZ	NY
JOSEFA	4	F	CHILD	PLZZZZ	NY
J	2	M	CHILD	PLZZZZ	NY
S	.06	M	INFANT	PLZZZZ	NY
PRZSIORA, JAR	29	M	LABR	PLZZZZ	NY
RUCIENSKI, M	42	M	LABR	PLZZZZ	NY
SOKOLA, LEBE	30	F	W	PLZZZZ	USA
R	6	F	CHILD	PLZZZZ	USA
A	3	M	CHILD	PLZZZZ	USA
STARGINSKY, A	42	M	LABR	PLZZZZ	PA
JOSEFA	11	F	CH	PLZZZZ	PA
THOMASCHEWSKY, S	22	M	LABR	PLZZZZ	NY
FISKOWSKI, H	29	M	LABR	PLZZZZ	NY

SHIP: WIELAND

FROM: HAMBURG
TO: NEW YORK
ARRIVED: 26 MARCH 1888

PASSENGER	AGE	SEX	OCCUPATION	PRVIL	DES
COSTKOW, JACOB	26	F	LABR	RRZZZZ	USA
PROSTEK, ANDJE	18	M	LABR	RRZZZZ	USA
RAKOWSKI, MARCIN	37	M	LABR	RRZZZZ	USA
SCHITZKOWSKY, JAN	22	M	LABR	RRZZZZ	USA
MORR, JACOB	26	M	LABR	RRZZZZ	USA
SWENSKI, VINCENTY	39	M	LABR	RRZZZZ	USA
TRUCHAN, JAN	22	M	LABR	RRZZZZ	USA
BOROTKI, JOSEF	46	M	LABR	RRZZZZ	USA
ANDERSON, JOH	25	F	SGL	FNZZZZ	USA
HEMMING, JOH	43	M	LABR	FNZZZZ	USA
KOSKI, OSCAR	29	M	LABR	FNZZZZ	USA
FRIMANN, KARL	21	M	UNKNOWN	FNZZZZ	USA
FORSLUND, ALEXANDER	28	M	UNKNOWN	FNZZZZ	USA
SKULVIK, JOH	22	M	UNKNOWN	FNZZZZ	USA
STROEMSHOHN, KARL	17	M	UNKNOWN	FNZZZZ	USA

PASSENGER	AGE	SEX	OCCUPATION	PRV VIL DES
VENTER, VICTOR	20	M	UNKNOWN	FNZZZZUSA
BLONQUEST, JOH	27	M	LABR	FNZZZZUSA
BASTIAN, EDUARD	19	M	LABR	FNZZZZUSA
NYMANN, JACOB	19	M	FARMER	FNZZZZUSA
PERHIDATTER, HILDA	24	F	SGL	FNZZZZUSA
JUNGELL, GIDEON	20	M	MCHT	FNZZZZUSA
WIKMAN, FRCYWILD	29	M	SLR	FNZZZZUSA
KARLSON, HENRIK	22	M	UNKNOWN	FNZZZZUSA
LITHEI, ALEXANDER	35	M	LABR	FNZZZZUSA
NORLUND, EMIL	20	M	SLR	FNZZZZUSA
BACHMANN, ALEXANDER	28	M	SLR	FNZZZZUSA
ALNAR, JOH	18	M	LABR	FNZZZZUSA
JOH	18	M	LABR	FNZZZZUSA
TORNBLUM, MATH	48	M	UNKNOWN	FNZZZZUSA
JOH	48	F	W	FNZZZZUSA
LOFS, JACOB	29	M	SLR	FNZZZZUSA
HANSEN, GUSTAV	43	M	UNKNOWN	FNZZZZUSA
HOFLAGER, JOH	28	M	LABR	FNZZZZUSA
JACOBSOHN, JACOB	29	M	LABR	FNZZZZUSA
TARGONSKA, CHAWE	26	F	W	RRZZZZUSA
SARA	.11	F	INFANT	RRZZZZUSA
LIPSCHITZ, ABRAH	9	M	CHILD	RRZZZZUSA
JERNCHEM	8	F	CHILD	RRZZZZUSA
REISEL	4	M	CHILD	RRZZZZUSA
RAISCHULSKI, CHANNE	36	F	W	RRZZZZUSA
TAUBE	3	F	CHILD	RRZZZZUSA
STUHLMACHER, ESTHER	30	F	WO	RRZZZZUSA
LIRS, CHEIE	9	F	CHILD	RRZZZZUSA
ABR	8	M	CHILD	RRZZZZUSA
MOSES	7	M	CHILD	RRZZZZUSA
WOLF	5	M	CHILD	RRZZZZUSA
URBAN, JANS	31	M	LABR	RRZZZZUSA
ARZBITA	26	F	W	RRZZZZUSA
WLADISLAW	3	M	CHILD	RRZZZZUSA
JAN	.09	M	INFANT	RRZZZZUSA
KAMINSKY, JOSEF	29	M	LABR	RRZZZZUSA
LEJEWSKI, ANTONIE	22	F	SGL	RRZZZZUSA
ZUPER, FELIX	22	M	LABR	RRZZZZUSA
BURCZAK, ALEXANDER	35	M	LABR	RRZZZZUSA
ANNA	9	F	CHILD	RRZZZZUSA
PRZEWINSKI, JOSEF	31	M	LABR	RRZZZZUSA
KILMANN, SIMON	33	M	LABR	RRZZZZUSA
PADAZOMA, ROMAN	20	M	LABR	RRZZZZUSA
PROSKOROWSKI, ELI	28	M	CBTMKR	RRZZZZUSA
LUBARSKI, LEIB	26	M	CBTMKR	RRZZZZUSA
GERSTEIN, ESTHER	25	F	W	RRZZZZUSA
SCHILEM	.11	M	INFANT	RRZZZZUSA
COSININZAK, JAN	28	M	LABR	RRZZZZUSA
TONSCHAK, ANDR	33	M	LABR	RRZZZZUSA
MICHALK, STANISL	29	M	LABR	RRZZZZUSA
CIESLA, JOHANN	25	M	LABR	RRZZZZUSA
WINKMANN, ERNESTINE	21	F	SGL	RRZZZZUSA
VIOTKOSSI, THOMAS	22	M	LABR	RRZZZZUSA
DOBUDA, STANISLAUS	31	M	LABR	RRZZZZUSA
LAZAROWICZ, ANTONIE	24	F	UNKNOWN	RRZZZZUSA
MILLARSKY, FRANZ	40	M	LABR	RRZZZZUSA
MICHALSK, IGNATZ	30	M	LABR	RRZZZZUSA
PUEWSZK, JAN	25	M	LABR	RRZZZZUSA
KRUZINSKY, JOSEF	39	M	LABR	RRZZZZUSA
WITTKOWSKY, STANISL	22	M	LABR	RRZZZZUSA
SEMSEWSKY, JOS	22	M	LABR	RRZZZZUSA
KOJATKOWSKY, JANS	22	M	LABR	RRZZZZUSA
LASKOWSKY, MARTIN	34	M	LABR	RRZZZZUSA
SLYROWSKY, ANTON	22	M	LABR	RRZZZZUSA
LEWANDOWSKY, JOSEF	31	M	LABR	RRZZZZUSA
SLATCHOVIAK, FRANZISCA	21	F	SGL	RRZZZZUSA
CZEMNETZKY, PETER	30	M	LABR	RRZZZZUSA
LEVJIERSKY, STANISL	29	M	LABR	RRZZZZUSA
KAWKA, ANDREAS	25	F	LABR	RRZZZZUSA
RIZEWSKI, ANTON	26	M	LABR	RRZZZZUSA
JECHA, JAN	28	M	LABR	RRZZZZUSA
MURCIIS, NUCIN	30	M	LABR	RRZZZZUSA
KUEHNE, DORA	18	M	SGL	RRZZZZUSA
GORNOLINSKI, JAN	23	M	LABR	RRZZZZUSA
KOTARSKI, FRANZ	44	M	LABR	RRZZZZUSA

PASSENGER	AGE	SEX	OCCUPATION	PRV VIL DES
NAGOWSKI, JAN	21	M	LABR	RRZZZZUSA
JAN	21	M	LABR	RRZZZZUSA
RUTESKI, SEMON	33	M	LABR	RRZZZZUSA
MACZKIEWICZ, ANTON	25	M	LABR	RRZZZZUSA
KORNATZKI, FRANZ	23	M	LABR	RRZZZZUSA
STRUZINA, VALENTI	40	M	LABR	RRZZZZUSA
LANDETZKI, JAN	28	M	LABR	RRZZZZUSA
KOTSCHKA, ANASTASIA	27	F	SGL	RRZZZZUSA
BARTHEL, MAX	23	M	JNR	RRZZZZUSA
GRIESKE, HINDE	29	F	W	RRZZZZUSA
MENNCHE	9	F	CHILD	RRZZZZUSA
JANOSCHEFSKY, MICHAEL	40	M	LABR	RRZZZZUNK
SULKOWSKY, THEOD	50	M	LABR	RRZZZZUNK
SULINSKY, BARTHOL	30	M	LABR	RRZZZZUNK
LARADOWSKY, JAN	21	M	LABR	RRZZZZUNK
ANTON	30	M	LABR	RRZZZZUNK
KALINOWSKY, JOSEF	27	M	LABR	RRZZZZUNK
RACINSKY, LADISLAUS	25	M	LABR	RRZZZZUNK
MIKALOWSKI, ANTONI	31	M	LABR	RRZZZZUNK
MILEWSKI, JOSEPH	22	M	LABR	RRZZZZUNK
SCHAIKOWSKI, FRANZ	22	M	LABR	RRZZZZUNK
DILON, LUCAS	40	M	MCHT	RRZZZZUNK
BEILSON, MARIE	19	F	SGL	RRZZZZUNK
KALISAK, JAN	31	M	LABR	RRZZZZUNK
MANSEK, IGNACZ	36	M	LABR	RRZZZZUNK
ADAMSKY, LUDWIG	21	M	LABR	RRZZZZUNK
SATKOWSKY, MARIAN	25	M	LABR	RRZZZZUNK
NOWACK, NUFRI	19	M	LABR	RRZZZZUNK
BOLECHOWICZ, STANISL	31	M	LABR	RRZZZZUNK
KASTEN, DANIEL	40	M	LABR	RRZZZZUNK
EMILIE	41	F	UNKNOWN	RRZZZZUNK
CARL	9	M	CHILD	RRZZZZUNK
JOHANN	8	M	CHILD	RRZZZZUNK
MARTHA	.09	F	INFANT	RRZZZZUNK
BUCHHOLZ, CAROLINE	27	F	W	RRZZZZUNK
EVA	2	F	CHILD	RRZZZZUNK
KRUSE, DETLEV	18	M	FARMER	RRZZZZUNK
SPIWIK, LAZAR	20	M	TCHR	RRZZZZUNK
SCHMANOWSKY, METTE	20	F	SGL	RRZZZZUNK
FABRIZKI, ADAMS	27	M	LABR	RRZZZZUNK
GARCELLA, STANISL	23	M	FARMER	RRZZZZUNK
KORTMANN, FRIEDR	38	M	LABR	RRZZZZUNK
KORDULASCHINSKI, JOSEF	33	M	LABR	RRZZZZUNK
TRUSCHINSKI, JOSEF	38	M	LABR	RRZZZZUNK
NEUDE, CHRISTIAN	27	M	LABR	RRZZZZUNK
GUSTAV	23	M	LABR	RRZZZZUNK
OCZIMKIEWICZ, IGNATZ	33	M	LABR	RRZZZZUNK
MALOWSKY, CASIMIR	24	M	LABR	RRZZZZUNK
RAJEWSKY, BERNHARD	46	M	LABR	RRZZZZUNK
KLENOWSKY, STEFAN	37	M	LABR	RRZZZZUNK
GRUENEMANN, NESCHE	27	M	LABR	RRZZZZUNK
DAMSCHEWITZ, JOSEPH	27	M	LABR	RRZZZZUNK
ANTON	30	M	LABR	RRZZZZUNK
JARKOWSKY, PETER	24	M	LABR	RRZZZZUNK
GRABESZ, MARCIN	27	M	LABR	RRZZZZUNK
DIRSZOWSKI, ADAM	31	M	LABR	RRZZZZUNK
GALONZI, THEOPH	28	M	LABR	RRZZZZUNK
PALIWODA, JAN	23	M	LABR	RRZZZZUNK
DUMKOWSKI, JAC	31	M	LABR	RRZZZZUNK
KORDEK, KASIMIR	28	M	LABR	RRZZZZUNK
UZAREWITSCH, FRANZ	33	M	LABR	RRZZZZUNK
MERTEWITZ, ANTON	28	M	LABR	RRZZZZUNK
DILEWSKI, JAN	20	M	LABR	RRZZZZUNK
DZIKOWSKI, JAN	30	M	LABR	RRZZZZUNK
RIFINSKI, JAN	18	M	LABR	RRZZZZUNK
SCHUMACHOWSKY, JOSEPH	28	M	LABR	RRZZZZUNK
KILOWITSCH, JAN	19	M	LABR	RRZZZZUNK
JABLONSKI, FRANZ	36	M	LABR	RRZZZZUNK
MATSCHIEWSKI, JAN	32	M	LABR	RRZZZZUNK
SCHUMACHOWSKI, MICHAEL	29	M	LABR	RRZZZZUNK
COHN, BLUME	22	F	W	RRZZZZUNK
JENTE	.06	F	INFANT	RRZZZZUNK
KANNER, DWORA	9	F	CHILD	RRZZZZUNK
ARBUSS, ISAAC	29	M	DLR	RRZZZZUNK
MALINOW, SZMIEL	26	M	LABR	RRZZZZUNK

PASSENGER	AGE	SEX	OCCUPATION	PRV VIL DES
WORLIN, THOMAS	31	M	LABR	FNZZZZUNK
MACKARI, JOH	40	M	LABR	FNZZZZUNK
WILLIG, MATS	30	M	LABR	FNZZZZUNK
OISTE, MATI	30	M	LABR	FNZZZZUNK
KARLIN, MATTS	36	M	LABR	FNZZZZUNK
APPEL, JOSEPH	27	M	LABR	FNZZZZUNK
MIKASI, HERRM	38	M	LABR	FNZZZZUNK
BERNATOWITZ, AGATHE	22	F	WO	RRZZZZUNK
MARTHA	.11	F	INFANT	RRZZZZUNK
STEPINSKI, ELIAS	18	M	FARMER	RRZZZZUNK
BERNATOWICZA, JER	33	M	LABR	RRZZZZUNK
PERNIKOW, JALCHE	27	F	WO	RRZZZZUNK
SCHEREUEWSKY, FRANZ	25	M	LABR	RRZZZZUNK
WALENTA, FRANZ	21	M	LABR	RRZZZZUNK
ZINKEWICZ, ST	23	M	LABR	RRZZZZUNK
WOLUBOWITZ, JOSEF	22	M	LABR	RRZZZZUNK
VANIS, ANDREAS	25	M	LABR	RRZZZZUNK
GURKOWSKI, WOYCIECH	36	M	LABR	RRZZZZUNK
BREGENZ, ADOLF	35	M	LABR	RRZZZZUNK
SAWUL, MARIN	36	M	LABR	RRZZZZUNK
GAMSER, JENNY	22	F	SGL	RRZZZZUSA

SHIP: ARIZONA

FROM: LIVERPOOL AND QUEENSTOWN
TO: NEW YORK
ARRIVED: 26 MARCH 1888

PASSENGER	AGE	SEX	OCCUPATION	PRV VIL DES
ANDRUSKIEWICZ, ANDREZ	30	M	LABR	PLZZZZUSA
FEITSON, MENDEL	29	M	LABR	PLZZZZUSA
SANDMOFSKY, WOLF	24	M	LABR	PLACBFUSA
BUNI	23	F	W	PLACBFUSA
MICK	3	M	CHILD	PLACBFUSA
MARKIEWICZ, STANISLAU	32	M	ART	PLZZZZUSA
TOTTLER, JERMEL	25	M	ART	PLZZZZUSA
SANDNOFSKY, NATHAN	.08	M	INFANT	PLACBFUSA
KOCHASKY, IGNAZ	40	M	ART	PLZZZZUSA
MICHOLASCHER, FRANZ	30	M	ART	PLZZZZUSA
WALUZKY, STANISLAW	25	M	LABR	PLZZZZUSA
MARCUS, ABRAHAM	25	M	ART	PLACBFUSA
BASCHE	20	F	W	PLACBFUSA
SANDLER, EFROIM	32	M	FARMER	RRZZZZUSA
CHANE	28	F	W	RRZZZZUSA
FRIEDE	3	F	CHILD	RRZZZZUSA
FEIGE	.05	F	INFANT	RRZZZZUSA
KORETZKI, MARIAM	18	F	W	RRZZZZUSA
JACOB	4	M	CHILD	RRZZZZUSA
RADUNSKY, TAUBE	33	F	W	PLZZZZUSA
DICKSTEIN, ABRAM	36	M	PNTR	RRZZZZUSA

SHIP: LAKE ONTARIO

FROM: LIVERPOOL
TO: BOSTON
ARRIVED: UNKNOWN

PASSENGER	AGE	SEX	OCCUPATION	PRV VIL DES
SAMUEL, LUDAS	43	M	LABR	RRZZZZNY
LAMONT, JOHN	29	M	SHMK	RRZZZZNY
HOWNITZ, GITTEL	19	F	W	PLZZZZNY
KALAPOOX, ISTWAN	43	M	TLR	PLZZZZNY
JACOBOWITZ, ADOLPH	18	M	TLR	RRZZZZNY
PEGUS, WAJCECK	44	M	LABR	RRZZZZNY
SABOMSKI, KARL	22	M	LABR	RRZZZZNY
KAGMANSKI, FELX.	31	M	TLR	RRZZZZNY
ANTONIA	28	M	TLR	RRZZZZNY
MINONSKI, JOHAN	27	M	BLDR	RRZZZZNY
KLOKES, ANTOINE	48	M	LABR	RRZZZZBO
KATRINA	28	F	W	RRZZZZBO
JERZRA	8	F	CHILD	RRZZZZBO

SHIP: PENNSYLVANIA

FROM: ANTWERP
TO: NEW YORK
ARRIVED: 27 MARCH 1888

PASSENGER	AGE	SEX	OCCUPATION	PRV VIL DES
ADAMOWIG, JOSEF	29	M	LABR	PLZZZZNY
BARINOWSKY, W.	36	M	LABR	PLZZZZNY
BARCEWSKI, JOSEF	21	M	LABR	PLZZZZNY
BEYANESKY, M.	24	M	LABR	PLZZZZNY
BONSZKOWSKI, J.	35	M	BKR	PLZZZZCH
U	30	F	W	PLZZZZCH
STANE.	5	F	CHILD	PLZZZZCH
THEO.	3	F	CHILD	PLZZZZCH
CATH.	2	F	CHILD	PLZZZZCH
AND.	.02	M	INFANT	PLZZZZCH
DUMALSKI, JACOB	29	M	LABR	PLZZZZUNK
DECKER, JACOB	40	M	LABR	PLZZZZNY
ELIZ.	36	F	W	PLZZZZNY
CARL	7	M	CHILD	PLZZZZNY
EMMA	5	F	CHILD	PLZZZZNY
FRANZISCHEK, PICH	23	M	CH	PLZZZZNY
GRAIEWSKI, JOSEF	24	M	LABR	PLZZZZNY
GISCHKOWIEZ, ANTON	39	M	LABR	PLZZZZNY
JANZEN, MICH.	28	M	LABR	PLZZZZNY
JOHNA	25	M	LABR	PLZZZZNY
KOEFZWTYZ, K.	23	M	LABR	PLZZZZNY
KALLENBORN, MICH.	66	M	LABR	PLZZZZBUF
KALAMAGKA, ANT.	24	M	LABR	PLZZZZWAR
KONSOWSKA, ANTN.	20	M	UNKNOWN	PLZZZZCH
LECHOWSKI, ANT.	21	M	LABR	PLZZZZNY
MATOSEWIZ, JOSEF	21	M	LABR	PLZZZZNY
MILOWSKY, J.	31	M	LABR	PLZZZZNY
POJCIANOWSKY, K.	25	M	LABR	PLZZZZNY
PULLES, DAN.	28	M	LABR	PLZZZZNY
RUGIOLA, WIN.	19	F	SVNT	PLZZZZNY
ROZANSKI, P.	36	M	LABR	PLZZZZNY
RUTKOWSKI, T.	21	M	LABR	PLZZZZNY
SELNZ, JOSIF	22	M	LABR	PLZZZZNY
SCHAPIRA, PIER	45	M	LABR	PLZZZZNY
FREIDE	9	M	CHILD	PLZZZZNY
SASENA, ANT.	50	M	LABR	PLZZZZNY
SALA, MATTES	24	M	LABR	PLZZZZNY
MENEGUZZI, VINCEN	31	M	LABR	PLZZZZNY
GRELIC, INO	23	M	LABR	PLZZZZPHI
KLOKOLI, JURE	37	M	LABR	PLZZZZPHI
KASMIEC, JANKO	27	M	LABR	PLZZZZPHI
BEIER, STEFAN	36	M	LABR	PLZZZZPHI
SPELIC, PETAR	18	M	LABR	PLZZZZPHI
LEO, VICO	37	M	LABR	PLZZZZPHI
KASMER, HANKO	36	M	LABR	PLZZZZPHI
KUFLER, STAN.	32	M	LABR	PLZZZZBAL
SWIEWITZ, JANN	33	M	LABR	PLZZZZNY
TOMORAK, JAN	26	M	LABR	PLZZZZCH
WOLKONES, YERM.	29	M	LABR	PLAIDXNY
WOLMEWIEZ, F.	30	M	LABR	PLAIDXOMA

PASSENGER	AGE	SEX	OCCUPATION	PRV	VIL	DES

SHIP: ANCHORIA

FROM: GLASGOW AND MOVILLE
TO: NEW YORK
ARRIVED: 27 MARCH 1888

PASSENGER	AGE	SEX	OCCUPATION	PRV	VIL	DES
HURWITZ, HIRSCH	23	M	HTR	RR	ZZZZ	USA
SCHEME	19	F	W	RR	AHTF	USA
SCHMUDEROWITZ, SAUFAN	25	M	LABR	RR	ZZZZ	USA
SCHIEVELANER, MAZSIE	31	M	LABR	RR	ZZZZ	USA
SCHMUDENOWITZ, PETER	28	M	LABR	RR	ZZZZ	USA
FEDEROWITZ, IGNATZ	30	M	LABR	RR	ZZZZ	USA
SCHIDLOWSKY, JEAN	19	M	LABR	RR	ZZZZ	USA
DELIAN, IGNAT	30	M	LABR	RR	ZZZZ	USA
MAKERSWITZ, PIOT.	40	M	LABR	RR	ZZZZ	USA
MOSGOLIS, PIOT.	22	M	LABR	RR	ZZZZ	USA
RADZEWSKI, JEAN	21	M	LABR	RR	ZZZZ	USA
SOKOLOWSKY, BART.	21	M	LABR	RR	ZZZZ	USA
FELDYSCH, ABRAM	38	M	PDLR	RR	AIAX	USA
TOMELWITZ, SIMON	21	M	LABR	RR	ZZZZ	USA
WILSROSKY, PIOT	31	M	PDLR	RR	ZZZZ	USA
TYWIZITZKI, MAR.	26	M	PDLR	RR	ZZZZ	USA
ALPERT, NAFTOLI	20	M	PDLR	RR	AGRT	USA
BUDNIK, JOSSEL	24	M	PDLR	RR	AGRT	USA
SCHORSCHER, WOLF	28	M	PDLR	RR	AHTU	USA
GINSBURG, MARKUS	20	M	PDLR	RR	ZZZZ	USA
MOROSCHOWSKY, LEON	26	M	PDLR	RR	ZZZZ	USA
LUNDBRIS, JOSEF	22	M	GDBT	RR	ZZZZ	USA
BIEDERMAN, BARTAL	30	M	FARMER	RR	AICF	USA
POSSEL, CHAIM	20	M	HTR	RR	ZZZZ	USA
SCHMIDT, DAN.	24	M	LABR	RR	ZZZZ	USA
KREMPETZ, MICH.	29	M	LABR	RR	ZZZZ	USA
WJENKOWSKY, JEAN	30	M	LABR	RR	ZZZZ	USA
JEAN	30	M	LABR	RR	ZZZZ	USA
BUDZYESKY, LUD.	24	M	LABR	RR	ZZZZ	USA
WEIMER, JENZIE	30	M	LABR	RR	ZZZZ	USA
SCHULZ, GOTTFRIED	28	M	LABR	RR	ZZZZ	USA
CZYZINSKI, JEAN	23	M	LABR	RR	ZZZZ	USA
MAKIEWICZ, JEAN	50	M	LABR	RR	ZZZZ	USA
WISNEOWSKY, FRANZ	30	M	LABR	RR	ZZZZ	USA
GZIELKOWSKI, WOCICH	22	M	LABR	RR	ZZZZ	USA
PRELOWSKY, TOBIAN	18	M	LABR	RR	ZZZZ	USA
FRANKOWSKI, JEAN	30	M	LABR	RR	ZZZZ	USA
KRUGER, FRANZ	50	M	LABR	RR	ZZZZ	USA
ZARNETZ, FRANZ	25	M	LABR	RR	ZZZZ	USA
HEDKE, LUDWIG	25	M	LABR	RR	ZZZZ	USA
BASUMAS, MIKES	24	M	LABR	RR	ZZZZ	USA
BERZINAR, JONAS	36	M	LABR	RR	ZZZZ	USA
ZAWETZKA, THOS.	23	M	LABR	RR	ZZZZ	USA
URBANOWITZ, JOSEF	28	M	LABR	RR	ZZZZ	USA
KRUGER, Z-ILIE	17	F	HP	RR	ZZZZ	USA

SHIP: NORWEGIAN

FROM: GLASGOW
TO: BOSTON
ARRIVED: VE UNKNOWN A CR

PASSENGER	AGE	SEX	OCCUPATION	PRV	VIL	DES
SILWIN, JOSEF	23	M	INWKR	PL	ZZZZ	UNK
VINGIL, WM.	23	M	INWKR	PL	ZZZZ	UNK
DEARANSKI, MICHL.	44	M	LABR	PL	ZZZZ	NY
KLEPARSKI, STAN.	33	M	LABR	PL	ZZZZ	NY
GRODOSKI, STAN.	25	M	LABR	PL	ZZZZ	NY
STANNY, VAL.	20	M	LABR	PL	ZZZZ	NY
SIEWECKI, FRANC.	29	M	LABR	PL	ZZZZ	NY
TOBAKO, KATIE	18	F	DMS	PL	ZZZZ	NY
SALENZKI, FRIZEK	25	F	DMS	PL	ZZZZ	NY
GISSY, KOHEN	17	F	DMS	PL	ZZZZ	NY
WILLEY, EDEL	49	F	DMS	PL	ZZZZ	NY
ISCHELSCHERSKY, JAN	29	M	LABR	PL	ZZZZ	NY
ROSENSTEIN, MOSES	45	M	LABR	PL	ZZZZ	NY
WOJEIECH, CHECHANOWSKY	44	M	LABR	PL	ZZZZ	NY
CHOJNATZKI, JOSEF	34	M	LABR	PL	ZZZZ	NY
MUELLERSKI, JOH.	33	M	LABR	PL	ZZZZ	NY
LEWINSOHN, JOHS.	50	M	LABR	PL	ZZZZ	NY
RICHTER, FRANC	24	M	LABR	PL	ZZZZ	UNK
GRZEIZKOWICK, ANT.	35	M	LABR	PL	ZZZZ	UNK
FABIESCHEWSKI, FRANZ	18	M	LABR	PL	ZZZZ	UNK

SHIP: STATE OF NEBRASKA

FROM: GLASGOW AND LARNE
TO: NEW YORK
ARRIVED: 28 MARCH 1888

PASSENGER	AGE	SEX	OCCUPATION	PRV	VIL	DES
LEFF, ARON	30	M	PDLR	RR	ZZZZ	USA
WERKSMANN, MOSES	22	M	PDLR	RR	ZZZZ	USA
GULINSKY, BREINEL	19	M	PDLR	RR	ZZZZ	USA
TRUB, ISAAC	24	M	TNSTH	RR	ZZZZ	USA
LEIKIA, KALLMAN	19	M	DYR	RR	ZZZZ	USA
SCHLOSSBERG, ISAAC	32	M	PNTR	RR	ZZZZ	USA
FREITELBERG, ISAAC	20	M	PNTR	RR	ZZZZ	USA
ZUCIKERMAN, ABRAHAM	34	M	CGRMKR	RR	ZZZZ	USA
ALPERN, LESER	38	M	JNR	RR	ZZZZ	USA
LAZEROWITZ, SIMON	38	M	TLR	RR	ZZZZ	USA
CHARLIP, MOSES	44	M	TLR	RR	ZZZZ	USA
RZEPPA, ADAM	35	M	LABR	RR	ZZZZ	USA
MAROSORD, PARFEY	32	M	LABR	RR	ZZZZ	USA
PUTOFIOW, SIMON	24	M	LABR	RR	ZZZZ	USA
DARWEANG, MARCUS	45	M	PDLR	RR	ZZZZ	USA
MEDUNCKI, MEINE	20	F	SP	RR	ZZZZ	USA
LAICHTER, MECHAINE	20	F	SP	RR	ZZZZ	USA
LEZOWA, MARIANNA	20	F	SP	RR	ZZZZ	USA
SCHNEIDER, SCHIFFRE	45	F	W	RR	ZZZZ	USA
MIREL	14	M	CH	RR	ZZZZ	USA
KRAUSTER, ROSE	21	F	W	RR	ZZZZ	USA
CHAPSEL	2	M	CHILD	RR	ZZZZ	USA
SCHNEIDER, NECHE	30	F	W	RR	ZZZZ	USA
ABRAHAM	7	M	CHILD	RR	ZZZZ	USA
CHAJE	2	F	CHILD	RR	ZZZZ	USA
NOCHEM	1	M	CHILD	RR	ZZZZ	USA
HORWITZ, LEA	26	F	W	RR	ZZZZ	USA
REBECCA	5	F	CHILD	RR	ZZZZ	USA
ABRAHAM	3	M	CHILD	RR	ZZZZ	USA
LILLY	1	F	CHILD	RR	ZZZZ	USA
KONWITZ, ANNA	32	F	W	PL	ZZZZ	USA
JOSEF	.09	M	INFANT	PL	ZZZZ	USA
LIDANSKY, DINA	55	F	W	PL	ZZZZ	USA
STEFANKOWITZCH, JULIAN	45	M	TLR	PL	ZZZZ	USA
MARIANNE	42	F	W	PL	ZZZZ	USA
MARIA	11	F	CH	PL	ZZZZ	USA
BARBARA	9	F	CHILD	PL	ZZZZ	USA
JUSCHKIS, DOMINICK	23	M	TLR	PL	ZZZZ	USA
PETRONELLA	16	F	W	PL	ZZZZ	USA
SCHUCHAT, SUSAMANN	25	M	MLR	PL	ZZZZ	USA
RISCHE	24	F	W	PL	ZZZZ	USA
FRIEDRICH, JACOB	24	M	LABR	PL	ZZZZ	USA
SCHWIDERSKY, ADAM	18	M	LABR	PL	ZZZZ	USA
SWIZLIKOWSKI, ANTON	32	M	LABR	PL	ZZZZ	USA
BOBITZKY, JAN	18	M	LABR	PL	ZZZZ	USA
DERHIN, FRANZ	28	M	LABR	PL	ZZZZ	USA
GAUGLENSKY, FRANZ	16	M	LABR	PL	ZZZZ	USA
MOLSKY, JANKO	27	M	LABR	PL	ZZZZ	USA
SLOTOZINSKY, JACOB	27	M	LABR	PL	ZZZZ	USA
KOZLOWSKI, JAN	29	M	LABR	PL	ZZZZ	USA
MINEWITZ, JULIAN	22	M	LABR	PL	ZZZZ	USA
KULESSA, WOICHECK	18	M	LABR	PL	ZZZZ	USA
ARASCHOMOWSKY, ALEXANDE	24	M	LABR	PL	ZZZZ	USA
SZUCZLIKOWSKI, FRANZ	27	M	LABR	PL	ZZZZ	USA

PASSENGER	AGE	SEX	OCCUPATION	PRIV	VIL	DES
OTZENSKI, JOSEF	49	M	LABR	PL	ZZZZ	USA
STAPONKO, IVAN	27	M	LABR	PL	ZZZZ	USA
RATOWSKI, JAN	42	M	LABR	PL	ZZZZ	USA
NOVITZKY, WLADISLAUS	18	M	LABR	PL	ZZZZ	USA
KELPS, JULIAN	30	M	LABR	PL	ZZZZ	USA
PIDUS, OSI	18	M	LABR	PL	ZZZZ	USA
GUDORSKY, ANTONA	21	M	LABR	PL	ZZZZ	USA
OSCHITZ, ANTONA	25	M	LABR	PL	ZZZZ	USA
TADYIS, OSI	21	M	LABR	PL	ZZZZ	USA
OSCHITZ, ANTONA	25	M	LABR	PL	ZZZZ	USA
TADYIS, KASPER	25	M	LABR	PL	ZZZZ	USA
KATSCHENOWSKY, ADAM	30	M	LABR	PL	ZZZZ	USA
OLLOF, FRANZ	32	M	LABR	PL	ZZZZ	USA
SZWCZLIKOWSKI, JOHANN	33	M	LABR	PL	ZZZZ	USA
KAMINSKY, ANTON	23	M	LABR	PL	ZZZZ	USA
ANDRUSCHKEWITZ, ANTON	30	M	LABR	PL	ZZZZ	USA
DARGEITZ, CASSIMIR	30	M	LABR	PL	ZZZZ	USA
MISSBERG, CHAIM	29	M	TLR	PL	ZZZZ	USA
JAWORSKI, ALEXANDER	33	M	CPTR	PL	ZZZZ	USA
JASCHINSKI, MARIAN	44	M	CPR	PL	ZZZZ	USA

SHIP: AUSTRALIA

FROM: HAMBURG
TO: NEW YORK
ARRIVED: 28 MARCH 1888

PASSENGER	AGE	SEX	OCCUPATION	PRIV	VIL	DES
RACHLIN, DWORE	28	F	WO	RR	ZZZZ	NY
MOSES	3	M	CHILD	RR	ZZZZ	NY
RUBEN	.08	M	INFANT	RR	ZZZZ	NY
BEKATZKI, JUTE	8	F	CHILD	RR	ZZZZ	NY
CHAPSE	7	M	CHILD	RR	ZZZZ	NY
LEICKE	2	F	CHILD	RR	ZZZZ	NY
MORDKE	.06	F	INFANT	RR	ZZZZ	NY
OLDERMANN, SARA	18	F	UNKNOWN	RR	ZZZZ	NY
KRAWCSEK, MARTIN	29	M	LABR	RR	ZZZZ	NY
ANTONIE	28	F	W	RR	ZZZZ	NY
SOPIHA	.04	M	INFANT	RR	ZZZZ	NY
KUERTZ, DANIEL	40	M	LABR	RR	ZZZZ	NY
PRAMP, ABR.	33	M	MLR	RR	ZZZZ	NY
LEWANDOFSKI, VALENTIN	29	M	LABR	RR	ZZZZ	NY
PIKOLKA, FRIEDRICH	23	M	LABR	RR	ZZZZ	NY
KALSCHEFSZKI, JOSEF	23	M	LABR	RR	ZZZZ	NY
PIPSZINSKI, MARTZIN	30	M	LABR	RR	ZZZZ	NY
WITKOFSZKY, FRANZ	35	M	LABR	RR	ZZZZ	NY
SZLATHOFSCKY, JOSEF	24	M	LABR	RR	ZZZZ	NY
FLEGEL, GOTTLIEB	49	M	SHMK	RR	ZZZZ	NY
KOWALSSKI, ADAM	30	M	LABR	RR	ZZZZ	NY
SCHOMITZKY, RUSOLF	35	M	LABR	RR	ZZZZ	NY
JOHAN	35	F	W	RR	ZZZZ	NY
WITKOFSZKY, JAN	33	M	LABR	RR	ZZZZ	NY
ADAMESYK, JOHAN	22	M	LABR	RR	ZZZZ	NY
JABSSINSKI, STANISLAUS	19	M	LABR	RR	ZZZZ	NY
GAYTKOFSKI, JOHAN	45	M	LABR	RR	ZZZZ	NY
SCHAUSERSKY, JULIAN	27	M	MSN	RR	ZZZZ	NY
NAPTAKOVITZ, LEON	19	M	SMH	RR	ZZZZ	NY
MUECHEVITZ, JOSEF	30	M	LABR	RR	ZZZZ	NY
BANASCSOFSKY, JAN	20	M	LABR	RR	ZZZZ	NY
LEWANDOFSCKY, FRANZ	31	M	LABR	RR	ZZZZ	NY
WASKIEVITZ, ANTON	27	M	LABR	RR	ZZZZ	NY
WICZKOFSZKI, MARTIN	31	M	LABR	RR	ZZZZ	NY
SINKIEVITZ, BALTROMI	33	M	LABR	RR	ZZZZ	NY
KLINOVITZ, ANDREY	30	M	LABR	RR	ZZZZ	NY
SCHNEDE, ROSALIA	23	M	LABR	RR	ZZZZ	NY
HIRKOVITZ, HERSCH	28	M	LABR	RR	ZZZZ	NY
WICEZBOWSKY, FRANZ	31	M	LABR	RR	ZZZZ	NY
INDJAVSKI, VITALIS	26	M	LABR	RR	ZZZZ	NY
KOZOWSKY, WLAD	27	M	LABR	RR	ZZZZ	NY
RATTENBERG, ADOLF	19	M	LABR	RR	ZZZZ	NY
WOLF, MAX	24	M	DLR	RR	ZZZZ	NY
PEHILIS, MARTIN	25	M	LABR	RR	ZZZZ	NY
LEUHN, AUGUSTE	27	M	LABR	RR	ZZZZ	NY
EMMERSCHON, JOSAM	32	M	LABR	RR	ZZZZ	NY
SCHILINSKY, FRANZ	23	M	LABR	RR	ZZZZ	NY
JOFFE, ROSA	26	F	WO	RR	ZZZZ	NY
STEINMANN, JANKEL	32	M	DLR	RR	ZZZZ	NY
GRUNBERG, HERSCH	46	M	DLR	RR	ZZZZ	NY
MARKUS	42	M	DLR	RR	ZZZZ	NY
IZCWSKY, JOSAM	22	M	DLR	RR	ZZZZ	NY
GUERIN, FEUVEL	26	M	LABR	RR	ZZZZ	NY
LIPPMANN, JAKOB	35	M	SDLR	RR	ZZZZ	NY
STRESSITTE, STEFAN	25	M	LABR	RR	ZZZZ	NY
ECPERN, SCHLOME	18	M	FARMER	RR	ZZZZ	NY
MARKUSZE, LEYSER	35	M	DLR	RR	ZZZZ	NY
TAS---KI, JAKOB	25	M	LABR	RR	ZZZZ	NY
SWILACZKY, IGNEZ	21	M	LABR	RR	ZZZZ	NY
TUROWSKY, PIETRO	20	M	LABR	RR	ZZZZ	NY
JELANITZ, IWAN	28	M	LABR	RR	ZZZZ	NY
LEKONITZ, OSIEP	26	M	LABR	RR	ZZZZ	NY
PLUNGAN, IGNEZ	18	M	LABR	RR	ZZZZ	NY
MIKOLANITZ, MICHAEL	18	M	LABR	RR	ZZZZ	NY
ELACHNOVITZ, IWAN	24	M	LABR	RR	ZZZZ	NY
KONSTANTIN, MICHAEL	22	M	LABR	RR	ZZZZ	NY
JAKUEBOVITZ, ALEXANDER	21	M	LABR	RR	ZZZZ	NY
SILANSKI, MATHIAS	25	M	LABR	RR	ZZZZ	NY
SCHMIEL, MOSES	21	M	FARMER	RR	ZZZZ	NY
PERL	15	M	FARMER	RR	ZZZZ	NY
HIRSCH, IZAK	21	M	FARMER	RR	ZZZZ	NY
FERCKSEN, PERSIDE	17	M	FARMER	RR	ZZZZ	NY
KUFFER, PAL	45	M	FARMER	RR	ZZZZ	USA
KOSMA, JANOS	35	M	FARMER	RR	ZZZZ	NY
MOLHRAUER, AUGUST	20	M	LABR	RR	ZZZZ	NY
WEISS, CHAI--	23	M	LABR	RR	ZZZZ	NY
KOBRZINSKI, CHUWE	22	M	LABR	RR	ZZZZ	NY
LAN, KALMAN	26	M	LABR	RR	ZZZZ	NY
GRIMGOLZ, MAX	20	M	LABR	RR	AAXL	NY
ELMANN, JANKEL	27	M	LABR	RR	AAXL	NY
LIDIE	23	F	W	RR	AAXL	NY
TREMMEL, JOHANN	33	M	UNKNOWN	RR	AAXL	NY
RUESS, JAKOB	28	M	LABR	RR	AAXL	NY
KAPRALET, AUGUST	33	M	LABR	RR	AAXL	NY
WISSKUF, JOSEF	18	M	LABR	RR	AAXL	NY
BERNATH, ISTREN	44	M	LABR	RR	AAXL	NY
ROGELSKI, CONTSTANTIN	32	M	LABR	RR	AAXL	NY
WOZTINA, LUZA	23	M	LABR	RR	AAXL	NY
PILENDER, JAN	26	M	LABR	RR	AAXL	NY
PETER	30	M	LABR	RR	AAXL	NY
LIMEZOWSKI, STANISLAUS	30	M	LABR	RR	AAXL	NY
BOGNA, STANILAUS	20	M	LABR	RR	AAXL	NY
ZUKOWSCKY, WLADISLAUS	20	M	LABR	RR	AAXL	NY
SKINOZILEWSKY, JAN	25	M	LABR	RR	AAXL	NY
KOZDIRSKY, ADAM	18	M	LABR	RR	AAXL	NY
RADZKICWICZ, VIKTOR	20	M	LABR	RR	AAXL	NY
POLLAK, FRANZ	40	M	LABR	RR	AAXL	NY
ZACHZSEDOWSKY, MICHAL	24	M	LABR	RR	AAXL	NY
U, U	30	M	LABR	RR	AAXL	NY
MALINOWSZKY, AN--	22	M	LABR	RR	AAXL	NY
HUNTZE, WILHELM	28	M	TLR	RR	AAXL	NY
BERTHE	20	F	W	RR	AAXL	NY
FARR, FRIDRICH	45	M	FARMER	RR	AAXL	NY
OTTO	14	M	CH	RR	AAXL	NY
HERMANN	9	M	CHILD	RR	AAXL	NY
ANNA	8	F	CHILD	RR	AAXL	NY
JOHANE.	4	F	CHILD	RR	AAXL	NY
ANKSLEIM, SALOME	30	M	TLR	RR	AAXL	USA
MACK, PETER	23	M	LABR	RR	AAXL	NY

PASSENGER	AGE	SEX	OCCUPATION	PRIV	VIL	DES

SHIP: PARISIAN

FROM: LIVERPOOL
TO: BALTIMORE
ARRIVED: 30 MARCH 1888

PASSENGER	AGE	SEX	OCCUPATION	PRIV	VIL	DES
LE---ITZKI, -IETRO	26	M	LABR	RR	ZZZZ	CLE
ROSENBAUM, BERT	23	M	TLR	RR	ZZZZ	BAL
LEIBERMANN, DAVID	36	M	BLKSMH	RR	ZZZZ	UNK
MANFIELD, A	36	M	LABR	RR	ZZZZ	BAL
COHN, MARCUS	23	M	CPMKR	RR	ZZZZ	BAL
ROSENBERG, MOSES	23	M	SDLR	RR	ZZZZ	BAL
LEFTITZ, SEMA	25	F	W	RR	ZZZZ	BAL
MESCHE	00	F	INF	RR	ZZZZ	BAL
CHAIM	17	M	TLR	RR	ZZZZ	BAL
CHANIE	16	F	UNKNOWN	RR	ZZZZ	BAL
BAERMAN, MORDCH	30	M	LABR	RR	ZZZZ	BAL
BAR, FANNY	16	F	DMS	RR	ZZZZ	BAL
RAPZENSKA, MARIE	30	F	W	PL	ZZZZ	CLE
ANTONIA	4	M	CHILD	PL	ZZZZ	CLE
MARTHA	3	F	CHILD	PL	ZZZZ	CLE
MARIE	00	F	INF	PL	ZZZZ	CLE
GOLDBERG, WOLF	40	M	CPTR	RR	ZZZZ	PIT

SHIP: RHEIN

FROM: BREMEN
TO: BALTIMORE
ARRIVED: 30 MARCH 1888

PASSENGER	AGE	SEX	OCCUPATION	PRIV	VIL	DES
SOBOCINSKY, ERASMUS	41	M	RE	RR	ZZZZ	MIL
KUHN, SILVESTER	39	M	RE	RR	ZZZZ	MIL
JEKA, STANISLAUS	43	M	RE	RR	ZZZZ	MIL
KIMBRUM, JOSEL	18	M	BRR	RR	ZZZZ	BAL
NARJEWSKA, MATEUSZ	26	M	LABR	RR	ZZZZ	BAL
GERNIALOWICZ, MATENZ	18	M	LABR	RR	ZZZZ	BAL
STEGIN, SAMEL	23	M	LABR	RR	ZZZZ	BAL
LINERSKI, ANTON	23	M	LABR	RR	ZZZZ	BAL
RUTKOWSKY, NICOLAS	26	M	LABR	RR	ZZZZ	BAL
LEWANDOWSKI, INGATZ	15	M	LABR	RR	ZZZZ	BAL
MARIANNA	40	F	NN	RR	ZZZZ	BAL
KATHA.	7	F	CHILD	RR	ZZZZ	BAL
STANKEWITZ, ANNA	20	F	NN	RR	ZZZZ	BAL
KALWAYTUS, MATHIAS	45	M	LABR	RR	ZZZZ	BAL
KONETZSCHINAK, NEPOMUCK	33	M	LABR	RR	ZZZZ	BAL
BULLOSCHEFSKI, JACOB	31	M	LABR	RR	ZZZZ	IL
KATARYNA	26	F	W	RR	ZZZZ	IL
ZWINSKI, JOSEF	23	M	LABR	RR	ZZZZ	IL
BALCEREK, LUCAS	35	M	LABR	RR	ZZZZ	IL
ADAMCZIK, MATHEUS	24	M	LABR	RR	ZZZZ	IL
PIETRAS, MARTIN	26	M	LABR	RR	ZZZZ	OH
SKONETZNE, WOJCIECH	22	M	LABR	RR	ZZZZ	OH
JESEWSKY, MATEY	21	M	LABR	RR	AIAP	BAL
KOTLEWSKY, THOMAS	30	M	LABR	RR	AIAP	BAL
KWIATKOWSKY, STANISL.	46	M	LABR	RR	AIAP	BAL
KARONOWSKI, PETER	32	M	LABR	RR	AIAP	BAL
LETOWNIK, JOS.	27	M	LABR	RR	AIAP	BAL
KAIDNASZ, TOMAS	38	M	LABR	RR	AIAP	BAL
PETRONELLA	31	F	W	RR	AIAP	BAL
MICHNIEWICZ, ANDREAS	40	M	LABR	RR	AIAP	BAL
STANSKI, FRITZ	28	M	LABR	RR	AIAP	BAL
IGNATOWSKA, FRANZISKA	21	F	NN	RR	AIAP	BAL
JOSEPHA	6	F	CHILD	RR	AIAP	BAL
KLAMMER, KARL	21	M	LABR	RR	AIAP	BAL
GOLDBERG, SALOMINE	18	M	GDNR	RR	AIAP	BAL
MODEZYNKEWITZ, ANTONI	40	M	LABR	RR	AIAP	IL

SHIP: ITALY

FROM: LIVERPOOL
TO: NEW YORK
ARRIVED: 30 MARCH 1888

PASSENGER	AGE	SEX	OCCUPATION	PRIV	VIL	DES
FUND, MORRIS	25	M	CGRMKR	RR	ADBQ	NY
MOSKOWSKY, C.M.	30	F	W	RR	ADBQ	NY
RACHEL	3	F	CHILD	RR	ADBQ	NY
RUBIN, C.	30	M	LABR	RR	ADBQ	NY
BERNSTEIN, N.	29	M	LABR	RR	ADBQ	NY
HILLPOND, MORRIS	30	M	LABR	RR	ADBQ	NY
KINSKY, SAM.L.	39	M	LABR	RR	ACBF	NY
GJUCKA, MORETZ	21	M	LABR	RR	ACBF	NY
JOSEPH	11	M	CH	RR	ACBF	NY
MARKSOHN, JOS.	17	M	LABR	RR	ACBF	NY
MINARSKY, BENG.	19	M	LABR	RR	ACBF	NY
SCLONDE, JULIAN	22	M	LABR	RR	ACBF	NY
LAMMER, AUGUST	24	M	LABR	RR	ACBF	NY
KURY, OTTO	24	M	LABR	RR	ACBF	NY
CHODOROWSKY, JON	26	M	LABR	RR	ACBF	NY
STLENDON, MOSES	20	M	LABR	RR	ACBF	NY
GINSTEVE, DIERO	38	M	LABR	RR	ACBF	CH
KOPPE, JERI	20	M	LABR	RR	ACBF	NY
ROSENHAUS, ABRAH	43	M	LABR	RR	ACBF	NY
OLSEN, LAURETZ	46	M	LABR	RR	ACBF	CH
AGESSIN, JOHAMES	29	M	LABR	RR	ACBF	CH
LYGESSON, AUGUST	19	M	LABR	RR	ACBF	NY
AUESSON, HANS	18	M	LABR	RR	ACBF	NY
MARK, CHRISTIN	19	M	LABR	RR	ACBF	MI
PETERSON, THEODOR	28	M	LABR	RR	ACBF	USA
WISCHNEWSKY, STANISL.	25	M	LABR	RR	ACBF	NY
KICEGESKY, ANTON	18	M	LABR	RR	ACBF	NY
WISCHENEWSKY, IGANT	22	M	LABR	RR	ACBF	NY
RODJETHNETUS, M.KRAIN	30	M	LABR	RR	ACBF	NY
KALYEWITZ, JOHAN	21	M	LABR	RR	ACBF	NY
THOMAS, ADAM	22	M	LABR	RR	ACBF	NY
DREWEKEWITZ, MARTIN	25	M	LABR	RR	ACBF	NY
WASKEITZ, JELIX	26	M	LABR	RR	ACBF	NY
LUKASCHEVITZ, ANDR.	28	M	LABR	RR	ACBF	NY
SHAWECKIS, JOHAN	66	M	LABR	RR	ACBF	NY
LOSVUSKY, ALEXAND.	37	M	LABR	RR	ACBF	NY
ANGEHMIAETIS, BORUH	20	M	LABR	RR	ACBF	NY
MEKALEWITZ, LEISCH	37	M	LABR	RR	ACBF	NY

SHIP: REPUBLIC

FROM: LIVERPOOL AND QUEENSTOWN
TO: NEW YORK
ARRIVED: 31 MARCH 1888

PASSENGER	AGE	SEX	OCCUPATION	PRIV	VIL	DES
ANDRITICHY, JOHN	36	M	LABR	PL	ZZZZ	USA
KOSEWRITZHY, KALMAN	27	M	LABR	PL	ZZZZ	USA
BUANOPHY, CHONA	22	M	LABR	PL	ZZZZ	USA
KREUCLEMUS, DELINSTER	30	M	LABR	PL	ZZZZ	USA
BLANK, A.F.	22	M	LABR	PL	ZZZZ	USA
SHYOLD, JACOB	23	M	LABR	PL	ZZZZ	USA
BIOSK, ANDRES-E.	25	M	LABR	PL	ZZZZ	USA
FORSELL, IVAN-A.	20	M	LABR	PL	ZZZZ	USA
BERYASK, ERIK-B.	36	M	LABR	PL	ZZZZ	USA
GIDMAN, JOHANZ	22	M	LABR	PL	ZZZZ	USA
LAUD, JOHAN	30	M	LABR	PL	ZZZZ	USA
JORNGOIST, AXEL	28	M	LABR	PL	ZZZZ	USA
NORDMAN, ISAK	43	M	LABR	PL	ZZZZ	USA
MAKAR, AUG.	20	M	LABR	PL	ZZZZ	USA
STANK, JOHN	38	M	LABR	PL	ZZZZ	USA
NORDMAN, AUG.	39	M	LABR	PL	ZZZZ	USA
RUSK, CHARLES	38	M	LABR	PL	ZZZZ	USA
FRANZ, AUG.	23	M	LABR	PL	ZZZZ	USA

PASSENGER	AGE	SEX	OCCUPATION	PRV VIL DES
PNITAK, MARIA	18	F	SP	PLZZZZUSA
HERRAMANN, MOSES	23	M	LABR	PLZZZZUSA
-EIFER, MOSES	29	M	LABR	PLZZZZUSA
RACHEL	29	F	W	PLZZZZUSA
JULIA	7	F	CHILD	PLZZZZUSA
JOSEPH	3	M	CHILD	PLZZZZUSA
NOWISKY, MATHIAS	32	M	LABR	PLZZZZUSA
REIZMER	29	M	LABR	PLZZZZUSA
FRANCESKA	26	F	W	PLZZZZUSA
VERONIKA	1	F	CHILD	PLZZZZUSA
ROSALIA	1	F	CHILD	PLZZZZUSA
KALITA, ELIZABETH	17	F	SVNT	PLZZZZUSA
VISSBERG, JACOB	18	M	LABR	PLZZZZUSA
MOSYEKOWITZ, JACOB	20	M	LABR	PLZZZZUSA
MILHSTEIN, MARCUS	24	M	LABR	PLZZZZUSA
ISSLER, ISAK	17	M	LABR	PLZZZZUSA
GEIGER, MOSES	22	M	LABR	PLZZZZUSA
PARTNOG, BEER	33	M	LABR	PLZZZZUSA
FENKLER, CHARGI	50	F	SVNT	PLZZZZUSA
FRIEDLAND, PESCHS	28	F	W	PLZZZZUSA
MOSCHKE	5	F	CHILD	PLZZZZUSA
KIRSCHLER	1	F	CHILD	PLZZZZUSA
MIEROWITZ, DAVID	10	M	CH	PLZZZZUSA
SKORN, LEA	20	F	SVNT	PLZZZZUSA
MIZIEKIS, ITE	28	F	W	PLZZZZUSA
CHARGI	5	F	CHILD	PLZZZZUSA
SORE	3	F	CHILD	PLZZZZUSA
OLSCHEWSKY, HENERITTE	28	F	W	PLZZZZUSA
WILHELMINA	3	F	CHILD	PLZZZZUSA
HENRIETTA	2	F	CHILD	PLZZZZUSA
PAUL	1	M	CHILD	PLZZZZUSA
MASCHLAWSKI, SCHLOME	23	M	LABR	PLZZZZUSA
GORKA, MICHAEL	28	M	LABR	PLZZZZUSA
KILIGORA, MICHAEL	30	M	LABR	PLZZZZUSA
UGOSKI, ABRAHAM	33	M	LABR	PLZZZZUSA
UKRENSKI, ISAK	18	M	LABR	PLZZZZUSA
DZIEBZIEK, VINCENTY	45	M	LABR	PLZZZZUSA
LOPALA, MARCIN	45	M	LABR	PLZZZZUSA
GRESIUS, ADELINA	22	F	SVNT	PLZZZZUSA
WEPFLI, JACOB	24	M	LABR	PLZZZZUSA

SHIP: CITY OF BERLIN

FROM: LIVERPOOL
TO: NEW YORK
ARRIVED: 31 MARCH 1888

PASSENGER	AGE	SEX	OCCUPATION	PRV VIL DES
DENLONSKI, FRANCYSKI	30	M	PDLR	PLAFWJNY
BLONKOUSKI, JAN	45	M	LABR	PLAFWJNY
WAISCHULTZ, JAN	28	M	LABR	PLAFWJNY
CHOWKIN, ISRAIL	25	M	TLR	PLACBFNY
HOLDURE, MAH	11	M	CH	PLACBFNY
BRONBERG, ABM.	25	M	LABR	PLACBFNY
GRUNES, SCHUM.	25	M	UNKNOWN	PLAFWJNY
LESCHWITZ, ARON	00	M	UNKNOWN	PLACBFPHI
ITZIG	8	M	CHILD	PLACBFPHI
KORSKA, GEO.	19	M	LABR	PLACBFNY
KAS, MENDEL	22	M	W	PLACBFNY
PROWZINER, CHIGE	22	M	LABR	PLACBFNY
ROTHBAUR, B.	35	M	W	PLACBFNY
LEIB	9	M	CHILD	PLACBFNY
HANA	7	F	CHILD	PLACBFNY
FINKILATEN, SISSEL	34	F	W	PLACBFNY
FRADEL	9	M	CHILD	PLACBFNY
GISILA	6	F	CHILD	PLACBFNY
KOHN, SOMDEL	44	M	TLR	PLACBFNY
EMMI	11	F	CH	PLACBFNY
BINDER, ML.	28	M	LABR	PLACBFNY
KOWITZ, BETTY	18	F	SVNT	PLACBFNY
BERNSTUNS, JOS	32	M	LABR	PLACBFNY
SCHUNDEL	21	F	W	PLACBFNY
BERL	00	M	INF	PLACBFNY
EISENBERG, CHAIJE	40	M	LABR	PLACBFNY
LEIB	18	F	SVNT	PLACBFNY
NACHOME	11	M	CH	PLACBFNY

SHIP: FULDA

FROM: BREMEN AND SOUTHAMPTON
TO: NEW YORK
ARRIVED: 31 MARCH 1888

PASSENGER	AGE	SEX	OCCUPATION	PRV VIL DES
GOLDSTEIN, LORE	28	M	LABR	RRZZZZUSA
ESTER	7	F	CHILD	RRZZZZUSA
NUEW	6	M	CHILD	RRZZZZUSA
HELENE	.04	F	INFANT	RRZZZZUSA
SHEMAN, GOLDE	28	M	PDLR	RRZZZZUSA
SEISER	14	M	LABR	RRZZZZUSA
SOSETE	7	M	CHILD	RRZZZZUSA
REBECCA	4	F	CHILD	RRZZZZUSA
ISKE	2	M	CHILD	RRZZZZUSA
SCHOLL, JACOB	27	M	BTMK	RRZZZZUSA
GRUENEWALD, BARBARA	25	F	UNKNOWN	RRZZZZUSA
MAZERER, KATHARINA	26	F	UNKNOWN	RRZZZZUSA
WERNER, FRANZ	25	M	PNTR	RRZZZZUSA
ROSENBERG, ISAAC	16	M	MCHT	RRZZZZUSA
WACKER, ANNA	23	F	UNKNOWN	RRZZZZUSA
BORCHERING, H.	21	M	PNTR	RRZZZZUSA
STREITMANN, LISETTE	23	F	UNKNOWN	RRZZZZUSA
PFANNEBECKER, BARBARA	22	F	UNKNOWN	RRZZZZUSA
FITTING, PHILIPP	54	M	FARMER	RRZZZZUSA
MARHARETHE	29	F	UNKNOWN	RRZZZZUSA
FETTING, CHRISTIAN	22	M	LABR	RRZZZZUSA
HEINRICH	15	M	LABR	RRZZZZUSA
KRANZ, SYBILLA	16	F	UNKNOWN	RRZZZZUSA
ZENBARKI, JOHANN	26	M	FARMER	RRZZZZUSA
JULIANNA	20	F	UNKNOWN	RRZZZZUSA
BELZER, MARTIN	26	M	FARMER	RRZZZZUSA
KAIER, JOSEPH	26	M	FARMER	RRZZZZUSA
LANG, CATHARINE	20	F	UNKNOWN	RRZZZZUSA
BOLINGER, MARY	22	F	UNKNOWN	RRZZZZUSA
EISEMANN, HEINRICH	24	M	CPTR	RRZZZZUSA
MESSER, MARIE	23	F	UNKNOWN	RRZZZZUSA
SCHOEFER, BERTHA	22	F	UNKNOWN	RRZZZZUSA
HERMANN	16	M	LABR	RRZZZZUSA
GOGEL, CAROLINE	22	F	UNKNOWN	RRZZZZUSA
SPERR, JOHANN	26	M	FARMER	RRZZZZUSA
KOENIG, JACOB	26	M	FARMER	RRZZZZUSA
HAEFNER, CHRISTIAN	27	M	FARMER	RRZZZZUSA
LEMER, MARIE	21	F	UNKNOWN	RRZZZZUSA
EJEKTER, FRIEDRICH	18	M	BCHR	RRZZZZUSA
SCHLEGEL, JACOB	15	M	LABR	RRZZZZUSA
STOLTZ, CHRISTIAN	16	M	LABR	RRZZZZUSA
MUENEBINGER, WILHELM	14	M	LABR	RRZZZZUSA
HEIDELBERGER, JULIUS	16	M	FARMER	RRZZZZUSA
ROTHLAGE, ELISE	20	F	UNKNOWN	RRZZZZUSA
LUEBKEN, LESETTE	36	F	UNKNOWN	RRZZZZUSA
PLETSCH, CAROLINE	18	F	UNKNOWN	RRZZZZUSA
JOHANNES	15	M	FARMER	RRZZZZUSA
GAUCH, HENRY	17	M	FARMER	RRZZZZUSA
PFAFF, KATHARINA	21	F	UNKNOWN	RRZZZZUSA
KAFERSTEIN, LISETTE	17	F	UNKNOWN	RRZZZZUSA
GRAEBNER, MARIE	14	F	UNKNOWN	RRZZZZUSA
VIERING, PAUL	18	M	LABR	RRZZZZUSA
WETTLAUFER, ELISE	15	F	UNKNOWN	RRZZZZUSA
BOCHULEIN, CONRAD	17	M	FARMER	RRZZZZUSA
WRAZDA, ROSA	14	F	UNKNOWN	RRZZZZUSA
GOTZ, ANNA	21	F	UNKNOWN	RRZZZZUSA
KRAUSE, GOTTLIEB	19	M	LABR	RRZZZZUSA
CAROLINE	58	F	UNKNOWN	RRZZZZUSA

PASSENGER	AGE	SEX	OCCUPATION	PRIV	VIL	DES
TUERPE, JOHANN	30	M	FARMER	RR	ZZZZ	USA
WILHELMINE	29	F	UNKNOWN	RR	ZZZZ	USA
ELSA	2	F	CHILD	RR	ZZZZ	USA
RICHARD	.09	M	INFANT	RR	ZZZZ	USA
SCHMIDT, CATHARINA	50	F	UNKNOWN	RR	ZZZZ	USA
CATHARINA	15	F	UNKNOWN	RR	ZZZZ	USA
GRAFENIA	8	F	CHILD	RR	ZZZZ	USA
STILLE	6	M	CHILD	RR	ZZZZ	USA
BENUS	5	M	CHILD	RR	ZZZZ	USA
STREIBERGER, XAVER	60	M	FARMER	RR	ZZZZ	USA
JOSEPHA	31	F	UNKNOWN	RR	ZZZZ	USA
JOHANN	8	M	CHILD	RR	ZZZZ	USA
XAVER	6	M	CHILD	RR	ZZZZ	USA
BERNHARDINE	2	F	CHILD	RR	ZZZZ	USA
KRAFT, THERESIA	24	F	UNKNOWN	RR	ZZZZ	USA
BORNBACHER, LEO	37	M	FARMER	RR	ZZZZ	USA
SCHULEIN, JOHANN	48	M	FARMER	RR	ZZZZ	USA
MARGARETHA	48	F	UNKNOWN	RR	ZZZZ	USA
ELBINGER, JOHANN	24	M	JNR	RR	ZZZZ	USA
SCHUELEIN, JOHANN	7	M	CHILD	RR	ZZZZ	USA
WILHELMINE	7	F	CHILD	RR	ZZZZ	USA
SOPHIE	8	F	CHILD	RR	ZZZZ	USA
LUDWIG	5	M	CHILD	RR	ZZZZ	USA
SOBKOWIAK, FRANZ	28	M	LABR	RR	ZZZZ	USA
MUEHLMICHL, GEORG	30	M	LABR	RR	ZZZZ	USA
BARBARA	25	F	UNKNOWN	RR	ZZZZ	USA
MICHAEL	.04	M	INFANT	RR	ZZZZ	USA
GEISSLER, JOHANN	23	M	FARMER	RR	ZZZZ	USA
KELLER, MARGARETHA	24	F	UNKNOWN	RR	ZZZZ	USA
KATHARINA	.06	F	INFANT	RR	ZZZZ	USA
JURZ, AUGUST	59	M	PNTR	RR	ZZZZ	USA
KUNIGUNDE	46	F	UNKNOWN	RR	ZZZZ	USA
JOHANN	19	M	LABR	RR	ZZZZ	USA
FRIEDRICH	16	M	LABR	RR	ZZZZ	USA
JOHANN	8	M	CHILD	RR	ZZZZ	USA
BARBARA	6	F	CHILD	RR	ZZZZ	USA
MARIA	4	F	CHILD	RR	ZZZZ	USA
SAYER, JOHANN	24	M	FARMER	RR	ZZZZ	USA
STIEGELMICHL, MARIANNE	20	F	UNKNOWN	RR	ZZZZ	USA
CHRISTEL, KATHARINA	16	F	UNKNOWN	RR	ZZZZ	USA
ZIEGLER, CASPER	26	M	FARMER	RR	ZZZZ	USA
KOEGLER, KUNIGUNDE	22	F	UNKNOWN	RR	ZZZZ	USA
JOHANN	.09	M	INFANT	RR	ZZZZ	USA
SCHLUCK, KASPAR	41	M	LABR	RR	ZZZZ	USA
VAMIAN	16	M	LABR	RR	ZZZZ	USA
HOFFMANN, JOSEF	26	M	FARMER	RR	ZZZZ	USA
LANDWEHR, GENOFEVA	25	F	UNKNOWN	RR	ZZZZ	USA
ZABERCK, FRANZ	32	M	GDNR	RR	ZZZZ	USA
THERESIA	30	F	UNKNOWN	RR	ZZZZ	USA
BERNHARD	3	M	CHILD	RR	ZZZZ	USA
THERESIA	.09	F	INFANT	RR	ZZZZ	USA
GANSS, JEAN	27	M	FARMER	RR	ZZZZ	USA
DREISSIGACKER, WILH.	24	M	FARMER	RR	ZZZZ	USA
MERRER, JOSEF	24	M	FARMER	RR	ZZZZ	USA
PLIDWINSKY, JOSEF	20	M	LABR	RR	ZZZZ	USA
BIEMIWICZ, THOMAS	17	M	LABR	RR	ZZZZ	USA
KLEBS, MARIE	24	F	UNKNOWN	RR	ZZZZ	USA
LOUISE	23	F	UNKNOWN	RR	ZZZZ	USA
KOZINSKY, JAN	20	M	LABR	RR	ZZZZ	USA
ZIELINSLY, SIGMUND	29	M	LABR	RR	ZZZZ	USA
MIZKIWICZ, VINCENT	23	M	LABR	RR	ZZZZ	USA
MALSKY, ZAN	24	M	LABR	RR	ZZZZ	USA
PRISSMANN, E.	38	M	LABR	RR	ZZZZ	USA
RETSCHEL	26	F	UNKNOWN	RR	ZZZZ	USA
ZEBSCHINSKY, JAN	45	M	BKR	RR	ZZZZ	USA
OSTROWSKY, WOJCIECH	37	M	LABR	RR	ZZZZ	USA
ZASLAWY, FRANZ	26	M	LABR	RR	ZZZZ	USA
LASKOWSKY, PITRO	31	M	LABR	RR	ZZZZ	USA
GRUDZINSKY, FRANZ	33	M	LABR	RR	ZZZZ	USA
TOMSKY, MARIAN	26	M	LABR	RR	ZZZZ	USA
STECHOWITZ, JAN	30	M	FARMER	RR	ZZZZ	USA
DALZ, MICHAEL	25	M	FARMER	RR	ZZZZ	USA
WESICKI, IGNATS	22	M	FARMER	RR	ZZZZ	USA
SZEMION, ANTOIN	32	M	LABR	RR	ZZZZ	USA
SZYMLEWSKI, JOSEF	25	M	LABR	RR	ZZZZ	USA
FEROMSKI, ANTONI	28	M	LABR	RR	ZZZZ	USA
PAWLOWSKY, MARJAN	31	M	LABR	RR	ZZZZ	USA
REINOW, WILLIAM	25	M	LABR	RR	ZZZZ	USA
EVA	25	F	UNKNOWN	RR	ZZZZ	USA
KOSEWSKI, STANISLAUS	40	M	LABR	RR	ZZZZ	USA
LUBISCH, DAVID	46	M	LABR	RR	ZZZZ	USA
ROTUSIUK, SAMUEL	22	M	LABR	RR	ZZZZ	USA
JANGROLSKY, ISAAK	39	M	LABR	RR	ZZZZ	USA
JANPOLSKY, LUBA	17	F	UNKNOWN	RR	ZZZZ	USA
PASCHE	6	F	CHILD	RR	ZZZZ	USA
BRUSTEIN, MERGER	25	M	PDLR	RR	ZZZZ	USA
DUBE	22	F	UNKNOWN	RR	ZZZZ	USA
WISACKY, WECENTY	29	M	LABR	RR	ZZZZ	USA
RUDNICKY, MAEIN	31	M	LABR	RR	ZZZZ	USA
FELDMANN, GOTTLIEB	29	M	LABR	RR	ZZZZ	USA
MACKIEWITZ, JAN	22	M	LABR	RR	ZZZZ	USA
ZIBLOWSKY, ANTONI	35	M	LABR	RR	ZZZZ	USA
JUSADOWSKY, FRANZ	37	M	LABR	RR	ZZZZ	USA
BURTZINSKY, JOSEF	31	M	LABR	RR	ZZZZ	USA
SADOWSKY, PIOTR	37	M	LABR	RR	ZZZZ	USA
WACZKIEWICZ, JOSEF	37	M	LABR	RR	ZZZZ	USA
SANDROWSKY, MARIAN	30	M	LABR	RR	ZZZZ	USA
SADOWSKY, FAKOB	34	M	LABR	RR	ZZZZ	USA
LEON, GOTTLIEB	29	M	LABR	RR	ZZZZ	USA
SARELANIEN, WILHELM	37	M	LABR	RR	ZZZZ	USA
PAPOLA, ANDREAS	33	M	LABR	RR	ZZZZ	USA
PISCHLER, MARTIN	42	M	LABR	RR	ZZZZ	USA
STEPHAN, AUGUST	22	M	LABR	RR	ZZZZ	USA
WESTERGAARD, ELLEN	17	F	FARMER	RR	ZZZZ	USA
ROSSEN, MARIA	20	F	FARMER	RR	ZZZZ	USA
SCHMIDT, PETER	15	M	FARMER	RR	ZZZZ	USA
JECHL, ANNA	16	F	UNKNOWN	RR	ZZZZ	USA
JEMEN, HANS	20	M	FARMER	RR	ZZZZ	USA
WELINSKY, EFRAIM	30	M	LABR	RR	ZZZZ	USA
RICHTER, ERNST	40	M	FARMER	RR	ZZZZ	USA

SHIP: PAVONIA

FROM: LIVERPOOL AND QUEENSTOWN
TO: BOSTON
ARRIVED: LW UNKNOWN Y AN

PASSENGER	AGE	SEX	OCCUPATION	PRIV	VIL	DES
KOPROWSKY, JEAN	28	M	LABR	RR	ZZZZ	NY
BETENAS, CARL	24	M	LABR	RR	ZZZZ	WI
NORWICH, JULIUS	28	M	FARMER	RR	ZZZZ	NY
SPRUZSTGLI--, IM---	25	M	LABR	RR	ZZZZ	NY
DEMBOUSKY, JOSEF	35	M	TLR	RR	ZZZZ	NY
WISOCHI, STANILAUS	22	M	LABR	RR	ZZZZ	NY
HOLTZ, HAIM	26	M	PDLR	RR	ZZZZ	NY
CHAIME, MOSES	24	M	PDLR	RR	ZZZZ	NY
SCHIMELEWITTZ, MOSES	25	M	JWLR	RR	ZZZZ	BO
JAKISI--N, JOH	37	M	LABR	FN	ZZZZ	MA
WERONON, NIKODEMUS	19	M	LABR	FN	ZZZZ	MA
KANGAS, KAW	25	M	LABR	FN	ZZZZ	MA
KLYMA, ISAK	42	M	LABR	FN	ZZZZ	MA
SANKKO, H-KKE	30	M	LABR	FN	ZZZZ	MA
ARMALA, KANS	36	M	GCR	FN	ZZZZ	MA
ESSELSTROM, AXEL	36	M	FARMER	FN	ZZZZ	CAN
-AURICKI, STAN	18	M	LABR	PL	ZZZZ	NY
PUREZIPKI, BRONI-LA-	20	M	LABR	PL	ZZZZ	NY
STATHWITZ, FRANCISCA	30	F	SP	PL	ZZZZ	NY
SUPO, THOS	35	M	LABR	FN	ZZZZ	MA
SUSANNA	36	F	W	FN	ZZZZ	MA
HANNA	10	M	CH	FN	ZZZZ	MA
OLIGA-SKI, KATE	28	F	MA	FN	ZZZZ	BO
HANNA	6	F	CHILD	FN	ZZZZ	BO
PAKKINSON, ANTI	30	F	SP	FN	ZZZZ	CAN
KARTALA, JAKKA	38	F	MA	FN	ZZZZ	MA
JUSSERUPOKKA, KUSTA	36	F	MA	FN	ZZZZ	CAN

SHIP: DEVONIA

FROM: GLASGOW
TO: NEW YORK
ARRIVED: 02 APRIL 1888

PASSENGER	AGE	SEX	OCCUPATION	PRV VIL DES
LAPUK, LIEB	24	M	LABR	FNACBFUSA
PESSE	18	F	NN	FNACBFUSA
JARUS, ANNA	20	F	HSMD	FNACBFUSA
ANDRE-IK, AUGUST	30	M	LABR	FNACBFUSA
BICK---, JAN	40	M	LABR	FNACBFUSA
BRADMIS, JEGER	22	M	LABR	FNACBFUSA
BRUEGER, SIMON	33	M	TLR	FNACBFUSA
BERIL, MISHEL	35	M	LABR	FNACBFUSA
BESSEL, AUGUST	25	M	LABR	FNACBFUSA
DOLIS, HEINRICH	45	M	LABR	FNACBFUSA
FRIEDMAN, JAKOB	37	M	DSTLR	FNACBFUSA
GODES, BE-E	38	M	TLR	FNACBFUSA
ME-Z	8	M	CHILD	FNACBFUSA
FAIL	6	M	CHILD	FNACBFUSA
GALOCO, JOSEF	37	M	LABR	FNACBFUSA
GORSKI, STANISLAW	26	M	LABR	FNACBFUSA
GOLSCHINSKI, AULEK	28	M	LABR	FNACBFUSA
-ISHINSKI, STAN	41	M	LABR	FNACBFUSA
DRI--ILSKI, JOSEF	17	M	LABR	FNACBFUSA
BLASCHKEWICZ, JEAN	48	M	LABR	FNACBFUSA
ANTON	9	M	CHILD	FNACBFUSA
GOLOMBESKI, ANTON	30	M	CH	FNACBFUSA
GAVERSCHEWITZ, MARZIAN	30	M	BTMKR	FNACBFUSA
STANKIEWIEZ, CONSTAN	26	M	GDNR	FNACBFUSA
JANOWITZ, DOMK	19	M	LABR	FNACBFUSA
JUSELINSKI, PIOLI	41	M	LABR	FNACBFUSA
KNIDER, ADAM	23	M	LABR	FNACBFUSA
KOSCIELNIAK, MICHAEL	27	M	LABR	FNACBFUSA
KOROLEWITZ, FRAN	23	M	LABR	FNACBFUSA
KRZNIRSKY, ANDREI	23	M	LABR	FNACBFUSA
KASARSKI, JOSEF	27	M	LABR	FNACBFUSA
KONGENDHSKY, SE-DER	14	M	LABR	FNACBFUSA
LANG, JAKOB	29	M	LABR	FNACBFUSA
LUDKE, JOHN	40	M	LABR	FNACBFUSA
DO-MAN, JNO	24	M	PLSTR	FNAIDLUSA
DOUGHERTY, JAS	21	M	TLR	FNAIDLUSA
SHOTH, KAROL	36	M	LABR	FNACBFUSA
STANKIEWITZ, FELIX	30	M	LABR	FNACBFUSA
STANINSKI, MA-IS	24	M	LABR	FNACBFUSA
S-LOW-ZICK, JELIG	24	M	LABR	FNACBFUSA
SKIZINSKI, ANDREAS	38	M	LABR	FNACBFUSA
LUDWIG	18	M	LABR	FNACBFUSA
ALVIN	24	M	LABR	FNACBFUSA
JANKIEWITZ, JAN	28	M	LABR	FNACBFUSA
TOMASZEWSKI, JAN	28	M	LABR	FNACBFUSA
WISCHLINSKI, CARUL	24	M	BTMKR	FNACBFUSA
WI-TIZENSKY, JURKRAUS	22	M	LABR	FNACBFUSA
ZANRULEWITZ, JAN	28	M	LABR	FNACBFUSA

SHIP: MORAVIA

FROM: HAMBURG AND HAVRE
TO: NEW YORK
ARRIVED: 02 APRIL 1888

PASSENGER	AGE	SEX	OCCUPATION	PRV VIL DES
TYKARSKI, JOSEF	25	M	LABR	RRZZZZUSA
KUEHN, LEOPOLD	48	M	LABR	RRZZZZUSA
URMANA-, LEOPOLD	28	M	LABR	RRZZZZUSA
ZAKRZEWSKI, FRANZ	25	M	LABR	RRAIHHUSA
KETERSEN, DORA	20	F	SGL	RRAFVGUSA
BOJENSKI, JOSEPH	18	M	LABR	RRZZZZUSA
MATUSZEWSKI, ROMAN	38	M	LABR	RRZZZZUSA
PETERSEN, PETER	17	M	FARMER	RRZZZZUSA
ANDRESEN, HANS	16	M	FARMER	RRZZZZUSA
SKINJELEWSKI, MARIAN	35	M	LABR	RRZZZZUSA
S--LINSKI, VINC	30	M	LABR	RRZZZZUSA
SLAVINSKI, JAN	24	M	LABR	RRZZZZUSA
GRIESASKI, FRANZ	22	M	LABR	RRZZZZUSA
ARASCHIN, FRANZ	30	M	LABR	RRZZZZUSA
JADEROWSKI, STANISL	25	M	LABR	RRZZZZUSA
KLIMAS, JOSEF	18	M	LABR	RRZZZZUSA
---WINZKI, GUST	30	M	LABR	RRZZZZUSA
MONT-YMOWICZ, IGNATZ	19	M	LABR	RRAHTFUSA
ANTONI	30	M	LABR	RRAHTFUSA
GABLONSKY, ANTON	23	M	LABR	RRZZZZUSA
WALOKOWSKA, FRANZISKA	20	F	SGL	RRZZZZUSA
WITKOWSKI, JACOB	19	M	LABR	RRAINVUSA
BROKOWSKI, VICENTY	19	M	LABR	RRAINUUSA
CHORNECZKI, VALENTY	23	M	LABR	RRZZZZUSA
-OZAMKI, VALENTY	25	M	LABR	RRAINVUSA
ZOTNOWSKI, MICHAL	40	M	LABR	RRAINVUSA
WASILANKAS, SYLVESTER	19	M	LABR	RRZZZZUSA
BREZENSKI, PETER	29	M	LABR	RRAHUIUSA
RIBINSKY, VALENTIN	19	M	LABR	RRAHUIUSA
WENZKEWITZ, WIZENTI	34	M	LABR	RRZZZZUSA
MARGR	23	F	W	RRZZZZUSA
ANNA	3	F	CHILD	RRZZZZUSA
OSSIP	.11	M	INFANT	RRZZZZUSA
KLIMOWITZ, ISCHATI	21	M	LABR	RRZZZZUSA
SINKEWITZ, OSSIP	19	M	LABR	RRZZZZUSA
RADWILEWICZ, MARTIN	28	M	LABR	RRZZZZUSA
GRABOWSKI, ALEXANDER	27	M	LABR	RRZZZZUSA
SZKLAR, SELIG	32	M	LABR	RRAIAVUSA
-ITLER, KALMEN	30	M	LABR	RRZZZZUSA
BEMERT, MARTIN	33	M	LABR	RRZZZZUSA
KATZONAS, IGNATZ	25	M	LABR	RRZZZZUSA
MAGDALENA	18	F	W	RRZZZZUSA
SCHWALA, HERZ	19	M	LABR	RRZZZZUSA
BIRG, SCHLOME	19	M	LABR	RRZZZZUSA
BENJAMIN	23	M	LABR	RRZZZZUSA
GALLIS, MARIUS	37	M	LABR	RRZZZZUSA
WIEMANN, ISAAC	35	M	DLR	RRZZZZUSA
DASCHE	19	F	W	RRZZZZUSA
SZYKODA, LUDWIG	26	M	LABR	RRZZZZUSA
WALIZAK, JOSEF	33	M	LABR	RRAIFXUSA
BAZANSKI, JACOB	26	M	LABR	RRZZZZUSA
SZUDTA, JAN	26	M	LABR	RRZZZZUSA
TUTZ, JOSEF	42	M	LABR	RRZZZZUSA
SOJKO, KARL	42	M	LABR	RRZZZZUSA
SZCZECH, JOSEF	33	M	LABR	RRZZZZUSA
PLEWA, JOSEF	25	M	LABR	RRZZZZUSA
GRUSZKA, PIOTR	23	M	LABR	RRZZZZUSA
HENZI--, WOJECIECH	27	M	LABR	RRZZZZUSA
PITOMAK, PHILIPP	38	M	LABR	RRZZZZUSA
JOHANNSEN, ALEXANDER	24	M	SMH	FNZZZZUSA
PERLIN, GEZEL	22	M	LABR	FNAHUIUSA
RITSCHKER, JACOB	33	M	LABR	RRZZZZUSA
KANZLER, STANISL	21	M	LABR	RRZZZZUSA
GIBITZKI, WLADISL	25	M	LABR	RRZZZZUSA
ANDR	30	M	LABR	RRZZZZUSA
DOMBROWSKI, ISAAC	21	M	LABR	RRZZZZUSA
STANISL	31	M	LABR	RRZZZZUSA
FRIEDRICH, FRANZ	26	M	LABR	RRZZZZUSA
MESKEWITZ, CONST	27	M	LABR	RRZZZZUSA
SUMCZACHI, JAN	28	M	LABR	RRAHUIUSA
GONSEROWSKI, BARTOLOMEU	24	M	LABR	RRAHUIUSA
MAGALSKI, JAN	20	M	LABR	RRAHUIUSA
KOWADSKI, MICHAL	29	M	LABR	RRZZZZUSA
MILEWSKY, NICODEM	54	M	LABR	RRAHUIUSA
SCZISZENSKY, SEWERIN	47	M	LABR	RRAHUIUSA
-ENEWSKY, EMILIE	20	F	W	RRZZZZUSA
-ILIPOWICZ, TEKLA	17	F	SGL	RRZZZZUSA
KSIAZKIAWICZ, VINCENTY	25	M	BRR	RRZZZZUSA
BARTEN, CARL	21	M	LABR	RRAHUIUSA
ZIEL, FRIEDRICH	24	M	LABR	RRAHUIUSA
MEYER, ADAM	25	M	LABR	RRAHUIUSA
RUBSCHAS	27	M	LABR	RRAHUIUSA
NARKAS, FRANZ	26	M	LABR	RRZZZZUSA

PASSENGER	AGE	SEX	OCCUPATION	PRIV	VIL	DES
WITKOWSKI, HEINR	32	M	LABR	RR	ZZZZ	USA
DAMILEWITZ, ANTON	32	M	LABR	RR	AEFL	USA
ZIELENSKI, SIMON	37	M	LABR	RR	ZZZZ	USA
CHMIELEWSKI, IGNATZ	28	M	LABR	RR	ZZZZ	USA
KRAJEWSKI, VA-LAW	35	M	LABR	RR	AHUL	USA
KANOPACKI, ANDRZEJ	30	M	LABR	RR	ZZZZ	USA
ZIELEWSKI, JOSEF	23	M	LABR	RR	ZZZZ	USA
ZELINSKI, MICHAEL	25	M	LABR	RR	AHUI	USA
K-EINOWSKI, ARCHELAUS	29	M	LABR	RR	AHUI	USA
GARDETZKI, FRANZ	20	M	LABR	RR	AHUI	USA
GRABOWSKI, -AOWEL	42	M	LABR	RR	AHUI	USA
BIBSCHINSKI, BO-N-ATZI	35	M	LABR	RR	AHUI	USA
HOFFMANN, LUDWIG	23	M	LABR	RR	AHUI	USA
BAAR, JOH	27	M	LABR	RR	AHUI	USA
SHERP, WILH	37	M	LABR	RR	AHUI	USA
ADAMOWICZ, KASIMIR	34	M	LABR	RR	AHUI	USA
CZACK, JAN	26	M	LABR	RR	AHUI	USA
PASICK, JOSEF	30	M	LABR	RR	AHUI	USA
PIACZEK, STANISL	36	M	LABR	RR	AHUI	USA
-IONKA, MICHAEL	23	M	LABR	RR	AHUI	USA
BURSTEIN, LEISEV	49	M	DLR	RR	AFVG	USA
POSCHIKOWITZ, JURGENS	21	M	LABR	RR	ZZZZ	USA
WILKENT, BJEDSCHI	22	M	LABR	RR	ZZZZ	USA
NARKEM	20	M	LABR	RR	ZZZZ	USA
LAJESKY, CHRISTIAN	36	M	LABR	RR	AHUI	USA
GOGOLIN, JAN	30	M	LABR	RR	AHUI	USA
GERLACH, CARL	25	M	LABR	RR	AHUI	USA
CAROLINE	30	F	W	RR	AHUI	USA
PESTA, JAN	44	M	LABR	RR	AHUI	USA
BEHNCKE, AUGUST	35	M	LABR	RR	AHUI	USA
-INDRIJEWSKY, ADAM	43	M	LABR	RR	AHUI	USA
BEHNCKE, MICHAEL	37	M	LABR	RR	AHUI	USA
STREISSMANN, STANISL	26	M	LABR	RR	AHUI	USA
STEIN, ABRAHAM	27	M	LABR	RR	ZZZZ	USA
BRATZKY, ALEX	18	M	LABR	RR	AIOH	USA
GRONDAT, AUGUST	42	M	UNKNOWN	RR	ZZZZ	USA
ANNA	14	F	D	RR	ZZZZ	USA
POWNKIEWI--, CONSTANTIN	26	M	LABR	RR	ZZZZ	USA
-E-NZALSKI, ANTON	27	M	LABR	RR	ZZZZ	USA
KAR-ASZEWSKI, ANDR	36	M	LABR	RR	ZZZZ	USA

SHIP: TRAVE

FROM: BREMEN AND SOUTHAMPTON
TO: NEW YORK
ARRIVED: 02 APRIL 1888

PASSENGER	AGE	SEX	OCCUPATION	PRIV	VIL	DES
HOFFMANN, ADOLF	35	M	LABR	RR	ZZZZ	USA
NAWIZKI, KAZMIR	24	M	LABR	RR	ZZZZ	USA
JAWARSKA, MARIANNE	26	F	UNKNOWN	RR	ZZZZ	USA
MONMKOWIES, JOHANN	25	M	LABR	RR	ZZZZ	USA
GERRIETS, EDUARD	17	M	LABR	RR	ZZZZ	USA
MUEHLER, ADOLF	28	M	BKR	RR	ZZZZ	USA
BASINSKI, VALENTIN	18	M	FARMER	RR	ZZZZ	USA
WOHLERS, HEINRICH	24	M	FARMER	RR	ZZZZ	USA
HERMINE	21	F	UNKNOWN	RR	ZZZZ	USA
JOHANN	4	M	CHILD	RR	ZZZZ	USA
KUCH, ADAM	29	M	FARMER	RR	ZZZZ	USA
LOUISE	26	F	UNKNOWN	RR	ZZZZ	USA
HERMANN	.03	M	INFANT	RR	ZZZZ	USA
SCHUH, GOTTLIEB	26	M	CPTR	RR	ZZZZ	USA
VALENTINA	24	F	UNKNOWN	RR	ZZZZ	USA
URSULA	.02	F	INFANT	RR	ZZZZ	USA
HEREM, ANTON	18	M	CL	RR	ZZZZ	USA
BODER, CARL-L.	21	M	SMH	RR	ZZZZ	USA

SHIP: AURANIA

FROM: LIVERPOOL AND QUEENSTOWN
TO: NEW YORK
ARRIVED: 02 APRIL 1888

PASSENGER	AGE	SEX	OCCUPATION	PRIV	VIL	DES
GOBROWSKA, MARY	22	F	SP	RR	ZZZZ	NY
DUGOLO, PETER	19	M	LABR	RR	ZZZZ	NY
BOHSLER	17	M	LABR	RR	ZZZZ	NY
MARIANNA	19	F	SP	RR	ZZZZ	NY
SUDEKEWITZ, BALESLAW	38	M	LABR	RR	ZZZZ	NY
AGATE	17	F	SP	RR	ZZZZ	NY
BOGUSCHEWITZ, BALESLAW	34	M	LABR	RR	ZZZZ	NY

SHIP: ELBE

FROM: BREMEN AND SOUTHAMPTON
TO: NEW YORK
ARRIVED: 05 APRIL 1888

PASSENGER	AGE	SEX	OCCUPATION	PRIV	VIL	DES
WODAREZAK, PIOTR.	34	M	LABR	RR	ZZZZ	NY
GOOSSEN, HEINR.	49	M	FARMER	RR	ZZZZ	NY
ELISAB.	49	F	W	RR	ZZZZ	NY
HEINR.	23	M	FARMER	RR	ZZZZ	NY
PETER	13	M	CH	RR	ZZZZ	NY
JOHANNES	7	M	CHILD	RR	ZZZZ	NY
MARIE	17	F	SVNT	RR	ZZZZ	NY
U	15	F	CH	RR	ZZZZ	NY
ANNA	9	F	CHILD	RR	ZZZZ	NY
JEZEWSKY, FRANZ	23	M	LABR	RR	ZZZZ	NY
CZIZMOR, GEORGY	34	M	LABR	RR	ZZZZ	NY
PUCHALA, JOS.	17	M	LABR	RR	ZZZZ	NY
SCHELKE, ADOLPH	17	M	LABR	RR	ZZZZ	NY
PINSEKA, FRANZ	21	M	LABR	RR	ZZZZ	NY
DOSKA	24	F	W	RR	ZZZZ	NY
WLADISL.	.09	M	INFANT	RR	ZZZZ	NY
PINKALLA, ANDR.	25	M	LABR	RR	ZZZZ	NY
STANISL.	18	M	LABR	RR	ZZZZ	NY
KENNSKY, KASIM.	25	M	LABR	RR	ZZZZ	NY

SHIP: HERMANN

FROM: BREMEN
TO: BALTIMORE
ARRIVED: 06 APRIL 1888

PASSENGER	AGE	SEX	OCCUPATION	PRIV	VIL	DES
MARANA, JOHANN	25	M	LABR	RR	ZZZZ	MD
HARASZIM, MACEZ	30	M	DLR	RR	AFVG	MD
BLEIWEISS, MEYER	26	M	DLR	RR	AFVG	MD
BECKMANN, JOSSEL	40	M	DLR	RR	AFVG	MD
GRZADZILESKI, JAN	44	M	LABR	RR	AFVG	MD
MEYER, CHRISTIAN	16	M	UNKNOWN	RR	AFVG	MD
JOHANNES	4	M	CHILD	RR	AFVG	MD
FRANZ	26	M	LABR	RR	AFVG	MD
CATHARINA	32	F	W	RR	AFVG	MD
HANNES	1	M	CHILD	RR	AFVG	MD
FRANZ	1	M	CHILD	RR	AFVG	MD
KALEWA, STANISLAUS	22	M	UNKNOWN	RR	AHOO	MD
KUEZMARZKI, KOJETAN	28	M	LABR	RR	AHOO	MD
SPIESS, PETER	29	M	LABR	RR	AHOO	MD
CHRISTINE	28	F	W	RR	AHOO	MD
PETER	4	M	CHILD	RR	AHOO	MD
HAMER	2	M	CHILD	RR	AHOO	MD
THEKLA	.06	F	INFANT	RR	AHOO	MD

PASSENGER	AGE	SEX	OCCUPATION	PRV VIL DES
KLUKORSKI, RANVILDE	32	M	LABR	RRZZZZNY
ARANNOWSKI, JEAN	30	M	DLR	RRZZZZPA
ELIAS, WLADISLAUS	28	M	DLR	RRZZZZUNK
FLECK, WILH	46	F	UNKNOWN	RRAIFLUNK
DOROTHEA	16	F	UNKNOWN	RRAIFLUNK
JOHANNA	10	F	CH	RRAIFLUNK
RUEDZIR, MARDZAN	27	M	LABR	RRAIFLUNK
JANKOOWSKY, KAZMIR	23	M	LABR	RRAIFLUNK
SINNOWITZ, WLADISLAUS	25	M	LABR	RRAIFLUNK
EICHHORN, GEORG	41	M	LKSH	RRAIFLKS
KAOWSKI, ANDENZG	29	M	LABR	RRAINRMD
LEWANDOWSKY, THOMAS	33	M	LABR	RRAINRMD
STABSKY, VINCENT	35	M	LABR	RRAINRMD
MOCZKIEWIEZ, JOSEF	18	M	UNKNOWN	RRAINRMD
FOLK, CONRAD	49	M	LABR	RRAINRIL
BARBARA	44	F	W	RRAINRIL
FRANZ	18	M	LABR	RRAHOOIL
ANTON	11	M	CH	RRAHOOIL
MAGDALENA	9	F	CHILD	RRAHOOIL
PHILIPPINE	8	F	CHILD	RRAHOOIL
REGINE	4	F	CHILD	RRAHOOIL

SHIP: ENGLAND

FROM: LIVERPOOL AND QUEENSTOWN
TO: NEW YORK
ARRIVED: 06 APRIL 1888

PASSENGER	AGE	SEX	OCCUPATION	PRV VIL DES
DOBRONALSKI, LEOKADIA	26	F	SVNT	RRZZZZNY
UNGAR, ESH	17	F	SVNT	RRZZZZNY
SUIZEZANSKY, ANTON	38	M	LABR	RRZZZZNY
CECILE	26	F	W	RRZZZZNY
KOLENDO, STANIL	23	M	LABR	RRZZZZNY
KAMISKY, ALEX	26	M	LABR	RRZZZZNY
SKORUPA, JOSEF	27	M	LABR	RRZZZZNY
RUKSMTIS, JANS	25	M	LABR	RRZZZZNY
ZEGORSKY, SIMON	20	M	LABR	RRZZZZNY
JAN	27	M	LABR	RRZZZZNY
PAVEL, GREGOR	24	M	LABR	RRZZZZNY
PRAVDIK, JAN	26	M	LABR	RRZZZZNY
ZINCHWOUSKY, JOSEF	20	M	LABR	RRZZZZNY
WASHLEWSKY, MICH	24	M	LABR	RRZZZZNY
UNZLUSKY, VINCENT	28	M	LABR	RRZZZZNY
MALSCHMONSKY, VINC	37	M	LABR	RRZZZZNY
PITNOW, JACOB	27	M	LABR	RRZZZZNY
WISCHKOWSKY, ANTON	24	M	LABR	RRZZZZNY
GREUSENSKY, ADAM	35	M	LABR	RRZZZZNY
MIELOWSKY, FRANZ	44	M	LABR	RRZZZZNY
KASCHNOWSKY, FRANZ	25	M	LABR	RRZZZZNY
RAKONESKY, MICH	24	M	LABR	RRZZZZNY
MARIUS, USCHER	24	M	LABR	RRZZZZNY
PHEILER, JOSEPH	26	M	LABR	RRZZZZNY
ANDILIZKES, ENDRES	27	M	LABR	RRZZZZNY
SHEDER, FREDRIC	25	M	LABR	RRZZZZNY
MITZKOWSITZ, BALMES	25	M	LABR	RRZZZZNY
BLASIR, JOSEF	28	M	LABR	RRZZZZNY
BUBA, JUNIS	23	M	LABR	RRZZZZNY
ZEBULSKY, FEDOR	30	M	LABR	RRZZZZNY
RAPOLY, THOMAS	25	M	LABR	RRZZZZNY
PASKO, LUDWIG	25	M	LABR	RRZZZZNY
KUEIM, UNGAR	24	M	LABR	RRZZZZNY
ZIBULSKY, BOCHOW	26	M	LABR	RRZZZZNY
LUPA, ISAAC	48	M	LABR	RRZZZZNY
GOLDSTEIN, ABEL	18	M	LABR	RRZZZZNY
TABAKEVEITZ, RUBIN	35	M	LABR	RRZZZZPHI
MEISILEWSKY, KAS	24	M	LABR	RRZZZZNY
KIMMITIS, MATH	22	M	LABR	RRZZZZNY
MATSELEWSKY, CONST	23	M	LABR	RRZZZZNY

SHIP: GALLIA

FROM: LIVERPOOL AND QUEENSTOWN
TO: NEW YORK
ARRIVED: 07 APRIL 1888

PASSENGER	AGE	SEX	OCCUPATION	PRV VIL DES
ROSEN, JANKEL	26	M	LABR	RRACBFUSA
SCHENKEL	22	F	W	RRACBFUSA
KELE	21	F	SVNT	RRACBFUSA
SWORL	51	F	WI	RRACBFUSA
RAHEL	11	F	CH	RRACBFUSA
BALE	10	F	CH	RRACBFUSA
RESEL	8	F	CHILD	RRACBFUSA
ABRAHAM	6	M	CHILD	RRACBFUSA
MOSES	3	M	CHILD	RRACBFUSA
CHAIE	.04	F	INFANT	RRACBFUSA
SOKOLOWSKY, ANTON	46	M	LABR	RRACBFUSA
RIZOZOWSKI, VOCEDI	22	M	TLR	RRACBFUSA
LANGET, ELKE	28	F	SVNT	RRACBFUSA
LAWIN, NILS	20	M	FARMER	RRAGUZUSA
KARGRI, GUST	20	M	FARMER	RRAGUZUSA

SHIP: CITY OF CHESTER

FROM: LIVERPOOL AND QUEENSTOWN
TO: NEW YORK
ARRIVED: 07 APRIL 1888

PASSENGER	AGE	SEX	OCCUPATION	PRV VIL DES
GUSYEWIN, K	26	M	LABR	RRAFVGNY
SULO, JACOB	45	M	LABR	RRACBFNY
OLANSEN, ARB	24	M	LABR	RRZZZZWI
KURUSCH, FRANK	10	M	CH	RRACBFPA
FRANK	9	M	CHILD	RRACBFPA
GERE, MICHAEL	20	M	LABR	RRACBFMI
ZYDEK, JOSEF	47	M	LABR	RRACBFNY
KNISKERVILL, ANT	34	M	BKLYR	RRACBFUNK
PETERNOVIL, JOHN	44	M	BKLYR	RRACBFUNK
POEZTKER, THOMAS	26	M	LABR	RRACBFPA
MICHADCK, MALIY	26	M	LABR	RRACBFPA
PERICCZ, JOSEF	50	M	BKLYR	RRACBFUNK
DANTROVSKI, ADAM	36	M	LABR	RRACBFBRO
KOLTOW, BIMM	32	M	TLR	RRACBFNY
WIESNEWSKI, FRANZ	33	M	LABR	RRACBFBRO
RADZINSKI, WAYTEK	29	M	LABR	RRACBFBRO
DEMBIENSKI, FRANZ	29	M	LABR	RRACBFBRO
BRIZEZIMSKI, MAGDALENA	16	M	LABR	RRACBFNY
ROSENFELD, HEINR	30	M	BKR	RRADEDNY
SARAH	24	F	W	RRADEDNY

SHIP: CALIFORNIA

FROM: HAMBURG
TO: NEW YORK
ARRIVED: 09 APRIL 1888

PASSENGER	AGE	SEX	OCCUPATION	PRV VIL DES
ABRAMOWICZ, ALEXANDER	25	M	LABR	RRZZZZNY
BUDNIK, MARZI	30	M	LABR	RRZZZZNY
DULCINBO, MARIE	25	M	LABR	RRZZZZWI
SERETZKI, JOSEF	36	M	LABR	RRZZZZSFC
MARYANNE	30	F	W	RRZZZZSFC
STANISLAUS	8	M	CHILD	RRZZZZSFC
JOSEF	7	M	CHILD	RRZZZZSFC
STEFAN	11	M	INF	RRZZZZSFC
SOHYDLOWSKI, VICTOR	28	M	LABR	RRZZZZSFC

PASSENGER	AGE	SEX	OCCUPATION	PRIV	DES
SMOKOWSKI, JAN	44	M	LABR	RRZZZZ	SFC
SOERENSEN, SOEREN	20	M	FARMER	RRZZZZ	SFC
CARL	16	M	FARMER	RRZZZZ	SFC
NIELSEN, ISOER	15	M	FARMER	RRZZZZ	SFC
HULINOWSKI, ANTONI	20	M	LABR	RRZZZZ	UNK
CIESIELSKI, ANTON	34	M	LABR	RRZZZZ	UNK
SCHIKOWSKI, FRANCISZEK	18	M	LABR	RRZZZZ	NY
KOPIENSKI, JAN	20	M	LABR	RRZZZZ	NY
KRSYZIKOWSKI, JAN	19	M	LABR	RRZZZZ	NY
LESZYNSKI, SZEPAN	25	M	LABR	RRZZZZ	NY
JARSEMBOWSKI, JAN	19	M	LABR	RRZZZZ	NY
ZAWITOWSKI, JOSEF	26	M	LABR	RRZZZZ	NY
WINNIEWICZ, STANISL	26	M	LABR	RRZZZZ	BUF
LEWANDOWSKI, PETER	27	M	LABR	RRZZZZ	BUF
BLUM, FRANCISKA	30	F	WO	RRZZZZ	BUF
WLADISLAV	4	M	CHILD	RRZZZZ	BUF
JOSEFA	.11	F	INFANT	RRZZZZ	BUF
HEIDELBERGER, BRUNO	24	M	BKBNDR	RRZZZZ	BUF
DAMIKAT, AUGUST	28	M	LABR	RRZZZZ	BUF
MUZIK, VACLAW	27	M	TLR	RRZZZZ	OH
PETRA, MIKOLA	30	F	FARMER	RRZZZZ	KS
MOTZKUS, JOH	28	M	LABR	RRZZZZ	KS
TOMASCHAIKI, ANTON	24	M	LABR	RRZZZZ	KS
NOVOS, FRANZ	19	M	LABR	RRZZZZ	KS
LIMANSKI, JOSEPH	29	M	LABR	RRZZZZ	KS
NOWATZKI, STEFAN	23	M	LABR	RRZZZZ	KS
STAHOSKI, ANDREUS	27	M	LABR	RRZZZZ	KS
ZEDERSKI, SIMON	27	M	LABR	RRZZZZ	KS
SIEBERT, MARIE	20	F	UNKNOWN	RRZZZZ	PUR
KOPCZYNSKI, ADAM	25	M	LABR	RRZZZZ	NY
DEMBOWSKI, JACOB	36	M	LABR	RRZZZZ	NY
SPIRKA, JOSEPH	45	M	LABR	RRZZZZ	NY
CONSTANTIA	33	F	W	RRZZZZ	NY
VINCENTE	9	M	CHILD	RRZZZZ	NY
STEFAN	7	M	CHILD	RRZZZZ	NY
ANNA	4	F	CHILD	RRZZZZ	NY
CATH	9	F	CHILD	RRZZZZ	NY
WLACHOWJAK, CASIMIR	22	M	LABR	RRZZZZ	NY
LISOTHA, JOSEPH	31	M	LABR	RRZZZZ	NY
JOSEFA	32	F	W	RRZZZZ	NY
THOMAS	7	M	CHILD	RRZZZZ	NY
CATH	4	F	CHILD	RRZZZZ	NY
MATUSZEWICZ, ADAM	26	M	LABR	RRZZZZ	CH
WAZLOWSKI, ROCH	28	M	LABR	RRZZZZ	NY
KIOK, ANTON	43	M	LABR	RRZZZZ	NY
JAN	33	M	LABR	RRZZZZ	NY
ZADORSKI, STANISL	23	M	LABR	RRZZZZ	NY
KRASUS, SEIDE	25	M	LABR	RRZZZZ	NY
STEGEMANN, AUGUST	41	M	LABR	RRZZZZ	NY
MARIE	36	F	W	RRZZZZ	NY
JDA	15	F	W	RRZZZZ	NY
OTTO	9	M	CHILD	RRZZZZ	NY
EMIL	8	M	CHILD	RRZZZZ	NY
AUGUST	4	M	CHILD	RRZZZZ	NY
NORUPSCHAWITZ, JOSEPH	28	M	LABR	RRZZZZ	NY
PULSCHEWSKI, ALEXANDER	27	M	LABR	RRZZZZ	NY
GOERDIN, MOSES	26	M	LABR	RRZZZZ	NY
KANTERWITZ, ALEXANDER	21	M	LABR	RRZZZZ	NY
HEIN, PAUL	28	M	LABR	RRZZZZ	NY
SALEWSKA, ROSA	35	F	UNKNOWN	RRZZZZ	NY
STUBECKI, FRANZ	30	M	LABR	RRZZZZ	NY
SZEPANSKI, ANTON	25	M	LABR	RRZZZZ	NY
BIALKOWSKI, FRANZ	26	M	LABR	RRZZZZ	NY
KOWALSKI, MARIEL	26	M	LABR	RRZZZZ	NY
OLENITSCHAK, JAN	20	M	LABR	RRZZZZ	NY
MATZCKIEWICZ, THOMAS	30	M	LABR	RRZZZZ	RAC

SHIP: SUEVIA

FROM: HAMBURG AND HAVRE
TO: NEW YORK
ARRIVED: 09 APRIL 1888

PASSENGER	AGE	SEX	OCCUPATION	PRIV	DES
SZ-KOWSKY, ANTON	30	M	LABR	RRAHUV	USA
SOSKO, JOH	26	M	LABR	RRZZZZ	USA
LEWANSKI, LEON	24	M	LABR	RRZZZZ	USA
OHRENSTEIN, MENDEL	30	M	LABR	RRZZZZ	USA
ALEXINAS, VINENTE	27	M	LABR	RRZZZZ	USA
HARLON, ANTON	24	M	LABR	RRZZZZ	USA
GOLOSCHEWSKI, PETERS	33	M	LABR	RRZZZZ	USA
NORSTOVRIS, JAN	27	M	LABR	RRZZZZ	USA
LECKER, SIMON	16	M	LABR	RRZZZZ	USA
REPPEN, HENRIETTE	54	F	WO	RRAFVG	USA
ADOLPH	23	M	MCHT	RRAFVG	USA
ROSENWI---, U	25	M	LABR	RRAHZS	USA
RAD--N, GUSTAV	29	M	LABR	RRZZZZ	USA
JUKEY-SY, JOSEFA	21	F	SGL	RRZZZZ	USA
SACK, JOSEPH	27	M	BCHR	RRZZZZ	USA
WEINROTH, ALTER	27	M	DLR	RRZZZZ	USA
-OSSIE	29	F	W	RRZZZZ	USA
LOUISE	13	F	CH	RRZZZZ	USA
ARON	9	M	CHILD	RRZZZZ	USA
MARIE	5	F	CHILD	RRZZZZ	USA
LEON	3	M	CHILD	RRZZZZ	USA
MOSES	.11	M	INFANT	RRZZZZ	USA
MARGUARDT, WILHELMINE	26	F	WO	RRZZZZ	USA
PAUL	.11	M	INFANT	RRZZZZ	USA
MURA-OSKI, ANTON	25	M	LABR	RRZZZZ	USA
CZURA--O, JAN	29	M	LABR	RRAHUI	USA
KAMENICKI, CHAP	43	F	WO	RRAHWQ	USA
ISAAC	15	M	CH	RRAHWQ	USA
WOLFF	8	M	CHILD	RRAHWQ	USA
RI-OKE	9	M	CHILD	RRAHWQ	USA
KAMENKI, RICH---	6	M	CHILD	RRAHWQ	USA
SILBERMANN, BEILE	18	F	SGL	RRAHWQ	USA
REISE	9	F	CHILD	RRAHWQ	USA
SCHULZ, CAROL	20	F	SGL	RRZZZZ	USA
WILH	18	M	FARMER	RRZZZZ	USA
SASS, KARL	29	M	TLR	RRZZZZ	USA
BERTHA	34	F	W	RRZZZZ	USA
STEK---, ANTON	30	M	LABR	RRAHZS	USA
SCHMIDT, RUDOLPH	26	M	LABR	RRZZZZ	USA
GEHLKE, SAMUEL	29	M	LABR	RRZZZZ	USA
EIMBINDER, JUHEEL	25	M	LABR	RRAHTU	USA
OKUNSKY, ANTONY	27	M	LABR	RRAHUI	USA
SZ-RROWSKI, JAN	27	M	LABR	RRAHUI	USA
KIANOWSKI, JACOB	38	M	LABR	RRAHUI	USA
ULENOWSKI, FRANZ	30	M	LABR	RRAHUI	USA
GUZEWSKY, FRANZ	42	M	LABR	RRAHUI	USA
TOBILEWICZ, VOYEND	27	M	LABR	RRZZZZ	USA
JUD--IENN, FRIEDERIKE	40	F	WO	RRZZZZ	USA
RIEFKE	9	F	CHILD	RRZZZZ	USA
REISEL	5	F	CHILD	RRZZZZ	USA
TEL	2	F	CHILD	RRZZZZ	USA
CHAIKEL	.09	F	INFANT	RRZZZZ	USA
HUSLAGER, FRANZ	33	M	LABR	FNZZZZ	USA
SCHWANENBERG, AUGUST	32	M	LABR	FNZZZZ	USA
SAMSANOWITZ, PIOTR	27	M	LABR	FNAINQ	USA
BORIS, ALEXANDER	24	M	LABR	FNAINQ	USA
SCHAUTA, ANTON	20	M	LABR	FNAINQ	USA
ABUKOWSKI, SURZEI	31	M	LABR	FNAINQ	USA
WASER, ANTON	23	M	LABR	FNAINQ	USA
SELNER, PIOTR	24	M	LABR	FNAINQ	USA
PAS-HNKO-IS, VINCENTY	18	M	LABR	FNAINQ	USA
GRIK, VINANTY	27	M	LABR	FNAINQ	USA
NORUSCHOWITZ, J	30	M	LABR	FNAINQ	USA
KIR---, ANTANAS	40	M	LABR	FNAHZS	USA
SWIRSKI, CHAM	20	M	LABR	FNAHZS	USA
DUKEWITZ, JANOS	37	M	LABR	FNAHZS	USA
PAKULIS, SUNDS	24	M	LABR	FNAHZS	USA
GIWARKOWSKY, SAMUEL	28	M	LABR	FNAHZS	USA

PASSENGER	AGE	SEX	OCCUPATION	PRVIL	DES
MICHLOITZKI, ADAM	30	M	LABR	RRZZZZ	USA
KIREITAIS, ZOH	29	M	LABR	RRZZZZ	USA
-EYBLEWSKI, TOMAS	25	M	LABR	RRZZZZ	USA
PIRCHWSKY, FRANZISKA	24	F	WO	RRZZZZ	USA
ADAM	.03	M	INFANT	RRZZZZ	USA
JANTON, ANDRAS	23	M	FARMER	FNZZZZ	USA
STENT--ES, JULIUS	25	M	FARMER	FNZZZZ	USA
TARP, ANDRAS	28	M	FARMER	FNZZZZ	USA
PELDAU, ANDRES	21	M	FARMER	FNZZZZ	USA
STEECHALUIK, ILDZIE	45	F	WO	RRZZZZ	USA
BAZIK	16	F	CH	RRZZZZ	USA
THEODOZIA	10	F	CH	RRZZZZ	USA
MALEKA, ANNA	20	F	SGL	RRZZZZ	USA
M-RIS, SIMON	25	M	LABR	RRAHZS	USA
SCHWI-KE, TAMADIUS	23	M	LABR	RRZZZZ	USA
WERNER, HEINRICH	19	M	LABR	RRZZZZ	USA
SCHUGOWSKI, VICTORIA	30	F	WO	RRAHZS	USA
VALERIA	5	M	CHILD	RRAHZS	USA
ALEXANDER	3	M	CHILD	RRAHZS	USA
JOS	.03	M	INFANT	RRAHZS	USA
JUDKIN, SCHADES	9	M	CHILD	RRAHOK	USA
MEYER, WILH	24	M	MCHT	RRAICJ	USA
WLADIMIR, B	34	M	BSP	RRZZZZ	USA
CH-DNOWSKI, GEORGI	45	M	MSNY	RRZZZZ	USA
DAKOW, NICOLAUS	28	M	MSNY	RRZZZZ	USA
GRINKEW--CH, NICOLAI	24	M	MSNY	RRZZZZ	USA
SHERWICH, ALEXANDER	20	M	MSNY	RRAFWJ	USA
MARTISCH, ALEXANDER	40	M	MSNY	RRZZZZ	USA
KATHA	35	F	W	RRZZZZ	USA
SOFIA	6	F	CHILD	RRZZZZ	USA
ROMAN	5	M	CHILD	RRZZZZ	USA
VASILIE	14	M	CH	RRZZZZ	USA
NICOLAI	9	M	CHILD	RRZZZZ	USA
BORTNOWSKI, IVAN	17	M	MSNY	RRAFWJ	USA
KRUDKOW, IVAN	25	M	MSNY	RRZZZZ	USA
THEOFFISTA	24	F	W	RRZZZZ	USA
BOBOWS--, ALEXANDER	18	M	MSNY	RRZZZZ	USA
SANE-KI, ANTON	18	M	MSNY	RRZZZZ	USA
KUDR---, NICOLAI	19	M	MSNY	RRAFWJ	USA
---ICHENKE, IVAN	19	M	MSNY	RRAFWJ	USA
KOR--LICH, ERTILI	14	M	MSNY	RRAFWJ	USA
H--NNOWSKI, ANTON	14	M	MSNY	RRAFWJ	USA
ALLAN, WILLIAM	19	M	MSNY	RRZZZZ	USA
LEVIN, BORIS	16	M	MSNY	RRAFWJ	USA

SHIP: WERRA

FROM: BREMEN AND SOUTHAMPTON
TO: NEW YORK
ARRIVED: 10 APRIL 1888

PASSENGER	AGE	SEX	OCCUPATION	PRVIL	DES
KIEDA, KAZIMIR	34	M	LABR	RRZZZZ	USA
WEISS, JOH.	37	M	LABR	RRZZZZ	UNK
FRIEDKE.	32	F	W	RRZZZZ	UNK
EMILIE	8	F	CHILD	RRZZZZ	UNK
JOH.	5	M	CHILD	RRZZZZ	UNK
ROSINA	4	F	CHILD	RRZZZZ	UNK
JACOB	.09	M	INFANT	RRZZZZ	UNK
KRUEGER, CARL	26	M	FARMER	RRZZZZ	UNK
DOROTHEA	22	F	W	RRZZZZ	UNK
EDUARD	4	M	CHILD	RRZZZZ	UNK
JACOB	15	M	NN	RRZZZZ	UNK
FUEDE, FRIEDR.	21	M	NN	RRZZZZ	UNK
MARGA.	19	F	W	RRZZZZ	UNK
NETZ, DAN.	18	M	LABR	RRZZZZ	UNK
MAEDER, ANDR.	27	M	LABR	RRZZZZ	UNK
MARGA	17	F	NN	RRZZZZ	UNK
MELLMGER, JOS.	25	M	FARMER	RRZZZZ	UNK
CATHA.	22	F	W	RRZZZZ	UNK
PAULE.	.06	F	INFANT	RRZZZZ	UNK
MARIE	7	F	CHILD	RRZZZZ	UNK
PIPKOWSKY, STANISL.	30	M	LABR	RRZZZZ	UNK

SHIP: NEVADA

FROM: LIVERPOOL AND QUEENSTOWN
TO: NEW YORK
ARRIVED: 11 APRIL 1888

PASSENGER	AGE	SEX	OCCUPATION	PRVIL	DES
DARBLINSKY, JOS.	32	M	SHMK	RRACBF	USA
FIED.	23	M	SHMK	RRACBF	USA
KUSCHENITZ, INSARO	31	M	FARMER	RRACBF	USA
RAKOWSKY, JULIAN	24	M	LABR	RRACBF	USA
WIZOTSKY, AUGUST	23	M	LABR	RRACBF	USA
MICHELOWSKY, ALEX	22	M	LABR	RRACBF	USA
URANOWITZ, DOMINIK	43	M	FARMER	RRACBF	USA
SCHIMANOWTZ, ALEXR.	27	M	LABR	RRACBF	USA
STANOWSKY, KASIMAR	17	M	LABR	RRACBF	USA
CZERMAUSKY, ISRAIZ	36	M	LABR	RRACBF	USA
RULHOWSKI, FRANTZISZEL	21	M	LABR	RRACBF	USA
SCHERKOWAS, JONAS	22	M	LABR	RRACBF	USA
LENOLSKI, ADAM	21	M	LABR	RRACBF	USA
ANDRASZKEIWIER, ADAM	19	M	LABR	RRACBF	USA
FISCHEN, MOSES	34	M	LABR	RRACBF	USA
STAROWSKY, JOHAN	24	M	LABR	RRACBF	USA
SARCHH, JUDEL	24	M	LABR	RRACBF	USA
BASCHE	24	F	W	RRACBF	USA
DUTEWITZ, TOMACH	32	M	FARMER	RRACBF	USA
MARIA	28	F	W	RRACBF	USA
JANKOWSKY, FRANZ	31	M	FARMER	RRACBF	USA
MARIAME	31	F	W	RRACBF	USA
FRANCISCE	.06	F	INFANT	RRACBF	USA

SHIP: DONAU

FROM: BREMEN
TO: BALTIMORE
ARRIVED: 11 APRIL 1888

PASSENGER	AGE	SEX	OCCUPATION	PRVIL	DES
CZIEJEIJNAS, EDUARD	20	M	LABR	RRZZZZ	IL
LUECKA, LEOPOLD	22	M	LABR	RRZZZZ	IL
SEJKMANN, LOUISE	35	F	NN	RRZZZZ	IL
ROBERT	.07	M	INFANT	RRZZZZ	IL
WAGNER, JACOB	21	M	MCHT	RRZZZZ	IL
MARIE	23	F	NN	RRZZZZ	IL
BUZA, JAN	25	M	LABR	RRZZZZ	IL
SCHULZ, ADOLF	26	M	MLR	RRZZZZ	PA
ANTON	23	M	MLR	RRZZZZ	PA
TRUSCINSKI, THEOPHIL	21	M	CPR	RRZZZZ	MD
MAKOWITZ, ANTON	38	M	LABR	RRZZZZ	KY
ZIELENSKA, ANNA	24	F	NN	RRZZZZ	PA
CHUNILEWSKI, FRANZISZEK	39	M	LABR	RRZZZZ	BAL
NIET-LICS, FRANZISZEK	35	M	LABR	RRZZZZ	BAL
CHUNILEWSKI, MAR---	26	M	LABR	RRZZZZ	BAL
NIETULICS, ANDERZEF	24	M	LABR	RRZZZZ	BAL
BULIT, JACOB	27	M	JNR	RRZZZZ	PA
OSZINCK, JOHAN	22	M	ENGR	RRZZZZ	PA
BAUER, CARL	22	M	ENGR	RRZZZZ	PA
SOSINSKY, FRANZ	37	M	LABR	RRZZZZ	BAL
ANTONIA	37	F	NN	RRZZZZ	BAL
EDUARD	3	M	CHILD	RRZZZZ	BAL
STEFANIE	.06	F	INFANT	RRZZZZ	BAL
STANISLAUS	36	M	LABR	RRZZZZ	BAL
-UREK, PETER	53	M	LABR	RRZZZZ	BAL

PASSENGER	AGE	SEX	OCCUPATION	PRIVL	DES

SHIP: STATE OF INDIANA

FROM: GLASGOW
TO: NEW YORK
ARRIVED: 12 APRIL 1888

PASSENGER	AGE	SEX	OCCUPATION	PRIVL	DES
PROBNESKY, DANEL	25	M	PDLR	RRAIDL	USA
RABINOWITZ, SCHASSE	28	M	PDLR	RRAIDL	USA
KUPPPERMANN, BERIZIAN	40	M	LABR	RRAIDL	USA
KOWSLKSI, MICHAEL	24	M	LABR	RRAIDL	USA
JESSEWICZ, MARTIN	25	M	LABR	RRAIDL	USA
KINATKOWSKY, FRANZ	29	M	LABR	RRAIDL	USA
SHAFFRAINSKY, ANTONI	22	M	LABR	RRAIDL	USA
ROSINSKY, JENKE	17	M	LABR	RRAIDL	USA
LEHWITZ, MARTIN	24	M	LABR	RRAIDL	USA
KRASCHINOWTZKY, JAN	24	M	LABR	RRAIDL	USA
KALLINOWSKY, VINCENT	25	M	TLR	RRAIDL	USA
NEOWULLES, MARTIN	22	M	TLR	RRAIDL	USA
DERESCHKEWITZ, MARTIN	23	M	TLR	RRAIDL	USA
KIPROSKY, SYLVESTER	22	M	TLR	RRAIDL	USA
LOWAS, JOSEF	30	M	PDLR	RRAIDL	USA
KRPEZA, JOSEF	35	M	PDLR	RRAIDL	USA
ISAACS, JORK	24	M	PDLR	RRAIDL	USA

SHIP: RHYNLAND

FROM: ANTWERP
TO: NEW YORK
ARRIVED: 13 APRIL 1888

PASSENGER	AGE	SEX	OCCUPATION	PRIVL	DES
MARTONSLIS, VINC.	29	M	TLR	RRZZZZ	NY
MAR.	26	F	UNKNOWN	RRZZZZ	NY
JOS.	00	M	INF	RRZZZZ	NY
STEIZEWIEZ, ANT.	47	M	LABR	RRZZZZ	NY
ANT.	18	M	LABR	RRZZZZ	NY
JOS.	30	M	LABR	RRZZZZ	NY
JAN	00	M	INF	RRZZZZ	NY
NARDONI, BAT.	27	M	LABR	RRZZZZ	NY

SHIP: WISCONSIN

FROM: LIVERPOOL AND QUEENSTOWN
TO: NEW YORK
ARRIVED: 14 APRIL 1888

PASSENGER	AGE	SEX	OCCUPATION	PRIVL	DES
LEIVERANT, LEISER	23	M	GZR	RRZZZZ	USA
JANAWIEZ, MICKEL	22	M	GZR	RRZZZZ	USA
BARANOWSKY, ANTON	17	M	UNKNOWN	RRZZZZ	USA
ALBOWIZ, ADAM	26	M	FARMER	RRZZZZ	USA
RADZWITOWITZ, JOHAN	37	M	FARMER	RRZZZZ	USA
ADOLPH	32	M	FARMER	RRZZZZ	USA
COHN, SIMON	22	M	PNTR	RRZZZZ	USA
SCHAPIRO, ELKE	32	F	W	RRZZZZ	USA
EISIK	7	M	CHILD	RRZZZZ	USA
SARA	.11	F	INFANT	RRZZZZ	USA
KULAK, ABRAM	18	M	JNR	RRZZZZ	USA
LEIVI, JANEL	25	M	GZR	RRZZZZ	USA
BARASCH, MOSES	24	M	GZR	RRZZZZ	USA

SHIP: ALLER

FROM: BREMEN AND SOUTHAMPTON
TO: NEW YORK
ARRIVED: 14 APRIL 1888

PASSENGER	AGE	SEX	OCCUPATION	PRIVL	DES
STANICKI, ANTON	26	M	FARMER	RRZZZZ	USA
BUCH, SAMUEL	20	M	FARMER	RRZZZZ	USA
DAMBENSKY, JIM	25	M	FARMER	RRZZZZ	USA
KOWALSKY, ANTONIE	25	F	UNKNOWN	RRZZZZ	USA
GRETT, CHRISTINE	27	F	UNKNOWN	RRZZZZ	USA
DORA	20	F	UNKNOWN	RRZZZZ	USA
DORSZJINSKA, AMALIE	25	F	UNKNOWN	RRZZZZ	USA
RAJEE, CATTRINE	25	F	UNKNOWN	RRZZZZ	USA
BERETSKY, MATTILDE	17	F	UNKNOWN	RRZZZZ	USA
SYETEK, PELAGIA	23	F	UNKNOWN	RRZZZZ	USA
JOHAN	5	M	CHILD	RRZZZZ	USA
HEER, CHRISTIAN	28	M	FARMER	RRZZZZ	USA
CHRISTINE	28	F	W	RRZZZZ	USA
REBECKA	3	F	CHILD	RRZZZZ	USA
CHRISTINE	2	F	CHILD	RRZZZZ	USA
EISLINGER, JOHAN	27	M	FARMER	RRZZZZ	USA
CATHERINE	22	F	W	RRZZZZ	USA
REBECKE	.05	F	INFANT	RRZZZZ	USA

SHIP: LEERDAM

FROM: ROTTERDAM
TO: NEW YORK
ARRIVED: 16 APRIL 1888

PASSENGER	AGE	SEX	OCCUPATION	PRIVL	DES
GERA--EVSKY, FRANS	22	M	UNKNOWN	RRZZZZ	USA
HERNANKUN, JAN	22	M	UNKNOWN	RRZZZZ	USA
BELANTS, ANTON	21	M	UNKNOWN	RRZZZZ	USA
PLOTZ, JOHAN	23	M	UNKNOWN	RRZZZZ	USA
SAAL, ANTON	22	M	UNKNOWN	RRZZZZ	USA
SCHRE-E, GOTLIEB	23	M	UNKNOWN	RRZZZZ	USA
SCHARTINOWITZ, SUSE	27	F	UNKNOWN	RRZZZZ	USA
WAYKE, AUG.	28	M	UNKNOWN	RRZZZZ	USA
SCHLEBEDURK, MARTIN	36	M	UNKNOWN	RRZZZZ	USA
HAYSEN, JOH.	37	M	UNKNOWN	RRZZZZ	USA
SCHLESELAWCHUS, SIMON	24	M	UNKNOWN	RRZZZZ	USA
ROSANOSKY, JOSEF	29	M	UNKNOWN	RRZZZZ	USA
SABULOWSKY, ALEX	27	M	UNKNOWN	RRZZZZ	USA
MA-SMA, PAUL	25	M	UNKNOWN	RRZZZZ	USA
JUTTA, JOSEF	35	M	UNKNOWN	RRZZZZ	USA
BAKSA, DOM.	32	M	UNKNOWN	RRZZZZ	USA
ANNA	24	F	UNKNOWN	RRZZZZ	USA
MALWAR, JONNES	26	M	UNKNOWN	RRZZZZ	USA
KONARS, ANDREAS	43	M	UNKNOWN	RRZZZZ	USA
MAWINKY, FRANS	29	M	UNKNOWN	RRZZZZ	USA
KATAZINKA	25	F	UNKNOWN	RRZZZZ	USA
JOSEFA	4	F	CHILD	RRZZZZ	USA
PASKAS, MICHALY	17	M	UNKNOWN	RRZZZZ	USA
VOSEN, ANDREAS	20	M	UNKNOWN	RRZZZZ	USA
PAWEL	40	M	UNKNOWN	RRZZZZ	USA
IWANWINSKY, MICHEL	30	M	UNKNOWN	RRZZZZ	USA
WELIACH, MICHEL	25	M	UNKNOWN	RRZZZZ	USA
WOLFSBAUER, MICH.	34	M	UNKNOWN	RRZZZZ	USA

PASSENGER	AGE	SEX	OCCUPATION	PRV VIL DES

SHIP: SERVIA

FROM: LIVERPOOL AND QUEENSTOWN
TO: NEW YORK
ARRIVED: 16 APRIL 1888

PASSENGER	AGE	SEX	OCCUPATION	PRV VIL DES
HARJIE, HEIKKI	40	M	LABR	RRZZZZNY
WISSMARK, ADOLF-F.	31	M	LABR	RRZZZZIL
WOLYSARK, INO	33	M	LABR	RRZZZZMN
BERTHA	30	F	W	RRZZZZMN
HOSEA	7	M	CHILD	RRZZZZMN
SIMON	5	M	CHILD	RRZZZZMN
EKELUND, BRAVO	34	F	LABR	RRZZZZIL
HELGA	3	F	CHILD	RRZZZZIL
VALHURG	.09	F	INFANT	RRZZZZIL

SHIP: CITY OF CHICAGO

FROM: LIVERPOOL AND QUEENSTOWN
TO: NEW YORK
ARRIVED: 16 APRIL 1888

PASSENGER	AGE	SEX	OCCUPATION	PRV VIL DES
ISAKSON, AUG	28	M	LABR	RRAGUZIL
SODERBERG, ERIK	23	M	LABR	RRAGUZNY
KARLSON, KARL	28	M	LABR	RRAGUZNY
PIMMAKI, JOHAN	33	M	LABR	RRAGUZNY
KIWMSKI, WILHELM	19	M	LABR	RRAGUZNY
KAWUMAKI, JOHR	31	M	LABR	RRAGUZNY
KUSBAKI, GUST	29	M	LABR	RRAGUZNY
FILLIPSON, ANDR	36	M	LABR	RRAGUZNY

SHIP: ALASKA

FROM: LIVERPOOL AND QUEENSTOWN
TO: NEW YORK
ARRIVED: 16 APRIL 1888

PASSENGER	AGE	SEX	OCCUPATION	PRV VIL DES
KAUNOSTA, MATTS.W.	28	M	LABR	FNZZZZUSA
JOHANSDOTTER, ANNA	41	F	MA	FNZZZZUSA
JENKKA, MATTS.A.	39	M	LABR	FNZZZZUSA
WUTA, MATTS.G.	36	M	LABR	FNZZZZUSA
SAARI, MATTS.J.	29	M	LABR	FNZZZZUSA
ISAKSSON, ISAK	45	M	LABR	FNZZZZUSA
HNITSA, WILL	38	M	MRNR	FNZZZZUSA
HAKOLA, HERMAN	32	M	LABR	FNZZZZUSA
HERNESINA, MATTS.	39	M	LABR	FNZZZZUSA
VIERNILS, JOHAN	40	M	MRNR	FNZZZZUSA
HELAKOWSKI, EMIL	19	M	MRNR	FNZZZZUSA
ROUTA, SIGFIN	28	M	LABR	FNZZZZUSA
SINILOOTS, JACOB	33	M	LABR	FNZZZZUSA
ANTOLA, HENRIK	24	M	LABR	FNZZZZUSA
MARGANJERDIN, HENRIK	00	M	FARMER	FNZZZZUSA
LATWALA, FREDRIK	26	M	PNTR	FNZZZZUSA
OTTE, JOHN	40	M	LABR	FNZZZZUSA
MEJESSAA, JOHAN	28	M	LABR	FNZZZZUSA
POPPIMAKI, JACOB	25	M	FARMER	FNZZZZUSA
PETTREN, JOHAN	27	M	LABR	FNZZZZUSA
HOPOSOLA, ANANIUS	41	M	TLR	FNZZZZUSA
SEPAALA, KALLE	45	M	PNTR	FNZZZZUSA
SEPPA, JOHN	43	M	PNTR	FNZZZZUSA
KARPI, OTTO	19	M	LABR	FNZZZZUSA
KORPI, ALEXN.	24	M	MRNR	FNZZZZUSA
SEPPA, MATTI	41	M	LABR	FNZZZZUSA
JOCKITALLO, ENOK	25	M	LABR	FNZZZZUSA
KLEBBESTER, ERIK	41	M	LABR	FNZZZZUSA
HORLIN, ANDERS	33	M	LABR	FNZZZZUSA
LILJESTROEM, FRED.	34	M	PNTR	FNZZZZUSA
JOHAN	41	M	LABR	FNZZZZUSA
CARRIERAS, A.	45	M	GENT	RRZZZZUSA

SHIP: RUGIA

FROM: HAMBURG AND HAVRE
TO: NEW YORK
ARRIVED: 16 APRIL 1888

PASSENGER	AGE	SEX	OCCUPATION	PRV VIL DES
MASSAL, CAROL	27	F	SGL	RRACBFUSA
ZAISER, GOTTL	29	M	FARMER	RRACBFUSA
CHRIST	26	F	W	RRACBFUSA
ROSINE	7	F	CHILD	RRACBFUSA
CHRIST	3	F	CHILD	RRACBFUSA
JACOB	18	M	UNKNOWN	RRACBFUSA
KRUEGER, FRIEDR	25	M	LABR	RRACBFUSA
FRD	25	F	W	RRACBFUSA
HILL, GEORG	28	M	FARMER	RRACBFUSA
CATH	24	F	W	RRACBFUSA
ANNA	8	F	CHILD	RRACBFUSA
CATH	2	F	CHILD	RRACBFUSA
ANNA	.06	F	INFANT	RRACBFUSA
FA, JACOB	32	M	FARMER	RRACBFUSA
ANNA	32	F	W	RRACBFUSA
MUELLER, JOSEF	23	M	LABR	RRACBFUSA
ELISABETH	24	F	W	RRACBFUSA
CONRAD	.06	M	INFANT	RRACBFUSA
GEORG	29	M	LABR	RRACBFUSA
CHRIST	26	F	W	RRACBFUSA
CHRIST	2	F	CHILD	RRACBFUSA
GEORG	.06	M	INFANT	RRACBFUSA
CHRISTIAN	25	M	LABR	RRACBFUSA
KEILES, GEDAYE	46	M	DLR	RRACBFUSA
BASSAN, FRANK	22	M	LABR	RRACBFUSA
SCHIKARSKI, STANISLAUS	21	M	LABR	RRACBFUSA
BOGDA, CARL	38	M	FARMER	RRACBFUSA
ERNEST	40	F	W	RRACBFUSA
SELMA	9	F	CHILD	RRACBFUSA
IDA	6	F	CHILD	RRACBFUSA
BERTHA	8	F	CHILD	RRACBFUSA
LOUISE	.01	F	INFANT	RRACBFUSA
FRD	56	F	WO	RRACBFUSA
WEGNER, CARL	15	M	FARMER	RRACBFUSA
ANISCHKIEWICZ, JOS	46	M	FARMER	RRACBFUSA
ROSALIE	45	F	W	RRACBFUSA
ANTONIE	15	F	D	RRACBFUSA
BRUNO	3	M	CHILD	RRACBFUSA
ERDMANN, HERM	29	M	FARMER	RRACBFUSA
AUGUSTE	29	F	W	RRACBFUSA
IDA	6	F	CHILD	RRACBFUSA
ALBERT	3	M	CHILD	RRACBFUSA
AUGUST	3	M	CHILD	RRACBFUSA
SCHMIDT, PAUL	23	M	LABR	RRACBFUSA
PLATZKI, BENZI	40	M	LABR	RRACBFUSA
NEKIRAS, MUTZE	40	M	LABR	RRACBFUSA
AMBROSCHEWITZ, KATALITZ	22	M	LABR	RRACBFUSA
KUBEEL, JULIUS	30	M	LABR	RRACBFUSA
PELZER, DANIEL	30	M	LABR	RRACBFUSA
BRAUN, FRIEDR	43	M	LABR	RRACBFUSA
SIEGLER, JOSEF	28	M	LABR	RRACBFUSA
KRENZ, ANTON	30	M	LABR	RRACBFUSA
DEMKO, KASIMIR	44	M	LABR	RRACBFUSA
FARMBRUCH, GEORG	19	M	FARMER	RRACBFUSA
HOFFMANN, HEINR	19	M	FARMER	RRACBFUSA
CATH	20	F	W	RRACBFUSA
MAGDAL	.06	F	INFANT	RRACBFUSA
SCHAEFFER, HEINR	19	M	FARMER	RRACBFUSA

PASSENGER	AGE	SEX	OCCUPATION	PRIV	VIL	DES
HILL, CONRAD	19	M	FARMER	RR	ACBF	USA
TORNASZEZIK, FERENZ	40	M	LABR	RR	ACBF	USA
LUKAEZ, SAHOL	16	M	LABR	RR	ACBF	USA
BOBACK, HRYE	16	M	LABR	RR	ACBF	USA
PATRICK, VASIL	47	M	LABR	RR	ACBF	USA
BACSA, JANOS	16	M	LABR	RR	ACBF	USA
FORKOS, PAULI	40	M	LABR	RR	ACBF	USA

SHIP: HAMMONIA

FROM: HAMBURG
TO: NEW YORK
ARRIVED: 17 APRIL 1888

PASSENGER	AGE	SEX	OCCUPATION	PRIV	VIL	DES
GROBOWSKY, FRITZ	23	M	CPTR	RR	ZZZZ	USA
BUNGSCHE, GUSTAV	23	M	BKLYR	RR	ZZZZ	USA
ZUECSER, JANOS	23	M	FARMER	RR	ZZZZ	USA
BLADT, ROMAN	30	M	MCHT	RR	AHQD	USA
ZERNAITIS, JURAS	45	M	LABR	RR	AHXH	USA
CLASSEN, VICTOR	21	M	LABR	RR	AHXH	USA
ARTHUR	18	M	LABR	RR	AHXH	USA
ZEMARTIS, DWORA	36	M	LABR	RR	AHXH	USA
SCHLINSKI, CAASIMIR	37	M	LABR	RR	AHXH	USA
STASULIS, ADOMAS	38	M	LABR	RR	AHXH	USA
BOMBLAWSKI, LEO	40	M	LABR	RR	AHXH	USA
WALZ, CAROL	33	M	LABR	RR	ACBR	USA
KICS, PHILIPP	32	M	FARMER	RR	ZZZZ	USA
WILH	32	F	W	RR	ZZZZ	USA
CATH	9	F	CHILD	RR	ZZZZ	USA
CHRISTIAN	8	M	CHILD	RR	ZZZZ	USA
JACOB	7	M	CHILD	RR	ZZZZ	USA
PHILIPP	5	M	CHILD	RR	ZZZZ	USA
JOHANNE	3	F	CHILD	RR	ZZZZ	USA
WILH	.11	M	INFANT	RR	ZZZZ	USA
NAUROD, PAULINE	22	F	SGL	RR	ZZZZ	USA
PLUNGE, AUGUSTE	23	M	LABR	RR	ZZZZ	USA
TOTJUNS, THOMACHIS	29	M	LABR	RR	ZZZZ	USA
MATZEWICZ, IGNATZ	26	M	LABR	RR	ZZZZ	USA
GESOLLIS, FRANZ	20	M	LABR	RR	ZZZZ	USA
PRONCKEFKAS, JOSIUS	26	M	LABR	RR	ZZZZ	USA
GALMENS, KASPAR	28	M	LABR	RR	ZZZZ	USA
SZANZENBACH, DANIEL	32	M	FARMER	RR	ZZZZ	USA
ROSINA	32	F	W	RR	ZZZZ	USA
DANIEL	9	M	CHILD	RR	ZZZZ	USA
JOHANN	8	M	CHILD	RR	ZZZZ	USA
GEORG	7	M	CHILD	RR	ZZZZ	USA
CHRISTINE	6	M	CHILD	RR	ZZZZ	USA
CHRISTIAN	5	M	CHILD	RR	ZZZZ	USA
JACOB	4	M	CHILD	RR	ZZZZ	USA
FRIEDRICH	3	M	CHILD	RR	ZZZZ	USA
ROSINA	.11	F	INFANT	RR	ZZZZ	USA
DANGINS, ANTON	26	M	LABR	RR	AHTF	USA
JUNKA, DOMINIK	26	M	LABR	RR	AHTF	USA
GROIS, PAWEL	25	M	LABR	RR	AHTF	USA
BALUTZKIS, CASIMIR	36	M	LABR	RR	AHTF	USA
PALISCHEIT, JURGAS	17	M	LABR	RR	AHTF	USA
SPORF, ANDERS	19	M	LABR	RR	ZZZZ	USA
HELLSTRAND, ANDERS	38	M	TLR	RR	ZZZZ	USA
NIY, ANDERS	26	M	LABR	RR	ZZZZ	USA
ALEXANDER	25	M	LABR	RR	ZZZZ	USA
FRANZ, ANDERS	23	M	LABR	RR	ZZZZ	USA
LOHOLM, JOHANN	26	M	LABR	RR	ZZZZ	USA
ESTE, JONAS	42	M	LABR	RR	ZZZZ	USA
ANDERSEN, CARL	26	M	LABR	RR	ZZZZ	USA
GULNILLER, JOHANN	26	M	LABR	RR	ZZZZ	USA
GREVE, HENRIK	32	M	LABR	RR	ZZZZ	USA
SOSNASKY, PALAS	30	M	LABR	RR	AHTF	USA
WLADISCHA, PATRAS	30	M	LABR	RR	AHTF	USA
SZEKIS, STANISLAW	26	M	LABR	RR	AHTF	USA
ANDRIANSKIS, JURGAS	40	M	LABR	RR	ZZZZ	USA
JOSEPS, ATTROP	35	M	LABR	RR	ZZZZ	USA
JURAS, WINCAS	27	M	LABR	RR	AHTF	USA
ROMPAWICZ, KASIS	36	M	LABR	RR	AHTF	USA
MASCOCHAS, JURGIS	26	M	LABR	RR	AHTF	USA
MIRNIKI, JEAN	26	M	LABR	RR	AHTF	USA
GRUENBERG, CARL	25	M	FARMER	RR	ZZZZ	USA
BECKER, FREDRICH	26	M	FARMER	RR	ZZZZ	USA
BADZIWILOWITZ, JAN	24	M	LABR	RR	ZZZZ	USA
ALUZA, SELVESTRA	21	M	LABR	RR	ZZZZ	USA
SAWLIANIS, KASIMIR	23	M	LABR	RR	ZZZZ	USA
MICHALEK, FRANZ	22	M	LABR	RR	ZZZZ	USA
WENZOT, JOHANN	26	M	LABR	RR	ZZZZ	USA
REH, JULIUS	25	M	SMH	RR	ZZZZ	USA
MARIE	26	F	W	RR	ZZZZ	USA
EMMA	3	F	CHILD	RR	ZZZZ	USA
MATILDE	.11	F	INFANT	RR	ZZZZ	USA
GUTTENTAG, TEOFILA	62	F	WO	RR	AIFZ	USA
KOHN, ANNA	53	F	WO	RR	AIFZ	USA
NATALIE	25	F	SGL	RR	AIFZ	USA
REGINA	22	F	SGL	RR	AIFZ	USA

SHIP: AMERICA

FROM: BREMEN
TO: BALTIMORE
ARRIVED: 17 APRIL 1888

PASSENGER	AGE	SEX	OCCUPATION	PRIV	VIL	DES
STEPNANKAS, JOSEF	18	M	LABR	RR	ZZZZ	MN
BERGER, ILIAS	31	M	FARMER	RR	ZZZZ	UNK
SUSA	31	F	UNKNOWN	RR	ZZZZ	UNK
JAKOB	5	M	CHILD	RR	ZZZZ	UNK
BERNHARD	2	M	CHILD	RR	ZZZZ	UNK
FRIMKE, JOH.	39	M	FARMER	RR	ZZZZ	UNK
HELENE	36	F	UNKNOWN	RR	ZZZZ	UNK
HELENE	13	F	UNKNOWN	RR	ZZZZ	UNK
ELISAB.	11	F	UNKNOWN	RR	ZZZZ	UNK
WIEBKE, GERHARD	41	M	FARMER	RR	AICK	IL
ELIDABETH	44	F	UNKNOWN	RR	AICK	IL
JOHANN	13	M	UNKNOWN	RR	AICK	IL
JACOB	10	M	CH	RR	AICK	IL
FRANZ	5	M	CHILD	RR	AICK	IL
ELISABETH	2	F	CHILD	RR	AICK	IL
FINCK, JOSEF	36	M	LABR	RR	AICK	CO
LAMUTHE, MICHAEL	38	M	LABR	RR	AICK	CO
KORETIC, GEORG	27	M	LABR	RR	AICK	CO
KOCINIGGY, ANTON	28	M	LABR	RR	AICK	MD
UERBANSKY, JOSEF	20	M	LABR	RR	AICK	MD
REMMERT, ANNA	46	F	SVNT	RR	AICK	MD
ELISABETH	17	F	UNKNOWN	RR	AICK	MD
LINA	15	F	UNKNOWN	RR	AICK	MD
WIEBKE, GERHD.	18	M	FARMER	RR	AICK	MD
REMMERT, CARL	11	M	FARMER	RR	AICK	MD
BRAUN, JOSEF	49	M	FARMER	RR	AICK	MD
BARBA.	33	F	UNKNOWN	RR	AICK	MD
MARGA.	10	F	CH	RR	AICK	MD
MARIA	4	F	CHILD	RR	AICK	MD
ANDREAS	3	M	CHILD	RR	AICK	MD
JOHANNES	1	M	CHILD	RR	AICK	MD
CATHA.	17	F	UNKNOWN	RR	AICK	MD
JUNKER, ANDR.	42	M	FARMER	RR	AICK	MD
KOHN, ANDR.	33	M	FARMER	RR	AICK	MD
MARGA.	25	F	UNKNOWN	RR	AICK	MD
KRAUSE, JOH.GEORG	37	M	FARMER	RR	AICK	MN
MARIA	34	F	UNKNOWN	RR	AICK	MN
GEORG	15	M	UNKNOWN	RR	AICK	MN
HEINR.	7	M	CHILD	RR	AICK	MN
ELISABETH	14	F	UNKNOWN	RR	AICK	MN
MARIA	13	F	UNKNOWN	RR	AICK	MN
ELIDABETH	11	F	UNKNOWN	RR	AICK	MN
FRIEDRICH	.02	M	INFANT	RR	AICK	MN

PASSENGER	AGE	SEX	OCCUPATION	PRV VIL DES
KUHN, HANNES	3	M	CHILD	RRAICKMD
LORENZ	.06	M	INFANT	RRAICKMD
GERMAND, CHR.	33	M	MSN	RRAICKNM
JAKUBIWIKA, MICH.	27	M	FARMER	RRAICKNE

SHIP: EIDER

FROM: BREMEN AND SOUTHAMPTON
TO: NEW YORK
ARRIVED: 18 APRIL 1888

PASSENGER	AGE	SEX	OCCUPATION	PRV VIL DES
RECHES, SAMUEL	28	M	MCHT	RRZZZZUSA
RUEVE	20	M	MCHT	RRZZZZUSA
OLSZEWSKI, ANTON	25	M	LABR	RRZZZZUSA
WASILEWSKI, STANISLAW	24	M	LABR	RRZZZZUSA
MELANIE	20	F	W	RRZZZZUSA
DOBRIAN, BETTI	18	F	UNKNOWN	RRZZZZUSA
JANOWSKI, MICH	27	M	LABR	RRZZZZUSA
JANETZKI, MICH	38	M	LABR	RRZZZZUSA
ROSZKI, CHRIST	25	M	LABR	RRZZZZUSA
BRISCHKE, FERD	18	M	LABR	RRZZZZUSA
WALLAT, MARIE	22	F	UNKNOWN	RRZZZZUSA
KOCH, FRANZ	35	M	LABR	RRZZZZUSA
CATHARINA	35	F	UNKNOWN	RRZZZZUSA
CATHARINA	11	F	UNKNOWN	RRZZZZUSA
ANNA	9	F	CHILD	RRZZZZUSA
HEINRICH	2	M	CHILD	RRZZZZUSA
MATHILDE	.06	F	INFANT	RRZZZZUSA
HORST, HERM	32	M	BBR	RRZZZZUSA
ANNA	28	F	W	RRZZZZUSA
ANDREAS	2	M	CHILD	RRZZZZUSA
HERMANN	.01	M	INFANT	RRZZZZUSA
KLETKE, WILH	24	M	LABR	RRZZZZUSA
EISSENBERG, ALB	25	M	LABR	RRZZZZUSA
FISCHER, MARIE	30	F	UNKNOWN	RRZZZZUSA
ADOLF	9	M	CHILD	RRZZZZUSA
JULIUS	7	M	CHILD	RRZZZZUSA
CATHARINE	.09	F	INFANT	RRZZZZUSA
KAVAS, JOHANN	28	M	LABR	RRZZZZUSA
SEMAUER, MAGAS	42	M	LABR	RRZZZZUSA
ZEBNAK, ANDRAS	18	M	LABR	RRZZZZUSA
SURGALA, PETER	20	M	LABR	RRZZZZUSA
BELALYKO, ANDR	28	M	LABR	RRZZZZUSA
GAZIK, MICHAL	28	M	LABR	RRZZZZUSA
IGNATZ, MICHAL	33	M	LABR	RRZZZZUSA
FISCHER, GEORG	25	M	LABR	RRZZZZUSA
BREZEL, ANDR	31	M	LABR	RRZZZZUSA
ANA	27	F	W	RRZZZZUSA
CATHI	50	F	UNKNOWN	RRZZZZUSA
CATHI	4	F	CHILD	RRZZZZUSA
ANNA	.08	F	INFANT	RRZZZZUSA
KOS---, ANDRES	16	M	LABR	RRZZZZUSA
KREMZ--, AGNES	24	F	UNKNOWN	RRZZZZUSA
GECZIK--, JURE	32	F	UNKNOWN	RRZZZZUSA
KOSKE, ANDRAS	19	M	LABR	RRZZZZUSA
KUZENKA, IGNATZ	38	M	LABR	RRZZZZUSA
KOMORNIK, MICHEL	45	M	LABR	RRZZZZUSA
MARIE	37	F	W	RRZZZZUSA
ELISE	.11	F	INFANT	RRZZZZUSA
ROBAK, CORDIAN	18	M	LABR	RRZZZZUSA
HLADIK, MARTIN	44	M	LABR	RRZZZZUSA
IMKOWITZ, MARTIN	20	M	LABR	RRZZZZUSA
GRUNIEWALD, IGNATZ	22	M	LABR	RRZZZZUSA
HABA--, MARTIN	32	M	LABR	RRZZZZUSA
VRABEL, RESARA	20	F	UNKNOWN	RRZZZZUSA
MATZEIKS, PAUL	26	M	LABR	RRZZZZUSA
KEALOWITZ, CATH	32	F	UNKNOWN	RRZZZZUSA
STEFAN	8	M	CHILD	RRZZZZUSA
MARIA	6	F	CHILD	RRZZZZUSA
PESCH, JOHANN	32	M	LABR	RRZZZZUSA

PASSENGER	AGE	SEX	OCCUPATION	PRV VIL DES
GYVKOWSKI, VINCYL	12	M	LABR	RRZZZZUSA
MICHELIK, STEFAN	19	M	LABR	RRZZZZUSA
DOICHA, JAN	36	M	LABR	RRZZZZUSA
SEMAN, RISKA	28	F	UNKNOWN	RRZZZZUSA

SHIP: SAALE

FROM: BREMEN AND SOUTHAMPTON
TO: NEW YORK
ARRIVED: 21 APRIL 1888

PASSENGER	AGE	SEX	OCCUPATION	PRV VIL DES
BOXTER, MILTON	30	M	CPTR	RRAHQDUSA
MUELLER, ALB.	30	M	CPTR	RRAHQDUSA
SCHONERT, OTTILIE	25	F	UNKNOWN	RRAHTNUSA
SPAMLEFSKI, JOSEF	22	M	LABR	RRAFWJUSA
ROLIKOWSKA, ANNA	26	F	UNKNOWN	RRAFWJUSA
MUELLER, FRIEDR.	28	M	LABR	RRAIEEUSA
CHRISTE.	27	F	W	RRAIEEUSA
JACOB	3	M	CHILD	RRAIEEUSA
MARIA	.11	F	INFANT	RRAIEEUSA
U, U	20	M	UNKNOWN	RRAIEEUSA
U	00	M	UNKNOWN	RRAIEEUSA
CATHA.	23	F	UNKNOWN	RRAIEEUSA
WILHNE.	2	F	CHILD	RRAIEEUSA
EHRET, JACOB	30	M	LABR	RRAIEEUSA
MAGDA.	27	F	W	RRAIEEUSA
FRIEDR.	2	M	CHILD	RRAIEEUSA
MAGDA.	6	F	CHILD	RRAIEEUSA
ELISAB.	.11	F	INFANT	RRAIEEUSA
ALDINGER, JACOB	20	M	LABR	RRAIEEUSA
WEISSHAR, JACOB	27	M	LABR	RRAIEEUSA
ELISAB.	25	F	W	RRAIEEUSA
RUD.	.11	M	INFANT	RRAIEEUSA
RECHTLAND, CHEWE	15	F	UNKNOWN	RRAFWJUNK
SCHADNER, CARL	33	M	LABR	RRAHQDUNK
FISCHER, JUL.	34	M	LABR	RRAHQDUNK
FECHTER, AUG.	34	M	LABR	RRAHQDUNK
KALWEIT, JOS.	26	M	LABR	RRAHQDUNK

SHIP: KANSAS

FROM: LIVERPOOL
TO: BOSTON
ARRIVED: ON UNKNOWN ON

PASSENGER	AGE	SEX	OCCUPATION	PRV VIL DES
SALOWIZIZ, LEISTER	28	M	MCHT	RRZZZZBO
MERCHA	23	F	W	RRZZZZBO
KLECAUSKI, JERMA	24	M	LABR	RRZZZZNY
ROSENFELD, MORRIS	22	M	LABR	RRZZZZNY
NOSCHEWITZKZ, MRAETO	44	M	LABR	RRZZZZNY
SEBERT, B.	26	M	LABR	PLZZZZNY
ABALSKY, JOSEPH	26	M	LABR	RRZZZZNY
BLACE, ABR.	40	M	LABR	RRZZZZNY
BERNARD, ISAAC	28	M	LABR	RRZZZZPHI
GRIZMONITZ, KAZINIO	29	M	LABR	RRZZZZNY
KLOBWITCH, MARTIN	33	M	LABR	RRZZZZNY

SHIP: ST. OF PENNSYLVANIA

FROM: GLASGOW AND LARNE
TO: NEW YORK
ARRIVED: 21 APRIL 1888

PASSENGER	AGE	SEX	OCCUPATION	PRV VIL DES
FALKASKI, JOSEF	23	M	LABR	RRZZZZUSA
JOHANA, ASDAM	26	M	LABR	RRZZZZUSA
MATY, NAHNY	25	M	LABR	RRZZZZUSA
JANOS, BENATE	25	M	LABR	RRZZZZUSA
ZWICKIE, JAN	30	M	LABR	RRZZZZUSA
BROSSINSKY, ERNSTOW	40	M	LABR	RRZZZZUSA
ALONE, ADAM	37	M	LABR	RRZZZZUSA
LINGEUS, WINGEUS	23	M	LABR	RRZZZZUSA
SCHULTENIS, JAN	30	M	LABR	RRZZZZUSA
GREDELIE, JAN	23	M	LABR	RRZZZZUSA
MIKISIS, SURGIS	30	M	LABR	RRZZZZUSA
BUKOFAKI, JOSEF	35	M	LABR	RRZZZZUSA
JOSEF, PATERKA	22	M	LABR	RRZZZZUSA
HERONIN, JOHN	23	M	LABR	RRZZZZUSA
STURZEK, JOHN	27	M	LABR	RRZZZZUSA
MATEY, SEPA	33	M	LABR	RRZZZZUSA
MUELLER, CLAUS	23	M	LABR	RRZZZZUSA
KRUEGER, EMMA	11	F	CH	RRZZZZUSA
PAZEWITZ, ADAM	45	M	LABR	RRZZZZUSA
TEKLE	38	F	W	RRZZZZUSA
ADAM	10	M	CH	RRZZZZUSA
JULIE	8	F	CHILD	RRZZZZUSA
TEWOSIE	.09	F	INFANT	RRZZZZUSA

SHIP: SCYTHIA

FROM: LIVERPOOL AND QUEENSTOWN
TO: NEW YORK
ARRIVED: 22 APRIL 1888

PASSENGER	AGE	SEX	OCCUPATION	PRV VIL DES
BLAUCHER, JOSEF	30	M	LABR	RRZZZZUSA
GUSSHONCKI, JOHANN	18	M	LABR	RRZZZZUSA
JVIZIS, JOSEF	22	M	LABR	RRZZZZUSA
JACABOK, RAFAEL	23	M	LABR	RRZZZZUSA
NERGUNS, FRANS	32	M	LABR	RRZZZZUSA
RIEZINSKI, IWAN	20	M	LABR	RRZZZZUSA
WARUWETZKI, DAVID	20	M	LABR	RRZZZZUSA
WARNAJUS, SIMON	22	M	LABR	RRZZZZUSA
ANNALU, JOHAN	25	M	LABR	FNZZZZUSA
HILTURA, ALBINUS	24	M	LABR	FNZZZZUSA
HAPPA, AUGUST	23	M	LABR	FNZZZZUSA
KOSKI, SAKRIS	27	M	LABR	FNZZZZUSA
U, MA--	00	M	LABR	FNZZZZUSA
OJO, TOMAS	30	M	LABR	FNZZZZUSA
SAMPI, CARL	27	M	LABR	FNZZZZUSA
TOLANIS, JOHAN	23	M	LABR	FNZZZZUSA
BARTINAKY, FRANS	26	M	LABR	PLZZZZUSA
ANNA	36	F	W	PLZZZZUSA
WANDA	8	F	CHILD	PLZZZZUSA
PASZEYAK, ANTONIO	28	M	MRNR	PLZZZZUSA
JOSEF	11	M	CH	PLZZZZUSA
STANISLAUS	10	M	CH	PLZZZZUSA
JULIA	8	F	CHILD	PLZZZZUSA
WHADISLAUS	4	M	CHILD	PLZZZZUSA
ANTON	.10	M	INFANT	PLZZZZUSA

SHIP: CITY OF RICHMOND

FROM: LIVERPOOL AND QUEENSTOWN
TO: NEW YORK
ARRIVED: 23 APRIL 1888

PASSENGER	AGE	SEX	OCCUPATION	PRV VIL DES
GATZA, MACEIZ	27	M	TLR	PLAHOOMI
BARANOWITZ, ANTON	38	M	LABR	PLAFVGPHI
GSEWITOWITZ, THOMAS	30	M	LABR	PLAEFLPA
MIASIKEWITZ, TH	18	M	LABR	PLAHOOBO
MASAKOWIZ, KASIS	25	M	LABR	PLAHOOBO
PETAITIS, ZAGES	23	M	LABR	PLAHOOPHI
DUDAK, STANISLAUS	27	M	LABR	PLAHOONJ
JASEWITZ, JOSEF	24	M	LABR	PLAHOONJ
HASABUTZKY, ADAM	33	M	TLR	PLAEFLOH
WIDSIKY, MATWEL	24	M	LABR	PLAHOONY
WIDEIKI, JOSEPH	22	M	LABR	PLAHOONY
JASKEWITZ, FELIX	36	M	LABR	PLAHOONY

SHIP: SIBERIAN

FROM: GLASGOW AND LIVERPOOL
TO: BOSTON
ARRIVED: UNKNOWN

PASSENGER	AGE	SEX	OCCUPATION	PRV VIL DES
MAKONSKI, FRANZ	25	M	LABR	PLZZZZNY
ZAGRABSKI, JOSEF	37	M	LABR	PLZZZZNY
RENZ, STANISLAUS	25	M	LABR	PLZZZZNY
ZERZATKONSKI, MICH	22	M	LABR	PLZZZZNY
GROCHSCKI, TH	22	M	LABR	PLZZZZNY
CHICHSCKI, FRANCIS	45	M	LABR	PLZZZZNY
JESICKI, STANISLAUS	21	M	LABR	PLZZZZNY
JANICKI, ANTON	26	M	LABR	PLZZZZNY
KWIATKOWSKY, M	39	M	LABR	PLZZZZNY
SZYMANNSKY, FRANZ	34	M	LABR	PLZZZZNY
FRANCISCA	46	F	UNKNOWN	PLZZZZPA
JOSEFA	15	F	UNKNOWN	PLZZZZPA
FAVENGA	14	F	UNKNOWN	PLZZZZPA
KATARZYNA	9	F	CHILD	PLZZZZPA
JAN	7	M	CHILD	PLZZZZPA
FRANCISCA	6	F	CHILD	PLZZZZPA

SHIP: ETHIOPIA

FROM: GLASGOW AND MOVILLE
TO: NEW YORK
ARRIVED: 24 APRIL 1888

PASSENGER	AGE	SEX	OCCUPATION	PRV VIL DES
RENY, EMIL	26	M	MLR	RRZZZZUSA
SOMMER, AMALIE	22	F	HP	RRZZZZUSA
ROBERT	17	M	UNKNOWN	RRZZZZUSA
JULIUS	11	M	UNKNOWN	RRZZZZUSA
RUTHA	10	F	CH	RRZZZZUSA
CLARA	9	F	CHILD	RRZZZZUSA
ANNA	3	F	CHILD	RRZZZZUSA
JOHN, WILHELM	52	M	TLR	RRZZZZUSA
WILHELMINE	50	F	UNKNOWN	RRZZZZUSA
SOMMER, WILHELM	18	M	TLR	RRZZZZUSA
HEWGER, MATHILDE	20	M	UNKNOWN	RRZZZZUSA
CAROLINE	50	M	UNKNOWN	RRZZZZUSA
WOJERSCHOWSKY, VALENTY	33	M	LABR	RRZZZZUSA
MARIANE	45	F	UNKNOWN	RRZZZZUSA
NOWASCHELSKY, HELENE	20	F	UNKNOWN	RRZZZZUSA
LEIBE	1	F	CHILD	RRZZZZUSA

PASSENGER	AGE	SEX	OCCUPATION	PRV VIL DES
URBANSKY, MICHAEL	25	M	LABR	PLZZZZUSA
ORSULA	25	F	UNKNOWN	PLZZZZUSA

SHIP: FULDA

FROM: BREMEN AND SOUTHAMPTON
TO: NEW YORK
ARRIVED: 24 APRIL 1888

PASSENGER	AGE	SEX	OCCUPATION	PRV VIL DES
DOENHOP, JOHANNA	23	M	FARMER	RRZZZZUSA
KUBIAK, MICHAEL	25	M	FARMER	RRZZZZUSA
FRANZISKA	20	F	UNKNOWN	RRZZZZUSA
FURKEWICZ, FRANZ	28	M	LABR	RRZZZZUSA
GANZINSKY, JAN	33	M	PNTR	RRZZZZUSA
KUR---NY, JANOS	29	M	LABR	RRZZZZUSA
LINDER, MAGDALENA	27	F	UNKNOWN	RRZZZZUSA
BERTHA	5	F	CHILD	RRZZZZUSA
CAROLINE	.07	F	INFANT	RRZZZZUSA
MARIA	3	F	CHILD	RRZZZZUSA
MARIA	20	F	UNKNOWN	RRZZZZUSA
WASIELEWSKA, MARIANNA	16	F	UNKNOWN	RRZZZZUSA
VERONIKA	8	F	CHILD	RRZZZZUSA
ZABUBAUIS, MARIA	16	F	CH	RRZZZZUSA
DREWES, BENJAMIN	39	M	FARMER	RRZZZZUSA
JESSE, JULIUS	23	M	FARMER	RRZZZZUSA
FERING, BENJAMIN	36	M	FARMER	RRZZZZUSA
BERENT, JOHANN	24	M	LABR	RRZZZZUSA
PRIBUDKEWICZ, ANTON	29	M	LABR	RRZZZZUSA
DRLEUZKY, FRANZ	48	M	LABR	RRZZZZUSA
STANKOWSKY, MICHAEL	41	M	LABR	RRZZZZUSA
KRAWULSKY, LEON	35	M	LABR	RRZZZZUSA
MILEWSKY, JOSEF	36	M	LABR	RRZZZZUSA
PESKY, HERMANN	22	M	LABR	RRZZZZUSA
KAZAKEWICZ, MARJAN	21	M	LABR	RRZZZZUSA
PAWLITZKI, STANISLAUS	26	M	LABR	RRZZZZUSA
BALITZKI, JOSEF	25	M	LABR	RRZZZZUSA
MARIAN	17	M	LABR	RRZZZZUSA
ORSCHEKOSKI, SIM	40	M	LABR	RRZZZZUSA
GOVETZKI, JAN	23	M	LABR	RRZZZZUSA
LAWANDOSKI, JAN	21	M	LABR	RRZZZZUSA
GRAPKOWSKI, FRANZ	17	M	FARMER	RRZZZZUSA
PESTA, JAN	20	M	FARMER	RRZZZZUSA
SABOLEWSKY, BARTLOMIN	28	M	FARMER	RRZZZZUSA
GRZYWINSKI, ANTONI	28	M	LABR	RRZZZZUSA
KUWONSKI, KAJETAN	23	M	LABR	RRZZZZUSA
IGNATOWSKI, FRANZISEK	40	M	LABR	RRZZZZUSA
GARABARDA, STANISLAUS	26	M	LABR	RRZZZZUSA
JAN	23	M	LABR	RRZZZZUSA
CHMIGEL, JOSEF	26	M	LABR	RRZZZZUSA
SIEDLOCKI, PIOTR	24	M	LABR	RRZZZZUSA
STRUGULEWSKI, FELIX	40	M	LABR	RRZZZZUSA
ALEX	23	M	LABR	RRZZZZUSA
LEWAKOWSKI, IGNAZY	45	M	LABR	RRZZZZUSA
PALCZEWSKI, FRANCISZE	31	M	LABR	RRZZZZUSA
GALIK, MASIMIR	24	M	LABR	RRZZZZUSA
PIETROWSKI, JAN	34	M	LABR	RRZZZZUSA
STRUGULEWSKI, PIOT	28	M	LABR	RRZZZZUSA
GRESCHKOWSKY, FRANTICZE	25	M	LABR	RRZZZZUSA
ESSLINGER, KARL	43	M	TLR	RRZZZZUSA
ROSINA	41	F	UNKNOWN	RRZZZZUSA
FRIEDRICH	17	M	FSHMN	RRZZZZUSA
SARAH	13	F	UNKNOWN	RRZZZZUSA
CAROLINE	8	F	CHILD	RRZZZZUSA
CHRISTINE	8	F	CHILD	RRZZZZUSA
MICHAEL	7	M	CHILD	RRZZZZUSA
KATHARINE	.09	F	INFANT	RRZZZZUSA
MICHAEL	33	M	PNTR	RRZZZZUSA
WILHELMINE	28	F	UNKNOWN	RRZZZZUSA
CHRISTIAN	8	M	CHILD	RRZZZZUSA
JOHANNES	7	M	CHILD	RRZZZZUSA
CHRISTINE	.09	F	INFANT	RRZZZZUSA
MUNDT, GOTTLIEB	37	M	GDNR	RRZZZZUSA
CHRISTINE	33	F	UNKNOWN	RRZZZZUSA
MAGDALENE	3	F	CHILD	RRZZZZUSA
CHRISTIAN	8	M	CHILD	RRZZZZUSA
CHRISTINE	7	F	CHILD	RRZZZZUSA
FRIEDERIKE	5	F	CHILD	RRZZZZUSA
ROSINE	3	F	CHILD	RRZZZZUSA
CAROLINE	2	F	CHILD	RRZZZZUSA
BARTEL, JOHANN	18	M	BCHR	RRZZZZUSA
MUNDT, FERDINAND	48	M	SMH	RRZZZZUSA
CHRISTINE	46	F	UNKNOWN	RRZZZZUSA
BARBARA	22	F	UNKNOWN	RRZZZZUSA
CHRISTIAN	16	M	LABR	RRZZZZUSA
CHRISTINE	13	F	UNKNOWN	RRZZZZUSA
DOROTHEA	7	F	CHILD	RRZZZZUSA
GOTTLIEB	4	M	CHILD	RRZZZZUSA
HEINZMANN, CHRISTIAN	27	M	FARMER	RRZZZZUSA
CHRISTINE	28	F	UNKNOWN	RRZZZZUSA
MAGDALENE	2	F	CHILD	RRZZZZUSA
ADAM, JOH	16	M	FARMER	RRZZZZUSA
FERDINAND	20	M	FARMER	RRZZZZUSA
BEGLAN, WILHELM	30	M	FARMER	RRZZZZUSA
CAROLINE	30	F	UNKNOWN	RRZZZZUSA
MARIA	3	F	CHILD	RRZZZZUSA
VIRGIN, FRIEDERIKE	60	F	UNKNOWN	RRZZZZUSA
CHRISTOF	16	M	PNTR	RRZZZZUSA
SAMUEL	19	F	PNTR	RRZZZZUSA
CAROLINE	18	F	UNKNOWN	RRZZZZUSA
RADKE, JOHANN	16	M	FARMER	RRZZZZUSA
KARWEL, JAN	29	M	FARMER	RRZZZZUSA
KORZENSKI, ROM	26	M	FARMER	RRZZZZUSA
KRIPA, MICHAEL	47	M	PDLR	RRZZZZUSA
KUSCHEMA, FRANZ	32	M	LABR	RRZZZZUSA
ANNA	28	F	UNKNOWN	RRZZZZUSA
BRONISLAWA	4	F	CHILD	RRZZZZUSA
JOSEF	3	M	CHILD	RRZZZZUSA
MARYANA	.05	F	INFANT	RRZZZZUSA
ZEBELKA, ANDREAS	29	M	PDLR	RRZZZZUSA
MARIANNE	21	F	UNKNOWN	RRZZZZUSA
FRIEDLER, LUDWIG	32	M	LABR	RRZZZZUSA
KOHCSINSKY, THOMAS	26	M	LABR	RRZZZZUSA
KUNZ, CHRIST	37	M	LABR	RRZZZZUSA
EVA	35	F	UNKNOWN	RRZZZZUSA
FRANZISKA	14	F	UNKNOWN	RRZZZZUSA
LINA	8	F	CHILD	RRZZZZUSA
ANNA	7	F	CHILD	RRZZZZUSA
MICHAEL	3	M	CHILD	RRZZZZUSA
EMILIE	.07	F	INFANT	RRZZZZUSA
BOHM, JOSEF	27	M	UNKNOWN	RRZZZZUSA
MAGDALENE	25	F	UNKNOWN	RRZZZZUSA
FRANZ	.06	M	INFANT	RRZZZZUSA
NATHAN, HEINRICH	24	M	LABR	RRZZZZUSA
SCHLOSSER, ADAM	38	M	LABR	RRZZZZUSA
LISAB	35	F	UNKNOWN	RRZZZZUSA
BARBARA	8	F	CHILD	RRZZZZUSA
PHILIPP	8	M	CHILD	RRZZZZUSA
MICHAEL	5	M	CHILD	RRZZZZUSA
HERMINE	4	F	CHILD	RRZZZZUSA
ROSA	3	F	CHILD	RRZZZZUSA
MARIANNE	2	F	CHILD	RRZZZZUSA
EVA	.06	F	INFANT	RRZZZZUSA
JACOB	46	M	LABR	RRZZZZUSA
MARIANNE	42	F	UNKNOWN	RRZZZZUSA
ELISABETH	19	F	UNKNOWN	RRZZZZUSA
ADAM	8	M	CHILD	RRZZZZUSA
PETER	6	M	CHILD	RRZZZZUSA
JOSEPHINE	.07	F	INFANT	RRZZZZUSA

SHIP: WYOMING

FROM: LIVERPOOL AND QUEENSTOWN
TO: NEW YORK
ARRIVED: 25 APRIL 1888

PASSENGER	AGE	SEX	OCCUPATION	PRV VIL DES
PONINERER, KARL	21	M	FARMER	RRZZZZUSA
ITZKOWITZ, DORA	28	F	W	RRZZZZUSA
IREAH	8	F	CHILD	RRZZZZUSA
FANNIE	6	F	CHILD	RRZZZZUSA
ESTHER	5	F	CHILD	RRZZZZUSA
SCHONBAUN, B.	21	F	W	RRZZZZUSA
ROSA	7	F	CHILD	RRZZZZUSA
BRUCHE	5	M	CHILD	RRZZZZUSA
KASAMINSKI, ELIZ.	22	F	SVNT	RRZZZZUSA
GUSTAVUS, MAGDAL.	23	F	SVNT	RRZZZZUSA
LINWOOD, ABON	22	M	LABR	RRZZZZUSA
GULLMANN, EIZCH	21	M	LABR	RRZZZZUSA
RIFKE	18	F	SVNT	RRZZZZUSA
SOVANOSIKK, FANIZ	24	M	LABR	RRZZZZUSA
KEIB, KORNKRANT	22	F	SVNT	RRZZZZUSA
MENDEL, ZABLON	20	M	LABR	RRZZZZUSA
MABWAYFFE, ADAM	22	M	LABR	RRZZZZUSA
SIGNAL, SARA	24	F	SVNT	RRZZZZUSA
LAMPORT, SUSANA	35	M	LABR	RRZZZZUSA
MINDEL	32	F	W	RRZZZZUSA
RYKE	5	M	CHILD	RRZZZZUSA
MIREL	4	M	CHILD	RRZZZZUSA
RACHAEL	1	M	CHILD	RRZZZZUSA
BANK, JESSE	28	F	SVNT	RRZZZZUSA
MAL.	18	F	SVNT	RRZZZZUSA
MINNIE	24	F	SVNT	RRZZZZUSA
HORN, ELISE	28	M	LABR	RRZZZZUSA
SCHONBAUN, GUNCHE	1	F	CHILD	RRZZZZUSA
RABY, ABRAM	28	M	LABR	RRZZZZUSA
NORDIKAN, KEIDE	22	F	SVNT	RRZZZZUSA
GRODE, EMELIA	25	F	SP	PLZZZZUSA
KOLKOWSKY, ROSA	20	F	SP	PLZZZZUSA
F.	25	M	LABR	PLZZZZUSA
KORGINE, H.	36	M	LABR	PLZZZZUSA
MADAUTS, WM.	30	M	LABR	PLZZZZUSA
TWAMSKINGA, A.	20	M	LABR	PLZZZZUSA
CATH.	30	F	W	PLZZZZUSA
RIDBERG, MAG.	4	F	CHILD	PLZZZZUSA
JENNY	00	F	INF	PLZZZZUSA
SORENTZ, F.	23	M	LABR	PLZZZZUSA
BECKER, A.	38	M	LABR	PLZZZZUSA
FRANZ	35	F	W	PLZZZZUSA
MARTIN	4	M	CHILD	PLZZZZUSA
JEAN	7	M	CHILD	PLZZZZUSA
MARGT.	00	F	INF	PLZZZZUSA
ANNA	00	F	W	PLZZZZUSA
MOLET--, FRANCOIS	27	M	LABR	PLZZZZUSA
SCHROEDER, JEAN	25	M	LABR	PLZZZZUSA
LIST--, N.	16	M	LABR	PLZZZZUSA
WEIMER, PIENS	22	M	LABR	PLZZZZUSA
SANDER, MICHEL	27	M	LABR	PLZZZZUSA
MANGEN, P.	29	M	LABR	PLZZZZUSA
HERBIN, M.	27	M	LABR	PLZZZZUSA
STROMBISSON, A.	19	M	LABR	PLZZZZUSA
FRANKOWSKI, V.	27	M	LABR	PLZZZZUSA
MARIA	23	F	W	PLZZZZUSA
LYIFRANSKY, J.	23	M	LABR	PLZZZZUSA
ANTOLINA	23	F	W	PLZZZZUSA
MARIANA	00	F	INF	PLZZZZUSA
STANISLAUS	00	M	INF	PLZZZZUSA
U	45	M	LABR	PLZZZZUSA
LEON	7	M	CHILD	PLZZZZUSA
REBECCA	7	F	CHILD	PLZZZZUSA
ARON	6	M	CHILD	PLZZZZUSA
ABEL	50	M	LABR	PLZZZZUSA
KIRNOWSKY, J.	20	M	LABR	PLZZZZUSA
ROBERT, MARENO	31	F	SP	PLZZZZUSA
ZWANZIGER, JOS.	17	M	LABR	PLZZZZUSA
KREZ, LEIB	26	M	LABR	PLZZZZUSA
HERCLOWITZ, LEIB	48	M	LABR	PLZZZZUSA
LAWATZY, JOHAN	35	M	LABR	PLZZZZUSA
LEWANDOSKY, JAN.	24	M	LABR	RRZZZZUSA
ORLOWSKY, M.	25	M	LABR	RRZZZZUSA
NARB-T, J.	38	F	SP	RRZZZZUSA
AREFITZ, J.	35	M	LABR	RRZZZZUSA
KILESKY, JOHANN	25	M	LABR	RRZZZZUSA
NEHL, CARL	51	M	LABR	RRZZZZUSA
SCHAFFERUS, WM.	22	M	LABR	RRZZZZUSA
JAROSSKY, J.	36	M	LABR	RRZZZZUSA
FRANCO.	22	F	W	RRZZZZUSA
MADELINA	7	F	CHILD	RRZZZZUSA
WADESLOWA	7	M	CHILD	RRZZZZUSA
STANISLAUS	00	M	INF	RRZZZZUSA
CAS.	00	F	INF	RRZZZZUSA
BARTH.	33	M	LABR	RRZZZZUSA
THERESA	18	F	W	RRZZZZUSA

SHIP: GELLERT

FROM: HAMBURG
TO: NEW YORK
ARRIVED: 26 APRIL 1888

PASSENGER	AGE	SEX	OCCUPATION	PRV VIL DES
GAWEITSCH, CASEMIR	43	M	UNKNOWN	RRZZZZNY
WIROSCH, IGNATZ	49	M	UNKNOWN	RRZZZZNY
WASNAK, JAN	28	M	UNKNOWN	RRZZZZNY
OLESA, SCHAFRAN	40	M	UNKNOWN	RRZZZZNY
SKIBA, FRANZ	33	M	UNKNOWN	RRZZZZNY
WOSNAK, JANESCHI	34	U	UNKNOWN	RRZZZZNY
PUSALSKY, ADAM	40	M	UNKNOWN	RRZZZZNY
MARIANNA	40	F	W	RRZZZZNY
AGNES	4	F	CHILD	RRZZZZNY
IGNATZ	3	M	CHILD	RRZZZZNY
SCHERLING, GEORG	48	M	LABR	RRAIOONY
BETHGE, JOHANN	54	M	LABR	RRAIOONY
GOTTLIEB	21	M	LABR	RRAIOONY
GOTTFRIED	9	M	CHILD	RRAIOONY
GUST, GOTTFRIED	32	M	LABR	RRAIOONY
PEHDE, CHRISTIAN	29	M	LABR	RRAIOONY
DITTBRENNER, JUL.	22	M	LABR	RRAIOONY
RUDOLF	25	M	LABR	RRAIOONY
BUSALSKY, FRANZ	9	M	CHILD	RRAIOONY
OSTROWKA, JOHA.	22	F	WO	RRZZZZNY
FRANZ	00	M	INF	RRZZZZNY
ZITOWICKI, JAN	20	M	LABR	RRZZZZNY
PASDRINSKY, ANTON	20	M	LABR	RRZZZZNY
LAMANSKY, CONSTANTIN	23	M	LABR	RRZZZZNY
WITKOWSKY, CARL	22	M	LABR	RRZZZZNY
DILIKAWSKY, JOS.	23	M	LABR	RRZZZZNY
LEWINSKY, VINCENT	25	M	LABR	RRAHZSNY
JELIONAWSKY, JOH.	20	M	LABR	RRAHZSNY
MARIANNA	25	F	W	RRAHZSNY
RATSCHAWSKY, WOYCECH	29	M	LABR	RRAHZSNY
BELAWSKY, JOHANN	20	M	LABR	RRAHZSNY
JANDRASKA, ANTON	34	M	LABR	RRAHZSNY
WILANSKY, JULIAN	30	M	LABR	RRAHZSNY
OSRTOWSKY, FRANTISEK	26	M	LABR	RRAHZSNY
ANTONIA	26	F	W	RRAHZSNY
JULIUS	00	M	INF	RRAHZSNY
SALEWSKY, VINCENT	30	M	LABR	RRAHZSNY
GOLOVSKY, JAN	30	M	LABR	RRAHZSNY
DOMBROWSKI, FRANZ	30	M	SGL	RRAHZSNY
BAIKOWSKY, JACOB	25	M	LABR	RRAHZSNY
BOLOWSKY, WOJCECH	33	M	LABR	RRZZZZNY
GOLAZINSKI, STANISL.	42	M	LABR	RRZZZZNY
PRCZEWSLY, PAWEL	37	M	LABR	RRZZZZNY
MIKOAESCH, WOJTECH	27	M	LABR	RRZZZZNY
PILARSKI, STANISL.	27	M	LABR	RRZZZZNY

PASSENGER	AGE	SEX	OCCUPATION	PRV VIL DES
SCHRAMM, GUSTAV	23	M	LABR	RRZZZZNY
EWERT, MARTON	30	M	LABR	RRZZZZNY
RACHWOLSKI, THOMAS	45	M	LABR	RRZZZZNY
JOHN	19	M	LABR	RRZZZZNY
GROMELSKI, STANISL.	22	M	LABR	RRZZZZNY
LUBLAK, FRANZ	27	M	LABR	RRZZZZNY
MILS, WOYCSCH	28	M	LABR	RRZZZZNY
SUNZIK, PETER	25	M	LABR	RRAICHNY
KANIA, PETER	41	M	LABR	RRAHTONY
LUCAS	9	M	CHILD	RRAHTONY
BARONOWSKY, FRANZ	31	M	LABR	RRAHTONY
KAWALCHIK, JAN	33	M	LABR	RRAHTONY
RUSZIK, JUL.	33	M	LABR	RRAHTONY
SAMMESKI, FRANZ	48	M	LABR	RRAHTONY
KORDEK, JOSEF	26	M	LABR	RRAHTONY
MARSCHEFSKI, FRANZ	38	M	LABR	RRAHTONY
TUMINS, FRANZ	42	M	LABR	RRAHTONY
KOWSALSCHIK, WOYCISCH	28	M	LABR	RRAHTONY
POPIELATZKI, VALENT	23	M	LABR	RRAHTONY
KORSCHANTZKI, FRANZ	27	M	LABR	RRAHTONY
SZINZIK, JAN	27	M	LABR	RRAHTONY
SCHILKOVSKY, JAN	23	M	LABR	RRAHTONY
GUROCKY, JOH.	27	M	LABR	RRZZZZNY
FRANKOWIAK, ANTON	42	M	LABR	RRZZZZNY
BUNIN, MENDEL	39	M	DLR	RRZZZZNY
NOACH	22	M	DLR	RRZZZZNY
HATHAN	18	M	DLR	RRZZZZNY
KOPSZEWSKI, FRANZ	20	M	DLR	RRZZZZNY
BYK, KOPEL	22	M	WCHMKR	RRZZZZNY
TROPOLSKI, NACHUME	36	F	WO	RRZZZZNY
BEILE	17	F	CH	RRZZZZNY
MORDCHE	9	F	CHILD	RRZZZZNY
CHAJE	7	F	CHILD	RRZZZZNY
SALOMON	5	M	CHILD	RRZZZZNY
ZASLAWSKI, SCHAJE	36	M	TLR	RRZZZZNY
KRAMER, ARON	40	M	MCHT	RRAIOONY
PETROFSKI, JOSEF	50	M	LABR	RRZZZZNY
MARIANNA	00	F	SGL	RRZZZZNY
GOLOMBIESKI, JAN	21	M	LABR	RRZZZZNY
KUWRONSKY, JAN	24	M	LABR	RRZZZZNY
SZYMANSKI, ADAM	29	M	LABR	RRAIEQNY
JOSEF	15	M	LABR	RRAIEQNY
LOEWENTHAL, BERNHA.	24	M	LABR	RRAIINNY
HARTWIG, JESS	59	M	FARMER	RRAHZSNY
GRETHE	54	F	W	RRAHZSNY
PIWSLEK, VINCENTY	26	M	LABR	RRAHZSNY
MIERZEJEWSKY, PIOTR	31	M	LABR	RRAHZSNY
ZELADOWSKI, KAPETAN	24	M	LABR	RRAHZSNY
GADZON, CASEMIR	34	M	LABR	RRAHZSNY
MROZINZWIEZ, MACEI	18	M	LABR	RRAHZSNY
RUSOWIEZ, ANTONI	28	M	LABR	RRAHZSNY
FISCHER, JESIN	25	M	SMH	RRAIINNY
CHRISTELEIT, ADAM	39	M	LABR	RRAHZSNY
BANASCHEWSKY, STANISL	43	M	LABR	RRZZZZNY
POLARSKY, LEON	24	M	LABR	RRZZZZNY
ARNIMSKI, JAN	40	M	LABR	RRZZZZNY
ROMMDT, JAN	42	M	LABR	RRZZZZNY
KUPETZKI, ANTON	26	M	LABR	RRZZZZNY
UTUP, AUG.	33	M	LABR	RRZZZZNY
PAWLITZKY, FRANZ	54	M	LABR	RRAIMENY
WISCHNEWSKY, MICHAL	23	M	LABR	RRZZZZNY
KRAPKOWSKY, ANDRAS	34	M	LABR	RRZZZZNY
CELKOWSKY, JOS.	23	M	LABR	RRAIMENY
DAWALSCHIN, ANTON	34	M	LABR	RRAHUINY
DRASDIBITZKY, JOS.	24	M	LABR	RRAHUINY
WARGREN, CARL	32	M	SLR	RRAIEKNY
GRANHOLM, OTTO	29	M	SLR	RRAIEKNY
GUSTAVSON, MARGA.	43	F	W	RRAIEKNY
EMILIE	9	F	CHILD	RRAIEKNY
HERIBAT	9	M	CHILD	RRAIEKNY
HOLM, MATS.	20	M	FARMER	RRAIEKNY
HOEGMANN, GUSTAV	22	M	FARMER	RRAIEKNY
LITEUR, ALEXANDER	28	M	FARMER	RRZZZZNY
BRASCH, ANDERS	29	M	FARMER	RRZZZZNY
ISCHONASKY, U	00	M	INF	RRAHZSNY
MAKSIMOWIZ, ANTONY	35	F	SGL	RRAHZSNY

SHIP: NORSEMAN

FROM: LIVERPOOL
TO: BOSTON
ARRIVED: UNKNOWN

PASSENGER	AGE	SEX	OCCUPATION	PRV VIL DES
RUBENSTEIN, DAVID	23	M	LABR	RRZZZZNY
BRAMORSKY, MORRIS	26	M	LABR	RRZZZZNY
FUCHS, ABRAHAM	45	M	MECH	RRZZZZBO
NY, PAUL	20	M	MECH	RRZZZZBO
WARAKA, PIOTR	28	M	MECH	RRZZZZBO
DOPKOWSKI, JOSEPH	23	M	MECH	RRZZZZBO
KUCHOWOROSKI, ABETANA	28	M	MECH	RRZZZZBO
JACOBOWITZ, KARIM---	28	M	MECH	RRZZZZBO
LUIKI, PETER	23	M	MECH	RRZZZZBO
GABL--, JOSEPH	00	M	MECH	RRZZZZBO
KASIMMA--, PETER	23	M	MECH	RRZZZZBO
MILKE, MICHAEL	24	M	MECH	RRZZZZBO
-ESHIPULOWITZ, JOHAN	24	M	MECH	RRZZZZBO
TISCHEWITZ, JULIUS	42	M	MECH	RRZZZZBO
BUTWILES, JULIUS	27	M	MECH	RRZZZZBO
TSCHIPULWITZ, JOSEPH	37	M	MECH	RRZZZZBO
MISCHNOWITZ, JULIUS	28	M	MECH	RRZZZZBO
DUI-E, AUGUST	33	M	MECH	RRZZZZUNK
ELECRA, CHRISTIAN	31	M	MECH	RRZZZZUNK
RAC--IMM-S, GEORGE	32	M	MECH	RRZZZZUNK
BRUSTUS, CHRISTOPHE	20	M	MECH	RRZZZZUNK
MALLWELL, FREA	29	M	MECH	RRZZZZUNK
NAPOUS, HENRY	30	M	MECH	RRZZZZUNK
PITZULAS, MICH	52	M	MECH	RRZZZZUNK
H-MMSDO-A, FERDINAND	16	M	UNKNOWN	RRZZZZUNK

SHIP: STATE OF GEORGIA

FROM: GLASGOW AND LARNE
TO: NEW YORK
ARRIVED: 26 APRIL 1888

PASSENGER	AGE	SEX	OCCUPATION	PRV VIL DES
ALLSCHEWSKI, OSIP	24	M	LABR	RRZZZZUSA
BANTZALL, JOHAN	26	M	LABR	RRZZZZUSA
RADOWA	40	F	W	RRZZZZUSA
KATARINA	19	F	SVNT	RRZZZZUSA
STEFAN	.09	M	INFANT	RRZZZZUSA
BARTSCHENSKI, JOHAN	25	M	LABR	RRZZZZUSA
BARZEFSKI, LEON	25	M	LABR	RRZZZZUSA
BEDNACK, JEAN	31	M	LABR	RRZZZZUSA
MAGDALENA	25	F	W	RRZZZZUSA
JOSEFA	1	F	CHILD	RRZZZZUSA
APOTKA, MICHAEL	28	M	LABR	RRZZZZUSA
MARIANNA	.03	F	INFANT	RRZZZZUSA
DUBENSOWE, KRISTINE	50	F	W	RRZZZZUSA
FILLIPOWAT, FRANZ	40	M	PDLR	RRZZZZUSA
THEODORA	30	F	W	RRZZZZUSA
BRONISLAW	2	M	CHILD	RRZZZZUSA
ADOLPH	.03	M	INFANT	RRZZZZUSA
GRAJEWSKI, JACOB	21	M	LABR	RRZZZZUSA
HARRIS, BENJ.	19	M	LABR	RRZZZZUSA
JARDOWSKI, VALENTIN	25	M	LABR	RRZZZZUSA
KALETTA, FRANCISCHEK	17	M	LABR	RRZZZZUSA
CONSTANTINE	23	F	SVNT	RRZZZZUSA
KAWANOWSKI, KITTON	26	M	LABR	RRZZZZUSA
KIVOWALSKY, FRANZ	21	M	LABR	RRZZZZUSA
KOLISKI, VALENTIN	45	M	LABR	RRZZZZUSA

PASSENGER	AGE	SEX	OCCUPATION	PRIV	VIL	DES
KANINSKI, ANDREZ	25	M	LABR	RR	ZZZZ	USA
KRAEMPER, JOHAN	37	M	LABR	RR	ZZZZ	USA
KRETZKA, KATZEN	21	F	W	RR	ZZZZ	USA
JOSEF	.03	M	INFANT	RR	ZZZZ	USA
KRUTISKOWSKI, FRANZISCH	32	M	LABR	RR	ZZZZ	USA
KRZYNOCIK, VALENTZ	25	M	LABR	RR	ZZZZ	USA
KOENIG, FRANZ	30	M	LABR	RR	ZZZZ	USA
JOHAN	29	M	LABR	RR	ZZZZ	USA
LIZEWSKI, THOMAS	37	M	LABR	RR	ZZZZ	USA
MACZINSKI, FRANZ	25	M	LABR	RR	ZZZZ	USA
MATHEOWITZ, MARIA	22	F	SVNT	RR	ZZZZ	USA
MAKOWSKI, ANTON	16	M	LABR	RR	ZZZZ	USA
THOMAS	4	M	CHILD	RR	ZZZZ	USA
MAPALIS, ANDRY	30	M	LABR	RR	ZZZZ	USA
NARKIEWICZ, AUGUSTINE	30	F	W	RR	ZZZZ	USA
PAVEL	6	M	CHILD	RR	ZZZZ	USA
STANISLAWA	3	F	CHILD	RR	ZZZZ	USA
DOMINIK	2	M	CHILD	RR	ZZZZ	USA
ANTON	.06	M	INFANT	RR	ZZZZ	USA
PAULUS, VALENTIN	34	M	LABR	RR	ZZZZ	USA
MARIANE	30	F	W	RR	ZZZZ	USA
THOMAS	5	M	CHILD	RR	ZZZZ	USA
LUDOVICA	3	F	CHILD	RR	ZZZZ	USA
PELAZIE	1	F	CHILD	RR	ZZZZ	USA
PIETROWICZ, STANISLAUS	24	M	LABR	RR	ZZZZ	USA
PILINSKI, PAWEL	25	M	LABR	RR	ZZZZ	USA
POPLAWSKI, JACOB	24	M	LABR	RR	ZZZZ	USA
PUTRIS, MICHEL	25	M	LABR	RR	ZZZZ	USA
ROGALSKI, FRANZ	40	M	MCHT	RR	ZZZZ	USA
ANNA	35	F	W	RR	ZZZZ	USA
FELIX	11	M	CH	RR	ZZZZ	USA
PETRONELLA	8	F	CHILD	RR	ZZZZ	USA
WILESIA	3	F	CHILD	RR	ZZZZ	USA
TONY	.06	F	INFANT	RR	ZZZZ	USA
SAVARSKI, ANSCHER	26	M	LABR	RR	ZZZZ	USA
SAVORSKI, PIOT.	23	M	LABR	RR	ZZZZ	USA
SCHAFRANSKI, JACOB	40	M	LABR	RR	ZZZZ	USA
LUDNYA	27	F	W	RR	ZZZZ	USA
ANTON	1	M	CHILD	RR	ZZZZ	USA
SCHNITKA, JACOB	31	M	LABR	RR	ZZZZ	USA
SCHWITSCHEK, VOJWOCK	30	M	LABR	RR	ZZZZ	USA
SKORDAN, JEAN	33	M	LABR	RR	ZZZZ	USA
SLOTOROWICZKI, FRANZ	27	M	LABR	RR	ZZZZ	USA
SZWERBINE, PETER	28	M	LABR	RR	ZZZZ	USA
WALKOWIAK, JACOB	30	M	LABR	RR	ZZZZ	USA
WALUKONIS, VICENTY	18	M	LABR	RR	ZZZZ	USA
ZIERKOWSKA, KATARINA	50	F	W	RR	ZZZZ	USA

SHIP: THE QUEEN

FROM: LIVERPOOL AND QUEENSTOWN
TO: NEW YORK
ARRIVED: 27 APRIL 1888

PASSENGER	AGE	SEX	OCCUPATION	PRIV	VIL	DES
SCHWARTZ, JOS.	26	M	LABR	RR	ZZZZ	NY
SECKEIM, N.	27	M	LABR	RR	ADBQ	NY
ROSENFIELD, B.	30	M	LABR	RR	ADBQ	NY
GOLDSTEIN, M.	30	M	LABR	RR	ZZZZ	NY
TOMCHOWSKI, B.	35	M	CH	RR	ZZZZ	NY
MALAKOFF, A.	27	M	LABR	RR	ZZZZ	NY
RUOSS, LUDWIG	24	M	LABR	RR	ZZZZ	NY
SUDIN, CONRAD	21	M	LABR	RR	ZZZZ	NY
VUSSELOFF, ADAM	52	M	LABR	RR	ZZZZ	NY
JASSON, HAROLD	39	M	LABR	RR	ZZZZ	NY
STRAPESTY, ANTON	40	M	LABR	RR	ZZZZ	NY
WUZLOVSKY, FRANZ	28	M	LABR	RR	ZZZZ	NY
ANTON	24	M	LABR	RR	ZZZZ	NY
KUPUTSKEY, NATHAN	34	M	LABR	RR	ZZZZ	NY
RUKOWSKY, JOHN	37	M	LABR	RR	ZZZZ	NY
WUESTAL, HERMAN	18	M	LABR	RR	ZZZZ	NY
PEPI	18	M	LABR	RR	ZZZZ	NY
CZGON-KI, HAUTEN	15	M	LABR	RR	ZZZZ	PHI
CLEV.	11	M	CH	RR	ZZZZ	PHI
ALBERT	8	M	CHILD	RR	ZZZZ	PHI
STEPHAN	6	M	CHILD	RR	ZZZZ	PHI
JOSEPHA	4	M	CHILD	RR	ZZZZ	PHI
ANTON	2	M	CHILD	RR	ZZZZ	PHI
ADMACK, ANTONIA	22	M	LABR	PL	ZZZZ	PHI
WANZ, GOTLIEB	36	M	LABR	RR	ZZZZ	PHI
HOLONSKY, THOMAS	32	M	LABR	RR	ZZZZ	PHI
SARAFINA, K.	27	M	LABR	RR	ZZZZ	DET
NICKKIN, K.	30	M	LABR	RR	ZZZZ	NY
MULLIRERI, JOHN	45	M	LABR	RR	ZZZZ	NY
WASLIE, JOHN	35	M	LABR	RR	ZZZZ	NY
NAWAWSKY, FRANTZ	32	M	LABR	RR	ZZZZ	NY
MARINA	23	F	W	RR	ZZZZ	NY
JOSEFA	8	F	CHILD	RR	ZZZZ	NY
THEKLA	4	F	CHILD	RR	ZZZZ	NY
HELENA	1	M	CHILD	RR	ZZZZ	NY
LEO	2	M	CHILD	RR	ZZZZ	NY
SAMBORCHI, M.	23	F	SP	RR	ZZZZ	NY

SHIP: TRAVE

FROM: BREMEN AND SOUTHAMPTON
TO: NEW YORK
ARRIVED: 27 APRIL 1888

PASSENGER	AGE	SEX	OCCUPATION	PRIV	VIL	DES
KWIATNOWSKI, FRANCIZEK	46	M	LABR	RR	ZZZZ	USA
ARGULSKA, HELENA	30	F	UNKNOWN	RR	ZZZZ	USA
SOPHIA	2	F	CHILD	RR	ZZZZ	USA
STODOWSKI, JOSEF	21	M	LABR	RR	ZZZZ	USA
KORSIRSKY, FRANZ	30	M	LABR	RR	ZZZZ	USA
BYNCEKI, JAN	24	M	LABR	RR	ZZZZ	USA
LAWINSKY, JAN	24	M	LABR	RR	ZZZZ	USA
WINDINGER, JAN	27	M	LABR	RR	ZZZZ	USA
JUDWICSI, ANDRAS	30	M	LABR	RR	ZZZZ	USA
MYCLINSKI, VALENTZ	30	M	LABR	RR	ZZZZ	USA
LASKOWSKY, LEON	34	M	LABR	RR	ZZZZ	USA
ISRAEL, DAVID	25	M	LABR	RR	ZZZZ	USA
OLIAN, MORITZ	16	M	LABR	RR	ZZZZ	USA
GARUNTZKY, ISRAEL	20	M	LABR	RR	ZZZZ	USA
HIRSCHOWITZ, JOSSEL	28	M	LABR	RR	ZZZZ	USA
KRADENSKY, JOSEF	33	M	CH	RR	ZZZZ	USA
SLAVINSKY, JOSEF	20	M	CH	RR	ZZZZ	USA
NARWIDOWNA, SAL.	24	M	CH	RR	ZZZZ	USA
ANELA	30	F	UNKNOWN	RR	ZZZZ	USA
CATHA.	.02	F	INFANT	RR	ZZZZ	USA
ERUGOWITZ, EVA	17	F	UNKNOWN	RR	ZZZZ	USA
STANISLAUS, IVAN	30	M	LABR	RR	ZZZZ	USA
RUTKAWSKY, JAN	30	M	LABR	RR	ZZZZ	USA
POLONIS, SIGM.	23	M	LABR	RR	ZZZZ	USA
BALSCHEWSKY, JUST.	23	M	LABR	RR	ZZZZ	USA
PAULA.	20	F	UNKNOWN	RR	ZZZZ	USA
STANISL.	1	M	CHILD	RR	ZZZZ	USA
BOBSL.	.06	M	INFANT	RR	ZZZZ	USA
POSCHKIS, JERZI	26	M	UNKNOWN	RR	ZZZZ	USA
PASCHEFRAWA, ROSALIE	45	M	UNKNOWN	RR	ZZZZ	USA
ROSALIE	7	F	CHILD	RR	ZZZZ	USA
ANTONIA	22	F	UNKNOWN	RR	ZZZZ	USA

PASSENGER	AGE	SEX	OCCUPATION	PRIVL	DES
SHIP: MAIN					
FROM: BREMEN					
TO: BALTIMORE					
ARRIVED: 28 APRIL 1888					
BOTT, CONR.	17	M	FARMER	RRZZZZ	BAL
DOMBEK, JOHANN	31	M	FARMER	RRZZZZ	BAL
RUMANOWSKI, WOJCIECH	21	M	FARMER	RRZZZZ	BAL
KAMINSKI, JAN	26	M	FARMER	RRZZZZ	MD
TRAUT, HEINR.	20	M	FARMER	RRAIIX	MD
BOTT, HEINR.	30	M	FARMER	RRAIIX	PA
LOUISE	33	F	W	RRAIIX	PA
LOUISE	3	F	CHILD	RRAIIX	PA
HEINR.	.01	M	INFANT	RRAIIX	PA
GLANZ, JACOB	44	M	FARMER	RRAIIX	PA
CATHARINE	44	F	W	RRAIIX	PA
WILHELM	21	M	FARMER	RRAIIX	PA
HEINR.	19	M	FARMER	RRAIIX	PA
ELISAB.	17	F	CH	RRAIIX	PA
CHRISTINE	14	F	CH	RRAIIX	PA
CATHR.	9	F	CHILD	RRAIIX	PA
JOHANNE	8	M	CHILD	RRAIIX	PA
ULBRICH, FRANZ	41	M	FARMER	RRAIIX	KY
ANNA	22	F	W	RRAIIX	KY
GIZWINSKA, KATARZYNA	21	F	MLNR	RRZZZZ	MD

PASSENGER	AGE	SEX	OCCUPATION	PRIVL	DES
SHIP: TAORMINA					
FROM: HAMBURG					
TO: NEW YORK					
ARRIVED: 28 APRIL 1888					
RUCHSCZO, ANDR	20	M	LABR	RRZZZZ	NY
WANDROWSKY, MAGDALA	16	F	SGL	RRZZZZ	NY
WAWROWSKI, ANTONIN	43	M	LABR	RRZZZZ	NY
RIKACZEWSKI, JULIAN	51	M	LABR	RRZZZZ	NY
KA-ECZYNKI, IGNATZ	19	M	LABR	RRZZZZ	NY
BABERSKY, ADAM	27	M	LABR	RRZZZZ	NY
SZULINSKI, PIOTR	24	M	LABR	RRZZZZ	NY
RULTISZEWIEZ, PIOTR	24	M	LABR	RRZZZZ	NY
MOSAITISZ, ADAM	30	M	LABR	RRZZZZ	NY
-IBISZ, KASIMIR	24	M	LABR	RRZZZZ	NY
EVANGELISCH, WRAWROZIN	40	M	FARMER	RRZZZZ	NY
SIETZAN, JOS	31	M	LABR	RRZZZZ	NY
ANNA	34	F	W	RRZZZZ	NY
WOND-OSKI, P---EL	41	M	LABR	RRZZZZ	NY
CINNANSKI, LEON	18	M	LABR	RRZZZZ	NY
ZWOLENSKY, DAMASY	19	M	LABR	RRZZZZ	NY
RAFALOVSKA, FRANZISZCK	23	M	LABR	RRAIDA	NY
BOROSSKI, MICHAL	29	M	LABR	RRAIDA	NY
PAWELOWSKY, LUDWIG	33	M	LABR	RRAIDA	NY
MARSCHALL, CHARL	27	M	LABR	RRAIDA	NY
DULKANSKI, BRONISLAW	26	M	LABR	RRAIDA	NY
BRADOWSKI, FRANZISZEK	23	M	LABR	RRAIDA	NY
BENKE, JULIUS	36	M	LABR	RRAIDA	NY
WELLING, GOTTLIEB	26	M	LABR	RRAIDA	NY
FRIED	23	M	LABR	RRAIDA	NY
SI--NIEWSKY, MARTIN	32	M	LABR	RRAIDA	NY
MAKIMO--SY, ANTON	35	M	LABR	RRAIDA	NY
ROSENKOWITZ, JOS	26	M	LABR	RRAIDA	NY
ZABLIK, ABRAHAM	26	M	LABR	RRAIDA	NY

PASSENGER	AGE	SEX	OCCUPATION	PRIVL	DES
SHIP: WIELAND					
FROM: HAMBURG					
TO: NEW YORK					
ARRIVED: 28 APRIL 1888					
LANGE, CARL	36	M	FARMER	RRZZZZ	USA
ROSALIE	26	F	W	RRZZZZ	USA
LYDIA	9	F	CHILD	RRZZZZ	USA
MARIE	7	F	CHILD	RRZZZZ	USA
MATHILDE	4	F	CHILD	RRZZZZ	USA
AMALIE	.11	F	INFANT	RRZZZZ	USA
KUNT, GOTTFRIED	31	M	FARMER	RRZZZZ	USA
EVA	31	F	W	RRZZZZ	USA
FRIEDR.	6	M	CHILD	RRZZZZ	USA
ADOLPHINE	4	F	CHILD	RRZZZZ	USA
ULMER, JACOB	40	M	FARMER	RRZZZZ	USA
RODE, JOHAMS	31	M	FARMER	RRZZZZ	USA
JOHAMS	31	M	FARMER	RRZZZZ	USA
MARIE	31	F	W	RRZZZZ	USA
EMILIE	4	M	CHILD	RRZZZZ	USA
ADOLF	.11	M	INFANT	RRZZZZ	USA
FAKLIN, WILH.	40	M	TDR	FNZZZZ	USA
MALINOFSKY, MOSES	18	M	DLR	RRZZZZ	USA
WISCHNOWSKY, ROMAN	18	M	LABR	RRZZZZ	USA
SMOLIKEWICZ, STANISL.	30	M	LABR	RRZZZZ	USA
MASCHKEWICZ, MICHAEL	28	M	LABR	RRZZZZ	USA
CHOCZKY, JAN	19	M	LABR	RRZZZZ	USA
MASCHKOWITZ, STANISL.	40	M	LABR	RRZZZZ	USA
KOWALSKY, MARTEN	27	M	LABR	RRZZZZ	USA
ZELMER, JOS.	33	M	LABR	RRZZZZ	USA
HONZEK, VACLAV	40	M	MNR	RRZZZZ	USA
WASZINSKI, WAWZINCE	30	M	LABR	RRZZZZ	***
STANISLAUS	22	M	LABR	RRZZZZ	***
MELLER, MARIAN	16	M	LABR	RRZZZZ	***
FABNISKI, IGNATZ	40	M	LABR	RRZZZZ	***
ZMESEWICZ, FRANZ	36	M	LABR	RRZZZZ	***
SCHOTKOWSKY, PETER	23	M	LABR	RRZZZZ	***
MOJEFSKY, FRANZ	35	M	LABR	RRZZZZ	***
WITKOVSKY, WLADISLAV	18	M	LABR	RRZZZZ	***
BUNETZKI, MARIAN	22	M	LABR	RRZZZZ	***
SCHETZKI, SCHIMO	22	M	LABR	RRZZZZ	***
MEIEFSKI, CASIMIR	33	M	LABR	RRZZZZ	***
JAN	29	M	LABR	RRZZZZ	***
ROTENBERG, ARON	36	M	LABR	RRZZZZ	***
PAULINE	16	F	SGL	RRZZZZ	***
HORULA, HERM.	28	M	LABR	FNZZZZ	***
ERICHSEN, JACOB	30	M	LABR	FNZZZZ	***
SUCHOSELSKI, MICHAEL	39	M	SHMK	RRZZZZ	***
SPIEGELMANN, CHAIM	40	M	DLR	RRZZZZ	***
GILBERT, SARA	22	F	WO	RRZZZZ	***
RAHEL	.11	F	INFANT	RRZZZZ	***
GURWITZ, LEA	20	F	WO	RRZZZZ	***
MICHEL	.11	M	INFANT	RRZZZZ	***
RYBAKEWICZ, ANTONY	36	M	LABR	RRZZZZ	***
FEDEROVITZ, ALEXANDER	20	M	LABR	RRZZZZ	***
DROSCH, PIOTR	18	M	LABR	RRZZZZ	***
KRUSCHINSKY, JAN	25	M	LABR	RRZZZZ	***
STANNELI, MARCUS	40	M	MCHT	RRZZZZ	***
SPIMANSKI, WAWZENI	22	M	LABR	RRZZZZ	***
SIKOVSKI, BRONISLAW	19	M	LABR	RRZZZZ	***
KOTNISKI, MARZEL	20	M	LABR	RRZZZZ	***
SAMIROWSKY, JOHAMS	20	M	LABR	RRZZZZ	***
SCHESCHEWSKY, JACOB	30	M	LABR	RRZZZZ	***
NORDOVSKA, MARIANNA	21	F	SGL	RRZZZZ	***
PETROWSKY, ANTON	42	M	LABR	RRZZZZ	***
GUMPEL, LEIB	45	M	DLR	RRZZZZ	***
SAMUEL	23	M	CH	RRZZZZ	***
ESTHER	17	F	CH	RRZZZZ	***
SELIG	9	M	CHILD	RRZZZZ	***
RIWKE	18	F	SGL	RRZZZZ	***
STINCH-, SCHMERL	43	M	TLR	RRZZZZ	***
KANTUROWICZ, LEISER	16	M	DLR	RRZZZZ	***
STEIN, BERL	36	M	DLR	RRZZZZ	***

PASSENGER	AGE	SEX	OCCUPATION	PRIV	VIL	DES
MANSKI, MINNA	20	F	SGL	RR	ZZZZ	***
NACHT, MOSES	23	M	LABR	RR	ZZZZ	***
KNORR, EMIL	23	M	LKSH	RR	ZZZZ	***
WELTMANN, NOCHEN	24	M	BKBNDR	RR	ZZZZ	***
HERZOG, MICHAEL	33	M	MCHT	RR	ZZZZ	***
MICHAEL	35	M	MCHT	RR	ZZZZ	***
KOBER, TEOFIL	26	M	MLR	RR	ZZZZ	***
JUZRAK, JAN	27	M	LABR	RR	ZZZZ	***
RYBAK, IGNATZ	22	M	LABR	RR	ZZZZ	***
BENDER, ABRAHAM	39	M	TLR	RR	ZZZZ	***
CHELTZT, FISCH	22	M	TLR	RR	ZZZZ	***
DANIELOWITZ, ABEL	43	M	DLR	RR	ZZZZ	***
GURNY, STANISLAUS	28	M	LABR	RR	ZZZZ	***
MILISCHONTZKI, BOLTERS	18	M	LABR	RR	ZZZZ	***
TUROWSKI, WLADISL.	21	M	LABR	RR	ZZZZ	***

SHIP: ANCHORIA

FROM: GLASGOW AND MOVILLE
TO: NEW YORK
ARRIVED: 30 APRIL 1888

PASSENGER	AGE	SEX	OCCUPATION	PRIV	VIL	DES
-ARNOWSKA, SOFIA	35	F	NN	RR	AEAB	USA
MAGDALENE	18	F	NN	RR	AEAB	USA
MICHAEL	10	M	CH	RR	AEAB	USA
FRANK	6	M	CHILD	RR	AEAB	USA
STANISLAUS	2	M	CHILD	RR	AEAB	USA
TARONOWSKY, FRANZ	50	M	LABR	RR	AEAB	USA
JOSE	24	M	LABR	RR	AEAB	USA
ZEREKYS, BARBARA	18	F	NN	RR	AEAB	USA
JOHN	2	M	CHILD	RR	AEAB	USA
PEATROWSKY, WAWIE	40	M	LABR	RR	AEAB	USA
FULKOWSKI, JAN	36	M	LABR	RR	AEAB	USA
BROZENSKI, ANTON	24	M	LABR	RR	AEAB	USA
DANESC-EFSKY, LIEB	28	M	PDLR	RR	AEAB	USA
SEWANDOWSKY, JANOS	33	M	PDLR	RR	AEAB	USA
SRALAMACHA, FRANZ	33	M	LABR	RR	AEAB	USA
GUZEFSKI, JENDY	28	M	LABR	RR	AEAB	USA
KOSIEWSKY, WLAD	22	M	LABR	RR	AEAB	USA
BRECHT, JAKOB	26	M	LABR	RR	AEAB	USA
JOSWALK, MICHAEL	27	M	LABR	RR	AEAB	USA
MERTEL, FRANCIS	30	M	LABR	RR	AEAB	USA
KLAUSENSKY, BRONISLA	26	M	LABR	RR	AEAB	USA
SIENKI--CZ, STANISL	25	M	LABR	RR	AEAB	USA
MIKOSLSCHIK, ANGT	25	M	LABR	RR	AEAB	USA
FILEND-, JEAN	35	M	LABR	RR	AEAB	USA
IVAN, VINCENTZ	42	M	LABR	RR	AEAB	USA
OLSCHEWSKY, FRANCIS	22	M	LABR	RR	AEAB	USA
RA-INSKY, WOICEICH	24	M	LABR	RR	AEAB	USA
RA--INKSI, SIMON	40	M	LABR	RR	AEAB	USA
TOVASCHKEWITZ, ANDRY	28	M	LABR	RR	AEAB	USA
BULAKOWSKY, STAN	25	M	LABR	RR	AEAB	USA
MICHALIE, MICHAL	21	M	LABR	RR	AEAB	USA
FANZEKAS, ANDREAS	25	M	LABR	RR	AEAB	USA
PAMAN, MICHAL	28	M	LABR	RR	AEAB	USA
MISCHSWIE, ANTON	21	M	LABR	RR	AEAB	USA
WORSCHMACK, MICHE	30	M	LABR	RR	AEAB	USA
RUDOLKA, FRANCIS	19	M	LABR	RR	AEAB	USA
ARESIN, STEPHAN	27	M	LABR	RR	AEAB	USA
KORACHEFSKY, KASIMIR	30	M	LABR	RR	AEAB	USA
LUKOWSKY, ANTON	25	M	LABR	RR	AEAB	USA
LUDNICK, TULKOMKI	25	M	LABR	RR	AEAB	USA
WOKOWIAK, WOICEK	16	M	LABR	RR	AEAB	USA
DOMINIAK, THO	24	M	LABR	RR	AEAB	USA
S-IAT--Z, THOS	30	M	LABR	RR	AEAB	USA
BOJANOWKSI, ANTONI	18	M	LABR	RR	AEAB	USA
SAWAROWSKY, MARIAN	22	F	HP	RR	AEAB	USA
LI-YNSKI, MARIAN	23	F	HP	RR	AEAB	USA
NOWINSKI, AGNES	19	F	HP	RR	AEAB	USA

SHIP: SPAIN

FROM: LIVERPOOL AND QUEENSTOWN
TO: NEW YORK
ARRIVED: 30 APRIL 1888

PASSENGER	AGE	SEX	OCCUPATION	PRIV	VIL	DES
BLEISIES, JP	30	F	SVNT	RR	AHOO	USA
O-DER, JP	35	F	SVNT	RR	AHOO	USA
WATSON, PETER	29	M	LABR	RR	AHOO	USA
ANTONORIE, MARIA	25	F	SVNT	RR	AHOO	USA
KANNECKY, MARIA	22	F	SVNT	RR	AHOO	USA
JUDALECKY, SIMON	26	M	LABR	RR	AHOO	USA
LIPPINSKY, U	26	M	LABR	RR	AHOO	USA
B---ES, ANTONI	22	M	LABR	RR	AHOO	USA
JEZEPKOWSKY, ALEX	23	M	LABR	RR	AHOO	USA
WISSEN, PETER	13	M	LABR	RR	AHOO	USA
PELATZ, ANDREAS	36	M	LABR	RR	AHOO	USA
SPEEN, JANOS	29	M	LABR	RR	AHOO	USA
-RIUSBAUS, LIEB	18	M	LABR	RR	AHOO	USA
-LANLENTO-, L	22	M	LABR	RR	AHOO	USA
JUDIS, JOSEF	29	M	LABR	RR	AHOO	USA
-AZEKS, JOSEPH	18	M	LABR	RR	AHOO	USA
SAHALANN--, JOSEPH	28	M	LABR	RR	AHOO	USA
GA--NOW--, PETER	33	M	LABR	RR	AHOO	USA
RAIS---, AUGST	28	M	LABR	RR	AHOO	USA
ANTIMON, AUGUST	39	M	LABR	RR	ZZZZ	USA
ZELKONSKY, ANTONI	40	M	LABR	RR	ZZZZ	USA
RE-BACKY, -RAINSICK	25	M	LABR	RR	ZZZZ	USA
BURGURSKY, SCH---L	23	M	LABR	RR	ZZZZ	USA
ANKONIC, HOBY	30	M	LABR	RR	ZZZZ	USA
RABABITZBY, ANTON	25	M	LABR	RR	ZZZZ	USA
MIG-TY, MICHAEL	26	M	LABR	RR	ZZZZ	USA
RICHENTZ, -RONG	23	M	LABR	RR	ZZZZ	USA
RASCHIS, THOS	28	M	LABR	RR	ZZZZ	USA
BREKINSKY, JOHAN	27	M	LABR	RR	ZZZZ	USA
PRYEPIERY, ANTON	20	M	LABR	RR	ZZZZ	USA
MIKINLANITZ, JOH	34	M	LABR	RR	ZZZZ	USA
MARG--ITZ, JURI	50	M	LABR	RR	ZZZZ	USA
STEINGAPPE, ENOCH	18	M	LABR	RR	ZZZZ	USA
BLOSCHST-N, -LIE	24	M	LABR	RR	ZZZZ	USA
DOPPE, PETER	21	M	LABR	RR	ZZZZ	USA
SCHERINCTZ, MARTIN	40	M	LABR	RR	ZZZZ	USA
BENEDCK, DAKIN	21	M	LABR	RR	ZZZZ	USA
KATZ, ABRAM	27	M	LABR	RR	ZZZZ	USA
SAMAITIS, KAUS	24	M	LABR	RR	ZZZZ	USA
PELVATIO, U	24	M	LABR	RR	ZZZZ	USA
----GYCK, JA-	39	M	LABR	RR	ZZZZ	USA
--BOB, JOSEF	20	M	LABR	RR	ZZZZ	USA
HAUSICK, S	22	M	LABR	RR	ZZZZ	USA
BARNOW, JACOB	31	M	LABR	RR	ZZZZ	USA
WISCH-USKY, ANTON	22	M	LABR	RR	ZZZZ	USA
MELANONSKY, AUSTIN	18	M	LABR	RR	ZZZZ	USA
LEWA---, JOS	24	M	LABR	RR	ZZZZ	USA
KAROLSKY, JAN	19	M	LABR	RR	ZZZZ	USA
SOLISKY, WEID	19	M	LABR	RR	ZZZZ	USA
RUSTIN, STAUSLAV	30	M	LABR	RR	ZZZZ	USA
S-E-CBYKY, B	20	M	LABR	RR	ZZZZ	USA
KUSTIAN, STEPHAN	24	M	LABR	RR	ZZZZ	USA
-OWS--ESTY, ADAM	23	M	LABR	RR	ZZZZ	USA
SCHAKING, VALENTIN	25	M	LABR	RR	ZZZZ	USA
LOVINKONISON, CARRIL	28	M	LABR	RR	ZZZZ	USA
JURARN, HANILUS	30	M	LABR	RR	ZZZZ	USA
PILVABIS, JES	28	M	LABR	RR	ZZZZ	USA
KAMB-KY, JOSEF	28	M	LABR	RR	ZZZZ	USA
-UDMOWBY, ANTON	28	M	LABR	RR	ZZZZ	USA
GALETSKY, FRANC	32	M	LABR	RR	ZZZZ	USA
LEDIRBERG, MARIER	26	M	LABR	RR	ZZZZ	USA
---SCHOL, JOSEF	25	M	LABR	RR	ZZZZ	USA
PACRSKAY, ANTON	23	M	LABR	RR	ZZZZ	USA
REIN, SOLOMAN	24	M	LABR	RR	ZZZZ	USA
KURSTKY, VAL---TO	38	M	LABR	RR	ZZZZ	USA
WLERTOSKY, JAN	34	M	LABR	RR	ZZZZ	USA
ALBERT	44	M	LABR	RR	ZZZZ	USA
ROSENSACK, MOSES	40	M	LABR	RR	ZZZZ	USA

PASSENGER	AGE	SEX	OCCUPATION	PRIV	VIL	DES
POLUPOUAL, PETER	24	M	LABR	RR	ZZZZ	USA
BERS--SKY, SELIG	22	M	LABR	RR	ZZZZ	USA
ULETYKY, AUTER	28	M	LABR	RR	ZZZZ	USA
BRIEKY, DOMUK	22	M	LABR	RR	ZZZZ	USA
KRISTIAN, PETER	20	M	LABR	RR	ZZZZ	USA
-LINCEGGEP, FRANZ	30	M	LABR	RR	ZZZZ	USA
WEIGKILA---, JO--UP	40	M	LABR	RR	ZZZZ	USA
WACHOLD--Y, S	23	M	LABR	RR	ZZZZ	USA
BOLSEN, SAM	19	M	LABR	RR	ZZZZ	USA
LINGVIST, GUSTEY	43	M	LABR	RR	ZZZZ	USA
KONCH, ANTON	25	M	LABR	RR	ZZZZ	USA
PENZIK, MAX	25	M	LABR	RR	ZZZZ	USA
JOSEF	18	M	LABR	RR	ZZZZ	USA

SHIP: ARABIC

FROM: LIVERPOOL AND QUEENSTOWN
TO: NEW YORK
ARRIVED: 30 APRIL 1888

PASSENGER	AGE	SEX	OCCUPATION	PRIV	VIL	DES
OALRABAUSOW, JUULIK	30	M	FARMER	RR	ADAX	USA
ANTONISON, SALOMON	18	M	FARMER	RR	ADAX	USA
SULRESON, BERENT	30	M	FARMER	RR	ADAX	USA
EGELUND, GINSE	17	F	SVNT	RR	ADAX	USA
BUSTAD, ABRAHAM	28	M	LABR	RR	ADAX	USA
WEIMBLADT, BRUNE	29	F	W	RR	ADAX	USA
PAPARKA, FIGE	36	F	HSKPR	RR	ADAX	USA
WINDOTTE, EPSBRASEN	4	M	CHILD	RR	ADAX	USA
DANIEL, KUNAGE	32	M	LABR	RR	ADAX	USA
JOHAN, VANGO	29	M	LABR	RR	ADAX	USA
HOGNEG, PAUL	29	M	LABR	RR	ADAX	USA
ANNE	22	F	W	RR	ADAX	USA
ELSA	00	F	INF	RR	ADAX	USA
THOMPSON, MARY	20	F	SVNT	RR	ADAX	USA
HOELZYSKE, JOHANNA	27	F	SVNT	RR	ADAX	USA
JOSEF.	32	F	SVNT	RR	ADAX	USA
ELLINEK, FRANISKA	25	F	SVNT	RR	ADAX	USA
HEINERIG, SERIE	30	F	SVNT	RR	ADAX	USA
ECHAGE	11	M	CH	RR	ADAX	USA
JERDAL	8	M	CHILD	RR	ADAX	USA
MABEL	6	F	CHILD	RR	ADAX	USA
MICHHAR	3	F	CHILD	RR	ADAX	USA
HEIRBIER, ROSA	34	F	SVNT	RR	ADAX	USA
GROUMON, SARA	19	F	SVNT	RR	ADAX	USA
MAUDZK, MARY	20	F	SVNT	RR	ADAX	USA
ZPEMER, GUTA	20	F	SVNT	RR	ADAX	USA
LEIBINGER, SIMON	17	M	LABR	RR	ADAX	USA
JORGENSEN, ANNA	28	F	W	RR	ADAX	USA
MARTIN	7	M	CHILD	RR	ADAX	USA
ANNA	4	F	CHILD	RR	ADAX	USA
LAUZA, GIOVANNI	43	M	LABR	RR	ADAX	USA
BIONDA, JELIA	33	F	SVNT	RR	ADAX	USA
KAFFEMANN, MATHILDA	24	F	SP	RR	ADAX	USA
BI--, HERMAN	24	M	LABR	RR	ADAX	USA
MARK	21	M	LABR	RR	ADAX	USA
AMSTERDAM, B--	26	M	LABR	RR	ADAX	USA
FART, BERT	21	M	LABR	RR	ADAX	USA
BIEM, SAMIL.	35	M	LABR	RR	ADAX	USA
ROSENBERG, MCHL.	18	M	LABR	RR	ADAX	USA
NERDAZER, MORDKE	25	M	LABR	RR	ADAX	USA
SALOMON	15	M	LABR	RR	ADAX	USA
BERGOWITZ, PINEBOR	32	M	LABR	RR	ADAX	USA
ROCHAD	20	F	W	RR	ADAX	USA
TAUST, MOSES	32	M	LABR	RR	ADAX	USA
BRODOS, JACOB	20	M	LABR	RR	ADAX	USA
BLEET, GITTEL	55	F	W	RR	ADAX	USA
MOSES	9	M	CHILD	RR	ADAX	USA
CLAUS	7	M	CHILD	RR	ADAX	USA
ISAK	5	M	CHILD	RR	ADAX	USA
ESTER	3	F	CHILD	RR	ADAX	USA
LURE	00	F	INF	RR	ADAX	USA
MITCHAEL, GEO.	27	M	LABR	RR	ADAX	USA
JORGNESON, ANNA	00	F	INF	RR	ADAX	USA
FRIGINCT, OBESCH	24	F	LABR	RR	ADAX	USA
GOST, BENJ.	24	M	LABR	RR	ADAX	USA
LANGBOUM, KUSCH	24	M	LABR	RR	ADAX	USA
KORPF, MORKER	36	M	LABR	RR	ADAX	USA
KOHM, JACOB	50	M	LABR	RR	ADAX	USA
ZINE	14	F	SP	RR	ADAX	USA
LETZTER, WOLF	50	M	LABR	RR	ADAX	USA
MAYER, VINZENT	29	M	LABR	RR	ADAX	USA
ANNA	11	F	CH	RR	ADAX	USA
KOFFEMANN, HANNA	18	F	SP	RR	ADAX	USA
RUNGALIN, JUDE	17	M	LABR	RR	ADAX	USA
HOAS, CLIMEN	30	M	LABR	RR	ADAX	USA
NEGTHE, KUNT	50	M	LABR	RR	ADAX	USA
BREGIT	58	F	W	RR	ADAX	USA
ROSALIELD	26	F	SP	RR	ADAX	USA
SIMON	22	M	LABR	RR	ADAX	USA
FREN	15	M	LABR	RR	ADAX	USA
EKENHAGEN, NILS	60	M	LABR	RR	ADAX	USA
JUGRI	55	F	SVNT	RR	ADAX	USA
OLICE	20	F	SVNT	RR	ADAX	USA
THORE	17	M	LABR	RR	ADAX	USA
ANNE	11	F	CH	RR	ADAX	USA
JUGER	7	F	CHILD	RR	ADAX	USA
NEZTTO, ELLEN	68	M	FARMER	RR	ADAX	USA
BARBRO	66	F	W	RR	ADAX	USA
ANNE	20	F	SP	RR	ADAX	USA
HUSET, OLE	22	M	LABR	RR	ADAX	USA
THORE	35	M	LABR	RR	ADAX	USA
KIEBAKKIN, ROZUHILD	20	F	SVNT	RR	ADAX	USA
KERO, KUND	30	M	LABR	RR	ADAX	USA
OLE	22	M	LABR	RR	ADAX	USA
LZKKEN, JUGO.	24	F	SVNT	RR	ADAX	USA
BARBRO	32	F	SVNT	RR	ADAX	USA
EVENSDOTTER, KRISTI	20	F	SVNT	RR	ADAX	USA
HALBROTHEN, EUGBERT	25	M	LABR	RR	ADAX	USA
MOSKEGARD, LARS	21	M	LABR	RR	ADAX	USA
MYBRER, NIELS	28	M	LABR	RR	ADAX	USA
NILSDOTTER, JUGLEGOR	72	F	HSKPR	RR	ADAX	USA
GORFF, OLE	42	M	LABR	RR	ADAX	USA

SHIP: ARIZONA

FROM: LIVERPOOL AND QUEENSTOWN
TO: NEW YORK
ARRIVED: 30 APRIL 1888

PASSENGER	AGE	SEX	OCCUPATION	PRIV	VIL	DES
KOHEN, LEPSIE	17	M	LABR	RR	ZZZZ	USA
BRASIDICH, GEORGE	25	M	PNTR	RR	ACBF	USA
KRULSE, ANNIE	25	F	W	RR	ACBF	USA
DRA--OLIN	3	M	CHILD	RR	ACBF	USA
KOHN, CHAIE	18	F	SP	RR	ACBF	USA
MERE	20	M	LABR	RR	ACBF	USA
CHATZKEL	21	F	SP	RR	ACBF	USA
BER-ER, HIRSCH	24	M	MECH	RR	ACBF	USA
KANOWITZ, HERSCH	15	M	LABR	RR	ACBF	USA
WISCHEISKI, JOSEPH	35	M	ATSN	RR	ACBF	USA
SCHIR--, ISAK	18	M	LABR	RR	ACBF	USA
TOPER, BRAINE	18	F	SP	RR	ACBF	USA
ORLOWITZ, FRANZ	24	M	LABR	RR	ACBF	USA
RONOWITZ, ANTONI	34	M	FARMER	PL	ZZZZ	USA
SCHIDKOWSKI, JOSEF	35	M	FARMER	PL	ACBF	USA
TINLEWSKY, -AIR	28	M	MSN	PL	ACBF	USA
LASCHKEWITZ, JAN	35	M	SDLR	PL	ACBF	USA
RISTA, JAN	28	M	PNTR	PL	ACBF	USA
FURMANN, MARITZ	24	M	LABR	PL	AILA	USA
MORDAS, LUDWIG	23	M	LABR	PL	AILA	USA
DUBYANSKI, JACHEL	25	M	ATSN	PL	AILA	USA

PASSENGER	AGE	SEX	OCCUPATION	PRIVL	DES
SCHINDER, JASSEL	18	M	FLABR	PLAIL	AUSA
BLUMENSTEIN, JOSEPH	56	M	ATSN	PLAFZ	DUSA
SKROD-ANNT, MA-INT	43	M	ATSN	PLAFZ	DUSA
URBAN, ISIDOR	43	M	ATSN	PLAFZ	DUSA
WOCKMAN, FRANZ	19	M	LABR	PLAFZ	DUSA
GAWSCHITZ, DORANICK	25	M	FLABR	PLAFZ	DUSA
JARNBOWSKY, SIDOR	24	M	PMBR	PLAFZ	DUSA
GAIDIMACHT, FRANZ	24	M	LABR	PLAIL	AUSA
MAR-EWITZ, JOSEPH	25	M	UNKNOWN	PLAIL	AUSA
MARKIEWITZ, NINCENTZ	28	M	UNKNOWN	PLAIL	AUSA
PODEZASKI, JAN	24	M	FLABR	PLAFZ	DUSA
SABEROWSKY, FRANZ	28	M	SDLR	PLAFZ	DUSA
KEMPRUSKI, LUDWIG	24	M	LABR	PLAFZ	DUSA
MATALSKI, BO-ES-AW	18	M	LABR	PLACB	FUSA
SA-OKWEITZEK, GER-ON	46	M	ATSN	PLACB	FUSA
KA-NIC-SANSKI, ABM	28	M	ATSN	PLACB	FUSA
SALAWE-TZK, JACOB	18	M	LABR	PLACB	FUSA
SELWANSKI, ABRAHAM	45	M	SMH	PLACB	FUSA
OSAWITZKI, ABRAM	36	M	UNKNOWN	PLACB	FUSA
SCHMERKES, LEISER	28	M	ATSN	RRZZZ	ZUSA
ZALEWITZ, ISRAEL	23	M	JNR	RRACB	FUSA
KROSMINTZ, SAMUEL	21	M	LABR	RRAFZ	DUSA
RIDZEWSKI, ANTONI	24	M	ATSN	RRACB	FUSA
ANRIS-CYKI, DOMINICK	23	M	ATSN	RRACB	FUSA
SOPRISKI, W-RENTZI	30	M	ATSN	RRACB	FUSA
URCZINSKI, --SSEL	36	M	ATSN	RRACB	FUSA
KRUKOWSKI, SIPAN	27	M	FLABR	RRAFZ	DUSA
-EELKAWOCTZ, ALEX	21	M	LABR	RRAFZ	DUSA
MACIJEWSKI, IVAN	22	M	MSN	RRAFZ	DUSA
SKALKOWKSI, SAME	18	F	SP	RRAFZ	DUSA
NEKRUNTMAN, ISRAEL	20	M	LABR	RRAFZ	DUSA
BACHER, -ARIS	35	M	ATSN	RRAFZ	DUSA
FUHRMAN, MO-ES	29	M	ATSN	RRAFZ	DUSA

SHIP: BRAUNSCHWEIG

FROM: BREMEN
TO: BALTIMORE
ARRIVED: 01 MAY 1888

PASSENGER	AGE	SEX	OCCUPATION	PRIVL	DES
DOMPKOWSKI, FRANZ	40	M	LABR	RRZZZ	ZUNK
KOWEDSKA, MARYANN	24	F	W	RRZZZ	ZUNK
ADAM	.09	M	INFANT	RRZZZ	ZUNK
FRANCISZEK	36	M	LABR	RRZZZ	ZUNK
KELL, JULIAN	29	M	LABR	RRZZZ	ZUNK
GLOWATZKY, THOMAS	22	M	LABR	RRZZZ	ZUNK
BEDNURSKY, LUDWIG	28	M	LABR	RRZZZ	ZUNK
BROWSKY, FRANZ	37	M	LABR	RRZZZ	ZUNK
ZAPEJEWSKI, WACZIM	37	M	LABR	RRZZZ	ZUNK
PALZEWSKI, EUPOZINA	30	F	UNKNOWN	RRZZZ	ZUNK
VAL.	5	F	CHILD	RRZZZ	ZUNK
U, U	00	F	CH	RRZZZ	ZUNK
--NYZNISKI, FRANZ	62	M	LABR	RRZZZ	ZUNK
JOSEFA	42	F	W	RRZZZ	ZUNK
ANTONIA	3	F	CHILD	RRZZZ	ZUNK
BENETZKI, JOSEF	26	M	LABR	RRAIJ	EUNK
BERLYNOSKI, JEAN	19	M	LABR	RRAIJ	EUNK
LUDZYCK, HEINRICH	26	M	LABR	RRAIJ	EBAL
POLLATZ, ADAM	24	M	LABR	RRAIJ	EBAL
SCHMIDT, ADAM	24	M	LABR	RRAIJ	EBAL
MILLMANN, MEYER	28	M	LABR	RRAIJ	EBAL
KOLINAKY, GEORG	43	M	FARMER	RRAIJ	EDAK
RISINE	38	F	W	RRAIJ	EDAK
LOUISE	20	F	D	RRAIJ	EDAK
BARBARA	19	F	D	RRAIJ	EDAK
GOERSCH, MARTIN	29	M	LABR	RRAIJ	EDAK
KOLNISKY, MARIE	13	F	D	RRAIJ	EDAK
GOERSCH, CATHARINA	28	F	W	RRAIJ	EDAK
MARIE	4	F	CHILD	RRAIJ	EDAK
KATHARINA	3	F	CHILD	RRAIJ	EDAK
HELENE	2	F	CHILD	RRAIJ	EDAK
GOLABECK, JACOB	52	M	LABR	RRAIJ	EKS
BERTHA	37	F	W	RRAIJ	EKS
HELENE	22	F	D	RRAIJ	EKS
CATHARINA	20	F	D	RRAIJ	EKS
JACOB	16	M	S	RRAIJ	EKS
ANNA	14	F	CH	RRAIJ	EKS
BERTHA	12	F	CH	RRAIJ	EKS
PETER	9	M	CHILD	RRAIJ	EKS
U	7	F	CHILD	RRAIJ	EKS
HENRICH	5	M	CHILD	RRAIJ	EKS
WILHELM	4	M	CHILD	RRAIJ	EKS
HERMANN	.06	M	INFANT	RRAIJ	EKS
EDUARD	3	M	CHILD	RRAIJ	EKS
GOLDBECK, JOHANN	25	M	LABR	RRAIJ	EKS
MARIE	29	F	W	RRAIJ	EKS
TISKA, ANAILA	26	F	SVNT	RRAIJ	EKS
PULAK, JOSEFA	22	F	SVNT	RRAIJ	EKS
SMUSKY, BOLESLAW	18	M	LABR	RRAIJ	EKS
CHAICH, ELISA	18	F	SVNT	RRAIJ	EKS
MILLMANN, ETE	30	F	UNKNOWN	RRAIJ	EKS
MOSES	9	M	CHILD	RRAIJ	EKS
JACOB	6	M	CHILD	RRAIJ	EKS
MALANOWSKA, ANASTASIA	20	F	SVNT	RRAIJ	EKS
CZAPANOWSKI, JOHAN	30	M	LABR	RRAIJ	EKS

SHIP: ELBE

FROM: BREMEN AND SOUTHAMPTON
TO: NEW YORK
ARRIVED: 02 MAY 1888

PASSENGER	AGE	SEX	OCCUPATION	PRIVL	DES
SLOPCYNSKI, JAN	19	M	UNKNOWN	RRAIL	ANY
GULKEZYNSKI, CLEM.	20	M	UNKNOWN	RRAIL	ANY
BOLESLAW	18	U	UNKNOWN	RRAIL	ANY
--JNAK, U	24	M	LABR	RRAIL	ANY
--BANSKI, U	35	M	LABR	RRAIL	ANY
---JEWSKI, U	19	M	LABR	RRAIL	ANY
U, U	33	M	LABR	RRAIL	ANY
BOLECHOWICZ, MARIE	26	F	W	RRZZZ	ZNY
SOPHIA	.09	F	INFANT	RRZZZ	ZNY
OPANOWIEZ, VICTORIA	30	F	W	RRAIL	ANY
VICTORIA	6	F	CHILD	RRAIL	ANY
JOHANN	.06	M	INFANT	RRAIL	ANY
WIWIAS, ALBERT	33	M	LABR	RRAIL	ANY
RINKI--, ANT.	29	M	LABR	RRAIL	ANY
---WICZ, KAZIM.	29	M	LABR	RRAIL	ANY
DOMBROWSKI, JOS.	26	M	LABR	RRAIG	VNY
SCHAFRINSKY, MARIE	14	F	SVNT	RRAIL	ANY
WILKANOWSKA, FRANZA.	37	F	W	RRAIL	ANY
STEFAN	11	M	CH	RRAIL	ANY
FRANZKA.	7	F	CHILD	RRAIL	ANY
ANTON	5	M	CHILD	RRAIL	ANY
JAKUBOWITZ, ANTON	25	F	SVNT	RRAIL	AIL
STOWRONSKI, PETER	30	M	LABR	RRAIL	AIL
CACKOWSKI, JOH.	19	M	LABR	RRAIL	AIL
NITSCHKE, WILHELM	47	M	CPTR	RRAIL	ADAK
CHRISTINE	40	F	W	RRAIL	ADAK
WILHELMINE	7	M	CHILD	RRAIL	ADAK
CHRISTINE	6	F	CHILD	RRAIL	ADAK
MATHILDE	4	F	CHILD	RRAIL	ADAK
DOBLER, JACOB	28	M	FARMER	RRAIL	ADAK
JOHANNE	28	F	W	RRAIL	ADAK
JOHANNE	28	F	W	RRAIL	ADAK
MATHILDE	6	F	CHILD	RRAIL	ADAK
JOHANNES	4	M	CHILD	RRAIL	ADAK
REINHARD	2	M	CHILD	RRAIL	ADAK
SUSANNE	.01	F	INFANT	RRAIL	ADAK
HERDER, JOHANN	26	M	TCHR	RRAIL	ADAK
BARBARA	24	F	W	RRAIL	ADAK

PASSENGER	AGE	SEX	OCCUPATION	PRV VIL DES
JOHANN	2	M	CHILD	RRAILADAK
GOTTB.	.01	M	INFANT	RRAILADAK
SCHRAMM, MATTHIAS	31	M	FARMER	RRAILADAK
LOUISE	31	F	W	RRAILADAK
SUSANNE	7	F	CHILD	RRAILADAK
CARL	6	M	CHILD	RRAILADAK
CATHARIN.	6	F	CHILD	RRAILADAK
SARAH	.10	F	INFANT	RRAILADAK
ZIELINSKY, FRANZ	27	M	LABR	RRAILANY
ROGINSKY, JOSEF	22	M	LABR	RRAILANY
OLISCHAITZA, JOS.	21	M	LABR	RRAFTMNY
LUSNEY, STANISL.	22	M	LABR	RRAFTMNY
SLABUSKY, LUDWIG	27	M	LABR	RRAILANY
CHONOWSKY, STANISLE.	26	M	LABR	RRAILANY
KACZENKOWSKY, FRANZ	23	M	LABR	RRAILANY
ANUSCHEWITZ, NADRAS	26	M	LABR	RRAILANY
DOMBROWSKY, JAN	40	M	LABR	RRAILANY
MARIE	30	F	W	RRAILANY
OLESCH	4	M	CHILD	RRAILANY
STASZ	.11	M	INFANT	RRAILANY
PANESCHKO, JAN	20	M	LABR	RRAILANY
KAMINSKY, JAN	34	M	LABR	RRAILANY
GEHLERT, JOHANN	21	M	LABR	RRAILADAK
BESLER, JOHANN	20	M	LABR	RRAILADAK
MARZ, THOMAS	64	M	FARMER	RRAILADAK
THOMAS	23	M	FARMER	RRAILADAK
CAROLINE	24	F	W	RRAILADAK
FRIEDERIKE	19	F	SVNT	RRAILADAK
ROSINE	2	F	CHILD	RRAILADAK
OTTILIE	.01	F	INFANT	RRAILADAK
HERMANN, GOTTF.	34	M	FARMER	RRAILADAK
MARGARETHE	28	F	W	RRAILADAK
FRIEDRICH	7	M	CHILD	RRAILADAK
MARIE	5	F	CHILD	RRAILADAK
OTTILIE	4	F	CHILD	RRAILADAK
SARAH	3	F	CHILD	RRAILADAK
FRIEDERIKE	2	F	CHILD	RRAILADAK
GOTTF.	.06	M	INFANT	RRAILADAK
NITSCHKE, JACOB	25	M	LABR	RRAILADAK
SCHEIKOWSKY, NICOLAI	33	M	LABR	RRAILANY
JARUSEWSKY, FRANZ	32	M	LABR	RRAILANY
ZEGELSKI, JAN	34	M	LABR	RRAILANY
OSTROSKI, FRANZ	28	M	LABR	RRAILANY
JASINISKI, ANTON	29	M	LABR	RRAILANY
JEZINSKI, JAN	24	M	LABR	RRAILANY
STRIBITZKI, VOJC.	48	M	LABR	RRAILANY
BOROWSKI, JAN	39	M	LABR	RRAILANY
BIALETZKI, JAN	38	M	LABR	RRAILANY
GONSIEROWSKY, JOS.	35	M	LABR	RRAILANY
KAZANCKI, MART.	33	M	LABR	RRAILANY
GRODKOWSKY, JAN	28	M	LABR	RRAILANY
SZULEZEWSKI, FRANZ	45	M	LABR	RRAILANY
PLAWINICH, ALEX	20	M	LABR	RRAILANY
MUHKEWIZ, ALEX	27	M	LABR	RRAILANY
MAJEWSKI, MART.	29	M	LABR	RRAILANY
FATTER, SIMON	19	M	LABR	RRAILANY
BERNATZKI, ANTON	32	M	LABR	RRAILANY
KISLAITIS, ANTON	30	M	UNKNOWN	RRAILADET
LUKOSCHEWITZ, WILHELM	25	M	UNKNOWN	RRAILADET
JEGUNAS, AMBRASCH	24	M	UNKNOWN	RRAILADET
KAIDAS, WILHELM	24	M	UNKNOWN	RRAILADET
KLEVZINSKI, BALT.	26	M	UNKNOWN	RRAILADET
AKRANUS, WINEENS	22	M	UNKNOWN	RRAILADET
SOHNRAITIS, WICLUTZ	25	M	UNKNOWN	RRAILADET
SCHUKIS, FRANZ	22	M	UNKNOWN	RRAILADET
OKOLIEZ, CARL	50	M	UNKNOWN	RRAILADET
SCHAUKER, ISRAEL	28	M	UNKNOWN	RRAILADET
MARTIANOWSKI, MICH.	24	M	UNKNOWN	RRAILADET
OKU--SKY, STANISL.	28	M	UNKNOWN	RRAILADET
JARTNIKA, JAN	29	M	UNKNOWN	RRAILADET
TATKOWSKY, WOJ	33	M	UNKNOWN	RRAILADET
--LEITA, ANDRAS	32	M	UNKNOWN	RRAILADET
MICHALINE	18	F	W	RRAILADET
SCHUGERLEWSKY, JOS.	24	M	LABR	RRAILANY
TIS, JULIA	28	F	SVNT	RRAILANY

PASSENGER	AGE	SEX	OCCUPATION	PRV VIL DES
SCHEBEL, JAN	46	M	LABR	RRAILANY
REDEWSKY, KASPER	24	M	LABR	RRAILANY
BAGNIK, ANTON	25	M	LABR	RRAILANY
KRAUKOWSKY, WINC.	24	M	LABR	RRAILANY
KOWALEWSKY, ANTON	25	M	LABR	RRAILANY
WIERZYLEWSKY, PETER	26	M	LABR	RRAILANY
WALUTKOWITZ, ANTON	30	M	LABR	RRAILANY
BETLEJESKI, JAN	26	M	LABR	RRAILANY
ZIOLKOWSKY, FRANZ	26	M	LABR	RRAILABUF
KALIKOWICZ, ADAM	27	M	LABR	RRAILANY
BRODJINSKI, MART.	39	M	LABR	RRAILANY
SZYMANNSKY, WOJ.	36	M	LABR	RRAILANY
SCHEDIG, MARIE	21	M	UNKNOWN	RRAILANY
RUSCHINSKY, VALENTIN	35	M	UNKNOWN	RRAILANY
MURASKI, THOMAS	28	M	UNKNOWN	RRAILANY
GRABKOWSKY, MICH.	25	M	UNKNOWN	RRAILANY
LEVY, HERMANN	44	M	DLR	RRAILAUNK
TIMKO, MAX	30	M	LABR	RRAILANY
---DARSKI, U	50	M	UNKNOWN	RRAILANY
---WSKA, U	32	F	UNKNOWN	RRAILANY
VICTORIA	5	F	CHILD	RRAILANY
MALINOWSKI, ANTON	23	M	LABR	RRAILANY
MACZKEWIECZ, STEPHAN	27	M	LABR	RRAILANY
WILKANOWSKI, FRANZ	3	M	CHILD	RRAILANY
ANNA	.09	F	INFANT	RRAILANY
SZEMNICZER, JANOS	30	F	LABR	RRAILANY
TUTLIS, MATHEUS	33	F	LABR	RRAILANY
KAZIMIR	24	F	LABR	RRAILANY
AGATHE	20	F	SVNT	RRAILANY
FISCHERING, HERSCH	30	M	DLR	RRAILANY
DRACHENBERG, JAN	20	M	DLR	RRAILANY
POWODZINSKI, FR.	27	M	LABR	RRAILANY
ARONOWICZ, LEIBE	21	M	LABR	RRAILANY

SHIP: IOWA

FROM: LIVERPOOL
TO: BOSTON
ARRIVED: 03 UNKNOWN 1888

PASSENGER	AGE	SEX	OCCUPATION	PRV VIL DES
GUNDEROFF, MENDALL	20	M	LABR	RRZZZZUSA
SARA	22	F	W	RRZZZZUSA
CHINOWITZ, HZIG	45	M	LABR	RRZZZZUSA
REBECCA	33	F	W	RRZZZZUSA
TAUBMAN, TONE	30	M	LABR	RRZZZZUSA
MALKE	20	F	W	RRZZZZUSA
LAMANZYKI, THOMAS	35	M	LABR	RRZZZZUSA
MARIA	27	F	W	RRZZZZUSA
WINITZKY, ISAAC	26	M	TLR	RRZZZZUSA
SARA	26	F	W	RRZZZZUSA
SARA	26	F	W	RRZZZZUSA
POLZIN, PAULINE	17	F	SP	PLZZZZUSA
HOROWITZ, BASSIE	16	F	SP	RRZZZZUSA
KLEIN, ROSA	18	F	SP	PLZZZZUSA
CHAIMOWITZ, JULIUS	11	M	CH	RRZZZZUSA
MATWIN	10	M	CH	RRZZZZUSA
GISELA	.11	F	INFANT	RRZZZZUSA
TAUBMAN, MATHILDE	.09	F	INFANT	RRZZZZUSA
HOROWITZ, ROSE	10	F	SCH	RRZZZZUSA
ABLESHON, SAMUEL	11	M	SCH	RRZZZZUSA
LEMANZYKI, MARTHA	4	F	CHILD	RRZZZZUSA
JOSEF	2	M	CHILD	RRZZZZUSA
BERKOWITZ, NOCHIN	18	M	TLR	RRZZZZUSA
BOHNEN, NAFTALI	21	M	SHMK	RRZZZZUSA
STUMBLER, WOLFF	35	M	TLR	RRZZZZUSA
BERNSHEIN, L.	21	M	SHMK	RRZZZZUSA
BECHENLINE, SAMUEL	25	M	TLR	RRZZZZUSA
KANTER, T.	35	M	PNTR	RRZZZZUSA
HARRIS, S.	25	M	TLR	RRZZZZUSA
HIRSHKOWITZ, BROCHE	19	M	LABR	PLZZZZUSA

PASSENGER	AGE	SEX	OCCUPATION	PV RI VL DES
JAKOBOWITZ, AARRON	16	M	LABR	RRZZZZUSA
KASTOWTZKY, BIRKE	29	M	SHMK	RRZZZZUSA
SWITALSKI, STEFAN	29	M	LABR	PLZZZZUSA
NOWAK, JAN	21	M	LABR	RRZZZZUSA
DOBRANSKY, JOSEF	60	M	LABR	PLZZZZUSA
HOROWITZ, MOSES	40	M	SMH	RRZZZZUSA
MOLLMANN, SAMUEL	38	M	LABR	RRZZZZUSA
BIRKOWSKY, ABRAM	23	M	CKCTR	RRZZZZUSA
MARGULEIS, PINKAS	20	M	HTR	RRZZZZUSA
KELLEWITZ, ABRAM	25	M	JNR	RRZZZZUSA
WEISMAN, JOSEF	21	M	TLR	RRZZZZUSA
CIGLAR, JANOS	24	M	LABR	RRZZZZUSA
SIRKE, ISTWAN	35	M	LABR	RRZZZZUSA
DUBEIE, JOSEF	32	M	LABR	RRZZZZUSA
RATULSKI, MARTIN	35	M	LABR	RRZZZZUSA
MARATACH, JOHN	22	M	LABR	RRZZZZUSA
U, LEIB	18	M	SHMK	RRZZZZUSA
KOVALEWSKI, ANDRE	24	M	LABR	RRZZZZUSA
SPENSIEL, SEBASTIAN	57	M	LABR	RRZZZZUSA
MIOCKLK, SAUL	24	M	LABR	RRZZZZUSA
SZAFANSKI, JOSEF	33	M	LABR	RRZZZZUSA
MIKARYZAK, IGNATZ	69	M	LABR	RRZZZZUSA
SOPALSKI, TOMAS	30	M	LABR	RRZZZZUSA
SACKOL, ABRAM	38	M	TLR	RRZZZZUSA
ABERSTEIN, DAVID	38	M	LABR	RRZZZZUSA
OLSCHEWITZ, LEIB	35	M	JNR	RRZZZZUSA
ANGORSCHWITZ, JANKEL	29	M	TLR	RRZZZZUSA
HAI, CHAIM	18	M	BKR	RRZZZZUSA
HURZROK, RAFAEL	20	M	BCHR	RRZZZZUSA
SPRUG, CHIM	24	M	BCHR	RRZZZZUSA
SELLAK, JOSEF	26	M	LABR	RRZZZZUSA
ALSZKI, STANISL.	22	M	LABR	RRZZZZUSA
RUBENSTEIN, DAVID	18	M	TLR	RRZZZZUSA
KROSA, J.KLIROT	22	M	LABR	RRZZZZUSA
HALPER, SIESAMOWITZ	22	M	LABR	RRZZZZUSA
SPAKANSKI, SILVESTER	28	M	LABR	RRZZZZUSA
STEPONKIS, VINCENTO	21	M	LABR	RRZZZZUSA
SAPHIR, EDIR	26	M	SHMK	RRZZZZUSA
BERNSTERN, ABEL	26	M	LABR	RRZZZZUSA
RUBENSTEIN, JACOB	25	M	LABR	RRZZZZUSA
DATNO, SIMON	28	M	CPRSMH	RRZZZZUSA
ROTMAN, MORDCHE	23	M	LABR	RRZZZZUSA
HALTMAN, LEON	23	M	LABR	RRZZZZUSA
BAUMANN, KARL	20	M	LABR	RRZZZZUSA
MOLEWSKY, KAZIONIER	20	M	CPTR	PLZZZZUSA
PETEKEWITZ, JOSEPH	23	M	LKSH	RRZZZZUSA
DOBRIOW, MATHEI	48	M	LABR	RRZZZZUSA
RASWITZ, VINCENTI	26	M	LABR	RRZZZZUSA
FRANSKI, ANTON	26	M	LABR	RRZZZZUSA
RUDROWSKY, VINCENTI	31	M	LABR	RRZZZZUSA
POLINICK, JOSEF	25	M	LABR	RRZZZZUSA
BOHAU, FRANZ	27	M	LABR	RRZZZZUSA
TROTZKI, JULIAN	23	M	LABR	RRZZZZUSA
ORLINSKI, SIEGMUND	22	M	LABR	RRZZZZUSA
WANTELOWITZ, ALPHONIS	22	M	LABR	RRZZZZUSA
SIPAWSKI, JOSSI	22	M	LABR	RRZZZZUSA
ROGASCH, WLADISLAUS	23	M	LABR	RRZZZZUSA
POPERSKI, VINCENTI	26	M	LABR	RRZZZZUSA
IVINSCHONSKI, VINCENTI	23	M	LABR	RRZZZZUSA
ROLKIS, ABRAM	23	M	LABR	RRZZZZUSA
REENTZWITZ, JOSEF	35	M	LABR	RRZZZZUSA
GAUGLE, MARTIN	32	M	LABR	RRZZZZUSA
SCHAMSKI, MATHEI	32	M	LABR	RRZZZZUSA
LEBAZIS, KASIMIR	30	M	LABR	RRZZZZUSA
MOSEL, VINCENTI	33	M	LABR	RRZZZZUSA
SAULAWITZ, JOHANN	20	M	LABR	RRZZZZUSA
BALTUSCHEWITZ, JOSEF	17	M	LABR	RRZZZZUSA
ORLOG, VINCENTI	17	M	LABR	RRZZZZUSA
PRUNTYKI, PIOTER	30	M	LABR	RRZZZZUSA
MASENES, VINCENTI	18	M	LABR	RRZZZZUSA
PELONINSKY, ANTON	14	M	LABR	RRZZZZUSA
TRIGELSKA, AGATA	20	M	LABR	RRZZZZUSA
GUDRANIS, MATHEI	38	M	LABR	RRZZZZUSA
KOCKOWSKY, SCHUME	33	M	LABR	RRZZZZUSA
SOSNOWSKY, STANISLAUS	39	M	LABR	RRZZZZUSA
JABR-CIUS, EMIL	29	M	LABR	RRZZZZUSA
PIENA	22	M	LABR	RRZZZZUSA
ROGOW, ISAAC	19	M	BLKSMH	RRZZZZUSA
KNISNIK, BULE	28	M	LABR	RRZZZZUSA
FREEDLANDER, HIRSCH	25	M	PNTR	RRZZZZUSA
GLARESKEE, JOSEPH	22	M	LABR	RRZZZZUSA
YEKONSKY, MICKOLY	24	M	LABR	RRZZZZUSA
ZIMMERMAN, WOLFF	21	M	LABR	RRZZZZUSA
JANISWICH, WM.	21	M	PNTR	RRZZZZUSA
LESSMAN, MARK	40	M	DRMR	PLZZZZUSA
GALLEN, MOSES-J.	46	M	CPTR	RRZZZZUSA

SHIP: LAHN

FROM: BREMEN AND SOUTHAMPTON
TO: NEW YORK
ARRIVED: 04 MAY 1888

PASSENGER	AGE	SEX	OCCUPATION	PV RI VL DES
HOFF, CHRIST	27	M	FARMER	RRAHUFUSA
GUTOWSKI, MICH	18	M	FARMER	RRAHUFUSA
HOFF, JOHANN	33	M	FARMER	RRAHUFUSA
RENN, GOTTLIEB	40	M	FARMER	RRAHUFUSA
DJUKOWSKI, FRIEDR	32	M	LABR	RRAHUFUSA
SLIWIANSKY, WALENTY	24	M	LABR	RRAHUFUSA
BICK, ANDREAS	21	M	LABR	RRAHUFUSA
BUCGHARSKI, JAN	29	M	LABR	RRAHUFUSA
TUROWSKI, JAN	29	M	LABR	RRAHUFUSA
ZBIKOWSKII, JOSEF	24	M	LABR	RRAHUFUSA
TABELKOWITSCH, KALMAN	40	M	LABR	RRAHUFUSA
KOSKO, ADELE	36	F	W	RRAHZSUSA
SIEGMUND	7	M	CHILD	RRAHZSUSA
WACLAW	6	M	CHILD	RRAHZSUSA
KASIMIRG	5	M	CHILD	RRAHZSUSA
MIECISLAW	3	M	CHILD	RRAHZSUSA
JADWIGA	11	F	INF	RRAHZSUSA
GALIAN, LUCINA	19	F	UNKNOWN	RRAHZSUSA
FELIX	7	M	CHILD	RRAHZSUSA

SHIP: GALLIA

FROM: LIVERPOOL AND QUEENSTOWN
TO: NEW YORK
ARRIVED: 04 MAY 1888

PASSENGER	AGE	SEX	OCCUPATION	PV RI VL DES
LOEWENTHAL, PHILIPP	22	M	TLR	RRZZZZUSA
BLONGUIST, EGBERT	36	M	SLR	FNZZZZUSA
ERIKSON, FRANZ	36	M	SLR	FNZZZZUSA
HABERLAND, CARL	32	M	LABR	FNZZZZUSA
HAGGESON, WILHELM	22	M	LABR	FNZZZZUSA
LENDBLOM, IDA	22	F	SVNT	FNZZZZUSA

SHIP: LESSING

FROM: HAMBURG
TO: NEW YORK
ARRIVED: 04 MAY 1888

PASSENGER	AGE	SEX	OCCUPATION	PV RI VL DES
LIPMANOWITZ, LESER	36	M	UNKNOWN	RRZZZZUSA
LEWIN	29	M	UNKNOWN	RRAHVUUSA
DEMAGOLSKY, ANTON	25	M	LABR	RRAHULUSA

PASSENGER	AGE	SEX	OCCUPATION	PRV VIL DES
GUSCHIHOWSKY, IGNATZ	30	M	LABR	RRAHTOUSA
KOWALSKY, JOS.	20	M	LABR	RRAHTOUSA
KUJANSKY, JOS.	30	M	UNKNOWN	RRAHUIUSA
KULINSKY, STEFAN	30	M	UNKNOWN	RRAHUIUSA
KILCZ, FRANZ	25	M	UNKNOWN	RRAHUIUSA
SZWANKOWKI, JOS.	26	M	UNKNOWN	RRAHUIUSA
POBILAVITSCH, FREIDE	22	F	WO	RRAHZHUSA
GRODZISKY, PESSER	27	F	W	RRAILFUSA
RACHEL	.11	F	INFANT	RRAILFUSA
BLANK, JOS.	18	M	LABR	RRAHUOUSA
MINES, MOSES	29	M	LABR	RRAHVUUSA
AUGEIST, ROSA	40	F	W	RRAHZHUSA
WOLF	9	M	CHILD	RRAHZHUSA
SARA	7	F	CHILD	RRAHZHUSA
SIMCKE	4	M	CHILD	RRAHZHUSA
SEMEL, CHAIM	36	M	SHMK	RRZZZZUSA
FURMANSCHICK, FEIWEL	26	M	TLR	RRAIHXUSA
BOGA, MOSES	27	M	UNKNOWN	RRAIHXUSA
LIESEROWICTZ, ABRAM	17	M	UNKNOWN	RRAIHXUSA
MARDER, BENJAMIN	31	M	UNKNOWN	RRZZZZUSA
BURTA, ISAAC	20	M	UNKNOWN	RRZZZZUSA
BELLER, SIMCHE	25	M	UNKNOWN	RRZZZZUSA
HORUSTEIN, ISAAC	42	M	UNKNOWN	RRAIESUSA
GUL, MICH.	26	M	LABR	RRZZZZUSA
SARAFIN, MICH.	26	M	LABR	RRZZZZUSA
OKO, FRANCISEK	27	M	LABR	RRZZZZUSA
HIRSCH, LEIB	20	M	LABR	RRZZZZUSA
SHOWRONSKY, JOS.	27	M	LABR	RRZZZZUSA
STABIRSKY, JOS.	25	M	LABR	RRAIKKUSA
SIEGELLACK, KALMAN	17	M	LABR	RRZZZZUSA
SPRUNG, JACOB	34	M	LABR	RRAHQUUSA
BOTWINIK, SALOMON	23	M	LABR	RRZZZZUSA
STANKEWITZ, CONSTANTIN	28	M	LABR	RRAHSPUSA
BOLWITZKI, ABRAM	26	M	LABR	RRAHSPUSA
CUCLSOHN, JUDA	28	M	LABR	RRZZZZUSA
WONSOWSKY, ABRAM	27	M	LABR	RRAHZSUSA
MILLER, SARA	22	F	WO	RRAHZSUSA
KONITZPOLSKY, BERNHA.	18	M	LABR	RRAHZSUSA
ELISTEIN, DAVID	27	M	LABR	RRAHZSUSA
BERKOWSKY, IGNATZ	37	M	LABR	RRAHZSUSA
SETIN, JOHANN	26	M	LABR	RRAHZSUSA
JESCHINOZIK, JACOB	38	M	LABR	RRAHZSUSA
SIEGMUND, PETRAS	26	M	LABR	RRZZZZUSA
HOFFMANN, MORITZ	20	M	CL	RRZZZZUSA
SCHIMBERG, JOSEF	18	M	TLR	RRZZZZUSA
SPEJANKOWSKY, MICHAEL	29	M	LABR	RRAHUIUSA
MORACZINKOWSKI, JAN	22	M	LABR	RRAHUIUSA
KOWAKOWSKI, MICH.	23	M	LABR	RRAHUIUSA
CHEIKOWSKI, FRANZISZEK	23	M	LABR	RRAHUIUSA
MOLINSKA, CATHA.	23	F	SGL	RRAHUIUSA
PRUSEMIK, PSOTZ.	25	M	LABR	RRAHTOUSA
BACULA, NIKOLAI	30	M	LABR	RRAHTOUSA
CHROSTEK, PIOTR	25	M	LABR	RRAHTOUSA
KOPREK, ALEXANDER	25	M	LABR	RRAHTOUSA
SUBELSCH, JOHANN	25	M	LABR	RRAHZSUSA
VALENTI, VINCENTI	26	M	LABR	RRAHZSUSA
RYBEK, SIMSCHEL	21	M	LABR	RRAHZSUSA
WOLIKANIS, CARL	22	M	LABR	RRAHZSUSA
RAMEIKA, FRANZ	20	M	LABR	RRAHZSUSA
JESCHMANN, ANDRAS	20	M	LABR	RRAHZSUSA
SOVATZKI, ANDRUS	21	M	LABR	RRAHZSUSA
GUDELEWITZ, JOSEF	23	M	LABR	RRZZZZUSA
SCHELANIS, JOSEF	25	M	LABR	RRZZZZUSA
TOLOB, JOHANN	18	M	LABR	RRZZZZUSA
BANDELEWITZ, KASIMIR	31	M	LABR	RRZZZZUSA
BUROWSKI, ANTON	26	M	LABR	RRZZZZUSA
BARTKEWIC, KASIMIR	50	M	LABR	RRZZZZUSA
SCHERKSMISS, JOSEF	25	M	LABR	RRZZZZUSA
KULSKOWSKI, MIHAL	21	M	LABR	RRZZZZUSA
KILIAN, JOSEF	32	M	LABR	RRZZZZUSA
FAMOLIS, JOSEF	24	M	LABR	RRZZZZUSA
SCHELANIS, ANTON	25	M	LABR	RRAHZSUSA
ZAVADKY, BEBEDICT	51	M	LABR	RRAIGHUSA
BOLISLAV	23	M	LABR	RRAIGHUSA
ANTON	18	M	LABR	RRAIGHUSA

PASSENGER	AGE	SEX	OCCUPATION	PRV VIL DES
PETER	9	M	CHILD	RRAIGHUSA
KARTSCHANSKY, MATHEUS	33	M	LABR	RRAHZSUSA
ZIMON, ANTON	38	M	LABR	RRAHZSUSA
SURWILL, JOSEF	19	M	LABR	RRAHZSUSA
DOBEL, PETER	18	M	LABR	RRAHZSUSA
ULRIK, SAVIL	22	M	LABR	RRZZZZUSA
BUDZIN, ANTON	29	M	LABR	RRAHZSUSA
PETRANSKY, HEROJIS	30	M	LABR	RRAHZSUSA
AGNES	22	F	UNKNOWN	RRAHZSUSA
KOLTESCHIS, ANTON	52	M	LABR	RRAHZSUSA
SUBATZKI, KASIMIR	40	M	LABR	RRAHZSUSA
LALANZINCUS, ULIAS	30	M	LABR	RRAHZSUSA
JOHN, ALEXANDER	40	M	LABR	RRAHZSUSA
LISTOKIN, MOSES	18	M	LABR	RRZZZZUSA
BRANDWEIN, HERSCH	20	M	LABR	RRAIGHUSA
FRUME	18	F	W	RRAIGHUSA
ZOBOTYNSKY, ISAAC	24	M	LABR	RRAIAEUSA
GORITZ, DANIEL	22	M	LABR	RRZZZZUSA
MIGATZ, LETSO	17	F	SGL	RRZZZZUSA
SCHWEIT, ISAAC	17	M	MCHT	RRZZZZUSA
KEYSA, PETER	19	M	LABR	RRZZZZUSA
PAKROPIS, JAN	28	M	LABR	RRZZZZUSA
MILLER, WIYRICH	24	M	LABR	RRZZZZUSA
UZDILO, ANTONI	20	M	LABR	RRZZZZUSA
ZWILLENBERG, CHOME	50	F	WO	RRZZZZUSA
MARIAN	16	F	CH	RRZZZZUSA
BEILE	6	F	CHILD	RRZZZZUSA
SZANDARSKI, ELSBETA	20	F	WO	RRZZZZUSA
MICHAEL	00	M	INF	RRZZZZUSA
BRUDNITZKI, JAN	27	M	LABR	RRAHUIUSA
BLANKSTEIN, ARON	34	M	LKSH	RRAIMVUSA
KOETLER, CHAIM	33	M	DLR	RRZZZZUSA
CEZCHOEVSKI, ZIEWE	23	F	SGL	RRZZZZUSA
DORFMAN, SAMUEL	17	M	LABR	RRAHTOUSA
KORECZINSKI, ISAAC	21	M	TLR	RRAIMWUSA
KRAWENETZ, CHANE	18	M	TLR	RRAIMWUSA
ROTTSTEIN, ABRAHAM	20	M	DLR	RRZZZZUSA
GRENCZAMSKI, JACOB	22	M	FARMER	RRAHRZUSA
SUMOWSKI, SCHEBSEL	23	M	DLR	RRAIMWUSA
JABLOK, BISCHKI	29	M	DLR	RRAIMWUSA
MILISCHEWSKI, MOSES	18	M	TLR	RRAIMWUSA
KUNIESPOLSKA, SCHMILKO	28	M	DLR	RRZZZZUSA
BELKIN, CHONON	22	M	MCHT	RRAIGHUSA
PEREZ, OSCHER	17	M	LABR	RRAIGHUSA
PUNDA, JOHANN	38	M	LABR	RRZZZZUSA
SAWITSKI, MATTWEI	44	M	LABR	RRZZZZUSA
KOSLAWSKI, MOZI	29	M	LABR	RRZZZZUSA
WENIS, CARL	24	M	LABR	RRZZZZUSA
SEKEWITZ, ALEXANDER	25	M	LABR	RRZZZZUSA
LOEIVIN, JODNA	19	M	LABR	RRAIHBUSA
GAREWITZ, ADAM	25	M	LABR	RRZZZZUSA
SCHULTZ, ANTON	25	M	LABR	RRZZZZUSA
ANNA	20	F	SGL	RRZZZZUSA
BRAUZEWITZ, ANTON	25	M	LABR	RRZZZZUSA
KAMINETZKI, AISIK	18	M	LABR	RRAHXIUSA
SARA	18	F	W	RRAHXIUSA
BONEWITZ, PETER	23	M	LABR	RRZZZZUSA
ROSSUKEWITZ, FAMA	40	M	LABR	RRZZZZUSA
GAZEWITZ, FLORIAN	23	M	LABR	RRZZZZUSA
JUSCHKO, ANDR.	37	M	LABR	RRZZZZUSA
JOSSOWITZ, CASIMIR	25	M	LABR	RRZZZZUSA
ILZEWITRY, SEMION	25	M	LABR	RRZZZZUSA
WILDSCHEWSKI, ABRAH.	17	M	LABR	RRZZZZUSA
SCHMIDT, AUGUST	23	M	LABR	RRAHULUSA
EMILIE	17	F	W	RRAHULUSA
LEBETZ, ALEXANDER	35	M	LABR	RRZZZZUSA
DONNA	35	F	W	RRZZZZUSA
WANA	00	F	INF	RRZZZZUSA
SCHMIDT, JACOB	28	M	LABR	RRAHULUSA
SANER, ISAAC	25	M	DLR	RRAHUIUSA
FEIGE	21	F	W	RRAHUIUSA
GLEIBERSCHN, ARON	19	M	UPHST	RRAIGHUSA
JASCHHEWITZ, VINCENTI	24	M	LABR	RRZZZZUSA
MAZINKEWITZ, VINCENTI	40	M	LABR	RRZZZZUSA
FALOWEG, CHACKEL	50	M	CPTR	RRAHVUUSA

PASSENGER	AGE	SEX	OCCUPATION	PRV	VIL	DES
REICHEL	19	F	CH	RR	AHVUU	USA
BEILE	9	F	CHILD	RR	AHVUU	USA
POLEIKA, KASIMIR	34	M	LABR	RR	ZZZZ	USA
GANZER, ADAM	26	M	LABR	RR	ZZZZ	USA
ANDREI	30	M	LABR	RR	ZZZZ	USA
HANDWERKER, HERM.	30	M	DLR	RR	ZZZZ	USA
KORSINEK, FRANZ	24	M	LABR	RR	AHTO	USA
POKALIS, JAN	26	M	LABR	RR	ZZZZ	USA
WASCHKIEWICZ, MICHAEL	30	M	LABR	RR	AHTO	USA
DULSKI, JURAS	43	M	LABR	RR	AHZS	USA
WINCEWITZ, MATH.	38	M	LABR	RR	AHZS	USA
KRAUSHAAR, HEINR.	16	M	LABR	RR	AFWJ	USA
ASCH, KALMAN	38	M	TDR	RR	AIEO	USA
GLASSNER, JOSEF	18	M	CL	RR	AIFP	USA
WOJEICHOWSKI, JAN	22	M	LABR	RR	AHUL	USA
MURAWSKI, FRANZ	23	M	LABR	RR	AHUL	USA
PANKOWSKI, JAN	30	M	LABR	RR	AHUL	USA
NOWINSKI, TOMAS	26	M	LABR	RR	AHUL	USA
PAWLICKI, STANISLAUS	26	M	LABR	RR	AHUL	USA
MODRACHOWSKI, JOS.	46	M	LABR	RR	AHUL	USA
KALINOWSKY, JOSEF	30	M	LABR	RR	AHUL	USA
GOERTH, FRIEDR.	32	M	LABR	RR	ZZZZ	USA
CAROLINE	25	F	W	RR	ZZZZ	USA
LAURA	5	F	CHILD	RR	ZZZZ	USA
ANNA	00	F	INF	RR	ZZZZ	USA
LUCIE	.01	F	INFANT	RR	ZZZZ	USA
JANGEIS, STANISLUS	30	M	LABR	RR	AIKS	USA
GOLDBERG, NISSEN	26	M	DLR	RR	AHTU	USA
KISEL, JULS.	37	M	LABR	RR	AHTF	USA
JARZOMBEK, MARIUS	24	M	TLR	RR	ZZZZ	USA
HITEL, BARUCH	26	M	DLR	RR	AIHX	USA
GAST, ISRAEL	25	M	TLR	RR	AIHX	USA
LOEWENTHAL, ISRAEL	17	M	DLR	RR	ZZZZ	USA
BLUM, MARCUS	23	M	DLR	RR	AIHX	USA
WISCHNE, BRAINE	25	F	W	RR	AIHX	USA
JACOB	.11	M	INFANT	RR	AIHX	USA
NESCHEK, RACHEL	26	F	W	RR	AIHX	USA
FEIGEL	6	F	CHILD	RR	AIHX	USA
RUDA, SALOMON	25	M	TLR	RR	ZZZZ	USA
BRANDE, SARA	23	F	LABR	RR	AIEP	USA
KAHN, LEISER	20	M	UNKNOWN	RR	AHRZ	USA
COHN, ABRAHAM	20	M	DLR	RR	AIHX	USA
BASCHNER, SCHIE	18	M	TLR	RR	ZZZZ	USA
KALENDER, SIMON	29	M	TLR	RR	AIHX	USA
MOSCHKOWITZ, ABRAHAM	19	M	TNM	RR	AIHX	USA
MIRDA, JOSEF	17	M	TLR	RR	AIHX	USA
KADISHEWITZ, MERE	20	F	SGL	RR	AIEQ	USA
FEIWEL	17	M	TLR	RR	AIEQ	USA
LISZINEWSKI, ANTON	22	M	LABR	RR	AHUI	USA
NEGEDLY, ANTON	21	M	SHMK	RR	ZZZZ	USA
BOHUMIL	21	M	BCHR	RR	ZZZZ	USA
KLEMPKIEWICZ, ANNA	30	F	WO	RR	AHXH	USA
MARTHA	9	F	CHILD	RR	AHXH	USA
HELENE	8	F	CHILD	RR	AHXH	USA
LANKOP, JOHANN	26	M	SMH	RR	AHXH	USA
PETKUS, MATHAUS	30	M	LABR	RR	AHXH	USA
CONRAD, JOSEF	23	M	LABR	RR	AHXH	USA
MOROSCHOWITZ, SCHEINE	17	M	LABR	RR	ZZZZ	USA
ADELSOHN, JACOB	25	M	LABR	RR	ZZZZ	USA
EPSTEIN, JACOB	28	M	LABR	RR	ZZZZ	USA
BREWDE, BERL.	37	M	LABR	RR	ZZZZ	USA
ZACHNOWITZ, MICHEL	19	M	LABR	RR	AGRT	USA
NAUMANN, HILLEL	18	M	LABR	RR	ZZZZ	USA
KAPLAN, FEIWEL	28	M	LABR	RR	ZZZZ	USA
BREWDE, MORDCHE	22	M	LABR	RR	ZZZZ	USA
POCKER, MEICR	25	M	MCHT	RR	ZZZZ	USA
MOCHMANOWITZ, ZODECK	43	M	TLR	RR	ZZZZ	USA
RASRAN, SCHLOME	38	M	LABR	RR	ZZZZ	USA
NATACH, CHAIM	22	M	LABR	RR	ZZZZ	USA
LUSCH, MESCHEL	40	M	LABR	RR	ZZZZ	USA
STOCK, ESRIEL	18	M	LABR	RR	AHTU	USA
SARCHE, LINA	23	F	SGL	RR	ZZZZ	USA

SHIP: RHAETIA

FROM: HAMBURG AND HAVRE
TO: NEW YORK
ARRIVED: 04 MAY 1888

PASSENGER	AGE	SEX	OCCUPATION	PRV	VIL	DES
GURELOWSKY, SCHULE	22	F	WO	RR	ZZZZ	USA
JACOB	9	M	CHILD	RR	ZZZZ	USA
WOWICKI, ANTON	22	M	LABR	RR	ZZZZ	USA
SURMAS, URSULA	22	F	WO	RR	ZZZZ	USA
OCHEN, ESTER	23	F	W	RR	ZZZZ	USA
ALERAP	3	M	CHILD	RR	ZZZZ	USA
SCHEINE	.09	F	INFANT	RR	ZZZZ	USA
RAINES, ITZIG	18	M	CL	RR	ZZZZ	USA
ANOLIK, JACOB	19	M	LABR	RR	ZZZZ	USA
MURAWSKY, EVA	26	F	W	RR	ZZZZ	USA
MINA	9	F	CHILD	RR	ZZZZ	USA
MARIE	8	F	CHILD	RR	ZZZZ	USA
GUSTAV	6	M	CHILD	RR	ZZZZ	USA
SCHULMANN, ISAAK	21	M	HTR	RR	ZZZZ	USA
SARA	18	F	W	RR	ZZZZ	USA
MEYER	17	M	HTR	RR	ZZZZ	USA
WEHDE, CHRISTIAN	42	M	FARMER	RR	ZZZZ	USA
MAGDALENA	45	F	W	RR	ZZZZ	USA
JOH.	14	M	CH	RR	ZZZZ	USA
HEINR.	9	M	CHILD	RR	ZZZZ	USA
DORIS	8	F	CHILD	RR	ZZZZ	USA
GUSTAV	7	M	CHILD	RR	ZZZZ	USA
SCHMULOWSKY, ISAAK	63	M	TDR	RR	ZZZZ	USA
MORITZ	16	M	CH	RR	ZZZZ	USA
GLATTER, SCHMUL	27	M	LABR	RR	ZZZZ	USA
BERGUENDE, ALBERT	27	M	WO	RR	ZZZZ	USA
STASZEWSKI, STANISL.	25	M	SMH	RR	ZZZZ	USA
WASICKY, MARCELLY	34	M	LABR	RR	ZZZZ	USA
KARPINSKA, VALERIA	18	F	WO	RR	ZZZZ	USA
MILIKOWSKI, ARON	28	M	LABR	RR	ZZZZ	USA
EPSTEIN, MOSES	30	M	LABR	RR	ZZZZ	USA
FRUDZINSKI, ANTON	33	M	LABR	RR	ZZZZ	USA
VEIT, VALENTIN	27	M	UNKNOWN	RR	ZZZZ	USA
GOLEWBIAK, FRANZ	25	M	UNKNOWN	RR	ZZZZ	USA
CASPAR	28	M	UNKNOWN	RR	ZZZZ	USA
MARIANSKI, FRANZ	26	M	UNKNOWN	RR	ZZZZ	USA
EVA	24	F	LABR	RR	ZZZZ	USA
JAN	.10	M	INFANT	RR	ZZZZ	USA
SENDZYKOWSKY, WOJCECH	20	M	LABR	RR	ZZZZ	USA
HELLER, HEINRICH	26	M	CPTR	RR	ZZZZ	USA
SCHISKAIT-, JOS.	22	M	CPTR	RR	ZZZZ	USA
TOMASZEWSKI, ANTONI	24	M	UNKNOWN	RR	ZZZZ	USA
KORALEWSKY, WOJCECH	32	M	UNKNOWN	RR	ZZZZ	USA
SURINSKI, STANISL.	24	M	UNKNOWN	RR	ZZZZ	USA
BUMKOWSKI, ANTON	23	M	UNKNOWN	RR	ZZZZ	USA
SWARDOWSKI, ANTON	34	M	UNKNOWN	RR	ZZZZ	USA
DSCHWIECKI, FELIX	40	M	UNKNOWN	RR	ZZZZ	USA
TOMASCHEWSKI, JAN	26	M	UNKNOWN	RR	ZZZZ	USA
MANKEWITZ, WLADISL.	25	M	UNKNOWN	RR	ZZZZ	USA
WIESCHNEWSKI, JAN	36	M	UNKNOWN	RR	ZZZZ	USA
GURETZKI, ANTON	27	M	UNKNOWN	RR	ZZZZ	USA
JOSEF	24	M	UNKNOWN	RR	ZZZZ	USA
JULITZKI, JOSEFA	22	M	UNKNOWN	RR	ZZZZ	USA
GODENSKI, ANTON	24	M	UNKNOWN	RR	ZZZZ	USA
MOELLER, JOSEF	37	M	UNKNOWN	RR	ZZZZ	USA
LO-----, ELISBETA	17	F	UNKNOWN	RR	ZZZZ	USA
STANHOVECZ, LEONHD.	23	M	LABR	RR	ZZZZ	USA
NAWOCKI, LAWRYN	40	M	LABR	RR	ZZZZ	USA
WOJTICHUS, PIETRO	25	M	LABR	RR	ZZZZ	USA
SZETBAR, ANTON	25	M	LABR	RR	ZZZZ	USA
GYBOWITZ, VINET	28	M	LABR	RR	ZZZZ	USA
GOTOWETZ, ANDR.	25	M	LABR	RR	ZZZZ	USA
GABREINAS, JOSES	22	M	LABR	RR	ZZZZ	USA
SLANIAVICZ, ADAM	24	M	LABR	RR	ZZZZ	USA
WOJTICHUS, OSYP	30	M	LABR	RR	ZZZZ	USA
UZBICHOWIEZ, THEODOR	23	M	LABR	RR	ZZZZ	USA
WOJTECHUS, SIMON	25	M	LABR	RR	ZZZZ	USA
WISMANSKI, JOSEF	28	M	LABR	RR	ZZZZ	USA

PASSENGER	AGE	SEX	OCCUPATION	PV RIVL	DES
KRAGLEWSKI, IGNATZ	61	M	LABR	RRZZZZ	USA
GALINSKA, JACOB	30	M	LABR	RRZZZZ	USA
JANUSKIWIECZ, FRANZ	26	M	LABR	RRZZZZ	USA
WENZLAU, VINCENT	28	M	LABR	RRZZZZ	USA
DOMBROWSKI, STANISLAUS	21	M	LABR	RRZZZZ	USA
STANISLAUS	21	M	LABR	RRZZZZ	USA
KONOPACKI, JOSEF	30	M	LABR	RRZZZZ	USA
SCHNEIDER, JAN	36	M	LABR	RRZZZZ	USA
WOVENETZKI, JOSEF	27	M	LABR	RRZZZZ	USA
JOCHLITZKI, KAETCHEN	19	F	SGL	RRZZZZ	USA
CIPERK, MARCIN	28	M	LABR	RRZZZZ	USA
MAREMKOWSKY, IGNATZ	23	M	LABR	RRZZZZ	USA
BALIZEROWICZ, JAN	28	M	LABR	RRZZZZ	USA
NOHLICZKY, IGNATZ	24	M	LABR	RRZZZZ	USA
KWIATKOWSKY, WLADISL.	28	M	LABR	RRZZZZ	USA
CZYRANOWITZ, ROMAN	20	M	LABR	RRZZZZ	USA
ABRAMSOHN, HEYMANN	18	M	SHMK	RRZZZZ	USA
ISIDOR	16	M	SHMK	RRZZZZ	USA
ULCZINSKY, JAN	29	M	DLR	RRZZZZ	USA
LEWIN, FERKEL	32	M	DLR	RRZZZZ	USA
BOLEWICZ, GERSEY	20	M	LABR	RRZZZZ	USA
GIBOWIC, ADAM	26	M	LABR	RRZZZZ	USA
ZUMOROWIEZ, STANISL.	36	M	LABR	RRZZZZ	USA
PASEWIC, VINCENTY	30	M	LABR	RRZZZZ	USA
GROCHOWICZ, JAN	27	M	LABR	RRZZZZ	USA
CHOMENTOWSKY, WLADISLAW	20	M	LABR	RRZZZZ	USA
MISZKO, JOH.	29	M	LABR	RRZZZZ	USA
FRANZISKA	30	F	W	RRZZZZ	USA
MANIKE	4	F	CHILD	RRZZZZ	USA
LEON	2	M	CHILD	RRZZZZ	USA
ZIELINSKY, ANTON	29	M	LABR	RRZZZZ	USA
PAULE.	28	F	W	RRZZZZ	USA
BOLESLAV	.04	M	INFANT	RRZZZZ	USA
SAWICKI, FRANZ	27	M	LABR	RRZZZZ	USA
DOMICELA	22	F	W	RRZZZZ	USA
BOLESLAV	.11	M	INFANT	RRZZZZ	USA
GORSKI, JAN	9	M	CHILD	RRZZZZ	USA
SAWICKI, IGNATZ	27	M	LABR	RRZZZZ	USA
KELLNER, MARIANNE	20	F	SGL	RRZZZZ	USA
BRESLAUER, SCHAJE	14	M	LABR	RRZZZZ	USA
SUSSMANN, DAVID	33	M	LABR	RRZZZZ	USA
LIT, BENJAMIN	25	M	LABR	RRZZZZ	USA
RISCHE	23	F	W	RRZZZZ	USA
BARUCH	24	M	LABR	RRZZZZ	USA
SOBOLANSKI, ANTON	29	M	LABR	RRZZZZ	USA
MURAWSKY, JAN	23	M	LABR	RRZZZZ	USA
SZATKOWSKY, JAN	29	M	LABR	RRZZZZ	USA
PARADOWSKI, JOSEF	29	M	LABR	RRZZZZ	USA
ZUEKOWSKA, SARA	22	F	WO	RRZZZZ	USA
DAVID	.11	M	INFANT	RRZZZZ	USA
DORTMANN, ISAAC	17	M	LKSH	RRZZZZ	USA
BEHRMANN, JESER	23	M	DLR	RRZZZZ	USA
BRADOWSKY, JOHANN	30	M	LABR	RRZZZZ	USA
LUDWIKA	29	F	W	RRZZZZ	USA
LINGULA, WILH.	24	M	LABR	RRZZZZ	USA
MINNA	19	F	W	RRZZZZ	USA
WAWRUGEWITZ, WLAD.	18	M	LABR	RRZZZZ	USA
FALTIM, FRANT.	20	M	LABR	RRZZZZ	USA
MAZALEWSKY, PAWEL	24	M	LABR	RRZZZZ	USA
ZOWNA, JOSEF	24	M	LABR	RRZZZZ	USA
WOJTASCHEK, JAN	24	M	LABR	RRZZZZ	USA
WRONOWSKY, FRANK	33	M	LABR	RRZZZZ	USA
BUDERNDORF, MARTIN	24	M	LABR	RRZZZZ	USA
BRZEZRENSKY, STEFAN	28	M	LABR	RRZZZZ	USA
WISCHNEWSKY, ANDR.	29	M	LABR	RRZZZZ	USA
SLESINSKI, ANDR.	21	M	LABR	RRZZZZ	USA
RIBUTZWIC, ANTON	19	M	LABR	RRZZZZ	USA
WINEWSKY, JOSEF	17	M	LABR	RRZZZZ	USA
KUEHLAK, STANIS.	26	M	LABR	RRZZZZ	USA
SCHIDER, HIRSCH	30	M	LABR	RRZZZZ	USA
HOLSTEIN, OWSCHI	17	M	LABR	RRZZZZ	USA
MISKIND, SAL.	26	M	LABR	RRZZZZ	USA
KETZELES, JANKEL	23	M	LABR	RRZZZZ	USA
SCHILOWSKY, ABR.	9	M	CHILD	RRZZZZ	USA
LEWADSKY, PETER	18	M	LABR	RRZZZZ	USA

PASSENGER	AGE	SEX	OCCUPATION	PV RIVL	DES
JATOWOC, IGNATZ	26	M	LABR	RRZZZZ	USA
SINAKOWSKY, KASIMIR	21	M	LABR	RRZZZZ	USA
PIETEREMSKI, JAN	52	M	LABR	RRZZZZ	USA
PICEWITZ, ANTONI	20	M	LABR	RRZZZZ	USA
MILANIS, SIMON	26	M	LABR	RRZZZZ	USA
GLATUSKEWICZ, FRANC.	26	M	LABR	RRZZZZ	USA
BOGDIAN, ANTONI	44	M	LABR	RRZZZZ	USA
RIDZIEWITZ, JOH.	26	M	LABR	RRZZZZ	USA
ZALSKOWSKY, FAUSTIN	25	M	LABR	RRZZZZ	USA
DRUICK, ANTONIN	30	M	LABR	RRZZZZ	USA
SCHLINSKI, JAN	24	M	LABR	RRZZZZ	USA
SCHELASKA, ANDR.	30	M	LABR	RRZZZZ	USA
FABIANSKI, JAN	40	M	LABR	RRZZZZ	USA
LULENSKI, VALENT.	20	M	UNKNOWN	RRZZZZ	USA
BARTNICKI, TOMAK	29	F	UNKNOWN	RRZZZZ	USA
GIMINLA, EVA	20	F	SGL	RRZZZZ	USA
BARBA.	18	F	SGL	RRZZZZ	USA
LEBOWSKY, JOSEF	23	M	LABR	RRZZZZ	USA
KARPINSKY, FRANZ	16	M	LABR	RRZZZZ	USA
WISCHMEWSKY, ELBITA	24	F	SGL	RRZZZZ	USA
JABLONSKI, ANTON	27	M	LABR	RRZZZZ	USA
BURSCHINSKY, FRANZ	23	M	LABR	RRZZZZ	USA
CHMILEWSKI, FRANZ	24	M	LABR	RRZZZZ	USA
JASZESKI, STANISL.	26	M	LABR	RRZZZZ	USA
BAZILA, JULIAN	22	M	LABR	RRZZZZ	USA
MISKEWICZ, JOHANN	36	M	LABR	RRZZZZ	USA
DUDOS, IWAN	22	M	LABR	RRZZZZ	USA
WISCHNEWSKY, JOSEF	55	M	LABR	RRZZZZ	USA
HREHOR, ANDRAS	26	M	LABR	RRZZZZ	USA
WANJER, JANOS	32	M	LABR	RRZZZZ	USA
KOMMENDA, JANOS	39	M	LABR	RRZZZZ	USA
KESCHKOWSKI, XAVER	23	M	LABR	RRZZZZ	USA
RADWANSKY, FRANZ	42	M	LABR	RRZZZZ	USA
WITKOWSKI, STANISL.	46	M	LABR	RRZZZZ	USA
GUERETZKI, MARIAN	27	M	LABR	RRZZZZ	USA
KOPROWSKA, MARIAN	32	M	LABR	RRZZZZ	USA
MRUFCZINSKI, ANDR.	22	M	LABR	RRZZZZ	USA
BUDZINSKI, STANISL.	25	M	LABR	RRZZZZ	USA
PATAN, VICTOR	26	M	LABR	RRZZZZ	USA
ETELARK, HENRIK	28	M	LABR	FNZZZZ	USA
AN--ILA, JOHANN	41	M	LABR	FNZZZZ	USA
KOPPELOSCHTATT, ERIK	26	M	LABR	FNZZZZ	USA
U, JOH.	27	M	LABR	FNZZZZ	USA
JARVINEN, HENRIKSEN	34	M	LABR	FNZZZZ	USA
LESKIMEN, AUGUSTON	25	M	LABR	FNZZZZ	USA
HERMESMANN, ALEXANDER	30	M	LABR	FNZZZZ	USA
MATTSON, HERMANN	29	M	LABR	FNZZZZ	USA
LEPONEN, TIMATEUS	27	M	LABR	FNZZZZ	USA
ROPONNEN, DAVID	28	M	LABR	FNZZZZ	USA
ANTIO, KARL	21	M	LABR	FNZZZZ	USA
MYLLYSILTA, MATS	33	M	LABR	FNZZZZ	USA
KAUPPI, KARL	33	M	LABR	FNZZZZ	USA
MOLLER, CHRISTIAN	42	M	JNR	FNZZZZ	USA
CHRISTENSEN, CHRESTEN	23	M	MSN	FNZZZZ	USA
JENSEN, PETER	47	M	BCHR	FNZZZZ	USA
LUCHKO, GUSTAV	19	M	LABR	FNZZZZ	USA
SUSPELTO, ANDERS	39	M	LABR	FNZZZZ	USA
MAKELA, KARL	33	M	LABR	FNZZZZ	USA
YTTEHODES, ESAFAS	26	M	LABR	FNZZZZ	USA
MATHISON, ZEFONIS	26	M	LABR	FNZZZZ	USA
ULTKODES, NIKODEMUS	22	M	LABR	FNZZZZ	USA
DIAMANT, FISCHEL	63	M	LABR	RRZZZZ	USA
HANNES	9	M	CHILD	RRZZZZ	USA
TOMACHOWITZ, ALEXANDER	25	M	LABR	RRZZZZ	USA
MISZKEWITZ, ANTON	25	M	LABR	RRZZZZ	USA
WLOCHOWITZ, VALENTY	20	M	LABR	RRZZZZ	USA
ROGINSKI, ANTON	30	M	LABR	RRZZZZ	USA
KIEWSKI, JAN	34	M	LABR	RRZZZZ	USA
PRUCHINSKY, MICH.	49	M	LABR	RRZZZZ	USA
KRAJEWSKI, ANDRY	36	M	LABR	RRZZZZ	USA
OLKIEWICZ, JAN	29	M	LABR	RRZZZZ	USA
WIELKOWSKI, IGNATZ	27	M	LABR	RRZZZZ	USA
TOMAZEWSKI, ANTON	22	M	LABR	RRZZZZ	USA
BUTZKI, IGNATZ	31	M	LABR	RRZZZZ	USA
SAMOWSKI, JAN	21	M	LABR	RRZZZZ	USA

PASSENGER	AGE	SEX	OCCUPATION	PRV VIL DES
MOSCHLOWSKI, ANDR.	48	M	LABR	RRZZZZUSA
KIVIATKOWSKI, ADAM	26	M	LABR	RRZZZZUSA
SOTRAWSKY, JURGIS	27	M	LABR	RRZZZZUSA
ABRAMOWITZ, SIMON	26	M	LABR	RRZZZZUSA
PERLOKONIS, PETER	38	M	LABR	RRZZZZUSA
KASCHIC, IGNATZ	30	M	LABR	RRZZZZUSA
BOKUEM, WAWRZYN	20	M	LABR	RRZZZZUSA
DEMUNDETSCH, BOLESLAW	30	M	LABR	RRZZZZUSA
WASILIS, OSIP	23	M	LABR	RRZZZZUSA
LOTZ, LUDWIG	27	M	LABR	RRZZZZUSA
RATKOWSKI, JAN	34	M	LABR	RRZZZZUSA
MARZIKA, FRANZ	34	M	LABR	RRZZZZUSA
JANTSOWICZ, JOS.	28	M	LABR	RRZZZZUSA
STADNESKI, JAN	34	M	LABR	RRZZZZUSA
SPITKA, ALEXANDER	28	M	LABR	RRZZZZUSA
GEZIK, FRANZ	23	M	LABR	RRZZZZUSA
BRZESKI, MEYER	18	M	LABR	RRZZZZUSA
OMSINSKI, STANISL.	25	M	LABR	RRZZZZUSA
SOLBE, FRANZ	22	M	LABR	RRZZZZUSA
REALISCHKI, TOMAS	29	M	LABR	RRZZZZUSA
GEREITIS, VINCENT	23	M	LABR	RRZZZZUSA
SAWITZKI, CHEIM	20	M	FARMER	RRZZZZUSA
SAMOLIS, CARL	23	M	FARMER	RRZZZZUSA
LEWANDOWSKY, JOS.	30	M	LABR	RRZZZZUSA
CHOCOZKY, WINCAS	22	M	LABR	RRZZZZUSA
SCHOLZ, JOS.	40	M	MCHT	RRZZZZUSA
DOBRICZ, STANISL.	23	M	SHMK	RRZZZZUSA
MEYERSOHN, BENJAMIN	30	M	MCHT	RRZZZZUSA
GOLD, RUBEL	16	M	TLR	RRZZZZUSA
KAPLAN, BENJAMIN	23	M	LABR	RRZZZZUSA
AUGUSTOWSKY, ARON	48	M	LABR	RRZZZZUSA
WOLKENSTEIN, CHRISTIAN	56	M	LABR	RRZZZZUSA
CHRISTIANE	51	F	W	RRZZZZUSA
WILH.	9	M	CHILD	RRZZZZUSA
CARL	8	M	CHILD	RRZZZZUSA
CZERNITZKI, ANTONIE	28	F	LABR	RRZZZZUSA
DZOUS, VALENTIN	40	M	LABR	RRZZZZUSA
GANG, PIOTR	26	M	LABR	RRZZZZUSA
NESWETZKI, VALENTIN	46	M	LABR	RRZZZZUSA
SCHITKOWSKI, FRANZ	23	M	LABR	RRZZZZUSA
KOTSCHINSKY, IGNATZ	26	M	LABR	RRZZZZUSA
KACZMARSKY, JOS.	26	M	LABR	RRZZZZUSA
SCHABLOWSKY, ROWAL	21	M	LABR	RRZZZZUSA
SIMON, LEIB	23	M	LABR	RRZZZZUSA
HUMERFELD, GEDALIA	30	M	LABR	RRZZZZUSA
SCHLESINGER, MOSES	21	M	LABR	RRZZZZUSA
KOSITZKI, MOSES	30	M	LABR	RRZZZZUSA
HOLLENSCH, MOSES	30	M	LABR	RRZZZZUSA
LEWANDOWSKY, SIGMUND	15	M	LABR	RRZZZZUSA
GLOWACKI, ANTON	33	M	LABR	RRZZZZUSA
SCHIDLOWSKY, STANISL.	29	M	LABR	RRZZZZUSA
KUBELSDORF, WLADISL.	40	M	LABR	RRZZZZUSA
SCHACH, JAN	30	M	LABR	RRZZZZUSA
GERZIG, JAN	28	M	LABR	RRZZZZUSA
DOMIAN, MARIAN	27	M	LABR	RRZZZZUSA
SCHOPPS, IGNATZ	30	M	LABR	RRZZZZUSA
ZERSCHATZKI, IGNATZ	40	M	LABR	RRZZZZUSA
SCHAIKOWSKI, MATH.	47	M	LABR	RRZZZZUSA
MAZIK, JAN	36	M	LABR	RRZZZZUSA
LAMPERSKI, JOS.	26	M	LABR	RRZZZZUSA
JENDRAZYCK, JOS.	17	M	LABR	RRZZZZUSA
KOBUS, JOS.	30	M	LABR	RRZZZZUSA
GLAS, FRANZ	37	M	LABR	RRZZZZUSA
GOLLASCH, FRANZ	22	M	LABR	RRZZZZUSA
SAKOLOWSKI, TEOFIL	25	M	LABR	RRZZZZUSA
SATRIP, JAN	27	M	LABR	RRZZZZUSA
DASCHWESKY, WLADISL.	25	M	LABR	RRZZZZUSA
FETERBAUM, LEIB	29	M	LABR	RRZZZZUSA
STABINSKY, SAM.	47	M	LABR	RRZZZZUSA
GRUENBERG, ABRAM	43	M	LABR	RRZZZZUSA
HOFZUK, MOSES	26	M	LABR	RRZZZZUSA
JANKATZ, MOSES	44	M	LABR	RRZZZZUSA
LUBINSKY, ANNA	24	M	LABR	RRZZZZUSA
REMSTEIN, JACOB	33	M	LABR	RRZZZZUSA
WISCHINSKY, ISRAEL	23	M	LABR	RRZZZZUSA
RUTKOWSKY, DAVID	26	M	LABR	RRZZZZUSA
KOWALEWSKY, DAVID	23	M	LABR	RRZZZZUSA
SCHNEIDER, JAN	40	M	LABR	RRZZZZUSA
HOLLAENDER, VALENTIN	24	M	LABR	RRZZZZUSA
CZANCZANAS, WINCZAS	23	M	LABR	RRZZZZUSA
HUERTSTAEDTER, MOSES	34	M	DLR	RRZZZZUSA
KLINOWSKY, FRANZ	25	M	LABR	RRZZZZUSA
SCHAPIRO, JANOS	17	M	LABR	RRZZZZUSA
FRIEDMANN, CHAJE	17	F	SGL	RRZZZZUSA
MILKOLET, LEOPOLD	28	M	LABR	RRZZZZUSA
HENRIETTE	20	F	W	RRZZZZUSA
JAKUBOWSKI, MAXEL	23	M	LABR	RRZZZZUSA
GRUENHAUS, ABRAM	17	M	LABR	RRZZZZUSA
TUENSKI, FRANZ	40	M	LABR	RRZZZZUSA
RACJONZER, SALOMON	27	M	TNM	RRZZZZUSA
KOEGLER, JULIE	8	F	CHILD	RRZZZZUSA
LANKOS, JOS.	27	M	LABR	RRZZZZUSA
VINCENT	25	M	LABR	RRZZZZUSA
LINDERTES, JONAS	26	M	LABR	RRZZZZUSA
WILEK, HENRI	28	M	LABR	RRZZZZUSA
MATWEKEWITZ, FRANK	22	M	LABR	RRZZZZUSA

SHIP: POLARIA

FROM: HAMBURG
TO: NEW YORK
ARRIVED: 04 MAY 1888

PASSENGER	AGE	SEX	OCCUPATION	PRV VIL DES
KRANZITZKY, SALAMAN	22	M	CL	RRZZZZUSA
SOBEZAK, JONAS	24	M	LABR	RRZZZZUSA
MARTHA	30	F	W	RRZZZZUSA
THEODORR	8	M	CHILD	RRZZZZUSA
HELENE	6	F	CHILD	RRZZZZUSA
LEA	3	F	CHILD	RRZZZZUSA
MARIE	.09	F	INFANT	RRZZZZUSA
KOZA, ALBERT	28	M	LABR	RRZZZZUSA
PIERSIALEK, VALENTIN	31	M	LABR	RRZZZZUSA
SZIZEPANSKY, MARINS	24	M	LABR	RRZZZZUSA
ROMANOWSKY, JOSEF	22	M	LABR	RRZZZZUSA
SCHECHWOWIZ, MICHAEL	25	M	LABR	RRZZZZUSA
MACKAY, MICHAEL	26	M	LABR	RRZZZZUSA
WITTZECK, AGATHE	22	F	SGL	RRZZZZUSA
LEWANDOWSKY, JOSEF	31	M	LABR	RRZZZZNY
ROSOWOOSKY, VINCENT	22	M	LABR	RRZZZZNY
BOROSKY, WLADIS	22	M	LABR	RRZZZZNY
WENGLIKOWSKY, JAKOB	27	M	LABR	RRZZZZNY
KUPREWITZ, FRANC	24	M	LABR	RRZZZZNY
GRAPEWSKY, JULIAN	35	M	LABR	RRZZZZNY
BABMANN, MODECH	30	M	TLR	RRZZZZNY
SCHURWITZ, KAPITAN	40	M	LABR	RRZZZZNY
KATZ, JAKOB	55	M	LABR	RRZZZZUSA
JAMBONITZ, ABRAH	26	M	LABR	RRZZZZUSA
KOPPELT, LEIB	27	M	LABR	RRZZZZUSA
JAMBONITZ, VINCENT	27	M	LABR	RRZZZZUSA
NARBERT, ALEX	30	M	LABR	RRZZZZUSA
STANKEWITZ, KASEMIR	33	M	LABR	RRZZZZUSA
LATUSCHEWITZ, JOSEF	24	M	LABR	RRZZZZUSA
WIRSCHKOWSKY, FRANZ	28	M	LABR	RRZZZZUSA
BRACHEITIS, IVAN	29	M	LABR	RRZZZZUSA
ARMENAITIS, ADAM	26	M	LABR	RRZZZZUSA
KALLAITES, JUERGI	27	M	LABR	RRZZZZUSA
STAWINSKY, STANISLAUS	29	M	LABR	RRZZZZUSA
SCHMITAEWSKY, JAN	24	M	LABR	RRZZZZUSA
RENNOWITZ, STANISLAV	21	M	LABR	RRZZZZUSA
ANNASTASI	23	M	LABR	RRZZZZUSA
DRABINS, KASEMIR	23	F	LABR	RRZZZZUSA
ROMANSKY, FRANZ	24	M	LABR	RRZZZZUSA
SZCREKANZKY, MAREK	28	M	LABR	RRZZZZUSA
RAPSKEWITZ, SIGMUND	27	M	LABR	RRZZZZUSA
NISSEN, SELIG	35	M	LABR	RRZZZZUSA

PASSENGER	AGE	SEX	OCCUPATION	PRIVL	DES
FEIN, FEIVEL	19	M	LABR	RRZZZZ	USA
RUINSKY, LEISER	18	M	LABR	RRZZZZ	USA
RASCHKOOSKY, RUBIN	27	M	LABR	RRZZZZ	USA
MINSK, LEIB	29	M	LABR	RRZZZZ	USA
SILBERGLAIT, MOSES	26	M	LABR	RRZZZZ	USA
SCHACE	18	M	LABR	RRZZZZ	USA
SCHWITRA, KASEMIR	18	M	LABR	RRZZZZ	NY
DOMELEWSKY, VINCENT	38	M	LABR	RRZZZZ	NY
MARKILAWITZ, STANISLAW	24	M	LABR	RRZZZZ	NY
BURDE, ABRAHAM	24	M	LABR	RRZZZZ	NY
ROBINSON, SALOMON	29	M	DLR	RRZZZZ	NY
BELLA	17	F	W	RRZZZZ	NY
JOSELOWSKY, SAUL	17	M	LABR	RRZZZZ	NY
SCHWEINGWEDER, FRIEDRIC	23	M	FARMER	RRZZZZ	NY
SCHWEINGWEDER, JELAMPHI	18	F	W	RRZZZZ	NY
SCHWEINGWEDER, LENE	.03	F	INFANT	RRZZZZ	NY
RADANSKY, ANTON	22	M	LABR	RRZZZZ	NY
SPAETEN, FEIGE	23	M	LABR	RRZZZZ	NY
WASCHENESKY, MICHAEL	33	M	SGL	RRZZZZ	NY
SPAETER, MINA	19	F	UNKNOWN	RRZZZZ	NY
MULKOSKA, STANISLAW	17	M	LABR	RRZZZZ	NY
NAPORSCHKA, STANISL	22	M	SGL	RRZZZZ	NY
ZELAKOWSKY, MATHIAS	55	M	LABR	RRZZZZ	NY
SCHMARE, JOSEF	25	M	LABR	RRZZZZ	NY
WILHBECK, CHAIM	30	M	LABR	RRZZZZ	NY
RADCZEWITZ, JULIAN	43	M	LABR	RRZZZZ	NY
KOLEWITZ, CYPRYAN	35	M	LABR	RRZZZZ	NY
SPERPRICH, ALEXANDER	22	M	LABR	RRZZZZ	NY
KARLINSKY, MAEKE	48	F	SGL	RRZZZZ	NY
SCHOLIN, WATZKY	17	F	SGL	RRZZZZ	NY
LEYEMANN, ADOLF	9	M	CHILD	RRZZZZ	NY
HERMANOWITZ, LINA	40	F	WO	RRZZZZ	NY
CHAIE	22	F	UNKNOWN	RRZZZZ	NY
NECHANE	3	F	CHILD	RRZZZZ	NY
HARRY	.06	M	INFANT	RRZZZZ	NY
SCHWATZ, SCHMUL	19	M	LABR	RRZZZZ	NY
BUTKOFSKY, FRANZ	43	M	LABR	RRZZZZ	NY
WISCHNESKY, MATHIAS	43	M	LABR	RRZZZZ	NY
JESIONKOWSKY, ANTON	37	M	LABR	RRZZZZ	NY
WOSCHKEWITZ, WOYCICH	19	M	LABR	RRZZZZ	NY
KOWIATKONKY, JAN	27	M	LABR	RRZZZZ	NY
BRICHA, LUDW	52	M	LABR	RRZZZZ	NY
ADOLF	21	M	LABR	RRZZZZ	NY
PEKUM, ANDR	22	M	LABR	RRZZZZ	NY
ZACHAZ, JAN	23	M	LABR	RRZZZZ	NY
WOLLSCHLAEGER, CARL	37	M	LABR	RRZZZZ	NY
PREICHEL, MICHEL	39	M	LABR	RRZZZZ	NY
FREIMUTH, MICHEL	56	M	LABR	RRZZZZ	NY
SENDROWSKY, JOSEF	19	M	LABR	RRZZZZ	NY
GOLKOWSKY, FRANZ	28	M	LABR	RRZZZZ	NY
DSTROWSKY, FRANZ	28	M	LABR	RRZZZZ	NY
CHMELWSKY, MARELLIN	56	M	LABR	RRZZZZ	NY
MEIER, MARIUS	34	M	LABR	RRZZZZ	NY
DWORE	24	F	W	RRZZZZ	NY
SARA	6	F	CHILD	RRZZZZ	NY
RAECHEL	2	F	CHILD	RRZZZZ	NY
MEINDEL	.10	M	INFANT	RRZZZZ	NY
MALKE	50	F	WO	RRZZZZ	NY
RECSKKA, ANDRZECH	33	M	LABR	RRZZZZ	NY
MAIKOOSKY, STANISLAUS	30	M	LABR	RRZZZZ	NY
VALENTY, JOSEF	45	M	LABR	RRZZZZ	NY
MINIKAS, JANAS	27	M	LABR	RRZZZZ	UNK
ANNA	26	F	W	RRZZZZ	UNK
GLUSWITSCHKY, MOSES	33	M	SHMK	RRZZZZ	NY
SCHLECHTMEISTER, ABRAHA	39	M	LABR	RRZZZZ	NY
RUPKO, ABR	32	M	LABR	RRZZZZ	NY
GOLDANSKY, MEIER	18	M	LABR	RRZZZZ	NY
FEIN, AZEK	18	M	LABR	RRZZZZ	NY
NACHAMANAWSKY, NACHUME	17	F	LABR	RRZZZZ	NY
ROWITZ, DAID	18	M	LABR	RRZZZZ	NY
JOSEF	15	M	LABR	RRZZZZ	NY
WISMIENSKA, LEONORE	27	F	WO	RRZZZZ	NY
SPARBEL, AUG	27	M	FARMER	RRZZZZ	NY
JOH	27	F	W	RRZZZZ	NY
JOH	6	M	CHILD	RRZZZZ	NY

PASSENGER	AGE	SEX	OCCUPATION	PRIVL	DES
SIEVERS, GERTRUDE	27	F	W	RRZZZZ	NY
MAREN	5	F	CHILD	RRZZZZ	NY
JOHS	00	M	INF	RRZZZZ	NY
SCHUCHARD, LOUISE	29	F	W	RRZZZZ	NY
ELISE	4	F	CHILD	RRZZZZ	NY
BREMER, ANNA	20	F	WO	RRZZZZ	NY
ALWINE	19	F	WO	RRZZZZ	NY
KOLUMBUS, ORSCHINI	6	M	CHILD	RRZZZZ	TOL
SCHAID	00	F	INF	RRZZZZ	TOL
STANIS, AUG	24	M	LABR	RRZZZZ	TOL
STRUDKAS, ANDREAS	25	M	LABR	RRZZZZ	TOL
KALTER, JAKOB	22	M	LABR	RRZZZZ	NY
BIYK, SENDEO	24	F	W	RRZZZZ	NY
ALIAJE	24	M	LABR	RRZZZZ	NY
DLSCHEFSKY, ANTON	22	M	LABR	RRZZZZ	NY
SUCKINSKI, ADAM	38	M	LABR	RRZZZZ	NY
JANKOWSKI, ANTON	38	M	LABR	RRZZZZ	NY
SABAROWSKY, FRANZ	23	M	LABR	RRZZZZ	NY
SASITSCHKY, FRANZ	44	M	LABR	RRZZZZ	NY
MUTIANOWSKY, NIKOLAI	40	M	LABR	RRZZZZ	NY
SUCZYNSKI, JAN	42	M	LABR	RRZZZZ	NY
OLSCHEFSKI, JOS	28	M	LABR	RRZZZZ	NY
JANKOWSKI, PAWEL	26	M	LABR	RRZZZZ	NY
LEWANSKY, THOMAS	59	M	LABR	RRZZZZ	NY
WISNEWSKY, FRANZ	28	M	LABR	RRZZZZ	NY
DSCHINSKY, ANTON	33	M	LABR	RRZZZZ	NY
PACYNNSKI, FRANZ	19	M	LABR	RRZZZZ	NY
PODZINSKI, JOS	24	M	LABR	RRZZZZ	NY
LUKINCK, MARIAN	23	M	LABR	RRZZZZ	NY
GURKOWSKI, ANTON	25	M	LABR	RRZZZZ	NY
KOPIOWSKI, LEON	26	M	LABR	RRZZZZ	NY
ZIEGEMITZKY, JOSSEL	23	M	LABR	RRZZZZ	NY
ECHILANSBERG, ABRAM	23	M	LABR	RRZZZZ	NY
LITSKI, JOSSEL	22	M	LABR	RRZZZZ	NY
JOSSELLOHM, LASE	18	M	LABR	RRZZZZ	NY
SCHALKOWSKI, STANISL	39	M	LABR	RRZZZZ	NY
KLEMCSAK, ANTON	30	M	LABR	RRZZZZ	NY
ANTON	30	M	LABR	RRZZZZ	PHI
GLAWIEWSKY, ANTON	27	M	LABR	RRZZZZ	NY
MALINOWSKI, VINCENTY	48	M	LABR	RRZZZZ	NY
SCHNIEGEL, MICHAEL	26	M	LABR	RRZZZZ	NY
SEMINSKY, MIDIAL	25	M	LABR	RRZZZZ	NY
GROIZINZKY, BLUME	40	M	LABR	RRZZZZ	NY
RACHEL	9	F	CHILD	RRZZZZ	NY
HINDE	7	F	CHILD	RRZZZZ	NY
REIBE, JOS	36	M	LABR	RRZZZZ	NY
BIALOBLOTZKI, THEODORE	23	M	LABR	RRZZZZ	NY
DESSIORSKI, FRANZ	34	M	LABR	RRZZZZ	NY
LINCEWSKI, FRANZ	24	M	LABR	RRZZZZ	NY
ANTONIE	16	F	LABR	RRZZZZ	NY
GLAWAKI, MICHAEL	29	F	LABR	RRZZZZ	NY
WENRSCH, MARTIN	24	F	LABR	RRZZZZ	NY
KAEZMANN, VALENTY	34	F	LABR	RRZZZZ	NY
BETNER, JOS	27	F	LABR	RRZZZZ	NY
CHNIWANZI, FRANZ	28	M	LABR	RRZZZZ	NY
PISEZACK, ANTON	30	M	LABR	RRZZZZ	NY
BRAUNSCHWEIG, JANKEL	34	M	LABR	RRZZZZ	NY
RIEWKE	24	F	W	RRZZZZ	NY
LEIB	00	M	INF	RRZZZZ	NY
BRAUNSTEIN, JUSSE	20	M	UNKNOWN	RRZZZZ	NY
KANIEKA, JOS	24	M	LABR	RRZZZZ	NY
MOSKOWITZ, SENDER	24	M	LABR	RRZZZZ	NY
KRESS, ABRAH	24	M	LABR	RRZZZZ	NY
FEIN, GESSEL	25	M	LABR	RRZZZZ	NY
MILLER, MOZEK	33	M	DLR	RRZZZZ	NY
HALLEL, CARL	32	M	LABR	RRZZZZ	NY
ERNST	35	F	W	RRZZZZ	NY
REICHARD	9	M	CHILD	RRZZZZ	NY
KOLANOWSKI, STANISL	35	M	LABR	RRZZZZ	NY
PIEPER, AUGUST	18	M	LABR	RRZZZZ	NY
ZLOMIZESKI, STANISL	42	M	JNR	RRZZZZ	NY
SKINBISKA, AGNISKA	25	M	WO	RRZZZZ	NY
WLADISLAUS	5	M	CHILD	RRZZZZ	NY
LEON	3	M	CHILD	RRZZZZ	NY
VERONA	.06	F	INFANT	RRZZZZ	NY

PASSENGER	AGE	SEX	OCCUPATION	PRIV	VIL	DES
FRANZ	.08	F	INFANT	RR	ZZZZ	NY
JANKOSKA, FRANZISKA	45	F	WO	RR	ZZZZ	NY
ENGEL, WILH	17	M	LABR	RR	ZZZZ	NY
WISMERSCHKY, MICHAEL	44	M	LABR	RR	ZZZZ	NY
JOSEFA	43	F	W	RR	ZZZZ	NY
MICHAL	16	M	CH	RR	ZZZZ	NY
PELAGIA	14	M	CH	RR	ZZZZ	NY
ALBERT	9	M	CHILD	RR	ZZZZ	NY
JOHN	8	M	CHILD	RR	ZZZZ	NY
JOSEF	6	M	CHILD	RR	ZZZZ	NY
VALENTIN	3	M	CHILD	RR	ZZZZ	NY
MABROSIUS	.11	M	INFANT	RR	ZZZZ	NY
KRUZKOWSKA, MARIN	38	M	LABR	RR	ZZZZ	NY
VERONIKA	36	F	W	RR	ZZZZ	NY
STEFAN	9	M	CHILD	RR	ZZZZ	NY
STANISLAUS	8	M	CHILD	RR	ZZZZ	NY
BERNHARD	6	M	CHILD	RR	ZZZZ	NY
VALERIA	4	F	CHILD	RR	ZZZZ	NY
SARA	3	F	CHILD	RR	ZZZZ	NY
FRANZISKA	.11	F	INFANT	RR	ZZZZ	NY
MARIAN	11	F	INF	RR	ZZZZ	NY
REIMER, CARL	19	M	SGL	RR	ZZZZ	NY
WOZNIEWSKI, JOHN	24	M	LABR	RR	ZZZZ	NY
BETLEPEWSKI, EVA	25	F	WO	RR	ZZZZ	NY
IGNATZ	.11	M	INFANT	RR	ZZZZ	NY
MARGALSKI, JAN	20	M	LABR	RR	ZZZZ	NY
KOLINSKI, JOSEF	21	M	LABR	RR	ZZZZ	NY
BASINOWITZ, LUDWIG	28	M	LABR	RR	ZZZZ	NY
SENETOWITZ, OLESSIA	21	F	SGL	RR	ZZZZ	NY
BARINDTZ, MARCUS	21	M	LABR	RR	ZZZZ	NY
HARKARTZKI, SIEGMUND	23	M	LABR	RR	ZZZZ	OMA
ROSENFELD, ARON	25	M	LABR	RR	ZZZZ	NY
ROSA	20	F	W	RR	ZZZZ	NY
SINKOWITZ, JOHAN	36	M	LABR	RR	ZZZZ	NY
RAMEL	9	M	CHILD	RR	ZZZZ	NY
PEKSHA, KASIMIR	32	M	LABR	RR	ZZZZ	CH
MUZKEWWITZ, OCIF	36	M	LABR	RR	ZZZZ	NY
KAIRAITIS, ANDREAS	31	M	LABR	RR	ZZZZ	NY
JESNLEWITZ, ANTONIAS	18	M	LABR	RR	ZZZZ	NY

SHIP: BRITANIC

FROM: LIVERPOOL AND QUEENSTOWN
TO: NEW YORK
ARRIVED: 04 MAY 1888

PASSENGER	AGE	SEX	OCCUPATION	PRIV	VIL	DES
JEDENAK, MARG	24	F	SVNT	RR	ADAX	USA
CZARHOUSHA, GUZANNA	29	F	W	RR	ADAX	USA
FRANZ	10	M	CH	RR	ADAX	USA
WADASLOW, U	2	M	CHILD	RR	ADAX	USA
SOFIA	4	F	CHILD	RR	ADAX	USA
CIARHOUSKI, JOHAN	20	M	MNR	RR	ADAX	USA
JOHAN	24	M	MNR	RR	ADAX	USA
DICH, BLUNE	52	M	MNR	RR	ADAX	USA
MILOHOLINCH, PEOTR	45	M	MNR	RR	ADAX	USA
STAGGEL, CHAIM	31	M	MNR	RR	ADAX	USA
DUAH, BENN	20	M	MNR	RR	ADAX	USA
RETTEN, SEIE	25	F	SVNT	RR	ADAX	USA
LANPAN, ALTE	19	F	SVNT	RR	ADAX	USA
WACHTEL, DOURE	56	F	W	RR	ADAX	USA
LOZER	18	M	FARMER	RR	ADAX	USA
FADEL	16	M	FARMER	RR	ADAX	USA
DABIE	11	M	CH	RR	ADAX	USA
GUCHEL	10	M	CH	RR	ADAX	USA
MOSES	.06	M	INFANT	RR	ADAX	USA
RASNA, MALLIE	21	M	SVNT	RR	ADAX	USA
BLOJER, ISRAEL	28	M	LABR	RR	ADAX	USA
PEHISOY, JOSEPH	24	M	LABR	RR	ADAX	USA
CLAV, THERESE	22	F	SVNT	RR	ADAX	USA
SCHLIGKIN, JEGE	50	F	W	RR	ADAX	USA
GERE	7	M	CHILD	RR	ADAX	USA
JEAN	6	M	CHILD	RR	ADAX	USA
U	.04	M	INFANT	RR	ADAX	USA

SHIP: NOVA SCOTIAN

FROM: LIVERPOOL
TO: BALTIMORE
ARRIVED: 05 MAY 1888

PASSENGER	AGE	SEX	OCCUPATION	PRIV	VIL	DES
CYEPLINSKY, JAN	28	M	LABR	PL	ZZZZ	PHI
SAVERNE, STAENLAU	30	M	LABR	PL	ZZZZ	PHI
PAULINE	26	F	W	PL	ZZZZ	PHI
STANISLAW	3	M	CHILD	PL	ZZZZ	PHI
JOSEPH	1	M	CHILD	PL	ZZZZ	PHI
BELLINSKY, LUDWIG	30	M	LABR	PL	ZZZZ	PHI
JOSEPH	26	F	W	PL	ZZZZ	PHI
JOSEPH	1	M	CHILD	PL	ZZZZ	PHI
GRAMARZKI, LEAH	50	F	CPMKR	RR	ZZZZ	NY
GERTIE	11	F	UNKNOWN	RR	ZZZZ	NY
BEURESKUTZ, CASS	30	M	LABR	PL	ZZZZ	PHI
LEWANDOUSKY, L	36	M	LABR	PL	ZZZZ	BAL
BRELSKY, JOHN	25	M	LABR	PL	ZZZZ	BAL
GORESKI, PETER	34	M	LABR	PL	ZZZZ	BAL
MESCHTINOL, JACOBS	25	M	LABR	PL	ZZZZ	BAL
KOSEOL, ANTON	37	M	LABR	PL	ZZZZ	BAL
STRENK, FRANZ	29	M	LABR	PL	ZZZZ	BAL
JOSEPHA	25	F	W	PL	ZZZZ	BAL
FRANCIZEK	1	F	CHILD	PL	ZZZZ	BAL
BARASZYNSKY, JULIAN	34	M	FIL	PL	ZZZZ	BAL
EVA	30	F	W	PL	ZZZZ	BAL
ADAMOSYSKY, SALOMON	25	M	FIL	PL	ZZZZ	BAL
BARANZYN, MECH	7	F	CHILD	PL	ZZZZ	BAL
KATARZYNA	4	F	CHILD	PL	ZZZZ	BAL
GROMELSKY, JOSEPH	29	M	LABR	PL	ZZZZ	BAL

SHIP: STATE OF NEVADA

FROM: GLASGOW AND LARNE
TO: NEW YORK
ARRIVED: 05 MAY 1888

PASSENGER	AGE	SEX	OCCUPATION	PRIV	VIL	DES
ANDRACZNIK, ANTONIO	28	M	LABR	RR	ZZZZ	USA
ANDREJOWSKY, FRANZ	31	M	LABR	RR	ZZZZ	USA
BROCZOWSKY, JOSEF	36	M	LABR	RR	ZZZZ	USA
BEHR, JOSEF	24	M	LABR	RR	ZZZZ	USA
BROCK, ABRAH.	18	M	LABR	RR	ZZZZ	USA
BORDOWITZ, SCH.	19	M	MCHT	RR	ZZZZ	USA
BISMARCK, MAX	42	M	TLR	RR	ZZZZ	USA
BIRDSCHIK, NACHUM	23	M	TLR	RR	ZZZZ	USA
COHN, SAMUEL	25	M	MCHT	RR	ZZZZ	USA
DERZWINSKI, FRANZ	17	M	LABR	RR	ZZZZ	USA
DECKSON, CHRISTIAN	35	M	LABR	RR	ZZZZ	USA
EVANOWITSCH, ISAK	37	M	TLR	RR	ZZZZ	USA
MEIER	11	M	CH	RR	ZZZZ	USA
FENERMAN, MORITZ	17	M	MCHT	RR	ZZZZ	USA
GILBOWICZ, ADAM	36	M	LABR	RR	ZZZZ	USA
GRINECK, ANNA	22	F	SVNT	RR	ZZZZ	USA
GRUENMAN, JACO	34	M	MCHT	RR	ZZZZ	USA
GISKI-, VICENTY	23	M	LABR	RR	ZZZZ	USA
GORDON, MEIER	21	M	LABR	RR	ZZZZ	USA
GABRIESKI, VALENTY	29	M	LABR	RR	ZZZZ	USA
GUTSTEIN, BARUCH	45	M	TLR	RR	ZZZZ	USA
GRZEZWEK, JACOB	24	M	LABR	RR	ZZZZ	USA
JOSEFA	23	F	W	RR	ZZZZ	USA

PASSENGER	A G E	S E X	OCCUPATION	P V R I V L	D E S
STANISLAWA	.09	F	INFANT	RRZZZZ	USA
GOSCZKA, MARIANNE	10	F	CH	RRZZZZ	USA
HELENA	8	F	CHILD	RRZZZZ	USA
GRODEWSKY, JOSEF	26	M	LABR	RRZZZZ	USA
GOLDSTEIN, MARCIN	20	M	LABR	RRZZZZ	USA
GERSCHENOWICZ, MENDEL	30	M	MCHT	RRZZZZ	USA
HADRICH, LEON	28	M	LABR	RRZZZZ	USA
JOSEFA	23	F	W	RRZZZZ	USA
WLADISLAWA	.06	M	INFANT	RRZZZZ	USA
HOLTZMAN, ADOLF	20	M	LABR	RRZZZZ	USA
HIRSCHKOWSKY, SARAH	22	F	MRNR	RRZZZZ	USA
HIRSCH	1	M	CHILD	RRZZZZ	USA
CHAIM	.03	M	INFANT	RRZZZZ	USA
ITZEKOWICZ, GERSCHEN	20	M	MCHT	RRZZZZ	USA
JASCHKO, FRANZ	22	M	LABR	RRZZZZ	USA
JERZINOWSKI, MIK--	26	M	LABR	RRZZZZ	USA
JONAS, DWILIS	27	M	LABR	RRZZZZ	USA
JUNCEWIZ, FRANCISAN	22	M	LABR	RRZZZZ	USA
JACOBOWICZ, ABR.	11	M	CH	RRZZZZ	USA
KONCEWITZ, FRANTZ	38	M	LABR	RRZZZZ	USA
MICHAEL	29	M	LABR	RRZZZZ	USA
KOSTOWSKY, JAN	30	M	LABR	RRZZZZ	USA
KURCZNIK, JACOBUS	30	M	LABR	RRZZZZ	USA
KRINSKI, ELY	30	M	LABR	RRZZZZ	USA
KAMELA, WOICZEK	19	M	LABR	RRZZZZ	USA
JOSEF	32	M	LABR	RRZZZZ	USA
VICTORIA	32	F	W	RRZZZZ	USA
ROSALIA	10	F	CH	RRZZZZ	USA
FADWI-G	8	F	CHILD	RRZZZZ	USA
ELIZABETH	3	F	CHILD	RRZZZZ	USA
MARIANNA	1	F	CHILD	RRZZZZ	USA
KRUSE, THEODOR	26	M	LABR	RRZZZZ	USA
FRANZISCA	23	F	W	RRZZZZ	USA
KORB, SCHLOME	22	F	W	RRZZZZ	USA
LASARCZIK, JOSEPH	39	M	MCHT	RRZZZZ	USA
JOHAN	28	M	LABR	RRZZZZ	USA
JOSEF	18	M	LABR	RRZZZZ	USA
LEIBOWITZ, ETHEL	24	F	MRNR	RRZZZZ	USA
SOLOMON	1	M	CHILD	RRZZZZ	USA
LASCHER, SCHOLEM	33	M	LABR	RRZZZZ	USA
HENNE	4	M	CHILD	RRZZZZ	USA
LEGNER, MORDSCHE	27	M	LABR	RRZZZZ	USA
MILKOWSKI, ANTON	24	M	LABR	RRZZZZ	USA
MISKIEWICZ, FRANZ	30	M	LABR	RRZZZZ	USA
MARSCHOW, KUSMAN	39	M	LABR	RRZZZZ	USA
MASIZINOS, FRANZ	20	M	LABR	RRZZZZ	USA
MIKOLOWSKI, MOTHE	33	M	LABR	RRZZZZ	USA
MENDELMAN, SCHMUL	30	M	TLR	RRZZZZ	USA
MAKOWIAK, JOHAN	44	M	LABR	RRZZZZ	USA
MAZID, MAUSCHE	18	M	LABR	RRZZZZ	USA
NOWAWINSKI, WOICZEK	24	M	LABR	RRZZZZ	USA
NABARTIS, JONAS	30	M	LABR	RRZZZZ	USA
POLUMIS, VICENTI	28	M	LABR	RRZZZZ	USA
IWANOW, PARIFINI	30	M	LABR	RRZZZZ	USA
PIATKOWSKI, MARCEL	38	M	LABR	RRZZZZ	USA
PERIN, SELIG	36	M	LABR	RRZZZZ	USA
PESTNOSKY, FEIGE	22	F	SVNT	RRZZZZ	USA
ROSENFELD, BRIDZET	23	F	SVNT	RRZZZZ	USA
REYNOLDS, WM.	25	M	LABR	RRZZZZ	USA
ROSENFELD, LEIB	20	M	SMH	RRZZZZ	USA
RISCHENSKY, FRANZ	26	M	SMH	RRZZZZ	USA
MARIANNE	28	F	W	RRZZZZ	USA
ANTON	.06	M	INFANT	RRZZZZ	USA
ROYLIN, JAN	22	M	LABR	RRZZZZ	USA
ROSENBERG, CHAIE	41	F	MRNR	RRZZZZ	USA
MATTE	7	F	CHILD	RRZZZZ	USA
MARIANNE	6	F	CHILD	RRZZZZ	USA
SCHWEIER, JOHAN	47	M	LABR	RRZZZZ	USA
SLOMOWICZ, WADISLAW	26	M	LABR	RRZZZZ	USA
SPRINGER, IVAN	28	M	LABR	RRZZZZ	USA
JOSEPH	18	M	LABR	RRZZZZ	USA
LEIKIS, JOSEF	26	M	LABR	RRZZZZ	USA
SCHACHTEL, ISAK	21	M	MCHT	RRZZZZ	USA
SIEMICKI, THS.	25	M	LABR	RRZZZZ	USA
ANTONIA	22	F	W	RRZZZZ	USA
SEKOLSKI, JOSEF	25	M	LABR	RRZZZZ	USA
SAKARSKY, ANDY	37	M	LABR	RRZZZZ	USA
SCHIEMENSKY, FRIEDEL	11	M	CH	RRZZZZ	USA
STARODETZKI, KILLEL	19	M	MCHT	RRZZZZ	USA
SLEIF, SAMUEL	17	M	MCHT	RRZZZZ	USA
SCHNEIDER, CHAIM	20	M	MCHT	RRZZZZ	USA
SCHAN, JOSEF	17	M	LABR	RRZZZZ	USA
SCHELASNI, FROM	27	M	TLR	RRZZZZ	USA
SALADUCH, SCHLOME	27	M	MCHT	RRZZZZ	USA
SELZER, JOSSEL	19	M	TNSTH	RRZZZZ	USA
SAMBORSKY, SCHMUL	30	M	MCHT	RRZZZZ	USA
SAMET, MORTIZ	18	M	TNR	RRZZZZ	USA
TRAJASKY, HILLEL	40	M	MCHT	RRZZZZ	USA
ILLAROWSKI, MARTIN	25	M	LABR	RRZZZZ	USA
CONSTANZE	22	F	W	RRZZZZ	USA
WITTKOWSKI, CARL	32	M	LABR	RRZZZZ	USA
WALICZKO, THS.	30	M	LABR	RRZZZZ	USA
WALLITIS, JOSEPH	25	M	LABR	RRZZZZ	USA
WEINERT, KARL	19	M	LABR	RRZZZZ	USA
WACHTEL, JOSEF	29	M	MCHT	RRZZZZ	USA
WORKIEWICZ, PIOT.	34	M	LABR	RRZZZZ	USA
WEINER, DAVID.B.	16	M	LABR	RRZZZZ	USA
ZINSKI, VINCENT	29	M	LABR	RRZZZZ	USA

SHIP: EMS

FROM: BREMEN
TO: NEW YORK
ARRIVED: 07 MAY 1888

PASSENGER	A G E	S E X	OCCUPATION	P V R I V L	D E S
KINAK, LUDW.	25	M	LABR	RRAHOO	BAL
JULIA	20	F	W	RRAHOO	BAL
EMILIA	.11	F	INFANT	RRAHOO	BAL
STANGLEWICZ, JOSEPH	31	M	DRVR	RRAAKH	BAL
KRAMP, ROSALIA	27	F	W	RRACBR	BAL
AUGUST	.11	M	INFANT	RRACBR	BAL
ELANDT, JOH.AUG.	27	M	WVR	RRZZZZ	BAL
KRAMP, AUGUST	27	M	MNR	RRACBR	BAL
MASCHOSTA, AUGUST	28	M	MNR	RRZZZZ	BAL
EMIL	26	M	MNR	RRZZZZ	BAL
GROTHA, JOSEPH	27	M	MNR	RRZZZZ	BAL
JENDRUSHAK, MARTIN	25	M	MNR	RRZZZZ	BAL
PLICZA, NICOLAUS	43	M	MNR	RRAARR	BAL
JENDRUSHAK, WOJCSECH	36	M	MNR	RRADGO	BAL
VALENTIN	37	M	MNR	RRADGO	BAL
MICHALINA	27	F	W	RRADGO	BAL
JAN	4	M	CHILD	RRADGO	BAL
STANISLAWA	3	F	CHILD	RRADGO	BAL
BERSMANN, CHANE	16	F	UNKNOWN	RRAHOO	BAL
LABOLEWSKI, THEOPHIL	40	M	LABR	RRAHOO	UNK
SAPIO, TAUBE	20	F	UNKNOWN	RRZZZZ	BAL
DOLKA, FRANZ	.11	M	INFANT	RRZZZZ	SOU
SWILER, FEIGE	38	F	W	RRAHOO	CH
NOCHEM	8	M	CHILD	RRAHOO	CH
CHANE	7	F	CHILD	RRAHOO	CH
ESTER	3	F	CHILD	RRAHOO	CH
ISAAC	.06	M	INFANT	RRAHOO	CH
RABINOWITZ, MARKOR	18	M	MCHT	RRAHOO	PIT
BARDZILOWSKI, ANTON	21	M	MCHT	RRAHOO	PIT
BERLIN, HANE	13	F	UNKNOWN	RRAHOO	BAL
PAULINE	11	F	UNKNOWN	RRAHOO	BAL
SEGAL, JACOB	12	M	PDLR	RRAHOO	CH
OSTROWSKI, FRANZITSEK	22	M	MNR	RRZZZZ	BAL
KLEIN, EMILIE	28	F	W	RRAIAW	CLE
KARL	.09	M	INFANT	RRAIAW	CLE
SORKAI, LEOPOLD	33	M	LABR	RRAIEJ	CLE
CAROLINE	27	F	W	RRAIEJ	CLE
FRITZ	5	M	CHILD	RRAIEJ	CLE
URSULA	.10	F	INFANT	RRAIEJ	CLE
YOTOMBIEWSKI, JOSEF	24	M	MNR	RRAIBN	BAL

PASSENGER	AGE	SEX	OCCUPATION	PRV VIL DES
DELINSKA, ANTONIA	25	F	W	RRAHOOUNK
SOFIA	3	F	CHILD	RRAHOOUNK
SOFA	.11	M	INFANT	RRAHOOUNK
SCHER, STZIG	26	M	PDLR	RRAHOOBAL
NEOBALSKY, FRANCZEK	23	F	LABR	RRAHOOCLE
PRELEWSKY, MICHAEL	45	M	PDLR	RRAEXKUNK
GEMLAT, GOTTLIEB	31	M	DRVR	RRAHOOCH
KLINAH, ANNA	24	F	UNKNOWN	RRAHOOCLE
EDUARD	2	M	CHILD	RRAHOOCLE
CARL	.11	M	INFANT	RRAHOOCLE
CAROLINE	25	F	UNKNOWN	RRAHOOCLE
FEDLIN, FROJIAN	24	M	LABR	RRAHOOSTL
TAUHE	23	F	W	RRAHOOSTL
EKE	3	F	CHILD	RRAHOOSTL
MINDEL	.05	M	INFANT	RRAHOOSTL
MINKEWICSZ, ANDREAS	44	M	LABR	RRAIJDDET
MARIANNE	44	F	W	RRAIJDDET
ELIONORE	11	F	CH	RRAIJDDET
MARIANNE	10	F	CH	RRAIJDDET
JOSEPH	8	M	CHILD	RRAIJDDET
ANNA	7	F	CHILD	RRAIJDDET
FRANZISKA	4	F	CHILD	RRAIJDDET
JOHANN	2	M	CHILD	RRAIJDDET
DANGIRDA, KLEMENCE	30	F	UNKNOWN	RRAHOOCH
SCHMICK, JAN	15	M	FARMER	RRAHOOUNK
NIEDERMEYER, MICHAEL	26	M	FARMER	RRAHOOUNK
SCHMIDT, LUDWIG	28	M	FARMER	RRAHOOBAL
SIOLKOWSKI, ADAM	36	M	LABR	RRAHOOBAL
HERR, FRIEDRICH	24	M	LABR	RRZZZZBAL
--IM, MICHAEL	22	M	LABR	RRZZZZBAL
ADOLF	17	M	LABR	RRZZZZBAL
SCHKNAZINSKI, JOSEF	29	M	LABR	RRZZZZBAL
KOPLAN, CESACH	45	M	PDLR	RRZZZZBAL
CZEWA	40	F	W	RRZZZZBAL
RASCHE	20	F	UNKNOWN	RRZZZZBAL
ISAAC	17	M	LABR	RRZZZZBAL
IRAEL	3	M	CHILD	RRZZZZBAL
GERSON	35	M	PDLR	RRZZZZBAL
ROSSMAR, ROSA	24	F	UNKNOWN	RRZZZZBAL
IDEL	3	F	CHILD	RRZZZZBAL
BASS, ABRAHAM	46	M	PDLR	RRZZZZBAL
JASELOWITZ, MALKE	18	F	UNKNOWN	RRZZZZBAL
SINGER, ARON	37	M	LABR	RRAHOOBAL
NAUENBURG, JOHAS	53	M	FARMER	RRAHOONY
JOHANN	25	M	FARMER	RRAHOONY
ELISABETH	27	F	W	RRAHOONY
CAROLINE	.04	F	INFANT	RRAHOONY
RASEMOWITZ, IGNATZ	24	M	PDLR	RRAHOONY
FRIEDRICH, ALEX	25	M	LABR	RRAHOONY
SCIERBACK, MOSES	10	M	CH	RRAHOONY
PJETROWSKI, ANTON	23	M	LABR	RRAHOONY
--MRAK, JOSEF	31	M	LABR	RRAHOOCH

SHIP: PENNSYLVANIA

FROM: ANTWERP
TO: NEW YORK
ARRIVED: 09 MAY 1888

PASSENGER	AGE	SEX	OCCUPATION	PRV VIL DES
BONAK, B	23	M	LABR	PLZZZZUSA
BUCH, J	18	M	LABR	PLZZZZNY
BALZAN, D	40	M	LABR	PLZZZZNY
BEANKEL, EIDEL	38	M	LABR	PLZZZZNY
L	41	M	LABR	PLZZZZNY
BECKER, C	24	M	LABR	PLZZZZNY
ANNA	23	F	W	PLZZZZNY
FRED	40	M	LABR	PLZZZZNY
BULINS, J	31	M	LABR	PLZZZZNY
BORECZEWSKY, J	31	M	LABR	PLZZZZNY
CHECKOWSKY, L	30	M	LABR	PLZZZZNY
DUNSKY, M	52	M	LABR	PLZZZZNY
DIMAND, D	26	M	LABR	PLZZZZNY
DOMANSKE, W	31	M	LABR	PLZZZZCH
ENGELHERT, S	19	M	LABR	PLZZZZNY
FREIDBERG, S	43	M	LABR	PLZZZZNY
H	24	M	LABR	PLZZZZNY
GOLDBERG, J	21	M	LABR	PLZZZZNY
GROSCHELSKY, V	18	M	LABR	PLZZZZNY
GESCHTAWT, J	23	M	LABR	PLZZZZNY
GWIEWITZ, J	18	M	LABR	PLZZZZNY
GIMJEWSKY, L	37	M	LABR	PLZZZZNY
GRONOWSKI, J	39	M	LABR	PLZZZZNY
GROCHOWSKA, AN	24	F	SP	PLZZZZNY
HELIGMANN, C	18	M	LABR	PLZZZZNY
HERSHKOWITZ, W	30	M	LABR	PLZZZZNY
HEER, W	35	M	LABR	PLZZZZNY
HONSKY, ITZ	21	M	LABR	PLZZZZNY
FEIGE	22	F	W	PLZZZZNY
HEER, F	20	M	LABR	PLZZZZNY
HAMMOESCHLAG, J	18	M	LABR	PLZZZZNY
HALINKA, P	26	M	LABR	PLZZZZNY
JOCZIS, J	20	M	LABR	PLZZZZCH
JAKULEWICZ, P	23	M	LABR	PLZZZZCH
JURCZAK, B	32	M	LABR	PLZZZZNY
KOSLAWSKY, V	38	M	LABR	PLZZZZNY
KRUSCHOWSKY, Y	22	M	LABR	PLZZZZNY
KLOTZ, F	46	M	LABR	PLZZZZNY
KESSLOE, B	32	M	LABR	PLZZZZNY
KOLINSKY, C	21	M	LABR	PLZZZZNY
KUPPOEMANN, J	16	M	LABR	PLZZZZNY
KREUTZVOGEL, J	30	M	LABR	RRZZZZNY
KOTZLAU, J	22	M	LABR	PLZZZZNY
KREVOWICZ, W	26	M	LABR	PLZZZZUNK
J	23	F	W	PLZZZZUNK
LEFKOVICK, S	28	M	LABR	PLZZZZNY
LEWANDOWSKY, C	22	M	LABR	PLZZZZNY
LINDENBAUM, M	38	M	LABR	PLZZZZNY
MISNIEWSKI, J	28	M	LABR	PLZZZZIL
ANT	24	F	W	PLZZZZIL
MARIE	4	F	CHILD	PLZZZZIL
JUD	2	F	CHILD	PLZZZZIL
W	6	M	CHILD	PLZZZZIL
MENDLESOHN, J	18	M	LABR	PLZZZZNY
MAJEK, P	48	M	LABR	PLZZZZNY
MAZUR, W	33	M	LABR	PLZZZZNY
MATIEWICZ, J	30	M	LABR	PLZZZZNY
MICHALOK, JAN	35	M	LABR	PLZZZZCH
OSTROWST, F	33	M	LABR	PLZZZZCH
PETRUSKEWICZ, M	28	M	LABR	PLZZZZCH
PUSITZ, S	46	M	LABR	PLZZZZCH
OFEFFER, N	45	M	LABR	PLZZZZCH
PIRZEK, W	18	M	LABR	PLZZZZNY
RUTKOWSKY, K	24	M	LABR	PLZZZZNY
RUDEWICH, V	26	M	LABR	PLZZZZNY
REICHBAUM, A	16	M	LABR	PLZZZZNY
RUBINSTEIN, L	25	M	LABR	PLZZZZNY
RAJCZYK, S	19	M	LABR	PLZZZZNY
RODNY, J	24	M	LABR	PLZZZZNY
SCHARKOWSKY, J	28	M	LABR	PLZZZZNY
SCHMIEL, R	16	M	LABR	PLZZZZNY
SCHUSTER, S	22	F	LABR	PLZZZZNY
SCHMERKOWITZ, J	22	M	LABR	PLZZZZNY
SILITZY, J	24	M	LABR	PLZZZZNY
SCHULMANN, S	23	M	LABR	PLZZZZNY
SCHINDEWITA, J	31	M	LABR	PLZZZZNY
SCHVEKIS, E	26	M	LABR	PLZZZZNY
SCHWARTZ, J	49	M	LABR	PLZZZZNY
SCHOTT, M	21	M	LABR	PLZZZZNY
SKIRBANOWSKY, H	33	M	LABR	PLZZZZNY
SAND, B	24	M	LABR	PLZZZZNY
SOH, F	26	M	LABR	PLZZZZNY
SCHMIDT, P	32	M	LABR	PLZZZZNY
TELINSKY, A	35	M	LABR	PLZZZZNY
TRUB, J	24	M	LABR	PLZZZZNY
WOJKHEWIEZ, S	25	M	LABR	PLZZZZNY

PASSENGER	AGE	SEX	OCCUPATION	PRV VIL DES
WIRZBINSKY, J	33	M	LABR	PLZZZZNY
WOSILEWSKY, J	38	M	LABR	PLZZZZNY
WOLIEWITSCH, J	25	M	LABR	PLZZZZNY
WIENER, C	24	M	LABR	PLZZZZNY
WISMEWSKA, V	28	M	LABR	PLZZZZNY
A	25	M	LABR	PLZZZZNY
J	24	M	LABR	PLZZZZNY
WILINISCHIEK, B	27	M	LABR	PLZZZZNY
WARZEK, J	27	M	LABR	PLZZZZNY
WASSERMANN, C	17	M	LABR	PLZZZZNY
WASCHILEWSKY, F	20	M	LABR	PLZZZZNY
WEINFELD, M	19	M	LABR	PLZZZZNY
WARZAK, T	28	M	LABR	PLZZZZNY
WISBAR, V	18	M	LABR	PLZZZZNY
WARIAS, J	28	M	LABR	PLZZZZNY
W	26	M	LABR	PLZZZZNY
WERBA, Y	27	M	LABR	PLZZZZNY
WELSCH, ANT	20	M	LABR	PLZZZZNY
WISCHNEWSKY, F	19	F	W	PLZZZZNY
AND	.06	M	INFANT	PLZZZZNY
WEINRICH, ANNA	17	F	SP	PLZZZZNY
YANDOWSKY, A	30	M	LABR	PLZZZZNY
YASZINSKA, D	45	M	LABR	PLZZZZNY
GROCHOWSKA, V	.02	M	INFANT	PLZZZZUNK

SHIP: DEVONIA

FROM: GLASGOW
TO: NEW YORK
ARRIVED: 09 MAY 1888

PASSENGER	AGE	SEX	OCCUPATION	PRV VIL DES
RECHTMANN, PESCHE	38	M	NN	PLAEABUSA
MOSES	16	M	NN	PLAEABUSA
ISRAEL	14	M	NN	PLAEABUSA
PEREL	11	M	NN	PLAEABUSA
BARUCH	7	M	CHILD	PLAEABUSA
ARON	5	M	CHILD	PLAEABUSA
RACHEL	1	F	CHILD	PLAEABUSA
SCHERMAN, RIWKE	23	F	NN	PLAEABUSA
GERSON	12	M	CH	PLAEABUSA
BLUME	11	F	CH	PLAEABUSA
ESTHER	2	F	CHILD	PLAEABUSA
JAKOB	.04	M	INFANT	PLAEABUSA
ROERS, SCHMUL	12	M	INF	PLAEABUSA
SCHERMAN, BEILE	1	F	CHILD	PLAEABUSA
KOSLIN, BERKE	40	M	LABR	PLAEABUSA
LEIE	11	F	CH	PLAEABUSA
MARKUS	9	M	CHILD	PLAEABUSA
REICH, MORRIS	38	M	TLR	PLAEABUSA
LEISER	16	M	NN	PLAEABUSA
LEWIN, KEILE-R.	24	F	NN	PLAEABUSA
SCHEINE	5	M	CHILD	PLAEABUSA
JOLUSSKA, LEA.	17	F	CH	PLAEABUSA
KAPLAN, BROCHE	17	F	CH	PLAEABUSA
PABELINSKY, HADES	16	F	CH	RRZZZZUSA
OWERBACH, LEON	45	M	LABR	RRZZZZUSA
BENACH, JAKOB-M.	18	M	TLR	RRZZZZUSA
BRAVERMAN, SCHIMER	24	M	BRR	RRZZZZUSA
BOBROWSKY, JANKEL	23	M	TLR	RRZZZZUSA
DZEKOWSKI, JOZES	25	M	LABR	RRZZZZUSA
LIBZKY, CHAIM	36	M	LABR	RRZZZZUSA
MACHLEWSKI, JAN	24	M	LABR	RRZZZZUSA
MARGIL, MENDEL	17	M	LABR	RRAEFLUSA
BERLOWITZ, PINEUS	11	M	LABR	RRAEFLUSA
ZEZNLEWICZ, KASEMIR	30	M	LABR	RRAEFLUSA
SCRANOWITSCH, CHAIM	37	M	LABR	RRAEFLUSA
STEIN, JAKOB	36	M	LABR	RRZZZZUSA
WIRZBA, JANKEL-M.	27	M	LABR	RRZZZZUSA
CZESCHAS, ANTON	24	M	LABR	RRZZZZUSA
DALSEWE, ANTON	30	M	LABR	RRZZZZUSA

PASSENGER	AGE	SEX	OCCUPATION	PRV VIL DES
FINKERBERG, SARAH	37	F	NN	RRZZZZUSA
MINDEL	6	F	CHILD	RRZZZZUSA
JAKOB	5	M	CHILD	RRZZZZUSA
CHANE	1	F	CHILD	RRZZZZUSA
GZEBINKI, FAVEL	23	M	TLR	RRZZZZUSA
GRUNER, ARON	45	M	TLR	RRZZZZUSA
HOFFMANN, BENZIG-H.	22	M	PDLR	RRZZZZUSA
MALKE	23	M	PDLR	RRZZZZUSA
LEVIN, HIRSCH	19	M	TNSTH	RRZZZZUSA
LIMANOWICZ, PETER	39	M	LABR	RRZZZZUSA
MAT, BERTHA	36	F	NN	RRZZZZUSA
LEIB	4	M	CHILD	RRZZZZUSA
MAWROCKI, MICHL.	27	M	LABR	RRZZZZUSA
MAJEWSKI, ALBERT	42	M	LABR	RRZZZZUSA
MONTKOWSKI, FRANZ	40	M	LABR	RRZZZZUSA
HUDELMANN, MOSCHE	50	M	LABR	RRZZZZUSA
CHAJE	45	F	NN	RRZZZZUSA
PESSCHE	20	F	NN	RRZZZZUSA
GENENDEL	18	F	NN	RRZZZZUSA
CHANE	16	F	NN	RRZZZZUSA
INDES	9	F	CHILD	RRZZZZUSA
JANKEL	4	F	CHILD	RRZZZZUSA
REISES	4	F	CHILD	RRZZZZUSA
PELRESSCHZANKI, MALUCH	28	M	LABR	RRZZZZUSA
SCHINSKOS, MATIAS	20	M	LABR	RRZZZZUSA
FEINSTEIN, VICTOR	20	M	JNR	RRZZZZUSA
SAPZENSKI, FRANZ	28	M	LABR	RRZZZZUSA
WOJINSKI, FELIX	24	M	DLR	RRZZZZUSA
EMMA	21	F	NN	RRZZZZUSA
JESLAVA	.06	F	INFANT	RRZZZZUSA
WIEMECK, CASPAR	51	M	LABR	RRZZZZUSA
WERITZKI, FRANZ	28	M	LABR	RRZZZZUSA
WERBITZKI, JOSE	25	M	SHMK	RRZZZZUSA

SHIP: RHEIN

FROM: BREMEN
TO: BALTIMORE
ARRIVED: 09 MAY 1888

PASSENGER	AGE	SEX	OCCUPATION	PRV VIL DES
SOKOLOWSKI, JOSEF	24	M	LABR	RRZZZZBAL
POTROWSKA, MARIA	24	F	UNKNOWN	RRZZZZBAL
JOHANN	.11	M	INFANT	RRZZZZBAL
MAINOWE, ETTA	15	F	UNKNOWN	RRZZZZBAL
POROWINSKI, JAN	32	M	LABR	RRZZZZBAL
MAZOWE, SWIL	25	F	UNKNOWN	RRZZZZBAL
ABRAHAM	.11	M	INFANT	RRZZZZBAL
HIMMELSTEIN, GOLDE	25	F	UNKNOWN	RRZZZZBAL
SOSCHE	25	F	UNKNOWN	RRZZZZBAL
FEIGE	2	F	CHILD	RRZZZZBAL
RACHEL	.07	M	INFANT	RRZZZZBAL
JASENOFF, EZKIEL	21	M	LABR	RRZZZZBAL
TODEROWITZ, SCHORE	44	F	UNKNOWN	RRZZZZBAL
ESTHER	21	F	UNKNOWN	RRZZZZBAL
JOSEF	7	M	CHILD	RRZZZZBAL
WOLF	5	M	CHILD	RRZZZZBAL
MOSES	2	M	CHILD	RRZZZZBAL
LEIB	.10	M	INFANT	RRZZZZBAL
ORLOWSKI, STANISLAW	24	M	LABR	RRZZZZUSA
BIELANOWSKI, MARG	24	F	UNKNOWN	RRZZZZUSA
WLADISLAWA	.04	F	INFANT	RRZZZZUSA
DOMBROWSKI, JAN	28	M	LABR	RRZZZZUSA
BLASKIEWICZ, JULIANNA	19	F	UNKNOWN	RRZZZZUSA
MARIANNA	18	F	UNKNOWN	RRZZZZUSA
WISNIEWSKA, THEOPHIL	20	M	LABR	RRZZZZUSA
ZAWISTOWSKI, JOSEF	27	M	LABR	RRZZZZUSA
ANNA	26	F	W	RRZZZZUSA
MARIANNA	4	F	CHILD	RRZZZZUSA
ZUZANNA	2	F	CHILD	RRZZZZUSA
STANISLAUS	.02	M	INFANT	RRZZZZUSA

PASSENGER	AGE	SEX	OCCUPATION	PRV VIL DES
SCHULZ, EMILIE	17	F	UNKNOWN	RRZZZZUSA
MASSA, ADAM	35	M	LABR	RRZZZZUSA
BRUDULIS, KOROL	26	M	LABR	RRZZZZUSA
MARYANNA	24	F	W	RRZZZZUSA
GOSZCZYCKI, JOH	22	M	LABR	RRZZZZMO
TAWCZYNSKI, WLADISL	32	M	LABR	RRZZZZMO
PIZEWORSKY, IGNACY	17	M	LABR	RRZZZZIL
BORDIN, FRANZ	20	M	LABR	RRZZZZIL
BULINCKI, MARIANNA	29	F	UNKNOWN	RRZZZZIL
FRANZ	.01	M	INFANT	RRZZZZIL
WISNIEWSKI, JACOB	37	M	LABR	RRZZZZIL
PRECK, AMALIA	20	F	UNKNOWN	RRZZZZIL
JULIUS	1	M	CHILD	RRZZZZIL
HEINR	.04	M	INFANT	RRZZZZIL
BARA, JAN	18	M	LABR	RRZZZZIL
PAWLUKOWSKI, WLADISLAW	23	M	LABR	RRZZZZIL
MELLER, ADAM	26	M	LABR	RRZZZZIL
BECKER, JAN	34	M	LABR	RRZZZZPA
HOFFMANN, AUG	24	M	LABR	RRZZZZPA
KOWALSKY, WLADISLAW	20	M	LABR	RRZZZZBAL
SKOWRINSKY, JOSEF	24	M	LABR	RRZZZZBAL
GURNY, JACOB	27	M	LABR	RRZZZZBAL
FISCHER, BAR	30	M	LABR	RRZZZZBAL
LAZKOZKIE, WALENTY	28	M	LABR	RRZZZZBAL
DEWINAIKIS, SIDOR	29	M	LABR	RRZZZZBAL
PETROWSKY, KAZMIR	36	M	LABR	RRZZZZBAL
WEISSBERG, BENJAMIN	16	M	LABR	RRZZZZIL
JESS, GOTTL	48	M	LABR	RRZZZZBAL
ERNSTINE	48	F	W	RRZZZZBAL
ATLIENA	6	F	CHILD	RRZZZZBAL
WILLNOCK, AUG	40	M	FARMER	RRZZZZMI
CAROLINE	37	F	W	RRZZZZMI
ROBERT	6	M	CHILD	RRZZZZMI
EMMA	2	F	CHILD	RRZZZZMI
MARIE	.11	F	INFANT	RRZZZZMI
JESS, OTTILIE	21	F	UNKNOWN	RRZZZZMI
BERTHA	2	F	CHILD	RRZZZZMI
HERMANN	.09	M	INFANT	RRZZZZMI
ESKERT, GOTTL	.06	M	INFANT	RRZZZZMI
PUFAHL, GOTTL	34	M	GDNR	RRZZZZMI
ZIEHLKE, HERM	25	M	LABR	RRZZZZMI
WILH	22	F	W	RRZZZZMI
EMMA	.03	F	INFANT	RRZZZZMI

SHIP: MICHIGAN

FROM: LIVERPOOL
TO: BOSTON
ARRIVED: 09 MAY 1888

PASSENGER	AGE	SEX	OCCUPATION	PRV VIL DES
STANISLAW, FRANZISCH	38	M	CRBLDR	PLZZZZUSA
BEILES, ABEL	35	M	BXMR	PLZZZZUSA
ORLAWSKI, STANS.	23	M	LABR	PLZZZZUSA
RASWASNICH, EUDRUG	37	M	TLR	PLZZZZUSA
SZEIN, KEZIMIR	30	M	HTR	PLZZZZUSA
NADABOX, JOSEPH	20	M	UNKNOWN	PLZZZZUSA
SCHIANLOWSKY, JOSEPH	27	M	JWLR	PLZZZZUSA
DOBRZYA, FRANZ	22	M	CPTR	PLZZZZUSA
SCHWARZ, JULIUS	42	M	LABR	PLZZZZUSA
KALINISKOW, VICTOIRE	23	M	LABR	PLZZZZUSA
EGIN, SALOMON	50	M	UNKNOWN	PLZZZZUSA
DUBRZYN, ANTON	18	M	LABR	PLZZZZUSA
KELCH, ANTON	30	M	LABR	PLZZZZUSA
DENISKI, STAULS	30	M	WCHMKR	PLZZZZUSA
JOFFIS, NACHAM	36	M	UNKNOWN	PLZZZZUSA
GUZKA, JOSEPH	20	M	BLKSMH	PLZZZZUSA
MARY	11	F	SCH	PLZZZZUSA
ABRAMOWIEZ, SARA	29	F	SP	PLZZZZUSA
BERKOWITZ, BELTZ	18	F	SP	PLZZZZUSA
JOFFIS, PAULINE	18	F	SP	PLZZZZUSA
EVA	16	F	SP	PLZZZZUSA
SCHIFIYZK, SHRIVE	18	F	SP	PLZZZZUSA
GNYKA, JOHN	40	M	BLKSMH	PLZZZZUSA
EDELSTIN, SIKEN	20	M	BTMKR	PLZZZZUSA
CHAJE	18	F	W	PLZZZZUSA
HARWITZ, MENDEL	17	M	WCHMKR	PLZZZZUSA
DORE	20	F	W	PLZZZZUSA
LOWENORTH, RACHEL	3	F	CHILD	PLZZZZUSA
ISAAC	2	M	CHILD	PLZZZZUSA

SHIP: WERRA

FROM: BREMEN AND SOUTHAMPTON
TO: NEW YORK
ARRIVED: 09 MAY 1888

PASSENGER	AGE	SEX	OCCUPATION	PRV VIL DES
DEMPSKI, WLADISLAW	21	M	FARMER	RRZZZZUSA
DENUB, ABRAHAM	24	M	LABR	RRZZZZUSA
TEKLENSKI, ROMAN	21	M	LABR	RRZZZZUSA
GRONOWALD, JOH.	22	M	LABR	RRZZZZUSA
PATKOWSKA, HELENE	16	M	NN	RRZZZZUSA
WALUSZKA, JERZY	26	M	LABR	RRZZZZUSA
RAU, ANNA	50	F	W	RRZZZZUSA
KANOKOSKI, PAUL	36	M	LABR	RRZZZZUSA
CAROLE.	25	F	W	RRZZZZUSA
PAULE.	6	F	CHILD	RRZZZZUSA
WILH.	4	M	CHILD	RRZZZZUSA
BERTHA	.11	F	INFANT	RRZZZZUSA
WENZUS, SELVESTER	23	M	LABR	RRZZZZUSA
JOSEF	23	M	LABR	RRZZZZUSA
KUKATIS, WICENTY	24	M	LABR	RRZZZZUSA
PAWILANIS, JOSEF	50	M	LABR	RRZZZZUSA
WISALKI, WICENTY	18	M	LABR	RRZZZZUSA
REVULT, IGNANCIO	34	M	LABR	RRZZZZUSA
PANGANIS, JULIAN	26	M	LABR	RRZZZZUSA
PAURLAIKA, MATWAI	36	M	LABR	RRZZZZUSA
KARPOWITZ, WICENZ	50	M	LABR	RRZZZZUSA
TERKOWSKI, WALENTI	28	M	LABR	RRZZZZUSA
ZEMENIELSKA, THOMAS	45	M	LABR	RRZZZZUSA
VJITOSLAWSKI, VALENTY	40	M	LABR	RRZZZZUSA
RADKA, AUGUST	43	M	LABR	RRZZZZUSA
JULIANE	40	F	W	RRZZZZUSA
SCHIEBERT, CARL	29	M	LABR	RRZZZZUSA
HOFFMANN, AUGUST	21	M	LABR	RRZZZZUSA
WYCKA, JOSEF	27	M	LABR	RRZZZZUSA
MAKOWSKI, FRANZ	26	M	LABR	RRZZZZUSA
WALKIEWICZ, JOSEF	27	M	LABR	RRZZZZUSA
ZALEWSKI, WOJCIECH	22	M	LABR	RRZZZZUSA
PESTA, VALENTY	32	M	LABR	RRZZZZUSA
STANISLAW	32	M	LABR	RRZZZZUSA
AGACUSKA, ADAM	22	M	LABR	RRZZZZUSA
LEWANDOWSKI, ANTON	22	M	LABR	RRZZZZUSA
KOWALSKI, JAN	36	M	LABR	RRZZZZUSA
MUGOROWSKI, KASIMIR	40	M	LABR	RRZZZZUSA
LURIA, GEORG	20	M	LABR	RRZZZZUSA
IGNATEWITZ, MAGUS	25	M	LABR	RRZZZZUSA
BALMIS, ANTON	19	M	LABR	RRZZZZUSA
WILARY, JAN	45	M	LABR	RRZZZZUSA
ZIELINSKY, JOSEF	40	M	LABR	RRZZZZUSA
MINKEWITZ, ANT.	40	M	LABR	RRZZZZUSA
JARELWITZ, CAS.	26	M	LABR	RRZZZZUSA
BUINSKI, PAWEL	24	M	LABR	RRZZZZUSA
MUZUKOJAK, PETER	30	M	LABR	RRZZZZUSA
BERKMANN, ROCHEL	18	M	LABR	RRZZZZUSA
FABER, HARRIS	31	M	LABR	RRZZZZUSA
BORSZEWSKI, RACHMAL	21	M	LABR	RRZZZZUSA
FUCHSEL, SCHAJE	34	M	LABR	RRZZZZUSA
GROSSMANN, AISIK	32	M	LABR	RRZZZZUSA
FUHRMANN, JOSEF	35	M	LABR	RRZZZZUSA
WOLTER, GOTTL.	36	M	LABR	RRZZZZUSA

PASSENGER	AGE	SEX	OCCUPATION	PRV	VIL	DES
CAROLE.	26	F	W	RR	ZZZZ	USA
GUST.	3	M	CHILD	RR	ZZZZ	USA
EMIL	.11	M	INFANT	RR	AEWM	USA
NOWAKOWSKI, JOSEF	39	F	NN	RR	ZZZZ	USA
SUCHORSKI, SCEPAN	31	M	FARMER	RR	ZZZZ	USA
SCHLACHTER, JUL.	32	M	FARMER	RR	ZZZZ	USA
JASTKOWIAK, STANISL.	27	M	FARMER	RR	ZZZZ	USA
MICHA.	23	F	W	RR	ZZZZ	USA
GERTWITA	.11	F	INFANT	RR	ZZZZ	USA
MARIA	.01	F	INFANT	RR	ZZZZ	USA
OLYNICZAK, VALENTIN	50	M	FARMER	RR	ZZZZ	USA
MARIANNA	45	F	W	RR	ZZZZ	USA
STANISL.	7	M	CHILD	RR	ZZZZ	USA
ANNA	5	F	CHILD	RR	ZZZZ	USA
PETER	3	M	CHILD	RR	ZZZZ	USA
IGNATTZ	.06	M	INFANT	RR	ZZZZ	USA
WALICKA, EMILIA	31	F	W	RR	ZZZZ	USA
MALWINA	6	F	CHILD	RR	ZZZZ	USA
IDA	4	F	CHILD	RR	ZZZZ	USA
MARTHA	.10	F	INFANT	RR	ZZZZ	USA
FAKOWSKI, PIETER	18	M	LABR	RR	ZZZZ	USA
POMEILIS, ANDREAS	22	M	LABR	RR	ZZZZ	USA
SZYMANSKI, WOJCIECH	21	M	LABR	RR	ZZZZ	USA
JOSEF	32	M	LABR	RR	ZZZZ	USA
LINORT, JARZI	18	M	LABR	RR	ZZZZ	USA
LUCIE, MINE	19	F	NN	RR	ZZZZ	USA
KLETCZEWSKI, TEHMOKA	28	F	W	RR	ZZZZ	USA
TEHMOKA	4	F	CHILD	RR	ZZZZ	USA
MINE	.11	F	INFANT	RR	ZZZZ	USA
MITONLEWICZ, ANTONI	40	M	LABR	RR	ZZZZ	USA
PAHL, LUDWIG	25	M	LABR	RR	ZZZZ	USA
WAIZEKAUZKUS, JURAS	24	M	LABR	RR	ZZZZ	USA
GUDINAS, PETRAS	35	M	LABR	RR	ZZZZ	USA
WITGETELI, JANOS	23	M	LABR	RR	ZZZZ	USA
KULANZKAS, PETRAS	23	M	LABR	RR	ZZZZ	USA
KESMER, VOJC.	33	M	LABR	RR	AHZS	USA
ANDRUSKEWITZ, ALEX	28	M	LABR	RR	AHZS	USA
SCHLEKIS, JURGES	26	M	LABR	RR	AHZS	USA
ALABNIC, JURAS	39	M	LABR	RR	AHZS	USA
KLINATZKAS, JOSAS	31	M	LABR	RR	AHZS	USA
FIRMAWITZ, ADAMAS	27	M	LABR	RR	AHZS	USA
MUSKEWITZ, CONST.	22	M	LABR	RR	AGRT	USA
MARCATIS, MATRAI	22	M	LABR	RR	AGRT	USA
ZURLANIS, ANTON	18	M	LABR	RR	ZZZZ	USA
GUSTAITIS, FRANZISA.	35	F	NN	RR	ZZZZ	USA
INNKEWITZ, WIKENTY	44	M	LABR	RR	ZZZZ	USA
BARNAS	26	M	LABR	RR	ZZZZ	USA
KOLINTA, AUGUST	17	M	LABR	RR	AGRT	USA
BALTINOWITZ, MATREI	25	M	LABR	RR	AGRT	USA
ZELENCZEWITZ, WICENTY	18	M	LABR	RR	AGRT	USA
KOSAITIS, JURGIS	20	M	LABR	RR	AHZS	USA
ULEWITZ, KASIO	27	M	LABR	RR	AHZS	USA
RAILINAITIS, PRUS	26	M	LABR	RR	AHZS	USA
SAMANOWITZ, STANISL.	30	M	LABR	RR	AHZS	USA
MACIDULSKY, OSIP	19	M	LABR	RR	AHZS	USA
BRELEWITZ, ANDREI	26	M	LABR	RR	AHZS	USA
MIKOLAINIS, WIKENTY	49	M	LABR	RR	AHZS	USA
BIELITZKY, PETER	40	M	LABR	RR	AHZS	USA
DARBITZKI, IWAN	30	M	LABR	RR	AHZS	USA
MOSCHENKA, MARTIN	33	M	LABR	RR	AHZS	USA
GERMALI, MIHAL	30	M	LABR	RR	AGRT	USA
ZAPLIK, JACOB	40	M	LABR	RR	AGRT	USA
LIPOWITZ, PETER	18	M	LABR	RR	AGRT	USA
KAMANN, OTTO	42	M	LABR	RR	AHXH	USA
BOROWITSCH, ANTON	28	M	LABR	RR	AHXH	USA
KOSTETZKY, LEONH.	28	M	LABR	RR	AHXH	USA
JENSEWSKI, JAN	27	M	LABR	RR	ZZZZ	USA
BIRGEL, JAN	26	M	LABR	RR	ZZZZ	USA
SMOLAREK, STANISL.	24	M	LABR	RR	ZZZZ	USA
LEMBICZ, MICH.	23	M	LABR	RR	ZZZZ	USA
JAKUBOWSKY, ANDR.	22	M	LABR	RR	ZZZZ	USA
KOSTANECKY, PETER	21	M	LABR	RR	ZZZZ	USA
ZALEWSKY, MARCIN	32	M	LABR	RR	ZZZZ	USA
IGNATZ	23	M	LABR	RR	ZZZZ	USA
JENSEWITZ, JAN	25	M	LABR	RR	ZZZZ	USA
SCHURAU, MICHAEL	25	M	LABR	RR	ZZZZ	USA
JANIK, ANTONI	33	M	LABR	RR	ZZZZ	USA
ZIMUNT, IVAN	36	M	LABR	RR	ZZZZ	USA
RAZOWSKY, OSIP	29	M	LABR	RR	ZZZZ	USA
PULUK, JOSES	30	M	LABR	RR	ZZZZ	USA
CHMIELEWSKI, VALENT	22	M	LABR	RR	AHUF	USA
CZARNECKI, JAN	27	M	LABR	RR	AHUF	USA
BLASCHKE, ANDR.	30	M	LABR	RR	AHUF	USA
CZARNECKI, LUDW.	42	M	LABR	RR	AHUF	USA
CARL	24	M	LABR	RR	AHUF	USA
STEFANSKI, VOJC.	28	M	LABR	RR	AHUF	USA
ZAKRZEWSKY, JAN	28	M	LABR	RR	AHUF	USA
KUPERMANN, MOSES	37	M	LABR	RR	AHUF	USA
GERZCHUNI, INDE	10	F	NN	RR	AHUF	USA
BOLL, FRIEDR.	27	M	FARMER	RR	ZZZZ	USA
MARGA.	21	F	W	RR	ZZZZ	USA
REUTER, CARL	17	M	W	RR	ZZZZ	USA
SCHAAL, JOH.	28	M	FARMER	RR	ZZZZ	USA
CHRISTE.	23	F	W	RR	ZZZZ	USA
MARGA.	.06	F	INFANT	RR	ZZZZ	USA
JAN	2	M	CHILD	RR	ZZZZ	USA
WAGNER, CHRIST.	15	M	NN	RR	ZZZZ	USA
HAEUSER, BARBA.	62	F	W	RR	ZZZZ	USA
KRIMMESSIN, GUST.	20	M	LABR	RR	ZZZZ	USA
BERGMANN, JOH.	25	M	LABR	RR	AIDV	USA
SCHWERINOS, TAMOSCH	23	M	LABR	RR	ZZZZ	USA

SHIP: WISCONSIN

FROM: LIVERPOOL AND QUEENSTOWN
TO: NEW YORK
ARRIVED: 10 MAY 1888

PASSENGER	AGE	SEX	OCCUPATION	PRV	VIL	DES
RAPLOWSKI, SHOLLA	32	F	SP	RR	ZZZZ	USA
SAHON, DAVID	32	M	GZR	RR	ZZZZ	USA
KUSSEL, NESCHE	21	F	W	PL	ZZZZ	USA
LIPE	.10	F	INFANT	PL	ZZZZ	USA
JESEPOTZKY, CHAIM	51	M	FARMER	RR	ZZZZ	USA
RECKER, CHAIM	26	M	FARMER	RR	ZZZZ	USA
HAKERMANN, PUDKA	24	F	W	PL	ZZZZ	USA
ABRAM	.09	M	INFANT	PL	ZZZZ	USA
SEGALL, JONES	26	M	PMBR	RR	ZZZZ	USA
GOLDBERG, ABRAM	37	M	PMBR	RR	ZZZZ	USA
DANOWSKI, LIEBE	30	F	W	PL	ZZZZ	USA
CHAIE	7	F	CHILD	PL	ZZZZ	USA
JOHN	3	M	CHILD	PL	ZZZZ	USA
JUDES	.08	M	INFANT	PL	ZZZZ	USA
CIREL	.08	M	INFANT	PL	ZZZZ	USA
LEWIN, ABRAM	21	M	MSN	RR	ZZZZ	USA
VIAROT, OSCAR	23	M	GZR	RR	ZZZZ	USA
PLOSCHOWSKI, CHAS	25	F	W	PL	ZZZZ	USA
CHANE	.10	F	INFANT	PL	ZZZZ	USA
SAUN, BLUME	00	M	CH	PL	ZZZZ	USA
ABERBERG, ELIS	00	M	LABR	RR	ZZZZ	USA
YLOTTOLON, AB	26	M	LABR	RR	ZZZZ	USA
MENDEL	24	F	W	RR	ZZZZ	USA
SABOLEWSKI, BEILE	37	M	FARMER	PL	ZZZZ	USA
RACHAL	27	F	W	PL	ZZZZ	USA
MARIAN	7	F	CHILD	PL	ZZZZ	USA
ISAAC	6	M	CHILD	PL	ZZZZ	USA
LEIB	3	F	CHILD	PL	ZZZZ	USA
KOLNICZANSKI, ITE	22	F	W	PL	ZZZZ	USA
ABRAM	3	M	CHILD	PL	ZZZZ	USA
SCHEINE	.11	F	INFANT	PL	ZZZZ	USA
BEKER, ABRAM	7	M	CHILD	PL	ZZZZ	USA
ZABATKEWITZ, CHAIE	3	F	CHILD	RR	ZZZZ	USA
MUEDOWITZ, BEIL	20	M	TLR	RR	ZZZZ	USA
SMARTINIK, ABR	37	M	LABR	RR	ZZZZ	USA
SOHNOWITZ, HORIN	18	M	FARMER	RR	ZZZZ	USA
MLETZINK, SCHEINE	42	F	W	RR	ZZZZ	USA

PASSENGER	AGE	SEX	OCCUPATION	PRV VIL DES
CHANE	7	F	CHILD	RRZZZZUSA
ESTER	6	F	CHILD	RRZZZZUSA
RIVKE	3	F	CHILD	RRZZZZUSA
HODORONIK, SACH	33	M	LABR	PLZZZZUSA
YREEWSKI, M	34	M	GZR	RRZZZZUSA
KOEZANSKI, FRANZ	30	M	PMBR	RRZZZZUSA
BEKER, LEIE	18	F	SP	RRZZZZUSA
SCHULTZ, JACOB	24	M	PMBR	RRZZZZUSA
BERZINSKI, NATHAN	17	M	PMBR	RRZZZZUSA
SUSMANOWITZ, HERSCH	6	M	CHILD	RRZZZZUSA
GIDANEZIK, SALOMON	29	M	GZR	RRZZZZUSA
MARYSON, MAX	18	M	PNTR	RRZZZZUSA
GOLDING, SELLY	17	F	SP	RRZZZZUSA
GRUNFELDT, KASEN	18	M	LABR	RRZZZZUSA
JACOBETZKY, MOSES	27	M	PMBR	RRZZZZUSA
ABRAM	6	M	CHILD	RRZZZZUSA

SHIP: ITALY

FROM: LIVERPOOL AND QUEENSTOWN
TO: NEW YORK
ARRIVED: 11 MAY 1888

PASSENGER	AGE	SEX	OCCUPATION	PRV VIL DES
SUEMANWISTA, A	30	M	LABR	RRADBQNY
MELINOWITZ, F	25	M	LABR	RRADBQNY
KONGTOWSKI, VALENTIN	28	F	W	RRACBFNY
FRANZ	2	M	CHILD	RRACBFNY
LADISLAW	00	M	INF	RRACBFNY
KOLUEB, JOHAN	25	M	LABR	RRACBFNY
WRIZINSKY, LEON	23	M	LABR	RRACBFNY
KAUES, JOSEF	30	M	LABR	RRACBFNY
MILUS, JONS	28	M	LABR	RRACBFNY
PAYILIS, ADAM	17	M	LABR	RRACBFNY
PELRUSKOWITZ, ANTON	18	M	LABR	RRACBFNY
GENIRYIS, AUGUSTIN	18	M	LABR	RRACBFNY
KIBLIS, ADAM	18	M	LABR	RRACBFNY
AROWITZ, SIMON	28	M	LABR	RRACBFNY
TRIP, FRANK	35	M	LABR	RRACBFNY
JARMULEWIE, MARTIN	25	M	LABR	RRACBFNY
GLOWSKY, IONA	22	M	LABR	RRACBFNY
BATKEWIES, WINCORT	26	M	LABR	RRACBFNY
PANOWITS, MICHAEL	28	M	LABR	RRACBFNY
BRAND, GUSCHEN	26	M	LABR	RRACBFNY
JAWLEWITZ, MENDEL	17	M	LABR	RRACBFNY
OSCAR	24	M	LABR	RRACBFNY
MUSOWITZ, MOSES	22	M	LABR	RRACBFNY
FLAUSAN, JOSEPH	18	M	LABR	RRACBFNY
MALTZ, NISSEN	37	M	LABR	RRACBFNY
KITZ, FRANZ	23	M	LABR	RRACBFNY
NIGER, SELIG	10	F	CH	RRACBFNY
MEYER	8	M	CHILD	RRACBFNY
WREUTI, AGELI	18	M	LABR	RRACBFNY
MICHALOWSKY, THOMAS	18	M	LABR	RRACBFNY
WIADOWSKY, ANTON	42	M	LABR	RRACBFNY
MIZANOWITZ, KAROL	22	M	LABR	RRACBFNY
PRACHOLD, STANIEL	25	M	LABR	RRACBFNY
KOLINGAVT, FRANZ	21	M	LABR	RRACBFNY
PIOTASYWITZ, PROLE	40	M	LABR	RRACBFNY
MISCHWITZ, JONT	28	M	LABR	RRACBFNY
KASIMIA	43	M	LABR	RRACBFNY
PICHAWTZ, ANTON	50	M	LABR	RRACBFNY
PETCHSUTAL, CHANDEL	18	M	LABR	RRACBFNY
JONNY	26	M	LABR	RRACBFNY
LEMMEL, MOSES	30	M	LABR	RRACBFNY
WADE, ABR	24	M	LABR	RRACBFNY
DRECHOLN, LUB	26	M	LABR	RRACBFNY
GRIESTEIN, SOLOMON	24	M	LABR	RRACBFNY
GOLDBERG, SCHAIM	22	M	LABR	RRACBFNY
BERKIN, J	19	M	LABR	RRACBFNY
GAM, PIECHEL	20	M	LABR	RRACBFNY
WITEYWSKY, IGNATZ	45	M	LABR	RRACBFNY
KALN, JANKEL	22	M	LABR	RRACBFNY
CHAN	20	M	LABR	RRACBFNY
JITZMANN, MEYER	20	M	LABR	RRACBFNY
LING, JOCTET	20	M	LABR	RRACBFNY
WERREN, FANNY	20	F	W	RRACBFNY
NATHAN	3	M	CHILD	RRACBFNY
FAYILSKA, KATHERINE	26	F	W	RRACBFNY
MARIANA	4	F	CHILD	RRACBFNY
FULKA	3	M	CHILD	RRACBFNY
ANTON	00	M	INF	RRACBFNY
WAZAWITZ, WILLIAM	25	M	LABR	RRACBFNY
MARKOSTOS, ANTON	25	M	LABR	RRACBFNY
ROYNI, MICHAEL	24	M	LABR	RRACBFNY
MOSES, M	32	M	LABR	RRACBFNY
ROMANESCHER, LEUGO	25	M	LABR	RRACBFNY
FYGARSKY, ANTON	32	M	LABR	RRADAXNY
KOLAMSKY, JOH	38	M	LABR	RRADAXNY
SCHIETY, ANTON	22	M	LABR	RRADAXNY
GONZYNSKA, MARTA	16	M	LABR	RRADAXNY
STABUESKI, ANTON	28	M	LABR	RRADAXNY
BALTEUSIETY, PAMSAI	20	M	LABR	RRADAXNY
KILIMAS, JOSEF	26	M	LABR	RRADAXNY
FARBER, JOEL	18	M	LABR	RRADAXNY
SCHAPIRO, GERSON	14	M	LABR	RRADAXNY
RANIAMOWSKY, IGNACZ	30	M	LABR	RRADAXNY
ROMANOSKY, MARTIN	30	M	LABR	RRADAXNY
KUWNEZ, MIKI	19	M	LABR	RRADAXNY
JUS	27	M	LABR	RRADAXNY
STABINSKA, FRANZ	26	M	LABR	RRADAXNY
WARAKONISKI, JAN	34	M	LABR	RRADAXNY
SUKOWSKI, FRANZ	45	M	LABR	RRADAXNY
WINKEL, MATHILDA	20	F	SP	RRADAXNY
OTTILIE	17	F	SP	RRADAXNY
ROSCILINK, JOHN	38	M	LABR	RRADAXNY
ABRAMOWITZ, IBYIG	17	M	LABR	RRADAXNY
WUSS, JOSSEL	40	M	LABR	RRADAXNY
DASKOL, HERMAN	50	M	LABR	RRADAXNY
LUTKOWSKI, THOS	20	M	LABR	RRADAXNY
L---, KASMIA	22	M	LABR	RRADAXNY
JACHMOWITZ, MERY	22	M	LABR	RRADAXNY
LICKMAN, CLAUS	19	M	LABR	RRADAXNY
KNIVIEY, JAN	24	M	LABR	RRADAXNY
ROMANSKY, PETER	41	M	LABR	RRADAXNY
STABINSKI, PETER	20	M	LABR	RRADAXNY
RURYWSKY, DANIEL	18	M	LABR	RRADAXNY
WUTZMAN, OTTO	38	F	W	RRADAXNY
TRYDER	10	M	CH	RRADAXNY
ARBYNSON, SIG	26	M	LABR	RRADAXNY
MIKKELNER, MIKAL	36	M	LABR	RRADAXNY
KAMINSKA, M	39	M	LABR	RRADAXNY
LUDOSKI, JANS	24	M	LABR	RRADAXNY
AMARTARA	19	F	W	RRADAXNY
BRONISLAUS	.05	M	INFANT	RRADAXNY
DRUINSKI, STANISLAW	32	M	LABR	RRADAXNY
PORKI, JAN	28	M	LABR	RRADAXNY
SNIOTKOSKI, BARTAG	24	M	LABR	RRACBFNY
NASADOWSKI, ANTON	30	M	LABR	RRACBFNY
MARY	24	F	W	RRACBFNY
STANISLAW	10	M	CH	RRACBFNY
ANTONI	8	M	CHILD	RRACBFNY
JAN	3	M	CHILD	RRACBFNY
KAISAULATLI, LARS	28	M	LABR	RRACBFNY
VALEKINGOS, CARL	33	M	LABR	RRACBFNY
LAIDI, DAVIE	21	M	LABR	RRACBFNY
GWELA, VITA	25	F	SP	RRACBFNY
WALBERG, ANNA	20	F	SP	RRACBFNY
RAISONEN, ISAK	34	M	LABR	RRACBFNY
BEAONER, CARLI	23	M	LABR	RRACBFNY
BYOSHAM, DANIEL	27	M	LABR	RRACBFNY
FASJUN, LARS	19	M	LABR	RRACBFNY
NILSON, HANS	33	M	LABR	RRACBFNY
TAUB, HANS	25	M	LABR	RRACBFNY
JORVELE, ERIK	23	M	LABR	RRACBFNY
ARETANDER, NIL	37	M	LABR	RRACBFNY

PASSENGER	AGE	SEX	OCCUPATION	PRV	VIL	DES
PAUSON, KARL	22	M	LABR	RR	AC	BFNY
RINKOWSKY, MATHERS	50	M	LABR	RR	AC	BFNY
ANTONI	30	F	W	RR	AC	BFNY
NALKER	12	M	CH	RR	AC	BFNY
JOHAN	7	M	CHILD	RR	AC	BFNY
MAKOWITZ, ITZIG	22	M	LABR	RR	AC	BFNY
HANNA	16	F	W	RR	AC	BFNY
S	15	M	LABR	RR	AC	BFNY
SBYALSKY, EMMA	18	M	LABR	RR	AC	BFNY
GEYLEWSKY, IVAN	33	M	LABR	RR	AC	BFNY
WROBLEWSKY, STANISL	33	M	LABR	RR	AC	BFNY

SHIP: ALLER

FROM: BREMEN AND SOUTHAMPTON
TO: NEW YORK
ARRIVED: 12 MAY 1888

PASSENGER	AGE	SEX	OCCUPATION	PRV	VIL	DES
GEHKHAR, GUSTAV	29	M	FARMER	RR	ZZZZ	USA
OTTO	17	M	FARMER	RR	ZZZZ	USA
CON---, CASPAR	18	M	FARMER	RR	ZZZZ	USA
-UDEIMS, ANTON	25	M	FARMER	RR	ZZZZ	USA
BRAK--ES, JOHAN	26	M	FARMER	RR	ZZZZ	USA
LE-V, CHRISTIAN	37	M	FARMER	RR	ZZZZ	USA
BAUM--ATES, ADAM	34	M	FARMER	RR	ZZZZ	USA
TONATES, JOSEF	21	M	FARMER	RR	ZZZZ	USA
BEISCHER, MARTIN	24	M	FARMER	RR	ZZZZ	USA
GOWATZKY, MICHAEL	30	M	FARMER	RR	ZZZZ	USA
SCHMAEL, GEORG	21	M	FARMER	RR	ZZZZ	USA
-ESSEBRADE, CARL	45	M	FARMER	RR	ZZZZ	USA
DZIECHOKWSKY, KORZ	36	M	FARMER	RR	ZZZZ	USA
-UV, JANOS	30	M	FARMER	RR	ZZZZ	USA
STAPAKOV, ISAAK	40	M	FARMER	RR	ZZZZ	USA
AUGAR, TAJE	50	M	FARMER	RR	ZZZZ	USA
--ZKOWIS, FRANCISCA	30	F	NN	RR	ZZZZ	USA
HELENE	7	F	CHILD	RR	ZZZZ	USA
FRANCISCA	6	F	CHILD	RR	ZZZZ	USA
ANNA	5	F	CHILD	RR	ZZZZ	USA
WLADISLAUS	3	M	CHILD	RR	ZZZZ	USA
AMANDA	2	F	CHILD	RR	ZZZZ	USA
WANDA	.11	F	INFANT	RR	ZZZZ	USA
MALI-OWICZ, MARIANE	31	F	NN	RR	ZZZZ	USA
WLADISLAWA	14	F	NN	RR	ZZZZ	USA
CUST-A--	7	M	CHILD	RR	ZZZZ	USA
BARBARA	5	F	CHILD	RR	ZZZZ	USA
-ICHUELA	3	F	CHILD	RR	ZZZZ	USA
STEPHAN	.09	M	INFANT	RR	ZZZZ	USA
GRAM---, JANE	30	F	NN	RR	ZZZZ	USA
JUDA	7	F	CHILD	RR	ZZZZ	USA
KATZ, LINA	26	F	NN	RR	ZZZZ	USA
ABRAHAM	6	M	CHILD	RR	ZZZZ	USA
RAM--ATES, JOHAN	30	M	FARMER	RR	ZZZZ	USA
HELENE	28	F	W	RR	ZZZZ	USA
JOSEF	6	M	CHILD	RR	ZZZZ	USA
JOHANNE	.04	F	INFANT	RR	ZZZZ	USA
RIEMER, T--T	21	M	FARMER	RR	ZZZZ	USA
BERTHA	21	F	W	RR	ZZZZ	USA
SOEMME---, ERNST	19	M	MCHT	RR	ZZZZ	USA
LOUISE	17	F	W	RR	ZZZZ	USA
KAM----, EVA	25	F	NN	RR	ZZZZ	USA
CARL	6	M	CHILD	RR	ZZZZ	USA
G-ENTZ, FRIDRICH	33	M	FARMER	RR	ZZZZ	USA
ROSINE	33	F	W	RR	ZZZZ	USA
JACOB	7	M	CHILD	RR	ZZZZ	USA
GOTTFRIED	4	M	CHILD	RR	ZZZZ	USA
CARL	.06	M	INFANT	RR	ZZZZ	UNK
GOTTFRIED	30	M	FARMER	RR	ZZZZ	USA
PETER	28	M	FARMER	RR	ZZZZ	USA
ELISABETH	3	F	CHILD	RR	ZZZZ	USA

SHIP: BOHEMIA

FROM: HAMBURG AND HAVRE
TO: NEW YORK
ARRIVED: 12 MAY 1888

PASSENGER	AGE	SEX	OCCUPATION	PRV	VIL	DES
MASCHELSKI, ROMAN	28	M	MLR	RR	ZZZZ	BUF
JAN	25	M	PNTR	RR	ZZZZ	BUF
SCHNEIDER, GUSTAV	15	M	FSHMN	RR	ZZZZ	BUF
MANDAU, FRIEDR	23	M	MLR	RR	ZZZZ	BUF
HAASE, JOH	28	M	JNR	RR	ZZZZ	IL
KNASKOWSKI, WAICIECH	24	M	LABR	RR	ZZZZ	IL
FELS, JOSEF	22	M	JNR	RR	ZZZZ	IL
SOKOLOWSKI, JOSEPH	43	M	FARMER	RR	AIDD	IL
GAJEWSKI, JOSEPH	28	M	FARMER	RR	AIDD	IA
REDLINSKI, CLEMENS	40	M	LABR	RR	ZZZZ	BUF
MARIANNA	27	F	W	RR	ZZZZ	BUF
FRANZ	9	M	CHILD	RR	ZZZZ	BUF
VERONICA	6	F	CHILD	RR	ZZZZ	BUF
DURNIAK, ANTON	28	M	LABR	RR	AIBH	BUF
BUCHALSKI, FRANZIZEK	24	M	LABR	RR	ZZZZ	IL
BRONISLAWA	22	F	W	RR	ZZZZ	IL
LIOFUSZYNSKI, STANISLAU	36	M	LABR	RR	ZZZZ	IL
LIOFUSZYNSKI, JULIANE	26	F	W	RR	ZZZZ	BUF
MICHALINE	8	F	CHILD	RR	ZZZZ	BUF
MARIANNE	2	F	CHILD	RR	ZZZZ	BUF
VICTORIA	.06	F	INFANT	RR	ZZZZ	BUF
STANISLAW	9	M	CHILD	RR	ZZZZ	BUF
KARPINSKI, ANDRES	36	M	LABR	RR	ZZZZ	BUF
LEKADIA	2	F	CHILD	RR	ZZZZ	BUF
ANTONIA	23	F	W	RR	ZZZZ	BUF
GRUDOWSKY, FRANZ	40	M	LABR	RR	ZZZZ	NY
SCHULZ, CHARLOTTE	25	F	SGL	RR	ZZZZ	NY
REDA, JAN	22	M	LABR	RR	ZZZZ	NY
GROGLEIT, JOHANN	28	M	LABR	RR	AIFN	NE
JELISKI, KLEMENS	30	M	LABR	RR	ZZZZ	IL
DARWENOWITZ, MARZIN	19	M	LABR	RR	ZZZZ	IL
WOTKEWITZ, MAZI	18	M	LABR	RR	ZZZZ	IL
SCHLEWENSKY, FRANZISCHE	25	M	LABR	RR	ZZZZ	IL
WARCHAUTZKY, JERS	36	M	LABR	RR	ZZZZ	IL
SBKOLOWSKY, ALEX	20	M	LABR	RR	AIDD	DET
SZELINSKI, JAN	40	M	LABR	RR	AIDD	UNK
JESCHINOWSKI, STANISL	47	M	LABR	RR	AIDD	UNK
KUSCHINSK, JOSEF	33	M	LABR	RR	AIDD	UNK
ORLOWSKI, KASIMIR	21	M	LABR	RR	AIDD	UNK
KOWALEWSKI, LEON	31	M	LABR	RR	AIDD	UNK
MEHLING, KATH	35	M	WO	RR	ZZZZ	NE
CONRAD	9	M	CHILD	RR	ZZZZ	NE
LISBETH	8	F	CHILD	RR	ZZZZ	NE
KATH	.11	F	INFANT	RR	ZZZZ	NE
MROCZZKOWSKI, ANTON	21	M	LABR	RR	AHUI	NY
KAROLEWSKI, ANTONI	21	M	LABR	RR	AHUI	NY
ARMANOWITZ, VINCENT	33	M	LABR	RR	ZZZZ	PA
WILHELMOWITZ, FRANCICEK	31	M	LABR	RR	ZZZZ	PA
DANGILEWITZ, JAN	20	M	LABR	RR	ZZZZ	PA
POSKOWITZE, VINCENTY	25	M	LABR	RR	ZZZZ	OH
LATCHITZKY, MICHAEL	28	M	LABR	RR	ZZZZ	OH
GARMANSKY, VINCENTY	22	M	LABR	RR	ZZZZ	OH
POZETULSKY, VITAL	31	M	LABR	RR	ZZZZ	OH
SAMEITIL, DINIZI	36	M	LABR	RR	ZZZZ	OH

SHIP: SERVIA

FROM: LIVERPOOL AND QUEENSTOWN
TO: NEW YORK
ARRIVED: 14 MAY 1888

PASSENGER	AGE	SEX	OCCUPATION	PRV	VIL	DES
METZLER, ZODEK	25	M	LABR	RR	ADAX	PA
KLEIN-CH--IE--, MOJSCHE	26	M	LABR	RR	ADAX	PA

PASSENGER	AGE	SEX	OCCUPATION	PRV VIL DES
CZELETZKI, FRANCISEK	25	M	LABR	RRADAXNY
ANTONIA	18	F	W	RRADAXNY
KRUSCHEN, PERCHES	36	M	TLR	RRADAXPHI
CHA--	37	F	W	RRADAXPHI
RIFKE	7	M	CHILD	RRADAXPHI
ROCHEL	5	F	CHILD	RRADAXPHI
CHAYE	.02	F	INFANT	RRADAXPHI
BROCHE	.11	F	INFANT	RRADAXPHI
CZELETZKI, BALEY----	00	M	INF	RRADAXNY

SHIP: SORRENTO

FROM: HAMBURG
TO: NEW YORK
ARRIVED: 14 MAY 1888

PASSENGER	AGE	SEX	OCCUPATION	PRV VIL DES
ZBYTNEWSKY, JULIAN	37	M	NN	RRZZZZUSA
KAPZINSKY, SIMON	43	M	NN	RRZZZZUSA
MALINOWSKI, VALENTI	24	M	NN	RRZZZZUSA
SAVAROWSKY, W.	23	M	NN	RRZZZZUSA
SCHOLDAR, ISRAEL	19	M	TLR	RRZZZZUSA
KONSKI, NICOLAI	38	M	TLR	RRZZZZUSA
SKAZANSKI, JANDZI	38	M	DLR	RRZZZZUSA
BUCHHOLZ, JOSEF	25	M	LABR	RRZZZZUSA
TENTZER, FRIEDR.	37	M	CTHR	RRZZZZUSA
ZDALINSKI, SOFIE	51	F	WO	RRZZZZUSA
BRONESCHKOWSKI, JACOB	33	M	LABR	RRZZZZUSA
LEHMANN, JULS.	32	M	LABR	RRZZZZUSA
MANKES, PAWEL	24	M	LABR	RRZZZZUSA
SLARSKI, BERIL	20	M	LABR	RRZZZZUSA
WULF	40	M	LABR	RRZZZZUSA
ABR.	25	M	LABR	RRZZZZUSA
TASSANSKI, NOCHIM	34	M	LABR	RRZZZZUSA
BUCKLER, JOSEF	30	M	LABR	RRZZZZUSA
MASITIS, CARL	27	M	LABR	RRZZZZUSA
SCHERKES, PETER	23	M	LABR	RRZZZZUSA
MALTIKOWSKI, FRANZ	22	M	LABR	RRZZZZUSA
KEILBOTZKY, JACOB	23	M	LABR	RRZZZZUSA
SOBELEWSKY, MICHAEL	30	M	LABR	RRZZZZUSA
WASCHULEWITZ, ALEX	21	M	LABR	RRZZZZUSA
DZEWILEWSKI, LEON	22	M	LABR	RRZZZZUSA
SOBELEWSKY, ANTON	22	M	LABR	RRZZZZUSA
BAJARSKIE, MEYER	29	M	LABR	RRZZZZUSA
WOLNICKI, SCHLOME	25	M	LABR	RRZZZZUSA
LIPINSKY, DAVID	20	M	LABR	RRZZZZUSA
SARA	21	F	W	RRZZZZUSA
BURASK, ABR.	40	M	LABR	RRZZZZUSA
BUSCH, LEIB	28	M	LABR	RRZZZZUSA
ABR.	25	M	LABR	RRZZZZUSA
KAPLAN, WOLF	34	M	LABR	RRZZZZUSA
RISK, WOLF	33	M	LABR	RRZZZZUSA
SEELKOWITZ, DAVID	17	M	LABR	RRZZZZUSA
BECKER, MOSES	17	M	LABR	RRZZZZUSA
GILTZIZ, MOSES	21	M	LABR	RRZZZZUSA
LEIBOWITZ, LEIB	18	M	LABR	RRZZZZUSA
ALESSANDROWITZ, SIMON	27	M	LABR	RRZZZZUSA
LEBOWITZ, CHAIM	18	M	JNR	RRZZZZUSA
NOSIK, JACOB	19	M	LABR	RRZZZZNY
MELER, MOSES	22	M	LABR	RRZZZZNY
SCHMIDT, LEIB	40	M	TLR	RRZZZZNY
BERMANN, LEIB	47	M	SHMK	RRZZZZNY
ELIOSCHOW, CHAIM	23	M	MLR	RRZZZZNY
PODBERCSKY, SCHEINE	57	M	DLR	RRZZZZNY
KRANZ, JACOB	22	M	DLR	RRZZZZNY
KATILAW, PIETRO	35	M	LABR	RRZZZZNY
POPLINSKI, VINCENTY	28	M	LABR	RRZZZZNY
BULSIMAS, ANTON	26	M	LABR	RRZZZZNY
GELLAS, JANOS	18	M	LABR	RRZZZZNY
KLEIN, JANKEL	19	M	TLR	RRZZZZNY
KURWITZ, ARON	34	M	DLR	RRZZZZNY
KLOMOWITSCH, TH.	25	M	LABR	RRZZZZNY
ABRULEWITZ, ADAM	26	M	LABR	RRZZZZNY
JURDISKY, CH.	22	M	DLR	RRZZZZNY
KANTOWICZ, MOSES	26	M	LABR	RRZZZZNY
FISCHKIN, BER.	46	M	LABR	RRZZZZNY
POSNAK, LEIB	23	M	LABR	RRZZZZNY
PANKWITZ, VASIL	23	M	LABR	RRZZZZNY
BLUM, HERM.	24	M	LABR	RRZZZZNY
JUDELOWITZ, INDE	9	M	CHILD	RRZZZZNY
HELWIZ, LUDWIG	49	M	MSN	RRZZZZDAK
WILHE.	42	F	W	RRZZZZDAK
AUGUST	9	M	CHILD	RRZZZZDAK
GUSTAV	8	M	CHILD	RRZZZZDAK
FERDINAND	7	M	CHILD	RRZZZZDAK
FRANZ	3	M	CHILD	RRZZZZDAK
ELISABETH	.09	F	INFANT	RRZZZZDAK
GIDEMANSKY, SPRINZE	15	F	SGL	RRZZZZNY
PAGELOWITZ, JANZEL	50	M	LABR	RRZZZZNY
GARBEROWA, D.	18	F	SGL	RRZZZZNY
EPSTEIN, REPECCA	17	F	SGL	RRZZZZNY
ALPER, MOSES	38	M	DLR	RRZZZZNY
RILMER, LEIB	23	M	DLR	RRZZZZNY
MALZMAN, LIEBE	17	F	SGL	RRZZZZNY
SPRINZE	.09	F	INFANT	RRZZZZNY
BARON, CHAMIE	20	F	SGL	RRZZZZNY
GRINBERG, PESCHE	15	F	SGL	RRZZZZNY
EPSTEIN, SCHEINE	18	F	SGL	RRZZZZNY
BURALIN, CHAP.	25	F	WO	RRZZZZNY
DAVID	.09	M	INFANT	RRZZZZNY
BLUMENTHAL, PEISACH	18	M	TLR	RRZZZZNY
SHERMAN, RIEFKE	17	F	SGL	RRZZZZNY
JANKEL	9	M	CHILD	RRZZZZNY
GROSSBORD, LEIB	15	M	CLGYMN	RRZZZZNY
AWRICK, IDA	19	F	SGL	RRZZZZNY
KLEIN, HIRSCH	25	M	DLR	RRZZZZNY
FACAN, AMA	20	F	SGL	RRZZZZNY
NOWAK, MICHAEL	52	M	LABR	RRZZZZNY
MARIANNA	22	M	JNR	RRZZZZNY
FILSOSEF, THOMAS	24	M	LABR	RRZZZZNY
SZEPANEK, PROSPER	25	M	LABR	RRZZZZNY
NOVAK, ANTON	.11	M	INFANT	RRZZZZNY
STANISLAUS	.11	M	INFANT	RRZZZZNY
CHUSANOWICZ, J.	31	M	LABR	RRZZZZNY
CHAIM	30	M	LABR	RRZZZZNY
GREULICH, RUDOLPH	24	M	CPTR	RRZZZZNY
BOCHLKE, EMILIE	33	F	WO	RRZZZZNY
MARSCHALEK, PETER	55	M	LABR	RRZZZZNY
KOWALSKI, VICTOR	40	M	LABR	RRZZZZNY
REHAK, THERESE	19	F	W	RRZZZZNY
CERNY, JOSEF	24	M	LABR	RRZZZZNY
STALLKOWITZ, FRANZ	26	M	LABR	RRZZZZNY
POOLCITIS, JOS.	22	M	LABR	RRZZZZNY
ROMANGAYTIS, S.	22	M	LABR	RRZZZZNY
MARTIN, JURGIS	35	M	LABR	RRZZZZNY
VALATIN, ELLA	60	F	WO	RRZZZZNY
AUGUST	9	M	CHILD	RRZZZZNY
GACIS, JOSEF	35	M	LABR	RRZZZZNY
SILBERMANN, SAMUEL	8	M	CHILD	RRAIIXBUF
BERY	7	M	CHILD	RRAIIXBUF
MINNA	4	F	CHILD	RRAIIXBUF
TAUBE	.11	M	INFANT	RRAIIXBUF
HEIDEL, GUSTAV	28	M	LABR	RRAIIXBUF
IDA	29	F	W	RRAIIXBUF
FRITZ	.06	M	INFANT	RRAIIXBUF
VENDORF, CHAS.	20	M	LABR	RRAIIXBUF
ZIESMER, LOUISE	60	F	WO	RRAIIXBUF
FRAHSE, VILHE.	60	F	WO	RRAIIXBUF
BOFINGER, ADOLF	3	M	CHILD	RRAIIXBUF
ZACHARIAS, OTTO	29	M	FARMER	RRAIIXBUF
MARGR.	28	F	W	RRAIIXBUF
PETER	7	M	CHILD	RRAIIXBUF
HEINRICH	4	M	CHILD	RRAIIXBUF
MARIE	2	F	CHILD	RRAIIXBUF
AUGUST	.03	F	INFANT	RRAIIXBUF
AMALIE	22	F	SGL	RRAIIXBUF

PASSENGER	AGE	SEX	OCCUPATION	PRIV	VIL	DES
JENSEN, CATHA.	19	F	SGL	RRAI	IX	BUF
SAPHIR, FEIGE	22	F	SGL	RRAI	IX	BUF
JACOBWICZ, EVA	26	F	WO	RRAI	IX	BUF
ERNE	4	F	CHILD	RRAI	IX	BUF
YRMANN, VICENTY	19	M	LABR	RRAI	IX	BUF
PILEWSKY, W.	22	M	LABR	RRAI	IX	BUF
KANNENGIESSER, ISAAC	45	M	TLR	RRAI	IX	BUF
GWILDIS, HASNER	28	M	LABR	RRAI	IX	BUF
WISNEWSKY, ELENA	17	F	SGL	RRAI	IX	BUF
GOLDMANN, NATHAN	36	M	LABR	RRAI	IX	BUF
PARISER, ETTEL	23	F	WO	RRAI	IX	BUF
LUSSIE	3	F	CHILD	RRAI	IX	BUF
KLEIN, SOLIE	18	F	SGL	RRAI	IX	BUF
SOFER, JUDEL	9	M	CHILD	RRAI	IX	BUF
MEHL, SELIG	9	M	CHILD	RRAI	IX	BUF
SIEDLOSKA, M.	30	F	WO	RRAI	IX	BUF
WOLESLAW	3	M	CHILD	RRAI	IX	BUF
ADAM	.11	M	INFANT	RRAI	IX	BUF
PLATA, FRIEDR.	40	M	LABR	RRAI	IX	BUF
SINKWITZ, VINCENTY	44	F	SGL	RRAI	IX	BUF
ELISABETH	40	F	WO	RRAI	IX	BUF
JAN	9	M	CHILD	RRAI	IX	BUF
ANNA	8	F	CHILD	RRAI	IX	BUF
JOSEFA	7	F	CHILD	RRAI	IX	BUF
STANISLAW	3	M	CHILD	RRAI	IX	BUF
HELPERN, ZODEK	42	M	DLR	RRAI	IX	BUF
BARUCH	9	M	CHILD	RRAI	IX	BUF
WENGROFSKY, ISAAC	28	M	DLR	RRAI	IX	BUF
KAATZ, MOSES	30	M	DLR	RRAI	IX	BUF
BUFF, MOSES	26	M	DLR	RRAI	IX	BUF
VITZBERG, ELOFE	25	M	DLR	RRAI	IX	BUF
PUESCHIN, JEKEL	30	M	DLR	RRAI	IX	BUF
BECHER, ARON	44	M	DLR	RRAI	IX	BUF
CHACKOWSKI, SCH.	34	M	LABR	RRAI	IX	BUF
ROMANOWSKI, JAN	20	M	LABR	RRAI	IX	BUF
JOVANOVSKI, JOSEF	22	M	LABR	RRAI	IX	BUF
HRYPSKI, ANTON	37	M	LABR	RRAI	IX	BUF
CHORZEY, JAN	30	M	LABR	RRAI	IX	BUF
JEMULAN, F.	20	M	LABR	RRAI	IX	BUF
BOCHENOWSKI, JULIAN	23	M	LABR	RRAI	IX	BUF
WILZINSKI, MICHAEL	22	M	LABR	RRAI	IX	BUF
BORIS, MOSES	21	M	LABR	RRAI	IX	BUF
SOSNOWSKI, JAN	21	M	LABR	RRAI	IX	BUF
BUCHANOWSKI, P.	28	M	LABR	RRAI	IX	BUF
DWORETZKI, WINCENTO	19	M	LABR	RRAI	IX	BUF
WITTKOWSKI, J.	33	M	LABR	RRAI	IX	BUF
BUCHANOWSKI, P.	29	M	LABR	RRAI	IX	BUF
MESCHKINIS, JULIAN	25	M	LABR	RRAI	IX	BUF
BUCHANOWSKI, V.	18	M	LABR	RRAI	IX	BUF
JANOWITZ, T.	34	M	LABR	RRAI	IX	BUF
MISKINS, LAWRENTZ	24	M	LABR	RRAI	IX	BUF
RUDNER, MIHAL	25	M	DLR	RRAI	IX	BUF
GOLDE	25	F	W	RRAI	IX	BUF
RUDZINSKI, JAN	19	M	UNKNOWN	RRAI	IX	BUF
SUEMPER, BENZE	30	M	DLR	RRAI	IX	BUF
JACOB	9	M	CHILD	RRAI	IX	BUF
RUZANSKI, SCH.	25	M	DLR	RRAI	IX	BUF
WASZKIEWICZ, JAN	22	M	LABR	RRAI	IX	BUF
DINOWICZ, GUTE	21	F	WO	RRAI	IX	BUF
WALDER, VICTOR	23	M	LABR	RRAI	IX	BUF
STOCKSCHEER, MOSES	19	M	LABR	RRAI	IX	BUF
PINCZUK, ITZKO	15	M	LABR	RRAI	IX	BUF
SPIELBERG, ASRIEL	18	M	LABR	RRAI	IX	BUF
BALINKA, ANTON	18	M	LABR	RRAI	IX	BUF
RUBIN, BARUCH	23	M	DLR	RRAI	IX	BUF
JASMANOWICZ, S.	22	M	LABR	RRAI	IX	BUF
POTOLENACZ, V.	28	M	LABR	RRAI	IX	NY
SIKUCZ, ANTONI	28	M	LABR	RRAI	IX	NY
KAROLONATZ, CASIMIR	28	M	LABR	RRAI	IX	NY
PIETROSKEWICZ, PAWEL	23	M	LABR	RRAI	IX	NY
GLASS, ISAAC	26	M	LABR	RRAI	IX	NY
WOLFERT, SELIG	20	M	LABR	RRAI	IX	NY
KLODKOWSKI, V.	25	M	LABR	RRAI	IX	NY
MONTIWITZ, HIPPOLIT	35	M	LABR	RRAI	IX	NY
SCHLOMOWITZ, ITZIG	42	M	DLR	RRAI	IX	NY
RACHEL	15	F	SGL	RRAI	IX	NY
BROSGE, SCHMUL	17	M	DLR	RRAI	IX	NY
LOSER, HERSCH	36	M	DLR	RRAI	IX	NY
KANTOWSKI, DOMINIK	19	M	LABR	RRAI	IX	NY
GOLDGAS, LEON	23	M	LABR	RRAI	IX	NY
LODZINSKI, JOSEF	18	M	LABR	RRAI	IX	NY
RAPFELS, PHILIPAS	23	M	LABR	RRAI	IX	NY
NASKIWICZ, DOMONIK	28	M	LABR	RRAI	IX	NY
ALEGANOW, PATZUS	18	M	LABR	RRAI	IX	NY
PAWLANTZKI, CASIMIR	36	M	LABR	RRAI	IX	NY
MEJOSCHUS, PETER	27	M	LABR	RRAI	IX	NY
DOMBROWSKI, ANTONIE	30	F	SGL	RRAI	IX	NY
KEMAR, MATHES	37	M	LABR	RRAI	IX	NY
ULGINSKY, MARIE	35	F	WO	RRAI	IX	NY
VINCENZ	9	M	CHILD	RRAI	IX	NY
MARTHA	7	F	CHILD	RRAI	IX	NY
EVA	3	F	CHILD	RRAI	IX	NY
CUSEROW, KATI	18	F	SGL	RRAI	IX	NY
ULCZINSKI, JAN	31	M	LABR	RRAI	IX	NY
SCHWARZBACH, CHAIM	9	M	CHILD	RRAI	IX	NY
WISNIENOSKY, M.	44	M	SMH	RRAI	IX	NY
REBARTZIK, JOSEF	25	M	SMH	RRAI	IX	NY
KISZINSKI, JOSEF	27	M	SMH	RRAI	IX	NY
RUCHKIAVICZ, JACOB	23	M	SMH	RRAI	IX	NY
LUEDKE, FRIEDR.	26	M	SMH	RRAI	IX	NY
MALOTZKI, NICOLAI	47	M	SMH	RRAI	IX	NY
MARKOWKSKI, JOSEF	23	M	SHMK	RRAI	IX	NY
RASCHKOWSKI, ALEX	30	M	LABR	RRAI	IX	NY
LUKASCHWITZ, STANISLAUS	26	F	LABR	RRAI	JR	NY
FRESS, GEORG	41	M	LABR	RRAI	JR	PHI
CISZ, GEORG	27	M	LABR	RRAI	JR	PHI
DOMAGOLSKI, MARIANNA	21	F	LDY	RRAI	JR	NY
ZIMANSKI, H.	19	M	LABR	RRAI	JR	NY
LINTNEV, LOUISE	28	F	WO	RRAI	JR	NY
GUSTAV	.11	M	INFANT	RRAI	JR	NY
ZILINSKI, SENDZE	23	M	LABR	RRAI	JR	NY
JAN	16	M	LABR	RRAI	JR	NY
PAVLOWSKI, JENDZE	23	M	LABR	RRAI	JR	NY
BE--MBUCH, DIETRICH	16	M	LABR	RRAI	JR	NY
OHRT, PETER	26	M	FARMER	RRAI	JR	CH
META	49	F	WO	RRAI	JR	CH
MARGR.	9	F	CHILD	RRAI	JR	CH
ROGACKI, F.	20	M	LABR	RRAI	JR	NY
STADING, CARL	33	M	FARMER	RRAI	JR	BUF
DOROTHEA	29	F	W	RRAI	JR	BUF
WILHELM	9	M	CHILD	RRAI	JR	BUF
PAULINE	7	M	CHILD	RRAI	JR	BUF
DOROTHEA	6	M	CHILD	RRAI	JR	BUF
MARIE	3	F	CHILD	RRAI	JR	BUF
LIDIA	2	F	CHILD	RRAI	JR	BUF
MATHILDE	.04	F	INFANT	RRAI	JR	BUF

SHIP: SUEVIA

FROM: HAMBURG AND HAVRE
TO: NEW YORK
ARRIVED: 14 MAY 1888

PASSENGER	AGE	SEX	OCCUPATION	PRIV	VIL	DES
MELZER, HIRCH	16	M	LABR	RRAH	VQ	USA
KLIMAWICZAWA, MARIANNE	25	F	W	RRZZ	ZZ	USA
SIMON	6	M	CHILD	RRZZ	ZZ	USA
JOSEPH	3	M	CHILD	RRZZ	ZZ	USA
NEUMARK, ISAAK	21	M	MCHT	RRAH	UI	USA
SCHUSTERMANN, SIEDE	38	M	LABR	RRZZ	ZZ	USA
NOVAKOWSKY, JAN	37	M	LABR	RRZZ	ZZ	USA
PETRONELLA	30	F	W	RRZZ	ZZ	USA
URSULA	8	F	CHILD	RRZZ	ZZ	USA
JAN	5	M	CHILD	RRZZ	ZZ	USA
FRANCISKA	4	F	CHILD	RRZZ	ZZ	USA
MICHAEL	2	M	CHILD	RRZZ	ZZ	USA

PASSENGER	AGE	SEX	OCCUPATION	PRV VIL DES
MICHAEL	00	M	INF	RRZZZZUSA
HURWITZ, MEYER	27	M	TDR	RRZZZZUSA
WALISCHOFSKY, JOSEF	28	M	LABR	RRZZZZUSA
BAROWIK, JOS	40	M	SHMK	RRAILZUSA
HIRSCHOWITZ, CHAIM	30	M	TDR	RRAIINUSA
LIDWINOWSKY, ISAAK	20	M	TLR	RRZZZZUSA
JALKUT, SALOMON	44	M	TLR	RRZZZZUSA
LATZNITZKI, ESTER	8	F	CHILD	RRZZZZUSA
ROSENBLUM, BEILE	24	F	W	RRZZZZUSA
CICIE	8	F	CHILD	RRZZZZUSA
WOLPERT, MOSES	38	M	LABR	RRZZZZUSA
PAUL, LISETTE	48	F	W	RRZZZZUSA
CAROLINE	16	F	D	RRZZZZUSA
PISKA, WAWIZIN	23	M	LABR	RRZZZZUSA
MICHALIK, IGNATZ	40	M	LABR	RRZZZZUSA
ZERBINOWSKY, RICH	23	M	LABR	RRZZZZUSA
DOMAGALSKI, FRANZ	23	M	LABR	RRZZZZUSA
ZABORSKI, JOSEF	34	M	LABR	RRZZZZUSA
DOMBROWSKY, LEON	34	M	LABR	RRZZZZUSA
JENDRZEWSKY, IGNATZ	20	M	LABR	RRZZZZUSA
GOLDENBERG, HERSCH	32	M	LABR	RRZZZZUSA
SILBERBLATT, ANNA	28	F	WO	RRZZZZUSA
PRIVA	9	F	CHILD	RRZZZZUSA
JANIO	7	M	CHILD	RRZZZZUSA
HELENE	4	F	CHILD	RRZZZZUSA
ETA	3	F	CHILD	RRZZZZUSA
BOAS	.11	U	INFANT	RRZZZZUSA
WISCHEWSKY, ANNE	32	F	SGL	RRZZZZUSA
SUSZYNSKI, JOSEF	16	M	LABR	RRZZZZUSA
PREITEL, GEDALIE	21	M	TLR	RRAHUIUSA
GUSTINSKY, ISIDOR	30	M	UNKNOWN	RRAIFSUSA
ARKIN, JOSEF	17	M	DLR	RRZZZZUSA
ISRAEL	9	M	CHILD	RRZZZZUSA
MINNESMANN, HIRSCH	55	M	LABR	RRAHWMUSA
EISENSTADT, WOLF	29	M	LABR	RRAHVUUSA
SL-TKI, FEIBUSCH	18	M	TLR	RRZZZZUSA
GODLEWSKI, ANTON	35	M	LABR	RRZZZZUSA
RAUS, STANISL	25	M	LABR	RRZZZZUSA
MURAWSKY, JOSEF	29	M	LABR	RRZZZZUSA
WASSOLOWSKY, JAN	40	M	LABR	RRAHUIUSA
MICOLAITSCHICK, JOSEF	20	M	LABR	RRAHUIUSA
MICHAEL	30	M	LABR	RRAHUIUSA
LEBOWITZ, ANTON	50	M	LABR	RRZZZZUSA
ALEXANDER	26	M	LABR	RRZZZZUSA
ANDERSEN, ANDERS	35	M	LABR	RRZZZZUSA
MATTHSON, MADS	34	M	LABR	RRZZZZUSA
HENRIKSON, JOH	34	M	LABR	RRZZZZUSA
HANSSON, MADS	34	M	LABR	RRZZZZUSA
JOHANSSON, MADS	35	M	LABR	RRZZZZUSA
BALKIN, RUBIN	16	M	TLR	RRZZZZUSA
KLEIN, MALI	16	F	SGL	RRZZZZUSA
MARIAM, CHAMME	55	F	WO	RRAIBOUSA
LATKEWICZ, SARAH	25	F	WO	RRAIBOUSA
JANKOWSKY, IGNATZ	22	M	LABR	RRZZZZUSA
WILMIWICZ, ANDRZY	30	M	LABR	RRZZZZUSA
-ZMISCHEWCTZKI, MOSES	30	M	LABR	RRZZZZUSA
GEITTEL	25	F	W	RRZZZZUSA
MORDCHE	.11	F	INFANT	RRZZZZUSA
ZELINSKY, JOSEF	21	M	LABR	RRZZZZUSA
ROSALIE	17	F	SGL	RRZZZZUSA
WEINBAUM, HERSCH	32	M	LABR	RRZZZZUSA
ABBELIN, GITTEL	21	F	WO	RRAIGJUSA
FELSCHNITZ, SOSSEL	40	M	TDR	RRAILRUSA
MINDSTECK, JACOB	28	M	TDR	RRZZZZUSA
SANTOR, ZINE	22	F	W	RRZZZZUSA
LINE	00	F	INF	RRZZZZUSA
RAKOWSKY, PERLE	17	F	WO	RRZZZZUSA
INSCHEROWSKI, STANISL	24	M	LABR	RRAICSUSA
KOCHANSKI, WOJCECH	37	M	LABR	RRAICSUSA
ROWALSKI, JOS	34	M	LABR	RRAHUIUSA
OLSCHEFSKI, IGNATZ	22	M	LABR	RRAICVUSA
HOLST, LUDWIG	34	M	LABR	RRZZZZUSA
ROGALSKI, ERNST	23	M	LABR	RRZZZZUSA
DIALKOW, ANNA	30	F	SGL	RRZZZZUSA
RAGOOIN, CHAJKEL	30	M	LABR	RRZZZZUSA

PASSENGER	AGE	SEX	OCCUPATION	PRV VIL DES
JASKUNER, MICHELE	48	F	SGL	RRZZZZUSA
SI-G, MARIE	20	F	SGL	RRZZZZUSA
KRAUSE, CAROLE	14	F	SGL	RRZZZZUSA
ITZBRANDT, ANNA	28	F	WO	RRZZZZUSA
MAREL	24	M	B	RRZZZZUSA
HELENE	.06	F	INFANT	RRZZZZUSA
DANIELEWICZ, JOSEF	35	M	LABR	RRAHUIUSA
SCHULMANN, HIRSCH	36	M	TNM	RRZZZZUSA
SCHENIN, LEIB	30	M	CGRTW	RRAHTUUSA
KLEINSBACH, ABRAHAM	28	M	LABR	RRAHYWUSA
---EINE	30	F	W	RRAHYWUSA
KATZ, LEA	9	F	CHILD	RRAHYWUSA
BINIMOWITZ, MOSES	9	M	CHILD	RRAHYWUSA
LINKOWITZ, FELIX	23	M	LABR	RRZZZZUSA
MARGOLIS, RIEPKE	30	M	LABR	RRZZZZUSA
JENNIE	36	F	W	RRZZZZUSA
SARA	9	F	CHILD	RRZZZZUSA
SATKEMANN, MENACHE	38	M	LABR	RRZZZZUSA
SINGMANN, ISRAEL	35	M	LABR	RRZZZZUSA
ZINKAWECKI, ISRAEL	39	M	LABR	RRZZZZUSA
CHUDESZ, JANKEL	45	M	LABR	RRZZZZUSA
SC-MEIDER, ASRIEL	44	M	LABR	RRZZZZUSA
LEA	42	F	W	RRZZZZUSA
SALOMON	9	M	CHILD	RRZZZZUSA
SEIGE	5	F	CHILD	RRZZZZUSA
SARA	3	F	CHILD	RRZZZZUSA
RIDKE	.09	F	INFANT	RRZZZZUSA
SPINEL, MOSES	24	M	LABR	RRZZZZUSA
GALINSKI, STANISLAUS	29	M	LABR	RRZZZZUSA
MINZ, FRANZ	26	M	LABR	RRZZZZUSA
STRIENGOWSKY, ANTONI	23	M	LABR	RRZZZZUSA
SCHUCHMANN, REBECCA	32	F	WO	RRZZZZUSA
RIWKE	9	F	CHILD	RRZZZZUSA
--OENE	8	F	CHILD	RRZZZZUSA
-EIGE	6	M	CHILD	RRZZZZUSA
REUBEN	5	M	CHILD	RRZZZZUSA
ITZIG	3	M	CHILD	RRZZZZUSA
GOLDE	.11	F	INFANT	RRZZZZUSA
ZIRKE	.01	F	INFANT	RRZZZZUSA
HERZENSOHN, MOSES	37	M	LABR	RRZZZZUSA
BEILE	34	F	W	RRZZZZUSA
SARA	9	F	CHILD	RRZZZZUSA
SALOMON	8	M	CHILD	RRZZZZUSA
MOUSZIEWICZ, FRANZISKA	34	F	WO	RRADIMUSA
JULIAN	5	F	CHILD	RRADIMUSA
GABR	3	F	CHILD	RRADIMUSA
TEOFILA	.11	F	INFANT	RRADIMUSA

SHIP: CIRCASSIA

FROM: GLASGOW AND MOVILLE
TO: NEW YORK
ARRIVED: 15 MAY 1888

PASSENGER	AGE	SEX	OCCUPATION	PRV VIL DES
BOMKOWSKI, EFRAIM	32	M	LABR	RRAIDLUSA
MEREAZSKI, FRANZ	40	M	LABR	RRAIDLUSA
MILLNER, BORACH	20	M	MLR	RRAIDLUSA
JANKELOWITZ, MOSES	26	M	JNR	RRAIDLUSA
KRIS-T-TZKY, ITZIE	32	M	DLR	RRAIDLUSA
SCHAFSKOFT, WOLF	20	M	MSN	RRAIDLUSA
ZIMM, HIRCH	17	M	TLR	RRAIDLUSA
KATZ, JOSEF	39	M	PNTR	RRAIDLUSA
SILBERSTEIN, CHAM	30	M	DLR	RRAIDLUSA
MICHLIAWIZ, JAKOB	12	M	DLR	RRAIDLUSA
LEVY, LEON	43	M	TLR	RRAIDLUSA
ZAGET, ERV	18	M	WCHMKR	RRAIDLUSA
KAPLAN, S	22	M	WCHMKR	RRAIDLUSA
KARLOWSKI, FRANZ	23	M	LABR	RRAIDLUSA
DONESCHEWSKI, ALBR	17	M	TU	RRAIDLUSA
SWIERZYNSKI, ANT	32	M	JNR	RRAIDLUSA

PASSENGER	AGE	SEX	OCCUPATION	PRV	VIL	DES
LEWIN, LIEB	18	M	GZR	RR	AIDL	USA
KOLOWSKI, JOSEF	24	M	LABR	RR	AIDL	USA
SAKHEIM, HEZ	17	M	DLR	RR	AIDL	USA
LIPMICKE, L-SER	17	M	DLR	RR	AIDL	USA
SCHABSAG, MICH	23	M	SMH	RR	AIDL	USA
OCHSENHORN, ABR	23	M	TLR	RR	AIDL	USA
MEDNICK, HERRS	32	M	TLR	RR	AIDL	USA
SACHS, ISRAEL	33	M	LABR	RR	AIDL	USA
GARIDSEN, WOLF	11	M	CH	RR	AIDL	USA
OCHSENSTEIN, M-GER	46	M	TLR	RR	AIDL	USA
KAPLAN, J	32	M	TLR	RR	AIDL	USA
CHAIM, ABR	20	M	DLR	RR	AIDL	USA
KUSCHMITZKY, CASIMO	28	M	LABR	RR	AIDL	USA
ISAKSOHN, MENDEL	16	M	LABR	RR	AIDL	USA
SINGER, -IPE	18	M	LABR	RR	AIDL	USA
GUTMAN, JANKEL	31	M	DLR	RR	AIDL	USA
STINBARK, ISRAEL	28	M	TU	RR	AIDL	USA
KUKISS, MODCHE	25	M	JNR	RR	AIDL	USA
PERNIK, ITZIG	24	M	JNR	RR	AIDL	USA
-OVE	18	M	JNR	RR	AIDL	USA
HOFFMANN, MORDUCH	29	M	FSHMN	RR	AIDL	USA
ROSENZWEIG, CHAIM	17	M	LABR	RR	AIDL	USA
KATZKOWSKI, CHAIM	20	M	BKR	RR	AIDL	USA
HOFFMANN, BORUK	17	M	LABR	RR	AIDL	USA
RASEKEWITZ, IVAN	22	M	SHMK	RR	AIDL	USA
KALMOWSKY, JAN	30	M	LABR	RR	AIDL	USA
KLEIN, ABR	26	M	PDLR	RR	AIDL	USA
KEVITKOWSKY, PETER	22	M	PDLR	RR	AIDL	USA
SKEAT, ELIAS	34	M	PDLR	RR	AIDL	USA
RUBIN, MODUCH	47	M	TLR	RR	AIDL	USA
BARWI--Z, JONAS	31	M	TLR	RR	AIDL	USA
CHA-T, CHONE	17	M	WCHMKR	RR	AIDL	USA
ARKIN, HERCHE	18	M	TLR	RR	AIDL	USA
FRADEL	20	M	TLR	RR	AIDL	USA
MANDELS, H	29	M	LABR	RR	AIDL	USA
MAZNEWS--, ANT	19	M	TLR	RR	AIDL	USA
RUDZIEWIZ, IGNATZ	31	M	LABR	RR	AIDL	USA
GOZAMEWSKI, KASSIMER	27	M	LABR	RR	AIDL	USA
MAKOWSKI, STANSL	23	M	LABR	RR	AIDL	USA
MALASCHURTZ, MARTIN	19	M	LABR	RR	AIDL	USA
ONUSZEK, MARYANE	24	F	HP	RR	AIDL	USA
KOSLOWSKY, VICTORIA	29	F	HP	RR	AIDL	USA
KROSKEMOWSKY, LIEBE	18	F	HP	RR	AIDL	USA
LIEBE	19	F	HP	RR	AIDL	USA
NALYWOTZKI, ROCHEL	20	M	TLR	RR	AIDL	USA
BARAN, CHAIE	19	F	HP	RR	AIDL	USA
TARBER, MERE	24	F	W	RR	AIDL	USA
M-CHE	2	F	CHILD	RR	AIDL	USA
DANOWICE, SARAH	26	F	W	RR	AIDL	USA
ISAK	2	M	CHILD	RR	AIDL	USA
GREZESKOWISK, M	28	M	LABR	RR	AIDL	USA
JOSEFA	25	F	W	RR	AIDL	USA
STEPHANA	16	F	HP	RR	AIDL	USA
URBANOWSKI, ANT	27	M	LABR	RR	AIDL	USA
MCHE	22	F	W	RR	AIDL	USA
S-ANA	.06	F	INFANT	RR	AIDL	USA
GAWRISZEWSKI, FRANZ	30	M	LABR	RR	AIDL	USA
FRANZA	28	F	W	RR	AIDL	USA
MARGTA	2	F	CHILD	RR	AIDL	USA
VERONIKA	.09	F	INFANT	RR	AIDL	USA
DR-Z-WINSKI, PELAGIA	18	F	W	RR	AIDL	USA
ALPERT, PERLE	35	F	W	RR	AIDL	USA
CHAIM	11	M	CH	RR	AIDL	USA
JOSSEL	8	M	CHILD	RR	AIDL	USA
LEIE	4	F	CHILD	RR	AIDL	USA
SIMKE	2	F	CHILD	RR	AIDL	USA
MENTLEWSKA, FRANCA	24	F	W	RR	AIDL	USA
MARY	4	F	CHILD	RR	AIDL	USA
VICTORIA	2	F	CHILD	RR	AIDL	USA
STANSA	3	F	CHILD	RR	AIDL	USA
CATH	.09	F	INFANT	RR	AIDL	USA
HELFANT, ALBE	50	F	W	RR	AIDL	USA
-EME	17	F	HP	RR	AIDL	USA
GAWOISZEWSKI, IGNATZ	23	M	LABR	RR	AIDL	USA

SHIP: HUNGARIA

FROM: HAMBURG
TO: NEW YORK
ARRIVED: 15 MAY 1888

PASSENGER	AGE	SEX	OCCUPATION	PRV	VIL	DES
KATZERGUNSKY, DWORE	40	F	WO	RR	ZZZZ	USA
GOLDSTEIN, SARAH	37	F	W	RR	ZZZZ	USA
JOSEF	9	M	CHILD	RR	ZZZZ	USA
WOLF	8	M	CHILD	RR	ZZZZ	USA
HAFF, ABRAHAM	50	M	LABR	RR	ZZZZ	USA
GOLDSTEIN, SCHEINE	7	F	CHILD	RR	ZZZZ	USA
BLEKICKI, ADOLF	23	M	LABR	RR	ZZZZ	USA
KROLL, LEIBUSCH	63	M	TCHR	RR	ZZZZ	USA
DOBIS, MARIE	20	F	SGL	RR	ZZZZ	USA
ZIMMERMANN, LEISER	30	M	LABR	RR	ZZZZ	USA
ROBINOWICZ, RUBIN	23	M	LABR	RR	ZZZZ	USA
-ELE	22	F	W	RR	ZZZZ	USA
GEMBOR, MASER	38	M	TLR	RR	ZZZZ	USA
MISNKIEWICZ, JAN	21	M	LABR	RR	ZZZZ	USA
BARTNIKOWSKY, PAUL	31	M	LABR	RR	ZZZZ	USA
MOLSCHASKI, JOHN	30	M	LABR	RR	ZZZZ	USA
NEUMANN, CARL	15	M	LABR	RR	ZZZZ	USA
DZULEWSKY, JAN	36	M	LABR	RR	ZZZZ	USA
THOMASZEWSKI, JANOS	46	M	LABR	RR	ZZZZ	USA
STEMCZINSKI, JOSEF	27	M	LABR	RR	ZZZZ	USA
POLENOWSKI, JOHANN	32	M	LABR	RR	ZZZZ	USA
FULKOWSKI, THOMAS	28	M	LABR	RR	ZZZZ	USA
GROSZKOWSKI, MICHAL	43	M	LABR	RR	ZZZZ	USA
POLENOWSKI, PAUL	27	M	LABR	RR	ZZZZ	USA
BUDZYNSKI, FRANTISZEK	34	M	LABR	RR	ZZZZ	USA
LINOWSKI, MARIAN	27	M	LABR	RR	ZZZZ	USA
STASEWITZ, MICHAL	33	M	FARMER	RR	ZZZZ	USA
ADAMINA	23	F	W	RR	ZZZZ	USA
STANISLAWA	3	F	CHILD	RR	ZZZZ	USA
VINCENTY	.03	M	INFANT	RR	ZZZZ	USA
ZETELNY, ANTON	30	M	FARMER	RR	ZZZZ	USA
CATHA	23	F	W	RR	ZZZZ	USA
VICTORIA	8	F	CHILD	RR	ZZZZ	USA
JOSEF	.11	M	INFANT	RR	ZZZZ	USA
FRICARICH, GOTTLIEB	40	M	LABR	RR	ZZZZ	USA
RAITER, FRIEDRICH	40	M	LABR	RR	ZZZZ	USA
BARTNIKOWSKA, AGNES	27	F	WO	RR	ZZZZ	USA
HELENE	.11	F	INFANT	RR	ZZZZ	USA
SAFCROWITZ, LEA	21	F	WO	RR	ZZZZ	USA
SARA	.11	F	INFANT	RR	ZZZZ	USA
MAROSS, MAREIN	32	M	LABR	RR	ZZZZ	USA
FRIEDLAENDER, JACOB	32	M	DLR	RR	ZZZZ	USA
MARE	23	F	W	RR	ZZZZ	USA
KUROWSKY, JAN	25	M	LABR	RR	ZZZZ	USA
LEWIN, ARON	18	M	LABR	RR	ZZZZ	USA
PUMPSTEIN, HERSCH	24	M	LABR	RR	ZZZZ	USA
SZADOWSKY, JAN	47	M	LABR	RR	ZZZZ	USA
LUKOWSKY, LEON	25	M	LABR	RR	ZZZZ	USA
LENG-ANSKI, STANISL	22	M	LABR	RR	ZZZZ	USA
BA-ER, SCHAJE	42	M	LABR	RR	ZZZZ	USA
KASELEWITZ, ALEX	33	M	LABR	RR	ZZZZ	USA
-AYTOWSKI, JULIUS	48	M	LABR	RR	ZZZZ	USA
JOSEF	44	M	LABR	RR	ZZZZ	USA
WREZINSKY, JAN	34	M	LABR	RR	ZZZZ	USA
CHIZEWSKY, WLADISLAV	38	M	LABR	RR	ZZZZ	USA
SZODOWSKY, MARIANNE	24	F	SGL	RR	ZZZZ	USA
DUSCHAK, CHLAWNE	28	M	LABR	RR	ZZZZ	USA
GINSBURG, LEIB	18	M	LABR	RR	ZZZZ	USA
SCHEIKER, ISAAC	20	M	LABR	RR	ZZZZ	USA
ROGOWIN, HIRSCH	25	M	LABR	RR	ZZZZ	USA
CZEWITZ, MARCIN	23	M	LABR	RR	ZZZZ	USA
KUZANOWSKY, CASIMIR	25	M	LABR	RR	ZZZZ	USA
-EINBLUM, JACOB	29	M	LABR	RR	ZZZZ	USA
WINKELMANN, SALOMON	20	M	LABR	RR	ZZZZ	USA
CHARMANES, BEILE	18	F	SGL	RR	ZZZZ	USA
GARNIK, MEYER	34	M	LABR	RR	ZZZZ	USA
PALONSKY, REWKE	32	F	W	RR	ZZZZ	USA
RIWA	9	F	CHILD	RR	ZZZZ	USA

PASSENGER	AGE	SEX	OCCUPATION	PRI VIL	DES
BERDINA	8	F	CHILD	RRZZZZ	USA
ABRAM	6	M	CHILD	RRZZZZ	USA
DINA	.09	F	INFANT	RRZZZZ	USA
RAFFE, ISAAC	23	M	DRG	RRZZZZ	USA
OWSCHINOWICZ, HIRSCH	38	M	TDR	RRZZZZ	USA
MALER, SCHMUL	18	M	TDR	RRZZZZ	USA
JAWERWITZ, JOSEF	20	M	TLR	RRZZZZ	USA
MEZEIKO, MICHAL	27	M	LABR	RRZZZZ	USA
STNEITIS, VINZENTY	45	M	LABR	RRZZZZ	USA
EVA	40	F	W	RRZZZZ	USA
MAGDA	8	F	CHILD	RRZZZZ	USA
ANDRAS	35	M	LABR	RRZZZZ	USA
ANDREAS	3	M	CHILD	RRZZZZ	USA
VINCENTY	.09	M	INFANT	RRZZZZ	USA
NANARTOWITSCH, ADAM	23	M	LABR	RRZZZZ	USA
SARTANAWITSCH, VINCENTY	26	M	LABR	RRZZZZ	USA
SAMATOWITSCH, JACOB	30	M	LABR	RRZZZZ	USA
TOMAZEWSKI, CONSTANTIN	23	M	LABR	RRZZZZ	USA
WISNEWSKY, FRANZ	40	M	LABR	RRZZZZ	USA
OLSCHEWSKY, IGNATZ	30	M	LABR	RRZZZZ	USA
WJIKOWSKA, MARIANNA	22	M	LABR	RRZZZZ	USA
BLUM, JACOB	30	M	LABR	RRZZZZ	USA
PUCETA, VINCENTY	26	M	LABR	RRZZZZ	USA
BRAUN, HEINR	29	M	LABR	RRZZZZ	USA
WOZAK, JOSEF	33	M	LABR	RRZZZZ	USA
JANKOWSKY, ANDRE	33	M	LABR	RRZZZZ	USA
AGNISKA	27	F	W	RRZZZZ	USA
FRANZ	4	M	CHILD	RRZZZZ	USA
JOSEF	3	M	CHILD	RRZZZZ	USA
JADWIGA	.10	F	INFANT	RRZZZZ	USA
WEDZIOFSKY, JOS	44	M	LABR	RRZZZZ	USA
KALISKY, MATHIAS	50	M	LABR	RRZZZZ	USA
MALIZEWZKY, JAN	30	M	LABR	RRZZZZ	USA
STRAGIS, MIKAS	21	M	LABR	RRZZZZ	USA
KASZALA, PETER	18	M	LABR	RRZZZZ	USA
BILLMAS, JACOB	23	M	LABR	RRZZZZ	USA
ZESTER, FRANZ	31	M	LABR	RRZZZZ	USA
SCHERR, BARUCH	26	M	LABR	RRZZZZ	USA
MOSES	34	M	LABR	RRZZZZ	USA
KASCHELJANIS, WIEBKE	22	F	WO	RRZZZZ	USA
DEMSKI, VICTOR	35	M	BCHR	RRZZZZ	USA
DUSCHINSKY, JACOB	27	M	LABR	RRZZZZ	USA
NAWRINSK, JAN	35	M	LABR	RRZZZZ	USA
APPEL, JOHS	46	M	FARMER	RRZZZZ	USA
LOUISE	42	F	W	RRZZZZ	USA
LEOPOLD	16	M	CH	RRZZZZ	USA
ROSALIA	8	F	CHILD	RRZZZZ	USA
EUGEN	7	M	CHILD	RRZZZZ	USA
MARIE	5	F	CHILD	RRZZZZ	USA
OSWALD	3	M	CHILD	RRZZZZ	USA
JOHANNES	.09	M	INFANT	RRZZZZ	USA
FUCHS, GEORG	32	M	FARMER	RRZZZZ	USA
SOFIA	32	F	W	RRZZZZ	USA
MARIA	8	F	CHILD	RRZZZZ	USA
HEINR	4	M	CHILD	RRZZZZ	USA
JOHANNES	.09	M	INFANT	RRZZZZ	USA
PTAFFENROTH, PETER	24	M	FARMER	RRZZZZ	USA
CATHA	24	F	W	RRZZZZ	USA
CATHA	3	F	CHILD	RRZZZZ	USA
MARIA	.10	F	INFANT	RRZZZZ	USA
LUFT, CONRAD	27	M	FARMER	RRZZZZ	USA
ANNA	20	F	W	RRZZZZ	USA
ANNA	.09	F	INFANT	RRZZZZ	USA
SCHMUECK, ADAM	19	M	FARMER	RRZZZZ	USA
SCHMIK, JOHANNES	32	M	FARMER	RRZZZZ	USA
MARIE	26	F	W	RRZZZZ	USA
ELISABETH	4	F	CHILD	RRZZZZ	USA
ADAM	2	M	CHILD	RRZZZZ	USA
HEINR	00	M	INF	RRZZZZ	USA
LANGLITZ, CONRAD	36	M	FARMER	RRZZZZ	USA
SCHENERMANN, HEINRICH	34	M	FARMER	RRZZZZ	USA
MARIE	34	F	W	RRZZZZ	USA
CATHA	3	F	CHILD	RRZZZZ	USA
HEINR	7	M	CHILD	RRZZZZ	USA
ELISABETH	6	F	CHILD	RRZZZZ	USA

PASSENGER	AGE	SEX	OCCUPATION	PRI VIL	DES
MARIA	4	F	CHILD	RRZZZZ	USA
JULIA	2	F	CHILD	RRZZZZ	USA
SCHEUERMANN, ADAM	38	M	FARMER	RRZZZZ	USA
MARIA	36	F	W	RRZZZZ	USA
MARIA	18	F	CH	RRZZZZ	USA
JOHANNES	16	M	CH	RRZZZZ	USA
MARIE	8	F	CHILD	RRZZZZ	USA
MARIANNE	4	F	CHILD	RRZZZZ	USA
HEINRICH	.09	M	INFANT	RRZZZZ	USA
LUFT, HEINRICH	19	M	FARMER	RRZZZZ	USA
MARGARETHE	19	F	W	RRZZZZ	USA
RABINER, JANKEL	25	M	LABR	RRZZZZ	USA
GOLDBERG, HIRCH	20	M	LABR	RRZZZZ	USA
BARTNIKOWSKI, PAUL	39	M	LABR	RRZZZZ	USA
MEISTER, LEIB	30	M	LABR	RRZZZZ	USA
RABINOWITZ, JANKEL	33	M	LABR	RRZZZZ	USA

SHIP: EIDER

FROM: BREMEN AND SOUTHAMPTON
TO: NEW YORK
ARRIVED: 16 MAY 1888

PASSENGER	AGE	SEX	OCCUPATION	PRI VIL	DES
BAEHR, EDUARD	35	M	NN	RRZZZZ	RSS
HARRID	33	F	W	RRZZZZ	RSS
ALFRED	13	M	NN	RRZZZZ	RSS
HARRIED	11	F	CH	RRZZZZ	RSS
HERMANN	10	M	CH	RRZZZZ	RSS
SZPAKOFSKI, STANISLAW	27	M	LABR	RRZZZZ	USA
PIETRONELA	26	F	W	RRZZZZ	USA
RUBINSON, HERSCH	18	M	CNF	RRZZZZ	USA
ORELOWITZ, ARON	50	M	MCHT	RRZZZZ	USA
MALKE	45	F	W	RRZZZZ	USA
MASCHEL	12	F	CH	RRZZZZ	USA
RUSCHEL	8	F	CHILD	RRZZZZ	USA
SOBOLEWSKI, STANISLAUS	32	M	LABR	RRZZZZ	USA
MARTANSWITZ, JOZEFA	21	F	NN	RRZZZZ	USA
JOSEFA	.03	F	INFANT	RRZZZZ	USA
SZUKOWSKI, ALEXANDER	18	M	LABR	RRZZZZ	USA
ALEXANDROWICZ, VALERIE	19	F	NN	RRZZZZ	USA
KOSAKOWSKA, VERONICA	32	F	NN	RRZZZZ	USA
KASCHMIR	5	M	CHILD	RRZZZZ	USA
LOCADIA	.11	F	INFANT	RRZZZZ	USA
FALKOWSKI, JAN	24	M	LABR	RRZZZZ	USA
JASKULSKI, JOH.	22	M	LABR	RRZZZZ	USA
SCHATKOFSKI, ISIDOR	25	M	MCHT	RRZZZZ	USA
USALAK, STEFAN	48	M	LABR	RRZZZZ	USA
KLEPS, FRITZ	21	M	LABR	RRZZZZ	USA
NEUMANN, JETTA	29	F	NN	RRZZZZ	USA
DORA	11	F	CH	RRZZZZ	USA
ANNA	8	F	CHILD	RRZZZZ	USA
ABRAHAM	8	M	CHILD	RRZZZZ	USA
GUSTA	6	F	CHILD	RRZZZZ	USA
MORITZ	4	M	CHILD	RRZZZZ	USA
BLUME	2	F	CHILD	RRZZZZ	USA
COHN, PESCHE	23	F	NN	RRZZZZ	USA
NOCHEM	4	M	CHILD	RRZZZZ	USA
SALACKI, PEISACH	22	M	MCHT	RRZZZZ	USA
KUNE	18	F	W	RRZZZZ	USA
KUCZM---KI, ALEX	38	M	LABR	RRZZZZ	USA
JULIANE	28	F	W	RRZZZZ	USA
WARZAW	6	M	CHILD	RRZZZZ	USA
KASCHMIRO	.06	M	INFANT	RRZZZZ	USA
WYSKE, STANISLAUS	31	M	MNR	RRZZZZ	USA
SWOLINSKA, CATHARINE	20	F	SVNT	RRZZZZ	USA
JAN	.09	M	INFANT	RRZZZZ	USA
ROJANOWSKA, EVA	22	F	NN	RRZZZZ	USA
MARIE	.11	F	INFANT	RRZZZZ	USA
KLENOWSKI, FRANZ	33	M	LABR	RRZZZZ	USA
ABRAHAM, ROCHINA	49	F	NN	RRZZZZ	USA

PASSENGER	AGE	SEX	OCCUPATION	PRIVL	DES
GILDE	17	M	MCHT	RRZZZZ	USA
SPINAL	15	M	MCHT	RRZZZZ	USA
TEME	12	M	CH	RRZZZZ	USA
GITL	8	M	CHILD	RRZZZZ	USA
DAMRAZ, DAVID	42	M	LABR	RRZZZZ	USA
CARL	16	M	LABR	RRZZZZ	USA
KRAGENSTREIN, JACOB	36	M	LABR	RRZZZZ	USA
JAN	23	M	LABR	RRZZZZ	USA
THIEL, JOHANN	37	M	LABR	RRZZZZ	USA
LAUCKA, MICHEL	35	M	LABR	RRZZZZ	USA
MUELLER, GUSTAV	24	M	LABR	RRZZZZ	USA
WERNER, AUGUST	19	M	LABR	RRZZZZ	USA
MODERSKI, JOSEF	23	M	LABR	RRZZZZ	USA
PILERSKI, LEON	27	M	LABR	RRZZZZ	USA
HARTALEWITSCH, JOH.	28	M	LABR	RRZZZZ	USA
ERDREICH, SELLMANN	17	M	MCHT	RRZZZZ	USA
RUBIN, LEIB	45	M	MCHT	RRZZZZ	USA
KORNBLUM, MOSES	29	M	MCHT	RRZZZZ	USA
JACOBI, JULIUS	6	M	CHILD	RRZZZZ	USA
WITUHSKI, MICH.	31	M	LABR	RRZZZZ	USA
ZIELENSKI, MICH.	34	M	LABR	RRZZZZ	USA
KURZEWSKI, IGNACZ	18	M	LABR	RRZZZZ	USA
RADKOWSKI, JOS.	24	M	LABR	RRZZZZ	USA
WISNIEWSKI, JOS.	18	M	LABR	RRZZZZ	USA
WASNIEWSKI, JAS.	18	M	LABR	RRZZZZ	USA
STRASZEWSKI, MIKOLAJ	28	M	LABR	RRZZZZ	USA
KURZENSKI, JAN	22	M	LABR	RRZZZZ	USA
KAMNISSKY, FANCIZEH	26	M	LABR	RRZZZZ	USA
ZUCHOWSKY, JOSEF	18	M	LABR	RRZZZZ	USA
ROMANOWISKA, KATARZYNA	8	F	CHILD	RRZZZZ	USA
SARNOWSKY, IGNACY	19	M	LABR	RRZZZZ	USA
LOSCHEFSKY, ANTON	30	M	LABR	RRZZZZ	USA
U, U	25	M	LABR	RRZZZZ	USA
LOWOMOWITZ, MATWEI	24	M	LABR	RRZZZZ	USA
PORDANSTA, VICENTY	36	M	LABR	RRZZZZ	USA
MILANTZKES, MATZASCHES	38	M	LABR	RRZZZZ	USA
KORAHINAS, MATEWITZ	25	M	LABR	RRZZZZ	USA
ALOWETZKY, JAN	24	M	LABR	RRZZZZ	USA
MIZELISCH, JOSAS	26	M	LABR	RRZZZZ	USA
SOHATAS, MIKAS	38	M	LABR	RRZZZZ	USA
NEUKULIN, VICENTY	24	M	LABR	RRZZZZ	USA
JAKEMEWITZ, EUDRENS	20	M	LABR	RRZZZZ	USA
MAZULACHIS, TAUWSCHCHES	28	M	LABR	RRZZZZ	USA
KOLODJEWSKI, BRONISLAW	21	M	LABR	RRZZZZ	USA
CZENY, THOMAS	36	M	LABR	RRZZZZ	USA
ADAMOWIZ, FRANZ	25	M	LABR	RRZZZZ	USA
JANKIEWICZ, ANTON	28	M	LABR	RRZZZZ	USA
NIEDZGORSKI, LUDWIG	35	M	LABR	RRZZZZ	USA
PLUTS------, MARTIN	28	M	LABR	RRZZZZ	USA
MAJEWSKI, JOSEF	30	M	LABR	RRZZZZ	USA
KUMCIZKA, JOSEF	31	M	LABR	RRZZZZ	USA
PIETSCHAK, JAN	34	M	LABR	RRZZZZ	USA
KULAWINSKI, IGNATZ	30	M	LABR	RRZZZZ	USA
MASCHAHOWSKI, FRANZISEK	30	M	LABR	RRZZZZ	USA
ROSALIE	31	F	W	RRZZZZ	USA
REDMERSKY, JOSEF	6	M	CHILD	RRZZZZ	USA
CECILIA	4	F	CHILD	RRZZZZ	USA
CHRISTOFOWICZ, CONSTANT	7	M	CHILD	RRZZZZ	USA
SOBRITZKY, JACOB	26	M	LABR	RRZZZZ	USA
MIRWITZ, BERL	32	M	LABR	RRZZZZ	USA
KOHN, ABEL	19	M	LABR	RRZZZZ	USA
BARAWCZIG, SOLOMON	26	M	LABR	RRZZZZ	USA
KARZMA, JANKEL	26	M	LABR	RRZZZZ	USA
GUNZBURG, BENJAM.	30	M	LABR	RRZZZZ	USA
MULLERMANN, JACOB	36	M	LABR	RRZZZZ	USA
DOMBROWSKY, VICENTY	46	M	LABR	RRZZZZ	USA
BOLEWSKY, ANTONIE	32	F	NN	RRZZZZ	USA
RICHMANNSKY, KASIMIR	30	M	LABR	RRZZZZ	USA
DONLONGOWSKY, FRANZ	24	M	LABR	RRZZZZ	USA
JADWIGA	30	F	W	RRZZZZ	USA
LEON	3	M	CHILD	RRZZZZ	USA
ANTONIA	.09	F	INFANT	RRZZZZ	USA
MATUSCHEFSKY, JAN	22	M	LABR	RRZZZZ	USA
MARIANNE	21	F	W	RRZZZZ	USA
BARANOWSKY, BARTONI	26	M	LABR	RRZZZZ	USA

PASSENGER	AGE	SEX	OCCUPATION	PRIVL	DES
KRAJEWSKY, MARYAN	26	M	LABR	RRZZZZ	USA
U, U	22	F	W	RRZZZZ	USA
ZUBRICKI, ANTON	40	M	LABR	RRZZZZ	USA
KOLOSZEWSKI, KLEMENS	44	M	LABR	RRZZZZ	USA
SWIERZLINOWITZ, FRANZ	32	M	LABR	RRZZZZ	USA
KAMINSKI, KAROL.	35	M	LABR	RRZZZZ	USA
SOBOLEWSKI, FRANZ	21	M	LABR	RRZZZZ	USA
----CHWEWITZ, KASIMIR	23	M	LABR	RRZZZZ	USA
KOWALEWSKY, ANTON	30	M	LABR	RRZZZZ	USA
BERDCHNA, STANISLAUS	21	M	LABR	RRZZZZ	USA
SROKOS, KAZIS	33	M	LABR	RRZZZZ	USA
ZAKIEBMYS, SYLVESTER	20	M	LABR	RRZZZZ	USA
BARTSCHEWITZ, FRANZISEK	27	M	LABR	RRZZZZ	USA
WOLOW, JOSEF	23	M	LABR	RRZZZZ	USA
MANNSCHAK, ANDRZI	30	M	LABR	RRZZZZ	USA
STANISLAUS	2	F	CHILD	RRZZZZ	USA
WLADISLAW	.09	M	INFANT	RRZZZZ	USA
KIEZWICKI, CASIMIR	23	M	LABR	RRZZZZ	USA
AMUCZINSKY, PIOTR	33	M	LABR	RRZZZZ	USA
KAMINSKY, OSIP	27	M	LABR	RRZZZZ	USA
PICKUNES, KAZMIR	30	M	LABR	RRZZZZ	USA
BENCEWITZ, WOJSISCH	23	M	LABR	RRZZZZ	USA
KUKALIS, JAN	23	M	LABR	RRZZZZ	USA
STANKOWSKY, TEOFIL	30	M	LABR	RRZZZZ	USA
JAKUBINCZEK, ANTONI	25	M	LABR	RRZZZZ	USA
MAKOWSKY, ANTONI	8	M	CHILD	RRZZZZ	USA
KRASCHEWSKY, MARYANNE	13	F	NN	RRZZZZ	USA
MILNA	7	F	CHILD	RRZZZZ	USA
POLSKA, LIEBE	61	F	NN	RRZZZZ	USA
MENDEL	7	M	CHILD	RRZZZZ	USA
DOMALEWSKY, FRANZ	33	M	LABR	RRZZZZ	USA
POMETEWSKY, JOSEF	35	M	LABR	RRZZZZ	USA
BOBIN, MICHAEL	18	M	LABR	RRZZZZ	USA
ROLF, AUGUST	21	M	LABR	RRZZZZ	USA
EVA	25	F	W	RRZZZZ	USA
U, WLAD----	32	M	LABR	RRZZZZ	USA
SKUBISCH, ADOLF	31	M	LABR	RRZZZZ	USA
HOHL, ADOLF	34	M	LABR	RRZZZZ	USA
MOESSEN, COLUMBUS	00	M	INF	RR****	USA
KOEPKOW, HERMANN	19	M	LABR	RRZZZZ	USA
SEEPKOWSKY, JOSEF	35	M	LABR	RRZZZZ	USA
KOZLOWSKY, MAREI	8	M	CHILD	RRZZZZ	USA

SHIP: STATE OF NEVADA

FROM: LIVERPOOL AND QUEENSTOWN
TO: NEW YORK
ARRIVED: 16 MAY 1888

PASSENGER	AGE	SEX	OCCUPATION	PRIVL	DES
SCHECHTER, ISRAEL	35	M	LABR	RRZZZZ	USA
KOSSEWITSKI, BEREL	31	M	LABR	RRZZZZ	USA
GOLDBERG, BENJAMIN	18	M	LABR	RRZZZZ	USA
KALMOWSKI, MICHAEL	28	M	LABR	RRZZZZ	USA
ISAACSOHN, BAR	17	M	LABR	RRZZZZ	USA
EISIKOWIZ, SAM	17	M	LABR	RRZZZZ	USA
ISAACSOHN, MORITZ	20	M	LABR	RRZZZZ	USA
GOLD, MOSES	20	M	LABR	RRZZZZ	USA
LANESKY, JOHN	27	M	TLR	RRZZZZ	USA
MESONSINK, ISRAEL	45	M	TLR	RRZZZZ	USA
SUPOSITY, BERL	19	M	LABR	RRZZZZ	USA
SMOLENSKI, ZODEK	19	M	LABR	RRZZZZ	USA
COHN, DAVID	35	M	WCHMKR	RRZZZZ	USA
ELIAS, SOLOMON	27	M	LABR	RRZZZZ	USA
MALZOTZKI, ANNA	18	F	SP	RRZZZZ	USA
JANKOWSKI, CHAINNE	17	F	SP	RRZZZZ	USA
SCHLIOMOWITZ, BLUME	24	F	SP	RRZZZZ	USA
LETIA	15	F	SP	RRZZZZ	USA
JACOBSOHN, ZEIGEL	40	F	W	RRZZZZ	USA
COPE	7	F	CHILD	RRZZZZ	USA
MOSES	6	M	CHILD	RRZZZZ	USA

PASSENGER	AGE	SEX	OCCUPATION	PRV	VIL	DES
MAYAKOWITZ, BEILA	7	F	CHILD	RR	ZZZZ	USA
GOLDSCHMIDT, KARL	35	F	W	RR	ZZZZ	USA
HENR	6	F	CHILD	RR	ZZZZ	USA
KRUG, CHAIE	46	F	W	RR	ZZZZ	USA
ISAAC	7	M	CHILD	RR	ZZZZ	USA
WOLF	5	M	CHILD	RR	ZZZZ	USA
CHAIN	3	M	CHILD	RR	ZZZZ	USA
DAVID	.06	M	INFANT	RR	ZZZZ	USA
KWIKEWITZ, BEILA	28	F	W	RR	ZZZZ	USA
FEIGE	7	F	CHILD	RR	ZZZZ	USA
MALKE	6	F	CHILD	RR	ZZZZ	USA
GONSKI, ESTER	23	F	SP	RR	ZZZZ	USA
ZEITZKI, JOHAN	39	M	LABR	RR	ZZZZ	USA
EMMA	29	F	W	RR	ZZZZ	USA
RABINOWITZ, CHAIM	24	M	LABR	RR	ZZZZ	USA
SOPHIE	21	F	W	RR	ZZZZ	USA
TROLLFEIST, JACOB	32	M	LABR	RR	ZZZZ	USA
MINGELGRIMER, MOSES	32	M	LABR	RR	ZZZZ	USA
HOSCHAUDER, GULL	55	F	MA	RR	ZZZZ	USA

SHIP: PERUVIAN

FROM: LIVERPOOL AND QUEENSTOWN
TO: BALTIMORE
ARRIVED: 17 MAY 1888

PASSENGER	AGE	SEX	OCCUPATION	PRV	VIL	DES
KLEWANSKY, NATHAN	17	M	LABR	RR	ZZZZ	BAL
SCHER, JOPE	18	M	LABR	RR	ZZZZ	BAL
DANELOWITZ, ABRAH	4	M	CHILD	RR	ZZZZ	BAL
JANKEL	19	M	LABR	RR	ZZZZ	BAL
KLEWANSKY, ABRAHAM	53	M	LABR	RR	ZZZZ	BAL
JOSEF	9	M	CHILD	RR	ZZZZ	BAL
KATZ, MEYER	18	M	LABR	RR	ZZZZ	IL
GRUNBERG, MICHL.	25	M	LABR	RR	ZZZZ	BAL
RIBAKIN, DOBE	30	F	HSWF	RR	ZZZZ	BAL
PERSACK	8	M	CHILD	RR	ZZZZ	BAL
HEUNE	6	M	CHILD	RR	ZZZZ	BAL
PAULE	3	M	CHILD	RR	ZZZZ	BAL
SCHUMANN, HIRSCH	43	M	SHMK	RR	ZZZZ	BAL
GINSBERG, SOPHIE	17	M	LABR	RR	ZZZZ	BAL
JENSEN, SOREN	26	M	LABR	RR	ZZZZ	NY
SAK, SAMUEL	25	M	LABR	RR	ZZZZ	BAL
GUSTAFSON, J.A.	16	M	LABR	RR	ZZZZ	PA
SEPANSKY, SCHRAL	18	M	LABR	RR	ZZZZ	BAL
PESCHKE, EDUARD	28	M	LABR	RR	ZZZZ	MN
PREAS, SCH.L.	16	M	LABR	RR	ZZZZ	BAL
OWSCHEY, LEISER	34	M	LABR	RR	ZZZZ	BAL
MIRWIS, IDA	20	F	DMS	RR	ZZZZ	BAL
U, FRUME	60	M	LABR	RR	ZZZZ	BAL
KLUNOWSKI, STANISLAW	36	M	LABR	RR	ZZZZ	OH
-UNO-LIEB, GOTT	67	M	LABR	RR	ZZZZ	BAL
JERRESCH, RIFKE	30	M	LABR	RR	ZZZZ	BAL
SCHESCHEFSKY, JOSEF	25	M	LABR	RR	ZZZZ	BAL
SCHER, BER.	11	M	CH	RR	ZZZZ	BAL
FISCHE, JOSSEF	16	M	LABR	RR	ZZZZ	USA
CHAIE	15	F	DMS	RR	ZZZZ	USA
MAUZKE, CAROLINE	25	F	HSWF	RR	ZZZZ	OH
FRANZ	.05	M	INFANT	RR	ZZZZ	OH
SCHRAMM, CARL	52	M	LABR	RR	ZZZZ	OH
ALBERTINA	51	F	W	RR	ZZZZ	OH
BERTHA	11	F	CH	RR	ZZZZ	OH
STOZMECKY, ROSALIA	22	F	DMS	RR	ZZZZ	MI
NIESPOTZIANA, ROSALIA	23	F	HSWF	RR	ZZZZ	BAL
FRANZ	2	M	CHILD	RR	ZZZZ	BAL
STANISLA	.03	F	INFANT	RR	ZZZZ	BAL

SHIP: ENGLAND

FROM: LIVERPOOL AND QUEENSTOWN
TO: NEW YORK
ARRIVED: 17 MAY 1888

PASSENGER	AGE	SEX	OCCUPATION	PRV	VIL	DES
KURDZEIDSKI, STAUS	21	M	LABR	PL	ZZZZ	SHN
MAZEITIS, J	26	M	LABR	PL	AIIX	SHN
WERONKA, PAUL	18	M	LABR	PL	AIIX	SHN
FLECK, JONS	30	M	LABR	PL	AIIX	SHN
MORITZ, MATTHEW	30	M	LABR	PL	AIIX	SHN
WERONKA, JOSEPH	28	M	LABR	PL	AIIX	SHN
STANISCHEWSKY, JANS	30	M	LABR	PL	AIIX	SHN
KRECINBES, ANTON	28	M	LABR	PL	AIIX	SHN
ROTHMAN, SOLOMAN	24	M	LABR	PL	AIIX	SHN
PAS--AMS, AUG	27	M	LABR	PL	AIIX	SHN
GRYWINSKI, THOMAS	35	M	LABR	PL	AIIX	PA
HA-ANOWITZ, ERNATH	38	M	LABR	PL	AIIX	NY
WALI-EZ, JOS	22	M	LABR	PL	AIIX	NY
KOLONKIEWIEZ, JOSEF	24	M	LABR	PL	AIIX	NY
WILKOFSKY, JOSEF	15	M	LABR	PL	AIIX	UNK
OLOWNEK, JAN	22	M	LABR	PL	AIIX	NY
WIELKOWSKY, WALENTY	29	M	LABR	PL	AIIX	NY
MALUSCH, JAN	28	M	LABR	PL	AIIX	PHI
MIKOSCH, T-KI	27	M	LABR	PL	AIIX	NY
KUPSTACZ, AND	40	M	LABR	PL	AIIX	PHI
STEFANOKI, FRANZ	25	M	LABR	PL	AIIX	NAT
RYPKOWSKI, MICH	25	M	LABR	PL	AIIX	SHN
FORTGANG, DAVID	26	M	LABR	PL	AIIX	SHN
BAUMAN, SERTE	17	M	LABR	PL	AIIX	PHI
KLINGHOFER, HERSCH	18	M	LABR	PL	AIIX	NY
SULIZKI, HERSCHEL	39	M	LABR	PL	AIIX	NY
KURESKOWSKI, VINE	25	M	LABR	PL	AIIX	NY
SARDOWSKI, JOSEF	30	M	LABR	PL	AIIX	NY
SIKORKI, LEON	23	M	LABR	PL	AIIX	NY
KLUCK, SYLVESTER	34	M	LABR	PL	AIIX	BUF
MICK--SY, JOSEF	20	M	LABR	PL	AIIX	BUF
WEINER, A	24	M	LABR	PL	AIIX	NY
RADOWSKI, JACOB	25	M	LABR	PL	AIIX	NY
PETKO, JEDELSOHN	15	M	LABR	PL	AIIX	PIT
MENZKOWSKI, ISAAC	27	M	LABR	PL	AIIX	PHI
MALENOW, JANKEL	23	M	LABR	PL	AIIX	NY
SULEWICZ, ANDREAS	20	M	LABR	PL	AIIX	NY
--ANZEO, G	32	M	LABR	PL	AIIX	NY
DINKEWISCH, JOSEPH	18	M	LABR	PL	AIIX	NY
BALLON, ADAM	25	M	LABR	PL	AIIX	PHI
BUZAROWSKI, FELIX	25	M	LABR	PL	AIIX	NY
KASELOWSKI, KASIMIR	24	M	LABR	PL	AIIX	NY
ANTON	22	M	LABR	PL	AIIX	NY
LISS, FRANK	20	M	LABR	PL	AIIX	NY
KOSELEWSKI, FRANZ	26	M	LABR	PL	AIIX	NY
-OBLONSKI, PETER	28	M	LABR	PL	AIIX	NY
SALIKLESS, JOSES	29	M	LABR	PL	AIIX	NY
KONOWISKY, MICH	25	M	LABR	PL	AIIX	NY
MISLUK, JAN	26	M	LABR	PL	AIIX	NY
KRUSGER, LOUIS	27	M	LABR	PL	AIIX	NY
ENTSKAR--IS, J	24	M	LABR	PL	AIIX	NY
BUDRAKIS, S	23	M	LABR	PL	AIIX	NY
MI-ULSKY, JURGES	23	M	LABR	PL	AIIX	NY
PETRONSKY, S	33	M	LABR	PL	AIIX	NY
SAVOICKSY, FRANZ	24	M	LABR	PL	AIIX	NY
BUCEIWICZ, MAR--N	27	M	LABR	PL	AIIX	NY
KAROL	11	M	CH	PL	AIIX	NY
ANZ-NIS, ANZEL	22	M	LABR	PL	AIIX	NY
-OSCHOWITZ, CHAIM	18	M	LABR	PL	AIIX	NY
GANINSKI, SOLOMAN	23	M	LABR	PL	AIIX	NY
DILOFSKI, MARTIN	37	M	LABR	PL	AIIX	NY
FALCORVITZ, ANTON	19	M	LABR	PL	AIIX	NY
WISNER, L	17	M	LABR	PL	AIIX	NY
INSKYKIEWIG, PETER	26	M	LABR	PL	AIIX	NY
ADAM, MORSCHAINS	21	M	LABR	PL	AIIX	PHI
JANOWSKI, JULIAN	21	M	LABR	PL	AIIX	PHI
KAR-ONWIEZ, JAN	18	M	LABR	PL	AIIX	PHI
FRIED, HIRSCH	16	M	LABR	PL	AIIX	BAL

PASSENGER	AGE	SEX	OCCUPATION	PRIV	VIL	DES
SEGAR, JOSEPH	18	M	LABR	PLA	II	XNY
SAB-ZANSKI, MARKS	20	M	LABR	PLA	II	XNY
SCHOMER, MELUK	20	M	LABR	PLA	II	XNY
KEISERMAN, NISZEL	20	M	LABR	PLA	II	XPHI
DRAUGINIS, VINC	28	M	LABR	PLA	II	XNY
EBBSCHITZ, ISAAC	16	M	LABR	PLA	II	XNY
-AKS, BERL	30	M	LABR	PLA	II	XNY
WERONKA, JACOB	18	M	LABR	PLA	II	XNY
MISENWITZ, JOSEPH	30	M	LABR	PLA	II	XNY
GURNY, SELIG	25	M	LABR	PLA	II	XNY
KOPPEL	35	M	LABR	PLA	II	XNY
RADINSKY	19	M	LABR	PLA	II	XNY
PODUTZ, ABRAH	33	M	LABR	PLA	II	XNY
WOJCIK, ANTONI	19	M	LABR	PLA	II	XNST
KATZ, NOTEL	46	M	LABR	PLA	II	XNY
-UESTERDAM, NAFTALI	19	M	LABR	PLA	II	XNY
BAVANOSKI, FRANN	17	M	LABR	PLA	II	XNY
WISOCKSI, JOHAN	18	M	LABR	PLA	II	XNY
RENKEWITZ, FRANZ	38	M	LABR	PLA	II	XNY
BENZINSKI, BARTUCHER	36	M	LABR	PLA	II	XNY
SCHIMANSKI, JAN	30	M	LABR	PLA	II	XNY
RANKELL, JH	23	M	LABR	PLA	II	XMI
EISIK, ABRAH	24	M	LABR	PLA	II	XBO
CZAPULISKI, ADAM	47	M	LABR	PLA	II	XNY
SITZWITKOWSKI, JOSEF	27	M	LABR	PLA	II	XNY
ROWALOWSKI, IGNATZ	27	M	LABR	PLA	II	XNY
BUSCHANZKES, ANTON	24	M	LABR	PLA	II	XBAL
SAGER, MAX	25	M	LABR	PLA	II	XNY
KAMMERMANN, JACOB	30	M	LABR	PLA	II	XNY
NEUMANN, JOSEF	28	M	LABR	PLA	II	XNY
MARK, CHAIM	33	M	LABR	PLA	II	XNY
DEUTCH, ABRAHAM	25	M	LABR	PLA	II	XNY
LANGMAN, SAME	28	M	LABR	PLA	II	XNY
ASERSKY, BEHR	29	M	LABR	PLA	II	XNY
KIRSCHK--, BENJAMIN	27	M	LABR	PLA	II	XNY
HAHN, JOSEL	26	M	LABR	PLA	II	XNY
LEITER, MEILACH	29	M	LABR	PLA	II	XNY
GRABOWSKI, KASIMER	23	M	LABR	PLA	II	XNY
KLINKOWSKI, REUBEN	30	M	LABR	PLA	II	XNY
MOSEWIZSKI, ABRAH	40	M	LABR	PLA	II	XNY
S--ETIZKIN, J	30	M	LABR	PLA	II	XNY
KAROSCH, JOSEF	40	M	LABR	PLA	II	XNY
KE--ATKOWSKI, ANTON	24	M	LABR	PLA	II	XNY
-OCKWITZKI, WLAD	28	M	LABR	PLA	II	XNY
-EPHAITES, JERSEI	24	M	LABR	PLA	II	XNY
BERG, ABRAHAM	22	M	LABR	PLA	II	XNY
ISRAELSON, C	27	M	LABR	PLA	II	XNY
FREIDA, RESI	20	F	SP	PLA	II	XNY
JENO	10	F	CH	PLA	II	XNY
ESTO	7	F	CHILD	PLA	II	XNY
WIS-O	5	M	CHILD	PLA	II	XNY
SOLMO	1	M	CHILD	PLA	II	XNY
KATZ, DORA	15	F	SP	PLA	II	XNY
APPE	11	F	CH	PLA	II	XNY
ROTHMAN, PERL	40	F	W	PLA	II	XNY
FEIGE	19	F	SP	PLA	II	XNY
JOSSEL	17	M	LABR	PLA	II	XNY
MICHE	11	M	CH	PLA	II	XNY
ISRAEL	7	M	CHILD	PLA	II	XNY
DIEGEL, DWORE	13	F	SP	PLA	II	XNY
ARTESCHUDSKI, JULIA	32	F	W	PLA	II	XNY
RUD	2	M	CHILD	PLA	II	XNY
KAPELORITZ, RACHEL	25	F	W	PLA	II	XNY
DEVORE	.09	F	INFANT	PLA	II	XNY
-AKTORSKY, REWKE	18	F	SVNT	PLA	II	XNY
DANK, RICHE	42	F	MA	PLA	II	XNY
CHAJE	17	F	SP	PLA	II	XNY
BUDZEK, ANNA	22	F	SP	PLA	II	XNY
TZORSKI, DOVRA	19	F	SP	PLA	II	XNY
GOLDSTERN, JENTO	27	F	W	PLA	II	XNY
HERCH	5	M	CHILD	PLA	II	XNY
DAWNEY, PAULINE	48	F	SVNT	PLA	II	XNY
GRAV, LEA	24	F	W	PLA	II	XNY
KOLMEA	4	F	CHILD	PLA	II	XNY
CHAIM	1	F	CHILD	PLA	II	XNY

PASSENGER	AGE	SEX	OCCUPATION	PRIV	VIL	DES
PEROWTCH, SORE	19	F	SVNT	PLA	II	XNY
SAGDOWSKY, MARIA	18	F	SVNT	PLA	II	XNY
LIEBKIND, SCHONE	18	F	SVNT	PLA	II	XNY
WENGROWITZ, FIEGE	30	F	W	PLA	II	XNY
S-RE	11	F	CH	PLA	II	XNY
RIFKE	10	M	CH	PLA	II	XNY
RACHEL	8	F	CHILD	PLA	II	XNY
CHAIME	4	F	CHILD	PLA	II	XNY
ZIMMERMANN, MOSES	42	M	LABR	PLA	II	XNY
FIRNT	40	F	W	PLA	II	XNY
SCHIEL	10	F	CH	PLA	II	XNY
HANNA	7	F	CHILD	PLA	II	XNY
FANNY	4	F	CHILD	PLA	II	XNY
BENJN	1	M	CHILD	PLA	II	XNY
DESSEV, CHANE	16	F	SP	PLA	II	XNY
JANKEL	11	M	CH	PLA	II	XNY
SILBER, HEINDE	18	F	SVNT	PLA	II	XNY
SNATO-, MOTE	50	F	SVNT	PLA	II	XNY
KLEIN, JONAS	56	M	LABR	PLA	II	XNY
HANI	42	F	W	PLA	II	XNY
ADOLPH	17	M	LABR	PLA	II	XNY
ROSE	11	F	CH	PLA	II	XNY
KAUMERAVICK, ALEX	20	M	LABR	PLA	II	XNY
JOHANNA	25	F	W	PLA	II	XNY
MOSKOWIT, JENNY	17	F	SVNT	PLA	II	XNY
MALMONSKY, MICH	40	M	LABR	PLA	II	XNY
PAULINE	34	F	W	PLA	II	XNY
WYCON--Y, FRANCISCA	8	F	CHILD	PLA	II	XNY
TEPPICK, ISAAC	36	M	LABR	PLA	II	XNY
FANNY	32	F	W	PLA	II	XNY
DEBORAH	7	F	CHILD	PLA	II	XNY
JETTA	5	F	CHILD	PLA	II	XNY
ESTER	1	F	CHILD	PLA	II	XNY
MOSKOWITZ, LINTA	16	F	SVNT	PLA	II	XNY
TRUDNOWKSY, JOSEPH	25	M	LABR	PLA	II	XBUF
MARYANN	27	F	W	PLA	II	XBUF
FRANZ	3	M	CHILD	PLA	II	XBUF
JOSEPH	1	M	CHILD	PLA	II	XBUF
JANOWSKY, FRANZ	28	M	LABR	PLA	II	XUNK
PENEWSKY, VICTORIA	30	F	SVNT	PLA	II	XUNK
-OBE, MATEL	15	F	SVNT	PLA	II	XNY
STOLEWITZKE, RACHEL	45	F	W	PLA	II	XNY
KAUF, MICHAEL	23	M	LABR	PLA	II	XNY
LEIB	.06	F	INFANT	PLA	II	XNY
KLEIN, FANNY	30	F	W	PLA	II	XNY
ADOLPH	9	M	CHILD	PLA	II	XNY
ESTE	6	F	CHILD	PLA	II	XNY
MISKA	1	F	CHILD	PLA	II	XNY
ROTH, ROSALI	20	M	LABR	PLA	II	XNY
FRIEDMAN, MARIE	11	F	CH	PLA	II	XNY
JACOB	10	M	CH	PLA	II	XNY
ESTHER	8	F	CHILD	PLA	II	XNY
S-ALSDA, FRANTESCH	38	M	LABR	PLA	II	XNY
JENNY	35	F	W	PLA	II	XNY
ANTONI	8	M	CHILD	PLA	II	XNY
MARY	3	F	CHILD	PLA	II	XNY
FRANTISCH	5	M	CHILD	PLA	II	XNY
JOSEPH	1	M	CHILD	PLA	II	XNY
TORMAN, ANTONIA	14	F	SP	PLA	II	XNY
WICKE, ROSA	25	F	SP	PLA	II	XNY
BEILE	6	F	CHILD	PLA	II	XNY
BRAVE	1	F	CHILD	PLA	II	XNY
MANUCHE	24	F	W	PLA	II	XNY
REIVE	1	F	CHILD	PLA	II	XNY
RASOK, ANNA	20	F	SVNT	PLA	II	XNY
SP-VAL, RIFKE	21	F	W	PLA	II	XNY
ESTHER	3	F	CHILD	PLA	II	XNY
LEIB	.07	F	INFANT	PLA	II	XNY
ERSTEIN, JOCHAMED	17	M	SVNT	PLA	II	XNY
CHEMIL, MARIA	26	F	W	PLA	II	XNY
DAVID	8	M	CHILD	PLA	II	XNY
JUDKI	6	M	CHILD	PLA	II	XNY
LEA	3	F	CHILD	PLA	II	XNY
RACHEL	1	F	CHILD	PLA	II	XNY
ELLIS, SARAH	23	F	W	PLA	II	XPHI

PASSENGER	AGE	SEX	OCCUPATION	PRIV	VIL	DES
CECILLE	.04	F	INFANT	PL	AIIX	PHI
STEIN, GETTA	30	F	W	PL	AIIX	CH
JOSEPH	10	M	CH	PL	AIIX	CH
SARAH	10	F	CH	PL	AIIX	CH
ALTEKE	.11	F	INFANT	PL	AIIX	CH
HELD, MARIA	30	F	W	PL	AIIX	NY
RIVKE	11	F	CH	PL	AIIX	NY
BOUTCH	8	M	CHILD	PL	AIIX	NY
RACHEL	.10	F	INFANT	PL	AIIX	NY
BIDERMANN, HANNA	38	F	W	PL	AIIX	NY
BETTY	17	F	SP	PL	AIIX	NY
DAVID	15	M	LABR	PL	AIIX	NY
FANNY	8	F	CHILD	PL	AIIX	NY
VERRARS	4	F	CHILD	PL	AIIX	NY
FRIEDMANN, JETTY	32	F	W	PL	AIIX	NY
HERMANN	6	M	CHILD	PL	AIIX	NY
ISAK	4	M	CHILD	PL	AIIX	NY
REGE	1	M	CHILD	PL	AIIX	NY
LITZER, CHAJE	23	F	W	PL	AIIX	NY
JOSSEL	.10	F	INFANT	PL	AIIX	NY
SCHNEWASEN, SALOMAN	39	M	LABR	PL	AIIX	NY
DINA	30	F	W	PL	AIIX	NY
SCHENDAL	11	M	CH	PL	AIIX	NY
BELA	9	F	CHILD	PL	AIIX	NY
WOWE	7	F	CHILD	PL	AIIX	NY
MOTTEL	.08	F	INFANT	PL	AIIX	NY
TILLES, MOTTEL	45	F	SVNT	PL	AIIX	PHI
BORGESS, JANE	18	F	SVNT	PL	AIIX	NY
LIEPCHITZ, CHAIN	30	M	LABR	PL	AIIX	NY
CHAIE	28	F	W	PL	AIIX	NY
LEZERYNSKY, MOSES	25	M	LABR	PL	AIIX	PHI
FUHRMANN, JESSEL	29	M	LABR	PL	AIIX	PHI
BAVANOWSKY, PETER	36	M	LABR	PL	AIIX	NY
KATRINA	26	F	W	PL	AIIX	NY
PETER	3	M	CHILD	PL	AIIX	NY
OLESCH	.09	M	INFANT	PL	AIIX	NY
BURDMAN, SLOME	26	M	LABR	PL	AIIX	PHI
RACHEL	21	F	W	PL	AIIX	PHI
WACKS, HIRSCH	31	M	LABR	PL	AIIX	PHI
FERGE	22	F	W	PL	AIIX	PHI
LEWINSOHN, BELZ	23	M	LABR	PL	AIIX	BAL
MODCHE	20	F	W	PL	AIIX	BAL
TISCHLER, HIRSCHE	25	M	LABR	PL	AIIX	PHI
ANDEITIS, MAGGIE	27	F	W	PL	AIIX	NY
MICHAEL	5	M	CHILD	PL	AIIX	NY
VINCENT	1	M	CHILD	PL	AIIX	NY
ANDETKI, WILLM	35	M	LABR	PL	AIIX	NY
HERSCHON, SARAH	19	F	SVNT	PL	AIIX	BO

SHIP: ROMAN

FROM: LIVERPOOL
TO: BOSTON
ARRIVED: 17 MAY 1888

PASSENGER	AGE	SEX	OCCUPATION	PRIV	VIL	DES
HYMAN, ABRAM	21	M	LABR	PL	ZZZZ	NY
LEUTSKY, ISAAC	00	M	LABR	PL	ZZZZ	NY
KAPAETRU, ABRAM	00	M	MCHT	RR	ZZZZ	USA
GOLDE	00	F	SP	RR	ZZZZ	USA
DROARCHE	27	F	SP	RR	ZZZZ	USA
SCHOLAN	24	F	SP	RR	ZZZZ	USA
DAVID	22	M	MCHT	RR	ZZZZ	USA
ISAAC	18	M	MCHT	RR	ZZZZ	USA
SALOMON	16	M	MCHT	RR	ZZZZ	USA
REBECCA	16	F	SP	RR	ZZZZ	USA
SCHNOZE, BACHE	26	F	W	RR	ZZZZ	BO
REBECCA	9	F	CHILD	RR	ZZZZ	BO
MAROS	6	F	CHILD	RR	ZZZZ	BO
MIRRAM	4	F	CHILD	RR	ZZZZ	BO
SALOMON	00	M	INF	RR	ZZZZ	BO
DHULL, SARAH	00	F	CH	RR	ZZZZ	BO
ARON	00	M	CH	RR	ZZZZ	BO
CAIN	00	M	CH	RR	ZZZZ	BO
ECK, WOLFF	19	M	MCHT	RR	ZZZZ	BO
SALZNIUS, ABRM.	19	M	MCHT	RR	ZZZZ	BO
SIALOWSKY, ELIUS	00	M	MCHT	RR	ZZZZ	BO
DHILL, ELLEN	00	F	W	RR	ZZZZ	BO
SGRUPAK, B.	00	M	MCHT	RR	ZZZZ	NY
MUTILINSKY, F.	00	M	MCHT	RR	ZZZZ	NY
WUROK, ABRAM	00	M	MCHT	RR	ZZZZ	USA
WIALENSKY, D.	38	M	LABR	RR	ZZZZ	BO
PAL---, CHARLES	90	M	HSWF	RR	ZZZZ	BO
ABRAM	16	M	UNKNOWN	RR	ZZZZ	BO
JULIS	6	M	CHILD	RR	ZZZZ	BO
ERSTEN, HERSCH	24	F	SP	RR	ZZZZ	BO
POSEN, SCHINNA	25	M	LABR	RR	ZZZZ	BO
SCHROTE, ITE	17	M	LABR	PL	ZZZZ	BO
GUPERNITSKIE, DAVID	16	M	LABR	PL	ZZZZ	BO
KASLINSKIE, SELIG	20	M	LABR	PL	ZZZZ	BO
SCHAPER, MOSES	20	M	LABR	PL	ZZZZ	BO
SALZBURG, LEIB	18	M	LABR	PL	ZZZZ	BO
STRUMM, ABR.	22	M	LABR	PL	ZZZZ	BO
BRUBCHOWSKY, MOSES	41	M	LABR	RR	ZZZZ	BO
ULH--, SCHIME	36	M	LABR	RR	ZZZZ	BO
RUGAL, DAVID	24	M	LABR	RR	ZZZZ	BO
HUROWITZ, MOSES	30	M	LABR	RR	ZZZZ	BO
DALMATOSKIE, GEROCHM	27	M	LABR	RR	ZZZZ	BO
JISMER, DAVID	28	M	LABR	RR	ZZZZ	BO
BERMSTON, ESSIG	18	M	LABR	RR	ZZZZ	BO
GRUNPAN, JOSEF	23	M	LABR	RR	ZZZZ	BO
SIBOWITZ, LEIB	16	M	LABR	RR	ZZZZ	BO
SCUDES, MOSES	24	M	LABR	RR	ZZZZ	BO
SCHWARZ, ABRAM	25	M	LABR	RR	ZZZZ	BO
JUNABITSKY, MARTIN	24	M	LABR	RR	ZZZZ	BO
SALTZ, JOHN	20	M	LABR	RR	ZZZZ	BO
SERGIUS, JOSEPH	40	M	LABR	RR	ZZZZ	BO
DEISCHKEWIZ, JOHAN	43	M	LABR	RR	ZZZZ	BO
ISHAMMISKIE, CONT.	23	M	MCHT	RR	ZZZZ	BO
JAN	50	M	LABR	RR	ZZZZ	BO
DRASCHPONKIE, MONSTSCHE	27	M	LABR	RR	ZZZZ	BO
ROPALOWSKUZ, FRANZ	28	M	UNKNOWN	RR	ZZZZ	BO
KAHN, MAX	38	M	UNKNOWN	RR	ZZZZ	BO
BOWARSKI, MOSES	10	M	CH	RR	ZZZZ	BO
LEIB	8	M	CHILD	RR	ZZZZ	BO
KORAPSCHICK, BOR.	54	M	LABR	RR	ZZZZ	BO
PRINPER, ANINE	18	F	UNKNOWN	RR	ZZZZ	BO
BENISCHT, DAVID	18	M	UNKNOWN	RR	ZZZZ	BO
DINUS, SCHLONIS	24	F	UNKNOWN	RR	ZZZZ	BO
DALINTCKIE, NECHUM	42	M	UNKNOWN	RR	ZZZZ	BO
LISTON, ABRAM	22	M	LABR	RR	ZZZZ	NY
BLISHE, MOSEUS	40	M	LABR	RR	ZZZZ	NY
MORRISON, JOS.	18	M	LABR	RR	ZZZZ	NY
MEYERSEN, LANE	42	F	SP	RR	ZZZZ	NY
EPSTENN, ESTHER	50	F	SP	RR	ZZZZ	NY
BENJAMIN	10	M	CH	RR	ZZZZ	NY
ROSE	8	F	CHILD	RR	ZZZZ	NY
LENDER, HARRIS	22	M	LABR	RR	ZZZZ	NY
PRISTON, DAN	53	M	LABR	RR	ZZZZ	PHI
DAIGER, I.	32	M	LABR	RR	ZZZZ	NY
BARNETT, E.	34	M	UNKNOWN	PL	ZZZZ	NY
SILVER, INANT	32	M	LABR	RR	ZZZZ	NY
SALOMAN, HACGAR	17	F	SP	RR	ZZZZ	NY
MILAFSKUZ, MATILDA	18	F	SP	RR	ZZZZ	NY
VOITCK, JATENLE	25	F	SP	RR	ZZZZ	PHI
HASKESKIE, ANTON	32	M	LABR	RR	ZZZZ	NY
ZOLNAKI, MATHAD	40	M	LABR	RR	ZZZZ	NY

SHIP: STATE OF INDIANA

FROM: GLASGOW AND LARNE
TO: NEW YORK
ARRIVED: 17 MAY 1888

PASSENGER	AGE	SEX	OCCUPATION	PRV VIL DES
MOKOWITZ, MEYER	33	M	TLR	RRZZZZUSA
EISENBERG, MOSES	24	M	TLR	RRZZZZUSA
KLOPPS, ISAAC	26	M	TLR	RRZZZZUSA
RUDNIK, ABRAHAM	44	M	TLR	RRZZZZUSA
JOSSELAWITZ, MORDOKE	15	M	PDLR	RRZZZZUSA
LEWIN, BETZE	21	M	PDLR	RRZZZZUSA
WOLOWITZ, MORDOKE	36	M	BKR	RRZZZZUSA
KAPLAN, CHAWE	28	M	SHMK	RRZZZZUSA
ZENTE	50	F	W	RRZZZZUSA
HOLLAND, MOSES	36	M	LABR	RRZZZZUSA
KERBEDIS, JOSEF	33	M	LABR	RRZZZZUSA
KRAUZUNS, HANS	24	M	LABR	RRZZZZUSA
MULLER, JONAS	23	M	LABR	RRZZZZUSA
ANDERSOHN, CARL	21	M	LABR	RRZZZZUSA
KOWALSKI, LEIBE	43	M	SMH	RRZZZZUSA
BLUM, MORITZ	16	M	PDLR	RRZZZZUSA
LEIKINT, DAVID	39	M	TLR	RRZZZZUSA
REMERT, LUDWIG	30	M	LABR	RRZZZZUSA
HAUSRATH, FRED	23	M	SMH	RRZZZZUSA
RUTUHIS, THOS	22	M	LABR	RRZZZZUSA
TAMOLANIS, JACOB	48	M	LABR	RRZZZZUSA
MEYER, WILHELM	40	M	LABR	RRZZZZUSA
JOSEF	19	M	LABR	RRZZZZUSA
TAROFI, IGNATZ	40	M	LABR	RRZZZZUSA
MEYER, FRED	24	M	LABR	RRZZZZUSA
BAGULEITIS, JOSEF	23	M	TLR	RRZZZZUSA
CHAOZINSKI, PITORE	50	F	LABR	RRZZZZUSA
SOSOHINSKAS, JOSEF	22	F	LABR	RRZZZZUSA
MALASCHKEWITZ, KASIMIR	25	M	TLR	RRZZZZUSA
ANDRUKOT, AUGUST	25	M	LABR	RRZZZZUSA
MARZIG, JUBA	28	M	LABR	RRZZZZUSA
BEHRATZKIS, ANTON	22	M	LABR	RRZZZZUSA
BARANOFSKI, ADOLF	22	M	LABR	RRZZZZUSA
TINDROWSKY, GOTTLIEB	30	M	CPTR	RRZZZZUSA
HOSS, ARON	18	M	TLR	RRZZZZUSA
YACOBSOHN, MAX	18	M	LABR	RRZZZZUSA
MATULSKI, ISAAK	33	M	TLR	RRZZZZUSA
ROBINOWITZ, MOSES	50	M	PDLR	RRZZZZUSA
HERMANN	16	M	PDLR	RRZZZZUSA
UMANSLKI, LIEBACH	18	M	TLR	RRZZZZUSA
MORIS	16	M	TLR	RRZZZZUSA
DUTSCHMANN, JEOHOLT	11	M	TLR	RRZZZZUSA
TISCHKOWSKA, HILLEL	18	M	TLR	RRZZZZUSA
BRUENWALSKI, MEYER	17	M	TLR	RRZZZZUSA
HOKON, HIRSCH	25	M	TLR	RRZZZZUSA
WILENSKI, SCHEINE	19	F	SVNT	RRZZZZUSA
FEUBE	17	M	LABR	RRZZZZUSA
HIRSCH	11	M	UNKNOWN	RRZZZZUSA
UNTERSCHATZ, WOLF	19	M	TLR	RRZZZZUSA
MARGULES, JACOB	23	M	SP	RRZZZZUSA
KOLAN, YANKEL	23	M	PDLR	RRZZZZUSA
WOLK, ITZIG	35	M	CPTR	RRZZZZUSA
SAWJELEWITZ, RIWIN	17	M	SDLR	RRZZZZUSA
KUSNITZKI, TODIES	19	M	LABR	RRZZZZUSA
KOHN, ABRAHAM	23	M	LABR	RRZZZZUSA
BERMANN, MICHAEL	39	M	TLR	RRZZZZUSA
SEZNPAOK, ISSER	35	M	LABR	RRZZZZUSA
ABRAMSON, ISRAEL	40	M	BCHR	RRZZZZUSA
PABLELINSKI, MOSES	18	M	LABR	RRZZZZUSA
DIKSTEIN, MOSCHE	17	M	LABR	RRZZZZUSA
RUCHITIS, JANKEL	15	M	BKBNDR	RRZZZZUSA
SALMENOWICH, FEIWEL	20	M	PDLR	RRZZZZUSA
JEINSTEIN, JOSEF	23	M	LABR	RRZZZZUSA
PAOKZIG, SALMEN	50	F	TLR	RRZZZZUSA
TUSCHIN, MALKE	18	F	DMS	RRZZZZUSA
NISSMAN, SIEME	24	F	DMS	RRZZZZUSA
GALUS, ZUSANA	15	F	DMS	RRZZZZUSA
KATZ, RAJNE	20	F	DMS	RRZZZZUSA
ZIEBERFART, MUSCHE	16	F	DMS	RRZZZZUSA
SCHAPIR, RELL	17	F	DMS	RRZZZZUSA
RJOKSOHNS, DOMINIKA	24	F	DMS	RRZZZZUSA
SILLBERSTEIN, MINNIE	20	F	DMS	RRZZZZUSA
FELDMANN, BRANE	53	F	UNKNOWN	RRZZZZUSA
BASCHE	6	F	CHILD	RRZZZZUSA
SKIRSBOLSKI, RACHEL	45	F	W	RRZZZZUSA
JEMEL	17	M	LABR	RRZZZZUSA
HURWITZ, HENNI	26	F	W	RRZZZZUSA
JOHNMEL	2	M	CHILD	RRZZZZUSA
JOSEF	1	M	CHILD	RRZZZZUSA
MASLAUSKI, ABRAHAM	27	M	CTW	RRZZZZUSA
FREIDE	27	F	W	RRZZZZUSA
KROMFELD, ABRAHAM	30	M	TLR	RRZZZZUSA
ESTLER	24	F	W	RRZZZZUSA
ELWOWSKI, JUDEL	42	M	LABR	RRZZZZUSA
BELL	40	F	W	RRZZZZUSA
ESTHER	40	F	W	RRZZZZUSA
ISRAEL	16	M	LABR	RRZZZZUSA
HENRI	11	F	UNKNOWN	RRZZZZUSA
TREODEL	8	M	CHILD	RRZZZZUSA
HERSCHEL	6	M	CHILD	RRZZZZUSA
BEREL	5	M	CHILD	RRZZZZUSA
MEBBEL, MOSES	51	M	CGRMKR	RRZZZZUSA
JIPPE	40	F	W	RRZZZZUSA
SINRE	22	M	LABR	RRZZZZUSA
ABRAHAM	1	M	CHILD	RRZZZZUSA
JACOB	.09	M	INFANT	RRZZZZUSA
WEIT, BECKE	22	F	W	RRZZZZUSA
MALE	2	F	CHILD	RRZZZZUSA
VILLI	.06	F	INFANT	RRZZZZUSA
KASOHN, HENDEL	40	M	TLR	RRZZZZUSA
SCHEINE	40	F	W	RRZZZZUSA
SARAH	8	F	CHILD	RRZZZZUSA
SCHLEIME	12	F	CH	RRZZZZUSA
SCHUANOWITZ, JAOBWET	26	F	W	RRZZZZUSA
MEIER	2	M	CHILD	RRZZZZUSA
HIRSCH	1	M	CHILD	RRZZZZUSA
SIEMINKIEWIEZ, SALAMEO	40	F	W	RRZZZZUSA
ALEXANDRA	26	F	SVNT	RRZZZZUSA
PETER	3	M	CHILD	RRZZZZUSA
U, GL--	21	F	W	RRZZZZUSA
SARAH	7	F	CHILD	RRZZZZUSA
RAHLE	3	M	CHILD	RRZZZZUSA
MEYER	2	M	CHILD	RRZZZZUSA
ABRAMOWITZ, ROSA	20	F	W	RRZZZZUSA
LINA	.06	F	INFANT	RRZZZZUSA
RATMAN, LEA	26	F	W	RRZZZZUSA
ELIE	9	F	CHILD	RRZZZZUSA
ISAH	6	F	CHILD	RRZZZZUSA
JOSEF	2	M	CHILD	RRZZZZUSA
SA---STEIN, ROCHEL	25	F	W	RRZZZZUSA
CHANE	3	F	CHILD	RRZZZZUSA
PROZER, LEA	36	F	W	RRZZZZUSA
HYMAN	5	M	CHILD	RRZZZZUSA
RACHAME	9	M	CHILD	RRZZZZUSA
NATAN	10	M	CH	RRZZZZUSA
KATZ	2	F	CHILD	RRZZZZUSA
MISSCHKOSSKI, PESOH	23	F	W	RRZZZZUSA
CHATZKEL	5	M	CHILD	RRZZZZUSA
CHAIKEL	1	F	CHILD	RRZZZZUSA
KOHN, REBECA	11	F	UNKNOWN	RRZZZZUSA

PASSENGER	AGE	SEX	OCCUPATION	PRIV	DES
SHIP: SAALE					
FROM: BREMEN AND SOUTHAMPTON					
TO: NEW YORK					
ARRIVED: 18 MAY 1888					
GOSZKE, STANISL.	26	M	LABR	RRZZZZ	USA
KWASCHNEWSKI, JAN	24	M	LABR	RRZZZZ	USA
TURSKI, JAN	33	M	LABR	RRZZZZ	USA
MELINSKI, JAN	27	M	LABR	RRZZZZ	USA
WITKOWSKI, ANT.	35	M	LABR	RRZZZZ	USA
BRZUSKI, ANTON	23	M	LABR	RRZZZZ	USA
JANKOWSKI, JAN	48	M	LABR	RRZZZZ	USA
DOBIENITZKI, FRANZ	23	M	LABR	RRZZZZ	USA
SIEMIONTKOWSKI, JOSEF	20	M	LABR	RRZZZZ	USA
FROMMER, WILH.	48	M	FARMER	RRZZZZ	USA
ROSALIE	46	F	W	RRZZZZ	USA
HERME.	7	F	CHILD	RRZZZZ	USA
ARMIN	6	M	CHILD	RRZZZZ	USA
BLEI---, GUEZA	18	F	NN	RRZZZZ	USA
HELMRICH, MARIE	19	F	NN	RRZZZZ	USA
HAKALA, JACOB	30	M	LABR	FNZZZZ	USA
ERKKILA, JAKOB	22	M	LABR	FNZZZZ	USA
KUJOA-, KARL	31	M	LABR	FNZZZZ	USA
GERTRUD	28	F	W	FNZZZZ	USA
MARIA	26	F	NN	FNZZZZ	USA
DREGER, JUL.	28	M	BCHR	RRZZZZ	USA
AUG.	23	M	BCHR	RRZZZZ	USA
HERSKA, JULIA	26	F	NN	FNZZZZ	USA
WEINSTEIN, STINA	19	F	NN	RRZZZZ	USA
ADASSA	16	F	NN	RRZZZZ	USA
OLAR-IK, ABRAH.	23	M	LABR	RRZZZZ	USA
MANKOSKA, MARYANNA	23	M	JNR	RRZZZZ	USA
WOYZECH	.01	M	INFANT	RRZZZZ	USA
MANELSKI, WOYCIECH	27	M	LABR	RRZZZZ	USA
MANKOWSKI, JAN	25	M	LABR	RRZZZZ	USA
FRIEDRICH, PELAGIA	30	F	W	RRZZZZ	USA
LUCIAN	6	M	CHILD	RRZZZZ	USA
SAGACKI, FRANZ	28	M	CPTR	RRZZZZ	USA
WITKOWSKI, STANISL.	25	M	CPTR	RRZZZZ	USA
BLEIWEISS, ANNA	23	F	W	RRZZZZ	USA
MARCUS	2	M	CHILD	RRZZZZ	USA
MORITZ	.10	M	INFANT	RRZZZZ	USA
GRABOWSKI, JOH.	45	M	LABR	RRZZZZ	USA
RABALEWSKI, JOH.	43	M	LABR	RRZZZZ	USA
JUCKLINSKI, FELIX	29	M	LABR	RRZZZZ	USA
CATHA.	20	F	NN	RRZZZZ	USA
SEVERINSKA, ELISAB.	17	F	NN	RRZZZZ	USA
PONIEWSKI, U	48	M	BCHR	RRZZZZ	USA
LEWANDOWSKI, MICH.	22	M	LABR	RRZZZZ	USA
ROSIN, IDEL	29	M	LABR	RRZZZZ	USA
KAMINSKI, ESTHER	22	M	LABR	RRZZZZ	USA
SCHITKO, CHAIM	50	M	LABR	RRZZZZ	USA
VOSIL, JAN	20	M	LABR	RRZZZZ	USA
BECIZOWICZ, MACIEJ	26	M	LABR	RRZZZZ	USA
KACZERIS, JAN	26	M	LABR	RRZZZZ	USA
SERGUS, VINCENTY	38	M	LABR	RRZZZZ	USA
JENOLAJTIS, EVA	42	F	W	RRZZZZ	USA
JAN	7	M	CHILD	RRZZZZ	USA
STANKIEWICZ, ADAM	40	M	LABR	RRZZZZ	USA
HEYER, U	44	M	LABR	RRZZZZ	USA
AUGSTE.	18	F	NN	RRZZZZ	USA
MESKE, AUG.	56	M	LABR	RRZZZZ	USA
SOWETZKI, JOH.	19	M	LABR	RRZZZZ	USA
KIESEL, GUST.	16	M	LABR	RRZZZZ	USA
VOIGT, JULIANNE	33	F	W	RRZZZZ	USA
ANNA	6	F	CHILD	RRZZZZ	USA
GUST.	.10	M	INFANT	RRZZZZ	USA
STRASDIS, GEORG	24	M	LABR	RRZZZZ	USA
JOSEWEIT, GEORG	17	M	LABR	RRZZZZ	USA
UNGEREUTH, HERM.	29	M	LABR	RRZZZZ	USA
ARBASCHAT, U	27	M	LABR	RRZZZZ	USA
EMMERLATT, JOH.	22	M	LABR	RRZZZZ	USA
GRAJEWSKI, FELIX	28	M	LABR	RRZZZZ	USA
GURSKI, STEPH.	58	M	LABR	RRZZZZ	USA
GERKENS, JOH.	14	M	NN	RRZZZZ	USA
BIALOBOTZKI, ABRAH.	40	M	LABR	RRZZZZ	USA
RICHTER, CARL	27	M	LABR	RRZZZZ	USA
CHRISTA.	24	F	W	RRZZZZ	USA
KUCH, KARL	44	M	LABR	RRZZZZ	USA
THERESIA	42	F	W	RRZZZZ	USA
CHRIST.	18	M	LABR	RRZZZZ	USA
EDW.	16	M	LABR	RRZZZZ	USA
NATH.	4	M	CHILD	RRZZZZ	USA
ADOLF, AUG.	26	M	LABR	RRZZZZ	USA
CATHE.	24	F	W	RRZZZZ	USA
DOMEL	2	M	CHILD	RRZZZZ	USA
CATHA.	.05	F	INFANT	RRZZZZ	USA
ANDR.	14	M	NN	RRZZZZ	USA
MANCH, FRIEDR.	28	M	LABR	RRZZZZ	USA
CHRISTA.	28	F	W	RRZZZZ	USA
DOROTHEA	7	F	CHILD	RRZZZZ	USA
MARIA	.05	F	INFANT	RRZZZZ	USA
KUCH, CHRIST.	32	M	LABR	RRZZZZ	USA
LOUISE	29	F	W	RRZZZZ	USA
CHRIST.	6	M	CHILD	RRZZZZ	USA
JACOB	3	M	CHILD	RRZZZZ	USA
BERNHD.	.08	M	INFANT	RRZZZZ	USA
LENZ, CHRIST.	29	M	LABR	RRZZZZ	USA
LYDIA	26	F	W	RRZZZZ	USA
REINHOLD	4	M	CHILD	RRZZZZ	USA
NATH.	.11	M	INFANT	RRZZZZ	USA
FRIEDE.	56	F	W	RRZZZZ	USA
MATHEIS, CHRIST.	30	M	LABR	RRZZZZ	USA
EVA	28	F	W	RRZZZZ	USA
BARBA.	3	F	CHILD	RRZZZZ	USA
STAMSZEWSKI, MARG.	30	M	LABR	RRZZZZ	USA
GERSCHMUND, STANISL.	27	M	LABR	RRZZZZ	USA
NOWIDZKY, LUDW.	19	M	LABR	RRZZZZ	USA
ROSCHVOSKY, WITOLT.	36	M	LABR	RRZZZZ	USA
MARGA	22	F	NN	RRZZZZ	USA
CONFALVA, MARIE	28	F	NN	RRZZZZ	USA
SHIP: RHYNLAND					
FROM: ANTWERP					
TO: NEW YORK					
ARRIVED: 18 MAY 1888					
WARZBURG, A	27	M	SLR	FNZZZZ	NY
SHIP: GOTHIA					
FROM: STETTIN					
TO: NEW YORK					
ARRIVED: 18 MAY 1888					
KULAK, ANDREAS	30	M	LABR	RRZZZZ	USA
LUDWIGA	23	F	W	RRZZZZ	USA
MUSAL, FRIEDRICH	17	M	LABR	RRZZZZ	USA
WEINHOLZ, DAVID	20	M	LABR	RRZZZZ	USA
BERG, AUGUST	20	M	LABR	RRZZZZ	USA
MAKOWSKI, FRANZ	20	M	LABR	RRZZZZ	USA
SCHRAUK, EMIL	27	M	LABR	RRZZZZ	USA
ROMMA, ANTON	37	M	STCTR	RRZZZZ	USA
KRAHM, MICHAEL	22	M	LABR	RRZZZZ	USA
MAREINOWSKY, JAN	29	M	LABR	RRZZZZ	USA
GEORGE	19	M	LABR	RRZZZZ	USA
IAUEZAITIR, MARY	22	F	W	RRZZZZ	USA

PASSENGER	AGE	SEX	OCCUPATION	PRV VIL DES
MYSZKOWSKI, WLADISLAUS	33	M	LABR	RRZZZZUSA
KUCHARSKI, JOHANN	28	M	LABR	RRZZZZUSA
GAUZ, LUDWIG	59	M	LABR	RRZZZZUSA
CAROLINE	61	F	W	RRZZZZUSA
AUGUST	23	M	CH	RRZZZZUSA
BERTHA	20	F	CH	RRZZZZUSA
FEUNER, WILHELMINE	22	F	SGL	RRZZZZUSA
JACOBSEN, CHRIST	39	M	LKSH	RRZZZZUSA
HEDWIG	12	F	CH	RRZZZZUSA
CARL	10	M	CH	RRZZZZUSA
PAUL	9	M	CHILD	RRZZZZUSA
LOUSE	4	F	CHILD	RRZZZZUSA
MARGARETHE	1	F	CHILD	RRZZZZUSA
GRIESBACH, MATHILDE	34	F	W	RRZZZZUSA
CHRISTIAN	1	M	CHILD	RRZZZZUSA
SAAGER, HERMANN	32	M	LABR	RRZZZZUSA
BERTHA	33	F	W	RRZZZZUSA
AUGUST	11	M	CH	RRZZZZUSA
WILHELLM	9	M	CHILD	RRZZZZUSA
EMIL	4	M	CHILD	RRZZZZUSA
FRIEDRICH	1	M	CHILD	RRZZZZUSA
WEIDEMANN, ADOLF	21	M	BKR	RRZZZZUSA
SKIBINSKA, CAICILIE	53	F	W	RRZZZZUSA
TARASCHINSKY, JACOB	28	M	LABR	RRZZZZUSA
JULIE	24	F	W	RRZZZZUSA
JACOB	3	M	CHILD	RRZZZZUSA
ANNA	.06	F	INFANT	RRZZZZUSA
SKIBICKE, JOHANN	24	M	LABR	RRZZZZUSA
REWOLDT, AUGUST	26	M	FARMER	RRZZZZUSA
LABAJ, JOSEF	30	M	LABR	RRZZZZUSA
JULIANA	28	F	W	RRZZZZUSA
MARIANNA	22	F	SI	RRZZZZUSA
FRANZ	3	M	CHILD	RRZZZZUSA
LEOKADIA	1	F	CHILD	RRZZZZUSA
IGNATZ	.06	M	INFANT	RRZZZZUSA
DAVID, OTILIE	21	F	SGL	RRZZZZUSA
HAASE, CARL	28	M	LABR	RRZZZZUSA
AUGUSTE	30	F	W	RRZZZZUSA
BERTHA	4	F	CHILD	RRZZZZUSA
FRIEDRICH	.03	M	INFANT	RRZZZZUSA
SOLOBODOWSKI, FRANZISKA	28	F	W	RRZZZZUSA
THEODOSIA	3	F	CHILD	RRZZZZUSA
ANASTASIA	2	F	CHILD	RRZZZZUSA
JOSEPHINE	.03	F	INFANT	RRZZZZUSA
KATH, AUGUSTE	40	F	W	RRZZZZUSA
MARIE	11	F	CH	RRZZZZUSA
EMMA	7	F	CHILD	RRZZZZUSA
ERICH	4	M	CHILD	RRZZZZUSA
NAATZ, EMILIE	19	F	SGL	RRZZZZUSA
SCHULZ, JACOB	49	M	LABR	RRZZZZUSA
JANKOWSKY, ANTON	19	M	LABR	RRZZZZUSA
WIEDEN, BERTHA	24	F	SGL	RRZZZZUSA
MARIE	20	F	SGL	RRZZZZUSA
DAMROW, CARL	34	M	LABR	RRZZZZUSA
EMILIE	33	F	W	RRZZZZUSA
HOSS, HENRIETTE	64	F	M	RRZZZZUSA
DAMROW, WILLI	1	M	CHILD	RRZZZZUSA
BEHRENT, LEOVI	31	M	LABR	RRZZZZUSA
JULIE	28	F	W	RRZZZZUSA
AUGUSTE	6	F	CHILD	RRZZZZUSA
ADOLF	4	M	CHILD	RRZZZZUSA
LUDWIG	2	M	CHILD	RRZZZZUSA
JUNGAIT, JOSEF	17	M	DLR	RRZZZZUSA
JANKELOWITZ, SCHABIE	17	M	SCHM	RRZZZZUSA
STEINBERG, DAVID	49	M	LABR	RRZZZZUSA
DARVINISS, JOHANN	17	M	LABR	RRZZZZUSA
GERIMMSCH, AUGUST	28	M	LABR	RRZZZZUSA
GOSSELWITZ, LOUIS	26	M	LABR	RRZZZZUNK
ROTTWITSCH, JOSEF	33	M	LABR	RRZZZZUNK
SESMANSKI, ALBERT	18	M	CH	RRZZZZUNK
AUGUSTE	11	F	CH	RRZZZZUNK
PAUL	.03	M	INFANT	RRZZZZUNK
WIRTALLA, WILHELMINE	30	F	W	RRZZZZUNK
RUDOLF	8	M	CHILD	RRZZZZUNK
HERMANN	5	M	CHILD	RRZZZZUNK
WILHELM	2	M	CHILD	RRZZZZUNK
FROEMSCHOLZ, FERDINAND	23	M	LABR	RRZZZZUNK
WILHELMINE	29	F	W	RRZZZZUNK
WILHELM	6	M	CHILD	RRZZZZUNK
HEYER, EDUARD	00	M	LABR	RRZZZZUNK
LIPSCHUETZ, LORE	22	F	SGL	RRZZZZUNK
POSCHKEWITZ, JOSEF	23	M	LABR	RRZZZZUNK
SCHIFFMANN, BORUCK	23	M	DLR	RRZZZZUNK
BORZUK, ANTON	26	M	LABR	RRZZZZUNK
SALACHUCHE, ISRAEL	23	M	LABR	RRZZZZUNK
LEA	20	F	W	RRZZZZUNK
TATARSKI, JOSSEL	20	M	DLR	RRZZZZUNK
REBECCA	20	F	W	RRZZZZUNK
GOLDBERG, REISACH	20	M	DLR	RRZZZZUNK
TASROPWITZ, FRANZ	24	M	DLR	RRZZZZUNK
KRULISCHOWSKY, ANTON	26	M	DLR	RRZZZZUNK
ENGROUN, CHANNE	27	M	LABR	RRZZZZUNK
ZIPLIWITZ, JAKOB	36	M	LABR	RRZZZZUNK
SIMCHE	19	M	LABR	RRZZZZUNK
CHANCE	18	F	SI	RRZZZZUNK
S-LDBERG, U	36	M	LABR	RRZZZZUNK
SILBERGUT, MOSES	27	M	LABR	RRZZZZUNK
LACHOWITZ, ISAAC	39	M	LABR	RRZZZZUNK
SILBERMANN, BORUCH	40	M	LABR	RRZZZZUNK
GERSCHOWITZ, DAVID	20	M	LABR	RRZZZZUNK
DWORKIN, RUBIN	37	M	LABR	RRZZZZUNK
FINKELMANN, KUSCHEL	36	M	LABR	RRZZZZUNK
DUEDMANN, ABRAHAM	25	M	LABR	RRZZZZUNK
SCHALOEWITZ, WIDGER	29	M	LABR	RRZZZZUNK
BERTMANN, JACOB	40	M	LABR	RRZZZZUNK
ZAKRZEWSKY, ANTONIE	22	F	W	RRZZZZUNK
STANISLAUS	4	M	CHILD	RRZZZZUNK
MASURKIEWITSCH, ANTON	35	M	LABR	RRZZZZUNK
LEONHARD	16	M	LABR	RRZZZZUNK
JOSEF	27	M	LABR	RRZZZZUNK
SOLACHUCHE, SCHAMUEL	2	M	CHILD	RRZZZZUNK
SCHIKE	.06	M	INFANT	RRZZZZUNK
PIETRAS, JACOB	20	M	LABR	RRZZZZUNK
SURTAY, JAN	22	M	LABR	RRZZZZUNK

SHIP: MARSALA

FROM: HAMBURG
TO: NEW YORK
ARRIVED: 19 MAY 1888

PASSENGER	AGE	SEX	OCCUPATION	PRV VIL DES
SCHESINSKE, NOCHUM	30	M	SMH	RRZZZZNY
KOLARSKI, WLADISLAUS	26	M	SMH	RRZZZZNY
TAUBE, JACOB	25	F	SGL	RRZZZZNY
KOLARSKI, ADAM	20	M	LABR	RRZZZZNY
PAPIERSKIE, PAWEL	40	M	SHMK	RRZZZZNY
MEHT, JOSEPH	21	M	LABR	RRZZZZNY
JOHANNA	9	F	CHILD	RRZZZZNY
GAVRONSKI, ANNA	15	F	SGL	RRZZZZNY
JORDANSKI, MOSES	23	M	LABR	RRZZZZNY
EYDZYN, CAREL	26	M	LABR	RRZZZZNY
SCHLOSS, ANNA	21	F	WO	RRZZZZNY
SAMUEL	2	M	CHILD	RRZZZZNY
KUSZULIS, JOSEPH	23	M	LABR	RRZZZZNY
CHRAPOT, MEYER	19	M	LABR	RRZZZZNY
VERDERBER, MARIE	21	F	SGL	RRZZZZNY
ROSSMANN, PETER	11	M	BY	RRZZZZNY
LEWANDOWSKI, FRANZ	22	M	LABR	RRZZZZNY
KRUCEWSKI, CHAN	17	F	SGL	RRZZZZNY
LEWIN, SCHLOME	31	M	MCHT	RRZZZZNY
SUCHAWITZKA, HANNA	18	F	SGL	RRZZZZNY
RANSKI, JOSCE	27	M	JNR	RRZZZZNY
DAVIDOWITZ, ISAAC	50	M	JNR	RRZZZZNY
SUSNITZKI, DAVID	32	M	LABR	RRZZZZNY
ABRAMOWITZ, BENZER	23	M	LABR	RRZZZZNY

PASSENGER	AGE	SEX	OCCUPATION	PRV VIL DES
CHRAPOT, BERL	50	M	TLR	RRZZZZNY
WATCHCLIS, U	17	M	LABR	RRZZZZNY
SCHIKORSKI, ROSA	20	F	SGL	RRZZZZNY
WALLINITZ, ADAM	28	M	LABR	RRZZZZNY
MORZEL, JAN	30	M	LABR	RRZZZZNY
PAROWSKI, MATZE	25	F	SGL	RRZZZZNY
BLOCH, CHAISE	20	F	SGL	RRZZZZNY
ELBERT, MOSES	30	M	LABR	RRZZZZNY
ROSENKRAUZ, CHUME	28	M	LABR	RRZZZZNY
SIMIANSKI, FISCHEL	30	M	LABR	RRZZZZNY
KOJTZAN, JOS	52	M	LABR	RRZZZZNY
BARTOL, STANISLAWA	19	F	SGL	RRZZZZNY
MAKOSKA, EMILIE	23	F	WO	RRZZZZNY
JULIAN	.11	M	INFANT	RRZZZZNY
STANISLAWA	.11	F	INFANT	RRZZZZNY
WALENKARSKA, FRANZISKA	25	F	SGL	RRZZZZNY
GLOWATZKI, MICHAEL	22	M	LABR	RRZZZZNY
GUSCHLEWITZ, UNEFRY	45	M	LABR	RRZZZZNY
LEIDER, IGNATZ	23	M	LABR	RRZZZZNY
POLIWNIK, WOLF	20	M	LABR	RRZZZZCIN
CHEISE	17	F	SGL	RRZZZZCIN
ANDROESICH, THAUDIUS	30	M	LABR	RRZZZZNY
OZEKELA, JAN	24	M	LABR	RRZZZZNY
CZICHOWSKI, JOSEF	26	M	LABR	RRZZZZNY
PJONTE, PAUL	23	M	LABR	RRZZZZNY
BRAUNSTEIN, OSIP	17	M	DLR	RRZZZZNY
REKAS, JEZI	21	M	LABR	RRZZZZNY
KWIATKOWSKI, MICHAEL	26	M	LABR	RRZZZZNY
ANNA	20	F	SGL	RRZZZZNY
HUGO, ANNA	58	F	WO	RRZZZZNY
KAWONIK, JOSSEL	25	M	LABR	RRZZZZNY
FRANK, ASCIEL	25	M	DLR	RRZZZZNY
KOZLOWSKI, FELIX	23	M	LABR	RRZZZZNY
DOELA, ANTON	24	M	DLR	RRZZZZNY
ANNA	30	F	UNKNOWN	RRZZZZNY
AGNESCA	8	F	CHILD	RRZZZZNY
MARIANNE	8	F	CHILD	RRZZZZNY
ZAHRZEWSKI, MICHAL	22	M	LABR	RRZZZZNY
KAROL	28	M	LABR	RRZZZZNY
LAJBINUS, ANTONY	19	M	LABR	RRZZZZNY
STRASCHUN, ARON	24	M	LABR	RRZZZZNY
WEINER, HIRSCH	18	M	LABR	RRZZZZNY
SEMSKI, DAVID	40	M	UNKNOWN	RRZZZZNY
CHAIM	17	M	UNKNOWN	RRZZZZNY
WISCHNOWSKI, JOHANN	24	M	LABR	RRZZZZNY
KUSMITZKI, MATTHIAS	22	M	LABR	RRZZZZNY
HELFMANN, OSCHER	20	M	DLR	RRZZZZNY
TIKOTZKI, ETTEL	16	F	SGL	RRZZZZNY
BIALOBLOTZKI, ESTHER	9	F	CHILD	RRZZZZNY
JACHNIK, IGNATZ	28	M	BKR	RRZZZZBUF
KAPLAN, ABRAHAM	25	M	TLR	RRZZZZBUF
SCHAIES, DUSCHE	17	F	SGL	RRZZZZBUF
KAPLAN, JACOB	21	M	TLR	RRZZZZSY
DOLEJSKA, ANTONIN	26	M	TLR	RRZZZZCH

SHIP: CITY OF CHICAGO

FROM: LIVERPOOL AND QUEENSTOWN
TO: NEW YORK
ARRIVED: 19 MAY 1888

PASSENGER	AGE	SEX	OCCUPATION	PRV VIL DES
CHERAGS, GILLIG	32	F	W	PLZZZZUSA
K--	6	M	CHILD	PLZZZZUSA
LESHENS	4	M	CHILD	PLZZZZUSA
FRIED	00	F	INF	PLZZZZUSA
SCHULEM	11	M	CH	PLZZZZUSA

SHIP: RUGIA

FROM: HAMBURG
TO: NEW YORK
ARRIVED: 19 MAY 1888

PASSENGER	AGE	SEX	OCCUPATION	PRV VIL DES
GRODZINSKI, DINA	34	F	W	RRZZZZUSA
HIRSCH	8	M	CHILD	RRZZZZUSA
SCHOLEM	7	M	CHILD	RRZZZZUSA
MENDEL	00	F	INF	RRZZZZUSA
ALTMAN, SALOMON	46	M	LABR	RRZZZZUSA
MALKE	40	F	W	RRZZZZUSA
NICZETZKI, SAM	39	M	TLR	RRZZZZUSA
GOLDBERG, JUDEL	21	M	TLR	RRZZZZUSA
SLAVINSKA, BALVINE	27	M	SGL	RRZZZZUSA
PIONTHOOSKI, AMALIE	47	F	WO	RRZZZZUSA
EMMA	9	F	CHILD	RRZZZZUSA
BERLA	7	F	CHILD	RRZZZZUSA
KERBAUM, HERMAN	25	M	UNKNOWN	RRZZZZUSA
STIEZINSKY, STANISLAUS	22	M	UNKNOWN	RRZZZZUSA
BRADZINSKY, JOSEF	37	M	LABR	RRZZZZUSA
KLANICKI, LUCAS	45	M	LABR	RRZZZZUSA
KATH	20	F	SGL	RRZZZZUSA
FERLEY, JOS	25	M	LABR	RRZZZZUSA
LEIBNER, DABE	30	F	W	RRZZZZUSA
GITTEL	5	F	CHILD	RRZZZZUSA
FIDEL	00	M	INF	RRZZZZUSA
PUSIC, ANDRZY	30	M	LABR	RRZZZZUSA
USZTOWINOWSKA, MASCA	20	M	LABR	RRZZZZUSA
FARESZEWICZ, ALEX	25	M	LABR	RRZZZZUSA
DRAGON, MATH	23	M	LABR	RRZZZZUSA
KAMINSKY, KASIS	42	M	LABR	RRZZZZUSA
SCHIFSLIKOWSKY, SALAMON	31	M	MCHT	RRZZZZUSA
GEBRSKI, JAN	24	M	MCHT	RRZZZZUSA
PADBEREWSKY, SCHEINE	24	F	WO	RRZZZZUSA
ABRAM	4	M	CHILD	RRZZZZUSA
SUSSI	.11	F	INFANT	RRZZZZUSA
MOSES	18	M	DLR	RRZZZZUSA
KOLTUM, JACOB	44	M	LABR	RRZZZZUSA
IDES	36	F	W	RRZZZZUSA
ANNA	16	F	CH	RRZZZZUSA
SARA	14	F	UNKNOWN	RRZZZZUSA
ROSA	5	F	CHILD	RRZZZZUSA
OSSI	9	F	CHILD	RRZZZZUSA
SALOMON	8	M	CHILD	RRZZZZUSA
FALIK	4	M	CHILD	RRZZZZUSA
MOSES	.11	M	INFANT	RRZZZZUSA
DWORSKY, CHAIM	14	M	LABR	RRZZZZUSA
NAPIURSKY, JAN	28	M	LABR	RRZZZZUSA
RESCHKA, FRANZ	28	M	LABR	RRZZZZUSA
JANKOWSKA, EMILIE	20	F	SGL	RRZZZZUSA
LEMKE, LOUISE	22	F	SGL	RRZZZZUSA
DAN, RACHEL	18	F	SGL	RRZZZZUSA
KUSCHINSKY, STANISLAV	25	M	LABR	RRZZZZUSA
NADRATOWSKY, FRANZ	23	M	LABR	RRZZZZUSA
FRIEDRIKOWICZ, JANDRE	28	M	LABR	RRZZZZUSA
BUDNIKA, FRUMA	22	F	WO	RRZZZZUSA
BERNSTEIN, ESTER	40	F	WO	RRZZZZUSA
ASNE	9	F	CHILD	RRZZZZUSA
MINDEL	5	F	CHILD	RRZZZZUSA
KATHISKI, ABEL	9	M	CHILD	RRZZZZUSA
BUSCH, SARA	26	F	LABR	RRZZZZUSA
HYMAN	6	M	CHILD	RRZZZZUSA
CHINKE	.11	F	INFANT	RRZZZZUSA
SILBERSTEIN, SCHEINE	38	F	WO	RRZZZZUSA
ESTHER	18	F	CH	RRZZZZUSA
TAUBE	9	F	CHILD	RRZZZZUSA
JOSEF	8	M	CHILD	RRZZZZUSA
MEYER	7	M	CHILD	RRZZZZUSA
NOCHEM	.11	M	INFANT	RRZZZZUSA
WOLKANSKY, WOLF	36	M	LABR	RRZZZZUSA
DEBORE	15	F	SGL	RRZZZZUSA
SIMAN	9	M	CHILD	RRZZZZUSA
KATZ, SCHIFFRE	18	F	SGL	RRZZZZUSA

PASSENGER	AGE	SEX	OCCUPATION	PRV	VIL	DES
SIERSCHK, JOSEF	29	M	LABR	RR	ZZZZ	USA
BASCHIG, JAN	23	M	LABR	RR	ZZZZ	USA
PLAGENS, FRIEDR	21	M	LABR	RR	ZZZZ	USA
NARUSIEWIC, STANISLAUS	28	M	LABR	RR	ZZZZ	USA
WALCKA, MIHAL	30	M	LABR	RR	ZZZZ	USA
BACKSZEE, JOSEF	14	M	LABR	RR	ZZZZ	USA
PIKARSKI, ABRAM	28	M	LABR	RR	ZZZZ	USA
SABICZYNSKA, VICTOR	25	M	LABR	RR	ZZZZ	USA
MARKIEWIZ, MARY	22	F	WO	RR	ZZZZ	USA
LIPPMAN, JOSEF	16	M	LABR	RR	ZZZZ	USA
ZAKREWSKA, MARIANNA	25	F	SGL	RR	ZZZZ	USA
LISOWSKI, MARIANNA	18	F	SGL	RR	ZZZZ	USA
JAN	14	M	LABR	RR	ZZZZ	USA
PATOCKI, VINCENTI	21	M	LABR	RR	ZZZZ	USA
SWIZEWICZ, ADAM	18	M	LABR	RR	ZZZZ	USA
SUGATO, ANTONI	35	M	LABR	RR	ZZZZ	USA
ORTLIEB, LUSWIG	19	M	LABR	RR	ZZZZ	USA
CASTENE	18	F	SGL	RR	ZZZZ	USA
DZETKOWSKY, JOHN	30	M	LABR	RR	ZZZZ	USA
BROST, MENUCHE	14	M	CH	RR	ZZZZ	USA
HENE	9	M	CHILD	RR	ZZZZ	USA
PICAN, JOSEF	23	M	LABR	RR	ZZZZ	USA
LISAKOWSLY, JAN	30	M	LABR	RR	ZZZZ	USA
CHRIST	30	F	WO	RR	ZZZZ	USA
JOSEF	.11	M	INFANT	RR	ZZZZ	USA
CHMILEWSKI, STANISLAUS	24	M	LABR	RR	ZZZZ	USA
SEID, KOPPEL	46	M	DLR	RR	ZZZZ	USA
BARCZYKOWSKY, ANTON	23	M	LABR	RR	ZZZZ	USA
MUELLER, MARIAN	19	M	LABR	RR	ZZZZ	USA
MASWICKEWISZ, RAIM	24	M	MLR	RR	ZZZZ	USA
SEEGERS, BALISLAV	18	M	SDLR	RR	ZZZZ	USA
SCHULZ, JOH	30	M	LABR	RR	ZZZZ	USA
MARIANNA	26	F	W	RR	ZZZZ	USA
GUSTAV	5	M	CHILD	RR	ZZZZ	USA
DANIEL	3	M	CHILD	RR	ZZZZ	USA
HOFFMANN, LUDWIG	24	M	LABR	RR	ZZZZ	USA
FADLAN, RUDOLF	24	M	LABR	RR	ZZZZ	USA
PLUEDDEMANN, ERNEST	25	F	W	RR	ZZZZ	USA
WILH	6	F	CHILD	RR	ZZZZ	USA
MICHAEL	2	M	CHILD	RR	ZZZZ	USA
BABANOW, VASILAV	20	M	LABR	RR	ZZZZ	USA
FLATKY, ISRAEL	19	M	TCHR	RR	ZZZZ	USA
KAMINSKY, TAUBE	29	F	W	RR	ZZZZ	USA
JOSEF	8	M	CHILD	RR	ZZZZ	USA
GEORG	6	M	CHILD	RR	ZZZZ	USA
RITKE	2	F	CHILD	RR	ZZZZ	USA
KANTISKORUM, DWORE	16	M	FARMER	RR	ZZZZ	USA
NOWEZALSKY, HERSCH	20	M	LABR	RR	ZZZZ	USA
BLUME	20	F	W	RR	ZZZZ	USA
ESTHER	00	F	INF	RR	ZZZZ	USA
KORZNAY, WELI	31	M	LABR	RR	ZZZZ	USA
RUBINSTEIN, GEDALIE	20	M	UNKNOWN	RR	ZZZZ	USA
GOLDE	22	F	W	RR	ZZZZ	USA
LINDENBLUETH, SIMON	20	M	LABR	RR	ZZZZ	USA
TOEPPERMAN, GOETTEL	24	F	WO	RR	ZZZZ	USA
FRAENKEL, BYNUM	25	M	LABR	RR	ZZZZ	USA
HEUSS, HENOCH	20	M	LABR	RR	ZZZZ	USA
SZULPETER, ISAAC	32	M	LABR	RR	ZZZZ	USA
DUNAJIWSKI, MICHAEL	40	M	LABR	RR	ZZZZ	USA
BRAUNSTEIN, WOLF	20	M	LABR	RR	ZZZZ	USA
ISCHIEL	8	M	CHILD	RR	ZZZZ	USA
SOKALSKI, SAM	22	M	LABR	RR	ZZZZ	USA
SAM	22	M	LABR	RR	ZZZZ	USA
HELENE	20	F	W	RR	ZZZZ	USA
DOBRING, FICHEL	21	M	LABR	RR	ZZZZ	USA
KARPUTAWSKY, JACOB	28	M	LABR	RR	ZZZZ	USA
CHEIVE	27	F	W	RR	ZZZZ	USA
SPRINE	8	F	CHILD	RR	ZZZZ	USA
RACHEL	5	F	CHILD	RR	ZZZZ	USA
ISRAEL	3	M	CHILD	RR	ZZZZ	USA
ISAAK	00	M	INF	RR	ZZZZ	USA
JALINSKI, SIMCHE	30	M	LABR	RR	ZZZZ	USA
RIVKE	29	F	W	RR	ZZZZ	USA
CHUNE	18	F	D	RR	ZZZZ	USA
BENIE	16	F	D	RR	ZZZZ	USA

PASSENGER	AGE	SEX	OCCUPATION	PRV	VIL	DES
CHAWE	6	F	CHILD	RR	ZZZZ	USA
MECHLE	4	M	CHILD	RR	ZZZZ	USA
FRUME	00	F	INF	RR	ZZZZ	USA
ZABLADZKI, BERL	25	M	LABR	RR	ZZZZ	USA
DWAPNE	16	F	SGL	RR	ZZZZ	USA
SERBITZKI, HOFLIDIS	23	M	LABR	RR	ZZZZ	USA
TYSSAR, INO	20	M	LABR	RR	ZZZZ	USA
TOMAZEWSKI, JOS	21	M	LABR	RR	ZZZZ	USA
MICHLOWSKI, MICHAEL	16	M	LABR	RR	ZZZZ	USA
FISS, RACHEL	22	F	WO	RR	ZZZZ	USA
GOLDBERG, BERTHA	15	F	WO	RR	ZZZZ	USA
LEWINTHAL, JANKEL	58	M	LABR	RR	ZZZZ	USA
COHEN, GITE	35	F	W	RR	ZZZZ	USA
ROCHE	8	F	CHILD	RR	ZZZZ	USA
PESSE	7	F	CHILD	RR	ZZZZ	USA
MICHAEL	5	M	CHILD	RR	ZZZZ	USA
HIRSCH	5	M	CHILD	RR	ZZZZ	USA
CHAJE	4	M	CHILD	RR	ZZZZ	USA
CHAPUR	2	M	CHILD	RR	ZZZZ	USA
SCHAPIRO, EIDE	16	F	WO	RR	ZZZZ	USA
COHEN, HAPPEL	20	M	LABR	RR	ZZZZ	USA
WILBUSHEWITZ, BENI	23	M	APTC	RR	ZZZZ	USA
BROTUNISHKI, SIMON	22	M	LABR	RR	ZZZZ	USA
KARPOWITZ, ALTER	26	M	LABR	RR	ZZZZ	USA
MARZINKEWITZ, JAN	21	M	LABR	RR	ZZZZ	USA
WOLSKI, FRANZ	31	M	LABR	RR	ZZZZ	USA
SCHMACKNER, AMALIE	28	F	WO	RR	ZZZZ	USA
RAGORD, ALEX	35	M	TLR	RR	ZZZZ	USA
GUTTER, JACOB	22	M	TLR	RR	ZZZZ	USA
KAUNI, MAYER	31	M	MCHT	RR	ZZZZ	USA
GENI	24	F	W	RR	ZZZZ	USA
ARON	5	F	CHILD	RR	ZZZZ	USA
GUJA	3	F	CHILD	RR	ZZZZ	USA
ESTER	00	F	INF	RR	ZZZZ	USA
KASSA	15	F	D	RR	ZZZZ	USA
BERNSTEIN, JANKEL	6	M	CHILD	RR	ZZZZ	USA
LEIB	4	M	CHILD	RR	ZZZZ	USA
ARONOWITZ, JOSEF	50	M	DLR	RR	ZZZZ	USA
SUEV, MOSES	19	M	UNKNOWN	RR	ZZZZ	USA
BRANDE, MOSES	17	M	UNKNOWN	RR	ZZZZ	USA
WOYZIK, SALA	33	M	MCHT	RR	ZZZZ	USA
WOLFACHOWITZ, SCHMUL	24	M	JNR	RR	ZZZZ	USA
BLESS, JUDEL	25	M	JNR	RR	ZZZZ	USA
HARDER	20	F	UNKNOWN	RR	ZZZZ	USA
SARAH	55	F	WO	RR	ZZZZ	USA
KRETZMAR, LEIB	35	M	DLR	RR	ZZZZ	USA
ILSE	19	F	W	RR	ZZZZ	USA
REINSTEIN, ETEL	22	F	SGL	RR	ZZZZ	USA
PRUSKI, ALEXANDER	21	M	LABR	RR	ZZZZ	USA
BLESS, CHEWE	22	F	WO	RR	ZZZZ	USA
ABR	3	M	CHILD	RR	ZZZZ	USA
BALDY, ANTON	42	M	FARMER	RR	ZZZZ	USA
AGNES	40	F	W	RR	ZZZZ	USA
HEDWIG	9	F	CHILD	RR	ZZZZ	USA
PAUL	9	M	CHILD	RR	ZZZZ	USA
BARTOL	4	M	CHILD	RR	ZZZZ	USA
PADLEWSKY, STANISLAUS	21	M	MLR	RR	ZZZZ	USA
LEMKE, CHRISTIAN	33	M	LABR	RR	ZZZZ	USA
HUTNER, EIDE	40	F	WO	RR	ZZZZ	USA
JACOB	9	M	CHILD	RR	ZZZZ	USA
FRANK, CHANNE	15	F	SGL	RR	ZZZZ	USA
WISCHINSKI, VICENTY	47	M	LABR	RR	ZZZZ	USA
FELIX	19	M	LABR	RR	ZZZZ	USA
JAN	16	M	LABR	RR	ZZZZ	USA
ARNASCHIM, PETER	30	M	LABR	RR	ZZZZ	USA
KLOCK, ALEX	45	M	LABR	RR	ZZZZ	USA
JOSEFE	40	F	W	RR	ZZZZ	USA
KATSCHUK, JAN	24	M	LABR	RR	ZZZZ	USA
BAUMGART, CARL	28	M	LABR	RR	ZZZZ	USA
CARL	24	M	LABR	RR	ZZZZ	USA
WIELSKI, WILH	21	M	LABR	RR	ZZZZ	USA
KRIEGER, HEINR	17	M	LABR	RR	ZZZZ	USA
GURIEZ, ANNA	18	F	SGL	RR	ZZZZ	USA
WEISSMAN, MARCUS	34	M	LABR	RR	ZZZZ	USA
BERNSTEIN, ITZIG	39	M	LABR	RR	ZZZZ	USA

PASSENGER	AGE	SEX	OCCUPATION	PRV VIL DES
FIELBERG, JOSIS	46	M	LABR	RRZZZZUSA
MATLA	36	F	W	RRZZZZUSA
GREGORIAS	9	M	CHILD	RRZZZZUSA
ANNA	9	F	CHILD	RRZZZZUSA
FITELBERG, LOUISE	7	F	CHILD	RRZZZZUSA
HUBER, MOSES	28	M	LABR	RRZZZZUSA
NATHANSON, ISRAEL	27	M	LABR	RRZZZZUSA
ROSEL, JOH	24	M	LABR	RRZZZZUSA
REISTAN, KARL	25	M	LABR	RRZZZZUSA
WODARSKI, THOS	31	M	LABR	RRZZZZUSA
FIEDLER, MARTIN	26	M	LABR	RRZZZZUSA
KNAPT, KARL	17	M	LABR	RRZZZZUSA
ROGOZINSKY, VINCENT	28	M	LABR	RRZZZZUSA
WOPECHOWSKY, JOSEF	33	M	LABR	RRZZZZUSA
CZUDNOWSKI, DAVID	35	M	LABR	RRZZZZUSA
RECKIW, MAILACH	29	M	TLR	RRZZZZUSA
CHAJI	19	F	W	RRZZZZUSA
BUREZINSKI, AGNES	54	F	UNKNOWN	RRZZZZUSA
CASEMIR	20	M	UNKNOWN	RRZZZZUSA
THEODOR	17	M	UNKNOWN	RRZZZZUSA
ADRIAN	8	M	CHILD	RRZZZZUSA
SILBERMANN, ELKE	25	F	WO	RRZZZZUSA
CHANNE	.11	F	INFANT	RRZZZZUSA
BANASCH, JOSEF	33	M	LABR	RRZZZZUSA
FRIEDERIKE	32	F	W	RRZZZZUSA
OTTO	.06	M	INFANT	RRZZZZUSA
SOBILISKI, ANTONIA	26	F	WO	RRZZZZUSA
ALEXANDER	2	M	CHILD	RRZZZZUSA
U	.11	M	INFANT	RRZZZZUSA
DAMBROWSKA, U	33	F	UNKNOWN	RRZZZZUSA
U	8	M	CHILD	RRZZZZUSA

SHIP: AMERICA

FROM: BREMEN
TO: BALTIMORE
ARRIVED: 20 MAY 1888

PASSENGER	AGE	SEX	OCCUPATION	PRV VIL DES
PAPKE, LOUISE	22	F	SVNT	RRZZZZIL
PABISZEWSKY, JOSEPH	25	M	MCHT	RRZZZZDAK
POSZKA, KAZENNEARS	25	M	LABR	RRZZZZOH
CATARZINA	20	F	UNKNOWN	RRZZZZOH
BARTKIEWITZ, PETER	30	M	BLKSMH	RRZZZZOH
LAGOCKI, IGNATZ	31	M	CPTR	RRZZZZOH
MARIE	29	F	UNKNOWN	RRZZZZOH
CZIVICKLINSKE, VERONICA	24	F	UNKNOWN	RRZZZZOH
ROSALIA	2	F	CHILD	RRZZZZOH
JOHANN	.10	M	INFANT	RRZZZZOH
RATAIVZAK, MARIANNE	33	F	UNKNOWN	RRZZZZNE
MARIANNE	6	F	CHILD	RRZZZZNE
ANTONIA	5	F	CHILD	RRZZZZNE
FRANZISKA	4	F	CHILD	RRZZZZNE
FRANZEK	2	M	CHILD	RRZZZZNE
WINCENTI	.11	M	INFANT	RRZZZZNE
LEZARSKY, JOSEF	27	M	MNR	RRZZZZUSA
ANNA	.09	F	INFANT	RRZZZZUSA
KUEHN, ERNESTINE	20	F	SVNT	RRZZZZUSA
WOLF, DANIEL	24	M	MCHT	RRZZZZUSA
LAMPARSKA, FRANZISCA	26	F	UNKNOWN	RRZZZZUSA
LUDISLAW	2	M	CHILD	RRZZZZUSA
HELENE	.10	F	INFANT	RRZZZZUSA
PRAUKE, ERNST	23	M	MCHT	RRZZZZUSA
BERLING, DINA	5	F	CHILD	RRZZZZUSA
GRUNDWALD, WILHELMINE	23	F	SVNT	RRZZZZUSA
LATAWSCHINSKI, MICHAEL	22	M	LABR	RRZZZZMO
BRZEUKWICZ, VALENTINA	18	F	UNKNOWN	RRZZZZMO
SCHMIDT, OTTILIE	23	F	UNKNOWN	RRZZZZMO
MARTHA	2	F	CHILD	RRZZZZMO
GEORG	.03	M	INFANT	RRZZZZMO
AUGUSTE	44	F	UNKNOWN	RRZZZZMO
OTTILIE	21	F	SVNT	RRZZZZMO
REINHARDT	7	M	CHILD	RRZZZZMO
HERMANN	6	M	CHILD	RRZZZZMO
MARTHA	2	F	CHILD	RRZZZZMO
KRAJECKI, IGNATZ	57	M	UNKNOWN	RRZZZZNE
MARIANNA	56	F	UNKNOWN	RRZZZZNE
LADISLAW	12	M	CH	RRZZZZNE
JOHAN	9	M	CHILD	RRZZZZNE
MARIANNA	7	F	CHILD	RRZZZZNE
ANNA	5	F	CHILD	RRZZZZNE
THEOPHILA	3	F	CHILD	RRZZZZNE
PIETSCHINNSKY, JOSEPH	14	M	CH	RRZZZZNE
KAMINSKY, JOSEPH	45	M	LABR	RRZZZZAL
WASBRICH, AUGUST	12	M	LABR	RRZZZZAL
BELZINSKY, JAN	42	M	FARMER	RRZZZZMO
MASLOWSKY, FELIX	25	M	TLR	RRZZZZMO
MODERSKY, JACOB	13	M	CH	RRZZZZMO
GREGOROWIECZ, ADELLA	35	F	UNKNOWN	RRZZZZUT
ADAM	6	M	CHILD	RRZZZZUT
EVA	4	F	CHILD	RRZZZZUT
POSLOWSKI, ELISABETH	36	F	CK	RRZZZZMD
SZIDLOWSKI, ANTON	24	M	LABR	RRZZZZMD
TOMASZEWSKI, MARZANA	23	F	LABR	RRZZZZAR
IGNATZ	25	M	LABR	RRZZZZAR
PUZNIK, FRANIZEK	26	M	LABR	RRZZZZAR
MAURORAROWITZ, FRANIZEK	50	M	LABR	RRZZZZAR
FRAENKEL, SIMON	32	M	LABR	RRZZZZAR
FLAX, LEISER	25	M	MCHT	RRZZZZAR
MAROWITZ, ABRAM	16	M	UNKNOWN	RRZZZZMI
WOLF, SOLOMON	25	M	MCHT	RRZZZZMI
MERENBLUM, SCHEYNE	25	F	UNKNOWN	RRZZZZMI
SCHEYNE	.09	F	INFANT	RRZZZZMI
LEVITZ, ABRAHAM	33	M	MCHT	RRZZZZMD
BLEECHER, SCHEINE	40	F	UNKNOWN	RRZZZZMD
WUNKZCHESOVA, JOSEFA	30	F	UNKNOWN	RRZZZZMD
MARIANA	3	F	CHILD	RRZZZZMD
SOPHIA	.06	F	INFANT	RRZZZZMD
SONNENBERG, FREDRICH	26	M	UNKNOWN	RRZZZZMD
LUEDE, WILHELM	27	M	FARMER	RRZZZZIL
SEIDEL, OTTILIE	42	F	UNKNOWN	RRZZZZPA
MINNA	13	F	UNKNOWN	RRZZZZPA
FRANZ	11	M	CH	RRZZZZPA
PAULINE	7	F	CHILD	RRZZZZPA
CUNO	6	M	CHILD	RRZZZZPA
EMMA	5	F	CHILD	RRZZZZPA
GUSTAV	4	M	CHILD	RRZZZZPA
HELENE	2	F	CHILD	RRZZZZPA
SZMAIDE, ANTONIA	30	F	MCHT	RRZZZZVA
LEWARTOWEECZ, FRANZ	22	M	MCHT	RRZZZZVA
KAZMIROWSKI, WARZIN	26	M	MCHT	RRZZZZVA
KRAWCZYN, ANDREZY	29	M	LABR	RRZZZZPA
FULTAWSKI, JOSEF	23	M	LABR	RRZZZZMD
LYDICHIZ, NATE	23	M	LABR	RRZZZZMD
KRASNAWSKY, JOEL	16	M	LABR	RRZZZZMD
ROMANOWSKI, FRANZISECK	29	M	LABR	RRZZZZMI
STAROLEWITZ, JURIE	28	M	LABR	RRZZZZMD
PUPKUS, ANTON	27	M	LABR	RRZZZZMD
LEDRONSKY, ISAAC	17	M	LABR	RRZZZZMD
LAGATZKY, INGATZ	37	M	LABR	RRZZZZMD
AGATHE	30	F	UNKNOWN	RRZZZZMD
SKOWSRONSKI, ANTON	25	M	LABR	RRZZZZBAL
SLIKY, JAN	42	M	LABR	RRZZZZBAL
HASENPUTH, MASKUD	32	M	LABR	RRZZZZBAL
KARTUN, SALOMON	17	M	LABR	RRZZZZBAL
SEDEL, ABRAHAM	21	M	LABR	RRZZZZBAL
WISNIEWSKI, FRANZ	38	M	LABR	RRZZZZMD
JANKOWSKY, MAROIAN	31	M	LABR	RRZZZZMD
CZEIKOWSKI, JACOB	29	M	LABR	RRZZZZMD
GABRIELSKI, WOJCIECH	31	M	LABR	RRZZZZMD
IZBRECHT, ANDREZY	23	M	LABR	RRZZZZMD
PAWLOWSKI, MARIAN	28	M	LABR	RRZZZZMD
NOWINSKI, JAN	38	M	LABR	RRZZZZMD

PASSENGER	AGE	SEX	OCCUPATION	PRV VIL DES

SHIP: ALASKA

FROM: LIVERPOOL AND QUEENSTOWN
TO: NEW YORK
ARRIVED: 21 MAY 1888

PASSENGER	AGE	SEX	OCCUPATION	PRV VIL DES
SAKOLSKI, REIB	16	M	TLR	RRZZZZUSA
GOLDBER, LEIB	21	M	LABR	RRZZZZUSA
AKSELROD, ISRAEL	22	M	LABR	RRZZZZUSA
STABINSKI, MORDCHE	30	M	LABR	RRZZZZUSA
SCHLIEFER, ISRAEL	20	M	PDLR	PLZZZZUSA
LEWITA, RIWKE	50	F	MA	RRZZZZUSA
LEHA	15	F	SP	RRZZZZUSA
SARA	11	F	CH	RRZZZZUSA
SARNOWSKI, SILVESTER	29	M	LABR	RRZZZZUSA
SONNACK, SLUTE	32	F	MA	RRZZZZUSA
SCHEINE	9	F	CHILD	RRZZZZUSA
ITTE	8	F	CHILD	RRZZZZUSA
NATHAN	5	M	CHILD	RRZZZZUSA
LISHON, ZALIK	18	M	LABR	RRZZZZUSA
LEWIN, ISRAEL	17	M	TLR	RRZZZZUSA
BRILAND, BERT.	30	M	LABR	RRZZZZUSA
SABIN, ROCHEL	21	M	TLR	RRZZZZUSA
SANDEL	20	F	W	RRZZZZUSA
SONNACK, SENDEL	10	M	CH	RRZZZZUSA
LESERSOHN, ISAAC	22	M	LABR	RRZZZZUSA
DITON, ZAN	25	M	DPR	PLZZZZUSA
SOPKIN, JACOB	25	M	FARMER	RRZZZZUSA

SHIP: UMBRIA

FROM: LIVERPOOL AND QUEENSTOWN
TO: NEW YORK
ARRIVED: 21 MAY 1888

PASSENGER	AGE	SEX	OCCUPATION	PRV VIL DES
SWATKOWSKI, JOSEF	30	M	LABR	RRAFWJUSA
NAHUMSKY, PERL	40	M	MA	RRAFWJUSA
HEUGE	9	M	CHILD	RRAFWJUSA
BELL	4	F	CHILD	RRAFWJUSA
ANNA	2	F	CHILD	RRAFWJUSA
BLID, JOHAN-E.	32	M	FARMER	RRAICBUSA

SHIP: FURNESSIA

FROM: GLASGOW AND MOVILLE
TO: NEW YORK
ARRIVED: 21 MAY 1888

PASSENGER	AGE	SEX	OCCUPATION	PRV VIL DES
ALISKREUSKY, MARIANNA	30	F	SVNT	RRZZZZUSA
ADJOVITCH, KAJIM	25	M	LABR	RRZZZZUSA
EVA	22	F	UNKNOWN	RRZZZZUSA
FRIDA	.09	F	INFANT	RRZZZZUSA
BERKOWITZ, EMMA	20	F	DMS	RRZZZZUSA
DILLON, ELIE	21	M	LABR	RRZZZZUSA
LEWIN, DESCHE	24	F	UNKNOWN	RRZZZZUSA
LEIB	5	F	CHILD	RRZZZZUSA
SCHMUL	1	M	CHILD	RRZZZZUSA
STERNFELD, FEIGE	10	M	CH	RRZZZZUSA
DREUSTER, AUGUSTE	27	F	SVNT	RRZZZZUSA
EMELIE	16	F	DMS	RRZZZZUSA
YRDZWEI, ANNA	28	F	DMS	RRZZZZUSA
JONAS	1	F	CHILD	RRZZZZUSA
BIRON, C	18	F	TLR	RRZZZZUSA
BALASCHRIK, SCHEINE	38	F	UNKNOWN	RRZZZZUSA
LEILE	10	M	CH	RRZZZZUSA
BOCKOWITZ, SARAH	17	F	TLR	RRZZZZUSA
CONTATIT, ADRIAN	18	F	TLR	RRZZZZUSA
JENNIE	20	F	TLR	RRZZZZUSA
GOSSMAN, FANNIE	25	F	DMS	RRZZZZUSA
GROLLMANN, SCHEINE	38	F	DMS	RRZZZZUSA
ROSA	12	F	DMS	RRZZZZUSA
MORITZ	9	M	CHILD	RRZZZZUSA
DORA	7	F	CHILD	RRZZZZUSA
HARA	3	F	CHILD	RRZZZZUSA
HABEN, KIVE	24	F	UNKNOWN	RRZZZZUSA
KRISTAL, SAMMUEL	23	M	LABR	RRZZZZUSA
NECHAME	33	F	UNKNOWN	RRZZZZUSA
LEIE	.09	F	INFANT	RRZZZZUSA
KANDEL, LEAH	20	F	UNKNOWN	RRZZZZUSA
CHAJE	1	F	CHILD	RRZZZZUSA
KASSIN, JOH	40	M	LABR	RRZZZZUSA
AUGUSTE	40	F	UNKNOWN	RRZZZZUSA
BARBARA	6	F	CHILD	RRZZZZUSA
LEWIHIAN, SAMUEL	25	M	LABR	RRZZZZUSA
HANNE	15	F	UNKNOWN	RRZZZZUSA
NATIL	9	F	CHILD	RRZZZZUSA
ASTER	1	F	CHILD	RRZZZZUSA
LURIE, NOTEL	18	M	LABR	RRZZZZUSA
LEWIN, JOSEL	50	M	MUSN	RRZZZZUSA
ESTER	45	F	UNKNOWN	RRZZZZUSA
MALICKA, REISEL	14	F	DMS	RRZZZZUSA
MEINKEN, JUIDEL	35	M	ENGR	RRZZZZUSA
HANNA	32	F	UNKNOWN	RRZZZZUSA
JINDA	11	F	CH	RRZZZZUSA
MENDEL	9	M	CHILD	RRZZZZUSA
BENZEL	7	M	CHILD	RRZZZZUSA
ISAK	3	M	CHILD	RRZZZZUSA
YSCHNE	.09	F	INFANT	RRZZZZUSA
MITZKEWICZ, MATES	40	M	LABR	RRZZZZUSA
MARIA	40	F	UNKNOWN	RRZZZZUSA
PITCHOKAIT, ANTON	30	M	LABR	RRZZZZUSA
MOWSHAI, ESTER	20	F	TLR	RRZZZZUSA
NUDELMANN, SIMON	50	M	LABR	RRZZZZUSA
FEIGE	40	F	UNKNOWN	RRZZZZUSA
ERIE	18	F	UNKNOWN	RRZZZZUSA
PIERISKI, HIRSCH	11	F	UNKNOWN	RRZZZZUSA
PEXAT, JOHANNA	25	F	DMS	RRZZZZUSA
PENSKEN, HANE	18	F	DMS	RRZZZZUSA
RAMES, FISCHEL	24	M	LABR	RRZZZZUSA
LEA	11	M	CH	RRZZZZUSA
ARON	9	M	CHILD	RRZZZZUSA
RUBIN, HIRSCH	38	M	LABR	RRZZZZUSA
SARAH	28	F	UNKNOWN	RRZZZZUSA
ROSA	7	F	CHILD	RRZZZZUSA
ESTHER	2	F	CHILD	RRZZZZUSA
JOSEPH	1	M	CHILD	RRZZZZUSA
ABRAM	6	M	CHILD	RRZZZZUSA
E	4	F	CHILD	RRZZZZUSA
FREDRICK	7	M	CHILD	RRZZZZUSA
PINKOWSKI, HIRSCH	18	F	UNKNOWN	RRZZZZUSA
SCHEER, JACOB	22	M	SHMK	RRZZZZUSA
SARAH	15	F	UNKNOWN	RRZZZZUSA
SINKOW, ALTER	41	M	LABR	RRZZZZUSA
MALKE	39	F	UNKNOWN	RRZZZZUSA
D	15	F	UNKNOWN	RRZZZZUSA
BERTHA	4	F	CHILD	RRZZZZUSA
RIWKE	1	F	CHILD	RRZZZZUSA
SABELNMAN, ISRAEL	27	M	LABR	RRZZZZUSA
BASCHE	19	F	UNKNOWN	RRZZZZUSA
SCHEMNESER, J	16	F	UNKNOWN	RRZZZZUSA
CHANE	10	F	CH	RRZZZZUSA
SCHADOWSKY, SPRING	15	M	TLR	RRZZZZUSA
JEGER, CHANE	27	M	DMS	RRZZZZUSA
LASCHMANN, ANNA	19	M	DMS	RRZZZZUSA
WADONSKY, LEA	16	M	DMS	RRZZZZUSA
WEITZ, LEIBE	50	F	UNKNOWN	RRZZZZUSA
CHAIE	22	F	UNKNOWN	RRZZZZUSA
P	10	F	CH	RRZZZZUSA
MALKE	1	M	CHILD	RRZZZZUSA

PASSENGER	A G E	S E X	OCCUPATION	P R V	V I L	D E S
LINLIN, DWIERIE	20	F	TLR	RRZ	ZZ	USA
ALMNITZKER, WALF	7	M	CHILD	RRZ	ZZ	USA
ALECHONES, ARTHUR	23	M	LABR	RRZ	ZZ	USA
KITTIE	28	M	LABR	RRZ	ZZ	USA
ABZAMCK, JUDEL	36	M	LABR	RRZ	ZZ	USA
BAERS, HIRSEMIR	27	M	LABR	RRZ	ZZ	USA
BLINTZIK, LEISER	46	M	TLR	RRZ	ZZ	USA
BERGMANN, M	28	M	LABR	RRZ	ZZ	USA
BAIKOWSKI, KOPEL	45	M	SCHM	RRZ	ZZ	USA
BERNAS, JANKEL	18	M	WCHMKR	RRZ	ZZ	USA
BENEZAR, G	32	M	WCHMKR	RRZ	ZZ	USA
CHINSKY, G	30	M	DLR	RRZ	ZZ	USA
DAVIDOWITZ, N	28	M	TLR	RRZ	ZZ	USA
DANEMARK, ABR	22	M	WCHMKR	RRZ	ZZ	USA
TALIZKY, ENACH	25	M	SHMK	RRZ	ZZ	USA
DEGERTES, JOSEF	24	M	TLR	RRZ	ZZ	USA
ZEEBKER, ITZIG	26	M	TLR	RRZ	ZZ	USA
ESTHER	3	F	CHILD	RRZ	ZZ	USA
FELDMANN, ABR	28	M	TLR	RRZ	ZZ	USA
FEIFER, KASIMIR	21	M	LABR	RRZ	ZZ	USA
FORSCHANSKI, JACOB	32	M	SHMK	RRZ	ZZ	USA
FELDSTEIN, ISAK	27	M	MCHT	RRZ	ZZ	USA
GOLDIN, HIRSCH	50	M	MCHT	RRZ	ZZ	USA
GRUNSKI, LEON	40	M	TLR	RRZ	ZZ	USA
GITLIN, ABR	38	M	LABR	RRZ	ZZ	USA
GORDAN, ELIE	37	M	TLR	RRZ	ZZ	USA
JORMANN, GITHEL	12	M	UNKNOWN	RRZ	ZZ	USA
GILSIN, ABRM	28	M	LABR	RRZ	ZZ	USA
GOLDSTEIN, HERMANN	54	M	LABR	RRZ	ZZ	USA
GRUNBERG, D	30	M	LABR	RRZ	ZZ	USA
GOLDSTEIN, ISIDOR	23	M	DLR	RRZ	ZZ	USA
ALINE	17	F	UNKNOWN	RRZ	ZZ	USA
GLUKMANN, JUDEL	17	M	UNKNOWN	RRZ	ZZ	USA
SCHOLME	10	M	CH	RRZ	ZZ	USA
GARMISE, MENDEL	17	M	TLR	RRZ	ZZ	USA
GLASER, ARON	22	M	SHMK	RRZ	ZZ	USA
GITTLIN, HIRSCH	19	M	TLR	RRZ	ZZ	USA
MICHELOWITZ, S	12	M	UNKNOWN	RRZ	ZZ	USA
HIRSCHBERG, T	13	M	UNKNOWN	RRZ	ZZ	USA
HACHBERG, LESER	35	M	LABR	RRZ	ZZ	USA
KLINOWITZ, H	21	M	LABR	RRZ	ZZ	USA
KAMELHAR, F	16	M	LABR	RRZ	ZZ	USA
KOWIENSKY, ABRAM	25	M	BCHR	RRZ	ZZ	USA
KATOK, LESER	55	M	LABR	RRZ	ZZ	USA
FEIGE	60	M	LABR	RRZ	ZZ	USA
KAPLAN, D	25	M	LABR	RRZ	ZZ	USA
KALECKI, JOSEL	16	M	LABR	RRZ	ZZ	USA
HARASCHINSKY, ISAK	44	M	LABR	RRZ	ZZ	USA
KRYKI, A	40	M	SHMK	RRZ	ZZ	USA
KIRMAN, Z	17	M	TLR	RRZ	ZZ	USA
KALONSKY, VALENTIN	21	M	LABR	RRZ	ZZ	USA
LEWIN, MORDECHI	28	M	PREST	RRZ	ZZ	USA
RESEIL	18	M	SMH	RRZ	ZZ	USA
LEIBLE, FRANZ	26	M	LABR	RRZ	ZZ	USA
LEW, LEIB	40	M	CPTR	RRZ	ZZ	USA
LEWY, SAMUEL	35	M	TLR	RRZ	ZZ	USA
LEVINOWITZ, HIRSCH	29	M	SLT	RRZ	ZZ	USA
LIEBERPARB, JOEL	40	M	TLR	RRZ	ZZ	USA
LAPATINSKI, ABR	24	M	UNKNOWN	RRZ	ZZ	USA
LURIN, JASEL	20	M	TLR	RRZ	ZZ	USA
NICHALOWITZ, T	44	M	PDLR	RRZ	ZZ	USA
MISEWITZ, JOHAN	28	M	LABR	RRZ	ZZ	USA
MIBTELMANN, MENHERT	26	M	LABR	RRZ	ZZ	USA
MEIERSON, ABRM	17	M	LABR	RRZ	ZZ	USA
MATUKEWITZ, KAROL	26	M	LABR	RRZ	ZZ	USA
MILHOF, SIMON	20	M	LABR	RRZ	ZZ	USA
MILWILSKI, CHANE	40	M	TLR	RRZ	ZZ	USA
MINGER, ANGEL	18	M	TLR	RRZ	ZZ	USA
NEHRING, AUGUST	21	M	LABR	RRZ	ZZ	USA
NORMAN, JOSSEL	19	M	SHMK	RRZ	ZZ	USA
NEURILIS, W	17	M	LABR	RRZ	ZZ	USA
PANTEL, MOSCHE	18	M	SHMK	RRZ	ZZ	USA
PISOZKE, LEISER	35	M	LABR	RRZ	ZZ	USA
ROSENBAUM, CHANE	22	M	LABR	RRZ	ZZ	USA
ROSENBERG, BENISCH	30	M	LABR	RRZ	ZZ	USA
ROZONKER, LEIB	23	M	TLR	RRZ	ZZ	USA
RESNIK, HIRSCH	37	M	TLR	RRZ	ZZ	USA
RUDNIK, HIRSCH	30	M	TLR	RRZ	ZZ	USA
RUSKER, ANTONI	27	M	LABR	RRZ	ZZ	USA
ROSENBLATT, WOLF	40	M	LABR	RRZ	ZZ	USA
PERLMAN, WOLF	25	M	LABR	RRZ	ZZ	USA
RUBIN, AKADI	21	M	LABR	RRZ	ZZ	USA
STUPKI, CHONE	23	M	CPTR	RRZ	ZZ	USA
STOLAI, MOSES	40	M	CPTR	RRZ	ZZ	USA
HINDE	17	M	TLR	RRZ	ZZ	USA
SCHEIE	10	M	CH	RRZ	ZZ	USA
SIEBERMANN, PESSE	50	F	UNKNOWN	RRZ	ZZ	USA
ISRAEL	17	M	TNM	RRZ	ZZ	USA
JOSSEL	10	M	CH	RRZ	ZZ	USA
SCHLESS, ABR	35	M	TLR	RRZ	ZZ	USA
SCHEIN, MICHEL	29	M	BCHR	RRZ	ZZ	USA
SKLAR, M	32	M	TLR	RRZ	ZZ	USA
SCHWARZ, JANKEL	43	M	SHMK	RRZ	ZZ	USA
KOHS	15	M	UNKNOWN	RRZ	ZZ	USA
SURESCHKI, HOSIAS	35	M	BCHR	RRZ	ZZ	USA
STRONG, PIOTR	45	M	UNKNOWN	RRZ	ZZ	USA
WITKISKI, BENZEL	37	M	LABR	RRZ	ZZ	USA
SCHEISKIERSH, SAMUEL	35	M	LABR	RRZ	ZZ	USA
WASILEWSKY, L	30	M	UNKNOWN	RRZ	ZZ	USA
WILANSKY, SCHLOME	16	M	LABR	RRZ	ZZ	USA
WABALAS, AUGUSTIN	28	M	LABR	RRZ	ZZ	USA
HERSCHOWSKY, CHIM	27	M	SHMK	RRZ	ZZ	USA
WILANSKI, MENDEL	50	M	TLR	RRZ	ZZ	USA
ABR	11	M	CH	RRZ	ZZ	USA
SEBURSKI, PAVEL	42	M	LABR	RRZ	ZZ	USA
BLITZSTEIN, ISAK	32	M	LABR	RRZ	ZZ	USA
ANDROWALAMEITZ, ANTONIA	28	M	LABR	RRZ	ZZ	USA
CHAJSAN, PETRIO	27	M	LABR	RRZ	ZZ	USA
KORDE, JOSEF	32	M	LABR	RRZ	ZZ	USA
MAREZUKEITIS, GEO	33	M	LABR	RRZ	ZZ	USA
PALUK, ANDREY	29	M	UNKNOWN	RRZ	ZZ	USA
STEC, JACOB	35	M	UNKNOWN	RRZ	ZZ	USA
WALINEZ, LEISER	20	M	HTR	RRZ	ZZ	USA

SHIP: FULDA

FROM: BREMEN AND SOUTHAMPTON
TO: NEW YORK
ARRIVED: 22 MAY 1888

PASSENGER	A G E	S E X	OCCUPATION	P R V	V I L	D E S
SCHOLIS, ADAM	28	M	LABR	RRZ	ZZ	USA
MASCHALAITIS, JURAS	24	M	LABR	RRZ	ZZ	USA
LOGIS, JOHANN	28	M	LABR	RRZ	ZZ	USA
STRUPINSKY, JOSEF	36	M	LABR	RRZ	ZZ	USA
JANOWSKY, ANTON	40	M	LABR	RRZ	ZZ	USA
WASIMES, JAN	45	M	LABR	RRZ	ZZ	USA
MIKNEWITZ, ANDER	32	M	LABR	RRZ	ZZ	USA
MARCINKEWITZ, PETER	27	M	LABR	RRZ	ZZ	USA
CZUPKOWITZ, MARTIN	28	M	LABR	RRZ	ZZ	USA
U, MATE	26	M	LABR	RRZ	ZZ	USA
BOLINSKY, JOSEF	31	M	LABR	RRZ	ZZ	USA
SOBESCHINSKY, JAN	19	M	LABR	RRZ	ZZ	USA
ZULOBSKY, CONSTANTIN	35	M	LABR	RRZ	ZZ	USA
ZENTARSKY, TOMASCH	38	M	LABR	RRZ	ZZ	USA
GLOWATZKY, THODOR	28	M	LABR	RRZ	ZZ	USA
KOLOZINSKI, WALERIA	20	F	UNKNOWN	RRZ	ZZ	USA
ZWISCHEFSKY, IGNATZ	33	M	FARMER	RRZ	ZZ	USA
NEUMANN, JAN	35	M	FARMER	RRZ	ZZ	USA
SEZAMKOWSKY, THEOFIL	26	M	FARMER	RRZ	ZZ	USA
NEUMANN, ANDRZI	29	M	FARMER	RRZ	ZZ	USA
MASCHITZKI, ISRAEL	26	M	LABR	RRZ	ZZ	USA
FREIDE	7	F	CHILD	RRZ	ZZ	USA
TAUBE, JACOB	45	M	PDLR	RRZ	ZZ	USA
ARONES, JANKEL	45	M	TLR	RRZ	ZZ	USA
KUSTROW, BARIS	36	M	SMH	RRZ	ZZ	USA

PASSENGER	AGE	SEX	OCCUPATION	PRV VIL DES
CECELIA	19	F	UNKNOWN	RRZZZZUSA
TENIA	.08	F	INFANT	RRZZZZUSA
FRIEDBERG, JACOB	17	M	LABR	RRZZZZUSA
THOM, LUDW.	26	M	LABR	RRZZZZUSA
WINTER, CARL	19	M	LABR	RRZZZZUSA
ITT, GUSTAV	22	M	LABR	RRZZZZUSA
MILKOWSKI, MACIEJ	29	M	LABR	RRZZZZUSA
FIEDELMANN, BERL	28	M	LABR	RRZZZZUSA
ZLOTKEWITZ, JACOB	30	M	LABR	RRZZZZUSA
U, KACHMEN	38	M	UNKNOWN	RRZZZZUSA
KAFKA, ISAAC	43	M	FARMER	RRZZZZUSA
WITOCKY, MICH.	24	M	PDLR	RRZZZZUSA
JANGRISCHKEWITZ, JAN	26	M	LABR	RRZZZZUSA
KRZYODA, MACEI	40	M	LABR	RRZZZZUSA
NEUMARKT, DORA	62	F	UNKNOWN	RRZZZZUSA
MARY	8	F	CHILD	RRZZZZUSA
R-D-OFF, ADAM	30	M	SMH	RRZZZZUSA
JOHANN, RADMACHER	38	M	FARMER	RRZZZZUSA
BARBARA	34	F	UNKNOWN	RRZZZZUSA
JULIE	7	F	CHILD	RRZZZZUSA
FRANZ	6	M	CHILD	RRZZZZUSA
ANNA	4	F	CHILD	RRZZZZUSA
LOUISE	3	F	CHILD	RRZZZZUSA
BARBARA	3	F	CHILD	RRZZZZUSA
FRIEDRICH	2	M	CHILD	RRZZZZUSA
JACOB	2	M	CHILD	RRZZZZUSA
FRIEDRICH, KNIELING	34	M	FARMER	RRZZZZUSA
LOUISE	29	F	UNKNOWN	RRZZZZUSA
CAROLINE	4	F	CHILD	RRZZZZUSA
JOHANN	3	M	CHILD	RRZZZZUSA
MICHAEL	2	M	CHILD	RRZZZZUSA
PETER	.03	M	INFANT	RRZZZZUSA
WILHELM, WENDLING	28	M	FARMER	RRZZZZUSA
WENDLING, CHRISTINE	27	F	UNKNOWN	RRZZZZUSA
JOHANNE	2	F	CHILD	RRZZZZUSA
CLAUS	.07	M	INFANT	RRZZZZUSA
HEINRICH, ART.	39	M	FSHMN	RRZZZZUSA
CAROLINE	32	F	UNKNOWN	RRZZZZUSA
HENRIETTE	8	F	CHILD	RRZZZZUSA
JOHANN	6	M	CHILD	RRZZZZUSA
FRANZ	4	M	CHILD	RRZZZZUSA
FILIP	3	M	CHILD	RRZZZZUSA
CARL	3	M	CHILD	RRZZZZUSA
KATHARINA	2	F	CHILD	RRZZZZUSA
JOHANN, SCHAEFFER	50	M	BCHR	RRZZZZUSA
LOUISE	45	F	UNKNOWN	RRZZZZUSA
FRIEDRICH, MOCK	23	M	JNR	RRZZZZUSA
MARTIN, KNAPP	48	M	GDNR	RRZZZZUSA
KELLER, MICHAEL	38	M	PNTR	RRZZZZUSA
CATHARINA	33	F	UNKNOWN	RRZZZZUSA
FRANZ	7	M	CHILD	RRZZZZUSA
JOHANN	7	M	CHILD	RRZZZZUSA
ADAM	6	M	CHILD	RRZZZZUSA
FILIP	4	M	CHILD	RRZZZZUSA
ANNA	2	F	CHILD	RRZZZZUSA
JOHANN, ZACHMANN	35	M	FARMER	RRZZZZUSA
CATHARINA	31	F	UNKNOWN	RRZZZZUSA
MARIE	4	F	CHILD	RRZZZZUSA
JOHANNA	3	F	CHILD	RRZZZZUSA
KOSCHUSKI, ADALBERT	23	M	LABR	RRZZZZUSA
ZACKHOFS, JOH.	22	M	LABR	RRZZZZUSA
LEBE, ARON-COHN	22	M	MCHT	RRZZZZUSA
WITKOCZKA, EVA	23	F	UNKNOWN	RRZZZZUSA
HEINRICH	.09	M	INFANT	RRZZZZUSA
JASKULSKA, ANTONIA	18	F	UNKNOWN	RRZZZZUSA
STODORSKI, JOSEF	21	M	LABR	RRZZZZUSA
PEK, PAULINE	19	F	UNKNOWN	RRZZZZUSA
LITKA, KAROL.	30	M	FARMER	RRZZZZUSA
KAMINSKI, JOSEF	17	M	FARMER	RRZZZZUSA
SAMUELSON, LIBE	48	M	LABR	RRZZZZUSA
ISRAEL	22	M	LABR	RRZZZZUSA
LESER	18	M	LABR	RRZZZZUSA
MARY	7	F	CHILD	RRZZZZUSA
RIFKE	5	F	CHILD	RRZZZZUSA
-----LING, EMMA	17	F	UNKNOWN	RRZZZZUSA
JAKRZEWSKI, ADAM	30	M	LABR	RRZZZZUSA
KATARZYNA	29	F	UNKNOWN	RRZZZZUSA
FRANZISZEK	7	M	CHILD	RRZZZZUSA
JABLONSKI, ADAM	29	M	LABR	RRZZZZUSA
SCHAPKOWSKI, M.	63	M	LABR	RRZZZZUSA
PUPEL, HENRIETTE	63	F	UNKNOWN	RRZZZZUSA
EMILIE	33	F	UNKNOWN	RRZZZZUSA
CAROLINE	34	F	UNKNOWN	RRZZZZUSA
JULIUS	3	M	CHILD	RRZZZZUSA
HEINRICH	.08	M	INFANT	RRZZZZUSA
KUTSCHIWITZKI, SIMON	19	M	LABR	RRZZZZUSA
URBANOWICZ, STANISLAUS	27	M	LABR	RRZZZZUSA
DOMINICA	25	F	UNKNOWN	RRZZZZUSA
SKURSKI, JOSEF	26	M	BCHR	RRZZZZUSA
ITZKO, JACOB	29	M	BCHR	RRZZZZUSA
SCHMEER, MARGA.	19	F	UNKNOWN	RRZZZZUSA
HEINRICH	27	M	JNR	RRZZZZUSA
WOSILEWSKI, JAN	32	M	FARMER	RRZZZZUSA
PALUCH, JOHANN	27	M	FARMER	RRZZZZUSA
ELISABETH	24	F	UNKNOWN	RRZZZZUSA
HEDWIG	.06	F	INFANT	RRZZZZUSA
JACOBSEN, BERNARD	26	M	LABR	RRZZZZUSA
FELIN, NATHAN	23	M	LABR	RRZZZZUSA
SENDOCZ, MENDEL	52	M	LABR	RRZZZZUSA
GRODITZKI, ALEXANDR	18	F	MCHT	RRZZZZUSA
STERZYPCY, ELIAS	36	M	LABR	RRZZZZUSA
ENIS, MADER	19	M	LABR	RRZZZZUSA
REDEMERSKY, JACOB	25	M	LABR	RRZZZZUSA
VASIONEK, MARIAN	27	M	LABR	RRZZZZUSA
SCHNEIDER, DUCHE	30	F	LABR	RRZZZZUSA
SURE	13	F	LABR	RRZZZZUSA
KIWIE	8	M	CHILD	RRZZZZUSA
CHAJE	7	F	CHILD	RRZZZZUSA
JACOB	4	M	CHILD	RRZZZZUSA
SARAH	.06	F	INFANT	RRZZZZUSA
SCHAEFER, BARBARA	27	F	CH	RRZZZZUSA
RADNETT, ELISABETH	23	F	CH	RRZZZZUSA
ELLER, ANDREAS	20	M	PNTR	RRZZZZUSA
GOETZINGER, ELISABETH	18	F	UNKNOWN	RRZZZZUSA
U, U	38	F	UNKNOWN	RRZZZZUSA
U	8	M	CHILD	RRZZZZUSA
ADALBERT	7	M	CHILD	RRZZZZUSA
LISSI	5	F	CHILD	RRZZZZUSA
KATHARINA	3	F	CHILD	RRZZZZUSA
HELENE	2	F	CHILD	RRZZZZUSA
EMMA	.02	F	INFANT	RRZZZZUSA
WLASIM, EDUARD	31	M	PNTR	RRZZZZUSA
LEOPOLDINE	26	F	UNKNOWN	RRZZZZUSA
ALBERTINE	6	F	CHILD	RRZZZZUSA
JULIUS	4	M	CHILD	RRZZZZUSA
PETER	3	M	CHILD	RRZZZZUSA
ANNA	.06	F	INFANT	RRZZZZUSA
SCHNELLER, JOSEF	70	M	LABR	RRZZZZUSA
THERESIA	64	F	UNKNOWN	RRZZZZUSA

SHIP: AUSTRALIA

FROM: HAMBURG
TO: NEW YORK
ARRIVED: 22 MAY 1888

PASSENGER	AGE	SEX	OCCUPATION	PRV VIL DES
ROSSMANN, BASSE	17	M	GLMK	RRZZZZNY
SZEGAL, CHAJEM	27	M	LABR	RRZZZZNY
SCHEINDEL	20	F	W	RRZZZZNY
U, U	00	U	UNKNOWN	RRZZZZNY
ROSSMANN, JUDEL	38	M	LABR	RRZZZZPHI
CHAINE	36	F	W	RRZZZZPHI
ISAAK	14	M	CH	RRZZZZPHI
SCHEME	9	M	CHILD	RRZZZZPHI
MENASSE	8	M	CHILD	RRZZZZPHI

PASSENGER	AGE	SEX	OCCUPATION	PRV VIL DES
BASCHE	.09	M	INFANT	RRZZZZPHI
WYNOKUR, SIMON	33	M	LABR	RRZZZZNY
EISENBERG, EISIGK	44	M	LABR	RRZZZZNY
GITTEL	38	F	W	RRZZZZNY
MOSES	5	M	CHILD	RRZZZZNY
CHAWE	2	M	CHILD	RRZZZZNY
FROIME	.06	M	INFANT	RRZZZZNY
GOLDSTEIN, GODEL	43	M	LABR	RRZZZZNY
MIREL	41	F	W	RRZZZZNY
MOSES	18	M	CH	RRZZZZNY
CHANNE	13	M	CH	RRZZZZNY
HILLEL	9	M	CHILD	RRZZZZNY
MEIER	8	M	CHILD	RRZZZZNY
MENNIE	26	F	SVNT	RRZZZZNY
NOWAK, CATHA.	28	F	WO	RRZZZZNY
WLADISLAWA	6	F	CHILD	RRZZZZNY
XAVER	2	M	CHILD	RRZZZZNY
ALEXANDER	.10	M	INFANT	RRZZZZNY
BERGER, CHAIE	25	F	WO	RRZZZZNY
LEIB	3	M	CHILD	RRZZZZNY
CHAIM, MOSES	17	M	SHMK	RRZZZZNY
WULF, MINE	20	F	FLWMKR	RRZZZZNY
SCHAFFMANN, JANOS	28	M	TLR	RRZZZZNY
DWYLYS, PIETER	24	M	LABR	RRZZZZNY
LOEB, CHAJEM	9	M	CHILD	RRZZZZNY
PICKEROWSKY, ISRAEL	25	M	LABR	RRZZZZNY
BENON, ROSA	20	F	SVNT	RRZZZZNY
GOLDSTEIN, FANNY	18	F	FLWMKR	RRZZZZNY
MANISOWITZ, GUTE	40	F	WO	RRZZZZNY
MORDSCHEL	9	M	CHILD	RRZZZZNY
BLUME	7	M	CHILD	RRZZZZNY
POLKA	5	M	CHILD	RRZZZZNY
SCHABSOWITZ, SCHMERL	22	M	BCHR	RRZZZZNY
ALTER, SIMCHE	36	M	TLR	RRZZZZNY
PAPUTZKI, GITTEL	20	F	SVNT	RRZZZZNY
AISAKOWSKY, ARON	9	M	CHILD	RRZZZZNY
COHN, LENE	20	F	SVNT	RRZZZZNY
KOWALEWSKY, WOYSINEC	24	M	LABR	RRZZZZNY
KUZMICKY, MICHAEL	31	M	LABR	RRZZZZNY
LASZER, ZALMEN	32	M	LABR	RRZZZZNY
GOERZ, JENTE	18	F	FLWMKR	RRZZZZNY
ROSENBLUM, WOLF	48	M	BKR	RRZZZZNY
BERTHA	48	F	W	RRZZZZNY
CHANNE	15	F	CH	RRZZZZNY
RIEFKE	2	F	CHILD	RRZZZZNY
WIDUTIS, ELSA	28	F	WO	RRZZZZNY
MARIE	3	F	CHILD	RRZZZZNY
ANNA	.09	F	INFANT	RRZZZZNY
ZUCKAR, BERENT	24	M	LABR	RRZZZZNY
WISCHNIEWSKY, JAN	50	M	LABR	RRZZZZNY
WISNEWETZKI, MARIE	50	F	DLR	RRZZZZNY
CHAIE	49	F	W	RRZZZZNY
ALTE	14	M	CH	RRZZZZNY
PINCHOS	9	M	CHILD	RRZZZZNY
LEIB	8	M	CHILD	RRZZZZNY
RIWE	7	M	CHILD	RRZZZZNY
GILNERSCH, BARUCH	24	M	LABR	RRZZZZNY
BRAUN, ROSA	21	F	FLWMKR	RRZZZZNY
STEIN, ISAAC	14	M	BCHR	RRZZZZNY
WESLER, NOACH	40	M	BCHR	RRZZZZNY
KOSLAWSKY, MICH.	35	M	LABR	RRZZZZNY
LEWIN, ISAAC	36	M	DLR	RRZZZZNY
HURWITZ, HIRSCH	23	M	DLR	RRZZZZNY
STEIN, ARON	17	M	DLR	RRZZZZNY
SCHWARZ, JESSEL	57	M	DLR	RRZZZZNY
FREUND, NOCHEM	35	M	DLR	RRZZZZNY
SUSSMANN, GEDALJE	26	M	TLR	RRZZZZNY
CHANNE	25	F	W	RRZZZZNY
KURTAN, MINE	22	F	WO	RRZZZZNY
SPRINCE	.11	F	INFANT	RRZZZZNY
ALPERN, SARA	20	F	WO	RRZZZZNY
CHAZEM	9	M	CHILD	RRZZZZNY
OTTO, HEINRICH	20	M	LABR	RRZZZZNY
KRAMPITZ, FLORENTE	28	F	DRSMKR	RRZZZZNY
BRESLAWSKA, LEA	18	F	SVNT	RRZZZZNY

PASSENGER	AGE	SEX	OCCUPATION	PRV VIL DES
ZERKOWSKY, CASIMIR	33	M	LABR	RRZZZZNY
LEIBINER, THOMAS	18	M	LABR	RRZZZZNY
WARKOWSKY, JOSEPH	30	M	LABR	RRZZZZNY
ZUCKERMANN, ABR.	33	M	LABR	RRZZZZNY
BILOROOSKY, MEYER	47	M	LABR	RRZZZZNY
ABRAMOWITZ, ABR.	19	M	JNR	RRZZZZNY
PREMBITZ, MOSES	27	M	TLR	RRZZZZNY
ROSENZWEIG, SARAH	25	F	WO	RRZZZZNY
ESTHER	.09	F	INFANT	RRZZZZNY
KLETZKI, MOSES	38	M	LABR	RRZZZZNY
JOSSEL	9	M	CHILD	RRZZZZNY
KULAVIA, ANTON	36	M	LABR	RRZZZZNY
KUPPERMANN, HERSCHEL	32	M	LABR	RRZZZZPHI
REISEL	25	F	W	RRZZZZPHI
GITTEL	.09	M	INFANT	RRZZZZPHI
WALSSOHN, PERETZ	24	M	LABR	RRZZZZPHI
ZEMERINSKY, ISAAC	36	M	DLR	RRZZZZNY
KRAWETZ, MAIER	17	M	DLR	RRZZZZNY
ZUCKERMANN, CHANNE	22	F	BKBNDR	RRZZZZNY
ONTEILER, MATUSCH	30	M	LABR	RRZZZZNY
GRUENWALD, MOSES	25	M	LABR	RRZZZZNY
PILICK, ALEX	26	M	LABR	RRZZZZNY
RADUSTER, DAVID	22	M	LKSH	RRZZZZNY
BULKIND, LIPPMANN	19	M	UPHST	RRZZZZNY
GREIS, FRUME	18	F	SVNT	RRZZZZNY
ISKY, DWORE	20	F	SVNT	RRZZZZNY
SOLEMISKY, CHAIM	25	M	JNR	RRZZZZNY
MAGDIS, ABR.	17	M	LABR	RRZZZZNY
SCHNEIDMANN, JENDEL	40	M	JNR	RRZZZZNY
BRODZINSKY, ANDRAS	37	M	LABR	RRZZZZNY
DZIZARSKY, ANTON	28	M	LABR	RRZZZZNY
KUSCHARSKY, ANDR.	25	M	LABR	RRZZZZNY
GOTHELF, WOLF	26	M	DLR	RRZZZZNY
WALZAC, MASCHE	31	M	DLR	RRZZZZNY
WOLINETZ, JUDELL	42	M	DLR	RRZZZZNY
GITTEL	16	M	CH	RRZZZZNY
HENE	9	M	CHILD	RRZZZZNY
NOCHEM	8	M	CHILD	RRZZZZNY
HOCHMANN, HIRSCH	20	M	DLR	RRZZZZNY
KRAMETZ, LEIB	28	M	DLR	RRZZZZNY
LEW, SEIBEL	23	M	DLR	RRZZZZNY
GRATZ, MOSES	23	M	DLR	RRZZZZNY
MOTELANSKY, SCHLOME	23	M	DLR	RRZZZZNY
LEW, MOSCHE	25	M	DLR	RRZZZZNY
RIBACK, LEGIE	25	M	DLR	RRZZZZNY
MAZURSKA, ABR.	25	M	DLR	RRZZZZNY
ALPERIN, JOSEL	25	M	DLR	RRZZZZNY
HICHMANN, BERIL	40	F	WO	RRZZZZNY
FREIDE	17	F	CH	RRZZZZNY
BALKUNSKY, ISAAC	26	M	LABR	RRZZZZNY
BUT, LEIB	34	M	DLR	RRZZZZNY
SCHEDREWITZKY, ABR.	32	M	DLR	RRZZZZNY
BLECHER, MOSCHE	38	M	DLR	RRZZZZNY
REISMANN, SELMAN	24	M	DLR	RRZZZZNY
MARCUS, SAL.	30	M	DLR	RRZZZZNY
KUSIL	24	M	DLR	RRZZZZNY
FLEXER, LEIB	26	M	DLR	RRZZZZNY
EDENBERG, HIRSCH	22	M	DLR	RRZZZZNY
SCHRAGE, EMAN	27	M	DLR	RRZZZZNY
JANITZKI, ROSALIE	49	F	FLWMKR	RRZZZZNY
ISAACSOHN, LEISER	23	M	LABR	RRZZZZNY
LEWIN, JUDE	29	M	LABR	RRZZZZNY
SCHNITTMANN, MICH.	28	M	LABR	RRZZZZNY
HURWITZ, LEISER	18	M	LABR	RRZZZZNY
SCHULMANN, ITZIG	22	M	TLR	RRZZZZNY
ISAAKSOHN, HIRSCH	30	M	JNR	RRZZZZNY
RABINOWITZ, RIEWN	28	M	SHMK	RRZZZZNY
GIDANSKY, MORDSCHE	20	M	DLR	RRZZZZNY
MARGOLIS, EFROIM	23	M	DLR	RRZZZZNY
GOLDENOWSKY, ARON	27	M	DLR	RRZZZZNY
GOTHELF, CHRISTE.	27	M	DLR	RRZZZZNY
CHRTE.	36	F	WO	RRZZZZNY
RINKE	14	F	CH	RRZZZZNY
RABINOWITZ, SARAH	24	F	SVNT	RRZZZZNY
GOLDBERG, SARAH	5	F	CHILD	RRZZZZNY

PASSENGER	AGE	SEX	OCCUPATION	PRIV	DES
MEIER	3	F	CHILD	RRZZZZ	NY
ZIREL	2	F	CHILD	RRZZZZ	NY
RIWE	.06	F	INFANT	RRZZZZ	NY
LIPSKI, BERE	32	M	DLR	RRZZZZ	NY
LEIB	9	M	CHILD	RRZZZZ	NY
RUDICK, SPRINZE	19	F	SVNT	RRZZZZ	NY
KARASCH, JACOB	17	M	DLR	RRZZZZ	UNK
RASCHKOWITZ, JOSEPH	20	M	DLR	RRZZZZ	UNK
ARKIN, BERL	43	M	DLR	RRZZZZ	UNK
MATYSKIES, PAWEL	26	M	DLR	RRZZZZ	UNK
JATZEK, WOYCICH	41	M	LABR	RRZZZZ	NY
BRUSSACK, CASIMIR	19	M	LABR	RRZZZZ	NY
RUBINSTEIN, JOS.	22	M	LABR	RRZZZZ	NY
HURDEROS, JUROS	23	M	LABR	RRZZZZ	NY
SAKOWSKY, OSIP	40	M	LABR	RRZZZZ	NY
CHALT, OREL	35	M	LABR	RRZZZZ	NY
WARNAGIRIS, ADAM	23	M	LABR	RRZZZZ	NY
MURIKANSKY, JOSSEL	24	M	BCHR	RRZZZZ	NY
BERKOWITZ, SAMUEL	30	M	BCHR	RRZZZZ	NY
MICHNOWITZ, RACHEL	15	F	SVNT	RRZZZZ	NY
ZARANOWSKY, WLADISLAW	22	M	LABR	RRZZZZ	NY
HUNKE, EDWARD	17	M	CH	RRZZZZ	NY
LEIPE, JULIANE	30	F	WO	RRZZZZ	NY
GUSTAV	9	M	CHILD	RRZZZZ	NY
BERTHA	8	F	CHILD	RRZZZZ	NY
ROGAZINSKY, CONSTANT.	18	M	LABR	RRZZZZ	NY
REISMANN, GUST.	40	M	LABR	RRZZZZ	NY
FLORA	36	F	W	RRZZZZ	NY
KUTZURUBA, EFIM	17	M	LABR	RRZZZZ	NY
LAUENBURG, SENDER	19	M	LABR	RRZZZZ	NY
EBBIN, WOLF	18	M	LABR	RRZZZZ	NY
NUSSENSOHN, ISAAC	19	M	LABR	RRZZZZ	NY
BERLIN, SAMUEL	16	M	LABR	RRZZZZ	NY
SCHUTZKOWER, FEITEL	19	M	TLR	RRZZZZ	NY
HILLMANN, SARAH	25	F	SVNT	RRZZZZ	NY
MELTZER, ISRAEL	19	M	SMH	RRZZZZ	NY
WYCISK, JOSEF	25	M	LABR	RRZZZZ	DYT
BOHAC, ALOISIE	.09	F	INFANT	RRZZZZ	NY

SHIP: WESTERLAND

FROM: ANTWERP
TO: NEW YORK
ARRIVED: 23 MAY 1888

PASSENGER	AGE	SEX	OCCUPATION	PRIV	DES
HERSCHCKOF, J	28	M	FARMER	PLZZZZ	NY
BARKEWSKI, M	20	M	LABR	PLZZZZ	NY
CERNITZKI, J	52	M	FARMER	PLZZZZ	NY
MARIE	42	F	UNKNOWN	PLZZZZ	NY
STEZAK, STEFAN	38	M	LABR	PLZZZZ	NY
FERENZ	24	F	UNKNOWN	PLZZZZ	NY
MALCHOWSKY, SAMUEL	27	M	LABR	PLZZZZ	NY
RIGNISKI, JOSEF	26	M	LABR	PLZZZZ	NY
OHSEN, ABEL	32	M	LABR	PLZZZZ	NY
COHN, ANNE	25	M	TLR	PLZZZZ	NY
ANNA	11	F	UNKNOWN	PLZZZZ	NY
JOSEF	22	M	CL	PLZZZZ	NY
DOMKOWSKI, JOSEF	32	M	LABR	PLZZZZ	NY
BORUCH, JAN	26	M	LABR	PLZZZZ	NY
COLON, FRANZ	34	M	LABR	PLZZZZ	NY
ROTTKEN, SCHAUDER	32	M	LABR	PLZZZZ	NY
LIEKOWSKY, ANDREAS	28	M	LABR	PLZZZZ	NY
GRUNSTEIN, ISAAC	35	M	FARMER	PLZZZZ	NY
BRANE	27	F	UNKNOWN	PLZZZZ	NY
MARIE	1	F	CHILD	PLZZZZ	NY
DAKARTK, HENRIETTE	22	F	UNKNOWN	PLZZZZ	NY
PUTTER, JOSSEL	26	M	MCHT	PLZZZZ	NY
DWOISICK, FRUMME	36	M	WCHMKR	PLZZZZ	NY
SCHEW, SCHOLEM	22	M	FARMER	PLZZZZ	NY
ETEL	22	F	UNKNOWN	PLZZZZ	NY
WARSCHOFKT, N	18	M	LABR	PLZZZZ	NY
PIRETZ	20	F	UNKNOWN	PLZZZZ	NY
BARNEFKI, ISRAEL	17	M	LABR	PLZZZZ	NY
JODZO, FRANZ	30	M	LABR	PLZZZZ	NY
JOSEFA	24	F	UNKNOWN	PLZZZZ	NY
MICHAEL	1	M	CHILD	PLZZZZ	NY
WISOSKI, MARIANNA	24	F	UNKNOWN	PLZZZZ	NY
JOSEF	36	M	FARMER	PLZZZZ	NY
PAULINE	2	F	CHILD	PLZZZZ	NY
KRAGULSKY, JOSEF	24	M	FARMER	PLZZZZ	NY
RUDNICKI, ANDR	19	M	CL	PLZZZZ	CH
KASSNER, MARIA	30	F	UNKNOWN	PLZZZZ	CH
BRADE, AUGUST	26	M	CL	PLZZZZ	CH
NORAZ, CARL	24	M	LABR	PLZZZZ	NY
VACHA, ANTON	22	M	CL	PLZZZZ	NY
LITOK, JOSEF	18	M	LABR	PLZZZZ	NY
LAHODWY, JOSEF	23	M	LABR	PLZZZZ	NY
FAUCECK, FRANZ	47	M	FARMER	PLZZZZ	NY
ANNA	36	F	UNKNOWN	PLZZZZ	NY
ANNA	16	F	UNKNOWN	PLZZZZ	NY
AMALIA	13	F	UNKNOWN	PLZZZZ	NY
BAZENA	9	F	CHILD	PLZZZZ	NY
UGSO, FRANZ	35	M	LABR	PLZZZZ	NY
ANNA	32	F	UNKNOWN	PLZZZZ	NY
MARIA	12	F	UNKNOWN	PLZZZZ	NY
RUZENA	9	F	CHILD	PLZZZZ	NY
HOZENA	7	F	CHILD	PLZZZZ	NY
EMILIE	5	F	CHILD	PLZZZZ	NY
FRANZ	4	M	CHILD	PLZZZZ	NY
ANNA	2	F	CHILD	PLZZZZ	NY
HENRIETTE	1	F	CHILD	PLZZZZ	NY
BURES, FRANCISCA	29	F	UNKNOWN	PLZZZZ	NY
MARTINCI, MARIA	16	F	UNKNOWN	PLZZZZ	NY
JOSEF	18	M	LABR	PLZZZZ	NY
APPELBAUM, B	20	M	TLR	PLZZZZ	NY
MARKENS, ISAAC	22	M	CL	PLZZZZ	NY
FALKOWITZ, CATH	18	F	UNKNOWN	PLZZZZ	NY
ASHER	32	M	FARMER	PLZZZZ	NY
HANNAH	30	F	UNKNOWN	PLZZZZ	NY
GINSBERG, JACOB	20	M	MECH	PLZZZZ	NY
SCHOCKER, AARON	26	M	CL	PLZZZZ	NY
PACKIN, MANDEL	19	M	FARMER	PLZZZZ	NY
LEWIN, SIMON	23	M	CTW	PLZZZZ	NY
BERNSTEIN, LAZARUS	20	M	CGRMKR	PLZZZZ	NY
ANTIN, JACOB	00	M	TLR	PLZZZZ	NY
RACHEL	25	F	UNKNOWN	PLZZZZ	NY
SAHNKA	2	F	CHILD	PLZZZZ	NY
BRINO	1	F	CHILD	PLZZZZ	NY
MILCHIKER, BENED	26	M	CNF	PLZZZZ	BO
MALCK, ANTON	39	M	LABR	PLZZZZ	NY
MARIE	32	F	UNKNOWN	PLZZZZ	NY
ANTON	11	M	UNKNOWN	PLZZZZ	NY
MARIE	9	F	CHILD	PLZZZZ	NY
JAROSLAUS	8	M	CHILD	PLZZZZ	NY
FRANZ	6	M	CHILD	PLZZZZ	NY
STANISLAUS	3	M	CHILD	PLZZZZ	NY
PANOWSKI, MARIE	36	F	UNKNOWN	PLZZZZ	NY
RUDOLF	7	M	CHILD	PLZZZZ	NY
OTOKAR	1	M	CHILD	PLZZZZ	NY
RUZICKA, JOH	49	M	LABR	PLZZZZ	NY
MARIE	48	F	UNKNOWN	PLZZZZ	NY
PAULINE	21	F	UNKNOWN	PLZZZZ	NY
JOSEF	17	M	UNKNOWN	PLZZZZ	NY
JOSEFINE	10	F	UNKNOWN	PLZZZZ	NY
HEINRICH	5	M	CHILD	PLZZZZ	NY
PAVETTO, JOSEF	35	M	LABR	PLZZZZ	NY
MASAR, ROSALIE	36	F	UNKNOWN	PLZZZZ	NY
ALANE	2	F	CHILD	PLZZZZ	NY
BURDA, JOSEF	32	M	FARMER	PLZZZZ	NY
BEGNISKA, ANTON	32	M	FARMER	PLZZZZ	NY
VOLSANSKA, FRZ	27	M	FARMER	PLZZZZ	NY
STIBOR, FRANZ	39	M	FARMER	PLZZZZ	NY
MARIE	36	F	UNKNOWN	PLZZZZ	NY
MARIE	11	F	UNKNOWN	PLZZZZ	NY
VINZ	9	M	CHILD	PLZZZZ	NY

PASSENGER	AGE	SEX	OCCUPATION	PRV VIL DES
ANAN	7	F	CHILD	PLZZZZNY
JOSEF	5	M	CHILD	PLZZZZNY
ANTONIE	2	F	CHILD	PLZZZZNY
FRANZ	.07	M	INFANT	PLZZZZNY
MALEK, JOHANN	50	M	FARMER	PLZZZZNY
CATHA	44	F	UNKNOWN	PLZZZZNY
FRANCISCA	22	F	UNKNOWN	PLZZZZNY
MARIA	11	M	UNKNOWN	PLZZZZNY
ANALOSIE	9	F	CHILD	PLZZZZNY
ANTONIE	6	F	CHILD	PLZZZZNY
ANNA	3	F	CHILD	PLZZZZNY
ALAI, ISAAC	16	M	LABR	PLZZZZNY
KROSCHEFSKY, JOSEF	28	M	LABR	PLZZZZNY
AMELEA	24	F	UNKNOWN	PLZZZZNY
HAUDELSMANN, ISAAC	25	M	LABR	PLZZZZNY
ZECHER, RUBIN	45	M	LABR	PLZZZZNY
REINER, JACOB	17	M	LABR	PLZZZZNY
FUCHS, D	17	M	LABR	PLZZZZNY
ABRAHAM	10	M	CH	PLZZZZNY
LEHMANN, RIGN	18	F	UNKNOWN	PLZZZZNY
KLEIN, A	19	F	UNKNOWN	PLZZZZNY
PAUZER, FRD	25	M	CL	PLZZZZNY
PASCHER, C	18	F	UNKNOWN	PLZZZZNY
KNEGMANN, A	45	M	LABR	PLZZZZNY
ESTER	00	F	UNKNOWN	PLZZZZNY
LEHMANN, GITTEL	18	F	UNKNOWN	PLZZZZNY
PENZOK, SERTISH	27	M	LABR	PLZZZZNY
FAUST, GEDALIO	24	M	LABR	PLZZZZNY
WOLITZER, HCH	31	M	LABR	PLZZZZNY
KNOBUL, DAVID	11	M	UNKNOWN	PLZZZZNY
CZOIZKAY, S	20	M	LABR	PLZZZZNY
SCRUGER, HIRSCH	26	M	LABR	PLZZZZNY
JANZER, GOTZEL	19	M	TLR	PLZZZZNY
KOWALSKI, SEFAN	27	M	FARMER	PLZZZZCH

SHIP: ST. OF PENNSYLVANIA

FROM: GLASGOW AND LARNE
TO: NEW YORK
ARRIVED: 23 MAY 1888

PASSENGER	AGE	SEX	OCCUPATION	PRV VIL DES
ZOFIN, ISAAC	16	M	PNTR	RRZZZZUSA
SEEMAN, JACOB	35	M	FLST	RRZZZZUSA
SCHAOK, HENDEL	19	M	CGRMKR	RRZZZZUSA
LITTERS, ISAAC	26	M	CPRSMH	RRZZZZUSA
FARBER, SUNDEL	25	M	JNR	RRZZZZUSA
ORLOWITZ, MOSES	22	M	JNR	RRZZZZUSA
GARBER, JOSSEL	48	M	TNR	RRZZZZUSA
MEROWITZ, LEIBE	25	M	TNR	RRZZZZUSA
PEWOWITZ, METE	21	M	TLR	RRZZZZUSA
COHEN, MEYER	17	M	TLR	RRZZZZUSA
RAFELOWITSCH, KALMAN	18	M	TLR	RRZZZZUSA
SCHWAIN, JULIUS	25	M	TLR	RRZZZZUSA
MACKINE, LEIB	24	M	TLR	RRZZZZUSA
DOCOWJANSKY, SELIG	21	M	TLR	RRZZZZUSA
KOLNIK, ISAAC	28	M	TLR	RRZZZZUSA
KRULEWITZ, LIPMANN	23	M	TLR	RRZZZZUSA
LEWIN, JACOB	28	M	TLR	RRZZZZUSA
GOLDSTEIN, SAML.	24	M	TLR	RRZZZZUSA
ABRAMOWITZ, BENJAMIN	19	M	PDLR	RRZZZZUSA
MISKI, SIMON	22	M	PDLR	RRZZZZUSA
SLAPAK, ABRAHAM	21	M	PDLR	RRZZZZUSA
SOROKIN, MOSES	18	M	PDLR	RRZZZZUSA
SCHMIDKIN, MORDCHE	26	M	PDLR	RRZZZZUSA
REBALSKI, SALOMON	17	M	PDLR	RRZZZZUSA
SMOLSKI, RUBIN	45	M	PDLR	RRZZZZUSA
GALASK, RUBIN	45	M	PDLR	RRZZZZUSA
LEISER	24	M	PDLR	RRZZZZUSA
RUPINSKI, ITALIE	35	M	PDLR	RRZZZZUSA
SABELINSKI, ISRAEL	39	M	PDLR	RRZZZZUSA
SALEDUSHE, SCHMUEL	18	M	PDLR	RRZZZZUSA
LEWIN, ZALLEL	19	M	PDLR	RRZZZZUSA
FRIEDMAN, MOSES	40	M	PDLR	RRZZZZUSA
GAMSON, LEON	19	M	PDLR	RRZZZZUSA
ROWARSKY, HENNE	42	M	PDLR	RRZZZZUSA
UNTERMANY, MOSES	23	M	PDLR	RRZZZZUSA
SOCKOL, MOSES	25	M	LABR	RRZZZZUSA
KUBELLIS, PIOK	19	M	LABR	RRZZZZUSA
ORLOWITZ, ARON	27	M	LABR	RRZZZZUSA
PEKER, DAVID	17	M	LABR	RRZZZZUSA
BICZYSKO, ANTONI	30	M	LABR	RRZZZZUSA
MISCHLOWSKY, JAN	26	M	LABR	RRZZZZUSA
TOBITZIG, PIALI	18	M	LABR	RRZZZZUSA
TEZEBACH, JOSEF	20	M	LABR	RRZZZZUSA
LEUTZIG, FRANZ	20	M	LABR	RRZZZZUSA
MARSALKO, JOSEF	25	M	LABR	RRZZZZUSA
PONITCHTER, STANISLAUS	24	M	LABR	RRZZZZUSA
MAXIMOWITCH, JAN	17	M	LABR	RRZZZZUSA
ROMOWSKY, ADAM	26	M	LABR	RRZZZZUSA
FRANCECK, JOSEF	26	M	LABR	RRZZZZUSA
BAMBOLA, STANISLAW	26	M	LABR	RRZZZZUSA
KELISCH, ELIE	37	M	LABR	RRZZZZUSA
SLATAGORSKY, DAVID	47	M	LABR	RRZZZZUSA
SCHROEDER, AUGUST	40	M	LABR	RRZZZZUSA
LEUTNER, JOHAN	23	M	LABR	RRZZZZUSA
AROMOWITZ, BEREL	26	M	TLR	RRZZZZUSA
ZIMON, ISRAEL	18	M	LABR	RRZZZZUSA
RUTZIA, ZODEK	20	M	LABR	RRZZZZUSA
HALIBOW, ABRAHAM	24	M	LABR	RRZZZZUSA
SIMON, JACOB	17	M	LABR	RRZZZZUSA
GOLDBERG, LEISER	30	M	LABR	RRZZZZUSA
KAHN, ABRAHAM	22	M	LABR	RRZZZZUSA
KUBELIS, MACE	25	M	LABR	RRZZZZUSA
BRADINSKY, PINCUS	30	M	LABR	RRZZZZUSA
WEGDOCKSHIK, ZODECH	25	M	LABR	RRZZZZUSA
KUNOWSKY, ISAAC	23	M	LABR	RRZZZZUSA
SOPOSNIK, MEYER	16	M	LABR	RRZZZZUSA
BISZODECKY, MICHAEL	58	M	LABR	RRZZZZUSA
MITTELDORF, DAVID	20	M	LABR	RRZZZZUSA
SCHINDELOWITZ, SCHLOME	18	M	LABR	RRZZZZUSA
SALOMON, ALEXANDER	27	M	LABR	RRZZZZUSA
KOPMAN, RUHMICH	26	M	LABR	RRZZZZUSA
DWORESKY, GEDALJE	20	M	LABR	RRZZZZUSA
MEYER, ABRAHAM	16	M	LABR	RRZZZZUSA
KUSCHNER, BENJAMIN	35	M	LABR	RRZZZZUSA
HOFFMAN, ALEX	29	M	LABR	RRZZZZUSA
FRIEDLAND, BEHR.	48	M	LABR	RRZZZZUSA
HELLER, SAML.	26	M	LABR	RRZZZZUSA
WEICHTER, KEILE	18	F	SP	RRZZZZUSA
KRULEWITZ, HIRSCH	20	F	SP	RRZZZZUSA
KOHL, HELENE	18	F	SP	RRZZZZUSA
HEIN, SABINA	17	F	SP	RRZZZZUSA
ROGIN, MARY	20	F	SP	RRZZZZUSA
PARANOWITZ, DENSOLIE	20	F	SP	RRZZZZUSA
HOLLANDER, DWORE	16	F	SP	RRZZZZUSA
ISAACHSON, RACHEL	18	F	SP	RRZZZZUSA
FESHMANN, ROSA	20	F	SP	RRZZZZUSA
HERZ, CHAJE	15	F	SP	RRZZZZUSA
RABINOWITZ, SOFIE	22	F	SP	RRZZZZUSA
REISNER, SARAH	20	F	SP	RRZZZZUSA
SCHWARZ, SCHEINE	20	F	SP	RRZZZZUSA
NOCHEMOWITZ, BASCHE	20	F	SP	RRZZZZUSA
SELSCHOWSKY, PAIL	20	F	SP	RRZZZZUSA
STARBECKER, FANNY	20	F	SP	RRZZZZUSA
BRANBERG, BEILE	18	F	SP	RRZZZZUSA
GILLMAN, PERKE	15	F	SP	RRZZZZUSA
SELSCHKOWSKY, HERL	20	F	SP	RRZZZZUSA
MARGOLINE, LEJE	15	F	SP	RRZZZZUSA
CYLKOWSKI, SUSANNE	18	F	SP	RRZZZZUSA
SHERMANN, SARAH	18	F	SP	RRZZZZUSA
CHAIM	16	M	TLR	RRZZZZUSA
DETTNER, SIMON	33	M	SMH	RRZZZZUSA
FLORENTINE	35	F	W	RRZZZZUSA
WRATZLAM	5	M	CHILD	RRZZZZUSA
MARIA	7	F	CHILD	RRZZZZUSA

PASSENGER	AGE	SEX	OCCUPATION	PRV	VIL	DES
SOHOR	3	M	CHILD	RR	ZZZ	USA
JOSEPH	.09	M	INFANT	RR	ZZZ	USA
MANEWITSCH, PAWEL	25	M	LABR	RR	ZZZ	USA
ANTONIA	18	F	UNKNOWN	RR	ZZZ	USA
MEIEROWSKI, SCHMUEL	41	M	TLR	RR	ZZZ	USA
ZERELUNKOW, LEISER	11	M	CH	RR	ZZZ	USA
LEWIN, ETTE	35	F	W	RR	ZZZ	USA
MAX	9	M	CHILD	RR	ZZZ	USA
BARUCH	2	M	CHILD	RR	ZZZ	USA
ZIPPE	1	F	CHILD	RR	ZZZ	USA
MESEROWITZ, SUSSKIN	30	F	W	RR	ZZZ	USA
MATHIAS	16	M	LABR	RR	ZZZ	USA
DROSNESS, ROCHE	21	F	SP	RR	ZZZ	USA
CHAMNE	34	F	W	RR	ZZZ	USA
RAASCHE	21	F	SP	RR	ZZZ	USA
ELIE	10	F	CH	RR	ZZZ	USA
BEILE	8	F	CHILD	RR	ZZZ	USA
KINDE	6	F	CHILD	RR	ZZZ	USA
SARAH	2	F	CHILD	RR	ZZZ	USA
GORBER, ISRAEL	24	M	FARMER	RR	ZZZ	USA
CHANNE	20	F	W	RR	ZZZ	USA
KOWAKE, HIRSCH	18	M	BKR	RR	ZZZ	USA
LORE	21	F	W	RR	ZZZ	USA
LIPNITZKI, JUSTINA	48	F	W	RR	ZZZ	USA
MARIA	10	F	CH	RR	ZZZ	USA
MASKEWITZ, DANIEL	38	M	LABR	RR	ZZZ	USA
MOTURNA	29	F	W	RR	ZZZ	USA
MARIA	5	F	CHILD	RR	ZZZ	USA
HELENE	2	F	CHILD	RR	ZZZ	USA
ALFONS	1	M	CHILD	RR	ZZZ	USA
KORTH, LIEB	28	M	LABR	RR	ZZZ	USA
ROCHE	30	F	W	RR	ZZZ	USA
RAFAEL	5	M	CHILD	RR	ZZZ	USA
BASCHE	.06	M	INFANT	RR	ZZZ	USA
KLEIN, LEA	60	F	WI	RR	ZZZ	USA
UPPIN, SORE	20	F	W	RR	ZZZ	USA
JOSEF	2	M	CHILD	RR	ZZZ	USA
CHANE	50	F	W	RR	ZZZ	USA
BURGEW, ANNA	22	F	SP	RR	ZZZ	USA
ELIAS	9	M	CHILD	RR	ZZZ	USA
BENJAMIN	11	M	CH	RR	ZZZ	USA
GERSON	3	M	CHILD	RR	ZZZ	USA
DAVID	1	M	CHILD	RR	ZZZ	USA
GOLDSTEIN, FRUMME	40	F	W	RR	ZZZ	USA
LEA	11	F	CH	RR	ZZZ	USA
ESTHER	10	F	CH	RR	ZZZ	USA
SORE	8	F	CHILD	RR	ZZZ	USA
ISAAC	7	M	CHILD	RR	ZZZ	USA
ELGE	5	F	CHILD	RR	ZZZ	USA
FEIGE	3	F	CHILD	RR	ZZZ	USA
BACHNER, SPRINGE	30	F	W	RR	ZZZ	USA
FANNY	11	F	CH	RR	ZZZ	USA
BERNHARD	10	M	CH	RR	ZZZ	USA
GOLE	8	F	CHILD	RR	ZZZ	USA
LINA	5	F	CHILD	RR	ZZZ	USA
GOLOWSKY, ANASTASIA	27	F	W	RR	ZZZ	USA
ROWAN	8	M	CHILD	RR	ZZZ	USA
EMMA	5	F	CHILD	RR	ZZZ	USA
MARY	3	F	CHILD	RR	ZZZ	USA
WLADISLAUS	.09	M	INFANT	RR	ZZZ	USA
SELZER, ESTHER	40	F	W	RR	ZZZ	USA
FERGE	10	F	CH	RR	ZZZ	USA
SCHWAUCK	8	F	CHILD	RR	ZZZ	USA
CHAIME	5	F	CHILD	RR	ZZZ	USA
ZUCKERMANN, HIRSCH	23	M	TLR	RR	ZZZ	USA
BEILE	25	F	W	RR	ZZZ	USA
HENNY	6	M	CHILD	RR	ZZZ	USA
SORE	3	F	CHILD	RR	ZZZ	USA
TAUFF, JARNE	32	F	W	RR	ZZZ	USA
SCHIE	1	F	CHILD	RR	ZZZ	USA
ZILKOWITZ, SCHMUEL	28	M	PDLR	RR	ZZZ	USA
TAUBE	18	F	W	RR	ZZZ	USA
ARON	2	M	CHILD	RR	ZZZ	USA
GOLDE-LEVIN	26	F	W	RR	ZZZ	USA
ARON	.09	M	INFANT	RR	ZZZ	USA
TRABINOWITZ, GEDALIE	57	M	PDLR	RR	ZZZ	USA
SCHEINE	30	F	W	RR	ZZZ	USA
MOSES	9	M	CHILD	RR	ZZZ	USA
ESTHER	5	F	CHILD	RR	ZZZ	USA
ABRAMOWITZ, ESTHER	23	F	W	RR	ZZZ	USA
ITZIG	1	M	CHILD	RR	ZZZ	USA
DURAS, SHEINE	28	F	W	RR	ZZZ	USA
GITEL	5	M	CHILD	RR	ZZZ	USA
MANASCHE	4	M	CHILD	RR	ZZZ	USA
MOTTLE	2	M	CHILD	RR	ZZZ	USA
BARUCH	.09	M	INFANT	RR	ZZZ	USA
STANAY, ERZEBEL	25	F	W	RR	ZZZ	USA
FANO	3	F	CHILD	RR	ZZZ	USA
JULIANE	.03	F	INFANT	RR	ZZZ	USA
KAPLAN, ZLAWE	40	F	W	RR	ZZZ	USA
FREILE	11	F	CH	RR	ZZZ	USA
MICHEL	10	M	CH	RR	ZZZ	USA
CHAIVE	8	F	CHILD	RR	ZZZ	USA
ABEL	6	M	CHILD	RR	ZZZ	USA
MATUSZ, JULIAN	17	F	F	RR	ZZZ	USA
FEWY	.09	M	INFANT	RR	ZZZ	USA
GOLDSTEIN, SARA	28	F	W	RR	ZZZ	USA
GIVE	5	M	CHILD	RR	ZZZ	USA
MOSES	3	M	CHILD	RR	ZZZ	USA
STERN, JETTE	25	F	W	RR	ZZZ	USA
MOSES	1	M	CHILD	RR	ZZZ	USA
FERWISCH, BRANE	40	F	W	RR	ZZZ	USA
ESTER	15	F	SP	RR	ZZZ	USA
WOLF	11	M	CH	RR	ZZZ	USA
ZIWE	9	M	CHILD	RR	ZZZ	USA
SCHERE	7	M	CHILD	RR	ZZZ	USA
RIVE	5	M	CHILD	RR	ZZZ	USA
SCHUDA	3	M	CHILD	RR	ZZZ	USA
AZIEL	2	M	CHILD	RR	ZZZ	USA
ISAAC	1	M	CHILD	RR	ZZZ	USA
LANDAU, MOSES	40	M	TLR	RR	ZZZ	USA
LEA	14	F	CH	RR	ZZZ	USA
KUROS, MASIEG	20	M	FRMN	RR	ZZZ	USA

SHIP: WESER

FROM: BREMEN
TO: BALTIMORE
ARRIVED: 24 MAY 1888

PASSENGER	AGE	SEX	OCCUPATION	PRV	VIL	DES
BUERNK, RACHEL	30	F	UNKNOWN	RR	ZZZ	MO
LEA	7	F	CHILD	RR	ZZZ	MO
CHAJEM	5	F	CHILD	RR	ZZZ	MO
HINDE	4	F	CHILD	RR	ZZZ	MO
LOEW, ABRAHAM	35	M	DLR	RR	ZZZ	MO
WISMIERSKI, ANDREAS	36	M	LABR	RR	ZZZ	PA
BANAZEWSKI, JOSEPH	26	M	LABR	RR	ZZZ	MO
KOPANSKY, JOSEPH	30	M	LABR	RR	ZZZ	MI
JUSTIN	24	F	UNKNOWN	RR	ZZZ	MI
WILHELMINA	4	F	CHILD	RR	ZZZ	MI
ANTON	3	M	CHILD	RR	ZZZ	MI
BAERKERT, PAULINA	32	F	UNKNOWN	RR	ZZZ	PA
AUGUST	7	M	CHILD	RR	ZZZ	PA
EPHRAIM	6	M	CHILD	RR	ZZZ	PA
THALMANN, FRRIEDR	45	M	LABR	RR	ZZZ	IL
ANNA	50	F	UNKNOWN	RR	ZZZ	IL
PAULINE	10	F	CH	RR	ZZZ	IL
JANKOWSKY, ANTON	21	M	LABR	RR	ZZZ	IA
KUCHARSKI, STANISLAUS	27	M	LABR	RR	ZZZ	PA
PADD, OTTO	18	M	BKR	RR	ZZZ	WI
KNOPF, WILHELM	22	M	LABR	RR	ZZZ	MI
POUSKI, FRANZ	17	M	PNTR	RR	ZZZ	MN
GRUBMANN, JULIUS	18	M	GDNR	RR	ZZZ	MD
GRAJEWSKY, STEFAN	48	M	LABR	RR	ZZZ	MD
MATWEI	19	M	LABR	RR	ZZZ	MD

PASSENGER	AGE	SEX	OCCUPATION	PRV VIL DES
VICENTY	16	M	LABR	RRZZZZMD
SKLAWSKI, ISAAC	21	M	LABR	RRZZZZMD
SCHAFERMANN, JANKEL	25	M	DLR	RRZZZZMD
SCHAWITZ, WOLF	27	M	DLR	RRZZZZMD
BURACK, HIRSCH	25	M	DLR	RRZZZZMD
BASCH, MASCHE	25	M	DLR	RRZZZZMD
ROSSMANN, AUG	14	M	DLR	RRZZZZMD
JUSIEFSIE, ROSALIA	20	F	UNKNOWN	RRZZZZMD
WOLINECK, ANNA	23	F	UNKNOWN	RRZZZZMD
KRUCHANIS, SIMON	28	M	LABR	RRZZZZMD
MILEWSKY, VICENTY	26	M	LABR	RRZZZZPA
MIEAZINSKI, JOSEPH	21	M	LABR	RRZZZZPA
WOLSKI, LEON	21	M	DLR	RRZZZZPA
ZINOWSKY, THOMAS	21	M	LABR	RRZZZZWI
MELLER, JOSEPH	30	M	LABR	RRZZZZMD
OLAVINSKY, JAN	29	M	LABR	RRZZZZMD
NADOLNY, U	36	F	UNKNOWN	RRZZZZMD
U	.11	M	INFANT	RRZZZZMD
HONOWSKI, U	44	M	LABR	RRZZZZMD
WILSCHINSKY, DAVID	17	M	LABR	RRZZZZIA
BILKE, CHANE	20	F	UNKNOWN	RRZZZZOH
JANKEL	3	M	CHILD	RRZZZZOH
DOEGE	9	M	CHILD	RRZZZZOH
WEINTRAUB, MARIA	50	F	UNKNOWN	RRZZZZOH
DRIEZIACK, JOHN	30	M	LABR	RRZZZZPA
GAMIEFSKY, MARGA	28	F	UNKNOWN	RRZZZZOH
WASIACK, STANISLAUS	25	M	LABR	RRZZZZPA
KONIZEWSKI, JOSEPH	32	M	LABR	RRZZZZMD
LULINSKI, JAN	30	M	LABR	RRZZZZOH
CICHOTZKY, IGNATZ	47	M	LABR	RRZZZZIL
LUTOWSKI, KASIMIR	37	M	LABR	RRZZZZIL

SHIP: ADRIATIC

FROM: LIVERPOOL AND QUEENSTOWN
TO: NEW YORK
ARRIVED: 25 MAY 1888

PASSENGER	AGE	SEX	OCCUPATION	PRV VIL DES
SCHEEKTMAN, LEA	21	F	SVNT	RRADAXUSA
RESSNEI, ABRAHAM	32	M	MNR	RRADAXUSA
KOENIGSBURG, ISRAEL	28	M	MNR	RRADAXUSA
KATZENBURG, ABRAHAM	18	M	MNR	RRADAXUSA
SCHMISDET, CHAFERGE	25	F	MNR	RRADAXUSA
RISI	24	F	MNR	RRADAXUSA
KNYASELZKY, CHANCHIL	15	F	MNR	RRADAXUSA
KNZASEKKY, JETTE	45	F	W	RRADAXUSA
NOCHAMH	15	M	MNR	RRADAXUSA
GISTL	13	M	CH	RRADAXUSA
RISAHEVE	11	F	CH	RRADAXUSA
BERST, MARIA	18	F	SVNT	RRADAXUSA
PILACHMONTY, JOSEF	26	M	LABR	RRADAXUSA
KABALIN, MARL	23	M	LABR	RRADAXUSA
HANDLER, ABRAM	15	M	LABR	RRADAXUSA
LANDAU, RITA	20	F	SVNT	RRADAXUSA

SHIP: TRAVE

FROM: BREMEN AND SOUTHAMPTON
TO: NEW YORK
ARRIVED: 26 MAY 1888

PASSENGER	AGE	SEX	OCCUPATION	PRV VIL DES
ROUDEL, RANZISCA	24	F	UNKNOWN	RRZZZZUSA
TIFIK, MARCSA	18	F	UNKNOWN	RRZZZZUSA
ALTMANOWICZ, ANTONY	19	F	UNKNOWN	RRZZZZUSA
ANNA	22	F	UNKNOWN	RRZZZZUSA
FRANKEWICZ, TOMASUS	26	M	LABR	RRZZZZUSA
KIRCHMANSKY, MASZE	68	M	LABR	RRZZZZUSA
OKUMIEWSKY, GITTEL	68	F	UNKNOWN	RRZZZZUSA
DRIKOWSKA, MATGOROTA	40	F	UNKNOWN	RRZZZZUSA

SHIP: LEERDAM

FROM: ROTTERDAM
TO: NEW YORK
ARRIVED: 28 MAY 1888

PASSENGER	AGE	SEX	OCCUPATION	PRV VIL DES
KLIMONICH, A.	26	F	FARMER	PLZZZZUSA
W.	15	F	FARMER	PLZZZZUSA
J.	3	F	CHILD	PLZZZZUSA
P.	00	F	INF	PLZZZZUSA
SOBERTER, J.	24	M	LABR	PLZZZZUSA
MANUSZENSKI, J.	57	M	LABR	PLZZZZUSA
A.	59	F	LABR	PLZZZZUSA
ROOSHEN, J.	37	M	LABR	PLZZZZUSA
B.	22	F	LABR	PLZZZZUSA
MANUZEWSKI, F.	27	M	LABR	PLZZZZUSA
DOBROK, A.	30	M	LABR	PLZZZZUSA
PIRMINSKI, F.	28	M	LABR	PLZZZZUSA
KOLINS, E.	24	M	LABR	PLZZZZUSA
RACZAK, S.	57	M	LABR	PLZZZZUSA
L.	45	F	LABR	PLZZZZUSA
F.	14	M	LABR	PLZZZZUSA
M.	1	M	CHILD	PLZZZZUSA
BOGONSKI, F.	21	M	UNKNOWN	PLZZZZUSA
WEISMAN, A.	41	M	UNKNOWN	PLZZZZUSA
ISZIBIATOWSKI, A.	26	M	UNKNOWN	PLZZZZUSA
ORZYKOWSKI, J.	12	M	CH	PLZZZZUSA
BRESKI, A.	30	M	LABR	PLZZZZUSA
J.	28	F	LABR	PLZZZZUSA
H.	20	F	LABR	PLZZZZUSA
V.	8	F	CHILD	PLZZZZUSA
L.	5	M	CHILD	PLZZZZUSA
P.	3	M	CHILD	PLZZZZUSA
P.	00	F	INF	PLZZZZUSA
J.	00	F	INF	PLZZZZUSA
WOGKOWSKI, W.	36	M	INF	PLZZZZUSA
G.	30	F	INF	PLZZZZUSA
MALINOWSKA, D.	30	F	INF	PLZZZZUSA
J.	27	M	INF	PLZZZZUSA
NAWOLSKA, B.	21	F	INF	PLZZZZUSA
WRONIECKI, P.	28	M	INF	PLZZZZUSA
GLOWECKI, M.	25	F	INF	PLZZZZUSA
M.	29	M	INF	PLZZZZUSA
K.	00	F	INF	PLZZZZUSA
KARCZUWSKI, J.	40	M	LABR	PLZZZZUSA
PUDINSKA, A.	25	M	LABR	PLZZZZUSA
KACZMARZCIK, J.	22	M	LABR	PLZZZZUSA
GRZYWEICK, J.	19	M	LABR	PLZZZZUSA
M.	18	M	LABR	PLZZZZUSA
PAWLAK, J.	17	M	LABR	PLZZZZUSA
MACHINSKY, A.	12	M	LABR	PLZZZZUSA
MICHAL, J.	16	M	LABR	PLZZZZUSA
JAGUSKI, J.	30	M	LABR	PLZZZZUSA
F.	28	F	LABR	PLZZZZUSA
J.	80	F	LABR	PLZZZZUSA
J.	5	F	CHILD	PLZZZZUSA
J.	3	F	CHILD	PLZZZZUSA
LABINSKI, J.	26	M	LABR	PLZZZZUSA
A.	26	F	LABR	PLZZZZUSA
J.	4	M	CHILD	PLZZZZUSA
AMSTARHUWSEZ, F.	28	M	CH	PLZZZZUSA
M.	23	F	CH	PLZZZZUSA
S.	2	F	CHILD	PLZZZZUSA
WOZEICH, B.	30	M	LABR	PLZZZZUSA
PONIATOWSKI, F.	30	M	LABR	PLZZZZUSA

PASSENGER	AGE	SEX	OCCUPATION	PRV	VIL	DES
E.	32	F	LABR	PL	ZZZZ	USA
H.	2	F	CHILD	PL	ZZZZ	USA
J.	00	F	INF	PL	ZZZZ	USA
WICHKOWSKY, F.	33	M	LABR	PL	ZZZZ	USA
ALEVSOREK, A.	27	F	LABR	PL	ZZZZ	USA
H.	4	F	CHILD	PL	ZZZZ	USA
VASANN, M.	20	F	CH	PL	ZZZZ	USA
MILESI, G.	42	M	CH	PL	ZZZZ	USA
GOVDI, D.	27	F	CH	PL	ZZZZ	USA
F.	4	F	CHILD	PL	ZZZZ	USA
CARVENTI, N.	27	M	LABR	PL	ZZZZ	USA
A.	20	F	LABR	PL	ZZZZ	USA
G.	00	F	INF	PL	ZZZZ	USA
FABIANO, A.	48	M	LABR	PL	ZZZZ	USA
CASANO, S.	28	M	LABR	PL	ZZZZ	USA
DI-CENZO, S.	31	M	LABR	PL	ZZZZ	USA
ARRIGHINI, A.	38	M	FARMER	PL	ZZZZ	USA
OBERTO, G.	42	M	LABR	PL	ZZZZ	USA
BERTOLEW, G.	22	M	LABR	PL	ZZZZ	USA
BOTTINELLI, B.	39	M	LABR	PL	ZZZZ	USA
PATRINI, C.	22	M	LABR	PL	ZZZZ	USA
GIOTTO, L.	27	M	LABR	PL	ZZZZ	USA
GARRO, B.	23	M	LABR	PL	ZZZZ	USA
ARIASI, B.	29	M	LABR	PL	ZZZZ	USA
GIANG-WE, L.	31	M	LABR	PL	ZZZZ	USA
A.	11	F	CH	PL	ZZZZ	USA
C.	8	F	CHILD	PL	ZZZZ	USA
R.	5	M	CHILD	PL	ZZZZ	USA
BOLLINE, R.	34	M	CH	PL	ZZZZ	USA
G.	28	M	CH	PL	ZZZZ	USA
NATALE, R.	25	M	CH	PL	ZZZZ	USA
RINALDO, S.	28	M	CH	PL	ZZZZ	USA
U, A.	33	M	CH	PL	ZZZZ	USA
BARTOLOMEO, R.	33	M	CH	PL	ZZZZ	USA
BLONINI, F.	28	M	CH	PL	ZZZZ	USA
MEINGER, M.	20	F	CH	PL	ZZZZ	USA
KOFFI-, F.	26	M	SLSMN	PL	ZZZZ	USA
HEBRICH, J.	30	M	LABR	PL	ZZZZ	USA
WEIDEMAN, C.	18	M	LABR	PL	ZZZZ	USA
HAHN, H.	24	M	FARMER	PL	ZZZZ	USA
JEHLE, C.	23	M	LABR	PL	ZZZZ	USA
WUNDER, N.	32	M	FARMER	PL	ZZZZ	USA
BREINS, B.	18	M	LABR	PL	ZZZZ	USA
BOSUK, W.	14	M	FARMER	PL	ZZZZ	USA
E.	12	F	CH	PL	ZZZZ	USA
HOFMANN, K.	39	M	FARMER	PL	ZZZZ	USA
H.	7	M	CHILD	PL	ZZZZ	USA
KNAPP, G.	16	M	FARMER	PL	ZZZZ	USA
JATH, J.	24	M	LABR	PL	ZZZZ	USA
KULLMAN, L.	24	M	LABR	PL	ZZZZ	USA
MULLER, M.	26	F	LABR	PL	ZZZZ	USA
N.	6	F	CHILD	PL	ZZZZ	USA
A.	4	M	CHILD	PL	ZZZZ	USA
J.	2	M	CHILD	PL	ZZZZ	USA
STREIB, F.	28	M	FARMER	PL	ZZZZ	USA
SCHAEFER, G.	27	M	FARMER	PL	ZZZZ	USA
HANEMANN, M.	18	M	LABR	PL	ZZZZ	USA
BERGER, S.	17	M	LABR	PL	ZZZZ	USA
DAUR, J.	17	M	FARMER	PL	ZZZZ	USA
WUNT, G.	27	M	FARMER	PL	ZZZZ	USA
WINTERMANTEL, C.	21	M	LABR	PL	ZZZZ	USA
DEUERBERG, K.	20	F	LABR	PL	ZZZZ	USA
LEISS, SOP.	15	M	LABR	PL	ZZZZ	USA
HEROLD, F.	19	M	LABR	PL	ZZZZ	USA
HINTZ, M.	28	F	LABR	PL	ZZZZ	USA
G.	6	M	CHILD	PL	ZZZZ	USA
REIMAN, F.	20	M	MCHT	PL	ZZZZ	USA
SCHERBER, W.	28	M	LABR	PL	ZZZZ	USA
BESCHOFF, G.	50	M	FARMER	PL	ZZZZ	USA
LINDAUER, G.	50	M	FARMER	PL	ZZZZ	USA
VERMER, F.	24	M	FARMER	PL	ZZZZ	USA
WEBER, G.	15	M	FARMER	PL	ZZZZ	USA
VOSS, F.	57	M	BRR	PL	ZZZZ	USA
LANG, G.	24	M	BRR	PL	ZZZZ	USA
KAESS, E.	8	F	CHILD	PL	ZZZZ	USA
BAUMBUSCH, R.	23	F	LABR	PL	ZZZZ	USA
MUNCH, R.	23	F	LABR	PL	ZZZZ	USA
SCH---, K.	13	F	LABR	PL	ZZZZ	USA
LOUIS, R.	57	M	LABR	PL	ZZZZ	USA
G.	56	F	LABR	PL	ZZZZ	USA
F.	21	M	LABR	PL	ZZZZ	USA
VOGT, G.	18	M	FARMER	PL	ZZZZ	USA
SPERLE, J.F.	24	M	LABR	PL	ZZZZ	USA
MASLER, F.	25	M	LABR	PL	ZZZZ	USA
HLIVANG, S.	20	M	LABR	PL	ZZZZ	USA
BREN, A.	26	M	LABR	PL	ZZZZ	USA
KARL, M.	44	F	FARMER	PL	ZZZZ	USA
J.	18	M	FARMER	PL	ZZZZ	USA
E.	13	F	FARMER	PL	ZZZZ	USA
C.	9	F	CHILD	PL	ZZZZ	USA
A.	7	F	CHILD	PL	ZZZZ	USA
LIEBNER, F.	26	F	LABR	PL	ZZZZ	USA
AZOGHOWSKI, A.	21	M	LABR	PL	ZZZZ	USA
MAIER, M.	15	F	LABR	PL	ZZZZ	USA
MAAG, S.	18	F	LABR	PL	ZZZZ	USA
KLEMP, M.	27	M	LABR	PL	ZZZZ	USA
VOGELMAN, P.	16	M	LABR	PL	ZZZZ	USA
REGNER, F.	13	F	LABR	PL	ZZZZ	USA
A.	13	F	LABR	PL	ZZZZ	USA
HEINSTEIN, M.	15	F	LABR	PL	ZZZZ	USA
EBERTSCH, K.	18	F	LABR	PL	ZZZZ	USA
HAAG, A.M.	65	F	LABR	PL	ZZZZ	USA
WEISE, F.	40	M	FARMER	PL	ZZZZ	USA
F.	40	F	FARMER	PL	ZZZZ	USA
A.	10	F	CH	PL	ZZZZ	USA
F.	6	M	CHILD	PL	ZZZZ	USA
A.	3	M	CHILD	PL	ZZZZ	USA
MERZ, V.	27	M	LABR	PL	ZZZZ	USA
BAKEMAN, H.	27	F	LABR	PL	ZZZZ	USA
SCHIMMEL, L.	18	F	UNKNOWN	PL	ZZZZ	USA
SCHREIBER, M.	28	M	UNKNOWN	PL	ZZZZ	USA
A.	23	F	UNKNOWN	PL	ZZZZ	USA
L.	4	M	CHILD	PL	ZZZZ	USA
WEIMER, D.	17	F	CH	PL	ZZZZ	USA
MOTZER, R.	38	F	CH	PL	ZZZZ	USA
U, C.	16	F	CH	PL	ZZZZ	USA
WERNER, A.	18	F	CH	PL	ZZZZ	USA
MONAH, E.	45	M	FARMER	PL	ZZZZ	USA
E.	44	F	FARMER	PL	ZZZZ	USA
M.	5	F	CHILD	PL	ZZZZ	USA
M.	4	F	CHILD	PL	ZZZZ	USA
B.	3	F	CHILD	PL	ZZZZ	USA
F.	00	F	INF	PL	ZZZZ	USA
SCHUDELIN, A.	20	F	LABR	PL	ZZZZ	USA
KLIPPEL, M.	16	F	LABR	PL	ZZZZ	USA
ALBRECHT, D.	17	F	LABR	PL	ZZZZ	USA
BULLING, K.	24	F	LABR	PL	ZZZZ	USA
HOFFMAN, A.G.	60	F	LABR	PL	ZZZZ	USA
M.M.	23	F	LABR	PL	ZZZZ	USA
GOERGEN, A.	18	F	LABR	PL	ZZZZ	USA
PRENER, B.C.	20	M	LABR	PL	ZZZZ	USA
BAYLER, J.	27	M	LABR	PL	ZZZZ	USA
BASKER, M.	29	F	LABR	PL	ZZZZ	USA
RIES, H.	18	F	LABR	PL	ZZZZ	USA
FILIPPE, P.	60	M	FARMER	PL	ZZZZ	USA
R.	60	F	FARMER	PL	ZZZZ	USA
C.	39	F	FARMER	PL	ZZZZ	USA
M.	20	F	FARMER	PL	ZZZZ	USA
R.	17	M	FARMER	PL	ZZZZ	USA
E.	7	M	CHILD	PL	ZZZZ	USA
ZEPP, J.	18	M	CH	PL	ZZZZ	USA
PABST, E.	19	F	LABR	PL	ZZZZ	USA
EHRAN, U	34	M	LABR	PL	ZZZZ	USA
BAYER, M.	25	M	LABR	PL	ZZZZ	USA
SMEENK, J.	25	M	LABR	PL	ZZZZ	USA
METHAMMER, J.	31	M	LABR	PL	ZZZZ	USA
BUCHHOLD, M.	42	M	LABR	PL	ZZZZ	USA
R.	40	F	LABR	PL	ZZZZ	USA
FINK, W.	40	M	FARMER	PL	ZZZZ	USA
C.	35	F	FARMER	PL	ZZZZ	USA

PASSENGER	AGE	SEX	OCCUPATION	PRV VIL DES
AQ.	7	F	CHILD	PLZZZZUSA
A.	10	M	CH	PLZZZZUSA
M.	4	F	CHILD	PLZZZZUSA
VOLLMAR, C.	51	F	LABR	PLZZZZUSA
D.	17	M	LABR	PLZZZZUSA
L.	9	M	CHILD	PLZZZZUSA
HEUSLE, A.	52	M	CH	PLZZZZUSA
REICHLE, W.	34	M	CH	PLZZZZUSA
HEEMSTR-, O.	30	M	FARMER	PLZZZZUSA
A.	30	F	FARMER	PLZZZZUSA
P.	7	F	CHILD	PLZZZZUSA
J.	4	M	CHILD	PLZZZZUSA
S.	.11	M	INFANT	PLZZZZUSA
METZEL, M.	24	F	INF	PLZZZZUSA
C.	6	F	CHILD	PLZZZZUSA
C.	4	M	CHILD	PLZZZZUSA
GUNSE, U	00	M	LABR	PLZZZZUSA
SCHLEGEL, S.	24	M	FARMER	PLZZZZUSA
OTTERBEIN, M.	26	M	LABR	PLZZZZUSA
M.	65	F	LABR	PLZZZZUSA
M.	6	F	CHILD	PLZZZZUSA
A.	3	M	CHILD	PLZZZZUSA
MUHL, K.	31	M	FARMER	PLZZZZUSA
MEHL, F.	31	F	FARMER	PLZZZZUSA
E.	10	F	CH	PLZZZZUSA
H.	8	F	CHILD	PLZZZZUSA
K.	7	M	CHILD	PLZZZZUSA
A.	4	F	CHILD	PLZZZZUSA
J.	00	F	INF	PLZZZZUSA
LEPPER, D.	53	F	INF	PLZZZZUSA
E.	14	F	INF	PLZZZZUSA
R.	10	M	INF	PLZZZZUSA
A.	9	M	CHILD	PLZZZZUSA
P.	20	F	FARMER	PLZZZZUSA
RIEBER, A.	22	F	FARMER	PLZZZZUSA
F.	17	M	LABR	PLZZZZUSA
KIFFEL, A.	20	F	LABR	PLZZZZUSA
MAYER, S.	22	F	LABR	PLZZZZUSA
KIRCHNER, N.	22	F	LABR	PLZZZZUSA
HAMMER, M.	25	F	LABR	PLZZZZUSA
FRITZ, M.	21	F	FARMER	PLZZZZUSA

SHIP: RICHMOND

FROM: LIVERPOOL AND QUEENSTOWN
TO: NEW YORK
ARRIVED: 28 MAY 1888

PASSENGER	AGE	SEX	OCCUPATION	PRV VIL DES
ROBBINOWITCH, D.	32	M	FARMER	PLAHOOMN
MIETKIERWIZ, WOYEICEK	22	M	FARMER	PLAFWJBUF
LAWIZIM, FR.	48	M	FARMER	PLAFWJPA
MASCHKAWIER, JAN	24	M	FARMER	PLAFWJPA
DIROYALLS, KONSTANZ	10	M	CH	PLAFWJPA
WLADISLAU	17	F	SP	PLAFWJPA
SIBLER, MELLER	18	M	LKSH	PLAHOOCIN
REIND, AMALIA	20	F	LABR	PLAGUZNY
MORTALS, CARL-KUSLAA	21	M	LABR	PLAGUZNY
RAUTA, ITT-M.J.	27	M	LABR	PLAGUZNY
HOOPULD, SOFIA-E.	27	M	LABR	PLAGUZNY
HAUNEPPT, MARY	29	F	W	PLAGUZMA
DAVID	3	M	CHILD	PLAGUZMA
MALIN, JOSEF	31	M	FARMER	PLAGUZBO
GABRIEL	27	M	FARMER	PLAGUZBO
JACOBSDOTTER, LISA	22	F	LABR	PLAGUZNY
PAJNUCT, JACOB	52	M	FARMER	PLAGUZNE
FYNGALE, JOHAN	19	M	LABR	PLAGUZMA
AUTOLA, HENRIK	27	M	LABR	PLAGUZMA
PAULUS, GUSTAF	31	M	LABR	PLAGUZMA
MACNUSSON, JOHAN	18	M	LABR	PLAGUZMA
YLISOLA, GABRIEL	27	M	FARMER	PLAGUZMA
HUKTAMAKI, HERMAN	35	M	LABR	PLAGUZMA
KAUGASMAKI, JACOB	28	M	LABR	PLAGUZBO
SURTALA, JOHAN	23	M	LABR	PLAGUZBO
ULIOLA, ISAK	19	M	FARMER	PLAGUZBO
SALOCUSTIDE, MATTS	27	M	FARMER	PLAGUZBO
NISULA, ISAK	20	M	LABR	PLAGUZBO
STOBACHR, ANDERS	31	M	LABR	PLAGUZBO
FULKA, JOHAN	37	M	LABR	PLAGUZBO
PER	40	M	UNKNOWN	PLAGUZBO
PER	30	M	UNKNOWN	PLAGUZBO
KARKIATRO, MATTS	19	M	UNKNOWN	PLAGUZBO
FRIEDMANN, JUDA	20	M	TLR	PLAFWJNY
BRIENE	25	F	W	PLACBFNY
ETHE	5	F	CHILD	PLACBFNY
ZETERA, JAN	27	M	LABR	PLAFWJNY
LAZZAK, THEOPHIL	25	M	FARMER	PLAFWJNY
RAGOWIN, TEMPKE	30	F	W	PLAHOONY
BISCHE	11	F	CH	PLAHOONY
BASCHE	7	F	CHILD	PLAHOONY
ARON	4	F	CHILD	PLAHOONY
HURWITZ, JOSEF	38	M	PNTR	PLAHOONY
BERWNIAK, JOSEF	38	M	LABR	PLAHOONY
HUSCHMAR, CHASKEL	36	M	SHPKR	PLAHOONY
WETSTERN, SIMON	35	M	FSHMN	PLAFWJNY
ZAUDERER, ISAC	52	M	GCR	PLAFWJNY
IDES	46	F	W	PLAFWJNY
ANNA	22	F	SVNT	PLAFWJNY
BETTY	20	F	SVNT	PLAFWJNY
MOSES	19	M	CL	PLAFWJNY
REBECCA	15	F	SVNT	PLAFWJNY
PEPPI	13	F	SVNT	PLAFWJNY
TROSCHYLO, JOSEF	24	M	LABR	PLAFWJPA

SHIP: AURANIA

FROM: LIVERPOOL AND QUEENSTOWN
TO: NEW YORK
ARRIVED: 28 MAY 1888

PASSENGER	AGE	SEX	OCCUPATION	PRV VIL DES
SUGLSI, JOHAN	45	M	LABR	FNZZZZNY
PAKININ, JACOB	25	M	LABR	FNZZZZNY
PERTHALA, JOH.	39	M	LABR	FNZZZZNY
PERTHENLA, JOH.JAKKA	28	M	LABR	FNZZZZNY
KOWPILLA, AND.	27	M	LABR	FNZZZZNY
PIESI, CARL	40	M	LABR	FNZZZZNY
PAPYN, AND.	26	M	LABR	FNZZZZNY
LETHERN, JOH.	32	M	LABR	FNZZZZNY
ANTTI, JOH.	32	M	LABR	FNZZZZNY
JOHANSON, OTTO	17	M	LABR	FNZZZZNY
NILS.B.	21	M	LABR	FNZZZZNY
PELGAHEMAKIE, MATTI	20	F	SP	FNZZZZNY
VAYALA, ELINA	18	F	SP	FNZZZZNY
MAHILA, ERIK	20	M	LABR	FNZZZZNY
WALLIN, TH.	20	M	LABR	FNZZZZNY
RANTIS, JOH.R.	30	M	LABR	FNZZZZNY
MEKALO, JOH.	20	M	LABR	FNZZZZNY
LAETALA, FELIX	20	M	LABR	FNZZZZNY
JOH.	27	M	LABR	FNZZZZNY
HEITELA, JOH.	44	M	LABR	FNZZZZNY
TYNZIKA, MATT	41	M	LABR	FNZZZZNY
JOHANSON, OLAF	47	M	LABR	FNZZZZNY
HEITELA, JOH.	26	M	LABR	FNZZZZNY
LASILA, ISAK	29	M	LABR	FNZZZZNY
ESKALA, GEORGA	29	M	LABR	FNZZZZNY
ISOKARTA, MERKO	25	M	LABR	FNZZZZNY
KIRTALA, JOH.	18	M	LABR	FNZZZZNY
ANTILA, THOMAS	30	M	LABR	FNZZZZNY
PISPANAN, ISRAEL	24	M	LABR	FNZZZZNY
LU-ALA, GUST.	34	M	LABR	FNZZZZNY
PESALO, ELIAS	36	M	LABR	FNZZZZNY

PASSENGER	AGE	SEX	OCCUPATION	PRV VIL DES
TXEKANGAS, HENR.	42	M	LABR	FNZZZZNY
TASTALA, ENEKE	23	M	LABR	FNZZZZNY
HANKANEN, ABR.	24	M	LABR	FNZZZZNY
HAKALA, EMIL	30	M	LABR	FNZZZZNY
KUSENIEM, HEIKI	43	M	LABR	FNZZZZNY
PYHILA, MIKKO	38	M	LABR	FNZZZZNY
HENTLA, JOH.	45	M	LABR	FNZZZZNY
REMALA, ED.	18	M	LABR	FNZZZZNY
KOKONEN, FRED.	27	M	LABR	FNZZZZNY
ECKELA, HUKI	34	M	LABR	FNZZZZNY
MALAKAWU, ANT.	37	M	LABR	FNZZZZNY
TAKKONEN, ERIK	31	M	LABR	FNZZZZNY
YLITALO, OTTO	30	M	LABR	FNZZZZNY
HATALA, JOH.	19	M	LABR	FNZZZZNY
REIM, SAKARIAS	30	M	LABR	FNZZZZNY
HENTLA, HERM.	20	M	LABR	FNZZZZNY
K--KALA, ADOLF	27	M	LABR	FNZZZZNY
REIMKA, JOH.	28	M	LABR	FNZZZZNY
SWENSEN, AND.	33	M	LABR	FNZZZZNY
MACHI, JOH-E.	50	M	LABR	FNZZZZNY
SOUKA, JAK.	20	M	LABR	FNZZZZNY
HEUNEMNEN, KUSSLI	32	M	LABR	FNZZZZNY
BAUWALO, JAN	18	M	LABR	FNZZZZNY
TALAGART, ERIK	40	M	LABR	FNZZZZNY
HENS, MATS	25	M	LABR	FNZZZZNY
MELKOS, JAKO	24	M	LABR	FNZZZZNY
VESTERBERG, AB.	26	M	LABR	FNZZZZNY
AYRON, JANK	36	M	LABR	FNZZZZNY
SELM, AUG.	24	M	LABR	FNZZZZNY
LAMBEN, SAM.	30	M	LABR	FNZZZZNY
LANEBIN, ISAK	25	M	LABR	FNZZZZNY
AHR, PEKKER	30	M	LABR	FNZZZZNY
KAWITZKY, ABRAHAM	35	M	LABR	RRZZZZNY
ZODERAS, BALTRUS	25	M	LABR	RRZZZZNY
KALINOWSKY, ANTON	20	M	LABR	RRZZZZNY
STROLIS, JERZI	40	M	LABR	RRZZZZNY
SCHLETTER, MARTIN	51	M	LABR	RRZZZZNY
LACKNER, ANDREAS	28	M	LABR	RRZZZZNY
BELKE, MICH.	30	M	LABR	RRZZZZNY
NARKUN, JOHANN	30	M	LABR	RRZZZZNY
MATTSCHIS, ANTON	26	M	LABR	RRZZZZNY
JEMSCHAITES, WINZAS	30	M	LABR	RRZZZZNY
SUSSMANN, LEISER	38	M	LABR	RRZZZZNY
CHAJE	35	F	W	RRZZZZNY
FEIGE	5	F	CHILD	RRZZZZNY
KOACZINSKY, WLADISLAW	22	M	LABR	RRZZZZNY
TIMMIK, JULIUS	30	M	LABR	RRZZZZNY
THERESE	28	F	W	RRZZZZNY
KARLITZKI, BERTHA	26	F	W	RRZZZZNY
JULIUS	4	M	CHILD	RRZZZZNY
LEVANDOWSKY, JACOB	27	M	LABR	RRZZZZNY
TOLODZIKI, MARCIN	22	M	LABR	RRZZZZNY
RYPINSKI, FRANZ	45	M	LABR	RRZZZZNY
GRZELECKI, ANDRZY	35	M	LABR	RRZZZZNY
JOSEFA	24	F	W	RRZZZZNY
LEVANDOWSKI, MARIAN	27	M	LABR	RRZZZZNY
GUTOWSKY, JULIUS	21	M	LABR	RRZZZZIL
PERTRICK, AUGUST	33	M	LABR	RRZZZZIL
SIEDLEWSKY, JOSEF	29	M	LABR	RRZZZZNY
BOGES, ADAM	28	M	LABR	RRZZZZNY
IGNAITIS, FRANZ	21	M	LABR	RRZZZZNY
WAITSCHANASS, ANDREAS	22	M	PNTR	RRZZZZNY
SCHIDOMIS, IVAN	20	M	TLR	RRZZZZNY
WOLLSEWITZ, WINZAS	40	M	LABR	RRZZZZNY
WOLFSON, LOUIS	25	M	CL	RRZZZZNY
GRABLIKAS, HANOS	27	M	LABR	RRZZZZNY
HANOS	25	M	LABR	RRZZZZNY

SHIP: ELBE

FROM: BREMEN AND SOUTHAMPTON
TO: NEW YORK
ARRIVED: 29 MAY 1888

PASSENGER	AGE	SEX	OCCUPATION	PRV VIL DES
POLOWSKA, CHAJE	43	M	TT	RRZZZZUSA
SCHAIET, CHAJE	30	M	FARMER	RRAHOKUSA
SCHIPOL, CONSTANTIN	40	M	FARMER	RRZZZZNY
BRUNSKAL, JOHANN	30	M	SMH	RRZZZZNY
KOZLAWSKA, MARIANNE	19	F	SVNT	RRZZZZNY
KOPROWSKI, JAN	55	M	FARMER	RRZZZZNY
FRAHN, EMIL	6	M	CHILD	RRZZZZNY
ALBERT	5	M	CHILD	RRZZZZNY
CARL	4	M	CHILD	RRZZZZNY
OBAROWSKI, JAN	45	M	LABR	RRZZZZNY
KAMINSKY, MOSES	28	M	LABR	RRZZZZNY
MANE	23	F	W	RRZZZZNY
PLANTIN, LEO	34	M	LABR	RRAFQVNY
MOLZAHN, JOSEF	34	M	LABR	RRAFQVNY
KOEHL, ADOLF	29	M	LABR	RRAFQVNY
FLEISCHMANN, FRANZISKA	20	F	SVNT	RRZZZZBUF
WUST, FRANZISKA	19	F	SVNT	RRZZZZBUF
FITTJE, GERHARD	23	M	LABR	RRZZZZNE
HORMANN, JOH.	25	M	LABR	RRZZZZCAL
KIEFER, JACOB	26	M	LABR	RRZZZZNY
JUNKER, KASPAR	25	M	LABR	RRZZZZNY
KAMINTZKY, STARCH	21	M	LABR	RRAIKKNY
VICTORIA	17	F	W	RRAIKKNY
WENTEL, JAN	26	M	PNTR	RRAIKKNY
KARDELL, ANTON	26	M	PNTR	RRAIKKNY
JOSEF, SCHORER	17	M	JNR	RRZZZZNY
ZERNEWSKY, JUERGES	30	M	LABR	RRZZZZNY
RICHTER, JOSES	20	M	LABR	RRZZZZNY
SIMANOWITZ, FRANZ	16	M	LABR	RRZZZZNY
ABRAHAMSOHN, ISRAEL	40	M	LABR	RRZZZZNY
JESSELOWITZ, JOSSEL	46	M	LABR	RRZZZZNY

SHIP: ETHIOPIA

FROM: GLASGOW
TO: NEW YORK
ARRIVED: 29 MAY 1888

PASSENGER	AGE	SEX	OCCUPATION	PRV VIL DES
KWIEMCKY, MECHAEL	24	M	LABR	RRZZZZUSA
BZAROWSKY, CONSTANTIN	33	M	LABR	RRZZZZUSA
LABOWSKY, FILEX	40	M	LABR	RRZZZZUSA
WOLKOWSKY, WOLEK	19	M	LABR	RRZZZZUSA
KARZOWSKY, JONAS	28	M	LABR	RRZZZZUSA
MROWEZALKY, FRANCHESCHE	33	M	LABR	RRZZZZUSA
KUBVEZNISKY, ANTON	28	M	LABR	RRZZZZUSA
FRENK, TAUBE	33	F	UNKNOWN	RRZZZZUSA
L.	6	M	CHILD	RRZZZZUSA
SEHERE	4	M	CHILD	RRZZZZUSA
ITZIG	1	M	CHILD	RRZZZZUSA
HIRSCH	.03	M	INFANT	RRZZZZUSA
RUDTMAN, ALTE	35	F	UNKNOWN	RRZZZZUSA
ALTER	11	F	UNKNOWN	RRZZZZUSA
CZARNE	7	F	CHILD	RRZZZZUSA
CHANE	3	F	CHILD	RRZZZZUSA
ROZAREK, SCHEME	17	F	UNKNOWN	RRZZZZUSA
OYENS, ROSA	24	F	UNKNOWN	RRZZZZUSA
DAVID	1	M	CHILD	RRZZZZUSA
MIHL, SORE	23	F	UNKNOWN	RRZZZZUSA
WOLF	1	M	CHILD	RRZZZZUSA
WINKMAN, HERSCH	17	M	DLR	RRZZZZUSA
GOLDBERG, RUBE	35	F	UNKNOWN	RRZZZZUSA
IDEL	9	M	CHILD	RRZZZZUSA
LEIB	7	M	CHILD	RRZZZZUSA
SCHLOME	5	F	CHILD	RRZZZZUSA
DCHAJE	3	F	CHILD	RRZZZZUSA
BRANE	1	F	CHILD	RRZZZZUSA

PASSENGER	AGE	SEX	OCCUPATION	PRV VIL DES
MEYER	45	M	UNKNOWN	RRZZZZUSA
ABRAHAM	15	M	UNKNOWN	RRZZZZUSA
LEIB	40	M	DLR	RRZZZZUSA
CHANE	9	M	CHILD	RRZZZZUSA
KREMAKY, RABA	38	F	UNKNOWN	RRZZZZUSA
GOLDE	11	F	UNKNOWN	RRZZZZUSA
RELH.	16	F	UNKNOWN	RRZZZZUSA
NOCHA	7	M	CHILD	RRZZZZUSA
KREMSKY, RIWE	5	F	CHILD	RRZZZZUSA
PHIL.	.03	F	INFANT	RRZZZZUSA
HALPERN, MOSES	28	M	DLR	RRZZZZUSA
SKLADOWSKY, ELZE	21	M	DLR	RRZZZZUSA
AUZUR, SMIE	17	F	UNKNOWN	RRZZZZUSA
SPREGELGLAS, BROKE	26	F	UNKNOWN	RRZZZZUSA
RESIE	5	M	CHILD	RRZZZZUSA
ABRAHAM	1	M	CHILD	RRZZZZUSA
NERHANSKY, BER	27	M	HTR	RRZZZZUSA
ROBINOWITZ, IDA	24	F	UNKNOWN	RRZZZZUSA
CHANI	2	M	CHILD	RRZZZZUSA
SCHAHNUN, LIEBE	28	M	DLR	RRZZZZUSA
KEARTURKIS, JOSEF	25	M	LABR	RRZZZZUSA
PRANAJTIS, BUAFRE	25	M	LABR	RRZZZZUSA
GUTAWIEZ, KAPEL	32	M	BCHR	RRZZZZUSA
SARAH	25	F	HP	RRZZZZUSA
SCHIKENS, LUDWIG	30	M	LABR	RRZZZZUSA
THOMAS, PILECHY	30	M	LABR	RRZZZZUSA
VINCINTY, OGENKIS	28	M	LABR	RRZZZZUSA
SARABA, KASIMIR	29	M	LABR	RRZZZZUSA
ANDRASUZIK, PETER	23	M	LABR	RRZZZZUSA
KOMUSKY, HAVER	22	M	LABR	RRZZZZUSA
EDEGER, ROBERT	16	M	LABR	RRZZZZUSA
KREMGLES, AGATHE	28	F	UNKNOWN	RRZZZZUSA
ANTON	2	M	CHILD	RRZZZZUSA
SMEDGVEST, GUSTAV	44	M	SEMN	FNZZZZUSA
G--, JOHAN	21	M	LABR	FNZZZZUSA
LORNEGVEST, MATS.AN.	29	M	FSHMN	FNZZZZUSA
RYNTOJERS, JOSEFINA	23	F	UNKNOWN	FNZZZZUSA
JOHN	3	M	CHILD	FNZZZZUSA
LAMERJETZ, MARTIN	26	M	LABR	PLZZZZUSA
SICAKOS, ANTON	32	M	LABR	PLZZZZUSA
JUNOWSKI, ALFRED	22	M	MCHT	RRZZZZUSA
KAMILA	18	F	UNKNOWN	RRZZZZUSA
ANTON	16	M	UNKNOWN	RRZZZZUSA

SHIP: MAIN

FROM: BREMEN
TO: BALTIMORE
ARRIVED: 30 MAY 1888

PASSENGER	AGE	SEX	OCCUPATION	PRV VIL DES
SEARBAK, MANSCHE	44	M	FARMER	RRZZZZMD
GUTMANN, JACOB	14	M	FARMER	RRZZZZMD
YANISKEL, SIMON	19	M	FARMER	RRZZZZMD
MONDIK, ANDRAS	20	M	FARMER	RRZZZZMD
PULKOWSKY, JOH.	39	M	FARMER	RRZZZZMD
URBANSKI, JOSEF	23	M	FARMER	RRZZZZMD
STORZALOWSKI, JORFIL	25	M	FARMER	RRZZZZMD
JUSTIN, ANDREAS	37	M	FARMER	RRZZZZMD
FUCHS, ERNST	23	M	FARMER	RRZZZZMD
MAAS, AUGUST	23	M	FARMER	RRZZZZMD
BORGNUS, KASMIR	25	M	FARMER	RRZZZZMD
WENBRI, ANTON	22	M	FARMER	RRZZZZMD
CIDERWITZ, BALTERMIJES	25	M	FARMER	RRZZZZMD
SPUKAWITZ, JULIAN	19	M	FARMER	RRZZZZMD
BLANZ, BALTRA	23	M	FARMER	RRZZZZMD
GRUENS, JURGES	30	M	FARMER	RRZZZZMD
ROSENBAUM, MOSES	30	M	MCHT	RRZZZZMD
JURIST, JOSEF	18	M	MCHT	RRZZZZMD
WEINTRANK, MORITZ	16	M	CK	RRZZZZMD
HILT, CARL	34	M	MCHT	RRZZZZMD
WILLMANN, MARTIN	34	M	MCHT	RRZZZZMD
ZUDELOWITZ, MOSES	24	M	MCHT	RRZZZZMD
FELDMANN, JACOB	28	M	FARMER	RRZZZZMD
FELENHAUER, ERNST	36	M	FARMER	RRZZZZMD
FREIMANN, LUDW.	18	M	FARMER	RRZZZZMD
KOSSEBURT, WOLF	22	M	FARMER	RRZZZZMD
LEWIN, RACHMIEL	20	M	MCHT	RRZZZZMD
ABRAHAM	32	M	MCHT	RRZZZZMD
WIHMISKUS, THEUSUS	35	M	MCHT	RRZZZZMD
SPERKEL, MOSES	27	M	FARMER	RRZZZZMD
BERENKEWITZ, ABRAHAM	22	M	FARMER	RRZZZZMD
OSTROWSKY, MENDEL	28	M	FARMER	RRZZZZMD
KIEFNER, BERTHOLD	17	M	FARMER	RRZZZZMD
THIEDE, CARL	17	M	FARMER	RRZZZZMI
PRAZAK, JOSEF	30	M	FARMER	RRZZZZMI
WALT, ADOLF	39	M	FARMER	RRZZZZMD
FRIEDENSBERG, WILH.	24	M	FARMER	RRZZZZMD
FRIEDRICH, CANNERTH	21	M	FARMER	RRZZZZMD
LASCHINSKY, IGNATZ	25	M	FARMER	RRZZZZMD
MAKOREK, MATHIAS	27	M	FARMER	RRZZZZMD
SOCZINSKI, WOJCIECH	58	M	NN	RRZZZZIL
JUSTRZYK, RUDOLF	32	M	NN	RRZZZZIL
JAFFER, ESTER	22	F	W	RRZZZZBAL
BERTE	.11	F	INFANT	RRZZZZBAL
KRASNOPOLE, GILLE	23	F	W	RRZZZZBAL
MORIS	3	M	CHILD	RRZZZZBAL
CHAJE	.11	M	INFANT	RRZZZZBAL
KRANZA, THEKLA	24	F	SVNT	RRZZZZBAL
TIEDEMANN, ESTER	30	F	W	RRZZZZBAL
JACOB	8	M	CHILD	RRZZZZBAL
MOSES	4	M	CHILD	RRZZZZBAL
BRINIE, REBECCA	36	F	W	RRZZZZBAL
LACA	9	F	CHILD	RRZZZZBAL
HERM.	7	M	CHILD	RRZZZZBAL
WILLY	2	M	CHILD	RRZZZZBAL
LEIB	4	F	CHILD	RRZZZZBAL
SELESNITZKY, ROCHEL-LEA	30	F	W	RRZZZZBAL
MATZE	8	F	CHILD	RRZZZZBAL
SELIG	5	M	CHILD	RRZZZZBAL
DOBRUS	4	M	CHILD	RRZZZZBAL
KUSLEWICZ, ARSZULIA	19	F	SVNT	RRZZZZBAL
MAJEWSKI, CONSTANTIN	25	M	FARMER	RRZZZZOH
RUWINSKY, LEMIL	28	M	FARMER	RRZZZZBAL
MARIA	22	F	W	RRZZZZBAL
MENDEL	.11	M	INFANT	RRZZZZBAL
LEITSCHINSKY, ELSE	27	F	W	RRZZZZBAL
KRASNE, MORDSCHE	38	M	FARMER	RRZZZZBAL
MAJEM	19	M	FARMER	RRZZZZBAL
AST, JACOB	60	M	FARMER	RRZZZZKS
CATHARINA	58	F	W	RRZZZZKS
FRANZ	24	M	FARMER	RRZZZZKS
JARABINE	21	F	W	RRZZZZKS
JOSEF	18	M	FARMER	RRZZZZKS
ADAM	14	M	NN	RRZZZZKS
MARY	.10	F	INFANT	RRZZZZKS
STICKEL, JACOB	46	M	FARMER	RRZZZZPA
WILHELMINE	49	F	W	RRZZZZPA
BERTHA	12	F	CH	RRZZZZPA
BERTSCH, SAMUEL	44	M	MCHT	RRZZZZDAK
SARAH	43	F	W	RRZZZZDAK
JOHANNES	20	M	MCHT	RRZZZZDAK
MARGR.	21	F	CH	RRZZZZDAK
SAMUEL	17	M	MCHT	RRZZZZDAK
CHRISTINE	16	F	CH	RRZZZZDAK
MARIA	14	F	CH	RRZZZZDAK
SARAH	10	F	CH	RRZZZZDAK
ROSALIE	6	F	CHILD	RRZZZZDAK
MAGA.	4	F	CHILD	RRZZZZDAK
FRIEDRICH	2	M	CHILD	RRZZZZDAK
FRIEDERIKE	.06	F	INFANT	RRZZZZDAK
KEMPF, MATHIAS	60	M	FARMER	RRZZZZDAK
CATHAR.	50	F	W	RRZZZZDAK
CATHAR.	17	F	CH	RRZZZZDAK
FRIEDKE.	15	F	CH	RRZZZZDAK
MICHAEL	26	M	FARMER	RRZZZZDAK

PASSENGER	AGE	SEX	OCCUPATION	PRV VIL DES
CATHARINE	22	F	W	RRZZZZDAK
NIEL, FRIEDR.	25	M	FARMER	RRZZZZDAK
OTTILIE	23	F	W	RRZZZZDAK
OTTILIE	.09	F	INFANT	RRZZZZDAK
SELBIG, CARL	40	M	FARMER	RRZZZZBAL
MARIA	39	F	W	RRZZZZBAL
CARL	12	M	CH	RRZZZZBAL
WILHELM	7	M	CHILD	RRZZZZBAL
RUDOLF	3	M	CHILD	RRZZZZBAL
ALWINE	2	F	CHILD	RRZZZZBAL
THEODOR	.06	M	INFANT	RRZZZZBAL
KOCKLIN, WILHELM	63	M	FARMER	RRZZZZBAL
FRIEDKE	46	F	W	RRZZZZBAL
CARL	16	M	FARMER	RRZZZZBAL
NATALIE	14	F	CH	RRZZZZBAL
REINHOLD	12	M	CH	RRZZZZBAL
OTTO	6	M	CHILD	RRZZZZBAL

SHIP: WIELAND

FROM: HAMBURG
TO: NEW YORK
ARRIVED: 31 MAY 1888

PASSENGER	AGE	SEX	OCCUPATION	PRV VIL DES
SCHULTZ, MATHILDE	20	F	WO	RRZZZZUSA
KRETZIG, CARL	24	M	WVR	RRZZZZUSA
MOGALSKI, JAN	26	M	LABR	RRZZZZUSA
ANTONIA	20	F	WO	RRZZZZUSA
RAUSCHMANN, HANS	22	M	LABR	RRZZZZUSA
BOSSIT, HEINR	23	M	LABR	RRZZZZUSA
WEINSTEIN, OLGA	21	F	SGL	RRZZZZUSA
HOFFMANN, KARL	24	M	LABR	RRZZZZUSA
CHAROWSKA, SARA	17	F	SGL	RRZZZZUSA
GOLDBERG, ROSA	32	F	WO	RRZZZZUSA
GITTEL	7	F	CHILD	RRZZZZUSA
LESKE, MARTHA	16	F	SGL	RRZZZZUSA
GUDMAS, ANNA	19	F	SGL	RRZZZZUSA
KURAPKA, STANISL	29	M	LABR	RRZZZZUSA
GUDCITIS, VINCENT	19	M	LABR	RRZZZZUSA
ANNA	18	F	SGL	RRZZZZUSA
KRASINCKE, SUZEP	26	M	LABR	RRZZZZUSA
SLAWIENSKA, CATH	37	F	WO	RRZZZZUSA
ANNA	7	F	CHILD	RRZZZZUSA
---RDA	8	F	CHILD	RRZZZZUSA
LIBERMANN, JANKEL	16	M	CH	RRZZZZUSA
MISIWICZ, MICHAL	30	M	UNKNOWN	RRZZZZUSA
PRESS, BASSIE	60	F	WO	RRZZZZUSA
ALTER	9	M	CHILD	RRZZZZUSA
GEDALJE	8	F	CHILD	RRZZZZUSA
WOLF	2	M	CHILD	RRZZZZUSA
CZUPRINSKA, VINCENTY	32	M	LABR	RRZZZZUSA
SASNOWSKY, JAN	19	M	LABR	RRZZZZUSA
HEMPEL, CHAIE	28	F	WO	RRZZZZUSA
LEVI	7	M	CHILD	RRZZZZUSA
LEISER	5	M	CHILD	RRZZZZUSA
POJADYS, MARIANNA	26	F	LABR	RRZZZZUSA
ANNA	4	F	CHILD	RRZZZZUSA
HAGEN, ADOLF	29	M	UNKNOWN	RRZZZZUSA
ROSALIE	24	F	W	RRZZZZUSA
HUGO	3	M	CHILD	RRZZZZUSA
OSCAR	.11	M	INFANT	RRZZZZUSA
WOLSKI, THOMAS	40	M	LABR	RRZZZZUSA
NAKELINEN, JUDIN	25	M	MCHT	RRZZZZUSA
BLINDER, U	37	M	CGRMKR	RRZZZZUSA
MINKIN, ISAAE	35	M	UNKNOWN	RRZZZZUSA
ANNA	17	F	UNKNOWN	RRZZZZUSA
HELENE	16	F	D	RRZZZZUSA
SCHWERESCHEWSKY, ISAAC	34	M	TNR	RRZZZZUSA
KARELIZ, SUNDEL	23	M	PNTR	RRZZZZUSA
PITKIEWITZ, CARL	44	M	LABR	RRZZZZUSA
JANUSCHEWSKY, ANTONIA	32	F	SGL	RRZZZZUSA
BORDEWITZ, SIEGMUND	22	M	LABR	RRZZZZUSA
PALZEWSKI, JOH	19	M	LABR	RRZZZZUSA
EMES, SCHEPSEL	28	M	LABR	RRZZZZUSA
ROESEL	7	F	CHILD	RRZZZZUSA
BAMGANIS, JERZE	29	M	LABR	RRZZZZUSA
ROMECKA, ANDRZEI	19	M	LABR	RRZZZZUSA
LIBIN, MAX	23	M	LABR	RRZZZZUSA
BEILMSOHN, NATHAN	20	M	JWLR	RRZZZZUSA
PETROWSKY, IGNATZ	26	M	LABR	RRZZZZUSA
FRUNZE, ALEXANDER	27	M	LABR	RRZZZZUSA
BLASZAK, JAN	25	M	LABR	RRZZZZUSA
NADROTOWSKY, JAN	42	M	LABR	RRZZZZUSA
CHUCHLAWSKY, JOSEF	23	M	LABR	RRZZZZUSA
REPEZEUESKI, IGNATZ	19	M	LABR	RRZZZZUSA
DOMINSKY, JAN	40	M	SHMK	RRZZZZUSA
ANTONIA	30	F	W	RRZZZZUSA
GROSSBERG, ISRAEL	50	F	TLR	RRZZZZUSA
BEILE	50	F	W	RRZZZZUSA
HERM	18	M	CH	RRZZZZUSA
MAR	7	M	CHILD	RRZZZZUSA
PEARLOWYCZENIC, AGATHE	30	F	WO	RRZZZZUSA
LAURA	7	F	CHILD	RRZZZZUSA
WOYCICHOWSKI, THEODOR	41	M	LABR	RRZZZZUSA
JOH	37	F	W	RRZZZZUSA
STANISLAW	7	M	CHILD	RRZZZZUSA
ANTONIE	6	F	CHILD	RRZZZZUSA
FRANZ	5	M	CHILD	RRZZZZUSA
MARIE	4	F	CHILD	RRZZZZUSA
ROSALIE	2	F	CHILD	RRZZZZUSA
JAN	.11	M	INFANT	RRZZZZUSA
KRAJNIOK, MARIANNA	19	F	SGL	RRZZZZUSA
LEWANDOWSKY, ANTONIA	28	F	SGL	RRZZZZUSA
BALUTA, FRANK	14	M	LABR	RRZZZZUSA
FRANZISCA	25	F	WO	RRZZZZUSA
LEON	3	M	CHILD	RRZZZZUSA
ANIELA	.11	F	INFANT	RRZZZZUSA
ALBANOWICZ, ROSALIE	17	F	SGL	RRZZZZUSA
LEXOW, FRIEDR	16	M	LABR	RRZZZZUSA
OSOLIN, KARL	18	M	LABR	RRZZZZUSA
ANNA	16	F	SGL	RRZZZZUSA
ELPE, JESIAS	25	M	LABR	FNZZZZUSA
ANDERSEN, KARL	30	M	LABR	FNZZZZUSA
HELLSTRAND, MATTES	41	M	LABR	FNZZZZUSA
KAPPELL, HERM	23	M	LABR	FNZZZZUSA
ABRAHAMSON, KARL	20	M	LABR	FNZZZZUSA
NOBB, SIMON	37	M	LABR	FNZZZZUSA
NORD, AUGUST	19	M	LABR	FNZZZZUSA
WESTERBAEK, AUGUST	28	M	LABR	FNZZZZUSA
KAPLAN, SZEPSEL	20	M	LABR	RRZZZZUSA
ZWENGEL, CHUNE	20	M	LABR	RRZZZZUSA
COHAN, ICHIEL	34	M	LABR	RRZZZZUSA
TROSTONECKA, JUTE	17	M	LABR	RRZZZZUSA
GILWARZ, ABRAM	22	M	LABR	RRZZZZUSA
WITTENSTEIN, MORITZ	57	M	LABR	RRZZZZUSA
GERUBURAD, MEIER	35	M	LABR	RRZZZZUSA
HEILPERN, SALOMON	40	M	LABR	RRZZZZUSA
SOLZ, ANNA	19	F	SGL	RRZZZZUSA
MILESKA, FRANZISKA	33	F	WO	RRZZZZUSA
ANTON	7	M	CHILD	RRZZZZUSA
WLADESLAW	8	M	CHILD	RRZZZZUSA
KURPIEWSKI, FRANZ	37	M	LABR	RRZZZZUSA
SCHILLER, ALBERT	36	M	SHMK	RRZZZZUSA
BLUMENSCHEID, ANNA	25	F	SGL	RRZZZZUSA
BAUMGART, PAUL	45	M	WO	RRZZZZUSA
HENRIETTE	21	M	WO	RRZZZZUSA
REBECCA	17	M	WO	RRZZZZUSA
MORITZ	19	M	WO	RRZZZZUSA
BERNHARD	7	M	CHILD	RRZZZZUSA
HILDA	7	F	CHILD	RRZZZZUSA
JENNY	6	F	CHILD	RRZZZZUSA
RUDOLF	8	M	CHILD	RRZZZZUSA
LOUIS	26	M	UNKNOWN	RRZZZZUSA
SCHILLER, GUSTAV	61	M	UNKNOWN	RRZZZZUSA
AGNES	64	F	W	RRZZZZUSA

PASSENGER	AGE	SEX	OCCUPATION	PRV VIL DES
ROSCHKANKAS, ANTON	33	M	LABR	RRZZZZUSA
SUNI, HILMA	25	F	SGL	FNZZZZUSA
SCHLESS, ZAHNAN	8	M	CHILD	RRZZZZUSA
PANIE	7	F	CHILD	RRZZZZUSA
ABBA, JOSEF	28	M	UNKNOWN	RRZZZZUSA
CHASSE	36	F	W	RRZZZZUSA
FINKELSTEIN, CHANNE	24	F	WO	RRZZZZUSA
JAEGER, CARL	23	M	BKR	RRZZZZUSA
WILENSKI, ASNE	25	F	WO	RRZZZZUSA
MSES	9	M	CHILD	RRZZZZUSA
ELKE	20	F	SGL	RRZZZZUSA
PEPLAU, MICH	24	M	LABR	RRZZZZUSA
BRANDT, MICH	26	M	LABR	RRZZZZUSA
WEISS, IGNATZ	24	M	LABR	FNZZZZUSA
HELLMAKI, F	26	M	LABR	FNZZZZUSA
TAANONEN, JACOB	24	M	LABR	RRZZZZUSA
TOFT, ANTON	38	M	LABR	FNZZZZUSA
SUESSBORKEN, NIKLES	36	M	LABR	FNZZZZUSA
REMTAMAKI, ISSAK	33	M	LABR	FNZZZZUSA
PIKKINEN, JOH	39	M	LABR	FNZZZZUSA
SIRONEN, ALSKRIS	29	M	LABR	FNZZZZUSA
LAURAMAKI, ALBANUS	24	M	LABR	FNZZZZUSA
STEMMAN, KARL	31	M	LABR	FNZZZZUSA
SULKO, JOHANN	34	M	LABR	FNZZZZUSA
FORIMAN, THOMAS	28	M	LABR	FNZZZZUSA
TRAINEN, JOHANN	34	M	LABR	FNZZZZUSA
LOITINEN, JOH	28	M	LABR	FNZZZZUSA
RUIDAMAKI, ISAAC	36	M	LABR	FNZZZZUSA
SKULKI, ANDERS	20	M	LABR	FNZZZZUSA
MACUPAA, JACOB	29	M	LABR	FNZZZZUSA
PUGTELARI, HENRIK	37	M	LABR	FNZZZZUSA
KAKKAMAKI, ANDERS	33	M	LABR	FNZZZZUSA
JAEGER, MAYER	55	M	MCHT	FNZZZZUSA
ZILINSKI, WOWRZYN	44	M	LABR	RRZZZZUSA

SHIP: NOORDLAND

FROM: ANTWERP
TO: NEW YORK
ARRIVED: 31 MAY 1888

PASSENGER	AGE	SEX	OCCUPATION	PRV VIL DES
SCHIRCK, FR.	28	F	W	RRZZZZCH
FR.	00	M	INF	RRZZZZCH
YURIZISAUSKY, M.	23	M	LABR	RRAINMNY
PERLUMANN, L.	18	M	LABR	RRAINMNY
HERSCHEL, M.	18	M	LABR	RRAINMNY
KOBOUSKY, J.	26	M	LABR	RRAINMNY
M.	26	F	W	RRAINMNY
BEDMORSKY, F.	28	M	LABR	RRAINMNY
S.	24	F	W	RRAINMNY
BRESLANER, P.	21	M	LABR	RRZZZZNY
KOSTKA, M.	44	M	LABR	RRZZZZNY
SPITZER, H.	17	M	LABR	RRZZZZNY
RABINOWITZ, S.	34	M	LABR	RRZZZZNY
FINGER, K.	27	M	LABR	RRZZZZNY
LEBOWITZ, J.	35	M	LABR	RRZZZZNY
J.	28	F	W	RRZZZZNY
J.	4	M	CHILD	RRZZZZNY
J.	00	F	INF	RRZZZZNY
SHWARWARER, A.	40	M	LABR	RRZZZZNY
ETTINGER, J.	44	M	LABR	RRZZZZNY
WAIESAITIS, M.	24	M	LABR	RRZZZZNY
MORGENSTIEN, L.	43	M	LABR	RRZZZZNY
M.	16	M	LABR	RRZZZZNY
RABULAK, J.	28	M	LABR	RRAEXKNY
OSICKY, V.	30	M	LABR	RRAEXKNY
RECHON, L.	28	M	LABR	RRAEXKNY
J.	23	F	W	RRAEXKNY
M.	2	F	CHILD	RRAEXKNY
F.	00	M	INF	RRAEXKNY

PASSENGER	AGE	SEX	OCCUPATION	PRV VIL DES
HOELL, J.	27	M	LABR	RRZZZZNY
HORWATH, J.	23	M	LABR	RRZZZZNY
RABUSE, J.	24	M	LABR	RRZZZZNY
GARNIK, J.	24	M	LABR	RRZZZZNY
FEINGERHECT, F.	18	M	LABR	RRAHOONY
RUDOWSKY, A.	21	M	LABR	RRZZZZNY
RESABEC, A.	24	M	LABR	RRZZZZNY
NERADO, A.	35	M	LABR	RRZZZZNY
A.	36	F	W	RRZZZZNY
A.	7	M	CHILD	RRZZZZNY
F.	6	M	CHILD	RRZZZZNY
M.	3	M	CHILD	RRZZZZNY
W.	00	M	INF	RRZZZZNY
RYCHTIC, J.	19	M	LABR	RRZZZZNY
F.	32	F	LABR	RRZZZZNY
V.	25	F	W	RRZZZZNY
M.	3	M	CHILD	RRZZZZNY
C.	2	M	CHILD	RRZZZZNY
J.	00	M	INF	RRZZZZNY
BERLIN, J.	43	M	LABR	RRZZZZNY
C.	31	F	W	RRZZZZNY
A.	11	M	UNKNOWN	RRZZZZNY
M.	9	F	CHILD	RRZZZZNY
F.	3	M	CHILD	RRZZZZNY
A.	00	M	INF	RRZZZZNY
MAHR, J.	24	M	LABR	RRZZZZNY
A.	23	F	W	RRZZZZNY
TESAR, J.	29	M	LABR	RRZZZZNY
LAUSTIL, M.	41	M	LABR	RRZZZZNY
M.	38	F	W	RRZZZZNY
M.	15	F	UNKNOWN	RRZZZZNY
J.	11	M	UNKNOWN	RRZZZZNY
A.	9	F	CHILD	RRZZZZNY
A.	7	F	CHILD	RRZZZZNY
F.	3	F	CHILD	RRZZZZNY
T.	00	F	INF	RRZZZZNY
KLEUMETZ, J.	32	M	LABR	RRZZZZNY
M.	25	F	W	RRZZZZNY
HEYTSKY, J.	19	M	LABR	RRZZZZNY
LEITHAM, M.	19	F	SVNT	RRZZZZNY
MINTOVORAC, B.	18	F	SVNT	RRZZZZNY
KOCEK, F.	36	M	LABR	RRZZZZNY
A.	32	F	W	RRZZZZNY
F.	3	M	CHILD	RRZZZZNY
J.	2	M	CHILD	RRZZZZNY
ZIKMUND, J.	26	M	LABR	RRZZZZNY
SCHELLE, A.	28	F	SVNT	RRZZZZNY
YAMMSCH, P.	50	M	LABR	RRZZZZNY
FASER, M.	28	M	LABR	RRZZZZNY
FEIN, J.	28	M	LABR	RRZZZZNY
BLUMENTHAL, S.	36	M	LABR	RRZZZZNY
SCHWARZ, N.	26	M	LABR	RRZZZZNY
P.	20	M	LABR	RRZZZZNY
H.	20	F	W	RRZZZZNY
H.	00	F	INF	RRZZZZNY
B.	21	M	LABR	RRZZZZNY
LEFKOVITZ, M.	20	M	LABR	RRZZZZNY
KAFKA, J.	48	M	LABR	RRZZZZNY
SZEZUTKOWSKY, K.	44	M	LABR	RRZZZZNY
M.	46	F	W	RRZZZZNY
F.	18	F	UNKNOWN	RRZZZZNY
C.	8	F	CHILD	RRZZZZNY
J.	4	F	CHILD	RRZZZZNY
J.	2	M	CHILD	RRZZZZNY
GRABOWSKI, F.	31	M	LABR	RRAIKRNY
MATKOWSKI, F.	29	M	LABR	RRAIKRNY
BOJARSKI, J.	58	M	LABR	RRAHULNY
HIRSCHREUTZEL, M.	35	M	LABR	RRACXZNY
KUPFERMANN, J.	18	M	LABR	RRACXZNY
EFFS, L.	37	M	LABR	RRZZZZNY
GOLDSTEIN, C.	30	M	LABR	RRZZZZNY
ZIMMERMANN, L.	16	F	SVNT	RRZZZZNY
KONOSSFUNKA, M.	26	F	SVNT	RRZZZZNY
WITTKUS, V.	26	M	LABR	RRAHTFNY
KIWALKOWSKI, J.	40	M	LABR	RRAHTFNY

PASSENGER	AGE	SEX	OCCUPATION	PRIV	VIL	DES
REIBIKS, TH.	28	M	LABR	RR	AHTF	NY
SCHOR, L.	25	M	LABR	RR	AHTF	NY
PUSSEL, S.	28	M	LABR	RR	AHTF	NY
GROSS, J.	17	M	LABR	RR	ZZZZ	NY
LOWIDMANN, S.	32	M	LABR	RR	ZZZZ	NY
KRAGNIAK, M.	23	F	W	RR	ZZZZ	NY
FUHNMANN, E.	13	M	LABR	RR	ZZZZ	NY
SUSSMANN, G.	20	F	SVNT	RR	ZZZZ	NY
BERKOWITZ, C.	17	F	SVNT	RR	ZZZZ	NY
FEUCHEL, G.	27	F	W	RR	ZZZZ	NY
R.	00	M	INF	RR	ZZZZ	NY
BLUMENTHAL, A.	23	M	LABR	RR	ZZZZ	CH
WIESE, P.	16	M	LABR	RR	ZZZZ	CH
REX, R.	29	M	LABR	RR	ZZZZ	CH
SCHETTEL, F.	11	M	LABR	RR	ZZZZ	CH
A.	9	F	CHILD	RR	ZZZZ	CH
SMITH, TH.	17	M	LABR	RR	ZZZZ	USA
M.	20	F	SVNT	RR	ZZZZ	USA
PETERSEN, P.	20	F	SVNT	RR	ZZZZ	IA
SZUNNIE, M.	19	F	SVNT	RR	ZZZZ	CLE
KATUSCHAK, A.	31	F	W	RR	ZZZZ	CLE
J.	4	M	CHILD	RR	ZZZZ	CLE
M.	3	M	CHILD	RR	ZZZZ	CLE
F.	00	M	INF	RR	ZZZZ	CLE
STEFANI, D.	40	F	W	RR	ZZZZ	CLE
A.	9	F	CHILD	RR	ZZZZ	CLE
PETZEL, G.	36	M	LABR	RR	ZZZZ	UNK
KRAZNIAK, L.	24	M	LABR	RR	ZZZZ	STL

SHIP: STATE OF GEORGIA

FROM: GLASGOW AND LARNE
TO: NEW YORK
ARRIVED: 31 MAY 1888

PASSENGER	AGE	SEX	OCCUPATION	PRIV	VIL	DES
ALKEWITZ, FREIDE	18	F	SVNT	RR	ZZZZ	USA
ANDROLAMS, STANISLAW	27	M	LABR	RR	ZZZZ	USA
BAIERMANN, HINDE	20	F	SVNT	RR	ZZZZ	USA
BALANIS, ANTONI	28	M	LABR	RR	ZZZZ	USA
BALTOZEWICK, KAROL.	45	M	LABR	RR	ZZZZ	USA
BEHREND, LEIB	55	M	PDLR	RR	ZZZZ	USA
GITTEL	24	F	W	RR	ZZZZ	USA
CHANE	10	F	CH	RR	ZZZZ	USA
BELLION, BETTY	20	F	SVNT	RR	ZZZZ	USA
BESSEL, ESTER	38	F	W	RR	ZZZZ	USA
SCHLOMA	5	F	CHILD	RR	ZZZZ	USA
SORE	2	F	CHILD	RR	ZZZZ	USA
BOLENDZETGIS, PIOTR	30	M	LABR	RR	ZZZZ	USA
BUCZENSKY, KASIMIR	23	M	LABR	RR	ZZZZ	USA
COHEN, WOLFE	21	M	TLR	RR	ZZZZ	USA
U-MRS	21	F	W	RR	ZZZZ	USA
ADA	2	F	CHILD	RR	ZZZZ	USA
SAMUEL	.06	M	INFANT	RR	ZZZZ	USA
U, PIOTR.	28	M	LABR	RR	ZZZZ	USA
DOPKOWSKI, MATIS	27	M	LABR	RR	ZZZZ	USA
DUNSKY, CHAJE	29	M	TLR	RR	ZZZZ	USA
EDELMANN, LEIB	25	M	TLR	RR	ZZZZ	USA
EPSTEIN, DINA	20	F	SVNT	RR	ZZZZ	USA
SCHLOME	15	M	SVNT	RR	ZZZZ	USA
JOSEPH	11	M	CH	RR	ZZZZ	USA
FRANK, LEAH	25	F	W	RR	ZZZZ	USA
SARAH	1	F	CHILD	RR	ZZZZ	USA
FRANKFORT, DINA	18	F	SVNT	RR	ZZZZ	USA
FRIEDMANN, BEOKE	21	F	W	RR	ZZZZ	USA
HINDE	1	F	CHILD	RR	ZZZZ	USA
JULIA	25	F	W	RR	ZZZZ	USA
HINDE	2	F	CHILD	RR	ZZZZ	USA
GARFINKEL, MOSES	35	M	LABR	RR	ZZZZ	USA
GITTER, SARAH	14	F	CH	RR	ZZZZ	USA
GLUCKMANN, MOSES	35	M	LABR	RR	ZZZZ	USA
GRUSHY, FEIGE	31	F	W	RR	ZZZZ	USA
LEIBE	3	F	CHILD	RR	ZZZZ	USA
SCHEINE	1	F	CHILD	RR	ZZZZ	USA
GUTTMANN, DANIEL	22	M	PDLR	RR	ZZZZ	USA
ILIONSKI, MAVKE	18	F	SVNT	RR	ZZZZ	USA
JACOBSOHN, ETTEL	19	F	SVNT	RR	ZZZZ	USA
MARIASCHE	10	F	CH	RR	ZZZZ	USA
JACOWANIS, ANTON	24	M	LABR	RR	ZZZZ	USA
JAMEBORICK, PIOTE	34	M	LABR	RR	ZZZZ	USA
JEDZINSKI, ANTON	38	M	LABR	RR	ZZZZ	USA
JEIN, TEMA	18	F	SVNT	RR	ZZZZ	USA
JURIST, ADOLF	32	M	LABR	RR	ZZZZ	USA
ROCHEL	20	F	W	RR	ZZZZ	USA
SAUL	40	M	LABR	RR	ZZZZ	USA
LEIBE	36	F	W	RR	ZZZZ	USA
KALINSKY, JAN	25	M	LABR	RR	ZZZZ	USA
MARIE	18	F	W	RR	ZZZZ	USA
KALMENISKES, NESHAME	18	F	SVNT	RR	ZZZZ	USA
KAPELOWITZ, SCHLOME	25	M	FARMER	RR	ZZZZ	USA
KOROLEVITZ, FRANZ	20	M	LABR	RR	ZZZZ	USA
KORALUNAS, JOSEF	27	M	LABR	RR	ZZZZ	USA
KERSOH, SARAH	40	F	W	RR	ZZZZ	USA
KERZMAN, MOSES	35	M	JNR	RR	ZZZZ	USA
KLEIN, ABRAHAM	34	M	TLR	RR	ZZZZ	USA
ISAAC	9	M	CHILD	RR	ZZZZ	USA
KAMMER, HIRSCH	26	M	MCHT	RR	ZZZZ	USA
KONRATZKY, JOSEF	19	M	LABR	RR	ZZZZ	USA
KONEZEL, JOHANNA	29	M	LABR	RR	ZZZZ	USA
KUSCHNIETZ, ELIZA	44	M	LABR	RR	ZZZZ	USA
KUSNER, SELDE	19	F	SVNT	RR	ZZZZ	USA
KUWES, RIWE	16	F	SVNT	RR	ZZZZ	USA
KIKOWITSCH, NAOHEM	32	M	LABR	RR	ZZZZ	USA
LESCH, MERE	25	F	SVNT	RR	ZZZZ	USA
LEW, DAVID	36	M	LABR	RR	ZZZZ	USA
LURIA, SCHEINE	15	F	SVNT	RR	ZZZZ	USA
LEIB	11	M	CH	RR	ZZZZ	USA
LEWIN, MARIE	18	F	SVNT	RR	ZZZZ	USA
U, U	15	F	SVNT	RR	ZZZZ	USA
LICHT, RUVE	17	M	LABR	RR	ZZZZ	USA
MARGOLIEG, ABRAHAM	43	M	PDLR	RR	ZZZZ	USA
MASSIE, ARON	50	M	TLR	RR	ZZZZ	USA
JACOB	8	M	CHILD	RR	ZZZZ	USA
MEDUCK, JOHEWE	19	F	SVNT	RR	ZZZZ	USA
MENDELSOHN, DAVID	16	M	LABR	RR	ZZZZ	USA
MIRKELMANN, ISAAC	40	M	LABR	RR	ZZZZ	USA
MICKELMANN, F.	51	M	PDLR	RR	ZZZZ	USA
MINNE	18	F	SVNT	RR	ZZZZ	USA
CHANNE	15	F	SVNT	RR	ZZZZ	USA
MAPZIKOW, DAVID	27	M	PDLR	RR	ZZZZ	USA
MUSANIS, FRANZ	17	M	LABR	RR	ZZZZ	USA
MUSCHKIN, SAMUEL	30	M	LABR	RR	ZZZZ	USA
MUSCHE	19	F	W	RR	ZZZZ	USA
ORKOWITSCH, DINA	28	F	W	RR	ZZZZ	USA
CHAJE	8	F	CHILD	RR	ZZZZ	USA
ITTE	5	F	CHILD	RR	ZZZZ	USA
MEIER	1	M	CHILD	RR	ZZZZ	USA
PALENIS, LEIB	33	M	LABR	RR	ZZZZ	USA
PASCHUKANIS, BERTHOL	23	M	LABR	RR	ZZZZ	USA
PILWALIS, AMATHEUS	30	M	LABR	RR	ZZZZ	USA
PJONTAC, SARAH	30	F	W	RR	ZZZZ	USA
DAVID	10	M	CH	RR	ZZZZ	USA
RIWKE	5	F	CHILD	RR	ZZZZ	USA
PLINER, LEIKE	28	M	LABR	RR	ZZZZ	USA
PINSTEIN, BENJAMIN	26	M	LABR	RR	ZZZZ	USA
PRZESTOWITZ, DAVID	22	M	LABR	RR	ZZZZ	USA
RELEP, ABRAHAM	18	M	TLR	RR	ZZZZ	USA
RESSEN, MIOKLE	22	F	SVNT	RR	ZZZZ	USA
ROSENBLOM, LOUIS	30	M	TLR	RR	ZZZZ	USA
ROZESUNSKI, ZIWIE	26	F	W	RR	ZZZZ	USA
SCHLOME	4	F	CHILD	RR	ZZZZ	USA
JOSEPH	2	M	CHILD	RR	ZZZZ	USA
LEA	18	F	SVNT	RR	ZZZZ	USA
DANIEL	.06	M	INFANT	RR	ZZZZ	USA
POSNACK, MEYER	32	M	LABR	RR	ZZZZ	USA
SAMUEL	12	M	CH	RR	ZZZZ	USA

PASSENGER	AGE	SEX	OCCUPATION	PRV	VIL	DES
SACK, SIMON	18	M	LABR	RR	ZZZZ	USA
SEFFIR, JANKEL	50	M	LABR	RR	ZZZZ	USA
MARIA	15	F	SVNT	RR	ZZZZ	USA
SAFRON, AMALIE	26	F	W	RR	ZZZZ	USA
HERMANN	2	M	CHILD	RR	ZZZZ	USA
SARA	1	F	CHILD	RR	ZZZZ	USA
SAPOZNIK, BASSE	25	F	W	RR	ZZZZ	USA
FEIGE	1	F	CHILD	RR	ZZZZ	USA
SAPPORSTEIN, ETTEL	17	M	LABR	RR	ZZZZ	USA
ZINKOLSTEIN, SCHLOME	11	F	CH	RR	ZZZZ	USA
SAVOKINAS, JAN	45	M	LABR	RR	ZZZZ	USA
SCHEFUR-, RECHAME	17	F	SVNT	RR	ZZZZ	USA
SCHERKINS, MIKAL	27	M	LABR	RR	ZZZZ	USA
SCHINSKI, ANDREAS	20	M	LABR	RR	ZZZZ	USA
SCHIVEIDEL, RITTEL	18	M	LABR	RR	ZZZZ	USA
SCHULZ, GITTEL	17	F	SVNT	RR	ZZZZ	USA
SCHWEDLOW, MARIE	20	F	SVNT	RR	ZZZZ	USA
SELIG, ARIE	23	M	CGRMKR	RR	ZZZZ	USA
MASCH	18	F	SVNT	RR	ZZZZ	USA
ETTKE	16	F	SVNT	RR	ZZZZ	USA
SKARZINSKY, JAN	28	M	LABR	RR	ZZZZ	USA
PAULINE	23	F	W	RR	ZZZZ	USA
SKIOR, NISSEN	36	M	TLR	RR	ZZZZ	USA
STASNIAWSKY, VINZENTI	33	M	LABR	RR	ZZZZ	USA
MARTHA	30	F	W	RR	ZZZZ	USA
JOSEF	3	M	CHILD	RR	ZZZZ	USA
VIETA	1	F	CHILD	RR	ZZZZ	USA
SONGAZLO, CARL	25	M	STDNT	RR	ZZZZ	USA
SOPINSKY, CHANNE	29	F	W	RR	ZZZZ	USA
FEIGE	1	F	CHILD	RR	ZZZZ	USA
RASSMANN, SCHLOME	11	M	CH	RR	ZZZZ	USA
SCHPULEVITZ, VICENTI	30	M	LABR	RR	ZZZZ	USA
STERLING, MICHAEL	11	M	CH	RR	ZZZZ	USA
SUSSMANN, FRIEDE	20	F	SVNT	RR	ZZZZ	USA
ULANIS, ANTON	31	M	LABR	RR	ZZZZ	USA
WALD, PINKAS	27	M	FARMER	RR	ZZZZ	USA
WEINMANN, JON.	34	M	LABR	RR	ZZZZ	USA
WESHTLER, MALKE	30	F	W	RR	ZZZZ	USA
RIEWKE	6	F	CHILD	RR	ZZZZ	USA
ABRAHAM	2	M	CHILD	RR	ZZZZ	USA
WISNEWSKI, WOLF	29	M	LABR	RR	ZZZZ	USA
RACHEL	1	F	CHILD	RR	ZZZZ	USA
WINKOWSKY, ANDRY	25	M	LABR	RR	ZZZZ	USA

SHIP: LAHN

FROM: BREMEN AND SOUTHAMPTON
TO: NEW YORK
ARRIVED: 01 JUNE 1888

PASSENGER	AGE	SEX	OCCUPATION	PRV	VIL	DES
RAPPHUHN, GOTTFR.	62	M	JNR	RR	ZZZZ	USA
JUSTINE	9	F	CHILD	RR	ZZZZ	USA
WILH.	18	M	JNR	RR	ZZZZ	USA
ALBERT	16	M	JNR	RR	ZZZZ	USA
MARTHA	24	F	W	RR	ZZZZ	USA
ANNA	.11	F	INFANT	RR	ZZZZ	USA
HAGEL, GOTTFR.	29	M	JNR	RR	ZZZZ	USA
THERESE	20	F	W	RR	ZZZZ	USA
RAPPHUHN, BERTHA	23	F	W	RR	ZZZZ	USA
OTTO	3	M	CHILD	RR	ZZZZ	USA
LANGE, EDUARD	24	M	FARMER	RR	ZZZZ	USA
BRADASCH, PAULINE	27	F	NN	RR	ZZZZ	USA
MINA	28	F	NN	RR	ZZZZ	USA
RADKE, CARL	23	M	JNR	RR	ZZZZ	USA
MOHR, BENNO	23	M	FARMER	RR	ZZZZ	USA
BUSCH, CHANE	27	F	NN	RR	ZZZZ	USA
GRODZICKI, FLORIAN	35	M	JNR	RR	ACSD	USA
JONDSCHUNKIS, JOSEF	20	M	LABR	RR	ADIM	USA
SPEDIS, ANTONI	22	M	LABR	RR	ADIM	USA
KALINAS, JONAS	33	M	LABR	RR	ADIM	USA
MILISCHANTKAS, JONAS	56	M	LABR	RR	ADIM	USA
RASCHENKI, ADAMAS	28	M	LABR	RR	ADIM	USA

SHIP: GALLIA

FROM: LIVERPOOL AND QUEENSTOWN
TO: NEW YORK
ARRIVED: 01 JUNE 1888

PASSENGER	AGE	SEX	OCCUPATION	PRV	VIL	DES
KERCZKI, JOHN	15	M	LABR	RR	ACBF	USA
USAK, ULTATZOTAN	12	M	CH	RR	ACBF	USA
COPELSWITZ, J.	21	M	LABR	RR	ACBF	USA
SEVIKOSKI, OTTMAN	19	M	LABR	RR	ACBF	USA
SELMAN, MERDCHI	15	M	LABR	RR	ACBF	USA
KORPI, GAKOBI	21	M	LABR	RR	ACBF	USA
BROYLAWSKI, VINCENTZ	29	M	LABR	RR	ACBF	USA
FILIPOWSKI, KASIMIR	30	M	LABR	RR	ACBF	USA
U, VICTOR	38	M	LABR	RR	ACBF	USA
CHAPSINSKY, JOHAS	29	M	LABR	RR	ACBF	USA
BUROJAS, CASES	26	M	LABR	RR	ACBF	USA
LUNKEWITSCH, JACOB	44	M	LABR	RR	ACBF	USA
ADAM	18	M	LABR	RR	ACBF	USA
AUSIS, JOHAS	24	M	FARMER	RR	ACBF	USA
WARMELIS, BOHAS	40	M	LABR	RR	ACBF	USA
BROSOKAS, DAHAS	30	M	LABR	RR	ACBF	USA
SHIRPEWITZ, ANDRAS	30	M	FARMER	RR	ACBF	USA
JMOSCHAITDES, MARCUS	24	M	LABR	RR	ACBF	USA
BENZAWESCHIER, VINCUS	26	M	LABR	RR	ACBF	USA
DEJUTSES, U	29	M	LABR	RR	ACBF	USA
BONKARL, STANISLAW	27	M	FARMER	RR	ACBF	USA
LUDVIG, ANDRAS	38	M	LABR	RR	ACBF	USA
REICH, HERSCH	38	M	PNTR	RR	ACBF	USA
ALISAUM, ANTON	20	M	LABR	RR	ACBF	USA
PLANKEWICZ, ALPHIND	40	M	LABR	RR	ACBF	USA
SCHLINUSKY, KASIMIR	28	M	LABR	RR	ACBF	USA
SZECHOWITZKI, ANTON	24	M	CPTR	RR	ACBF	USA
BUCHOLZ, MENDEL	32	M	TLR	RR	ACBF	USA
HARTWIZ, LUDWIG	26	M	LABR	RR	ACBF	USA
LUCK, MICH.	26	M	LABR	RR	ACBF	USA
JACOBOWSKY, JOSEF	20	M	LABR	RR	ACBF	USA
MAZIKEWITSCH, JON	20	M	LABR	RR	ACBF	USA
TOCKER, JACOB	21	M	CPTR	RR	ACBF	USA
ZURAWSKI, JAN	33	M	LABR	RR	ACBF	USA
FETZAN, FELIX	36	M	LABR	RR	ACBF	USA
TANIPOLSKY, LOVY	20	M	TLR	RR	ACBF	USA
SROKA, GREGOR	38	M	LABR	RR	ACBF	USA
NAWALANA, MARIA	25	F	SVNT	RR	ACBF	USA
ANCHESEGER, MARIA	16	F	SVNT	RR	ACBF	USA
MALMOSSKY, ROCHULA	20	F	SVNT	RR	ACBF	USA
KERCOCH, HEO.	19	M	LABR	RR	ACBF	USA
MAGJU	26	F	SVNT	RR	ACBF	USA
SCHWEBEBLUTA, BEILE	45	F	MA	RR	ACBF	USA
JAN	11	M	CH	RR	ACBF	USA
GREGOLOWSKY, ADAM	26	M	LABR	RR	ACBF	USA
PANKKOLA, L.	27	M	LABR	RR	ACBF	USA
PASRAJA, JAN	30	M	LABR	RR	ACBF	USA
WIRKOLA, M.	28	M	LABR	RR	ACBF	USA
KALLABACKA, T.	46	M	LABR	RR	ACBF	USA
KANTRAINEN, M.	32	M	LABR	RR	ACBF	USA
KALTAPACKA, E.	33	M	LABR	RR	ACBF	USA
ULITALA, T.	30	M	LABR	RR	ACBF	USA
HONKAKOSKI, O.	23	M	LABR	RR	ACBF	USA
TOKKILCHTO, A.	50	M	LABR	RR	ACBF	USA
U, M.PIN.	23	M	LABR	RR	ACBF	USA
U	34	M	LABR	RR	ACBF	USA
KANARSKNOSKY, M.	19	M	LABR	RR	ACBF	USA
MANNE, JOSEPH	30	M	LABR	RR	ACBF	USA
ROGERS, PHILIP	26	M	BKBNDR	RR	ACBF	USA
BRANDO, ARON	42	M	SLR	RR	ACBF	USA
POLIWAY, ELIAS	14	M	UNKNOWN	RR	ACBF	USA

PASSENGER	AGE	SEX	OCCUPATION	PRV VIL DES
WAITTAN, JOHAN	40	M	LABR	RRACBFUSA
KALLABACCA, WILLIAM	30	M	LABR	RRACBFUSA
SALPUKKA, ANDREU	18	M	LABR	RRACBFUSA
POLE, AUGUST	20	M	LABR	RRACBFUSA
SAUKKS, MATTI	50	M	LABR	RRACBFUSA
KORSTINER, U	20	M	LABR	RRACBFUSA
LAINPSER, JOHAN	35	M	LABR	RRACBFUSA
KULZANMER, MIKUS	24	M	LABR	RRACBFUSA
JABLONSKI, ANTON	24	M	LABR	RRACBFUSA
STUTYKSEWISZ, UELAD	26	M	LABR	RRACBFUSA
GOEJORAWITZ, WINCENTZ	38	M	LABR	RRACBFUSA
BULONOWICZ, LONGEN	23	M	LABR	RRACBFUSA
GAKULAITIS, JONAS	26	M	LABR	RRACBFUSA
GESOLEIT, JONAS	20	M	LABR	RRACBFUSA
SCHONBAUM, DAVID	28	M	LABR	RRAHTBUSA
SUROTZKI, MOSES	32	M	LABR	RRAHOKUSA
POKRANY, HILLEL	29	M	LABR	RRAHOKUSA
DIONZIG, ELIAS	18	M	BKR	RRADXWUSA
KRONAY, TEZIANGO	18	M	LABR	RRACBFUSA
GRUNKER, GANDER	16	M	TNSTH	RRACBFUSA
HELLEVAT, GEO	25	M	LABR	RRACBFUSA
ORLAN, LEIB	19	M	LABR	RRAHOKUSA
SARAH	15	F	SVNT	RRAHOKUSA
KAMIENA, RIFKE	25	F	W	RRAHOKUSA
NIDEL, FROMME	32	F	SVNT	RRACBFUSA
KARMEL, TAUBE	22	F	MA	RRACBFUSA
LEA	20	F	SVNT	RRACBFUSA
SURE	8	F	CHILD	RRACBFUSA
TEIGI	.11	F	INFANT	RRACBFUSA
CAMICKA, ANNA	21	F	SVNT	RRACBFUSA
JENDRUST, PALHE	20	M	LABR	RRACBFUSA
HANNILA, JAN	25	M	LABR	RRAEWSUSA
NISSELAA, M.	35	M	LABR	RRAEWSUSA
MOLLER, CARL	33	M	SLR	RRAGUZUSA
AHLOTIAM, OLE	33	M	SLR	RRAGUZUSA
GAGAMAS, A.	17	M	LABR	RRAEWSUSA
JUAPOKANGAS, T.	40	M	LABR	RRAEWSUSA
PASONEN, H.	28	M	LABR	RRAEWSUSA
PARHIOLA, T.	26	M	LABR	RRAEWSUSA
HAGGLUND, TOR.	28	M	LABR	RRAEWSUSA
JANSON, E.	20	M	LABR	RRAEWSUSA
MATTSON, CARL	19	M	LABR	RRAEWSUSA
JOHANSON, MAR.	21	M	LABR	RRAEWSUSA
J.A.	17	M	LABR	RRAEWSUSA
MATSON, SALOMON	21	M	LABR	RRAEWSUSA
MASHA, HENIK	18	M	LABR	RRAEWSUSA
PERRAIREN, MATH.	21	M	LABR	RRAEWSUSA
SANDKALLA, CARL	29	M	LABR	RRAEWSUSA
SANEL, JOHAN	19	M	LABR	RRAEWSUSA
KARJULA, ALEX	18	M	LABR	RRAEWSUSA
SODARBERG, J.A.	19	M	LABR	RRAEWSUSA
KIHCHLIKEWITZ, JOSEF	24	M	LABR	RRAEWSUSA
MADLETZKY, JANOS	40	M	LABR	RRAEWSUSA
KALPANEN, TOBIAS	28	M	LABR	RRAEWSUSA
MATTSON, MATH.	29	M	LABR	RRAEWSUSA
KORPISA, LEANDER	29	M	MNR	RRAEWSUSA
PINELA, ANDERS	19	M	LABR	RRAEWSUSA
BLUGTILA, EFRAIM	29	M	LABR	RRAEWSUSA
NILMELA, ANDERS	21	M	LABR	RRAEWSUSA
GUNDERSON, LEONARD	19	M	LABR	RRAEWSUSA
MIKINEN, CARL	29	M	LABR	RRAEWSUSA
GREKILA, GUSTAF	41	M	LABR	RRAEWSUSA
PETAGA, SEVER	24	M	LABR	RRAEWSUSA
TOKOLA, MATH.	34	M	LABR	RRAEWSUSA
PESOLA, LEANDER	20	M	LABR	RRAEWSUSA
LUSMALA, THOMAN	51	M	LABR	RRAEWSUSA
KIVISTS, JACOB	21	M	LABR	RRAEWSUSA
ALAKANGAS, ELISABETH	30	F	SVNT	RRAEWSUSA
JANKEN, ELISABETH	18	F	SVNT	RRAEWSUSA
KULABACA, JOSEPHINE	23	F	SVNT	RRAEWSUSA
SAPOLA, MARIA	25	F	SVNT	RRAEWSUSA
KORVELA, MARIA	19	F	SVNT	RRAEWSUSA
KERANEN, SOFIA	23	F	SVNT	RRAEWSUSA
RASAKKA, FRIDERIKA	19	F	SVNT	RRAEWSUSA
KARLING, BRITA	28	F	SVNT	RRAEWSUSA
ALSLOCKA, PELAGIA	20	F	SP	RRAEWSUSA
TAMMINEN, ALEXANDRA	28	F	SVNT	RRAEWSUSA

SHIP: AMALFI

FROM: HAMBURG
TO: NEW YORK
ARRIVED: 01 JUNE 1888

PASSENGER	AGE	SEX	OCCUPATION	PRV VIL DES
DOBCZYNSKI, SARAH	20	F	SGL	RRZZZZUSA
ESTHER	15	F	SGL	RRZZZZUSA
PUSTELBAUM, MOSES	23	M	LABR	RRZZZZUSA
KORB, DAVID	25	M	TLR	RRAIOOPA
REIZESCH, FEIWEL	26	M	LABR	RRAHTUWI
WILDNER, ABRAHAM	25	M	LABR	RRAHTUWI
REIZESCH, LEON	19	M	LABR	RRAHTUWI
FRIEDMANN, ABRAHAM	42	M	JNR	RRAHTUWI
SMUSCHKOWITZ, BENJAMIN	40	M	LABR	RRZZZZWI

SHIP: NORSEMAN

FROM: LIVERPOOL AND LONDON
TO: BOSTON
ARRIVED: 02 JUNE 1888

PASSENGER	AGE	SEX	OCCUPATION	PRV VIL DES
FRENZEL, JULIAN	23	F	SP	PLZZZZPA
KAIMUTZKE, L.	23	M	LABR	PLZZZZUSA
LEVIN, BEZ.	30	M	LABR	PLZZZZNY
CHAIT, A.	29	M	LABR	RRZZZZNY
SOLOTOW, JOSEF	30	M	LABR	RRZZZZNY
PESURT, U	20	F	SP	PLZZZZUSA
LEVIN, HENRY	30	M	MACH	RRZZZZUSA
WENIFELD, WOLF	25	M	LABR	RRZZZZUSA
SCHARAFSKY, BE--	40	M	MACH	RRZZZZUSA
ISAAC	28	M	MACH	RRZZZZUSA
CHAJE	16	M	CH	RRZZZZUSA
MOSES	11	M	CH	RRZZZZUSA
CHAJENER	10	M	CH	RRZZZZUSA
CHAUM	9	M	CHILD	RRZZZZUSA
JEHIE, JECHEAL	23	M	MACH	PLZZZZBO
SCHLULTZ, CHEYNE	30	M	MACH	RRZZZZBO
SLATODKIN, SCHEINAN	35	M	MACH	PLZZZZBO
DODOWSKY, BRUME	40	M	MACH	PLZZZZBO
WILD, SARAH	22	F	SVNT	RRZZZZBO
WRIME, ISAAC	35	M	LABR	RRZZZZIL
ISARIEL	32	F	W	RRZZZZIL
LINTORA, KAZFA	28	M	LABR	RRZZZZIL
LISTO, ALFRD.	22	M	LABR	RRZZZZOH
JACKS	18	M	LABR	RRZZZZOH
STENIBACKER, ABRAHAM	48	M	LABR	RRZZZZDAK
ANNIE	48	F	W	RRZZZZDAK
ESCOLA, ANDREW	17	M	LABR	RRZZZZDAK
LENOVA, HENRICK	19	M	LABR	RRZZZZUSA
GUSTAFEN, JOHN	40	M	LABR	RRZZZZUSA
RAOVA, GIORIA	27	M	LABR	RRZZZZUSA
WASADNAIKI, T.	27	M	LABR	RRZZZZUSA
LUNFISI, JOHN	26	M	LABR	RRZZZZUSA
BRUNLA, ANTON	25	M	LABR	PLZZZZNY
WALLACE, ESAAC	22	M	LABR	RRZZZZBO
COHEN, MEYER	28	M	LABR	RRZZZZNY
LEIBER, ALEX	36	M	LABR	RRZZZZNY
TODERSTROM-, JACOB	45	M	LABR	RRZZZZNY
BULTZVORSKI, JOHN	23	M	LABR	RRZZZZNY
CARLSON, AUGUST	26	M	LABR	RRZZZZNY
LEKKINSON, JOHN	28	M	LABR	RRZZZZNY

PASSENGER	AGE	SEX	OCCUPATION	PRV VIL DES
MYLLYKISKI, CATTARINE	35	F	W	RRZZZZNY
JOHAN	2	M	CHILD	RRZZZZNY
HEIKKI	32	M	LABR	RRZZZZNY
HORM, ABRAHAM	20	M	LABR	RRZZZZNY
KYBUNSKA, GEO.	21	M	LABR	RRZZZZNY
ABRAHAMSON, DANIEL	27	M	LABR	RRZZZZNY
BEYANIANIS, HORNA	25	F	SP	RRZZZZUSA
RESSEDAI, CASPLE	36	M	LABR	RRZZZZUSA
KLEIM, SAM	36	M	LABR	RRZZZZNY
LAUSCOSARAFE, FRN.	25	M	LABR	PLZZZZPA
VASITIS, MARTIN	23	M	LABR	PLZZZZPA
JALMITHE, JOS.	25	M	LABR	PLZZZZPA
LASLAWAKIE, EPH.	25	M	LABR	RRZZZZNY
PIREMUTTER, SAM	31	M	LABR	RRZZZZNY
PERLMUTTER, ARIMATTIEA	18	M	LABR	RRZZZZNY
MENS, GEA	41	M	LABR	RRZZZZNY
LAUFMAN, FRAN	22	M	LABR	RRZZZZNY
BRU--, ARTTI.	27	M	LABR	RRZZZZUSA
BESSANT, A.	37	M	LABR	RRZZZZUSA
DUBIANSKIZ, BEN	18	M	LABR	RRZZZZNY
GORS, HENRY	50	M	LABR	RRZZZZNY
WENFULD, JANNY	19	M	LABR	RRZZZZBO
GOLDENBERG, J.	17	M	LABR	RRZZZZNY
LAWENKALI, S.	44	M	LABR	RRZZZZNY
PITICHA, CH.	18	M	LABR	RRZZZZNY
MALZATZKY, ANNA	18	F	SP	RRZZZZNY
PEKARAWETZ, M.	18	M	UNKNOWN	PLZZZZNY
LAWENKOFF, SAVA	20	M	LABR	RRZZZZNY
GUTMAN, SAM	26	M	LABR	RRZZZZNY
CHLS.	24	F	W	RRZZZZNY
MICH.	3	M	CHILD	RRZZZZNY
PAULINE	00	F	INF	RRZZZZNY
N.	26	M	LABR	RRZZZZNY
FANNY	24	F	W	RRZZZZNY
SALOMON	9	M	CHILD	RRZZZZNY
ANNETTIE	00	F	INF	RRZZZZNY
LAHAUSKIA, BEN	28	M	LABR	RRZZZZNY
SCHERFER, A.	40	M	LABR	RRZZZZNY
SCHWERDLAW, A.	44	M	LABR	RRZZZZNY
ROSCHEL	28	F	SP	RRZZZZNY
MONHE	18	F	SP	RRZZZZNY
LEIB	10	M	CH	RRZZZZNY
MASCHE	9	M	CHILD	RRZZZZNY
ROSEKKI	7	F	CHILD	RRZZZZNY
ROSA	5	F	CHILD	RRZZZZNY
CHOSKEL	3	M	CHILD	RRZZZZNY
GELTTE	00	M	INF	RRZZZZNY
GANS, C.	25	M	LABR	RRZZZZNY
LEAER, J.	28	M	LABR	RRZZZZNY
MENGALOWSKY, J.	23	M	LABR	RRZZZZNY
HINZANSKI, H.	22	M	LABR	RRZZZZNY
SCHARER, M.	36	M	LABR	RRZZZZPHI
FREYDE	27	F	W	RRZZZZPHI
CHANIN	00	M	INF	RRZZZZPHI
GOLD, S.	23	M	LABR	RRZZZZPHI
FIKOWITZ, J.	21	M	LABR	PLZZZZNY
HOLMAN, Z.	25	M	LABR	RRZZZZNY
SCHULMAN, M.	23	M	LABR	RRZZZZNY
HOLMAN, LELI	18	F	UNKNOWN	RRZZZZNY
HISCHEVE, A.	34	M	LABR	RRZZZZNY
BLAZK, J.	19	M	LABR	RRZZZZNY
WEITZMESAN, DAVID	18	M	LABR	RRZZZZNY
LUDWIG	11	M	CH	RRZZZZNY
BAUN, LEIB	16	M	UNKNOWN	RRZZZZNY
MINDELSTHIN, JOSEF	24	M	LABR	RRZZZZNY
JANERWEDZ, MARIA	35	F	SP	RRZZZZNY
PESSER	25	F	SP	RRZZZZNY
PALSKY, LEON	35	M	MACH	PLZZZZNY
WALTER, MICHEAL	60	M	MACH	PLZZZZNY
POLSKY, WINSNIUTZ	24	M	MACH	PLZZZZNY
GUTTMAN, MOSES	24	M	LABR	RRZZZZNY
WALDIYNOKY, WOLF	32	M	LABR	RRZZZZNY
KLAFCOUSKIL, JANCOF	37	M	LABR	RRZZZZNY
WEDA, JOSEPHINA	44	F	W	RRZZZZNY
LOWINSTI--, WELMOSAH	25	M	LABR	RRZZZZNY

PASSENGER	AGE	SEX	OCCUPATION	PRV VIL DES
JOCHRANN, IWAN	32	F	W	RRZZZZNY
WRAK, MICHEAL	32	M	MACH	PLZZZZNY
JANNSCH, EILIS	25	M	MACH	PLZZZZNY
ZUFE, ABRAM	33	M	MACH	PLZZZZNY
RAPPAPERT, LEMER	44	M	MACH	RRZZZZNY
JULIE	38	F	W	RRZZZZNY
ROLUV, ABRAM	63	M	MACH	RRZZZZUNK
ZETIE	60	F	W	RRZZZZUNK
ROSALIE	11	F	CH	RRZZZZUNK
RUSZKAW, SALMER	28	M	LABR	RRZZZZNY
GOLDE	23	M	LABR	RRZZZZNY
SCHIPSEL	40	M	LABR	RRZZZZNY
SYPER, JOSEF	16	M	LABR	RRZZZZNY
SCHOFF, LE---	24	M	LABR	RRZZZZNY
BEALOWITZ, JOHN	16	M	LABR	PLZZZZNY
ZAWASISSKI, JOHN	17	M	LABR	PLZZZZNY
GUTKIMSKI, MOSCHE	18	M	LABR	RRZZZZNY
HOLLANDER, MOLKE	17	M	LABR	RRZZZZNY
DAMILEWITZ, ESTER	60	F	W	RRZZZZNY
MASON, PAULL	28	M	LABR	PLZZZZNY
HIWITZKI, JOS.	27	M	LABR	RRZZZZBO
KARILITZ, EL.	46	M	LABR	RRZZZZBO
KOSOWSKI, BEN	36	M	LABR	RRZZZZBO
WOLF, GERSON	29	M	LABR	RRZZZZBO
MUK, JAN	19	M	LABR	RRZZZZBO
KANTER, JACOB	18	M	LABR	RRZZZZBO
WIECHAW, JOS	30	M	LABR	RRZZZZBO
ZETIE	30	F	W	RRZZZZBO
MADEL	3	M	CHILD	RRZZZZBO
M.	00	F	INF	RRZZZZBO
MICHELAW, M.	19	M	MACH	RRZZZZBO
SWALUKAUSKI, EL.	19	M	MACH	RRZZZZBO
ROSA	18	F	W	RRZZZZBO
WASCHWISKY, M.	28	M	LABR	PLZZZZBO
WIKINEUETZ, H.	22	M	LABR	PLZZZZBO
RAIDKAUSKI, SIMON	24	M	LABR	PLZZZZBO
POKSCHAWSKI, W.	18	M	LABR	PLZZZZBO
LEWELSZ, ISREAL	27	M	LABR	RRZZZZBO
BASSE	23	F	W	RRZZZZBO
HAMIEL	00	F	INF	RRZZZZBO
SCHAPERO, JACOB	18	M	LABR	RRZZZZBO
WOLF, ARON	31	M	LABR	RRZZZZBO
LIEMOWIEZ, J.	32	M	LABR	PLZZZZBO
ALSTRAN	32	F	W	PLZZZZBO
RU.	12	F	CH	PLZZZZBO
THAN.	7	F	CHILD	PLZZZZBO
BAL.	3	F	CHILD	PLZZZZBO
SLAN	00	M	INF	PLZZZZBO
GANS, M.	40	M	LABR	PLZZZZBO
PALATIWETCH, RUBEN	49	M	LABR	PLZZZZBO
ROSALIE	38	F	W	PLZZZZBO
MANY	8	F	CHILD	PLZZZZBO
SARAH	10	F	CH	PLZZZZBO
THOMIKUS, MACE	30	M	LABR	PLZZZZBO
ANBRIS, KAS	34	M	LABR	PLZZZZBO
GINMER, BERKE	28	M	LABR	PLZZZZBO
LAMBE	20	M	LABR	PLZZZZBO
RESERE	6	M	CHILD	PLZZZZBO
BEREWUTOHN, L.	23	M	LABR	RRZZZZBO
MAHLMAN, M.	23	M	LABR	RRZZZZBO
KRIPLIK, L.	30	M	LABR	RRZZZZBO
ADELSOHN, M.	22	M	LABR	RRZZZZBO
STERN, G.	35	M	LABR	RRZZZZBO
GRUN, L.	44	M	LABR	RRZZZZBO
LEBAUSTINN, L.	24	M	LABR	RRZZZZBO
REME	10	M	CH	RRZZZZBO
JACOB	2	M	CHILD	RRZZZZBO
WELTZ	00	M	INF	RRZZZZBO
ESKMUD, EL.	16	M	CH	RRZZZZBO
MATUSAN, M.	26	M	LABR	RRZZZZBO
LALKAWSKY, J.	24	M	LABR	PLZZZZBO
BERTOMY, A.	31	M	LABR	PLZZZZBO
KUSANKOWITZ, S.	26	M	LABR	PLZZZZNY
KRAWIZIK, JOS.	38	M	LABR	RRZZZZNY
BUDZINSKI, JAN	23	M	LABR	PLZZZZNY

PASSENGER	AGE	SEX	OCCUPATION	PRV VIL DES
WINOFULD, WOLF	35	M	LABR	RRZZZZNY
ABRAHAMOWITZ, J.	25	M	LABR	RRZZZZNY
SUAL, S.	38	M	LABR	RRZZZZNY
CHAIE	38	F	W	RRZZZZNY
CHANNE	3	M	CHILD	RRZZZZNY
RIWKE	00	F	INF	RRZZZZNY
LISKINS, PLUIS	23	M	LABR	PLZZZZNY
KAIGIBAN, BEN	10	M	CH	RRZZZZNY
MUDWARD, MOSIEHE	18	M	LABR	RRZZZZNY
LUN, ABRAM	36	M	LABR	RRZZZZNY
LISUIZKI, JONET	19	M	LABR	RRZZZZNY
MELAMA, MOSES	20	M	LABR	RRZZZZNY
KUSZINSKI, ZIABYER	33	M	LABR	RRZZZZNY
CELLI	10	M	CH	RRZZZZNY
HALERMAN, SITINEUL	42	M	LABR	RRZZZZNY
MACHAM	10	M	CH	RRZZZZNY
KOFIZINSIKI, MARIAM	25	F	SP	PLZZZZNY
WILLIAMS, FRAZ	31	M	LABR	PLZZZZNY
RINISKY, ISAAC.C.	34	M	LABR	RRZZZZNY
ARSIK, HERM.	25	M	LABR	RRZZZZNY
BARWAM, JOS	33	M	LABR	PLZZZZNY
JENKELSHEM, BARUK	29	M	LABR	RRZZZZNY
PULMAN, ISREAL	30	M	LABR	RRZZZZNY
SACKS, BELIS	23	M	LABR	RRZZZZNY
BIERMAN, M.	30	M	LABR	RRZZZZNY
INKERITIZ, BEN	25	M	LABR	RRZZZZNY
WOLINSKI, MENDEL	19	M	LABR	RRZZZZNY
BUSOWSKY, LIEB	22	M	LABR	RRZZZZNY
MFURA, WOSUL	30	M	LABR	PLZZZZNY
LEKURA, LEON	28	M	LABR	RRZZZZNY
BALYER, CHAIME	18	M	LABR	RRZZZZNY
SEPLBOUM, R.	30	M	LABR	RRZZZZNY
RIPPNER, WOLF	23	M	LABR	RRZZZZNY
ROSA	21	F	W	RRZZZZNY
WIERS, BERUTH	17	M	LABR	RRZZZZNY
RABINOWITZ, MARK	26	M	LABR	RRZZZZNY
LOZCLKEWITZ, MARSCHA	23	M	LABR	RRZZZZNY
SCHOGEWSKI, LEIB	22	M	LABR	RRZZZZNY
BLANK, HUSCHE	25	M	LABR	RRZZZZNY
MARIA	23	F	W	RRZZZZNY
SCKATNER, ABRAM	34	M	LABR	RRZZZZNY
SEKUFNITZ, ARON	32	M	LABR	RRZZZZNY
ZELANIS, VERI	48	M	LABR	PLZZZZNY
GOLIS, MATTE	26	M	LABR	PLZZZZNY
CASEWITZ, KASIMER	26	M	LABR	PLZZZZNY
HANEBUNY, KALMIER	54	M	LABR	PLZZZZBO
JUNCHS	6	F	CHILD	PLZZZZBO
FRINTE	9	F	CHILD	PLZZZZBO
FEWEL	8	F	CHILD	PLZZZZBO
RATZIN, JORE	18	M	LABR	PLZZZZBO
NICKLISCHANSKI, RUMEN	18	M	LABR	PLZZZZBO
HAMBURG, MOLKE	35	M	LABR	RRZZZZBO
PISCHE	14	M	CH	RRZZZZBO
ROSNIK, MOSCHE	24	M	LABR	RRZZZZNY
IBE	18	F	W	RRZZZZNY
LEMOSSITES, LARFIS	27	M	LABR	PLZZZZNY
BODOWOSKI, MERE--	38	M	LABR	PLZZZZNY
SZUB, SIM	27	M	LABR	PLZZZZNY
ACHALA, CRISTOW	24	M	LABR	PLZZZZNY
WASLOWIEZ, JAN	31	M	LABR	PLZZZZNY
WENGZIN, PLITE	30	M	LABR	PLZZZZNY
MARIANNE	25	F	W	PLZZZZNY
BICHZAWITSCHI, BZKA	26	M	LABR	PLZZZZNY
GURTITZ, JAZUASKA	17	M	LABR	PLZZZZNY
KEILSIKA, MASCH	15	M	LABR	PLZZZZNY
FRAISZA, FRANK	15	M	LABR	PLZZZZNY
ADMIZYKI, BURTON	17	M	LABR	PLZZZZNY
MIMON, LIEB	35	M	LABR	PLZZZZBO
LEHSPIRO, MOSCHE	27	M	LABR	RRZZZZBO
GIEBMAN, ISREAL	25	M	LABR	RRZZZZBO
NIDMISKI, PETRE	24	M	LABR	PLZZZZNY
WEBINOWITZ, NICKAS	26	M	LABR	PLZZZZNY
LISCHKIN, DAVID	30	M	LABR	RRZZZZNY
ASRIEL, BORISCHE	26	M	LABR	RRZZZZBO
LEWIN, TOMA	18	M	LABR	RRZZZZNY

PASSENGER	AGE	SEX	OCCUPATION	PRV VIL DES
KRAWITZ, BERKA	20	M	LABR	RRZZZZNY
GLOS, SRAWNA	18	M	LABR	RRZZZZNY
RAGULIS, RINN	24	M	LABR	PLZZZZNY
MASEMOWITZ, SLANN	23	M	LABR	PLZZZZNY
EVA	20	F	W	PLZZZZNY
JACKSON, J.	25	M	UNKNOWN	PLZZZZBO
SLIAW, THOS.	28	M	UNKNOWN	PLZZZZBO
BOLAND, JOS.	29	M	UNKNOWN	PLZZZZBO
GETTLINY, WM.	30	M	UNKNOWN	PLZZZZBO
CEARNY, J.	24	M	UNKNOWN	PLZZZZBO
COBLINS, E.	25	M	UNKNOWN	PLZZZZBO
FELLOW, A.	23	M	UNKNOWN	PLZZZZBO
MIRPHY, THO.	29	M	UNKNOWN	PLZZZZBO
JYNEH, J.	40	M	UNKNOWN	PLZZZZBO
NILSON, ALEX	29	M	UNKNOWN	PLZZZZBO
DEAN, F.	30	M	UNKNOWN	PLZZZZBO
HINDLE, S.	35	M	UNKNOWN	PLZZZZBO
HARRIYTON, J.	32	M	UNKNOWN	PLZZZZBO
DELANY, DANIL	29	M	UNKNOWN	PLZZZZBO
DUFFY, J.	26	M	UNKNOWN	PLZZZZBO
BERRY, P.	30	M	UNKNOWN	PLZZZZBO
H--, J.ME.	32	M	UNKNOWN	PLZZZZBO
U, RICHARD	28	M	UNKNOWN	PLZZZZBO
HOLMAN, Z.	00	M	LABR	RRZZZZBO
HEIDINGESKI, C.	35	M	LABR	RRZZZZBO
PALALOWITCH, JADEL	16	F	SP	PLZZZZBO
KARELITZ, S.	36	M	MACH	RRZZZZNY
GOLDMAN, THOS.	28	M	LABR	RRZZZZBO
POTCHAVICK, JOSEF	18	M	LABR	PLZZZZBO
LALCOWAICSHIL, JOSEF	23	M	LABR	PLZZZZBO
ALAKEWICK, BALTROV	25	M	LABR	PLZZZZBO

SHIP: ANCHORIA

FROM: GLASGOW
TO: NEW YORK
ARRIVED: 04 JUNE 1888

PASSENGER	AGE	SEX	OCCUPATION	PRV VIL DES
BERGER, SARA	30	F	UNKNOWN	PLAIAKUSA
GERSM	10	F	CH	PLAIAKUSA
FANNI	8	F	CHILD	PLAIAKUSA
PEVE	6	F	CHILD	PLAIAKUSA
FEIGE	7	F	CHILD	PLAIAKUSA
EISING	2	F	CHILD	PLAIAKUSA
TRUBISCHOK, ELKE	40	F	UNKNOWN	PLAGRTUSA
RACHEL	21	F	UNKNOWN	PLAGRTUSA
LEIB	18	F	UNKNOWN	PLAGRTUSA
MOSCHI	11	F	UNKNOWN	PLAGRTUSA
CHANE	7	F	CHILD	PLAGRTUSA
FRICHTELBERG, SAM	50	M	TLR	PLAGRTUSA
JETTE	30	F	W	PLAGRTUSA
MARCUS	11	M	UNKNOWN	PLAGRTUSA
MEYER	4	M	CHILD	PLAGRTUSA
MOSES	1	M	CHILD	PLAGRTUSA
TOSSENOWSKY, GIMPEL	33	F	UNKNOWN	PLAGRTUSA
LEISER	6	F	CHILD	PLAGRTUSA
ISRAEL	2	M	CHILD	PLAGRTUSA
MEINRICH	.03	M	INFANT	PLAGRTUSA
KREINER, BEILE	26	M	BCHR	PLAGRTUSA
LEA	9	F	CHILD	PLAGRTUSA
CHANE	1	F	CHILD	PLAGRTUSA
ASER, FRIEDKE	40	F	UNKNOWN	PLAGRTUSA
RIVE	11	F	CH	PLAGRTUSA
SLIRE	8	M	CHILD	PLAGRTUSA
LEISER	7	M	CHILD	PLAGRTUSA
REISMAN, REISEL	26	F	UNKNOWN	PLAGRTUSA
RUBIN	10	M	CH	PLAGRTUSA
FRIEDA	8	F	CHILD	PLAGRTUSA
LENA	1	F	CHILD	PLAGRTUSA
FRIEDNER, CHORNA	28	F	UNKNOWN	PLAGRTUSA

PASSENGER	AGE	SEX	OCCUPATION	PRIVL	DES
MORITZ	17	M	UNKNOWN	PLAGR	TUSA
LEON	9	M	CHILD	PLAGR	TUSA
HOCHFELD, ARON	12	M	UNKNOWN	PLACT	CUSA
ROSENFELD, MISCHE	30	F	UNKNOWN	PLACT	CUSA
ISAK	11	M	UNKNOWN	PLACT	CUSA
FEIGE	7	F	CHILD	PLACT	CUSA
KREINE	1	M	CHILD	PLACT	CUSA
BRANN, KEILE	40	F	UNKNOWN	PLACT	CUSA
MESCHE	4	M	CHILD	PLACT	CUSA
MINDEL	8	M	CHILD	PLACT	CUSA
LAKOWSKY, BORUCH	50	M	DR	PLACT	CUSA
ESTER	50	F	W	PLACT	CUSA
SCHIFRE	23	F	HP	PLACT	CUSA
REIS, SCHEINE	22	F	UNKNOWN	PLACT	CUSA
CHANE	1	F	CHILD	PLACT	CUSA
LEWY, RIVE	30	F	UNKNOWN	PLAGR	TUSA
ITTE	1	F	CHILD	PLAGR	TUSA
PECKER, DINA	25	F	UNKNOWN	PLAGR	TUSA
MOSES	5	M	CHILD	PLAGR	TUSA
HENESCH	1	M	CHILD	PLAGR	TUSA
WOLZENIK, NOCHEM	27	M	PDLR	PLAGR	TUSA
NECHAME	25	F	W	PLAGR	TUSA
BEIR	.02	M	INFANT	PLAGR	TUSA
LANDSMANN, RIVE	16	F	UNKNOWN	PLAGR	TUSA
ROCHI	11	F	UNKNOWN	PLAGR	TUSA
SCHOCHET, GERSON	19	M	JNR	PLAEA	BUSA
FEIGE	20	F	HP	PLAGR	TUSA
MULLER, LEISER	23	M	UNKNOWN	PLAGR	TUSA
TAMASE	18	M	PNTR	PLAGR	TUSA
MOISBERG, MAX	22	M	BLKSMH	PLAGR	TUSA
HELENA	21	F	W	PLAGR	TUSA
MOWSCHOWITZ, CHANE	25	F	W	PLAHO	OUSA
CHAJE	.10	F	INFANT	PLAHO	OUSA
JEMPULSKI, JENNIE	24	F	HP	PLAHO	OUSA
ANNI	20	F	HP	PLAHO	OUSA
KOPELIEWICZ, SAROCH	25	M	W	PLAHO	OUSA
JAKOB	1	M	CHILD	PLAHO	OUSA
FLEXER, LEIB	38	F	W	PLAHO	OUSA
CHAIM	9	F	CHILD	PLAHO	OUSA
BRIN, LEISER	30	M	LABR	PLAHO	OUSA
TAUB, ZARIL	40	M	BRWKR	PLAHO	OUSA
PIXMAN, CALEB	17	M	WCHMKR	PLAHO	OUSA
LEWIN, SCHLAM	28	M	JNR	PLAGR	TUSA
SPRINGER, HERMAN	12	M	CH	PLAGR	TUSA
HUSSMAN, JAKOB	37	M	BCHR	PLAGR	TUSA
PUTOLSKI, JOSEF	29	M	LABR	PLAGR	TUSA
MECHIN, PERSACK	35	M	LABR	PLAGR	TUSA
BURSTSIN, SALOMON	19	M	JNR	PLAGR	TUSA
FELITZKI, MOSCHE	40	M	SMH	PLAGR	TUSA
EPSTEIN, ARON	18	M	SHMK	PLAGR	TUSA
BRAVERMAN, MOSES	39	M	PDLR	PLAGR	TUSA
KALINOSKI, DAVID	24	M	SHMK	PLAGR	TUSA
ELIASCHOWITZ, MENDEL	37	M	MUSN	PLAGR	TUSA
TABACZNIK, JAKOB	29	M	LABR	PLAGR	TUSA
PALEI, WOLF	25	M	TLR	PLAGR	TUSA
GURALNIK, JAKOB	40	M	LABR	PLAGR	TUSA
ROMER, ABRAH	18	M	SMH	PLAGR	TUSA
WISEN, GUTMAN	42	M	TLR	PLAGR	TUSA
ROBINOWIEZ, MOSES	30	M	BKBNDR	PLAGR	TUSA
KAHN, MOSSEL	17	M	JNR	PLAGR	TUSA
HANDLER, SCHALE	22	M	PPHGR	PLAGR	TUSA
HIRSCH	18	M	PPHGR	PLAGR	TUSA
PETROCH, SCHOLEM	22	M	PRNTR	PLAGR	TUSA
SOSSEK, WOLF	16	M	LABR	PLAGR	TUSA
SILETZKI, ISAK	26	M	LABR	PLAGR	TUSA
HELLER, CHAIM	26	M	LABR	PLAGR	TUSA
MILKOWSKY, ISAK	22	M	LABR	PLAGR	TUSA
JOSELOWITZ, JOSEL	30	M	JNR	PLAGR	TUSA
JACOB, SALOMON	17	M	SMH	PLAGR	TUSA
BLEIWEIS, DARIEL	24	M	LABR	PLAGR	TUSA
LOSSER, ASRIEL	25	M	WCHMKR	PLAHQ	UUSA
BRUCK, SALOMON	18	M	LABR	PLAHQ	UUSA
WEINSTEIN, MORDUCH	58	M	TLR	PLAHQ	UUSA
LIFTSCHITZ, SALOMON	27	M	LABR	RRZZZ	ZUSA
RESCHER, SELIG	24	M	TLR	RRZZZ	ZUSA
WOLFSOHN, JAKOB	37	M	TLR	RRAGR	TUSA
ISAK	14	M	TLR	RRAGR	TUSA
WOLEWIK, SCHMUL	28	M	JNR	RRAGR	TUSA
ROSENHEIM, ISSAC	34	M	GZR	RRAHT	FUSA
PLASCHEK, MOSES	47	M	TLR	RRAHT	FUSA
KITAJOWITZ, ITZIG	28	M	LABR	RRAGR	TUSA
WOLF, LEISER	28	M	PDLR	RRAGR	TUSA
SZABO, MICHAEL	33	M	LABR	RRAGR	TUSA
SZALAK, ANDREAN	36	M	LABR	RRAGR	TUSA
SUZEL, GEORG	25	M	LABR	RRAGR	TUSA
KLAMISKA, MICH	27	M	LABR	RRAGR	TUSA
MASEKULAK, PAUL	24	M	LABR	RRAGR	TUSA
SZALAK, JANOS	17	M	LABR	RRAGR	TUSA
STOLAR, SAL	44	M	LABR	RRAGR	TUSA
SENKOS, ADAM	25	M	LABR	RRAGR	TUSA
EISNER, MARKUS	26	M	LABR	RRAGR	TUSA
ABRAMOWITZ, SARAH	36	F	UNKNOWN	RRAGR	TUSA
WEISER, ROSA	17	F	UNKNOWN	RRACT	CUSA
SLUTZKI, FEIGE	19	F	HP	RRAGR	TUSA
POTRUCK, SANIE	20	F	HP	RRAGR	TUSA
SCHAPIRA, MIRE	20	F	HP	RRAGR	TUSA
ROSENFELD, REGI	10	F	CH	RRAGR	TUSA
SLITOWITZ, HENE	28	F	HP	RRAGR	TUSA
DEDA, YENDRZYN	30	F	HP	RRAGR	TUSA
LECKOWITZ, AUGUSTIN	43	M	MUSN	RRZZZ	ZUSA
IRENE	42	F	W	RRZZZ	ZUSA
MARIE	9	F	CHILD	RRZZZ	ZUSA
OLIMPA	1	F	CHILD	RRZZZ	ZUSA
GEZEWIEZ, ANTON	38	M	LABR	RRAHT	FUSA
NISEMAN, PIETR	30	M	LABR	RRAHT	FUSA
MARIAN	24	F	W	RRAHT	FUSA
NEWALD, CHRIS	35	M	LABR	RRAHT	FUSA
LENORE	18	F	W	RRAHT	FUSA
LYKEWSKI, JOSEF	29	M	SHMK	RRAHT	FUSA
OLSTEIN, MICH	45	M	LABR	RRAHT	FUSA
BARKOWITZ, STANSL	30	M	LABR	RRAHT	FUSA
LEESNY, TOMAS	21	M	LABR	PLZZZ	ZUSA
DOBRYTE, MATEWS	27	M	LABR	PLZZZ	ZUSA
KUKOWSKY, JOSEF	24	M	LABR	RRZZZ	ZUSA
DANOWSKY, JEAN	31	M	LABR	RRZZZ	ZUSA
WIZSNIESKI, FRANC	34	M	LABR	RRZZZ	ZUSA
GIRDWOJ, SILVESTER	40	M	LABR	RRZZZ	ZUSA
OWEZAZAK, PETER	40	M	LABR	RRZZZ	ZUSA
MOSKOWITZ, MEYER	17	M	LABR	RRZZZ	ZUSA
SMIKOWSKI, ANTON	24	M	LABR	RRZZZ	ZUSA
SEATERESICO, ANTONIO	31	M	LABR	RRZZZ	ZUSA
OLESEZKY, JAN	23	M	LABR	RRZZZ	ZUSA
CHROMIK, JANOS	23	M	LABR	RRZZZ	ZUSA
KILINSKI, FRANZ	33	M	LABR	PLZZZ	ZUSA
SKLIPKO, STEFAN	24	M	LABR	PLZZZ	ZUSA
ZUSKA, ADDARKO	25	M	LABR	PLZZZ	ZUSA
MILHIGER, SCHMUL	28	M	LABR	PLZZZ	ZUSA
KAMMINSKI, LEISER	31	M	LABR	PLZZZ	ZUSA
HOPTA, VASIL	20	M	LABR	PLZZZ	ZUSA
MAZKEWICZ, FRANZ	39	M	LABR	PLZZZ	ZUSA
ZAMITYS, MARIA	27	F	HP	PLZZZ	ZUSA
SZARKOSKI, EMMA	14	F	HP	PLZZZ	ZUSA
JOHANNISTALI, ERIK	40	M	LABR	FNZZZ	ZUSA
KAISER	21	M	LABR	FNZZZ	ZUSA
TJARO, VICTOR	20	M	LABR	FNZZZ	ZUSA
MYLYKOSKI, KARL	27	M	LABR	FNZZZ	ZUSA
EHINTALA, MATTS	19	M	LABR	FNZZZ	ZUSA
HILTUNEN, ANTI	27	M	LABR	FNZZZ	ZUSA

SHIP: ARIZONA

FROM: LIVERPOOL AND QUEENSTOWN
TO: NEW YORK
ARRIVED: 04 JUNE 1888

PASSENGER	AGE	SEX	OCCUPATION	PRV VIL DES
ERIKSSON, E.	18	M	LABR	FNZZZZUSA
OJALA, EUSCH	41	M	ATSN	FNZZZZUSA
ZALMONOWITZ, RUSKE	40	F	W	FNACBFUSA
LINEWITZ, SCHLOMA	46	F	W	FNACBFUSA
MILEZIN, SCHMUEL	19	M	FARMER	FNACBFUSA
WAINES, ARON	30	M	PNTR	FNACBFUSA
LEID, JOSSEL	16	M	LABR	FNACBFUSA
BARTKOWSKI, OFEL	34	M	ATSN	FNACBFUSA
MITTELMAN, IGNATZ	17	M	LABR	FNACBFUSA
LUBITZKY, MOSES	18	M	LABR	FNACBFUSA
LIBLANG, HERTZ	55	M	ATSN	FNACBFUSA
KRUPINTZKI, FERGEL	24	M	FARMER	FNACBFUSA
MUTT, FRANNIE	18	F	SP	FNACBFUSA
JACOB	7	M	CHILD	FNACBFUSA
ISAAC	7	M	CHILD	FNACBFUSA
GITEL	6	M	CHILD	FNACBFUSA
DAVID	5	M	CHILD	FNACBFUSA
ROBIN, CARL	50	M	ATSN	FNACBFUSA
WILLIAM	25	M	ATSN	FNACBFUSA
LOUISA	25	F	W	FNACBFUSA
WILHELMINA	20	F	SP	FNACBFUSA
FREDRIKA	16	F	SP	FNACBFUSA
AMRY	70	F	MA	FNACBFUSA
WEINER, ISAAC	17	M	LABR	FNACBFUSA
ERNESTINA	7	F	CHILD	FNACBFUSA
DANIEL	6	M	CHILD	FNACBFUSA
LUBOLOMOWITZ, MARIA	52	F	W	FNACBFUSA
NENMARK, MOSES	45	M	ATSN	FNACBFUSA
BERTHA	43	F	W	FNACBFUSA
MATE	7	M	CHILD	FNACBFUSA
RACHEL	6	F	CHILD	FNACBFUSA
SNAPPIER, HINDE	20	F	SP	FNACBFUSA
LEBKORICK, CHAIE	33	F	W	FNACBFUSA
MARITZ	22	M	MSN	FNACBFUSA
SOLOMON	16	M	LABR	FNACBFUSA
RASMUSEN, SEREN	19	M	LABR	FNACBFUSA
EISIK, MORITZ	27	M	SDLR	FNACBFUSA
KATSAN, SARAH	46	F	W	FNACBFUSA
GUESCHE	16	F	SP	FNACBFUSA
RAHEL	7	M	CHILD	FNACBFUSA
RAHES	.10	M	INFANT	FNACBFUSA
HAVRILYAK, GEORG	44	M	ATSN	FNACBFUSA
MAFID, CHAIE	50	F	W	FNACBFUSA
LEHA	21	F	SP	FNACBFUSA
RIWKE	7	F	CHILD	FNACBFUSA
LEIBE	6	F	CHILD	FNACBFUSA
KOTLAR, ABRAM	26	M	MSN	FNACBFUSA
KAZISCHACK, JAN	16	M	LABR	FNACBFUSA
DANTZIG, CHANNA	18	F	SP	FNACBFUSA
LUDKOLM, EBRAIM	40	M	ATSN	FNAGUZUSA
JOHAN	35	M	ATSN	FNAGUZUSA
ERIK	45	M	ATSN	FNAGUZUSA
JOKELATTA, JOHAN	30	M	SEMN	FNAGUZUSA
HOSLOOTA, MALTS	25	M	PNTR	FNAGUZUSA
PAJKAJSKI, JAKOR	45	M	FARMER	FNAGUZUSA
LUDKONER, ELIAS	26	M	LABR	FNAGUZUSA
PALKOKORJON, MATTS	27	M	LABR	FNAGUZUSA
KORHONER, HENRIK	27	M	SMH	FNAGUZUSA
PIETELA, GUSTAF	18	M	CL	FNAGUZUSA
JOKILA, LEANDER	34	M	CPTR	FNAGUZUSA
PIERDARA, FRANS	25	M	SHPMN	FNAGUZUSA
LENKENAJA, AUGUST	27	M	PNTR	FNAGUZUSA
KYROLE, LEANDER	33	M	ATSN	FNAGUZUSA
GUSTAFSSON, ALEXR.	27	M	PMBR	FNAGUZUSA
HOFFSTEDT, FERTHROF	21	M	SHPMN	FNAGUZUSA
LILFA, OLOF	20	M	FARMER	FNAGUZUSA
CARLSSON, CARL	18	M	LABR	FNAGUZUSA
JANSSON, ERIK	33	M	MNR	FNAGUZUSA

PASSENGER	AGE	SEX	OCCUPATION	PRV VIL DES
ERIKSSON, KARL	37	M	FARMER	FNAGUZUSA
MATTSON, CARL	30	M	MSN	FNAGUZUSA
SODERLUND, JOHAN	14	M	LABR	FNAGUZUSA
HEDBLONS, CARL	35	M	SDLR	FNAGUZUSA
KARLSSON, MATTS	22	M	PNTR	FNAGUZUSA
JANSSON, MATTS	28	M	WVR	FNAEWSUSA
RUNDBERG, CARL	27	M	SMH	FNAGUZUSA
BLOMBERG, JOHAN	18	M	LABR	FNAGUZUSA
SODERLUND, KARL	23	M	SHMK	FNAGUZUSA
GUSTAFSSON, CARL	22	M	FARMER	FNAGUZUSA
ANDERSSON, ERNST	22	M	FARMER	FNAGUZUSA
KARLSSON, CARL	22	M	CL	FNAGUZUSA
CARLSSON, JOHAN	22	M	LABR	FNAGUZUSA
SJOSTROM, EMIL	19	M	LABR	FNAGUZUSA
EKSTROM, AUGUST	21	M	PMBR	FNAGUZUSA
MANNERSTROM, EMIL	17	M	FARMER	FNAGUZUSA
CARLSSON, VICTOR	52	M	ATSN	FNAGUZUSA
LEANDERSSON, CARL	23	M	JNR	FNAGUZUSA
CARLSSON, CARL	22	M	JNR	FNAGUZUSA
KARLSSON, JOHAN	19	M	GDNR	FNAGUZUSA
ANDERSSON, CARL	23	M	PNTR	FNAGUZUSA
JOHANSSON, CARL	21	M	FARMER	FNAGUZUSA
MATTASON, JOHAN	23	M	FARMER	FNAGUZUSA
METTSON, JOHAN	36	M	CPTR	FNAGUZUSA
ANDERSSON, CARL	29	M	BKLYR	FNAGUZUSA
DANIELSON, OTTO	39	M	SMH	FNAGUZUSA
SJOLUND, FREDRIK	26	M	SDLR	FNAGUZUSA
BJORKMANN, ERIK	53	M	MCHT	FNAGUZUSA
LAHDENPERA, JOHAN	31	M	MSN	FNAGUZUSA
TYHR, MATTS	19	M	LABR	FNAGUZUSA
KURKKI, HENRICH	32	M	MNR	FNAGUZUSA
KAARI, JOHAN	34	M	FIL	FNAGUZUSA
VICMILI, JOHAN	34	M	SEMN	FNAGUZUSA
BROSON, THOMAS	30	M	FARMER	FNAGUZUSA
JOHANSSON, ERIK	19	M	CL	FNAGUZUSA
GOLDIN, RAJEL	28	F	W	FNACBFUSA
BENJAMIN	3	M	CHILD	FNACBFUSA
ENE	.07	F	INFANT	FNACBFUSA
HEDLER, CHRE	26	F	SP	FNACBFUSA
HOLLER, JACOB	25	M	JNR	FNACBFUSA
ISACHES, SARA	24	F	W	FNACBFUSA
BERIL	7	M	CHILD	FNACBFUSA
KAHN, CARL	27	M	ATSN	FNACBFUSA
CARL	4	M	CHILD	FNACBFUSA
LINA	3	F	CHILD	FNACBFUSA
GUSTAV	2	M	CHILD	FNACBFUSA
EILHELM	.10	M	INFANT	FNACBFUSA
MED, CHRIC	30	F	W	FNACBFUSA
MOTTEL	7	M	CHILD	FNACBFUSA
ARON	6	M	CHILD	FNACBFUSA
SCHNAPPER, CHAIE	.08	F	INFANT	FNACBFUSA
MUTT, LIPE	.11	F	INFANT	FNACBFUSA
KRUPNISKI, TAUBE	.05	F	INFANT	FNACBFUSA
LIBKOWITZ, MARIE	.06	F	INFANT	FNACBFUSA
SCHNEIDER, ROSA	22	F	W	FNACBFUSA
SALOMON	6	M	CHILD	FNACBFUSA
KOWALZIK, JEAN	22	M	LABR	FNACBFUSA
PRAWDRIECK, ANTON	30	M	MSN	FNACBFUSA
MALESCHEWSKY, JAN	20	M	FARMER	FNACBFUSA
KATCH, JOSEPH	49	M	MCHT	FNACBFUSA
WITKANTZKAS, KASIS	45	M	ATSN	FNACBFUSA
JECNSCHEWITZKOS, FELIX	25	M	ATSN	FNACBFUSA
BUNANCZUS, JOSA	26	M	SMH	FNACBFUSA
PETKEWITZKOS, BARN	32	M	PNTR	FNACBFUSA
MAGID, OSIA	24	M	CPTR	FNACBFUSA
RABONOWITZ, GILEB	25	F	W	FNACBFUSA
SCHLENIE	.07	F	INFANT	FNACBFUSA
MAGID, BENE	.10	F	INFANT	FNACBFUSA

PASSENGER	AGE	SEX	OCCUPATION	PRIVL	DES

SHIP: WERRA

FROM: BREMEN AND SOUTHAMPTON
TO: NEW YORK
ARRIVED: 05 JUNE 1888

PASSENGER	AGE	SEX	OCCUPATION	PRIVL	DES
GRIEWING, CARL	38	M	FARMER	RRZZZZ	USA
ALIDE	27	F	UNKNOWN	RRZZZZ	USA
SCHAEFER, VALENTIN	45	M	LABR	RRZZZZ	USA
ELISE	42	F	W	RRZZZZ	USA
HEIN	22	M	LABR	RRZZZZ	USA
GEORG	14	M	UNKNOWN	RRZZZZ	USA
BORKOSKI, VALENTIN	28	M	FARMER	RRZZZZ	USA
BAUMANN, MARKUS	59	M	LABR	RRZZZZ	USA
CHAJE	21	F	UNKNOWN	RRZZZZ	USA
ROCHEL	20	F	UNKNOWN	RRZZZZ	USA
COHEN, JACOB	28	M	FARMER	RRZZZZ	USA
DINKWALD, AUG	32	M	LABR	RRZZZZ	USA
BERENDT, JAKOB	37	M	LABR	RRZZZZ	USA
SCHIEWI, FRANZ	31	M	FARMER	RRZZZZ	USA
HENRIETTE	28	F	W	RRZZZZ	USA
HENRIETTE	.11	F	INFANT	RRZZZZ	USA
FRANZ	2	M	CHILD	RRZZZZ	USA
MICH	18	M	FARMER	RRZZZZ	USA
AUGUSTE	17	F	UNKNOWN	RRZZZZ	USA
BERTHA	.03	F	INFANT	RRZZZZ	USA
MURACH, WILH	28	M	FARMER	RRZZZZ	USA
MARIA	21	F	W	RRZZZZ	USA
ADOLF	.11	M	INFANT	RRZZZZ	USA
WAGNER, GEORG	20	M	FARMER	RRZZZZ	USA
BARB	23	F	W	RRZZZZ	USA
MEIER, MARG	48	F	LABR	RRZZZZ	USA
JACOB	17	M	LABR	RRZZZZ	USA
FRIEDR	11	M	CH	RRZZZZ	USA
FRIED	10	F	CH	RRZZZZ	USA
JOHANN	4	M	CHILD	RRZZZZ	USA
CHR	25	M	LABR	RRZZZZ	USA
CATH	24	F	W	RRZZZZ	USA
JOH	.11	M	INFANT	RRZZZZ	USA
CHR	28	M	LABR	RRZZZZ	USA
BARB	27	F	W	RRZZZZ	USA
SABINE	4	F	CHILD	RRZZZZ	USA
FRIEDR	2	M	CHILD	RRZZZZ	USA
CHRIST	33	M	LABR	RRZZZZ	USA
MARG	33	F	W	RRZZZZ	USA
CATH	11	F	CH	RRZZZZ	USA
FRIED	6	F	CHILD	RRZZZZ	USA
CHR	4	M	CHILD	RRZZZZ	USA
MAG	3	F	CHILD	RRZZZZ	USA
ROSINE	.11	F	INFANT	RRZZZZ	USA
ANNA	76	F	W	RRZZZZ	USA
SISELOWITZ, WOLF	25	M	LABR	RRZZZZ	USA
SALOMON	22	M	LABR	RRZZZZ	USA
MILKOWSKY, ZEMESCH	20	M	LABR	RRZZZZ	USA
SELOWITZ, ABRAHAM	18	M	LABR	RRZZZZ	USA
MUELLER, GERD	24	M	LABR	RRAHUF	USA
BEHNKE, JACOB	43	M	LABR	RRAHUF	USA
PLINES, FRINNE	20	F	W	RRZZZZ	USA
ROSA	.09	F	INFANT	RRZZZZ	USA
SUESSEL	18	M	LABR	RRZZZZ	USA
HERMANN, EISIG	24	M	LABR	RRZZZZ	USA
MOSESSOHN, WOLF	42	M	LABR	RRZZZZ	USA
BICZYSKA, STANISL	30	M	LABR	RRZZZZ	USA
SCHOTTLAND, HEINR	15	F	W	RRZZZZ	USA
MACHINSKA, MARYANNA	26	F	UNKNOWN	RRZZZZ	USA
WASCHWEDDOWSKY, HANE	32	F	W	RRZZZZ	USA
GITTA	4	F	CHILD	RRZZZZ	USA
LIBJECKA, ANNIELA	31	M	LABR	RRZZZZ	USA
LUKOWSKA, JOSEFA	19	F	UNKNOWN	RRZZZZ	USA
MEYER, IDA	14	F	UNKNOWN	RRZZZZ	USA
ROEHLING, SOPHIE	17	F	UNKNOWN	RRZZZZ	USA
SIECKOECKA, JOH	53	M	LABR	RRZZZZ	USA
MORGENSTERN, HARRIS	30	M	LABR	RRZZZZ	USA
LAPIDES, GITEL	20	M	LABR	RRZZZZ	USA
GRIMBERG, SAM	26	M	LABR	RRZZZZ	USA
ROSALIE	23	F	W	RRZZZZ	USA
STINKES, WILH	19	M	LABR	RRZZZZ	USA
DANITSCHEWITZ, KASIS	20	M	LABR	RRZZZZ	USA
GUTANZKAS, ANDREAS	48	M	LABR	RRZZZZ	USA
MATJES, WINZENS	27	M	LABR	RRZZZZ	USA
BERKOWITZ, JANKEL	18	M	LABR	RRZZZZ	USA
LABOWITZ, SCHEPSEL	48	M	LABR	RRZZZZ	USA
KLIBANSKY, KOPEL	33	M	LABR	RRZZZZ	USA
SCHAGATIS, WALCIAN	23	M	LABR	RRZZZZ	USA
BIRKAS, KAZMIR	23	M	LABR	RRZZZZ	USA
WELLER, PADRES	48	M	LABR	RRZZZZ	USA
MARGELITE, ISAAC	37	M	LABR	RRZZZZ	USA
MICHALOWSKY, ADAM	23	M	LABR	RRZZZZ	USA
JURKZAJTIS, JURGIS	26	M	LABR	RRZZZZ	USA
KANNE, ALB	60	M	LABR	RRZZZZ	USA
MARIE	45	F	W	RRZZZZ	USA
SAKAMBOSKY, DANIEL	18	M	LABR	RRZZZZ	USA
FESCO, CATH	19	F	UNKNOWN	RRZZZZ	USA
LESCHINSKY, FRITZ	23	M	LABR	RRZZZZ	USA
SCHABEL, ARON	34	M	LABR	RRZZZZ	USA
ROSA	30	F	W	RRZZZZ	USA
BASCHE	9	F	CHILD	RRZZZZ	USA
FRIEDE	7	F	CHILD	RRZZZZ	USA
FROME	4	F	CHILD	RRZZZZ	USA
MALKE	2	F	CHILD	RRZZZZ	USA
ABRAMOWITZ, MATE	19	M	LABR	RRZZZZ	USA
TUCIWITZ, MICHAEL	39	M	LABR	RRZZZZ	USA
DOMBROWSKY, WAJCIECH	20	M	LABR	RRZZZZ	USA
SCHUDINK, KAZMIR	24	M	LABR	RRAHTF	USA
EPELBAUM, CHAIM	20	M	LABR	RRAHTF	USA
KLEINHAN, ISAAC	30	M	LABR	RRAHTF	USA
GUTTERMANN, TENWUS	28	M	LABR	RRAHTF	USA
LAZAR, SZOBEL	19	M	MCHT	RRAHTF	USA
BRANDE, HELLER	32	M	MCHT	RRZZZZ	USA
LEWIN, DAVID	32	M	MCHT	RRZZZZ	USA

SHIP: THE QUEEN

FROM: LIVERPOOL AND QUEENSTOWN
TO: NEW YORK
ARRIVED: 06 JUNE 1888

PASSENGER	AGE	SEX	OCCUPATION	PRIVL	DES
PILILHEAVALTA, H.	29	M	LABR	RRZZZZ	NY
MATTILA, AUGUST	29	M	LABR	RRZZZZ	NY
PETTOMAN, JOHAN	30	M	LABR	RRZZZZ	NY
HELSNIG, G.J.SARRIS	24	M	LABR	RRZZZZ	NY
HAHLMAN, GUSTAF	20	M	LABR	RRZZZZ	NY
PLAZIG, AUG.	29	M	LABR	RRZZZZ	NY
JENENZENSKY, W.	26	M	LABR	RRZZZZ	NY
PIRI, AUGUST	20	M	LABR	RRZZZZ	NY
KOBISTA, HEIKKI	24	M	LABR	RRZZZZ	NY
LIMPEN, JOHN-P.	35	M	LABR	RRZZZZ	NY
PALTANGUS, ALBERT	31	M	LABR	RRZZZZ	NY
BIRGAINEN, SOFIA	35	F	SP	RRZZZZ	NY
KNORIEL, LEIBE	18	F	SP	RRZZZZ	NY
EPSTEIN, S.H.	28	M	LABR	RRZZZZ	NY
GOLDS, N.	28	F	W	RRZZZZ	NY
M.	3	M	CHILD	RRZZZZ	NY
ALIN, OTTO	20	M	LABR	RRZZZZ	NY
STEROCHER, SAUNE	26	M	LABR	RRZZZZ	NY
RUDEMSKEY, S.	34	M	LABR	RRZZZZ	NY
ROSCHANEL, S.	24	M	LABR	RRZZZZ	NY
BRITZKOWSKY, ESEIR	28	M	LABR	RRZZZZ	NY
ZEMIK, BER.	24	F	W	RRZZZZ	NY
ROCHE	4	F	CHILD	RRZZZZ	NY
WEISS, ELLE	22	F	W	RRZZZZ	NY
PER	1	F	CHILD	RRZZZZ	NY
SAPPERSTEIN, BAS.	32	F	W	RRZZZZ	STL
SCHAGE	5	F	CHILD	RRZZZZ	STL

PASSENGER	AGE	SEX	OCCUPATION	PRIV	VIL	DES
KISSEL	3	F	CHILD	RR	ZZZZ	STL
BER.	1	M	CHILD	RR	ZZZZ	STL
DOBRZYNISKI, MIG.	17	F	SP	RR	ZZZZ	STL
BASS, MORDEL	25	M	LABR	RR	ZZZZ	STL
LEWIN, CHAIM	26	M	LABR	RR	ZZZZ	STL
SCHWARZMAN, A.	29	M	LABR	RR	ZZZZ	STL
HELSTEIN, B.	55	F	W	RR	ZZZZ	STL
HENRY	11	M	CH	RR	ZZZZ	STL
KACKIZ	10	M	CH	RR	ZZZZ	STL
ROCKLAN	7	M	CHILD	RR	ZZZZ	STL
DUVERE	4	M	CHILD	RR	ZZZZ	STL
SAGOEL	2	M	CHILD	RR	ZZZZ	STL
SOLENM	1	M	CHILD	RR	ZZZZ	STL
MALONOWSKI, J.	26	M	LABR	RR	ZZZZ	STL
RUBENSTEIN, W.	28	M	LABR	RR	ZZZZ	STL
ROBAT, JOHAN	16	M	LABR	RR	ZZZZ	STL
LEWIN, ITZIG	23	M	LABR	RR	ZZZZ	STL
JALOWICZ, M.	29	F	W	RR	ZZZZ	STL
W.	7	F	CHILD	RR	ZZZZ	STL
J.	4	F	CHILD	RR	ZZZZ	STL
W.	2	F	CHILD	RR	ZZZZ	STL
ROBINSON, CHAIM	15	M	LABR	RR	ZZZZ	STL
KRAUSS, E.	26	M	LABR	RR	ZZZZ	CH
THERESA	24	F	W	RR	ZZZZ	CH
STRAEASKI, JOS.	27	M	LABR	RR	ZZZZ	BO
KUSOWSKY, JOHAN	27	M	LABR	RR	ZZZZ	NY
MARTHA	25	F	W	RR	ZZZZ	NY
CATH.	20	F	SP	RR	ZZZZ	NY
MARTHA	1	F	CHILD	RR	ZZZZ	NY
HANOLA, ELIAS	30	M	LABR	RR	ZZZZ	CH
KESKIL, HANNA	20	F	SP	RR	ZZZZ	CH
ALZ, JACOB	40	M	LABR	RR	ZZZZ	CH
WISTI, JACOB	35	M	LABR	RR	ZZZZ	CH
RERSONEN, SAMUEL	18	M	LABR	RR	ZZZZ	CH
SAUL, ANT.	30	M	LABR	RR	ZZZZ	CH
ANT.	18	M	LABR	RR	ZZZZ	CH
PITTI, JOHAN	40	M	LABR	RR	ZZZZ	CH
KLEMALA, JOHAN	40	M	LABR	RR	ZZZZ	CH
JOHAN	30	M	LABR	RR	ZZZZ	CH
LAMMONKOSKI, JACOB	30	M	LABR	RR	ZZZZ	NY
PENTOLA, JOHAN	40	M	LABR	RR	ZZZZ	NY
PESPA, JOHAN	30	M	LABR	RR	ZZZZ	NY
SUNDBERG, ISAK	30	M	LABR	RR	ZZZZ	NY
PEUKANASKI, GUTA.	27	M	LABR	RR	ZZZZ	NY
OHO, HEIKE	27	M	LABR	RR	ZZZZ	NY
ANT.	30	M	LABR	RR	ZZZZ	NY
PYKARI, MATH.	21	M	LABR	RR	ZZZZ	NY
SGOLINID, HERMAN	30	M	LABR	RR	ZZZZ	NY
GROMAS, JACOB	24	M	LABR	RR	ZZZZ	NY
KAUKAWONA, MATH.	24	M	LABR	RR	ZZZZ	NY
SARKAGOROI, ERKI	35	M	LABR	RR	ZZZZ	NY
PETTAKANGAS, JOHAN	25	M	LABR	RR	ZZZZ	NY
MEINE, JOHAN	40	M	LABR	RR	ZZZZ	NY
TALEY, ERLAND	50	M	LABR	RR	ZZZZ	NY
WISKALI, MATH.	19	M	LABR	RR	ZZZZ	NY
ROSENBERG, JOHAN	20	M	LABR	RR	ZZZZ	NY
KAUGAS, ANT.	23	M	LABR	RR	ZZZZ	NY
NATILA, ISAK	36	M	LABR	RR	ZZZZ	NY
ESKONSIVA, ISAK	36	M	LABR	RR	ZZZZ	NY
HARHS, ISAK	30	M	LABR	RR	ZZZZ	NY
WIKLAND, JARD.	28	M	LABR	RR	ZZZZ	NY
KARIN, ANT.	31	M	LABR	RR	ZZZZ	NY
SETTOR, JONA	29	M	LABR	RR	ZZZZ	NY
KAUGAS, OTTE	34	M	LABR	RR	ZZZZ	NY
LUNDGWIST, JOHAN	18	M	LABR	RR	ZZZZ	NY
PERLA, JAKARIS	31	M	LABR	RR	ZZZZ	NY
RATALA, JOHAN	42	M	LABR	RR	ZZZZ	NY
RAUTIS, PEKKA	28	M	LABR	RR	ZZZZ	NY
OLLART, GUST.	26	M	LABR	RR	ZZZZ	NY
RACKMAN, ERIK	44	M	LABR	RR	ZZZZ	NY
HASTRUN	43	F	W	RR	ZZZZ	NY
KARL	12	M	CH	RR	ZZZZ	NY
ANNA	9	F	CHILD	RR	ZZZZ	NY
JOHANSDOTTER, SIGNE	26	M	LABR	RR	ZZZZ	NY
GRIFE, KARL	22	M	LABR	RR	ZZZZ	NY
SVENSDOTTER, EMMA	23	F	SP	RR	ZZZZ	IL
ADOLPDO, AUGUSTE	22	M	LABR	RR	ZZZZ	IL
POLLERDOTTER, EMMA	18	F	SP	RR	ZZZZ	NY
BONNAN, KARL	35	M	LABR	RR	ZZZZ	NY
MANISTI, LEANDER	30	M	LABR	RR	ZZZZ	NY
PAGOLA, ESAIAS	48	M	LABR	RR	ZZZZ	NY
KARELA, ANTE	21	M	LABR	RR	ZZZZ	NY
KAUKAS, MATT	18	M	LABR	RR	ZZZZ	NY
LARIN, ANTI	17	M	LABR	RR	ZZZZ	NY
KARLELA, JUHEN	25	F	SP	RR	ZZZZ	NY
MARITAENEN, JUHEN	40	F	SP	RR	ZZZZ	NY
WATAMAKI, JOHAN	30	M	LABR	RR	ZZZZ	NY
PENUS, JOH.	19	M	LABR	RR	ZZZZ	NY
BERGREM, LARS	23	M	LABR	RR	ZZZZ	NY
ROSCHOFSKY, DINE	20	M	LABR	RR	ZZZZ	NY
LEVINSTEIN, SORE	42	F	W	RR	ZZZZ	NY
MEIER	16	M	LABR	RR	ZZZZ	NY
DOBERE	18	M	LABR	RR	ZZZZ	NY
SCHIE	10	M	CH	RR	ZZZZ	NY
RIWKE	3	M	CHILD	RR	ZZZZ	NY
ZIPKE	5	M	CHILD	RR	ZZZZ	NY
ROSENBLUM, MOSEN	27	M	LABR	RR	ZZZZ	NY
WINTEVCHE, ITE	20	M	LABR	RR	ZZZZ	NY
WEINSTOCK, DAVID	20	M	LABR	RR	ZZZZ	NY
SCHEINE	20	F	W	RR	ZZZZ	NY
KRAUS, JOSEF	58	M	LABR	RR	ZZZZ	NY
FABRI	25	M	LABR	RR	ZZZZ	NY
SCHWARZENFELD, SALI	20	M	LABR	RR	ZZZZ	NY
HEMMI	18	F	W	RR	ZZZZ	NY
SCHWARTZ, GITEL	38	M	LABR	RR	ZZZZ	NY
DRUSCHKEWITZ, DUM.	36	M	LABR	RR	ZZZZ	NY
DELPUS, AUGUST	39	M	LABR	RR	ZZZZ	NY
PETRANZKA, ZERODIS	25	M	LABR	RR	ZZZZ	NY
KAULA, KATHARINA	22	F	SP	RR	ZZZZ	NY
KRUKLATS, DWORE	25	F	W	RR	ZZZZ	NY
PAULUS	.01	F	INFANT	RR	ZZZZ	NY
CHINSKI, MOSES	38	M	LABR	RR	ZZZZ	NY
KATZ, MARCUS	47	M	LABR	RR	ZZZZ	NY
META	38	F	W	RR	ZZZZ	NY
BERTA	18	F	SP	RR	ZZZZ	NY
SOFIA	16	F	SP	RR	ZZZZ	NY
SIGMUND	11	M	CH	RR	ZZZZ	NY
RUBIN	8	M	CHILD	RR	ZZZZ	NY
SU---A	6	M	CHILD	RR	ZZZZ	NY
BURICH	4	M	CHILD	RR	ZZZZ	NY
SEGALL, G.CHAIM	23	M	LABR	RR	ZZZZ	NY
CHANE	24	F	W	RR	ZZZZ	NY
ROSENZWEIG, MARIE	16	F	SP	RR	ZZZZ	NY
AMALIE	15	F	SP	RR	ZZZZ	NY
PFLAUZER, SLATE	47	F	W	RR	ZZZZ	NY
ISAK	11	M	CH	RR	ZZZZ	NY
RUXEL	7	F	CHILD	RR	ZZZZ	NY
MARKUS	1	M	CHILD	RR	ZZZZ	NY
FRIEDMANN, CHANE	46	F	W	RR	ZZZZ	BO
ROSAWSKY, WOSSIE	18	M	LABR	RR	ZZZZ	BO
FRIEDMANN, MISCHKET	10	M	CH	RR	ZZZZ	BO
CARL	10	M	CH	RR	ZZZZ	BO
MUEL	8	M	CHILD	RR	ZZZZ	BO
HEUDEL	1	M	CHILD	RR	ZZZZ	BO
SARA	1	F	CHILD	RR	ZZZZ	BO
WEISS, DAVID	16	M	LABR	RR	ZZZZ	BO
SCHUHMAN, E.	14	M	LABR	RR	ZZZZ	BO
MOSES	28	M	LABR	RR	ZZZZ	BO
KOTTINEY, SAML.	37	M	LABR	RR	ZZZZ	BO
TIEVNER, EISIG	19	M	LABR	RR	ZZZZ	BO
ETTE	17	F	SP	RR	ZZZZ	BO
SANKOWSKA, D.	28	F	W	RR	ZZZZ	NY
C.	9	M	CHILD	RR	ZZZZ	NY
B.	6	M	CHILD	RR	ZZZZ	NY
R.	3	M	CHILD	RR	ZZZZ	NY
J.	1	M	CHILD	RR	ZZZZ	NY
C.	1	M	CHILD	RR	ZZZZ	NY
EISEN, MOSES	18	M	LABR	RR	ZZZZ	NY
BATTERSEN, ANN	25	F	SP	RR	ZZZZ	NY
JACUBOWITZ, RISI	18	M	LABR	RR	ZZZZ	NY

PASSENGER	A G E	S E X	OCCUPATION	P R V / V I L / D E S
UNGAR, KIND	28	F	W	RRZZZZNY
MCHL.	11	F	CH	RRZZZZNY
LEDER, LEI	10	F	CH	RRZZZZNY
SOLINDER, ABM.	24	M	LABR	RRZZZZNY
MAURER, PHILIP	29	M	LABR	RRZZZZPIT
SCHLESINGER, P.	20	M	LABR	RRZZZZPIT
ROSENBAUM, M.	17	M	LABR	RRZZZZPIT
STEINER, GITTEL	27	F	W	RRZZZZNY
EMMA	8	F	CHILD	RRZZZZNY
F.	6	M	CHILD	RRZZZZNY
BETTY	1	F	CHILD	RRZZZZNY
FELONFELD, M.	26	M	LABR	RRZZZZNY
HORORSSKY, C.D.	36	M	LABR	RRZZZZNY
R.D.	27	F	W	RRZZZZNY
ARON-H.	10	M	CH	RRZZZZNY
MOSES	5	M	CHILD	RRZZZZNY
HORRORSKY, J.	1	M	CHILD	RRZZZZNY
SMELSKY, GUSTAV	21	M	LABR	RRZZZZNY
SCHWARZ, JOSEF	50	M	LABR	RRZZZZNY
M.	6	M	CHILD	RRZZZZNY
KOLTWIETZ, SARA	16	F	SP	RRZZZZNY
TUCHFELD, RACHEL	35	F	W	RRZZZZNY
ABRAM	11	M	CH	RRZZZZNY
VICTOR	9	M	CHILD	RRZZZZNY
KREPLEK, M.	20	F	W	RRZZZZNY
F.	9	F	CHILD	RRZZZZNY
B.	7	F	CHILD	RRZZZZNY
ULANOWITZ, V.	40	M	LABR	RRZZZZNY
SCHELINSKY, M.	24	M	LABR	RRZZZZNY
GRUNWALD, H.	48	M	LABR	RRZZZZNY
KAFCONSKI, J.	27	M	LABR	RRZZZZNY
FISCHER, JACOB	23	M	LABR	RRZZZZNY
KREMER, AUG.	43	M	LABR	RRZZZZNY
LEO	30	F	W	RRZZZZNY
AMILIE	9	F	CHILD	RRZZZZNY
ALBERT	5	M	CHILD	RRZZZZNY
HEDWIG	1	M	CHILD	RRZZZZNY
LONDON, SORE	38	F	W	RRZZZZNY
NOTTE	11	M	CH	RRZZZZNY
NOACH	10	M	CH	RRZZZZNY
H.J.	6	M	CHILD	RRZZZZNY
J.	4	M	CHILD	RRZZZZNY
HORNSTEIN, BETZY	28	F	W	RRZZZZNY
MOCHE	8	M	CHILD	RRZZZZNY
R.BERG	28	F	W	RRZZZZNY
M.	3	M	CHILD	RRZZZZNY
LEIB	2	M	CHILD	RRZZZZNY
SORE	1	F	CHILD	RRZZZZNY
FEINSTEIN, B.	47	F	W	RRZZZZNY
N.	18	F	SP	RRZZZZNY
C.	7	M	CHILD	RRZZZZNY
G.	4	M	CHILD	RRZZZZNY
D.	2	M	CHILD	RRZZZZNY
CHELONSKY, MOSES	24	M	LABR	RRZZZZNY
SPIEWAK, J.	43	M	LABR	RRZZZZNY
HOLZHAGEL, A.	7	M	CHILD	RRZZZZNY
TOLORCZYK, ANDREAS	40	M	LABR	RRZZZZNY
ROSOWSKY, NATIA	17	F	SP	RRZZZZNY
ABRAHAM, JACOB	46	M	LABR	RRZZZZNY
S.	31	F	W	RRZZZZNY
N.	11	M	CH	RRZZZZNY
KOLINKIWICZ, JOSEF	30	M	LABR	RRZZZZNY
SNIEL, P.	40	M	LABR	RRZZZZNY
RAROWEIS, GEO	22	M	LABR	RRZZZZBO
DRONICUS, MICHL.	22	M	LABR	RRZZZZBO
GRACZHOWSKI, J.	22	M	LABR	RRZZZZNY
OSLOWAR, ANTON	27	M	LABR	RRZZZZNY
MARY	00	F	W	RRZZZZNY
AMELIA	3	F	CHILD	RRZZZZNY
B.	1	M	CHILD	RRZZZZNY
RAHYZYNA, M.	20	F	W	RRZZZZNY
J.	11	M	CH	RRZZZZNY
ANCA, WATSKA	20	M	LABR	RRZZZZNY
SITSAK, S.	23	M	LABR	RRZZZZNY
OBERATH, DORA	16	F	SP	RRZZZZNY

PASSENGER	A G E	S E X	OCCUPATION	P R V / V I L / D E S
ROSSTER, JOHANNA	18	F	SP	RRZZZZNY
TRAGIL, JACHOW	45	M	LABR	RRZZZZNY
DANIELOWITZ, E.	60	M	LABR	RRZZZZNY
GODEK, MICHL.	21	M	LABR	RRZZZZNY
KARDESWOTSKI, J.	32	M	LABR	RRZZZZNY
REKIEWIEZ, MARIANA	22	F	SP	RRZZZZNY
POWLOWIC, MILE	32	M	LABR	RRZZZZNY
KWIATKOWSKY, W.	38	M	LABR	RRZZZZNY
GORGEWITSCH, ROB.	23	M	LABR	RRZZZZNY
LEIGREYNICHT, GEO	14	M	LABR	RRZZZZNY
CISELIK, FRANK	32	M	LABR	RRZZZZNY
KUBLACHI, ANDR.	26	M	LABR	RRZZZZNY
LASKOWSKI, EVA	26	F	SP	RRZZZZNY
FANULONIS, P.	19	M	LABR	RRZZZZNY
CAPIGA, STAINE	26	M	LABR	RRZZZZNY
JANIE, JOS.	16	M	LABR	RRZZZZNY
MALZGA, JOHN	35	M	LABR	RRZZZZNY
MICHL.	32	M	LABR	RRZZZZNY
KOWALSKI, M.	24	M	LABR	RRZZZZNY
JOSEF	29	M	LABR	RRZZZZNY
MISKILL, JERZY	26	M	LABR	RRZZZZNY
KOWALEWSKI, S.	30	M	LABR	RRZZZZNY
MITOI, RABADO	26	M	LABR	RRZZZZNY
FREIKS, ELIZA	25	F	SP	RRZZZZNY
SATHOFF, JOHN	17	M	LABR	RRZZZZNY
LUKOWIEZ, J.	23	M	LABR	RRZZZZNY
MICHAL, HUDAK	24	M	LABR	RRZZZZNY
JOLT, JOHAN	22	M	LABR	RRZZZZNY
LECANY, MICO	29	M	LABR	RRZZZZBO
MACAN, GEORG	34	M	LABR	RRZZZZBO
SAMOWZSKA, H.	41	M	LABR	RRZZZZBO
ROSENSTRAUSS, R.	20	M	LABR	RRZZZZBO
BUCHHOLZ, MARTIN	57	F	LABR	RRZZZZBO
AUG.	20	F	LABR	RRZZZZBO
IDA	18	F	SP	RRZZZZBO
KLISZES, MAGA.	30	F	W	RRZZZZNY
MAGA	10	F	W	RRZZZZNY
PARZI	4	M	CHILD	RRZZZZNY
MARGANE	3	M	CHILD	RRZZZZNY
RUKSCHELZ, ANT.	26	M	LABR	RRZZZZNY
MOHRHARDT, JACOB	37	M	LABR	RRZZZZNY
WEMRAUB, KAL.	28	M	LABR	RRZZZZNY
HOBSGARTEN, WOLF	34	M	LABR	RRZZZZNY
REIZEMAN, SARA	19	F	SP	RRZZZZNY
KLEIN, MOSCHE	50	M	LABR	RRZZZZNY
BILE	45	F	W	RRZZZZNY
STERNBERG, EDD	20	M	LABR	RRZZZZNY
BRAUN, CHIEL	16	M	LABR	RRZZZZNY
KALCHSTEIN, D.	53	M	LABR	RRZZZZNY
LENI	43	F	W	RRZZZZNY
SALI	16	F	SP	RRZZZZNY
FAUNE	8	F	CHILD	RRZZZZNY
MSCHKOWITZ, MORITZ	38	M	LABR	RRZZZZNY
LELOWITZ, SAM.	26	M	LABR	RRZZZZNY
ROSENTHAL, D.	21	M	LABR	RRZZZZPHI
LITKAVET, ESTER	23	F	SP	RRZZZZPHI
EPSTEIN, SARA	10	F	CH	RRZZZZPHI
LEWITZKI, JANKEL	30	M	LABR	RRZZZZNY
CHANE	24	F	W	RRZZZZNY
BEILE	4	F	CHILD	RRZZZZNY
JOSSIE	1	F	CHILD	RRZZZZNY
LEWIN, B.	41	F	W	RRZZZZNY
G.	11	F	CH	RRZZZZNY
PAPE, HERM.	36	M	LABR	RRZZZZNY
LEWIN, SARA	27	F	W	RRZZZZNY
MOSES	6	M	CHILD	RRZZZZNY
PETEL	1	F	CHILD	RRZZZZNY
RAWZNIE, SENDOR	27	M	LABR	RRZZZZNY
PRUGAU, JUL.	28	F	SP	RRZZZZNY
PATZ, ADOLF	30	M	LABR	RRZZZZNY
HERBST, FRIED.	24	M	LABR	RRZZZZNY
JAGLER, AUG.	19	M	LABR	RRZZZZNY
TIN, TAUBE	22	F	W	RRZZZZNY
ITZIC	4	M	CHILD	RRZZZZNY
GUTTMAN, EISIC	19	M	LABR	RRZZZZNY

PASSENGER	AGE	SEX	OCCUPATION	PRV VIL DES
LUKS, ANNA	18	F	SP	RRZZZZNY
ANDR.	16	M	LABR	RRZZZZNY
JUSTINA	10	F	CH	RRZZZZNY
G.	4	M	CHILD	RRZZZZNY
STEF	3	M	CHILD	RRZZZZNY
BUDZISEK, ANNA	20	F	SP	RRZZZZNY
WERNER, AMALIE	25	F	SP	RRZZZZNY
HARNIG, FRED.	19	M	LABR	RRZZZZSTL
PRIESCHKOWSKY, SLATE	24	M	LABR	RRZZZZSTL
NIDECH, SCHKE	48	F	W	RRZZZZNY
MOSCHE	15	M	LABR	RRZZZZNY
SARA	14	F	SP	RRZZZZNY
ARON	10	M	CH	RRZZZZNY
CHAFE	9	M	CHILD	RRZZZZNY
RACHEL	7	F	CHILD	RRZZZZNY
JAKOB	4	M	CHILD	RRZZZZNY
ASCHER	3	M	CHILD	RRZZZZNY
LEIE	2	F	CHILD	RRZZZZNY
LICHENSTEIN, JETEL	17	M	LABR	RRZZZZNY
ROEWER, AUGUST	29	M	LABR	RRZZZZNY
MOZDZIECHZ, ADALLE	25	F	SP	RRZZZZNY
WIJCIECHOWSKI, ALEXR.	27	M	LABR	RRZZZZNY
MAKAREWITZ, TOMAS	27	M	LABR	RRZZZZNY
IMELKO, MICHAL	22	M	LABR	RRZZZZNY
MAKAREWITZ, ANTON	24	M	LABR	RRZZZZNY
IROMA, KAROL.	26	M	LABR	RRZZZZNY

SHIP: BRAUNSCHWEIG

FROM: BREMEN
TO: BALTIMORE
ARRIVED: 06 JUNE 1888

PASSENGER	AGE	SEX	OCCUPATION	PRV VIL DES
BEUMAN, ARRON	11	M	UNKNOWN	RRZZZZOH
KOSTOWSKY, MARYANNA	19	F	SVNT	RRZZZZIL
DURKOWSKA, PAULINE	25	F	UNKNOWN	RRZZZZIL
JACOB	.11	M	INFANT	RRZZZZIL
KLEIWS, KASIMUR	38	M	FARMER	RRZZZZIL
KOROLOWSKI, JOHANN	22	M	FARMER	RRZZZZIL
KIBIERT, PETER	30	M	FARMER	RRZZZZIL
ZENKICUREZ, IGNAZ	22	M	FARMER	RRZZZZNE
NARWELA, PAULINE	23	F	SVNT	RRZZZZNE
KOLASINSKI, IGNAZ	28	M	FARMER	RRZZZZNE
BREDES, MIKOLAY	23	M	FARMER	RRZZZZNE
PRISEWIEZ, JAN	30	M	FARMER	RRZZZZNE
KONATOWSKY, IWAN	26	M	FARMER	RRZZZZNE
TERACKIEWIEZ, JOSEF	36	M	FARMER	RRZZZZNE
WASILOWSKI, JAN	26	M	FARMER	RRZZZZNE
GLUZA, GERSCH	22	M	FARMER	RRZZZZWI
HELENA	16	F	SVNT	RRZZZZWI
JULIANA	50	F	M	RRZZZZWI
RADKOWITCH, JOHANN	43	M	FARMER	RRZZZZWI
SIEJA, VARZYN	39	M	FARMER	RRZZZZWI
BALBENA	28	F	W	RRZZZZWI
CARL	5	M	CHILD	RRZZZZWI
PETER	.06	M	INFANT	RRZZZZWI

SHIP: STATE OF NEVADA

FROM: GLASGOW AND LARNE
TO: NEW YORK
ARRIVED: 06 JUNE 1888

PASSENGER	AGE	SEX	OCCUPATION	PRV VIL DES
ARONSTEIN, JOSEF	28	M	MCHT	RRAIDLUSA
RELBER, SELR-	48	M	MCHT	RRAIDLUSA
MINNE	34	F	UNKNOWN	RRAIDLUSA
HERSCHEL	17	M	UNKNOWN	RRAIDLUSA
CHANE	11	F	UNKNOWN	RRAIDLUSA
ARON	10	M	CH	RRAIDLUSA
MANI	6	F	CHILD	RRAIDLUSA
REBEKKE	2	F	CHILD	RRAIDLUSA
TH.	1	F	CHILD	RRAIDLUSA
MOSES	.03	M	INFANT	RRAIDLUSA
BROTZKY, FREIDE	35	F	M	RRAIDLUSA
U, U	28	M	MCHT	RRAIDLUSA
ROSA	19	F	UNKNOWN	RRAIDLUSA
SOLOMON	20	M	UNKNOWN	RRAIDLUSA
MICHEL	1	M	CHILD	RRAIDLUSA
HIRSCH	.03	M	INFANT	RRAIDLUSA
BREKSTTIN, JOSEF	19	M	MCHT	RRAIDLUSA
DEITZ, EMMA	28	F	M	RRAIDLUSA
BASCHI	5	F	CHILD	RRAIDLUSA
ESTHER	2	F	CHILD	RRAIDLUSA
CHAJE	1	F	CHILD	RRAIDLUSA
DRAHOSEL, JOSEF	18	M	LABR	RRAIDLUSA
DALOW, SALOMON	28	M	MCHT	RRAIDLUSA
EHRLICH, ESTHER	40	F	M	RRAIDLUSA
SARAH	15	F	UNKNOWN	RRAIDLUSA
MOSES	11	M	CH	RRAIDLUSA
ABRAHAM	10	M	CH	RRAIDLUSA
RIEWKE	8	F	CHILD	RRAIDLUSA
TAUBE	6	F	CHILD	RRAIDLUSA
FASSEL	4	M	CHILD	RRAIDLUSA
DWORE	2	F	CHILD	RRAIDLUSA
MORDSCHE	1	M	CHILD	RRAIDLUSA
EJPSLEIN, SARAH	17	F	SVNT	RRAIDLUSA
SCHULE	13	F	UNKNOWN	RRAIDLUSA
JETE	10	F	CH	RRAIDLUSA
GINS, SCHINDIR	26	M	MCHT	RRAIDLUSA
GARZOW, REISEL	50	F	M	RRAIDLUSA
ABRAH	18	M	UNKNOWN	RRAIDLUSA
SALOMON	15	M	UNKNOWN	RRAIDLUSA
RACHEL	9	F	CHILD	RRAIDLUSA
GAWLE, JOSEF	40	M	MCHT	RRAIDLUSA
ENTE	25	F	UNKNOWN	RRAIDLUSA
CHAJE	2	F	CHILD	RRAIDLUSA
JOHANNE	.09	F	INFANT	RRAIDLUSA
GERBER, WOLF	23	M	PNTR	RRAIDLUSA
GROPPEN, SALOMON	31	M	TLR	RRAIDLUSA
GONB, LINA	22	F	SVNT	RRAIDLUSA
HESCHKE, SARAH	30	F	M	RRAIDLUSA
ISAK	4	M	CHILD	RRAIDLUSA
HENNAK, JANOS	24	M	LABR	RRAIDLUSA
HARZAN, MEYER	24	M	MCHT	RRAIDLUSA
CHAJE	20	F	W	RRAIDLUSA
HOFMAN, BERTHA	20	F	SVNT	RRAIDLUSA
JASTRONG, SCHN.	50	M	MCHT	RRAIDLUSA
PATZKOWSKY, M.	00	F	SVNT	RRAIDLUSA
ANTON	18	M	LABR	RRAIDLUSA
JENITZKY, FRANCYCZEK	40	M	LABR	RRAIDLUSA
GUTKEWICZ, JOSEF	24	M	LABR	RRAIDLUSA
JOCHMUD, CZERNE	20	F	SVNT	RRAIDLUSA
KAUFMANN, NACHUM	22	M	MCHT	RRAIDLUSA
RACHEL	20	F	W	RRAIDLUSA
KLEIN, IGNATZ	36	M	MCHT	RRAIDLUSA
RACHEL	23	F	UNKNOWN	RRAIDLUSA
MALWIN	2	M	CHILD	RRAIDLUSA
KILBORN, DWORE	36	F	M	RRAIDLUSA
MARIE	11	F	CH	RRAIDLUSA
LEB	2	M	CHILD	RRAIDLUSA
SAML.	1	M	CHILD	RRAIDLUSA
KOTZKO, JANKO	26	M	LABR	RRAIDLUSA
KATZENKLATSCHER, LEISER	37	M	MCHT	RRAIDLUSA
HIRSCHE	28	F	UNKNOWN	RRAIDLUSA
JANKEL	27	M	UNKNOWN	RRAIDLUSA
BARUCH	11	M	CH	RRAIDLUSA
ELZI	10	M	CH	RRAIDLUSA
KAPLAN, ROCHE	20	F	SVNT	RRAIDLUSA
KATZENHLATSCHER, BARUCH	21	M	MCHT	RRAIDLUSA
KILINSER, HIRSCH	27	M	MCHT	RRAIDLUSA

PASSENGER	AGE	SEX	OCCUPATION	PRVL	VIL	DES
LEMBERG, HINDE	26	F	M	RR	AIDL	USA
LEWIEN, RENZEL	27	M	MCHT	RR	AIDL	USA
LEIKIND, RACHEL	51	F	M	RR	AIDL	USA
DIRSKE	50	F	M	RR	AIDL	USA
GNOCHE	28	F	UNKNOWN	RR	AIDL	USA
MARIANNA	25	F	UNKNOWN	RR	AIDL	USA
ANNE	17	F	UNKNOWN	RR	AIDL	USA
ROTHEL	16	F	UNKNOWN	RR	AIDL	USA
RIEWKA	2	F	CHILD	RR	AIDL	USA
SARAH	.09	F	INFANT	RR	AIDL	USA
RACHEL	20	F	UNKNOWN	RR	AIDL	USA
LASER, HERMAN	28	M	MCHT	RR	AIDL	USA
LEWIEN, JOSSEL	19	M	MCHT	RR	AIDL	USA
HAMES	65	M	MCHT	RR	AIDL	USA
U	30	F	M	RR	AIDL	USA
GEO	10	M	CH	RR	AIDL	USA
SARAH	3	F	CHILD	RR	AIDL	USA
NARERKIS, JOSEF	35	M	LABR	RR	AIDL	USA
NELSON, BORCHE	17	F	SVNT	RR	AIDL	USA
JPESCHTIN, JANOS	10	M	CH	RR	AIDL	USA
PARSNEWSKY, WLADISLAW	24	M	LABR	RR	AIDL	USA
JOSEPHA	20	F	W	RR	AIDL	USA
ROSENBLATH, MIRIAM	55	F	UNKNOWN	RR	AIDL	USA
CHANE	21	F	UNKNOWN	RR	AIDL	USA
CZERNE	8	F	CHILD	RR	AIDL	USA
SUNDEL	28	M	UNKNOWN	RR	AIDL	USA
RIPOZOWSKI, MORDSCHE	26	M	MCHT	RR	AIDL	USA
ROZAZINSKY, ABR.	18	M	MCHT	RR	AIDL	USA
SLABOGEN, JOSSEL	33	M	MCHT	RR	AIDL	USA
JAKOB	25	M	MCHT	RR	AIDL	USA
BROSCHE	24	F	W	RR	AIDL	USA
SCHIME	1	F	CHILD	RR	AIDL	USA
SCHASINSKY, LERE	50	F	M	RR	AIDL	USA
SKLOW, GEDALJE	32	M	MCHT	RR	AIDL	USA
SCHAJE	30	M	MCHT	RR	AIDL	USA
SUJEKA, FRANCISCA	18	F	M	RR	AIDL	USA
SCZEWCZAK, JAN	30	M	LABR	RR	AIDL	USA
FRANCYCZEK	25	M	LABR	RR	AIDL	USA
SELISKY, ATSAH	30	M	MCHT	RR	AIDL	USA
ARON	18	M	MCHT	RR	AIDL	USA
MENSCHE	17	M	MCHT	RR	AIDL	USA
JALL	16	M	MCHT	RR	AIDL	USA
SAPHIR, RAPHAEL	33	M	MCHT	RR	AIDL	USA
OILBERSTEIN, VICTOR	36	M	MCHT	RR	AIDL	USA
STEHBERG, JANCKEL	36	M	MCHT	RR	AIDL	USA
SOPHIE	26	F	W	RR	AIDL	USA
TEDILKOWSKY, NIRSCH	29	M	MCHT	RR	AIDL	USA
TCZIASKI, MORDSCHE	30	M	MCHT	RR	AIDL	USA

SHIP: CITY OF ROME

FROM: LIVERPOOL AND QUEENSTOWN
TO: NEW YORK
ARRIVED: 07 JUNE 1888

PASSENGER	AGE	SEX	OCCUPATION	PRVL	VIL	DES
PAPKIN, ABIN	22	M	SHMK	RR	ADAX	USA
MEYERS, HARRIS	28	M	TLR	RR	ADAX	USA
GOLDSTER, JOH	22	M	TLR	RR	ADAX	USA
MARDEL, TRINKER	26	M	LABR	RR	ADAX	USA
SCHIENKMAN, DOBE	35	F	W	RR	ADAX	USA
MOWE	19	F	SVNT	RR	ADAX	USA
CLAM	16	F	SVNT	RR	ADAX	USA
SCHEINKMAN, ZEDIDIE	8	F	CHILD	RR	ADAX	USA
ZECHNE	1	F	CHILD	RR	ADAX	USA
OLKENTZKY, RODE	21	F	W	RR	ADAX	USA
DABE	2	F	CHILD	RR	ADAX	USA
BLOCK, MARGASCHE	19	F	SVNT	RR	ADAX	USA
RUDMICKI, JUDEL	38	M	CL	RR	ADAX	USA

SHIP: WAESLAND

FROM: ANTWERP
TO: NEW YORK
ARRIVED: 08 JUNE 1888

PASSENGER	AGE	SEX	OCCUPATION	PRVL	VIL	DES
STEPANOWKSI, ANAST.	20	M	LABR	RR	ZZZZ	NY
EISENBERG, CHRIS-J.	35	M	MCHT	RR	ZZZZ	NY
GRABOWSKI, CAROLINE	26	F	SVNT	RR	ZZZZ	NY
RANKE, CARL	28	M	BKR	RR	ZZZZ	NY
GERTD.	20	F	BKR	RR	ZZZZ	NY
HORENBERG, MOISE	27	M	CGRMKR	RR	ZZZZ	NY
ABRAMOWITZ, ABRAM	26	M	CGRMKR	RR	ZZZZ	NY
WEINTTSCHMIDT, MATTH.	26	M	MCHT	RR	ZZZZ	NY
KURZ, CHAJE	16	F	TLR	PL	ZZZZ	NY
SCHEIN	11	M	TLR	PL	ZZZZ	NY
WEIL, SARA	9	F	CHILD	PL	ZZZZ	NY
ZUECKER, CHEIDEL	26	F	CH	PL	ZZZZ	NY
ITER	5	F	CHILD	PL	ZZZZ	NY
SCHLUERER, JOSEPH	25	M	LABR	RR	ZZZZ	NY
SABIK, JOHANN	36	M	LABR	RR	ZZZZ	NY
KOPELOWITZ, ANELE	26	M	CBTMKR	RR	ZZZZ	NY
SCHMUTOVITZ, MOISCHE	45	M	BCHR	RR	ZZZZ	NY
SEW-EW, SCHMERL	25	M	LABR	RR	ZZZZ	NY
PEISHO, LEVIN	24	M	WCHMKR	RR	ZZZZ	NY
OLEWINSKI, FRANZ	33	M	LABR	PL	ZZZZ	NY
GLODFKI, HEINR.	22	M	LABR	RR	ZZZZ	NY

SHIP: CALIFORNIA

FROM: HAMBURG
TO: NEW YORK
ARRIVED: 08 JUNE 1888

PASSENGER	AGE	SEX	OCCUPATION	PRVL	VIL	DES
PETROWIN, AGATHE	18	M	LABR	RR	ZZZZ	NY
BLONSTROTZ, WITOLIJI	20	M	LABR	RR	ZZZZ	NY
WAYSKEWEZ, TEKLA	18	F	UNKNOWN	RR	ZZZZ	NY
PAWLOWSKA, ANIELA	20	F	UNKNOWN	RR	ZZZZ	NY
SIEGFRIED	.11	M	INFANT	RR	ZZZZ	NY
DENSKI, JULIUS	19	M	LABR	RR	ZZZZ	NY
PSZYBYLSKA, MARIANNA	20	F	SVNT	RR	ZZZZ	NY
GIRAITIS, JOAHNN	35	M	LABR	RR	ZZZZ	NY
ROMANSWIEZ, FABIAN	26	M	LABR	RR	ZZZZ	NY
KARLOWICZ, ANTON	24	M	LABR	RR	ZZZZ	NY
GOCTOLSKY, LEON	25	M	LABR	RR	ZZZZ	NY
ANIELA	24	F	W	RR	ZZZZ	NY
SCHAPIRO, RACHEL	45	F	CK	RR	ZZZZ	NY
RUBEN	15	M	FARMER	RR	ZZZZ	NY
JACOB	9	M	CHILD	RR	ZZZZ	NY
CHANNE	8	M	CHILD	RR	ZZZZ	NY
LEBANZ, CARL	34	M	LABR	RR	ZZZZ	NY
RYPCZENSKI, JAN	34	M	LABR	RR	ZZZZ	NY
RODKIEWICZ, PETER	31	M	LABR	RR	ZZZZ	NY
JETKE, CAROL	19	M	BKR	RR	AIIX	USA
BARAS, ANDRUS	39	M	LABR	RR	AIIX	NY
HOWARTOWICZ, JAN	28	M	LABR	RR	AIIX	NY
SZANDZOWA, ANNA	35	F	WO	RR	AIIX	NY
ANNA	2	F	CHILD	RR	AIIX	NY
JUREWICZ, ALEXANDER	25	M	LABR	RR	AIIX	NY
BULEKA, ANNA	19	F	UNKNOWN	RR	AIIX	NY
ANTON	14	M	UNKNOWN	RR	AIIX	NY
JAN	9	M	CHILD	RR	AIIX	NY
ARVULATIC, HAMIELA	16	M	FARMER	RR	AIIX	NY
NIMILANY, RAHEL	30	F	UNKNOWN	RR	AIIX	NY
MAGID, CHANNE	38	M	LABR	RR	AIIX	NY
SOFIA	34	F	SVNT	RR	AIIX	NY
MARK	4	M	CHILD	RR	AIIX	NY
SCHLODOWSKY, ISIDOR	27	M	LABR	RR	AIIX	NY
PINTSCHER, ABRAHAM	31	M	LABR	RR	AIIX	NY

PASSENGER	AGE	SEX	OCCUPATION	PRIVIL	DES
GERSCHANSTEIN, JOSSEL	39	M	LABR	RRAIIXNY	
ZONIE	34	F	UNKNOWN	RRAIIXNY	
SCHLOME	8	M	CHILD	RRAIIXNY	
MOSES	4	M	CHILD	RRAIIXNY	
GOLDE	2	M	CHILD	RRAIIXNY	
STASZKA, JOSEF	30	M	FARMER	RRAIIXUSA	
GRUENBLATH, DAVID	28	M	FARMER	RRAIIXNY	
CHAJS	26	F	UNKNOWN	RRAIIXNY	
JACOB	10	M	CH	RRAIIXNY	
FEIWEL	8	F	CHILD	RRAIIXNY	
RACHEL	7	F	CHILD	RRAIIXNY	
TAUBE	5	F	CHILD	RRAIIXNY	
RINKE	3	F	CHILD	RRAIIXNY	
GAIDA, CAROLINA	18	F	SVNT	RRAIIXNY	
HERMANN	20	M	FARMER	RRAIIXNY	
ELISABETH	16	F	UNKNOWN	RRAIIXNY	
EUGENIE	9	F	CHILD	RRAIIXNY	
FRITZ	8	M	CHILD	RRAIIXNY	
SANDLER, PAVUEL	32	M	SHMK	RRAIIXNY	
ANTALEK, KASPER	25	M	LABR	RRAIIXNY	
MYER, SOPHIE	21	F	SVNT	RRAIIXNY	
WISMIESKA, ROSALIE	18	F	SVNT	RRAIIXNY	
SLAWIENSKI, WOJICICH	30	M	UNKNOWN	RRAIIXNY	
KAZINSNISKI, FRANZISZEK	40	M	LABR	RRAIIXNY	
WEINSTEIN, LAZAR	32	M	LABR	RRAIIXNY	
AMRASAILIS, KASIMIR	27	M	LABR	RRAIIXNY	
KAPITROSKI, KASIMIR	24	M	LABR	RRAIIXNY	
WEINSTEIN, FEIZ	25	M	SHMK	RRAIIXNY	
ARANCWICZ, MENDEL	30	M	TLR	RRAIIXNY	
DEBORAH	26	F	W	RRAIIXNY	
SZEMANSKI, FRANZISZEK	41	M	LABR	RRAIIXNY	
WSZELAKI, VACLAW	14	M	LABR	RRAIIXNY	
LIETZKE, JOHANN	24	M	SHMK	RRAIIXNY	
SMISZYNSKA, CONSTANTIN	44	M	LABR	RRAIIXNY	
WISNIEWSKI, ALEXANDER	27	M	UNKNOWN	RRAIIXNY	
CZOZOSKI, JOSEF	23	M	LABR	RRAIIXSP	
SCJOCLER, CHRISTIAN	23	M	LABR	RRAIIXUSA	
PUWAZERSIS, VINCENTI	25	M	LABR	RRAIIXUSA	
KOSLOWSKI, KARL	36	M	LABR	RRAIIXUSA	
KIRSHBAUM, BENJAMIN	23	M	PNTR	RRAIIXUSA	
MARTIN, PENJUK	24	M	LABR	RRAIIXUSA	
KALINOWSKI, JOSEF	21	M	LABR	RRAIIXUSA	
JANKOWSKI, MARTIN	24	M	LABR	RRAIIXUSA	
KOSLAWSKI, STANISLAW	25	M	LABR	RRAIIXUSA	
TRATZKEVITZ, ANTON	24	M	LABR	RRAIIXUSA	
FALKENBERG, FERDINAND	27	M	LABR	RRAIIXUSA	
PAULINE	21	F	W	RRAIIXUSA	
MOGDANY, EMILIE	17	F	SGL	RRAIIXUSA	
SCHALLER, GUSTAV	23	M	LABR	RRAIIXUSA	
JOHANNA	24	F	W	RRAIIXUSA	
KALLIN, LOUISE	21	F	SGL	RRAIIXUSA	
GASTER, JOHANNA	16	F	SGL	RRAIIXUSA	
GOTTFRIED	46	M	SMH	RRAIIXUSA	
AMALIE	42	F	W	RRAIIXUSA	
WILHELM	11	M	CH	RRAIIXUSA	
JOHANN	4	M	CHILD	RRAIIXUSA	
TEOFILA	.09	F	INFANT	RRAIIXUSA	
WILLWORK, HEINRICH	43	M	UNKNOWN	RRAIIXUSA	
JOHANNA	16	F	D	RRAIIXUSA	
GLAESKE, JOHANNA	53	F	SVNT	RRAIIXUSA	
MATHILDE	16	F	CH	RRAIIXUSA	
HERMANN	14	M	CH	RRAIIXUSA	
GASTER, WILHELM	14	F	SGL	RRAIIXUSA	
SCHAMMHA, AUGUST	30	M	LABR	RRAIIXUSA	
ERNESTINE	66	F	WO	RRAIIXUSA	
KLATH, FERDINAND	24	M	FARMER	RRAIIXUSA	
JULIANE	25	F	W	RRAIIXUSA	
GUSTAV	.09	M	INFANT	RRAIIXUSA	

SHIP: GELLERT

FROM: HAMBURG AND HAVRE
TO: NEW YORK
ARRIVED: 09 JUNE 1888

PASSENGER	AGE	SEX	OCCUPATION	PRIVIL	DES
ACKERMANN, MECLACH	18	M	LABR	RRZZZZUSA	
FINKELSTEIN, FRANC	19	F	SGL	RRZZZZUSA	
HAUTANEN, MATTI	40	M	LABR	FNZZZZUSA	
HIROCLAM, ISAAC	38	M	LABR	FNZZZZUSA	
ULISCLA, TOMAS	40	M	LABR	FNZZZZUSA	
HAMAKA, ELIAS	18	M	LABR	FNZZZZUSA	
HIETCKKO, OSCAR	23	M	LABR	FNZZZZUSA	
DEUTSCH, ADOLPH	31	M	SHMK	FNZZZZUSA	
HERGWICH, BARIE	16	M	LABR	RRZZZZUSA	
SABAS, ANNA	21	F	W	RRZZZZUSA	
MILERIS, JANOS	21	M	LABR	RRZZZZUSA	
WARHAFTIG, ARNOLD	21	M	MCHT	RRZZZZUSA	
MINZ, ALEXANDER	20	M	MCHT	RRZZZZUSA	
FORSBUKA, JACOB	24	M	LABR	FNZZZZUSA	
FORSTBOUD, KARL	34	M	LABR	FNZZZZUSA	
SAROISTA, JOHANN	26	M	LABR	FNZZZZUSA	
KOSOLA, KARL	19	M	LABR	FNZZZZUSA	
PAPIHATO, MATTS	23	M	LABR	FNZZZZUSA	
WICORI, HERMANN	19	M	LABR	FNZZZZUSA	
RINTA, MICHAEL	17	M	LABR	FNZZZZUSA	
TURJA, MATTS	19	M	LABR	FNZZZZUSA	
MUSTUMAKI, GABRIEL	19	M	LABR	FNZZZZUSA	
KASARI, MATTS	23	M	LABR	FNZZZZUSA	
FORSBACKA, ANNA	22	F	SGL	FNZZZZUSA	
WARU, SIMON	20	M	LABR	FNZZZZUSA	
WARNA, JOHANN	35	M	LABR	FNZZZZUSA	
ANDERSEN, TOMAS	26	M	LABR	FNZZZZUSA	
LOEBENSTEIN, ABRAM	15	M	DLR	RRZZZZUSA	
TOMASZEWSKI, ADOLF	36	M	LABR	RRZZZZUSA	
HELENE	31	F	W	RRZZZZUSA	
EDUARD	2	M	CHILD	RRZZZZUSA	
ZADIKOWITZ, CHIO	18	M	LABR	RRZZZZUSA	
ESTHER	9	F	CHILD	RRZZZZUSA	
JOFFA, LOTTA	24	F	WO	RRZZZZUSA	
LEIB	.11	M	INFANT	RRZZZZUSA	
SCHWARTZ, DAVID	55	M	LABR	RRZZZZUSA	
EVA	55	F	W	RRZZZZUSA	
EMILIE	16	F	D	RRZZZZUSA	
SCHIMANSKI, KARL	23	M	LABR	RRZZZZUSA	
FIEDLER, GUSTAV	13	M	LABR	RRZZZZUSA	
KATKIWICZ, ANDREW	20	M	LABR	RRZZZZUSA	
SIGEL, CHAIM	44	M	TLR	RRZZZZUSA	
ANTERLOWICZ, ANTONI	23	M	LABR	RRZZZZUSA	
KATZ, NACHEM	19	M	CL	RRZZZZUSA	
SERMANN, BARUCH	17	M	DLR	RRZZZZUSA	
WITTEN, JOSEPH	19	M	LABR	RRZZZZUSA	
MIKLISCHAUSKI, MORDCHE	50	M	LABR	RRZZZZUSA	
SILBERMANN, ABRAM	25	M	LABR	RRZZZZUSA	
FERGENSON, CIRLA	20	F	SGL	RRZZZZUSA	
REICH, CARL	31	M	LABR	RRZZZZUSA	
GUTSTEIN, ABRAM	55	M	DLR	RRZZZZUSA	
DWORE	50	F	W	RRZZZZUSA	
SCHAPIRA, TAUBE	17	F	SGL	RRZZZZUSA	
MORKOUSKI, SARAH	18	F	SGL	RRZZZZUSA	
GUTSTEIN, ISAAC	20	M	LABR	RRZZZZUSA	
FINKELSTEIN, NAPHTOLI	9	M	CHILD	RRZZZZUSA	
GUBEROWA, URSULA	40	F	WO	RRZZZZUSA	
ANTON	9	M	CHILD	RRZZZZUSA	
MARIANNA	4	F	CHILD	RRZZZZUSA	
SEYER, CARL	44	M	FARMER	RRZZZZUSA	
SCHWEIG, JACOB	30	M	SMH	RRZZZZUSA	
PADEREWSKY, JULI	30	M	ACHTT	RRZZZZUSA	
SALOMEA	18	F	SGL	RRZZZZUSA	
SZCZESNA, MARTHA	20	F	SGL	RRZZZZUSA	
PEPEKE, CHANNE	26	F	WO	RRZZZZUSA	
SARAH	18	F	SGL	RRZZZZUSA	
BERESCH	7	M	CHILD	RRZZZZUSA	
BERLE	5	M	CHILD	RRZZZZUSA	

PASSENGER	AGE	SEX	OCCUPATION	PRIV	DES
MORDCHE	6	M	CHILD	RRZZZZ	USA
ROTHBERG, WOLF	17	M	DLR	RRZZZZ	USA
GERMAN, NOCHEM	37	M	SMH	RRZZZZ	USA
WOYTOWICZ, VINCENZ	29	M	LABR	RRZZZZ	USA
SCHWARZ, LEA	25	F	WO	RRZZZZ	USA
LIDA	.11	F	INFANT	RRZZZZ	USA
ZIELEWICOWA, ANTONIA	44	F	WO	RRZZZZ	USA
JULIE	22	F	SGL	RRZZZZ	USA
MARIANNA	15	F	SGL	RRZZZZ	USA
MESCHKUTZ, NOSSEL	25	M	DLR	RRZZZZ	USA
MARIAKIEWICZ, ADOLF	36	M	LABR	RRZZZZ	USA
RISMANN, MR.	26	M	LABR	RRZZZZ	USA
JACOB	9	M	CHILD	RRZZZZ	USA
GUDANSKY, MENDEL	40	M	LABR	RRZZZZ	USA
SCHITKOWSKY, MERLECH	40	M	LABR	RRZZZZ	USA
STAROSZINSKI, PESCHE	16	F	SGL	RRZZZZ	USA
MIEL, MALKE	35	F	WO	RRZZZZ	USA
ROCHE	9	F	CHILD	RRZZZZ	USA
MORDCHE	8	M	CHILD	RRZZZZ	USA
ALBE	4	M	CHILD	RRZZZZ	USA
JANKEL	.11	M	INFANT	RRZZZZ	USA
TEPLITZ, SALOMON	18	M	CL	RRZZZZ	USA
PUSSEN, JANE	23	F	SGL	RRZZZZ	USA
FRANK, JANKEL	18	M	TLR	RRZZZZ	USA
SCHUKLAWSKY, WOLF	13	M	LABR	RRZZZZ	USA
KRIEGER, KASSRIEL	18	M	SHMK	RRZZZZ	USA
WEITENSTEIN, ABRAM	23	M	TLR	RRZZZZ	USA
SCHAPIRSKY, MEYER	20	M	DLR	RRZZZZ	USA
MICHEL, ISRAEL	28	M	DLR	RRZZZZ	USA
MICHELOW, JANKEL	28	M	DLR	RRZZZZ	USA
GORDON, SALMEN	17	M	DLR	RRZZZZ	USA
MIRSKY, ISRAEL	29	M	DLR	RRZZZZ	USA
LAZAR, SARAH	36	F	WO	RRZZZZ	USA
GITE	59	F	WO	RRZZZZ	USA
ISAAC	8	M	CHILD	RRZZZZ	USA
JENTE	6	F	CHILD	RRZZZZ	USA
MENDEL	5	M	CHILD	RRZZZZ	USA
NESCHE	.11	M	INFANT	RRZZZZ	USA
MAEKELA, MATTS	19	M	FARMER	FNZZZZ	USA
GILLMANN, ROSA	25	F	WO	RRZZZZ	USA
PAUZA, THOMAS	48	M	LABR	RRZZZZ	USA
SCHMOLKOWITZ, JUDES	18	F	SGL	RRZZZZ	USA
ORKIN, SAMUEL	29	M	TLR	RRZZZZ	USA
BAROL, ISAAC	25	M	LABR	RRZZZZ	USA
GOTTHOLD, PEISACH	18	M	DLR	RRZZZZ	USA
FEIN, EISIG	23	M	DLR	RRZZZZ	USA
MEIERSCH, EISIG	27	M	DLR	RRZZZZ	USA
LAWANDOWSKI, MIECISLAW	18	M	LABR	RRZZZZ	USA
TIBURSKI, ANTON	32	M	LABR	RRZZZZ	USA
ARDANOWSKI, JAN	35	M	LABR	RRZZZZ	USA
MALINOWSKI, IGNATZ	17	M	LABR	RRZZZZ	USA
WEINTRAUB, GMUNDEL	26	F	WO	RRZZZZ	USA
HANNE	8	F	CHILD	RRZZZZ	USA
MOSES	.11	M	INFANT	RRZZZZ	USA
KOPCZANSKI, SARAH	25	F	WO	RRZZZZ	USA
JACOB	5	M	CHILD	RRZZZZ	USA
DOBE	.11	F	INFANT	RRZZZZ	USA
TOBIAS, ADOLPH	24	M	MCHT	RRZZZZ	USA
WILDSBEIN, ABRAHAM	30	M	MCHT	RRZZZZ	USA
SARAH	20	F	W	RRZZZZ	USA
ZERWANSKI, RUWEN	18	M	MCHT	RRZZZZ	USA
ULUCK, ITZIG	35	M	LABR	RRZZZZ	USA
REIMANN, WILHELM	26	M	LABR	RRZZZZ	USA
RESCHEINSKA, CHAIM	23	M	LABR	RRZZZZ	USA
TISCHLER, WILHELM	28	M	BKBNDR	RRZZZZ	USA
MIESKAWSKI, ALPHONS	26	M	FARMER	RRZZZZ	USA
LEWIN, REBECCA	44	F	WO	RRZZZZ	USA
ROSALIE	8	F	CHILD	RRZZZZ	USA
MAX	6	M	CHILD	RRZZZZ	USA
ANNA	20	F	SGL	RRZZZZ	USA
AMALIE	18	F	SGL	RRZZZZ	USA
AXELROD, RISCHE	40	F	WO	RRZZZZ	USA
NECHAME	17	F	CH	RRZZZZ	USA
DWORSCHE	15	F	CH	RRZZZZ	USA
ROCHE	7	F	CHILD	RRZZZZ	USA
ITZIK	5	M	CHILD	RRZZZZ	USA
RAKOW, LEIB	19	M	DLR	RRZZZZ	USA
ROSHITZKI, ABRAM	18	M	DLR	RRZZZZ	USA
PETREWITZ, OSIF	24	M	LABR	RRZZZZ	USA
SIGMUND, JOSEPH	27	M	LABR	RRZZZZ	USA
SCHIASKO, BONIFAC.	20	M	LABR	RRZZZZ	USA
MESIS, IGNATZ	27	M	LABR	RRZZZZ	USA
PRAUIS, VINCENTI	24	M	LABR	RRZZZZ	USA
ROCH, GILIS	26	M	LABR	RRZZZZ	USA
CANNER, FRANZ	25	M	LABR	RRZZZZ	USA
BREWA, CASIMIR	26	M	LABR	RRZZZZ	USA
SOFOS, CASIMIR	45	M	LABR	RRZZZZ	USA
MICKUS, JAN	24	M	LABR	RRZZZZ	USA
MIOSUS, MATIAS	35	M	LABR	RRZZZZ	USA
ALIOSUS, U	15	M	LABR	RRZZZZ	USA
U, U	22	M	WO	RRZZZZ	USA
WOJTKMAAS, JIRZI	22	M	WO	RRZZZZ	USA
PRILULAS, ALEXANDER	26	M	WO	RRZZZZ	USA
JULIE	26	M	WO	RRZZZZ	USA
SPULGUNAS, GAB	27	M	WO	RRZZZZ	USA
ROSEWITSCH, JORGI	24	M	WO	RRZZZZ	USA
MOTISAL, CHRISTOPH	28	M	WO	RRZZZZ	USA
GOLDSTEIN, CIRRIL	18	M	TNM	RRZZZZ	USA
SMILISKY, LINE	20	F	SGL	RRZZZZ	USA
SPRINTZ, AUGUSTE	19	F	SGL	RRZZZZ	USA
GRUENBLATT, CATHARINA	20	F	SGL	RRZZZZ	USA
SILKAS, ANDRAS	49	M	LABR	RRZZZZ	USA
KARBOWICZ, ANTON	24	M	LABR	RRZZZZ	USA
SCHLOSSER, AUGUST	39	M	LABR	RRZZZZ	USA
DAMSCHARL, LUDWIG	20	M	LABR	RRZZZZ	USA
JOSEFA	18	M	LABR	RRZZZZ	USA
JESSEN, ANNA	58	F	WO	RRZZZZ	USA
ANNIE	26	F	SGL	RRZZZZ	USA
ODIN, JULIE	28	F	SGL	RRZZZZ	USA
KRAUSE, WILHELM	16	M	MCHT	RRZZZZ	USA

SHIP: CITY OF BERLIN

FROM: LIVERPOOL AND QUEENSTOWN
TO: NEW YORK
ARRIVED: 09 JUNE 1888

PASSENGER	AGE	SEX	OCCUPATION	PRIV	DES
GEMIA, WYCIK	20	M	LABR	RRAFWJ	NY
ZEMINSKI, JOSEPH	20	M	LABR	RRAFWJ	NY
KRUIK, WOICI	20	M	LABR	RRAFWJ	NY
LENMAN, ADOLF	38	M	LABR	RRAFWJ	NY
KUKI, SLIK	30	M	LABR	RRAFWJ	NY
ROLUB, ML	14	M	LABR	RRAFWJ	NY
FRINSIKI, JACOB	32	M	LABR	RRAFWJ	NY
EINIS, LILIE	30	F	W	RRAFWJ	NY
U	5	F	CHILD	RRAFWJ	NY
U	3	F	CHILD	RRAFWJ	NY
ORANSTEIN, MOSES	42	M	LABR	RRAFWJ	NY
LUSSI	19	F	SVNT	RRAFWJ	NY
ISRAEL	17	M	LABR	RRAFWJ	NY
HANNI	15	F	NRS	RRAFWJ	NY
GALNSTEIN, WOLF	36	M	LABR	RRAFWJ	NY
GOLDA	10	F	CH	RRAFWJ	NY
MORS, MOSES	29	M	LABR	RRACBF	PHI
HAIMZES, JACOB	21	M	LABR	RRACBF	PHI
FRANKELL, JOS	16	M	LABR	RRACBF	PHI
AUGENSTEIN, JOS	11	M	LABR	RRACBF	PHI
MAKAMA, V	45	F	W	RRACBF	PHI
FEEN, MINA	28	F	W	RRACBF	PHI
PESCHE	00	F	INF	RRACBF	PHI
WEINBERG, MARIA	18	F	LABR	RRACBF	PHI
HERSCHOWITZ, DAVID	25	M	LABR	RRACBF	PHI
ROSA	22	F	W	RRACBF	PHI
BELSER, CHAIE	43	F	W	RRACBF	PHI
AMELIE	36	F	W	RRACBF	PHI

PASSENGER	AGE	SEX	OCCUPATION	PRIVL	VIL	DES
FANNY	21	F	LABR	RRACBFPHI		
SOFIE	20	F	LABR	RRACBFPHI		
JACOB	19	M	LABR	RRACBFPHI		
ARTHUR	00	M	LABR	RRACBFPHI		
ISRAEL	10	M	CH	RRACBFPHI		
TIMI	4	M	CHILD	RRACBFPHI		
RUCK, FREAK	41	M	LABR	RRACBFPHI		
HENRIETTE	36	F	W	RRACBFPHI		
BERTHA	9	F	CHILD	RRACBFPHI		
ALBT	7	M	CHILD	RRACBFPHI		
ADOLPH	3	M	CHILD	RRACBFPHI		
ERNEST	00	M	INF	RRACBFPHI		
DUNCYEWITZ, SCHMAL	46	M	LABR	RRACBFPHI		
JUDIS	45	F	W	RRACBFPHI		
ESTHER	20	F	LABR	RRACBFPHI		
PERL	18	M	LABR	RRACBFPHI		
ELKE	16	F	LABR	RRACBFPHI		
ISRAEL	11	M	CH	RRACBFPHI		
TYNNE	9	F	CHILD	RRACBFPHI		

SHIP: ALLER

FROM: BREMEN
TO: NEW YORK
ARRIVED: 09 JUNE 1888

PASSENGER	AGE	SEX	OCCUPATION	PVD
SIPNITSKY, ISIDOR	23	M	FARMER	RRZZZZUSA
MATUSCHEWITZ, IGNATZ	45	M	FARMER	RRZZZZUSA
GURONIA, CASIMIR	41	M	FARMER	RRZZZZUSA
CZWITMINSKI, MARCUS	46	M	FARMER	RRZZZZUSA
HIRSCH, ABRAHAM	20	M	FARMER	RRZZZZUSA
NIRWITZ, ISAAK	26	M	FARMER	RRZZZZUSA
SCHUSTER, ISER	20	M	FARMER	RRZZZZUSA
MANOWITZ, STANISL.	22	M	FARMER	RRZZZZUSA
BECKMANN, S--BE	27	M	FARMER	RRZZZZUSA
BERNSTEIN, BERUH	00	M	FARMER	RRZZZZUSA
SCHAPIRO, HILLER	29	M	FARMER	RRZZZZUSA
WASKOWITZ, MAJEM	25	M	FARMER	RRZZZZUSA
MELLER, ISAAK	36	M	FARMER	RRZZZZUSA
LEWI, SALKE	20	M	FARMER	RRZZZZUSA
NIE-LBALSKI, ADAM	46	M	FARMER	RRZZZZUSA
SULKA, AUGUST	35	M	FARMER	RRZZZZUSA
ROSENFELD, SELIG	29	M	FARMER	RRZZZZUSA
KAMINSKI, ISRAEL	35	M	FARMER	RRZZZZUSA
OLOREWSKI, JOSEF	27	M	FARMER	RRZZZZUSA
BADENKOWITZ, ANDR.	22	M	FARMER	RRZZZZUSA
WANAZIRN, JONAS	25	M	FARMER	RRZZZZUSA
SEGINSKY, JAN	30	M	FARMER	RRZZZZUSA
ZEGINZKAS, WINZAS	25	M	FARMER	RRZZZZUSA
BRAZULIS, FRONERS	33	M	FARMER	RRZZZZUSA
LEGUS, WINCAS	22	M	FARMER	RRZZZZUSA
ZEGINKUS, ISIDOR	24	M	FARMER	RRZZZZUSA
BASTIN, ANTON	20	M	FARMER	RRZZZZUSA
JUDISCKY, JOSES	24	M	FARMER	RRZZZZUSA
KONWISSER, MOSES	50	M	FARMER	RRZZZZUSA
ZIPL, JAN	35	M	FARMER	RRZZZZUSA
SCHUMANITZKY, ABRAH.	26	M	FARMER	RRZZZZUSA
LEVIN, CHANI	23	M	FARMER	RRZZZZUSA
SCHMEHE, NATHAN	27	M	FARMER	RRZZZZUSA
ZURWIETZ, BENZE	28	M	FARMER	RRZZZZUSA
JOJA, CATHI	28	F	UNKNOWN	RRZZZZUSA
FENNER, EVA	23	F	UNKNOWN	RRZZZZUSA
SLACH, MARIE	16	F	UNKNOWN	RRZZZZUSA
ULRIANEK, ANNA	20	F	UNKNOWN	RRZZZZUSA
GOLLABOCK, MELANIE	18	F	UNKNOWN	RRZZZZUSA
BROCKMANN, MINNA	17	F	UNKNOWN	RRZZZZUSA
MUENDE, CHAJEM	34	M	FARMER	RRZZZZUSA
SARAH	16	F	UNKNOWN	RRZZZZUSA
SALOMON	7	M	CHILD	RRZZZZUSA
BLOCH, HILLA	21	F	UNKNOWN	RRZZZZUSA

PASSENGER	AGE	SEX	OCCUPATION	PVD
DORE	23	F	UNKNOWN	RRZZZZUSA
BELER, PAULINE	23	F	UNKNOWN	RRZZZZUSA
IRMA	2	F	CHILD	RRZZZZUSA
SCHAKSEN, ABRAHAM	28	M	MCHT	RRZZZZUSA
SALOMONA	25	F	W	RRZZZZUSA
HORDON, ELIJUS	22	M	MCHT	RRZZZZUSA
NESHME	18	F	W	RRZZZZUSA
LANDAU, ISAAK	53	M	GDNR	RRZZZZUSA
U	00	M	CH	RRZZZZUSA
KAPERTA, KATE	30	F	UNKNOWN	RRZZZZUSA
MARIE	.09	F	INFANT	RRZZZZUSA
HANTLIC, JPETER	49	M	FARMER	RRZZZZUSA
MATHES	16	M	CH	RRZZZZUSA
KIVAS, MARIE	25	F	UNKNOWN	RRZZZZUSA
ROSA	7	F	CHILD	RRZZZZUSA

SHIP: REPUBLIC

FROM: LIVERPOOL
TO: NEW YORK
ARRIVED: 11 JUNE 1888

PASSENGER	AGE	SEX	OCCUPATION	PVD
BJORKLUND, M.	21	M	LABR	RRZZZZUSA
STAAL, VICTOR	00	M	LABR	PLZZZZUSA
DRYKOLASKE, J.E.	00	M	LABR	PLZZZZUSA
SKAFEN, PEDER-O.	16	M	MNR	PLZZZZUSA
FOSSE, JOHANNES-J.	20	M	LABR	PLZZZZUSA
ORZECHOWYKI, FRAULY	00	M	LABR	PLZZZZUSA
FILDERFINI, GITTEL-F.	36	F	W	PLZZZZUSA
STULL	16	M	MNR	PLZZZZUSA
CHAGUS	7	M	CHILD	PLZZZZUSA
CHONE	5	F	CHILD	PLZZZZUSA
FELDESTERN, M.	36	M	LABR	PLZZZZUSA
SHEFLER, BERL	18	M	LABR	PLZZZZUSA
HERSCH, DAVID	26	M	LABR	PLZZZZUSA
BENN, SAMUEL	17	M	LABR	PLZZZZUSA
KELBER, M.	30	M	LABR	PLZZZZUSA
PLATE, ZAKNIAS	44	M	LABR	PLZZZZUSA
TRYGG, FRANTZ-A.	23	M	LABR	PLZZZZUSA
CHRISTINA	66	F	HSKPR	PLZZZZUSA
ROSENYARITZ, MOSES	22	M	LABR	PLZZZZUSA
OSCHEROWITZ, LEISER	26	M	LABR	PLZZZZUSA

SHIP: SERVIA

FROM: LIVERPOOL AND QUEENSTOWN
TO: NEW YORK
ARRIVED: 11 JUNE 1888

PASSENGER	AGE	SEX	OCCUPATION	PVD
SCHAPIRO, HENECK	20	M	LABR	RRZZZZPA
BORROWSKY, MOSES	18	M	LABR	RRZZZZNY
GUTTMAN, MOSES	30	M	LABR	RRZZZZNY
BLECHER, ISAK	40	M	LABR	RRZZZZNY
KOLLOWSKY, JOSEPH	25	M	LABR	RRZZZZNY
KOCINSKY, LUDWIG	27	M	LABR	RRZZZZNY
ROJDANSKY, JOHAN	29	M	LABR	RRZZZZNY
ENDRICH, DOMMINICH	27	M	LABR	RRZZZZNY
RUEBANDWITZ, PETER	21	M	LABR	RRZZZZNY
ROSKOWSKY, JONAS	25	M	LABR	RRZZZZNY
SOFIS, KAZ	45	M	LABR	RRZZZZNY
ELISCHEWITZ, JANKEL	20	M	LABR	RRZZZZNY
TWIANSKIF, MARCIN	40	M	LABR	RRZZZZNY
RIEMGEIL, FRITZ	31	M	LABR	RRZZZZNY
SONEID, JOHAN	55	M	LABR	RRZZZZNY
RUNKOWSKY, FRANZ	44	M	LABR	RRZZZZNY

PASSENGER	AGE	SEX	OCCUPATION	PRV VIL DES
FELDMAN, JACOB	33	M	LABR	RRZZZZNY
FRANZ	10	M	CH	RRZZZZNY
KRAULIS, ANDRE	31	M	LABR	RRZZZZNY
FELDMAN, KARL	28	M	LABR	RRZZZZNY
WILSON, ADAM	25	M	LABR	RRZZZZNY
ORSON, PERT	27	M	LABR	RRZZZZNY
GNITAL, LYNAZ	28	M	LABR	RRZZZZNY
SOLOWAG, PERSON	20	M	LABR	RRZZZZNY
KARPET, EISIG	10	M	CH	RRZZZZNY
SILZNOW, LIPAM	30	M	LABR	RRZZZZNY
LONOWZEWSKI, HAZNI	45	M	LABR	RRZZZZNY
FRIEDMANN, ESTER	19	F	SP	RRZZZZNY
GUMENCHAS, DOLGAURH	45	M	LABR	RRZZZZNY
GRUNOWSKI, JONAS	26	M	LABR	RRZZZZNY
VALVADA, JOSEF	28	M	LABR	RRZZZZNY
GAWAS, PETER	27	M	LABR	RRZZZZNY
CHWILOWSKI, MOSES	17	M	LABR	RRZZZZNY
ROSENBLUM, ISAAC	23	M	CGRMKR	RRZZZZNY
DWOR, BASCHE	20	F	SP	RRZZZZNY
SOLZ, ROSA	22	F	SP	RRZZZZNY
MARIENHOFF, ETTE	17	F	SP	RRZZZZNY
SELBERMAN, SELDE	26	F	W	RRZZZZNY
HJADE	6	F	CHILD	RRZZZZNY
GESE	4	F	CHILD	RRZZZZNY
CHAJE	.10	F	INFANT	RRZZZZNY
LEA	28	F	W	RRZZZZNY
GODEL	6	M	CHILD	RRZZZZNY
CHAJE	4	F	CHILD	RRZZZZNY
ABRAHAM	.10	M	INFANT	RRZZZZNY
GOLDBERG, DAORE	32	F	W	RRZZZZNY
DAVID	10	M	CH	RRZZZZNY
CHAJE	8	F	CHILD	RRZZZZNY
ROCHEL	6	F	CHILD	RRZZZZNY
SARAH	4	F	CHILD	RRZZZZNY
REBECCA	.10	F	INFANT	RRZZZZNY
BUCGHRACH, JULIUS	22	M	BKPR	RRZZZZNY
IDA	22	F	W	RRZZZZNY
EICHENBAUM, CATARINA	20	F	SP	RRZZZZIL
CARL	16	M	LABR	RRZZZZIL
REGINE	10	F	CH	RRZZZZIL
CILLA	9	F	CHILD	RRZZZZIL
ROSENBERG, MARY	50	F	W	RRZZZZNY
LEHAH	16	F	SP	RRZZZZNY
KANGAS, JOHAN	26	M	LABR	RRZZZZMN
REUTHER, WILLIAM	18	M	LABR	RRZZZZMI
KOSKI, JAKOB	28	M	LABR	RRZZZZCAL
JOH	19	M	LABR	RRZZZZCAL
SIBAKKA, LUEKMIUS	31	M	LABR	RRZZZZCAL
BRZOZOWSKI, JOSEF	18	M	PNTR	RRZZZZNY
STUEZKA, ANTON	32	M	LABR	RRZZZZNY
BASINSKA, MARIANNE	21	F	SP	RRZZZZNY
FORUTA, KASIMIR	57	M	LABR	RRZZZZNY
HELENA	57	F	W	RRZZZZNY
ADILE	14	F	SP	RRZZZZNY
JOSEPH	10	M	CH	RRZZZZNY

SHIP: DEVONIA

FROM: GLASGOW AND MOVILLE
TO: NEW YORK
ARRIVED: 11 JUNE 1888

PASSENGER	AGE	SEX	OCCUPATION	PRV VIL DES
ROM, CHNE	30	F	UNKNOWN	RRAIDLUSA
RIFKE	12	F	UNKNOWN	RRAIDLUSA
FREIDE	11	F	UNKNOWN	RRAIDLUSA
ASRAN	9	M	CHILD	RRAIDLUSA
HERRMAN	6	M	CHILD	RRAIDLUSA
SCHER	2	M	CHILD	RRAIDLUSA
GOLDBERG, SORE	30	F	UNKNOWN	RRAIDLUSA
HIRSCH	10	M	CH	RRAIDLUSA
JOCHE	5	F	CHILD	RRAIDLUSA
HENNE	2	F	CHILD	RRAIDLUSA
JUDE	1	M	CHILD	RRAIDLUSA
CHEHNIEWOJS, CATH.	38	F	UNKNOWN	RRAIDLUSA
JOS.	7	M	CHILD	RRAIDLUSA
JULIA	4	F	CHILD	RRAIDLUSA
THERESE	.10	F	INFANT	RRAIDLUSA
FRANKINSKY, CLARA	18	F	UNKNOWN	RRAIDLUSA
PUNSKI, DWIRE	50	F	UNKNOWN	RRAIDLUSA
RIFKE	30	F	UNKNOWN	RRAIDLUSA
SARAH	8	F	CHILD	RRAIDLUSA
HIRSCH	3	F	CHILD	RRAIDLUSA
LUSEROWA, BLUME	25	F	UNKNOWN	RRAIDLUSA
JANKEL	2	M	CHILD	RRAIDLUSA
SORE	1	F	CHILD	RRAIDLUSA
PRENSKE, PAULINE	36	F	UNKNOWN	RRAIDLUSA
BLANDIE	3	F	CHILD	RRAIDLUSA
ALFRED	1	M	CHILD	RRAIDLUSA
ZIMERMAN, KREINE	35	F	UNKNOWN	RRAIDLUSA
FIESEL	10	F	CH	RRAIDLUSA
NATHAN	8	M	CHILD	RRAIDLUSA
DERENGOWSKI, JOSEF	25	M	MNR	RRAIDLUSA
SUSANNA	19	F	UNKNOWN	RRAIDLUSA
SCHBERSTEIN, ZIPE	18	F	UNKNOWN	RRAIDLUSA
DAVID	1	M	CHILD	RRAIDLUSA
URDANG, BEILE	26	F	UNKNOWN	RRAIDLUSA
ABR.	1	M	CHILD	RRAIDLUSA
BLANSTEIN, ESTER	18	F	UNKNOWN	RRAIDLUSA
HENNE	18	F	UNKNOWN	RRAIDLUSA
BUNJAKOWSKI, THEKLA	24	F	SVNT	RRAIDLUSA
HARTMAN, CHANE	17	F	SVNT	RRAIDLUSA
JAFFE, ASNE	45	F	SVNT	RRAIDLUSA
LEWIN, SUSCHE	35	F	SVNT	RRAIDLUSA
LITOWITZ, FRUME	20	F	SVNT	RRAIDLUSA
LEISEROWITZ, ROCHE	21	F	SVNT	RRAIDLUSA
ZELKA, EMMA	18	F	SVNT	RRAIDLUSA
BLOZYP, JOKOB	26	M	LABR	RRAIDLUSA
BARHENELSKY, ISAK	28	M	LABR	RRAIDLUSA
BARANEKTAS, KAZIS	18	M	LABR	RRAIDLUSA
BROLINZKY, DAV.	21	M	LABR	RRAIDLUSA
BERGMAN, ELIAS	36	M	SHMK	RRAIDLUSA
BIELOWSKY, FRANZ	23	M	CPTR	RRAIDLUSA
CHAN, JOS	34	M	LABR	RRAIDLUSA
CAJKOWSKY, LEON	20	M	LABR	RRAIDLUSA
DAVIDOWITZ, HIRSCH	43	M	LABR	RRAIDLUSA
GRATOWSKY, ANTONAS	30	M	LABR	RRAIDLUSA
GONCHAREWITSCH, CONSTAN	20	M	LABR	RRAIDLUSA
GRINEWITSCH, CONST.	38	M	LABR	RRAIDLUSA
GOTTHOLD, JANKEL	33	M	LABR	RRAIDLUSA
HARRIS, HYMAN	31	M	LABR	RRAIDLUSA
HEBEL, JOH.	44	M	LABR	RRAIDLUSA
JOFSOREK, AUGT.	33	M	LABR	RRAIDLUSA
JAFFE, ADOLF	24	M	LABR	RRAIDLUSA
HURA, JANOS	11	M	UNKNOWN	RRAIDLUSA
JONASS, BENJ.	38	M	LABR	RRAIDLUSA
JAHN, NACHUNN	40	M	LABR	RRAIDLUSA
KOHN, GEDALJE	18	M	LABR	RRAIDLUSA
KASIMIRSKY, VICTOR	21	M	LABR	RRAIDLUSA
KUNKRO, JANKEL	27	M	LABR	RRAIDLUSA
KOSSEMAR, ABRAHAM	13	M	UNKNOWN	RRAIDLUSA
KLUSEITIS, VICENTY	25	M	LABR	RRAIDLUSA
KOSLAWSKY, PETER	22	M	LABR	RRAIDLUSA
LARIN, PESACH	18	M	LABR	RRAIDLUSA
JUDEL	22	M	LABR	RRAIDLUSA
LENDUESKI, RUVM	26	M	LABR	RRAIDLUSA
MANIOR, SAVEL	30	M	CPTR	RRAIDLUSA
MABULA, ADAM	22	M	LABR	RRAIDLUSA
MOREKA, ADAM	23	M	LABR	RRAIDLUSA
MOWSOWITZ, URIE	45	M	LABR	RRAIDLUSA
MEIEROWITZ, ELIE	33	M	LABR	RRAIDLUSA
MATUKEITIS, JONAS	24	M	LABR	RRAIDLUSA
MERSCHOWITZ, WOLF	21	M	LABR	RRAIDLUSA
NETSCHINSKY, LEON	38	M	LABR	RRAIDLUSA
PLAZKIN, NIKOLAI	24	M	LABR	RRAIDLUSA
PATAGINSKY, IGNATZ	20	M	LABR	RRAIDLUSA

PASSENGER	AGE	SEX	OCCUPATION	PRIV	DES
RIBEN, CHAIM	25	M	LABR	RRAIDL	USA
RENNIS, MATHEUS	21	M	MNR	RRAIDL	USA
RAND, HERRY	35	M	TLR	RRAIDL	USA
REIDER, BEINISCH	22	M	LABR	RRAIDL	USA
SALOMON, CHAIM	19	M	LABR	RRAIDL	USA
SCHAUFER, MOSES	35	M	LABR	RRAIDL	USA
SOBALOWSKY, JURGIS	20	M	LABR	RRAIDL	USA
SOLOGUL, BARTOLOMIS	22	M	LABR	RRAIDL	USA
SCHEWZSELD, MATHIUS	28	M	LABR	RRAIDL	USA
SZEMANIEK, MERE	23	F	UNKNOWN	RRAIDL	USA
SAMULIS, SASEMIR	24	M	LABR	RRAIDL	USA
STUDNETZKY, LEIE	40	F	UNKNOWN	RRAIDL	USA
SIRUSAS, FERENION	19	M	LABR	RRAIDL	USA
URDANG, BEHR.	37	M	SHMK	RRAIDL	USA
URSTINOWITSCH, KASIMIR	24	M	LABR	RRAIDL	USA
WENZULUS, PETRAS	26	M	LABR	RRAIDL	USA

SHIP: EIDER

FROM: BREMEN AND SOUTHAMPTON
TO: NEW YORK
ARRIVED: 12 JUNE 1888

PASSENGER	AGE	SEX	OCCUPATION	PRIV	DES
MARLINKAJTIS, JOSEF	25	M	FARMER	RRZZZZ	USA
KRINZLER, SALI	30	M	UNKNOWN	RRZZZZ	USA
HERM	8	M	CHILD	RRZZZZ	USA
ADOLF	6	M	CHILD	RRZZZZ	USA
MARGA	4	F	CHILD	RRZZZZ	USA
LEOPOLD	.11	M	INFANT	RRZZZZ	USA
BERGER, IDA	24	F	UNKNOWN	RRZZZZ	USA
HELENE	.11	F	INFANT	RRZZZZ	USA
KLUNEWSKI, LUDW	23	M	FARMER	RRZZZZ	USA
CIESIENZKEMMBRENI, JOH	24	M	LABR	RRZZZZ	USA
POSPIECK, JOH	24	M	LABR	RRZZZZ	USA
MENZINSKY, RINA	32	F	UNKNOWN	RRZZZZ	USA
CSYZE	10	F	CH	RRZZZZ	USA
CHAJE	9	F	CHILD	RRZZZZ	USA
ESTER	7	F	CHILD	RRZZZZ	USA
ABRAHAM	5	M	CHILD	RRZZZZ	USA
HERBST, ALMA	17	F	UNKNOWN	RRZZZZ	USA
PALMBAUM, BASCHE	55	F	MLR	RRZZZZ	USA
U, U	16	M	TLR	RRZZZZ	USA
---HAMSON, ANDR	18	M	MCHT	RRZZZZ	USA
SOSSKIN, SALOMON	30	M	DLR	RRZZZZ	USA
BASCHE	25	F	W	RRZZZZ	USA
JONIEF, ISAAK	23	M	TNM	RRZZZZ	USA
ZIMERKA, MATRIA	27	F	UNKNOWN	RRZZZZ	USA
LUCKNEWITZ, VICENTY	20	M	LABR	RRZZZZ	USA
WISURDY, WICES	26	M	LABR	RRZZZZ	USA
ZAPLA, VICETTY	26	M	LABR	RRZZZZ	USA
KOIWITZKY, TAMUSCH	23	M	LABR	RRZZZZ	USA
BIEBER, CARL	28	M	LABR	RRZZZZ	USA
REGINE	25	F	W	RRZZZZ	USA
LOUISE	.11	F	INFANT	RRZZZZ	USA
WILH	19	M	LABR	RRZZZZ	USA
KLAR, SAM	52	M	MCHT	RRZZZZ	USA
MATEL	28	M	MCHT	RRZZZZ	USA
CHEICKE	20	F	UNKNOWN	RRZZZZ	USA
HERSCH	11	M	UNKNOWN	RRZZZZ	USA
RIFKE	8	F	CHILD	RRZZZZ	USA
ARON	.11	M	INFANT	RRZZZZ	USA
HARM, HEINRICH	35	M	LABR	RRZZZZ	USA
MARIANNE	32	F	W	RRZZZZ	USA
EMMA	9	F	CHILD	RRZZZZ	USA
ADOLF	8	M	CHILD	RRZZZZ	USA
FERDINAD	7	M	CHILD	RRZZZZ	USA
FELIX	4	M	CHILD	RRZZZZ	USA
JOHANN	2	M	CHILD	RRZZZZ	USA
OLGA	.11	F	INFANT	RRZZZZ	USA
KARPINSKI, WICENTY	21	M	LABR	RRZZZZ	USA
VOLKMANN, WILH	42	M	LABR	RRZZZZ	USA
CHICEK, JONDEL	40	M	LABR	RRZZZZ	USA
BIRKI, CHAWO	22	M	LABR	RRZZZZ	USA
ZUCHOSAIT, MOTCHE	18	F	UNKNOWN	RRZZZZ	USA
LEIB---, HIRSCH	00	M	MCHT	RRZZZZ	USA
STEFANOWITZ, JOS	41	M	MCHT	RRZZZZ	USA
RUSSKI, ANTON	26	M	LABR	RRZZZZ	USA
WALMTOMOWITZ, PAWEL	23	M	LABR	RRZZZZ	USA
OLMINSKY, BER	20	M	LABR	RRZZZZ	USA
ROSENHOLZ, ISER	19	M	LABR	RRZZZZ	USA
HORWITZ, MARKUS	18	M	LABR	RRZZZZ	USA
KRUGLAK, MOSES	33	M	LABR	RRZZZZ	USA
LANDEMANN, ABRAH	24	M	LABR	RRZZZZ	USA
HURWITZ, SCHLOMA	18	F	UNKNOWN	RRZZZZ	USA
ELMESSKY, ROCHEL	20	F	UNKNOWN	RRZZZZ	USA
SAMAROW, ISAAK	31	M	FARMER	RRZZZZ	USA
HJASCHEWITZ, JOSEF	23	M	LABR	RRZZZZ	USA
PALOTZEK, REBECCA	17	F	UNKNOWN	RRZZZZ	USA
EDELMANN, FENOMIA	27	F	UNKNOWN	RRZZZZ	USA
LEWIN, PAULE	17	F	UNKNOWN	RRZZZZ	USA
ABELOWITZ, MOSES	24	M	CNF	RRZZZZ	USA
POLATZEK, KANE	20	F	UNKNOWN	RRZZZZ	USA
KLIBEMSKY, ELIAS	48	M	LABR	RRZZZZ	USA
KOSCHMANN, LUDWIG	29	M	LABR	RRZZZZ	USA
STAHE, CARL	29	M	LABR	RRZZZZ	USA
AMETNIK, RUDOLF	28	M	LABR	RRZZZZ	USA
HINVER, JOSEPH	30	M	LABR	RRZZZZ	USA
NEWIGRADSKY, HIRSCH	25	M	LABR	RRZZZZ	USA
DRANJELES, WINCENTE	30	M	LABR	RRZZZZ	USA
BECKEWITSCH, WINZES	28	M	LABR	RRZZZZ	USA
SUHAITSCH, AGATHE	21	F	UNKNOWN	RRZZZZ	USA
BREWEK, JANKEL	34	M	LABR	RRZZZZ	USA

SHIP: SPAIN

FROM: LIVERPOOL AND QUEENSTOWN
TO: NEW YORK
ARRIVED: 12 JUNE 1888

PASSENGER	AGE	SEX	OCCUPATION	PRIV	DES
HESSEN, CARL	24	M	LABR	RRAHOO	USA
FREEDHOFF, HERMAN	21	M	LABR	RRAHOO	USA
OKIN, MOSES	18	M	LABR	RRAHOO	USA
KERN, ABRAM	29	M	LABR	RRAHOO	USA
PORBRAND, ESIK	40	M	LABR	RRAHOO	USA
FREEDMAN, MEAUL.	30	M	LABR	RRAHOO	USA
SPRIDY, SAML.	33	M	LABR	RRAHOO	USA
YAFFEN, JOSEPH	27	M	LABR	RRAHOO	USA
GOBLEST, JANKEL	29	M	LABR	RRAHOO	USA
NYLANER, LAZAR	26	M	LABR	RRAHOO	USA
LERRTS, LEIB	40	M	LABR	RRAHOO	USA
HASHMAN, JULUS	29	M	LABR	RRAHOO	USA
MULLEKANGAS, MATTE	33	M	LABR	RRAHOO	USA
STUSKARN, JOHN	26	M	LABR	RRAHOO	USA
WAHTELM, JAKOB	30	M	LABR	RRAHOO	USA
SOBOLENSKY, W.	24	M	LABR	RRAHOO	USA
KENIAJHE, MORRIS	20	M	LABR	RRAHOO	USA
SEVANHELDER, ENGLE	24	M	LABR	RRAHOO	USA
KRUNAN, J.	29	M	LABR	RRAHOO	USA
SANGER, M.E.	20	M	LABR	RRAHOO	USA
BARCHE, ABRAHAM	16	M	LABR	RRAHOO	USA
PESIN, ABRAHAM	19	M	LABR	RRAHOO	USA
BEGORK, CARL	38	M	LABR	RRAHOO	USA
BELBER, CARL	21	M	LABR	RRAHOO	USA
GELDERT, S.	22	M	LABR	RRAHOO	USA
HOLTMANN, JOHAN	50	M	LABR	RRAHOO	USA
DRYNSKA, JUDA	48	M	LABR	RRAHOO	USA
SHERMAN, MENDEL	20	M	LABR	RRAHOO	USA
TOPPER, S.	21	M	LABR	RRAHOO	USA
JOHENSKIS, B.	20	M	LABR	RRAHOO	USA
BITMEDECH, ISAC	36	M	LABR	RRAHOO	USA

PASSENGER	AGE	SEX	OCCUPATION	PRV	VIL	DES
DORBECK, SAML.	35	M	LABR	RR	AHOO	USA
KINLANDER, JAK.	25	M	LABR	RR	AHOO	USA
HORN, PETER	24	M	LABR	RR	AHOO	USA
G-GOWER, C.	26	F	LABR	RR	AHOO	USA
DROBESCH, B.	26	F	LABR	RR	AHOO	USA
KOHSIN, C.	19	F	LABR	RR	AHOO	USA
GRENBERG, H.	35	F	LABR	RR	AHOO	USA
SHARY, W.	20	F	LABR	RR	AHOO	USA
TESCHER, WOLF	40	F	LABR	RR	AHOO	USA
TURBE	17	F	LABR	RR	AHOO	USA
SAMAR	19	F	LABR	RR	AHOO	USA
COLIN, BAIL	20	F	LABR	RR	AHOO	USA
SALASEN, J.	28	F	LABR	RR	AHOO	USA
ARSHBELL, A.	20	F	LABR	RR	AHOO	USA
KAMPMAN, GITTE	17	F	LABR	RR	AHOO	USA
LEIB	11	M	CH	RR	AHOO	USA
BALSAM, ESTHER	18	F	SVNT	RR	AHOO	USA
LOSENSKEY, S.	45	M	LABR	RR	AHOO	USA
PENKE	18	M	LABR	RR	AHOO	USA
WALLMER, JETTE	20	M	LABR	RR	AHOO	USA
ZWAIG, CHAI	18	F	SVNT	RR	AHOO	USA
KAMFARAN, CLARE	55	F	W	RR	AHOO	USA
EVE	18	F	SVNT	RR	AHOO	USA
MARRDA	11	F	CH	RR	AHOO	USA
SPREDY, CHAEN	22	F	SVNT	RR	AHOO	USA
SPENAK, CHAS.	26	M	LABR	RR	AHOO	USA
BUZE	22	F	W	RR	AHOO	USA
M.	6	F	CHILD	RR	AHOO	USA
S.	.06	F	INFANT	RR	AHOO	USA
GABRIELSEN, G.A.	30	M	LABR	RR	AHOO	USA
HEESTREIN	47	F	W	RR	AHOO	USA
JENNY	11	F	CH	RR	AHOO	USA
LEEBKIN, N.	22	F	SVNT	RR	AHOO	USA
SARIN, LEESER	35	F	SVNT	RR	AHOO	USA
SPEGER, JADEL	40	M	LABR	RR	AHOO	USA
SARAH	40	F	W	RR	AHOO	USA
ABE	12	M	CH	RR	AHOO	USA
MOSES	9	M	CHILD	RR	AHOO	USA
MALKA	7	M	CHILD	RR	AHOO	USA
VICTOR	5	M	CHILD	RR	AHOO	USA
ERIKSEN, ANNA-M.	2	F	CHILD	RR	AHOO	USA
HESTELHEIN, E.A.	31	M	LABR	RR	AHOO	USA
OHNE	28	F	W	RR	AHOO	USA
ANDRES	10	M	CH	RR	AHOO	USA
LAVINA	3	F	CHILD	RR	AHOO	USA
U	.03	F	INFANT	RR	AHOO	USA
ZUCKARMAN, E.	27	M	LABR	RR	AHOO	USA
STENBER, C.	20	M	LABR	RR	AHOO	USA
WASSENBERG, HANNAH	38	F	W	RR	AHOO	USA
JETTY	3	F	CHILD	RR	AHOO	USA
DEETSCH, BASCHE	18	F	SVNT	RR	AHOO	USA
ZIPE	11	F	CH	RR	AHOO	USA
DUNBREN, J.	26	M	LABR	RR	AHOO	USA
FEELDMAN, SLATER	23	M	LABR	RR	AHOO	USA
GRUMSPAIN, ALEX	20	M	LABR	RR	AHOO	USA
SCHULLYKE, JOHAN	43	M	LABR	RR	AHOO	USA
COHEN, RAHEL	22	F	SVNT	RR	AHOO	USA
SEEGAN	21	F	SVNT	RR	AHOO	USA
COHN, SIMON	52	M	LABR	RR	AHOO	USA
SLIVA	44	F	W	RR	AHOO	USA
GESTEL	17	F	SVNT	RR	AHOO	USA
FANNY	15	F	SVNT	RR	AHOO	USA
JADAL	14	F	SVNT	RR	AHOO	USA
REDAL	11	F	CH	RR	AHOO	USA
ABE	9	M	CHILD	RR	AHOO	USA
MALLY	6	F	CHILD	RR	AHOO	USA
HENRY	2	M	CHILD	RR	AHOO	USA
HEINRICH	.10	M	INFANT	RR	AHOO	USA
FLUMAN, C.	24	F	W	RR	AHOO	USA
ABE	2	M	CHILD	RR	AHOO	USA
HERSCH	.08	M	INFANT	RR	AHOO	USA
RAPPEPORT, HERSCH	45	M	LABR	RR	AHOO	USA
BARRAVSKY, BENN	35	F	W	RR	AHOO	USA
A.	7	M	CHILD	RR	AHOO	USA
LEAH	6	F	CHILD	RR	AHOO	USA
COHN, ROSA	20	F	SVNT	RR	ZZZZ	USA
BOSKERTEH, ELEN	10	F	CH	RR	ZZZZ	USA
SANATISKY, MASECAS	10	F	CH	RR	ZZZZ	USA
SPERAK, DAVID	35	M	LABR	RR	ZZZZ	USA
MANGEL, ESTHER	16	F	SVNT	RR	ZZZZ	USA
SCHURKEN, JETCHEN	38	M	LABR	RR	ZZZZ	USA
RASCHI	38	F	W	RR	ZZZZ	USA
CHAST	15	F	SVNT	RR	ZZZZ	USA
WOLF	8	M	CHILD	RR	ZZZZ	USA
EKEL	4	M	CHILD	RR	ZZZZ	USA
HERVEL	2	M	CHILD	RR	ZZZZ	USA
BERNSTEIN, BLUME	22	F	W	RR	ZZZZ	USA
CLARA	.06	F	INFANT	RR	ZZZZ	USA
ILIEN, ALINE	19	F	SVNT	RR	ZZZZ	USA
ABERSTEIN, NATHAN	20	M	LABR	RR	ZZZZ	USA
HEINSTETE, SCHEIN	29	F	W	RR	ZZZZ	USA
JANKEL	5	M	CHILD	RR	ZZZZ	USA
SIMON	.10	M	INFANT	RR	ZZZZ	USA
SPANTZ, JANKEL	56	M	LABR	RR	ZZZZ	USA
PERL	54	F	W	RR	ZZZZ	USA
LEIB	26	M	LABR	RR	ZZZZ	USA
BRACH	22	F	SVNT	RR	ZZZZ	USA
JANET	.10	F	INFANT	RR	ZZZZ	USA
KERRA, OVA	36	F	SVNT	RR	ZZZZ	USA
RACHEL	21	F	SVNT	RR	ZZZZ	USA
KINE	23	F	SVNT	RR	ZZZZ	USA
SOLOMAN	19	M	LABR	RR	ZZZZ	USA
ARENTES, SCHEIN	47	F	W	RR	ZZZZ	USA
ORENWETZ, SANTEL	47	M	LABR	RR	ZZZZ	USA
WOLBRAND, CLARA	20	F	SVNT	RR	ZZZZ	USA
ROTHWEN, LESSER	60	M	LABR	RR	ZZZZ	USA
ROTHMAN, ALTA	32	F	W	RR	ZZZZ	USA
SARAH	10	F	CH	RR	ZZZZ	USA
U	.06	F	INFANT	RR	ZZZZ	USA
LEPSTETZ, CLARA	50	F	W	RR	ZZZZ	USA
RACHEL	20	F	SVNT	RR	ZZZZ	USA
GRESTE	18	F	SVNT	RR	ZZZZ	USA
PORANESKY, FLORENCE	19	F	SVNT	RR	ZZZZ	USA
F.DUSALATZ	25	M	LABR	RR	ZZZZ	USA
U	20	F	W	RR	ZZZZ	USA
-ACT--L	.06	F	INFANT	RR	ZZZZ	USA
BERKOWITZ, B.	23	F	SVNT	RR	ZZZZ	USA
RACHEL	22	F	SVNT	RR	ZZZZ	USA
SARAH	18	F	SVNT	RR	ZZZZ	USA
SCHACHTER, CLARA	20	F	SVNT	RR	ZZZZ	USA
ELLEN	11	F	CH	RR	ZZZZ	USA
SEGALL, G.	19	F	SVNT	RR	AHOO	USA
GAHE.	25	F	SVNT	RR	AHOO	USA
GREMBERG, ETEL	18	M	LABR	RR	AHOO	USA
CATER.	10	F	CH	RR	AHOO	USA

SHIP: WISCONSIN

FROM: LIVERPOOL AND QUEENSTOWN
TO: NEW YORK
ARRIVED: 13 JUNE 1888

PASSENGER	AGE	SEX	OCCUPATION	PRV	VIL	DES
KRANT, CHANNA	16	F	SP	RR	ZZZZ	USA
WOOLF, AZRIEL	18	F	SP	RR	ZZZZ	USA
GAPENSKY, CINE	32	F	SP	RR	ZZZZ	USA
KOZENITZKI, OSIP	49	M	GLSR	PL	ZZZZ	USA
MILOKANIS, FRANZ.	23	F	SP	PL	ZZZZ	USA
FRIEDHEIM, PINCUS	44	M	TLR	RR	ZZZZ	USA
ZALMINOWITZ, RACHL.	15	F	SP	RR	ZZZZ	USA
RUBENSTEIN, MOSES	36	M	FARMER	RR	ZZZZ	USA
LIPKE, FEIGE	45	F	MA	RR	ZZZZ	USA
BROTMAN, LSATE	24	F	W	RR	ZZZZ	USA
CHANE	.08	F	INFANT	RR	ZZZZ	USA
AKSEBROD, NOCHEM	18	M	LABR	RR	ZZZZ	USA
ONIKELSKI, HERTZ	7	M	CHILD	RR	ZZZZ	USA

PASSENGER	AGE	SEX	OCCUPATION	PRV VIL DES
LEWIN, FANNY	24	F	SP	RRZZZZUSA
AZLMANWITZ, ABRAM	16	M	FARMER	RRZZZZUSA
BERLINSKI, MEIR	18	M	FARMER	RRZZZZUSA
DWORA	18	F	SP	RRZZZZUSA
FRANK, RACHEL	19	F	SP	RRZZZZUSA
FEIGENBAUMM, ISAAC	29	M	PMBR	RRZZZZUSA
ROSENZWEIG, CHAIM	22	M	PMBR	RRZZZZUSA
MAGERKEWITZ, JACOB	23	M	PMBR	RRZZZZUSA
BENJAMIN, AMALIE	55	F	MA	RRZZZZUSA
JOSEPH	13	M	PNTR	RRZZZZUSA
SCHONBERG, JUDES	.09	M	INFANT	RRZZZZUSA
RUOKSE	.10	F	INFANT	RRZZZZUSA
HURWITZ, LEHA	.11	F	INFANT	RRZZZZUSA
MENSON, ARON	.08	M	INFANT	RRZZZZUSA
LEHA	.10	F	INFANT	RRZZZZUSA
ROSEN, LEUB	18	M	TLR	RRZZZZUSA
COHEN, SIMON	30	M	TLR	RRZZZZUSA
SNERJEH, SIMON	10	M	CH	RRZZZZUSA
EHRENBERG, JETTE	45	F	W	RRZZZZUSA
MOSCHE	7	F	CHILD	RRZZZZUSA
ARON	6	M	CHILD	RRZZZZUSA
CHLEBORICH, CHANA	18	F	SP	RRZZZZUSA
SCHERNMAN, SCHEINE	15	F	SP	RRZZZZUSA
WITPINSI, MOYSCHE	25	F	SP	RRZZZZUSA
LEBESENEY, FRUME	30	F	SP	RRZZZZUSA
LERLANTY, WALKE	32	F	W	RRZZZZUSA
HINDE	30	F	SP	RRZZZZUSA
LION	18	M	PMBR	RRZZZZUSA
CHASKEL	8	M	CHILD	RRZZZZUSA
MASURICH, LISER	28	M	LABR	RRZZZZUSA
CUTTS, JAINOS	18	M	LABR	RRZZZZUSA
LACKER, N.	36	M	LABR	RRZZZZUSA
PRECUCH, SIC	26	M	LABR	RRZZZZUSA
MICHOL	32	M	LABR	RRZZZZUSA
KUMERTRICH, JACOB	48	M	LABR	RRZZZZUSA
ABRAMSON, SERE	30	F	SP	RRZZZZUSA
CHIVELOWSKY, ROSE	30	F	W	RRZZZZUSA
CHAGE	11	M	CH	RRZZZZUSA
RACHEL	7	F	CHILD	RRZZZZUSA
MAX	5	M	CHILD	RRZZZZUSA
GASSMAN, LED	26	M	LABR	RRZZZZUSA
FRIEVEL	8	F	CHILD	RRZZZZUSA
LUZA	8	F	CHILD	RRZZZZUSA
GNENSKY, PHILIP	31	M	TKR	RRZZZZUSA
KLEIDMAN, MOSCHE	34	F	MA	RRZZZZUSA
YERESPOLSKY, MENDEL	19	M	SDLR	RRZZZZUSA
PELLER, R.	7	M	CHILD	RRZZZZUSA
MULLER, ROSA	15	F	SP	RRZZZZUSA
HACKMAN, HERMAN	47	M	TLR	RRZZZZUSA
RESY	44	F	W	RRZZZZUSA
BERNHARD	11	M	CH	RRZZZZUSA
ROSA	8	F	CHILD	RRZZZZUSA
AMALIE	7	F	CHILD	RRZZZZUSA
KATHIE	6	F	CHILD	RRZZZZUSA
MARKUS	3	M	CHILD	RRZZZZUSA
ISIDOR	.07	M	INFANT	RRZZZZUSA
WEISSBERGER, HANE	16	F	SP	RRZZZZUSA
ERZ, MOSES	20	M	TKR	RRZZZZUSA
MARIE	20	F	W	RRZZZZUSA
ARSENSOHN, SAML.	15	M	GZR	RRZZZZUSA
WEINDITCH, FRANZ	31	M	PMBR	RRZZZZUSA
MARIE	27	F	W	RRZZZZUSA
SCHNEIDER, FISCHEL	15	M	LABR	RRZZZZUSA
MOSKOWITZ, ISRAEL	20	M	LABR	RRZZZZUSA
BERKOWITZ, FISCHEL	45	M	FARMER	RRZZZZUSA
GITTEL	40	F	W	RRZZZZUSA
MOSES	20	M	FARMER	RRZZZZUSA
PIREL	14	M	FARMER	RRZZZZUSA
JAMBO	7	M	CHILD	RRZZZZUSA
SCHATZEN, LEIE	24	F	SP	RRZZZZUSA
DON, JANKEL	58	M	FARMER	RRZZZZUSA
SCHEINMAN, IDES	29	F	W	RRZZZZUSA
RICHEL	7	F	CHILD	RRZZZZUSA
SCHACHER, ABRAM	28	M	LABR	RRZZZZUSA
RICH, GITTEL	20	F	SP	RRZZZZUSA
KRANT, VICTOR	25	M	LABR	RRZZZZUSA
SCHMEDEL	22	F	W	RRZZZZUSA
RAND, BERISCH	26	M	TLR	RRZZZZUSA
ABRAMSON, DAWED	39	M	GZR	RRZZZZUSA
ARON	16	M	GZR	RRZZZZUSA
KAMERTRICH, TAUBE	.11	F	INFANT	RRZZZZUSA
SIMLAK, SIMON	35	M	LABR	RRZZZZUSA
MAYER, SAMUL	26	M	LABR	RRZZZZUSA
DLEISKI, JOSEF	25	M	LABR	RRZZZZUSA
RUBINSKI, FEIGE	22	M	LABR	RRZZZZUSA
RUZOWSKI, PEREL	25	M	LABR	RRZZZZUSA
PRAMPER, HANE	21	F	SP	RRZZZZUSA
JUNTUNEA, ALBERT	25	M	TLR	RRZZZZUSA
LEWIN, HIRSCH	22	M	TKR	RRZZZZUSA
WISNAWITZ, CHARE	3	F	CHILD	RRZZZZUSA
BRULL, LENSER	28	M	LABR	RRZZZZUSA
FINCHER, MOSE	17	M	LABR	RRZZZZUSA
SCHENEGEWKY, ALEA	25	M	LABR	RRZZZZUSA
SANEWKY, ADAM	25	M	LABR	RRZZZZUSA
LIBOWITZ, DAVID	23	M	LABR	RRZZZZUSA
GROBMAN, BARUCH	40	M	LABR	RRZZZZUSA
GRUMBLATT, MART.	19	M	LABR	RRZZZZUSA
KUSEN, SALMEN	36	M	LABR	RRZZZZUSA
SCHMULOWITZ, DAVID	16	M	LABR	RRZZZZUSA
KASCHUL, MASCJE	35	F	MA	RRZZZZUSA
SCHENINSI, SCHERN	24	M	FARMER	RRZZZZUSA
RABAZINK, MOSES	17	M	TLR	RRZZZZUSA
SCHUSTER, GEDOLIA	22	F	SP	RRZZZZUSA
RISCHWAG, HEINRICH	30	M	LABR	RRZZZZUSA
SAETAS, FEIWEL	20	M	LABR	RRZZZZUSA
HATERMAN, ABRAM	35	M	FARMER	RRZZZZUSA
SOPHIE	30	F	W	RRZZZZUSA
LEWIN, FEIZE	38	F	W	RRZZZZUSA
HERSCH	.07	M	INFANT	RRZZZZUSA
HARN, SANI	32	M	FARMER	RRZZZZUSA
MICHAEL	17	M	FARMER	RRZZZZUSA
SCHSELROD, JULIUS	20	M	FARMER	RRZZZZUSA
CHASEN, BASCHE	20	F	SP	RRZZZZUSA
ISIS, ELKE	18	M	GZR	RRZZZZUSA
ROSENBUM, DWORE	18	F	SP	RRZZZZUSA
CHAIMWITZ, NECHE	43	F	W	RRZZZZUSA
ESTER	7	F	CHILD	RRZZZZUSA
HOFMAN, KUSIEL	23	M	TKR	RRZZZZUSA
KEILE	22	F	W	RRZZZZUSA
SWETNIK, LEIB	31	M	FARMER	RRZZZZUSA
ISAAC	19	M	FARMER	RRZZZZUSA
HOFFMAN, SCHUNEL	30	M	LABR	RRZZZZUSA
ASH, ICHIEL	29	M	LABR	RRZZZZUSA
SCHOMBERG, ESTER	34	F	W	RRZZZZUSA
CHANE	15	F	SP	RRZZZZUSA
SOLOMON	7	M	CHILD	RRZZZZUSA
MICHAEL	4	M	CHILD	RRZZZZUSA
PRENOWITZ, CHANE	19	F	SP	RRZZZZUSA
HURWITZ, LOIN	23	M	MSN	RRZZZZUSA
NECHEMIE	4	F	CHILD	RRZZZZUSA
MENSON, ESTER	24	F	SP	RRZZZZUSA
DAICZ, DAVID	15	M	JNR	RRZZZZUSA
ZEBENDOW, MACHLE	30	F	W	RRZZZZUSA
SCHLAVLEM	7	M	CHILD	RRZZZZUSA
JACOB	6	M	CHILD	RRZZZZUSA
POLLAK, MENDEL	17	M	LABR	RRZZZZUSA
SOVA, ESRIEL	27	M	LABR	RRZZZZUSA
FEINSOD, ISRAEL	28	M	LABR	RRZZZZUSA
KURTZICH, MARTIN	20	M	LABR	RRZZZZUSA
WISNEWITZ, CHANE	50	F	MA	RRZZZZUSA
RIFKE	19	F	SP	RRZZZZUSA
HARRIS	22	M	FARMER	RRZZZZUSA
EPSTEIN, MOJSCHE	17	F	SP	RRZZZZUSA
ROSE	19	F	SP	RRZZZZUSA
SUKAWARSKI, JOSEF	35	M	FARMER	RRZZZZUSA
ZARNOV, EFRAINA	28	M	FARMER	RRZZZZUSA
FRESTOFF, SARAH	20	F	SP	RRZZZZUSA
JACKEN, ABRAM	18	M	TKR	RRZZZZUSA
MIKALOWITZ, AGALA	22	M	PNTR	RRZZZZUSA
SIMELOVETE, ESEL	34	M	GZR	RRZZZZUSA

PASSENGER	AGE	SEX	OCCUPATION	PRV VIL DES
OGENSTERN, RACHEL	29	F	W	RRZZZZUSA
MOSES	7	M	CHILD	RRZZZZUSA
FRADA	6	F	CHILD	RRZZZZUSA
ZELDA	5	F	CHILD	RRZZZZUSA
KOSKA, TEOLA	22	F	SP	RRZZZZUSA
JANSSON, JOHAN	39	M	JNR	FNZZZZUSA
WIKLAND, WILHELM	27	M	LABR	FNZZZZUSA
FRIDLUND, NILS	29	M	LABR	FNZZZZUSA
BACKE, WM.	24	M	LABR	FNZZZZUSA
WIKLUND, NIKLAS	20	M	LABR	FNZZZZUSA
HARPOK, ISAK	26	M	FARMER	FNZZZZUSA
PELANT, CARL	21	M	FARMER	FNZZZZUSA
BARTILO, JAKOR	19	M	FARMER	FNZZZZUSA
BACK, AUGUST	24	M	JNR	FNZZZZUSA
WAST, JOHAN	21	M	CPTR	FNZZZZUSA
ABOYMAN, ERIK	38	M	PNTR	FNZZZZUSA
ENGBLOM, JOHAN	36	M	FARMER	FNZZZZUSA
KATARINA	33	F	W	FNZZZZUSA
OSTERHOLM, GRETA	23	F	W	FNZZZZUSA
ERIKA	.09	F	INFANT	FNZZZZUSA
ZUNDBERG, JOHAN	22	M	MSN	FNZZZZUSA
AUGUSTA	21	F	W	FNZZZZUSA
KPONGA, HK.HENRIK	24	M	FARMER	FNZZZZUSA
JOHANSON, CARL	22	M	FARMER	FNZZZZUSA
KALLMAN, ANDERS	33	M	MCHT	FNZZZZUSA
LOUISA	29	F	W	FNZZZZUSA
GUSTAF	4	M	CHILD	FNZZZZUSA
JOHAN	.07	M	INFANT	FNZZZZUSA
NYLUND, CARL	31	M	GENT	FNZZZZUNK
AHLBERG, J.	39	M	GENT	FNZZZZUNK
M.	39	F	LDY	FNZZZZUNK
KORALOINEN, A.	22	F	LDY	FNZZZZUNK
ST.	.08	F	INFANT	FNZZZZUNK

SHIP: DONAU

FROM: BREMEN
TO: BALTIMORE
ARRIVED: 13 JUNE 1888

PASSENGER	AGE	SEX	OCCUPATION	PRV VIL DES
ZUKOWSKI, KONSTANTY	33	M	LABR	RRZZZZMO
SAMALOWSKA, ANNA	20	F	UNKNOWN	RRZZZZMA
GRAZOMA, K---	24	M	LABR	RRZZZZMA
HIRSCHBERG, JANKE	19	M	MCHT	RRZZZZMA
GUTMANN, ISAAC	20	M	TLR	RRZZZZIL
HITTELMANN, LUDW	19	M	LABR	RRZZZZMD
BURGINSKI, JOSEPH	20	M	LABR	RRZZZZMI
GROOSD, OSHER	45	M	LABR	RRZZZZPA
ROTH, ESTI	22	F	UNKNOWN	RRZZZZPA
ETELKA	.11	F	INFANT	RRZZZZPA
WAGNER, JULIANE	21	F	UNKNOWN	RRZZZZMI
PETZEL, MATHILDE	17	F	UNKNOWN	RRZZZZMI
HEIRSCHBERG, DINA	29	F	UNKNOWN	RRZZZZIL
HERMAN	11	M	UNKNOWN	RRZZZZIL
MARCUS	9	M	CHILD	RRZZZZIL
JOSEPH	8	M	CHILD	RRZZZZIL
SAMUEL	4	M	CHILD	RRZZZZIL
JOSSEL	3	M	CHILD	RRZZZZIL
ROSENBERG, BALLE	33	F	UNKNOWN	RRZZZZIL
JACOB	5	M	CHILD	RRZZZZIL
ISAC	9	M	CHILD	RRZZZZIL
SARA	5	F	CHILD	RRZZZZIL
RAHLE	3	F	CHILD	RRZZZZIL
LISS, SCHFRA.	18	F	UNKNOWN	RRZZZZIL
KARMINEWSKI, LEON	31	M	FARMER	RRZZZZNE
KISSELMANN, KATH	27	F	UNKNOWN	RRZZZZCO
LIND, MARIE	39	F	UNKNOWN	RRZZZZCO
LEWANDOWSKI, JAN	24	M	MLR	RRZZZZOH
ZEINUS, JONAS	26	M	LABR	RRZZZZMD
IMGI	29	M	LABR	RRZZZZMD

PASSENGER	AGE	SEX	OCCUPATION	PRV VIL DES
BLECH, IGNATZI	28	M	TLR	RRZZZZMD
REDZILINSKI, GERSON	52	M	MCHT	RRZZZZMD
DAILIDONIS, JUSTIN	21	M	LABR	RRZZZZIL
BLOCHKIS, KAZMIR	18	M	LABR	RRZZZZMD
DAKNIS, ELISABETH	21	F	UNKNOWN	RRZZZZMD
RADZINSKY, NIKOLAY	23	M	TNM	RRZZZZMD
LINKOWITZ, JAN	29	M	LABR	RRZZZZMD
REWLUSCHOWITZ, JOSEPH	18	F	UNKNOWN	RRZZZZMD
BREMERMANN, ROCHEL	18	F	UNKNOWN	RRZZZZMD
ZUCKER, MORDCHE	30	M	MCHT	RRZZZZMD
PERKUSCH, ABRAHAM	19	M	BCHR	RRZZZZMD
STRANDSKY, SCHOLOME	23	F	UNKNOWN	RRZZZZPA
SCHULZ, CHAJE	20	F	UNKNOWN	RRZZZZPA
MOSES	11	M	CH	RRZZZZPA
MONSON, CHRISTIAN	49	M	BKLYR	RRZZZZIL
CHRISTIAN	19	M	BKLYR	RRZZZZIL
OTTO	17	M	BKLYR	RRZZZZIL
MAGNUS	10	M	CH	RRZZZZIL
THERESE	8	F	CHILD	RRZZZZIL
LORENZ	4	M	CHILD	RRZZZZIL
KITELSACK, JOHANNE	19	F	UNKNOWN	RRZZZZMD
SCHLEI, JOHAN	47	M	FARMER	RRZZZZDAK
ANNA	47	F	UNKNOWN	RRZZZZDAK
ANNA	19	F	UNKNOWN	RRZZZZDAK
JUSTINE	17	F	UNKNOWN	RRZZZZDAK
MARIA	16	F	UNKNOWN	RRZZZZDAK
HELENE	11	F	UNKNOWN	RRZZZZDAK
PETER	10	M	CH	RRZZZZDAK
WERLE, JOSEPH	42	M	JNR	RRZZZZDAK
ELISABETH	27	F	UNKNOWN	RRZZZZDAK
FRIEDA	3	F	CHILD	RRZZZZDAK
CHRIST	1	F	CHILD	RRZZZZDAK
SCHROEHLER, JOHAN	34	M	LABR	RRZZZZDAK
ELISABETH	30	F	UNKNOWN	RRZZZZDAK
ANNA	6	F	CHILD	RRZZZZDAK
HERMAN	4	M	CHILD	RRZZZZDAK
JACOB	2	M	CHILD	RRZZZZDAK
JOHAN	.08	M	INFANT	RRZZZZDAK
DREIER, ABRAHAM	23	M	MCHT	RRZZZZMI
U, U	00	U	UNKNOWN	RRZZZZMI
STANSKY, SCHEINE	33	F	UNKNOWN	RRZZZZMD
JACOBSON, ABEL	17	M	PDLR	RRZZZZMD
BETHER, NECHEMINE	42	F	UNKNOWN	RRZZZZMD
JANKELOWITZ, CHAJE	20	F	UNKNOWN	RRZZZZMD
ANDRZEJESKI, WOJICECH	34	M	LABR	RRZZZZIL
NOWAK, STANILAUS	30	M	LABR	RRZZZZPA
SZYDLOWSKI, JOSEF	35	M	FARMER	RRZZZZIL
MARIANNA	33	F	UNKNOWN	RRZZZZIL
ANASTASIA	7	F	CHILD	RRZZZZIL
MARIANNA	3	F	CHILD	RRZZZZIL
FELIX	5	M	CHILD	RRZZZZIL
ANGELA	.11	F	INFANT	RRZZZZIL
ROSKOSKI, KA--IR	40	M	LABR	RRZZZZMI
AGNITZKA	30	F	UNKNOWN	RRZZZZMI
MARTHA	4	F	CHILD	RRZZZZMI
ANTONIE	15	F	UNKNOWN	RRZZZZMI
GOGOLIN, AUGUST	53	M	FARMER	RRZZZZPA
FRANZISKA	54	F	UNKNOWN	RRZZZZPA
GUSTAV	15	M	UNKNOWN	RRZZZZPA
WLADILAUS	11	M	UNKNOWN	RRZZZZPA
JOSEPH	9	M	CHILD	RRZZZZPA
VICTORIA	19	F	UNKNOWN	RRZZZZPA
KOTHE, FRANZISKA	25	F	UNKNOWN	RRZZZZIL
ANTONIA	20	F	UNKNOWN	RRZZZZIL
UTAS, JULIANE	23	F	MNR	RRZZZZIL
JOHAN	23	M	UNKNOWN	RRZZZZIL
SAPIKOWSKI, MARIA	25	F	UNKNOWN	RRZZZZPA
DROZYNSKI, JOHN	36	M	LABR	RRZZZZMI
KARTUN, SLEIME	18	M	MCHT	RRZZZZMD
POBSCHAFER, ROSA	25	F	UNKNOWN	RRZZZZPA
ESTHER	3	F	CHILD	RRZZZZPA
LINDE	1	M	CHILD	RRZZZZPA
RAGROKI, MORDCHE	44	F	UNKNOWN	RRZZZZMO
FERZE	20	F	UNKNOWN	RRZZZZMO
ABRAHAM	11	M	CH	RRZZZZMO

PASSENGER	AGE	SEX	OCCUPATION	PRV VIL DES
LEIB, JUDE	.11	M	INFANT	RRZZZZMO
ROGALSKI, ADOLF	26	M	LABR	RRZZZZMD
GRYNKIEWICZ, PIETRONELL	16	F	UNKNOWN	RRZZZZMD
FEUERMANN, OSIAS	38	M	MCHT	RRZZZZMD
ISAAC	12	M	UNKNOWN	RRZZZZMD
FRAENKEL, MARJEUM	16	M	MCHT	RRZZZZMD
STERNFELD, DAVID	18	M	MCHT	RRZZZZMD
MIKELANIS, FRANC	25	M	LABR	RRZZZZPA
MACIEWSKY, ANDRAS	30	M	LABR	RRZZZZNY
GOTOWASKY, ANDRAS	27	M	LABR	RRZZZZNY
OKSCON, ADAM	24	M	LABR	RRZZZZNY
MIZKUS, MICHEL	24	M	LABR	RRZZZZNY
HORN, WILH	28	M	LABR	RRZZZZNY
SCHATAS, ANTONIE	30	F	UNKNOWN	RRZZZZMD
MICHAEL	18	M	LABR	RRZZZZMD
HIRSCHFELD, BERNH.	27	M	LABR	RRZZZZMD

SHIP: STATE OF NEBRASKA

FROM: GLASGOW AND LARNE
TO: NEW YORK
ARRIVED: 13 JUNE 1888

PASSENGER	AGE	SEX	OCCUPATION	PRV VIL DES
LEISEROWITZ, ZIWIE	35	F	W	RRZZZZUSA
FEIGE	10	F	CH	RRZZZZUSA
ASSINSKY, TOBIA	20	M	SP	RRZZZZUSA
ESTER	18	M	SP	RRZZZZUSA
SUSSMANN, CHANNE	17	M	SP	RRZZZZUSA
ROTH, SARAH	18	M	SP	RRZZZZUSA
LEWTTEN, JETTE	15	M	SP	RRZZZZUSA
DRUSKY, LIZZIE	18	M	SP	RRZZZZUSA
SIMANOWITZ, ROSA	20	M	SP	RRZZZZUSA
BLUME	17	M	SP	RRZZZZUSA
BROCKMANN, HINDE	17	M	SP	RRZZZZUSA
MAPARTICK, DWORE	19	M	SP	RRZZZZUSA
SUMAKER, CHANE	18	M	SP	RRZZZZUSA
SARAH	55	F	WI	RRZZZZUSA
GORDON, ERNESTINE	20	F	SP	RRZZZZUSA
PERSKY, CHASCHE	25	F	W	RRZZZZUSA
BLUMBERG, ROSA	22	F	W	RRZZZZUSA
PULTAWE, ESTHER	48	F	WI	RRZZZZUSA
ROSENTHAL, HENZE	46	F	WI	RRZZZZUSA
BERLINSKY, LEIL	30	F	W	RRZZZZUSA
MARKS	10	M	CH	RRZZZZUSA
JACOB	8	M	CHILD	RRZZZZUSA
SUTH, MINNA	35	F	W	RRZZZZUSA
EL.	10	M	CH	RRZZZZUSA
HERSCHEL	7	M	CHILD	RRZZZZUSA
SCHMUEL	5	M	CHILD	RRZZZZUSA
DWARSOWITZ, BEILE	50	F	W	RRZZZZUSA
TAUBE	7	F	CHILD	RRZZZZUSA
CHASKIN, JETTE	29	F	W	RRZZZZUSA
BASCHE	8	F	CHILD	RRZZZZUSA
GRIECHE	5	M	CHILD	RRZZZZUSA
SCHEINE	2	M	CHILD	RRZZZZUSA
MANE	1	F	CHILD	RRZZZZUSA
MELZEI, JACOB	50	M	LABR	RRZZZZUSA
SORE	48	F	W	RRZZZZUSA
LEA	25	F	SP	RRZZZZUSA
ARON	11	M	CH	RRZZZZUSA
DWERE	6	F	CHILD	RRZZZZUSA
HIRSCH	5	M	CHILD	RRZZZZUSA
BERGER, MOSCHE	22	M	BCHR	RRZZZZUSA
CHAJE	24	F	W	RRZZZZUSA
ABE	9	M	CHILD	RRZZZZUSA
DWORE	11	F	CH	RRZZZZUSA
BRODKIN, ABRAHAM	40	M	JNR	RRZZZZUSA
ROSE	40	F	W	RRZZZZUSA
ARON	11	M	CH	RRZZZZUSA
JACOB	6	M	CHILD	RRZZZZUSA
MAWSCHE	1	M	CHILD	RRZZZZUSA
HIRSCH	.02	M	INFANT	RRZZZZUSA
KASLOWSKY, JOSSEL	30	M	SDLR	RRZZZZUSA
DRISE	23	F	W	RRZZZZUSA
BASCHE	.11	F	INFANT	RRZZZZUSA
SCHAJEWITZ, ISRAEL	23	M	TLR	RRZZZZUSA
SPRINZE	24	F	W	RRZZZZUSA
POTASNIK, CHONON	23	M	STDNT	RRZZZZUSA
SCHONE	20	F	W	RRZZZZUSA
KOSEHMSKY, ABRAHAM	45	M	LKSH	RRZZZZUSA
JOCHEBET	42	F	W	RRZZZZUSA
JOSEF	22	M	SMH	RRZZZZUSA
NISSEN	19	M	UNKNOWN	RRZZZZUSA
ISAAC	17	M	UNKNOWN	RRZZZZUSA
RAKOWSKY, SANE	25	M	LABR	RRZZZZUSA
SALAMENSKY, MARTIN	22	M	LABR	RRZZZZUSA
SUSKIND, JEHOR	27	M	LABR	RRZZZZUSA
BUDIL, IGNATZ	24	M	LABR	RRZZZZUSA
MICHALON, FEODOR	29	M	LABR	RRZZZZUSA
WEHRIK, ADAM	25	M	LABR	RRZZZZUSA
BOKSTANSKY, ELJE	30	M	LABR	RRZZZZUSA
OSSIM, MOSES	22	M	LABR	RRZZZZUSA
BROCKMANN, DAVID	49	M	TLR	RRZZZZUSA
BALANIS, VINCENT	50	M	LABR	RRZZZZUSA
SKUNDA, JOHAN	50	M	LABR	RRZZZZUSA
BALANIS, MICHEL	29	M	LABR	RRZZZZUSA
GRABLUN, VINCENTI	45	M	LABR	RRZZZZUSA
SZAMETATIS, KONSTANTIN	21	M	LABR	RRZZZZUSA
SKOWRONSKY, LEON	25	M	LABR	RRZZZZUSA
KOSBEL, STANISLAUS	24	M	LABR	RRZZZZUSA
CZUWETZKA, JAN	24	M	LABR	RRZZZZUSA
GURLEWSKY, JOSEF	27	M	LABR	RRZZZZUSA
HUSER, JURI	43	M	LABR	RRZZZZUSA
SCHEINMANN, SALOMON	30	M	LABR	RRZZZZUSA
WASKELASSE, JAKOB	54	M	TLR	RRZZZZUSA
SACHNESS, MAUSCHE	48	M	TLR	RRZZZZUSA
MALKES, WOLF	28	M	TLR	RRZZZZUSA
COHN, ITSCHE	32	M	TLR	RRZZZZUSA
WINOGRODOW, RAWEN	42	M	TLR	RRZZZZUSA
ISKIN, SELIG	28	M	TLR	RRZZZZUSA
DRUSKY, SCHLOME	48	M	TLR	RRZZZZUSA
GROSS, SCHMUEL	19	M	JNR	RRZZZZUSA
ABENDETZ, ARON	27	M	JNR	RRZZZZUSA
JUBELERAR, ISAAC	17	M	JNR	RRZZZZUSA
WOLF, JOSEF	23	M	PDLR	RRZZZZUSA
KATZ, ITZIG	27	M	PDLR	RRZZZZUSA
LIDEKER, JAKOB	17	M	PDLR	RRZZZZUSA
OSCHEROWSKI, BERNHARDT	19	M	PDLR	RRZZZZUSA
LEPKOWITZ, ISSER	23	M	PDLR	RRZZZZUSA
STEINHOLZ, ITZCHAK	32	M	PDLR	RRZZZZUSA
ISAACSOHN, SAMUEL	36	M	PDLR	RRZZZZUSA
SCHMID, BENJAMIN	21	M	PDLR	RRZZZZUSA
KALM, JOSEPH	20	M	PDLR	RRZZZZUSA
KATZ, SAMUEL	40	M	PDLR	RRZZZZUSA
KLEIN, FEIWEL	55	M	PDLR	RRZZZZUSA
SCHEBSEL	19	M	PDLR	RRZZZZUSA
SCHAPIR, BEHR	21	M	PDLR	RRZZZZUSA
SWORSKI, NATHAN	25	M	CL	RRZZZZUSA
ARINS, EPHRAIM	19	M	CL	RRZZZZUSA
SKLONEWSKY, HIRSCH	28	M	LKSH	RRZZZZUSA
KAHN, BARUCH	18	M	WCHMKR	RRZZZZUSA
KUMKIN, ISRAEL	28	M	SHMK	RRZZZZUSA
DUCKSCHITZKY, HIRSCH	23	M	BCHR	RRZZZZUSA
SIGALSKI, MEYER	17	M	TNSTH	RRZZZZUSA
FELLER, ABRAHAM	38	M	CGRMKR	RRZZZZUSA
SCHUFF, JOSEPH	20	M	BRR	RRZZZZUSA
BENDER, MORDCHE	30	M	RPR	RRZZZZUSA
KLUTZKO, ABRAHAM	47	M	MLR	RRZZZZUSA
PETTE, JAKOB	18	M	LABR	FNZZZZUSA
JAKOBSON, JAKOB	24	M	LABR	FNZZZZUSA
HARTULL, JOHAN	31	M	LABR	FNZZZZUSA
KLEMETS, ABRAHAM	19	M	LABR	FNZZZZUSA
GRABBEL, MICKEL	21	M	LABR	FNZZZZUSA
ISAKAS, JOHAN	32	M	LABR	FNZZZZUSA

PASSENGER	AGE	SEX	OCCUPATION	PRV	VIL	DES

SHIP: BELGENLAND

FROM: ANTWERP
TO: NEW YORK
ARRIVED: 14 JUNE 1888

PASSENGER	AGE	SEX	OCCUPATION	PRV	VIL	DES
KUKLOWSKI, ANTON	19	M	LABR	RR	ZZZZ	UNK
BRESLAU, ISRAEL	19	M	CL	RR	ZZZZ	NY
ZAY, ULICH	43	M	LABR	PL	ZZZZ	BUF
MARIANNA	43	F	UNKNOWN	PL	ZZZZ	BUF
MARIANNA	19	F	UNKNOWN	PL	ZZZZ	BUF
FRANCKA.	17	F	UNKNOWN	PL	ZZZZ	BUF
CATH.	10	F	CH	PL	ZZZZ	BUF
STANISL.	7	M	CHILD	PL	ZZZZ	BUF
KLIMKA, MARTIN	33	M	LABR	PL	ZZZZ	BUF
ANELA	30	F	UNKNOWN	PL	ZZZZ	BUF
MARIANNA	4	F	CHILD	PL	ZZZZ	BUF
ANDRZY	2	M	CHILD	PL	ZZZZ	BUF
SKOZYPEE, ROSALIE	28	F	UNKNOWN	PL	ZZZZ	NY
ANTONIN, AUG.	31	M	FARMER	PL	AIED	NY
KUPKOWSKA, REGINA	00	F	SVNT	PL	ZZZZ	NY
ABRAMSON, MARK	22	M	CKCTR	RR	ZZZZ	NY
HOLKOWITZ, SOLOMON	23	M	CGRMKR	RR	ZZZZ	NY
GOLDMANN, HEYMAN	22	M	TLR	RR	ZZZZ	NY
UZLANER, JACOB	20	M	WCHMKR	RR	ZZZZ	NY
LIPKOWSKI, HYMAN	20	M	TNSTH	RR	ZZZZ	NY
TAISCHNER, GOTH.	20	M	WCHMKR	RR	ZZZZ	NY
PERLMAN, DAVID	20	M	FUR	RR	ZZZZ	NY
KIRSCHBERG, BENJ.	22	M	TNR	RR	ADBQ	NY
WONDEL-ORT, DAVID	25	M	PNTR	RR	ADBQ	NY
TURNER, ELIAS	23	M	HTR	RR	ADBQ	NY
SCHAFER, ABRA-JAC.	25	M	TCHR	RR	ADBQ	NY
LENERSON, ABRA-JAC.	25	M	TCHR	RR	ADBQ	NY
GOLDBERG, SIMON	22	M	LABR	RR	ADBQ	NY
TONKIN, B.	20	M	SMH	RR	ADBQ	NY
BERGER, SOLOMON	24	M	TLR	RR	ADBQ	PHI
HODAS	24	F	UNKNOWN	RR	ADBQ	PHI
DAVIS	00	M	INF	RR	ADBQ	PHI
SARA	20	F	UNKNOWN	RR	ADBQ	PHI
U, U	25	M	UNKNOWN	RR	ADBQ	PHI
U	22	F	UNKNOWN	RR	ADBQ	PHI
HODA	3	F	CHILD	RR	ADBQ	PHI
SARAH	00	F	INF	RR	ADBQ	PHI
ANNIE	20	F	INF	RR	ADBQ	PHI
JADOWSKY, MARK	22	M	BTMKR	RR	ADBQ	BO
OSERPWOTSCJH, MOSCHE	24	M	LABR	RR	ZZZZ	NY
JUDE	24	M	LABR	RR	ZZZZ	NY
HANNE	10	M	CH	RR	ZZZZ	NY
NADELMANN, ZIPPE	22	F	UNKNOWN	RR	AIMP	NY
U	00	M	INF	RR	AIMP	NY
KLEMMANN, U	32	M	LABR	RR	AHTQ	NY
LEBENSTEIN, LEIB	14	M	LABR	RR	AHXL	NY
BEILES, HIRSCH	29	M	LABR	RR	AHXL	NY
GLASSNER, SELIG	48	M	LABR	RR	ZZZZ	NY
GLUECK, MOSES	28	M	LABR	RR	ZZZZ	UNK
SOFER, NOCHEM	17	M	LABR	RR	AHXL	UNK
RIKLER, CHONE	16	M	UNKNOWN	RR	AINM	UNK
BENISON, MARCUS	20	M	UNKNOWN	RR	AINM	UNK
SCHAPIRO, BERNHARD	24	M	UNKNOWN	RR	AHTF	UNK
ABWALT, SCHULEM	27	M	JNR	RR	ZZZZ	NY
HERSCHKOWITZ, MEIER	25	M	LABR	RR	ZZZZ	NY
KACMAREC, JULIAN	33	M	GDNR	RR	AICT	NY
TRINTOWSKI, JOHAN	28	M	LABR	RR	ZZZZ	NY
GNIDERS, HIRONIMUS	36	M	LABR	RR	AHTF	NY
JACKOS, LEO	24	M	LABR	RR	AHTF	NY
JACKS, FRIED.	29	M	LABR	RR	AHTF	NY
GUDJAHN, JOHAN	27	M	LABR	RR	AHTF	NY
GUDJONES, CASIMIR	31	M	LABR	RR	AHTF	NY
SCHMANSTEIN, JOH.	36	M	LABR	RR	AHTF	NY
ANSCHE, LAURENTINO	29	M	LABR	RR	AHTF	NY
JAKOWITZ, ALOIS	44	M	LABR	RR	AHTF	NY
RUTTKOWSKI, PETER	26	M	LABR	RR	ZZZZ	NY
SLEPICKA, WZL.	26	M	LABR	RR	ZZZZ	NY
KATH.	28	F	UNKNOWN	RR	ZZZZ	NY
FRZ.	9	M	CHILD	RR	ZZZZ	NY
WZL.	7	M	CHILD	RR	ZZZZ	NY
CERNY, MARIA	30	F	SVNT	RR	ZZZZ	NY
DOTLAVIL, ANNA	27	F	UNKNOWN	RR	ZZZZ	NY
MARIA	5	F	CHILD	RR	ZZZZ	NY
ANNA	9	F	CHILD	RR	ZZZZ	NY
DROZINSKI, WADISL.	28	M	LABR	RR	ZZZZ	NY
JOSEFA	22	F	UNKNOWN	RR	ZZZZ	NY
SIGM.	4	M	CHILD	RR	ZZZZ	NY
ZBOVIL, FRZ.	48	M	LABR	RR	ZZZZ	NY
FRED.	41	F	UNKNOWN	RR	ZZZZ	NY
FRZ.	14	M	CH	RR	ZZZZ	NY
FRZKA.	11	F	CH	RR	ZZZZ	NY
JOSEPHINE	5	F	CHILD	RR	ZZZZ	NY
U, U	4	M	CHILD	RR	ZZZZ	NY
U	3	U	CHILD	RR	ZZZZ	NY
U	.09	U	INFANT	RR	ZZZZ	NY
PATRICK, ANTON	32	M	LABR	RR	ZZZZ	NY
ALOISIE	19	F	UNKNOWN	RR	ZZZZ	NY
ZBOVIL, JOH.	54	M	LABR	RR	ZZZZ	NY
FRZ.	43	F	UNKNOWN	RR	ZZZZ	NY
THERESE	18	F	UNKNOWN	RR	ZZZZ	NY
RUDOLF	4	M	CHILD	RR	ZZZZ	NY
FRZ.	.09	M	INFANT	RR	ZZZZ	NY
BRODA, JAN	35	M	BBR	RR	ZZZZ	NY
HEDWIG	34	F	UNKNOWN	RR	ZZZZ	NY
FRZ.	10	M	CH	RR	ZZZZ	NY
THOS.	6	M	CHILD	RR	ZZZZ	NY
MONIKA	4	F	CHILD	RR	ZZZZ	NY
U	.09	F	INFANT	RR	ZZZZ	NY
DZIEWECZINSKI, MARTIN	60	M	UNKNOWN	RR	ZZZZ	NY
MELARZ, STANLS.	48	M	LABR	RR	ZZZZ	NY
KOSCZWIA, AGNES	19	F	UNKNOWN	RR	ZZZZ	NY
DZIEWECZUNSKI, FRZ.	23	M	UNKNOWN	RR	ZZZZ	NY
WOLNIAK, BARB.	18	F	UNKNOWN	RR	ZZZZ	NY
JAGLA, JOHANN	24	M	LABR	RR	ZZZZ	NY
RESCHEWITZ, GEORGE	18	M	LABR	RR	ZZZZ	NY
HEMSBERG, BERL	40	M	LABR	RR	ZZZZ	NY
JOSSEL	29	M	LABR	RR	ZZZZ	NY
JAMSCHERKY, REMAHL	30	M	LABR	RR	AHUI	NY
SPIEGEL, HEIN	24	M	LABR	RR	ZZZZ	NY
CHAREHULIN, CHAIM	27	M	LABR	RR	ZZZZ	NY
DETHER, SCHEPEL	42	M	PDLR	RR	ZZZZ	NY
PECHEL	38	F	UNKNOWN	RR	ZZZZ	NY
U	12	F	CH	RR	ZZZZ	NY
U	3	M	CHILD	RR	ZZZZ	NY
STRASBURG, AB.	56	M	LABR	RR	AFWJ	NY
FEIGE	36	F	UNKNOWN	RR	AFWJ	NY
TAUBE	19	M	UNKNOWN	RR	AFWJ	NY
INDA	17	F	UNKNOWN	RR	AFWJ	NY
DEUTSCH, MAIL	24	M	UNKNOWN	RR	AEFL	NY
KOHLI, ELISE	21	F	SVNT	RR	AIAZ	UNK

SHIP: EMS

FROM: BREMEN AND SOUTHAMPTON
TO: NEW YORK
ARRIVED: 14 JUNE 1888

PASSENGER	AGE	SEX	OCCUPATION	PRV	VIL	DES
KAPLANSKI, DAVID	20	M	LABR	RR	AHOO	USA
PUMLUC	26	F	UNKNOWN	RR	AHOO	USA
HALANA	19	F	UNKNOWN	RR	AHOO	USA
MATYCHEWITZ, MOSES	30	M	TLR	RR	AHOO	NY
MISCHKUNIS, KASIS	23	M	LABR	RR	AHOO	NY
RUSSETZKI, ANTON	24	M	LABR	RR	AHOO	NY
KENSKANAS, ANDR.	20	M	LABR	RR	AHOO	NY
JODES, MATHES	25	M	LABR	RR	AHOO	NY
SCHIPENIHRA, MARTHA	36	F	UNKNOWN	RR	AHQD	NY
JEWA	18	F	UNKNOWN	RR	AHQD	NY
RUBINSTEIN, LEJE	20	F	W	RR	ZZZZ	NY

PASSENGER	AGE	SEX	OCCUPATION	PRV VIL DES
RUBIN	.05	M	INFANT	RRZZZZNY
LEJE	.05	F	INFANT	RRZZZZNY
WAJZULOWIS, WINZAS	16	M	LABR	RRAHZSNY
KRUPNICK, ISAAK	28	M	LABR	RRAHZSNY
RABINOWICZ, ELISE	.09	F	INFANT	RRAHZSNY
ZIPPE	20	M	LABR	RRAHQDNY

SHIP: NOVA SCOTIAN

FROM: LIVERPOOL
TO: BALTIMORE
ARRIVED: 14 JUNE 1888

PASSENGER	AGE	SEX	OCCUPATION	PRV VIL DES
BLUMBERG, HIRACTO	20	M	LABR	RRZZZZBAL
FINKETSLUEM, RACHEL	25	F	DRSMKR	RRZZZZBAL
PETRORAITIS, JURE	30	M	LABR	RRZZZZBAL
SYPCEZYNSKA, JANACY	20	M	LABR	RRZZZZPIT
DORFORNANN, MINI	4	F	CHILD	RRAIIESP
SOFIA	25	F	W	RRAIIESP
SCHUMSLOW, LEA	35	F	W	RRAIIECIN
ROSA	10	F	CH	RRAIIECIN
EPHRIM	8	M	CHILD	RRAIIECIN
KIENE	4	M	CHILD	RRAIIECIN

SHIP: POLYNESIA

FROM: HAMBURG
TO: NEW YORK
ARRIVED: 15 JUNE 1888

PASSENGER	AGE	SEX	OCCUPATION	PRV VIL DES
WINIKASTIS, MAXCIM	22	M	LABR	RRZZZZNY
MARIANIS, FRANZ	25	M	LABR	RRZZZZNY
MILOSMICKI, JAN	25	M	LABR	RRZZZZNY
BALUBIS, IGNATZ	24	M	LABR	RRZZZZNY
ZAGALSKI, JOS	45	M	LABR	RRZZZZNY
DOMBROWSKI, ANTON	23	M	LABR	RRZZZZNY
SAROKE, MICHEL	22	M	LABR	RRZZZZNY
JORKUM, IGNATZ	24	M	LABR	RRZZZZNY
LEWANECZYK, VINCENTY	26	M	LABR	RRZZZZNY
LUTKEITIS, IWAN	24	M	LABR	RRZZZZNY
GERGEL, JOS	27	M	LABR	RRZZZZNY
RAZWEIELKA, CASIMIR	27	M	LABR	RRZZZZNY
JASIMOVETS, ANTON	23	M	LABR	RRZZZZNY
CERNALIS, MATH	35	M	LABR	RRZZZZNY
LOBSEVSKY, CASIMIR	31	M	LABR	RRZZZZNY
JASENOWSKY, MARY	35	M	LABR	RRZZZZNY
NECZBRUETZ, GEORG	23	M	LABR	RRZZZZNY
ZELARSKY, VINCENT	27	M	LABR	RRZZZZNY
WASILEWSKY, JAN	20	M	LABR	RRZZZZNY
CHOJNOWSKI, WOJCECH	21	M	LABR	RRZZZZNY
KURWITS, SCHEINE	16	F	WO	RRZZZZNY
FRACHMOWITZ, JOS	23	M	LABR	RRZZZZNY
PCZKOSKA, JOSEFA	20	F	W	RRZZZZNY
ANTONIE	8	F	CHILD	RRZZZZNY
STANISLAV	6	M	CHILD	RRZZZZNY
JOSEF.	2	F	CHILD	RRZZZZNY
PAULIXE	00	M	INF	RRZZZZNY
JONAKEIT, CHRISTINE	21	F	WO	RRZZZZNY
SIMANZIG, SARA	33	F	W	RRZZZZNY
SLATE	8	F	CHILD	RRZZZZNY
MOSES	7	M	CHILD	RRZZZZNY
LISE	6	F	CHILD	RRZZZZNY
LIPSKY, CHAJE	30	F	W	RRZZZZNY
ABRAM	8	M	CHILD	RRZZZZNY
DWORE	7	F	CHILD	RRZZZZNY
BERL	4	M	CHILD	RRZZZZNY
PERLE	00	F	INF	RRZZZZNY
KOSZEWSKI, ADAM	2	M	CHILD	RRZZZZNY
GANSLICKI, JOSEFA	36	F	WO	RRZZZZNY
MINGER, DOBRE	35	F	W	RRZZZZNY
JACOB	8	M	CHILD	RRZZZZNY
DAVID	4	M	CHILD	RRZZZZNY
CHAJE	7	F	CHILD	RRZZZZNY
SALOMON	6	M	CHILD	RRZZZZNY
JUDKE	00	F	INF	RRZZZZNY
WEINBERG, ROSA	23	F	WO	RRZZZZNY
RUMOWICZ, NASTASY	40	M	LABR	RRZZZZNY
GREIDZINSKY, SLADY	18	F	WO	RRZZZZNY
BORNSTEIN, SALOMON	20	M	TLR	RRZZZZNY
ABRAM	43	M	TLR	RRZZZZNY
LEWIN, DWORE	25	F	W	RRZZZZNY
JANKEL	7	M	CHILD	RRZZZZNY
ZIPE	7	F	CHILD	RRZZZZNY
BERNH	5	M	CHILD	RRZZZZNY
PROSKUS, JESZI	25	M	LABR	RRZZZZNY
JENSCHECZAK, JOSEFA	30	F	WO	RRZZZZNY
JOSEFA	4	F	CHILD	RRZZZZNY
STANISLAUS	.11	M	INFANT	RRZZZZNY
SLISMON, SALOMON	40	M	DLR	RRZZZZNY
BEIER, JANKO	22	M	DLR	RRZZZZNY
GOLDBLATT, ROSA	23	F	SGL	RRZZZZNY
PULINSKI, MARIE	16	F	SGL	RRZZZZNY
KAHN, ZIWIE	9	F	CHILD	RRZZZZNY
PETROFSKI, MORITZ	16	M	LABR	RRZZZZUSA
JECHELWITZ, LEIE	30	F	WO	RRZZZZUSA
CHAIE	5	F	CHILD	RRZZZZUSA
MORDCHEL	3	F	CHILD	RRZZZZUSA
JECHELOWITZ, ESTER	.11	F	INFANT	RRZZZZUSA
BECKER, MORDCHEL	32	M	LABR	RRZZZZUSA
WISCHTART, ANTON	18	M	LABR	RRZZZZUSA
DINGFELD, CARL	33	M	LABR	RRZZZZUSA
HEYSE, JOHANN	50	M	LABR	RRZZZZUSA
GRAEBER, FRIEDR	31	M	LABR	RRZZZZUSA
DANKERWITZ, FRITZ	31	M	SHMK	RRZZZZUSA
SIEWERT, JOHANN	22	M	LABR	RRZZZZUSA
SCHOENBERG, ROBERT	30	M	LABR	RRZZZZUSA
IWANOWO, GEORG	39	M	LABR	RRZZZZUSA
JULIE	30	F	W	RRZZZZUSA
JACOB	9	M	CHILD	RRZZZZUSA
ANNA	8	F	CHILD	RRZZZZUSA
ELSA	.11	F	INFANT	RRZZZZUSA
POHDNECK, WILH	9	M	CHILD	RRZZZZUSA
HORSMANN, ARIE	28	M	UNKNOWN	RRZZZZUSA
FRAENKEL, JOSEF	29	M	UNKNOWN	RRZZZZUSA
KAHN, SAMUEL	20	M	UNKNOWN	RRZZZZUSA
BUERGER, OAH	48	M	MCHT	RRZZZZUSA
ESTHER	45	F	W	RRZZZZUSA
LEA	15	M	CH	RRZZZZUSA
ETHEL	9	F	CHILD	RRZZZZUSA
SIMON	3	M	CHILD	RRZZZZUSA
LIEBE	9	M	CHILD	RRZZZZUSA
SARA	5	F	CHILD	RRZZZZUSA
GRASSER, OSCAR	26	M	TCHR	RRZZZZUSA
WIESEN, TRAUGOTT	21	M	LABR	RRZZZZUSA
LAWE, WILH	23	M	LABR	RRZZZZUSA
HEIDAN, JOH	27	M	LABR	RRZZZZUSA
BENKE, KRISCH	24	M	LABR	RRZZZZUSA
DEKIND, CHRISTOF	23	M	BCHR	RRZZZZUSA
BECKER, ISIDOR	19	M	MCHT	RRZZZZUSA
RAUDOWICZ, JOH	35	M	LABR	RRZZZZUSA
NIEZGADSKA, MARIANNA	21	F	SGL	RRZZZZUSA
SAELLUSKI, MARGARETHA	17	F	SGL	RRZZZZUSA
PUKSZTOWA, FELICIA	23	F	WO	RRZZZZUSA
HELENE	.09	F	INFANT	RRZZZZUSA
ZAWICKI, ANTON	22	M	LABR	RRZZZZUSA
DZENDIDLOWSKA, KATH	23	F	WO	RRZZZZUSA
SOFIE	3	F	CHILD	RRZZZZUSA
BRONISLAW	.11	M	INFANT	RRZZZZUSA
RARIMIESWKI, DOMINICKA	31	F	WO	RRZZZZUSA
JOSEF	7	M	CHILD	RRZZZZUSA

PASSENGER	A G E	S E X	OCCUPATION	P V D R I E V L S
FILOMENA	2	F	CHILD	RRZZZZUSA
PREUS, ADOLF	20	M	LABR	RRZZZZUSA

SHIP: SAALE

FROM: BREMEN AND SOUTHAMPTON
TO: NEW YORK
ARRIVED: 16 JUNE 1888

PASSENGER	AGE	SEX	OCCUPATION	PV DES
TERAPOLSKI, WOLF	42	M	FARMER	RRAFWJUSA
ZIELINSKI, FRANZ	24	M	LABR	RRAARRUSA
STANIS	22	M	LABR	RRAARRUSA
TAUB, LINA	17	F	UNKNOWN	RRAHZSUSA
KREITMANN, BENJ	27	M	FARMER	RRAIEZUSA
DINA	22	F	W	RRAIEZUSA
SCHWARZMANN, RIFKA	50	F	UNKNOWN	RRAIEZUSA
GLIEKEL	11	M	UNKNOWN	RRAIEZUSA
KORUBLUM, MEYER	40	M	FARMER	RRAFWJUSA
JEKEWITSCH, FRANZ	28	M	FARMER	RRAHQDUSA
MARIANNA	25	F	W	RRAHQDUSA
ANTONIE	.09	F	INFANT	RRAHQDUSA
EIDUKINESS, IWAN	22	M	SMH	RRAHQDUSA
MARTUSCHEWITZ, ALEX	30	M	SMH	RRAHQDUSA
LAFESIZOLOWITZ, CASPAR	30	M	SMH	RRAHQDUSA
BARZDAIKIS, ANTON	24	M	FARMER	RRAHQDUSA
RAINES, JOSES	28	M	FARMER	RRAHQDUSA
SCHMIEDELIS, PINES	21	M	FARMER	RRAFWJUSA
JOIDWIS, ALEX	32	M	FARMER	RRAFWJUSA

SHIP: SCYTHIA

FROM: LIVERPOOL AND QUEENSTOWN
TO: NEW YORK
ARRIVED: 16 JUNE 1888

PASSENGER	AGE	SEX	OCCUPATION	PV DES
JANSON, NATALIA	32	F	SP	RRZZZZUSA
NASS, ALINA	16	F	SP	RRZZZZUSA
PITTERSON, LENOR	20	F	SP	RRZZZZUSA
SAHAMYLYMAKI, AMALIA	19	F	SP	RRZZZZUSA
AKESON, SAMUEL	32	M	LABR	RRZZZZUSA
BECONITZ, JEAN	24	M	LABR	RRZZZZUSA
HANSON, ERIK	24	M	LABR	RRZZZZUSA
HECTAOJA, VICTOR	18	M	LABR	RRZZZZUSA
HONGISTO, JACOB	26	M	LABR	RRZZZZUSA
HISTARJA, ALFRED	20	M	LABR	RRZZZZUSA
ISCHAROS, PAULUS	23	M	LABR	RRZZZZUSA
JANSON, JOH.J.	28	M	LABR	RRZZZZUSA
KOHBALA, MATTE	32	M	LABR	RRZZZZUSA
KUJOGNAA, IVAN	25	M	LABR	RRZZZZUSA
LULNFOLK, ERIK	26	M	LABR	RRZZZZUSA
LAUTUHWINA, JOHAN	26	M	LABR	RRZZZZUSA
LINDHOLM, ERIC	27	M	MUSN	RRZZZZUSA
MIKKA--FAKA, JUHR	22	M	LABR	RRZZZZUSA
MALTSON, CARL	26	M	LABR	RRZZZZUSA
OMASSA, HERMAN	24	M	LABR	RRZZZZUSA
PATILLA, CARL	29	M	LABR	RRZZZZUSA
PETTERFULA, IVAR	33	M	LABR	RRZZZZUSA
PENTTI, JACOB	28	M	LABR	RRZZZZUSA
RUNDBERG, ALBERT	24	M	LABR	RRZZZZUSA
RYIBERG, CARL	29	M	LABR	RRZZZZUSA
SAHEWITZ, MORLIN	22	M	LABR	RRZZZZUSA
ZAKIMAKA, MALTS	35	M	LABR	RRZZZZUSA
VESL, JOHAN	28	M	LABR	RRZZZZUSA
WEKOJA, ALEY	52	M	LABR	RRZZZZUSA
BRITA	20	F	SP	RRZZZZUSA
ZULS, NICHOLAS	22	M	LABR	RRZZZZUSA
BANDEL, ELIAS	33	M	LABR	RRZZZZUSA
BURSTEIN, NOCHEM	24	M	LABR	RRZZZZUSA
DAUSKI, ELIAS	18	M	LABR	RRZZZZUSA
HAUFMANN, JOSEF	23	M	LABR	RRZZZZUSA
LANDAN, JOSEF	19	M	LABR	RRZZZZUSA
SPRINGE	18	F	SP	RRZZZZUSA
BASCHE	18	F	SP	RRZZZZUSA
LEWIN, ABRAHAM	32	M	LABR	RRZZZZUSA
BALANUT, PESSEL	11	F	CH	RRZZZZUSA
LEWITZ, MICHAL	20	M	LABR	RRZZZZUSA
BELLA	24	F	SP	RRZZZZUSA
MATINFRANKA, OSKAR	19	M	LABR	RRZZZZUSA
PILLAS, MICHEAL	35	M	LABR	RRZZZZUSA
SCHMINKER, SCHMERL	22	M	LABR	RRZZZZUSA
SCHAFIRI, MOSES	18	M	LABR	RRZZZZUSA
SAPERSTEIN, SCHAFSSE	36	M	LABR	RRZZZZUSA
ABRAHAM	19	M	LABR	RRZZZZUSA
STRANSSBRG, SUSSMAN	28	M	LABR	RRZZZZUSA
JAMSE, MIZEL	11	F	CH	RRZZZZUSA
FENERSTIN, MEIER	18	M	LABR	RRZZZZUSA
FARBER, CHAJE	44	F	SVNT	RRZZZZUSA
SARA	19	F	SP	RRZZZZUSA
FIEFE	17	F	SP	RRZZZZUSA
EISIK	10	M	CH	RRZZZZUSA
ABRAHAM	6	M	CHILD	RRZZZZUSA
DEBORAH	4	F	CHILD	RRZZZZUSA
HOROWITZ, DAWID	24	M	LABR	RRZZZZUSA
CHAJI	20	F	W	RRZZZZUSA
SMARDIN, DAVID	14	M	LABR	RRZZZZUSA
MINA	24	F	SP	RRZZZZUSA
HIJA	20	F	SP	RRZZZZUSA
BICKER, REBECCA	18	F	SP	RRZZZZUSA
GOLDENBERG, ROSA	18	F	SP	RRZZZZUSA
RUDOWIKI, CHAJE	19	F	SP	RRZZZZUSA
STRAUSBERG, HENDEL	18	F	SP	RRZZZZUSA
JORMENERD, SARA	20	F	SP	PLZZZZUSA
LEWIN, LEVI	11	M	BY	PLZZZZUSA
TARRS, WILHAIM	35	M	LABR	PLZZZZUSA
AGGIE	30	F	W	PLZZZZUSA
KLAPIOWZKA, KUNDUNDA	30	F	SP	PLZZZZUSA
SOFIE	26	F	SP	PLZZZZUSA
JOSEPH	1	M	CHILD	PLZZZZUSA
SCHUSIDER, ESTER	28	F	SVNT	PLZZZZUSA
LEHULIN	3	M	CHILD	PLZZZZUSA
LEIBICH	.04	M	INFANT	PLZZZZUSA
COHN, MARKUS	44	M	LABR	PLZZZZUSA
SCHWARZ, HERMANN	11	M	BY	PLZZZZUSA
GUSCHINZKI, ROMAN	19	M	LABR	PLZZZZUSA
JUZRIGAUSKI, JOSSEL	18	M	LABR	PLZZZZUSA
WIGDOWITZ, GILLE	34	M	LABR	PLZZZZUSA
HIRSCH	27	M	LABR	PLZZZZUSA
CHEIB	23	F	W	PLZZZZUSA
DAVID	7	M	CHILD	PLZZZZUSA
SUSIE	4	F	CHILD	PLZZZZUSA
KOHL, EISIK	18	M	LABR	PLZZZZUSA
MORGORGE, SALOMON	45	M	LABR	PLZZZZUSA
ROMANOWSKY, FRANZ	25	M	LABR	PLZZZZUSA
KRAKOWZKY, ADAM	28	M	LABR	PLZZZZUSA
SACHS, MARENS	11	M	BY	PLZZZZUSA
HIRSCH	11	M	BY	PLZZZZUSA
WASHEWITZ, JULES	24	M	LABR	PLZZZZUSA
ZUZINAKI, JOSIL	19	M	LABR	PLZZZZUSA
NIMKIN, HIRSCH	24	M	LABR	PLZZZZUSA

PASSENGER	AGE	SEX	OCCUPATION	PRIV	VIL	DES

SHIP: CITY OF CHESTER

FROM: LIVERPOOL AND QUEENSTOWN
TO: NEW YORK
ARRIVED: 16 JUNE 1888

PASSENGER	AGE	SEX	OCCUPATION	PV VIL	DES
HENINKSON, JOSEPH	21	M	LABR	PLAIDE	NY
LAHTI, JOHAN	43	M	LABR	PLAIDE	NY
BRUSI, OTTO	30	M	LABR	PLAIDE	NY
CARL	20	M	LABR	PLAIDE	NY
REIKITA, MATS	39	M	LABR	PLAIDE	BO
LOVILMER, FRANS	24	M	LABR	PLAIDE	BO
YTTERKODAS, JOH	23	M	LABR	PLAIDE	BO
LEIWMEN, JOHAN	29	M	LABR	PLAIDE	NY
TOLKOWSKI, MATITUS	31	M	TLR	PLAIDE	NY
MUNDERS, LENI	13	M	LABR	PLAFZD	NY
GOLDBAUM, DAVID	26	M	TLR	PLAFZD	NY
RUKAS, JOS	20	M	LABR	PLAFZD	NY
M---, U	41	M	SHMK	PLAFZD	NY
GINSTERG, BENT	30	M	CGRMKR	PLAFZD	NY
FIMKOWSKY, M	35	M	LABR	PLAFZD	NY
MEHLMANN, JANKEL	30	M	SHMK	PLAEFL	NY
BORKOWSKI, THD.	21	M	LABR	PLAFZD	NY
ANT	32	M	LABR	PLAFZD	NY
PINKAS, MENDEL	34	M	TLR	PLAFZD	NY
LETWIST, ANTONI	22	M	LABR	PLAFZD	NY
SELIKOWSKI, BENNIS	35	M	STKPR	PLAFZD	NY
WIDLANSKI, SIMON	27	M	SMH	PLAFZD	NY
SGERL, SCHOLME	16	M	LABR	PLAFZD	NY
KALIN, MEIER	17	M	LABR	PLAFZD	NY
DAMSKI, JOSEPH	24	M	TLR	PLAFZD	PHI
ROSEMANN, SCH	32	M	LABR	PLAFZD	NY
PERNLA, MATTS	19	M	LABR	PLAIDE	BO
ULALLIN, MATTS	44	M	LABR	PLAIDE	BO
LAMMINPAN, JONAS	21	M	LABR	PLAIDE	SFC
SIMDOHL, WALDEMAR	21	M	LABR	PLAIDE	NY
BAR, MEIER	15	M	LABR	PLAIDE	NY
MARWILL, KALMAN	18	M	TLR	PLAIDE	NY
BARTINK, ROMAN	22	M	LABR	PLAIDE	NY
LIMIK, MARTIN	35	M	LABR	PLAIDE	NY
ROSCHETZKY, ANTON	25	M	LABR	PLAIDE	NY
PLOTKIN, MEIER	23	M	LABR	PLAIDE	NY
WISCHOFSKY, JAN	23	M	LABR	PLAIDE	NY
HOCHSTEIN, MOSCHE	30	M	TLR	PLAIDE	NY
SCHIGERNOPSKI, JAN	30	M	LABR	PLAFZD	NY
RIBAK, JOSEPH	28	M	TLR	PLAFZD	BAL
DOSCHKEWITZ, LUD	23	M	LABR	PLAFZD	NY
MAMMAKI, SUS	23	F	W	PLAFZD	DAK
BABITSCH, ESTER	59	F	W	PLAFZD	IL
PRAWZ, CLER	53	F	W	PLAFZD	PHI
JUHASKA, E	20	M	SP	PLAHVL	USA
GETZAR, RISCHE	17	F	SP	PLAHVL	NY
ELTERMANN, DWOSCHE	18	F	SP	PLAHVL	NY
BAR, FANNE	18	F	SP	RRZZZZ	NY
WIDLANSKI, GITEL	20	F	SP	RRZZZZ	PHI
ZELENYNKI, ANNA	21	F	SP	RRZZZZ	NY
ROLTMANN, HESSEL	22	F	CGRMKR	RRZZZZ	BAL
CHANS	18	F	CGRMKR	RRZZZZ	BAL
GOEDBAUM, FEIGE	25	F	W	RRAINM	NY
ZIRIL	5	F	CHILD	RRAINM	NY
KATZ, GERSEN	50	M	TLR	RRAINM	NY
SORE	44	F	W	RRAINM	NY
CHAIM	9	M	CHILD	RRAINM	NY
ZAPHUND, M	32	F	W	RRAINM	IL
STAUS	6	M	CHILD	RRAINM	IL
JAN	4	M	CHILD	RRAINM	IL
JOSEPH	.10	M	INFANT	RRAINM	IL
CHECHOWITZ, VIC	22	F	W	RRAINM	IL
JOH	3	M	CHILD	RRAINM	IL
MARY	.08	F	INFANT	RRAINM	IL
ZANDSKA, ANNA	26	F	W	RRAINM	IL
JOH	3	M	CHILD	RRAINM	IL
ANNA	.09	F	INFANT	RRAINM	IL
POSTILMIK, CH	46	M	LABR	RRAINM	IL
SCH	47	F	W	RRAINM	IL
RUBEN	26	F	SP	RRAINM	IL
SILDE	22	F	SP	RRAINM	IL
LIEBE	4	M	CHILD	RRAINM	IL
ROSA	.11	F	INFANT	RRAINM	IL
KORENFILD, RACHE	45	F	W	RRAINM	PA
ALRA	18	M	LABR	RRAINM	PA
USCHEN	11	M	CH	RRAINM	PA
SEMEL	8	M	CHILD	RRAINM	PA
GITTEL	7	F	CHILD	RRAINM	PA
ABOWITZ, CHANE	38	M	LABR	RRAINM	PA
SCHIE	11	F	CH	RRAINM	PA
GOLDE	3	M	CHILD	RRAINM	PA
CHAIE	.10	F	INFANT	RRAINM	PA
SAPOSINSKA, ALBE	39	F	W	RRAFVG	NY
HINDE	10	F	CH	RRAFVG	NY
GRISCHE	8	M	CHILD	RRAFVG	NY
SIMKE	14	F	CH	RRAFVG	NY
FEIGE	.08	F	INFANT	RRAFVG	NY
BLUME	.10	F	INFANT	RRAFVG	NY
IMIDEWITSCH, JOS	25	M	MLR	RRAFVG	PHI
PAWLACZIK, JOH	35	M	SMH	RRZZZZ	PA
SOWA, FRIED	60	M	CPTR	RRZZZZ	PA
GOTH	53	F	W	RRZZZZ	PA
AUG	10	M	CH	RRZZZZ	PA
TIMBULSKI, ST.	30	M	LABR	RRZZZZ	PA
SVODA, JULIA	18	F	SVNT	RRZZZZ	PA
BARANSKI, MARIA	21	F	SVNT	RRZZZZ	PA
NIPPICH, WILH	25	F	SVNT	RRZZZZ	PA
MELADICK, GOETH	23	F	SVNT	RRZZZZ	PA

SHIP: RHAETIA

FROM: HAMBURG AND HAVRE
TO: NEW YORK
ARRIVED: 18 JUNE 1888

PASSENGER	AGE	SEX	OCCUPATION	PV VIL	DES
KUEKKOMANN, JOH.	15	M	LABR	FNZZZZ	USA
KROTOPSKY, MICHEL	17	M	TLR	RRZZZZ	USA
NATHAN	16	M	TLR	RRZZZZ	USA
ISZGAUZUTI, ROSZIA	20	F	SGL	RRZZZZ	USA
BUDUKIEWICZ, FELIX	21	M	LABR	RRZZZZ	USA
LEVITEMSKI, SALOMON	38	M	UNKNOWN	RRZZZZ	USA
ERSON, ANIE	14	F	SGL	RRZZZZ	USA
FELLER, CHAIE	56	F	WO	RRZZZZ	USA
PISMENTZER, MORITZ	24	M	LABR	RRZZZZ	USA
HALPERN, ESTHER	20	F	SGL	RRZZZZ	USA
HERRMANN, ABRAM	42	M	LABR	RRZZZZ	USA
PERLOW, MOSES	21	M	LABR	RRZZZZ	USA
ULANOWSKA, HIRSCH	16	M	LABR	RRZZZZ	USA
REHER, WILH.	47	M	LABR	RRZZZZ	USA
PARUWER, SZUEL	43	M	LABR	RRZZZZ	USA
ABRAM	17	M	LABR	RRZZZZ	USA
GALIKS, BENZIAN	40	M	LABR	RRZZZZ	USA
SZLEISEN, NACHMEN	20	M	LABR	RRZZZZ	USA
HOSLER, HERZ	35	M	LABR	RRZZZZ	USA
OLDZIEWSKI, MARIANE	37	F	W	RRZZZZ	USA
STANISL.	8	M	CHILD	RRZZZZ	USA
BRONISL.	2	M	CHILD	RRZZZZ	USA
SCHWARZ, MOSES	60	M	LABR	RRZZZZ	USA
SARLINSKY, ANTON	24	M	LABR	RRZZZZ	USA
MARKUNAS, ANTON	21	M	LABR	RRZZZZ	USA
PUTZKA, HELENE	45	F	W	RRZZZZ	USA
HECSE, ANDREY	50	M	LABR	RRZZZZ	USA
TESSMANN, LOUISE	21	F	WO	RRZZZZ	USA
STANIZEWSKY, FRANZ	26	M	LABR	RRZZZZ	USA
BERGER, FRIEDR.	26	M	CPTR	RRZZZZ	USA
LACKA, CLEMENTINE	33	F	W	RRZZZZ	USA
SOFIE	7	F	CHILD	RRZZZZ	USA
LUZDGOWNA, MAGDA.	30	F	WO	RRZZZZ	USA

PASSENGER	AGE	SEX	OCCUPATION	PRV VIL DES
KUNDROTKAS, ANDRZY	20	M	LABR	RRZZZZUSA
CYTEWICZ, LEONARD	20	M	LABR	RRZZZZUSA
ENDLER, LEA	18	F	WO	RRZZZZUSA
STACHINDITZ, SCHIMKE	25	F	SGL	RRZZZZUSA
KROM, BARUCH	17	M	LABR	RRZZZZUSA
GOLDBERG, ABRAM	17	M	LABR	RRZZZZUSA
WATEJIJANOWSKY, OSIM	28	M	LABR	RRZZZZUSA
ANTON	25	M	LABR	RRZZZZUSA
SMIELYEIR, JURIS	50	M	LABR	RRZZZZUSA
EUTER, CARL	15	M	LABR	RRZZZZUSA
KANAROOGEL, LEA	28	F	W	RRZZZZUSA
UHLMANN, BERTHA	19	F	WO	RRZZZZUSA
URBACH, LOUIS	18	M	LABR	RRZZZZUSA
SCHWENDNER, AUGE.	15	F	WO	RRZZZZUSA
SCHAPNIAK, CHAJE	16	F	SGL	RRZZZZUSA
ZICH, ROSA	21	F	SGL	RRZZZZUSA
ARONOWITZ, MEYER	17	M	DLR	RRZZZZUSA
SOCKEL, ALTER	16	M	TLR	RRZZZZUSA
MANDLEIN, SLATE	18	F	SGL	RRZZZZUSA
KOSLAWSKY, KARL	27	M	LABR	RRZZZZUSA
LOSONSKI, VICTOR	22	M	LABR	RRZZZZUSA
LEVINSOHN, CHAIM	16	M	LABR	RRZZZZUSA
MESIS, FRANZ	30	M	LABR	RRZZZZUSA
ALKSCHNIS, JOSEF	27	M	LABR	RRZZZZUSA
MILNER, HIRSCH	20	M	LABR	RRZZZZUSA
KRAM, OREL	20	M	LABR	RRZZZZUSA
TALWACHS, FRANZ	36	M	LABR	RRZZZZUSA
BLUMENZWEIG, GELLA	17	F	SGL	RRZZZZUSA
BERKOWITZ, JUDEL	20	M	JNR	RRZZZZUSA
WALTANA, JOSEF	20	M	LABR	RRZZZZUSA
NARUMSKI, ARON	17	M	SHMK	RRZZZZUSA
LURJE, CHANE	23	M	DLR	RRZZZZUSA
ZERKOWSKY, JULIAN	26	M	LABR	RRZZZZUSA
BUMKUS, IGNATZ	19	M	LABR	RRZZZZUSA
WISNEWSKI, BERL	30	M	DLR	RRZZZZUSA
LEIB	9	M	CHILD	RRZZZZUSA
GELBERT, MATIS	33	M	DLR	RRZZZZUSA
SCHACK, NOSSEN	27	M	LABR	RRZZZZUSA
ROMANOWSKI, BOLESLAW	24	M	LABR	RRZZZZUSA
KORCI, JAN	17	M	LABR	RRZZZZUSA
TIETZ, AUGUST	35	M	SHMK	RRZZZZUSA
MORDCHELISWIECZ, ABR.	26	M	DLR	RRZZZZUSA
FREIBERG, ARON	16	M	DLR	RRZZZZUSA
ROSENSOHN, DAVID	21	M	LABR	RRZZZZUSA
FRIDA	18	F	W	RRZZZZUSA
SAWIALIS, MARIA	21	F	WO	RRZZZZUSA
ISERSKI, HENE	18	F	SGL	RRZZZZUSA
KWIAT, ABRAM	18	M	DLR	RRZZZZUSA
MORDCHIEL, FRANZ	38	M	DLR	RRZZZZUSA
BROSAROSKY, VINCENTY	22	M	DLR	RRZZZZUSA
PALESTIN, SCHLOMA	32	M	DLR	RRZZZZUSA
HINDE	28	F	WO	RRZZZZUSA
CZUPRINSKI, ANNA	40	F	WO	RRZZZZUSA
KOWALSKA, MARIANNE	22	F	WO	RRZZZZUSA
MARIANNE	1	F	CHILD	RRZZZZUSA
FELIX	.01	M	INFANT	RRZZZZUSA
SUZYNSKI, CHRISTIAN	24	M	LABR	RRZZZZUSA
LEDER, JOSEF	43	M	JNR	RRZZZZUSA
FRANZ	13	M	CH	RRZZZZUSA
THADEN, UDE	15	M	FARMER	RRZZZZUSA
ZALONIS, VINCENTI	18	M	LABR	RRZZZZUSA
SECKAWIEZ, JOSEF	37	M	LABR	RRZZZZUSA
ORNOTOWICZ, JOSEF	37	M	LABR	RRZZZZUSA
CARSTEIN, CATHA.	16	F	SGL	FNZZZZUSA
SLAHAMULA, KONSTANTIN	28	F	SGL	FNZZZZUSA
HARPN, SUTTI	34	F	SGL	FNZZZZUSA
LABUTIS, JAN	33	F	SGL	FNZZZZUSA
BIELSKA, ANNA	16	F	SGL	RRZZZZUSA
ROSENTHAL, LEISER	17	M	DLR	RRZZZZUSA
KLASKE, HANNE	30	F	WO	RRZZZZUSA
DIME	15	F	CH	RRZZZZUSA
ESTHER	9	F	CHILD	RRZZZZUSA
DAVID	8	M	CHILD	RRZZZZUSA
HEIE	7	F	CHILD	RRZZZZUSA
IDELAIDE	6	F	CHILD	RRZZZZUSA

PASSENGER	AGE	SEX	OCCUPATION	PRV VIL DES
LOSER	4	M	CHILD	RRZZZZUSA
LIPOLATZKI, BERKO	20	M	DLR	RRZZZZUSA
LAMMI, OSCAR	24	M	LABR	FNZZZZUSA
HAEKALA, CONSTANTIN	18	M	LABR	FNZZZZUSA
ECKLOEF, JACOB	34	M	LABR	FNZZZZUSA
PERLMUTTER, MAX	24	M	DLR	RRZZZZUSA
SCHIENHAUSEN, MEILECH	23	M	LABR	RRZZZZUSA
GABSKY, LADISLAWA	21	F	SGL	RRZZZZUSA
YRSILA, ISMAEL	27	M	LABR	FNZZZZUSA
JAGERSTROEM, JOHANN	34	M	LABR	FNZZZZUSA
SAAREMPA, JUHA	21	M	LABR	FNZZZZUSA
KAARA, MARIA	26	F	WO	FNZZZZUSA
TIA	19	F	SGL	FNZZZZUSA
WIHTORI	4	F	CHILD	FNZZZZUSA
IDA	.09	F	INFANT	FNZZZZUSA
HEITKINPOCKO, JOHANN	24	M	LABR	FNZZZZUSA
SARAANPAA, HEUTRIK	44	M	LABR	FNZZZZUSA
KLEINOKOSKI, NESTOR	19	M	LABR	FNZZZZUSA
KOVERSA, HEUTRIK	26	M	LABR	FNZZZZUSA
SCHULZ, MARIA	19	F	SGL	FNZZZZUSA
BACKER, PESCHE	19	F	SGL	RRZZZZUSA
KANTZIPOWITZ, RACHEL	16	F	SGL	RRZZZZUSA
CHAI	9	F	CHILD	RRZZZZUSA
POLEY, ANNIE	17	F	SGL	RRZZZZUSA
SCHICHOTSKI, CASIMIR	22	M	LABR	RRZZZZUSA
NOWOWRYKY, BERKO	24	M	LABR	RRZZZZUSA
SCHAPIRA, DAVID	19	M	LABR	RRZZZZUSA
KANOWITZ, BARUCH	18	M	LABR	RRZZZZUSA
WEINER, ROSA	40	F	SGL	RRZZZZUSA
MISCHKOLZ, MENDEL	18	M	LABR	RRZZZZUSA
WERNER, FEIWEL	55	F	DLR	RRZZZZUSA
FRUME	41	F	W	RRZZZZUSA
CHATZKEL	18	M	CH	RRZZZZUSA
SLOME	9	F	CHILD	RRZZZZUSA
JUDE	8	M	CHILD	RRZZZZUSA
SAMUEL	5	M	CHILD	RRZZZZUSA
MOSES	3	M	CHILD	RRZZZZUSA
MECKE	9	F	CHILD	RRZZZZUSA
WEBER, EFRAIM	19	M	DLR	RRZZZZUSA
SAWLINAS, KONSTANTIN	28	M	JNR	RRZZZZUSA
WEITSCHULIS, ANTON	25	M	LABR	RRZZZZUSA
LEUKOWSKI, FRANZICZEK	24	M	LABR	RRZZZZUSA
LIBOWSKY, JOSEF	22	M	LABR	RRZZZZUSA
MAKSTUETZ, MARCUS	21	M	FARMER	RRZZZZUSA
DLUNSKI, ISRAEL	32	M	LABR	RRZZZZUSA
LASAR	9	M	CHILD	RRZZZZUSA
GILDENBERG, HIRSCH	27	M	DLR	RRZZZZUSA
GRESSER, WOLFF	33	M	FUR	RRZZZZUSA
GARMAISL, MERSES	41	M	DLR	RRZZZZUSA
GRAESSER, TEWIE	36	M	FUR	RRZZZZUSA
RIWKIN, MEYER	20	M	JNR	RRZZZZUSA
JACOB	28	M	JNR	RRZZZZUSA
GUSTAITIS, JOSES	17	M	LABR	RRZZZZUSA
KARPOWITZ, PETRAS	29	M	LABR	RRZZZZUSA
KASIS	20	M	LABR	RRZZZZUSA
IDELZIK, RAFAEL	40	M	FUR	RRZZZZUSA
SMICAKSKOSKI, CARL	21	M	LABR	FNZZZZUSA
KOTKA, MATTS	18	M	LABR	FNZZZZUSA
ARALA, HENRIK	18	M	LABR	FNZZZZUSA
CAROLSCHUK, PETER	30	M	LABR	RRZZZZUSA
BROSMOWSKY, JACOB	30	M	LABR	RRZZZZUSA
WERBIN, MARIE	25	F	WO	RRZZZZUSA
ZIWJE	.09	F	INFANT	RRZZZZUSA
LEWIN, TAUBE	3	F	CHILD	RRZZZZUSA
KOVODA, KALLE	25	M	LABR	FNZZZZUSA
LONTO, JOH.	21	M	LABR	FNZZZZUSA
FRIEDELSOHN, JACOB	27	M	DLR	RRZZZZUSA
WOLLBERG, LENA	23	F	WO	RRZZZZUSA
CLARA	.11	F	INFANT	RRZZZZUSA
KAMINSKA, JOSEFA	32	F	WO	RRZZZZUSA
SINDER, CHANNE	50	F	WO	RRZZZZUSA
FEDAK, MARCIA	17	F	SGL	RRZZZZUSA
KANOBSKIN, HEYMANN	34	M	JNR	RRZZZZUSA
MEUSCHAR	9	M	CHILD	RRZZZZUSA
NEUMANN, SLOME	35	F	LABR	RRZZZZUSA

PASSENGER	AGE	SEX	OCCUPATION	PRIVL	DES
GRUB, LEVY	27	F	LABR	RRZZZZ	USA
KIENBERG, SZIMIEL	26	F	LABR	RRZZZZ	USA
BURD, RIWE	46	F	WO	RRZZZZ	USA
LEA	19	F	CH	RRZZZZ	USA
BRZODKA, JAN	35	M	LABR	RRZZZZ	USA
KOENIGSBERG, NATHAN.	20	M	LABR	RRZZZZ	USA
WEISS, SALOMON	20	M	LABR	RRZZZZ	USA
MERSENOWA, SARAH	21	F	WO	RRZZZZ	USA
INDESKE	.11	F	INFANT	RRZZZZ	USA
SZEPANOWA, KARL	32	M	LABR	RRZZZZ	USA
ANTANAS, PAUL	29	M	LABR	RRZZZZ	USA
DABENECKA, FILOMELA	22	F	WO	RRZZZZ	USA
JOSEF	.09	M	INFANT	RRZZZZ	USA
FRIEDEBERG, ARTHUR	23	M	APTC	RRZZZZ	USA
JAWEIN, OSCAR	23	M	MCHT	RRZZZZ	USA

SHIP: CIRCASSIA

FROM: GLASGOW AND MOVILLE
TO: NEW YORK
ARRIVED: 19 JUNE 1888

PASSENGER	AGE	SEX	OCCUPATION	PRIVL	DES
OLDAKOWSKY, ADOLF	23	M	LABR	RRZZZZ	USA
CHONES, ABR	18	M	WCHMKR	RRZZZZ	USA
PIKEL, FRANKEL	29	M	LABR	RRZZZZ	USA
OPPENHEIM, ISRAEL	19	M	TLR	RRZZZZ	USA
SILBERMAN, CH	19	M	LABR	RRZZZZ	USA
TOKIER, KOPEL	23	M	TLR	RRZZZZ	USA
STASOKINAS, MICHAEL	28	M	LABR	RRZZZZ	USA
BALKUM, ADAM	23	M	DLR	RRZZZZ	USA
BRUCHANSKY, CHASKEL	45	M	TLR	RRZZZZ	USA
MCTR.	16	M	TLR	RRZZZZ	USA
BALTRUKONIS, LUKAS	21	M	LABR	RRZZZZ	USA
SKOWRONSKY, MICHAEL	19	M	LABR	RRZZZZ	USA
KALCHA, LIPMAN	50	M	LABR	RRZZZZ	USA
SORE	16	M	LABR	RRZZZZ	USA
SALSE	14	M	LABR	RRZZZZ	USA
SCHEPENOR, SIMON	31	M	LABR	RRZZZZ	USA
LIEB	9	M	CHILD	RRZZZZ	USA
ZILSUSKAS, KASIMIR	20	M	CH	RRZZZZ	USA
EIDLEMAN, HOSSIAS	19	M	DLR	RRZZZZ	USA
SCHNOCKLY, VICTOR	22	M	LABR	RRZZZZ	USA
LAM, JOACHIM	23	M	TLR	RRZZZZ	USA
KANNER, KIRSCH	39	M	DLR	RRZZZZ	USA
HARFER, MASCHOK	53	M	DLR	RRZZZZ	USA
PALLER, BORUCK	29	M	LABR	RRZZZZ	USA
WIRNSCH, ANSER	16	M	LABR	RRZZZZ	USA
LUBEDKIN, ARON	30	M	LABR	RRZZZZ	USA
OLDYNSKI, PAVIL	22	M	LABR	RRZZZZ	USA
KRASEWITZ, MEYER	30	M	TLR	RRZZZZ	USA
KOHN, SCHLOME	10	M	CH	RRZZZZ	USA
BORKY, ABR	34	M	DLR	RRZZZZ	USA
WASEBE, LUKJEN	40	M	LABR	RRZZZZ	USA
BROSOWITZ, MISKPO	39	M	LABR	RRZZZZ	USA
IVAN	28	M	LABR	RRZZZZ	USA
JACOBINAS, ANTON	28	M	LABR	RRZZZZ	USA
FEDEROWITZ, KASEMIR	24	M	LABR	RRZZZZ	USA
FISCHER, CHEIN	25	M	LABR	RRZZZZ	USA
NIERENSTEIN, SCHLOME	24	M	CGRMKR	RRZZZZ	USA
GOLDBERG, MOSES	19	M	LABR	RRZZZZ	USA
WERMUTH, JAEGNES	21	M	LABR	RRZZZZ	USA
RABINOWITZ, MICH	35	M	MACH	RRZZZZ	USA
KOHN, MOSES	31	M	HTLKPR	RRZZZZ	USA
KUSNETZ, SCHLOME	37	M	TLR	RRZZZZ	USA
OLKOWSKY, WODESLAU	30	M	LKSH	RRZZZZ	USA
ANDUSKISWICZ, MARCIN	33	M	LABR	RRZZZZ	USA
LEIMANOWITZ, BOCH	44	M	LABR	RRZZZZ	USA
GNEAZDOWSKI, WITALIS	32	M	DLR	RRZZZZ	USA
SCHKOLNIK, SCHAPSE	23	M	BKBNDR	RRZZZZ	USA
GOLDBERG, RUWEN	38	M	TLR	RRZZZZ	USA

PASSENGER	AGE	SEX	OCCUPATION	PRIVL	DES
BERNSTEIN, JAKOB	27	M	BTMKR	RRZZZZ	USA
LEWANDOWSKY, WAUZYAN	26	M	LABR	RRZZZZ	USA
AGNES	25	F	W	RRZZZZ	USA
FRQNCISCA	1	F	CHILD	RRZZZZ	USA
TUCHNEWIEZ, ANDREAS	41	M	LABR	RRZZZZ	USA
AGATA	30	F	W	RRZZZZ	USA
DOMINIK	1	M	CHILD	RRZZZZ	USA
ROSENBERG, DAVID	24	M	DLR	RRZZZZ	USA
CHAJE	23	F	W	RRZZZZ	USA
ZARNA, ISAK	36	M	DLR	RRZZZZ	USA
LEA	36	F	W	RRZZZZ	USA
HIRSCH	10	M	CH	RRZZZZ	USA
BERRIEL	6	M	CHILD	RRZZZZ	USA
HANNS	4	M	CHILD	RRZZZZ	USA
KUNCEWITZKI, WOLF	44	M	DLR	RRZZZZ	USA
ESTER	43	F	W	RRZZZZ	USA
KRISTINE	22	F	HP	RRZZZZ	USA
RIWKE	7	F	CHILD	RRZZZZ	USA
ITKE	6	F	CHILD	RRZZZZ	USA
LIEBE	1	F	CHILD	RRZZZZ	USA
LIES	.04	M	INFANT	RRZZZZ	USA
EFFRON, MOSES	22	M	DLR	RRZZZZ	USA
CHAIE	20	F	W	RRZZZZ	USA
LEIS	.09	M	INFANT	RRZZZZ	USA
SOMENSKY, SCHAJE	29	F	W	RRZZZZ	USA
SCHEWACK	7	M	CHILD	RRZZZZ	USA
ROOKE	5	M	CHILD	RRZZZZ	USA
ETTEL	18	F	HP	RRZZZZ	USA
SAREMBA, ETTE	19	F	HP	RRZZZZ	USA
GOLDE	17	F	HP	RRZZZZ	USA
HERZOG, GUSTA	19	F	HP	RRZZZZ	USA
WESJE, ROSA	20	F	HP	RRZZZZ	USA
SCHONBBANN, RACHEL	17	F	HP	RRZZZZ	USA
MARG	15	F	HP	RRZZZZ	USA
PERLMAN, BEILE	18	F	HP	RRZZZZ	USA
FOLTSKINE, ARENSTINE	17	F	HP	RRZZZZ	USA
EPSTEIN, MASCHE	20	F	HP	RRZZZZ	USA
SARAH	21	F	HP	RRZZZZ	USA
STEIN, LIEB	43	F	HP	RRZZZZ	USA
WISNEROSKA, MARIANA	20	F	HP	RRZZZZ	USA
KNEATZINSKY, MORDCHE	24	F	HP	RRZZZZ	USA
CHANE	17	F	HP	RRZZZZ	USA
ROSENBAUM, ROSA	33	F	W	RRZZZZ	USA
MALKE	10	F	CH	RRZZZZ	USA
ETTE	6	F	CHILD	RRZZZZ	USA
MOSES	1	M	CHILD	RRZZZZ	USA
GILLIS, PESSE	30	F	HP	RRZZZZ	USA
CHAJE	33	F	HP	RRZZZZ	USA
BASSE	12	F	UNKNOWN	RRZZZZ	USA
ROCHE	11	F	UNKNOWN	RRZZZZ	USA
SCHMUL	8	M	CHILD	RRZZZZ	USA
ELKE	1	F	CHILD	RRZZZZ	USA
FESZE	1	F	CHILD	RRZZZZ	USA
MISCHALOWITZ, MARTA	19	F	HP	RRZZZZ	USA
WERSDEC, MINDE	20	F	HP	RRZZZZ	USA
KONIG, SCHIFNE	25	F	HP	RRZZZZ	USA
GOLDLISH, HANE	20	F	HP	RRZZZZ	USA
DLOSH, FEIGE	18	F	HP	RRZZZZ	USA
MADOGENSKY, LESSE	26	F	W	RRZZZZ	USA
RIFKE	3	M	CHILD	RRZZZZ	USA
OLE	.06	F	INFANT	RRZZZZ	USA
SCHALE, SCHEINE	17	M	HP	RRZZZZ	USA
KAHN, GALI	17	M	HP	RRZZZZ	USA
ZISLISKY, KAROLINE	50	F	HP	RRZZZZ	USA
KAUFMANN, DREISKE	20	F	W	RRZZZZ	USA
SALIG	.10	M	INFANT	RRZZZZ	USA
ISAK, LEIB	18	M	LABR	RRZZZZ	USA
TAUBA	20	M	HP	RRZZZZ	USA
GOLDENBERG, RESIL	15	F	HP	RRZZZZ	USA
BLANCK, CHAIE	45	F	HP	RRZZZZ	USA
BRUSHA	14	F	HP	RRZZZZ	USA
WENDELOWITZ, LIEB	18	M	LABR	RRZZZZ	USA
GOLDENBERG, SENDEL	15	M	LABR	RRZZZZ	USA
BLANK, SCHMUL	24	M	LABR	RRZZZZ	USA

SHIP: FULDA

FROM: BREMEN AND SOUTHAMPTON
TO: NEW YORK
ARRIVED: 19 JUNE 1888

PASSENGER	AGE	SEX	OCCUPATION	PRV VIL DES
NESTOROWITSCH, ALESYS	43	M	TT	RRZZZZUSA
CONSTANZ	7	F	CHILD	RRZZZZUSA
WADENTYERNA, WALFRIED	31	M	MCHT	RRZZZZUSA
FLINKMANOWA, SOSCHE	40	M	FARMER	RRZZZZUSA
LESER	7	M	CHILD	RRZZZZUSA
NISZEN	5	M	CHILD	RRZZZZUSA
PEZE	4	M	CHILD	RRZZZZUSA
COHN, ESTER-REFKE	18	M	LABR	RRZZZZUSA
KORENBLUEH, ZILLI	6	M	CHILD	RRZZZZUSA
SCHERMANN, GERSON	21	M	FARMER	RRZZZZUSA
MARSCHAWSKY, PERL	7	M	CHILD	RRZZZZUSA
FISCHER, SARAH	19	F	UNKNOWN	RRZZZZUSA
ARON	52	M	LABR	RRZZZZUSA
JENNIE	49	F	UNKNOWN	RRZZZZUSA
SCHEINE	7	F	CHILD	RRZZZZUSA
FUERTOS, REBECKA	40	F	CH	RRZZZZUSA
HELLMANN, WILHELM	20	M	FARMER	RRZZZZUSA
DAASE, AUGUST	22	M	LABR	RRZZZZUSA
GONTARSKY, ANTON	27	M	PNTR	RRZZZZUSA
JONASZ, FELIX	26	M	PNTR	RRZZZZUSA
FUCHS, LEOPOLD	59	M	FARMER	RRZZZZUSA
CAROLINE	57	F	UNKNOWN	RRZZZZUSA
GUSTAV	18	M	FARMER	RRZZZZUSA
THEOPHIL	16	M	FARMER	RRZZZZUSA
LUDWIG	7	M	CHILD	RRZZZZUSA
KOSTRZEWSKY, KAZIMIR	25	M	LABR	RRZZZZUSA
DOBIERZ, JAN	22	M	LABR	RRZZZZUSA
JAN	22	M	LABR	RRZZZZUSA
ROMELSKI, ADAM	28	M	LABR	RRZZZZUSA
SABSOWITSCH, HIRSCH	28	M	LABR	RRZZZZUSA
CATHARINE	28	F	UNKNOWN	RRZZZZUSA
MARIA	4	F	CHILD	RRZZZZUSA
WERA	.09	F	INFANT	RRZZZZUSA
DAVIDOFF, MARCUS	21	M	LABR	RRZZZZUSA
FLIKMANORE, MASCHE	18	M	LABR	RRZZZZUSA
ROSENTHAL, DAVID	25	M	LABR	RRZZZZUSA
SAMUEL	27	M	LABR	RRZZZZUSA
GUSTAITIS, TOMASCHE	24	M	LABR	RRZZZZUSA
GOLDSTEIN, ARON	18	M	LABR	RRZZZZUSA
ROCHELSOHN, FEIGE	19	M	BKR	RRZZZZUSA
GOLUB, CHAJEM	27	M	BKR	RRZZZZUSA
RODAK, MENDEL	27	M	DYR	RRZZZZUSA
MICHALOWICZ, DWORE	53	M	LABR	RRZZZZUSA
ARONSOHN, HANNA	33	F	UNKNOWN	RRZZZZUSA
BERTHA	7	F	CHILD	RRZZZZUSA
REBECCA	6	F	CHILD	RRZZZZUSA
MANE	5	F	CHILD	RRZZZZUSA
BELLA	3	F	CHILD	RRZZZZUSA
HERMANN	.09	M	INFANT	RRZZZZUSA
COHN, LESE	29	F	UNKNOWN	RRZZZZUSA
JONAS	4	M	CHILD	RRZZZZUSA
JOSSEL	5	F	CHILD	RRZZZZUSA
SUESSEL	18	F	UNKNOWN	RRZZZZUSA
BALSTEIN, LESE	17	F	UNKNOWN	RRZZZZUSA
MICKIEWICZ, JONAS	23	M	LABR	RRZZZZUSA
EVA	22	F	UNKNOWN	RRZZZZUSA
JAK, SCHIMAN	70	M	LABR	RRZZZZUSA
SCHISTRA	7	F	CHILD	RRZZZZUSA
ABRAHAM	6	M	CHILD	RRZZZZUSA
OPPENLAENDER, FRIEDRICH	20	M	BKR	RRZZZZUSA
MARIE	19	F	UNKNOWN	RRZZZZUSA
WOLEISCHO, JONATZ	20	M	FARMER	RRZZZZUSA
MARIE	19	F	UNKNOWN	RRZZZZUSA
LUDWIG	17	M	FARMER	RRZZZZUSA
POLIANSKY, ABRAM	37	M	LABR	RRZZZZUSA
WIRSTEIN, ABRAHAM	32	M	LABR	RRZZZZUSA
PARMETZ, SCHLOME	20	F	UNKNOWN	RRZZZZUSA
SEGALOF, ELSE	28	F	UNKNOWN	RRZZZZUSA
RACHEL	22	F	UNKNOWN	RRZZZZUSA

SHIP: NEVADA

FROM: LIVERPOOL AND QUEENSTOWN
TO: NEW YORK
ARRIVED: 20 JUNE 1888

PASSENGER	AGE	SEX	OCCUPATION	PRV VIL DES
STYF, ABRAHAM	40	M	FARMER	RRACBFUSA
LILIKOWSKY, LEIB	36	M	FARMER	RRACBFUSA
KUDBLISKY, ABRAHAM	27	M	FARMER	RRACBFUSA
SCHAPIRO, ABRAHAM	18	M	FARMER	RRACBFUSA
WEISS, SCHAIE	19	M	FARMER	RRACBFUSA
SCHAKER, MARCUS	35	M	FARMER	RRACBFUSA
GOLDREICK, HANNA	7	F	CHILD	RRACBFUSA
SLUNAK, BARUCH	15	M	LABR	RRACBFUSA
TAFFE, ABRAHAM	20	M	LABR	RRACBFUSA
GARLENLAND, HERSCH	47	M	FARMER	RRACBFUSA
ISAAC	20	M	FARMER	RRACBFUSA
KLONGELAND, PEDER	36	M	FARMER	RRACBFUSA
POKARSKI, JANKEL	21	M	FARMER	RRACBFUSA
BENJAMIN, JULIUS	18	M	FARMER	RRACBFUSA
CESELSKI, SAMUEL	7	M	CHILD	RRACBFUSA
JACUBOWITZ, KATI	18	M	LABR	RRACBFUSA
SLAWINSKI, NESIE	18	M	LABR	RRACBFUSA
ABRAMOWICZ, NACHAM	16	M	LABR	RRACBFUSA
WECHSTER, ISRAEL	27	M	LABR	RRACBFUSA
HOLMGVIST, FREDERICK	27	M	LABR	RRACBFUSA
FREIDEL, ISAAC	26	M	FARMER	RRACBFUSA
KREI, ARON	23	M	FARMER	RRACBFUSA
WOLKOWITZ, FRUNE	26	F	W	RRACBFUSA
RIWKE	6	F	CHILD	RRACBFUSA
MICHLE	5	M	CHILD	RRACBFUSA
SCHWARTZ, FANNY	23	F	SP	RRACBFUSA
SCHEIERMAN, RACHEL	23	F	W	RRACBFUSA
ABRAHAM	.06	M	INFANT	RRACBFUSA
MESCHORER, SCHMERL	.06	M	INFANT	RRACBFUSA
KRAWCZUK, ELKE	28	M	FARMER	RRACBFUSA
RINE	26	F	W	RRACBFUSA
CHONE	.06	F	INFANT	RRACBFUSA
ISRAEL	.06	M	INFANT	RRACBFUSA
ROSENSTEIN, ESTER	6	F	CHILD	RRACBFUSA
SMAIDERMAN, LEAH	24	F	W	RRACBFUSA
GASHEN	4	M	CHILD	RRACBFUSA
MESHEL	.06	F	INFANT	RRACBFUSA
EPSKIN, PESCHE	58	F	W	RRACBFUSA
TAUBE	28	F	W	RRACBFUSA
MENDEL	4	F	CHILD	RRACBFUSA
JUDAS	.09	M	INFANT	RRACBFUSA

SHIP: RHEIN

FROM: BREMEN
TO: BALTIMORE
ARRIVED: 21 JUNE 1888

PASSENGER	AGE	SEX	OCCUPATION	PRV VIL DES
HITTELMANN, L.	19	M	FARMER	RRZZZZBAL
SCHIRMER, MARIE	7	F	CHILD	RRZZZZBAL
MILEWSKI, MACEJ	24	M	FARMER	RRZZZZBAL
STENKEWICZ, MARYANNA	22	F	NN	RRZZZZBAL
STERNFELD, JENTE	40	M	FARMER	RRZZZZBAL
ROLKE	9	M	CHILD	RRZZZZBAL
NOCHUM	7	M	CHILD	RRZZZZBAL
MANE	.01	F	INFANT	RRZZZZBAL
BRODY, LOEB	20	M	LABR	RRZZZZBAL

PASSENGER	AGE	SEX	OCCUPATION	PRV	VIL	DES
SCHIKOWITZ, MEISCHE	15	F	NN	RR	ZZZZ	BAL
HOROZINSKI, JOSEF	25	M	LABR	RR	ZZZZ	BAL
GRATKOWSKI, WLADISL.	17	M	LABR	RR	ZZZZ	BAL
BARTEL, LUDW.	19	M	LABR	RR	ZZZZ	BAL
LANG, JOHANN	26	M	LABR	RR	ZZZZ	BAL
KLEMWITZ, ANNA	17	F	NN	RR	ZZZZ	BAL
SIBEK, ANNA	48	M	LABR	RR	ZZZZ	BAL
ROSENBERG, ALTER	23	M	LABR	RR	ZZZZ	BAL
FRIEDLAENDER, MALE	18	F	NN	RR	ZZZZ	BAL
RUBINSOHN, LIBE	20	F	NN	RR	ZZZZ	BAL
KIRPTON, VINCENT	25	M	SMH	RR	ZZZZ	BAL
CHONIC, JOSEFATO	30	F	NN	RR	ZZZZ	BAL
CZERWINSKY, JAN	45	M	LABR	RR	ZZZZ	BAL
MARIA	37	F	W	RR	ZZZZ	BAL
GENACH, SEPPE	22	F	NN	RR	ZZZZ	BAL
FRIEDMANN, HINDE	26	F	NN	RR	ZZZZ	BAL
ROZE	8	F	CHILD	RR	ZZZZ	BAL
HERM.	6	M	CHILD	RR	ZZZZ	BAL
PAUL	1	M	CHILD	RR	ZZZZ	BAL
KAUFMANN, MEIR	26	M	TRVLR	RR	ZZZZ	BAL
GROSCHOWSKA, SCHEINE	44	F	NN	RR	ZZZZ	BAL
ESTHER	16	F	NN	RR	ZZZZ	BAL
CHAJE	8	F	CHILD	RR	ZZZZ	BAL
JACOB	6	M	CHILD	RR	ZZZZ	BAL
LINDARS, ROBERT	27	M	LABR	RR	ZZZZ	BAL
LEMESCHIS, BALTREMES	26	M	LABR	RR	ZZZZ	BAL
KRZUYZPMANCZIK, KAZIS	21	M	LABR	RR	ZZZZ	BAL
MIELKER, CARL	47	M	DYR	RR	ZZZZ	KS
MARIE	46	F	W	RR	ZZZZ	KS
FRIEDR.	17	M	PNTR	RR	ZZZZ	KS
ALBERT	13	M	CH	RR	ZZZZ	KS
AUGUSTE	10	F	CH	RR	ZZZZ	KS
ADOLPHINE	7	F	CHILD	RR	ZZZZ	KS
KOLATH, CARL	56	M	LABR	RR	ZZZZ	BAL
DEMBINSKI, FRANZ	23	M	LABR	RR	ZZZZ	BAL
WIRAITES, SIMON	25	M	LABR	RR	ZZZZ	BAL
ROSENBLUT, EIWUSCH	18	M	LABR	RR	ZZZZ	OH
NEBESLER, LEIB	30	M	NN	RR	ZZZZ	BAL
BISCHKE	22	F	W	RR	ZZZZ	BAL
ROSEN, LUDW.	37	M	FARMER	RR	ZZZZ	BAL
GOLDSTEIN, FEIGE	26	F	NN	RR	ZZZZ	BAL
IDA	5	F	CHILD	RR	ZZZZ	BAL
MANTWILL, WINZENTY	35	M	LABR	RR	ZZZZ	BAL
MARJANNA	24	F	W	RR	ZZZZ	BAL
WINZENTY	6	M	CHILD	RR	ZZZZ	BAL
MAJET, MAJENI	15	M	CH	RR	ZZZZ	BAL
KUCHMEL, MARIE	26	F	NN	RR	ZZZZ	BAL
BUENTE, WILH.	11	M	CH	RR	ZZZZ	OH
SILBERMANN, ROCHE-L.	30	F	NN	RR	ZZZZ	OH
CHAJE	6	F	CHILD	RR	ZZZZ	OH
ESTER	4	F	CHILD	RR	ZZZZ	OH
INDA	2	F	CHILD	RR	ZZZZ	OH
KRANTZBERG, MERE	40	F	NN	RR	ZZZZ	IA
ABRAHAM	9	M	CHILD	RR	ZZZZ	IA
CHAWE	14	F	CH	RR	ZZZZ	IA
CHAJE	11	F	CH	RR	ZZZZ	IA
NESSER	16	M	CH	RR	ZZZZ	IA
SCHEWCE	7	F	CHILD	RR	ZZZZ	IA
KRISKO, JOH.	29	M	SDLR	RR	ZZZZ	IL
GART, SCHOLEN	16	M	GDR	RR	ZZZZ	IL
BELUK, JOSEPH	21	M	CPTR	RR	ZZZZ	MN

SHIP: RHYNLAND

FROM: ANTWERP
TO: NEW YORK
ARRIVED: 21 JUNE 1888

PASSENGER	AGE	SEX	OCCUPATION	PRV	VIL	DES
MIKULINE, MARIANNE	36	F	M	RR	AIHO	NAT
ANTONIE	4	M	CHILD	RR	AIHO	NAT
ANNA	3	F	CHILD	RR	AIHO	NAT
BARBA.	00	F	INF	RR	AIHO	NAT
PLAEJKAITIS, MARIANNA	26	F	M	RR	AIHO	NAT
MAGDA.	4	F	CHILD	RR	AIHO	NAT
TRABEL, LEWIN	21	M	CBTMKR	RR	AIHO	CH
CHEMISCH, ADAM	19	M	LABR	RR	AIHO	NY
BLEZINSKY, ITZE	28	M	LKSH	RR	AIHO	NY
KONOFSKY, HIRSCH	22	M	LABR	RR	AIHO	NY
KOMERLOWSKY, JOSEF	27	M	SHMK	RR	AIHO	NY
MARNOARNSKY, BERNH.	30	M	LABR	RR	AIHO	NY
KREMSKI, SIMON	23	M	LABR	RR	AIHO	NY
DIVORE	18	F	SVNT	RR	AIHO	NY
LACHMANN, HERMANN	22	M	TLR	RR	AIHO	NY
MARIE	22	F	W	RR	AIHO	NY
PINKUS, JOSEF	18	M	TLR	RR	AIHO	NY
KLEIN, SAMUEL	19	M	LABR	RR	AIHO	NY
BAER, JACOB	19	M	LABR	RR	AIHO	NY
NOWATNY, ANNA	18	F	SVNT	RR	AIHO	NY
LEBENSOHN, SARAH	20	F	W	RR	AIHO	CH
BOSCHITZKY, ISRAEL	49	M	DLR	RR	ZZZZ	NY
STIESCHE	47	F	W	RR	ZZZZ	NY
PESACH	11	M	CH	RR	ZZZZ	NY
LISSE	9	F	CHILD	RR	ZZZZ	NY
NESSCHE	7	M	CHILD	RR	ZZZZ	NY
HULPNISKY, GELDALJA	29	M	LABR	RR	ZZZZ	NY
SLATE	28	F	W	RR	ZZZZ	NY
RUDOLPH	6	M	CHILD	RR	ZZZZ	NY
ANNA	3	F	CHILD	RR	ZZZZ	NY
GOLDBERG, WOLF	30	M	LABR	RR	ZZZZ	NY
ESCHENBERG, MOSES	24	M	LABR	RR	ZZZZ	NY
MAGILEWITZ, SOFIE	25	M	CBTMKR	RR	ZZZZ	NY
MARSCHAK, NOAH	20	M	TLR	RR	ZZZZ	NY
KOBVOLAWSKY, ADAM	34	M	LABR	RR	ZZZZ	NY
BERNSTEIN, DAVID	21	M	MCHT	RR	ZZZZ	NY
PETERSEN, MORTON	28	M	BKLYR	RR	ZZZZ	NY
JOHANN	19	M	LABR	RR	ZZZZ	NY
PANTSEN, JOACHIM	25	M	LABR	RR	ZZZZ	NY
STRUHATSCH, MENDEL	23	M	MLR	RR	ZZZZ	NY
SCHLEMTHER, THEOD.	34	M	SMH	RR	ZZZZ	UNK
COHN, MOSES	24	M	CPTR	RR	ZZZZ	UNK
DURST, FRANZ	55	M	LABR	RR	ZZZZ	UNK
JANKEWITZ, JOSEF	19	M	LABR	RR	ZZZZ	UNK
PERLMANN, DAVID	27	M	CBTMKR	RR	ZZZZ	UNK
LEODANSKY, BOINE	23	F	W	RR	ZZZZ	UNK
LOWE, SARA	16	F	SVNT	RR	ZZZZ	UNK
LEVDANSKY, NACHUM	58	M	FARMER	RR	ZZZZ	CH
ROSA	47	F	W	RR	ZZZZ	CH
FEIGE	9	M	CHILD	RR	ZZZZ	CH
HORWITZ, BARUCH	17	M	TLR	RR	ZZZZ	CH

SHIP: ROMAN

FROM: LIVERPOOL AND LONDON
TO: BOSTON
ARRIVED: 21 JUNE 1888

PASSENGER	AGE	SEX	OCCUPATION	PRV	VIL	DES
KEDIK, MARTIN	25	M	LABR	RR	ZZZZ	NY
PESCHLER, JOHN	25	M	LABR	RR	ZZZZ	NY
SALMER, ISAAC	27	M	LABR	RR	ZZZZ	NY
SOFER, MENDEL	30	M	LABR	RR	ZZZZ	NY
WENICK, SIMON	26	M	LABR	RR	ZZZZ	NY
LOBIN, SOURCH	20	M	LABR	RR	ZZZZ	NY
GLADSTEIN, LETA	44	F	W	RR	ZZZZ	BO
CHAJE	16	M	LABR	RR	ZZZZ	BO
BASCHE	13	M	LABR	RR	ZZZZ	BO
RITCHELL	10	M	CH	RR	ZZZZ	BO
ALDERSOHN, CHANE	24	M	LABR	RR	ZZZZ	BO
NEUSTETIZ, RUBIN	20	M	LABR	PL	ZZZZ	BO
JAKUBOSKY, ISRAEL	26	M	LABR	RR	ZZZZ	BO
WAEBZIKYS, SINCHE	30	M	LABR	RR	ZZZZ	BO

PASSENGER	AGE	SEX	OCCUPATION	PRV VIL DES
LEIB	6	M	CHILD	RRZZZZBO
GERSTIN, ALTER	18	M	LABR	RRZZZZBO
CHUTOW, CHIPPE	50	F	W	RRZZZZBO
RACHE	17	M	LABR	RRZZZZBO
SCHEINE	9	M	CHILD	RRZZZZBO
OLSCHINITZKY, MERE	16	F	SP	RRZZZZBO
JENNI	8	F	CHILD	RRZZZZBO
LOUIS	6	F	CHILD	RRZZZZBO
BROMOWSKY, THOMAS	24	M	LABR	RRZZZZBO
HOLOPZA, MICH	25	M	LABR	RRZZZZBO
WANISCH	50	M	LABR	RRZZZZBO
BERSONSKY, ABRM.	50	M	LABR	RRZZZZBO
SCHAPIRO, MOSES	26	M	LABR	RRZZZZBO
D.	37	M	LABR	RRZZZZBO
MEIR	10	M	CH	RRZZZZBO
REMGOLD, ABM.	40	M	LABR	RRZZZZBO
ZOKILAWSKY, S	35	M	LABR	RRZZZZBO
ZUCKERMAN, B	32	M	LABR	RRZZZZBO
BEITZ, J	26	M	LABR	RRZZZZBO
CHEITOW, M	24	M	LABR	RRZZZZBO
GOLDENEY, S.	20	M	LABR	RRZZZZBO
FRANCIS	.10	M	INFANT	RRZZZZBO
CLIFFE, JOHN	35	M	FTR	RRZZZZPHI
BURNLEZ, CHARLES	19	M	LABR	RRZZZZPHI
CHAPPELL, MICHAEL	31	M	LABR	RRZZZZPHI
RIZMAN, BEN	20	M	LABR	RRZZZZPHI
HELLER, JOSEPH	20	M	ATSN	RRZZZZNY
WELHELBAUM, MICHAEL	33	M	LABR	RRZZZZBO
CHANE	25	F	W	RRZZZZBO
DOMMELLY, T	29	F	W	RRZZZZBO
RILEY, C	33	F	W	RRZZZZBO
PHILIP, P	21	F	W	RRZZZZBO
BURNS, E	25	F	W	RRZZZZBO
PSONECH, J	25	F	W	RRZZZZBO
SMITH, T	29	F	W	RRZZZZBO
BROWN, T	31	F	W	RRZZZZBO

SHIP: ITALY

FROM: LIVERPOOL AND QUEENSTOWN
TO: NEW YORK
ARRIVED: 21 JUNE 1888

PASSENGER	AGE	SEX	OCCUPATION	PRV VIL DES
SARATA, MORRIS	42	M	TLR	RRADAXPHI
HENEY, NATHAN	30	M	LABR	RRACBFNY
GELLAR, KALMAN	18	M	SHMK	RRADBQNY
PRESS, MOSES-J.	26	M	TLR	RRAIHANY
GOLDENBURG, SARA	26	F	W	RRADAXNY
JOSEF	2	M	CHILD	RRADAXNY
JOHANNA	1	F	CHILD	RRADAXNY
S.SEIDEL	16	M	LABR	RRADAXNY
U	9	M	CHILD	RRADAXNY
BOGGIN, P.	36	F	W	RRACBFNY
U	10	M	CH	RRACBFNY
LEIMER, S.	19	M	LABR	RRACBFNY
JACOBSON, FELIX	30	M	LABR	RRACBFNY
BEELA	28	F	W	RRACBFNY
SARA	10	F	CH	RRACBFNY
SALOMON	8	M	CHILD	RRACBFNY
MATHE	6	M	CHILD	RRACBFNY
ETH-GER, S.	30	M	TLR	RRACBFNY
U-MRS	30	F	W	RRACBFNY
SCHACHER, G.	26	M	CBTMKR	RRACBFNY
TEIN, G.	16	M	CBTMKR	RRACBFNY
CHAJKIN, SOLOMON	30	M	CBTMKR	RRACBFNY
SARAH	28	F	W	RRACBFNY
CHANE-LEAH	6	M	CHILD	RRACBFNY
GOLDSTEIN, ADELE	45	F	W	RRACBFNY
KOIWALA, ISAK	19	M	LABR	RRACBFNY
ABILEWITZ, M.	19	M	LABR	RRACBFNY
HOWITZ, S.W.	26	M	LABR	RRACBFNY
SWISKEWITZ, S.	30	M	TLR	RRACBFNY
KORNBLUM, S.	19	M	PDLR	RRACBFNY
EDELMANOWA, ESTER	20	F	W	RRACBFNY
HODE	20	M	CH	RRACBFNY
-IR	9	M	CHILD	RRACBFNY
SELIG	7	M	CHILD	RRACBFNY
MISININ, J.	18	M	LABR	RRACBFNY
AXELROD, CHAJE	18	F	SP	RRACBFNY
KAPELOWITZ, ISRAEL	50	M	LABR	RRACBFNY
KLEINER, JETTE	18	M	LABR	RRACBFNY
SEGALOWITZ, L.R.	45	F	W	RRACBFNY
SCHAMIEL	11	M	CH	RRACBFNY
ISRAEL	10	M	CH	RRACBFNY
JOSEPH	9	M	CHILD	RRACBFNY
WOLF	7	M	CHILD	RRACBFNY
GOLDIN	5	F	CHILD	RRACBFNY
RIFKA	3	F	CHILD	RRACBFNY
LEWY, L.	32	M	TLR	RRZZZZNY
COHEN, ABRAHAM	34	M	TLR	RRADBQNY
GOLDMEYER, RACHEL	26	F	W	RRADBQNY
U	00	M	INF	RRADBQNY
GUDREWICH, JAN	30	M	LABR	RRACBFNY
SCHITZ, ALBRECHT	26	M	LABR	RRACBFNY
MARIE	21	F	SP	RRACBFNY
SJASTROM, MAT.	23	M	SLR	RRACBFNY
HAGGBLAD, AUGUST	24	M	SLR	RRACBFNY
SILLOMBA, JOHAN	42	M	LABR	RRACBFNY
WRABMEN, JAKOB	28	M	LABR	RRACBFNY
SCHTONEN, JOHAN	20	M	LABR	RRACBFNY
ALPAKKA, HEIKKI	26	M	LABR	RRACBFNY
KOLLIJONEIME, MATTI	23	M	LABR	RRACBFNY
HEIKKOLA, HEKTOR	18	M	LABR	RRACBFNY
BRAVERMANN, B.	32	M	BRR	RRACBFNY
DUCHATTER, ISAAC	25	M	LABR	RRACBFPHI
PETREKINS, KASMIER	23	M	LABR	RRACBFPHI
MEDEROWITZ, LEIB	50	M	LABR	RRACBFPHI
KASPAROWSKY, NATHANE	20	F	SP	RRZZZZPHI
RIKOWITZ, SOLOMON	29	M	LABR	RRACBFPHI
SCHEWENJLOW, FEIGE	24	F	SP	RRACBFPHI
SCHWARZ, SAM.	28	M	TLR	RRACBFPHI
RUPKEWITZ, RACHEL	58	F	W	RRACBFPHI
KAMELBAUM, HERMAN	26	M	LABR	RRACBFCH
GREIGIN, SAMUEL	28	M	BKR	RRACBFNY
KROSNACHY, MORDCHE	17	M	LABR	RRACBFNY
LUKASZEWITZ, NEBOKIN	25	M	LABR	RRACBFNY
LEFSCHEUTZ, SORE	26	F	W	RRACBFNY
ZADECK	4	M	CHILD	RRACBFNY
WANIZROSHA, CHIE	24	F	SP	RRACBFNY
OTTINGER, BEILLE	8	F	CHILD	RRACBFNY
SELIG	6	M	CHILD	RRACBFNY
PLETONSTAG, CHANE	10	M	CH	RRACBFNY
KOHEN, MARX	31	M	CGRMKR	RRACBFPHI
ROSA	22	F	W	RRACBFPHI
LOUIS	00	M	INF	RRACBFPHI
KOHAN, HENI	20	M	LABR	RRACBFPA
GOLDE	18	F	SP	RRACBFPA
KOHEN, HODEF	16	M	TLR	RRACBFPA
SCHOLEM	14	M	TLR	RRACBFPA
KAHAN, HACHMAN	47	M	TLR	RRACBFPA
MARIE	37	F	W	RRACBFPA
ARON	10	M	CH	RRACBFPA
CHAIE	8	M	CHILD	RRACBFPA
ITTE	5	M	CHILD	RRACBFPA
MASSBA	00	F	INF	RRACBFPA
MARTZ, MOSES	26	M	TLR	RRZZZZPHI
DUBINSKI, MODCHE	26	M	TLR	RRZZZZPHI
SARETZKY, DORE	22	F	W	RRACBFPA
LEIBE	00	M	INF	RRACBFPA
SEGAL, CHAIM	42	M	LABR	RRACBFPA
HAJJBLOM, CARL-AUG.	28	M	SLR	RRACBFNY
HOLMBERG, JOHAN	25	M	SLR	RRACBFNY
ELKING, SARAH	28	F	SP	RRAGUZNY
MICK, MICHAEL	17	M	LABR	RRAGUZNY

PASSENGER	AGE	SEX	OCCUPATION	PRIVL	DES
SHIP: TRAVE					
FROM: BREMEN AND SOUTHAMPTON					
TO: NEW YORK					
ARRIVED: 22 JUNE 1888					
KUGLINSKY, JOSEF	22	M	FARMER	RRZZZZ	USA
STRAREPALSKY, CHANE	34	M	LABR	RRZZZZ	USA
KAPITZA, JANKEL	53	M	LABR	RRZZZZ	USA
HACKMANN, NATHAN	18	M	LABR	RRZZZZ	USA
RINALDO, HIRSCH	62	M	LABR	RRZZZZ	USA
CHAJE	59	F	UNKNOWN	RRZZZZ	USA
RUCHEL	20	F	UNKNOWN	RRZZZZ	USA
JULIE	18	F	UNKNOWN	RRZZZZ	USA
WOLF	6	M	CHILD	RRZZZZ	USA
KURZBAND, FEIGE	20	M	LABR	RRZZZZ	USA
FRANK, WOCHEM	21	M	LABR	RRZZZZ	USA
CHRONE	7	F	CHILD	RRZZZZ	USA
LEWIT, MEYER	6	M	CHILD	RRZZZZ	USA
ALLENSTEIN, BUM	20	M	FARMER	RRZZZZ	USA
SASMITZKI, ESTER	18	F	UNKNOWN	RRZZZZ	USA
CHORONZINSKI, MICHEL	16	M	UNKNOWN	RRZZZZ	USA
ROSENFELD, ABR	16	M	UNKNOWN	RRZZZZ	USA
SCHWARZ, MORITZ	32	M	UNKNOWN	RRZZZZ	USA
SARE	30	F	UNKNOWN	RRZZZZ	USA
JETTJ	7	F	CHILD	RRZZZZ	USA
FEIGE	14	M	CH	RRZZZZ	USA
NAPASTINK, JACOB	25	M	FARMER	RRZZZZ	USA
MARJEM	24	F	UNKNOWN	RRZZZZ	USA
JOSSEL	.11	M	INFANT	RRZZZZ	USA
SHIP: STATE OF INDIANA					
FROM: GLASGOW AND LARNE					
TO: NEW YORK					
ARRIVED: 22 JUNE 1888					
LEDERHANDLER, HIRSCH	43	M	LABR	RRZZZZ	USA
RANN, BENJAMIN	40	M	LABR	RRZZZZ	USA
ROBINSKY, -OSCKE	20	M	DMS	RRZZZZ	USA
GROSS, MOSES	24	M	GDNR	RRZZZZ	USA
LEWIN, CHATZKEL	17	M	FARMER	RRZZZZ	USA
KAPITZSKY, LEIB	20	M	PDLR	RRZZZZ	USA
KANTOROWITZ, SAML.	30	M	FARMER	RRZZZZ	USA
MOKLER, AISIK-MEIER	34	M	FARMER	RRZZZZ	USA
DIAMONT, ISIDOR	31	M	PDLR	RRZZZZ	USA
SCHOVASCH, RAPHAEL	16	M	FARMER	RRZZZZ	USA
MEHLMANN, JACOB	22	M	PDLR	RRZZZZ	USA
SCHNEIDER, SIMON	47	M	PDLR	RRZZZZ	USA
RUFF, LESER	27	M	PDLR	RRZZZZ	USA
ARENBAUN, GEDALJA	21	M	PDLR	RRZZZZ	USA
BECKER, HERMANN	18	M	LABR	RRZZZZ	USA
MEZARKIS, ANTON	40	M	PDLR	RRZZZZ	USA
GLAS, EFRAIM	21	M	JNR	RRZZZZ	USA
OTKINITZSKY, CHAZIN	38	M	LABR	RRZZZZ	USA
JANNBOICH, THOMAS	34	M	LABR	RRZZZZ	USA
ADAMONITZ, STANISLAW	21	M	PDLR	RRZZZZ	USA
SCHUSTER, STEFAN	25	M	JNR	RRZZZZ	USA
SCHWEICKLER, SANDER	38	M	LABR	RRZZZZ	USA
HULLMANN, MOSE	41	M	LABR	RRZZZZ	USA
BRONUKOSIN, JANKEL	19	M	LABR	RRZZZZ	USA
HACK, ITZIG	35	M	LABR	RRZZZZ	USA
KAHN, ABRAHAM	31	M	LABR	RRZZZZ	USA
TUMA, LEIB	24	M	UNKNOWN	RRZZZZ	USA
DAVID	8	M	CHILD	RRZZZZ	USA
ETTE	6	F	CHILD	RRZZZZ	USA
HENE	1	F	CHILD	RRZZZZ	USA
KESLINSKY, WOLF	24	M	LABR	RRZZZZ	USA
ROSA	24	F	W	RRZZZZ	USA
SLATE	.04	F	INFANT	RRZZZZ	USA
LARN, JANKEL	22	M	PDLR	RRZZZZ	USA
SARAH	19	F	W	RRZZZZ	USA
GROPPER, LIZA	25	F	W	RRZZZZ	USA
LASER	.06	M	INFANT	RRZZZZ	USA
MORGOWSKY, FREIDE	30	F	W	RRZZZZ	USA
JACOB	9	M	CHILD	RRZZZZ	USA
LEAH	7	F	CHILD	RRZZZZ	USA
RACHEL	2	F	CHILD	RRZZZZ	USA
RESEL	1	M	CHILD	RRZZZZ	USA
SCHLEFERT, JERNAM	50	M	LABR	RRZZZZ	USA
ANNA	50	F	W	RRZZZZ	USA
DOTRANSKIS, ANTON	46	M	FARMER	RRZZZZ	USA
BRONASKA	15	F	CH	RRZZZZ	USA
CEZADLOWSKY, CRESLAW	11	M	CH	RRZZZZ	USA
ROBINOWITZ, CLAWE	35	F	W	RRZZZZ	USA
LEIB	10	M	CH	RRZZZZ	USA
BASCHE	9	F	CHILD	RRZZZZ	USA
MOSES	8	F	CHILD	RRZZZZ	USA
RISCHE	6	F	CHILD	RRZZZZ	USA
SCHOLEN	1	M	CHILD	RRZZZZ	USA
GERDISCHIK, LIPPE	25	F	W	RRZZZZ	USA
LEIB	1	M	CHILD	RRZZZZ	USA
BERMANN, CHINE	40	F	W	RRZZZZ	USA
RACHEL	20	F	DMS	RRZZZZ	USA
ISRAEL	16	M	DMS	RRZZZZ	USA
BEILE	7	F	CHILD	RRZZZZ	USA
RASCHE	4	F	CHILD	RRZZZZ	USA
ESTHER	1	F	CHILD	RRZZZZ	USA
LEID, LANE	28	F	W	RRZZZZ	USA
CHAWE	6	F	CHILD	RRZZZZ	USA
ISAAC	2	M	CHILD	RRZZZZ	USA
MONCH, BETTY	5	F	CHILD	RRZZZZ	USA
CHAIN	1	F	CHILD	RRZZZZ	USA
WERSHOWSKI, JENTE	33	F	W	RRZZZZ	USA
MALKE	10	F	CH	RRZZZZ	USA
CHAIE	8	F	CHILD	RRZZZZ	USA
MATHEL	1	M	CHILD	RRZZZZ	USA
SPERHER, ALTER	50	M	CH	RRZZZZ	USA
SOPHIE	18	F	DMS	RRZZZZ	USA
HANNA	16	F	DMS	RRZZZZ	USA
FANNY	11	F	CH	RRZZZZ	USA
ARONZIK, DAVID	18	M	PDLR	RRZZZZ	USA
MARCHE	20	F	W	RRZZZZ	***
ROSENTHAL, TAUBE	20	F	W	RRZZZZ	USA
HOISCH	9	M	CHILD	RRZZZZ	USA
MARCHTALITZKY, ISOTUK	27	M	PDLR	RRZZZZ	USA
CHAIE	28	F	W	RRZZZZ	USA
MERKE	1	F	CHILD	RRZZZZ	USA
SARKE	.03	F	INFANT	RRZZZZ	USA
JENIE	45	F	DMS	RRZZZZ	USA
KLENOFSKY, PESOKE	10	F	CH	RRZZZZ	USA
KOHNS	8	M	CHILD	RRZZZZ	USA
BORSCHEFSKY, ITTE	45	F	W	RRZZZZ	USA
KEILE	18	F	DMS	RRZZZZ	USA
KONOPOWSE, DOMINICA	36	F	DMS	RRZZZZ	USA
KOHER, MATTE	15	F	DMS	RRZZZZ	USA
GAWRILZAWN, FELICIA	36	F	DMS	RRZZZZ	USA
HABER, SARAH	15	F	DMS	RRZZZZ	USA
SCHEWE	19	F	DMS	RRZZZZ	USA
FRIEDMANN, BAR.	17	F	DMS	RRZZZZ	USA
KAPLAN, DWEIRE	20	F	DMS	RRZZZZ	USA
ARCSRAD, JOHANN	15	F	DMS	RRZZZZ	USA
KAPOLEWITZ, GOLOT	17	F	DMS	RRZZZZ	USA
SUMINOWITZ, LINAKE	18	F	DMS	RRZZZZ	USA

PASSENGER	AGE	SEX	OCCUPATION	PRIV	VIL	DES

SHIP: CITY OF CHICAGO

FROM: LIVERPOOL AND QUEENSTOWN
TO: NEW YORK
ARRIVED: 23 JUNE 1888

PASSENGER	AGE	SEX	OCCUPATION	PV RI VL	D E S
SCHULO, FRED	29	M	UNKNOWN	RRACBF	NY
WINBERG, SALOMON	25	M	UNKNOWN	RRACBF	MA
STONFEILD, BURHT	38	M	UNKNOWN	RRACBF	NY
HUSS, AB	21	M	UNKNOWN	RRACBF	NY
SWISSKY, ISRAEL	26	M	UNKNOWN	RRACBF	PA
SCHOHN, CHAIM	36	M	UNKNOWN	RRACBF	PA
OSTROWSKY, JOCH	36	M	UNKNOWN	RRACBF	PA
DOMBROWSKY, STANISLAW	17	M	FARMER	RRADAX	NY
ROMBROWSKY, JACOB	27	M	FARMER	RRADAX	NY
PINKUS, SEME	38	M	FARMER	RRADAX	NY
CHRUCHER, ARN	38	M	FARMER	RRADAX	NY
SEFENOFF, JAK	30	M	FARMER	RRADAX	NY
HELFAND, JOCHEM	23	M	FARMER	RRADAX	NY
MUERKA, MICHAL	29	M	FARMER	RRADAX	NY
KOEBOF, FRANZ	24	M	FARMER	RRADAX	NY
SCHEIWYCK, WOLF	42	M	UNKNOWN	RRADAX	PA
FERUBLITT, ARON	24	M	UNKNOWN	RRADAX	NY
SALOMON	11	M	UNKNOWN	RRADAX	NY
LEWEK, FRANCISEK	38	M	LABR	RRADAX	NY
SIMMAWITZ, BEN	20	M	LABR	RRADAX	NY
SCHAPIRO, HESSEL	23	M	LABR	RRADAX	NY
MASIE, MORDOCK	26	M	LABR	RRADAX	NY
PUANKA, JANKEL	29	M	LABR	RRADAX	NY
SCHAUPSTEIN, ISRAEL	27	M	LABR	RRADAX	NY
OLRIN, PAUL	12	M	CH	RRADAX	IL
KRIMBERG, LEIB	40	M	LABR	RRADAX	NY
OGERBIVIK, FEN.	32	M	LABR	RRADAX	NY
BLOCK, SIMON	18	M	LABR	RRADAX	NY
KREINES, MORDOCH	30	M	LABR	RRADAX	NY
STERYN, SCHLEMI	45	M	LABR	RRADAX	NY
KORLAWSKY, ISRAEL	32	M	LABR	RRADAX	NY
KOZLOWSKY, ANTON	35	M	LABR	RRADAX	NY
BRENNER, BERTH	27	M	LABR	RRADAX	NY
LUBANSKI, SIMON	38	M	LABR	RRADAX	NY
FRIEDMAN, MORDOCH	18	M	LABR	RRADAX	NY
RODSOWITZ, HERM.	17	M	LABR	RRADAX	NY
KEPSLEWITZ, CHAIM	45	M	LABR	RRADAX	NY
ZUCKS, JANKEL	40	M	LABR	RRADAX	NY
BULIN, HIP--	42	M	LABR	RRADAX	NY
SIMON	12	M	CH	RRADAX	NY
D---	10	M	CH	RRADAX	NY
WINNIK, SERGEI	17	M	LABR	RRADAX	NY
GILHERT, ARON	24	M	LABR	RRADAX	NY
SAMUEL, AB.	43	M	LABR	RRADAX	NY
DOVIESCHEWITZ, INNDERT	25	M	LABR	RRADAX	NY
ORLSENITZKY, ARON	26	M	LABR	RRADAX	NY
LEZIRT, ARON	36	M	LABR	RRADAX	NY
MARK, LEISER	26	M	LABR	RRADAX	NY
BRUS, ISBET	18	M	LABR	RRADAX	NY
SOKOLOWSKY, SOFIO	26	M	LABR	RRADAX	NY
CHOMOWITZ, AB.	22	M	LABR	RRADAX	NY
SMOLOWSKY, AB.	28	M	LABR	RRADAX	NY
FELDMANN, MOSCHE	25	M	LABR	RRADAX	NY
POPSKI, SILIG	41	M	LABR	RRADAX	NY
KOPELOWITZ, ARON	22	M	LABR	RRADAX	NY
RUST, JOSEP	27	M	LABR	RRADAX	NY
DANISCHEWSKY, NOCHEM	36	M	LABR	RRADAX	NY
GORDE, JUDE	27	M	UNKNOWN	RRADAX	NY
ROSEN, BRO.	18	M	UNKNOWN	RRADAX	NY
SCHUTUSBERG, SALOMON	19	M	UNKNOWN	RRADAX	NY
STOFERMANN, HIERSH	55	M	UNKNOWN	RRADAX	NY
RUBIN, LEIB	32	M	CNF	RRADAX	OH
STOHL, B	40	F	W	RRADAX	MN
ROSA	9	F	CHILD	RRADAX	MN
SCHLESONIK, SCHIENE	22	F	UNKNOWN	RRADAX	PA
WEST, AUGUSTE	18	F	UNKNOWN	RRADAX	NY
HELSINGER, AMALIA	18	F	UNKNOWN	RRADAX	NY
FRANZBLAER, MOLKE	15	F	UNKNOWN	RRADAX	NY
ARONSTEIN, EMSLAW	22	F	UNKNOWN	RRADAX	NY
PINKAS, JOSEP	19	F	UNKNOWN	RRADAX	NY
CHAIE	12	F	CH	RRADAX	NY
RUSBURSKI, MARY	21	F	SP	RRADAX	NY
AROTZKER, HUS.	18	F	SP	RRADAX	NY
BRENER, CHANE	48	F	W	RRADAX	NY
LIEBENTHAL, TAUBE	20	F	W	RRADAX	NY
KINGERMANN, SARA	45	F	W	RRADAX	NY
KNUFMANN, ZEPE	22	F	SP	RRADAX	NY
GOLDBERG, LOUISE	16	F	SP	RRADAX	NY
GAUS, HENE	17	F	SP	RRADAX	NY
STEINHOLZ, CHASCHE	20	F	SP	RRADAX	NY
BLUM, JOHANNA	24	F	SP	RRADAX	NY
GARFINKIS, GEN.	30	F	SP	RRADAX	NY
KIDEZER, SELMA	47	M	PDLR	RRADAX	PA
HERT.	18	F	SP	RRADAX	PA
SCHOLOM	16	M	PDLR	RRADAX	PA
AB.	10	M	CH	RRADAX	PA
ROTENFELD, FANNY	27	F	W	RRADAX	NY
SIEGMUND	9	M	CHILD	RRADAX	NY
ROSE	6	F	CHILD	RRADAX	NY
BUNTAR	.10	M	INFANT	RRADAX	NY
KIDINGER, MOSES	48	M	PDLR	RRADAX	PA
CHANNE	33	F	W	RRADAX	PA
ROHL	20	F	SP	RRADAX	PA
JOSEF	19	M	PDLR	RRADAX	PA
ESTER	9	F	CHILD	RRADAX	PA
BRAN.	6	M	CHILD	RRADAX	PA
LEIB	5	M	CHILD	RRADAX	PA
KUGEL, FEIGE	27	F	W	RRADAX	NY
TIMECH	4	M	CHILD	RRADAX	NY
CHANNE	00	F	INF	RRADAX	NY
KOSCHINSKY, DWASEK	50	F	W	RRACBF	NY
THUBE	25	F	W	RRACBF	NY
BERN.	8	M	CHILD	RRACBF	NY
MAX	3	M	CHILD	RRACBF	NY
ROCHI	00	F	INF	RRACBF	NY
LUKEZEWSKI, ANTONIA	28	F	W	RRACBF	NY
STANISLAW	10	M	CH	RRACBF	NY
KAZIMIR	7	M	CHILD	RRACBF	NY
STANISLAWA	5	F	CHILD	RRACBF	NY
WAEGERED	3	M	CHILD	RRACBF	NY
JOSEF	00	M	INF	RRACBF	NY
LIZA	00	F	INF	RRACBF	NY
LANDSNER, SARA	38	F	W	RRACBF	NY
ROCHL	11	F	CH	RRACBF	NY
BEIL	3	F	CHILD	RRACBF	NY
SVHEINE	00	F	INF	RRACBF	NY
BERTSOHN, CHASKE	20	M	LABR	RRACBF	NY
RIEWE	20	F	W	RRACBF	NY
SCHILT, ANNA	19	F	UNKNOWN	RRACBF	PHI

SHIP: ZAANDAM

FROM: AMSTERDAM
TO: NEW YORK
ARRIVED: 25 JUNE 1888

PASSENGER	AGE	SEX	OCCUPATION	PV RI VL	D E S
KIRSNER, SELIG	34	M	LABR	RRZZZZ	USA
BLUMENTHAL, MAYER	27	M	LABR	RRZZZZ	USA
BERDOWSKY, NOCHMANN	22	M	LABR	RRZZZZ	USA
TEIBOWITZ, DAVID	50	M	LABR	RRZZZZ	USA
ANNA	28	F	SVNT	RRZZZZ	USA
SCHLOECHTER, ARIL	11	M	CH	RRZZZZ	USA
KATZ, ARON	29	M	LABR	RRZZZZ	USA
LEWIN, DAVID	38	M	LABR	RRZZZZ	USA
ANNES, CHAMIE	30	F	SVNT	RRZZZZ	USA
DWORE	3	F	CHILD	RRZZZZ	USA
ADEL	1	F	CHILD	RRZZZZ	USA
RADKEWITZ, SALOMON	17	M	MCHT	RRZZZZ	USA

PASSENGER	AGE	SEX	OCCUPATION	PRV VIL DES
PINSK, SELIG	25	M	LABR	RRZZZZUSA
DOLNI, ANDRE	17	M	LABR	RRZZZZUSA
CHONSKI, JACOB	23	M	LABR	RRZZZZUSA
LASCHWON, LEIB	25	M	LABR	RRZZZZUSA
WUERBEL, MOSES	36	M	LABR	RRZZZZUSA
JAFFE, MOSES	17	M	LABR	RRZZZZUSA
SANDROWSKI, JOS.	35	M	LABR	RRZZZZUSA
KAJAK, ADAM	00	M	LABR	RRZZZZUSA
MERZESOSKI, JON	00	M	LABR	RRZZZZUSA
MATULEWITZ, ADAM	00	M	LABR	RRZZZZUSA
BEWIS, JERSEY	00	M	LABR	RRZZZZUSA
KLIMAS, JON	31	M	LABR	RRZZZZUSA
MATTHEI	28	M	LABR	RRZZZZUSA
KWETKOWSKY, MATTHEW	38	M	LABR	RRZZZZUSA
HOSACVICZ, ISAC	20	M	MCHT	RRZZZZUSA
DOMIN, SALOMON	26	M	LABR	RRZZZZUSA
PAULIKANIS, JOS.	21	M	LABR	RRZZZZUSA
BLECHER, CHANE	18	F	SVNT	RRZZZZUSA
BAER, PESCHE	37	F	SVNT	RRZZZZUSA
CHIENA	16	F	SVNT	RRZZZZUSA
GITEL	11	F	CH	RRZZZZUSA
DOBRE	8	F	CHILD	RRZZZZUSA
ZABEL	10	M	CH	RRZZZZUSA
MAJONER, BER.	10	M	CH	RRZZZZUSA
GAZLE	19	M	LABR	RRZZZZUSA
SUCHANOWIC, JACOB	25	M	LABR	RRZZZZUSA
LOZOWSKY, JON	23	M	LABR	RRZZZZUSA
PRERADOWSKY, ARON	46	M	LABR	RRZZZZUSA
SAONTIS, ANTON	30	M	LABR	RRZZZZUSA
JACOBNO, ONANI	22	M	LABR	RRZZZZUSA
PILASCHEWITZ, JACOB	00	M	LABR	RRZZZZUSA
LEBERMANN, LIBER	00	M	MCHT	RRZZZZUSA
U, U	00	M	LABR	RRZZZZUSA
U	00	M	LABR	RRZZZZUSA
U	00	M	LABR	RRZZZZUSA
U	00	M	LABR	RRZZZZUSA
U	00	M	LABR	RRZZZZUSA
U	00	M	LABR	RRZZZZUSA
U	00	M	LABR	RRZZZZUSA
U	00	M	LABR	RRZZZZUSA
U	00	M	MCHT	RRZZZZUSA
U	00	M	LABR	RRZZZZUSA
U	00	M	BLKSMH	RRZZZZUSA
U	00	M	LABR	RRZZZZUSA
U	00	M	LABR	RRZZZZUSA
U	00	M	LABR	RRZZZZUSA
U	00	M	LABR	RRZZZZUSA
U	00	M	LABR	RRZZZZUSA
U	00	M	LABR	RRZZZZUSA
U	00	M	NN	RRZZZZUSA
U	00	F	NN	RRZZZZUSA
U	00	M	MCHT	RRZZZZUSA
U	00	F	SVNT	RRZZZZUSA
U	00	F	NN	RRZZZZUSA
U	00	M	NN	RRZZZZUSA
U	00	F	NN	RRZZZZUSA
U	00	M	LABR	RRZZZZUSA
-UMMELBRAU, SCHLOME	00	M	MCHT	RRZZZZUSA
DAVID	17	M	TLR	RRZZZZUSA
MORTEL	15	M	TLR	RRZZZZUSA
DINZEN, ABRAHAM	26	M	LABR	RRZZZZUSA
ROSTUGIAN, GRUT	35	F	SVNT	RRZZZZUSA
BERBERIAN, AR-T	18	M	LABR	RRZZZZUSA
JANEGA, DAVID	30	M	LABR	RRZZZZUSA
KAPIKIAN, GARABET	45	M	LABR	RRZZZZUSA
MUSIKIAN, BEDROW	26	M	LABR	RRZZZZUSA
HOLZMAN, BERL.	35	M	LABR	RRZZZZUSA
ROGORELSKI, SAMUEL	30	M	TLR	RRZZZZUSA
BERGER, GITEL	20	F	SVNT	RRZZZZUSA
CHAI	18	F	SVNT	RRZZZZUSA
KLISKELSKY, LIPE	27	F	SVNT	RRZZZZUSA
DEITZ, AARON-WALFKA	22	M	TLR	RRZZZZUSA
LUBZEWSKI, GITEL	19	F	SVNT	RRZZZZUSA
KASH, ABRAHAM	34	M	LABR	RRZZZZUSA
PINANSKI, VINCENZ	42	M	LABR	RRZZZZUSA

PASSENGER	AGE	SEX	OCCUPATION	PRV VIL DES
ZIPKIN, JOSEF	24	M	MCHT	RRZZZZUSA
BLACHER, MOSES	24	M	BTMKR	RRZZZZUSA
KOVARIKOVA, MARIA	16	F	SVNT	RRZZZZUSA
U, U	00	M	LABR	RRZZZZUSA
PAUFIL, JULIANA	35	F	SVNT	RRZZZZUSA
JOSEF	23	M	LABR	RRZZZZUSA
JOSEPHA	14	F	SVNT	RRZZZZUSA
FRANCISCA	5	F	CHILD	RRZZZZUSA
TEWS, AUGUSTA	38	F	SVNT	RRZZZZUSA
RUTKES, ALWINE	18	F	SVNT	RRZZZZUSA
SPIEGELSTEIN, SALOMON	22	M	LABR	RRZZZZUSA
BUCH, ARON	18	M	LABR	RRZZZZUSA
NOWETOWSKI, FEIGE	17	M	LABR	RRZZZZUSA
MOGINSKI, SUSSEL	17	F	SVNT	RRZZZZUSA
SCHAIKIN, SCHMULL	24	M	LABR	RRZZZZUSA
BLUMEN, CHAJAM	18	M	LABR	RRZZZZUSA
HIRSCHMUEL, ABRAHAM	25	M	LABR	RRZZZZUSA
KACKTHUM, ITZIG-LEIB	33	M	LABR	RRZZZZUSA
ABELOW, SORE	20	F	SVNT	RRZZZZUSA
RACHEL	10	F	NN	RRZZZZUSA
LEBOWITZ, ZIPRE	18	F	SVNT	RRZZZZUSA
MICHENSE, MAIER	00	M	LABR	RRZZZZUSA
U, U	00	U	UNKNOWN	RRZZZZUSA
LEWINSKI, LEIBEL	00	M	LABR	RRZZZZUSA
JAMBOS, ANNA	50	F	SVNT	RRZZZZUSA
LAILA, KAISA	25	F	SVNT	FNZZZZUSA
LIMA	3	F	CHILD	FNZZZZUSA
KETS, JACOB	18	M	SLR	FNZZZZUSA
HEITHIKILA, MATHILDE	28	F	SVNT	FNZZZZUSA
KAISER, HEINRICH	19	M	LABR	FNZZZZUSA
LAHLBOE, JOH.GABR.	38	M	LABR	FNZZZZUSA
NORDBECK, RODOLF.O.G.	19	M	LABR	FNZZZZUSA
KOJA, MATH.MATHSON	29	M	LABR	FNZZZZUSA
NORDBECK, K.A.HERM.	39	M	LABR	FNZZZZUSA
LAHLBO, C.J.CH.	25	M	LABR	FNZZZZUSA
RISBERG, JOS.E.JOH.	33	M	LABR	FNZZZZUSA
NORDSTROM, JOH.	36	M	LABR	FNZZZZUSA
NYEGARD, ABRAHAM	19	M	LABR	FNZZZZUSA
LASSILA, JOH.E.	32	M	LABR	FNZZZZUSA
NYEGGARD, HERM.	35	M	LABR	FNZZZZUSA
GIMMELGARD, JOHANN	25	M	LABR	FNZZZZUSA
STROEM, EMMA	24	F	SVNT	FNZZZZUSA

SHIP: TAORMINA

FROM: HAMBURG
TO: NEW YORK
ARRIVED: 25 JUNE 1888

PASSENGER	AGE	SEX	OCCUPATION	PRV VIL DES
WOZNIALIS, DOMINIK	30	M	UNKNOWN	RRZZZZNY
SKLAW, SARA	18	F	UNKNOWN	RRZZZZNY
BRANDSTEITTER, ANNA	19	F	UNKNOWN	RRZZZZNY
JAWOROWSKI, ADOLF	18	M	UNKNOWN	RRZZZZNY
SLUTZKI, CHAIM	18	M	UNKNOWN	RRZZZZNY
PIETRUZEWSKI, ADAM	21	M	LABR	RRZZZZNY
SCHWARTZ, ISAAK	32	M	LABR	RRZZZZNY
JOHANNSEN, JOHANN	33	M	LABR	RRZZZZNY
SAKOLOWITZ, RIFKE	22	F	W	RRZZZZNY
SAMUEL	00	M	INF	RRZZZZNY
MEYROWITZ, HATHAN	19	M	LABR	RRZZZZNY
CHAIE	16	F	UNKNOWN	RRZZZZNY
SCHEER, MORDSHE	29	M	TLR	RRZZZZNY
SCHWARZ, LIEBE	22	M	TDR	RRZZZZNY
LANG, LUDWIG	24	M	TDR	RRZZZZNY
DAVIDOWITSCH, ELIAS	25	M	TDR	RRZZZZNY
SKORZYNKAS, VINCENT	26	M	LABR	RRZZZZNY
WOLGON, ISRAEL	19	M	LABR	RRZZZZNY
BERSECK, MENASCHE	38	F	WO	RRZZZZNY
SCHIFFRE	13	F	CH	RRZZZZNY
ABRAM	9	M	CHILD	RRZZZZNY

PASSENGER	AGE	SEX	OCCUPATION	PRV VIL DES
NACHEM	7	M	CHILD	RRZZZZNY
DORSKE	5	F	CHILD	RRZZZZNY
SMIELKO	3	M	CHILD	RRZZZZNY
JELLKE	9	F	CHILD	RRZZZZNY
KRUPA, WOLF	26	M	LABR	RRZZZZNY
BODWITZKI, JOSSIE	17	F	SGL	RRZZZZNY
NOVICKO, STEFAN	20	M	LABR	RRZZZZNY
MORRIS, ISRAEL	50	M	LABR	RRZZZZNY
SELIG	48	M	LABR	RRZZZZNY
ZIPPE	16	F	SGL	RRZZZZNY
CEBULARZ, LEIB	28	M	LABR	RRZZZZNY
SALMEN	9	M	CHILD	RRZZZZNY
SZCZEK, FRANZISKA	30	F	SGL	RRZZZZNY
POLAK, PAUL	31	M	LABR	RRZZZZROC
SCHLUMPERT, LEIB	28	M	TLR	RRZZZZROC
EVA	24	F	UNKNOWN	RRZZZZROC
MORITZ	20	M	UNKNOWN	RRZZZZROC
CHUDISCHLOW, GITTEL	17	M	SGL	RRZZZZROC
SZERTOK, ABRAM	28	M	MCHT	RRZZZZROC
ANNA	24	F	W	RRZZZZROC
JPROJITZKI, NICOLAI	39	M	CPR	RRZZZZROC
STANKOWSKI, JOSEF	40	M	BCHR	RRZZZZROC
KASMIKEITIS, THOMAS	34	M	LABR	RRZZZZROC
ANNA	24	F	W	RRZZZZROC
SINKEWITZ, IGNATZ	35	M	LABR	RRZZZZROC
WITKO, VICTORIA	17	F	SGL	RRZZZZROC
FEINSILBER, OSIAS	18	M	LABR	RRZZZZROC
HIRSCHSOHN, ETTE	35	F	WO	RRZZZZROC
GOLDSTEIN, ROCHE	25	F	WO	RRZZZZROC
LIEBE	.11	F	INFANT	RRZZZZROC
FREIMANN, SARA	53	F	WO	RRZZZZROC
MARIE	21	F	SGL	RRZZZZROC
URIANA	13	F	SGL	RRZZZZROC
BERMANN, ISSER	23	M	LABR	RRZZZZROC
MILNER, MOSES	29	M	LABR	RRZZZZROC
SCHMUL	9	M	CHILD	RRZZZZROC
SALZMANN, LEISER	30	M	LABR	RRZZZZROC
MOROS, EISER	26	M	UNKNOWN	RRZZZZROC
HIRSCHSOHN, GOLDE	50	F	WO	RRZZZZROC
GOEMBZIK, ISRAEL	25	M	TLR	RRZZZZROC
NAPORSNIK, BENJAMIN	26	M	TLR	RRZZZZROC
LOCHBER, SCHMUL	25	M	FUR	RRZZZZROC
JANKEL	47	M	FUR	RRZZZZROC
GRANN, MOSES	25	M	LABR	RRZZZZROC
METWEZKI, MOSES	25	M	TLR	RRZZZZROC
MATUSCHEWITZ, ANTON	26	M	LABR	RRZZZZROC
WIDKIDAJEC, FRANZ	25	M	LABR	RRZZZZROC
ROFALOWSKI, ADAM	18	M	LABR	RRZZZZROC
KONICKI, VINCINTI	32	M	LABR	RRZZZZROC
SCHEMBORSKI, CZESLAW	20	M	LABR	RRZZZZROC
CISCHEWA, SCHMUL	21	M	LABR	RRZZZZROC
MAKOWSKI, MARTIN	37	M	LABR	RRZZZZROC
KREIDEL, JOSEFE.	48	F	WO	RRZZZZROC
ELISABETH	21	F	SGL	RRZZZZROC
BRZEZINSKI, MICHALINE	43	F	SGL	RRZZZZROC
SCHIMANOWICZ, LEISER	20	M	LABR	RRZZZZROC
CHANNE	22	F	W	RRZZZZROC
SORENSOHN, BEILE	22	F	WO	RRZZZZROC
ITZIG	16	M	LABR	RRZZZZROC
NOVSELSKI, LEIB	18	M	LABR	RRZZZZROC
CHEVATAU, TAUBE	20	F	SGL	RRZZZZROC
NIVES, SCHMUL	21	M	LABR	RRZZZZROC
SARA	21	F	W	RRZZZZROC
YLLMANN, ROSA	19	F	SGL	RRZZZZROC
MEYER, JACOB	22	M	PNTR	RRZZZZROC
KANTOROWITZ, ABRAM	24	M	BCHR	RRZZZZROC
LEIFER, SELIG	30	M	LABR	RRZZZZROC
KREIDER, HIRSCH	22	M	UNKNOWN	RRZZZZROC
ROSINSKI, JANKEL	26	M	UNKNOWN	RRZZZZROC
SELZ, FEINDEL	28	M	LABR	RRZZZZROC
CZINA, REBECCA	19	F	SGL	RRZZZZROC
KAPLAN, ABRAM	16	M	CK	RRZZZZROC
GUTMANN, LAMUEL	19	M	TLR	RRZZZZROC
RAUSBOR, M.	16	M	LABR	RRZZZZROC
LURAFSOWO, AMALIA	28	F	WO	RRZZZZROC

PASSENGER	AGE	SEX	OCCUPATION	PRV VIL DES
FRANZ	3	M	CHILD	RRZZZZROC
ANTON	.02	M	INFANT	RRZZZZROC
ELSBETH	.11	F	INFANT	RRZZZZROC
PLUSKAT, CHRIST.	42	M	LKSH	RRZZZZROC
KWIATKOWSKI, VALENTIN	39	M	LABR	RRZZZZROC
RUTKOWSKI, TEOFIL	24	M	LABR	RRZZZZNY
MARSELLI	22	M	LABR	RRZZZZNY
STROTZKI, ANTON	25	M	LABR	RRZZZZNY
JUDOMIR, ABRAHAM	29	M	MCHT	RRZZZZNY
SCHILLER, LUDWIG	21	M	MLR	RRZZZZNY
DIBURSKI, WOYNCH	23	M	LABR	RRZZZZNY
MARKOW, WOLF	47	M	DLR	RRZZZZNY
BRANE	45	F	W	RRZZZZNY
SCHLOMA	18	M	CH	RRZZZZNY
JOHE.	16	F	CH	RRZZZZNY
HESCHE	14	F	CH	RRZZZZNY
IDEL	9	F	CHILD	RRZZZZNY
TAUBE	9	F	CHILD	RRZZZZNY
JENTE	7	F	CHILD	RRZZZZNY
ESTHER	4	F	CHILD	RRZZZZNY
GORITZ, AUG.	24	M	LABR	RRZZZZNY
KALVARISKI, ISIDOR	16	M	TLR	RRZZZZNY
ODESES, MEISCHE	28	M	TLR	RRZZZZNY
RASCHE	22	F	W	RRZZZZNY
MEYER	.11	M	INFANT	RRZZZZNY
ESTHER	.01	F	INFANT	RRZZZZNY
BAERKER, HEINR.	42	M	SMH	RRZZZZNY
ERNESTE.	48	F	W	RRZZZZNY
NARKEWITZ, JACOB	21	M	LABR	RRZZZZNY
ZUBOROWSKI, ANTONI	20	M	LABR	RRZZZZNY
APIN, MARTIN	37	M	LABR	RRZZZZNY
SERTISCHONAS, ANTONI	24	M	LABR	RRZZZZNY
JOSEF	28	M	LABR	RRZZZZNY
KLIDAS, BALTRONI	40	M	LABR	RRZZZZNY
LOWECKA, CASIMIR	28	M	LABR	RRZZZZNY
LAWREISCHEK, MICHAEL	23	M	LABR	RRZZZZNY
GEJETSKY, ANTON	23	M	LABR	RRZZZZNY
PONIKOWSKI, DANIEL	30	M	LABR	RRZZZZNY
DABROWLINSKI, JOH.	21	M	LABR	RRZZZZNY
STUHLMANN, REBECCA	23	F	SGL	RRZZZZNY
WEISSBARTH, LOUISE	18	F	D	RRZZZZNY
JACOB	20	M	S	RRZZZZNY
ANNA	20	F	D	RRZZZZNY
HEISMANN, REBECCA	19	F	SGL	RRZZZZNY
WEINER, ABRAM	21	M	DLR	RRZZZZNY
RESCHE	20	F	W	RRZZZZNY
CHAWE	8	F	CHILD	RRZZZZNY
SURE	.09	F	INFANT	RRZZZZNY
DAVID	19	M	DLR	RRZZZZNY
RRIER, NOCHEM	37	M	DLR	RRZZZZNY
DOMBROWSKI, JOSEPH	55	M	LABR	RRZZZZNY
SCHER, RACHMIEL	37	M	TLR	RRZZZZNY
ROGARTEN, SAMUEL	29	M	TLR	RRZZZZNY
KRAPOWITZ, JEIZE	29	F	WO	RRZZZZNY
ROSENBERGER, ABRAH.	26	M	WO	RRZZZZNY
BENSOHN, MORITZ	32	M	WO	RRZZZZNY
ZAINKEL, SAPHIR	40	M	WO	RRZZZZNY
WAIZEL, LEISER	25	M	WO	RRZZZZNY
GOLNICK, CHAIM	28	M	WO	RRZZZZNY
JUGBERG, NISSEN	24	M	WO	RRZZZZNY
ABRAMOWITZ, HIRSCH	46	M	WO	RRZZZZNY
GERSTEIN, ABR.	33	M	WO	RRZZZZNY
KIWE	23	M	WO	RRZZZZNY
FUELLNER, CARL	21	M	LKSH	RRZZZZNY
WAINAGIRYS, LUDWIG	24	M	FARMER	RRZZZZNY

SHIP: ALASKA

FROM: LIVERPOOL AND QUEENSTOWN
TO: NEW YORK
ARRIVED: 25 JUNE 1888

PASSENGER	AGE	SEX	OCCUPATION	PRV VIL DES
ROSENBUM, ABRAHAM	35	M	LABR	RRZZZZUSA
AZERSKY, JUDAH	18	M	LABR	RRZZZZUSA
LEWINSKI, KALSE	21	F	SP	RRZZZZUSA
REIZ, SAM.	60	M	LABR	PLZZZZUSA
CAHIM	21	M	LABR	PLZZZZUSA
BOROWSKI, LEIB	18	F	SP	PLZZZZUSA
BLANKENSTEIN, ISRAEL	19	M	LABR	RRZZZZUSA
SCHNEIDER, CHAIE	17	F	SP	RRZZZZUSA
FLUKS, RIWKE	22	F	SP	RRZZZZUSA
ZADWADOWITZ, JANKEL	54	M	GZR	PLZZZZUSA
BEKER, ETLEB	17	F	SP	RRZZZZUSA
KAPLUN, MOSES	50	M	LABR	RRZZZZUSA
GOLDENTHAL, MOSES	25	M	GZR	RRZZZZUSA
WIWRINEN, AUGUST	24	M	LABR	FNZZZZUSA
HANTANCUKI, JOHAN	25	M	LABR	FNZZZZUSA
STLUBACKA, ERIK	17	M	LABR	FNZZZZUSA
BYGAR, MATH.	23	M	MRNR	FNZZZZUSA
MATH.	26	M	MRNR	FNZZZZUSA
BACKLUND, JOHAN	28	M	LABR	FNZZZZUSA
SODERLUND, ELIA	32	M	MRNR	FNZZZZUSA
ESSELSTROM, ANDERS	28	M	MRNR	FNZZZZUSA
FLINK, MATH.J.	37	M	LABR	FNZZZZUSA
NYGANOD, ANDERS	20	M	FARMER	FNZZZZUSA
MATTSSON, MATH.	21	M	LABR	FNZZZZUSA
JOHANSON, HERMAN	19	M	PNTR	FNZZZZUSA
JAPARS, BIETA	26	F	SP	FNZZZZUSA
HEDMAN, JACOB	22	M	LABR	FNZZZZUSA
HAGGLOF, SIMON	47	M	LABR	FNZZZZUSA
HOGHAMAKI, JAKOB	36	M	FARMER	FNZZZZUSA
PALLARI, MATTHIAS	21	M	LABR	FNZZZZUSA
BORGEN, JOHAN	19	M	LABR	FNZZZZUSA
PALLA, JONULS	18	M	LABR	FNZZZZUSA
PETTERSKOW, MATTS	18	M	PDLR	FNZZZZUSA
SANDSTROUN, CHARLOTTE	37	F	MA	FNZZZZUSA
MARIA	13	F	SP	FNZZZZUSA
REZVAUS, LISA	22	F	SP	FNZZZZUSA
LUNDZREN, MATHEAS	20	M	FARMER	RRZZZZUSA
SFOBLOM, JOHAN	21	M	LABR	FNZZZZUSA
BLOMGVIST, DANL.	39	M	LABR	FNZZZZUSA
WIKMAN, ERIK	31	M	CPTR	FNZZZZUSA
MSCHALSKY, JAN	27	M	LABR	RRZZZZUSA
MOMGELGRIN, SARA	18	F	SP	RRZZZZUSA
MEDANSKY, BENJ.	19	M	LABR	RRZZZZUSA
POKAMINSKI, LEPPE	24	F	SP	RRZZZZUSA
SALOMON, MANIL	11	F	CH	RRZZZZUSA
ARON	10	M	CH	RRZZZZUSA
BACKSTEIN, ADOLPH	25	M	LABR	RRZZZZUSA
KUROSHNER, CHRM	28	M	LABR	RRZZZZUSA
GRUNBLATT, GLENDEL	53	F	MA	PLZZZZUSA
LINA	27	F	SP	PLZZZZUSA
GLISCHEWSKY, MOSES	25	M	LABR	RRZZZZUSA
MINDEL	20	M	LABR	RRZZZZUSA
MATLIN, MARKUS	34	M	LABR	RRZZZZUSA
PAULINA	24	F	SP	RRZZZZUSA
AMRUSCH, BARBARA	26	F	SP	RRZZZZUSA
RITG, SUSANNA	18	F	SP	RRZZZZUSA
MISZUKEWITZ, KASSIMIR	36	M	LABR	RRZZZZUSA
SCHARKIN, ZERE	17	F	SP	RRZZZZUSA
SERMUAK, MOSES	21	M	LABR	RRZZZZUSA
DALSUSKY, CHONE	19	M	LABR	RRZZZZUSA
ROOKE	20	M	LABR	RRZZZZUSA
LEWIN, ELSAS	20	M	LABR	RRZZZZUSA
BERMANN, MORODRE	24	M	GZR	RRZZZZUSA
HAINBERG, LEIB	20	M	LABR	RRZZZZUSA
KRAWETZ, MOEDCHE	25	M	LABR	RRZZZZUSA
BLOCH, SELIG	21	M	GZR	RRZZZZUSA
SCHAMSDREN, RAHEL	18	F	SP	RRZZZZUSA
FEINSTEIN, JOCHEL	18	M	GZR	RRZZZZUSA
SCHMICLERSKY, SCHMISH	29	M	LABR	RRZZZZUSA
GORDON, ELIOKUM	25	M	LABR	RRZZZZUSA
SUCHAWOLSKI, CHAIM	11	M	CH	RRZZZZUSA
MANERBERGER, MOSES	19	M	LABR	RRZZZZUSA
FLUKS, JOSEL	10	M	CH	RRZZZZUSA
SCHNEIDER, JOSEL	10	M	CH	RRZZZZUSA
KASCHAWER, SCHOLEM	26	M	LABR	RRZZZZUSA
ROSEN, ESTER	2	F	CHILD	RRZZZZUSA
ROSENZWEIG, ETTI	.05	F	INFANT	RRZZZZUSA
MATTSDOTTER, SANNA	21	F	SP	FNZZZZUSA
LUNDBERG, JOHAN	33	M	MRNR	FNZZZZUSA
MARIA	21	F	SP	FNZZZZUSA
STEN, JOHAN	33	M	FARMER	FNZZZZUSA
NORMAN, ERIK	40	M	LABR	FNZZZZUSA
STEFANUS	38	M	LABR	FNZZZZUSA
MARKUS	29	M	LABR	FNZZZZUSA
ABRAMSON, JOHANES	21	M	LABR	FNZZZZUSA
MYRSKOG, HANS	28	M	LABR	FNZZZZUSA
ATHEBERG, ALEX.	28	M	LABR	FNZZZZUSA
BACK, JOHA.L.	23	M	SHMK	FNZZZZUSA
HAYSTRAIN, GUSTAF	29	M	FARMER	FNZZZZUSA
ANNA	26	F	SP	FNZZZZUSA
RUNDELL, JOHAN	38	M	LABR	FNZZZZUSA
STAGNUS, ANDREAS	34	M	LABR	FNZZZZUSA
FRANKSHOHN, JAKOB	28	M	LABR	FNZZZZUSA
FANTAN, ANDERS	19	M	LABR	FNZZZZUSA
WAST, KARL	19	M	LABR	FNZZZZUSA
FAUT, ANDERS	22	M	LABR	FNZZZZUSA
LABIKAUZAS, JOHAN	46	M	LABR	FNZZZZUSA
JOS, ANDERS	18	M	LABR	FNZZZZUSA
KONTONEN, MICKEL	17	M	LABR	FNZZZZUSA
WERNE, BRITTE	18	M	FARMER	FNZZZZUSA
JARVI, GUSTAF	32	M	FARMER	FNZZZZUSA
MAKI, JOHAN	32	M	LABR	FNZZZZUSA
AKERS, F.	23	M	LABR	FNZZZZUSA
JAKOBSON, M.	35	M	LABR	FNZZZZUSA
MYGAARD, J.	17	M	FARMER	FNZZZZUSA
HAGA, A.	30	M	LABR	FNZZZZUSA
ROMAS, J.	11	M	CH	FNZZZZUSA
HOBUS, ERIK	19	M	LABR	FNZZZZUSA
BLUSI, MARTIN	20	M	LABR	FNZZZZUSA
SODERGAND, SOFIA	19	F	SP	FNZZZZUSA
ROSENBERG, MATJAS	35	M	LABR	RRZZZZUSA
SEMSOLIN, MOSES	28	M	FLST	RRZZZZUSA
BESSIE	21	F	W	RRZZZZUSA
MATT.	2	M	CHILD	RRZZZZUSA
M.LACHS.	.04	M	INFANT	RRZZZZUSA
FILKOWITZ, MAYEN	35	M	LABR	RRZZZZUSA
IROLICZ, DORE	25	F	MA	RRZZZZUSA
MORDCHE	.10	M	INFANT	RRZZZZUSA
GERSTENKERW, FRIED	11	M	CH	RRZZZZUSA

SHIP: SLAVONIA

FROM: SWINEMUNDE
TO: NEW YORK
ARRIVED: 25 JUNE 1888

PASSENGER	AGE	SEX	OCCUPATION	PRV VIL DES
LOUIS, SCHLOMA	18	M	LABR	RRZZZZUSA
GILLIES, JULIUS	18	M	TRDSMN	RRZZZZUSA
GROHMANN, LOUIS	19	M	TRDSMN	RRZZZZUSA
MAJEWSKA, MAGDALENA	35	F	WO	RRZZZZUSA
KASPAR	11	M	CH	RRZZZZUSA
URSULA	10	F	CH	RRZZZZUSA
JOSEPH	8	M	CHILD	RRZZZZUSA
ANTON	7	M	CHILD	RRZZZZUSA
ROSALIE	4	F	CHILD	RRZZZZUSA
ALOIS	2	M	CHILD	RRZZZZUSA
KASIMIR	.11	M	INFANT	RRZZZZUSA
PAJEWSKY, JOSEPH	29	M	JNR	RRZZZZUSA

PASSENGER	AGE	SEX	OCCUPATION	PRIVL	DES
HARRMANN, EMMA	20	F	UNKNOWN	RRAEFL	USA
KOSLOWSKA, THEOFILA	45	F	WO	RRAHYM	USA
JULIANE	10	F	CH	RRAHYM	USA
JAN	3	M	CHILD	RRAHYM	USA
HENSELET, AUGUST	52	M	WHLR	RRAEFL	USA
WALDEMAR	17	M	S	RRAEFL	USA
FRIEDERIKE	45	F	W	RRAEFL	USA
JULIA	20	F	CH	RRAEFL	USA
FRIEDERIKE	9	F	CHILD	RRAEFL	USA
MARTHA	4	F	CHILD	RRAEFL	USA
ALADOWSKY, RACHEL	25	F	WO	RRZZZZ	USA
SARAH	2	F	CHILD	RRZZZZ	USA
MAYER	1	M	CHILD	RRZZZZ	USA
GEFKEN, BUNNIE	43	F	WO	RRZZZZ	USA
RICKE	17	F	CH	RRZZZZ	USA
PINDOS	10	M	CH	RRZZZZ	USA
BRAINE	6	F	CHILD	RRZZZZ	USA
KURIEL	4	M	CHILD	RRZZZZ	USA
SCHARIE	2	F	CHILD	RRZZZZ	USA
DAUGELOWITZ, ANNE	32	F	WO	RRZZZZ	UNK
JENIG, WILHELM	43	M	LABR	RRZZZZ	UNK
ADOLPH	19	M	S	RRZZZZ	UNK
THIEDE, JULIANE	43	F	WO	RRZZZZ	UNK
LUDWIG	15	M	CH	RRZZZZ	UNK
JULIA	11	F	CH	RRZZZZ	UNK
TYLDA	8	F	CHILD	RRZZZZ	UNK
TWARSKOWSKA, JULIANA	16	F	SVNT	RRZZZZ	UNK
WIEDNICKY, VALENTIN	20	M	LABR	RRZZZZ	UNK
BAKANAS, JOSEPH	23	M	LABR	RRZZZZ	UNK
SONNTAG, WILHELMINE	23	F	UNKNOWN	RRAEFL	UNK
SCHAUBY, ANDREAS	25	M	LABR	RRZZZZ	UNK
LAVAL, MATHILDE	37	F	WO	RRAEFL	UNK
ARTHUR	8	M	CHILD	RRAEFL	UNK
BERZYNS, ANTONO	34	M	LABR	RRZZZZ	UNK
EVA	31	F	W	RRZZZZ	UNK
ANDREAS	9	M	CHILD	RRZZZZ	UNK
ANNA	5	F	CHILD	RRZZZZ	UNK
BALZIEROSKY, MALGAZATA	28	F	WO	RRAIOC	UNK
ANIELA	00	F	CH	RRAIOC	UNK
CAECILIE	00	F	CH	RRAIOC	UNK
VALENTIN	00	M	CH	RRAIOC	UNK
SPERLING, JACOB	28	M	WCHMKR	RRZZZZ	UNK
CLAWA	28	F	W	RRZZZZ	UNK
FELSCHE	4	F	CHILD	RRZZZZ	UNK
REGINE	3	F	CHILD	RRZZZZ	UNK
EISIG	1	M	CHILD	RRZZZZ	UNK
MANN, ISAAC	51	M	LABR	RRZZZZ	UNK
FEIWUSCH	11	M	CH	RRZZZZ	UNK
BLUME	6	F	CHILD	RRZZZZ	UNK
BARANOWITZ, ZIVIC	20	F	UNKNOWN	RRAHVQ	UNK
HURWITZ, JOSEPH	25	M	GDSM	RRAINM	UNK
BERTHA	22	F	W	RRAINM	UNK
HELFER, HODIOS	11	M	BY	RRAINM	UNK
KOPOLOWITZ, MENDEL	27	M	TLR	RRZZZZ	UNK
WOLPIANSKY, CHAIM	40	M	TRDSMN	RRZZZZ	UNK
EIERWEISS, CHAZKEL	56	M	LABR	RRAGRT	UNK
SCHUSTER, JACOB	24	M	BCHR	RRZZZZ	UNK
BABUSCH, ABRAHAM	25	M	SHMK	RRZZZZ	UNK
ASKENASI, SCHOLEM	19	M	GDR	RRZZZZ	UNK
SZESKO, FRACZISCECK	26	M	LABR	RRAHSP	UNK
MUELLER, VALERIAN	18	M	FARMER	RRAEFL	UNK
OSCHKOWITSCH, EPHRAIM	48	M	TNR	RRAILY	UNK
SCHUBANSKY, JAN	25	M	JNR	RRAHXI	UNK
DAVID, FALK	40	M	TRDSMN	RRAIDN	UNK
ESTERLIEBE	9	F	CHILD	RRAIDN	UNK
BARANSKI, JOHANN	22	M	LABR	RRAIGB	UNK
KRUSINSKA, ANNA	19	F	SVNT	RRZZZZ	UNK
WASCHKOWSKY, WLADISLAUS	20	M	LABR	RRZZZZ	UNK
KLAWONSKY, MAYER	45	M	MCHT	RRZZZZ	UNK
CHALIASKY, MARTIN	29	M	LABR	RRZZZZ	UNK
GERSCHOWITZ, MAROUS	25	M	CPRSMH	RRZZZZ	UNK
ADAM, JUDES	20	M	LABR	RRZZZZ	UNK
SCHERMAN, JANKEL	36	M	TLR	RRAGRT	UNK
SCHNEIDER, MAYR	32	M	GZR	RRAGRT	UNK
MENDEL, GERSCHEN	32	M	PNTR	RRAGRT	UNK
STRANIES, GEORG	40	M	JNR	RRZZZZ	UNK
KESCHL, JOSEPH	30	M	LABR	RRZZZZ	UNK
BODWIT, JOHANN	25	M	LABR	RRZZZZ	UNK
BERNOTH, ZODER	25	M	LABR	RRZZZZ	UNK
KEPLAN, MAX	40	M	TLR	RRZZZZ	UNK
DANGELOWITZ, ANELA	4	M	CHILD	RRZZZZ	UNK
CHEMINSKY, JACOB	30	M	CPTR	RRZZZZ	UNK
HALPERU, SALOMON	40	M	SHMK	RRZZZZ	UNK
KATZMANN, RUBEN	34	M	TLR	RRAGRT	UNK
HIROCH	8	M	CHILD	RRAGRT	UNK
WOITKUWITZ, KESAREY	26	M	LABR	RRAHTU	UNK
BYDZEWSKY, JOSEPH	37	M	LABR	RRAHTU	UNK
KANTEROWITZ, SAWEL	36	M	BCHR	RRAIKY	UNK
HAHN, SELIG	27	M	TRDSMN	RRAIKY	UNK
ABRAMSOHN, CHANE	17	M	TLR	RRZZZZ	UNK
SALZ, ISAAC	52	M	BLKSMH	RRZZZZ	UNK
SKLAROWSKY, DAVID	30	M	GZR	RRZZZZ	UNK
LYTSCHKOWSKY, SIMON	23	M	LABR	RRAHTU	UNK
FERDMANN, LEIB	25	M	LABR	RRAGRT	UNK
MUSCHE	19	F	S	RRAGRT	UNK
JEKURSKA, BRONISLAWA	22	F	WO	RRAINY	UNK
BRUNISLAW	2	M	CHILD	RRAINY	UNK
KARBOWSKY, JAN	20	M	LABR	RRAINY	UNK
KAMEROWSKA, MARIANNE	29	F	WO	RRZZZZ	UNK
MARIANNE	8	F	CHILD	RRZZZZ	UNK
ANTONIE	4	F	CHILD	RRZZZZ	UNK
JAN	.09	M	INFANT	RRZZZZ	UNK
WOISCHIKOWSKY, JAN	20	M	LABR	RRZZZZ	UNK

SHIP: BOHEMIA

FROM: HAMBURG AND HAVRE
TO: NEW YORK
ARRIVED: 25 JUNE 1888

PASSENGER	AGE	SEX	OCCUPATION	PRIVL	DES
KOPPILOW, CARL	37	M	UNKNOWN	RRAHQU	NE
WOLOTZKI, ETTE	28	M	UNKNOWN	RRAHQU	NE
CHANE	7	F	CHILD	RRAHQU	NE
HIRSCH	5	M	CHILD	RRZZZZ	CAL
TERTIC, FILIPPO	28	M	LABR	RRZZZZ	CAL
GREC, JOSEPH	18	M	LABR	RRZZZZ	CAL
KOGIK, ALOJZY	41	M	LABR	RRZZZZ	PA
SLAHTA, JAKO	26	M	LABR	RRZZZZ	PA
CZEKAN, MIHAL	25	M	LABR	RRZZZZ	PA
CZILKA, FEDOR	16	M	LABR	RRZZZZ	PA
CIGON, FEDOR	20	M	LABR	RRZZZZ	PA
U, MATEJ	15	M	LABR	RRZZZZ	PA
KERTH, CARL	23	M	MCHT	RRAIIN	NE
PENTSAK, AGATHE	27	F	UNKNOWN	RRZZZZ	NY
JOSEF	4	M	CHILD	RRAIGH	NY
FRIEDMANN, ADOLF	21	M	CL	RRAINM	NE
LEIB	73	M	LABR	RRAINM	NE
SIFRE	57	F	W	RRAINM	NE
BEILE	19	F	CH	RRAINM	NE
SARA	17	F	CH	RRAINM	NE
LIPSCHITZ, SARA	40	F	WO	RRZZZZ	NE
KEPLER, AUGUST	40	M	LABR	RRZZZZ	NE
COHN, LINE	20	F	SGL	RRZZZZ	NE
SCHENE	16	F	SGL	RRZZZZ	NE
BERMANN	9	M	CHILD	RRZZZZ	NE
HERMANN	8	M	CHILD	RRZZZZ	NE
PRZYBILSKI, MARTIN	24	M	LABR	RRAIAJ	UNK
ANTONI	71	M	LABR	RRAIAJ	UNK
FRANZISKA	68	F	W	RRAIAJ	UNK
RADOSCHKOWSKI, LEIB	18	M	LABR	RRZZZZ	MI
LIPSCHITZ, BEILE	8	F	CHILD	RRZZZZ	MI
ROSENTHAL, MARIANNE	25	F	WO	RRAHQU	MI
ROSENFELD, JENTE	25	F	WO	RRAHQU	MI
JOSEF	.11	M	INFANT	RRAHQU	MI
JERUCHIM	.01	M	INFANT	RRAHQU	MI

PASSENGER	AGE	SEX	OCCUPATION	PRV VIL DES
GLAESER, HERZ	27	M	DLR	RRAIMCNE
POTASCHNIK, ISRAEL	17	M	DLR	RRAIMCNE
DANISCHEWSKI, DANIEL	9	M	CHILD	RRAIMCNE
MARCHEL, ANNA	24	F	SGL	RRAIKANE
ZIMMER, CARL	27	M	GDNR	RRZZZZUNK
ROSENZWEIG, MIREL	29	F	SGL	RRZZZZNY
DUKATENZAEHLER, LEIB	33	M	LABR	RRAILINY
BONE, SIMON	29	M	LABR	RRAICANY
HENIE	20	F	W	RRAICANY
STANISLAWSKI, ABRAM	47	M	LABR	RRZZZZNE
ITZSCHOK	18	M	LABR	RRZZZZNE
BAREZ, MOSES	38	M	LABR	RRAHWQNE
NOTHER, SCHEWACH	26	M	LABR	RRAHWQNE
STANISLAWSKI, MENIE	58	F	WO	RRZZZZNE
RIEFKE	18	M	CH	RRZZZZNE
LISA	18	F	CH	RRZZZZNE
AETE	14	M	CH	RRZZZZNE
MARCUS	9	M	CHILD	RRZZZZNE
CHAIM	8	M	CHILD	RRZZZZNE
LEON	7	M	CHILD	RRZZZZNE
MALKE	5	F	CHILD	RRZZZZNE
RAFAEL	3	F	CHILD	RRZZZZNE
ABERBUCH, ITZIG	52	M	LABR	RRZZZZNE
HERSCH	25	M	LABR	RRZZZZNE
CHAJES, ABRAM	20	M	LABR	RRZZZZNE
SIERKA	22	F	W	RRZZZZNE
FENNER, MAX	20	M	LABR	RRZZZZNE
BLAUZWIRN, JACOB	42	M	TLR	RRACONIL
TITEFSKI, ETEL	16	F	SGL	RRZZZZNY
GLUECKSMANN, SARA	24	F	WO	RRAFWJNY
PEISACH	4	M	CHILD	RRAFWJNY
LEIBUSCH	3	M	CHILD	RRAFWJNY
LEA	.11	F	INFANT	RRAFWJNY
FRIEDLAENDER, ERNESTINE	22	F	SGL	RRAEFLIL
SCHNEIDER, FEIGE	15	F	SGL	RRZZZZIL
OPPENHEIM, ABR.	22	M	DLR	RRZZZZNE
APTER, JANKEL	19	M	LABR	RRZZZZNE
PESCHE	9	F	CHILD	RRZZZZNE
GUTMANN, ZIPE	22	F	WO	RRAFWJNE
CHAJE	9	F	CHILD	RRAFWJNE
LEIB	8	M	CHILD	RRAFWJNE
RACHEL	5	F	CHILD	RRAFWJNE
MIREL	.11	M	INFANT	RRAFWJNE
ZAROMB, DWORE	38	F	WO	RRAIIBNE
SCHEI	8	F	CHILD	RRAIIBNE
MOSES	4	M	CHILD	RRAIIBNE
ULLRICH, CARL	20	M	TLR	RRAINZNE
BIELINSKI, AUGUSTE	26	F	WO	RRAIOGNY
WILH.	8	M	CHILD	RRAIOGNY
ADOLF	4	M	CHILD	RRAIOGNY
GUSTAV	2	M	CHILD	RRAIOGNY
JUDZITZKI, ALTE	16	F	SGL	RRZZZZNE
PLOTZNIK, FEIGE	24	F	WO	RRZZZZNE
HERZ	2	M	CHILD	RRZZZZNE
CJHAJE	.11	F	INFANT	RRZZZZNE
JUDELOWSKY, SCHEI	23	F	SGL	RRAHVANE
STOLPE, ANNA	44	F	WO	FNZZZZNY
HEILIKMANN, MENDEL	18	F	DLR	FNAHTFNY
KAPELOW, FREIDE	20	F	SGL	FNAHTUNY
SAWEFSKI, MICHAEL	27	M	LABR	RRZZZZNY
GOLDSTEIN, JOSSEL	19	M	LABR	RRAHZUNE
EPSTEIN, EDUARD	9	M	CHILD	RRAHZUNE
WILLONSKY, AETE	18	M	LABR	RRZZZZNE
BELINSKI, PETER	53	M	CPTR	RRZZZZNE
CAROLE.	59	F	W	RRZZZZNE
PAULINE	20	F	CH	RRZZZZNE
REINHARD	.11	M	INFANT	RRZZZZNE
KOHAN, CHAIM	20	M	LABR	RRAILPNE
CZARNOWSKI, PAUL	26	M	BKR	RRZZZZNE
DOLASTA, MATHILDE	22	F	WO	RRZZZZNE
ARTHUR	.11	M	INFANT	RRZZZZNE
FORGASCH, ARTHUR	15	M	STDNT	RRZZZZNE
ELIENBERG, ISRAEL	21	M	TLR	RRAILLUNK
KUPPERWASSER, DAVID	23	M	TLR	RRAILLUNK
PASSOLL, ARON	35	M	LABR	RRAHVLNE

PASSENGER	AGE	SEX	OCCUPATION	PRV VIL DES
RACHWALSKI, ARON	17	M	MCHT	RRZZZZNE
HENSENBERG, LEIER	37	F	WO	RRZZZZNY
BOROWSKI, SCHEINE	19	F	SGL	RRZZZZNY
RABINOWITZ, MICHLE	23	F	WO	RRAILRNY
DWORE	.11	F	INFANT	RRAILRNY
GRABEROWITZ, SORE	22	M	DLR	RRAHXLNY
RECHAME	3	F	CHILD	RRAHXLNY
BAKOS, STEPHAN	18	M	LABR	RRAHXLNY
SCHNIPISKI, DWORE	48	F	WO	RRAHXLNE
NOCHIM	9	M	CHILD	RRAHXLNE
MARGREIT, FRUMMET	18	F	SGL	RRAFWJNE
CHILKES, ESTHER	27	F	WO	RRAHQUNE
HIRSCH	7	M	CHILD	RRAHQUNE
MORDSCHE	5	M	CHILD	RRAHQUNE
SCHEINE	.11	F	INFANT	RRAHQUNE
NORDMAND, ISAAC	26	M	LABR	RRZZZZNE
NORSKI, CASIS	31	M	LABR	RRZZZZNY
LAKS, JOHANN	20	M	LABR	RRZZZZNY
DROSDANSKY, JOH.	19	M	LABR	RRZZZZNY
ANDRUSCHKEWICZ, JAN	23	M	LABR	RRZZZZNY
MICHAEL	48	M	LABR	RRZZZZNY
GOLDBERG, MOSES	34	M	DLR	RRAFVGNY
NUDELMANN, CHAJEN	60	M	DLR	RRAIGHNY
TURTULSKI, RIWE	27	F	WO	RRAIGHNY
CHAJE	3	F	CHILD	RRAIGHNY
DINA	.11	F	INFANT	RRAIGHNY
HELPER, GERMAN	26	M	DLR	RRAHTUNY
SLATE	7	F	CHILD	RRAHTUNY
BLUMBERG, ALEX	22	M	DLR	RRAHOKNY
BROSLAWSKI, ROSA	.11	F	INFANT	RRAICINY
ESTHER	.01	F	INFANT	RRAICINY
NORGUSKI, CHAJE	.11	F	INFANT	RRAICINY
HINE	.01	F	INFANT	RRAICINY
KLEIZEWSKI, IDA	17	F	SGL	RRZZZZOH
MATINPOIKA, JOHANN	17	M	LABR	FNZZZZOMA
SIMOPOIKA, JOHANN	15	M	LABR	FNZZZZOMA
NIELSEN, VENDLA	22	F	WO	FNZZZZOMA
GUSTAV	.07	M	INFANT	FNZZZZOMA
CARLSEN, CARL	20	M	LABR	FNZZZZOMA
JOHNSEN, ERRIC	19	M	LABR	FNZZZZOMA
PELTOMAC, NIKKARI	19	M	LABR	FNZZZZOMA
ALOYOKI, IDA	18	F	SGL	FNZZZZOMA
HERMANNSON, HERM.	30	M	LABR	FNZZZZOMA
RAINE, JOHANN	35	M	LABR	FNZZZZOMA
KOSKI, MARIE	30	F	SGL	FNZZZZOMA
DOTTER, BRITON-AND.	33	F	SGL	FNZZZZOMA
HAUSEN, CHR.A.	32	M	LABR	FNZZZZUNK
JOHS.	2	M	CHILD	FNZZZZUNK
JAKKU, MATTS	20	M	FARMER	FNZZZZOH
GOLDBLATT, RUWEN	32	M	DLR	RRZZZZNE
HELPER, ITE	45	F	WO	RRZZZZNE
JUDELOWSKI, BLUME	17	F	SGL	RRZZZZNE
HALPERN, JOSEF	21	M	DLR	RRAHXRNE
DOBROVICZ, HERMAN	34	M	DLR	RRAHXRUNK
RUDOLF, JOSEF	23	M	MUSN	RRAHOONY
ISAKOWITZ, HERM.	17	M	DLR	RRAIGHNY
HANNE	15	F	SGL	RRAIGHNY
STEINMANN, ABRAM	18	M	TLR	RRAIBONY
MUELLER, THOMAS	49	M	LABR	RRAIOFNE
FRANZ, DAVID	19	M	LABR	RRAIOFNE
TASCHEK, JOHANN	25	M	LABR	RRAIOFNE
KEMPKA, JOSEF	28	M	LABR	RRAIOFNE
LITHA	20	F	W	RRAIOFNE
ALBERT	.06	M	INFANT	RRAIOFNE
KOENIGSBERG, HENNY	18	F	SGL	RRAHXLNE
PRIZEWITZ, WAZLAW	18	M	LABR	RRAGRTNE
FRIEDMANN, REGI	17	F	SGL	RRZZZZNE
SALI	6	F	CHILD	RRZZZZNE
KLASCHKI, CHANNE	36	F	WO	RRAIGHMO
MASCHE	18	F	CH	RRAIGHMO
MOSES	9	M	CHILD	RRAIGHMO
ESTHER	8	F	CHILD	RRAIGHMO
SAMUEL	4	M	CHILD	RRAIGHMO
KURJULA, HINRISCH	39	M	LABR	FNZZZZOH
EKOLA, MAJO	20	M	SGL	FNZZZZOH

PASSENGER	AGE	SEX	OCCUPATION	PRV VIL DES
ALEX	30	M	LABR	FNZZZZOH
LAMINATO, HENRIK	47	M	LABR	FNZZZZOH
HUNSILA, GUSTAV	53	M	LABR	FNZZZZOH
ISAMESTAJOOM, ANZEJORN	19	M	LABR	FNZZZZOH
TOKOLA, ALEX	17	M	LABR	FNZZZZOH
ROMSILA, MATTS	44	M	LABR	FNZZZZOH
WILAMO, ALEX	19	M	LABR	FNZZZZUNK
KULJES, ALEXANDER	22	M	LABR	FNZZZZUNK
OSANKAS, ANTON	23	M	LABR	RRZZZZNE
ARMINOWITZ, MIHAEL	52	M	LABR	RRZZZZNE
WASILEWSKI, MARIANNE	22	F	SGL	RRZZZZNE
ANTON	20	M	LABR	RRZZZZNE
NEUMANN, EDUARD	25	M	LABR	RRZZZZPA
LICHT, MARIE	18	F	WO	RRAIOPNY
MEJZER, MOSES	36	M	LABR	RRAIOPNY
DOBRISACH	8	M	CHILD	RRAIOPNY
LANDAU, BERIL	19	M	LABR	RRAICZNY
BAZICZ, ABRAM	19	M	LABR	RRAICZNY
TODRESCH, JOS.	50	M	LABR	RRAHXHPA
SARA	50	F	W	RRAHXHPA
LINA	20	F	CH	RRAHXHPA
IDA	16	F	CH	RRAHXHPA
MAX	8	M	CHILD	RRAHXHPA
ADAMEC, MARIE	30	F	W	RRAHXHPA
BENES, JAN	6	M	CHILD	RRAHXHIL
SOFIE	7	F	CHILD	RRAHXHIL
SZBERTSKI, DOMINIK	27	M	LABR	RRAHTGNE
POSZKIEWICZ, JOHN	29	M	LABR	RRZZZZOH
DUDJIA, GERSCH	20	M	LABR	RRZZZZODE
STEIN, DINE	19	F	SGL	RRZZZZNY
JUBOWSKI, GRUNE	20	F	SGL	RRZZZZNY
HOCHMANN, HERM.	39	M	LABR	RRAFVGNY
FANNY	38	F	W	RRAFVGNY
MARCUS	7	M	CHILD	RRAFVGNY
ISRAEL	6	M	CHILD	RRAFVGNY
DORA	5	F	CHILD	RRAFVGNY
JONNI	3	M	CHILD	RRAFVGNY
MALEMATOWA, MALKE	40	F	WO	RRAHTFIL
CHANNE	16	F	CH	RRAHTFIL
Z--E	8	F	CHILD	RRAHTFIL
OLSCHEWSKI, MICHALINE	30	F	W	RRZZZZNE
JOS.	8	M	CHILD	RRZZZZNE
CATHA.	6	F	CHILD	RRZZZZNE
JAN	.04	M	INFANT	RRZZZZNE
BULZUNAS, JAN	19	M	LABR	RRZZZZNE
MARIE	24	F	SGL	RRZZZZNE
KORDON, DWORE	20	F	W	RRZZZZIA
IDES	8	F	CHILD	RRZZZZIA
SAM.	.07	M	INFANT	RRZZZZIA
WALD, ABRAHAM	26	M	LABR	RRAHXHNY
BATKIN, SAMUEL	27	M	LABR	RRZZZZNY
BERTHA	22	F	W	RRZZZZNY
KAPNER, JANKEL	20	M	DLR	RRAIMGNE
ZAHLE, OTTO	36	M	LABR	RRAIINNE
LISETTE	30	F	W	RRAIINNE
SAWITZKA, KATHA.	30	F	WO	RRAIINNE
BONKFELD, CHRISTIAN	36	M	LABR	RRAIINNE
CHENSIN, BERKO	28	M	DLR	RRZZZZNE
RADNIK, MOSES	20	M	DLR	RRAIEQNE
BUT, VINCENTZ	28	M	LABR	RRAHQUNE
STEINBERG, GEDALIE	34	M	LABR	RRAHQUNE
SCHMIDT, HENRIETTE	24	F	WO	RRAIFNIL
ELLA	.07	F	INFANT	RRAIFNIL
LEWIN, LEIB	22	M	LABR	RRZZZZIL
ZINNE	20	F	W	RRZZZZIL
DILDE, PINKUS	16	M	LABR	RRAIGHNY
KATZ, TAUBE	15	F	SGL	RRAIGHNY
KAPLAN, BASCHBE	59	F	WO	RRAFVGNY
CHAIMOWITZ, PINCUS	18	M	DLR	RRAFVGNY
AGULNIK, REBECCA	18	F	SGL	RRAFVGNY
HOMMA, FRANZ	28	M	LABR	RRAHQUNY
NETTER, ZALLEL	22	M	CL	RRAGRTNY
KAMINOWITZ, CHINKE	25	F	WO	RRAHTONY
LEIB	.07	M	INFANT	RRAHTONY
BERLOWITZ, CHAIM	20	M	WCHMKR	RRAILRNY

PASSENGER	AGE	SEX	OCCUPATION	PRV VIL DES
LOEWY, HIRSCH	28	M	TLR	RRZZZZNE
LINE	18	F	W	RRZZZZNE
ISAAC	.11	M	INFANT	RRZZZZNE
BERKOWITZ, SCHOLEM	28	M	TKR	RRAEFLNE
CHASSE	26	F	W	RRAEFLNE
SAMUEL	3	M	CHILD	RRAEFLNE
JETTE	.11	F	INFANT	RRAEFLNE
POLIYANSKI, WLADISLAW	21	M	LABR	RRZZZZNE
KOBILINSKI, JAN	40	M	LABR	RRZZZZNE
PAWEL	23	M	LABR	RRZZZZNE
PYSIREWSKI, KASIMIR	22	M	LABR	RRZZZZNE
ZAREW, BENJAMIN	18	M	APTC	RRAHVUNE
WASENKO, SIMON	16	M	APTC	RRZZZZIA
RUSIN, JEDREK	40	M	APTC	RRZZZZIA
KNOTHA, STEFAN	40	M	APTC	RRZZZZIA
MYSZLEIN, CONSTANTIN	20	M	LABR	RRZZZZPA
PIZIK, MOSCHE	22	M	LABR	RRAHVUPA
JUDE	16	M	LABR	RRAHVUPA
RAUSUCK, LINDA	23	F	SGL	RRAHVJIN
IKOLDE, ARON	40	M	DLR	RRZZZZNY
DOBRE	32	F	W	RRZZZZNY
ROSALIE	19	F	SGL	RRZZZZNY
ISRAEL	9	M	CHILD	RRZZZZNY

SHIP: AURANIA

FROM: LIVERPOOL AND QUEENSTOWN
TO: NEW YORK
ARRIVED: 25 JUNE 1888

PASSENGER	AGE	SEX	OCCUPATION	PRV VIL DES
HER, JORCH	19	F	SP	RRZZZZPHI
HARTMAN, MARY	22	F	SP	RRZZZZNY
SENGMAN, BERL	23	M	LABR	RRZZZZNY
LAZAROSKY, RIFKE	34	F	MA	RRZZZZNY
CHAIM	11	M	CH	RRZZZZNY
CHESCHE	9	F	CHILD	RRZZZZNY
FRIEDR.	6	M	CHILD	RRZZZZNY
WULF	3	F	CHILD	RRZZZZNY
LIPSSCHITZ, SIMON	3	M	CHILD	RRZZZZNY
SORE	28	F	MA	RRZZZZNY
BASCHE	17	F	SP	RRZZZZNY
JOSEL	13	M	NN	RRZZZZNY
RANTEV, AUGUSTI	30	M	LABR	RRZZZZNY
ELIZA	27	F	W	RRZZZZNY
GRUGUROWITSCH, ANTON	20	M	LABR	RRZZZZNY
WOCZHOWSKY, MANUH	30	M	LABR	RRZZZZNY
CZERNEWITZ, CONSTANTIN	22	M	LABR	RRZZZZNY
FRANZ	22	M	LABR	RRZZZZNY
FLEITZER, WILHELM	23	M	LABR	RRZZZZNY
RABINOWITZ, MAREN	28	M	LABR	RRZZZZNY
JANETTE	20	F	W	RRZZZZNY
MOSENBERG, JOFENDEL	19	M	LABR	RRZZZZNY
DWOATZKY, BEREL	19	M	LABR	RRZZZZNY
WEINSTEIN, JUDEL	28	M	LABR	RRZZZZNY
EFRON, BENJAMIN	19	M	LABR	RRZZZZNY
CHANCE	20	M	LABR	RRZZZZNY
KAHAN, LEIB	17	M	LABR	RRZZZZNY
KUTZMOKY, JOHAN	24	M	LABR	RRZZZZNY
HOCHMANN, TOCHIL	43	M	LABR	RRZZZZNY
ISAAC	17	M	LABR	RRZZZZNY
LAHWALLAMPE, MATTS	24	M	LABR	RRZZZZMN
KYNDBURG, ISAK	36	M	LABR	RRZZZZMA
HYRDEN, ISAK	49	M	LABR	RRZZZZMA
GIVARA, SALOMON	43	M	LABR	RRZZZZMA
POHDE, MARK	31	M	LABR	RRZZZZMA
SODERBACH, MICKEL	22	M	LABR	RRZZZZMA
CZIERNIE, JOH.	32	M	LABR	RRZZZZMA
SJOLUND, FRED.	30	M	LABR	RRZZZZMA
LALLVICK, JOH.	45	M	LABR	RRZZZZMA
TRIMAN, HERMAN	28	M	LABR	FNZZZZMA

PASSENGER	AGE	SEX	OCCUPATION	PRV VIL DES
SODERBACH, JOHN	20	M	LABR	FNZZZZMA
ANDERSON, AND.	32	M	LABR	FNZZZZMA
KOBILAIMEN, SELMA	24	M	LABR	FNZZZZNY
GORDMAN, MORRIS	39	M	LABR	FNZZZZNY
LARSEN, JOH.	45	M	LABR	FNZZZZNY
LINDSTEDT, IVER	25	M	LABR	FNZZZZNY
THOLLEN, J.A.	26	M	LABR	FNZZZZNY
MATTILA, JOSEF	18	M	LABR	FNZZZZMN
LIPSCHITZ, MENDEL	24	M	LABR	FNZZZZNY
GRAZULEWITZ, VINCENTZ	27	M	LABR	FNZZZZNY
ANNA	19	F	SP	FNZZZZNY
HABER, BERL	42	M	LABR	FNZZZZNY
GITEL	36	F	W	FNZZZZNY
MOSES	13	M	CH	FNZZZZNY
LEON	11	M	CH	FNZZZZNY
ALTE	9	F	CHILD	FNZZZZNY
CHASE	7	F	CHILD	FNZZZZNY
MAYER	5	F	CHILD	FNZZZZNY
CHASKEL	.08	F	INFANT	FNZZZZNY
BRECHSLER, BAPTIST	26	F	INF	FNZZZZNY
CATH.	22	F	W	FNZZZZNY
MALZ, SALOMON	18	M	LABR	FNZZZZNY
HURLESHA, JAN	25	M	LABR	FNZZZZNY
BRONISLAWA	20	M	LABR	FNZZZZNY
WESAGARSKI, CONSTANTIN	16	M	LABR	FNZZZZNY
SMOLINSKI, ANTON	25	M	LABR	FNZZZZNY
MLOWIEZ, DANIEL	32	M	LABR	FNZZZZNY
BUZANIN, PETER	38	M	LABR	FNZZZZNY
ROVSTZ, JAN-C.	21	M	LABR	FNZZZZNY
RUSENBEN, OTTO	23	M	LABR	FNZZZZNY
LEANTER, JACOB	20	M	LABR	FNZZZZNY
URLAHAS, STANISLAW	22	M	LABR	FNZZZZNY
MANNA, ANNA-S.	36	F	MA	FNZZZZBO
ANDERS	8	M	CHILD	FNZZZZBO
ANNA	3	F	CHILD	FNZZZZBO
WYMBERG, JOHANA	21	F	MA	FNZZZZMA
INO	34	M	LABR	FNZZZZMA
JACOB	.10	M	INFANT	FNZZZZMA
CIZORCKAY, WILLIAM	25	M	LABR	FNZZZZNY
NEHONERN, AND.	40	M	LABR	FNZZZZNY
KAYSA	19	F	SP	FNZZZZNY
ZANNULA, CAROLINA	23	F	SP	FNZZZZMA
SINNA, IDA	19	F	SP	FNZZZZMA
KOTILA, SAKARWIS	18	F	SP	FNZZZZMA
KOUPPAHANGAS, JACOB	37	M	LABR	FNZZZZMA
POTTASKAGAS, SATRIS	56	M	LABR	FNZZZZMA
ANNA	48	F	W	FNZZZZMA
JAMSA, AND.	32	M	LABR	FNZZZZMA
MAMEROD, CARL	20	M	LABR	FNZZZZBO
WASTER, JOH.	20	M	LABR	FNZZZZBO
HAFERKUT, U	30	M	LABR	FNZZZZBO
LEWICK, VICTOR	20	M	LABR	FNZZZZWI
KLEMONT, HENRIK	30	M	LABR	FNZZZZNY
BACKMAN, LINA	25	F	SP	FNZZZZNY
WILATA, NESTOR	21	M	LABR	FNZZZZNY
T--ARMAN, SAMUEL	19	M	LABR	FNZZZZNY
UPOKKO, HARRICK	35	M	LABR	FNZZZZBO
LEHTONEN, JACOB	35	M	LABR	FNZZZZNY
SILVAN, HENRIK	22	M	LABR	FNZZZZNY
SANDELIUS, ANDEN-JOH.	25	M	LABR	FNZZZZNY
AYSTE, SAMUEL	27	M	LABR	FNZZZZBO
HEINEBONRA, SAMUEL	36	M	LABR	FNZZZZNY
PARALA, JOHAN	20	M	LABR	FNZZZZBO
SAXBERG, JOHN	43	M	LABR	FNZZZZBO
WILLIAMS, ULRIKA	30	M	LABR	FNZZZZVA
D.HELDA	8	M	CHILD	FNZZZZVA
S.JOHANNES	6	M	CHILD	FNZZZZVA
D.OLZA	.06	M	INFANT	FNZZZZVA
HECKEN, TREHA	20	F	SP	FNZZZZNY
PARALO, ANTI	36	F	SP	FNZZZZBO
SUKSI, ISAK	42	M	LABR	FNZZZZBO
PARAH, MATTI	25	F	SP	FNZZZZBO
KIKERT, JAKOB	38	M	LABR	FNZZZZBO
LINDSTROM, OTTO-W.	41	M	LABR	FNZZZZPA
KAROLINA	33	F	W	FNZZZZPA
SOZKER	10	F	CH	FNZZZZPA
VICTOREN	3	F	CHILD	FNZZZZPA
FORMAS, HENRIK	24	M	LABR	FNZZZZMN
CARLSON, CARL-F.	34	M	LABR	FNZZZZMI
EKLUND, JOSEF	33	M	LABR	FNZZZZNY
PELLFOEK, AUGT.	33	M	LABR	FNZZZZMI
BLOMGVEST, JOSEF	20	M	LABR	FNZZZZMI
LEBVEK, CARL	32	M	LABR	FNZZZZMI
KLOCKAS, TAMA-M.	30	M	LABR	FNZZZZIL
ASTRANIO, ANDRES	43	M	LABR	FNZZZZNY
BERTA	34	F	W	FNZZZZNY
SALLY	11	F	CH	FNZZZZNY
CARL	8	M	CHILD	FNZZZZNY
INGRID	4	F	CHILD	FNZZZZNY
OLGAS	.11	M	INFANT	FNZZZZNY

SHIP: PERUVIAN

FROM: LIVERPOOL
TO: BALTIMORE
ARRIVED: 26 JUNE 1888

PASSENGER	AGE	SEX	OCCUPATION	PRV VIL DES
CZERNIN, BENJ	32	M	TLR	RRZZZZPA
KNOBLAND, FELIX	26	M	TLR	RRZZZZBAL
LORENZ, VERONIKA	24	M	LABR	RRZZZZUNK
JULIUS	00	M	INF	RRZZZZUNK
ZIOLKOWSKY, M.	23	M	CGRMKR	RRZZZZUNK
KUMMOWIETZ, ABRAHAM	24	M	CGRMKR	RRZZZZBAL
MOKE	24	F	W	RRZZZZBAL
ARON	00	M	INF	RRZZZZBAL
KORNEKISIK, JANKEN	33	M	GZR	RRZZZZBAL
CHIENNE	20	M	GZR	RRZZZZBAL

SHIP: RUGIA

FROM: HAMBURG
TO: NEW YORK
ARRIVED: 26 JUNE 1888

PASSENGER	AGE	SEX	OCCUPATION	PRV VIL DES
MACZOKOS, MACDALENE	30	F	WO	RRAIAUUSA
ALZIBETH	16	F	CH	RRAIAUUSA
ANDRAS	8	M	CHILD	RRAIAUUSA
JONAS	6	M	CHILD	RRAIAUUSA
DRAUGELIS, ANTONIE	40	M	LABR	RRZZZZUSA
METZNER, GERSON	69	M	LABR	RRAIGHUSA
MENACHE	00	M	UNKNOWN	RRAIGHUSA
BOROWSKY, U	29	U	UNKNOWN	RRZZZZUSA
ETTEL	15	F	SGL	RRAHZSUSA
BIEBER, ELIE	30	M	DLR	RRAHTUUSA
TURTELTAUB, BREINE	30	F	UNKNOWN	RRAFWJUSA
GITTE	28	F	WO	RRAFWJUSA
SARA	9	F	CHILD	RRAFWJUSA
ABRAM	8	M	CHILD	RRAFWJUSA
HELSCHA	7	F	CHILD	RRAFWJUSA
GITTE	2	F	CHILD	RRAFWJUSA
JANKEL	.11	M	INFANT	RRAFWJUSA
KAPLAN, LENE	30	F	WO	RRAHXLUSA
PHILIPP	8	M	CHILD	RRAHXLUSA
SALOMON	6	M	CHILD	RRAHXLUSA
LEISER	4	M	CHILD	RRAHXLUSA
JETTE	3	F	CHILD	RRAHXLUSA
ISAAC	.09	M	INFANT	RRAHXLUSA
CHODOSSOWA, GITTE	22	F	WO	RRAINDUSA
LEA	.11	F	INFANT	RRAINDUSA
JUDELOWSKY, ETTE	22	F	SGL	RRZZZZUSA

PASSENGER	AGE	SEX	OCCUPATION	PRV	VIL	DES
GERSCHNOVICZ, ESTHER	17	F	SGL	RR	ZZZZ	USA
CHEYAD, CHAIE	9	F	CHILD	RR	ZZZZ	USA
LEWINSON, CHAIE	40	F	WO	RR	ADIM	USA
ALTER	9	F	CHILD	RR	ADIM	USA
RACHEL	8	F	CHILD	RR	ADIM	USA
HIRSCH	6	M	CHILD	RR	ADIM	USA
ZALLEL, EZE	17	F	SGL	RR	ZZZZ	USA
FINKELSTEIN, BEILE	19	F	SGL	RR	ADIM	USA
LIEBERMANN, REBECCA	15	F	SGL	RR	ZZZZ	USA
WIERZBROWICZ, SIMON	44	M	UNKNOWN	RR	AHTO	USA
KAPLAN, HERSCH	35	M	UNKNOWN	RR	AHTF	USA
MAGNER, LEA	50	F	WO	RR	ZZZZ	USA
ROSENBLUM, CHINNE	40	F	WO	RR	AHTF	USA
KONOWITSCH, ESTHER	20	F	UNKNOWN	RR	ZZZZ	USA
ADELSOHN, RACHEL	20	F	UNKNOWN	RR	ZZZZ	USA
KOSLOWSKI, JUDEL	18	M	SHMK	RR	ZZZZ	USA
KETENSEN, NISS	42	M	PNTR	RR	AIJA	USA
BRODOW, MOSES	26	M	JNR	RR	AHTN	USA
SALAUSKI, CHIM	19	M	DLR	RR	ADOI	USA
EPHROIM, EISER	19	M	UNKNOWN	RR	AIOK	USA
SIMONSOHN, GABRIEL	27	M	UNKNOWN	RR	AIOK	USA
BAECK, BENJAMIN	51	M	UNKNOWN	RR	AIOK	USA
HAUPMANN, HERSCH	19	M	TLR	RR	ZZZZ	USA
KARLINSKI, LIEBE	27	F	WO	RR	ZZZZ	USA
MENDEL	4	M	CHILD	RR	ZZZZ	USA
JUDZEWITZ, ANTON	29	M	LABR	RR	ZZZZ	USA
JANKELEWITZ, FRADE	21	F	SGL	RR	AIIS	USA
MIEDOWICZ, SOSCHE	25	F	WO	RR	ZZZZ	USA
JASE	9	F	CHILD	RR	ZZZZ	USA
SZUL	5	F	CHILD	RR	ZZZZ	USA
RABINOWITZ, SIMCHE	18	M	UNKNOWN	RR	ZZZZ	USA
CHAIM	23	M	LABR	RR	ZZZZ	USA
BINDOCKES, JOSEPH	20	M	LABR	RR	ZZZZ	USA
NAMITZKES, THOMAS	18	M	LABR	RR	ZZZZ	USA
HEISEL, FRIEDR	35	M	LABR	RR	AIOO	USA
STANK, SAMUEL	28	M	FARMER	RR	AIOO	USA
CHARLOTTE	18	F	W	RR	AIOO	USA
POKOWA, SAMUEL	64	M	FARMER	RR	AIOO	USA
CHARLOTTE	56	F	W	RR	AIOO	USA
SWIENTY, FRIEDR	55	M	FARMER	RR	AIOO	USA
MARIE	51	F	W	RR	AIOO	USA
WILH	20	F	UNKNOWN	RR	AIOO	USA
LOUISE	17	F	CH	RR	AIOO	USA
AMALIE	9	F	CHILD	RR	AIOO	USA
AUGUSTE	9	F	CHILD	RR	AIOO	USA
SWIENTAY, GOTTL	37	M	LABR	RR	AIOO	USA
CAROLINE	32	F	W	RR	AIOO	USA
BERTHA	9	F	CHILD	RR	AIOO	USA
AUGUSTE	8	F	CHILD	RR	AIOO	USA
THEODOR	6	M	CHILD	RR	AIOO	USA
CAROLINE	3	F	CHILD	RR	AIOO	USA
FRIEDR	.03	M	INFANT	RR	AIOO	USA
PATZ, ADAM	33	M	LABR	RR	AIOO	USA
WILH	29	F	W	RR	AIOO	USA
AUGUSTE	9	F	CHILD	RR	AIOO	USA
BERTHA	7	F	CHILD	RR	AIOO	USA
JOH	4	M	CHILD	RR	AIOO	USA
ADAM	36	M	LABR	RR	AIOO	USA
REGINA	28	F	W	RR	AIOO	USA
HERMANN	7	M	CHILD	RR	AIOO	USA
GUSTAV	9	M	CHILD	RR	AIOO	USA
AUGUSTE	4	F	CHILD	RR	AIOO	USA
EMIL	2	M	CHILD	RR	AIOO	USA
WILH	.06	M	INFANT	RR	AIOO	USA
DUDEK, JOH	25	M	FARMER	RR	AIOO	USA
LOUISE	23	F	W	RR	AIOO	USA
JOH	2	M	CHILD	RR	AIOO	USA
FRIEDRICH	.09	M	INFANT	RR	AIOO	USA
BEDNATZ, WILH	25	M	FARMER	RR	AIOO	USA
REGINA	26	F	W	RR	AIOO	USA
MARIE	2	F	CHILD	RR	AIOO	USA
AUGUST	.06	M	INFANT	RR	AIOO	USA
MEYER, CARL	16	M	FARMER	RR	ZZZZ	USA
LORENZ, ANNA	25	F	WO	RR	AIBT	USA
REIMER, JOH	.11	M	INFANT	RR	AIBT	USA

PASSENGER	AGE	SEX	OCCUPATION	PRV	VIL	DES
RICKE, AUGUSTE	38	F	SGL	RR	ZZZZ	USA
ABRAMOWITSCH, MINNA	18	F	SGL	RR	ZZZZ	USA
ROSA	15	F	SGL	RR	ZZZZ	USA
LEWIN, ANNA	18	F	SGL	RR	ZZZZ	USA
LASCHIROWITZ, JUDEL	23	M	DLR	RR	ZZZZ	USA
ABRAMOWITSCH, CHIM	18	M	UNKNOWN	RR	ZZZZ	USA
KRAMER, FANNY	26	F	WO	RR	AIIM	USA
ROLLA	4	M	CHILD	RR	AIIM	USA
MICHEL	3	M	CHILD	RR	AIIM	USA
ERNESTINE	.06	F	INFANT	RR	AIIM	USA
KRIKSLANSKY, LEA	18	F	SGL	RR	AHTS	USA
SIMON, MARKS	19	M	MCHT	RR	ZZZZ	USA
MAJKUNICK, MICH	25	M	LABR	RR	ZZZZ	USA
AMBROSSEWICZ, ANDR	24	M	LABR	RR	AHZS	USA
WOLKOWITZ, JOS	20	M	LABR	RR	AHZS	USA
SAMEITIS, MIKOLAY	20	M	LABR	RR	AHZS	USA
IMGELEITIS, ANTON	24	M	UNKNOWN	RR	AHZS	USA
JAAKKOLA, OTTO	25	M	LABR	FN	ZZZZ	USA
INDOWITZ, DEBORAH	22	F	WO	FN	AICI	USA
DWEIRE	9	F	CHILD	FN	AICI	USA
DANILEWSKI, JOSEF	30	M	LABR	RR	ZZZZ	USA
ANASCHEWSKA, CATH	25	F	SGL	RR	ZZZZ	USA
EFROIMOWICZ, JOSSEL	30	M	DLR	RR	AHTU	USA
SUSCHE	27	F	W	RR	AHTU	USA
SARA	8	F	CHILD	RR	AHTU	USA
SCHHLOMAN	.11	M	INFANT	RR	AHTU	USA
CHAJE	.01	F	INFANT	RR	AHTU	USA
WISCHEWSKI, CASIMIR	29	M	LABR	RR	ZZZZ	USA
FILIPOWSKI, CHANNE	55	F	WO	RR	AHZS	USA
DUBITZKI, ABRAM	29	M	LABR	RR	ZZZZ	USA
RUSSANSKI, SALOMON	20	M	LABR	RR	AIIF	USA
MEIEWSKI, FRANZ	39	M	LABR	RR	ZZZZ	USA
RABINOWITZ, CHEWE	18	F	SGL	RR	ZZZZ	USA
HEISKA, ISAAK	23	M	LABR	FN	ZZZZ	USA
JOHANNSON, MICHEL	20	M	LABR	FN	ZZZZ	USA
FLUGRATH, WILH	54	M	FARMER	RR	ZZZZ	USA
RENATE	52	F	W	RR	ZZZZ	USA
EMMA	20	F	CH	RR	ZZZZ	USA
OTTILIE	18	F	CH	RR	ZZZZ	USA
IDA	9	F	CHILD	RR	ZZZZ	USA
CARL	8	M	CHILD	RR	ZZZZ	USA
AUGUST	3	M	CHILD	RR	ZZZZ	USA
EMILIE	.11	F	INFANT	RR	ZZZZ	USA
WILH	.01	M	INFANT	RR	ZZZZ	USA
HASSEL, MARCUS	18	M	LABR	RR	ZZZZ	USA
SARA	21	F	W	RR	ZZZZ	USA
JANKEL	.11	M	INFANT	RR	ZZZZ	USA
PAUSESKI, MOSES	18	M	LABR	RR	ZZZZ	USA
SCHLANDINISKI, MOSES	17	M	LABR	RR	ZZZZ	USA
URISCHN, JOSSEL	17	M	LABR	RR	ZZZZ	USA
RUTELONIS, MATEUS	24	M	LABR	RR	ZZZZ	USA
FRIEDMANN, RADES	18	M	LABR	RR	AHWM	USA
RATSCHUNA, ROSZT.	35	F	SGL	RR	ZZZZ	USA
ORNSTEIN, SALOMON	17	M	LABR	RR	ACTC	USA
BURAN, CHAGEN	30	M	LABR	RR	ZZZZ	USA
BARAN, MINNA	20	F	SGL	RR	ZZZZ	USA
HOFF, AMALIE	30	F	WO	RR	AHVA	USA
MERSON, MALKE	50	F	WO	RR	ZZZZ	USA
RIVKE	9	F	CHILD	RR	ZZZZ	USA
HENE	7	F	CHILD	RR	ZZZZ	USA
STANKOWITZ, JURAS	36	M	LABR	RR	ZZZZ	USA
NASCHELSKY, CHAJEM	39	M	MCHT	RR	AIKD	USA
OLSCHINSKA, DAVID	42	M	MCHT	RR	AIKD	USA
SINFELD, KAROLINE	40	F	WO	RR	AINZ	USA
WICKLICZ, JOSEF	15	M	LABR	RR	AINZ	USA
KARMELL, EISSEIE	29	M	DLR	RR	AINZ	USA
ARON	56	M	DLR	RR	AINZ	USA
REISEL	21	F	SGL	RR	AINZ	USA
FEIWELSCHN, JIZE	30	F	WO	RR	ZZZZ	USA
SARA	.11	F	INFANT	RR	ZZZZ	USA
TOLCZENSKY, LEA	39	F	WO	RR	AFVG	USA
HARRIS, SALOMON	18	M	LABR	RR	AINZ	USA
POZISKI, SCHLOME	15	M	LABR	RR	AINZ	USA
LEWY, ARON	19	M	LABR	RR	AINZ	USA
TEPLITZ, RACHEL	35	F	WO	RR	AIMR	USA

PASSENGER	AGE	SEX	OCCUPATION	PRV VIL DES
SALI	9	M	CHILD	RRAIMRUSA
FREIDE	4	F	CHILD	RRAIMRUSA
KUBILUS, MAGDALENE	22	F	SGL	RRZZZZUSA

SHIP: ELBE

FROM: BREMEN AND SOUTHAMPTON
TO: NEW YORK
ARRIVED: 27 JUNE 1888

PASSENGER	AGE	SEX	OCCUPATION	PRV VIL DES
KRIEGER, FRIEDR.	57	M	LABR	RRZZZZNY
CAROLINE	52	F	W	RRZZZZNY
BORINSTEIN, MOSES	30	M	TLR	RRZZZZNY
KIRSCHBAUM, CARL	19	M	BRR	RRZZZZNY
LOEWENSTEIN, SIEGMUND	24	M	BRR	RRZZZZNY
KOEHLER, JOH.	15	M	LABR	RRZZZZNY
SACHS, FRANZ	18	M	FARMER	RRZZZZNY
ZEIER, FERD.	18	M	FARMER	RRZZZZNY
DETIG, FRANZ	18	M	FARMER	RRZZZZNY
BECKHUSEN, GESINE	23	F	UNKNOWN	RRAIBGNY
FRIEDR.	00	F	UNKNOWN	RRAIBGNY
ZIELINSKY, MATUS	30	M	UNKNOWN	RRZZZZNY
PAJESKA, MARIANNE	26	F	UNKNOWN	RRZZZZNY
STENZEL, AMALIE	20	F	W	RRZZZZNY
MELIDA	.07	F	INFANT	RRZZZZNY
MARIE	22	F	UNKNOWN	RRZZZZNY
JAEGER, GOTTL.	22	M	LABR	RRAHTNBRO
SKAISGRIES, GEORG	20	M	MCHT	RRZZZZNY
RASCHEWICZ, HEINR.	28	M	UNKNOWN	RRZZZZMO
BALTOZAK, HEIM.	37	M	UNKNOWN	RRZZZZMO
ESSER, AUGUST	37	M	UNKNOWN	RRZZZZMO
DOROLAH, GEORG	23	M	UNKNOWN	RRZZZZMO
KOERBER, JOH.	40	M	FARMER	RRZZZZNY
HENRIETTE	38	F	UNKNOWN	RRZZZZNY
JOH.	9	M	CHILD	RRZZZZNY
WILH.	9	M	CHILD	RRZZZZNY
HEIM.	7	M	CHILD	RRZZZZNY
HULDA	3	M	CHILD	RRZZZZNY
ANNA	2	F	CHILD	RRZZZZNY
MARIA	.06	F	INFANT	RRZZZZNY
KIELISZEK, WAWRZYN	45	M	LABR	RRAIDZNY
PAWLOWSKY, MARIE	34	F	UNKNOWN	RRZZZZNY
GROBERMANN, HERSEZ	38	M	LABR	RRZZZZNY
WIEBE	28	F	UNKNOWN	RRZZZZNY
JUSTUS	.11	M	INFANT	RRZZZZNY
HOFFMANN, BERIE	28	M	LABR	RRZZZZNY
SOMMER, ELIAS-D.	30	M	LABR	RRZZZZNY
HINDE	22	F	UNKNOWN	RRZZZZNY
ELIAS	.03	M	INFANT	RRZZZZNY
MUELLER, MELCHIOR	57	M	FARMER	RRZZZZNY
MELCHIOR	17	M	FARMER	RRZZZZNY
FRUHAUF, CARL	38	M	FARMER	RRZZZZOR
CATHARINE	37	F	UNKNOWN	RRZZZZOR
CATHA.	13	F	UNKNOWN	RRZZZZOR
CARL	8	M	CHILD	RRZZZZOR
PAULINE	7	F	CHILD	RRZZZZOR
ALEX	4	M	CHILD	RRZZZZOR
ELISE	2	F	CHILD	RRZZZZOR
CZERMIAWSKI, JOSEF	34	M	DRVR	RRZZZZNY
FRUMME, SARAH	11	F	CH	RRZZZZNY
ZIEGLER, EMIL	21	M	UNKNOWN	RRZZZZCH
JAFFE, F.R.	24	M	UNKNOWN	RRZZZZCH
F.	10	M	CH	RRZZZZCH
SZLASK, RIWE	17	M	LABR	RRZZZZNY
BURWIN, LEBER	21	M	LABR	RRZZZZNY
SEWEINSKY, TAUBE	21	M	LABR	RRZZZZNY
RING, SARAH	25	F	UNKNOWN	RRZZZZNY
BEILE	4	M	CHILD	RRZZZZNY
KIBARTSKY, CHAJE	17	M	LABR	RRZZZZNY
LEA, FREIDE	26	M	LABR	RRZZZZNY
RUDKOWSKY, ADAM	16	M	LABR	RRZZZZNY
BUDLADSKY, STANISL.	30	M	LABR	RRZZZZNY
KRAUS, CARL	30	M	CGRMKR	RRZZZZNY
TAUER, ISIDOR	23	M	CGRMKR	RRZZZZNY
TRINKAUS, EDUARD	24	M	LABR	RRZZZZNY
BZOWA, JOSEFA	43	F	UNKNOWN	RRZZZZNY
STANISLAW	4	M	CHILD	RRZZZZNY
MOREIHE, JANOS	30	M	LABR	RRZZZZNY
WILKANIS, IGNATI	28	F	UNKNOWN	RRZZZZNY
KAZIMIR	6	F	CHILD	RRZZZZNY
ISABELLA	.06	F	INFANT	RRZZZZNY
SAPSE, JENNY	40	F	UNKNOWN	RRZZZZNY
CHAJKE	7	M	CHILD	RRZZZZNY
REISE	5	F	CHILD	RRZZZZNY
ESTER	2	F	CHILD	RRZZZZNY
ABE	.02	M	INFANT	RRZZZZNY

SHIP: AMERICA

FROM: BREMEN
TO: BALTIMORE
ARRIVED: 27 JUNE 1888

PASSENGER	AGE	SEX	OCCUPATION	PRV VIL DES
LEVIN, ISAAC	20	M	MCHT	RRZZZZUNK
GRALKE, FRANZ	13	M	UNKNOWN	RRZZZZMI
LEIFLAKDER, GETE	20	M	FARMER	RRZZZZMD
STUPELMANN, CHASCHE	20	M	FARMER	RRZZZZMD
SEYDE, TAUBE	18	M	FARMER	RRZZZZMD
SCHEIDERMANN, PHILIP	36	M	FARMER	RRZZZZOH
ELISABETH	28	F	UNKNOWN	RRZZZZOH
HEINRICH	6	M	CHILD	RRZZZZOH
ELISABETH	2	F	CHILD	RRZZZZOH
MARIA	.11	F	INFANT	RRZZZZOH
WAOLFORITZ, ZAMEL	26	M	MCHT	RRZZZZMD
SZERAPIOROKI, CLEMENS	40	M	LABR	RRZZZZOH
SCHRODER, LUDWIG	27	M	FARMER	RRZZZZMD
ANNA	27	F	UNKNOWN	RRZZZZMD
HERMANN	2	M	CHILD	RRZZZZMD
ZOAR, JULIANNA	19	F	SVNT	RRZZZZMD
KUEHN, GUSTAV	33	M	FARMER	RRZZZZMI
BUKOWSKI, WLADISLAW	19	M	FARMER	RRZZZZMI
PATWITSS, JOSEF	35	M	BRR	RRZZZZNE
MARIANNA	30	F	UNKNOWN	RRZZZZNE
LEKIN, SAMUEL	18	M	MLR	RRZZZZNE
FRIEDMANN, ARON	23	M	FARMER	RRZZZZNE
KULBERG, WILHELM	39	M	FARMER	RRZZZZNE
CICHOWSKIE, MICHAEL	38	M	FARMER	RRZZZZNE
SARN, CARL	27	M	FARMER	RRZZZZNE
PRISS, WILHELM	24	M	FARMER	RRZZZZNE
GRIGA, STANISLAUS	25	M	FARMER	RRZZZZNE
BESLER, GOTTLIEB	32	M	FARMER	RRZZZZNE
AUGUSTE	28	F	UNKNOWN	RRZZZZNE
WUTKIEWIECZ, WICENTY	25	M	FARMER	RRZZZZIL
SCHATZ, FRIEDRICH	43	M	FARMER	RRZZZZDAK
FRIEDRIKE	40	F	UNKNOWN	RRZZZZDAK
CHRISTIAN	13	M	CH	RRZZZZDAK
ANDREAS	11	M	CH	RRZZZZDAK
CHRISTIAN	8	M	CHILD	RRZZZZDAK
SUSANNA	6	F	CHILD	RRZZZZDAK
CATHARINA	.11	F	INFANT	RRZZZZDAK
JOHANNES	3	M	CHILD	RRZZZZDAK
MAGDALENA	.11	F	INFANT	RRZZZZDAK
HORST, FRIEDRICH	52	M	FARMER	RRZZZZDAK
LOUISE	50	F	UNKNOWN	RRZZZZDAK
JOHANN	25	M	FARMER	RRZZZZDAK
ELISABETH	26	F	UNKNOWN	RRZZZZDAK
JACOB	17	M	FARMER	RRZZZZDAK
LOUISE	11	F	CH	RRZZZZDAK
FRIEDRICH	10	M	CH	RRZZZZDAK
PETER	8	M	CHILD	RRZZZZDAK

PASSENGER	AGE	SEX	OCCUPATION	PRV VIL DES
JOHANN	2	M	CHILD	RRZZZZDAK
WILHELM	.11	M	INFANT	RRZZZZDAK
ULAZEWSKI, JOHN	18	M	LABR	RRZZZZMN
SPRUNG, CAROLINE	49	F	UNKNOWN	RRZZZZMD
ANNA	10	F	CH	RRZZZZMD
SEES, MATTHIAS	16	M	UNKNOWN	RRZZZZMD
INDELEWITZ, PESSE	47	F	UNKNOWN	RRZZZZIL
U	00	M	FARMER	RRZZZZIL
HENDE	22	F	UNKNOWN	RRZZZZIL
ABRAHAM	17	M	UNKNOWN	RRZZZZIL
MEYER	11	M	CH	RRZZZZIL
SARAH	8	F	CHILD	RRZZZZIL
MOSES	5	M	CHILD	RRZZZZIL
FRINOWSKY, MOSES	50	M	MCHT	RRZZZZIL
GAZAN, MASCHA	26	F	UNKNOWN	RRZZZZIL
RUWANN	4	M	CHILD	RRZZZZIL
JACOB	.11	M	INFANT	RRZZZZIL
SUNKLER, CHAYN	28	M	UNKNOWN	RRZZZZIL
BERGMANN, ROSALIA	22	F	UNKNOWN	RRZZZZIL
ANNA	50	F	UNKNOWN	RRZZZZIL
KIRSTEIN, MARRY	36	F	UNKNOWN	RRZZZZOH
MOSES	11	M	CH	RRZZZZOH
HERSCH	10	M	CH	RRZZZZOH
SAMUEL	8	M	CHILD	RRZZZZOH
LEISER	6	M	CHILD	RRZZZZOH
BEILE	6	F	CHILD	RRZZZZOH
MINNA	4	F	CHILD	RRZZZZOH
LEISE	1	F	CHILD	RRZZZZOH
GRIMM, ANNA	29	F	UNKNOWN	RRZZZZMN
JOSEF	6	M	CHILD	RRZZZZMN
ANNA	.06	F	INFANT	RRZZZZMN
UCHER, LUDWIG	19	M	BLKSMH	RRZZZZIL
GRIMWALD, JOSEF	19	M	FUR	RRZZZZIL
WIENERT, ANNA	25	F	SVNT	RRZZZZWI
BAUER, LEONHARD	29	M	UNKNOWN	RRZZZZWI
MARGARETHA	64	F	UNKNOWN	RRZZZZWI
BLUMENTHAL, FRANZ	28	M	LABR	RRZZZZMI
ZSCHENDERLEIN, FRIEDRIK	60	F	UNKNOWN	RRZZZZIL
ERDMANN, CLEMENS	16	M	TU	RRZZZZMN
GRZESKA, JOSEFA	21	F	UNKNOWN	RRZZZZUNK
HEDWIG	.11	F	INFANT	RRZZZZUNK
THOMAS	.01	M	INFANT	RRZZZZUNK
MUEHLHANS, MARTHA	22	F	UNKNOWN	RRZZZZIL
SCHONERT, WILHELM	29	M	LABR	RRZZZZMN
BRAESINGER, GEORG	19	M	SHMK	RRZZZZWI
SCHAMBERG, LUDWIG	23	M	JNR	RRZZZZPA
JOHANNSEN, PAUL	17	M	MCHT	RRZZZZMD
BUCHENAU, DORA	19	F	SVNT	RRZZZZOH
INDELSWITZ, LEISE	24	F	SVNT	RRZZZZOH
HAFFMAN, CATHARINE	36	F	UNKNOWN	RRZZZZIL
HINGKUNZ, MARTHA	20	F	SVNT	RRZZZZIL
SUCHOCKI, CARL	37	M	LABR	RRZZZZIL
ZEELINSKA, EMMA	11	F	UNKNOWN	RRZZZZMD
ADLER, REFE	20	F	UNKNOWN	RRZZZZOH
BEISE	.05	F	INFANT	RRZZZZOH
FABIEZ, SUGA	18	F	UNKNOWN	RRZZZZOH
LIPSCHITZ, FEIGE	58	M	MCHT	RRZZZZOH
SUGSDAS, JOSES	30	M	MCHT	RRZZZZOH
META	18	F	UNKNOWN	RRZZZZOH
GREGASCHAT, CARL	38	M	LABR	RRZZZZOH
ARZEWATZHAS, WIPZES	38	F	SVNT	RRZZZZOH
GUDAITYS, WIPZES	25	F	SVNT	RRZZZZOH

SHIP: ENGLAND

FROM: LIVERPOOL AND QUEENSTOWN
TO: NEW YORK
ARRIVED: 27 JUNE 1888

PASSENGER	AGE	SEX	OCCUPATION	PRV VIL DES
AHO, HENRY	28	M	LABR	RRAIIJUSA
PYKAN, MATTS	30	M	LABR	RRAIIJUSA
AHOLA, HENRY	30	M	LABR	RRAIIJNY
HUMSLANEN, JAKOB	26	M	LABR	RRAIIJNY
WIBERG, OSKAR	20	M	LABR	RRAIIJNY
HARO, JOHAN	25	M	LABR	RRAIIJNY
PIHLOJA, BOVAL	25	M	LABR	RRAIIJNY
KORPI, JOHAN	35	M	LABR	RRAIIJNY
HEDEN, MATTI	31	M	LABR	RRAIIJNY
SEVALAMBI, ANTI	37	M	LABR	RRAIIJNY
JYKHA, MANNA	34	M	LABR	RRAIIJBO
NYGARD, MATTI	40	M	LABR	RRAIIJNY
KUNNARI, JOHAN	19	M	LABR	RRAIIJNY
SETTENBACKA, JOHAN	25	M	LABR	RRAIIJNY
LAHTI, ENOK	28	M	LABR	RRAIIJNY
PISPANEN, MATTI	32	M	LABR	RRAIIJNY
KINOLA, ANTI	28	M	LABR	RRAIIJNY
HARPI, MATTI	48	M	LABR	RRAIIJNY
KARJOLA, KATTE	23	M	LABR	RRAIIJNY
PARSOLA, ANTI	22	M	LABR	RRAIIJNY
JAIBALLS, TUAMES	30	M	LABR	RRAIIJNY
MAYOLA, MATTI	48	M	LABR	RRAIIJBO
WAHASARJA, JACOB	35	M	LABR	RRAIIJBO
JARVENLA, ERKI	25	M	LABR	RRAIIJBO
NEIMI, JACOB	45	M	LABR	RRAIIJBO
JARVI, ELIAS	32	M	LABR	RRAIIJMN
LEASKA, JOHAN	26	M	LABR	RRAIIJMN
DEMKARI, JOHAN	19	M	LABR	RRAIIJOR
HORIGHTAMKI, SOLOMAN	46	M	LABR	RRAIIJNY
WARPOTA, SAMUEL	31	M	LABR	RRAIIJNY
HURVI, GUSTAV	45	M	LABR	RRAIIJNY
KAHAMA, JAKOB	30	M	LABR	RRAIIJNY
KAARAVMEX, SAM	26	M	LABR	RRAIIJNY
ROM, C.	24	M	LABR	RRAIIJNY
RUDOWSKY, L.	55	M	LABR	RRAIIJNY
GOLDBERG, DAVID	30	M	LABR	RRAIIJNY
BERMAN, SOLOMAN	25	M	LABR	RRAIIJNY
PERKSKY, W.	18	M	LABR	RRAIIJNY
MESLER, J.	24	M	LABR	RRAIIJNY
S.	19	M	LABR	RRAIIJNY
KASMINSKY, J.	29	M	LABR	RRAIIJNY
SRUTOWEN, S.	35	M	LABR	RRAIIJNY
A.	11	M	CH	RRAIIJNY
FRIEDMAN, J.	25	M	LABR	RRAIIJNY
PERLSKEIN, J.	18	M	LABR	RRAIIJNY
SCHADOHER, S.	20	M	LABR	RRAIIJNY
GRUGEVITCH, KASIMIR	24	M	LABR	RRAIIJNY
LINOWSKY, MOSES	22	M	LABR	RRAIIJNY
ABRAMITIS, HARRIS	30	M	LABR	RRAIIJNY
ROCK, JOSEF	38	M	LABR	RRAIIJNY
STEMPLE, SOLOMAN	32	M	LABR	RRAIIJUNK
MERINSCH, SCHEWEL	40	M	LABR	RRAIIJNY
GIDIN, ABRAHAM	22	M	LABR	RRAIIJNY
BUEKOWITZ, ANTON	44	M	LABR	RRAIIJNY
KALIKAUZKAS, JOSAS	20	M	LABR	RRAIIJNY
GODISKY, MEYER	18	M	LABR	RRAIIJNY
GURCZA, ANDREI	44	M	LABR	RRAIIJNY
GARELSWITZ, SIMON	24	M	LABR	RRAIIJNY
JANEZAKAS, JOSEF	26	M	LABR	RRAIIJNY
SKAISUKINAS, JOSEF	41	M	LABR	RRAIIJNY
NISSEL, SCHAJE	28	M	LABR	RRAIIJNY
SOLLEM, SALOMAN	23	M	LABR	RRAIIJNY
ZIMMERMANN, MOSES	26	M	LABR	RRAIIJNY
BARISDAITES, ANTONIS	20	M	LABR	RRAIIJNY
SEGALL, MANOCHE	38	M	LABR	RRAIIJPHI
JOITZKY, ISAAC	22	M	LABR	RRAIIJPHI
ELISBERG, MARSCHE	30	M	LABR	RRAIIJNY
CHAJET, BEHR	25	M	LABR	RRAIIJNY

PASSENGER	AGE	SEX	OCCUPATION	PRIV	VIL	DES
SEIDE, CHAIM	17	M	LABR	RRAI	IJ	NY
BIALSKY, ABRAHAM	27	M	LABR	RRAI	IJ	PHI
BERLIN, MOSES	18	M	LABR	RRAI	IJ	PHI
JWORAGER, MORRIS	29	M	LABR	RRAI	IJ	PHI
BUDINSK, WOLKO	34	M	LABR	RRAI	IJ	PHI
PERLUTZKY, ISRAEL	30	M	LABR	RRAI	IJ	NY
FURST, LEIB	37	M	LABR	RRAI	IJ	PHI
WASSERMAN, MOSES	35	M	LABR	RRAI	IJ	NY
CHAIM	30	M	LABR	RRAI	IJ	NY
MEYER	10	M	CH	RRAI	IJ	NY
RUDBERG, BERL	18	M	LABR	RRAI	IJ	NY
DAVIDOWISS, ABRAM	46	M	LABR	RRAI	IJ	NY
KUPOWITZ, NOCHEM	40	M	LABR	RRAI	IJ	PHI
SCHWARTZ, ABRAHAM	31	M	LABR	RRAI	IJ	NY
RODZANSKY, ISRAEL	24	M	LABR	RRAI	IJ	NY
WISOTZECHIK, BEREL	25	M	LABR	RRAI	IJ	NY
BARKER, ISAK	22	M	LABR	RRAI	IJ	NY
SIMNE, DAVID	56	M	LABR	RRAI	IJ	NY
LEWIN, ITZIG	36	M	LABR	RRAI	IJ	NY
MUNDEL, MOSES	28	M	LABR	RRAI	IJ	NY
STERN, ARON	21	M	LABR	RRAI	IJ	CLE
PINEZUK, MOSES	26	M	LABR	RRAI	IJ	NY
RELLER, HIRSCH	14	M	LABR	RRAI	IJ	NY
HUSIK, ABRAHAM	38	M	LABR	RRAI	IJ	PHI
ITZIG	17	M	LABR	RRAI	IJ	PHI
JANKEL	11	M	CH	RRAI	IJ	PHI
PISACH	8	M	CHILD	RRAI	IJ	PHI
MEIER	6	M	CHILD	RRAI	IJ	PHI
FRUME	48	F	MA	RRAI	IJ	PHI
SALOMON	17	M	LABR	RRAI	IJ	PHI
LEIKE	15	F	SP	RRAI	IJ	PHI
JEZIK	11	M	CH	RRAI	IJ	PHI
RISSEL	6	M	CHILD	RRAI	IJ	PHI
LOPOTSKY, NATHAN	29	M	LABR	RRAI	IJ	NY
SARAH	21	F	W	RRAI	IJ	NY
ZERNOBINSKY, ASRIEL	26	M	LABR	RRAI	IJ	PHI
BREINE	24	F	W	RRAI	IJ	PHI
HODDREL	.06	M	INFANT	RRAI	IJ	PHI
ISOLEHTO, CHRISTINE	24	F	SVNT	RRAI	IJ	NY
GELLER, ABRAHAM	55	M	LABR	RRAI	IJ	NY
ADE-	50	F	W	RRAI	IJ	NY
ZLATE	30	F	W	RRAI	IJ	NY
BASCHE	4	M	CHILD	RRAI	IJ	NY
MICHE.	9	M	CHILD	RRAI	IJ	NY
GERSON	4	M	CHILD	RRAI	IJ	NY
JIRSCHE	1	M	CHILD	RRAI	IJ	NY
KOSCHES, REGINA	24	F	SVNT	RRAI	IJ	NY
DOROSOW, SAMUEL	48	M	LABR	RRAI	IJ	NY
BEILE	35	F	W	RRAI	IJ	NY
LEIBE	17	M	LABR	RRAI	IJ	NY
SCHLOME	14	M	LABR	RRAI	IJ	NY
MOSES	9	M	CHILD	RRAI	IJ	NY
BERE	6	M	CHILD	RRAI	IJ	NY
JANKEL	4	M	CHILD	RRAI	IJ	NY
NOCHAME	2	F	CHILD	RRAI	IJ	NY
MENDEL	.10	M	INFANT	RRAI	IJ	NY
MAMLIN, FEIWASCH	22	M	LABR	RRAI	IJ	NY
BLUME	19	F	W	RRAI	IJ	NY
BIALOSKANSKI, SLATA	18	F	SVNT	RRAI	IJ	NY
KOSCHERT, MIRA	18	F	SVNT	RRAI	IJ	NY
JANOWING, ANNA	16	F	SVNT	RRAI	IJ	NY
HIEK, SARAH	23	F	SVNT	RRAI	IJ	PIT
MINDEESOHN, SARA	50	F	SVNT	RRAI	IJ	NY
FANNY	16	F	SVNT	RRAI	IJ	NY
KOKUSCH, SOLOMON	55	M	LABR	RRAI	IJ	NY
FEIGE	45	F	W	RRAI	IJ	NY
SARA	11	F	CH	RRAI	IJ	NY
MALI	7	F	CHILD	RRAI	IJ	NY
HAYSKOFF, RACHEL	20	F	SVNT	RRAI	IJ	NY
ESTER	18	F	SVNT	RRAI	IJ	NY
GOLDBERG, RACHEL	17	F	SVNT	RRAI	IJ	NY
FEIGE	20	F	SVNT	RRAI	IJ	NY
LEIM, FRUMA	16	F	SVNT	RRAI	IJ	NY
WRERZERUSKY, DAVID	60	M	LABR	RRAI	IJ	CH
JEME	20	F	SVNT	RRAI	IJ	NY

PASSENGER	AGE	SEX	OCCUPATION	PRIV	VIL	DES
RAJOWITZER, MARIEM	26	F	W	RRAI	IJ	PHI
MACKE	8	M	CHILD	RRAI	IJ	PHI
HIRSCH	5	M	CHILD	RRAI	IJ	PHI
RAZMSKY, CHAJE	19	F	SVNT	RRAI	IJ	NY
SHILLEL	11	F	CH	RRAI	IJ	NY
ROMITS, LEIB	45	M	LABR	RRAI	IJ	PHI
SALI	19	F	W	RRAI	IJ	PHI
ANTPOLSKI, ELLEN	15	F	SVNT	RRAI	IJ	PHI
PIKORSKY, BINE	22	F	W	RRAI	IJ	NY
LIEB	3	M	CHILD	RRAI	IJ	NY
HAUPT, ANNA	23	F	W	RRAI	IJ	NY
MARTHA	.10	F	INFANT	RRAI	IJ	NY
KRAWCON, CHANA	25	F	W	RRAI	IJ	NY
BERL	11	M	CH	RRAI	IJ	NY
CHAJE	9	M	CHILD	RRAI	IJ	NY
LERBE	4	M	CHILD	RRAI	IJ	NY
SARA	1	F	CHILD	RRAI	IJ	NY
FLEMMEYER, JETTE	40	F	W	RRAI	IJ	NY
BLUME	18	F	SP	RRAI	IJ	NY
ABRAH	10	M	CH	RRAI	IJ	NY
GELBIN, MENDEL	18	F	SVNT	RRAI	IJ	NY
STURMANN, TAUBE	29	F	W	RRAI	IJ	NY
CHOWE	8	F	CHILD	RRAI	IJ	NY
ESTER	1	F	CHILD	RRAI	IJ	NY
BINE	18	F	SVNT	RRAI	IJ	NY
WOLSON, ITTE	16	F	SVNT	RRAI	IJ	NY
DUBLISKI, FREIDE	28	F	SVNT	RRAI	IJ	NY
REZMIK, RACHEL	15	F	SVNT	RRAI	IJ	NY
HIRSCH	14	M	LABR	RRAI	IJ	NY
WOLSON, ISRAEL	23	M	LABR	RRAI	IJ	NY
KLEMBERG, MARKUS	32	M	LABR	RRAI	IJ	NY
SCHULUM	11	M	CH	RRAI	IJ	NY
JUTKA	10	M	CH	RRAI	IJ	NY
LSIBOWITZ, ROSA	19	F	SVNT	RRAI	IJ	NY
FINKELSTEIN, CHANE	52	F	SVNT	RRAI	IJ	NY
FEIGE	19	F	SVNT	RRAI	IJ	NY
SILBERMANN, SARA	18	F	SVNT	RRAI	IJ	NY
FEIGE	20	F	SVNT	RRAI	IJ	NY
MEISNEN, NOCHE	18	F	SVNT	RRAI	IJ	NY
ADLER, CYCEI	18	F	SVNT	RRAI	IJ	NY
KARP, MALIE	16	F	SVNT	RRAI	IJ	NY
CHAIT, CH.	25	F	SVNT	RRAI	IJ	NY
GOLDSTEIN, JACOB	52	M	LABR	RRAI	IJ	NY
BETSY	45	F	W	RRAI	IJ	NY
JOSEPH	15	M	LABR	RRAI	IJ	NY
JOEL	11	M	CH	RRAI	IJ	NY
SOLORINSKI, FANNY	35	F	W	RRAI	IJ	NY
RACHEL	7	F	CHILD	RRAI	IJ	NY
LEWIS	6	M	CHILD	RRAI	IJ	NY
ESTHER	5	F	CHILD	RRAI	IJ	NY
SARAH	2	F	CHILD	RRAI	IJ	NY
AMELIA	55	F	MA	RRAI	IJ	NY
FRANKS, MARY	33	F	W	RRAI	IJ	NY
LAZARUS	11	M	CH	RRAI	IJ	NY
ABRAHAM	10	M	CH	RRAI	IJ	NY
SARAH	8	F	CHILD	RRAI	IJ	NY
MICHAEL	6	M	CHILD	RRAI	IJ	NY
MOSES	3	M	CHILD	RRAI	IJ	NY
DORA	.11	F	INFANT	RRAI	IJ	NY
FOCHNOWITZ, SCHENDEL	29	F	W	RRAI	IJ	NY
RIFKE	19	F	SP	RRAI	IJ	NY
MOSES	8	M	CHILD	RRAI	IJ	NY
SAMUEL	6	M	CHILD	RRAI	IJ	NY
SARAH	5	F	CHILD	RRAI	IJ	NY
ADOLF	2	M	CHILD	RRAI	IJ	NY
HELENA	.06	F	INFANT	RRAI	IJ	NY
SILLANPAA, NILMA	20	F	SVNT	RRAI	IJ	NY
FINOLA, ELIEL	40	M	LABR	RRAI	IJ	NY
EVELINA	38	F	W	RRAI	IJ	NY
JOHANNES	11	F	CH	RRAI	IJ	NY
IDA	4	F	CHILD	RRAI	IJ	NY
HENRIK	1	M	CHILD	RRAI	IJ	NY
HERMAN	7	M	CHILD	RRAI	IJ	NY
ALAGOKI, HILDA	18	F	SVNT	RRAI	IJ	NY
BERHOWITZ, SARA	22	F	SVNT	RRAI	IJ	NY

PASSENGER	AGE	SEX	OCCUPATION	PRIV	VIL	DES
SHIP: ST. OF PENNSYLVANIA						
FROM: GLASGOW AND LARNE						
TO: NEW YORK						
ARRIVED: 27 JUNE 1888						
RASUNSKI, MERI	18	F	SP	RR	ZZZZ	USA
WEISSER, RACHEL	19	F	SP	RR	ZZZZ	USA
HOLFEN, CHAIE	20	F	SP	RR	ZZZZ	USA
ROCHEL	11	F	SP	RR	ZZZZ	USA
WEISS, CHAIE	39	F	SP	RR	ZZZZ	USA
GARTENLAUB, GOLDINE	21	F	SP	RR	ZZZZ	USA
ROTHSTEIN, CLARA	21	F	SP	RR	ZZZZ	USA
GRODNIK, SCHLAUME	18	F	SP	RR	ZZZZ	USA
LEVINSON, BERTHA	20	F	SP	RR	ZZZZ	USA
SIEGMANN, U	17	F	SP	RR	ZZZZ	USA
KOLDENZ, GITEL	16	F	SP	RR	ZZZZ	USA
ABRAMOWITZ, ETTE	19	F	SP	RR	ZZZZ	USA
IDELOWITZ, FEIGE	26	F	SP	RR	ZZZZ	USA
COLIA, CECILIE	22	F	SP	RR	ZZZZ	USA
MOLGRAMM, REISIL	16	F	SP	RR	ZZZZ	USA
REIDISCH, SCHEWE	18	F	SP	RR	ZZZZ	USA
GEISEROWITZ, MARIE	22	F	SP	RR	ZZZZ	USA
ROEHSE, ESTHER	18	F	SP	RR	ZZZZ	USA
SPIRO, ELIE	20	F	SP	RR	ZZZZ	USA
ELINBINDER, CHAJE	18	F	SP	RR	ZZZZ	USA
CHATZKEWITZ, ESTHER-L.	19	F	SP	RR	ZZZZ	USA
MARKEWITSCH, ROSE	18	F	SP	RR	ZZZZ	USA
ISRAEL	15	M	CH	RR	ZZZZ	USA
DEMBA, HIRSCH	16	M	CH	RR	ZZZZ	USA
LIPKOWITZ, MOSES	16	M	CH	RR	ZZZZ	USA
HURWITZ, DAVID	16	M	TLR	RR	ZZZZ	USA
BERNSTIN, DAVID	17	M	TLR	RR	ZZZZ	USA
NAGEL, JOSEF	48	M	TLR	RR	ZZZZ	USA
TAUB, MARCUS	17	M	TLR	RR	ZZZZ	USA
HERCHHOWITZ, PINKOS	44	M	TLR	RR	ZZZZ	USA
BROSOWSKY, HIRSCH	19	M	TLR	RR	ZZZZ	USA
KAPLAN, MARCUS	18	M	TLR	RR	ZZZZ	USA
MILRAD, CHAIM	20	M	TLR	RR	ZZZZ	USA
JASWANSKY, MASE	40	M	RFMK	RR	ZZZZ	USA
SUPMANN, HIRSCH	18	M	TCHR	RR	ZZZZ	USA
POTACHINSKY, ISAAC	17	M	HTR	RR	ZZZZ	USA
HUNTZEL, HENRY	18	M	BKR	RR	ZZZZ	USA
FARBER, MARK	23	M	CMST	RR	ZZZZ	USA
SEGAR, MAX	19	M	WCHMKR	RR	ZZZZ	USA
HABERMANN, SCHLOME	30	M	BKBNDR	RR	ZZZZ	USA
KRAWITZ, MARCUS	20	M	CL	RR	ZZZZ	USA
ALWITSKY, ISAAC	22	M	JNR	RR	ZZZZ	USA
GOLDBERG, SCHUMEL	24	M	JNR	RR	ZZZZ	USA
CHAIM	18	M	JNR	RR	ZZZZ	USA
HAMBURG, MENASCHE	30	M	GDSM	RR	ZZZZ	USA
KARFUNKEL, BERE	19	M	GDSM	RR	ZZZZ	USA
SPRITZER, MOSES	31	M	SHMK	RR	ZZZZ	USA
OCKINANN, JOACHIM	35	M	LABR	RR	ZZZZ	USA
RASANECKY, RAPSCHIK	29	M	LABR	RR	ZZZZ	USA
HRUSZNA, JOSEF	25	M	LABR	RR	ZZZZ	USA
JENOSKRATZ, MATHIAS	27	M	LABR	RR	ZZZZ	USA
KOWALEWSKI, ANTONI	40	M	LABR	RR	ZZZZ	USA
MENDLEWITZ, LEOPOLD	47	M	PDLR	RR	ZZZZ	USA
ROTZKOWSKY, SIMAR	28	M	PDLR	RR	ZZZZ	USA
BECKER, CHAIM	25	M	PDLR	RR	ZZZZ	USA
DAMOWSKY, SOLOMON	22	M	PDLR	RR	ZZZZ	USA
RUSSIAN, LOUIS	20	M	PDLR	RR	ZZZZ	USA
ALPER, ISRAEL	24	M	PDLR	RR	ZZZZ	USA
ZIEGLER, JACOB	17	M	PDLR	RR	ZZZZ	USA
LEWITA, U	56	M	PDLR	RR	ZZZZ	USA
WESAN, ISRAEL	21	M	PDLR	RR	ZZZZ	USA
HIRSCHBLERA	39	M	PDLR	RR	ZZZZ	USA
REISS, WOLFF	18	M	PDLR	RR	ZZZZ	USA
FEIWUSCH, MENDEL	25	M	PDLR	RR	ZZZZ	USA
GOLDENBERG, DAVID	20	M	PDLR	RR	ZZZZ	USA
FEIVEL, ABE	23	M	PDLR	RR	ZZZZ	USA
BEIZIKOWSKY, JOSEF	23	M	PDLR	RR	ZZZZ	USA
LEWITAN, PESACH	23	M	PDLR	RR	ZZZZ	USA
BEIZEL	28	M	PDLR	RR	ZZZZ	USA
FUDELOWITSCH, JACOB	25	M	PDLR	RR	ZZZZ	USA
RUBENSTEIN, LEIB	27	M	PDLR	RR	ZZZZ	USA
SEID, SIMON	50	M	PDLR	RR	ZZZZ	USA
ISAAC	10	M	CH	RR	ZZZZ	USA
BEILE	4	M	CHILD	RR	ZZZZ	USA
SILBERMAN, MEYER	50	M	PDLR	RR	ZZZZ	USA
JOSE	50	F	W	RR	ZZZZ	USA
MENDEL	18	M	PDLR	RR	ZZZZ	USA
EISIEK	16	M	PDLR	RR	ZZZZ	USA
FREIDI	8	F	CHILD	RR	ZZZZ	USA
LEBOWITSCH, MARIE	48	M	PDLR	RR	ZZZZ	USA
CHAIE	48	F	W	RR	ZZZZ	USA
HANNE	18	F	SP	RR	ZZZZ	USA
ETTEL	14	F	SP	RR	ZZZZ	USA
SENDER	10	M	CH	RR	ZZZZ	USA
DAVID	28	M	JNR	RR	ZZZZ	USA
GELBERG, CHAIM	28	M	JNR	RR	ZZZZ	USA
CHAJE	23	F	W	RR	ZZZZ	USA
LEIKE	6	F	CHILD	RR	ZZZZ	USA
RIWKE	4	F	CHILD	RR	ZZZZ	USA
NOCHEM	1	F	CHILD	RR	ZZZZ	USA
FANNY	20	F	SP	RR	ZZZZ	USA
LIVOW, CHAIM	35	M	PDLR	RR	ZZZZ	USA
MARIAN	9	F	CHILD	RR	ZZZZ	USA
LISA	5	F	CHILD	RR	ZZZZ	USA
ESTHER	1	F	CHILD	RR	ZZZZ	USA
BORAAS, BESSE-MINDEL	26	F	W	RR	ZZZZ	USA
SCHEIM	5	F	CHILD	RR	ZZZZ	USA
ESTHER	2	F	CHILD	RR	ZZZZ	USA
DAVID	1	M	CHILD	RR	ZZZZ	USA
ROTANNSKI, LEISH	30	F	W	RR	ZZZZ	USA
EFRAIM	11	M	CH	RR	ZZZZ	USA
HENNOCH	10	F	CH	RR	ZZZZ	USA
NEOPANNA	1	F	CHILD	RR	ZZZZ	USA
PRESIL, CHAIE	35	F	W	RR	ZZZZ	USA
TAUBE	18	F	SP	RR	ZZZZ	USA
ANNI	10	F	CH	RR	ZZZZ	USA
ROCHE	9	F	CHILD	RR	ZZZZ	USA
DRECKZER, BASSE	27	F	W	RR	ZZZZ	USA
RESSE	1	F	CHILD	RR	ZZZZ	USA
U	6	F	CHILD	RR	ZZZZ	USA
BENJAMIN	7	M	CHILD	RR	ZZZZ	USA
ITZIG	4	M	CHILD	RR	ZZZZ	USA
NISSUR	.03	M	INFANT	RR	ZZZZ	USA
SAGJARSKY, SCHEWE	30	F	W	RR	ZZZZ	USA
KALMANN	9	M	CHILD	RR	ZZZZ	USA
LEIBOWITZ, ROSA	22	F	W	RR	ZZZZ	USA
MOSES	1	M	CHILD	RR	ZZZZ	USA
ISAAC	.03	M	INFANT	RR	ZZZZ	USA
GRUNBERG, LIPPE	35	F	W	RR	ZZZZ	USA
BEROSCH	19	F	SP	RR	ZZZZ	USA
MAUSCHE	10	F	CH	RR	ZZZZ	USA
ROSA	1	F	CHILD	RR	ZZZZ	USA
WALDMANN, MERE	22	F	W	RR	ZZZZ	USA
WOLFF	4	M	CHILD	RR	ZZZZ	USA
REVKE	1	F	CHILD	RR	ZZZZ	USA
BERMANN, CHAIE	26	F	W	RR	ZZZZ	USA
SIMON	4	M	CHILD	RR	ZZZZ	USA
MORITZ	.09	M	INFANT	RR	ZZZZ	USA
BLOCK, SARAH	35	F	W	RR	ZZZZ	USA
BERE	11	F	CH	RR	ZZZZ	USA
LEIB	10	F	CH	RR	ZZZZ	USA
DAVID	1	M	CHILD	RR	ZZZZ	USA
ROCKEL	1	F	CHILD	RR	ZZZZ	USA
WEINBERG, RIWKE	27	F	UNKNOWN	RR	ZZZZ	USA
LEIB	8	F	CHILD	RR	ZZZZ	USA
ETTE	2	F	CHILD	RR	ZZZZ	USA

SHIP: KANSAS

FROM: LIVERPOOL AND LONDON
TO: BOSTON
ARRIVED: 28 JUNE 1888

PASSENGER	AGE	SEX	OCCUPATION	PRV VIL DES
BOSK, CARL	19	M	LABR	RRZZZZNY
NEWGARD, JULIUS	17	M	LABR	RRZZZZNY
DEQUIT, LENI	24	M	LABR	RRZZZZBO
RAUMSCHI, PETER	24	M	LABR	RRZZZZBO
GLUCK, EISIK	21	M	LABR	RRZZZZBO
SCHWARZ, AB--	45	M	LABR	RRZZZZBO
KLIMAS, JOSEPH	28	M	LABR	RRZZZZBO
SER, SOLOMON	20	M	LABR	RRZZZZUSA
LEWIES, SEIMON	20	M	LABR	PLZZZZUSA
DUNKLER, ADOLPH	23	M	LABR	RRZZZZPHI
EMILIE	22	F	W	RRZZZZPHI
KOWSKY, NOTE	24	M	LABR	RRZZZZBO
SARAH	20	F	W	RRZZZZBO
SCHMIDT, CARL	45	M	LABR	RRZZZZBO
MATHILDA	30	F	W	RRZZZZBO
LAUES, ALTER	48	M	LABR	RRZZZZBO
EIDEL	48	F	W	RRZZZZBO
HERSCH	11	M	CH	RRZZZZBO
RIVKE	8	F	CHILD	RRZZZZBO
IKE	.01	M	INFANT	RRZZZZBO
ROSENBERG, MICKA	28	M	LABR	RRZZZZBO
CHAGE	28	F	W	RRZZZZBO
ROSEL	.07	F	INFANT	RRZZZZBO
PITUWA, SARAH	.03	F	INFANT	RRZZZZBO
SLATE	00	F	INF	RRZZZZBO
OLSCHWITZKY, EIDI	41	F	W	RRZZZZBO
MIKI	.09	M	INFANT	RRZZZZBO
KOBILKOWSKY, RACHEL	44	F	SP	RRZZZZBO
FEINBERG, CHANE	30	F	W	RRZZZZBO
HERSCH, MORDOCH	5	M	CHILD	RRZZZZBO
SISSELMAN, SOMMY	4	M	CHILD	RRZZZZBO
ESTER	2	F	CHILD	RRZZZZBO
KUTZER, BETSY	18	F	SP	RRZZZZNY
GOLDSTEIN, LEIB	42	F	W	RRZZZZBO
CHAJE	10	F	CH	RRZZZZBO
LEWIN, MOLKE	22	F	SP	RRZZZZBO
LAUES, ROSA	18	F	SP	RRZZZZBO
BRAWDERS, THOMAS	6	M	CHILD	RRZZZZBO
PICTOW, BENY	38	M	LABR	RRZZZZBO
DOBRE	24	M	LABR	RRZZZZBO
SLATE	35	M	LABR	RRZZZZBO
HUBIS, MOSES	15	M	LABR	RRZZZZBO
FEINBERG, LEIB	35	M	MECH	RRZZZZBO
JUDES	11	M	CH	RRZZZZBO
SISSELMAN, JUDES	30	M	LABR	RRZZZZBO
SAM	34	M	MECH	RRZZZZBO
FEME	50	M	MECH	RRZZZZBO
SINVALSKY, LEIB	25	M	LABR	RRZZZZBO
ABRAMOWITZ, MAX	28	M	LABR	RRZZZZBO
WOLOWSKY, SCHEM	19	M	LABR	PLZZZZNY
YORNIZKI, ZALMA	25	M	LABR	RRZZZZNY
SHAVINSKY, MATHIAS	26	M	LABR	RRZZZZPHI
GOLDBERG, M	20	M	LABR	RRZZZZNY

SHIP: LAHN

FROM: BREMEN AND SOUTHAMPTON
TO: NEW YORK
ARRIVED: 29 JUNE 1888

PASSENGER	AGE	SEX	OCCUPATION	PRV VIL DES
MEISCHAK, JACOB	40	M	FARMER	RRAICPUSA
JACOB	40	M	FARMER	RRAICPUSA
BENARECK, JOSEPH	22	M	FARMER	RRAICPUSA
SCHULMANN, GODEL	45	M	CGRMKR	RRAFWJUSA
BROCHE	20	F	NN	RRAFWJUSA
RODGER, JOSEF	4	M	CHILD	RRAFWJUSA
F-ORKE, HEINR	33	M	BCHR	RRACBFUSA
CAROLE	25	F	W	RRACBFUSA
FRIDA	.01	F	INFANT	RRACBFUSA
STUMME, MINNA	47	F	NN	RRACBFUSA
KOCH, JOSEF	28	M	FARMER	RRAIIYUSA
MINDERMANN, JOH	16	M	NN	RRZZZZUSA
SCHRETTENBRUNNER, PETER	18	M	LABR	RRZZZZUSA
KAMMERER, EUGEN	23	M	FARMER	RRZZZZUSA
MAGDA	26	F	W	RRZZZZUSA
JODWIRSCHES, WINZENS	21	M	LABR	RRAICPUSA
MLAMED, WOLF	30	M	LABR	RRAICPUSA
KRAUSE, CARL	25	M	LABR	RRAICPUSA
TELSKE, JACOB	20	M	LLD	RRAFWJUSA
RICHTER, JACOB	29	M	LLD	RRAFWJUSA
SCHWERTEN, ERNST	39	M	LABR	RRAFWJUSA
DOROTHEA	31	F	W	RRAFWJUSA
EDWARD	1	M	CHILD	RRAFWJUSA
CLARA	.03	F	INFANT	RRAFWJUSA
CELA	18	F	NN	RRAFWJUSA
BAUMGART, OSCAR	37	M	LABR	RRAFWJUSA
ROTGER, TESSE	32	M	LABR	RRAFWJUSA
FEIGE	14	F	NN	RRAFWJUSA
ISAAK	8	M	CHILD	RRAFWJUSA
LEWANDOWSKY, ROMAN	17	M	FARMER	RRAFWJUSA
JANOZEWICZ, ALZBIETA	50	F	W	RRZZZZUSA
FRENZEL, JOSSEL	28	M	LABR	RRZZZZUSA
EPSTEIN, ARON	17	M	LABR	RRZZZZUSA

SHIP: GALLA

FROM: LIVERPOOL AND QUEENSTOWN
TO: NEW YORK
ARRIVED: 29 JUNE 1888

PASSENGER	AGE	SEX	OCCUPATION	PRV VIL DES
CHRISTOFFERSON, ANNE	4	F	CHILD	FNZZZZUSA
VENORI, FRANZ	29	M	LABR	FNACBFUSA
ESIOLA, MATT.	35	M	LABR	FNACBFUSA
ANNA	32	F	W	FNACBFUSA
ALEXANDER	3	M	CHILD	FNACBFUSA
KUMMERRA, SALOMAN	20	M	LABR	FNACBFUSA
JOHANSON, JOHAN	19	M	LABR	FNAEWSUSA
HAPPAWIN, JOHAN	36	M	LABR	FNAEWSUSA
GUSTAFSON, SAMUEL	27	M	LABR	FNAEWSUSA
MALLSON, JOHAN	39	M	LABR	FNAEWSUSA
JUSSILLA, AND.	30	M	LABR	FNAEWSUSA
LANGRER, JAKOB	45	M	LABR	FNACBFUSA
GILLMAN, GUST.	33	M	LABR	FNAEWSUSA
SANRIKOSHE, AND.	34	M	LABR	FNAEWSUSA
BUTRENSONITZ, JAN	22	M	LABR	FNAEWSUSA
ISONIAHI, JOHAN	25	M	LABR	FNAEWSUSA
ERICKSON, JOHN	27	M	SEMN	FNAEWSUSA
JOKILCHTE, AUGT.	30	M	CPR	FNAEWSUSA
TOROMEN, CARLE	40	M	LABR	FNAEWSUSA
JUNDUREN, ISAAC	50	M	LABR	FNAEWSUSA
ABRALA	20	M	LABR	FNAEWSUSA
HENDRIKSON, ERIK	60	M	LABR	FNZZZZUSA
NIBEL, FERGE	20	F	SVNT	FNZZZZUSA
KOUTALA, SEROFIA	26	F	SVNT	FNACBFUSA
CONTALA, SANNA	23	F	SVNT	FNACBFUSA
JALA, ANNA	20	F	SVNT	FNACBFUSA
KANFFIR, WILHELMINA	24	F	SVNT	FNACBFUSA
KRASI, MARIA	25	F	SVNT	FNACBFUSA
SRARRIA, LISA	36	F	SVNT	FNACBFUSA
ENILA, SUSANNA	16	F	SVNT	FNACBFUSA
ELFA, ANNA	25	F	SVNT	FNACBFUSA
LARTINEN, OSCAR	30	M	LABR	FNZZZZUSA
MINA	22	F	W	FNZZZZUSA

PASSENGER	AGE	SEX	OCCUPATION	PRV VIL DES
LUNSUA, OLOF	38	M	LABR	FNZZZZUSA
ARMANDE	27	F	W	FNZZZZUSA
HORDINAN, ANIA	18	F	SVNT	FNZZZZUSA
WINTER, SERAFINA	27	F	W	FNACBFUSA
BERNHARD	.11	M	INFANT	FNACBFUSA
BINDER, SALOMAN	16	M	MACH	FNACBFUSA
ROBJENSKY, ISRAEL	25	M	LABR	FNACBFUSA
RAMUSKY, JUDES	27	M	TLR	FNACBFUSA
BROSY, HERSH	52	M	LABR	FNACBFUSA
KOSCHYLEPKY, OSCHER	20	M	TLR	FNACBFUSA
EJAIM	10	M	CH	FNACBFUSA
LUNKANEN, WASELI	20	M	FARMER	FNACBFUSA
MOSAIR, DAVID	19	M	PDLR	RRZZZZUSA
SCHALIT, LEISER	17	M	TLR	RRACBFUSA
BERLOWSKY, WOLF	18	M	LABR	RRACBFUSA
JAROTZKI, IVAN	22	M	LABR	RRACBFUSA
GRUNSTEIN, BENJ	48	M	LABR	RRACBFUSA
DD.	23	M	LABR	RRACBFUSA
GLOWITZ, NOTTE	28	M	TLR	RRACBFUSA
CHICKAWSKY, MAX	19	M	TLR	RRACBFUSA
SOLODOWITZ, SAL.	30	M	LABR	RRACBFUSA
CHAUNKIN, LUE	16	M	LABR	RRACBFUSA
LEWIN, MORDECAI	34	M	LABR	RRACBFUSA
SKETAJOWITZ, SIMON	25	M	LABR	RRACBFUSA
BLOCK, EDWARD	21	M	MCHT	RRACBFUSA
MERSEN, BANICH	22	M	TLR	RRACBFUSA
BAURAK, LANUL	25	M	LABR	RRACBFUSA
ASIMON, WOLF	26	M	TLR	RRACBFUSA
HOLAPPA, JACOB	30	M	WHR	RRACBFUSA
LEHTE, HENDRIK	22	M	CPR	RRACBFUSA
KWIKAUGAS, ABRAM	26	M	LABR	RRACBFUSA
KUTIK, SARAH	23	F	SVNT	RRACBFUSA
KATZERIELLO--, MARTA	20	F	TLR	RRACBFUSA
KAUFMAN, KAROLINA	15	F	SP	RRACBFUSA
BORSCHAY, BEILE	17	F	TLR	RRACBFUSA
RAMBOLIUSKY, ROSA	22	F	SP	RRACBFUSA
HIMMELFART, KELA	28	F	TLR	RRACBFUSA
KOJA, ANNA	18	F	SVNT	RRACBFUSA
SILLANKORWA, MARJA	19	F	SVNT	RRACBFUSA
SCHLOSSMAN, NISSA	30	F	MA	RRACBFUSA
MOSES	6	M	CHILD	RRACBFUSA
ELISE	4	F	CHILD	RRACBFUSA
SIMON	.11	M	INFANT	RRACBFUSA
BARE, MATH.	30	M	FARMER	RRACBFUSA
RUTA	32	F	MA	RRACBFUSA
HENDRIK	7	M	CHILD	RRACBFUSA
MARIA	4	F	CHILD	RRACBFUSA
PAJO, HILMA	4	F	CHILD	RRACBFUSA
KAYSA	2	F	CHILD	RRACBFUSA
LANGAS, KAJSA	40	F	SVNT	RRACBFUSA
LINE, CHARJE	20	F	MA	RRACBFUSA
TAUBE	.10	M	INFANT	RRACBFUSA
HONKAWANA, MARIA	22	F	MA	RRACBFUSA
GRETHA	.07	F	INFANT	RRACBFUSA
JABINOWSKY, JANKEL	21	M	TLR	RRACBFUSA
ROSENFIELD, MASO	29	M	TLR	RRACBFUSA
KOCHAFF, JACOB	24	M	LABR	RRACBFUSA
FIEDMAN, SAML.	17	M	TLR	RRACBFUSA
BARANOWITZ, ITLE	16	F	TLR	RRACBFUSA
GROSSNOWITZ, SORIE	21	F	SP	RRACBFUSA

SHIP: HAMMONIA

FROM: HAMBURG AND HAVRE
TO: NEW YORK
ARRIVED: 29 JUNE 1888

PASSENGER	AGE	SEX	OCCUPATION	PRV VIL DES
BUCKSHAN, MARIE	22	F	UNKNOWN	RRAFWJUSA
BREINE	3	F	CHILD	RRAFWJUSA
DOBE	.06	F	INFANT	RRAFWJUSA
FELBROWSKY, JOH.	22	M	UNKNOWN	RRAHUUUSA
BUCHSTEIN, DOBRA	22	F	W	RRAHUUUSA
WASSERDAM, CHAIM	54	M	LABR	RRZZZZUSA
STERINSKY, JOHANN	23	M	UNKNOWN	RRAFWJUSA
GRUNAUER, LUDWIG	27	M	LABR	RRADATUSA
MOLAWSKY, FREIDE	30	F	W	RRAIFIUSA
ELIAS	2	M	CHILD	RRAIFIUSA
SARAH	.10	F	INFANT	RRAIFIUSA
KUSCHELOW, BEILE	36	F	W	RRAIFIUSA
REISEL	9	F	CHILD	RRAIFIUSA
SAMUEL	8	M	CHILD	RRAIFIUSA
CHANNE	6	F	CHILD	RRAIFIUSA
NATAN	.11	M	INFANT	RRAIFIUSA
STOLOW, ESTHER	30	F	W	RRAIFIUSA
MOSES	9	M	CHILD	RRAIFIUSA
BENZEL	6	M	CHILD	RRAIFIUSA
MAIER	.05	M	INFANT	RRAIFIUSA
BLACHMANN, SARA	21	F	SGL	RRZZZZUSA
BIRKER, RACHEL	21	F	SGL	RRZZZZUSA
JUNG, SCHEINE	17	F	SGL	RRZZZZUSA
SOBOLOWSKY, VINCENT	25	M	LABR	RRZZZZUSA
JANKOWSKY, MARIANNA	24	F	SGL	RRZZZZUSA
JANKANYCITIA, ELISABETH	24	F	SGL	RRZZZZUSA
SANKOWSKI, STANISLAUS	25	M	LABR	RRZZZZUSA
MUNDELWITZ, ESTER	37	F	W	RRZZZZUSA
ROSALIE	8	F	CHILD	RRZZZZUSA
TEOFIL	7	M	CHILD	RRZZZZUSA
HERSCH	6	M	CHILD	RRZZZZUSA
SIMME	5	M	CHILD	RRZZZZUSA
MOSES	3	M	CHILD	RRZZZZUSA
MARGR.	.06	M	INFANT	RRZZZZUSA
BOGEMANN, LUDWIG	25	M	UNKNOWN	RRZZZZUSA
HESAN, MARIE	23	F	UNKNOWN	RRZZZZUSA
FRAN-ENSLEIN, BARBARA	26	F	UNKNOWN	RRZZZZUSA
BANK, ROSA	18	F	SGL	RRAIKVUSA
WARTELSKI, CHAIE	48	F	SGL	RRAHZSUSA
NECHAME	14	F	CH	RRAHZSUSA
HENNE	16	F	CH	RRAHZSUSA
ELIAS	8	M	CHILD	RRAHZSUSA
SLATRINSKI, LEA	19	F	SGL	RRAHZSUSA
BERLOWITZ, CHAIM	30	M	MCHT	RRAHZSUSA
HERSCHTRICH, HERM.	24	M	UNKNOWN	RRAHZSUSA
BOTWIENCKY, ESTHER	28	F	W	RRAHZSUSA
BOTWIENEK, CZERNE	9	M	CHILD	RRAHTUUSA
ARON	7	M	CHILD	RRAHTUUSA
CHAIM	4	M	CHILD	RRAHTUUSA
RATNESOW, SPRINGE	20	F	SGL	RRAHTUUSA
CHALSHI, ISRAEL	45	M	LABR	RRAHTUUSA
CZECHANOWSKY, AISIK	26	M	LABR	RRAHTUUSA
CHAJE	23	F	W	RRAHTUUSA
GOLDBERG, OSCHER	29	M	UNKNOWN	RRAHTUUSA
RATNER, AABRAM	39	M	UNKNOWN	RRAHTUUSA
DOBROWSKA, MARIANNA	15	F	SGL	RRZZZZUSA
STRZYNSKI, BRONISLAV	31	M	UNKNOWN	RRZZZZUSA
GELER, DAVID	25	M	DLR	RRZZZZUSA
SARA	23	F	W	RRZZZZUSA
ISAAC	.10	M	INFANT	RRZZZZUSA
GOLGNER, MINDEL	30	F	W	RRZZZZUSA
SARA	9	F	CHILD	RRZZZZUSA
PEREZ	8	M	CHILD	RRZZZZUSA
JANOS	7	M	CHILD	RRZZZZUSA
LAZAR	6	M	CHILD	RRZZZZUSA
MENDEL	4	M	CHILD	RRZZZZUSA
CHAJE	.10	M	INFANT	RRZZZZUSA
SOSCHNER, SHEINE	28	F	W	RRZZZZUSA
BASTE	.10	F	INFANT	RRZZZZUSA
ISER	.01	F	INFANT	RRZZZZUSA
MISCHHOWITZ, LIRE	25	F	W	RRZZZZUSA
MEYER	4	M	CHILD	RRZZZZUSA
AISIK	.11	M	INFANT	RRZZZZUSA
SILBERHEIT, SALOMON	20	M	DLR	RRZZZZUSA
ROSEW, SARAH	16	F	SGL	RRZZZZUSA
BACZANSKI, MALKE	22	F	W	RRZZZZUSA
GITTEL	8	F	CHILD	RRZZZZUSA
MERE	.06	F	INFANT	RRZZZZUSA

PASSENGER	AGE	SEX	OCCUPATION	PRV VIL DES
ARONSOHN, AISIK	15	M	CL	RRZZZZUSA
KAMINSKI, SIMCHE	27	M	CGRMKR	RRZZZZUSA
LAZAROWICZ, MINA	24	F	W	RRZZZZUSA
GOLDE	.11	M	INFANT	RRZZZZUSA
JESZER, CLARA	20	F	SGL	RRZZZZUSA
SNOJANIM, FERD.	17	M	FARMER	RRZZZZUSA
BERHENITZ, ELIAS	19	M	BCHR	RRZZZZUSA
BRESNIAK, JACOB	29	M	LABR	RRZZZZUSA
POMERANZ, GABRIEL	26	M	LABR	RRZZZZUSA
BERESMAK, ABA	24	M	LABR	RRZZZZUSA
FARBER, SALOMON	50	M	LABR	RRZZZZUSA
EWIN, SIMON	28	M	UNKNOWN	RRZZZZUSA
LISE	22	F	W	RRZZZZUSA
WEITZMANN, SALOMON	23	M	LABR	RRZZZZUSA
EISEMANN, RUBIN	22	M	LABR	RRZZZZUSA
HEIT, ASIAS	29	M	LABR	RRZZZZUSA
FUCHS, JUDA	24	M	LABR	RRZZZZUSA
GARBOSIK, WOYCECH	30	M	LABR	RRZZZZUSA
BARENBLUTH, SEIDE	37	F	W	RRZZZZUSA
MALKE	35	M	LABR	RRZZZZUSA
FESREL	18	M	CH	RRZZZZUSA
MISEL	16	M	CH	RRZZZZUSA
SAMUEL	9	M	CHILD	RRZZZZUSA
BIEFHE	8	M	CHILD	RRZZZZUSA
MOSES	7	M	CHILD	RRZZZZUSA
KRISTALL, -IMCHE	39	M	LABR	RRZZZZUSA
CHANNA	35	F	W	RRZZZZUSA
LEA	15	F	CH	RRZZZZUSA
FANNY	9	F	CHILD	RRZZZZUSA
SHEINDEL	8	M	CHILD	RRZZZZUSA
BARUCH	4	M	CHILD	RRZZZZUSA
SMUL	.09	M	INFANT	RRZZZZUSA
BECK, WOLF	40	M	LABR	RRZZZZUSA
SANDER, JOEL	37	M	LABR	RRZZZZUSA
LATER, RICHEL	15	F	W	RRZZZZUSA
ENECK	9	F	CHILD	RRZZZZUSA
WOLF	6	M	CHILD	RRZZZZUSA
BILIK, JANKO	15	M	LABR	RRZZZZUSA
SZOTEK, MIHAL	32	M	LABR	RRZZZZUSA
KOVATZ, GYNRY	30	M	LABR	RRZZZZUSA
DANKO, ANDR.	26	M	LABR	RRZZZZUSA
JENESURA, MIHAL	25	M	LABR	RRZZZZUSA
WEISFELD, PESCHE	18	F	SGL	RRZZZZUSA
SUDOWITZ, ABRAM	22	M	LABR	RRZZZZUSA
HENOCK	27	M	LABR	RRAIBOUSA
PISKIN, SCHINE	30	F	WO	RRAIBOUSA
HINDE	9	F	CHILD	RRAIBOUSA
SCIFFRE	8	F	CHILD	RRAIBOUSA
SCHOLE	7	F	CHILD	RRAIBOUSA
ABRAM	3	M	CHILD	RRAIBOUSA
MONT, STANISLAW.	18	F	WO	RRAIBOUSA
ZEWCKA, MARIANNE	25	F	WO	RRAIBOUSA
ANTONIE	.11	F	INFANT	RRAIBOUSA
SINDERMANN, CHAJE	23	F	WO	RRAIBOUSA
CHAZE	3	F	CHILD	RRAIBOUSA
NECHAME	.09	F	INFANT	RRAIBOUSA
RADZEWITZ, ADAM	28	M	LABR	RRAIBOUSA
RADUSCHKEWSKY, JAN	17	M	UNKNOWN	RRAIBOUSA
CHANE, TELY	22	F	SGL	RRAIBOUSA
BRODINSLEI, KUBA	22	M	LABR	RRAIBOUSA
GUSET, MOSES	9	M	CHILD	RRAIBOUSA
LEWIN, ESTHER	15	F	SGL	RRAHTFUSA
SALMWEITSCHLIK, LIPPE	21	F	UNKNOWN	RRAHTFUSA
POLAK, ROCHE	30	F	UNKNOWN	RRAHTFUSA
LEIB	9	M	CHILD	RRAHTFUSA
FREIDE	8	M	CHILD	RRAHTFUSA
JOSUL	6	M	CHILD	RRAHTFUSA
JOSEF	.11	M	INFANT	RRAHTFUSA
FELLMANN, DAVID	35	M	UNKNOWN	RRZZZZUSA
LEIBERMANN, MENDEL	24	M	UNKNOWN	RRZZZZUSA
DOBRENKO, SIMON	26	M	UNKNOWN	RRZZZZUSA
SARA	22	F	W	RRZZZZUSA
MANIF	2	F	CHILD	RRZZZZUSA
WOLF	.09	M	INFANT	RRZZZZUSA
JEHZERS, FRANZ	43	M	LABR	RRZZZZUSA
SABETZKI, ANDRES	44	M	LABR	RRZZZZUSA
RUS, BALTICH	32	M	LABR	RRZZZZUSA

SHIP: SCHIEDAM

FROM: AMSTERDAM
TO: NEW YORK
ARRIVED: 02 JULY 1888

PASSENGER	AGE	SEX	OCCUPATION	PRV VIL DES
PEECHOWSKY, AUGUST	30	M	LABR	RRZZZZUSA
WOYCEHOWSKY, JOSEF	18	M	LABR	RRZZZZUSA
OHAMBA, FRANZ	18	M	LABR	RRZZZZUSA
STEPAT, KARL	27	M	LABR	RRZZZZUSA
KANNENG--, ROBERT	19	M	LABR	RRZZZZUSA
MARESAK, JOSEPHA	38	F	UNKNOWN	RRZZZZUSA
STANSLAW	4	M	CHILD	RRZZZZUSA
GOLDNER, ISRAEL	18	M	LABR	RRZZZZUSA
FIESE	21	M	LABR	RRZZZZUSA
HALTUM, ELTJE	33	M	LABR	RRZZZZUSA
LILASIO, JOSAS	25	M	LABR	RRZZZZUSA
HABRUNIS, PETER	25	M	LABR	RRZZZZUSA
BARBERRIG, ARON	25	M	LABR	RRZZZZUSA
KUNI	23	M	LABR	RRZZZZUSA
PRUSKI, DWORA	20	F	UNKNOWN	RRZZZZUSA
BAISBERING, KUNE	.03	F	INFANT	RRZZZZUSA
RAMANOEWSKI, VINE	30	M	LABR	RRZZZZUSA
UXUK, VINE	28	M	LABR	RRZZZZUSA
SAMORLINSKI, DAVID	19	M	LABR	RRZZZZUSA
GESELWITZ, PAWEL	28	F	SVNT	RRZZZZUSA
JOEL	21	M	LABR	RRZZZZUSA
MALEK, HERSCH	50	M	LABR	RRZZZZUSA
RAM, WILHELM	38	M	LABR	RRZZZZUSA
POLANT, MOSES	35	M	LABR	RRZZZZUSA
GOLDFELD, CHANE	50	F	SVNT	RRZZZZUSA
LOENBURG, JACOB	23	M	LABR	RRZZZZUSA
MICHAEL	17	M	LABR	RRZZZZUSA
MEISNER, MAX	38	M	LABR	RRZZZZUSA
BASIWSKI, BARUCH	28	M	LABR	RRZZZZUSA
CHARE	27	F	UNKNOWN	RRZZZZUSA
BASCHE	.07	F	INFANT	RRZZZZUSA
MOGULIEWSKI, MOSES	45	M	LABR	RRZZZZUSA
LEIE	30	F	UNKNOWN	RRZZZZUSA
MIRL	4	F	CHILD	RRZZZZUSA
BACHE	1	F	CHILD	RRZZZZUSA
ABRAHAM	.08	M	INFANT	RRZZZZUSA
CHLURECKOWA, CH.	30	F	UNKNOWN	RRZZZZUSA
SCHIL	9	M	CHILD	RRZZZZUSA
BORUCH	8	M	CHILD	RRZZZZUSA
SPUNTZE	.10	F	INFANT	RRZZZZUSA
SCHEIMAN, MOSES	18	M	LABR	RRZZZZUSA
CHALANDZUMAS, ANTON	21	M	LABR	RRZZZZUSA
MICH.	56	M	LABR	RRZZZZUSA
KISSEIS, JACOB	34	M	LABR	RRZZZZUSA
BECK, LELIG	24	F	SVNT	RRZZZZUSA
SCHLOSSBERG, CHJAJE	23	F	UNKNOWN	RRZZZZUSA
SANDE	4	F	CHILD	RRZZZZUSA
FRIED	.05	M	INFANT	RRZZZZUSA
GOLDMAN, LINA	31	F	UNKNOWN	RRZZZZUSA
MORITZ	10	M	CH	RRZZZZUSA
HEINAN	9	M	CHILD	RRZZZZUSA
GROSS, JALI	11	M	UNKNOWN	RRZZZZUSA
GOLDMAN, BERL	.08	F	INFANT	RRZZZZUSA
KREMDAL	10	M	CH	RRZZZZUSA
SINGER, MARCUS	22	M	LABR	RRZZZZUSA
SRLER	19	F	UNKNOWN	RRZZZZUSA
ISAAHSON, MORITZ	46	M	LABR	RRZZZZUSA
JETTE	35	F	UNKNOWN	RRZZZZUSA
AUGUSTA	7	F	CHILD	RRZZZZUSA
SALOMON	4	M	CHILD	RRZZZZUSA
AMALIA	.03	F	INFANT	RRZZZZUSA

PASSENGER	AGE	SEX	OCCUPATION	PRV VIL DES
PICHAESHI, ISAH	38	M	LABR	RRZZZZUSA
CHORE	40	F	UNKNOWN	RRZZZZUSA
LINA	14	F	SVNT	RRZZZZUSA
HULDA	11	F	UNKNOWN	RRZZZZUSA
SAMUEL	9	M	CHILD	RRZZZZUSA
DORA	7	F	CHILD	RRZZZZUSA
MAMITZ	4	F	CHILD	RRZZZZUSA
FRIDA	2	F	CHILD	RRZZZZUSA
REBECKA	.04	F	INFANT	RRZZZZUSA
ALBRECHT, WILH.	19	M	LABR	RRZZZZUSA
SCHARNENGHAUSE, WILH.	36	M	LABR	RRZZZZUSA
SCHMULEWITZ, JANKEL	20	M	LABR	RRZZZZUSA
KREINER, HILLER	26	M	LABR	RRZZZZUSA
KUNAWITZ, STEFAN	27	M	LABR	RRZZZZUSA
KLINKOWSKY, VINCENTY	28	M	LABR	RRZZZZUSA
LEWIN, CHANE	27	F	SVNT	RRZZZZUSA
MORDASCH, RAFAEL	40	M	LABR	RRZZZZUSA
LEVI, ABRAH.	29	M	LABR	RRZZZZUSA
DITTERDORF, PINHUS	31	M	LABR	RRZZZZUSA
LEWANDOWSKY, JACOB	24	M	LABR	RRZZZZUSA
HEPPEL, JACOB	18	M	LABR	RRZZZZUSA
GREGOR, JOH.	24	M	LABR	RRZZZZUSA
KATZ, EMIL	23	M	LABR	RRZZZZUSA

SHIP: CITY OF RICHMOND

FROM: LIVERPOOL AND QUEENSTOWN
TO: NEW YORK
ARRIVED: 02 JULY 1888

PASSENGER	AGE	SEX	OCCUPATION	PRV VIL DES
SCHOKET, LINI	50	F	W	RRAFVGNY
ZYDRAK, YLKO	26	M	LABR	RRACBFPA
BIALOSTOCKA, SARA	20	F	LABR	RRAFVGCLE
MAZNUZKWITZ, MARYAN	23	M	LABR	PLZZZZNY
RAPAPORT, URIA	14	M	LABR	RRZZZZNY
RUBENSTEIN, MARC	18	M	LABR	RRZZZZNY
KURLANGUNG, LEISER	18	M	PNTR	RRZZZZNY
ROPKIN, MORITZ	18	M	LABR	RRZZZZNY
MERLIS, ESTER	30	F	W	RRZZZZNY
CHANNA	6	F	CHILD	RRZZZZNY
RUATSALA, ANDREU	23	M	LABR	RRACBFMI
ULUTAUC, MARIA	25	F	LABR	RRACBFNY
ABRAHAMSON, JACOB	30	M	FSHMN	FNZZZZMI
JAKOLA, WILHELM	23	M	LABR	FNZZZZNY
KATISARI, JOHAN	18	M	LABR	FNZZZZMI
KOHAN, JOSEF	35	M	MECH	FNAFVGNY
LOWENSTEIN, ARON	27	M	TLR	FNAFVGNY
MALKE	19	F	W	FNAFVGNY
GILBEL, SABSCHEL	38	M	BKR	FNACBFNY
LAUGFELD, ISAC	27	M	LABR	FNACBFNY
MIRKE	20	F	LABR	FNACBFNY
LIPSKIN, ABRAM	17	M	PRNTR	FNAHOONY
GUTTMANN, ABRAM	16	M	PNTR	FNAHQDNY
MASCHAL, ROMAN	36	M	BKR	FNACBFNY
WILK, CHAIM	18	M	TLR	FNACBFNY
MAZURKEWIZ, VICTORIA	25	F	LABR	FNAHOOBUF
BAUK, SALET	42	M	BKR	RRZZZZBAL
CHASCHE	44	F	W	RRZZZZBAL
SCHLOIME	20	M	BKR	RRZZZZBAL
MARCUS	12	M	CH	RRZZZZBAL
ELIAS	8	M	CHILD	RRZZZZBAL
HODE	7	M	CHILD	RRZZZZBAL
GEDALJE	5	M	CHILD	RRZZZZBAL
HABERMANN, CHAIM	32	M	SMH	RRAFVGBAL
HOLDERMANN, USCHER	28	M	TLR	RRAHOOBAL
SCHLINSKY, LEISER	20	M	GZR	RRAHOOBAL
TAUBE	18	F	W	RRAHOOBAL
MARIE	.10	F	INFANT	RRAHOOBAL
WOLF	40	M	GZR	RRAHOOBAL
CHAJE	46	F	W	RRAHOOBAL
ARON	11	M	CH	RRAHOOBAL
SCHART, MOSES	20	M	TLR	RRAFVGNY
GRIFF, ARON	45	M	TLR	RRACBFNY
MARIANNE	17	F	LABR	RRACBFNY
WALTER, MAX	27	M	LABR	RRACBFNY
PERELMITTER, MECEL	37	M	LABR	RRACBFNY
BRAUMANN, HETEL	18	F	SVNT	RRAFVGNY
KURLAUZIG, JADEL	11	M	CH	RRAHOONY
BOEMRIZ, STANISLAW	27	M	LABR	RRACBFNY
RANBO, BOLESLAV	38	M	LABR	RRACBFNY
MICKELOW, MOSCHE	30	M	LABR	RRACBFNY
GOLDFARB, SAMUEL	29	M	CPTR	RRAFWJNY
SCHLIMOWITZ, JOSSEL	24	M	LABR	RRACBFNY
ISRAEL, WOLF	33	M	LABR	RRACBFBAL
SCHMUL	42	M	GDNR	RRACBFBAL
SAWILEWSKY, SAUL	22	M	GDNR	RRACBFBAL
ISRAEL, MOSES	39	M	TLR	RRACBFNY
PULJAK, SAUL	33	M	LABR	RRACBFNY
BRUCKMANN, MORDCHE	55	M	LABR	RRACBFPA
HINDE	45	F	W	RRACBFPA
ESTHER	19	F	LABR	RRACBFPA
NACHLE	17	F	LABR	RRACBFPA
MARIE	10	F	CH	RRACBFPA
BEILE	7	F	CHILD	RRACBFPA
BORUCH	4	F	CHILD	RRACBFPA
RUBMANN, MARCUS	27	M	FARMER	RRAFVGNY
BASCHKEWITZKI, BERL	23	M	FARMER	RRAFVGNY
TEITILBAUM, MINUSCH	17	M	FARMER	RRAFVGNY
KAPLAN, JOSCHNA	18	M	LABR	RRACBFNY
GORMANN, AUSCHEL	24	M	LABR	RRACBFNY
KAUN, MORITZ	19	M	TLR	RRAFVGNY
ROLANDSKY, BERKO	54	M	TLR	RRAFVGNY
BEHRMAN, MAXMILLIAM	32	M	CL	RRAFVGNY
CHASAN, MARISCHE	15	M	LABR	RRACBFNY
SCHIMANSKI, SCHIPOLIK	52	M	CPR	RRACBFNY
FRIEDA, JAN	42	M	LABR	RRACBFNY
ZENIZITZKY, STANISLAUS	50	M	LABR	RRACBFNY
GORMANN, HIRSCHBERG	28	M	LABR	RRACBFNY
AKIN, ASCHEL	25	M	LABR	RRACBFNY
KRUPNITZKI, ARON	35	M	LABR	RRACBFPA
MALULIS, KASIMIR	25	M	LABR	RRACBFPA
REISEN, MICHAEL	45	M	GDNR	RRAHOONY
NISSEN	19	F	LABR	RRAHOONY
MOSCHE	11	M	CH	RRAHOONY
WASILI, JOSEF	32	M	LABR	RRACBFNY
SNIRER, MARREC	21	M	LABR	RRACBFNY
MELZER, CHAIM	30	M	JNR	RRACBFNY
ZAKEAWEZ, ANDRE	30	M	GDNR	RRACBFNY
LEWINOWEIZ, MICHAS	36	M	GDNR	RRACBFNY
REZINA, FRIEDE	18	F	W	RRACBFNY
ELISSOHN, THEODOR	47	M	TLR	RRACBFPHI
KLUEZYSKY, JOSEF	40	M	PLMN	RRACBFWAS

SHIP: POLARIA

FROM: HAMBURG
TO: NEW YORK
ARRIVED: 02 JULY 1888

PASSENGER	AGE	SEX	OCCUPATION	PRV VIL DES
KOCH, JAN	22	M	LABR	RRAHTOUNK
SOBUSICUSKY, ADAM	34	M	LABR	RRAHTOUNK
POLTINOWITS, ANTON	24	M	LABR	RRAHYNUNK
DOWIDAJTIS, VINCENT	21	M	LABR	RRAHYNUNK
INKOTIS, ANDRY	21	M	LABR	RRAHYNUNK
KEYBERT, STEFAN	22	M	LABR	RRAHTOUNK
STANILSAUS	9	M	CHILD	RRAHTOUNK
SILWERMANN, PERL	22	F	SGL	RRAHWMUNK
ROGOW, ELIAS	18	M	SHMK	RRAHVLUNK
SMUTOFSKY, DOBE	35	F	WO	RRZZZZUNK
ARON	18	M	CH	RRZZZZUNK

PASSENGER	AGE	SEX	OCCUPATION	PRV VIL	DES
SCHLOME	8	F	CHILD	RRZZZZ	UNK
BLUME	.11	F	INFANT	RRZZZZ	UNK
BRANDEL	9	F	CHILD	RRZZZZ	UNK
ABRAHAM, GOLDE	50	F	WO	RRAIDD	UNK
JUDITH	20	F	CH	RRAIDD	UNK
FRADE	18	F	CH	RRAIDD	UNK
LEA	16	F	CH	RRAIDD	UNK
MORRIS, ESTHER	23	F	WO	RRAIDD	UNK
DWORE	.11	F	INFANT	RRAIDD	UNK
EDELMANN, LEA	50	F	WO	RRAHTU	UNK
SARA	18	F	SGL	RRAHTU	UNK
HERSCH	17	M	LABR	RRAHTU	UNK
SCHLAKMANN, ABRAM	25	M	DLR	RRAHTU	UNK
MASCHE	25	F	W	RRAHTU	UNK
GOLDE	4	F	CHILD	RRAHTU	UNK
GODEL	.11	M	INFANT	RRAHTU	UNK
CHASCHE	.01	F	INFANT	RRAHTU	UNK
ETEL	50	F	WO	RRAHTU	UNK
SLATE	9	F	CHILD	RRAHTU	UNK
WEISSBERGER, LEIB	56	M	DLR	RRZZZZ	UNK
GITTEL	53	F	W	RRZZZZ	UNK
OSTROMETZKI, SCHLOME	24	M	DLR	RRZZZZ	UNK
WASLAWSKI, JAN	41	M	LABR	RRAHUF	UNK
MURAFSKI, STANISL.	25	M	LABR	RRAHUF	UNK
KOLAKOWSKI, WLASCHEK	28	M	LABR	RRAHUF	UNK
BRETZ, LEISER	52	M	LABR	RRAGRT	UNK
SCHUFERSTEIN, HERM.	18	M	TLR	RRAGRT	UNK
KOKOLSKI, LEWEKE	23	M	TLR	RRAIIT	UNK
SOPHIE	18	F	W	RRAIIT	UNK
FALKOWITSCH, HERM.	35	M	TLR	RRZZZZ	UNK
MASULKEWITZ, VINCENTE	27	M	LABR	RRZZZZ	UNK
LEIPZERSAK, CHAIM	39	M	JNR	RRAHVU	UNK
STEIN, LEIB	26	M	TLR	RRZZZZ	UNK
POPER, OSIAS	25	M	LABR	RRZZZZ	UNK
MATULL, AUGUST	40	M	LABR	RRAEFL	UNK
HIRSCH, AUGUSTE	18	F	SGL	RRAHVA	UNK
BRATZ, FRIEDR.	40	M	JNR	RRAHVA	UNK
NAPIERSKY, VALENTIA	40	M	CPTR	RRAHUI	UNK
KLIMAZEWSKY, JAN	38	M	SHMK	RRAHUI	UNK
KORB, IDA	24	F	WO	RRZZZZ	UNK
SIMON	.11	M	INFANT	RRZZZZ	UNK
KRAWCSWICSZ, JOSEF	18	M	INF	RRZZZZ	UNK
BAY, ABEL	45	M	LABR	RRAIAR	UNK
CHAIC	42	F	W	RRAIAR	UNK
JOSEF	19	M	CH	RRAIAR	UNK
SARA	9	F	CHILD	RRAIAR	UNK
CHEIE	8	F	CHILD	RRAIAR	UNK
BEHR	7	M	CHILD	RRAIAR	UNK
DWORSKI, JERUCHEM	9	M	CHILD	RRAIHQ	UNK
KATZ, MAYER	30	M	DLR	RRAIHQ	OH
GUTMANN, MARCUS	38	M	LABR	RRZZZZ	OH
JULIE	31	F	W	RRZZZZ	OH
REGI	9	F	CHILD	RRZZZZ	OH
MANUEL	8	M	CHILD	RRZZZZ	OH
ARON	7	M	CHILD	RRZZZZ	OH
MALOC	6	F	CHILD	RRZZZZ	OH
CHANI	.11	F	INFANT	RRZZZZ	OH
FRIEDMANN, HERM.	7	M	CHILD	RRZZZZ	OH
RAFELOWICZ, MOSES	31	M	TLR	RRZZZZ	OH
GUTMANN, IDA	19	F	W	RRZZZZ	OH
MANNE	.11	F	INFANT	RRZZZZ	OH
LEBANOWITH, GISELA	18	F	SGL	RRZZZZ	OH
HEISCHOWITZ, ABRAM	25	M	DLR	RRAHZS	OH
MARCINHAUSKI, JANKEL	27	M	SMH	RRAHZS	OH
FREID, BERKO	52	M	DLR	RRAHZS	OH
ROBKOWSKY, ABRAM	40	M	LABR	RRAHSP	OH
BASCHE	18	F	SGL	RRAHSP	OH
ESTHER	20	F	SGL	RRAHSP	OH
MASCHE	18	F	SGL	RRAHSP	OH
GINSBURG, INDEL	14	M	LABR	RRAHZS	OH
EISIKOWICZ, ROAL-W.	40	F	W	RRAIFJ	OH
ELIE	7	F	CHILD	RRAIFJ	OH
IONA	9	F	CHILD	RRAIFJ	OH
MOSES	.11	M	INFANT	RRAIFJ	OH
SCHALMACH, SARA	13	F	SGL	RRZZZZ	OH
FILMEISTER, SCHEPSEL	19	M	DLR	RRZZZZ	OH
ERDMANN, HUDES	19	F	SGL	RRAIGH	OH
LEWESOHN, ISAAC	19	M	CL	RRAIFH	OH
RASMANN, MORDCHE	20	M	CL	RRAIFH	OH
SOOLOVITZ, SANDEL	27	M	DLR	RRZZZZ	OH
CHASCHE	9	F	CHILD	RRZZZZ	OH
LUDIN, ABE	22	F	W	RRZZZZ	OH
PESCHE	20	F	SGL	RRZZZZ	OH
ISAAC, ETEL	15	F	SGL	RRZZZZ	OH
PRINZINSKI, MICHAEL	33	M	LABR	RRZZZZ	OH
RADYPEWSKA, BERTHA	40	F	WO	RRZZZZ	OH
ROSALIE	16	F	CH	RRZZZZ	OH
HERM.	9	M	CHILD	RRZZZZ	OH
SARA	7	F	CHILD	RRZZZZ	OH
JACOBSOHN, MOSES	16	M	DLR	RRAIGH	OH
KATOWITZ, CHAJE	18	F	SGL	RRAIGH	OH
SCHATTENSTEIN, JACOB	22	M	DLR	RRZZZZ	OH
KISCHKO, SIMON	26	M	LABR	RRAILK	OH

SHIP: ETRURIA

FROM: LIVERPOOL AND QUEENSTOWN
TO: NEW YORK
ARRIVED: 02 JULY 1888

PASSENGER	AGE	SEX	OCCUPATION	PRV VIL	DES
MARGULIS, SIMON	22	M	LABR	RRACBF	PHI
ALFERN, FISCHEL	51	M	LABR	RRACBF	PHI
KAGAN, MEYER	18	M	LABR	RRACBF	PHI
MOTZENOW, ARON	26	M	LABR	RRACBF	PHI
BATEWNIK, GERSON	16	F	SP	RRAFWJ	PA
FRIEDMANN, BARUCH	29	M	CGRMKR	RRACBF	NY
HANHE	28	F	W	RRACBF	NY
PURSIS, HANNAH	14	F	SP	RRACBF	NY
BALL	11	F	SP	RRACBF	NY
SIWIN, U	60	M	MCHT	RRADAX	NY

SHIP: WYOMING

FROM: LIVERPOOL AND QUEENSTOWN
TO: NEW YORK
ARRIVED: 02 JULY 1888

PASSENGER	AGE	SEX	OCCUPATION	PRV VIL	DES
DOBBS, JANE	26	F	W	PLZZZZ	USA
HARRIETT	4	M	CHILD	PLZZZZ	USA
EDITH	00	F	INF	PLZZZZ	USA
KERMER, PAT.	21	M	FARMER	PLZZZZ	USA
IRONI, TERESEA	18	F	W	PLZZZZ	USA
PAFT, GEO	40	F	SP	PLZZZZ	USA
MCELNY, J	21	M	LABR	PLZZZZ	USA
MARY	19	F	W	PLZZZZ	USA
BYRENT, P	26	U	UNKNOWN	PLZZZZ	USA
GRAF, L	16	U	UNKNOWN	PLZZZZ	USA
DERANEY, PAT.	22	U	UNKNOWN	PLZZZZ	USA
DANGIKI, M	27	M	LABR	PLZZZZ	USA
THOM, J	20	M	LABR	PLZZZZ	USA
HUDSEN, F	21	F	SP	PLZZZZ	USA
PAGGERT, MAGGD.	25	U	LABR	PLZZZZ	USA
VUNGHUM, R	19	M	LABR	PLZZZZ	USA
NILSON, A.F.	20	F	SP	PLZZZZ	USA
ANDERSON, J	18	M	LABR	PLZZZZ	USA
ALMA	20	F	CH	PLZZZZ	USA
ERICKSON, CARL	19	M	LABR	PLZZZZ	USA
ENGLAND, CARL.	17	F	W	PLZZZZ	USA
BERGLUND, ERIKA	21	F	CH	PLZZZZ	USA
SO----, VICTOR	00	U	UNKNOWN	PLZZZZ	USA

PASSENGER	AGE	SEX	OCCUPATION	PRV VIL DES
GELEN, HILDA	22	U	LABR	PLZZZZUSA
KAUMEN, MARIA	19	U	LABR	PLZZZZUSA
KUGUSKOWSKI, TEKLA	16	F	SP	RRZZZZUSA
MARKIN, POLINA	16	M	LABR	RRZZZZUSA
KORPYEL, ESTER	7	F	CHILD	RRZZZZUSA
JEISSEL	7	F	CHILD	RRZZZZUSA
KELLUN, F	53	M	LABR	RRZZZZUSA
CHRIST	48	F	W	RRZZZZUSA
RUHEL	22	M	LABR	RRZZZZUSA
ABRAHAM	17	M	LABR	RRZZZZUSA
ESTER	7	F	CHILD	RRZZZZUSA
CL---, CHAIM	25	M	FARMER	RRZZZZUSA
NOAH	15	M	FARMER	RRZZZZUSA
BUNOND, LEA	16	F	SP	RRZZZZUSA
LER, CHAIM	7	M	CHILD	RRZZZZUSA
PARKER, HIRSCH	34	F	SP	RRZZZZUSA
OLIN, JOH	23	M	LABR	RRZZZZUSA
CATH	26	F	W	RRZZZZUSA
SCHULT, CARL	15	M	LABR	RRZZZZUSA
KOHN, JONAS	52	M	LABR	RRZZZZUSA
ANNA	49	F	W	RRZZZZUSA
EDLA	14	F	SP	RRZZZZUSA
JONAS	7	M	CHILD	RRZZZZUSA
WATAZOM, GUSTAF	25	M	LABR	RRZZZZUSA
PELKULU, JOHAN	36	M	LABR	RRZZZZUSA
LARIN, SIMON	26	M	LABR	RRZZZZUSA
LUBINA, JOHAN	39	M	LABR	RRZZZZUSA
KOSKI, MU--	20	M	LABR	RRZZZZUSA
PIKI, GUSTAF	20	M	LABR	RRZZZZUSA
LAORA, EMMANUEL	22	M	LABR	RRZZZZUSA
GURMOD, JOHANN	53	M	LABR	RRZZZZUSA
SNOWEANTIN, J	44	M	LABR	RRZZZZUSA
KYONIP, A	16	M	LABR	PLZZZZUSA
SUROND, MARIA	20	F	SP	PLZZZZUSA
FELDMAN, SURA	17	F	SP	PLZZZZUSA
KEPLIR, ABRAM	17	M	LABR	PLZZZZUSA
MARKUS, JACKEL	17	F	W	PLZZZZUSA
REYENSBURG	00	F	INF	PLZZZZUSA
ABRAMOWITZ, ARON	45	M	LABR	PLZZZZUSA
ESTER	38	F	W	PLZZZZUSA
ABRAHAM	18	M	LABR	PLZZZZUSA
DAVID	16	M	LABR	PLZZZZUSA
ISRAEL	14	M	LABR	PLZZZZUSA
MARYANNA	57	F	SP	PLZZZZUSA
RIWKE	7	F	CHILD	PLZZZZUSA
JOCKEWELD	6	F	CHILD	PLZZZZUSA
DEBORA	3	F	CHILD	PLZZZZUSA
RUCHE	00	F	INF	PLZZZZUSA
JUDO	00	M	INF	PLZZZZUSA
ILANOWITZ, S	20	M	LABR	PLZZZZUSA
STUNECEWIZ, J	50	M	LABR	PLZZZZUSA
RATEIM	16	M	LABR	PLZZZZUSA
MARGEWSKI, PAUL	25	M	LABR	PLZZZZUSA
LEA	22	F	W	PLZZZZUSA
RAHEL	00	F	INF	PLZZZZUSA
LEWIN, HERMAN	17	F	SP	PLZZZZUSA
VAHN, ABRAHAM	32	M	LABR	PLZZZZUSA
KROD, M	18	M	LABR	PLZZZZUSA
SCHWAZ, JOSEPH	20	M	LABR	PLZZZZUSA
LAHMANOWITZ, HITEL	27	M	LABR	PLZZZZUSA
WYER, LEBA	16	F	SP	PLZZZZUSA
LEIBISKI, M	26	F	SP	PLZZZZUSA
KOSOWSKI, ISAAC	38	M	LABR	PLZZZZUSA
BOTURAK, ELIAS	25	M	LABR	PLZZZZUSA
CHANE	25	F	SP	PLZZZZUSA
KLUPE, CHANNE	20	F	SP	PLZZZZUSA
VAHN, DINA	50	F	SP	PLZZZZUSA
PAKN, DAVID	22	M	FARMER	FNZZZZUSA
BOIMAN, MIREL	7	M	CHILD	FNZZZZUSA
CURBOTA, ABRAM	00	M	INF	FNZZZZUSA
GOTTLIEBOWN, FEISS	00	M	INF	FNZZZZUSA
BRYZOWSKI, REWKE	00	M	INF	FNZZZZUSA
DENKE, R	20	M	FARMER	FNZZZZUSA
EDELSTEIN, J	17	M	FARMER	FNZZZZUSA
GROSS, J	28	M	FARMER	FNZZZZUSA
KUBELL, H	30	M	FARMER	FNZZZZUSA
BERMAN, MIREL	55	F	SP	FNZZZZUSA
LEWIN, F	20	M	LABR	FNZZZZUSA
JUDELOW, A	16	M	LABR	FNZZZZUSA
HURWITZ, J	26	M	LABR	FNZZZZUSA
KOCHMAN, A	24	M	LABR	FNZZZZUSA
MYERJAK, MARIA	26	F	SP	FNZZZZUSA
SAUMBEWIZ, JOSES	31	M	LABR	PLZZZZUSA
ERDEMAN, S	37	M	LABR	PLZZZZUSA
TYOTRICK, MEYER	36	M	LABR	PLZZZZUSA
BERSOHN, ABRAM	34	M	LABR	PLZZZZUSA
JACOB, ISRAEL	25	M	LABR	PLZZZZUSA
BEHRMAN, ARON	3	M	CHILD	PLZZZZUSA
ERNST, FRANS	20	M	LABR	PLZZZZUSA
LARNIG, JOHAN	00	M	INF	PLZZZZUSA
KOENITCKA, S	27	M	LABR	PLZZZZUSA
LEYNON, L	25	M	LABR	PLZZZZUSA
LEWIN, HANNA	19	F	SP	PLZZZZUSA
RHEIM, M	16	M	LABR	PLZZZZUSA
MARKWELL, L	30	M	LABR	PLZZZZUSA
JANNA	27	F	W	PLZZZZUSA
WALTER	9	M	CHILD	PLZZZZUSA
REBECCA	00	F	INF	PLZZZZUSA
GUMNOWITZ, PERL	20	M	LABR	PLZZZZUSA
TIDMAN, D	22	M	LABR	PLZZZZUSA
SCHINBEWIZ, BESSE	20	F	SP	PLZZZZUSA
WELLSCHIN, BLYME	29	F	W	PLZZZZUSA
JENKAS	8	F	CHILD	PLZZZZUSA
DON, FRICKEL	35	M	LABR	PLZZZZUSA
BARDRIN, F	47	M	LABR	PLZZZZUSA
HECHT, HESSIE	21	F	SP	PLZZZZUSA
PERSON, BEU-	32	F	SP	PLZZZZUSA
PERMEYS	4	F	CHILD	PLZZZZUSA
GRUSKIN, S	26	F	SP	PLZZZZUSA
BERLE, CHARY	4	M	CHILD	PLZZZZUSA
SCHECHTER, S	18	F	SP	PLZZZZUSA
BRANDT, S	47	M	LABR	PLZZZZUSA
JORGENSEN, B	24	M	LABR	PLZZZZUSA
JACOB	27	M	LABR	PLZZZZUSA
SOENHAUSEN, HENDEL	26	M	LABR	PLZZZZUSA
ZEMMIN, WOLF	26	M	LABR	PLZZZZUSA
ZUMA, DAVID	23	M	LABR	PLZZZZUSA
BRUESTOTT, ALEX.	22	M	LABR	PLZZZZUSA
MARCUS, MOSES	17	M	LABR	PLZZZZUSA
GERSMAN, ROTKE	27	F	SP	PLZZZZUSA
KURT, LIEB	24	M	LABR	PLZZZZUSA
GOTTLIEB, S	18	M	LABR	PLZZZZUSA
MARKOWITZ, C	3	F	CHILD	PLZZZZUSA
BESSE	00	F	INF	PLZZZZUSA
LEIB	17	F	SP	PLZZZZUSA
LENA	8	F	CHILD	PLZZZZUSA
DANZIGER, LEOPOLD	19	M	LABR	PLZZZZUSA
ROSENFELD, MARCUS	18	M	LABR	PLZZZZUSA
SCHOCHET, ISAK	32	M	LABR	PLZZZZUSA
SCHUMMUELOWITZ, CHANE	00	F	INF	PLZZZZUSA
PERSON, FRED.	00	M	INF	PLZZZZUSA
MOROSCHEWITZ, ROSA	19	F	SP	PLZZZZUSA
EWEN, LEISA	35	F	SP	PLZZZZUSA
GRUSCHKA, T	3	F	CHILD	PLZZZZUSA
WEINSBURGER, ERNESTINE	18	F	CH	PLZZZZUSA
KRASCHOWSKA, MARIA	24	F	CH	PLZZZZUSA
TABULSCHACK, MOSES	40	M	LABR	PLZZZZUSA
CHANNE	17	F	SP	PLZZZZUSA
RUMSCHISKI, JOS	22	M	LABR	PLZZZZUSA
ALBMAN, MOS	52	M	LABR	PLZZZZUSA
BAUCH, FRED.	30	F	W	PLZZZZUSA
BERNHARD	6	F	CHILD	PLZZZZUSA
FRED.	00	F	INF	PLZZZZUSA

SHIP: NORSEMAN

FROM: LIVERPOOL AND QUEENSTOWN
TO: BOSTON
ARRIVED: 04 JULY 1888

PASSENGER	AGE	SEX	OCCUPATION	PRV VIL DES
SCHNUR, JACOB	45	M	MECH	RRZZZZNY
CZERENY, CHAINE	23	M	MECH	RRZZZZNY
SOCHER, BERT.	18	M	LABR	RRZZZZNY
REIMAN, ABRAM	19	M	LABR	RRZZZZNY
DADJOCK, MARCUS	19	M	LABR	RRZZZZNY
WEISS, BERECHARD	32	M	LABR	RRZZZZNY
RAUDA, HIEREH	25	M	LABR	RRZZZZNY
HEIBLUS, NATHAN	30	M	MECH	RRZZZZBO
ROSIE	30	F	W	RRZZZZBO
ADOLF	3	M	CHILD	RRZZZZBO
HYMAN	2	M	CHILD	RRZZZZBO
SOLOMON	.09	M	INFANT	RRZZZZBO
MEYEROWITZ, MEYER	28	M	LABR	RRZZZZBO
MUCZE	26	F	W	RRZZZZBO
SELDE	3	F	CHILD	RRZZZZBO
SELIG	18	F	SP	RRZZZZBO
GOLDBERG, FRITZ	45	F	W	RRZZZZBO
FRIEDE	19	M	LABR	RRZZZZBO
MERE	9	F	CHILD	RRZZZZBO
BELLE	6	F	CHILD	RRZZZZBO
SCHIEME	4	M	CHILD	RRZZZZBO
BARR, MORIS	23	M	LABR	RRZZZZBO
BILEMN, ROSE	15	F	SP	RRZZZZBO
SWENSCHEN, ABR.	40	M	LABR	RRZZZZNY
JACOBS, ABR.	22	M	LABR	RRZZZZNY
SHUFAK, RUBEN	21	M	LABR	RRZZZZNY
SCHURMERT, KARL	26	M	LABR	RRZZZZPHI
PIERRE, MANUS	23	M	LABR	RRZZZZPIT
NICHOLAS, CONRAD	27	M	LABR	RRZZZZPIT
WALFMANN, HIRMAN	28	M	LABR	RRZZZZPHI
BROMOUSKY, CARL	40	M	LABR	RRZZZZBO
KASIER, WOLF	31	M	LABR	RRZZZZBO
PAGALEWSKI, NATHAN	16	M	LABR	RRZZZZBO
BORMANN, RACHEL	16	F	SP	RRZZZZBO
STAHL, RIFKE	30	M	LABR	RRZZZZBO
ESTHER	7	F	CHILD	RRZZZZBO
ZEUKLER, FISCHEL	50	M	LABR	RRZZZZBO
ALTE	49	F	W	RRZZZZBO
GIRNBERT, CHANE	55	M	LABR	RRZZZZBO
CHAFFER, SCHMUEL	49	M	LABR	RRZZZZBO
STALL, ABR.	32	M	LABR	RRZZZZBO
MESEROWITZ, SAM.	00	M	INF	RRZZZZBO
GOLDBERG, LESER	.08	F	INFANT	RRZZZZBO
DABIES, BRAHAM	40	M	LABR	PLZZZZNY
MORRIS	3	M	CHILD	PLZZZZNY
ANNIE	.10	F	INFANT	PLZZZZNY
SOKOLOFSKY, FRANK	26	M	LABR	RRZZZZPHI
DIETROWSKY, ROBERT	25	M	LABR	RRZZZZPHI
PALURAS, ANAED	23	M	LABR	RRZZZZPHI
COHEN, WOLF	52	M	LABR	RRZZZZBO
FEINSTEIN, GEIGEL	18	F	SP	RRZZZZBO

SHIP: WERRA

FROM: BREMEN AND SOUTHAMPTON
TO: NEW YORK
ARRIVED: 05 JULY 1888

PASSENGER	AGE	SEX	OCCUPATION	PRV VIL DES
ROZDZEIL, REG.	25	F	W	RRZZZZUSA
REG.	.09	F	INFANT	RRZZZZUSA
KERSCHENBAUM, SARAH	21	F	UNKNOWN	RRZZZZUSA
SIMANSKI, SCHEINE	18	M	FARMER	RRZZZZUSA
SALINGER, RUBIN	42	M	LABR	RRZZZZUSA
CHANE	28	F	W	RRZZZZUSA
RESA	5	F	CHILD	RRZZZZUSA
CHAJE	3	F	CHILD	RRZZZZUSA
HIRSCH	.11	M	INFANT	RRZZZZUSA
CHODOROFSKI, E	22	M	LABR	RRZZZZUSA
BOZEK, BARTOLOMY	27	M	TLR	RRZZZZUSA
NISELEWITZ, SCHLEIME	25	M	LABR	RRZZZZUSA
DWORE	25	M	LABR	RRZZZZUSA
SCHLEIMOWITZ, JUDEL	20	M	LABR	RRZZZZUSA
CHACHE	22	M	LABR	RRZZZZUSA
KRISNANSKY, SCHIMAN	16	M	LABR	RRZZZZUSA
KRUSACH, FRANZISKAS	30	M	LABR	RRZZZZUSA
GOLDSTEIN, NATTALIE	26	F	UNKNOWN	RRZZZZUSA
LENCZEWSKI, THEOPHIL	34	M	LABR	RRZZZZUSA
GRODZINSKI, SORA	39	F	UNKNOWN	RRZZZZUSA
FANNY	17	F	UNKNOWN	RRZZZZUSA
DAVID	14	M	UNKNOWN	RRZZZZUSA
BERTHA	11	F	UNKNOWN	RRZZZZUSA
ARON	10	M	CH	RRZZZZUSA
MARTHA	8	F	CHILD	RRZZZZUSA
EMMA	4	F	CHILD	RRZZZZUSA
BAWIRSKI, MALKE	66	F	W	RRZZZZUSA
NENNCHE	20	F	UNKNOWN	RRZZZZUSA
LIEBE	19	F	UNKNOWN	RRZZZZUSA
ROSUK, ROCHEL	49	M	LABR	RRZZZZUSA
GAILEWICH, FEIGE	22	F	UNKNOWN	RRZZZZUSA
KRAMER, ESTHER	28	F	W	RRZZZZUSA
MERE	6	F	CHILD	RRZZZZUSA
BEILE	4	F	CHILD	RRZZZZUSA
ZLATE	.09	F	INFANT	RRZZZZUSA
KADISZKI, BAS	30	M	LABR	RRZZZZUSA
ROCHEL	4	F	CHILD	RRZZZZUSA
LEWIN, ABRAH.	23	M	LABR	RRZZZZUSA
BECKER, SELIG	35	M	LABR	RRZZZZUSA
RUBINOWITZ, SALOMON	37	M	LABR	RRZZZZUSA
DAVID, BARNY	35	M	LABR	RRZZZZUSA
SEIDEL, LEZER	16	M	LABR	RRZZZZUSA
KOHN, ROCHEL	16	M	LABR	RRZZZZUSA
CIEZNIESKA, AGNISKA	20	F	UNKNOWN	RRZZZZUSA
MICHALOWITZ, LEO	58	M	LABR	RRZZZZUSA
KANTOROTT, AGATA	22	F	UNKNOWN	RRZZZZUSA
PIESLAK, WAZLAW	28	M	LABR	RRZZZZUSA
MICHALOWIK, BENJ.	9	M	CHILD	RRZZZZUSA
RISKE, CHAJE	8	M	CHILD	RRZZZZUSA
BOWSEWITZ, LUDWIG	24	M	LABR	RRZZZZUSA
KOSAKEWITZ, JAN	25	M	LABR	RRZZZZUSA
ZIWINSKI, BOLESLAW	30	M	LABR	RRZZZZUSA
KATZ, RACHEL	53	F	W	RRZZZZUSA
MOSE	9	M	CHILD	RRZZZZUSA
LINA	7	F	CHILD	RRZZZZUSA
ERNA	5	F	CHILD	RRZZZZUSA
MARIA	3	F	CHILD	RRZZZZUSA

SHIP: STATE OF GEORGIA

FROM: GLASGOW AND LARNE
TO: NEW YORK
ARRIVED: 05 JULY 1888

PASSENGER	AGE	SEX	OCCUPATION	PRV VIL DES
BARABAA, ABRAHAM	28	M	PDLR	RRAIDLUSA
SONIE	19	F	W	RRAIDLUSA
BARANKAFSKY, BERE	17	F	SVNT	RRAIDLUSA
BONNE, RACHEL	23	F	UNKNOWN	RRAIDLUSA
BARTUSCHEWITZ, RODE	23	F	W	RRAIDLUSA
MASCHE	18	F	SVNT	RRAIDLUSA
SARAH	4	F	CHILD	RRAIDLUSA
ARON	.09	M	INFANT	RRAIDLUSA
BARDELOWITZ, WILH.	22	M	LABR	RRAIDLUSA
--TELON, GILBER	33	M	LABR	RRAIDLUSA
HANIZ, BOTH	27	M	LABR	RRAIDLUSA

PASSENGER	AGE	SEX	OCCUPATION	PRIV	VIL	DES
SCHARLOTA, GAB.	.03	F	INFANT	RR	AIDL	USA
REGINA, ROTH.	21	M	LABR	RR	AIDL	USA
MORITZ, GELB.	.03	F	INFANT	RR	AIDL	USA
KOLOMAN, BRUCK	24	M	LABR	RR	AIDL	USA
ZARCK, JOHEN	14	M	SVNT	RR	AIDL	USA
BAIN, ISAAC	18	M	LABR	RR	AIDL	USA
BERLINSKY, MORDSCHE	8	F	CHILD	RR	AIDL	USA
ISRAEL	51	M	PDLR	RR	ZZZZ	USA
DWORE	50	F	W	RR	ZZZZ	USA
REISSEL	14	M	BY	RR	ZZZZ	USA
RACHEL	10	F	CH	RR	ZZZZ	USA
BICHAKY, SCHALENS	20	M	PNTR	RR	ZZZZ	USA
BLANKFELD, ROCHE	18	F	SVNT	RR	ZZZZ	USA
BOWN, FEIWEL	22	M	LABR	RR	ZZZZ	USA
BRIMAR, JOSEPH	23	M	LABR	RR	ZZZZ	USA
BAKE	19	M	LABR	RR	ZZZZ	USA
BUTANSKY, R.	20	M	KEMK	RR	ZZZZ	USA
BRICKMANN, JOSELL	27	M	LABR	RR	ZZZZ	USA
LEIB	18	M	LABR	RR	ZZZZ	USA
JOSEL	18	M	LABR	RR	ZZZZ	USA
LARNER, CHAVE	17	F	SVNT	RR	ZZZZ	USA
CHAVES, ABRAHM	28	M	SHMK	RR	ZZZZ	USA
CHIVIDON, MALKE	17	F	SVNT	RR	ZZZZ	USA
CHAIN, SALOMON	39	M	TNM	RR	ZZZZ	USA
COHEN, DAVID	31	M	BCHR	RR	ZZZZ	USA
COHN, JACOB	40	M	PDLR	RR	ZZZZ	USA
DA--, U	32	F	SVNT	RR	ZZZZ	USA
DELATITSKY, JUDES	19	M	LABR	RR	ZZZZ	USA
ERZOWSKI, KIWE	19	M	CPTR	RR	ZZZZ	USA
FENISEW, MICHAEL	19	M	LABR	RR	ZZZZ	USA
SALK	18	M	LABR	RR	ZZZZ	USA
FLITTMANN, MAX	16	M	LABR	RR	ZZZZ	USA
FRIED, JACOB	20	M	LABR	RR	ZZZZ	USA
GLASER, LEIB	18	M	TLR	RR	ZZZZ	USA
GRANJANSKY, MORDSCHE	20	F	SVNT	RR	ZZZZ	USA
FEIGE	20	F	UNKNOWN	RR	ZZZZ	USA
GABERSKI, JOSEF	25	M	UNKNOWN	RR	ZZZZ	USA
GUTMAN, DAVID	19	M	UNKNOWN	RR	ZZZZ	USA
HENDLER, MOSCHE	20	M	LABR	RR	ZZZZ	USA
RACHEL	20	F	SVNT	RR	ZZZZ	USA
HERZETROWITZ, SARAH	17	F	SVNT	RR	ZZZZ	USA
HIRSCH, BARUCH	26	M	LABR	RR	ZZZZ	USA
JANATIS, MATZLIN	27	M	LABR	RR	ZZZZ	USA
MARATATZKI, MEYER	29	M	LABR	RR	ZZZZ	USA
JEALOWSKY, LEAH	48	F	W	RR	ZZZZ	USA
CHANE	9	F	CHILD	RR	ZZZZ	USA
PINKUS	50	M	SHMK	RR	ZZZZ	USA
ANNA	11	F	CH	RR	ZZZZ	USA
JOSEFSOHN, H.	35	M	LABR	RR	ZZZZ	USA
KOHMANSON, CHAJE	29	F	W	RR	ZZZZ	USA
SCHNEAN	5	M	CHILD	RR	ZZZZ	USA
RACHEL	1	F	CHILD	RR	ZZZZ	USA
ASSUNOWSKI, MENDEL	23	M	BKBNDR	RR	ZZZZ	USA
KANTOR	25	M	WCHMKR	RR	ZZZZ	USA
KAPLAN, WOLF	21	M	TLR	RR	ZZZZ	USA
ZIPPE	25	F	W	RR	ZZZZ	USA
SCHILIEN	2	M	CHILD	RR	ZZZZ	USA
SORE	1	M	CHILD	RR	ZZZZ	USA
KATSCHINSKY, SACHME	54	F	SVNT	RR	ZZZZ	USA
KATZEWSKY, ARON	22	M	SHMK	RR	ZZZZ	USA
RACHEL	25	F	SVNT	RR	ZZZZ	USA
KAZWINSKY, MATTHIAS	18	M	LABR	RR	ZZZZ	USA
KLEIMANN, JACHONAN	34	M	LABR	RR	ZZZZ	USA
KONKEWITSCH, MEYER	36	M	LABR	RR	ZZZZ	USA
KOPELSCHN, VICTOR	19	M	LABR	RR	ZZZZ	USA
KOWALLY, ANNA	17	F	SVNT	RR	ZZZZ	USA
KRAWITZ, ISAAC	16	M	PNTR	RR	ZZZZ	USA
CHAUNOWITZ, PINKOS	35	M	LABR	RR	ZZZZ	USA
LAIR, DAVID	17	M	SHMK	RR	AIDL	USA
LEHR, PERE	45	F	W	RR	AIDL	USA
BEILE	17	F	SVNT	RR	AIDL	USA
BEHR	11	M	BY	RR	AIDL	USA
ISAAC	9	M	CHILD	RR	AIDL	USA
LEHRNMANN, ABRAHAM	23	M	LABR	RR	AIDL	USA
LEWIEN, ARON	20	M	LABR	RR	AIDL	USA

PASSENGER	AGE	SEX	OCCUPATION	PRIV	VIL	DES
GITTEL	23	M	LABR	RR	AIDL	USA
LEWINSOHN, HIRSCH	42	M	BKBNDR	RR	AIDL	USA
LEWIT, NOACH	31	M	TLR	RR	AIDL	USA
LEIPZIG, MARIUS	40	M	LABR	RR	AIDL	USA
LEHR, NEHR	17	M	LABR	RR	AIDL	USA
LUBEROW, MOSCHE	26	M	LABR	RR	AIDL	USA
LUXENBURG, MOSES	25	M	LABR	RR	AIDL	USA
MARSCH, FROIE	55	F	W	RR	AIDL	USA
MOSES	7	M	CHILD	RR	AIDL	USA
MICHAWAR, CHAUN	17	M	LABR	RR	AIDL	USA
MERBLUM, FRIEDE	38	F	W	RR	AIDL	USA
LINA	16	F	SVNT	RR	AIDL	USA
MENDEL	2	M	CHILD	RR	AIDL	USA
MILNER, ITZIG	20	M	LABR	RR	AIDL	USA
KURCK, MALKE	33	F	W	RR	AIDL	USA
FEIGE	9	F	CHILD	RR	AIDL	USA
ESTER	4	F	CHILD	RR	AIDL	USA
NAHZAR, HIRSCH	54	M	TLR	RR	AIDL	USA
NAWETZKI, IWAN	30	M	SHMK	RR	AIDL	USA
NEWADOWSKI, MENDEL	40	M	TLR	RR	AIDL	USA
ORENSTEIN, CHAIE	24	F	SVNT	RR	AIDL	USA
CHAIE	50	F	W	RR	AIDL	USA
HITTEL	6	M	CHILD	RR	AIDL	USA
JANKEL	3	M	CHILD	RR	AIDL	USA
SAUCHE	11	F	CH	RR	AIDL	USA
CHAUN	1	M	CHILD	RR	AIDL	USA
OSCHEROWSKI, ABR.	18	M	PNTR	RR	AIDL	USA
PACKMANN, HIRSCH	19	M	LABR	RR	AIDL	USA
PACHTSCHAR, LEIBE	18	M	FARMER	RR	AIDL	USA
PALANSKI, ISAAC	20	M	LABR	RR	AIDL	USA
PODROFFSKY, ROCHE	19	F	SVNT	RR	AIDL	USA
PINA, ARON	30	M	TNM	RR	AIDL	USA
PERLMANN, ---HNE	27	M	CPTR	RR	AIDL	USA
U	20	M	CPTR	RR	AIDL	USA
PODGURNY, LORENZ	22	M	LABR	RR	AIDL	USA
RADUNSKY, SORE	20	F	SVNT	RR	AIDL	USA
RAKOWITSCH, LEISER	34	M	BCHR	RR	AIDL	USA
RIBISKY, BASCHE	30	F	W	RR	AIDL	USA
DAVID	10	M	CH	RR	AIDL	USA
FUERSCHE	9	F	CHILD	RR	AIDL	USA
CHAJE	.09	F	INFANT	RR	AIDL	USA
ROSENSTEIN, CHAJE	16	F	SVNT	RR	AIDL	USA
RIEBOCK, JACOB	30	M	LABR	RR	AIDL	USA
ROBJENSKY, ISRAEL	25	M	LABR	RR	AIDL	USA
KONLOWITZ, E.	25	F	SVNT	RR	AIDL	USA
RUBINSTEIN, MICHAEL	29	M	TLR	RR	AIDL	USA
RUBIN, TRADE	24	F	SVNT	RR	AIDL	USA
RUDISCHEWSKY, IDEL	23	M	PNTR	RR	AIDL	USA
SOPOTKINSKI, CHAJE	22	F	W	RR	AIDL	USA
U	1	F	CHILD	RR	AIDL	USA
LINDELMANN, U	37	M	TLR	RR	AIDL	USA
SCHAFFER, U	57	M	TLR	RR	AIDL	USA
CHAWA	38	F	W	RR	AIDL	USA
MIRA	18	F	SVNT	RR	AIDL	USA
MICHAEL	16	M	LABR	RR	AIDL	USA
MARCUS	3	M	CHILD	RR	AIDL	USA
LOTTA	2	F	CHILD	RR	AIDL	USA
DINA	.06	F	INFANT	RR	AIDL	USA
SCHAPIRA, JOSSEL	17	M	TLR	RR	AIDL	USA
HARRY	38	M	LABR	RR	AIDL	USA
SCHAUER, ANTON	37	M	PDLR	RR	AIDL	USA
U	10	M	CH	RR	AIDL	USA
SCHEINBERG, ALLE	29	F	W	RR	AIDL	USA
TAUBE	7	F	CHILD	RR	AIDL	USA
FEIGE	5	F	CHILD	RR	AIDL	USA
SCHLOME	3	F	CHILD	RR	AIDL	USA
SCHERMANN, KLARA	25	F	W	RR	AIDL	USA
DWORE	6	F	CHILD	RR	AIDL	USA
RACHEL	1	F	CHILD	RR	AIDL	USA
ACHIMOWITZ, S.	36	M	LABR	RR	AIDL	USA
SCHONERSOHN, ABRELI	30	M	LABR	RR	AIDL	USA
SCHULEIN, JEANETTE	18	F	SVNT	RR	AIDL	USA
U	00	M	LABR	RR	AIDL	USA
SEGALL, ABRAHAM	18	M	LABR	RR	AIDL	USA
ESTER	22	F	SVNT	RR	AIDL	USA

PASSENGER	AGE	SEX	OCCUPATION	PRV VIL DES
SIVIRSKY, SIMON	36	M	LABR	RRAIDLUSA
SKODSKI, LEISER	22	M	TLR	RRAIDLUSA
SKLOWSKY, DAVID	24	M	LABR	RRAIDLUSA
SPOLANSKY, SAMUEL	29	M	LABR	RRAIDLUSA
SRUBNIK, ISRAEL	25	M	LABR	RRAIDLUSA
STERN, CHAMINA	23	F	SVNT	RRAIDLUSA
SUSSMANN, LEIB	45	M	LABR	RRAIDLUSA
SUNDELOWITZ, BENZE	20	M	LABR	RRAIDLUSA
TABAKER, TRUNNE	26	F	SVNT	RRAIDLUSA
TORIK, SCHEIE	33	F	TLR	RRAIDLUSA
WAGNER, BERTHA	16	F	SVNT	RRAIDLUSA
WEGDEROWITZ, ESTER	24	F	W	RRAIDLUSA
DAVID	.03	M	INFANT	RRAIDLUSA
WEINER, ANNA	28	F	W	RRAIDLUSA
SARA	7	F	CHILD	RRAIDLUSA
FEIGE	5	F	CHILD	RRAIDLUSA
REISE	1	M	CHILD	RRAIDLUSA
WEISS, MAX	17	M	LABR	RRAIDLUSA
ZAVTOWIEZ, NICOLAY	28	M	LABR	RRAIDLUSA
ILM, IWAN	26	M	LABR	RRAIDLUSA
ZECHENOWITZ, FRANZISCHE	36	M	LABR	RRAIDLUSA

SHIP: CITY OF ROME

FROM: LIVERPOOL AND QUEENSTOWN
TO: NEW YORK
ARRIVED: 06 JULY 1888

PASSENGER	AGE	SEX	OCCUPATION	PRV VIL DES
STOLKER, FRAK	22	M	CGRMKR	RRADAXUSA
SCHIFFENHAUS, MORDE	31	M	LABR	RRADAXUSA
REINE	31	F	W	RRADAXUSA
JANKAL	.11	M	INFANT	RRADAXUSA
IRAD, ANNA	21	F	SVNT	RRADAXUSA
JUSTAFSON, P.	19	M	LABR	RRADAXUSA
IRE, JAKOB	45	M	LABR	RRADAXUSA
BACHMAN, KENRK.	24	M	LABR	RRADAXUSA
HANENBURG, LEIB	20	M	TLR	RRADAXUSA
SARAH	17	F	SVNT	RRADAXUSA
REISE	20	F	SVNT	RRADAXUSA
BJORK, ISRAEL	20	M	LABR	RRADAXUSA
WUKE, JAKOB	25	M	LABR	RRADAXUSA
WIRSOLA, IND.	21	M	LABR	RRADAXUSA
SOBUTZ, JOREF	23	M	LABR	RRADAXUSA
KJABVI, LIPE	19	M	BCHR	RRADAXUSA
RABINOWITZ, MINE	31	M	TLR	RRADAXUSA
KUPER, NOTHIM	26	M	SHMK	RRADAXUSA
BLAATNEK, SOLOMON	45	M	LABR	RRADAXUSA
POTASHNEK, LEID	18	F	SVNT	RRADAXUSA
JASGNE, JAKOB	27	M	LABR	RRADAXUSA
KJABVI, OSCHER	16	M	LABR	RRADAXUSA
MOSKOWITZ, ARON	32	M	LABR	RRADAXUSA
WILENSKY, JOSSEL	27	M	TLR	RRADAXUSA
HEPMSKI, FRANS	22	M	LABR	RRADAXUSA
MEINKA, S.	20	M	CPTR	RRADAXUSA
GREIZER, FRANKEL	17	M	CPTR	RRADAXUSA
HABEROWITZ, MICHL.	25	M	TLR	RRADAXUSA
HELPERN, ARON	26	M	LABR	RRADAXUSA
SCHPOSNIK, JAKOB	20	M	LABR	RRADAXUSA
SAKIR, TODUS	23	M	LABR	RRADAXUSA
SCHMUELSOHN, MODCHE	25	M	LABR	RRADAXUSA
WILIN, JAKOB	27	M	LABR	RRADAXUSA
SIMEINSKY, JAKOB	26	M	LABR	RRADAXUSA
FENSTEIN, MOCHEN	20	M	SHMK	RRADAXUSA
ESTER	18	F	W	RRADAXUSA
LIPPI, PIPI	20	F	SVNT	RRADAXUSA
ADOLF	10	M	CH	RRADAXUSA

SHIP: WESER

FROM: BREMEN
TO: BALTIMORE
ARRIVED: 07 JULY 1888

PASSENGER	AGE	SEX	OCCUPATION	PRV VIL DES
CIZESKI, STANISLAUS	20	M	NN	RRZZZZMD
BALIRMAS, JOHANN	15	M	NN	RRZZZZMD
HOCK, FERDINAND	34	M	PNTR	RRZZZZNE
ROSENBLUM, RACHEL	40	F	NN	RRAIILOH
TAUBE	17	F	NN	RRAIILOH
CHAJE	15	F	NN	RRAIILOH
LEIB	10	M	NN	RRAIILOH
LIEBE	8	F	CHILD	RRAIILOH
CHAJIM	7	M	CHILD	RRAIILOH
ROSE	5	F	CHILD	RRAIILOH
RAFALOWICZ, TROME	19	F	NN	RRAIILOH
OSTROWSKY, MALKE	45	F	NN	RRAIILIL
JACOB	10	M	CH	RRAIILIL
GITTE	.08	F	INFANT	RRAIILIL
GOLDSTEIN, TAUBE	20	F	NN	RRAIILIL
OSCHER	8	M	CHILD	RRAIILIL
SOLOVEY, SAYENE	29	F	NN	RRAIILIL
SLATE	9	M	CHILD	RRAIILIL
HIRSCH	7	M	CHILD	RRAIILIL
FANNY	5	F	CHILD	RRAIILIL
CEBULA, HANNAH	27	F	NN	RRAIILOH
WOLF	8	M	CHILD	RRAIILOH
JACOB	6	M	CHILD	RRAIILOH
CHAJE	3	F	CHILD	RRAIILOH
SUE	.08	F	INFANT	RRAIILOH
OSTROFSKY, CHAIA	24	F	INF	RRAIILOH
WOLF	.01	M	INFANT	RRAIILOH
HILBER, ISAAC	18	M	MCHT	RRAIILOH
HUBER, WILH.	26	M	MLR	RRAIILMN
CONSTANCE	36	F	NN	RRAIILMN
MAEDEL, OTTO	24	M	CNF	RRAIILIN
TABACK, ANDREAS	50	M	LABR	RRAIILIL
BLEMBERG, EMILIE	23	F	NN	RRAIILIL
RAUBA, NORBERT	43	M	LABR	RRAIILIL
LIEBENSTEIN, SAMUEL	20	M	PDLR	RRAIILMO
JENY	22	F	NN	RRAIILMO
RETUSCHINK, CHAJE	25	F	NN	RRAIILPA
WIRBULSKY, MENNSCHE	48	F	NN	RRAIILMD
HIRSCH	13	M	NN	RRAIILMD
BREINE	8	F	CHILD	RRAIILMD
GRAMS, AUGUST	22	M	FARMER	RRAIILNE
NEUMANN, LUDWIG	22	M	FARMER	RRAIILMN
MILANSIS, GEORG	21	M	LABR	RRAIILMD
CHAID, CHYE	20	M	TLR	RRAIILMD
REBENBLUT, ISAAC	17	M	WCHMKR	RRAIILPA
RABINEVIS, MEYER	50	M	MCHT	RRAIILPA
CHAJE	43	F	NN	RRAIILPA
ABRAHAM	8	M	CHILD	RRAIILPA
CZISZEWSKI, MICH.	38	M	LABR	RRAIILMD
WELLIWIS, PETER	36	M	LABR	RRAIILMD
ADAM	25	M	LABR	RRAIILMD
JAGODZINSKI, WOYECIECH	25	M	LABR	RRAIILMD
PALLIWODA, JOSEPH	32	M	LABR	RRAIILIL
WLADISLAW	5	M	CHILD	RRAIILIL
HELENA	3	F	CHILD	RRAIILIL
PIOTS	36	M	LABR	RRAIILIL
MAKIEWICZ, MAREIN	47	M	LABR	RRAIILIL
RABINOWICZ, PERETZ	42	M	LABR	RRAIILPA
TAUBE	17	F	NN	RRAIILPA
MILLER, JOHANN	33	M	FARMER	RRAIILOH
MARIE	32	F	NN	RRAIILOH
ZILZ, CARL	15	M	NN	RRAIILKS
MILLER, MARIE	3	F	CHILD	RRAIILOH
PELKE, HERMANN	21	M	FARMER	RRAIILOH
MORAWSKA, MARIANNA	25	F	NN	RRAIILVA
MACZKIEWITZ, MATHIAS	55	M	PDLR	RRAIILMO
EVA	55	F	NN	RRAIILMO
MASZKIEWICZ, JOSEFA	18	F	NN	RRAIILMO

PASSENGER	AGE	SEX	OCCUPATION	PRV VIL DES
FRANZ	14	M	NN	RRAIILMO
BAYNE, ROSINA	52	F	NN	RRAIILIL
TAUBE	14	F	NN	RRAIILIL
ESTER	11	F	NN	RRAIILIL
SARAH	9	F	CHILD	RRAIILIL
U	6	F	CHILD	RRAIILIL
SCHWARTZ, LEA	25	F	NN	RRAIILIL
ITZIGSOHN, RIWE	17	F	NN	RRAIILIL
LASEROW, MOSES	18	M	MCHT	RRAIILIL
TAUBE	17	F	NN	RRAIILIL
LESSER, SIMKE	40	F	NN	RRAIILMO
LIEBE	9	F	CHILD	RRAIILMO
OSCAR	5	M	CHILD	RRAIILMO
NECHAME	3	F	CHILD	RRAIILMO
LEWIN, RACHEL	25	F	CH	RRAIILIL
FEIGE	4	F	CHILD	RRAIILIL
DOEBRI, GERSON	42	M	PDLR	RRAIILOH
SCHWARTZ, IDA	20	F	NN	RRAIILMD
GLUECK, MALKE	26	F	NN	RRAIILMD
DANIEL	5	M	CHILD	RRAIILMD
ISAAC	3	M	CHILD	RRAIILMD
SCHARTZ, MERI	32	F	CH	RRAIILMD
LEA	7	F	CHILD	RRAIILMD
SCHWARTZ, ISAAC	3	M	CHILD	RRAIILMD
ESECK	.10	M	INFANT	RRAIILMD
SCHNEIDERMANN, BELE	12	F	CH	RRAIILMD
LEWINSOHN, CHANE	35	F	UNKNOWN	RRAIILOH
EISIG	11	M	CH	RRAIILOH
CHAJEM	10	F	CH	RRAIILOH
NATHAN	8	M	CHILD	RRAIILOH
ISAAC	.10	M	INFANT	RRAIILOH
SCHMUEKLER, PIMCHES	30	M	DLR	RRAIILPA
PARTNOI, MOSES	28	M	DLR	RRAIILPA
NEUDRISCH, HIRSCH	19	M	DLR	RRAIILPA

SHIP: ALLER

FROM: BREMEN AND SOUTHAMPTON
TO: NEW YORK
ARRIVED: 07 JULY 1888

PASSENGER	AGE	SEX	OCCUPATION	PRV VIL DES
NARUSCHEWSKY, FAVEL	28	M	FARMER	RRZZZZUSA
TSCHOERNER, GUST.	23	M	FARMER	RRZZZZUSA
RIPINSKI, ANTON	22	M	LABR	RRZZZZUSA
BUCHNER, WILH.	21	M	LABR	RRZZZZUSA
RIPS, ISAAK	22	M	FARMER	RRZZZZUSA
DENNER	26	M	LABR	RRZZZZUSA
ROSZKOWSKI, AUG.	40	M	FARMER	RRZZZZUSA
FREDREKSEN, BER.	26	M	FARMER	RRZZZZUSA
BAJKOWSKY, JOH.	31	M	FARMER	RRZZZZUSA
MILONIS, JAN	22	M	FARMER	RRZZZZUSA
RECHLIER, FERL	19	M	FARMER	RRZZZZUSA
HENNING, SALOMON	20	M	FARMER	RRZZZZUSA
DAYN, AMAND	56	M	FARMER	RRZZZZUSA
BUZANOWSKA, FRANCA.	18	F	NN	RRZZZZUSA
BLAZANIS, MARIE	18	F	NN	RRZZZZUSA
KUPELES, HELENE	17	F	NN	RRZZZZUSA
SCHWARZ, SOPHIE	25	F	NN	RRZZZZUSA
HEINR.	.11	M	INFANT	RRZZZZUSA
REBECCA	27	F	NN	RRZZZZUSA
BERNH.	4	M	CHILD	RRZZZZUSA
MATHILDE	1	F	CHILD	RRZZZZUSA
GASZINZYK, KATTI	24	F	CH	RRZZZZUSA
URSULA	.11	F	INFANT	RRZZZZUSA
AUTKOWSKY, ARILA	28	F	NN	RRZZZZUSA
ELWIS	7	F	CHILD	RRZZZZUSA
WISEK	.07	M	INFANT	RRZZZZUSA
LASEEMBERG, RACHEL	40	F	NN	RRZZZZUSA
JACOB	7	M	CHILD	RRZZZZUSA
JOHANNE	6	F	CHILD	RRZZZZUSA

SHIP: SORRENTO

FROM: HAMBURG
TO: NEW YORK
ARRIVED: 07 JULY 1888

PASSENGER	AGE	SEX	OCCUPATION	PRV VIL DES
BESCHINSKI, BENGAMIN	19	M	MCHT	RRZZZZNY
BRONSKY, CHAWE	45	M	MCHT	RRZZZZNY
NASCHE	39	F	W	RRZZZZNY
LENDER	15	M	CH	RRZZZZNY
ESTHER	16	F	CH	RRZZZZNY
REBECCA	9	F	CHILD	RRZZZZNY
BERTHA	4	F	CHILD	RRZZZZNY
LAUGEN, JACOB	26	M	LKSH	RRZZZZNY
JARMULOWITZ, JOH.	26	M	LABR	RRZZZZNY
ANDEROSKOWITZ, JOSEF	23	M	LKSH	RRZZZZNY
WENDSLOVA, ANTON	25	M	LABR	RRZZZZNY
SCHARAISAWSNI, IGNATZ	36	M	LABR	RRZZZZNY
GORODISCHT, ROZINA	25	F	SGL	RRZZZZNY
MUTKOWSKY, FRANZ	35	M	LABR	RRZZZZNY
RUBENSTEIN, JOHANNE	18	F	SGL	RRZZZZNY
BARTHAN, NATHAN	28	M	DLR	RRZZZZNY
CHAPON, MOSES	17	M	LABR	RRZZZZNY
MISKOWSKY, ESTER	50	F	WO	RRZZZZNY
MENDEL	16	F	WO	RRZZZZNY
ROCHEL	15	F	WO	RRZZZZNY
SLOVA	9	F	CHILD	RRZZZZNY
SIMCHI	8	M	CHILD	RRZZZZNY
WOLKA	6	F	CHILD	RRZZZZNY
OKUM, OSCHER	22	M	DLR	RRZZZZNY
NEIRMANN, MORDICHEL	20	F	W	RRZZZZNY
LAIBE	9	M	CHILD	RRZZZZNY
MENUCHE	7	F	CHILD	RRZZZZNY
ESTER	28	F	W	RRZZZZNY
LIBA	4	F	CHILD	RRZZZZNY
SARA	.06	F	INFANT	RRZZZZNY
SCHWARTMANN, ISRAEL	17	M	SHMK	RRZZZZNY
FRUMMER, ISAAC	40	M	LABR	RRZZZZNY
RIFKI	32	F	W	RRZZZZNY
CHAWE	6	M	CHILD	RRZZZZNY
SAITS, MOSES	22	M	LABR	RRZZZZNY
SIMONSEN, DAVID	30	M	LABR	RRZZZZNY
RUDOW, WOLF	25	M	LKSH	RRZZZZNY
ZIEHL, GOTTFRIED	23	M	LABR	RRZZZZNY
SZULAK, FEIGE	23	F	SGL	RRZZZZNY
LAVITZKI, FELIX	33	M	SHMK	RRZZZZNY
WAIZMANN, DAVID	20	M	DLR	RRZZZZNY
DORA	18	F	SGL	RRZZZZNY
SARGMANN, BENISCH	46	M	DLR	RRZZZZNY
ROSENBERG, RUWEL	20	M	LABR	RRZZZZNY
SARA	20	F	W	RRZZZZNY
PIRREY, GEORG	22	M	LABR	RRZZZZNY
KARSCHEL, GUSTAV	21	M	LABR	RRZZZZNY
DUTKEWITZ, JAN	24	M	LABR	RRZZZZNY
JUGELEWITZ, JAN	50	M	LABR	RRZZZZNY
SIEGEL, TAUBE	50	M	LABR	RRZZZZNY
BLUMBERG, MENDEL	28	M	LABR	RRZZZZNY
LEWINSON, HIRSCH	32	M	LABR	RRZZZZNY
BERLOWITZ, BENZE	34	M	LABR	RRZZZZNY
JORDAN, MARK	22	M	LABR	RRZZZZNY
GRUENSPAN, TAUBE	15	F	SGL	RRZZZZNY
GARBARSKI, MALKE	25	F	W	RRZZZZNY
MORRIS	4	M	CHILD	RRZZZZNY
LESSER	2	M	CHILD	RRZZZZNY
HORBAL, TEKLA	22	F	SGL	RRZZZZNY
BILIZNIEWSKY, JULIE	16	F	SGL	RRZZZZNY
WISSOTZKY, ISRAEL	18	M	LABR	RRZZZZNY
DANIEL, ABE	16	M	LABR	RRZZZZNY
BIALSKA, ANNA	19	F	SGL	RRZZZZNY
LIBORSKY, LIEBE	18	F	SGL	RRZZZZNY
MELACHOWSKI, JANKEL	45	M	DLR	RRZZZZNY
U, JOSSEL	30	M	GZR	RRZZZZNY
MOSELEWSKY, TAUBE	58	F	SGL	RRZZZZNY
FISCHMANN, SAMUEL	41	M	DLR	RRZZZZNY

PASSENGER	AGE	SEX	OCCUPATION	PRV VIL DES
KAPLAN, SALOMON	24	M	DLR	RRZZZZNY
GOLDBERG, KIWE	41	M	DLR	RRZZZZNY
-AWEZIK, U	28	M	SLR	RRZZZZNY
BARANKEWITZ, HERSCH	32	M	SLR	RRZZZZNY
GOLDSTEIN, WIGDER	24	M	TNM	RRZZZZNY
EFFER, ISRAEL	26	M	DLR	RRZZZZNY
KENDLER, BASCHE	20	F	SGL	RRZZZZNY
LAPOWITZ, SELDE	20	F	SGL	RRZZZZNY
NEUMANN, EWA	18	F	SGL	RRZZZZNY
STAVISKOFSKY, CHANNE	22	F	SGL	RRZZZZNY
FEIWE, JETTE	20	F	SGL	RRZZZZNY
STEINBERG, MEYER	18	M	DLR	RRZZZZIA
DINABURG, ISRAEL	30	M	DLR	RRZZZZNY
SEGALL, SARA	22	F	SGL	RRZZZZNY
MICHEL	9	M	CHILD	RRZZZZNY
GOTTFRIED, HIRSCH	30	M	LABR	RRZZZZNY
LEWIN, JUDEL	16	M	LABR	RRZZZZNY
NATELSCHN, MARIANNA	18	F	SGL	RRZZZZNY
KARPOWITZ, JONAS	25	M	LABR	RRZZZZNY
BABINOWITZ, ISRAEL	41	M	LABR	RRZZZZNY
LUBKOWITZ, SUSSMANN	40	M	LABR	RRZZZZNY
BIER, HANNE	22	F	SGL	RRZZZZNY
FRIEDMANN, KIEWE	42	M	LABR	RRZZZZNY
KELLERMANN, KERSCHEL	18	M	LABR	RRZZZZNY
STASZOWLA, HERSCH	50	M	LABR	RRZZZZNY
ARON	18	M	LABR	RRZZZZNY
UNROTH, NUTL	18	M	LABR	RRZZZZNY
GRUNHAUS, U	18	F	SGL	RRZZZZNY
ROSANSKY, ZIREL	19	M	LABR	RRZZZZNY
RIBAK, BEHR.	40	M	LABR	RRZZZZNY
PINKUS	9	M	CHILD	RRZZZZNY
BRICK, ITZKO	22	M	SLR	RRZZZZNY

SHIP: CATALONMIA

FROM: LIVERPOOL AND QUEENSTOWN
TO: BOSTON
ARRIVED: 09 JULY 1888

PASSENGER	AGE	SEX	OCCUPATION	PRV VIL DES
ARVOLA, HENRIK	32	M	LABR	RRZZZZUSA
WALLO, MARIA	19	F	SVNT	RRZZZZUSA
HAUTALA, CARL	40	M	LABR	RRZZZZUSA
HOHN, ALFRED	15	M	LABR	RRZZZZUSA
HAFAKAUGAS, ERIK	28	M	LABR	RRZZZZUSA
KERTTEE, JOHAN	20	M	LABR	RRZZZZUSA
KARFILA, MATTI	19	M	LABR	RRZZZZUSA
KUGAUPAA, GUST.	29	M	LABR	RRZZZZUSA
LAKTE, ANDREW	20	M	LABR	RRZZZZUSA
LEPPCKAGAS, MATTI	24	M	LABR	RRZZZZUSA
MAUGMANN, JACOB	19	M	LABR	RRZZZZUSA
MUSHKAMEN, JOH.	42	M	LABR	RRZZZZUSA
OGREN, MATS.	35	M	LABR	RRZZZZUSA
PERTRILA, JOH.	18	M	LABR	RRZZZZUSA
PIKKONES, MATHIAS	29	M	LABR	RRZZZZUSA
POCKHALM, JOH.	22	M	LABR	RRZZZZUSA
SOORREAR, JONAS	27	M	LABR	RRZZZZUSA
SIPILA, HUKKI	25	M	LABR	RRZZZZUSA
SWOM, KARL	20	M	LABR	RRZZZZUSA
SAARCLA, SAKOT	30	M	LABR	RRZZZZUSA
TAUSHALA, JOH.	37	M	LABR	RRZZZZUSA
ULFAES, ERIK	20	M	LABR	RRZZZZUSA
ASKUKARE, IDA	28	F	SVNT	RRZZZZUSA
SAARELA, MARIA	21	F	SVNT	RRZZZZUSA
SARKKMER, CATH.	22	F	SVNT	RRZZZZUSA
RAUHALD, LECUA	25	F	SVNT	RRZZZZUSA

SHIP: SERVIA

FROM: LIVERPOOL AND QUEENSTOWN
TO: NEW YORK
ARRIVED: 09 JULY 1888

PASSENGER	AGE	SEX	OCCUPATION	PRV VIL DES
RAKUSEN, ISAAC	15	M	LABR	RRADAXPA
GUTMAN	10	M	CH	RRADAXPA
BIRZANSKI, JOSEPH	24	M	CL	RRADAXNY
BLUDEN, MARCUS	35	M	LABR	RRAIFKNY
ISRAELSKY, MOSES	25	M	LABR	RRAIFKNY
MIRSKY, JOSEL	38	M	CL	RRAIFKNY
KAPLAN, BARUCH	22	M	LABR	RRAIFKNY
KLETZKIN, JACOB	26	M	TLR	RRAIFKNY
BONIS, MEYER	25	M	LABR	RRAIFKNY
SUSKIS, DAVID	46	M	BKR	RRAIFKNY
MALLER, CHAZKEL	30	M	LABR	RRAIFKNY
BRODSANSKY, JUDEL	20	M	LABR	RRAIFKNY
KAPCLOWITZ, MORDECAI	28	M	JNR	RRAIFKNY
ROSENBLOM, ABRAHAM	29	M	LABR	RRAIFKNY
SELIKOWSKI, DAVID	20	M	LABR	RRAIFKNY
GOLDMAN, ABRAHAM	20	M	MCHT	RRAIFKNY
ELPEROWITSCH, GREGOR	29	M	LABR	RRAIFKNY
JAKIESKY, MIHALY	32	M	LABR	RRAIFKNY
STEIN, IGNATZ	16	M	LABR	RRADAXNY
EMMANUEL	17	M	LABR	RRADAXNY
RESUMNI, SIMON	16	M	LABR	RRADAXNY
LEIBLOWICZ, SCHAGE	40	M	LABR	RRADAXNY
KAHN, WOLFF	36	M	BCHR	RRADAXNY
LUBER, DAVID	28	M	TLR	RRADAXNY
BERLOWITZ, NATHAN	38	M	TLR	RRADAXNY
KIRSCHENBAUM, SALOM	22	M	LABR	RRADAXNY
RUFF, DAVID	35	M	LABR	RRADAXNY
SPECKLER, BERL	30	M	CL	RRADAXNY
GEBBES, BERL	24	M	CL	RRADAXNY
AHONSON, CARL	26	M	LABR	RRADAXNY
FRANK, JACOB	34	M	TRVLR	RRADAXNY
GEROMIN, SALOMON	25	M	MCHT	RRADAXNY
ROSA	15	F	SP	RRADAXNY
FISCHANT, HANNE	21	F	SP	RRADAXNY
SUWENTISKI, ETTEL	16	F	SP	RRADAXNY
GORDON, CHYENE	29	F	SP	RRADAXNY
KRUBELNIK, FEIGE	17	F	SP	RRADAXNY
KUTNER, SITKA	6	F	CHILD	RRADAXNY
MILA	3	F	CHILD	RRADAXNY
ANOWSKI, ABRAHAM	40	M	LABR	RRADAXNY
REIVE	40	F	W	RRADAXNY
ISER	11	M	CH	RRADAXNY
BEILLE	11	F	UNKNOWN	RRADAXNY
SZYPPE	9	F	CHILD	RRADAXNY
SANCLOWITZ, ZACHARIAS	55	M	TLR	RRADAXNY
SARA	50	F	W	RRADAXNY
JANKEL	16	M	LABR	RRADAXNY
ETTEL	14	F	SP	RRADAXNY
HEIMANN, MINE	32	M	MA	RRADAXNY
FEIGE	7	F	CHILD	RRADAXNY
DABIE	3	F	CHILD	RRADAXNY
KAPLAN, CHAJE	25	F	MA	RRADAXNY
ABRAHAM	.07	M	INFANT	RRADAXNY
HIRSCHWITZ, PHILIPP	25	M	LABR	RRADAXNY
JOHNNA	20	F	W	RRADAXNY
KUTNER, INGA	40	F	MA	RRADAXPA
FEIVELMANN, EFRAIM	42	M	CL	RRADAXPA
PERLE	26	F	W	RRADAXPA
GITEL	11	F	CH	RRADAXPA
MEIER	10	M	CH	RRADAXPA
RAHEL	7	F	CHILD	RRADAXPA
MASCHE	3	F	CHILD	RRADAXPA
MOSES	2	M	CHILD	RRADAXPA
LEIB	.07	M	INFANT	RRADAXPA
ISTRANKIS, JOHN	25	M	LABR	RRADAXPA

SHIP: OHIO

FROM: LIVERPOOL AND QUEENSTOWN
TO: NEW YORK
ARRIVED: 09 JULY 1888

PASSENGER	AGE	SEX	OCCUPATION	PRV VIL DES
ASIGIWIEZ, S.	21	M	LABR	PLZZZZUNK
BLACHMANN, J.	23	M	LABR	RRZZZZNY
BASCHEL, M.	32	M	LABR	PLZZZZNY
BLECHOVSKI, B.	18	M	LABR	PLZZZZNY
BARONOWSK, W.	20	M	LABR	PLZZZZNY
CZISKA, J.	46	M	LABR	PLZZZZPA
CZALLALA, A.	22	M	LABR	PLZZZZPA
DOBRATZOVA, ELIE	20	F	SVNT	PLZZZZNY
HOOLGO, P.	25	M	LABR	PLZZZZNY
HOLZ, A.	25	M	LABR	PLZZZZNY
PEZIERKI, F.	36	M	LABR	PLZZZZNY
THELKA	35	F	W	PLZZZZNY
A.	.07	F	INFANT	PLZZZZNY
KERSCHNER, MAL.	22	F	W	PLZZZZNY
G.	.08	F	INFANT	PLZZZZNY
KAWINSKI, NIKE	25	F	W	PLZZZZNY
ABR.	4	M	CHILD	PLZZZZNY
P.	.06	F	INFANT	PLZZZZNY
KOSSEHMANN, F.	36	M	LABR	PLZZZZNY
LEBORWITZ, C.	18	M	LABR	PLZZZZNY
LAMERSDORF, LEWGEN	16	F	SVNT	PLZZZZPA
B.	11	M	CH	PLZZZZPA
F.	9	F	CHILD	PLZZZZPA
G.	8	M	CHILD	PLZZZZPA
LENOMSKY, SAM	17	M	LABR	PLZZZZNY
LEIBISKY, A.	18	M	LABR	PLZZZZNY
CHANE	22	F	SVNT	PLZZZZNY
MECK, CACILIE	20	M	LABR	PLZZZZNY
PAASELA, GUSTA	27	F	W	PLZZZZNY
ANNA	7	F	CHILD	PLZZZZNY
GUSTA	4	F	CHILD	PLZZZZNY
MARIA	.10	F	INFANT	PLZZZZNY
POAUSKEWIEZ, P.	20	M	LABR	PLZZZZNY
PESTLG, MARI	48	F	W	PLZZZZNY
P.	6	M	CHILD	PLZZZZNY
PERETZ, SCHIL	18	M	LABR	PLZZZZMT
PINKUS, SARA	18	F	SVNT	PLZZZZNY
ROGASCHASSKE, B.	18	M	LABR	PLZZZZOH
RAZLEWITZ, P.	28	M	LABR	PLZZZZNY
SCHUBACK, G.	34	M	LABR	PLZZZZNY
SIELE, F.	46	M	LABR	PLZZZZPA
SCHOLT, JON	28	M	LABR	PLZZZZPA
SPITALNA, J.	20	M	LABR	PLZZZZNY
SALEWITZ, L.	11	M	CH	PLZZZZNY
STEFAN, M.	33	M	LABR	PLZZZZPA
SAHOLSKE, J.M.	18	M	LABR	PLZZZZNY
LUDAR, MARIA	20	F	SVNT	PLZZZZNY
ABRAM	1	M	CHILD	RRACBFUSA
SEGALOWSKY, HIRSCH	16	M	PDLR	RRACBFUSA
WOLF	19	M	PDLR	RRACBFUSA
LAUFER, ABRAM-H.	20	M	LABR	RRAICFUSA
PFEIFFER, JOSEF	25	M	PDLR	RRACBFUSA
FINKELSTEIN, J.F.	21	M	LABR	RRACBFUSA
RASTENBAUM, NOCHEM	20	M	PDLR	RRACBFUSA
LUDMAN, JULIUS	24	M	PDLR	RRACBFUSA
RUBENSTEIN, JACOB	29	M	TCHR	RRACBFUSA
BORKOWSKI, SOLOMON	20	M	TLR	RRACBFUSA
SCHAPIRA, LEISER-T.	41	M	LABR	RRACBFUSA
RABINOWITZ, SCH.	46	M	PDLR	RRACBFUSA
WORCELIEWSKY, ZISSEL	18	M	SHMK	RRACBFUSA
SABRONITZI, PALTIE	33	M	BCHR	RRACBFUSA
JACOBSOHN, DEWIS	21	M	SMH	RRACBFUSA
POLLACK, LEIB	17	M	LABR	RRACBFUSA
NELZAR, MORDCHE	20	M	SHMK	RRACBFUSA
ABRAHAM, JANKEL	16	M	BCHR	RRACBFUSA
BLAUFEDER, MOSES	45	M	TLR	RRACBFUSA
KINOWITZ, JOSSEL	29	M	DLR	RRAHTUUSA
RUPERSTEIN, TOBIAS	40	M	TLR	RRACBFUSA
LISWAK, SCHLOME	49	M	TLR	RRACBFUSA
WOLFF, FUCHS	26	M	PDLR	RRAFWJUSA
BRENDER, CHASE	18	F	NN	RRACBFUSA
EDELMAN, SCHEINE	24	F	NN	RRACBFUSA
KLEIN, ESTER-BEHR	20	F	NN	RRACBFUSA
POSTON, LARS-GISEL	20	F	NN	RRACBFUSA
SINCY, SPRINZE	18	F	NN	RRACBFUSA
ROSENBLUM, CHERE	19	F	NN	RRACBFUSA
BRANDO, OLGA	24	F	NN	RRACBFUSA
SZUMIGALA, ANAST.	27	F	NN	RRACBFUSA
MARIAN	6	F	CHILD	RRACBFUSA
ANTONIE	5	F	CHILD	RRACBFUSA
HANKELESCHKE, SARAH	38	F	CH	RRACBFUSA
SISSE	17	F	CH	RRACBFUSA
DANIEL	10	M	CH	RRACBFUSA
BOGOTAWSKY, FREIDE	22	F	NN	RRACBFUSA
SORE	2	F	CHILD	RRACBFUSA
RESI	1	F	CHILD	RRACBFUSA
SULVIKOPKI, MARIAN	26	M	NN	RRACBFUSA
JOSEF	2	M	CHILD	RRACBFUSA
MARIAN	1	F	CHILD	RRACBFUSA
SZEWITZ, JOHAN	45	M	LABR	RRACBFUSA
JOSEPH	11	M	CH	RRACBFUSA
PUTRUSCHKE, ESTER	28	F	NN	RRACBFUSA
FEIGE	1	F	CHILD	RRACBFUSA
MEDWECZ, ANNA	20	F	HP	RRACBFUSA
MARIA	14	F	UNKNOWN	RRACBFUSA
POPLAWSKY, ANTON	35	M	LABR	RRZZZZUSA
ASSAREWEK, ALEX	38	M	LABR	RRZZZZUSA
BUTOWSKI, JOHAN	34	M	LABR	RRZZZZUSA
DUBISCH, MICH.	30	M	LABR	RRAEABUSA
PADZINSKI, ADAM	40	M	LABR	RRZZZZUSA
LIPMAN, CHAJE-R.	16	F	HP	RRACBFUSA

SHIP: ANCHORIA

FROM: GLASGOW AND MOVILLE
TO: NEW YORK
ARRIVED: 09 JULY 1888

PASSENGER	AGE	SEX	OCCUPATION	PRV VIL DES
BRANEY, CHAJE-LEA	32	F	NN	RRZZZZUSA
ABRAM	7	M	CHILD	RRZZZZUSA
MENNE-C.	4	F	CHILD	RRZZZZUSA
BEHR	2	F	CHILD	RRACBFUSA
RUBINSTEIN, FEIGE	50	F	NN	RRACBFUSA
JACOB	10	M	CH	RRACBFUSA
SARAH	8	F	CHILD	RRACBFUSA
LEWY, HENNE	23	F	CH	RRACBFUSA
ARON	2	M	CHILD	RRACBFUSA

SHIP: MORAVIA

FROM: HAMBURG AND HAVRE
TO: NEW YORK
ARRIVED: 09 JULY 1888

PASSENGER	AGE	SEX	OCCUPATION	PRV VIL DES
PNSKY, AMALIE	25	F	WO	RRAEFLUSA
WILH	3	M	CHILD	RRAEFLUSA
ALEXANDER	.11	M	INFANT	RRAEFLUSA
JESERSKY, LEWIK	29	M	WRT	RRAEFLUSA
MARIE	25	F	W	RRAEFLUSA
LINA	2	F	CHILD	RRAEFLUSA
EMMA	.03	F	INFANT	RRAEFLUSA
KAHANA, FREIDE	23	F	SGL	RRZZZZUSA
WEINSTOCK, MORITZ	17	M	TLR	RRZZZZUSA

PASSENGER	AGE	SEX	OCCUPATION	PRV VIL DES
LEICHTER, SCHLOME	51	M	MCHT	RRAHUVUSA
DUBIN, MOSES	25	M	SHMK	RRAHTBUSA
KRUG, MORITZ	20	M	DLR	RRAHTBUSA
NEUMANN, DAVID	25	M	LABR	RRZZZZUSA
KARNAUSKY, ROSA	21	F	WO	RRAHTFUSA
REBECCA	.11	F	INFANT	RRAHTFUSA
PINKELSTEIN, CHAIM	18	M	LABR	RRZZZZUSA
STARK, MARIE	32	F	WO	FNZZZZUSA
MARG.	9	F	CHILD	FNZZZZUSA
HIEKKILA, MATTI	20	M	LABR	FNZZZZUSA
HERLEVI, SOFIE	33	F	SGL	FNZZZZUSA
HUHTELIN, HILDA	22	F	SGL	FNZZZZUSA
PIETILA, ALEXANDER	20	M	LABR	FNZZZZUSA
PAUTTILA, ISAK	40	M	LABR	FNAIJHUSA
NEMQUIST, VICTOR	41	M	LABR	FNAIJHUSA
FUISKULA, JACOB	38	M	LABR	FNAIJHUSA
OJALA, JOH.	27	M	LABR	FNAIJHUSA
JOSEFINE	27	F	W	FNAIJHUSA
MARIE	.06	F	INFANT	FNAIJHUSA
NIKONEN, KRISTINE	20	F	SGL	FNZZZZUSA
JOHANNE	24	F	SGL	FNZZZZUSA
SORONEN, KARL	20	M	LABR	FNZZZZUSA
EISENSTADT, HEINR.	36	M	MCHT	FNAFVGUSA
PERSF, ISAAK	36	M	BKR	FNAFVGUSA
ESTES, MOSES	47	M	MCHT	FNAFVGUSA
SOFIA	42	F	W	FNAFVGUSA
LEON	16	M	CH	FNAFVGUSA
JACOB	14	M	CH	FNAFVGUSA
MAMSTOFF, FISCHEL	42	M	MCHT	FNAFVGUSA
FRIEDLAND, DORA	18	F	SGL	RRZZZZUSA
BLUMENFELD, ERNEST	24	M	SGL	RRZZZZUSA
HAUDKE, JULIANE	17	F	SGL	RRAHTFUSA
KORPAS, CHAIE	22	F	SGL	RRAHTFUSA
PESCHE	17	F	SGL	RRAHTFUSA
ROSA	9	F	CHILD	RRAHTFUSA
JACOB	8	M	CHILD	RRAHTFUSA
GORFINKEL, FEIGE	20	F	SGL	RRZZZZUSA
KRAUTZ, SCHEWE	22	F	WO	RRAFWJUSA
SALOMON	6	M	CHILD	RRAFWJUSA
ROSA	4	F	CHILD	RRAFWJUSA
SCHWEFELBLUM, MALKE	25	F	WO	RRAFWJUSA
MANDELKORN, PAULINE	25	F	WO	RRAHVUUSA
LISE	4	F	CHILD	RRAHVUUSA
PARADOWSKI, IWAN	18	M	LABR	RRAHUIUSA
SPYCHOWSKA, APOLLONIA	22	F	WO	RRACTCUSA
FRANCISCA	3	F	CHILD	RRACTCUSA
EDUARD	.11	M	INFANT	RRACTCUSA
BROT, ZULKIND	42	M	DLR	RRAINFUSA
MATSCHUNAS, BALTRAS	24	M	LABR	RRZZZZUSA
SEKLAMBERG, DEBORA	18	F	W	RRZZZZUSA
SCHEFFLER, JOH.	24	F	SGL	RRAHZSUSA
ADELINE	23	F	SGL	RRAHZSUSA
EDUARD	9	M	CHILD	RRAHZSUSA
RUTKOWSKI, BONIFACI	45	M	LABR	RRAHZSUSA
HELENE	40	F	W	RRAHZSUSA
ANTONIA	15	F	CH	RRAHZSUSA
JOSEF	9	M	CHILD	RRAHZSUSA
BONI.	.09	M	INFANT	RRAHZSUSA
ABELOW, BARUCH	19	M	DLR	RRAHZSUSA
GIETEL	50	F	LABR	RRAHZSUSA
FACKEL, RACHEL	46	F	WO	RRAHZSUSA
PAULINE	19	F	SGL	RRAHZSUSA
CHOLADENKI, ZIPE	27	F	WO	RRAIOOUSA
ABR.	4	M	CHILD	RRAIOOUSA
CHURGIN, SCHEINE	16	F	SGL	RRZZZZUSA
MEYERSOHN, MOSES	25	M	LABR	RRAHTFUSA
STIEZENICKI, ABR.	41	M	LABR	RRZZZZUSA
SOPHIE	37	F	W	RRZZZZUSA
PESSE	7	F	CHILD	RRZZZZUSA
BABER, SZUL	31	M	LABR	RRAIOOUSA
SZERMANN, HENOCH	25	M	LABR	RRAIOOUSA
WEINER, SZUL	36	M	LABR	RRAIOOUSA
SCHNEIDMANN, MORDCHE	31	M	LABR	RRZZZZUSA
KATZ, JANKEL	36	M	TLR	RRZZZZUSA
ZOLANSKI, REISEL	20	F	SGL	RRAHTFUSA
JANKELSOHN, RACHEL	15	F	SGL	RRAGRTUSA
BOROCH	9	M	CHILD	RRAGRTUSA
LEWIN, LEA	15	F	SGL	RRAHTUUSA
SIMON	9	M	CHILD	RRAHTUUSA
DAVID, KOHANNE	34	M	LABR	RRZZZZUSA
GRUENBERG, LISCHE	34	M	LABR	RRZZZZUSA
WOJCICECH, BARNA	29	M	LABR	RRZZZZUSA
MARKOWITZ, NISSEL	26	M	LABR	RRAHZSUSA
JOSSEL	9	M	CHILD	RRAHZSUSA
SCHEPSEL	9	M	CHILD	RRAHZSUSA
WENGROWSKY, LEGA	30	F	WO	RRAHRZUSA
HIRSCH	8	M	CHILD	RRAHRZUSA
SARA	6	F	CHILD	RRAHRZUSA
LEIB	4	M	CHILD	RRAHRZUSA
BRECKSTEIN, ESTER	17	F	SGL	RRAHRZUSA
RECHANE	8	M	CHILD	RRAHTQUSA
WASELOWSKA, HEINR.	30	M	LABR	RRAIMBUSA
POLLAK, GITTEL	30	F	WO	RRAIMBUSA
MINKE	9	F	CHILD	RRAIMBUSA
JUDE	5	F	CHILD	RRAIMBUSA
BERL	3	F	CHILD	RRAIMBUSA
KELE, JECHIEL	20	M	DLR	RRAHUSUSA
SIDELNIK, SARA	38	F	WO	RRZZZZUSA
WELWEL	9	F	CHILD	RRZZZZUSA
CHANNE	7	F	CHILD	RRZZZZUSA
KEILE	4	F	CHILD	RRZZZZUSA
NOSSEM	.11	F	INFANT	RRZZZZUSA
KOHAN, RIWKE	25	F	WO	RRAIBOUSA
JOSSEL	7	M	CHILD	RRAIBOUSA
DWORSCHE	5	F	CHILD	RRAIBOUSA
SVHOENBAUM, TAUBE	17	F	SGL	RRZZZZUSA
STOLDITZKI, ELKE	9	F	CHILD	RRZZZZUSA
SCHAPIRO, LIPE	9	F	CHILD	RRZZZZUSA
JUDELNITZKY, SOSCHE	18	F	SGL	RRZZZZUSA
BERBMAN, LEISER	45	M	LABR	RRAHSPUSA
CZICHOWSKI, ANNA	35	F	WO	RRAHVUUSA
RIVE	16	F	CH	RRAHVUUSA
WENWEL	7	F	CHILD	RRAHVUUSA
RACKEL	5	F	CHILD	RRAHVUUSA
DINAS, DINA	24	F	WO	RRAHQUUSA
CLARA	.11	F	INFANT	RRAHQUUSA
WOLF, IDA	22	F	WO	RRAHQUUSA
SALOMON	.11	M	INFANT	RRAHQUUSA
MARKIN, EPHRAIM	9	M	CHILD	RRAHQUUSA
STANEIKA, ANNA	20	F	SGL	RRAHZSUSA
SLAVINSKI, HERSCH	55	M	DLR	RRAHZSUSA
GOLDE	50	F	W	RRAHZSUSA
HINDE	18	F	D	RRAHZSUSA
OTT, WILH.	36	M	CPTR	RRAHTKUSA
WILMANSKI, ANTON	43	M	JNR	RRZZZZUSA
GILDE, ALBERT	16	M	STDNT	RRZZZZUSA
SCHWARZ, ADOLF	43	M	SHMK	RRAHUIUSA
GRAJEWSKI, STANISL.	23	M	TLR	RRAHZSUSA
HEYDEMANN, AUGUSTE	40	F	WO	RRAHZSUSA
NARKEWICZ, LUDWIG	20	M	LABR	RRZZZZUSA
FUDELSOHN, JANKEL	17	M	LABR	RRAHTFUSA
EISERIG, MARKUS	48	M	LABR	RRAIFRUSA
FEIGE	16	F	D	RRAIFRUSA
SCHAPIRO, LENA	28	F	WO	RRZZZZUSA
ANNA	4	F	CHILD	RRZZZZUSA
SUSEL	3	F	CHILD	RRZZZZUSA
KALMAN	.09	M	INFANT	RRZZZZUSA
BERNBERG, MAX	18	M	TLR	RRAIINUSA
WESATOWSKA, LUDWIKA	18	F	SGL	RRAIIRUSA
NICODEM	16	M	LABR	RRAIIRUSA
WILSLOW, NIC	17	M	LABR	RRAIFTUSA
MARANIAK, KATH.	16	F	SGL	RRZZZZUSA
MOSKOWITZ, MINNA	22	F	SGL	RRZZZZUSA
SALDUK, MATH.	19	M	LABR	RRZZZZUSA
GLUSGOLD, FEIWICH	37	M	LABR	RRAIOOUSA
BEHRMANN, CHR.	19	M	LABR	RRZZZZUSA
GERSCHEN, FEINGOLD	34	M	LABR	RRAILYUSA
MOSES, ROSEN	24	M	LABR	RRZZZZUSA
SCHWARTZMAN, RUBEN	27	M	LABR	RRZZZZUSA
EPSTEIN, CHAIM	30	M	LABR	RRZZZZUSA

PASSENGER	AGE	SEX	OCCUPATION	PRV VIL DES
BRILAWSKY, SIMON	28	M	LABR	RRZZZZUSA
SERMULEWICZ, ANDRZEY	53	M	LABR	RRZZZZUSA
MARKIELIS, ANDRZEY	38	M	LABR	RRZZZZUSA
PIKUS, TOMAS	36	M	LABR	RRAHZSUSA
ZANOWICZ, MIHAEL	33	M	LABR	RRAHZSUSA
ZIELANIS, ANTON	27	M	LABR	RRAHZSUSA
KIJEWSKY, ANDRZEY	28	M	LABR	RRAHZSUSA

SHIP: ARIZONA

FROM: LIVERPOOL AND QUEENSTOWN
TO: NEW YORK
ARRIVED: 09 JULY 1888

PASSENGER	AGE	SEX	OCCUPATION	PRV VIL DES
KUNNARI, TAPANI	26	M	PNTR	RRAGUZUSA
SELKAATO, AUTTI	27	M	PNTR	RRAGUZUSA
KYLLONER, SIGFRID	31	M	ART	RRAGUZUSA
ROSENTHAL, LEA-R.	25	F	W	RRACBFUSA
CHAJIM	5	F	CHILD	RRACBFUSA
JOSIFER, L.	25	M	PNTR	RRACBFUSA
MITSCOOSKY, SHEA-M.	30	M	FARMER	RRACBFUSA
SIZEBRIER, EIDE	30	F	W	RRACBFUSA
LEA	11	F	CH	RRACBFUSA
ROCHEL	9	F	CHILD	RRACBFUSA
JANKEL	7	M	CHILD	RRACBFUSA
MOESCHA	3	F	CHILD	RRACBFUSA
SOLLENER, WOLF	.10	M	INFANT	RRACBFUSA
SIZEBRIER, NECHOME	31	F	W	RRACBFUSA
JITZCHOK	9	M	CHILD	RRACBFUSA
KAMINSKI, LEIBE	27	M	ART	RRACBFUSA
PINSBURG, MARIASCHE	00	F	W	RRACBFUSA
MENDEL	4	M	CHILD	RRACBFUSA
HOTKIN, JOSEPH	20	M	FLABR	RRACBFUSA
DAWDROWITZ, FANNY	17	F	SP	RRACBFUSA
TIRSCHWELL, SINCHE	43	M	SMH	RRACBFUSA
SCHREIBER, CHAIE	10	F	CH	RRACBFUSA
NAVOHR, SUSANNE	15	F	SP	RRACBFUSA
GEORG	11	M	CH	RRACBFUSA
SODERBRACK, JOSEF-H.	26	M	JNR	RRAGUZUSA
BOLING, JOHAN-S.	43	M	ART	RRAGUZUSA
BERNAS, JOHAN	18	M	LABR	RRAGUZUSA
HEIKFOEN, MATTS	19	M	LABR	RRAGUZUSA
WIKSTROM, FREDRIK	15	M	LABR	RRAGUZUSA
KJELLMAR, JOHAN	23	M	MSN	RRAGUZUSA
FORSBACKA, HENRIK	19	M	LABR	RRAGUZUSA
MINDERS, JAKOB	34	M	PNTR	RRAGUZUSA
KAPALONEIN, ANANIAS	22	M	JNR	RRAGUZUSA
WELKE, EDWARD	35	M	BKR	RRAGUZUSA
HAKLIN, JAKOB	28	M	PNTR	RRAGUZUSA
ULLVILA, JOHAN	36	M	FTR	RRAGUZUSA
NORDBACH, KAREL	27	M	BCHR	RRAGUZUSA
TOMASCHEK, THOMAS	26	M	ART	RRACBFUSA
EIDENBAUM, BREINE	22	F	SP	RRACBFUSA
OCH, VITALIS	22	M	LABR	RRACBFUSA
HOLDMIKE, HERSCH	41	M	CPTR	RRACBFUSA
RIFKE	24	F	W	RRACBFUSA
CHARE	.11	F	INFANT	RRACBFUSA
POLITINSKY, ZIPPE	40	F	W	RRACBFUSA
ISAAC	11	M	CH	RRACBFUSA
F.	7	M	CHILD	RRACBFUSA
ROFKE	3	F	CHILD	RRACBFUSA
ELTIE	2	F	CHILD	RRACBFUSA
KALLMANN, ABRAHAM	50	M	ART	RRACBFUSA
SOLOMAN	14	M	LABR	RRACBFUSA
ILKE	10	M	CH	RRACBFUSA
LOFFLER, MARITZ	16	M	LABR	RRACBFUSA
BONDMEH, ISAAC	33	M	MECH	RRACBFUSA
POLDE	31	F	W	RRACBFUSA
TAUBE	11	F	CH	RRACBFUSA
MARIA	7	F	CHILD	RRACBFUSA
FEIGE	6	M	CHILD	RRACBFUSA
ETTY	6	F	CHILD	RRACBFUSA
BRUCHE	4	F	CHILD	RRACBFUSA
BENZION	.11	M	INFANT	RRACBFUSA
SAMUEL	.02	M	INFANT	RRACBFUSA
KISKOWSKA, CHAVE	16	F	SP	RRACBFUSA
SCHENECK, MARTIN	37	M	PRNTR	RRACBFUSA
KRENES, ELLI	54	M	SDLR	RRACBFUSA
NALEZNY, PAWEL	29	M	LABR	RRACBFUSA
SEIDMAN, MAKE	37	F	W	RRACBFUSA
JACOB	16	M	LABR	RRACBFUSA
SARA	10	F	CH	RRACBFUSA
JUDEL	7	F	CHILD	RRACBFUSA
SIMON	.10	M	INFANT	RRACBFUSA
SAMUEL	.10	M	INFANT	RRACBFUSA
MEIEROWITZ, NOCHEM	25	M	JNR	RRACBFUSA
KAHN, LEON	20	M	LABR	RRACBFUSA
KNOPERMAN, GEDALIE	20	M	LABR	RRACBFUSA
MAZOWSKY, BEILE	21	F	SP	RRACBFUSA
HOFENBERG, CHAIE	19	F	SP	RRACBFUSA
SEIDMANN, DAVID	17	M	LABR	RRACBFUSA
ALPER, DAVID	20	M	LABR	RRACBFUSA
LELIKOWITZ, SCHAIE	29	M	BKLYR	RRACBFUSA
SCHPIRO, SIMON	20	M	SHPMN	RRACBFUSA
HIRSCHKOWITZ, ISAC	39	M	MECH	RRACBFUSA
BERMAN, BORIS	26	M	PMBR	RRACBFUSA
RABINOWITZ, SORE	26	F	SP	RRACBFUSA
KOPULEWITZ, ISAAC	18	M	LABR	RRACBFUSA
SZERE-SER, DAVID	.10	M	INFANT	RRACBFUSA
GINZBURG, JAHER	.03	M	INFANT	RRACBFUSA

SHIP: LEERDAM

FROM: ROTTERDAM
TO: NEW YORK
ARRIVED: 10 JULY 1888

PASSENGER	AGE	SEX	OCCUPATION	PRV VIL DES
GRAMERY, ANREL	21	F	MCHT	RRZZZZUSA
LIBSKY, GIRSCH	16	F	MCHT	RRZZZZUSA
SENTA, M	30	F	MCHT	RRZZZZUSA
-LLURIN, JAN	40	F	MCHT	RRZZZZUSA
MOJOZEJEM, SAL	28	F	MCHT	RRZZZZUSA
PEREL	20	F	MCHT	RRZZZZUSA
PAULINE	.03	F	INFANT	RRZZZZUSA
FINKELSTEIN, ABRAH	24	M	INF	RRZZZZUSA
KRUMBOCH, FERD	17	M	LABR	RRZZZZUSA
DUDA, A	26	M	LABR	RRZZZZUSA
MAJCHRZYCHI, M	20	M	LABR	RRZZZZUSA
-ORMANE-, JOS	24	M	LABR	RRZZZZUSA
-IPERKA, JAN	30	M	LABR	RRZZZZUSA
HERM	33	F	NN	RRZZZZUSA
ANNA	10	F	CH	RRZZZZUSA
PAULINE	6	F	CHILD	RRZZZZUSA
MARIA	3	F	CHILD	RRZZZZUSA
MINKA	1	F	CHILD	RRZZZZUSA
MARIANNA	17	F	NN	RRZZZZUSA
KAROLINA	.01	F	INFANT	RRZZZZUSA
AUSTRAVOC, PATROP	25	M	MCHT	RRZZZZUSA
MICHAEL, DAVID	22	M	LABR	RRZZZZUSA
NATHAN	21	M	LABR	RRZZZZUSA
SCHWARZ, M	35	M	LABR	RRZZZZUSA
WILDER, LEITER	30	M	LABR	RRZZZZUSA
BEILER, SCHMULL	27	M	LABR	RRZZZZUSA

SHIP: EIDER

FROM: BREMEN AND SOUTHAMPTON
TO: NEW YORK
ARRIVED: 10 JULY 1888

PASSENGER	AGE	SEX	OCCUPATION	PRI	VL	DES
LISEWICZ, BRONISLAW	28	M	LABR	RR	ZZZZ	USA
ADAMETZ, ANTON	39	M	FARMER	RR	ZZZZ	USA
AMALIE	44	F	W	RR	ZZZZ	USA
ANNA	6	F	CHILD	RR	ZZZZ	USA
BLACHAIM	5	M	CHILD	RR	ZZZZ	USA
ANTON	.06	M	INFANT	RR	ZZZZ	USA
LISEWICZ, SALEMEJE	24	F	FARMER	RR	ZZZZ	USA
HOLSTEIN, PINCKES	42	M	MCHT	RR	ZZZZ	USA
SCHJE	11	F	UNKNOWN	RR	ZZZZ	USA
THOLKAN, NISEN	35	M	FARMER	RR	ZZZZ	USA
GOLDSTEIN, MAWEL	13	M	MCHT	RR	ZZZZ	USA
OSWIL, WITEL	25	M	MCHT	RR	ZZZZ	USA
STARESINSKY, JOSEF	50	M	MCHT	RR	ZZZZ	USA
SIRKIN, HESSEL	52	M	MCHT	RR	ZZZZ	USA
IWNICKY, DZIOL	28	M	MCHT	RR	ZZZZ	USA
SILBERMANN, CHAJE	25	F	UNKNOWN	RR	ZZZZ	USA
SCHIRINOWSKY, ISAAC	32	M	CNF	RR	ZZZZ	USA
LEWY, JACOB	25	M	CNF	RR	ZZZZ	USA
LEWIN, TAUBE	26	F	UNKNOWN	RR	ZZZZ	USA
ALIASBERG, BAROCH	59	M	FARMER	RR	ZZZZ	USA
ESTHER	55	F	W	RR	ZZZZ	USA
POLLACK, MICHAEL	26	M	FARMER	RR	ZZZZ	USA
SEMERTISCH, KASIS	29	M	FARMER	RR	ZZZZ	USA
KIRZYNSKA, VERONIKA	25	F	UNKNOWN	RR	ZZZZ	USA
JOSEPH	.10	M	INFANT	RR	ZZZZ	USA
ALISCHKEWITZ, LEA	24	F	UNKNOWN	RR	ZZZZ	USA
MAJKE	2	F	CHILD	RR	ZZZZ	USA
JACOB	.09	M	INFANT	RR	ZZZZ	USA
MEIROWITZ, CILLI	60	F	UNKNOWN	RR	ZZZZ	USA
PHILIPP	13	M	UNKNOWN	RR	ZZZZ	USA
NODIE, RACHMIEL	30	M	MCHT	RR	ZZZZ	USA
DOMBROWSKY, MICHAEL	28	M	MCHT	RR	ZZZZ	USA
TURTELTAUB, LEISER	22	M	MCHT	RR	ZZZZ	USA
GRUBE, CARL	26	M	PNTR	RR	ZZZZ	USA
OZBERG, NIKITA	26	F	LABR	RR	ZZZZ	USA
SCHEINBERG, GOTTFRIED	28	M	LABR	RR	ZZZZ	USA
WIETEPSKI, MAX	24	M	LABR	RR	ZZZZ	USA
PAULINE	22	F	UNKNOWN	RR	ZZZZ	USA
THEOPHILE	18	F	UNKNOWN	RR	ZZZZ	USA
SALSNIGER, TOMO	44	M	TLR	RR	ZZZZ	USA
PAULO	26	M	CNF	RR	ZZZZ	USA
OGUZAWOCA, MICO	24	M	LABR	RR	ZZZZ	USA
AGUSTUS	.05	M	INFANT	RR	ZZZZ	USA
RIZWIK, ISRAEL	5	M	CHILD	RR	ZZZZ	USA
QUINT, REBECCA	6	F	CHILD	RR	ZZZZ	USA
GETTIL	3	F	CHILD	RR	ZZZZ	USA
RACHEL	.11	F	INFANT	RR	ZZZZ	USA
OLENISKY, RACHEL	11	F	SCH	RR	ZZZZ	USA
KAPLAN, JONAS	10	M	SCH	RR	ZZZZ	USA
RABIN, ISRAEL	11	F	SCH	RR	ZZZZ	USA
SOLOMON	8	M	CHILD	RR	ZZZZ	USA
ABRAM	6	M	CHILD	RR	ZZZZ	USA
ASPER	.09	M	INFANT	RR	ZZZZ	USA
ROTHMAN, MEYER	.06	M	INFANT	RR	ZZZZ	USA
SWIRSKY, PESAIH	36	M	LABR	RR	ZZZZ	USA
LAIMAN, HARRIS	27	M	BCHR	RR	ZZZZ	USA
SCHIFFMAN, MARCUS	22	M	TLR	RR	ZZZZ	USA
NACHMAN, LEIMAN	56	M	LABR	RR	ZZZZ	USA
KEASEWICZ, LIBE	43	M	TLR	RR	ZZZZ	USA
JACOB	15	M	TLR	RR	ZZZZ	USA
LEBUMBAUM, SELIG	54	M	TLR	RR	ZZZZ	USA
COHEN, L.	28	M	BKLYR	RR	ZZZZ	USA
SAMUELSKY, ISAAK	50	M	TLR	RR	ZZZZ	USA
FORMAN, ABRAM	34	M	FARMER	RR	ZZZZ	USA
KIRSTEIN, NATHAN	30	M	TLR	RR	ZZZZ	USA
KRENZON, ABRAM	22	M	TLR	RR	ZZZZ	USA
BABER, HARRIS	46	M	TLR	RR	ZZZZ	USA
GOLDSTEIN, RAMET	21	M	BLKSMH	RR	ZZZZ	USA
LEVY, SIMON	15	M	TLR	RR	ZZZZ	USA
URDANG, BEN	31	M	LABR	RR	ZZZZ	USA
WINER, SAMUEL	20	M	CLKMKR	RR	ZZZZ	USA
MACHEL, FEWEL	17	M	CLKMKR	RR	ZZZZ	USA
HARBLITT, HIRSCH	26	M	CLKMKR	RR	ZZZZ	USA
LIPSKY, HIRSCH	41	M	SLR	RR	ZZZZ	USA
HERCHMAN, LEID	17	M	BKR	RR	ZZZZ	USA
ROTHEMAN, ABRAM	24	M	CLKMKR	RR	ZZZZ	USA
SCHOBEL, DAVID	22	M	LABR	RR	ZZZZ	USA
ALBERT, BARUCH	30	M	UNKNOWN	RR	ZZZZ	USA
KAPLAN, MOSES	20	M	BLKSMH	RR	ZZZZ	USA
WESSELL, WOLF	19	M	BLKSMH	RR	ZZZZ	USA
RABIN, WOLF	19	M	LABR	RR	ZZZZ	USA
MANCHI	18	M	LABR	RR	ZZZZ	USA
NOVNEIG, HERSCHALL	27	M	TLR	RR	ZZZZ	USA
HELLYNER, MOSES	24	M	CPTR	RR	ZZZZ	USA
GULKER, BIER	28	M	TLR	RR	ZZZZ	USA
GERSCHOWSKY, GESKEL	23	M	LABR	RR	ZZZZ	USA
GOLDBER, ZODEK	16	M	TLR	RR	ZZZZ	USA
KEMER, DAVID	45	M	TLR	RR	ZZZZ	USA
ISTKOWSKY, SONE	50	M	LABR	RR	ZZZZ	USA
LEWIN, NOACH	20	M	MRNR	RR	ZZZZ	USA

SHIP: IOWA

FROM: LIVERPOOL
TO: BOSTON
ARRIVED: 11 JULY 1888

PASSENGER	AGE	SEX	OCCUPATION	PRI	VL	DES
WESSEL, LAZARUS	30	F	W	RR	ZZZZ	USA
LEVY, ELIAS	58	M	TLR	RR	ZZZZ	USA
REBECCA	55	F	W	RR	ZZZZ	USA
SCHOSE, RIZWIK	37	F	W	RR	ZZZZ	USA
CIPPI, QUINT	28	F	W	RR	ZZZZ	USA
OLEMSKI, AARON	28	M	CGRMKR	RR	ZZZZ	USA
SARAH	48	F	W	RR	ZZZZ	USA
RABBIN, BEN	44	M	LABR	RR	ZZZZ	USA
ESTHER	44	F	W	RR	ZZZZ	USA
ROTHMAN, ETHEL	20	F	W	RR	ZZZZ	USA
JESSIE, BLU	18	F	SP	RR	ZZZZ	USA
SCHIMI, ITSKOWSKY	19	F	SP	RR	ZZZZ	USA
WESSEL, LEAH	3	F	CHILD	RR	ZZZZ	USA
HANNAH	4	F	CHILD	RR	ZZZZ	USA

SHIP: MAIN

FROM: BREMEN
TO: BALTIMORE
ARRIVED: 12 JULY 1888

PASSENGER	AGE	SEX	OCCUPATION	PRI	VL	DES
KOPACEWSKI, STANISL.	21	M	FARMER	RR	ZZZZ	BAL
ZALEWSKI, JAN	13	M	CH	RR	ZZZZ	BAL
KVITZ, RUBIN	24	M	FARMER	RR	ZZZZ	BAL
ABRONOWITZ, ABRAHAM	26	M	MCHT	RR	ZZZZ	BAL
BRANDLAW, MARKAN	23	M	TLR	RR	ZZZZ	BAL
WOLKOP, MOSES	19	M	MCHT	RR	ZZZZ	BAL
KALM, HERM.	18	M	MCHT	RR	ZZZZ	BAL
SAMM, MOSES	40	M	MCHT	RR	ZZZZ	BAL
HERZ, RUBIN	17	M	FARMER	RR	ZZZZ	BAL
JASSE, NAI	19	M	MCHT	RR	ZZZZ	OH
LIBUSCH, DAVID	25	M	TLR	RR	ZZZZ	OH
ABRAHAM, KUSCH	25	M	FARMER	RR	ZZZZ	IL
SEGAL, BENJE	23	M	FARMER	RR	ZZZZ	IL
WOLF, HEINR.	44	M	FARMER	RR	ZZZZ	IL
LISS, MATTEL	30	F	W	RR	ZZZZ	BAL

PASSENGER	AGE	SEX	OCCUPATION	PRV VIL DES
CHAJE	10	F	CH	RRZZZZBAL
SCHEINE	7	F	CHILD	RRZZZZBAL
AMBRUSEWICZ, WERONIKA	22	F	SVNT	RRZZZZBAL
KOEHN, LIEBE	30	F	W	RRZZZZBAL
BAHRA	4	F	CHILD	RRZZZZBAL
DOROTHEA	3	F	CHILD	RRZZZZBAL
DAVID	2	M	CHILD	RRZZZZBAL
GOLANT, LIBE	26	F	W	RRZZZZBAL
RAFALOWICZ, TRUMA	20	F	SVNT	RRZZZZBAL
BUCK, KATH.	27	F	SVNT	RRZZZZBAL
METHA	22	F	SVNT	RRZZZZBAL
ALTSCHULER, THRASSE	24	F	SVNT	RRZZZZBAL
LIBUS, LEAH	27	F	W	RRZZZZBAL
PADRACZEK, CHAJE	25	F	W	RRZZZZBAL
SCHEINE	6	F	CHILD	RRZZZZBAL
GITTAH	4	M	CHILD	RRZZZZBAL
SCHWARZMANN, DANE	21	F	SVNT	RRZZZZBAL
HERMANN, HENNE	14	F	SVNT	RRZZZZBAL
SCHWARTZMANN, CHAIE	27	F	W	RRZZZZBAL
MARIE	3	F	CHILD	RRZZZZBAL
CHAJEM	10	M	CH	RRZZZZBAL
MIRE	.01	F	INFANT	RRZZZZBAL
MANEKUM, MINE	16	F	SVNT	RRZZZZBAL
ABELOWITZ, ELISA	12	F	CH	RRZZZZBAL
FRIEDMANN, CHAJE	25	F	W	RRZZZZBAL
PESSE	.04	F	INFANT	RRZZZZBAL
CHAJET, JANHEL	22	F	SVNT	RRZZZZBAL
ESTER	22	F	SVNT	RRZZZZBAL
POWEDZEL, ISRAEL	62	M	MCHT	RRZZZZCH
MARY	50	F	W	RRZZZZCH
ESTER	18	F	D	RRZZZZCH
VON	11	F	CH	RRZZZZCH
ISAAK	10	M	CH	RRZZZZCH
FRIEDMANN, WHAWSTHE	26	M	MCHT	RRZZZZBAL
ESTHA	24	F	W	RRZZZZBAL
WOLF	50	M	MCHT	RRZZZZBAL
DEOORE	50	F	W	RRZZZZBAL
CHAJEM	11	M	CH	RRZZZZBAL
SARAH	3	F	CHILD	RRZZZZBAL
CHAJEM	.09	M	INFANT	RRZZZZBAL
LEAH	10	F	CH	RRZZZZBAL
JODETZKES, MOSES	30	M	MCHT	RRZZZZBAL
CHWASS, SAMUEL	36	M	MCHT	RRZZZZBAL
JOPPE, DANNE	38	F	W	RRZZZZNE
HIRSCH	8	M	CHILD	RRZZZZNE
JACOB	3	M	CHILD	RRZZZZNE
NISEN	.10	M	INFANT	RRZZZZNE

SHIP: WIELAND

FROM: HAMBURG
TO: NEW YORK
ARRIVED: 12 JULY 1888

PASSENGER	AGE	SEX	OCCUPATION	PRV VIL DES
SZULZ, JOSEPH	45	M	UNKNOWN	RRAIGDUSA
FRANCISCA	17	F	UNKNOWN	RRAIGDUSA
ZUBYCKI, PETER	35	M	UNKNOWN	RRZZZZUSA
LABUTIS, JURAS	30	M	LABR	RRZZZZUSA
UKASIK, ANIELA	20	F	SGL	RRZZZZUSA
LAGRO, ISIDOR	52	M	LABR	RRAICMUSA
BERTHA	49	F	W	RRAICMUSA
FLORENTINE	17	F	D	RRAICMUSA
CWIOK, FRANZ	26	M	LABR	RRAICHUSA
PICHWINSKI, WLADISL.	19	M	LABR	RRAICHUSA
RAKOWSKY, MIHAL	22	M	LABR	RRZZZZUSA
CITRON, ELKE	28	F	WO	RRAHVUUSA
MOTTEL	6	M	CHILD	RRAHVUUSA
LEISER	5	M	CHILD	RRAHVUUSA
RYCHEL	4	F	CHILD	RRAHVUUSA
MOSES	.05	M	INFANT	RRAHVUUSA

PASSENGER	AGE	SEX	OCCUPATION	PRV VIL DES
KLEIN, CHEIE	57	F	WO	RRZZZZUSA
PRZETOSKI, ANTON	40	M	LABR	RRZZZZUSA
ADAMOWICZ, MARIANNA	22	F	WO	RRZZZZUSA
BRONISIA	3	F	CHILD	RRZZZZUSA
JADWIGA	.05	F	INFANT	RRZZZZUSA
TATROWSKI, LUDWIKA	20	F	WO	RRZZZZUSA
VINCENT	2	M	CHILD	RRZZZZUSA
JPETRO	.11	M	INFANT	RRZZZZUSA
KUPLINSKY, SELIG	34	M	FARMER	RRAHVUUSA
SALMIN	29	M	JNR	RRAHVUUSA
RUBINOWSKI, JACOB	27	M	JNR	RRAHTUUSA
DIBIN, EUGEN	30	M	MCHT	RRAHTBUSA
PEREPLOZCK, MORDCHE	33	M	MCHT	RRAHTBUSA
GRINDLAND, DINA	20	F	SGL	RRAHTBUSA
SIWIG, KEIBE	20	F	SGL	RRAHTBUSA
MOSCHITZ, PERL	27	F	SGL	RRAHTBUSA
SHCEMINITZKI, LUDWIKA	18	F	SGL	RRAHXLUSA
SCHAPIRO, MORDCHE	26	M	DLR	RRAHTUUSA
GOLDHAAR, ARON	27	M	LABR	RRAHTUUSA
MATIKANSKY, BEER	35	M	LABR	RRAGRTUSA
BARK, ABRAM	16	M	DLR	RRZZZZUSA
SAPIR, CHANE	18	F	SGL	RRZZZZUSA
KAUFMANN, SEELIG	15	M	LABR	RRZZZZUSA
GORDAN, NATHAN	29	M	LABR	RRAGRTUSA
GOLDHAAR, MANOW	52	M	LABR	RRAHTUUSA
JULS	17	M	LABR	RRAHTUUSA
EVA	9	F	CHILD	RRAHTUUSA
ISAAC	16	M	LABR	RRAHTUUSA
SAARI, THILDA	19	F	SGL	FNZZZZUSA
ENGERT, ALBERTINE	37	F	WO	RRZZZZUSA
IDA	8	F	CHILD	RRZZZZUSA
HULDA	7	F	CHILD	RRZZZZUSA
MARIE	6	F	CHILD	RRZZZZUSA
LYDIA	3	F	CHILD	RRZZZZUSA
LINEWITZ, SORE	19	F	SGL	RRAHQUUSA
KURETZKY, ESCHKE	23	F	SGL	RRAHQUUSA
BERLOWITZ, ABRAM	17	M	TDR	RRZZZZUSA
HANISCHHAUS, AUG.	21	M	BBR	RRAHZSUSA
SPIRT, JUNNY	20	F	SGL	RRZZZZUSA
FANNY	17	F	SGL	RRZZZZUSA
GUSCHE	15	F	SGL	RRZZZZUSA
MOSES	8	M	CHILD	RRZZZZUSA
SCHUSTER, ABE	20	M	LABR	RRAGRTUSA
HINDE	20	F	W	RRAGRTUSA
RATTNER, MORDCHE	27	M	LABR	RRZZZZUSA
LEA	27	F	W	RRZZZZUSA
KAPELOWITZ, BASSE	43	F	WO	RRAGRTUSA
SCHEPSEL	8	M	CHILD	RRAGRTUSA
FREIDE	6	F	CHILD	RRAGRTUSA
MIRL	5	F	CHILD	RRAGRTUSA
SISSE	4	F	CHILD	RRAGRTUSA
PESACH	3	M	CHILD	RRAGRTUSA
BILZIG, MOSES	27	M	SMH	RRAHWMUSA
GUTER, JACOB	26	M	LABR	RRAHWMUSA
MEJROWITZ, MARIE	19	F	SGL	RRAEFLUSA
STOLNITZKY, MORDCHE	18	M	TDR	RRZZZZUSA
LEIB	8	M	CHILD	RRZZZZUSA
WARNEZ, VINCENTY	50	M	LABR	RRZZZZUSA
ARECHOWSKY, VINCENT	20	M	LABR	RRAHZSUSA
LIBOWSKI, RACHEL	35	F	WO	RRAHZSUSA
ABRAM	9	M	CHILD	RRAHZSUSA
CHEIE	8	M	CHILD	RRAHZSUSA
BOCIAN, B.	40	F	WO	RRZZZZUSA
GITTEL	18	M	S	RRZZZZUSA
MENDEL	9	M	CHILD	RRZZZZUSA
HEYMANN	7	M	CHILD	RRZZZZUSA
DAVID	3	M	CHILD	RRZZZZUSA
PRICETER, JOSEF	29	M	LABR	RRZZZZUSA
GRUNWALD, HIRSCHEL	48	M	LABR	RRZZZZUSA
RIEBOWSKI, SARAH	24	F	SGL	RRZZZZUSA
BERLHMANN, ISAAC	48	M	SHMK	RRAIHQUSA
HENWITZ, EIDE	19	F	SGL	RRZZZZUSA
BASCHE	16	F	SGL	RRZZZZUSA
FEINZOLD, KOPPEL	35	M	LABR	RRZZZZUSA
GLAZER, ABRAM	36	M	TLR	RRZZZZUSA

PASSENGER	AGE	SEX	OCCUPATION	PRIVL	DES
MATULSKE, RICKE	20	F	SGL	RRAHZS	USA
ISENKO, ROMAN	28	M	LABR	RRZZZZ	USA
REISMANN, ZAWEL	28	M	LABR	RRZZZZ	USA
FRANK, LEISER	50	M	LABR	RRZZZZ	USA
JOSEPH	28	M	LABR	RRZZZZ	USA
GOLDE	16	F	SGL	RRZZZZ	USA
FRIEDE	14	F	SGL	RRZZZZ	USA
GABEL, LEIB	50	M	TLR	RRAFVG	USA
SARA	49	F	W	RRAFVG	USA
MOSES	9	M	CHILD	RRAFVG	USA
BARUCH	8	M	CHILD	RRAFVG	USA
RABOWSKY, JUDEL	53	M	DLR	RRAHZS	USA
NOWIASKY, ISIDOR	19	M	CL	RRAIGD	USA
SUCHER, ABRAM	16	M	WCHMKR	RRAIGD	USA
MENDELSOHN, ABRAM	70	M	LABR	RRAHZS	USA
ESTHER	56	F	W	RRAHZS	USA
FOLTYNAK, ANNA	28	F	WO	RRZZZZ	USA
HELENE	4	F	CHILD	RRZZZZ	USA
OLKOWSKA, JOHANNA	26	F	WO	RRZZZZ	USA
JOHANN	3	M	CHILD	RRZZZZ	USA
WLADISLAV	.11	M	INFANT	RRZZZZ	USA
FRANZ	1	M	CHILD	RRZZZZ	USA
KUHL, CAROLINE	24	F	SGL	RRZZZZ	USA
PACZIKOWIEZ, ELKE	34	F	WO	RRAGRT	USA
TSDVHR	9	F	CHILD	RRAGRT	USA
JUDA	6	F	CHILD	RRAGRT	USA
ABRAM	5	M	CHILD	RRAGRT	USA
ZIRL	.11	M	INFANT	RRAGRT	USA
CHIMATZKI, MORDCHE	17	M	UNKNOWN	RRZZZZ	USA
NISSILIN, LUCCA	28	M	UNKNOWN	RRAIKJ	USA
CUCUCH, PIETRO	50	M	UNKNOWN	RRAIKJ	USA
SIMOWICH, PAUL	29	M	UNKNOWN	RRAIKJ	USA
MEJESIEWICK, JEWA	25	M	UNKNOWN	RRAIKJ	USA
ABRAMSKI, ABRAM	16	M	UNKNOWN	RRAHZS	USA
LALIXIL, ANTON	29	M	UNKNOWN	RRZZZZ	USA
KOPOLEWICZ, ABRAM	18	M	UNKNOWN	RRAGRT	USA
RUBIN, SIMKE	24	M	UNKNOWN	RRAGRT	USA
JANTHEL	4	M	CHILD	RRAGRT	USA
FRANEC	.11	F	INFANT	RRAGRT	USA
SCHINSCHIN, FANNY	19	F	WO	RRAGRT	USA
SAM	.11	M	INFANT	RRAGRT	USA
FKEUSCHMANN, IGNATZ	28	M	UNKNOWN	RRZZZZ	USA
JANOSHCEVSKI, HAVER	26	M	UNKNOWN	RRZZZZ	USA
LUSKIN, HINDE	18	F	SGL	RRZZZZ	USA
BANNICK, MAGDALENA	16	F	SGL	RRAADE	USA
WEINBERG, FRIDA	30	F	WO	RRZZZZ	USA
HIRSCH	5	M	CHILD	RRZZZZ	USA
KOTLARSCH, ESTHER	18	F	SGL	RRZZZZ	USA
GELLA	40	F	WO	RRZZZZ	USA
BLIMA	8	F	CHILD	RRZZZZ	USA
LEIB	8	M	CHILD	RRZZZZ	USA
GOLDBERG, ZLATE	38	F	WO	RRZZZZ	USA
JANKEL	9	M	CHILD	RRZZZZ	USA
MEINCH	8	M	CHILD	RRZZZZ	USA
BARUCH	7	M	CHILD	RRZZZZ	USA
LEIB	6	M	CHILD	RRZZZZ	USA
HINDE	5	M	CHILD	RRZZZZ	USA
RINKE	3	M	CHILD	RRZZZZ	USA
LUSKIN, RAUHAEL	22	M	TLR	RRZZZZ	USA
MUR, DAVID	38	M	LABR	RRZZZZ	USA
IWRENGANES, IGNATZ	31	M	LABR	RRZZZZ	USA
WANAGAS, JONAS	20	M	LABR	RRAHZS	USA
DOMEZIS, JOSES	20	M	LABR	RRAHZS	USA
ZAMATOPLES, FRANZ	20	M	LABR	RRAHZS	USA
GOLUBIZIK, SUDEL	17	M	LABR	RRAHQU	USA
ARONOWSKI, RESCHE	35	F	WO	RRAGRT	USA
SELDE	9	F	CHILD	RRAGRT	USA
LIPE	8	F	CHILD	RRAGRT	USA
HINDE	7	F	CHILD	RRAGRT	USA
RUBENSTEIN, DAVID	31	M	LABR	RRAHTO	USA
SLUTZKI, JUDEL	30	M	LABR	RRAHTO	USA
ALSCHANSKI, SCHEPE	30	M	LABR	RRAHTU	USA
RACHEL	28	F	W	RRAHTU	USA
CHANNE	9	M	CHILD	RRAHTU	USA
FEIGE	8	M	CHILD	RRAHTU	USA

PASSENGER	AGE	SEX	OCCUPATION	PRIVL	DES
MICHEL	3	M	CHILD	RRAHTU	USA
CHAIM	.01	M	INFANT	RRAHTU	USA
KLIMBORA, STEPHAN	25	M	LABR	RRAILK	USA
LESSMANN, ROSA	25	F	SGL	RRAEFL	USA
KOWINZKI, GITTEL	15	F	SGL	RRZZZZ	USA
JAFFE, SCHMUL	46	M	LABR	RRZZZZ	USA
BEILE	42	F	W	RRZZZZ	USA
LENNE	15	F	D	RRZZZZ	USA
ZIPRE	18	F	D	RRZZZZ	USA
RASCHE	17	F	D	RRZZZZ	USA
ISAAC	16	M	S	RRZZZZ	USA
TAUBE	8	M	CHILD	RRZZZZ	USA
FEIGE	4	F	CHILD	RRZZZZ	USA
SCHERMER, MARIE	15	F	SGL	RRZZZZ	USA
IGNATZ	9	M	CHILD	RRZZZZ	USA
PUMPOWSKY, CHAIE	27	F	WO	RRZZZZ	USA
ELISE	7	F	CHILD	RRZZZZ	USA
GUTENBERG, MALKE	18	F	SGL	RRZZZZ	USA
KAUFMANN, FANNY	20	F	SGL	RRAHTN	USA
SEGAL, ISRAEL	19	M	LABR	RRZZZZ	USA
SMOLNISKY, FRIEDE	20	F	SGL	RRAHZS	USA
CHAIE	.11	F	INFANT	RRAHZS	USA
WEINGARTEN, MINCHE	33	F	WO	RRZZZZ	USA
GEDALIC	15	F	CH	RRZZZZ	USA
RACHEL	14	F	CH	RRZZZZ	USA
ROSEL	9	F	CHILD	RRZZZZ	USA
ETTEL	8	F	CHILD	RRZZZZ	USA
ALIKSZEWIEZ, HEMRYK	37	M	LABR	RRZZZZ	USA
PETRIKAUSKE, ARON	19	M	LABR	RRZZZZ	USA
DORFMANN, BREINDEL	21	F	SGL	RRAIHS	USA
ZACHMANN, SALOMON	38	M	LABR	RRZZZZ	USA
LEO	19	M	JNR	RRZZZZ	USA
ROTHBARTH, ANNA	17	F	SGL	RRZZZZ	USA
URYSON, SCHINE	30	F	WO	RRZZZZ	USA
MOSES	6	M	CHILD	RRZZZZ	USA
ISRAEL	3	M	CHILD	RRZZZZ	USA
GERSON, SALOMON	17	M	LABR	RRAHZU	USA
GOLDMANN, MARIACHE	52	F	WO	RRAIGH	USA
MENUSCH, GROSO	18	M	LABR	RRZZZZ	USA
GROSS, ELIUS	27	M	LABR	RRAIKI	USA
ULLAKKO, MENNTA	24	F	SGL	FNZZZZ	USA
WESTWLAND, ERIK	32	M	LABR	FNAIER	USA
RADDENBERG, ANNA	27	F	WO	RRZZZZ	USA
JACOB	7	M	CHILD	RRZZZZ	USA
HIRSCH	5	M	CHILD	RRZZZZ	USA
NOVAK, JOSEPH	24	M	FARMER	RRZZZZ	USA
BUZENA	20	F	W	RRZZZZ	USA
SISKIND, CHAJE	18	F	SGL	RRZZZZ	USA
GURRING, LEISSER	20	M	FARMER	RRZZZZ	USA
CHAJE	18	F	W	RRZZZZ	USA
SZEKREWIEZ, LEIB	38	M	LABR	RRZZZZ	USA
CATORANSKI, ISRAEL	36	M	LABR	RRZZZZ	USA
LUNJEWSKI, LIEBE	32	F	WO	RRAGRT	USA
FRIEDEL	4	F	CHILD	RRAGRT	USA
MIEZINLIS, JAN	20	M	LABR	RRZZZZ	USA
ABRAMOWIEZ, ANTON	25	M	LABR	RRAIGI	USA
KUPIEKA, FRANZ	30	M	LABR	RRZZZZ	USA
SOBOLEWSKI, IGNATZ	15	M	LABR	RRZZZZ	USA
ROCHOW, MINNA	14	F	SGL	RRAIGH	USA
SIMON, SOPHIE	18	F	SGL	RRAIGH	USA
WOLLE, ISAAC	27	M	WTR	RRAHVU	USA
GROSSMANN, REISEL	17	F	SGL	RRAHVU	USA
FRIEDMANN, MORSCHE	59	M	TLR	RRAIOA	USA
SAMUIL	9	M	CHILD	RRAIOA	USA
PERILMANN, MERL	20	F	SGL	RRAIGH	USA
SCHILMANN, FEIGE	18	F	SGL	RRAIGH	USA
ALEXANDROWITSCH, HERMAN	31	M	LABR	RRZZZZ	USA
MOSOLEUSKY, STEPHAN	35	M	LABR	RRAIBD	USA
GABRIELE	35	F	W	RRAIBD	USA
JOH.	9	M	CHILD	RRAIBD	USA
FRANZ	8	M	CHILD	RRAIBD	USA
MARIE	4	F	CHILD	RRAIBD	USA
CASIMIR	3	M	CHILD	RRAIBD	USA
STANISLAVA	.09	F	INFANT	RRAIBD	USA
KOHAN, BEILE	48	F	WO	RRAGRT	USA

PASSENGER	AGE	SEX	OCCUPATION	PRVL	VIL	DES
MALKE	18	F	CH	RR	AGRT	USA
SIME	4	F	CHILD	RR	AGRT	USA
JAWB	9	M	CHILD	RR	AGRT	USA
LUBZKY, NATHAN	32	M	LABR	RR	AHTU	USA
CZERZIS, MOSES	30	M	LABR	RR	AHTU	USA
CHANNE	21	F	W	RR	AHTU	USA
ROSENBERG, LIEBE	20	F	SGL	RR	AHTU	USA
HATTOWSKY, CH.	20	F	SGL	RR	AIHB	USA
KATZENELLENBOGEN, MOSES	18	M	LABR	RR	AIHB	USA
MOSES	18	M	LABR	RR	AIHB	USA
KUPERMANN, ESTHER	46	F	WO	RR	ZZZZ	USA
SOSCHE	8	F	CHILD	RR	ZZZZ	USA
LESSIN, ISRAEL	18	M	LABR	RR	AFVG	USA
ABRAMSOHN, NISSEN	26	M	LABR	RR	AFWJ	USA
WEINSTEIN, JACOB	18	M	LABR	RR	AHVU	USA
SABWIENSCH, CHAIE	18	F	SGL	RR	AIGH	USA
JALOWITZ, MOSES	9	M	CHILD	RR	ZZZZ	USA
SUNDELOWITZ, ELKE	19	F	SGL	RR	ZZZZ	USA
LIPPSCHITZ, HIRSCH	36	M	UNKNOWN	RR	ZZZZ	USA
KRAWITZ, JETTE	20	F	SGL	RR	ZZZZ	USA
BLANSTEIN, LENOSCH	23	M	WTR	RR	ZZZZ	USA
LIPPSCHEITZ, RACHEL	25	F	WO	RR	ZZZZ	USA
CHANNE	6	M	CHILD	RR	ZZZZ	USA
SAMUEL	2	M	CHILD	RR	ZZZZ	USA
LIEBOWITZ, SAMUEL	23	M	LABR	RR	AIHV	USA
FRUMME	22	F	W	RR	AIHV	USA
KIENER, SALOMON	40	M	LABR	RR	AIAH	USA
MOSZWICK, ABRAM	25	M	LABR	RR	AIAH	USA
KIPER, LEZAR	40	M	LABR	RR	AIAH	USA
HAKNER, KALMANN	24	M	LABR	RR	AGRT	USA
WOLASINSKI, HIRSCH	17	M	SHMK	RR	AIGH	USA
GELFENSTEIN, SALOMON	22	M	MCHT	RR	AFVG	USA

SHIP: STATE OF NEVADA

FROM: GLASGOW AND LARNE
TO: NEW YORK
ARRIVED: 12 JULY 1888

PASSENGER	AGE	SEX	OCCUPATION	PRVL	VIL	DES
ANDOLOWICZ, SCHEPSEL	50	M	MCHT	RR	AIDL	USA
CHASCHE	45	F	W	RR	AIDL	USA
SLOME	22	F	CH	RR	AIDL	USA
ESTHER	18	F	CH	RR	AIDL	USA
ROCHE	17	F	CH	RR	AIDL	USA
LEIKE	11	F	CH	RR	AIDL	USA
MORKE	8	F	CHILD	RR	AIDL	USA
MARIAM	6	F	CHILD	RR	AIDL	USA
SCHMUL	4	M	CHILD	RR	AIDL	USA
LEISER	11	M	CH	RR	AIDL	USA
WASSEL, ABRAHAM	27	M	MCHT	RR	AIDL	USA
BRENNSCHIER, DEBORAH	26	F	UNKNOWN	RR	AIDL	USA
ROSA	26	F	UNKNOWN	RR	AIDL	USA
MORDSCHE	1	F	CHILD	RR	AIDL	USA
RAZDANOWICZ, AUTUST	38	M	LABR	RR	AIDL	USA
BERGMAN, JANCKEL	29	M	MCHT	RR	AIDL	USA
BLEIHEISER, EMIL	20	M	MCHT	RR	AIDL	USA
BRANERSCHIER, HIRSCHEL	19	M	MCHT	RR	AIDL	USA
BENZEL	11	M	CH	RR	AIDL	USA
RACKOWICZ, CHAJE	20	F	SVNT	RR	AIDL	USA
BRANDE, BEILE	14	F	SVNT	RR	AIDL	USA
RILLET, MINNE	30	F	UNKNOWN	RR	AIDL	USA
MEYER	1	M	CHILD	RR	AIDL	USA
U	.05	M	INFANT	RR	AIDL	USA
CORMALI, ALEX	27	M	LABR	RR	AIDL	USA
COHEN, HELEN	19	F	SVNT	RR	AIDL	USA
COHN, ETHEL	23	F	UNKNOWN	RR	AIDL	USA
MOSES	2	M	CHILD	RR	AIDL	USA
LOEB	.09	M	INFANT	RR	AIDL	USA
DWOR, ISRAEL	35	M	SHMK	RR	AIDL	USA
DAVIDOWICZ, HENRIETTA	22	F	SVNT	RR	AIDL	USA
CHAINE	11	M	CH	RR	AIDL	USA
DIAMOND, HELLA	25	F	UNKNOWN	RR	AIDL	USA
REGINA	26	F	UNKNOWN	RR	AIDL	USA
JANOS	1	F	CHILD	RR	AIDL	USA
DUBINSKY, ROSA	35	F	UNKNOWN	RR	AIDL	USA
SORA	11	F	CH	RR	AIDL	USA
FREIDE	8	F	CHILD	RR	AIDL	USA
LEJE	6	F	CHILD	RR	AIDL	USA
FEIGE	26	F	UNKNOWN	RR	AIDL	USA
EIDTMAN, ABR.	36	M	MCHT	RR	AIDL	USA
FRANKFURTER, HANNA	17	F	SVNT	RR	AIDL	USA
FEIERMAN, ADOLPH	24	M	LABR	RR	AIDL	USA
FLEISCHMAN, LEWI	24	M	LABR	RR	AIDL	USA
FEINBERG, BENJAMIN	15	M	MCHT	RR	AIDL	USA
FRIEDMAN, BENJAMIN	18	M	SHMK	RR	AIDL	USA
ZIGNE	20	F	W	RR	AIDL	USA
GROSSMAN, K.L.	35	M	MCHT	RR	AIDL	USA
GOR, MOSES	18	M	LABR	RR	AIDL	USA
MERE	17	F	SVNT	RR	AIDL	USA
GOLDSCHMIDT, SAML.	49	M	JNR	RR	AIDL	USA
GRIENMAN, SANDER	45	M	CPR	RR	AIDL	USA
GRENSTEIN, PHILIP	18	M	MCHT	RR	AIDL	USA
GRIBINSCHICK, MANSCHE	40	M	MCHT	RR	AIDL	USA
GARNOTZKI, HENE	40	F	SVNT	RR	AIDL	USA
GRIENBERG, HENE	24	F	UNKNOWN	RR	AIDL	USA
SORE	6	F	CHILD	RR	AIDL	USA
ROCHE	11	F	CH	RR	AIDL	USA
SISSLE	1	F	CHILD	RR	AIDL	USA
HERSCHKOWITZ, SORE	59	F	UNKNOWN	RR	AIDL	USA
HOLTZHEN, DAVID	19	M	CL	RR	AIDL	USA
HERSCHMAN, BENJAMIN	30	M	MCHT	RR	AIDL	USA
HURWITZ, ISRAEL	18	M	MCHT	RR	AIDL	USA
HATZBERG, JOHANNA	21	F	SVNT	RR	AIDL	USA
HEYMAN, ROSE	27	F	UNKNOWN	RR	AIDL	USA
ANNETH	.06	F	INFANT	RR	AIDL	USA
JACOB, FENWEL	27	M	TLR	RR	AIDL	USA
KASTANOWICZ, ISAK	32	M	SMH	RR	AIDL	USA
KLEIN, LEOPOLD	20	M	SMH	RR	AIDL	USA
KARABAS, ANDRAS	45	M	LABR	RR	AIDL	USA
KACZMARIK, JANOS	18	M	MCHT	RR	AIDL	USA
KASSOWSKY, JOSEF	18	M	LABR	RR	AIDL	USA
KOLOSKY, ISRAEL	18	M	CL	RR	AIDL	USA
KANTOR, HIRSCH	39	M	TLR	RR	AIDL	USA
KARDAN, RAPPEL	40	M	MCHT	RR	AIDL	USA
KAPLAN, ABR.	25	M	TLR	RR	AIDL	USA
KONIGSBERG, JOSEF	35	M	MCHT	RR	AIDL	USA
KITT, GERSON	26	M	MCHT	RR	AIDL	USA
KANDEROWICZ, WIGDOROWIT	18	M	LABR	RR	AIDL	USA
KAMEROWSKY, LEON	26	M	MCHT	RR	AIDL	USA
KITT, CHANNE	20	F	SVNT	RR	AIDL	USA
GISSE	18	F	SVNT	RR	AIDL	USA
LEA	16	F	SVNT	RR	AIDL	USA
KATZ, SPINGE	16	F	SVNT	RR	AIDL	USA
KASERSKY, BERLLE	45	F	UNKNOWN	RR	AIDL	USA
CHATZKEL	17	M	LABR	RR	AIDL	USA
KAUFMAN, SARAH	24	F	SVNT	RR	AIDL	USA
KLEIN, SALLY	16	F	SVNT	RR	AIDL	USA
LEWINTON, RUBIN	25	M	MCHT	RR	AIDL	USA
LANFER, MOSES	18	M	MCHT	RR	AIDL	USA
LEWIEN, MOSES	19	M	MCHT	RR	AIDL	USA
LEITER, LEOPOLD	36	M	MCHT	RR	AIDL	USA
LESCHINSKY, CHANNE	34	F	UNKNOWN	RR	AIDL	USA
ISRAEL	11	M	CH	RR	AIDL	USA
SELDE	10	F	CH	RR	AIDL	USA
LEWIEN, FRANNE	17	F	SVNT	RR	AIDL	USA
LIPOWITZ, MENSCHE	20	F	SVNT	RR	AIDL	USA
LEWINSOHN, SEBINA	22	F	SVNT	RR	AIDL	USA
MARGARETHA	19	F	SVNT	RR	AIDL	USA
MALEWIEZ, MEYER	16	M	MCHT	RR	AIDL	USA
MILER, JACOB	30	M	JNR	RR	AIDL	USA
MINSE, MICHAEL	28	M	LABR	RR	AIDL	USA
MALOWICZ, CHASKEL	24	M	MCHT	RR	AIDL	USA
VINCENT	36	M	LABR	RR	AIDL	USA
MORRIS, ANTRE	22	M	LABR	RR	AIDL	USA
MENDEBOHN, FEIGE	19	F	SVNT	RR	AIDL	USA

PASSENGER	AGE	SEX	OCCUPATION	PRV VIL DES
MILLER, SARAH	16	F	SVNT	RRAIDLUSA
NARONEWICZ, ALEX	45	M	LABR	RRAIDLUSA
NEULAND, RIEWKE	35	F	UNKNOWN	RRAIDLUSA
SARA	11	F	CH	RRAIDLUSA
LEISER	10	M	CH	RRAIDLUSA
BEHR	8	M	CHILD	RRAIDLUSA
SELIG	6	M	CHILD	RRAIDLUSA
ITZIG	1	M	CHILD	RRAIDLUSA
MEIER	2	M	CHILD	RRAIDLUSA
PINOHASCHEK, ABR.	22	M	LABR	RRAIDLUSA
POLSKOW, LEIB	29	M	JNR	RRAIDLUSA
PASSCHINSKY, CHANE	32	M	MCHT	RRAIDLUSA
FEIGE	30	F	UNKNOWN	RRAIDLUSA
SELIG	11	M	CH	RRAIDLUSA
SCHMUL	9	M	CHILD	RRAIDLUSA
ELIZA	7	F	CHILD	RRAIDLUSA
SORE	2	F	CHILD	RRAIDLUSA
SANE	40	M	MCHT	RRAIDLUSA
GITTEL	40	F	UNKNOWN	RRAIDLUSA
ALTE	11	M	CH	RRAIDLUSA
ABR.	53	M	MCHT	RRAIDLUSA
MEYER	17	M	LABR	RRAIDLUSA
CHAEM	11	M	CH	RRAIDLUSA
PAS-----, L.	17	F	SVNT	RRAIDLUSA
RACHEL	15	F	SVNT	RRAIDLUSA
NOACH	10	M	CH	RRAIDLUSA
RABINOWICZ, SELDE	15	F	SVNT	RRAIDLUSA
SORSSMAN, DAVD.	24	M	MCHT	RRAIDLUSA
SCHAPIRO, MICHLA	20	F	UNKNOWN	RRAIDLUSA
ABRAH	14	M	LABR	RRAIDLUSA
SACHS, HERM.	17	M	TLR	RRAIDLUSA
SARAKOWICZ, FRANZISCHEK	23	M	LABR	RRAIDLUSA
SALASCHITZ, EISIK	24	M	MCHT	RRAIDLUSA
SCHALNER, MOSES	39	M	MCHT	RRAIDLUSA
SENDEROWICZ, SOLIM	20	M	MCHT	RRAIDLUSA
SKUDSKY, JAKOB	19	M	MCHT	RRAIDLUSA
SELKOWICZ, KANDAL	23	M	LABR	RRAIDLUSA
SCHELKOWICZ, ANTON	27	M	MCHT	RRAIDLUSA
SANFER, BERMOIN	11	M	CH	RRAIDLUSA
SEDLOWSKY, FEIGE	30	F	UNKNOWN	RRAIDLUSA
ANNIE	11	F	CH	RRAIDLUSA
JOSSEL	9	M	CHILD	RRAIDLUSA
RIEWKA	7	F	CHILD	RRAIDLUSA
SELDE	5	F	CHILD	RRAIDLUSA
SCHEPSE	2	F	CHILD	RRAIDLUSA
SCHNEHAT, DWORE	22	F	SVNT	RRAIDLUSA
SCHEYER, ROSALIE	23	F	SVNT	RRAIDLUSA
SCHMUIN, MINNA	26	F	SVNT	RRAIDLUSA
ZIPURA, ASIZE	20	M	LABR	RRAIDLUSA
ZALANITZKY, MEYER	43	M	MCHT	RRAIDLUSA
ZANNICHE, MOSES	58	M	MCHT	RRAIDLUSA
ABR.	11	M	CH	RRAIDLUSA
ZAPLINSKY, JAN	37	M	LABR	RRAIDLUSA
ZUCKERMAN, NOACH	28	M	MCHT	RRAIDLUSA
LEIBE	1	F	CHILD	RRAIDLUSA
NACHAME	23	F	W	RRAIDLUSA
Z---IK, RIEWKA	18	F	SVNT	RRAIDLUSA
ZIRMAK, RICKEL	21	F	SVNT	RRAIDLUSA
GOLDBURG, HERM.	30	M	CMST	RRAIDLUSA

SHIP: WAESLAND

FROM: ANTWERP
TO: NEW YORK
ARRIVED: 13 JULY 1888

PASSENGER	AGE	SEX	OCCUPATION	PRV VIL DES
MO-ILEWSKY, ABRAHAM	49	M	PDLR	RRZZZZNY
NOSSE-	26	F	PDLR	RRZZZZNY
RISCHE	16	F	PDLR	RRZZZZNY
GISSE	9	M	CHILD	RRZZZZNY
ROMIA, HIRSCH	18	M	LABR	RRZZZZNY
SUSCHMANN, SZCHOK	51	M	WCHMKR	RRZZZZNY
RABINOWITZ, ARON	25	M	WCHMKR	RRZZZZNY
LUCHTIGER, SAMUEL	23	M	LABR	RRZZZZNY
LEVY, DAVID	18	M	UNKNOWN	RRZZZZNY
S--ONEF, MAURISE	25	M	MACH	RRZZZZNY
GLAZIER, MICHEL	23	M	TLR	RRZZZZNY
GLESSNER, PERA-	27	M	CPMKR	RRZZZZNY
ESTHER	21	M	CPMKR	RRZZZZNY
WEIN, ALTA	21	M	TLR	RRZZZZNY
SCHAPIRO, LAIUS	23	M	RVR	RRZZZZNY
TEICH, DAVIS	25	M	TLR	RRZZZZNY
SARA	19	F	TLR	RRZZZZNY
LEAH	00	M	INF	RRZZZZNY
BUSCHEL, MARCUS	28	M	BKR	RRZZZZNY
GASWA--, MARK	18	M	PLN	RRZZZZNY
SILVERMAN, ABRAHAM	24	M	TLR	RRZZZZNY
BELLAKOWSKY, RA-LEIN	20	M	TLR	RRZZZZNY
GREENSPAN, J	20	M	TLR	RRZZZZNY
JACOB, SAUL	18	M	TLR	RRZZZZNY
KATZEN, MARIA	31	F	NN	RRZZZZNY
CH	00	M	INF	RRZZZZNY
POMERANTZ, SAMUEL	18	M	TLR	RRZZZZNY
FRIEDMAN, ISAAC	25	M	STMAKR	RRAIDJNY
MARY	23	F	STMAKR	RRAIDJNY
JOSEF	3	M	CHILD	RRAIDJNY
LOUIS	00	M	INF	RRAIDJNY
LUBASCH, SAML	34	M	PDLR	RRZZZZNY
GIETEL	23	F	PDLR	RRZZZZNY
ISAACSON, LEOP	19	M	UNKNOWN	RRZZZZNY
BROWN, LEWIS	21	M	BKR	RRZZZZNY
-USCHAN, KAR	18	M	TLR	RRZZZZNY
CAPLAN, NATHAN	18	M	CPTR	RRZZZZNY
RE-KSCHAFFER, MIREL	16	M	TLR	RRZZZZNY
KAUFMANN, H	20	M	NN	RRZZZZUNK
BENJ	16	M	NN	RRZZZZUNK
RATTENBERG, JONAS	21	M	TLR	RRZZZZUNK
ALTE	21	F	TLR	RRZZZZUNK
CHONA	4	F	CHILD	RRZZZZUNK
SARAH	3	F	CHILD	RRZZZZUNK
JARUSKI, ELIE	45	M	LABR	RRZZZZUNK
KAUSTORON, MORDCH	30	M	LABR	RRZZZZUNK
ROSENWASSER, H	17	F	SVNT	RRZZZZUNK
WESNIK, LEISER	45	M	LABR	RRZZZZUNK
WEISSALT, S	23	M	TLR	RRZZZZUNK
SALI	19	F	TLR	RRZZZZUNK
J---WILOWICZ, JACOB	35	M	UNKNOWN	RRZZZZUNK
F	30	F	UNKNOWN	RRZZZZUNK
CHANE	7	F	CHILD	RRZZZZUNK
NACHEM	6	U	CHILD	RRZZZZUNK
SCHUAL	00	U	UNKNOWN	RRZZZZUNK
ETTE	00	F	INF	RRZZZZUNK
MOSELINSKY, JACOB	23	M	LABR	RRZZZZUNK
WACHTEL, RACHEL	15	F	NN	RRZZZZUNK
MIKOLA---, J	20	M	LABR	RRZZZZCH
GISZEWIEZ, FRANCISZIK	20	M	LABR	RRZZZZCH

SHIP: EMS

FROM: BREMEN AND SOUTHAMPTON
TO: NEW YORK
ARRIVED: 13 JULY 1888

PASSENGER	AGE	SEX	OCCUPATION	PRV VIL DES
SINAI, BORIS	30	M	MCHT	RRAILANY
MATHE	23	F	W	RRAILANY
ZAILSKA, EVA	18	F	NN	RRAILANY
CZARNIAWSKA, HELENA	16	F	NN	RRAILANY
BAROTZ, AUGUSTE	22	F	W	RRAILANY
SALOM	.11	M	INFANT	RRAILANY
KEDIS, ADONAS	23	M	LABR	RRAFWJNY

PASSENGER	AGE	SEX	OCCUPATION	PRI	VIL	DES
WOJTSCHIRRAS, ALEX	21	M	LABR	RRA	FWJ	NY
G-MOVSKY, JANA	20	F	NN	RRA	FWJ	NY
ZESCHEKOS, FRANCISKA	28	F	NN	RRA	FWJ	NY
PAUSA, ROSIS	22	M	LABR	RRA	FWJ	NY
CHENILEWSKY, ROSALIA	19	F	NN	RRA	FWJ	NY
ZEILSKAS, FRANZ	20	M	LABR	RRA	FWJ	NY
KOSTNIRSKY, MARCUS	40	M	LABR	RRA	FWJ	NY
GRAUSTEIN, ESPHR	29	M	LABR	RRA	HQD	NY
JAFFE, HIRSCH	30	M	LABR	RRA	HQD	NY
ARENDT, BEHR	62	M	LABR	RRA	HQD	NY
CERANKOWSKI, PAVEL	21	M	LABR	RRA	HQD	NY
GOLDSTEIN, IDA	26	F	W	RRA	HQD	NY
DAVID	3	M	CHILD	RRA	HQD	NY
SEJANKO, JUDEL	28	F	NN	RRA	HQD	NY
SARAMBOWSKY, ABRAH	26	M	LABR	RRA	HQD	NY
KOWALEWSKI, MARIANA	20	F	NN	RRA	FWJ	MA
STOFFER, GITEL	22	M	FARMER	RRA	FWJ	CH
BORKEWITZ, APOLONIA	35	F	NN	RRA	FWJ	NY
MAJEWSKA, MARIANA	25	F	NN	RRA	FWJ	NY
KAPUSCHTIRSKY, MART	29	M	LABR	RRA	FWJ	NY
RODLEWITZ, STANISL	16	M	LABR	RRA	FWJ	NY
KOWRECZKA, PAVEL	60	M	LABR	RRA	FWJ	NY
ELISAB	55	F	W	RRA	FWJ	NY
JANSHARSKY, BECKE	41	M	LABR	RRZ	ZZZ	TX
DAVID	10	M	CH	RRZ	ZZZ	TX
FREIMANN, LINA	23	F	W	RRZ	ZZZ	NY
FANNY	.01	F	INFANT	RRZ	ZZZ	NY
STAVINSKY, ADAM	50	M	LABR	RRA	HZS	NY
SERGI, STANISLAUS	50	M	LABR	RRA	HZS	NY
SAILOWSKA, PAVEL	24	M	LABR	RRA	HZS	NY
REINSCHREIBER, LOUIS	19	M	LABR	RRZ	ZZZ	NY
BASA, MATEVA	22	F	NN	RRZ	ZZZ	NY
TWERDZIK, KATARZYNA	25	F	NN	RRA	FWJ	NY

SHIP: EDAM

FROM: AMSTERDAM
TO: NEW YORK
ARRIVED: 16 JULY 1888

PASSENGER	AGE	SEX	OCCUPATION	PRI	VIL	DES
BUCZIN, MOISSHE	43	M	TLR	RRZ	ZZZ	NY
JACOBOWITZ, REGINA	33	F	UNKNOWN	RRZ	ZZZ	NY
DAVID	9	M	CHILD	RRZ	ZZZ	NY
DEBORA	10	F	CH	RRZ	ZZZ	NY
HANNI	.04	M	INFANT	RRZ	ZZZ	NY
TOLMAT, VILMAS	9	M	CHILD	RRZ	ZZZ	NY
GRUNFELD, EMILIE	35	F	UNKNOWN	RRZ	ZZZ	NY
LENE	.06	F	INFANT	RRZ	ZZZ	NY
ELHIN, MAWSCHE	25	F	SVNT	RRZ	ZZZ	NY
DORENTER, ROSE	22	F	SVNT	RRZ	ZZZ	NY
UCZYKHEN, HENNIE	18	F	SVNT	RRZ	ZZZ	NY
SELJER, SCHLOME	19	M	LABR	RRZ	ZZZ	NY
BRESFLER, JOSEF	18	M	LABR	RRZ	ZZZ	NY
SABLUD, JOCHE	30	F	UNKNOWN	RRZ	ZZZ	NY
LIEBE	11	F	UNKNOWN	RRZ	ZZZ	NY
GUTE	9	F	CHILD	RRZ	ZZZ	NY
CHAJE	5	F	CHILD	RRZ	ZZZ	NY
MICHEL	.07	M	INFANT	RRZ	ZZZ	NY
SIMON, JUDEL	40	M	MCHT	RRZ	ZZZ	NY
BALIE, GERWATIE	33	M	MCHT	RRZ	ZZZ	NY

SHIP: REPUBLIC

FROM: LIVERPOOL
TO: NEW YORK
ARRIVED: 16 JULY 1888

PASSENGER	AGE	SEX	OCCUPATION	PRI	VIL	DES
BJOEK, CHARLOTTA	00	F	SP	RRA	DAX	USA
RJAMNA, KALLE	00	F	SVNT	RRA	DAX	USA
SKOLD, EVA	36	F	W	RRA	DAX	USA
JENNY	7	F	CHILD	RRA	DAX	USA
STEN	5	M	CHILD	RRA	DAX	USA
ELNWI	3	F	CHILD	RRA	DAX	USA
BJOEKGRIST, VICTOR	25	M	LABR	RRA	DAX	USA
KJELBERTZ, CLARA	23	F	SP	RRA	DAX	USA
FEUG, EMELIA	21	F	SP	RRA	DAX	USA
JACOBSON, CASPAR	22	M	LABR	RRA	DAX	USA
ABRAMOWITZ, TAUBE	19	F	SP	RRA	DAX	USA
KESEMOAPER, IGNATZ	20	M	LABR	RRA	DAX	USA
FRAMZBLAND, FOE	17	M	LABR	RRA	DAX	USA
NEUMARK, TEL.	18	M	LABR	RRA	DAX	USA
WERPBERGER, M.	19	M	LABR	RRA	DAX	USA
SOMMER, MOSSEL	18	M	LABR	RRA	DAX	USA
SCURFMAN, RJFKE	11	M	CH	RRA	DAX	USA
LAUFER, CAZIL	32	F	W	RRA	DAX	USA
MALKE	11	F	UNKNOWN	RRA	DAX	USA
KALMAN	9	M	CHILD	RRA	DAX	USA
ITZAK	6	F	CHILD	RRA	DAX	USA
MALKE	20	F	SP	RRA	DAX	USA
BRARTSWLER, R.	16	M	LABR	RRA	DAX	USA
BRARKWER, T.	11	M	CH	RRA	DAX	USA
REINZACK, MERL	17	M	LABR	RRA	DAX	USA
DEARSKY, JOEL	40	M	LABR	RRA	DAX	USA
TEINGOLD, ABR.	28	M	LABR	RRA	DAX	USA
WITTERMARK, ANTONIE	30	F	W	RRA	DAX	USA
ROMAN	10	M	CH	RRA	DAX	USA
COHN, LEVER	23	F	W	RRA	DAX	USA
JOSEPH	4	M	CHILD	RRA	DAX	USA
SCHWEL, MARIDAL	30	M	LABR	RRA	DAX	USA
MAUEL, SALI	18	F	SP	RRA	DAX	USA
CHARGE	14	F	SP	RRA	DAX	USA
CHARGE	26	F	W	RRA	DAX	USA
LERB.	5	M	CHILD	RRA	DAX	USA
HAMER, AVOROCHE	40	M	LABR	RRA	DAX	USA
STROCK, SOLOMON	20	M	LABR	RRA	DAX	USA
TUCHLINKI, ANNA	32	F	SP	RRA	DAX	USA
SUPPERSOHN, LINA	30	F	SP	RRA	DAX	USA
BOCHAUCK, A.	17	M	LABR	RRA	DAX	USA
LELZER, MARIE	14	F	SVNT	RRA	DAX	USA
JOESINSKY, MAREM	25	F	SVNT	RRA	DAX	USA
SACHARAVY, DIANA	18	F	SP	RRA	DAX	USA
DIRSKY, FROEDE	18	M	LABR	RRA	DAX	USA
FRITZ, EMMA	43	F	W	RRA	DAX	USA
JOHN	11	M	CH	RRA	DAX	USA
HULDA	9	F	CHILD	RRA	DAX	USA
KAPLAN, BEILE	50	F	W	RRA	DAX	USA
BLUME	17	F	SP	RRA	DAX	USA
ESTER	10	F	CH	RRA	DAX	USA
CHAIE	9	F	CHILD	RRA	DAX	USA
HER.	6	M	CHILD	RRA	DAX	USA
FLESCHER, GOLDE	19	F	SVNT	RRA	DAX	USA
BLATT, REGINE	20	F	SVNT	RRA	DAX	USA
LUTIN, MAYER	22	M	LABR	RRA	DAX	USA
GOLDMANN, SILDE	18	M	LABR	RRA	DAX	USA
SCHADBLACH, MOSES	27	M	LABR	RRA	DAX	USA
AUDRACHLM, TRIM	32	M	FARMER	RRA	DAX	USA
MOULOUSTIE, BERNHARD	25	M	FARMER	RRA	DAX	USA
FITELYSKI, SEUDER	26	M	FARMER	RRA	DAX	USA
GOLDMANN, REGA	24	F	W	RRA	DAX	USA
LALE	3	F	CHILD	RRA	DAX	USA
GERLZA	1	F	CHILD	RRA	DAX	USA
HAUNSER, LAIE	16	F	SVNT	RRA	DAX	USA
SCHLAUGER, SCHAGE	14	F	SVNT	RRA	DAX	USA
BEER, MOSES	24	M	LABR	RRA	DAX	USA
THAIN, SAUL	23	M	LABR	RRA	DAX	USA

PASSENGER	AGE	SEX	OCCUPATION	PRVL	VIL	DES
HIRSCHBERG, TRINNET	9	M	CHILD	RR	ADAX	USA
DOBENZKI, MOSES	20	M	LABR	RR	ADAX	USA
TSEYMAISKE, CHAGE	21	M	LABR	RR	ADAX	USA
KORB, GITTEL	17	M	LABR	RR	ADAX	USA
LAIFER, MATTI	1	F	CHILD	RR	ADAX	USA
THINEB	1	M	CHILD	RR	ADAX	USA
RICKENTY, RENE	19	M	LABR	RR	ADAX	USA
BORSTEIN, PASSE	14	M	LABR	RR	ADAX	USA
BARACH, GUSTA	19	M	LABR	RR	ADAX	USA
PASSE	17	F	SVNT	RR	ADAX	USA
DURK, HIRSCH	45	M	MNR	RR	ADAX	USA
FRIEDE	44	F	W	RR	ADAX	USA
CHAGE	15	M	MNR	RR	ADAX	USA
PESSEL	11	F	CH	RR	ADAX	USA
HERNE	7	M	CHILD	RR	ADAX	USA
PENTRAS	5	F	CHILD	RR	ADAX	USA
KRESCH, JOSEPH	56	M	LABR	RR	ADAX	USA
STEPIN, SRUL	30	M	LABR	RR	ADAX	USA
ROTHSTEIN, TAUBE	15	F	SVNT	RR	ADAX	USA
DUBON, ITZKE	62	F	SVNT	RR	ADAX	USA
BORSTEIN, HESSEL	21	M	LABR	RR	ADAX	USA
GELEYNSKI, VICTORIA	20	F	SVNT	RR	ADAX	USA
KLEIN, SIMON	58	M	LABR	RR	ADAX	USA
MATHILDA	20	F	SVNT	RR	ADAX	USA
MAUTEL, MARKUS	1	F	CHILD	RR	ADAX	USA
WEXTER, SEIN.	50	M	LABR	RR	ADAX	USA
MARIE	48	F	W	RR	ADAX	USA
COHN, DAVID	40	M	LABR	RR	ADAX	USA
KAMBER, MOLDACHE	19	M	LABR	RR	ADAX	USA
KAMINKOUSKY, ABRAHAM	20	M	LABR	RR	ADAX	USA
WRABEL, MARIA	30	F	W	RR	ADAX	USA
HAMIN	11	M	CH	RR	ADAX	USA
ISSAC	10	M	CH	RR	ADAX	USA
SARIM	6	M	CHILD	RR	ADAX	USA
GROSS, AMANUEL	37	M	LABR	RR	ADAX	USA
KALTY	11	F	CH	RR	ADAX	USA
RELS	10	F	CH	RR	ADAX	USA
LAUFER, ESEYTE	16	M	LABR	RR	ADAX	USA
KELMMALET, MORITA	36	F	SVNT	RR	ADAX	USA
RETGER, ELIAS	35	M	LABR	RR	ADAX	USA
LAEBOURTEY, ISRAEL	24	M	LABR	RR	ADAX	USA
KLEIN, JACOB	25	M	LABR	RR	ADAX	USA
SIEGMONOUTEY, ROSA	20	F	SVNT	RR	ADAX	USA
FIELDMANN, SAUL	45	M	LABR	RR	ADAX	USA
KRAMMSTEIN, BERL	33	M	LABR	RR	ADAX	USA
TEMIN, MEYER	27	M	LABR	RR	ADAX	USA
SORE	26	M	LABR	RR	ADAX	USA
KOBRE, JOSEF	21	M	LABR	RR	ADAX	USA
HORYLOUSKY, ELIE	17	M	LABR	RR	ADAX	USA
FISCHMAN, CHAEGE	22	M	LABR	RR	ADAX	USA
SCHEINE	25	F	SVNT	RR	ADAX	USA
ESTER	16	F	SVNT	RR	ADAX	USA
KAMBLUM, PAUL	23	M	LABR	RR	ADAX	USA
MASTER, ISAK	24	M	LABR	RR	ADAX	USA
GOLDSCHLAZER, LASER	28	M	LABR	RR	ADAX	USA
BEILE	24	F	SVNT	RR	ADAX	USA

SHIP: DEVONIA

FROM: GLASGOW AND MOVILLE
TO: NEW YORK
ARRIVED: 16 JULY 1888

PASSENGER	AGE	SEX	OCCUPATION	PRVL	VIL	DES
WOLFF, SHINE	40	F	UNKNOWN	RR	ZZZZ	USA
ABRAHAMSOHN, SIMSCH	27	F	LABR	RR	ZZZZ	USA
SCHIFRE	16	F	UNKNOWN	RR	ZZZZ	USA
ABRM.	12	M	UNKNOWN	RR	ZZZZ	USA
BASS, MOSES	19	M	DLR	RR	ZZZZ	USA
ROSALIE	19	F	UNKNOWN	RR	ZZZZ	USA
BERLINER, RIFFE	42	F	UNKNOWN	RR	ZZZZ	USA
ABRAHAM	11	M	UNKNOWN	RR	ZZZZ	USA
BLUMBERG, RITE	25	F	UNKNOWN	RR	ZZZZ	USA
HANNA	6	F	CHILD	RR	ZZZZ	USA
SCHILM	1	M	CHILD	RR	ZZZZ	USA
KAPLINSKI, ABRAHAM	20	M	CPTR	RR	ZZZZ	USA
RACHEL	19	F	UNKNOWN	RR	ZZZZ	USA
SISSERMAN, MOSES	29	M	SHMK	RR	ZZZZ	USA
ROSALIA	30	F	UNKNOWN	RR	ZZZZ	USA
MEYER	.05	M	INFANT	RR	ZZZZ	USA
BULL, LEA	18	F	SVNT	RR	ZZZZ	USA
BEER, ESTER	20	M	UNKNOWN	RR	ZZZZ	USA
LIEBE	1	F	CHILD	RR	ZZZZ	USA
GRODZINSKA, ANNA	16	F	SVNT	RR	ZZZZ	USA
SUSANNA	19	F	SVNT	RR	ZZZZ	USA
GINSBWIG, SASE	20	F	SVNT	RR	ZZZZ	USA
GERACHENOWITZ, CHENJA	24	M	SHMK	RR	ZZZZ	USA
KAUFMAN, MINDEL	23	M	LABR	RR	ZZZZ	USA
MLUEZKOWA, MARIANNA	21	F	SVNT	RR	ZZZZ	USA
ROSITZKY, DORA	18	F	SVNT	RR	ZZZZ	USA
SMORGON, CHAZKIL	16	M	MUSN	RR	ZZZZ	USA
SONNENBERG, HINDE	26	F	UNKNOWN	RR	ZZZZ	USA
ROCHLE	.06	F	INFANT	RR	ZZZZ	USA
BERLINER, HIRSCH	50	M	LABR	RR	ZZZZ	USA
BRENNER, ISAK	18	M	LABR	RR	ZZZZ	USA
FISCH, CHANES	36	M	LABR	RR	ZZZZ	USA
GLAP, MICHAEL	25	M	LABR	RR	ZZZZ	USA
KRAPOTNISKI, JOSEF	20	M	LABR	RR	ZZZZ	USA
KATZEN, LEISER	22	M	LABR	RR	ZZZZ	USA
KOWALSKY, ANTON	26	M	LABR	RR	ZZZZ	USA
MIKOPA, MAXMILIAN	23	M	LABR	RR	ZZZZ	USA
MILLER, SCHMUL	18	M	LABR	RR	ZZZZ	USA
MALESCHEWSKY, GEJEL	23	M	LABR	RR	ZZZZ	USA
RABINASHON, A.	35	M	LABR	RR	ZZZZ	USA
SERETOROW, ANR.	33	M	LABR	RR	ZZZZ	USA
SEYCHE, JOHAN	30	M	LABR	RR	ZZZZ	USA
SCHNEIDER, GUSTAV	26	M	LABR	RR	ZZZZ	USA
SWERDBOWITZ, MORDECH	32	M	LABR	RR	ZZZZ	USA
WOETLAUES, ROSALIE	15	F	SVNT	RR	ZZZZ	USA
SIMANOWIC, YERSIE	21	F	SVNT	RR	ZZZZ	USA
ZEYNESKI, CHATZKI	22	M	LABR	RR	ZZZZ	USA
WOLFF, CHASKEL	5	F	CHILD	RR	ZZZZ	USA

SHIP: UMBRIA

FROM: LIVERPOOL AND QUEENSTOWN
TO: NEW YORK
ARRIVED: 16 JULY 1888

PASSENGER	AGE	SEX	OCCUPATION	PRVL	VIL	DES
AUSENBERG, GEIZEL	21	M	LABR	RR	AHOO	USA
ADAMOWICH, JAN	41	M	UNKNOWN	RR	AIHY	USA
SELIG	19	M	UNKNOWN	RR	AHOO	USA
BRANDES, MAX	20	M	UNKNOWN	RR	AHOO	USA
DUMAN, BEJNIX	16	M	LABR	RR	ACBF	USA
FILCHMAN, ISAAC	34	M	TLR	RR	AIHR	USA
HECKEL, CARL	32	M	TLR	RR	AAKH	USA
HEDWIG	28	F	W	RR	AAKH	USA
ELSA	8	F	CHILD	RR	AAKH	USA
KLEUNMANN, JITE	32	M	LABR	RR	ACBF	USA
KORSING, MORDESEI	25	M	LABR	RR	AIFL	USA
FAK--OSKY, ABRAM	28	M	LABR	RR	ZZZZ	USA
JANN, HIRSCH	54	M	LABR	RR	ZZZZ	USA
MOSES	18	M	LABR	RR	ZZZZ	USA
-UROK, JOSEF	18	M	LABR	RR	ZZZZ	USA
JOSEF	22	M	LABR	RR	ZZZZ	USA
KURBOTZKE, THOMAS	11	M	CH	RR	ZZZZ	USA
ROSNIKOW, SALOMON	23	M	TLR	RR	ADAX	USA
SCHAPIN, GITEL	28	F	MA	RR	ZZZZ	USA
BELE	7	F	CHILD	RR	ZZZZ	USA
ISRAEL	8	M	CHILD	RR	ZZZZ	USA
SAWITZKE, JOSEF	28	M	LABR	RR	ZZZZ	USA

PASSENGER	AGE	SEX	OCCUPATION	PRI	VIL	DES
SCHAUROKI, SCHOLEM	55	M	FARMER	RR	ZZZZ	USA
MALKI	55	F	W	RR	ZZZZ	USA
LUNDEL	26	M	LABR	RR	ZZZZ	USA
ALLI	11	M	CH	RR	ZZZZ	USA
SPECTOR, DAVID	25	M	WCHMKR	RR	AHOO	USA
SKLAR, SAMUEL	28	M	CPTR	RR	ZZZZ	USA
VORSCHAU, ERNST	21	M	JWLR	RR	AINJ	USA
JACOB	30	M	LABR	RR	AINJ	USA
WEGDORIK, BEN	23	M	LABR	RR	ACBF	USA
WALPE, LESER	28	M	LABR	RR	ACBF	USA

SHIP: FULDA

FROM: BREMEN AND SOUTHAMPTON
TO: NEW YORK
ARRIVED: 17 JULY 1888

PASSENGER	AGE	SEX	OCCUPATION	PRI	VIL	DES
LECH, ANNA	40	F	UNKNOWN	RR	ZZZZ	USA
JOSEF	6	M	CHILD	RR	ZZZZ	USA
SILBERMANN, JOSEF	26	M	FARMER	RR	ZZZZ	USA
EVA	20	F	UNKNOWN	RR	ZZZZ	USA
SALAMON	21	M	FARMER	RR	ZZZZ	USA
JUDIE	15	M	FARMER	RR	ZZZZ	USA
BAY, LEISER	23	M	MCHT	RR	ZZZZ	USA
GITTELSOHN, MEYER	50	M	LABR	RR	ZZZZ	USA
MARYEN	40	F	LABR	RR	ZZZZ	USA
ELIJAS	17	M	LABR	RR	ZZZZ	USA
ALTE	6	M	CHILD	RR	ZZZZ	USA
HIRSCH	5	M	CHILD	RR	ZZZZ	USA
BARMUS, JURGIS	26	M	LABR	RR	ZZZZ	USA
ROSENFELD, HENA	25	F	UNKNOWN	RR	ZZZZ	USA
KOHN, SARAH	23	F	UNKNOWN	RR	ZZZZ	USA
SEIDE	4	F	CHILD	RR	ZZZZ	USA
RUSCHNICK, ALTE	28	F	UNKNOWN	RR	ZZZZ	USA
ZUCKERMANN, ABRAHAM	40	M	LABR	RR	ZZZZ	USA
ROLNIK, MOSES	21	M	LABR	RR	ZZZZ	USA
FRIT, ABRAHAM	34	M	LABR	RR	ZZZZ	USA
GERMANSKY, CHA--	30	M	LABR	RR	ZZZZ	USA

SHIP: THE QUEEN

FROM: LIVERPOOL AND QUEENSTOWN
TO: NEW YORK
ARRIVED: 18 JULY 1888

PASSENGER	AGE	SEX	OCCUPATION	PRI	VIL	DES
BELEWISC, ISAAC	50	M	LABR	RR	ADBQ	PHI
VILINSKI, MYER	33	M	LABR	RR	ADBQ	PHI
KACEW, SAML.	22	M	LABR	RR	ADBQ	BAL
CELESTI, RAMELLE	16	M	LABR	RR	ADBQ	BO
LAZARUS, HANNAH	39	F	W	RR	ADBQ	NY
REBECCA	11	F	CH	RR	ADBQ	NY
MORIS	10	M	CH	RR	ADBQ	NY
HARRIS	9	M	CHILD	RR	ADBQ	NY
ESTHER	8	M	CHILD	RR	ADBQ	NY
DORA	6	M	CHILD	RR	ADBQ	NY
LEWIS	4	M	CHILD	RR	ADBQ	NY
SOPHIA	1	F	CHILD	RR	ADBQ	NY
HYMAN, ESTHER	20	F	SP	RR	ADBQ	NY
RABONOWITZ, M.	22	M	LABR	RR	ZZZZ	NY
HORTZ, M.	24	M	LABR	RR	ZZZZ	NY
ZWILLENBERG, ISRAEL	27	M	LABR	RR	ZZZZ	NY
BORSZOWAJ, MHAR.	11	M	CH	RR	ZZZZ	NY
KATZ, MEYER	50	F	W	RR	ZZZZ	NY
SPITZ, ARNOLD	18	M	LABR	RR	ZZZZ	NY
NATHAN	16	M	LABR	RR	ZZZZ	NY
PESASCHJE, HALJE	17	M	LABR	RR	ZZZZ	NY
ALLMAN, ROME	18	M	LABR	RR	ZZZZ	NY
LECHNER, LEISE	20	F	SP	RR	ZZZZ	NY
BOROWSKY, PERSCHE	42	M	LABR	RR	ZZZZ	NY
CHAJE	10	F	CH	RR	ZZZZ	NY
CHANE	7	F	CHILD	RR	ZZZZ	NY
NUTE	5	M	CHILD	RR	ZZZZ	NY
JURA, ISAAC	22	M	LABR	RR	ZZZZ	NY
CZEDROCLUNK, GOLDE	6	M	CHILD	RR	ZZZZ	NY
DAVID	5	M	CHILD	RR	ZZZZ	NY
WECHSLER, WOLF	20	M	LABR	RR	ZZZZ	NY
WESLER, JOHANN	19	M	LABR	RR	ZZZZ	NY
WILLIG, MARIA	23	F	SP	RR	ZZZZ	NY
ROSENBERG, SAM.	22	M	LABR	RR	ZZZZ	NY
SCHUERDEROWSKY, ITZKI	23	M	LABR	RR	ZZZZ	NY
ISAAC	17	M	LABR	RR	ZZZZ	NY
SCHNERDERMAN, JOS.	31	M	LABR	RR	ZZZZ	PHI
CHANE	30	F	W	RR	ZZZZ	PHI
ESTHER	17	F	SP	RR	ZZZZ	PHI
ABRAM	11	M	CH	RR	ZZZZ	PHI
FREID, FEITEL	18	M	LABR	RR	ZZZZ	PHI
MICHALOWSKA, MICHAEL	19	M	LABR	RR	ZZZZ	PHI
FRIECHMAN, GEDL	25	M	LABR	RR	ZZZZ	PHI
RISCHE	20	F	W	RR	ZZZZ	PHI
DAVIDSOHN, ELIE	14	F	SP	RR	ZZZZ	PHI
ROSAK, RUCKE	20	M	LABR	RR	ADAX	NY
BOMSTEIN, LISA	16	F	SP	RR	ADAX	NY
GLESER, CALMEN	20	M	LABR	RR	ADAX	NY
FREIDE	40	F	W	RR	ADAX	NY
KANTAVE, ELAONE	19	F	SP	RR	ADAX	NY
WEINBERG, JENTE	24	F	W	RR	ADAX	NY
GOLD	3	M	CHILD	RR	ADAX	NY
KEILE	1	F	CHILD	RR	ADAX	NY
ROSISADI, JOHAN	26	M	LABR	RR	ADAX	PHI
WOSKOLLINKY, JANKEL	37	M	LABR	RR	ADAX	NY
MEYE	8	F	CHILD	RR	ADAX	NY
FELDMAER, SAMUEL	25	M	LABR	RR	ADAX	NY
DUEBES, PETER	33	M	LABR	RR	ADAX	NY
RUCHINSKY, MATHEI	37	M	LABR	RR	ADAX	NY
MACEIS, ANTON	30	M	LABR	RR	ADAX	NY
ANNA	30	F	W	RR	ADAX	NY
ALBERT	4	M	CHILD	RR	ADAX	NY
FUHR, SCHEINE	22	M	LABR	RR	ADAX	NY
JANKEL	21	F	W	RR	ADAX	NY
SAMUELSON, SCHLOME	52	M	LABR	RR	ADAX	NY
SCHEINE	20	M	LABR	RR	ADAX	NY
BRAVITZ, MOSES	22	M	LABR	RR	ADAX	NY
NOHOSY, JOSEF	29	M	LABR	RR	ADAX	NY
MOSKOWITZ, MORITZ	17	M	LABR	RR	ADAX	NY
HELLGERS, HENRICK	45	M	LABR	RR	ADAX	NY
PIETRSEWITZ, KARL	22	M	LABR	RR	ADAX	NY
ZEKAITIS, FLAREN	19	M	LABR	RR	ADAX	NY
DUCHBINDER, DEBORA	24	F	W	RR	ADAX	NY
SCHIE	36	M	LABR	RR	ADAX	NY
BIENLAS, JAN	21	M	LABR	RR	ADAX	NY
MOSCHKOWITZ, FISCHER	22	M	LABR	RR	ADAX	NY
HERCHEL	5	M	CHILD	RR	ADAX	NY
KAHLA, FANNE	30	F	SP	RR	ADAX	NY
CHIN, ADELE	24	F	SP	RR	ADAX	NY
LESINK, MALVINA	18	F	SP	RR	ADAX	NY
SCHARGORODSKA, GUSTAF	22	M	LABR	RR	ADAX	NY
STEINBERG, ISAK	20	M	LABR	RR	ADAX	NY
ALADERT, MEYER	28	M	LABR	RR	ADAX	NY
FANNY	26	F	W	RR	ADAX	NY
ROSA	4	F	CHILD	RR	ADAX	NY
LEO	3	M	CHILD	RR	ADAX	NY
MICHALOWSKY, EVE	17	F	SP	RR	ADAX	NY
BRAILIAN, SAM.	26	M	LABR	RR	ADAX	NY
BASIS, ABRAH	18	M	LABR	RR	ADAX	NY
KWZINSKY, BEHR	26	M	LABR	RR	ADAX	NY
PARTNOW, BENEION	26	M	LABR	RR	ADAX	NY
ADELSOHN, SCHLOME	40	M	LABR	RR	ADAX	NY
SCHIEMELMAN, CHAJE	15	M	LABR	RR	ADAX	NY
LEHTER, SALOMEA	34	M	LABR	RR	ADAX	NY
FERDINAND, DAVID	37	M	LABR	RR	ADAX	NY

PASSENGER	AGE	SEX	OCCUPATION	PRV VIL DES
JUDELOW, JOEL	30	M	LABR	RRADAXNY
GOLDENBERG, MARCUS	30	M	LABR	RRADAXNY
LIFCHITZ, EPHRAIM	40	M	LABR	RRADAXNY
LAUTIS, ANTON	25	M	LABR	RRADAXNY
OSWET, S.	26	M	LABR	RRADAXNY
LLISCHOWSKY, FRANZ	25	M	LABR	RRADAXNY
BUEDONAS, JURGES	21	M	LABR	RRADAXNY
ZWIGOITES, A.	18	M	LABR	RRADAXNY
SCHVISTONSKES, JURGES	55	M	LABR	RRADAXNY
JACKUKA, WASILIE	27	M	LABR	RRADAXNY
SAVAFIN, JOSEF	29	M	LABR	RRADAXNY
PAUSNER, ISRAEL	18	M	LABR	RRADAXNY
SCHARF, LEISER	21	M	LABR	RRADAXNY
FINKELSTEIN, HIRSCH	31	M	LABR	RRADAXNY
BRANNE	20	F	W	RRADAXNY
BERCOWITZ, ANNA	18	F	SP	RRADAXNY
LEVIS, JACOB	20	M	LABR	RRADAXNY
ROSENER, LIPITZ	32	M	LABR	RRADAXNY
STEINFELD, SIMA	28	M	LABR	RRADAXNY
BLUMENFELD, ISAAC	47	M	LABR	RRADAXNY
ABRAHAMSOHN, E.	20	M	LABR	RRADAXNY
JACOB, LUCINIE	35	F	W	RRZZZZNY
SIMON	3	M	CHILD	RRZZZZNY

SHIP: WISCONSIN

FROM: LIVERPOOL AND QUEENSTOWN
TO: NEW YORK
ARRIVED: 18 JULY 1888

PASSENGER	AGE	SEX	OCCUPATION	PRV VIL DES
ROZENKRANZ, HIRSCH	30	M	PMBR	PLZZZZUSA
MAIKILA, NILS	20	M	TKR	FNZZZZUSA
GRINBERG, ROCHE	22	F	W	RRZZZZUSA
RUIVEN	4	F	CHILD	RRZZZZUSA
KRAWITZ, SCHLEIM	7	M	CHILD	RRZZZZUSA
RATBOMAN, CHAIE	19	F	SP	RRZZZZUSA
FRIEDMAN, ISRAEL	38	M	TLR	RRZZZZUSA
LAWEL	35	F	W	RRZZZZUSA
NECHE	23	F	SP	RRZZZZUSA
JANKEL	7	M	CHILD	RRZZZZUSA
FISCHER, ISAAC	30	M	PNTR	RRZZZZUSA
GRIMBERG, FANNY	16	F	SP	RRZZZZUSA
SAMUEL, ADELEL	23	F	SP	RRZZZZUSA
BIWIZINSKI, CHAIE	17	F	SP	RRZZZZUSA
GOLDZEIGER, LEIZER	18	F	SP	RRZZZZUSA
SCHITLES, ZISEL	18	F	SP	RRZZZZUSA
KATZ, SCHMUEL	18	M	TLR	PLZZZZUSA
HERRING, WOLF	45	M	BLKSMH	RRZZZZUSA
SARAH	40	F	W	RRZZZZUSA
JOSEPH	7	M	CHILD	RRZZZZUSA
CHANE	6	F	CHILD	RRZZZZUSA
NESCHE	4	F	CHILD	RRZZZZUSA
BRONSWEIN, JACOB	29	M	TKR	RRZZZZUSA
TENEBAUM, MINDEL	13	F	SP	RRZZZZUSA
MANNESCHEWITZ, ZIPPI	17	F	SP	RRZZZZUSA
BELANSKY, CHAIM	18	M	FARMER	RRZZZZUSA
HOMISCH, JOSEPH	34	M	FARMER	RRZZZZUSA
MATHILDE	25	F	W	RRZZZZUSA
SCHAPIRO, ABR.	29	M	TKR	RRZZZZUSA
JAGER, FRIEDR.	19	M	TKR	RRZZZZUSA
COHON, SCHLOME	22	M	GZR	RRZZZZUSA
ROXER, PETER	24	M	FARMER	RRZZZZUSA
SARA	50	F	MA	RRZZZZUSA
GROWOAS, EDLA	33	F	SP	RRZZZZUSA
GRUNHOHN, WM.	26	M	MSN	FNZZZZUSA
HAERING, BAER	.10	F	INFANT	RRZZZZUSA
BINMCHSKY, FRANZ	24	M	FARMER	RRZZZZUSA
KOHN, ABRAM	31	M	FARMER	RRZZZZUSA
LATTE	23	F	W	RRZZZZUSA
DINA	19	F	SP	RRZZZZUSA

PASSENGER	AGE	SEX	OCCUPATION	PRV VIL DES
ROSA	7	F	CHILD	RRZZZZUSA
ROSA	.08	F	INFANT	RRZZZZUSA
FELDMAN, TORINE	38	F	W	RRZZZZUSA
GITTEL	7	F	CHILD	RRZZZZUSA
JENKE	6	F	CHILD	RRZZZZUSA
SARA	3	F	CHILD	RRZZZZUSA
BARDOWITZ, BETTY	27	F	W	RRZZZZUSA
RASCHE	.11	F	INFANT	RRZZZZUSA
SCHARGORSKY, CHAINE	27	F	W	RRZZZZUSA
ABRAH.	7	M	CHILD	RRZZZZUSA
LUBE	6	F	CHILD	RRZZZZUSA
DAVID	5	M	CHILD	RRZZZZUSA
DOMBROWSKY, TAUBE	58	F	MA	RRZZZZUSA
SCHULKIN, MATE	37	M	LABR	RRZZZZUSA
KRONBERG, CARL	25	M	LABR	RRZZZZUSA
SAMUELZ, SALOMON	26	M	LABR	RRZZZZUSA
GRIMBERG, LEIB	.10	F	INFANT	RRZZZZUSA
BEN	.10	M	INFANT	RRZZZZUSA

SHIP: STATE OF NEBRASKA

FROM: GLASGOW AND LARNE
TO: NEW YORK
ARRIVED: 18 JULY 1888

PASSENGER	AGE	SEX	OCCUPATION	PRV VIL DES
ADAMSKI, CHAIM	10	M	CH	RRZZZZUSA
CHAIE	8	F	CHILD	RRZZZZUSA
NEKRITSCH, ISSER	35	M	PDLR	RRZZZZUSA
LEIBMANN, WOLF	29	M	PDLR	RRZZZZUSA
KRAWETZKI, SAMUEL	23	M	TLR	RRZZZZUSA
WARTMANN, JOSEPH	53	M	TLR	RRZZZZUSA
MASKOWITZ, MARCUS	26	M	TLR	RRZZZZUSA
ZUCKERMANN, MOSES	18	M	TLR	RRZZZZUSA
FARBMANN, LEIB	33	M	TLR	RRZZZZUSA
JACOB, GLAS	42	M	TLR	RRZZZZUSA
MOWACHOWITZ, BORUCH	19	M	TLR	RRZZZZUSA
FEIGNI, NISSEN	18	M	TLR	RRZZZZUSA
GRINSTEIN, BEHR.	48	M	TLR	RRZZZZUSA
HUCH, JANKEL	17	M	TLR	RRZZZZUSA
ROSTAIZER, BEREL	28	M	TLR	RRZZZZUSA
KURAN, CHAIM	17	M	APDST	RRZZZZUSA
MARIENHOF, WOLFF	22	M	BRR	RRZZZZUSA
SCHAPIRO, MOSES	37	M	GZR	RRZZZZUSA
WARSLAWSKI, CHANYNA	22	M	CGRMKR	RRZZZZUSA
KAPLAN, RAPHAEL	31	M	CPMKR	RRZZZZUSA
KANTROWITZ, KUSCHEL	25	M	BKLYR	RRZZZZUSA
DUGMANN, ISAAC	29	M	CL	RRZZZZUSA
SKILKEN, CHAIM	19	M	TNR	RRZZZZUSA
MASLAWSKY, MORRIS	33	M	MUSN	RRZZZZUSA
ORSCHOWSKY, ISRAEL	19	M	SHMK	RRZZZZUSA
KRAMER, GERSCHON	17	M	SHMK	RRZZZZUSA
MENDELBAUM, JACOB	43	M	CPTR	RRZZZZUSA
SANDLEI, SAMUEL	22	M	JNR	RRZZZZUSA
GRUENWALD, ISRAEL	30	M	JNR	RRZZZZUSA
SALZMANN, CHAIM	26	M	JNR	RRZZZZUSA
STOLER, WOLF	35	M	JNR	RRZZZZUSA
ZIMMERMANN, ABRAHAM	36	M	JNR	RRZZZZUSA
MELTZER, ITZIG	36	M	SMH	RRZZZZUSA
GOLDFARB, MOSES	17	M	SMH	RRZZZZUSA
RABINOSSE, LEIB	23	M	SMH	RRZZZZUSA
ZECHER, ABRAHAM	24	M	SMH	RRZZZZUSA
CHEIFITZ, ABRAHAM	20	M	LABR	RRZZZZUSA
ISRAEL	17	M	LABR	RRZZZZUSA
KARPAS, MAX	17	M	LABR	RRZZZZUSA
KAPUSTA, JAN	24	M	LABR	RRZZZZUSA
SCHLIEMANN, LEIB	13	M	LABR	RRZZZZUSA
KAMINSKY, GERSCHON	16	M	LABR	RRZZZZUSA
ANOP, FEODOR	24	M	LABR	RRZZZZUSA
JACOBSOHN, WOLF	21	M	LABR	RRZZZZUSA
LEWIN, BENJAMIN	21	M	LABR	RRZZZZUSA

PASSENGER	AGE	SEX	OCCUPATION	PRV VIL DES
GEFFEN, PINCHES	20	M	LABR	RRZZZZUSA
KAMINSKI, MARKNE	43	M	LABR	RRZZZZUSA
MELKOWSKY, MICHEL	22	M	LABR	RRZZZZUSA
SCHAPIRO, HENRY	22	M	LABR	RRZZZZUSA
HEN, GERSCH-	30	M	LABR	RRZZZZUSA
KARMENGIESSER, GETZE	46	M	LABR	RRZZZZUSA
MELL, MEYER	18	M	LABR	RRZZZZUSA
NOEL, MIREL	24	F	W	RRZZZZUSA
WOLFF	1	M	CHILD	RRZZZZUSA
BINDER, ISRAEL	24	M	LABR	RRZZZZUSA
KURTKOWSKY, ABRAHAM	20	M	LABR	RRZZZZUSA
ZUCKERMANN, ARIE	30	M	TLR	RRZZZZUSA
BASCHE	28	F	W	RRZZZZUSA
SCHMUEL	7	M	CHILD	RRZZZZUSA
BROWN, MOSES	26	M	SHMK	RRZZZZUSA
RIWE	26	F	W	RRZZZZUSA
ABRAM	3	M	CHILD	RRZZZZUSA
UMANSKI, MOSES	22	M	TLR	RRZZZZUSA
ROSA	19	F	W	RRZZZZUSA
WILMYK, MAX	38	M	TCHR	RRZZZZUSA
NATALIE	35	F	W	RRZZZZUSA
JOSEF	5	M	CHILD	RRZZZZUSA
ALEXANDRA	2	F	CHILD	RRZZZZUSA
ISIDOR	2	M	CHILD	RRZZZZUSA
ELIZABETH	.06	F	INFANT	RRZZZZUSA
AFRAIMOWITSCH, LEVY	23	M	PDLR	RRZZZZUSA
MINE	21	F	W	RRZZZZUSA
SORE	25	F	SP	RRZZZZUSA
KONIGSBERG, BREINE	17	F	SP	RRZZZZUSA
SORA	45	F	W	RRZZZZUSA
MORAWNI, GITTEL	25	F	SP	RRZZZZUSA
NEKRETZ, GITTEL	14	F	SP	RRZZZZUSA
HINDE	11	F	CH	RRZZZZUSA
PEISSERT, ITTE	16	F	SP	RRZZZZUSA
ELIE	7	M	CHILD	RRZZZZUSA
LAMASCHIN, STESSE	16	F	SP	RRZZZZUSA
GAFFAN, CHASSE	17	F	SP	RRZZZZUSA
SORE	17	F	SP	RRZZZZUSA
LEWIN, JOHANNA	22	F	SP	RRZZZZUSA
LINA	18	F	SP	RRZZZZUSA
TEITZ, ROCHE	28	F	W	RRZZZZUSA
KAPLAN, GOLDE	21	F	W	RRZZZZUSA
RUBENSTEIN, BASCHE	22	F	W	RRZZZZUSA
PONZ, BASCHE	30	F	SP	RRZZZZUSA
TONKE	30	F	W	RRZZZZUSA
SARAH	8	F	CHILD	RRZZZZUSA
FEIGE	6	F	CHILD	RRZZZZUSA
GOLDFART, RIFKE	35	F	W	RRZZZZUSA
BEILE	16	F	SP	RRZZZZUSA
CHEIKE	10	F	CH	RRZZZZUSA
ISAAC	9	M	CHILD	RRZZZZUSA
MARIAN	6	F	CHILD	RRZZZZUSA
BASCHE	4	F	CHILD	RRZZZZUSA
DWORE	1	F	CHILD	RRZZZZUSA
MASLAWSKY, CHAIE	21	F	W	RRZZZZUSA
ISSER	1	M	CHILD	RRZZZZUSA
ZUCKERMANN, GUTE	20	F	W	RRZZZZUSA
LEIBE	.06	F	INFANT	RRZZZZUSA
ROD, SORE	30	F	W	RRZZZZUSA
BERKE	9	M	CHILD	RRZZZZUSA
NOSKE	6	M	CHILD	RRZZZZUSA
JANKEL	5	M	CHILD	RRZZZZUSA
JASKEL	1	M	CHILD	RRZZZZUSA
BERGER, MARIE	45	F	W	RRZZZZUSA
ROSA	1	F	CHILD	RRZZZZUSA
COHN, SCHLOME	26	M	LABR	PLZZZZUSA
WISNEFSKY, JOSEPH	29	M	LABR	PLZZZZUSA
BINSCHEFSKY, JAN	23	M	LABR	PLZZZZUSA
SAMSKY, JOSEPH	22	M	LABR	PLZZZZUSA
SCHLENKS, MICHAEL	25	M	LABR	PLZZZZUSA
SCHELKO, MADESLAW	36	M	LABR	PLZZZZUSA
SEDLETZKY, STANISLAW	28	M	LABR	PLZZZZUSA
HERDMANN, MORDCHE	20	M	LABR	PLZZZZUSA
KURDAN, MATHEUS	26	M	LABR	PLZZZZUSA
KERSTON, JAN	27	M	LABR	PLZZZZUSA
NUDELMAN, MOSES	27	M	TLR	PLZZZZUSA
KRIETALL, ARON	21	M	TLR	PLZZZZUSA
HECHT, BERL	26	M	TLR	PLZZZZUSA
HOMOSTOWITSCH, JANKEL	27	M	SHMK	PLZZZZUSA
GUTTERMANN, DAVID	27	M	SHMK	PLZZZZUSA
PIRKEWITSCH, DAVID	36	M	PNTR	PLZZZZUSA
WUCKAUF, ABRAM	40	M	PNTR	PLZZZZUSA
BARWITSCH, JACOB	29	M	JWLR	PLZZZZUSA
BLUMENKOP, CHAIM	24	M	BCKM	PLZZZZUSA
LAMPERT, SCHOLEM	22	M	PDLR	PLZZZZUSA
SCHIMMER, FISCHEL	49	M	PDLR	PLZZZZUSA
AMALIA	22	F	SP	PLZZZZUSA
GOLDSTEIN, LIEBE	18	F	SP	PLZZZZUSA
CHANE	15	F	SP	PLZZZZUSA
CHENKE	11	F	CH	PLZZZZUSA
DREWAKO, AUGUSTA	23	F	W	PLZZZZUSA
BERTHA	6	F	CHILD	PLZZZZUSA
EMMA	1	F	CHILD	PLZZZZUSA
LICHTENSTEIN, ETTEL	26	F	W	PLZZZZUSA
LESER	6	M	CHILD	PLZZZZUSA

SHIP: BELGENLAND

FROM: ANTWERP
TO: NEW YORK
ARRIVED: 19 JULY 1888

PASSENGER	AGE	SEX	OCCUPATION	PRV VIL DES
ISCHITZKI, ABR.	27	M	SMH	PLADBQNY
SCHAPIRO, MORRIS	23	M	BLKSMH	PLADBQNY
BISTRETZKI, LEWIS	37	M	LABR	PLADBQNY
ROSENTHAL, ELIAS	18	M	LABR	PLADBQPHI
LEWIN, BARUCH	27	M	CPTR	PLADBQPHI
RUBIN, JACOB	22	M	TLR	PLADBQBO
KUFATZ, REBECCA	19	F	STDNT	PLADBQBO
GRADZINOWSKY, ESTER	20	F	UNKNOWN	PLAHTWNY
ISAAC	18	M	TLR	PLAHTWNY
RACHEL	15	F	UNKNOWN	PLAHTWNY
ABRAM	11	M	UNKNOWN	PLAHTWNY
BEILE	9	M	CHILD	PLAHTWNY
PALTER, TAUBE	18	F	UNKNOWN	PLAHVUNY
WRONSKY, JOSEF	28	M	LABR	RRZZZZNY
FORSKY, SOTTE	34	F	UNKNOWN	RRZZZZNY
ESCHKA	9	F	CHILD	RRZZZZNY
RACHEL	5	F	CHILD	RRZZZZNY
RURKE	4	M	CHILD	RRZZZZNY
BORKOWIEZ, JACOB	23	M	LABR	RRAIHZCH

SHIP: GOTHIA

FROM: STETTIN
TO: NEW YORK
ARRIVED: 19 JULY 1888

PASSENGER	AGE	SEX	OCCUPATION	PRV VIL DES
ARNDT, CARL	30	M	LABR	RRZZZZUSA
MARIE	29	F	W	RRZZZZUSA
ORENCEWITS, MACE	17	M	LABR	RRZZZZUSA
CINMKOWSKI, ANTON	17	M	LABR	RRZZZZUSA
DWOJAKOWSKA, ANNA	12	F	CH	RRZZZZUSA
ZACEK, KAREL	19	M	LABR	RRZZZZUSA
MILBRNDT, WILHELM	35	M	FARMER	RRZZZZUSA
SAWULKAJTYS, ANTONI	20	M	LABR	RRZZZZUSA
MARKOWITZ, ANNIS	23	F	W	RRZZZZUSA
AUSTRO, FRANZICEK	21	M	LABR	RRZZZZUSA
SALOMON, MICHAEL	30	M	DLR	RRZZZZUSA
BUFER, NUSSE	34	M	DLR	RRZZZZUSA

PASSENGER	AGE	SEX	OCCUPATION	PRIV	VIL	DES
JANKOWSKY, FRDR.	48	M	DLR	RR	ZZZZ	USA
RAKACZA, PAULINA	20	F	SGL	RR	ZZZZ	USA
SCHILLBERG, GOTTFRIED	43	M	FARMER	RR	ZZZZ	USA
MARIE	24	F	W	RR	ZZZZ	USA
ADOLF	4	M	CHILD	RR	ZZZZ	USA
MARTHA	.06	F	INFANT	RR	ZZZZ	USA
SCHOEN, SAMUEL	19	M	TLR	RR	ZZZZ	USA
ALTSCHULER, JACOB	28	M	TLR	RR	ZZZZ	USA
GOLUB, MOSES	28	M	GZR	RR	ZZZZ	USA
HORWITZ, ABRAHAM	31	M	GZR	RR	ZZZZ	USA
MICHELKER, HIRSCH	18	M	TLR	RR	ZZZZ	USA
POLZINSKY, LUDWIG	32	M	SHMK	RR	ZZZZ	USA
LOEWS, MENDEL	18	M	TLR	RR	ZZZZ	USA
RAMIG, JOHANNES	21	M	GZR	RR	ZZZZ	USA
LUTZKE, HERMANN	28	M	BCKM	RR	ZZZZ	USA
TREPTOW, WILHELM	27	M	LABR	RR	ZZZZ	USA
WOZNY, MARIE	18	F	SGL	RR	ZZZZ	USA
AGNES	15	F	SGL	RR	ZZZZ	USA
MILEWSKI, JAN	47	M	MCHT	RR	ZZZZ	USA
WINSCHKY, THOMAS	47	M	MCHT	RR	ZZZZ	USA
BARSUCK, ELIAS	37	M	SHMK	RR	ZZZZ	USA
KARSKY, VINCENT	49	M	SHMK	RR	ZZZZ	USA
OKROGLY, CONSTANTIN	28	M	LABR	RR	ZZZZ	USA
PLOTTKIN, LEIB	27	M	TLR	RR	ZZZZ	USA
HINDE	22	F	W	RR	ZZZZ	USA
KAPLAN, LEIWE	44	M	JNR	RR	ZZZZ	USA
KOWARSKE, IDIK	27	M	JNR	RR	ZZZZ	USA
WEIN, SALOMON	25	M	TNR	RR	ZZZZ	USA
BASCHKA, IGNATZ	37	M	LABR	RR	ZZZZ	USA
STANTSCHIN, PETER	26	M	TLR	RR	ZZZZ	USA
GRADOWSKI, KALMEN	27	M	TLR	RR	ZZZZ	USA
MARKOWITZ, ITTE	23	F	W	RR	ZZZZ	USA
FANNY	3	F	CHILD	RR	ZZZZ	USA
SALOMON	3	M	CHILD	RR	ZZZZ	USA
WOLF	1	M	CHILD	RR	ZZZZ	USA
LESKE, MARTHA	.03	F	INFANT	RR	ZZZZ	USA

SHIP: SAALE

FROM: BREMEN AND SOUTHAMPTON
TO: NEW YORK
ARRIVED: 20 JULY 1888

PASSENGER	AGE	SEX	OCCUPATION	PRIV	VIL	DES
JORDAN, ELIAS	21	M	LABR	RR	ZZZZ	USA
ROSA	20	F	W	RR	ZZZZ	USA
SCHIRMER, CARL	52	M	FARMER	RR	ZZZZ	USA
HENRIETTE	37	F	W	RR	ZZZZ	USA
EMILIE	5	F	CHILD	RR	ZZZZ	USA
ANNA	3	F	CHILD	RR	ZZZZ	USA
KAPPLER, REB.	37	M	SHMK	RR	ZZZZ	USA
CHARLOTTE	39	F	W	RR	ZZZZ	USA
CARL	8	M	CHILD	RR	ZZZZ	USA
JOHNE.	5	F	CHILD	RR	ZZZZ	USA
MATHILDE	.07	F	INFANT	RR	ZZZZ	USA
KOHN, HERM.	32	M	FARMER	RR	ZZZZ	USA
AUGUSTE	32	F	W	RR	ZZZZ	USA
K-ELS, FRIEDR.	71	M	FARMER	RR	ZZZZ	USA
ANNA	69	F	W	RR	ZZZZ	USA
MARGNARDT, ALB.	19	M	FARMER	RR	ZZZZ	USA
HARTWIG, AMALIE	18	F	UNKNOWN	RR	ZZZZ	USA
NOWINSKI, THOMAS	34	M	FARMER	RR	ZZZZ	USA
RUSKE, ALB.	23	M	MCHT	RR	ZZZZ	USA
MANHAMS, FRANZ	28	M	FARMER	RR	ZZZZ	USA
ANTON	25	M	FARMER	RR	ZZZZ	USA
MANSCHIK, USCHER	37	M	FARMER	RR	ZZZZ	USA
SAIWEL, KRONHOLZ	29	M	WCHMKR	RR	ZZZZ	USA
WACHMANN, FRANCISCA	29	F	UNKNOWN	RR	ZZZZ	USA
DOROTHEA	9	F	CHILD	RR	ZZZZ	USA
IWINSKY, LUDW.	24	M	FARMER	RR	ZZZZ	USA
VOGH, AD.	33	M	FARMER	RR	ZZZZ	USA

PASSENGER	AGE	SEX	OCCUPATION	PRIV	VIL	DES
GRIKETIS, PETRES	23	M	FARMER	RR	ZZZZ	USA
CZESIEWSKY, WINZENS	29	M	FARMER	RR	ZZZZ	USA
RABINOWITZ, MOSES	45	M	LABR	RR	ZZZZ	USA
ROSENGARDT, TOBIAS	20	M	LABR	RR	ZZZZ	USA
SCHIEWE, ADOLPH	29	M	LABR	RR	ZZZZ	USA
ADOLPHINE	24	F	W	RR	ZZZZ	USA
ANNA	.06	F	INFANT	RR	ZZZZ	USA
MART.	38	M	SMH	RR	ZZZZ	USA
ANNA	35	F	W	RR	ZZZZ	USA
ROB.	11	M	CH	RR	ZZZZ	USA
BERTHA	10	F	CH	RR	ZZZZ	USA
RICH.	9	M	CHILD	RR	ZZZZ	USA
ENR.	6	M	CHILD	RR	ZZZZ	USA
THEODOR	4	M	CHILD	RR	ZZZZ	USA
LEOKADIA	.06	F	INFANT	RR	ZZZZ	USA
KESSLER, ISAAC	19	M	FARMER	RR	ZZZZ	USA
RAPPOPORT, JOSEPH	45	M	FARMER	RR	ZZZZ	USA
KURKEWICH, SAM.	30	M	SP	RR	ZZZZ	USA
SCHONKOPF, JACOB	19	M	SP	RR	ZZZZ	USA
BIALER, MORITZ	19	M	SP	RR	ZZZZ	USA
ROGEL, SALIMON	35	M	FARMER	RR	ZZZZ	USA
ROGOSINSKI, CHAIN	21	M	FARMER	RR	ZZZZ	USA
TROZKY, ABEL	40	M	FARMER	RR	ZZZZ	USA

SHIP: ADRIATIC

FROM: LIVERPOOL AND QUEENSTOWN
TO: NEW YORK
ARRIVED: 20 JULY 1888

PASSENGER	AGE	SEX	OCCUPATION	PRIV	VIL	DES
SCHOR, ESTER	45	F	W	RR	ADAX	USA
ESCILIA	19	F	SVNT	RR	ADAX	USA
HAUFF, LEMIL	17	M	MNR	RR	ADAX	USA
SCHOR, ANETE	17	F	SP	RR	ADAX	USA
REBECKA	15	F	UNKNOWN	RR	ADAX	USA
SCHUSTER, BENJ.	10	M	CH	RR	ADAX	USA
FRIEDMANN, JOSEPH	54	M	MNR	RR	ADAX	USA
ESTER	52	F	W	RR	ADAX	USA
MIKSCHE	18	M	MNR	RR	ADAX	USA
JACOBOWITZ, LINA	18	F	SVNT	RR	ADAX	USA
HOMIAK, JAMOSCH	32	M	LABR	RR	ADAX	USA
JULIA	25	F	W	RR	ADAX	USA
ARZENTRY, CHAJE	17	F	SVNT	RR	ADAX	USA
MOSES	10	M	CH	RR	ADAX	USA
PEDKOWIETZKI, CHAJE	18	F	SVNT	RR	ADAX	USA
HURTWIZ, HANNE	18	F	SVNT	RR	ADAX	USA
LEUW, YERZCH	42	M	LABR	RR	ADAX	USA
LEIBJEWARKOWSKI, MOSES	41	M	LABR	RR	ADAX	USA
JEWARKOWSKI, MENDEL	11	M	CH	RR	ADAX	USA
FREIMARK, GUTE	22	F	W	RR	ADAX	USA
LESA	1	F	CHILD	RR	ADAX	USA
HALPERN, FEGE	11	F	CH	RR	ADAX	USA
BORECK	5	M	CHILD	RR	ADAX	USA
CHANE	10	F	CH	RR	ADAX	USA
PESSEIE	6	M	CHILD	RR	ADAX	USA
BERKOWITZ, HERSCH	20	M	LABR	RR	ADAX	USA
ANCHEL	11	F	CH	RR	ADAX	USA
BRUTHOFF, HITEL	30	M	LABR	RR	ADAX	USA
SAMUEL	3	M	CHILD	RR	ADAX	USA
ERDRICH, N.C.	22	M	LABR	RR	ADAX	USA
NEULAN, JOHAN	40	M	LABR	RR	ADAX	USA
GELBISCH, CHAJE	18	F	DMS	RR	ADAX	USA
JOSEPH	14	M	MNR	RR	ADAX	USA
LEIB	9	M	CHILD	RR	ADAX	USA
MAYER, FRED	18	M	LABR	RR	ADAX	USA
ENGER, B.	30	F	W	RR	ADAX	USA
ROSA	4	F	CHILD	RR	ADAX	USA
JACOBSEN, HARNE	24	F	SVNT	RR	ADAX	USA
THARSEN, A.T.	47	M	LABR	RR	ADAX	USA
BRECK, JOHANNE	20	M	LABR	RR	ADAX	USA

PASSENGER	AGE	SEX	OCCUPATION	PRV VIL DES
BERG, JOHANNES	24	M	LABR	RRADAXUSA
LUGHT, LUDWIG	30	M	LABR	RRADAXUSA
STEDEFEDER, GUSTAV	37	M	LABR	RRADAXUSA

SHIP: AMSTERDAM

FROM: ROTTERDAM
TO: NEW YORK
ARRIVED: 20 JULY 1888

PASSENGER	AGE	SEX	OCCUPATION	PRV VIL DES
WAGENHEIM, ABRAM	21	M	MCHT	RRZZZZUSA
U, U	00	M	MCHT	RRZZZZUSA
MOSTEL	16	M	MCHT	RRZZZZUSA
ISBITCHI, MENCHE	42	M	MCHT	RRZZZZUSA
SIME	40	F	NN	RRZZZZUSA
ARONOWICZ, CHANE	20	F	NN	RRZZZZUSA
ROMALD	3	M	CHILD	RRZZZZUSA
BRENNER, ABRAM	18	M	MCHT	RRZZZZUSA
BENGELOWICZ, SCHWEIE	28	M	MCHT	RRZZZZUSA
MALKE	26	F	NN	RRZZZZUSA
BLITZNER, JANKEL	22	M	MCHT	RRZZZZUSA
DAVIDOWICZ, JACOB	59	M	MCHT	RRZZZZUSA
MALY	49	F	NN	RRZZZZUSA
CHAIES, CHAIM	40	M	MCHT	RRZZZZUSA
STEIN, ELIAS	17	M	MCHT	RRZZZZUSA
NEROWICZ, ISAAC	37	M	MCHT	RRZZZZUSA
LASCHENER, MOSES	48	M	MCHT	RRZZZZUSA
ABRAM	18	M	MCHT	RRZZZZUSA
GERSACHAU, ABRAM	24	M	MCHT	RRZZZZUSA
EILINEY, GEREL	28	M	MCHT	RRZZZZUSA
MANDL, LOUIS	26	M	LABR	RRZZZZUSA
KANTOWITZ, SIMON	18	M	LABR	RRZZZZUSA
TARBER, BEUKE	38	M	MCHT	RRZZZZUSA
BAUCH, SAMUEL	21	M	TLR	RRZZZZUSA
OESTEREICHER, M.	24	M	MCHT	RRZZZZUSA
NUSSBAUM, LORENZ	20	M	MCHT	RRZZZZUSA
ROWZINKOW, ABRAM	19	M	MCHT	RRZZZZUSA
VONSCZAPSKI, JOSEF	18	M	LABR	RRZZZZUSA
STUEWACH, SARAH	28	F	NN	RRZZZZUSA
KOPELMAN, JAL	17	M	MCHT	RRZZZZUSA
MORGANITSKI, JANKEL	33	M	MCHT	RRZZZZUSA
KRAZER, HIRSCH	16	M	MCHT	RRZZZZUSA
PIENES, RUBEN	29	M	MCHT	RRZZZZUSA
GALEWITZ, MORIS	29	M	MCHT	RRZZZZUSA
PERLOWITZ, NATHAN	29	M	MCHT	RRZZZZUSA
NISEN, CHAJES	29	M	MCHT	RRZZZZUSA
PANKEWITZ, JONAS	30	M	MCHT	RRZZZZUSA
DOMBROWSKA, MARYANA	23	F	NN	RRZZZZUSA
MARENSOHN, ISAAC	20	M	MCHT	RRZZZZUSA
BUCZAK, KATHA.	24	F	NN	RRZZZZUSA

SHIP: RHAETIA

FROM: HAMBURG AND HAVRE
TO: NEW YORK
ARRIVED: 23 JULY 1888

PASSENGER	AGE	SEX	OCCUPATION	PRV VIL DES
WEITZ, OSCAR	37	M	UNKNOWN	RRZZZZUSA
MARIA	36	F	UNKNOWN	RRZZZZUSA
PAUL	3	M	CHILD	RRZZZZUSA
ERNST	2	M	CHILD	RRZZZZUSA
EDUARD	.11	M	INFANT	RRZZZZUSA
LABLUDOWSKI, ISRAEL	25	M	STDNT	RRZZZZUSA
TASCH, ARTHUR	19	M	WCHMKR	RRZZZZUSA
KRAMER, JOSEF	27	M	LABR	RRZZZZUSA
MARIE	21	F	W	RRZZZZUSA
CHANCHET, MICHEL	35	M	LABR	RRZZZZUSA
CHAJE	24	F	W	RRZZZZUSA
GOODSTEIN, SAM	30	M	JNR	RRZZZZUSA
STELS, CARL	44	M	LABR	RRZZZZUSA
CHARLOTTE	57	F	W	RRZZZZUSA
KOLUBNER, BERYL	18	M	LABR	RRZZZZUSA
MANIAK, ABRAHAM	28	M	LABR	RRZZZZUSA
ESTTHER	23	F	W	RRZZZZUSA
RABINOWITZ, ITZIG	36	M	DLR	RRZZZZUSA
KLINBORT, MALWINE	40	F	WO	RRZZZZUSA
SOFIE	16	F	CH	RRZZZZUSA
KATIE	15	F	CH	RRZZZZUSA
LOFKE	9	F	CHILD	RRZZZZUSA
NIANKE	8	F	CHILD	RRZZZZUSA
LUOMA, LISA	30	F	WO	FNZZZZUSA
LINJIA, SOFIE	20	F	SGL	FNZZZZUSA
SANDHOLM, MARIE	23	F	SGL	FNZZZZUSA
SACKSBERG, A.GUSTAV	27	M	LABR	FNZZZZUSA
PARKOWIAKR, OPPUDUS	19	M	LABR	FNZZZZUSA
SALO, HILMA	18	F	SGL	FNZZZZUSA
AURICH, JULS	29	M	MCHT	RRZZZZUSA
SCHALNIKOFF, FRUME	21	F	SGL	RRZZZZUSA
PORT, GOLDE	36	F	WO	RRZZZZUSA
DAVID	9	M	CHILD	RRZZZZUSA
MARY	4	F	CHILD	RRZZZZUSA
CHAIE	3	F	CHILD	RRZZZZUSA
RESIE	.11	F	INFANT	RRZZZZUSA
SCHALNIKOFF, ESTHER	22	F	WO	RRZZZZUSA
CZERMANN, TAUBE	20	F	SGL	RRZZZZUSA
WOLNIR, CHASKEL	48	M	LABR	RRZZZZUSA
FRANK, JONAS	40	M	LABR	RRZZZZUSA
SOKOLAW, ABRAM	30	M	LABR	RRZZZZUSA
RADAN, JACOB	45	M	LABR	RRZZZZUSA
LUOMA, JACOB	29	M	LABR	FNZZZZUSA
SELMA	4	F	CHILD	FNZZZZUSA
HOLT, ELIAS	32	M	LABR	FNZZZZUSA
STROMBERG, JOH.	29	M	LABR	FNZZZZUSA
SELINGER, RICHARD	20	M	LKSH	RRZZZZUSA
RIBACK, ARON	27	M	LABR	RRZZZZUSA
PJANKER, RACHEL	26	F	WO	RRZZZZUSA
CHAIM	6	M	CHILD	RRZZZZUSA
FREIDE	.11	F	INFANT	RRZZZZUSA
LEWIN, MORITZ	33	M	LABR	RRZZZZUSA
RULAVICZ, PETER	18	M	LABR	RRZZZZUSA
KOPLONSKI, JOHANN	22	M	LABR	RRZZZZUSA
LOT, ISAAC	23	M	LABR	FNZZZZUSA
ISERSKY, BARUCH	55	M	SMH	RRZZZZUSA
KARASCH, JOSSEL	18	M	LABR	RRZZZZUSA
LIPOWITZKI, FANNY	24	F	WO	RRZZZZUSA
MINE	20	F	SGL	RRZZZZUSA
SOFIE	7	F	CHILD	RRZZZZUSA
BERL	.04	M	INFANT	RRZZZZUSA
SARA	3	F	CHILD	RRZZZZUSA
DELSON, JEANOT	17	M	STDNT	RRZZZZUSA
BLIMENTHAL, CHANE	58	F	WO	RRZZZZUSA
JOH.	18	F	D	RRZZZZUSA
WOLFSOHN, MINNA	18	F	SGL	RRZZZZUSA
GOSCHIEB, HERRM.	20	M	TCHR	RRZZZZUSA
STANOWITZ, JUERGEN	23	M	BKR	RRZZZZUSA
CHYCINSKI, JOSEF	25	M	CPR	RRZZZZUSA
HELENE	17	F	SGL	RRZZZZUSA
KISSLER, SCHOLEM	26	M	LABR	RRZZZZUSA
PLUCKIN, ABRAM	34	M	LABR	RRZZZZUSA
KAHAN, JUDES	40	F	WO	RRZZZZUSA
SCHEINE	6	F	CHILD	RRZZZZUSA
MOTTEL	3	M	CHILD	RRZZZZUSA
RAUCHFEUER, FRANZ	21	M	LABR	RRZZZZUSA
WISLAUSKY, GOLDE	45	F	WO	RRZZZZUSA
STEINBERG, CHEIE	19	F	CL	RRZZZZUSA
MEZINCKOWSKY, ANTON	25	M	LABR	RRZZZZUSA
GLANTERNIK, CHAJE	20	F	SGL	RRZZZZUSA
COHN, LIEBE	16	F	SGL	RRZZZZUSA
WEISELS, GITTEL	18	F	SGL	RRZZZZUSA
BRAWLOSSKY, FEUWEL	40	M	TLR	RRZZZZUSA

PASSENGER	AGE	SEX	OCCUPATION	PRV VIL DES
SARA	35	F	W	RRZZZZUSA
GLAT, ESTHER	14	F	SGL	RRZZZZUSA
BLOCH, LEILE	66	M	TNM	RRZZZZUSA
TEWE	52	F	W	RRZZZZUSA
LIEBE	20	F	CH	RRZZZZUSA
FREIDE	18	F	CH	RRZZZZUSA
MENDEL	11	M	CH	RRZZZZUSA
MALKE	9	F	CHILD	RRZZZZUSA
SARA	8	F	CHILD	RRZZZZUSA
JOSEF	7	M	CHILD	RRZZZZUSA
RACHEL	6	F	CHILD	RRZZZZUSA
RENDEL, OSCHER	47	M	LABR	RRZZZZUSA
LEWIN, JACOB	18	M	LABR	RRZZZZUSA
BRODE, MINNA	19	F	SGL	RRZZZZUSA
FREITMANN, JENKE	36	F	WO	RRZZZZUSA
ABRAM	18	M	CH	RRZZZZUSA
MOSCHE	9	M	CHILD	RRZZZZUSA
SARA	8	F	CHILD	RRZZZZUSA
BRUESCHICK, JOSEF	19	M	TLR	RRZZZZUSA
SCHWINGLER, HEDZ.	23	M	TLR	RRZZZZUSA
BINDER, SCHAPSEL	31	M	LABR	RRZZZZUSA
MILIKOWSKI, JOSSEL	25	M	LABR	RRZZZZUSA
KOHAN, MOSCHE	25	M	JNR	RRZZZZUSA
SCHAPIRO, ISRAEL	24	M	LABR	RRZZZZUSA
GRUENBERG, SENDER	23	M	SHMK	RRZZZZUSA
GORDEN, MAX	40	M	LABR	RRZZZZUSA
SIDERMANN, ABRAM	31	M	TLR	RRZZZZUSA
LEWITAS, MENDEL	27	M	TLR	RRZZZZUSA
BRENDE, REISE	20	F	SGL	RRZZZZUSA
ANDRUSZEWITZ, JADWIGA	20	F	SGL	RRZZZZUSA
MALUKIEWICZ, KAZIMIR	40	M	LABR	RRZZZZUSA
WEINSTEIN, ARON	15	M	LABR	RRZZZZUSA
WEINHAUS, CHAJE	25	F	WO	RRZZZZUSA
FRIEDA	.11	F	INFANT	RRZZZZUSA
ROSENBLUM, MOSES	20	F	LABR	RRZZZZUSA
ZWIE	20	F	W	RRZZZZUSA
FELDSTEIN, HIRSCH	19	M	LABR	RRZZZZUSA
RAWINIS, JAN	24	M	LABR	RRZZZZUSA
CEDERHOHN, OLAF	52	M	LABR	FNZZZZUSA
OLAF	23	M	LABR	FNZZZZUSA
MAROCHIS, ARCADIA	16	F	SGL	RRZZZZUSA
KAPELUSZ, ISAAC	23	M	LABR	RRZZZZUSA
KIRINE	18	F	SGL	RRZZZZUSA
LAPIDESS, CHAIM	23	M	LABR	RRZZZZUSA
SEGALL, ABRAM	17	M	LABR	RRZZZZUSA
STUTSCHINSKI, MENDEL	15	M	LABR	RRZZZZUSA
MENKUS, PESCHE	20	F	SGL	RRZZZZUSA
CHAJE	18	F	SGL	RRZZZZUSA
ZUEHN, BENJAMIN	30	M	LABR	RRZZZZUSA
RAHEL	22	F	W	RRZZZZUSA
SALOMON	.01	M	INFANT	RRZZZZUSA
LANDSMANN, MOSES	27	M	LABR	RRZZZZUSA
SALTZMANN, SZMIL	19	M	LABR	RRZZZZUSA
PODATER, SIMCHE	19	M	LABR	RRZZZZUSA
BUED, NOCHEM	36	M	LABR	RRZZZZUSA
WEINSTEIN, CHAPELL	18	M	LABR	RRZZZZUSA
BEUSMANN, MENDEL	28	M	DLR	RRZZZZUSA
LEA	27	F	W	RRZZZZUSA
RASCHE	.09	F	INFANT	RRZZZZUSA
MINE	22	F	SGL	RRZZZZUSA
FELDE	22	F	SGL	RRZZZZUSA
GILBER, MOSES	40	M	JNR	RRZZZZUSA
ARLUCK, FEIGE	21	F	SGL	RRZZZZUSA
MEYCROWITZ, DAVID	14	M	CH	RRZZZZUSA
ELI	9	M	CHILD	RRZZZZUSA
MACKWOWSKY, DOMENIK	18	M	LABR	RRZZZZUSA
ZDANCZIEWICZ, JOSEFA	22	F	SGL	RRZZZZUSA
GIRDWAJM, KASIMIR	40	F	W	RRZZZZUSA
FRANZISKA	18	F	D	RRZZZZUSA
RACZKOWSKY, REWE	27	F	SGL	RRZZZZUSA
RADIS, BROCHE	26	F	W	RRZZZZUSA
ROCHE	10	F	CH	RRZZZZUSA
RRIER, SCHEINE	6	F	CHILD	RRZZZZUSA
SARA	4	F	CHILD	RRZZZZUSA
MAROTOWICZ, ANTON	34	M	LABR	RRZZZZUSA
GIRDMAGIN, PETRONELY	15	F	SGL	RRZZZZUSA
FRANCISEK	9	M	CHILD	RRZZZZUSA
ZADAWATZKAS, JOSAZ	27	M	LABR	RRZZZZUSA
BREITMANN, LEIB	19	M	LABR	RRZZZZUSA
BRAMA, CHMUL	18	M	LABR	RRZZZZUSA
ABRAMOVICZ, ELIE	20	M	LABR	RRZZZZUSA
HILL, JACOB	48	M	LABR	RRZZZZUSA
GITTEL	38	F	W	RRZZZZUSA
CHARLOTTE	9	F	CHILD	RRZZZZUSA
FANNY	7	F	CHILD	RRZZZZUSA
CHAJE	3	F	CHILD	RRZZZZUSA
HOBIN, RACHEL	28	F	SGL	RRZZZZUSA
BARANEK, GYURA	28	M	LABR	RRZZZZUSA

SHIP: AURANIA

FROM: LIVERPOOL AND QUEENSTOWN
TO: NEW YORK
ARRIVED: 23 JULY 1888

PASSENGER	AGE	SEX	OCCUPATION	PRV VIL DES
KISHI, PETER	27	M	LABR	FNZZZZNY
ROTTHANEN, OLOF	30	M	LABR	FNZZZZNY
KRITA	33	F	W	FNZZZZNY
HAHNIAR	2	M	CHILD	FNZZZZNY
MARIA	8	F	CHILD	FNZZZZNY
LOHEBOHLI, SARA	22	F	SP	FNZZZZNY
ANDERS	27	M	LABR	FNZZZZNY
RUNTRKAINAN, LUNARD	30	M	LABR	FNZZZZNY
ROKKET, ANDREN	50	M	LABR	FNZZZZNY
JUNTTE, OSKAR	14	M	LABR	FNZZZZNY
ANNA	15	F	SP	FNZZZZNY
WASMEN, SARAFINE	25	F	UNKNOWN	FNZZZZNY
WASKELAMHI, SURFAS	46	F	MA	FNZZZZNY
KARJARJA, CHRISTIAN	24	M	LABR	FNZZZZNY
HAUSEN, MISKEL	30	M	LABR	FNZZZZNY
LAHTI, IVAR	43	M	LABR	FNZZZZNY
JANSE, JOH	29	M	LABR	FNZZZZNY
RANTUFOA, ANRIA	31	M	LABR	FNZZZZNY
ABRAMORER, MAREN	29	F	MA	FNZZZZNY
JOHAN	3	M	CHILD	FNZZZZNY
WELHAM	2	M	CHILD	FNZZZZNY
AUGUST	.06	M	INFANT	FNZZZZNY
KNITTI, LISU	33	M	LABR	FNZZZZNY
KOCKE, ANNA	19	F	SP	FNZZZZMN
LIGTBY, CARL	36	M	LABR	FNZZZZNY
MATTALO, HERM.	37	M	LABR	FNZZZZMI
SILIZKOFKY, BENJAMIN	18	M	LABR	RRZZZZNY
PHRING, SANIE	32	F	MA	RRZZZZNY
ELLA	11	F	CH	RRZZZZNY
BADANN	7	M	CHILD	RRZZZZNY
DORFELD, FHGL.	46	M	LABR	RRZZZZNY
SINI	11	M	CH	RRZZZZNY
KOHAN, MOSES	30	M	LABR	RRZZZZNY
BLERNSTEIN, BERTHA	19	F	SP	RRZZZZNY
BARSCHAN, LITMAN	25	M	LABR	RRZZZZNY
CHARAD, JUDEL	37	M	LABR	RRZZZZNY
JAFFE, DEBORA	36	F	MA	RRZZZZNY
FLIGL	11	M	CH	RRZZZZNY
MARKUS	9	M	CHILD	RRZZZZNY
SALLY	3	F	CHILD	RRZZZZNY
SCHNEIDER, MENDEL	27	M	LABR	RRZZZZNY
SIMONS, JOHAN	40	M	LABR	RRZZZZUT
ENGES, JOHAN	42	M	LABR	RRZZZZMI
JIWI, PETER	19	M	LABR	RRZZZZMI
FISCHER, MAX	19	M	JWLR	RRZZZZOH
SAM.	19	M	JWLR	RRZZZZOH

SHIP: AMALFI

FROM: HAMBURG
TO: NEW YORK
ARRIVED: 24 JULY 1888

PASSENGER	AGE	SEX	OCCUPATION	PRV VIL DES
STRIKO, JOSEFA	26	F	WO	RRZZZZUSA
JULIAN	6	M	CHILD	RRZZZZUSA
BONISLAW	4	M	CHILD	RRZZZZUSA
SINSKOWSKI, THOMAS	13	M	BY	RRZZZZUSA
HORNITZKI, IZIMI	37	F	WO	RRZZZZUSA
TONI	11	F	CH	RRZZZZUSA
RINOK	6	M	CHILD	RRZZZZUSA
JANKEL	4	M	CHILD	RRZZZZUSA
LEA	.11	F	INFANT	RRZZZZUSA
STOLAKI, ROCHEL	24	F	SGL	RRZZZZUSA
BRAWMANN, MASCHE	25	F	WO	RRZZZZUSA
RIWKE	.11	F	INFANT	RRZZZZUSA
WURMANN, JOSEF	18	M	LABR	RRZZZZUSA
NIMSKI, SIMI	19	F	SGL	RRZZZZUSA
SELKER, SARAH	42	F	WO	RRZZZZUSA
HERSCH	6	M	CHILD	RRZZZZUSA
DAVID	8	M	CHILD	RRZZZZUSA
RIWKE	10	F	CH	RRZZZZUSA
LEIB	7	M	CHILD	RRZZZZUSA
SAMUEL	.11	M	INFANT	RRZZZZUSA
LAZNIG, BAREL	16	M	LABR	RRZZZZUSA
SALLOWICZ, ABRAM	24	M	LABR	RRZZZZUSA
LABASZ, DEONZY	14	M	LABR	RRZZZZUSA
KALSTEIN, ISAAC	17	M	LABR	RRZZZZUSA
KUEZYNSKI, TAUBE	16	F	SGL	RRZZZZUSA
GOETZENBERG, ABRAHAM	46	M	LABR	RRZZZZUSA
RUSCHEL	35	F	W	RRZZZZUSA
WELLE	18	F	CH	RRZZZZUSA
TAUBE	9	F	CHILD	RRZZZZUSA
SCHMUL	8	M	CHILD	RRZZZZUSA
SUSS	7	F	CHILD	RRZZZZUSA
EHAIM	5	M	CHILD	RRZZZZUSA
KOLTEN, JANKEL	19	M	LABR	RRZZZZUSA
BASSE	26	F	W	RRZZZZUSA
MITTELMANN, MOSES	18	M	LABR	RRZZZZUSA
BESEMIAN, OSCHER	34	M	FARMER	RRZZZZUSA
BESSES, CHMUL	22	M	FARMER	RRZZZZUSA
RABIMOWITZ, SARA	45	F	WO	RRZZZZUSA
LEIB	12	M	CH	RRZZZZUSA
MOSCHE	9	F	CHILD	RRZZZZUSA
SHANNE	8	F	CHILD	RRZZZZUSA
MISCHUZKI, ELKE	00	F	UNKNOWN	RRZZZZUSA
EHAIE	17	M	CH	RRZZZZUSA
MARIE	9	F	CHILD	RRZZZZUSA
SCHIMEL	6	F	CHILD	RRZZZZUSA
PERL	.10	M	INFANT	RRZZZZUSA
SALEK	17	M	CH	RRZZZZUSA
BESMANN, HARY	35	M	LABR	RRZZZZUSA
GOLDSTEIN, ISRAEL	22	M	LABR	RRZZZZUSA
SANDES, ABE	22	M	LABR	RRZZZZUSA
DWORL	18	F	UNKNOWN	RRZZZZUSA
BESSACH	28	M	LABR	RRZZZZUSA
SCHORR, BEILE	14	F	SGL	RRZZZZUSA
DWORL	18	F	SGL	RRZZZZUSA
PERLMUTTER, MEYER	29	M	LABR	RRZZZZUSA
SLOMNIK, EIBISCH	30	M	LABR	RRZZZZUSA
BAUM, FEIGE	24	F	SGL	RRZZZZUSA
TURONY, SARA	19	F	SGL	RRZZZZUSA
GOLDBERG, CHAIM	24	M	TNM	RRZZZZUSA
ZERULNIK, MENUCHE	50	F	W	RRZZZZUSA
ELIE	60	M	MCHT	RRZZZZUSA
VICKTOR	25	M	CH	RRZZZZUSA
CHASHE	21	F	CH	RRZZZZUSA
MOSES	19	M	CH	RRZZZZUSA
SELIG	16	M	CH	RRZZZZUSA
ABRAHAM	11	M	CH	RRZZZZUSA
MANDEL, MOSES	28	M	TLR	RRZZZZUSA
LIPPE	24	F	W	RRZZZZUSA
KEIB	25	F	SGL	RRZZZZUSA
LISS, JACOB	26	M	LABR	RRZZZZUSA
MAGOLIAS, MEYER	18	M	LABR	RRZZZZUSA
RABINOWITZ, ITZKO	18	M	LABR	RRZZZZUSA
WINZMIR, MEIER	33	M	LABR	RRZZZZUSA
HENE	23	F	W	RRZZZZUSA
BERLINER, ISAAC	23	M	LABR	RRZZZZUSA
ESTHER	25	F	W	RRZZZZUSA
BERTHA	4	F	CHILD	RRZZZZUSA
ALEX	11	M	CH	RRZZZZUSA
BALIENER, BERTHA	21	F	WO	RRZZZZUSA
EMILIE	.11	F	INFANT	RRZZZZUSA
SCHLAMESOHN, LIPA	30	M	BCHR	RRZZZZUSA
TAUBE	28	F	W	RRZZZZUSA
ABRAM	11	M	S	RRZZZZUSA
LEVIN, ISRAEL	17	M	LABR	RRZZZZUSA
PROPANOWSKI, JACKOB	53	M	LABR	RRZZZZUSA
MEYER, CHRISTIAN	55	M	FARMER	RRZZZZUSA
WAGNER, JOHS.	39	M	FARMER	RRZZZZUSA
MARIE	38	F	W	RRZZZZUSA
CONRAD	14	M	CH	RRZZZZUSA
JOHS.	7	M	CHILD	RRZZZZUSA
ADOLF	.09	M	INFANT	RRZZZZUSA
GOLDER, BEINHOLD	20	M	FARMER	RRZZZZUSA
BARBARA	21	F	W	RRZZZZUSA
OTTO	.06	M	INFANT	RRZZZZUSA
EBERLING, HEINRICH	20	M	FARMER	RRZZZZUSA
BIERGRAFF, PHILIPP	30	M	FARMER	RRZZZZUSA
RUBIN, CACILLIA	22	F	W	RRZZZZUSA
KATZ, SLATE	40	F	WO	RRZZZZUSA
BAUKER, RIWKE	12	F	SGL	RRZZZZUSA
GOLDBERG, MINDEL	30	F	WO	RRZZZZUSA
CHAIME	1	F	CHILD	RRZZZZUSA
SCHUWALSKY, NISSEN	21	M	LABR	RRZZZZUSA
MIDWIDOWSKY, JOCHNE	27	F	WO	RRZZZZUSA
BEISEL	3	F	CHILD	RRZZZZUSA
ZARNIKOWA, BEILE	70	F	WO	RRZZZZUSA
SALZ, MARIE	18	F	SGL	RRZZZZUSA
SCHIRR, SCHOLEM	42	M	LABR	RRZZZZUSA
PENNENBAUM, JACOB	40	M	LABR	RRZZZZUSA
CHANE	42	F	W	RRZZZZUSA
ITTE	18	F	CH	RRZZZZUSA
HEINE	6	F	CHILD	RRZZZZUSA
BAGESNITZKI, DAVID	32	M	LABR	RRZZZZUSA
JURASDITZKI, JACOB	32	M	LABR	RRZZZZUSA
HERSCHKOWITZ, ADAM	17	M	SMH	RRZZZZUSA
RESZCZYNSKA, JOSEFA	27	F	SGL	RRZZZZUSA
PODORSCHIK, SEIB	35	M	DLR	RRZZZZUSA
BRUNNE	35	F	W	RRZZZZUSA
WOLF	9	M	CHILD	RRZZZZUSA
PODORSCHICK, SAMUEL	7	M	CHILD	RRZZZZUSA
ROAGOWSKA, ZOLMAN	38	M	DLR	RRZZZZUSA
KOWSRSKI, ASCHER	19	M	UNKNOWN	RRZZZZUSA
BAUMFELD, SALOMON	39	M	DLR	RRZZZZUSA
SCHIRKOBRODA, SCHMUL	55	M	SMH	RRZZZZUSA

SHIP: GELLERT

FROM: HAMBURG
TO: NEW YORK
ARRIVED: 25 JULY 1888

PASSENGER	AGE	SEX	OCCUPATION	PRV VIL DES
DEKTOR, JETTE	21	F	WO	RRAEFLUSA
PAULINE	2	F	CHILD	RRAEFLUSA
BERTHA	.06	F	INFANT	RRAEFLUSA
GELBERT, HERIKLY	25	M	TLR	RRZZZZUSA
DICEWSKY, JOSEF	28	M	LABR	RRZZZZUSA
ALISYEWSKY, ANTON	18	M	LABR	RRZZZZUSA
WOLCK, REBECCA	16	F	SGL	RRAIGHUSA
DEKTOR, ERNSTINE	19	F	SGL	RRAEFLUSA

PASSENGER	AGE	SEX	OCCUPATION	PRV VIL DES
GOLDINGER, SARA	30	F	WO	RRAEFLUSA
LITJE	4	F	CHILD	RRAEFLUSA
DORFMANN, ROSIA	30	F	WO	RRAEFLUSA
CHASKE	9	M	CHILD	RRAEFLUSA
BENJAMIN	7	M	CHILD	RRAEFLUSA
FREIDE	7	F	CHILD	RRAEFLUSA
FOIKEL	5	M	CHILD	RRAEFLUSA
LUSCHE	.11	F	INFANT	RRAEFLUSA
ETTINGER, VICENT	27	M	MCHT	RRAHOKUSA
ARON, MICHEL	23	M	WCHMKR	RRAHOKUSA
SEGALOWITZ, ABEL	42	M	APTC	RRAHOKUSA
SOPHIE	28	F	W	RRAHOKUSA
HUGO	5	M	CHILD	RRAHOKUSA
JEPHINE	4	F	CHILD	RRAHOKUSA
KATH.	.11	F	INFANT	RRAHOKUSA
BIRCINSKI, WLADISLAUS	18	M	LABR	RRZZZZUSA
RIKLIS, ABE	26	M	LABR	RRAILXUSA
SELAZYKIN, HELENE	24	F	SGL	RRAIOOUSA
JAIKONIS, JAN	28	M	UNKNOWN	RRZZZZUSA
BREZGIL, VINCENT	26	M	LABR	RRAHZSUSA
KAZIMIK, KASIMIR	21	M	LABR	RRAHZSUSA
GOLDBERG, MOSES	54	M	LABR	RRAEFLUSA
PRASKOWSKI, DREIZE	18	F	SGL	RRAIMBUSA
BREMER, HANNA	18	F	SGL	RRZZZZUSA
LAFRENTZ, CHRISTIANE	45	F	WO	RRZZZZUSA
GERTRUDE	20	F	WO	RRZZZZUSA
EMMA	9	F	CHILD	RRZZZZUSA
JOH.	6	M	CHILD	RRZZZZUSA
PETER	3	M	CHILD	RRZZZZUSA
MATHS	.10	M	INFANT	RRZZZZUSA
NICOLAUS	.03	M	INFANT	RRZZZZUSA
SCHILLINAT, JULS	40	M	LABR	RRZZZZUSA
JAFFER, BENJAMIN	16	M	LABR	RRZZZZUSA
WABNIK, FREIDEL	40	F	WO	RRZZZZUSA
JOPPE	20	F	WO	RRZZZZUSA
CHAIE	14	F	WO	RRZZZZUSA
SIMCHE	9	M	CHILD	RRZZZZUSA
PESSACH	7	M	CHILD	RRZZZZUSA
WOLFF	.11	M	INFANT	RRZZZZUSA
GLUMBOTZKA, FEIGE	20	F	SGL	RRAHQUUSA
DRUCKER, BRANE	30	F	WO	RRZZZZUSA
CALEL	6	M	CHILD	RRZZZZUSA
SISCHE	4	F	CHILD	RRZZZZUSA
CHINE	.11	M	INFANT	RRZZZZUSA
BRAZINSKI, CHANNE	25	F	SGL	RRZZZZUSA
GRYBOWSKI, STEFAN	24	M	LABR	RRAHUFUSA
STOWIZKNONA, MARIANNA	19	M	LABR	RRZZZZUSA
BACHRACH, CHAIM	45	M	WCHMKR	RRZZZZUSA
HONIGSTOCK, SELIG	27	M	BKBNDR	RRAFWJUSA
WIMOKLE, PELTAN	16	M	LABR	RRAFWJUSA
WIRBOLOWSKY, LEISER	48	M	MCHT	RRZZZZUSA
SCHEWE	38	F	W	RRZZZZUSA
SCHEINE	9	F	CHILD	RRZZZZUSA
CHERZLOWITZKI, PESCHE	30	F	WO	RRZZZZUSA
FEIGE	9	F	CHILD	RRZZZZUSA
DAVID	8	M	CHILD	RRZZZZUSA
ANDSCHE	5	F	CHILD	RRZZZZUSA
BENJAMIN	3	F	CHILD	RRZZZZUSA
NACHMANN	.11	F	INFANT	RRZZZZUSA
FERDINAND, MOSES	19	M	LABR	RRZZZZUSA
SCHWARZ, ROSI	18	F	SGL	RRZZZZUSA
SUNDBERG, DWORSCHE	19	F	SGL	RRAIMEUSA
SCHOLOMOWITZ, LEIB	18	M	LABR	RRAGRTUSA
BLUME	25	F	SGL	RRAGRTUSA
GORDON, FEIGE	40	F	WO	RRAGRTUSA
RACHEL	9	F	CHILD	RRAGRTUSA
MALKE	8	F	CHILD	RRAGRTUSA
CHANNE	7	M	CHILD	RRAGRTUSA
ALTER	3	M	CHILD	RRAGRTUSA
HOLZHACKER, LIEBIE	25	F	WO	RRAGRTUSA
PERL	6	M	CHILD	RRAGRTUSA
PIKAWSKY, WOLF	18	M	LKSH	RRAHOKUSA
RACIAZA, REGINA	24	F	WO	RRAHUFUSA
JACOB	.07	M	INFANT	RRAHUFUSA
SOBOCZYNSKI, JOSEF	40	M	LABR	RRAHUFUSA

PASSENGER	AGE	SEX	OCCUPATION	PRV VIL DES
KAVALANTZKENE, AGATHA	30	F	W	RRAHUFUSA
JANOS	.11	M	INFANT	RRAHUFUSA
NIMIGANSKY, SARAH	24	M	WO	RRAHTUUSA
DRESE	7	F	CHILD	RRAHTUUSA
MICHLE	4	F	CHILD	RRAHTUUSA
GRUENBERG, LEO	25	M	MCHT	RRAFVGUSA
CHARLOTTE	23	F	W	RRAFVGUSA
WALDEMAR	3	M	CHILD	RRAFVGUSA
MELNIK, CHAINE	21	M	LABR	RRAGRTUSA
LISSNER, FERDINAND	32	M	LABR	RRZZZZUSA
JOSEFA	29	F	W	RRZZZZUSA
HELENA	9	F	CHILD	RRZZZZUSA
FERD.	8	M	CHILD	RRZZZZUSA
ANNA	4	F	CHILD	RRZZZZUSA
HILDEGARD	3	M	CHILD	RRZZZZUSA
EMIL	.10	M	INFANT	RRZZZZUSA
STEINERT, WILHELM	64	M	FARMER	RRZZZZUSA
CAROLE	54	F	W	RRZZZZUSA
PAULINE	21	F	W	RRZZZZUSA
BERTHA	9	F	CHILD	RRZZZZUSA
WILHELM	7	M	CHILD	RRZZZZUSA
PRESENT, GERSON	62	M	LABR	RRZZZZUSA
ROSAWETZKI, ABRAM	30	M	LABR	RRAIKTUSA
WELIZKIN, ALTER	25	M	LABR	RRAIMBUSA
DWORE	24	F	W	RRAIMBUSA
KANEKE, JOSEPH	24	M	LABR	RRAHUEUSA
DWORE	20	F	W	RRAHUEUSA
BAKST, MOSES	39	M	LABR	RRZZZZUSA
MILLER, AUGUST	32	M	LABR	RRAHZSUSA
GREWE, ANDREI	30	M	LABR	RRAHZSUSA
GRUENBERG, CHAIM	42	M	LABR	RRAFWJUSA
PERL	35	F	W	RRAFWJUSA
WEINBERG, FEIWEL	36	M	LABR	RRAFWJUSA
DINA	22	F	W	RRAFWJUSA
LEA	5	F	CHILD	RRAFWJUSA
SARA	3	F	CHILD	RRAFWJUSA
MOSES	.11	M	INFANT	RRAFWJUSA
PASO, PETER	26	M	LABR	FNZZZZUSA
ISOMETTA, JOHANS	25	M	LABR	FNZZZZUSA
MATJUSSI, HILMA	21	F	SGL	FNZZZZUSA
MEROWITZ, HERM.	35	M	WCHMKR	FNAEFLUSA
PLOEFKA, MOSES	27	M	TLR	FNAHTUUSA
RUDZINSKI, HERZ	45	M	TLR	FNAHTUUSA
POLIKOWSKI, OLI	20	F	SGL	FNAFVGUSA
PAETZOLDT, AUGUST	31	M	LABR	FNAIDCUSA
REIFOWICH, SALOMON	16	M	LABR	FNAHXLUSA
PINCHUS	9	M	CHILD	FNAHXLUSA
SEGAL, DAVID	46	M	LABR	FNAHXZUSA
WISKI, ABRAM	42	M	LABR	FNAHVUUSA
ARON	9	M	CHILD	FNAHVUUSA
LEWIS, RACHEL	18	F	SGL	RRZZZZUSA
JUNGERMANN, CHAIM	.06	M	INFANT	RRZZZZUSA
PANITZ, MORRIS	37	M	LABR	RRAHVUUSA
FRIEDLAND, SARA	30	F	WO	RRAHTFUSA
SALOMON	3	M	CHILD	RRAHTFUSA
SARA	.11	F	INFANT	RRAHTFUSA
LUBELSKY, CHAIM	46	M	LABR	RRAHZSUSA
SCHROEDER, JEFIN	24	M	TLR	RRAIBYUSA
SCHMAL, ADOLF	22	M	SMH	RRZZZZUSA
WOSKOLONIK, MARKU	36	M	LABR	RRZZZZUSA
PESSIE	23	F	W	RRZZZZUSA
JUDA	.11	F	INFANT	RRZZZZUSA
KOSCHER, MEIER	50	M	LABR	RRAFVGUSA
CHAIE	40	F	W	RRAFVGUSA
SCHIE	19	F	CH	RRAFVGUSA
BASSE	18	F	CH	RRAFVGUSA
HENE	.11	F	INFANT	RRAFVGUSA
KAROL, OSCHER	63	M	LABR	RRZZZZUSA
LEA	25	F	W	RRZZZZUSA
JANKEL	3	M	CHILD	RRZZZZUSA
CHANNE	.11	M	INFANT	RRZZZZUSA
JANUSCHEWSKI, WILH.	26	M	LABR	RRZZZZUSA
CHRISTINE	23	F	W	RRZZZZUSA
JABLONSKI, FABIAN	32	M	LABR	RRZZZZUSA
SOMBECK, JAN	30	M	LABR	RRZZZZUSA

PASSENGER	AGE	SEX	OCCUPATION	PRV VIL DES
RUSCHEL, JOSEF	30	M	LABR	RRZZZZUSA
MALINAT, LUDWIG	57	M	LABR	RRZZZZUSA
SCHILLER, LUDWIG	55	M	LABR	RRZZZZUSA
TEMCZA, GEORG	27	M	LABR	RRZZZZUSA
SOROKACZ, STEFAN	24	M	LABR	RRZZZZUSA
BERL, ISRAEL	37	M	LABR	RRAIATUSA
SAPELIANSKI, MALKE	20	F	SGL	RRAHVUUSA
DILITZKI, BASCHE	20	F	SGL	RRAHVUUSA
LISKIS, DWORSCHE	18	F	SGL	RRAHVUUSA
MANDELBAUM, ALTE	16	F	SGL	RRAHVUUSA
MOSES	9	M	CHILD	RRAHVUUSA
FRANKFURT, JACOB	27	M	DLR	RRAGRTUSA
FEIZELMANN, CHASKEL	28	M	LABR	RRAGRTUSA
LJUBIEZ, RACHEL	43	F	WO	RRAHRZUSA
HELENE	9	F	CHILD	RRAHRZUSA
MOSES	4	M	CHILD	RRAHRZUSA
LUTLER, SCHUCHER	35	M	CGRMKR	RRAHQUUSA
POLAKIOWSKI, MARKUS	21	M	DLR	RRAHZSUSA
BAKUNAS, ANTANAS	43	M	LABR	RRAHZSUSA
KAKANOWSKI, KASIS	19	M	LABR	RRAHZSUSA
LIPNIECKO, JOSEFA	40	F	WO	RRAGRTUSA
FRANZISKA	14	F	WO	RRAGRTUSA
PALATZ, ESTHER	22	F	SGL	RRAHTFUSA
NEMJO, MIHAL	17	M	LABR	RRZZZZUSA
SCHMITTKOWSKI, WLADISLA	19	M	LABR	RRAHZDUSA
ZAMOFSKI, THOMAS	20	M	BKR	RRAHWOUSA
MANN, LEWIN	22	M	TLR	RRAFWJUSA
BARKOWITZ, EFROIM	33	M	LABR	RRAIFRUSA

SHIP: NEVADA

FROM: LIVERPOOL AND QUEENSTOWN
TO: NEW YORK
ARRIVED: 25 JULY 1888

PASSENGER	AGE	SEX	OCCUPATION	PRV VIL DES
MEIEROWITZ, IGNATZ	13	M	LABR	RRACBFUSA
HERSCHINOWITZ, JOSEPH	18	M	LABR	RRACBFUSA
GOLDNMANN, MOSES	7	M	CHILD	RRACBFUSA
POSALSKY, JOSEPH	24	M	LABR	RRACBFUSA
LACHTANOWICZ, PETER	23	M	LABR	RRACBFUSA
WISCHNOOISKY, JARTEL	15	M	LABR	RRACBFUSA
REIDIEL, SALOMON	25	M	LABR	RRACBFUSA
OBEBNITZSKY, ARON	19	M	LABR	RRACBFUSA
LUKASCHEWICZ, ARON	28	M	LABR	RRACBFUSA
KLINSKY, WLADISLAW	29	M	LABR	RRACBFUSA
COHN, JACOB	15	M	LABR	RRACBFUSA
PALINSKY, GISRAEL	21	M	LABR	RRACBFUSA
RABINOWITZ, JUDEL	19	F	SP	RRACBFUSA
KUSAUSKI, CHAIE	25	F	W	RRACBFUSA
MOSES	.10	M	INFANT	RRACBFUSA
RABINOWITZ, SORE	17	F	SP	RRACBFUSA
MORDESOWITZ, FEIGE	28	F	W	RRACBFUSA
ITE	18	F	SP	RRACBFUSA
ABRAM	.10	M	INFANT	RRACBFUSA
SISKOWICZ, MALKE	19	F	SP	RRACBFUSA
SAMUEL	7	M	CHILD	RRACBFUSA
KOHN, CHAJE	20	F	W	RRACBFUSA
ITE	.06	F	INFANT	RRACBFUSA
JACOBS, FRUNE	7	F	CHILD	RRACBFUSA
MEIROWITZ, LEISER	50	M	FARMER	RRACBFUSA
ROSI	45	F	W	RRACBFUSA
WOLICINER, JONOFF	44	M	FARMER	RRACBFUSA
RIFKE	44	F	W	RRACBFUSA
GIPPE	21	F	SP	RRACBFUSA
ABRAHAM	17	M	LABR	RRACBFUSA
HENE	7	F	CHILD	RRACBFUSA
CHANNE	6	F	CHILD	RRACBFUSA
BEILE	4	F	CHILD	RRACBFUSA

SHIP: ELBE

FROM: BREMEN AND SOUTHAMPTON
TO: NEW YORK
ARRIVED: 25 JULY 1888

PASSENGER	AGE	SEX	OCCUPATION	PRV VIL DES
SIMELOWITZ, M.	50	M	UNKNOWN	RRAILANY
MENE	45	F	UNKNOWN	RRAILANY
ZORECH	15	F	UNKNOWN	RRAILANY
LIPE	10	F	CH	RRAILANY
JENSE	8	M	CHILD	RRAILANY
HIRSCH	6	M	CHILD	RRAILANY
TER, EMIELIA	24	F	UNKNOWN	FNZZZZOH
KAYAMA, ALEX	25	M	FARMER	FNZZZZOH
KOSKI, HERM.	22	M	UNKNOWN	FNZZZZOH
HAKALA, ISAK	28	M	UNKNOWN	FNZZZZOH
HAANE, G.	25	M	UNKNOWN	FNZZZZNY
MARIA	26	F	UNKNOWN	FNZZZZNY
MARIA	.02	F	INFANT	FNZZZZNY
HULTIN, HILDEGARD	26	M	FARMER	FNZZZZNY
SANBERG, FRANZISKA	23	F	UNKNOWN	FNZZZZNY
LOUIS	22	M	FARMER	FNZZZZNY
FRANS	17	M	FARMER	FNZZZZNY
JERRISJAWI, ALLI	48	F	UNKNOWN	FNZZZZOR
ANNA	40	F	UNKNOWN	FNZZZZOR
THYRA	2	F	CHILD	FNZZZZOR
NIWA, ABRAHAM	31	M	LABR	FNZZZZMI
HILDA	24	F	UNKNOWN	FNZZZZMI
NIELSSON, NIELS	33	M	LABR	FNZZZZNY
SELL, HEINR.	35	M	UNKNOWN	FNAILANY
CATHA.	31	F	UNKNOWN	FNAILANY
MARIA	11	F	UNKNOWN	FNAILANY
CATHARINE	3	F	CHILD	FNAIEGNY
JACOB	.08	M	INFANT	FNAIEGNY
SCHEUBEL, GEORG	33	M	TLR	FNAIEGNY
ANNA	30	F	UNKNOWN	FNAIEGNY
MARIE	4	F	CHILD	FNAIEGNY
CATHARINE	2	F	CHILD	FNAIEGNY
OSTOWSY, FISCHEL	15	M	LABR	FNAILANY
GUENBERG, MORITZ	37	M	MCHT	FNAILANY
GASEN, GERSON	50	M	DLR	FNAILANY
WIEZBICKY, JAN	40	M	BBR	FNAILANY
ZAHORSKY, LEONH.	27	M	DLR	FNAILANY
LEHMANN, CHAIN	25	M	DLR	FNAILANY
HOROWITZ, MACHA	14	F	UNKNOWN	FNAILANY
EUGENIE	3	F	CHILD	FNAILANY
INSELWITZ, EUGENIE	21	F	UNKNOWN	FNAILANY
WOJNIECHOWSKY, MICHAEL	55	M	LABR	FNAILANY
ZULTOWSKA, ISABELLA	60	F	UNKNOWN	FNAILANY
KRITSCHMAS, JOSEF	46	M	LABR	FNAILANY
SCHUBECKA, MIKAS	33	M	LABR	FNAILANY
ALZBETA	28	F	UNKNOWN	FNAILANY
GAIFENKEL, ZIRE	16	F	UNKNOWN	FNAILANY
BERENSTEIN, SCHORE	19	F	UNKNOWN	FNAILANY
COHN, MOSES	41	M	LABR	FNAILANY
MISCHOK, CATHA.	21	F	UNKNOWN	FNAILANY
SCHADWEIL, JULIAN	23	M	LABR	FNAILANY
KRAEMER, ANNA	20	F	UNKNOWN	FNAILANY
SIMOLOWITZ, CHAIEM	45	M	LABR	FNAILANY
---DINOW, U	40	M	LABR	FNAILANY
PERLE	17	F	UNKNOWN	FNAILANY
ZIGANSKY, STANISL.	26	M	LABR	FNAILANY
BERNOTAYTES, KAZMIR	34	M	LABR	FNAILANY
POYTENIS, WICENTY	24	M	LABR	FNAILANY
SCHUBINSKY, PIOTRO	25	M	LABR	FNAILANY
BAYOWIS, JOSEF	27	M	LABR	FNAILANY
DRANGELIS, KAZMIR	23	M	LABR	FNAILANY
HELFER, BARACH	20	M	LABR	FNAILANY
SCHAPIERE, JOSSEL	36	M	LABR	FNAILANY
LEVY, HERM.	45	M	DLR	FNAILANY
HAVUNEN, MAJA	33	F	UNKNOWN	FNZZZZOH
ISAK	10	M	CH	FNZZZZOH
MATHIAS	9	M	CHILD	FNZZZZOH
LASKOWSKA, JOSEFA	31	F	UNKNOWN	RRZZZZNY

PASSENGER	AGE	SEX	OCCUPATION	PRIV	VIL	DES
JAN	7	M	CHILD	RR	ZZZZ	NY
CONSTANTIN	5	M	CHILD	RR	ZZZZ	NY
ANNA	3	F	CHILD	RR	ZZZZ	NY
RZEPCZINSKI, JOH.	27	M	LABR	RR	ZZZZ	WI
BOROWSKY, ALEX	22	M	LABR	RR	ZZZZ	WI
PETERS, GUST.	25	M	LABR	RR	ZZZZ	WI
BERGMANN, ADOLF	33	M	LABR	RR	ZZZZ	WI
BESSER, MARIA	28	F	UNKNOWN	RR	AEAB	NY
CILLY	2	F	CHILD	RR	AEAB	NY
KESSELMANN, WELE	30	M	UNKNOWN	RR	ZZZZ	BAL
SURKE	10	M	CH	RR	ZZZZ	BAL
RASEL	8	M	CHILD	RR	ZZZZ	BAL
DWOJRE	5	M	CHILD	RR	ZZZZ	BAL
PAUBE	.06	M	INFANT	RR	ZZZZ	BAL
SCHLOJEWITZ, JACOB	44	M	LABR	RR	ZZZZ	NY
RAMASZEWSKY, JOHA.	14	F	UNKNOWN	RR	ZZZZ	NY
BALGIKIS, JURAS	25	M	LABR	RR	ZZZZ	NY
SCHLECHTER, ABRAHAM	32	M	LABR	RR	ACBR	NY
SCHMIDT, ADAM	31	M	LABR	RR	ZZZZ	NY
WOLOWITZ, ISRAEL	35	M	LABR	RR	AIOE	NY
ABRAHAM	.10	M	INFANT	RR	ZZZZ	NY
SALZMANN, EISIG	33	M	LABR	RR	ZZZZ	NY
DOBE	26	F	UNKNOWN	RR	ZZZZ	NY
NECHAME	6	F	CHILD	RR	AIEG	NY
MOSES	5	M	CHILD	RR	AILA	NY
WOLF	2	M	CHILD	RR	AILA	NY
MARIA	.10	F	INFANT	RR	AILA	NY

SHIP: DONAU

FROM: BREMEN
TO: BALTIMORE
ARRIVED: 25 JULY 1888

PASSENGER	AGE	SEX	OCCUPATION	PRIV	VIL	DES
BLUMERMANN, DWEINE	19	F	UNKNOWN	RR	ZZZZ	MD
GOLDBERG, ISRAEL	16	M	UNKNOWN	RR	ZZZZ	MD
COHN, ASHER	19	M	UNKNOWN	RR	ZZZZ	MD
U	25	F	UNKNOWN	RR	ZZZZ	MD
U	.03	F	INFANT	RR	ZZZZ	MD
RUDO, JOSEF	30	M	MCHT	RR	ZZZZ	MD
SARG	20	F	UNKNOWN	RR	ZZZZ	MD
WEISBERG, SIEBE	40	F	UNKNOWN	RR	ZZZZ	MI
ABRAHAM	10	M	CH	RR	ZZZZ	MI
MOSES	10	M	CH	RR	ZZZZ	MI
CHANE	9	F	CHILD	RR	ZZZZ	MI
HINDE	8	F	CHILD	RR	ZZZZ	MI
REINE	5	F	CHILD	RR	ZZZZ	MI
SARAH	3	F	CHILD	RR	ZZZZ	MI
SAIONTZ, ESTER	28	F	UNKNOWN	RR	ZZZZ	MI
MEARSCHE	.06	F	INFANT	RR	ZZZZ	MI
HERSCH	7	M	CHILD	RR	ZZZZ	MI
SCHKLAV, LINE	25	F	UNKNOWN	RR	ZZZZ	MI
LIBE	5	F	CHILD	RR	ZZZZ	MI
REBECKA	3	F	CHILD	RR	ZZZZ	MI
SCHKLER, SALE	19	F	UNKNOWN	RR	ZZZZ	MI
SOLUTKITZKI, CHAJE	25	F	UNKNOWN	RR	ZZZZ	IL
KUESCHE	5	F	CHILD	RR	ZZZZ	IL
ESTER	3	F	CHILD	RR	ZZZZ	IL
BEILE	2	F	CHILD	RR	ZZZZ	IL
AUGUSTAT, AMALIA	43	F	UNKNOWN	RR	ZZZZ	MD
EDUARD	11	M	UNKNOWN	RR	ZZZZ	MD
GUSTAV	9	M	CHILD	RR	ZZZZ	MD
HERMAN	7	M	CHILD	RR	ZZZZ	MD
OTTO	6	M	CHILD	RR	ZZZZ	MD
EMIL	4	M	CHILD	RR	ZZZZ	MD
EMMA	2	F	CHILD	RR	ZZZZ	MD
ADOLF	.11	M	INFANT	RR	ZZZZ	MD
SCHKLAR, HIRSCH	.11	M	INFANT	RR	ZZZZ	MD
MEYER, AUGUSTE	29	F	UNKNOWN	RR	ZZZZ	MD
DOMUKAJTIS, PETER	35	M	FARMER	RR	ZZZZ	MD
DOMINICA	30	F	UNKNOWN	RR	ZZZZ	MD
ROKOWSKI, JAN	30	M	FARMER	RR	ZZZZ	IL
MENDJUK, LEIB	47	M	UNKNOWN	RR	ZZZZ	IL
ABRAHAM	9	M	CHILD	RR	ZZZZ	IL
GUREWICH, SONJE	19	F	UNKNOWN	RR	ZZZZ	IL
DROHN, CHAIM	24	M	FARMER	RR	ZZZZ	IL
KACZPEREWITZ, JOHAN	30	M	LABR	RR	ZZZZ	WI
LEIB, RLEIN	30	M	MCHT	RR	ZZZZ	MD
SCHMEISSER, CASPAR	25	M	CGRMKR	RR	ZZZZ	UNK
MARMER, JOSEPH	26	M	LABR	RR	ZZZZ	MD
ESTHER	21	F	UNKNOWN	RR	ZZZZ	MD
HIRSCH	.05	M	INFANT	RR	ZZZZ	MD
MLINDIKOVA, BEILE	16	F	UNKNOWN	RR	ZZZZ	MD
KARBALSKY, ABRAHAM	19	M	FARMER	RR	ZZZZ	MD
SACHS, LEIB	27	M	FARMER	RR	ZZZZ	MD
U, M.	29	M	FARMER	RR	ZZZZ	MD
ROGOV, CHEINE	28	F	UNKNOWN	RR	ZZZZ	IA
LEOPOLD	12	M	UNKNOWN	RR	ZZZZ	IA
PAULINE	8	F	CHILD	RR	ZZZZ	IA
FANNI	6	F	CHILD	RR	ZZZZ	IA
HERMAN	6	M	CHILD	RR	ZZZZ	IA
JULIUS	4	M	CHILD	RR	ZZZZ	MD
SCHOCHERT, ISRAEL	32	M	FARMER	RR	ZZZZ	MI
GRODANS, ITZIG	22	M	MCHT	RR	ZZZZ	MI
PAUL	22	M	MCHT	RR	ZZZZ	MI
ROSENSTEIN, U	42	F	UNKNOWN	RR	ZZZZ	MI
MALKE	18	F	UNKNOWN	RR	ZZZZ	MI
SAMUEL	11	M	UNKNOWN	RR	ZZZZ	MI
JACOB	9	M	CHILD	RR	ZZZZ	MI
TAUBE	7	F	CHILD	RR	ZZZZ	MI
BLUMBERG, LIBBIE	34	F	UNKNOWN	RR	ZZZZ	MD
--CHEL	7	F	CHILD	RR	ZZZZ	MD
ESTER	1	F	CHILD	RR	ZZZZ	MD
LINDEMANN, HELENE	24	F	UNKNOWN	RR	ZZZZ	MD
ELISABETH	3	F	CHILD	RR	ZZZZ	MD
ANNA	.09	F	INFANT	RR	ZZZZ	MD
FLEYER, FREYDE	45	F	UNKNOWN	RR	ZZZZ	PA
KEWIZOVA, B.	23	F	UNKNOWN	RR	ZZZZ	PA
GREIS, U	20	M	LABR	RR	ZZZZ	IL

SHIP: SPAIN

FROM: LIVERPOOL AND QUEENSTOWN
TO: NEW YORK
ARRIVED: 25 JULY 1888

PASSENGER	AGE	SEX	OCCUPATION	PRIV	VIL	DES
AROWERIZ, LEIH	40	M	LABR	RR	AEFL	USA
KASUSCHEAITZ, DAVID	19	M	LABR	RR	AEFL	USA
BEELE	19	F	LABR	RR	AEFL	USA
GERUSKIN, M.	24	M	LABR	RR	AEFL	USA
KENCHEIE, FRANZE	19	M	LABR	RR	AEFL	USA
SYKSTEEN, ABR.	20	M	LABR	RR	AEFL	USA
WERHBERGER, JOS.	16	M	LABR	RR	AEFL	USA
FANNY	18	F	SVNT	RR	AEFL	USA
GOLDBERG, JANKEL	42	M	LABR	RR	AEFL	USA
MARGUS, JOSEL	33	M	LABR	RR	AEFL	USA
KAUGANG, O.B.	17	M	LABR	RR	AEFL	USA
WITTLER, JAM	45	M	LABR	RR	AEFL	USA
SPADE, J.	28	M	LABR	RR	AEFL	USA
MAUKOWSKA, GEDALIE	28	M	LABR	RR	AEFL	USA
SCHUNKORE, MENDEL	29	M	LABR	RR	AEFL	USA
SAPPERSTEIN, DONES	39	M	LABR	RR	AEFL	USA
GRINBERGE, JUTKE	57	M	LABR	RR	AEFL	USA
SCHIFFMANORTIZY, E.	23	M	LABR	RR	AEFL	USA
SCHILLENGER, AUGUST	21	M	LABR	RR	AEFL	USA
WISTEENIZKY, MOSES	20	M	LABR	RR	AEFL	USA
RITTSLORF, T.J.	50	M	LABR	RR	AEFL	USA
SAUSER, LUDWIG	32	M	LABR	RR	AEFL	USA
LOKOLONSK, LEISER	32	M	LABR	RR	AEFL	USA
MICHALOAN, MORDCHE	44	M	LABR	RR	AEFL	USA

PASSENGER	AGE	SEX	OCCUPATION	PRV VIL DES
SOPOLISKI, HYAN	35	M	LABR	RRAEFLUSA
ATTSCHESLEE, LEEBE	19	M	LABR	RRAEFLUSA
SVENLEN, E.	26	M	LABR	RRAEFLUSA
YAGUNKY, SAM	26	M	LABR	RRAEFLUSA
SALSEGE, JACOB	40	M	LABR	RRAEFLUSA
CUS, JACOB	19	M	LABR	RRAEFLUSA
COENELIS, CHR.	39	M	LABR	RRAEFLUSA
FRACKEL, FRED	40	M	LABR	RRAEFLUSA
KAUTARE, J.	28	M	LABR	RRAEFLUSA
LESOW, MENDEL	16	M	LABR	RRAEFLUSA
ANDRAWSKY, BACH.	40	M	LABR	RRAEFLUSA
BRADAK, ANDREAS	36	M	LABR	RRAEFLUSA
DROINKAU, FRANZ	28	M	LABR	RRAEFLUSA
BENKS, JANOSCH	38	M	LABR	RRAEFLUSA
EBERSTEIN, MOSES	14	M	LABR	RRAEFLUSA
SCHRAGER, JACOB	49	M	LABR	RRAEFLUSA
YAMABINS, JOSES	21	M	LABR	RRAEFLUSA
KUSCHENHUDER, ADOLF	20	M	LABR	RRAEFLUSA
LAND, JOHAN	47	M	LABR	RRAEFLUSA
SALAKKA, J.W.	28	M	LABR	RRAEFLUSA
JEKAUEN, EDWARD	18	M	LABR	RRAEFLUSA
KANGOS, ANETE	18	M	LABR	RRAFVGUSA
ANOLA, HUKA	39	M	LABR	RRAFVGUSA
WINLEF, JUHAN	28	M	LABR	RRAFVGUSA
LEBAMA, EUKKA	21	M	LABR	RRAFVGUSA
JULILA, GUSTAF	28	M	LABR	RRAFVGUSA
MATH.	21	M	LABR	RRAFVGUSA
JAKOLA, KANE	28	M	LABR	RRAFVGUSA
HERRI, ANTI	21	M	LABR	RRAFVGUSA
GOLDSTEIN, JACOB	33	M	LABR	RRAFVGUSA
LINDSTEIN, JOHAN	13	M	LABR	RRAFVGUSA
WILHIDEN, OTTO	11	M	CH	RRAFVGUSA
LYM, C.M.	26	M	LABR	RRAFVGUSA
LEPANSKI, JOSE	51	M	LABR	RRAFVGUSA
MILLAND, H.	33	M	LABR	RRAFVGUSA
WISKARN, SEVNESH	22	M	LABR	RRAFVGUSA
JUSELA, NATA	21	M	LABR	RRAFVGUSA
OBEESTADT, CHAS.	15	M	LABR	RRAFVGUSA
PAULINE	18	F	SVNT	RRAFVGUSA
STEIN, OLOGA	30	F	SVNT	RRAFVGUSA
RUSKA, KAISER	23	M	LABR	RRAFVGUSA
PUITAMA, ELSI	36	F	SVNT	RRAFVGUSA
GUMLOR, PAUL	28	M	LABR	RRAFVGUSA
KRAUSIL, G.M.	20	F	SVNT	RRAFVGUSA
BERBARCH, LESSER	28	M	LABR	RRAFVGUSA
MINA	55	F	W	RRAFVGUSA
SCHEORTZ, SIMON	40	M	LABR	RRAFVGUSA
SOPHIE	32	F	W	RRAFVGUSA
REID, SCHENENDES	29	F	SVNT	RRAFVGUSA
LAUTS, KISIK	15	F	SVNT	RRAFVGUSA
HELENA	11	F	CH	RRAFVGUSA
VERTYMAN, CLARE	17	F	SVNT	RRAFVGUSA
MASSEL	11	F	CH	RRAFVGUSA
MEGINA, VER..	40	F	W	RRAFVGUSA
ALEX	.06	M	INFANT	RRAFVGUSA
KALUTZKY, SARAH	17	F	SVNT	RRAFVGUSA
WASCHTEL, REBECCA	40	F	W	RRAFVGUSA
SARRAH	18	F	SVNT	RRAFVGUSA
ROSA	11	F	CH	RRAFVGUSA
JETEL	.06	F	INFANT	RRAFVGUSA
TENESER, JANETE	17	F	SVNT	RRAFVGUSA
GOLDSTEIN, ADOLF	23	M	LABR	RRAFVGUSA
SAUDES, LEA	18	F	SVNT	RRAFVGUSA
PENER	16	F	SVNT	RRAFVGUSA
KRUTZBERG, ISIDOR	26	M	LABR	RRAFVGUSA
SARAH	22	F	W	RRAFVGUSA
BERNSTEIN, S.	20	F	SVNT	RRAFVGUSA
ROSENBERG, SAM	14	M	LABR	RRAFVGUSA
SALI	30	F	W	RRZZZZUSA
JENI	8	M	CHILD	RRZZZZUSA
SIMON	3	M	CHILD	RRZZZZUSA
CELKA	5	F	CHILD	RRZZZZUSA
MAFI	.08	F	INFANT	RRZZZZUSA
FAUDMAN, HARRIS	39	M	UNKNOWN	RRZZZZUSA
ANNELA	34	F	W	RRZZZZUSA
SOLOMON	11	M	CH	RRZZZZUSA
HYMAN	3	M	CHILD	RRZZZZUSA
MARTHA	.11	F	INFANT	RRZZZZUSA
EINHOON, HERMAN	19	M	LABR	RRZZZZUSA
GRUMBERG, R.	24	M	LABR	RRZZZZUSA
ROSENSTEIN, MEYER	28	M	LABR	RRZZZZUSA
MALKA	22	F	W	RRZZZZUSA
JOSEF	.06	M	INFANT	RRZZZZUSA
MOSSEL, FRANCES	30	F	W	RRZZZZUSA
LANGANSON, JACOB	33	M	LABR	RRZZZZUSA
LIMA	23	F	W	RRZZZZUSA
BERNHARD	2	M	CHILD	RRZZZZUSA
ANNA	.09	F	INFANT	RRZZZZUSA
SCHUNDER, ARON	18	M	LABR	RRZZZZUSA
MOGULMSKY, S.	23	F	SVNT	RRZZZZUSA
GRUNBERG, SCHUML	40	M	LABR	RRZZZZUSA
IPOLITEY	24	F	W	RRZZZZUSA
SCHERBURG, CLARA	30	F	W	RRZZZZUSA
JOSEPH	8	M	CHILD	RRZZZZUSA
KASSMAN, MINA	20	F	SVNT	RRZZZZUSA
WEMBERG, JULIUS	30	M	LABR	RRZZZZUSA
ROSA	24	F	W	RRZZZZUSA
VIGRETT	3	M	CHILD	RRZZZZUSA
SAMUEL	.11	M	INFANT	RRZZZZUSA
WILHELM	.01	M	INFANT	RRZZZZUSA
KAPPER, LUBE	50	M	LABR	RRZZZZUSA
GILLESON, FREDE	20	F	SVNT	RRZZZZUSA
GOLDENBERG, RACHEL	20	F	SVNT	RRZZZZUSA
HERCHLOWULSKY, R.	26	F	W	RRZZZZUSA
SEBA	19	F	SVNT	RRZZZZUSA
SIMON	.11	M	INFANT	RRZZZZUSA
JUGE	14	M	CH	RRZZZZUSA
HOULKOUSKY, USFA	45	F	W	RRZZZZUSA
KOHEN, RACHEL	16	F	SVNT	RRZZZZUSA
ADOLF	11	M	CH	RRZZZZUSA
KOYAN, ABRAM	37	M	LABR	RRZZZZUSA
DORA	32	F	W	RRZZZZUSA
GALVE	10	F	CH	RRZZZZUSA
PRISEL	8	M	CHILD	RRZZZZUSA
CHAIE	4	M	CHILD	RRZZZZUSA
RENER	.11	M	INFANT	RRZZZZUSA
KIESMAN, SCHEN	22	F	W	RRZZZZUSA
JACOB	6	M	CHILD	RRZZZZUSA
SARAH	4	F	CHILD	RRZZZZUSA
JOE	.11	M	INFANT	RRZZZZUSA
LOKOLOUSKE, LIEB	32	M	LABR	RRZZZZUSA
SARE	26	F	W	RRZZZZUSA
CHANE	7	F	CHILD	RRZZZZUSA
H.	5	F	CHILD	RRZZZZUSA
MOSSES	3	M	CHILD	RRZZZZUSA
KAHANE	.10	F	INFANT	RRZZZZUSA

SHIP: RHYNLAND

FROM: ANTWERP
TO: NEW YORK
ARRIVED: 26 JULY 1888

PASSENGER	AGE	SEX	OCCUPATION	PRV VIL DES
YOZER, CEPLA	27	M	FARMER	RRAIMIUNK
PAWLOWSKI, HERSCH	22	M	BCHR	RRZZZZNY
ZORING, DANIEL	36	M	LABR	RRZZZZNY
TRIEB, SALOMON	25	M	SHMK	RRZZZZNY
GOLDE	22	F	W	RRZZZZNY
CHANE	10	F	CH	RRZZZZNY
JACOB	9	M	CHILD	RRZZZZNY
BRANE	00	F	INF	RRZZZZNY
GERLAU, CARL	25	M	LABR	RRZZZZNY
BALINSKY, JAN	23	M	LABR	RRZZZZNY
GUTLEWSKY, JULIAN	24	M	FARMER	RRZZZZNY
KOPELOWITZ, JANKEL	35	M	PNTR	RRAICDNY

PASSENGER	AGE	SEX	OCCUPATION	PV RI VL	DES
BARKINA, MEYER	35	M	TLR	RRAIC	DNY
SUBRISS, MORDEKE	39	M	TLR	RRAIC	DNY
CRAWES, CHAIM	37	M	TLR	RRAIC	DNY
KAJEKOWSKI, FLORIAN	16	F	NN	RRAIL	UNY
MEIER, MARIA	20	F	SVNT	RRAIL	UUNK

SHIP: ROMAN

FROM: LIVERPOOL
TO: BOSTON
ARRIVED: 26 JULY 1888

PASSENGER	AGE	SEX	OCCUPATION	PV RI VL	DES
COHEN, ELKE	23	F	W	RRZZZ	ZNY
DISCHE	.06	F	INFANT	RRZZZ	ZNY
BLEYER, MART	59	M	LABR	RRZZZ	ZNY
JILLY	47	F	W	RRZZZ	ZNY
KROKIN, SCHL.	18	M	LABR	RRZZZ	ZNY
ABRAMOWITZ, CHANA	14	M	LABR	RRZZZ	ZNY
CHOLT, YANKEL	22	M	LABR	RRZZZ	ZNY
PERAN, EMANUEL	16	M	LABR	RRZZZ	ZNY
FISCHER, MINE	19	M	LABR	RRZZZ	ZNY
LIKTEROWITZ, GOLDE	23	F	SP	RRZZZ	ZUNK
NARSAWITZKY, INGE	30	F	SP	RRZZZ	ZUNK
HYMAN, HENNY	19	F	SP	RRZZZ	ZNY
RIGOKIN, LOSER	21	M	LABR	RRZZZ	ZNY
SPINGAL, WOLF	28	M	LABR	RRZZZ	ZNY
HURIO, ITZCHOK	2	M	CHILD	RRZZZ	ZNY
DERTER, ESPRAIM	30	M	LABR	RRZZZ	ZNY
OLIMSKI, SAM	43	M	LABR	RRZZZ	ZBO
SARA	40	F	W	RRZZZ	ZBO
ABRAM	10	M	CH	RRZZZ	ZBO
MOSES	4	M	CHILD	RRZZZ	ZBO
SMUTZKY, TAUBE	22	F	W	RRZZZ	ZBO
SCHINE	.04	F	INFANT	RRZZZ	ZBO
SMOLAUSKY, DRISSEL	12	M	LABR	RRZZZ	ZBO
LEIB	11	M	CH	RRZZZ	ZBO
BENAWITZ, CHAJE	23	M	LABR	RRZZZ	ZBO
SILBERT, JOSEPH	24	M	LABR	RRZZZ	ZBO
WOLINSKY, SCHIFRE	16	M	LABR	RRZZZ	ZBO
GOLDBERG, BEN	36	M	LABR	RRZZZ	ZBO
MOSES	17	M	LABR	RRZZZ	ZBO
WILENSKY, CHAINE	19	M	LABR	RRZZZ	ZBO
EDELSTIEN, REIVEN	42	M	LABR	RRZZZ	ZBO
SCHENE	32	F	W	RRZZZ	ZBO
SCHMEAL	10	F	CH	RRZZZ	ZBO
CHANE	8	F	CHILD	RRZZZ	ZBO
FRUME	.07	F	INFANT	RRZZZ	ZBO
GORDON, DD.	29	M	LABR	RRZZZ	ZBO
DAWN, ALEX	25	M	LABR	RRZZZ	ZBO
TAKLIMONWITZ, P.	30	M	LABR	RRZZZ	ZBO
SCHMILANSKY, N.	27	M	LABR	RRZZZ	ZBO
KARTCHEN, WOLF	20	M	LABR	RRZZZ	ZBO
SUKICIN, MOSES	20	M	LABR	RRZZZ	ZBO
TALKEWITZ, HIR.	26	M	LABR	RRZZZ	ZBO
RAMGONSKY, SEL.	30	M	LABR	RRZZZ	ZBO
ROBNIK, MOSCHE	39	M	LABR	RRZZZ	ZBO
ROLNIK, HERKN	50	M	LABR	RRZZZ	ZBO
SILBERBLUTT, TLKA.	18	F	SP	RRZZZ	ZBO
TIKTOROWITSCH, CHANE	.05	F	INFANT	RRZZZ	ZBO
NASSOWITZKY, ARON	.04	M	INFANT	RRZZZ	ZBO
SCHWUTZKY, PESCHE	.05	M	INFANT	RRZZZ	ZBO
BOTREY, G.	26	M	LABR	PLZZZ	ZBO
FRANCISCO, W.	32	M	LABR	RRZZZ	ZNY
PARLERI, IRI	40	M	LABR	RRZZZ	ZNY
ANTON, K.	30	M	LABR	RRZZZ	ZNY
MYEROVITCH, ABM.	25	M	LABR	RRZZZ	ZNY
PRIESTEIN, BEREL	18	M	LABR	RRZZZ	ZNY
STEIN, DD.	16	M	LABR	RRZZZ	ZNY
FRIEDMAN, ROSA	32	F	SP	RRZZZ	ZNY
FERMAN, ALEX	25	M	LABR	RRZZZ	ZNY

PASSENGER	AGE	SEX	OCCUPATION	PV RI VL	DES
KISCHNER, BROCK	34	M	LABR	RRZZZ	ZNY

SHIP: STATE OF INDIANA

FROM: GLASGOW AND LARNE
TO: NEW YORK
ARRIVED: 26 JULY 1888

PASSENGER	AGE	SEX	OCCUPATION	PV RI VL	DES
SUFFRIN, A.M.	28	M	PDLR	RRZZZ	ZUSA
CHAZDOWITSCH, ISAK	29	M	PDLR	RRZZZ	ZUSA
SCHADOWIK, MOSES	32	M	PDLR	RRZZZ	ZUSA
KREUTZER, HEYMANN	32	M	PDLR	RRZZZ	ZUSA
KARAPSIK, HIRSCH	22	M	LABR	RRZZZ	ZUSA
KASEPES, SANDEL	37	M	PDLR	RRZZZ	ZUSA
NACHSEIW, DOCHEM	38	M	PDLR	RRZZZ	ZUSA
SCHULMANN, LEISEN	38	M	PDLR	RRZZZ	ZUSA
HELFZOTH, ISRAEL	29	M	LABR	RRZZZ	ZUSA
SIDLOWSKY, LEIB	19	M	PDLR	RRZZZ	ZUSA
SYESGALL, OSSYEN	22	M	PDLR	RRZZZ	ZUSA
BASSIMON, ABR.	43	M	LABR	RRZZZ	ZUSA
KOSUWEN, JOSEF	37	M	LABR	RRZZZ	ZUSA
STRASGIN, ISRAEL	11	M	CH	RRZZZ	ZUSA
SAABEMANN, KOLMAN	27	M	PDLR	RRZZZ	ZUSA
WEINSTEIN, ABRAHAM	17	M	PDLR	RRZZZ	ZUSA
LOHER, JOHN	56	M	FARMER	RRZZZ	ZUSA
JEAN, DONSTER	24	M	PDLR	RRZZZ	ZUSA
WERROTZSKI, JOSEPH	26	M	LABR	RRZZZ	ZUSA
PETRNEY, R.	26	M	LABR	RRZZZ	ZUSA
ZAWASSKY, MAYENT	26	M	LABR	RRZZZ	ZUSA
MUSCHEWITZ, JOSEF	17	M	PDLR	RRZZZ	ZUSA
NEBELOW, JACOB	20	M	LABR	RRZZZ	ZUSA
ZEDBAWSKY, MEYER	36	M	FARMER	RRZZZ	ZUSA
GRINBERG, JOSEPH	18	M	PDLR	RRZZZ	ZUSA
SCHLOSSBERG, HARRIEL	20	M	PDLR	RRZZZ	ZUSA
MASCHE	20	F	W	RRZZZ	ZUSA
FRERMANN, HERSCH	21	M	PDLR	RRZZZ	ZUSA
FEIGE	19	F	W	RRZZZ	ZUSA
GRENDA, CHANE	25	F	W	RRZZZ	ZUSA
CHAJE	8	F	CHILD	RRZZZ	ZUSA
MOSES	5	M	CHILD	RRZZZ	ZUSA
HERSCH	1	M	CHILD	RRZZZ	ZUSA
RIEBNER, CHAJE	30	F	W	RRZZZ	ZUSA
SARAH	10	F	CH	RRZZZ	ZUSA
DAVID	7	M	CHILD	RRZZZ	ZUSA
ISAAC	1	M	CHILD	RRZZZ	ZUSA
RIWKE	.03	F	INFANT	RRZZZ	ZUSA
GOLDENSTEIN, BARUCH	30	M	LABR	RRZZZ	ZUSA
GORDON, ERDE	45	F	W	RRZZZ	ZUSA
HULDA	20	F	DMS	RRZZZ	ZUSA
RACHEL	11	F	CH	RRZZZ	ZUSA
SCHEENE	9	F	CHILD	RRZZZ	ZUSA
BER.	6	M	CHILD	RRZZZ	ZUSA
SARETZSKY, REBECCA	20	F	DMS	RRZZZ	ZUSA
BAY, ITZKA	50	F	DMS	RRZZZ	ZUSA
SJUNNA-, SCHIE	19	F	DMS	RRZZZ	ZUSA
ROBERT, CATH.	53	F	DMS	RRZZZ	ZUSA
SCHEMELEWITZ, OTTE	45	F	DMS	RRZZZ	ZUSA
MAKOFSKY, ZOFIEL	15	F	DMS	RRZZZ	ZUSA
MEHROKWITSCHOW, CATH.	26	F	DMS	RRZZZ	ZUSA

PASSENGER	AGE	SEX	OCCUPATION	PRIV	VIL	DES

SHIP: GALLIA

FROM: LIVERPOOL AND QUEENSTOWN
TO: NEW YORK
ARRIVED: 27 JULY 1888

PASSENGER	AGE	SEX	OCCUPATION	PRIV	VIL	DES
SINIWITZKI, MOSES	43	M	TLR	RR	ACBF	USA
DEMANZKA, PETER	22	M	PDLR	RR	ACBF	USA
RIFKIN, EFRAIM	29	M	TLR	RR	ACBF	USA
ROSENFELD, PAISACK	45	M	TLR	RR	ACBF	USA
MOSERANSKY, SAML	28	M	FARMER	RR	ACBF	USA
LEVY, BERNARD	19	M	SHMK	PL	ZZZZ	USA
TURFULSKI, ISAAC	19	M	TLR	PL	AFWJ	USA
OSTAWITZKI, MAYER	15	M	TLR	PL	ACBF	USA
MINDE	18	F	SVNT	PL	ACBF	USA
CHAHUSKY, RAHEL	23	F	MACH	PL	ACBF	USA
WOLFF, JENNY	19	F	SVNT	PL	ACBF	USA
SAKOWITZ, JOSEL	10	M	CH	PL	ACBF	USA
LEISEROWITZ, ROSA	23	F	SVNT	PL	ACBF	USA
OSTARWITZKI, ISAAC	48	M	SHMK	PL	ACBF	USA
GITEL	40	F	W	PL	ACBF	USA
CHAIM	21	F	SVNT	PL	ACBF	USA
SOLOMON	11	M	CH	PL	ACBF	USA
RAHIL	8	F	CHILD	PL	ACBF	USA
SCHURGANI, CHAZKE	30	M	HRSB	PL	ACBF	USA
FREIDI	19	F	W	PL	ACBF	USA
PLOTNIK, JOSEL	50	M	PDLR	PL	ACBF	USA
JASKEL	.11	M	INFANT	PL	ACBF	USA
WIEMER, LISSER	10	M	CH	PL	ACBF	USA
KOLOMAKI, GUST.	27	M	LABR	FN	ZZZZ	OH
KULMINGI, MIKKE	20	M	LABR	FN	ZZZZ	OH
WANHOPIKA, JOHS	18	M	FARMER	FN	ZZZZ	OH
KAUPPI, PETTER	35	M	FARMER	FN	ZZZZ	OH
PLETILA, PETER	25	M	LABR	FN	ZZZZ	OH
MEDINK, ABRAM	30	M	LABR	FN	ACBF	OH
KOSTINRE, ALDRICH	22	M	LABR	FN	ACBF	OH
KUNHER, ESAJAS	27	M	LABR	FN	ACBF	OH
BAKKILA, MATTI	36	M	LABR	FN	ACBF	OH
SUNTARI, ERIK	21	M	LABR	FN	ACBF	OH
POLO, JOHAN	27	M	FARMER	FN	ACBF	OH
HYTTMEN, ABRAHAM	30	M	LABR	FN	ACBF	OH
NIVA, PETER	27	M	LABR	FN	ACBF	OH
OIVA, ANDERS	30	M	LABR	FN	ACBF	OH
NIVA, KARL	24	M	LABR	FN	ACBF	OH
TAPAIN, PETER	17	M	LABR	FN	ACBF	OH
LOHTE, AARON	40	M	FARMER	FN	ACBF	OH
NIHENEN, KALLI	18	M	LABR	FN	ACBF	OH
LUHSUA, ALEX	20	M	LABR	FN	ACBF	OH
KALPAKKA, BRITA	19	F	SP	FN	ACBF	UNK
KARKELA, GUSTAVA	21	F	SP	FN	ACBF	UNK
NISHA, HILDA	21	F	SVNT	FN	ACBF	UNK
HILTERNEN, LISA	33	F	W	FN	ACBF	UNK
MARIA	9	F	CHILD	FN	ACBF	UNK
PAPAIN, EVA	23	F	SP	FN	ACBF	UNK
JAHTILA, KAISA	16	F	SP	FN	ACBF	UNK
KANGUS, LEA	15	F	SP	FN	ACBF	UNK
SLAND, ANNA	52	F	W	FN	ACBF	UNK
MARIE	20	F	SP	FN	ACBF	UNK
HERMANN	16	M	LABR	FN	ACBF	UNK
GUSTAF	14	M	LABR	FN	ACBF	UNK
AMALA, HEDWIG	40	F	MA	FN	ACBF	OH
HENDRIK	12	M	CH	FN	ACBF	OH
FANNY	8	F	CHILD	FN	ACBF	OH
HILMA	6	F	CHILD	FN	ACBF	OH

SHIP: NOVA SCOTIAN

FROM: LIVERPOOL
TO: BALTIMORE
ARRIVED: 27 JULY 1888

PASSENGER	AGE	SEX	OCCUPATION	PRIV	VIL	DES
KAIN, DAVID	22	M	LABR	RR	ZZZZ	BAL
SARA	20	F	W	RR	ZZZZ	BAL
SCHUSDOWITZ, EPHRAIM	18	M	LABR	RR	ZZZZ	BAL
CAJE	19	F	W	RR	ZZZZ	BAL
LANDSMAN, ITZIG	19	F	DRSMKR	RR	ZZZZ	BAL
CEREY	20	M	LABR	RR	ZZZZ	BAL
SUSSKIND, ROCHE	19	F	DRSMKR	RR	ZZZZ	BAL
PISCHOWITZ, ISRAEL	38	M	LABR	RR	ZZZZ	BAL
MELUN, ISRAEL	33	M	LABR	RR	ZZZZ	BAL
HEVREVITZ, ISRAEL	37	M	MCHT	RR	ZZZZ	BAL
ROSENBERG, JOSEPH	27	M	MCHT	RR	ZZZZ	CLE
JENTE	27	F	W	RR	ZZZZ	CLE
ISRAEL	4	M	CHILD	RR	ZZZZ	CLE
BETTY	3	F	CHILD	RR	ZZZZ	CLE
LUBINAN	2	F	CHILD	RR	ZZZZ	CLE
SAMUEL	.09	F	INFANT	RR	ZZZZ	CLE
BERKOWITZ, ESTHE	18	M	UNKNOWN	RR	ZZZZ	CLE

SHIP: CITY OF CHICAGO

FROM: LIVERPOOL AND QUEENSTOWN
TO: NEW YORK
ARRIVED: 28 JULY 1888

PASSENGER	AGE	SEX	OCCUPATION	PRIV	VIL	DES
BERGER, SAML	18	M	LABR	RR	ZZZZ	NY
NABRIAWITZ, MARTIN	42	M	LABR	RR	ZZZZ	NY
JANYZEWSKA, ANTONIA	20	F	W	RR	ZZZZ	NY
FRANCAW	2	F	CHILD	RR	ZZZZ	BUF
RAASACZNUAS, RASALIA	30	F	W	RR	ZZZZ	UNK
MICHL.	6	M	CHILD	RR	ZZZZ	UNK
ANTONI	4	M	CHILD	RR	ZZZZ	UNK
FRANZISCHIK	.08	F	INFANT	RR	ZZZZ	UNK
SCHVEKEL, TAMBI	18	M	SHMK	RR	ZZZZ	NY
PODUNEASKI, JOSEF	30	M	TLR	RR	AFWJ	NY
JAMES, HENRIK	18	M	LABR	RR	ZZZZ	NY
SINCOMAN, MARIA	20	F	SP	RR	ZZZZ	NY
KAAS, JOHANNES	18	M	LABR	RR	ZZZZ	NY
PERSONN, ELIS.	26	F	LABR	RR	ZZZZ	NY
SODERMAN, WILHELMINA	22	M	LABR	RR	ZZZZ	NY
LOMDMAN, JOHAN	17	M	LABR	RR	ZZZZ	NY
PERSON, ANDERS	44	M	LABR	RR	ZZZZ	NY
NOODSTROM, CHARLOTTE	46	F	W	RR	ZZZZ	JAK
WRITHEN, WAHEBOJ	36	M	LABR	RR	ZZZZ	MN
DAMICUS, H.	30	M	LABR	RR	ZZZZ	MN
DAHL, JOHAN	30	M	LABR	RR	ZZZZ	NY
GOLDBAUM, SAM.	36	M	LABR	RR	AFWJ	NY
BERNSTEIN, ANNA	40	F	W	RR	AFWJ	NY
HJE	8	F	CHILD	RR	AFWJ	NY
GERSCHEN	5	M	CHILD	RR	AFWJ	NY
SEIBRIDA, VINCENT	24	M	LABR	RR	AFWJ	NY
GRODZINSKY, MOSES	27	M	PRNTR	RR	ZZZZ	BO
SOPHIE	20	F	W	RR	ZZZZ	BO
CHAIM	9	F	CHILD	RR	ZZZZ	BO
DALINSKI, MOYE	16	M	TLR	FN	ZZZZ	NY
MARK, CHAWE	16	F	SP	RR	ZZZZ	NY
HEINROT, DAVID	27	M	LABR	RR	ZZZZ	NY
LUDWIG, LOUISE	28	F	SVNT	PL	ZZZZ	NY
RUMBERGER, LESER	35	M	LABR	RR	ZZZZ	NY
SOFIE	45	F	W	RR	ZZZZ	NY
ISRAEL	25	M	LABR	RR	ZZZZ	NY
SEAMUND	24	F	SVNT	RR	ZZZZ	NY
WILLI	16	M	CPR	RR	ZZZZ	NY
GETTEL	12	M	CH	RR	ZZZZ	NY

PASSENGER	AGE	SEX	OCCUPATION	PRIVIL	DES
NECHEMI	9	F	CHILD	RRZZZZ	NY
JOEL	4	M	CHILD	RRZZZZ	NY
MARQUIS, ALHA	26	M	LABR	RRAHOO	NY
GREENBURG, FEIGE	25	F	W	RRAFWJ	NY
JULIE	.03	F	INFANT	RRAFWJ	NY
LAPIDUS, JACOB	20	M	PNTR	RRAFWJ	NY
DARLENTSKIE, JACOB	27	M	TLR	RRAINK	BO
ABRAHAM	19	M	TLR	RRAINK	BO

SHIP: TRAVE

FROM: BREMEN AND SOUTHAMPTON
TO: NEW YORK
ARRIVED: 28 JULY 1888

PASSENGER	AGE	SEX	OCCUPATION	PRIVIL	DES
PARSONS, HENRY	72	M	TT	RRZZZZ	USA
CLARA	18	F	UNKNOWN	RRZZZZ	USA
KLAUSE, ADOLF	21	M	LABR	RRZZZZ	USA
AUG.	23	M	LABR	RRZZZZ	USA
EHN, ABRAM	21	M	BCHR	RRZZZZ	USA
BERGSTROEM, ANDERS	22	M	LABR	RRZZZZ	USA
WIKSTROEM, JOH.	30	M	LABR	RRZZZZ	USA
WELIN, ANNA	53	F	W	RRZZZZ	USA
ELIN	6	M	CHILD	RRZZZZ	USA
ANNA	5	F	CHILD	RRZZZZ	USA
JOHANNSON, AXEL	26	M	LABR	RRZZZZ	USA
ANNA	33	F	W	RRZZZZ	USA
CHODKOWSKI, JOS.	22	M	FARMER	RRZZZZ	USA
LIBOWITZ, ETEL	27	M	FARMER	RRZZZZ	USA
FRUME	6	F	CHILD	RRZZZZ	USA
JOSEF	6	M	CHILD	RRZZZZ	USA
SALI	4	F	CHILD	RRZZZZ	USA
JACOBE	.10	M	INFANT	RRZZZZ	USA
STRAS, ELA	17	F	UNKNOWN	RRZZZZ	USA
KATZ, MENDEL	19	M	LABR	RRZZZZ	USA
LEVY, SALOMON	16	M	LABR	RRZZZZ	USA
PERENDANTZKOS, MATEUS	40	M	LABR	RRZZZZ	USA
JAKUBOWSKY, JAN	24	M	LABR	RRZZZZ	USA
HIRSCH, SALOMON	19	M	LABR	RRZZZZ	USA
FRUME	21	F	W	RRZZZZ	USA
BRAKER, JOS.	29	M	LABR	RRZZZZ	USA
KAPUS, ADOLF	20	F	FARMER	RRZZZZ	USA
LOEWEN, FRANZ	37	M	FARMER	RRZZZZ	USA
SUSANNA	32	F	W	RRZZZZ	USA
FRANZ	7	M	CHILD	RRZZZZ	USA
DIEDR.	5	M	CHILD	RRZZZZ	USA
KATH.	2	F	CHILD	RRZZZZ	USA
FISCH, MARIA	30	F	W	RRZZZZ	USA
DAVID	7	M	CHILD	RRZZZZ	USA
WOLF	6	M	CHILD	RRZZZZ	USA
NISEL	3	M	CHILD	RRZZZZ	USA
LOUISE	.11	F	INFANT	RRZZZZ	USA

SHIP: ALASKA

FROM: LIVERPOOL AND QUEENSTOWN
TO: NEW YORK
ARRIVED: 30 JULY 1888

PASSENGER	AGE	SEX	OCCUPATION	PRIVIL	DES
LAKA-LI, K	32	M	LABR	FNZZZZ	USA
BU-TIO, SANKA	19	F	SP	FNZZZZ	USA
GORDON, JANKEL	32	M	TLR	RRZZZZ	USA
BOMSTEIN, P	23	F	SP	RRZZZZ	USA
EIDMAN, MASCHE	15	F	SP	RRZZZZ	USA
PUTASCHUICK, LEIBE	50	F	MA	RRZZZZ	USA
EIDMAN, ARON	20	M	LABR	RRZZZZ	USA
NUDLEMAN, FROIM	14	M	CPR	RRZZZZ	USA
METZNICK, MALKE	26	F	SP	RRZZZZ	USA
EIDMAN, SARA	50	F	MA	RRZZZZ	USA
WOLPEN, ABRAM	57	M	TLR	RRZZZZ	USA
MASSOSNICK, ELIAS	3	M	CHILD	RRZZZZ	USA
BERMAN, SENDEL	20	F	SP	RRZZZZ	USA
-EPPAM-----, ANNA	30	F	SP	FNZZZZ	USA
IANUSE, KAISA	28	F	SP	FNZZZZ	USA
BLONGVIST, SOFIA	27	F	SP	FNZZZZ	USA
BACKMAN, KAROLINA	35	F	SP	FNZZZZ	USA
ENGLAND, EMILIA	37	F	SP	FNZZZZ	USA
SICK--EN, GUSTAF	26	M	LABR	FNZZZZ	USA
WURT--AMEN, KARL	26	M	LABR	FNZZZZ	USA
ELIKASKI, ELIAS	36	M	FARMER	FNZZZZ	USA
ROGOWN, MARDOKE	40	M	FMGR	RRZZZZ	USA
SENDEL, HIRSCH	19	M	MUSN	RRZZZZ	USA
WEISMANN, ITZIG	21	M	TLR	RRZZZZ	USA
KORMANN, BLASIUS	36	M	PDLR	PLZZZZ	USA
MITZNIK, BENZIN	2	M	CHILD	RRZZZZ	USA
MASOSNIK, SCHINDE	00	F	MA	RRZZZZ	USA
CHAIE	3	F	CHILD	RRZZZZ	USA
VICTOR	.08	M	INFANT	RRZZZZ	USA
FELDMAN, NECHANE	30	F	MA	RRZZZZ	USA
LEIBE	9	M	CHILD	RRZZZZ	USA
--NE	3	M	CHILD	RRZZZZ	USA
BARNCH	.10	M	INFANT	RRZZZZ	USA
LEPZINSKY, IGNAZ	21	M	LABR	RRZZZZ	USA
SKUKOWSKY, PIESCH	29	M	LABR	RRZZZZ	USA
NACHAMIOWICZ, RACHEL	32	F	MA	RRZZZZ	USA
LEA	6	M	CHILD	RRZZZZ	USA
SARA	3	F	CHILD	RRZZZZ	USA
LEISER	.08	M	INFANT	RRZZZZ	USA
GILMAN, HIRSCH	28	M	MACH	RRZZZZ	USA
HURWITZ, JOSSEL	48	M	PDLR	RRZZZZ	USA
HILLEL	16	M	PDLR	RRZZZZ	USA
PASSELL, MATH	51	M	LABR	FNZZZZ	USA
JOHANSON, JULIUS	26	M	LABR	FNZZZZ	USA
HONGELL, JULIUS	28	M	LABR	FNZZZZ	USA
JOHANSON, U	20	M	LABR	FNZZZZ	USA
SWEILA, JOHAN	20	M	LABR	FNZZZZ	USA
HENDRICKSON, JOHAN	26	M	LABR	FNZZZZ	USA
FREEDMAN, HY	29	M	BKBNDR	RRZZZZ	USA
JOSEPH, P	33	M	TLR	PLZZZZ	USA
JADERLAND, ANDERS	33	M	MNR	FNZZZZ	USA

SHIP: ETRURIA

FROM: LIVERPOOL AND QUEENSTOWN
TO: NEW YORK
ARRIVED: 30 JULY 1888

PASSENGER	AGE	SEX	OCCUPATION	PRIVIL	DES
KOHANE, MAREA	25	M	LABR	FNAHOO	NY
CHASS--, SALONA	28	M	LABR	FNAHOO	NY
EPSTEIN, SALONA	25	M	LABR	FNAHOO	NY
WEINESS, SELIG	50	M	LABR	FNAHOO	NY
PAWLOWSKI, VALERIA	23	M	LABR	FNAHOO	NY
SCHAPINO, ABRAHAM	25	M	LABR	FNAHOO	NY
BACK, JOHN	27	M	SEMN	FNZZZZ	NY
PABATZACK, SCHENDER	20	M	LABR	FNAHOO	PHI
RUSUK, SIMON	29	M	MCHT	PLZZZZ	NY

SHIP: FURNESSIA

FROM: GLASGOW AND MOVILLE
TO: NEW YORK
ARRIVED: 30 JULY 1888

PASSENGER	AGE	SEX	OCCUPATION	PRV VIL DES
DONISKI-TY, LEONARD	23	M	LABR	PLAIDLUSA
GLADIS, ANDRES	18	M	LABR	PLAIDLUSA
KANYNCH, JOHANN	22	M	LABR	PLAIDLUSA
KARPUS, TARGIS	23	M	LABR	PLAIDLUSA
SCHERMANN, SCHM--	33	M	TLR	PLAIDLUSA
VITKA, STEPHAN	20	M	LABR	PLAIDLUSA
ZYRWA, GEORG	30	M	LABR	PLAIDLUSA
HORT, ANNA	20	F	HP	PLAIDLUSA
MO--CINK, CHAJE	18	F	HP	PLAIDLUSA
JACOBS, BESSIE	21	F	HP	PLAIDLUSA
WM	19	M	TLR	PLAIDLUSA
ABRAHAM	45	M	TLR	PLAIDLUSA
MRS	46	F	NN	PLAIDLUSA
DAVID	17	M	TLR	PLAIDLUSA
SOLOMON	11	M	CH	PLAIDLUSA
ISRAEL	9	M	CHILD	PLAIDLUSA
SARAH	7	F	CHILD	PLAIDLUSA
SZYEPANSKI, MARY	24	F	NN	PLAIDLUSA
JOHN	.06	M	INFANT	PLAIDLUSA
VICENTY	.06	F	INFANT	PLAIDLUSA

SHIP: WERRA

FROM: BREMEN AND SOUTHAMPTON
TO: NEW YORK
ARRIVED: 31 JULY 1888

PASSENGER	AGE	SEX	OCCUPATION	PRV VIL DES
BARONOWSKY, JUL.	35	M	MCHT	RRZZZZUSA
RYBINSKA, MARYANNA	24	F	W	RRZZZZUSA
WALATHA	.11	F	INFANT	RRZZZZUSA
GREJMAS, POTSZ	20	M	FARMER	RRZZZZUSA
GROSCINSKI, FRANCISZEK	30	M	LABR	RRZZZZUSA
PRUSAKOWSKI, TOMASZ	24	M	LABR	RRZZZZUSA
TUELLIKKA, JOSEF.	30	F	UNKNOWN	FNZZZZUSA
ERLANDSON, MARIA	28	F	UNKNOWN	FNZZZZUSA
LANDBERG, ALB.	25	M	LABR	FNZZZZUSA
NILSSON, CARL	37	M	LABR	FNZZZZUSA
PETTERSON, NILS	34	M	LABR	FNZZZZUSA
ZAWACKA, ROZALIA	26	F	W	RRZZZZUSA
BRONISLAUS	2	M	CHILD	RRZZZZUSA
HOLDACK, EVA	28	F	W	RRZZZZUSA
ALEX	.10	M	INFANT	RRZZZZUSA
JASCENSKA, ROSALIA	23	F	UNKNOWN	RRZZZZUSA
LAUDE, DINE	45	F	W	RRZZZZUSA
CHANE	17	F	W	RRZZZZUSA
DAVID	10	M	CH	RRZZZZUSA
MEHL, FRIEDR.	32	M	LABR	RRZZZZUSA
LOUISE	32	F	W	RRZZZZUSA
GORODONOWITZ, DAVID	32	M	LABR	RRZZZZUSA
MIGOWSKY, WICENTY	19	M	LABR	RRZZZZUSA
STOLOWSKY, BEILE	38	F	W	RRZZZZUSA
LEIBE	14	F	UNKNOWN	RRZZZZUSA
REBECCA	13	F	CH	RRZZZZUSA
CHAJE	6	M	CHILD	RRZZZZUSA
MOSES	4	M	CHILD	RRZZZZUSA
DAVID	.07	M	INFANT	RRZZZZUSA
STADALNISK, JANOS	20	M	LABR	RRZZZZUSA
FRAJANOW, ANNA	25	F	W	RRZZZZUSA
BERTHA	10	F	CH	RRZZZZUSA
ADOLF	3	M	CHILD	RRZZZZUSA
MARIE	.11	F	INFANT	RRZZZZUSA
POWELL, VAN	22	M	LABR	RRAHZSUSA
LOHNTA	24	M	LABR	RRAHZSUSA

PASSENGER	AGE	SEX	OCCUPATION	PRV VIL DES
PIEGER, MICHAEL	26	M	LABR	RRZZZZUSA

SHIP: SUEVIA

FROM: HAMBURG AND HAVRE
TO: NEW YORK
ARRIVED: 31 JULY 1888

PASSENGER	AGE	SEX	OCCUPATION	PRV VIL DES
THORNER, GUSTAV	21	M	LABR	RRZZZZUSA
JANUS--OIC, ANTONY	21	M	LABR	RRZZZZUSA
MA--TEWICZ, ANNA	27	F	SGL	RRZZZZUSA
KAPIENSKY, PIOTER	26	M	WO	RRAHTOUSA
JOSOWSKY, PAULINE	21	F	SGL	RRAHTOUSA
ROGOW, ELIAS	23	M	LABR	RRAIGDUSA
TRACHTER, HERSCH	48	M	LABR	RRZZZZUSA
HINKA	30	F	W	RRZZZZUSA
CHAIM	3	M	CHILD	RRZZZZUSA
SAMUEL	.11	M	INFANT	RRZZZZUSA
SCHMICHE	19	M	LABR	RRZZZZUSA
MARIE	18	F	SGL	RRZZZZUSA
WEINSTEIN, MENDEL	17	M	LABR	RRZZZZUSA
HOSMACK, ELISE	40	F	WO	RRAFWJUSA
MAX	8	M	CHILD	RRAFWJUSA
ROSA	6	F	CHILD	RRAFWJUSA
LEON	3	M	CHILD	RRAFWJUSA
HERMAN, ROSA	.11	F	INFANT	RRAFWJUSA
RINGSALOWSKI, JOH	30	M	LABR	RRZZZZUSA
ANNA	25	F	W	RRZZZZUSA
BUSCH, RUDOLF	30	M	JNR	RRZZZZUSA
GUDELLA, CARL	15	M	LABR	RRAHVUUSA
MISCH-H--SKY, JULS	32	M	LABR	RRZZZZUSA
CHRISTINE	32	F	W	RRZZZZUSA
THEODOR	9	M	CHILD	RRZZZZUSA
ELENORE	4	F	CHILD	RRZZZZUSA
OTTILIE	3	F	CHILD	RRZZZZUSA
MARIE	.09	F	INFANT	RRZZZZUSA
MULTACH, JACOB	26	M	LABR	RRZZZZUSA
KAPLAN, WOLFF	20	M	LABR	RRAIGHUSA
MOKTOWER, ABRAHAM	9	M	CHILD	RRZZZZUSA
RUDNITZKA, BRONIE	20	F	SGL	RRZZZZUSA
SCHORK, RACHEL	16	F	SGL	RRZZZZUSA
BLUME	44	F	WO	RRZZZZUSA
FEIGE	17	F	SGL	RRZZZZUSA
SCHAPIRO, ITZIG	28	M	LABR	RRZZZZUSA
SCHNEIDERMAN, MIRKE	35	F	WO	RRZZZZUSA
MORDSCHE	9	F	CHILD	RRZZZZUSA
BROCHE	5	F	CHILD	RRZZZZUNK
MOSES	3	M	CHILD	RRZZZZUSA
MARIAN	.11	F	INFANT	RRZZZZUSA
SCHALANK, ISRAEL	30	M	LABR	RRAILJUSA
PERL, BAER	18	M	LABR	RRZZZZUSA
JOKIP-, -ALOMON	27	M	LABR	FNZZZZUSA
KRYZNIANSKY, JARA	18	F	SGL	FNAHZSUSA
GOLDSTEIN, SOSCHE	16	F	SGL	FNAHVUUSA
JOHANSON, VICTOR	23	M	LABR	FNZZZZUSA
MALLIN, ANNA	17	F	SGL	FNZZZZUSA
KAHLROTH, ELOINE	27	F	SGL	FNAIDSUSA
SOLARSKE, MICHAEL	28	M	LABR	RRZZZZUSA
COHN, ISRAEL	29	M	LABR	RRAHXLUSA
DOGIR, HIRSCH	50	M	LABR	RRAINMUSA
SEZPSZIWSKY, ISAAK	26	M	TLR	RRAIIUUSA
KEILE	20	F	W	RRAIIUUSA
TEWI-	.11	F	INFANT	RRAIIUUSA
MAIN, BRIDA	18	F	SGL	RRAHTFUSA
NORMANN, MEYER	28	M	LABR	RRAINMUSA
BUBENSTEIN, SIMON	22	M	LABR	RRAHTOUSA
-EUDKERMANN, JANKEL	16	M	LABR	RRAGRTUSA
HALPERN, RA--EL	19	F	SGL	RRAEFLUSA
GILLIONSKY, JOSSEL	26	M	LABR	RRAHTBUSA
FREDIS, KIWE	17	M	STDNT	RRZZZZUSA

PASSENGER	AGE	SEX	OCCUPATION	PRIVIL	DES
MEDWEDOWSKY, MENDEL	22	M	MCHT	RRZZZZ	USA
HUDEL	20	M	MCHT	RRZZZZ	USA
ZIMMERMANN, GELDE	40	F	WO	RRZZZZ	USA
MEIER	16	M	CH	RRZZZZ	USA
EFROIM	9	M	CHILD	RRZZZZ	USA
GERSON	8	M	CHILD	RRZZZZ	USA
RIEFKE	3	M	CHILD	RRZZZZ	USA
SMIL	.11	F	INFANT	RRZZZZ	USA
MENGOWSKI, JACK	35	F	WO	RRAEFL	USA
JETTE	9	F	CHILD	RRAEFL	USA
ADOLF	8	M	CHILD	RRAEFL	USA
SAMUEL	5	M	CHILD	RRAEFL	USA
ZILLE	3	F	CHILD	RRAEFL	USA
CHANNE	.09	F	INFANT	RRAEFL	USA
JOSEPH, MASSE	16	F	SGL	RRAIIN	USA
GORITZKY, WOLF	45	M	LABR	RRZZZZ	USA
JETTES, JOSEPH	23	M	LABR	RRZZZZ	USA
NA-A-INE, MO-EL	28	M	LABR	RRAIBB	USA
EHRLICH, SPRINGE	17	F	SGL	RRZZZZ	USA

SHIP: WESTERLAND

FROM: ANTWERP
TO: NEW YORK
ARRIVED: 01 AUGUST 1888

PASSENGER	AGE	SEX	OCCUPATION	PRIVIL	DES
SOUBNER, LEIB	46	M	MCHT	PLZZZZ	NY
HAISSE	46	F	UNKNOWN	PLZZZZ	NY
HANNE	20	F	UNKNOWN	PLZZZZ	NY
MANASE	17	F	UNKNOWN	PLZZZZ	NY
LEWIE	13	M	UNKNOWN	PLZZZZ	NY
HANNA	2	F	CHILD	PLZZZZ	NY
EDLE	8	F	CHILD	PLZZZZ	NY
LEYE	7	F	CHILD	PLZZZZ	NY
ZIMMERMANN, CH.	65	F	UNKNOWN	PLZZZZ	NY
RADETZKA, MICH.	25	M	LABR	PLZZZZ	NY
SONKENIK, SCHEPSEL	34	M	MECH	PLZZZZ	NY
CHAKIN, ELZE	23	M	LABR	RRZZZZ	NY
LICKOMOWITZ, E.	43	M	MCHT	RRZZZZ	NY
RACHEL	42	F	UNKNOWN	RRZZZZ	NY
FREME	18	F	UNKNOWN	RRZZZZ	NY
RIWE	11	F	UNKNOWN	RRZZZZ	NY
MASCHE	6	F	CHILD	RRZZZZ	NY
JACOB	4	M	CHILD	RRZZZZ	NY
MAUSCHE	1	F	CHILD	RRZZZZ	NY
ASSORSOHN, SAMUEL	33	M	LABR	RRZZZZ	NY
MUSHARER, JOSEF	38	M	FARMER	RRZZZZ	NY
MADOLSKI, STANISL.	21	M	LABR	PLZZZZ	CH
GORKI, STANISL.	20	M	FARMER	PLZZZZ	CH
JANNENHEISEN, ISAAC	54	M	FARMER	PLZZZZ	NY
HANNAH	48	F	UNKNOWN	PLZZZZ	NY
MARIA	28	F	UNKNOWN	PLZZZZ	NY
NATHAN	21	M	UNKNOWN	PLZZZZ	NY
AMALIE	26	F	UNKNOWN	PLZZZZ	NY
TAUBE	11	M	UNKNOWN	PLZZZZ	NY
MARSEN, ANNIE	22	F	UNKNOWN	PLZZZZ	NY
NOVORK, THOMAS	33	M	FARMER	PLZZZZ	NY
MARIE	21	F	UNKNOWN	PLZZZZ	NY
EMILIE	11	F	UNKNOWN	PLZZZZ	NY
MARSIK, JOSEF	41	M	FARMER	PLZZZZ	NY
ZALL, JOSEF	42	M	LABR	PLZZZZ	NY
RUTKOWSKY, STANISLAUS	43	M	LABR	PLZZZZ	NY
HERSCHMOWITZ, R.	20	M	FARMER	PLZZZZ	NY
DREWS, MAX	23	M	FARMER	PLZZZZ	NY
ULONSKE, JOHANNES	24	M	CL	PLZZZZ	TRA
JANSKY, JAN	24	M	LABR	PLZZZZ	NY

SHIP: ST. OF PENNSYLVANIA

FROM: GLASGOW AND LARNE
TO: NEW YORK
ARRIVED: 01 AUGUST 1888

PASSENGER	AGE	SEX	OCCUPATION	PRIVIL	DES
SOMMER, MAX	19	M	CL	RRZZZZ	USA
ZUCKERMANN, NATTAH	30	M	BLDR	RRZZZZ	USA
WEREBIAVSKY, EFHRAIM	28	M	FARMER	RRAIDL	USA
MAUOWITZ, SAMUEL	24	M	GZR	RRAIDL	USA
SCHAGIN, LEWI	55	M	BCHR	RRAIDL	USA
KAPLAN, MORDCHE	33	M	LITGR	RRAIDL	USA
AKUHAN, SALOMON	30	M	JNR	RRAIDL	USA
SFEETER, MOSES	19	M	GDSM	RRAIDL	USA
GOLDIN, MICHEL	53	M	GDSM	RRAIDL	USA
MASCHE	14	F	SVNT	RRAIDL	USA
SEIDLER, BORRIS	48	M	PDLR	RRAIDL	USA
PRIGONIGER, CHAIME	22	M	PDLR	RRAIDL	USA
GUTMAN, ALEXANDER	30	M	PDLR	RRAIDL	USA
GROSSBARA, LEIB	20	M	PDLR	RRAIDL	USA
GEIBER, TOBIAS	22	M	PDLR	RRAIDL	USA
GRUENBERG, MOSES	21	M	PDLR	RRAIDL	USA
REUD, LAUMEL	18	M	TLR	RRAIDL	USA
PAUTEL, ISRAEL	28	M	TLR	RRAIDL	USA
GIRSCHOWSKY, BARUCH	20	M	TLR	RRAIDL	USA
RICHENLOWITZ, DAVID	18	M	TLR	RRAIDL	USA
FERDINAND, MUIER	41	M	TLR	RRAIDL	USA
CHASANOWITZ, ZIWIE	11	M	BY	RRAIDL	USA
AMALIN, SAMUEL	28	M	TLR	RRAIDL	USA
ROBE	26	F	W	RRAIDL	USA
SORE	1	F	CHILD	RRAIDL	USA
GOLDGART, MALE	46	F	W	RRAIDL	USA
CHIEL	18	M	SLSMN	RRAIDL	USA
SEIDY	16	M	SLSMN	RRAIDL	USA
STAUKEWITZ, JAN	42	M	LABR	RRAIDL	USA
SZEBEDO, AUGUST	23	M	LABR	RRAIDL	USA
SCHWAK, WOLF	26	M	LABR	RRAIDL	USA
ZIBILINSKY, SCHOLEM	36	M	LABR	RRAIDL	USA
SENDERMANN, SHIGE	26	M	LABR	RRAIDL	USA
PODLOWSKY, BENJAMIN	17	M	LABR	RRAIDL	USA
MATAKIS, VINCENT	21	M	LABR	RRAIDL	USA
BAMEIWYTZ, KASIMIR	20	M	LABR	RRAIDL	USA
LESSELONIS, SIMON	19	M	LABR	RRAIDL	USA
BOKDAM, GEORG	21	M	LABR	RRAIDL	USA
WOLTER, JOHAN	31	M	LABR	RRAIDL	USA
EMILIE	28	F	W	RRAIDL	USA
WILHELM	1	M	CHILD	RRAIDL	USA
RUDOLF	.01	M	INFANT	RRAIDL	USA
KRUGER, MICHAEL	36	M	LABR	RRAIDL	USA
ANNA	41	F	W	RRAIDL	USA
HERMAN	16	M	LABR	RRAIDL	USA
AUGUST	5	M	CHILD	RRAIDL	USA
EMILIE	.04	F	INFANT	RRAIDL	USA
GOLDIN, SORE	25	F	SP	RRAIDL	USA
ALEXANDER, MENUCHE	19	F	SP	RRAIDL	USA
GERSCHEWITZ, HINDI	18	F	SP	RRAIDL	USA
ROSMARIN, SARA	18	F	SP	RRAIDL	USA
ROKOMZY, MIRKE	17	F	SP	RRAIDL	USA
SILVER, GASSE	30	F	SP	RRAIDL	USA
KASSEL, ETTEL	23	F	SP	RRAIDL	USA
SILBERT, OTTILIE	20	F	W	RRAIDL	USA
RICHARD	1	M	CHILD	RRAIDL	USA
GOLDSMIDT, SCHOLEM	11	F	CH	RRAIDL	USA
MALE	50	F	W	RRAIDL	USA
CHAJE	26	F	W	RRAIDL	USA
LIEBE	1	F	CHILD	RRAIDL	USA
GROSSMANN, BASSE	38	F	W	RRAIDL	USA
RUIVEN	8	M	CHILD	RRAIDL	USA
GABRIEL	9	M	CHILD	RRAIDL	USA
AUGLAWSKY, FEIWEL	11	M	CH	RRAIDL	USA
LEIB	9	M	CHILD	RRAIDL	USA
GOLDJARB, RABA	11	F	CH	RRAIDL	USA
SORE	9	F	CHILD	RRAIDL	USA
MIREL	2	F	CHILD	RRAIDL	USA

PASSENGER	AGE	SEX	OCCUPATION	PRV	VIL	DES
BERKOWITZ, HENCI	9	F	CHILD	RR	AIDL	USA
SCHIRK, SARAH	40	F	W	RR	AIDL	USA
MENDE	4	M	CHILD	RR	AIDL	USA
CHAJE	7	M	CHILD	RR	AIDL	USA
FINKELSTEIN, CHAJE	18	F	W	RR	AIDL	USA
ARMELIND, ISRAEL	2	M	CHILD	RR	AIDL	USA
ALEXANDER, MERE	40	F	W	RR	AIDL	USA
GITTE	11	F	CH	RR	AIDL	USA
ROCHE	9	F	CHILD	RR	AIDL	USA
HARRY	6	M	CHILD	RR	AIDL	USA
LIMCHE	2	M	CHILD	RR	AIDL	USA
GRUENBERG, CHAJE	40	F	W	RR	AIDL	USA
RACHEL	15	F	SP	RR	AIDL	USA
ARON	4	M	CHILD	RR	AIDL	USA
SARAH	2	F	CHILD	RR	AIDL	USA
SCHEINDEL	1	M	CHILD	RR	AIDL	USA
SARAH	20	F	W	RR	AIDL	USA
MINCE	7	F	CHILD	RR	AIDL	USA
ZIRD	.03	M	INFANT	RR	AIDL	USA
RUBIN, MATLE	40	F	W	RR	AIDL	USA
LEIB	10	M	CH	RR	AIDL	USA
FELDMANN, BASSE	40	F	W	RR	AIDL	USA
ESTHER	11	F	CH	RR	AIDL	USA
SELDE	7	F	CHILD	RR	AIDL	USA
WAGMANN, ETTEL	26	F	W	RR	AIDL	USA
GOLDE	11	F	CH	RR	AIDL	USA
GOLDE	1	F	CHILD	RR	AIDL	USA
RISSAN, ROCHE	36	F	W	RR	AIDL	USA
ROSA	9	F	CHILD	RR	AIDL	USA
JACOB	1	M	CHILD	RR	AIDL	USA
ARONSTEIN, REBECCA	27	F	W	RR	AIDL	USA
BEHR	24	M	LABR	RR	AIDL	USA
JETTI	18	F	SP	RR	AIDL	USA
NACUA	1	F	CHILD	RR	AIDL	USA
ABRAHM	.03	M	INFANT	RR	AIDL	USA
LEIBOWITZ, SORE	48	F	W	RR	AIDL	USA
TAUBE	30	F	CH	RR	AIDL	USA
CHAJE	3	F	CHILD	RR	AIDL	USA
WOLFF	2	M	CHILD	RR	AIDL	USA
SCHEIM	1	M	CHILD	RR	AIDL	USA
MARIE	.03	F	INFANT	RR	AIDL	USA
BENJAMIN, GILSE	30	F	W	RR	AIDL	USA
FEIGE	11	M	CH	RR	AIDL	USA
ESTHER	8	F	CHILD	RR	AIDL	USA
MATTES	.03	F	INFANT	RR	AIDL	USA

SHIP: LAHN

FROM: BREMEN AND SOUTHAMPTON
TO: NEW YORK
ARRIVED: 03 AUGUST 1888

PASSENGER	AGE	SEX	OCCUPATION	PRV	VIL	DES
SZILINSKA, DUMICLA	26	F	NN	RR	ZZZZ	USA
COHRS, WILHELM	17	M	LABR	RR	ZZZZ	USA
BROWARSKA, MARYANNA	31	F	W	RR	ZZZZ	USA
WICENTY	9	M	CHILD	RR	ZZZZ	USA
FRANZISKA	.07	F	INFANT	RR	ZZZZ	USA
GOELDNER, LYDIA	18	F	NN	RR	ZZZZ	USA
CLARA	16	F	NN	RR	ZZZZ	USA
PREISS, LEONID	29	M	LABR	RR	ZZZZ	USA
CONSTANTE.	26	F	W	RR	ZZZZ	USA
OJALA, DANIEL	32	M	LABR	RR	AAYK	USA
SITKIA, JAKOB	30	M	LABR	RR	AAYK	USA
RAUTIO, ANDERS	40	M	LABR	RR	AAYK	USA
HARJUKOSKI, ANNA	26	F	NN	RR	AAYK	USA
SALO, MARIA	24	F	W	RR	AAYK	USA
ANDERS	.01	M	INFANT	RR	AAYK	USA
PURANTOKA, JOH.	21	M	LABR	RR	AAYK	USA
HERRSMANN, LINA	28	F	W	RR	ZZZZ	USA
ABRAHAM	2	M	CHILD	RR	ZZZZ	USA
GARMASCH, ROMAN	30	M	LABR	RR	ZZZZ	USA
EISNISS, SALOMON	33	M	LABR	RR	AFWJ	USA
OLGA	24	F	W	RR	AFWJ	USA
JACOB	11	M	CH	RR	AFWJ	USA
SOPHIE	15	F	NN	RR	AFWJ	USA
BERGEND, EMIL	25	M	LABR	RR	AHTU	USA
THIELEMANN, MORITZ	48	M	LABR	RR	AHTU	USA
ROSNISLOWITZ, ADOLF	23	M	LABR	RR	AHTU	USA
GRODEK, JAN	18	M	LABR	RR	AHTU	USA
HINZ, OTTO	18	M	LABR	RR	AHTU	USA
SOKOLSKY, SALOMON	37	M	LABR	RR	AFWJ	USA
GARFINKEL, KAPEL	15	M	NN	RR	AFWJ	USA
MIETZ, AUGUST	32	M	FARMER	RR	ZZZZ	USA
MARIE	28	F	W	RR	ZZZZ	USA
AUGUSTE	9	F	CHILD	RR	ZZZZ	USA
OTTILIE	7	F	CHILD	RR	ZZZZ	USA
RUDOLF	4	M	CHILD	RR	ZZZZ	USA
OTTO	.11	M	INFANT	RR	ZZZZ	USA
HASENPUSCH, FERD.	67	M	FARMER	RR	ZZZZ	USA
CHARLOTTE	67	F	W	RR	ZZZZ	USA
HERZBERG, FRIEDR.	43	M	FARMER	RR	ZZZZ	USA
AUGUSTE	37	F	W	RR	ZZZZ	USA
ANNA	16	F	NN	RR	ZZZZ	USA
CARL	15	M	NN	RR	ZZZZ	USA
GUSTAV	6	M	CHILD	RR	ZZZZ	USA
SAMUEL, AUGUST	29	M	DLR	RR	ZZZZ	USA
GERSCHOWSKY, JACOB	18	M	LABR	RR	ZZZZ	USA
SEDLETZKY, SCHOLEM	22	M	LABR	RR	ZZZZ	USA
SCHACHT, LUDWIG	40	M	DLR	RR	ZZZZ	USA
RATTNER, SIMON	42	M	DLR	RR	ZZZZ	USA
RESNICK, R.L.	30	M	LABR	RR	ZZZZ	USA
MOSES	10	M	CH	RR	ZZZZ	USA
ISRAEL	7	M	CHILD	RR	ZZZZ	USA
JOSEF	5	M	CHILD	RR	ZZZZ	USA
ROSA	.06	F	INFANT	RR	ZZZZ	USA
KAJERSKI, STANISLAUS	21	M	LABR	RR	ZZZZ	USA
PALWNIK, ROCHEL	48	M	LABR	RR	AHZS	USA
FEIGE	11	F	NN	RR	AHZS	USA
URISAN, ISAAC	16	M	LABR	RR	AHZS	USA
SUESSKIND, JOSEF	18	M	LABR	RR	AHZS	USA

SHIP: NORSEMAN

FROM: LIVERPOOL
TO: BOSTON
ARRIVED: 03 AUGUST 1888

PASSENGER	AGE	SEX	OCCUPATION	PRV	VIL	DES
BROWN, LIEBE	14	F	UNKNOWN	RR	AIIC	USA
BENJ.	19	M	LABR	RR	AIIC	USA
SCHAMFELD, MARIA	22	F	SVNT	RR	AIIC	USA
SCHWIAT, SCHLOWIN	25	M	LABR	RR	AIIC	NY
MCHORN, MICHAEL	17	M	LABR	RR	AIIC	MA
EGAN, EDWARD	17	M	LABR	RR	AIIC	MA
BEINON, JANE	30	F	UNKNOWN	RR	AIIC	NY
MARG.	9	F	CHILD	RR	AIIC	NY
JOHN	7	M	CHILD	RR	AIIC	NY
ELISAB.	5	F	CHILD	RR	AIIC	NY
ELLEN	3	F	CHILD	RR	AIIC	NY
PATTON, GEORGE	21	M	LABR	RR	AIIC	CH
PRIEL, GEORGE	21	M	LABR	RR	AIIC	UNK
SLATTERY, MARY	22	F	LABR	RR	AIIC	NY
BRAMSTEIN, LEHA	25	F	W	RR	AIIC	NY
SOLOMON	00	M	INF	RR	AIIC	NY
TARHISH, JACOB	22	M	LABR	RR	AIIC	NY
FEUCH, JOHN	25	M	LABR	RR	AIIC	PHI
WOZOWSKY, D.	23	M	LABR	RR	ZZZZ	NY
BERKOWSKY, RAPHEL	24	M	LABR	RR	ZZZZ	NY
LEVY, ISAC	28	M	LABR	RR	ZZZZ	NY
L.	28	F	W	RR	ZZZZ	NY
MARK	5	M	CHILD	RR	ZZZZ	NY

PASSENGER	AGE	SEX	OCCUPATION	PRV VIL DES
SIMON	00	M	INF	RRZZZZNY
U	00	M	INF	RRZZZZNY
GHESTER, ISIDOR	22	M	LABR	RRZZZZNY
BABENORITSH, H.D.	31	M	LABR	RRZZZZPHI
SCHLAMINSKY, LIEBE	50	F	LABR	RRZZZZNY
SCHAP, LIEB	18	F	LABR	RRZZZZNY
CHAIE	20	F	LABR	RRZZZZNY
ABROMOWITZ, ARON	27	F	LABR	RRZZZZNY
HALHERIN, D.	18	M	LABR	RRZZZZNY
SCHEDLETZKY, MALKE	38	M	LABR	RRZZZZNY
CHANE	17	M	LABR	RRZZZZNY
CHAIE	15	F	CH	RRZZZZNY
SARAH	13	F	CH	RRZZZZNY
BECKER, BERL	15	M	LABR	RRZZZZBO
JASELSOHN, ABEL	36	M	LABR	RRZZZZBO
BERNSTEIN, CHAEL	20	M	LABR	RRZZZZBO
BEREL	18	M	LABR	RRZZZZBO
LEIB	11	M	CH	RRZZZZBO
SILBERMANN, JACOB	30	M	LABR	RRZZZZBO
ROSA	25	F	W	RRZZZZBO
KONIG, CORSIP	18	M	LABR	RRZZZZBO
KAVANY, JOSEF	28	M	LABR	RRZZZZBO

SHIP: MARSALLA

FROM: HAMBURG
TO: NEW YORK
ARRIVED: 04 AUGUST 1888

PASSENGER	AGE	SEX	OCCUPATION	PRV VIL DES
ARONSTAM, MODEST	17	M	PNTR	RRAHTFNY
LESSNIK, ZADICK	36	M	WCHMKR	RRAHTUNY
SAPERS, CHAI	24	M	LABR	RRZZZZNY
SLONIMSKI, SALOMON	17	M	LABR	RRZZZZNY
KASCHER, ADOLF	63	M	SHMK	RRAILSNY
IGLINSKI, ALEXANDER	16	M	LABR	RRZZZZNY
BELFORT, DWORE	20	F	WO	RRAFVGBAL
ANTINOWSKY, LEON	19	M	LABR	RRAHWQNY
LIPMANOWITZ, GIDE	50	F	WO	RRAEFLNY
HANNE	16	F	WO	RRAEFLNY
JANKE	14	F	WO	RRAEFLNY
WOLF	13	M	WO	RRAEFLNY
MICHEL	9	M	CHILD	RRAEFLNY
LINE	8	F	CHILD	RRAEFLNY
ZALLEN	4	M	CHILD	RRAEFLNY
ISAAC	2	M	CHILD	RRAEFLNY
SILVERMANN, PESCHE	28	F	WO	RRAHTSNY
MOSES	7	M	CHILD	RRAHTSNY
MINNIE	5	F	CHILD	RRAHTSNY
SCHEPSEL	3	M	CHILD	RRAHTSNY
BIRKAU, LEON	16	M	MCHT	RRAHOONY
JACOB	24	M	MCHT	RRAHOONY
GELHERD, MENDEL	20	M	LABR	RRAIFINY
RAUSIK, MORIS	16	M	LABR	RRZZZZNY
HINDSBURTH, ABR.	30	M	LABR	RRZZZZNY
BRAUNSTEIN, CHEIM	37	F	WO	RRAIFANY
SARAH	.11	F	INFANT	RRAIFANY
KANOWAL, CHAWE	36	F	WO	RRAIASNY
LEA	.11	F	INFANT	RRAIASNY
FUCHTMANN, DAVID	30	M	LABR	RRAIASNY
ELPERN, ELIAS	23	M	LABR	RRAIIUNY
CHAJE	55	F	WO	RRAIIUNY
CHANNE	17	F	D	RRAIIUNY
SCHAWELSOHN, DANIEL	9	M	CHILD	RRAIIUNY
STOLGOITIS, JURGI	38	M	LABR	RRZZZZNY
LEWITZKI, HERM.	24	M	LABR	RRZZZZNY
KUPPERMANN, SIEGMUND	31	M	LABR	RRAHWNNY
RIEFKE	31	F	W	RRAHWNNY
ISRAEL	33	M	LABR	RRAHWNNY
LEIB	4	M	CHILD	RRAHWNNY
AWNER	.09	M	INFANT	RRAHWNNY
MEIEWSKI, ANTON	21	M	LABR	RRAHUFNY
BIGANSKA, EMMA	27	F	SGL	RRAFWJNY
MARTINSOHN, JOSEF	32	M	MCHT	RRAEFLNY
RUBENSOHN, LEIB	20	M	LABR	RRAEFLNY
MERZ, HEINR.	24	M	LABR	RRZZZZNY
KNJUTH, DANIEL	51	M	LABR	RRZZZZNY
JULIANNE	51	F	W	RRZZZZNY
HENRIETTE	21	F	UNKNOWN	RRZZZZNY
WILHELMINE	14	F	UNKNOWN	RRZZZZNY
FRIEDRICH	16	M	UNKNOWN	RRZZZZNY
CARL	9	M	CHILD	RRZZZZNY
KNISPEL, JULIUS	23	M	LABR	RRACONNY
HRBECK, STEFANI	24	F	SGL	RRAFWJNY
GOLDBERG, RIEFKE	9	F	CHILD	RRAFWJNY
LEA	8	F	CHILD	RRAFWJNY
PAUKSCHEN, REINHOLD	22	M	SHMK	RRAEFLNY
KLIMOWITSCH, PETER	9	M	CHILD	RRAHZSNY
ZABOROWSKY, FRANZ	27	M	LABR	RRZZZZNY
GRAVIEWSKY, VALENTY	31	M	LABR	RRZZZZNY
RABINOWITZ, WOLF	22	M	LABR	RRZZZZNY
DORFMANN, BENJAMIN	21	M	LABR	RRZZZZNY
GELHAR, LUCAS	26	M	SHMK	RRAIDMNY
ROLLNIK, MOSES	20	M	LABR	RRAHOKNY
CHAIM, CHIME	22	M	LABR	RRZZZZNY
OTTO, MARIE	20	F	SGL	RRAHVUNY
MATHILDE	16	F	SGL	RRAHVUNY
GROSSMANN, CHANE	20	F	UNKNOWN	RRAHVUNY
GRIMPLASCH, ISAC	19	M	PRNTR	RRAIBONY
HIRSCHSOHN, ISAAC	26	M	LABR	RRZZZZNY
KLEINMMANN, JACOB	40	M	LABR	RRAHWQPHI
CHAJE	36	F	W	RRAHWQPHI
ZIW.	18	F	CH	RRAHWQPHI
ISRAEL	16	M	CH	RRAHWQPHI
FEIGE	9	F	CHILD	RRAHWQPHI
GITTEL	7	F	CHILD	RRAHWQPHI
LEA	.11	F	INFANT	RRAHWQPHI
JABLOWSKI, ABEL	18	M	MCHT	RRZZZZPHI
LEWGOLD, MARIE	24	F	SGL	RRAHXHPHI
RATNER, ESTER	22	F	SGL	RRAIBOPHI
ELEFANT, MOSES	46	M	LABR	RRAIBOPHI
LEBEUSBAUM, LEA	18	F	SGL	RRAIBOPHI
MAZUR, BORIS	22	M	LABR	RRZZZZPHI
GRIMBERG, GRIES	24	M	CPTR	RRZZZZPHI
CHRISTOPH	25	M	CPTR	RRZZZZPHI
KALMIN, THEOD.	25	M	UNKNOWN	RRZZZZPHI
SILBERMANN, MAX	12	M	UNKNOWN	RRZZZZPHI

SHIP: ITALY

FROM: LIVERPOOL AND QUEENSTOWN
TO: NEW YORK
ARRIVED: 04 AUGUST 1888

PASSENGER	AGE	SEX	OCCUPATION	PRV VIL DES
BENGELL, BARNET	20	M	UNKNOWN	RRZZZZNY
DOLDT, CHRIST.VOICHACH	23	M	LABR	PLZZZZNY
STAHONICZ, J.	25	M	BCHR	PLZZZZPLY
SHAVARIUS, JUERGEN	23	M	LABR	PLZZZZNY
URBANOWITSCH, PAVA	27	M	LABR	PLZZZZNY
TRANK, KASEL	24	M	SLSMN	RRZZZZNY
LJUCK, DAVID	21	M	TLR	RRADAXPHI
GREEN, GUSTAF	18	M	LABR	PLZZZZNY
HELBERG, CAARLE	24	F	LABR	PLACBFNY
MAIKKA, JULI	18	F	SP	PLAGUZNY
ROCHNA, TIMKO	35	F	LABR	PLACBFNY
TIBA, SCHNERDEF.	35	F	W	PLAFVGNY
MOSCHE	10	M	CH	PLAFVGNY
CHADES, SCHM.	26	M	LABR	PLACBFNY
JOSSEL	10	M	CH	PLACBFNY
JOHNSEN, OLOF	32	M	LABR	PLACBFBO
JOHANSON, DAVID	21	M	LABR	PLACBFBO

PASSENGER	AGE	SEX	OCCUPATION	PRV VIL DES
ANNANDA	20	F	SP	PLACBFBO
CAIRSON, PETER	23	M	SP	PLACBFBO
ORGALA, JOHN	26	M	UNKNOWN	PLACBFBO
KAUKONEN, MILKA	17	F	SP	PLACBFUSA
ERGALA, SOPHIE	26	F	W	PLACBFMI
BLESSARD, ANNA	33	F	W	PLACBFMI
HANK, ELLA	19	F	SP	PLACBFMI
KOGHOGNOI, MATTE	24	M	LABR	PLACBFMI
WASHMAN, ALFRED	20	M	LABR	PLACBFMI
WEATBOCKA, ALEX	30	M	LABR	PLACBFUNK
WESTBACKA, MALTS	20	M	LABR	PLACBFUNK
BANOLA, EMLI	38	M	LABR	PLAGUZSFC
TUNBCEBACKI, ALEX	26	M	LABR	PLAGUZSFC
TALLBACKU, JOHN	18	M	LABR	PLAGUZSFC
BEMALU, JACOB	17	M	LABR	PLAGUZSFC
KOEGONEN, ISAAK	38	M	LABR	PLAGUZSFC
RAUNOKI, J.GARKEZ	20	M	LABR	PLACBFNY
PERCHALSKI, ADAM	20	M	LABR	PLACBFNY
HERBERT, JOS.	20	M	LABR	PLACBFNY
GREVEVIZ, ARON	27	M	LABR	PLAFVGNY
SKENAK, JOSEF	28	M	LABR	PLACBFNY
LEISE	30	F	W	PLACBFNY
ASOTNYLSEY, CHAIM	20	M	LABR	PLZZZZNY
SARA	20	F	W	PLZZZZNY
ROSEL, ADOLF	30	M	LABR	PLACBFNY
STERPENSTEI, ALEX	36	M	LABR	PLACBFNY
HECKLER, JACOB	30	M	LABR	PLACBFNY
EDIN, NOCHM	24	M	LABR	PLACBFNY
FANNY	22	F	SP	PLACBFNY
ROCHEL	17	F	SP	PLAFVGNY
ZEADAUT, ANTON	38	M	LABR	PLACBFNY
GRITZKI, AMALIE	40	M	LABR	PLACBFNY
RUDOLF	21	M	LABR	PLACBFNY
WENDELOWSKY, FRANZ	24	M	LABR	PLACBFNY
KIKLOWITZ, MOSES	41	M	LABR	PLACBFNY
LIBECHITZ, LEIB	45	M	LABR	PLACBFNY
LYAMERDYK, JOSEFA	24	F	W	PLACBFNY
U	00	F	INF	PLACBFNY
MALINSKI, ANDREA	31	M	LABR	PLACBFNY
ANTMANN, PETTER	16	M	LABR	PLACBFNY
SCHLON, MOSES	29	M	LABR	PLACBFNY
IGADINSKY, D.	40	M	GCR	PLACBFNY
GRAUVAS, HEIM.	44	M	LABR	PLACBFMI
BODONOGEL, LEIBE	27	M	LABR	PLACBFNY

SHIP: RUGIA

FROM: HAMBURG AND HAVRE
TO: NEW YORK
ARRIVED: 04 AUGUST 1888

PASSENGER	AGE	SEX	OCCUPATION	PRV VIL DES
RUTELONIS, AGATHE	33	F	WO	RRZZZZUSA
MAGDALENE	8	F	CHILD	RRZZZZUSA
CATHA.	7	F	CHILD	RRZZZZUSA
JAN	5	M	CHILD	RRZZZZUSA
FRIEDRICH	.09	M	INFANT	RRZZZZUSA
KAURAPESFER, ERIK	37	M	LABR	FNZZZZUSA
LAIHOMA, IDA	30	F	WO	FNZZZZUSA
IDA	6	F	CHILD	FNZZZZUSA
MICKELSEN, ULRIKE	58	F	WO	FNZZZZUSA
BALO, MARIE	38	F	WO	FNZZZZUSA
MARIE	15	F	CH	FNZZZZUSA
JOH.	9	M	CHILD	FNZZZZUSA
JOSEFINE	7	F	CHILD	FNZZZZUSA
SMEDS, JACOB	16	M	LABR	FNZZZZUSA
HAEGGBLOM, MARTINUS	32	M	LABR	FNZZZZUSA
HENRIKE	36	F	W	FNZZZZUSA
HIRSCHSON, BENNO	21	M	UNKNOWN	FNAIDMUSA
SAFKIR, ELIAS	45	M	MCHT	RRZZZZUSA
CHANNE	22	F	W	RRZZZZUSA

PASSENGER	AGE	SEX	OCCUPATION	PRV VIL DES
COHN, ELKE	27	F	WO	RRAFWJUSA
FREIDE	3	F	CHILD	RRAFWJUSA
STOODIG, KARL	22	M	LABR	FNZZZZUSA
MASTAB, MALKE	26	F	UNKNOWN	FNAFWJUSA
MOSES	9	M	CHILD	FNAFWJUSA
SCHIFFRE	6	F	CHILD	FNAFWJUSA
MAKI, FRDK.	40	F	WO	FNZZZZUSA
LISE	9	F	CHILD	FNZZZZUSA
ANDRAS	9	M	CHILD	FNZZZZUSA
TEKLA	8	F	CHILD	FNZZZZUSA
SERAFINE	5	F	CHILD	FNZZZZUSA
WALKOWICZOWA, ELISABETH	23	F	SGL	FNAGRTUSA
SOSCHKOWICZ, ALEXANDER	22	M	LABR	FNAGRTUSA
MICHALINE	20	F	W	FNAGRTUSA
WITEBSKY, HELENE	25	F	SGL	FNAIGHUSA
WOLIANSKY, REISE	23	F	SGL	RRZZZZUSA
LIPNIK, REICHEL	24	F	WO	RRAHQUUSA
CHAIM	3	M	CHILD	RRAHQUUSA
FILE	.11	F	INFANT	RRAHQUUSA
KATZ, ARON	19	M	LABR	RRZZZZUSA
BYGOZYNSKA, JOSEFA	23	F	WO	RRZZZZUSA
WLADISLAWA	.11	F	INFANT	RRZZZZUSA
SELBERBERG, SALO	28	M	PNTR	RRAHTNUSA
WADIN, JULIANA	22	F	SGL	RRZZZZUSA
ZAKOWICZ, FELIX	26	M	LABR	RRZZZZUSA
RIEMCZAL, JOSEF	26	M	LABR	RRZZZZUSA
ABRAMOWICZ, JAN	43	M	LABR	RRAIEUUSA
SUKONSKI, FRANZ	22	M	LABR	RRZZZZUSA
JWASKONSKY, JETZIL	20	M	LABR	RRAHZLUSA
RATZKOWSKY, SARA	32	F	WO	RRAHZLUSA
GERSON	9	M	CHILD	RRAHZLUSA
LEISER	8	M	CHILD	RRAHZLUSA
ETTE	4	F	CHILD	RRAHZLUSA
KINAVIAK, ANTON	18	M	LABR	RRZZZZUSA
M--GIRD, JOSEF	27	M	LABR	RRZZZZUSA
BILANSKI, OSEW	25	M	LABR	RRZZZZUSA
WOLFSCHN, LEIBE	23	F	SGL	RRZZZZUSA
GOTTLIEB, TILI	22	F	SGL	RRZZZZUSA
SCHAPIRO, MOSES	27	M	LABR	RRZZZZUSA
SCHEGANSKY, RESE	17	F	SGL	RRAIABUSA
ZWINGEL, HERSCH	26	M	LABR	RRZZZZUSA
MIROSZNIK, JANKEL	27	M	LABR	RRZZZZUSA
SIEGEL, ELIAS	27	M	LABR	RRZZZZUSA
BREITNER, MALAC	27	F	WO	RRZZZZUSA
ITZIG	6	M	CHILD	RRZZZZUSA
LEIB	.11	M	INFANT	RRZZZZUSA
WEINEROWITSCH, LADKI	18	F	SGL	RRAIDWUSA
BERYNTE, ILTKO	19	F	SGL	RRAHTUUSA
ORSCHMANN, ISRAEL	20	M	LABR	RRZZZZUSA
BRESLAU, FEIGE	28	F	WO	RRAHVUUSA
SCHIFFRE	5	F	CHILD	RRAHVUUSA
ABR.	.11	M	INFANT	RRAHVUUSA
MOLLER, HERSCH	41	M	LABR	RRZZZZUSA
BRANNE	21	F	W	RRZZZZUSA
ABRAM	.11	M	INFANT	RRZZZZUSA
SARA	.01	F	INFANT	RRZZZZUSA
POOENHEIMER, LEIB	31	M	LABR	RRAHTNUSA
POBILIS, VINCENTI	43	M	LABR	RRAICUUSA
BREICK, OSCHER	27	M	MCHT	RRAIJYUSA
ADELHEID	22	F	W	RRAIJYUSA
HONI--AUM, RACHEL	16	F	SGL	RRZZZZUSA
GRUMBECKER, MOSES	23	M	MCHT	RRAGRTUSA
MEISEL, NIKOL	26	M	MCHT	RRAGRTUSA
WILKAMS, AUGUST	32	M	MCHT	RRZZZZUSA
ROMME, CHAWE	18	F	SGL	RRAHTFUSA
GERSTNER, OTTO	30	M	LKSH	RRZZZZUSA
JORDAN, CARL	41	M	LABR	RRZZZZUSA
SILBERMANN, ARON	49	M	BCHR	RRZZZZUSA
RUTKEWICZ, ALFER	35	M	LABR	RRAIFRUSA

PASSENGER	AGE	SEX	OCCUPATION	PRV	VIL	DES

SHIP: SERVIA

FROM: LIVERPOOL AND QUEENSTOWN
TO: NEW YORK
ARRIVED: 06 AUGUST 1888

PASSENGER	AGE	SEX	OCCUPATION	PRV VIL DES
STOMAKER, AUG.	30	M	LABR	RRADAXMI
FREDA	30	F	W	RRADAXMI
FREDA	2	F	CHILD	RRADAXMI
LEWY, SIMON	19	M	LABR	RRADAXMI
SMJALSKI, ANTON	26	M	LABR	RRADAXPA
STULING, MOSES	20	M	LABR	RRADAXPA
KASLOWSKY, IS.	40	M	LABR	RRADAXPA
FUTZEWETZ, SILVESTER	25	M	LABR	RRADAXPA
MARTIN, MOSES	32	M	JWLR	RRADAXIL
BACHFINK, LIA	21	F	SP	RRADAXPA
LIEBA	18	F	SP	RRADAXPA
LEPSCHITZ, MERE	18	F	SP	RRADAXPA
SOKOLOWSKI, RABEL	18	F	SP	RRADAXPA
GROSSMAN, RULI	36	F	MA	RRADAXNY
FEIGE	14	F	SP	RRADAXNY
SAMUEL	11	M	CH	RRADAXNY
MASCHKOWITZ, ESTER	36	F	W	RRADAXPA
HANNA	11	F	CH	RRADAXPA
LIPSCHITZ, SELIG	40	M	LABR	RRADAXPA
MARIE	38	F	W	RRADAXPA
LIEBE	3	F	CHILD	RRADAXPA
NECHAUL	2	M	CHILD	RRADAXPA
WILKOWSKY, JOSEFINI	17	F	SP	RRADAXNY
ANTON	14	M	LABR	RRADAXNY
ZYEZYMAN	11	M	CH	RRADAXNY
LEVI, LEWIS	25	M	SHMK	RRADAXIL
ANNIE	18	F	W	RRADAXIL
GOLDSTEIN, RACHEL	35	F	W	RRADAXIL
MOTTEL	16	M	LABR	RRADAXIL
MOYSCH	14	M	LABR	RRADAXIL
MENDEL	9	F	CHILD	RRADAXIL
HINDE	7	F	CHILD	RRADAXIL
DAVID	3	M	CHILD	RRADAXIL
SUSTES, NATHAN	18	M	LABR	RRADAXMA
KAHN, JACOB	36	M	LABR	RRADAXNY
WOOD, MARY	30	F	W	RRADAXIL
BAUMANN, EDWARD	28	M	GENT	RRADAXIL
JONES, EDWARD	30	M	GENT	RRADAXIL

SHIP: CITY OF RICHMOND

FROM: LIVERPOOL AND QUEENSTOWN
TO: NEW YORK
ARRIVED: 06 AUGUST 1888

PASSENGER	AGE	SEX	OCCUPATION	PRV VIL DES
ASTROG, J.K.	35	M	LABR	RRZZZZNY
GOLDMANN, ROSA	20	F	SVNT	RRZZZZNY
HUNYODI, V.	17	F	SP	PLZZZZNY
MAYERS, A.	30	M	MECH	PLAIIXNY
FANNY	20	F	W	PLAIIXNY

SHIP: BOTHNIA

FROM: LIVERPOOL AND QUEENSTOWN
TO: BOSTON
ARRIVED: 06 AUGUST 1888

PASSENGER	AGE	SEX	OCCUPATION	PRV VIL DES
HENDRIKSON, JOHN	26	M	LABR	FNZZZZMI
ALAKITTI, JOHAN	30	M	LABR	FNZZZZMA
RANNA, ERICK	29	M	LABR	FNZZZZMA
PETAIA, OFLI	29	M	LABR	FNZZZZMA
RANNA, GRETAR	30	M	LABR	FNZZZZMA
ZESS, HENRY	25	M	LABR	FNZZZZMA
JOHN	10	M	CH	FNZZZZMA
ASPEGREN, FREAK	19	M	LABR	FNZZZZMI
TEKKALA, MARIA	17	F	SP	FNZZZZMA
GRAU, EDLA	29	F	SP	FNZZZZOH
HANNA, KRETTA	26	F	MA	FNZZZZMA
HANNA	3	F	CHILD	FNZZZZMA
JENNY	.06	F	INFANT	FNZZZZMA
RUSODELI, ANNA	27	F	MA	FNZZZZMA
GASTA	.06	F	INFANT	FNZZZZMA
RANNA, BRITA	4	F	CHILD	FNZZZZMA
HILDA	2	F	CHILD	FNZZZZMA
GRETA	.06	F	INFANT	FNZZZZMA

SHIP: EIDER

FROM: BREMEN AND SOUTHAMPTON
TO: NEW YORK
ARRIVED: 07 AUGUST 1888

PASSENGER	AGE	SEX	OCCUPATION	PRV VIL DES
ECKSTEIN, AMAL.	23	F	UNKNOWN	RRZZZZUSA
KANN, LIBE	27	F	UNKNOWN	RRZZZZUSA
ESTER	5	F	CHILD	RRZZZZUSA
JACOB	3	M	CHILD	RRZZZZUSA
BALKOW.	.11	M	INFANT	RRZZZZUSA
ROMITO, REISEL	18	F	UNKNOWN	RRZZZZUSA
DAMBACH, EMIL	18	M	LABR	RRZZZZUSA
ZABERONSKY, CHAI.	35	M	FARMER	RRZZZZUSA
FREIDE	10	F	CH	RRZZZZUSA
CHEPSE	8	F	CHILD	RRZZZZUSA
CHANE	7	F	CHILD	RRZZZZUSA
RACHEL	6	F	CHILD	RRZZZZUSA
ZACHEL	.03	F	INFANT	RRZZZZUSA
DALOWITZ, SORE	20	F	UNKNOWN	RRZZZZUSA
ROSENHOLZ, NESCHE	19	F	UNKNOWN	RRZZZZUSA
FELDMANN, TAUBE	18	F	UNKNOWN	RRZZZZUSA
KANTEROWA, CHGE.	69	F	UNKNOWN	RRZZZZUSA
SCHANER, LUDW.	30	M	LABR	RRZZZZUSA
KOSTENBORSKY, SARA	20	F	UNKNOWN	RRZZZZUSA
LEWTANSKY, JACOB	36	M	UNKNOWN	RRZZZZUSA
MALISCHEWS, THOM.	25	M	LABR	RRZZZZUSA
TENKEWITZ, JURGIO	25	F	UNKNOWN	RRZZZZUSA
SCHMITTE, LUDW.	38	M	LABR	RRZZZZUSA
EMIL	33	F	W	RRZZZZUSA
ANNA	8	F	CHILD	RRZZZZUSA
KRUEGER, JOH.	26	M	LABR	RRZZZZUSA
WILH.	27	F	UNKNOWN	RRZZZZUSA
JOHA.	.02	F	INFANT	RRZZZZUSA
ROBHART, JANKEL	40	M	MCHT	RRZZZZUSA
MARKEL	17	F	UNKNOWN	RRZZZZUSA
SARAH	20	F	UNKNOWN	RRZZZZUSA
GLEICH, HERSCH	27	M	LABR	RRZZZZUSA
LADIN, LEIB	42	M	LABR	RRZZZZUSA
JANKELWITZ, LINA	22	F	UNKNOWN	RRZZZZUSA
KAHN, MORITZ	53	M	MCHT	RRZZZZUSA
CHANE	53	F	W	RRZZZZUSA
BENJAMIN	8	M	CHILD	RRZZZZUSA

PASSENGER	AGE	SEX	OCCUPATION	PRV VIL DES

SHIP: ETHIOPIA

FROM: GLASGOW AND MOVILLE
TO: NEW YORK
ARRIVED: 07 AUGUST 1888

PASSENGER	AGE	SEX	OCCUPATION	PRV VIL DES
ABERG, ALFRED	27	M	SEMN	RRZZZZUSA
BURNSTEIN, S.	44	M	LABR	RRZZZZUSA
WAJWODA, SIMON	47	M	LABR	RRZZZZUSA
SADONIS, JURGES	40	M	LABR	RRZZZZUSA
RECKOFSKY, LE.	20	M	UNKNOWN	RRZZZZUSA
KRIWASEWA, ABRH.	73	M	TLR	RRZZZZUSA
BARS, ISAK	43	M	TLR	RRZZZZUSA
DEMBROWCKY, NECHANIE	70	F	UNKNOWN	RRZZZZUSA
RAGELMAN, BORIS	27	M	MCHT	RRZZZZUSA
NOEOGRODSKY, LEIB	36	M	LABR	RRZZZZUSA
BRANDE---, CHANE	17	F	HP	RRZZZZUSA
BLUME	70	F	HP	RRZZZZUSA
RUCASOVICH, LAZZARE	70	M	LABR	RRZZZZUSA
ANNINE	15	F	HP	RRZZZZUSA

SHIP: HERMANN

FROM: BREMEN
TO: BALTIMORE
ARRIVED: 08 AUGUST 1888

PASSENGER	AGE	SEX	OCCUPATION	PRV VIL DES
HOFFMANN, FERD.	19	M	FARMER	RRZZZZMD
SZURPITA, STANISL.	28	M	FARMER	RRZZZZMD
KATARZINA	16	F	UNKNOWN	RRZZZZMD
KEBBEL, KARL	20	M	UNKNOWN	RRZZZZMD
ULOZYNSKI, JURGI	21	M	FARMER	RRZZZZMD
BOJNOWSKI, JOSEF	27	M	FARMER	RRZZZZMD
ZIRANSKY, NECHORNE	40	M	FARMER	RRZZZZMD
EITZIK	23	M	FARMER	RRZZZZMD
KRELINGER, JOHANNA	28	F	UNKNOWN	RRZZZZMD
ALEXANDER	5	M	CHILD	RRZZZZMD
BERTHA	4	F	CHILD	RRZZZZMD
EDUARD	2	M	CHILD	RRZZZZMD
KURALEWSKA, ANTONIA	36	F	W	RRZZZZMD
VALENTIN	17	M	W	RRZZZZMD
MAXIM	12	M	CH	RRZZZZMD
STANISLAW	9	M	CHILD	RRZZZZMD
PELAGIA	7	F	CHILD	RRZZZZMD
MARZELLI	5	M	CHILD	RRZZZZMD
WLADISLAW	.01	M	INFANT	RRZZZZMD
TURKOWSKI, MICHAEL	40	M	FARMER	RRZZZZMD
PICHOKI, JOSEF	36	M	LABR	RRZZZZMI
DREIMANN, FRITZ	19	M	LABR	RRZZZZMD
EWALDSEN, FRITZ	40	M	BKLYR	RRZZZZMD
RUSANOK, LEBER	38	M	PDLR	RRZZZZMD
RACHEL	30	F	W	RRZZZZMD
ROSA	8	F	CHILD	RRZZZZMD
ESTER	5	F	CHILD	RRZZZZMD
SARAH	.11	F	INFANT	RRZZZZMD
VONFIELD, GEORG	32	M	FARMER	RRZZZZMD
CATHARINA	33	F	W	RRZZZZMD
JOSEF	12	M	CH	RRZZZZMD
MICHAEL	9	M	CHILD	RRZZZZMD
MARIA	7	F	CHILD	RRZZZZMD
GEORG	5	M	CHILD	RRZZZZMD
CATHARINA	3	F	CHILD	RRZZZZMD
HANNES	1	M	CHILD	RRZZZZMD
PETER	.01	M	INFANT	RRZZZZMD
KARABINOWITZ, VALERIA	24	F	W	RRZZZZMD
ALEXANDER	4	M	CHILD	RRZZZZMD
MARIA	3	F	CHILD	RRZZZZMD
KULERCHO, HEINR.	18	M	UNKNOWN	RRZZZZMD
HECKERT, SAMUEL	23	M	FARMER	RRZZZZMD
FEINBERG, SCHEINE	19	F	UNKNOWN	RRZZZZMD
VERSAU, RALE	20	F	UNKNOWN	RRZZZZMD
SCHAITKIN, JETTE	26	F	UNKNOWN	RRZZZZMD
DAVID	5	M	CHILD	RRZZZZMD
MOSES	3	M	CHILD	RRZZZZMD
LOUIS	1	M	CHILD	RRZZZZMD
MARIANOW, CHAINE	18	M	PDLR	RRZZZZMD
ROSENBAUM, BEILE	34	F	W	RRZZZZMD
JESCHE	15	F	UNKNOWN	RRZZZZMD
LEIE	8	F	CHILD	RRZZZZMD
CHASKEL	6	F	CHILD	RRZZZZMD
WOLF	4	M	CHILD	RRZZZZMD
CHANNE	3	F	CHILD	RRZZZZMD
SPIEGELMANN, SCHORE	88	F	UNKNOWN	RRZZZZMD
DAVID	14	M	CH	RRZZZZMD
SCHAJEM	11	M	CH	RRZZZZMD
CIREL	5	M	CHILD	RRZZZZMD
MAREUS	3	M	CHILD	RRZZZZMD
GUBERMANN, FRUNE	16	M	UNKNOWN	RRZZZZMD
MALINSKA, MARIANNE	27	F	UNKNOWN	RRZZZZMD
JOSEF	3	M	CHILD	RRZZZZMD
JULIANE	2	F	CHILD	RRZZZZMD
SOFIA	1	F	CHILD	RRZZZZMD
MICHELEWSKY, NISEN	18	M	UNKNOWN	RRZZZZMD
BLOCH, LUDWIG	30	M	FARMER	RRZZZZMD
GARBER, BASSE	35	F	W	RRZZZZMD
SARAH	14	F	UNKNOWN	RRZZZZMD
STERE	10	F	CH	RRZZZZMD
MARIA	7	F	CHILD	RRZZZZMD
DINA	4	F	CHILD	RRZZZZMD
CHORNSKY, FRUNE	20	F	UNKNOWN	RRZZZZMD

SHIP: IOWA

FROM: LIVERPOOL
TO: BOSTON
ARRIVED: 08 AUGUST 1888

PASSENGER	AGE	SEX	OCCUPATION	PRV VIL DES
BLITZER, MARIANN	40	F	W	PLZZZZUSA
DOETERWOEITZ, ROSE	45	F	W	RRZZZZUSA
NULTSLONE, ABRAM	25	M	TLR	RRZZZZUSA
ELLY	24	F	W	RRZZZZUSA
PALKIN, M.	36	F	W	RRZZZZUSA
ZUCKER, KAROLINA	16	F	SP	PLZZZZUSA
BLITZER, JETTY	19	F	SP	PLZZZZUSA
MIGLIN, RACHEL	20	F	SP	PLZZZZUSA
ROSENBEIN, ESTHER	18	F	SP	PLZZZZUSA
BLITZER, LEON	11	M	CH	PLZZZZUSA
JACOB	10	M	CH	PLZZZZUSA
ANETY	7	F	CHILD	PLZZZZUSA
PEPI	4	M	CHILD	PLZZZZUSA
DOETEROWITZ, JULA	11	M	CH	RRZZZZUSA
SCHLAME	9	M	CHILD	RRZZZZUSA
DAVID	7	M	CHILD	RRZZZZUSA
MIRCHAL	3	M	CHILD	RRZZZZUSA
FABER	1	M	CHILD	RRZZZZUSA
NULSTONE, HUMAN	3	M	CHILD	RRZZZZUSA
JOSEPH	.11	M	INFANT	RRZZZZUSA
SALKIN, ISRAEL	11	M	INF	RRZZZZUSA
JOSEPH	10	M	INF	RRZZZZUSA
LEWIS	7	M	CHILD	RRZZZZUSA
LUBIN, ABRAM	25	M	MECH	RRZZZZUSA
BUSELL, J.	18	M	TLR	RRZZZZUSA
GALLENFALL, NATHAN	25	M	JNR	RRZZZZUSA
DOETEROWITZ, BUKA	14	M	LABR	RRZZZZUSA
SAMSKY, PHILLIP	24	M	UNKNOWN	RRZZZZUSA
ROSENBEIN, CHAUM	22	M	TLR	PLZZZZUSA
GOLDSKATA, AIRSH	19	M	JNR	RRZZZZUSA
WOLFFSHOEN, AIRSH	18	M	SMH	RRZZZZUSA
ROSENTHALL, HRY.	35	M	TLR	RRZZZZUSA

PASSENGER	AGE	SEX	OCCUPATION	PRV VIL DES
MOTTELINSKY, JAN	30	M	BCHR	PLZZZZUSA
SALKIN, HENRY	18	M	UNKNOWN	RRZZZZUSA
JAMUSCHIS, KASIM	24	M	LABR	PLZZZZUSA
FINK, NACHEN	20	M	SMH	RRZZZZUSA
SIMON	18	M	SMH	RRZZZZUSA
BEK, ISRAEL	25	M	PNTR	RRZZZZUSA

SHIP: STATE OF GEORGIA

FROM: GLASGOW AND LARNE
TO: NEW YORK
ARRIVED: 08 AUGUST 1888

PASSENGER	AGE	SEX	OCCUPATION	PRV VIL DES
BERKOWITSCH, ISAAC	54	M	PDLR	RRAIDLUSA
CHANKALIN, OHAN	90	M	PDLR	RRAIDLUSA
MERIONS	49	M	LABR	RRAIDLUSA
THOMAS	18	M	LABR	RRAIDLUSA
L.	32	M	LABR	RRAIDLUSA
THOMAS	20	M	LABR	RRAIDLUSA
BEDROS	10	M	BY	RRAIDLUSA
THOMAS	10	M	BY	RRAIDLUSA
SAITINI	7	F	CHILD	RRAIDLUSA
SHAJEIR, U	00	F	W	RRAIDLUSA
CHAIKE	9	F	CHILD	RRAIDLUSA
GESSIL	5	F	CHILD	RRAIDLUSA
SARAH	2	F	CHILD	RRAIDLUSA
HENOCH	1	M	CHILD	RRAIDLUSA
CHOUCHIAA, OHAN	21	M	LABR	RRAIDLUSA
SACHAN	40	M	LABR	RRAIDLUSA
COHEN, PORE	28	F	W	RRAIDLUSA
LEIBE	10	F	CH	RRAIDLUSA
SCHOME	4	F	CHILD	RRAIDLUSA
SCHAIE	1	M	CHILD	RRAIDLUSA
DEWEROSSES, MASCHA	18	F	SVNT	RRAIDLUSA
GOLDMANN, LEISA	24	F	W	RRAIDLUSA
JACOB	5	M	CHILD	RRAIDLUSA
ISAAC	3	M	CHILD	RRAIDLUSA
SCHEINDEL	1	M	CHILD	RRAIDLUSA
HASIN, ELIZ	90	F	W	RRAIDLUSA
JOSEPH	34	M	LABR	RRAIDLUSA
MILHAM	23	M	LABR	RRAIDLUSA
SALIN	6	M	CHILD	RRAIDLUSA
KAPLAN, FENTA	22	F	UNKNOWN	RRAIDLUSA
LASGOWER, MENDEL	46	M	LABR	RRAIDLUSA
BEILE	36	F	W	RRAIDLUSA
JANKEL	00	M	UNKNOWN	RRAIDLUSA
MANHOF, MANNIE	16	F	SVNT	RRAIDLUSA
ROCHE	11	F	CH	RRAIDLUSA
BASSE	7	F	CHILD	RRAIDLUSA
PRUDIAN, AZOB	22	M	LABR	RRAIDLUSA
ALTONI	30	M	LABR	RRAIDLUSA
BEDROS, SABANGIAN	30	M	LABR	RRAIDLUSA
RASUMNA, SIMON	36	M	PDLR	RRAIDLUSA
HASLE, HER.	16	M	TLR	RRAIDLUSA
BEILE	19	F	SVNT	RRAIDLUSA
HOLZ, GITHL	17	F	SVNT	RRAIDLUSA
HIRSCHFELD, MIRE	17	F	SVNT	RRAIDLUSA
JELENSKY, EHE	40	M	LABR	RRAIDLUSA
JAFFE, MARCUS	22	M	MCHT	RRAIDLUSA
JAKOBOWIZ, JANKEL	17	M	TLR	RRAIDLUSA
JAFFE, F.	17	F	SVNT	RRAIDLUSA
JUDOWICZ, MICHEL	37	M	MCHT	RRAIDLUSA
SCHEINE	28	F	W	RRAIDLUSA
JOWELL, LERE	18	F	SVNT	RRAIDLUSA
KATRAN, PEREZ	19	M	CL	RRAIDLUSA
KURS, MARENS	25	M	MCHT	RRAIDLUSA
KOROWICZ, MOSES	23	M	MCHT	RRAIDLUSA
ELIAS	17	M	MCHT	RRAIDLUSA
KAHAN, LIEBE	36	F	M	RRAIDLUSA
FREIDE	6	F	CHILD	RRAIDLUSA
MENDEL	2	M	CHILD	RRAIDLUSA
KATZ, TAUBE	18	F	SVNT	RRAIDLUSA
KLAVANSKY, BERNHARD	11	M	CH	RRAIDLUSA
KAPLAN, NACHEME	20	F	SVNT	RRAIDLUSA
KUSS, ITZIG	29	M	LABR	RRAIDLUSA
LORE	31	F	UNKNOWN	RRAIDLUSA
ESTHER	9	F	CHILD	RRAIDLUSA
MOSES	5	M	CHILD	RRAIDLUSA
ROBECCA	2	F	CHILD	RRAIDLUSA
ELKE	.06	F	INFANT	RRAIDLUSA
LIEBSCHUTZ, SCHMUL	23	M	MCHT	RRAIDLUSA
LEWIEN, RACHEL	20	F	SVNT	RRAIDLUSA
RIEWKE	18	F	SVNT	RRAIDLUSA
CHANNE	17	F	SVNT	RRAIDLUSA
LIPKOWITSCH, HENI	20	F	SVNT	RRAIDLUSA
LEWIN, SCHOLEM	20	M	MCHT	RRAIDLUSA
SPRINJE	16	F	SVNT	RRAIDLUSA
LAKOWITSCH, LIPPE	39	M	MCHT	RRAIDLUSA
LEWIEN, LEIB	30	M	MCHT	RRAIDLUSA
LARGE, RACHE.	17	F	SVNT	RRAIDLUSA
MEYEROWISCH, NACHUM	21	M	MCHT	RRAIDLUSA
MORDIKINZ, CHAJE	18	F	SVNT	RRAIDLUSA
MACHAL, CHAIM	25	M	BBR	RRAIDLUSA
MIKLITZKY, HILLEL	17	M	MCHT	RRAIDLUSA
MATZ, CHANNE	17	U	UNKNOWN	RRAIDLUSA
MOWSCHOWITZ, MEYER	50	M	MCHT	RRAIDLUSA
REILE	48	F	UNKNOWN	RRAIDLUSA
JANCKEL	15	M	UNKNOWN	RRAIDLUSA
FEIGE	11	F	UNKNOWN	RRAIDLUSA
CHANE	9	F	CHILD	RRAIDLUSA
MORRITZ, ESTHER	33	F	MSN	RRAIDLUSA
MESSINGER, SCHOLEM	24	M	MCHT	RRAIDLUSA
MAGRIL, ROSA	30	F	M	RRAIDLUSA
FREDA	2	F	CHILD	RRAIDLUSA
SORE	1	F	CHILD	RRAIDLUSA
MEYERSAHR, MASSE	19	F	SVNT	RRAIDLUSA
MANN, BERLE	48	F	M	RRAIDLUSA
LIPE	18	F	UNKNOWN	RRAIDLUSA
ELIE	16	F	UNKNOWN	RRAIDLUSA
SESSE	11	F	UNKNOWN	RRAIDLUSA
MORDSCH	7	M	CHILD	RRAIDLUSA
PERE	2	F	CHILD	RRAIDLUSA
MALINOWSKY, ELIAS	23	M	MCHT	RRAIDLUSA
MOWSHER, HIRSCH	22	M	MCHT	RRAIDLUSA
MENDELOWITZ, MOSES	22	M	JNR	RRAIDLUSA
NUSO, ISAK	20	M	MCHT	RRAIDLUSA
ITZIGSOHN, SAML.	18	M	MCHT	RRAIDLUSA
NURITZKY, LEIB	26	M	SHMK	RRAIDLUSA
ITZKEWITZ, ARON	16	M	CL	RRAIDLUSA
PROPISOHN, ITZIG	20	M	MCHT	RRAIDLUSA
POJANEW, NOSSUM	35	M	MCHT	RRAIDLUSA
PRUSS, DWORE	17	F	SVNT	RRAIDLUSA
PARTNERZ, ZIREL	24	F	M	RRAIDLUSA
ROCHEL	2	F	CHILD	RRAIDLUSA
SORE	1	F	CHILD	RRAIDLUSA
PERLMAN, ROSA	19	F	SVNT	RRAIDLUSA
PARASCH, MASSE	27	M	TLR	RRAIDLUSA
PESTIN, CHRISTIAN	29	M	MCHT	RRAIDLUSA
POTASCH, ABRAHAM	18	M	MCHT	RRAIDLUSA
PO--K, WOLF	18	M	MCHT	RRAIDLUSA
ROSENFELD, ABR.	20	M	MCHT	RRAIDLUSA
RESNIK, ESTHER	25	F	M	RRAIDLUSA
BASSE	2	F	CHILD	RRAIDLUSA
RUSIK, MARIA	29	F	SVNT	RRAIDLUSA
RENSCHASKY, BERTHA	25	F	M	RRAIDLUSA
JITTEL	1	F	CHILD	RRAIDLUSA
CHAIM	.03	M	INFANT	RRAIDLUSA
RUSNIKOW, ABR.	35	M	MCHT	RRAIDLUSA
SIMKE, FRANZ	31	M	LABR	RRAIDLUSA
SCHUMAN, HIRSCH	30	M	MCHT	RRAIDLUSA
SLOBODSKY, ISAK	19	M	MCHT	RRAIDLUSA
SANRICH, NACHUAN	18	M	SHMK	RRAIDLUSA
SHEREN, HIRSCH	28	M	MCHT	RRAIDLUSA
SCHIFFER, SOLOMON	25	M	MCHT	RRAIDLUSA
SAPIRO, MEYER	20	M	MCHT	RRAIDLUSA

PASSENGER	AGE	SEX	OCCUPATION	PRV	VIL	DES
SMOLE, RASSE	22	F	SVNT	RR	AIDL	USA
SCHNEIDER, JACOB	28	M	MCHT	RR	AIDL	USA
SNIGER, MOSES	30	M	MCHT	RR	AIDL	USA
STEIN, MARIA	14	F	SVNT	RR	AIDL	USA
SAHUVECZIK, JACOB	28	M	SMH	RR	AIDL	USA
SCHINDER, RIEWKE	18	F	SVNT	RR	AIDL	USA
SUBLITZK-, BREIM	36	F	UNKNOWN	RR	AIDL	USA
RACHEL	7	F	CHILD	RR	AIDL	USA
ABRAHAM	1	M	CHILD	RR	AIDL	USA
SOSNISKI, SCHLOM	20	M	CL	RR	AIDL	USA
SOCKET, FEANET	19	F	SVNT	RR	AIDL	USA
SUSAN, LIEBE	20	F	SVNT	RR	AIDL	USA
SAMECK, ROCHE	25	F	M	RR	AIDL	USA
ABR.	11	M	CH	RR	AIDL	USA
FREIDE	9	F	CHILD	RR	AIDL	USA
MICHEL	8	M	CHILD	RR	AIDL	USA
SCHEINE	6	F	CHILD	RR	AIDL	USA
ELTE	2	F	CHILD	RR	AIDL	USA
SEIDEL, SALKUW	17	M	UNKNOWN	RR	AIDL	USA
SAZALOWIEZ, JACOB	36	M	TLR	RR	AIDL	USA
SAR, LIEBE	17	F	SVNT	RR	AIDL	USA
SCHINOWSKY, ESTHER	28	F	M	RR	AIDL	USA
TERZE	2	F	CHILD	RR	AIDL	USA
JARUH	6	F	CHILD	RR	AIDL	USA
SACH, MENDEL	20	M	MCHT	RR	AIDL	USA
SCHAPIRO, JOSSEL	22	M	MCHT	RR	AIDL	USA
SCHUMLOWICZ, MOSES	18	M	MCHT	RR	AIDL	USA
SENDER, SCHMUL	18	M	TLR	RR	AIDL	USA
UPIN, HIRSCH	17	M	MCHT	RR	AIDL	USA
WOJCZAK, LEIB	20	M	SHMK	RR	AIDL	USA
WEISKOPF, MOSES	34	M	MCHT	RR	AIDL	USA
WOHLGEMUK, JACOB	46	M	MCHT	RR	AIDL	USA
ZENSCHSOHN, SANDER	26	M	MCHT	RR	AIDL	USA
ZIMMERMAN, LEIB	48	M	MCHT	RR	AIDL	USA
HADISCH	11	M	CH	RR	AIDL	USA
ZALKOWITZ, HENE	40	F	M	RR	AIDL	USA
SCHONE	18	F	CH	RR	AIDL	USA
ZIFFE	16	F	CH	RR	AIDL	USA
SOMLE	8	M	CHILD	RR	AIDL	USA
SUSSKIEW, MOSES	38	M	BKBNDR	RR	AIDL	USA

SHIP: WYOMING

FROM: LIVERPOOL AND QUEENSTOWN
TO: NEW YORK
ARRIVED: 08 AUGUST 1888

PASSENGER	AGE	SEX	OCCUPATION	PRV	VIL	DES
ANDERSON, HEDDA	22	F	CH	PL	ZZZZ	USA
PARKER, GEO.	24	M	LABR	PL	ZZZZ	USA
IMINSDOW, MARY	22	F	UNKNOWN	PL	ZZZZ	USA
ASHTON, J.	25	U	UNKNOWN	PL	ZZZZ	USA
KEUST, C.	20	U	UNKNOWN	PL	ZZZZ	USA
BILLINGTON, D.	39	U	UNKNOWN	PL	ZZZZ	USA
MARY	30	F	UNKNOWN	PL	ZZZZ	USA
ELISA	7	F	CHILD	PL	ZZZZ	USA
ARON	6	M	CHILD	PL	ZZZZ	USA
LYBIL	3	U	CHILD	PL	ZZZZ	USA
GERTRUDE	00	F	INF	PL	ZZZZ	USA
WALKER, E.	40	U	UNKNOWN	PL	ZZZZ	USA
ROY, M.	36	U	UNKNOWN	PL	ZZZZ	USA
SLOYD, WM.	25	U	UNKNOWN	PL	ZZZZ	USA
CULLEN, J.	32	U	UNKNOWN	PL	ZZZZ	USA
ZUSKOWITZ, SAML.	15	M	LABR	RR	ZZZZ	USA
HERMAN	7	M	CHILD	RR	ZZZZ	USA
EHRLICH, MEILICH	00	M	INF	RR	ZZZZ	USA
PESCHE	00	F	INF	RR	ZZZZ	USA
LEIBNER, CHARE	00	F	INF	RR	ZZZZ	USA
ROSENTHAL, A.	22	M	LABR	RR	ZZZZ	USA

SHIP: HAMMONIA

FROM: HAMBURG AND HAVRE
TO: NEW YORK
ARRIVED: 09 AUGUST 1888

PASSENGER	AGE	SEX	OCCUPATION	PRV	VIL	DES
TROJANOWSKI, LEONIDA	9	F	CHILD	RR	ZZZZ	USA
MARIANNA	7	F	CHILD	RR	ZZZZ	USA
JOSEF	5	M	CHILD	RR	ZZZZ	USA
LESSMANN, REGINA	21	F	SGL	RR	ZZZZ	USA
WERTELSKY, BERH.	20	M	SLR	RR	ZZZZ	USA
BARTUL, CARL	25	M	CNF	RR	AEFL	USA
KALISKI, NATALIE	32	F	W	RR	ZZZZ	USA
JETTE	9	F	CHILD	RR	ZZZZ	USA
JOSEF	3	M	CHILD	RR	ZZZZ	USA
ITZIG	.11	M	INFANT	RR	ZZZZ	USA
ROSENSOHN, CHAJE	35	F	W	RR	AHXL	USA
FEIGE	9	F	CHILD	RR	AHXL	USA
GITEL	6	F	CHILD	RR	AHXL	USA
JANKEL	4	F	CHILD	RR	AHXL	USA
STUPSKA, RIEKE	27	F	W	RR	AHTW	USA
CHEINE	4	F	CHILD	RR	AHTW	USA
CHAJE	3	F	CHILD	RR	AHTW	USA
ANGELZIK, MOSES	18	M	LABR	RR	AHTW	USA
WOLLACK, FREIDE	16	F	SGL	RR	ZZZZ	USA
GOLIBRODSKI, MARCUS	28	M	MCHT	RR	ZZZZ	USA
KLEMH, MACHLE	45	F	W	RR	ZZZZ	USA
SEBA, SHEINE	48	F	W	RR	AFWJ	USA
DEWORE	6	F	CHILD	RR	AFWJ	USA
HURWITZ, ISRAEL	26	M	APTC	RR	ZZZZ	USA
FANNY	23	F	W	RR	ZZZZ	USA
SALI	.11	F	INFANT	RR	ZZZZ	USA
WALKER, NAUM	22	M	BBR	RR	ZZZZ	USA
MINNA	19	F	W	RR	ZZZZ	USA
ABOWITZ, DWORE	39	F	SGL	RR	AHTF	USA
WAHEG, LEIBE	29	F	W	RR	AIIN	USA
BUCHDAHL, JOHANN	25	M	CPTR	RR	AIIN	USA
VAN, DISUS	43	M	FARMER	RR	ZZZZ	USA
POMERANK, F.	34	M	SLR	RR	ZZZZ	USA
JARESZKY, MEZA	14	F	SGL	RR	AIOL	USA
FRANCK, JACOB	28	M	LABR	RR	ZZZZ	USA
BENDA, MARIE	17	F	SGL	RR	ZZZZ	USA
ERTZ, SAMUEL	25	M	LABR	RR	ZZZZ	USA
DONGINEK, FRANZ	18	M	LABR	RR	ZZZZ	USA
JOSEF	16	M	LABR	RR	ZZZZ	USA
HOROWITZ, RACHEL	19	F	SGL	RR	AHTF	USA
CHAIMOWITZ, SAMUEL	28	M	LABR	RR	AGRT	USA
RACHEL	16	F	W	RR	AGRT	USA
KARSON, MERE	14	F	SGL	RR	AGRT	USA
SCHULTZ, CHANNE	18	F	SGL	RR	AGRT	USA
BERMAN, ESSER	25	F	LABR	RR	ZZZZ	USA
FREIDE	.10	F	INFANT	RR	ZZZZ	USA
GRODZINSKY, RACHEL	30	F	W	RR	ZZZZ	USA
CHANE	6	F	CHILD	RR	ZZZZ	USA
BOBE	9	F	CHILD	RR	ZZZZ	USA
MENDEL	8	M	CHILD	RR	ZZZZ	USA
ALTER	.11	M	INFANT	RR	ZZZZ	USA
PERSKY, CHAJE	21	F	SGL	RR	ZZZZ	USA
LEWIN, SCHALE	35	F	SGL	RR	ZZZZ	USA
REBECCA	3	F	CHILD	RR	ZZZZ	USA
LEIB	.10	M	INFANT	RR	ZZZZ	USA
DESSAN, CHAIME	29	M	MCHT	RR	ZZZZ	USA
HUSWITZ, MORDACH	16	M	LABR	RR	ZZZZ	USA
GRUENE	14	F	SGL	RR	AFWJ	USA
KOMER, LEA	16	F	SGL	RR	AFWJ	USA
PRUEHLING, CHAJE	17	F	SGL	RR	ZZZZ	USA
MOSES	17	M	B	RR	ZZZZ	USA
BRUZKOWITSCH, URSULA	17	F	SGL	RR	ZZZZ	USA
KIGOL, PETER	21	M	LABR	RR	ZZZZ	USA
STEIN, ESTHER	40	F	W	RR	AIEO	USA
SCHLOME	9	F	CHILD	RR	AIEO	USA
HENE	7	F	CHILD	RR	AIEO	USA
REISZE	6	F	CHILD	RR	AIEO	USA
MAGID, JESCHE	40	M	LABR	RR	ZZZZ	USA

PASSENGER	AGE	SEX	OCCUPATION	PRV VIL DES
LICHSENKUM, ARON	26	M	LABR	RRZZZZUSA
JELSAND, JOEL	9	M	CHILD	RRZZZZUSA
SPISALNIK, JACOB	23	M	LABR	RRZZZZUSA
KRAFTZINSKY, ISAAC	25	M	LABR	RRZZZZUSA
MASGOLD, BARUCH	22	M	LABR	RRZZZZUSA
LEBOWITZ, ISRAEL	38	M	LABR	RRZZZZUSA
WERSCHANSKY, RACHEL	55	F	W	RRZZZZUSA
PERCE	15	F	CH	RRZZZZUSA
JACUBOWITZ, LENE	40	F	W	RRZZZZUSA
BEN.	16	F	CH	RRZZZZUSA
FANNY	9	F	CHILD	RRZZZZUSA
REGI	8	F	CHILD	RRZZZZUSA
MENGES	7	F	CHILD	RRZZZZUSA
MORITZ	6	M	CHILD	RRZZZZUSA
DAVID	.11	M	INFANT	RRZZZZUSA
SKORBIN, RESEL	25	F	W	RRZZZZUSA
RASCHEWE	3	F	CHILD	RRZZZZUSA
SCHLOMA	.11	F	INFANT	RRZZZZUSA
KREMER, RIFKE	26	F	W	RRZZZZUSA
CHEIE	9	F	CHILD	RRZZZZUSA
MENUCHE	8	F	CHILD	RRZZZZUSA
MENDEL	6	F	CHILD	RRZZZZUSA
TAUBE	3	F	CHILD	RRZZZZUSA
DAWIDOW, ISAC	51	M	MCHT	RRAFVGUSA
SHEINDEL	51	F	W	RRAFVGUSA
MASSE	26	M	CH	RRAFVGUSA
MALKE	13	M	CH	RRAFVGUSA
COHN, MARK	6	M	CHILD	RRAFVGUSA
FRISCHMANN, BASCHE	72	M	WCHMKR	RRZZZZUSA
SCHAMAI, JANKEL	58	M	TLR	RRZZZZUSA
SEBACH, SH.	31	M	LABR	RRAFWJUSA
HORWITZ, ISAAC	24	M	LABR	RRAGRTUSA
CHAVE	9	F	CHILD	RRAGRTUSA
KROHNSOHN, MEIER	19	M	LABR	RRZZZZUSA
REINGOLD, CHAJE	18	F	SGL	RRAHTBUSA
GERSCHENOWITZ, MORDCHE	24	M	MCHT	RRAHTBUSA
REBECCA	24	F	W	RRAHTBUSA
ISRAEL	9	M	CHILD	RRAHTBUSA
MUNZ, ISLE	28	F	W	RRAHTBUSA
MALKE	.10	F	INFANT	RRAHTBUSA
RAHLELS, RACHMIEL	24	M	MCHT	RRAHTBUSA
DICK, HINDE	19	F	SGL	RRZZZZUSA
RESMHOW, RACHEL	21	F	SGL	RRZZZZUSA
BRENNER, JENNY	21	F	SGL	RRZZZZUSA
GRUENBAUM, RIWKE	24	F	W	RRAHVUUSA
REISE	.06	F	INFANT	RRAHVUUSA
KOTHOWSKY, SPRINZE	18	F	SGL	RRAHVUUSA
WEINSTEIN, RACHEL	20	F	SGL	RRAIMEUSA
HARPACK, JULIANE	19	F	SGL	RRZZZZUSA
SEGALL, ELKE	20	F	W	RRAIDWUSA
SARA	.11	F	INFANT	RRAIDWUSA
SCHLOME	.01	F	INFANT	RRAIDWUSA
SCHMIDT, ISAAC	38	M	TLR	RRAIDWUSA
DIZEK, SELKA	26	F	W	RRAIDWUSA
FLORA	8	F	CHILD	RRAIDWUSA
MARKUS	3	M	CHILD	RRAIDWUSA
LEWITAN, ETE	35	F	W	RRAHTFUSA
PESCHE	16	F	CH	RRAHTFUSA
MICHEL	14	F	CH	RRAHTFUSA
RIWE	19	F	CH	RRAHTFUSA
WOLF	8	F	CHILD	RRAHTFUSA
JACOB	6	F	CHILD	RRAHTFUSA
KUPINSKI, HIRSCH	9	M	CHILD	RRAHTFUSA
STRAUB, BERTA	20	F	SGL	RRAHTFUSA
KLATZ, ALFRED	25	M	MCHT	RRAHTFUSA
ARNOLD, ROBERT	29	M	JNR	RRAHTFUSA
RUF, FR.J.	16	M	LABR	RRAHTFUSA
ULJENS, CARL	42	M	LABR	RRAIDSUSA
GENIEFF, JETTEN	29	M	LABR	RRAIDSUSA
ARENT	26	M	LABR	RRAIDSUSA
PILIKOFF, SIMON	22	M	LABR	RRAIDSUSA
ROSMAN, WOLF	18	M	TDR	RRZZZZUSA
HELENE	18	F	W	RRZZZZUSA
LEWIN, DORA	18	F	SGL	RRAEFLUSA
KAPLAN, LEIB	17	M	TLR	RRZZZZUSA
ISKOWITZ, DAVID	28	M	MCHT	RRABQBUSA
JACOBSON, IS.	25	M	MCHT	RRABQBUSA
LICHTESTEIN, EFRAIM	28	M	MCHT	RRZZZZUSA
STANG, ITZIG	34	M	TDR	RRZZZZUSA
NACHME	13	M	TDR	RRZZZZUSA
SORSMANN, WOLF	35	M	MLR	RRZZZZUSA
GOLDBERG, BETI	20	F	SGL	RRZZZZUSA
PLATAN, WIGDOR	25	M	LABR	RRZZZZUSA
FUND, CHAIM	28	M	TLR	RRZZZZUSA
PROBECK, GROV.	31	M	TLR	RRZZZZUSA
BERMAN, GITE	18	F	SGL	RRZZZZUSA
ABRAMOWITZ, ROSA	24	F	W	RRAIBUUSA
CHAWE	.09	F	INFANT	RRAIBUUSA
BERNSTEIN, ROCHE	19	F	SGL	RRAHTUUSA
HER, ARIC	54	F	MCHT	RRAHTFUSA
GINZBURG, ABRAM	31	F	MCHT	RRAHTFUSA
SAMASZYN, LEON	22	F	MCHT	RRAHTFUSA
ROSALIE	30	F	W	RRAHTFUSA
JOACHIM, REBECCA	34	F	W	RRAHTFUSA
LEON	14	M	SGL	RRAHTFUSA
SALOMON	9	M	CHILD	RRAHTFUSA
MARIE	7	F	CHILD	RRAHTFUSA
SOSSNA, FEIGE	40	F	W	RRAHTOUSA
RIWKE	5	F	CHILD	RRAHTOUSA
SONA	4	F	CHILD	RRAHTOUSA
DINGFELD, MARIE	32	F	W	RRZZZZUSA
MATH.	8	F	CHILD	RRZZZZUSA
WM.	6	M	CHILD	RRZZZZUSA
AUGUST	4	M	CHILD	RRZZZZUSA
KRASSER, ITE	30	F	W	RRZZZZUSA
LIKI	7	F	CHILD	RRZZZZUSA
CHAJE	8	F	CHILD	RRZZZZUSA
LEISER	.11	F	INFANT	RRZZZZUSA
SALOMON, SHIFFRE	27	F	W	RRZZZZUSA
CHAJE	5	F	CHILD	RRZZZZUSA
ISRAEL	3	M	CHILD	RRZZZZUSA
BARTOZKA, AUGUSTIN	26	M	LABR	RRZZZZUSA
MEYER, SARA	35	F	W	RRAHTFUSA
CHANNE	18	F	CH	RRAHTFUSA
JANKEL	8	M	CHILD	RRAHTFUSA
LEIB	4	M	CHILD	RRAHTFUSA
ANEN, IDA	19	F	SGL	RRAHTFUSA
SZARENKA, MIRE	17	F	SGL	RRAHTFUSA
PRIKANSKI, JESSE	17	M	LABR	RRAHWMUSA
OSTROWSKI, BALBINA	25	F	W	RRAHWMUSA
ANTONI	.06	M	INFANT	RRAHWMUSA
ABRANSKI, CHEIE	45	F	W	RRAHWMUSA
SARA	24	F	CH	RRAHWMUSA
FREME	7	F	CHILD	RRAHWMUSA
ABRAM.	7	M	CHILD	RRAHWMUSA
MOSES	6	M	CHILD	RRAHWMUSA
GOLDE	3	F	CHILD	RRAHWMUSA
ARON	.11	M	INFANT	RRAHWMUSA
POLINE, CHANNE	17	F	SGL	RRAHTOUSA
BOEHMER, JOHNNA	58	F	W	RRAHTOUSA
ASMUS, HEINR.	25	M	BCHR	RRZZZZUSA
FRIEDMANN, MARY	50	F	W	RRAHXHUSA
MOSES	20	M	LABR	RRAHXHUSA
LEVIS	18	F	SGL	RRAHXHUSA
SCHMUEL	17	M	LABR	RRAHXHUSA
KISSINGER, FRIEDR.	28	M	FARMER	RRZZZZUSA
GRUENN, SARA	9	F	CHILD	RRAIBUUSA
BREETZ, MICHNE	35	F	W	RRZZZZUSA
NACHME	4	M	CHILD	RRZZZZUSA
MOLHEWITZ, JURE	25	F	W	RRAIHGUSA
SOWIE	6	F	CHILD	RRAIHGUSA
MEYER	3	M	CHILD	RRAIHGUSA
LEIBISCH	.04	M	INFANT	RRAIHGUSA
HOLIDORSKY, MORDCHE	47	M	MCHT	RRZZZZUSA
SIMONSEN, AUG.	24	M	LABR	RRZZZZUSA
LEFKOWITZ, RACHEL	15	F	SGL	RRAFWJUSA
BALSKI, JENTE	23	F	SGL	RRAFWJUSA
NACHTIGALL, LEIB	66	M	LABR	RRAIFBUSA
PETERSEN, CHRISTIAN	58	M	FARMER	RRZZZZUSA
GERLACH, AUGUST	24	M	TLR	RRAIBAUSA

PASSENGER	AGE	SEX	OCCUPATION	PV D RI E VL S
KORTHALS, WILH.	20	M	STDNT	RRAAKHUSA
RICKON, FRIED.	36	F	SGL	RRAAKHUSA
SHERNUSKY, NACHEM	20	M	LLD	RRAAKHUSA
SHUPHIN, U	19	F	SGL	RRAAKHUSA
WERJINSKY, -ILLEL	20	M	MCHT	RRAAKHUSA
LEWIN, SHOLEM	19	M	LABR	RRAAKHUSA
MENACHE	19	M	LABR	RRAAKHUSA
GUDMASKI, MATH.	20	M	LABR	RRAAKHUSA
HERMANN, ARON	20	M	LABR	RRAAKHUSA
TAUBE	20	F	W	RRAAKHUSA
KATZENELLASCHER, SAMUEL	23	M	LABR	RRAAKHUSA
FRANKEL, BASCHE	20	F	SGL	RRAFWJUSA
SARA	19	F	SGL	RRAFWJUSA
PUESSKER, FRANZ	40	M	LABR	RRAHTUUSA
GOLDMANN, CHAJE	32	F	W	RRAHTUUSA
BASCHE	9	F	CHILD	RRAHTUUSA
LIPE	8	F	CHILD	RRAHTUUSA
JACOB	3	M	CHILD	RRAHTUUSA
SALOUCSNEK, CHAJE	19	F	SGL	RRAHTUUSA
MEISTER, ROSA	44	F	UNKNOWN	RRAIBOUSA
DINA	9	F	CHILD	RRAIBOUSA
CHAJE	7	F	CHILD	RRAIBOUSA
LEWIN, SARA	25	F	W	RRAIBOUSA
MISCHKE	.11	M	INFANT	RRAIBOUSA
U, U	39	F	W	RRAIGGUSA
PESCHE	6	F	CHILD	RRAIGGUSA
ENTE	.11	F	INFANT	RRAIGGUSA
BREITERMANN, MOSES	23	M	LABR	RRAFWJUSA
MOSES	18	M	LABR	RRAFWJUSA
EMILIE	17	F	SGL	RRAFWJUSA
BER	8	M	CHILD	RRAFWJUSA
MRNDEL	.06	M	INFANT	RRAFWJUSA
ZILULSKI, MARTIN	56	M	LABR	RRZZZZUSA
JORINSKI, CHAJE	29	F	W	RRZZZZUSA
LITMAN	7	M	CHILD	RRZZZZUSA
RACHEL	5	F	CHILD	RRZZZZUSA
LEIB.	.03	M	INFANT	RRZZZZUSA
ZUKOWA, MARIANNE	29	F	W	RRAHZSUSA
BARBARA	5	F	CHILD	RRAHZSUSA
MARIANNE	.04	F	INFANT	RRAHZSUSA
U, BALTRI--	25	M	LABR	RRAHZSUSA
BAESEWICZ, ---ON	24	M	LABR	RRAHZSUSA
BLANTIS, JANOS	25	M	LABR	RRAHZSUSA
LENAWERT, ANDREAS	20	M	LABR	RRAHZSUSA
KUSAITCS, JOSEF	20	M	LABR	RRAHZSUSA
ELJANIN, ELTE	25	M	LABR	RRAICMUSA
SACHAWITZKY, HANNE	19	M	LABR	RRZZZZUSA
ZABANITZKY, LEB	29	M	LABR	RRZZZZUSA
HURWITZ, MOSES	42	M	LABR	RRZZZZUSA
ARLUK, STEFAN	30	M	LABR	RRZZZZUSA
GOTTESLEBEN, FRANZ	23	M	LABR	RRZZZZUSA

SHIP: ENGLAND

FROM: LIVERPOOL AND QUEENSTOWN
TO: NEW YORK
ARRIVED: 09 AUGUST 1888

PASSENGER	AGE	SEX	OCCUPATION	PV D RI E VL S
BREEYOWITZ, BENAS	22	M	LABR	RRZZZZNY
NUBORSKY, ISRAEL	37	M	LABR	RRZZZZSY
HEMPEL, ISAAC	24	M	LABR	RRAIIXSY
HOLLENDERSKY, SOLOMON	23	M	LABR	RRAIIXSY
SUKIER, JAN	30	M	LABR	RRAIIXSY
JOS	23	M	LABR	RRAIIXSY
PAUL	23	M	LABR	RRAIIXSY
CIEZEWSKY, ALEXANDER	28	M	LABR	RRAIIXSY
ZURYLOMAN, JESCHIE	22	M	LABR	RRAIIXSY
YAHER, JUDE	40	M	LABR	RRAIIXSY
HANES, SAMUEL	19	M	LABR	RRAIIXSY
MENDELOWIC, CHASEL	24	M	LABR	RRAIIXPHI
SOFIAS, JANKEL	19	M	LABR	RRAIIXNY
BASCHKOWSKY, CHAIM	24	M	LABR	RRAIIXNY
SCHNEIDER, BARUCH	29	M	LABR	RRAIIXNY
WEIRE, JOHN	26	M	LABR	RRAIIXNY
KENNY, JOHN	26	M	LABR	RRAIIXNY
GOLDSTEIN, MOSES	53	M	LABR	RRAIIXNY
SCORNE	10	F	CH	RRAIIXNY
ELKE	9	F	CHILD	RRAIIXNY
NOCHAM	8	M	CHILD	RRAIIXNY
ROSENWEIG, ROSA	40	F	W	RRAIIXNY
BLUMA	16	F	SP	RRAIIXNY
GOLDMANN, ANNIE	26	F	W	RRAIIXNY
MORRIS	3	M	CHILD	RRAIIXNY
KLEBANSKY, HARRIS	10	M	CH	RRAIIXNY
NEWMAN	8	M	CHILD	RRAIIXNY
THAPVIS, JACOB	33	M	LABR	RRAIIXNY
SARAH	31	F	W	RRAIIXNY
JOSEPH	9	M	CHILD	RRAIIXNY
KATE	5	F	CHILD	RRAIIXNY
ELISAS	2	M	CHILD	RRAIIXNY
RACHEL	.05	F	INFANT	RRAIIXNY
PERLMANN, ROSA	23	F	W	RRAIIXNY
KOHN, FANNY	24	F	W	RRAIIXNY
GALLER, FEIGE	32	F	W	RRAIIXNY
ITZIG	9	M	CHILD	RRAIIXNY
ISRAEL	7	M	CHILD	RRAIIXNY
MUREL	1	F	CHILD	RRAIIXNY
SCHILLING, LIEBE	19	F	SVNT	RRAIIXNY
FIXMAN, SAMUEL	25	M	LABR	RRAIIXNY
ZIPPE	27	F	W	RRAIIXNY
IWAN	.06	M	INFANT	RRAIIXNY
AHS, HENRIK	39	M	LABR	RRAIIXNY
MATHILDA	40	F	W	RRAIIXNY
JOHANNA	11	F	CH	RRAIIXNY
ARTHUR	9	M	CHILD	RRAIIXNY
MARIE	6	F	CHILD	RRAIIXNY
JOHAN	2	M	CHILD	RRAIIXNY
HILDEN, MARTI	26	M	LABR	RRAIIXMI
CHRISTINE	25	F	W	RRAIIXMI
ALEXANDRA	4	F	CHILD	RRAIIXMI
ALFA	1	M	CHILD	RRAIIXMI

SHIP: GERMANIC

FROM: LIVERPOOL AND QUEENSTOWN
TO: NEW YORK
ARRIVED: 10 AUGUST 1888

PASSENGER	AGE	SEX	OCCUPATION	PV D RI E VL S
KYNSIGARUS, AUGUST	27	M	MNR	RRADAXUSA
TEEFAN, LEA	27	F	W	RRADAXUSA
TOMMY	9	M	CHILD	RRADAXUSA
REBECKA	7	F	CHILD	RRADAXUSA
SAMUEL	5	M	CHILD	RRADAXUSA
PEPPE	3	F	CHILD	RRADAXUSA
KRELS, CHARGE	50	F	SVNT	RRADAXUSA
ROSA	22	F	SVNT	RRADAXUSA
EISNER, M.	13	F	SP	RRADAXUSA
STOPIEN, TAMBIE	25	F	W	RRADAXUSA
MARM.	4	M	CHILD	RRADAXUSA
BLITEY, SARAH	24	F	W	RRADAXUSA
SELIG	3	M	CHILD	RRADAXUSA
STERPHOLBER, LEIEBY	00	M	LABR	RRADAXUSA
BINBER, TOBIA	00	F	SVNT	RRADAXUSA
LIPEHARTY, FISCHE.	35	M	LABR	RRADAXUSA
FIENBURG, B.	20	F	W	RRADAXUSA
GAMBERG, EPHRIAM	21	M	LABR	RRADAXUSA
MASSANA, ROSA	00	F	W	RRADAXUSA
ARM.	8	M	CHILD	RRADAXUSA
U	7	F	CHILD	RRADAXUSA
-EMEL	5	M	CHILD	RRADAXUSA

PASSENGER	AGE	SEX	OCCUPATION	PRIVL	DES
BREHM, MATIEAS	00	M	LABR	RRADAX	USA
TAMIG, JOHANNA	28	F	SVNT	RRADAX	USA
JOHNSON, SUSAN	33	M	LABR	RRADAX	USA
MAREN	19	F	SVNT	RRADAX	USA
BITTLEAG, A.	26	M	LABR	RRADAX	USA
SORGGFIED, JENS	25	M	LABR	RRADAX	USA
TENNING, JOHANNES	18	M	LABR	RRADAX	USA
JAKRE, DOMMNIC	18	M	LABR	RRADAX	USA
JOENSTER, G.	00	M	LABR	RRADAX	USA
POHKA, FRED.	26	M	LABR	RRADAX	USA
HENGA, PHILLIP	26	M	LABR	RRADAX	USA
VERMANKI, A.	29	M	TT	RRADAX	USA
PARKKAISENI, ANNA	30	F	SP	RRADAX	USA
RIVELA, BERTHA	32	F	SP	RRADAX	USA
VAST, JOHAN	27	M	LABR	RRADAX	USA
HJORT, J.	23	M	LABR	RRADAX	USA
JACOB	23	M	LABR	RRADAX	USA
MICHOLADKI, ABRAHAM	34	M	LABR	RRADAX	USA
GERGER, GITTE	24	M	LABR	RRADAX	USA
ZOMOKI, LEWERZI	50	F	W	RRADAX	USA
MORDCHE	17	F	SP	RRADAX	USA
ZOMEKI, MOSES	11	M	CH	RRADAX	USA
CHAROI	10	F	CH	RRADAX	USA
HERSCH	7	M	CHILD	RRADAX	USA
GRUNCHOWORTZ, MOSEHE	35	M	LABR	RRADAX	USA
GOLD, SALOMON	25	M	LABR	RRADAX	USA
GOUCHOWITZ, RIFKI	32	F	W	RRADAX	USA
FROLKE	10	F	CH	RRADAX	USA
NICHE	9	F	CHILD	RRADAX	USA
RACHAEL	7	F	CHILD	RRADAX	USA
CHARGI	6	F	CHILD	RRADAX	USA
DOLI	4	F	CHILD	RRADAX	USA
JOHANNE	1	F	CHILD	RRADAX	USA
ADOLPHSON, THEODORE	28	M	LABR	RRADAX	USA
KURONSKI, ANONIA	22	F	SVNT	RRADAX	USA
GERALSKI, JOSEF	37	M	LABR	RRADAX	USA
RASDWILLE, MICHAEL	17	M	LABR	RRADAX	USA
MOSESOHN, JULIE	28	F	SVNT	RRADAX	USA
GROWITZ, BRURE	50	F	SVNT	RRADAX	USA
PROZE, SIMON	38	M	LABR	RRADAX	USA
HANDLER, ELIAS	30	M	LABR	RRADAX	USA
KRUSCHISKI, SENDER	22	M	LABR	RRADAX	USA
SAPIRO, CHAIM	17	M	LABR	RRADAX	USA
KIRSCHOWITZ, FEWEL	28	M	LABR	RRADAX	USA
ABRAMROITZ, RACHEL	18	F	SP	RRADAX	USA
BLITZ, BRUI	1	F	CHILD	RRADAX	USA
EHRLICH, WOLF	25	M	LABR	RRADAX	USA
ROTH, HERSCH	21	M	LABR	RRADAX	USA
FREDURAMM, ARIM	28	M	FARMER	RRADAX	USA
ROSILIA	24	F	W	RRADAX	USA
MANDOR	3	M	CHILD	RRADAX	USA
HELM.	1	F	CHILD	RRADAX	USA
BRENNER, HIRSCH	24	M	LABR	RRADAX	USA
KOSSURMANN, CHAGENI	16	M	LABR	RRADAX	USA
SHACHUER, ISAAK	14	M	LABR	RRADAX	USA
PANDERBOCK, EMISTINA	24	F	SVNT	RRADAX	USA
MADSL, CICELA	24	F	SVNT	RRADAX	USA
JACABROWITZ, MOSES	24	M	LABR	RRADAX	USA
KOMINSEG, IGNATZ	20	M	LABR	RRADAX	USA
SOMMER, ELKE	36	F	SVNT	RRADAX	USA
MASSAWOR, HERSCH	5	M	CHILD	RRADAX	USA
LEIB	1	F	CHILD	RRADAX	USA
PROSELLER, HENOCH	32	M	LABR	RRADAX	USA
TRIED, COBLIE	15	F	SP	RRADAX	USA
GROSS, TONI	14	F	SP	RRADAX	USA
PERLMAN, JACOB	19	M	LABR	RRADAX	USA
SCHUWAL, SCHACHM	35	M	LABR	RRADAX	USA
GOSSMANN, SUMM	21	M	LABR	RRADAX	USA
LAPIDER, REVE	40	F	W	RRADAX	USA
MARAGETES	9	F	CHILD	RRADAX	USA
LIEBE	4	F	CHILD	RRADAX	USA
BUEL	2	F	CHILD	RRADAX	USA
TRUEV, LEPOLD.	24	M	LABR	RRADAX	USA
TEDESCHI, JOHN.	28	M	LABR	RRADAX	USA
LEGMAN, JOSEF	24	M	LABR	RRADAX	USA
MELCHORISKI, JAMNENA	24	F	SVNT	RRADAX	USA
EISNER, IGNALY	24	M	LABR	RRADAX	USA
LURCHI, ANDREY	31	M	LABR	RRADAX	USA
KASPEROWITZ, MART.	23	M	LABR	RRADAX	USA
RAZIN, IBGIZ	18	M	LABR	RRADAX	USA
SUSENETZ, RUOWU	16	M	LABR	RRADAX	USA
TOKASSKI, BIGLI	17	F	SP	RRADAX	USA
POLONSKI, ESTED	18	F	SP	RRADAX	USA
FRANKOWSKY, MENDEL	36	M	LABR	RRADAX	USA
ONSOW, ANDRES	35	M	FARMER	RRADAX	USA
NILS	9	M	CHILD	RRADAX	USA
LYNING, HILDING	2	M	CHILD	RRADAX	USA
ZOUSKI, CHARKEL	45	M	LABR	RRADAX	USA

SHIP: CITY OF NEW YORK

FROM: LIVERPOOL AND QUEENSTOWN
TO: NEW YORK
ARRIVED: 10 AUGUST 1888

PASSENGER	AGE	SEX	OCCUPATION	PRIVL	DES
MANEK, JOHN	53	M	LABR	FNZZZZ	IL
MARINSON, JANS	21	M	LABR	FNAGUZ	IL
ANDERSON, ERIK	49	M	LABR	FNAGUZ	IL
JOHAN	9	M	CHILD	FNAGUZ	IL
FROCK, HERSEL	25	M	UNKNOWN	FNACBF	IL
CZAEVKOWITZ, GOT.	28	M	UNKNOWN	FNACBF	IL
GUOGRAV, SAEMD	10	M	CH	FNACBF	IL
SHERR, JAS.	22	M	UNKNOWN	FNACBF	IL
HOWELL, HELEN	19	F	SP	FNACBF	NY
WARTH, SUSAN	20	F	SP	FNACBF	MI
JUL.	18	F	SP	FNACBF	MI
OLSEN, GATH.	16	F	SP	FNACBF	MI
KUIMLARNIZ, ELISE	25	F	W	FNACBF	MI
JOS.	00	F	INF	FNACBF	MI
KANDFRIP-, CHANA	25	F	SP	FNACBF	NY
DOTROVSKI, MARY	16	F	SP	FNACBF	NY
BERG, PALAME	28	M	LABR	FNACBF	NY
LISKOW, KATH.	42	M	UNKNOWN	FNACBF	NY
JIHREN	31	F	UNKNOWN	FNACBF	NY
SZAGREN, HENIS	55	F	UNKNOWN	FNACBF	NY
LEOPOLD	60	M	LABR	FNACBF	NY

SHIP: ALLER

FROM: BREMEN AND SOUTHAMPTON
TO: NEW YORK
ARRIVED: 10 AUGUST 1888

PASSENGER	AGE	SEX	OCCUPATION	PRIVL	DES
KRONENBERG, SCHEIM	44	M	FARMER	RRZZZZ	USA
MAGILEWSKY, ISAAK	21	M	FARMER	RRZZZZ	USA
KADILZAK, MICHAL	40	M	FARMER	RRZZZZ	USA
FRIEDMANN, FAUCHEM	18	M	FARMER	RRZZZZ	USA
STRAWEC, MARCUS	24	M	FARMER	RRZZZZ	USA
KLIBANSKI, LOSER	16	M	FARMER	RRZZZZ	USA
SAREFSKI, SANTE	21	M	FARMER	RRZZZZ	USA
KAHN, MICHEL	19	M	FARMER	RRZZZZ	USA
ORLOWSKY, SCHMAJE	27	M	FARMER	RRZZZZ	USA
RATHORSEN, DAVID	24	M	FARMER	RRZZZZ	USA
LIBOWITZ, MOSES	25	M	FARMER	RRZZZZ	USA
BASS, CHEMJE	19	M	FARMER	RRZZZZ	USA
SAVATZKY, NOCHEM	57	M	FARMER	RRZZZZ	USA
SCHNEIDEROWITZ, CHONE	20	M	FARMER	RRZZZZ	USA
RABINOWITZ, MOSES	36	M	FARMER	RRZZZZ	USA
SCHAITKIN, MICHEL	18	M	FARMER	RRZZZZ	USA
GOLUBAK, HERZ	33	M	FARMER	RRZZZZ	USA

PASSENGER	AGE	SEX	OCCUPATION	PRV VIL DES
ABRAMSON, SCHLAMA	20	M	FARMER	RRZZZZUSA
JURKEWITZ, WORZ	23	M	FARMER	RRZZZZUSA
FIUMPOWSKY, JOSEL	30	M	FARMER	RRZZZZUSA
FUCZINSKIS, JURAS	20	M	FARMER	RRZZZZUSA
KAPLAN, CHAJE	40	F	NN	RRZZZZUSA
ABRAHAM	11	M	CH	RRZZZZUSA
FONKAFF	6	M	CHILD	RRZZZZUSA
JUDEL	5	F	CHILD	RRZZZZUSA
CHAINE	3	F	CHILD	RRZZZZUSA
GORSKOW, SORE	34	F	CH	RRZZZZUSA
LIEBVE	7	F	CHILD	RRZZZZUSA
LEIB	6	M	CHILD	RRZZZZUSA
NACHEL	5	F	CHILD	RRZZZZUSA
DAVID	4	M	CHILD	RRZZZZUSA
MARCUS	2	M	CHILD	RRZZZZUSA
JUBE	29	F	CH	RRZZZZUSA
LEIE	7	F	CHILD	RRZZZZUSA
NACHEM	4	F	CHILD	RRZZZZUSA
REBECCA	3	F	CHILD	RRZZZZUSA
MOREC, CHRISTE.	30	F	CH	RRZZZZUSA
EMMA	5	F	CHILD	RRZZZZUSA
RICHARD	2	M	CHILD	RRZZZZUSA
RUINSKY, SIMON	25	M	LABR	RRZZZZUSA
FRIEDE	20	F	W	RRZZZZUSA
MAKIEL, SELIG	55	M	LABR	RRZZZZUSA
SOPHIE	50	F	W	RRZZZZUSA
MEYER	11	M	CH	RRZZZZUSA
IDA	7	F	CHILD	RRZZZZUSA
MINNA	5	F	CHILD	RRZZZZUSA
EHME	3	F	CHILD	RRZZZZUSA
CANTHER, LEIE	23	F	NN	RRZZZZUSA
MARCUS	3	M	CHILD	RRZZZZUSA

SHIP: POLUNESIA

FROM: HAMBURG
TO: NEW YORK
ARRIVED: 10 AUGUST 1888

PASSENGER	AGE	SEX	OCCUPATION	PRV VIL DES
STERNBERG, JENNY	20	F	UNKNOWN	RRZZZZNY
SARA	22	F	UNKNOWN	RRZZZZNY
WASSERMANN, MEIER	25	M	UNKNOWN	RRZZZZNY
HENNI	17	F	SGL	RRZZZZNY
LECKA	22	F	SGL	RRZZZZNY
CHWASCHZEWSKY, ANZE	23	M	LABR	RRZZZZNY
SUNDELOWITZ, NATHAN	28	M	MCHT	RRZZZZNY
ANNA	28	F	W	RRZZZZNY
TOBIAS	.06	M	INFANT	RRZZZZNY
CHOSSID, REBECCA	20	F	UNKNOWN	RRZZZZNY
LEA	.11	F	INFANT	RRZZZZNY
MOSES	23	M	LABR	RRZZZZNY
JETTE	9	F	CHILD	RRZZZZNY
HIRSCH	.11	M	INFANT	RRZZZZNY
TODOJEWSKY, MARTIN	21	M	SMH	RRZZZZNY
KOWSKI, IGNATZ	26	M	LABR	RRZZZZNY
HENRIK	19	M	LABR	RRZZZZNY
ASGED, MOSES	17	M	LABR	RRZZZZNY
ABRAMOCHIUSKI, JETTE	21	F	SGL	RRZZZZNY
FELDSTEIN, ZEMACH	18	M	LABR	RRZZZZNY
ROTTENBERG, MOSES	20	M	LABR	RRZZZZNY
LEWY, JUDEL	16	M	LABR	RRZZZZNY
FRISCH, HENE	33	F	WO	RRZZZZNY
TRADEL	4	F	CHILD	RRZZZZNY
MAZINKIEWITZ, ANNA	20	F	WO	RRZZZZNY
ANTON	.11	M	INFANT	RRZZZZNY
GOLDMANN, SIMCHE	45	F	WO	RRZZZZNY
SARAH	17	F	CH	RRZZZZNY
LEIB	9	M	CHILD	RRZZZZNY
SALOMON	8	M	CHILD	RRZZZZNY
ENOCH	7	M	CHILD	RRZZZZNY
ITZIG	5	M	CHILD	RRZZZZNY
GALIEWICZ, OLESIA	17	F	SGL	RRZZZZNY
GALDSTEIN, ABRAM	60	M	LABR	RRZZZZNY
GOLDE	50	F	W	RRZZZZNY
HELZER, LIEBE	15	F	SGL	RRZZZZNY
SCHNEIDEMANN, SCHIFFRE	36	F	WO	RRZZZZNY
BERTHA	16	F	CH	RRZZZZNY
JOSEF	9	M	CHILD	RRZZZZNY
ISAAC	6	M	CHILD	RRZZZZNY
GOLDSTEIN, GOLDE	30	F	SGL	RRZZZZNY
BIALIG, TASCHE	30	F	WO	RRZZZZNY
MOSES	9	M	CHILD	RRZZZZNY
BLOCH, CHASSE	28	F	WO	RRZZZZNY
LEIB	4	M	CHILD	RRZZZZNY
ABRAM	3	M	CHILD	RRZZZZNY
OSCHER	.11	M	INFANT	RRZZZZNY
RADZINSKI, JOSEF	17	M	LABR	RRZZZZNY
LEVY, SARA	20	F	SGL	RRZZZZNY
EISENBERG, SARA	17	F	SGL	RRZZZZNY
WEISSBERG, LEA	29	F	WO	RRZZZZNY
BLUME	9	F	CHILD	RRZZZZNY
ITZE	8	M	CHILD	RRZZZZNY
DAVID	3	M	CHILD	RRZZZZNY
CHAEW	.11	F	INFANT	RRZZZZNY
ARONSOHN, HESSE	40	F	WO	RRZZZZNY
SAMUEL	8	M	CHILD	RRZZZZNY
MARIE	5	F	CHILD	RRZZZZNY
LEIB	.11	M	INFANT	RRZZZZNY
MAIER, MORDCHE	19	M	UNKNOWN	RRZZZZNY
FALK, MINNA	20	F	SGL	RRZZZZNY
DWORETZKI, MARCUS	23	M	MCHT	RRZZZZNY
NIEPORENT, TEKLA	30	F	WO	RRZZZZNY
GARNIESKY, STANISLAV	27	M	LABR	RRZZZZNY
ROSENBAUM, MEYER	17	M	TLR	RRZZZZNY
MARGOLIES, MUSCHE	16	F	SGL	RRZZZZNY
FREINKEL, HERMANN	15	M	UNKNOWN	RRZZZZNY
SCHLAMM	9	M	CHILD	RRZZZZNY
ALTSCHULER, BARUCH	35	M	UNKNOWN	RRZZZZNY
RABINOWITSCH, RACHEL	18	F	SGL	RRZZZZNY
GOLDSTEIN, JACOB	17	M	WCHMKR	RRZZZZNY
LEWIN, JOSEF	18	M	TLR	RRZZZZNY
KRZOSSA, FRIEDRICH	54	M	FARMER	RRZZZZNY
LOUISE	47	F	W	RRZZZZNY
MARTHA	17	F	CH	RRZZZZNY
MINNA	14	F	CH	RRZZZZNY
GUSTAV	9	M	CHILD	RRZZZZNY
RICHARD	8	M	CHILD	RRZZZZNY
AUGUST	4	M	CHILD	RRZZZZNY
WIERZLA, ABDRAS	37	M	FARMER	RRZZZZNY
MARIE	31	F	W	RRZZZZNY
ALBERT	4	M	CHILD	RRZZZZNY
THERESE	2	F	CHILD	RRZZZZNY
OSSOW	.06	F	INFANT	RRZZZZNY
ADOLF	15	M	CH	RRZZZZNY
GUSEK, GOTLIEB	32	M	FARMER	RRZZZZNY
BERTHA	24	F	W	RRZZZZNY
FRIEDRICH	6	M	CHILD	RRZZZZNY
GUSTAV	4	M	CHILD	RRZZZZNY
ROBERT	3	M	CHILD	RRZZZZNY
LYDIA	.06	F	INFANT	RRZZZZNY
JACOB	24	M	FARMER	RRZZZZNY
MONDSCHEIN, SIMON	34	M	LABR	RRZZZZNY
NAUMOWICZ, JOS.	23	M	LABR	RRZZZZNY
DAVID, ISAAK	23	M	TLR	RRZZZZNY
ELISE	23	F	W	RRZZZZNY
TOBIAS	4	M	CHILD	RRZZZZNY
SARAH	.09	F	INFANT	RRZZZZNY
KASPER, HEINRICH	47	M	FARMER	RRZZZZNY
ALOWITZ, RACHEL	44	F	WO	RRZZZZNY
JETTE	16	F	CH	RRZZZZNY
SCHOENE	9	F	CHILD	RRZZZZNY
JOSET	6	M	CHILD	RRZZZZNY
SIDER, ZIWIC	25	M	LABR	RRZZZZNY
SCHMANN, MORITZ	35	M	MCHT	RRZZZZNY
KRICKPAN, WILH.	23	M	LABR	RRZZZZNY

PASSENGER	AGE	SEX	OCCUPATION	PRIV	VIL	DES
STANK, JOHANN	33	M	MCHT	RR	ZZZZ	NY
WILHELE.	28	F	W	RR	ZZZZ	NY
AMALIE	2	F	CHILD	RR	ZZZZ	NY
ANNA	.09	F	INFANT	RR	ZZZZ	NY
KREGER, CHRISTIAN	23	M	LABR	RR	ZZZZ	NY
HEISER, GOTTLIEB	52	M	LABR	RR	ZZZZ	NY
JAN	56	M	LABR	RR	ZZZZ	NY
HENRIETTE	47	F	W	RR	ZZZZ	NY
GUSTAV	17	M	CH	RR	ZZZZ	NY
LUDWIG	16	M	CH	RR	ZZZZ	NY
WILHELME.	9	F	CHILD	RR	ZZZZ	NY
EMILIE	8	F	CHILD	RR	ZZZZ	NY
ADOLF	7	M	CHILD	RR	ZZZZ	NY
ZISKA, SAMUEL	29	M	LABR	RR	ZZZZ	NY
SACUBAITC, JUERGENS	34	M	LABR	RR	ZZZZ	NY
MACHSON, HIRSCH	23	M	LABR	RR	ZZZZ	NY
WEISSFELD, ANNIE	17	F	SGL	RR	ZZZZ	NY
HERBSTMANN, SAMUEL	29	M	LABR	RR	ZZZZ	NY
SCHORR, LEIB	37	M	LABR	RR	ZZZZ	NY
DANN, MIHAL	21	M	SHMK	RR	ZZZZ	NY
BLOCH, ARON	38	M	TNM	RR	ZZZZ	NY
LOMSKY, FRIMET	30	F	WO	RR	ZZZZ	NY
SARAH	2	F	CHILD	RR	ZZZZ	NY
LEFSCHER	.09	M	INFANT	RR	ZZZZ	NY
FRIEDMANN, CHIENE	23	F	SGL	RR	ZZZZ	NY
SCHIMBERG, EFRAIM	28	M	LABR	RR	ZZZZ	NY
BLOCH, ROSALIE	18	F	SGL	RR	ZZZZ	NY
GROSS, CHRISTIAN	30	M	LABR	RR	ZZZZ	NY
LUDIA	23	F	W	RR	ZZZZ	NY
LEISCHNER, LOUISE	38	F	WO	RR	ZZZZ	NY
MARIE	19	F	CH	RR	ZZZZ	NY
CAROLINE	16	F	CH	RR	ZZZZ	NY
JOHANN	9	M	CHILD	RR	ZZZZ	NY
GOTTHILF	8	M	CHILD	RR	ZZZZ	NY
DANIEL	7	M	CHILD	RR	ZZZZ	NY
LYDIA	4	F	CHILD	RR	ZZZZ	NY
MATHILDE	3	F	CHILD	RR	ZZZZ	NY
JOHANNES	.11	M	INFANT	RR	ZZZZ	NY
KUDRAVO, MARIE	18	F	SGL	RR	ZZZZ	NY
ROGATZ, MARIUS	37	M	LABR	RR	ZZZZ	NY

SHIP: NOORDLAND

FROM: ANTWERP
TO: NEW YORK
ARRIVED: 10 AUGUST 1888

PASSENGER	AGE	SEX	OCCUPATION	PRIV	VIL	DES
LAZINSKI, A.	28	M	LABR	RR	AAHU	NY
DEBOROWSKI, J.	22	M	LABR	RR	AAHU	NY
S.	18	F	W	RR	AAHU	NY
J.	00	F	INF	RR	AAHU	NY

SHIP: SLAVONIA

FROM: SWINEMUNDE
TO: NEW YORK
ARRIVED: 13 AUGUST 1888

PASSENGER	AGE	SEX	OCCUPATION	PRIV	VIL	DES
SZYMANSKA, TWOFILA	27	F	UNKNOWN	RR	ZZZZ	USA
VERSS, MAX	17	M	LABR	RR	AIFV	USA
OBERJAT, ADOLPH	44	M	MLR	RR	ZZZZ	USA
ZWEIGHAFT, RAPHAEL	27	M	LMNFTR	RR	ZZZZ	USA
LEIBMANN, DAVID	18	M	UNKNOWN	RR	ZZZZ	USA
BILKOWSKY, FRANZISCEK	26	M	LABR	RR	ZZZZ	UNK
ILWINSKA, VICTORIA	35	F	WO	RR	ZZZZ	UNK
MARIANNE	11	F	CH	RR	ZZZZ	UNK
LUSIA	9	F	CHILD	RR	ZZZZ	UNK
JOSEPH	7	M	CHILD	RR	ZZZZ	UNK
BAGESKER, BEILE	22	F	WO	RR	AHZP	UNK
JANKOWITZA	3	F	CHILD	RR	AHZP	UNK
STUCZKA, KATATZYNA	38	F	WO	RR	AIIZ	UNK
MARIANNE	11	F	CH	RR	AIIZ	UNK
MAGDALENE	11	F	CH	RR	AIIZ	UNK
JOHANNA	9	F	CHILD	RR	AIIZ	UNK
ALEXANDER	7	M	CHILD	RR	AIIZ	UNK
PA-MBAUM, JOSEPH	28	M	TRDSMN	RR	ZZZZ	UNK
SISKINDEL, WOLFF	24	M	LABR	RR	ZZZZ	UNK
BASCHE	21	F	W	RR	ZZZZ	UNK
LEWIN, ISCHAJE	24	M	LABR	RR	ZZZZ	UNK
WEIDEROWITZ, PALTIEL	18	M	BLKSMH	RR	ZZZZ	UNK
CHAROWITZ, JACOB	20	M	TRDSMN	RR	ADOI	UNK
KOST-WSKA, JOSEPHA	28	F	WO	RR	AIGL	UNK
LEONARDO	10	M	CH	RR	AIGL	UNK
JOSALOWITZ, SCHEWE	20	F	UNKNOWN	RR	AIEP	UNK
MALISKA, JOHN	35	M	LABR	RR	AIEP	UNK
RABINOWITZ, ROPEL	28	M	TLR	RR	ZZZZ	UNK
SCHUMANSKY, LEIB	17	M	BKPR	RR	ZZZZ	UNK
BAGESKER, CHAIJE	2	F	CHILD	RR	ZZZZ	UNK
MALKUS, FREIDE	25	F	WO	RR	AIMD	UNK
CHEIKE	.11	F	INFANT	RR	AIMD	UNK
LIPOWITZ, MENDEL	25	M	TRDSMN	RR	ZZZZ	UNK
WINIK, LIEBE	21	F	W	RR	ZZZZ	UNK
JOSEPH	22	M	TRDSMN	RR	ZZZZ	UNK
BASSISTA, WOLF	20	M	TRDSMN	RR	ZZZZ	UNK
SAWITZKY, NORBERT	25	M	TLR	RR	AHTU	UNK
SCHUKUWITZ, STEPHAN	26	M	CK	RR	AHTU	UNK
MELZER, ABRAHAM	30	M	TLR	RR	AIMD	UNK
BURMANN, HIRSCH	38	M	TLR	RR	AIMD	UNK
ISRAEL	15	M	S	RR	AIMD	UNK
RAKOTZ, HERZ	23	M	WVR	RR	AHTN	UNK
MICHAELS, ABRAHAM	34	M	UNKNOWN	RR	ZZZZ	UNK
RABINSOHN, JUDEL	45	M	UNKNOWN	RR	ZZZZ	UNK
GORDON, NACHUM	18	M	SHMK	RR	AIMD	UNK
SIUVA, ADAM	21	M	LABR	RR	ZZZZ	UNK
SOIWA, JOSEPH	19	M	LABR	RR	ZZZZ	UNK
IGNAZ	10	M	CH	RR	ZZZZ	UNK
KOSLOWSKA, FRANZISKA	.09	F	INFANT	RR	ZZZZ	UNK
REGUTER, BERNHARD	30	M	UNKNOWN	RR	ZZZZ	UNK

SHIP: UMBRIA

FROM: LIVERPOOL
TO: NEW YORK
ARRIVED: 13 AUGUST 1888

PASSENGER	AGE	SEX	OCCUPATION	PRIV	VIL	DES
AMMADOW, ROSA	14	F	SVNT	RR	AFVG	USA
BECKMAN, EMILIE	22	F	SVNT	RR	AFVG	USA
BLOME, MARIA	27	F	MA	RR	AHOK	USA
JOHANNA	3	F	CHILD	RR	AHOK	USA
BEMBEL, AAREN	17	M	LABR	RR	AIEF	USA
BLACHMANN, BEER	35	M	TLR	RR	ZZZZ	USA
CHAJE	35	F	W	RR	ZZZZ	USA
FANNY	15	F	SVNT	RR	ZZZZ	USA
SOCHE	11	M	CH	RR	ZZZZ	USA
HIRSCH	10	M	CH	RR	ZZZZ	USA
RAHEL	9	F	CHILD	RR	ZZZZ	USA
SARA	7	F	CHILD	RR	ZZZZ	USA
ZIPPE	3	F	CHILD	RR	ZZZZ	USA
SALOMON	2	M	CHILD	RR	ZZZZ	USA
FEIMEL	.11	M	INFANT	RR	ZZZZ	USA
CROCKITT, MARY	20	F	SVNT	RR	ADAX	USA
COPLAK, JACOB	40	M	LABR	RR	ADAX	USA
FAROTZKI, ITZKA	19	M	LABR	RR	ADAX	USA
HEIKKA, LISE	16	F	SVNT	RR	ADAX	USA
GORTON, HEIN.	37	F	MA	RR	ZZZZ	USA

PASSENGER	AGE	SEX	OCCUPATION	PRIV	VIL	DES
LIEBE	17	F	SVNT	RR	ZZZZ	USA
GUESCHE	10	F	CH	RR	ZZZZ	USA
CHAIM	7	F	CHILD	RR	ZZZZ	USA
KRASZEWITZ, ABRAM	36	M	LABR	RR	ZZZZ	USA
MOSES	40	M	LABR	RR	ZZZZ	USA
KAELITZ, MURDOCHAI	17	M	LABR	RR	ZZZZ	USA
ESTHER	10	F	CH	RR	ZZZZ	USA
KAHN, CHANE	20	F	MA	RR	ZZZZ	USA
SARA	28	F	MA	RR	ZZZZ	USA
LEA	.10	M	INFANT	RR	ZZZZ	USA
LEPORSKY, NATAN	20	M	LABR	RR	ZZZZ	USA
LAUAILA, BRITA	24	F	SVNT	RR	AINM	USA
LEWIN, PETER	24	M	TLR	RR	AINM	USA
ROSA	20	F	W	RR	AINM	USA
LEPOOSKY, SARAH	20	F	MA	RR	ZZZZ	USA
MINIE	3	F	CHILD	RR	ZZZZ	USA
ABRAM	.11	M	INFANT	RR	ZZZZ	USA
LUBANSKY, GEDULZE	28	M	LABR	RR	ZZZZ	USA
LIEBMAN, ANNIE	20	F	MA	RR	ZZZZ	USA
SARA	.07	F	INFANT	RR	ZZZZ	USA
MOLLER, ANNA	27	F	MA	RR	ZZZZ	USA
MINNIE	4	F	CHILD	RR	ZZZZ	USA
CARL	2	M	CHILD	RR	ZZZZ	USA
ELIS.	.07	F	INFANT	RR	ZZZZ	USA
MARTENSEN, JOH.	22	M	MNR	RR	ZZZZ	USA
MAESCHINK, WILHELM	45	M	TLR	RR	AFWJ	USA
TAUBE	11	M	CH	RR	AFWJ	USA
MINEZINSKY, DAVID	36	M	TLR	RR	AFWJ	USA
MAURRIS, REBECCA	18	F	SVNT	RR	AFWJ	USA
MILLUCK, JOS.	45	M	LABR	RR	AFWJ	USA
NANTI, FERD.	23	M	LABR	RR	AFWJ	USA
PAIRIPPE, HENDRIK	18	M	LABR	RR	AFWJ	USA
PYAKINEN, SOFIA	30	F	SVNT	RR	AFWJ	USA
PAINZIN, ADOLF	36	M	LABR	RR	AFWJ	USA
RUTKOWSKY, ISAAC	40	M	LABR	RR	AFWJ	USA
FUMMEL	13	F	SVNT	RR	AFWJ	USA
SUTTMAN, BRITA	31	F	SVNT	RR	AFWJ	USA
SACK, ESTHER	18	F	MA	RR	AFWJ	USA
GEDALZE	.11	M	INFANT	RR	AFWJ	USA
SUERMA, MARCIA	28	M	LABR	RR	AFWJ	USA
SPIELMAN, MOSES	17	M	JWLR	RR	AFWJ	USA
SAFER, RACHMIEL	26	M	JWLR	RR	AFWJ	USA
SCHIFAL	22	F	W	RR	AFWJ	USA
RINE	.10	F	INFANT	RR	AFWJ	USA
HANNIEN, BENJAMIN	11	M	CH	RR	AFWJ	USA
SALAMERZYKI, SIMON	34	M	MSN	RR	AAKH	USA
SCHIFF, HIRSCH	20	M	LABR	RR	AIEF	USA
RAHEL	22	M	LABR	RR	AIEF	USA
TUKEINTZ, ISAAC	24	M	SHMK	RR	ZZZZ	USA
TOMZIK, JAN	24	M	LABR	RR	ZZZZ	USA
MARIE	19	F	W	RR	ZZZZ	USA
TANNINBAUM, FUMMEL	25	F	MA	RR	ZZZZ	USA
BEILE	00	F	MA	RR	ZZZZ	USA
ESTHER	4	F	CHILD	RR	ZZZZ	USA
AMDURSKY, ABRAM	.04	M	INFANT	RR	ZZZZ	USA
TIPKOV, LISI	32	M	LABR	RR	AIEF	USA
ZUNE, JACOB	40	M	LABR	RR	AIEF	USA

SHIP: EMS

FROM: BREMEN AND SOUTHAMPTON
TO: NEW YORK
ARRIVED: 13 AUGUST 1888

PASSENGER	AGE	SEX	OCCUPATION	PRIV	VIL	DES
BRUSTI, ANDERS	20	M	LABR	FN	ZZZZ	NY
HANNI, MARIA	26	F	UNKNOWN	FN	ZZZZ	NY
LEITINEN, MARIE	18	F	UNKNOWN	FN	ZZZZ	NY
BROUD, JAWEL	22	F	UNKNOWN	FN	AHOO	NY
MERKER, ADOLPH	16	M	CL	FN	AHOO	NY
SZACHNOWICZ, MENNCHE	55	M	LABR	FN	AHOO	NY
SZCZALKE, ESTER	30	F	W	FN	AHOO	NY
SCHEINE	6	M	CHILD	FN	AHOO	NY
ISAAK	4	M	CHILD	FN	AHOO	NY
HERSCH	2	M	CHILD	FN	AHOO	NY
REISER, TEYE	23	F	W	FN	AHOO	NY
CHANE	.09	F	INFANT	FN	AHOO	NY
LEWYN, SARA	20	F	UNKNOWN	FN	AHOO	NY
MORIL, SELMA	48	M	LABR	FN	AHOO	UNK
NAUELIS, AUGUST	45	M	LABR	FN	AHOO	UNK
SLOVENA, MICUS	35	M	LABR	FN	AHOO	UNK
CHAJET, HIRSCH	52	M	LABR	FN	AHOO	UNK
KATZ, SAMUEL	30	M	LABR	FN	AHOO	NY
FEIGE	17	F	UNKNOWN	FN	AHOO	NY
SCHKARER, SORCH	50	M	LABR	FN	AHOO	NY
ARMANOWSKY, ABRAHAM	26	M	LABR	FN	AHOO	NY
KATZWITZKY, EFRAIM	18	M	LABR	FN	AHOO	NY
GORDON, JACOB	20	M	LABR	FN	AHOO	NY
RACHEL	18	F	W	FN	AHOO	NY
WEINRICH, EVA	30	F	W	FN	AHQD	NY
LEON	3	M	CHILD	FN	AHQD	NY
ANNA	19	F	UNKNOWN	FN	AHQD	NY
LISA	19	F	UNKNOWN	FN	AHQD	NY
PRAG, JOSSEL	20	M	JNR	FN	AHQD	NY
KARP, JACOB	22	M	LABR	RR	ZZZZ	NY
ORLIN, FREIDE	28	F	W	RR	ZZZZ	NY
LIBE	2	F	CHILD	RR	ZZZZ	NY
LISSE	.09	F	INFANT	RR	ZZZZ	NY

SHIP: ANCHORIA

FROM: GLASGOW AND MOVILLE
TO: NEW YORK
ARRIVED: 13 AUGUST 1888

PASSENGER	AGE	SEX	OCCUPATION	PRIV	VIL	DES
LIPERNER, DIVERE	40	F	UNKNOWN	RR	ZZZZ	USA
SELDE	18	F	UNKNOWN	RR	ZZZZ	USA
SORE	7	F	CHILD	RR	ZZZZ	USA
CHAINE	3	M	CHILD	RR	ZZZZ	USA
FRUME	1	F	CHILD	RR	ZZZZ	USA
CHOLMINSKA, JOSEFA	24	F	UNKNOWN	RR	ZZZZ	USA
ANDRE	4	M	CHILD	RR	ZZZZ	USA
JOAEF	.10	M	INFANT	RR	ZZZZ	USA
MICHAL	.01	M	INFANT	RR	ZZZZ	USA
KRAMER, DAVID	48	M	PDLR	RR	ZZZZ	USA
ROSA	19	F	UNKNOWN	RR	ZZZZ	USA
PAULINE	17	F	UNKNOWN	RR	ZZZZ	USA
ZAFF, MACH.ELKE	23	F	UNKNOWN	RR	ZZZZ	USA
PERL	2	F	CHILD	RR	ZZZZ	USA
BOREL	1	F	CHILD	RR	ZZZZ	USA
KAZINCEW, JOEL.	50	M	TLR	RR	ZZZZ	USA
SCHMUL	10	M	CH	RR	ZZZZ	USA
PRIESTER, BORUCH	34	M	SMH	RR	ZZZZ	USA
MENDEL	15	M	SMH	RR	ZZZZ	USA
LEWANOWSKY, ARIEL	15	M	TLR	RR	ZZZZ	USA
JAZIBE	12	F	CH	RR	ZZZZ	USA
NITSCHINN, CHAIM	40	M	TLR	RR	ZZZZ	USA
SCHMUL	18	M	TLR	RR	ZZZZ	USA
LINETZKY, EMANUL	22	M	SMH	RR	ZZZZ	USA
ROSALIE	19	F	W	RR	ZZZZ	USA
JAFFE, ABR.LAU.	18	M	TLR	RR	ZZZZ	USA
MEYER	11	M	TLR	RR	ZZZZ	USA
GOLDENBERG, IDEL	22	M	TLR	RR	ZZZZ	USA
BARKOW, MORITZ	28	M	LABR	RR	ZZZZ	USA
BERNSTEIN, LEOPOLD	24	M	BCHR	RR	ZZZZ	USA
SCHNEIDER, SCHOLM	32	M	SHMK	RR	ZZZZ	USA
PORTNIJ, NISSEN	40	M	TLR	RR	ZZZZ	USA
KANTAROWIEZ, BORUCH	16	M	TLR	RR	ZZZZ	USA
PECKEL, ABRAM	36	M	TLR	RR	ZZZZ	USA
LIPSCHITZ, MARITZ	19	M	UNKNOWN	RR	ZZZZ	USA
KARINCEW, MOSCHE	18	M	TLR	RR	ZZZZ	USA

PASSENGER	AGE	SEX	OCCUPATION	PRV VIL DES
SCHWINCKY, BORUCH	17	M	TLR	RRZZZZUSA
KRENNER, JAKOB	28	M	UNKNOWN	RRZZZZUSA
DIAMANT, MORDCHE	28	M	UNKNOWN	RRZZZZUSA
BRAVERMAN, SALOMON	20	M	UNKNOWN	RRZZZZUSA
LAPIDUS, ITZKA	40	M	UNKNOWN	RRZZZZUSA
HANDEL, KIVE	20	M	UNKNOWN	RRZZZZUSA
KRISTEL, PESCHE	16	F	UNKNOWN	RRZZZZUSA
FROIM	11	F	CH	RRZZZZUSA
LUSMAN, IDA	16	F	UNKNOWN	RRZZZZUSA
BERREL, JEATE	18	F	UNKNOWN	RRZZZZUSA
BROSSMAN, J.	21	F	UNKNOWN	RRZZZZUSA
LIEW, CHAE	21	F	UNKNOWN	RRZZZZUSA
KATZ, PESCHE	50	M	MA	RRZZZZUSA
MAREZAK, CH.	43	F	W	PLZZZZUSA
RIENK	11	F	CH	PLZZZZUSA
FUGE	10	F	CH	PLZZZZUSA
FOERD	7	M	CHILD	PLZZZZUSA
CHANE	2	M	CHILD	PLZZZZUSA
SENSAEZ, SAMEL	36	M	UNKNOWN	PLZZZZUSA
AMALIE	26	F	W	PLZZZZUSA
LEMHEN	4	F	CHILD	PLZZZZUSA
JONA	1	F	CHILD	PLZZZZUSA
LEWIN, SELIG	27	M	LABR	PLZZZZUSA
WIEF, LEIBNUH	22	M	UNKNOWN	PLZZZZUSA
LIBIZ, ESTER	19	F	HP	PLZZZZUSA
BURGAN, FEIGE	33	F	UNKNOWN	PLACBRUSA
ROSA	3	F	CHILD	PLACBRUSA
RACHEL	1	F	CHILD	PLACBRUSA

SHIP: ARIZONA

FROM: LIVERPOOL AND QUEENSTOWN
TO: NEW YORK
ARRIVED: 13 AUGUST 1888

PASSENGER	AGE	SEX	OCCUPATION	PRV VIL DES
HENDRIKEN, HERMAN	33	M	ART	FNZZZZUSA
JOHN	18	M	LABR	FNZZZZUSA
KRON, CHANE	24	F	SP	FNACBFUSA
STEIN, NECHEM	21	M	LABR	FNACBFUSA
ZUSTMAN, ZUSKIND	10	M	CH	FNACBFUSA
KREINEL	9	F	CHILD	FNACBFUSA
PERTMAN, HENE	27	F	W	FNACBFUSA
MARIAM	7	F	CHILD	FNACBFUSA
CHIMKE	3	F	CHILD	FNACBFUSA
EPSTEIN, JOSEF	7	M	CHILD	FNACBFUSA
CIPE	10	F	CH	FNACBFUSA
RAIGROTZKI, SALMEN	16	M	LABR	FNACBFUSA
WILK, AEVADIE	34	F	W	FNACBFUSA
ALPERAVITZ, FRIEME	36	F	W	FNACBFUSA
CHAIE	11	F	CH	FNACBFUSA
BEILE	10	F	CH	FNACBFUSA
SCHADINE	7	F	CHILD	FNACBFUSA
CHAIM	3	F	CHILD	FNACBFUSA
GREENBERG, MARIA	15	F	SP	FNACBFUSA
GRUDZINSKY, GRITTYE	20	F	SP	FNACBFUSA
HORWITZ, SHIMON	17	M	LABR	FNACBFUSA
LAPCHIM, JUDEL	17	M	LABR	FNACBFUSA
SCHLOME, HERSCH	43	M	PRNTR	FNACBFUSA
SCHAN, HODES	15	F	SP	FNACBFUSA
ABRAMOWITZ, ARON	32	M	SMH	FNACBFUSA
ALPERT, SIMON	13	M	LABR	FNACBFUSA
GLEICHENHAUS, MASCHE	18	F	SP	FNACBFUSA
HINDE	16	F	SP	FNACBFUSA
GILLES, SCHLOM	50	M	CPTR	FNACBFUSA
GOLDSTEIN, SARAH	24	F	W	FNACBFUSA
FEIGE	4	F	CHILD	FNACBFUSA
ARON	3	M	CHILD	FNACBFUSA
OFFCHINSKY, ETTKY	18	F	SP	FNACBFUSA
FISCHER, JACOB	56	M	ART	FNACBFUSA
RAHEL	44	F	W	FNACBFUSA
ISAAC	7	M	CHILD	FNACBFUSA
HERSCH	6	M	CHILD	FNACBFUSA
SCHELIN, CARL	22	M	LABR	FNAGUZUSA
HAGZBLAM, ERIK	40	M	ART	FNAGUZUSA
CINACHOWITZ, SCHIE	17	M	LABR	FNACBFUSA
BINNIN, MINNA	23	F	SP	FNACBFUSA
MIKALSKI, TAUBE	20	F	SP	FNACBFUSA
GRINWALD, SARA	11	F	CH	FNACBFUSA
PERLMAN, JACOB	.10	M	INFANT	FNACBFUSA
BROCHES, RACHEL	32	F	W	FNACBFUSA
CHANE	30	F	SP	FNACBFUSA
CIFRE	11	F	CH	FNACBFUSA
ARON	7	M	CHILD	FNACBFUSA
OSCHER	4	M	CHILD	FNACBFUSA
DAVID	3	M	CHILD	FNACBFUSA
REIVE	.08	F	INFANT	FNACBFUSA
ALPEROWITZ, KOPEL	.04	M	INFANT	FNACBFUSA
LEFKOWICZ, CLARA	16	F	SP	FNACBFUSA
ALPERN, PATTEIL	7	M	CHILD	FNACBFUSA
GRIMBERG, MOSES	16	M	LABR	FNACBFUSA
KOMGSBERGER, ISAAC	40	M	SMH	FNACBFUSA
ALEXANDROWICZ, ARON	49	M	SMH	FNACBFUSA
KALETZKY, RAHEL	20	F	SP	FNACBFUSA
SUKOWSKY, FEIGE	44	F	W	FNACBFUSA
ESTER	11	F	CH	FNACBFUSA
MOSES	7	M	CHILD	FNACBFUSA
JACOB	6	M	CHILD	FNACBFUSA
BEREL	3	F	CHILD	FNACBFUSA
MARIA	.09	F	INFANT	FNACBFUSA
FINKEL, SAMUEL	50	M	FARMER	FNACBFUSA
JUDES	50	F	W	FNACBFUSA
ABRAHAM	20	M	FARMER	FNACBFUSA
TAUBE	22	F	SP	FNACBFUSA
GOLDSTEIN, ARON	24	M	PRNTR	FNACBFUSA
SARAH	20	F	W	FNACBFUSA
KOLLER, RIWSKE	20	F	SP	FNACBFUSA

SHIP: AMERICA

FROM: BREMEN
TO: BALTIMORE
ARRIVED: 14 AUGUST 1888

PASSENGER	AGE	SEX	OCCUPATION	PRV VIL DES
BITE, AGATHE	20	F	SVNT	RRZZZZMD
OMILANOWSKI, CASIMIR	28	M	LABR	RRZZZZMD
DIETZ, JANO	14	F	UNKNOWN	RRZZZZMD
JANOT, RASAH	18	M	FARMER	RRZZZZMD
FEIGE	15	F	UNKNOWN	RRZZZZMD
BESLECHEMN, TAUBE	18	F	UNKNOWN	RRZZZZMD
ZORDEIWSKY, KENACH	14	M	UNKNOWN	RRZZZZMD
ROSENFELD, BEILE	25	F	UNKNOWN	RRZZZZMD
LISA	00	F	UNKNOWN	RRZZZZMD
DAVID	3	M	CHILD	RRZZZZMD
BANK, AARON	20	M	FARMER	RRZZZZMD
WONDOLAWS, FRANZ	18	M	FARMER	RRZZZZMD
BRUNGARDT, JOHANN	53	M	LABR	RRZZZZMD
CATHARINA	53	F	UNKNOWN	RRZZZZMD
ANTON	15	M	UNKNOWN	RRZZZZMD
MICHAEL	9	M	CHILD	RRZZZZMD
CATHARINA	68	F	UNKNOWN	RRZZZZMD
ZIMANTIS, SIMON	23	M	FARMER	RRZZZZMD
AMALIE	14	F	UNKNOWN	RRZZZZMD
FROMPINSKI, JOHANN	11	M	UNKNOWN	RRZZZZMD
ZEMANTIS, MARIANNA	.06	F	INFANT	RRZZZZMD
ISAJTYS, EVAS	24	M	FARMER	RRZZZZMD
HEINRICH, AMALIA	18	F	SVNT	RRZZZZMD
WIRBICKI, ANTONI	24	F	SVNT	RRZZZZMD
PANKAFSKI, JAN	14	M	UNKNOWN	RRZZZZMN
FRANZ	11	M	CH	RRZZZZMN
WALTSCHAU, NATEL	38	M	MCHT	RRZZZZMD

PASSENGER	AGE	SEX	OCCUPATION	PV RIVL	D E S
KLEWANSKI, SALOMON	50	M	MCHT	RRZZZZ	MD
CHARLOTTE	50	F	UNKNOWN	RRZZZZ	MD
MANOSCHEWITZ, PAULINE	19	F	SVNT	RRZZZZ	MD
WINKELMANN, CHAJKE	25	F	UNKNOWN	RRZZZZ	MD
SCHMUL	5	M	CHILD	RRZZZZ	MD
RIFKE	7	F	CHILD	RRZZZZ	MD
ESTHER	6	F	CHILD	RRZZZZ	MD
MAREUS	.11	M	INFANT	RRZZZZ	MD
ELISE	.03	F	INFANT	RRZZZZ	MD
KAZIMERKIEWICZ, ANTON	29	M	FARMER	RRZZZZ	AR
ZIMMERMANN, JULIANNA	17	F	SVNT	RRZZZZ	AR
LEWIKE, MARIE	48	F	UNKNOWN	RRZZZZ	MD
JOSEFA	38	F	UNKNOWN	RRZZZZ	MD
LAURA	17	F	UNKNOWN	RRZZZZ	MD
STEFAN	10	M	CH	RRZZZZ	MD
STEFANIE	6	F	CHILD	RRZZZZ	MD
VALERIA	3	F	CHILD	RRZZZZ	MD
PONTOWSKA, ANTONIA	14	F	UNKNOWN	RRZZZZ	BAL
BIERMANN, CIENNA	30	F	UNKNOWN	RRZZZZ	MD
SIMON	12	M	CH	RRZZZZ	MD
ISRAEL	9	M	CHILD	RRZZZZ	MD
SARAH	7	F	CHILD	RRZZZZ	MD
ARON	5	M	CHILD	RRZZZZ	MD
HERMANN	2	M	CHILD	RRZZZZ	MD
LAMP, DWORE	30	F	UNKNOWN	RRZZZZ	OH
BLUME	12	F	CH	RRZZZZ	OH
KLATE	11	F	CH	RRZZZZ	OH
RACHEL	6	F	CHILD	RRZZZZ	OH
ARON	3	M	CHILD	RRZZZZ	OH
BOGNATZ, JITZCHAK	18	M	FARMER	RRZZZZ	IL
SCHULTZ, BAER	15	M	UNKNOWN	RRZZZZ	IL
FALMUND, BAER	15	M	UNKNOWN	RRZZZZ	IL
GOLAMBIK, BLUME	30	F	UNKNOWN	RRZZZZ	OH
LIEBE	13	F	UNKNOWN	RRZZZZ	OH
SCHAJE	10	F	UNKNOWN	RRZZZZ	OH
BAROCH	8	F	CHILD	RRZZZZ	OH
SCHARPE	5	F	CHILD	RRZZZZ	OH
ZEINACH	4	M	CHILD	RRZZZZ	OH
MOLATZNIK, ETZEK	19	M	MCHT	RRZZZZ	OH
ADES, MARKS	14	M	UNKNOWN	RRZZZZ	OH
SCHULMANN, MIRE	20	F	UNKNOWN	RRZZZZ	OH
KAPLAN, RALE	20	F	UNKNOWN	RRZZZZ	OH
HAAS, ETTE	30	F	UNKNOWN	RRZZZZ	MD
MALKE	8	F	CHILD	RRZZZZ	MD
SARAH	6	F	CHILD	RRZZZZ	MD
JACOB	.10	M	INFANT	RRZZZZ	MD
PELMISKY, ROSE	30	F	UNKNOWN	RRZZZZ	MD
ISAAC	4	M	CHILD	RRZZZZ	MD
MARCUS	2	M	CHILD	RRZZZZ	MD
FAIN	.06	F	INFANT	RRZZZZ	MD
FUCKSMANN, CHAIEN	55	M	PDLR	RRZZZZ	MD
JOCHE	24	F	UNKNOWN	RRZZZZ	MD
MOSES	5	M	CHILD	RRZZZZ	MD
FISCHEL	3	M	CHILD	RRZZZZ	MD
BERLIA, JOSEL	31	M	MCHT	RRZZZZ	MD
WAGENER, ANTON	37	M	LABR	RRZZZZ	MN
CERNITRZ, MOSES	20	M	MCHT	RRZZZZ	MD
FELDBAUM, ISRAEL	28	M	MCHT	RRZZZZ	MD
WOLINER, ISRAEL	23	M	MCHT	RRZZZZ	MD
WOSTERMANN, ISAAK	21	M	MCHT	RRZZZZ	MD
MEISEROWITZ, JETTE	18	F	UNKNOWN	RRZZZZ	MD
WINBVLEWSKY, VICTOR	23	M	MCHT	RRZZZZ	MD
ARNT, AUGUST	23	M	MCHT	RRZZZZ	MI
PETT, ANDREAS	24	M	MCHT	RRZZZZ	MI
KAMINSKA, JOSEFA	21	F	UNKNOWN	RRZZZZ	PA
CONSTANTIA	17	F	UNKNOWN	RRZZZZ	PA
GRASCHKEWITZ, FRANZ	30	M	LABR	RRZZZZ	OH
HURWITZ, DAVID	52	M	FARMER	RRZZZZ	OH
NORWILL, PETER	29	M	TLR	RRZZZZ	OH
MARIE	28	F	UNKNOWN	RRZZZZ	OH
EMILIE	7	F	CHILD	RRZZZZ	OH
WAZLAWA	3	F	CHILD	RRZZZZ	OH
MUSIKANSKY, ANNA	26	F	UNKNOWN	RRZZZZ	OH
ETTE	.11	F	INFANT	RRZZZZ	OH
BAR, NECHANIE	30	F	UNKNOWN	RRZZZZ	OH
REBECCA	6	F	CHILD	RRZZZZ	OH
FEIGE	4	F	CHILD	RRZZZZ	OH
ADES, DORA	20	F	UNKNOWN	RRZZZZ	OH
LEISER	11	M	CH	RRZZZZ	OH
MOSES	8	M	CHILD	RRZZZZ	OH
GREEN, EMMA	22	F	UNKNOWN	RRZZZZ	OH
SCHAPIRO, TAUBE	33	F	UNKNOWN	RRZZZZ	MD
HIRSCH	11	M	CH	RRZZZZ	MD
MAX	9	M	CHILD	RRZZZZ	MD
MORITZ	7	M	CHILD	RRZZZZ	MD
SALY	5	F	CHILD	RRZZZZ	MD
SCHEINE	18	F	UNKNOWN	RRZZZZ	MD
LEISER, ITZIG	15	M	UNKNOWN	RRZZZZ	MD
FRIEDMANN, SCHMUL	15	M	UNKNOWN	RRZZZZ	MD
GODLENIK, JACOB	20	M	LABR	RRZZZZ	MD
FUKSMANN, NISEN	40	M	LABR	RRZZZZ	MD
KAPLAN, LEISER	14	M	LABR	RRZZZZ	MD
BASAWSKY, JAKE	17	F	UNKNOWN	RRZZZZ	MD
LEWINSOHN, JUDEL	25	M	MCHT	RRZZZZ	MD
SWEDLAW, ANNA	20	F	UNKNOWN	RRZZZZ	MD
ALF, BENJAMIN	19	M	SHMK	RRZZZZ	VA
EWERT, DAVID	18	M	FARMER	RRZZZZ	VA
MALINSKA, MARIANNA	27	F	UNKNOWN	RRZZZZ	MD
JOSEF	3	M	CHILD	RRZZZZ	MD
JULIANNA	2	F	CHILD	RRZZZZ	MD
SOPHIE	.11	F	INFANT	RRZZZZ	MD
LEVIN, ANNE	18	F	UNKNOWN	RRZZZZ	OH
LEWIN, IDA	10	F	CH	RRZZZZ	OH
HARMOSER, JOSEF	22	M	MCHT	RRZZZZ	OH
BRATI, JONAS	22	M	MCHT	RRZZZZ	OH
WELOMISCHKE, FRANZ	24	M	FARMER	RRZZZZ	OH

SHIP: KANSAS

FROM: LIVERPOOL
TO: BOSTON
ARRIVED: 15 AUGUST 1888

PASSENGER	AGE	SEX	OCCUPATION	PV RIVL	D E S
BURDIN, HIRSCH	38	M	LABR	RRZZZZ	NY
SCHEWE	36	F	W	RRZZZZ	NY
JOSEPH	.11	M	INFANT	RRZZZZ	NY
DWORE	3	F	CHILD	RRZZZZ	NY
CIBULSKY, MOSES	48	M	LABR	RRZZZZ	BO
CHANE	46	F	W	RRZZZZ	BO
SOLOMON	11	M	CH	RRZZZZ	BO
PEWEL	10	M	CH	RRZZZZ	BO
ISAAC	8	M	CHILD	RRZZZZ	BO
SCHEIM	4	M	CHILD	RRZZZZ	BO
OLEONISKY, JACOB	23	M	LABR	RRZZZZ	BO
MARY	23	F	W	RRZZZZ	BO
MORITZ	3	M	CHILD	RRZZZZ	BO
JARCH, MARK	22	M	ATSN	RRZZZZ	NY
RACFIL	20	F	W	RRZZZZ	NY
JPHILLIP	.09	M	INFANT	RRZZZZ	NY
HERR, LOIUS	31	M	LABR	RRZZZZ	UNK
SARAH	22	F	W	RRZZZZ	UNK
ARAN	9	M	CHILD	RRZZZZ	UNK
JACOB	3	M	CHILD	RRZZZZ	UNK
ABRAMOWITZ, BER	47	M	LABR	PLZZZZ	NY
LIEBE	45	F	W	PLZZZZ	NY
ESTHER	20	F	SP	PLZZZZ	NY
GITTLEL	18	M	LABR	PLZZZZ	NY
LEIB	11	M	CH	PLZZZZ	NY
GOLDMAN, MARIA	11	F	CH	RRZZZZ	NY
CHATZEK	7	M	CHILD	RRZZZZ	NY
WLOSCAUSKY, DOBI	40	F	W	RRZZZZ	BO
IDA	9	F	CHILD	RRZZZZ	BO
NACHMAN	7	M	CHILD	RRZZZZ	BO
MALKO	3	M	CHILD	RRZZZZ	BO
IENSTER, DWORE	18	F	SP	RRZZZZ	NY

PASSENGER	AGE	SEX	OCCUPATION	PRV VIL DES
SILBERSCHLAG, BRUIN	14	F	SP	RRZZZZNY
GREM, SARAH	14	F	SP	RRZZZZNY
KOHNO, ESTHER	24	F	SP	RRZZZZBO
LEISEROWITZ, RACHEL	38	F	W	RRZZZZBO
BASCHE	11	M	CH	RRZZZZBO
BLUME	10	M	CH	RRZZZZBO
WAMKOWITZ, FEIGE	33	F	W	RRZZZZBO
JACOB	14	M	CH	RRZZZZBO
CHAM	10	F	CH	RRZZZZBO
DAVID	9	M	CHILD	RRZZZZBO
MIRA	3	F	CHILD	RRZZZZBO
DWORA	.07	F	INFANT	RRZZZZBO
KAPIHOWITZ, FEIGE	24	F	SP	RRZZZZBO
WELLER, CIDI	48	F	W	RRZZZZBO
SOLOMON	11	M	CH	RRZZZZBO
ODO	9	M	CHILD	RRZZZZBO
DULIDIG, ANTONIA	21	F	W	PLZZZZBO
GOLDON, SARAH	30	F	W	RRZZZZBO
ANNA	9	F	CHILD	RRZZZZBO
ABRAHAM	7	M	CHILD	RRZZZZBO
ISIDOR	6	M	CHILD	RRZZZZBO
ISAAC	5	M	CHILD	RRZZZZBO
SIMON	3	M	CHILD	RRZZZZBO
DEILEDY, ANTONINA	2	F	CHILD	RRZZZZBO
SCHMUETOWITZ, SARAH	50	F	HSKPR	RRZZZZNY
CLARA	18	F	SP	RRZZZZNY
JEWEROWITZ, HETTE	18	F	W	RRZZZZBO
ABEL	1	M	CHILD	RRZZZZBO
CHAS.	24	M	CPTR	RRZZZZBO
MERE	3	M	CHILD	RRZZZZBO
SCH.	.06	M	INFANT	RRZZZZBO
SCHALONIS, MINNA	20	F	SP	RRZZZZBO
JANWISKY, MORRIS	26	M	LABR	RRZZZZNY
LONIS, DEREA	25	M	LABR	RRZZZZNY
BOOKDANER, A.	18	M	LABR	PLZZZZNY
FRIEDMAN, SCH.	18	M	LABR	RRZZZZUNK
GODUR, MOS.	42	M	LABR	RRZZZZUNK
GLASS, LEISER	29	M	LABR	RRZZZZUNK
FUHMAN, MICH.	29	M	LABR	RRZZZZNY
MULFER, MEYER	21	M	LABR	RRZZZZNY
BEHR, SONE	18	M	LABR	RRZZZZNY
GLUCKSTEIN, NACH.	18	M	LABR	RRZZZZNY
BLOCH, I.	22	M	LABR	RRZZZZNY
PRUGININ, WOLF	30	M	LABR	RRZZZZNY
POLATZKI, SAM.	26	M	LABR	RRZZZZNY
MOSES	14	M	LABR	RRZZZZNY
LANGER, JOS.	42	M	LABR	RRZZZZBO
LAPOSKY, MICH.	33	M	LABR	RRZZZZBO
BURAL, BEREL	32	M	LABR	RRZZZZBO
MESINGER, JACOB	25	M	LABR	RRZZZZBO
DORIN, CH.	33	M	LABR	RRZZZZBO
WALLACK, JAN	33	M	LABR	RRZZZZBO
HERMAN, MOS.	31	M	LABR	RRZZZZBO
SUCHO, CH.	24	M	LABR	RRZZZZBO
WIENCH, JOHAH	27	M	LABR	RRZZZZBO
ELIASCHEWITZ, JACOB	16	M	LABR	RRZZZZBO
LEZINSKI, ARD.	20	M	LABR	RRZZZZBO
WASSCHEWSKY, MICH.	30	M	LABR	RRZZZZBO
SCHIRDLIN, MENDEL	23	M	LABR	RRZZZZBO
WAGTOWITZ, JOS.	33	M	LABR	PLZZZZBO
STURM, ALBERT	25	M	LABR	RRZZZZBO
SIEBERG, JACOB	35	M	LABR	RRZZZZBO
SCHOFL, NACHMAN	34	M	LABR	RRZZZZNY
VICTOROWITZ, JACOB	25	M	LABR	RRZZZZMA
CRUSCHTER, ISRAEL	22	M	LABR	RRZZZZMA
LUBERMAN, JONES	29	M	LABR	RRZZZZNY
WERKLEICH, BEIL	24	M	LABR	RRZZZZNY
SHEIUMAN, B.	26	M	LABR	RRZZZZNY
SELBERMAN, F.	28	M	LABR	RRZZZZNY
WEIROKUR, S.	16	M	LABR	RRZZZZNY
SCHWARZ, LEZER	30	M	LABR	RRZZZZNY
STEIN, SAM.	25	M	LABR	RRZZZZNY
BROTMAN, MICHAEL	34	M	LABR	PLZZZZNY
HOFFMAN, JACOB	18	M	LABR	RRZZZZBO
BRENER, CHAYINN	33	M	LABR	RRZZZZBO

PASSENGER	AGE	SEX	OCCUPATION	PRV VIL DES
FORK, RUBIN	22	M	LABR	RRZZZZBO
ESTHER	10	M	SCH	RRZZZZBO
FRAILIK, BENZEL	34	M	LABR	RRZZZZBO
SLEPIAN, JACOB	24	M	LABR	RRZZZZBO
CALDER, MARKS	21	M	LABR	RRZZZZBO
SLONISKY, ISAK	40	M	LABR	PLZZZZBO
YAKUBOWSKY, LEIB	30	M	LABR	RRZZZZBO
MULLER, DIETRICH	21	M	LABR	RRZZZZMO
SERIKUTIS, JOSEPH	32	M	LABR	RRZZZZPHI
LIBSCHMITZ, L.	30	M	LABR	RRZZZZNY
PERSER, JACOB	29	M	LABR	RRZZZZNY
KAVALISKY, PETRO	30	M	LABR	PLZZZZPHI
WILDNER, FRANK	48	M	LABR	RRZZZZNY

SHIP: SCHIEDAM

FROM: AMSTERDAM
TO: NEW YORK
ARRIVED: 15 AUGUST 1888

PASSENGER	AGE	SEX	OCCUPATION	PRV VIL DES
BUHRMANN, MOSES	29	M	LABR	RRZZZZUSA
KOSMOSHUY, ALEXANDER	21	M	LABR	RRZZZZUSA
KAWALEWSHY, JOSEF	40	M	LABR	RRZZZZUSA
ZISALIS, MATH.	30	M	LABR	RRZZZZUSA
KROC, MATH.	22	M	LABR	RRZZZZUSA
SPEDER, AUGUST	24	M	LABR	RRZZZZUSA
ASEWITZ, MATH.	40	M	LABR	RRZZZZUSA
KATZ, LIBE	40	F	UNKNOWN	RRZZZZUSA
WILANSKY, ISRAEL	22	M	LABR	RRZZZZUSA
GILDBERG, SCHMUL	18	M	LABR	RRZZZZUSA
KATZ, SORECH	22	M	LABR	RRZZZZUSA
GRIEDFELD, ISRAEL	30	M	LABR	RRZZZZUSA
BECKER, ABRAHAM	18	M	LABR	RRZZZZUSA
DUART, ARON	24	M	LABR	RRZZZZUSA
KITNI, JEMACH	19	M	LABR	RRZZZZUSA
WEIMER, ITZIG	23	M	LABR	RRZZZZUSA
MASLACH, ABRAH	26	M	LABR	RRZZZZUSA
SAVADITZ, HIRSCH	21	M	LABR	RRZZZZUSA
TENZER, SIMON	38	M	LABR	RRZZZZUSA
KRALENSHA, JULIANE	20	F	SVNT	RRZZZZUSA
RADKE, GUSTAV	21	M	FARMER	RRZZZZUSA
ROZENZWEICH, M.	30	M	UNKNOWN	RRZZZZUSA
PERFELSOHN, LEIB	26	M	MCHT	RRZZZZUSA
ENFENSTEIN, ISRAEL	35	M	LABR	RRZZZZUSA
HERMANN, RUDOLPH	35	M	UNKNOWN	RRZZZZUSA
CROLDBERG, ABRAH	00	M	UNKNOWN	RRZZZZUSA
SPOROWSKY, ITZIG	20	M	LABR	RRZZZZUSA
BAMBEIN, DAVID	25	M	LABR	RRZZZZUSA
BORISOWSKY, LEISER	20	M	LABR	RRZZZZUSA
SCHUSTER, LEISER	20	M	LABR	RRZZZZUSA
WIRNIH, ITZIG	25	M	LABR	RRZZZZUSA
LEO, JOSEL	35	M	LABR	RRZZZZUSA
COHN, FREIDE	45	F	UNKNOWN	RRZZZZUSA
CHARE	15	F	UNKNOWN	RRZZZZUSA
LEIB	18	M	UNKNOWN	RRZZZZUSA
GEDWILL, ROB	35	M	LABR	RRZZZZUSA

SHIP: BOHEMIA

FROM: HAMBURG
TO: NEW YORK
ARRIVED: 15 AUGUST 1888

PASSENGER	AGE	SEX	OCCUPATION	PRV VIL DES
SCHAPIRO, LINE	19	F	SGL	RRZZZZPA
BIBLIN, META	40	F	SGL	RRZZZZPA

PASSENGER	AGE	SEX	OCCUPATION	PRV	VIL	DES
SARA	19	F	SGL	RR	ZZZZ	PA
LIEBE	9	F	CHILD	RR	ZZZZ	PA
ESCHE	8	F	CHILD	RR	ZZZZ	PA
HANNA	7	F	CHILD	RR	ZZZZ	PA
WEIDNER, THEODOR	15	M	UNKNOWN	RR	ACBF	PA
JANKOWSKA, ANNA	30	F	UNKNOWN	RR	ZZZZ	PA
KAZMIER	7	M	CHILD	RR	ZZZZ	PA
LEOKADA	4	F	CHILD	RR	ZZZZ	PA
MARIANNA	.01	F	INFANT	RR	ZZZZ	PA
FRIEDMANN, MOSES	28	M	UNKNOWN	RR	ZZZZ	PA
KALINSKI, DAVID	50	M	LABR	RR	ZZZZ	PA
ESTHER	18	F	SGL	RR	ZZZZ	PA
ELIAS	56	M	LABR	RR	ZZZZ	PA
SCHIFRA	55	F	LABR	RR	ZZZZ	PA
MERE	18	F	CH	RR	ZZZZ	PA
ISAAC	9	M	CHILD	RR	ZZZZ	PA
ROSIN, HENRY	30	M	CH	RR	ZZZZ	UNK
REISE	7	F	CHILD	RR	ZZZZ	UNK
MALKE	.11	F	INFANT	RR	ZZZZ	UNK
MEHROW, ETTE	33	F	SGL	RR	AHWE	UNK
KEILE	8	F	CHILD	RR	AHWE	UNK
RACHEL	7	F	CHILD	RR	AHWE	UNK
FALK	5	M	CHILD	RR	AHWE	UNK
HEILIGBERG, HENNIE	20	F	UNKNOWN	RR	ZZZZ	UNK
DOBRE	.11	F	INFANT	RR	ZZZZ	UNK
BOGENSTEIN, JANKEL	26	M	LABR	RR	ZZZZ	NY
LEWIN, DAVID	21	M	LABR	RR	AHUE	NY
RIWE	21	F	UNKNOWN	RR	AHUE	NY
GRUENDLICH, ROSINE	61	F	WO	RR	ZZZZ	NY
FRIEDMANN, CHAJE	26	F	WO	RR	ZZZZ	PA
CHANNE	2	F	CHILD	RR	ZZZZ	PA
PESKE	.06	F	INFANT	RR	ZZZZ	PA
ROTKOWITZ, JERUCHEM	50	M	LABR	RR	ZZZZ	PA
IDA	9	F	CHILD	RR	ZZZZ	PA
MARKOWSKI, JOSEF	30	M	LABR	RR	ZZZZ	PA
IGNATZ	27	M	LABR	RR	AHTW	PA
ROENNE, CARL	23	M	STDNT	RR	AIIM	PA
RIFKE, JETTE	17	F	SGL	RR	AHVA	PA
POLNITZKI, MOSES	18	M	LABR	RR	AHWM	PA
ROSENBERG, MALKE	35	F	WO	RR	ZZZZ	PA
SCHEINE	9	F	CHILD	RR	ZZZZ	PA
SALOMON	8	M	CHILD	RR	ZZZZ	PA
HERTZBERG, SALOMON	36	M	UNKNOWN	RR	ZZZZ	NY
ISRAEL	9	M	CHILD	RR	ZZZZ	NY
BERKUBEN, FRIEDR.	30	M	LABR	RR	ZZZZ	NY
DONIM, ANNA	21	F	SGL	RR	ZZZZ	NY
EICHENBERG, MERE	40	F	WO	RR	ZZZZ	NY
ZALMEN	9	F	CHILD	RR	ZZZZ	NY
RUWEN	8	M	CHILD	RR	ZZZZ	NY
MOSES	3	M	CHILD	RR	ZZZZ	NY
NEUMANN, FRUME	50	F	UNKNOWN	RR	ZZZZ	NY
CORNIEWSKI, ANDREW	19	M	LABR	RR	ZZZZ	NE
STEIN, PAULINE	22	F	SGL	RR	ZZZZ	NE
GOLDSTEIN, SARA	39	F	WO	RR	ZZZZ	NE
ITZIG	8	M	CHILD	RR	ZZZZ	NE
CHAJE	6	F	CHILD	RR	ZZZZ	NE
ANDURSKY, MEIHAL	18	M	LABR	RR	ZZZZ	NE
WILENSKY, SCHOLEM	55	M	UNKNOWN	RR	AHXL	PA
ZIMBROSKY, FLRY	30	M	LABR	RR	AIJI	PA
IDA	3	F	CHILD	RR	AIJI	PA
TIKOTZKY, ZIPE	21	F	SGL	RR	AHQU	IL
RUBIN, MENDEL	18	M	LABR	RR	AHTU	PA
JOSELOWITZ, JACOB	17	M	LABR	RR	AIFM	PA
CHMILEWSKY, JACOB	17	M	LABR	RR	ZZZZ	PA
MIKABOLSKY, REBECCA	18	F	SGL	RR	ZZZZ	KS
GOLDBERG, CHAIM	42	M	LABR	RR	AIJK	PA
GOLDE	42	F	W	RR	AIJK	PA
ISRAEL	14	M	UNKNOWN	RR	AIJK	PA
MATIS	8	M	CHILD	RR	AIJK	PA
JUDA	6	F	CHILD	RR	AIJK	PA
ZEHMANOWITZ, CHIEL	22	M	LABR	RR	AIJK	PA
SOBEL, ARON	25	M	LABR	RR	ZZZZ	PA
BERSIK, BENJAMIN	17	M	UNKNOWN	RR	AIGH	PA
PEREMONSKY, GOLDE	26	F	WO	RR	ZZZZ	NE
ABRAHAM	.11	M	INFANT	RR	ZZZZ	NE
BUCH, SALOMON	24	M	LABR	RR	ZZZZ	NE
PISKIN, CZERNA	30	F	UNKNOWN	RR	AIBO	KS
ALTE	9	F	CHILD	RR	AIBO	KS
BARUCH	.01	M	INFANT	RR	AIBO	KS
SELNERER, LINE	27	F	WO	RR	ZZZZ	KS
MOSES	2	M	CHILD	RR	ZZZZ	KS
MORDCHE	.06	F	INFANT	RR	ZZZZ	KS
LEWITAN, SIME	26	F	SGL	RR	AIIO	KS
EVA	20	F	SGL	RR	AIIO	KS
ARON	19	M	MCHT	RR	AIIO	KS
SABROWSKI, MEYER	42	M	BBR	RR	AFWJ	NY
DAVID	9	M	CHILD	RR	AFWJ	NY
GRENKE, JOHANN	22	M	MLR	RR	ZZZZ	NJ
GUENTHER, WILH.	24	M	MLR	RR	ZZZZ	NJ
BERKUBEN, ANNA	19	F	WO	RR	ZZZZ	NY
SILBERSTEIN, ANNA	17	F	SGL	RR	ZZZZ	NY
FACKTOR, JACOB	20	M	LABR	RR	ZZZZ	NY
DRESNER, OSIAS	26	M	DLR	RR	ZZZZ	NY
RATHKE, WILHELMINE	28	F	WO	RR	ZZZZ	NY
MIKABOLSKY, ZETTE	9	F	CHILD	RR	ZZZZ	KS
BUKE, MORDCHE	18	M	LABR	RR	AHQU	KS
GARFUNKEL, JOSEPH	30	M	LABR	RR	ZZZZ	IL
KURLENKAS, KAZIMIR	42	M	LABR	RR	AHZS	IL
NIESZUKAITIS, IVAN	26	M	LABR	RR	AHZS	KS
HABER, SORE	16	F	SGL	RR	AHYQ	KS
WOLFF, REISEL	19	F	SGL	RR	AHVU	KS
FEITELBERG, LEWIN	31	M	LABR	RR	ZZZZ	PA
LAMPE, MARYA	36	F	WO	RR	AIKN	NY

SHIP: WAESLAND

FROM: ANTWERP
TO: NEW YORK
ARRIVED: 16 AUGUST 1888

PASSENGER	AGE	SEX	OCCUPATION	PRV	VIL	DES
HUPPMANN, U	26	F	UNKNOWN	RR	ZZZZ	NY
J.	.02	M	INFANT	RR	ZZZZ	NY
POPLER, FANNY	40	F	UNKNOWN	RR	ZZZZ	CH
CHARLES	21	M	UNKNOWN	RR	ZZZZ	PIT
JOSEPH	11	M	CH	RR	ZZZZ	PIT
ROSA	9	F	CHILD	RR	ZZZZ	PIT
ANNIE	7	F	CHILD	RR	ZZZZ	PIT
STEPHAN	5	M	CHILD	RR	ZZZZ	PIT
WLADISL.	1	M	CHILD	RR	ZZZZ	PIT
KAWAWALSKI, S.	36	M	CPR	RR	ZZZZ	NY
DEOLWJID, OTTO	27	M	SHMK	RR	ZZZZ	NY
ELISAB.	29	F	SHMK	RR	ZZZZ	NY
KAPLAN, SCHIFRE	20	F	SVNT	RR	ZZZZ	NY
PERLOWICZ, GIETEL	19	F	SVNT	RR	ZZZZ	NY
BREDMETZKI, MENDEL	42	M	CBTMKR	RR	ZZZZ	NY

SHIP: STATE OF NEVADA

FROM: GLASGOW AND LARNE
TO: NEW YORK
ARRIVED: 16 AUGUST 1888

PASSENGER	AGE	SEX	OCCUPATION	PRV	VIL	DES
ARONSTEIN, SANDEL	56	M	TLR	RR	AIDL	USA
ABRAHAMOWIEZ, ARON	25	M	MCHT	RR	AIDL	USA
DAVID	51	M	MCHT	RR	AIDL	USA
MENDEL	11	M	CH	RR	AIDL	USA
ANTOWIL, SCHOLEM	28	M	BBR	RR	AIDL	USA
ARONSKY, JUDISCH	23	F	M	RR	AIDL	USA
CHANE	1	F	CHILD	RR	AIDL	USA
ALPERIN, ROSSE	25	F	M	RR	AIDL	USA

PASSENGER	AGE	SEX	OCCUPATION	PRV	VIL	DES
SALLY	1	F	CHILD	RR	AID	LUSA
ALEXAND, CHAIM	00	M	UNKNOWN	RR	AID	LUSA
ALPER, SAMUEL	51	M	TLR	RR	AID	LUSA
BLOCH, JUDEL	19	M	BLKSMH	RR	AID	LUSA
REST, WELEN	30	M	TLR	RR	AID	LUSA
BERENS, JOSSEL	32	M	FSHMN	RR	AID	LUSA
BINGER, HINDE	60	F	M	RR	AID	LUSA
BERSCHOWSKY, LERER	19	M	UNKNOWN	RR	AID	LUSA
JOSSEL	22	M	UNKNOWN	RR	AID	LUSA
BERKMAN, HINDE	34	F	M	RR	AID	LUSA
ITZASCHECH	15	M	CH	RR	AID	LUSA
LEIB	10	M	CH	RR	AID	LUSA
MOSCHE	1	M	CHILD	RR	AID	LUSA
BERMAN, CHAIM	29	M	MCHT	RR	AID	LUSA
BANK, SARAH	20	F	SVNT	RR	AID	LUSA
CHAST, CHAINE	28	M	BLKSMH	RR	AID	LUSA
CHAIT, RUBEN	40	M	TLR	RR	AID	LUSA
OLGA	26	F	W	RR	AID	LUSA
CHASERM, MARIA	17	F	SVNT	RR	AID	LUSA
DAVIDSOHN, ISRAEL	15	M	MCHT	RR	AID	LUSA
DANZIG, ROCHEL	22	F	SVNT	RR	AID	LUSA
EVERT, GERSCHON	22	M	MCHT	RR	AID	LUSA
EICHENBREMER, SELIG	28	M	TLR	RR	AID	LUSA
EPSTEIN, SORE	38	F	M	RR	AID	LUSA
SCHLOME	9	F	CHILD	RR	AID	LUSA
FUNK, ISRAEL	17	M	MCHT	RR	AID	LUSA
FALLMAN, JUTE	23	F	SVNT	RR	AID	LUSA
FERGER, JACOB	14	M	TLR	RR	AID	LUSA
FEMSILBER, AMMA	31	F	M	RR	AID	LUSA
ROSA	6	F	CHILD	RR	AID	LUSA
FRIETMAN, OTTO	10	M	CH	RR	AID	LUSA
GORZKA, JOSEFA	32	F	SVNT	RR	AID	LUSA
GUSTAVE, MOSES	21	M	CL	RR	AID	LUSA
GORM, SALOMON	29	M	TLR	RR	AID	LUSA
GONIANSKY, BENJ	19	M	MCHT	RR	AID	LUSA
GONT, FERWEL	48	M	MCHT	RR	AID	LUSA
CHAJE	18	F	SVNT	RR	AID	LUSA
GOLDBERG, CHANER	40	M	MCHT	RR	AID	LUSA
CHAJE	17	F	W	RR	AID	LUSA
GEILIK, SELDE	20	F	SVNT	RR	AID	LUSA
GRAILN, SIMON	18	M	MCHT	RR	AID	LUSA
GUZIK, PEISAK	19	M	MCHT	RR	AID	LUSA
GRANTSTEIN, SCHMUL	32	M	MCHT	RR	AID	LUSA
GERSTMAN, MOSES	38	M	SMH	RR	AID	LUSA
GORUNATZKY, JANCKEL	30	F	SVNT	RR	AID	LUSA
GERSCHOWICZ, FREIDE	30	F	M	RR	AID	LUSA
ITZIG	2	M	CHILD	RR	AID	LUSA
CHAJE	1	F	CHILD	RR	AID	LUSA
HANIS, MORITZ	38	M	TLR	RR	AID	LUSA
RABIN, TAUBE	28	F	W	RR	AID	LUSA
TAEL	18	F	SVNT	RR	AID	LUSA
NOLE	5	F	CHILD	RR	AID	LUSA
ISRAEL	2	M	CHILD	RR	AID	LUSA
MOSES	1	M	CHILD	RR	AID	LUSA
SCHENKER, PINENS	42	M	PDLR	RR	AID	LUSA
PERL	30	F	W	RR	AID	LUSA
RIWKE	4	F	CHILD	RR	AID	LUSA
GITTEL	1	M	CHILD	RR	AID	LUSA
SCHALOMOWITZ, TOCHA	40	F	W	RR	AID	LUSA
SCHIPPE	11	F	CH	RR	AID	LUSA
DWOSCHA	8	F	CHILD	RR	AID	LUSA
MONSCHA	6	F	CHILD	RR	AID	LUSA
PERACH	2	M	CHILD	RR	AID	LUSA
DWORE	1	F	CHILD	RR	AID	LUSA
STENBERG, DAVID	24	M	LABR	RR	AID	LUSA
TOMEA, CHRISTIAN	32	M	LABR	RR	AID	LUSA
WEINERMANN, POLIE	21	F	W	RR	AID	LUSA
JACOB	.08	M	INFANT	RR	AID	LUSA
WOLFMANN, PAIE	20	F	SVNT	RR	AID	LUSA
ZARNA, MALTHE	25	F	W	RR	AID	LUSA
CHANN	11	M	CH	RR	AID	LUSA
TAUBE	5	F	CHILD	RR	AID	LUSA
GELE	2	F	CHILD	RR	AID	LUSA
ZIPPE	.06	F	INFANT	RR	AID	LUSA

SHIP: TAORMINA

FROM: HAMBURG
TO: NEW YORK
ARRIVED: 17 AUGUST 1888

PASSENGER	AGE	SEX	OCCUPATION	PRV	VIL	DES
KARLOWSKA, ELZBITA	33	F	CGRMKR	RR	ZZZ	ZNY
ANNA	5	F	CHILD	RR	ZZZ	ZNY
GERSCHENOWITZ, GITTEL	22	F	WO	RR	ZZZ	ZNY
BENSIAN	5	M	CHILD	RR	ZZZ	ZNY
DAVID	.09	M	INFANT	RR	ZZZ	ZNY
BUSAKOWSKY, SARA	25	F	CH	RR	ZZZ	ZNY
DAVID	4	M	CHILD	RR	ZZZ	ZNY
KUBE	2	M	CHILD	RR	ZZZ	ZNY
MIHAL	.11	M	INFANT	RR	ZZZ	ZNY
BROSDE, CHAIM	43	M	LABR	RR	ZZZ	ZNY
GISCHE	2	F	CHILD	RR	ZZZ	ZNY
DUMISCH, MEIER	16	M	LABR	RR	ZZZ	ZNY
KRAJETZKI, RASCHE	53	F	UNKNOWN	RR	ZZZ	ZNY
KROWJETZKY, TAUBE	12	F	SGL	RR	ZZZ	ZNY
CHANNE	2	F	CHILD	RR	ZZZ	ZNY
KATZ, LEON	26	M	LABR	RR	ZZZ	ZCH
SZEPANSKI, ANTONIE	25	M	LABR	RR	ZZZ	ZNY
JAN	23	M	LABR	RR	ZZZ	ZNY
LEPIEWSKI, EMIL	24	M	LABR	RR	ZZZ	ZNY
MALISCHEMSKY, ANDR.	29	M	LABR	RR	ZZZ	ZNY
DAHLMANN, AUG.	19	M	LABR	RR	ZZZ	ZNY
MUELLER, U	22	F	W	RR	ZZZ	ZNY
KORNBLUM, GUSTAV	36	M	LABR	RR	ZZZ	ZNY
PAULINE	36	F	W	RR	ZZZ	ZNY
CAROLINE	9	F	CHILD	RR	ZZZ	ZNY
AUGUSTE	2	F	CHILD	RR	ZZZ	ZNY
JOSSIN, SARAH	22	F	SGL	RR	ZZZ	ZNY
REBECCA	20	F	SGL	RR	ZZZ	ZNY
KURTSCHPEL, PERL	24	F	WO	RR	ZZZ	ZNY
JOSEF	6	M	CHILD	RR	ZZZ	ZNY
GOLDSTEIN, ESTHER	40	F	WO	RR	ZZZ	ZNY
CHAJE	2	F	CHILD	RR	ZZZ	ZNY
VITTEN	7	F	CHILD	RR	ZZZ	ZNY
JOTTI	6	F	CHILD	RR	ZZZ	ZNY
MILLER, TONIE	22	F	SGL	RR	ZZZ	ZNY
SLOTOWSKA, TAUBE	34	F	WO	RR	ZZZ	ZNY
MALKE	2	F	CHILD	RR	ZZZ	ZNY
ARON	7	M	CHILD	RR	ZZZ	ZNY
PEISACK	5	M	CHILD	RR	ZZZ	ZNY
MORDCHE	.11	F	INFANT	RR	ZZZ	ZNY
BASENBLATT, MEYER	39	M	LABR	RR	ZZZ	ZNY
GARFINKEL, ABRAHAM	34	M	LABR	RR	ZZZ	ZNY
ASZENHAGEN, EPHRAIM	25	M	DLR	RR	ZZZ	ZNY
BESNIK, BREINE	20	F	WO	RR	ZZZ	ZUSA
WEISSMANN, DOBRISCH	35	F	SGL	RR	ZZZ	ZOMA
DOBRISCH	35	F	SGL	RR	ZZZ	ZOMA
JOVKOWETZKI, FRIEDR.	26	M	LABR	RR	ZZZ	ZOMA
KNICZORZEK, JON	30	M	FARMER	RR	ZZZ	ZOMA
ANNA	32	F	W	RR	ZZZ	ZOMA
CARL	3	M	CHILD	RR	ZZZ	ZOMA
REGINE	.11	M	INFANT	RR	ZZZ	ZOMA
DOLESCH, JOS.	21	M	FARMER	RR	ZZZ	ZOMA
NATHANSOHN, HERSCH	26	M	DLR	RR	ZZZ	ZNY
HATSCHINSKI, MECHIEL	36	M	DLR	RR	ZZZ	ZNY
KESTELMANN, MASCHE	44	M	DLR	RR	ZZZ	ZNY
LEIPNER, NATHAN	37	M	DLR	RR	ZZZ	ZNY
SCHIMEL, SCHEINKE	17	F	W	RR	ZZZ	ZNY
SCHOLUTKER, HALKA	27	M	LABR	RR	ZZZ	ZNY
BEHRENDT, THEODOR	6	M	CHILD	RR	ZZZ	ZNY
STECHERT, HERM.	19	M	MCHT	RR	ZZZ	ZNY
MAIWALD, HEINRICH	64	M	MLR	RR	ZZZ	ZUNK
BLUMENTHAL, WULF	20	M	LABR	RR	ZZZ	ZUNK
COHN, LEA	26	F	WO	RR	ZZZ	ZUNK
JUDES	.11	M	INFANT	RR	ZZZ	ZUNK
MARKS, ABRAM	16	M	LABR	RR	ZZZ	ZUNK
WOLF	8	M	CHILD	RR	ZZZ	ZUNK
BRZISKER, SELIG	16	M	LABR	RR	ZZZ	ZUNK
WINETZKY, TAUBE	35	F	WO	RR	ZZZ	ZUNK

PASSENGER	AGE	SEX	OCCUPATION	PV D RIE VLS
ELSE	8	F	CHILD	RRZZZZUNK
HIRSCH	7	M	CHILD	RRZZZZUNK
BENJAMIN	6	M	CHILD	RRZZZZUNK
ABRAM	5	M	CHILD	RRZZZZUNK
BASCHE	.11	F	INFANT	RRZZZZUNK
RAWITZKY, CHAJE	26	F	WO	RRZZZZUNK
FANNY	4	F	CHILD	RRZZZZUNK
FRIEDMANN, EMANUEL	9	M	CHILD	RRZZZZUNK
GOTTHOFER, JENTO	20	F	SGL	RRZZZZNY
JURA, TELZA	22	F	WO	RRZZZZNY
PINCHOS	4	M	CHILD	RRZZZZNY
CHAIM	.11	F	INFANT	RRZZZZNY
COHN, HIRSCH	57	M	DLR	RRZZZZNY
JURA, SCHEINE	18	F	SGL	RRZZZZNY
CHAIM	8	M	CHILD	RRZZZZNY
JANKEL	8	M	CHILD	RRZZZZNY
LEWY, CHAJE	23	F	WO	RRZZZZNY
CHANE	4	F	CHILD	RRZZZZNY
SCHEBSEL	.11	F	INFANT	RRZZZZNY
MILBRAD, KARL	23	M	LABR	RRZZZZNY
GANSCHIROFSKI, ISIDOR	22	M	DLR	RRZZZZNY
CHANNE	29	F	W	RRZZZZNY
SALOMON	4	M	CHILD	RRZZZZNY
HELLER	.11	M	INFANT	RRZZZZNY
KNISPEL, RACHEL	.11	F	INFANT	RRZZZZNY
EHRKE, GOTTFRIED	51	M	TLR	RRZZZZNY
GEILPERN, THEODOR	22	M	TLR	RRZZZZNY
U, U	00	U	UNKNOWN	RRZZZZNY
SCHWARZMANN, DAVID	25	M	DLR	RRZZZZNY

SHIP: WIELAND

FROM: HAMBURG AND HAVRE
TO: NEW YORK
ARRIVED: 17 AUGUST 1888

PASSENGER	AGE	SEX	OCCUPATION	PV D RIE VLS
LASAROWITZ, A.	42	M	DLR	RRZZZZUSA
LINGERMANN, JOEL	28	M	WO	RRZZZZUSA
RACHEL	4	F	CHILD	RRZZZZUSA
TAUBE	.11	F	INFANT	RRZZZZUSA
BARNOWSKY, ISAAC	14	M	UPHST	RRZZZZUSA
LICHTER, ADELE	29	F	WO	RRAGRTUSA
JOH.	7	M	CHILD	RRAGRTUSA
CARL	4	M	CHILD	RRAGRTUSA
EMMA	3	F	CHILD	RRAGRTUSA
MARIE	.06	F	INFANT	RRAGRTUSA
LENZNER, BERTHA	28	F	WO	RRAGRTUSA
PAULINE	5	F	CHILD	RRAGRTUSA
ROGOSCHINSKI, MICHAEL	24	M	MCHT	RRZZZZUSA
STRUWE, PAUL	75	M	CPTR	RRZZZZUSA
META	68	F	W	RRZZZZUSA
SUSSMANN, ITZIG	14	M	LABR	RRAIJYUSA
COHN, RENA	22	F	WO	RRZZZZUSA
SARAH	2	F	CHILD	RRZZZZUSA
EISENBERG, RACHEL	19	F	SGL	RRZZZZUSA
KOOACS, JANOS	38	M	LABR	RRZZZZUSA
GAZSY, ANDREAS	50	M	LABR	RRZZZZUSA
PJETRAK, CARL	35	M	JNR	RRZZZZUSA
MARIE	30	F	W	RRZZZZUSA
BRONISLAWA	7	F	CHILD	RRZZZZUSA
LUDWIG	3	M	CHILD	RRZZZZUSA
BOLESLAV	.09	M	INFANT	RRZZZZUSA
BRZOSTOWSKI, PAUL	23	M	LABR	RRZZZZUSA
LUTJE, MARGR.	20	F	SGL	RRAIDRUSA
SCHNEIDER, AUGUSTE	20	F	SGL	RRZZZZUSA
LASCHKOWITZ, JOSEPH	21	M	LABR	RRZZZZUSA
KRUEGER, AUGUSTE	27	F	WO	RRZZZZUSA
GEBHARD	2	M	CHILD	RRZZZZUSA
MARTHA	.06	F	INFANT	RRZZZZUSA
BLULMENFELD, SZENA	43	F	WO	RRAIGQUSA
RADUTZKY, BASCHE	23	F	WO	RRAHOKUSA
BRUCHE	.11	F	INFANT	RRAHOKUSA
MUEHLBERG, OSIAS	31	M	TLR	RRAHOKUSA
REBACCA	24	F	W	RRAHOKUSA
GRAD, IDA	25	F	SGL	RRZZZZUSA
BERNSTEIN, SOPHIE	20	F	SGL	RRZZZZUSA
NAFTALIN, FRENDE	40	F	WO	RRZZZZUSA
TEWJE	7	F	CHILD	RRZZZZUSA
SARA	6	F	CHILD	RRZZZZUSA
ROSENZWEIG, PEPI	23	F	SGL	RRZZZZUSA
CHARAK, FEIGE	24	F	WO	RRZZZZUSA
ARSOHN, LEIB	17	M	LABR	RRAHSLUSA
ROMONISKY, ABRAH	42	M	MCHT	RRAHSLUSA
ROZNISKY, TAUBE	32	F	WO	RRAHSLUSA
BEILE	7	F	CHILD	RRAHSLUSA
BER	5	M	CHILD	RRAHSLUSA
SARAH	.11	F	INFANT	RRAHSLUSA
LICHTANFELD, REICHEL	23	F	SGL	RRAIFOUSA
BIENENTHAL, MARIUS	37	M	MCHT	RRAFWJUSA
SAWELSOHN, MOSES	22	M	MCHT	RRAHTFUSA
EMMA	21	F	W	RRAHTFUSA
FROEHLICH, CARL	50	M	FARMER	RRAIOOUSA
DOROTHEA	43	F	W	RRAIOOUSA
HULDA	17	F	CH	RRAIOOUSA
HERRM.	17	M	CH	RRAIOOUSA
RUDOLPH	9	M	CHILD	RRAIOOUSA
ROBERT	8	M	CHILD	RRAIOOUSA
ROCHILIN, ABRAH.	60	M	LABR	RRAHWAUSA
SOPHIE	40	F	W	RRAHWAUSA
MENDEL	15	M	CH	RRAHWAUSA
RACHEL	16	F	CH	RRAHWAUSA
RESEL	8	F	CHILD	RRAHWAUSA
HIRSCH	7	M	CHILD	RRAHWAUSA
PODLUBING, CHAIM	35	M	LABR	RRAHXXUSA
CHAJE	18	F	W	RRAHXXUSA
MENASSE	16	F	SGL	RRAHXXUSA
ZIPE	16	F	SGL	RRAHXXUSA
DAVID	4	M	CHILD	RRAHXXUSA
NOCHEM	2	M	CHILD	RRAHXXUSA
ETTEL	.11	F	INFANT	RRAHXXUSA
RESEL	.04	F	INFANT	RRAHXXUSA
FEINMANN, ISAAC	30	M	DLR	RRAHTFUSA
SPOLA, JACOB	27	M	LABR	FNZZZZUSA
SKARRA, MISKA	19	M	LABR	FNAINOUSA
HEKLER, ELIESER	24	M	LABR	FNAGRTUSA
SPINZE	22	F	W	FNAGRTUSA
POPKO, DAVID	17	M	LABR	FNAGRTUSA
GEWIERZMANN, JOSEF	18	M	LABR	FNAFWJUSA
SAPOROWSKY, CHAJE	19	F	SGL	RRZZZZUSA
GOLDONOFSKY, EIDLE	28	F	LABR	RRZZZZUSA
ABRAM	5	M	CHILD	RRZZZZUSA
KATJE	3	F	CHILD	RRZZZZUSA
MOSES	.11	M	INFANT	RRZZZZUSA
FRANKOWSKI, NISSEN	47	M	BCHR	RRZZZZUSA
ZISCHAK, ITZECK	18	M	DLR	RRAHWUUSA
FEIWISCHOWITZ, REISE	22	F	SGL	RRAHTUUSA
SOBOL, MOSES	31	M	LABR	RRZZZZUSA
REPHULN, JACOB	18	M	LABR	RRAHSNUSA
MARKOWITZ, RIWKE	14	F	SGL	RRZZZZUSA
LICHTNFELD, SCHOLEM	22	M	DLR	RRAIFOUSA
KOPOTER, NOSSEN	18	M	DLR	RRAHUIUSA
MEYER	20	M	DLR	RRAHUIUSA
JARKAUSKE, SAMUEL	18	M	LABR	RRZZZZUSA
REHUMKEWICZ, CASIMIR	22	M	LABR	RRAHTFUSA
KOHAN, CHAIM	33	M	TLR	RRAICWUSA
STEIN, ABRAHAM	30	M	DLR	RRAHTFUSA
HANNA	30	F	W	RRAHTFUSA
JESSE	.09	M	INFANT	RRAHTFUSA
NANYUNACZ, JOHN	22	M	LABR	RRAHXLUSA
SCHERMANN, ELI	22	M	TLR	RRZZZZUSA
REISCHINSKI, MEYER	43	M	MCHT	RRZZZZUSA
KOHAN, ABRAHAM	17	M	TLR	RRAHTOUSA
GERSCHENSTEIN, SCHMUEL	24	M	DLR	RRAFVGUSA
RIWKE	19	F	W	RRAFVGUSA
SCHOLEM	.09	M	INFANT	RRAFVGUSA

PASSENGER	AGE	SEX	OCCUPATION	PRVIL	DES
HERZMANN, SOWIE	24	F	WO	RRAFVG	USA
SCHOLEM	.01	M	INFANT	RRAFVG	USA
SCHAPIRA, FEIWEL	28	M	DLR	RRAHTF	USA
STRAUBE, LUDWIG	37	M	SDLR	RRZZZZ	USA
LEVIN, SENDER	17	M	MCHT	RRAHOO	USA
SILBERMANN, LEW	20	M	MCHT	RRAHOO	USA
FRANZISKA	22	F	W	RRAHOO	USA
OWZINSKY, ISRAEL	40	M	DLR	RRAHTU	USA
GLUCK, SALOMON	26	M	APTC	RRAHWE	USA
SILBERMANN, CHAJE	20	F	WO	RRAHWE	USA
RIZBICKY, FEIGE	21	F	SGL	RRAIGA	USA
KASCHNIETZKY, U	26	M	LABR	RRZZZZ	USA
SCHMERIN, JOSSEL	37	M	BKBNDR	RRAHYN	USA
MICHELSON, ROWE	23	M	TLR	RRZZZZ	USA
LIPMANN, PLEIN	24	M	BCHR	RRAIIM	USA
HERSCHMANN, MARIE	25	F	W	RRZZZZ	USA
MINNA	.09	F	INFANT	RRZZZZ	USA
GHUCKMANN, JETTE	18	F	SGL	RRAHTF	USA
BHUNENTHAL, ISAAK	50	M	BCHR	RRAHTF	USA
BEILE	45	F	W	RRAHTF	USA
MIREL	19	F	D	RRAHTF	USA
JANKEL	9	M	CHILD	RRAHTF	USA
LICHTENFELD, LEIBCHE	.09	F	INFANT	RRAIFO	USA
KANONOW, ANNA	15	F	SGL	RRAHQD	USA

SHIP: SAALE

FROM: BREMEN AND SOUTHAMPTON
TO: NEW YORK
ARRIVED: 18 AUGUST 1888

PASSENGER	AGE	SEX	OCCUPATION	PRVIL	DES
WARSCHAWSKY, SCHALOM	43	M	BKBNDR	RRZZZZ	USA
LEIBISCH	11	M	CH	RRZZZZ	USA
SCHERWINSKY, NISSEN	18	M	FARMER	RRZZZZ	USA
KARINSKY, SEMAN	42	M	CPTR	RRZZZZ	USA
OIRICH, FISCHEL	41	M	CPTR	RRZZZZ	USA
OBERSANSKY, SALOM	33	M	CPTR	RRZZZZ	USA
----KY, U	51	M	FARMER	RRZZZZ	USA
BLUME	51	F	W	RRZZZZ	USA
BLEICHER, MEYER	31	M	LABR	RRZZZZ	USA
ZGELSKI, ISAAC	52	M	FARMER	RRZZZZ	USA
HINDA	44	F	W	RRZZZZ	USA
HELENE	23	F	UNKNOWN	RRZZZZ	USA
REBECCA	20	F	UNKNOWN	RRZZZZ	USA
JOSEPH	18	M	FARMER	RRZZZZ	USA
JULIUS	16	M	FARMER	RRZZZZ	USA

SHIP: CITY OF BERLIN

FROM: LIVERPOOL AND QUEENSTOWN
TO: NEW YORK
ARRIVED: 18 AUGUST 1888

PASSENGER	AGE	SEX	OCCUPATION	PRVIL	DES
KLODOWSKY, DAVID	19	M	LABR	RRAFWJ	NY
LEIB	18	M	LABR	RRAFWJ	NY
KAPICE, CON	23	M	LABR	RRAFWJ	NY
AULINGER, FAWEL	21	M	LABR	RRAFWJ	NY
RUSCHMAN, SELIG	35	M	LABR	RRAFWJ	NY
KAMEREA, JETTE	36	F	LABR	RRAFWJ	NY
CIRSLIEKZ, FRANCEZ	37	F	W	RRAFWJ	NY
JUDWIGA	3	F	CHILD	RRAFWJ	NY
STANISLAW	00	M	INF	RRAFWJ	NY
KATZ, REBECCA	14	F	NRS	RRAFWJ	NY
JOHANA	11	F	CH	RRAFWJ	NY
HERSCHSOHN, HERMAN	17	M	LABR	RRZZZZ	USA
BARUCH	11	M	LABR	RRZZZZ	USA
MICHALOWITZ, MORITZ	17	M	LABR	RRZZZZ	USA
ZUNDELIR, HENE	20	M	LABR	RRZZZZ	USA
FALMAN, ISAAK	19	M	LABR	RRZZZZ	USA
PIKUS, SCHMIL	27	M	LABR	RRZZZZ	USA
KANTOWCIER, JOSEF	25	M	SMH	RRZZZZ	USA
GRUNFEILD, MOSES	18	M	LABR	RRAFWJ	USA
RAMUN, HERSCH	24	M	LABR	RRAFWJ	USA
BERMANN, SCHMUL	20	M	LABR	RRAFWJ	USA
PLUSHMAN, ABEL	51	M	LABR	RRAFWJ	USA
COHN, RICHMEL	51	M	TLR	RRAFWJ	USA
JANKLEWITZ, ABM	35	M	LABR	RRAFWJ	USA
MUROWITZ, ISAAK	30	M	LABR	RRZZZZ	USA
SULEK, ABM.	20	M	LABR	RRZZZZ	USA
SZEBMK, GNESCHE	20	F	LABR	RRZZZZ	USA
MANEWITZ, LEEBA	25	F	SVNT	RRZZZZ	USA
FLEISCHMAN, SCHIM	47	F	W	RRZZZZ	USA
HERSCH	40	M	CH	RRZZZZ	USA
MATTEL	10	M	CH	RRZZZZ	USA
SARA	4	M	CHILD	RRZZZZ	USA
CHANE	25	M	CH	RRZZZZ	USA
HERTZ	4	M	CHILD	RRZZZZ	USA
SCHEWSFLD, SARA	34	F	W	RRAFWJ	USA
ROHL	15	M	CH	RRAFWJ	USA
RIPPE	14	M	CH	RRAFWJ	USA
ESTER	6	M	CHILD	RRAFWJ	USA
CHAIM, J.	9	M	CHILD	RRAFWJ	USA
MICHJEZ, ABM.	48	M	UNKNOWN	RRAFWJ	USA
Z.	28	F	W	RRAFWJ	USA
FEIGE	9	F	CHILD	RRAFWJ	USA
NISSE	4	F	CHILD	RRAFWJ	USA
JOSEF	3	M	CHILD	RRAFWJ	USA
ARON	00	M	INF	RRAFWJ	USA
JANUSCHEWSKY, ANTON	26	M	LABR	RRZZZZ	USA
ANNA	28	F	W	RRZZZZ	USA
JERUSALINSKY, ISAAC	20	M	LABR	RRZZZZ	USA
BELIE	16	M	LABR	RRZZZZ	USA

SHIP: LEERDAM

FROM: ROTTERDAM
TO: NEW YORK
ARRIVED: 20 AUGUST 1888

PASSENGER	AGE	SEX	OCCUPATION	PRVIL	DES
KETZMAN, ELIAS	22	M	JNR	PLZZZZ	USA
KETO, JAC.	44	M	TLR	RRZZZZ	USA
PITSKAJARA, S.E.	27	F	UNKNOWN	RRZZZZ	USA
HANTISOSKI, M.	25	F	UNKNOWN	RRZZZZ	USA
HUTTA, M.	53	M	FARMER	RRZZZZ	USA
ULATOWSKI, A.	18	M	LABR	RRZZZZ	USA
TURNADJIEFF, D.	21	M	LABR	PLZZZZ	USA
M.	17	F	UNKNOWN	PLZZZZ	USA
PRESS, SARA	25	F	UNKNOWN	PLZZZZ	USA
SSRAEL, WEINRAH	25	M	LABR	PLZZZZ	USA
HORWITZ, OFS.	39	M	UNKNOWN	PLZZZZ	USA
ROSENSTEIN, E.	25	M	TLR	RRZZZZ	USA
JOCOBSON, T.	25	M	TLR	RRZZZZ	USA
LUTTKE, S.	30	M	MCHT	RRZZZZ	USA
R.	25	F	UNKNOWN	RRZZZZ	USA
B.	9	F	CHILD	RRZZZZ	USA
MALIMANEK, JOS.	46	M	LABR	RRZZZZ	USA
BOROCHITCHOROWITZ, H.	46	M	BCHR	RRZZZZ	USA

SHIP: REPUBLIC

FROM: LIVERPOOL
TO: NEW YORK
ARRIVED: 20 AUGUST 1888

PASSENGER	AGE	SEX	OCCUPATION	PRV VIL DES
ROHONREY, JOSEF	34	M	LABR	RRADAXUSA
ANNA	32	F	W	RRADAXUSA
ANNE	11	F	CH	RRADAXUSA
MARY	3	F	CHILD	RRADAXUSA
PETTERSON, OLAF	30	M	LABR	RRADAXUSA
NAPARTSLEK, NICHE	28	F	W	RRADAXUSA
BLUME	5	M	CHILD	RRADAXUSA
JACOB	3	M	CHILD	RRADAXUSA
HIRSCH	.10	M	INFANT	RRADAXUSA
BALIS, TAUBE	50	M	LABR	RRADAXUSA
ISAAC	9	M	CHILD	RRADAXUSA
GERSCHEN	11	F	CH	RRADAXUSA
BRUTMANN, ADORF	24	M	LABR	RRADAXUSA
NEUMANN, ESZLIR	.10	F	INFANT	RRADAXUSA
ROSENBLATH, RIFKE	17	F	SVNT	RRADAXUSA
BERALOWITZ, SAUL	38	M	LABR	RRADAXUSA
MULNER, JAUL	21	F	SVNT	RRADAXUSA
STERNBORCH, SAUL	36	M	LABR	RRADAXUSA
ROTH, MINDA	25	M	LABR	RRADAXUSA
KAUZKA, NAFTR.	22	M	LABR	RRADAXUSA
CROBALYK, MICHAEL	18	M	LABR	RRADAXUSA
SACHS, IGNATZ	31	M	LABR	RRADAXUSA
SCHWARZMANN, FEIGE	46	F	W	RRADAXUSA
WOLF	10	M	CH	RRADAXUSA
JENNIE	6	F	CHILD	RRADAXUSA
ALFE	3	M	CHILD	RRADAXUSA
GOLDENBERG, RUSSET	18	F	SVNT	RRADAXUSA
GROFOWSKI, SAMUEL	38	M	LABR	RRADAXUSA
MILSKSASKI, JUDEL	17	F	SVNT	RRADAXUSA
GRIMBERG, SCHAJO	20	F	SVNT	RRADAXUSA
NAIMAN, ARAJIT	18	M	LABR	RRADAXUSA
LERMAN, ALTER	19	M	LABR	RRADAXUSA
AVELSOHN, MOSES	45	M	LABR	RRADAXUSA
LESY, LEISER	16	M	LABR	RRADAXUSA
WUBERG, RIV.	33	F	W	RRADAXUSA
GETTLE	8	F	CHILD	RRADAXUSA
LEAH	6	F	CHILD	RRADAXUSA
GRIMBLATT, ABRAHAM	16	M	LABR	RRADAXUSA
KATZ, SAMUEL	42	M	LABR	RRADAXUSA
ANETTE	30	F	W	RRADAXUSA
SOBALKOWITZ, MOSES	48	M	LABR	RRADAXUSA
JAKOSKY, ANTON	18	M	LABR	RRADAXUSA
LEIGINN, JOHAN	17	M	LABR	RRADAXUSA
SCHEFF, ROSA	22	F	SVNT	RRADAXUSA
WILHELM	11	M	CH	RRADAXUSA
KREHANISK, CHAJE	18	F	SVNT	RRADAXUSA
MARKOWITZ, JETTE	25	F	W	RRADAXUSA
ARON	11	M	CH	RRADAXUSA
SILDDA	3	F	CHILD	RRADAXUSA
RISEL	.09	F	INFANT	RRADAXUSA
MALINE, MALKE	18	F	SVNT	RRADAXUSA

SHIP: DEVONIA

FROM: GLASGOW
TO: NEW YORK
ARRIVED: 20 AUGUST 1888

PASSENGER	AGE	SEX	OCCUPATION	PRV VIL DES
BERGER, RIWKE	28	F	UNKNOWN	RRZZZZUSA
ABRAHAM	5	M	CHILD	RRZZZZUSA
FANNY	2	F	CHILD	RRZZZZUSA
EDELSTEIN, BENJAMIN	18	M	LABR	RRZZZZUSA
MAGDALINE	18	F	UNKNOWN	RRZZZZUSA
GOLDINES, MARYANE	50	F	UNKNOWN	RRZZZZUSA
DINE	19	F	UNKNOWN	RRZZZZUSA
DAVID	11	M	UNKNOWN	RRZZZZUSA
GERCHUNG, BASSIE	20	F	UNKNOWN	RRZZZZUSA
MORDCHE	3	F	CHILD	RRZZZZUSA
MARIE	2	F	CHILD	RRZZZZUSA
GUSCHNEROW, ABRAHAM	45	M	LABR	RRZZZZUSA
RIFKE	17	F	UNKNOWN	RRZZZZUSA
HAPMAN, CHANE	22	F	UNKNOWN	RRZZZZUSA
BARNET	1	M	CHILD	RRZZZZUSA
KAUFFMAN, ANNA	35	F	UNKNOWN	RRZZZZUSA
ADA	8	F	CHILD	RRZZZZUSA
ISAK	3	M	CHILD	RRZZZZUSA
BORUCH	.06	M	INFANT	RRZZZZUSA
KUBERSKI, ANTONIA	22	F	UNKNOWN	RRZZZZUSA
MICHALINA	.11	M	INFANT	RRZZZZUSA
JOSEPHO	.02	M	INFANT	RRZZZZUSA
LEWENSOHN, ANNIE	17	F	UNKNOWN	RRZZZZUSA
ELLIK	16	M	UNKNOWN	RRZZZZUSA
RAFALOWITZ, LEIBE	45	F	UNKNOWN	RRZZZZUSA
ROCHE	30	F	UNKNOWN	RRZZZZUSA
ALTER	9	M	CHILD	RRZZZZUSA
SIMCHE	2	F	CHILD	RRZZZZUSA
KAULAROWITZ, BENJ	17	M	UNKNOWN	RRZZZZUSA
KATZ, HELKE	23	F	UNKNOWN	RRZZZZUSA
CHANE	2	F	CHILD	RRZZZZUSA
HARIS	1	M	CHILD	RRZZZZUSA
ROSENFELD, BRAIGE	23	F	UNKNOWN	RRZZZZUSA
HESTER	8	F	CHILD	RRZZZZUSA
SANKE	2	F	CHILD	RRZZZZUSA
WOLF	1	M	CHILD	RRZZZZUSA
SCHARZMAN, DAVID	26	M	LABR	RRZZZZUSA
REISE	21	F	UNKNOWN	RRZZZZUSA
ZIKLIK, MOSES	25	M	TLR	RRZZZZUSA
LIBE	18	F	UNKNOWN	RRZZZZUSA
BASS, RIVE	18	F	UNKNOWN	RRZZZZUSA
BIRESHITZ, ROCHE	45	F	HSMD	RRZZZZUSA
EISE, CHANE	21	F	UNKNOWN	RRZZZZUSA
JACHWED	21	F	UNKNOWN	RRZZZZUSA
CHAJE	.03	F	INFANT	RRZZZZUSA
FABER, CHAJE	21	F	HSMD	RRZZZZUSA
KATZ, FEIWE	50	F	UNKNOWN	RRZZZZUSA
LIEBE	19	F	UNKNOWN	RRZZZZUSA
KOPELOWITZ, RAHEL	20	F	HSMD	RRZZZZUSA
MECHALER, MECHE	20	F	HSMD	RRZZZZUSA
MORGEUSTERN, MARJEM	18	F	HSMD	RRZZZZUSA
MELLER, SUSSH	19	F	HSMD	RRZZZZUSA
ROSENBLUM, HENE	18	F	HSMD	RRZZZZUSA
SCHMEIDER, FANNY	20	F	HSMD	RRZZZZUSA
SRIBNIK, ESTER	50	F	UNKNOWN	RRZZZZUSA
SAPUROWSKY, BEILE	22	F	HSMD	RRZZZZUSA
SLUTZKI, ROSE	17	F	HSMD	RRZZZZUSA
SELIN, RIWKE	20	F	HSMD	RRZZZZUSA
SCHIMANSWITSCH, LISE	18	F	HSMD	RRZZZZUSA
JIKOTZKY, BEILE	22	F	HSMD	RRZZZZUSA
BOLUSNIK, MORDSHE	26	M	LABR	RRZZZZUSA
STAROSELSKI, LEWI	28	M	LABR	RRZZZZUSA
BECKER, SCHLOME	21	M	UNKNOWN	RRZZZZUSA
FLAUM, OSIAS	11	M	UNKNOWN	RRZZZZUSA
BRONSLEIN, ISAK	30	M	LABR	RRZZZZUSA
CHRONAWITZ, MAX	28	M	LABR	RRZZZZUSA
CASPE, ISAAC	17	M	LABR	RRZZZZUSA
DREINETZKY, ISRAEL	20	M	LABR	RRZZZZUSA
DIMAN, CHAIM	20	M	LABR	RRZZZZUSA
ELLIN, JACOB	35	M	LABR	RRZZZZUSA
GRODZENSKY, GERSON	20	M	LABR	RRZZZZUSA
HEROMIN, JOS.	21	M	LABR	RRZZZZUSA
HERZKES, JOSSEL	18	M	LABR	RRZZZZUSA
KOWALSKI, JOHN	24	M	LABR	RRZZZZUSA
KOHN, LEIB	17	M	LABR	RRZZZZUSA
DAVID	40	M	LABR	RRZZZZUSA
KLOSS, JOSEF	25	M	LABR	RRZZZZUSA
KLAPKU, FRE.	18	M	LABR	RRZZZZUSA
KRAWITZ, JUDEL	17	M	LABR	RRZZZZUSA
KRAKOW, ISAAK	43	M	LABR	RRZZZZUSA

PASSENGER	AGE	SEX	OCCUPATION	PRV VIL DES
KRAWITZ, CHATZKEL	19	M	LABR	RRZZZZUSA
LIKER, MANES	23	M	LABR	RRZZZZUSA
MORGENSTERN, FROIM	20	M	LABR	RRZZZZUSA
PERLBERG, CHATZKEL	25	M	LABR	RRZZZZUSA
PALON, SCHLOME	25	M	LABR	RRZZZZUSA
POLLONOWICZ, PAUL	20	M	LABR	RRZZZZUSA
PARSCKI, LIPE	35	M	LABR	RRZZZZUSA
PIKUSCH, RUBEN	35	M	LABR	RRZZZZUSA
SASLAWSKY, JAKOB	20	M	LABR	RRZZZZUSA
STADULEWISH, IGNATZ	30	M	LABR	RRZZZZUSA
SCHULMAN, NOCHEM	20	M	LABR	RRZZZZUSA
SIW, ARON	16	M	LABR	RRZZZZUSA
JAGANSKI, RIWKE	15	F	UNKNOWN	RRZZZZUSA
ULER, OSER	35	M	FARMER	RRZZZZUSA

SHIP: AURANIA

FROM: LIVERPOOL AND QUEENSTOWN
TO: NEW YORK
ARRIVED: 20 AUGUST 1888

PASSENGER	AGE	SEX	OCCUPATION	PRV VIL DES
REMMELHOV, MORRIS	26	M	TLR	PLZZZZNY
RUBIN, HODES	15	F	SP	PLZZZZNY
DAMOWITZ, ESTER	22	F	MA	PLZZZZNY
ERNST	.06	M	INFANT	PLZZZZNY
KOHEN, RYFKE	23	M	LABR	PLZZZZNY
LEAH	20	F	W	PLZZZZNY
JOHNA, GUSTAFSON	27	F	SP	PLZZZZNY
KOHEN, MEYER	.06	M	INFANT	PLZZZZNY
RUBIN, CHAGE	26	F	MA	PLZZZZNY
SCHLINE	3	F	CHILD	PLZZZZNY
ARON	.10	M	INFANT	PLZZZZNY
FENKELSTEIN, JUDETH	14	F	SP	PLZZZZNY
SEFFALA, JOB.	28	M	TLR	PLZZZZNY
BASEK, PETER	30	M	LABR	PLZZZZNY
ZURAK, SIMON	40	M	LABR	PLZZZZNY
WILINSKER, BARACH	50	M	LABR	PLZZZZNY
REINE	45	F	W	PLZZZZNY
BEILE	18	F	SP	PLZZZZNY
CHANE	5	M	CHILD	PLZZZZNY
FEINSTEIN, ISRAEL	40	M	LABR	PLZZZZNY
SCHAFIER, BEILE	19	F	SP	PLZZZZNY
LEWINSKY, ISSER	38	M	LABR	PLZZZZNY
LEIBOWITZ, LEIB	25	M	LABR	PLZZZZNY
ANNA	25	F	W	PLZZZZNY
SEGAL, HIRSCH	40	M	LABR	PLZZZZNY
KIVLDRODITZ, KASIMIR	26	M	LABR	PLZZZZNY

SHIP: FULDA

FROM: BREMEN AND SOUTHAMPTON
TO: NEW YORK
ARRIVED: 21 AUGUST 1888

PASSENGER	AGE	SEX	OCCUPATION	PRV VIL DES
HIRSCHMANN, FANNY	21	F	NN	RRZZZZUSA
BLAUSTEIN, SAMUEL	19	M	LABR	RRZZZZUSA
DORA	16	F	NN	RRZZZZUSA
SMITH, ARON	30	M	FARMER	RRZZZZUSA
KOPETULSKY, NAFTALIE	35	F	NN	RRZZZZUSA
SILVERMANN, LOUIS	34	M	DLR	RRZZZZUSA
GOLDSTEIN, CHA-EM	44	M	DLR	RRZZZZUSA
BURNSTEIN, RAPHAEL	00	M	MCHT	RRZZZZUSA
STOLPER, SALOMON	40	M	DLR	RRZZZZUSA
VOLKOBOWSKY, TAUBE	22	F	NN	RRZZZZUSA
LASCHEWITZ, BERNHARD	19	M	LABR	RRZZZZUSA

PASSENGER	AGE	SEX	OCCUPATION	PRV VIL DES
ZURANSKI, THEODOR	23	M	LABR	RRZZZZUSA
FRANZ	26	M	LABR	RRZZZZUSA
KO-ZMIRZEK, THOMAS	22	M	LABR	RRZZZZUSA
LENZ, FRIEDRICH	28	M	LABR	RRZZZZUSA
SZYKOWSKA, JOSEFA	00	F	NN	RRZZZZUSA
KWIATKOWSKA, MICHAL----	17	F	NN	RRZZZZUSA
LISESKA, BERTHA	00	F	NN	RRZZZZUSA
KWIATKOWSKA, FRANZISKA	35	F	NN	RRZZZZUSA
MICHAELENA	7	F	CHILD	RRZZZZUSA
JAN	.06	M	INFANT	RRZZZZUSA
SCHWARZ, LOUIS	15	M	LABR	RRZZZZUSA
ROSENBERG, PONNE	25	F	NN	RRZZZZUSA
ILLE	6	F	CHILD	RRZZZZUSA
LAIBSON, GITEL-	17	F	NN	RRZZZZUSA
RUBINSTEIN, SALOMON	20	M	SMH	RRZZZZUSA

SHIP: MAIN

FROM: BREMEN
TO: BALTIMORE
ARRIVED: 22 AUGUST 1888

PASSENGER	AGE	SEX	OCCUPATION	PRV VIL DES
LEVIN, HADDE	17	M	TLR	RRZZZZBAL
GROLLMANN, YAEL	21	M	PDLR	RRZZZZBAL
ISAAESON, ISAAC	17	M	PDLR	RRZZZZBAL
WORTH, JULA	52	M	FARMER	RRZZZZBAL
MUTZ, FRIEDR.	23	M	MLR	RRZZZZBAL
MANCZYNSKI, FRANZ	18	M	MLR	RRZZZZBAL
KLINOWSKI, FRANZ	17	M	FARMER	RRZZZZOH
WARSZAWITZ, ISRAEL	41	M	LABR	RRZZZZMD
SIEGELMANN, JANKEL	13	M	CH	RRZZZZMD
ZIMMERMANN, HERSCH	65	M	MCHT	RRZZZZMD
MEYER	13	M	CH	RRZZZZMD
BLASHKE, WEZL	24	M	PDLR	RRZZZZWI
BELTER, GABRIEL	27	M	PDLR	RRZZZZUSA
WALPERT, ISRAEL	21	M	MCHT	RRZZZZUSA
SPIES, CARL	44	M	LABR	RRZZZZMI
ZIMMERMANN, BRUNO	46	M	PDLR	RRZZZZBAL
CHOINATZKI, JOHANN	28	M	FARMER	RRZZZZBAL
RAIBMANN, MORCHEL	57	M	FARMER	RRZZZZBAL
WEILMANN, LIESE	21	F	SVNT	RRZZZZBAL
SZAEFFER, BERTHA	23	F	SVNT	RRZZZZBAL
JERKE, ROSA	28	F	SVNT	RRZZZZBAL
MILKEREIT, CHRISTINE	22	F	W	RRZZZZBAL
AUGUSTE	.06	F	INFANT	RRZZZZBAL
ANGUSTADT, KAROLINE	35	F	W	RRZZZZBAL
ANNA	7	F	CHILD	RRZZZZBAL
JOSEF	8	M	CHILD	RRZZZZBAL
WACKS, FAGE	40	F	W	RRZZZZBAL
VESCHE	8	F	CHILD	RRZZZZBAL
ESTER	7	F	CHILD	RRZZZZBAL
SELDE	7	F	CHILD	RRZZZZBAL
ESRIEL	5	M	CHILD	RRZZZZBAL
SARAH	.11	F	INFANT	RRZZZZBAL
COHEN, CERNE	17	F	SVNT	RRZZZZBAL
TZUKER, SCHEINE	16	F	SVNT	RRZZZZBAL
KAHN, BERE	44	F	W	RRZZZZBAL
JOEL	11	M	CH	RRZZZZBAL
BORE, MINA	20	F	SVNT	RRZZZZPA
BERDICEWSKY, FEIGE	25	F	W	RRZZZZBAL
TIMDETES, MARIANNA	27	F	W	RRZZZZPA
GUSTAV	.11	M	INFANT	RRZZZZPA
APOLONIA	3	F	CHILD	RRZZZZPA
ZILACHOWSKA, FRANZISCA	40	F	W	RRZZZZBAL
WADISLAW	10	M	CH	RRZZZZBAL
PRONTA	7	F	CHILD	RRZZZZBAL
CATHARINA	2	F	CHILD	RRZZZZBAL
MORITZ, JOHANN	32	M	MCHT	RRZZZZBAL
MARIA	26	F	W	RRZZZZBAL
MARIA	3	F	CHILD	RRZZZZBAL

PASSENGER	AGE	SEX	OCCUPATION	PRV VIL DES
AUGUSTE	.01	F	INFANT	RRZZZZBAL

SHIP: MICHIGAN

FROM: LIVERPOOL
TO: BOSTON
ARRIVED: 22 AUGUST 1888

PASSENGER	AGE	SEX	OCCUPATION	PRV VIL DES
LEBARTOSKY, VICTOR	32	M	TLR	RRZZZZUSA
---MMAKEDICZ, NOYECH	25	M	UNKNOWN	RRZZZZUSA
ROSENBAUM, SAM	26	M	UNKNOWN	RRZZZZUSA
JOGG, MORRIS	21	M	CVR	RRZZZZUSA
MORSHOW, ITZIG	35	M	SHMK	RRZZZZUSA
MARCUS, ABRAHAM	16	M	TLR	RRZZZZUSA
LALLEL	11	M	SCH	RRZZZZUSA
WASSERTHAL, ABRAHAM	39	M	TRVLR	RRZZZZUSA
MICHAL, S-A	18	M	BCHR	RRZZZZUSA
GROSS, SAM	16	M	BLKSMH	RRZZZZUSA
KATAWOUSKI, WA-	20	M	SMH	RRZZZZUSA
NIXON, MACH	22	M	LKSH	RRZZZZUSA
KALURN, GUSTAV	25	M	BCHR	RRZZZZUSA
KATZ, VICTOR	25	M	TLR	RRZZZZUSA
HACHS, LEVY	17	M	TLR	RRZZZZUSA
ROSENFELD, SOLOMON	30	M	TLR	RRZZZZUSA
DREY-AR, JULIUS	35	M	BKLYR	RRZZZZUSA
VARSHAVYICK, SAMUEL	21	M	TLR	RRZZZZUSA
WEDOLKY, HIRSH	00	M	UNKNOWN	RRZZZZUSA
KUELHT, OSCAR	40	M	TLR	RRZZZZUSA
BECKER, MENDEL	30	M	BCHR	RRZZZZUSA
MEYAR, JOSEPH	43	M	TLR	RRZZZZUSA
H---DE	16	M	TLR	RRZZZZUSA
BLACHER, BENJAMIN	25	M	PRNTR	RRZZZZUSA
LANGDORF, JACOB	55	M	TLR	RRZZZZUSA
SCHNEIDER, WOLF	23	M	TLR	RRZZZZUSA
SCHERER, ABRAHAM	19	M	TLR	RRZZZZUSA
WERTER, LEIB	33	M	TLR	RRZZZZUSA
BACH, MOSES	26	M	TLR	RRZZZZUSA
ROSENSTOCK, ELY	26	M	TLR	RRZZZZUSA
LABOWITZ, MENDEL	26	M	TLR	RRZZZZUSA
ROSENFEL, ABRAHAM	28	M	TLR	RRZZZZUSA
L--INI, ELIA	38	M	SHMK	RRZZZZUSA
SKLA-, MENDEL	24	M	TLR	RRZZZZUSA
GRUMPCHAW, MARIA	20	F	SP	RRZZZZUSA
ROTHFELD, ROSA	20	F	SP	RRZZZZUSA
WERNER, DORA	18	F	SP	RRZZZZUSA
AMSTERDAM, MIMMIE	16	F	SP	RRZZZZUSA
RU-EL	18	F	SP	RRZZZZUSA
JACOB, CHA--A	19	F	SP	RRZZZZUSA
SCHRAGER, MALKE	20	F	SP	RRZZZZUSA
BIRUBACH, P--EL	15	F	SP	RRZZZZUSA
LISBURN, MARTIN	23	M	SHMK	RRZZZZUSA
CATHERINE	23	F	W	RRZZZZUSA
MORRIS, U	18	M	SHMK	RRZZZZUSA
LEAH	22	F	W	RRZZZZUSA
MADEL-ANN, ABRAHAM	19	M	BCHR	RRZZZZUSA
CHANE-	19	F	W	RRZZZZUSA
WIC-, ABRAHAM	27	M	TLR	RRZZZZUSA
REBECCA	28	F	W	RRZZZZUSA
LANGDORF, MALKE	50	F	NN	RRZZZZUSA
FRANKEL, GITTEL	24	F	NN	RRZZZZUSA
SCHERER, HIRSCH	57	M	TLR	RRZZZZUSA
SARAH	48	F	W	RRZZZZUSA
LEAH	32	F	W	RRZZZZUSA

SHIP: STATE OF NEBRASKA

FROM: GLASGOW AND LARNE
TO: NEW YORK
ARRIVED: 22 AUGUST 1888

PASSENGER	AGE	SEX	OCCUPATION	PRV VIL DES
GETZ, FEIWEL	25	M	MLR	RRAIDLUSA
KORB, MENDEL	38	M	BCHR	RRAIDLUSA
LEISEROWITZ, MOSES	32	M	GCR	RRAIDLUSA
FELTER, LEIB	18	M	GCR	RRAIDLUSA
PAGER, MORITZ	27	M	CL	RRAIDLUSA
ELIAS	45	M	TLR	RRAIDLUSA
SKLARGEWITZ, MEYER	52	M	GZR	RRAIDLUSA
LEVIT, MENDEL	30	M	PDLR	RRAIDLUSA
BORDOWITZ, SIRUCHE	30	M	PDLR	RRAIDLUSA
HUSCHKIN, CHAIM	27	M	TLR	RRAIDLUSA
ANDREISSER, ITZIG	27	M	TLR	RRAIDLUSA
HIRSCH, SIMON	30	M	TLR	RRAIDLUSA
CHAID, JANKEL	19	M	TLR	RRAIDLUSA
HENDEL, JANKEL	19	M	TLR	RRAIDLUSA
MINEWSKI, ABRAM	21	M	TLR	RRAIDLUSA
KANTROWITZ, SAMUEL	31	M	TLR	RRAIDLUSA
SWIRSKY, ORE	17	M	LABR	RRAIDLUSA
PARIGOLDI, CHAIM	40	M	LABR	RRAIDLUSA
GOTTLIEB, SCHLAUME	18	M	LABR	RRAIDLUSA
GURIN, KESIEL	17	M	LABR	RRAIDLUSA
CHOCHOW, MEIER	20	M	LABR	RRAIDLUSA
KROPOLSKI, JANKEL	35	M	LABR	RRAIDLUSA
SCHAPIRO, CONSTANTIN	33	M	LABR	RRAIDLUSA
ANATOLIE	3	M	CHILD	RRAIDLUSA
ABRAMSON, MOSES	11	M	CH	RRAIDLUSA
BAWERSAUSKY, CHOWE	10	M	CH	RRAIDLUSA
EISIK	50	M	LABR	RRAIDLUSA
SCHWANN, CHANE	20	F	W	RRAIDLUSA
BAR, LEIE	40	F	W	RRAIDLUSA
NEMZINSKY, PEREL	22	F	W	RRAIDLUSA
PLUMBERG, CHAJE	18	F	SP	RRAIDLUSA
WOLFBERG, ZIPPE	18	F	SP	RRAIDLUSA
AUGUSTIN, CHENKE	18	F	SP	RRAIDLUSA
SARAH	16	F	SP	RRAIDLUSA
MELECHSON, SOSCHE	20	F	SP	RRAIDLUSA
GARFINKEL, HODES	20	F	SP	RRAIDLUSA
BOIFERT, DINE	20	F	SP	RRAIDLUSA
GROTZKY, SCHIFFRE	17	F	SP	RRAIDLUSA
BARITSCH, VASI	32	F	W	RRAIDLUSA
DORAH	5	F	CHILD	RRAIDLUSA
FUNDILLA, GRUNE	50	F	W	RRAIDLUSA
ZIPPE	20	F	SP	RRAIDLUSA
ROCHEL	9	F	CHILD	RRAIDLUSA
FEINSTEIN, ESTHER	30	F	W	RRAIDLUSA
CHAIE	11	F	CH	RRAIDLUSA
LEIE	7	F	CHILD	RRAIDLUSA
JACOB	2	M	CHILD	RRAIDLUSA
PHILIP, ROCHEL	27	F	W	RRAIDLUSA
HANNA	6	F	CHILD	RRAIDLUSA
HIRSCHEL	5	M	CHILD	RRAIDLUSA
BERL.	2	M	CHILD	RRAIDLUSA
SEGULOWITZ, NECHAME	28	F	W	RRAIDLUSA
JANKEL	11	M	CH	RRAIDLUSA
SPRINGE	6	F	CHILD	RRAIDLUSA
SANIE	4	F	CHILD	RRAIDLUSA
RIWE	2	F	CHILD	RRAIDLUSA
KOSEL, GOLDE	36	F	W	RRAIDLUSA
MOSES	8	M	CHILD	RRAIDLUSA
ISAAC	7	M	CHILD	RRAIDLUSA
JUDEL	1	M	CHILD	RRAIDLUSA
LURIA, SORE	26	F	W	RRAIDLUSA
CHANE	5	F	CHILD	RRAIDLUSA
SEGAL, RIWE	24	F	W	RRAIDLUSA
FREIDE	1	F	CHILD	RRAIDLUSA
HELPERIN, FREIDE	30	F	W	RRAIDLUSA
RIWKE	11	F	CH	RRAIDLUSA
MINNE	8	F	CHILD	RRAIDLUSA
MOSES	2	M	CHILD	RRAIDLUSA

PASSENGER	AGE	SEX	OCCUPATION	PRV	VIL	DES
SCHLOME	2	M	CHILD	RR	AIDL	USA
ROSCHEL	36	F	W	RR	AIDL	USA
ESTER	8	F	CHILD	RR	AIDL	USA
SIMCHE	6	M	CHILD	RR	AIDL	USA
HIRSCH	5	M	CHILD	RR	AIDL	USA
KAUFMANN, MARIAN	36	F	W	RR	AIDL	USA
BEILE	10	F	CH	RR	AIDL	USA
BERTHA	2	F	CHILD	RR	AIDL	USA
ABRAHAM	1	M	CHILD	RR	AIDL	USA
GRUNSPAN, MIRKE	26	F	W	RR	AIDL	USA
SCHIE	8	F	CHILD	RR	AIDL	USA
ESTHER	6	F	CHILD	RR	AIDL	USA
CHAWE	2	F	CHILD	RR	AIDL	USA
ISRAEL	.09	M	INFANT	RR	AIDL	USA
GOLDSMITH, CHJENNE	32	F	W	RR	AIDL	USA
JANKEL	8	M	CHILD	RR	AIDL	USA
SLAK, NECHAME	24	F	W	RR	AIDL	USA
JAEL	7	M	CHILD	RR	AIDL	USA
MALKE	5	F	CHILD	RR	AIDL	USA
ROWINSKO, CINA	38	F	W	RR	AIDL	USA
MOTTEL	10	M	CH	RR	AIDL	USA
BEILE	6	F	CHILD	RR	AIDL	USA
JACUBOWITZ, JENTE	40	F	W	RR	AIDL	USA
SASCHE	11	M	CH	RR	AIDL	USA
ROSA	7	F	CHILD	RR	AIDL	USA
JOEL	2	M	CHILD	RR	AIDL	USA
ISAAC	1	M	CHILD	RR	AIDL	USA
LEIB	.02	M	INFANT	RR	AIDL	USA
CIESPELSKIN, MIECZYSLAW	32	M	UNKNOWN	RR	AIDL	USA
HELENA	17	F	W	RR	AIDL	USA

SHIP: BELGENLAND

FROM: ANTWERP
TO: NEW YORK
ARRIVED: 23 AUGUST 1888

PASSENGER	AGE	SEX	OCCUPATION	PRV	VIL	DES
EDELMANN, BERKO	26	M	LABR	RR	ZZZZ	NY
RECH, PETER	27	M	LABR	RR	ZZZZ	NY
SCHNEIDER, JOHANN	36	M	LABR	RR	ZZZZ	NY
MARGA.	29	F	UNKNOWN	RR	ZZZZ	NY
MARGA.	8	F	CHILD	RR	ZZZZ	NY
JACOB	7	M	CHILD	RR	ZZZZ	NY
WILH.	3	M	CHILD	RR	ZZZZ	NY
ELISAB.	1	M	CHILD	RR	ZZZZ	NY
DEBUS, KATCHEN	26	F	UNKNOWN	RR	ZZZZ	NY
SPITZNAGEL, MARIE	26	F	CK	RR	ZZZZ	NY
KEIL, OTTO	18	M	LABR	RR	ZZZZ	CH
GANZ, FREID	17	M	BKR	RR	ADOI	CH
BERGNER, ELISA	22	F	SVNT	RR	ZZZZ	PIT
MAUER, BARBA.	28	F	CK	RR	AIGZ	PIT
GREFFIN, BARBA.	28	F	CK	RR	AIGZ	PIT
HYPTE.	26	M	BLKSMH	RR	AILE	PIT
DRIESCHER, AUG.	25	M	LABR	RR	ZZZZ	CH
MAUD, MATH.	45	M	CPTR	RR	ZZZZ	AUS
PROBST, CARL	27	M	BCHR	RR	ZZZZ	MIL
SCHMEHEL, REINH.	21	M	BLKSMH	RR	ZZZZ	NY
GOLDE, AUGUST	27	M	CPTR	RR	ABHT	NY
KAUBZ, RICH.	16	M	UNKNOWN	RR	ZZZZ	NY
KOENIG, JACOB	19	M	BKR	RR	ZZZZ	NY
FAUZER, WILH.	30	M	CPTR	RR	AIMK	NY
FITZEK, RUD.	23	M	LABR	RR	ZZZZ	CH
EME.	21	M	LABR	RR	ZZZZ	CH
HESTEN, B.	27	M	CL	RR	ZZZZ	STL
BRUEHLE, GOTTL.	17	M	LABR	RR	ZZZZ	PHI
ORSOLACK, JOH.	39	M	LABR	RR	AIEB	NY
EKEL, FRITZ	22	M	BKR	RR	ZZZZ	NY
VONRAPELSHOFER, FRIED	22	M	LABR	RR	ZZZZ	NY
PFEIFER, NICOLAS	25	M	BCHR	RR	AIHU	NY
DEBUS, EDW.	23	M	BKBNDR	RR	ZZZZ	NY

PASSENGER	AGE	SEX	OCCUPATION	PRV	VIL	DES
HAUDLER, ELKE	40	F	UNKNOWN	RR	ZZZZ	NY
CHAWE	12	F	CH	RR	ZZZZ	NY
NOECH	10	M	CH	RR	ZZZZ	NY
HERSCH	8	M	CHILD	RR	ZZZZ	NY
JOSSEL	6	M	CHILD	RR	ZZZZ	NY
ABRAHAM	5	M	CHILD	RR	ZZZZ	NY
JITE	1	F	CHILD	RR	ZZZZ	NY
WILLOWSKY, HYMAN	19	M	TLR	RR	ADBQ	NY
COHEN, NEWLY	19	M	PRNTR	RR	ADBQ	NY
ANNE	23	F	UNKNOWN	RR	ADBQ	NY
JAMSOLANSKY, RAPHAEL	00	M	SLR	RR	ADBQ	NY
LEVENE, SIMON	22	M	MECH	RR	ADBQ	NY
JAFFE, HYMAN	35	M	MECH	RR	ADBQ	NY
BROWN, DEBORAH	30	F	UNKNOWN	RR	ADBQ	NY
NACHME	10	M	CH	RR	ADBQ	NY
OSCAR	3	M	CHILD	RR	ADBQ	NY
SCHATZ, RUD.	24	M	LABR	RR	ADBQ	NY
CHOBRONITZKY, AARON	21	M	TLR	RR	ADBQ	NY
ZEIZERMACHER, CALMAN	27	M	TLR	RR	ADBQ	NY
RACHEL	22	F	UNKNOWN	RR	ADBQ	NY
SILBERMANN, BARNETT	34	M	TLR	RR	ADBQ	NY
DEBORAH	27	F	UNKNOWN	RR	ADBQ	NY
CIMAMAN, LAZARUS	18	M	TLR	RR	ADBQ	BO
JOSSER, ELIAS	22	M	LABR	RR	ADBQ	BO
GOLD, SAML.	21	M	LABR	RR	ADBQ	BO
SCHWARZ, ALTER	16	M	CL	RR	AHXH	NY
OSTROWSKY, MICHEL	23	M	CL	RR	AINH	NY
MEYER, WILH.	21	M	LABR	RR	ZZZZ	NY
ZEŻEWSKI, NAFTALI	18	M	LABR	RR	ZZZZ	NY
RASCHOLOF--, U	24	M	TLR	RR	ZZZZ	NY
ROSENFELD, PESACH	34	M	LABR	RR	ZZZZ	NY
ASADOUR, HABECHIAN	34	M	LABR	RR	AIDR	SFC
HAGOPOS, KILIDPAN	45	M	LABR	RR	AIDR	SFC
MIHALI, SZAVENSKI	36	M	LABR	RR	ZZZZ	CH
ROFFMANN, ABRAH.	25	M	BBR	RR	AHXH	CIN
LEA	20	F	UNKNOWN	RR	AHXH	CIN
SCHARZE, RACHEL	22	F	UNKNOWN	RR	AHXH	CIN

SHIP: GALLIA

FROM: LIVERPOOL AND QUEENSTOWN
TO: NEW YORK
ARRIVED: 24 AUGUST 1888

PASSENGER	AGE	SEX	OCCUPATION	PRV	VIL	DES
SMOLUSKI, MOSES	21	M	LABR	RR	ACBF	USA
WIRSCHBOWITZ, LEA	32	M	PDLR	RR	ACBF	USA
BARANOWSKY, ABRAHAM	45	M	LABR	RR	ACBF	USA
GELLEMAN, BARUCH	17	F	SVNT	RR	ACBF	USA
HAN, REBECCA	20	F	SVNT	RR	ACBF	USA
TAGGE, CHANE	21	F	SMSTS	RR	ACBF	USA
WENMANN, FRANS	26	M	LABR	RR	AEWS	USA
HEDVIG	24	F	W	RR	AEWS	USA
WEMBERG, RESCHE	32	F	MA	RR	ACBF	USA
ISAAC	9	M	CHILD	RR	ACBF	USA
NECHANE	10	F	CH	RR	ACBF	USA
MINA	1	F	CHILD	RR	ACBF	USA
GOARDON, DEBORAH	35	F	MA	RR	ACBF	USA
MARIE	15	F	SVNT	RR	ACBF	USA
JACOB	10	M	CH	RR	ACBF	USA
EPHRAIM	9	M	CHILD	RR	ACBF	USA
SALOMON	2	M	CHILD	RR	ACBF	USA
LEVELAUSKY, ADIS	50	F	WI	RR	AEWS	USA

SHIP: WISCONSIN

FROM: LIVERPOOL AND QUEENSTOWN
TO: NEW YORK
ARRIVED: 24 AUGUST 1888

PASSENGER	AGE	SEX	OCCUPATION	PRV VIL DES
FINN, SUVE	15	M	LABR	RRZZZZUSA
RUDKOSKI, ISRAEL	40	M	TLR	RRZZZZUSA
RANTNOWITZ, MOSES	50	M	TLR	RRZZZZUSA
REINER, HINDE	13	F	SP	RRZZZZUSA
AKSELROD, SARA	20	F	SP	RRZZZZUSA
KAPLAN, ARON	22	M	PMBR	RRZZZZUSA
RICKLES, HENE	32	F	W	RRZZZZUSA
NOCHEM	7	F	CHILD	RRZZZZUSA
CHAWS	3	F	CHILD	RRZZZZUSA
KAUFMAN, SARA	26	F	W	RRZZZZUSA
ETTEL	6	F	CHILD	RRZZZZUSA
PERLMUTTER, TAUBE	31	F	W	RRZZZZUSA
DWORE	7	F	CHILD	RRZZZZUSA
MENRO	3	M	CHILD	RRZZZZUSA
REMBA, EFRAIM	7	M	CHILD	RRZZZZUSA
LEWITZ, JEHA	52	F	MA	RRZZZZUSA
WILENEZIK, MARDEK	33	M	GZR	RRZZZZUSA
CHAIET, BERL	26	M	GZR	RRZZZZUSA
HURWITZ, SCHAJS	7	M	CHILD	RRZZZZUSA
ESTER	6	F	CHILD	RRZZZZUSA
ABRAMOWITZ, RUIVEN	19	M	PNTR	RRZZZZUSA
BIALESTOFKI, SCHEINE	28	M	PNTR	RRZZZZUSA
RCZRICHOWSKI, BEILE	7	F	CHILD	RRZZZZUSA
SCHILMAN, SARAH	15	F	SP	RRZZZZUSA
ZIVITZ, MOSES	38	M	TLR	RRZZZZUSA
ICLIN, ELJA	22	M	TLR	RRZZZZUSA
SEIN, SORE	20	M	TLR	RRZZZZUSA
BROZIN, ZEDKA	29	F	W	RRZZZZUSA
HILDA	6	F	CHILD	RRZZZZUSA
SAMUEL	4	M	CHILD	RRZZZZUSA
CHAIM	2	M	CHILD	RRZZZZUSA
ROUSE, ISAK	18	M	MSN	RRZZZZUSA
BERKEWITZ, CHAIM	46	F	W	RRZZZZUSA
BERKA	20	F	SP	RRZZZZUSA
MARIA	7	F	CHILD	RRZZZZUSA
WIDALFSKY, RUWKE	50	F	MA	RRZZZZUSA
CHAWE	20	F	SP	RRZZZZUSA
SELDE	18	F	SP	RRZZZZUSA
ELIE	7	F	CHILD	RRZZZZUSA
JUDA	7	F	CHILD	RRZZZZUSA
KESSLER, CERESTINA	28	F	SP	RRZZZZUSA
FALATZK, JOHANNA	16	F	SP	RRZZZZUSA
JESSELSOHN, FEIWEL	34	F	SP	RRZZZZUSA
NEMANA, ISAAC	52	M	FARMER	RRZZZZUSA
FEIGE	50	F	W	RRZZZZUSA
RAHEL	18	F	SP	RRZZZZUSA
SCHLOMEN	6	M	CHILD	RRZZZZUSA
ESTER	7	F	CHILD	RRZZZZUSA
LIDSCHOWITZ, WAKEL	40	M	TLR	RRZZZZUSA
COHN, CHONER	25	M	TLR	RRZZZZUSA
BERKOWITZ, ISIDOR	7	M	CHILD	RRZZZZUSA
BERL	6	M	CHILD	RRZZZZUSA
SOPHIE	.11	F	INFANT	RRZZZZUSA
NEISENTREIF, LEA	17	F	SP	RRZZZZUSA
RISCHE	3	F	CHILD	RRZZZZUSA
RURLANDER, RUBEN	23	M	FARMER	RRZZZZUSA
KESSLER, SOPHIE	.10	F	INFANT	RRZZZZUSA
RAEKOWSKI, MAX	15	M	TLR	PLZZZZUSA
ANGER, JANKEL	40	M	GZR	RRZZZZUSA
KALETZKY, JUDEL	38	M	FARMER	RRZZZZUSA
BEILE	24	F	W	RRZZZZUSA
DORA	2	F	CHILD	RRZZZZUSA
KUNE	.09	F	INFANT	RRZZZZUSA
CLARA	.09	F	INFANT	RRZZZZUSA
KOPELOWITZ, SACHARA	22	F	SP	RRZZZZUSA
SCHAFINA, ISRAEL	46	M	TLR	RRZZZZUSA
REZRIK, SCHAIE	36	M	TLR	RRZZZZUSA
RERLMUTTER, JERIMAS	.10	M	INFANT	RRZZZZUSA
RIALOSTOZKY, CTRSSK.	.10	M	INFANT	RRZZZZUSA
LEVY, VICTOR	22	M	LABR	RRZZZZUSA
RABINOWITZ, NATHAN	27	M	LABR	RRZZZZUSA

SHIP: TRAVE

FROM: BREMEN AND SOUTHAMPTON
TO: NEW YORK
ARRIVED: 24 AUGUST 1888

PASSENGER	AGE	SEX	OCCUPATION	PRV VIL DES
HUENE, BARON	36	M	TT	RRAARRUSA
KONACKA, MARTHA	19	F	UNKNOWN	RRAILAUSA
SIFSCHITZ, F.	26	M	LABR	RRAILAUSA
KALMANN, RACHEL	63	M	UNKNOWN	RRAILAUSA
--HEL	24	U	UNKNOWN	RRAILAUSA
SIFSCHITZ, ISRAEL	24	M	UNKNOWN	RRAILAUSA
KERT, ERNESTINE	29	F	UNKNOWN	RRAILAUSA
GUSTAV	3	M	CHILD	RRAILAUSA
NEITZ, AUGUSTE	16	F	UNKNOWN	RRAILAUSA
KUEBLER, CHR.	34	M	FARMER	RRAILAUSA
MARGA.	27	F	UNKNOWN	RRAILAUSA
CHRISTE.	7	F	CHILD	RRAILAUSA
CAROLE.	3	F	CHILD	RRAILAUSA
ADAM	.09	M	INFANT	RRAILAUSA
CHRIST.	77	M	FARMER	RRAILAUSA
HENRIETTE	60	F	UNKNOWN	RRAILAUSA
CATHA.	21	F	UNKNOWN	RRAILAUSA
SARAH	19	F	UNKNOWN	RRAILAUSA
GALL, ELISAB.	21	F	UNKNOWN	RRAILAUSA
TESMANN, SUSANNA	29	F	UNKNOWN	RRAILAUSA
WOROBEICZIK, MOSES	50	M	LABR	RRAILAUSA
CHAJE	49	F	UNKNOWN	RRAILAUSA
BEILE	16	F	UNKNOWN	RRAILAUSA
GOLSBERG, JOCHEL	18	M	LABR	RRAILAUSA
JERKE, EMMA	24	F	UNKNOWN	RRAILAUSA
LACHERT, WILHE.	37	F	UNKNOWN	RRAILAUSA
ADELE	7	F	CHILD	RRAILAUSA
REINHOLD	5	M	CHILD	RRAILAUSA
AUTHUR	6	M	CHILD	RRAILAUSA
FEIST, DOROTHEA	38	F	UNKNOWN	RRAILAUSA
DREWS, EMIL	24	M	TCHR	RRAILAUSA
ZEIDLER, AUG.	48	M	MLR	RRAILAUSA
NATALIE	36	F	UNKNOWN	RRAILAUSA
REINHOLD	16	M	UNKNOWN	RRAILAUSA
AMALIE	14	F	UNKNOWN	RRAILAUSA
EMIL	6	M	CHILD	RRAILAUSA
OSCAR	5	M	CHILD	RRAILAUSA
SCHMIDT, FLORTA.	28	F	UNKNOWN	RRAILAUSA
ZACHERT, ED.	27	M	MCHT	RRAILAUSA
BLEIWEISS, BORUCH	40	M	DLR	RRAILAUSA
RYTKIN, OTIAS	30	M	DLR	RRAILAUSA
KOCHANSKI, CHAIN	40	M	LABR	RRAILAUSA
HELLER, CHAIN	23	M	LABR	RRAILAUSA
BLOCH, JOSEF	47	M	LABR	RRAHTFUSA
NACHAME	16	F	UNKNOWN	RRAHTFUSA
FINKETSTEIN, CHAJEM	25	M	LABR	RRAHZSUSA
SOBORDA, CHAIM	50	M	LLD	RRAHUFUSA
EIBSCHUETZ, GUSTJE	22	F	UNKNOWN	RRAIJSUSA
JETTY	3	F	CHILD	RRAIJSUSA
SOKAKEWSKY, JUDEE	28	F	UNKNOWN	RRAINZUSA

SHIP: CITY OF CHESTER

FROM: LIVERPOOL AND QUEENSTOWN
TO: NEW YORK
ARRIVED: 25 AUGUST 1888

PASSENGER	AGE	SEX	OCCUPATION	PRV VIL DES
ROSINDAHL, MEIZER	32	M	TCHR	RRZZZZBO
NYERECHOWSKY, ANTON	25	M	UNKNOWN	RRZZZZNY
WENUS, ANTON	35	M	UNKNOWN	RRZZZZNY
SZAPIRO, ABR.D.	17	M	UNKNOWN	RRZZZZNY
GRUNDFEST, M.	30	M	BLKSMH	RRAHTUNY
STUEBERG, BORIS	29	M	CL	RRAHTUPHI
AKITZER, JOSSEL	4	M	CHILD	RRZZZZNY
MORDCHE, KIZELARY	18	M	TLR	RRZZZZNY
GRIN, MOSES	26	M	TLR	RRZZZZNY
GERDMANN, SCHLOME	26	M	TLR	RRZZZZPHI
FRORMEZYKI, EFRAIM	17	M	TLR	RRZZZZNY
TILE, JACOB	36	M	TNSTH	RRZZZZNY
KETAIN, MISCHER	28	M	LABR	RRZZZZNY
SZOPIRO, LEISER	17	M	MECH	RRZZZZNY
TILL, HERMANN	26	M	TLR	RRZZZZNY
TARENSKY, L.MRS	25	M	BKBNDR	RRZZZZNY
ACKITSON, BAYLA-R.	26	F	UNKNOWN	RRZZZZNY
ATKINSON, ROSE	20	F	SP	RRZZZZPA
KAHN, FREIDE	19	F	SP	RRZZZZMD
DRAHBRUNAN, FRESDE	50	F	UNKNOWN	RRZZZZNY
RACHEL	10	F	CH	RRZZZZNY
JENKEL, DAVID	19	F	HTR	RRZZZZNY
CHAYE	18	F	HTR	RRZZZZNY
BISCHKOWICZ, KALMAN	10	M	CH	RRZZZZNY
DZIKOWIE, MARY	24	F	W	RRZZZZNY
JOHN	.09	M	INFANT	RRZZZZNY
ATKENSIN, MARIA	57	F	W	RRZZZZPA
MARKA	7	F	CHILD	RRZZZZPA
STEINBRUCK, TISET	30	F	W	RRZZZZNY
MERCK	.11	M	INFANT	RRZZZZNY
KIRSCHNER, FREIDE	25	F	TLR	RRZZZZNY
LEIB	5	M	CHILD	RRZZZZNY
KRAWSCHICK, RESEL	49	F	W	RRZZZZNY
JALKE	24	F	W	RRZZZZNY
SCHMRIL	3	M	CHILD	RRZZZZNY
RACHIL	.10	F	INFANT	RRZZZZNY
DEDA, MADALENA	30	F	W	RRZZZZNY
KATAZYNA	4	F	CHILD	RRZZZZNY
MARCIN	2	F	CHILD	RRZZZZNY
JOSEPH	.08	M	INFANT	RRZZZZNY
JORAELSKI, LEIB	24	F	W	RRZZZZNY
FREISNISKY, ISRAEL	12	M	CH	RRZZZZNY
ISRAELSKY, JANKEL	.09	F	INFANT	RRZZZZNY

SHIP: EDAM

FROM: AMSTERDAM
TO: NEW YORK
ARRIVED: 27 AUGUST 1888

PASSENGER	AGE	SEX	OCCUPATION	PRV VIL DES
BLANK, MICHEL	19	M	LABR	RRZZZZNY
KUMMERS---, LEISER	20	M	LABR	RRZZZZNY
SCHAPIRA, JANNE	23	F	MSVNT	RRZZZZNY
ROCHE	20	F	MSVNT	RRZZZZNY
GERSON, LOUIS	18	M	LABR	RRZZZZNY
KLEIN, JUDEL	37	M	LABR	RRZZZZNY
FRIEDMAN, JUDEL	20	M	LABR	RRZZZZNY
SCHMULEWITZ, ISAK	21	M	LABR	RRZZZZNY
HILLMAN, HIRSCH	20	M	LABR	RRZZZZNY
LUKIAN, ABRAH	22	M	LABR	RRZZZZNY
GRINSBERG, SALOMON	20	M	LABR	RRZZZZNY
GLANTZ, MO-TZ	19	M	LABR	RRZZZZNY
DU-IET, NEILE	15	F	MSVNT	RRZZZZNY
FRIEDMAN, M--CHEN	35	F	MSVNT	RRZZZZNY
WASSERMANN, JETTIE	10	F	CH	RRZZZZNY
CHADERS, DAVID	26	M	LABR	RRZZZZNY
SELIKOWITZ, MOSES	37	M	LABR	RRZZZZNY
FERNBERG, ABRAH	17	M	LABR	RRZZZZNY
SCHWARTZ, ARON	20	M	LABR	RRZZZZNY
STEN, BEILA	18	F	CK	RRZZZZNY
PAP-E, WILH	25	M	LABR	RRZZZZNY
SCHUBERT, GUSTAV	24	M	LABR	RRZZZZNY
EDUARD	20	M	LABR	RRZZZZNY
HECKEL, ANNA	18	F	MSVNT	RRZZZZNY
HEIN, HERM	21	M	LABR	RRZZZZNY
JULIUS	34	M	LABR	RRZZZZNY
HOPPE, KATH	33	F	NN	RRZZZZNY
KATH	9	F	CHILD	RRZZZZNY
MATELSOHN, ROBERT	15	M	LABR	RRZZZZNY
KORMAN, H	18	M	LABR	RRZZZZUNK
IBVORMAN, DANIEL	19	M	LABR	RRZZZZUNK
KLIBANSKY, DAVID	18	M	LABR	RRZZZZNY
KLEINMANN, A	20	M	LABR	RRZZZZNY

SHIP: CIRCASSIA

FROM: GLASGOW AND MOVILLE
TO: NEW YORK
ARRIVED: 27 AUGUST 1888

PASSENGER	AGE	SEX	OCCUPATION	PRV VIL DES
BORNE, ISRAEL	33	M	TLR	RRZZZZUSA
JURCK, MOSES	48	M	DLR	RRZZZZUSA
SCHLAFROCK, PESSACK	55	M	DLR	RRZZZZUSA
GRUN, BEILE	19	M	UNKNOWN	RRZZZZUSA
KALMANBUSSLOTH, ARON	28	M	DLR	RRZZZZUSA
SCHILEWSKI, JAKOB	11	M	DLR	RRZZZZUSA
JACOB	11	M	DLR	RRZZZZUSA
BERNSTEIN, MISSL	51	M	DLR	RRZZZZUSA
MOSCHE	16	M	DLR	RRZZZZUSA
KANAL, HIRSCH	27	M	TLR	RRZZZZUSA
ARONOWITZ, ARON	46	M	DLR	RRZZZZUSA
HERONE, CHAJE	11	M	UNKNOWN	RRZZZZUSA
SCHULKLUSTER, ABR.	45	M	DLR	RRZZZZUSA
SCHULLER, BR.	45	M	BKBNDR	RRZZZZUSA
KNIPERUECKOW, CHAIM	24	M	DLR	RRZZZZUSA
KOTZEN, SCHUMEL	22	M	DLR	RRZZZZUSA
LITTER, GEO	27	M	FLSH	RRZZZZUSA
GRIZMAN, MOSES	18	M	DLR	RRZZZZUSA
SALMAN, BLUME	40	M	LABR	RRZZZZUSA
JOSSEL	9	M	CHILD	RRZZZZUSA
MENDEL	7	M	CHILD	RRZZZZUSA
LEIB	3	M	CHILD	RRZZZZUSA
BIRICH, ANTON	27	M	LABR	RRZZZZUSA
MARGUIS, MASSE	11	M	UNKNOWN	RRZZZZUSA
MICH	9	M	CHILD	RRZZZZUSA
HURITZ, MOSES	27	M	DLR	RRZZZZUSA
LUBMAN, M	32	M	JNR	RRZZZZUSA
WEODHALS, D.	16	M	UNKNOWN	RRZZZZUSA
GUSNAN, ELIE	14	M	LABR	RRZZZZUSA
BAR.	11	M	LABR	RRZZZZUSA
GLUER, JUDE	40	M	GZR	RRZZZZUSA
LIBMAN, GEZAL	38	M	DLR	RRZZZZUSA
SCHIZNEZINSKI, PAUL	20	M	FLSH	RRZZZZUSA
WARSCHARZIG, CHAIM	52	M	FLSH	RRZZZZUSA
DERN, MEER	26	M	DLR	RRZZZZUSA
RUCHNER, ISAK	16	M	BBR	RRZZZZUSA
MISCHOLOWSKY, ALTER	25	M	LABR	RRZZZZUSA
KROWEIN, MOSES	28	M	DLR	RRZZZZUSA
GRASSMAN, MEYER	34	M	DLR	RRZZZZUSA
CZERHOWIN, MAYER	36	M	BCHR	RRZZZZUSA
SILBERBLUSS, JOHN	28	M	DLR	RRZZZZUSA
THUDER, CHRIS.	50	M	JNR	RRZZZZUSA
BEHRMAN, ISRAEL	25	M	BRR	RRZZZZUSA

PASSENGER	AGE	SEX	OCCUPATION	PRV VIL DES
KOHAN, ANTON	20	M	LABR	RRZZZZUSA
WISCHNEW, ELIE	18	M	LABR	RRZZZZUSA
ALEXROD, WOLF	36	M	LABR	RRZZZZUSA
RACHLIN, HIRSCH	18	M	LABR	RRZZZZUSA
KITAEZ, JUDEH	20	M	LABR	RRZZZZUSA
GETEL	18	F	W	RRZZZZUSA
CORDETZKI, CAROL	44	M	LABR	RRZZZZUSA
JADWIGA	30	F	W	RRZZZZUSA
ED.	3	M	CHILD	RRZZZZUSA
BOLHSTEIN, SCHUEL	18	M	DLR	RRZZZZUSA
CHAJE	20	F	W	RRZZZZUSA
SCHUARD, CHANE	16	F	HP	RRZZZZUSA
HEIN, SCHEINE	18	F	HP	RRZZZZUSA
JUDES	20	F	HP	RRZZZZUSA
HODESS, JUDE	21	F	HP	RRZZZZUSA
KRAWITZ, BEILE	24	F	HP	RRZZZZUSA
FEUBMANN, HANNE	20	F	HP	RRZZZZUSA
JAKOBWITZ, BERTHA	20	F	HP	RRZZZZUSA
GRYNNFEST, RIFKE	20	F	HP	RRZZZZUSA
SACHMANN, DORIS	16	F	W	RRZZZZUSA
MUCHESS, FEIGE	25	F	HP	RRZZZZUSA
SIMON, RWEBECA	22	F	HP	RRZZZZUSA
JEISCHOFF, MALKE	17	F	HP	RRZZZZUSA
WILKOWSKA, SOLE	21	F	HP	RRZZZZUSA
BUISTEIN, BETTY	25	F	HP	RRZZZZUSA
BIRMAN, CHAIM	21	F	HP	RRZZZZUSA
GIPKNOWSKI, MARIAN	21	F	W	RRZZZZUSA
BIENI	.06	F	INFANT	RRZZZZUSA
WRENSTEL, SARAH	45	F	W	RRZZZZUSA
SAL.	11	F	UNKNOWN	RRZZZZUSA
TULMANN, MARIA	28	F	W	RRZZZZUSA
MAX	5	M	CHILD	RRZZZZUSA
MINE	3	M	CHILD	RRZZZZUSA
WOLF	1	M	CHILD	RRZZZZUSA
OGISKI, BLUME	32	F	W	RRZZZZUSA
CHANE	3	M	CHILD	RRZZZZUSA
BASSA	1	M	CHILD	RRZZZZUSA
MELSON, HELENA	22	F	W	RRZZZZUSA
OLGA	5	F	CHILD	RRZZZZUSA
NICOLSEN	4	M	CHILD	RRZZZZUSA
SEGMUND	3	M	CHILD	RRZZZZUSA
WLADIMIR	1	M	CHILD	RRZZZZUSA
OKUR, CHAIE	36	F	W	RRZZZZUSA
BORACH	11	M	CH	RRZZZZUSA
MOSES	8	M	CHILD	RRZZZZUSA
RACHEL	3	F	CHILD	RRZZZZUSA
MAROCZNIK, JENTE	50	F	W	RRZZZZUSA
SCHUMEL	11	M	UNKNOWN	RRZZZZUSA
ISAK	6	M	CHILD	RRZZZZUSA
ZARNE, FEIGE	50	F	W	RRZZZZUSA
RAECHE	17	F	W	RRZZZZUSA
SELIG	7	M	CHILD	RRZZZZUSA
CHEMSKA, ETTEL	46	F	W	RRZZZZUSA
OLINSKI, JAHLE	36	F	W	RRZZZZUSA
CHAJE	8	M	CHILD	RRZZZZUSA
LEIB	8	F	CHILD	RRZZZZUSA
JOSEF	3	M	CHILD	RRZZZZUSA
BLUME	2	F	CHILD	RRZZZZUSA
DAVID	1	M	CHILD	RRZZZZUSA
SCHWARZMAN, DINE	16	F	HP	RRZZZZUSA
ELIAS	9	M	CHILD	RRZZZZUSA
DAVID	5	M	CHILD	RRZZZZUSA
JACOB	40	M	DLR	RRZZZZUSA
CHERJOWSKA, JUDEL	18	M	DLR	RRZZZZUSA
OLINSKI, SORE	14	M	DLR	RRZZZZUSA

SHIP: SAMARIA

FROM: LIVERPOOL AND QUEENSTOWN
TO: BOSTON
ARRIVED: 28 AUGUST 1888

PASSENGER	AGE	SEX	OCCUPATION	PRV VIL DES
KATZ, HINNA	45	F	W	RRZZZZMA
CHAIE	15	F	SP	RRZZZZMA
EITEL	10	F	CH	RRZZZZMA
HIRSCH	8	M	CHILD	RRZZZZMA
SWIDSCHE, ELLI	19	M	LABR	RRZZZZMA
TOMMINE, IDA	34	F	W	RRZZZZMA
AUGUSTA	9	F	CHILD	RRZZZZMA
OTTO	5	M	CHILD	RRZZZZMA
LYDIA	3	F	CHILD	RRZZZZMA
BERHOWITZ, JULIUS	20	M	CL	RRZZZZME

SHIP: GELLERT

FROM: HAMBURG AND HAVRE
TO: NEW YORK
ARRIVED: 28 AUGUST 1888

PASSENGER	AGE	SEX	OCCUPATION	PRV VIL DES
HIMMELHOCH, SARA	20	F	SGL	RRZZZZUSA
FEHRS, EMMA	19	F	SGL	RRACBFUSA
ARONSON, SARA	48	F	WO	RRAHTSUSA
PRENSKI, HERTZ	8	M	CHILD	RRAHTSUSA
WOLF	7	M	CHILD	RRAHTSUSA
GODOWSKI, LEIB	52	M	DLR	RRAHTSUSA
RIDLEWSKI, BEILE	18	F	SGL	RRAHTSUSA
EDELSTEIN, ISRAEL	22	M	LABR	RRZZZZUSA
GLUECK, KALMAN	24	M	LABR	RRAHTFUSA
LEWINSOHN, MOSES	22	M	DLR	RRAHUEUSA
SCHAFFER, LEA	40	F	WO	RRAHUEUSA
SAMUEL	16	M	CH	RRAHUEUSA
FRENDE	8	M	CHILD	RRAHUEUSA
SARA	7	F	CHILD	RRAHUEUSA
KODISCH	5	M	CHILD	RRAHUEUSA
REBECCA	4	F	CHILD	RRAHUEUSA
KRESTOF, MIHAL	18	M	UNKNOWN	RRZZZZUSA
ANNA	16	F	SGL	RRZZZZUSA
HOROWITZ, OFSCHI	33	M	LABR	RRAFWJUSA
TOGOWNIK, SCHLOME	31	M	LABR	RRAIIFUSA
ARKIN, JULIUS	46	M	DLR	RRZZZZUSA
BAEH.	30	M	GZR	RRZZZZUSA
HELSEN, LEIB	34	M	LABR	RRZZZZUSA
ROBINSON, ESTHER	43	F	WO	RRAIIGUSA
IDA	8	F	CHILD	RRAIIGUSA
DOLNITZTHY, JACOB	30	M	LABR	RRZZZZUSA
PAULE	28	F	W	RRZZZZUSA
ABL.	6	M	CHILD	RRZZZZUSA
RACHEL	.09	F	INFANT	RRZZZZUSA
BERKOWITZ, HARRIS	19	M	TLR	RRZZZZUSA
FELTENSTEIN, MARIE	18	F	SGL	RRZZZZUSA
JOGNITI, AGNISKA	19	F	SGL	RRZZZZUSA
SCHNEIDER, MARIE	30	F	WO	RRZZZZUSA
ALEXANDER	4	M	CHILD	RRZZZZUSA
GREGOR	.11	M	INFANT	RRZZZZUSA
LIN, CHAIE	22	F	WO	RRZZZZUSA
BEIRUCH	5	M	CHILD	RRZZZZUSA
JACOB	.11	M	INFANT	RRZZZZUSA
ARNOWSKY, MOSES	27	M	LABR	RRZZZZUSA
JACOB	25	M	LABR	RRZZZZUSA
COHEN, SARAH	30	F	SGL	RRAIHQUSA
MOSES	8	M	CHILD	RRAIHQUSA
NEIMARK, LEA	19	F	SGL	RRAHUPUSA
LEWITAN, CHAJE	50	F	WO	RRAHZSUSA
EFRAIM	8	M	CHILD	RRAHZSUSA
JECHIEL	7	M	CHILD	RRAHZSUSA

PASSENGER	AGE	SEX	OCCUPATION	PRV VIL DES
KNJZENOJT, ANNA	18	F	SGL	RRAHTFUSA
WENZJT, ANNA	19	F	SGL	RRAHTFUSA
SEIFERT, AUG.	33	M	LABR	RRAHTFUSA
HODESMANN, HDES.	60	F	WO	RRAHTWUSA
TREISAU, MORDCHE	17	F	SGL	RRZZZZUSA
KRISTOL, JOSEPH	39	M	UNKNOWN	RRZZZZUSA
BEILE	32	F	W	RRZZZZUSA
SCHEINE	8	M	CHILD	RRZZZZUSA
REBECCA	4	F	CHILD	RRZZZZUSA
JACOB	2	M	CHILD	RRZZZZUSA
SIEFERS, ERWIN	22	M	LABR	RRAHOOUSA
TREISAU, MORDCHE	23	F	SGL	RRZZZZUSA
MATUCZEWICZ, VACLAV	36	M	CL	RRZZZZUSA
NUDCE, MORITZ	15	M	TLR	RRZZZZUSA
GORDON, CHANNE	35	F	WO	RRZZZZUSA
RUWEN	.11	M	INFANT	RRZZZZUSA
MIRIOS, PERE	50	F	WO	RRZZZZUSA
WATSTEIN, MOSES	38	M	LABR	RRZZZZUSA
LANDE, JANKEL	23	M	LABR	RRAIONUSA
SILBERMANN, MALKE	45	F	WO	RRZZZZUSA
JENKE	23	M	CH	RRZZZZUSA
BROCHE	15	M	CH	RRZZZZUSA
HANNE	8	F	CHILD	RRZZZZUSA
FEGELE	7	F	CHILD	RRZZZZUSA
WEER, CLARA	33	F	WO	RRZZZZUSA
HEDWIG	8	F	CHILD	RRZZZZUSA
FELIX	4	M	CHILD	RRZZZZUSA
VALERIA	2	F	CHILD	RRZZZZUSA
ANNA	.11	F	INFANT	RRZZZZUSA
KOZMINSKI, GITTEL	19	F	SGL	RRZZZZUSA
WOLHEYN, ELIAS	40	M	LABR	RRAFWJUSA
CHASEN, BASCHE	24	F	WO	RRAIEQUSA
ISRAEL	.09	F	INFANT	RRAIEQUSA
LEA	20	F	SGL	RRAIEQUSA
FUCHS, RIEFKE	32	F	WO	RRZZZZUSA
JUDEL	8	M	CHILD	RRZZZZUSA
HERSCHEL	7	M	CHILD	RRZZZZUSA
ZIPPE	6	F	CHILD	RRZZZZUSA
SCHAJE	5	F	CHILD	RRZZZZUSA
FEIWUSCH	4	M	CHILD	RRZZZZUSA
ROSENBERG, SARAH	19	F	SGL	RRAHTFUSA
LAZYNSKI, MATHIAS	35	F	SGL	RRAHTFUSA
SOPHIE	25	F	W	RRAHTFUSA
HELENE	4	F	CHILD	RRZZZZUSA
KONSTANTIA	3	F	CHILD	RRZZZZUSA
PLACIDA	.05	F	INFANT	RRZZZZUSA
RISKIN, SIMON	25	M	TLR	RRAEFLUSA
TOMBACHER, SIMON	21	M	MCHT	RRAHRZUSA
BOLSKI, MOSES	32	M	MCHT	RRAHZSUSA
GANS, ABEL	50	M	LABR	RRAEFLUSA
LINA	54	F	W	RRAEFLUSA
SARA	8	F	CHILD	RRAEFLUSA
SCHMITT, RACHEL	23	F	WO	RRAEFLUSA
BENJAMIN	.11	M	INFANT	RRAEFLUSA
PARWER, MEYER	25	M	TLR	RRZZZZUSA
MECHOWER, MOSES	8	M	CHILD	RRZZZZUSA
SWIRSKY, ISAAC	26	M	LABR	RRZZZZUSA
GORDON, TANCHEN	25	M	LABR	RRAGRTUSA
MEKLER, MARCUS	36	M	LABR	RRZZZZUSA
JURKANSKE, DEBORA	19	F	SGL	RRZZZZUSA
WALDMANN, SIMCHE	46	M	TLR	RRAGRTUSA
GADON, HERRMAN	47	M	LABR	RRZZZZUSA
CHOSAN, MICHEL	20	M	DLR	RRAIGHUSA
IMCKES, DWORA	42	F	WO	RRAFVGUSA
EFRAIM	20	M	S	RRAFVGUSA
CLARA	8	F	CHILD	RRAFVGUSA
SARA	8	F	CHILD	RRAFVGUSA
BERGER, MIHAL	30	F	WO	RRAHTFUSA
NOSSEN	8	M	CHILD	RRAHTFUSA
ABRAHAM	7	M	CHILD	RRAHTFUSA
HILLEL	6	F	CHILD	RRAHTFUSA
WOLF	.11	M	INFANT	RRAHTFUSA
MICHALOWITZ, MARG.	20	F	SGL	RRAHTFUSA
EPSTEIN, SAMUEL	20	M	DLR	RRAHTFUSA
GLUECKLICH, ITZIG	56	M	DLR	RRAFVGUSA

PASSENGER	AGE	SEX	OCCUPATION	PRV VIL DES
RIEFKE	55	F	W	RRAFVGUSA
SOSSEL	17	M	CH	RRAFVGUSA
ETEL	8	F	CHILD	RRAFVGUSA
ABRAHAM	7	M	CHILD	RRAFVGUSA
JUDE	6	M	CHILD	RRAFVGUSA
SCHENDE	5	F	CHILD	RRAFVGUSA
KRIGSTEIN, FRUME	19	F	SGL	RRAFVGUSA
TACHNE	17	F	SGL	RRAFVGUSA
ROSENBERG, DORA	18	F	SGL	RRAHTFUSA
RICKE	16	F	SGL	RRAHTFUSA
RACHEL	14	F	SGL	RRAHTFUSA
STRZELINSKI, MORITZ	18	M	LABR	RRZZZZUSA
OLSZEWSKI, STANISLAUS	30	M	LABR	RRZZZZUSA
ANZULAEJTIS, ANTONI	26	M	LABR	RRAIBFUSA
LEVIN, PESCHE	26	F	WO	RRAGRTUSA
LEIBE	8	M	CHILD	RRAGRTUSA
SILLBERSTEIN, BESSIE	15	F	SGL	RRAHUVUSA
SARA	8	F	CHILD	RRAHUVUSA
PIKUS, JANKEL	19	M	LABR	RRZZZZUSA
WORINKO, CAROLINE	30	F	WO	RRZZZZUSA
PELONIA	4	F	CHILD	RRZZZZUSA
LUDWIGA	.03	F	INFANT	RRZZZZUSA
BADIAN, JOSEF	40	M	MCHT	RRAIOOUSA
SZENKOLOWSKA, JAN	28	M	LABR	RRZZZZUSA
KRAWCA, ROSA	20	F	SGL	RRAGRTUSA
REITMANN, BERNDEL	23	M	HRCTR	RRZZZZUSA
ROSSMEYER, OSWALD	38	M	MCHT	RRAIHDUSA
FRISCHMANN, NACHME	60	M	MCHT	RRAIOOUSA
WIRCHOWSKI, CHONE	37	M	TLR	RRAHTBUSA
ESTHER	33	F	W	RRAHTBUSA
ABRAHAM	16	M	CH	RRAHTBUSA
WOLF	8	M	CHILD	RRAHTBUSA
SARA	8	F	CHILD	RRAHTBUSA
MOSES	6	M	CHILD	RRAHTBUSA
GESE	.03	F	INFANT	RRAHTBUSA
SCHWUNG, WILH.	28	M	BLKSMH	RRZZZZUSA
AMALIE	29	F	W	RRZZZZUSA
SCHOLOMOWITZ, DAVID	40	M	LABR	RRAINMUSA
KRONOWSKY, LEIB	30	M	DLR	RRZZZZUSA
SEIDMANN, DAOZIK	18	M	DLR	RRZZZZUSA
ANDURSKY, SARA	17	F	SGL	RRZZZZUSA
LEWIN, JOSSEL	54	M	LABR	RRAGRTUSA
CHAIM	18	M	LABR	RRAGRTUSA
CHANNE	14	F	SGL	RRAGRTUSA
LEIB	45	M	LABR	RRAGRTUSA
OSSIPOWSKY, SCHOLEM	22	M	LABR	RRZZZZUSA
PULISCHEWSKY, SCHLOME	24	M	LABR	RRZZZZUSA
FRAENKEL, MEYER	46	M	LABR	RRZZZZUSA
MOSES	18	M	LABR	RRZZZZUSA
GOLDSTEIN, TANCHE	34	M	DLR	RRAHXLUSA
SCHAPIRO, TANCHE	17	M	DLR	RRAHXLUSA
SKLARSKY, TANCHE	26	M	DLR	RRAHXLUSA
ALEXANDROWITZ, HIRSCH	53	M	DLR	RRAHZSUSA
JUDITZKY, CHAJE	30	F	WO	RRZZZZUSA
BEREL	8	M	CHILD	RRZZZZUSA
SCHOLEM	7	M	CHILD	RRZZZZUSA
ANDURSKY, ABRAHAM	18	M	LABR	RRZZZZUSA
SAPERSTEIN, LINA	16	F	SGL	RRZZZZUSA
RUDNIK, JACOB	25	M	LABR	RRAGRTUSA
FRUMIN, MENDEL	20	M	LABR	RRZZZZUSA
SLISRACH, DAVID	28	M	DLR	RRAHQUUSA
SEDRANSKI, CHAJE	23	F	WO	RRAHVUUSA
CHAJE	4	F	CHILD	RRAHVUUSA
EISENBERG, DAVID	16	M	LABR	RRAHVUUSA
DUKAREWIG, RIWE	28	F	WO	RRAIIOUSA
ESTHER	8	M	CHILD	RRAIIOUSA
ABRAH	7	M	CHILD	RRAIIOUSA
ETEL	3	F	CHILD	RRAIIOUSA
JACOB	.11	M	INFANT	RRAIIOUSA
LASAR	.01	M	INFANT	RRAIIOUSA
KUTSCHAUCK, ALEXANDER	22	M	LABR	RRAIJVUSA
GES, JAN	47	M	LABR	RRZZZZUSA
KOSTROWSKI, BENJAMIN	26	M	DLR	RRAHVUUSA
BOZDANOWITZ, BARTLOMEY	30	M	LABR	RRZZZZUSA
MAGDA	20	F	W	RRZZZZUSA

PASSENGER	AGE	SEX	OCCUPATION	PRV VIL DES
GOLDUHR, PERE	20	F	WO	RRZZZZUSA
LELISCH	.11	F	INFANT	RRZZZZUSA
KROLL, CHAJE	21	F	WO	RRZZZZUSA
ALEXANDER	.11	M	INFANT	RRZZZZUSA
KOPSICZ, CAROLINE	22	F	WO	RRZZZZUSA
FRIEDMANN, GNESCHE	25	F	WO	RRZZZZUSA
ITZIG	.11	M	INFANT	RRZZZZUSA
BRAUNSTEIN, TEMA	35	F	WO	RRZZZZUSA
BRANDEL	14	M	CH	RRZZZZUSA
BEILE	8	F	CHILD	RRZZZZUSA
SARA	6	F	CHILD	RRZZZZUSA
DATNOW, LINE	23	F	WO	RRAIINUSA
MOHNAT, ARON	30	M	DLR	RRAHTFUSA
HOFFNER, SALOMON	35	M	DLR	RRZZZZUSA
WOLLERSTEIN, NOACH	28	M	MCHT	RRZZZZUSA
KAMENITZKI, BASCHE	20	F	WO	RRAIBOUSA
ISRAEL	.11	M	INFANT	RRAIBOUSA
WOLFF	.01	M	INFANT	RRAIBOUSA
SIMANSKI, STANISLAW	42	M	LABR	RRAIHNUSA
WOLTMANN, CHLOME	50	M	TNM	RRAHTFUSA
DWORE	50	F	W	RRAHTFUSA
BENZI	14	F	CH	RRAHTFUSA
BASCHE	8	F	CHILD	RRAHTFUSA
KRIEGEL, MOSES	40	M	SLR	RRAHTUUSA
KAPLAN, ABRAM	17	M	TLR	RRAHTUUSA
PORTMANN, HODE	17	F	SGL	RRAHTUUSA
FEIBUSCH, ABRAHAM	17	M	MCHT	RRAHULUSA
WOLF, SARA	22	F	SGL	RRAHOKUSA
HOCHENBERG, THERESE	25	F	WO	RRAHXHUSA
JETTE	4	F	CHILD	RRAHXHUSA
BETTI	.11	F	INFANT	RRAHXHUSA
KREMESSIER, LOUISE	40	F	WO	RRZZZZUSA
AUGUST	16	M	CH	RRZZZZUSA
MARIE	8	F	CHILD	RRZZZZUSA
OTTILIE	3	F	CHILD	RRZZZZUSA
GUSTAV	1	M	CHILD	RRZZZZUSA
CITRYN, SARA	30	F	SGL	RRACONUSA
LEIBUSCH	23	M	PNTR	RRACONUSA
SCHAPIRO, RUWEN	21	M	TLR	RRADOIUSA
CHAJE	20	F	W	RRADOIUSA
ZION, CHAIN	16	M	LABR	RRADOIUSA
CHANE	44	F	W	RRADOIUSA
ABL.	8	M	CHILD	RRADOIUSA
CHANNE	.11	F	INFANT	RRADOIUSA
PETEREIT, AUGUSTE	29	F	W	RRADOIUSA
MALWINE	.06	F	INFANT	RRADOIUSA
HIZIGRATH, ANNA	29	F	SGL	RRADOIUSA
SUBBOTNIK, MOSES	20	M	TLR	RRAINCUSA
ELIASCHKEWITZ, BENJAMIN	30	M	LABR	RRAGRTUSA
SONEK, CLARA	20	F	SGL	RRZZZZUSA
GITEL, ITZIG	17	M	FARMER	RRAGRTUSA
KREZMER, HIRSCH	16	M	DLR	RRZZZZUSA
PESKIN, JANKEL	21	M	BKR	RRAHOOUSA
GOLDE	24	F	W	RRAHOOUSA
JAWETZ, MARKUS	36	M	DLR	RRZZZZUSA
SILBERMANN, CHAJE	28	F	WO	RRZZZZUSA
GITTEL	.11	F	INFANT	RRZZZZUSA
BUCZYNSKI, MICHAEL	8	M	CHILD	RRAHTBUSA
GLINSKY, ANTON	21	M	LABR	RRZZZZUSA
HORN, JUDE	30	F	SGL	RRAHTFUSA
EPELBLAT, MAJE	8	M	CHILD	RRAHTFUSA
TURNIANSKI, FREIDE	20	F	WO	RRAHTFUSA
ABRAHAM	.11	M	INFANT	RRAHTFUSA
DANE	.01	M	INFANT	RRAHTFUSA
CHORASCHER, SCHEINE	25	F	WO	RRAFWJUSA
MINDEL	3	F	CHILD	RRAFWJUSA
BECKSTEIN, SISKIN	20	M	DLR	RRAGRTUSA
KAMINKER, U	37	M	TCHR	RRZZZZUSA
RAIVICH, SAMUEL	17	M	LABR	RRAHVUUSA
WEISS, JANKEL	20	M	TLR	RRZZZZUSA
KUSZINSKI, HENRY	24	F	WO	RRAHXHUSA
MAYER	.11	M	INFANT	RRAHXHUSA
ARCZEWSKI, ANTON	25	M	LABR	RRZZZZUSA

SHIP: ELBE

FROM: BREMEN AND SOUTHAMPTON
TO: NEW YORK
ARRIVED: 28 AUGUST 1888

PASSENGER	AGE	SEX	OCCUPATION	PRV VIL DES
FRUMES, ROSALIE	28	F	UNKNOWN	RRZZZZNY
MARIE	11	F	UNKNOWN	RRZZZZNY
GOLDE	8	F	CHILD	RRZZZZNY
KROJANSKI, SCHEINE	28	M	LABR	RRZZZZNY
OSIAS	11	M	UNKNOWN	RRZZZZNY
FEIGE	.01	M	INFANT	RRZZZZNY
JONAJTIS, MAGDALENE	24	F	UNKNOWN	RRZZZZNY
URSULA	3	F	CHILD	RRZZZZNY
WICHMANN, ELISE	19	F	UNKNOWN	RRAIECNY
NEUMANN, CLARA	40	F	UNKNOWN	RRAIECNY
HAHN, FRIEDRIKE	70	F	UNKNOWN	RRAIECNY
SCHRAGE, SOPHIE	45	F	UNKNOWN	RRZZZZNY
SOPHIE	11	F	UNKNOWN	RRZZZZNY
GRABOW, RUDOLF	34	M	MLR	RRZZZZNY
DAMMEIER, HEIN.	37	M	FARMER	RRZZZZNY
WILHELMINE	24	F	UNKNOWN	RRZZZZNY
ROWOLD, CONRAD	48	M	UNKNOWN	RRZZZZNY
WILHELMINE	52	F	UNKNOWN	RRZZZZNY
ERNST	14	M	UNKNOWN	RRZZZZNY
WESEMANN, FERD.	16	M	UNKNOWN	RRZZZZNY
GUTERMUTH, SOPHIE	38	F	UNKNOWN	RRZZZZNY
KATHIE	6	F	CHILD	RRZZZZNY
EMMA	11	F	CH	RRZZZZNY
WILLY	1	M	CHILD	RRZZZZNY
GROESCH, MARIA	20	F	UNKNOWN	RRZZZZNY
KNECHT, MICH.	67	M	FARMER	RRAIDUNY
WENGER, WILHELMINE	17	F	UNKNOWN	RRAIDUNY
REICHERT, MARIE	21	F	UNKNOWN	RRAIDUNY
WARSCHEWSKY, HEUL	18	F	LABR	RRZZZZNY
CETERSKA, FRANCISKA	23	F	UNKNOWN	RRZZZZNY
ROSALIE	3	F	CHILD	RRZZZZNY
BLAKOWIAK, SOFIA	30	F	UNKNOWN	RRZZZZNY
JAN	8	M	CHILD	RRZZZZNY
JADWIGA	3	F	CHILD	RRZZZZNY
ROSENBERG, LEA	22	M	UNKNOWN	RRZZZZNY
KURZ, CARL	23	M	TU	RRZZZZOH
JORE, ABRAHAM	19	M	LABR	RRZZZZNY
GOLDSTEIN, JOS.	24	M	LABR	RRZZZZNY
MARKOWIC, CLAUS	33	M	LABR	RRZZZZNY
RACHEL	9	M	CHILD	RRZZZZNY
MEYER	7	M	CHILD	RRZZZZNY
RIFKE	5	M	CHILD	RRZZZZNY
GITEL	2	M	CHILD	RRZZZZNY
LICHTSTEIN, ROSE	10	F	CH	RRZZZZNY
ROSENBERG, MARIE	3	F	CHILD	RRZZZZNY
LINA	3	F	CHILD	RRZZZZNY
STALLER, MOSES	36	M	DLR	RRZZZZOH
ZLATE	37	F	UNKNOWN	RRZZZZOH
CHENKE	20	F	UNKNOWN	RRZZZZOH
FANNI	8	F	CHILD	RRZZZZOH
DAVID	6	M	CHILD	RRZZZZOH
MARENS	5	M	CHILD	RRZZZZOH
SAMSON	2	M	CHILD	RRZZZZOH
ALEXANDER	.06	M	INFANT	RRZZZZOH
MENAKER, MORDUSCH	15	M	UNKNOWN	RRZZZZNY
LUTZEWSKY, JURIE	36	F	UNKNOWN	RRZZZZNY
PIVOVARSKI, FRANZIS	28	M	LABR	RRZZZZNY
TEITZ, CHAJEM	27	F	UNKNOWN	RRZZZZNY
RUBEN	.06	F	INFANT	RRZZZZNY
GRUENBLAT, JONAS	25	M	FARMER	RRZZZZNY
ELKE	25	F	UNKNOWN	RRZZZZNY
SESSE	.05	F	INFANT	RRZZZZNY
BOCK, RIEWE	18	F	UNKNOWN	RRZZZZNY
ZADIKOW, ESTHER	37	M	FARMER	RRZZZZNY
BENJAMON	9	M	CHILD	RRZZZZNY
ELKE	5	F	CHILD	RRZZZZNY
STEINBERG, CHAJE	10	F	CH	RRZZZZNY
GABLONSKY, TYNCHES	24	M	FARMER	RRZZZZNY

PASSENGER	AGE	SEX	OCCUPATION	PRIV	VIL	DES
ALMINE	25	F	UNKNOWN	RR	ZZZZ	NY
JUKUBLONIS, J.J.	26	M	LABR	RR	ZZZZ	NY
PETRINE	22	F	UNKNOWN	RR	ZZZZ	NY
KATZ, FREIDE	36	F	UNKNOWN	RR	ZZZZ	NY
ZULKOWSKA, MARYANNA	26	F	UNKNOWN	RR	ZZZZ	BUF
STEFAN	7	M	CHILD	RR	ZZZZ	BUF
KAZIMA	6	F	CHILD	RR	ZZZZ	BUF
ANNA	.09	F	INFANT	RR	ZZZZ	BUF
MINARSKI, ELIAS	16	M	LABR	RR	ZZZZ	IL
NEUMANN, JUDEL	36	M	DLR	RR	ZZZZ	PA
KAPLAN, BEREL	47	M	DLR	RR	ZZZZ	PA
FEIGE	44	M	DLR	RR	ZZZZ	PA
MARE	17	M	DLR	RR	ZZZZ	PA
CHAIM	11	M	DLR	RR	ZZZZ	PA
MOSSESSOHN, HESSER	20	M	DLR	RR	ZZZZ	PA
AUSIEBEWITZ, LIEBE	23	F	UNKNOWN	RR	ZZZZ	NY
STEINBERG, CHAJEM	23	M	CPR	RR	ZZZZ	NY
SCHWARZ, MATHAUS	24	M	LABR	RR	ZZZZ	NY
AUSIEBEWITZ, ANNA	.01	F	INFANT	RR	ZZZZ	NY
JACKHEIM, WOLF	27	M	LABR	RR	ZZZZ	NY
LEBOWITZ, SCHULEM	35	M	LABR	RR	ZZZZ	NY
U	32	F	UNKNOWN	RR	ZZZZ	NY
KRAIBACH, ISAAK	18	M	UNKNOWN	RR	ZZZZ	NY
GROSS, ENDRICKE	23	F	UNKNOWN	RR	ZZZZ	NY
ZOFFE, BERNH.	20	M	SMH	RR	ZZZZ	NY
BUNOVIUS, MATEWISCH	38	M	FARMER	RR	ZZZZ	NY
U	35	F	UNKNOWN	RR	ZZZZ	NY
STAMM, ISAAC	32	M	BCHR	RR	ZZZZ	NY
KOSRTURA, HANNA	28	F	UNKNOWN	RR	ZZZZ	NY
HANNA	4	F	CHILD	RR	ZZZZ	NY
HRASKO, MARIA	29	F	UNKNOWN	RR	ZZZZ	NY
MARIA	6	F	CHILD	RR	ZZZZ	NY
GERGELY, PAVEL	29	M	LABR	RR	ZZZZ	NY
SKRPAN, ANNA	25	F	UNKNOWN	RR	ZZZZ	NY
FRANZ	.09	M	INFANT	RR	ZZZZ	NY
LUKACS, JANOS	26	M	LABR	RR	ZZZZ	NY

SHIP: NEVADA

FROM: LIVERPOOL AND QUEENSTOWN
TO: NEW YORK
ARRIVED: 29 AUGUST 1888

PASSENGER	AGE	SEX	OCCUPATION	PRIV	VIL	DES
DEBBESKY, CHINANIA	16	M	LABR	RR	ACBF	USA
EKONOR, LEVI	35	M	LABR	RR	ACBF	USA
KATZ, JACOB	22	M	LABR	RR	ACBF	USA
BOKSCHITZKY, JOS.	18	M	LABR	RR	ACBF	USA
KLIWANSKI, LOUIS	17	M	LABR	RR	ACBF	USA
PESERIETY, ENNE	19	F	SP	RR	ACBF	USA
SCHWARTZ, LEIE	18	F	SP	RR	ACBF	USA
ARESSA	19	F	SP	RR	ACBF	USA
UDEL	17	F	SP	RR	ACBF	USA
LEBOWITZ, HANE	23	F	W	RR	ACBF	USA
DAVID	.09	M	INFANT	RR	ACBF	USA
PRIBZ, MEIER	18	M	LABR	RR	ACBF	USA
RACHEL	20	F	SP	RR	ACBF	USA
SPALINETZ, LEBE	18	F	SP	RR	ACBF	USA
BASCHE	16	F	SP	RR	ACBF	USA
SARAH	7	F	CHILD	RR	ACBF	USA
KARLOWSKI, SARA	18	F	SP	RR	ACBF	USA
BREZINSKI, CHAIE	38	F	W	RR	ACBF	USA
GOLDE	7	F	CHILD	RR	ACBF	USA
SARA	6	F	CHILD	RR	ACBF	USA
ABRAM	3	M	CHILD	RR	ACBF	USA
MELOWITZ, MOSES	7	M	CHILD	RR	ACBF	USA
MEICHASCHOW, TUNCHE	40	F	W	RR	ACBF	USA
ISAAC	25	M	LABR	RR	ACBF	USA
ROCHEL	18	F	SP	RR	ACBF	USA
SARAH	19	F	SP	RR	ACBF	USA

SHIP: STETE OF INDIANA

FROM: GLASGOW AND LARNE
TO: NEW YORK
ARRIVED: 30 AUGUST 1888

PASSENGER	AGE	SEX	OCCUPATION	PRIV	VIL	DES
RILTSON, NILS	26	M	LABR	RR	AIDL	USA
HAFFENBERG, SCHMUEL	34	M	UNKNOWN	RR	AIDL	USA
LAMMER, NATHAN	20	M	LABR	RR	AIDL	USA
HELTERMANN, WALF	48	M	LABR	RR	AIDL	USA
CHIWSKY, TOBIAS	19	M	PDLR	RR	AIDL	USA
ITZKOWITZ, HERSCH	17	M	LABR	RR	AIDL	USA
HELTELMANN, SAMUEL	2	M	CHILD	RR	AIDL	USA
ZIPTIKOW, U	45	F	W	RR	AIDL	USA
BLITZKY, -ASCHE	28	F	W	RR	AIDL	USA
HIRSCH	2	M	CHILD	RR	AIDL	USA
MOSES	1	M	CHILD	RR	AIDL	USA
SCHINERNITZSKY, RIFKE	26	F	W	RR	AIDL	USA
MORDSCHE	6	M	CHILD	RR	AIDL	USA
MUNSCHE	4	M	CHILD	RR	AIDL	USA
FRIMMIE	2	F	CHILD	RR	AIDL	USA
HERZBERG, CHAJE	10	F	CH	RR	AIDL	USA
HELTERMANN, SAMUEL	16	M	PDLR	RR	AIDL	USA
OEB.	8	F	CHILD	RR	AIDL	USA
SARAH	10	F	CH	RR	AIDL	USA
BRODSKY, SCHIFFRE	9	F	CHILD	RR	AIDL	USA
PEISASH	1	M	CHILD	RR	AIDL	USA
SALOMON	.03	M	INFANT	RR	AIDL	USA
AUBBUK, ISAAC	11	M	CH	RR	AIDL	USA
MENASCHE	9	F	CHILD	RR	AIDL	USA
MEKOWAITZ, FEIGE	45	F	W	RR	AIDL	USA
ZIPPE	9	F	CHILD	RR	AIDL	USA
MIFLOWSKY, PAULINE	35	F	W	RR	AIDL	USA
MARIA	9	F	CHILD	RR	AIDL	USA
BRODSKY, BLUME	30	F	W	RR	AIDL	USA
BASOHE	14	F	CH	RR	AIDL	USA
SOPIRO, CHASSE	34	F	W	RR	AIDL	USA
CHANE	10	F	CH	RR	AIDL	USA
ABRAHAM	11	M	CH	RR	AIDL	USA
CHAIE	8	F	CHILD	RR	AIDL	USA
MEIR	6	M	CHILD	RR	AIDL	USA
HODES	2	M	CHILD	RR	AIDL	USA
HOSCHENAU, R.	28	F	W	RR	AIDL	USA
NELBONU	9	F	CHILD	RR	AIDL	USA
BENJAMIN	7	M	CHILD	RR	AIDL	USA
SARAH	5	F	CHILD	RR	AIDL	USA
MOSES	2	M	CHILD	RR	AIDL	USA
SELDE	.03	F	INFANT	RR	AIDL	USA
RALE	1	F	CHILD	RR	AIDL	USA
BARANOWITSCH, CHAWE	40	F	W	RR	AIDL	USA
MAUSCHE	6	M	CHILD	RR	AIDL	USA
MARIASOHE	5	F	CHILD	RR	AIDL	USA
KURTZEN, RIWKE	17	F	DMS	RR	AIDL	USA
LEBOWITZ, RIWKE	18	F	DMS	RR	AIDL	USA
HERZBERG, ABRAHAM	22	M	DMS	RR	AIDL	USA
BAUCH, ZEIK	19	F	DMS	RR	AIDL	USA

SHIP: LAHN

FROM: BREMEN
TO: NEW YORK
ARRIVED: 31 AUGUST 1888

PASSENGER	AGE	SEX	OCCUPATION	PRIV	VIL	DES
WOLFSOHN, JENNY	19	F	UNKNOWN	RR	AIIN	RSS
RAPPAPORT, DAVID	19	M	LABR	RR	AFWJ	USA
ZUERNDROFER, MAX	17	M	LABR	RR	ZZZZ	USA
HIRNER, GOTTLOB	15	M	UNKNOWN	RR	AIBJ	USA
KINZER, HERM.	31	M	BKR	RR	ZZZZ	USA
BRODHAG, PAULE.	32	F	W	RR	ZZZZ	USA

PASSENGER	A G E	S E X	OCCUPATION	P V D R I E V L S
CHRIST.	9	M	CHILD	RRZZZZUSA
ADOLF	7	M	CHILD	RRZZZZUSA
EDUARD	2	M	CHILD	RRZZZZUSA
CARL	.06	M	INFANT	RRZZZZUSA
KERNER, NANE	20	F	UNKNOWN	RRZZZZUSA
ROLLER, JACOB	28	M	MLR	RRAIBJUSA
KLEIN, MARIE	26	F	UNKNOWN	RRZZZZUSA
BEERKIROHER, GOTTLOB	17	M	LABR	RRZZZZUSA
JAUSS, MINA	18	F	UNKNOWN	RRAIKMUSA
MUELLER, FRIDA	16	F	UNKNOWN	RRAIKMUSA
PFAENDER, EMILIA	43	F	W	RRAIKMUSA
CATHA.	20	F	UNKNOWN	RRAIKMUSA
LINA	15	F	UNKNOWN	RRAIKMUSA
GEORG	11	M	CH	RRAIKMUSA
MATHAEUS	4	M	CHILD	RRAIKMUSA
SCHMITZLER, JOHANN	25	M	LABR	RRZZZZUSA
SCHWARZ, LEOPOLD	18	M	MCHT	RRZZZZUSA
LOEWENSTEIN, MARKUS	16	M	MCHT	RRZZZZUSA
RUDOLPH, OTTO	28	M	LABR	RRZZZZUSA
STAIGER, HERME.	18	F	UNKNOWN	RRZZZZUSA
SIEBERT, AUGUST	26	M	LABR	RRZZZZUSA
SCHWAPPACHER, MARGE.	22	F	UNKNOWN	RRZZZZUSA
DUSEL, LORENZ	28	M	FARMER	RRAIBCUSA
ABLEMANN, LEHA	16	F	UNKNOWN	RRZZZZUSA
MINNA	26	F	UNKNOWN	RRZZZZUSA
ZOELLER, ELISE	18	F	UNKNOWN	RRZZZZUSA
FRIEDR.	16	M	BKLYR	RRZZZZUSA
BECKER, CARGE.	22	F	UNKNOWN	RRZZZZUSA
WOLF, GOTTLIEB	16	M	FARMER	RRZZZZUSA
KROTKI, MARKS	20	M	MCHT	RRZZZZUSA
BIDERMANN, ESTER	18	F	UNKNOWN	RRAILAUSA
ROSENTHAL, JOSSEL	49	M	LABR	RRAILAUSA
JANKEL	11	M	CH	RRAILAUSA
ANDERSSON, CARL	22	M	LABR	FNZZZZUNK
SOEDERMAN, EMILIA	24	F	UNKNOWN	FNZZZZUNK
BRUNE, GUSTAF	20	M	LABR	FNZZZZUNK
FRANSSON, FRANS	18	M	LABR	FNZZZZUNK
SPANN, JOHANNES	19	M	LABR	FNZZZZUNK
GUSTAFSON, ANNA	23	F	UNKNOWN	FNZZZZUNK
JOHANASSON, ANNA	22	F	UNKNOWN	FNZZZZUNK
SPANN, ELIAS	23	M	LABR	FNZZZZUNK
ERIKSSON, HJOLMAR	19	M	LABR	FNZZZZUNK
ADAMSSON, EMMA	32	F	UNKNOWN	FNZZZZUNK
HOLM, CAROLA.	23	F	UNKNOWN	FNZZZZUNK
JONASDOFFER, MATHA.	40	F	UNKNOWN	FNZZZZUNK
BORGSBROEM, MATHA.	47	F	W	FNZZZZUNK
HULDA	23	F	UNKNOWN	FNZZZZUNK
GOLDERSSOHN, BERNHD.	16	M	UNKNOWN	FNZZZZUNK
LUNDOTROEM, HILDA	28	F	UNKNOWN	FNZZZZUNK
HOPPENHEIM, PAULE.	32	F	W	FNAFWJUNK
NOCHEM	16	M	LABR	FNAFWJUNK
FANNY	15	F	UNKNOWN	FNAFWJUNK
FRIEDA	9	F	CHILD	FNAFWJUNK
BRODSKY, SELIG	25	M	MCHT	FNAFWJUNK
RIWKE	23	F	W	FNAFWJUNK
ROSENTHAL, HENACH	8	M	CHILD	FNAFWJUNK
CHANE	4	M	CHILD	FNAFWJUNK
HOLZMAN, M.J.	21	M	LABR	FNAFWJUNK
CHAJE	20	M	LABR	FNAFWJUNK
WERTELEWSKY, BENJAMIN	28	M	LABR	FNAIINUNK
WULFSOHN, BENJAMIN	42	M	LABR	FNAIINUNK
ARON	14	M	UNKNOWN	FNAIINUNK
SANAPEL, ISAAK	30	M	LABR	FNAIINUNK
HAMUTA, FRIEDR.	28	M	LABR	FNAFWJUNK
GOLDMANN, MOSES	42	M	LABR	FNAIINUNK
JETTE	32	F	W	FNAIINUNK
HERCH	16	M	UNKNOWN	FNAIINUNK
ROCHEL	11	F	CH	FNAIINUNK
MOTTEL	9	M	CHILD	FNAIINUNK
SIMON	7	M	CHILD	FNAIINUNK
LEAH	5	F	CHILD	FNAIINUNK
REBECCA	.09	F	INFANT	FNAIINUNK
SARAH	3	F	CHILD	FNAIINUNK
PERLSTEIN, MENDEL	38	M	LABR	FNAIINUNK
BENJAMIN	8	M	CHILD	FNAIINUNK
FELDMANN, DAVID	69	M	LABR	FNAIINUNK
LEAH	55	F	W	FNAIINUNK
REBECCA	22	F	UNKNOWN	FNAIINUNK
SCHEREPOVSKI, FRIDA	16	F	UNKNOWN	FNAHOKUNK

SHIP: WESER

FROM: BREMEN
TO: BALTIMORE
ARRIVED: 31 AUGUST 1888

PASSENGER	A G E	S E X	OCCUPATION	P V D R I E V L S
KAPLAN, GITTE	27	F	UNKNOWN	RRZZZZOH
HIRSCH	5	M	CHILD	RRZZZZOH
SAUL	3	M	CHILD	RRZZZZOH
LEISER	.02	M	INFANT	RRZZZZOH
HIRSCH, SCHEINE	50	F	UNKNOWN	RRZZZZOH
CHEIM, ADOLF	18	M	FARMER	RRZZZZOH
SCHWITKOWER, SCHULEM	20	M	MCHT	RRZZZZOH
GROSS, JUDITH	28	F	UNKNOWN	RRZZZZMN
LEIB	8	M	CHILD	RRZZZZMN
HERZ	4	M	CHILD	RRZZZZMN
TURMANN, SCHIFFKE	30	F	UNKNOWN	RRZZZZMN
TAUBE	10	F	UNKNOWN	RRZZZZMN
HERZ	7	M	CHILD	RRZZZZMN
JUDEL	4	F	CHILD	RRZZZZMN
BASCHE	.09	F	INFANT	RRZZZZMN
SILBERMANN, SCHORKE	19	M	DLR	RRZZZZIL
KAHN, DORA	18	F	UNKNOWN	RRZZZZIL
FANNY	16	F	UNKNOWN	RRZZZZIL
ELIAS	10	M	CH	RRZZZZIL
BISKOMMLER, HINDE	42	F	UNKNOWN	RRZZZZPA
BERL	25	M	DLR	RRZZZZPA
DISCHKE	11	F	UNKNOWN	RRZZZZPA
JANKEL	8	M	CHILD	RRZZZZPA
SCHEINDEL	5	M	CHILD	RRZZZZPA
SAMI	3	F	CHILD	RRZZZZPA
GUDELKE, EMIL	18	M	MCHT	RRZZZZMI
KLISS, JAN	12	M	UNKNOWN	RRZZZZPA
CAJETAN	10	M	CH	RRZZZZPA
KRASINSKA, ANNA	28	F	UNKNOWN	RRZZZZPA
VALERIA	.10	F	INFANT	RRZZZZPA
MICHALKOWSKY, JAN	30	M	LABR	RRZZZZMD
PUCHANOWSKI, VICTOR	18	M	FARMER	RRZZZZUNK
JWRSONSKY, STANISLAUS	23	M	FARMER	RRZZZZUNK
SKUPKI, ANTON	40	M	LABR	RRZZZZUNK
GUTKIN, JOSEPH	36	M	MCHT	RRZZZZPA
CHIGER, SALOMON	26	M	MCHT	RRZZZZMD
KAHNUS, TURGERS	35	M	LABR	RRZZZZMD
LOEWINSOHN, ISAAC	31	M	DLR	RRZZZZMD
SAUL	13	M	UNKNOWN	RRZZZZMD
HERZ, BERN	25	M	MCHT	RRZZZZMD
ZENDRICKE, ELIAS	28	M	PNTR	RRZZZZPA
VICTORIA	4	F	CHILD	RRZZZZPA
CASIMIR	3	M	CHILD	RRZZZZPA
MARIANNA	.10	F	INFANT	RRZZZZPA
JAGIELSKI, JOSEPH	41	M	MCHT	RRZZZZPA
KLEYS, ELISABETH	35	F	UNKNOWN	RRZZZZMA
CASIMIR	4	M	CHILD	RRZZZZMA
SIGMUND	.11	M	INFANT	RRZZZZMA
KASINSKY, FELIX	22	M	LABR	RRZZZZKY
LAZAROWIEZS, MAJE	30	F	UNKNOWN	RRZZZZMO
GOLDE	10	F	CH	RRZZZZMO
LIEBE	8	F	CHILD	RRZZZZMO
LAZARUS	6	M	CHILD	RRZZZZMO
HADE	3	F	CHILD	RRZZZZMO
KUREWITZ, JANKEL	18	M	LABR	RRZZZZOH
GITTA	16	F	UNKNOWN	RRZZZZOH
BERLIN, FEIGE	39	F	UNKNOWN	RRZZZZPA
ZAMEL	10	M	CH	RRZZZZPA
SARAH	8	F	CHILD	RRZZZZPA

PASSENGER	AGE	SEX	OCCUPATION	PV VIL DES
ESTER	6	F	CHILD	RRZZZZPA
MINSCHE	3	F	CHILD	RRZZZZPA
SEIDERMANN, LOUIS	43	M	ENGR	RRZZZZPA
FRIED, KODUSCH	18	M	LABR	RRZZZZPA
ETTEL	19	F	UNKNOWN	RRZZZZPA
BREUER, ELIAS	31	M	BCHR	RRZZZZIL
MILKEREIST, CHRISTINE	18	F	UNKNOWN	RRZZZZIL
AUGUSTE	.02	F	INFANT	RRZZZZIL
DACHSLAGER, CHAIM	18	M	MCHT	RRZZZZMD
SPACK, JULIANA	21	F	UNKNOWN	RRZZZZNY
WEINKRANTZ, JOIL	26	M	PDLR	RRZZZZOH
MOEL, CHAJE	58	F	UNKNOWN	RRZZZZOH
MAJEM	18	M	PDLR	RRZZZZOH
SEMP	11	M	CH	RRZZZZOH
ELKE	5	F	CHILD	RRZZZZOH
MALKE	15	F	UNKNOWN	RRZZZZOH
WEINKRANTZ, BASE	38	F	UNKNOWN	RRZZZZOH
SAMUEL	19	M	PDLR	RRZZZZOH
GITTE	2	F	CHILD	RRZZZZOH
SCHEINDEL	8	F	CHILD	RRZZZZOH
ROSA	8	F	CHILD	RRZZZZOH
CHAJE	7	F	CHILD	RRZZZZOH
LERE	4	M	CHILD	RRZZZZOH
BEILE	.11	F	INFANT	RRZZZZOH
GLUCKMANN, FANNY	50	F	UNKNOWN	RRZZZZOH

SHIP: RHYNLAND

FROM: ANTWERP
TO: NEW YORK
ARRIVED: 31 AUGUST 1888

PASSENGER	AGE	SEX	OCCUPATION	PV VIL DES
GROCOFSKY, STANISLAS	50	M	PNTR	RRZZZZUNK
BOEUR, BERER	30	M	HTR	RRZZZZPHI
ADM--K	11	M	CH	RRZZZZNY
ROSENBLUM, NATHAN	27	M	CGRMKR	RRZZZZNY

SHIP: ROMAN

FROM: LIVERPOOL
TO: BOSTON
ARRIVED: 31 AUGUST 1888

PASSENGER	AGE	SEX	OCCUPATION	PV VIL DES
SAROWSKY, MOSES	59	M	LABR	RRZZZZNY
CHAIE	59	F	W	RRZZZZNY
RANCH, HASCH	46	M	LABR	RRZZZZNY
GOLDBERG, FEIGE	26	F	W	RRZZZZNY
SARAH	3	F	CHILD	RRZZZZNY
ABOM	.03	M	INFANT	RRZZZZNY
NEWMAN, BLUM	22	M	LABR	RRZZZZNY
HIENDE	17	F	W	RRZZZZNY
UNGER, SAM.	18	M	LABR	RRZZZZNY
BALSAM, ESTER	18	F	SP	RRZZZZNY
COHEN, CHANE	33	F	W	RRZZZZNY
MOSES	6	M	CHILD	RRZZZZNY
WASSERZIHER, LOUISA	20	F	SP	RRZZZZNY
ZIGELM, ABRM.J.	28	M	LABR	RRZZZZNY
TOLOTORE-, SCHERNY	24	F	SP	RRZZZZCLE
MALLE	20	F	SP	RRZZZZCLE
SANDLOWITZ, FRAGDA	44	M	LABR	RRZZZZNY
BRAURUNAN, SAMUEL	16	M	LABR	RRZZZZBO
ABRM.	20	M	LABR	RRZZZZBO
FORRCKER, RACHAEL	25	F	W	RRZZZZBO
LEAH	.03	F	INFANT	RRZZZZBO
EIDE	40	F	W	RRZZZZBO
NECHE	11	F	CH	RRZZZZBO
SARAH	8	F	CHILD	RRZZZZBO
SCHEINE	7	F	CHILD	RRZZZZBO
ISRAEL	5	M	CHILD	RRZZZZBO
ISAAC	3	M	CHILD	RRZZZZBO
GUTMAN, CHAYEM	23	M	LABR	RRZZZZBO
LIPSHON, HIRSCH	18	M	LABR	RRZZZZBO
CHANE	18	M	LABR	RRZZZZBO
GUDUSKY, HEUNA	25	F	W	RRZZZZBO
MOSES	7	M	CHILD	RRZZZZBO
BEIL	6	M	CHILD	RRZZZZBO
JACOBSOHN, MOSES	19	M	LABR	RRZZZZBO
HARTMAN, IGNATZ	48	M	LABR	RRZZZZBO
MARY	35	F	W	RRZZZZBO
HENNY	8	M	CHILD	RRZZZZBO
RUBIN	6	M	CHILD	RRZZZZBO
ESTHER	.06	F	INFANT	RRZZZZBO
MUTNIK, ANNIE	23	F	W	RRZZZZBO
JENNIE	.05	F	INFANT	RRZZZZBO
PELZ, ARON	29	M	LABR	RRZZZZNY
KAPLAN, MEYER	11	M	CH	RRZZZZNY
LITMAN, WILLIAM	27	M	LABR	RRZZZZNY
BLOCK, A.	18	M	LABR	RRZZZZBO
U, JESSIE	34	F	W	RRZZZZBO
ROSE	8	F	CHILD	RRZZZZBO
SARAH	6	F	CHILD	RRZZZZBO
RICHSTEIN, ABRAM	28	M	DYR	RRZZZZBO
LIPSCHUTZ, CHAIM	27	M	LABR	RRZZZZBO
TIXPE	26	F	W	RRZZZZBO
MIREL	18	F	SP	RRZZZZBO
BARCHE	8	M	CHILD	RRZZZZBO
MACKE	7	M	CHILD	RRZZZZBO
JACHIEL	2	M	CHILD	RRZZZZBO
WLF.	.05	M	INFANT	RRZZZZBO
JERMAN, SCH.	40	M	LABR	RRZZZZBO
MASSE	40	F	W	RRZZZZBO
JAL.	27	M	LABR	RRZZZZBO
JACOB	17	M	LABR	RRZZZZBO
JAM.	5	M	CHILD	RRZZZZBO
RACHAEL	8	F	CHILD	RRZZZZBO
ISRAEL	2	M	CHILD	RRZZZZBO
RABINOWITZ, ISRAEL	20	M	LABR	RRZZZZBO
RATNER, MANSCHE	18	M	LABR	RRZZZZBO
MANSCHE	18	M	LABR	RRZZZZBO
POTASNIK, LIEB	44	M	LABR	RRZZZZSTL
INO	22	M	LABR	RRZZZZSTL
ETTEL	17	M	LABR	RRZZZZSTL
TEIZE	15	M	LABR	RRZZZZSTL
JOHN	9	M	CHILD	RRZZZZSTL
DEBORA	8	F	CHILD	RRZZZZSTL
NEUNA	5	F	CHILD	RRZZZZSTL
SPRINZE	44	F	W	RRZZZZSTL
KRENER, SCH.	25	M	LABR	RRZZZZBO
JETTI	22	F	W	RRZZZZBO
JUROWSKY, NECHE	3	F	CHILD	RRZZZZBO
GROSMAN, SARAH	18	F	SP	RRZZZZBO
LEIB	40	M	LABR	RRZZZZBO
ZUREL	18	M	LABR	RRZZZZBO
HARTMAN, HARRY	14	M	LABR	RRZZZZBO
PATES, LIER	20	F	SP	RRZZZZBO
ZORN, ARON	26	M	LABR	RRZZZZBO
KAPLAN, MEYER	18	M	LABR	RRZZZZBO
WESSCARD, MORRIS	17	M	LABR	RRZZZZNY
BAZAN, PATK.	21	M	LABR	RRZZZZNY
HOFMAN, EPHRAIM	25	M	LABR	RRZZZZNY
SHOPEN, JACOB	23	M	LABR	RRZZZZNY
KOOHLER, MENDEL	30	M	LABR	RRZZZZNY
SOLOMAN, MOSES	35	M	LABR	RRZZZZBO

PASSENGER	AGE	SEX	OCCUPATION	PRV	VIL	DES
SHIP: AMSTERDAM						
FROM: ROTTERDAM						
TO: NEW YORK						
ARRIVED: 01 SEPTEMBER 1888						
GOSPER, MARIA	16	F	NN	RR	ZZZZ	USA
STASZENLEWITZ, ANNA	17	F	LABR	RR	ZZZZ	USA
PRUELOWSKY, ANNA	15	F	NN	RR	ZZZZ	USA
GOTOWKA, ROSALIA	22	F	NN	RR	ZZZZ	USA
STANISLAUS	18	M	LABR	RR	ZZZZ	USA
NEUMANN, SARAH	59	F	NN	RR	ZZZZ	USA
VELOWSKY, JAN	60	M	PREST	RR	ZZZZ	USA
SHIP: CEPHALONIA						
FROM: LIVERPOOL AND QUEENSTOWN						
TO: BOSTON						
ARRIVED: 03 SEPTEMBER 1888						
GRAU, CARL	30	M	LABR	FN	ZZZZ	USA
MUTKE, JAKOB	24	M	LABR	FN	ZZZZ	USA
KJOURN, JAKOB	26	M	LABR	FN	ZZZZ	USA
MAHI, JOHAN	26	M	LABR	FN	ZZZZ	USA
LUKKARI, PETER	50	M	LABR	FN	ZZZZ	USA
KALHOHOSHI, JOHAN	42	M	LABR	FN	ZZZZ	USA
MERVILLA, JAKOB	28	M	LABR	FN	ZZZZ	USA
SIRVIA, JAKOB	27	M	LABR	FN	ZZZZ	USA
LINNDSTROM, OSK	16	M	LABR	FN	ZZZZ	USA
LUND, JOHAN	28	M	LABR	FN	ZZZZ	USA
LUNA, SHRINA	40	F	W	FN	ZZZZ	USA
CLAUS	11	M	CH	FN	ZZZZ	USA
MGA.	10	F	CH	FN	ZZZZ	USA
JOHAN	8	M	CHILD	FN	ZZZZ	USA
ELVIGA	4	F	CHILD	FN	ZZZZ	USA
EMELIA	3	F	CHILD	FN	ZZZZ	USA
OTTO	.10	M	INFANT	FN	ZZZZ	USA
SHIP: CITY OF CHICAGO						
FROM: LIVERPOOL AND QUEENSTOWN						
TO: NEW YORK						
ARRIVED: 03 SEPTEMBER 1888						
ROTTENBACH, ELLIE	27	F	W	FNA	CBF	NY
SCHEURCH	4	M	CHILD	FNA	CBF	NY
SCHEURCH	00	M	INF	FNA	CBF	NY
PHILIPS, ABRAM	20	M	WCHMKR	FNA	CBF	NY
ANNA	19	F	W	FNA	CBF	NY
UEWITZ, SCHEINE	18	F	SP	FNA	CBF	NY
KETTUNEAR, ARTIE	20	M	LABR	FNA	CBF	MI
WOLFRON, JACOB	68	M	MCHT	FNA	CBF	MI
TAIVOLA, ASASIAS	31	M	LABR	FNA	CBF	NY
CHAZKOWITZ, IZRAEL	35	M	LABR	FNA	CBF	PHI
RACHEL	30	F	W	FNA	CBF	PHI
BUSHIN, CHANE	20	M	LABR	FNA	CBF	PHI
KAHANS, SUNDEL	3	M	CHILD	FNA	CBF	NY
KORHENEL, SAMUEL	47	M	LABR	FNA	CBF	NY
RUBRUCKIN, MARIE	22	F	UNKNOWN	FNA	CBF	NY
GOLDFART, LEIB	22	M	UNKNOWN	FNA	CBF	NY
SCHUESTER, ITZIG	41	M	UNKNOWN	FNA	CBF	NY
HORACH, ALTER	52	M	UNKNOWN	FNA	CBF	BO
CHAIE	45	F	W	FNA	CBF	BO
MONICKA	17	F	UNKNOWN	FNA	CBF	BO
PINHUS	9	M	CHILD	FNA	CBF	BO
HEMTSCHILO, RISCHI	19	M	CH	FNA	CBF	NY
PORENSTEIN, LULIE	29	F	W	FNA	CBF	PHI
POSEL	9	F	CHILD	FNA	CBF	PHI
RAHEL	7	F	CHILD	FNA	CBF	PHI
PESACH	2	M	CHILD	FNA	CBF	PHI
LENENBAUM, ARON	25	M	UNKNOWN	FNA	CBF	NY
BRANDE, NOA	24	M	UNKNOWN	FNA	CBF	NY
ROSA	18	F	W	FNA	CBF	NY
SCHEE	00	F	INF	FNA	CBF	NY
MELGNER, CHESEL	49	M	LABR	FNA	CBF	NY
CHAJE	49	F	W	FNA	CBF	NY
ISRAIL	11	M	CH	FNA	CBF	NY
HERSCH, ZEME	22	F	SP	FNA	CBF	NY
GELIAS, OLEAS	49	M	BKR	FNA	CBF	NY
KAHN, AWIGDE	48	M	TLR	FNA	CBF	BO
LEIBMANN, NATE	20	M	SHMK	FNA	CBF	USA
ROSSKIND, JOSEL	28	M	UNKNOWN	FNA	CBF	NY
KAHN, HIRSCH	21	M	PNTR	FNA	CBF	NY
ELIAS	20	M	PDLR	FNA	CBF	NY
BARS, REUBEN	16	M	SHMK	FNA	CBF	NY
SENNA, ABRAHAM	15	M	TLR	FNA	CBF	NY
KNEIN, JAN	30	M	LABR	FNA	CBF	NY
HOLLMAN, CHEVAT	22	F	W	FNA	CBF	PHI
U	00	M	INF	FNA	CBF	PHI
U	00	F	INF	FNA	CBF	PHI
GROSSMANN, ROSE	30	F	W	FNA	CBF	PTL
DAVID	22	M	TLR	FNA	CBF	PTL
WOLF	11	M	CH	FNA	CBF	PTL
ZACHARIAS	8	M	CHILD	FNA	CBF	PTL
CHAIM	5	M	CHILD	FNA	CBF	PTL
NOCHEM	3	M	CHILD	FNA	CBF	PTL
FEINSHROEDER, MOSES	20	M	LABR	FNA	CBF	PTL
HISHAWL, CHASKEL	19	M	PDLR	FNA	CBF	PTL
LENGER, SALOM	40	M	BCHR	FNA	CBF	PTL
BERMANN, MINNE	46	F	W	FNA	CBF	PTL
CANTOROWITZ, ISAAC	28	M	LABR	FNA	CBF	PTL
FRUCHTMAN, MICHEL	30	M	LABR	FNA	CBF	PTL
ELIE	10	F	CH	FNA	CBF	PTL
GRIENBLAT, PRAIL	16	M	LABR	FNA	CBF	PTL
HARPATS, BLUME	28	F	W	FNA	CBF	PTL
SAMUEL	9	M	CHILD	FNA	CBF	PTL
ESTER	5	F	CHILD	FNA	CBF	PTL
MEENE	00	F	INF	FNA	CBF	PTL
SOLOMON	28	M	TNSTH	FNA	CBF	PTL
BOROWSKI, JOSEF	22	M	PDLR	FNA	CBF	PTL
INNANZ	18	F	W	FNA	CBF	PTL
SCHAFIE, BEILE	26	F	W	FNA	CBF	NY
ELEAS	00	M	INF	FNA	CBF	NY
KLEINE, ABEL	38	M	PDLR	FNA	CBF	NY
FREIDLAND, SCHEINE	35	F	W	FNA	CBF	NY
ANNETTE	8	F	CHILD	FNA	CBF	NY
SAMUEL	7	M	CHILD	FNA	CBF	NY
JUDEL	2	F	CHILD	FNA	CBF	NY
LINA	00	F	INF	FNA	CBF	NY
LEWIN, TAUBE	21	F	SP	FNA	CBF	NY
GOLDFEIN, ISAAC	27	M	BLKSMH	FNA	CBF	NY
GOLDSTEIN, BURUCH	23	M	UNKNOWN	FNA	CBF	NY
REBECCA	21	F	W	FNA	CBF	NY
NAFLALOWITZ, JOSSEL	45	M	SHMK	FNA	CBF	NY
GOLDBERG, JENTE	15	F	SP	FNA	CBF	NY
KEIFFER, GABEL	18	F	SP	FNA	CBF	NY
LEWIN, SUSSMANNES	20	M	LABR	FNA	CBF	NY
LIPSCHERDONCH, INDEL	17	M	LABR	FNA	CBF	NY
REICHMANN, SALOMON	18	M	SMH	FNA	CBF	NY
BETTYRUSKE, STANISLAUS	27	M	LABR	FNA	CBF	NY
DISZESKI, ABRAHAM	50	M	HTR	FNA	CBF	NY
GUEMSKE, SHALNE	43	F	W	FNA	CBF	NY
WOLF	11	M	CH	FNA	CBF	NY
SBIA	3	F	CHILD	FNA	CBF	NY
LEMMENER, LEA	38	F	W	FNA	CBF	NY
ROHIL	8	F	CHILD	FNA	CBF	NY
MORDICHIA	2	F	CHILD	FNA	CBF	NY
GOLDRING, MAX	30	M	LABR	FNA	CBF	BO
FISCHER, ISRAEL	26	F	SVNT	FNA	CBF	NY

PASSENGER	AGE	SEX	OCCUPATION	PRIVL	DES
SOLLER, JAMES	22	M	LABR	FNACBF	NY
STADULSKI, ANTONIA	40	F	W	FNACBF	MIN
JAN	9	F	CHILD	FNACBF	MIN
ADAM	7	M	CHILD	FNACBF	MIN
GENNES	00	F	INF	FNACBF	MIN
WILDMAN, DAVID	42	M	TLR	FNACBF	NY
BARON, BERNET	42	M	LABR	FNACBF	NY
MEUDSCHENI, JACOB	20	M	GDSM	FNACBF	NY
BAUM, LEWE	15	M	MACH	FNACBF	BO
HUBNER, HUGO	46	M	TLR	FNACBF	CAL
DOLISCH, ISAAC	25	M	LABR	FNACBF	CAL
BERGLIS, SOLOMON	11	M	CH	FNACBF	CAL
KESTENBAUM, MEYER	28	M	BCHR	FNACBF	CAL
WALLACH, ISRAEL	25	M	CPTR	FNACBF	CAL
EISEN, JENE	00	M	INF	FNACBF	CAL
WEISSBART, SCHEINE	00	M	INF	FNACBF	CAL
ARBEIT, MARCKUS	18	M	LABR	FNACBF	CAL
SARACHEN, ITKE	46	F	W	FNACBF	CAL
HENKE	11	M	CH	FNACBF	CAL
HIRSCH	8	M	CHILD	FNACBF	CAL
SARA	7	F	CHILD	FNACBF	CAL
TOGELFANGER, MOSES	30	M	LABR	FNACBF	CAL
SCHRURISKI, BLUME	20	F	LABR	FNACBF	CAL
TODEMANN, GERSON	50	M	PDLR	FNACBF	CAL
SCHEME	18	M	PDLR	FNACBF	CAL
BERKOWITZ, LEON	20	M	PDLR	FNACBF	CAL
LEU, ISCHIE	24	M	TLR	FNACBF	CAL
POLONSKY, TAHL	23	M	PDLR	FNACBF	CAL
PERAKOWICZ, BACHY	18	F	SMH	FNACBF	CAL
WESCHERSKARD, DENA	20	F	SMH	FNACBF	CAL
ROLMAN, M.	25	M	LABR	FNACBF	CAL
EISEN, MENDEL	38	F	W	FNACBF	CAL
RIFKE	19	F	SVNT	FNACBF	CAL
SIMSCHE	11	F	CH	FNACBF	CAL
RACHEL	8	F	CHILD	FNACBF	CAL
WEISSBERT, PERL	41	F	W	FNACBF	CAL
ELKE	9	F	CHILD	FNACBF	CAL
MALKE	7	F	CHILD	FNACBF	CAL
STRAPE, GOLIE	16	F	SP	FNACBF	CAL
LEMPEL, WIFL.	40	F	W	FNACBF	CAL
BASSIE	10	F	CH	FNACBF	CAL
WOLF	11	M	CH	FNACBF	CAL
JOSEL	5	M	CHILD	FNACBF	CAL
MEINKES	7	F	CHILD	FNACBF	CAL
ABR.M.	24	M	TLR	FNACBF	CAL
SPIEHMAN, JOSEF	22	M	TLR	FNACBF	NY
REISEL	17	F	W	FNACBF	NY
LEMPEL, NECHE	18	F	SP	FNACBF	NY
BERZYNUSKI, S.	16	F	SP	FNACBF	NY
MULTEMAN, CHAJE	17	M	LABR	FNACBF	NY
WILLNER, JACOB	25	M	TLR	FNACBF	NY
SCHAPERO, LEVIE	20	F	SP	FNACBF	NY

SHIP: SUEVIA

FROM: HAMBURG AND HAVRE
TO: NEW YORK
ARRIVED: 03 SEPTEMBER 1888

PASSENGER	AGE	SEX	OCCUPATION	PRIVL	DES
KRALNICK, CHAM	34	F	WO	RRZZZZ	NY
BARBA	8	F	CHILD	RRZZZZ	NY
JENTE	7	F	CHILD	RRZZZZ	NY
MARIE	4	F	CHILD	RRZZZZ	NY
ZERREL	3	F	CHILD	RRZZZZ	NY
ETJE	8	F	CHILD	RRZZZZ	NY
SKARZINSKA, PIETRUSZA	18	F	SGL	RRZZZZ	NY
MENKIEWICZ, ADAM	8	M	CHILD	RRZZZZ	NY
RECA, JAN	19	M	LABR	RRZZZZ	NY
SKARSINSKAS, JANOS	50	M	LABR	RRZZZZ	NY
JABLOWSKY, JENE	60	F	WO	RRAIFO	NY
HUDES	19	F	SGL	RRAIFO	NY
ZEMBLER, ABRAM	24	M	LABR	RRAIGQ	NY
WERZBOLOWSKY, HENRY	20	M	LABR	RRAINZ	NY
ARNSTEIN, MENASCHE	28	M	UNKNOWN	RRAFWJ	NY
BRANDWEINBRENNER, SAMUE	38	M	LABR	RRZZZZ	NY
VETTER, JULIE	29	F	SGL	RRAHVU	NY
AUGUSTE	22	F	SGL	RRAHVU	NY
GERSOHN, LOTTE	18	F	SGL	RRAEFL	NY
KIESSER, PAULINE	37	F	WO	RRZZZZ	NY
EMMA	5	F	CHILD	RRZZZZ	NY
IDA	3	F	CHILD	RRZZZZ	NY
ROSENBERG, CHANNE	19	F	SGL	RRAHXL	NY
JACOB	8	M	CHILD	RRAHXL	NY
IZEKOWITZ, SCHEWE	40	F	WO	RRAHVA	NY
SCHIFRE	18	F	SGL	RRAHVA	NY
HEIMANN, CHAJE	18	F	SGL	RRAFWJ	NY
FEDERMANN, WOLF	20	M	LABR	RRADOI	NY
BERL	17	M	LABR	RRADOI	NY
WOSOLEW, ESRIEL	20	M	LABR	RRADOI	NY
ESTHER	20	F	SGL	RRADOI	NY
WEINSTEIN, CHAIE	18	F	SGL	RRAHZS	NY
FINN, REBECCA	24	F	WO	RRAHZN	NY
BLUNGARD, HAWUSCH	18	M	UNKNOWN	RRAINZ	NY
WERZBOLOWSKI, HEIBUSCH	20	M	UNKNOWN	RRAINZ	NY
GOLLUB, CHAIE	19	F	WO	RRAHWM	NY
FRUME	.11	F	INFANT	RRAHWM	NY
BROROWSKY, FRUME	18	F	SGL	RRAHWM	NY
WERZBALOWSKI, RACHEL	20	F	WO	RRAINZ	NY
SLABEDOWSKY, SAMUEL	25	M	LABR	RRZZZZ	NY
DEUTSCHMANN, EDUARD	26	M	BLKSMH	RRAHZS	NY
RUWELSKY, SAMUEL	16	M	LABR	RRAHWM	NY
BELLA	18	F	SGL	RRAHWM	NY
GRODZIENSKI, BEDANIE	19	F	SGL	RRZZZZ	NY
SCHERESCHEWSKY, ISAAC	60	M	LABR	RRAHQU	NY
HOLMSTOEM, MARIE	19	F	SGL	RRAINO	NY
WISE, FOINE	36	F	WO	RRZZZZ	NY
ALBERT	7	M	CHILD	RRZZZZ	NY
ZALE	8	M	CHILD	RRZZZZ	NY
SEBCZAZKI, CZARNE	44	F	WO	RRAHQU	NY
ARON	8	M	CHILD	RRAHQU	NY
FELD, ESTHER	21	F	WO	RRZZZZ	NY
MARIE	.11	F	INFANT	RRZZZZ	NY
KOTARSKI, ANNA	23	F	UNKNOWN	RRAHUF	NY
JOSEFA	21	F	S	RRAHUF	NY
BRONOSLAW	8	M	CHILD	RRAHUF	NY
MARIANNE	.11	F	INFANT	RRAHUF	NY
MUCHNICKA, ELEONORE	60	F	WO	RRZZZZ	NY
NACHUNWOWSKI, CHONNE	48	F	LABR	RRAGRT	NY
SZCZENNOWICZ, FELIX	24	M	LABR	RRAHTF	NY
FELD, REISEL	20	F	WO	RRAHQU	NY
SCHUENE	.09	F	INFANT	RRAHQU	NY
MIROWITZ, TAUBE	50	F	WO	RRAIMS	NY
CHASKEL	22	M	S	RRAIMS	NY
MARIE	19	F	D	RRAIMS	NY
RUPINSKI, MOSES	15	M	UNKNOWN	RRZZZZ	NY
MER	8	M	CHILD	RRZZZZ	NY
DRUKERMANN, LOSER	19	M	UNKNOWN	RRAIOJ	NY
RIWER, JANKEL	27	M	UNKNOWN	RRAGRT	NY
LUCI	21	F	W	RRAGRT	NY
MINE	8	F	CHILD	RRAGRT	NY
MIREL	25	F	WO	RRAGRT	NY
MOSES	.06	M	INFANT	RRAGRT	NY
LUCA, HIRSCH	29	M	HRDRS	RRAFWJ	NY
SARA	22	F	W	RRAFWJ	NY
MALKE	.06	F	INFANT	RRAFWJ	NY
ETTEL	58	F	WO	RRAFWJ	NY
NADELMANN, CHAIM	44	M	LABR	RRZZZZ	NY
NOCHEM	16	M	CH	RRZZZZ	NY
ITZSCHAK	8	M	CHILD	RRZZZZ	NY
MORATZKI, REBECCA	22	F	SGL	RRAIMX	NY
EMMA	20	F	SGL	RRAIMX	NY
LEWOWA, JULIE	24	F	WO	RRAHUF	NY
JULIE	.06	F	INFANT	RRAHUF	NY
JOSSER, CHAJE	20	F	UNKNOWN	RRAHTF	NY
GABRILOWITZ, ELIE	30	F	WO	RRAHSL	NY

PASSENGER	AGE	SEX	OCCUPATION	PRV VIL DES
SCHOLEM	3	M	CHILD	RRAHSLNY
GILINSKY, SARAH	27	F	WO	RRAIEWNY
SROJE	.11	F	INFANT	RRAIEWNY
BRODZINSKI, JACOB	36	M	LABR	RRAFVGNY
STURCHISCH, ABRAH	27	M	DLR	RRAGRTNY
CHANE	27	F	W	RRAGRTNY
HUBE	.02	F	INFANT	RRAGRTNY
JENSEN, JENSINE	18	F	SGL	RRZZZZNY
ANDERSON, WILLIAN	27	M	MCHT	RRAHQDNY

SHIP: WERRA

FROM: BREMEN AND SOUTHAMPTON
TO: NEW YORK
ARRIVED: 04 SEPTEMBER 1888

PASSENGER	AGE	SEX	OCCUPATION	PRV VIL DES
JOSEF, ANNA	16	F	UNKNOWN	RRZZZZUSA
DORA	14	F	UNKNOWN	RRZZZZUSA
PRAIDT, REBECCA	30	F	UNKNOWN	RRZZZZUSA
DRACHENBERG, PAUL.	32	F	W	RRZZZZUSA
ANNA	5	F	CHILD	RRZZZZUSA
OLGA	1	F	CHILD	RRZZZZUSA
LYDIA	4	F	CHILD	RRZZZZUSA
SPICK, WLADISLAW	11	M	UNKNOWN	RRZZZZUSA
DLOGULINSKI, SEELIG	34	M	MCHT	RRZZZZUSA
RUBIN, LIBE	50	F	W	RRZZZZUSA
ZEWALTOW, MARIE	40	F	W	RRZZZZUSA
REBECCA	18	F	UNKNOWN	RRZZZZUSA
MARY	17	F	UNKNOWN	RRZZZZUSA
SAMUEL	10	M	CH	RRZZZZUSA
WOLFSOHN, CHAJE	30	F	W	RRZZZZUSA
OFSCHE	9	F	CHILD	RRZZZZUSA
BENZIN	8	M	CHILD	RRZZZZUSA
LISIE	3	F	CHILD	RRZZZZUSA
CHARASOTEL, GITE	20	F	UNKNOWN	RRZZZZUSA
WEINSTEIN, ASCKER	53	M	LABR	RRZZZZUSA
DORA	55	F	W	RRZZZZUSA
ROSALIA	11	F	CH	RRZZZZUSA
HEYMANN	34	M	LABR	RRZZZZUSA
WILHELM	10	M	CH	RRZZZZUSA
DILLON, SOPHIE	33	F	W	RRZZZZUSA
FANNY	15	F	UNKNOWN	RRZZZZUSA
ADELE	12	F	UNKNOWN	RRZZZZUSA
JACOB	10	M	CH	RRZZZZUSA
HIRSCH	8	M	CHILD	RRZZZZUSA
ARONSOHN, BEILE	26	F	W	RRZZZZUSA
CHANE	7	F	CHILD	RRZZZZUSA
HIRSCH	5	M	CHILD	RRZZZZUSA
MENNCHE	.10	M	INFANT	RRZZZZUSA
FELDNMANN, LIEBE	20	F	UNKNOWN	RRZZZZUSA
WILENSKI, MOSES	40	M	LABR	RRZZZZUSA
WISIENSKI, EMILIE	29	F	W	RRZZZZUSA
FRANZ	9	M	CHILD	RRZZZZUSA
MARIANNA	6	F	CHILD	RRZZZZUSA
BOLESLAV	.09	M	INFANT	RRZZZZUSA
NATELWITZ, SALMEN	24	M	LABR	RRZZZZUSA
RACHE	21	F	W	RRZZZZUSA
COHEN, SINDEL	16	M	UNKNOWN	RRZZZZUSA
JERLAT, JOSEF	30	M	DLR	RRZZZZUSA
WEINBRANDT, SCHLOMME	25	F	UNKNOWN	RRZZZZUSA
HAVERMAASS, EMILIE	24	F	W	RRZZZZUSA
EMMA	.06	F	INFANT	RRZZZZUSA
BRUEDNER, BROCHE	20	M	DLR	RRZZZZUSA
UTAK, CONAGA	18	F	UNKNOWN	RRZZZZUSA
BLUMENTHAL, HERM.	32	M	LABR	RRZZZZUSA
BOROSDIN, PHILIPP	26	M	LABR	RRZZZZUSA
LINETZKY, DAVID	19	M	LABR	RRZZZZUSA
KOMSKY, ABR.	65	M	LABR	RRZZZZUSA
MINDEL	60	M	LABR	RRZZZZUSA
MARIA	18	F	UNKNOWN	RRZZZZUSA

PASSENGER	AGE	SEX	OCCUPATION	PRV VIL DES
DAVID	16	M	UNKNOWN	RRZZZZUSA
ITTA	10	F	CH	RRZZZZUSA
MOSES	.08	M	INFANT	RRZZZZUSA
GUTTMANN, JOSEF	38	M	LABR	RRZZZZUSA
OSCAR	11	M	CH	RRZZZZUSA
MAYER	10	M	CH	RRZZZZUSA
SAPORNIK, JEOCHIA	26	M	LABR	RRZZZZUSA
HALPIRA, JOS.	25	M	LABR	RRZZZZUSA
SAKOLOWSKI, MARIE	30	F	W	RRZZZZUSA
FRANZ	.10	M	INFANT	RRZZZZUSA
TANNENBAUM, JANKEL	30	M	FARMER	RRZZZZUSA
HOCHSTEIN, MOSES	30	M	FARMER	RRZZZZUSA

SHIP: SORRENTO

FROM: HAMBURG
TO: NEW YORK
ARRIVED: 04 SEPTEMBER 1888

PASSENGER	AGE	SEX	OCCUPATION	PRV VIL DES
ORDZECHOWSKY, MORTIZ	18	M	TLR	RRZZZZNY
CARMEL, JUDEL	19	M	TLR	RRZZZZNY
FRIEDMANN, SARAH	16	F	SGL	RRZZZZNY
LINDENBERG, SARAH	40	F	WO	RRZZZZNY
HYMANN	8	M	CHILD	RRZZZZNY
MEYER	3	M	CHILD	RRZZZZNY
FANNY	.11	F	INFANT	RRZZZZNY
JANKELOWITZ, HENE	15	F	SGL	RRZZZZNY
HOCHMANN, ANNA	18	F	WO	RRZZZZNY
ZELINSKA, FRANZISKA	29	F	WO	RRZZZZNY
ADAM	.11	M	INFANT	RRZZZZNY
MOSES, RACHEL	52	F	WO	RRZZZZNY
LENE	8	F	CHILD	RRZZZZNY
BENJAMIN	7	M	CHILD	RRZZZZNY
SAMUEL	5	M	CHILD	RRZZZZNY
HELM, WILHELMINE	58	F	WO	RRZZZZNY
ALWINE	19	F	WO	RRZZZZNY
RIV-VITZ, PORA	35	F	WO	RRZZZZNY
RIVCOVITZ, HANNA	8	F	CHILD	RRZZZZNY
NELLI	7	F	CHILD	RRZZZZNY
NATHAN	6	M	CHILD	RRZZZZNY
RACHWIEL	3	M	CHILD	RRZZZZNY
KULIK, RIWKE	30	F	WO	RRZZZZNY
LEA	16	F	CH	RRZZZZNY
ISAAC	7	M	CHILD	RRZZZZNY
SARA	4	F	CHILD	RRZZZZNY
ARKIESCH, MORITZ	18	M	LABR	RRZZZZNY
STRINKOWSKY, LEISER	52	M	LABR	RRZZZZNY
MOSES	14	M	CH	RRZZZZNY
SCHOENBAUM, SARAH	25	F	WO	RRZZZZNY
CHOWE	.11	F	INFANT	RRZZZZNY
WEISSMANN, ESTHER	17	F	SGL	RRZZZZNY
FRIEDMANN, MOSES	24	M	LABR	RRZZZZNY
ORDZECHOWSKY, MORITZ	18	M	TLR	RRZZZZNY
CARMEL, JUDEL	19	M	LABR	RRZZZZNY
FRIEDMANN, SARAH	16	F	SGL	RRZZZZNY
LINDENBERG, SARAH	40	F	WO	RRZZZZNY
HEYMANN	8	M	CHILD	RRZZZZNY
MEYER	3	M	CHILD	RRZZZZNY
FANNY	.11	F	INFANT	RRZZZZNY
KANKELOWITZ, HENE	15	F	SGL	RRZZZZNY
HOCHMANN, ANNA	18	F	WO	RRZZZZNY
ZELINSKA, FRANZISKA	29	F	WO	RRZZZZNY
ADAM	.11	M	INFANT	RRZZZZNY
MOSES, RACHEL	52	F	WO	RRZZZZNY
LENE	8	F	CHILD	RRZZZZNY
BENJAMIN	7	M	CHILD	RRZZZZNY
SAMUEL	5	M	CHILD	RRZZZZNY
RIV-VITZ, PARA	35	F	WO	RRZZZZNY
RIVCOVITZ, HANNA	8	F	CHILD	RRZZZZNY
NELLI	7	F	CHILD	RRZZZZNY

PASSENGER	AGE	SEX	OCCUPATION	PRV VIL DES
NATHAN	6	M	CHILD	RRZZZZNY
RACHWIEL	3	M	CHILD	RRZZZZNY
KULIK, RIWKE	30	F	WO	RRZZZZNY
LEA	16	F	CH	RRZZZZNY
ISAAC	7	M	CHILD	RRZZZZNY
SARA	4	F	CHILD	RRZZZZNY
ARKIESCH, MORITZ	18	M	LABR	RRZZZZNY
JAPKOWICH, SCHLOME	20	M	LABR	RRZZZZNY
BESCHE	18	F	SGL	RRZZZZNY
JEROM	8	M	CHILD	RRZZZZNY
BENNIR	6	M	CHILD	RRZZZZNY
ZIEWE, GITTE	38	F	WO	RRZZZZNY
JOSEPH	15	M	CH	RRZZZZNY
RACHMINE	8	F	CHILD	RRZZZZNY
JOCHE	7	M	CHILD	RRZZZZNY
JACOB	6	M	CHILD	RRZZZZNY
STRINKOWSKY, LEISER	52	M	LABR	RRZZZZNY
MOSES	14	M	CH	RRZZZZNY
SCHOENBAUM, CHOWE	.11	F	INFANT	RRZZZZNY
WEISSMANN, ESTHER	17	F	SGL	RRZZZZNY
FRIEDMANN, MOSES	24	M	LABR	RRZZZZNY
DUGLITZKY, MOSES	21	M	LABR	RRZZZZNY
GORSON, SCHLOME	19	M	BLKSMH	RRZZZZNY
GRODZINSKY, RACHEL	33	F	WO	RRZZZZNY
RIWKE	8	M	CHILD	RRZZZZNY
ELIAS	7	M	CHILD	RRZZZZNY
RUBIN	6	M	CHILD	RRZZZZNY
ISRAEL	5	M	CHILD	RRZZZZNY
BEREK	4	M	CHILD	RRZZZZNY
LURIA, FANNY	20	F	SGL	RRZZZZNY
ZELANSKY, CHANE	18	F	SGL	RRZZZZNY
POSNERT, TOBIAS	27	M	DLR	RRZZZZNY
STREIT, TILE	33	F	WO	RRZZZZNY
ELKE	8	F	CHILD	RRZZZZNY
CHAWE	7	F	CHILD	RRZZZZNY
SIME	.11	M	INFANT	RRZZZZNY
KATZ, LEIB	23	M	TLR	RRZZZZNY
WISACKY, WOICZEK	34	M	LABR	RRZZZZNY
ANNA	38	F	W	RRZZZZNY
ANTON	8	M	CHILD	RRZZZZNY
WLADISLAUS	7	M	CHILD	RRZZZZNY
MARIANNE	5	F	CHILD	RRZZZZNY
WALIRKA	.11	F	INFANT	RRZZZZNY
GARFINKEL, JOSEPH	50	M	DLR	RRZZZZNY
RAWIN, SCHLOME	37	M	CLGYMN	RRZZZZNY
JOCHELSOHN, JOSEPH	30	M	DLR	RRZZZZNY
KAPLAN, CHANE	20	F	SGL	RRZZZZNY
ORZECHOWSKY, ABRAHAM	19	M	TLR	RRZZZZNY
SZCZEPINSKA, ANNAIE	57	F	WO	RRZZZZBO
KAZIMIR	15	F	CH	RRZZZZBO
KATHAR.	13	F	CH	RRZZZZBO
OXMANN, JILKA	45	F	WO	RRZZZZBO
PINA	35	F	WO	RRZZZZBO
KORASSECK, MALKE.	30	F	WO	RRZZZZBO
GUSTAV	8	M	CHILD	RRZZZZBO
MAX	7	M	CHILD	RRZZZZBO
SALOMON	6	M	CHILD	RRZZZZBO
KARASSECK, LEOSZA	5	F	CHILD	RRZZZZNY
RABINOWITZ, IGLOWITZ	52	M	DLR	RRZZZZNY
FELDMANN, CHASSE	28	F	WO	RRZZZZNY
MEYER	4	M	CHILD	RRZZZZNY
BOSNE	.11	F	INFANT	RRZZZZNY
RABINOWITZ, BASCHE	18	F	SGL	RRZZZZNY
WALLENSTEIN, ROSA	20	F	SGL	RRZZZZNY
FRIEDMANN, JACHWED	19	F	SGL	RRZZZZNY
FEIGE	15	F	SGL	RRZZZZNY
SOMMERFELD, SALOMON	17	M	TLR	RRZZZZNY
KRAMER, MOSES	16	M	LABR	RRZZZZNY
WOLFENSOHN, FROME	16	F	SGL	RRZZZZNY
BRUMBERG, JOCHWED	30	F	WO	RRZZZZNY
MERKE	8	F	CHILD	RRZZZZNY
PINCHES	7	M	CHILD	RRZZZZNY
ESTHER	4	F	CHILD	RRZZZZNY
CHASKEL	.09	F	INFANT	RRZZZZNY
FRAIDEN, LIEBE	35	F	WO	RRZZZZNY
JENTE	15	F	CH	RRZZZZNY
RACHEL	8	F	CHILD	RRZZZZNY
SLATTIE	7	F	CHILD	RRZZZZNY
JANKEL	6	M	CHILD	RRZZZZNY
SALOMON	5	M	CHILD	RRZZZZNY
SCHOENHAUS, SCHMUEL	16	M	LABR	RRZZZZNY
BASCHE	8	F	CHILD	RRZZZZNY
KADISZEWITZ, JOSSEL	8	M	CHILD	RRZZZZNY
GLUGOWSKA, HENRIETTE	26	F	SGL	RRZZZZNY
STRENKOWSKI, KEILE	28	F	WO	RRZZZZNY
FRUME	.10	F	INFANT	RRZZZZNY
APOTHEKER, DAVID	39	M	PRNTR	RRZZZZNY
KOEGON, LEIB	35	M	TLR	RRZZZZNY
HALPERIN, FALK	48	M	DLR	RRZZZZNY
LENATOWITZ, IGNATZ	30	M	JNR	RRZZZZNY
ZUCHER, ITZIG	58	M	MCHT	RRZZZZNY
LEWIS, JOHN	47	M	FARMER	RRZZZZNY
MATIJONES, STANISLAUS	30	M	LABR	RRZZZZNY
AGATHE	24	F	W	RRZZZZNY
REMES, NUCHIM	31	M	DLR	RRZZZZNY
FAKTAKE, RIFKE	22	F	SGL	RRZZZZNY
HARRIS, ASNE	42	F	WO	RRZZZZNY
REBECCA	16	F	CH	RRZZZZNY
MOSES	8	M	CHILD	RRZZZZNY
JACOB	7	M	CHILD	RRZZZZNY
LIEBE	5	F	CHILD	RRZZZZNY
GRUENBERG, BERNARD	16	M	LABR	RRZZZZNY
SILBERMANN, LEIZER	18	M	LABR	RRZZZZNY
RUDNER, FEIWUSCH	37	M	DLR	RRZZZZNY
APEROWITZ, LEIB	30	M	LABR	RRZZZZNY
BUCHHALTER, JANKEL	19	M	BKBNDR	RRZZZZNY
PODSTROWSKI, RIEWE	18	F	SGL	RRZZZZCH
GOLDOWSKY, GOLDE	20	F	SGL	RRZZZZCH
BENSON, RACHEL	19	F	SGL	RRZZZZNY
BLUMBERG, RUDOLPH	31	M	FARMER	RRZZZZNY
TOBIAS, FANNY	20	F	SGL	RRZZZZNY
PAKUSCHEWSKY, DWORE	46	F	WO	RRZZZZNY
ROSA	18	F	WO	RRZZZZNY
JUDEL	16	F	WO	RRZZZZNY
SCHLOMA	8	F	CHILD	RRZZZZNY
HIRSCH	7	M	CHILD	RRZZZZNY
CHAIM	6	M	CHILD	RRZZZZNY
NOSSEN	5	M	CHILD	RRZZZZNY
LIDWINOWSKI, JANKEL	17	M	CL	RRZZZZNY
CZUDMOWSKA, CHIME	25	M	MCHT	RRZZZZNY
RIEFKE	26	F	W	RRZZZZNY
JEAN	4	M	CHILD	RRZZZZNY
BAREL	.11	M	INFANT	RRZZZZNY
MARIA	.01	F	INFANT	RRZZZZNY
ZRODELNY, JOSEF	42	M	LABR	RRZZZZCH
MILOSLAWSKY, RUBIN	50	M	LABR	RRZZZZCH
SCHOLEM	20	M	LABR	RRZZZZCH
BEILE	18	F	SGL	RRZZZZCH
SARA	19	F	SGL	RRZZZZCH
HILLEL	8	M	CHILD	RRZZZZCH
MIELIMONKA, ANTON	28	M	PNTR	RRZZZZCH
ABRAMOWITZ, GITTEL	29	F	SGL	RRZZZZCH
FINKELSTEIN, ESTHER	18	F	SGL	RRZZZZNY
GOLDSTEIN, MARKUS	19	M	DLR	RRZZZZNY
BANOWITSCH, LEIB	30	M	BKBNDR	RRZZZZNY
KAPLAN, MICHAEL	30	M	DLR	RRZZZZNY
ESTHER	18	F	W	RRZZZZNY
GOLDBERG, SAMUEL	27	M	LABR	RRZZZZNY
GOLDE, VICTOR	40	M	LABR	RRZZZZNY
HOFFMANN, GLASER	18	M	DLR	RRZZZZNY
RAIOWER, CHAIM	32	M	DLR	RRZZZZNY
MEROWITZ, SCHEINE	20	F	WO	RRZZZZNY
MALAGIN, ABRAHAM	20	M	UNKNOWN	RRZZZZNY
POLACK, ABRAHAM	18	M	DLR	RRZZZZNY
MILLNER, JAKOB	22	M	DLR	RRZZZZNY
FRIEDMANN, MORDCHE	8	M	CHILD	RRZZZZNY
WEISS, JOSSEL	25	M	DLR	RRZZZZNY
SPIRO, MORITZ	18	M	DLR	RRZZZZNY
FREIMANN, GITTEL	20	F	SGL	RRZZZZPHI
PINZECK, MOSES	19	M	BKBNDR	RRZZZZCH

PASSENGER	AGE	SEX	OCCUPATION	PRV VIL DES
SCHIEST-ER, HIRSCH	22	M	DLR	RRZZZZCH
BRANE	17	F	W	RRZZZZNY
GORKAWI, SCHMUEL	17	M	LABR	RRZZZZNY
DWORKIN, MINIE	8	F	CHILD	RRZZZZNY
JUDA, ABRAHAM	25	M	DLR	RRZZZZNY
NASSBERG, LEIB	24	M	LABR	RRZZZZNY
SZKERINSKI, ARON	26	M	LABR	RRZZZZNY
ELKA	20	F	W	RRZZZZNY
PUNE, MORDCHE	62	M	DLR	RRZZZZNY
PRINCEN, JOCHEL	44	M	DLR	RRZZZZPHI
LEISER	19	M	DLR	RRZZZZPHI
JUDELOWITZ, ZLATE	26	F	WO	RRZZZZPHI
RUBEN	.09	M	INFANT	RRZZZZPHI
BURSTEIN, CHAIM	26	M	LABR	RRZZZZPHI
JUDELOWITZ, REBECCA	14	F	SGL	RRZZZZPHI
KOHN, SUCHER	15	M	TLR	RRZZZZPHI

SHIP: FURNESSIA

FROM: GLASGOW AND MOVILLE
TO: NEW YORK
ARRIVED: 04 SEPTEMBER 1888

PASSENGER	AGE	SEX	OCCUPATION	PRV VIL DES
PLATUSCH, ITZIG	19	M	TLR	RRZZZZUSA
SCHISGOLL, SOLM.	25	M	WCHMKR	RRZZZZUSA
MISCHKOWSKIE, BERIL	18	M	WCHMKR	RRZZZZUSA
MITZRIAN, MARDUCH	24	M	LABR	RRZZZZUSA
JOHANSON, SOLM.	30	M	BBR	RRZZZZUSA
PRANZIG, MICHL.	27	M	LABR	RRZZZZUSA
BRIASZUSTTA, MARYANE	19	F	HP	RRZZZZUSA
KATZ, JUSKA	18	F	HP	RRZZZZUSA
KRAINAK, MARGIE	20	F	HP	RRZZZZUSA
MA-A-Z, BARBARA	22	F	HP	RRZZZZUSA
MISLIANSKI, GOLDE	45	F	HP	RRZZZZUSA
PIETRSKSIMA, MAZDALINA	20	F	HP	RRZZZZUSA
SZERSKY, SELMAN	40	M	DSTLR	RRZZZZUSA
PRESDE	30	F	HP	RRZZZZUSA
ISRAEL	17	M	NN	RRZZZZUSA
CHAN	2	F	CHILD	RRZZZZUSA
FR.	.06	F	INFANT	RRZZZZUSA

SHIP: WESTERNLAND

FROM: ANTWERP
TO: NEW YORK
ARRIVED: 05 SEPTEMBER 1888

PASSENGER	AGE	SEX	OCCUPATION	PRV VIL DES
LEVSKY, HAN.	29	F	UNKNOWN	PLZZZZNY
LEAH	9	F	CHILD	PLZZZZNY
HARRIS	6	M	CHILD	PLZZZZNY
HOBLENZ, MENDEL	20	M	TLR	PLZZZZNY
MOLER, MINA	25	F	UNKNOWN	PLZZZZNY
ROANSCH, MEYER	26	M	TLR	PLZZZZNY
CHOWAS, ATHEL	26	F	UNKNOWN	PLZZZZNY
MORRIS	3	M	CHILD	PLZZZZNY
DEBORAH	1	F	CHILD	PLZZZZNY
ISAAC, JACOB	25	M	TLR	PLZZZZNY
BERNSTEIN, HY.	20	M	SHMK	PLZZZZNY
PRICET, ARTHUR	35	M	MCHT	PLZZZZNY
ELISE	38	F	UNKNOWN	PLZZZZNY
PAKOVA, W	22	M	SHMK	PLZZZZNY
EISENBERG, L.	34	M	PNTR	PLZZZZNY
CHL.	26	F	UNKNOWN	PLZZZZNY
LOUISA	7	F	CHILD	PLZZZZNY
GOLDA	6	F	CHILD	PLZZZZNY

PASSENGER	AGE	SEX	OCCUPATION	PRV VIL DES
POTOCHINSKY, VINC.	23	M	LABR	PLZZZZPHI
WETOWSKY, VINC.	28	M	LABR	PLZZZZPHI
LORG--, LOUISE	58	F	UNKNOWN	PLZZZZUNK
OTTO	24	M	FARMER	PLZZZZUNK
APMAS, JOHANN	23	M	MNR	RRZZZZNY
HART, WENZL	43	M	LABR	RRZZZZNY
SVARZ, JOSEF	36	M	LABR	RRZZZZNY
MERESE	14	F	UNKNOWN	RRZZZZNY
JOSA	12	F	UNKNOWN	RRZZZZNY
BOGASIAN, LUCAS	38	M	LABR	RRZZZZNY
ASWERDZADONSKI, K.	25	M	LABR	RRZZZZNY
BAGLULIKIAN, R.	38	M	LABR	RRZZZZNY
GARHEDIEN, J.	17	M	LABR	RRZZZZNY
SARKIESSIAN, G.	18	M	LABR	RRZZZZNY
NEGIB, C.	23	M	MNR	RRZZZZNY
JUNG, MARIE	16	F	UNKNOWN	RRZZZZNY
HORN, MARIA	42	F	UNKNOWN	RRZZZZNY
NUGER, ELISAB.	25	F	UNKNOWN	RRZZZZNY
BAUM, CHRISTINE	21	F	UNKNOWN	RRZZZZNY
BAUSCH, OTTO	16	M	LABR	RRZZZZNY
ELLIG, GUSTAV	34	M	LABR	RRZZZZPIT
HOOG, FRIED.	17	M	CL	RRZZZZUNK
HUBLER, FRIED.	26	M	FARMER	RRZZZZUNK
OSSMANN, CAROLINE	30	F	UNKNOWN	RRZZZZSTL
CARL	3	M	CHILD	RRZZZZSTL
CARTHENSER, CHRISTINA	32	F	UNKNOWN	RRZZZZIN
LINA	4	F	CHILD	RRZZZZIN
LOUISE	3	F	CHILD	RRZZZZIN
EUDERLE, JOHANNE	16	F	UNKNOWN	RRZZZZPHI
WALZ, FRED.	17	M	CL	RRZZZZCH
GRIMM, GERTRUDE	27	F	UNKNOWN	RRZZZZCH
CARL	6	M	CHILD	RRZZZZCH
OTTO	4	M	CHILD	RRZZZZCH
OFSTENBUSCH, JOH.	23	M	SMH	RRZZZZNY
VEIT, CARL	52	M	MCHT	RRZZZZNY
SELINA	32	F	UNKNOWN	RRZZZZNY
WALTHER	8	M	CHILD	RRZZZZNY
ERICH	6	M	CHILD	RRZZZZNY
HERMANN	5	M	CHILD	RRZZZZNY
PROCHT, AUG.	43	M	FARMER	RRZZZZNY
LORENZ, LIDIA	21	F	UNKNOWN	RRZZZZNY
SCHAAFER, HCH.	24	M	FARMER	RRZZZZNY
STUMMPF, MARTIN	28	M	FARMER	RRZZZZNY
GRAUBOCH, GUSTAV	12	M	CH	RRZZZZNY
RUTH, BARB.	64	F	UNKNOWN	RRZZZZNY
EISEMANN, LOUISE	5	F	CHILD	RRZZZZNY

SHIP: DONAU

FROM: BREMEN
TO: BALTIMORE
ARRIVED: 05 SEPTEMBER 1888

PASSENGER	AGE	SEX	OCCUPATION	PRV VIL DES
KUEHNER, RICHARD	39	M	MCHT	RRZZZZIL
TOMASZEWSKA, JOSEFA	20	F	UNKNOWN	RRZZZZIL
STANISLAUS	11	M	CH	RRZZZZIL
LEIB, ANNA	40	F	UNKNOWN	RRZZZZIL
AMALIA	19	F	UNKNOWN	RRZZZZIL
SACHS, MARIE	30	F	UNKNOWN	RRZZZZIL
DORIS	4	F	CHILD	RRZZZZIL
FRIEDMANN, PAULINE	25	F	UNKNOWN	RRZZZZIL
HENE	55	F	UNKNOWN	RRZZZZIL
MEYER	8	M	CHILD	RRZZZZIL
REIE	5	F	CHILD	RRZZZZIL
SENY	5	F	CHILD	RRZZZZIL
BERTHA	4	F	CHILD	RRZZZZIL
ISACOWICH, SARA	33	F	UNKNOWN	RRZZZZIL
MALKE	11	F	UNKNOWN	RRZZZZIL
FRADE	8	F	CHILD	RRZZZZIL
BEINISCH	5	U	CHILD	RRZZZZIL

PASSENGER	AGE	SEX	OCCUPATION	PRV VIL DES
FLORENCE	3	F	CHILD	RRZZZZIL
ORENFELD, GOLDE	60	F	UNKNOWN	RRZZZZIL
JUDELOWITZ, MINNA	25	F	UNKNOWN	RRZZZZIL
CHANE	4	F	CHILD	RRZZZZIL
MOTTEL	3	M	CHILD	RRZZZZIL
SAMUEL	.09	M	INFANT	RRZZZZIL
GARFINKEL, BRAINE	40	F	UNKNOWN	RRZZZZIL
MITZNIK, SENDLE	21	M	MCHT	RRZZZZIL
LIEBE	12	F	UNKNOWN	RRZZZZIL
ELY	.03	F	INFANT	RRZZZZIL
FRIEDMANN, SIMKE	30	F	UNKNOWN	RRZZZZIL
MERKE	10	M	CH	RRZZZZIL
EFRAIM	1	M	CHILD	RRZZZZIL
FRADE	1	F	CHILD	RRZZZZIL
ABRAHAM	6	M	CHILD	RRZZZZIL
MILLER, FRADE	30	F	UNKNOWN	RRZZZZIL
JOSEPH	6	M	CHILD	RRZZZZIL
BULANOVA, REGINA	25	F	UNKNOWN	RRZZZZIL
ANNA	.07	F	INFANT	RRZZZZIL
MIBRIEKIWICZ, LUCIA	25	F	UNKNOWN	RRZZZZIL
GARFINKEL, PRINE	29	F	UNKNOWN	RRZZZZIL
---IB	7	M	CHILD	RRZZZZIL
U	3	F	CHILD	RRZZZZIL
SALOMON	.10	M	INFANT	RRZZZZIL
LICHTENSTEIN, ESTHER	12	F	UNKNOWN	RRZZZZIL
MILLER, WOLF	12	M	UNKNOWN	RRZZZZIL
HOFFMANN, ROCHEL	28	F	UNKNOWN	RRZZZZIL
MINDEL	.05	F	INFANT	RRZZZZIL
SOREK	30	M	UNKNOWN	RRZZZZIL
MINDEL	8	F	CHILD	RRZZZZIL
JANDIGAS, ANNA	20	F	UNKNOWN	RRZZZZMD
GORODKOWITZ, BENJAMIN	21	M	MCHT	RRZZZZMD
GOLDMANN, ETHEL	21	F	UNKNOWN	RRZZZZMD
KALMAN	.03	M	INFANT	RRZZZZMD
FEGE, ----E	35	F	UNKNOWN	RRZZZZMD
AXEL	11	M	CH	RRZZZZMD
REIZE	9	F	CHILD	RRZZZZMD
MEMMSCHE	7	M	CHILD	RRZZZZMD
TAUBE	4	F	CHILD	RRZZZZMD
LISS, EPRAIM	23	M	FARMER	RRZZZZMD
MATZ, LINA	16	F	UNKNOWN	RRZZZZMD
POLAK, DAVID	22	M	FARMER	RRZZZZMD
ROSENTHAL, BANC.	19	M	FARMER	RRZZZZMD
SEIDMANN, SALOMON	35	M	FARMER	RRZZZZMD
ROM, JOSEF	38	M	FARMER	RRZZZZMD
JUDELOWITZ, ROSE	23	F	UNKNOWN	RRZZZZMD
SCHAPERSTEIN, NACHAME	45	F	UNKNOWN	RRZZZZMD
FROME	13	F	UNKNOWN	RRZZZZMD
PEISEL	10	M	CH	RRZZZZMD
ABRAHAM	7	M	CHILD	RRZZZZMD
SUESSEL	4	F	CHILD	RRZZZZMD
ISRAEL	3	F	CHILD	RRZZZZMD
RUBIN, ESTHER	18	F	UNKNOWN	RRZZZZMD
SARNECH, CARL	24	M	LABR	RRZZZZMD
ELFENSTEIN, HIRSCH	42	M	MCHT	RRZZZZPA
PESSE	38	F	UNKNOWN	RRZZZZPA
CHAJE	16	F	UNKNOWN	RRZZZZPA
MARCUS	13	M	UNKNOWN	RRZZZZPA
JACOB	9	M	CHILD	RRZZZZPA
LEA	7	F	CHILD	RRZZZZPA
PAULA	.03	F	INFANT	RRZZZZPA
GRUSMANN, ISRAEL	19	M	PDLR	RRZZZZMO
SEROWITZ, SCHAINE	30	F	UNKNOWN	RRZZZZMD
HILEL	8	M	CHILD	RRZZZZMD
CHAJE	7	F	CHILD	RRZZZZMD
ZIRRI	4	F	CHILD	RRZZZZMD
GOETZ, STANISLAW	40	M	SHMK	RRZZZZPA
SCHERR, JETTE	28	F	UNKNOWN	RRZZZZMO
JACOB	9	M	CHILD	RRZZZZMO
HERMAN	8	M	CHILD	RRZZZZMO
MAX	5	M	CHILD	RRZZZZMO
OSCAR	3	M	CHILD	RRZZZZMO
BEGEL, MALKE	19	F	UNKNOWN	RRZZZZMO
JESSEN, JETTE	19	F	UNKNOWN	RRZZZZMO
BLOSSTEIN, BESSE	27	F	UNKNOWN	RRZZZZMO

PASSENGER	AGE	SEX	OCCUPATION	PRV VIL DES
TAUBE	27	F	UNKNOWN	RRZZZZMO
TORF, FREIDE	33	F	UNKNOWN	RRZZZZMD
ROSA	11	F	UNKNOWN	RRZZZZMD
JETTE	8	F	CHILD	RRZZZZMD
SAMUEL	3	M	CHILD	RRZZZZMD
BLUM, SCHORE	34	F	UNKNOWN	RRZZZZMD
OSIAS	6	M	CHILD	RRZZZZMD
ISAAC	3	M	CHILD	RRZZZZMD
LIBE	.11	F	INFANT	RRZZZZMD
COHN, MOSES	34	M	MCHT	RRZZZZMN
KEMERZUNE, PETRUS	20	M	MCHT	RRZZZZMD
HAKAN, EPHAIM	31	M	MCHT	RRZZZZIL
BUCHORIK, U	00	M	INF	RRZZZZIL
STANISLAWSKA, FRANZ.	00	M	INF	RRZZZZIL

SHIP: NORSEMAN

FROM: LIVERPOOL
TO: BOSTON
ARRIVED: 05 SEPTEMBER 1888

PASSENGER	AGE	SEX	OCCUPATION	PRV VIL DES
RAPAPORT, SPRINZE	20	F	W	RRZZZZNY
HIRSCH	3	M	CHILD	RRZZZZNY
FROIM	.08	M	INFANT	RRZZZZNY
EPSTEIN, IZRELL	60	M	MACH	RRZZZZNY
LOMINSKY, ABRAM	19	M	TLR	RRZZZZBO
LISINTZKY, CHAJE	17	F	SVNT	RRZZZZBO
SIMON, GIRSCHE	16	F	SVNT	RRZZZZBO
WOLF, BARCHE	18	F	SVNT	RRZZZZBO
FRCH.	10	M	CH	RRZZZZBO
JOKOWITZ, DAVOSE	28	F	W	RRZZZZBO
EPSTEIN, PAUL	27	M	MACH	RRZZZZBO
MARY	23	F	W	RRZZZZBO
LIZZA	3	F	CHILD	RRZZZZBO
ROZELBLACK, FRANZ	38	F	LABR	RRZZZZPHI
RADMINSKY, LOUIS	22	M	MACH	RRZZZZBO
GLUCKMANN, ABRAHAM	55	M	MACH	RRZZZZBO
LEABE	46	F	W	RRZZZZBO
LEBAMNAN, BERNETT	22	M	LABR	RRZZZZBO
GLASBURG, BARUCHE	23	M	MCHT	RRZZZZNY
DREYER, ROCHE	25	F	W	RRZZZZOH
SARAH	2	F	CHILD	RRZZZZOH
GRENFELD, ROSA	32	F	W	RRZZZZBO
ROBT.	2	M	CHILD	RRZZZZBO
DEUTCHLAUDER, JULIANA	35	M	FARMER	PLZZZZBO
GRYESKY, ALEX	39	M	FARMER	PLZZZZBO
JOSEPHA	35	F	W	PLZZZZBO
LEUCIMSKY, GRITEL	22	F	W	RRZZZZBO
LEIBOWSKY, ITZIG	30	M	MECH	RRZZZZBO

SHIP: ALLER

FROM: BREMEN AND SOUTHAMPTON
TO: NEW YORK
ARRIVED: 07 SEPTEMBER 1888

PASSENGER	AGE	SEX	OCCUPATION	PRV VIL DES
HALPERN, JOHAN	18	M	LABR	RRZZZZUSA
TOPELBAUM, SIMON	28	M	LABR	RRZZZZUSA
KOCKERICH, JACOB	25	M	LABR	RRZZZZUSA
LITMAN, LIPE	36	M	LABR	RRZZZZUSA
AUERBACH, EFRAM	29	M	LABR	RRZZZZUSA
MASE, ARON	18	M	LABR	RRZZZZUSA
OKE, JOSEF	18	M	LABR	RRZZZZUSA
RONANAK, PAUL	21	M	LABR	RRZZZZUSA
KUHTALA, AMANDA	21	F	UNKNOWN	RRZZZZUSA

PASSENGER	AGE	SEX	OCCUPATION	PRV VIL DES
NIMONEN, ANNA	24	F	UNKNOWN	RRZZZZUSA
ERKKIL-, EVA	18	F	UNKNOWN	RRZZZZUSA
JUNKLA, SUSA	27	F	UNKNOWN	RRZZZZUSA
RUBOVITZ, ERZSA	28	F	UNKNOWN	RRZZZZUSA
GUILA	3	F	CHILD	RRZZZZUSA
ISTVAN	.10	M	INFANT	RRZZZZUSA
GRUENBERG, FRITZ	38	M	FARMER	RRZZZZUSA
CZARNE	16	F	W	RRZZZZUSA
MEIER	7	M	CHILD	RRZZZZUSA
SARAH	5	F	CHILD	RRZZZZUSA
HULDA	3	F	CHILD	RRZZZZUSA
MARGALOS, FANNY	30	F	UNKNOWN	RRZZZZUSA
WILH.	.11	F	INFANT	RRZZZZUSA
KOCKERICHE, SENDER	46	M	FARMER	RRZZZZUSA
SURE	46	F	W	RRZZZZUSA
NIETSEN	14	M	CH	RRZZZZUSA
NACHME	12	F	CH	RRZZZZUSA
DANIEL	7	M	CHILD	RRZZZZUSA
CHAJEM	6	M	CHILD	RRZZZZUSA
BETTY	5	F	CHILD	RRZZZZUSA
MARIE	4	F	CHILD	RRZZZZUSA
TRUDEL	2	F	CHILD	RRZZZZUSA
CHAJE	.06	F	INFANT	RRZZZZUSA
HESSLER, LUDW.	39	M	TLR	RRZZZZUSA
ELISE	35	F	W	RRZZZZUSA
JOHAN	14	M	CH	RRZZZZUSA
JACOB	8	M	CHILD	RRZZZZUSA
MARY	6	F	CHILD	RRZZZZUSA
EVA	4	F	CHILD	RRZZZZUSA
ELISE	2	F	CHILD	RRZZZZUSA
BARBA.	.03	F	INFANT	RRZZZZUSA
HEMZ, ANTON	48	M	GDNR	RRZZZZUSA
ELISE	34	F	W	RRZZZZUSA
MICHEL	12	M	CH	RRZZZZUSA
JOHAN	8	M	CHILD	RRZZZZUSA
JOSEF	6	M	CHILD	RRZZZZUSA
ROCHUS	4	M	CHILD	RRZZZZUSA
TONI	2	F	CHILD	RRZZZZUSA
FRANZE.	.10	F	INFANT	RRZZZZUSA
RICHTER, ADAM	29	M	FARMER	RRZZZZUSA
EVA	28	F	W	RRZZZZUSA
JOHAN	4	M	CHILD	RRZZZZUSA
PETER	2	M	CHILD	RRZZZZUSA
JACOB	.04	M	INFANT	RRZZZZUSA
THOMAS, MARTIN	52	M	GDNR	RRZZZZUSA
LATTI	45	F	W	RRZZZZUSA
WEDLIN	12	M	CH	RRZZZZUSA
WILH.	7	M	CHILD	RRZZZZUSA
MICHEL	5	M	CHILD	RRZZZZUSA
CATI	4	F	CHILD	RRZZZZUSA
LISE	2	F	CHILD	RRZZZZUSA
ANNA	.09	F	INFANT	RRZZZZUSA
SCHEREPANSKY, CHAJE	58	F	UNKNOWN	RRZZZZUSA
ANNA	32	F	UNKNOWN	RRZZZZUSA
WALLER, MICHEL	40	M	FARMER	RRZZZZUSA
BARBA.	35	F	W	RRZZZZUSA
JOSEF	11	M	CH	RRZZZZUSA
ANTON	7	M	CHILD	RRZZZZUSA
CARL	6	M	CHILD	RRZZZZUSA
JOHAN	4	M	CHILD	RRZZZZUSA
MARIE	2	F	CHILD	RRZZZZUSA

SHIP: NOVA SCOTIAN

FROM: LIVERPOOL
TO: BALTIMORE
ARRIVED: 07 SEPTEMBER 1888

PASSENGER	AGE	SEX	OCCUPATION	PRV VIL DES
CHESSER, SCHEINE	27	F	SVNT	RRZZZZBAL
ZOOLLE	14	F	CH	RRZZZZBAL
ISRAEL	11	M	CH	RRZZZZBAL
HENNE	9	M	CHILD	RRZZZZBAL
FAUBO	6	F	CHILD	RRZZZZBAL
RUVE	4	F	CHILD	RRZZZZBAL
GUTTMENN, GUVESZE	60	F	UNKNOWN	RRZZZZBAL
CHARKOWIEZ, GITTEL	22	M	SHMK	RRZZZZBAL
FOIDEL.	1	M	CHILD	RRZZZZBAL
NYERMANN, LEA	31	M	UNKNOWN	RRZZZZBAL
MOEZE	4	M	CHILD	RRZZZZBAL
ABRAHAMSON, JENKE	16	F	DRSMKR	RRZZZZBAL
BERILOWITZ, CHAIM	22	M	BKR	RRZZZZBAL
FUGE	22	F	W	RRZZZZBAL
ABRAMOWITZ, JOSCKEL	24	M	LABR	RRZZZZBAL
LESCHKOWSKI, WOFLECH	24	M	SVNT	RRZZZZUSA
REPKA	22	F	W	RRZZZZUSA
ANNA	1	F	CHILD	RRZZZZUSA
MARIE	3	F	CHILD	RRZZZZUSA
BLOND, F.M.	55	M	TLR	RRZZZZNY
JACKES, CHAIM	14	M	LABR	RRZZZZPIT
WERKSMANN, CHENIE	17	M	LABR	RRZZZZBAL
JACHNOWITZ, ARON	30	M	TLR	RRZZZZBAL
MESKOWIEZ, WLADESLAW	19	M	LABR	RRZZZZCLE
BIWKOWITZ, ITZIG	15	M	TLR	RRZZZZBAL

SHIP: POLARIA

FROM: HAMBURG
TO: NEW YORK
ARRIVED: 08 SEPTEMBER 1888

PASSENGER	AGE	SEX	OCCUPATION	PRV VIL DES
WIKENS, HIRSCH	37	M	LABR	RRADBQUSA
MANDELSKI, PAUL	33	M	LABR	RRZZZZUSA
HOLINSKY, LEA	30	F	WO	RRAHOKUSA
ZLATE	8	F	CHILD	RRAHOKUSA
JOEL	7	M	CHILD	RRAHOKUSA
ABRAHAM	6	M	CHILD	RRAHOKUSA
ROSA	5	F	CHILD	RRAHOKUSA
GOLDE	.11	F	INFANT	RRAHOKUSA
APOTHEKER, DAVID	39	M	MCHT	RRAIIKUSA
SEIDMANN, JOSEPH	17	M	TLR	RRZZZZUSA
NORWITZ, GUTKE	24	F	WO	RRAFVGUSA
ABRAH.	3	M	CHILD	RRAFVGUSA
RACHEL	.03	F	INFANT	RRAFVGUSA
JACOBINAS, JOSEF	23	M	LABR	RRAHTFUSA
BACHRACH, DAVID	20	M	LABR	RRAIFUUSA
SCHEINKERT, FEIWEL	26	M	LABR	RRZZZZUSA
RITTENBERG, SCHMERIL	18	M	LABR	RRZZZZUSA
KLIGMAN, ROSA	26	F	WO	RRZZZZUSA
LEIB	5	M	CHILD	RRZZZZUSA
CHANNE	.11	F	INFANT	RRZZZZUSA
BURNISKI, RAULIN	53	M	FARMER	RRAIBQUSA
WOLPERT, MARKUS	20	M	LABR	RRZZZZUSA
WINKELSTEIN, IDA	20	F	SGL	RRZZZZUSA
LEVY	8	M	CHILD	RRZZZZUSA
MOSES	6	M	CHILD	RRZZZZUSA
SCHAB, NELLY	26	M	TLR	RRAHRKUSA
DAVIDOWITZ, ABR.	20	M	LABR	RRAHWQUSA
KIRTLA, LIPMANN	40	M	LABR	RRAILNUSA
KALKOWSKA, JULIANE	22	F	WO	RRAHZSUSA
MARIE	.06	F	INFANT	RRAHZSUSA
BOLKOWSKY, ANTONY	28	M	LABR	RRAHZSUSA
INIEKIEWICZ, JOS.	8	M	CHILD	RRAHZSUSA
SUNDELWITZ, BEREL	34	M	DLR	RRAHTFUSA
REMS, WOLF	34	M	DLR	RRZZZZUSA
NURWITZ, ABRA.	30	M	DLR	RRZZZZUSA
RUBINSTEIN, SARAH	00	F	WO	RRAGRTUSA
GERSON	.06	M	INFANT	RRAGRTUSA
SLONINSKY, TOB.	37	F	WO	RRAHVUUSA
EDELSTEIN, MOSES	37	M	LABR	RRAHVUUSA
GUSTATIS, PETRUS	20	M	LABR	RRZZZZUSA

PASSENGER	AGE	SEX	OCCUPATION	PRV VIL DES
ARKMANN, AUDREPAS	20	M	LABR	RRZZZZUSA
ZDAWCZYK, MARTIN	22	M	SHMK	RRZZZZUSA
WADZINSKI, ANTON	22	M	LABR	RRZZZZUSA
TECHLER, CHARLOTTE	45	F	WO	RRZZZZUSA
ERNST	26	M	S	RRZZZZUSA
CESAR	19	M	S	RRZZZZUSA
WOLAWITZ, STATE	30	F	WO	RRZZZZUSA
JOSEPH	5	M	CHILD	RRZZZZUSA
GRIEBENSOHN, HENRIETTE	40	F	WO	RRAEFLUSA
METT, AMALIE	17	F	SGL	RRAHXLUSA
REITER, ROSALIE	20	F	SGL	RRAHXLUSA
NARKUNSKI, EDLI	26	F	WO	RRAHTFUSA
SCHLOME	6	F	CHILD	RRAHTFUSA
MENDEL	.11	M	INFANT	RRAHTFUSA
ISRAEL	.11	M	INFANT	RRAHTFUSA
JAKUBOWSKY, ROSALIE	25	F	WO	RRAIIOUSA
JULIUS	.11	M	INFANT	RRAIIOUSA
SLOTOWSKY, JOSSEL	30	M	DLR	RRZZZZUSA
APPELBAUM, PESCHE	17	F	WO	RRZZZZUSA
SUSMID, PAUL	32	M	LABR	RRZZZZUSA
ZODIKOW, SCHMUEL	38	M	BKR	RRAHTFUSA
SALZBERG, ARON	44	M	DLR	RRZZZZUSA
SILBERSTEIN, CHAINE	23	M	DLR	RRAFWJUSA
FUNK, HIRSCH	20	M	DLR	RRAFWJUSA
ENESSMANN, JACOB	22	F	W	RRAFWJUSA
MARIA	.09	F	INFANT	RRAFWJUSA
SOBEL, ELIAS	43	M	DLR	RRZZZZUSA
RIWKE	40	F	W	RRZZZZUSA
MALKE	18	F	CH	RRZZZZUSA
LEISER	16	M	CH	RRZZZZUSA
MOSES	14	M	CH	RRZZZZUSA
JUDEL	11	M	CH	RRZZZZUSA
CHAIE	5	F	CHILD	RRZZZZUSA
HERSCHEL	3	M	CHILD	RRZZZZUSA
ISRAEL	2	M	CHILD	RRZZZZUSA
APELBAUM, AUSER	28	M	DLR	RRZZZZUSA
BERKOWITZ, LESER	27	M	TLR	RRAIINUSA
LUKAS, BEHR	20	M	LABR	RRZZZZUSA
KRIEGER, MICHNE	19	F	SGL	RRAHTFUSA
FEINBERG, EISER	25	M	LABR	RRAHTUUSA
MICHLE	.11	M	INFANT	RRAHTUUSA
LIFSCHITZ, RACHEL	25	F	WO	RRAHTUUSA
JACOB	.06	M	INFANT	RRAHTUUSA
LEIZERIN, SARA	29	F	WO	RRAHZNUSA
PESCHE	3	F	CHILD	RRAHZNUSA
PREISS, ROSA	28	F	WO	RRAHWUUSA
RECH.	8	M	CHILD	RRAHWUUSA
ESTHER	.11	F	INFANT	RRAHWUUSA
BERNSTEIN, MALE	38	F	WO	RRAHTFUSA
LENE	7	F	CHILD	RRAHTFUSA
TEITELBAUM, EISIK	47	M	DLR	RRAHWOUSA
RIVE	47	F	W	RRAHWOUSA
ISRAEL	8	M	CHILD	RRAHWOUSA
RACHEL	7	F	CHILD	RRAHWOUSA
SARA	6	F	CHILD	RRAHWOUSA
ABRAM	5	M	CHILD	RRAHWOUSA
MAX	4	M	CHILD	RRAHWOUSA
STORR, NOVAH	55	M	DLR	RRZZZZUSA
DOBRA	53	F	W	RRZZZZUSA
ESTHER	17	F	CH	RRZZZZUSA
ABRAM	8	M	CHILD	RRZZZZUSA
SAMUEL	6	M	CHILD	RRZZZZUSA
MARIE	7	F	CHILD	RRZZZZUSA
DIBOWSKY, LUDW.	25	M	LABR	RRZZZZUSA
WOLOWITZ, SAMUEL	30	M	LABR	RRZZZZUSA
LIFSCHUETZ, SCHMEREL	27	M	DLR	RRAHVUUSA
BASCHE	22	F	W	RRAHVUUSA
FEIGE	.03	F	INFANT	RRAHVUUSA
MARKOWSKY, BELE	40	M	DLR	RRAFVGUSA
MOSES	22	M	CH	RRAFVGUSA
RACHEL	16	M	CH	RRAFVGUSA
JOSEF	8	M	CHILD	RRAFVGUSA

SHIP: BOTHNIA

FROM: LIVERPOOL AND QUEENSTOWN
TO: NEW YORK
ARRIVED: 08 SEPTEMBER 1888

PASSENGER	AGE	SEX	OCCUPATION	PRV VIL DES
SCHWARZ, WIEL.	18	F	SP	RRZZZZUSA
POLINSKY, CHANE	20	F	SP	RRZZZZUSA
GUTMANN, ROSE	14	F	SP	RRZZZZUSA
GORDON, ELISA	17	F	SP	RRZZZZUSA
ALEXANDROWITZ, SORE	17	F	SP	RRZZZZUSA
WIESFENFIFR, BROCHE	18	F	SP	RRZZZZUSA
RATRIER, FREIDE	20	F	SP	RRZZZZUSA
GROSS, DINE	20	F	SP	RRZZZZUSA
COHN, JOSEF	50	F	MA	RRZZZZUSA
GORDON, RISCKE	55	F	MA	RRZZZZUSA
CORDT, ELIZ.	21	F	SP	PLZZZZUSA
WEINSTEIN, BRITE	15	F	SP	PLZZZZUSA
GOESTEIN, MAX	24	M	LABR	RRZZZZUSA
ESTER	24	F	W	RRZZZZUSA
HOCHERSEN, SCHEUDE	19	F	SP	RRZZZZUSA
FRIEDMAN, SELIG	24	M	LABR	RRZZZZUSA
GOLDB--, JANKEL	45	M	LABR	RRZZZZUSA
KRAWITZ, ITZIG	18	M	TLR	RRZZZZUSA
KOWERTZKY, LEIBE	36	M	LABR	RRZZZZUSA
RASIN, RACHEL	21	F	SP	RRZZZZUSA
SOCHS, ISAK	30	M	LABR	FNZZZZUSA
HAKKO, AUGUST	23	M	LABR	FNZZZZUSA
MEINSTRI, ALFRED	23	M	LABR	PLZZZZUSA
ZORUCH, CRON	18	M	LABR	PLZZZZUSA
DOBROWALSKY, STANISLAUS	31	M	LABR	PLZZZZUSA
PERLZWEIG, ABRAHAM	48	M	APTC	RRZZZZUSA
MORDKO	54	M	APTC	RRZZZZUSA
VLADIMIR	14	M	STDNT	RRZZZZUSA
NICOLAUS	11	M	STDNT	RRZZZZUSA
SCHEBERG, GUSTAV	34	M	SEMN	FNZZZZUSA

SHIP: CITY OF RICHMOND

FROM: LIVERPOOL AND QUEENSTOWN
TO: NEW YORK
ARRIVED: 10 SEPTEMBER 1888

PASSENGER	AGE	SEX	OCCUPATION	PRV VIL DES
HEIRWITZ, JANKIL	40	M	LABR	RRZZZZUSA
PITSEL, WILLEY	35	M	LABR	RRACBFNY
PELER, MATES	28	M	LABR	RRACBFNY
ABM.	10	M	CH	RRACBFNY
SAM	9	M	CHILD	RRACBFNY
SCHWARZMAN, ISRAEL	20	M	LABR	RRACBFNY
SCHIT, WULF	20	M	LABR	RRACBFNY
ROSSUNAER, ELIAS	29	M	LABR	RRACBFNY
GOLDFEIN, KUSEIL	18	M	LABR	RRACBFNY
SCHMUL	11	M	CH	RRACBFNY
KRIEGER, MOSES	21	M	LABR	RRACBFNY
GOLAR	21	M	LABR	RRACBFNY
FUCHS, MADSOL	30	M	LABR	RRACBFNY
NYLECK, WOLF	50	M	LABR	RRACBFNY
LEWY, SCHLAN	23	M	LABR	RRACBFNY
SCH, HESSEL	38	M	LABR	RRACBFPHI
KLEGSPPER, JOHN	20	M	LABR	FNZZZZNY
LOWENSTEIN, MALKE	48	F	W	RRZZZZNY
PROCK, SPENGER	30	F	W	RRACBFUSA
MIRSEL	10	F	CH	RRACBFUSA
BELE	6	F	CHILD	RRACBFUSA
HERSCHEL	3	F	CHILD	RRACBFUSA
CHAIM	00	F	INF	RRACBFUSA
BRANDEL	18	F	SP	RRACBFUSA
JEINE	15	F	SP	RRACBFUSA
SAKO, LENI	12	F	CH	RRACBFNY

PASSENGER	AGE	SEX	OCCUPATION	PRV VIL DES
LEON	10	M	CH	RRACBFNY
BODIK, SOPHIN	24	F	W	RRACBFNY
SIMCHE	6	F	CHILD	RRACBFNY
ISRAEL	3	F	CHILD	RRACBFNY
SORE	00	F	INF	RRACBFNY
HEIMERLING, GUSTI	24	F	W	RRACBFNY
GISA	3	F	CHILD	RRACBFNY
MORITZ	00	M	INF	RRACBFNY
FERNSCHURTEN, JUL.	11	M	CH	RRACBFNY
SCHENSIL, CHAIN	15	F	SP	RRACBFWI
SORE	24	F	W	RRACBFWI
CHAM	3	F	CHILD	RRACBFWI
JULEN	00	M	INF	RRACBFWI
SUFESKA, MART.	25	F	W	RRADAXNY
SORES	3	M	CHILD	RRADAXNY
STAN	00	M	INF	RRADAXNY
SPIELMANN, GILDI	35	F	W	RRADAXNY
DREN	00	F	INF	RRADAXNY
CZERTOK, CHAIN	36	F	W	RRADAXNY
FRUN	7	F	CHILD	RRADAXNY
SEADKA, ANN	25	F	W	RRADAXNY
ZURKEZ	00	F	INF	RRADAXNY
KAMENSKY, SAM	17	M	LABR	RRADAXNY
HENNE	17	F	SP	RRADAXNY
BRUMER, BOER	10	M	CL	RRADAXNY
PALINNSKA, LEON	28	M	LABR	RRADAXNY
SURKA	20	F	W	RRADAXNY
KOHN, SCHELEM	20	F	W	RRACBFNY
IDOR	20	M	LABR	RRACBFNY
MARKOWITZ, JUDAS	48	F	W	RRADAXNY
PAUL.	17	F	SP	RRADAXNY

SHIP: GOTHIA

FROM: STETTIN
TO: NEW YORK
ARRIVED: 10 SEPTEMBER 1888

PASSENGER	AGE	SEX	OCCUPATION	PRV VIL DES
EMMERICH, PETER	65	M	JNR	RRZZZZUSA
ELISABETH	65	F	W	RRZZZZUSA
ZANISKA, VALERIA	20	F	SGL	RRZZZZUSA
SAKS, LEIB	16	M	WCHMKR	RRZZZZUSA
KLAWONSKY, GLUESKE	40	F	W	RRZZZZUSA
LEIBE	23	F	W	RRZZZZUSA
SUNDE	12	F	CH	RRZZZZUSA
CHANE	10	F	CH	RRZZZZUSA
FREIDE	.09	F	INFANT	RRZZZZUSA
ZULKOWSKA, MARIANA	63	F	W	RRZZZZUSA
KAHN, JACOB	25	M	SHMK	RRZZZZUSA
SORKIN, CHANNE	25	M	TLR	RRZZZZUSA
CHANNE	23	F	W	RRZZZZUSA
BARUCH	.11	M	INFANT	RRZZZZUSA
KALINOWSKY, JOHN	26	M	LABR	RRZZZZUSA
SEDLITZKY, KASIMIR	28	M	LABR	RRZZZZUSA
KATZ, ELIAS	27	M	DLR	RRZZZZUSA
HERZBERG, HERZ	19	M	LKSH	RRZZZZUSA
ABRAMOWITZ, ABRAHAM	18	M	UNKNOWN	RRZZZZUSA
PEIKON, LEIBE	20	F	W	RRZZZZUSA
MARKOWSKY, SARA	15	F	SGL	RRZZZZUSA
HANNE	2	F	CHILD	RRZZZZUSA
TAUBE	37	F	W	RRZZZZUSA
NECHUNNE	10	F	CH	RRZZZZUSA
KLIMOWSKA, FRANZISKA	37	F	W	RRZZZZUSA
DUMAGALSKA, ANASTASIA	25	F	W	RRZZZZUSA
HELENA	.06	F	INFANT	RRZZZZUSA
KURASKOWSKA, MARIA	20	F	S	RRZZZZUSA
ALPEROWITZ, ABE	18	M	LABR	RRZZZZUSA
SAZKEWER, DEBORAH	20	F	W	RRZZZZUSA
KLAWONSKY, CHANITA	5	F	CHILD	RRZZZZUSA
GARSZTASKA, HELENE	1	F	CHILD	RRZZZZUSA

PASSENGER	AGE	SEX	OCCUPATION	PRV VIL DES
PRUGER, REIMUND	40	M	SHMK	RRZZZZUSA

SHIP: EIDER

FROM: BREMEN AND SOUTHAMPTON
TO: NEW YORK
ARRIVED: 11 SEPTEMBER 1888

PASSENGER	AGE	SEX	OCCUPATION	PRV VIL DES
HERTUB, JAN	20	M	LABR	RRZZZZUSA
LANGE, MARIA	19	F	SWMKR	RRZZZZUSA
SOPHIE	18	F	SMSTS	RRZZZZUSA
SCHRADER, WILH.	11	M	UNKNOWN	RRZZZZUSA
DAMBROWSKA, INZEFATA	25	F	UNKNOWN	RRZZZZUSA
JOSEF	2	M	CHILD	RRZZZZUSA
VONTUNGELN, HELENE	26	F	W	RRZZZZUSA
HARMS, JOHANNE	22	F	SWR	RRZZZZUSA
H----BERGER, U	40	M	MCHT	RRZZZZUSA
RATZ, LOUISE	22	F	SMSTS	RRZZZZUSA
RUNBERGER, MARIE	23	F	SMSTS	RRZZZZUSA
WALZ, CATHAR.	17	F	SMSTS	RRZZZZUSA
WEIT, JOHS.	23	M	BRR	RRZZZZUSA
SALZGEBER, JOH.	43	M	FARMER	RRZZZZUSA
JOS.	10	M	CH	RRZZZZUSA
HAUSMANN, GEORG	25	M	HTR	RRZZZZUSA
STERN, SARAH	20	F	UNKNOWN	RRZZZZUSA
HILDEBRECHT, ANNA	10	F	CH	RRZZZZUSA
GOTTSCHALK, JOH.	63	M	MCHT	RRZZZZUSA
ANNA	62	F	W	RRZZZZUSA
-FENNATZ, U	18	M	TLR	RRZZZZUSA
SCHULZ, MARTHA	25	F	SWR	RRZZZZUSA
KOEHLER, JOHS.	17	M	LABR	RRZZZZUSA
KANN, LUDW.	14	M	LABR	RRZZZZUSA
EMANNEL, SYBILLA	20	F	UNKNOWN	RRZZZZUSA
LUNDBERG, CARL	34	M	FARMER	RRZZZZUSA
GRULER, ADOLF	22	M	FARMER	RRZZZZUSA
GRATHWOKE, PAUL	15	M	UNKNOWN	RRZZZZUSA
LENSBERGER, ELISAB.	65	F	UNKNOWN	RRZZZZUSA
GALDBACH, CARG.	39	F	UNKNOWN	RRZZZZUSA
HAAG, HEMR.	34	M	FARMER	RRZZZZUSA
VOGT, JUL.	21	M	FARMER	RRZZZZUSA
EBNER, EMIL	26	M	MCHT	RRZZZZUSA
THOME, MARG.	15	F	UNKNOWN	RRZZZZUSA
HAASE, MART.	36	M	BKR	RRZZZZUSA
JACOB, JACOB	18	M	UNKNOWN	RRZZZZUSA
WIELER, SARAH	28	F	UNKNOWN	RRZZZZUSA
SCHOEB, ELISAB.	21	F	UNKNOWN	RRZZZZUSA
MORITZ, THEOD.	36	M	MCHT	RRZZZZUSA
ROCSKOVSKY, -RNT.	31	M	LABR	RRZZZZUSA
WACKIEWICZ, WAJEIECH	28	M	LABR	RRZZZZUSA
RUBINSKI, BENZ.	35	M	LABR	RRZZZZUSA
GLUCKFELD, ROB.	10	M	CH	RRZZZZUSA
NARNICHHOWICZ, FRANZ	46	M	LABR	RRZZZZUSA
PAULINE	33	F	W	RRZZZZUSA
STANISLAUS	2	M	CHILD	RRZZZZUSA
HUEBNER, JOSEF	46	M	LABR	RRZZZZUSA
BANK, ELIAS	36	M	MCHT	RRZZZZUSA
ISAAC	11	M	UNKNOWN	RRZZZZUSA
LEWERMANN, ELISE	26	F	UNKNOWN	RRZZZZUSA
ANCHEL	19	F	UNKNOWN	RRZZZZUSA
GLUECKFELD, LIEBE	35	F	UNKNOWN	RRZZZZUSA
MAJE	25	F	UNKNOWN	RRZZZZUSA
MANE	2	F	CHILD	RRZZZZUSA
JOSEF	.09	M	INFANT	RRZZZZUSA

SHIP: ETHIOPIA

FROM: GLASGOW AND MOVILLE
TO: NEW YORK
ARRIVED: 11 SEPTEMBER 1888

PASSENGER	AGE	SEX	OCCUPATION	PRV VIL DES
ITUELA, WILE	20	M	LABR	FNZZZZUSA
NORKIN, MENDEL	21	M	LABR	FNZZZZUSA
HENNE	22	M	LABR	FNZZZZUSA
ABRAHAM	10	M	CH	FNZZZZUSA
RUBINSTEIN, MOSES	18	M	LKSH	RRZZZZUSA
MORADKO, CHANIE	10	M	CH	RRZZZZUSA
SEGALL, JEIDEL	20	M	SHMK	RRZZZZUSA
WETASCHKY, INNG	40	F	UNKNOWN	RRZZZZUSA
JELLY	.11	F	INFANT	RRZZZZUSA
SENGER, LEA	42	F	UNKNOWN	RRZZZZUSA
ADELA	17	F	UNKNOWN	RRZZZZUSA
ROSA	10	F	CH	RRZZZZUSA
MOSES	6	M	CHILD	RRZZZZUSA
ESTER	.06	F	INFANT	RRZZZZUSA
KOLOMESKA, FREIDE	50	F	UNKNOWN	RRZZZZUSA

SHIP: WYOMING

FROM: LIVERPOOL AND QUEENSTOWN
TO: NEW YORK
ARRIVED: 11 SEPTEMBER 1888

PASSENGER	AGE	SEX	OCCUPATION	PRV VIL DES
KORNBLEIM, IDW.	19	F	SP	PLZZZZUSA
KUSHUBA, GEDRUTE	22	F	SP	PLZZZZUSA
SEIDL, F.	30	F	W	PLZZZZUSA
FRANK	3	M	CHILD	PLZZZZUSA
BARBARA	00	F	INF	PLZZZZUSA
PEDRILA, SUSANNA	24	F	SP	PLZZZZUSA
SILBERMANN, H.	29	M	LABR	PLZZZZUSA
NOLZEY, W.	24	M	LABR	PLZZZZUSA
MULKE, A.	15	M	LABR	PLZZZZUSA
MARIE	22	F	SP	PLZZZZUSA
SCHMIDT, MARIA	18	F	UNKNOWN	PLZZZZUSA
MILKA, MARTHA	19	F	UNKNOWN	PLZZZZUSA
KERPTZANKOW, MARIA	23	F	UNKNOWN	PLZZZZUSA
HOKU, SARAH	19	F	W	PLZZZZUSA
WM.	00	M	INF	PLZZZZUSA
JERMERMANN, L.	20	F	SP	PLZZZZUSA
KRUMAR, S.	29	M	LABR	PLZZZZUSA
GRATZ, R.	40	F	W	PLZZZZUSA
JUER, CHANNE	30	F	W	PLZZZZUSA
JACOB	7	M	CHILD	PLZZZZUSA
SCHOE	3	M	CHILD	PLZZZZUSA
POLLUCK, C.	48	F	W	PLZZZZUSA
EITEL	7	M	CHILD	PLZZZZUSA
BERA, M.	38	F	W	PLZZZZUSA
PREIDE	7	F	CHILD	PLZZZZUSA
FEIGE	6	F	CHILD	PLZZZZUSA
TAUBE	4	M	CHILD	PLZZZZUSA
AITSTZKI, MALKA	34	F	W	PLZZZZUSA
ABRAHAMSON, SARA	33	F	UNKNOWN	PLZZZZUSA
NECHE	8	M	CHILD	PLZZZZUSA
IDA	7	F	CHILD	PLZZZZUSA
ROCHE	6	M	CHILD	PLZZZZUSA
ABRAHAMSOHN, LEIB	5	M	CHILD	PLZZZZUSA
ISAAC	4	M	CHILD	PLZZZZUSA
ESTER	2	F	CHILD	PLZZZZUSA
ABRAM	00	M	INF	PLZZZZUSA

SHIP: HERMANN

FROM: BREMEN
TO: BALTIMORE
ARRIVED: 12 SEPTEMBER 1888

PASSENGER	AGE	SEX	OCCUPATION	PRV VIL DES
SCHWAND, AUGUST	34	M	FARMER	PLAIFDMD
MARIA	37	F	W	PLAIFDMD
THEODOR	8	M	CHILD	PLAIFDMD
CARL	6	M	CHILD	PLAIFDMD
ALWINE	2	F	CHILD	PLAIFDMD
FREIDES, SZIMEN	22	M	CL	PLAIFDMD
GOLDSTEIN, ICEAK	18	M	CL	PLAIFDMD
BROOKS, AFE.	20	F	UNKNOWN	PLAIFDMD
KOMETA, JONAS	16	M	UNKNOWN	PLAIFDMD
ZUBLIN, SAMUEL	20	M	UNKNOWN	PLAIFDMD
SULMANN, CHASSE	45	F	UNKNOWN	PLAIFDMD
BASE	18	F	UNKNOWN	PLAIFDMD
CHAJE	14	F	UNKNOWN	PLAIFDMD
ISRAEL	10	M	CH	PLAIFDMD
KATZ, BERE	17	F	UNKNOWN	PLAIFDMD
HOFMANN, JOSEF	15	M	UNKNOWN	PLAIFDMD
FAKLER, ELISE	22	F	UNKNOWN	PLAIFDMD
NATHANSEN, RACHEL	25	F	UNKNOWN	PLAIFDMD
NATHAN	3	M	CHILD	PLAIFDMD
GOSLAWSKA, MARYANA	31	F	UNKNOWN	PLAIFDMD
ANNA	.09	F	INFANT	PLAIFDMD
SCHWAND, EMILIE	16	F	UNKNOWN	PLAIFDMD
MIECZYNSKI, ANTONIE	25	M	MCHT	PLAIFDMD
CHATIN, SCHMIESCHE	35	F	UNKNOWN	PLAIFDMD
JACOB	9	M	CHILD	PLAIFDMD
JOSEF	8	M	CHILD	PLAIFDMD
MOSES	.11	M	INFANT	PLAIFDMD
LEWITAN, DOBRE	27	F	UNKNOWN	PLAIFDMD
MONIE	.01	F	INFANT	PLAIFDMD
OBREZENY, SAM.	24	M	FARMER	PLAIFDMD
BUCH, LEAH.	50	F	UNKNOWN	PLAIFDMD
ORLOWSKY, STANL.	16	M	UNKNOWN	PLAIFDMI
DUBOVIS, FESCHEL	23	F	UNKNOWN	PLAIFDMD
MATHEIS, FERDINAND	38	M	FARMER	PLAIFDCO
--DINANDE	40	F	W	PLAIFDCO
JOHANNA	11	F	CH	PLAIFDCO
JULIA	6	F	CHILD	PLAIFDCO
FERDINAND	4	M	CHILD	PLAIFDCO
JOSEF	2	M	CHILD	PLAIFDCO
FRANZ	.06	M	INFANT	PLAIFDCO
FEIDES, SUSE	17	F	UNKNOWN	PLAIFDMD
BRODE, FRIEDA	19	F	UNKNOWN	PLAIFDIL
COLOMB, DAVID	16	M	UNKNOWN	PLAIFDMD

SHIP: CALIFORNIA

FROM: HAMBURG
TO: NEW YORK
ARRIVED: 13 SEPTEMBER 1888

PASSENGER	AGE	SEX	OCCUPATION	PRV VIL DES
SCHIR, BELE	22	F	SGL	PLAHTFUSA
GUROWITZ, BASSIE	18	F	SGL	PLAHTFUSA
REMPEL, ISRAEL	17	M	LABR	PLAFVGUSA
ENGEL, FRIEDRICH	38	M	BRR	PLACONUSA
SCHEPES, ABRAHAM	20	M	TLR	PLAHVUUSA
MECHANIK, WOLF	27	M	TLR	RRZZZZUSA
ZIPPE	21	F	W	RRZZZZUSA
JERUSALIMSKI, ISAAC	28	M	FSHMN	RRAHVUUSA
SPOLIANSKI, JACOB	23	M	LABR	RRAFVGUSA
GABRIEL, LEIB	20	M	TLR	RRZZZZUSA
KORMANN, MENDEL	26	M	TLR	RRZZZZUSA
LIPHABBE, ABRAHAM	25	M	MCHT	RRZZZZUSA
ROTHSTADT, JACOB	42	M	BBR	RRZZZZUSA

PASSENGER	AGE	SEX	OCCUPATION	PRIVL	VILS	DES
GILLENA	22	F	W	RR	ZZZZ	USA
LENO, HEINRICH	50	M	FARMER	RR	ZZZZ	USA
CATH.	49	F	W	RR	ZZZZ	USA
HEINRICH	14	M	CH	RR	ZZZZ	USA
MAGDALENE	8	F	CHILD	RR	ZZZZ	USA
BRAEUDE, MINNA	19	F	SGL	RR	ZZZZ	USA
CILIE	25	F	WO	RR	ZZZZ	USA
MARIE	.09	F	INFANT	RR	ZZZZ	USA
LIBSCHUETZ, BERNHARD	29	M	LKSH	RR	AHTN	USA
WILK, LEA	23	F	WO	RR	ZZZZ	USA
SEEDE	.09	F	INFANT	RR	ZZZZ	USA
ROSENTHAL, NENNE	22	M	AGNT	RR	AFWJ	USA
NACHAME	23	F	W	RR	AFWJ	USA
LOEFFEL, ZIWIE	25	F	WO	RR	AHTU	USA
PESCHE	.11	F	INFANT	RR	AHTU	USA
RIMANOWSKY, STANISLAUS	23	M	LABR	RR	AHTF	USA
GRUENBERG, JOHEL	18	M	DLR	RR	AFWJ	USA
GANS, NACHUM	22	F	SGL	RR	AFWJ	USA
DALLIN, MAX	25	M	DRG	RR	AIIN	USA
KUBULKA, JANOS	26	M	LABR	RR	ZZZZ	USA
ANDRUSCHEITES, ANTON	27	M	LABR	RR	ZZZZ	USA
BURANTZKY, PETER	24	M	LABR	RR	ZZZZ	USA
ADLER, FANNY	18	F	SGL	RR	AHTF	USA
ROSEN, REISEL	30	F	WO	RR	ZZZZ	USA
SIMON	8	M	CHILD	RR	ZZZZ	USA
RIFKE	4	F	CHILD	RR	ZZZZ	USA
SPIWACK, FEIGE	27	F	UNKNOWN	RR	AHTO	USA
HERSCH	6	M	CHILD	RR	AHTO	USA
CHAJE	3	M	CHILD	RR	AHTO	USA
CHAINE	.11	F	INFANT	RR	AHTO	USA
LEA	.01	F	INFANT	RR	AHTO	USA

SHIP: IOWA

FROM: LIVERPOOL
TO: BOSTON
ARRIVED: 13 SEPTEMBER 1888

PASSENGER	AGE	SEX	OCCUPATION	PRIVL	VILS	DES
BURTMAN, PERI	17	M	LABR	RR	ZZZZ	USA
SCHARAPSKY, CHANE	24	M	LABR	RR	ZZZZ	USA
MILZER, ABRAM	31	M	LABR	RR	ZZZZ	USA
DOGITES, MICHOEH	25	M	LABR	RR	ZZZZ	USA
KATYMAZIK, FRANZ	23	M	LABR	RR	ZZZZ	USA
DIMCEK, VINCENTZ	27	M	LABR	RR	ZZZZ	USA
BIERMAN, BEILE	18	M	LABR	RR	ZZZZ	USA
ISRAEL	15	M	LABR	RR	ZZZZ	USA
RENEWSIKY, B.ROMPS.	25	M	FARMER	RR	ZZZZ	USA
JPERKOWSKY, WAY	30	M	LABR	RR	ZZZZ	USA
CHAMETIZ, JAN	20	M	LABR	RR	ZZZZ	USA
FR.	28	M	LABR	RR	ZZZZ	USA
DRAGAN, JOHAN	26	M	LABR	RR	ZZZZ	USA
KORLI, LAILI	24	M	LABR	RR	ZZZZ	USA
DELSKY, CARLE	27	M	LABR	RR	ZZZZ	USA
DUDEN, FRITZ	24	M	LABR	RR	ZZZZ	USA
SCHMEGER, ED.	36	M	LABR	RR	ZZZZ	USA
BROCTZEK, JAN	28	M	LABR	RR	ZZZZ	USA
ELLEMAN, SCH.	19	M	LABR	RR	ZZZZ	USA
BROWNLOR, ROBERT	22	M	LABR	RR	ZZZZ	USA
KOHEN, BESSIE	28	F	W	RR	ZZZZ	USA
BARETMAN, MARIA	40	F	W	RR	ZZZZ	USA
SCHMIDT, ST.	00	M	LABR	RR	ZZZZ	USA
MOY	39	F	W	RR	ZZZZ	USA
ZLOLMUSKY, CHAYEM	21	M	LABR	RR	ZZZZ	USA
FERINA	21	F	W	RR	ZZZZ	USA
GRAPS, SAMAEL	44	M	LABR	RR	ZZZZ	USA
ROSA	24	F	W	RR	ZZZZ	USA
NURIKANSKY, DWOSCHE	24	F	W	RR	ZZZZ	USA
SACK, LENA	24	F	SP	RR	ZZZZ	USA
GOLDSCHARIDT, LEA	21	F	SP	RR	ZZZZ	USA
SCHMIDT, ALMA	26	F	SP	RR	ZZZZ	USA
ALMA	20	F	SP	RR	ZZZZ	USA
KOHEN, CHASSIE	10	M	CH	RR	ZZZZ	USA
PINNIE	9	F	CHILD	RR	ZZZZ	USA
ZENSE	6	M	CHILD	RR	ZZZZ	USA
SAWA	5	F	CHILD	RR	ZZZZ	USA
BRATMAN, ELIUS	12	M	CH	RR	ZZZZ	USA
CHANGE	9	M	CHILD	RR	ZZZZ	USA
MUSIKANSKY, CLAYAN	3	M	CHILD	RR	ZZZZ	USA
REBACA	1	F	CHILD	RR	ZZZZ	USA
SCHMIDT, KAS.	11	M	CH	RR	ZZZZ	USA
GRUP, JULIUS	.03	F	INFANT	RR	ZZZZ	USA
BIERMAN, BEREL	3	M	CHILD	RR	ZZZZ	USA
FLINK, O.	3	M	CHILD	RR	ZZZZ	USA

SHIP: ITALY

FROM: LIVERPOOL AND QUEENSTOWN
TO: NEW YORK
ARRIVED: 13 SEPTEMBER 1888

PASSENGER	AGE	SEX	OCCUPATION	PRIVL	VILS	DES
DARR, JOHN	44	M	TLR	RR	ADBQ	STL
AMELIA	38	F	W	RR	ADBQ	STL
ABRAHAM	14	M	TLR	RR	ADBQ	STL
HANNAH	9	F	CHILD	RR	ADBQ	STL
ETTEL	.06	F	INFANT	RR	ADBQ	STL
LEFASHIN, LINA	48	F	W	RR	ADAX	PHI
REBECCA	11	F	CH	RR	ADAX	PHI
LEWIN, LEIB	17	M	LABR	RR	ZZZZ	NY
SARAH	23	F	W	RR	ZZZZ	NY
U	00	F	INF	RR	ZZZZ	NY
TREMONT, CATHARINE	35	F	SP	RR	ADAX	NY
DARCY, E.	26	F	W	RR	ADAX	DET
CHRISTINA	11	F	CH	RR	ADAX	DET
GEORGE	00	M	INF	RR	ADAX	DET
JOSEPHINE	00	F	INF	RR	ADAX	DET
SAUBORSKI, M.	18	M	LABR	RR	AGUZ	DET
GOLDBERG, MEYER	27	M	LABR	RR	AGUZ	DET
ROSA	26	F	UNKNOWN	RR	AGUZ	DET
LEIB	4	M	CHILD	RR	AGUZ	DET
EDEL	3	M	CHILD	RR	AGUZ	DET
U	00	M	INF	RR	AGUZ	DET
MOSCHKOWITZ, BASCHE	38	F	W	RR	ACBF	NY
RIFKE	11	M	CH	RR	ACBF	NY
SARA	9	F	CHILD	RR	ACBF	NY
LEA	10	F	CH	RR	ACBF	NY
KRAWITZ, SOLOMON	16	M	LABR	RR	ACBF	NY
SCHOCHET, GISCHE	25	F	W	RR	ZZZZ	NY
BER	6	M	CHILD	RR	ZZZZ	NY
ISTE	5	M	CHILD	RR	ZZZZ	NY
AND.	00	M	INF	RR	ZZZZ	NY
MASSOT, KARK	19	M	LABR	RR	ZZZZ	NY
SVENSON, HULDA	00	F	INF	RR	ZZZZ	NY
MALLEY, TADIN	26	M	LABR	RR	ACBF	NY
WILHELM	28	M	LABR	RR	ACBF	NY
MOYELUNSKY, RODKI	36	M	LABR	RR	ACBF	NY
BUCKOWSKY, FRANCIS	35	M	LABR	RR	ACBF	NY
STALKEWIE, GOLDA	35	F	W	RR	ACBF	PHI
ERIE	18	F	SP	RR	ACBF	PHI
ROSA	8	F	CHILD	RR	ACBF	PHI
LINE	4	F	CHILD	RR	ACBF	PHI
CHURTS	1	M	CHILD	RR	ACBF	PHI
STOH.	00	M	INF	RR	ACBF	PHI
TISCHUS, MICHAEL	42	M	LABR	PL	ZZZZ	NY
CHAJE	42	F	W	PL	ZZZZ	NY
SILVIE	24	M	LABR	PL	ZZZZ	NY
WOLKA	20	M	LABR	PL	ZZZZ	NY
ZANKEL	16	M	LABR	PL	ZZZZ	NY
ESTER	14	F	SP	PL	ZZZZ	NY
CHANE	6	F	CHILD	PL	ZZZZ	NY
TISCHKIS, OSCHEN	11	M	CH	PL	AILA	NY

PASSENGER	AGE	SEX	OCCUPATION	PRV VIL DES
ABRAH.	4	M	CHILD	PLAILANY
MARIAN	00	F	INF	PLAILANY
KURSCHWERD, GOLDE	43	F	W	PLACBFBO
MOERDCHA	8	M	CHILD	PLACBFBO
MIKE	7	M	CHILD	PLACBFBO
GRABOWSKI, MUSE	18	M	LABR	PLACBFBO
TIEDLER, BUEL	46	M	LABR	PLACBFNY
DANOFF, LUSER	24	M	LABR	PLACBFNY
MESSNER, WOLF	25	M	LABR	PLACBFNY
CAROLINE	24	F	W	PLACBFNY
ZABLER, JOSEF	44	M	LABR	PLACBFNY
GLASER, MOSES	42	M	LABR	PLACBFPHI
ZESAK, MENDEL	26	M	LABR	PLACBFNY
MENDEL, LEIB	32	M	LABR	PLACBFCH
LEIBOMS, BLUOCH	20	M	LABR	PLACBFCH
GRUMBERG, ARON	28	M	LABR	PLACBFNY
SCHERASCHEWSKY, MORT.	48	M	LABR	PLACBFNY
BLUM	47	F	W	PLACBFNY
MOSES	10	M	CH	PLACBFNY
SCHLIAT, PETER	23	M	LABR	PLAHQUNY
KURSCHAN, ABRAHAM	47	M	LABR	PLAHQUNY

SHIP: STATE OF GEORGIA

FROM: GLASGOW AND LARNE
TO: NEW YORK
ARRIVED: 13 SEPTEMBER 1888

PASSENGER	AGE	SEX	OCCUPATION	PRV VIL DES
ABRANOWITZ, TYKS	21	M	BCHR	PLAIDLUSA
APIRIA, ISRAEL	24	M	JNR	PLAIDLUSA
SORE	24	F	W	PLAIDLUSA
ARONSOHN, RACHEL	22	F	SVNT	PLAIDLUSA
BASS, REBECCA	33	F	W	PLAIDLUSA
JOSEPH	8	M	CHILD	PLAIDLUSA
FREIDE	1	F	CHILD	PLAIDLUSA
BERKOWITSCH, JOSEPH	16	M	TLR	PLAIDLUSA
BERTAM, MATHIAS	28	M	TLR	PLAIDLUSA
COHEN, MOSES	25	M	PDLR	PLAIDLUSA
DANITZKY, SCHMUEL	55	M	SHMK	PLAIDLUSA
ELISCHKA, SCHIFFRE	21	F	W	PLAIDLUSA
GEANETTE	1	F	CHILD	PLAIDLUSA
FIKOWSKY, LEIB	28	M	LABR	PLAIDLUSA
GINSBURG, CHANE	18	M	LABR	PLAIDLUSA
GUTMANN, FEI--	37	M	SHMK	PLAIDLUSA
KAHN, MICHLI	42	M	PDLR	PLAIDLUSA
JOSEPH	11	M	BY	PLAIDLUSA
KAMELKAR, SARAH	30	F	W	PLAIDLUSA
FEIWUSCH	11	M	BY	PLAIDLUSA
FEIGE	10	F	CH	PLAIDLUSA
SCHAUME	6	M	CHILD	PLAIDLUSA
REBECCA	2	F	CHILD	PLAIDLUSA
KANNENGIESA, MUSCHE	40	M	TLR	PLAIDLUSA
KAPOTZKY, LEAH	50	F	W	PLAIDLUSA
REIGORDETZKY, FEIGE	25	F	W	PLAIDLUSA
JUDE	7	M	CHILD	PLAIDLUSA
RUBEN	5	M	CHILD	PLAIDLUSA
RUWE	.03	F	INFANT	PLAIDLUSA
KAHN, ELIAS	50	M	PDLR	PLAIDLUSA
KOPOLOWITZ, FREIDE	24	F	SVNT	PLAIDLUSA
TAUKEROWITZ, CHLANE	30	F	SVNT	PLAIDLUSA
LAPIDES, REFKE	18	F	SVNT	PLAIDLUSA
LEWIN, SORE	18	F	SVNT	PLAIDLUSA
LEWOWE, MERI	19	F	SVNT	PLAIDLUSA
MANISCHEWITZ, RAPHAEL	23	F	W	PLAIDLUSA
SCHAPIRO, ARON	11	M	BY	PLAIDLUSA
MOSES	9	M	CHILD	PLAIDLUSA
PRESS, CHANE	11	M	BY	PLAIDLUSA
MARKOWITZ, CHAIE	30	F	W	PLAIDLUSA
WULFF	2	M	CHILD	PLAIDLUSA
SCHOLEM	1	M	CHILD	PLAIDLUSA

PASSENGER	AGE	SEX	OCCUPATION	PRV VIL DES
EMMA	.03	F	INFANT	PLAIDLUSA
NEDELMAN, TAUBE	22	F	W	PLAIDLUSA
REWKA	.09	F	INFANT	PLAIDLUSA
REMGELSDORF, BREINE	22	F	W	PLAIDLUSA
REWKE	1	M	CHILD	PLAIDLUSA
SCHERMANN, BELLY	24	F	W	PLAIDLUSA
ABRAHAM	.06	M	INFANT	PLAIDLUSA
SCHNEIDER, LEIBER	28	M	TLR	PLAIDLUSA
SCHWARZ, SCHEIMEN	17	M	LABR	PLAIDLUSA
BEILE	40	F	SVNT	PLAIDLUSA
HEYMANN	1	M	CHILD	PLAIDLUSA
STOLOWITZ, TANSHEN	20	M	TLR	PLAIDLUSA
CHAIE	22	F	W	PLAIDLUSA
SUSS, LOUISE	18	F	SVNT	PLAIDLUSA
TERUSCHOWITZ, RACHEL	56	F	SVNT	PLAIDLUSA
DEBORE	24	F	SVNT	PLAIDLUSA
LEVY	26	M	TLR	PLAIDLUSA
ABRAHAM	18	M	TLR	PLAIDLUSA
LAZARUS	16	M	TLR	PLAIDLUSA
ZUCKERMANN, BADANE	20	F	SVNT	PLAIDLUSA

SHIP: SALE

FROM: BREMEN AND SOUTHAMPTON
TO: NEW YORK
ARRIVED: 14 SEPTEMBER 1888

PASSENGER	AGE	SEX	OCCUPATION	PRV VIL DES
EPSTEIN, SOLOMON	20	M	FARMER	RRZZZZUSA
RUBINSTEIN, NECHE	38	F	NN	RRZZZZUSA
ISRAEL	11	M	CH	RRZZZZUSA
ESTHER	10	F	CH	RRZZZZUSA
CHAIM	9	M	CHILD	RRZZZZUSA
WIZDOR	7	M	CHILD	RRZZZZUSA
FRAME	6	F	CHILD	RRZZZZUSA
HERSCH	4	M	CHILD	RRZZZZUSA
MANI	2	F	CHILD	RRZZZZUSA
PINCHUS	.05	M	INFANT	RRZZZZUSA

SHIP: HAMMONIA

FROM: HAMBURG AND HAVRE
TO: NEW YORK
ARRIVED: 14 SEPTEMBER 1888

PASSENGER	AGE	SEX	OCCUPATION	PRV VIL DES
INGWES, BONDEN	39	M	FARMER	FNZZZZNY
KORNOS, CHAJE	45	F	W	FNAFVGNY
GITTEL	8	F	CHILD	FNAFVGNY
FEIGE	7	F	CHILD	FNAFVGNY
TOFT, CHRISTINE	31	F	W	FNAFWJNY
CARL	.11	M	INFANT	FNAFWJNY
ALEXANDER	14	M	CH	FNAFWJNY
HIRSCH	8	M	CHILD	FNAFWJNY
JACOB	3	M	CHILD	FNAFWJNY
ANNA	7	F	CHILD	FNAFWJNY
JENNY	5	F	CHILD	FNAFWJNY
WEISS, SALOMON	35	M	LABR	FNAGRTNY
FIN-ELSEIN, LEIL	31	M	MCHT	FNAHTFNY
CHA-T, RUBIN	17	M	LABR	FNAGRTNY
KUDIG, ELIAS	41	M	SLR	FNAFWJNY
NACUM	18	M	SLR	FNAFWJNY
REISER, DAVID	44	M	PNTR	FNAFVGNY
LEW---, SALOMON	.06	M	INFANT	RRZZZZNY
RUBINSTEIN, GETZEL	26	M	DLR	RRAHXHNY
CHAMME	22	F	W	RRAHXHNY
RAPPEPORT, RACHEL	19	F	SGL	RRAHXHNY

PASSENGER	AGE	SEX	OCCUPATION	PRIVL	DES
GAWRONSKI, LINE	18	F	SGL	RRAHXH	NY
KATZEL, ERNESTINE	20	F	SGL	RRAHXH	NY
ANGELNIK, MARKUS	44	M	LABR	RRAGRT	NY
LEWADANSKY, IVAN	45	M	LABR	RRZZZZ	NY
FONDILLA, RACHEL	24	F	W	RRAHTU	NY
ESTHER	9	M	CHILD	RRAHTU	NY
ISAAC	3	M	CHILD	RRAHTU	NY
WILLE	.10	M	INFANT	RRAHTU	NY
BRAND, SARA	20	F	SGL	RRZZZZ	NY
KRAMER, SAMUEL	8	M	CHILD	RRZZZZ	NY
ZADIHOWITZ, CHASI	40	F	W	RRZZZZ	NY
BLOCH-ZADIHOWITZ, JOSEF	30	M	LABR	RRZZZZ	NY
HANSEN, OTTO	24	M	GDNR	RRZZZZ	NY
E--LAS, MARY	28	F	W	RRZZZZ	NY
CHAIM	3	F	CHILD	RRZZZZ	NY
ISAAC	4	F	CHILD	RRZZZZ	NY
KAROTOSINSKY, ARON	30	M	LABR	RRZZZZ	NY
CZARNE, BEILE	20	F	SGL	RRAHVL	NY
KRAVETZ, RACHEL	19	F	SGL	RRAHVL	NY
BRAMSON, MUSCHI	40	F	W	RRAHVL	NY
ABRAHAM	8	M	CHILD	RRAHVL	NY
LEIB	7	M	CHILD	RRAHVL	NY
CHAIE	6	M	CHILD	RRAHVL	NY
SARA	.11	F	INFANT	RRAHVL	NY
ZUCHERMANN, ABRAH	18	M	LABR	RRAGRT	NY
H	18	F	W	RRAGRT	NY
DUDJUS, ISAAC	24	M	DLR	RRZZZZ	NY
HAUSMANN, JOSEF	25	M	MUSN	RRZZZZ	NY
WEJRIK, JA----ELL	30	M	DLR	RRZZZZ	NY
DINITZ, PE--	19	M	DLR	RRZZZZ	NY
DEUTSCHMANN, SALKE	22	F	W	RRAFWJ	NY
MORITZ	2	M	CHILD	RRAFWJ	NY
ROSA	.06	F	INFANT	RRAFWJ	NY
STRESCHER, ISKE	17	F	SGL	RRAFWJ	NY
LEVIN, SALOMON	36	M	LABR	RRAFWJ	NY
ROSA	34	F	W	RRAFWJ	NY
KATZ, LIEBE	26	F	W	RRAHVU	NY
UNGER, BER	45	M	LABR	RRAHZS	NY
FRANKEL, MIECZYLAV	33	M	MCHT	RRZZZZ	NY
GOLOLEN-IEWSKA, VERONIK	24	F	SGL	RRZZZZ	NY

SHIP: ADRIATIC

FROM: LIVERPOOL AND QUEENSTOWN
TO: NEW YORK
ARRIVED: 14 SEPTEMBER 1888

PASSENGER	AGE	SEX	OCCUPATION	PRIVL	DES
CZECT, ABRAHAM	19	M	LABR	RRADAX	USA
GLUCHOWSKI, SALOMON	37	M	LABR	RRADAX	USA
LEON	10	M	CH	RRADAX	USA
KSONSOWSKI, GEDALGI	43	M	LABR	RRADAX	USA
MOSES	29	M	LABR	RRADAX	USA
SOHN, DOBRE	30	F	W	RRADAX	USA
BREDEL	3	F	CHILD	RRADAX	USA
DWORE	1	F	CHILD	RRADAX	USA
HERVELLING, EMIL	34	M	LABR	RRADAX	USA
NEUMANN, CHASSIE	24	F	W	RRADAX	USA
NOFTALI	2	F	CHILD	RRADAX	USA
SARA	2	F	CHILD	RRADAX	USA
ABRAMM	1	M	CHILD	RRADAX	USA
BROWSTRON, SARA	29	F	W	RRADAX	USA
MOSES	3	M	CHILD	RRADAX	USA
KEWE	1	F	CHILD	RRADAX	USA
POLACKI, KERNACK	27	M	LABR	RRADAX	USA
MICHTEN, HERSEL	30	M	LABR	RRADAX	USA
TUCHAN, HERMINE	3	F	CHILD	RRADAX	USA
JOSEPH	1	M	CHILD	RRADAX	USA
BLOCH, PENCHAS	21	M	LABR	RRADAX	USA
MICHLA	20	M	LABR	RRADAX	USA
RURZYK, SELIG	59	M	LABR	RRADAX	USA
FUGE	50	F	W	RRADAX	USA
BIRN, SIMON	56	M	LABR	RRADAX	USA
RESI	47	F	W	RRADAX	USA
SAMI	8	M	CHILD	RRADAX	USA
STILLAR, RIFKE	25	M	LABR	RRADAX	USA
STEIN, MICHEL	24	M	LABR	RRADAX	USA
RABINOWITZ, SCHEINDEL	26	F	W	RRADAX	USA
NACHMEIR	8	M	CHILD	RRADAX	USA
BREMER, SOFIE	19	F	W	RRADAX	USA
DWORE	1	F	CHILD	RRADAX	USA
STENMUTZ, RESSEL	16	F	SP	RRADAX	USA
LYUNGDAHL, CARL	2	M	CHILD	RRADAX	USA
HILMA	1	F	CHILD	RRADAX	USA
EKESTEDT, ANNA	9	F	CHILD	RRADAX	USA
MATILDA	4	F	CHILD	RRADAX	USA
LYDIA	2	F	CHILD	RRADAX	USA
HOHN, HANNA	30	F	SP	RRADAX	USA
LINDGREN, T.F.	25	M	LABR	RRADAX	USA
JOHAN	2	M	CHILD	RRADAX	USA
HANSON, FRANZ	1	M	CHILD	RRADAX	USA
JOHANNESON, OLE	27	M	LABR	RRADAX	USA
BEDI, M.T.	31	M	LABR	RRADAX	USA
ALTH, ANDREAS	19	M	LABR	RRADAX	USA
SCHWARZ, LUCIA	17	F	SVNT	RRADAX	USA
GRYNBORG, MARIANNE	18	F	UNKNOWN	RRADAX	USA
GOLDJARL, KINE	15	M	LABR	RRADAX	USA
BERKOWITZ, FAIN.	29	M	LABR	RRADAX	USA
DOM.	6	M	CHILD	RRADAX	USA
SCHACHNE	4	M	CHILD	RRADAX	USA
SALI	2	M	CHILD	RRADAX	USA
JESSIE	1	F	CHILD	RRADAX	USA
TRADIE	11	M	CH	RRADAX	USA
BERNHOFF, JOSEPH	19	M	LABR	RRADAX	USA
SILLBERMANN, LEON	19	M	LABR	RRADAX	USA
ENGEL, ADELE	19	M	LABR	RRADAX	USA
PRAUL, ESTER	17	M	LABR	RRADAX	USA
RIVE	15	M	LABR	RRADAX	USA

SHIP: EMS

FROM: BREMEN AND SOUTHAMPTON
TO: NEW YORK
ARRIVED: 14 SEPTEMBER 1888

PASSENGER	AGE	SEX	OCCUPATION	PRIVL	DES
KOPINDLOFSKY, SIMON	20	M	LABR	RRAHOO	NY
RULLMANN, GUSTAV	16	M	LABR	RRAHOO	NY
HUCHTHANSEN, ANNA	16	F	NN	RRAARR	NY
KUNZ, RUDOLF	11	M	CH	RRAARR	NY
BRAND, JULIUS	16	M	BCK	RRZZZZ	NY
LUDWIG, ELISABETH	23	F	W	RRAIEC	NY
EMMA	3	F	CHILD	RRAIEC	NY
WALTHER	.10	M	INFANT	RRAIEC	NY
KUZ, JOSEF	23	M	SHMK	RRAIEC	NY
RUTKOWSKY, JOSEF	46	M	FARMER	RRAHOO	NY
CATHARINA	25	F	W	RRAHOO	NY
CORSSEN, JOHANN	16	M	SHMK	RRACBR	NY
LESEMKANN, WILHELM	42	M	FARMER	RRZZZZ	NY
SOPHIE	33	F	W	RRZZZZ	NY
CARLO	13	M	CH	RRZZZZ	NY
WILHELM	11	M	CH	RRZZZZ	NY
AUGUSTE	9	F	CHILD	RRZZZZ	NY
CARL	5	M	CHILD	RRZZZZ	NY
MARIE	3	F	CHILD	RRZZZZ	NY
KARSCH, CARL	17	M	BCK	RRZZZZ	NY
WILHELM, EDUARD	26	M	JNR	RRZZZZ	NY
WEISS, MARIE	18	F	NN	RRZZZZ	NY
RAN, MAX	17	M	TNM	RRZZZZ	UNK

PASSENGER	AGE	SEX	OCCUPATION	PRV VIL DES

SHIP: ANCHORIA

FROM: GLASGOW
TO: NEW YORK
ARRIVED: 18 SEPTEMBER 1888

PASSENGER	AGE	SEX	OCCUPATION	PRV VIL DES
BARAN, C.JACOB	26	M	JNR	RRZZZZUSA
JETTE	26	F	W	RRZZZZUSA
ABRAHAM	2	M	CHILD	RRZZZZUSA
GLASS, SALOM	25	M	PDLR	RRZZZZUSA
ESTER	22	F	W	RRAIKLUSA
SCHER, SAML.	26	M	PDLR	RRAIKLUSA
PASCKE	23	F	W	RRZZZZUSA
SUSSMANN, ABRAM	27	M	SHMK	RRZZZZUSA
SARAH	20	F	W	RRAICFUSA
WEICHSELBRAUN, BEILE	30	M	LABR	RRAICFUSA
KEMPER, SOPHIE	20	F	UNKNOWN	RRZZZZUSA
LEWIN, PESCHE	27	F	W	RRZZZZUSA
CHAIM	3	F	CHILD	RRZZZZUSA
ISAK	1	M	CHILD	RRAHTUUSA
BORISZPOLSKI, LEIE	43	F	W	RRAHOKUSA
SORE	17	F	UNKNOWN	RRAHOKUSA
MALKE	10	F	CH	RRAHOKUSA
WEINSTEIN, VICTOR	32	M	LABR	RRAICCUSA
RUBURZEK, FROIM	15	M	LABR	RRAICCUSA
GROSS, MICHL.	23	M	TLR	RRAICCUSA
JURITZ, HERMAN	21	M	TLR	RRZZZZUSA
RUBENSTEIN, SCHLOME	23	M	TLR	RRZZZZUSA
KAHN, ISAK	23	M	SHMK	RRZZZZUSA
BERGERN, STANISLAUS	27	M	LABR	PLZZZZUSA
SISNOLE	24	F	W	PLZZZZUSA
SKOPIC, TOMA	26	M	LABR	PLZZZZUSA
ANDREI	28	M	LABR	PLZZZZUSA
NANJETIS, JEAN	28	M	LABR	PLZZZZUSA
RODOWITZ, EDUARD	24	M	WCHMKR	PLAHTFUSA
JELEP, SIDOR	31	M	LABR	PLZZZZUSA

SHIP: ARIZONA

FROM: LIVERPOOL AND QUEENSTOWN
TO: NEW YORK
ARRIVED: 18 SEPTEMBER 1888

PASSENGER	AGE	SEX	OCCUPATION	PRV VIL DES
FREIDMAN, L.	36	F	W	PLACBFUSA
SALOMON	22	M	LABR	PLACBFUSA
RIFKE	17	F	SP	PLACBFUSA
FRANK, SAML.J.	17	M	LABR	PLACBFUSA
LEWIN, ESTER-R.	40	F	W	PLACBFUSA
KUPERSTEIN, HILLET	20	M	JNR	PLACBFUSA
LEWIN, CHAINE	30	F	W	PLACBFUSA
NOWDSCHE	6	M	CHILD	PLACBFUSA
HENE-DOBE	3	F	CHILD	PLACBFUSA
JENCZYK, ALWIN	39	M	ART	PLACBFUSA
WILCYAK, MARIA	24	F	SP	PLACBFUSA
JENCZYK, FRANZ	6	M	CHILD	PLACBFUSA
LEWENSBERG, IDA	19	F	SP	PLACBFUSA
SCHECHT, ARON	15	M	LABR	PLACBFUSA
LEIB	11	M	CH	PLACBFUSA
ANTEKOLSKI, HODE	22	F	SP	PLACBFUSA
GANSBERG, C.	18	M	LABR	PLACBFUSA
ELKE	4	F	CHILD	PLACBFUSA
KRAFTZUK, SINCHE	18	F	SP	PLACBFUSA
OLENT, MASCHE	20	F	SP	PLACBFUSA
LEWIN, MALKE	.10	F	INFANT	PLACBFUSA
CHAITOWICZ, BEILE	30	F	W	PLACBFUSA
SLATE	7	F	CHILD	PLACBFUSA
CHAIM	5	F	CHILD	PLACBFUSA
MEORET	.04	M	INFANT	PLACBFUSA
LEWIN, RIFKE	.05	F	INFANT	PLACBFUSA

PASSENGER	AGE	SEX	OCCUPATION	PRV VIL DES
RICH, PAHUKE	26	M	PNTR	PLACBFUSA
WOSTRAKOF, R.	39	M	GENT	PLADAXRSS

SHIP: FULDA

FROM: BREMEN AND SOUTHAMPTON
TO: NEW YORK
ARRIVED: 18 SEPTEMBER 1888

PASSENGER	AGE	SEX	OCCUPATION	PRV VIL DES
LOEFGVIST, ERIK	30	M	FARMER	RRZZZZUSA
LINDEVALL, AMALIA	38	F	UNKNOWN	RRZZZZUSA
FILPPULA, ADOLFINA	17	F	UNKNOWN	RRZZZZUSA
EKOLA, MATTS	28	M	LABR	RRZZZZUSA
PORRASMAKI, JOHANN	40	M	LABR	RRZZZZUSA
WOLLTI, LISA	15	F	UNKNOWN	RRZZZZUSA
JANNA	13	F	UNKNOWN	RRZZZZUSA
GOLDHAAR, ADOLF	15	M	UNKNOWN	RRZZZZUSA
KREUZVOGEL, SANDEL	17	M	FARMER	RRZZZZUSA
DORFMANN, JETTE	28	F	UNKNOWN	RRZZZZUSA
RUDIAK, JUDIE	20	F	UNKNOWN	RRZZZZUSA
SCHWARSTEIN, MARIE	28	F	UNKNOWN	RRZZZZUSA
BRUCHE	25	M	LABR	RRZZZZUSA
ESTHER	3	F	CHILD	RRZZZZUSA
JOSEF	.08	M	INFANT	RRZZZZUSA
BERKAUSCHKAS, JOH.	23	M	LABR	RRZZZZUSA
MENNRAPSKA, JOS.	15	M	LABR	RRZZZZUSA
VINZENS	20	M	LABR	RRZZZZUSA
LUSTO, DAVID-S.	48	M	LABR	RRZZZZUSA
SALMISEN, PETTER	36	M	LABR	RRZZZZUSA
SANDELL, FANY	23	F	UNKNOWN	RRZZZZUSA
JOHANNSEN, V.	26	F	UNKNOWN	RRZZZZUSA
SANDELL, DAVID	18	M	LABR	RRZZZZUSA

SHIP: KANSAS

FROM: LIVERPOOL
TO: BOSTON
ARRIVED: 19 SEPTEMBER 1888

PASSENGER	AGE	SEX	OCCUPATION	PRV VIL DES
LUBINSKY, JACOB	39	M	LABR	RRZZZZUNK
BETSY	40	F	W	RRZZZZUNK
ROSA	23	F	SP	RRZZZZUNK
MICHAEL	19	M	LABR	RRZZZZUNK
REBECCA	15	F	SP	RRZZZZUNK
MOSES	11	M	CH	RRZZZZUNK
LEIB	10	M	CH	RRZZZZUNK
RACHEMIL	8	M	CHILD	RRZZZZUNK
EFRAIM	6	M	CHILD	RRZZZZUNK
HYMAN	3	M	CHILD	RRZZZZUNK
DANZEL, SARAH	47	F	SP	RRZZZZBO
PORTNOI, PERETZ	24	M	LABR	RRZZZZBO
EDELSTEIN, MICH.	25	M	LABR	RRZZZZBO
WOLFSOHN, JOS.	20	M	LABR	RRZZZZBO
KAPOLOWITZ, JOS.	20	M	LABR	RRZZZZBO
SHIMANSKY, ARON	14	M	LABR	RRZZZZBO
JAMESHOEN, SCH.	43	M	LABR	RRZZZZBO
KRAUSE, WIL.	39	M	LABR	RRZZZZBO
IPERS, JACOB	26	M	LABR	RRZZZZBO
PLISCHAN, ELIAS	33	M	LABR	RRZZZZNY
SILBERMANN, JOS.	18	M	LABR	RRZZZZNY
COHEN, MENDEL	26	M	LABR	RRZZZZNY
MAXOFSKY, GERGUS	28	M	LABR	RRZZZZPHI
SCHWINSKY, IVAN	26	M	LABR	RRZZZZPHI

SHIP: RHAETIA

FROM: HAMBURG AND HAVRE
TO: NEW YORK
ARRIVED: 19 SEPTEMBER 1888

PASSENGER	AGE	SEX	OCCUPATION	PV RIVL DES
WEINBERG, PAULA	25	F	SGL	RRACBFUSA
BUTRIMOWITSCH, ISAAC	24	M	DLR	RRACBFUSA
BAKULA, FRANZ.	27	F	LABR	RRACBFUSA
SILBERMANN, LINE	18	F	SGL	RRACBFUSA
JUDELSOHN, SARA	40	F	WO	RRACBFUSA
ADROSZITZ, JOSEF	25	M	LABR	RRACBFUSA
RAGOVSKY, LOUIS	16	M	FARMER	RRACBFUSA
LUBALIN, HANNA	20	F	SGL	RRACBFUSA
APPELBAUM, SOPHIE	20	F	SGL	RRACBFUSA
HUEDELMANN, MOSES	18	M	LABR	RRACBFUSA
GITTEL	19	F	SGL	RRACBFUSA
ISIDOR	7	M	CHILD	RRACBFUSA
TAUBE, GETZEL	22	M	TLR	RRACBFUSA
BERMANN, JOCHNE	17	M	TLR	RRACBFUSA
KRIWERNZKI, PEREL	40	F	WO	RRACBFUSA
GOLDE	13	F	WO	RRACBFUSA
ABRAH.	7	M	CHILD	RRACBFUSA
ZIWIE	6	F	CHILD	RRACBFUSA
MARCIN	5	M	CHILD	RRACBFUSA
ELIAS	4	M	CHILD	RRACBFUSA
HORIAS	.11	M	INFANT	RRACBFUSA
SCHULSINGER, JACOB	22	M	MCHT	RRACBFUSA
LIBOWITZ, MARTIN	27	M	LABR	RRACBFUSA
BURAGAS, ANTON	19	M	LABR	RRACBFUSA
DOMBROWSKY, PIOTR	30	M	LABR	RRACBFUSA
MARIANNE	7	F	CHILD	RRACBFUSA
KOMIENSKY, GREGOR	29	M	LABR	RRACBFUSA
STAUKEWICZ, EVAN	24	M	LABR	RRACBFUSA
SAKALSKI, ESTHER	22	F	WO	RRACBFUSA
SARAH	.11	F	INFANT	RRACBFUSA
GREGOROWSKI, ANGELIKA	19	F	SGL	RRACBFUSA
FRANZISKA	16	F	SGL	RRACBFUSA
KRIWERNZKI, FREIN	12	M	CH	RRACBFUSA
VANMERTZENFELD, ANATOL	26	M	ENGR	RRACBFUSA
DEGERHOHN, EDUARD	22	M	ENGR	RRACBFUSA

SHIP: RHEIN

FROM: BREMEN
TO: BALTIMORE
ARRIVED: 19 SEPTEMBER 1888

PASSENGER	AGE	SEX	OCCUPATION	PV RIVL DES
OGRODOWICZ, JOHANN	25	M	FARMER	RRZZZZMD
BORKOWSKY, VALENTY	30	M	LABR	RRZZZZMD
LUBOWICKY, LUDWIG	24	M	LABR	RRZZZZMD
ANDRUZKIEWICZ, OZEF	20	M	FARMER	RRZZZZMD
WARBAT, STANISLAWA	27	F	NN	RRZZZZMD
JAN	60	M	FARMER	RRZZZZMD
FOTYSZELOSKA, ANNA	60	F	NN	RRZZZZMD
MARIANNA	17	F	NN	RRZZZZMD
JOSEF	.05	M	INFANT	RRZZZZMD
ALEXANDER	.04	M	INFANT	RRZZZZMD
JOUNKER, ANNA	41	F	NN	RRZZZZMD
JOHANNES	18	M	FARMER	RRZZZZMD
ADAM	10	M	CH	RRZZZZMD
PETER	10	M	CH	RRZZZZMD
ANDREAS	2	M	CHILD	RRZZZZMD
ANNA	5	F	CHILD	RRZZZZMD
CATHA.	.10	F	INFANT	RRZZZZMD
TOMASZEWSKI, JACOB	30	M	LABR	RRZZZZMD
CATHE.	22	F	W	RRZZZZMD
U, JOSEPH	33	M	LABR	RRZZZZMD
JOSEFINE	4	F	CHILD	RRZZZZMD
ADAM	5	M	CHILD	RRZZZZMD
NAVROCKI, MACIEJ	22	M	FARMER	RRZZZZMD
RACZUS, CATHA.	25	F	NN	RRZZZZMD
CATHA.	.04	F	INFANT	RRZZZZMD
MILEWSKY, EWA	25	F	NN	RRZZZZMD
JULIANE	.02	F	INFANT	RRZZZZMD
LUDZIS, ADAM	21	M	BKR	RRZZZZMD

SHIP: STATE OF NEVADA

FROM: GLASGOW AND LARNE
TO: NEW YORK
ARRIVED: 20 SEPTEMBER 1888

PASSENGER	AGE	SEX	OCCUPATION	PV RIVL DES
BURLANN, JONA	20	M	LABR	RRZZZZUSA
BREMER, CHAIME	18	M	MCHT	RRZZZZUSA
CANTOR, LEIB	60	M	TLR	RRZZZZUSA
SARAH	15	F	NN	RRZZZZUSA
GLOWITZ, CHAJE	19	M	FARMER	RRZZZZUSA
RACHEL	16	M	FARMER	RRZZZZUSA
JUDDSOHN, JUDEL	35	M	TLR	RRZZZZUSA
KANTROWICZ, MISCHE	40	M	MCHT	RRZZZZUSA
KAPLAN, SCHLOME	55	M	MCHT	RRZZZZUSA
KRETZNER, EDLE	50	F	UNKNOWN	RRZZZZUSA
LITTMAN, LEA	16	F	SVNT	RRZZZZUSA
LOBJASNIK, JETTE	60	F	W	RRZZZZUSA
GITTEL	16	M	LABR	RRZZZZUSA
MACZEJIMACZ, JOSEF	27	M	LABR	RRZZZZUSA
OSBEITES, JANOS	20	M	LABR	RRZZZZUSA
PATNOI, WOLF	15	M	LABR	RRZZZZUSA
ROSERBLUM, JOSSEL	19	M	SHMK	RRZZZZUSA
SCHEIN, NOCHEN	40	M	TLR	RRZZZZUSA
SALTZ, SELIG	38	M	TNSTH	RRZZZZUSA
SARAH	24	F	UNKNOWN	RRZZZZUSA
LOTHE	8	F	CHILD	RRZZZZUSA
RACHEL	1	F	CHILD	RRZZZZUSA
JEWINDS, ROCHEL	26	F	UNKNOWN	RRZZZZUSA
SCHOLEM	2	M	CHILD	RRZZZZUSA
BEILE	1	F	CHILD	RRZZZZUSA
SCHWER, ELIAS	26	M	TLR	RRZZZZUSA
TISS, JUSTINA	23	F	UNKNOWN	RRZZZZUSA
JULIE	1	F	CHILD	RRZZZZUSA
TURTELBAUM, ZILLI	19	F	SVNT	RRZZZZUSA
ZOLL, SCHEINE	30	M	MRNR	RRZZZZUSA
LEIB	9	M	CHILD	RRZZZZUSA
SARAH	7	F	CHILD	RRZZZZUSA
NISSEN	1	F	CHILD	RRZZZZUSA

SHIP: PERUVIAN

FROM: LIVERPOOL
TO: BALTIMORE
ARRIVED: 21 SEPTEMBER 1888

PASSENGER	AGE	SEX	OCCUPATION	PV RIVL DES
KOPEL, TORRES	18	M	GZR	FNZZZZPIT
MARKARAWICK, MUTENI	27	M	GZR	FNZZZZOMA

PASSENGER	AGE	SEX	OCCUPATION	PRIVL	DES
SHIP: CITY OF BERLIN					
FROM: LIVERPOOL					
TO: NEW YORK					
ARRIVED: 21 SEPTEMBER 1888					
STEPHANOWSTTE, VICENT	21	M	LABR	FNACBF	NY
ANDEKSON, CARL	24	M	LABR	FNACBF	NY
SHIP: TRAVE					
FROM: BREMEN AND SOUTHAMPTON					
TO: NEW YORK					
ARRIVED: 21 SEPTEMBER 1888					
RUSAKROW, IGUZAFENA	33	F	UNKNOWN	RRZZZZ	USA
ALEXANDER	7	M	CHILD	RRZZZZ	USA
ROETHELMANN, JOS.	28	M	MCHT	RRZZZZ	USA
ASCHKENAX, SAUL	32	M	DLR	RRZZZZ	USA
ESTHER	30	F	UNKNOWN	RRZZZZ	USA
MIREL	20	M	DLR	RRZZZZ	USA
FREIDE	7	F	CHILD	RRZZZZ	USA
CHAWE	6	F	CHILD	RRZZZZ	USA
MEYER	5	M	CHILD	RRZZZZ	USA
SANJE	4	M	CHILD	RRZZZZ	USA
ISAC	2	M	CHILD	RRZZZZ	USA
RABINOWITZ, LEISER	38	M	DLR	RRZZZZ	USA
DWORA	33	F	UNKNOWN	RRZZZZ	USA
MARCUS	7	M	CHILD	RRZZZZ	USA
BEER	6	M	CHILD	RRZZZZ	USA
MOSES	4	M	CHILD	RRZZZZ	USA
BOSCHE	.11	M	INFANT	RRZZZZ	USA
PINKASSOHN, LEIB	25	M	LABR	RRZZZZ	USA
BADER, ISAAC	30	M	DLR	RRZZZZ	USA
HOFMANN, MARG.	24	F	UNKNOWN	RRZZZZ	USA
EMMA	.11	F	INFANT	RRZZZZ	USA
BAELULIS, JOSEF	23	M	FARMER	RRZZZZ	USA
SHIP: AMALFI					
FROM: HAMBURG					
TO: NEW YORK					
ARRIVED: 22 SEPTEMBER 1888					
BIEGEMANN, AUGUSTE	23	F	SGL	RRZZZZ	NY
SIMSON, SIMON	18	M	LABR	RRZZZZ	NY
HSWANY, SHAIKEL	26	M	LABR	RRZZZZ	NY
SAWEYKA, SIGISMUND	23	M	FARMER	RRZZZZ	NY
SMAGZINSKI, VICENTY	28	M	FARMER	RRZZZZ	CH
OISTEITH, KLARA	17	F	SGL	RRZZZZ	NY
BRUCHE	15	F	SGL	RRZZZZ	NY
MOSES	9	M	CHILD	RRZZZZ	NY
JAMPOLSKY, ROSA	42	F	SGL	RRZZZZ	NY
ANNE	4	F	CHILD	RRZZZZ	NY
RUDSTEIN, JANKEL	48	M	DLR	RRZZZZ	NY
WEISS, WILLE	39	M	GDNR	RRZZZZ	NY
LEIPSTEDT, EISI	25	F	WO	RRZZZZ	NY
LUKAITINI, MARIE	49	F	WO	RRZZZZ	NY
GUTZKI, EMILIE	25	F	SGL	RRZZZZ	NY
RADATZ, JOHANN	51	M	WHLR	RRZZZZ	NY
FRDKE.	57	F	W	RRZZZZ	NY
ANNA	19	F	CH	RRZZZZ	NY
AUGUSTE	17	F	CH	RRZZZZ	NY
PAUL	7	M	CHILD	RRZZZZ	NY
FIEFS, ANNA	34	F	WO	RRZZZZ	NY
FERDINAND	4	M	CHILD	RRZZZZ	NY
WILHELM	3	M	CHILD	RRZZZZ	NY
HIRSCHFELD, JETTY	23	F	SGL	RRZZZZ	NY
ROTKIN, CHAIME	14	F	SGL	RRZZZZ	NY
MEYERWITZ, CIREL	35	F	WO	RRZZZZ	NY
MAX	6	M	CHILD	RRZZZZ	NY
PAULINE	5	F	CHILD	RRZZZZ	NY
GROSCHUPP, HERMANN	30	M	WVR	RRZZZZ	NY
SCHNUR, ISAAC	27	M	DLR	RRZZZZ	NY
SARAH	22	F	W	RRZZZZ	NY
LEA	.09	F	INFANT	RRZZZZ	NY
EWS, EMMA	20	F	WO	RRZZZZ	NY
GUTMANN, ITZIG	35	M	LABR	RRZZZZ	NY
MUSIKANT, MEIER	35	M	LABR	RRZZZZ	NY
GERMIN, ITZIG	21	M	LABR	RRZZZZ	NY
MIELKITZ, JOHANN	21	M	LABR	RRZZZZ	NY
BENDELIUS, ALBERT	42	M	LABR	RRZZZZ	NY
KARETZKI, JAN	29	M	LABR	RRZZZZ	NY
KEROWSKI, JOSEF	45	M	LABR	RRZZZZ	NY
JATKOWSKI, STANISLAUS	26	M	LABR	RRZZZZ	NY
MAPELBEIM, ISAAC	30	M	MCHT	RRZZZZ	NY
GUPRINSKI, FRANZ	24	M	LABR	RRZZZZ	NY
SHIP: DEVONIA					
FROM: GLASGOW					
TO: NEW YORK					
ARRIVED: 24 SEPTEMBER 1888					
LEWESCH, GITEL	23	M	NN	RRZZZZ	USA
MORSCHINK, JUTEL	50	M	NN	RRZZZZ	USA
SCHMUL	11	M	CH	RRZZZZ	USA
ISAK	6	M	CHILD	RRZZZZ	USA
TOGGER, SCHEINE	15	F	NN	RRZZZZ	USA
SHIP: WISCONSIN					
FROM: LIVERPOOL AND QUEENSTOWN					
TO: NEW YORK					
ARRIVED: 25 SEPTEMBER 1888					
DAVIDOV, EFRAIM	23	M	GZR	RRZZZZ	USA
ZABENZANSKA, ZODEK	7	M	CHILD	RRZZZZ	USA
GRIMBER, LEHA	.09	F	INFANT	RRZZZZ	USA
BRACLAWSKI, PINCHOS	.08	M	INFANT	RRZZZZ	USA
ABRM.	.07	M	INFANT	RRZZZZ	USA
SLOMINSKY, SARAH	40	F	W	RRZZZZ	USA
MORDECHE	7	F	CHILD	RRZZZZ	USA
CHASCHE	4	F	CHILD	RRZZZZ	USA
JETTE	3	F	CHILD	RRZZZZ	USA
HESCHE	.10	F	INFANT	RRZZZZ	USA
GULLANS, CARL	40	M	MNR	FNZZZZ	USA
JOHAN	39	M	MSN	FNZZZZ	USA
WALDMAN, SABEZANSKI	25	F	MSN	RRZZZZ	USA
ULBERG, HELIE	25	F	MSN	RRZZZZ	USA
GRINBERG, RACHEL	25	F	W	RRZZZZ	USA
BENJ.	3	M	CHILD	RRZZZZ	USA
BRACHLOWSKI, LEIB	30	F	W	RRZZZZ	USA
RASCHE	7	F	CHILD	RRZZZZ	USA
BROCHE	3	F	CHILD	RRZZZZ	USA
SUCHOVALSKY, CHIEL	24	F	SP	RRZZZZ	USA
GUREWITZ, IKE	20	M	MNR	RRZZZZ	USA
F-OLA, KARLS	17	M	MNR	FNZZZZ	USA
NISULA, MAGNUS	39	M	FARMER	FNZZZZ	USA

PASSENGER	AGE	SEX	OCCUPATION	PV RIV DES

SHIP: ELBE

FROM: BREMEN AND SOUTHAMPTON
TO: NEW YORK
ARRIVED: 25 SEPTEMBER 1888

PASSENGER	AGE	SEX	OCCUPATION	PV RIV DES
HEIKIN, AUGUSTE	24	F	UNKNOWN	FNAILANY
META	.06	F	INFANT	FNAILANY
MIECZKOWSKA, EVA	30	F	UNKNOWN	FNAILANY
FRANZISKA	9	F	CHILD	FNAILANY
KOPEKE, MENJE	21	F	UNKNOWN	FNAILAUSA
WEISSMANN, MOSCHKE	17	F	UNKNOWN	FNAILANY
SCHERMANN, CHANE	22	F	UNKNOWN	FNAILANY
KUEHN, ALBERT	24	M	FARMER	FNAILANY
RASCHKEN, MINNA	20	F	UNKNOWN	FNAILANY
RABINOWITZ, ELENA	20	F	UNKNOWN	FNAILANY
WESTERBACH, JOH.	23	M	LABR	FNAIDENY
HELLSBERG, HELENE	46	F	UNKNOWN	FNAIDENY
VIKTOR	11	M	CH	FNAIDENY
LAUGSJO, JACOB	15	M	LABR	FNAIDENY
EHRENGREEN, ANDRAS	41	M	LABR	FNAIDENY
HANSEN, HERMANN	37	M	LABR	FNAIDENY
SAARI, ANNA	21	F	UNKNOWN	FNAIDENY
HILDA	.08	F	INFANT	FNAIDENY
KURTLILA, MARSA	33	F	UNKNOWN	FNAIDENY
GRAUVIK, EDLA	19	F	UNKNOWN	FNAIDENY
RADBERG, AUGUSTE	45	F	UNKNOWN	FNAIDENY
LOEFGREEN, JOH.	31	M	LABR	FNAIDENY

SHIP: AMERICA

FROM: BREMEN
TO: BALTIMORE
ARRIVED: 25 SEPTEMBER 1888

PASSENGER	AGE	SEX	OCCUPATION	PV RIV DES
SUEPALA, IDA	18	F	UNKNOWN	RRZZZZMD
LYDIA	11	F	CH	RRZZZZMD
SCHWARZ, JULIUS	36	M	FARMER	RRZZZZKS
ELISABETH	32	F	UNKNOWN	RRZZZZKS
ELISABETH	10	F	CH	RRZZZZKS
JOHANN	5	M	CHILD	RRZZZZKS
PETER	3	M	CHILD	RRZZZZKS
ANNA	.10	F	INFANT	RRZZZZKS
ANESZKA, JOSEPH	23	M	LABR	RRZZZZKS
SCHWARZ, CATHARINE	8	F	CHILD	RRZZZZKS
WIMSIKOWSKA, JULIANNE	40	F	UNKNOWN	RRZZZZMI
JOSEPH	19	M	FARMER	RRZZZZMI
LARIE, HANNE	32	F	UNKNOWN	RRZZZZOH
ZILE	9	F	CHILD	RRZZZZOH
MEYER	5	M	CHILD	RRZZZZOH
LURIE, PAULINE	2	F	CHILD	RRZZZZOH
TALMALJANAS, ERNST	20	M	STDNT	RRZZZZUNK
BIEBERSDORF, FRIEDRICH	40	M	FARMER	RRZZZZKS
JUSTINE	40	F	UNKNOWN	RRZZZZKS
ADOLFINE	16	F	UNKNOWN	RRZZZZKS
EMILIE	11	F	CH	RRZZZZKS
HELENE	8	F	CHILD	RRZZZZKS
FRIEDRICH	6	M	CHILD	RRZZZZKS
HERMANN	3	M	CHILD	RRZZZZKS
WILHELMINE	1	F	CHILD	RRZZZZKS
KLEBE, FRIEDRICH	32	M	FARMER	RRZZZZKS
OTTILIE	20	F	UNKNOWN	RRZZZZKS
AUGUST	2	M	CHILD	RRZZZZKS
AUGUSTO	.06	F	INFANT	RRZZZZKS
HEINRICH	23	M	FARMER	RRZZZZKS
KRANSCHEFSKY, MARIA	35	F	UNKNOWN	RRZZZZMD
FEIGE	6	F	CHILD	RRZZZZMD
LAINB	4	M	CHILD	RRZZZZMD
MUSENKAMP, MINNA	18	F	UNKNOWN	RRZZZZMD

PASSENGER	AGE	SEX	OCCUPATION	PV RIV DES
BECKER, HODE	22	F	UNKNOWN	RRZZZZMD
MOISCH	1	F	CHILD	RRZZZZMD

SHIP: STATE OF NEBRASKA

FROM: GLASGOW AND LARNE
TO: NEW YORK
ARRIVED: 26 SEPTEMBER 1888

PASSENGER	AGE	SEX	OCCUPATION	PV RIV DES
MANKOWSKY, CHAIM	26	M	LABR	RRAIDLUSA
CHAIE	24	F	LABR	RRAIDLUSA
MOTTEL	1	F	CHILD	RRAIDLUSA
HAUDMANN, HILLEL	17	M	PDLR	RRAIDLUSA
RESEL	15	F	SP	RRAIDLUSA
SEWIN, ETTE	17	F	SP	RRAIDLUSA
MANKOWSKY, FREIDE	54	F	WI	RRAIDLUSA
PENDIK, SAMUEL	15	M	BKBNDR	RRAIDLUSA
SKORKOWSKY, MADESLAW	24	M	LABR	RRAIDLUSA
KLIKULSKY, ANTONI	28	M	LABR	RRAIDLUSA
DZIKOWSKY, STANISLAW	18	M	LABR	RRAIDLUSA

SHIP: CITY OF CHESTER

FROM: LIVERPOOL AND QUEENSTOWN
TO: NEW YORK
ARRIVED: 29 SEPTEMBER 1888

PASSENGER	AGE	SEX	OCCUPATION	PV RIV DES
WAINER, JANKEL	18	M	UNKNOWN	RRZZZZUSA
ABRAMINAN, NICH.	28	M	UNKNOWN	RRZZZZNY
HUARD, JOHAN	24	M	UNKNOWN	RRZZZZNY
BORANKA, FRANS	25	M	UNKNOWN	RRZZZZUSA
SZILDEWIEZ, JAN	19	M	UNKNOWN	RRZZZZNY
MILSKULSKY, JOSEF	30	M	UNKNOWN	RRZZZZNY
SOLJONDER, KARL	23	M	UNKNOWN	RRAINOWY
JONSSON, EPR.A.	19	M	UNKNOWN	RRAINOWY
FARVINEN, ELIAS	25	M	UNKNOWN	RRAINOWY
PEGOLA, JOHAN	26	M	UNKNOWN	RRAINOWY
STRTSCHABOR, JOHAN	20	M	UNKNOWN	RRAINOWY
MSONSKY, DAVID	19	M	JNR	RRZZZZWY
KLIPPO, GRETA	18	F	SP	RRZZZZWY
RON, MARIA	27	F	SP	RRZZZZNY
HANNUKSLA, MARIA	24	F	SP	RRZZZZNY
CALLATON, WOLF.	30	F	W	RRZZZZNY
RONSBI, MARIA	20	F	SP	RRZZZZNY

SHIP: MAIN

FROM: BREMEN
TO: BALTIMORE
ARRIVED: 01 OCTOBER 1888

PASSENGER	AGE	SEX	OCCUPATION	PV RIV DES
KRATUSCHEFSKY, CHAJE	18	F	SVNT	RRZZZZBAL
SW-NOWNE, KALINE	20	F	SVNT	RRZZZZBAL
BAUMGARTH, BERTHA	29	F	W	RRZZZZNE
MARANOWSKI, ANNA	33	F	W	RRZZZZPA
KAZIMIR	7	M	CHILD	RRZZZZPA
APPELSTEIN, FRIEDR	25	F	W	RRZZZZBAL
CHAJE	3	F	CHILD	RRZZZZBAL
CHANE	1	F	CHILD	RRZZZZBAL
BUDUCKI, FRANZICEK	36	M	CPTR	RRZZZZPA

PASSENGER	AGE	SEX	OCCUPATION	PRV VIL DES
FRANZISKA	36	F	W	RRZZZZPA
NARCIS	.11	F	INFANT	RRZZZZPA
FRANZISCA	.11	F	INFANT	RRZZZZPA

SHIP: MARSALA

FROM: HAMBURG
TO: NEW YORK
ARRIVED: 01 OCTOBER 1888

PASSENGER	AGE	SEX	OCCUPATION	PRV VIL DES
MORASEWSKI, JEAN	37	M	LABR	RRAHVUNY
WILHE.	36	F	W	RRAHVUNY
OLGA	7	F	CHILD	RRAHVUNY
JAWOROWSKI, ANTON	32	M	LKSH	RRAHVUNY
JOSEFA	34	F	W	RRAHVUNY
WILAMOWSKI, ALEXANDER	27	M	LABR	RRAHVUNY
KONSTANZIA	20	F	W	RRAHVUNY
ALEXANDER	.11	M	INFANT	RRAHVUNY
JAROTZLAWSKA, ANNA	30	F	WO	RRZZZZNY
LEON	7	M	CHILD	RRZZZZNY
ZALLE, JOHANN	23	M	PNTR	RRAEFLBUF
MESSER, NATHAN	18	M	DLR	RRACONNY
BABILEWICZ, KATHA.	28	F	SGL	RRAHWMNY
BRUSKA, JOSEPFA	26	F	WO	RRZZZZNY
AUGUST	6	M	CHILD	RRZZZZNY
JACOB	4	M	CHILD	RRZZZZNY
RACHEL	.11	F	INFANT	RRZZZZNY
LIPIESKA, VERONIKA	22	F	WO	RRACONNY
LEON	.09	M	INFANT	RRACONNY
LAUTER, FRIDR.	23	M	LABR	RRAIAMNY
SARNOWSKI, JAN	26	M	LABR	RRAIEONY
ELIASOHN, HIRSCH	26	M	MCHT	RRAHOKCH
ABRAHAM	38	M	MCHT	RRAHOKCH
KLOT, JACOB	25	M	MCHT	RRAGRTCH
SCHAPIRO, U	39	M	LABR	RRAHOKCH
LEA	43	F	W	RRAHOKCH
GOLDE	16	F	CH	RRAHOKCH
MALKE	14	F	CH	RRAHOKCH
EKI	13	F	CH	RRAHOKCH
RUBEN	7	M	CHILD	RRAHOKCH
GOD.	6	M	CHILD	RRAHOKCH
SCHEINE	.11	F	INFANT	RRAHOKCH
PREUSS, EDUARD	20	M	FARMER	RRAHTFNY
SPINGATH, EMIL	26	M	MLR	RRAIOFNY
AUGUSTE	21	F	W	RRAIOFNY
HELENE	.09	F	INFANT	RRAIOFNY
HOFFMANN, DANIEL	27	M	CPTR	RRZZZZSP
EMILIE	26	F	W	RRZZZZSP
GUSTAV	4	M	CHILD	RRZZZZSP
PINNOW, FRIEDR.	21	M	LABR	RRAHZSSP
GELLMANN, ESTER	20	F	SGL	RRAHXXNY
MISCIVITSCH, JOSEF	28	M	TLR	RRZZZZNY
CHAWEINSKY, CIVIE	25	F	WO	RRAHTFNY
HENDE	3	F	CHILD	RRAHTFNY
EISIK	.11	M	INFANT	RRAHTFNY
JENISSEF, JACOB	18	M	DLR	RRAHOONY
WILMINSKY, MICHAL	32	M	FARMER	RRZZZZNY
ROTHSTEIN, WOLH	39	M	DLR	RRZZZZNY
GITTEL	34	F	W	RRZZZZNY
CHEIN	2	M	CHILD	RRZZZZNY
GREINERT, LEIB	7	M	CHILD	RRZZZZNY
BARTNIK, SARA	16	F	SGL	RRZZZZNY
BIELNAS, ANNA	24	F	SGL	RRAHZSNY
MIZORITZKA, MINDEL	20	F	SGL	RRAHUEPHI

SHIP: LEERDAM

FROM: ROTTERDAM
TO: NEW YORK
ARRIVED: 01 OCTOBER 1888

PASSENGER	AGE	SEX	OCCUPATION	PRV VIL DES
MOROZOW, LUISCHE	32	M	MCHT	RRZZZZUSA
GRABSKI, JOSEPH	20	M	LABR	PLZZZZUSA
BIYNOK, SOPHIE	18	F	UNKNOWN	PLZZZZUSA
DEPENBROCH, OTTO	15	M	UNKNOWN	PLZZZZUSA

SHIP: SLAVONIA

FROM: SWINEMUNDE
TO: NEW YORK
ARRIVED: 01 OCTOBER 1888

PASSENGER	AGE	SEX	OCCUPATION	PRV VIL DES
GROBKOWSKA, EVA	30	F	WO	RRZZZZUSA
JOHANN	3	M	CHILD	RRZZZZUSA
RETKOWSKY, JAN	42	M	TLR	RRZZZZUSA

SHIP: MORAVIA

FROM: HAMBURG AND HAVRE
TO: NEW YORK
ARRIVED: 01 OCTOBER 1888

PASSENGER	AGE	SEX	OCCUPATION	PRV VIL DES
GEBAUER, O.	35	F	WO	RRAIDPUSA
GOLDENBERG, JACOB	27	M	DLR	RRZZZZUSA
MARIETTE	22	F	W	RRZZZZUSA
DINA	3	F	CHILD	RRZZZZUSA
ZIPORA	.06	F	INFANT	RRZZZZUSA
SARAH	54	F	WO	RRZZZZUSA
EPPLESTEIN, KANE	50	M	LABR	RRAHTFUSA
ESTHER	45	F	W	RRAHTFUSA
AKIALIS, ANTON	33	M	LABR	RRZZZZUSA
BAERMANN, MOSES	25	M	TLR	RRZZZZUSA
SZAFRANSKA, AGATHE	22	F	SGL	RRZZZZUSA
ZULEWSKI, ADAM	20	M	LABR	RRAHUFUSA
KALMANOWITZ, JOSSEL	58	M	LABR	RRAHOKUSA
GORDON, DWORE	28	F	WO	RRZZZZUSA
UNTERMANN, MOSCHE	26	M	DLR	RRZZZZUSA
LIBA	28	F	W	RRZZZZUSA
RIWKA	7	F	CHILD	RRZZZZUSA
NECHENAJE	6	F	CHILD	RRZZZZUSA
DORA	4	F	CHILD	RRZZZZUSA
CHANNE	.11	F	INFANT	RRZZZZUSA
PUTSCHINSKI, JONAS	28	M	LABR	RRAIMHUSA
KOKAUSKI, MATJUSCHES	29	M	LABR	RRAIMHUSA
GRODZKY, GITE	23	F	SGL	RRAFVGUSA
GRABALIS, JAN	18	M	LABR	RRZZZZUSA
WASILEWSKY, STANISLAV	21	M	LABR	RRZZZZUSA
ROMANOWSKY, VINCENTY	26	M	LABR	RRZZZZUSA
ANNA	19	F	W	RRZZZZUSA
ZEBRONSKY, FRANZ	31	M	LABR	RRAHZSUSA
PISEV, FRANZ	52	M	SHMK	RRAHZSUSA
KALMANOWITZ, SARA	54	F	W	RRAHOKUSA
MOTTE	17	M	CH	RRAHOKUSA
MENNCHE	15	M	CH	RRAHOKUSA
SZOLTINKA, MARIANNE	20	F	SGL	RRZZZZUSA
MARIANNA	20	F	SGL	RRAINKUSA
BRZEZINA, ABRAHAM	23	M	BKBNDR	RRAFWJUSA
BORUCHOWICZ, SCHLEINE	20	M	DLR	RRAHUEUSA
GITTELMANN, RIWKE	55	F	WO	RRAHUEUSA

PASSENGER	AGE	SEX	OCCUPATION	PRV VIL DES
PESCHE	28	F	WO	RRAHUEUSA

SHIP: CIRCASSIA

FROM: GLASGOW AND MOVILLE
TO: NEW YORK
ARRIVED: 02 OCTOBER 1888

PASSENGER	AGE	SEX	OCCUPATION	PRV VIL DES
DE, A.	27	F	WI	RRZZZZUSA
RAPPAPORT, SARA	30	F	W	RRZZZZUSA
MUNKEL	11	M	UNKNOWN	RRZZZZUSA
JASSEL	8	M	CHILD	RRZZZZUSA
PERIL	7	M	CHILD	RRZZZZUSA
BASSIE	11	F	CH	RRZZZZUSA
MACHINE	.09	F	INFANT	RRZZZZUSA
PAWELESKA, MAGDALENE	22	F	W	RRZZZZUSA
FEDOR	2	M	CHILD	RRZZZZUSA
ANNA	1	F	CHILD	RRZZZZUSA
DOMBROWSKA, JULIANA	19	F	HP	RRZZZZUSA
ZAPIENSKI, TEOPILIS	22	F	HP	RRZZZZUSA
JAIVE, MATILDA	23	F	HP	RRZZZZUSA
DOWKOUSKA, MARIANNA	35	F	W	RRZZZZUSA
ANT.	1	M	CHILD	RRZZZZUSA
DRZELJA, VIOLIE	10	F	CH	RRZZZZUSA
FECOWICH, GIOVANI	16	M	LABR	RRZZZZUSA
LINDGVIST, GUST.	29	M	LABR	RRZZZZUSA
LONDHOLM, W.	30	M	LABR	RRZZZZUSA
SALMEN, FRED	25	M	LABR	RRZZZZUSA
HENDEKSEN, JACOB	24	M	LABR	RRZZZZUSA
GLAWISKY, STEFEN	16	M	LABR	RRZZZZUSA
DESEWITSCH, VAWS.	26	M	LABR	RRZZZZUSA
SZELECKA, BERNARD	35	M	LABR	RRZZZZUSA
SPIELHOLZ, SALOMON	17	M	TLR	RRZZZZUSA
GEDMAN, EFRAM	55	M	DLR	RRZZZZUSA
ESTER	50	F	W	RRZZZZUSA
HESAR	15	M	UNKNOWN	RRZZZZUSA
REBECKA	10	F	CH	RRZZZZUSA
RACHEL	9	F	CHILD	RRZZZZUSA
SMOLAK, MEIS	35	M	DLR	RRZZZZUSA
BELE	34	F	W	RRZZZZUSA
BLUME	15	F	UNKNOWN	RRZZZZUSA
JACOB	11	M	CH	RRZZZZUSA
HERSCH	8	M	CHILD	RRZZZZUSA
DWENE	.09	F	INFANT	RRZZZZUSA
STJERNE, ISAK	23	M	SP	RRZZZZUSA
MARIA	20	F	W	RRZZZZUSA
TANCICH, MARCO	28	M	WCHMKR	RRZZZZUSA
MARGT.	27	F	W	RRZZZZUSA

SHIP: RHYNLAND

FROM: ANTWERP
TO: NEW YORK
ARRIVED: 04 OCTOBER 1888

PASSENGER	AGE	SEX	OCCUPATION	PRV VIL DES
STRANSKY, ANTON	25	M	NN	RRZZZZNY
HOROWITZ, SOPHIE	43	F	W	RRZZZZNY

SHIP: GELLERT

FROM: HAMBURG AND HAVRE
TO: NEW YORK
ARRIVED: 06 OCTOBER 1888

PASSENGER	AGE	SEX	OCCUPATION	PRV VIL DES
DIAMANT, KATHA.	17	F	SGL	RRZZZZUSA
OSTEIN, MOSES	40	M	MCHT	RRAFVGUSA
THESCHMOBSKY, ELIAS	35	M	DLR	RRAGRTUSA
PAKONEN, MARIE	33	F	SGL	RRZZZZUSA
ARENS, HERRM.	53	M	LABR	RRAIAGUSA
KOTOSIRJESKA, JAGNISKA	21	F	SGL	RRZZZZUSA
KAUFMANN, HATTI	24	F	SGL	RRAAKHUSA
BERNSTEIN, MOSES	19	M	MCHT	RRAHVUUSA
KLEIN, RACHEL	30	F	WO	RRZZZZUSA
DORA	4	F	CHILD	RRZZZZUSA
WAROZEWSKI, ORE	17	M	DLR	RRAIMGUSA
ESKELINEN, MARIE	25	F	DLR	FNZZZZUSA
BLUMKIN, SAMUEL	20	M	DLR	FNAHTFUSA
DAVIDOVICZ, BERNHARD	25	M	MCHT	FNAHQDUSA
NOVAGRADER, ETKA	37	F	WO	FNAIHMUSA
JUDKA	7	F	CHILD	FNAIHMUSA
MOSES	6	M	CHILD	FNAIHMUSA
KRAJWENAS, ANTONY	39	M	LABR	FNAHWMUSA
SIMON	22	M	LABR	FNAHWMUSA
PETROWSKI, ANTON	18	M	LABR	RRZZZZUSA

SHIP: CITY OF CHICAGO

FROM: LIVERPOOL AND QUEENSTOWN
TO: NEW YORK
ARRIVED: 06 OCTOBER 1888

PASSENGER	AGE	SEX	OCCUPATION	PRV VIL DES
STULTMANN, RACHAEL	30	F	W	RRACBFNY
U	00	F	INF	RRACBFNY
JYKARSKA, AMELA	22	F	SVNT	RRACBFNY
EHRLIEH, CHANCE	35	F	W	PLZZZZNY
DAVID	9	M	CHILD	PLZZZZNY
ARBAN, MARIANNIA	28	F	W	PLACBFNY
ANTHONY	00	M	INF	PLACBFNY
KRALIP, RIVIE	15	F	SLR	PLAHTUNY
KRABIK, SIZA	22	F	DRSMKR	PLAHTUNY
KLUSCAR, AMALIA	30	F	W	PLZZZZUSA
AMALIA	4	F	CHILD	PLZZZZUSA
ARM, P.	38	F	W	PLZZZZUSA
U	11	F	CH	PLZZZZUSA
U	9	M	CHILD	PLZZZZUSA
DEINARD, EFRAIN	43	M	TLR	PLAFVGNY
MARIA	42	F	W	PLAFVGNY
WANKATATAS, HELENA	26	F	SVNT	FNZZZZNY
SOBOL, JAN	30	M	TLR	FNACBFNY
YIMGROD, SALOMON	16	M	TLR	FNAFZDNY
CISCHER, LEIN	26	M	TU	FNACBFNY
MAKURAK, NICKOLAY	24	M	BTMKR	FNAFVGNY
DEINARD, ROSA	11	F	CH	FNAFVGNY
REBECCA	8	M	CHILD	FNAFVGNY
OLIE	4	F	CHILD	FNAFVGNY
ESTER	6	F	CHILD	FNAFVGNY
JULES	4	M	CHILD	FNAFVGNY
SPATY, ABRA.	19	F	SVNT	FNACBFNY
BECHER, DAVID	28	M	BTMKR	PLZZZZNY
SKOKAN, JANOS	40	M	TLR	PLAFVGNY
BANDOLA, MARIE	18	F	SVNT	PLAFZDNY
JANOSKA, ERGIE	19	F	SVNT	PLAFZDNY
WIETKOWSKA, CATHA	18	F	SVNT	PLACBFNY
JYKARSKY, FRANZ	2	M	CHILD	PLACBFNY
PSAR, JAMES	28	M	TLR	PLAFVGNY
DWANESAK, MARIA	25	F	SVNT	PLZZZZUSA
UNGAR, MOSES	22	M	PDLR	PLAFWJNY

PASSENGER	AGE	SEX	OCCUPATION	PRV	VIL	DES
KURIZ, MARIA	14	F	SVNT	PL	AID	HNY

SHIP: ALLER

FROM: BREMEN AND SOUTHAMPTON
TO: NEW YORK
ARRIVED: 06 OCTOBER 1888

PASSENGER	AGE	SEX	OCCUPATION	PRV	VIL	DES
WOLF, MORITZ	36	M	FARMER	RR	ZZZ	USA
RUSZYK, ANT	42	M	LABR	RR	ZZZ	USA
ROSENSTEIN, LUDW	34	M	LABR	RR	ZZZ	USA
BENDORA----, ANTON	28	M	LABR	RR	ZZZ	USA
WOY-KIEWICZ, -IENANZ	30	M	LABR	RR	ZZZ	USA
MAKIWICKI, JAN	27	M	MCHT	RR	ZZZ	USA
BANOU-, MICH	40	M	FARMER	RR	ZZZ	USA
B--TKIN, FRIEDR	16	M	LABR	RR	ZZZ	USA
WISNIEWSKI, JOSEF	20	M	LABR	RR	ZZZ	USA
PODAISKI, JULEK	21	M	LABR	RR	ZZZ	USA
WAGNER, ALB	30	M	FARMER	RR	ZZZ	USA
BRETLIN, EMILIE	19	F	NN	RR	ZZZ	USA
-YDO, ---BERTA	20	F	NN	RR	ZZZ	USA
BALI-, MORITZ	33	M	FARMER	RR	ZZZ	USA
PA--	30	F	W	RR	ZZZ	USA
HOPPER, JOH	56	F	FARMER	RR	ZZZ	USA
MARIA	49	F	W	RR	ZZZ	USA
HEINR	22	M	FARMER	RR	ZZZ	USA
AUG	7	M	CHILD	RR	ZZZ	USA
ELISAB	6	F	CHILD	RR	ZZZ	USA
KELLER, JOSEF	25	M	FARMER	RR	ZZZ	USA
FRANZKA	25	F	W	RR	ZZZ	USA
MARGA	4	F	CHILD	RR	ZZZ	USA
LORENZ	.06	M	INFANT	RR	ZZZ	USA
ROSENBERG, ROSALIE	20	F	NN	RR	ZZZ	USA
ROB	.08	M	INFANT	RR	ZZZ	USA
KO-U----, ANNA	24	F	NN	RR	ZZZ	USA
ANNA	.01	F	INFANT	RR	ZZZ	USA

SHIP: POLYNESIA

FROM: HAMBURG
TO: NEW YORK
ARRIVED: 06 OCTOBER 1888

PASSENGER	AGE	SEX	OCCUPATION	PRV	VIL	DES
JURDEWICZ, JAN	23	M	LABR	RR	ZZZ	ZNY
BOGDANSKI, LOUISE	35	F	WO	RR	ZZZ	ZNY
ANNA	7	F	CHILD	RR	ZZZ	ZNY
WILH.	6	M	CHILD	RR	ZZZ	ZNY
CARL	3	M	CHILD	RR	ZZZ	ZNY
MARIE	.06	F	INFANT	RR	ZZZ	ZNY
MOISCHNECK, JAN	23	M	LABR	RR	AHZ	SNY
LEINAT, KRIS	20	M	LABR	RR	AHZ	SNY
BUCHMANN, ESTER	24	F	SGL	RR	ZZZ	ZNY
BERMANN, CHAIE	21	F	SGL	RR	ZZZ	ZNY
SCHMIDT, HEIMAN	20	M	LABR	RR	AIM	RNY
BERMANN, MORDCHE	20	M	LABR	RR	ZZZ	ZNY
PSIROTZKY, SAMUEL	34	M	LABR	RR	AFW	JNY
BOBMANN, BOBE	27	F	WO	RR	AHV	UNY
MALKE	7	F	CHILD	RR	AHV	UNY
ROCKMACHER, ZIREL	20	F	SGL	RR	ZZZ	ZNY
HIRSCH	16	M	LABR	RR	ZZZ	ZUSA
ABEL	7	M	CHILD	RR	ZZZ	ZUSA
JAFFE, HERM.	18	M	DLR	RR	AHV	UUSA
JASINSKI, ROMAN	20	M	STDNT	RR	AFW	JUSA
BLUMENBERG, SARA	19	F	SGL	RR	ZZZ	ZUSA
SACHONITZKY, CIPPE	45	M	LABR	RR	AHQ	UUSA
SARA	18	F	D	RR	AHQ	UUSA
PHILIPOWITSCH, BRONSIL	24	M	MLR	RR	AHU	IUSA
GASKULSKI, ROMAN	27	M	GDNR	RR	AHU	IUSA
HELLSTRAND, HENRICK	36	M	SLR	FN	ZZZ	ZUSA
BEILMANN, ISAAC	45	M	MCHT	RR	ZZZ	ZUSA
KRABOWSKI, JAN	24	M	LABR	RR	AIG	TUSA
KAMERASS, JANNY	20	F	SGL	RR	ABQ	BUSA
CHACHLOWITZ, TEVEL	18	M	MCHT	RR	AGR	TUSA
SAMUEL	21	M	MCHT	RR	AGR	TUSA
OSYCO, JANOS	33	M	DLR	RR	ZZZ	ZUSA
MATULAJTES, ANTON	22	M	LABR	RR	ZZZ	ZUSA
STROJNIS, BARTHOLOMEUS	21	M	LABR	RR	ZZZ	ZUSA
JUZENEWSKY, ANTON	26	M	LABR	RR	AIE	XUSA
GRUENSTEIN, SESSER	33	M	LABR	RR	AFV	GUSA
SARA	25	F	W	RR	AFV	GUSA
CICENSK, ALEXANDER	23	M	LABR	RR	AHS	PUSA
ANDRAKO, MICHAEL	30	M	LABR	RR	AHQ	UUSA
RADSCHEWA, SIMON	22	M	LABR	RR	AHQ	UUSA
SKIROLSKY, BARHOLOMAUS	32	M	LABR	RR	AFW	JUSA
JARGO, JEAN	45	M	LABR	RR	AHQ	UUSA
RADSHEVA, CASIMIR	27	M	LABR	RR	AHQ	UUSA
STRAGE, CHAIE	17	F	SGL	RR	AIJ	JUSA

SHIP: ALASKA

FROM: LIVERPOOL AND QUEENSTOWN
TO: NEW YORK
ARRIVED: 08 OCTOBER 1888

PASSENGER	AGE	SEX	OCCUPATION	PRV	VIL	DES
MARGOLIES, A.	22	M	LABR	RR	ZZZ	USA
MELNIKOWA, R.	30	F	SP	RR	ZZZ	USA
ROSIN, HERSCH	46	M	FORMN	RR	ZZZ	USA
KRYWIEZ, ARON	24	M	LABR	RR	ZZZ	USA
AINSBURG, JOS.	20	M	LABR	RR	ZZZ	USA
SILVER, SAML.	35	M	SHPMN	PL	ZZZ	USA
WUTANILURI, GABRIEL	26	M	LABR	FN	ZZZ	USA
ROSIN, ARON	9	M	CHILD	RR	ZZZ	USA
MELNIKOWA, LEIB	.11	M	INFANT	RR	ZZZ	USA

SHIP: EIDER

FROM: BREMEN AND SOUTHAMPTON
TO: NEW YORK
ARRIVED: 09 OCTOBER 1888

PASSENGER	AGE	SEX	OCCUPATION	PRV	VIL	DES
SCHWERSOHN, JUDEL	32	M	MCHT	RR	ZZZ	USA
GRIMBERG, ROB.	33	M	LABR	RR	ZZZ	USA
SEGAL, MOSES	26	M	MCHT	RR	ZZZ	USA
MOGILINSKI, JOHN	24	M	LABR	RR	ZZZ	USA
ANNA	39	F	UNKNOWN	RR	ZZZ	USA
KWIATKOWSKA, FRANZISKA	16	F	UNKNOWN	RR	ZZZ	USA
GOBIEN, BERTHA	21	F	UNKNOWN	RR	ZZZ	USA
CHAMIN, HIRSCH.	23	M	MCHT	RR	ZZZ	USA
KAMZES, JANKEL	44	M	MCHT	RR	ZZZ	USA
FRIEDMAN, DAVID	25	M	MCHT	RR	ZZZ	USA
MALINOWSKI, STANISLAUS	40	M	LABR	RR	ZZZ	USA
KWIATKOWSKA, MARIANNE	39	F	UNKNOWN	RR	ZZZ	USA
JOHANN	13	M	UNKNOWN	RR	ZZZ	USA
CASIMIR	6	M	CHILD	RR	ZZZ	USA
WACLAW	.10	M	INFANT	RR	ZZZ	USA
DAYLIDANOS, MAGDALENA	32	F	UNKNOWN	RR	ZZZ	USA
PIJIS	10	M	CH	RR	ZZZ	USA
JOSEF	8	M	CHILD	RR	ZZZ	USA
ALZLUCTA	2	F	CHILD	RR	ZZZ	USA
JANKAJTIS, JAN	30	M	FARMER	RR	ZZZ	USA

SHIP: BOHEMIA

FROM: HAMBURG
TO: NEW YORK
ARRIVED: 09 OCTOBER 1888

PASSENGER	AGE	SEX	OCCUPATION	PRV	VIL	DES
PALEI, CEISEL	22	F	WO	RR	AHOK	NY
SCHIMEN	.11	F	INFANT	RR	AHOK	NY
BRUSKE, WILH.	25	M	LABR	RR	AIOG	NY
PAULINE	20	F	W	RR	AIOG	NY
BERTHA	.11	F	INFANT	RR	AIOG	NY
SLEZAT, ANNA	20	F	SGL	RR	ZZZZ	NY
SATULA, MARIANNE	19	F	SGL	RR	ZZZZ	NY
WEST, MATTS	28	M	CPTR	FN	ZZZZ	NY
FREDLUND, CARL	36	M	CPTR	FN	ZZZZ	NY
OLEK, ANNA	18	F	SGL	RR	ZZZZ	NY
EVA	7	F	CHILD	RR	ZZZZ	NY
JEGENDORF, SCHEINE	20	F	WO	RR	ZZZZ	NY
ROCHE	.09	F	INFANT	RR	ZZZZ	NY

SHIP: THE QUEEN

FROM: LIVERPOOL AND QUEENSTOWN
TO: NEW YORK
ARRIVED: 10 OCTOBER 1888

PASSENGER	AGE	SEX	OCCUPATION	PRV	VIL	DES
PASKUNSKY, P.	36	F	W	RR	ADBQ	NY
MARY	8	F	CHILD	RR	ADBQ	NY
SVEEN, OLINE	25	F	SP	RR	ZZZZ	NY
KOXENSK, ANNA	22	F	SP	RR	ZZZZ	NY
KURTH, HELENA	24	F	SP	RR	ADAX	NY
LUKAS, A.	23	F	SP	RR	ADBQ	NY
J.	19	F	SP	RR	ADBQ	NY
HAWRELA, M.	27	F	SP	RR	ZZZZ	NY
LIMDGREEN, ANNA	37	F	SP	RR	ZZZZ	NY
GRAUTE, OLINE	30	F	W	RR	ZZZZ	NY
OLINE	4	F	CHILD	RR	ZZZZ	NY
KATZ, LENA	19	F	SP	RR	ZZZZ	NY
KAMFSKA, T.	55	F	W	RR	ZZZZ	NY
J.	20	F	SP	RR	ZZZZ	NY
G.	18	F	SP	RR	ZZZZ	NY
FEMSTEIN, R.	27	F	W	RR	ZZZZ	NY
FRIEDE	4	F	CHILD	RR	ZZZZ	NY
MULLER, JOHAN	57	M	LABR	RR	ZZZZ	NY
SCHWARTZ, SOPHIA	28	F	W	RR	ZZZZ	NY
SARA	6	F	CHILD	RR	ZZZZ	NY
SAML.	5	M	CHILD	RR	ZZZZ	NY
ANDRE	1	M	CHILD	RR	ZZZZ	NY
LEWY, M.	17	M	LABR	RR	ZZZZ	NY
SIVAK, STEFAN	32	M	LABR	RR	ZZZZ	NY
NIRSENBAUN, CHAINE	27	M	LABR	RR	ADBQ	NY
FELDMAN, S.	25	M	LABR	RR	ADBQ	NY
FENDRISKI, C.	28	M	LABR	RR	ADBQ	BO
TEDELBAUM, B.	24	M	LABR	RR	ADBQ	BO
HERMAN, H.	28	M	LABR	RR	ZZZZ	BO
SCEDBLUM, H.	24	M	LABR	RR	ZZZZ	BO
CRIBB, J.	22	M	LABR	RR	ADBQ	NY
ZICKI, JOSES	18	M	LABR	RR	ZZZZ	NY
ANTON	23	M	LABR	RR	ZZZZ	NY
WASHIEVITZ, N.	38	M	LABR	RR	ZZZZ	NY
ELIASON, QUEMUCH	39	F	W	RR	ZZZZ	NY
ZELDA	19	F	SP	RR	ZZZZ	NY
SPRINZA	11	F	CH	RR	ZZZZ	NY
HYMAN	10	M	CH	RR	ZZZZ	NY
BORUCH	8	M	CHILD	RR	ZZZZ	NY
HINDA	4	F	CHILD	RR	ZZZZ	NY
LAZ.	1	M	CHILD	RR	ZZZZ	NY

SHIP: NORSEMAN

FROM: LIVERPOOL
TO: BOSTON
ARRIVED: 10 OCTOBER 1888

PASSENGER	AGE	SEX	OCCUPATION	PRV	VIL	DES
ZIRKASKY, SCHMER	27	M	LABR	PL	ZZZZ	NY
AUGUSTA, REBECCA	24	F	W	PL	ZZZZ	USA
GEORGE	25	M	LABR	PL	ZZZZ	USA
LOPSZA, SILVESTA	30	M	MCHT	PL	ZZZZ	USA
KIRSETER, JOSCHAN	22	M	TLR	PL	ZZZZ	NY
KUKLIN, ARON	25	M	LABR	PL	ZZZZ	NY
GROCKMAN, WOLFF	19	M	TLR	PL	ZZZZ	BO
RATRA, ISACA	22	M	TLR	PL	ZZZZ	BO
REFTLIUNSKI, K.	39	M	MCHT	PL	AIIX	BO
ENYRSKY, D.	23	M	MCHT	PL	AIIX	BO
LAFANELL, GEO.	30	M	MCHT	PL	AIIX	BO
BREAKES, BOSBI	30	F	UNKNOWN	PL	AIIX	BO
SARAH	22	F	UNKNOWN	PL	AIIX	BO
RIVELKY, EBRAHAM	28	M	LABR	PL	AAXL	BO

SHIP: ST. OF PENNSYLVANIA

FROM: GLASGOW AND LARNE
TO: NEW YORK
ARRIVED: 10 OCTOBER 1888

PASSENGER	AGE	SEX	OCCUPATION	PRV	VIL	DES
PIRL, HIRSCH	19	M	TLR	RR	ZZZZ	USA
SJANKO, MAUSCHE	26	M	TLR	RR	ZZZZ	USA
REWIS, ISRAEL	17	M	LABR	RR	ZZZZ	USA
SILBER, SIMON	38	M	LABR	RR	ZZZZ	USA
WIKLOWSKY, TARY	22	M	LABR	RR	ZZZZ	USA
PIETKOWITZ, ANTONI	19	M	LABR	RR	ZZZZ	USA
TENERSTEIN, GOLDE	21	F	SP	RR	ZZZZ	USA
GREGOR, MARIA	25	F	SP	RR	ZZZZ	USA
SJANKO, RIVE	50	F	W	RR	ZZZZ	USA
PESCHE	15	F	SP	RR	ZZZZ	USA
MALKE	26	F	W	RR	ZZZZ	USA
NISSEN	3	M	CHILD	RR	ZZZZ	USA
CHATZKELOWITZ, RIVKE	2	F	CHILD	RR	ZZZZ	USA
FEIGE	50	F	W	RR	ZZZZ	USA
PASCHE	28	F	W	RR	ZZZZ	USA
TOSSEL	18	M	LABR	RR	ZZZZ	USA
WOSCHINSKA, JULIANNA	27	F	W	RR	ZZZZ	USA
MONIKA	6	F	CHILD	RR	ZZZZ	USA
SOPHIA	22	F	W	RR	ZZZZ	USA
CHAJNOSKI, ELISABETH	22	F	W	RR	ZZZZ	USA
HELENE	1	F	CHILD	RR	ZZZZ	USA

SHIP: EMS

FROM: BREMEN AND SOUTHAMPTON
TO: NEW YORK
ARRIVED: 11 OCTOBER 1888

PASSENGER	AGE	SEX	OCCUPATION	PRV	VIL	DES
SEIFERT, KARL	46	M	LABR	RR	AHOO	NY
WILHE.	46	F	W	RR	AHOO	NY
GUSTAV	23	M	LABR	RR	AHOO	NY
WACLAV	20	M	LABR	RR	AHOO	NY
MARIE	10	F	CH	RR	AHOO	NY

SHIP: CITY OF RICHMOND

FROM: LIVERPOOL AND QUEENSTOWN
TO: NEW YORK
ARRIVED: 13 OCTOBER 1888

PASSENGER	AGE	SEX	OCCUPATION	PRV VIL DES
KRUSCHOLD, J.	50	M	LABR	FNZZZZUSA
LARSON, AL.	18	F	SP	FNZZZZMI
STENBACHER, ANNA	19	F	SP	FNZZZZIL
KRUSIMAKI, S.	34	F	SP	FNZZZZIL
SALLI, ANNA	36	F	W	FNZZZZNY
HILDA	4	F	CHILD	FNZZZZNY
FURNEY, HEDVIG	29	F	SP	FNZZZZNY
LAUREN, SERAFIA	22	F	SP	FNZZZZMT
ERIKSON, SEREFEA	26	F	W	FNZZZZMT
A.	00	F	INF	FNZZZZMT
LAY, JOHANNA	22	F	W	FNZZZZMI
MALLS	00	F	INF	FNZZZZMI
DUBINCKY, ANN	48	F	W	FNACBFNY
LUCINA	18	F	SP	FNACBFNY
KAULAREK, MARIAN	18	F	W	FNACBFNY
U	00	F	INF	FNACBFNY
POSTAR, U	20	F	SP	FNACBFNY
KARTAREK, ABE	48	M	LABR	FNADAXNY
LEA	28	F	W	FNADAXNY
U	9	M	CHILD	FNADAXNY
SAMUEL	6	M	CHILD	FNADAXNY
MOSES	4	M	CHILD	FNADAXNY
JENKEL	00	M	INF	FNADAXNY

SHIP: AMSTERDAM

FROM: ROTTERDAM
TO: NEW YORK
ARRIVED: 13 OCTOBER 1888

PASSENGER	AGE	SEX	OCCUPATION	PRV VIL DES
WOLF, HEINRICH	28	M	LABR	RRZZZZUSA
BOLEWICZ, PETER	22	M	LABR	RRZZZZUSA
TARBAS, PAUL	17	M	LABR	RRZZZZUSA
KOPEZO, PAUL	20	M	LABR	RRZZZZUSA
JANKOWSKY, ASIF	25	M	LABR	RRZZZZUSA
CHOROSZ, SAMUEL	22	M	LABR	RRZZZZUSA
JASATOWITZ, OSIF	28	M	LABR	RRZZZZUSA

SHIP: SCYTHIA

FROM: LIVERPOOL AND QUEENSTOWN
TO: BOSTON
ARRIVED: 15 OCTOBER 1888

PASSENGER	AGE	SEX	OCCUPATION	PRV VIL DES
KOSKI, MATH	25	M	LABR	RRZZZZUNK
KAWAMEN, HENRY	29	M	LABR	RRZZZZUNK
MAILEMEN, --OMAS	28	M	LABR	RRZZZZUNK
NIKKALA, ANDERS	18	M	LABR	RRZZZZUNK
SADINKANGAS, CARL	25	M	LABR	RRZZZZUNK
SEFANIAS	18	M	LABR	RRZZZZUNK
HARPULA, MATTI	30	M	LABR	RRZZZZUNK

SHIP: SUEVIA

FROM: HAMBURG AND HAVRE
TO: NEW YORK
ARRIVED: 15 OCTOBER 1888

PASSENGER	AGE	SEX	OCCUPATION	PRV VIL DES
CHIMIK, SELIG	23	M	LITGR	RRAFVGIL
FANNY	19	F	W	RRAFVGIL
KOZLOWSKA, MARIANNE	21	F	SGL	RRZZZZNE
SUBOCZAS, HIPPOLIT	17	M	LABR	RRZZZZNY
KARPEL, JOSEF	30	M	LABR	RRZZZZPA
GULAU, JAN	22	M	LABR	RRZZZZPA
GERSCHOWSKY, VICTOR	32	M	LABR	RRZZZZPA
KUCHLIK, VINCENT	25	M	LABR	RRAHQUPA
BIELAWSKY, THOMAS	27	M	LABR	RRZZZZNY
CHODOROWSKY, STEFAN	23	M	LABR	RRZZZZNY
JABLONSKI, ANTON	18	M	LABR	RRZZZZIA
BERKOWITZ, FEIWE	21	F	PNTR	RRAHTUNE
BUDWEIS, ANTON	28	M	LABR	RRAHTFNE
BARNOWSKI, ANDREAS	45	M	LABR	RRAHTFNE
USZELOWA, ANNA	20	F	WO	RRAHTFNE
VICENTY	.11	M	INFANT	RRAHTFNE
BAUMANN, FERD.	22	M	MCHT	RRAINNNE
EDUARD	20	M	BRR	RRAINNNE
ELIBOWITZ, LAWREN	44	M	LABR	RRZZZZNY
MICHEL	21	M	LABR	RRZZZZNY
ZIMMERMANN, AUGUSTE	18	F	SGL	RRZZZZNY
WIECZOREK, JACOB	26	M	LABR	RRZZZZNY
LEOCADIA	19	F	W	RRZZZZNY
STANISLAUS	.08	M	INFANT	RRZZZZNY
PETRIKA, JONAS	25	M	LABR	RRZZZZNY
PAKUNAS, OSIF	27	M	LABR	RRZZZZNY
MATULES, ANTON	24	M	LABR	RRZZZZNY
EVA	21	F	W	RRZZZZNY

SHIP: GALLIA

FROM: LIVERPOOL
TO: NEW YORK
ARRIVED: 16 OCTOBER 1888

PASSENGER	AGE	SEX	OCCUPATION	PRV VIL DES
AKSELING, MIKKI	25	M	LABR	FNZZZZUSA
ENBURK, CARL	21	M	LABR	FNZZZZUSA
FOX, DAVID	25	M	UNKNOWN	RRZZZZUSA
HARWITZ, LOUIS	28	M	LABR	RRZZZZUSA
KRAMER, RACHMIEL	46	M	SPM	RRACBFUSA
SCHATZ, BENJ	36	M	GZR	RRACBFUSA
WRAMOCHEWSKY, JOHAN	36	M	UNKNOWN	RRACBFUSA
ZINKERMAN, ISRAEL	38	M	TLR	RRACBFUSA
BRONDE, JENNY	18	F	TLR	RRACBFUSA
OLIANSKY, RISCHE	22	F	TLR	RRACBFUSA
SEGUALL, HODES	59	F	WI	RRACBFUSA
KALIN, RAHIL	40	F	MA	RRACBFUSA
CHANE	.03	F	INFANT	RRACBFUSA
FRANK, BADAM	40	F	MA	RRACBFUSA
CHANE	20	F	SVNT	RRACBFUSA
ISRAEL	11	M	CH	RRACBFUSA
M.	8	M	CHILD	RRACBFUSA
MERE	4	F	CHILD	RRACBFUSA
PIERETZNY, ABRAM	35	M	TLR	RRACBFUSA
SLODOWIZ, SAMUEL	33	M	TLR	RRACBFUSA
SOHOSTACK, M.	40	M	LABR	RRACBFUSA
WARSOHAUSKY, RAFHAEL	18	M	WCHMKR	RRACBFUSA
JASCHOVER, FRIEDE	22	F	MA	RRACBFUSA
CHANE	2	F	CHILD	RRACBFUSA
BRENNER, CHAIE	23	F	MA	RRACBFUSA
FREIDE	2	F	CHILD	RRACBFUSA
WARSENGASCH, ESTER	21	F	MA	RRACBFUSA
CAHNE	1	F	CHILD	RRACBFUSA

PASSENGER	AGE	SEX	OCCUPATION	PRIV	VIL	DES

SHIP: RUGIA

FROM: HAMBURG AND HAVRE
TO: NEW YORK
ARRIVED: 16 OCTOBER 1888

PASSENGER	AGE	SEX	OCCUPATION	PRIV	VIL	DES
FEINSCHTEIN, LEIB	18	M	MCHT	RR	AFVG	USA
DEGNER, MICHAEL	23	M	MLR	RR	AIOJ	USA
KASPAR, HERSCH	17	M	LABR	RR	AHUL	USA
SZEMING, JACHS	29	M	LABR	RR	ZZZZ	USA
GRASMANN, MIKIRER	23	M	LABR	RR	ZZZZ	USA
PETARSKE, PIOTR	30	M	LABR	RR	ZZZZ	USA
JWANOW, WASIL	18	M	LABR	RR	ZZZZ	USA
HALPERN, SALOMON	30	M	LABR	RR	AGRT	USA
ALT, ROBERT	20	M	BKLYR	RR	ACON	USA
SCHERR, SCHAIE	19	M	TLR	RR	ACON	USA
KAHN, SAMUEL	48	M	TLR	RR	AHTF	USA
WILINSKY, CHAJE	30	F	WO	RR	AHTF	USA
STAROKENSTANDIWONSKIARR	20	M	LABR	RR	AFVG	USA
PERKIOMAKI, JOHANN	22	M	LABR	FN	ZZZZ	USA
RUSSETZKY, JULS.	14	M	LABR	FN	AIGA	USA
BEHMKE, AUGUSTE	18	F	SGL	RR	ZZZZ	USA
NATHALIE	16	F	SGL	RR	ZZZZ	USA
LOGWINERCKO, MICHAEL	23	M	MCHT	RR	ZZZZ	USA
MOZLAWSKI, JULIAN	25	M	LABR	RR	ZZZZ	USA
RUTKOWSKI, MARTIN	32	M	LABR	RR	ZZZZ	USA
TRUTTLER, HERSCH	9	M	CHILD	RR	ZZZZ	USA
SCHEINKOPF, SALOMON	24	M	DLR	RR	AHTO	USA
LONDONER, LEON	21	M	LABR	RR	ZZZZ	USA
DANITONICZ, STANG	19	M	LABR	RR	AHZS	USA

SHIP: FULDA

FROM: BREMEN AND SOUTHAMPTON
TO: NEW YORK
ARRIVED: 16 OCTOBER 1888

PASSENGER	AGE	SEX	OCCUPATION	PRIV	VIL	DES
ZIRANSKY, JETTE	21	F	UNKNOWN	RR	ZZZZ	USA
MARCIAN, MARIA	18	F	UNKNOWN	RR	ZZZZ	USA
TORMANN, JOCHEL	22	M	BBR	RR	ZZZZ	USA
ZURNANSKY, FRIEDKE.	65	F	UNKNOWN	RR	ZZZZ	USA
FRIEDMANN, DOBE	7	F	CHILD	RR	ZZZZ	USA
PROST, HENRIETTE	56	F	UNKNOWN	RR	ZZZZ	USA
ANDR.	26	M	LABR	RR	ZZZZ	USA
DZIERWINSKA, WILHE.	52	F	UNKNOWN	RR	ZZZZ	USA
ANNA	7	F	CHILD	RR	ZZZZ	USA
LENKARIA	6	F	CHILD	RR	ZZZZ	USA
SCHAPIRN, MOSES	3	M	CHILD	RR	ZZZZ	USA
WISZMEWSKI, PAWEL	18	M	LABR	RR	ZZZZ	USA
KOWALEWSKI, ROMAN	22	M	LABR	RR	ZZZZ	USA
KOLOWSKI, FRANZ	22	M	LABR	RR	ZZZZ	USA
KOHEN, JAC.	26	M	CPTR	RR	ZZZZ	USA
SALONI	23	M	LABR	RR	ZZZZ	USA
BRAESE, AUG.	27	M	LABR	RR	ZZZZ	USA
HAUF, H.JOH.	66	M	LABR	RR	ZZZZ	USA
MARIE	65	F	UNKNOWN	RR	ZZZZ	USA
JOH.	19	M	LABR	RR	ZZZZ	USA
LISBETH	18	F	UNKNOWN	RR	ZZZZ	USA
WIGDOROWICZ, BEITE	18	F	UNKNOWN	RR	ZZZZ	USA
RUSZKOWSKI, JOH.	21	M	LABR	RR	ZZZZ	USA

SHIP: WYOMING

FROM: LIVERPOOL AND QUEENSTOWN
TO: NEW YORK
ARRIVED: 16 OCTOBER 1888

PASSENGER	AGE	SEX	OCCUPATION	PRIV	VIL	DES
GUSELKA, ANNA	33	F	UNKNOWN	PL	ZZZZ	USA
EHLEN, H.	22	M	LABR	PL	ZZZZ	USA
ANNA	22	F	SP	PL	ZZZZ	USA
KLANERBERG, E.	27	M	UNKNOWN	PL	ZZZZ	USA
HOCHMAN, JANKEL	3	M	CHILD	PL	ZZZZ	USA
GOLDE	00	M	INF	PL	ZZZZ	USA
BERNKRANT, LELIA	33	F	UNKNOWN	PL	ZZZZ	USA
STUSCHANER, D.	7	M	CHILD	PL	ZZZZ	USA
SELKOWITZ, ROSE	7	F	CHILD	PL	ZZZZ	USA
CHANE	6	F	CHILD	PL	ZZZZ	USA
SCHEINE	00	F	INF	PL	ZZZZ	USA
SCHLISCHKA, ANNA	16	F	SP	RR	ZZZZ	USA
MIGOSINIS, JORGE	27	M	LABR	RR	ZZZZ	USA
KUGMANZKA, CONST.	37	F	SP	RR	ZZZZ	USA
ZAPRINSKI, FRANS.	30	F	SP	RR	ZZZZ	USA
JOSEFA	27	F	SP	RR	ZZZZ	USA
KUSKA, SUSANNA	25	F	SP	RR	ZZZZ	USA
LAMPERT, LEO	23	M	LABR	RR	ZZZZ	USA
MARIE	21	F	W	RR	ZZZZ	USA
STRANCHLIR, ARON	18	M	LABR	RR	ZZZZ	USA
JACHAROWITZ, CHANE	30	F	W	RR	ZZZZ	USA
SCHLOME	8	M	CHILD	RR	ZZZZ	USA
BELL	7	M	CHILD	RR	ZZZZ	USA
SISIK	3	M	CHILD	RR	ZZZZ	USA
RASCHE	00	F	INF	RR	ZZZZ	USA
LAPIS, OSIUS	20	M	LABR	RR	ZZZZ	USA
DONNE	18	F	SP	RR	ZZZZ	USA
MASUSTER, MAX	28	M	LABR	RR	ZZZZ	USA
FEIGE	27	F	W	RR	ZZZZ	USA
H.	8	M	CHILD	RR	ZZZZ	USA
ROCHE	7	M	CHILD	RR	ZZZZ	USA
KUJPOREVATZ, JOHAN	21	M	LABR	RR	ZZZZ	USA
KLACH, AUGTE.	24	F	SP	RR	ZZZZ	USA
SCHWARZA, PAUL	25	M	LABR	RR	ZZZZ	USA
SCHIFFERMANN, MOSES	17	M	LABR	RR	ZZZZ	USA
DURCKELBERG, HERSCH	27	M	LABR	RR	ZZZZ	USA
STERN, SISIDOR	38	M	LABR	RR	ZZZZ	USA
ODROBMAH, JOS.	24	M	LABR	RR	ZZZZ	USA
MARIA	24	F	W	RR	ZZZZ	USA
GREBLER, MATH.	39	F	W	RR	ZZZZ	USA
MARTHA	8	F	CHILD	RR	ZZZZ	USA
OTTO	5	M	CHILD	RR	ZZZZ	USA
CARL	3	M	CHILD	RR	ZZZZ	USA
DORA	00	F	INF	RR	ZZZZ	USA
TOBJERS, JERFI	17	F	SP	RR	ZZZZ	USA
PAULZ, RIGV.	26	M	LABR	RR	ZZZZ	USA
ANGLI, J.	28	M	LABR	RR	ZZZZ	USA
KIRKOR, J.	29	M	LABR	RR	ZZZZ	USA
ARON, B.	7	M	CHILD	RR	ZZZZ	USA
AURMER, J.	7	M	CHILD	RR	ZZZZ	USA

SHIP: SPAIN

FROM: LIVERPOOL AND QUEENSTOWN
TO: NEW YORK
ARRIVED: 17 OCTOBER 1888

PASSENGER	AGE	SEX	OCCUPATION	PRIV	VIL	DES
TELECH, NASTA.	20	M	LABR	RR	AHQD	USA
M.	18	M	LABR	RR	AHQD	USA
SOLSI, KRISHAN	20	M	LABR	RR	AHQD	USA
LIPECHITIG, SOL.	21	M	LABR	RR	AHQD	USA
SCHUTABN, C.	32	M	LABR	RR	AHQD	USA
SEVENSON, ETHEL	25	F	W	RR	AHQD	USA

PASSENGER	AGE	SEX	OCCUPATION	PRIVL	DES
M.	3	F	CHILD	RRAHQD	USA
J.	2	F	CHILD	RRAHQD	USA
M.	.06	F	INFANT	RRAHQD	USA
DENISKA, RUDOLF	28	M	UNKNOWN	RRAHQD	USA
MARIA	24	F	W	RRAHQD	USA
SURASEY, SAND.	23	M	LABR	RRAHQD	USA
CHURSATY, RACHEL	40	F	W	RRAHOK	USA
ABRAHAM	10	M	CH	RRAHOK	USA
CHAIM	8	M	CHILD	RRAHOK	USA
DWORA	7	M	CHILD	RRAHOK	USA
BEN	3	M	CHILD	RRAHOK	USA
ANN	2	F	CHILD	RRAHOK	USA
FRIGALUMES, F.	23	M	LABR	RRAHOK	USA
DOHEL, WILHELM	29	M	LABR	RRAHOK	USA
PAGOLA, JACOB	27	M	LABR	RRAHOK	USA
WANKE, GUSTAF	39	M	LABR	RRAHOK	USA
RANHALLEN, SEBAN	23	M	LABR	RRAHOK	USA
BUCKLOTY, JULS	43	M	LABR	RRAFVG	USA
BASS, JEAN	36	M	GENT	RRADBQ	USA

SHIP: HAMMONIA

FROM: HAMBURG AND HAVRE
TO: NEW YORK
ARRIVED: 19 OCTOBER 1888

PASSENGER	AGE	SEX	OCCUPATION	PRIVL	DES
NEUHOF, CHAJE	35	F	W	RRZZZZ	USA
GEILE	6	F	CHILD	RRZZZZ	USA
SADOWSKY, JOHANN	46	M	FARMER	RRZZZZ	USA
ALEXANDER	14	M	FARMER	RRZZZZ	USA
GLLUCKMANN, LEIBEL	22	M	BKR	RRZZZZ	USA
SCHABSIN, TAUBE	26	F	W	RRAIIO	USA
CHASHEL	7	F	CHILD	RRAIIO	USA
JOSEF	.06	M	INFANT	RRAIIO	USA
BRODZINER, PHILIPP	14	M	DLR	RRZZZZ	USA
STEINER, MOSES	27	F	W	RRAHTF	USA
NATHAN	.11	M	INFANT	RRAHTF	USA
FEIGE	.01	F	INFANT	RRAHTF	USA
SHAPIRO, LINA	17	F	SGL	RRAHSL	USA
BRAUN, HERMAN	33	M	FARMER	RRAICO	USA
EMILIE	33	F	W	RRAICO	USA
JACOB	7	M	CHILD	RRAICO	USA
FRIEDR.	6	M	CHILD	RRAICO	USA
BERNH.	5	M	CHILD	RRAICO	USA
FERDINAND	3	M	CHILD	RRAICO	USA
MARIE	.11	F	INFANT	RRAICO	USA
RUGE, ERNST	24	M	MCHT	RRAHQD	USA
STORIN, GUSTAV	27	M	UNKNOWN	RRZZZZ	USA
MARIA	32	F	W	RRZZZZ	USA
FEISELBAUM, RACHEL	34	F	W	RRZZZZ	USA
CHANNE	7	F	CHILD	RRZZZZ	USA
LIEBE	4	F	CHILD	RRZZZZ	USA
RECHAME	3	F	CHILD	RRZZZZ	USA
ISAAC	.11	M	INFANT	RRZZZZ	USA
LEWIN, LEISER	15	M	DLR	RRZZZZ	USA
LEIB	40	M	DLR	RRZZZZ	USA
GROSSMANN, GOLDE	35	F	W	RRZZZZ	USA
RUWEN	7	M	CHILD	RRZZZZ	USA
SARA	5	F	CHILD	RRZZZZ	USA
JOSEF	4	M	CHILD	RRZZZZ	USA
JACOB	3	M	CHILD	RRZZZZ	USA
KUPPERMAN, MEYER	57	M	DLR	RRAIGP	USA
KATZ, BARUCH	19	M	LABR	RRZZZZ	USA
KRUEGER, LINA	18	F	SGL	RRZZZZ	USA
PERLSTEIN, ANNA	25	F	SGL	RRZZZZ	USA
HILLEL, BODZE	17	F	SGL	RRZZZZ	USA
KRAMANITHZ, SAVEL	18	M	LABR	RRZZZZ	USA
BRUEN, ROSA	20	F	SGL	RRZZZZ	USA
RUDIANSKY, ABRAHAM	17	M	DLR	RRAIBO	USA
BORRES	20	M	DLR	RRAIBO	USA

PASSENGER	AGE	SEX	OCCUPATION	PRIVL	DES
STEINBERG, MOSES	30	M	LABR	RRAHTU	USA
MORAMOWIZ, CHAIM	16	M	LABR	RRAHTU	USA
ZEMBROWSHY, MOSES	25	M	LKSH	RRAHTS	USA
BURAK, FEIGE	40	F	W	RRAFVG	USA
CHANE	9	F	CHILD	RRAFVG	USA
MARTINE, DANIEL	20	M	LABR	RRAFVG	USA
LEHMAN, HEINRICH	27	M	LABR	RRZZZZ	USA
LUSZE, PRIEDR.	24	M	LABR	RRZZZZ	USA
SCHIKOWSHI, ADAM	20	M	LABR	RRZZZZ	USA
MOCHOWSKI, WASEL	26	M	LABR	RRZZZZ	USA
PESO, IWAN	42	M	LABR	RRZZZZ	USA
SCHIHOWSKI, JULIAN	20	M	LABR	RRZZZZ	USA
SABOL, JANOS	20	M	LABR	RRZZZZ	USA
WASSERMANN, MICHAEL	26	M	LABR	RRZZZZ	USA
BEMAN, STERIGO	16	M	LABR	RRZZZZ	USA
PISHEWSKI, FRANZ	27	M	LABR	RRZZZZ	USA
LEFKOWITZ, ABR.	23	M	SHMK	RRAFWJ	USA
SEIDENSCHNUR, NADIE	21	F	SGL	RRAFVG	USA
FREINHELSTEIN, ESTER	18	F	SGL	RRZZZZ	USA
LEWITAN, JACOB	19	M	LABR	RRAHSL	USA
PECARCIK, MICHAEL	30	M	LABR	RRZZZZ	USA
RADZIEWICZ, STANISL.	58	M	LABR	RRAHTF	USA
SUSANNE	60	F	W	RRAHTF	USA
ANNA	7	F	CHILD	RRAHTF	USA

SHIP: TRAVE

FROM: BREMEN AND SOUTHAMPTON
TO: NEW YORK
ARRIVED: 19 OCTOBER 1888

PASSENGER	AGE	SEX	OCCUPATION	PRIVL	DES
LADVAMAKI, JACOB	30	M	FARMER	RRZZZZ	USA
LACHDETKORPI, MARIE	25	F	UNKNOWN	RRZZZZ	USA
NAUKKI, JOSEPHE	25	F	UNKNOWN	RRZZZZ	USA
SUERO, JOSEPHE	30	F	UNKNOWN	RRZZZZ	USA
TEUTLILA, HILDA	19	F	UNKNOWN	RRZZZZ	USA
LARSSON, LOFIE	32	F	UNKNOWN	RRZZZZ	USA
LINDELL, ANNA	19	F	UNKNOWN	RRZZZZ	USA
OSTERGREEN, JOHN	44	M	LABR	RRZZZZ	USA
MINAR, MICHEL	31	M	FARMER	RRZZZZ	USA
KOMAKIWICZ, JOSEF	28	M	FARMER	RRZZZZ	USA
CIRPINSKY, STANISL.	39	M	FARMER	RRZZZZ	USA
FRANZA.	37	F	W	RRZZZZ	USA
HEDWIG	18	F	CH	RRZZZZ	USA
MATHILDE	3	F	CHILD	RRZZZZ	USA
PAULA	.09	F	INFANT	RRZZZZ	USA
HERZBERG, SAMUEL	20	M	MCHT	RRZZZZ	USA
GALDINGER, JOSEF	23	M	MCHT	RRZZZZ	USA
EMMA	23	F	W	RRZZZZ	USA
SACHAREWITZ, CASIMIR	21	M	FARMER	RRZZZZ	USA
GERSZMANN, JOH.	21	M	FARMER	RRZZZZ	USA
OSILUTE, ELSE	24	F	UNKNOWN	RRZZZZ	USA
WEISSMANN, LEIE	46	F	UNKNOWN	RRZZZZ	USA
CISSE	20	F	UNKNOWN	RRZZZZ	USA
BENLSTEIN, BEILE	14	F	UNKNOWN	RRZZZZ	USA
SUBRICKI, MICH.	23	M	FARMER	RRZZZZ	USA
KUSCHEWSKY, IGNATZ	31	M	FARMER	RRZZZZ	USA
GAYAN, BERKE	46	M	FARMER	RRZZZZ	USA
MILKOWISKY, JAN	27	M	FARMER	RRZZZZ	USA
BRANDT, MARIE	19	F	UNKNOWN	RRZZZZ	USA
ZIPT, FRITZ	21	M	FARMER	RRZZZZ	USA
SCHATZ, FRANCISCA	48	F	UNKNOWN	RRZZZZ	USA
CHRISTIAN	17	M	CH	RRZZZZ	USA
EUGENE	19	F	CH	RRZZZZ	USA
MICHAEL	7	M	CHILD	RRZZZZ	USA
JOHANNE	4	F	CHILD	RRZZZZ	USA
ANTON	27	M	FARMER	RRZZZZ	USA
EVA	23	F	W	RRZZZZ	USA
MAGDA	2	F	CHILD	RRZZZZ	USA
HUEPFNER, JOHAN	47	M	FARMER	RRZZZZ	USA

PASSENGER	AGE	SEX	OCCUPATION	PRIVL	DES
GENAFEFA	46	F	W	RRZZZZ	USA
REGINE	22	F	CH	RRZZZZ	USA
JOSEF	18	M	CH	RRZZZZ	USA
ELIAS	16	M	CH	RRZZZZ	USA
JACOB	14	M	CH	RRZZZZ	USA
GABRIEL	7	M	CHILD	RRZZZZ	USA
JOHAN	6	M	CHILD	RRZZZZ	USA
HELENE	5	F	CHILD	RRZZZZ	USA
IGNATZ	3	M	CHILD	RRZZZZ	USA
ANTON	.11	M	INFANT	RRZZZZ	USA
MASTL, ROBERT	31	M	FARMER	RRZZZZ	USA
MARIE	25	F	W	RRZZZZ	USA
PETER	4	M	CHILD	RRZZZZ	USA
JOHAN	2	M	CHILD	RRZZZZ	USA
ROCHUS	.11	M	INFANT	RRZZZZ	USA
SCHERR, JACOB	19	M	FARMER	RRZZZZ	USA
GEFNE, ROCHYS	28	M	FARMER	RRZZZZ	USA
VERONICA	24	F	W	RRZZZZ	USA
JOHAN	7	M	CHILD	RRZZZZ	USA
STEPHAN	5	M	CHILD	RRZZZZ	USA
LUIPOLD	3	M	CHILD	RRZZZZ	USA
JOSEPH	1	M	CHILD	RRZZZZ	USA
WALD, MARTIN	16	M	GDNR	RRZZZZ	USA
BECKER, CARL	49	M	FARMER	RRZZZZ	USA
MARIA	45	F	W	RRZZZZ	USA
PAUL	23	M	CH	RRZZZZ	USA
MAGDA	21	F	CH	RRZZZZ	USA
REGINE	18	F	CH	RRZZZZ	USA
PETER	16	M	CH	RRZZZZ	USA
ELISE	11	F	CH	RRZZZZ	USA
FETRICH, ANTON	35	M	FARMER	RRZZZZ	USA
THERESE	33	F	W	RRZZZZ	USA
BARBARA	3	F	CHILD	RRZZZZ	USA
PETER	.06	M	INFANT	RRZZZZ	USA
SCHMIDT, LEONHARD	30	M	FARMER	RRZZZZ	USA
JULIE	22	F	W	RRZZZZ	USA
THEKLA	6	F	CHILD	RRZZZZ	USA
PETER	4	M	CHILD	RRZZZZ	USA
MICHEL	.03	M	INFANT	RRZZZZ	USA
KRAFFT, JACOB	50	M	FARMER	RRZZZZ	USA
JULIE	49	F	W	RRZZZZ	USA
ANDREAS	17	M	CH	RRZZZZ	USA
ADELHEIT	12	F	CH	RRZZZZ	USA
CATHI	7	F	CHILD	RRZZZZ	USA
GABRIEL	5	M	CHILD	RRZZZZ	USA
MARIA	3	F	CHILD	RRZZZZ	USA
BARTSCH, MATTH.	36	M	FARMER	RRZZZZ	USA
ELISE	35	F	W	RRZZZZ	USA
MARIE	7	F	CHILD	RRZZZZ	USA
ANTON	6	M	CHILD	RRZZZZ	USA
BENEDICT	5	M	CHILD	RRZZZZ	USA
MARG.	.06	F	INFANT	RRZZZZ	USA
STAUSS, ANTON	30	M	FARMER	RRZZZZ	USA
JOHANNE	25	F	W	RRZZZZ	USA
JOHANNE	6	F	CHILD	RRZZZZ	USA
THILEMON	.09	M	INFANT	RRZZZZ	USA
KUEHN, FLORIAN	25	M	GDNR	RRZZZZ	USA
CATHI	24	F	W	RRZZZZ	USA
JOSEF	.06	M	INFANT	RRZZZZ	UNK
KNAFT, JOSEF	28	M	LABR	RRZZZZ	USA
HELENE	28	F	W	RRZZZZ	USA
MAGDA	2	F	CHILD	RRZZZZ	USA
WALD, SEBASTIAN	39	M	FARMER	RRZZZZ	USA
ELISE	39	F	W	RRZZZZ	USA
CONRAD	15	M	CH	RRZZZZ	USA
STANISL.	6	M	CHILD	RRZZZZ	USA
CATHI	4	F	CHILD	RRZZZZ	USA
SEBART	3	M	CHILD	RRZZZZ	USA
MATTH.	.08	M	INFANT	RRZZZZ	USA
ANTON	28	M	FARMER	RRZZZZ	USA
AGNES	29	F	W	RRZZZZ	USA
MARIANNE	2	F	CHILD	RRZZZZ	USA
PAUL	.06	M	INFANT	RRZZZZ	USA
SCHALL, NICOLAUS	60	M	MCHT	RRZZZZ	USA
MARIANNE	52	F	W	RRZZZZ	USA
WERLINGER, HELENE	35	F	UNKNOWN	RRZZZZ	USA
ANNA	.07	F	INFANT	RRZZZZ	USA
SCHALL, JOSEF	34	M	FARMER	RRZZZZ	USA
BARBARA	30	F	W	RRZZZZ	USA
MICHAEL	5	M	CHILD	RRZZZZ	USA
CAROLA	3	F	CHILD	RRZZZZ	USA
MARIE	.08	F	INFANT	RRZZZZ	USA
SCHMAB, LORENZ	28	M	FARMER	RRZZZZ	USA
REGINE	25	F	W	RRZZZZ	USA
CATHI	2	F	CHILD	RRZZZZ	USA
EVA	.11	F	INFANT	RRZZZZ	USA
KERTLER, NICOLAUS	37	M	FARMER	RRZZZZ	USA
MARIE	35	F	W	RRZZZZ	USA
JOHANNE	7	F	CHILD	RRZZZZ	USA
CATHI	5	F	CHILD	RRZZZZ	USA
MARTIN	3	M	CHILD	RRZZZZ	USA
JACOB	.04	M	INFANT	RRZZZZ	USA
WEISSBACH, VALENTIN	17	M	GCR	RRZZZZ	USA
KRAFT, FERDIN	38	M	FARMER	RRZZZZ	USA
CHRISTE.	25	F	W	RRZZZZ	USA
MARTHA	4	F	CHILD	RRZZZZ	USA
ANNA	3	F	CHILD	RRZZZZ	USA
JOHAN	.08	M	INFANT	RRZZZZ	USA
UHL, WILHELM	23	M	BCHR	RRZZZZ	USA
LECHNER, ANTON	24	M	MLR	RRZZZZ	USA
WALKERS, MATHILDE	32	F	UNKNOWN	RRZZZZ	USA
ANNA	15	F	UNKNOWN	RRZZZZ	USA
RETTER, HELENE	23	F	UNKNOWN	RRZZZZ	USA
DEMETER, HANIK	38	M	FARMER	RRZZZZ	USA
JOSEF, VALI	20	M	LABR	RRZZZZ	USA
ANNFER, MIHALY	18	M	LABR	RRZZZZ	USA
WALKA, SARAH	15	F	UNKNOWN	RRZZZZ	USA
HIRSCH, JUDEL	7	F	CHILD	RRZZZZ	USA
SLATE, SCHEINE	5	F	CHILD	RRZZZZ	USA
SABZBERG, JANKEL	40	M	FARMER	RRZZZZ	USA
KLEIN, HERMAN	18	M	FARMER	RRZZZZ	USA
RAHLENZ, FRANCISCA	26	F	UNKNOWN	RRZZZZ	USA
STADERMANN, GUSTAV	26	M	FARMER	RRZZZZ	USA
KURZER, JENETTE	36	F	UNKNOWN	RRZZZZ	USA
NOPOLSKY, STANISL.	24	M	LABR	RRZZZZ	USA
TRABE, AUGUST	22	M	LABR	RRZZZZ	USA
FUTA, JACOB	20	M	LABR	RRZZZZ	USA
MARCINIK, PAUL	26	M	LABR	RRZZZZ	USA
KAWZINSKI, JAN	21	M	LABR	RRZZZZ	USA
SORAVIK, JOHAN	44	M	LABR	RRZZZZ	USA
MARIE	16	F	UNKNOWN	RRZZZZ	USA
PETRA	18	F	UNKNOWN	RRZZZZ	USA
MANSCHEN, JOHN	21	M	LABR	RRZZZZ	USA

SHIP: TAORMINA

FROM: HAMBURG
TO: NEW YORK
ARRIVED: 22 OCTOBER 1888

PASSENGER	AGE	SEX	OCCUPATION	PRIVL	DES
DAGLA-, MARIE	26	F	SGL	RRZZZZ	NY
KOHN, GERSON	34	M	DLR	RRZZZZ	NY
NOVIZKA, MARIANNE	25	F	SGL	RRZZZZ	CH
KANZAK, CAROLE	30	F	WO	RRZZZZ	NY
ARTHUR	.11	M	INFANT	RRZZZZ	NY
MATISCHWITZ, FRANZ	28	M	LABR	RRZZZZ	NY
STREIT, SALOMA	20	F	SGL	RRZZZZ	NY
HAMMER, ABRAM	19	M	MCHT	RRZZZZ	NY
KOPMANN, JANKEL	23	M	DLR	RRZZZZ	NY
LEWY, GREGORI	20	M	DLR	RRZZZZ	NY
GURSKY, HIND-	56	F	WO	RRZZZZ	NY
MENUCHE	9	F	CHILD	RRZZZZ	NY
PERL	7	F	CHILD	RRZZZZ	NY
FISCHER, ISIDOR	25	M	LKSH	RRZZZZ	NY
TEOFILA	25	F	W	RRZZZZ	NY

PASSENGER	AGE	SEX	OCCUPATION	PRV VIL DES

SHIP: ANCHORIA

FROM: GLASGOW AND MOVILLE
TO: NEW YORK
ARRIVED: 22 OCTOBER 1888

PASSENGER	AGE	SEX	OCCUPATION	PRV VIL DES
MAGURKIEWICZ, SIMON	23	M	LABR	RRAILRUSA
PRYZWTOWSKI, TEOFIL	25	M	CCHBLDR	RRAILRUSA
NOVAKOWSKA, JOSEF	26	M	LABR	RRAILRUSA
MARTHA	23	F	W	RRAILRUSA

SHIP: ARIZONA

FROM: LIVERPOOL AND QUEENSTOWN
TO: NEW YORK
ARRIVED: 22 OCTOBER 1888

PASSENGER	AGE	SEX	OCCUPATION	PRV VIL DES
SALOMONZIK, GOLDE	50	F	W	RRACBFUSA
JACOB	58	M	ART	RRACBFUSA
OSCHER	11	M	CH	RRACBFUSA
BER, RASCHE	18	F	SP	RRACBFUSA
ROSSEIN, BENJEL	19	M	LABR	RRACBFUSA
SCHNEIDER, JANKEL	17	M	LABR	RRACBFUSA
ZELDE	22	F	SP	RRACBFUSA
MORDUSOWITZ, IDA	18	F	SP	RRACBFUSA
BRENER, LEWEN	17	M	LABR	RRACBFUSA
FLACKS, ISRAEL	19	M	LABR	RRACBFUSA
FURMANSKI, SORE	30	F	W	RRACBFUSA
MOSES	11	M	CH	RRACBFUSA
RAME	10	F	CH	RRACBFUSA
LEISER	7	F	CHILD	RRACBFUSA
HIRSCH	5	M	CHILD	RRACBFUSA
GRINFOS, DWORE	17	F	SP	RRACBFUSA
KLEZMER, TAUBE	16	F	SP	RRACBFUSA
LEIB	4	M	CHILD	RRACBFUSA
PROZER, BERL	18	M	FLABR	RRACBFUSA
GLAZER, JACOB	20	M	FLABR	RRACBFUSA
BLERDER, JACOB	24	M	MSN	RRACBFUSA
KATZ, ROSE	55	F	W	RRACBFUSA
DOLINSKY, SALOMON	19	M	LABR	RRACBFUSA
GLUCKMAR, LOUIS	18	M	LABR	RRACBFUSA
LAZAR, ABRAHAM	17	M	LABR	RRACBFUSA
PENI, JULIE	19	F	SP	RRACBFUSA
MARCK, SALLY	18	F	SP	RRACBFUSA
MULIVICZ, LEOPOLD	19	M	MSN	RRACBFUSA
ALBAUM, ROCHEL	17	F	SP	RRACBFUSA
M.	16	F	SP	RRACBFUSA
MIKELOWICZ, NACHE	27	F	SP	RRACBFUSA
GOLDSTEIN, ESTER	34	F	W	RRACBFUSA
FEYE	.10	F	INFANT	RRACBFUSA
LATTAN, PER	34	M	PRNTR	RRACBFUSA
SCHAIE	11	F	CH	RRACBFUSA
HARRIS	7	M	CHILD	RRACBFUSA
JACOB	5	M	CHILD	RRACBFUSA
SPEYEL, PHILIPP	19	M	LABR	RRACBFUSA
HERSCHENSTRAUSS, ITTE	9	F	CHILD	RRACBFUSA
HENNE	11	F	CH	RRACBFUSA
ABRAMOFSKY, HERMAN	22	M	MSN	RRACBFUSA
STINKLEYEYER, PAUL	58	M	ART	RRACBFUSA
THERESE	58	F	W	RRACBFUSA
JECHINOWSKY, ESTER	24	F	SP	RRACBFUSA
ROBINSON, SOLOMON	20	M	LABR	RRACBFUSA
LEIGLER, ZILLI	15	F	SP	RRACBFUSA
JUGMAN, HERMAN-G.	30	M	MECH	RRAGUZUSA
ANDERS-G.	35	M	MECH	RRAGUZUSA
ANGELZIG, SELIG	42	M	ART	RRACBFUSA
KATZ, CHAIM	43	M	ART	RRACBFUSA
ESTHER	38	F	W	RRACBFUSA
ALTER	14	M	LABR	RRACBFUSA
LEIB	10	F	CH	RRACBFUSA
ARON	7	M	CHILD	RRACBFUSA
ALTKE	4	F	CHILD	RRACBFUSA
TAUBE	.11	F	INFANT	RRACBFUSA
ISAAC	.02	M	INFANT	RRACBFUSA
FURMANSKI, LEIZER	7	F	CHILD	RRACBFUSA
ISRAEL	.10	M	INFANT	RRACBFUSA
HINDE	00	F	INF	RRACBFUSA
PROZER, MALKE	11	F	CH	RRACBFUSA
BEREL, CHANE	16	F	SP	RRACBFUSA
LEWIN, GERSCHON	23	M	LABR	RRACBFUSA
ZXALKOWITZ, RELKE	38	F	W	RRACBFUSA
LEA	11	F	CH	RRACBFUSA
GITLE	9	F	CHILD	RRACBFUSA
BREINDEL	7	M	CHILD	RRACBFUSA
ROCKE	3	M	CHILD	RRACBFUSA
HINDE	.10	F	INFANT	RRACBFUSA
THOMSEN, HEINRICH	31	M	FTR	RRACBFUSA
SACHT, HEINRICH	21	M	SHPMN	RRACBFUSA
KIRST, LIPPE	18	F	SP	RRACBFUSA
SINGER, CHONE	22	M	LABR	RRACBFUSA
MICHALOWICZ, SCHIFFRE	.04	F	INFANT	RRACBFUSA
TESCHINOWSKY, KOPEL	.08	M	INFANT	RRACBFUSA
WEUNMAR, JOSSEL	52	M	MECH	RRACBFUSA
DASSLER, MAX	22	M	LABR	RRACBFUSA
DAMENSTEIN, ARON	59	M	ART	RRACBFUSA
ROSA	55	F	W	RRACBFUSA
JETTE	21	F	SP	RRACBFUSA
SAMUEL	9	M	CHILD	RRACBFUSA
GISTMANN, HENNE	18	F	SP	RRACBFUSA
JUDELSOHN, MARIANNE	40	F	W	RRACBFUSA
ROCHEL	18	F	SP	RRACBFUSA
PALMROTH, CARL	24	M	FLABR	RRAGUZUSA
LASSENCUS, FRANS	22	M	SHPMN	RRAGUZUSA
KIWETZ, JOS.	40	M	SMH	RRACBFUSA
LEWIN, JOSEPH	21	M	LABR	RRADBQUSA
PEPPERMAN, U-MRS	35	F	W	RRADBQUSA
SABEL	11	F	CH	RRADBQUSA
SABEL	4	F	CHILD	RRADBQUSA
JANE	2	F	CHILD	RRADBQUSA
FRANK	.05	M	INFANT	RRADBQUSA
SCHMER, BERNT	19	M	LABR	RRACBFUSA
GLAVICZ, JOSEFA	22	F	W	RRACBFUSA
MARY	2	F	CHILD	RRACBFUSA
GROSS, CZANER	17	F	SP	RRACBFUSA
BAUER, BEILE	20	F	SP	RRACBFUSA
FELMANN, ZATTEL	36	F	W	RRACBFUSA
SCHILLBERG, LUDERG	35	M	ART	RRACBFUSA

SHIP: STATE OF GEORGIA

FROM: GLASGOW
TO: NEW YORK
ARRIVED: 22 OCTOBER 1888

PASSENGER	AGE	SEX	OCCUPATION	PRV VIL DES
ABRAMS, S.	23	M	TLR	RRZZZZUSA
BELL, EUGEN	19	M	JNR	RRZZZZUSA
BEZOZOWSKI, MATHIAS	23	M	LABR	RRZZZZUSA
GOLDSCHMIDT, FEIGE	25	F	W	RRZZZZUSA
GERDAN, SINE	20	F	SVNT	RRZZZZUSA
HOROS, ANDRASZ	45	M	LABR	RRZZZZUSA
MEKISIS, MAGDALENA	26	F	W	RRZZZZUSA
MARDA	.09	F	INFANT	RRZZZZUSA
NEWSCHEILE, ANNIE	62	F	W	RRZZZZUSA
RIWELES, ABBE	22	M	TLR	RRZZZZUSA
ROSAKOWSKY, STANISLAUS	15	M	LABR	RRZZZZUSA
SCHEINDLING, JACOB	22	M	CL	RRZZZZUSA
SDHWARZ, MEYER	17	M	LABR	RRZZZZUSA
SRENICK, PALOW	18	M	PDLR	RRZZZZUSA
WARSHEL, SCHECHTER	18	F	SVNT	RRZZZZUSA

PASSENGER	AGE	SEX	OCCUPATION	PRV VIL DES
SCHLECHTER, FLENE	16	F	SVNT	RRZZZZUSA

SHIP: HERMANN

FROM: BREMEN
TO: BALTIMORE
ARRIVED: 24 OCTOBER 1888

PASSENGER	AGE	SEX	OCCUPATION	PRV VIL DES
PUVAL, EMILIE	27	F	UNKNOWN	RRZZZZMD
ALBERT	8	M	CHILD	RRZZZZMD
EMIL	5	M	CHILD	RRZZZZMD
ALFRED	4	M	CHILD	RRZZZZMD
HELENE	.01	F	INFANT	RRZZZZMD
KLINGBED, JULIANE	70	F	UNKNOWN	RRZZZZMD
ORKEN, FRIEDR.	25	M	UNKNOWN	RRZZZZMD
WULFSOHN, CHAIE	16	F	UNKNOWN	RRZZZZMD
JUDE	11	F	CH	RRZZZZMD
ZEIDEL, MOSES	49	M	FARMER	RRZZZZMD
KANOWITZ, RASSE	22	F	UNKNOWN	RRZZZZMD
JUDELWITZ, BETY	20	F	UNKNOWN	RRZZZZMD
OSTROW, REBECCA	20	F	UNKNOWN	RRZZZZMD
CHEW, BINIOME	19	F	UNKNOWN	RRZZZZMD
MEYER	17	M	UNKNOWN	RRZZZZMD
MARGOSSIM, ESTER	22	F	UNKNOWN	RRZZZZMD
BRUCHE	.09	F	INFANT	RRZZZZMD
FADENWECHT, RUDOLF	31	M	JNR	RRZZZZNE
--IANDA	24	F	W	RRZZZZNE
RUDOLF	6	M	CHILD	RRZZZZNE
BERNHARD	5	M	CHILD	RRZZZZNE
KASTEN, SAMUEL	28	M	FARMER	RRZZZZNE
JULIANE	22	F	W	RRZZZZNE
JUSTINE	4	F	CHILD	RRZZZZNE
PAULINE	3	F	CHILD	RRZZZZNE
BERTHA	.11	F	INFANT	RRZZZZNE
MEYEROWITZ, ABRH.	34	M	MCHT	RRZZZZIL
SOFIA	31	F	W	RRZZZZIL
SAMUEL	8	M	CHILD	RRZZZZIL
MEYER	4	M	CHILD	RRZZZZIL
REBECCA	3	F	CHILD	RRZZZZIL
RANOWITZ, FEIGE	45	M	UNKNOWN	RRZZZZIL
CHAJE	8	F	CHILD	RRZZZZIL
RAPHAEL	.09	M	INFANT	RRZZZZIL
KAROWITZ, LOGER	20	M	TLR	RRZZZZMD
WEINER, NOSER	37	M	MCHT	RRZZZZMD
RACHEL	34	F	W	RRZZZZMD
MARCUS	11	M	CH	RRZZZZMD
BLUMENTHAL, LESER	48	M	PDLR	RRZZZZMD
MEILER, RINKE	40	F	UNKNOWN	RRZZZZMD
RACHEL	10	F	CH	RRZZZZMD
ABEL	8	M	CHILD	RRZZZZMD
LEIB	6	F	CHILD	RRZZZZMD
HODE	.05	F	INFANT	RRZZZZMD
BERLINSKI, NONNI	24	F	UNKNOWN	RRZZZZMD
JUDEL	10	M	CH	RRZZZZMD
LEIBE	.01	F	INFANT	RRZZZZMD
SLABASINE, CHAJE	35	F	UNKNOWN	RRZZZZMD
ROCHE	11	F	CH	RRZZZZMD
ABRAHAM	9	M	CHILD	RRZZZZMD
GUTE	.11	F	INFANT	RRZZZZMD
JAERSBSOHN, U	00	M	UNKNOWN	RRZZZZMD
KOHN, CHAWE	32	F	UNKNOWN	RRZZZZMD
TAUBE	8	F	CHILD	RRZZZZMD
KASPEL	6	F	CHILD	RRZZZZMD
BASCHE	4	F	CHILD	RRZZZZMD
PESSE	.11	F	INFANT	RRZZZZMD
GOTHEICH, SALI	18	M	UNKNOWN	RRZZZZMD
MOSESCHAWI, ROMAN	20	M	UNKNOWN	RRZZZZMD
SZERMINSKI, MICHEL	22	M	UNKNOWN	RRZZZZMD
BOLTAJLIS, WLADISLAWA	21	F	UNKNOWN	RRZZZZMD

SHIP: STATE OF NEVADA

FROM: GLASGOW AND LARNE
TO: NEW YORK
ARRIVED: 25 OCTOBER 1888

PASSENGER	AGE	SEX	OCCUPATION	PRV VIL DES
APIRAN, REBECCA	25	F	SVNT	RRAIGXUSA
DUSCHAN, SENDER	23	M	GDSM	RRAIDLUSA
HIRSCHFELD, CHAJE	40	F	UNKNOWN	RRAIDLUSA
SORE	16	F	UNKNOWN	RRAIDLUSA
ESTHER	10	F	CH	RRAIDLUSA
GITHL	4	F	CHILD	RRAIDLUSA
KARB, EISIZ	25	M	FARMER	RRAIDLUSA
KAPLAN, MENDEL	15	M	SMH	RRAIDLUSA
LEBOWITZ, RIEFKE	22	F	SVNT	RRAIDLUSA
MATIS, OCI	25	M	FARMER	RRAIDLUSA
U	24	F	UNKNOWN	RRAIDLUSA
ANNIE	2	F	CHILD	RRAIDLUSA
MARY	.06	F	INFANT	RRAIDLUSA
MENDEL, DAVID	18	M	MCHT	RRAIDLUSA
U, U	58	F	UNKNOWN	RRAIDLUSA
SLEIF, MALKE	15	F	SVNT	RRAIDLUSA
SCHUSTERMAN, JOSSEL	27	M	SLR	RRAIDLUSA
ZERISE	25	F	W	RRAIDLUSA
WISCHATZKY, KASIMIR	37	M	FARMER	RRAIDLUSA
SUSANNE	37	F	UNKNOWN	RRAIDLUSA
BELCZYK, PAUL	24	M	LABR	RRAIDLUSA
BRAUNSTEIN, BLUME	26	F	SVNT	RRAIDLUSA

SHIP: LAHN

FROM: BREMEN AND SOUTHAMPTON
TO: NEW YORK
ARRIVED: 26 OCTOBER 1888

PASSENGER	AGE	SEX	OCCUPATION	PRV VIL DES
TERGUSON, ANNIE	50	F	UNKNOWN	RRAFWJUSA
NAWIKAUCKINTE, MAGDA.	21	F	UNKNOWN	RRAFWJUSA
ZARUKA, GEORG	28	M	LABR	RRAILAUSA
VINCENT	20	M	LABR	RRAILAUSA
GOLDEIN, BENJAMIN	32	M	LABR	RRAFWJUSA
SZEPANKOWICZ, FRANZ	33	M	LABR	RRAFWJUSA
KAZINSKI, WIZISLAW	36	M	LABR	RRAFWJUSA
WOLFSDORF, BENNO	48	M	LABR	RRAFWJUSA
BORNSTEIN, AUGUSTE	27	F	W	RRAFWJUSA
JOSEF	2	M	CHILD	RRAFWJUSA
MORITZ	.06	M	INFANT	RRAFWJUSA
MAKOWSKI, JOSEF	64	M	LABR	RRAILAUSA
PETERS, ISBRAND	32	M	LABR	RRAILAUSA
AGATHE	29	F	W	RRAILAUSA
JACOB	6	M	CHILD	RRAILAUSA
FRANZ	4	M	CHILD	RRAILAUSA
MARGA.	3	F	CHILD	RRAILAUSA
WIEBE, JOHANN	37	M	FARMER	RRAILAUSA
ANNA	37	F	W	RRAILAUSA
JOHANN	14	M	UNKNOWN	RRAILAUSA
JACOB	8	M	CHILD	RRAILAUSA
HEINR.	7	M	CHILD	RRAILAUSA
ANNA	4	F	CHILD	RRAILAUSA
MARIE	2	F	CHILD	RRAILAUSA
HELENE	.06	F	INFANT	RRAILAUSA
MEZNER, BER	18	M	LABR	RRAILAUSA
LUTZ, JOSEF	33	M	FARMER	RRAILHUSA
MAGDA.	30	F	W	RRAILHUSA
ANNA	8	F	CHILD	RRAILHUSA
XAVER	4	M	CHILD	RRAILHUSA
GEORG	2	M	CHILD	RRAILHUSA
ANTON	.03	M	INFANT	RRAILHUSA
ZIEGLERSEN, CHRIST.	57	M	FARMER	RRAILHUSA
FRANZKA.	54	F	W	RRAILHUSA

PASSENGER	AGE	SEX	OCCUPATION	PRIVL	DES
JOSEF	14	M	UNKNOWN	RRAILH	USA
JOSEFE.	22	F	UNKNOWN	RRAILH	USA
SILBERNAGEL, JOHANN	37	M	FARMER	RRAILH	USA
ELISABETH	34	F	W	RRAILH	USA
SUGARDE	8	F	CHILD	RRAILH	USA
CHRIST.	4	M	CHILD	RRAILH	USA
JOSEF	3	M	CHILD	RRAILH	USA
FRANZKA.	1	F	CHILD	RRAILH	USA
JACOB	.03	M	INFANT	RRAILH	USA
WIETERS, OTTO	23	M	FARMER	RRAIDK	USA
LOIKAU, JACOB	39	M	FARMER	RRAIDK	USA
SOPHIE	40	F	W	RRAIDK	USA
JOHANN	14	M	UNKNOWN	RRAIDK	USA
KARLICH, HEINR.	41	M	FARMER	RRAIDK	USA
AGNES	40	F	W	RRAIDK	USA
JACOB	19	M	FARMER	RRAIDK	USA
DOROTHEA	15	F	UNKNOWN	RRAIDK	USA
MARIA	9	F	CHILD	RRAIDK	USA
SOPHIA	3	F	CHILD	RRAIDK	USA
FRANZ	2	M	CHILD	RRAIDK	USA
KAMINSKI, KASIMIR	24	M	FARMER	RRAIDK	USA
GALOC, ABRAHAM	26	M	LABR	RRAIDK	USA
KATZ, HERZ	29	M	LABR	RRAIDK	USA
WITTE, FRIEDR.	45	M	LABR	RRAHTU	USA
SARAH	25	F	UNKNOWN	RRAHTU	USA
MARIA	20	F	UNKNOWN	RRAHTU	USA
ISAAK	11	M	CH	RRAHTU	USA
MARTA	9	F	CHILD	RRAHTU	USA
IDA	8	F	CHILD	RRAHTU	USA
REIGER	3	M	CHILD	RRAHTU	USA
HELENA	2	F	CHILD	RRAHTU	USA
PHILIPOWSKI, JACOB	19	M	LABR	RRAHTF	USA
GOLDSTEIN, REISEL	44	F	W	RRAHUF	USA
SARAH	15	F	UNKNOWN	RRAHUF	USA
DAVID	11	M	CH	RRAHUF	USA
BEIMISCH	10	M	CH	RRAHUF	USA
CHASKEL	8	M	CHILD	RRAHUF	USA
FRUME	6	F	CHILD	RRAHUF	USA
BER	.11	M	INFANT	RRAHUF	USA
ZOCHED	.11	F	INFANT	RRAHUF	USA

SHIP: WIELAND

FROM: HAMBURG
TO: NEW YORK
ARRIVED: 26 OCTOBER 1888

PASSENGER	AGE	SEX	OCCUPATION	PRIVL	DES
CHAJE	26	F	WO	RRAHWQ	USA
JANKEL	.11	M	INFANT	RRAHWQ	USA
KENDIS, ALTE	30	F	WO	RRAIOO	USA
TAUBE	7	F	CHILD	RRAIOO	USA
CHANNE	6	F	CHILD	RRAIOO	USA
NECHAME	5	M	CHILD	RRAIOO	USA
SCHOIL	3	M	CHILD	RRAIOO	USA
URBANOWICH, EVA	24	F	WO	RRAHZS	USA
WINZI	6	M	CHILD	RRAHZS	USA
PETER	5	M	CHILD	RRAHZS	USA
JOHANN	3	M	CHILD	RRAHZS	USA
ANTON	.06	M	INFANT	RRAHZS	USA
GLUCKOWSKI, ANTON	20	M	LABR	RRAHZS	USA
HERSOHN, VICTOR	7	M	CHILD	RRAIGK	USA
FEIGENBAUM, SARA	35	F	WO	RRAHTU	USA
SALMEN	15	M	CH	RRAHTU	USA
RIEWE	7	F	CHILD	RRAHTU	USA
GITTEL	6	M	CHILD	RRAHTU	USA
GOLDIN, MEYER	20	M	JNR	RRAHTU	USA
WARNEZEUSKY, FREDERIK	22	M	JNR	RRZZZZ	USA
KAZENELSEN, BASSE	30	F	WO	RRAHOK	USA
SLATE	2	F	CHILD	RRAHOK	USA
MALKE	.09	F	INFANT	RRAHOK	USA

PASSENGER	AGE	SEX	OCCUPATION	PRIVL	DES
NIEMROWITZ, THERESE	20	F	SGL	RRZZZZ	USA
SZMANIA, BRIGITTE	22	F	WO	RRZZZZ	USA
IGNATZ	3	M	CHILD	RRZZZZ	USA
MARIANNA	.11	F	INFANT	RRZZZZ	USA
GABRYELOWICZ, WLADISLAW	21	F	SGL	RRZZZZ	USA
GENSELOWITZ, HERSCHEL	18	M	TLR	RRAIMA	USA
BRIARSKI, GEDALIA	20	F	SGL	RRAGRT	USA
BROZKY, MINDEL	58	M	LABR	RRAHRK	USA
LEYE	48	F	W	RRAHRK	USA
GOLDSTEIN, ROSA	19	F	WO	RRAHWQ	USA
DOBE	.06	F	INFANT	RRAHWQ	USA
TSICHRIEB, HEINR.	36	M	LABR	RRAFVG	USA
ELISABETH	28	F	UNKNOWN	RRAFVG	USA
HEINR.	5	M	CHILD	RRAFVG	USA
LEONHARDT	4	M	CHILD	RRAFVG	USA
KATHA.	.11	F	INFANT	RRAFVG	USA
THEODOR	.01	M	INFANT	RRAFVG	USA
DANIELS, ANNA	24	F	SGL	RRZZZZ	USA
ROSE, ESTER	25	F	WO	RRZZZZ	USA
JONE	.11	M	INFANT	RRZZZZ	USA
KOMIRCARSKI, MINNA	17	F	SGL	RRAINZ	USA
REICHEL	16	F	SGL	RRAINZ	USA
ROSE, SINE	20	F	SGL	RRZZZZ	USA
HURWICZ, SALOMON	39	M	BBR	RRZZZZ	USA
SINOLINSKY, BERL	15	M	LABR	RRAHZS	USA
CZERKOW, AISIK	28	M	LABR	RRZZZZ	USA
RESE	22	F	W	RRZZZZ	USA
MOSES	.11	M	INFANT	RRZZZZ	USA
SEIDEL, ESTER	23	F	SGL	RRAHTU	USA
BRUM, LEIB	23	M	LKSH	RRAHTU	USA
KRAZEWSKY, IWAN	40	M	TLR	RRAHTO	USA
ROSALIE	38	F	W	RRAHTO	USA
MARIANNA	4	F	CHILD	RRAHTO	USA

SHIP: ITALY

FROM: LIVERPOOL AND QUEENSTOWN
TO: NEW YORK
ARRIVED: 26 OCTOBER 1888

PASSENGER	AGE	SEX	OCCUPATION	PRIVL	DES
RATCUZCKI, JON	46	M	LABR	RRADBQ	CIN
LANSGE, M.	20	M	LABR	RRADAX	NY
JEKOWITZ, M.	22	M	LABR	RRADAX	NY
JELECH, A.	26	M	LABR	RRADAX	NY
LAPIDUS, DAVID	26	M	UPHST	RRADAX	NY
KUKKE, SALMON	24	M	LABR	RRADAX	SFC
OFFIS, SOLOMON	24	M	LABR	RRACBF	NY
CHEZ	17	M	LABR	RRACBF	NY
ZIUDM--, LIME	30	M	LABR	RRACBF	NY
GRUNBERG, M.	29	F	W	RRADAX	NY
MALKE	8	F	CHILD	RRADAX	NY
RIFKE	7	F	CHILD	RRADAX	NY
BENY	00	M	INF	RRADAX	NY
NOVESK, BORESCH	20	M	LABR	RRACBF	NY
LEEG, IGNATZ	21	M	LABR	RRACBF	NY
GURBET, NIKOLAY	28	M	LABR	PLZZZZ	NY
GELL, ABRAHAM	18	M	LABR	RRZZZZ	NY
DWORKOWSKY, MOSES	48	M	TLR	RRZZZZ	NY
RIJEOM, MARLIS	17	M	LABR	RRACBF	NY
KLAUSNER, MARKUS	30	M	JNR	RRACBF	NY
ZUIDMAN, JACOB	20	M	FARMER	RRACBF	NY
SHEHL----, MAX	18	M	LABR	RRACBF	NY
METARSKY, WOLF	18	M	STDNT	RRACBF	NY
MENARSKI, WOLF	18	M	LABR	RRACBF	NY
RONE, SIMON	18	M	BKBNDR	RRACBF	NY
KORGOLA, WILHELIM	27	M	LABR	RRZZZZ	NY
SYCHOHN, JOHNN	26	M	LABR	RRZZZZ	NY

PASSENGER	AGE	SEX	OCCUPATION	PRV VIL DES

SHIP: DEVONIA

FROM: GLASGOW
TO: NEW YORK
ARRIVED: 29 OCTOBER 1888

PASSENGER	AGE	SEX	OCCUPATION	PRV VIL DES
FRAM, CHAME	20	F	SVNT	RRZZZZUSA
GOLDENBERG, MALKE	25	F	NN	RRZZZZUSA
GOLDE	.06	M	INFANT	RRZZZZUSA
GRINFELD, CHAJE	33	F	NN	RRZZZZUSA
HIRSCH	3	M	CHILD	RRZZZZUSA
KANTOR, ROCHE	18	F	SVNT	RRZZZZUSA
LIPMANOWITZ, JUDEL	19	F	SVNT	RRZZZZUSA
-RANG, MARIA	58	F	NN	RRZZZZUSA
KORAES, ANNA	10	F	CH	RRZZZZUSA
MILTON, DAR.	38	M	JNR	RRZZZZUSA
PERSTZ, NOCHEM	19	M	LABR	RRZZZZUSA
STEPHEN, MORDSCHE	10	F	CH	RRZZZZUSA
PESCHE	8	F	CHILD	RRZZZZUSA
MENDELSOHN, SORE	16	F	SVNT	RRZZZZUSA
MLINORTZ, SCHEINE	16	F	SVNT	RRZZZZUSA
MOSCHE	13	M	CH	RRZZZZUSA
OBERMANN, ENJE	50	F	CH	RRZZZZUSA
PUNSKY, REISEL	15	F	SVNT	RRZZZZUSA
RUNKIN, MEISCHE	26	M	LABR	RRZZZZUSA
MINE	20	F	NN	RRZZZZUSA
STOLAR, ROSA	20	F	SVNT	RRZZZZUSA
WILSTEIN, MARKUS	28	M	BKR	RRZZZZUSA
LALKA	2	F	CHILD	RRZZZZUSA
ADELAW, SCHMUEL	19	M	LABR	RRZZZZUSA
ROSENBERG, JACOB	24	M	LABR	RRZZZZUSA
BERNIKER, LIPPE	25	M	LABR	RRZZZZUSA
BORKAN, PINCHUS	33	M	LABR	RRZZZZUSA
BRENNER, ISAK	26	M	LABR	RRZZZZUSA
BAUMANN, ISRAEL	23	M	LABR	RRZZZZUSA
BEITZES, HIRSCH	18	M	LABR	RRZZZZUSA
BENNDERSOHN, HIRSCH	23	M	LABR	RRZZZZUSA
CHOROWSKI, BENZIEN	18	M	LABR	RRZZZZUSA
DAULZ, ENOCH	19	M	LABR	RRZZZZUSA
FICHEL, AUGT.	38	M	LABR	RRZZZZUSA
GUTMAN, HIRSCH	45	M	LABR	RRZZZZUSA
GROSSBAUM, ITZIG	20	M	LABR	RRZZZZUSA
KAWON, MASCHE	30	M	LABR	RRZZZZUSA
KRAUTSTEIN, LEISER	27	M	LABR	RRZZZZUSA
KNAPP, FEIVEL	33	M	LABR	RRZZZZUSA
OSINSKY, MOSCHE	26	M	LABR	RRZZZZUSA
RUBIN, NATHAN	26	M	LABR	RRZZZZUSA
SCHUDNOWSKI, ISAK	19	M	LABR	RRZZZZUSA
SCHEFTELSOHN, SALOMON	34	M	LABR	RRZZZZUSA
STOLOW, PESACH	18	M	LABR	RRZZZZUSA
STRUMPF, JOEL	18	M	LABR	RRZZZZUSA
WISZOMBERG, JANKEL	23	M	LABR	RRZZZZUSA
BALKEN, FEIGE	26	F	WO	RRAHZIUSA
KURIZKY, ESTHER	20	F	SGL	RRAHVUUSA
KAPICE, LENE	21	F	WO	RRZZZZUSA
MOSES	.09	M	INFANT	RRZZZZUSA
JIKOWITZ, REINE	30	F	WO	RRZZZZUSA
MOSES	7	M	CHILD	RRZZZZUSA
JACOB	6	M	CHILD	RRZZZZUSA
CHACE	5	F	CHILD	RRZZZZUSA
SARA	4	F	CHILD	RRZZZZUSA
SCHALIT, EMANUEL	19	M	FARMER	RRZZZZUSA
HERNSTEIN, ELIAS	18	M	BKBNDR	RRZZZZUSA
ALENIK-, ARON	18	M	LABR	RRZZZZUSA
KAPELOWITZ, MARK	17	M	MCHT	RRAHQDUSA
GUTMANN, ALTER	26	M	DLR	RRAHVUUSA
EPSTEIN, RACHEL	30	F	WO	RRAHTFUSA
RINA	4	F	CHILD	RRAHTFUSA
SCHAPIRO, MARIA	26	F	WO	RRAHTFUSA
RIESMANN, MOSES	19	M	DLR	RRZZZZUSA
BONNER, WOLF	23	M	UNKNOWN	RRAHXHUSA
KANUNKOWSKY, ZALLEL	35	M	DLR	RRZZZZUSA
NENDENBERG, ZADECK	23	M	DLR	RRAHTFUSA
ZADOWSKOI, FRANZ	50	M	LABR	RRZZZZUSA
VICTORIA	30	F	W	RRZZZZUSA
KIAKULAITIS, ANTANAS	38	M	LABR	RRZZZZUSA
ANDREWAITIS, ANDREUS	30	M	LABR	RRZZZZUSA
HESS, AMALIE	18	F	SGL	RRZZZZUSA
SCHAWEN, FREIDE	40	F	WO	RRAFVGUSA
WIKE	7	F	CHILD	RRAFVGUSA
PESCHE	6	F	CHILD	RRAFVGUSA
SCHLOME	5	F	CHILD	RRAFVGUSA
ITE	4	F	CHILD	RRAFVGUSA
FROMBERG, MARIE	28	F	SGL	RRAHQDUSA
RIFKIN, ELIUS	30	F	BRR	RRZZZZUSA
MARIE	30	F	W	RRZZZZUSA
FANNY	4	F	CHILD	RRZZZZUSA
HEISEL, LUDW.	40	M	FARMER	RRZZZZUSA
AUGUSTE	33	F	W	RRZZZZUSA
GUSTAV	7	M	CHILD	RRZZZZUSA
MARTHA	6	F	CHILD	RRZZZZUSA
EMILIE	4	F	CHILD	RRZZZZUSA
HERMANN	3	M	CHILD	RRZZZZUSA
RUDOLF	.09	M	INFANT	RRZZZZUSA
SUEDOWITZ, JESCHEL	40	M	MNFTR	RRAHTFUSA
HANNE	44	F	W	RRAHTFUSA
GITTEL	17	F	CH	RRAHTFUSA
MENDEL	7	M	CHILD	RRAHTFUSA
PESCHE	4	F	CHILD	RRAHTFUSA
SLOWSKOWSKI, JOSEF	22	M	LABR	RRAHZSUSA
GAJLEWICZ, ADAM	20	M	LABR	RRZZZZUSA
DANELICZ, ANT.	21	M	LABR	RRAHZSUSA
MOESCHOWITZ, WAWERD.	37	M	LABR	RRZZZZUSA
WEIMANER, JANKEL	20	M	LABR	RRAIFIUSA
HOFSCHA, MORRIS	30	M	LABR	RRAHTFUSA
PAUSNER, TENNE	19	M	MCHT	RRZZZZUSA
SMELKIN, RUBIN	19	M	MCHT	RRAHTXUSA

SHIP: POLARIA

FROM: HAMBURG
TO: NEW YORK
ARRIVED: 29 OCTOBER 1888

PASSENGER	AGE	SEX	OCCUPATION	PRV VIL DES
DORFMANN, MARE	24	F	SGL	RRAFVGUSA
AMOLKY, TAUBE	17	F	SGL	RRAHTFUSA
GROLL, SALOMON	16	M	LABR	RRZZZZUSA
MARKS, ABRAHAM	15	M	LABR	RRZZZZUSA
FANNY	16	F	SGL	RRZZZZUSA
LUBLUIER, CHANNE	27	M	DLR	RRAIHRUSA
GOLDSTEIN, LINE	32	F	WO	RRZZZZUSA
HERSCH	3	M	CHILD	RRZZZZUSA
ITZIG	.11	M	INFANT	RRZZZZUSA
BUDREWICZ, TEOFIL	28	M	LABR	RRZZZZUSA

SHIP: WERRA

FROM: BREMEN AND SOUTHAMPTON
TO: NEW YORK
ARRIVED: 30 OCTOBER 1888

PASSENGER	AGE	SEX	OCCUPATION	PRV VIL DES
SCHLICKMANN, MOSES	30	M	LABR	RRZZZZUSA
REICHENSTEIN, INDA	33	F	NN	RRZZZZUSA
BONNSEWICZ, MECSISLAW	35	M	LABR	RRZZZZUSA
GRUEN, SAM.	24	M	LABR	RRZZZZUSA
SORG, ISAAC	36	M	LABR	RRZZZZUSA
PERLMANN, CHANE	16	F	NN	RRZZZZUSA
IDJAL, ISAAC	28	M	FARMER	RRAHZSUSA
ZIEGLER, JOHANN	38	M	LABR	RRZZZZUSA

PASSENGER	AGE	SEX	OCCUPATION	PRV VIL DES
MARIA	37	F	W	RRZZZZUSA
JOSEF	7	M	CHILD	RRZZZZUSA
JOACHIM	4	M	CHILD	RRZZZZUSA
JACOB, LORENZ	28	M	FARMER	RRZZZZUSA
ANNA	26	F	W	RRZZZZUSA
JOSEF	2	M	CHILD	RRZZZZUSA
FLIEGER, BERNHD.	42	M	FARMER	RRZZZZUSA
ELEONORE	28	F	W	RRZZZZUSA
PETER	19	M	FARMER	RRZZZZUSA
JACOB	17	M	FARMER	RRZZZZUSA
BERNH.	15	M	NN	RRAHYKUSA
MATHES	13	M	NN	RRAHYKUSA
FRANZ	4	M	CHILD	RRAHYKUSA
MARGA.	3	F	CHILD	RRAHYKUSA
ELISAB.	2	F	CHILD	RRAHYKUSA
MARIANNE	.11	F	INFANT	RRAHYKUSA
ZIEGLER, EMANUEL	2	M	CHILD	RRAHYKUSA
MORGNART, GABRIEL	40	M	FARMER	RRABIJUSA
REGINA	39	F	W	RRABIJUSA
MARTIN	11	M	CH	RRABIJUSA
ELISABETH	9	F	CHILD	RRABIJUSA
BALZER	7	M	CHILD	RRABIJUSA
NIC.	4	M	CHILD	RRABIJUSA
CATHA.	2	F	CHILD	RRABIJUSA
GRETA	.11	F	INFANT	RRABIJUSA
MARGUART, LUKAS	64	M	INF	RRACOVUSA
CATHA.	67	F	W	RRACOVUSA
PETER	29	M	FARMER	RRACOVUSA
CATHA.	26	F	W	RRACOVUSA
CASIMIR	4	M	CHILD	RRACOVUSA
MARGA.	3	F	CHILD	RRACOVUSA
ALTMANN, SARA	23	F	NN	RRZZZZUSA
LIEBERMANN, PESSE	40	M	LABR	RRZZZZUSA
MOSES	17	M	LABR	RRZZZZUSA
DETNIK, JUNKER	59	M	LABR	RRZZZZUSA
ZIEGLER, CHRIST.	24	M	LABR	RRZZZZUSA
MAGDA.	20	F	W	RRZZZZUSA
JOSEF	.06	M	INFANT	RRZZZZUSA
BARTEL, DAVID	34	M	FARMER	RRAHZSUSA
EI, FERDINAND	44	M	FARMER	RRAHZSUSA
CAROLE.	33	F	W	RRAHZSUSA
EMILIE	10	F	CH	RRAHZSUSA
BERTHA	10	F	CH	RRAHZSUSA
ADOLF	.06	M	INFANT	RRAHZSUSA
BERTHA	1	F	CHILD	RRAHZSUSA
KOHANSKY, ANNA	33	F	W	RRAHTNUSA
REGINA	10	F	CH	RRAHTNUSA
SOSCHA	11	F	CH	RRAHTNUSA
SEFKE, WOLF	32	M	LABR	RRAHTOUSA
WEISSBERG, FROME	34	F	W	RRAHTOUSA
SARAH	9	F	CHILD	RRAHTOUSA

SHIP: RHEIN

FROM: BREMEN
TO: BALTIMORE
ARRIVED: 30 OCTOBER 1888

PASSENGER	AGE	SEX	OCCUPATION	PRV VIL DES
MILLNER, MEYER	18	M	LABR	RRZZZZUNK
WILANSKY, FRIDA	23	F	NN	RRZZZZUNK
CHAJE	5	F	CHILD	RRZZZZUNK
BELE	4	F	CHILD	RRZZZZUNK
BARKE	.09	F	INFANT	RRZZZZUNK
ISTWA-, PARANAI	19	M	LABR	RRZZZZUNK
R-SICECKI, M	19	M	LABR	RRZZZZUNK
BORNER, BERTHA	22	F	CK	RRZZZZUNK
WESTENFELD, HEINR	36	M	FARMER	RRZZZZUNK
HENRIETTE	36	F	W	RRZZZZUNK
LUISE	6	F	CHILD	RRZZZZUNK
ANNA	.10	F	INFANT	RRZZZZUNK
TELLEN, JANKEL	17	M	SDLR	RRZZZZUNK
WARRECKER, OTTO	23	M	JNR	RRZZZZUNK
ROBINOWITZ, HAIM	11	M	CH	RRZZZZUNK
NACHIMSOHN, DAVID	45	M	LABR	RRZZZZUNK
SCHER, JANKEL	20	M	MCHT	RRZZZZUNK
MARTIN, BO-IFACI-RS	23	M	LABR	RRZZZZMI
BULLER, ELISABETH	31	F	NN	RRZZZZMI
HELENA	29	F	NN	RRZZZZMI
-ONDRIS, FREIDE	20	F	NN	RRZZZZUNK
MARY	.11	F	INFANT	RRZZZZUNK
ITTE	.11	F	INFANT	RRZZZZUNK
JOSCHELOWITZ, ITTE	20	F	NN	RRZZZZUNK
KAMIROWITZ, MENDRA	20	M	NN	RRZZZZUNK
RAPPAPORT, HARRIS	42	M	MCHT	RRZZZZUNK
FERGE	36	F	W	RRZZZZUNK
MAYER	17	M	CH	RRZZZZUNK
ELKE	15	F	CH	RRZZZZUNK
ISAAC	11	M	CH	RRZZZZUNK
JOSEL	9	M	CHILD	RRZZZZUNK
WOLF	7	M	CHILD	RRZZZZUNK
BEILE	.01	F	INFANT	RRZZZZUNK
STEINBERG, RIFKE	19	F	NN	RRZZZZUNK
MANDUSCHOW, CHAJIM	18	M	BCHR	RRZZZZUNK
BINDER, BELE	19	F	NN	RRZZZZUNK
GOLDSTEIN, BELE	15	F	NN	RRZZZZUNK
BLOOMINTHAL, JOSSEL	19	M	LABR	RRZZZZUNK
CHAIET, BEILE	40	F	NN	RRZZZZUNK
DAVID	18	M	MCHT	RRZZZZUNK
SURE	16	F	NN	RRZZZZUNK
SCHULEM	9	M	CHILD	RRZZZZUNK
GUTMACHER, CHAIM	17	F	NN	RRZZZZUNK
BALIMOW, ABRAHAM	44	M	MCHT	RRZZZZUNK
CURKLINSKI, JOSEF	56	M	MCHT	RRZZZZUNK
ANNA	17	F	NN	RRZZZZUNK
FRANZ	15	M	NN	RRZZZZUNK
GUTTMANN, LEO	6	M	CHILD	RRZZZZIL
ROSA	4	F	CHILD	RRZZZZIL
ALEX	.07	M	INFANT	RRZZZZIL
SAMUEL	.07	M	INFANT	RRZZZZIL
LEVIN, AARON	17	M	CL	RRZZZZUNK
STRELKA, PILIPINA	10	F	CH	RRZZZZUNK

SHIP: MICHIGAN

FROM: LIVERPOOL
TO: BOSTON
ARRIVED: 30 OCTOBER 1888

PASSENGER	AGE	SEX	OCCUPATION	PRV VIL DES
GOLDSTEIN, SOLOMON	35	M	TLR	RRZZZZUSA
KONRAT, O.	22	M	TLR	RRZZZZUSA
SCHAPIRE, SCH.	21	M	SHMK	RRZZZZUSA
BLUMENSTOCK, BAR.	27	M	TLR	RRZZZZUSA
HIRSCH, ISRAEL	14	M	SCH	RRZZZZUSA
HELLER, SAMUEL	20	M	TLR	RRZZZZUSA
ROSIN, ITZIG	50	M	TLR	RRZZZZUSA
ABRAHAM	17	M	TLR	RRZZZZUSA
DAVIDOW, AIRSCH	45	M	TLR	RRZZZZUSA
ELLINA, DORAH	18	F	SP	RRZZZZUSA
NADJEDA	17	F	SP	RRZZZZUSA
WELENSJY, MENDEL	44	M	TLR	RRZZZZUSA
DUNE	40	F	W	RRZZZZUSA
ELLINA, ANNA	66	F	W	RRZZZZUSA
WELENSKY, CHEIKE	8	F	CHILD	RRZZZZUSA
ISAAC	7	M	CHILD	RRZZZZUSA
MALTKE	3	F	CHILD	RRZZZZUSA
ELLINA, VASSILE	8	F	CHILD	RRZZZZUSA

PASSENGER	AGE	SEX	OCCUPATION	PRV	VIL	DES

SHIP: PERUVIAN

FROM: HALIFAX AND LIVERPOOL
TO: BALTIMORE
ARRIVED: 31 OCTOBER 1888

PASSENGER	AGE	SEX	OCCUPATION	PRV VIL DES
ROSENBLATT, SCHLOME	35	M	TLR	RRZZZZBAL
STRYSZEWSKI, ANTON	20	M	TLR	RRZZZZBAL
WEINER, HIRSCH	28	M	MLR	RRZZZZPIT
KELLER, ABRAM	28	M	MLR	PLZZZZPIT

SHIP: WISCONSIN

FROM: LIVERPOOL AND QUEENSTOWN
TO: NEW YORK
ARRIVED: 31 OCTOBER 1888

PASSENGER	AGE	SEX	OCCUPATION	PRV VIL DES
NOWAK, JENTE	55	F	MA	RRZZZZUSA
LEGAE, SARA	20	F	SP	RRZZZZUSA
WINOGRODIN, YINWIE	25	F	SP	RRZZZZUSA
KUNNER, LEIB	20	F	SP	RRZZZZUSA
EFROM	19	M	PMBR	RRZZZZUSA
MARKSON, JACOB	30	M	PMBR	RRZZZZUSA
FRIEDMAN, FEIWEL	20	M	PMBR	RRZZZZUSA
YREIFOLD, JOS.	20	M	GZR	RRZZZZUSA
ROSENHALTZ, ETTIE	17	F	SP	PLZZZZUSA
ZALTOFSKY, DAVID	17	M	LABR	PLZZZZUSA
SANDERZY, MARIANA	18	F	SP	PLZZZZUSA
GOLDING, LEIB	21	F	SP	PLZZZZUSA
FRADA	20	F	SP	PLZZZZUSA
HALLADA, JOHN	18	M	GZR	RRZZZZUSA
ESKILI, MATTS	31	M	JNR	FNZZZZUSA
ZEHTIKANGAS, ERIK	33	M	FARMER	FNZZZZUSA
SCHGUT, SENDER	7	F	CHILD	RRZZZZUSA
KARKLINSKI, YESIE	7	F	CHILD	RRZZZZUSA
NOWAK, ETTE	7	F	CHILD	RRZZZZUSA
KATZ, JANOS	27	M	PMBR	RRZZZZUSA
KANENGIESER, CHATZKEL	20	F	SP	RRZZZZUSA
SCHMIGELSKI, YROWIE	.10	F	INFANT	RRZZZZUSA
PASCHELINSKI, ABRAM	.09	M	INFANT	RRZZZZUSA
ZEIGLER, ZILLI	15	F	SP	PLZZZZUSA
SCHIMELNITZKI, BENJ	16	M	GZR	RRZZZZUSA
MILLER, LOSA	20	F	SP	RRZZZZUSA
GEROWSKI, MOSES	54	M	PMBR	RRZZZZUSA
JACOB	12	M	CH	RRZZZZUSA
SCHINIGELSKI, ITE	22	F	SP	RRZZZZUSA
KAHANOW, PAGE	20	M	PNTR	RRZZZZUSA
GOLDREICH, LEIB	52	F	MA	PLZZZZUSA
REBA	7	F	CHILD	PLZZZZUSA
BLUME	3	F	CHILD	PLZZZZUSA
PASCHELINSKI, SARA	40	F	MA	PLZZZZUSA
DAVID	7	M	CHILD	PLZZZZUSA
MERE	6	F	CHILD	PLZZZZUSA

SHIP: GOTHIA

FROM: STETTIN
TO: NEW YORK
ARRIVED: 31 OCTOBER 1888

PASSENGER	AGE	SEX	OCCUPATION	PRV VIL DES
PAHL, ANNA	21	F	SGL	RRZZZZUSA
K--OEREL, MASCHEL	18	F	SGL	RRZZZZUSA
PERE-HSON, MARIE	60	F	W	RRZZZZUSA
CHELMIENIEWICZ, JOSEPHA	40	F	W	RRZZZZUSA
ANTONIA	12	F	CH	RRZZZZUSA
JULIA	8	F	CHILD	RRZZZZUSA
PAULINE	6	F	CHILD	RRZZZZUSA
WLADISLAW	3	M	CHILD	RRZZZZUSA
GAGEROSKA, KATHARINA	22	F	W	RRZZZZUSA
HELENE	.11	F	INFANT	RRZZZZUSA
SONIEN, CHAIM	27	M	DLR	RRZZZZUSA
SCHILOW, ABRAHAM	45	M	TLR	RRZZZZUSA
FREIDE	35	F	W	RRZZZZUSA
MALKE	15	F	CH	RRZZZZUSA
CHAME	11	F	CH	RRZZZZUSA
DINA	5	F	CHILD	RRZZZZUSA
REINE	3	F	CHILD	RRZZZZUSA
ARON	1	M	CHILD	RRZZZZUSA

SHIP: PENNLAND

FROM: ANTWERP
TO: NEW YORK
ARRIVED: 01 NOVEMBER 1888

PASSENGER	AGE	SEX	OCCUPATION	PRV VIL DES
LINDSTROM, ERICK	21	M	TLR	RRZZZZNY

SHIP: WERRA

FROM: BREMEN AND SOUTHAMPTON
TO: NEW YORK
ARRIVED: 02 OCTOBER 1888

PASSENGER	AGE	SEX	OCCUPATION	PRV VIL DES
JANOTAJTIS, MAGDA.	22	F	NN	RRZZZZUSA
JANOS, KOVAL	26	M	LABR	RRZZZZUSA
GYORG, RYNYO	31	M	LABR	RRZZZZUSA
SMAISTZKI, BRAINE	23	F	W	RRZZZZUSA
SALOMON	.01	M	INFANT	RRZZZZUSA
LABODA, ISAAC	28	M	LABR	RRZZZZUSA
KISSIN, RAICHEL	35	M	LABR	RRZZZZUSA
SOPHIE	16	F	NN	RRZZZZUSA
ROSA	10	F	CH	RRZZZZUSA
WEICHERT, ANNA	23	F	NN	RRAHTKUSA
CHOROSINSKI, JOSA	28	F	W	RRZZZZUSA
PESA	6	F	CHILD	RRZZZZUSA
ISAAC	13	F	CH	RRZZZZUSA
REBECCA	17	F	NN	RRZZZZUSA
MEDOWNIK, ESTHER	43	M	FARMER	RRZZZZUSA
SCHEINE	23	F	W	RRZZZZUSA
SALOMON	.11	M	INFANT	RRZZZZUSA
GRUENBLAT, ROCHE	20	F	W	RRZZZZUSA
DORI	.06	F	INFANT	RRZZZZUSA
ZABINSKA, JOSEFA	26	F	NN	RRZZZZUSA
JAKUBOWSKA, REBECKA-Z.	20	F	NN	RRZZZZUSA
ROMALSKI, WACLAW	23	M	FARMER	RRZZZZUSA

SHIP: ROMAN

FROM: LIVERPOOL
TO: BOSTON
ARRIVED: 02 NOVEMBER 1888

PASSENGER	AGE	SEX	OCCUPATION	PRV VIL DES
GOERTNER, DAVID	15	M	LABR	RRZZZZUSA
LITWILL, ABRAM-L.	23	M	LABR	PLZZZZNY

PASSENGER	AGE	SEX	OCCUPATION	PV RIVL	DES
MIDMITZKY, HIRSCH	24	M	LABR	RRZZZZ	NY
GREEN, CHANE	23	M	LABR	PLZZZZ	NY
FUCHS, JACOB	20	M	LABR	PLZZZZ	NY
PARMET, ABRAM	18	M	LABR	PLZZZZ	NY
STRAYTER, S.	20	M	LABR	PLZZZZ	NY
LINBOZKY, CHAINE-B.	22	M	LABR	RRZZZZ	CH
SCHUFRA, SCAETNE	20	M	LABR	RRZZZZ	BO
LAISEROWITZ, SCHAYE	20	M	LABR	RRZZZZ	BO
WASSERMAN, RIWKE	33	F	W	RRZZZZ	BO
ESCHRAINE	10	F	CH	RRZZZZ	BO
ISSAC	7	F	CHILD	RRZZZZ	BO
FUGE	5	F	CHILD	RRZZZZ	BO
JACOB	3	M	CHILD	RRZZZZ	BO
BASSIE	.06	M	INFANT	RRZZZZ	BO
STUNIKE, BASCHE	16	M	LABR	RRZZZZ	BO
GOLDMAN, VICTOR	20	F	W	RRZZZZ	BO
PESSE	.04	F	INFANT	RRZZZZ	BO
NATHAN, LOUIS	23	M	LABR	RRZZZZ	NY
COHEN, ARON	19	M	LABR	RRZZZZ	NY
SEIGMAN, LEO	26	M	LABR	PLZZZZ	NY
SOLOMSON, HIRSCH	35	M	LABR	RRZZZZ	PHI
BRANDE, ETHEL	25	M	LABR	RRZZZZ	BO
SCHAPIRO, BERL	43	M	LABR	RRZZZZ	NY
BECKERSONB, H.	22	M	LABR	RRZZZZ	NY
MINNA	21	F	W	RRZZZZ	NY
COHEN, CHAS.	24	M	LABR	RRZZZZ	CH
ESTHER	4	F	CHILD	RRZZZZ	CH
MARIAN	2	F	CHILD	RRZZZZ	CH
SCH.	.05	F	INFANT	RRZZZZ	CH
BUSCH, HARRIS	36	M	LABR	PLZZZZ	NY
PHILIPPS, MOSES	32	M	LABR	PLZZZZ	NY

SHIP: SORRENTO

FROM: HAMBURG
TO: NEW YORK
ARRIVED: 02 NOVEMBER 1888

PASSENGER	AGE	SEX	OCCUPATION	PV RIVL	DES
CHOCHAMOWITZ, SALOMON	30	M	TLR	RRZZZZ	NY
KAPITOWSKY, ENTE	35	F	W	RRZZZZ	NY
SCHIME	7	F	CHILD	RRZZZZ	NY
JOSEF	6	M	CHILD	RRZZZZ	NY
LIEBE	5	F	CHILD	RRZZZZ	NY
MEYER	3	M	CHILD	RRZZZZ	NY
SELDE	.09	F	INFANT	RRZZZZ	NY
RASTATT, MARTIN	45	M	LABR	RRZZZZ	NY
ANNA	44	F	W	RRZZZZ	NY
BERTHA	2	F	CHILD	RRZZZZ	NY
BRONNER, SARA	45	F	WO	RRZZZZ	NY
HELENE	7	F	CHILD	RRZZZZ	NY
LEA	6	F	CHILD	RRZZZZ	NY
GORDON, TOMARE	35	F	WO	RRZZZZ	NY
JOSEF	7	M	CHILD	RRZZZZ	NY
HASCHE	6	F	CHILD	RRZZZZ	NY
ELKE	4	F	CHILD	RRZZZZ	NY
KOWALEWSKA, MARIANNE	30	F	WO	RRZZZZ	CH
SOSA	3	F	CHILD	RRZZZZ	CH
MARTHA	.06	F	INFANT	RRZZZZ	CH
WASKOWSKA, JOSEFA	17	F	SGL	RRZZZZ	NY
ROSENSOHN, HEYMAN	18	M	LABR	RRZZZZ	NY
PRUSKINSKY, MARCUS	20	M	LABR	RRZZZZ	NY
KURITZKY, ABRAM	25	M	LABR	RRZZZZ	NY
KUPILSKY, SCHIME	19	F	SGL	RRZZZZ	NY
SZIK, SARA	18	F	SGL	RRZZZZ	NY
KALIN, SENDER	30	M	LABR	RRZZZZ	NY
REINBERG, GITTEL	50	F	WO	RRZZZZ	NY
PALIWANSKY, JANKEL	20	M	LABR	RRZZZZ	NY
SUGALOWITZ, JOEL	25	M	LABR	RRZZZZ	NY
CHANNE	20	F	W	RRZZZZ	NY
LUZUKI, MORITZ	16	M	LABR	RRZZZZ	NY
KINKEL, NOSSEN	21	M	WCHMKR	RRZZZZ	NY
JUN, LINCKE	25	M	TLR	RRZZZZ	NY
MOEDE, MARTIN	65	M	LABR	RRZZZZ	NY
FREILACH, MORDCHE	38	M	LABR	RRZZZZ	NY
ROTTENBERG, HERSCH	25	M	LABR	RRZZZZ	NY
BUCKSPAN, NAFTALI	21	M	LABR	RRZZZZ	NY
SADONSKY, ANTON	21	M	GDNR	RRZZZZ	NY
PLANT, FEIGE	36	F	WO	RRZZZZ	NY
CHAWE	14	F	CH	RRZZZZ	NY
MICHAEL	7	M	CHILD	RRZZZZ	NY
JOSEF	6	M	CHILD	RRZZZZ	NY
CHAWE	6	F	CHILD	RRZZZZ	NY
SAMUEL	5	M	CHILD	RRZZZZ	NY
ISRAEL	4	M	CHILD	RRZZZZ	NY
GITTEL	.11	F	INFANT	RRZZZZ	NY
BEILE	.01	F	INFANT	RRZZZZ	NY
JAPBONSKA, ANNA	51	F	WO	RRZZZZ	NY
JACOB	22	M	S	RRZZZZ	NY
JOH.	7	M	CHILD	RRZZZZ	NY
SCHROEDER, HERMAN	27	M	LABR	RRZZZZ	NY
SKELTIS, FRANZISKUS	25	M	LABR	RRZZZZ	NY
GAROLIS, SZUMANTIS	26	M	LABR	RRZZZZ	NY
SILBER, ROSALIE	30	F	WO	RRZZZZ	NY
SAZKI, ANNA	36	F	WO	RRZZZZ	NY
CHAIM	7	M	CHILD	RRZZZZ	NY
CHANE	6	F	CHILD	RRZZZZ	NY
LEIB	5	M	CHILD	RRZZZZ	NY
BENZE	7	F	CHILD	RRZZZZ	NY
BRAUNGOLD, SCHMUL	30	M	MCHT	RRZZZZ	NY
LEGERZIK, JANKEL	35	M	MCHT	RRZZZZ	NY
ADAMI, ISAAC	49	M	LABR	RRZZZZ	NY
SARA	48	F	W	RRZZZZ	NY
MEYER	30	M	S	RRZZZZ	NY
GITTEL	18	F	D	RRZZZZ	NY
CHABE	16	F	D	RRZZZZ	NY
CHANNE	7	F	CHILD	RRZZZZ	NY
JOSEL	5	M	CHILD	RRZZZZ	NY
LEBEL	3	M	CHILD	RRZZZZ	NY
CHAIKE	.11	M	INFANT	RRZZZZ	NY
SEGALL, JESKA	16	F	SGL	RRZZZZ	NY
PIRAGOS, ROSALIE	38	F	WO	RRZZZZ	NY
JAN	18	M	UNKNOWN	RRZZZZ	NY
ANDRO	7	M	CHILD	RRZZZZ	NY
MICHAEL	6	M	CHILD	RRZZZZ	NY
ABERBUCH, BRAINE	40	F	WO	RRZZZZ	NY
HOPP, ADAM	21	M	LABR	RRZZZZ	NY
HUKMOSKI, LEIB	43	M	MCHT	RRZZZZ	NY
ROSA	24	F	W	RRZZZZ	NY
BARONSKY, CHANNE	18	F	SGL	RRZZZZ	NY
GOLDSTEIN, RACHEL	59	F	WO	RRZZZZ	NY
BERIL	61	M	LABR	RRZZZZ	NY
ABRAMOVIC, ROSA	19	F	SGL	RRZZZZ	NY
ISSERSOHN, DAVID	24	M	TCHR	RRZZZZ	NY
REPAZKY, MICHALY	30	M	HTR	RRZZZZ	NY

SHIP: CITY OF CHESTER

FROM: LIVERPOOL AND QUEENSTOWN
TO: NEW YORK
ARRIVED: 03 NOVEMBER 1888

PASSENGER	AGE	SEX	OCCUPATION	PV RIVL	DES
ADLER, PETER	30	M	LABR	RRAGRT	NY
SORZETZKI, NOCHEM	28	M	LABR	RRAGRT	NY
WERBER, WILL	26	M	LABR	RRAGRT	MA
SLY-ZAK, MEYER	35	M	TLR	RRAFWJ	NY
ROSENFELD, JOSEF	18	M	TLR	RRAFWJ	NY
GINZBURG, LEIB	39	M	LABR	RRAFWJ	NY
WEIN, ARSCHEI	35	M	LABR	RRAFWJ	NY
JECHIEL	18	M	LABR	RRAFWJ	NY
LACK, MOSES	16	M	LABR	RRAFWJ	NY

PASSENGER	AGE	SEX	OCCUPATION	PRV	VIL	DES
LENECHETZKY, NOACH	25	M	LABR	RRAF	WJ	NY
ANLAND, HERSCH	18	M	LABR	RRAF	WJ	NY
ISEWEL, BER.	20	M	LABR	RRAF	WJ	BAL
SCHEN, JOSSEL	21	M	LABR	RRAF	WJ	NY
FARMANN, L.	19	M	LABR	RRAF	WJ	NY
ACKERMANN, HELENA	18	F	SP	RRAF	WJ	NY
BORNETEIN, LEA	21	F	SP	RRAF	WJ	UNK
DISTALAT-, S.	45	M	LABR	RRAF	WJ	UNK
WEL-E	20	F	W	RRAF	WJ	UNK
GOLDBERG, MOSES	24	M	LABR	RRAF	WJ	UNK
ROSA	23	F	W	RRAF	WJ	UNK
DWORE	.08	M	INFANT	RRAF	WJ	UNK
LISCHINSKY, CHAJE	31	F	W	RRAF	WJ	ODE
ALBER	11	M	CH	RRAF	WJ	ODE
SORE	5	F	CHILD	RRAF	WJ	ODE
LIBE	.02	F	INFANT	RRAF	WJ	ODE

SHIP: ALLER

FROM: BREMEN AND SOUTHAMPTON
TO: NEW YORK
ARRIVED: 03 NOVEMBER 1888

PASSENGER	AGE	SEX	OCCUPATION	PRV	VIL	DES
SENDERS, ABRAH.SCHLOME	28	M	MCHT	RRZZ	ZZ	USA
GANTNER, CARL	17	M	LABR	RRZZ	ZZ	USA
SCHMALZ, LUDWIG	20	F	FARMER	RRZZ	ZZ	USA
BOCHMANN, GEORG	19	F	FARMER	RRZZ	ZZ	USA
SILBERNAGEL, JOSEPH	17	F	FARMER	RRZZ	ZZ	USA
BERJE, GUSTAV	18	M	FARMER	RRZZ	ZZ	USA
ULANTZKIS, JOSES	20	M	FARMER	RRZZ	ZZ	USA
KEPPLIN, MICH.	22	M	FARMER	RRZZ	ZZ	USA
MARKS, PEILE	26	M	FARMER	RRZZ	ZZ	USA
SENKERMANN, ISRAEL	31	M	FARMER	RRZZ	ZZ	USA
KLUDS, HEINR.	20	M	FARMER	RRZZ	ZZ	USA
LINDEMANN, PHILIPP	22	M	FARMER	RRZZ	ZZ	USA
WOLFSON, MARIE	16	F	UNKNOWN	RRZZ	ZZ	USA
LEWETS, HELENE	18	F	UNKNOWN	RRZZ	ZZ	USA
EVANCHO, ELLA	20	F	UNKNOWN	RRZZ	ZZ	USA
SABOL, MARIE	21	F	UNKNOWN	RRZZ	ZZ	USA
PETRILLOCK, MARY	22	F	UNKNOWN	RRZZ	ZZ	USA
BROSDR, JOHS.	31	M	LABR	RRZZ	ZZ	USA
FRZKA	22	F	W	RRZZ	ZZ	USA
JOHS.	.11	M	INFANT	RRZZ	ZZ	USA
SEITZ, JOHS.	26	M	LABR	RRZZ	ZZ	USA
MARGE.	25	F	W	RRZZ	ZZ	USA
MADLEN	.11	F	INFANT	RRZZ	ZZ	USA
MIKLER, JOHS.	29	M	LABR	RRZZ	ZZ	USA
MARIE	27	F	W	RRZZ	ZZ	USA
VALENTIN	2	M	CHILD	RRZZ	ZZ	USA
MARIANNA	.03	F	INFANT	RRZZ	ZZ	USA
SCHMALZ, SEBASTIAN	31	M	LABR	RRZZ	ZZ	USA
MADLENE	29	F	W	RRZZ	ZZ	USA
LEIER, JACOB	44	M	LABR	RRZZ	ZZ	USA
CATHE.	38	F	W	RRZZ	ZZ	USA
ED	7	M	CHILD	RRZZ	ZZ	USA
HEINR.	6	M	CHILD	RRZZ	ZZ	USA
MATHE.	5	F	CHILD	RRZZ	ZZ	USA
CHRISTE.	4	F	CHILD	RRZZ	ZZ	USA
HELENE	1	F	CHILD	RRZZ	ZZ	USA
HELD, MICHEL	68	M	FARMER	RRZZ	ZZ	USA
MARIANNA	60	F	W	RRZZ	ZZ	USA
LUCAS	20	M	FARMER	RRZZ	ZZ	USA
STEPHAN	18	M	FARMER	RRZZ	ZZ	USA
RIEDLINGER, PETER	23	M	LABR	RRZZ	ZZ	USA
ROSINE	23	F	W	RRZZ	ZZ	USA
MATHEUS	.11	M	INFANT	RRZZ	ZZ	USA
PFEIL, JOH.	54	M	LABR	RRZZ	ZZ	USA
CHRISTE.	46	F	W	RRZZ	ZZ	USA
MARIA	7	F	CHILD	RRZZ	ZZ	USA
FRIEDR.	20	M	LABR	RRZZ	ZZ	USA
JOH.	6	M	CHILD	RRZZ	ZZ	USA
HEINR.	4	M	CHILD	RRZZ	ZZ	USA
MANNE	.09	M	INFANT	RRZZ	ZZ	USA
MARGUARD, CHRIST.	26	M	LABR	RRZZ	ZZ	USA
ROSALIE	18	F	W	RRZZ	ZZ	USA
LUDWIG	.11	M	INFANT	RRZZ	ZZ	USA
RUDIRKA, JOSEF	50	M	LABR	RRZZ	ZZ	USA
JOSEF	7	M	CHILD	RRZZ	ZZ	USA
DOHN, CARL	35	M	FARMER	RRZZ	ZZ	USA
CAROLE.	34	F	W	RRZZ	ZZ	USA
WILHE.	7	M	CHILD	RRZZ	ZZ	USA
CHRIST.	4	M	CHILD	RRZZ	ZZ	USA
CARL	.06	M	INFANT	RRZZ	ZZ	USA
CAROLE.	6	F	CHILD	RRZZ	ZZ	USA
JACOBE.	2	F	CHILD	RRZZ	ZZ	USA
SCHRENK, JACOB	39	M	FARMER	RRZZ	ZZ	USA
FRIEDERKE.	35	F	W	RRZZ	ZZ	USA
JACOB	13	M	CH	RRZZ	ZZ	USA
CHRISTIAN	11	M	CH	RRZZ	ZZ	USA
EMANUEL	4	M	CHILD	RRZZ	ZZ	USA
KARL	3	M	CHILD	RRZZ	ZZ	USA
HEINR.	.06	M	INFANT	RRZZ	ZZ	USA
SOPHIE	14	F	UNKNOWN	RRZZ	ZZ	USA
MAGDAL.	7	F	CHILD	RRZZ	ZZ	USA
BREDSEL, CARL	30	M	FARMER	RRZZ	ZZ	USA
GERTRUD	23	F	W	RRZZ	ZZ	USA
JOH.	62	M	FARMER	RRZZ	ZZ	USA
CHRISTINE	57	M	W	RRZZ	ZZ	USA
PHILIPP	26	M	FARMER	RRZZ	ZZ	USA
CHRISTE.	23	F	D	RRZZ	ZZ	USA
CATHE.	16	F	D	RRZZ	ZZ	USA
JOHE.	16	F	D	RRZZ	ZZ	USA
ADAM	21	M	FARMER	RRZZ	ZZ	USA
GOTTL.	13	M	FARMER	RRZZ	ZZ	USA
MARGE.	27	F	D	RRZZ	ZZ	USA
KAHLENBERGER, JOSEPH	34	M	FARMER	RRZZ	ZZ	USA
ELIDABETH	34	F	W	RRZZ	ZZ	USA
JOH.	6	M	CHILD	RRZZ	ZZ	USA
CATHE.	2	F	CHILD	RRZZ	ZZ	USA
BARBARA	.06	F	INFANT	RRZZ	ZZ	USA
SELBERMANN, U	25	M	LABR	RRZZ	ZZ	USA
ROMANER, SAM.	34	M	LABR	RRZZ	ZZ	USA
FRIEDKE.	34	F	W	RRZZ	ZZ	USA
HUGO	7	M	CHILD	RRZZ	ZZ	USA
FANNY	6	F	CHILD	RRZZ	ZZ	USA
ABRAH.	4	M	CHILD	RRZZ	ZZ	USA
ANNA	.11	F	INFANT	RRZZ	ZZ	USA
BETTY	.02	F	INFANT	RRZZ	ZZ	USA
JAWSOHN, JOCHEL	16	M	UNKNOWN	RRZZ	ZZ	USA
BEER	11	M	UNKNOWN	RRZZ	ZZ	USA
MARKS, LEISER	4	M	CHILD	RRZZ	ZZ	USA
MAIER, PHILIPP	32	M	LABR	RRZZ	ZZ	USA
CATH.	30	F	W	RRZZ	ZZ	USA
JACOB	7	M	CHILD	RRZZ	ZZ	USA
CHRISTINE	3	F	CHILD	RRZZ	ZZ	USA
PHILIPP	.06	M	INFANT	RRZZ	ZZ	USA
PELWINSKIZ, FEYE	31	F	UNKNOWN	RRZZ	ZZ	USA
ZIWJA	8	F	CHILD	RRZZ	ZZ	USA
BRANE	6	M	CHILD	RRZZ	ZZ	USA
SENDERMANN, NORA	7	F	CHILD	RRZZ	ZZ	USA

SHIP: BOTHNIA

FROM: LIVERPOOL AND QUEENSTOWN
TO: NEW YORK
ARRIVED: 03 NOVEMBER 1888

PASSENGER	AGE	SEX	OCCUPATION	PRV	VIL	DES
ISENBERG, ABRAM	32	M	LABR	RRAF	WJ	USA
AFTENAS, PANKO	35	M	LABR	RRAF	WJ	USA
GLESER, BENZE	18	M	LABR	RRAF	VG	USA

PASSENGER	AGE	SEX	OCCUPATION	PRVIL	DES
JOFFE, MOSES	22	M	LABR	RRAFVG	USA
STANOLEWITZ, JOSEF	26	M	LABR	RRAEFL	USA
PETROWSKI, VIKTOR	23	M	LABR	RRAEFL	USA
GINTOWT, SIGISMUND	24	M	LABR	RRAEFL	USA
WIZANTSKI, SOLOMON	16	M	LABR	RRAEFL	USA
KAISER, PIOTO	22	M	LABR	RRAGRT	USA
JEMOLOSKY, MARTIN	23	M	LABR	RRAGRT	USA
KOTZEN, ISAAC	38	M	LABR	RRAFWJ	USA
SCHEFTELWITZ, MACHEN	48	M	LABR	RRAFWJ	USA
OSTER, ISAAC	60	M	LABR	RRAFWJ	USA
SACHO, ISRAEL	35	M	LABR	RRAEFL	USA
JACOBSON, ELIAS.	18	M	LABR	RRAEFL	USA
BERSEAN, LIERSE	30	M	LABR	RRAEFL	USA
BUHR, AUSCHEL	18	M	LABR	RRAEFL	USA
BLAUSTEIN, BOLTE	47	M	LABR	RRAEFL	USA
MASA, RIMER	22	M	LABR	RRAEFL	USA
SCHLANDER, ISRAEL	52	M	LABR	RRZZZZ	USA
BARNOK, SUSANNA	23	F	LABR	PLZZZZ	USA
CARLSON, ERIKA	20	F	LABR	FNZZZZ	USA
NEWMAN, CHAJE	17	F	LABR	RRZZZZ	USA
PERLBERG, FEIGE	16	F	LABR	RRZZZZ	USA
CREWITZ, ROSE	18	F	LABR	RRZZZZ	USA
MORENS, MENDEL	17	F	LABR	RRZZZZ	USA
GRUNGOWSKY, DEBORA	20	F	LABR	RRZZZZ	USA
BAREWITZ, FRADE	23	F	LABR	RRZZZZ	USA
LIPSCHITZ, PINCOS	30	M	LABR	RRZZZZ	USA
ETTA	23	F	W	RRZZZZ	USA

SHIP: RHAETIA

FROM: HAMBURG AND HAVRE
TO: NEW YORK
ARRIVED: 05 NOVEMBER 1888

PASSENGER	AGE	SEX	OCCUPATION	PRVIL	DES
NESWETZKI, LEA	20	F	SGL	RRZZZZ	USA
LOROFSKI, JOHN	25	M	LABR	RRZZZZ	USA
KARKLINSKY, GRUNE	30	F	WO	RRZZZZ	USA
REINE	4	F	CHILD	RRZZZZ	USA
SUSEL	.11	F	INFANT	RRZZZZ	USA
MARCINKICWIA, LEOKADIA	27	F	WO	RRZZZZ	USA
STEFAN	.11	M	INFANT	RRZZZZ	USA
WAHL, DOROTHEA	70	F	WO	RRZZZZ	USA
JANTZ, PETER	64	M	LABR	RRZZZZ	USA
MARIE	65	F	W	RRZZZZ	USA
BRZCZYNSKY, ARON	37	M	LABR	RRZZZZ	USA
DOBRES, CHAJE	17	F	SGL	RRZZZZ	USA
MATISEWICZ, SARA	26	F	WO	RRZZZZ	USA
FISCHEL	8	F	CHILD	RRZZZZ	USA
JOSSEL	.11	M	INFANT	RRZZZZ	USA
PRZEWORSKYH, FRANZ	19	M	LABR	RRZZZZ	USA
HURWITZ, EDDA	25	F	WO	RRZZZZ	USA
MOSES	2	M	CHILD	RRZZZZ	USA
KOLLNER, SELIG	23	M	LABR	RRZZZZ	USA
FINGEROWSKY, CHAJE	18	F	SGL	RRZZZZ	USA
WENZOLINSKI, RIWE	18	F	SGL	RRZZZZ	USA
APPELBAUM, WOLFF	18	M	TNR	RRZZZZ	USA
RAILSKY, NISSEN	26	M	GLSR	RRZZZZ	USA
SLAWENICZ, MARCILAWY	30	F	WO	RRZZZZ	USA
DEMBAT, JOH.	19	M	FARMER	RRZZZZ	USA
BASCHUCKEWICZ, JOSEF	21	M	JNR	RRZZZZ	USA
KELI, GOLDE	22	F	WO	RRZZZZ	USA
RIWE	.09	F	INFANT	RRZZZZ	USA
WASLENTZKY, MANNE	21	M	TLR	RRZZZZ	USA
KRASSUJANSKI, ISAAC	16	M	MCHT	RRZZZZ	USA
SIRR, FRANZ	39	M	FARMER	RRZZZZ	USA
HELENE	41	F	W	RRZZZZ	USA
MARIE	17	F	CH	RRZZZZ	USA
AGNEZKA	15	F	CH	RRZZZZ	USA
JOSEF	4	M	CHILD	RRZZZZ	USA
FRANZ	.09	M	INFANT	RRZZZZ	USA
ROSENBERG, PESSY	16	F	SGL	RRZZZZ	USA
ARBUS, CHAJE	34	F	WO	RRZZZZ	USA
TAUBE	4	F	CHILD	RRZZZZ	USA
BERL	3	M	CHILD	RRZZZZ	USA
MOSES	.11	M	INFANT	RRZZZZ	USA
ROSENKRAZ, MARJEM	50	F	WO	RRZZZZ	USA
SCHROEDER, MARIE	20	F	SGL	RRZZZZ	USA
KURAPKAT, EMILIA	17	F	SGL	RRZZZZ	USA
ZAX, ISAAC	20	M	LABR	RRZZZZ	USA
BEILE	20	F	W	RRZZZZ	USA
ABERSTEIN, BENJAMIN	38	M	LABR	RRZZZZ	USA
WELICSTEIN, ETKA	32	F	WO	RRZZZZ	USA
MEIER	6	M	CHILD	RRZZZZ	USA
HANNE	4	F	CHILD	RRZZZZ	USA
DUNKELMANN, LEA	32	F	WO	RRZZZZ	USA
HERSCH	3	M	CHILD	RRZZZZ	USA
LAUFER, JOSEF	22	M	TLR	RRZZZZ	USA
SYRYP, MOSES	28	M	TLR	RRZZZZ	USA
LEIBOW, JACOB	17	M	LABR	RRZZZZ	USA
SPIWAK, MOSES	18	M	LABR	RRZZZZ	USA
ROTHMANN, ROSA	21	F	SGL	RRZZZZ	USA
OWSZEWICZ, M.	35	M	LABR	RRZZZZ	USA
LOTTER, BERIL	36	M	LABR	RRZZZZ	USA
ESTER	34	F	W	RRZZZZ	USA
ESRAM	8	M	CHILD	RRZZZZ	USA
SCHEINDEL	5	F	CHILD	RRZZZZ	USA
ABRAM	4	M	CHILD	RRZZZZ	USA
CHANNE	.09	F	INFANT	RRZZZZ	USA
VOLK, JOSEF	53	M	FARMER	RRZZZZ	USA
MARGA	47	F	W	RRZZZZ	USA
FRANZ	19	M	CH	RRZZZZ	USA
SEBASTIAN	14	M	CH	RRZZZZ	USA
FRANCISCA	9	F	CHILD	RRZZZZ	USA
MAGDALENA	8	F	CHILD	RRZZZZ	USA
MARIE	4	F	CHILD	RRZZZZ	USA
DOSCH, WENDELIN	18	M	FARMER	RRZZZZ	USA
ELISABETH	22	F	SGL	RRZZZZ	USA
REGINA	19	F	SGL	RRZZZZ	USA
GOLDATA, JOHANES	27	M	FARMER	RRZZZZ	USA
MAGDA.	24	F	W	RRZZZZ	USA
ELISABETH	.09	F	INFANT	RRZZZZ	USA
THOMAS, THERESE	18	F	SGL	RRZZZZ	USA
GRUBER, JOSEF	60	M	FARMER	RRZZZZ	USA
JOSEF	33	M	FARMER	RRZZZZ	USA
ROSALIE	26	F	W	RRZZZZ	USA
MAGDLA.	3	F	CHILD	RRZZZZ	USA
EVA	2	F	CHILD	RRZZZZ	***
LUCKARTHA	.09	F	INFANT	RRZZZZ	USA
HENINGSOHN, HERSCH	50	M	LABR	RRZZZZ	USA
ADLER, CHANNE	17	F	SGL	RRZZZZ	USA
KILCKEWITZ, JOSES	22	M	FARMER	RRZZZZ	USA
KESSLER, ROCHUS	33	M	FARMER	RRZZZZ	USA
BREGITA	36	F	W	RRZZZZ	USA
FELIX	.09	M	INFANT	RRZZZZ	USA
AGNESIA	4	F	CHILD	RRZZZZ	USA
STEFAN	20	M	FARMER	RRZZZZ	USA
DOMINIK	17	M	FARMER	RRZZZZ	USA
WENDELIN	22	M	FARMER	RRZZZZ	USA
GRUENSTEINER, GABRIEL	56	M	LABR	RRZZZZ	USA
BARBA.	54	F	W	RRZZZZ	USA
ADAM	9	M	CHILD	RRZZZZ	USA
ANTON	4	M	CHILD	RRZZZZ	USA
ANNA	19	F	CH	RRZZZZ	USA
CATHA.	15	F	CH	RRZZZZ	USA
EVA	8	F	CHILD	RRZZZZ	USA
WARZEWSKI, ISIDOR	23	M	LABR	RRZZZZ	USA
BLUM, ETTE	38	F	WO	RRZZZZ	USA
IDA	9	F	CHILD	RRZZZZ	USA
MAJK	.11	M	INFANT	RRZZZZ	USA
RAHLE	.01	F	INFANT	RRZZZZ	USA
MEROWITSCH, GEMHAM	52	M	LABR	RRZZZZ	USA
ELLE	9	F	CHILD	RRZZZZ	USA
JOSSEL	8	M	CHILD	RRZZZZ	USA
PIETRIEWICZ, MICHAS	32	M	LABR	RRZZZZ	USA
GLASER, ITZIG	47	M	LABR	RRZZZZ	USA

PASSENGER	AGE	SEX	OCCUPATION	PRIVL	DES
RABYANSKY, JANKEL	33	M	LABR	RRZZZZ	USA
ZWICHLINSKY, WOJCIECH	20	M	LABR	RRZZZZ	USA
KADISKY, ABRAM	24	M	LABR	RRZZZZ	USA
KAHN, DAVID	27	M	LABR	RRZZZZ	USA
SEEF, ALEXANDER	30	M	LABR	RRZZZZ	USA
REBECCA	6	F	CHILD	RRZZZZ	USA
SCHELLENGOWSKI, SARAH	18	F	SGL	RRZZZZ	USA
GOOD, NOSSE	22	M	BCHR	RRZZZZ	USA
HOLDE	20	F	W	RRZZZZ	USA
FEIGE	.11	F	INFANT	RRZZZZ	USA
MONCIT, RAFAEL	38	M	MCHT	RRZZZZ	USA
ISAAC	9	M	CHILD	RRZZZZ	USA
KASCHTAU, CHAIE	17	F	SGL	RRZZZZ	USA
GADACHEWICZ, WOLF	30	M	MCHT	RRZZZZ	USA
KLORIN, CHANE	24	F	SGL	RRZZZZ	USA
GERBASS, ETTE	20	F	W	RRZZZZ	USA
CHANE	.09	F	INFANT	RRZZZZ	USA
ZANAT, ROBERT	21	M	LABR	RRZZZZ	USA
HAMMER, BEREK	34	M	LABR	RRZZZZ	USA
ULM, SYLVESTER	60	M	FARMER	RRZZZZ	USA
CATHA.	59	F	W	RRZZZZ	USA
MEYER, PETER	42	M	FARMER	RRZZZZ	USA
MARIA	39	F	W	RRZZZZ	USA
MICHAEL	5	M	CHILD	RRZZZZ	USA
MARIA	2	F	CHILD	RRZZZZ	USA
BARBA.	.06	F	INFANT	RRZZZZ	USA
REISS, ANTON	17	M	FARMER	RRZZZZ	USA
GRUENSTEINER, AD.	20	M	FARMER	RRZZZZ	USA

SHIP: EIDER

FROM: BREMEN AND SOUTHAMPTON
TO: NEW YORK
ARRIVED: 07 NOVEMBER 1888

PASSENGER	AGE	SEX	OCCUPATION	PRIVL	DES
LAUDSBERG, ISAAK	20	M	MCHT	RRZZZZ	USA
RUDNIK, PESCHE	23	F	NN	RRZZZZ	USA
RA-FF, MARIA	21	F	SMSTS	RRZZZZ	USA
NOLDE, HENRIETTE	66	F	NN	RRZZZZ	USA
MASCHULAST, MATH	48	M	FARMER	RRZZZZ	USA
LIPSKA, HASKIEL	52	M	LABR	RRZZZZ	USA
MENDEL	16	F	NN	RRZZZZ	USA
KROUN, ELIAS	17	M	LABR	RRZZZZ	USA
BERN	14	M	LABR	RRZZZZ	USA
EISENBERG, FEIGE	18	F	NN	RRZZZZ	USA
AUSCHKELSOHN, MALKE	20	F	NN	RRZZZZ	USA
SEHKOLNICK, GERSON	28	M	FARMER	RRZZZZ	USA
SCHENKMANN, ROSE	18	F	NN	RRZZZZ	USA
HLAPOSKA, ELZBETA	32	F	NN	RRZZZZ	USA
MICHE	6	F	CHILD	RRZZZZ	USA
STANISLAW	3	M	CHILD	RRZZZZ	USA
PETER	2	M	CHILD	RRZZZZ	USA
ZA--ISZEWSKA, ZOFIA	27	F	NN	RRZZZZ	USA
LATZLAWA	3	F	CHILD	RRZZZZ	USA
UTRECHT, MARYANNA	35	F	NN	RRZZZZ	USA
JACOB	11	M	CH	RRZZZZ	USA
FRANCISCA	8	F	CHILD	RRZZZZ	USA
TEKLA	5	F	CHILD	RRZZZZ	USA
ALEX	3	M	CHILD	RRZZZZ	USA
LOCADA	.11	F	INFANT	RRZZZZ	USA
ROSELLA	.11	F	INFANT	RRZZZZ	USA
BOKSER, HERSCH	20	M	MCHT	RRZZZZ	USA
CHAJEM	23	M	MCHT	RRZZZZ	USA
BLINDER, JANKEL	36	M	MCHT	RRZZZZ	USA
BRISMIK, S--JE	18	M	MCHT	RRZZZZ	USA
BAYER, WILH	32	M	LABR	RRZZZZ	USA
MARIA	26	F	W	RRZZZZ	USA
ANDRAS	5	M	CHILD	RRZZZZ	USA
CARL	3	M	CHILD	RRZZZZ	USA
BEYER, CATHARINE	.06	F	INFANT	RRZZZZ	USA

PASSENGER	AGE	SEX	OCCUPATION	PRIVL	DES
LINDE, JOHANN	37	M	FARMER	RRZZZZ	USA
ELISABETH	32	F	W	RRZZZZ	USA
ELISE	7	F	CHILD	RRZZZZ	USA
PHILIPP	5	M	CHILD	RRZZZZ	USA
JOHANNES	3	M	CHILD	RRZZZZ	USA
MICHAEL	.06	M	INFANT	RRZZZZ	USA
MICHAEL	57	M	FARMER	RRZZZZ	USA
ELISE	54	F	W	RRZZZZ	USA
PHILIPP	20	M	FARMER	RRZZZZ	USA
MARIA	19	F	NN	RRZZZZ	USA
MICHAEL	17	M	FARMER	RRZZZZ	USA
PETERS, CAROLINE	24	F	NN	RRZZZZ	USA
MARIA	2	F	CHILD	RRZZZZ	USA
INGODZKI, JOHANN	50	M	FARMER	RRZZZZ	USA
PAVOLIC, MICH	25	M	LABR	RRZZZZ	USA
BUERBALYAK, EVA	26	F	NN	RRZZZZ	USA

SHIP: CIRCASSIA

FROM: GLASGOW AND MOVILLE
TO: NEW YORK
ARRIVED: 07 NOVEMBER 1888

PASSENGER	AGE	SEX	OCCUPATION	PRIVL	DES
RASCHKMEL, WENDEL	19	M	LABR	RRAIDL	USA
KRUPER, CHANE	18	M	LABR	RRAIDL	USA
SCHUB, JACOB	21	M	DLR	RRAIDL	USA
JUSKINSKI, BORIS	34	M	LABR	RRAIDL	USA
JARABEK, JANOS	26	M	BTMKR	RRAIDL	USA
PAPESH, JACOB	20	M	LABR	RRAIDL	USA
ROCK, EISOG	45	M	DLR	RRAIDL	USA
NOOVAK, MATHEAS	20	M	LABR	RRAIDL	USA
HOSIE, ANTON	20	M	LABR	RRAIDL	USA
BLATNIK, ANTON	26	M	LABR	RRAIDL	USA
ISRAEL, WOLF	48	M	DLR	RRAIDL	USA
SCHEWELEWITZ, NORACH	20	M	DLR	RRAIDL	USA
KULENSKY, JOSEL	19	M	LABR	RRAIDL	USA
SLAKOSZAT, JOSEF	20	M	LABR	RRAIDL	USA
SALZSTEIN, WOLF	24	M	LABR	RRAIDL	USA
BLEICH, ADOLF	17	M	MCHT	RRAIDL	USA
ROSENTHAL, HERSCH	16	M	LABR	RRAIDL	USA
ERNESTINE	17	F	HP	RRAIDL	USA
SALASAS, ANTON	20	M	LABR	RRAIDL	USA
POKRANZ, ABRAHAM	40	M	DLR	RRAIDL	USA
MARJORM	40	F	W	RRAIDL	USA
MERCZA	15	F	UNKNOWN	RRAIDL	USA
TAUBE	16	F	UNKNOWN	RRAIDL	USA
LINA	8	F	CHILD	RRAIDL	USA
CHANKA	3	F	CHILD	RRAIDL	USA
PAPESCH, HELENE	20	F	HP	RRAIDL	USA
HAKUP, PAUL	21	M	LABR	RRAIDL	USA
MARIE	24	F	W	RRAIDL	USA
ANNA	.09	F	INFANT	RRAIDL	USA
ZIMMERMANN, MARTIN	34	M	LABR	RRAIDL	USA
MARGT.	30	F	W	RRAIDL	USA
JACOB	9	F	CHILD	RRAIDL	USA
PETER	5	M	CHILD	RRAIDL	USA
ELISABETH	.09	F	INFANT	RRAIDL	USA
KAHANOWOEZ, JACHKE	20	F	HP	RRAIDL	USA
RACHEL	18	F	HP	RRAIDL	USA
GUSTAFSDOTTER, EDLA	22	F	HP	RRAIDL	USA
PAPESCH, FRANZ	20	F	HP	RRAIDL	USA
OBERSTA, NEZE	29	F	HP	RRAIDL	USA
MARKOWITZ, JALYA	15	F	HP	RRAIDL	USA
FENKAS, EWA	18	F	HP	RRAIDL	USA
KAROWITZ, MESCHKA	19	F	HP	RRAIDL	USA
ROSENTHAL, LEA	17	F	HP	RRAIDL	USA

SHIP: AMERICA

FROM: BREMEN
TO: BALTIMORE
ARRIVED: 08 NOVEMBER 1888

PASSENGER	AGE	SEX	OCCUPATION	PRI VIL DES
KATZEN, MERE	24	F	NN	RRZZZZUNK
KAFITKIN, BEILE	24	F	NN	RRZZZZUNK
SCHNEIDER, CHANE	23	F	NN	RRZZZZUNK
BALSER, MOSES	20	M	MCHT	RRZZZZUNK
STEIN, LORE	50	F	NN	RRZZZZUNK
SCHULEN	11	M	CH	RRZZZZUNK
BAR	10	M	CH	RRZZZZUNK
EPHRAIM	8	M	CHILD	RRZZZZUNK
RACHEL	6	F	CHILD	RRZZZZUNK
BERMANN, DI--ENE	43	F	NN	RRZZZZUNK
SCHAUL	5	M	CHILD	RRZZZZUNK
SCHNEIDER, MA--SCHE	16	F	NN	RRZZZZUNK
SACHS, LEIBS	14	F	NN	RRZZZZUNK
WOSASKY, JACOB	23	M	GDNR	RRZZZZUNK
AARON, FOSSEL	16	M	NN	RRZZZZUNK
KLEIN, AUGUSTE	23	F	NN	RRZZZZUNK
GUSTAV	3	M	CHILD	RRZZZZUNK
GEORG	.09	M	INFANT	RRZZZZUNK
DOLBERT, DOROTHEA	40	F	CK	RRZZZZUNK
KAUFMANN, BE-G	28	M	FARMER	RRZZZZUNK
REZNITZKY, AMALIA	18	F	SVNT	RRZZZZUNK
ROSA	16	F	SVNT	RRZZZZUNK
ROSENTHAL, JACOB	19	M	FARMER	RRZZZZUNK
LEWENSOHN, LIEBE	26	F	NN	RRZZZZUNK
MINNA	7	F	CHILD	RRZZZZUNK
GERSOHN	6	M	CHILD	RRZZZZUNK
MARCUS	2	M	CHILD	RRZZZZUNK
ALTER	.05	M	INFANT	RRZZZZUNK
WASELNEK, JOHANN	23	M	FARMER	RRZZZZUNK
STEIN, SCHEINE	19	F	NN	RRZZZZUNK
SULEZEWSKI, ANTON	21	M	LABR	RRZZZZPA
WISNEWSKI, BALBINA	22	F	NN	RRZZZZPA
RYEZKOW, NICOLAUS	25	M	FARMER	RRZZZZMI
LORENZ, PHILIPP	23	M	JNR	RRZZZZCOL
MARGARETHE	26	F	NN	RRZZZZCOL
DANIEL	.09	M	INFANT	RRZZZZCOL
BRUCKNER, GEORG	23	M	BKR	RRZZZZMD
MOSER, CHRISTIAN	43	M	FARMER	RRZZZZCOL
BARBARA	40	F	NN	RRZZZZCOL
CATHARINA	21	F	NN	RRZZZZCOL
CHRISTIANNA	17	F	NN	RRZZZZCOL
CHRISTIAN	13	M	CH	RRZZZZCOL
ELISABETH	9	F	CHILD	RRZZZZCOL
BARBARA	7	F	CHILD	RRZZZZCOL
HEINRICH	4	M	CHILD	RRZZZZCOL
CAROLINE	2	F	CHILD	RRZZZZCOL
JACOB	2	M	CHILD	RRZZZZCOL
KRUMMING, REINHOLD	24	M	SHFM	RRZZZZWI
KLAWING, JOHANN	22	M	GDNR	RRZZZZWI
HERZEL, JACOB	35	M	FARMER	RRZZZZDAK
ROSINE	36	F	NN	RRZZZZDAK
MARGARETHE	11	F	CH	RRZZZZDAK
JACOB	9	M	CHILD	RRZZZZDAK
WILHELM	7	M	CHILD	RRZZZZDAK
HEINRICH	5	M	CHILD	RRZZZZDAK
ROSINE	3	F	CHILD	RRZZZZDAK
CATHARINE	.11	F	INFANT	RRZZZZDAK
MASER, JOHANN	27	M	LABR	RRZZZZNE
ELISABETH	26	F	NN	RRZZZZNE
ELISABETH	3	F	CHILD	RRZZZZNE
CARL	.01	M	INFANT	RRZZZZNE
OSTER, CHRISTIAN	51	M	FARMER	RRZZZZCOL
FREDRIKE	51	F	NN	RRZZZZCOL
JACOB	28	M	FARMER	RRZZZZCOL
CAROLINE	24	F	NN	RRZZZZCOL
CATHARINE	2	F	CHILD	RRZZZZCOL
JACOB	.08	M	INFANT	RRZZZZCOL
CHRISTIAN	24	M	FARMER	RRZZZZCOL
CATHARINA	23	F	NN	RRZZZZCOL
ELISABETH	.01	F	INFANT	RRZZZZCOL
FREDRIKE	19	F	NN	RRZZZZCOL
CHRISTINE	17	F	NN	RRZZZZCOL
JOHANN	13	M	NN	RRZZZZCOL
CATHERINE	2	F	CHILD	RRZZZZCOL
GUENTHER, ADAM	48	M	FARMER	RRZZZZCOL
CATHERINE	48	F	NN	RRZZZZCOL
JACOB	34	M	FARMER	RRZZZZCOL
JOHANN	22	M	FARMER	RRZZZZCOL
CHRISTIAN	17	M	FARMER	RRZZZZCOL
PHILIPP	15	M	NN	RRZZZZCOL
GUSTAV	11	M	CH	RRZZZZCOL
CATHERINE	20	F	NN	RRZZZZCOL
EVA	13	F	CH	RRZZZZCOL
LYDIA	3	F	CHILD	RRZZZZCOL
ELISABETH	.01	F	INFANT	RRZZZZCOL
BOLAENDER, CHRIST	51	M	FARMER	RRZZZZCOL
ANNA	37	F	NN	RRZZZZCOL
JACOB	19	M	FARMER	RRZZZZCOL
GUSTAV	15	M	NN	RRZZZZCOL
JOHANN	9	M	CHILD	RRZZZZCOL
AUGUST	7	M	CHILD	RRZZZZCOL
PHILIPP	6	M	CHILD	RRZZZZCOL
LOUISE	16	F	SVNT	RRZZZZCOL
DOROTHEA	6	F	CHILD	RRZZZZCOL
CHRISTINE	2	F	CHILD	RRZZZZCOL
SCHADIN, RIVEN	17	M	FARMER	RRZZZZUNK
HABEL, FEIGE	20	F	NN	RRZZZZUNK
PUDWINSKI, JOHANN	33	M	FARMER	RRZZZZUNK
WIEHARDT, AUGUST	29	M	FARMER	RRZZZZCOL
FRIERIKE	24	F	NN	RRZZZZCOL

SHIP: SAALE

FROM: BREMEN AND SOUTHAMPTON
TO: NEW YORK
ARRIVED: 10 NOVEMBER 1888

PASSENGER	AGE	SEX	OCCUPATION	PRI VIL DES
FOHSTROEM, ALMA	22	F	UNKNOWN	RRZZZZUSA
VANDAR, ELLA	20	F	UNKNOWN	RRZZZZUSA
TENENBAUM, SALOMEA	20	F	UNKNOWN	RRZZZZUSA
BOGOLEWSKY, ROSE	23	F	UNKNOWN	RRZZZZUSA
CHAJE	6	F	CHILD	RRZZZZUSA
ISRAEL	3	F	CHILD	RRZZZZUSA
KOZLOWSKI, ANTON	28	M	FARMER	RRZZZZUSA
SACHS, BERE	35	M	FARMER	RRZZZZUSA
JANKEL	30	M	FARMER	RRZZZZUSA
KAUR, JOSSEL	18	M	FARMER	RRZZZZUSA
MAJEWSKI, ANTON	28	M	FARMER	RRZZZZUSA

SHIP: BELGENLAND

FROM: ANTWERP
TO: NEW YORK
ARRIVED: 12 NOVEMBER 1888

PASSENGER	AGE	SEX	OCCUPATION	PRI VIL DES
BOLTIIMSKI, JANKEL	28	M	BBR	RRAIADNY
HINDE	27	F	UNKNOWN	RRAIADNY
SIESSENHOFF, DAVID	30	M	UNKNOWN	RRADBQNY
FANNY	23	F	UNKNOWN	RRADBQNY
ABRAHAM	2	M	CHILD	RRADBQNY
ESTHER	00	F	INF	RRADBQNY
TOMAK, RUD.	31	M	FRMKR	RRADBQNY
MECHIVEWITSCH, ISSAC	32	M	TLR	RRADBQNY

PASSENGER	AGE	SEX	OCCUPATION	PRV VIL DES
U	30	F	UNKNOWN	RRADBQNY
U	2	F	CHILD	RRADBQNY
LIFKOWITZ, DAVID	23	M	WCHMKR	RRADBQNY
MABZ, CH.	36	M	GLSCTR	RRADBQNY
GOLDENBERG, FANNY	23	F	TLR	RRADBQNY

SHIP: GELLERT

FROM: HAMBURG
TO: NEW YORK
ARRIVED: 12 NOVEMBER 1888

PASSENGER	AGE	SEX	OCCUPATION	PRV VIL DES
BERKOWITZ, HANNE	28	F	SGL	RRAHTDUSA
ERCKSDOTTER, OLGA	21	F	SGL	FNZZZZUSA
BASCH, MARCUS	56	M	LABR	FNZZZZUSA
MARIANNE	60	F	W	FNZZZZUSA
MUELLER, INDES	58	F	WO	FNAIMUUSA
PUSKELNY, CHAIE	58	F	WO	FNAHXLUSA
LUNEL, SOREN	17	M	MCHT	RRZZZZUSA
AAKJAAR, JENS	24	M	MCHT	RRZZZZUSA
JENNY, MARY	46	F	WO	RRZZZZUSA
SOERENSEN, DOROTHEA	60	F	WO	RRAIMUUSA
DETLEFSEN, MORITZ	19	M	FARMER	RRZZZZUSA
MANSKY, IDA	23	F	SGL	RRAIDYUSA
GREGOR, PAUL	31	M	MUSN	RRAIBNUSA
KIEWE, MARIE	22	F	SGL	RRZZZZUSA
GRABOWSKI, PAULA.	33	F	SGL	RRZZZZUSA
NEUENKIRCH, AUGUST	66	M	LABR	RRZZZZUSA
MARIE	60	F	W	RRZZZZUSA
MARIE	33	F	CH	RRZZZZUSA
ANNA	23	F	CH	RRZZZZUSA
ADAM, CARL	30	M	LABR	RRZZZZUSA
BASCH, BERTH	20	F	SGL	RRZZZZUSA
MIKULSKI, ANTON	20	M	LABR	RRZZZZUNK
GOREIKY, JOSEPH	23	M	LABR	RRZZZZUNK
KUHN, ADOLF	27	M	MCHT	RRABQBUNK
DOMBROWSKA, ROSALIA	20	F	WO	RRZZZZUNK
JOSEF	.03	M	INFANT	RRZZZZUNK
ZEFF, IDA	28	F	WO	RRAHWOUNK
PERICS	7	M	CHILD	RRAHWOUNK
LEIB	5	M	CHILD	RRAHWOUNK
GROSSMANN, FRANZ	37	M	PHRS	RRZZZZUNK
PASCHUR, HERZ	15	M	TNM	RRAGRTUNK
SCHMIDT, MOSES	21	M	LABR	RRZZZZUNK
FREEMANN, MARCUS	7	M	CHILD	RRZZZZUNK
KOPELOWIEZ, MOSES	20	M	LABR	RRAHTSUNK
GOLISZ, MANES	32	M	STDNT	RRZZZZUNK
ZOELEK, MATES	34	M	SHMK	RRAHTFUNK
ALTSCHULLER, PESCHE	39	F	WO	RRAHXLUNK
SLATE	18	F	CH	RRAHXLUNK
MOSES	16	F	CH	RRAHXLUNK
LEIB	7	F	CHILD	RRAHXLUNK
BLUMBERG, JOSNA	44	M	LABR	RRAGRTUNK
SIEDERSOHN, LEIB	18	M	LABR	RRAGRTUNK
CHAIE	20	F	SGL	RRAGRTUNK
BARTOLIS, JOSES	18	M	LABR	RRAHZSUNK
BRANDT, SAMUEL	32	M	LABR	RRZZZZUNK
ORNSTEIN, FEIGE	17	F	SGL	RRAIBOUNK
FLAKSMANN, MOTE	18	M	LABR	RRZZZZUNK
LEITELBAUM, JACOB	28	M	LABR	RRAHVUUNK
COHN, CH-S.	17	F	SGL	RRAHVUUNK
MIRMANN, SCHMUL	22	M	TLR	RRZZZZUNK
FRIEDA	20	F	W	RRZZZZUNK
BLECHMANN, JACOB	20	M	LABR	RRAIEKUNK
MENDELSOHN, BLUME	20	F	SGL	RRAIEKUNK
FLEISCHER, MOSES	24	M	LABR	RRAIEKUNK
GOLDBERG, MICHEL	21	M	TLR	RRAIHJUNK
SIDOWJANSKY, ITZIG	22	M	TLR	RRAIHJUNK
LEIB	38	M	TLR	RRAIHJUNK
KATZEN, REBECCA	20	F	SGL	RRAGRTUNK

PASSENGER	AGE	SEX	OCCUPATION	PRV VIL DES
DATEL, RACHMIEL	17	M	TLR	RRZZZZUNK
MIUSCHKES, ARON	26	M	LABR	RRAIBOUNK
PAROIN, EATE	53	F	WO	RRZZZZUNK
SOPHIE	23	F	CH	RRZZZZUNK
LASLOFFSKY, FANY	18	F	SGL	RRZZZZUNK
NEYETTE	16	F	SGL	RRZZZZUNK
NUNJE	16	M	LABR	RRZZZZUNK
LANDAU, NATHAN	40	M	LABR	RRAFWJUNK
COHN, CHAIE	30	F	WO	RRAHZSUNK
FEIGE	7	F	CHILD	RRAHZSUNK
WITKOWSKI, JAN	24	M	LABR	RRAHZSUNK
VAVICKY, MICHAEL	18	M	LABR	RRAHZSUNK

SHIP: CITY OF CHICAGO

FROM: LIVERPOOL AND QUEENSTOWN
TO: NEW YORK
ARRIVED: 12 NOVEMBER 1888

PASSENGER	AGE	SEX	OCCUPATION	PRV VIL DES
JOSEF, HENRICH	40	M	LABR	RRACBFNY
WILHELMINE	38	F	W	RRACBFNY
WILHELM	14	M	CH	RRACBFNY
KORE	12	M	CH	RRACBFNY
MAX	9	M	CHILD	RRACBFNY
LOUISA	8	F	CHILD	RRACBFNY
AUGUST	4	M	CHILD	RRACBFNY
WILHELMINE	6	F	CHILD	RRACBFNY
FRITT	4	M	CHILD	RRACBFNY
ANNA	2	F	CHILD	RRACBFNY
U	00	M	INF	RRACBFNY
ZERFNIKIEWICZ, ANNA	24	F	SVNT	RRACBFNY
STINGOVONSKA, HANKA	20	F	SVNT	RRACBFNY
SKAIRDRA, INALIA	50	F	W	RRACBFNY
SITILIA	11	F	CH	RRACBFNY
ISAAS	5	M	CHILD	RRACBFNY
DEUSEHEN, RIGINE	23	F	TCHR	RRACBFNY
GOLDSCHMIDT, LEIB	30	M	PDLR	RRACBFNY
EISENBERG, MAX	15	M	LABR	RRACBFNY
SUCHBERG, SCHENDEL	11	F	CH	RRACBFNY
LEWIN, MENDEL	17	F	SVNT	RRACBFNY
MENDEL	11	F	CH	RRACBFNY
HIRSCH	10	M	CH	RRACBFNY
BABAZNISKY, JOHANN	45	M	LABR	RRACBFWI
JUDWIGA	40	F	W	RRACBFWI
MICHOLAS	30	M	LABR	RRACBFWI
VINCENT	17	M	LABR	RRACBFWI
LUDWIG	10	M	CH	RRACBFWI
WAGTICH	6	M	CHILD	RRACBFWI
STANISLAWS	4	F	CHILD	RRACBFWI
BANAZINSKY, FRANZ	26	M	LABR	RRACBFWI
STANILAUS	22	F	W	RRACBFWI
JOSEF	00	M	INF	RRACBFWI
ABRAMOWIC, FISCHEL	35	M	TLR	RRACBFNY
JOSEBERVITZ, ABE	40	M	TLR	RRACBFNY
GERSCHEN, SARACH	19	F	SVNT	RRACBFNY
PERL	20	M	BRM	RRACBFNY
MARK, JANKEL	30	M	BKR	RRACBFNY
SCHMANS, SORE	18	F	SVNT	RRACBFNY
SCHER, HIRSCH	23	M	TLR	RRACBFNY
KRIGERSKAJA, SOFIA	19	F	TCHR	RRACBFNY
FRIEDMANN, CHAIE	29	F	W	RRACBFNY
ABRAM	00	M	INF	RRACBFNY
MANOWIC, BRONISLAVA	28	F	W	RRACBFNY
STAFANIE	00	F	INF	RRACBFNY
KOTIK, IVAN	23	M	LABR	RRACBFNY
ROYAK, JOSEF	32	M	LABR	RRACBFNY
GROSMANN, SOLDI	22	F	W	RRACBFNY
ROCHEL	2	F	CHILD	RRACBFNY
JIRKENTAUB, HIRSCH	27	M	PDLR	RRACBFNY
BLUMB, ABRAM	22	M	PDLR	RRACBFNY

PASSENGER	AGE	SEX	OCCUPATION	PRV	VIL	DES
SELIG	20	F	W	RR	AC	BFNY
ETTIE	20	M	LABR	RR	AC	BFNY
CHOW, CHASKE	22	M	LABR	RR	AC	BFNY
SIMCHE	60	M	LABR	RR	AC	BFNY
SILSBERSTEIN, SCHEME	40	F	W	RR	AC	BFNY
CHAIE	21	F	SVNT	RR	AC	BFNY
DOBE	10	F	CH	RR	AC	BFNY
GITTEL	9	M	CHILD	RR	AC	BFNY
ROSE	4	F	CHILD	RR	AC	BFNY
SCHEPSEL	00	M	INF	RR	AC	BFNY

SHIP: ALASKA

FROM: LIVERPOOL AND QUEENSTOWN
TO: NEW YORK
ARRIVED: 12 NOVEMBER 1888

PASSENGER	AGE	SEX	OCCUPATION	PRV	VIL	DES
HERSCHKAUDTZ, JEKLER	11	M	PDLR	RR	ZZ	ZUSA
MEKLER, LEIB	36	M	PDLR	RR	ZZ	ZUSA
WEISKOP, SCHEINDEL	28	F	MA	RR	ZZ	ZUSA
DAVID	10	M	CH	RR	ZZ	ZUSA
GRINBLUTT, SARA	39	F	MA	RR	ZZ	ZUSA
GESTENKERN, CHANE	16	F	SP	RR	ZZ	ZUSA
SOFIA, SITKO	34	M	LABR	RR	ZZ	ZUSA
IRIWETZ, LEIB	30	F	SP	RR	ZZ	ZUSA
SCHANDER, RUVE	19	F	SP	RR	ZZ	ZUSA
NEUBOF, MARCUS	50	M	LABR	RR	ZZ	ZUSA
SCHOSCHE	55	M	LABR	RR	ZZ	ZUSA
DOBKIN, CHAIE	19	F	SP	RR	ZZ	ZUSA
SILBERMAN, NECHAME	28	F	SP	RR	ZZ	ZUSA
GRINFIELD, ZELIK	18	M	LABR	RR	ZZ	ZUSA
KIRSCHENBAUM, REITIL	20	F	SP	RR	ZZ	ZUSA
BERNBAUM, BERKO	36	M	LABR	RR	ZZ	ZUSA
BERNER, MOSES	32	M	LABR	RR	ZZ	ZUSA
GOLDFARB, CHEINE	29	M	LABR	PL	ZZ	ZUSA
FRANKEL, BENJM.	30	M	TLR	RR	ZZ	ZUSA
SCHLOM, MEIER	18	M	TLR	RR	ZZ	ZUSA
CHALEF, LINA	50	F	MA	RR	ZZ	ZUSA
LACHER, RATZ	50	F	MA	PL	ZZ	ZUSA
MENDEL	11	M	CH	PL	ZZ	ZUSA
JACOB	8	M	CHILD	PL	ZZ	ZUSA
BAILA	7	M	CHILD	PL	ZZ	ZUSA
WILTZUSKY, ABRAM	18	M	LABR	PL	ZZ	ZUSA
HERMAN	15	M	LABR	PL	ZZ	ZUSA
ZODEKOW, SITFERFIN	18	M	PDLR	PL	ZZ	ZUSA
RABINOWIZ, RACHEL	20	F	SP	PL	ZZ	ZUSA
BRANSILBER, SCHOLEN	20	M	PDLR	PL	ZZ	ZUSA
ONIGER, LEOB	35	M	LABR	RR	ZZ	ZUSA
JUNDELIER, JOCHUL	19	M	LABR	PL	ZZ	ZUSA
BRUTKY, MENDEL	21	M	PDLR	PL	ZZ	ZUSA
LEIB	18	M	PDLR	PL	ZZ	ZUSA
GINYBURY, SARA	44	F	MA	PL	ZZ	ZUSA
DIZKULS, JAN	22	M	MRNR	RR	ZZ	ZUSA
SINGER, KREINE	7	M	CHILD	RR	ZZ	ZUSA
POTOSCHANSKY, MOSES	20	M	LABR	PL	ZZ	ZUSA
HABER, MIRDEL	17	F	SP	RR	ZZ	ZUSA
GINZBURG, HENE	18	F	SP	PL	ZZ	ZUSA
PESCHE	17	F	SP	PL	ZZ	ZUSA
SCHLOWA	15	F	SP	PL	ZZ	ZUSA
PESCHE	10	F	CH	PL	ZZ	ZUSA
MENDE	9	M	CHILD	PL	ZZ	ZUSA
KOWKA	3	M	CHILD	PL	ZZ	ZUSA
GOLD, BASCHE	18	F	SP	RR	ZZ	ZUSA
MOSCHKOWITZ, IDEL	26	M	LABR	RR	ZZ	ZUSA
SILBERMAN, FEIGE	3	F	CHILD	RR	ZZ	ZUSA
RACHEL	.07	F	INFANT	RR	ZZ	ZUSA
CHOLEF, CHATZKEL	10	F	CH	RR	ZZ	ZUSA
LIEBE	8	M	CHILD	RR	ZZ	ZUSA
JEK-, MIHUL	45	M	LABR	RR	ZZ	ZUSA
ZIEWATZ, CHAIE	3	F	CHILD	RR	ZZ	ZUSA

PASSENGER	AGE	SEX	OCCUPATION	PRV	VIL	DES
CHAIM	2	F	CHILD	RR	ZZ	ZUSA
GRINBLATT, GITEL	2	F	CHILD	RR	ZZ	ZUSA
FRUME	.11	F	INFANT	RR	ZZ	ZUSA

SHIP: SAALE

FROM: BREMEN AND SOUTHAMPTON
TO: NEW YORK
ARRIVED: 13 OCTOBER 1888

PASSENGER	AGE	SEX	OCCUPATION	PRV	VIL	DES
FRIEDLUNSKI, BARUCH	20	M	FARMER	RR	ZZ	ZUSA
BEILE	23	F	W	RR	ZZ	ZUSA
ROSA	.11	F	INFANT	RR	ZZ	ZUSA
BACZUNAS, JAN	35	M	FARMER	RR	ZZ	ZUSA
ROSALIE	24	F	W	RR	ZZ	ZUSA
BRONISLAW	3	M	CHILD	RR	ZZ	ZUSA
JOHNE.	.11	F	INFANT	RR	ZZ	ZUSA
TINGARTEN, RIVKE	20	F	NN	RR	ZZ	ZUSA
ROSA	.09	F	INFANT	RR	ZZ	ZUSA
SCHOR, ABRAHAM	26	M	FARMER	RR	ZZ	ZUSA
STRASBURG, LURE	60	M	FARMER	RR	ZZ	ZUSA
ADAM, BERNICKI	26	M	FARMER	RR	ZZ	ZUSA
GEORGE, LATT	30	M	FARMER	RR	ZZ	ZUSA
PEL, HENRIETTE	25	F	NN	RR	ZZ	ZUSA
OTTILIE	3	F	CHILD	RR	ZZ	ZUSA
AUGUST	.11	M	INFANT	RR	ZZ	ZUSA
COLISH, MARIA	26	F	NN	RR	ZZ	ZUSA
ANDREW	7	M	CHILD	RR	ZZ	ZUSA
PETER	4	M	CHILD	RR	ZZ	ZUSA
HERMANN	.10	M	INFANT	RR	ZZ	ZUSA
ASKANAS, HANNA	24	F	INF	RR	ZZ	ZUSA
ADELINA	6	F	CHILD	RR	ZZ	ZUSA
REBECCA	5	F	CHILD	RR	ZZ	ZUSA
JACOB	3	M	CHILD	RR	ZZ	ZUSA
SONNENSCHEIN, CARL	28	M	FARMER	RR	ZZ	ZUSA
HOLZHEIMER, JOH.	26	M	FARMER	RR	ZZ	ZUSA

SHIP: FULDA

FROM: BREMEN AND SOUTHAMPTON
TO: NEW YORK
ARRIVED: 14 NOVEMBER 1888

PASSENGER	AGE	SEX	OCCUPATION	PRV	VIL	DES
FINKEL, RACHEL	22	F	UNKNOWN	RR	AH	QDVA
PAVIAN, NEIBA	21	F	UNKNOWN	RR	AH	OONY
COHN, ABRAHAM	39	M	DLR	RR	AH	OONY
SALOMON	12	M	CH	RR	AH	OONY
SAHRA	18	F	CH	RR	AH	OONY
KARASCHEK, MAX	23	M	LABR	RR	AH	OONY
SCHOENBECK, FRIEDR.	31	M	FARMER	RR	AH	OOMN
CAROLINE	26	F	W	RR	AH	OOMN
LIESBETH	4	F	CHILD	RR	AH	OOMN
WILHELMINE	.01	F	INFANT	RR	AH	OOMN
WYSIENWICZ, DOMINIK	26	M	FARMER	RR	AH	OOPA
MUELLER, LEIE	17	M	TILM	RR	AH	OONY
KOBRINSKY, ANNA	23	F	W	RR	AH	OONY
MARIE	7	F	CHILD	RR	AH	OONY
SCHLOME	4	F	CHILD	RR	AH	OONY
CHAJE	1	F	CHILD	RR	AH	OONY
RAJGORODECKA, CILIA	20	F	UNKNOWN	RR	AH	OONY
SZPUKOWSKA, MARYANNA	22	F	W	RR	AH	OONY
MARYANNA	.09	F	INFANT	RR	AH	OONY
WESOLOFSKY, SIMON	20	M	LABR	RR	AH	OONY
ROSLOWITZ, JONAS	25	M	SHMK	RR	AH	ZSPA
SORTSKI, KOSES	25	M	LABR	RR	AH	ZSPA

PASSENGER	AGE	SEX	OCCUPATION	PRI	VIL	DES
MEIEZSIK, KEILE	28	M	LABR	RR	AHVZ	NY
ISAAK	5	M	CHILD	RR	AHVZ	NY
BENJAMIN	3	M	CHILD	RR	AHVZ	NY
ROSA	.06	F	INFANT	RR	AHVZ	NY

SHIP: MAIN

FROM: BREMEN
TO: BALTIMORE
ARRIVED: 15 NOVEMBER 1888

PASSENGER	AGE	SEX	OCCUPATION	PRI	VIL	DES
PIETRAS, ANNA	27	F	W	RR	ZZZZ	BAL
JOHANN	6	M	CHILD	RR	ZZZZ	BAL
VICTORIA	3	F	CHILD	RR	ZZZZ	BAL
SALZMANN, JUDE	17	F	SVNT	RR	ZZZZ	BAL
KINSBRUNN, SARA	22	F	SVNT	RR	ZZZZ	BAL
DINOWITZ, FEIGE	45	F	W	RR	ZZZZ	BAL
BARNHARD	11	M	CH	RR	ZZZZ	BAL
SCHEINE	4	F	CHILD	RR	ZZZZ	BAL
MOKATOW, SIRSCHA	21	F	SVNT	RR	ZZZZ	BAL
GREMBLET, BEILE	40	F	W	RR	ZZZZ	BAL
RIFLKE	18	F	D	RR	ZZZZ	BAL
BREINE	15	F	D	RR	ZZZZ	BAL
BASKE	12	M	CH	RR	ZZZZ	BAL
NIZKE	9	F	CHILD	RR	ZZZZ	BAL
HAIM	7	M	CHILD	RR	ZZZZ	BAL
RACHEL	5	F	CHILD	RR	ZZZZ	BAL
ISAAC	3	M	CHILD	RR	ZZZZ	BAL
MERKE	2	F	CHILD	RR	ZZZZ	BAL
KARP, SARAH	20	F	SVNT	RR	ZZZZ	BAL
GORSCHOWSKA, SOSIE	47	F	W	RR	ZZZZ	BAL
MARIA	15	F	D	RR	ZZZZ	BAL
MOSES	11	M	CH	RR	ZZZZ	BAL
SCHLOME	9	M	CHILD	RR	ZZZZ	BAL
BURRIS	7	M	CHILD	RR	ZZZZ	BAL
SCHAIM	5	M	CHILD	RR	ZZZZ	BAL
KLAEFF, CHAINE	18	F	SVNT	RR	ZZZZ	BAL
SANDER, ANTON	42	M	MLR	RR	ZZZZ	KS
DOROTHEA	42	F	W	RR	ZZZZ	KS
ANTON	5	M	CHILD	RR	ZZZZ	KS
JOHANNES	.11	M	INFANT	RR	ZZZZ	KS

SHIP: FURNESSIA

FROM: GLASGOW AND MOVILLE
TO: NEW YORK
ARRIVED: 15 NOVEMBER 1888

PASSENGER	AGE	SEX	OCCUPATION	PRI	VIL	DES
AJENLIS, JOSEF	25	M	LABR	RR	ZZZZ	USA
BRODNOZKI, PENKUS	18	M	LABR	RR	ZZZZ	USA
BUTRUNOVIZ, THOMAS	18	M	LABR	RR	ZZZZ	USA
CHMILEWSKY, JOSEPH	20	M	LABR	RR	ZZZZ	USA
EPSTEIN, CHAIM	19	M	LABR	RR	ZZZZ	USA
GRAJEWSKY, HANISLAW	21	M	LABR	RR	ZZZZ	USA
KER--R, LESER	17	M	NN	RR	ZZZZ	USA
HERSCH	10	M	NN	RR	ZZZZ	USA
KWAK, JAN	26	M	LABR	RR	ZZZZ	USA
LEWIN, ABRAHAM	20	M	LABR	RR	ZZZZ	USA
MASLOWATI, JONAS	48	M	LABR	RR	ZZZZ	USA
METH, HERMAN	18	M	LABR	RR	ZZZZ	USA
RAHUSE, WLADIMIR	20	M	LABR	RR	ZZZZ	USA
ROSENKOWITZ, RAFAEL	24	M	LABR	RR	ZZZZ	USA
RAHTRSKEIN, MONSCHE	17	M	LABR	RR	ZZZZ	USA
SCHELITZKI, LEIB	25	M	LABR	RR	ZZZZ	USA
TRAKUNOWITZ, MICHAEL	24	M	LABR	RR	ZZZZ	USA
ZEZULKA, JOSEF	18	M	LABR	RR	ZZZZ	USA
JEDZURKA, MARIANNA	11	F	NN	RR	ZZZZ	USA
PELIAN	8	M	CHILD	RR	ZZZZ	USA
KAGELIZKA, PELAZIA	35	F	CH	RR	ZZZZ	USA
KO--, BERTHA	18	F	DMS	RR	ZZZZ	USA
TUZIER, CHAJE	50	F	NN	RR	ZZZZ	USA
ORONSKY, PESCHE	30	F	NN	RR	ZZZZ	USA
CHAIM	7	M	CHILD	RR	ZZZZ	USA
JEAH.	1	M	CHILD	RR	ZZZZ	USA
ZIJSKIN, LEIB.	17	M	DMS	RR	ZZZZ	USA
KORZENSKIEL, DAVID	36	M	TLR	RR	ZZZZ	USA
MELKA	24	F	NN	RR	ZZZZ	USA
KATZENELLBOGIN, SCHOME	20	M	TLR	RR	ZZZZ	USA
ABRAMOWSKY, SARAH	20	M	TLR	RR	ZZZZ	USA
LUBOWSKI, MICHAEL	19	M	NN	RR	ZZZZ	USA
KOLTINSKA, THERESIA	53	F	NN	RR	ZZZZ	USA
MINNA	22	F	NN	RR	ZZZZ	USA
JEHTE	11	F	CH	RR	ZZZZ	USA
LOWENSTEIN, CHAIM	32	M	TLR	RR	ZZZZ	USA
GOLDE	20	F	NN	RR	ZZZZ	USA
JACOB	8	M	CHILD	RR	ZZZZ	USA
CHAJE	3	F	CHILD	RR	ZZZZ	USA
ADLERSTEIN, MINDEL	17	F	DMS	RR	ZZZZ	USA
ANBRAHAM	11	M	CH	RR	ZZZZ	USA
ARANOWIZ, MOSCHE	52	M	LABR	RR	ZZZZ	USA
KORN, SCHINE	30	F	NN	RR	ZZZZ	USA
SCHMUL	3	M	CHILD	RR	ZZZZ	USA
JOSEF	2	M	CHILD	RR	ZZZZ	USA
SACH, LEVIE	19	F	DMS	RR	ZZZZ	USA
ROSEMAN, LEIE	35	F	NN	RR	ZZZZ	USA
CHAJE	16	F	NN	RR	ZZZZ	USA
SA-S-	12	F	NN	RR	ZZZZ	USA
GOLDE	10	F	NN	RR	ZZZZ	USA
SCHMUEL	6	M	CHILD	RR	ZZZZ	USA
SEILE	1	F	CHILD	RR	ZZZZ	USA
SCHLOME	3	F	CHILD	RR	ZZZZ	USA
KOZLECKO, LUDWIE	.06	M	INFANT	RR	ZZZZ	USA
STANISLAW	.06	M	INFANT	RR	ZZZZ	USA

SHIP: LEERDAM

FROM: ROTTERDAM
TO: NEW YORK
ARRIVED: 16 NOVEMBER 1888

PASSENGER	AGE	SEX	OCCUPATION	PRI	VIL	DES
MUSIKANT, NOACH.	20	M	LABR	RR	ZZZZ	USA
CHAIE	21	F	UNKNOWN	RR	ZZZZ	USA
U, FR.	00	F	UNKNOWN	RR	ZZZZ	USA
GRUNBERG, SCHULI	18	F	UNKNOWN	PL	ZZZZ	USA
GHUWKO, ABRAH.	19	F	UNKNOWN	PL	ZZZZ	USA
SETCHANEK, HARRE	19	F	UNKNOWN	PL	ZZZZ	USA
MUSHOWITZ, JONK.GITZEL	29	M	BKR	RR	ZZZZ	USA
ROSENBLATT, JETCHIM	24	M	DLR	RR	ZZZZ	USA
BERNSTEIN, WOLF	50	M	BKR	RR	ZZZZ	USA
MIKSIA, LEWOY	32	M	LABR	RR	ZZZZ	USA
LAPEI, ULSEN	17	M	LABR	RR	ZZZZ	USA
BERNSTEIN, ISRAEL	18	M	UNKNOWN	RR	ZZZZ	USA
GELBERG, MOSES	24	M	UNKNOWN	RR	ZZZZ	USA
LABOWITZ, IDA	22	F	UNKNOWN	RR	ZZZZ	USA
DAMLA, JOAN	24	M	DLR	PL	ZZZZ	USA
PAWLAK, ANDRI	24	M	DLR	PL	ZZZZ	USA

PASSENGER	AGE	SEX	OCCUPATION	PRV	VIL	DES

SHIP: DONAU

FROM: BREMEN
TO: BALTIMORE
ARRIVED: 17 NOVEMBER 1888

PASSENGER	AGE	SEX	OCCUPATION	PRV	VIL	DES
ANCHSCHUM, U	20	M	UNKNOWN	RR	ZZZZ	MD
QUILIAM, KATHERINA	21	F	UNKNOWN	RR	ZZZZ	MD
WITKOWICZ, JOSEPH	23	M	LABR	RR	ZZZZ	UNK
NEUMANN, GOTTLIEB	40	M	FARMER	RR	ZZZZ	UNK
ALBERTINE	30	F	UNKNOWN	RR	ZZZZ	UNK
ELIDIA	11	F	CH	RR	ZZZZ	UNK
ADOLF	7	M	CHILD	RR	ZZZZ	UNK
ERNESTINE	3	F	CHILD	RR	ZZZZ	UNK
GUSTAV	2	M	CHILD	RR	ZZZZ	UNK
EMILIE	.05	F	INFANT	RR	ZZZZ	UNK
ZELENIAK, VINCENTY	63	M	LABR	RR	ZZZZ	MD
MARYANNE	55	F	UNKNOWN	RR	ZZZZ	MD
FRIEDMANN, HERMANN	21	M	FARMER	RR	ZZZZ	MD
ZAKRZEWSKA, JULIA	21	F	UNKNOWN	RR	ZZZZ	MD
ANNA	.06	F	INFANT	RR	ZZZZ	MD
BURDIN, ADOLF	43	M	CPTR	RR	ZZZZ	MD
LOUISE	37	F	UNKNOWN	RR	ZZZZ	MD
ALEXANDER	19	M	UNKNOWN	RR	ZZZZ	MD
JOHAN	14	M	UNKNOWN	RR	ZZZZ	MD
EMILIE	5	F	CHILD	RR	ZZZZ	MD
FREUND, STANISL.	24	M	JNR	RR	ZZZZ	MD
WISCOCKI, FRANZISZEK	35	M	TNM	RR	ZZZZ	MD
GUTOWSKI, JAN	23	M	LABR	RR	ZZZZ	MD
DERRATH, MINNA	28	F	UNKNOWN	RR	ZZZZ	MD
STACK, JOSEPH	40	M	LABR	RR	ZZZZ	MD

SHIP: IOWA

FROM: LIVERPOOL
TO: BOSTON
ARRIVED: 17 NOVEMBER 1888

PASSENGER	AGE	SEX	OCCUPATION	PRV	VIL	DES
BERMAN, MEYER	32	M	WCHMKR	RR	ZZZZ	USA
MERKS, JACOB	22	M	TLR	RR	ZZZZ	USA
DABOVITZ, GES.	23	M	LABR	RR	ZZZZ	USA
WILK, GEORGE	33	M	LABR	RR	ZZZZ	USA
DIEMAN, SOLOMAN	23	M	GZR	RR	ZZZZ	USA
NABIN, SIMON	32	M	LABR	RR	ZZZZ	USA
ARPINN, JULIUS	19	M	PRNTR	RR	ZZZZ	USA
PUPYIN, M.	28	M	BKR	RR	ZZZZ	USA
MALLINSK-, M.	20	M	BKR	RR	ZZZZ	USA
BURSCHKIN, ABM.	29	M	WCHMKR	RR	ZZZZ	USA
SCHNIEDER, GEO	24	M	WCHMKR	RR	ZZZZ	USA
SKENRIL, JOS.	25	M	FARMER	RR	ZZZZ	USA
AMLOS-, F.	24	M	FARMER	RR	ZZZZ	USA
STER--NG, IWAC	16	M	SCH	RR	ZZZZ	USA
GUTZ, FANNY	45	F	SP	RR	ZZZZ	USA
STERING, LEONH.	36	F	W	RR	ZZZZ	USA
GOLD, BETSY	24	F	W	RR	ZZZZ	USA
HERMAN, MARKO	38	M	TLR	RR	ZZZZ	USA
PAULINE	22	F	W	RR	ZZZZ	USA
SOLOTONENJON, M.	25	F	W	RR	ZZZZ	USA
SIMON, ABRAHAM	23	M	PRSR	RR	ZZZZ	USA
TILLEY	23	F	W	RR	ZZZZ	USA
JONES, HENRY	32	M	MNR	RR	ZZZZ	USA
SARAH	25	M	MNR	RR	ZZZZ	USA
SCHASHEN, JACOB	3	M	CHILD	RR	ZZZZ	USA
AUGUSTA	.10	M	INFANT	RR	ZZZZ	USA
GOLA, BELLA	2	F	CHILD	RR	ZZZZ	USA
MEYER	1	M	CHILD	RR	ZZZZ	USA
SARAH	3	F	CHILD	RR	ZZZZ	USA
HERMAN, BENARD	.07	M	INFANT	RR	ZZZZ	USA
GOLDOTOYRON, MOS.	6	M	CHILD	RR	ZZZZ	USA
JAS.	5	M	CHILD	RR	ZZZZ	USA
ORILLA	3	F	CHILD	RR	ZZZZ	USA
ABR.	2	F	CHILD	RR	ZZZZ	USA
MAYA	1	M	CHILD	RR	ZZZZ	USA
LEIB	.03	M	INFANT	RR	ZZZZ	USA
BLECHNER, SALIA	.03	M	INFANT	RR	ZZZZ	USA
HERM.	.01	M	INFANT	RR	ZZZZ	USA

SHIP: RHYNLAND

FROM: ANTWERP
TO: NEW YORK
ARRIVED: 19 NOVEMBER 1888

PASSENGER	AGE	SEX	OCCUPATION	PRV	VIL	DES
CAPELEWIEZ, ISAAC	24	M	LABR	RR	ZZZZ	NY
STRAS, REBECCA	22	F	FSHMN	RR	ZZZZ	NY
SAND, DAVID	18	M	LABR	RR	ZZZZ	NY
ELA	17	F	W	RR	ZZZZ	NY
AMELIEN, MICHEL	25	M	LABR	RR	ZZZZ	NY
INNDREES, NICOLAI	40	M	LABR	RR	ZZZZ	NY
KASAWITZ, ANTONI	25	M	LABR	RR	ZZZZ	NY

SHIP: ST.OF PENNSYLVANIA

FROM: GLASGOW AND LARNE
TO: NEW YORK
ARRIVED: 19 NOVEMBER 1888

PASSENGER	AGE	SEX	OCCUPATION	PRV	VIL	DES
WAIN, ISRAEL	17	M	MNFTR	RR	ZZZZ	USA
STEINBACH, ALBERT	19	M	PNTR	RR	ZZZZ	USA
GOLLOBOCK, LEIBER	20	M	SHMK	RR	ZZZZ	USA
SUPOWITZ, SCHMUL	22	M	LABR	RR	ZZZZ	USA
SUHAN, FECKO	23	M	LABR	RR	ZZZZ	USA
GELERUTER, ABRAHAM	25	M	LABR	RR	ZZZZ	USA
EVA	24	F	W	RR	ZZZZ	USA
HERMANN	.11	M	INFANT	RR	ZZZZ	USA
PINKUS, FEWUSCH	44	M	PDLR	RR	ZZZZ	USA
ENDE	40	F	W	RR	ZZZZ	USA
LEA	15	F	SP	RR	ZZZZ	USA
LOB.	10	M	CH	RR	ZZZZ	USA
SCHEINDEL	9	F	CHILD	RR	ZZZZ	USA
NOACK	8	M	CHILD	RR	ZZZZ	USA
GOLDE	5	F	CHILD	RR	ZZZZ	USA
CHUNE	3	M	CHILD	RR	ZZZZ	USA

SHIP: TRAVE

FROM: BREMEN
TO: NEW YORK
ARRIVED: 20 NOVEMBER 1888

PASSENGER	AGE	SEX	OCCUPATION	PRV	VIL	DES
KASZOSKA, FELDEDA	24	F	UNKNOWN	RR	ZZZZ	RSS
GRUETZHAENDLER, SIGMD.	26	M	MCHT	RR	ZZZZ	RSS
ENGALITCHEFF, FRIOTIN	40	F	UNKNOWN	RR	ZZZZ	RSS
MAEKLEN, H.	24	M	UNKNOWN	RR	ZZZZ	RSS
SEGAL, FANNY	25	F	UNKNOWN	RR	ZZZZ	RSS
ANNA	6	F	CHILD	RR	ZZZZ	RSS
HIRSCH	5	M	CHILD	RR	ZZZZ	RSS
AUSENBERG, MALKE	30	F	UNKNOWN	RR	ZZZZ	RSS
LOUIS	7	M	CHILD	RR	ZZZZ	RSS

PASSENGER	AGE	SEX	OCCUPATION	PRV VIL DES
JACOB	6	M	CHILD	RRZZZZRSS
DAVID	.01	M	INFANT	RRZZZZRSS
FAEGER, JANETA	24	F	UNKNOWN	RRZZZZUSA
MAX	3	M	CHILD	RRZZZZUSA
PARCOVICIE, CECILIA	18	F	UNKNOWN	RRZZZZUSA
CODIK, LINA	18	F	UNKNOWN	RRZZZZUSA
SCHAUER, MATHE.	28	F	UNKNOWN	RRZZZZUSA
FRIEBERG, JOH.	22	M	FARMER	RRZZZZUSA
BAUM, CLARA	20	F	UNKNOWN	RRZZZZUSA
ELIZUR, ISRAEL	17	M	LABR	RRZZZZUSA
PILLER, CES.GEORG	65	M	LABR	RRZZZZUSA
HELENE	35	F	UNKNOWN	RRZZZZUSA
JAC.	15	M	LABR	RRZZZZUSA
GEORG	4	M	CHILD	RRZZZZUSA
CARL	6	M	CHILD	RRZZZZUSA
MARIE	2	F	CHILD	RRZZZZUSA
JOH.	1	M	CHILD	RRZZZZUSA
STEIN, JOH.	28	M	LABR	RRZZZZUSA
CATHA.	30	F	UNKNOWN	RRZZZZUSA
PETER	5	M	CHILD	RRZZZZUSA
MARIE	3	F	CHILD	RRZZZZUSA
PHILIPP	1	M	CHILD	RRZZZZUSA
CAROLE.	.02	F	INFANT	RRZZZZUSA
HARDE	35	F	UNKNOWN	RRZZZZUSA
MARGE.	69	F	UNKNOWN	RRZZZZUSA
ANDR.	14	M	LABR	RRZZZZUSA
JAC.	4	M	CHILD	RRZZZZUSA
FRANZ	2	M	CHILD	RRZZZZUSA
CATHA.	.01	F	INFANT	RRZZZZUSA
BRAUN, OSCHER	35	M	LABR	RRZZZZUSA
GLATT, FRANZ	26	M	FARMER	RRZZZZUSA
KLARA	25	F	UNKNOWN	RRZZZZUSA
WILHELM	2	M	CHILD	RRZZZZUSA
BARBARA	.11	F	INFANT	RRZZZZUSA
PETER	20	M	FARMER	RRZZZZUSA
SCHUMACHER, NOCOL.	17	M	FARMER	RRZZZZUSA
MARTEL, DONAT	29	M	LABR	RRZZZZUSA
ROSA	30	F	UNKNOWN	RRZZZZUSA
PETER	.02	M	INFANT	RRZZZZUSA
WERNER, JOHANNES	26	M	FARMER	RRZZZZUSA
AGATHE	24	F	UNKNOWN	RRZZZZUSA
ANTON	.11	M	INFANT	RRZZZZUSA
FREHSCHERER, JOH.	31	M	LABR	RRZZZZUSA
WALPURGA	22	F	UNKNOWN	RRZZZZUSA
BAUMGAERTNER, JOS.	20	M	FARMER	RRZZZZUSA
HARTMANN, PIUS	20	M	FARMER	RRZZZZUSA
WENZ, FRANZ	20	M	FARMER	RRZZZZUSA
THOMAS, FRANZ	45	M	FARMER	RRZZZZUSA
VERONICA	38	F	UNKNOWN	RRZZZZUSA
CASPAR	20	M	FARMER	RRZZZZUSA
SALOMEA	7	F	CHILD	RRZZZZUSA
VERONICA	4	F	CHILD	RRZZZZUSA
ANDREAS	.09	M	INFANT	RRZZZZUSA
BURKHARDT, JOSEF	20	M	FARMER	RRZZZZUSA
FEIST, JACOB	20	M	FARMER	RRZZZZUSA
MARTJAHN, JOHANNES	21	M	FARMER	RRZZZZUSA
WALD, ANTON	25	M	FARMER	RRZZZZUSA
MAGDALENA	22	F	UNKNOWN	RRZZZZUSA
JACOB	.01	M	INFANT	RRZZZZUSA
KRAFFT, JOSEF	20	M	FARMER	RRZZZZUSA
MARTIN, WILH.	53	M	LABR	RRZZZZUSA
MARIA	52	F	UNKNOWN	RRZZZZUSA
WILHELM	21	M	LABR	RRZZZZUSA
FRIEDR.	19	M	LABR	RRZZZZUSA
FRIESANN, BALTHASAR	27	M	FARMER	RRZZZZUSA
FELLER, ELISABETH	17	F	UNKNOWN	RRZZZZUSA
WAGNER, ADAM	24	M	LABR	RRZZZZUSA
ROSENA	22	F	UNKNOWN	RRZZZZUSA
ADAM	4	M	CHILD	RRZZZZUSA
DOROTHEA	.03	F	INFANT	RRZZZZUSA
MARTIN, JOHANN	24	M	LABR	RRZZZZUSA
CHRISTINE	23	F	UNKNOWN	RRZZZZUSA
MAGDALENA	2	F	CHILD	RRZZZZUSA
CATHA.	.03	F	INFANT	RRZZZZUSA
PILLER, JACOB	35	M	LABR	RRZZZZUSA
MARGARETHA	31	F	UNKNOWN	RRZZZZUSA
FRIEDRICH	7	M	CHILD	RRZZZZUSA
MARIE	6	F	CHILD	RRZZZZUSA
MALVINE	7	F	CHILD	RRZZZZUSA
JACOB	5	M	CHILD	RRZZZZUSA
CATHA.	3	F	CHILD	RRZZZZUSA
MARGARETTE	1	F	CHILD	RRZZZZUSA
GRAF, FELISE	28	M	FARMER	RRZZZZUSA
ANNA	26	F	UNKNOWN	RRZZZZUSA
MARGAR.	69	F	UNKNOWN	RRZZZZUSA
JACOB	2	M	CHILD	RRZZZZUSA
JOHANN	.01	M	INFANT	RRZZZZUSA
STEIN, FRANZ	24	M	LABR	RRZZZZUSA
CATHA.	24	F	UNKNOWN	RRZZZZUSA
PETER	2	M	CHILD	RRZZZZUSA
CATHA.	.01	F	INFANT	RRZZZZUSA
SCHWEIZER, ELISABETH	60	F	UNKNOWN	RRZZZZUSA
FRANZ	7	M	CHILD	RRZZZZUSA
GINNRUNSKY, SMEREL	21	M	LABR	RRZZZZUSA
PRESZAK, KAROLA.	43	F	UNKNOWN	RRZZZZUSA
FRANZ	7	M	CHILD	RRZZZZUSA
ANTON	6	M	CHILD	RRZZZZUSA
HEDWIG	4	F	CHILD	RRZZZZUSA
WRINLER, WILLIBALD	23	M	LABR	RRZZZZUSA
JOSEF	18	M	UNKNOWN	RRZZZZUSA
TORNEK, MAREY	30	F	UNKNOWN	RRZZZZUSA
WOLLMUTH, MARIA	19	F	UNKNOWN	RRZZZZUSA
STERNISSE, JOS.	31	M	LABR	RRZZZZUSA
BERNATOWISCH, TEOFIL	31	M	LABR	RRZZZZUSA
ADAM	30	M	LABR	RRZZZZUSA
ALTMANN, BERKE	51	F	UNKNOWN	RRZZZZUSA
ITTA	20	F	UNKNOWN	RRZZZZUSA
SAM.	16	M	FARMER	RRZZZZUSA
GRAF, CONRAD	32	M	FARMER	RRZZZZUSA
MARIE	28	F	UNKNOWN	RRZZZZUSA
FRIEDR.	7	M	CHILD	RRZZZZUSA
MARGARTH.	13	F	UNKNOWN	RRZZZZUSA
PHILLIPP	5	M	CHILD	RRZZZZUSA
CATHARINE.	2	F	CHILD	RRZZZZUSA
JACOB	.01	M	INFANT	RRZZZZUSA

SHIP: SLAVONIA

FROM: STETTIN
TO: NEW YORK
ARRIVED: 21 NOVEMBER 1888

PASSENGER	AGE	SEX	OCCUPATION	PRV VIL DES
KORK, SCHAJER	19	M	LABR	RRZZZZUSA
BERNSTEIN, FANNY	17	F	UNKNOWN	RRAIITUSA
ABBELBOM, SARAH	18	F	UNKNOWN	RRAIIBUSA
KOLWAT, ANNA	21	F	UNKNOWN	RRZZZZUSA
HAMANN, HENRIETTE	16	F	SVNT	RRZZZZUSA
ZUDKEWICZ, BARUCH	38	M	MLR	RRZZZZUSA
MITGANG, JANKEL	30	M	TLR	RRZZZZUSA
SCHROT, LAIB	30	M	MLR	RRAIITUSA
MOLINER, BARUCH	35	M	SHMK	RRAIITUSA
KORZENNER, JANKEL	24	M	BLKSMH	RRAIITUSA
BERNSTEIN, PINNOCHUS	38	M	TRDSMN	RRAIITUSA
BROCZTOWSKY, HUPOLIT	45	M	TLR	RRAFZDUSA
AINSTEIN, SAMUEL	16	M	LABR	RRZZZZUSA

PASSENGER	AGE	SEX	OCCUPATION	PRV	VIL	DES

SHIP: ELBE

FROM: BREMEN AND SOUTHAMPTON
TO: NEW YORK
ARRIVED: 21 NOVEMBER 1888

PASSENGER	AGE	SEX	OCCUPATION	PV VL DES
WOLFSON, TAUBE	46	F	W	RRZZZZNY
BUNIEWICZ, JULES	40	F	W	RRZZZZNY
ADAM	8	M	CHILD	RRZZZZNY
ROSALIE	6	F	CHILD	RRZZZZNY
MARSCHAK, JUDEL	25	M	DLR	RRZZZZNY
GESAITIS, MICHAEL	23	M	DLR	RRZZZZNY
WEINREICH, CHAJEM	68	M	TT	RRZZZZNY

SHIP: WYOMING

FROM: LIVERPOOL AND QUEENSTOWN
TO: NEW YORK
ARRIVED: 22 NOVEMBER 1888

PASSENGER	AGE	SEX	OCCUPATION	PV VL DES
SISKILZTI, WOLF	45	M	LABR	PLZZZZUSA
KOSENFELD, S.	44	M	LABR	PLZZZZUSA
ZIREL	34	F	W	PLZZZZUSA
CHAJE	7	F	CHILD	PLZZZZUSA
JOSSEL	3	M	CHILD	PLZZZZUSA
JAWAROWSKI, J.	24	M	LABR	PLZZZZUSA
RONDACH, J.	19	M	LABR	PLZZZZUSA
PAILET, S.	50	M	LABR	PLZZZZUSA
ZELIG	7	M	CHILD	PLZZZZUSA
NEIJMANN, A.	32	M	LABR	PLZZZZUSA
HEHMAN, ABRAM	58	M	LABR	PLZZZZUSA
PESCHE	30	F	W	PLZZZZUSA
MICHEL	7	M	CHILD	PLZZZZUSA
ISAAC	7	M	CHILD	PLZZZZUSA
GROSS, LINA	17	F	SP	PLZZZZUSA
BROCHES, J.	55	M	LABR	PLZZZZUSA
LENA	55	F	W	PLZZZZUSA
CHRIST.	7	M	CHILD	PLZZZZUSA
GUTENBERG, J.	40	M	LABR	PLZZZZUSA
MARAT, J.	7	M	CHILD	PLZZZZUSA
ELLA	7	F	CHILD	PLZZZZUSA
REPMANN, MARG.	19	F	SP	PLZZZZUSA
JARIK, J.	44	M	LABR	PLZZZZUSA
FRED.	40	F	W	PLZZZZUSA
CARL	16	M	LABR	PLZZZZUSA
JOHN	14	M	LABR	PLZZZZUSA
M.	7	M	CHILD	PLZZZZUSA
ALONIA	7	F	CHILD	PLZZZZUSA
MOURCHWITZ, M.	19	M	LABR	PLZZZZUSA
KLJSOI, A.	34	M	LABR	PLZZZZUSA
TINKELSTEIN, C.	36	M	LABR	PLZZZZUSA
MIORYNGWIN, MARIA	18	F	SP	PLZZZZUSA
LIEBOWICZ, RUDE	25	F	SP	PLZZZZUSA
GRANVIK, ANNA	21	F	SP	RRZZZZUSA
KASS, ADOLF	21	M	LABR	RRZZZZUSA
KLOCHARS, J.	22	M	LABR	RRZZZZUSA
LILLAM, H.	23	M	LABR	RRZZZZUSA
SCHAAFF, P.	24	M	LABR	RRZZZZUSA
HANSEN, C.	20	M	LABR	RRZZZZUSA
JENSEN, T.	37	M	LABR	RRZZZZUSA
HUSSHIND, C.	46	F	W	RRZZZZUSA
STEINER, H.	22	M	LABR	RRZZZZUSA
BISKRITZKI, R.	45	F	W	PLZZZZUSA
CHAIM	6	M	CHILD	PLZZZZUSA
ABRAM	3	M	CHILD	PLZZZZUSA
JEREMIAS	2	M	CHILD	PLZZZZUSA
PICKAR, G.	15	M	LABR	PLZZZZUSA
ZAS, LEIB	15	M	LABR	PLZZZZUSA
PALET, EIGE	7	F	CHILD	PLZZZZUSA
JASPAN, N.	26	M	LABR	PLZZZZUSA
ROSENFELD, J.	00	M	INF	PLZZZZUSA
UTESCHS, C.	41	M	LABR	PLZZZZUSA
SOPHIA	45	F	W	PLZZZZUSA
WILHELMINE	15	F	CH	PLZZZZUSA
AUGUST	6	M	CHILD	PLZZZZUSA

SHIP: ELBE

FROM: BREMEN AND SOUTHAMPTON
TO: NEW YORK
ARRIVED: 23 OCTOBER 1888

PASSENGER	AGE	SEX	OCCUPATION	PV VL DES
ZEDERBAUM, AD.	39	M	UNKNOWN	RRZZZZNY
WERGMANN, MAUSCHE	54	F	UNKNOWN	RRZZZZNY
SPIRO, TEOPHILA	25	F	UNKNOWN	RRZZZZMO
ROSA	3	F	CHILD	RRZZZZMO
U	.02	M	INFANT	RRZZZZMO
POSTMANN, ISAAC	17	M	FARMER	RRZZZZMO
VENTIOSKA, MARIANNE	40	F	UNKNOWN	RRZZZZNY
ADAM	14	M	CH	RRZZZZNY
ANNA	11	F	CH	RRZZZZNY
JOH.	7	M	CHILD	RRZZZZNY
WADISLAW	3	M	CHILD	RRZZZZNY
MARIANNE	.09	F	INFANT	RRZZZZNY
SCHAPIRO, HELENE	33	F	UNKNOWN	RRZZZZROC
ISAAC	12	M	CH	RRZZZZROC
KRZCSYUSKI, MICH.	48	M	LABR	RRAARRNY
BEHR, WILHELM	28	M	LABR	RRZZZZNY
ANNA	21	F	UNKNOWN	RRZZZZNY
SKUDIC, MARTIN	46	M	UNKNOWN	RRZZZZNY
FRIEDRIKE	26	F	UNKNOWN	RRZZZZNY
MICH.	17	M	UNKNOWN	RRZZZZNY
WENDEL, ANNA	18	F	UNKNOWN	RRZZZZNY
PRESSE, ED.	25	M	FARMER	RRZZZZIL
WOJSCHILLUS, JOS.	24	M	LABR	RRZZZZIL
LEWIN, MICHAEL	28	M	LABR	RRZZZZIL
MARIE	25	F	UNKNOWN	RRZZZZIL
SUSDINES, JOH.	23	M	BKR	RRZZZZIL
POSILA, JOSEFA	38	F	UNKNOWN	RRZZZZPA
BARTOZEK, STANISLAW	41	M	TLR	RRZZZZPA
FRIEDMANN, ISAAC	32	M	LABR	RRZZZZNY
LEBA	46	F	UNKNOWN	RRZZZZNY
KIEWE	34	M	LABR	RRZZZZNY
SALOWEICZE, ISRAEL	23	M	LABR	RRZZZZNY
IRKA--, EMMA	20	F	UNKNOWN	RRZZZZNY
MICHAEL	3	M	CHILD	RRZZZZNY
MARIE	.04	F	INFANT	RRZZZZNY
RUDEMANN, ARON	27	M	MCHT	RRZZZZNY
ABRAMSON, MEYER	34	M	DLR	RRZZZZNY
MARYANNE	27	F	UNKNOWN	RRZZZZNY
JETTE	7	F	CHILD	RRZZZZNY
WOLF	5	M	CHILD	RRZZZZNY
BENJAMIN	2	M	CHILD	RRZZZZNY
ARON, HERZ	30	M	CH	RRZZZZNY
WOLF	7	M	CHILD	RRZZZZNY
GOLDBERG, ROSA	12	F	CH	RRZZZZNY
SCHUDRASKY, SIMON	23	M	LABR	RRZZZZNY
BIELYKOWSKY, CHAIM	23	M	LABR	RRZZZZNY
SUCHCZIKI, BAJUMED	19	M	LABR	RRZZZZNY
JUCHNEWSKI, MARCEL	29	M	LABR	RRZZZZNY
DZELCZ, MICHAEL	18	M	LABR	RRZZZZNY

PASSENGER	AGE	SEX	OCCUPATION	PRV VIL DES

SHIP: AMALFI

FROM: HAMBURG
TO: NEW YORK
ARRIVED: 23 NOVEMBER 1888

PASSENGER	AGE	SEX	OCCUPATION	PRV VIL DES
MIRKEN, HADIES	17	M	TLR	RRZZZZUSA
KASPROW, THERESE	39	F	WO	RRZZZZUSA
AGNES	11	F	CH	RRZZZZUSA
FELIX	10	M	CH	RRZZZZUSA
JOSEF	8	M	CHILD	RRZZZZUSA
RAEZKOWSKI, SILVESTER	22	M	LABR	RRZZZZUSA
MISZHUER, JANKEL	45	M	LABR	RRZZZZUSA
ROCHEL	42	F	W	RRZZZZUSA
LORE	11	F	CH	RRZZZZUSA
ABRAM	9	M	CHILD	RRZZZZUSA
CHANE	14	F	CH	RRZZZZUSA
PAGEL, GUSTAV	19	M	JNR	RRZZZZUSA
GOLDBERG, ABRAM	17	M	DLR	RRZZZZUSA
GOLDANOWSKA, REINE	40	F	WO	RRZZZZUSA
MAX	18	M	CH	RRZZZZUSA
JAC	16	M	CH	RRZZZZUSA
EKAT	7	M	CHILD	RRZZZZUSA
GRUEN, FEIGE	20	F	SGL	RRZZZZUSA
PIETSZAK, JULIANNA	27	F	W	RRZZZZUSA
JOHANN	36	M	LABR	RRZZZZUSA
LEON	8	M	CHILD	RRZZZZUSA
HELENE	1	F	CHILD	RRZZZZUSA
VICTORIA	.06	F	INFANT	RRZZZZUSA
EISICKOWITZ, ITTE	30	F	WO	RRZZZZUSA
SIMON	10	M	CH	RRZZZZUSA
RECHAME	7	F	CHILD	RRZZZZUSA
TAUBE	1	F	CHILD	RRZZZZUSA
RUDNITZKI, REISE	25	F	WO	RRZZZZUSA
MIRKE	5	F	CHILD	RRZZZZUSA
BRESAND, FRANE	26	F	WO	RRZZZZUSA
CHAIE	6	F	CHILD	RRZZZZUSA
BEILE	4	F	CHILD	RRZZZZUSA
MATLE	2	F	CHILD	RRZZZZUSA
TAUBE	.09	F	INFANT	RRZZZZUSA
FISCH, GISZE	17	F	SGL	RRZZZZUSA
KALMANOWSKI, CHAIE	30	F	WO	RRZZZZUSA
SARA	9	F	CHILD	RRZZZZUSA
BATONOWITSCH, SOPHIE	35	F	WO	RRZZZZUSA
PRISLAW	9	M	CHILD	RRZZZZUSA
JAN	5	M	CHILD	RRZZZZUSA
WLADISLAW	2	M	CHILD	RRZZZZUSA
ADELI	.03	F	INFANT	RRZZZZUSA
BERKMANN, HIRSCHEL	20	M	LABR	RRZZZZUSA
ABOY, MORSCHE	16	M	WCHMKR	RRZZZZUSA
HELENE	19	F	SGL	RRZZZZUSA
WIRBICKINTE, MARYANE	21	F	SGL	RRZZZZUSA
RIEGEL, ABRAM	24	M	LABR	RRZZZZUSA
GINGOLD, CHANE	20	F	WO	RRZZZZUSA
SIMSCHE	3	F	CHILD	RRZZZZUSA
KARBOWIAK, MARYANE	43	F	WO	RRZZZZUSA
BARBARA	19	F	CH	RRZZZZUSA
WEDNI	10	M	CH	RRZZZZUSA
GUSNOFSKY, ABRAM	19	M	LABR	RRZZZZUSA
RITSCHKOWSKY, CHAJE	22	F	SGL	RRZZZZUSA
SAPERSTEIN, EMIL	11	M	BY	RRZZZZUSA
EPSTEIN, FEIWEL	46	M	LABR	RRZZZZNY
CHON, HENOCK	23	M	LABR	RRZZZZNY
HOCHMANN, BETTY	37	F	WO	RRZZZZNY
CHEESE	12	F	CH	RRZZZZNY
ISAAC	10	M	CH	RRZZZZNY
ARTHUR	9	M	CHILD	RRZZZZNY
FELDMANN, ANNA	22	F	SGL	RRZZZZNY
SKOWORSKI, JOSEF	28	M	LABR	RRZZZZNY
GOTTWALD, OTTO	16	M	LABR	RRZZZZNY
BASCHAINE, JOSEL	22	M	LABR	RRZZZZNY
MOREM, SCHIE	15	M	LABR	RRZZZZNY
DURST, OSIAS	23	M	LABR	RRZZZZNY
PICKRON, MARAM	33	M	LABR	RRZZZZNY
JUSCHKALIS, JNJE	28	M	LABR	RRZZZZNY
SOLTENOWITZ, IGNATZ	22	M	LABR	RRZZZZNY
GWOSDINSKY, ANTON	28	M	BCHR	RRZZZZNY
PRIKOZI, NACHIM	36	M	CHMKR	RRZZZZMA
DEIBO, NATHAN	28	M	BBR	RRZZZZNY
ANSULEWIZ, JAN	25	M	LABR	RRZZZZNY
STRUTZENBERG, HEINRICH	22	M	LABR	RRZZZZIL
BARTOLOM, TABOLA	26	M	LABR	RRZZZZNY
KUZENKA, PAULINE	33	F	SGL	RRZZZZPA

SHIP: LAHN

FROM: BREMEN AND SOUTHAMPTON
TO: NEW YORK
ARRIVED: 24 NOVEMBER 1888

PASSENGER	AGE	SEX	OCCUPATION	PRV VIL DES
MUEHLENTHAL, MARL	24	M	CMST	RRZZZZUNK
KNOCH, ARTHUR	22	M	CMST	RRAEFLUNK
RUDOWSKY, ADAM	31	M	LABR	RRAHZSUNK
BOGUSZEWSKY, SILVESTER	31	M	LABR	RRAHZSUNK
SCHNEIDER, ANTON	57	M	LABR	RRAFVGUNK
CATHA.	54	F	W	RRAFVGUNK
CATHA.	17	F	UNKNOWN	RRAFVGUNK
MARIA	8	F	CHILD	RRAFVGUNK
BAUMGARTNER, JOHS.	18	M	LABR	RRAFVGUNK
BRAUNNAGE, WENDELIN	24	M	LABR	RRAFVGUNK
LISBETH	22	F	W	RRAFVGUNK
HOPFEINGER, MARGA.	54	F	WI	RRAFVGUNK
JOSEF	20	M	LABR	RRAFVGUNK
JACOB	15	M	LABR	RRAFVGUNK
WARLIKOWSKI, MARIANNA	40	F	UNKNOWN	RRZZZZUNK
CZACHOWSKI, FRANZ	30	M	JNR	RRZZZZUNK
TUCHEWITZ, JOSEF	27	M	LABR	RRZZZZUNK
ZMYEWSKI, FELIX	27	M	LABR	RRZZZZUNK
ALUKIEWICZ, MATH.	30	M	LABR	RRZZZZUNK
URSULA	30	F	W	RRZZZZUNK
ANNA	4	F	CHILD	RRZZZZUNK
BRUNS, ELISE	26	F	UNKNOWN	RRZZZZUNK
SIES, MARIE	24	F	UNKNOWN	RRZZZZUNK
WEHLAU, CHRISTE.	15	F	UNKNOWN	RRZZZZUNK
FELDHUS, MARGE.	54	F	UNKNOWN	RRZZZZUNK
OTJENBRUNNS, HELENE	27	F	W	RRZZZZUNK
MARIE	3	F	CHILD	RRZZZZUNK
WILHM.	.11	M	INFANT	RRZZZZUNK
HAAKE, CARL	15	M	UNKNOWN	RRZZZZUNK
WIECHHORST, CAECILIE	18	F	UNKNOWN	RRZZZZUNK
LICHTSIN, HERM.	23	M	FARMER	RRZZZZUNK
OLDACH, FRANCISZEK	21	M	LABR	RRAFWJUNK
EIN, FEIGE	26	F	UNKNOWN	RRAFWJUNK
NOSIETZKY, BARKA	24	M	BRM	RRAFWJUNK
BERNSTEIN, JACOB	20	M	UNKNOWN	RRZZZZUNK
FRIEDE	21	F	W	RRZZZZUNK
SCHNITKIN, LOUIS	50	M	DLR	RRAHTFUNK
DEICHES, JUDES	25	M	UNKNOWN	RRAHTFUNK
ROSENBERG, JANKEL	27	M	LABR	RRAHTFUNK
SCHMUEL	11	M	CH	RRAHTFUNK
IMANSKI, KALMEN	63	M	DLR	RRAHTFUNK
GELENEK, JOHANNA	21	F	UNKNOWN	RRZZZZUNK

SHIP: HAMMONIA

FROM: HAMBURG
TO: NEW YORK
ARRIVED: 24 NOVEMBER 1888

PASSENGER	AGE	SEX	OCCUPATION	PRIVL	DES
SEEBERG, SELIG	15	M	LABR	RRZZZZ	USA
BLUME	20	F	SGL	RRZZZZ	USA
KWOLHOWITZ, BALSROMEY	24	M	LABR	RRZZZZ	USA
MITUS, ANNA	16	F	SGL	RRZZZZ	USA
JOSEF	7	M	CHILD	RRZZZZ	USA
LASHOWSKI, ANTON	28	M	LABR	RRZZZZ	USA
SCHMIDT, STEFANIE	20	F	SGL	RRAHTK	USA
KITERS, GENIE	15	F	SGL	RRZZZZ	USA
REIGENDORF, CHAIM	25	M	SHMK	RRZZZZ	USA
BAILEW, ITZIG	27	M	TLR	RRZZZZ	USA
WANCHOFSKY, BENZIEN	20	M	LABR	RRAINB	USA
RATZE	18	F	W	RRAINB	USA
BECKER, SARA	26	F	SGL	RRAIIG	USA
JAHNEWICZ, STANISLAW	21	M	LABR	RRZZZZ	USA
KLATSCHHIN, RACHEL	17	F	SGL	RRAGRT	USA
ETERMANN, ABRAM	19	M	LABR	RRAGRT	USA
SCHUMLIVIZ, DAVID	45	M	LABR	RRAGRT	USA
SACHARIAS, LISA	23	F	SGL	RRZZZZ	USA
LEIB	18	M	LABR	RRZZZZ	USA
SCHALMEN, SCHLOME	17	M	MLR	RRZZZZ	USA
KARPOWITSCH, FELIX	22	M	LABR	RRZZZZ	USA
BUKELWICZ, MACY	30	M	LABR	RRZZZZ	USA
WILBENBERG, ASNE	28	F	W	RRZZZZ	USA
CHAJE	7	F	CHILD	RRZZZZ	USA
FEIGE	6	F	CHILD	RRZZZZ	USA
RACHEL	5	F	CHILD	RRZZZZ	USA
MAX	4	M	CHILD	RRZZZZ	USA
SALMEN	.11	M	INFANT	RRZZZZ	USA
WORK, ETTIE	20	F	SGL	RRZZZZ	USA
TISCHLLER, SAMUEL	29	M	LABR	RRAIGA	UNK
HELENE	24	F	W	RRAIGA	UNK
BUTSOWE, RUDOLF	31	M	BKR	RRZZZZ	UNK
ROSENBAUM, JACOB	28	M	LABR	RRZZZZ	UNK
MUELLER, CHRISTIANE	17	F	SGL	RRZZZZ	UNK
WOLFF, WILH.	22	M	MCHT	RRZZZZ	UNK
STUMACH, JANKEL	50	M	MCHT	RRZZZZ	UNK
SLATE	40	F	W	RRZZZZ	UNK
MOSES	17	M	CH	RRZZZZ	UNK
GOLDE	9	F	CHILD	RRZZZZ	UNK
ROCHE	6	F	CHILD	RRZZZZ	UNK
RASI	4	F	CHILD	RRZZZZ	UNK
SARA	.01	F	INFANT	RRZZZZ	UNK
MOSES	.11	M	INFANT	RRZZZZ	UNK
BLUME	30	F	UNKNOWN	RRZZZZ	UNK
BALTRUSCHAT, JURGAS	32	M	LABR	RRZZZZ	UNK
ELISABETH	28	F	W	RRZZZZ	UNK
JOSEF	.01	M	INFANT	RRZZZZ	UNK
ARONOWITZ, MORDACH	25	M	PRNTR	RRZZZZ	UNK
BARKOWSKY, SIMON	28	M	LABR	RRZZZZ	UNK
PETRONI	30	F	W	RRZZZZ	UNK
ANNA	.01	F	INFANT	RRZZZZ	UNK
SELINCHENE, PETRONI	26	F	W	RRZZZZ	UNK
MATEJUS	.09	M	INFANT	RRZZZZ	UNK
JUSSILA, ALBERS	35	M	LABR	FNZZZZ	UNK
SOFIE	3	F	CHILD	FNZZZZ	UNK
MARTA	3	F	CHILD	FNZZZZ	UNK
OLGA	.11	F	INFANT	FNZZZZ	UNK
HEIKCSA, MARIE	65	F	W	FNZZZZ	UNK
BAKALENIK, HERSCH	42	M	LABR	FNAHWQ	UNK

SHIP: THE QUEEN

FROM: LIVERPOOL AND QUEENSTOWN
TO: NEW YORK
ARRIVED: 24 NOVEMBER 1888

PASSENGER	AGE	SEX	OCCUPATION	PRIVL	DES
HYMAN, M.	30	F	W	FNADBQ	BO
SWEET, JOHN	19	M	LABR	FNADBQ	NY
GRUMBERGER, BETTE	20	F	SP	FNADBQ	NY
BLANKENFELD, G.	17	M	LABR	RRZZZZ	NY
STOSLEIN, OLE	60	M	LABR	RRZZZZ	NY
BESITH	55	F	W	RRZZZZ	NY
OLINE	20	F	SP	RRZZZZ	NY
SCHWARZ, HANI	17	F	SP	RRZZZZ	NY
KESTERBAUM, ANNA	21	F	SP	RRZZZZ	NY
MENDELSACK, D.	26	M	LABR	RRZZZZ	NY
RUMINSKA, TEOFILA	34	F	W	RRZZZZ	NY
ULAD	11	F	CH	RRZZZZ	NY
LEONORA	4	F	CHILD	RRZZZZ	NY
CECILIE	2	F	CHILD	RRZZZZ	NY
JAN	1	M	CHILD	RRZZZZ	NY
BAMBAUM, JEINE	19	M	LABR	RRZZZZ	NY
SCHWERSKY, HUSCH	27	M	LABR	RRZZZZ	NY
SINGER, RIVKE	26	F	W	RRZZZZ	NY
ROSA	5	F	CHILD	RRZZZZ	NY
SARA	1	F	CHILD	RRZZZZ	NY
LIBOWICZ, CLARA	18	F	SP	RRZZZZ	NY
GRUMBERG, CLARA	20	F	W	RRZZZZ	NY
HERMAN	3	M	CHILD	RRZZZZ	NY
KAHN, RACHEL	45	F	W	RRZZZZ	NY
BASIL	9	M	CHILD	RRZZZZ	NY
CHANE	7	M	CHILD	RRZZZZ	NY
LIBOWIECZ, LEA	50	F	W	RRZZZZ	PHI
FANNY	26	F	SP	RRZZZZ	PHI
M.	7	F	CHILD	RRZZZZ	PHI
AMALIE	4	F	CHILD	RRZZZZ	PHI
BLUME	3	F	CHILD	RRZZZZ	PHI
EISENBERG, PAULINE	18	F	SP	RRZZZZ	NY
HALZMANN, CHAIM	44	M	SP	RRZZZZ	NY
SICHERMANN, BEIN	21	M	LABR	RRZZZZ	BO
MOSKOWIEZ, G.	34	M	LABR	RRZZZZ	NY
KASTIN, ESTER	24	F	SP	RRZZZZ	NY
KAPLAN, SCHLOME	23	M	LABR	RRZZZZ	NY
NOWICK, MEIER	20	M	LABR	RRZZZZ	NY
LAPRENZ, PETER	20	M	LABR	RRZZZZ	NY
KORPINSKA, BRAN.	26	F	SP	RRZZZZ	NY
SCHWARZ, HUDEL	24	F	SP	RRZZZZ	NY
KLENE, CHAIME	24	M	LABR	RRZZZZ	NY
GOLDBERG, PRIDE	19	F	SP	RRZZZZ	NY
KOSLOWSKY, SIMON	27	M	LABR	RRZZZZ	NY
EMMA	24	F	W	RRZZZZ	NY
MARIE	1	F	CHILD	RRZZZZ	NY
ANNA	1	F	CHILD	RRZZZZ	NY
ETZEKOWITZ, BLUME	17	F	SP	RRZZZZ	NY
DORA	10	F	CH	RRZZZZ	NY
SINOLKA, SCHULEM	33	M	LABR	RRZZZZ	NY
RAFAEL, BENZEL	19	M	LABR	RRZZZZ	NY
SCHOLHNAS, O.	20	M	LABR	RRZZZZ	BAL
LEWANDOWSKY, P.	22	M	LABR	RRZZZZ	NY
BREIT, CHAJE	20	F	SP	RRZZZZ	NY
SILICOWIEZ, GEIGE	22	M	LABR	RRZZZZ	NY
TISKI, FRANZ	33	M	LABR	RRZZZZ	NY
MANA, STANSLOW	19	M	LABR	RRZZZZ	NY
K.	23	F	W	RRZZZZ	NY
SELICHOWICZ, FEIGE	22	F	SP	RRZZZZ	NY
INGBER, JUDA	55	F	W	RRZZZZ	NY
ESTHER	28	F	SP	RRZZZZ	NY
TAUBE	17	F	SP	RRZZZZ	NY
FRIACCA, PETER	64	M	LABR	RRADBQ	NY
LORETTA	19	F	SP	RRADBQ	NY

PASSENGER	AGE	SEX	OCCUPATION	PRV	VIL	DES

SHIP: CITY OF RICHMOND

FROM: LIVERPOOL AND QUEENSTOWN
TO: NEW YORK
ARRIVED: 26 NOVEMBER 1888

PASSENGER	AGE	SEX	OCCUPATION	PRV	VIL	DES
SCHIEFER, ELEE	18	M	LABR	RR	ACBF	NY
LIPINSKY, GEO.	45	M	LABR	RR	ACBF	PA
SAKATSUSKI, SOMON	31	M	LABR	RR	ACBF	STL
PLANKE, VEN.	22	M	LABR	RR	ACBF	STL
SERSTERAGE, BASSE	23	M	LABR	RR	ACBF	STL
MAREUS, LAZAR	16	M	LABR	RR	ACBF	NY
MATEZ, DD.	37	M	LABR	RR	ACBF	NY
FLEISCHER, JON	59	M	LABR	RR	ACBF	NY
STEIN, BARUST	29	M	LABR	RR	ACBF	NY
SUTHED, R.	17	M	LABR	RR	ACBF	NY
KENNELHER, BER.	18	M	LABR	RR	ACBF	NY
BAROV, BORELK	18	M	LABR	RR	ACBF	NY
FUKS, ISAAC	28	M	LABR	RR	ACBF	NY
JANKELOWITZ, MOSES	28	M	LABR	RR	ACBF	NY
BEKER, IT.	26	M	LABR	RR	ACBF	NY
JAVESSERZORG, TEOFIL	36	M	LABR	RR	ACBF	NY
WOLFF, ITZEK	52	M	LABR	RR	ACBF	NY
KLIMMERMANN, MORDCH	17	M	LABR	RR	ACBF	NY
GUROWITZ, EL.	20	M	LABR	RR	ACBF	NY
SCHENSKI, STEF.	46	M	LABR	RR	ACBF	NY
ERONS, H.	31	M	LABR	RR	ACBF	NY
ANDRA, MAHER	28	M	LABR	RR	ACBF	NY
GABA, GUS.	42	M	LABR	RR	ACBF	NY
MOSS, MOSCHE	36	M	LABR	RR	ACBF	NY
EDZENBERGT, REBECCA	15	F	SP	RR	ACBF	NY
SPIEGEL, BELLY	17	F	SP	RR	ACBF	NY
JACOBSOHN, SARAH	28	F	SP	RR	ACBF	NY
GLEICH, HYG.	17	F	SP	RR	ACBF	NY
NALZBRATZKY, S.	19	F	SP	RR	ACBF	NY
MILTHEN, MIRE	22	F	SP	RR	ACBF	NY
BAB.	17	F	SP	RR	ACBF	NY
BRENER, CHAIE	18	F	SP	RR	ACBF	NY
LIEBNER, DWORE	30	F	W	RR	ACBF	NY
RAHEL	00	F	INF	RR	ACBF	NY
MEIRLAESETIZ, ROSE	18	F	SP	RR	ACBF	NY
SALZMAN, R.	19	F	SP	RR	ACBF	NY
FISCHMAN, FANNY	17	F	SP	RR	ACBF	NY
PESTAES, ZOFEN	30	M	LABR	RR	ACBF	NY
JAN	10	M	CH	RR	ACBF	NY
GARENBERG, SAML.	30	F	LABR	RR	ACBF	USA
MALF.	30	F	W	RR	ACBF	USA
U	00	F	INF	RR	ACBF	USA
BASSILL, CHAIM	33	F	W	RR	ACBF	NY
MALKE	11	F	CH	RR	ACBF	NY
CH.	9	F	CHILD	RR	ACBF	NY
BUSEL	4	F	CHILD	RR	ACBF	NY
SACKAROWITZ, MOUSHE	22	M	LABR	RR	ACBF	NY
MINNE	20	F	W	RR	ACBF	NY
STESAK, ITH.	36	F	W	RR	ACBF	NY
BRUNEL	12	M	CH	RR	ACBF	NY
ANNA	11	F	CH	RR	ACBF	NY
REISE	8	F	CHILD	RR	ACBF	NY
RACHEL	5	M	CHILD	RR	ACBF	NY
SAM.	00	F	INF	RR	ACBF	NY
NACH.	00	F	INF	RR	ACBF	NY
RUBEVAER, SCHUMER	19	M	LABR	RR	ACBF	NY
ETHEL	18	F	W	RR	ACBF	NY
LEZKOWSKY, JOSEFA	19	F	W	RR	ACBF	NY
M.	00	F	INF	RR	ACBF	NY
ROSENMONZEL, MOSES	32	M	LABR	RR	ACBF	NY
MALKE	30	F	W	RR	ACBF	NY
JACOB	5	M	CHILD	RR	ACBF	NY
B.	1	M	CHILD	RR	ACBF	NY
GERMOIZE, J.	27	M	LABR	RR	ACBF	NY
REGINA	18	F	W	RR	ACBF	NY
ZEIM, SAMIL	48	M	TLR	RR	ACBF	NY
L.	48	F	W	RR	ACBF	NY
ABRA.	18	F	SP	RR	ACBF	NY
LENA	16	F	SP	RR	ACBF	NY
JOH.	10	M	CH	RR	ACBF	NY
WOLFF	7	M	CHILD	RR	ACBF	NY

SHIP: GALLIA

FROM: LIVERPOOL AND QUEENSTOWN
TO: NEW YORK
ARRIVED: 27 NOVEMBER 1888

PASSENGER	AGE	SEX	OCCUPATION	PRV	VIL	DES
HERMANSON, HERM.	24	M	LABR	RR	ACBF	USA
BERNSTEIN, NICOLAI	21	M	TLR	FN	ZZZZ	USA
LINA	20	F	SP	FN	ZZZZ	USA
OLSON, CAROLINA	24	F	SP	FN	AEFL	USA
SILAKINSKY, ANDREAS	26	M	TLR	FN	ACBF	USA
HARWITZ, CHAINE	18	M	SHMK	FN	ACBF	USA
JANOWSKY, MOSES	21	M	SHMK	RR	ZZZZ	USA
SALSON, JOSEL	33	M	ENGR	RR	ACBF	USA
KOMINAD, MENDEL	14	F	SVNT	RR	ACBF	USA
OJIUS, HODE	19	F	TLR	RR	ACBF	USA
FERGI	20	F	TLR	RR	ACBF	USA
METZ, PESIL	16	F	SP	RR	AEFL	USA
BUNIN, HENNE	30	F	MA	RR	ACBF	USA
PESCHE	11	F	CH	RR	ACBF	USA
BASCHE	6	F	CHILD	RR	ACBF	USA
LOUISE	.11	F	INFANT	RR	ACBF	USA
JWANITZKA, PETRONELLO	22	F	SP	RR	AEFL	USA

SHIP: POLYNESIA

FROM: HAMBURG
TO: NEW YORK
ARRIVED: 27 NOVEMBER 1888

PASSENGER	AGE	SEX	OCCUPATION	PRV	VIL	DES
ALPEIN, RIWE	50	F	WO	RR	ZZZZ	NY
CHAJE	22	F	CH	RR	ZZZZ	NY
SCHEINE	18	F	CH	RR	ZZZZ	NY
SELIG	23	M	CH	RR	ZZZZ	NY
JACOB	20	M	CH	RR	ZZZZ	NY
CHAIM	7	M	CHILD	RR	ZZZZ	NY
BEILE	6	M	CHILD	RR	ZZZZ	NY
GALLER, ISRAEL	19	M	LABR	RR	ZZZZ	NY
KORSZTKOWSKY, JAN	33	M	LABR	RR	AIEN	NY
KORECKI, MAREIN	27	M	LABR	RR	ZZZZ	NY
NAPIEWOCKI, JOSEF	33	M	LABR	RR	AIEN	NY
BROMKOWSKI, ALFONS	35	M	LABR	RR	AHZD	NY
RZYMKOWSKY, JOSEF	33	M	LABR	RR	AHUL	NY
RUBINSTEIN, ISRAEL	27	M	LABR	RR	ZZZZ	NY
ROTHSTEIN, DEBORAH	15	F	SGL	RR	ZZZZ	NY
RATZEWITZ, AGATHE	28	F	WO	RR	ZZZZ	NY
JENDRACH	5	M	CHILD	RR	ZZZZ	NY
DREWYATZKY, ARON	19	M	LABR	RR	AGRT	NY
GRUENBERG, FEIGE	40	F	WO	RR	ZZZZ	NY
PAVEL	7	M	CHILD	RR	ZZZZ	NY
JAN	.11	M	INFANT	RR	ZZZZ	NY
TEIKEF, DEBORAH	30	F	WO	RR	AFWJ	NY
MOSES	4	M	CHILD	RR	AFWJ	NY
SAHRA	.11	M	INFANT	RR	AFWJ	NY
HENNE	.01	M	INFANT	RR	AFWJ	NY
SONNINGSON, LEOPOLD	23	M	TLR	RR	AIKN	NY
SCHEUSAL, MAX	20	M	TLR	RR	AIKN	NY
HAEMISCH, MOSES	23	M	PNTR	RR	AIEZ	NY
SCHELL, GEORG	31	M	FARMER	RR	ABIJ	NY
JOSEFINE	24	F	W	RR	ABIJ	NY
JOSEF	7	M	CHILD	RR	ABIJ	NY

PASSENGER	A G E	S E X	OCCUPATION	P R V	V I L	D E S
FRANZISCA	3	F	CHILD	RR	ABIJ	NY
VINCENZ	2	M	CHILD	RR	ABIJ	NY
CONRAD	.06	M	INFANT	RR	ABIJ	NY
MEYER, VINCENZ	30	M	FARMER	RR	ABIJ	NY
RICHARDA	24	F	W	RR	ABIJ	NY
CATHA.	.09	F	INFANT	RR	ABIJ	NY
VOLK, THEODOR	30	M	FARMER	RR	ABIJ	NY
ELISABETH	19	F	W	RR	ABIJ	NY
BRAUN, JACOB	60	M	FARMER	RR	ABIJ	NY
CATHA.	47	F	W	RR	ABIJ	NY
OHRS, JOHANN	20	M	FARMER	RR	AIAN	NY
SEDELKA, VAERONIKA	20	F	SGL	RR	ZZZZ	NY
KISTELMANN, SAMUEL	19	M	CL	RR	AIOO	NY
UGER, YESSAJE	16	M	CL	RR	AIOO	NY
JANUSCHAD, VINCENTZ	50	M	CL	RR	ZZZZ	NY
MAATHE, EMMA	21	F	SGL	FN	ZZZZ	NY
KRAWITZ, MEYER	23	M	TLR	RR	ZZZZ	NY
BIRK, ABRAM	25	M	JNR	RR	ZZZZ	NY
SOKOLOWSKI, STANILSAW	28	M	LABR	RR	ZZZZ	NY
SALTYS, MARIANNE	19	F	SGL	RR	AHZS	NY
SMOLITZ, FILARY	16	M	LABR	RR	AHZS	NY
MALEWSKY, B--ISLAW	19	M	LABR	RR	AHZS	NY
QUAST, RUDOLF	28	M	BCHR	RR	AAKH	NY
GERIN, MOSES	17	M	CL	RR	AHOO	NY
LUOMALA, MATHS.	19	M	LABR	FN	ZZZZ	NY
PIHLAJAMAA, JOH.	38	M	LABR	FN	ZZZZ	NY
HANTISALO, ALEXANDER	35	M	LABR	FN	ZZZZ	NY
SIKALA, ALEXANDER	19	M	LABR	FN	ZZZZ	NY
LAENTHA, JOH.	44	M	LABR	FN	ZZZZ	NY
SIKALA, KARL	19	M	LABR	FN	ZZZZ	NY
MATTSEN, MATTS	47	M	LABR	FN	ZZZZ	NY
CARLSEN, JACOB	34	M	LABR	FN	ZZZZ	NY
LAUTHA, JOH.	19	M	LABR	FN	ZZZZ	NY
ANDERS	35	M	LABR	FN	ZZZZ	NY
LUAMALA, JOHANN	19	M	LABR	FN	ZZZZ	NY
NIKKORIKOSKI, JACOB	18	M	LABR	FN	ZZZZ	NY
KUSICK, AUGUST	31	M	MCHT	FN	ZZZZ	NY
EMMA	23	F	W	FN	ZZZZ	NY
SIMKOWSKA, JULIE	30	F	WO	FN	AHRZ	NY
KLAT, AUGUST	29	M	LABR	FN	ZZZZ	NY
MATHILDE	23	F	W	FN	ZZZZ	NY
FRIEDRICH	.09	M	INFANT	FN	ZZZZ	NY
FRIED, KLARA	16	F	SGL	RR	ZZZZ	NY
SAWIK, ADAM	19	M	LABR	RR	AICR	NY
TODRESOWITZ, SARA	28	F	WO	RR	AIAE	NY
RUBEN	7	F	CHILD	RR	AIAE	NY
SEINZE	4	F	CHILD	RR	AIAE	NY
KEILE	.11	F	INFANT	RR	AIAE	NY
WAWRA, AGNES	47	F	WO	RR	AGRT	NY
JENTE	20	F	W	RR	AGRT	NY
KADISKI, ELIAS	21	M	MCHT	RR	ZZZZ	NY
DSCHUWIGER, MORDCHE	34	M	TLR	RR	ZZZZ	NY
SCHELL, VINCENZ	30	M	FARMER	RR	ZZZZ	NY
CATHA.	24	F	W	RR	ZZZZ	NY
GERTRUDE	4	F	CHILD	RR	ZZZZ	NY
BARBA.	2	F	CHILD	RR	ZZZZ	NY
SEBASTIAN	00	M	INF	RR	ZZZZ	NY

SHIP: ARIZONA

FROM: LIVERPOOL AND QUEENSTOWN
TO: NEW YORK
ARRIVED: 27 NOVEMBER 1888

PASSENGER	A G E	S E X	OCCUPATION	P R V	V I L	D E S
BERGMAN, EMIL	22	M	MSN	RR	AGUZ	USA
TRAPSKI, MICHEL	19	M	LABR	RR	ACBF	USA
JUDES	17	F	SP	RR	ACBF	USA
PISAR, WOLF	33	M	ATSN	RR	ACBF	USA
NACHMAN	11	M	CH	RR	ACBF	USA
SOBOLENSKI, MIRKE	26	F	W	RR	ACBF	USA
MARIASCHE	4	F	CHILD	RR	ACBF	USA
ELIAS	3	M	CHILD	RR	ACBF	USA
MOSCHOWITZ, BANWEL	19	M	LABR	RR	ACBF	USA
JOSEPH	17	M	LABR	RR	ACBF	USA
NEMOWITZ, SORE	21	M	LABR	RR	ACBF	USA
HINERMAN, BORUCH	58	M	MECH	RR	ACBF	USA
RACHEL	19	F	W	RR	ACBF	USA
SANDELMAN, RIWEN	21	F	SP	RR	ACBF	USA
GITEL	25	F	SP	RR	ACBF	USA
BRENER, ARON	16	M	LABR	RR	ACBF	USA
SORTMAN, LEWIS	21	M	SHPMN	RR	ACBF	USA
HILLOWITZ, MALKA	18	F	SP	RR	ACBF	USA
LEWINOWITZ, LASER	21	M	PMBR	RR	ACBF	USA
KATZ, CERNA	32	F	W	RR	ACBF	USA
CHAIE	14	F	SP	RR	ACBF	USA
SORE	11	M	CH	RR	ACBF	USA
CINKE	7	F	CHILD	RR	ACBF	USA
ABE	6	M	CHILD	RR	ACBF	USA
LEIBE	4	F	CHILD	RR	ACBF	USA
FEIVEL	3	F	CHILD	RR	ACBF	USA
SALMON, GITTEL	16	F	SP	RR	ACBF	USA
FENDEL, MIRE	23	F	SP	RR	ACBF	USA
SCHWARTZ, SARE	22	F	SP	RR	ACBF	USA
RIBBLER, LEIBOWITZ	16	M	TLR	RR	ACBF	USA
SUFFRA, MICHAEL	58	M	SMH	RR	ACBF	USA
HODE	56	F	W	RR	ACBF	USA
PORTNOI, SARAH	16	F	SP	RR	ACBF	USA
HINEMAN, MARIE	6	F	CHILD	RR	ACBF	USA
KARLSON, ANDERS	41	M	FARMER	RR	AGUZ	USA
KATZ, KNNE.I.	.10	M	INFANT	RR	ACBF	USA
LINDSMANN, FRAMME	17	F	SP	RR	ACBF	USA
GASHVIRTH, BEILE	18	F	SP	RR	ACBF	USA

SHIP: WERRA

FROM: BREMEN AND SOUTHAMPTON
TO: NEW YORK
ARRIVED: 28 NOVEMBER 1888

PASSENGER	A G E	S E X	OCCUPATION	P R V	V I L	D E S
EMERTH, ANNA	26	F	UNKNOWN	RR	AILA	USA
KRAFT, FRIEDA	42	F	W	RR	AILA	USA
FRIEDEN, MOSES	42	M	MCHT	RR	ZZZZ	USA
NEUMANN, CATHA.	49	F	W	RR	ZZZZ	USA
JACOB	18	M	LABR	RR	ZZZZ	USA
LUDIA	11	F	CH	RR	ZZZZ	USA
CATHA.	9	F	CHILD	RR	ZZZZ	USA
SLOMONIA	7	F	CHILD	RR	ZZZZ	USA
STARL, FRANZISKUS	21	M	FARMER	RR	AILA	USA
SCHAPUS, ANTON	21	M	FARMER	RR	AILA	USA
WEINSTEIN, LUDW.	35	M	FARMER	RR	AILA	USA
ROSENTHAL, JOSEF	34	M	FARMER	RR	AILA	USA
EISIK	29	M	FARMER	RR	AILA	USA
STEIN, JACOB	19	M	FARMER	RR	AILA	USA
WELNER, SALOM.	37	M	BCHR	RR	AILA	USA
PAULINE	32	F	W	RR	AILA	USA
MORITZ	11	M	CH	RR	AILA	USA
ALB.	9	M	CHILD	RR	AILA	USA
WOLF	9	M	CHILD	RR	AILA	USA
MICHEL	4	M	CHILD	RR	AILA	USA
GABRIEL	.06	M	INFANT	RR	AILA	USA
CIESINSKI, JOHN	26	M	LABR	RR	AILA	USA
HUCK, ADOLF	20	M	LABR	RR	ZZZZ	USA
SZAFFRAMSKI, SCHMOL	19	M	BCHR	RR	AHQU	USA
ROCHEL	22	M	UNKNOWN	RR	AHQU	USA
JORSTMANN, MINNA	39	F	W	RR	AHQU	USA
DOBE	3	F	CHILD	RR	AHQU	USA
ABRAHAM	2	M	CHILD	RR	AHQU	USA
JETTE	.11	F	INFANT	RR	AHQU	USA

SHIP: ANCHORIA

FROM: GLASGOW AND MOVILLE
TO: NEW YORK
ARRIVED: 30 NOVEMBER 1888

PASSENGER	AGE	SEX	OCCUPATION	PRV VIL DES
KAPLAN, LEIBE	35	F	UNKNOWN	RRZZZZUSA
SCHEINE	6	F	CHILD	RRZZZZUSA
ISRAEL	1	M	CHILD	RRZZZZUSA
SORE	1	F	CHILD	RRZZZZUSA
KLAPP, LEA	43	F	UNKNOWN	RRZZZZUSA
FANNY	12	F	UNKNOWN	RRZZZZUSA
ROSA	10	F	CH	RRZZZZUSA
RISIKO, NACHMAN	35	M	BKBNDR	RRZZZZUSA
BUSCH, ITZIG	24	M	JNR	RRZZZZUSA
HINDE	25	F	W	RRZZZZUSA
OBELSCH, ASCHEL	40	M	LABR	RRZZZZUSA
LEA	40	F	W	RRZZZZUSA
KAPLAN, SCHMERL	35	M	SMH	RRZZZZUSA
ESRAS, ITZIG	42	M	LABR	RRZZZZUSA
LACHNOWITZ, CHONE	18	M	BBR	RRZZZZUSA
INOLKE, ANTONI	24	M	LABR	RRAIIVUSA
KALIKOWSKI, JAN	25	M	LABR	RRAHTFUSA
SIDONAS, KASEMIR	26	M	LABR	RRAHTFUSA
GASZUNIS, ANTON	26	M	LABR	RRAHTFUSA
BERTASKA, ANTON	26	M	LABR	RRAHTFUSA
KARDZINICE, KARL	21	M	LABR	RRAHTFUSA

SHIP: SPAIN

FROM: LIVERPOOL
TO: NEW YORK
ARRIVED: 30 NOVEMBER 1888

PASSENGER	AGE	SEX	OCCUPATION	PRV VIL DES
NOKENEN, SOPHIA	22	M	LABR	RRAEXKUSA
STORCH, FEIGE	17	M	LABR	RRAEXKUSA
SEIDEL, MATILDE	18	F	SP	RRAEXKUSA
WEISSLER, PAGE	22	M	LABR	RRAEXKUSA
BLANES, JOHS	36	M	LABR	RRAEXKUSA
NAKKOLA, M.	35	M	LABR	RRAEXKUSA
BAKKA, JOHAN	45	M	LABR	RRAEXKUSA
LESYEVRYTIS, B.	18	M	LABR	RRAEXKUSA
JACOB, OMAN	43	M	LABR	RRAEXKUSA
WUPEN, JANKEL	21	M	LABR	RRAEXKUSA
BOTEINIK, L.	20	F	SP	RRAEXKUSA
KIRASNERSKI, K.	36	F	W	RRAEXKUSA
W.	9	F	CHILD	RRAEXKUSA
HELENE	7	F	CHILD	RRAEXKUSA
AUSTIN	4	F	CHILD	RRAEXKUSA
JOSEF	.11	M	INFANT	RRAEXKUSA
FREDRICK, R.	20	M	LABR	RRAEXKUSA
U	20	F	W	RRAEXKUSA
RICKUINRATH, LORE	21	M	LABR	RRAEXKUSA
KALINA, M.	20	M	LABR	RRAEXKUSA
CITSEN, N.	24	F	W	RRZZZZUSA
U	.10	F	INFANT	RRZZZZUSA
MELUTOFF, B.	30	M	LABR	RRZZZZUSA
LUNDBERG, A.	19	M	LABR	RRZZZZUSA
HANCHAN, A.	18	M	LABR	RRZZZZUSA
PINICK, JOHN	24	M	LABR	RRZZZZUSA
LEIPYRIGER, SOL.	28	M	LABR	RRZZZZUSA
MANSKOPT, D.	26	M	LABR	RRZZZZUSA
WELIKKA, VICTOR	30	M	LABR	RRZZZZUSA
SCHEVVY, HEIN.	22	F	W	RRZZZZUSA
U	1	F	CHILD	RRZZZZUSA
SCHWARTZ, BESIL	26	F	SP	RRZZZZUSA
MARKUSUS, E.	20	F	SP	RRZZZZUSA

SHIP: CITY OF BERLIN

FROM: LIVERPOOL
TO: NEW YORK
ARRIVED: 01 DECEMBER 1888

PASSENGER	AGE	SEX	OCCUPATION	PRV VIL DES
SESPINER, DAVID	36	M	LABR	RRACBFNY
IWANOW, PIFAN	19	M	LABR	RRACBFNY
ROSENTHAL, LOUISE	32	M	LABR	RRACBFNY
BACKWORTH, JOSEPH	19	M	TLR	RRACBFNY
NATHEUSEN, MAUER	17	M	LABR	RRACBFNY
KAHUN, ERIK	17	M	FARMER	RRAICENY
DERGETUTIES, MICHAEL	23	M	LABR	RRACBFNY
ERISUEK, JOHN	23	M	LABR	RRACBFNY
KASPEEWING, PETERON	28	M	LABR	RRACBFNY
KIAWUNG, JAN	18	F	W	RRACBFWI
JAN	6	F	CHILD	RRACBFWI
KEMERN, JULIAN	25	F	LABR	RRACBFNY
DERGILESHEL, JEAGI	52	M	LABR	RRACBFNY
BRANNSTEIN, ANNA	20	M	LABR	RRACBFMN
ROTHESCHULET, REWKIE	18	F	LABR	RRACBFNY
JENTE	16	F	LABR	RRACBFNY
DRIZIENICH, ANDERZ	24	M	LABR	RRACBFNY
MUCHOLEWSKI, KEZINEL	21	M	LABR	RRACBFNY
SNOFS, TEIVEL	30	M	LABR	RRACBFNY
HOLEERNE, JOHN	18	M	LABR	RRACBFALB
ICOTES, H.	47	F	W	RRACBFNY
LEIB	15	M	CH	RRACBFNY
ANN	9	F	CHILD	RRACBFNY
KURTENWIK, CHINE	24	M	LABR	RRACBFNY
WEICH, FREDRICH	38	M	LABR	RRACBFNY
STEIN, HENERICH	18	M	LABR	RRACBFNY
RINKENUES, IWAN	39	M	LABR	RRACBFNY
HAFFEMANN, LOUISE	32	M	LABR	RRACBFNY
LEAVY, ROSALIE	10	F	CH	RRACBFNY
GLASEN, KEIL	17	M	LABR	RRACBFNY
HOLOFGINET, SCHEINE	36	F	W	RRACBFNY
JEWIE	11	F	CH	RRACBFNY
ISSAK	10	M	CH	RRACBFNY
LEIB	8	M	CHILD	RRACBFNY
FEIGEL	5	M	CHILD	RRACBFNY
MARK, HERSCH	17	M	CH	RRACBFNY
REN, J.BERL	21	M	LABR	RRACBFNY
GOLDENBERG, EISKI	18	M	TLR	RRACBFNY

SHIP: ALLER

FROM: BREMEN
TO: NEW YORK
ARRIVED: 01 DECEMBER 1888

PASSENGER	AGE	SEX	OCCUPATION	PRV VIL DES
JANKOWSKI, JAN	45	M	FARMER	RRZZZZUSA
VOIGT, WALTER	24	M	FARMER	RRZZZZUSA
JONAS, JULIUS	33	M	FARMER	RRZZZZUSA
DYLINSKI, JAN	20	M	LABR	RRZZZZUSA
FRUEHSAM, MICHEL	18	M	FARMER	RRZZZZUSA
SZAFRANSKI, VICTORIA	30	F	NN	RRZZZZUSA
MARIA	8	F	CHILD	RRZZZZUSA
HEINR.	5	M	CHILD	RRZZZZUSA
JAMINA	3	F	CHILD	RRZZZZUSA
SIEGMUND	.09	M	INFANT	RRZZZZUSA
SENGER, JOSEF	58	M	FARMER	RRZZZZUSA
AGATHE	48	F	W	RRZZZZUSA
MARIE	18	F	CH	RRZZZZUSA
PHILOME	17	F	CH	RRZZZZUSA
CHRISTINE	9	F	CHILD	RRZZZZUSA
JOSEFA	8	F	CHILD	RRZZZZUSA
ANGELA.	7	F	CHILD	RRZZZZUSA
JOSEF	4	M	CHILD	RRZZZZUSA

PASSENGER	AGE	SEX	OCCUPATION	PRV VIL DES
MARTHA	3	F	CHILD	RRZZZZUSA
FRANZISKA	2	F	CHILD	RRZZZZUSA
RICHTER, HYRONIMUS	44	M	FARMER	RRZZZZUSA
LISBETH	39	F	W	RRZZZZUSA
JACOB	14	M	CH	RRZZZZUSA
BARBA.	4	F	CHILD	RRZZZZUSA
CHRIST.	2	M	CHILD	RRZZZZUSA
CAULIA	.06	F	INFANT	RRZZZZUSA
MATH.	39	M	FARMER	RRZZZZUSA
MARG.	39	F	W	RRZZZZUSA
FRANZ	9	M	CHILD	RRZZZZUSA
VALENT.	.06	M	INFANT	RRZZZZUSA
JOHS.	18	M	FARMER	RRZZZZUSA
JACOB	18	M	FARMER	RRZZZZUSA
ROHDE, WILH.	34	M	FARMER	RRZZZZUSA
GOTTL.	23	M	FARMER	RRZZZZUSA
LYDIA	6	F	CHILD	RRZZZZUSA
EMILIE	4	F	CHILD	RRZZZZUSA
MATHE.	2	F	CHILD	RRZZZZUSA
SAMUEL	.09	M	INFANT	RRZZZZUSA
SORZKONY, ANNA	30	F	NN	RRZZZZUSA
ELISE	9	F	CHILD	RRZZZZUSA
PETER	3	M	CHILD	RRZZZZUSA
ANNY	.04	F	INFANT	RRZZZZUSA
ANTON	24	M	FARMER	RRZZZZUSA
SCHMIDT, HEINR.	35	M	FARMER	RRZZZZUSA
GENOFEVA	28	F	W	RRZZZZUSA
FRANZKA.	9	F	CHILD	RRZZZZUSA
MAGDAL.	7	F	CHILD	RRZZZZUSA
BARBA.	6	F	CHILD	RRZZZZUSA
MARIANNE	4	F	CHILD	RRZZZZUSA
GEORG	2	M	CHILD	RRZZZZUSA
AGNES	.05	F	INFANT	RRZZZZUSA
VETTER, AUG.	43	M	FARMER	RRZZZZUSA
JOSEFINA	37	F	W	RRZZZZUSA
JOHA.	18	F	CH	RRZZZZUSA
THOMAS	15	M	CH	RRZZZZUSA
ROSALIE	13	F	CH	RRZZZZUSA
MAGDAL.	11	F	CH	RRZZZZUSA
MARGA.	9	F	CHILD	RRZZZZUSA
ANTON	7	M	CHILD	RRZZZZUSA
VALENTIN	48	M	FARMER	RRZZZZUSA
FRANZKA	44	F	W	RRZZZZUSA
JOHA.	13	F	CH	RRZZZZUSA
BALTH.	11	M	CH	RRZZZZUSA
JULIE	17	F	CH	RRZZZZUSA
MARGA.	13	F	CH	RRZZZZUSA
MARIA	9	F	CHILD	RRZZZZUSA
FRUEHSAM, JOH.	28	M	FARMER	RRZZZZUSA
MAGD.	26	F	W	RRZZZZUSA
MARIA	4	F	CHILD	RRZZZZUSA
THERESIA	.05	F	INFANT	RRZZZZUSA
MICHEL	19	M	FARMER	RRZZZZUSA
GOLDADE, PETER	20	M	FARMER	RRZZZZUSA
VALENT.	29	M	FARMER	RRZZZZUSA
CATH.	23	F	W	RRZZZZUSA
BERNH.	.11	M	INFANT	RRZZZZUSA

SHIP: NOORDLAND

FROM: ANTWERP
TO: NEW YORK
ARRIVED: 01 DECEMBER 1888

PASSENGER	AGE	SEX	OCCUPATION	PRV VIL DES
BECK, R.	35	M	LABR	RRAHOOPVX
TURSIK, J.	26	M	FARMER	RRAHOONY
HAUZLIK, J.	55	M	FARMER	RRAHOONY
M.	53	F	W	RRAHOONY
B.	15	F	SVNT	RRAHOONY
KUBAT, J.	26	M	LABR	RRAHOONY
KLAG, A.	23	F	SVNT	RRAHOOUNK

SHIP: STATE OF NEVADA

FROM: GLASGOW AND LARNE
TO: NEW YORK
ARRIVED: 01 DECEMBER 1888

PASSENGER	AGE	SEX	OCCUPATION	PRV VIL DES
BASCHKER, SAML.	20	M	TLR	RRZZZZUSA
DWORE	19	F	W	RRZZZZUSA
DAVIDOFF, MOSES	50	M	LABR	RRZZZZUSA
U	20	F	CH	RRZZZZUSA
MARIA	14	F	CH	RRZZZZUSA
SOWINSKY, ISRAEL	37	M	TLR	RRZZZZUSA
DAMOWITSCH, ANTON	20	M	LABR	RRZZZZUSA
--UTSTEIN, U	45	M	TLR	RRZZZZUSA
LUKOWITZ, ABR.	50	M	TLR	RRZZZZUSA
PIETZKA, SALOMEA	20	F	UNKNOWN	RRZZZZUSA
FELIX	.06	M	INFANT	RRZZZZUSA
WOLOZOWICZ, EVA	21	F	W	RRZZZZUSA
VINCENTY	.11	M	INFANT	RRZZZZUSA

SHIP: HERMANN

FROM: BREMEN
TO: BALTIMORE
ARRIVED: 03 DECEMBER 1888

PASSENGER	AGE	SEX	OCCUPATION	PRV VIL DES
SALKENVIZ, ANELLA	19	F	UNKNOWN	RRZZZZMD
WATNER, SCHORE	12	F	UNKNOWN	RRZZZZMD
KNOPS, PAULINE	21	F	UNKNOWN	RRZZZZMD
HERZ, BAREL	41	F	UNKNOWN	RRZZZZMD
FUEKS, HERM.	00	U	UNKNOWN	RRZZZZMD
U, U	00	U	UNKNOWN	RRZZZZMD
GRAFENBERG, ANNA	19	F	UNKNOWN	RRZZZZMD
EULER, U	11	M	CH	RRZZZZMD
POBOLINSKI, PEISACH	50	M	DLR	RRZZZZMD
HENE	50	F	W	RRZZZZMD
FEIGE	11	F	CH	RRZZZZMD
DIVORE	9	F	CHILD	RRZZZZMD
KANZAR, MARG.	26	F	UNKNOWN	RRZZZZMD
JAZE	5	F	CHILD	RRZZZZMD
JOSEF	.01	M	INFANT	RRZZZZMD
KRAJEWSKA, SLANE	26	M	LABR	RRZZZZMD
ROESSEL, CHRIST.	20	M	LABR	RRZZZZMI
FEDER, WOLF	33	M	DLR	RRZZZZMD
CHAJE	27	F	W	RRZZZZMD
JOSEF	4	M	CHILD	RRZZZZMD
ELIAS	3	M	CHILD	RRZZZZMD
GALI	.11	F	INFANT	RRZZZZMD
KAHN, MICHEL	27	M	UNKNOWN	RRZZZZMD
ABRAM, JOHANN	22	M	LABR	RRZZZZMD
SCHLAPOVERSKI, BENJ.	22	F	UNKNOWN	RRZZZZMD
ZWEIG, SCHAESE	22	F	UNKNOWN	RRZZZZMD
STARK, MICHAEL	50	M	FARMER	RRZZZZMD
AUGUSTE	50	F	W	RRZZZZMD
PAUL	25	M	FARMER	RRZZZZMD
EMIL	15	M	UNKNOWN	RRZZZZMD
GALZKI, ROBERT	17	M	UNKNOWN	RRZZZZMD
KARNZA, FRANZ	27	M	FARMER	RRZZZZMD
HAVERMANN, HENRIETT	50	M	UNKNOWN	RRZZZZMD
ANNA	20	F	UNKNOWN	RRZZZZMD
GRUENBERG, BEDASI	50	M	UNKNOWN	RRZZZZMD
WELERI	11	M	CH	RRZZZZMD
BRUNZINSKI, MOSES	20	M	FARMER	RRZZZZMD

PASSENGER	AGE	SEX	OCCUPATION	PV RI VL DES
BERGER, MENASCHE	57	M	UNKNOWN	RRZZZZMD
LIEBE	11	F	CH	RRZZZZMD
U, U	00	U	UNKNOWN	RRZZZZMD

SHIP: NOVA SCOTIAN

FROM: LIVERPOOL
TO: BALTIMORE
ARRIVED: 03 DECEMBER 1888

PASSENGER	AGE	SEX	OCCUPATION	PV RI VL DES
SHEROTTE, MOSES	51	M	SHMK	RRZZZZBAL
BASCHE	40	F	W	RRZZZZBAL
ISTRAEL	16	M	SHMK	RRZZZZBAL
CHAIE	15	M	SHMK	RRZZZZBAL
ABRAHAM	11	M	CH	RRZZZZBAL
DAVID	10	M	CH	RRZZZZBAL
ETHE	8	F	CHILD	RRZZZZBAL
FANNIE	5	F	CHILD	RRZZZZBAL
ARON	3	M	CHILD	RRZZZZBAL
SUSE	1	F	CHILD	RRZZZZBAL
GASMIS, DOMINIK	24	M	LABR	RRZZZZBAL
TOMASCHENDT, HANISL	22	M	LABR	RRZZZZBAL
KURTIS, JACOB	24	M	SMH	RRZZZZBAL
LEDOWSKY, ADAM	21	M	LABR	RRZZZZUSA
KISE, JIRSCHIM	21	F	SVNT	RRZZZZBAL
LASHS, MALKE	23	F	SVNT	RRZZZZBAL

SHIP: RUGIA

FROM: HAMBURG
TO: NEW YORK
ARRIVED: 03 DECEMBER 1888

PASSENGER	AGE	SEX	OCCUPATION	PV RI VL DES
ALCZOWSKY, MACY	21	M	LABR	RRZZZZUSA
ZOCHAROW, ANNA	16	F	SGL	RRZZZZUSA
STEFANOWSKY, LUDWIG	19	M	LABR	RRAHZSUSA
ANDRUKAT, PAULINE	26	F	WO	RRZZZZUSA
OSWALD	.10	M	INFANT	RRZZZZUSA
KALTOWSKI, ANDRE.	14	M	LABR	RRZZZZUSA
ANNA	16	F	SGL	RRZZZZUSA
BLANK, SIEGMUND	21	M	LABR	RRAFWJUSA
MOSESOHN, MORDCHE	28	M	UNKNOWN	RRAHZSUSA
KASTRAUSKI, ITZIG	20	M	LABR	RRAIBOUSA
STANISKI, JAN	26	M	LABR	RRAICXUSA
WONZOWICZ, CARL	29	M	SMH	RRAHUFUSA
TENENBERG, LEON	22	M	CL	RRZZZZUSA
TOKAUSKY, HIRSCH	17	M	TLR	RRAFWJUSA
WARSCHAWSKY, SIGMUND	26	M	TNM	RRZZZZUSA
BROGOWSKY, JAN	20	M	MCHT	RRZZZZUSA
KRUPUTOJTYS, JOS.	23	M	MCHT	RRAHZSUSA
BAUNERMANN, TAUBE	7	F	CHILD	RRAIFRUSA
JASINSKY, ANTON	21	M	LABR	RRZZZZUSA
SKUTSCHAS, VINCENTI	23	M	LABR	RRAHXLUSA
MARIANNA	23	F	W	RRAHXLUSA
MIDLER, CHAZKEL	17	M	LABR	RRZZZZUSA
SCHILINGAWSKY, MOSES	19	M	LABR	RRZZZZUSA
MIDLER, MICHEL	18	M	SMH	RRZZZZUSA
RUBEN, MEIER	49	M	LABR	RRZZZZUSA
KATIN, MICHEL	45	M	LABR	RRZZZZUSA

SHIP: MARSALA

FROM: HAMBURG
TO: NEW YORK
ARRIVED: 06 DECEMBER 1888

PASSENGER	AGE	SEX	OCCUPATION	PV RI VL DES
LEWITZKI, MARTIN	28	M	LABR	RRAINXNY
LICHT, PESCHE	18	F	SGL	RRAHTUNY
SEIL, MARGARETHE	20	F	SGL	RRZZZZNY
PLOTNIK, BENSMEN	27	M	LABR	RRZZZZNY
SCHOLEM	4	M	CHILD	RRAIEMNY
FEIGERSOHN, KEILE	20	F	SGL	RRAHWENY
NEUMANN, ALEX	18	M	BKR	RRZZZZNY
DONEKER, BALDIN	25	M	APTC	RRAIKNNY
GROTT, FRANZ	37	M	LABR	RRAHYKNY
HELENE	7	F	CHILD	RRAHYKNY
LEWITA, ELLA	18	F	SGL	RRAIINNY
CHAIKELOWITZ, BEILE	16	F	SGL	RRAHXLNY
DAVIED	7	M	CHILD	RRAHXLNY
ROSENWASSER, REFINA	22	F	SGL	RRAFWJNY
DIAMAND, LIEBE	45	F	WO	RRAHTNNY
JACOB	7	M	CHILD	RRAHTNNY
SALOMON	19	M	UNKNOWN	RRAHTNNY
KAZIMIR, ALEX	30	M	LABR	RRAHZSNY
GOLDMANN, LIEBE	17	F	SGL	RRAIGHNY
SILBERSTEIN, SARA	23	F	WO	RRAHTSNY
LEIB	.11	M	INFANT	RRAHTSNY
CHONE	.02	F	INFANT	RRAHTSNY
POLLIN, BRARES	23	M	MCHT	RRAIGCNY
TRACHELSKY, TAUBE	60	F	WO	RRADOINY
NUNEWITZ, STANISLAV	22	M	SHMK	RRAIKBNY
BENZIC, JOSEF	23	M	LABR	RRZZZZNY
MARBER, HINDE	53	F	WO	RRZZZZNY
U	18	F	WO	RRZZZZNY
ETTE	7	F	CHILD	RRZZZZNY
PECAR, ANTON	21	M	LABR	RRZZZZUNK
SEMANZIK, LEA	50	F	WO	RRZZZZNY
MARIE	5	F	CHILD	RRZZZZNY
LOGANKA, ULIANNA	21	F	WO	RRZZZZNY
FRANZ	.11	M	INFANT	RRZZZZNY
JAN	.01	M	INFANT	RRZZZZNY
LEWANDOWSKY, JOSEF	23	M	LABR	RRZZZZNY
BERKOWITZ, ROSA	45	F	WO	RRAHUONY
LEWANDOWSKA, JEAN	28	M	LABR	RRZZZZNY
WOZNIAK, ROSALLIE	38	F	WO	RRZZZZNY
MARIANNE	16	F	CH	RRZZZZNY
WLADISLAUS	4	M	CHILD	RRZZZZNY
STEFAN	.11	M	INFANT	RRZZZZNY
BIEDERMANN, MORITZ	34	M	MCHT	RRZZZZNY
NEUMANN, HEINR.	21	M	LABR	RRZZZZNY
APESZINSKY, ABR.	16	M	LABR	RRZZZZNY
HAIMBUCKEL, ADELHEID	19	F	SGL	RRZZZZPIT
WILLNER, BEILE	30	F	WO	RRZZZZPIT
HIRSCH	7	M	CHILD	RRZZZZPIT
JANKEL	4	M	CHILD	RRZZZZPIT
NOAH	.11	M	INFANT	RRZZZZPIT

SHIP: DEVONIA

FROM: GLASGOW
TO: NEW YORK
ARRIVED: 06 DECEMBER 1888

PASSENGER	AGE	SEX	OCCUPATION	PV RI VL DES
ABRAMOWITZ, JUDEL	25	M	PDLR	RRZZZZUSA
CHAJE	23	F	UNKNOWN	RRZZZZUSA
SESCHZINSKY, ABRAHAM	35	M	TLR	RRZZZZUSA
MINA	18	F	SVNT	RRZZZZUSA
ZIPE	16	F	SVNT	RRZZZZUSA
STRACH, GIRSCH	42	M	LABR	RRZZZZUSA

PASSENGER	AGE	SEX	OCCUPATION	PRIVIL	DES
CHANE	22	F	SVNT	RRZZZZ	USA
BORUCH	20	M	LABR	RRZZZZ	USA
SINTMAN, CHANE	30	F	UNKNOWN	RRZZZZ	USA
PESCHE	.09	F	INFANT	RRZZZZ	USA
WINZKOWSKY, LEB.	30	M	LABR	RRZZZZ	USA
MINE	18	F	SVNT	RRZZZZ	USA
WASBUTSKI, SCHLOME	19	M	PDLR	RRZZZZ	USA
ISAK	16	M	PDLR	RRZZZZ	USA
ETTEL	15	F	UNKNOWN	RRZZZZ	USA
EISIK	10	M	CH	RRZZZZ	USA
GOLDMAN, SLATE	17	F	SVNT	RRZZZZ	USA
LEWIN, MICHL.	24	M	SVNT	RRZZZZ	USA
BARANOSKI, JOSEF	23	M	LABR	RRZZZZ	USA
BERENSTEIN, SAUL	18	M	LABR	RRZZZZ	USA
GOLDBERG, SCHLOME	23	M	LABR	RRZZZZ	USA
FELDMAN, HIRSCH	30	M	LABR	RRZZZZ	USA
JUCHNEDCTZKI, BARUCH	43	M	LABR	RRZZZZ	USA
IDELSOHN, MOSES	20	M	LABR	RRZZZZ	USA
KASDAN, LEIB	23	M	LABR	RRZZZZ	USA
KRAMETZ, JUDEL	18	M	LABR	RRZZZZ	USA
RAGOW, ISAK	41	M	LABR	RRZZZZ	USA
STRAUS, MARKUS	21	M	LABR	RRZZZZ	USA

SHIP: WISCONSIN

FROM: LIVERPOOL AND QUEENSTOWN
TO: NEW YORK
ARRIVED: 06 DECEMBER 1888

PASSENGER	AGE	SEX	OCCUPATION	PRIVIL	DES
SAPIRA, MOSSEL	20	M	GZR	RRZZZZ	USA
KARROL, REBECCA	24	F	W	RRZZZZ	USA
ABRAM	.09	M	INFANT	RRZZZZ	USA
BERNSTEIN, RACHEL	29	F	UNKNOWN	RRZZZZ	USA
FR--E	4	F	CHILD	RRZZZZ	USA
BEILE	3	F	CHILD	RRZZZZ	USA
BELITZKY, JOHANNA	16	F	UNKNOWN	RRZZZZ	USA
LASNITZKY, ROSA	45	F	UNKNOWN	RRZZZZ	USA
SLOTSKY, GOLDE-	22	M	MSN	RRZZZZ	USA
KURTZ, PESACH	17	M	MSN	RRZZZZ	USA
ROSENSTREICH, CHAIME	18	F	SP	RRZZZZ	USA
WESTERMAN, JOHAN	21	M	FARMER	FNZZZZ	USA

SHIP: STATE OF NEBRASKA

FROM: GLASGOW AND LARNE
TO: NEW YORK
ARRIVED: 06 DECEMBER 1888

PASSENGER	AGE	SEX	OCCUPATION	PRIVIL	DES
BLANKENBERG, ITZIG	36	M	PDLR	FNAIDL	USA
MECK, NISSON	36	M	PDLR	FNAIDL	USA
GOLD, HILLEL	19	M	PNTR	FNAIDL	USA
GILMAN, BER	35	M	LABR	FNAIDL	USA
SCHWOSEN, LEISER	19	M	BCHR	FNAIDL	USA
RABINOWITSCH, SONNE	24	M	JNR	FNAIDL	USA
WARSCHAWZYK, ISSE	19	M	CL	FNAIDL	USA
REICH, ABRAHAM	23	M	MLR	FNAIDL	USA
SCHMEROWITZ, MEYER	30	M	LKSH	FNAIDL	USA
GLICK, MENDEL	17	M	CL	FNAIDL	USA
MARTRUSOHN, HIRSCH	18	M	LABR	FNAIDL	USA
BENJAMIN	15	M	LABR	FNAIDL	USA
WIRSCH, INDEL	11	M	CH	FNAIDL	USA
KRAKINOWSKI, ISRAEL	11	M	UNKNOWN	FNAIDL	USA
SORE	9	F	CHILD	FNAIDL	USA
WIRSCHBA, RIFKE	15	F	SP	FNAIDL	USA
WILK, FEIGE	25	F	W	FNAIDL	USA

PASSENGER	AGE	SEX	OCCUPATION	PRIVIL	DES
CHANE	4	F	CHILD	FNAIDL	USA
U, U	00	U	CH	FNAIDL	USA
NEMAROFSKY, REITZE	35	F	W	FNAIDL	USA
LIPI	11	M	CH	FNAIDL	USA
MOSES	8	M	CHILD	FNAIDL	USA
SIMON	.11	M	INFANT	FNAIDL	USA
KANTER, SCHOLEM	25	M	PDLR	FNAIDL	USA
BEILE	25	F	W	FNAIDL	USA
SCHAPERA, ELLIAS	40	M	BKR	FNAIDL	CAN
ESTHER	40	F	W	FNAIDL	CAN
PHOREZ	7	M	CHILD	FNAIDL	CAN
KWITNISKI, FRANZISIK	18	M	LABR	FNAIDL	USA
SOBESTRIEL, VOICHECK	45	M	LABR	FNAIDL	USA
URBAN, VOICHECK	33	M	LABR	FNAIDL	USA
HEYACEK, MATHES	31	M	LABR	FNAIDL	USA
PETRUSINSKY, JOACHIM	29	M	SP	FNAIDL	USA
QUARTNER, DEBORA	17	F	SP	FNAIDL	USA
LISNEWSKA, ANNA	22	F	W	FNAIDL	USA
GIZESKKOWIAK, ANNA	30	F	W	FNAIDL	USA
STANISLAWA	6	F	CHILD	FNAIDL	USA
MARTINA	2	F	CHILD	FNAIDL	USA
FRANZISKA	2	F	CHILD	FNAIDL	USA
ANTONY	.04	M	INFANT	FNAIDL	USA

SHIP: WIELAND

FROM: HAMBURG
TO: NEW YORK
ARRIVED: 07 DECEMBER 1888

PASSENGER	AGE	SEX	OCCUPATION	PRIVIL	DES
POKALSKI, JOSEF	27	M	LABR	FNAAKH	USA
KOPEL, MOSES	24	M	MCHT	FNAHTF	USA
RIFKE	22	F	W	FNAHTF	USA
JACOBSOHN, RAHAEL	7	M	CHILD	FNAHTU	USA
AISIK	54	M	DLR	FNAHTU	USA
SCHIRER, JANKEL	43	M	LABR	RRZZZZ	USA
STARKMMEITT, LISA	18	F	SGL	RRAFVG	USA
KIERAJSZIE, ANTHONY	31	M	FARMER	RRZZZZ	USA
SEGALOWSKY, PESCHE	50	F	WO	RRAIHB	USA
BEILE	19	F	CH	RRAIHB	USA
RIWKE	7	F	CHILD	RRAIHB	USA
MENTZ, FERD.	24	M	TNR	RRACBF	USA
GERTRUDE	22	F	W	RRACBF	USA
LEWINSOHN, SAMUEL	50	M	DLR	RRAHZS	USA
GITTEL	50	F	W	RRAHZS	USA
TONIE	17	F	CH	RRAHZS	USA
RACHEL	15	M	CH	RRAHZS	USA
LEIB	14	M	CH	RRAHZS	USA
LEA	7	F	CHILD	RRAHZS	USA
KATZ, ABRAHAM	45	M	MCHT	RRZZZZ	USA
GUTMANN, ABRAHAM	20	M	LABR	RRAHXL	USA
LICHTMANN, CHAJE	15	F	SGL	RRZZZZ	USA
SEGALL, CHANNE	32	F	WO	RRAHTF	USA
MOSES	7	M	CHILD	RRAHTF	USA
JOSEF	6	M	CHILD	RRAHTF	USA
HIRSCH	4	M	CHILD	RRAHTF	USA
HURWITZ, LEIB	19	M	DLR	RRAHWE	USA
KORACH, HUGO	24	M	MCHT	RRACBF	USA
OSCHWANGER, ELIAS	46	M	MCHT	RRZZZZ	USA
STANKOWSKA, OLIANNA	24	F	SGL	RRZZZZ	USA
SERLIN, LEA	32	F	WO	RRZZZZ	USA
CHONE	7	F	CHILD	RRZZZZ	USA
SARA	6	F	CHILD	RRZZZZ	USA
REBEKKA	4	F	CHILD	RRZZZZ	USA
JACOB	3	M	CHILD	RRZZZZ	USA
MARIE	.11	F	INFANT	RRZZZZ	USA
MARCINKEWICZ, INOZAS	21	M	LABR	RRAHZS	USA
KALISZEFSKI, JOSEF	22	M	LABR	RRZZZZ	USA
MARIE	24	F	W	RRZZZZ	USA
STANISL.	16	M	CH	RRZZZZ	USA

PASSENGER	AGE	SEX	OCCUPATION	PRV	VIL	DES
ANTONIA	.07	F	INFANT	RR	ZZZZ	USA
BEHRMANN, HIRSCH	24	M	LABR	RR	ZZZZ	USA
PIOZ, WENDELIN	24	M	LABR	RR	ZZZZ	USA
MAGDALENA	23	F	W	RR	ZZZZ	USA
JACOB	3	M	CHILD	RR	ZZZZ	USA
PH.	.11	M	INFANT	RR	ZZZZ	USA
BEDNARSKI, IGNATZ	34	M	LABR	RR	ZZZZ	USA
WILDEMANN, MICHAEL	23	M	TLR	RR	AHUI	USA
FRIEDRICH	17	M	TLR	RR	AHUI	USA
SERHN, JACOB	20	M	DLR	RR	AHQU	USA
WEINSTEIN, BEILE	26	F	WO	RR	AHVU	USA
MICHLE	4	M	CHILD	RR	AHVU	USA
RUTKOWSKI, ADAM	27	M	LABR	RR	AHTO	USA
WISZNEWSKI, JAN	39	M	LABR	RR	AHTO	USA
JENIKOWZKI, VICENTI	26	M	LABR	RR	AHTO	USA
STALLMUS, JONAS	24	M	LABR	RR	ZZZZ	USA
AWENT, JOHANN	24	M	LABR	RR	ZZZZ	USA
STEINKE, JULS	22	M	LABR	RR	ZZZZ	USA
DRESSLER, FRITZ	20	M	CPTR	RR	AHXH	USA
GERSCHOWSKY, JOHANN	23	M	LABR	RR	AIDN	USA
KADZINSKA, HELENE	17	F	SGL	RR	AIDN	USA
JOSEF	7	M	CHILD	RR	AIDN	USA
ALBRECHT, LOUISE	24	F	SGL	RR	ZZZZ	USA
WENZLAN, MARIE	26	F	SGL	RR	ZZZZ	USA
SCHEWE, WILH.	18	M	LABR	RR	ZZZZ	USA
BUETTNER, GUSTAV	23	M	LABR	RR	ZZZZ	USA
FIELBRAND, FRIEDRICH	26	M	LABR	RR	ZZZZ	USA
PFEIFFER, MINNA	26	F	WO	RR	AAKH	USA
STREICHERT, LUDWIG	24	M	LABR	RR	ZZZZ	USA
LITTMANMN, LOUIS	16	M	CL	RR	AIIV	USA
RUBEN, JOSEPH	20	M	LABR	RR	AHTU	USA
MINKO, JOSEPH	20	M	LABR	RR	AHZP	USA
SPITZER, URIEL	23	M	MCHT	RR	ZZZZ	USA
ANNA	22	F	W	RR	ZZZZ	USA
BEILIN, RACHEL	20	F	SGL	RR	AHTU	USA
ARENDARSKY, VINCENTY	27	M	LABR	RR	ZZZZ	USA
WASINSKY, STANISL.	43	M	CK	RR	ZZZZ	USA
ROLLNIK, JOSEPH	27	M	MCHT	RR	AHTU	USA
RITTENBAND, CHAIME	25	M	MCHT	RR	AHTU	USA
ROSENBERG, JACOB	16	M	MCHT	RR	ZZZZ	USA

SHIP: WAESLAND

FROM: ANTWERP
TO: NEW YORK
ARRIVED: 08 DECEMBER 1888

PASSENGER	AGE	SEX	OCCUPATION	PRV	VIL	DES
MISCH-K, NATHAN	45	M	TCHR	RR	ZZZZ	NY
NATTKEMPER, E	19	M	SLSMN	RR	ZZZZ	BAL

SHIP: CITY OF CHESTER

FROM: LIVERPOOL AND QUEENSTOWN
TO: NEW YORK
ARRIVED: 08 DECEMBER 1888

PASSENGER	AGE	SEX	OCCUPATION	PRV	VIL	DES
KOBIN, SELKE	30	M	LABR	RR	AGRT	NY
GUTTMANN, NACH.	22	M	LABR	RR	AGRT	NY
MORAWSKI, STANISL.	23	M	LABR	RR	AGRT	CH
JONOWITZ, MICHAL	47	M	SHMK	RR	AEFL	NY
GEDDORL, ELIUS	30	M	LABR	RR	AEFL	IL
PITIN, CHMERL	35	M	LABR	RR	AEFL	NY
SASS, SALOMON	23	M	LABR	RR	AEFL	PHI
SCHPIRA, HENOCH	40	M	TLR	RR	AEFL	NY
JOSEL	9	M	CHILD	RR	AEFL	NY
CUBACHINSK, ML.	24	M	BKR	RR	AEFL	PA
FELBER, JUDA	20	M	LABR	RR	AEFL	NY
GOTTOM, ABE.	23	M	TLR	RR	AEFL	NY
KALINSKY, ABR.	24	M	TLR	RR	AHXH	NY
NIEMOZAK, SIMON	24	M	LABR	RR	AHXH	NY
FRIEDMANN, LEIB	24	M	PDLR	RR	AHXH	USA
KYSKO, ISAAC	18	M	BLKSMH	RR	AHXH	NY
GOLDBEITUS, BORIS	26	M	TLR	RR	AHXH	NY
LAURENCE, WM.P.	16	M	WCHMKR	RR	AHQD	NY
BERKOWIEZ, BERND.	26	M	TLR	RR	AHQD	IL
ZUBECK, MOSES	23	M	WCHMKR	RR	ZZZZ	NY
GOLBEIN, DAVED	26	M	TLR	RR	ZZZZ	IL
GUTTMANN, NACH.	21	M	LABR	RR	ZZZZ	NY
RABINERSOHN, SUSS.	18	M	TLR	RR	ZZZZ	NY
JUMASCHKO, VIN.	26	M	BLKSMH	RR	ZZZZ	NW
ROSENBLATT, FEIGE	31	F	W	RR	ZZZZ	NW
KOBIN, FANNY	30	F	W	RR	ZZZZ	NY
JAYB, MARIE	20	F	W	RR	ZZZZ	NY
CHANNE	.11	F	INFANT	RR	ZZZZ	NY
SCHATSKY, PESCHE	17	F	SP	RR	ZZZZ	NY
RESNICK, CHAJE	20	F	DRSMKR	RR	ZZZZ	NY
PALLOCK, BREINE	40	F	W	RR	ZZZZ	NY
OSACK, FRANCES	52	M	LABR	RR	ZZZZ	PA
STOCKAWZAK, S.J.	35	F	SVNT	RR	ZZZZ	PA
SIEBERSTEIN, BERL.	40	M	CPTR	RR	AHQD	NY
PESCHE	38	F	W	RR	AHQD	NY
BRUCHMANN, WILFF	28	M	PDLR	RR	AHQD	NY
BETTE	25	F	W	RR	AHQD	NY
ANNA	32	F	SVNT	RR	AHQD	NY
DALTZ, ZIREL	22	F	W	RR	ZZZZ	NY
WANE	2	M	CHILD	RR	ZZZZ	NY
ABRAHAM	.08	M	INFANT	RR	ZZZZ	NY
GOLDENBERG, TAUBE	28	F	W	RR	ZZZZ	NY
BLINE	5	F	CHILD	RR	ZZZZ	NY
MANNIE	3	F	CHILD	RR	ZZZZ	NY
MITTE	.11	F	INFANT	RR	ZZZZ	NY

SHIP: IOWA

FROM: LIVERPOOL
TO: BOSTON
ARRIVED: ET UNKNOWN IN

PASSENGER	AGE	SEX	OCCUPATION	PRV	VIL	DES
LAVENHAM, MAX	31	M	TLR	RR	ZZZZ	USA
HEBIA	28	F	W	RR	ZZZZ	USA
RACHEL	11	F	SCH	RR	ZZZZ	USA
FANNY	8	F	CHILD	RR	ZZZZ	USA
BETTSY	6	F	CHILD	RR	ZZZZ	USA
HARRIS	2	M	CHILD	RR	ZZZZ	USA
MARY	.07	F	INFANT	RR	ZZZZ	USA
SHOSHUSLY, JACOB	18	M	PDLR	RR	ZZZZ	USA
ANDERSON, NEIL	25	M	SHMK	RR	ZZZZ	USA
KAIZERMAN, U	25	M	SHMK	RR	ZZZZ	USA

SHIP: P. CALAND

FROM: AMSTERDAM
TO: NEW YORK
ARRIVED: 10 DECEMBER 1888

PASSENGER	AGE	SEX	OCCUPATION	PRV	VIL	DES
BERN-HEIM, HIRSCH	26	M	SHMK	RR	ZZZZ	USA
MAXYNOKI, DAVID	26	M	LABR	RR	ZZZZ	USA
LABRAUSKI, SEND--	20	M	TLR	RR	ZZZZ	USA
SIRMISK, STEFAN	21	M	LABR	RR	ZZZZ	USA
ANDRY	23	M	LABR	RR	ZZZZ	USA

SHIP: ITALY

FROM: LIVERPOOL AND QUEENSTOWN
TO: NEW YORK
ARRIVED: 10 DECEMBER 1888

PASSENGER	AGE	SEX	OCCUPATION	PRV	VIL	DES
GOLDBERG, DORA	32	F	SP	RR	ADAX	BAL
ROGOZINSKI, H.	43	M	CPMKR	RR	ADBQ	CH
GANDZCHNEIDER, H.	23	M	TLR	RR	ADBQ	KS
KEYGERMAN, M.	24	F	SP	RR	ADAX	NY
WALTER, MARIE	26	F	SP	RR	ACBF	NY
KLEIN, ZILLI	20	F	W	RR	ACBF	NY
HERMAN	12	M	CH	RR	ACBF	NY
LEIB	8	M	CHILD	RR	ACBF	NY
SHUZALIS, JOSEF	25	M	LABR	RR	ACBF	NY
WALYEWSKY, L.	47	M	LABR	RR	AARR	NY
KATHERINE	35	F	W	RR	AARR	NY
FRANSISKA	14	M	LABR	RR	AARR	NY
MARIA	11	F	CH	RR	AARR	NY
JOHANNA	5	F	CHILD	RR	AARR	NY
JULIA	00	F	INF	RR	AARR	NY
WEISS, JENNY	23	F	SP	RR	ACBF	NY
GITTEL	13	M	CH	RR	ACBF	NY
GREICKER, PAWRON	33	M	LABR	RR	ACBF	PHI
DANKO, MARIE	24	M	LABR	RR	ACBF	UNK
BERGMAN, ISAAC	20	M	TLR	RR	ADBQ	UNK
SCHLANWEITZ, BER.	20	M	TLR	RR	ACBF	NY
RABINOWITZ, SCHIMEL	39	M	PDLR	RR	ACBF	NY
HIRSCHAN, BEREL	45	M	LABR	RR	ACBF	NY
BARKAS, JOSUS	21	M	LABR	RR	ACBF	NY
IBESCHEUESKY, JONAS	21	M	LABR	RR	ACBF	NY
GRASIGMACCY, U	39	M	LABR	RR	ACBF	NY

SHIP: AURANIA

FROM: LIVERPOOL AND QUEENSTOWN
TO: NEW YORK
ARRIVED: 10 DECEMBER 1888

PASSENGER	AGE	SEX	OCCUPATION	PRV	VIL	DES
SCHLOKIWITZ, CHANE	20	M	LABR	RR	ZZZZ	NY
CHANE	18	M	LABR	RR	ZZZZ	NY
KRAMER, ELKE	44	F	MA	RR	ZZZZ	NY
PELAEL	11	F	CH	RR	ZZZZ	NY
SUSKIN, MOSES	19	M	LABR	RR	ZZZZ	NY
KUGEL, CHAZKEL	21	M	LABR	RR	ZZZZ	NY
JACOBSON, BEILE	19	F	SP	RR	ZZZZ	NY
OKUM, HANNA	24	F	SP	RR	ZZZZ	NY
BERTHA	18	F	SP	RR	ZZZZ	NY
ROSA	16	F	SP	RR	ZZZZ	NY
SCHNUSTER, MECHAEL	19	M	LABR	RR	ZZZZ	NY
HERLPERN, SCHEINE	25	F	MA	RR	ZZZZ	NY
SARA	7	F	CHILD	RR	ZZZZ	NY
SZYAKIEWIZ, S.	37	M	LABR	RR	ZZZZ	NY
FRUDBERG, ADOLPH	42	M	LABR	RR	ZZZZ	NY
NOGNE, LOUIS	35	M	FARMER	RR	ZZZZ	NY
SOPHIE	40	F	W	RR	ZZZZ	NY
GROSS, REBECCA	19	F	SP	RR	ZZZZ	NY

SHIP: CIRCASSIA

FROM: GLASGOW AND MOVILLE
TO: NEW YORK
ARRIVED: 11 DECEMBER 1888

PASSENGER	AGE	SEX	OCCUPATION	PRV	VIL	DES
WUETALE, ANDREAS	30	M	TLR	RR	ZZZZ	USA
WAVANAUCLY, R.	22	M	TLR	RR	ZZZZ	USA
KAPLANSKIE, SAWEL	24	M	DLR	RR	ZZZZ	USA
WACKEE, JOHAN	55	M	FARMER	RR	ZZZZ	USA
PAVLICKE, ADAM	33	M	DLR	RR	ZZZZ	USA
GIENDHAUSEN, SAE	19	M	DLR	RR	ZZZZ	USA
RAF, ABRAHAM	18	M	DLR	RR	ZZZZ	USA
WEIN, REIE	19	M	MSN	RR	ZZZZ	USA
URBAUS, ANTANCES	23	M	LABR	RR	ZZZZ	USA
LUBWIES, SUNOW	38	M	DLR	RR	ZZZZ	USA
WUIE, HERSCH	24	M	TLR	RR	ZZZZ	USA
RUIE	23	F	UNKNOWN	RR	ZZZZ	USA
DWORKIN, LEIE	50	F	UNKNOWN	RR	ZZZZ	USA
SCHMALE	12	M	UNKNOWN	RR	ZZZZ	USA
JANKEL	10	M	CH	RR	ZZZZ	USA
CHAIE	9	F	CHILD	RR	ZZZZ	USA
SHUE	8	M	CHILD	RR	ZZZZ	USA
JOHELAM, AISIK	36	M	DLR	RR	ZZZZ	USA
RASCHE	36	F	UNKNOWN	RR	ZZZZ	USA
MATHAIS	20	M	UNKNOWN	RR	ZZZZ	USA
HEISCHE	18	F	UNKNOWN	RR	ZZZZ	USA
HERSCH	12	F	UNKNOWN	RR	ZZZZ	USA
GILLIE	11	F	UNKNOWN	RR	ZZZZ	USA
ELKIE	10	F	CH	RR	ZZZZ	USA
JOCKS	4	M	CHILD	RR	ZZZZ	USA
SCHMUEL	3	M	CHILD	RR	ZZZZ	USA
ZIUS, SCHAIGE	55	M	TLR	RR	ZZZZ	USA
IDES	58	F	UNKNOWN	RR	ZZZZ	USA
KOPEL, MINDEL	21	M	TLR	RR	ZZZZ	USA
ESTER	24	F	UNKNOWN	RR	ZZZZ	USA
HARWITZ, M.	55	M	TLR	RR	ZZZZ	USA
SLATA	55	F	UNKNOWN	RR	ZZZZ	USA
WEUNSTEIN, RESLAES	28	F	UNKNOWN	RR	ZZZZ	USA
RASELIE	7	F	CHILD	RR	ZZZZ	USA
SCHMAL	3	M	CHILD	RR	ZZZZ	USA
LEISER	2	M	CHILD	RR	ZZZZ	USA
SCHUR, RASSIE	40	F	UNKNOWN	RR	ZZZZ	USA
WOLF	12	M	UNKNOWN	RR	ZZZZ	USA
SCHOLEM	10	M	CH	RR	ZZZZ	USA
U	9	F	CHILD	RR	ZZZZ	USA
ENDELMAN, LEIBE	33	M	TCHR	RR	ZZZZ	USA
NICHAME	7	M	CHILD	RR	ZZZZ	USA

SHIP: EMS

FROM: BREMEN AND SOUTHAMPTON
TO: NEW YORK
ARRIVED: 11 DECEMBER 1888

PASSENGER	AGE	SEX	OCCUPATION	PRV	VIL	DES
LENGGELLFY, JANNY	24	F	UNKNOWN	RR	ZZZZ	USA
HOLM, GEORG	25	M	TT	RR	ZZZZ	USA
WART, SOPHIE	18	F	SVNT	RR	ZZZZ	USA
HEISLER, HERMANN	24	M	FARMER	RR	ZZZZ	USA
TALPIS, RAPHAEL	20	M	MCHT	RR	ZZZZ	USA
KASSELBERG, MINDEL	15	M	UNKNOWN	RR	ZZZZ	USA
GITEL	14	M	UNKNOWN	RR	ZZZZ	USA
JUTTA	9	F	CHILD	RR	ZZZZ	USA
WEISS, M.	55	M	FARMER	RR	ZZZZ	USA

SHIP: NEVADA

FROM: LIVERPOOL AND QUEENSTOWN
TO: NEW YORK
ARRIVED: 13 DECEMBER 1888

PASSENGER	AGE	SEX	OCCUPATION	PRI VIL DES
IMSOFFOWICZ, FEIWEL	26	M	LABR	RRACBFUSA
KROKOTZKY, LIEB	34	M	LABR	RRACBFUSA
MENDELOWITZ, JACOB	28	M	LABR	RRACBFUSA
PAUDRAVICH, MICHAEL	23	M	PDLR	RRACBFUSA
MALKOWSKI, LEINE	23	M	LABR	RRACBFUSA
BALBETZKI, CHANE	35	F	W	RRACBFUSA
WOLFF	9	M	CHILD	RRACBFUSA
HENZEPOWITZ, LEA	19	F	SP	RRACBFUSA
JENTE	11	F	CH	RRACBFUSA
PEGULES, ARIZEBETH	16	F	SP	RRACBFUSA

SHIP: RHEIN

FROM: BREMEN
TO: BALTIMORE
ARRIVED: 13 DECEMBER 1888

PASSENGER	AGE	SEX	OCCUPATION	PRI VIL DES
HRABLIKOWSKY, THOMAS	30	M	FARMER	RRZZZZMD
MICHAELSOHN, MICH.	23	M	LABR	RRZZZZMD
KRUEWIC, WINCENTY	33	M	LABR	RRZZZZMD
MARIE	21	F	W	RRZZZZMD
LINA	.11	F	INFANT	RRZZZZMD
SCHER, FREIDE	23	F	UNKNOWN	RRZZZZMD
NASCHELSKY, JACOB	17	M	LABR	RRAIJNMD
GOLDENBERG, BERNHD.	18	M	CL	RRAIJNMI
BALRZAR, FREIDE	22	F	CK	RRAIJNMD
ANSCHROTH, JOSEF	24	M	FARMER	RRAIJNPA
SIMPER, JOH.	60	M	FARMER	RRAIJNIN
CATHA.	34	F	W	RRAIJNIN
ROSALIE	19	F	UNKNOWN	RRAIJNIN
FRANZ	11	M	CH	RRAIJNIN
EMILIE	7	F	CHILD	RRAIJNIN
HMIELEWSKI, JAN	29	M	FARMER	RRAIJNMD
GORDON, MEYER	30	M	SDLR	RRAIJNMD
BERCZIMSKI, FEIWEL	18	M	LABR	RRAIJNMD
STUCKSCHISCH, JOSEF	21	M	LABR	RRAIJNMD
SAGOWSKY, HERSCHEL	30	M	MCHT	RRAIJNMD
SCHWARZ, SORE	30	F	UNKNOWN	RRAIJNMD
CHANE	10	F	CH	RRAIJNMD
CHAJE	.11	F	INFANT	RRAIJNMD
MIROSLAWSKY, STANISL.	31	M	PNTR	RRAIJNIL
JHELENE	24	F	W	RRAIJNIL
TRAPPE, HERMANN	.01	M	INFANT	RRZZZZIL
EMMA	.01	F	INFANT	RRZZZZIL

SHIP: AUSTRALIA

FROM: HAMBURG
TO: NEW YORK
ARRIVED: 13 DECEMBER 1888

PASSENGER	AGE	SEX	OCCUPATION	PRI VIL DES
LEANDER, MATTS.	21	M	LABR	FNZZZZUSA
SCHAFRANSKY, HIRSCH	28	M	LABR	RRZZZZUSA
PRATESEWITZ, STANISLAUS	56	M	LABR	RRZZZZUSA
KURSEL, CHAIM	18	M	LABR	RRZZZZUSA
GOBULOW, KUSMA	23	M	LABR	RRZZZZUSA
KULLIAMENIC, HENDRIK	30	M	LABR	FNZZZZUSA
PRUSAITIS, ANDRAS	20	M	LABR	RRZZZZUSA
WICKMANN, JACOB	40	M	LABR	FNZZZZUSA
KANTER, ITZIG	32	M	LABR	FNAHTQUSA
BADIN, SALOMON	16	M	LABR	FNADOIUSA
SCHEERSCHNEIDER, NACHUA	30	M	SHMK	FNAIIGUSA
GOLDBERG, HAYMAM	20	M	LABR	RRZZZZUSA
OLZEWSKI, ANTON	36	M	LABR	RRZZZZUSA
WIEDBAUM, MOSES	21	M	MLR	RRAIIGUSA
KAMINSKI, MOSES	37	M	LABR	RRAHWKUSA
KORZINSKI, JAN	28	M	LABR	RRAHZSUSA
ANTON	24	M	LABR	RRAHZSUSA
KANTZKAS, ANTANY	24	M	LABR	RRZZZZUSA
MURAWIEW, CHARITON	33	M	LABR	RRAIEXUSA
FISCHMANN, CHAIM	26	M	LABR	RRAIIGUSA
WEINSTOCK, MARCUS	25	M	LABR	RRZZZZUSA
PASLATZ, MORITZ	7	M	CHILD	RRZZZZUSA
STRENDERN, MAX	16	M	LABR	RRAIIVUSA
BIHARSJAS, MINNA	47	F	WO	RRZZZZUSA
LIELBRANDA, SOFIA	20	F	SGL	FNZZZZUSA
ADOMITSCH, AGATHE	20	F	SGL	RRZZZZUSA
HIBSCHMANN, FESSIE	19	F	SGL	RRAHQUUSA
RACHEL	7	F	CHILD	RRAHQUUSA
PUDLEWSKI, WOYCIEK	35	M	LABR	RRZZZZUSA
ANTONIE	36	F	W	RRZZZZUSA
BELLKOWSKI, VALENTIN	34	M	LABR	RRZZZZUSA
EVA	29	F	W	RRZZZZUSA
ADAM	5	M	CHILD	RRZZZZUSA
MARIANNA	.11	F	INFANT	RRZZZZUSA
CIARKOWSKI, ANTON	26	M	LABR	RRZZZZUSA
ANNA	23	F	W	RRZZZZUSA
ROSALIE	.11	F	INFANT	RRZZZZUSA
MIRANSKA, SUSANNE	45	F	WO	RRZZZZUSA
KWIATKOWSKI, MARTIN	26	M	LABR	RRZZZZUSA
KATHARINA	26	F	W	RRZZZZUSA
BOLESLAV	.11	M	INFANT	RRZZZZUSA
GLESKA, FRIEDRICH	37	M	LABR	RRZZZZUSA
JULIANNA	35	F	W	RRZZZZUSA
JAN	00	M	INF	RRZZZZUSA
SCHIBSIL, FERDINAND	40	M	LABR	RRZZZZUSA
HENRIETHE	38	F	W	RRZZZZUSA
HELLMANN, ESTER	21	F	SGL	RRZZZZUSA
ELLMANN, FEIGE	48	F	WO	RRZZZZUSA
RINDKE	7	F	CHILD	RRZZZZUSA
MORDCHE	6	F	CHILD	RRZZZZUSA
NEUMANN, CARL	35	M	FARMER	RRZZZZUSA
ANNA	32	F	W	RRZZZZUSA
MARIE	7	F	CHILD	RRZZZZUSA
LOUISE	5	F	CHILD	RRZZZZUSA
BLAESCHKE, ERNST	21	M	FARMER	RRZZZZUSA
GLASS, ETTE	30	F	WO	RRZZZZUSA
DWORE	.11	F	INFANT	RRZZZZUSA
ARON, LEIB	30	M	TLR	RRZZZZUSA
SARA	28	F	W	RRZZZZUSA
FALKOWSKI, MALKE	22	F	WO	RRZZZZUSA
MORDCHE	.09	M	INFANT	RRZZZZUSA
REGALSKA, ANNA	57	F	WO	RRZZZZUSA
ALBERT	22	M	S	RRZZZZUSA
FINK, CHOSZA	45	F	WO	RRADOIUSA
PINKUS	19	M	BCHR	RRADOIUSA
MITILKEWITZ, WINZOS	29	M	LABR	RRZZZZUSA
ANNA	20	F	W	RRZZZZUSA

SHIP: PENNLAND

FROM: ANTWERP
TO: NEW YORK
ARRIVED: 17 DECEMBER 1888

PASSENGER	AGE	SEX	OCCUPATION	PRI VIL DES
ROMANOFSKI, JOS.	26	M	BKR	RRAHXLNY
F.	26	F	UNKNOWN	RRAHXLNY
DYMYTRO	1	M	CHILD	RRAHXLNY

PASSENGER	AGE	SEX	OCCUPATION	PRIV	VIL	DES
JEKATRUM	.04	F	INFANT	RR	AHX	LNY

SHIP: CITY OF CHICAGO

FROM: LIVERPOOL AND QUEENSTOWN
TO: NEW YORK
ARRIVED: 17 DECEMBER 1888

PASSENGER	AGE	SEX	OCCUPATION	PRIV	VIL	DES
KARP, R.	36	F	W	RR	AFWJ	PA
BEILE	4	F	CHILD	RR	AFWJ	PA
ABRAM	3	M	CHILD	RR	AFWJ	PA
U	00	F	INF	RR	AFWJ	PA
LUSCORVUGG, HENE	27	F	SP	RR	AHOO	PA
GRAGOK, KARTARGUS	50	F	W	RR	AHOO	PA
FOLKE, KEEVER	16	M	TLR	RR	AFWJ	MRL
SAML	19	M	TLR	RR	AFWJ	MRL
FILDMANN, JOSHUA	25	M	BRM	PL	ZZZZ	NY
JASINOFSKY, HIRSCH	25	M	LABR	PL	AFVG	NY
HOIS	28	M	MCHT	PL	AFVG	NY
VICHHANDLER, ARGOLD	15	M	PDLR	PL	AFVG	NY
JOAS, LEOPOLD	60	M	LABR	PL	AFVG	NY
SOKOTOUSKI, CATH.	25	F	SVNT	PL	AIEG	UNK
ORSGAK, FERENZ	30	M	LABR	PL	ZZZZ	NY
AMSTERDAM, CHEVER	18	F	SVNT	PL	ZZZZ	NY
KAPLAN, BEREL	19	M	JNR	PL	AFVG	NY
KOCHANOWITZ, AGNISKA	17	M	LABR	PL	AFVG	NY
HIRSCHNOWITZ, JACOB	29	M	PDLR	PL	AFVG	BAL
DING, JOSEPH	33	M	LABR	PL	ZZZZ	NY
KIBISCH, FRANZ	29	M	BKR	PL	ZZZZ	UNK
MALSCHUTEER, ANTONI	35	M	LABR	PL	ZZZZ	UNK
DANILWIEG, STANISLAW	23	M	LABR	PL	ZZZZ	UNK
SCHIERGHIN, JAN	30	M	LABR	PL	ZZZZ	UNK
RACHECKESSKI, FRANASEK	21	M	LABR	PL	ZZZZ	UNK
RASCHECHEFSKI, JAN	33	M	LABR	PL	ZZZZ	UNK
SEPSCHETZ, MOSES	22	M	SHMK	PL	ZZZZ	BAL
FREYDE	18	F	SVNT	PL	ZZZZ	BAL
KANENERA, FELECIA	16	F	SVNT	PL	ZZZZ	PA
KANTRONETY, ISAAC	21	M	CL	PL	AFVG	NY
GREENBERG, HIRSCH	33	M	BLKSMH	PL	AFVG	NY
STOMECINSKEY, ELKE	21	F	SVNT	PL	ZZZZ	NY
HOVRILG, ABRAH.	23	M	CGRMKR	PL	ZZZZ	IA
BAUER, AUGUST	34	M	UNKNOWN	PL	ZZZZ	NY
FRIEDERIKA	32	F	W	PL	ZZZZ	NY
MINNIE	6	F	CHILD	PL	ZZZZ	NY
GEORGINE	3	F	CHILD	PL	ZZZZ	NY
FREDERECK	2	M	CHILD	PL	ZZZZ	NY
ROSENBERG, ISAC	21	M	PDLR	RR	ZZZZ	NY
MASSELL, SCHREFEG	20	F	W	RR	ZZZZ	NY
SAFRENULATER, ABRAHAM	26	M	WTR	PL	ZZZZ	NY

SHIP: TRAVE

FROM: BREMEN AND SOUTHAMPTON
TO: NEW YORK
ARRIVED: 17 DECEMBER 1888

PASSENGER	AGE	SEX	OCCUPATION	PRIV	VIL	DES
STRASSUM, JOSEF	25	M	MCHT	RR	ZZZZ	RSS
MACKEDOWIZ, MARGANA	23	F	UNKNOWN	RR	ZZZZ	USA
CONSTANTIN	.04	M	INFANT	RR	ZZZZ	USA
RUBKOWSKA, ANTONIA	18	F	UNKNOWN	RR	ZZZZ	USA
BUNIERKA, FRANCISCA	21	F	UNKNOWN	RR	ZZZZ	USA
SCHAEFER, KARL	25	M	FARMER	RR	ZZZZ	USA
ERNST	16	M	FARMER	RR	ZZZZ	USA
BUECHNER, JOH.	24	M	FARMER	RR	ZZZZ	USA
GERKE, FR.	30	M	FARMER	RR	ZZZZ	USA
JAKUBOWSKI, PIOTR	44	M	LABR	RR	ZZZZ	USA
KARZEBSKI, JOSEF	22	M	LABR	RR	ZZZZ	USA
PIELKIWICZ, FRANCISCA	23	F	UNKNOWN	RR	ZZZZ	USA
BUNLOWITZ, ABRAHAM	21	M	UNKNOWN	RR	ZZZZ	USA
LOCKEZOWITZ, CH.	27	M	LABR	RR	ZZZZ	USA
LEISSER, SCHALRIE	45	M	LABR	RR	ZZZZ	USA
ZURTRIN, MOSES	34	M	LABR	RR	ZZZZ	USA
KUHERT, MOSES	14	M	LABR	RR	ZZZZ	USA
WURZEL, MOSES	14	M	LABR	RR	ZZZZ	USA
JODAZTISZON, AND.	24	M	LABR	RR	ZZZZ	USA
GOEDICHE, ERNST	27	M	JNR	RR	ZZZZ	USA

SHIP: RHAETIA

FROM: HAMBURG
TO: NEW YORK
ARRIVED: 18 DECEMBER 1888

PASSENGER	AGE	SEX	OCCUPATION	PRIV	VIL	DES
DULINSKINTE, ANNA	20	F	SGL	RR	ACBF	USA
GRAZUT, KAZMIR	28	M	LABR	RR	ACBF	USA
MITKOSKA, FEOFILA	23	F	SGL	RR	ACBF	USA
BLUE, SIMON	20	M	LABR	RR	ACBF	USA
BYGMESTER, CATH.	29	F	SGL	RR	ACBF	USA
HOOSNAS, BRITTE	24	F	SGL	RR	ACBF	USA
BAGNIK, MARIANE	22	F	WO	RR	ACBF	USA
SACHARZKI, THOMAS	25	M	LABR	RR	ACBF	USA
BIEBERT, HENRIETTE	22	F	SGL	RR	ACBF	USA
LIKAT, AMALIE	21	F	SGL	RR	ACBF	USA
JAFFA, JACOB	42	M	JWLR	RR	ACBF	USA
SARAH	30	F	W	RR	ACBF	USA
GRUENBERG, CHANNE	24	F	SGL	RR	ACBF	USA
HAGEL, BRAINEL	32	F	WO	RR	ACBF	USA
WOLF	7	M	CHILD	RR	ACBF	USA
SISSEL	6	F	CHILD	RR	ACBF	USA
JOSSEL	5	M	CHILD	RR	ACBF	USA
MEISCHE	4	M	CHILD	RR	ACBF	USA
MINDEL	3	M	CHILD	RR	ACBF	USA
CHAIM	.11	M	INFANT	RR	ACBF	USA
WISNEWSKA, ANNA	17	F	SGL	RR	ACBF	USA
HILLER, CHANNE	22	F	SGL	RR	ACBF	USA
ITZIKOWICZ, MARKUS	39	M	TCHR	RR	ACBF	USA
POSNANSKY, MOSCHE	18	M	LABR	RR	ACBF	USA
KUPUSTEIN, JEREMIR	26	M	LABR	RR	ACBF	USA
RUDKEWITZ, KASIMIR	27	M	LABR	RR	ACBF	USA
JANKELOW, WOLF	30	M	LABR	RR	ACBF	USA
FIKOTZKI, ESTHER	17	F	SGL	RR	ACBF	USA
SACHS, TAUBE	38	F	WO	RR	ACBF	USA
MOSES	7	M	CHILD	RR	ACBF	USA
MOTTEL	6	M	CHILD	RR	ACBF	USA
LEIB	4	M	CHILD	RR	ACBF	USA
SLATE	1	M	CHILD	RR	ACBF	USA
MEYER, CARL	23	M	FARMER	RR	ACBF	USA
HOWAK, JOSEF	31	M	LABR	RR	ACBF	USA
FRANZISKA	17	F	SI	RR	ACBF	USA
COHN, HENRY	14	M	BY	RR	ACBF	USA
SELIG	11	M	BY	RR	ACBF	USA
KALETZKI, CHANNE	30	F	SGL	RR	ACBF	USA
BENDER, GEORG	52	M	FARMER	RR	ACBF	USA
MARG.	50	F	W	RR	ACBF	USA
CHRIST.	20	F	CH	RR	ACBF	USA
JOHANN	17	M	CH	RR	ACBF	USA
MARG.	5	F	CHILD	RR	ACBF	USA
ELISAB.	1	F	CHILD	RR	ACBF	USA
GIESSE, JOHANNES	43	M	FARMER	RR	ACBF	USA
EVA	39	F	W	RR	ACBF	USA
JOSEPH	18	M	CH	RR	ACBF	USA
BALTHASAR	15	M	CH	RR	ACBF	USA
WILHELM	11	M	CH	RR	ACBF	USA
GREGOR	4	M	CHILD	RR	ACBF	USA
CATH.	.09	F	INFANT	RR	ACBF	USA

PASSENGER	AGE	SEX	OCCUPATION	PRV VIL DES
DREYER, SARAH	21	F	SGL	RRACBFUSA
DORITZKI, POLAK	21	M	LABR	RRACBFUSA
SCHILISCHOSSKI, ISAAC	29	M	LABR	RRACBFUSA

SHIP: ROTTERDAM

FROM: ROTTERDAM
TO: NEW YORK
ARRIVED: 18 DECEMBER 1888

PASSENGER	AGE	SEX	OCCUPATION	PRV VIL DES
WINTER, B.	52	M	MCHT	RRZZZZUSA
CIKHANOWSKEN, A.	30	F	UNKNOWN	RRZZZZUSA
F.	3	F	CHILD	RRZZZZUSA
J.	.10	F	INFANT	RRZZZZUSA
SCHMIDKES, J.	28	M	LABR	RRZZZZUSA
E.	24	F	UNKNOWN	RRZZZZUSA
WEINBERG, P.	53	M	LABR	RRZZZZUSA
S.	48	F	UNKNOWN	RRZZZZUSA
F.	24	F	UNKNOWN	RRZZZZUSA
B.	22	F	UNKNOWN	RRZZZZUSA
M.	20	F	UNKNOWN	RRZZZZUSA
R.	9	F	CHILD	RRZZZZUSA
H.	7	F	CHILD	RRZZZZUSA
R.	.01	F	INFANT	RRZZZZUSA
KRET, H.	40	M	LABR	RRZZZZUSA
ZOLAN, W.	25	M	LABR	RRZZZZUSA
BUBNICZCH, W.	25	M	LABR	RRZZZZUSA
PYSZ, F.	23	M	LABR	RRZZZZUSA
GRAHAN, W.	40	M	LABR	RRZZZZUSA
SZERBA, P.	18	M	LABR	RRZZZZUSA
MOLNAR, J.	46	M	LABR	RRZZZZUSA
MAMANKO, J.	43	M	LABR	RRZZZZUSA
JOKA, D.	24	M	LABR	RRZZZZUSA
SLAWISCHEH, A.	27	M	LABR	RRZZZZUSA
MYKLINSKI, J.	28	M	LABR	RRZZZZUSA
A.	24	M	LABR	RRZZZZUSA
KUBIALE, J.	24	M	LABR	RRZZZZUSA
BORUMAS, J.	20	M	LABR	RRZZZZUSA
SWIDERSKI, J.	40	M	LABR	RRZZZZUSA
BERGER, E.	50	M	LABR	RRZZZZUSA
WILCZALE, M.	45	M	LABR	RRZZZZUSA
FEDAH, M.	32	F	UNKNOWN	PLZZZZUSA
M.	9	F	CHILD	PLZZZZUSA
TH.	7	M	CHILD	PLZZZZUSA
J.	3	F	CHILD	PLZZZZUSA
J.	1	F	CHILD	PLZZZZUSA

SHIP: FURNESSIA

FROM: GLASGOW AND MOVILLE
TO: NEW YORK
ARRIVED: 18 DECEMBER 1888

PASSENGER	AGE	SEX	OCCUPATION	PRV VIL DES
ANUROWITZ, MARTIN	26	M	LABR	RRZZZZUSA
LABONOWSKY, WM.	21	M	LABR	RRZZZZUSA
PLATKUS, ALEXANDER	40	M	LABR	RRZZZZUSA
WICHOFSKY, MATTIAS	24	M	LABR	RRZZZZUSA
GOLDBERG, FUME	21	F	UNKNOWN	RRZZZZUSA
BEILE	11	F	CH	RRZZZZUSA
LEIE	9	F	CHILD	RRZZZZUSA
MOWSCHE	2	F	CHILD	RRZZZZUSA

SHIP: BELGENLAND

FROM: ANTWERP
TO: NEW YORK
ARRIVED: 21 DECEMBER 1888

PASSENGER	AGE	SEX	OCCUPATION	PRV VIL DES
MEYEROWITZ, RUWIN	35	M	PDLR	RRAHTFNY
ROSA	24	F	UNKNOWN	RRAHTFNY
SARAH	3	F	CHILD	RRAHTFNY
REUKAZISKY, MOSES	43	M	HTR	RRAINMNY
KANTER, DAVID	38	M	TU	RRZZZZKS
ALPEROWITZ, GATTE	18	F	UNKNOWN	RRADBQNY
BERRICK, F.	20	M	SHMK	RRADBQNY
BUGNE, GELDA	26	M	UNKNOWN	RRADBQNY
KOLTON, MEYER	23	M	TLR	RRADBQNY
TEPER, BENJAMIN	23	M	TLR	RRADBQNY
FEIN, BENZION	25	M	PDLR	RRADBQBO

SHIP: AMERICA

FROM: BREMEN
TO: BALTIMORE
ARRIVED: 21 DECEMBER 1888

PASSENGER	AGE	SEX	OCCUPATION	PRV VIL DES
GUSEWER, PALIFERIA	44	F	UNKNOWN	RRAIJEKS
KATARINA	22	F	UNKNOWN	RRAIJEKS
MAFRA	5	F	CHILD	RRAIJEKS
ARTJEM	.10	M	INFANT	RRAIJEKS
SZERANIEWICZ, MARY	34	F	CK	RRAIJEOH
FRUBB, JOHANNES	35	M	FARMER	RRAIJEOH
MARIE	33	F	UNKNOWN	RRAIJEOH
ANNA	9	F	CHILD	RRAIJEOH
CATHARINA	5	F	CHILD	RRAIJEOH
JOHANNES	7	M	CHILD	RRAIJEOH
CONRAD	3	M	CHILD	RRAIJEOH
MARIE	.11	F	INFANT	RRAIJEOH
CELMA	.02	F	INFANT	RRAIJEOH
HAUFMANN, ESTER	22	F	UNKNOWN	RRAIJEOH
MESCHE	.11	F	INFANT	RRAIJEOH
JABLOWSKA, JADWIGA	25	F	UNKNOWN	RRAIJEOH
ADAM	9	M	CHILD	RRAIJEOH
SOPHIE	8	F	CHILD	RRAIJEOH
ANNA	6	F	CHILD	RRAIJEOH
RABINOWITZ, GITL	22	F	UNKNOWN	RRAIJEOH
ESTHER	1	F	CHILD	RRAIJEOH
ADLER, GITTEL	35	F	UNKNOWN	RRAIJEOH
OSIAS	11	M	UNKNOWN	RRAIJEOH
SUESSMANN	9	M	CHILD	RRAIJEOH
JENNY	7	F	CHILD	RRAIJEOH
TISCH, SELIG	37	M	MCHT	RRAIJEOH
KURLOWIEZ, ADAM	23	M	LABR	RRAIJEMD
WILEZEWSKI, ADOLF	23	M	LABR	RRAIJEMD
JANICKE, JULIAN	24	M	LABR	RRAIJEMD
GUERTLER, EWALD	15	M	LABR	RRAIJEMD
HARACZKIEWIEZ, VICTOR	21	M	LABR	RRAIJEMD
STEIN, CHRISTIAN	22	M	FARMER	RRAIJEOH
CATHARINA	20	F	UNKNOWN	RRAIJEOH
CHRISTIAN	.08	M	INFANT	RRAIJEOH
WOLF, CHRISTIAN	38	M	FARMER	RRAIJEOH
MAGARETHE	35	F	UNKNOWN	RRAIJEOH
MATTHIAS	11	M	UNKNOWN	RRAIJEOH
ELISABETH	10	F	CH	RRAIJEOH
CHRISTIAN	5	M	CHILD	RRAIJEOH
JOHANNES	4	M	CHILD	RRAIJEOH
FRIEDRICH	2	M	CHILD	RRAIJEOH
AWELKI, HUSIEF	26	M	LABR	RRAIJEOH
IMBER, MINDEL	38	M	MCHT	RRAIJEMD
ISAAC	11	M	MCHT	RRAIJEMD
BIEZA, SAWORY	22	M	MCHT	RRAIJEPA

PASSENGER	AGE	SEX	OCCUPATION	PRV VIL DES
JOSEFA	21	F	UNKNOWN	RRAIJEPA
MAEZENKA, MICHAEL	24	M	MCHT	RRAIJEOH
ZALEPKA, MARIA	19	F	SVNT	RRAIJEOH
KLUKA, MARIA	20	F	UNKNOWN	RRAIJEOH
FRANZ	.08	M	INFANT	RRAIJEOH

SHIP: POLARIA

FROM: HAMBURG
TO: NEW YORK
ARRIVED: 21 DECEMBER 1888

PASSENGER	AGE	SEX	OCCUPATION	PRV VIL DES
GINDSBERGER, ZIWIE	30	F	WO	RRAHQUUSA
CHAJE	7	F	CHILD	RRAHQUUSA
BICZDZECKI, WANG.	18	M	LABR	RRZZZZUSA
OLCZAK, LEON	22	M	LABR	RRZZZZUSA
TSCHERUUS, MIKAS	26	M	LABR	RRZZZZUSA
WILGAKKALA, JOH.	20	M	LABR	FNZZZZUSA
KLEIN, HENOCH	42	M	DLR	FNAIKFUSA
REIN	32	F	W	FNAIKFUSA
ZWIE	3	F	CHILD	FNAIKFUSA
ROCHE	.11	F	INFANT	FNAIKFUSA
DOBROWSKI, MEYER	23	M	MCHT	RRZZZZUSA
GOLDMANN, ABRAHAM	29	M	TLR	RRZZZZUSA
PERLMANN, MOSES	18	M	LABR	RRAIMFUSA
PLAUSKY, LEIB	35	M	LABR	RRZZZZUSA
GRUTZKI, PESE	38	F	WO	RRAHTFUSA
CHAJE	7	F	CHILD	RRAHTFUSA
NIRSCHBERG, TOTZE	48	F	WO	RRZZZZUNK
HERSCH	3	M	CHILD	RRZZZZUNK
BEILE	.11	F	INFANT	RRZZZZUNK
FRANK, BASCHE	40	F	WO	RRZZZZUNK
REBECCA	8	F	CHILD	RRZZZZUNK
LIFSCHUETZ, AISIK	20	M	LABR	RRZZZZUNK
JOHNA, JUDITH	17	F	SGL	RRZZZZUNK
LEVI, CHACENA	25	M	LABR	RRAHZSUNK
WOLOZIA, BENJAMIN	25	M	LABR	RRAHWEUNK
SHAUSS, SCHIE	48	M	LABR	RRZZZZUNK
KASKA, KROLITZKA	20	M	LABR	RRAIJZUNK
MICHLOWSKA, LEIB	48	M	LABR	RRAHZSUNK
RUMINSKI, ANTON	21	M	LABR	RRZZZZUNK
ERKNOW, LOUISE	25	F	SGL	RRAHZSUNK
KOCKSTETTER, JULIANE	25	F	LABR	RRAHZSUNK
LEWIN, LEISER	21	M	MCHT	RRAHTOUNK
EISENSTADT, NECHAME	39	F	WO	RRZZZZUNK
NECHAME	39	F	WO	RRZZZZUNK
BASCHE	20	F	CH	RRZZZZUNK
ABRAHAM	16	M	CH	RRZZZZUNK
DINE	14	F	CH	RRZZZZUNK
BENJAMIN	5	M	CHILD	RRZZZZUNK
CHAIM	.03	M	INFANT	RRZZZZUNK
GUTTMANN, CHAIM	54	M	PNTR	RRAHTFUNK
NECHE	17	F	SGL	RRAHTFUNK

SHIP: LAHN

FROM: BREMEN AND SOUTHAMPTON
TO: NEW YORK
ARRIVED: 22 DECEMBER 1888

PASSENGER	AGE	SEX	OCCUPATION	PRV VIL DES
GOTZ, ISIDOR	34	M	TT	RRAFWJGR
JURSZAJEZINTE, MAGD.	17	F	UNKNOWN	RRAHZSUSA
JURKSZAITSOWA, KOSTANCY	23	F	W	RRAHZSUSA
JURKSZAITSOWA, JOHANNES	.01	M	INFANT	RRAHZSUSA
RZEPINCKA, FRANZISKA	26	F	W	RRAHZSUSA
BRUENISLAW	.01	M	INFANT	RRAHZSUSA
RUCZKOWSKA, ANIELLA	23	F	UNKNOWN	RRAINMUSA
FRISINSKI, NOCHIM	21	M	TLR	RRAHZSUSA
SIMON, PINCHUS	21	M	TLR	RRAHZSUSA
SKORSKI, JAN	20	M	LABR	RRAGRTUSA
BAUER, HIRSCH	52	M	FARMER	RRAGRTUSA
LEYBL	52	F	W	RRAGRTUSA
CHAJE	18	F	UNKNOWN	RRAGRTUSA
ROCHEL	16	F	UNKNOWN	RRAGRTUSA
KEWSKI, ABRAM	21	M	LABR	RRZZZZUSA
TIKTIN, ELISE	26	F	UNKNOWN	RRAFWJUSA
KIPERMANN, KUNO	30	M	TLR	RRAGRTUSA
MELAMED, ISRAEL	20	M	PNTR	RRAGRTUSA
MIDWED, ROHDE	32	F	W	RRAHVUUSA
SARAH	7	F	CHILD	RRAHVUUSA
RUWEN	6	M	CHILD	RRAHVUUSA
JOSEF	3	M	CHILD	RRAHVUUSA
ISAAC	.11	M	INFANT	RRAHVUUSA
SCHLESINGER, LAI	34	F	W	RRZZZZUSA
JENTE	3	F	CHILD	RRZZZZUSA
FELIX, JAN	28	M	LABR	RRAHZSUSA
PROTR, IWANOW	33	M	LABR	RRAHZSUSA
MICHALEWSKY, MAX	32	M	LABR	RRAHZSUSA
GONKOWA, MARIA	18	F	UNKNOWN	RRAHZSUSA
CHICH, LUDWIG	23	M	LABR	RRAHZSUSA
FELLMANN, HENRIETTE	23	F	W	RRZZZZUSA
AUGUSTE	.09	F	INFANT	RRZZZZUSA
POSTAWELSKI, ROSCHEN	26	F	W	RRAHZSUSA
APE.	5	F	CHILD	RRAHZSUSA

SHIP: ENGLAND

FROM: LIVERPOOL
TO: NEW YORK
ARRIVED: 22 DECEMBER 1888

PASSENGER	AGE	SEX	OCCUPATION	PRV VIL DES
SILROWSKI, PAULINA	48	F	SVNT	RRZZZZNE
FREEDMANN, CHAIE	23	F	W	RRZZZZNY
RIVKE	2	F	CHILD	RRZZZZNY
MOSES	1	M	CHILD	RRZZZZNY
JANOSEWS, HODA	28	F	SVNT	RRZZZZNY
LEVI, SOSSEL	19	F	SVNT	RRZZZZNY
TINPIANSKY, HINDE	20	F	SVNT	RRZZZZNY
DIMENTMANN, CHAIE	20	F	SVNT	RRZZZZNY
STURNOCH, CHAIE	35	F	W	RRZZZZNY
JANKEL	.09	M	INFANT	RRZZZZNY
KURGER, HIRCH	59	M	LABR	RRZZZZNY
AMDE	22	F	SVNT	RRZZZZNY
SARA	25	F	SVNT	RRZZZZNY
JABLOWSKI, ELKE	17	F	SVNT	RRZZZZNY
GOLDSTEIN, SCHEINE	19	F	SVNT	RRZZZZNY
KALINA, MOSES	50	M	LABR	RRZZZZNY
SARA	45	F	W	RRZZZZNY
BARUCH	11	M	CH	RRZZZZNY
HERSCHE	10	M	CH	RRZZZZNY
SCHEINE	7	F	CHILD	RRZZZZNY
SCIME	5	M	CHILD	RRZZZZNY
ITTE	4	M	CHILD	RRZZZZNY
GOLDE	1	F	CHILD	RRZZZZNY
JASGER, GERCHN	16	M	LABR	RRZZZZNY
ARGEWIEZ, BENI	44	M	LABR	RRZZZZNY
SUABASTIS, JOSEF	20	M	LABR	RRZZZZNY
MICHALOWICZ, NICHOLAS	22	M	LABR	RRZZZZNY
KEYSER, JAIDE	21	M	LABR	RRZZZZPHI
ZIBECK, JOSEF	20	M	LABR	RRZZZZNY
LEWKE, BERL	44	M	LABR	RRZZZZNY
ABRAHAM	11	M	CH	RRZZZZNY
DANIELS, FERDINAND	23	M	LABR	RRZZZZNY
KLENOWN, JAN	20	M	LABR	RRZZZZNY
SLAHOWSKY, VINCENT	24	M	LABR	RRZZZZNY

PASSENGER	AGE	SEX	OCCUPATION	PRV	VIL	DES
PORCELLAN, JOSEL	24	M	LABR	RR	ZZZZ	NY

SHIP: SERVIA

FROM: LIVERPOOL AND QUEENSTOWN
TO: NEW YORK
ARRIVED: 24 DECEMBER 1888

PASSENGER	AGE	SEX	OCCUPATION	PRV	VIL	DES
MISCHRUSKI, MOSES	53	M	TLR	RR	ZZZZ	NY
KEUDICH, SCHAGE	30	M	TLR	RR	ZZZZ	NY
YOWURCK, ANDREAS	19	M	LABR	RR	ZZZZ	NY
JOSEF	10	M	CH	RR	ZZZZ	NY
ROSNER, JESSEL	40	M	BCHR	RR	ZZZZ	NY
MEIERS, MENDEL	17	M	LABR	RR	ZZZZ	NY
SARDYSKY, JOHN	15	M	LABR	RR	ZZZZ	NY
MARONER, AXEL	34	M	LABR	RR	ZZZZ	NY
HOLMBERG, JOHS	20	M	LABR	RR	ZZZZ	NY
JUELSON, CARL	23	M	LABR	RR	ZZZZ	NY
EDELMAN, NOCHUM	49	M	LABR	RR	ZZZZ	NY
JUTTLIEB, ROSE	19	F	SP	RR	ZZZZ	NY
SCHURGOTT, SOFIE	30	F	MA	RR	ZZZZ	NY
VICTORIA	4	F	CHILD	RR	ZZZZ	NY
KEROLA, MARIA	32	F	MA	RR	ZZZZ	NY

SHIP: OHIO

FROM: LIVERPOOL AND QUEENSTOWN
TO: NEW YORK
ARRIVED: 24 DECEMBER 1888

PASSENGER	AGE	SEX	OCCUPATION	PRV	VIL	DES
ALIBER, LINE	20	F	SVNT	RR	ACBF	NY
ALPES, SCHAME	50	M	BCHR	RR	ACBF	NY
JARKO, BOIVA	23	M	LABR	RR	ACBF	NY
BUCHANN, MOSE	18	M	TLR	RR	ACBF	NY
FEEAR, JAN	30	M	LABR	RR	ACBF	PHI
GRATZ, NECHAME	18	M	LABR	RR	ACBF	PHI
GRINZAK, GABRIEL	19	M	LABR	RR	ACBF	PHI
MARKO	40	M	LABR	RR	ACBF	PHI
GENKEL, HAWSCHE	16	M	UNKNOWN	RR	ACBF	NY
JACOB, SCHMUL	8	M	CHILD	RR	ACBF	NY
PUTRISKA, STANISL.	30	M	LABR	RR	ACBF	NY
RURERMANN, LEIBE	10	M	CH	RR	ACBF	NY
ROCHE	9	F	CHILD	RR	ACBF	NY
DREESE	00	F	W	RR	ACBF	NY
ZIFE	00	M	LABR	RR	ACBF	NY
SOBOLEWSKY, SINDEL	21	M	TLR	RR	ACBF	NY
SUNIZKE, ABRAHAM	32	M	LABR	RR	ACBF	PHI
SCHVENHAUS, CHAJE	11	F	CH	RR	ACBF	NY
SCHENDLING, JUDEL	18	M	LABR	RR	ACBF	NY
LIRT, ARON	35	M	LABR	RR	ACBF	NY
BENG.	10	M	CH	RR	ACBF	NY
VAWALWIZKI, ANZI	00	M	LABR	RR	ACBF	NY
WELLER, MEIER	18	M	LABR	RR	ZZZZ	BO
WEKSLIN, CHAIM	00	M	GENT	RR	ACBF	NY

SHIP: ETHIOPIA

FROM: GLASGOW AND MOVILLE
TO: NEW YORK
ARRIVED: 26 DECEMBER 1888

PASSENGER	AGE	SEX	OCCUPATION	PRV	VIL	DES
MICLACZEWSKI, ROCH	33	M	LABR	RR	ZZZZ	USA
FRANCISCHEK	20	M	LABR	RR	ZZZZ	USA
AGNOWSKI, JEAN	29	M	LABR	RR	ZZZZ	USA
RUBINOWITZ, ELIAS	28	M	DLR	RR	ZZZZ	USA
KAPLAN, ISRAEL	22	M	DLR	RR	ZZZZ	USA
BASCH, JOSSEL	20	M	TLR	RR	ZZZZ	USA
RAUTBERG, FRIEDE	27	F	UNKNOWN	RR	ZZZZ	USA
PAJE	19	F	UNKNOWN	RR	ZZZZ	USA
JANKEL	4	M	CHILD	RR	ZZZZ	USA
LUBE	1	F	CHILD	RR	ZZZZ	USA
CZARMIAK, ELZBUTA	41	F	UNKNOWN	RR	ZZZZ	USA
ANTON	10	M	CH	RR	ZZZZ	USA
STAFAN	9	M	CHILD	RR	ZZZZ	USA
STANISLAVA	3	F	CHILD	RR	ZZZZ	USA
WLODELOWSKI, EZECHRAB	18	M	LABR	RR	ZZZZ	USA
PIKARSKI, WOJEICH	18	M	LABR	RR	ZZZZ	USA
DEWANDDORIS, ALEX	21	M	LABR	RR	ZZZZ	USA
MULER, DAVID	18	M	TLR	RR	ZZZZ	USA

SHIP: WYOMING

FROM: LIVERPOOL AND QUEENSTOWN
TO: NEW YORK
ARRIVED: 27 DECEMBER 1888

PASSENGER	AGE	SEX	OCCUPATION	PRV	VIL	DES
ROTH, J.	18	M	LABR	PL	ZZZZ	USA
JOELSOHN, M.	35	F	W	PL	ZZZZ	USA
GAZBARSKY, J.	17	M	LABR	PL	ZZZZ	USA
LUDWINOWITZ, E.	56	F	W	PL	ZZZZ	USA
BEILE	18	F	SP	PL	ZZZZ	USA
ROSEN, E.	22	M	LABR	PL	ZZZZ	USA
LAONISBERG, C.	30	F	W	PL	ZZZZ	USA
REWE	7	F	CHILD	PL	ZZZZ	USA
MEIE	3	F	CHILD	PL	ZZZZ	USA
DELNITSKI, A.	27	M	LABR	PL	ZZZZ	USA
MUK, AUG.	32	F	W	PL	ZZZZ	USA
GOTAR	7	M	CHILD	PL	ZZZZ	USA
HELEN	6	F	CHILD	PL	ZZZZ	USA
ADOLPH	4	M	CHILD	PL	ZZZZ	USA
WALTER	00	M	INF	PL	ZZZZ	USA
GOLDENBURG, M.	23	M	LABR	PL	ZZZZ	USA
DESATNIK, M.	19	M	LABR	PL	ZZZZ	USA
BERN, HANA	35	F	W	PL	ZZZZ	USA
DIAMANLSTEIN, W.	20	M	LABR	PL	ZZZZ	USA
REISS, G.	21	M	LABR	PL	ZZZZ	USA
OLYA	17	F	SP	PL	ZZZZ	USA
WOLFF, W.	17	F	SP	PL	ZZZZ	USA
GOLDSTEIN, M.	17	F	SP	PL	ZZZZ	USA
NAFTHIN, O.	36	M	LABR	PL	ZZZZ	USA
SCHWARTZ, SARA	7	F	CHILD	PL	ZZZZ	USA
SAPIRA, B.	33	F	W	PL	ZZZZ	USA
SCHLOME	7	M	CHILD	PL	ZZZZ	USA
SARA	6	F	CHILD	PL	ZZZZ	USA
JOELSOHN, C.	7	M	CHILD	PL	ZZZZ	USA
LESKEWITZ, J.	30	M	LABR	PL	ZZZZ	USA
HELENA	17	F	SP	PL	ZZZZ	USA
HESS, H.	20	M	LABR	PL	ZZZZ	USA
MIRK, T.	00	M	INF	PL	ZZZZ	USA
SAPIRA, A.	00	M	INF	PL	ZZZZ	USA
SCHMIDT, C.	22	M	LABR	PL	ZZZZ	USA
WISSOSKA, NATALIA	34	F	W	RR	ZZZZ	USA
NATALIA	7	F	CHILD	RR	ZZZZ	USA
GIEL, J.	22	M	LABR	RR	ZZZZ	USA

PASSENGER	AGE	SEX	OCCUPATION	PRV VIL DES
JASKNIEKI, A.	23	M	LABR	PLZZZZUSA

SHIP: TAORMINA

FROM: HAMBURG
TO: NEW YORK
ARRIVED: 28 DECEMBER 1888

PASSENGER	AGE	SEX	OCCUPATION	PRV VIL DES
RALAS, JOSEFA	30	M	LABR	RRZZZZNY
LYKOSKI, ANTONI	22	M	LABR	RRZZZZNY
HORAS, ANNA	30	F	WO	RRZZZZNY
HISKOL	7	M	CHILD	RRZZZZNY
BREEDE, MARTIN	24	M	LABR	RRZZZZNY
KAMMENSKY, BARTHAMM	65	M	LABR	RRZZZZNY
ANNA	56	F	W	RRZZZZNY
ALKS, WOLF	40	M	LABR	RRZZZZNY
ABRAHAMSOHN, ETTE	50	F	WO	RRZZZZNY
LIBOWSKY, ISAAK	20	M	TLR	RRZZZZNY
KLIWANSKY, LEIE	19	F	SGL	RRZZZZNY
ROSENBERG, WOLF	26	M	LABR	RRZZZZPHI
NASCHEN, JUDEL	33	F	LABR	RRZZZZPHI
GOLDBLATT, SCHLOMER	45	M	LABR	RRZZZZNY
CHAIM	7	M	CHILD	RRZZZZNY
BRAUN, PETER	20	M	FARMER	RRZZZZNY
MARIE	19	F	W	RRZZZZNY
ABRAMSOHN, SCHOLEM	7	M	CHILD	RRZZZZCH
ITZIG	6	M	CHILD	RRZZZZCH
ROHN, BEILE	32	F	WO	RRZZZZCH
ABRAHAM	7	M	CHILD	RRZZZZCH
MOSES	6	M	CHILD	RRZZZZCH
JOSSEL	3	M	CHILD	RRZZZZCH
RACHEL	.11	F	INFANT	RRZZZZCH
PREIS, WILH.	23	M	LABR	RRZZZZNY
BLABIS, ELISE	40	F	WO	RRZZZZNY
ERNST	7	M	CHILD	RRZZZZNY
MAGDAL.	6	F	CHILD	RRZZZZNY
---ARD	3	M	CHILD	RRZZZZNY
ELISE	14	F	CH	RRZZZZNY
MERZOWSKY, ANDRY	37	M	LABR	RRZZZZPA
BRZOOSKI, JERZIE	20	M	LABR	RRZZZZPA
HIRSCHOWITZ, JUDEL	16	M	TLR	RRZZZZPA
KLEMAS, MALIAS	20	M	LABR	RRZZZZPA
MOSESSOHN, SCHOLEM	32	F	CPTR	RRZZZZPA
SCHEUSAL, JOSEPH	29	M	TLR	RRZZZZPA
KRZLOSKA, JULIE	21	F	WO	RRZZZZPA
WACLAWA	00	F	INF	RRZZZZPA
RABINOWITZ, JOSEPH	28	M	TLR	RRZZZZPA
ESER, JOHANN	21	M	GDNR	RRZZZZPA
RUDMANN, SAMUEL	21	M	WCHMKR	RRZZZZPA
LIPPERT, MORITZ	23	M	LABR	RRZZZZPA
GOLDSTEIN, WEHREL	28	M	TLR	RRZZZZPA
DEPHILIPPI, BERTIS	22	M	MNR	RRZZZZNY
MATHIAS, JOSEPH	22	M	LABR	RRZZZZNY
BUDNITZKY, JAN	20	M	LABR	RRZZZZNY

SHIP: SCHIEDAM

FROM: AMSTERDAM
TO: NEW YORK
ARRIVED: 28 DECEMBER 1888

PASSENGER	AGE	SEX	OCCUPATION	PRV VIL DES
MULLER, C.F.	28	M	MCHT	RRZZZZUSA
KRUCKENBERG, GOTTLIEB	42	M	LABR	RRZZZZUSA
DOROTHEA	42	F	UNKNOWN	RRZZZZUSA
JOHAN	19	M	LABR	RRZZZZUSA
JACOB	17	M	LABR	RRZZZZUSA
MARIE	15	F	SVNT	RRZZZZUSA
KATARINE	9	F	CHILD	RRZZZZUSA
GOTTLIEB	7	M	CHILD	RRZZZZUSA
FRIEDRICH	3	M	CHILD	RRZZZZUSA
BERNHARD, ALFRED	21	M	LABR	RRAEFLUSA
KLEIN, MATH	18	F	SVNT	RRAEFLUSA
ELIAS, JULIUS	21	M	LABR	RRAEFLUSA
FRIEDMAN, MEYER	23	M	LABR	RRAEFLUSA
CHAIM, FASSLICH	27	M	MCHT	RRAEFLUSA
GRODNIK, LEIB	40	M	MCHT	RRAEFLUSA
SLAWKOWSKY, HU.	23	M	LABR	RRAEFLUSA
FOIMILEWICZ, ANTON	20	M	LABR	RRAEFLUSA
HERMAN, JOSEL	42	M	MCHT	RRAEFLUSA

SHIP: RHYNLAND

FROM: ANTWERP
TO: NEW YORK
ARRIVED: 31 DECEMBER 1888

PASSENGER	AGE	SEX	OCCUPATION	PRV VIL DES
VINOKUR, SALOMON	21	M	TLR	RRAIIXUSA

SHIP: CITY OF BERLIN

FROM: LIVERPOOL
TO: NEW YORK
ARRIVED: 31 DECEMBER 1888

PASSENGER	AGE	SEX	OCCUPATION	PRV VIL DES
CHINILEWSKE, JOSEF	22	M	LABR	RRACBFPHI
WESELOWSKIE, STANSLINE	26	M	LABR	RRACBFNY
RUKAWICZKA, FROCEOS	19	M	LABR	RRACBFNY
ADAMSKY, JOSEF	21	M	LABR	RRACBFCH
BLASZYK, JOSAFA	26	M	LABR	RRACBFIL
KUKELAWSKY, JOSE	36	M	FARMER	RRACBFNY
STARON, JOHANN	25	M	FARMER	RRACBFNY
HOWDCHOL, ACAFER	18	M	LABR	RRACBFCH
GABOR, KRYSTINE	19	F	SVNT	RRACBFPA
WISNEWSKEY, ANNA	19	F	SVNT	RRACBFPA
KOFOKA, THEODORE	18	F	SVNT	RRACBFKIN
STANTAUERONY, MARCELA	26	F	W	RRACBFNY
STEFANIA	00	F	INF	RRACBFNY
CHWALNA, F.	25	F	W	RRACBFNY
MARIA	5	F	CHILD	RRACBFNY
VALERIA	4	F	CHILD	RRACBFNY
HELENA	3	F	CHILD	RRACBFNY
WALIYK, BYOFIA	20	F	W	RRACBFNY
JADWIGA	6	F	CHILD	RRACBFNY
KASPRICK, MAYA	22	F	W	RRACBFNY
MARIA	2	F	CHILD	RRACBFNY
STANS.	00	F	INF	RRACBFNY
MIRETOWITZ, BARIL	53	M	LABR	RRACBFPHI
DREBIZAKE, FELIX	26	M	LABR	RRACBFPHI
ROKALYK, CONSTANTINE	16	F	CH	RRACBFPHI
MARENISCHEK, STEFAN	11	F	CH	RRACBFPHI
LEWINSKAUSKY, REWIN	20	M	LABR	RRACBFNY
ZECYENBOCK, LEIB	10	M	CH	RRACBFNY
SINGEL, BARUCH	18	M	LABR	RRAEFLNY
WEINEL, HERICH	34	M	LABR	RRAEFLNY
WELLECHOMCKEY, FRANCIES	24	M	LABR	RRAEFLNY
MYER, AMALIE	38	F	LABR	RRAEFLNY
BRINDGER, A.	19	F	LABR	RRAEFLNY
FLENESTEIN, BEUSCH	38	F	LABR	RRAEFLNY
KRINSKIE, CHAIM	29	F	FARMER	RRAEFLNJ
J.	40	M	FARMER	RRAEFLPHI

PASSENGER	AGE	SEX	OCCUPATION	PRI VIL	DES
ANNA	17	F	CH	RRAEFL	PHI
KAKOLD, MATILDE	35	F	W	RRAEFL	NY
HENRY	6	M	CHILD	RRAEFL	NY
MARY	3	F	CHILD	RRAEFL	NY
SCHUNDEL, REUBEN	50	M	LABR	RRAEFL	NY
RIVE	48	F	W	RRAEFL	NY
SOOE	10	M	CH	RRAEFL	NY
ITZIG	7	M	CHILD	RRAEFL	NY

SHIP: ALLER

FROM: BREMEN
TO: NEW YORK
ARRIVED: 31 DECEMBER 1888

PASSENGER	AGE	SEX	OCCUPATION	PRI VIL	DES
SCHLIFKA, MOSES	24	M	LABR	RRZZZZ	USA
SIKORSKI, ED.	20	M	LABR	RRZZZZ	USA
KANTER, SCHMUEL	34	M	LABR	RRZZZZ	USA
SCHANDINISZKI, JACOB	9	M	CHILD	RRZZZZ	USA
MAKOWSKY, JENNE	18	F	UNKNOWN	RRZZZZ	USA
KWACIEWSKI, ANTONIE	22	F	UNKNOWN	RRZZZZ	USA
ROSENBAUM, SCHENE	32	F	UNKNOWN	RRZZZZ	USA
SAFKE	5	F	CHILD	RRZZZZ	USA
ABELOW, CARL	23	M	LABR	RRZZZZ	USA
DWORE	5	F	CHILD	RRZZZZ	USA
SAMUEL	.11	M	INFANT	RRZZZZ	USA

SHIP: UMBRIA

FROM: LIVERPOOL AND QUEENSTOWN
TO: NEW YORK
ARRIVED: 31 DECEMBER 1888

PASSENGER	AGE	SEX	OCCUPATION	PRI VIL	DES
HERMAN, DAVID	23	M	PNTR	RRAFZD	NY
GRUNBERG, SEHIE	22	M	LABR	RRAFZD	NY
CURSON, SIMON	30	M	LABR	RRAFZD	NY
HAOK, ISRME	16	M	TLR	RRAFZD	NY
BURNETT, GEORGE	20	M	TLR	RRAFZD	NY
ZONECKER, SCHRINE	30	F	MA	RRAFZD	NY
SHIE	1	M	CHILD	RRAFZD	NY
MOSES	10	M	CH	RRAFZD	NY
SURA	4	F	CHILD	RRAFZD	NY
DOMMA, ETTE	17	F	SP	RRAFZD	NY
MENDEL	10	M	CH	RRAFZD	NY
GIDOORRIG, GITE	36	F	MA	RRAFZD	NY
NECHANE	11	F	CH	RRAFZD	NY
WILLY	5	M	CHILD	RRAFZD	NY

SHIP: SUEVIA

FROM: HAMBURG
TO: NEW YORK
ARRIVED: 01 JANUARY 1889

PASSENGER	AGE	SEX	OCCUPATION	PRI VIL	DES
JANKOWSKA, MAGDALENA	20	F	SGL	RRZZZZ	PA
JABLOSKI, STANISLAW	22	M	LABR	RRZZZZ	PA
WOICICHOWSKA, JOSEF	25	M	LABR	RRAHXH	IL
KAMINSKY, MARIAN	22	M	LABR	RRZZZZ	IL
BEISTER, ANNA	20	F	WO	RRZZZZ	IL
GUSTAV	.11	M	INFANT	RRZZZZ	IL
VOGT, KAROLINE	24	F	SGL	RRZZZZ	IL
BERTHA	7	F	CHILD	RRZZZZ	IL
KMIESIAK, MICHAEL	23	M	LABR	RRACBF	UNK
BLUM, CHANNE	54	F	WO	RRAHXZ	MA
CHAJE	18	F	D	RRAHXZ	MA
HUREWITZ, JACOB	25	M	LABR	RRZZZZ	PA
STERNSOHUSS, LINE	37	F	WO	RRZZZZ	PA
MISCHE	.11	M	INFANT	RRZZZZ	PA
PRAODA, ABRAM	50	M	LABR	RRAFWJ	PA
TAUBE	18	F	SGL	RRAFWJ	PA
SOHMUGLER, PAUL	23	M	LKSH	RRAFVG	PA
BUYEWSKI, JOSEFSITIS	21	M	LABR	RRAHZS	PA
FRISCHKO, JOHANN	30	M	LABR	RRAHTF	PA
LIPSCHITZ, GERSON	22	M	MCHT	RRZZZZ	PA
ADAMSKI, ANNA	59	F	WO	RRACON	PA
ANIELA	30	F	CH	RRACON	PA
ROMAN	19	M	CH	RRACON	PA
MALYNEWSKY, ANIELA	48	F	WO	RRACON	PA
KAHANN, CHANNE	29	F	WO	RRAFWJ	PA
SALMEN	5	M	CHILD	RRAFWJ	PA
SCHALKE	.11	M	INFANT	RRAFWJ	PA
SEKANOWSKI, KASIMIR	25	M	LABR	RRZZZZ	PA
JOKUBAT, KASIMIR	27	M	LABR	RRZZZZ	PA
HAROHOWSKY, CHAINE	23	F	SGL	RRAHTU	NY
PAPIER, LOAV	30	M	LABR	RRZZZZ	PA
LIZZIE	20	F	W	RRZZZZ	PA
SAMUEL	8	M	CHILD	RRZZZZ	PA
SUSSIE	9	F	CHILD	RRZZZZ	PA
KOTSCHANOWITZ, MEYER	45	M	LABR	RRZZZZ	IA
SAMBERG, MOSES	29	M	TLR	RRAHRK	IA
LASINSKI, ELIAR	21	M	MCHT	RRAIBI	IA
DOWIAK, VINCENTY	30	M	LABR	RRZZZZ	IA
MESCHKOWSKY, JAN	26	M	LABR	RRZZZZ	IA
DIAMANT, MOSES	33	M	LABR	RRAHXX	IA
LEONCZYK, THEOFIL	25	M	LABR	RRAHZS	NY
DANIELOWICZ, ANNA	24	F	SGL	RRAIIN	NY

SHIP: ANCHORIA

FROM: GLASGOW AND MOVILLE
TO: NEW YORK
ARRIVED: 02 JANUARY 1889

PASSENGER	AGE	SEX	OCCUPATION	PRI VIL	DES
SLAWONSKI, CHAIE	18	F	NN	RRZZZZ	USA
ETTEL	1	F	CHILD	RRZZZZ	USA
LIEBE	30	F	CH	RRZZZZ	USA
RUBEN	5	M	CHILD	RRZZZZ	USA
WOLF	2	M	CHILD	RRZZZZ	USA
MERE	1	M	CHILD	RRZZZZ	USA
BREMRES, FANNY-G.	19	F	HP	RRZZZZ	USA
GITTEL	10	F	CH	RRZZZZ	USA
BABIN, LEISER	18	M	TLR	RRZZZZ	USA
MOSES	28	M	TLR	RRABQB	USA
BANK, BENJAMIN	22	M	DLR	RRABQB	USA
LEIB	21	F	W	RRABQB	USA
BISINEWICZ, ANTON	21	M	BCHR	RRABQB	USA
ANDRUICHEWITZ, IGNACI	21	M	TLR	RRZZZZ	USA
WULFOWITZ, A.M.	36	M	TLR	RRZZZZ	USA
GEDIMIN, RAINOLD	27	M	TLR	RRAHTU	USA
JACOBSOHN, JOHAN	26	M	SMH	RRAIAR	USA
SALTZMANN, GETIEL	40	M	BCHR	RRZZZZ	USA
KLUNASCHEWITZNER, BENJ.	22	M	TLR	RRZZZZ	USA
NUDEL, ABRAM-J.	28	M	TLR	RRZZZZ	USA
SBAR, MOSES	19	M	CPTR	RRAFWJ	USA
KOSKEVICH, KARL	44	M	SHMK	PLZZZZ	USA
MARIA	22	F	HP	PLZZZZ	USA
KAROLINA	13	F	HP	PLZZZZ	USA
JOHAN	11	M	CH	PLZZZZ	USA
EDMUNDA	9	F	CHILD	PLZZZZ	USA

PASSENGER	AGE	SEX	OCCUPATION	PRIV	VIL	DES

SHIP: ARIZONA

FROM: LIVERPOOL AND QUEENSTOWN
TO: NEW YORK
ARRIVED: 02 JANUARY 1889

PASSENGER	AGE	SEX	OCCUPATION	PRIV	VIL	DES
RACRUKAITIS, THOMAS	22	M	LABR	PL	ACBF	USA
BRAND, ADAM	49	M	ATSN	PL	ACBF	USA
JAFFER, JULIE	18	M	LABR	PL	ACBF	USA
URI, IDES	16	F	SP	PL	ACBF	USA
DRUCK, MUSSLE	25	F	W	PL	ACBF	USA
HENRY	.08	M	INFANT	PL	ACBF	USA
BADANE, ANE	25	F	SP	PL	ACBF	USA
BARANOWITZ, EISK	45	M	PNTR	PL	ACBF	USA
NACH, RUIVE	47	M	ATSN	PL	ACBF	USA
CHAIE	27	F	W	PL	ACBF	USA
RACHMIEL	11	F	CH	PL	ACBF	USA
JOSEPH	9	M	CHILD	PL	ACBF	USA
ISRAEL	7	M	CHILD	PL	ACBF	USA
SUSMAN	3	M	CHILD	PL	ACBF	USA
STROLUK, RACHEL	23	F	SP	PL	ACBF	USA
MELAWJAK, ITTE	19	F	SP	PL	ACBF	USA
OSUR, ETTE	22	F	SP	PL	ACBF	USA

SHIP: SORRENTO

FROM: HAMBURG
TO: NEW YORK
ARRIVED: 03 JANUARY 1889

PASSENGER	AGE	SEX	OCCUPATION	PRIV	VIL	DES
ADELMANN, REBECCA	19	F	SGL	RR	ZZZZ	NY
MOSCHIWITZKY, ELIAS	20	M	TLR	RR	ZZZZ	NY
BAAKLUND, ANDERS	19	M	LABR	FN	ZZZZ	NE
SILVERMANN, EIDEL	20	F	SGL	RR	ZZZZ	NE
KOPKO, KASIMIR	26	M	LABR	RR	ZZZZ	NY
AL-ELROTH, ELIE	41	M	PNTR	RR	ZZZZ	NY
POLLACK, ALEXANDER	25	M	LABR	RR	ZZZZ	NY
KAMINSKI, JAN	37	M	LABR	RR	ZZZZ	NY
GOLDIN, CHONE	25	M	DLR	RR	ZZZZ	NY
ZILNETZKI, M	19	F	SGL	RR	ZZZZ	NY
-LABODOWSKY, -RUME	19	F	SGL	RR	ZZZZ	NY
PORTECK, B	22	M	LABR	RR	ZZZZ	NY
SUTZEWIS, WINZAS	32	M	LABR	RR	ZZZZ	NY
BOBAN--, JOSEF	21	M	LABR	RR	ZZZZ	NY
WALENTOVIEZ, -EOFIE	26	M	LABR	RR	ZZZZ	PHI
MAR-ELLY	28	M	LABR	RR	ZZZZ	NY
FRITSCHAL, PAWELL	35	M	MLR	RR	ZZZZ	NY
GOETZ, JANKEL	42	M	LABR	RR	ZZZZ	NY
LOEWENTHAL, MORDCHE	19	M	LABR	RR	ZZZZ	NY
POZOLOMSKI, MORDCHE	33	M	LABR	RR	ZZZZ	NY
FRANKEL, MEYER	22	M	LABR	RR	ZZZZ	NY

SHIP: WESTERNLAND

FROM: ANTWERP
TO: NEW YORK
ARRIVED: 05 JANUARY 1889

PASSENGER	AGE	SEX	OCCUPATION	PRIV	VIL	DES
KLOSKOSKY, ISRAEL	21	M	CL	RR	AIMM	NY
PERLEMANN, ISAAC	23	M	UNKNOWN	RR	AIMM	NY
JAKOBOWSKY, LOUIS	23	M	SLR	RR	AIMM	NY
HIRSCH, PERETZ	23	M	SHMK	RR	AIMM	NY
PASCH, ISAAC	20	M	SLR	RR	AIMM	NY
KAFLANSKY, ABRAHAM	22	M	PRSR	RR	AIMM	NY

SHIP: THE QUEEN

FROM: LIVERPOOL
TO: NEW YORK
ARRIVED: 05 JANUARY 1889

PASSENGER	AGE	SEX	OCCUPATION	PRIV	VIL	DES
CHARNIEWICK, V.	27	F	SP	RR	ADBQ	PA
KAWEZYNSKA, A.	40	F	W	RR	AILA	PA
JOHANNA	4	F	CHILD	RR	AILA	PA
BERKOWITZ, M.	25	M	LABR	RR	AILA	PA
KAWEZYNSKA, J.	18	F	SP	RR	AILA	PA
HELENA	10	F	CH	RR	AILA	PA
WOLLER, JACOB	26	M	LABR	RR	AILA	PA
MINA	26	F	W	RR	AILA	PA
ISRAEL	3	M	CHILD	RR	AILA	PA
NATHAN	1	M	CHILD	RR	AILA	PA
HOWITZ, JOSEF	6	M	CHILD	RR	AILA	PA
SILBERT, SALMEN	35	M	LABR	RR	AILA	NY
BIER, MOSES	18	M	LABR	RR	AILA	NY
BRANDE	16	M	LABR	RR	AILA	NY
HEINAN, ALWIS	26	F	SP	RR	AILA	NY
MADAME	30	F	SP	RR	AILA	NY
HIBONI, JOSEF	24	M	LABR	RR	AILA	NY
SCHMUSCH, MORITZ	20	M	LABR	RR	AILA	NY
FANNY	19	F	W	RR	AILA	NY
TEDDRY, SCHUCK	26	M	LABR	RR	AILA	NY
HORBAL, KISLENA	19	F	SP	RR	AILA	NY
SCHACH, MACIEF	25	M	LABR	RR	AILA	NY
GORDIN, MOSES	29	M	LABR	RR	AILA	NY
BAICHE	27	F	W	RR	AILA	NY
LUZNER, GITTEL	50	F	W	RR	AILA	NY
BEILE	30	F	W	RR	AILA	NY
HERSCH	1	M	CHILD	RR	AILA	NY

SHIP: LLOYD

FROM: BREMEN AND SOUTHAMPTON
TO: NEW YORK
ARRIVED: 05 JANUARY 1889

PASSENGER	AGE	SEX	OCCUPATION	PRIV	VIL	DES
LOSCKIN, ALEXANDER	30	M	FARMER	RR	AHOO	USA
BLAGAVESCHENSKY, WLADIM	34	M	FARMER	RR	AHOO	USA
VOLKOFF, NICOLAUS	36	M	FARMER	RR	AHOO	USA
KAPORSKY, MICHAEL	32	M	FARMER	RR	AHOO	USA
POTNICOF, ALEXIS	40	M	FARMER	RR	AHOO	USA
TIMOFEEV, ALEXIUS	29	M	FARMER	RR	AHOO	USA
KRIWASCHEIN, BASILIUS	23	M	FARMER	RR	AHOO	USA
KALASCHNICOF, NICOLAUS	10	M	CH	RR	AHOO	USA
VASSILIEFF, ALEXANDRINE	21	F	W	RR	AHOO	USA
PAOLOFF, AGRIPPINE	26	F	W	RR	AHOO	USA
PASNIKOFF, OLGA	19	F	W	RR	AHOO	USA
ASLAMASOFF, CATHARINA	24	F	W	RR	AHOO	USA
LOCKIN, WLADIMIR	3	M	CHILD	RR	AHOO	USA
WILDOFSKY, ROSE	18	F	NN	RR	AHQD	USA
HAMMER, LEIBUCZ	35	M	LABR	RR	AHOO	USA
LIPSCHITZ, CHAJE	34	F	W	RR	AHOO	USA
ETTEL	5	F	CHILD	RR	AHOO	USA
KOKNY, RESHEY	16	M	LABR	RR	AHOO	IN
MOSES	26	M	LABR	RR	AHOO	IN
SKORKA, URSULA	23	F	NN	RR	AHOO	PA
MAIER, PHILIPP	21	M	FARMER	RR	AHOO	DAK
ARINOWITZ, MAREUS	22	M	LABR	RR	AHOO	NY
RABINOWITZ, ISRAEL	22	M	LABR	RR	AHQD	NY
GITTA	20	F	W	RR	AHQD	NY
WILENSKI, ROCHEL	45	M	LABR	RR	AHQD	NY
TEW, SCHAGE	32	M	TLR	RR	AHQD	NY
ASCHER, LIEBE	40	F	W	RR	AHQD	NY
DWORE	11	F	CH	RR	AHQD	NY
CHAIN	9	M	CHILD	RR	AHQD	NY

PASSENGER	AGE	SEX	OCCUPATION	PRV VIL DES
MOSES	5	M	CHILD	RRAHQDNY
CHANE	3	M	CHILD	RRAHQDNY
BERIL	.01	M	INFANT	RRAHQDNY
ROSENSTEIN, FEIGE	65	M	LABR	RRAHQDNY
DAVIDSOHN, CHAJE	20	F	W	RRAHQDNY
FREIDE	.01	F	INFANT	RRAHQDNY
LIPSCHUETZ, CHANE	3	M	CHILD	RRAHQDNY
SUMRZIK, MEYER	24	M	LABR	RRAHQDNY
SMIRLE, SARA	35	F	NN	RRAHQDNY
SCHMIED, MOSES	22	M	MCHT	RRAHOONY
GARNETZ, MORDCHE	22	F	NN	RRAHOONY
JASCHINOWSKY, SAUL	21	M	LABR	RRAHOONY
ANTONOWITZ, KOZIMIR	28	M	BCHR	RRAHOONY
ANNA	18	F	W	RRAHOONY
GRUENFELD, MENASSE	22	M	LABR	RRAHOONY
ESTER	17	F	W	RRAHOONY

SHIP: MAIN

FROM: BREMEN
TO: BALTIMORE
ARRIVED: 06 JANUARY 1889

PASSENGER	AGE	SEX	OCCUPATION	PRV VIL DES
BRENER, SCHAUL	18	M	LABR	RRZZZZBAL
DAEJEWSKA, FRANZISCA	26	F	W	RRZZZZMO
LADISLAWA	2	F	CHILD	RRZZZZMO
MARTHA	5	F	CHILD	RRZZZZMO
BANK, DORA	18	F	SVNT	RRZZZZMO
LEIENSEN, EDDE	34	F	W	RRZZZZMO
JOSEF	10	M	CH	RRZZZZMO
MEYER	7	M	CHILD	RRZZZZMO
CELYE	3	F	CHILD	RRZZZZMO
LANDSMANN, BECKE	20	F	SVNT	RRZZZZMO
GINSBERG, GENEVA	50	F	W	RRZZZZMO
CHAIE	16	F	CH	RRZZZZMO
MILLER, SARA	25	F	W	RRZZZZIL
MEYER	6	M	CHILD	RRZZZZIL
COHN, BEILE	19	F	SVNT	RRZZZZIL
MARBITZ, DEMEIRE	34	F	W	RRZZZZIL
SORE	11	F	CH	RRZZZZIL
LAH	9	F	CHILD	RRZZZZIL
BINE	2	F	CHILD	RRZZZZIL
ROCHEL	19	M	FARMER	RRZZZZIL
PRZYGODINSKI, JOHANN	38	M	LABR	RRZZZZMI
MARIA	30	F	W	RRZZZZMI
DAHN, HEINRICH	46	M	FARMER	RRZZZZKS
FRIEDERIKE	40	F	W	RRZZZZKS

SHIP: PAVONIA

FROM: LIVERPOOL
TO: BOSTON
ARRIVED: 08 JANUARY 1889

PASSENGER	AGE	SEX	OCCUPATION	PRV VIL DES
BAZAWSKY, HASSAL	28	M	PDLR	RRZZZZNY
FRANIC	25	M	PDLR	RRZZZZNY
KALEKLER, MOSES	21	M	PDLR	RRZZZZNY
BULSKI, FRANZ	37	M	PDLR	RRZZZZNY
URIUSNITZ, STANISLAW	33	M	LABR	RRZZZZNY
KALINOWSKY, KAZIMIL	22	M	LABR	RRZZZZNY
RUTKOUSKY, ALEX	22	M	LABR	RRZZZZNY
BIEWENSTOCK, ELEAS	22	M	LABR	RRZZZZNY
MARDELBAUM, SAUD.	22	M	LABR	RRZZZZNY
NERKKUA, ANNA	37	F	MA	RRZZZZNY
ERIKKI	00	M	CH	RRZZZZNY

PASSENGER	AGE	SEX	OCCUPATION	PRV VIL DES
BUEDUSON, ALLEN	28	F	MA	RRZZZZNY
ADA	5	F	CHILD	RRZZZZNY
ISAAC	3	M	CHILD	RRZZZZNY
LEWIN, RAHEL	35	F	MA	RRZZZZNY
MENE	6	F	CHILD	RRZZZZNY
LUSIA	3	F	CHILD	RRZZZZNY

SHIP: RUGIA

FROM: HAMBURG
TO: NEW YORK
ARRIVED: 08 JANUARY 1889

PASSENGER	AGE	SEX	OCCUPATION	PRV VIL DES
PRUSTIN, JOSEPH	23	M	MLR	RRAIGHUSA
ZILNETZKI, MUCHLY	19	F	SGL	RRZZZZUSA
DUSCHKIN, GITTEL	19	F	SGL	RRZZZZUSA
EUEHNER, RIWKE	18	F	SGL	RRZZZZUSA
PRUSLIN, CHAIE	22	F	SGL	RRZZZZUSA
CHAIE	22	F	SGL	RRZZZZUSA
CHMZICKI, VALENTY	35	M	LABR	RRZZZZUSA
DOROTHEA	29	F	W	RRZZZZUSA
PETWITZ, PETER	24	M	LABR	RRAIGHUSA
DOMBROWSKY, PETER	28	M	LABR	RRZZZZUSA
WEWAK, WLADISLAV	23	M	LABR	RRZZZZUSA
KAPLAN, OSCHER	22	M	LABR	RRAHVUUSA
EDELKIND, LIPPMANN	46	M	LABR	RRZZZZUSA
ROSEWITZ, MICHAEL	30	M	LABR	RRZZZZUSA
BARKOWSKY, ZALLY	36	M	LABR	RRAHWMUSA
ROSALIE	37	F	W	RRAHWMUSA
PETER	7	M	CHILD	RRAHWMUSA
JOSES	6	M	CHILD	RRAHWMUSA
MAGDALENE	4	F	CHILD	RRAHWMUSA
JONNER	.11	M	INFANT	RRAHWMUSA
WIZENTY	26	M	LABR	RRAHWMUSA
KEPLER, EVA	24	F	SGL	RRAHXLUSA
DANKSZIO, ORSZULIA	20	F	SGL	RRAHZSUSA
BEREURCOWA, MARIANNA	12	F	SGL	RRZZZZUSA
WURBU, ANTON	23	M	LABR	RRAHZSUSA
KOSSETZKI, WLADISLAV	30	M	LABR	RRAHTUUSA
GRUENWALD, PAULINE	26	F	SGL	RRAHTUUSA
BOGDANOFF, ANDREAS	33	M	LABR	FNZZZZUSA
ABOWITSCH, LAIA	18	F	SGL	FNAHTOUSA
JANKOWSKA, MONIA	41	F	WO	FNAFWJUSA
APPOLLONIA	5	F	CHILD	FNAFWJUSA
HURWITZ, ABRAM	35	M	LABR	FNAHXLUSA
AKNOVICH, JECHWED	65	F	WO	FNAHXLUSA
MERENCE, MOSES	36	M	LABR	FNAIIOUSA
SZLONAKY, DINKE	17	F	SGL	RRZZZZUSA
ABRAMOWICZ, MOSCHE	18	F	SGL	RRAHTUUSA
ROSOWSKY, SOPHIE	21	F	SGL	RRAHTUUSA
CLASEN, ERNST	23	M	MCHT	RRAEFLUSA
SULSKY, JACOB	24	M	MCHT	RRAHOOUSA
KOTURWOLUZKY, JUDEL	20	M	MCHT	RRZZZZUSA
RACZINSKI, JOHANN	27	M	LABR	RRZZZZUSA
SCHUB, MARGR.	35	F	WO	RRZZZZUSA
MALKE	7	F	CHILD	RRZZZZUSA
BASCHE	6	F	CHILD	RRZZZZUSA
PESSEL	5	F	CHILD	RRZZZZUSA
WEISGOTZKY, ABRAHAM	17	M	CTHR	RRAHVUUSA
HERZFINKEL, LEBA	22	M	LABR	RRAFWJUSA
MAWSZA	24	F	W	RRAFWJUSA
ANNITHA	.06	F	INFANT	RRAFWJUSA
GOLDSTEIN, PESY	28	F	WO	RRAFWJUSA
GUTMANN, EPHROIM	45	M	HTR	RRAHWQUSA
GOLDSTEIN, SAMUEL	24	M	CPTR	RRZZZZUSA
ZTOZENSKI, ANTON	24	M	LABR	RRAHZSUSA
GOLUBEK, ANTON	22	M	LABR	RRAHZSUSA
SMYDA, HARRY	26	M	LABR	RRAHZSUSA
KUEBARTH, AUGUSTE	22	F	WO	RRAHXLUSA
BERTHA	.09	F	INFANT	RRAHXLUSA

PASSENGER	AGE	SEX	OCCUPATION	PRV	VIL	DES
ARHIS, OTTO	26	M	MLR	RR	AIFJ	USA
ROSENFELD, JOSEPH	28	M	MCHT	RR	ZZZZ	USA

SHIP: DEVONIA

FROM: GLASGOW
TO: NEW YORK
ARRIVED: 09 JANUARY 1889

PASSENGER	AGE	SEX	OCCUPATION	PRV	VIL	DES
EHRENSTEIN, CHAIE	30	F	UNKNOWN	RR	ZZZZ	USA
SLOME	8	M	CHILD	RR	ZZZZ	USA
ANAN	6	F	CHILD	RR	ZZZZ	USA
LEISER	3	M	CHILD	RR	ZZZZ	USA
HILLERMANN, BEREL	26	M	TLR	RR	ZZZZ	USA
ESTER	20	F	UNKNOWN	RR	ZZZZ	USA
ILESCHEWITZ, ABE	20	M	TLR	RR	ZZZZ	USA
CHAIE	20	F	UNKNOWN	RR	ZZZZ	USA
KARP, CHANE	30	F	UNKNOWN	RR	ZZZZ	USA
INDES	11	M	CH	RR	ZZZZ	USA
HIRSCH	8	M	CHILD	RR	ZZZZ	USA
BERL	3	M	CHILD	RR	ZZZZ	USA
RIBAKEWITSCH, DAVID	25	M	TLR	RR	ZZZZ	USA
SCHEPSEL	18	M	LABR	RR	ZZZZ	USA
SCHMULEWITZ, LEISER	60	M	BLKSMH	RR	ZZZZ	USA
SORE	8	F	CHILD	RR	ZZZZ	USA
BEIMEUROSCH, SCHLOME	30	M	UNKNOWN	RR	ZZZZ	USA
MATLIN, MESCHE	35	F	UNKNOWN	RR	ZZZZ	USA
OGULNIK, ROSCHE	21	F	UNKNOWN	RR	ZZZZ	USA
BROSEWSKY, NOCHEL	16	M	TLR	RR	ZZZZ	USA
DAVIDOWITZ, BENZEL	42	M	FARMER	RR	ZZZZ	USA
GERDNY, MATESO	27	M	LABR	RR	ZZZZ	USA
KRUNOWSKY, BERNARD	21	M	LABR	RR	ZZZZ	USA
KUPPERSTEIN, RUBEN	59	M	LABR	RR	ZZZZ	USA
DAVID	28	M	LABR	RR	ZZZZ	USA

SHIP: BOTHNIA

FROM: LIVERPOOL AND QUEENSTOWN
TO: NEW YORK
ARRIVED: 09 JANUARY 1889

PASSENGER	AGE	SEX	OCCUPATION	PRV	VIL	DES
BLECHOOSKY, ABRAM	20	M	LABR	RR	AINL	USA
KOBELKOWSKY, HIRSCH	17	M	LABR	RR	AINL	USA
SAUDELEWITZ, MARIE	15	F	SP	RR	AINL	USA
PULAREWITZ, SARA	44	F	MA	RR	AINL	USA
HANNE	15	F	SP	RR	AINL	USA
ETE	11	F	CH	RR	AINL	USA
CZESAKAS, KAZIMIR	22	M	LABR	FN	ZZZZ	USA
JOGA, MARTIN	39	M	LABR	FN	AFWJ	USA
HULITA, MATTI	25	M	LABR	FN	AFWJ	USA
SANNAMAKI, HEIKI	37	M	LABR	FN	AHOO	USA
SZTELCZYK, MARIANNA	40	F	MA	FN	AIIH	USA
AGNES	4	F	CHILD	FN	AIIH	USA

SHIP: LEERDAM

FROM: AMSTERDAM
TO: NEW YORK
ARRIVED: 10 JANUARY 1889

PASSENGER	AGE	SEX	OCCUPATION	PRV	VIL	DES
MAI, FRANZ	28	M	LABR	RR	ZZZZ	USA
GUMPIETZ, NATHAN	35	M	LABR	RR	ZZZZ	USA
FLECK, GOLDI	16	M	LABR	RR	ZZZZ	USA
MAIEROSKI, JULIAN	25	M	LABR	RR	ZZZZ	USA
STEMMER, SIG.	33	M	MCHT	RR	ZZZZ	USA
KARPMANN, S.	25	M	MCHT	RR	ZZZZ	USA
RICHOW, EMOND	25	M	CNF	RR	ZZZZ	USA
PODOLSKI, CHAIE	18	M	LABR	RR	ZZZZ	USA
FOMULANUS, THOMAS	43	M	LABR	RR	ZZZZ	USA
ALBACHEWITZ, FRANZ	24	M	LABR	RR	ZZZZ	USA
KLEIN, MARIE	17	F	UNKNOWN	RR	ZZZZ	USA
KOCIK, KAREL	35	M	LABR	RR	ZZZZ	USA
GUNTHER, LUDWIG	29	M	LABR	RR	ZZZZ	USA

SHIP: WISCONSIN

FROM: LIVERPOOL AND QUEENSTOWN
TO: NEW YORK
ARRIVED: 10 JANUARY 1889

PASSENGER	AGE	SEX	OCCUPATION	PRV	VIL	DES
MEYERSON, MARY	19	F	SP	RR	ZZZZ	USA
STENER, MAGDALENE	47	F	W	PL	ZZZZ	USA
JOHANN	7	M	CHILD	PL	ZZZZ	USA
FRANZ	7	M	CHILD	PL	ZZZZ	USA
LEVINSON, ISRAEL	23	M	PMBR	RR	ZZZZ	USA
RABINSKI, DEBORE	17	F	SP	RR	ZZZZ	USA
LEIB	15	F	SP	RR	ZZZZ	USA
MILL, CHTZKEL	18	M	TLR	RR	ZZZZ	USA

SHIP: MICHIGAN

FROM: LIVERPOOL
TO: BOSTON
ARRIVED: 11 JANUARY 1889

PASSENGER	AGE	SEX	OCCUPATION	PRV	VIL	DES
FOX, LUUIS	23	M	LKSH	RR	ZZZZ	USA
KABINOWITZ, ISRAEL	57	M	TLR	RR	ZZZZ	USA
KULKIN, LEIB	28	M	CNF	RR	ZZZZ	USA
ROSENSTEIN, ISRAEL	22	M	TLR	RR	ZZZZ	USA
SACK, JOHAN	35	M	LABR	RR	ZZZZ	USA
JONOWILOTCH, JAN	18	M	TLR	RR	ZZZZ	USA
BLUMBERG, LERY	38	M	WCHMKR	RR	ZZZZ	USA
WINTLAND, FERDINAND	32	M	LABR	RR	ZZZZ	USA
KATZ, JACOB	21	M	LABR	RR	ZZZZ	USA
BLUMBERG, MORRIS	34	M	BCHR	RR	ZZZZ	USA
GORDON, WOLF	16	M	BCHR	RR	ZZZZ	USA
GOLDSMITH, BARNET	20	M	TLR	RR	ZZZZ	USA
ASPIS, CHARLES	30	M	TLR	RR	ZZZZ	USA
GOTECHIN, ISER	22	M	WCHMKR	RR	ZZZZ	USA
DIAMOND, RACHEL	34	F	W	RR	ZZZZ	USA
KEIBETZKY, CHARLES	19	M	JNR	RR	ZZZZ	USA
BADANE	20	F	W	RR	ZZZZ	USA
ABELOW, FEIGEE	23	F	W	RR	ZZZZ	USA
GITEL	23	F	W	RR	ZZZZ	USA
DIAMOND, MACEL	4	F	CHILD	RR	ZZZZ	USA
ABELOW, SARAH	2	F	CHILD	RR	ZZZZ	USA
FREIDE	.09	F	INFANT	RR	ZZZZ	USA
SONY	2	F	CHILD	RR	ZZZZ	USA

PASSENGER	AGE	SEX	OCCUPATION	PRIVIL DES
KARCHE	.08	F	INFANT	RRZZZZUSA
STEIN, FRIEDR.	38	M	LABR	RRZZZZNY

SHIP: CITY OF CHESTER

FROM: LIVERPOOL AND QUEENSTOWN
TO: NEW YORK
ARRIVED: 14 JANUARY 1889

PASSENGER	AGE	SEX	OCCUPATION	PRIVIL DES
JERDELWITSCH, DAVID	17	M	LABR	RRZZZZNY
FRIEDMANN, GOLDE	43	M	LABR	RRZZZZNY
FUHMANSKI, LEAH	16	M	LABR	RRZZZZNY
FREDMANN, JACOB	43	M	LABR	RRZZZZNY
FALLIG, JUDEL	55	M	LABR	RRAGRTNY
GINSER, KOPPEL	30	M	LABR	RRAGRTNY
CHASWITOCH, HIRSCH	35	M	LABR	RRAGRTNY
JESCHER, MAUSCHE	21	M	LABR	RRAHTUNY
KATZ, ISAAC	17	M	LABR	RRAHTUNY
JECHIA	21	M	LABR	RRAHTUNY
BLETZ, SILY	33	M	TLR	RRAFWJNY
GUMBERNS, NACH.	29	M	SMH	RRAFWJNY
BERKOWITZ, JAEL	29	M	BKBNDR	RRAFWJNY
BRUM, M.	20	F	SP	RRZZZZNY
JOHN	34	M	FTR	RRZZZZNY
LOWE, SARAH	37	F	W	RRZZZZNY
SARAH	37	F	W	RRZZZZNY
ELLEN	14	F	SP	RRZZZZNY
FRED	10	M	CH	RRZZZZNY
HENRY	9	M	CHILD	RRZZZZNY
BROOK, WM.	35	M	DPR	RRZZZZFL
BRONGHTON, GEO	39	M	LABR	RRZZZZNY
ALICE	27	F	W	RRZZZZNY
REEMAN, F.J.	32	M	FARMER	RRADBQNY
J.	28	F	W	RRADBQNY
MEDHURSCH, GEO	56	M	UNKNOWN	RRADBQNY
U	56	F	W	RRADBQNY
RUSCHFERTH, WALTER	21	M	UNKNOWN	RRADEDOH
PRIER, F.	31	M	CCHMN	RRZZZZFL
U	29	F	W	RRZZZZFL
PAINTER, JAS.C.	24	M	CL	RRZZZZFL

SHIP: ELBE

FROM: BREMEN AND SOUTHAMPTON
TO: NEW YORK
ARRIVED: 14 JANUARY 1889

PASSENGER	AGE	SEX	OCCUPATION	PRIVIL DES
GLAUZKOPF, ROSALIE	42	F	TT	RRZZZZNY
REG.	20	F	TT	RRZZZZNY
JACOB	25	M	TT	RRZZZZNY
MECHKOWITZ, ABRAHAM	24	M	LABR	RRZZZZUSA
HENNE	28	F	UNKNOWN	RRZZZZUSA
EIDE	6	F	CHILD	RRZZZZUSA
BARKIEWICZ, JAN	25	M	LABR	RRZZZZUSA
SCHMULEWITZ, DAVID	35	M	LABR	RRZZZZUSA
ROCHEL, SARA	30	F	UNKNOWN	RRZZZZUSA
JACOB	.10	M	INFANT	RRZZZZUSA
ELLERT, MARKUS	30	M	SHMK	RRZZZZUSA
GEMBER, RACHEL	29	F	UNKNOWN	RRZZZZUSA
ZARIE	4	F	CHILD	RRZZZZUSA
FEIGE	.08	M	INFANT	RRZZZZUSA
KREIPZIO, WINZENT	38	M	LABR	RRZZZZNY
DZIEDZICH, JAN	24	M	LABR	RRZZZZNY
POSWITOWIZ, JAN	22	M	LABR	RRZZZZNY
WALICHEWICZ, FRANZ	28	M	LABR	RRZZZZNY
STRENKOWSKI, ANDR.	45	M	LABR	RRZZZZNY

SHIP: NOVA SCOTIAN

FROM: LIVERPOOL
TO: BALTIMORE
ARRIVED: 14 JANUARY 1889

PASSENGER	AGE	SEX	OCCUPATION	PRIVIL DES
SCHINELOWITZ, REUBEN	22	M	TLR	PLZZZZBAL
DRUMBELOWSKI, MADES	22	M	LABR	PLZZZZPIT

SHIP: GALLIA

FROM: LIVERPOOL AND QUEENSTOWN
TO: NEW YORK
ARRIVED: 16 JANUARY 1889

PASSENGER	AGE	SEX	OCCUPATION	PRIVIL DES
DELSCHOW, MAX	23	M	TLR	PLACBFUSA
WAGNISISHER, DD.	22	M	LABR	PLACBFUSA
WAVEZULIS, JOS.	20	M	LABR	PLACBFUSA
LIFFMAN, SARA	18	F	SP	RRZZZZUSA
KRUSCHELSKA, ETTE	18	F	SP	RRZZZZUSA
SABINSKY, WOLF	25	M	BLKSMH	RRZZZZUSA
SURE	23	F	W	RRZZZZUSA
KENTZ, MARK	22	M	TLR	RRADBQUSA

SHIP: NEVADA

FROM: LIVERPOOL AND QUEENSTOWN
TO: NEW YORK
ARRIVED: 19 JANUARY 1889

PASSENGER	AGE	SEX	OCCUPATION	PRIVIL DES
VOGTEK, ANDREW	23	M	LABR	RRZZZZUSA
SOBEL, HARRIS	34	M	LABR	PLZZZZUSA
COHN, ISAAC	2	M	CHILD	RRZZZZUSA
DOMBROSKY, ANTONY	25	M	LABR	RRZZZZUSA

SHIP: CITY OF CHICAGO

FROM: LIVERPOOL
TO: NEW YORK
ARRIVED: 19 JANUARY 1889

PASSENGER	AGE	SEX	OCCUPATION	PRIVIL DES
WOJEICH, KRASON	36	M	LABR	RRACBFKIN
KAROL, GOLOS	9	M	CHILD	RRACBFKIN
ZOKARZ, JOS.	42	M	LABR	RRACBFPA
KATH.	9	F	CHILD	RRACBFPA
POTOPINSKY, ST.	15	M	LABR	RRACBFNY
GUILEKOWSKA, A.	21	F	W	RRACBFMI
PUCHORSKA, K.	17	F	W	RRACBFMI
ANTO	10	F	CH	RRACBFMI
CALLICK, E.	24	M	LABR	RRACBFPA
GOROKE, JOH.	28	M	LABR	RRACBFPA
ROMANCUSKI, J.	31	M	LABR	PLZZZZPA
COATTAS, J.	31	M	LABR	PLZZZZPA

PASSENGER	AGE	SEX	OCCUPATION	PRV VIL DES
VAGS, M.	35	M	LABR	PLZZZZPA
MAJESSING, KATA	16	M	LABR	PLACBFCT
SINDENISKI, KONRAD	26	M	TLR	PLACBFUNK
FRANCISCA	26	F	W	PLACBFUNK
SCHMELEWIEZ, ISRAEL	33	M	JNR	PLACBFNY
JENKEL	10	M	CH	PLACBFNY
MOSCH	2	M	CHILD	PLACBFNY
ALTER, JOSEF	47	M	TLR	PLACBFNY
GOLDE	47	F	W	PLACBFNY
SARA	17	F	SVNT	PLACBFNY
ISAAK	.11	M	INFANT	PLACBFNY
AROWITZ, MACHM.	38	M	SHMK	PLACBFNY
SCHMELGING, FRANCIS	40	F	W	PLACBFOH
CHANNA	8	M	CHILD	PLACBFOH
MENACHE	3	F	CHILD	PLACBFOH
MOSES	2	M	CHILD	PLACBFOH
CHENE	.10	M	INFANT	PLACBFOH
BRUZEK, JOSEF	38	M	LABR	PLACBFNY
KESTINGER, SOLOMON	55	M	LABR	PLACBFNY
WALLACH, MARCUS	18	M	LABR	PLACBFNY
HANDIKE, FRANZ	48	M	BLKSMH	PLACBFNY
KATALZKI, ABRAM	20	M	LABR	PLACBFNY
SCHIFF, REIN.	25	F	W	PLACBFNY
CHANA	.01	F	INFANT	PLACBFNY
TROMKIN, ABRAM	30	M	TLR	PLACBFNY
MARCUS	11	M	BY	PLACBFNY
PEIAKENT, MOCHRIN	46	M	PDLR	PLACBFNY
PERECKONI, ROCHE	39	F	W	PLACBFNY
MOSES	5	M	CHILD	PLACBFNY
SCHMAN	5	M	CHILD	PLACBFNY
MOLE	.10	M	INFANT	PLACBFNY
PERWER, SELIG	45	M	FARMER	PLACBFBAL
PERMMEUSKI, CHAIN	16	M	UNKNOWN	PLACBFNY
LIPKOWITZ, BASCHE	19	F	SVNT	PLACBFNY
LEVY, HYMAN	39	M	TLR	PLACBFNY
SACHS, SAM	22	M	PDLR	PLADAXBAL

SHIP: ROMAN

FROM: LIVERPOOL
TO: BOSTON
ARRIVED: 20 JANUARY 1889

PASSENGER	AGE	SEX	OCCUPATION	PRV VIL DES
OLSCHENETZKY, SARAH	38	F	SVNT	PLZZZZBO
JOS.	10	M	CH	PLZZZZBO
ZANNEF	3	F	CHILD	PLZZZZBO
HALHERN, ALK	30	M	LABR	RRZZZZCIN
LEAH	20	F	W	RRZZZZCIN
ZANRET, ANDRIES	21	M	LABR	RRZZZZCH
PUREN, MARTIN	25	M	LABR	RRZZZZCH
MEYROVITCH, BEHR.	25	M	LABR	RRZZZZNY
SZIERSCEWSKY, PAUL	24	M	LABR	PLZZZZSHN
SCHWARZ, ADOLPH	26	M	TLR	RRZZZZNY
EDLEMAN, N.	21	M	TLR	RRZZZZNY
ARFA, ESTER	18	F	SP	PLZZZZNY
FETBRAND, BENJ.	18	F	SP	PLZZZZNY
COHEN, JACOB	29	M	LABR	RRZZZZNY

SHIP: WERRA

FROM: BREMEN AND SOUTHAMPTON
TO: NEW YORK
ARRIVED: 21 JANUARY 1889

PASSENGER	AGE	SEX	OCCUPATION	PRV VIL DES
TIEDEMANN, WILHELM	25	M	MCHT	RRZZZZUSA
GRASS, AUGUST	23	M	CL	RRZZZZUSA
KANZLER, EUGEN	16	M	CL	RRZZZZUSA
VON, ERNST	21	M	ACHTT	RRZZZZUSA
LAN--, CARL	28	M	MCHT	RRZZZZUSA
KAPLAN, RESER	60	M	FARMER	RRZZZZUSA
SCHMIDT, HERMINE	24	F	NN	RRZZZZUSA
WINKLER, LORE	26	F	NN	RRZZZZUSA
JOSEF	18	M	LABR	RRZZZZUSA
CHAJA	15	F	NN	RRZZZZUSA
FEUVEL	5	F	CHILD	RRZZZZUSA
FREIDA	3	F	CHILD	RRZZZZUSA
LEVIN, MAKE	22	M	MCHT	RRZZZZUSA
GESINE	18	F	NN	RRZZZZUSA
KOLOWITZ, WOLF	29	M	DLR	RRZZZZUSA
VISOZKI, MARTIN	18	M	DLR	RRZZZZUSA
SELIKOWITZ, ITZIG	20	M	LABR	RRZZZZUSA
KOTLER, SCHMEREL	45	M	LABR	RRZZZZUSA
JARMASCH, LIEBA	35	F	NN	RRZZZZUSA
HEINRICH	7	M	CHILD	RRZZZZUSA
CHAME	5	F	CHILD	RRZZZZUSA
GERSCHMANN, DAVID	19	M	BKR	RRZZZZUSA
SARAH	20	F	NN	RRZZZZUSA
LETTEL, ODES	30	M	FARMER	RRZZZZUSA
HUNA	6	F	CHILD	RRZZZZUSA
ISRAEL	5	M	CHILD	RRZZZZUSA
BERNHARD	4	M	CHILD	RRZZZZUSA
SARA	.01	F	INFANT	RRZZZZUSA
BERKOWITZ, SCHEINDEL	18	M	LABR	RRZZZZUSA
KA-ASLIWAS, ANNA	25	F	NN	RRZZZZUSA
PATKEWICZ, FELIX	28	M	GDNR	RRZZZZUSA

SHIP: SERVIA

FROM: LIVERPOOL AND QUEENSTOWN
TO: NEW YORK
ARRIVED: 21 JANUARY 1889

PASSENGER	AGE	SEX	OCCUPATION	PRV VIL DES
TOSSELOWITZ, WOLFF	27	M	LABR	RRZZZZCAN
ROSENKRAUZ, ISRAEL	26	M	LABR	RRZZZZCAN
SEGALL, JACOB	18	M	CL	RRZZZZCAN
BECK, DANIEL	15	M	CL	RRZZZZCAN
STEINBERG, FRANKEL	18	M	TLR	RRZZZZCAN
MATUSEWICZ, KASIMIR	19	M	LABR	RRZZZZCAN
TARZENIK, ANTON	32	M	LABR	RRZZZZCAN
TOIVALA, JOHAN	40	M	LABR	RRZZZZCAN
NIKKILA, JAKOB	44	M	LABR	RRZZZZCAN
KUSKINER, ROBERT	34	M	FARMER	RRZZZZCAN
LEONHARD	44	M	LABR	RRZZZZCAN
MAZKOWICZ, BARUCH	20	M	LABR	RRZZZZCAN
AUGUSTENSKY, CHAIM	40	M	LABR	RRZZZZCAN
MICHAELS, DAVID	27	M	TRVLR	RRZZZZMA
HANKILA, HENDRIK	30	M	FARMER	RRZZZZMI
WINOGRADOW, LEIB	30	M	TLR	RRZZZZNY
RAHEL	11	F	CH	RRZZZZNY
ABRAHAM	9	M	CHILD	RRZZZZNY
KAPAND, FLIGE	35	F	MA	RRZZZZNY
HANNACH	12	F	CH	RRZZZZNY
SAMUEL	9	M	CHILD	RRZZZZNY
HANOCH	8	M	CHILD	RRZZZZNY
BARUCH	6	M	CHILD	RRZZZZNY
MAYER	5	M	CHILD	RRZZZZNY
ZIPPE	4	M	CHILD	RRZZZZNY

PASSENGER	AGE	SEX	OCCUPATION	PRV	VIL	DES
FANNY	7	F	CHILD	RR	ZZZZ	NY
KALINOWSKA, TEKLA	19	F	SP	RR	ZZZZ	NY

SHIP: WAESLAND

FROM: ANTWERP
TO: NEW YORK
ARRIVED: 22 JANUARY 1889

PASSENGER	AGE	SEX	OCCUPATION	PRV	VIL	DES
LIPOWSKI, MOSES	45	M	PDLR	RR	ZZZZ	NY
SVATOS, JOHAN	45	M	MSN	PL	ZZZZ	NY
JOSEFA	35	F	MSN	PL	ZZZZ	NY
JOHAN	9	M	CHILD	PL	ZZZZ	NY
ANNA	8	F	CHILD	PL	ZZZZ	NY
JOSEF	6	M	CHILD	PL	ZZZZ	NY
WENZL	3	M	CHILD	PL	ZZZZ	NY
AGNES	1	F	CHILD	PL	ZZZZ	NY
HEILPERT, SIMON	30	M	LABR	PL	ZZZZ	NY

SHIP: CIRCASSIA

FROM: GLASGOW AND MOVILLE
TO: NEW YORK
ARRIVED: 22 JANUARY 1889

PASSENGER	AGE	SEX	OCCUPATION	PRV	VIL	DES
GOLDFAM, JACOB	58	M	GENT	PL	ZZZZ	USA
MARY	28	F	W	PL	ZZZZ	USA
EDWIN	1	M	CHILD	PL	ZZZZ	USA
SCOHN, MICH.	34	M	FARMER	RR	ZZZZ	USA
CHASANOWITZ, SABATIS	18	M	DLR	RR	ZZZZ	USA
REISBERG, BERND.	16	M	LABR	RR	ZZZZ	USA
STANKEIWITZ, JAN	30	M	JNR	RR	ZZZZ	USA
RYMARZUK, FRANZ	24	M	JNR	RR	ZZZZ	USA
HAWITSKI, POWIL	30	M	LABR	RR	ZZZZ	USA
ALRAHAMOWITZ, GOLDE	40	F	W	RR	ZZZZ	USA
PAULINE	16	F	HP	RR	ZZZZ	USA
WENICHEL, ESTER	23	F	W	RR	ZZZZ	USA
GETEL	6	F	CHILD	RR	ZZZZ	USA

SHIP: ITALY

FROM: LIVERPOOL
TO: NEW YORK
ARRIVED: 22 JANUARY 1889

PASSENGER	AGE	SEX	OCCUPATION	PRV	VIL	DES
BENER, ABRAH.	22	M	CGRMKR	RR	ACBF	NY
WENJBOTER, CHAIM	23	M	CGRMKR	RR	ACBF	NY
BLATH, CHAIM	23	M	CGRMKR	RR	ACBF	NY
LABIEKE, ISAAC	27	M	CGRMKR	RR	ADAX	NY
RACHILES, MOSES	19	M	LABR	RR	ACBF	NY
FEINGSEK, ZALLE	21	M	CGRMKR	RR	ACBF	NY
GOLDMANN, MEIR	47	M	LABR	RR	ACBF	NY

SHIP: BOHEMIA

FROM: HAMBURG
TO: NEW YORK
ARRIVED: 23 JANUARY 1889

PASSENGER	AGE	SEX	OCCUPATION	PRV	VIL	DES
GRUENBERG, ROSA	20	F	SGL	RR	AEFL	USA
MAGOLIES, MOSES	40	M	MCHT	RR	AHUV	USA
NIDRE	20	F	CH	RR	AHUV	USA
SALOMON	7	M	CHILD	RR	AHUV	USA
RADEZKY, ESTHER	47	F	WO	RR	ZZZZ	USA
RACHEL	17	F	CH	RR	ZZZZ	USA
IONE	14	F	CH	RR	ZZZZ	USA
STEIN, HANNE	19	F	SGL	RR	ZZZZ	USA
BLACKSTEIN, MICHAEL	22	M	LABR	RR	ZZZZ	USA
KUPPER, SARA	22	F	WO	RR	AHVU	USA
SCHMUL	.11	M	INFANT	RR	AHVU	USA
TISCHBEIN, BEILE	21	F	SGL	RR	AIHR	USA
LIEBOWITZ, ELKE	30	F	WO	RR	AHVU	USA
CHANE	8	F	CHILD	RR	AHVU	USA
PERL	3	F	CHILD	RR	AHVU	USA
RACHE	2	F	CHILD	RR	AHVU	USA
CHOJE	.01	F	INFANT	RR	AHVU	USA
JULINSKY, JOSEF	21	M	LABR	RR	AHVU	USA
MILEWIEZ, SCHLONE	21	M	LABR	RR	AHVU	USA
DWORKOWITZ, HERRM.	17	M	LABR	RR	AHZP	USA
EMMA	46	F	WO	RR	AHZP	USA
PAUL	22	M	LABR	RR	AHZP	USA
JOH.	15	M	LABR	RR	AHZP	USA
LINE	14	F	SGL	RR	AHZP	USA
SABLUDWSKY, ROSA	18	F	SGL	RR	AEFL	USA
SUBERSKY, PESACK	21	M	JNR	RR	AHTO	USA
AUGUSTENOWIEZ, JOSEF	23	M	LABR	RR	AIGH	USA
KONKEL, JOSEF	25	M	BKR	RR	ZZZZ	USA
SADOWSKY, ANTON	19	M	LABR	RR	ZZZZ	USA
MAGED, RAPHAL	20	M	CL	RR	AHZJ	USA
RUBINOWITZ, LOEB	14	M	LABR	RR	ZZZZ	USA
SILBERMANN, MARIE	48	F	WO	RR	ZZZZ	USA
LIBBY	9	F	CHILD	RR	ZZZZ	USA
ACKIZER, BARNEY	18	M	LABR	RR	AIGH	USA
RUBINSTEIN, DAVID	32	M	SHMK	RR	AHQD	USA
PINNESKOCKI, JOH.	34	M	LABR	FN	ZZZZ	USA
JOH.	40	M	LABR	FN	ZZZZ	USA
KORPELA, MATTS	18	M	LABR	FN	ZZZZ	USA
POETILA, ALRIK	14	M	LABR	FN	ZZZZ	USA
MATILA, ANDRES	18	M	LABR	FN	ZZZZ	USA
WISOCKI, MATEL	40	F	WO	RR	ZZZZ	USA
BRANDIS, DOROTHEA	40	F	WO	RR	ZZZZ	USA
IDA	13	F	CH	RR	ZZZZ	USA
MARTHA	9	F	CHILD	RR	ZZZZ	USA
OSCAR	6	M	CHILD	RR	ZZZZ	USA
LURIC, ISRAL	19	M	LABR	RR	ZZZZ	USA
CHILEKA, ABRAM	37	M	LABR	RR	ZZZZ	USA
JAMPOLSKY, ABRAM	19	M	LABR	RR	ZZZZ	USA

SHIP: NECKAR

FROM: BREMEN
TO: BALTIMORE
ARRIVED: 25 JANUARY 1889

PASSENGER	AGE	SEX	OCCUPATION	PRV	VIL	DES
ZIECH, JOHANN	30	M	FARMER	RR	ZZZZ	BAL
ELISABETH	31	F	W	RR	ZZZZ	BAL
MATHILDE	7	F	CHILD	RR	ZZZZ	BAL
MARIE	4	F	CHILD	RR	ZZZZ	BAL
FRIEDRICH	.01	M	INFANT	RR	ZZZZ	BAL
DURAWA, JOHANN	34	M	LABR	RR	ZZZZ	BAL
NUELLER, AUGUSTE	24	F	W	RR	ZZZZ	BAL
WILHELM	2	M	CHILD	RR	ZZZZ	BAL

PASSENGER	AGE	SEX	OCCUPATION	PRIVIL	DES
CLARA	.08	F	INFANT	RRZZZZ	BAL
KIRWAITIE, MARIA	24	F	SVNT	RRZZZZ	BAL
FINKELSTEIN, RAHEL	30	F	W	RRZZZZ	BAL
JETTE	4	F	CHILD	RRZZZZ	BAL
NATHAN	3	M	CHILD	RRZZZZ	BAL
BERNHARD	1	M	CHILD	RRZZZZ	BAL
SAERNICKI, JOHANN	40	M	FARMER	RRZZZZ	BAL
MARGARETHA	30	F	W	RRZZZZ	BAL
ANNA	10	F	CH	RRZZZZ	BAL
JOSEF	7	M	CHILD	RRZZZZ	BAL
ANTON	3	M	CHILD	RRZZZZ	BAL
CONSTANTIN	.11	M	INFANT	RRZZZZ	BAL
BUMSCHAFT, BAER	48	M	FARMER	RRZZZZ	BAL
ISRAEL	17	M	FARMER	RRZZZZ	BAL
SCHEPK	10	F	CH	RRZZZZ	BAL
ITZIGSON, LEISER	33	M	PDLR	RRZZZZ	BAL
ROSENBERG, LEIB	11	M	UNKNOWN	RRZZZZ	BAL
KLEINOWITZ, MORSCHEL	59	F	W	RRZZZZ	BAL
BLOCH, MARIE	36	F	W	RRZZZZ	BAL
ISAAC	5	M	CHILD	RRZZZZ	BAL
BENJAMIN	.11	M	INFANT	RRZZZZ	BAL
GRUENBLATT, MAUSCHE	19	F	SVNT	RRZZZZ	BAL
BALTE, CHASEM	17	F	UNKNOWN	RRZZZZ	BAL
FRIEDMANN, LEIB	15	M	FARMER	RRZZZZ	BAL
ROSA	20	F	SVNT	RRZZZZ	BAL
BUSCHKA, MARIA	30	F	W	RRZZZZ	BAL
JOSEF	8	M	CHILD	RRZZZZ	BAL
FRANZ	6	M	CHILD	RRZZZZ	BAL
BERTHA	3	F	CHILD	RRZZZZ	BAL
HERMINE	.11	F	INFANT	RRZZZZ	BAL
BAGDOWIZ, VLADISLAUS	24	M	LABR	RRZZZZ	BAL
GUTTMANN, MENACHIM	40	M	LABR	RRZZZZ	BAL
SAMUEL	18	M	LABR	RRZZZZ	BAL
JACOB	8	M	CHILD	RRZZZZ	BAL
LEIB	16	M	CH	RRZZZZ	BAL
BUNDSCHAFT, GITTEL	48	F	W	RRZZZZ	BAL
MARIE	25	F	SVNT	RRZZZZ	BAL
EITEL	18	M	LABR	RRZZZZ	BAL
FRIEDMANN, JOSEF	14	M	LABR	RRZZZZ	BAL
HIRSCH	15	M	LABR	RRZZZZ	BAL
EIDING, MARIE	32	F	W	RRZZZZ	PA
CLARA	10	F	CH	RRZZZZ	PA
LEO	2	M	CHILD	RRZZZZ	PA
BERTHA	.11	F	INFANT	RRZZZZ	PA
KRICK, HIRSH	22	M	LABR	RRZZZZ	BAL
PIORONAK, ERNST	24	M	LABR	RRZZZZ	BAL
BOBSKI, THERESE	23	F	SVNT	RRZZZZ	BAL
LOCKE, MARIA	18	F	SVNT	RRZZZZ	BAL

SHIP: NORSEMAN

FROM: LIVERPOOL
TO: BOSTON
ARRIVED: 25 JANUARY 1889

PASSENGER	AGE	SEX	OCCUPATION	PRIVIL	DES
SILBERSTEIN, ISAAC	23	M	TLR	RRZZZZ	BO
LOPLAN, LEWIS	22	M	TLR	RRZZZZ	BO
WALKOWSKY, JOS.	28	M	LABR	RRZZZZ	NY
OPERHEIM, SOLOMON	25	M	LABR	RRZZZZ	NY
BEYMAN, LEIZER	22	M	LABR	RRZZZZ	BO
DEIMAN, KAN.	00	M	INF	RRZZZZ	BO
MELLER, MEYER	22	M	BKR	RRZZZZ	NY
HOTKEY, MEYER	21	M	LABR	RRZZZZ	NY
COHEN, L.	27	M	BKR	RRZZZZ	NY
HELEN	23	F	W	RRZZZZ	NY
HENRY	00	M	INF	RRZZZZ	NY
BLOCKS, MORRIS	22	M	LABR	RRAIIQ	NY
AMONITZ, MORRIS	32	M	MCHT	RRAIIQ	NY
LANK, LEO	25	M	TLR	RRAIIQ	NY
DESANT, CH.	22	M	TLR	RRAIIQ	PA
LEAJAWSKY, JOB.	22	M	UNKNOWN	RRAIIQ	NY
CHEFEY, ISAAC	22	M	TLR	RRAIIQ	NY
ABRAHAM, JACOB	24	M	TLR	RRAIIQ	NY
LASEWITZ, W.	20	M	TLR	RRAIIQ	BO
BARKER, JAS.	38	M	MCHT	RRAIIQ	USA
ITKOWSKY, SAUR	14	M	TLR	RRAIIQ	BO
GUTMAN, BAS.	40	F	W	RRAIIQ	BO
ESTHER	15	F	SP	RRAIIQ	BO
G.	10	M	CH	RRAIIQ	BO
GERSON	8	M	CHILD	RRAIIQ	BO
DORMAN, SARA	20	F	SVNT	RRAIIX	BO
KAPENSKIE, R.L.	35	M	BKR	RRAIIX	NY
LANDAU, S.	23	M	TLR	RRAIIX	NY

SHIP: AMALFI

FROM: HAMBURG
TO: NEW YORK
ARRIVED: 26 JANUARY 1889

PASSENGER	AGE	SEX	OCCUPATION	PRIVIL	DES
BREN, ITZIG	52	M	LABR	RRZZZZ	NY
ABRAMOWITZ, FEIGE	24	F	SGL	RRZZZZ	NY
CHASSE	22	F	WO	RRZZZZ	NY
MAYNE	5	F	CHILD	RRZZZZ	NY
HALPERN, SARA	18	F	SGL	RRZZZZ	NY
RUBINSTEIN, HIRSCH	16	M	LABR	RRZZZZ	NY
STROMSKI, JAN	28	M	LABR	RRZZZZ	NY
ADELSEN, FAGIE	16	F	SGL	RRAHWM	NY
MACZULSKI, MARIE	18	F	SGL	RRAHWM	NY
ABRAMOWITZ, WOLF	17	M	LABR	RRZZZZ	NY
FRIEDLAND, SAMUEL	25	M	LABR	RRAGRT	NY
GARDON, CHAJE	30	F	WO	RRAIGH	NY
SCHEWE	8	F	CHILD	RRAIGH	NY
BOMSTEIN, CHAIM	34	M	CL	RRZZZZ	NY
RESNIKEWITZ, JOSEF	21	M	LABR	RRAIMC	NY
NEUMANN, MICH.	24	M	LABR	RRAIOH	NY
LANGE, JUL.	21	M	LABR	RRAIOH	NY
ANNA	22	F	W	RRAIOH	NY
MICHELSEN, MICKEL	18	M	FARMER	FNZZZZ	NY
EIDELATEIN, ABRAM	16	M	LABR	FNAHWM	NY
ZARENSKY, DWOSSE	24	F	WO	RRZZZZ	NY
RUBIN	.11	M	INFANT	RRZZZZ	NY
SUSSMANN, LIPMANN	49	M	MCHT	RRZZZZ	NY
STOLTNITZ, LEA	28	F	WO	RRAHTO	NY
KASZINKEWITZ, FLORIAN	27	M	LABR	RRAGRT	NY
WASCHKILAI, JOSEF	21	M	LABR	RRAGRT	NY
KLUTSCHNIK, WILKENTY	24	M	LABR	RRAGRT	NY
LEWIN, CHAJE	19	F	TLR	RRAHTU	NY
ALPERN, SALY	19	F	LKSH	RRAHTU	NY
SCHWENTASZURL, STANISLA	27	M	LABR	RRZZZZ	NY
PRISTAWIEN, SITONAS	26	M	LABR	RRZZZZ	NY
CHOZ, RUWKE	37	F	WO	RRAIBO	NY
GITTEL	18	F	CH	RRAIBO	NY
CHAIM	9	M	CHILD	RRAIBO	NY
MOSCHE	8	F	CHILD	RRAIBO	NY
ELISE	7	F	CHILD	RRAIBO	NY
CHASCHE	3	F	CHILD	RRAIBO	NY
PESCHE	.11	M	INFANT	RRAIBO	NY
BOCZWAR, ABRAHAM	21	M	LABR	RRAIBO	NY
FREUND, CHASKEL	26	M	LKSH	RRZZZZ	NY
WILFSOHN, LEIB	23	M	LABR	RRZZZZ	NY
STACH, JOHANN	22	M	FARMER	RRAIDG	NY
HUMANN, HEINRICH	19	M	FARMER	RRAIDG	NY
NUDELMANN, JODDI	68	F	WO	RRZZZZ	NY
DORFMANN, DAVID	24	M	MCHT	RRAHXH	NY
KRAUSE, CARL	22	M	LABR	RRAFWJ	NY
AMALIE	22	F	W	RRAFWJ	NY
WLADISLAWE	3	M	CHILD	RRAFWJ	NY
BARWICKI, JAN	17	M	LABR	RRZZZZ	NY
OELENZWEIG, HELEZ	23	M	LABR	RRAIIG	NY

PASSENGER	AGE	SEX	OCCUPATION	PRV	VIL	DES
RASCHIN, CHAJE	54	F	WO	RR	ZZZZ	NY
MATUCKEN, JOSEF	16	M	LABR	RR	ZZZZ	NY

SHIP: EMS

FROM: BREMEN AND SOUTHAMPTON
TO: NEW YORK
ARRIVED: 26 JANUARY 1889

PASSENGER	AGE	SEX	OCCUPATION	PRV	VIL	DES
JANKOWSKY, AUG.	32	M	LABR	RR	ZZZZ	USA
BARLINEKA, FRANZA.	36	F	WO	RR	ZZZZ	USA
FRANKEL, WOLF	21	M	LABR	RR	ZZZZ	USA
SCHNEIDER, NATHAN	22	M	TLR	RR	ZZZZ	USA
BRANDT, AUG.	33	M	LABR	RR	ZZZZ	USA
FLORA	26	F	W	RR	ZZZZ	USA
AUGE.	16	F	LABR	RR	ZZZZ	USA
MATHE.	6	F	CHILD	RR	ZZZZ	USA
OTTILIE	4	F	CHILD	RR	ZZZZ	USA
ALBERT	1	M	CHILD	RR	ZZZZ	USA
ROMANN, JAN	22	M	LABR	RR	ZZZZ	USA
WASCHKELA, MICH.	18	M	LABR	RR	ZZZZ	USA
ROSENZWEIG, GERSON	30	M	FARMER	RR	ZZZZ	USA
ANNA	28	F	W	RR	ZZZZ	USA
LIBE	8	F	CHILD	RR	ZZZZ	USA
MORITZ	6	F	CHILD	RR	ZZZZ	USA
DWORE	3	F	CHILD	RR	ZZZZ	USA
CHAJE	.11	M	INFANT	RR	ZZZZ	USA
MASCHE	22	F	TLR	RR	ZZZZ	USA
ESTER	.01	F	INFANT	RR	ZZZZ	USA
SEREIDKI, CHANN	17	M	FARMER	RR	ZZZZ	USA
FINKELBERG, ROSE	16	F	TLR	RR	ZZZZ	USA

SHIP: STATE OF INDIANA

FROM: GLASGOW AND LARNE
TO: NEW YORK
ARRIVED: 26 JANUARY 1889

PASSENGER	AGE	SEX	OCCUPATION	PRV	VIL	DES
MOLSK, PETER	22	M	PDLR	RR	AIDL	USA
HANSEN, KATI	40	F	W	RR	AIGX	USA

SHIP: RHAETIA

FROM: HAMBURG
TO: NEW YORK
ARRIVED: 28 JANUARY 1889

PASSENGER	AGE	SEX	OCCUPATION	PRV	VIL	DES
MITTNICK, BERNHD.	23	M	WCHMKR	RR	ZZZZ	USA
MALKE	20	F	W	RR	ZZZZ	USA
ROSENBERG, HEIMAN	20	M	LABR	RR	ZZZZ	USA
MAX	18	M	LABR	RR	ZZZZ	USA
BERLIN, SCHEWEL	35	M	MCHT	RR	ZZZZ	USA
SOBLOCKY, JOSEF	26	M	LABR	RR	ZZZZ	USA
DARCZINSKY, ANTONI	35	M	LABR	RR	ZZZZ	USA
DAMELSEN, JOH.	25	M	LABR	FN	ZZZZ	USA
WILHELMSEN, ERITZ	28	M	LABR	FN	ZZZZ	USA
HEMRICKSEN, JACOB	25	M	LABR	FN	ZZZZ	USA
SLABOTZKY, STEFAN	18	M	LABR	RR	ZZZZ	USA
RABINOWITZ, BOBIL	25	F	WO	RR	ZZZZ	USA
ABRAHAM	.11	M	INFANT	RR	ZZZZ	USA

PASSENGER	AGE	SEX	OCCUPATION	PRV	VIL	DES
MIRAUSKI, SCHMUL	20	M	LABR	RR	ZZZZ	USA
GOLDSTUECK, ABRAM	23	M	LABR	RR	ZZZZ	USA
TALESYZO, MARIANNE	21	F	SGL	RR	ZZZZ	USA
WALINEC, JAN	24	M	LABR	RR	ZZZZ	USA
ASSIEWITZSCH, ANDR.	40	M	LABR	RR	ZZZZ	USA

SHIP: OHIO

FROM: LIVERPOOL
TO: NEW YORK
ARRIVED: 28 JANUARY 1889

PASSENGER	AGE	SEX	OCCUPATION	PRV	VIL	DES
HANIG, ISSAC	23	M	STCTR	RR	ACBF	NY
BERSALS, SOSCHE	20	F	SVNT	RR	ACBF	NY
NOREMBER, CHAGE	20	F	SVNT	RR	ACBF	NY
HERZ, FEIZR	18	F	SVNT	RR	ACBF	NY
LANKISKY, INDLE	15	M	UNKNOWN	RR	ACBF	NY
GINZBURG, RIWEN	23	M	CGRMKR	RR	ZZZZ	NY
REZAVITZ, HIRSCH	44	M	PDLR	RR	ACBF	BO
DROSEK, WALLEN	45	M	LABR	RR	ACBF	NY
PIECHOLSKA, BARBRA	19	F	SVNT	RR	ACBF	BAL
FASCHOWISK, WANZYN	26	M	LABR	RR	ACBF	BAL
JULIANNA	18	F	W	RR	ACBF	BAL
BEMBEAWER, CHAIM	30	M	TLR	RR	ACBF	NY
GRINBERG, MOSCHE	17	M	SHMK	RR	ACBF	NY
CHAEKLIS, SOLOMON	26	M	LABR	RR	ACBF	PHI
ROKOLINZE, CHAIM	18	M	FARMER	RR	ACBF	NY
STOCKMANN, ISAAC	18	M	TLR	RR	ACBF	NY
FUND, RIEL	20	M	LABR	RR	ACBF	NY
BREMEN, BRILL	26	M	LABR	RR	ZZZZ	NY
COHEN, CHILL	21	M	LABR	RR	ACBF	NY
SCHAFER, ISRAEL	33	M	LABR	RR	ACBF	NY
MASOTSCH, MOSES	22	M	LABR	RR	ACBF	PHI
RUKAWICNEK, JACOB	25	M	LABR	RR	ACBF	NY
SUSSELL	25	F	W	RR	ACBF	NY

SHIP: POLAND

FROM: AMSTERDAM
TO: NEW YORK
ARRIVED: 28 JANUARY 1889

PASSENGER	AGE	SEX	OCCUPATION	PRV	VIL	DES
ROSSIB, VALENTIN	60	F	UNKNOWN	PL	ZZZZ	USA
CATARYNE	50	F	UNKNOWN	PL	ZZZZ	USA
FRANZ	11	M	CH	PL	ZZZZ	USA
WINCENTY	9	F	CHILD	PL	ZZZZ	USA
TOMASZEWSKY, MAGDALENA	28	F	UNKNOWN	PL	ZZZZ	USA
RIDLE, MAX	21	M	TLR	PL	ZZZZ	USA
LUCANEK, LOUOS	26	M	TLR	RR	ZZZZ	USA
STEIN, ABRAHAM	24	M	LABR	RR	ZZZZ	USA
RIWKE	23	F	LABR	RR	ZZZZ	USA

SHIP: ETRURIA

FROM: LIVERPOOL AND QUEENSTOWN
TO: NEW YORK
ARRIVED: 28 JANUARY 1889

PASSENGER	AGE	SEX	OCCUPATION	PRV	VIL	DES
LAPPAILA, KATHARINA	34	F	MA	RR	AEWS	NY
JOHANN	7	M	CHILD	RR	AEWS	NY

PASSENGER	AGE	SEX	OCCUPATION	PRIVL	DES
IDA	9	F	CHILD	RRAEWS	NY
OLGA	3	F	CHILD	RRAEWS	NY
WOIZNIEZKA, MARIANNA	22	F	MA	RRAEWS	UNK
MAGDALENA	11	F	CH	RRAEWS	UNK
JACOB	3	M	CHILD	RRAEWS	UNK
VERONIKA	1	M	CHILD	RRAEWS	UNK
JEAN	.02	F	INFANT	RRAEWS	UNK
EIDELMANN, PESCHE	32	F	MA	RRAEWS	NY
EFRAIM	8	M	CHILD	RRAEWS	NY
SOLOMON	7	M	CHILD	RRAEWS	NY
LEIB	3	M	CHILD	RRAEWS	NY
SAMEROGA, CARL	42	M	LABR	RRAGUZ	NY
ANNA	55	F	W	RRAGUZ	NY

SHIP: AUSTRALIA

FROM: HAMBURG
TO: NEW YORK
ARRIVED: 28 JANUARY 1889

PASSENGER	AGE	SEX	OCCUPATION	PRIVL	DES
FRAENKEL, RACHEL	18	F	SGL	RRAIGH	USA
LITKA, AUGUST	27	M	LABR	RRZZZZ	USA
BEYER, SELIG	27	M	LABR	RRAHOK	USA
KLAVANSKYES, REBECCA	33	F	SGL	RRAIKA	USA
KLIGERMANN, SCHIE	19	M	LABR	RRAHOK	USA
KARIGANSKY, LEOPOLD	16	M	LABR	RRZZZZ	USA
BRENGTMANN, DAVID	38	M	CH	RRZZZZ	USA
JACOB	7	M	CHILD	RRZZZZ	USA
SALOPICHIN, CHANNE	58	F	WO	RRAHZD	USA
KAPEAN, FEIDEL	19	M	LABR	RRAHZD	USA
PETO, WLADISLAW	25	M	MCHT	RRAIHC	CH
MARIE	21	F	W	RRAIHC	CH
POKRESNEWITZ, GEORG	45	M	LABR	RRZZZZ	UNK
LUTKEWITZ, PIUS	19	M	LABR	RRZZZZ	UNK
BJORKHOLTS, GUSTAV	38	M	LABR	FNZZZZ	UNK
HAKOLA, JOHS.	25	M	LABR	FNZZZZ	UNK
HIETALA, ISAACV	25	M	LABR	FNZZZZ	UNK
HELLBERG, JACOB	25	M	LABR	FNZZZZ	UNK
SUN, SARA	20	F	SGL	RRZZZZ	UNK
KOHURT, FRANZ	24	M	FARMER	RRZZZZ	UNK
PRODTMANN, AMALIA	38	F	WO	RRZZZZ	USA
MARIE	4	F	CHILD	RRZZZZ	USA
CLARA	2	F	CHILD	RRZZZZ	USA
SZUMANSKI, JOHANN	16	M	LABR	RRZZZZ	USA
SUCHINSKI, DANIEL	33	M	LABR	RRZZZZ	USA
ROSMANN, JACOB	23	M	TLR	RRAHTF	USA
UMITSCH, SALOMON	22	M	TLR	RRAHTF	USA
SELIGMANN, REICH	48	M	MCHT	RRAHTF	USA
NACHSTERN, MORITZ	26	M	SMH	RRAFWJ	USA

SHIP: IOWA

FROM: LIVERPOOL
TO: BOSTON
ARRIVED: 31 JANUARY 1889

PASSENGER	AGE	SEX	OCCUPATION	PRIVL	DES
SEDONITZ, CHAIN	33	M	BKLYR	RRZZZZ	USA
BENZYKORSKY, LOR--IN	30	M	LKSH	RRZZZZ	USA
JOFFON, BARUCH	30	M	TLR	RRZZZZ	USA
SEGEL, ABRAM	25	M	MLDR	RRZZZZ	USA
HRISE---Z, HIRSCH	14	M	MUSN	RRZZZZ	USA
BARIN, ALBERT	18	M	MUSN	RRZZZZ	USA
SCHMIDT, HENRICH	26	M	GZR	RRZZZZ	USA
BORYA, JOSEPH	24	M	BKLYR	RRZZZZ	USA
KIRSCHNER, SELIG	21	M	CRT	RRZZZZ	USA

PASSENGER	AGE	SEX	OCCUPATION	PRIVL	DES
ROZKE	22	M	CRT	RRZZZZ	USA
INGNATIS, JOSEPH	10	M	SCH	RRZZZZ	USA
SOLDMAN, SAMUEL	27	M	TLR	RRZZZZ	USA
MYERS, MARK	23	M	SHMK	RRZZZZ	USA
RUSGON, JACOB	27	M	CBTMKR	RRZZZZ	USA
OLCHENBRYKY, GEDALJE	44	M	GZR	RRZZZZ	USA
RUPELOWITZ, ROSA	9	F	CHILD	RRZZZZ	USA
CHANE	17	F	CH	RRZZZZ	USA
U, U	23	F	CH	RRZZZZ	USA
CASSONAM, CHANE	20	F	SP	RRZZZZ	USA
SCHAPIER, HIRSCH	19	F	SP	RRZZZZ	USA
RUPELOWITZ, BER.	7	M	CHILD	RRZZZZ	USA

SHIP: ROTTERDAM

FROM: ROTTERDAM
TO: NEW YORK
ARRIVED: 01 FEBRUARY 1889

PASSENGER	AGE	SEX	OCCUPATION	PRIVL	DES
BOBER, MARTIN	30	M	LABR	RRZZZZ	OH
ROZDZIELSKI, PROKOP	22	M	LABR	RRZZZZ	NY
VECHAR, MICHAL	45	M	LABR	RRZZZZ	IL
TOKAREZYEB, JAN	32	M	LABR	RRZZZZ	IL
MITIT, WASIL	16	M	LABR	RRZZZZ	IL
JAGODZINSKI, SOMON	53	M	LABR	RRZZZZ	NY
MARYANNE	50	F	LABR	RRZZZZ	NY
STANISLAW	15	M	LABR	RRZZZZ	NY
JAN	10	M	CH	RRZZZZ	NY
ANTONI	8	M	CHILD	RRZZZZ	NY
MACKOWICH, JAN	26	M	LABR	RRZZZZ	NY
MARYANNA	34	F	UNKNOWN	RRZZZZ	NY
AGNES	8	F	CHILD	RRZZZZ	NY
MARYANNE	6	F	CHILD	RRZZZZ	NY
STANISLAW	3	M	CHILD	RRZZZZ	NY
KATHARINA	.11	F	INFANT	RRZZZZ	NY
PIACHOWSKI, ANTON	26	M	LABR	RRZZZZ	IL
STANISLAWSKI, ANTON	25	M	LABR	RRZZZZ	UNK
KONWELT, JAN	33	M	LABR	RRZZZZ	NY
PAWLAT, STANISL.	29	M	LABR	RRZZZZ	UNK

SHIP: CITY OF BERLIN

FROM: LIVERPOOL
TO: NEW YORK
ARRIVED: 02 FEBRUARY 1889

PASSENGER	AGE	SEX	OCCUPATION	PRIVL	DES
FISCHEL, JERNE	20	M	SVNT	RRACBF	BAL
BRISKEL, ISAAK	22	M	TLR	RRACBF	NY
SPITALIN, IWALL	21	M	SVNT	RRACBF	BAL
FRESSEL, FRIDEL	18	F	SVNT	RRACBF	NY
DANWICK, SCHEINE	22	F	W	RRACBF	PHI
DEFTEL, SARA	21	F	W	RRACBF	NY
CHANE	00	F	INF	RRACBF	NY
KAEISLUKIE, ANNA	28	F	W	RRACBF	NY
MARIA	4	F	CHILD	RRACBF	NY
JAN	2	M	CHILD	RRACBF	NY
JANUCH, HENRY	41	M	FARMER	FNZZZZ	NY

SHIP: TAORMINA

FROM: UNKNOWN
TO: NEW YORK
ARRIVED: 27 FEBRUARY 1889

PASSENGER	AGE	SEX	OCCUPATION	PRIVL	DES
SIRONEN, MARIA	29	F	UNKNOWN	RRZZZZ	USA
ALEX	3	M	CHILD	RRZZZZ	USA
MARIA	.01	F	INFANT	RRZZZZ	USA
PADTTIMAKI, ELINA	29	F	UNKNOWN	RRZZZZ	USA
GOELDNER, GUST.	27	M	LABR	RRZZZZ	USA
REPPKE, AUG.	33	M	LABR	RRZZZZ	USA
SCHVARZ, DAVID	29	M	LABR	RRZZZZ	USA
WOPHENSKY, MOSES	18	M	LABR	RRZZZZ	USA
BACHRACH, LEIB	30	M	LABR	RRZZZZ	USA
KWIATKOWSKI, JAN	24	M	BCHR	RRZZZZ	USA
WELE-, ANTON	26	M	FARMER	RRZZZZ	USA
KLANOSKA, JULIANA	19	F	UNKNOWN	RRZZZZ	USA
KURZEVA, LEIZER	30	M	MCHT	RRZZZZ	USA
LOSSER, ISRAEL	19	M	LABR	RRZZZZ	USA
PANLOWSKY, STANISLAUS	25	M	LABR	RRACBF	NY
JANITZKY, JOSEF	40	M	LABR	RRACBF	NY
SCHMIDT, EMILIE	19	F	SGL	RRACBF	NY
HALWINE	16	F	SGL	RRACBF	NY
KANTOR, DAVID	45	M	TLR	RRACBF	NY
ROITMANN, HERCH	30	M	LABR	RRACBF	NY
ZWICKEL, MARCUS	30	M	TLR	RRACBF	NY
TANNEBAUM, DANIEL	22	M	WCHMKR	RRACBF	NY

SHIP: ARIZONA

FROM: LIVERPOOL AND QUEENSTOWN
TO: NEW YORK
ARRIVED: 04 FEBRUARY 1889

PASSENGER	AGE	SEX	OCCUPATION	PRIVL	DES
KAPLANSKI, DAMAZIN	22	M	FLABR	FNZZZZ	USA
MELLER, FRITZ	38	M	FLABR	PLZZZZ	USA
WANISLAWSKY, RAHEL	27	F	W	RRZZZZ	USA
RIFKE	3	F	CHILD	RRZZZZ	USA
AUGRIS, RIFKE	36	F	W	RRZZZZ	USA
JOSSEL	10	M	CH	RRZZZZ	USA
THEA	8	F	CHILD	RRZZZZ	USA
ESTER	8	F	CHILD	RRZZZZ	USA
JENNY	7	F	CHILD	RRZZZZ	USA
ABRAHAM	3	M	CHILD	RRZZZZ	USA
BUZANSKY, SCHOLEN	43	M	FARMER	RRZZZZ	USA
SPINSE, LEA	23	F	W	PLZZZZ	USA
DAVID	.04	M	INFANT	PLZZZZ	USA
STEIN, ESTER	30	F	W	PLZZZZ	USA
JOSEPH	8	M	CHILD	PLZZZZ	USA
SUSSEL	6	F	CHILD	PLZZZZ	USA
MORDCHE	.09	M	INFANT	PLZZZZ	USA
HAUSEN, ANDERS	32	M	FLABR	FNZZZZ	USA
HAVES-A, VIKALA	35	M	UNKNOWN	FNZZZZ	USA
HAVESBA, VIKALA	35	M	MSN	FNZZZZ	USA
ABRAHAMSEN, ABRAHAM	19	M	FLABR	FNZZZZ	USA
STEINAS, OSAK	46	M	ART	FNZZZZ	USA
P--UVES, OLLE	41	M	ART	FNZZZZ	USA
FORSUABBA, MATTS	19	M	FLABR	FNZZZZ	USA
KEVIAHS, ABRAHAM	27	M	UNKNOWN	FNZZZZ	USA
SLONOLA, AUGUST	45	M	FARMER	FNZZZZ	USA
SICOLA, MICHAEL	35	M	JNR	FNZZZZ	USA
JACOBSEN, AUBI	22	M	FLABR	FNZZZZ	USA
ULLAKKA, ELSA	22	F	SP	FNZZZZ	USA
EPSTEIN, SCHLIMA	48	M	TLR	RRZZZZ	USA
SHANBUM, MARKS	29	M	TLR	RRZZZZ	USA

SHIP: LAKE SUPERIOR

FROM: LIVERPOOL
TO: BOSTON
ARRIVED: 05 FEBRUARY 1889

PASSENGER	AGE	SEX	OCCUPATION	PRIVL	DES
MARKUSKY, DAVID	20	M	LABR	RRACBF	CH
FEIN, DOBRIE	43	F	W	RRACBF	CH
PESCHIE	11	F	CH	RRACBF	CH
KOHN, LIBE	16	F	SP	RRACBF	CH
RISS, BLUME	30	F	W	RRACBF	MIL
JOSEPH	11	M	BY	RRACBF	MIL
JORE	9	M	CHILD	RRACBF	MIL
NAFTOLE	5	F	CHILD	RRACBF	MIL
ROGUJINSKY, JACOB	18	M	BKR	RRACBF	CH
DAVIDSON, ABRAM	19	M	LABR	RRACBF	CH
STUHLMAN, MERHEL	21	M	JNR	RRACBF	CH
NETTY	15	F	SP	RRACBF	CH
ODENZ, LAZER	30	M	CPTR	RRACBF	MIL
ARKIN, MENATHIN	21	M	LABR	RRACBF	CH
GENNA, JOHN	44	M	LABR	RRACBF	CH
SALONA	32	F	W	RRACBF	CH
MARGARETH	12	F	SP	RRACBF	CH
URSILA	11	F	SP	RRACBF	CH
FREDRICK, JOHN	8	M	CHILD	RRACBF	CH
MARTINA	5	F	CHILD	RRACBF	CH
JOHN	2	M	CHILD	RRACBF	CH
JOHN	1	M	CHILD	RRACBF	CH
DRAPA, PETER	22	M	LABR	RRACBF	NY
SCHUSTER, MOSES	30	M	SMH	RRACBF	CH

SHIP: ANCHORIA

FROM: GLASGOW AND MOVILLE
TO: NEW YORK
ARRIVED: 05 FEBRUARY 1889

PASSENGER	AGE	SEX	OCCUPATION	PRIVL	DES
BROSGOLB, ISAAK	21	M	DRG	RRZZZZ	USA
WALKO, SOPHIA	30	F	W	RRZZZZ	USA
JAN	.09	M	INFANT	RRZZZZ	USA
PETRASCHEK, MARIA	30	F	W	RRZZZZ	USA
HILKA	.09	M	INFANT	RRZZZZ	USA
MAUER, LUNACH	27	M	CGRMKR	RRZZZZ	USA
SZWELLOFF, JOH.	20	M	TLR	RRZZZZ	USA
BALICNUK, ANTON	27	M	LABR	RRZZZZ	USA
SCHWERBINN, JOHAN	23	M	LABR	RRZZZZ	USA
SCHEMEN, ANTON	47	M	LABR	RRZZZZ	USA
WORBALEWSKY, ANTON	37	M	CNF	RRZZZZ	USA
CASIMIR	25	M	CNF	RRZZZZ	USA
SZOCHITZKY, JACOB	48	M	LABR	RRZZZZ	USA
INKEITIS, IGNATZ	26	M	LABR	RRZZZZ	USA
MEYEK, MINNA	18	F	HP	RRZZZZ	USA

SHIP: AURANIA

FROM: LIVERPOOL AND QUEENSTOWN
TO: NEW YORK
ARRIVED: 05 FEBRUARY 1889

PASSENGER	AGE	SEX	OCCUPATION	PRIVL	DES
SPULHOLZ, GITMAN	25	M	LABR	RRZZZZ	PHI
SCHWARZ, JACOB	38	M	LABR	RRZZZZ	PA
ESTHER	19	F	SP	RRZZZZ	PA
KOESIL, JACOB	26	M	BKLYR	PLZZZZ	PA
MAMAK, STANISLAW	55	M	LABR	PLZZZZ	PA

PASSENGER	AGE	SEX	OCCUPATION	PRV	VIL	DES
KATARINA	34	F	W	PL	ZZZZ	PA
JOSEF	3	M	CHILD	PL	ZZZZ	PA
ADISLAW	2	F	CHILD	PL	ZZZZ	PA
MARKOWSKY, WLADISLAW	23	F	SP	PL	ZZZZ	PA
LUDOWIKA	17	F	UNKNOWN	PL	ZZZZ	PA
WAITORS, EDWAN	19	M	LABR	FN	ZZZZ	NY
HAUTAHESKE, ALF.	24	M	LABR	FN	ZZZZ	NY
SFEFULO, GUS.	27	M	LABR	FN	ZZZZ	NY
FOOHANSOW, HUNNA	49	M	LABR	FN	ZZZZ	NY
HAVAMAKI, GUST.	26	M	LABR	FN	ZZZZ	NY
NAUTI, GUST.	17	M	LABR	FN	ZZZZ	NY
HANNINGER, ANNILI	33	M	LABR	FN	ZZZZ	NY
AMALA, NICKOLAI	17	M	LABR	FN	ZZZZ	NY
HANINGI, JOHI	38	M	LABR	FN	ZZZZ	NY
HASKIMAKI, JOH.	25	M	LABR	FN	ZZZZ	NY
LINTHI, JACOB	40	M	LABR	FN	ZZZZ	NY
MUKKALA, ALF.	36	M	LABR	FN	ZZZZ	NY
LANA	33	F	W	FN	ZZZZ	NY
HILKA	11	F	CH	FN	ZZZZ	NY

SHIP: WYOMING

FROM: LIVERPOOL
TO: NEW YORK
ARRIVED: 05 FEBRUARY 1889

PASSENGER	AGE	SEX	OCCUPATION	PRV	VIL	DES
MEKOWLEWICZUS, ROSALIA	22	F	SP	PL	ZZZZ	USA
SCHAPOIZ, MORDSCHE	22	F	SP	PL	ZZZZ	USA
TRIWAKE, D.	16	M	LABR	PL	ZZZZ	USA
SCHOCHEL, RACHEL	32	F	W	PL	ZZZZ	USA
SALOMON	7	M	CHILD	PL	ZZZZ	USA
HODE	6	M	CHILD	PL	ZZZZ	USA
CHANS	5	M	CHILD	PL	ZZZZ	USA
ABRAHAM	4	M	CHILD	PL	ZZZZ	USA
AWISCHARITZ, ANNA	17	F	SP	RR	ZZZZ	USA
PALUTZ, ISAAC	18	M	LABR	RR	ZZZZ	USA
HOP, ROCH.	47	M	LABR	RR	ZZZZ	USA
MOSES	7	M	CHILD	RR	ZZZZ	USA
SCHAPIRA, ZUIRE	20	F	SP	PL	ZZZZ	USA
MEKAKOLEWIZARA, B.	3	F	CHILD	PL	ZZZZ	USA
BUCHAINIS, GEO	21	M	LABR	PL	ZZZZ	USA
HEINRICH, H.	39	M	LABR	PL	ZZZZ	USA
BULLMANN, PETER	22	M	LABR	PL	ZZZZ	USA

SHIP: AMERICA

FROM: BREMEN
TO: BALTIMORE
ARRIVED: 06 FEBRUARY 1889

PASSENGER	AGE	SEX	OCCUPATION	PRV	VIL	DES
CHARIF, ETEL	18	F	UNKNOWN	RR	ZZZZ	MD
GRAIS, MASLIA	25	F	UNKNOWN	RR	ZZZZ	MD
ELKE	4	F	CHILD	RR	ZZZZ	MD
LAIB, SAMUEL	.11	M	INFANT	RR	ZZZZ	MD
GREIS, CZERNA	20	F	UNKNOWN	RR	ZZZZ	MD
SUEPELLAT, MARIE	50	F	UNKNOWN	RR	ZZZZ	MD
ANNA	16	F	UNKNOWN	RR	ZZZZ	MD
BLUMENFELD, JAKER	37	M	MCHT	RR	ZZZZ	MD
KRUSE	30	M	MCHT	RR	ZZZZ	MD
SARE	17	F	UNKNOWN	RR	ZZZZ	MD
JACOB	9	M	CHILD	RR	ZZZZ	MD
ZOCHEWED	3	M	CHILD	RR	ZZZZ	MD
BIBER, ROBERT	16	M	UNKNOWN	RR	ZZZZ	OH
KRUT, CHANE	30	F	UNKNOWN	RR	ZZZZ	OH
SCHI-E	11	F	CH	RR	ZZZZ	OH

PASSENGER	AGE	SEX	OCCUPATION	PRV	VIL	DES
BREINE	9	F	CHILD	RR	ZZZZ	OH
ISRAEL	7	M	CHILD	RR	ZZZZ	OH
BENJAMIN	4	M	CHILD	RR	ZZZZ	OH
GROSSKOWSKY, JOSEF	40	M	FARMER	RR	ZZZZ	OH
AGULSKY, ROCHEL	40	F	UNKNOWN	RR	ZZZZ	PA
LIBE	16	F	UNKNOWN	RR	ZZZZ	PA
ZWINAKOWI, THOMAS	26	M	FARMER	RR	ZZZZ	IL
VICTORIA	23	F	UNKNOWN	RR	ZZZZ	IL
NANKI---, SALMANN	21	M	LABR	RR	ZZZZ	IL
SEGLOWITZ, ABRAHAM	19	M	LABR	RR	ZZZZ	IL
MUMSCHE	22	F	UNKNOWN	RR	ZZZZ	IL
GRONTOWITZ, JOSEF	32	M	LABR	RR	ZZZZ	MD
BLUMENFELD, MOSER	3	M	CHILD	RR	ZZZZ	MD
MAKOWSKI, JOHANN	16	M	UNKNOWN	RR	ZZZZ	MD
BRZUSLOOSKI, MALKE	50	F	UNKNOWN	RR	ZZZZ	OH
REBECCA	24	F	SVNT	RR	ZZZZ	OH
J-FFER, U	9	M	CHILD	RR	ZZZZ	IL
-ODA, REBECCA	27	F	SVNT	RR	ZZZZ	IL

SHIP: FULDA

FROM: BREMEN AND SOUTHAMPTON
TO: NEW YORK
ARRIVED: 06 FEBRUARY 1889

PASSENGER	AGE	SEX	OCCUPATION	PRV	VIL	DES
LUSCHINSKI, MORITZ	40	M	PDLR	RR	ZZZZ	NY
OLSINA, HENECH	25	M	PDLR	RR	AHXZ	NY
TAENZER, CHASKEL	28	M	PDLR	RR	AIJJ	NY
BRZOZA, WOLF	36	M	MCHT	RR	AFWJ	NY
ROSALIE	26	F	W	RR	AFWJ	NY
AMALIE	6	F	CHILD	RR	AFWJ	NY
ORLIK, DWORE	28	F	W	RR	ZZZZ	NY
RIFKO	3	F	CHILD	RR	ZZZZ	NY
KONTROVITSCH, PINCUS	29	M	LABR	RR	AHTF	NY
CHAJETT, NOACH	57	M	UNKNOWN	RR	AHTF	NY
WOLFF	18	M	UNKNOWN	RR	AHTF	NY
ZOFFIN, SALOMON	16	M	UNKNOWN	RR	AHTF	NY
BLIEDEN, MAX	18	M	BRK	RR	AEFL	NY

SHIP: MASSALA

FROM: HAMBURG
TO: NEW YORK
ARRIVED: 08 FEBRUARY 1889

PASSENGER	AGE	SEX	OCCUPATION	PRV	VIL	DES
LOBOWITZ, CHAIN.	30	M	LABR	RR	ZZZZ	NY
BABINKI, MATE.	22	M	LABR	RR	ZZZZ	NY
NICOLAJUWKI, LOF.	19	M	CGRMKR	RR	ZZZZ	NY
MIZKWEITZ, JOSEF	42	M	LABR	RR	ZZZZ	NY
MAPUSKI, THEOFIEL	22	M	LABR	RR	ZZZZ	NY
SZIMBROWSKI, JOHN	26	M	LABR	RR	ZZZZ	NY
WIDAL, FRANZ	20	M	LABR	RR	ZZZZ	NY

PASSENGER	AGE	SEX	OCCUPATION	PRV	VIL	DES
SHIP: RHYNLAND						
FROM: ANTWERP						
TO: NEW YORK						
ARRIVED: 08 FEBRUARY 1889						
DRAGASOWICH, GATEANA	25	M	BKR	PL	ZZZZ	BAL
MARTERICH, VINCENZO	25	M	UNKNOWN	PL	ZZZZ	BAL
SWEDERICH, VINCENZO	29	M	UNKNOWN	PL	ZZZZ	BAL
BOZARICH, NICOLAS	29	M	UNKNOWN	PL	ZZZZ	BAL
WIDAWICH, MICHEL	24	M	UNKNOWN	PL	ZZZZ	BAL
GERREDINO	28	M	UNKNOWN	PL	ZZZZ	BAL
SOMARICH, GERANDSA	25	M	UNKNOWN	PL	ZZZZ	BAL
STANOVICH, FRANK	33	M	UNKNOWN	PL	ZZZZ	USA
MARINIOVICH, ANDREA	30	M	UNKNOWN	PL	ZZZZ	USA
KOLANOWSKI, JACOB	37	M	LABR	PL	AICL	NY
KOFFMANN, JOSEF	46	M	MCHT	PL	AICL	NY
JENNY	40	F	MCHT	PL	AICL	NY
ACHENY	18	F	MCHT	PL	AICL	NY
GOLDY	8	M	CHILD	PL	AICL	NY
JACOB	17	M	MCHT	PL	AICL	NY
BENJAMIN	3	M	CHILD	PL	AICL	NY
JUEDEL	00	M	INF	PL	AICL	NY
ABRAHAM, ANNIE	7	F	CHILD	PL	AICL	NY
MORRIS	5	M	CHILD	PL	AICL	NY
SIMON	3	M	CHILD	PL	AICL	NY
LOUIS	2	M	CHILD	PL	AICL	NY
RACHEL	00	F	INF	PL	AICL	NY
JANKEWITZ, J.	66	M	LABR	PL	AICL	NY
SHIP: UMBRIA						
FROM: LIVERPOOL						
TO: NEW YORK						
ARRIVED: 11 FEBRUARY 1889						
KRAKOMSCH, KAT.	20	F	SVNT	PL	AHUE	USA
MALISDUF, OLGA	16	M	LABR	PL	AHUE	USA
LANISA	18	F	SVNT	PL	AHUE	USA
SCHAGE	17	M	TLR	PL	AFWJ	USA
MUSCHER, JAME	40	M	FARMER	PL	AFWJ	USA
MERA	11	M	CH	PL	AFWJ	USA
KITTAS, JOHAN	29	M	LABR	PL	AHOK	USA
JUAKOWSKY, LENING	33	M	LABR	PL	AHOK	USA
KRISTAK, ADAM	46	M	LABR	PL	AHOK	USA
GOLDMANN, ISAAC	42	M	LABR	PL	AHQD	USA
STOTNIK, JOMKEL	15	M	LABR	PL	AHQD	USA
KRIGEL, SEREFINE	17	F	SVNT	PL	AHQD	USA
EPSTIN, CSIAS	21	M	LABR	PL	AHOK	USA
SHIP: SUEVIA						
FROM: HAMBURG AND HAVRE						
TO: NEW YORK						
ARRIVED: 11 FEBRUARY 1889						
ARYES, PEISSACH	18	M	LABR	RR	ZZZZ	NY
LIEDKE, ERNET	24	M	MCHT	RR	AEFL	NY
KARKLING, DANIEL	21	M	MCHT	RR	AEFL	NY
KAOPPILA, MICHEL	25	M	LABR	FN	ZZZZ	PA
MARIE	25	F	W	FN	ZZZZ	PA
HAUTEMAKI, JOH.	27	M	LABR	FN	ZZZZ	PA
HAUTALA, SEFANIUS	31	M	LABR	FN	ZZZZ	PA
KANNASTO, ESAJAS	25	M	LABR	FN	ZZZZ	PA
JARDI, GORG	18	M	LABR	FN	ZZZZ	PA
HARJU, MATHS.	24	M	LABR	FN	ZZZZ	PA
LECH, ADAM	27	M	LABR	FN	AIKP	NY
KALBER, SIMON	48	M	JNR	RR	ZZZZ	NY
LESZINSKI, MARIAN	45	M	LABR	RR	AHUI	NY
BERG, REINHOLD	27	M	SMH	RR	AHUI	NY
ALUNAS, ANTONIS	21	M	LABR	RR	ZZZZ	NY
LANDINITIS, JONAS	30	M	LABR	RR	ZZZZ	NY
BERTACZIS, JONAS	25	M	LABR	RR	ZZZZ	NY
RUBIN, MARK	38	M	LABR	RR	ZZZZ	NY
KAHN, JOSSEL	40	M	LABR	RR	ZZZZ	NY
MERSON, DINKO	52	M	LABR	RR	AHTU	PA
NUDELMANN, HANNA	52	F	WO	RR	AIFC	PA
ROSA	18	F	CH	RR	AIFC	PA
DINA	9	F	CHILD	RR	AIFC	PA
KAUFMANN, LIPPE	38	M	LABR	RR	ZZZZ	PA
SCHAPIRO, CHANNE	25	F	WO	RR	ZZZZ	PA
HAIE	2	M	CHILD	RR	ZZZZ	PA
ABRAHAMSON, JOH.	18	M	LABR	FN	ZZZZ	MI
KEJRO, JOH.	19	M	LABR	FN	ZZZZ	MI
HAHLUBA, MALACHIAS	25	M	LABR	FN	ZZZZ	WY
LAPIDES, SCHMUL	34	M	JNR	FN	AHTU	NY
GAKOMSKI, IGNATZ	52	M	UNKNOWN	FN	AGRT	NY
GROSCHOWSKI, FRANZ	28	M	TLR	FN	AHUL	NY
BRAUN, JACOB	40	M	LABR	FN	AHUL	NY
SHIP: ELBE						
FROM: BREMEN AND SOUTHAMPTON						
TO: NEW YORK						
ARRIVED: 12 FEBRUARY 1889						
BELKO, WICENTE	16	F	SVNT	RR	ZZZZ	NY
MARIE	14	F	SVNT	RR	ZZZZ	NY
CATH.	11	F	SVNT	RR	ZZZZ	NY
KRASUCKI, STANISL.	17	M	LABR	RR	ZZZZ	NY
NARCZENSKY, JOS.	31	M	LABR	RR	ZZZZ	NY
LEEBECK, GOTTL.	41	M	LABR	RR	ZZZZ	NY
BADOWSKI, JOS.	21	M	LABR	RR	ZZZZ	NY
WERGER, FRIED.	46	M	LABR	RR	ZZZZ	NY
SZTRILAM, BENJ.	29	M	LABR	RR	ZZZZ	NY
TREICHER, MICH.	42	M	LABR	RR	ZZZZ	NY
RUNOZEI, STANISL.	38	M	LABR	RR	ZZZZ	NY
GLODANSKI, MICH.	21	M	LABR	RR	ZZZZ	NY
RUDY, MART.	22	M	LABR	RR	ZZZZ	NY
KATZ, CHAIM	29	M	LABR	RR	ZZZZ	NY
GERSCHENOWITZ, B.	33	M	LABR	RR	ZZZZ	NY
DEMORST, M.	37	M	LABR	RR	ZZZZ	NY
NAJEWSKY, BART.	22	M	LABR	RR	ZZZZ	NY
ZULKOWSKI, JAN	32	M	LABR	RR	ZZZZ	NY
WAJEZAK, JOS.	27	M	LABR	RR	ZZZZ	CLE
KAWIZEWSKI, JOS.	26	M	LABR	RR	ZZZZ	CLE
SHIP: WESTERLAND						
FROM: ANTWERP						
TO: NEW YORK						
ARRIVED: 13 FEBRUARY 1889						
MUSILAK, ANTON	23	M	SDLR	PL	ZZZZ	USA
AUGUST	16	M	SDLR	PL	ZZZZ	USA
SKEUTNY, WILHELM	18	M	LABR	PL	ZZZZ	CH
STAVIZIK, JULIANNA	44	F	UNKNOWN	PL	ZZZZ	CH
MAX	10	M	CH	PL	ZZZZ	CH
STANISLAS	5	M	CHILD	PL	ZZZZ	CH

PASSENGER	AGE	SEX	OCCUPATION	PRIVL	DES
PETER	23	M	LABR	PLZZ	ZZCH
PRAETZKY, HY.	22	M	LABR	PLZZ	ZZCH
RACHEL	20	F	UNKNOWN	PLZZ	ZZCH

SHIP: WISCONSIN

FROM: LIVERPOOL AND QUEENSTOWN
TO: NEW YORK
ARRIVED: 14 FEBRUARY 1889

PASSENGER	AGE	SEX	OCCUPATION	PRIVL	DES
KRAVER, JANKEL	00	M	INF	PLAEFL	USA
MEISKI, NICALIAS	55	M	FARMER	PLAEFL	USA
BLECHER, RIFKE	20	F	SP	PLAEFL	USA
KRASER, ZELDA	23	F	SP	PLAEFL	USA
FRUPITZI, CHAIE	33	F	W	RRZZZZ	USA
JACOB	9	M	CHILD	RRZZZZ	USA
ELLERMAN, RUCKE	19	F	SP	RRZZZZ	USA
KRUPITZKI, DWORE	18	F	SP	RRZZZZ	USA
EROIMOWITZ, SCHIMEN	34	M	UNKNOWN	RRZZZZ	USA

SHIP: THE QUEEN

FROM: LIVERPOOL
TO: NEW YORK
ARRIVED: 16 FEBRUARY 1889

PASSENGER	AGE	SEX	OCCUPATION	PRIVL	DES
SMOLARZ, WOLF	27	M	LABR	RRAIL	APA
JORAS, SIMON	25	M	LABR	RRAIL	APA
SCHWARTZ, SAM	24	M	LABR	RRAIL	APA
WAGAHEIM, J.	20	M	LABR	RRAIL	APA
NASSEMOWITZ, ABE	22	M	LABR	RRAIL	APA
BLUM, SAM	25	M	LABR	RRAIL	APA
PERLOWGETZ, MOSES	42	M	LABR	RRAIL	APA
RIWKE	40	F	W	RRAIL	APA
ABRAH	10	M	CH	RRAIL	APA
FENZER, CHAZKEL	21	M	LABR	RRAIL	APA
TEMOMA	20	F	W	RRAIL	APA
PIZESTELSKY, ABM.	27	M	LABR	RRAIL	APA
PAWENBROWSKY, S.	25	M	LABR	RRAIL	APA
RABINOWITZ, HEUMAN	25	M	LABR	RRAIL	APA
RIFKE	24	F	W	RRAIL	APA
BRODICZ, GOLDE	15	F	SP	RRAIL	APA
BYISCHBE, BERL	26	M	LABR	RRAIL	ANY
KOBMALRISKI, CHAZ	24	M	LABR	RRAIL	ANY
WEINBERG, HERMAN	40	M	LABR	RRAIL	ANY
LUPIOS, DWORE	34	F	W	RRAIL	ANY
HERSCH	4	F	CHILD	RRAIL	ANY
MERE	1	F	CHILD	RRAIL	ANY
TROMPETER, DAVK.	20	M	LABR	RRAIL	ANY
STEIGN, MATHES	25	M	LABR	RRAIL	ANY
MESCHINSKI, ALEX	30	M	LABR	RRAIL	ANY
SCHUMBOWITZ, ROCHE	37	F	SP	RRAIL	ANY
STEIN, GUTMAN	20	M	LABR	RRAIL	ANY
ROSA	18	F	W	RRAIL	ANY
NAWOGRUSKI, CHAS	20	M	LABR	RRAIL	ANY
BEREUTSKI, NUSCHEM	20	M	LABR	RRAIL	ANY
NISSENBAUNN, SAMOL	36	M	LABR	RRAIL	ANY
SAROWICZ, GEORG	42	M	LABR	RRAIL	ANY
GARCZAR, ANTON	34	M	LABR	RRAIL	ANY
TARSUCHUNSKI, ANNA	23	F	W	RRAIL	ANY
ANNA	1	F	CHILD	RRAIL	ANY
MARI	1	F	CHILD	RRAIL	ANY
PRISCH, CATHARINA	23	F	SP	RRAIL	ANY
KASTELUNG, ANNA	22	F	SP	RRAIL	ANY
SYSUK, IWAN	24	M	LABR	RRAIL	ANY
SISULA, JOHAN	30	M	LABR	RRAIL	ANY
FEDORKAUTZ, MECHEL	30	M	LABR	RRAIL	ANY
SRUMSA, JANO	34	M	LABR	RRAIL	ANY
JUKOS, MICHEL	31	M	LABR	RRAIL	ANY
OLBOWICZ, MORITZ	16	M	LABR	RRAIL	ANY
FANNY	18	F	SP	RRAIL	ANY
STEIN, GINA	27	F	SP	RRAIL	ANY
WEISS, ROCHEL	40	F	W	RRAIL	ANY
LIBE	15	F	SP	RRAIL	ANY
TANCHEL	11	M	CH	RRAIL	ANY
ABEL	5	M	CHILD	RRAIL	ANY
WOVGAI, SCHEIMDEL	20	M	LABR	RRAIL	ANY
KOSLOWSKY, F.	48	F	W	RRAIL	ANY
JUDE	16	M	LABR	RRAIL	ANY
LEAH	11	F	CH	RRAIL	ANY
JOSEPH	9	M	CHILD	RRAIL	ANY
JOSEPH, ABM.	18	M	LABR	RRADAX	BAL

SHIP: MICHIGAN

FROM: LIVERPOOL
TO: BOSTON
ARRIVED: 16 FEBRUARY 1889

PASSENGER	AGE	SEX	OCCUPATION	PRIVL	DES
ROSENFELD, HARRIS	22	M	TLR	RRZZZZ	USA
BAS, NATHAN	46	M	TLR	RRZZZZ	USA
BERLOWITZ, BENJAMIN	24	M	TLR	RRZZZZ	USA
BRAUN, HERMANN	36	M	TLR	PLZZZZ	USA
JOFFA, JOHN	22	M	PNTR	RRZZZZ	USA
GUNSBERG, RAPHAEL	29	M	TLR	RRZZZZ	USA
LEWIN, RUBIN	25	M	TLR	RRZZZZ	USA
GLASER, MORRIS	20	M	TLR	RRZZZZ	USA
SHINLAK, CHIA	44	M	TLR	RRZZZZ	USA
ISSEL	17	M	TLR	RRZZZZ	USA
MECZJEWSKY, V.	22	M	CPTR	RRZZZZ	USA
DAIEN, LELIA	22	F	SP	RRZZZZ	USA
RUBIN	10	M	CH	RRZZZZ	USA
ALBARSCH, MICHAEL	48	M	TLR	RRZZZZ	USA
SCH.	24	F	W	RRZZZZ	USA

SHIP: WIELAND

FROM: HAMBURG
TO: NEW YORK
ARRIVED: 16 FEBRUARY 1889

PASSENGER	AGE	SEX	OCCUPATION	PRIVL	DES
HORWITZ, MEYER	20	M	TLR	RRZZZZ	USA
BERENOFSKY, MICHAEL	24	M	LABR	RRZZZZ	USA
MATIANOWSKI, JAN	27	M	LABR	RRZZZZ	USA
GERMANSKY, SORA	45	F	WO	RRZZZZ	USA
KORSUN, LEON	22	M	LABR	RRAIGJ	USA
WILKOWSKI, PAUL	28	M	LABR	RRZZZZ	USA
KONIKOWSKI, JOSEF	30	M	LABR	RRZZZZ	USA
MICHALINA	28	F	W	RRZZZZ	USA
RUZANSKA, MARJEIN	30	F	WO	RRAHTB	USA
ESTHER	9	F	CHILD	RRAHTB	USA
MEISCHE	7	F	CHILD	RRAHTB	USA
FRUME	.11	F	INFANT	RRAHTB	USA
EIDEL	.11	F	INFANT	RRAHTB	USA
HOLDER, SARA	23	F	WO	RRAHWE	USA
EIDE	6	F	CHILD	RRAHWE	USA
KOWALSKI, FRANZ	23	M	LABR	RRAFWJ	USA
NEUMARK, MERE	28	F	WO	RRAHWE	USA
SELDE	9	F	CHILD	RRAHWE	USA
KAUFMANN	7	M	CHILD	RRAHWE	USA

PASSENGER	AGE	SEX	OCCUPATION	PRV VIL DES
SISSEL	4	F	CHILD	RRAHWEUSA
PAIE	.11	M	INFANT	RRAHWEUSA
GESCHE	.11	F	INFANT	RRAHWEUSA
ROSEN, MORDCHE	24	M	LABR	RRZZZZUSA
PILAS, NOCHIM	31	M	LABR	RRZZZZUSA
GURNI, JOSEPH	38	M	LABR	RRAHUFUSA
AUGUCZAK, MARCIN	28	M	LABR	RRAHUFUSA
RUTKOWSKI, JAN	36	M	LABR	RRAHUFUSA
KANTRIMAS, DOMINIK	18	M	LABR	RRAHTFUSA
PETRUCHAS, BALTREMAS	24	M	LABR	RRAHTFUSA
WILKOWSKI, SARA	26	F	WO	RRZZZZUSA
LEWIN	.11	M	INFANT	RRZZZZUSA
NIGIN, ARON	25	M	LABR	RRAHTUUSA
PLOPLIS, WICKANTY	21	M	LABR	RRZZZZUSA
KUDICKA, WICKANTY	19	M	LABR	RRZZZZUSA
RUTHS, ERIK	19	M	LABR	RRAINOUSA
KRISHNE	30	F	SGL	RRAINOUSA
BLURI, JOHANN	28	M	LABR	RRAINOUSA
MASA, ISAAC	27	M	LABR	FNZZZZUSA
SVAHN, MATHS.	20	M	LABR	FNZZZZUSA
SUNDQUIST, JOHANN	38	M	LABR	FNAINOUSA
SKOGS, JOHANN	21	M	LABR	FNZZZZUSA
KNOB, JOHANN	22	M	LABR	FNZZZZUSA
ROSENGARTEN, SELDE	40	F	WO	FNAHTFUSA
MEYER	5	M	CHILD	FNAHTFUSA
ESSIG	1	M	CHILD	FNAHTFUSA
ROCHEL	5	M	CHILD	FNAHTFUSA
CHAIE	3	M	CHILD	FNAHTFUSA
HIRSCHBATCK, JOSEF	10	M	CH	FNAHTFUSA
GITE	.06	F	INFANT	FNAHTFUSA

SHIP: ALLER

FROM: BREMEN AND SOUTHAMPTON
TO: NEW YORK
ARRIVED: 16 FEBRUARY 1889

PASSENGER	AGE	SEX	OCCUPATION	PRV VIL DES
MOROS, SOPHIA	24	F	NN	FNAHQDUSA
HANNE	6	F	CHILD	FNAHQDUSA
SAMUEL	4	M	CHILD	FNAHQDUSA
MICHAEL	3	M	CHILD	FNAHQDUSA
CAROLINE	.09	F	INFANT	FNAHQDUSA
LENZ, JACOB	28	M	LABR	FNAFWJUSA
FINKELSTEIN, WOLF	44	M	LABR	FNAEFLUSA
SORE	45	F	W	FNAEFLUSA
LEIS	7	F	CHILD	FNAEFLUSA
RAZEL	6	F	CHILD	FNAEFLUSA
LEIB	5	F	CHILD	FNAEFLUSA
MEYROWITZ, NACHMANN	29	M	LABR	FNAEFLUSA
RABINOWITZ, LEISER	25	M	LABR	FNAEFLUSA
RAMER, WOLF	52	M	LABR	FNAEFLUSA
FARTMANN, SIMON	19	M	LABR	FNAEFLUSA

SHIP: STATE OF NEVADA

FROM: GLASGOW AND LARNE
TO: NEW YORK
ARRIVED: 16 FEBRUARY 1889

PASSENGER	AGE	SEX	OCCUPATION	PRV VIL DES
BLUM, JOSEF	42	M	TLR	RRZZZZUSA
RINTZEKEWICZ, JOSEF	18	M	LABR	RRZZZZUSA
BOLDON, ANTON	25	M	LABR	RRZZZZUSA
BABKIN, ABR.	30	M	TLR	RRZZZZUSA
DOROZKER, JOSEFA	40	F	W	RRZZZZUSA
JOHN	14	M	UNKNOWN	RRZZZZUSA
STANISLAUS	10	M	CH	RRZZZZUSA
JOSEF	8	M	CHILD	RRZZZZUSA
ANTON	00	M	CH	RRZZZZUSA
ESKIR, LEA	17	F	SVNT	RRZZZZUSA
DAVID	11	M	CH	RRZZZZUSA
NISSEN	9	M	CHILD	RRZZZZUSA
BERL	5	M	CHILD	RRZZZZUSA
ESTHER	2	F	CHILD	RRZZZZUSA
MORDSCHE	1	F	CHILD	RRZZZZUSA
ERSTEIN, CHAJE	30	F	W	RRZZZZUSA
SCHLOME	10	M	CH	RRZZZZUSA
HANNAH	7	F	CHILD	RRZZZZUSA
LUSIE	5	F	CHILD	RRZZZZUSA
GRONER, BARUCH	21	M	FARMER	RRZZZZUSA
GRASBERG, MORITZ	21	M	MCHT	RRZZZZUSA
GLASER, SCHOLEM	21	M	TLR	RRZZZZUSA
IWANOWITSCH, LORENZO	37	M	LABR	RRZZZZUSA
KATARINA	25	F	UNKNOWN	RRZZZZUSA
EMINA	1	F	CHILD	RRZZZZUSA
KOSLOWSKI, MICHEL	24	M	LABR	RRZZZZUSA
KRISTIAN, MICHAEL	18	M	LABR	RRZZZZUSA
KRASKOWSKI, PETER	30	M	LABR	RRZZZZUSA
KUPPERMAN, SCHLOME	25	M	TLR	RRZZZZUSA
KRANTZIG, ISRAEL	25	M	TLR	RRZZZZUSA
KREINSKY, JAKOB	21	M	WCHMKR	RRZZZZUSA
KRAKANER, FEIMEL	18	M	TLR	RRZZZZUSA
LISCHETSKY, VALENTIN	24	M	LABR	RRZZZZUSA
MARIANNE	18	F	W	RRZZZZUSA
LOEWENBERG, LAZAR	33	M	UNKNOWN	RRZZZZUSA
LIPIENSKY, BOREK	22	M	TLR	RRZZZZUSA
LEWANDOWSKI, ANDIG	60	M	LABR	RRZZZZUSA
KATARINA	50	F	W	RRZZZZUSA
ROSALIN	25	F	CH	RRZZZZUSA
WLADISLAW	.09	M	INFANT	RRZZZZUSA
MAWSOWITZ, MOSER	38	M	MCHT	RRZZZZUSA
MARANZOWITZ, GIOWANNI	38	M	LABR	RRZZZZUSA
NICOLO	23	M	LABR	RRZZZZUSA
PETROWSKY, MICHEL	24	M	LABR	RRZZZZUSA
RATZMILLERSOHN, NEDANJI	20	F	SVNT	RRZZZZUSA
RUDK, SARAH	20	F	SVNT	RRZZZZUSA
ROSENBAUM, ETTI	15	F	SVNT	RRZZZZUSA
ROSENBERG, SARKMA	20	M	TLR	RRZZZZUSA
BERTHA	25	F	W	RRZZZZUSA
SCHNEIDER, PETER	24	M	TLR	RRZZZZUSA
SCHENNAN, ABR.	21	M	TLR	RRZZZZUSA
SAPMER, FRANCISCA	35	F	SVNT	RRZZZZUSA
WIZOTZKI, EIDEL	24	F	W	RRZZZZUSA
GOLDE	.06	F	INFANT	RRZZZZUSA

SHIP: CITY OF CHESTER

FROM: LIVERPOOL AND QUEENSTOWN
TO: NEW YORK
ARRIVED: 18 FEBRUARY 1889

PASSENGER	AGE	SEX	OCCUPATION	PRV VIL DES
BRITWITZ, MORITZ	34	M	FARMER	RRZZZZUSA
PIETZAK, MARCIN	40	M	FARMER	RRZZZZUSA
CORN, JOEL	21	M	FARMER	RRZZZZUSA
JACOB	20	M	TLR	RRZZZZUSA
PIETZAK, MICHAL	16	M	TLR	RRAEFLMI
KERCHENBAUM, MOSES	22	M	TLR	RRAEFLBAL
KLEIN, JOSEF	31	M	TLR	RRAEFLNY
SCHUCHER, SCHAJE	32	M	TLR	RRAEFLNY
BEHELFER, MOSES	24	M	TLR	RRAEFLNY
LEWIN, ELIANKIN	18	M	BCHR	RRAHTFNY
ALPH.	18	M	BCHR	RRAHTFNY
COHN, SAMUEL	22	M	LABR	RRAHTFNY
ZONIARDER, MOSES	28	M	TLR	RRAHTFNY
GOLDENBERG, ADOLPH	20	M	BKR	RRAHTUNY
POPPER, MICHAEL	48	M	LABR	RRAHTUPHI

PASSENGER	AGE	SEX	OCCUPATION	PRI VL	V I L	DES
SAM.	12	M	W	RR	AHT	UPHI
ELDA	11	F	CH	RR	AHT	UPHI
MORITZ	10	M	CH	RR	AHT	UPHI

SHIP: SERVIA

FROM: LIVERPOOL AND QUEENSTOWN
TO: NEW YORK
ARRIVED: 20 FEBRUARY 1889

PASSENGER	AGE	SEX	OCCUPATION	PRI VL	V I L	DES
NILSSON, JONAS	37	M	SLR	RR	ADA	XIL
HOLDENGRAEBER, BERNARD	20	M	MCHT	RR	ADA	XNY
KOZELNIK, WOLF	25	M	LABR	RR	ADA	XNY
MACINKOWSKY, FRANZ	26	M	LABR	RR	ADA	XNY
HAUFARB, ABRAM	28	M	TLR	RR	ADA	XNY
KUMER, CHAIM	27	M	TLR	RR	ADA	XNY
DOBEL, SOLOMON	22	M	LABR	RR	ADA	XNY
GOLDMANN, ABRAHAM	21	M	LABR	RR	ADA	XNY
JUNSALA, JOHAN	29	M	LABR	RR	ADA	XNY
PETKOLA, GUST.	19	M	LABR	RR	ADA	XNY
KONTULA, MATH.	29	M	LABR	RR	ADA	XNY
YSOJARVI, MATH.	32	M	LABR	RR	ADA	XNY
NJANPAA, JAKOB	26	M	LABR	RR	ADA	XNY
GINZBURG, WOLF	24	M	LABR	RR	ADA	XNY
ZAARIKOSKI, JAKOB	29	M	LABR	RR	ADA	XMI
LEIMMUKKA, JOH.	24	M	LABR	RR	ADA	XMI
KAMPILA, ELIAS	20	M	LABR	RR	ADA	XMI
LAUTAMOS, IRKO	22	M	LABR	RR	ADA	XMI
RAUKALA, GUST.	20	M	LABR	RR	ADA	XMI
LANTAMOS, GUST.	25	M	LABR	RR	ADA	XIL
MARIA	22	F	W	RR	ADA	XIL
SPAAF, JAKOB	25	M	LABR	RR	ADA	XMI
LASSILA, JOH.	26	M	LABR	RR	ADA	XMI
KLEENDLA, NIKOLAI	29	M	LABR	RR	ADA	XNY
IYRJAMAKI, JAKOB	25	M	LABR	RR	ADA	XNY
KAKIMAKI, JOH.	32	M	LABR	RR	ADA	XNY
SATO, ISAAK	46	M	LABR	RR	ADA	XNY
PETKALA, ANTI	25	M	LABR	RR	ADA	XMI
REUTTALA, ELIAS	28	M	LABR	RR	ADA	XMI
LUMMUKKA, MATTI	20	M	LABR	RR	ADA	XMI
WINIKKA, ALF.	22	M	LABR	RR	ADA	XMI
OSTMAN, AND.	44	M	LABR	RR	ADA	XMI
DUDD, LEANDER	17	M	LABR	RR	ADA	XMI
GRAUBERG, HENRIK	22	M	LABR	RR	ADA	XMI
JOHANSEN, ALFRED	20	M	LABR	RR	ADA	XMI
RAIAL, CARL	27	M	LABR	RR	ADA	XCAL
KOSIKOWA, THERESA	17	F	SP	RR	ADA	XIL
TOFFARI, ANNA	19	F	SP	RR	ADA	XNY
FINNI, MINA	31	F	SP	RR	ADA	XNY

SHIP: DEVONIA

FROM: GLASGOW
TO: NEW YORK
ARRIVED: 20 FEBRUARY 1889

PASSENGER	AGE	SEX	OCCUPATION	PRI VL	V I L	DES
ADLES, MICHAEL	28	M	LABR	RR	ZZZ	USA
BALSARAGE, JOS.	20	M	TLR	RR	ZZZ	USA
BRANDE, ELIE	26	M	TLR	RR	ZZZ	USA
DEITZ, EISIK	31	M	TLR	RR	ZZZ	USA
CHAJE	25	F	UNKNOWN	RR	ZZZ	USA
DUCHMOWSKI, NICK.	35	M	PNTR	RR	ZZZ	USA
FEIGELSOHN, PESE	38	F	UNKNOWN	RR	ZZZ	USA
ABRAHAM	18	M	TLR	RR	ZZZ	USA
KLEWANSKI, ASCHER	21	M	LABR	RR	ZZZ	USA
MASELEWICZ, MARIE	22	F	SVNT	RR	ZZZ	USA
PATASCHMIK, KUSIEL	17	M	TLR	RR	ZZZ	USA
SCHNEIDMAN, BENONS	26	M	SHMK	RR	ZZZ	USA
SWEDAR, MIK	23	M	LABR	RR	ZZZ	USA
ANDREAS	20	M	LABR	RR	ZZZ	USA
STACKEWITZ, IGNATZ	40	M	LABR	RR	ZZZ	USA
SCHEUDERNMANN, MOSCHE	50	M	LABR	RR	ZZZ	USA
INDE	22	M	LABR	RR	ZZZ	USA
ISRAEL	18	M	LABR	RR	ZZZ	USA

SHIP: MAIN

FROM: BREMEN
TO: BALTIMORE
ARRIVED: 21 FEBRUARY 1889

PASSENGER	AGE	SEX	OCCUPATION	PRI VL	V I L	DES
SCHMITTMANN, SAMUEL	10	M	CH	RR	ZZZ	BAL
HUEGEL, SIMON	32	M	SHMK	RR	ZZZ	BAL
GOLDBERG, JANKEL	24	M	LABR	RR	ZZZ	BAL
PYBACK, HERGEL	17	M	LABR	RR	ZZZ	BAL
KOZELSKI, FRANZIZEK	26	M	LABR	RR	ZZZ	BAL
REZDLOWSKA, SEIDFR.	44	M	LABR	RR	ZZZ	BAL
ZINORGEWSKI, JOHANN	10	M	CH	RR	ZZZ	BAL
ALBERT	3	M	CHILD	RR	ZZZ	BAL
BESZT, FRANZIZEK	21	M	FARMER	RR	ZZZ	BAL
PAWOCENSKA, ANTONIA	24	F	SVNT	RR	ZZZ	BAL
BERMANN, HINDE	20	F	SVNT	RR	ZZZ	BAL
ESTHER	16	F	SVNT	RR	ZZZ	BAL

SHIP: NEVADA

FROM: LIVERPOOL AND QUEENSTOWN
TO: NEW YORK
ARRIVED: 21 FEBRUARY 1889

PASSENGER	AGE	SEX	OCCUPATION	PRI VL	V I L	DES
EHUAMAMAKI, GUSTAF	25	M	LABR	RR	ZZZ	USA
GRIBUSH, LEAN	16	F	SP	RR	ZZZ	USA
FRIEDLANDER, SIMON	46	M	BCHR	RR	ZZZ	USA
FUEDMAN, MORIS	25	M	TLR	RR	ZZZ	USA
PALAMMI, JOHANN	32	M	LABR	RR	ZZZ	USA
LORDEN, JOEL	34	M	UNKNOWN	RR	ZZZ	USA
LAUKKI, GUSTAF	22	M	LABR	RR	ZZZ	USA
LOAMAMAKI, JACOB	27	M	LABR	RR	ZZZ	USA
LILLVIS, ANDERS	23	M	LABR	RR	ZZZ	USA
KVALMEN, KARL	19	M	LABR	RR	ZZZ	USA
MARKAUSKI, VINCENTI	27	M	SLR	RR	ZZZ	USA
KONHAINEN, ERIK	26	M	LABR	RR	ZZZ	USA
PERTSNEN, ELIA	23	M	LABR	RR	ZZZ	USA
ANDERSEN, ANDERS	20	M	LABR	RR	ZZZ	USA
YLLEKOSKI, GUSTAF	26	M	LABR	RR	ZZZ	USA
NYLAND, JOHANN	25	M	CL	RR	ZZZ	USA
SARIN, ANDERS	36	M	LABR	RR	ZZZ	USA
KALKASARI, ERIK	25	M	LABR	RR	ZZZ	USA
RUNBACKER, ANDERS	26	M	TLR	RR	ZZZ	USA
ENGLUND, ERIK	30	M	LABR	RR	ZZZ	USA
SIMONS, GUSTAF	29	M	PNTR	RR	ZZZ	USA
LAUKEWITZ, ELKE	16	M	UNKNOWN	RR	ZZZ	USA
FERN, SLATE	17	F	SP	RR	ZZZ	USA
BAUSKE, FIEGE	17	M	LABR	RR	ZZZ	USA
ABAGANSKE, BETTE	40	F	MA	RR	ZZZ	USA
STRUNK, DEBORA	24	F	W	RR	ZZZ	USA
GUNDUK, BER	20	M	WCHMKR	RR	ZZZ	USA
PAUSKY, ROCHE	20	F	W	RR	ZZZ	USA
JIN, RACHAEL	34	F	W	RR	ZZZ	USA
RACHAEL	.05	F	INFANT	RR	ZZZ	USA

PASSENGER	AGE	SEX	OCCUPATION	PRIVL	DES
KARN, BARUCH	58	M	CPTR	RRZZZZ	USA
KAHN, JUDES	16	M	UNKNOWN	RRZZZZ	USA
ISSER	18	F	SP	RRZZZZ	USA
KRIER	7	M	CHILD	RRZZZZ	USA

SHIP: LAKE HURON

FROM: LIVERPOOL
TO: BOSTON
ARRIVED: 22 FEBRUARY 1889

PASSENGER	AGE	SEX	OCCUPATION	PRIVL	DES
HIRSCHNER, D.	35	F	W	RRZZZZ	CH
ROCHE	12	F	CH	RRZZZZ	CH
ABRON.	00	F	CH	RRZZZZ	CH
SCHENE	5	F	CHILD	RRZZZZ	CH
PINE, MARY	40	F	W	RRZZZZ	CH
SOREN	11	M	CH	RRZZZZ	CH
BIOCKLEY	9	M	CHILD	RRZZZZ	CH
YANKEL	12	M	CH	RRZZZZ	CH
WIRE, CHAJE	18	F	W	RRZZZZ	CH
SCHONBEKER, CHAI	34	F	W	RRZZZZ	CH
ZEBA	11	M	CH	RRZZZZ	CH
BERL	9	M	CHILD	RRZZZZ	CH
EISIG	4	M	CHILD	RRZZZZ	CH
COHEN, MOCHEM	18	M	TLR	RRZZZZ	MIL
PINKOWSKI, JEW.	26	M	TLR	RRZZZZ	CH
HIRSCHNER, CIZIP	35	F	W	RRZZZZ	CH
CHAJE	10	F	CH	RRZZZZ	CH
SCHENE	7	F	CHILD	RRZZZZ	CH
MELL, SELIG	16	M	CH	RRZZZZ	CH

SHIP: SAALE

FROM: BREMEN AND SOUTHAMPTON
TO: NEW YORK
ARRIVED: 23 FEBRUARY 1889

PASSENGER	AGE	SEX	OCCUPATION	PRIVL	DES
LITTMANN, HEIN.	19	M	CL	RRZZZZ	USA
NASKEWITZ, MARIA	25	F	UNKNOWN	RRZZZZ	USA
JOSEPHA	3	F	CHILD	RRZZZZ	USA
FRANCISKA	.01	F	INFANT	RRZZZZ	USA
SCHNITTER, MARIA	24	F	UNKNOWN	RRZZZZ	USA
HURWITZ, TAUBE	23	M	SMH	RRZZZZ	USA
SCHNEIDERMANN, ALKE	20	F	UNKNOWN	RRZZZZ	USA
FUZINSKA, ANTONIE	34	F	UNKNOWN	RRZZZZ	USA
ANDR.	7	M	CHILD	RRZZZZ	USA
BERKOWITZ, JOSEPH	25	M	SMH	RRZZZZ	USA
SUMMOWICZ, DAVID	29	M	SMH	RRZZZZ	USA
MATESOW, ROSE	30	F	UNKNOWN	RRZZZZ	USA
CHAJE	8	F	CHILD	RRZZZZ	USA
FROME	6	F	CHILD	RRZZZZ	USA
LEW, MEYER	26	M	FARMER	RRZZZZ	USA
GRABOWSKY, MOSES	16	M	FARMER	RRZZZZ	USA
MILLER, ISREL	17	M	FARMER	RRZZZZ	USA
WEINER, LINA	18	F	UNKNOWN	RRZZZZ	USA
SULSKI, JOH.	33	M	SMH	RRZZZZ	USA
MECHANEK, MENDEL	19	M	SMH	RRZZZZ	USA
KLEID, LAW	33	M	FARMER	RRZZZZ	USA
ZALEWITZ, DAVID	36	M	FARMER	RRZZZZ	USA
LUEOSCHE, FRENLAN	16	M	FARMER	RRZZZZ	USA
GOLDSTEIN, DAVID	18	M	FARMER	RRZZZZ	USA
GOMONDSKY, MATES	16	M	FARMER	RRZZZZ	USA
MACHLISCH, NOAH	31	M	FARMER	RRZZZZ	USA
TARFEL, ABRAH.	28	M	FARMER	RRZZZZ	USA
SCHLENKRUG, LEISER	26	M	FARMER	RRZZZZ	USA
TERREKAN, SCHOLEM	26	M	FARMER	RRZZZZ	USA
DIRK	26	M	FARMER	RRZZZZ	USA
JACOB	7	M	CHILD	RRZZZZ	USA
MARDIKAL, FEIGE	22	M	LABR	RRZZZZ	USA
EKELGICK, CHANE	35	M	LABR	RRZZZZ	USA
STEINMANN, MAUSCHE	31	M	LABR	RRZZZZ	USA
FERNWISCHOW, MORITZ	35	M	TLR	RRZZZZ	USA
KAUFFMANN, JUDEL	23	M	TLR	RRZZZZ	USA
FEIN, FEIGE	19	M	TLR	RRZZZZ	USA
AKSELBAUB, MAX	22	M	FARMER	RRZZZZ	USA
SOLDINSKI, VALENT.	20	M	FARMER	RRZZZZ	USA
KRYSTINAK, JOS.	18	M	FARMER	RRZZZZ	USA
MARGOWSKI, FRANZ	22	M	FARMER	RRZZZZ	USA
PROCHLAN, JOH.	25	M	FARMER	RRZZZZ	USA
ELING, JOH.	24	M	FARMER	RRZZZZ	USA
ROF, ALEX	26	M	FARMER	RRZZZZ	USA
CHMIELEWSKY, JOH.	28	M	FARMER	RRZZZZ	USA
ROF, JOSEPH	30	M	FARMER	RRZZZZ	USA
UKOWSKI, ANTONIA	25	F	UNKNOWN	RRZZZZ	USA
WEISSBLUTH, JENNY	38	F	UNKNOWN	RRZZZZ	USA
FANNY	7	F	CHILD	RRZZZZ	USA
WOLODY	4	F	CHILD	RRZZZZ	USA
ROSNIZKY, HEIN.	57	M	FARMER	RRZZZZ	USA

SHIP: ROMAN

FROM: LIVERPOOL
TO: BOSTON
ARRIVED: 23 FEBRUARY 1889

PASSENGER	AGE	SEX	OCCUPATION	PRIVL	DES
FINNIN, BENJAMIN	21	M	LABR	RRZZZZ	BO
LEVIN, SARAH	19	F	SP	RRZZZZ	BO
LAPENSKY, ISRAEL	23	M	LABR	RRZZZZ	BO
SCHINSOWITZ, JULIA	30	F	SP	RRZZZZ	BO
PIENWZ, MEKORDUS	45	M	LABR	RRZZZZ	BO
SOLOMON, MAX	28	M	LABR	RRZZZZ	BO
LERRIN, MOSES	11	M	CH	RRZZZZ	BO
SCHINDEL, JENKEL	16	M	LABR	RRZZZZ	BO
PERMETT, SOLOMON	43	M	LABR	RRZZZZ	BO
FIELDMANN, BAROCH	25	M	LABR	RRZZZZ	BO
FRESCHMANN, CHAJA	36	M	ATSN	RRZZZZ	PHI
GOSCHENSKY, MARY	27	F	SP	RRZZZZ	PHI

SHIP: NOORDLAND

FROM: ANTWERP
TO: NEW YORK
ARRIVED: 23 FEBRUARY 1889

PASSENGER	AGE	SEX	OCCUPATION	PRIVL	DES
RECHT, ISAAC	18	M	TLR	RRAIIX	NY

SHIP: CELTIC

FROM: LIVERPOOL AND QUEENSTOWN
TO: NEW YORK
ARRIVED: 25 FEBRUARY 1889

PASSENGER	AGE	SEX	OCCUPATION	PRIVL	DES
KEZZNISKE, JOWOAEN	26	M	LABR	PLZZZZ	USA
GOSTONSKY, FRANK	23	M	LABR	PLZZZZ	USA
JORDNIUM, PEDER	22	M	LABR	PLZZZZ	USA

PASSENGER	AGE	SEX	OCCUPATION	PRV	VIL	DES
HANSON, IVER	28	M	LABR	PL	ZZZZ	USA
SETTERGREN, U	18	M	LABR	PL	ZZZZ	USA
REMISNER, BOMCH	26	M	LABR	PL	ZZZZ	USA
SCHUSTER, IGNATZ	16	M	LABR	PL	ZZZZ	USA
GRIEDMANN, MOSES	20	M	LABR	PL	ZZZZ	USA
KEZUSKI, JOSEPH	1	M	CHILD	PL	ZZZZ	USA
WITTNER, ABRAHAM	35	M	LABR	PL	ZZZZ	USA
SCHIF, ELLET	22	M	LABR	PL	ZZZZ	USA
BALLTUCK, MARKUS	50	M	LABR	PL	ZZZZ	USA
BLUNE	16	F	SP	PL	ZZZZ	USA
ELKE	11	F	CH	PL	ZZZZ	USA
MENDEL	10	M	CH	PL	ZZZZ	USA
KYNOE, SYNECOW	20	M	LABR	PL	ZZZZ	USA
OJALA, ISAK	40	M	LABR	PL	ZZZZ	USA
KWALA, HULSKI	28	M	LABR	PL	ZZZZ	USA
HAKOLA, SAMUEL	20	M	LABR	PL	ZZZZ	USA
WALLI, JACOB	40	M	LABR	PL	ZZZZ	USA
LEPPANER, MATTI	38	M	LABR	PL	ZZZZ	USA
WEKOJA, ERIK	42	M	LABR	PL	ZZZZ	USA
WELENEW, JOHAN	26	M	LABR	PL	ZZZZ	USA
REKILA, LEANDER	27	M	LABR	PL	ZZZZ	USA
HAKOLA, MATTI	26	M	LABR	PL	ZZZZ	USA
WENTALA, JOHAN	24	M	LABR	PL	ZZZZ	USA
HERIKOSKI, AXEL	26	M	LABR	PL	ZZZZ	USA

SHIP: CITY OF CHICAGO

FROM: LIVERPOOL AND QUEENSTOWN
TO: NEW YORK
ARRIVED: 25 FEBRUARY 1889

PASSENGER	AGE	SEX	OCCUPATION	PRV	VIL	DES
LEOPLD, SAUL	18	M	LABR	PL	ADAX	NY
GOLDEN, INDEL	21	M	LABR	PL	ADAX	NY
KALUMOWSKY, ABRAM	36	M	LABR	PL	ADAX	NY
HERSCHKOWITZ, JOSEL	22	M	LABR	PL	ADAX	NY
LASCHNO, PUECH	20	M	LABR	PL	ADAX	NY
BUSCHBACK, JUSTHEN	21	M	LABR	PL	ADAX	NY
CASONMOWITZ, MARTIN	33	M	LABR	PL	ADAX	NY
POBIETZ, STANISLAW	18	M	LABR	PL	ADAX	NY
JANTEGEL, JOHAN	22	M	LABR	PL	ADAX	NY
BURBS, ADAMS	27	M	LABR	PL	ADAX	NY
WERTGKA, VINCENT	31	M	LABR	PL	ADAX	NY
VURSAL, ANDERS	32	M	LABR	PL	ADAX	NY
WILSER, H.	27	M	LABR	PL	ADAX	NY
RUK, CHASE	18	F	SP	PL	ACBF	NY
QUICK, ANN	20	F	SP	PL	AIHK	NY
TEASCHE, SOFIA	52	F	W	PL	AIHK	NY
SAUSGET, JOSEF	32	F	W	PL	AIHK	NY
U	4	M	CHILD	PL	AIHK	NY
ELISKI, ROSA	15	F	UNKNOWN	PL	AIHK	NY
ED.	00	M	INF	PL	AIHK	NY
AHRAMOWITZ, FANNY	28	F	W	PL	AIHK	NY
ANNEH	8	F	CHILD	PL	AIHK	NY
ROSA	7	F	CHILD	PL	AIHK	NY
ELSSKI, EH.	38	F	W	PL	ACBF	NY
RACHEL	20	F	SP	PL	ACBF	NY
MARI	18	F	SP	PL	ACBF	NY
MARSSILL, MARIA	18	F	SP	PL	ACBF	NY
HINDA	17	F	SP	PL	ACBF	NY
HORNGRIST, GUST.	27	M	LABR	PL	ACBF	NY

SHIP: CIRCASSIA

FROM: GLASGOW AND MOVILLE
TO: NEW YORK
ARRIVED: 26 FEBRUARY 1889

PASSENGER	AGE	SEX	OCCUPATION	PRV	VIL	DES
GUNGLEWSKY, RAZMUCZ	26	M	LABR	RR	ZZZZ	USA
BEHR, DAVID	21	M	DLR	RR	ZZZZ	USA
FRIEDMAN, LIEB	28	M	LABR	RR	ZZZZ	USA
BATSCHEWSKI, BERT	22	M	SHMK	RR	ZZZZ	USA
GRENBURG, HIRSCH	30	M	DLR	RR	ZZZZ	USA
JANKELEWITZ, CHAIN	17	M	DLR	RR	ZZZZ	USA
KOWALKOWSKI, JOSEF	28	M	MSN	RR	ZZZZ	USA
MUSNETZKI, MIKOL	22	M	LABR	RR	ZZZZ	USA
RAFAEL	20	M	LABR	RR	ZZZZ	USA
SAPINSKY, JAN	28	M	LABR	RR	ZZZZ	USA
MILEWESKI, WINSENTZ	29	M	LABR	RR	ZZZZ	USA
KUHL, LASER	26	M	LABR	RR	ZZZZ	USA
JOSEF	1	M	CHILD	RR	ZZZZ	USA
SUKEWICZ, MATZEY	35	M	LABR	RR	ZZZZ	USA
ARBISTER, ISRAEL	23	M	DLR	RR	ZZZZ	USA
SEGALL, WOLF	30	M	JNR	RR	ZZZZ	USA
REZESINSKY, ANTONI	28	M	LABR	RR	ZZZZ	USA
SCHMIELONSKY, STANISLAW	36	M	LABR	RR	ZZZZ	USA
WOJCIECH, ALEYA	33	M	LABR	RR	ZZZZ	USA
KANOWITZ, CHAIE	19	F	TLR	RR	ZZZZ	USA
SEIDLOWISKI, CHAIE	28	F	W	RR	ZZZZ	USA
ITTE	3	F	CHILD	RR	ZZZZ	USA
OGORENKO, LEONARD	28	M	JNR	RR	ZZZZ	USA
HELENE	22	F	W	RR	ZZZZ	USA

SHIP: SLAVONIA

FROM: SWINEMUNDE
TO: NEW YORK
ARRIVED: 26 FEBRUARY 1889

PASSENGER	AGE	SEX	OCCUPATION	PRV	VIL	DES
GOLDSTEIN, JANKOFF	19	M	WCHMKR	RR	ZZZZ	WI
KOPITCH, DANIEL	23	M	LABR	RR	AFZD	NY
ELSNER, CHARLOTTE	00	F	INF	RR	ZZZZ	NY

SHIP: EMS

FROM: BREMEN AND SOUTHAMPTON
TO: NEW YORK
ARRIVED: 26 FEBRUARY 1889

PASSENGER	AGE	SEX	OCCUPATION	PRV	VIL	DES
LEWIN, BROCHE	20	M	PNTR	RR	ZZZZ	USA
WINIK, REISEL	11	F	CH	RR	ZZZZ	USA
MOSES	9	M	CHILD	RR	ZZZZ	USA
GUTMAN, FRIEDE	28	F	W	RR	ZZZZ	USA
MOSES	9	M	CHILD	RR	ZZZZ	USA
SOLOWEITSCHYK, J.	26	M	DR	RR	ZZZZ	USA
DRYEWIEZKA, NAPAN	35	M	LABR	RR	ZZZZ	USA
CATHE.	14	F	TLR	RR	ZZZZ	USA
VERONICA	11	F	CH	RR	ZZZZ	USA
MARIE	9	F	CHILD	RR	ZZZZ	USA
VALERIE	7	F	CHILD	RR	ZZZZ	USA
NAPOLINA	4	F	CHILD	RR	ZZZZ	USA
JULIANA	3	F	CHILD	RR	ZZZZ	USA
HELENA	2	F	CHILD	RR	ZZZZ	USA
NATASIA	16	F	LABR	RR	ZZZZ	USA
BANER, BENZEL	23	M	UNKNOWN	RR	ZZZZ	USA
GREBIN, ISAAC	37	M	LABR	RR	ZZZZ	USA

PASSENGER	AGE	SEX	OCCUPATION	PRIV	DES
LELIGMANN, CIPE	49	M	LABR	RRZZZZ	USA
ANNA	20	F	TLR	RRZZZZ	USA
DOBE	19	M	LABR	RRZZZZ	USA
ROGOWSKY, SAM.	48	M	LABR	RRZZZZ	USA
SALOMON	20	M	LABR	RRZZZZ	USA
WARDANDKI, JOSEF	24	M	LABR	RRZZZZ	USA
LUKINSKY, PIOTR	33	M	LABR	RRZZZZ	USA
PRICHARKIEMIZ, JAN	31	M	LABR	RRZZZZ	USA
ZABLOWSKI, JAN	23	M	LABR	RRZZZZ	USA

SHIP: TAORMINA

FROM: UNKNOWN
TO: NEW YORK
ARRIVED: 27 FEBRUARY 1889

PASSENGER	AGE	SEX	OCCUPATION	PRIV	DES
SIRONEN, MARIA	29	F	UNKNOWN	RRZZZZ	USA
ALEX	3	M	CHILD	RRZZZZ	USA
MARIA	.01	F	INFANT	RRZZZZ	USA
PADTTIMAKI, ELINA	29	F	UNKNOWN	RRZZZZ	USA
GOELDNER, GUST.	27	M	LABR	RRZZZZ	USA
REPPKE, AUG.	33	M	LABR	RRZZZZ	USA
SCHVARZ, DAVID	29	M	LABR	RRZZZZ	USA
WOPHENSKY, MOSES	18	M	LABR	RRZZZZ	USA
BACHRACH, LEIB	30	M	LABR	RRZZZZ	USA
KWIATKOWSKI, JAN	24	M	BCHR	RRZZZZ	USA
WELE-, ANTON	26	M	FARMER	RRZZZZ	USA
KLANOSKA, JULIANA	19	F	UNKNOWN	RRZZZZ	USA
KURZEVA, LEIZER	30	M	MCHT	RRZZZZ	USA
LOSSER, ISRAEL	19	M	LABR	RRZZZZ	USA
PANLOWSKY, STANISLAUS	25	M	LABR	RRACBF	NY
JANITZKY, JOSEF	40	M	LABR	RRACBF	NY
SCHMIDT, EMILIE	19	F	SGL	RRACBF	NY
HALWINE	16	F	SGL	RRACBF	NY
KANTOR, DAVID	45	M	TLR	RRACBF	NY
ROITMANN, HERCH	30	M	LABR	RRACBF	NY
ZWICKEL, MARCUS	30	M	TLR	RRACBF	NY
TANNEBAUM, DANIEL	22	M	WCHMKR	RRACBF	NY

SHIP: NORSEMAN

FROM: LIVERPOOL
TO: BOSTON
ARRIVED: 27 FEBRUARY 1889

PASSENGER	AGE	SEX	OCCUPATION	PRIV	DES
KONWISKI, HAYMAN	27	M	UNKNOWN	RRZZZZ	NY
ETRIGEITOS, SIMON	29	M	PDLR	RRZZZZ	NY
MAUCHINSKI, VINCENT	22	M	PDLR	RRZZZZ	NY
ALEXANDER, MORRIS	30	M	UNKNOWN	RRZZZZ	NY
SOLOMONS, SOLOMON	23	M	TLR	RRZZZZ	PHI
GRISTROWSKY, LIVE	32	M	TLR	RRZZZZ	BO
SAKOWISKY, MATIS	17	M	TLR	RRZZZZ	BO
HATHAN, LEISER	40	M	TLR	RRZZZZ	NY
SITIRLES, SIMON	29	M	TLR	RRZZZZ	NY
JARBICA, SHIME	20	F	SVNT	RRZZZZ	NY
MEYER, FRK.	29	M	TLR	RRZZZZ	USA
ROSENBLATT, ROLPH	27	M	TLR	RRZZZZ	NY
BALTIRIMS, B.	24	M	LABR	RRZZZZ	BO
USEMETZKY, LISIR	19	M	TLR	RRZZZZ	BO
GOTTLIEB, SAM.	25	M	UNKNOWN	RRZZZZ	BO
TIMIETZ, GESDEN	44	M	TLR	RRZZZZ	BO
SMIRSKY, JAN	44	M	TLR	RRZZZZ	BO
BRUEG, MARTIN	44	M	TLR	RRZZZZ	BO
CHASANOWITZ, MEYER	15	M	UNKNOWN	RRZZZZ	BO
GINSLENG, LOUIS	20	M	TLR	RRZZZZ	BO

SHIP: LEERDAM

FROM: AMSTERDAM
TO: NEW YORK
ARRIVED: 29 FEBRUARY 1889

PASSENGER	AGE	SEX	OCCUPATION	PRIV	DES
CYRAN, M.	24	F	UNKNOWN	RRZZZZ	USA
S.	.10	F	INFANT	RRZZZZ	USA
STELKA, F.	24	M	LABR	RRZZZZ	USA
V.	22	F	UNKNOWN	RRZZZZ	USA
AUCH, J.	40	M	MCHT	RRZZZZ	USA
GROSSMANN, J.	21	M	LABR	RRZZZZ	USA
JECHSMOWICZ, J.	39	M	LABR	RRZZZZ	USA
BONESINSKY, J.	29	M	LABR	RRZZZZ	USA
BURTA, M.	25	M	LABR	RRZZZZ	USA
GAUTSCH, J.	26	M	LABR	RRZZZZ	USA
WERNINTE, J.	30	M	LABR	RRZZZZ	USA
BECIVAR, M.	30	F	UNKNOWN	RRZZZZ	USA
LOBALE, G.	29	M	LABR	RRZZZZ	USA
ROSIPALY, J.	24	M	LABR	RRZZZZ	USA
MALAKONIES, G.	38	M	LABR	RRZZZZ	USA
KINEC, J.	30	M	LABR	RRZZZZ	USA
MATEJ, J.	30	M	LABR	RRZZZZ	USA
FUDA, J.	23	M	UNKNOWN	RRZZZZ	USA
KAPLAR, J.	24	M	UNKNOWN	RRZZZZ	USA
PANKULICZ, M.	24	M	UNKNOWN	RRZZZZ	USA
HOCKO, J.	20	M	UNKNOWN	RRZZZZ	USA
FROSKA, A.	24	M	UNKNOWN	RRZZZZ	USA
GALONKA, M.	20	F	UNKNOWN	RRZZZZ	USA
PARAKSKA, M.	29	F	UNKNOWN	RRZZZZ	USA

SHIP: TRAVE

FROM: BREMEN AND SOUTHAMPTON
TO: NEW YORK
ARRIVED: 01 MARCH 1889

PASSENGER	AGE	SEX	OCCUPATION	PRIV	DES
BLYWASS, SAM.	55	M	PDLR	RRZZZZ	USA
WITI	35	F	UNKNOWN	RRZZZZ	USA
SCHIERSOHN, JOSEF	45	M	DLR	RRZZZZ	USA
FANNI	40	F	UNKNOWN	RRZZZZ	USA
BERTHA	16	F	UNKNOWN	RRZZZZ	USA
SOPHIE	14	F	UNKNOWN	RRZZZZ	USA
DORA	6	F	CHILD	RRZZZZ	USA
HIRSCH	7	M	CHILD	RRZZZZ	USA
RAPHAEL	.11	M	INFANT	RRZZZZ	USA
KINSBERG, ISRAEL	54	M	LABR	RRZZZZ	USA
PTASCHINSKY, WLADISLAW	17	M	LABR	RRZZZZ	USA
MUTULOWICZ, CARL	34	M	LABR	RRZZZZ	USA
SCHRUMKOWSICZ, ATON	18	M	LABR	RRZZZZ	USA
GLASS, CARL	45	M	LABR	RRZZZZ	USA
JOSEF	15	M	LABR	RRZZZZ	USA
MUTULOWICZ, MART.	18	M	LABR	RRZZZZ	USA
OROWICZ, ADAM	30	M	LABR	RRZZZZ	USA
KALINKOWSKI, WICENTY	23	M	LABR	RRZZZZ	USA
LASKOWSKI, FRANZ	23	M	LABR	RRZZZZ	USA
OROWICZ, CARL	28	M	LABR	RRZZZZ	USA
BOBARSKY, ALEX	18	M	DLR	RRZZZZ	USA
JOSEF	17	M	DLR	RRZZZZ	USA
CZERKAJES, FRANZ	25	M	LABR	RRZZZZ	USA
PISAROWITZ, ABZBIETA	30	F	UNKNOWN	RRZZZZ	USA
CHINA, MATHILDE	21	F	UNKNOWN	RRZZZZ	USA
SABORNI, JOHANN	20	M	LABR	RRZZZZ	USA
BUSCHKOWSKI, CONST.	29	M	DLR	RRZZZZ	USA
JABLONSKI, JOH.	29	M	DLR	RRZZZZ	USA
NOSOWITZKI, HARRIS	24	M	CL	RRZZZZ	USA

PASSENGER	AGE	SEX	OCCUPATION	PRIV	VIL	DES

SHIP: LAKE ONTARIO

FROM: LIVERPOOL
TO: BOSTON
ARRIVED: 04 MARCH 1889

PASSENGER	AGE	SEX	OCCUPATION	PRIV	VIL	DES
BERNSTEIN, SELIG	31	M	SHMK	PL	ZZZZ	NY
BERNBAUM, F.	21	M	CL	RR	ZZZZ	MIL
HELMAN, HARRY	20	M	LABR	RR	ZZZZ	CH
KUSEL, BORRECK	21	M	LABR	RR	ZZZZ	CH
FERMBERG, CHAGE	39	F	W	RR	ZZZZ	MIL
DOBRE	12	F	CH	RR	ZZZZ	MIL
MERE	8	F	CHILD	RR	ZZZZ	MIL
ARON	6	M	CHILD	RR	ZZZZ	MIL
GOLDBERG, LESMAN	17	M	LABR	PL	ZZZZ	CH
PRFKOWITZ, TH.	18	M	LABR	PL	ZZZZ	MIL
S.	15	F	SP	PL	ZZZZ	MIL
RUVEN	10	M	CH	PL	ZZZZ	MIL
WOLF	8	M	CHILD	PL	ZZZZ	MIL
CHASE	6	F	CHILD	PL	ZZZZ	MIL
ZAPLUTZ--, ELI	38	M	LABR	PL	ZZZZ	NY
FITO, CARL	35	M	LABR	PL	ZZZZ	NY
LETUREN, MORCHE-J.	16	M	LABR	PL	ZZZZ	CH
WEL------, JACOB	29	M	LABR	PL	ZZZZ	NY

SHIP: ETHIOPIA

FROM: GLASGOW AND MOVILLE
TO: NEW YORK
ARRIVED: 04 MARCH 1889

PASSENGER	AGE	SEX	OCCUPATION	PRIV	VIL	DES
ZESLOR, MASCHE	29	M	DLR	RR	ZZZZ	USA
JERASCHUKAS, ANDREAS	27	M	LABR	RR	ZZZZ	USA
SAROKA, SCHANAH	21	M	LABR	RR	ZZZZ	USA
LOOSER, JONAS	16	M	LABR	RR	ZZZZ	USA
WILKUS, KASEMIR	24	M	LABR	RR	ZZZZ	USA
PLO---S, SIMON	25	M	LABR	RR	ZZZZ	USA
U, ALEXANDER	23	M	LABR	RR	ZZZZ	USA
LANGER, DORI	19	F	HP	RR	ZZZZ	USA
LUBEL, MOSES	33	M	TLR	RR	ZZZZ	USA
GOLDSTEIN, JULIUS	28	M	TLR	RR	ZZZZ	USA
SORE	30	F	TLR	RR	ZZZZ	USA
ABRAHAM	9	M	CHILD	RR	ZZZZ	USA
D---ACK, MARIA	21	F	HP	RR	ZZZZ	USA
STEFAN, PINDAS	11	F	CH	RR	ZZZZ	USA
STRERNBERG, JACOB	25	M	TLR	RR	ZZZZ	USA
LESVERK, MEYER	22	M	TLR	RR	ZZZZ	USA
HEMGWELCH, MORDCHE	23	M	TLR	RR	ZZZZ	USA
BOTHURA, JOHAN	28	M	TLR	RR	ZZZZ	USA
POMERANZ, JANON	40	M	TLR	RR	ZZZZ	USA
ZIPE	12	M	CH	RR	ZZZZ	USA
GOLDBERG, SCHMUEL	27	M	TLR	RR	ZZZZ	USA
MORANZ, JOSEF	20	M	TLR	RR	ZZZZ	USA
SCHNEIDERSCHER, SIMON	26	M	SDLR	RR	ZZZZ	USA
BUROK, S-NCHE	22	M	TLR	RR	ZZZZ	USA
KRAWCEWICZ, SCHOLEM	18	M	TLR	RR	ZZZZ	USA
TABACZWIEZ, CHASKEL	20	M	TLR	RR	ZZZZ	USA
KAMMIEZKE, ISRAEL	12	M	TLR	RR	ZZZZ	USA
OFFENBACH, RACHEL	18	F	HP	RR	ZZZZ	USA
WOLAF, JEAN	37	M	LABR	RR	ZZZZ	USA
BIERMAN, JANKEL-BEER	29	M	LABR	RR	ZZZZ	USA
JALEL, MEYER-WOLF	22	M	SMH	RR	ZZZZ	USA
ZELECHOWSKI, ABRAHAM	25	M	TLR	RR	ZZZZ	USA

SHIP: AURANIA

FROM: LIVERPOOL
TO: NEW YORK
ARRIVED: 04 MARCH 1889

PASSENGER	AGE	SEX	OCCUPATION	PRIV	VIL	DES
GROSS, SIMON	16	M	LABR	PL	ZZZZ	NY
DABOLSKY, ADAM	20	M	LABR	PL	ZZZZ	NY
PALAWSKY, SYMON	28	M	LABR	PL	ZZZZ	NY
PAPSYILASZ, JOSEFR	25	M	LABR	PL	ZZZZ	NY
KORLENSKY, JAKOB	27	M	LABR	PL	ZZZZ	NY
ANDRYZYH, ANDRY	31	M	LABR	PL	ZZZZ	NY
KOBRYCH, PETER	40	M	LABR	PL	ZZZZ	NY
BROD, JOSSEL	45	M	LABR	PL	ZZZZ	NY
ALEXANDER, JACOB	25	M	LABR	RR	ZZZZ	NY
GOLDBERG, AB.	17	M	LABR	RR	ZZZZ	NY
-CHLUR---, SAML.	50	M	UNKNOWN	PL	ZZZZ	NY
MOSES	29	M	UNKNOWN	PL	ZZZZ	NY
PULKONEN, WM.	20	M	UNKNOWN	FN	ZZZZ	NY

SHIP: RHAETIA

FROM: HAMBURG
TO: NEW YORK
ARRIVED: 04 MARCH 1889

PASSENGER	AGE	SEX	OCCUPATION	PRIV	VIL	DES
ALEMLICK, SABINE	20	F	SGL	RR	ZZZZ	USA
REDEN, GUSTAV	26	M	SLR	RR	ZZZZ	USA
DRUDE, CARL	24	M	CL	RR	ZZZZ	USA
DOMBROWSKY, ANTONY	28	M	LABR	RR	ZZZZ	USA
KIMONT, POLIKART	26	M	LABR	RR	ZZZZ	USA
KORINO, CONSTANTIN	26	M	LABR	RR	ZZZZ	USA
SABIN, HIRSCH	36	M	TU	RR	ZZZZ	USA
ETIA	32	F	W	RR	ZZZZ	USA
DAVID	9	M	CHILD	RR	ZZZZ	USA
GOLDE	4	F	CHILD	RR	ZZZZ	USA
MOTJE	.11	M	INFANT	RR	ZZZZ	USA
WIEGER, KARL	39	M	WO	RR	ZZZZ	USA
LANGE, CARL	22	M	LABR	RR	ZZZZ	USA
ROZOWSKI, SCHEINE	29	F	SGL	RR	ZZZZ	USA
BALTROSCHANSKI, RACHEL	50	F	WO	RR	ZZZZ	USA
DAN, ZODEK	9	M	CHILD	RR	ZZZZ	USA
BANK, HINC	28	M	WO	RR	ZZZZ	USA
ELIAS	3	M	CHILD	RR	ZZZZ	USA
SIWE	1	M	CHILD	RR	ZZZZ	USA
CHAIE	22	F	SGL	RR	ZZZZ	USA
BALTOSCHANSKI, JANKEL	9	M	CHILD	RR	ZZZZ	USA
BLACZUWICZ, KOMOLD	17	M	CL	RR	ZZZZ	USA
DUDZINSKY, ANTON	23	M	LABR	RR	ZZZZ	USA
BRODZIK, JULIANNE	20	F	SGL	RR	ZZZZ	USA
KOCHNA, ANDERS	41	M	LABR	FN	ZZZZ	USA
PIHLMANN, JOHANN	25	M	LABR	FN	ZZZZ	USA
SILLAMPAA, JACOB	30	M	LABR	FN	ZZZZ	USA
ABY, MATTS	25	M	LABR	FN	ZZZZ	USA
WACKUNIN, HERMAN	24	M	LABR	FN	ZZZZ	USA
LIENAMAA, JOH.	25	M	LABR	FN	ZZZZ	USA
KNUTH, GABRIEL	25	M	LABR	FN	ZZZZ	USA
SVAMA, ANDERS	23	M	LABR	FN	ZZZZ	USA
WIK, JOH.	22	M	LABR	FN	ZZZZ	USA
SIMONSEN, HENRIK	20	M	LABR	FN	ZZZZ	USA
PESOLA, ANDERS	30	M	LABR	FN	ZZZZ	USA
LEWKKO, THOMAS	20	M	LABR	FN	ZZZZ	USA
KONIEVIMEN, MATTS	27	M	LABR	FN	ZZZZ	USA
MAKALA, MATTS	24	M	LABR	FN	ZZZZ	USA
PESOLA, GABRIEL	37	M	LABR	FN	ZZZZ	USA
OJALA, MATTS	39	M	LABR	FN	ZZZZ	USA
PUSKALA, JOH.	20	M	LABR	FN	ZZZZ	USA
PLOKKI, JACOB	20	M	LABR	FN	ZZZZ	USA
WRASTI, ESAIAS	44	M	LABR	FN	ZZZZ	USA

PASSENGER	AGE	SEX	OCCUPATION	PRIV	DES
PLOKKI, JOH.	27	M	LABR	FNZZZZ	USA
MAKALA, HENRIK	30	M	LABR	FNZZZZ	USA
PLOEKKI, JACOB	19	M	LABR	FNZZZZ	USA
KORPELA, GABRIEL	18	M	LABR	FNZZZZ	USA
PESOLA, ANNA	18	F	SGL	FNZZZZ	USA
SEGALOWITSCH, MERE	21	F	WO	RRZZZZ	USA
RICKLE	.09	F	INFANT	RRZZZZ	USA
SCHREIER, BERNHD.	34	M	MUSN	RRZZZZ	USA
KASCH, SARA	26	F	WO	RRZZZZ	USA
JABLONSKI, ANDRAS	21	F	SGL	RRZZZZ	USA
TSCHOCK, JOSEF	35	M	LABR	RRZZZZ	USA
MATUSCHEFSKY, JAN	37	M	LABR	RRZZZZ	USA
BRADZICK, FRANZ	33	M	LABR	RRZZZZ	USA
ROSALIE	22	F	W	RRZZZZ	USA
TREPASKA, WIKENTY	25	M	JNR	RRZZZZ	USA
SKLUT, ISRAEL	37	M	LABR	RRZZZZ	USA
PERSKY, ITZIG-J.	31	M	LABR	RRZZZZ	USA
MELKIK, ABRAHAM	40	M	MLR	RRZZZZ	USA
KAMIENSKA, PELAGIA	24	F	WO	RRZZZZ	USA
MARIANE	.11	F	INFANT	RRZZZZ	USA
VERONIKA	.01	F	INFANT	RRZZZZ	USA
ADLER, JUDES	32	F	WO	RRZZZZ	USA
MARIASCHE	9	F	CHILD	RRZZZZ	USA
MENUSCHE	8	M	CHILD	RRZZZZ	USA
JACOB	7	M	CHILD	RRZZZZ	USA
ARON	6	M	CHILD	RRZZZZ	USA
BERNSTEIN, ROCHE	16	F	SGL	RRZZZZ	USA
WASSIKANISCH, MATHS.	34	M	LABR	RRZZZZ	USA
GEDROVITZ, JOSEF	18	M	LABR	RRZZZZ	USA
SCHWARZ, ITZIG	46	M	SHMK	RRZZZZ	USA
MARTEL	18	M	LABR	RRZZZZ	USA
ROGUSKI, NICOLAUS	25	M	LABR	RRZZZZ	USA
SONPPI, JOH.	22	M	LABR	FNZZZZ	USA
ESSMUND, TEOFIL	30	M	LABR	RRZZZZ	USA
MARIANNE	30	F	W	RRZZZZ	USA
BRONKE	.11	F	INFANT	RRZZZZ	USA
NISSEL, MIHAL	20	M	LABR	FNZZZZ	USA
KULKID, SIMON	20	M	LABR	FNZZZZ	USA
YLINAKTALA, JOH.	42	M	LABR	FNZZZZ	USA
GOLICKY, MOSES	25	M	LABR	RRZZZZ	USA
PESCHE	22	F	W	RRZZZZ	USA
MOELLNER, FEIWEL	27	M	TLR	RRZZZZ	USA

SHIP: OHIO

FROM: LIVERPOOL
TO: NEW YORK
ARRIVED: 04 MARCH 1889

PASSENGER	AGE	SEX	OCCUPATION	PRIV	DES
SALI, KATE	43	F	W	RRACBD	NY
ALLI	16	F	NN	RRACBD	NY
REGI	11	M	CH	RRACBD	NY
MORITZ	9	M	CHILD	RRACBD	NY
BLEICHLEX, MALKE	00	U	UNKNOWN	RRACBD	NY
LIBE	.06	F	INFANT	RRACBD	NY
GOLDBERG, MOSCHE	00	M	TLR	RRACBD	NY
JENVIL	23	M	TLR	RRACBD	NY
ZECHNOWEZKA, RACHEL	25	F	W	RRACBD	NY
GEDALIE	.07	F	INFANT	RRACBD	NY
HIRSCHMAN, JANKEL	20	M	LABR	RRACBD	BAL
CHEESE	20	F	W	RRACBD	BAL
SCHLOME, ABRAMSKY	00	M	LABR	RRACBD	NY
KLINGES, BENJ.	16	M	NN	RRACBD	NY
NECHAME, ANDRESES	23	F	W	RRACBD	NY
ELIE	.08	F	INFANT	RRACBD	NY
STAKES, SE-S	24	M	LABR	RRACBD	NY
RACHMELOWIEZ, DWANE	18	F	SVNT	RRACBD	NY
PAWLOWSKY, LUDWIG	25	M	LABR	RRACBD	NY
LAMPER, ABRAM	28	M	LABR	RRACBD	NY
LAHN, HIRSCH	27	M	LABR	RRACBD	NY
KUCHELSKY, JACOB	35	M	LABR	RRACBD	NY
SCHWARZKOPF, JODERICK	36	M	TLR	RRACBD	BAL
JASAREN, STANISLAW	35	M	LABR	RRACBD	NY
SLALMOSKY, FRANZISEK	25	M	LABR	RRACBD	NY
MABULINSKY, JULIAN	23	M	LABR	RRACBD	NY
LEMINSKY, KALMAN	28	M	TLR	RRACBD	NY
LISTER, MANUEL	27	M	LABR	RRACBD	NY
BLEICH, SARAH	23	F	W	RRACBD	NY

SHIP: NECKAR

FROM: BREMEN
TO: BALTIMORE
ARRIVED: 05 MARCH 1889

PASSENGER	AGE	SEX	OCCUPATION	PRIV	DES
PFEIFFER, FRANZ	16	M	LABR	RRZZZZ	BAL
WILIZKY, MATZEI	20	M	FARMER	RRZZZZ	BAL
KRAJENZKY, HEMRICH	18	M	FARMER	RRZZZZ	BAL
MIDLER, RACHEL	25	F	SVNT	RRZZZZ	BAL
ADASKOW, RACHEL	25	F	W	RRZZZZ	BAL
TAUBE	3	M	CHILD	RRZZZZ	BAL
LAZAROW, LEVIN	22	M	LABR	RRZZZZ	BAL
KIRKAS, DAVID	39	M	LKSH	RRZZZZ	BAL
RUDMANN, JOSEF	35	M	PDLR	RRZZZZ	BAL
JETTE	20	F	W	RRZZZZ	BAL
SCHER, SALOMON	25	M	PDLR	RRZZZZ	BAL
SMILTNAK, JOHANN	27	M	LABR	RRZZZZ	IL
BORISIEWITZ, FRANZ	32	M	LABR	RRZZZZ	PA
BAGINSKY, ANTON	34	M	LABR	RRZZZZ	BAL
IVANKOWSKY, JAN	24	M	LABR	RRZZZZ	BAL
SLUMBARSKI, JAN	28	M	LABR	RRZZZZ	BAL
MALINOWSKY, STANISLAUS	26	M	LABR	RRZZZZ	BAL
ZUSCHKO, NIKIFER	18	M	LABR	RRZZZZ	BAL

SHIP: WYOMING

FROM: LIVERPOOL AND QUEENSTOWN
TO: NEW YORK
ARRIVED: 05 MARCH 1889

PASSENGER	AGE	SEX	OCCUPATION	PRIV	DES
LEWIN, S.	35	M	LABR	RRZZZZ	USA
ABRAMOWITZ, KIRSCH	35	M	LABR	RRZZZZ	USA
CHAIJE	19	F	SP	RRZZZZ	USA
RABINOWITZ, J.	7	F	CHILD	RRZZZZ	USA
BESSICH, P.	30	M	LABR	RRZZZZ	USA
COHN, JENNY	16	F	SP	RRZZZZ	USA
LEWIN, B.	17	F	SP	RRZZZZ	USA
MUCKSTOINSKI, J.	18	M	LABR	RRZZZZ	USA
OPPENHEIM, MOSIS	17	M	LABR	RRZZZZ	USA
KOCH, CHRISTINE	25	F	W	RRZZZZ	USA
HELWIG, GEO	4	M	CHILD	RRZZZZ	USA
SHURMANN, J.	24	M	LABR	RRZZZZ	USA
GEFINA	17	M	LABR	RRZZZZ	USA
NIWKE	25	M	LABR	RRZZZZ	USA
MUESINSKY, R.	39	F	W	RRZZZZ	USA
MORDCHE	15	F	SP	RRZZZZ	USA
ITTE	7	F	CHILD	RRZZZZ	USA
MUERSINSKY, U	6	F	CHILD	RRZZZZ	USA
LEBO	7	M	CHILD	RRZZZZ	USA
STELUS, HINDE	28	F	W	RRZZZZ	USA
HIRSCH	6	M	CHILD	RRZZZZ	USA
ESTER	4	F	CHILD	RRZZZZ	USA
KAHN, RUSSE	20	F	SP	RRZZZZ	USA
LEWIN, LEW	16	F	SP	RRZZZZ	USA

SHIP: FULDA

FROM: BREMEN AND SOUTHAMPTON
TO: NEW YORK
ARRIVED: 05 MARCH 1889

PASSENGER	AGE	SEX	OCCUPATION	PRV VIL DES
WERNER, MOSES	21	M	BKR	RRAHOONY
BIEDERMANN, PISSIE	22	F	UNKNOWN	RRAHQDNY
ZORANSKY, LEIB	38	M	MCHT	RRAHOKNY
SOPHIE	33	F	W	RRAHOKNY
CHAJE	13	F	CH	RRAHOKNY
JACOB	11	F	CH	RRAHOKNY
HIRSCH	7	M	CHILD	RRAHOKNY
SARAH	6	M	CHILD	RRAHOKNY
BERE	3	F	CHILD	RRAHOKNY
REBECCA	.01	F	INFANT	RRAHOKNY
SUWADE, PAULINE	43	F	W	RRZZZZNY
JADKOWSKI, EISICK	29	F	W	RRAHOKNY
SCHMIEL	11	M	CH	RRAHOKNY
SISKIN	10	F	CH	RRAHOKNY
ROCHMEL	18	F	CH	RRAHOKNY
SAKIN, MORITZ	27	M	MCHT	RRAHOKNY
FISCHER, JANI	25	F	UNKNOWN	RRAHOKNY
SCHATZKY, HENE	22	F	UNKNOWN	RRAHOKNY
FEINSTEIN, SEINE	40	F	W	RRAHOKNY
SCHEINE	16	F	CH	RRAHOKNY
SUSSEL	6	F	CHILD	RRAHOKNY
SAPROWITZ, CHASKE	25	F	UNKNOWN	RRAHOKNY
OLDOWITZ, MARCUS	30	M	MCHT	RRAHOKNY
MICHALSON, CHENYE	40	M	LABR	RRAHOKNY
SADJEL, SELIG	30	M	LABR	RRAHOKNY
WEIGL, GOTTLIEB	37	M	LABR	RRAHOKNY
JESKE, MARTIN	30	M	LABR	RRAHOKNY
SIEWERZ, ERNST	25	M	LABR	RRAHOKNY
ZEBJURA, FRANZ	30	M	LABR	RRAHOKNY
MARGUAS, FRANZISCEK	33	F	UNKNOWN	RRAHOKNY
CHANOWITZ, MORITZ	25	M	LABR	RRAHOONY
MATOFSKY, ISRAEL	45	M	LABR	RRAHOONY
SZANI, MAUSCHL	32	M	LABR	RRAHOONY
SOSZENSKY, ANDRY	26	M	LABR	RRZZZZNY
BERCHOW, BENJAMIN	28	M	LABR	RRAHZSNY
EPSTEIN, SIMON	17	M	LABR	RRAHTUNY
ASS, GERSON	33	M	LABR	RRAHTUNY
LICHSTEIN, MEYER	17	M	LABR	RRAHTFNY
LATKEWICZ, WOLF	21	M	LABR	RRAHTFNY
CHAEJE	21	F	W	RRAHTFNY
BIERMANN, ESCHE	19	F	UNKNOWN	RRZZZZNY
JOSEF, DAVID	17	M	MCHT	RRZZZZNY
SCHULLMANN, BARUCH	42	M	MCHT	RRZZZZNY
RAPHE	23	F	W	RRZZZZNY
METTE	17	F	UNKNOWN	RRZZZZNY
ALTE	11	F	CH	RRZZZZNY
SCHMIEL	4	M	CHILD	RRZZZZNY
BUDKUX, ABZANDER	23	M	LABR	RRZZZZNY
RUSANSKY, LEISER	24	M	LABR	RRZZZZNY
SEEPANSKY, ADAM	26	M	LABR	RRZZZZNY
CATHARINA	30	F	W	RRZZZZNY
RABOWSKY, WLADEK	25	M	LABR	RRZZZZNY
ANDA	20	F	W	RRZZZZNY
EISENBERG, GITTEL	24	M	FARMER	RRAHOKNY
PRZAESKI, JOSEF	43	M	LABR	RRZZZZNY
LUSCHINSKI, FRANZ	26	M	LABR	RRZZZZNY
KUNZEWSKI, ANDREAS	31	M	LABR	RRZZZZNY
LESCHINSKI, LEON	24	M	LABR	RRZZZZNY
ZALENSKI, MICHAEL	24	M	LABR	RRZZZZNY
LACH, AUGUST	23	M	BKR	RRZZZZNY
JAWSCHEWSKI, ADAM	36	M	BKR	RRZZZZNY
KOWALSKI, FRANZ	18	M	PNTR	RRZZZZNY
MOELLER, FRIEDR	22	M	BBR	RRZZZZNY
BEIFUSS, CARL	22	M	CPTR	RRZZZZNY
GOSCHEROWSKI, JOH.	23	M	CPTR	RRZZZZNY
BEIFUSS, JOHANN	19	M	CPTR	RRZZZZNY
PITROWSKA, JUSTINA	18	F	UNKNOWN	RRZZZZNY
KRYNICK, VICTORIA	22	F	UNKNOWN	RRZZZZNY

SHIP: ITALY

FROM: LIVERPOOL AND QUEENSTOWN
TO: NEW YORK
ARRIVED: 06 MARCH 1889

PASSENGER	AGE	SEX	OCCUPATION	PRV VIL DES
COHEN, AUGUST	25	M	TLR	RRADBQPHI
SOHLER, MEYER	25	M	TLR	RRADBQPHI
DZEWONIG, S.	18	M	LABR	RRADBQNY
KAPKIN, H.	26	M	LABR	RRADBQNY
RUBECK, ESTHER	12	F	CH	RRADBQNY
RUDA	8	F	CHILD	RRADBQNY
SARA	00	F	INF	RRADBQNY
GERTER, JESEN	52	M	LABR	RRADBQNY
CHANNE	16	M	LABR	RRADBQNY
ALB.	40	F	W	RRADBQNY
SASSET	10	M	CH	RRADBQNY
MAX	7	M	CHILD	RRADBQNY
GREENBERG, SOLOMON	24	M	LABR	RRADBQNY
BLUMM, ANNA	18	F	SP	RRADBQNY
KAPLAN, BIWIE	19	F	SP	RRACBFNY
HOPPIE, RUTHA	20	F	SP	RRACBFNY
PASTON, HINDERK	38	F	W	RRACBFNY
HERMANN	11	M	CH	RRACBFNY
G.	9	M	CHILD	RRACBFNY
HARRUKA	7	M	CHILD	RRACBFNY
DINA	4	F	CHILD	RRACBFNY
LAZAROWITZ, LESSER	51	M	LABR	RRACBFNY
KERSCHEDEWITZ, M.	40	M	LABR	RRACBFNY
MEDOWITZ, DAVID	25	M	LABR	RRACBFNY
WASILKOWSKY, ANDREAS	29	M	LABR	RRACBFNY
BEHRMAN, SCHEEM	18	M	LABR	RRACBFNY
OTTINSTEIN, JURE	27	M	LABR	RRACBFNY
RLETZNER, REWKE	35	F	W	RRACBFNY
GOLDE	13	F	CH	RRACBFNY
JANKEL	9	M	CHILD	RRACBFNY
ROCHEL	7	F	CHILD	RRACBFNY
BERLE	5	M	CHILD	RRACBFNY
ABRAM	2	M	CHILD	RRACBFNY
ARONSTEIN, JOS.	27	M	LABR	RRACBFNY
DEMBY, HIRSCH	44	F	LABR	RRACBFNY
BIDER, MOSES	18	F	LABR	RRACBFNY
KOSHICK, JOHANNA	23	F	W	RRACBFNY
JOHANNA	24	F	W	RRACBFNY
CARL	8	M	CHILD	RRACBFNY
POGGETE, CAROLINE	28	F	SP	RRACBFNY
ROTBELLIE, MOSES	20	M	LABR	RRACBFNY
RAWIANEK, JACOB	20	M	LABR	RRACBFNY
SCHEMITEWITZ, ISSEK	20	M	LABR	RRACBFNY
FAAM, JUDE	28	M	LABR	RRACBFNY
WOOLKERT, ISAAC	21	M	LABR	RRACBFNY
BRENNY	23	F	W	RRACBFNY
SALTENBERG, BERL	45	M	LABR	RRACBFNY
WEISS, BARUCH	38	M	LABR	RRACBFNY
INEBITZ, SILY	22	M	LABR	RRACBFNY
SILVERNAI, MORITZ	27	M	LABR	RRACBFNY
DAWEDESLE, SOLOMON	32	M	LABR	RRACBFNY
IWSERISKY, CHINNE	44	M	LABR	RRACBFNY
MEDEL, JOSSEL	37	M	LABR	RRACBFBO
KOZEUKT, SCHAIM	19	M	LABR	RRACBFNY
MOUCHWIT, JOSEF	26	M	LABR	RRACBFNY
MARIANNA	24	F	W	RRACBFNY
SIKINMOLD, JACOB	22	M	LABR	RRACBFNY
CHITZKIEWITZ, JOHAN	22	M	LABR	RRACBFNY
SZERBA, DIMITRE	47	M	LABR	RRACBFNY
SCHAPENI, LUKAS	25	M	LABR	RRACBFNY
TABIAN, DAVID	35	M	LABR	RRACBFNY
BERTRONIE, KUNEI	31	M	LABR	RRACBFNY
RUMANOWSKY, VICENTI	45	M	LABR	RRACBFNY
NAUWTEGLIE, FRAN.	31	M	LABR	RRACBFNY
HEISCHOWITZ, ARON	23	M	LABR	RRACBFNY
BUENMANY, CARL	18	M	LABR	RRACBFNY
REEBOLT, WALTER	20	M	LABR	RRACBFNY

PASSENGER	AGE	SEX	OCCUPATION	PRV VIL DES

SHIP: ST OF PENNSYLVANIA

FROM: GLASGOW AND LARNE
TO: NEW YORK
ARRIVED: 06 MARCH 1889

PASSENGER	AGE	SEX	OCCUPATION	PRV VIL DES
KATZ, MICHAEL	17	M	SDLR	RRAIDLUSA
RICKEL, LAZARUS	30	M	TLR	RRAIDLUSA
KASDAN, LUSSE	41	M	PDLR	RRAIDLUSA
GELAZELLA, JACOB	17	M	LABR	RRAIDLUSA
LATKEWITZ, ANTON	31	M	LABR	RRAIDLUSA
SCHEIL, WULF	17	M	LABR	RRAIDLUSA
RAGOWIN, JACOB	42	M	LABR	RRAIDLUSA
RUDINSKY, ISRAEL	20	M	LABR	RRAIDLUSA
LUDVINSKY, ADAM	23	M	LABR	RRAIDLUSA
MARIANNE	18	F	SP	RRAIDLUSA
PIEKER, FRUME	22	F	SP	RRAIDLUSA
PERLMANN, KRISCHE	23	F	SP	RRAIDLUSA
FRIEDBERG, CHAJE	18	F	SP	RRAIDLUSA
GOLDBERG, MERE	21	F	SP	RRAIDLUSA
SUKENIK, KREINDEL	18	F	SP	RRAIDLUSA
LEWITZKY, MENDEL	56	M	PDLR	RRAIDLUSA
LINE	8	F	CHILD	RRAIDLUSA
RACHEL	6	F	CHILD	RRAIDLUSA
ELIE	2	F	CHILD	RRAIDLUSA
KABELINSKY, ESTER	48	F	W	RRAIDLUSA
SORE	26	F	SP	RRAIDLUSA
BAER	10	M	CH	RRAIDLUSA
LEIB	5	F	CHILD	RRAIDLUSA
BASCHE	2	F	CHILD	RRAIDLUSA
ANOLK, RIFKE	26	F	W	RRAIDLUSA
MAUSCHE	11	M	CH	RRAIDLUSA

SHIP: SORRENTO

FROM: HAMBURG
TO: NEW YORK
ARRIVED: 06 MARCH 1889

PASSENGER	AGE	SEX	OCCUPATION	PRV VIL DES
UTER, JACOB	26	M	SHMK	RRZZZZNY
MARIE	22	F	WO	RRZZZZNY
ZATEWITZ, GITTEL	20	F	UNKNOWN	RRZZZZNY
WAGNER, LOUISE	34	F	WO	RRZZZZNY
EMIL	7	M	CHILD	RRZZZZNY
ADELINE	6	F	CHILD	RRZZZZNY
THEODORE	4	M	CHILD	RRZZZZNY
AUGUSTE	3	F	CHILD	RRZZZZNY
SICHLIN, ITZIG	50	M	UNKNOWN	RRZZZZNY
PRZYBOROWSKY, JULIANE	22	M	LABR	RRZZZZNY
STANICZAK, ANTON	26	M	LABR	RRZZZZPA
RYCZINSKY, FRANZ	39	M	LABR	RRZZZZNY
NATELEITES, JOSEPH	30	M	LABR	RRZZZZPHI
MUMMES, BARUCH	54	M	TLR	RRZZZZPHI
SIGLIN, SAMUEL	19	M	TLR	RRZZZZPHI
FAIM, CHAIM	30	M	LABR	RRZZZZPHI
BRATLONSKY, ISRAEL	16	M	TLR	RRZZZZPHI
LANGOWSKY, FRANZ	23	M	LABR	RRZZZZPHI
BOGDANOWITZ, STANISLAUS	27	M	LABR	RRZZZZPHI
GRUENBAUM, ITZIG	20	M	TLR	RRZZZZNY
FERCHT, LITMANN	30	M	MCHT	RRZZZZNY
MARIE	30	F	W	RRZZZZNY
BERTHA	4	F	CHILD	RRZZZZNY
NATHAN	.11	M	INFANT	RRZZZZNY
JOSEPH	.01	M	INFANT	RRZZZZNY
SAUERBACH, GITTEL	21	F	SGL	RRZZZZNY
EKLUND, CARL	27	M	TLR	FNZZZZNY
LAGERSTRONE, OSCAR	23	M	TLR	FNZZZZNY
MUHELSEN, CARL	26	M	LABR	FNZZZZNY
BARK, JONAS	27	M	LABR	FNZZZZNY
BYOERKAS, JOH.	24	M	LABR	FNZZZZNY
ERICHHOLM, ERIK	24	M	WCHMKR	FNZZZZNY
ASCHOLM, ANDERS	27	M	LABR	FNZZZZNY
LESSILA, ABRAHAM	25	M	LABR	FNZZZZNY
JOHANNSDOTTER, SUSANNE	24	F	SGL	FNZZZZNY
HOLSO, ESEYAS	20	M	LABR	FNZZZZNY
DUENDER, JOH.	20	M	LABR	FNZZZZNY
STAL, ADRIAN	48	M	LABR	FNZZZZNY
LANG, JOH.	19	M	LABR	FNZZZZNY
DUNDER, ANDERS	26	M	LABR	FNZZZZNY
BYORK, KRISTIAN	40	M	LABR	FNZZZZNY
KELLBERG, ERIK	38	M	LABR	FNZZZZNY
GREF, EMANUEL	36	M	LABR	FNZZZZNY
BATES, EMMA	19	M	LABR	FNZZZZNY
ARIOLA, KARL	19	M	LABR	FNZZZZNY
HOUKALA, ALEXANDER	22	M	LABR	FNZZZZNY
PURNESTAKA, ISMAEL	25	M	LABR	FNZZZZNY
ABRAHAMSON, ABRAHAM	40	M	LABR	FNZZZZNY
OLKKOLA, SEFONIAS	18	M	LABR	FNZZZZNY
PORKOLA, ALEXANDER	18	M	LABR	FNZZZZNY
ASIALA, HERM.	18	M	LABR	FNZZZZNY
PROST, KARL	27	M	LABR	FNZZZZNY
RYSS, JOH.	39	M	LABR	FNZZZZNY
NAGWAN, JOH.	42	M	LABR	FNZZZZNY
GENAS, JOH.	29	M	LABR	FNZZZZNY
SATTI, ULRIKE	19	F	SGL	FNZZZZNY
ANAS, KARL	38	M	LABR	FNZZZZNY
JONAS	33	M	LABR	FNZZZZNY
GOL, JONAS	20	M	LABR	FNZZZZNY
GOMMELGART, JONAS	18	M	LABR	FNZZZZNY
EDELMANN, KIWE	17	M	DLR	RRZZZZNY
SCHAPIRO, FEIGE	19	F	SGL	RRZZZZNY
EDELMANN, GERSON	58	M	MCHT	RRZZZZNY
WIEBENRUT, FRDR.	26	M	LABR	RRZZZZNY
MUNICHIS, ABR.	28	M	LABR	RRZZZZNY
KASCH, ALTE	15	F	SGL	RRZZZZNY
JANKEL	9	M	CHILD	RRZZZZNY
GITTELMANN, HEYMANN	21	M	UNKNOWN	RRZZZZNY
CHANE	21	F	SGL	RRZZZZNY

SHIP: CITY OF BERLIN

FROM: LIVERPOOL AND QUEENSTOWN
TO: NEW YORK
ARRIVED: 08 MARCH 1889

PASSENGER	AGE	SEX	OCCUPATION	PRV VIL DES
RIMGAILA, ANTONY	35	M	LABR	RRACBFIA
ARBOLINSKY, SORE	44	F	W	RRACBFBUF
KAMINSKI, CHANE	40	F	M	RRACBFNY
SARA	10	F	CH	RRACBFNY
FREIDE	9	M	CHILD	RRACBFNY
SCHMERT	6	M	CHILD	RRACBFNY
LIEBE	3	M	CHILD	RRACBFNY
SAMPALINSKI, MANOCHI	22	M	TLR	RRACBFNY
HULDA	23	F	W	RRACBFNY
KACZINSKI, JOSEF	36	M	LABR	RRAFZDNY
WINSKOWA, JULIA	30	F	SVNT	RRAGUZCH
MARKOWSKY, PAWEL	26	M	LABR	RRACBFCH
SELZAK, FRANCISEK	23	M	LABR	RRACBFCH
URIRE, ALEXANDER	26	M	MLDR	RRACBFCH
LUBOWITZ, VINCENTY	30	M	LABR	RRACBFMN
PODNERGA, FRANCISEK	36	M	TLR	RRACBFMN
BULKIN, BASCHE	4	M	CHILD	RRACBFMN
DUOJE	.11	M	INFANT	RRACBFMN
WECHTER, ABRAHAM	40	M	LABR	RRACBFMN
JAFFE, CHONE	29	M	TLR	RRACBFPHI
BRANDS, ABRAM	22	M	SHMK	RRACBFCIN
ECKSTEIN, PETER	16	M	LABR	RRACBFNY
GROSSY, BENDEL	23	M	LABR	RRACBFNY
NASELSON, MUSCHE	19	M	LABR	RRACBFNY

PASSENGER	AGE	SEX	OCCUPATION	PRV	VIL	DES
IDOWISCH, CHAINI	28	M	LABR	RR	ACBF	NY
FRIEDMANN, CHONE	23	M	TLR	RR	ACBF	PHI
SART, ELIE	24	M	SHMK	RR	ACBF	NY
BULKNOVA, CHANE	24	F	W	RR	ACBF	NY

SHIP: LAHN

FROM: BREMEN AND SOUTHAMPTON
TO: NEW YORK
ARRIVED: 08 MARCH 1889

PASSENGER	AGE	SEX	OCCUPATION	PRV	VIL	DES
WISBICKA, KATHA	26	F	NRS	RR	ZZZZ	USA
SAMET, EDUARD	29	M	LABR	RR	ZZZZ	USA
KRZISTUNIS, JUSTIN	26	M	LABR	RR	ZZZZ	USA
BALINSKY, PLOETS	26	M	LABR	RR	ZZZZ	USA
SWUSCHKAWITZ, IGNAZ	26	M	LABR	RR	ZZZZ	USA
REMKUNAS, OSIP	30	M	LABR	RR	ZZZZ	USA
SUNDINKE, BARB.	30	F	UNKNOWN	RR	ZZZZ	USA
BLUZUS, JUSTIN	34	M	LABR	RR	ZZZZ	USA
DACHNIS, ANTON	30	M	LABR	RR	ZZZZ	USA
DIEVIDADIS, LUDWIG	30	M	LABR	RR	ZZZZ	USA
WENIGEL, JOSEF	26	M	LABR	RR	AHZS	USA
RIMKEWITZ, LUDWIG	25	M	LABR	RR	AHZS	USA
KATZEK, NATHAN	32	M	DLR	RR	AHZS	USA
DISSADSKY, DWEIRE	27	M	LABR	RR	AHZS	USA
MEYER	7	M	CHILD	RR	AHZS	USA
CHAJEM	6	M	CHILD	RR	AHZS	USA
BACHRACH, CHANE	25	F	UNKNOWN	RR	AHZS	USA
HENDEL, JACOB	20	M	LABR	RR	AHZS	USA
JARKIEWICZ, FRANZ.	28	F	W	RR	ZZZZ	USA
MARIANNA	7	F	CHILD	RR	ZZZZ	USA
JAN	5	M	CHILD	RR	ZZZZ	USA
WINCENTY	3	M	CHILD	RR	ZZZZ	USA
JAGNISCHKA	.01	F	INFANT	RR	ZZZZ	USA
TRUSCHKOWSKI, WADISL.	25	M	LABR	RR	ZZZZ	USA
SOKOWSKI, STANISLAUS	27	M	LABR	RR	ZZZZ	USA
PIETROWSKI, JERZI	25	M	LABR	RR	ZZZZ	USA
DODA, ADAM	28	M	LABR	RR	ZZZZ	USA
JERMOLOWICZ, MICH.	25	M	LABR	RR	ZZZZ	USA
KAUSCH, FRIEDRICH	34	M	LABR	RR	ZZZZ	USA
MAIK, GERMAN	23	M	LABR	RR	ZZZZ	USA
KELLER, JOSEF	22	M	LABR	RR	ZZZZ	USA
GRUBICWICZ, JAKOB	25	M	LABR	RR	ZZZZ	USA
SALIMKO, ANDREA	22	F	UNKNOWN	RR	AFWJ	USA
KWIATKOWSKI, WLADISL.	22	M	LABR	RR	AFWJ	USA
JUDELOWITZ, SCHMUL	31	M	UNKNOWN	RR	ABIJ	USA
STEGAL, JORAEL	36	M	LABR	RR	ZZZZ	USA
JASKOWSKY, ADAM	32	M	LABR	RR	ZZZZ	USA
GOLDSTEIN, JACOB	45	M	MCHT	RR	ZZZZ	USA
ZUKOWSKI, ANTONI	18	F	UNKNOWN	RR	ZZZZ	USA
BRISZKA, HELENA	53	F	UNKNOWN	RR	ZZZZ	USA
KLEBS, EVA	22	F	UNKNOWN	RR	ZZZZ	USA

SHIP: RUGIA

FROM: HAMBURG AND HAVRE
TO: NEW YORK
ARRIVED: 11 MARCH 1889

PASSENGER	AGE	SEX	OCCUPATION	PRV	VIL	DES
LAFKOWITZ, SCHOLOM	14	M	LABR	RR	ZZZZ	USA
ALKIEWICZ, KASIMIR	24	M	LABR	RR	AHZS	USA
POTSCHUSKI, TEOFIL	19	M	LABR	RR	AHZS	USA
TSCHELADONIS, FRANZ	23	M	LABR	RR	AHZS	USA
MADJEJANIS, MADJE	23	M	LABR	RR	AHZS	USA
BLASNIELICZ, JOSEF	24	M	LABR	RR	AHZS	USA
URBANOWICZ, VINCENT	41	M	LABR	RR	AHZS	USA
CZUSKI, JAN	30	M	LABR	RR	AHZS	USA
NATIES, JACOB	27	M	LABR	RR	AHQD	USA
DENTSCH, MOSES	30	M	LABR	RR	AHQD	USA
MINNA	30	F	W	RR	AHQD	USA
DON, ELJEKUM	40	F	WO	RR	AHQD	USA
FRUME	15	F	CH	RR	ZZZZ	USA
CHANNE	9	F	CHILD	RR	ZZZZ	USA
MALKE	8	F	CHILD	RR	ZZZZ	USA
SILBER, SCHAJE	29	M	FUR	RR	ZZZZ	USA
HERSCHKOWICZ, FEIWEL	40	M	MCHT	RR	ZZZZ	USA
MUYLLYTA, GUSTAV	27	M	UNKNOWN	FN	ZZZZ	USA
KYSZOGRONSKY, ISAAC	59	M	TLR	FN	AHWU	USA
RACHEL	55	F	W	FN	AHWU	USA
JACOB	16	M	CH	FN	AHWU	USA
ABRAHAM	8	M	CHILD	FN	AHWU	USA
MUHELBACH, BERTHA	19	F	SGL	FN	AHXL	USA
EFFINOW, DORA	20	F	SGL	RR	ZZZZ	USA
LOSICSKY, SIME	40	F	WO	RR	AHXL	USA
MOSES	9	M	CHILD	RR	AHXL	USA
JOSSEL	6	M	CHILD	RR	AHXL	USA
GOGOELIN, JACOB	40	M	LABR	RR	ZZZZ	USA
CZERNAKOFSKI, FRANZ	40	M	FARMER	RR	AHUF	USA
ROSZINSKI, JAN	26	M	LABR	RR	AHUF	USA
GRABOWSKI, JULIAN	23	M	LABR	RR	AHUF	USA
CZICHOWSKI, ANTON	23	M	LABR	RR	AHUF	USA
MAKAUZKI, FRANZ	38	M	LABR	RR	AHUF	USA
WUDARSKI, OLEX	20	M	LABR	RR	AHUF	USA
DAMROSI, FRANZ	19	M	LABR	RR	AHUF	USA
LEVIN, RACHEL	44	F	WO	RR	AHTU	USA
JOSEF	9	M	CHILD	RR	AHTU	USA
NATHAN	7	M	CHILD	RR	AHTU	USA
KLAUS, ANNA	27	F	WO	RR	ZZZZ	USA
MALKE	8	F	CHILD	RR	ZZZZ	USA
FREIDE	.11	F	INFANT	RR	ZZZZ	USA
WOLKOWITZKI, SCHEINE	22	F	WO	RR	AHTB	USA
BENZEL	.11	M	INFANT	RR	AHTB	USA
ROSENBAUM, RIFKE	18	F	SGL	RR	AFWJ	USA
HOUDMANN, CHAJE	48	F	WO	RR	ZZZZ	USA
SARA	9	F	CHILD	RR	ZZZZ	USA
FEIGE	8	F	CHILD	RR	ZZZZ	USA
ABR.	5	M	CHILD	RR	ZZZZ	USA
NAHIM	3	M	CHILD	RR	ZZZZ	USA
MOYEROWITZ, JACOB	17	M	LABR	RR	AHUM	USA
SKAWIGOLSKY, CHIWA	24	M	LABR	RR	ZZZZ	USA
HOUDMANN, HERSCH	16	M	LABR	RR	ZZZZ	USA
IDAAC	24	M	LABR	RR	ZZZZ	USA
HANDRIK, KANIEL	25	M	LABR	RR	ZZZZ	USA
KOHN, PINKUS	19	M	LABR	RR	AFWJ	USA
ROSENBAUM, ARON	25	M	LABR	RR	AFWJ	USA
CZEPTE, ANTON	16	M	LABR	RR	AHWM	USA
LIEBMANN, CHANNE	18	M	LABR	RR	ZZZZ	USA
WOISCHNITZKI, JAN	31	M	LABR	RR	AHZS	USA
JELINSKI, JAN	28	M	LABR	RR	AHZS	USA
DOMBROWSKI, MICHAEL	25	M	LABR	RR	AHZS	USA
CZERWINSKI, STEFAN	40	M	LABR	RR	AIGH	USA
JWANOWSKI, JAN	26	M	LABR	RR	AIGH	USA
TOMTA, ANDJE	25	M	LABR	RR	ZZZZ	USA
MAZURKEWICZ, KASIMIR	28	M	LABR	RR	AIKX	USA
GILZEWSKY, PAWEL	27	M	LABR	RR	ZZZZ	USA
ANDROW, ALEXANDER	44	M	SHMK	RR	AHZS	USA
MICHELMANN, JOSEF	20	M	LABR	RR	AIGH	USA
WISCHMOVSKI, JOSEF	20	M	LABR	RR	ZZZZ	USA
BJARONSKI, RACHEL	19	F	SGL	RR	AILX	USA
URBAN, GUSTAV	22	M	LABR	RR	ZZZZ	USA
SCHUELL, ANNA	20	F	SGL	RR	AHZS	USA
TURNEWICZ, PAULINE	22	F	WO	RR	AHZS	USA
LUDWIG	.06	M	INFANT	RR	AHZS	USA
PAWLOWITZ, KATHA.	23	F	SGL	RR	AIDB	USA
NOVAKOVSKI, ANTON	20	M	LABR	RR	AHUF	USA
DARNATZKI, SCHLATTE	23	F	WO	RR	ZZZZ	USA
RAGSVAL, K.H.	27	M	LABR	RR	AIDS	USA
HEIN, ANTON	36	M	LABR	RR	AHXL	USA
ELISABETH	29	F	W	RR	AHXL	USA
FRANZ	8	M	CHILD	RR	AHXL	USA

PASSENGER	AGE	SEX	OCCUPATION	PRV VIL DES
ANNA	4	F	CHILD	RRAHXLUSA
GRAJEWSKA, ANTONIA	17	F	SGL	RRAHYQUSA
GADJEWSKI, PAWEL	45	M	LABR	RRAHZSUSA
KALEIDA, WOYCICH	30	M	LABR	RRAHZSUSA
WISOTZKI, KASIMIR	28	M	LABR	RRAHZSUSA
JABLONSKI, JOSEF	27	M	LABR	RRAHZSUSA
FABERKOWSKI, JESEFA	26	F	WO	RRZZZZUSA
ALFONS	.03	M	INFANT	RRZZZZUSA

SHIP: UMBRIA

FROM: LIVERPOOL AND QUEENSTOWN
TO: NEW YORK
ARRIVED: 11 MARCH 1889

PASSENGER	AGE	SEX	OCCUPATION	PRV VIL DES
ABRAHAMSOHN, ELFANT	18	M	LABR	RRADAXUSA
BENNA, SUSANNA	17	F	SVNT	RRADAXUSA
BJOCKUND, KATHA	18	F	SVNT	RRADAXUSA
SHUCHEL, LEIB	24	M	LABR	RRACBFUSA
CITKOWSKI, JOHAN	24	M	LABR	RRACBFUSA
HIEMEN, NOLE	26	M	LABR	RRACBFUSA
GATKAWSKY, ANTON	25	M	LABR	RRACBFUSA
GUSCHAW, MEIER	32	M	LABR	RRACBFUSA
GOLDSCHMIDT, ARON	27	M	LABR	RRACBFUSA
HELFANT, GEISEN	18	F	SVNT	RRAINMUSA
GOLDE	18	F	SVNT	RRAINMUSA
HENING, JOEL	22	M	LABR	RRAINMUSA
NARAGELSKY, SOLOMON	11	M	CH	RRAINMUSA
ISAKOWSKI, JOSEF	29	M	LABR	RRACBFUSA
JACKOWSKI, JOSEF	25	M	LABR	RRACBFUSA
IGELSKI, CHAIM	22	F	SVNT	RRAHOKUSA
KNIPINSKY, JOSEF	28	M	LABR	RRACBFUSA
KACZELSKY, JANKEL	24	M	LABR	RRACBFUSA
LIENEN, ANNI	46	F	MA	RRZZZZUSA
SENNE	17	F	LABR	RRZZZZUSA
MOSES	10	F	CH	RRZZZZUSA
BEN.	6	M	CHILD	RRZZZZUSA
ISAAC	.09	M	INFANT	RRZZZZUSA
MORISKOW, RACHMIEL	34	M	LABR	RRZZZZUSA
MARIENSTRANZ, JACOB	26	M	LABR	RRZZZZUSA
OLIN, GUSTAV	31	M	LABR	RRZZZZUSA
CAROLINE	30	F	W	RRZZZZUSA
GUSTAV	3	M	CHILD	RRZZZZUSA
CARL	9	F	CHILD	RRZZZZUSA
RITERSEIL, MOSES	24	M	FARMER	RRZZZZUSA
SALLY	23	F	W	RRZZZZUSA
PUSKAN, ANNA	17	F	SVNT	RRZZZZUSA
POERS, MISSEN	33	F	MA	RRZZZZUSA
RISSA, CARAN	25	M	LABR	RRZZZZUSA
CHANNE	54	F	MA	RRZZZZUSA
RISCHUKOW, MALKE	20	F	MA	RRZZZZUSA
FEIGE	2	M	CHILD	RRZZZZUSA
U	9	M	CHILD	RRZZZZUSA
KINKIND, ISRAEL	26	M	LABR	RRAIFLUSA
BEILE	26	F	W	RRAIFLUSA
RABINOWITSCH, LEIB	23	M	LABR	RRAIFLUSA
SAGALOWITZ, BEILE	23	M	LABR	RRACBFUSA
TATA, MICH.	18	M	LABR	RRACBFUSA
ULLISS, ANTON	21	M	LABR	RRACBFUSA
WILLACHOWSKY, LEA	18	F	SVNT	RRAIJOUSA
WATKOWSKI, JOSEF	22	M	LABR	RRAFVGUSA
ILESCHOWSKY, FLORIAN	27	M	LABR	RRAFVGUSA
VINCENT	30	M	LABR	RRAFVGUSA

SHIP: ARIZONA

FROM: LIVERPOOL AND QUEENSTOWN
TO: NEW YORK
ARRIVED: 11 MARCH 1889

PASSENGER	AGE	SEX	OCCUPATION	PRV VIL DES
GOLSMAN, SISCHE	45	F	W	RRZZZZUSA
ESTER	7	F	CHILD	RRZZZZUSA
ITZKOWITZ, CIZE	59	F	W	RRZZZZUSA
LINDENBAUM, LEISER	48	F	W	PLZZZZUSA
KOLBAUSKY, JANKEL	30	M	MCHT	PLZZZZUSA
JEVINSON, ISVINA	20	F	SP	RRZZZZUSA
SURGE, HARWITZ	30	M	GZR	PLZZZZUSA
WINOGRAD, LEIB	50	M	SMH	PLZZZZUSA
HAZIG, SCHEINDEL	40	M	SMH	RRZZZZUSA
MALKA	19	F	SP	RRZZZZUSA
ESTER	7	F	CHILD	RRZZZZUSA
MOTEL	4	F	CHILD	RRZZZZUSA
BUCH, SARA	22	F	SP	RRZZZZUSA
BENJAMIN	11	M	CH	RRZZZZUSA
RATHMUN, MOSES	18	M	MECH	PLZZZZUSA
SOLOMON, ISAAC	45	M	TLR	PLZZZZUSA
MONTEN, UNOK	23	M	GENT	FNZZZZUSA

SHIP: ANCHORIA

FROM: GLASGOW AND MOVILLE
TO: NEW YORK
ARRIVED: 12 MARCH 1889

PASSENGER	AGE	SEX	OCCUPATION	PRV VIL DES
NATANSOHN, ROSA	48	F	W	RRZZZZUSA
AMALIE	19	F	HP	RRZZZZUSA
SARA	16	F	UNKNOWN	RRZZZZUSA
JULIUS	11	M	CH	RRZZZZUSA
DANIEL	9	M	CHILD	RRZZZZUSA
POCH, ISRAEL	44	M	LABR	RRZZZZUSA
SORE	40	F	W	RRZZZZUSA
TEINE	9	M	CHILD	RRZZZZUSA
LEIB	22	F	HP	RRZZZZUSA
RUCKA	20	F	UNKNOWN	RRZZZZUSA
ORMLAND, CHIRCHE	25	F	W	RRZZZZUSA
LEIB	11	M	CH	RRZZZZUSA
JACOB	1	M	CHILD	RRZZZZUSA
HURWITZ, FRUME	30	F	W	RRZZZZUSA
HENNE	1	F	CHILD	RRZZZZUSA
SCHKWIATOWSKA, JANKEL	50	M	TLR	RRZZZZUSA
SORE	45	F	W	RRAHOKUSA
MALETZKEJ, FRUME	43	F	W	RRAHOKUSA
MEER	9	M	CHILD	RRAHOKUSA
GREENBERG, HENNE	11	F	CH	RRAIFGUSA
KRESKOW, GREGOR	27	M	TLR	RRZZZZUSA
PLATCK, ARON	28	M	TLR	RRAFWJUSA
GOLUBCZIK, ABR.	50	M	TLR	RRZZZZUSA
SUCHOWITZKI, SCHMUL	23	M	TLR	RRZZZZUSA
SOLODUCHOW, RUBEN	37	M	TLR	RRAGRTUSA
CHURGIL, JOSSEL	40	M	TLR	RRAGRTUSA
BASCHE	15	F	HP	RRAHTUUSA
GRINBERG, JACONB	19	M	TLR	RRAIGNUSA
TYSZKOWSKY, MEIER	46	M	TLR	RRAIGNUSA
LEW, JUDEL	40	M	TLR	RRZZZZUSA
JEDNAWINSKI, ISAK	24	M	SHMK	RRZZZZUSA
WEPINCKI, WOLF	36	M	SHMK	RRZZZZUSA
MALETZKY, GABRIEL	60	M	LABR	RRZZZZUSA
GRUNKAUS, ISAK	21	M	LABR	RRAHTUUSA
MILNARZYK, WALENT	24	M	LABR	RRZZZZUSA
MARCH-RKA, ANDR.	26	M	LABR	RRZZZZUSA
WUANTA, U	25	F	W	RRZZZZUSA
GSZOMIEZIEL, ED.	30	F	W	RRZZZZUSA
ARATOBSKI, JANKEL	26	F	W	RRZZZZUSA

PASSENGER	AGE	SEX	OCCUPATION	PRV VIL DES
MISGASSKI, STANS	24	F	W	RRZZZZUSA
ASCHKENAZE, MAX	21	F	W	RRAFWJUSA
BALTROMEI, ADOM	22	F	W	RRAIGEUSA
STALB, DOMINIK	22	F	W	RRAIGEUSA
ROZULIS, MICHE.	27	F	W	RRAIGEUSA
KOSEL, ABRAM	34	F	W	RRAGRTUSA
BORNCHOWITZ, DAVID	20	M	JWLR	RRAGRTUSA
POTAS, JACOB	40	M	LABR	RRAIDHUSA
GABER, NOTE	32	M	WCHMKR	RRABQBUSA
HOVANZETZ, BARBALO	18	F	HP	RRABQBUSA
STACHOWITZ, JOSEFA	20	F	HP	RRABQBUSA
NEMETZ, MARIAN	28	F	HP	RRABQBUSA
HOLPER, LIEBE	25	F	NN	RRZZZZUSA
ROCHEL	1	F	CHILD	RRZZZZUSA
MIEZLINSKI, WALENTY	24	M	LABR	RRZZZZUSA
PLONA, ANTONI	23	M	LABR	RRADATUSA
HANDLANGER, BELE	15	F	HP	RRZZZZUSA
FEIGELMAN, SORE	17	F	HP	RRAIKKUSA

SHIP: ELBE

FROM: BREMEN AND SOUTHAMPTON
TO: NEW YORK
ARRIVED: 12 MARCH 1889

PASSENGER	AGE	SEX	OCCUPATION	PRV VIL DES
YANCZEWSKY, JUS.	18	M	LABR	RRZZZZNY
WITKOWSKY, JUL.	18	M	LABR	RRZZZZNY
PETROWITZ, FRANZ	24	M	LABR	RRZZZZNY
JANISZEWSKY, ULYAN	24	M	SVNT	RRZZZZNY
LANDROWSKEY, DAVID	18	M	DLR	RRZZZZNY
WILKOWSKY, THEOPHIL	21	M	SVNT	RRZZZZPA
SEROKA, JOS.	23	M	LABR	RRZZZZPA
ZEGLARSKI, CLEM.	42	M	LABR	RRZZZZNY
STACHERSKI, KAZIMIR	26	M	LABR	RRZZZZNY
BUDZITEK, KONST.	30	M	LABR	RRZZZZNY
BEDNARZIK, FRANZ	26	M	LABR	RRZZZZNY
SZMUGEL, VALENTY	29	M	LABR	RRZZZZNY
PLONA, VALENTY	26	M	LABR	RRZZZZNY
PRUSAZYK, JAN	16	M	LABR	RRZZZZNY
STEIN, PHILIPP	31	M	LABR	RRZZZZIA
SELIG	11	M	LABR	RRZZZZNY
NOSEG, MATH.	37	M	LABR	RRZZZZNY
SWITAJ, JOS.	29	M	LABR	RRZZZZNY
GOGOLY, JAN	30	M	LABR	RRZZZZNY
JANISCHOFSKY, JOS.	24	M	LABR	RRZZZZNY
PELKOWSKY, FRANZ	20	M	LABR	RRZZZZNY
KLEINOWSKY, ANTON	44	M	LABR	RRZZZZNY
BUCZKOWSKY, PAWEL	33	M	LABR	RRZZZZNY
DECZEWSKI, LEON	21	M	LABR	RRZZZZNY
KALINOWSKY, STANISL.	18	M	WCHMKR	RRZZZZNY
DALDRUP, FERD.	30	M	SEMN	RRZZZZNY
JENSEN, LORENZ	27	M	MCHT	RRZZZZNY
KRAITZVOGEL, PERL	30	M	FARMER	RRZZZZNY
SZAFURSKI, WLADISLAW	22	F	SVNT	RRZZZZNY
JATWESKI, MOSES	29	M	SDLR	RRZZZZNY
LEWANDOWSKY, LEON	25	M	LABR	RRZZZZNY
KUNIANOWSKY, JAN	19	M	LABR	RRZZZZNY
ANTON	27	M	LABR	RRZZZZNY

SHIP: PENNLAND

FROM: ANTWERP
TO: NEW YORK
ARRIVED: 14 MARCH 1889

PASSENGER	AGE	SEX	OCCUPATION	PRV VIL DES
SKOVIEZKOCKZYCKI, HERSC	30	M	MCHT	RRZZZZNY

SHIP: KANSAS

FROM: LIVERPOOL
TO: BOSTON
ARRIVED: 14 MARCH 1889

PASSENGER	AGE	SEX	OCCUPATION	PRV VIL DES
BRENNER, CARL	30	M	LABR	RRZZZZBO
LINA	29	F	W	RRZZZZBO
GERBER, M.	55	M	SP	RRZZZZNY
HANCHOW, J.D.	46	M	LABR	RRZZZZNY
WALSKOWSKY, M.	19	M	LABR	RRZZZZBO
STEIN, W.	40	M	LABR	RRZZZZBO
SELZER, HYMAN	54	M	LABR	PLZZZZNY
PORTNOI, ISAAC	25	M	LABR	RRZZZZNY
WEINSCHENKER, B.	32	M	LABR	RRZZZZBO
KOSCHELMK, J.	32	M	LABR	RRZZZZBO
AUDLEK, W.	35	M	LABR	RRZZZZBO
SAMKOWITZ, JOS.	26	M	LABR	RRZZZZBO
KATZ, DD.	28	M	LABR	RRZZZZBO
JUKOFSKI, WOLF	19	M	LABR	RRZZZZBO

SHIP: CALIFORNIA

FROM: HAMBURG
TO: NEW YORK
ARRIVED: 14 MARCH 1889

PASSENGER	AGE	SEX	OCCUPATION	PRV VIL DES
GOLOMBICSKI, VINCENTI	30	M	LABR	RRAHYNUSA
SCHILLER, NECHE	46	F	WO	RRZZZZUSA
RACHEL	16	F	CH	RRZZZZUSA
DWORE	15	F	CH	RRZZZZUSA
SLATE	9	F	CHILD	RRZZZZUSA
FEIGE	8	F	CHILD	RRZZZZUSA
PHILIPOWITZ, LENI	45	F	WO	RRZZZZUSA
JENNI	9	F	CHILD	RRZZZZUSA
BERSANTZKIS, JAVAS	43	M	LABR	RRZZZZUSA
LEON	17	M	LABR	RRZZZZUSA
RADZINSKI, JAN	41	M	LABR	RRZZZZUSA
SZEMISOWA, ELSBETA	20	F	SGL	RRAIIAUSA
MARIANNE	18	F	SGL	RRADIMUSA
ABRAMOWITZ, ZALMEN	23	F	SGL	RRADIMUSA
KOPROWSKI, KATHRA.	49	F	WO	RRZZZZUSA
KATHRA.	17	F	CH	RRZZZZUSA
JOH.	14	M	CH	RRZZZZUSA
JOSEF	9	M	CHILD	RRZZZZUSA
JOSEFA	8	F	CHILD	RRZZZZUSA
OSTROWSKY, ESTHER	24	F	WO	RRZZZZUSA
NECHAMKE	4	F	CHILD	RRZZZZUSA
SCHLOME	2	F	CHILD	RRZZZZUSA
CHIZINSKY, JAN	31	M	LABR	RRAHUTUSA
FABISCHINSKY, MODAZ	25	M	LABR	RRAHUTUSA
SIKST, JACOB	28	M	LABR	RRZZZZUSA
CAROLINE	26	F	W	RRZZZZUSA
CRESELSKY, MICJHAEL	32	M	LABR	RRAHUTUSA
PLUCZINSKY, FRANCISCHEK	32	M	LABR	RRAHUTUSA
JANUSKOWITZ, WLADISLAW	25	M	LABR	RRAHTUUSA

PASSENGER	AGE	SEX	OCCUPATION	PRVL	VIL	DES
SCHURAWSKY, ANTON	33	M	FARMER	RR	AGRT	USA
POLACK, SIMCHE	17	M	PNTR	RR	AHTU	USA
BERCLOWITSCH, CHAIE	23	F	SGL	RR	ZZZZ	USA
OBERMANN, JACOB	18	M	TLR	RR	AION	USA
JACUBOWSKY, ADAM	33	M	LABR	RR	AGRT	USA
MARIE	22	F	W	RR	AGRT	USA
JOH.	22	M	LABR	RR	AIMB	USA
KOSSONEN, AUG.	24	M	TLR	RR	AINS	USA
WALUS, PETER	30	M	TLR	RR	AHQD	USA
KARAJTIS, ANDREAS	25	M	LABR	RR	AHZS	USA
BRAZENSKY, JOSEF	31	M	LABR	RR	ZZZZ	USA
HANSEN, HANS	55	M	FARMER	RR	ZZZZ	USA
MARIE	47	F	W	RR	ZZZZ	USA
ANNA	16	F	CH	RR	ZZZZ	USA
CARL	14	M	CH	RR	ZZZZ	USA
MARTHA	9	F	CHILD	RR	ZZZZ	USA
HANS	8	M	CHILD	RR	ZZZZ	USA
WILHELM	6	M	CHILD	RR	ZZZZ	USA
GROOTHOFF, HERMINE	23	F	SGL	RR	ZZZZ	USA
HANSEN, FRIEDR.	23	M	FARMER	RR	ZZZZ	USA
HARM	18	M	UNKNOWN	RR	ZZZZ	USA
LAND, PAWEL	23	M	BKBNDR	RR	AHTF	USA
ISIDORTSCHI, MICHAEL	24	M	LABR	RR	ACON	USA
MATSCHEWSKI, JOSEF	19	M	LABR	RR	ACON	USA
MAKOWSKI, ANTONIS	21	M	LABR	RR	ACON	USA
PAWNOWSKY, ANTONI	19	M	LABR	RR	ACON	USA
SKIWISCHUDSKI, JOSEF	30	M	LABR	RR	ACON	USA
JANDSCHOFSKA, KATHR.	9	F	CHILD	RR	ZZZZ	USA
MNILBRAT, JULIUS	29	M	JNR	RR	AEAB	USA
GOECKLER, WILHELM	24	M	LABR	RR	AIJJ	USA
BOEHM, ALEXANDER	20	M	LABR	RR	AIJX	USA
SCHAFULIN, MANASCHE	38	M	TLR	RR	ZZZZ	USA

SHIP: CITY OF NEW YORK

FROM: LIVERPOOL AND QUEENSTOWN
TO: NEW YORK
ARRIVED: 14 MARCH 1889

PASSENGER	AGE	SEX	OCCUPATION	PRVL	VIL	DES
BLUMBERG, ABR.	24	M	FARMER	RR	ZZZZ	NY
HALKANEN, H.	25	M	FARMER	RR	ZZZZ	NY
KINMIEAN, BENJ.	39	M	LABR	RR	ZZZZ	NY
KALLIN, JOHN-J.	30	M	LABR	RR	ZZZZ	NY
LAMPERT, HERSCH	48	M	FARMER	RR	ZZZZ	NY
MENDEL	10	M	CH	RR	ZZZZ	NY
PAIVARIULA, JOHAN	26	M	LABR	RR	ZZZZ	NY

SHIP: ROTTERDAM

FROM: ROTTERDAM
TO: NEW YORK
ARRIVED: 15 MARCH 1889

PASSENGER	AGE	SEX	OCCUPATION	PRVL	VIL	DES
KRUSKE, MICH.	25	M	FARMER	RR	ZZZZ	USA
WOJOLNUSKI, MARCILLE	25	M	LABR	RR	ZZZZ	PET
KABCIWICZ, KAT.	17	M	LABR	RR	ZZZZ	PET

SHIP: ALLER

FROM: BREMEN AND SOUTHAMPTON
TO: NEW YORK
ARRIVED: 16 MARCH 1889

PASSENGER	AGE	SEX	OCCUPATION	PRVL	VIL	DES
FRIEDMANN, S.N.	32	M	TT	RR	ZZZZ	USA
STONIEWSKY, M.	34	M	LABR	RR	ZZZZ	USA
BEATRITZ, CHEPES	23	M	LABR	RR	ZZZZ	USA
STRACKS, FISCHEL	27	M	FARMER	RR	ZZZZ	USA
KOSACK, GRYGORY	52	M	FARMER	RR	ZZZZ	USA
JACHINEWITZ, GEORG	28	M	FARMER	RR	ZZZZ	USA
SLOWINSKY, VALENZ	26	M	LABR	RR	ZZZZ	USA
GILLUS, AR.	19	F	NN	RR	ZZZZ	USA
DUMMER, LOUISE	25	F	NN	PL	ZZZZ	USA
SCHMIDT, ROSA	23	F	NN	PL	ZZZZ	USA
PFEIFFER, HELENE	23	F	NN	PL	ZZZZ	USA
SPIES, LINA	24	F	NN	PL	ZZZZ	USA
BECKER, EMMA	24	F	NN	PL	ZZZZ	USA
STUHLMUELLER, ANNA	20	F	NN	PL	ZZZZ	USA
SEMMLER, JOH.	27	M	FARMER	RR	ZZZZ	USA
MARIE	20	F	W	RR	ZZZZ	USA
GUSTAW	.09	M	INFANT	RR	ZZZZ	USA
HERMANN, JANO	28	M	LABR	RR	ZZZZ	USA
MINNA	30	F	W	RR	ZZZZ	USA
MELUSK, BENJAMIN	37	M	MCHT	RR	ZZZZ	USA
SONE	38	F	W	RR	ZZZZ	USA
SALOMON	.09	M	INFANT	RR	ZZZZ	USA
BECHER, HODE	17	M	NN	RR	ZZZZ	USA
SALEMON	10	M	FARMER	RR	ZZZZ	USA
LEIB	7	F	CHILD	RR	ZZZZ	USA
JOSEF	.11	M	INFANT	RR	ZZZZ	USA
BREINE	33	F	UNKNOWN	RR	ZZZZ	USA
SAINKOSKY, JOSEF	25	M	LABR	RR	ZZZZ	USA
ELISABETH	26	F	W	RR	ZZZZ	USA

SHIP: LAKE SUPERIOR

FROM: LIVERPOOL
TO: BOSTON
ARRIVED: 18 MARCH 1889

PASSENGER	AGE	SEX	OCCUPATION	PRVL	VIL	DES
LENTIN, JENNE	45	F	W	RR	ZZZZ	CH
MICHAEL	21	M	TLR	RR	ZZZZ	CH
SALMEN	10	M	CH	RR	ZZZZ	CH
CHAJE	8	M	CHILD	RR	ZZZZ	CH
ROYNEYA, MARIA	19	F	SP	RR	ZZZZ	NY
BECKER, MALKE	23	F	W	RR	ZZZZ	CH
BRAUNSTEIN, MARGE.	27	F	W	RR	ZZZZ	MIL
MARGE.	1	F	CHILD	RR	ZZZZ	MIL
BECKER, FYE	4	M	CHILD	RR	ZZZZ	CH

SHIP: SERVIA

FROM: LIVERPOOL AND QUEENSTOWN
TO: NEW YORK
ARRIVED: 18 MARCH 1889

PASSENGER	AGE	SEX	OCCUPATION	PRVL	VIL	DES
KONITZ, SOLOMON	23	M	MACH	RR	ZZZZ	PA
FRIEDMAN, SAML.	40	M	LABR	RR	ZZZZ	PA
GRINBERG, MOSES	28	M	TBCNST	RR	ZZZZ	NY
CELECKI, BAKER	28	M	BLKSMH	RR	ZZZZ	NY
RABINOWITZ, SAMUEL	38	M	LABR	RR	ZZZZ	NY
SIDERSKY, KINE	20	M	LABR	RR	ZZZZ	PA

PASSENGER	A G E	S E X	OCCUPATION	P R V	V I L	D E S
ROSGIS, MARTIN	45	M	WVR	RR	ZZZZ	NY
BLAUSEKIS, KASIMIR	23	M	LABR	RR	ZZZZ	NY
GATHUTZ, LAURENZ	23	M	LABR	RR	ZZZZ	NY
KRAUZIS, ANTONIO	40	M	LABR	RR	ZZZZ	NY
PETRAS	27	M	LABR	RR	ZZZZ	NY
INDIS, JOSEPH	24	M	LABR	RR	ZZZZ	NY
BINKUS, PAWELS	25	M	LABR	RR	ZZZZ	NY
DWERIONS, STANISLAUS	19	M	MNR	RR	ZZZZ	NY
KAWECKIS, STANISLAUS	30	M	LABR	RR	ZZZZ	NY
BARDAUSKIS, JOSEF	30	M	LABR	RR	ZZZZ	NY
SURSKENDOWITSCH, SAUL	23	M	TBCNST	RR	ZZZZ	NY
SCHONSWITH, CHAIM	43	M	TLR	RR	ZZZZ	NY
SPIEGEL, MOSCHE	28	M	TLR	RR	ZZZZ	NY
ANGAPEL, MUJER	28	M	TLR	RR	ZZZZ	NY
PORTER, JOSEF	41	M	TLR	RR	ZZZZ	NY
LEWIT, OSIP	18	M	TBCNST	RR	ZZZZ	NY
STEMPEL, ISAK	32	M	TLR	RR	ZZZZ	NY
PRZECIALSKY, MORITZ	24	M	TLR	RR	ZZZZ	NY
KAPLAN, ISRAEL	21	M	JWLR	RR	ZZZZ	NY
TOPP, MOSES	36	M	LABR	RR	ZZZZ	PA
ROLNIK, FEIGE	11	F	CH	RR	ZZZZ	PA
KOHAN, ISRAEL	24	M	TLR	RR	ZZZZ	NY
SARA	21	F	W	RR	ZZZZ	NY
STAPONKEZO, CONSTANZO	30	F	W	RR	ZZZZ	NY
STANISLAUS	.11	M	INFANT	RR	ZZZZ	NY
RABINOWITZ, NAUME	18	F	SP	RR	ZZZZ	NY

SHIP: MORAVIA

FROM: HAMBURG AND HAVRE
TO: NEW YORK
ARRIVED: 19 MARCH 1889

PASSENGER	A G E	S E X	OCCUPATION	P R V	V I L	D E S
SCHAN, CHANE	43	F	WO	RR	ZZZZ	PHI
PAPE	20	F	CH	RR	ZZZZ	PHI
SCHOLEM	8	M	CHILD	RR	ZZZZ	PHI
KAZCOKIWICZ, JOSEF	18	M	LABR	RR	AHXL	USA
KLOTZWY, ESTHER	28	F	WO	RR	ZZZZ	PHI
LINCHEN	2	F	CHILD	RR	ZZZZ	PHI
GITTEL	.09	M	INFANT	RR	ZZZZ	PHI
HINKELMANN, MARIE	19	F	SGL	RR	AIDF	CAL
FLOD, JACOB	32	M	LABR	FN	ZZZZ	NY
OWSCHEY, LINE	21	F	SGL	RR	ZZZZ	CH
KUTZNER, ANTON	28	M	LABR	RR	ZZZZ	CH
AMMA	30	F	W	RR	ZZZZ	CH
HUTGRA, MICHAEL	31	M	GDNR	RR	ZZZZ	UNK
KINIOWSKI, VINCENTI	19	M	LABR	RR	AHZS	IA
MARKS, JA-E	16	M	LABR	RR	AIGH	IA
SACHMANN, HANNA	36	F	WO	RR	ZZZZ	IA
DORA	7	F	CHILD	RR	ZZZZ	IA
LINE	5	F	CHILD	RR	ZZZZ	IA
SILBERMANN, ALTE	24	F	SGL	RR	ZZZZ	IA
LACHMANN, MARKUS	.09	M	INFANT	RR	ZZZZ	IA
STERNFELD, JACOB	19	M	LABR	RR	ZZZZ	IA
BARAM, ABRAM	22	M	LABR	RR	ZZZZ	NY
MAWE	21	F	W	RR	ZZZZ	NY
MARIL, ESTHER	21	F	SGL	RR	ZZZZ	NY
SELIG	14	M	LABR	RR	ZZZZ	NY
SELIG	14	M	LABR	RR	ZZZZ	NY
LEVINSOHN, PESSE	27	F	SGL	RR	AHTF	UNK
SOWELON, BERL	22	M	LABR	RR	AIGM	PHI
MELZER, SALOMON	50	F	MCHT	RR	AHVU	NY
BERACH	9	M	CHILD	RR	AHVU	NY
SARAH	22	F	SGL	RR	AHVU	NY
KARTUN, JUDE	17	F	SGL	RR	AHVU	BO
KLATSCHKE, MARIE	20	F	SGL	RR	ZZZZ	PHI
GUTMANN, ESTHER	24	F	WO	RR	AFWJ	NY
RIVKE	5	F	CHILD	RR	AFWJ	NY
SCHLOME	.05	M	INFANT	RR	AFWJ	NY
HURSKI, FREIDE	30	F	WO	RR	AHTU	NY
BASHE	8	F	CHILD	RR	AHTU	NY
BENZIN	54	M	CH	RR	AHTU	NY
DWORE	.06	F	INFANT	RR	AHTU	NY
NEUCZINSKI, VALENTIN	27	M	LABR	RR	ZZZZ	NY
STEINEROSKA, SALOMINE	37	F	SGL	RR	ZZZZ	NY
ANTON	4	M	CHILD	RR	ZZZZ	NY
EMILIE	3	F	CHILD	RR	ZZZZ	NY
REGINA	.11	F	INFANT	RR	ZZZZ	NY
CHAZINOWICZ, ISAACS	35	M	LABR	RR	AIAI	NY
BARTKOWSKI, THOMAS	00	M	LABR	RR	ZZZZ	PA
SCHINBECKER, PINCUS	38	M	LABR	RR	ZZZZ	CAL
ROBINSON, RIWA	30	F	WO	RR	AHTU	CAL
MOSES	8	M	CHILD	RR	AHTU	CAL
ILIA	6	F	CHILD	RR	AHTU	CAL
RACHEL	.08	F	INFANT	RR	AHTU	CAL
STAROSOLIN, CHAIN	36	M	MCHT	RR	ZZZZ	NY
KRUCHSCH, JOSEF	28	M	MSN	RR	ZZZZ	NY
S-ADON, FRIEDRICH	15	M	FARMER	RR	AIBT	WAL
SCHWARTZ, FRIEDRICH	15	M	FARMER	RR	AIBT	WAL
RASMUS, FERDINAND	15	M	FARMER	RR	ZZZZ	WAL
MEISLAHN, WILHELM	14	M	FARMER	RR	ZZZZ	IL
SEYER, NICOLAUS	14	M	FARMER	RR	AIBT	IA
IDEN, FRITZ	14	M	FARMER	RR	AIBT	IA
OSIKI, ADAM	32	M	LABR	RR	ZZZZ	NY
DOROTHEA	23	F	W	RR	ZZZZ	NY
ANASTASIA	.11	F	INFANT	RR	ZZZZ	NY
JOHANN	.11	M	INFANT	RR	ZZZZ	NY
KOEPP, BERTHA	16	F	SGL	RR	AIIW	NY
SCHMIDS, LUDWIG	31	M	FARMER	RR	AIIW	NY
ANNA	27	F	W	RR	AIIW	NY
FRIEDA	3	F	CHILD	RR	AIIW	NY
MARTHA	.11	F	INFANT	RR	AIIW	NY
FEODOROF, AMILIAN	21	M	LABR	RR	ZZZZ	UNK
LEW	22	M	LABR	RR	ZZZZ	UNK
SCHIBOF, RIVEL	22	M	LABR	RR	ZZZZ	UNK
LAWANOW, ANANIAN	31	M	LABR	RR	ZZZZ	UNK
KUNBAS, MATH.	27	M	FARMER	RR	ZZZZ	PHI
TINEBOR, GEORG	28	M	FARMER	RR	ZZZZ	PHI
MEISSAK, ALEXANDER	25	M	FARMER	RR	ZZZZ	NY
PUCKNOWICZ, JOSSEL	20	M	LABR	RR	ZZZZ	NY
RAASI, ANANIAS	21	M	LABR	FN	ZZZZ	NY
MUHRNECK, JOHANN	21	M	LABR	RR	ZZZZ	NY

SHIP: IOWA

FROM: LIVERPOOL
TO: BOSTON
ARRIVED: 19 MARCH 1889

PASSENGER	A G E	S E X	OCCUPATION	P R V	V I L	D E S
BIERMANN, NOAH	21	M	TLR	RR	ZZZZ	EN
NODELL, SIMON	21	M	BLKSMH	RR	ZZZZ	EN
KLEINBERG, JOSEPH	28	M	BKR	RR	ZZZZ	EN
TOLTRELS, MINSTEL	28	M	CUR	PL	ZZZZ	EN
SHERMAN, J.P.	31	M	TLR	PL	ZZZZ	EN
POTWISWANIKE, ITTZY	18	M	TLR	RR	ZZZZ	EN
SCHEER, KISSEVE	35	M	TLR	RR	ZZZZ	EN
ASPRIEL	25	M	TLR	RR	ZZZZ	EN
ALEVANIRTZKY, G.	23	M	TLR	RR	ZZZZ	EN
DARSCHISA, LEIB	20	M	JNR	RR	ZZZZ	EN
WIGER, ABRAHAM	55	M	FARMER	RR	ZZZZ	EN
KUZMENN, MOSES	35	M	TLR	RR	ZZZZ	EN
ROSENSHALL, WOLFE	20	M	BRFHR	RR	ZZZZ	EN
HENRY	18	F	W	RR	ZZZZ	EN

PASSENGER	AGE	SEX	OCCUPATION	PRV	VIL	DES
SHIP: MICHIGAN						
FROM: LIVERPOOL						
TO: BOSTON						
ARRIVED: 20 MARCH 1889						
LASKOWSKI, JAN	31	M	TLR	RR	ZZZZ	USA
COHEN, MAX	29	M	TLR	PL	ZZZZ	USA
SWARTZBURG, CHARLES	36	M	PDLR	PL	ZZZZ	USA
BLUCK, ABRAHAM	42	M	FRMKR	RR	ZZZZ	USA
EWALD, MAX	21	M	TLR	PL	ZZZZ	USA
VIGDOR, WOLFF	20	M	TLR	PL	ZZZZ	USA
KASMARUTES, HAVER	30	M	LABR	RR	ZZZZ	USA
POYETRYKEY, JOSEPH	25	M	UNKNOWN	RR	ZZZZ	USA
GROBOWSKY, LEYER	23	M	LABR	RR	ZZZZ	USA
DANELZIG, MICHEL	28	M	LABR	RR	ZZZZ	USA
ZILIRA, JOSEPH	30	M	TLR	RR	ZZZZ	USA
TEMUSCHOWITZ, SCHMUEL	19	M	TLR	RR	ZZZZ	USA
STAUCKOWSKY, ALEX	24	M	LABR	RR	ZZZZ	USA
KRCZYSETOYKI, JOSEPH	22	M	LABR	RR	ZZZZ	USA
GARAL, ANTON	25	M	LABR	RR	ZZZZ	USA
SLOKENSKI, JOHANNE	26	M	LABR	RR	ZZZZ	USA
ANDRYAWARA, ANTON	27	M	LABR	RR	ZZZZ	USA
RARELLO, IVAN	29	M	LABR	RR	ZZZZ	USA
ROTT, STANISLAUS	28	M	LABR	RR	ZZZZ	USA
LEWIE, JACOB	21	M	BRR	RR	ZZZZ	USA
HERSHMAN, SIMON	22	M	CPTR	PL	ZZZZ	USA
BLEDARSKY, ZIPPE	18	F	SP	PL	ZZZZ	USA
GOLD, GUTZE	20	F	SP	PL	ZZZZ	USA
AUGASHEUWITZ, ELSKE	15	F	UNKNOWN	PL	ZZZZ	USA
SHIP: WERRA						
FROM: BREMEN AND SOUTHAMPTON						
TO: NEW YORK						
ARRIVED: 20 MARCH 1889						
SZLIWINSKIENE, ALZBETA	25	F	UNKNOWN	RR	ZZZZ	USA
JOSEF	.11	M	INFANT	RR	ZZZZ	USA
ZEFF, DEISER	28	M	MCHT	RR	ZZZZ	USA
DEHMANN, MATHIAS	33	M	LABR	RR	ZZZZ	USA
KRANZOHN, MOSES	35	M	MCHT	RR	ZZZZ	USA
GRUNEWITZ, MATHIAS	23	M	MCHT	RR	ZZZZ	USA
DEWIN, LINA	25	F	UNKNOWN	RR	ZZZZ	USA
SCHENDE	3	F	CHILD	RR	ZZZZ	USA
FEIGE	.11	F	INFANT	RR	ZZZZ	USA
SARNOWSKY, JAN	23	M	MCHT	RR	ZZZZ	USA
GORDON, SALOMON	7	M	CHILD	RR	ZZZZ	USA
URANSKY, SCHOLEM	50	M	SHMK	RR	ZZZZ	USA
ALTSCHUELLER, JAKEL	21	M	LABR	RR	ZZZZ	USA
MATUSCHEWITZ, ABRAHAM	22	M	LABR	RR	ZZZZ	USA
EPSTEIN, HINKE	12	M	SCH	RR	ZZZZ	USA
MATUSCHEWITZ, ARON	49	M	LABR	RR	ZZZZ	USA
LEVITER, LEIE	19	M	LABR	RR	ZZZZ	USA
MATUSCHEWITZ, IDEL	19	M	LABR	RR	ZZZZ	USA
KAWCZUSKY, ANTONI	35	M	LABR	RR	ZZZZ	USA
SEBKE, CARL	41	M	LABR	RR	ZZZZ	USA
STIERLE, ANDREAS	39	M	LABR	RR	ZZZZ	USA
RISTAR, JULIAN	30	M	LABR	RR	ZZZZ	USA
GUSOVSKI, DANIEL	26	M	LABR	RR	ZZZZ	USA
DOEDE, JULIUS	35	M	LABR	RR	ZZZZ	USA
MARINSKI, FRIEDRICH	23	M	LABR	RR	ZZZZ	USA
WARNITZ, CHRISTIAN	49	M	LABR	RR	ZZZZ	USA

PASSENGER	AGE	SEX	OCCUPATION	PRV	VIL	DES
SHIP: VEERDAM						
FROM: ROTTERDAM						
TO: NEW YORK						
ARRIVED: 21 MARCH 1889						
JANTOWSKI, J.	34	M	MSN	PL	ZZZZ	USA
FARBER, BRAINE	48	M	SVNT	PL	ZZZZ	USA
CHAWE	18	F	SVNT	PL	ZZZZ	USA
CAICREDNISKY, J.	35	M	MCHT	PL	ZZZZ	USA
SINPANSKY, JOS.	26	M	MCHT	PL	ZZZZ	USA
BOMBLINSKY, KAT.	26	F	SVNT	PL	ZZZZ	USA
PFEIFFER, MARIANA	52	F	WTR	PL	ZZZZ	USA
JAN	16	M	PNTR	PL	ZZZZ	USA
BURZINSKA, MARIANNA	22	F	SVNT	PL	ZZZZ	USA
RITTER, C.	26	M	MCHT	PL	ZZZZ	USA
ROTHSTEIN, ELIAS	26	M	MCHT	PL	ZZZZ	USA
SHIP: STATE OF NEVADA						
FROM: GLASGOW AND LARNE						
TO: NEW YORK						
ARRIVED: 22 MARCH 1889						
CHAIMANEWSKY, FEIWEL	18	M	MCHT	RR	ZZZZ	USA
CHAIWE, MENDEL	19	M	TLR	RR	ZZZZ	USA
GNOTENFELD, JASSEL	11	M	UNKNOWN	PL	ZZZZ	USA
HARPIN, LEIB	11	M	UNKNOWN	RR	ZZZZ	USA
ITZKOWITZ, JAKAH	23	M	MCHT	RR	ZZZZ	USA
LEIE	25	F	W	RR	ZZZZ	USA
SAND	2	M	CHILD	RR	ZZZZ	USA
KUSCHAK, SCHAPSEL	26	M	LABR	RR	ZZZZ	USA
KUSCHINSKI, ABE	24	M	MCHT	RR	ZZZZ	USA
KUSCHAK, SCHAPSEL	26	M	LABR	RR	ZZZZ	USA
KUSCHNIK, MUNSCHE	28	M	TLR	RR	ZZZZ	USA
KOBOLSKY, SCHIMEN	24	M	MCHT	RR	ZZZZ	USA
KABATZNIK, MORDSCHE	11	M	UNKNOWN	RR	ZZZZ	USA
PEVTKEN, H.	26	M	FARMER	RR	ZZZZ	USA
MASCHE	20	F	W	RR	ZZZZ	USA
RAGOVIN, CHANE	18	F	SVNT	RR	ZZZZ	USA
RUDMAN, ARON	24	M	TLR	RR	ZZZZ	USA
SCHWIRZANER, FREIDE	35	F	W	RR	ZZZZ	USA
RIFKE	11	F	CH	RR	ZZZZ	USA
CHAIKE	10	F	CH	RR	ZZZZ	USA
ITKE	9	F	CHILD	RR	ZZZZ	USA
LEKE	7	F	CHILD	RR	ZZZZ	USA
U	7	M	CHILD	RR	ZZZZ	USA
BERKS	6	M	CHILD	RR	ZZZZ	USA
ISAK	1	M	CHILD	RR	ZZZZ	USA
SHIP: ENGLAND						
FROM: LIVERPOOL AND QUEENSTOWN						
TO: NEW YORK						
ARRIVED: 22 MARCH 1889						
KAHN, CHAIE	18	F	SVNT	RR	ZZZZ	NY
SASE	19	M	LABR	RR	ZZZZ	NY
GOLDMANN, ECKUMER	11	M	CH	RR	ZZZZ	NY
KATZINSKY, CHAIE	18	F	SVNT	RR	ZZZZ	NY
ALNJIELOK, ANTON	29	M	LABR	RR	ZZZZ	NY
FRANZISKA	23	F	W	RR	ZZZZ	NY
ANTONIA	.04	F	INFANT	RR	ZZZZ	NY
MARKOS, CHAIE	20	F	SVNT	RR	ZZZZ	NY

PASSENGER	AGE	SEX	OCCUPATION	PRIV	VIL	DES
WOLF	18	M	LABR	RRZZZZ		NY
RAHINOWITZ, ELI	18	M	LABR	RRZZZZ		NY
KASCHEWITZ, SCHEINE	18	F	SVNT	RRZZZZ		NY
LEWIN, KAILE	19	F	SVNT	RRZZZZ		NY
JAFFE, LISA	18	F	SVNT	RRZZZZ		NY
MIKOWITZ, SP.	19	F	SVNT	RRZZZZ		NY
KACZINSKY, KASIMIR	18	M	LABR	RRZZZZ		NY
TRAJSIENEZ, ANTON	33	M	LABR	RRZZZZ		NY
BERKOWITZ, MOSES	24	M	LABR	RRZZZZ		NY
CHAIM	18	M	LABR	RRZZZZ		NY
OLADEER, BERIL	54	M	LABR	RRZZZZ		NY
TYROWITZSKY, ARAM	20	M	LABR	RRZZZZ		NY
ELKSCHER, JOSEF	38	M	LABR	RRZZZZ		NY
VOLKI, BENZION	18	M	LABR	RRZZZZ		NY
LEWIN, SIMON	24	M	LABR	RRZZZZ		NY
ROCHEL	20	M	LABR	RRZZZZ		NY
SAMCLOWITZ, SCHUNE	23	M	LABR	RRZZZZ		NY
BERKOWITSCH, ELE	25	M	LABR	RRZZZZ		NY
CHARET, SUSSMAN	43	M	LABR	RRZZZZ		NY
RUBOK, ABRAHAM	18	M	LABR	RRZZZZ		NY
LEWIN, JANKEL	22	M	LABR	RRZZZZ		NY
WEIZKANKAS, DAVID	28	M	LABR	RRZZZZ		NY
DARGILI, ANTONI	26	M	LABR	RRZZZZ		NY
HUDA--, STEFAN	00	M	LABR	RRZZZZ		NY
RABINOWITZ, ISRAEL	19	M	LABR	RRZZZZ		NY
SCHAFSKOPT, ELIASSON	18	M	LABR	RRZZZZ		NY
PORTING, ABRAHAM	41	M	LABR	RRZZZZ		NY
HEIZOG, SAUL	25	M	LABR	RRZZZZ		NY
LIPPMANN, SAMUEL	18	M	LABR	RRZZZZ		NY
PICKUS, HILLEL	19	M	LABR	RRZZZZ		NY

SHIP: AMERICA

FROM: BREMEN
TO: BALTIMORE
ARRIVED: 22 MARCH 1889

PASSENGER	AGE	SEX	OCCUPATION	PRIV	VIL	DES
-UTMANN, U	33	F	UNKNOWN	RRZZZZ		OH
U	10	F	CH	RRZZZZ		OH
U	4	M	CHILD	RRZZZZ		OH
U	2	F	CHILD	RRZZZZ		OH
MAGER, U	40	M	MCHT	RRZZZZ		OH
HERMANN, U	17	M	MCHT	RRZZZZ		OH
SCHMIDT, JOHANNES	26	M	FARMER	RRZZZZ		OH
WALK, MOSES	19	M	LABR	RRZZZZ		OH
NEIROWITZ, BETTY	18	F	SVNT	RRZZZZ		OH
PLOUSKI, MATHIAS	58	M	LABR	RRZZZZ		OH
MARIANNE	50	F	UNKNOWN	RRZZZZ		OH
JULIA	20	F	UNKNOWN	RRZZZZ		OH
VOREZEWSKI, MACIG	22	M	TLR	RRZZZZ		OH
PRUSAKOWSKY, JOSEF	54	M	FARMER	RRZZZZ		MI
SANDSTROM, JULIUS	29	M	FARMER	RRZZZZ		MI
CAROLINE	44	F	UNKNOWN	RRZZZZ		MI
BOBROWA, PAUL	29	M	LABR	RRZZZZ		MD
LAWENDOWSKI, MARIAN	20	M	LABR	RRZZZZ		MD
GANOSINSKI, JOHANN	18	M	LABR	RRZZZZ		MD
PRUSAKOWSKI, JOHANN	30	M	LABR	RRZZZZ		MD
SZUCHOWSKY, STANISL.	21	M	LABR	RRZZZZ		MD
NIEDBELOKI, JOHANN	19	M	LABR	RRZZZZ		MD
RUITEK, ADALBERT	18	M	LABR	RRZZZZ		MD
ZAWSLISA, KAZIMIR	28	M	LABR	RRZZZZ		MD
DEMBEK, JOHANN	45	M	LABR	RRZZZZ		MD
DYELINSKI, ANDREAS	40	M	LABR	RRZZZZ		MD
RUSCHKOSKI, JOSEF	23	M	LABR	RRZZZZ		MD
PLONZKI, FRANZ	19	M	LABR	RRZZZZ		MD
SCHLAGOSKI, ALEXANDER	28	M	LABR	RRZZZZ		MD
BILVER, AUGUST	29	M	LABR	RRZZZZ		MD
LUDWIG	23	M	LABR	RRZZZZ		MD
WANJNAK, NEPOMUCEN	23	M	LABR	RRZZZZ		MD
STECHNISKI, FRANZIS	30	M	LABR	RRZZZZ		MD
MICHEL	26	M	LABR	RRZZZZ		MD
KANUSKI, JOSEF	25	M	JNR	RRZZZZ		MD
GOLDBERG, ABRAHAM	30	M	ENGR	RRZZZZ		PA
PAULA	31	F	UNKNOWN	RRZZZZ		PA
PESSI	10	F	CH	RRZZZZ		PA
TUBA	5	F	CHILD	RRZZZZ		PA
MORTJE	.10	F	INFANT	RRZZZZ		PA
KARNER, JOSELOWITZ	28	M	LABR	RRZZZZ		MD
LEVY, SEMECH	20	M	LABR	RRZZZZ		MN
SCHWARZMANN, ISRAEL	48	M	LABR	RRZZZZ		MD
SAMUEL	36	M	LABR	RRZZZZ		MD
GNAD, ULRICH	23	M	LABR	RRZZZZ		WI
HOHN, WOLFY	45	M	LABR	RRZZZZ		WI
WEIZER, PETER	24	M	LABR	RRZZZZ		WI
ENGLERT, ANNA	18	F	SVNT	RRZZZZ		PA
RIEGER, ROSINE	22	F	UNKNOWN	RRZZZZ		PA
FURST, LOTTE	19	F	UNKNOWN	RRZZZZ		PA
BOESE, WILHELM	36	M	FARMER	RRZZZZ		NE
SOPHIE	39	F	UNKNOWN	RRZZZZ		NE
MARIE	8	F	CHILD	RRZZZZ		NE
DIEDRICH	4	M	CHILD	RRZZZZ		NE
HEINRICH	3	M	CHILD	RRZZZZ		NE
ANNA	.11	F	INFANT	RRZZZZ		NE
WATNER, FEIGE	25	F	UNKNOWN	RRZZZZ		MD
IDA	2	F	CHILD	RRZZZZ		MD
LEVIN, LOUIS	17	M	LABR	RRZZZZ		MD
TUCKSMANN, CHARLI	48	F	UNKNOWN	RRZZZZ		MD
LOCKE	8	F	CHILD	RRZZZZ		MD
MOSES	5	M	CHILD	RRZZZZ		MD
GNETLEINICK, EATTEL	20	F	UNKNOWN	RRZZZZ		MD
BERMANN, ESTER	23	F	UNKNOWN	RRZZZZ		MD
BENJAMIN	3	M	CHILD	RRZZZZ		MD
FRIDA	.11	F	INFANT	RRZZZZ		MD
LEBERSTEIN, CHAIE	18	F	UNKNOWN	RRZZZZ		MD
STELANASCHUCK, VINCENT	37	M	MCHT	RRZZZZ		OH
BETKOSOSKI, MATHIAS	20	M	JNR	RRZZZZ		OH
SULMANSWITZ, GIDEL	14	F	UNKNOWN	RRZZZZ		OH
OMATUS, MICHAEL	42	M	SMH	RRZZZZ		OH
JULIA	34	F	UNKNOWN	RRZZZZ		OH
PAULINE	6	F	CHILD	RRZZZZ		OH
ADAMS	.03	M	INFANT	RRZZZZ		OH
EVA	.03	F	INFANT	RRZZZZ		OH
SACHS, LEINE	26	F	UNKNOWN	RRZZZZ		MD
KALINOWSKY, JAN	18	M	MCHT	RRZZZZ		MD

SHIP: WISCONSIN

FROM: LIVERPOOL AND QUEENSTOWN
TO: NEW YORK
ARRIVED: 22 MARCH 1889

PASSENGER	AGE	SEX	OCCUPATION	PRIV	VIL	DES
AURUZIN, ABRAM	22	M	LABR	RRZZZZ		USA
BERETICH, ANDREA	22	M	LABR	RRZZZZ		USA
BLATT, BEREL	29	M	LABR	RRZZZZ		USA
REHE, PAULORIUS	23	M	LABR	RRZZZZ		USA
BOCH, LEIB	8	F	CHILD	RRZZZZ		USA
RUBIN, MINA	6	F	CHILD	RRZZZZ		USA
FLINT, CHAIE	40	F	WI	RRZZZZ		USA
RUSEL, CHAIE	40	F	WI	RRZZZZ		USA
JOKARSKI, CHANNE	10	F	CH	RRZZZZ		USA
RESNIK, PAJE	45	F	W	RRZZZZ		USA
TAUBE	10	F	CH	RRZZZZ		USA
BEILE	7	F	CHILD	RRZZZZ		USA
JOSSEL	3	M	CHILD	RRZZZZ		USA
LATZKI, MAURICE	25	M	LABR	RRZZZZ		USA
SOFIE	24	F	W	RRZZZZ		USA
EGMOND	2	M	CHILD	RRZZZZ		USA
ALBERT	2	M	CHILD	RRZZZZ		USA
WOLLOWSKI, MARCIANNA	40	M	TIR	RRZZZZ		USA
MARIA	30	F	W	RRZZZZ		USA

PASSENGER	AGE	SEX	OCCUPATION	PRV VIL DES
AUGUST	17	M	SP	RRZZZZUSA
POLLASCHEK, JAQUES	27	M	MCHT	RRZZZZUSA
JOSEFINE	25	F	W	RRZZZZUSA

SHIP: INDIANA

FROM: ANTWERP
TO: NEW YORK
ARRIVED: 22 MARCH 1889

PASSENGER	AGE	SEX	OCCUPATION	PRV VIL DES
BARTKOWIAK, WOJ.	56	M	LABR	PLZZZZWI
PALOF, GEORGES	29	M	LABR	PLZZZZPA
ZAPP, GYORGY	38	M	FARMER	RRZZZZNY

SHIP: SAALE

FROM: BREMEN AND SOUTHAMPTON
TO: NEW YORK
ARRIVED: 23 MARCH 1889

PASSENGER	AGE	SEX	OCCUPATION	PRV VIL DES
GEZANG, JOSEPH	30	M	SP	RRZZZZUSA
MAGD.	24	F	UNKNOWN	RRZZZZUSA
ABRAMOWICH, MAX	25	M	TLR	RRZZZZUSA
GREDOWICZ, LEISER	33	M	TLR	RRZZZZUSA
KAVOR, JOSEPH	23	M	TLR	RRZZZZUSA
KLACZKOWSKY, MOSES	19	M	TLR	RRZZZZUSA
RAWINSKY, DAVID	39	M	TLR	RRZZZZUSA
DECHAND, MAGD.	2	F	CHILD	RRZZZZUSA
ADAM	.04	M	INFANT	RRZZZZUSA
SCHER, ROTE	34	M	FARMER	RRZZZZUSA
ITTE	29	F	W	RRZZZZUSA
ABRAHAM	9	M	CHILD	RRZZZZUSA
ISAAC	4	M	CHILD	RRZZZZUSA
FREIDE	3	F	CHILD	RRZZZZUSA
ZURALL, CHRIST.	30	M	FARMER	RRZZZZUSA
OSMEHA, JOSEF	32	M	SMH	RRZZZZUSA
SASTER, SIMON	30	M	FARMER	RRZZZZUSA
LANGER, CHAIE	26	M	FARMER	RRZZZZUSA
SIMON	24	M	FARMER	RRZZZZUSA
SUMMOWICH, JOSEPH	22	M	FARMER	RRZZZZUSA
SOFEROWICH, MAX	28	M	FARMER	RRZZZZUSA
RUDAKY, CLEMON	26	M	FARMER	RRZZZZUSA
TUCKOKI, DWORE	48	M	FARMER	RRZZZZUSA
ROSENFELD, CHAJE	27	F	UNKNOWN	RRZZZZUSA
BLUME	4	F	CHILD	RRZZZZUSA

SHIP: CELTIC

FROM: LIVERPOOL AND QUEENSTOWN
TO: NEW YORK
ARRIVED: 23 MARCH 1889

PASSENGER	AGE	SEX	OCCUPATION	PRV VIL DES
OVEYICHOUSKY, IGNAC	31	M	LABR	PLZZZZUSA
DRAGOBLIAH, LAZARUS	31	M	LABR	PLZZZZUSA
REYNFLAUDEN, O.O.	28	M	LABR	PLZZZZUSA
IRUDLUND, A.H.	24	M	LABR	PLZZZZUSA
KARSTEN, J.L.	20	M	LABR	PLZZZZUSA
DOWITZ, HEKL.BAR.	17	F	SP	PLZZZZUSA
METRAL, JURSCHAK	30	M	LABR	PLZZZZUSA
KNOBAL, MEMES	28	F	W	PLZZZZUSA
SUKE	7	F	CHILD	PLZZZZUSA
LIMA	4	F	CHILD	PLZZZZUSA
PEOOI	1	F	CHILD	PLZZZZUSA
KLEIN, HERSCH	32	M	LABR	PLZZZZUSA
KOPF, JETTY	26	F	W	PLZZZZUSA
SAMI	3	F	CHILD	PLZZZZUSA
JULINNA	1	F	CHILD	PLZZZZUSA
SCHWARZ, JENNITTE	17	F	SP	PLZZZZUSA
FISCHER, MARKUS	8	M	CHILD	PLZZZZUSA
MARGATUS, JACOB	34	M	LABR	PLZZZZUSA
SAMOJEA, JOSEPH	28	M	LABR	PLZZZZUSA
LEPSE	31	F	SVNT	PLZZZZUSA
POLAND, HIRSCH	30	M	LABR	PLZZZZUSA
BORSZ, GOLDE	16	M	LABR	PLZZZZUSA
KARKLENSKI, JOSEPH	24	M	LABR	PLZZZZUSA
TINK, MENDEL	17	M	LABR	PLZZZZUSA
KATZ, SENDER	20	M	LABR	PLZZZZUSA
KOLTON, JAN	28	M	LABR	PLZZZZUSA
TOBIASSON, THEODOR	23	M	LABR	PLZZZZUSA
TOLLA	28	F	SVNT	PLZZZZUSA
JESSION, TOMEAS	18	M	LABR	PLZZZZUSA
EILERTSON, EILERT	00	M	LABR	PLZZZZUSA
MORTENSON, NIELS	27	M	LABR	PLZZZZUSA
JANSON, LAURITZ	25	M	LABR	PLZZZZUSA
CHRISTIANSON, MADS	26	M	LABR	PLZZZZUSA
VINDER, HENDINE	28	F	SP	PLZZZZUSA
NIELSON, MARIA	20	F	SP	PLZZZZUSA
TJOSTEN, OLE--	28	M	FARMER	PLZZZZUSA
VALBORG	20	F	W	PLZZZZUSA
LANDE, OHR.N.	21	M	LABR	PLZZZZUSA

SHIP: POLYNESIA

FROM: HAMBURG
TO: NEW YORK
ARRIVED: 25 MARCH 1889

PASSENGER	AGE	SEX	OCCUPATION	PRV VIL DES
HERTZ, MARKUS	16	M	LABR	PLACBFUSA
PETRANIS, THOMAS	27	M	LABR	PLACBFUSA
POCHUTZKY, WLADISLAW	18	M	LABR	PLACBFUSA
HEINRICH, JULIUS	26	M	LABR	PLACBFUSA
GREJANTZKAS, IWAS	32	M	LABR	PLACBFUSA
HEINRICH, CARL	29	M	LABR	PLACBFUSA
KLUTZAK, JOSEPH	33	M	LABR	PLACBFUSA
BEIGELMANN, MARCUS	24	M	LABR	PLACBFUSA
MISSKEWITZ, JURGIS	24	M	LABR	PLACBFUSA
HIATAHLETI, MATTS	22	M	LABR	PLACBFUSA
JARDZIESSKI, PIETRO	23	M	LABR	PLACBFUSA
KOSEALSKA, MAGOCZALA	19	F	SGL	PLACBFUSA
LASKIN, NECHE	15	F	SGL	PLACBFUSA
RIFKE	20	F	SGL	PLACBFUSA
ELISCHOW, ELIE	16	M	LABR	PLACBFUSA
RASRAN, NACHMAN	20	M	LABR	PLACBFUSA
SCHWET, ABRAHAM	30	M	LABR	PLACBFUSA
GRESSMANN, GERSON	58	M	LABR	PLACBFUSA
BEILE	58	F	W	PLACBFUSA
WOLFF	18	M	CH	PLACBFUSA
RUBIN	9	M	CHILD	PLACBFUSA
SZCZEPANIAK, LEOKADIA	20	F	WO	PLACBFUSA
ROSALIA	.11	F	INFANT	PLACBFUSA
GRACIALNY, JAN	26	M	LABR	PLACBFUSA
VICTORIA	23	F	W	PLACBFUSA
WEINER, JOSEF	24	M	TLR	PLACBFUSA
FLISIAK, IGNATZ	26	M	LABR	PLACBFUSA
SCHOENFELD, SCHIMCHON	28	M	TLR	PLACBFUSA
ALTEROWITZ, NECHE	30	F	WO	PLACBFUSA
MORDCHE	.11	M	INFANT	PLACBFUSA
KAHAN, KUSSEL	36	M	MCHT	PLACBFUSA
HERSCHKOWITZ, MIRE	22	F	SGL	PLACBFUSA
WINEMETZKI, JAN	28	M	LABR	PLACBFUSA

PASSENGER	AGE	SEX	OCCUPATION	PRVIL	DES
MOROSSKI, JOSEF	24	M	LABR	PLACBF	USA
KARASCHESSKI, FRIEDR.	28	M	JWLR	PLACBF	USA
KAPAZ, GEORG	38	M	LABR	PLACBF	USA
PSCHIBOROWSKI, JOSEPF	32	M	LABR	PLACBF	USA
OEGLICKG, LEON	28	M	SGL	PLACBF	USA
DARAWCHINSKI, REISEL	18	F	SGL	PLACBF	USA
KLAHN, DAVID	40	M	LABR	PLACBF	USA
BELINSKI, STANISLAUS	37	M	LABR	PLACBF	USA
ROSALSKI, MICHAEL	18	M	LABR	PLACBF	USA
KRAJEWSKI, JAN	40	M	LABR	PLACBF	USA
WADIN, ANNA	21	F	SGL	PLACBF	USA
WIDOWSKY, SCHIE	29	M	LABR	PLACBF	USA
KOENIG, ETZIG	36	M	LABR	PLACBF	USA
KUWENT, LEISER	30	M	LABR	PLACBF	USA
LUKASZEWITZ, KASEMIR	23	M	LABR	PLACBF	USA
STERLING, DINA	35	F	WO	PLACBF	USA
PESCHE	9	F	CHILD	PLACBF	USA
MOTE	8	F	CHILD	PLACBF	USA
KATKEWICZ, FRANZ	28	M	LABR	PLACBF	USA
JABLONSKI, EVA	33	F	SGL	PLACBF	USA
KOLKOWSKY, VICENTI	34	M	LABR	PLACBF	USA
BUKOWSKY, SIMON	28	M	LABR	PLACBF	USA
GABNALANIS, JURAS	14	M	LABR	PLACBF	USA
KALKEWSKY, PETER	9	M	CHILD	PLACBF	USA
DIENERSTEIN, CHALZ	30	M	TLR	PLACBF	USA
WEINBERG, ESTHER	28	F	WO	PLACBF	USA
KASRIEL	4	F	CHILD	PLACBF	USA
WOLFF	3	M	CHILD	PLACBF	USA
SCSSENSKY, FRIEDE	22	F	SGL	PLACBF	USA
HANNE	15	F	SGL	PLACBF	USA
MARCTZNIK, CHAIRE	20	F	SGL	PLACBF	USA
BRUDE, SCHEFFEL	41	M	LABR	PLACBF	USA
ROFFES, CHAIM	40	M	TLR	PLACBF	USA
CISARECK, PETER	18	M	LABR	PLACBF	USA
DRANZEK, FRANZ	26	M	LABR	PLACBF	USA
BUSTRY, JOSEPH	30	M	LABR	PLACBF	USA
KULIS, FRANZ	26	M	LABR	PLACBF	USA
SIPKA, VALENTIN	27	M	LABR	PLACBF	USA
STARKI, ANTON	49	M	LABR	PLACBF	USA
ANTONIA	48	F	WO	PLACBF	USA
FRANZ	9	M	CHILD	PLACBF	USA
SCHOSSINSKY, NESSEN	17	M	TLR	PLACBF	USA
MALECEWITZ, AISEK	27	M	LABR	PLACBF	USA
LENECSINSKY, NECHE	25	F	WO	PLACBF	USA
MICHEL	1	M	CHILD	PLACBF	USA

SHIP: CITY OF CHICAGO

FROM: LIVERPOOL AND QUEENSTOWN
TO: NEW YORK
ARRIVED: 25 MARCH 1889

PASSENGER	AGE	SEX	OCCUPATION	PRVIL	DES
BURKIEWITZ, BALENTY	21	M	LABR	PLACBF	PA
WAEFTASIAK, MOZACH	25	M	LABR	PLACBF	PA
ROGOWITZ, P.	29	M	LABR	PLACBF	PA
HENIG, ANT.	24	M	LABR	PLACBF	PA
MASLOWSKI, P.	16	M	LABR	PLACBF	PA
GOTOSIESKI, MICHAEL	24	M	LABR	PLACBF	PA
GABER, IRZEG	40	M	LABR	PLACBF	PA
ABRAMOWSKY, MOSCHE	31	M	LABR	PLACBF	PA
SZETSCHAN, MARKUS	21	M	LABR	PLACBF	PA
POSAESBOWITZ, ANDR.	24	M	LABR	PLACBF	PA
KAWALKER, B.	30	M	LABR	PLACBF	PA
GALOMH, HAN	24	M	LABR	PLACBF	PA
WULTZ, FRED	24	M	LABR	PLACBF	PA
PAWLOWSKI, U	30	M	LABR	PLACBF	PA
GAZAMSKI, L.	26	M	LABR	PLACBF	PA
BUBA, JOSEF	25	M	LABR	PLACBF	PA
RODELSKI, JOSEPF	40	M	LABR	PLACBF	PA
KAGAT, S.	41	M	LABR	PLACBF	PA
KACNAAIK, ANDR.	19	M	LABR	PLACBF	PA
HEGEDUS, GEO.	35	M	LABR	PLACBF	PA
LECKASCH, MEYER	21	M	LABR	PLACBF	PA
KENELSKY, SCHEMIL	21	M	LABR	PLACBF	PA
WAGTASIAK, A.	22	F	SP	PLACBF	PA
MIKOLENZAK, CATH.	23	F	SP	PLACBF	PA
ZEDLAK, AGATHA	24	F	SP	PLACBF	PA
MAGOR, EVA	22	F	SP	PLACBF	PA
WYGONIK, VALERIA	24	F	SP	PLACBF	PA
SZREKAN, ZOPEA	30	F	SP	PLACBF	PA
KNEIZKA, AGANTHA	24	F	SP	PLACBF	PA
BARAN, JOSEFA	23	F	SP	PLACBF	PA
KRUK, SALEN	26	M	BKR	PLACBF	PA
SARA	22	F	W	PLACBF	PA
BELAI, MOSES	28	M	LABR	PLACBF	PA
FREIDA	24	F	W	PLACBF	PA
PETRUS, FRED	36	M	LABR	PLACBF	PA
CAROL.	28	F	W	PLACBF	PA
H.	5	M	CHILD	PLACBF	PA
GUSKOWSKI, W.	21	F	W	PLACBF	PA
M.	2	F	CHILD	PLACBF	PA
WLADZSLA.	00	F	INF	PLACBF	PA
FRANC.	00	F	INF	PLACBF	PA
DROZEWSKA, ANN	25	F	SP	PLACBF	PA

SHIP: BOHEMIA

FROM: HAMBURG AND HAVRE
TO: NEW YORK
ARRIVED: 26 MARCH 1889

PASSENGER	AGE	SEX	OCCUPATION	PRVIL	DES
SARTONWICZ, ELZBITA	25	F	W	RRZZZZ	USA
ANNA	.10	F	INFANT	RRZZZZ	USA
SOKOTOWSKIENA, JANOWI	18	M	LABR	RRAHZS	USA
PAWILONIS, LEON	28	M	LABR	RRZZZZ	USA
ANNA	20	F	W	RRZZZZ	USA
GUDIK, ANTONIA	20	F	SGL	RRZZZZ	USA
LEWIN, JACOB	17	M	GZR	RRAHZD	USA
HURWITZ, JUDES	20	F	SGL	RRAIGH	USA
KONIECHOWSKY, SARA	40	F	WO	RRZZZZ	USA
MOSES	9	M	CHILD	RRZZZZ	USA
RUWEN	6	M	CHILD	RRZZZZ	USA
REBECCA	15	F	SGL	RRZZZZ	USA
BAIKOWSKY, FEIGE	15	F	SGL	RRAHRZ	USA
MOSES	8	M	CHILD	RRAHRZ	USA
MECHABER, MIRIAM	40	F	WO	RRAHRZ	USA
SARA	18	F	CH	RRAHRZ	USA
LEIZER	7	F	CHILD	RRAHRZ	USA
CHANNE	5	F	CHILD	RRAHRZ	USA
REIZEL	32	F	WO	RRAHRZ	USA
SARA	7	F	CHILD	RRAHRZ	USA
CHAIM	5	M	CHILD	RRAHRZ	USA
GIWERSKI, MEIER	47	M	LABR	RRAIEX	USA
FURMANSKI, LEIB	40	M	UNKNOWN	RRZZZZ	USA
PAUBE	18	F	W	RRZZZZ	USA
HERZIG, LEISER	40	M	LABR	RRZZZZ	USA
KATZ, MENASSE	23	M	UPHST	RRAHTU	USA
LEWIN, ISKEL	17	M	CNF	RRZZZZ	USA
RABBER, ESTHER	20	F	SGL	RRZZZZ	USA
ELTERMANN, HANNE	30	F	WO	RRAGRT	USA
BEHR	9	M	CHILD	RRAGRT	USA
DOBE	8	M	CHILD	RRAGRT	USA
EIDEL	5	F	CHILD	RRAGRT	USA
ISSER	.11	F	INFANT	RRAGRT	USA
COHN, CHANNE	28	F	WO	RRZZZZ	USA
CHAIE	5	F	CHILD	RRZZZZ	USA
ABRAHAM	3	M	CHILD	RRZZZZ	USA
GITEL	28	F	WO	RRZZZZ	USA
ABRAHAM	5	M	CHILD	RRZZZZ	UNK
LEWIN, KADISZ	9	M	CHILD	RRAIGH	USA

PASSENGER	AGE	SEX	OCCUPATION	PRV VIL DES
FREID, ABEL	17	M	TLR	RRAHRZUSA
KOLNICZANSKI, ABRAHAM	28	M	BKR	RRAHRZUSA
BECKER, BEILE	37	F	WO	RRAHRZUSA
SCHEBSEL	.11	M	INFANT	RRAHRZUSA
DANEMARK, ABRAHAM	22	M	TLR	RRAHRZUSA
BERCZAK, PERIL	39	F	WO	RRZZZZUSA
PAUBE	19	F	CH	RRZZZZUSA
JOSEF	17	M	CH	RRZZZZUSA
ZISLE	9	F	CHILD	RRZZZZUSA
PINENCZ	8	M	CHILD	RRZZZZUSA
DOBRISCH	7	M	CHILD	RRZZZZUSA
ABRAM	6	M	CHILD	RRZZZZUSA
WIEDOW, FRIEDRICH	36	M	FARMER	RRZZZZUSA
MARIE	36	F	W	RRZZZZUSA
OTTO	7	M	CHILD	RRZZZZUSA
MARTHA	6	F	CHILD	RRZZZZUSA
ERNST	4	M	CHILD	RRZZZZUSA
ROBERT	3	M	CHILD	RRZZZZUSA
ANNA	.11	F	INFANT	RRZZZZUSA
LASARNIK, MORITZ	36	M	LABR	RRAFWJUSA
KORNBLUM, PERL	40	F	WO	RRAFWJUSA
WOLF	7	M	CHILD	RRAFWJUSA
ETHE	9	F	CHILD	RRAFWJUSA
FREEDMANN, CHAVE	59	F	WO	RRAHZUUSA
KUBINSKI, FRANZ	37	M	LABR	RRAHUFUSA
NIESCHK, MARTIN	52	M	LABR	RRAHUFUSA
ZIEMANSKI, JEAN	23	M	LABR	RRAHUFUSA
OLANDER, PETER	20	M	LABR	RRAHUFUSA
BRUDNO, ESTER	17	F	SGL	RRAHVQUSA
GROEVSKI, JACOB	9	M	CHILD	RRAHVQUSA
MICHELMANN, SARA	26	F	SGL	RRZZZZUSA
GOLDBERG, MALKE	20	F	SGL	RRAHUVUSA
SEGELBAUM, RACHEL	20	F	SGL	RRZZZZUSA
BOTNIK, FEIGE	19	F	SGL	RRAIGHUSA
LUDKIEWICZ, MARIANNE	30	F	WO	RRAHXLUSA
MAGDAL.	4	F	CHILD	RRAHXLUSA
MARIANNE	3	F	CHILD	RRAHXLUSA
SCHABALINSKI, JOSEF	20	M	LABR	RRAHTUUSA
ELINSKI, ABRAHAM	21	M	LABR	RRAGRTUSA
WIRZBA, HIRSCH	47	M	LABR	RRAHWEUSA
MEYER	20	M	LABR	RRAHWEUSA
ZESIN, JOSEF	38	M	LABR	RRAGRTUSA
LOEB.	9	M	CHILD	RRAGRTUSA
WIRTH, HIRSCH	44	M	FARMER	RRAILHUSA
GANZHORN, GEORG	36	M	FARMER	RRAILHUSA
KISZCLEWSKY, PETER	45	M	LABR	RRAHUIUSA
MALKOWITZ, FRANZ	28	M	LABR	RRAHUIUSA
MICHELMANN, JANKEL	45	M	LABR	RRZZZZUSA
ALTER	18	M	LABR	RRZZZZUSA
PELTENOWITSCH, JACOB	20	M	TNR	RRAHTOUSA
ZCHNER, ROCHE	40	F	WO	RRAGRTUSA
GITTEL	15	M	CH	RRAGRTUSA
CHAIM	9	M	CHILD	RRAGRTUSA
JETTKE	8	M	CHILD	RRAGRTUSA
MORDCHE	7	M	CHILD	RRAGRTUSA
ESTHER	5	F	CHILD	RRAGRTUSA
RIEFKE	3	F	CHILD	RRAGRTUSA
LOEBEL	.11	M	INFANT	RRAGRTUSA
BRODSTEIN, ABRAM	22	M	LABR	RRZZZZUSA
KORNBLUM, ESTHER	.11	F	INFANT	RRAFWJUSA
DITKOWSKI, DISMON	22	M	LABR	RRAGRTUSA
MATUJESKI, FRANZ	22	M	LABR	RRACONUSA
PAUL	25	M	LABR	RRACONUSA
GUGAS, STANISLAUS	19	M	LABR	RRACONUSA
NOWACK, MICHAEL	25	M	LABR	RRACONUSA
KRULL, MAIZIC	24	M	LABR	RRACONUSA
KOSOWSKY, FRANZ	33	M	LABR	RRACONUSA
ANUSZEWSKI, FRANZ	31	M	LABR	RRAHUFUSA
NADULSKI, JOSEF	44	M	LABR	RRAHUFUSA
BLASZAK, ANTON	35	M	LABR	RRAHUFUSA
BUDKA, JOSEF	28	M	LABR	RRAHUFUSA
JOSEF	27	M	LABR	RRAHUFUSA
LEMPNITZKI, ALEX	24	M	LABR	RRAHTOUSA
KUBZAK, VALT.	31	M	LABR	RRAHUFUSA
KALUSCHEWSKI, PAWEL	29	M	LABR	RRAHTOUSA
GRABOWSKI, JAN	26	M	LABR	RRAHUFUSA
BROSEWSKI, STEFAN	38	M	LABR	RRAHUFUSA
KOBSCHINSKI, WLADISL.	31	M	LABR	RRAHTOUSA
KAMEKOWITZ, ELIAS	27	M	LABR	RRAHTUUSA
POLAZCK, SAMUEL	20	M	LABR	RRAGRTUSA
LACKZINSKI, TOBIAS	19	M	LABR	RRAIGHUSA
ROCHE	19	F	W	RRAIGHUSA
PIWILATIS, JACOB	37	M	LABR	RRZZZZUSA
JAKIMOWITZ, MIKES	24	M	LABR	RRZZZZUSA
KOBULUTO, ANNUS	20	M	LABR	RRAHXLUSA
PUDINAT, MATEJUS	55	M	LABR	RRZZZZUSA
ASCHATZKI, MARIAN	20	M	LABR	RRAHTOUSA
GAWRISCH, WOYCUCH	30	M	LABR	RRAHTOUSA
KRISTKOWITZ, ERNST	25	M	LABR	RRAHTOUSA
GAWRISCH, VALENTIN	42	M	LABR	RRAHTOUSA
WELS, ANDZE	36	M	LABR	RRAHTOUSA
PROMTNITZKI, FRANZ	19	M	LABR	RRAHUFUSA
SADOWSKI, LUCAS	37	M	LABR	RRAHUFUSA
ZUMERATZKI, JAN	25	M	LABR	RRAHUFUSA
KILLA, JRANZ	35	M	LABR	RRAHUFUSA
SZCSKIEWICZ, JRANZ	19	M	LABR	RRAHUFUSA
ZIRTKOWSKI, ALEXI	42	M	LABR	RRAHUFUSA
ROHOWITSCH, COURT	30	M	LABR	RRAHUFUSA
KOJAWSKI, JOSEF	20	M	LABR	RRAHUFUSA
SZESKIEWICZ, ANTON	25	M	LABR	RRAHUFUSA
JASTRZIMSKI, FRANZ	38	M	LABR	RRAHUFUSA
CIZELSKI, ADAM	22	M	LABR	RRAHUFUSA
BUDKA, NICOLAI	30	M	LABR	RRAHUFUSA
JAN	19	M	LABR	RRAHUFUSA
MARKEWICZ, ANTON	27	M	LABR	RRAHUFUSA
DETTNER, ANTON	28	M	LABR	RRAHUFUSA
RUTKOWSKI, IGNATZ	25	M	LABR	RRAHUFUSA
KLINNEK, MADJE	30	M	LABR	RRAHUFUSA
IGNATOWSKI, ADAM	24	M	LABR	RRAHTOUSA
KORNBLUM, ABR.	28	M	LABR	RRAFWJUSA
RIWKE	20	F	W	RRAFWJUSA
MALKE	16	F	SGL	RRAFWJUSA
FREIDEL	4	F	CHILD	RRAFWJUSA
ISAAC	.09	M	INFANT	RRAFWJUSA
KRANTZ, SALOMEA	30	F	WO	RRAFWJUSA
WAKMERZ, KEILE	56	F	WO	RRAFWJUSA
STROHSCHIN, JOSEF	39	M	TCHR	RRAHOOUSA
EUGENIA	33	F	W	RRAHOOUSA
ADRIAN	4	M	CHILD	RRAHOOUSA
PAMULEWITZ, PARSCHNITZ	27	M	LABR	RRAHZSUSA
MAKOWITZ, WAWRINETZ	39	M	LABR	RRAHZSUSA
ORGELSKY, JOSEF	36	M	LABR	RRAHZSUSA
WINKELMANN, ISAAK	46	M	LABR	RRAHZSUSA
BRENNER, AISIK	22	M	LABR	RRAHZSUSA
GORTSCHINSKI, JAN	29	M	LABR	RRACONUSA
KRISTEUF, JACOB	35	M	LABR	RRZZZZUSA
KONISCHOSKA, REBECCA	15	F	SGL	RRZZZZUSA
WINOGRAD, ZABIEL	37	M	LABR	RRAHTOUSA

SHIP: EMS

FROM: BREMEN AND SOUTHAMPTON
TO: NEW YORK
ARRIVED: 26 MARCH 1889

PASSENGER	AGE	SEX	OCCUPATION	PRV VIL DES
WAJTANOWSKA, ALEXANDRA	24	F	UNKNOWN	RRZZZZUSA
CATHA.	30	F	UNKNOWN	RRZZZZUSA
CIESIELSKI, ANDR.	24	M	LABR	RRZZZZUSA
WITMKI, WILH.	26	M	LABR	RRZZZZUSA
FIZNO, BERTHA	30	F	SVNT	RRZZZZUSA
MICH.	.01	M	INFANT	RRZZZZUSA
FIZUR, THERESA	.01	F	INFANT	RRZZZZUSA
VOGT, WLADISLAUS	30	M	LABR	RRZZZZUSA
JAGUEZINSKI, FRANZ	15	M	LABR	RRZZZZUSA
KLAPECKI, AGNES	60	F	LABR	RRZZZZUSA

PASSENGER	AGE	SEX	OCCUPATION	PRV	VIL	DES
FRANZ	12	M	LABR	RR	ZZZZ	USA
SOPHIE	6	F	CHILD	RR	ZZZZ	USA
JAGODZINSKI, HAVER	32	M	LABR	RR	ZZZZ	USA
U, ANNA	18	F	SMSTS	RR	ZZZZ	USA
STRCHOWSKI, FRIEDR.	49	M	LABR	RR	ZZZZ	USA
OMICKINSKI, AGNES	27	F	SMSTS	RR	ZZZZ	USA
WEIROWSKY, ANNA	20	F	SMSTS	RR	ZZZZ	USA
BUSCHEK, ANNA	57	F	SMSTS	RR	ZZZZ	USA
BUDSCHEK, JOHANN	24	M	LABR	RR	ZZZZ	USA
THEODOR	12	M	LABR	RR	ZZZZ	USA
RANTALA, NICODEMUS	33	M	LABR	FN	ZZZZ	USA
ANDRAS	25	M	LABR	FN	ZZZZ	USA
KIERZESCHEWSKI, THOMAS	25	M	LABR	RR	ZZZZ	USA
STANISL.	23	M	LABR	RR	ZZZZ	USA
SAKOBOCHAK, MICH.	26	M	LABR	RR	ZZZZ	USA
KRASNITZKI, LEO	38	M	LABR	RR	ZZZZ	USA
MARIE	22	F	W	RR	ZZZZ	USA
STROMSKI, FRANZ	22	M	LABR	RR	ZZZZ	USA
U, SELI	22	M	LABR	RR	ZZZZ	USA
KANETZKI, JOS.	28	M	FARMER	RR	ZZZZ	USA
REITKOFSKA, VICTORIA	25	F	SMSTS	RR	ZZZZ	USA
RATTNER, CHAIM	27	M	LABR	RR	ZZZZ	USA
WOLFFSOHN, WOLF	17	M	LABR	RR	ZZZZ	USA
LISCHKOWSKY, FINICK	27	M	SHMK	RR	ZZZZ	USA
RATTNER, JOSEL	18	M	LABR	RR	ZZZZ	USA
LANDZEWITZ, SIMON	40	M	FARMER	RR	ZZZZ	USA
PODIMEITIS, ADAM	30	M	FARMER	RR	ZZZZ	USA
LABOSCHANSKY, SIMON	41	M	FARMER	RR	ZZZZ	USA
SUL, ISRAEL	19	M	DLR	RR	ZZZZ	USA
RIFKA	21	F	W	RR	ZZZZ	USA
SREJON, FREIWUSCH	18	M	LABR	RR	ZZZZ	USA
WOZNIAK, JALENTY	32	M	LABR	RR	ZZZZ	USA
SIEMIZEWSKY, LEON	25	M	SHMK	RR	ZZZZ	USA
SEUZIMSKI, PAVEL	24	M	FARMER	RR	ZZZZ	USA
KALENZ, MARZIN	23	M	FARMER	RR	ZZZZ	USA
SZIDROWITZ, JOSEF	24	M	FARMER	RR	ZZZZ	USA
BOSZKIEWICZ, JAN	27	M	FARMER	RR	ZZZZ	USA
GOLOZEWSKY, PAVEL	21	M	FARMER	RR	ZZZZ	USA
ROGOWSKY, JAN	30	M	FARMER	RR	ZZZZ	USA
MICKILSKY, U	40	M	FARMER	RR	ZZZZ	USA
SCHARSKA, JAN	27	M	SMH	RR	ZZZZ	USA
SABOLEWSKY, PETER	27	M	SMH	RR	ZZZZ	USA
JABLOWSKI, FRANZ	37	M	SMH	RR	ZZZZ	USA
KUBRACZ, JAN	22	M	SMH	RR	ZZZZ	USA
KOKOSCHKA, FRANZ	26	M	SMH	RR	ZZZZ	USA
BAREWSKI, PETER	36	M	SMH	RR	ZZZZ	USA
CHRIST, JOS.	22	M	SMH	RR	ZZZZ	USA
JAROWSKI, MARTIN	27	M	SMH	RR	ZZZZ	USA
ANNA	23	F	W	RR	ZZZZ	USA
GEARS, MAISEY	22	M	LABR	RR	ZZZZ	USA
BASCHE	14	F	SMSTS	RR	ZZZZ	USA
RIFKE	11	F	CH	RR	ZZZZ	USA
ORZOL, SALOMON	22	F	CH	RR	ZZZZ	USA
PACKUNAS, MARIANNA	20	F	SMSTS	RR	ZZZZ	USA
POKULINE, TINDON	30	M	LABR	RR	ZZZZ	USA
DYLTKANCKICKO, ARONI	63	F	UNKNOWN	RR	ZZZZ	USA
MEGGI	20	F	SVNT	RR	ZZZZ	USA
MATHIAS	.10	M	INFANT	RR	ZZZZ	USA
PRAWAZICK, FRANZISAK	31	M	LABR	RR	ZZZZ	USA
GRANACKI, STANISL.	28	M	LABR	RR	ZZZZ	USA
ZIEMBA, ALEXANDER	19	M	LABR	RR	ZZZZ	USA
BROZNOWSKI, THOM.	19	M	LABR	RR	ZZZZ	USA
KARP, ANTONI	24	M	LABR	RR	ZZZZ	USA
RYSZKIEWICZ, KAZIMIRZ	18	M	LABR	RR	ZZZZ	USA
MANEZNIK, FRANZ	24	M	LABR	RR	ZZZZ	USA
JEROCZ, TEOFIL	36	M	LABR	RR	ZZZZ	USA
GRAJEWSKI, ALEX	26	M	LABR	RR	ZZZZ	USA
KOSCHEWITZ, SALOMON	48	M	LABR	RR	ZZZZ	USA
GLUECKMANN, SCHOLEM	48	M	LABR	RR	ZZZZ	USA

SHIP: DEVONIA

FROM: GLASGOW
TO: NEW YORK
ARRIVED: 26 MARCH 1889

PASSENGER	AGE	SEX	OCCUPATION	PRV	VIL	DES
EHRLICH, MINDEL	23	F	UNKNOWN	RR	ZZZZ	USA
MARK	18	F	UNKNOWN	RR	ZZZZ	USA
CAYE	3	F	CHILD	RR	ZZZZ	USA
IRIBE	.10	F	INFANT	RR	ZZZZ	USA
GLASER, BORE	36	M	LABR	RR	ZZZZ	USA
GRUNBERG, SLATI	24	F	UNKNOWN	RR	ZZZZ	USA
SCHIM	4	M	CHILD	RR	ZZZZ	USA
LORA	2	F	CHILD	RR	ZZZZ	USA
KANTOR, MINA	40	F	UNKNOWN	RR	ZZZZ	USA
RIWA	15	F	UNKNOWN	RR	ZZZZ	USA
FRIEDE	12	F	UNKNOWN	RR	ZZZZ	USA
LEIB	9	F	CHILD	RR	ZZZZ	USA
MAX	5	M	CHILD	RR	ZZZZ	USA
LEWINZON, JENTA	20	F	UNKNOWN	RR	ZZZZ	USA
MILLNOWITSCH, MICHAEL	26	M	LABR	RR	ZZZZ	USA
OLGA	8	F	CHILD	RR	ZZZZ	USA
WIRSCHKOWSKY, PIOTR	20	M	LABR	RR	ZZZZ	USA
SCHNERIN, MARJE	29	F	UNKNOWN	RR	ZZZZ	USA
JERKE	8	F	CHILD	RR	ZZZZ	USA
ISROLKE	7	F	CHILD	RR	ZZZZ	USA
IDA	3	F	CHILD	RR	ZZZZ	USA
LIEBE	2	F	CHILD	RR	ZZZZ	USA
CHAIM	1	M	CHILD	RR	ZZZZ	USA
ZERNIN, SOL.	25	M	LABR	RR	ZZZZ	USA
BEYLA	20	F	UNKNOWN	RR	ZZZZ	USA
BARZEUSKI, STANIL.	26	M	LABR	RR	ZZZZ	USA
CHATZKELEWITZ, JANKEL	24	M	LABR	RR	ZZZZ	USA
DWORZAUSKI, FRANS	17	M	LABR	RR	ZZZZ	USA
DRAT, ERDAM	35	M	LABR	RR	ZZZZ	USA
FINKELSTEIN, EISIK	23	M	LABR	RR	ZZZZ	USA
MORRIS	30	M	SHMK	RR	ZZZZ	USA
GALASCHIN, MARTIN	31	M	LABR	RR	ZZZZ	USA
GELBERG, SOL.	16	M	LABR	RR	ZZZZ	USA
KUGEL, ABEL	39	M	LABR	RR	ZZZZ	USA
KLEPACKI, JEAN	31	M	LABR	RR	ZZZZ	USA
AB.	27	M	LABR	RR	ZZZZ	USA
KAPLAN, ARON	22	M	LABR	RR	ZZZZ	USA
KAPELUCHNIK, MOSCHE	20	M	LABR	RR	ZZZZ	USA
KOTINSKI, ADAM	31	M	LABR	RR	ZZZZ	USA
LEWANZEWITZ, FRANZ	38	M	LABR	RR	ZZZZ	USA
MORCHEL, JOSEF	40	M	LABR	RR	ZZZZ	USA
MORROSY, JOSEF	30	M	LABR	RR	ZZZZ	USA
ORSCHOCHOWSKY, SYVESTER	22	M	LABR	RR	ZZZZ	USA
ORLOWSKI, FRANCISH	37	M	LABR	RR	ZZZZ	USA
EDWD.	24	M	LABR	RR	ZZZZ	USA
ANTON	24	M	LABR	RR	ZZZZ	USA
RANTNER, JANKEL	20	M	LABR	RR	ZZZZ	USA
ROSEAETTI, J.	20	M	LABR	RR	ZZZZ	USA
RUSTAKOWSKI, MANIE	39	M	LABR	RR	ZZZZ	USA
RUBINSTEIN, CALMAN	26	M	LABR	RR	ZZZZ	USA
STEFAN, FRIEDR.	36	M	LABR	RR	ZZZZ	USA
SCHWARZ, LIESER	40	M	LABR	RR	ZZZZ	USA
STEFANOWSKY, JAKOB	21	M	LABR	RR	ZZZZ	USA
SCHESCHEWSKI, JEAN	43	M	LABR	RR	ZZZZ	USA
SLACHINSKI, ROMALDI	26	M	LABR	RR	ZZZZ	USA
SUCHOWSKI, WOJEIECH	34	M	LABR	RR	ZZZZ	USA
VINCENTY	45	M	LABR	RR	ZZZZ	USA
TRUCHAN, MATHUS	31	M	LABR	RR	ZZZZ	USA
WOJTKOWSKI, FRE.	30	M	LABR	RR	ZZZZ	USA
WAITKOLEWICZ, JOHAN	18	M	LABR	RR	ZZZZ	USA
ZOLEWSKI, FRANC	29	M	LABR	RR	ZZZZ	USA
ZELESNAK, PESACH	21	M	LABR	RR	ZZZZ	USA
ZIELNISKA, JAM.	40	M	LABR	RR	ZZZZ	USA

PASSENGER	AGE	SEX	OCCUPATION	PV RI VL	DES
SHIP: LLOYD					
FROM: BREMEN AND SOUTHAMPTON					
TO: NEW YORK					
ARRIVED: 05 JANUARY 1889					
LOPATCA, FRANZ	19	M	TLR	RRZZZZ	USA
SED, HIRSCH	18	M	LABR	RRZZZZ	USA
WIDEWA, NATHAN	27	M	LABR	RRZZZZ	USA
FUCHS, BASS	36	M	LABR	RRZZZZ	USA
LEPSCHITZ, BORKIN	19	M	LABR	RRZZZZ	USA
MICHEL	7	M	CHILD	RRZZZZ	USA
THOMSKI, BORKIN	16	M	LABR	RRZZZZ	USA
GOLDSTEIN, SERE	25	M	LABR	RRZZZZ	USA
MERE	7	M	CHILD	RRZZZZ	USA
GLAZIER, CHAIM	25	M	LABR	RRZZZZ	USA
PAULINE	21	F	W	RRZZZZ	USA
LANZMAN, CHANNER	18	F	SP	RRZZZZ	USA
BENAL	7	M	CHILD	RRZZZZ	USA
LABOWITZ, LORA	32	F	W	RRZZZZ	USA
LEOPOLD	7	M	CHILD	RRZZZZ	USA
ROSA	6	F	CHILD	RRZZZZ	USA
SAMI	3	M	CHILD	RRZZZZ	USA
MARITZ	.06	F	INFANT	RRZZZZ	USA
SHIP: STATE OF NEBRASKA					
FROM: GLASGOW AND LARNE					
TO: NEW YORK					
ARRIVED: 27 MARCH 1889					
GORODOWITSCH, ROCHEL	47	F	W	RRAIDL	USA
JANKEL	11	M	CH	RRAIDL	USA
SORE	6	F	CHILD	RRAIDL	USA
CHANE	2	F	CHILD	RRAIDL	USA
LIEBE	2	F	CHILD	RRAIDL	USA
AUSCHEL	1	M	CHILD	RRAIDL	USA
LITZKY, PESCHE	20	F	SP	RRAIDL	USA
RASCHWALD, MARKUS	24	M	LABR	RRAIDL	USA
ESPL, LIEISER	23	M	TLR	RRAIDL	USA
PERSKY, SCHAIE	18	M	TLR	RRAIDL	USA
WASRKEWICZ, KAZIMIR	44	M	LABR	RRAIDL	USA
KUBREN, MENDEL	28	M	TLR	RRAIDL	USA
SZERMINSKY, ANTONI	34	M	LABR	RRAIDL	USA
PAWEL	36	M	LABR	RRAIDL	USA
JOSEPH	38	M	LABR	RRAIDL	USA
SHIP: ROMAN					
FROM: LIVERPOOL					
TO: BOSTON					
ARRIVED: 28 MARCH 1889					
LITKOWSKY, SCHIFRE	18	M	LABR	RRZZZZ	BO
TANNENBAUM, G.	19	M	LABR	RRZZZZ	BO
SCHNEIDER, ABRAHAM	38	M	LABR	RRZZZZ	BO
LEISONOWIKY, OREL	28	M	LABR	RRZZZZ	BO
SARAH	25	F	SP	RRZZZZ	BO
ZIPPE	25	F	HSWF	RRZZZZ	BO
EPHRAIM	3	M	CHILD	RRZZZZ	BO
SARAH	.11	F	INFANT	RRZZZZ	BO
SUMMERMAN, LEIB	45	M	LABR	RRZZZZ	BO
LOUIS, N.	36	F	SP	RRZZZZ	BO
CHANE	19	M	LABR	RRZZZZ	BO
SARAH	15	F	SP	RRZZZZ	BO
SROLEWITZ, C.	35	M	LABR	RRZZZZ	BO
BASSIE	10	F	CH	RRZZZZ	BO
LEIB	5	F	CHILD	RRZZZZ	BO
ROSA	4	F	CHILD	RRZZZZ	BO
RELBE, LEAH	30	F	SP	RRZZZZ	UNK
GETTE	23	F	SP	RRZZZZ	UNK
MINNA	.10	F	INFANT	RRZZZZ	UNK
PIEPERT, DORE	50	F	HSWF	RRZZZZ	NY
MOSES	11	M	CH	RRZZZZ	NY
ISRAEL	7	M	CHILD	RRZZZZ	NY
SOKOLOWSKY, CHASSE	17	M	LABR	RRZZZZ	NY
GILMAN, SELIG	17	M	LABR	RRZZZZ	NY
REKPYER, HARRIS	22	M	LABR	RRZZZZ	NY
POLENSPOLMETZ, SAMUEL	64	M	LABR	RRZZZZ	BO
LEIS, TOCHAM	21	M	LABR	RRZZZZ	BO
SAKOWITZ, ADAM	35	M	LABR	RRZZZZ	BO
BERMAN, ELAS	24	M	LABR	RRZZZZ	BO
MOSCHWITZ, S.	28	M	LABR	RRZZZZ	BO
SLO----, M.	48	M	LABR	RRZZZZ	BO
FEITEL, ISAAC	22	M	LABR	RRZZZZ	BO
BERNSTEIN, SORE	32	F	HSWF	RRZZZZ	BO
SCH.	10	F	CH	RRZZZZ	BO
PEDIE	10	F	CH	RRZZZZ	BO
LEIBE	3	F	CHILD	RRZZZZ	BO
KOSLIK, ABRAHAM	32	M	LABR	RRZZZZ	BO
LANKOW, A.	30	M	LABR	RRZZZZ	BO
SAGULL, BETTSY	20	F	SP	RRZZZZ	BO
COHAN, M.	25	M	TLR	PLZZZZ	NY
LEWIS, ADA	9	F	CHILD	RRZZZZ	BO
BECCA	6	F	CHILD	RRZZZZ	BO
SHIP: QUEEN					
FROM: LIVERPOOL AND QUEENSTOWN					
TO: NEW YORK					
ARRIVED: 28 MARCH 1889					
VELVICK, WM.	20	M	LABR	RRZZZZ	NY
MULLER, A.	23	M	LABR	RRADBQ	NY
KNOPP, C.	45	M	LABR	RRZZZZ	NY
LEWITAS, L.	40	M	LABR	RRZZZZ	NY
GILDE, L.	19	F	SP	RRZZZZ	NY
KOCKIE, JOSEF	32	M	LABR	RRZZZZ	NY
FREDMAN, JOSEFE	23	M	LABR	RRZZZZ	NY
DRIBIN, G.	6	F	CHILD	RRZZZZ	NY
L.	6	F	CHILD	RRZZZZ	NY
DEMBY, SEGAL	17	F	SP	RRZZZZ	NY
KAUBER, M.	49	M	LABR	RRZZZZ	NY
NOCHEM	16	M	LABR	RRZZZZ	NY
TRIBLIN, CH.	23	F	W	RRZZZZ	NY
SCHOSSE	5	F	CHILD	RRZZZZ	NY
STRINK, FR.	50	M	LABR	RRZZZZ	NY
ELIAS	11	M	CH	RRZZZZ	NY
RUBINSTEIN, P.	8	F	CHILD	RRZZZZ	NY
SCHWARTZ, ISIDOR	31	M	LABR	RRZZZZ	NY
IDER	21	F	W	RRZZZZ	NY
IRENE	1	F	CHILD	RRZZZZ	NY
KOPPEL, JENKEL	26	M	LABR	RRZZZZ	NY
GERSCHOWITZ, ABE	19	M	LABR	RRZZZZ	NY
CHAJE	12	F	CH	RRZZZZ	NY
SCHWARTZ, WOLF	25	M	LABR	RRZZZZ	NY
GULINSKI, ANTON	24	M	LABR	RRZZZZ	NY
BUSTER, NOSGEN	18	M	LABR	RRZZZZ	NY
HOLDER, JOH.G.	22	M	LABR	RRZZZZ	NY
KATTKOWSKI, ANTON	35	M	LABR	RRZZZZ	NY
PEKINIAS, JOSEF	23	M	LABR	RRZZZZ	NY
TELIANS, JOSEF	23	M	LABR	RRZZZZ	NY
STRUCK, BORUSCH	58	F	SP	RRZZZZ	NY
ZIREL	25	F	SP	RRZZZZ	NY

PASSENGER	AGE	SEX	OCCUPATION	PRV VIL DES
SHIP: HERMANN				
FROM: BREMEN				
TO: BALTIMORE				
ARRIVED: 28 MARCH 1889				
JESCHILEWITZ, CHAME	20	F	W	RRZZZZUNK
MOSES	20	M	PDLR	RRZZZZUNK
FISCHER, ROSCHE	27	F	NN	RRZZZZUNK
ETTE	.11	F	INFANT	RRZZZZUNK
MILLER, JACOB	32	M	LABR	RRZZZZUNK
ELISABETH	35	F	W	RRZZZZUNK
JACOB	8	M	CHILD	RRZZZZUNK
ELOISABETH	7	F	CHILD	RRZZZZUNK
JOHANN	4	M	CHILD	RRZZZZUNK
LYDIA	3	F	CHILD	RRZZZZUNK
BARBARA	2	F	CHILD	RRZZZZUNK
U, U	00	F	CH	RRZZZZUNK
SCHILBERG, SPRINGE	30	F	CH	RRZZZZUNK
MEYER	9	M	CHILD	RRZZZZUNK
FREIDE	5	F	CHILD	RRZZZZUNK
HIRSCH	.11	M	INFANT	RRZZZZUNK
SCHWARZMANN, LEIB	48	M	NN	RRZZZZUNK
BEDANE	60	F	W	RRZZZZUNK
MEIER	8	M	CHILD	RRZZZZUNK
SCHAJE	6	F	CHILD	RRZZZZUNK
KATZ, RUBEN	47	M	NN	RRZZZZUNK
GUTMANN, SCHORE	55	F	NN	RRZZZZUNK
RIWKE	17	F	NN	RRZZZZUNK
GOLDOFF, ABRAM	30	M	PTR	RRZZZZUNK
KLEIWANSKI, MOTE	46	F	NN	RRZZZZUNK
GUTMANN, WOLF	23	M	FARMER	RRZZZZUNK
SCHLOME	27	M	LABR	RRZZZZUNK
HARSCHEL	20	M	LABR	RRZZZZUNK
MATESEVITZ, JOSEF	29	M	LABR	RRZZZZUNK
MALUSDE, VINCENZ	30	M	LABR	RRZZZZUNK
WILWANIS, ANTON	36	M	LABR	RRZZZZUNK
RUDKOWSKY, BERNARD	21	M	LABR	RRZZZZUNK
NESINSKI, FRANZ	17	M	FARMER	RRZZZZUNK
SIWOWLOS, ABRH.	18	M	PDLR	RRZZZZUNK
ZAKRZEWSKI, THOMAS	22	M	BLKSMH	RRZZZZUNK
TRRZYNSKI, ANTON	31	M	LABR	RRZZZZUNK
SIMON, ANASTASIUS	21	M	JNR	RRZZZZUNK
RADKE, EVA	20	F	NN	RRZZZZUNK
BERKOWINSKI, FRANCISEK	24	M	LABR	RRZZZZUNK
UMILYAN, PIOTER	40	M	LABR	RRZZZZUNK
LOPINSKI, JOSEF	21	M	LABR	RRZZZZUNK
SCJHMIDT, JOHANN	42	M	FARMER	RRZZZZNE
CHRISTINE	40	F	W	RRZZZZNE
MARGARETHE	15	F	NN	RRZZZZNE
BRAUER, JOHANN	21	M	FARMER	RRZZZZNE
U, SIMON	18	F	NN	RRZZZZNE
RUDECKI, ANTON	22	M	UNKNOWN	RRZZZZNY
OLCZEWSKI, LEO	16	M	UNKNOWN	RRZZZZMI
KOLSCHINDER, CARL	30	M	UNKNOWN	RRZZZZUNK
ZUDINEK, JOSEF	36	M	UNKNOWN	RRZZZZUNK
JACOBSOHN, MEYER	45	M	PDLR	RRZZZZUNK
ROCHEL	45	F	W	RRZZZZUNK
SAMUEL	19	M	NN	RRZZZZUNK
RIEWE	8	F	CHILD	RRZZZZUNK
LEA	6	F	CHILD	RRZZZZUNK
ISRAEL	5	M	CHILD	RRZZZZUNK
CHAJE	2	F	CHILD	RRZZZZUNK
HERWISCH, MEYER	38	M	PDLR	RRZZZZUNK
EYDUS, SAMUEL	37	M	PDLR	RRZZZZUNK
FRIEDLANDER, RIWKE	11	M	CH	RRZZZZUNK
EISENBERG, SCHOLEM	19	M	PDLR	RRZZZZUNK
MORAWSKA, KATARZA	34	F	NN	RRZZZZUNK
ANNA	5	F	CHILD	RRZZZZUNK
ALBERTINE	.11	F	INFANT	RRZZZZUNK
FRANK, SALOMON	19	M	TLR	RRZZZZUNK
FRIEDLAENDER, MARKUS	22	M	PDLR	RRZZZZUNK
PAGLINSKI, EDE	21	F	NN	RRZZZZUNK
SHARLINSKI, KAZMIRZ	20	M	LABR	RRZZZZUNK
PIERADSKI, JOSEF	33	M	LABR	RRZZZZUNK
DOCZKAS, JOSEF	40	M	LABR	RRZZZZUNK
GERDAT, MATIJAS	22	M	LABR	RRZZZZUNK
BUDNIK, FRITZ	22	M	LABR	RRZZZZUNK
DULBIS, KAZMISZ	27	M	LABR	RRZZZZUNK
U, U	00	M	LABR	RRZZZZUNK
SKARLINSKI, BOLESLAW	5	M	CHILD	RRZZZZOH
SERGINSKI, MOSES	17	M	NN	RRZZZZKY
SHIP: WIELAND				
FROM: HAMBURG				
TO: NEW YORK				
ARRIVED: 29 MARCH 1889				
GALATZKA, KASES	25	M	LABR	RRZZZZUSA
MARIE	23	F	W	RRZZZZUSA
MARIE	.11	F	INFANT	RRZZZZUSA
BLUMENTHAL, SARAH	39	F	W	RRAFVGUSA
BONNI	9	F	CHILD	RRAFVGUSA
ETTEL	8	F	CHILD	RRAFVGUSA
CHANNE	4	F	CHILD	RRAFVGUSA
LEO	4	M	CHILD	RRAFVGUSA
SCHLOME	.11	M	INFANT	RRAFVGUSA
LEWIN, MINNA	19	F	SGL	RRZZZZUSA
BRZYKOWSKI, JOS.	27	M	LABR	RRZZZZUSA
GRYGO, JAN	36	M	LABR	RRZZZZUSA
SCHNEIDER, FRANK	20	M	LABR	RRZZZZUSA
ZARETZKI, LOUISE	29	F	SGL	RRZZZZUSA
BALENSON, MENDEL	23	M	UNKNOWN	RRZZZZUSA
GOLDKIND, ISAAC	33	M	UNKNOWN	RRAHQDUSA
PETER	9	M	CHILD	RRAHQDUSA
OLINE, NISSEN	27	M	LABR	RRAHTUUSA
BORMANN, MOSES	16	M	LABR	RRZZZZUSA
MARGUARDT, TEKLA	27	F	WO	RRZZZZUSA
MAX	.11	M	INFANT	RRZZZZUSA
THEKLA	.01	F	INFANT	RRZZZZUSA
GRAMSE, IDA	20	F	SGL	RRZZZZUSA
STUEWE, OTTO	26	M	MUSN	RRZZZZUSA
SCHULER, AETE	19	F	SGL	RRZZZZUSA
PITROWSKI, FRANZ	17	M	LABR	RRAHUFUSA
DODRICH, SAMULE	26	M	MCHT	RRAHOKUSA
WISOTZKY, RUSKE	42	F	WO	RRAHVUUSA
SCHLOME	9	M	CHILD	RRAHVUUSA
JELENEWICZ, BATZE	24	F	WO	RRZZZZUSA
ISRAEL	8	M	CHILD	RRZZZZUSA
CHANNE	.11	F	INFANT	RRZZZZUSA
BOLBER, MAGGIE	26	F	WO	RRZZZZUSA
SARAH	5	F	CHILD	RRZZZZUSA
GOLDE	3	F	CHILD	RRZZZZUSA
TORSKI, CARL	24	M	LABR	RRZZZZUSA
BLUMENTHAL, WILH.	17	M	LKSH	RRADDQUSA
MEYER, HANS	61	M	FARMER	RRZZZZUSA
CATHA.	62	F	W	RRZZZZUSA
PLITT, MICHAEL	34	M	FARMER	RRAHUFUSA
GOTTLIEB	22	M	FARMER	RRAHUFUSA
RUCKS, MICHEL	43	M	FARMER	RRAHUFUSA
EMIL	16	M	FARMER	RRAHUFUSA
JANZEW, FRIEDRICH	39	M	FARMER	RRAHUFUSA
LEWANDOWSKI, VALENTIN	23	M	LABR	RRZZZZUSA
PETROSCHEFSKI, MICHEL	25	M	LABR	RRZZZZUSA
GROSSNITZ, JASSEL	18	M	LABR	RRZZZZUSA
RUDSCHEWITZ, PETRAS	34	M	LABR	RRZZZZUSA
KASLANTSKAS, JONAS	30	M	LABR	RRZZZZUSA
HOFFMANN, MALKE	27	F	WO	RRZZZZUSA
REBECCA	9	F	CHILD	RRZZZZUSA
BERKO, SORKE	20	F	SGL	RRZZZZUSA
SCHABLOWSKY, MATHIAS	26	M	LABR	RRZZZZUSA
HANNEMANN, FRIEDR.	24	M	LABR	RRZZZZUSA
WESCHLEFSKY, JACOB	29	M	LABR	RRZZZZUSA

PASSENGER	AGE	SEX	OCCUPATION	PRV VIL DES
ROSULIS, PETER	24	M	LABR	RRZZZZUSA
EGEZKY, PETER	27	M	LABR	RRZZZZUSA
ROSULIS, LUDWIG	30	M	LABR	RRZZZZUSA
KRENOWSKY, JENS	25	M	LABR	RRZZZZUSA
KOENEWSKY, ANTON	23	M	LABR	RRZZZZUSA
GONISCHEWSKY, ANTON	27	M	LABR	RRZZZZUSA
MIKELAUSKIS, STANISLAUS	24	M	LABR	RRZZZZUSA
ZIPEITIS, JOSEF	50	M	LABR	RRZZZZUSA
ALMA	30	F	W	RRZZZZUSA
MARIAN	15	F	D	RRZZZZUSA
ANGELIA	.11	F	INFANT	RRZZZZUSA
MATINER, MEYER	26	M	LABR	RRAHTOUSA
DICKELMANN, HELENA	19	F	SGL	RRAHTNUSA
SERWATKA, MATHIAS	26	M	LABR	RRZZZZUSA
SZEMAN, STANISLAV	45	M	LABR	RRZZZZUSA
SITKA, JOSEF	30	M	LABR	RRZZZZUSA
KRUSEWSKI, STANIL.	27	M	LABR	RRZZZZUSA
KAMINSKI, KARL	33	M	LABR	RRZZZZUSA
KECZMER, JAN	38	M	LABR	RRAHUIUSA
SIEDLECKI, ANTON	30	M	LABR	RRZZZZUSA
COHN, CHANNE	46	F	WO	RRZZZZUSA
RIFKE	9	F	CHILD	RRZZZZUSA
JACOB	8	M	CHILD	RRZZZZUSA
ESTER	6	F	CHILD	RRZZZZUSA
ROSA	4	F	CHILD	RRZZZZUSA
LANDSMANN, SARAH	25	F	WO	RRZZZZUSA
HERSCH	2	M	CHILD	RRZZZZUSA
INKEL	.05	M	INFANT	RRZZZZUSA
SISSKOWITZ, JECHE	16	F	SGL	RRAIMCUSA
TYFOLWICZ, MARIANNE	27	F	SGL	RRZZZZUSA
LEWITZKI, CHAIE	45	F	WO	RRAHRZUSA
SARA	9	F	CHILD	RRAHRZUSA
ISSER	8	M	CHILD	RRAHRZUSA
ESCHKE	7	F	CHILD	RRAHRZUSA
BREINE	6	F	CHILD	RRAHRZUSA
NECHANNE	3	F	CHILD	RRAHRZUSA
DAVID	.11	M	INFANT	RRAHRZUSA
BROD, SCHLOME	17	M	LABR	RRZZZZUSA
LUPINSKY, JANKEL	19	M	TLR	RRAIEOUSA
JARMULOWSKI, MEYER	9	M	CHILD	RRZZZZUSA
BERNATH, LOUIS	46	M	TLR	RRZZZZUSA
KROCHMALIK, ISRAEL	28	M	MCHT	RRAHTNUSA
BUKONIEWICZ, ANTON	46	M	LABR	RRAHZSUSA
WAWORKIEWICZ, FRANZ	47	M	LABR	RRAHZSUSA
BROZOWSKY, JOSEF	23	M	LABR	RRAHZSUSA
LEINAL, JOSEF	45	M	LABR	RRAHZSUSA
BALSCHUN, FRANZ	27	M	LABR	RRZZZZUSA
SAWISTANOWITZ, MATON	24	M	LABR	RRZZZZUSA
STEINGROB, BARUCH	22	M	LABR	RRZZZZUSA
RABINOWICZ, MEYER	27	M	MCHT	RRAHTOUSA
LUPEC, MATWY	32	M	LABR	RRZZZZUSA
SABIN, GEORG	32	M	TCHR	RRZZZZUSA

SHIP: TRAVE

FROM: BREMEN AND SOUTHAMPTON
TO: NEW YORK
ARRIVED: 29 MARCH 1889

PASSENGER	AGE	SEX	OCCUPATION	PRV VIL DES
KRIPAS, MATTHEUS	17	M	LABR	RRZZZZUSA
LIPSITZ, HENE	8	F	CHILD	RRZZZZUSA
ITE	42	F	UNKNOWN	RRZZZZUSA
ETTEL	11	M	CH	RRZZZZUSA
TEWEL	6	M	CHILD	RRZZZZUSA
HANECZIE, CASIMIR	26	M	LABR	RRZZZZUSA
FRANZ	24	M	LABR	RRZZZZUSA
VINE	25	M	LABR	RRZZZZUSA
LESNUOSKI, ANT.	24	M	LABR	RRZZZZUSA
SALANOWSKI, JAN.	24	M	LABR	RRZZZZUSA
SCHAVEL, GEORG	56	M	LABR	RRZZZZUSA
BALKO	25	M	LABR	RRZZZZUSA
STOVINI, JANO	24	M	LABR	RRZZZZUSA
GROSSMANN, NOACH	21	M	PDLR	RRZZZZUSA
TEHENAVIZOWA, MARYANNE	32	F	UNKNOWN	RRZZZZUSA
KLIBANSKY, SALOM.	35	M	DLR	RRZZZZUSA
DAVID	11	M	UNKNOWN	RRZZZZUSA
JACOBSEN, WM.	32	M	DLR	RRZZZZUSA
CHAJE	31	F	UNKNOWN	RRZZZZUSA
NECHE	18	F	UNKNOWN	RRZZZZUSA
MOSES	10	M	CH	RRZZZZUSA
JOSEF	6	M	CHILD	RRZZZZUSA
KURLANSKY, CHAJE	35	F	UNKNOWN	RRZZZZUSA
ITZKE	26	M	DLR	RRZZZZUSA
POWELSKI, BENJ.	16	M	LABR	RRZZZZUSA
BERMUN, MENDEL	29	M	LABR	RRZZZZUSA
KANAUK, RUEVKE	29	F	UNKNOWN	RRZZZZUSA
ABRAHAM	7	M	CHILD	RRZZZZUSA
SCHEPSEL	3	M	CHILD	RRZZZZUSA
WELINSKY, ISAAK	26	F	UNKNOWN	RRZZZZUSA
MARIE	7	M	CHILD	RRZZZZUSA
MALE	.11	M	INFANT	RRZZZZUSA
SELLEN, JOSEF	28	M	LABR	RRZZZZUSA

SHIP: GERMANIC

FROM: LIVERPOOL AND QUEENSTOWN
TO: NEW YORK
ARRIVED: 29 MARCH 1889

PASSENGER	AGE	SEX	OCCUPATION	PRV VIL DES
FREEDMAN, ROSA	24	F	SVNT	PLZZZZUSA
PORTEGGI, N.	32	M	LABR	PLZZZZUSA

SHIP: MARSALA

FROM: HAMBURG
TO: NEW YORK
ARRIVED: 29 MARCH 1889

PASSENGER	AGE	SEX	OCCUPATION	PRV VIL DES
SOKOLOWSKI, VINCENTY	29	M	LABR	RRZZZZNY
GREGOSSKI, FRANCISCHEK	21	M	LABR	RRZZZZNY
GULU-SKI, SCHLOMA	17	M	LABR	RRZZZZNY
MELSUK, VINZENTI	31	M	LABR	RRZZZZNY
PASKEWITZ, U	39	M	LABR	RRZZZZNY
GRODZINSKA, JOSEF	48	M	LABR	RRZZZZNY
WICENTY, JOSEFA	22	M	LABR	RRZZZZNY
MARGEWITZ, JOSEF	24	M	LABR	RRZZZZNY
GOLDBERG, JU--EL	28	M	MCHT	RRZZZZNY
GLASNA-, JOH	35	M	BBR	RRAFWJNY
SE--BU, FRANZ	36	M	LABR	RRZZZZNY
KROPECKI, FRANZ	29	M	LABR	RRZZZZNY
SPEJ-OSKY, INGNUS	20	M	LABR	RRZZZZNY
RACKOWSKI, ANDREJ	17	M	LABR	RRZZZZNY
SCHERMANN, ESTHER	45	F	WO	RRAIGHNY
WOLF	15	M	CH	RRAIGHNY
LEIB	9	M	CHILD	RRAIGHNY
CA--JE	7	M	CHILD	RRAIGHNY
HERSCH	5	M	CHILD	RRAIGHNY
ANDR-SZHI--ICZ, WLADILS	17	M	LABR	RRZZZZNY
P-LIPALY, ANNA	20	F	SGL	RRAHZSNY
GOLATSCH, JOS	33	M	LABR	RRAHZSNY
SZAKA, STANISL	25	M	LABR	RRZZZZNY
KLEEMAN, MORDCHE	33	M	MCHT	RRZZZZNY
BR-OSTEK, JAN	27	M	LABR	RRZZZZNY
-ORSKY, PETER	27	M	LABR	RRADATNY
-RISKA, JAN	27	M	LABR	RRAHWCNY

PASSENGER	AGE	SEX	OCCUPATION	PRIVL	DES
HERSDA, IGNATZ	29	M	LABR	RRZZZZ	NY
BALDIGA, KASIMAR	29	M	LABR	RRADAT	NY
SOCHELN, STANISLAV	22	M	LABR	RRZZZZ	NY
SCHOCK, PAVEL	30	M	LABR	RRZZZZ	NY
PIKORA, JOSEF	31	M	LABR	RRZZZZ	NY
BROOKY, JOSEF	28	M	LABR	RRZZZZ	NY
WARAKSA, FRANZ	21	M	LABR	RRZZZZ	NY
BE-TMARCK, MARTIN	34	M	LABR	RRZZZZ	NY
POPELOSCH, JOSEF	27	M	LABR	RRZZZZ	NY
WILKOWSKI, FRANZ	23	M	LABR	RRZZZZ	NY
DOMALE, VALENTIN	17	M	LABR	RRZZZZ	NY
GRABECK, INGNATZ	26	M	LABR	RRZZZZ	NY
STANISLAV	32	M	LABR	RRZZZZ	NY
ITIN, MARCUS	22	M	LABR	RRZZZZ	NY
U	25	F	W	RRZZZZ	NY
SELZER, BEILE	42	F	WO	RRZZZZ	NY
MAXIM	5	M	CHILD	RRZZZZ	NY
ALBERT	3	M	CHILD	RRZZZZ	NY
KUJINSKI, JAN	31	M	FARMER	RRZZZZ	NY
PETRIK, JAN	24	M	FARMER	RRZZZZ	NY
SCHWARZ, JULIAN	17	M	FARMER	RRZZZZ	NY
W-ITKOVSKI, JOSEF	37	M	LABR	RRAIJJ	NY
KRAIN, VICTOR	18	M	LABR	RRZZZZ	NY
BAEDAZEWSKA, FRANZISKA	19	F	SGL	RRZZZZ	NY
IGLEWSKA, SALOM	15	F	SGL	RRAIJJ	NY
MAT---INAK, ALBERT	27	M	LABR	RRZZZZ	NY
KROLL, FRANZ	29	M	LABR	RRZZZZ	NY
JANKOWIKI, LORENZ	39	M	LABR	RRZZZZ	NY
ANSTOK, LORENZ	30	M	LABR	RRZZZZ	NY
MICHOLK, FRANZ	19	M	LABR	RRZZZZ	NY
WELTMANN, HERSCHEL	16	M	LABR	RRZZZZ	NY
SCHAPIRO, CHAJE	33	M	NN	RRZZZZ	NY
ABRAM	9	M	CHILD	RRZZZZ	NY
-EWIE	.11	M	INFANT	RRZZZZ	NY
LEWANDOWSKI, ANTON	24	M	LABR	RRZZZZ	PA
STACHOWICZ, VICTOR	17	M	LABR	RRZZZZ	PA
LEWANDOWSKI, JAN	31	M	LABR	RRZZZZ	PA
SELZER, MARIN	5	M	CHILD	RRZZZZ	NY
ALBERT	3	M	CHILD	RRZZZZ	NY
KUJINSKI, JAN	31	M	FARMER	RRZZZZ	NY
PETRICK, JAN	24	M	FARMER	RRZZZZ	NY
SCHWARZ, JULIAN	17	M	FARMER	RRZZZZ	NY

SHIP: CITY OF CHESTER

FROM: LIVERPOOL
TO: NEW YORK
ARRIVED: 30 MARCH 1889

PASSENGER	AGE	SEX	OCCUPATION	PRIVL	DES
AK-ESTROM, VICTOR	36	M	SMH	RRACBF	NY
ANTOMP--KE, JACOB-A.	28	M	FARMER	RRACBF	NY
MACKTELLA, SAMUEL	18	M	LABR	RRACBF	NY
JANSER, NIKO	21	M	LABR	RRACBF	NY
PEUTO--EL, JOHN	26	M	LABR	RRACBF	NY
MAENPESON, K.	23	M	FARMER	RRACBF	BO
MILIKE, IWA	18	M	LABR	RRACBF	NY
KANKEWPAID, M.J.	20	M	FARMER	RRACBF	NY
KANKAS, JANKO	44	M	FARMER	RRACBF	NY
JANKORPSKE, SAMUEL	17	M	FARMER	RRACBF	NY
MORKE-GEAN, ELIAS	19	M	FARMER	RRACBF	NY
KANKEYIAN, JOHAN	23	M	FARMER	RRACBF	NY
HAKKALA, SAMEL	31	M	FARMER	RRACBF	NY
KAROILA, ERIK	18	M	FARMER	RRACBF	NY
KENTKAECEN, ERIK	23	M	FARMER	RRACBF	NY
PEERLA, JAKE	46	M	FARMER	RRACBF	NY
KAEMCKE, JAKE	34	M	FARMER	RRACBF	NY
KACEKOS, JANNKO	48	M	LABR	RRACBF	NY
KAAPAMCKE, GUSTAF	20	M	LABR	RRACBF	NY
MACEIS, LEONARD	28	M	FARMER	RRACBF	NY
HIKKITO, JOHAN	33	M	LABR	RRACBF	NY
MADET-GE, SIFANI-E	26	M	LABR	RRACBF	BO
MINTIRPRIKE, JAKOL	19	M	LABR	RRACBF	BO
BELENIWSKY, DAVID	28	M	LABR	RRACBF	NY
FREDMANN, SEIFER	19	M	LABR	RRACBF	NY
PRIABERGE, MICHAL	22	M	LABR	RRACBF	NY
FRIDEL	11	M	CH	RRACBF	NY
ZEBONSKIE, BRONSL.	46	M	LABR	RRACBF	NY
JOZEVICK, MARY	52	M	LABR	RRACBF	BUF
ONTOWIK, JODETEIN	18	M	LABR	RRACBF	NY
KERALSKY, ANTONI	21	M	LABR	RRACBF	NY
BRIESWOSKY, INNO	24	M	LABR	RRACBF	NY
FR-S, MANY	29	M	LABR	RRACBF	NY
KOPIASK, JOHANNA	33	M	SMH	RRACBF	PHI
U, ANEK	24	M	LABR	RRACBF	UNK
BRIENAU, FRANEY	27	M	LABR	RRACBF	NY
BEZECYENCIRSKY, JOSEF	28	M	LABR	RRACBF	NY
MACKONENZ, JOSEF	25	M	LABR	RRACBF	NY

SHIP: AURANIA

FROM: LIVERPOOL AND QUEENSTOWN
TO: NEW YORK
ARRIVED: 01 APRIL 1889

PASSENGER	AGE	SEX	OCCUPATION	PRIVL	DES
HAHES, MEYER	24	M	STMSN	RRZZZZ	NY
BANNER, SCHMAJE	24	M	TLR	RRZZZZ	NY
WOLFFSOHN, ABRAM	19	M	LABR	RRZZZZ	PHI
GRIMFELD, JETTER	15	F	SP	RRZZZZ	NY
KIRSCOW, HIRSCH	19	M	LABR	RRZZZZ	PHI
LEGAL, LEIB	40	M	LABR	RRZZZZ	NY
FUCHS, ALEX	23	M	LABR	RRZZZZ	NY
SCHOLMAN, DORA	19	F	SP	RRZZZZ	NY
HURWITZ, JACOB	30	M	LABR	RRZZZZ	PHI
MAKOWISKY, MATUS	37	M	LABR	RRZZZZ	NY
BRAZDA, WOJCIECH	38	M	LABR	RRZZZZ	NY
KEWETRICH, KASEMER	24	M	LABR	RRZZZZ	NY
KOWITZ, BENIDICT	24	M	LABR	RRZZZZ	NY
SETZER, CHAIM	28	M	LABR	RRZZZZ	NY
KOWALEWSKY, STANISLAUS	23	M	LABR	RRZZZZ	NY
MAXIMOWSKY, ANTON	22	M	TLR	RRZZZZ	NY
ULICK, GEDALJE	26	M	TLR	RRZZZZ	NY
CALLSON, HANS	30	M	LABR	RRZZZZ	NY
LEPSCHUTZ, CHAJE	28	F	MA	RRZZZZ	NY
RACHAEL	4	F	CHILD	RRZZZZ	NY
HOBZMAN, SARA	13	F	SP	RRZZZZ	NY
CHARLIP, LEIBE	48	M	LABR	PLZZZZ	NY
ELLKE	46	F	W	PLZZZZ	NY
RACHAEL	16	F	SP	PLZZZZ	NY
LASER	11	M	CH	PLZZZZ	NY
ANDITSKY, ISKA	20	M	LABR	PLZZZZ	NY
NACHT, ESTER	19	F	SP	PLZZZZ	NY
SCHAPIRS, BARUCH	35	M	JNR	PLZZZZ	NY
MOLESKA, MAY	10	F	CH	PLZZZZ	NY
DJEMENURKI, KASEMIR	44	M	LABR	PLZZZZ	NY
LANDGUSH, JOHN	27	M	LABR	FNZZZZ	NY

SHIP: ALASKA

FROM: LIVERPOOL AND QUEENSTOWN
TO: NEW YORK
ARRIVED: 01 APRIL 1889

PASSENGER	AGE	SEX	OCCUPATION	PRIVL	DES
SCHAPIRO, SARACH	52	F	SP	RRZZZZ	USA
JODARSKI, PESCHE	41	F	MA	RRZZZZ	USA
JACOB	11	M	CH	RRZZZZ	USA

PASSENGER	AGE	SEX	OCCUPATION	PRV VIL DES
ABRAM	8	M	CHILD	RRZZZZUSA
KAPLAN, SAML.	22	M	LABR	RRZZZZUSA
SPECTER, SCHIE	38	M	LABR	PLZZZZUSA
SORE	28	F	MA	PLZZZZUSA
HENE	8	M	CHILD	PLZZZZUSA
PESCHE	3	M	CHILD	PLZZZZUSA
JURMAN, CHAS	18	M	LABR	RRZZZZUSA
WILCHORSKY, WOGE	42	M	PDLR	PLZZZZUSA
JUDLOWITZ, MOSES	16	M	LABR	PLZZZZUSA
SAGRE, ESTER	37	F	MA	RRZZZZUSA
EITKE	9	M	CHILD	RRZZZZUSA
CHAJE	7	F	CHILD	RRZZZZUSA
KATE	3	F	CHILD	RRZZZZUSA
GOLDSTEIN, HIRSCH	17	M	LABR	PLZZZZUSA
BARUCH	26	M	LABR	PLZZZZUSA
LEWJENSKY, NOCHEM	29	M	LABR	PLZZZZUSA
BYAIL, FRANCIS	24	M	PDLR	PLZZZZUSA
SAGALL, JEATE	.10	F	INFANT	RRZZZZUSA
PERTTOLA, JOHAN	25	M	LABR	FNZZZZUSA
KAJSA	21	F	W	FNZZZZUSA

SHIP: FULDA

FROM: BREMEN AND SOUTHAMPTON
TO: NEW YORK
ARRIVED: 02 APRIL 1889

PASSENGER	AGE	SEX	OCCUPATION	PRV VIL DES
N---, HEINRICH	00	M	MCHT	RRZZZZNY
MAYER, SOPHIE	20	F	UNKNOWN	RRZZZZNY
CHYENKERS, ADA	29	F	W	RRZZZZNY
ANNA	47	F	W	RRZZZZNY
MINNA	8	F	CHILD	RRZZZZNY
ANNA	4	F	CHILD	RRZZZZNY
HIRSCH	.11	M	INFANT	RRZZZZNY
THIEL, DOBE	32	F	W	RRZZZZNY
SAMUEL	11	M	CH	RRZZZZNY
RACHEL	6	F	CHILD	RRZZZZNY
BEITE	3	F	CHILD	RRZZZZNY
ABRAHAM	.10	M	INFANT	RRZZZZNY
WO--AMS, IGNATZ	19	M	UNKNOWN	RRZZZZUSA
LITKE, JOSEF	18	M	UNKNOWN	RRZZZZUSA
OLECHEWSKI, JAN	37	M	UNKNOWN	RRZZZZUSA
CLOLEWINSKI, JAN	26	M	LABR	RRZZZZUSA
SZATWIEWSKI, JAN	21	M	LABR	RRZZZZNY
SCHRAGE, ROSALIE	15	F	UNKNOWN	RRZZZZNY
MICHALSKY, WOJEGESCH	32	M	LABR	RRZZZZNY
ZYIVISKI, PAWET	29	M	LABR	RRZZZZNY
JOZ-VIK, JAN	26	M	LABR	RRZZZZNY
SCHWANKOWSKI, ANDR.	29	M	LABR	RRZZZZNY
RAJTKOWSKI, FRANZ	19	M	LABR	RRZZZZNY
KWIATKOWSKI, MICH.	20	M	LABR	RRZZZZNY
KASDAN, KASCHE	27	F	W	RRZZZZNY
CHAWE	9	F	CHILD	RRZZZZNY
JENTE	7	F	CHILD	RRZZZZNY
CIRKE	.11	F	INFANT	RRZZZZNY
RUDOLPH, JOHHH	22	M	LABR	RRZZZZNY
DOROTHEA	32	F	W	RRZZZZNY
DOROTHEA	9	F	CHILD	RRZZZZNY
KATHARINA	7	F	CHILD	RRZZZZNY
JOHANN	6	M	CHILD	RRZZZZNY
MATHIAS	4	M	CHILD	RRZZZZNY
GEORG	2	M	CHILD	RRZZZZNY
JACOB	.11	M	INFANT	RRZZZZNY
BAUMGART, JULIUS	30	M	FARMER	RRZZZZNY
MARIE	26	F	W	RRZZZZNY
MINNA	4	F	CHILD	RRZZZZNY
ANNA	2	F	CHILD	RRZZZZNY
U	.11	F	INFANT	RRZZZZNY
KLEMER, JOHANN	26	M	FARMER	RRZZZZNY
JULIE	23	F	W	RRZZZZNY
LUDWIG	24	M	FARMER	RRZZZZNY
HIRSCHBERG, JUDA	44	M	DLR	RRZZZZNY
DWORE	44	F	W	RRZZZZNY
LEIB	10	M	CH	RRZZZZNY
ROSA	3	F	CHILD	RRZZZZNY
B----, HANI	3	F	CHILD	RRZZZZNY
ETTEL	3	F	CHILD	RRZZZZNY
MARIE	.11	F	INFANT	RRZZZZNY
PINKOWSKI, ARON	47	M	LABR	RRZZZZNY
REICHMANN, CHAIN	46	M	LABR	RRZZZZNY
SCHMILOW, CIT	32	M	LABR	RRZZZZNY
GLUMBOWSKI, NAZAR	24	M	LABR	RRZZZZNY
SEMIONOW, STIKITA	48	M	LABR	RRZZZZNY
TRAFIMOW, IWAN	23	M	LABR	RRZZZZNY
KARCZAVSKI, VICTOR	44	M	LABR	RRZZZZNY
SIMAWICZ, MARTIN	38	M	LABR	RRZZZZNY
CIBULSKA, NATALIA	27	F	W	RRZZZZNY
U	3	M	CHILD	RRZZZZNY
KO----, ANTONI	29	F	UNKNOWN	RRZZZZNY
TOTS-LOWSKI, ALEX	29	M	LABR	RRZZZZNY
MATINOWSKI, TOMAS	26	M	LABR	RRZZZZNY
GLOGOSNEWSKI, STANISL.	26	M	LABR	RRZZZZNY
GRODZINSKI, FRANZ	30	M	LABR	RRZZZZNY
KUBECKI, VIEDLAI	21	M	LABR	RRZZZZNY
ROBAKEWICZ, PAUL	30	M	LABR	RRZZZZNY
PICHOWSKI, WLADISL.	25	M	LABR	RRZZZZNY
SEWERIN	17	M	LABR	RRZZZZNY
CURLANIS, JAN	23	M	GDNR	RRZZZZNY
WOLONGEWIZ, JERZY	21	F	UNKNOWN	RRZZZZNY
WENGIS, KARNN	25	M	LABR	RRZZZZNY
MARBUT, JOSEF	33	M	LABR	RRZZZZNY
BRONGERT, MARIA	26	M	UNKNOWN	RRZZZZNY
ZAMBRZUSKI, STANIL.	24	M	LABR	RRZZZZNY
GLOWASKI, JAN	22	M	LABR	RRZZZZNY
JOWOCSKI, LEON	24	M	LABR	RRZZZZNY
SOBICCKI, STEFAN	19	M	LKSH	RRZZZZNY
TEOFILA	24	F	UNKNOWN	RRZZZZNY
CISZEWSKI, CLEMENS	22	M	LABR	RRZZZZNY
DAWJERT, ANTONIA	47	F	W	RRZZZZNY
RIWOZUNSKI, ANTON	32	M	LABR	RRZZZZNY
ANTONIA	25	F	W	RRZZZZNY
HAMS	3	M	CHILD	RRZZZZNY
SMIONTKOWICZ, ADAM	21	M	LABR	RRZZZZNY
BIDKINZKI, FRANZ	22	M	LABR	RRZZZZNY
KOWALSKI, JAN	38	M	LABR	RRZZZZNY
FORAMSKI, JENDR.	24	M	LABR	RRZZZZNY
GRANISCH, ANTONI	27	F	UNKNOWN	RRZZZZNY
TIZKOWSKI, JOSEF	26	M	FARMER	RRZZZZNY
KAZMIRA	25	F	W	RRZZZZNY
BARANOWSKI, WICENTZ	24	M	LABR	RRZZZZNY
ALABURDA, ADOLF	30	M	LABR	RRZZZZNY
GREBOWSKI, PIOTR	24	M	LABR	RRZZZZNY
WOHWIECZ, JERZI	38	M	LABR	RRZZZZNY
KOZLOWSKI, BALZ	30	M	LABR	RRZZZZNY
TELENDE, MICH.	16	M	LABR	RRZZZZNY
MORAWSKI, KLEMENS	22	M	LABR	RRZZZZNY
SINKEWICZ, VINCENTY	21	M	LABR	RRZZZZNY
SUPCZYNSKI, ANTON	24	M	LABR	RRZZZZNY
KOWALEWSKI, ANDR.	24	M	LABR	RRZZZZNY
SOCOTOWSKI, FRANZ	25	M	LABR	RRZZZZNY
LENDA, JOSEF	25	M	LABR	RRZZZZNY
ZAMBROWICZ, VICENTY	23	M	LABR	RRZZZZNY
GURSKI, MEELAN	28	M	LABR	RRZZZZNY
KARMIVSKI, STANISL.	18	M	LABR	RRZZZZNY
KUSTARSKI, KAZMIR	19	M	LABR	RRZZZZNY
STACKOWSKI, FRANZ	20	M	LABR	RRZZZZNY
STANISL.	30	M	LABR	RRZZZZNY
SCHIPERAK, JOSEF	18	M	LABR	RRZZZZNY
MEBROCH, JOSEF	29	M	LABR	RRZZZZNY
RUTKOWSKI, MATH.	22	M	LABR	RRZZZZNY
BLAZOWSKI, ANT.	25	M	LABR	RRZZZZNY
SUJE, ADAM	21	M	LABR	RRZZZZNY
ARUSZKIEWCZ, SIMON	27	M	LABR	RRZZZZNY
OLINKOWSKI, JOSEF	11	M	LABR	RRZZZZNY
CICSIEWSKI, ANDR.	21	M	LABR	RRZZZZNY

PASSENGER	AGE	SEX	OCCUPATION	PRVL	VIL	DES
SUMIL, WAASIL	19	M	LABR	RR	ZZZ	ZNY
HERMANN, RUD.	30	M	LABR	RR	ZZZ	ZNY
SUMIL, CEHAN	26	M	LABR	RR	ZZZ	ZNY
ROSEN, HABRIEL	18	M	LABR	RR	ZZZ	ZNY
JUSZEZAK, VALENTIN	32	M	LABR	RR	ZZZ	ZNY
BUGGEL, AELX	29	M	LABR	RR	ZZZ	ZNY
BILINSKI, ADAM	20	M	LABR	RR	ZZZ	ZNY
CZASSLIK, PIOTR	26	M	LABR	RR	ZZZ	ZNY
HOLEWSKI, ALEXANDER	30	M	LABR	RR	ZZZ	ZNY
ROMANTOWSKI, FELIX	39	M	LABR	RR	ZZZ	ZNY
KORNELA	38	F	W	RR	ZZZ	ZNY
ROBALINOWSKI, ZOFYA	29	F	UNKNOWN	RR	ZZZ	ZNY
POLLAK, ANNI	20	F	UNKNOWN	RR	ZZZ	ZNY
LERANDOWSKIE, EVA	20	F	UNKNOWN	RR	ZZZ	ZNY
WISNICSKA, MARYANNA	18	F	UNKNOWN	RR	ZZZ	ZNY
ROSHIS, THOMAS	37	M	LABR	RR	ZZZ	ZNY
MARIA	37	F	W	RR	ZZZ	ZNY
MONSKY, ADAM	29	M	LABR	RR	ZZZ	ZNY
BACEIE, ADAM	22	M	LABR	RR	ZZZ	ZNY
THREL, JOSEF	9	M	CHILD	RR	ZZZ	ZNY

SHIP: CIRCASSIA

FROM: GLASGOW AND MOVILLE
TO: NEW YORK
ARRIVED: 03 APRIL 1889

PASSENGER	AGE	SEX	OCCUPATION	PRVL	VIL	DES
GINSBURG, ISAK	47	M	LABR	RR	ZZZ	ZUSA
BAUER, CHATZ	39	M	TLR	RR	ZZZ	ZUSA
DOMBROSKY, JOSEF	37	M	LABR	RR	ZZZ	ZUSA
SZEKOWICZ, STEFAN	30	M	LABR	RR	ZZZ	ZUSA
ABRAMOWITZ, SAM.	27	M	LABR	RR	ZZZ	ZUSA
TOMESCHEK, AND.	27	M	LABR	RR	ZZZ	ZUSA
LITHOWET, AND.	30	M	LABR	RR	ZZZ	ZUSA
FRANCISCHEK, D.	28	M	LABR	RR	ZZZ	ZUSA
GRUNBERG, LEIG	35	M	LABR	RR	ZZZ	ZUSA
ARON	11	M	CH	RR	ZZZ	ZUSA
BERL----, JACOB	30	M	CH	RR	ZZZ	ZUSA
KLIGB--, JANOS	40	M	CH	RR	ZZZ	ZUSA
BEISER, SCH.	22	M	CH	RR	ZZZ	ZUSA
LADA, ALEX	29	M	CH	RR	ZZZ	ZUSA
SALKS, JOSEF	38	M	CH	RR	ZZZ	ZUSA
ANDERS	28	M	CH	RR	ZZZ	ZUSA
KRAWANSKI, M.	12	M	NN	RR	ZZZ	ZUSA
STARBEKER, ABRAM	27	M	LABR	RR	ZZZ	ZUSA
BACHINSKI, CHATZ	42	M	LABR	RR	ZZZ	ZUSA
SCHIPAR-, CHAIM	25	M	LABR	RR	ZZZ	ZUSA
ROTHESTEIN, SOB.	50	M	TLR	RR	ZZZ	ZUSA
MOSES	18	M	TLR	RR	ZZZ	ZUSA
U, U	18	M	TLR	RR	ZZZ	ZUSA
FRAWETZ, JOHAN	22	M	TLR	RR	ZZZ	ZUSA
SUDNIK, ANTON	30	M	TLR	RR	ZZZ	ZUSA
LAPUCH, JOHAN	25	M	TLR	RR	ZZZ	ZUSA
WAWSHENIK, STAS.	42	M	TLR	RR	ZZZ	ZUSA
BEUMOWICZ, M.	38	M	JNR	RR	ZZZ	ZUSA
SMIEK, VOY	40	M	JNR	RR	ZZZ	ZUSA
JOSEF	12	M	NN	RR	ZZZ	ZUSA
JEAN	12	M	NN	RR	ZZZ	ZUSA

SHIP: SPAIN

FROM: LIVERPOOL AND QUEENSTOWN
TO: NEW YORK
ARRIVED: 04 APRIL 1889

PASSENGER	AGE	SEX	OCCUPATION	PRVL	VIL	DES
BRULBODY, J.	30	F	W	RR	AIE	FUSA
F.	11	F	CH	RR	AIE	FUSA
MICHOL, SEGN.	37	M	LABR	RR	AIE	FUSA
SALA, M.	29	M	LABR	RR	AIE	FUSA
ALKERTEZ, LEON	22	M	LABR	RR	AIE	FUSA
TAYLUSCH, B.	20	M	LABR	RR	AIE	FUSA
KEPEN, PAUL	30	M	LABR	RR	AIE	FUSA
PHU-H--, HERMAN	25	M	LABR	RR	AIE	FUSA
ANDREAS, BACH	30	M	LABR	RR	AIE	FUSA
GLUERFELD, MAYER	27	M	LABR	RR	AIE	FUSA
MELGRON, MOSES	49	M	LABR	RR	AIE	FUSA
POSCHNAM, ADOLF	25	M	LABR	RR	AIE	FUSA
KOCH, M.	21	M	LABR	RR	AIE	FUSA
SOLIN, U	26	M	LABR	RR	AIE	FUSA
J--SE, JOSE	33	M	LABR	RR	AIE	FUSA
SARN, W.	29	M	LABR	RR	AIE	FUSA
SCHWARTZ, S.	45	M	LABR	RR	AIE	FUSA
WETNER, F.	43	M	LABR	RR	AIE	FUSA
GULENSKI, J.	47	M	LABR	RR	AIE	FUSA
MOLSKY, J.	24	M	LABR	RR	AIE	FUSA
HAUSKOPKY, F.	25	M	LABR	RR	AIE	FUSA
JALLEK, W.	25	M	LABR	RR	AIE	FUSA
CEBULKES, A.	29	M	LABR	RR	AIE	FUSA
RLEKAUS, A.	30	M	LABR	RR	AIE	FUSA
DORSKORSKY, M.	30	M	LABR	RR	AIE	FUSA
J.	20	M	LABR	RR	AIE	FUSA
CYRUSYESKY, F.	30	M	LABR	RR	AIE	FUSA
SEUZLAL, J.	38	M	LABR	RR	AIE	FUSA
KLERS, M.	38	M	LABR	RR	AIE	FUSA
VICTOR, P.	28	M	LABR	RR	AIE	FUSA
BARGARECSKY, A.	23	M	LABR	RR	AIE	FUSA
ROMAPEA, M.	26	M	LABR	RR	AIE	FUSA
LYDSIENATIS, JAN	21	M	LABR	RR	AIE	FUSA
IWANOWITZ, M.	26	M	LABR	RR	AIE	FUSA
PELAKAW, ALEX	30	M	LABR	RR	AIE	FUSA
MARTENOWITZ, A.	29	M	LABR	RR	AIE	FUSA
-AUSBERG, J.	52	M	LABR	RR	AIE	FUSA
M.	19	F	SVNT	RR	AIE	FUSA
JACOB	15	M	LABR	RR	AIE	FUSA
DAVID	11	M	CH	RR	AIE	FUSA
CUZEGRUSKA, M.	23	F	SVNT	RR	AIE	FUSA
CH-MER, C.	30	F	W	RR	AIE	FUSA
R.	6	F	CHILD	RR	AIE	FUSA
C.	.10	M	INFANT	RR	AIE	FUSA
JOSSELOVOVTY, ASNE	20	F	SVNT	RR	AIE	FUSA
GOLDFIST, H.	25	F	SVNT	RR	AIE	FUSA
DELLKOWITZ, D.	18	F	SVNT	RR	AIE	FUSA
MACHUT, D.	16	F	SVNT	RR	AIE	FUSA
FRESKIEN, E.	15	F	SVNT	RR	AIE	FUSA
SCHWAENTZ, J.	29	F	W	RR	AIE	FUSA
M.	11	M	CH	RR	AIE	FUSA
G.	9	F	CHILD	RR	AIE	FUSA
SALFO, K.	38	F	W	RR	AIE	FUSA
P.	11	M	CH	RR	AIE	FUSA
R.	9	M	CHILD	RR	AIE	FUSA
C.	5	M	CHILD	RR	AIE	FUSA
D.	.10	F	INFANT	RR	AIE	FUSA
SCHAUSCH, M.	21	F	SVNT	RR	AIE	FUSA
LEW, C.	11	F	CH	RR	AIE	FUSA
SLOTIN, T.	29	F	W	RR	AIE	FUSA
IDA	3	F	CHILD	RR	AIE	FUSA
SARL	.11	F	INFANT	RR	AIE	FUSA
ASTLET, SORE	33	F	W	RR	AIE	FUSA
HRCH.	10	M	W	RR	AIE	FUSA
MLKA.	8	M	CHILD	RR	AIE	FUSA
DOBE	4	M	CHILD	RR	AIE	FUSA
SOSOREK, REESEL	27	F	W	RR	AIE	FUSA
ISAK	4	M	CHILD	RR	AIE	FUSA

PASSENGER	AGE	SEX	OCCUPATION	PRI	VIL	DES
SOLAN	2	M	CHILD	RR	AIE	FUSA
SPE.	.10	F	INFANT	RR	AIE	FUSA
BLUM, H.	45	M	LABR	RR	AIE	FUSA
SORE	40	F	W	RR	AIE	FUSA
SKINI	.11	F	INFANT	RR	AIE	FUSA
L.	10	F	INF	RR	AIE	FUSA
L.	7	M	CHILD	RR	AIE	FUSA
VEIN	8	M	CHILD	RR	AIE	FUSA
PAULINE	.09	F	INFANT	RR	AIE	FUSA
LEW, F.	32	F	W	RR	AIE	FUSA
CHAIS.	11	F	CH	RR	AIE	FUSA
ROCH.	9	F	CHILD	RR	AIE	FUSA
M.	8	M	CHILD	RR	AIE	FUSA
SEIB	6	M	CHILD	RR	AIE	FUSA
JANKEL	3	M	CHILD	RR	AIE	FUSA
BOSENWE-G, E.	25	F	W	RR	AIE	FUSA
DWORE	16	F	SVNT	RR	AIE	FUSA
MANDELL	3	F	CHILD	RR	AIE	FUSA
CHAIN	.11	M	INFANT	RR	AIE	FUSA

SHIP: NORSEMAN

FROM: LIVERPOOL
TO: BOSTON
ARRIVED: 04 APRIL 1889

PASSENGER	AGE	SEX	OCCUPATION	PRI	VIL	DES
WISBOERKART, A.	19	M	UNKNOWN	RR	ZZZ	ZBO
BURYNEE, LAURNA	37	F	SVNT	RR	ZZZ	ZBO
JENSEN, A.	21	M	UNKNOWN	RR	ZZZ	ZBO
CHANDORSKY, A.	36	M	LABR	RR	ZZZ	ZBO
KONKOWSKY, P.	28	M	LABR	RR	ZZZ	ZBO
SOUBUM, J.	22	M	LABR	RR	ZZZ	ZBO
SCHALINSKY, F.	24	M	TLR	RR	ZZZ	ZBO
J.	21	M	TLR	RR	ZZZ	ZBO
BANDISH, J.	24	M	TLR	RR	ZZZ	ZBO
WISCHOWSKY, A.	26	M	TLR	RR	ZZZ	ZBO
HALWEITIS, J.	29	M	UNKNOWN	RR	ZZZ	ZBO
SCHAVENTSKY, P.	28	M	TLR	RR	ZZZ	ZBO
GINGEL, J.	29	M	PDLR	RR	ZZZ	ZBO
TARASCHEITIS, F.	26	M	PDLR	RR	ZZZ	ZBO
PELETZKY, J.	33	M	PDLR	RR	ZZZ	ZBO
ROSCHOWSKY, F.	36	M	PDLR	RR	ZZZ	ZBO
SKIBA, V.	15	M	PDLR	RR	ZZZ	ZBO
LASKO, N.	26	M	TLR	RR	ZZZ	ZBO
THON, H.	27	M	TLR	RR	ZZZ	ZBO
DARON, F.	24	M	TLR	RR	ZZZ	ZBO
PADUSKY, J.	25	M	PDLR	RR	ZZZ	ZBO
TOPAMDUSKY, J.	17	M	LABR	RR	ZZZ	ZBO
MISCHEWITZ, J.	21	M	LABR	RR	ZZZ	ZBO
WATZLAWISKY, J.	26	M	LABR	RR	ZZZ	ZBO
SAWITSKY, A.	27	M	LABR	RR	ZZZ	ZBO
LATOWSKY, LEZER	22	M	TLR	RR	ZZZ	ZBO
WILDEN, ITZIG	40	M	TLR	RR	ZZZ	ZBO
SCHWIDERSKY, JAN	24	M	TLR	RR	ZZZ	ZBO
GARDETZKY, M.	32	M	TLR	RR	ZZZ	ZBO
STURGULSKY, JOSEPH	30	M	TLR	RR	ZZZ	ZBO
SCHIDLETZKY, Y.	38	M	TLR	RR	ZZZ	ZBO
LEIDIWSKY, P.	27	M	TLR	RR	ZZZ	ZBO
WANZEIN, F.	18	M	LABR	RR	ZZZ	ZBO
TRUSPOWSKY, J.	32	M	LABR	RR	ZZZ	ZBO
BLIZEK, Y.	20	M	LABR	RR	ZZZ	ZBO
LUBEIS, JANOS	20	M	LABR	PL	ZZZ	ZBO
RAEWSKY, P.	21	M	LABR	RR	ZZZ	ZBO
PAKISCHANSKY, JUDEL	20	M	LABR	RR	ZZZ	ZBO
BIRFFMANN, JONAS	18	M	LABR	RR	ZZZ	ZBO
CHAIS	19	M	LABR	RR	ZZZ	ZBO
SAWARSKY, ARON	19	M	UNKNOWN	RR	ZZZ	ZNY
ASCHNE	19	M	TLR	RR	ZZZ	ZNY
BITSHOW, SALOMON	38	M	LABR	RR	ZZZ	ZNY
MOSES	42	M	LABR	RR	ZZZ	ZNY
SCHWACZBURG, FEIGE	17	M	UNKNOWN	PL	ZZZ	ZNY
KATOW, DAVID	00	M	INF	PL	ZZZ	ZBO
BEREL	00	F	INF	PL	ZZZ	ZBO
HEUPT, M.	24	M	LABR	RR	ZZZ	ZBO
CHESCHANSKY, C.	28	M	LABR	RR	ZZZ	ZBO
GOLDAMNN, SIMON	23	M	PDLR	RR	ZZZ	ZNY
HOLSCHAYNE, LEWIS	25	M	TLR	RR	ZZZ	ZNY
HEUSMANN, JUEL	29	M	LABR	RR	ZZZ	ZNY
LERWITZ, WERMINE	28	M	LABR	RR	ZZZ	ZBO
STERPEIKAS, JULIAN	56	M	LABR	RR	ZZZ	ZBO
DAIEULOWITZ, BALES	35	F	W	RR	ZZZ	ZBO
CEYENEY	8	F	CHILD	RR	ZZZ	ZBO
LENA	5	F	CHILD	RR	ZZZ	ZBO
ISAAC	00	M	INF	RR	ZZZ	ZBO
LEW, HILLEL	28	M	LABR	PL	ZZZ	ZUSA
CHAYETT, BENY	27	M	LABR	RR	ZZZ	ZNY
TAUBE	25	F	W	RR	ZZZ	ZNY
HENOCH	00	M	INF	RR	ZZZ	ZNY
DRESNER, PEREL	16	F	SVNT	PL	ZZZ	ZNY
JETTE	19	F	SVNT	PL	ZZZ	ZNY
SCHWARZ, MORITZ	19	M	LABR	RR	ZZZ	ZNY
HOTON, BLUMES	22	F	W	RR	ZZZ	ZNY
GORDON, ARON	16	M	LABR	RR	ZZZ	ZNY
OXENKRUG, H.	22	M	LABR	RR	ZZZ	ZNY
BEIMOWITZ, HIRSCH	30	M	TLR	RR	ZZZ	ZNY

SHIP: MAIN

FROM: BREMEN
TO: BALTIMORE
ARRIVED: 04 APRIL 1889

PASSENGER	AGE	SEX	OCCUPATION	PRI	VIL	DES
KOTKOWSKI, FRANZICEK	50	M	UNKNOWN	RR	ZZZ	ZBAL
DILKOWSKI, JOSEF	24	M	UNKNOWN	RR	ZZZ	ZBAL
KLEVEITYR, GEORG	35	M	UNKNOWN	RR	ZZZ	ZBAL
MICZKO, JOHN	27	M	UNKNOWN	RR	ZZZ	ZBAL
GAZKOWIAK, WLADISL.	17	M	LABR	RR	ZZZ	ZBAL
TURIWUSCH, CHAIM	16	M	LABR	RR	ZZZ	ZBAL
ZBIERAYEWSKY, FRANK	23	M	FARMER	RR	ZZZ	ZBAL
ZACMINSKI, MARCELI	22	M	FARMER	RR	ZZZ	ZBAL
SUCHOTZKI, U	41	M	FARMER	RR	ZZZ	ZBAL
BOGOSCHEFSKY, WILD	22	M	FARMER	RR	ZZZ	ZBAL
KUSNEREITIS, ANTON	20	M	FARMER	RR	ZZZ	ZBAL
GRIZANKOWSKY, WAWR	40	M	FARMER	RR	ZZZ	ZBAL
KOWALSKI, FRANZ	30	M	FARMER	RR	ZZZ	ZBAL
KONIETZNY, JAN	40	M	FARMER	RR	ZZZ	ZBAL
GREZANKOWSKY, MARIAN	28	M	FARMER	RR	ZZZ	ZBAL
PLOETZ, WACLAW	27	M	FARMER	RR	ZZZ	ZBAL
GAJEWSKY, JULIAN	37	M	FARMER	RR	ZZZ	ZBAL
SIEDECHO, JAN	38	M	FARMER	RR	ZZZ	ZBAL
SZARNECKY, STANIL.	30	M	FARMER	RR	ZZZ	ZBAL
ZOTORSKY, MARIAN	30	M	FARMER	RR	ZZZ	ZBAL
SLIWSKA, M.FRANZ	33	M	FARMER	RR	ZZZ	ZBAL
WILKOWSKA, JAN	31	M	FARMER	RR	ZZZ	ZBAL
SZALACZYNSKI, WACL.	27	M	FARMER	RR	ZZZ	ZBAL
SZWEDE, ANTON	26	M	FARMER	RR	ZZZ	ZBAL
INDICHI, ANTON	32	M	FARMER	RR	ZZZ	ZBAL
GRYGO, JUSTIN	43	M	FARMER	RR	ZZZ	ZPA
ZAKOZEWSKI, MICHEL	30	M	FARMER	RR	ZZZ	ZPA
KASZENSKI, WOJECEK	25	M	FARMER	RR	ZZZ	ZPA
BROWAREK, JOSEF	22	M	FARMER	RR	ZZZ	ZPA
SLOMA, FRANZ	30	M	FARMER	RR	ZZZ	ZPA
SWIRBLISCH, STANISL.	28	M	LABR	RR	ZZZ	ZBAL
LZNKEITISCH, JOSES	33	M	LABR	RR	ZZZ	ZBAL
BUKOWSKI, MARTIN	27	M	LABR	RR	ZZZ	ZBAL
STANESIC, ADAM	24	M	LABR	RR	ZZZ	ZBAL
URBAN, IGNATZ	27	M	LABR	RR	ZZZ	ZBAL
BARNOWSKI, SIMON	48	M	LABR	RR	ZZZ	ZBAL
SKIRAT, JOSEF	45	M	LABR	RR	ZZZ	ZBAL
KORSSMAN, SOLEM	27	M	FARMER	RR	ZZZ	ZBAL

PASSENGER	AGE	SEX	OCCUPATION	PRV	VIL	DES
SPERLING, CHAJE	23	M	FARMER	RR	ZZZZ	BAL
KLITZKY, ALBERT	21	M	FARMER	RR	ZZZZ	BAL
GURCZENSKY, JAN	30	M	FARMER	RR	ZZZZ	BAL
GRALIKOWSKI, MICHEL	35	M	FARMER	RR	ZZZZ	BAL
RACHEL, EMIL	31	M	FARMER	RR	ZZZZ	BAL
WALTER, EMIL	26	M	FARMER	RR	ZZZZ	BAL
RUSIEN, HEINR.	30	M	FARMER	RR	ZZZZ	BAL
MACHOSSACK, JAN	26	M	FARMER	RR	ZZZZ	BAL
RACHEL, BERNH.	30	M	FARMER	RR	ZZZZ	BAL
RUDOLPH	26	M	FARMER	RR	ZZZZ	BAL
RESCHKEN, HEINR.	34	M	FARMER	RR	ZZZZ	BAL
WOJCIECHOWSKI, ANDREAS	25	M	FARMER	RR	ZZZZ	BAL
FAMCZAK, FRANCIZEK	30	M	FARMER	RR	ZZZZ	IL
SCHIKOSKI, FELIX	28	M	FARMER	RR	ZZZZ	IL
KECK, EDUARD	39	M	FARMER	RR	ZZZZ	IL
LINKE, ERNST	29	M	FARMER	RR	ZZZZ	IL
SORIN, ERNST	26	M	FARMER	RR	ZZZZ	OH
LEWINSON, MINNA	17	F	SVNT	RR	ZZZZ	BAL
BRAUENBURGER, JASSE	16	F	SVNT	RR	ZZZZ	BAL
SCHTABRUSKY, CHANE	17	F	SVNT	RR	ZZZZ	BAL
KUBOWSKY, VICENTA	32	F	W	RR	ZZZZ	BAL
ZBIERAYEWSKY, APOLENA	23	F	W	RR	ZZZZ	BAL
TANKELEWITZ, KATHRA.	22	F	SVNT	RR	ZZZZ	BAL
JOFFE, FREIDA	22	F	SVNT	RR	ZZZZ	BAL
JACOBSEN, HANNE	24	F	W	RR	ZZZZ	BAL
REBECCA	.10	F	INFANT	RR	ZZZZ	BAL
WEILES, ITTE	33	F	W	RR	ZZZZ	BAL
SISSE	11	F	CH	RR	ZZZZ	BAL
GURZENSKY, MARIANNE	19	F	SVNT	RR	ZZZZ	BAL
KLEIN, CHANE	19	F	SVNT	RR	ZZZZ	BAL
OSER, GITTE	27	F	W	RR	ZZZZ	BAL
TOMASCHEWSKI, KASIMIR	23	M	LABR	RR	ZZZZ	BAL
SULWESTER	48	F	W	RR	ZZZZ	BAL

SHIP: LAKE HURON

FROM: LIVERPOOL
TO: BOSTON
ARRIVED: 04 APRIL 1889

PASSENGER	AGE	SEX	OCCUPATION	PRV	VIL	DES
RUDKOWSKI, WOLF	23	M	LABR	PL	ZZZZ	NY
ZIWES, JACOB	25	M	LABR	PL	ZZZZ	NY
MARCUS	14	M	UNKNOWN	RR	ZZZZ	CH
SCHITZNITZKY, LEA	24	F	LABR	RR	ZZZZ	CH
ELICH	23	F	LABR	RR	ZZZZ	CH
DAVID	3	M	CHILD	RR	ZZZZ	CH

SHIP: OBDAM

FROM: ROTTERDAM
TO: NEW YORK
ARRIVED: 05 APRIL 1889

PASSENGER	AGE	SEX	OCCUPATION	PRV	VIL	DES
WITKOWSKI, ANTON	56	F	SLR	RR	ZZZZ	USA
ST.	18	F	UNKNOWN	RR	ZZZZ	USA
JADWIGA	10	F	CH	RR	ZZZZ	USA
KOMMER, WILH.	16	M	CH	RR	ZZZZ	USA
SEGALOWITZ, CHARNE	17	F	CH	RR	ZZZZ	USA
PERWAJ, FRANZ	42	M	LABR	RR	ZZZZ	USA
FERDIN	17	M	LABR	RR	ZZZZ	USA
STUDEMEYER, IMR.	24	M	LABR	RR	ZZZZ	USA
WIDA, MICHAEL	26	M	LABR	RR	ZZZZ	USA
HEIM, WILLI	19	M	CGRMKR	RR	ZZZZ	USA
GIERSON, JOH.	37	M	CHMKR	RR	ZZZZ	USA
JOHANNA	22	F	UNKNOWN	RR	ZZZZ	USA
DAVID	15	M	UNKNOWN	RR	ZZZZ	USA

SHIP: GOTHIA

FROM: HAMBURG
TO: BALTIMORE
ARRIVED: 05 APRIL 1889

PASSENGER	AGE	SEX	OCCUPATION	PRV	VIL	DES
HANALE, KAIS	45	F	WO	FN	ZZZZ	BAL
EMS, GUSTAV	28	M	LABR	FN	ZZZZ	BAL
STENBAKA, ELISAS	26	M	LABR	FN	ZZZZ	BAL
PERKHIAMAK, MATH.	26	M	LABR	FN	ZZZZ	BAL
ELYBACKA, ANDERS	26	M	LABR	FN	ZZZZ	BAL
KNEKLISALO, GUSTAV	18	M	LABR	FN	ZZZZ	BAL
HANTELA, JACOB	17	M	LABR	FN	ZZZZ	BAL
HILLI, JOH.	26	M	LABR	FN	ZZZZ	BAL
PERKHIAMAK, JOH.	26	M	LABR	FN	ZZZZ	BAL
JACOBSEN, KARL	19	M	LABR	FN	ZZZZ	BAL
FURSBERG, JACOB	36	M	LABR	FN	ZZZZ	BAL
KOEGGBLAU, JOH.	42	M	FARMER	FN	ZZZZ	BAL
ZELMANSKY, ADAM	30	M	LABR	RR	ZZZZ	BAL
GOENRING, CARL	25	M	LABR	RR	ZZZZ	BAL
KRUSELAN, SIMON	60	M	LABR	RR	ZZZZ	BAL
MAGDALENA	58	F	W	RR	ZZZZ	BAL
SOBOL, JOS.	44	M	LABR	RR	ZZZZ	BAL
BJOERCKBARKA, MATH.	60	M	LABR	FN	ZZZZ	BAL
HANTEMAKI, ELIAS	35	M	LABR	FN	ZZZZ	BAL
HANTEKETO, MATH.	37	M	LABR	FN	ZZZZ	BAL

SHIP: LAHN

FROM: BREMEN AND SOUTHAMPTON
TO: NEW YORK
ARRIVED: 05 APRIL 1889

PASSENGER	AGE	SEX	OCCUPATION	PRV	VIL	DES
BASSBOGEN, JACOB	40	M	TT	FN	AARR	RSS
BURBUZKA, URSULA	25	F	UNKNOWN	FN	AILA	USA
WROBEL, BOCH	34	M	LABR	FN	AFWJ	USA
BASTOZEK, VINZENT	32	M	LABR	FN	AFWJ	USA
ANTON	37	M	LABR	FN	AFWJ	USA
OSSINWATA, MARTIN	22	M	LABR	FN	AFWJ	USA
SJOELBLOM, EMIL	25	M	FARMER	FN	ZZZZ	USA
KOCHANOWSKI, STEFAN	18	M	LABR	RR	ZZZZ	USA
ULINSKI, JULIAN	28	M	LABR	RR	ZZZZ	USA
BOBOL, JAN	24	M	LABR	RR	ZZZZ	USA
MEDIKOZO, LEO	20	M	LABR	RR	ZZZZ	USA
JOSEF	28	M	LABR	RR	ZZZZ	USA
JAKOWICZ, JUSTIN	16	M	LABR	RR	ZZZZ	USA
PORINO, JAN	31	M	LABR	RR	ZZZZ	USA
SZLAPOHERSKI, MEYER	50	M	LABR	RR	ZZZZ	USA
SCHIKORESITZ, SCHLEME	16	M	UNKNOWN	RR	ZZZZ	USA

SHIP: CITY OF BERLIN

FROM: LIVERPOOL AND QUEENSTOWN
TO: NEW YORK
ARRIVED: 06 APRIL 1889

PASSENGER	AGE	SEX	OCCUPATION	PRV	VIL	DES
RUTHOWSKA, MALGORAT	45	M	LABR	RR	ACBF	NY
INOSUCHOSKI	30	M	LABR	RR	ACBF	NY

PASSENGER	AGE	SEX	OCCUPATION	PV RI VL	DES
KICKOZA	26	M	LABR	RRACBF	NY
KATERYNA	4	F	CHILD	RRACBF	NY
MARYONA	00	F	INF	RRACBF	NY
VINCENT	00	F	INF	RRACBF	NY
KONESKI, VALENTIN	27	M	LABR	RRACBF	NY
KAWETZKI, JANKER	30	M	TLR	RRAEFL	NY
KINO	4	M	CHILD	RRAEFL	NY
KRUGER, JEDEL	20	M	TLR	RRAEFL	HAM
ROGALA, MAC.	24	M	LABR	RRAEFL	HAM
BEINSTEIN, FUGL	50	F	W	RRAEFL	HAM
PESCHE	20	F	SVNT	RRAEFL	HAM
MOTE	9	F	CHILD	RRAEFL	HAM
RINE	5	F	CHILD	RRAEFL	HAM
LOGELAIN, ROSINA	20	F	SVNT	RRAEFL	HAM
CZETKOWSKY, FRANZ	24	M	LABR	RRACBF	NY
NADROSKI, ANTONI	20	M	LABR	RRACBF	NY
SKOWRAN, JAN	27	M	LABR	RRACBF	NY
WOISCHITZKY, STANISLAUS	31	M	LABR	RRACBF	BUF
WUSCH, JAN	31	M	LABR	RRACBF	CH
KOPERA, STANISLAS	52	M	LABR	RRACBF	NY
BISTREK, VICTORIA	25	F	UNKNOWN	RRACBF	NY
SZELZEK, ROSALIE	18	F	UNKNOWN	RRACBF	NY
KOWALSKY, THOMAS	30	M	LABR	RRACBF	NY
SCHW--TEK, JAN	30	M	LABR	RRACBF	NY
POKROSCKEK, PETER	30	M	LABR	RRACBF	BUF
SACK, SH.	45	M	GZR	RRACBF	NY
KLEINMAN, BARUCH	16	M	SLR	RRACBF	NY
PIGUT, WOIZECH	38	M	LABR	RRACBF	NY
ROGOZINSKI, JAN	31	M	LABR	RRACBF	NY
KLAGA, FRANCISCHEK	38	M	LABR	RRACBF	NY
SHERNIAS, FRANCIS	26	M	LABR	RRACBF	NY
SABORA, VALENTIA	30	M	LABR	RRACBF	NY
BERNSTEIN, CHANE	5	F	CHILD	RRACBF	NY

SHIP: CEPHALONIA

FROM: LIVERPOOL AND QUEENSTOWN
TO: BOSTON
ARRIVED: 08 APRIL 1889

PASSENGER	AGE	SEX	OCCUPATION	PV RI VL	DES
CHAMPLEN, MICH.	27	M	LABR	FNZZZZ	USA
ABICITIS, ADOMAS	27	M	LABR	FNZZZZ	USA
KRUKOWSKY, FRANS	22	M	LABR	FNZZZZ	USA
WAMAWITCH, JACOB	69	M	LABR	FNZZZZ	USA
MUND, RASMUS	25	M	LABR	FNZZZZ	USA
KINDERGUARD, JENS	24	M	LABR	FNZZZZ	USA
DESSER, SAMUEL	44	M	LABR	RRZZZZ	USA
ROSA	43	F	W	RRZZZZ	USA
CHAIM	10	M	CH	RRZZZZ	USA
LEA	8	F	CHILD	RRZZZZ	USA
FEIVEL	5	F	CHILD	RRZZZZ	USA
ZAHSGUSZKA, JAGA	20	M	LABR	RRZZZZ	USA
KLAIN, DORA	24	F	W	RRZZZZ	USA
ISRAEL	6	M	CHILD	RRZZZZ	USA
ANNA	4	F	CHILD	RRZZZZ	USA
Z.	.06	F	INFANT	RRZZZZ	USA
ZOCILOWSKY, ALEX	30	M	LABR	RRZZZZ	USA

SHIP: ETHIOPIA

FROM: GLASGOW AND MOVILLE
TO: NEW YORK
ARRIVED: 09 APRIL 1889

PASSENGER	AGE	SEX	OCCUPATION	PV RI VL	DES
KALWEILIS, ALEXANDER	20	M	LABR	RRZZZZ	USA
KARDEL, ANTON	48	M	LABR	RRZZZZ	USA
KUZ, LUDWIG	25	M	LABR	RRZZZZ	USA
WEBAN, MATUS	27	M	LABR	RRZZZZ	USA
GREEHOWZKI, PAVEL	24	M	LABR	RRZZZZ	USA
KARLOWSKI, STANISLAW	20	M	LABR	RRZZZZ	USA
LISZWENSKI, STANISLAW	21	M	LABR	RRZZZZ	USA
ORBICK, FRANZ	26	M	LABR	RRZZZZ	USA
SKOWRONSKI, FRANZ	24	M	LABR	RRZZZZ	USA
JEAN	25	M	LABR	RRZZZZ	USA
FRANZ	24	M	LABR	RRZZZZ	USA
SZARKO, PIOTR	23	M	LABR	RRZZZZ	USA
TUKA, VOJCICH	22	M	LABR	RRZZZZ	USA
SIKALSKI, MARIAN	28	M	LABR	RRZZZZ	USA
TEMBOWSKI, ANTON	28	M	LABR	RRZZZZ	USA
POCHALSKI, JEAN	19	M	LABR	RRZZZZ	USA
ADAMZESKI, JOSEF	33	M	LABR	RRZZZZ	USA
TUBDUSKI, MICHAEL	25	M	LABR	RRZZZZ	USA
NOWACKI, WLADISLAW	35	M	LABR	RRZZZZ	USA
SITOBRSKI, JOSEF	23	M	LABR	RRZZZZ	USA
VEN, PEOTR	27	M	LABR	RRZZZZ	USA
TAENBOWSKI, EMILIE	17	F	HP	RRZZZZ	USA
ORLINSKI, LISBI.	20	F	HP	RRZZZZ	USA
MORDUCH	8	M	CHILD	RRZZZZ	USA
FEIGE	1	F	CHILD	RRZZZZ	USA
NAVESKI, HELENA	20	F	HP	RRZZZZ	USA
FRIEDMAN, ROCH	44	F	HP	RRZZZZ	USA
SELIG	18	M	UNKNOWN	RRZZZZ	USA
POSCHE	12	F	UNKNOWN	RRZZZZ	USA
NIESCHE	1	F	CHILD	RRZZZZ	USA
ARNOWSKI, LEA	19	F	HP	RRZZZZ	USA
BELMANN, EITE	20	F	HP	RRZZZZ	USA
ROCHE	3	F	CHILD	RRZZZZ	USA
BRYNDZA, JEAN	25	M	LABR	RRZZZZ	USA
BUTENAS, ANTON	37	M	LABR	RRZZZZ	USA
SABOLIS, PEOTR	21	M	LABR	RRZZZZ	USA
STANKEWICZ, PEOTR	21	M	LABR	RRZZZZ	USA
DZUKA, FRANZ	23	M	LABR	RRZZZZ	USA
FAFLYGYN, JEGOR	27	M	LABR	RRZZZZ	USA
EDCURS, JEAN	20	M	LABR	RRZZZZ	USA
JAENBOWICZ, ALEX	18	M	LABR	RRZZZZ	USA
WAGNER, MICHAEL	26	M	LABR	RRZZZZ	USA
KATRINA	26	F	UNKNOWN	RRZZZZ	USA
STANISLAW	1	M	CHILD	RRZZZZ	USA

SHIP: ELBE

FROM: BREMEN AND SOUTHAMPTON
TO: NEW YORK
ARRIVED: 10 APRIL 1889

PASSENGER	AGE	SEX	OCCUPATION	PV RI VL	DES
HESSE, AUG.	35	M	MCHT	RRZZZZ	CH
SOKOLOWSKY, CORIM.	33	M	FARMER	RRZZZZ	CH
GILIWITZ, NASTAS	18	M	FARMER	RRZZZZ	CH
ZITTKUS, VINEENS	21	M	FARMER	RRZZZZ	NY
BARANTZKI, JOS.	21	M	FARMER	RRZZZZ	NY
SELZER, CARL	20	M	FARMER	RRZZZZ	PA
POJAWJAS, JOS.	29	M	LABR	RRZZZZ	PA
EISRAT, AUG.	27	M	LABR	RRZZZZ	PA
CZESKA, MARCIN	37	M	LABR	RRZZZZ	IL
LYSTER, ANDREAS	36	M	LABR	RRZZZZ	IL
GLINKA, ADAM	43	M	LABR	RRZZZZ	IA
DYMSKI, PIOTR	29	M	LABR	RRZZZZ	IA

PASSENGER	AGE	SEX	OCCUPATION	PRIVL	DES
LENZA, MICH.	28	M	LABR	RRZZZZ	IA
NAWROTZKY, AND.	42	M	LABR	RRZZZZ	IA
BUNKOWSKI, CAZIMIR	43	M	FARMER	RRZZZZ	IA
ZAPOLSKY, VINCENTY	26	M	FARMER	RRZZZZ	NY
LOEW, EPHR.	22	M	FARMER	RRZZZZ	NY
LURY, MOSES	22	M	FARMER	RRZZZZ	NY
HERZ	36	M	FARMER	RRZZZZ	NY
ROWAKOWSKY, JOS.	17	M	LABR	RRZZZZ	NY
KURZEWSKY, FRANZ	30	M	LABR	RRZZZZ	NY
POZONDNY, WASIL	26	M	LABR	RRZZZZ	NY
WOJTASZ, ANT.	42	M	LABR	RRZZZZ	NY
POZONDNY, U	37	M	FARMER	RRZZZZ	NY
SMOLSKY, JOS.	29	M	FARMER	RRZZZZ	NY
ABRAMOWITZ, MATT.	26	M	FARMER	RRZZZZ	NY
TAMOLNICZ, JOS.	26	M	FARMER	RRZZZZ	NY
ALCHINES, JOS.	48	M	FARMER	RRZZZZ	NY
WEICZCKOWSKI, THOM.	20	M	FARMER	RRZZZZ	NY
KAEZKAMER, CASIM.	31	M	FARMER	RRZZZZ	NY
MECZKELIWIZ, NIEL	26	M	FARMER	RRZZZZ	NY
JOUNNAS, PAWEL	25	M	FARMER	RRZZZZ	NY
HOLL, AUG.	26	M	FARMER	RRZZZZ	NY
SAWULIS, ANT.	47	M	LABR	RRZZZZ	NY
AKULCITIS, WIE.	25	M	LABR	RRZZZZ	NY
GRUENBLATT, HIRSCH	23	M	MCHT	RRZZZZ	NY
BLASZAK, VALENT.	29	M	FARMER	RRZZZZ	NY
ZIELINSKI, MICH.	37	M	LABR	RRZZZZ	NY
PIETRZI, ANT.	24	M	LABR	RRZZZZ	NY
HALPERN, LEIB	19	M	LABR	RRZZZZ	IL
PERLMANN, HENDEL	55	M	LABR	RRZZZZ	IL
MORASKI, ALEXANDER	32	M	LABR	RRZZZZ	IL
KRZYZANSKI, ALEXANDER	28	M	LABR	RRZZZZ	IL
SMOLINSKY, CLEM.	29	M	LABR	RRZZZZ	IL
LAENER, FRANZ	31	M	GDNR	RRZZZZ	IL
DOLITZKI, JOH.	22	M	FARMER	RRZZZZ	IL
BURKOWSKI, SIMON	35	M	FARMER	RRZZZZ	IL
LEWANDOWSKY, LEONH.	18	M	LABR	RRZZZZ	IL
KIVIATKOWSKI, JAN	34	M	LABR	RRZZZZ	IL
KANJEWSKI, JOS.	46	M	LABR	RRZZZZ	IL
MAKIEWICZ, PETER	26	M	LABR	RRZZZZ	IL
JAN	33	M	LABR	RRZZZZ	IL
KANJERSKI, FRANK	23	M	LABR	RRZZZZ	IL
KWIATKOWSKI, ANT.	25	M	LABR	RRZZZZ	NY
LEWANDOWSKI, U	23	M	LABR	RRZZZZ	NY
JENDRZUSKY, MART.	23	M	LABR	RRZZZZ	NY
HOFFMANN, CHAIM	18	M	LABR	RRZZZZ	NY
FLINDER, FRIED.	40	M	LABR	RRZZZZ	NY
MISCHKOWITZ, ANTON	22	M	LABR	RRZZZZ	NY
SZMELEWSKI, JAN	26	M	LABR	RRZZZZ	NY
JUKOWSKI, JOS.	24	M	LABR	RRZZZZ	NY
---AB--, U	36	M	LABR	RRZZZZ	NY
CZANDOR, MICH.	22	M	LABR	RRZZZZ	NY
VICT.	28	M	LABR	RRZZZZ	NY
ROMANOWSKI, LADISL.	32	M	LABR	RRZZZZ	NY
GABRIEKZEK, JOS.	41	M	LABR	RRZZZZ	NY
MEDWICZKI, ALEX	24	M	LABR	RRZZZZ	NY
OSEWSKI, LUD.	32	M	LABR	RRZZZZ	NY
BILLAWSKI, LADISL.	21	M	LABR	RRZZZZ	NY
MIJEWSKI, VICTOR	26	M	LABR	RRZZZZ	NY
BIERJEWSKI, FRANZ	47	M	LABR	RRZZZZ	NY
DONDAK, WAICZEK	32	M	LABR	RRZZZZ	NY
GLICKOT, STANISL.	28	M	LABR	RRZZZZ	NY
SOKOLOWSKI, PETER	29	M	LABR	RRZZZZ	NY
GREWJUKOWSKI, STANISL.	29	M	LABR	RRZZZZ	NY
PEEZADA, ALEX	31	M	LABR	RRZZZZ	NY
KUSSINSKI, MART.	29	M	LABR	RRZZZZ	NY
KUPLINSKI, PETER	30	M	LABR	RRZZZZ	NY
CZOSNIKOWSKI, A.	26	M	LABR	RRZZZZ	NY
POTOLSKI, LEON	26	M	LABR	RRZZZZ	NY
BRANOWSKI, JAN	22	M	LABR	RRZZZZ	NY
GOLDSTEIN, SCATE	34	F	W	RRZZZZ	IN
SARAH	7	F	CHILD	RRZZZZ	IN
ROCKE	3	F	CHILD	RRZZZZ	IN
DWERE	.08	F	INFANT	RRZZZZ	IN
KISSLER, JOH.	31	M	CPTR	RRZZZZ	NE
MARIE	30	F	W	RRZZZZ	NE
OCHS, ANTON	38	M	FARMER	RRZZZZ	DAK
CATH.	26	F	W	RRZZZZ	DAK
U	7	M	CHILD	RRZZZZ	DAK
U	6	M	CHILD	RRZZZZ	DAK
JOHANES	4	M	CHILD	RRZZZZ	DAK
MICH.	3	M	CHILD	RRZZZZ	DAK
BERNH.	2	M	CHILD	RRZZZZ	DAK
JOS.	.03	M	INFANT	RRZZZZ	DAK
SEBASTIAN	49	M	FARMER	RRZZZZ	DAK
MARG.	47	F	W	RRZZZZ	DAK
KATH.	20	F	SVNT	RRZZZZ	DAK
MARG.	18	F	SVNT	RRZZZZ	DAK
MARIE	13	F	SVNT	RRZZZZ	DAK
WENDOLIN	7	M	CHILD	RRZZZZ	DAK
U	4	M	CHILD	RRZZZZ	DAK
JULIE	2	F	CHILD	RRZZZZ	DAK
LORENZ	.03	M	INFANT	RRZZZZ	DAK
JOHANNES	37	M	FARMER	RRZZZZ	DAK
MAGD.	36	F	W	RRZZZZ	DAK
KATH.	14	F	UNKNOWN	RRZZZZ	DAK
ANNA	11	F	UNKNOWN	RRZZZZ	DAK
REGINE	7	F	CHILD	RRZZZZ	DAK
BERNH.	4	M	CHILD	RRZZZZ	DAK
PAUL	2	M	CHILD	RRZZZZ	DAK
GERTRUDE	.11	F	INFANT	RRZZZZ	DAK
SENGE, JACOB	37	M	FARMER	RRZZZZ	DAK
MAGD.	33	F	W	RRZZZZ	DAK
PAUL.	5	F	CHILD	RRZZZZ	DAK
HELENE	4	F	CHILD	RRZZZZ	DAK
FRANZ	.10	F	INFANT	RRZZZZ	DAK
ANDR.	7	M	CHILD	RRZZZZ	DAK
WEISSBECK, MATHIAS	35	M	FARMER	RRZZZZ	DAK
MAGD.	30	F	W	RRZZZZ	DAK
JOSEF	4	M	CHILD	RRZZZZ	DAK
JOH.	3	M	CHILD	RRZZZZ	DAK
PETER	.11	M	INFANT	RRZZZZ	DAK
GEFRAEK, JACOB	38	M	FARMER	RRZZZZ	DAK
KATH.	36	F	W	RRZZZZ	DAK
ANTON	15	M	FARMER	RRZZZZ	DAK
SYLVESTER	9	M	CHILD	RRZZZZ	DAK
KATH.	7	F	CHILD	RRZZZZ	DAK
JACOB	4	M	CHILD	RRZZZZ	DAK
JOH.	2	M	CHILD	RRZZZZ	DAK
ALBIN	.01	M	INFANT	RRZZZZ	DAK
HUMEYER, JOH.	37	M	FARMER	RRZZZZ	DAK
MAGD.	33	F	W	RRZZZZ	DAK
GENOFEFA	7	F	CHILD	RRZZZZ	DAK
KATH.	7	F	CHILD	RRZZZZ	DAK
KONRAD	5	M	CHILD	RRZZZZ	DAK
MAGD.	3	F	CHILD	RRZZZZ	DAK
U	2	M	CHILD	RRZZZZ	DAK
U	.08	F	INFANT	RRZZZZ	DAK
RAPP, AUG.	20	M	FARMER	RRZZZZ	CAL
ELISAB.	20	F	W	RRZZZZ	CAL
CHRIST.	55	F	W	RRZZZZ	CAL
REN, CONRAD	27	M	FARMER	RRZZZZ	NE
CATH.	28	F	W	RRZZZZ	NE
HUBERT, PHILIPP	35	M	FARMER	RRZZZZ	CAL
ANNA	35	F	W	RRZZZZ	CAL
MARIE	3	F	CHILD	RRZZZZ	CAL
SCHESSLER, GEORG	25	M	FARMER	RRZZZZ	NY
ELISAB.	25	F	UNKNOWN	RRZZZZ	NY
HEINR.	18	M	FARMER	RRZZZZ	NY
BERNHARD, CONRAD	25	M	FARMER	RRZZZZ	NE
CATH.	25	F	UNKNOWN	RRZZZZ	NE
U	5	F	CHILD	RRZZZZ	NE
KLE--, ---RE	47	M	FARMER	RRZZZZ	NE
GRETE	41	F	UNKNOWN	RRZZZZ	NE
ANNA	10	F	CH	RRZZZZ	NE
FRIED.	7	M	CHILD	RRZZZZ	NE
MARIE	4	F	CHILD	RRZZZZ	NE
CARL	2	M	CHILD	RRZZZZ	NE
GRETE	.10	F	INFANT	RRZZZZ	NE
LIEDER, PETER	34	M	FARMER	RRZZZZ	NE
MARG.	30	F	UNKNOWN	RRZZZZ	NE

PASSENGER	AGE	SEX	OCCUPATION	PRV	VIL	DES
PETER	7	M	CHILD	RR	ZZZZ	NE
CARL	4	M	CHILD	RR	ZZZZ	NE
U	.10	M	INFANT	RR	ZZZZ	NE
ENGELMANN, FRIED.	55	M	FARMER	RR	ZZZZ	NE
CATH.	52	F	UNKNOWN	RR	ZZZZ	NE
PETER	15	M	FARMER	RR	ZZZZ	NE
ANNA	18	F	UNKNOWN	RR	ZZZZ	NE
DIEKL, HEINR.	21	M	FARMER	RR	ZZZZ	NY
CHRIST.	20	F	UNKNOWN	RR	ZZZZ	NY
HEINR.	.01	M	INFANT	RR	ZZZZ	NY
ADLER, VALENT.	58	M	FARMER	RR	ZZZZ	IL
CATH.	55	F	UNKNOWN	RR	ZZZZ	IL
CATH.	18	F	SVNT	RR	ZZZZ	IL
CATH.	9	F	CHILD	RR	ZZZZ	IL
--ALIE	6	F	CHILD	RR	ZZZZ	IL
PETER	30	M	FARMER	RR	ZZZZ	IL
ANNIE	29	F	UNKNOWN	RR	ZZZZ	IL
ANNA	3	F	CHILD	RR	ZZZZ	IL
PETER	3	M	CHILD	RR	ZZZZ	IL
HEINR.	.01	M	INFANT	RR	ZZZZ	IL
CONRAD	21	M	FARMER	RR	ZZZZ	IL
CATH.	26	F	UNKNOWN	RR	ZZZZ	IL
AMOND, JACOB	31	M	FARMER	RR	ZZZZ	NE
CATH.	26	F	UNKNOWN	RR	ZZZZ	NE
WILH.	19	M	FARMER	RR	ZZZZ	NE
CATH.	.01	F	INFANT	RR	ZZZZ	NE
WEBER, ADAM	21	M	FARMER	RR	ZZZZ	NY
MAGD.	20	F	UNKNOWN	RR	ZZZZ	NY
CATH.	.07	F	INFANT	RR	ZZZZ	NY
JACOB	19	M	FARMER	RR	ZZZZ	NY
KANZLER, WILH.	28	M	FARMER	RR	ZZZZ	NY
CATH.	23	F	UNKNOWN	RR	ZZZZ	NY
WILH.	.08	M	INFANT	RR	ZZZZ	NY
HEINR.	00	M	FARMER	RR	ZZZZ	NY
DIEHL, PETER	38	M	FARMER	RR	ZZZZ	NE
CATH.	35	F	UNKNOWN	RR	ZZZZ	NE
FRIED.	7	M	CHILD	RR	ZZZZ	NE
CARL	3	M	CHILD	RR	ZZZZ	NE
U	2	F	CHILD	RR	ZZZZ	NE
U	.02	M	INFANT	RR	ZZZZ	NE
WAKER, GEORG	25	M	FARMER	RR	ZZZZ	NE
ANNA	25	F	UNKNOWN	RR	ZZZZ	NE
GEORG	4	M	CHILD	RR	ZZZZ	NE
HEINR.	3	M	CHILD	RR	ZZZZ	NE
RISSLER, ANNA	3	F	CHILD	RR	ZZZZ	NY
HANNES	2	M	CHILD	RR	ZZZZ	NY
GEORG	.10	M	INFANT	RR	ZZZZ	NY
RADUNG, CARL	71	M	FARMER	RR	ZZZZ	NY
HAUCKSTEIN, NACHAME	48	F	W	RR	ZZZZ	NY
HATE	7	F	CHILD	RR	ZZZZ	NY
BAUMGARTEN, JACOB	32	M	FARMER	RR	ZZZZ	NY
CHRIST.	28	F	UNKNOWN	RR	ZZZZ	NY
FRANZ.	2	F	CHILD	RR	ZZZZ	NY
JOH.	4	M	CHILD	RR	ZZZZ	NY
ANTON	.11	M	INFANT	RR	ZZZZ	NY
EVA	.11	F	INFANT	RR	ZZZZ	NY
FEIST, KASPAR	33	M	FARMER	RR	ZZZZ	NY
KATH.	29	F	UNKNOWN	RR	ZZZZ	NY
MAGD.	6	F	CHILD	RR	ZZZZ	NY
JOS.	3	M	CHILD	RR	ZZZZ	NY
JOH.	3	M	CHILD	RR	ZZZZ	NY
MARG.	1	F	CHILD	RR	ZZZZ	NY
KASPAR	.05	M	INFANT	RR	ZZZZ	NY
FRANZ	34	M	FARMER	RR	ZZZZ	NY
CHRIST.	32	F	UNKNOWN	RR	ZZZZ	NY
WEND.	7	M	CHILD	RR	ZZZZ	NY
FRANZ.	4	F	CHILD	RR	ZZZZ	NY
ELISAB.	2	F	CHILD	RR	ZZZZ	NY
FRANZ.	.07	M	INFANT	RR	ZZZZ	NY
---EDER, U	43	M	FARMER	RR	ZZZZ	NY
U	41	F	UNKNOWN	RR	ZZZZ	NY
JOS.	11	M	CH	RR	ZZZZ	NY
CATH.	9	F	CHILD	RR	ZZZZ	NY
WEND.	7	M	CHILD	RR	ZZZZ	NY
ELISAB.	5	F	CHILD	RR	ZZZZ	NY
BENED.	3	F	CHILD	RR	ZZZZ	NY
BAUMGAERTNER, JOH.	40	M	FARMER	RR	ZZZZ	DAK
MARG.	38	F	UNKNOWN	RR	ZZZZ	DAK
MARG.	12	F	UNKNOWN	RR	ZZZZ	DAK
MICH.	9	F	CHILD	RR	ZZZZ	DAK
JOH.	7	M	CHILD	RR	ZZZZ	DAK
U	5	M	CHILD	RR	ZZZZ	DAK
LEOP.	3	M	CHILD	RR	ZZZZ	DAK
BARB.	1	F	CHILD	RR	ZZZZ	DAK
EVA	.10	F	INFANT	RR	ZZZZ	DAK
JOSEFINE	.10	F	INFANT	RR	ZZZZ	DAK
FRANZ	23	M	FARMER	RR	ZZZZ	DAK
MARG.	36	F	UNKNOWN	RR	ZZZZ	DAK
ANTON	9	M	CHILD	RR	ZZZZ	DAK
JOS.	7	M	CHILD	RR	ZZZZ	DAK
BARB.	5	F	CHILD	RR	ZZZZ	DAK
MARG.	3	F	CHILD	RR	ZZZZ	DAK
JULIE	1	F	CHILD	RR	ZZZZ	DAK
MARIANNA	.11	F	INFANT	RR	ZZZZ	DAK
PETER	.01	M	INFANT	RR	ZZZZ	DAK
GANJE, CARL	23	M	FARMER	RR	ZZZZ	DAK
EVA	22	F	UNKNOWN	RR	ZZZZ	DAK
BRIGITTE	.06	F	INFANT	RR	ZZZZ	DAK
PETROLEIT, JOHANN	42	M	LABR	RR	ZZZZ	DAK
U	37	F	UNKNOWN	RR	ZZZZ	DAK
U	29	M	FARMER	RR	ZZZZ	CAL
MARG.	29	F	UNKNOWN	RR	ZZZZ	CAL
CARL	4	M	CHILD	RR	ZZZZ	CAL
AUG.	2	M	CHILD	RR	ZZZZ	CAL
MAX	.10	M	INFANT	RR	ZZZZ	CAL
MEYER, GEORG	33	M	UNKNOWN	RR	ZZZZ	CAL
MARIE	33	F	UNKNOWN	RR	ZZZZ	CAL
CONRAD	20	M	FARMER	RR	ZZZZ	CAL
HEINR.	18	M	FARMER	RR	ZZZZ	CAL
HEININGER, FRIED.	32	M	FARMER	RR	ZZZZ	CAL
CATH.	24	F	UNKNOWN	RR	ZZZZ	CAL
WILH.	20	M	FARMER	RR	ZZZZ	CAL
ANNA	.06	F	INFANT	RR	ZZZZ	CAL
WEIGL, ANDR.	35	M	FARMER	RR	ZZZZ	NY
ANNA	32	F	UNKNOWN	RR	ZZZZ	NY
LUD.	6	M	CHILD	RR	ZZZZ	NY
FRIED.	4	M	CHILD	RR	ZZZZ	NY
EMILIE	.11	F	INFANT	RR	ZZZZ	NY
HACKMANN, HENACH	47	M	FARMER	RR	ZZZZ	BUF
FEIGE	49	F	UNKNOWN	RR	ZZZZ	BUF
BARNATEUS, MARIA	24	F	W	RR	ZZZZ	BUF
U	.11	M	INFANT	RR	ZZZZ	BUF
---ABOWITZ, U	25	F	W	RR	ZZZZ	BUF
BERNSTEIN, DWEIRE	25	F	W	RR	ZZZZ	BUF
FRADEL	.11	M	INFANT	RR	ZZZZ	BUF
S---, U	22	F	SVNT	RR	ZZZZ	NY
U, U	18	F	SVNT	RR	ZZZZ	NY
SARALEINER, FRIED.	38	F	W	RR	ZZZZ	NY
TAPOLLE, ANNA	27	F	W	RR	ZZZZ	NY
HEININE, MARIE	33	F	W	RR	ZZZZ	NY
EISRAT, HENRIETTE	22	F	SVNT	RR	ZZZZ	NY
OBROMSKA, MARIE	19	F	SVNT	RR	ZZZZ	PA
FISCHER, TAUBE	22	F	SVNT	RR	ZZZZ	BAL
GRINBERG, MARG.	25	F	SVNT	RR	ZZZZ	NY
PIALKOWSKA, MARG.	25	F	SVNT	RR	ZZZZ	NY
JELINSKA, MARIE	18	F	SVNT	RR	ZZZZ	NY
BRANOWSKA, ANNA	19	F	SVNT	RR	ZZZZ	NY

SHIP: LAKE ONTARIO

FROM: LIVERPOOL
TO: BOSTON
ARRIVED: 11 APRIL 1889

PASSENGER	AGE	SEX	OCCUPATION	PRV VIL DES
MECHANK, OLGA	14	M	MECH	RRZZZZCH
MISCHEWSKY, JAN	28	M	MECH	RRZZZZCH
CZUEVAN, MOR.L.	15	M	MECH	RRZZZZCH
BLEIER, LIBE	30	F	W	PLZZZZCH
FEGE	11	M	CH	PLZZZZCH
DAVID	10	M	CH	PLZZZZCH
CHAJE	5	M	CHILD	PLZZZZCH
JACHET	4	M	CHILD	PLZZZZCH
TIZ.	3	M	CHILD	PLZZZZCH
FEGE	31	F	W	PLZZZZCH
AB.	5	M	CHILD	PLZZZZCH
RACHEL	3	F	CHILD	PLZZZZCH
KAPLER, CHANE	30	M	FARMER	RRZZZZCH
SCH.	10	M	CH	RRZZZZCH
SUN.	4	M	CHILD	RRZZZZCH
MARIE	1	F	CHILD	RRZZZZCH
MARIE	1	F	CHILD	RRZZZZCH
RIDEN, WATEULZ	27	M	MECH	RRZZZZCH
JANSKOWSKY, JOSEF	24	M	MECH	RRZZZZCH
SCHMIWSKY, WAW	27	M	MECH	RRZZZZCH
ALBRECHT, JULIUS	22	M	MECH	RRZZZZNY
KRYER, JOHANN	31	M	MECH	RRZZZZNY
PLISKA, F.	20	M	MECH	RRZZZZNY
SOBUS, JOSEF	43	M	MECH	RRZZZZNY
BOGDAM, JOSEF	34	M	MECH	RRZZZZNY
SWOITZEN, JURKA	40	M	FARMER	PLZZZZNY
BERNASCH, PITTRO	40	M	FARMER	PLZZZZNY
ZEWAFSKY, WLAD.	22	M	FARMER	PLZZZZNY
KRAKOWSKY, WALENT	38	M	FARMER	PLZZZZNY
KASCKEWITZ, WAW	27	M	FARMER	PLZZZZNY
JASTHENSKY, JOSEF	28	M	FARMER	PLZZZZNY

SHIP: PENNSYLVANIA

FROM: ANTWERP
TO: NEW YORK
ARRIVED: 11 APRIL 1889

PASSENGER	AGE	SEX	OCCUPATION	PRV VIL DES
DOMARACK, J.	27	M	LABR	RRZZZZNY
PAWLOWSKI, F.	23	M	LABR	PLZZZZPIT
PRARDIK, J.	32	M	LABR	PLZZZZNY
RENWARSKI, PAULINE	24	F	SVNT	PLZZZZNY
SCHERBINZKY, W.	31	M	LABR	PLZZZZNY
JUROVSKY, F.	37	M	LABR	RRZZZZNY
WITKOWSKI, M.	35	M	LABR	PLZZZZBUF
MARIE	24	F	W	PLZZZZBUF
J.	5	M	CHILD	PLZZZZBUF
W.	2	M	CHILD	PLZZZZBUF
ZIPERSKI, A.	36	M	LABR	PLZZZZMIL
A.	36	F	W	PLZZZZMIL
R.	9	F	CHILD	PLZZZZMIL
AUG.	4	M	CHILD	PLZZZZMIL
BERN.	2	M	CHILD	PLZZZZMIL
M.	.06	F	INFANT	PLZZZZMIL

SHIP: ST. OF PENNSYLVANIA

FROM: GLASGOW AND LARNE
TO: NEW YORK
ARRIVED: 12 APRIL 1889

PASSENGER	AGE	SEX	OCCUPATION	PRV VIL DES
LONGRAN, WM.	36	M	SLR	FNZZZZUSA
BASCHUKEWITZ, SELIG	40	M	GZR	RRZZZZUSA
SAMSON, BORUCH	26	M	BTMKR	RRZZZZUSA
JARUSKI, JOEL	24	M	BTMKR	RRZZZZUSA
RABINOWITZ, SCHAJE	38	M	MLR	RRZZZZUSA
MANEROITZ, SCHMUEL	43	M	HRCTR	RRZZZZUSA
SLOSUETZKI, GIMPEL	24	M	CPRSMH	RRZZZZUSA
FAUBLES, BARUCH	20	M	TLR	RRZZZZUSA
SCHUMAKER, MOSES	18	M	TLR	RRZZZZUSA
SCHMUEL	16	M	TLR	RRZZZZUSA
ALTMANN, JANKEL	28	M	TLR	RRZZZZUSA
ANIS, GEDALJE	30	M	TLR	RRZZZZUSA
ROBOTIUK, EISIK	18	M	PDLR	RRZZZZUSA
DRESNER, SALOMON	16	M	PDLR	RRZZZZUSA
JAKON, MAWSCHE	38	M	PDLR	RRZZZZUSA
AWENBERG, SCHMUEL	17	M	PDLR	RRZZZZUSA
BARK, NOACH	16	M	PDLR	RRZZZZUSA
PERSK, RACHMIEL	18	M	PDLR	RRZZZZUSA
KRUBSKIWIN, JACOB	26	M	PDLR	RRZZZZUSA
SPIES, VICENTI	24	M	LABR	RRZZZZUSA
STUREZINSKY, JAN	30	M	LABR	RRZZZZUSA
HIELPERN, JACOB	15	M	LABR	RRZZZZUSA
LICHTENFELD, JACOB	19	M	LABR	RRZZZZUSA
GLASER, MOSES	18	M	LABR	RRZZZZUSA
PERK, WULFF	20	M	LABR	RRZZZZUSA
JANZKOWSKY, JOSEPH	20	M	LABR	RRZZZZUSA
GUTSCHOWSKY, STAUL	23	M	LABR	RRZZZZUSA
JAGASCHINSKI, JAN	25	M	LABR	RRZZZZUSA
GORNY, JOSEPH	50	M	LABR	RRZZZZUSA
BIELINSKI, ANTON	30	M	LABR	RRZZZZUSA
KRAFT, GOTTFRIED	45	M	LABR	RRZZZZUSA
GIRODOWSKY, ALBERT	47	M	LABR	RRZZZZUSA
LUKASZ, MICHAL	23	M	LABR	RRZZZZUSA
SZEPANEK, PAWEL	28	M	LABR	RRZZZZUSA
TWASCHKEURTSCH, MICHAEL	35	M	LABR	RRZZZZUSA
DRAUGLIS, MATAUSCH	30	M	LABR	RRZZZZUSA
SWININKA, FEDOR	31	M	LABR	RRZZZZUSA
KERYLA, MICHAL	27	M	LABR	RRZZZZUSA
GRAJEWSKY, SIMON	11	M	BY	RRZZZZUSA
DOGVILLE, ANTON	12	M	BY	RRZZZZUSA
STAAKEWITZ, MICHAL	32	M	LABR	RRZZZZUSA
POLINOFSKY, ADOLPH	22	M	LABR	RRZZZZUSA
SOLYGOUR, OSIP	36	M	LABR	RRZZZZUSA
PATRA, ANDRAS	32	M	LABR	RRZZZZUSA
WEREB, ISTWAN	21	M	LABR	RRZZZZUSA
BOBAY, JANOS	25	M	LABR	RRZZZZUSA
MAGA, JAN	23	M	LABR	RRZZZZUSA
JANOWITSH, KAZIMIR	27	M	LABR	RRZZZZUSA
KNUFSKI, JOSEPH	30	M	LABR	RRZZZZUSA
JEAN	12	M	LABR	RRZZZZUSA
MAZIKA, VICTORIA	19	F	SP	RRZZZZUSA
ARRENBERG, HENE	18	F	SP	RRZZZZUSA
KRAUZ, FREIDE	15	F	SP	RRZZZZUSA
STEMSCHUSS, ENTE	27	F	SP	RRZZZZUSA
MORGULIS, ROCHE	20	F	SP	RRZZZZUSA
ROSENBAUM, ELKE	22	F	SP	RRZZZZUSA
CLODESCH, SHAJE	20	F	SP	RRZZZZUSA
JANOWITZKY, DEBRUSCHE	18	F	SP	RRZZZZUSA
LICHTERMANN, NECHANNE	22	F	SP	RRZZZZUSA
MOGA, MARIA	16	F	SP	RRZZZZUSA
KAZOWITZ, ELKE	11	F	CH	RRZZZZUSA
GENISON, MENDEL	20	M	JNR	RRZZZZUSA
FEIGE	22	F	W	RRZZZZUSA
GOLDSTEIN, ISRAEL	60	M	PDLR	RRZZZZUSA
SORE	18	F	SP	RRZZZZUSA
DIKAT, PAUL	22	M	LABR	RRZZZZUSA
KAROL	18	F	W	RRZZZZUSA
BOROWSKY, JOSEPH	41	M	LABR	RRZZZZUSA

PASSENGER	AGE	SEX	OCCUPATION	PRIV	VIL	DES
MARIANNE	40	F	W	RR	ZZZ	USA
NOWICKI, JAN	25	M	LABR	RR	ZZZ	USA
ANTONIE	21	F	W	RR	ZZZ	USA
PAZDERSKI, BARTHOLOMY	34	M	LABR	RR	ZZZ	USA
KATI	28	F	W	RR	ZZZ	USA
ROSEDORE, JULIUS	22	M	LABR	RR	ZZZ	USA
ROCHEL	20	F	W	RR	ZZZ	USA
CHAJE	.09	F	INFANT	RR	ZZZ	USA
PLOTNIKOW, GIHEL	23	M	TLR	RR	ZZZ	USA
MENASCHE	18	F	W	RR	ZZZ	USA
JEUNNE	6	F	CHILD	RR	ZZZ	USA
ITZIG	.09	M	INFANT	RR	ZZZ	USA
DESCHATZKY, FREIDEL	24	F	W	RR	ZZZ	USA
MARKE	2	M	CHILD	RR	ZZZ	USA
OSCHER	2	M	CHILD	RR	ZZZ	USA
MOSES	9	M	CHILD	RR	ZZZ	USA
PAZDERSKY, MARIE	4	F	CHILD	RR	ZZZ	USA
STEFAN	2	M	CHILD	RR	ZZZ	USA
LEONORE	.03	F	INFANT	RR	ZZZ	USA
FRIED, FRIEDE	28	F	W	RR	ZZZ	USA
MOSES	2	M	CHILD	RR	ZZZ	USA
RACHMIEL	.06	M	INFANT	RR	ZZZ	USA
LEWITAN, RIWKE	25	F	W	RR	ZZZ	USA
CHASKEL	.09	F	INFANT	RR	ZZZ	USA
RABINOWITSCH, CHANNE	60	F	W	RR	ZZZ	USA
JOSCHE	40	F	W	RR	ZZZ	USA
RASCHE	18	F	SP	RR	ZZZ	USA
ZALLE	11	M	CH	RR	ZZZ	USA
BASCHE	9	F	CHILD	RR	ZZZ	USA
ABRAHAM	8	M	CHILD	RR	ZZZ	USA
JANKEL	7	M	CHILD	RR	ZZZ	USA
BROYDE, MALKE	47	F	W	RR	ZZZ	USA
SAMUEL	11	M	CH	RR	ZZZ	USA
SCHEINE	10	M	CH	RR	ZZZ	USA
MEYER	7	M	CHILD	RR	ZZZ	USA
CHAJE	2	F	CHILD	RR	ZZZ	USA
BONSTEIN, CHANY	30	F	W	RR	ZZZ	USA
SARA	2	F	CHILD	RR	ZZZ	USA
ELIAS	1	M	CHILD	RR	ZZZ	USA
GITERMANN, CHAJE	23	F	W	RR	ZZZ	USA
ZIMCHE	6	M	CHILD	RR	ZZZ	USA
ITZIG	2	M	CHILD	RR	ZZZ	USA
ABRAHAM	.09	M	INFANT	RR	ZZZ	USA
HERZKOPF, HINDE	25	F	W	RR	ZZZ	USA
ROCHEL	5	F	CHILD	RR	ZZZ	USA
ZERUCHIM	1	M	CHILD	RR	ZZZ	USA
HADE	.03	M	INFANT	RR	ZZZ	USA
JOLUGOW, BONOFACI	34	F	W	RR	ZZZ	USA
KALMIRA	9	F	CHILD	RR	ZZZ	USA
MARIA	7	F	CHILD	RR	ZZZ	USA
WALIGORA, VYKTORIA	29	F	W	RR	ZZZ	USA
MARYANNE	3	F	CHILD	RR	ZZZ	USA
ROSALIE	1	F	CHILD	RR	ZZZ	USA
HOLZBERG, RICHLIN	25	F	W	RR	ZZZ	USA
MEYER	5	M	CHILD	RR	ZZZ	USA
SHAJE	1	F	CHILD	RR	ZZZ	USA
GOLAFEIN, DOBRE	22	F	W	RR	ZZZ	USA
CHAJE	23	F	SP	RR	ZZZ	USA
SIMACHE	.09	F	INFANT	RR	ZZZ	USA
DESCHATSKY, JUDEL	27	M	LABR	RR	ZZZ	USA

SHIP: WESER

FROM: BREMEN
TO: BALTIMORE
ARRIVED: 12 APRIL 1889

PASSENGER	AGE	SEX	OCCUPATION	PRIV	VIL	DES
LEKEMANN, CHAJE	28	F	LABR	RR	ZZZ	BAL
CHAJE	7	F	CHILD	RR	ZZZ	BAL
HUS, SARA	22	F	UNKNOWN	RR	ZZZ	BAL
SCHMUL	.11	M	INFANT	RR	ZZZ	BAL
SCHER, ENTE	45	F	UNKNOWN	RR	ZZZ	BAL
BELTE, BALE	32	F	UNKNOWN	RR	ZZZ	BAL
REBECCA	16	F	UNKNOWN	RR	ZZZ	BAL
SCHEINE	11	F	UNKNOWN	RR	ZZZ	BAL
GUSTI	8	F	CHILD	RR	ZZZ	BAL
SAMUEL	6	M	CHILD	RR	ZZZ	BAL
PHILIPP	4	M	CHILD	RR	ZZZ	BAL
BETTY	.11	F	INFANT	RR	ZZZ	BAL
LAJETZKY, CHAJE	16	F	UNKNOWN	RR	ZZZ	BAL
SCHMIDT, WILHELM	18	M	LABR	RR	ZZZ	BAL
MARTIN	60	M	LABR	RR	ZZZ	BAL
EMILIE	30	F	UNKNOWN	RR	ZZZ	BAL
MARYANNA	4	F	CHILD	RR	ZZZ	BAL
PRAKENINGE, ANNA	31	F	UNKNOWN	RR	ZZZ	BAL
ALBERT	14	F	UNKNOWN	RR	ZZZ	BAL
FINE, CHANNE	25	F	UNKNOWN	RR	ZZZ	BAL
FEIGE	2	F	CHILD	RR	ZZZ	BAL
LEA, REBECCA	19	F	UNKNOWN	RR	ZZZ	BAL
MOLIN, BENI.NOCH.	45	M	SMH	RR	ZZZ	BAL
RIVE	45	F	UNKNOWN	RR	ZZZ	BAL
JAKOB	23	M	UNKNOWN	RR	ZZZ	BAL
FROME	18	F	UNKNOWN	RR	ZZZ	BAL
SIMON	9	M	CHILD	RR	ZZZ	BAL
CHAJE	8	F	CHILD	RR	ZZZ	BAL
ROCHE	6	F	CHILD	RR	ZZZ	BAL
KUZLARCK, STANISL.	45	M	LABR	RR	ZZZ	BAL
PROTOSIEWICZ, FRANK	25	M	LABR	RR	ZZZ	BAL
MENDEL, JOHANN	18	M	FARMER	RR	ZZZ	BAL
CIERNICKI, STANISL.	24	M	FARMER	RR	ZZZ	MN
GRATH, WILH.	40	M	FARMER	RR	ZZZ	IL
GITTELSOHN, JETTE	19	F	UNKNOWN	RR	ZZZ	IL
MESSMANN, SPRINCE	15	F	SVNT	RR	ZZZ	IL
HURWITZ, ESTER	25	F	SVNT	RR	ZZZ	IL
BOLCERECK, JOSEF	30	F	SVNT	RR	ZZZ	IL
BORUCKI, ANDREAS	18	F	SVNT	RR	ZZZ	IL
OLSZEWSKA, FRANZ.	18	F	SVNT	RR	ZZZ	IL
DOBRZYNSKI, ANTON	25	M	TLR	RR	ZZZ	IL
CELKOSKI, WICENTY	25	M	SMH	RR	ZZZ	IL
OLSZEWSKA, PRAKSEDA	21	F	SVNT	RR	ZZZ	IL
NOKRACKI, JOSEFA	19	F	SVNT	RR	ZZZ	IL
BULERA, JOSEF	26	M	LABR	RR	ZZZ	IL
WROBLEWSKI, FRANZ	25	M	LABR	RR	ZZZ	IL
NOKRACKI, VALENTIN	30	M	FARMER	RR	ZZZ	IL
NADREJ	20	M	FARMER	RR	ZZZ	IL
PEADA, CASIMIR	27	M	FARMER	RR	ZZZ	BAL
PEZA, FRANZ	26	M	LABR	RR	ZZZ	BAL
HANS, ROCHE	48	F	UNKNOWN	RR	ZZZ	BAL
REINHARDT, LUDWIG	29	M	FARMER	RR	ZZZ	BAL
PREUSS, FRIEDR.	27	M	UNKNOWN	RR	ZZZ	BAL
CAROL.	26	F	UNKNOWN	RR	ZZZ	BAL
CHOINACKI, SZCZEP.	30	M	FARMER	RR	ZZZ	DAK
HAPPERLE, JOH.	31	M	UNKNOWN	RR	ZZZ	DAK
MARG.	27	F	UNKNOWN	RR	ZZZ	DAK
JOHANN	6	M	CHILD	RR	ZZZ	DAK
MAGD.	4	F	CHILD	RR	ZZZ	DAK
WILH.	.11	F	INFANT	RR	ZZZ	DAK
FRIED, JAKOB	25	M	FARMER	RR	ZZZ	DAK
BARB.	23	F	UNKNOWN	RR	ZZZ	DAK
MARG.	2	F	CHILD	RR	ZZZ	DAK
ELISABETH	.04	F	INFANT	RR	ZZZ	DAK
WOLFER, FRIEDR.	50	M	FARMER	RR	ZZZ	DAK
MARGA.	48	F	UNKNOWN	RR	ZZZ	DAK
ADAM	18	M	UNKNOWN	RR	ZZZ	DAK
CARL	8	M	CHILD	RR	ZZZ	DAK
MATHIAS	4	M	CHILD	RR	ZZZ	DAK
KOHN, CHAJE	18	F	SVNT	RR	ZZZ	IN
NACHEMOWICZ, FROME	13	F	UNKNOWN	RR	ZZZ	BAL
KISSLING, JOSEF	72	M	FARMER	RR	ZZZ	CAL
JULIA	60	F	UNKNOWN	RR	ZZZ	CAL
FRANZ	44	M	FARMER	RR	ZZZ	CAL
CAROLINE	42	F	UNKNOWN	RR	ZZZ	CAL
EMMA	16	F	UNKNOWN	RR	ZZZ	CAL
LUDWIGA	5	F	CHILD	RR	ZZZ	CAL
ZULEWSKY, ADAM	27	M	LABR	RR	ZZZ	PA

PASSENGER	AGE	SEX	OCCUPATION	PRV	VIL	DES
BREINER, JOSEF	27	M	LABR	RR	ZZZZ	PA
LAWONNI, JOSEF	44	M	LABR	RR	ZZZZ	PA
MALKOWSKY, WOJ.	24	M	LABR	RR	ZZZZ	PA
WESSOLOWSKY, JOH.	27	F	UNKNOWN	RR	ZZZZ	PA
KOBYLINSKY, LEOF.	24	M	LABR	RR	ZZZZ	BAL
KOLSKY, ANTONI	18	M	LABR	RR	ZZZZ	BAL
STEPANZKY, JAKOB	33	M	LABR	RR	ZZZZ	BAL
CIESZINSKY, ANT.	53	M	LABR	RR	ZZZZ	BAL
KAENNENSKY, ARND.	20	M	LABR	RR	ZZZZ	BAL
KOBYLINSKY, STANISL.	37	M	LABR	RR	ZZZZ	BAL
STAN.	23	M	FARMER	RR	ZZZZ	BAL
OLSZLA, IGNAZ	27	M	FARMER	RR	ZZZZ	BAL
VINCENT	18	M	FARMER	RR	ZZZZ	BAL
BUZANOWSKY, FRANZ	26	M	FARMER	RR	ZZZZ	BAL
JENDLER, GUSTAV	26	M	FARMER	RR	ZZZZ	MI
APFELMANN, JOHANN	26	M	FARMER	RR	ZZZZ	MI
KRISCHEWICZ, KARM.	22	M	FARMER	RR	ZZZZ	PA
ZIELINSKY, STAN.	27	M	FARMER	RR	ZZZZ	PA
WAWRIKEWICZ, ANT.	30	M	FARMER	RR	ZZZZ	BAL
KRUSKY, PETER	24	M	FARMER	RR	ZZZZ	BAL
KRIMPISKY, AND.	40	M	FARMER	RR	ZZZZ	BAL

SHIP: EIDER

FROM: BREMEN AND SOUTHAMPTON
TO: NEW YORK
ARRIVED: 12 APRIL 1889

PASSENGER	AGE	SEX	OCCUPATION	PRV	VIL	DES
CHINK, FRANZISZEK	28	M	LABR	RR	ZZZZ	USA
WITEZKA, ROZALIA	20	F	UNKNOWN	RR	ZZZZ	USA
ZIEDANIS, ANNA	20	F	UNKNOWN	RR	ZZZZ	USA
ZAMBLOSKI, JAN	23	M	LABR	RR	ZZZZ	USA
BAZEWICS, KSAWERZ	30	M	LABR	RR	ZZZZ	USA
KORNPATWA, FRANZ	26	M	LABR	RR	ZZZZ	USA
PIOTRKIEWICZ, WOJ.	23	M	LABR	RR	ZZZZ	USA
WOJCIECHOWSKY, MARIAN	21	M	LABR	RR	ZZZZ	USA
BLUKEWICZ, WASL.	25	M	LABR	RR	ZZZZ	USA
ROZISEWSKY, RAPOL.	21	M	LABR	RR	ZZZZ	USA
JANOS, GAVALIER	29	M	LABR	RR	ZZZZ	USA
ROWALSKY, JOS.	28	M	LABR	RR	ZZZZ	USA
RACZEWSKY, VINZ	28	M	LABR	RR	AIEG	USA
BOLAKOWSKY, JURA	24	M	LABR	RR	AIEG	USA
FASCA, STAN.	33	M	LABR	RR	AIEG	USA
BRZOZOWSKY, JAC.	31	M	LABR	RR	ZZZZ	USA
BARANOWSKY, JAN	28	M	LABR	RR	ZZZZ	USA
BRZOZOWSKY, STAN.	30	M	LABR	RR	ZZZZ	USA
WIRBICKY, JOSEF	28	M	FARMER	RR	ZZZZ	USA
GULAN, ANDRZI	28	M	FARMER	RR	ZZZZ	USA
MADERA, WOJCIECH	30	M	FARMER	RR	ZZZZ	USA
GULAN, PIOTR	25	M	FARMER	RR	ZZZZ	USA
OLSZIELSKI, JACOB	38	M	FARMER	RR	ZZZZ	USA
KUBIK, ANDR.	29	M	FARMER	RR	ZZZZ	USA
STEFANOWSKY, MARY	33	F	UNKNOWN	RR	AIEG	USA
LANZKOWSKY, JOSEF	27	M	LABR	RR	ZZZZ	USA
GRIMSKY, ANTON	32	M	LABR	RR	ZZZZ	USA
SIBINSKY, ANDR.	28	M	LABR	RR	ZZZZ	USA
PIEMLEWICZ, SAMOLEJA	24	F	W	RR	ZZZZ	USA
JOSEF	2	M	CHILD	RR	ZZZZ	USA
KAZMIEZ	28	M	LABR	RR	ZZZZ	USA
ANTONIE	20	M	LABR	RR	ZZZZ	USA
ILOWINSKA, TEKLA	20	F	UNKNOWN	RR	ZZZZ	USA
BESSLER, AUGUST	28	M	LABR	RR	ZZZZ	USA
JELASZYNSKY, JAN	26	M	LABR	RR	ZZZZ	USA
JANITZKY, WM.	21	F	UNKNOWN	RR	ZZZZ	USA
SELANIS, ANTON	22	M	FARMER	RR	ZZZZ	USA
BUDKEWITZ, JOSEF	24	M	FARMER	RR	ZZZZ	USA
KADRASZ, JURAS	27	M	FARMER	RR	ZZZZ	USA
MICHALOW, JOSEF	25	M	FARMER	RR	ZZZZ	USA
BLOGIN, JANOS	25	M	FARMER	RR	ZZZZ	USA
JUSRAL, JOSEF	19	M	FARMER	RR	ZZZZ	USA

PASSENGER	AGE	SEX	OCCUPATION	PRV	VIL	DES
SIMKEWITZ, JAN	35	M	FARMER	RR	AIEG	USA
WINZEWITZ, ANTON	26	M	FARMER	RR	AIEG	USA
KROLIKOWSKI, WLAD.	27	M	FARMER	RR	AIEG	USA
ANIELA	26	F	W	RR	AIEG	USA
JAN	4	M	CHILD	RR	AIEG	USA
MARIA	3	F	CHILD	RR	AIEG	USA
KURZYANA, ADAM	35	M	FARMER	RR	AIEG	USA
ZYGOWSKA, MARG.	32	F	UNKNOWN	RR	AIEG	USA
BALCIKEWITZ, WIC.	35	M	FARMER	RR	AIEG	USA
JESULEWITZ, WIC.	24	M	FARMER	RR	AIEG	USA
HARAHURDA, JOSEF	26	M	FARMER	RR	AIEG	USA
KLEMENS	25	M	FARMER	RR	AIEG	USA
BACZKOWSKY, FRANZ	30	M	FARMER	RR	AIEG	USA
ANDRAKA, IGNATZ	38	M	FARMER	RR	AIEG	USA
BARTHOLOMANS, WICTOR	28	M	FARMER	RR	ZZZZ	USA
OLSCHEFSKY, VICTOR	29	M	FARMER	RR	ZZZZ	USA
BARTSCH, JACOB	50	M	FARMER	RR	AIEG	USA
MARG.	47	F	W	RR	AIEG	USA
PETER	21	M	FARMER	RR	AIEG	USA
MELANI	18	F	UNKNOWN	RR	AIEG	USA
JOH.	15	F	UNKNOWN	RR	AIEG	USA
BARB.	11	F	CH	RR	AIEG	USA
ANTON	7	M	CHILD	RR	AIEG	USA
MALSAM, LORENZ	24	M	FARMER	RR	ZZZZ	USA
ELISABETH	21	F	W	RR	ZZZZ	USA
PETER	.03	M	INFANT	RR	ZZZZ	USA
BRZOYOWSKY, KAZIM.	30	M	LABR	RR	ZZZZ	USA
FRANKENBERG, ALEXANDER	31	M	LABR	RR	ZZZZ	USA

SHIP: ALLER

FROM: BREMEN AND SOUTHAMPTON
TO: NEW YORK
ARRIVED: 13 APRIL 1889

PASSENGER	AGE	SEX	OCCUPATION	PRV	VIL	DES
PIDGORSKI, ANTON	48	M	SMH	RR	ZZZZ	USA
FRANK, ESTER	25	M	LABR	RR	ZZZZ	USA
LEIBESKIND, FR.	73	M	LABR	RR	ZZZZ	USA
GEMINDEN, ISRAEL	20	M	LABR	RR	ZZZZ	USA
GOLDBERG, VICTOR	23	M	LABR	RR	ZZZZ	USA
KORDRZEWSKY, JOSEF	38	M	LABR	RR	ZZZZ	USA
OZRAZEWSKY, FRANZ	32	M	LABR	RR	ZZZZ	USA
MUSCHA, JOSEF	37	M	LABR	RR	ZZZZ	USA
PRZESIAK, FRANZ	35	M	LABR	RR	ZZZZ	USA
GORLEWSKI, JOSEF	21	M	LABR	RR	ZZZZ	USA
JONOWSKY, FRANZ	32	M	LABR	RR	ZZZZ	USA
MROCZYNSKI, IGNATZ	21	M	LABR	RR	ZZZZ	USA
UZINSKI, WACLAW	45	M	LABR	RR	ZZZZ	USA
GOLENIEWSKI, JAN	26	M	LABR	RR	ZZZZ	USA
KWABUKOWSKI, LUDWIG	33	M	LABR	RR	ZZZZ	USA
NAWORSKI, JOSEF	29	M	LABR	RR	ZZZZ	USA
WASILEWSKI, JOSEF	23	M	LABR	RR	ZZZZ	USA
POPLASKI, ANTON	21	M	LABR	RR	ZZZZ	USA
NEUFELD, JAN	33	M	FARMER	RR	ZZZZ	USA
KUCZINSKI, VINCANT	33	M	FARMER	RR	ZZZZ	USA
JAKRZEWSKI, U	36	M	FARMER	RR	ZZZZ	USA
KISZELEWSKA, JAN	28	M	LABR	RR	ZZZZ	USA
DAZOA, JOSEF	32	M	LABR	RR	ZZZZ	USA
KAPROLAH, JOSEF	25	M	LABR	RR	ZZZZ	USA
WERZBICHI, JULIAN	25	M	LABR	RR	ZZZZ	USA
WEISS, ELISABETH	19	F	UNKNOWN	RR	ZZZZ	USA
SCHMIDT, CATHA.	18	F	UNKNOWN	RR	ZZZZ	USA
KURLE, ELISAB.	25	F	UNKNOWN	RR	ZZZZ	USA
ROEPOWSKI, FRANCISKA	29	F	UNKNOWN	RR	ZZZZ	USA
BABECKI, ANTONI	21	F	UNKNOWN	RR	ZZZZ	USA
EIDELBERG, MARY	24	F	UNKNOWN	RR	ZZZZ	USA
HOFFMANN, CHRISTE.	28	F	UNKNOWN	RR	ZZZZ	USA
CAROLE.	30	F	UNKNOWN	RR	ZZZZ	USA
JACOB	5	M	CHILD	RR	ZZZZ	USA
CAROLE.	.06	F	INFANT	RR	ZZZZ	USA

PASSENGER	AGE	SEX	OCCUPATION	PRV VIL DES
WOLF, GEORG	35	M	FARMER	RRZZZZUSA
MARGA.	28	F	W	RRZZZZUSA
MAGDE.	.06	F	INFANT	RRZZZZUSA
STEIN, CHRIST.	23	M	LABR	RRZZZZUSA
CATHA.	23	F	W	RRZZZZUSA
CATHA.	.05	F	INFANT	RRZZZZUSA
RUSSMANL, CHRIST.	22	M	FARMER	RRZZZZUSA
CATHA.	20	F	W	RRZZZZUSA
JOHA.	16	F	UNKNOWN	RRZZZZUSA
HANKS, JOH.	50	M	FARMER	RRZZZZUSA
MAGDE.	32	F	W	RRZZZZUSA
MAGDE.	9	F	CHILD	RRZZZZUSA
CAROLE.	7	F	CHILD	RRZZZZUSA
LISBETH	5	F	CHILD	RRZZZZUSA
FISCHER, JOH.	32	M	FARMER	RRZZZZUSA
ELISAB.	28	F	W	RRZZZZUSA
JOH.	5	M	CHILD	RRZZZZUSA
ROSINE	2	F	CHILD	RRZZZZUSA
CHRIST.	27	M	FARMER	RRZZZZUSA
FRIEDE	22	F	W	RRZZZZUSA
BENDER, PHIL.	37	M	FARMER	RRZZZZUSA
ROSINE	35	F	W	RRZZZZUSA
ROSINE	15	F	CH	RRZZZZUSA
GEORG	10	M	CH	RRZZZZUSA
PHIL.	8	M	CHILD	RRZZZZUSA
CHRISTE.	5	F	CHILD	RRZZZZUSA
JACOB	4	M	CHILD	RRZZZZUSA
CARL	3	M	CHILD	RRZZZZUSA
JOHA.	.03	M	INFANT	RRZZZZUSA
GOLDBERG, DAVID	36	M	FARMER	RRZZZZUSA
GUSTE.	30	F	W	RRZZZZUSA
SAMUEL	8	M	CHILD	RRZZZZUSA
JOH.	7	M	CHILD	RRZZZZUSA
VICTOR	2	M	CHILD	RRZZZZUSA
SALY	.03	F	INFANT	RRZZZZUSA
KLEIN, KATHA.	29	M	PNTR	RRZZZZUSA
FRIEDE	21	F	W	RRZZZZUSA
CHRISTE.	.04	F	INFANT	RRZZZZUSA
ZADEER, ONISCHE	23	F	UNKNOWN	RRZZZZUSA
MALKE	24	F	UNKNOWN	RRZZZZUSA
WOLF, JACOB	41	M	FARMER	RRZZZZUSA
CATHA.	29	F	W	RRZZZZUSA
CATHA.	7	F	CHILD	RRZZZZUSA
CHRISTE.	6	F	CHILD	RRZZZZUSA
JAC	2	M	CHILD	RRZZZZUSA
URSINE	.01	F	INFANT	RRZZZZUSA
RAU, JAC	28	M	LABR	RRZZZZUSA
LOUISE	25	F	W	RRZZZZUSA
FENNER, JAC	28	M	FARMER	RRZZZZUSA
MAGDA.	28	F	W	RRZZZZUSA
CHRISTE.	2	F	CHILD	RRZZZZUSA
MAGDA.	3	F	CHILD	RRZZZZUSA
SAREMBOWSKI, CHASE	36	F	UNKNOWN	RRZZZZUSA
JACOB	11	M	UNKNOWN	RRZZZZUSA
SCHLEISE	7	F	CHILD	RRZZZZUSA
PEITACH	6	M	CHILD	RRZZZZUSA
SAREMBOWSKY, BELIE	.03	F	INFANT	RRZZZZUNK

SHIP: POLARIA

FROM: HAMBURG
TO: NEW YORK
ARRIVED: 15 APRIL 1889

PASSENGER	AGE	SEX	OCCUPATION	PRV VIL DES
BRUNOWSKI, JOHN	24	M	LABR	RRZZZZNY
POLL, NOCHEM	36	M	MCHT	RRZZZZNY
RUSKEWICZOWA, ANNA	19	F	SGL	RRZZZZNY
LASKI, LEONARDY	22	M	LABR	RRAHZSNY
WOZMALIS, MACY	24	M	LABR	RRZZZZNY
ZAWATZKY, WLADISLAW	17	M	LABR	RRAHZSNY
MILEWSKY, FRANZ	23	M	LABR	RRAHZSNY
WOYCICH	27	M	LABR	RRAHZSNY
MILENOWSKY, ADOLF	20	M	LABR	RRAHZSNY
ROZZIS, STANISL.	25	M	LABR	RRAHZSNY
URBAN, FRANZ	22	M	LABR	RRAHZSNY
OROWITZ, JOSEF	26	M	LABR	RRZZZZNY
SCHULMANN, DAVID	49	M	UNKNOWN	RRZZZZNY
ROSA	43	F	UNKNOWN	RRZZZZNY
ANNA	16	F	SGL	RRZZZZNY
BENJAMIN	9	M	CHILD	RRZZZZNY
LINE	7	F	CHILD	RRZZZZNY
IDA	5	F	CHILD	RRZZZZNY
SARA	3	F	CHILD	RRZZZZNY
MERKOWSKY, JANEK	22	M	UNKNOWN	RRZZZZNY
SADOWSKY, FRANZ	30	M	UNKNOWN	RRZZZZNY
GLIMSKY, ANDRI	30	M	UNKNOWN	RRZZZZNY
CZICHOTZKY, ANTON	25	M	UNKNOWN	RRZZZZNY
FROTZKY, ANTON	26	M	UNKNOWN	RRZZZZNY
STEPANSKY, KASIMIR	23	M	UNKNOWN	RRZZZZNY
JECZWISKY, MATWEI	25	M	UNKNOWN	RRZZZZNY
LAGORSKY, IGANTZ	25	M	UNKNOWN	RRAIEQNY
BANISCHEWSKY, STEFAN	25	M	UNKNOWN	RRAIEQNY
WOUDSZINSKY, SZEPAN	24	M	LABR	RRAHUINY
JURSDITZKY, JACOB	19	M	LABR	RRAHTUNY
OPPENHEIM, ITZIG	41	M	LABR	RRAHTUNY
ROSENBLUM, DAVID	56	M	UNKNOWN	RRZZZZNY
SCHEINE	50	F	UNKNOWN	RRZZZZNY
BASSE	16	F	CH	RRZZZZNY
SARA	9	F	CHILD	RRZZZZNY
KAHN, JACOB	38	M	LABR	RRAHOKNY
ANTIKOCZ, MANNE	19	F	SGL	RRAGRTNY
ADAMOWITZ, JOSES	19	M	LABR	RRZZZZNY
MARZINKEWIT, ZMICAS	22	M	LABR	RRZZZZNY
LEWENGELA, MICHAL	33	M	LABR	RRZZZZNY
DREKO, VASIL	25	M	LABR	RRZZZZNY
SCHULIKOWSKY, KAJETAN	27	M	LABR	RRAHZSNY
MERESCHKEWITZ, KASIMIR	26	M	LABR	RRZZZZNY
KASCHKAU, THOMAS	22	M	LABR	RRZZZZNY
SELAINIS, KASIMIR	24	M	LABR	RRZZZZNY
GLAMBOTZKI, ALEXANDER	26	M	LABR	RRZZZZNY
JUDKEWITZ, JACOB	42	M	LABR	RRZZZZNY
KASCHKAU, THOMAS	25	M	LABR	RRZZZZNY
BUCHENKO, JAN	22	M	LABR	RRAHQUNY
MIKOLOWSKI, JOSEF	22	M	LABR	RRAHZSNY
CASPAROWICZ, BAITER	20	M	LABR	RRAHZSNY
KAMOSZA, MIHAL	24	M	LABR	RRZZZZNY
KLEBANOWICZ, ANTON	26	M	LABR	RRAHZSNY
TRISCHINSKI, FRANZ	29	M	LABR	RRAHQUNY
SNAROWSKI, PAWEL	26	M	LABR	RRAHTONY
FIEDLER, FRIEDR.	39	M	LABR	RRAHUFNY
SNAROWSKI, JOSEF	34	M	LABR	RRAHTONY
PLITT, WILH.	31	M	LABR	RRAHUFNY
ZUSKO, WOYCICH	22	M	LABR	RRAHQUNY
GUSTEITIS, MARCIN	28	M	LABR	RRAHZSNY
IWANOWSKI, MATHAUS	27	M	LABR	RRAHZSNY
MARCINKEWICZ, THOMAS	24	M	LABR	RRAHZSNY
MUZKAS, ANTON	26	M	LABR	RRAHZSNY
KLEBANOWSKI, JAN	25	M	LABR	RRAHZSNY
KASCZKAS, PETER	24	M	LABR	RRAHZSNY
DERKE, CHRISTIAN	27	M	LABR	RRAHUFNY
RUTKOWSKI, STANISL.	42	M	LABR	RRAHUFNY
GSELINSKI, JACOB	34	M	LABR	RRAHUFNY
BRUDZINSKI, STANISL.	26	M	LABR	RRAHZSNY
STANKIEWICZ, JOHAS	18	M	LABR	RRAHZSNY
KRAKOWSKY, FRANZ	22	M	LABR	RRAHUFNY
CHRISTOFEK, CONST.	33	M	LABR	RRAHTONY
HAGEMEIES, STANISL.	22	M	LABR	RRAHTONY
DOBEROWSKI, BEIJAI	26	M	LABR	RRAHTONY
LEWANDOWSKY, FRANZ	32	M	LABR	RRAHUIUNK
DREWITZ, JAN	24	M	LABR	RRAHUIUNK
LUCHOPARSKI, JACOB	20	M	LABR	RRZZZZUNK
KANKOWSKA, AUGUSTE	18	F	SGL	RRZZZZUNK
SYPNIEWSKA, ANTE.	22	F	SGL	RRZZZZUNK
LAJANOWICE, NADEZDA	26	F	SGL	RRZZZZUNK
GARNFIEDLER, ESTHER	32	F	WO	RRZZZZUNK

PASSENGER	AGE	SEX	OCCUPATION	PRV VIL DES
BERTHA	9	F	CHILD	RRZZZZUNK
LEISER	8	M	CHILD	RRZZZZUNK
K.	7	M	CHILD	RRZZZZUNK
RAHEL	6	F	CHILD	RRZZZZUNK
AARON	4	M	CHILD	RRZZZZUNK
ROSA	.11	F	INFANT	RRZZZZUNK
MOSES, CHAIM	9	M	CHILD	RRAHTUUNK
SEGALOWITZ, FREIDE	17	F	SGL	RRAHTUUNK
MERETZKY, LEIB	42	M	LABR	RRZZZZUNK
GRUENWALD, CHAJE	42	F	WO	RRAHRZUNK
ALTE	9	M	CHILD	RRAHRZUNK
SETHER	7	F	CHILD	RRAHRZUNK
DAVID	.11	M	INFANT	RRAHRZUNK
GROSBAUM, ISRAEL	19	M	TLR	RRAHQUUNK
RUTENBERG, RACHEL	60	F	WO	RRAHZSUNK
SADLOWSKY, VALT.	28	M	LABR	RRAHTOUNK
KUN, AD.	25	M	LABR	RRAHTOUNK
BOJANKI, FRANZ	28	M	LABR	RRAHTOUNK
WRZINSNI, JOSEF	23	M	LABR	RRZZZZNY
GROBNER, RACHEL	17	F	SGL	RRAHQUNY
WIERWINSKI, STANISL.	21	M	LABR	RRZZZZNY
ALICHANTZKAS, ERDNIS	28	M	LABR	RRZZZZNY
WELIWISS, MATHS.	23	M	LABR	RRZZZZNY
MIKA	25	M	LABR	RRZZZZNY
LITWIRSKI, ANDRE	16	M	LABR	RRZZZZNY
KARUZEWICZ, MICHAEL	32	M	LABR	RRAHUFNY
ZATARSKI, JAN	32	M	LABR	RRAHUFNY
JANKOWSKI, JAN	42	M	LABR	RRAHUFNY
BUNEWSKI, COSTANT.	23	M	LABR	RRAHUFNY
JANKOWSKI, MATH.	32	M	LABR	RRAHUFNY
OLOFF, GREGOR	26	M	LABR	RRAHZSNY
SCHOSCHUCKI, WASIL	20	M	LABR	RRAHZSNY
SNITOFF, ALEXANDER	45	M	LABR	RRAHZSNY
SAMUEL	55	M	LABR	RRAHZSNY
CHUCHAKOF, HATOP	48	M	LABR	RRAHZSNY
OLOFF, MERKEN	23	M	LABR	RRAHZSNY
ISTAELSON, KERT	27	M	LABR	FNZZZZNY
MATSON, ESKET	42	M	LABR	FNZZZZNY
JOHANNSON, MATHS.	31	M	LABR	FNZZZZNY
KONECK, AUGUSTE	45	F	WO	FNZZZZNY
LAPINOJA, JOH.	28	M	LABR	FNZZZZNY
HENRICHSEN, ALBERT	38	M	LABR	FNZZZZNY
ANDERSEN, GUSTAV	19	M	LABR	FNZZZZNY
HENRIKSEN, ANDERS	26	M	LABR	FNZZZZNY
MATTSON, JOHN	29	M	LABR	FNZZZZNY
HEIKINPOIKA, OTTO	18	M	LABR	FNZZZZNY
OTLIKA, AUGUST	38	M	LABR	FNZZZZNY
OJALA, HEIKI	32	M	LABR	FNZZZZNY
POSKLIN, FELIX	19	M	LABR	FNZZZZNY
ASO, JOH.	21	M	LABR	FNZZZZNY
LEWIN, SAM.	16	M	LABR	FNAHZSNY
PUDLACEK, JACOB	33	M	LABR	FNAHWNNY
BUKOWITZ, PETER	25	M	LABR	RRZZZZNY
ALTSCHULER, BENJAMIN	36	M	LABR	RRAHOKNY
KRAJEWSKI, JOSEF	25	M	LABR	RRAHTONY
JENTZKO, JOSEF	25	M	LABR	RRAHTONY
SUHR, ALEX	37	M	LABR	RRAHTONY
RUTKOWSKI, STANISL.	30	M	LABR	RRZZZZNY
WARCZIKOWSKI, THEODOSSI	28	M	LABR	RRZZZZNY
ILZONSKY, BENJAMIN	26	M	LABR	RRZZZZNY
BEIGROWITSCH, JAN	26	M	LABR	RRAHUFNY
KILANOWSKI, FRANZ	20	M	LABR	RRAHUFNY
KAMINSKI, THOMAS	26	M	LABR	RRAHUFNY
HEIZEL, PETER	39	M	LABR	RRAHUFNY
KROTALSKI, JAN	30	M	LABR	RRAHUFNY
PEITSCH, MICHAEL	40	M	LABR	RRAHUFNY
KOWALSKI, FRANZ	25	M	LABR	RRAHUFNY
CESLUKOWSKI, JAN	31	M	LABR	RRAHZSNY
WALLUS, ANTON	33	M	LABR	RRAHTFNY
MARVILLE, JAN	27	M	LABR	RRAHTFNY
BUTZNOWICZ, DOMINIK	23	M	LABR	RRAHZSNY
LITKEWITZ, JOSEF	25	M	LABR	RRAHZSNY
BUSCHINSKI, JOSEF	19	M	LABR	RRAHZSNY
SCHESCHLUKOWITZ, SIMON	18	M	LABR	RRAHZSNY
JURAIZ, LUDWIG	30	M	LABR	RRAHZSNY
MOIKA, ANTON	31	M	LABR	RRAHTUNY
ROMAN, OSI	30	M	LABR	RRAHTUNY
DSEZSECKI, JOSEF	22	M	LABR	RRAHZSNY
URBAN, SYLVESTER	27	M	LABR	RRAHZSNY
SCHIFF, BENJAMIN	20	M	LABR	RRZZZZNY
URBANSKI, JAN	30	M	LABR	RRAHZSNY
JESSYRESKY, PETER	36	M	MD	RRAHOONY
HERSZEL, FAKTOR	28	M	LABR	RRAHVUNY
BYLARSKI, JOHN	23	M	LABR	RRAHUINY
STIPILMANN, MEIER	23	M	LABR	RRZZZZNY
HUKINPOCKA, JOH.	21	M	LABR	FNZZZZNY
ADAMOWITZ, JOS.	20	M	LABR	RRZZZZNY

SHIP: SUEVIA

FROM: HAMBURG
TO: NEW YORK
ARRIVED: 15 APRIL 1889

PASSENGER	AGE	SEX	OCCUPATION	PRV VIL DES
FORMANN, SCHELDE	32	F	WO	RRZZZZIL
KOLMANN	16	M	CH	RRZZZZIL
FIWE	8	F	CHILD	RRZZZZIL
SCHAPIRE, ASNE	38	F	WO	RRZZZZIL
CHANNE	17	F	CH	RRZZZZIL
MERKE	9	F	CHILD	RRZZZZIL
ZIWIE	8	M	CHILD	RRZZZZIL
CZAFNEWSKI, WLADISL.	30	M	LABR	RRZZZZWI
CZEFENEWSKY, MARIE	30	M	LABR	RRZZZZWI
MIOHNOWITZ, JEROMIE	40	F	SGL	RRZZZZWI
SACHS, ELLA	28	F	SGL	RRZZZZWI
ZEITE, ERNESTE	53	F	WO	RRZZZZNY
OTTO	16	M	LABR	RRZZZZNY
BURKHARDT, LOUIS	14	M	SCH	RRZZZZNY
GLUECKMANN, PETTE	18	F	SGL	RRZZZZNE
BASSEBATZKI, MORDCHE	45	M	LABR	RRZZZZNE
ALEXANDROWITZ, MARTEI	29	M	LABR	RRZZZZIL
MARSKELIS, ANTON	23	M	LABR	RRZZZZNY
ALEXANDROWITZ, PETER	41	M	LABR	RRZZZZNY
SELINSKY, DOMINIK	30	M	LABR	RRZZZZNY
PITZULIS, WIKENTY	30	M	LABR	RRZZZZNY
STANNLIS, ANTONAS	19	M	LABR	RRZZZZNY
KURTULIS, MAZUS	19	M	LABR	RRZZZZNY
MALINOWSKI, KARL	28	M	LABR	RRZZZZNY
NOTSLA, DOMINAS	29	M	LABR	RRZZZZNY
BJALKOWSKY, ANTON	30	M	LABR	RRAHUICAL
ANTONIA	25	F	W	RRAHUICAL
WITTKOWSKY, ANDREY	40	M	LABR	RRAHUICAL
JULIE	25	F	W	RRAHUICAL
BIALKOWSKY, FRANZ	38	M	LABR	RRAHUICAL
KATZLOWSKY, PETER	23	M	LABR	RRAHUICAL
KRAJEWSKY, ANTONIA	20	F	SGL	RRAHUICAL
PAWLOWSKY, STANISLAV	30	M	LABR	RRAHUICAL
DERENSOWSKY, SIMON	30	M	LABR	RRAHUIIA
BAROFSKY, JOSEF	32	M	LABR	RRAHUIPA
CZAPLINSKY, JAN	22	M	LABR	RRAHUIPA
JAN	22	M	LABR	RRAHUIPA
MARKOWITZ, ADAM	30	M	LABR	RRAHUIPA
MANDELSKY, ANTONI	30	M	LABR	RRAHUIPA
BRODZENSKY, ADAM	23	M	LABR	RRAHUIPA
LISEWSKY, MARON	23	M	LABR	RRAHUIPA
RAMUTKOWSKI, ANTONI	28	M	LABR	RRAHUIPA
GEMNIERSKY, ANTON	37	M	LABR	RRAHUIPA
SZADOWSKY, ANDRY	42	M	LABR	RRAHUINY
JANKOSKI, FRANZ	30	M	LABR	RRAHULNY
BOLICHOWITZ, ANIELA	24	F	SGL	RRAHULNY
PIETUZKA, JAN	18	M	LABR	RRAHZSNY
MARIANNE	16	F	SGL	RRAHZSNY
WACH, CHRISTIAN	26	M	LABR	RRACONPA
MANHEIM, CHRISTIAN	21	M	LABR	RRACONPA
SCHANTZKEWITZ, DAVID	18	M	LABR	RRZZZZPA

PASSENGER	AGE	SEX	OCCUPATION	PRV	VIL	DES
KUROWSKI, MARIANNE	35	F	WO	RR	AFWJ	PA
BADOJN	9	M	CHILD	RR	AFWJ	PA
VICTORIA	5	F	CHILD	RR	AFWJ	PA
KAMOWSKI, JAN	32	M	LABR	RR	ZZZZ	PA
BROMNIRSKI, ANTON	22	M	LABR	RR	ZZZZ	PA
KAMONS, FRANZ	26	M	LABR	RR	ZZZZ	NY
ONIZKI, SYBILLA	15	F	SGL	RR	AHZS	NY
WILK, ANDREAS	24	M	LABR	RR	ZZZZ	NY
BIDER, MEYER	17	M	TLR	RR	ZZZZ	NY
GECHANOWSKY, MARIE	20	F	SGL	RR	ZZZZ	NY
ONISKI, CHLAWNY	24	M	LABR	RR	AHZS	NY
SPIRT, BERMAN	42	M	LABR	RR	ZZZZ	PA
SCHEINDEL	40	F	W	RR	ZZZZ	PA
JESSE	4	F	CHILD	RR	ZZZZ	PA
SELDE	6	F	CHILD	RR	ZZZZ	PA
HINDE	4	F	CHILD	RR	ZZZZ	PA
DEBORA	.06	F	INFANT	RR	ZZZZ	PA
WOLF	40	M	LABR	RR	ZZZZ	PA
PUDLIK, DAVID	20	M	MCHT	RR	AIGH	NY
GROSZEWSKI, LUDWIG	29	M	SDLR	RR	ZZZZ	OH
KORSTEIN, ZIWJE	20	F	SGL	RR	AHTU	PA
GELENTON, LEISER	21	M	LABR	RR	AHTU	PA
DJAGELLER, ARON	28	M	LABR	RR	ZZZZ	PA
SEMENISKI, ADAM	30	M	LABR	RR	ZZZZ	PA
PETRUSCHAINIT, IVAN	33	M	LABR	RR	ZZZZ	PA
TSCHESCHAINIS, MARTIN	26	M	LABR	RR	ZZZZ	PA
SUDKKO, PETER	20	M	LABR	FN	ZZZZ	IL
KOWALSKI, PAWEL	39	M	LABR	FN	AHTF	IL
PSHOSKOWSKY, NIKODEM	26	M	LABR	RR	ZZZZ	PA
KUCHANOWSKY, JOSEPH	26	M	LABR	RR	ZZZZ	PA
INKNEWITZ, GERSHI	27	M	LABR	RR	ZZZZ	PA
RASIMAS, MATWEY	24	M	LABR	RR	ZZZZ	PA
MAGDE	25	M	LABR	RR	ZZZZ	PA
STEFANOWITZ, STANISLAUS	26	M	LABR	RR	ZZZZ	PA
STALDINSKY, JOSEPH	24	M	LABR	RR	ZZZZ	PA
NEDSINSKY, STEFAN	25	M	LABR	RR	ZZZZ	PA
KSHESANOWSKY, ANTON	29	M	LABR	RR	ZZZZ	PA
SLICH, ANDREW	34	M	LABR	RR	ZZZZ	IL
RASIMAS, JONNAS	22	M	LABR	RR	ZZZZ	IL
NEDTINSKY, WIZENTZ	25	M	LABR	RR	ZZZZ	IL
KASINIOWSKY, JAN	22	M	LABR	RR	ZZZZ	IL
GUDELSKY, BULTWIM	30	M	LABR	RR	ZZZZ	IL
BERNATOWITZ, ALFONS	26	M	LABR	RR	ZZZZ	IL
BUCHACKY, ALEXANDER	32	M	LABR	RR	ZZZZ	IA
PIRDROZ, DAVID	65	M	LABR	RR	ZZZZ	IA
CZECHOWSKY, JAN	30	M	LABR	RR	ZZZZ	IL
BACEFICH, MARTIN	40	M	LABR	RR	ZZZZ	IL
SCHMIDT, ADOLF	22	M	LABR	RR	ZZZZ	IL
PANOREU, MATH.	39	M	LABR	RR	AIDS	IL
KLEIN, JULIUS	27	M	LABR	RR	AHUI	IL
GLODOWSKY, FRIEDR.	39	M	LABR	RR	AHUI	IL
STAWICKI, IHNATZ	18	M	LABR	RR	ZZZZ	IL

SHIP: IOWA

FROM: LIVERPOOL
TO: BOSTON
ARRIVED: 15 APRIL 1889

PASSENGER	AGE	SEX	OCCUPATION	PRV	VIL	DES
SCESCHONSKY, S.	20	F	SP	RR	ZZZZ	USA
DOGKLOKER, SARA	17	F	SP	RR	ZZZZ	USA
BRONDL, MARION	16	F	SP	RR	ZZZZ	USA
KRENNER, FEIGE	15	F	SP	RR	ZZZZ	USA
BEILAS, HINRIK	15	F	SP	RR	ZZZZ	USA
GOLDE	12	F	SP	RR	ZZZZ	USA
BILMEISON, SCHURE	11	F	UNKNOWN	RR	ZZZZ	USA
KREMER, SOLOMON	10	F	UNKNOWN	RR	ZZZZ	USA
SALEWSKY, FRANZ	20	M	TLR	RR	ZZZZ	USA
SCHER, W.	20	M	LABR	RR	ZZZZ	USA
KASZARIN, LECLIS	19	M	LABR	RR	ZZZZ	USA
SEGAL, L.	20	M	LABR	RR	ZZZZ	USA
BIMMNER, J.	42	M	LABR	RR	ZZZZ	USA
JEAKIEMOSA, F.	37	M	LABR	RR	ZZZZ	USA
HORINEWITZ, K.	18	M	LABR	RR	ZZZZ	USA
HARE	11	M	SCH	RR	ZZZZ	USA
SNABOWSKY, C.	32	M	LABR	RR	ZZZZ	USA
SCHALANARS, FR.	25	M	LABR	RR	ZZZZ	USA
SHUHOLZ, S.	24	M	TLR	RR	ZZZZ	USA
MESCHITNIUS, J.	25	M	LABR	RR	ZZZZ	USA
LEWIN, DAN	49	M	LABR	RR	ZZZZ	USA
SCH.	19	M	LABR	RR	ZZZZ	USA
BISCHINEWKO, A.	23	M	LABR	RR	ZZZZ	USA
KOWALEWSKY, A.	39	M	LABR	RR	ZZZZ	USA
SELETZKY, K.	30	M	LABR	RR	ZZZZ	USA
ROSENTHAL, DAN	14	M	SCH	RR	ZZZZ	USA
HORIC	10	M	CH	RR	ZZZZ	USA
SCHENIC, A.B.	32	M	LABR	RR	ZZZZ	USA
RIBAK, J.	22	M	TLR	RR	ZZZZ	USA
ERCRSKY, WILE	21	M	LABR	RR	ZZZZ	USA
MEVIAS, TOBIAT	18	M	LABR	RR	ZZZZ	USA
GEIND, LEAH	28	M	LABR	RR	ZZZZ	USA
LARES, JOS.	20	M	LABR	RR	ZZZZ	USA
KAZWARIK, EISIK	18	M	LABR	RR	ZZZZ	USA
BERTA	17	F	W	RR	ZZZZ	USA
BROWDER, M.	38	M	TLR	RR	ZZZZ	USA
LEIN	32	F	W	RR	ZZZZ	USA
RASENTHAL, FREIDE	45	F	W	RR	ZZZZ	USA
BENJAMER, JOS.	23	M	W	RR	ZZZZ	USA
HANORA	21	F	W	RR	ZZZZ	USA
BILMIAN, GUTE	42	M	UNKNOWN	RR	ZZZZ	USA
KREMER, CHAJE	42	M	UNKNOWN	RR	ZZZZ	USA
BEILAS, RIVSE	34	M	UNKNOWN	RR	ZZZZ	USA
ROSENTHAL, ABRAM	9	M	CHILD	RR	ZZZZ	USA
MOSES	7	M	CHILD	RR	ZZZZ	USA
BILMANN, LASER	9	F	CHILD	RR	ZZZZ	USA
LEIE	8	F	CHILD	RR	ZZZZ	USA
KRENNER, ESTHER	9	F	CHILD	RR	ZZZZ	USA
CHATAY	6	F	CHILD	RR	ZZZZ	USA
BERTINA	3	F	CHILD	RR	ZZZZ	USA

SHIP: SERVIA

FROM: LIVERPOOL AND QUEENSTOWN
TO: NEW YORK
ARRIVED: 15 APRIL 1889

PASSENGER	AGE	SEX	OCCUPATION	PRV	VIL	DES
WYROMBER, FRANCISZEK	46	M	LABR	RR	ZZZZ	PA
BALDYGA, JANEK	45	M	LABR	RR	ZZZZ	PA
FILIPCZAK, JACOB	40	M	LABR	RR	ZZZZ	PA
PALASZEWSKI, JAN	30	M	LABR	RR	ZZZZ	PA
PRZCZYNSKI, IGNATZ	35	M	LABR	RR	ZZZZ	PA
DOMPKOWSKY, JOHN	46	M	LABR	RR	ZZZZ	PA
LENEKEG, WALENTIZ	19	M	LABR	RR	ZZZZ	MN

SHIP: CARTHGINIAN

FROM: UNKNOWN
TO: BOSTON
ARRIVED: 15 APRIL 1889

PASSENGER	AGE	SEX	OCCUPATION	PRV	VIL	DES
CAPUL, RACHEL	18	F	W	RR	ZZZZ	PIT
MOSES	00	M	INF	RR	ZZZZ	PIT
MERE	26	F	W	RR	ZZZZ	PIT
RACHAEL	00	F	INF	RR	ZZZZ	PIT
TROLISKY, MONZEL	17	M	LABR	RR	ZZZZ	PIT

PASSENGER	AGE	SEX	OCCUPATION	PRI	VIL	DES
MADSEN, DAVID	25	M	LABR	RR	ZZZZ	PTL
ANDERSEN, HULDA	23	F	LABR	RR	ZZZZ	PTL
LEWITAN, CHASKEL	17	F	SP	RR	ZZZZ	PIT
MERVIS, JANKEL	55	M	FARMER	RR	ZZZZ	PIT
ANDERSEN, L.P.	23	M	LABR	RR	ZZZZ	PIT
SVENSEN, HELENA	37	F	DMS	RR	ZZZZ	BO
A.	15	F	SP	RR	ZZZZ	BO
JOHANSON, ADA	15	F	SP	RR	ZZZZ	BO
CARL	41	M	LABR	RR	ZZZZ	BO
NILLSON, ERIK	19	M	LABR	RR	ZZZZ	BO
ANDERSEN, LE.M.	28	M	LABR	RR	ZZZZ	BO
TOLKOF, MINNE	63	M	LABR	RR	ZZZZ	BO
REWE	16	F	CH	RR	ZZZZ	BO
MINCHE	16	F	CH	RR	ZZZZ	BO
ABRAHAM	11	M	CH	RR	ZZZZ	BO
RAFALEL	7	M	CHILD	RR	ZZZZ	BO
ELKEN	9	M	CHILD	RR	ZZZZ	BO
LOPONZKA, MOSES	31	M	LABR	RR	ZZZZ	BO

SHIP: HAMMONIA

FROM: HAMBURG
TO: NEW YORK
ARRIVED: 15 APRIL 1889

PASSENGER	AGE	SEX	OCCUPATION	PRI	VIL	DES
BUTSKUS, DAN	26	M	LABR	RR	ZZZZ	USA
IGNATZIS, ANTON	28	M	LABR	RR	ZZZZ	USA
BULANOWSKI, JOS.	39	M	LABR	RR	ZZZZ	USA
POPHA, PRETR	21	M	LABR	RR	ZZZZ	USA
JAURKSCKE, KAN.	19	M	LABR	RR	ZZZZ	USA
LITZKOWITZ, OSSIP	25	M	LABR	RR	ZZZZ	USA
BAROWSKI, OSSIP	23	M	LABR	RR	ZZZZ	USA
ROMANOWSKI, JOS.	35	M	LABR	RR	ZZZZ	USA
RUDO, IGN.	26	M	LABR	RR	ZZZZ	USA
TOMACHUMAS, B.	34	M	LABR	RR	ZZZZ	USA
DOWAROWITZ, JOS.	18	M	LABR	RR	ZZZZ	USA
LIPNITZKI, BALT	34	M	LABR	RR	ZZZZ	USA
BALOKENITZ, W.	23	M	LABR	RR	ZZZZ	USA
WITOWSKY, JUL.	26	M	LABR	RR	ZZZZ	USA
SAMOLIS, J.	18	M	LABR	RR	ZZZZ	USA
RUDKOWSKI, MACI	24	M	LABR	RR	ZZZZ	USA
MIKALOWSKI, ANT.	26	M	LABR	RR	ZZZZ	USA
WAL-----, U	26	M	LABR	RR	ZZZZ	USA
MISAWITZ, JONAS	28	M	LABR	RR	ZZZZ	USA
JUSEPH, VALENT.	29	M	LABR	RR	ZZZZ	USA
HOWIKAS, JURA	20	M	LABR	RR	ZZZZ	USA
PETER	30	M	LABR	RR	ZZZZ	USA
JANHERTZ, PETRAS	18	M	LABR	RR	ZZZZ	USA
STACHURA, FRANZ	28	M	LABR	RR	AHTF	USA
JANHAL, JAN	25	M	LABR	RR	AHTF	USA
JESZEWIK, JOS.	36	M	LABR	RR	AHTF	USA
BALTISSING, PAUL	24	M	LABR	RR	AHTF	USA
MUDRIZKI, JOSEF	23	M	LABR	RR	AHTF	USA
KEGONSKI, IVAN	24	M	LABR	RR	AHTF	USA
SLOPARY, JORGES	28	M	LABR	RR	AHTF	USA
MAZULIS, R.	36	M	LABR	RR	AHTF	USA
SCHUB, SISSE	45	F	W	RR	AHTF	USA
SARA	14	F	CH	RR	AHTF	USA
HIBL	9	F	CHILD	RR	AHTF	USA
POULOSKY, JOS.	31	M	LABR	RR	ZZZZ	USA
CHOJNACHY, JOS.	30	M	LABR	RR	ZZZZ	USA
MIGOLSKA, JAN	18	M	LABR	RR	AIJV	USA
KLEKNY, WL.	18	M	LABR	RR	AIJV	USA
MIKOLANSKY, A.	26	M	LABR	RR	AIJV	USA
WOYCICHHOWSKY, JAN	29	M	LABR	RR	AIJV	USA
ROMANOFSKY, A.	32	M	LABR	RR	AIJV	USA
LENCOFSKY, JOS.	33	M	LABR	RR	AIJV	USA
WISCHNEWSKY, JOS.	46	M	LABR	RR	AIJV	USA
PELANK, JAN	29	M	LABR	RR	AIJV	USA
WORNITZKY, BRON.	28	M	LABR	RR	AHUI	USA
NAGRATOWSKY, JAN	27	M	LABR	RR	AHUI	USA
PESTA, WLAD.	23	M	LABR	RR	AHUI	USA
MARG.	21	M	LABR	RR	AHUI	USA
WOIZNITZKI, JAN	21	M	LABR	RR	AHUI	USA
CHENCHINSKY, J.	21	M	LABR	RR	AHUI	USA
LUNGEWSKY, JAN	28	M	LABR	RR	AHUI	USA
BREDAC, ANTON	24	M	LABR	RR	AHUI	USA
KWIATHOWSKY, CONST.	28	M	LABR	RR	AHUI	USA
KNUTHINSEN, K.	35	M	LABR	FN	ZZZZ	USA
KARHN, JOH.	28	M	LABR	FN	ZZZZ	USA
ARANOWITZ, RIVE	34	F	W	FN	AFVG	USA
ABE	7	M	CHILD	FN	AFVG	USA
CHAIE	5	M	CHILD	FN	AFVG	USA
MEYER	3	M	CHILD	FN	AFVG	USA
GRODKOWITZ, JAN	35	M	LABR	RR	ZZZZ	USA
SZEZECZAK, SIMON	29	M	LABR	RR	ZZZZ	USA
PAWELCE, JACOB	29	M	LABR	RR	ZZZZ	USA
KRAJEWSKI, CAS.	42	M	LABR	RR	ZZZZ	USA
CIHURKA, ANTON	37	M	LABR	RR	ZZZZ	USA
LISKEWSKI, JAN	27	M	LABR	RR	ZZZZ	USA
BLOCHI, ANTON	34	M	LABR	RR	ZZZZ	USA
PAWELA, ANTON	29	M	LABR	RR	ZZZZ	USA
SZYMANSKI, FRANZ	27	M	LABR	RR	ZZZZ	USA
KRIWANEK, JAN	36	M	LABR	RR	ZZZZ	USA
KOSEBUD, JOSEF	22	M	LABR	RR	ZZZZ	USA
MALY, VACLAV	28	M	LABR	RR	ZZZZ	USA
JOSEFA	34	F	W	RR	ZZZZ	USA
KOTLALA, JAN	25	M	LABR	RR	ZZZZ	USA
KULHANEK, MATEJ	29	M	LABR	RR	ZZZZ	USA
SAZERSKI, SIMON	29	M	LABR	RR	ZZZZ	USA
REPNITZKY, ALEX	38	M	LABR	RR	ZZZZ	USA
KARKOWSKY, CONST.	31	M	LABR	RR	ZZZZ	USA
KAMINSKY, VINCENT	25	M	LABR	RR	ZZZZ	USA
RAUHARDT, FRIEDR	20	M	LABR	RR	ZZZZ	USA
SKEWINA, ANNA	29	F	SGL	RR	ZZZZ	USA
DOBRZYNSKI, FRANZISKA	26	F	SGL	RR	ZZZZ	USA
WISNIEWSKI, PETER	22	M	LABR	RR	ZZZZ	USA
DELINEZKI, JAN	29	M	LABR	RR	ZZZZ	USA
DOBUSSINSKI, BOLISLAV	26	M	LABR	RR	ZZZZ	USA
GROCHOWSKY, VINCENT	25	M	LABR	RR	ZZZZ	USA
SAKNOWSKI, ULIANA	17	F	SGL	RR	ZZZZ	USA
SENDLINKA, SALOMON	23	M	LABR	RR	AGRT	USA

SHIP: AMSTERDAM

FROM: ROTTERDAM
TO: NEW YORK
ARRIVED: 15 APRIL 1889

PASSENGER	AGE	SEX	OCCUPATION	PRI	VIL	DES
PLAGE, REIFER	30	M	UNKNOWN	RR	ZZZZ	USA
LEAS	34	M	UNKNOWN	RR	ZZZZ	USA
SZABO, MICHEL	28	M	UNKNOWN	RR	ZZZZ	USA
MACHAL, GULA	32	M	UNKNOWN	RR	ZZZZ	USA
JOHANSEN, JOHAN	24	M	UNKNOWN	RR	ZZZZ	USA
MICHAL, GARRIE	30	M	UNKNOWN	RR	ZZZZ	USA
KRAFZINSKI, CHANE	25	F	UNKNOWN	RR	ZZZZ	USA
GETE	10	F	CH	RR	ZZZZ	USA
GERZEL	3	F	CHILD	RR	ZZZZ	USA
MARTUS, JUDA	30	M	LABR	RR	ZZZZ	USA
MERLINSKI, CHANE	20	M	LABR	RR	ZZZZ	USA
WEINER, LIPPLE	24	F	UNKNOWN	RR	ZZZZ	USA
CESINE	1	F	CHILD	RR	ZZZZ	USA
WAGNER, FRANZ	23	M	LABR	RR	ZZZZ	USA
FRINKEL, MOISCHE	41	M	MCHT	RR	ZZZZ	USA
HANSER, HANS	22	M	MCHT	RR	ZZZZ	USA
BERL, VOGEL	25	M	LABR	RR	ZZZZ	USA
REMSE, ABBIARO	25	M	UNKNOWN	RR	ZZZZ	USA
GERNWAL, JOSEF	22	M	UNKNOWN	RR	ZZZZ	USA
WIERZCHWITZ, BRONISLAW	22	M	LABR	RR	ZZZZ	USA
MALECKE, KONSTANCY	24	M	LABR	RR	ZZZZ	USA

PASSENGER	AGE	SEX	OCCUPATION	PRV VIL DES
JADWIGO, JURECK	22	M	LABR	RRZZZZUSA
PANKWSKY, FRANZ	33	M	LABR	RRZZZZUSA
HOLZEN, HERMANN	19	M	LABR	RRZZZZUSA
CZERNETSKY, ANTON	31	M	LABR	RRZZZZUSA
BELDA, SIMON	40	M	LABR	RRZZZZUSA
MATELEWICZ, MAJIZ	24	M	UNKNOWN	RRZZZZUSA
SUSENSKI, STANISLAW	35	M	LABR	RRZZZZUSA
OMILIAN, JOHAN	24	M	LABR	RRZZZZUSA
SURKOWSKY, FRANZ	22	M	LABR	RRZZZZUSA
MAJESKI, MATECHE	46	M	UNKNOWN	RRZZZZUSA
MATKOW, ANDREAS	27	M	UNKNOWN	RRZZZZUSA
MUSULAIS, JERSEI	27	M	LABR	RRZZZZUSA
SZERNEWSKI, PAUL	35	M	LABR	RRZZZZUSA
LANGE, ALBERT	21	M	LABR	RRZZZZUSA
KUBIAZ, CASUNI	26	M	LABR	RRZZZZUSA
THOMAZEWK, ANDREAS	19	M	LABR	RRZZZZUSA
CEGELSKY, JOHN	20	M	LABR	RRZZZZUSA
URSKI, ADAM	22	M	LABR	RRZZZZUSA
MAVRIGY, FRANZ	26	M	LABR	RRZZZZUSA
U	28	M	LABR	RRZZZZUSA
KRACHON, VACLOW	23	M	LABR	RRZZZZUSA
SCHALTI, JACOBUS	22	M	LABR	RRZZZZUSA
WOJESK, JANOS	28	M	LABR	RRZZZZUSA
MIESFER, JOSEPH	22	M	LABR	RRZZZZUSA
DELDKWITZ, JAN	27	M	LABR	RRZZZZUSA
SEIKER, STEFFAN	37	M	LABR	RRZZZZUSA
HOLLEND	.02	M	INFANT	RRZZZZUSA
LUIDA, JOSEPH	21	M	LABR	RRZZZZUSA
MOROSOW, U	27	M	LABR	RRZZZZUSA
-ERSCHNEID, U	20	M	LABR	RRZZZZUSA
MIESLMEC, JOSEF	40	M	LABR	RRZZZZUSA
SOKOLOWSKI, JOSEF	28	M	LABR	RRZZZZUSA
SIMON, ARON	18	M	LABR	RRZZZZUSA
OLOF, STANISLAW	24	M	LABR	RRZZZZUSA
JUSKEWIEZ, JAN	22	M	LABR	RRZZZZUSA
VISLIC, GEORGE	30	M	LABR	RRZZZZUSA
SOKALOWS, ANTON	28	M	LABR	RRZZZZUSA
STILLER, SCHITGE	18	M	LABR	RRZZZZUSA
SCHALYZEN, JACOB	4	M	CHILD	RRZZZZUSA
NOVRATEL, MICHAEL	31	M	CH	RRZZZZUSA
MARIE	31	F	UNKNOWN	RRZZZZUSA
JOSEPH	23	M	UNKNOWN	RRZZZZUSA
MARIE	3	F	CHILD	RRZZZZUSA
NEPH, ANTON	16	M	UNKNOWN	RRZZZZUSA

SHIP: ANCHORIA

FROM: GLASGOW AND MOVILLE
TO: NEW YORK
ARRIVED: 15 APRIL 1889

PASSENGER	AGE	SEX	OCCUPATION	PRV VIL DES
GINTER, JOSEPH	30	M	LABR	PLZZZZUSA
WINCINTY	24	M	TLR	PLZZZZUSA
SMOKOWSKI, ANTON	30	M	LABR	PLZZZZUSA
MARGOWITZ, PITR	26	M	DR	PLZZZZUSA
KOCZUNSKI, ANTON	36	M	JNR	PLZZZZUSA
PUGOTSKI, MICHAEL	32	M	LABR	PLZZZZUSA
SCHEREIKIS, INRIE	22	M	TLR	PLZZZZUSA
LEWANDOWSKI, JANAS	30	M	LABR	PLZZZZUSA
WINCLAW, TOMAS	26	M	LABR	PLZZZZUSA
LOBANOWSKY, ANTON	22	M	CTR	PLZZZZUSA
SILZ, INRIE	24	M	CPTR	PLZZZZUSA
BOLZOSIS, OSIF	23	M	CPTR	PLAHTFUSA
JUSEPOWITZ, USTIN	20	M	SHMK	PLAHTFUSA
GAGAJEWSKI, FELIX	23	M	FARMER	PLAHTFUSA
SCHAPULIS, KASIMIR	26	M	SDLR	PLAHTFUSA
SIGMOND, S.W.	36	M	LABR	PLAHTFUSA
SAULINSKY, MICHE.	18	M	LABR	PLAHTFUSA
LAZANES, VINCENTY	21	M	LABR	PLAHTFUSA
WOLMEWITZ, JOSEF	21	M	TILM	PLAHTFUSA

PASSENGER	AGE	SEX	OCCUPATION	PRV VIL DES
DAKUNIS, INRIE	19	M	TLR	PLAHTFUSA
GLIZEZYNCK, JOSEF	60	M	LABR	PLAHTFUSA
WALENTENOWITZ, RAMERT	20	M	LABR	PLAHTFUSA
JANASIK, ALBERT	28	M	LABR	PLAHTFUSA
PETRUSCHKEWICZ, VIN.	22	M	LABR	PLAHTFUSA
BONASCHEFSKI, ANTON	26	M	FARMER	PLZZZZUSA
NOVAK, FRANZ	28	M	LABR	PLZZZZUSA
ASAGOWSKI, MICHL.	36	M	LABR	PLZZZZUSA
JOKSCHEWITZ, STEFAN	24	M	LABR	PLZZZZUSA
PIOTRE, ZISIS	18	M	LABR	PLZZZZUSA
FEIZERSKI, JOSEF	20	M	LABR	PLZZZZUSA
BLIKENES, PIOTRE	20	M	LABR	PLZZZZUSA
SZEZPANIAK, JAN	29	M	LABR	PLAIKSUSA
STARISKA, MARYN	34	M	GDNR	PLAHUFUSA
PULICANOS, IGNATZ	28	M	LABR	PLZZZZUSA
SCHIBANIS, OSIP	20	M	LABR	PLZZZZUSA
BORISNEWITZ, STAN.	34	M	JNR	RRZZZZUSA
ANNA	25	F	W	RRZZZZUSA
STEFAN	9	M	CHILD	RRZZZZUSA
AMELIE	5	F	CHILD	RRZZZZUSA
SCHILINSKY, VERONIKA	20	F	HP	RRZZZZUSA
SIKORSKI, PAULINE	21	F	HP	RRZZZZUSA
ROBINSON, DANIEL	19	M	BCHR	RRZZZZUSA
ZITTRON, SCHMUL	19	M	SDLR	RRZZZZUSA
LEWMSOHN, RIVE	33	F	UNKNOWN	RRZZZZUSA
CHAJE	9	F	CHILD	RRZZZZUSA
JUDEL	3	M	CHILD	RRZZZZUSA
SCHMUL	2	M	CHILD	RRZZZZUSA
KOHN, NOCHIM	18	M	TLR	RRZZZZUSA
NEYASCH	11	M	CH	RRZZZZUSA
KRAUESE, MALKE	10	F	CH	RRZZZZUSA
GREINETZ, SCHMUL	12	M	CH	RRZZZZUSA
BEHRE	11	M	CH	RRZZZZUSA
COHEN, JACOB	35	M	LABR	RRZZZZUSA
ZALMEN	18	M	LABR	RRZZZZUSA
ROTHSLEIN, BEREL	40	M	GCR	RRZZZZUSA
LOVOSKY, ISAK	19	M	WCHMKR	RRZZZZUSA
OSWISCZINSKI, CHAIM	19	M	TLR	RRZZZZUSA
GUSTER, JACOB	22	M	LABR	RRZZZZUSA
FEINGOLD, SIMCHE	25	M	LABR	RRZZZZUSA
REMANOW, JUDEL	19	M	UNKNOWN	RRZZZZUSA
PERZOWIICZ, RACHEL	18	F	HP	RRZZZZUSA
AMSTERDAM, SISEL	15	F	HP	RRZZZZUSA
RUTENBERG, CHALINE	20	F	HP	RRZZZZUSA

SHIP: SLAVONIA

FROM: SWINEMUNDE
TO: NEW YORK
ARRIVED: 16 APRIL 1889

PASSENGER	AGE	SEX	OCCUPATION	PRV VIL DES
JAWORSKI, WALENTY	30	M	LABR	RRZZZZNY
IGNATZ	22	M	LABR	RRZZZZNY
MIELITZ, CARL	47	M	BCKM	RRZZZZNY
HENRIETTE	45	F	W	RRZZZZNY
ERNST	10	M	CH	RRZZZZNY
HEINRICH	12	M	CH	RRZZZZNY
FRITZ	7	M	CHILD	RRZZZZNY
LUDWIG	5	M	CHILD	RRZZZZNY
DRAZBA, BERBARA	22	F	UNKNOWN	RRZZZZNY
GRUNWALD, ISAAC	22	M	LABR	RRZZZZNY
YESELAN, PAWLINGE	18	F	UNKNOWN	RRZZZZNY
RIWAL, AUGUST	23	M	LABR	RRZZZZNY
BEGGEROW, ERNST	31	F	LABR	RRZZZZNY
LOUISE	41	M	UNKNOWN	RRZZZZNY
WILHELM	8	M	CHILD	RRZZZZNY
FRANZ	7	M	CHILD	RRZZZZNY
KNAPP, JOHANN	28	M	UNKNOWN	RRZZZZNY
BERTHA	28	F	UNKNOWN	RRZZZZNY
PAUL	2	M	CHILD	RRZZZZNY

PASSENGER	AGE	SEX	OCCUPATION	PRV VIL DES
JOHANN	43	M	UNKNOWN	RRZZZZNY
ZYWICKA, ANNASTASIA	17	F	UNKNOWN	RRZZZZNY
AGNES	15	F	UNKNOWN	RRZZZZNY
JOSEFINE	9	F	CHILD	RRZZZZNY
BIDKOWSKY, JOSEFINE	21	F	CH	RRZZZZNY
EMILIE	18	F	CH	RRZZZZNY
BECKMANN, WILHELM	40	M	UNKNOWN	RRZZZZNY
EMMA	38	F	W	RRZZZZNY
CARL	14	M	CH	RRZZZZNY
AUGUST	13	M	CH	RRZZZZNY
GUSTAV	11	M	CH	RRZZZZNY
ANNA	10	F	CH	RRZZZZNY
EMMA	8	F	CHILD	RRZZZZNY
BERTHA	5	F	CHILD	RRZZZZNY
MARTHA	4	F	CHILD	RRZZZZNY
HERMANN	1	M	CHILD	RRZZZZNY
FRIESE, ROSALIA	21	F	UNKNOWN	RRZZZZNY
GRADZYK, MARIE	25	F	UNKNOWN	RRZZZZNY
NEHRING, MARTHA	22	F	UNKNOWN	RRAEWMNY
BREMER, EMILIE	15	F	UNKNOWN	RRZZZZNY
DITHBERNER, MATHILDE	20	F	UNKNOWN	RRADZUNY
SCHAUER, AMALIA	30	F	WO	RRZZZZNY
FLORENTINE	8	F	CHILD	RRZZZZNY
EMILIE	2	F	CHILD	RRZZZZNY
MARTHA	1	F	CHILD	RRZZZZNY
RUDZINKY, FRANZISZEK	35	M	JNR	RRAFWJNY
U, HENSCHEL	24	F	W	RRAIHRNY
GOTTLIEB	38	M	LABR	RRAIHRNY
BENJAMEN	.09	M	INFANT	RRAIHRNY
SAJORSKY, JACOB	13	M	LABR	RRZZZZNY
KOWALEWSKI, NICODEM	19	M	LABR	RRZZZZNY
WISCNIEWSKI, ADAM	20	M	LABR	RRZZZZUSA
MITZHOWITZ, ALBERT	32	M	FARMER	RRZZZZUSA
KAROLAK, EDMUND	23	M	JNR	RRZZZZUSA
GRABBAUTZKAS, WINZES	32	M	LABR	RRZZZZUSA
MEIER, JOSEPH	58	M	LKSH	RRAFVGUSA
BRENNHAUDRN, JOSEPH	26	M	LABR	RRZZZZUSA
NUSJA, JOSEF	28	M	UNKNOWN	RRAFZDUSA
KUBATZKI, ANTON	32	M	UNKNOWN	RRAFZDUSA
BARSCHT, NOCOLAI	25	M	UNKNOWN	RRAFZDUSA
SCHIFFZETZKI, STANISLAU	42	M	UNKNOWN	RRAFZDUSA

SHIP: CITY OF RICHMOND

FROM: LIVERPOOL AND QUEENSTOWN
TO: NEW YORK
ARRIVED: 17 APRIL 1889

PASSENGER	AGE	SEX	OCCUPATION	PRV VIL DES
ARONIKIS, PETRIO	39	M	FARMER	RRZZZZNY
CHAIESKI, LORENZ	25	M	FARMER	RRZZZZNY
DOMANSKI, JAN	40	M	FARMER	RRZZZZNY
EWA	35	F	W	RRZZZZNY
JOSEF	22	M	FARMER	RRZZZZNY
PALINTZ	17	M	FARMER	RRZZZZNY
MAICIN	10	F	CH	RRZZZZNY
KATARZJNA	5	F	CHILD	RRZZZZNY
DRENDA, JACOB	55	M	FARMER	RRZZZZNY
ANTONIA	52	F	W	RRZZZZNY
JOSEFA	10	F	CH	RRZZZZNY
STUNZIK, JOSEF	26	M	FARMER	RRZZZZNY
FRANSISKA	20	F	W	RRZZZZNY
FABRIKEWICZ, VALENTIN	37	M	FARMER	RRZZZZNY
KLAUS, ANDREAS	24	M	FARMER	RRZZZZNY
STREMPA, WOJCIEB	25	M	FARMER	RRZZZZNY
MICHALITSCH, JOSEF	31	M	FARMER	RRZZZZNY
MARTONJAK, IVANNY	29	M	FARMER	RRZZZZNY
MICKAR, ANNA	11	F	CH	RRZZZZNY
PANKEWIECZ, JOHN	25	M	FARMER	RRZZZZMI
REZENSTEACK, CH.	55	M	FARMER	RRZZZZMI
RACHNATSKI, ANA	27	F	SVNT	RRZZZZNY
SAPIIEZA, MARTIN	21	M	FARMER	RRZZZZNY
SPINGER, JOHN	33	M	FARMER	RRZZZZBUF
ANNA	50	F	M	RRZZZZBUF
SPRINGER, ANTONIA	32	F	W	RRZZZZBUF
JADWIGA	4	F	CHILD	RRZZZZBUF
JOSEF	.10	M	INFANT	RRZZZZBUF
SCHEDLING, ADAM	56	M	FARMER	RRZZZZNY
TEIKOWSKY, JAN	28	M	LABR	RRZZZZNY
GLEB, KISNNI	23	M	LABR	RRZZZZNY
JEROMIN, ANTON	22	M	LABR	RRZZZZNY
SLAPKING, KNUZEK	18	M	LABR	RRZZZZNY
URBAN, KLOMIR	22	M	LABR	RRZZZZNY
WIBERSKI, VINCENT	46	M	FARMER	RRZZZZBUF
MINTOWSKI, FRAN.	20	M	FARMER	RRZZZZBUF

SHIP: ARIZONA

FROM: LIVERPOOL AND QUEENSTOWN
TO: NEW YORK
ARRIVED: 17 APRIL 1889

PASSENGER	AGE	SEX	OCCUPATION	PRV VIL DES
WEEDER, OTTO	17	M	LABR	FNZZZZUSA
WOLDMAN, STAF.	40	M	ATSN	RRZZZZUSA
HEIMIK, ABRAM	17	M	LABR	RRZZZZUSA
NIEFELD, DWOSCHE	24	F	W	RRZZZZUSA
ABRAM	6	M	CHILD	RRZZZZUSA
JANKELSEN, MORDCHE	55	M	MECH	RRZZZZUSA
BRAUNSTEIN, SCHEFTEL	22	M	JNR	RRZZZZUSA
REIZLEWITZ, LEIL	30	F	W	RRZZZZUSA
ZALEL	7	F	CHILD	RRZZZZUSA
RUBIN	3	M	CHILD	RRZZZZUSA
SCHEIE	5	F	CHILD	RRZZZZUSA
MOSCHOWITZ, PAIL	30	F	W	RRZZZZUSA
ZALEL	7	F	CHILD	RRZZZZUSA
BRANDENBURGER, HANNA	48	F	W	RRZZZZUSA
DANIEL	11	M	CH	RRZZZZUSA
WOLF	9	M	CHILD	RRZZZZUSA
HIRSCH	7	M	CHILD	RRZZZZUSA
LIEBE	7	F	CHILD	RRZZZZUSA
SARA	6	F	CHILD	RRZZZZUSA
GOTTLIEB	3	M	CHILD	RRZZZZUSA
REBECCA	3	F	CHILD	RRZZZZUSA
PILCHER, ARON	20	M	LABR	RRZZZZUSA
IDA	20	F	W	RRZZZZUSA
NEUSTADT, MEIER	24	M	TLR	RRZZZZUSA
REIZLEWITZ, GIRSEN	.08	M	INFANT	RRZZZZUSA
MOSCHKOWITZ, HENE	.04	F	INFANT	RRZZZZUSA
ERIKSON, C.	22	M	LABR	FNZZZZUSA
KINLANDER, G.F.	30	M	ATSN	FNZZZZUSA
DREICER, JACOB	30	M	GENT	RRZZZZUSA
JACOB	35	F	LDY	RRZZZZUSA

SHIP: KANSAS

FROM: LIVERPOOL
TO: BOSTON
ARRIVED: 18 APRIL 1889

PASSENGER	AGE	SEX	OCCUPATION	PRV VIL DES
ROBINSON, R.	28	M	LABR	RRZZZZBO
FRUME	18	F	W	RRZZZZBO
WOLSON, L.	24	M	LABR	PLZZZZBO
SETE	24	F	W	PLZZZZBO
GINETZKY, VALENTIN	25	M	LABR	PLZZZZBO
JOSEPHA	23	F	W	PLZZZZBO
PLAWENSKY, THOMAS	28	M	LABR	RRZZZZBO

PASSENGER	A G E	S E X	OCCUPATION	P V D R I E V L S
MARGARET	36	F	W	RRZZZZBO
MENIA	11	F	CH	RRZZZZBO
STAN	9	M	CHILD	RRZZZZBO
ANT.	3	M	CHILD	RRZZZZBO
FR.	00	F	INF	RRZZZZBO
KOZOCHOWSKY, S.	27	M	LABR	RRZZZZBO
KUHFERMANN, J.	18	M	LABR	PLZZZZBO
BORSCHATZ, S.	20	M	LABR	RRZZZZBO
GRUNBERG, S.	25	M	LABR	PLZZZZNY
MOBLE, J.	19	M	LABR	RRZZZZNY
DROBIG, JOHN	24	M	LABR	RRZZZZBO
PERSKY, J.	24	M	LABR	RRZZZZBO
JORZIK, J.	25	M	LABR	PLZZZZBO
SAKALOWSKY, J.	44	M	LABR	RRZZZZBO
STEPHANOWSKY, F.	37	M	LABR	RRZZZZBO
GUSCHEWSKY, M.	17	M	LABR	RRZZZZBO
KRUPA, J.	33	M	LABR	RRZZZZBO
WOROLOSKY, F.	28	M	LABR	RRAAQHBO
WAGOLEWSKY, P.	34	M	LABR	RRAAQHBO
SHERUSKA, A.	24	M	LABR	RRAAQHBO
WOROLOLEWSKY, H.	25	M	LABR	RRAAQHBO
WILKEWITZ, A.	28	M	LABR	RRAAQHBO
UBIS, F.	25	M	LABR	RRAAQHBO
WOLIS, A.	34	M	LABR	RRAAQHBO
LUTCHISKA, J.	24	M	LABR	RRAAQHBO
WILKUS, V.	20	M	LABR	RRAAQHBO
KELBSH, J.	32	M	LABR	RRAAQHBO
PAGEL, J.	28	M	LABR	RRAAQHBO
SWENDEN, M.	32	M	LABR	RRAAQHBO
STRUDARA, JOHN	30	M	LABR	RRAAQHCH
NYLAND, CARL	35	M	LABR	RRAAQHNY
DANNES, FR.	26	M	LABR	RRAAQHNY
SORIS, OSIP	28	M	LABR	RRAAQHNY
PZTZEL, M.	18	M	LABR	RRAAQHNY
REIMISS, E.	23	M	LABR	RRAAQHNY

SHIP: BOTHNIA

FROM: LIVERPOOL AND QUEENSTOWN
TO: NEW YORK
ARRIVED: 19 APRIL 1889

PASSENGER	A G E	S E X	OCCUPATION	P V D R I E V L S
BASEZHICIOCZOWA, TEOFIL	31	F	MA	RRZZZZUSA
BASEZHICIOCZOWA, FRANZ	8	M	CHILD	RRZZZZUSA
JOHAN	5	M	CHILD	RRZZZZUSA
STANISLAUS	1	M	CHILD	RRZZZZUSA
BUKOWSKI, JOSEF	26	M	LABR	RRZZZZUSA
MAXIMILIAN	24	M	LABR	RRZZZZUSA
DILTER, ANTON	30	M	LABR	RRZZZZUSA
ANTONIA	24	F	W	RRZZZZUSA
WOCYIEK	8	M	CHILD	RRZZZZUSA
DAUBROWSKY, MICHAEL	26	M	LABR	RRZZZZUSA
SEVERINA	23	F	W	RRZZZZUSA
MARIANNA	1	F	CHILD	RRZZZZUSA
VICTORIA	.03	F	INFANT	RRZZZZUSA
NEDWEDOWSKY, ISAK	43	M	LABR	RRZZZZUSA
SCHERA	40	F	W	RRZZZZUSA
ESTER	11	F	CH	RRZZZZUSA
RIFKE	10	F	CH	RRZZZZUSA
DAVID	8	M	CHILD	RRZZZZUSA
MOJISCH	7	M	CHILD	RRZZZZUSA
MOLKE	3	M	CHILD	RRZZZZUSA
ZILINSKIEWSKY, ANTONIA	30	F	MA	RRZZZZUSA
STANS.	7	M	CHILD	RRZZZZUSA
MARIANNA	5	F	CHILD	RRZZZZUSA
ANEITE	3	F	CHILD	RRZZZZUSA
HELENA	.08	F	INFANT	RRZZZZUSA
HEYMANN, JETTA	17	F	SP	RRZZZZUSA
MAUSHALLET, MARIA	48	F	W	RRZZZZUSA
MARIA	18	F	SP	RRZZZZUSA
SCHACHNOWSKY, SONE	17	F	SP	RRZZZZUSA
ANDRYEWSKI, KARL	29	M	LABR	RRZZZZUSA
BILEWSKY, MICHAEL	22	M	LABR	RRZZZZUSA
BLOZIK, JOHAN	34	M	LABR	RRZZZZUSA
DZORBICKI, JOSEF	20	M	LABR	RRZZZZUSA
EZERSKI, MARTIN	35	M	LABR	RRZZZZUSA
HEYMANN, MOSES	18	M	LABR	RRZZZZUSA
HUKNURSKA, MICHEL	38	M	LABR	RRZZZZUSA
KORGE, FREDRICK	40	M	LABR	RRZZZZUSA
KNYGER, JOHAN	57	M	LABR	RRZZZZUSA
KONRAD, AUGUST	35	M	LABR	RRZZZZUSA
MACIEZEWSKI, VORITH	30	M	LABR	RRZZZZUSA
MONDRY, HIPPOLD	19	M	LABR	RRZZZZUSA
NOWACK, JAN	37	M	LABR	RRZZZZUSA
STEFANIAK, STEFAN	24	M	LABR	RRZZZZUSA
SCHWOATAK, JAN	40	M	LABR	RRZZZZUSA
SHEBRCUSKY, FELIX	32	M	LABR	RRZZZZUSA
SCHRAWOSKY, PIOTER	27	M	LABR	RRZZZZUSA
STAUREN, JULIUS	23	M	LABR	RRZZZZUSA
SCHWIKLINSKY, PETER	33	M	LABR	RRZZZZUSA
STACKOWICK, THOMAS	32	M	LABR	RRZZZZUSA
SINGER, ADOLF	22	M	LABR	RRZZZZUSA
ZAPONCZKOWSKY, KONSTANT	38	M	LABR	RRZZZZUSA

SHIP: ITALY

FROM: LIVERPOOL AND QUEENSTOWN
TO: NEW YORK
ARRIVED: 19 APRIL 1889

PASSENGER	A G E	S E X	OCCUPATION	P V D R I E V L S
COHN, EFRAIM	16	M	LABR	RRACBFNY
EUGERYLYNSKA, W.	17	M	LABR	RRACBFNY
BARWONSKI, ANTON	22	M	LABR	RRACBFNY
JANKOWSKI, JOHAN	22	M	LABR	RRACBFBRO
KONIGASCHI, JENTE	33	F	W	RRACBFNY
SOLOMON	5	M	CHILD	RRACBFNY
DOBRATZKI, KASIMIR	26	M	LABR	RRACBFNY
WOLOWEL, VICTORIA	22	F	SP	RRACBFCH
WILK, AUGUST	34	M	LABR	RRACBFNY
AITUKOWSKI, JONAS	30	M	LABR	RRACBFNY
DEPWSKI, STANISL.	23	M	LABR	RRACBFUSA
JAUCTZAK, ANTON	26	M	LABR	RRACBFUNK
PALUNAP, PETER	24	M	LABR	RRACBFUNK
STAWOSKY, ANTON	24	M	LABR	RRACBFUNK
RADSCHUSKY, KARL	17	M	LABR	RRACBFUNK
IKLUTTI, JOHANN	21	M	LABR	RRACBFCH
BOLTAMIE, KOLENDA	23	M	LABR	RRACBFCH
RADOSCHEWSKY, SIMON	33	M	LABR	RRACBFNY
KARATZKI, JULIUS	19	M	LABR	RRACBFNY
OLEGMIS, MARTIN	22	M	LABR	RRACBFNY
BARONOWSKY, PAUL	4	M	CHILD	RRACBFNY
SCHMEKAIS, VINCENT	30	M	LABR	RRACBFNY
JUSKANIS, MATHIAS	25	M	LABR	RRACBFNY
LIBERMANN, D.	30	M	LABR	RRACBFNY
HASAK, R.	26	M	LABR	RRACBFNY
JAKOTIS, JAN	20	M	LABR	RRAFVGNY
SAVAN, J.	21	M	LABR	RRACBFNY
GRABE, KOPPITE	26	M	LABR	RRACBFNY
AFBIDA, JUDA	30	M	LABR	RRACBFNY
IRMCHEL, FRIEDA	34	M	LABR	RRACBFCH
WILHELMINE	28	F	W	RRACBFCH
AUGUSTE	6	M	CHILD	RRACBFCH
CARL	00	M	INF	RRACBFCH
MILLAK, BARTOMEY	30	M	LABR	RRACBFNY
ANTONIO	26	M	LABR	RRACBFNY
MARIANNA	28	F	W	RRACBFNY
WALURBE	3	M	CHILD	RRACBFNY
JOSEPH	00	M	INF	RRACBFNY
MARYANNA	5	F	CHILD	RRACBFNY
GALWAGER, A.	30	M	LABR	RRACBFNY

PASSENGER	AGE	SEX	OCCUPATION	PRIVL	DES
WAIDOWSKY, W.	36	M	LABR	RRACBF	NY
RECKUS, M.	18	M	LABR	RRACBF	NY
SCHWABT, HIRSCH	25	M	LABR	RRACBF	NY
FUGAR, H.	27	M	LABR	RRACBF	NY
MICHALSKY, J.	30	M	LABR	RRACBF	NY
RINIE	7	F	CHILD	RRACBF	NY
ARIE	4	F	CHILD	RRACBF	NY
ETTE	00	F	INF	RRACBF	NY
LIGM, F.	20	M	LABR	RRACBF	NY
KUZA, BARBARA	25	F	W	RRACBF	NY
U	3	F	CHILD	RRACBF	NY
U	00	F	INF	RRACBF	NY
POPOLSKY, P.	30	M	LABR	RRACBF	NY
SEMMELKACK, MICHOLAS	23	M	LABR	RRACBF	IL
TIRCNER, G.	28	M	LABR	RRACBF	NY
MUSKOWITZ, JANS	30	M	LABR	RRACBF	MI

SHIP: HELVETIA

FROM: LIVERPOOL
TO: NEW YORK
ARRIVED: 19 APRIL 1889

PASSENGER	AGE	SEX	OCCUPATION	PRIVL	DES
JAUSASKI, JAN	29	M	LABR	PLZZZZ	NY
POLLAKI, JOSEPH	26	M	LABR	PLZZZZ	NY
GOLOLSKI, CHRISTIAN	30	M	LABR	PLZZZZ	NY
FORZNALSKI, ANTON	23	M	LABR	PLZZZZ	NY
NOHARIOWICZ, SIMON	25	M	LABR	PLZZZZ	NY
ZOBIZYOSKI, J.	38	M	LABR	PLZZZZ	NY
LEWANDOWSKI, JAN	26	M	LABR	PLZZZZ	NY
LANDLE, F.	30	M	LABR	PLZZZZ	NY
SCHLAZ, FRIEDRICK	22	M	LABR	PLZZZZ	NY
KAZULA, JAN	14	M	LABR	PLZZZZ	NY
JAUKOWSKI, ADAM	30	M	LABR	PLZZZZ	OH
MACIEZEWSKI, ANTON	28	M	LABR	PLZZZZ	CH
REGER, MERE	45	F	W	RRZZZZ	NY
BEILE	15	F	SP	RRZZZZ	NY
JACOB	8	M	CHILD	RRZZZZ	NY
ABRAHAM	4	M	CHILD	RRZZZZ	NY
SAMUEL	00	M	INF	RRZZZZ	NY
RUBENZIF, P.	29	F	W	RRZZZZ	NY
LINNIE	7	F	CHILD	RRZZZZ	NY
CHJENE	4	F	CHILD	RRZZZZ	NY
ROCHE	3	M	CHILD	RRZZZZ	NY
MERE	00	F	INF	RRZZZZ	NY
SCHENFELD, RACHEL	22	F	SP	RRZZZZ	NY
HOLSTEIN, FIEJA	38	F	W	RRZZZZ	NY
FAIE	17	F	SP	RRZZZZ	NY
ERCHANE	10	F	CH	RRZZZZ	NY
ABRAHAM	8	M	CHILD	RRZZZZ	NY
WIRSOK, S.	26	F	W	RRZZZZ	IL
BERTHE	00	F	INF	RRZZZZ	NY
MILCHANES, F.	25	F	SP	RRZZZZ	NY
BRON, R.	28	M	LABR	RRZZZZ	NY
GLAGEN, F.	26	M	LABR	RRZZZZ	NY
ALPESON, ZELLA	21	M	LABR	RRZZZZ	NY
SAMERLOWITZ, MEME	28	F	W	RRZZZZ	BRO
ESTHER	18	F	SP	RRZZZZ	BRO
SCHEINE	20	F	SP	RRZZZZ	BRO
SCHIE	8	F	CHILD	RRZZZZ	BRO
EISEK	4	M	CHILD	RRZZZZ	BRO
MOUSCHE	2	M	CHILD	RRZZZZ	BRO
FALK, G.	20	F	SP	RRZZZZ	NY
SCHAUSTOWITZ, M.	19	F	SP	RRZZZZ	NY
RIFKIN, O.	18	F	SP	RRZZZZ	NY
GRANDES, MAJI	30	F	W	RRZZZZ	NY
HENACH	10	M	CH	RRZZZZ	NY
CHANIE	8	F	CHILD	RRZZZZ	NY
ITZIG	6	F	CHILD	RRZZZZ	NY
HEUSCHEL	3	M	CHILD	RRZZZZ	NY

PASSENGER	AGE	SEX	OCCUPATION	PRIVL	DES
RACHAEL	1	F	CHILD	RRZZZZ	NY
JACOBSKI, A.	27	M	LABR	RRZZZZ	NY
GLAZER, H.	25	M	LABR	RRZZZZ	NY
CZERMESKI, PETER	22	M	LABR	RRZZZZ	NY
GRINBERG, L.	25	M	LABR	RRZZZZ	CH
RUBENZK, S.	23	M	LABR	RRZZZZ	ROC
ROCHE	18	M	LABR	RRZZZZ	ROC
PEOLE	11	M	CH	RRZZZZ	ROC
CHAM	10	M	CH	RRZZZZ	ROC
BURSTEIN, D.	27	M	LABR	RRZZZZ	NY
WILK, A.	28	M	LABR	RRZZZZ	NY
ALXELLBRODE, JACOB	39	M	LABR	RRZZZZ	NY
BUTOWITZ, FRENZEL	23	M	LABR	RRZZZZ	NY
RUZERNESKI, ANTON	37	M	LABR	RRZZZZ	NY
ANOWITZ, ARON	35	M	LABR	RRZZZZ	NY
FREME	26	F	W	RRZZZZ	NY
MEME	8	F	CHILD	RRZZZZ	NY
ERNA	00	F	INF	RRZZZZ	NY

SHIP: TAORMINA

FROM: HAMBURG
TO: NEW YORK
ARRIVED: 20 APRIL 1889

PASSENGER	AGE	SEX	OCCUPATION	PRIVL	DES
OHERBERG, ANTONIE	30	F	SGL	RRZZZZ	NY
LIBINSKY, SCHLEPPAU	48	M	LABR	RRZZZZ	NY
BUDZALAWSKY, KONSTANTI	20	M	LABR	RRZZZZ	NY
DALGOW, HERM.	24	F	WO	RRZZZZ	NY
BARUCH	3	M	CHILD	RRZZZZ	NY
WIESNISOSKY, JAN	44	M	LABR	RRZZZZ	NY
BOGACKI, VICTOR	22	M	LABR	RRZZZZ	NY
SCHERISKY, ELIAS	19	M	LABR	RRZZZZ	NY
BLOCK, IGNATZ	32	M	LABR	RRZZZZ	NY
APOLLINA	28	F	W	RRZZZZ	NY
VALENTIN	5	M	CHILD	RRZZZZ	NY
STANISLAV	.06	M	INFANT	RRZZZZ	NY
SCHERISKY, RESE	26	F	WO	RRZZZZ	NY
ISRAEL	3	M	CHILD	RRZZZZ	NY
SCHNIGGEL, FRANZ	38	M	LABR	RRZZZZ	NY
KORDECK, TOMAS	40	M	LABR	RRZZZZ	NY
KOWALCZICK, JOSEF	30	M	LABR	RRZZZZ	NY
KULAS, MARCELL	24	M	LABR	RRZZZZ	NY
KERNOSEK, PIETER	34	M	LABR	RRZZZZ	NY
BERENT, HEINR.	39	M	LABR	RRZZZZ	NY
WISCHNEWSKI, FRANZ	28	M	LABR	RRZZZZ	NY
GOERTZ, ANDREWE	44	M	LABR	RRZZZZ	NY
CHEISE, ALEXANDER	23	M	LABR	RRZZZZ	NY
TOMASZEWSKY, STANISLAUS	37	M	LABR	RRZZZZ	NY
NADROWSKY, LUDWIG	23	M	LABR	RRZZZZ	NY
BZALNOWSKY, PETER	21	M	LABR	RRZZZZ	NY
FILISOWSKY, FRANZ	40	M	LABR	RRZZZZ	NY
DOMAGALSKI, STANISLAUS	21	M	LABR	RRZZZZ	NY
COFFERS, THEODOR	29	M	JNR	RRZZZZ	NY
FRANZ	22	M	JNR	RRZZZZ	NY
MALECKI, ANTON	56	M	CPTR	RRZZZZ	NY
MARG.	45	F	W	RRZZZZ	NY
THEODOR	22	M	UNKNOWN	RRZZZZ	NY
KROTZANO, VALENTY	24	M	LABR	RRZZZZ	NY
MARIANNE	22	F	W	RRZZZZ	NY
MARIANNE	.06	F	INFANT	RRZZZZ	NY
SZELOSZYK, JADWIGA	21	F	SGL	RRZZZZ	NY
ZAGURSKY, JAN	27	M	LABR	RRZZZZ	NY
PIOTR	24	M	LABR	RRZZZZ	NY
FOMA, FRANZ	24	M	LABR	RRZZZZ	NY
GRENEWITZ, LEONARD	27	M	LABR	RRZZZZ	NY
WOJNITZ, PAWEL	26	M	LABR	RRZZZZ	NY
KAULIANIS, OSSIP	21	M	LABR	RRZZZZ	NY
PZEBIKI, WICENTY	24	M	LABR	RRZZZZ	NY
MATLANON, ALEXANDER	30	M	LABR	FNZZZZ	NY

PASSENGER	AGE	SEX	OCCUPATION	PRV VIL DES
JAPPINEN, MATIKIJAS	20	M	LABR	FNZZZZNY
LEIONSKA, JOH.	33	M	LABR	FNZZZZNY
KROG, MATTH.	25	M	LABR	FNZZZZNY
PALIKA, MIKKEL	27	M	LABR	FNZZZZNY
PRETANER, ELYAS	32	M	LABR	FNZZZZNY
PERTTANEN, JACOB	38	M	LABR	FNZZZZNY
PRAESTANEN, ELYAS	32	M	LABR	FNZZZZNY
REISS, CARL	19	M	LABR	FNZZZZNY
PLUT, RINDKE	17	F	SGL	RRZZZZNY
BOROWSKY, IGNATZ	32	M	LABR	RRACBFNY
PAULE	34	F	W	RRACBFNY
WIRZINSKY, JOSEF	32	M	SHMK	RRACBFNY
REDNECKY, ANNA	19	F	SGL	RRACBFNY
PUSCHAKOWSKY, JOS	29	F	SGL	RRACBFNY
WISCHNEWSKY, JAN	30	F	SGL	RRACBFNY
RASTUBOWITZ, ADAM	28	F	SGL	RRACBFNY
RANITZKY, IVAN	32	F	SGL	RRACBFNY
OSCHLEWSKY, STANISL.	25	F	SGL	RRACBFNY
BLUKOWSKY, JAN	24	F	SGL	RRACBFNY
BRUDOWITZ, JAN	25	F	SGL	RRACBFNY

SHIP: P.CALAND

FROM: AMSTERDAM
TO: NEW YORK
ARRIVED: 20 APRIL 1889

PASSENGER	AGE	SEX	OCCUPATION	PRV VIL DES
SPYDLOWSKA, ANNA	20	F	UNKNOWN	RRZZZZUSA
ANTON	2	M	CHILD	RRZZZZUSA
MICHELINA	.08	F	INFANT	RRZZZZUSA
REJNIEWICZ, ANTON	33	M	LABR	RRZZZZUSA
BREZNIEWICZ, HERI	22	M	LABR	RRZZZZUSA
MARKUS, STEIN	18	M	LABR	RRZZZZUSA
JUNGERMAN, BABY	18	F	UNKNOWN	RRZZZZUSA
NOEICKI, MARCUS	30	M	LABR	PLZZZZUSA
FRANCISKA	19	F	UNKNOWN	PLZZZZUSA
ANTONIA	.03	F	INFANT	PLZZZZUSA
WUGZCHELSKI, BALENTIN	30	M	LABR	PLZZZZUSA
AGMISKE	28	F	UNKNOWN	PLZZZZUSA
STANISLAW	4	F	CHILD	PLZZZZUSA
KRASKA, WOJIECK	24	F	UNKNOWN	PLZZZZUSA
STANISLAS	.06	F	INFANT	PLZZZZUSA
NOWICK, FRANCISZEK	27	M	LABR	PLZZZZUSA
ANOMINA	25	F	UNKNOWN	PLZZZZUSA
RUBALIK, JOZEF	26	M	LABR	PLZZZZUSA
NOWICKI, AGNES	.06	F	INFANT	PLZZZZUSA
HILKOWSKI, JOHANN	30	M	LABR	PLZZZZUSA
AGNES	26	F	UNKNOWN	PLZZZZUSA
STAN	.06	M	INFANT	PLZZZZUSA
JUDITZKI, ALENANDER	20	M	LABR	PLZZZZUSA
KARCSMARCSYK, ALENANDER	18	M	LABR	PLZZZZUSA
JVANITZKI, STANISLAV	26	M	FARMER	PLZZZZUSA
SCHALINSKY, MARTIN	39	M	FARMER	PLZZZZUSA
TIMINSKY, FRANZ	38	M	FARMER	PLZZZZUSA
WILZEWSKI, JAN	40	M	FARMER	PLZZZZUSA
SCHUPA, ANTONI	25	M	FARMER	PLZZZZUSA
JARMOLOWITZ, STANISLAV	40	M	FARMER	PLZZZZUSA
SCHALENSKY, MARTEN	29	M	FARMER	PLZZZZUSA
BUEZINSKY, STANISLAV	23	M	FARMER	PLZZZZUSA
MODLINSKI, MICHEL	29	M	FARMER	PLZZZZUSA
SIEGMUND, MICHEL	33	M	FARMER	PLZZZZUSA
MAZUKOWSKI, ANDRES	38	M	FARMER	PLZZZZUSA
KARESMARCZYK, ULION	19	M	FARMER	PLZZZZUSA
REMERS, OSSCHACH	39	M	FARMER	PLZZZZUSA
PLONKOS, IGNAZ	30	M	FARMER	PLZZZZUSA
HANE, STANISLAV	24	M	FARMER	PLZZZZUSA
MARUNSKY, JAN	23	M	FARMER	PLZZZZUSA
BRANKNECKI, STAN.	27	M	FARMER	PLZZZZUSA
WARYCK, FRANZ	28	M	FARMER	PLZZZZUSA
FRANZ	26	M	FARMER	PLZZZZUSA
ZYTKOWSKI, FRANZ	28	M	FARMER	PLZZZZUSA
KOZEN, JAN	23	M	FARMER	PLZZZZUSA
LUKAWSKI, FRANZ	26	M	FARMER	PLZZZZUSA
TISCARNY, NIC	25	M	FARMER	PLZZZZUSA
KABATZKI, ANTONI	24	M	FARMER	PLZZZZUSA
DOMINIAN, VELENTI	23	M	FARMER	PLZZZZUSA
KLORIATKOWSKI, JOSEPH	50	M	FARMER	PLZZZZUSA
SULUSKI, ANDREA	25	F	UNKNOWN	PLZZZZUSA
STEPAN	9	M	CHILD	PLZZZZUSA
FRANCISCA	30	F	UNKNOWN	PLZZZZUSA
KUDZINSKY, JAN	20	M	LABR	PLZZZZUSA
ANNA	23	F	UNKNOWN	PLZZZZUSA
ODBURZYCHLEB, JOSEF	25	M	LABR	PLZZZZUSA
KOSTOWSKY, FRANZ	21	M	LABR	PLZZZZUSA
CZECHANUSKY, THOMES	26	M	LABR	PLZZZZUSA
PIOTROWSKI, BONIFACIUS	30	M	LABR	PLZZZZUSA
WIONIEWSKI, JOSEF	19	M	LABR	PLZZZZUSA
KAGNOWITSCH, JOSEF	23	M	LABR	PLZZZZUSA
EISEK, PAWEL	23	M	LABR	PLZZZZUSA
TOMAMSKY, JOSEF	39	M	LABR	PLZZZZUSA
KARDOWSKY, KASIMUS	23	M	LABR	PLZZZZUSA
NOLOVITZ, FRANZ	20	M	LABR	PLZZZZUSA
BEEMSKA, CATHERINA	29	F	UNKNOWN	PLZZZZUSA
OWSIAMY, ANTONI	18	M	FARMER	PLZZZZUSA
GURBACKI, THEODOR	40	M	FARMER	PLZZZZUSA
JADWIGA	35	F	UNKNOWN	PLZZZZUSA
KARIMIS	13	M	UNKNOWN	PLZZZZUSA
KARGANNE-	8	F	CHILD	PLZZZZUSA
LEONORA	3	F	CHILD	PLZZZZUSA
ROMAN	.11	M	INFANT	PLZZZZUSA
LEON	5	M	CHILD	PLZZZZUSA
PETESVITZ, JOSEF	22	M	LABR	PLZZZZUSA
VEMIESZ, WALENTY	24	M	LABR	PLZZZZUSA
NOWAKOWSKI, STANISLAV	24	M	FARMER	PLZZZZUSA
POKRYSKA, JOHANN	24	M	FARMER	PLZZZZUSA
ANDREAS	30	M	FARMER	PLZZZZUSA
SIURNSKI, PRAKZEDE	19	F	UNKNOWN	PLZZZZUSA
ZWIERSKA, MARCYAMA	30	F	UNKNOWN	PLZZZZUSA
MOWZYN	4	F	CHILD	PLZZZZUSA
JOSEFA	2	F	CHILD	PLZZZZUSA

SHIP: RHEIN

FROM: BREMEN
TO: BALTIMORE
ARRIVED: 20 APRIL 1889

PASSENGER	AGE	SEX	OCCUPATION	PRV VIL DES
ZYKENS, CH	30	F	NN	RRZZZZUSA
JOSEF	3	M	CHILD	RRZZZZUSA
CATH	.11	F	INFANT	RRZZZZUSA
MARIA	24	F	NN	RRZZZZUSA
BRODA, SCHEFE	38	F	NN	RRZZZZUSA
TOBA	17	F	NN	RRZZZZUSA
LEAH	14	F	NN	RRZZZZUSA
SELIA	7	F	CHILD	RRZZZZUSA
TERESE	5	F	CHILD	RRZZZZUSA
LEVIN, FIZK-	19	M	TLR	RRZZZZUSA
FA--ETH, FEIDE	38	F	NN	RRZZZZUSA
GITTEL	16	F	NN	RRZZZZUSA
SCHEMDEL	7	F	CHILD	RRZZZZUSA
MA-EM	5	M	CHILD	RRZZZZUSA
CZYMLEWSKI, JULIUS	28	M	LABR	RRZZZZUSA
BURKA, HENDEL	29	M	LABR	RRZZZZUSA
BERNSTEIN, HERM	17	M	CL	RRZZZZUSA
SCHELDEN, AUG	29	M	FARMER	RRZZZZUSA
LEWIN, U	30	F	NN	RRZZZZUSA
MARCUS	7	M	CHILD	RRZZZZUSA
BROEDE, T	16	F	NN	RRZZZZUSA
GRABO-TSKY, PETER	25	M	DLR	RRZZZZUSA
T-ADEN, H	31	M	FARMER	RRZZZZUSA

PASSENGER	AGE	SEX	OCCUPATION	PRV VIL DES
FOLKE	34	F	NN	RRZZZZUSA
DINA	7	F	CHILD	RRZZZZUSA
-ALTJE	6	F	CHILD	RRZZZZUSA
JOHA	4	F	CHILD	RRZZZZUSA
-ADE	.10	F	INFANT	RRZZZZUSA
DIMMER, FR	17	M	TLR	RRZZZZUSA
-AGERER, JOSEF	16	M	LABR	RRZZZZUSA
BO-BERTH, FRITZ	28	M	NN	RRZZZZUSA
SCHUMANN, H	26	M	MNR	RRZZZZUSA
F--KE, WILHE	24	M	MNR	RRZZZZUSA
FRANZ--ZIK, FRANZ	26	M	LABR	RRZZZZUSA
GRUBER, ROSINE	19	F	NN	RRZZZZUSA
NACHREINER, MARIE	20	F	NN	RRZZZZUSA
KREITNER, TERESE	19	F	NN	RRZZZZUSA
MUHLBAUER, ANNA	15	F	NN	RRZZZZUSA
JOSEF	7	M	CHILD	RRZZZZUSA
F--KE, GUSTAV	27	M	FARMER	RRZZZZUSA
EMIL	23	M	FARMER	RRZZZZUSA
SCHULZ, AUGUST	27	M	FARMER	RRZZZZUSA
ANDRE-, MARIE	22	F	NN	RRZZZZUSA
PRZYLYSKI, JAN	26	M	FARMER	RRZZZZUSA
STANASLAWKI, JOSEF	27	M	FARMER	RRZZZZUSA
DORB--T, GEORG	22	M	FARMER	RRZZZZUSA
SCHMIDT, GG	43	M	FARMER	RRZZZZUSA
ELIS	46	F	NN	RRZZZZUSA
ELIS	15	F	NN	RRZZZZUSA
SIMON	7	M	CHILD	RRZZZZUSA
HEINR	6	M	CHILD	RRZZZZUSA
PH	5	M	CHILD	RRZZZZUSA
MARGA	73	F	NN	RRZZZZUSA
BISCHOFF, CHR	24	M	FARMER	RRZZZZUSA
OSTER, WILH	32	M	CPR	RRZZZZUSA
CHRIST	36	F	NN	RRZZZZUSA
LISBETH	15	F	NN	RRZZZZUSA
JOH	7	M	CHILD	RRZZZZUSA
WILH	.10	M	INFANT	RRZZZZUSA
FA-L, JOH	28	M	FARMER	RRZZZZUSA
CATH	28	F	NN	RRZZZZUSA
KLUCZKOWSKI, ANNA	24	F	NN	RRZZZZUSA
ALBERT	16	M	LABR	RRZZZZUSA
SCHULTZ, CONRAD	24	M	CPR	RRZZZZUSA
STRANZ, FRANCA	21	F	NN	RRZZZZUSA
BLACHOWIAK, MICH	25	M	FARMER	RRZZZZUSA
WENDLAND, ROBERT	15	M	CL	RRZZZZUSA
GRAZOZAK, J	23	F	NN	RRZZZZUSA
VALENTZ	2	M	CHILD	RRZZZZUSA
ST.	4	M	CHILD	RRZZZZUSA
GOMOLSKI, ST	30	M	LABR	RRZZZZUSA
AGNES	28	F	NN	RRZZZZUSA
CACILIE	.09	F	INFANT	RRZZZZUSA
OWSZAN, THOMAS	7	M	CHILD	RRZZZZUSA
KNUSCH, THERESE	28	F	NN	RRZZZZUSA
JOHANN	2	M	CHILD	RRZZZZUSA
MARIE	.06	F	INFANT	RRZZZZUSA
SCHMIDT, CHRIST	16	M	MCHT	RRZZZZUSA
WESTWALL, JOH	34	M	FARMER	RRZZZZUSA
ANNA	34	F	NN	RRZZZZUSA
MARIANNA	7	F	CHILD	RRZZZZUSA
ANTON	6	M	CHILD	RRZZZZUSA
FRANCA	5	F	CHILD	RRZZZZUSA
MICHAEL	3	M	CHILD	RRZZZZUSA
KOTTINA--, JULIUS	32	M	LABR	RRZZZZUSA
STRUSS, MARIE	24	F	NN	RRZZZZUSA
HOR-ENGA, F	56	M	LABR	RRZZZZUSA
BORENDJE	52	F	NN	RRZZZZUSA
KRILL, JOS	16	M	MCHT	RRZZZZUSA
ROSIN, ALOIS	18	M	LABR	RRZZZZUSA
SCHMAUSS, FRANZ	19	M	LABR	RRZZZZUSA
DOEMKE, RUDOLF	28	M	MCHT	RRZZZZUSA
ADOLF	7	M	CHILD	RRZZZZUSA
NATALI	24	F	NN	RRZZZZUSA
MAX	2	M	CHILD	RRZZZZUSA
SCHWANDT, EMILIE	31	F	NN	RRZZZZUSA
HOZMIDER, A	30	F	NN	RRZZZZUSA
MICHAEL	7	M	CHILD	RRZZZZUSA
JACOB	4	M	CHILD	RRZZZZUSA
CONSTANTINA	2	F	CHILD	RRZZZZUSA
JOHAN	.04	M	INFANT	RRZZZZUSA
KOT, JAN	26	M	FARMER	RRZZZZUSA
ANDZEJEWSKI, THOMAS	24	M	LABR	RRZZZZUSA
ANDTKOWIAK, JOSEFA	31	F	NN	RRZZZZUSA
NAPERIALA, FRANZ	19	M	LABR	RRZZZZUSA
ADKOWIAK, ST	24	M	LABR	RRZZZZUSA
MARIA	21	F	NN	RRZZZZUSA

SHIP: NOORDLAND

FROM: ANTWERP
TO: NEW YORK
ARRIVED: 22 APRIL 1889

PASSENGER	AGE	SEX	OCCUPATION	PRV VIL DES
BURESKI, GULEPSK	44	M	LABR	RRZZZZNY
CUDAGEFSKA, JULIANA	30	F	SVNT	RRZZZZCH
SOLENSKA, FRANCISCA	19	F	SVNT	RRZZZZCH

SHIP: RHAETIA

FROM: HAMBURG AND HAVRE
TO: NEW YORK
ARRIVED: 22 APRIL 1889

PASSENGER	AGE	SEX	OCCUPATION	PRV VIL DES
WESOLOLOWSKA, STEFANIA	26	F	WO	RRZZZZUSA
MICHAL	6	M	CHILD	RRZZZZUSA
KASIMIRA	5	F	CHILD	RRZZZZUSA
PELAGIA	3	F	CHILD	RRZZZZUSA
ADAM	.09	M	INFANT	RRZZZZUSA
RONTSCHKA, CHANNE	34	F	WO	RRZZZZUSA
JOSEF	7	M	CHILD	RRZZZZUSA
BERTHA	5	F	CHILD	RRZZZZUSA
GOLDEN, MENDEL	35	M	LABR	RRZZZZUSA
GRODZISKY, HIRSCH	21	M	LABR	RRZZZZUSA
RUSITZKA, JOSEF	34	M	LABR	RRZZZZUSA
META	32	F	W	RRZZZZUSA
KANTROWITZ, MOSES	22	M	LABR	RRZZZZUSA
SYRECK, SOLOMEA	20	F	SGL	RRZZZZUSA
KARBOWICZ, AGATHE	18	F	SGL	RRZZZZUSA
JAN	24	M	LABR	RRZZZZUSA
NAWROCKI, ANTON	42	M	LABR	RRZZZZUSA
MUSZEYNSKI, JOHANN	22	M	LABR	RRZZZZUSA
SEBURECHI, FELIX	20	M	LABR	RRZZZZUSA
RUBENSTEIN, SAMUEL	29	M	MCHT	RRZZZZUSA
MERE	27	F	W	RRZZZZUSA
BLUMBERG, SARAH	25	F	WO	RRZZZZUSA
MOSES	3	M	CHILD	RRZZZZUSA
ROSLE	.11	F	INFANT	RRZZZZUSA
SCHULTZ, AUGSTE.	62	F	WO	RRZZZZUSA
SABKOWIAK, SIMON	40	M	UNKNOWN	RRZZZZUSA
BARBA.	40	F	W	RRZZZZUSA
MARIANNE	14	F	CH	RRZZZZUSA
MICHAEL	7	M	CHILD	RRZZZZUSA
SIMON	6	M	CHILD	RRZZZZUSA
JACOB	4	M	CHILD	RRZZZZUSA
JADWIGA	18	F	SGL	RRZZZZUSA
BAHN, FRIEDR.	17	M	FARMER	RRZZZZUSA
MARIE	7	F	CHILD	RRZZZZUSA
TREPTOW, FRIEDR.	72	M	FARMER	RRZZZZUSA
ALWINE	57	F	W	RRZZZZUSA
ZIMMERMAN, MAROSCHE	49	F	WO	RRZZZZUSA
IDA	17	F	D	RRZZZZUSA
KOWALIK, WOYCICH	30	M	LABR	RRZZZZUSA

PASSENGER	AGE	SEX	OCCUPATION	PRV VIL DES
ADAM	17	M	LABR	RRZZZZUSA
GAWRONSKI, FELIX	35	M	LABR	RRZZZZUSA
RAJANSKI, JOSEF	25	M	LABR	RRZZZZUSA
BARTUZEWSKI, JAN	25	M	LABR	RRZZZZUSA
GAIKOWSKI, WLADISL.	24	M	LABR	RRZZZZUSA
TEDEUS, PETROKUS	48	M	LABR	RRZZZZUSA
MARTINKUS, ISIDORUS	50	M	LABR	RRZZZZUSA
KIRSCHGALLIS, JOSEF	44	M	LABR	RRZZZZUSA
WALL, JOHANN	34	M	LABR	RRZZZZUSA
SIDOBRA, KASIS	18	M	LABR	RRZZZZUSA
AMBROSEWITZ, BONTRAS	34	M	LABR	RRZZZZUSA
ANNA	31	F	W	RRZZZZUSA
NORBUNELIS, ANDREAS	19	M	LABR	RRZZZZUSA
SCHIFFER, WILH.	43	M	LABR	RRZZZZUSA
WAXHKATIS, KASIMIR	24	M	LABR	RRZZZZUSA
SIMONS, JURAS	24	M	LABR	RRZZZZUSA
FRIEDMANN, LEIB	30	M	TLR	RRZZZZUSA
LETKOWITSCH, HERRM.	47	M	DLR	RRZZZZUSA
HERZOG, HERRM.	36	M	DLR	RRZZZZUSA
BERLYN, SCHMUL	28	M	DLR	RRZZZZUSA
NOSSEM	14	M	DLR	RRZZZZUSA
KANTEROWA, CHANNE	24	F	SGL	RRZZZZUSA
HERZSTEIN, LEOPOLD	14	M	DLR	RRZZZZUSA
MALE	7	F	CHILD	RRZZZZUSA
HOASULA, GRETE	24	F	SGL	FNZZZZUSA
ASUPAMAA, MARIE	28	F	SGL	FNZZZZUSA
TIKIPRNIKI, JACOB	30	M	UNKNOWN	FNZZZZUSA
SAVILA, JOH.	24	M	UNKNOWN	FNZZZZUSA
WOSUKOWIS, MARIE	26	F	WO	RRZZZZUSA
ANTONY	3	M	CHILD	RRZZZZUSA
WOLTMANN, DAVID	28	M	FARMER	RRZZZZUSA
PAULINE	22	F	W	RRZZZZUSA
LYDIA	.02	F	INFANT	RRZZZZUSA
ORTLIEB, ADOLF	24	M	LABR	RRZZZZUSA
NASS, JACOB	25	M	LABR	RRZZZZUSA
TOPPER, HENOCH	50	M	TLR	RRZZZZUSA
HANNE	40	F	W	RRZZZZUSA
MALE	7	M	CHILD	RRZZZZUSA
KNOPT, ZACHARIAS	7	M	CHILD	RRZZZZUSA
GRUNSPARA, JOSEF	39	M	TLR	RRZZZZUSA
LEA	7	F	CHILD	RRZZZZUSA
KNITO, JAN	31	M	LABR	RRZZZZUSA
JERMOSKA, JOSEF	24	M	LABR	RRZZZZUSA
ORNDROLESZ, VINCENT	42	M	LABR	RRZZZZUSA
GEDWALS, PETER	30	M	LABR	RRZZZZUSA
JUSKIS, PETER	35	M	LABR	RRZZZZUSA
KASIMIR	45	M	LABR	RRZZZZUSA
SOLDUKOWSKY, MICHAEL	43	M	LABR	RRZZZZUSA
LAZAROWITZ, JEGEL	26	M	LABR	RRZZZZUSA
ZDROJAK, HYPOLIT	31	M	LABR	RRZZZZUSA
JANIESKOWSKI, JOSEF	24	M	LABR	RRZZZZUSA
KWIATKOWSKY, FRANZ	23	M	LABR	RRZZZZUSA
PALEWSKY, JOSEF	14	M	LABR	RRZZZZUSA
MILLOSKA, ANTON	32	M	LABR	RRZZZZUSA
BIGUN, BEIRACH	43	M	LABR	RRZZZZUSA
HENCHENBERG, JACOB	14	M	LABR	RRZZZZUSA
GINZBURG, GITTEL	23	F	WO	RRZZZZUSA
ZIREL	4	F	CHILD	RRZZZZUSA
LEA	.11	F	INFANT	RRZZZZUSA
FRIEDMANN, SCHOLEM	48	M	DLR	RRZZZZUSA
KAPLAN, MIRIAM	20	F	SGL	RRZZZZUSA
LAZARUS, JOSEF	18	M	LABR	RRZZZZUSA
CHANNE	54	F	W	RRZZZZUSA
BUJEWSKA, MARIANNE	18	F	SGL	RRZZZZUSA
SCHEIM, MARKUS	37	M	BCHR	RRZZZZUSA
SACKSOHN, BEILE	22	F	WO	RRZZZZUSA
MOSCHE	7	M	CHILD	RRZZZZUSA
SARA	5	F	CHILD	RRZZZZUSA
HERSCH	.11	M	INFANT	RRZZZZUSA
ROSENBAUM, SCHLOME	19	F	LABR	RRZZZZUSA
KASENELSOHN, SAMUEL	20	M	LABR	RRZZZZUSA
MARGOLJIS, HINDE	16	F	SGL	RRZZZZUSA
MOSES	7	M	CHILD	RRZZZZUSA
WEITZMANN, MOSES	19	M	LABR	RRZZZZUSA
SCHAJE	15	F	LABR	RRZZZZUSA

PASSENGER	AGE	SEX	OCCUPATION	PRV VIL DES
HILLELSOHN, LEIB	17	M	LABR	RRZZZZUSA
LEWINSON, LEIE	6	F	CHILD	RRZZZZUSA
NAWRENETZKI, ABRAH.	18	M	CL	RRZZZZUSA
ZANDERA, EMILIE	24	M	UNKNOWN	RRZZZZUSA
LOEWENSTEIN, EMANUEL	17	M	UNKNOWN	RRZZZZUSA
FEIWES, SARA	20	F	SGL	RRZZZZUSA
STERN, LEISER	14	M	LABR	RRZZZZUSA
JUDOWITZ, HERSCH	47	M	LABR	RRZZZZUSA
FELD, ISRAEL	40	M	LABR	RRZZZZUSA
STARK, ABRAHAM	26	M	LABR	RRZZZZUSA
STEZ, FEDIO	26	M	LABR	RRZZZZUSA
SEW, BER	34	M	DLR	RRZZZZUSA
TIEL, AUGUST	17	M	CL	RRZZZZUSA
KRULIKOWSKI, FRANZ	31	M	SDLR	RRZZZZUSA
STEPHAN	22	M	SDLR	RRZZZZUSA
WOITOWITZ, AUGUST	21	M	LABR	RRZZZZUSA
BERMANN, SARA	23	F	SGL	RRZZZZUSA
SELIGMANN, ZIREL	18	F	SGL	RRZZZZUSA
ROLLNIK, LIEBE	36	F	WO	RRZZZZUSA
IDEL	15	F	CH	RRZZZZUSA
CHASSE	13	F	CH	RRZZZZUSA
RACHEL	7	F	CHILD	RRZZZZUSA
BEILE	6	F	CHILD	RRZZZZUSA
ASSE	5	M	CHILD	RRZZZZUSA
NATKIN, LEISER	31	M	DLR	RRZZZZUSA
MER, PINCUS	22	M	DLR	RRZZZZUSA
KONOTOPSKI, SCHAJE	25	M	TLR	RRZZZZUSA
SCHLECHTMANN, SISSEL	19	F	WO	RRZZZZUSA
MILNER, SARA	29	F	WO	RRZZZZUSA
CHANNE	.11	F	INFANT	RRZZZZUSA
SARYN, SLATE	26	F	WO	RRZZZZUSA
ESTHER	5	F	CHILD	RRZZZZUSA
ISRAEL	4	M	CHILD	RRZZZZUSA
MENDEL	.11	M	INFANT	RRZZZZUSA
LUXEMBURG, CHAJE	17	F	SGL	RRZZZZUSA
FEINSTEIN, DWORE	20	F	WO	RRZZZZUSA
MARIANNE	.11	F	INFANT	RRZZZZUSA
REIBSCHEID, SOMON	28	M	DLR	RRZZZZUSA
GRUNBERG, RIFKE	24	F	WO	RRZZZZUSA
HIRSCH	6	M	CHILD	RRZZZZUSA
LOEL	5	M	CHILD	RRZZZZUSA
SINE	.09	F	INFANT	RRZZZZUSA
MALINOWITZ, SORE	29	F	WO	RRZZZZUSA
HUDES	5	F	CHILD	RRZZZZUSA
CHAJE	.02	F	INFANT	RRZZZZUSA
GANTZ, JOHANN	40	M	FARMER	RRZZZZUSA
ADOLF	19	M	FARMER	RRZZZZUSA
AUGUSTE	17	F	SGL	RRZZZZUSA
CARL	14	M	FARMER	RRZZZZUSA
STROEBEL, ADOLF	32	M	FARMER	RRZZZZUSA
FISCHBACH, GOTTLB.	36	M	FARMER	RRZZZZUSA
CAROLE.	34	F	W	RRZZZZUSA
AUGST.	7	M	CHILD	RRZZZZUSA
GOTTLB.	4	M	CHILD	RRZZZZUSA
SERAPHIN, EVA	20	F	SGL	RRZZZZUSA
SECLIGER, AUGUST	26	M	FARMER	RRZZZZUSA
EMILIE	23	F	W	RRZZZZUSA
ALBECHT	2	M	CHILD	RRZZZZUSA
ELFRIEDE	.11	F	INFANT	RRZZZZUSA
JANSEWITZ, URSULA	40	F	WO	RRZZZZUSA
ANTONI	7	M	CHILD	RRZZZZUSA
DOMINIK	6	M	CHILD	RRZZZZUSA
KAMILLA	5	F	CHILD	RRZZZZUSA
SELINSKY, RACHEL	17	F	SGL	RRZZZZUSA
ARRIOLO, AUGST.	31	M	LABR	FNZZZZUSA
TEJZENISKA, FEIGE	22	F	WO	RRZZZZUSA
LEA	.11	F	INFANT	RRZZZZUSA
GUSTOMZIK, PAUL	40	M	LABR	RRZZZZUSA
ZILINSKY, FRANZ	26	M	LABR	RRZZZZUSA
MARIE	15	F	SGL	RRZZZZUSA
ROBINSON, EDUARD	20	M	LABR	RRZZZZUSA
WIESZORECK, ANDREAS	26	M	LABR	RRZZZZUSA
TEISEMITZKI, MARCUS	29	M	LABR	RRZZZZUSA
HEWITZ, NOCHEM	40	M	LABR	RRZZZZUSA
CHAJE	15	F	D	RRZZZZUSA

PASSENGER	AGE	SEX	OCCUPATION	PRV VIL DES
EISCHOWITZ, MICHEL	21	M	LABR	RRZZZZUSA
KRASNOPOLSKI, CHAJE	18	M	LABR	RRZZZZUSA
KIRINSKY, SCHMUEL	20	M	LABR	RRZZZZUSA
KATZ, JANKEL	62	M	LABR	RRZZZZUSA
STAROPOLSKY, ABRAHAM	33	M	LABR	RRZZZZUSA
SCHILAMM, MALKE	19	F	SGL	RRZZZZUSA
MANDELBAUM, ITKE	35	F	WO	RRZZZZUSA
SIMON	7	M	CHILD	RRZZZZUSA
DWORE	7	F	CHILD	RRZZZZUSA
STOTZENBERG, LEISER	18	M	LABR	RRZZZZUSA
AWROSCHENKE, SLATE	42	F	WO	RRZZZZUSA
MALKE	23	F	WO	RRZZZZUSA
ISAAC	29	M	BKBNDR	RRZZZZUSA
MEYER	22	M	BKBNDR	RRZZZZUSA
HAGER, KATHA.	30	F	WO	RRZZZZUSA
MARIE	3	F	CHILD	RRZZZZUSA
JACOB	.11	M	INFANT	RRZZZZUSA
KRISTMANN, WULH.	56	M	FARMER	RRZZZZUSA
ANNA	56	F	W	RRZZZZUSA
WILH.	7	M	CHILD	RRZZZZUSA
HOFFMANN, JOH.	23	M	FARMER	RRZZZZUSA
CARLE.	20	F	W	RRZZZZUSA
FRDKE.	.11	F	INFANT	RRZZZZUSA
CATHA.	.11	F	INFANT	RRZZZZUSA
ACKERMANN, PHILIPP	27	M	FARMER	RRZZZZUSA
DOROTHEA	22	F	W	RRZZZZUSA
KRISTENSEN, WILH.	33	M	FARMER	RRZZZZUSA
ELISABETH	30	F	W	RRZZZZUSA
ANNA	7	F	CHILD	RRZZZZUSA
CHRISTIAN	4	M	CHILD	RRZZZZUSA
PETER	.11	M	INFANT	RRZZZZUSA
JACOB	.01	M	INFANT	RRZZZZUSA
KALMBACH, FRIEDR.	31	M	FARMER	RRZZZZUSA
DOROTHEA	27	F	W	RRZZZZUSA
RASEWITZ, CASIMIR	28	M	LABR	RRZZZZUSA
BALTRANY	26	M	LABR	RRZZZZUSA
WARAKOWICZ, CASEMIR	28	M	LABR	RRZZZZUSA
KOROTZKY, ANTON	25	M	LABR	RRZZZZUSA
GADYZIS, JOH.	25	M	LABR	RRZZZZUSA
DZABERS, JOSEF	23	M	LABR	RRZZZZUSA
JOHANN	19	M	LABR	RRZZZZUSA
RAHN, AUGUSTE	.07	F	INFANT	RRZZZZUSA
MALINOEITZ, DORA	.06	F	INFANT	RRZZZZUSA

SHIP: EMS

FROM: BREMEN AND SOUTHAMPTON
TO: NEW YORK
ARRIVED: 22 APRIL 1889

PASSENGER	AGE	SEX	OCCUPATION	PRV VIL DES
FLEUNNER, PHILIPP	22	M	LABR	RRZZZZUSA
RAN, GOTHLIEB	31	M	LABR	RRZZZZUSA
LOUISE	31	F	W	RRZZZZUSA
JOHANN	3	M	CHILD	RRZZZZUSA
MAGDA.	4	F	CHILD	RRZZZZUSA
DAVID	.03	M	INFANT	RRZZZZUSA
KLEIN, GOTTLIEB	23	M	LABR	RRZZZZUSA
BARBA.	23	F	W	RRZZZZUSA
KATHA.	2	F	CHILD	RRZZZZUSA
JOH.	.04	M	INFANT	RRZZZZUSA
GROSS, HEINR.	33	M	LABR	RRZZZZUSA
CHRIST.	29	F	W	RRZZZZUSA
JACOB	6	M	CHILD	RRZZZZUSA
ROSINE	4	F	CHILD	RRZZZZUSA
HEINR.	1	M	CHILD	RRZZZZUSA
SCHUHMACHER, JOH.	43	M	LABR	RRZZZZUSA
SCHUHNACHER, ROSINE	38	F	W	RRZZZZUSA
SCHUHMACHER, JOHANN	18	M	LABR	RRZZZZUSA
LUDWIG	17	M	LABR	RRZZZZUSA
ROSINA	15	F	SMSTS	RRZZZZUSA
CHRISTA.	13	F	SMSTS	RRZZZZUSA
CATHA.	10	F	CH	RRZZZZUSA
CAROL.	8	F	CHILD	RRZZZZUSA
CHRIST.	7	M	CHILD	RRZZZZUSA
JACOB	4	M	CHILD	RRZZZZUSA
CHRIST.	2	M	CHILD	RRZZZZUSA
PETER	.06	M	INFANT	RRZZZZUSA
KAUB, MATHIAS	34	M	LABR	RRZZZZUSA
RAUB, CATHA.	29	F	W	RRZZZZUSA
JOHANN	3	M	CHILD	RRZZZZUSA
CHRISTIAN	2	M	CHILD	RRZZZZUSA
CHRISTINE	.03	F	INFANT	RRZZZZUSA
HACKSTATZ, JOHANN	26	M	LABR	RRZZZZUSA
ROSINE	24	F	W	RRZZZZUSA
CAROLINE	2	F	CHILD	RRZZZZUSA
HOFFMANN, DAVID	31	M	LABR	RRZZZZUSA
CATHA.	29	F	W	RRZZZZUSA
DAVID	4	M	CHILD	RRZZZZUSA
CATHA.	2	F	CHILD	RRZZZZUSA
ROSINE	15	F	SMSTS	RRZZZZUSA
STOCK, JOH.	26	M	LABR	RRZZZZUSA
HAUSMAUER, JOH.	26	M	BKLYR	RRZZZZUSA
MARGA.	25	F	W	RRZZZZUSA
HAUSA-ER, MARYA	.03	F	INFANT	RRZZZZUSA
KUGEL, CHRIST.	25	M	PNTR	RRZZZZUSA
CATHA.	20	F	W	RRZZZZUSA
JACOB	.03	M	INFANT	RRZZZZUSA
JOHANN	15	M	LABR	RRZZZZUSA
GROSS, GEORG	32	M	CPTR	RRZZZZUSA
ELISABETH	30	F	W	RRZZZZUSA
JOHANN	8	M	CHILD	RRZZZZUSA
JACOB	7	M	CHILD	RRZZZZUSA
CHRIST.	7	M	CHILD	RRZZZZUSA
GOTTL.	3	M	CHILD	RRZZZZUSA
CHRIST.	2	M	CHILD	RRZZZZUSA
HEINR.	.11	M	INFANT	RRZZZZUSA
NIESS, JACOB	50	M	MLR	RRZZZZUSA
NIES, CHRISTE.	49	F	W	RRZZZZUSA
ROSINE	24	F	SVNT	RRZZZZUSA
DOROTHE.	22	F	NN	RRZZZZUSA
JOH.	18	M	LABR	RRZZZZUSA
HEINR.	13	M	LABR	RRZZZZUSA
MARGA	8	F	CHILD	RRZZZZUSA
CATHARINA	4	F	CHILD	RRZZZZUSA
JACOB	23	M	LABR	RRZZZZUSA
FRIEDR.	20	F	W	RRZZZZUSA
ROSINE	.02	F	INFANT	RRZZZZUSA
GROSS, MATH.	30	M	LABR	RRZZZZUSA
CHRIST.	26	F	W	RRZZZZUSA
CHRISTINE	64	F	NN	RRZZZZUSA
SCHOCK, JOH.	22	M	LABR	RRZZZZUSA
JOHE.	26	F	W	RRZZZZUSA
ROSINE	3	F	CHILD	RRZZZZUSA
FOEDERER, JOH.	43	M	FARMER	RRZZZZUSA
MAGDA.	45	F	W	RRZZZZUSA
FRANZ	18	M	LABR	RRZZZZUSA
JOH.F.	17	M	LABR	RRZZZZUSA
JACOB	8	M	CHILD	RRZZZZUSA
ROSINE	6	F	CHILD	RRZZZZUSA
DAVID	3	M	CHILD	RRZZZZUSA
NELLICH, JACOB	27	M	SMH	RRZZZZUSA
NRELLICH, MAGDA.	26	F	W	RRZZZZUSA
MAGDA.	2	F	CHILD	RRZZZZUSA
CATHA.	.06	F	INFANT	RRZZZZUSA
NELLICH, CHRIST.	22	M	LABR	RRZZZZUSA
SCHBABEL, PETER	41	M	LABR	RRZZZZUSA
SCHNABEL, ELISABETH	40	F	W	RRZZZZUSA
PETER	19	M	LABR	RRZZZZUSA
JOH.	17	M	LABR	RRZZZZUSA
CATH.	14	F	NN	RRZZZZUSA
JACOB	6	M	CHILD	RRZZZZUSA
FRIEDERIKE.	.02	F	INFANT	RRZZZZUSA
GROSS, CHRIST.	42	F	INF	RRZZZZUSA
CATHA.	41	F	W	RRZZZZUSA
CATHA.	17	F	NN	RRZZZZUSA

PASSENGER	AGE	SEX	OCCUPATION	PRV VIL DES
JACOB	16	M	LABR	RRZZZZUSA
JOHS.	13	M	LABR	RRZZZZUSA
HEINR.	7	M	CHILD	RRZZZZUSA
CHRIST.	4	M	CHILD	RRZZZZUSA
GROHS, ROSINE	.11	F	INFANT	RRZZZZUSA
KREUTZLER, GOTTLIEB	54	M	LABR	RRZZZZUSA
MARIA	54	F	W	RRZZZZUSA
GOTTL.	26	M	LABR	RRZZZZUSA
U	23	F	W	RRZZZZUSA
L-KIFFER, P.	38	M	LABR	RRZZZZUSA
CHRISTE.	28	F	W	RRZZZZUSA
SCHIFFER, CATHA.	7	F	CHILD	RRZZZZUSA
LEKIFFER, CHRISTE.	6	F	CHILD	RRZZZZUSA
DREFT, JACOB	42	M	LABR	RRZZZZUSA
DOROTHEA	38	F	W	RRZZZZUSA
HEINR.	18	M	PNTR	RRZZZZUSA
JACOB	14	M	LABR	RRZZZZUSA
CATHA.	8	F	CHILD	RRZZZZUSA
ROSINE	7	F	CHILD	RRZZZZUSA
JOH.	4	M	CHILD	RRZZZZUSA
CARL	.06	M	INFANT	RRZZZZUSA
DOLLINGER, PHILIPP	48	M	TLR	RRZZZZUSA
BARBA.	48	F	W	RRZZZZUSA
CATHA.	26	F	NN	RRZZZZUSA
ROSINE	20	F	SVNT	RRZZZZUSA
JOHAN	18	M	LABR	RRZZZZUSA
CATHA.	16	F	NN	RRZZZZUSA
JENOB	14	M	NN	RRZZZZUSA
ELISABETH	10	F	CH	RRZZZZUSA
CHRIST.	8	M	CHILD	RRZZZZUSA
CHRISTE.	7	F	CHILD	RRZZZZUSA
MAGDA.	4	F	CHILD	RRZZZZUSA
JEHL, JACOB	25	M	LABR	RRZZZZUSA
CATHA.	23	F	W	RRZZZZUSA
WEYELER, JOH.	31	M	LABR	RRZZZZUSA
DEISS, GEORG	36	M	PNTR	RRZZZZUSA
DEI-S, JOHANNA	26	F	W	RRZZZZUSA
DEISS, JACOB	.06	M	INFANT	RRZZZZUSA
JACOBES, JOHANN	32	M	BKLYR	RRZZZZUSA
CATHA.	28	F	W	RRZZZZUSA
MAGDA.	3	F	CHILD	RRZZZZUSA
CATHA.	1	F	CHILD	RRZZZZUSA
ELISAB.	.03	F	INFANT	RRZZZZUSA
HOLLWEGER, FR.	25	M	LABR	RRZZZZUSA
HOLLWEYER, MARGA.	30	F	W	RRZZZZUSA
JACOB	8	M	CHILD	RRZZZZUSA
FRIED	6	M	CHILD	RRZZZZUSA
ROSINE	3	F	CHILD	RRZZZZUSA
PAULE.	.06	F	INFANT	RRZZZZUSA
HASART, JACOB	23	M	FARMER	RRZZZZUSA
ROSINE	21	F	W	RRZZZZUSA
TOBIAS	.11	M	INFANT	RRZZZZUSA
RAEMLE, JOH.	22	M	MCHT	RRZZZZUSA
KAEMLE, PAULE	21	F	W	RRZZZZUSA
JOHS.	.11	M	INFANT	RRZZZZUSA
KRAUSE, WILH.	61	M	BRR	RRZZZZUSA
ELISAB.	42	F	W	RRZZZZUSA
ELISAB.	21	F	NN	RRZZZZUSA
PETER	27	M	LABR	RRZZZZUSA
SOPFIE	23	F	W	RRZZZZUSA
ADINA	2	F	CHILD	RRZZZZUSA
LEONHARDIA	1	F	CHILD	RRZZZZUSA
FLE-K, JOSEF	31	M	LABR	RRZZZZUSA
JOHANNA	28	F	W	RRZZZZUSA
FLECK, EMILIE	3	F	CHILD	RRZZZZUSA
OTTILIE	2	F	CHILD	RRZZZZUSA
JOHANNA	.03	F	INFANT	RRZZZZUSA
AMANN, JANOB	28	M	LABR	RRZZZZUSA
ELISAB.	20	F	W	RRZZZZUSA
RAPHAEL	20	M	LABR	RRZZZZUSA
FRANZ	26	M	LABR	RRZZZZUSA
BALANOV	25	M	LABR	RRZZZZUSA
-INKELMEIER, JACOB	49	M	LABR	RRZZZZUSA
STUEKELMAIER, MARIA	46	F	W	RRZZZZUSA
CATHA.	18	F	NN	RRZZZZUSA

PASSENGER	AGE	SEX	OCCUPATION	PRV VIL DES
CAROLE.	15	F	NN	RRZZZZUSA
MARIE	7	F	CHILD	RRZZZZUSA
LOUISE	4	F	CHILD	RRZZZZUSA
MAGDA.	3	F	CHILD	RRZZZZUSA
JACOB	26	M	PNTR	RRZZZZUSA
ROSINE	27	F	W	RRZZZZUSA
EVA	3	F	CHILD	RRZZZZUSA
MARIA	2	F	CHILD	RRZZZZUSA
ELISAB.	.06	F	INFANT	RRZZZZUSA
WAGNER, ADAM	53	M	FARMER	RRZZZZUSA
CATHA.	41	F	W	RRZZZZUSA
JOHANN	18	M	FARMER	RRZZZZUSA
CHRISTE	14	F	NN	RRZZZZUSA
BENJAMIN	13	M	NN	RRZZZZUSA
CHRIST.	11	M	NN	RRZZZZUSA
LYDIA	8	F	CHILD	RRZZZZUSA
CATHA.	7	F	CHILD	RRZZZZUSA
EDUARD	6	M	CHILD	RRZZZZUSA
ANDREAS	4	M	CHILD	RRZZZZUSA
FRIEDR.	.06	M	INFANT	RRZZZZUSA
PETER	2	M	CHILD	RRZZZZUSA
KAUB, JOSEF	32	M	LABR	RRZZZZUSA
CHRISTE.	24	F	W	RRZZZZUSA
JACOB	25	M	LABR	RRZZZZUSA
BRAUER, JOH.	21	M	BRR	RRZZZZUSA
ADOLF, KARL	67	M	FARMER	RRZZZZUSA
EVA	62	F	W	RRZZZZUSA
ZANK, GOTTF.	17	M	LABR	RRZZZZUSA
DASE, ANNA	30	F	NN	RRZZZZUSA
WENNER, AUGE.	16	F	NN	RRZZZZUSA
RENNER, EDW.	29	M	TLR	RRZZZZUSA
POOS, JULIUS	24	M	LABR	RRZZZZUSA
MARIANNE	23	F	W	RRZZZZUSA
WROBLEWSKI, JAN	23	M	LABR	RRZZZZUSA
WINKUS, JAN	27	M	LABR	RRZZZZUSA
MITTELSBACH, JACOB	28	M	LABR	RRZZZZUSA
LENGER, ANTON	35	M	LABR	RRZZZZUSA
JOHANNA	35	F	W	RRZZZZUSA
PETER	7	M	CHILD	RRZZZZUSA
BARBA.	4	F	CHILD	RRZZZZUSA
ANDR.	.04	M	INFANT	RRZZZZUSA
GEFFRE, JOSEF	59	M	LABR	RRZZZZUSA
LISB.	57	F	W	RRZZZZUSA
ANTON	18	M	NN	RRZZZZUSA
URSULA	16	F	NN	RRZZZZUSA
ADAM	34	M	LABR	RRZZZZUSA
CATHA.	33	F	W	RRZZZZUSA
LISB.	8	F	CHILD	RRZZZZUSA
SEBAST.	7	M	CHILD	RRZZZZUSA
MARIE	4	F	CHILD	RRZZZZUSA
MAREUS	3	M	CHILD	RRZZZZUSA
JULIA	.11	F	INFANT	RRZZZZUSA
HARTMANN, PETER	44	M	LABR	RRZZZZUSA
THERESE	44	F	W	RRZZZZUSA
FLORIAN	23	M	LABR	RRZZZZUSA
JOHANN	18	M	NN	RRZZZZUSA
JOSEPH	16	M	NN	RRZZZZUSA
JACOB	6	M	CHILD	RRZZZZUSA
ROSE	2	F	CHILD	RRZZZZUSA
AMANN, JACOB	58	M	LABR	RRZZZZUSA
DOMINIKO	54	M	LABR	RRZZZZUSA
RODUS	18	M	LABR	RRZZZZUSA
MICHAEL	18	M	NN	RRZZZZUSA
JOHANN	8	M	CHILD	RRZZZZUSA
ANTON	7	M	CHILD	RRZZZZUSA
JEFFRE, ANDR.	22	M	LABR	RRZZZZUSA
GEFFRE, MARIE	20	F	LABR	RRZZZZUSA
LIEB	.11	M	INFANT	RRZZZZUSA
ADOLD, DANIEL	45	M	LABR	RRZZZZUSA
ADOLF.	43	F	W	RRZZZZUSA
ADOLF, FRIEDR.	20	M	LABR	RRZZZZUSA
PAULINA	17	F	NN	RRZZZZUSA
HEINR.	7	M	CHILD	RRZZZZUSA
MARTIN	6	M	CHILD	RRZZZZUSA
NEUMANN, MICH.	19	M	LABR	RRZZZZUSA

PASSENGER	AGE	SEX	OCCUPATION	PRV VIL DES
CHRIST.	18	M	LABR	RRZZZZUSA
RIETSTER, HEINR.	32	M	LABR	RRZZZZUSA
RICHTER, BARBA.	28	F	W	RRZZZZUSA
JOHA.	4	F	CHILD	RRZZZZUSA
AUG.	2	M	CHILD	RRZZZZUSA
EDUARD	.06	M	INFANT	RRZZZZUSA
NEUMANN, GOTTFR.	27	M	LABR	RRZZZZUSA
CHRISTA.	24	F	W	RRZZZZUSA
HAMEYER, WILH.	30	M	LABR	RRZZZZUSA
HOMEYER, MARIA	31	F	W	RRZZZZUSA
CARL	7	M	CHILD	RRZZZZUSA
HEINR.	3	M	CHILD	RRZZZZUSA
MARIA	.09	F	INFANT	RRZZZZUSA
LUDW.	28	M	LABR	RRZZZZUSA
TESKE, JOH.	40	M	LABR	RRZZZZUSA
GOTTL.	28	M	LABR	RRZZZZUSA
JOZUNDKIZ, JUERGIS	30	M	LABR	RRZZZZUSA
SCHUS-KY, MAGDA.	27	F	NN	RRZZZZUSA
JOZUNKIS, MATHAEUS	18	M	LABR	RRZZZZUSA
JEN-BINAS, PETRAS	22	M	LABR	RRZZZZUSA
BURMANN, JOHANN	56	M	LABR	RRZZZZUSA
MARIE	57	F	W	RRZZZZUSA
GOLOMBIEWSKY, THOMAS	28	M	LABR	RRZZZZUSA
GEISLER, FRIEDR.	16	M	LABR	RRZZZZUSA
KOZIORENSKI, THEOFIL	28	M	MLR	RRZZZZUSA
IGNAC	20	M	MLR	RRZZZZUSA
GEFFRE, PETER	31	M	LABR	RRZZZZUSA
LISE	29	M	W	RRZZZZUSA
GRETE	6	F	CHILD	RRZZZZUSA
JACOB	4	M	CHILD	RRZZZZUSA
BARBEL	3	M	CHILD	RRZZZZUSA
LISBETH	.11	F	INFANT	RRZZZZUSA
LEIBEL, ANTON	36	M	LABR	RRZZZZUSA
BARBA.	33	F	W	RRZZZZUSA
BARBA.	8	F	CHILD	RRZZZZUSA
MAGA.	7	F	CHILD	RRZZZZUSA
HEINR.	.06	M	INFANT	RRZZZZUSA
MATERI, THEKLA	17	F	NN	RRZZZZUSA
HEINS, FRANZ	13	M	NN	RRZZZZUSA
MATERI, RAM	13	M	NN	RRZZZZUSA
SHAEFER, HCH.	32	M	LABR	RRZZZZUSA
CATHA.	28	F	W	RRZZZZUSA
SCHAEFER, CLEIN	4	M	CHILD	RRZZZZUSA
LUISE	3	F	CHILD	RRZZZZUSA
BARBARA	.04	F	INFANT	RRZZZZUSA
MOSER, WILH.	24	M	CPTR	RRZZZZUSA
JOHA.	21	F	W	RRZZZZUSA
WILH.	4	M	CHILD	RRZZZZUSA
CATHA.	1	F	CHILD	RRZZZZUSA
JACOB	.07	M	INFANT	RRZZZZUSA
MAZURKIEWICZ, JOHA.	22	F	NN	RRZZZZUSA
KANTORSKI, WLAD.	18	M	LABR	RRZZZZUSA
SCHINKI, FRANZ	30	M	LABR	RRZZZZUSA
MAKSTUTIS, IWAN	26	M	LABR	RRZZZZUSA
KASULIN, ADAM	30	M	LABR	RRZZZZUSA
KULKOWSKI, WOJE	35	M	LABR	RRZZZZUSA
KOLIHONSKI, ANDO	31	M	LABR	RRZZZZUSA
KANTOLA, NICOLAI-CARLSO	22	M	LABR	FNZZZZUSA
NIL---, JOH.GUST.	31	M	LABR	FNZZZZUSA
JANISZEWSKI, PIOTR.	45	M	LABR	RRZZZZUSA
U, U	00	M	LABR	RRZZZZUSA
DASE, PETER	35	M	LABR	RRZZZZUSA
PETRUK, AWORIK	43	M	LABR	RRZZZZUSA

SHIP: DRESDEN

FROM: BREMEN
TO: BALTIMORE
ARRIVED: 23 APRIL 1889

PASSENGER	AGE	SEX	OCCUPATION	PRV VIL DES
BIALOSKI, FRANZ	34	M	LABR	RRZZZZMI
KOWALKOWSKI, ANDREAS	24	M	LABR	RRZZZZMI
U, G.	27	M	FARMER	RRZZZZDAK
-AWLINA	30	F	NN	RRZZZZDAK
JULIUS	10	M	CH	RRZZZZDAK
HULDA	4	F	CHILD	RRZZZZDAK
EDUARD	.11	M	INFANT	RRZZZZDAK
EMMA	8	F	CHILD	RRZZZZDAK
TRAUCK, WILH.	30	M	FARMER	RRZZZZDAK
OTTILIA	32	F	NN	RRZZZZDAK
JOHANN	10	M	CH	RRZZZZDAK
ALBERT	8	M	CHILD	RRZZZZDAK
DANIEL	6	M	CHILD	RRZZZZDAK
PAUL	4	M	CHILD	RRZZZZDAK
SCHOPP, ADAM	38	M	PNTR	RRZZZZDAK
WILHELM	35	F	NN	RRZZZZDAK
EVA	3	F	CHILD	RRZZZZDAK
JACOB	.05	M	INFANT	RRZZZZDAK
BITTMANN, FRIEDR.	25	M	LABR	RRZZZZDAK
EVA	20	F	NN	RRZZZZDAK
FRIEDRICH	.10	M	INFANT	RRZZZZDAK
GALLAS, ADAM	26	M	TLR	RRZZZZPA
BARTH, ANDREAS	54	M	LABR	RRZZZZUNK
DEZEWSKI, FR.	25	M	LABR	RRZZZZPA
KOWALKOWSKA, TH.	19	F	NN	RRZZZZPA
WILAMOMSKA, JAN	27	M	GDNR	RRZZZZPA
WOICIECH	11	M	CH	RRZZZZPA
STAMPKOWIAK, EVA	20	F	CH	RRZZZZPA
WROZOWSKI, PIOT.	28	M	LABR	RRZZZZPA
MARAM--SKI, JAN	46	M	LABR	RRZZZZPA
PIWORECK, WOYCIECH	24	M	LABR	RRZZZZPA
FRANZA.	22	F	NN	RRZZZZPA
ORG, BARTHOLOMEUS	37	M	LABR	RRZZZZPA
PRUEPP-L, JOHS.	22	M	LABR	RRZZZZIA
OTTILIA	49	F	NN	RRZZZZIA
ZMIGAUBA, MARTHA.	23	F	NN	RRZZZZIA
KLEINOWSKI, ANTON	30	M	LABR	RRZZZZUNK
URBANSKI, STRANISLAUS	26	M	LABR	RRZZZZMI
BOLONDER, CHRISTIAN	30	M	FARMER	RRZZZZUNK
CATH.	27	F	NN	RRZZZZUNK
JACOB	.03	M	INFANT	RRZZZZUNK
LEWANDOWSKI, JOSEPH	28	M	LABR	RRZZZZDAK
U, FRANZ	38	M	LABR	RRZZZZDAK
FRANZISKA	28	F	NN	RRZZZZDAK
GRISKMUSITZ, ANNA	24	F	NN	RRZZZZDAK
MASIJEWSKA, STANISLAUS	25	M	LABR	RRZZZZDAK
GRIZINKOWSKI, WOYCICH	26	M	LABR	RRZZZZDAK
ERDMANN, ADAM	42	M	FARMER	RRZZZZDAK
BERTHA	40	F	NN	RRZZZZDAK
JOSEPH	14	M	NN	RRZZZZDAK
GOTTFRIED	10	M	CH	RRZZZZDAK
DANIEL	8	M	CHILD	RRZZZZDAK
ADOLF	5	M	CHILD	RRZZZZDAK
EMILIA	3	F	CHILD	RRZZZZDAK
JULIANA	.06	F	INFANT	RRZZZZDAK
KIENZLER, JOH.	30	M	LABR	RRZZZZMT
CHRISTINA	30	F	NN	RRZZZZMT
WILHELM	3	M	CHILD	RRZZZZMT
EMILIE	.04	F	INFANT	RRZZZZMT
MAJANSSKI, JOHANN	31	M	LABR	RRZZZZMI
ANTONIA	27	F	NN	RRZZZZMI
JOSEPH	5	M	CHILD	RRZZZZMI
AGNES	4	F	CHILD	RRZZZZMI
FRANCISCA	2	F	CHILD	RRZZZZMI
ADAM	.03	M	INFANT	RRZZZZMI

PASSENGER	AGE	SEX	OCCUPATION	PRV	VIL	DES

SHIP: MICHIGAN

FROM: LIVERPOOL
TO: BOSTON
ARRIVED: 24 APRIL 1889

PASSENGER	AGE	SEX	OCCUPATION	PRV VIL	DES
LUBOWITZ, HYMEN	21	M	TLR	RRZZZZ	USA
GOURSA, A	25	M	TLR	RRZZZZ	USA
PETROUSKEWITZ, P	26	M	TLR	RRZZZZ	USA
SUCHOTZKY, FRANK	26	M	HTR	RRZZZZ	USA
JOSEPH	25	M	HTR	RRZZZZ	USA
TOFEL	21	M	TLR	RRZZZZ	USA
SMA-SKY, FR	21	M	TLR	RRZZZZ	USA
ORONOWITZ, FR	28	M	TLR	RRZZZZ	USA
BULSKY, CARL	25	M	TLR	RRZZZZ	USA
LEON	27	M	TLR	RRZZZZ	USA
MA-KEWITZ, A	23	M	TLR	RRZZZZ	USA
B--KEWITZ, P	28	M	LABR	RRZZZZ	USA
STEIN--, N	25	M	TLR	RRZZZZ	USA
WALMETZ, S	28	M	TLR	RRZZZZ	USA
KRANA-S, LEON	20	M	TLR	RRZZZZ	USA
LAFASKY, RACHEL	22	F	SP	RRZZZZ	USA

SHIP: WISCONSIN

FROM: LIVERPOOL AND QUEENSTOWN
TO: NEW YORK
ARRIVED: 25 APRIL 1889

PASSENGER	AGE	SEX	OCCUPATION	PRV VIL	DES
DOMKOWITZ, VINCENTY	24	M	PMBR	RRACBF	USA
REISNER, ISIDOR	24	M	GZR	RRACBF	USA
PINSCHOSAK, VAZCECH	40	M	TLR	RRACBF	USA
MAZESKI, THOMAS	28	M	LABR	RRACBF	USA
OSTROSSKY, FRNCIS	19	M	LABR	RRACBF	USA
MIZENSKY, THEOPHIL	23	M	UNKNOWN	RRACBF	USA
LICHTANSKY, ANTON	37	M	LABR	RRACBF	USA
HORWITZ, JACOB	30	M	LABR	RRACBF	USA
GASEOL, JOSEPH	36	M	LABR	RRACBF	USA
KALINSKA, MARIANNA	17	F	SP	RRACBF	USA
JANKEWITSCH, CONSTANTIN	27	M	BKR	RRACBF	USA
KATARINA	21	F	W	RRACBF	USA
LUDWIG	00	M	INF	RRACBF	USA
BRUESENSKI, JOHAN	44	M	TLR	RRACBF	USA
PELAGIA	16	F	SP	RRACBF	USA
HALENA	8	F	CHILD	RRACBF	USA
NAVICKA, EVA	16	F	SP	RRACBF	USA

PASSENGER	AGE	SEX	OCCUPATION	PRV VIL	DES
LEDUNN, JAN	25	M	FARMER	RRZZZZ	NY
KIRTZ, WILHELM	26	M	FARMER	RRZZZZ	NY
KULIESKY, ELIJAS	30	M	FARMER	RRZZZZ	NY
WALEGAKERS, JOSEF	40	M	FARMER	RRZZZZ	NY
SIRLEKOWSKI, L.	34	M	FARMER	RRZZZZ	NY
WARSZOWSKI, A.	18	M	FARMER	RRZZZZ	NY
BANK, AUGUSTIN	36	M	FARMER	RRZZZZ	NY
SZARBURES, ANT.	30	M	FARMER	RRZZZZ	NY
JYLA, ANTONI	00	M	FARMER	RRZZZZ	NY
NOWN--, JOSEPH	00	M	FARMER	RRZZZZ	NY
HIMKEWIEZ, U	00	U	FARMER	RRZZZZ	NY
KIRCHANSKI, ANTIN	00	U	FARMER	RRZZZZ	NY
MOWINSKI, JENI	28	U	FARMER	RRZZZZ	NY
LAMKISKI, ALEX	26	M	FARMER	RRZZZZ	NY
PAPROLA, AUB.	29	M	FARMER	RRZZZZ	NY
GROSKY, SRENTKA	28	M	FARMER	RRZZZZ	NY
GIBLOWSKEY, C.K.	29	F	W	RRZZZZ	NY
SIMON	.09	M	INFANT	RRZZZZ	NY
SRENN--, JOHANNE	40	F	UNKNOWN	RRZZZZ	NY
JINKOWSKA, AUST.	21	F	UNKNOWN	RRZZZZ	NY
ADAMSKY, MY.A.	20	F	UNKNOWN	RRZZZZ	NY
BRINK, PETRONELLA	35	F	W	RRZZZZ	NY
MARGANNA	.11	F	INFANT	RRZZZZ	NY
POWIEKA, ANDIN	24	F	SP	RRZZZZ	NY
CHIMARA, ANNE	18	F	SP	RRZZZZ	NY
MARSGAEKOSKA, A.	28	F	W	RRZZZZ	NY
LUD.	.09	M	INFANT	RRZZZZ	NY
KUROWSKA, F.	19	F	SP	RRZZZZ	NY
HERINGER, LUISE	30	F	SP	RRZZZZ	NY
WRYNK, THOMAS	26	M	LABR	RRZZZZ	NY
MARINNA	24	F	W	RRZZZZ	NY
STANISLAUS	00	U	UNKNOWN	RRZZZZ	NY
AWIZDZINSKE, AGNISZKA	24	F	UNKNOWN	RRZZZZ	NY
STANISLA	3	M	CHILD	RRZZZZ	NY
MARIAM	.06	F	INFANT	RRZZZZ	NY
BRODSKI, VALENTINE	33	M	LABR	RRZZZZ	NY
FRANCISKA	22	F	W	RRZZZZ	NY
JOSEF	4	M	CHILD	RRZZZZ	NY
KASIMER	3	M	CHILD	RRZZZZ	NY
JOSEF	.08	M	INFANT	RRZZZZ	NY
KOP----, A.	00	U	UNKNOWN	RRZZZZ	NY
ANTONIA	00	U	UNKNOWN	RRZZZZ	NY
MY.A.	18	U	UNKNOWN	RRZZZZ	NY
JAN	12	M	UNKNOWN	RRZZZZ	NY
FRIMSKA	10	M	CH	RRZZZZ	NY
KATH.	5	F	CHILD	RRZZZZ	NY
OVEKOWSKI, SARAH	35	F	W	RRZZZZ	NY
HURST.	23	F	SP	RRZZZZ	NY
JACOB	9	M	CHILD	RRZZZZ	NY
MANDEL	7	M	CHILD	RRZZZZ	NY
CRSCH	5	F	CHILD	RRZZZZ	NY
DAVID	3	M	CHILD	RRZZZZ	NY
BEHR.	2	M	CHILD	RRZZZZ	NY
RACHEL	.07	F	INFANT	RRZZZZ	NY

SHIP: CITY OF NEW YORK

FROM: LIVERPOOL AND QUEENSTOWN
TO: NEW YORK
ARRIVED: 25 APRIL 1889

PASSENGER	AGE	SEX	OCCUPATION	PRV VIL	DES
AZINSKI, A.CAWY	00	U	UNKNOWN	RRZZZZ	NY
BRENK, W.	00	U	UNKNOWN	RRZZZZ	NY
MANZALKOWSKI, JACOB	25	M	UNKNOWN	RRZZZZ	NY
KLISKOWSKI, K.	17	M	UNKNOWN	RRZZZZ	NY
BIZEZINSKI, VALENTI	11	M	UNKNOWN	RRZZZZ	NY
B.	35	M	UNKNOWN	RRZZZZ	NY
WIBONSKI, C.	32	M	LABR	RRZZZZ	NY
GALAMEK, ROCH.	30	M	LABR	RRZZZZ	NY
OLEZINZAK, A.	22	M	LABR	RRZZZZ	NY
KLAMOWSKY, FRANZ	22	M	LABR	RRZZZZ	NY
KOZITZSKY, MICHAEL	22	M	LABR	RRZZZZ	NY

SHIP: TRAVE

FROM: BREMEN AND SOUTHAMPTON
TO: NEW YORK
ARRIVED: 26 APRIL 1889

PASSENGER	AGE	SEX	OCCUPATION	PRV VIL	DES
ALBERS, JOH.	15	M	FARMER	RRZZZZ	USA
KELLER, SEBAST.	35	M	FARMER	RRZZZZ	USA
MAGDA.	30	F	UNKNOWN	RRZZZZ	USA
MAX	7	M	CHILD	RRZZZZ	USA
SCHWAB, MARTIN	49	M	FARMER	RRZZZZ	USA
CATHA.	48	F	UNKNOWN	RRZZZZ	USA
LISABETH	18	F	UNKNOWN	RRZZZZ	USA
MICH.	14	M	FARMER	RRZZZZ	USA
JOS.	7	M	CHILD	RRZZZZ	USA

PASSENGER	AGE	SEX	OCCUPATION	PRIV	VIL	DES
SEBASTIAN	6	M	CHILD	RR	ZZZ	USA
GERTRUDE	.03	F	INFANT	RR	ZZZ	USA
GIESSENGER, FRANZ	40	M	FARMER	RR	ZZZ	USA
CATHA.	39	F	UNKNOWN	RR	ZZZ	USA
AMBROSIUS	17	M	FARMER	RR	ZZZ	USA
MARIA	14	F	UNKNOWN	RR	ZZZ	USA
EVA	4	F	CHILD	RR	ZZZ	USA
ANNA	7	F	CHILD	RR	ZZZ	USA
REGINA	5	F	CHILD	RR	ZZZ	USA
LIESBETH	2	F	CHILD	RR	ZZZ	USA
CATHA.	.06	F	INFANT	RR	ZZZ	USA
SELZLER, JOSEF	46	M	FARMER	RR	ZZZ	USA
ROSINA	45	F	UNKNOWN	RR	ZZZ	USA
BARBA.	6	F	CHILD	RR	ZZZ	USA
MICHEL	7	M	CHILD	RR	ZZZ	USA
KELLER, JOSEF	29	M	FARMER	RR	ZZZ	USA
MONICA	28	F	UNKNOWN	RR	ZZZ	USA
DORA	7	F	CHILD	RR	ZZZ	USA
MAGDA.	3	F	CHILD	RR	ZZZ	USA
VERONICA	.03	F	INFANT	RR	ZZZ	USA
ZENZ, ANTON	40	M	FARMER	RR	ZZZ	USA
MAGDE.	38	F	UNKNOWN	RR	ZZZ	USA
ANDR.	18	M	FARMER	RR	ZZZ	USA
PETER	15	M	UNKNOWN	RR	ZZZ	USA
ANTON	6	M	CHILD	RR	ZZZ	USA
OTTILIE	4	F	CHILD	RR	ZZZ	USA
FRANZ	3	M	CHILD	RR	ZZZ	USA
KILLER, CASPAR	39	M	FARMER	RR	ZZZ	USA
ROSINE	35	F	UNKNOWN	RR	ZZZ	USA
JOHS.	14	M	FARMER	RR	ZZZ	USA
CATHA.	7	F	CHILD	RR	ZZZ	USA
MAGDA.	4	F	CHILD	RR	ZZZ	USA
BARBA.	3	F	CHILD	RR	ZZZ	USA
USSELMANN, ALEX	45	M	FARMER	RR	ZZZ	USA
MARGA.	40	F	UNKNOWN	RR	ZZZ	USA
JOHS.	21	M	FARMER	RR	ZZZ	USA
VALENTIN	18	M	FARMER	RR	ZZZ	USA
ANNA	19	F	UNKNOWN	RR	ZZZ	USA
MARGA	14	F	UNKNOWN	RR	ZZZ	USA
ANTON	6	M	CHILD	RR	ZZZ	USA
JULIE	4	F	CHILD	RR	ZZZ	USA
JOSEF	7	M	CHILD	RR	ZZZ	USA
ADAM	.07	M	INFANT	RR	ZZZ	USA
EGIDIE	38	F	UNKNOWN	RR	ZZZ	USA
AGATHE	36	F	UNKNOWN	RR	ZZZ	USA
JOSEF	9	M	CHILD	RR	ZZZ	USA
JOHANN	7	M	CHILD	RR	ZZZ	USA
CARL	.06	M	INFANT	RR	ZZZ	USA
WALD, BARBA.	19	F	UNKNOWN	RR	ZZZ	USA
KRAFT, PETER	42	M	FARMER	RR	ZZZ	USA
CATHA.	40	F	UNKNOWN	RR	ZZZ	USA
STEFAN	19	M	FARMER	RR	ZZZ	USA
CATHA.	17	F	UNKNOWN	RR	ZZZ	USA
CACILIE	15	F	UNKNOWN	RR	ZZZ	USA
GREGOR	6	M	CHILD	RR	ZZZ	USA
ADAM	7	M	CHILD	RR	ZZZ	USA
CACILIE	3	F	CHILD	RR	ZZZ	USA
FERD.	2	M	CHILD	RR	ZZZ	USA
PETER	.03	M	INFANT	RR	ZZZ	USA
BALZ, LOUISE	23	F	UNKNOWN	RR	ZZZ	USA
JAEGER, JULIE	25	F	UNKNOWN	RR	ZZZ	USA
KURZ, CHRISTE.	27	F	UNKNOWN	RR	ZZZ	USA
GOTTLOB	.09	M	INFANT	RR	ZZZ	USA
KOCH, WILHELMINE	36	F	UNKNOWN	RR	ZZZ	USA
WINKELMANN, HCH.	23	M	FARMER	RR	ZZZ	USA
GOROZEWSKY, JAN	24	M	FARMER	RR	ZZZ	USA
KRUEGER, FRANZ	42	M	FARMER	RR	ZZZ	USA
HINTRA, KALLE	28	M	UNKNOWN	RR	ZZZ	USA
WAIMANEN, HENRICH	19	M	UNKNOWN	RR	ZZZ	USA
HOKKANEN, VICTOR	32	M	UNKNOWN	RR	ZZZ	USA
FREDERIKSON, BANDER	21	M	UNKNOWN	RR	ZZZ	USA
HOKKANA, U	26	M	UNKNOWN	RR	ZZZ	USA
JOH.MATTSON	25	M	UNKNOWN	RR	ZZZ	USA
FRAST, MATTD.KURTAANPOE	23	M	UNKNOWN	RR	ZZZ	USA
RUHIMAKI, OSCAR	16	M	UNKNOWN	RR	ZZZ	USA
RIDANPAA, TEOPILUS	3	M	CHILD	RR	ZZZ	USA
WARISMAKI, JOH.JOHARYRO	30	M	UNKNOWN	RR	ZZZ	USA
LAPP, FRANZ	18	M	UNKNOWN	RR	ZZZ	USA
KACKMEN, ELIAS	21	M	UNKNOWN	RR	ZZZ	USA
LAMALIN, JOH.GUSTAFSSON	24	M	UNKNOWN	RR	ZZZ	USA
KOCARI, JACOB	23	M	UNKNOWN	RR	ZZZ	USA
MINDER, ALFRED	35	M	UNKNOWN	RR	ZZZ	USA
BLANK, KARL	19	M	UNKNOWN	RR	ZZZ	USA
U, ALBRECHT	21	M	UNKNOWN	RR	ZZZ	USA
KELLER, JAC	24	M	UNKNOWN	RR	ZZZ	USA

SHIP: WERRA

FROM: BREMEN AND SOUTHAMPTON
TO: NEW YORK
ARRIVED: 26 APRIL 1889

PASSENGER	AGE	SEX	OCCUPATION	PRIV	VIL	DES
DANIELSKA, VICTORIA	23	F	UNKNOWN	RR	ZZZ	USA
TICTINS, JOHANN-E.	.11	M	INFANT	RR	ZZZ	USA
DIPIENSKI, FRANZISKA	22	F	UNKNOWN	RR	ZZZ	USA
MARIE	.11	F	INFANT	RR	ZZZ	USA
LESINSKA, MARIANNA	23	F	UNKNOWN	RR	ZZZ	USA
MARIANNA	.11	F	INFANT	RR	ZZZ	USA
KORZYEKOWSKA, VVERONIKA	18	F	UNKNOWN	RR	ZZZ	USA
STANISLAUS	.11	M	INFANT	RR	ZZZ	USA
WASS, GOTTFRIED	32	M	SHMK	RR	ZZZ	USA
JASTRZEBSKI, JAN	30	M	LABR	RR	ZZZ	USA
MILUM, VINCENT	33	M	LABR	RR	ZZZ	USA
PHILIPPOWITZ, ANTONIA	33	F	UNKNOWN	RR	ZZZ	USA
SOBOLEWSKI, FRANZ	26	M	LABR	RR	ZZZ	USA
MILEWSKI, VINCENT	28	M	LABR	RR	ZZZ	USA
SOKOLSKI, FRANZ	24	M	LABR	RR	ZZZ	USA
MARKOWSKI, ANTON	22	M	LABR	RR	ZZZ	USA
BARANSKI, VALENTIN	20	M	LABR	RR	ZZZ	USA
ORGEL, ANTON	49	M	LABR	RR	ZZZ	USA
SZANORKY, JOSEF	31	M	LABR	RR	ZZZ	USA
MARSCHEWSKY, STANISLAUS	23	M	LABR	RR	ZZZ	USA
HEVKER, WILHELM	34	M	LABR	RR	ZZZ	USA
YRONI, ANDREAS	20	M	LABR	RR	ZZZ	USA
NOWICKI, FRANZ	29	M	LABR	RR	ZZZ	USA
SCHOENKE, JOHANN	30	M	FARMER	RR	ZZZ	USA
DOEGER, FERDINAND	24	M	FARMER	RR	ZZZ	USA
GRIMM, GOTTLIEB	35	M	FARMER	RR	ZZZ	USA
LOSZECKI, ALER	49	M	FARMER	RR	ZZZ	USA
KAMINSKY, JOSEF	50	M	FARMER	RR	ZZZ	USA
MARINOWSKY, MARIAN	55	M	LABR	RR	ZZZ	USA
STAWSKI, STANISLAUS	22	M	SMH	RR	ZZZ	USA
KURCZEWSKY, VAN	24	M	LABR	RR	ZZZ	USA
GULEWSKY, RICHARD	24	M	LABR	RR	ZZZ	USA
PAUTER, ANNA	25	F	UNKNOWN	RR	ZZZ	USA
MARIA	.11	F	INFANT	RR	ZZZ	USA
LUCZAK, SZIMON	48	M	FARMER	RR	ZZZ	USA
WYSOCKI, MICHAEL	50	M	FARMER	RR	ZZZ	USA
SZAJKOWSKI, PAWEL	43	M	FARMER	RR	ZZZ	USA
ANTKOVICZ, JOSEF	46	M	FARMER	RR	ZZZ	USA
SZOTOWICZ, JACOB	31	M	FARMER	RR	ZZZ	USA
WERNEROWSKY, KONSTANZ	27	M	FARMER	RR	ZZZ	USA
GRENZECK, WAWCZYNIE	23	M	LABR	RR	ZZZ	USA
KELMA, CAROLINA	30	F	UNKNOWN	RR	ZZZ	USA
EISSNER, COTTLIEB	27	M	SHMK	RR	ZZZ	USA
SCHENKER, SCHMUL	30	M	LABR	RR	ZZZ	USA
JENNER, JOHANN	17	M	LABR	RR	ZZZ	USA
RAN, JOHANNES	20	M	LABR	RR	ZZZ	USA
WOLF	16	M	LABR	RR	ZZZ	USA
ALPERN, BEILE	28	F	UNKNOWN	RR	ZZZ	USA
LISLE	6	F	CHILD	RR	ZZZ	USA
BEILE	2	F	CHILD	RR	ZZZ	USA
WOLLMERS, HEINRICH	26	M	LABR	RR	ZZZ	USA

SHIP: CALIFORNIA

FROM: HAMBURG
TO: NEW YORK
ARRIVED: 26 APRIL 1889

PASSENGER	AGE	SEX	OCCUPATION	PRV VIL DES
TOMOLEWICZ, STANISLAW	25	M	LABR	RRAIGHUSA
LUDKEWICZ, SIMON	40	M	LABR	RRAIGHUSA
ADAM	40	M	LABR	RRAIGHUSA
WARANOWICZ, AMBROSIES	27	M	LABR	RRAIGHUSA
RUDZEWICZ, JOSEF	46	M	LABR	RRAIGHUSA
KILKUTZKI, LUDWIG	30	M	LABR	RRAIGHUSA
SASETZKI, WLADISLAV	27	M	LABR	RRAIGHUSA
DAWICZUK, JAN	27	M	LABR	RRAIGHUSA
GOSTANCZYK, LEON	39	M	LABR	RRZZZZUSA
MARIA	30	F	W	RRZZZZUSA
PAULE	9	F	CHILD	RRZZZZUSA
VICTORIA	7	F	CHILD	RRZZZZUSA
ROSALIE	.09	F	INFANT	RRZZZZUSA
BURZYNSKA, ANASTASIA	29	F	SGL	RRZZZZUSA
GADOMSKY, JOH.	30	M	LABR	RRZZZZUSA
SKIBA, FRANZ	24	M	LABR	RRZZZZUSA
SCHIBEK, VALENTIN	31	M	LABR	RRZZZZUSA
KORBUS, VALENTIN	26	M	LABR	RRZZZZUSA
ROLKA, ADAM	20	M	LABR	RRZZZZUSA
ROMANDOWSKY, FRANZ	19	M	LABR	RRZZZZUSA
PETROWSKY, FRANZ	33	M	LABR	RRZZZZUSA
SARNOWSKI, FRANZ	31	M	LABR	RRZZZZUSA
GRABECK, FRANZ	33	M	LABR	RRAIHNUSA
JURECK, JACOB	32	M	LABR	RRAIHNUSA
CHENTNIK, STANISL.	44	M	LABR	RRAIHNUSA
WALUKAINS, MICH	22	M	LABR	RRAHZSUSA
JAN	24	M	LABR	RRAHZSUSA
MARIANNE	26	F	W	RRAHZSUSA
CATH.	24	F	W	RRAHZSUSA
CZAMOWSKI, THOMAS	36	M	LABR	RRZZZZUSA
ANNA	27	F	W	RRZZZZUSA
SCHULZ, JULIE	21	F	SGL	RRAIDNUSA
CEGULSKI, STANISL.	40	M	LABR	RRZZZZUSA
AMALIE	32	F	W	RRZZZZUSA
JOSEF	7	M	CHILD	RRZZZZUSA
FRANZ	3	M	CHILD	RRZZZZUSA
ALBERT	.11	M	INFANT	RRZZZZUSA
JAN	.01	M	INFANT	RRZZZZUSA
RYBINSKI, STANISL.	18	M	LABR	RRAIKPUSA
FILARSKA, PELAGIA	16	F	SGL	RRAIKPUSA
ZYSKOWSKI, JAN	18	M	LABR	RRZZZZUSA
MEYER, CATH	17	F	SGL	RRZZZZUSA
ANNA	26	F	WO	RRZZZZUSA
JEDRZY	.11	M	INFANT	RRZZZZUSA
STOLLBERG, ADAM	30	M	LABR	RRAHZSUSA
EICKERT, JAN	35	M	LABR	RRAHZSUSA
WRUBLINSKY, JOSEF	27	M	LABR	RRAHUFUSA
CZECHINSKY, JOSEFA	24	F	SGL	RRAHUFUSA
MIKOLAJONOSKY, LUDWIG	38	M	LABR	RRAHUFUSA
GIGLOWSKI, WOYCEK	32	M	LABR	RRAHZSUSA
STENDOOSKI, JAN	28	M	LABR	RRAHUFUSA
CONSTANTINA	25	F	W	RRAHUFUSA
JOSEFA	.11	F	INFANT	RRAHUFUSA
JOSEF	3	M	CHILD	RRAHUFUSA
LIPINZICK, WOYCEK	26	M	LABR	RRAFWJUSA
JOSEFA	18	F	W	RRAFWJUSA
DURABA, ANDJE	39	M	LABR	RRAFWJUSA
KALINOWSKI, VICENTY	28	M	LABR	RRAFWJUSA
PESKA, JAN	38	M	LABR	RRAFWJUSA
WYNEVIC, JOSEF	29	M	LABR	RRAHTFUSA
JANIKAS, ANTON	23	M	LABR	RRAHTFUSA
KOWALSKI, ANTON	26	M	LABR	RRAHUFUSA
FRANZ	17	M	LABR	RRAHUFUSA
WELOT, WOYTECK	24	M	LABR	RRAHUFUSA
WITTKOWSKY, STEPHAN	40	M	LABR	RRAHUFUSA
KOWALCZYK, JACOB	32	M	LABR	RRAHTFUSA
OSTAS, JOSEF	38	M	LABR	RRAHTFUSA
KERNA, ANNA	23	F	SGL	RRZZZZUSA
MATHIA, MARTIN	30	M	LABR	RRZZZZUSA
POGLAN, HEINR.	49	M	FARMER	RRZZZZUSA
AMALIE	42	F	W	RRZZZZUSA
RUDOLF	16	M	CH	RRZZZZUSA
IDA	15	F	CH	RRZZZZUSA
MARIE	9	F	CHILD	RRZZZZUSA
BERTHA	5	F	CHILD	RRZZZZUSA
SCZECHOWSKY, ANTONY	30	M	LABR	RRZZZZUSA
APPOLONIA	34	F	W	RRZZZZUSA
JOSEFA	7	F	CHILD	RRZZZZUSA
ANDREY	.11	M	INFANT	RRZZZZUSA
VALENTIN	.01	M	INFANT	RRZZZZUSA
MATUSAK, KASIMIR	49	M	LABR	RRZZZZUSA
FEIERABEND, WILH.	30	M	LABR	RRZZZZUSA
NOWACK, MICHAL	34	M	LABR	RRZZZZUSA
BECKER, MICHAL	30	M	LABR	RRZZZZUSA
JOHA	30	F	W	RRZZZZUSA
SCHAERMAK, VICTOR	30	M	LABR	RRZZZZUSA
BLASCHKE, GUSTAV	21	M	BKR	RRZZZZUSA
IDA	23	F	SGL	RRZZZZUSA
LUKAZEWICZ, SIMON	39	M	LABR	RRAHTFUSA
SZAPUTIS, STANISL.	22	M	LABR	RRAHTFUSA
BELSKI, ANTON	42	M	LABR	RRAHTFUSA
DRUKTEN, ANTON	43	M	LABR	RRAHTFUSA
JOCIS, JAN	45	M	LABR	RRAHTFUSA
SCZYMANZICK, PAWEL	24	M	LABR	RRAHTFUSA
KREMER, JAN	31	M	LABR	RRAHTFUSA
SCZYMANKEWICZ, FRANZ	35	M	LABR	RRAHTFUSA
SENKEWITSCH, JOSEF	32	M	LABR	RRAGRTUSA
JULIE	24	F	W	RRAGRTUSA
ALBIN	3	M	CHILD	RRAGRTUSA
SCHMIDT, ADAM	26	M	LABR	RRZZZZUSA
STRECKER, FRIEDR.	35	M	LABR	RRZZZZUSA
SCHLITZKA, ADAM	36	M	LABR	RRZZZZUSA
TROMMER, RICH.	23	M	WVR	RRZZZZUSA
KOWALSKI, MARIAM	30	M	LABR	RRAHZDUSA
SCHMIDT, GOTTFR.	27	M	MCHT	RRZZZZUSA
MILBRANDT, MICHL	27	M	MCHT	RRZZZZUSA
SZESZ, LUDWIG	18	M	MCHT	RRZZZZUSA
CZILKI, LUDWIG	18	M	MCHT	RRZZZZUSA
DRESCHER, AUG.	52	M	LABR	RRZZZZUSA
RUTKIS, OTTO	25	M	LABR	RRZZZZUSA
KRAHN, DANIEL	23	M	LABR	RRAHUFUSA
ANDRE	26	F	W	RRAHUFUSA
SZAZINSKI, JAN	22	M	LABR	RRAHUFUSA
THOMAZEWSKI, ANDRE	48	M	LABR	RRAHZSUSA
GINZEWSKI, ANDRE	28	M	LABR	RRAHZSUSA
KRUTZE, WILH.	23	M	MCHT	RRAHXHUSA
RESZELA, JOSEF	29	M	WHR	RRZZZZUSA
HEESE, CONRAD	24	M	LABR	RRAAKHUSA
WOLFF, DOROTHEA	23	F	SGL	RRZZZZUSA
SANGER, MARIANNE	25	F	SGL	RRZZZZUSA
SCHLEISS, FRIEDR.	30	M	MSN	RRAEFLUSA
KOLEMANSKI, MATHIAS	40	M	LABR	RRZZZZUSA
DESECHKANTZ, WINZES	40	M	LABR	RRZZZZUSA
KURNEWICZ, PAULUS	20	M	LABR	RRZZZZUSA
TURSKY, THADEUS	40	M	LABR	RRZZZZUSA
EVA	20	F	W	RRZZZZUSA
WARNIAK, FRANZ	30	M	LABR	RRZZZZUSA
KOSCHMIOJ, HERRM.	31	M	LABR	RRZZZZUSA

SHIP: FULDA

FROM: BREMEN AND SOUTHAMPTON
TO: NEW YORK
ARRIVED: 01 MAY 1889

PASSENGER	AGE	SEX	OCCUPATION	PRV VIL DES
ZECHMEISTER, JOHANN	51	M	FARMER	RRZZZZUSA
ELISABETH	51	F	W	RRZZZZUSA
GEORG	14	M	CH	RRZZZZUSA

PASSENGER	AGE	SEX	OCCUPATION	PRV	VIL	DES
JOHANN	9	M	CHILD	RR	ZZZZ	USA
SCHWADERER, FRIEDRICH	22	M	FARMER	RR	ZZZZ	USA
ELISABETH	24	F	W	RR	ZZZZ	USA
CHRISTINE	2	F	CHILD	RR	ZZZZ	USA
GEORG	.06	M	INFANT	RR	ZZZZ	USA
SCHEID, GOTTLIEB	34	M	FARMER	RR	ZZZZ	USA
SUSANNE	33	F	W	RR	ZZZZ	USA
MARIE	4	F	CHILD	RR	ZZZZ	USA
FRIEDERIKE	.08	F	INFANT	RR	ZZZZ	USA
FRIEDERIKE	16	F	UNKNOWN	RR	ZZZZ	USA
FROESCHLE, CHRISTOPH	43	M	FARMER	RR	ZZZZ	USA
DOROTHEA	43	F	W	RR	ZZZZ	USA
CHRISTOPH	.07	F	INFANT	RR	ZZZZ	USA
CATHARINA	8	F	CHILD	RR	ZZZZ	USA
MATDALENA	3	F	CHILD	RR	ZZZZ	USA
WEHLHOF, JACOB	29	M	FARMER	RR	ZZZZ	USA
MARIE	29	F	W	RR	ZZZZ	USA
CATHARINA	.11	F	INFANT	RR	ZZZZ	USA
ORTWINS, LUDWIG	29	M	FARMER	RR	ZZZZ	USA
ROSINA	28	F	W	RR	ZZZZ	USA
FRIEDRICH	.04	M	INFANT	RR	ZZZZ	USA
SCHAEFER, JACOB	41	M	FARMER	RR	ZZZZ	USA
JACOB	16	M	FARMER	RR	ZZZZ	USA
SCHELSKE, WILHELM	38	M	FARMER	RR	ZZZZ	USA
CATHARINA	41	F	W	RR	ZZZZ	USA
JOHANN	18	M	FARMER	RR	ZZZZ	USA
WILHELM	16	M	FARMER	RR	ZZZZ	USA
GOTTFRIED	14	M	FARMER	RR	ZZZZ	USA
GOTTLIEB	12	M	CH	RR	ZZZZ	USA
CATHARINA	15	F	CH	RR	ZZZZ	USA
CAROLINE	7	F	CHILD	RR	ZZZZ	USA
MARGARETHA	2	F	CHILD	RR	ZZZZ	USA
JOHANN	3	M	CHILD	RR	ZZZZ	USA
CHARLOTTE	8	F	CHILD	RR	ZZZZ	USA
MERKLE, JOHANN	42	M	FARMER	RR	ZZZZ	USA
UNTERSCHER, GOTTLIEB	38	M	FARMER	RR	ZZZZ	USA
MARGARETHA	37	F	W	RR	ZZZZ	USA
LOUISE	13	F	CH	RR	ZZZZ	USA
GOTTLIEB	9	M	CHILD	RR	ZZZZ	USA
FRIEDRICH	8	M	CHILD	RR	ZZZZ	USA
HEINRICH	6	M	CHILD	RR	ZZZZ	USA
JOHANN	3	M	CHILD	RR	ZZZZ	USA
PAULINE	.11	F	INFANT	RR	ZZZZ	USA
JOHANN	28	M	FARMER	RR	ZZZZ	USA
MARGARETHA	26	F	W	RR	ZZZZ	USA
JOHANN	.04	M	INFANT	RR	ZZZZ	USA
SCHAEFER, JACOB	46	M	FARMER	RR	ZZZZ	USA
MAGDALENA	44	F	W	RR	ZZZZ	USA
PAUL	19	M	FARMER	RR	ZZZZ	USA
SEBESTIA	18	M	FARMER	RR	ZZZZ	USA
FRANZ	9	M	CHILD	RR	ZZZZ	USA
JOHANNES	7	M	CHILD	RR	ZZZZ	USA
KUNIGUNDE	15	F	CH	RR	ZZZZ	USA
MAGDALENA	13	F	CH	RR	ZZZZ	USA
DUFILIA	.06	F	INFANT	RR	ZZZZ	USA
MICHEL	73	M	UNKNOWN	RR	ZZZZ	USA
FISCHER, OSEF	27	M	FARMER	RR	ZZZZ	USA
THERESIA	26	F	W	RR	ZZZZ	USA
MICHAEL	.06	M	INFANT	RR	ZZZZ	USA
JOHANN	59	M	FARMER	RR	ZZZZ	USA
ELISABETH	54	F	W	RR	ZZZZ	USA
ROSALIE	18	F	CH	RR	ZZZZ	USA
CATHARINA	17	F	CH	RR	ZZZZ	USA
JOHANN	13	M	CH	RR	ZZZZ	USA
MARIE	9	F	CHILD	RR	ZZZZ	USA
SEBESTIAN	11	M	CH	RR	ZZZZ	USA
ADAM	7	M	CHILD	RR	ZZZZ	USA
GOLDADE, GEORG	50	M	FARMER	RR	ZZZZ	USA
MARIA	49	F	W	RR	ZZZZ	USA
CATHARINA	17	F	CH	RR	ZZZZ	USA
CLARA	10	F	CH	RR	ZZZZ	USA
JOAEF	9	M	CHILD	RR	ZZZZ	USA
ROSA	2	F	CHILD	RR	ZZZZ	USA
ISSLER, GOTTLIEB	25	M	FARMER	RR	ZZZZ	USA
CATHARINA	27	F	W	RR	ZZZZ	USA

PASSENGER	AGE	SEX	OCCUPATION	PRV	VIL	DES
CATHARINA	.11	F	INFANT	RR	ZZZZ	USA
WUEST, VINSENZ	28	M	FARMER	RR	ZZZZ	USA
MARHARETHA	30	F	W	RR	ZZZZ	USA
JOSEF	2	M	CHILD	RR	ZZZZ	USA
CARL	.06	M	INFANT	RR	ZZZZ	USA
FOETH, LUDWIG	30	M	FARMER	RR	ZZZZ	USA
REGINA	26	F	W	RR	ZZZZ	USA
THERESE	4	F	CHILD	RR	ZZZZ	USA
WENDELIN	2	M	CHILD	RR	ZZZZ	USA
MAGDALENA	.06	F	INFANT	RR	ZZZZ	USA
SCHMID, GEORG	32	M	FARMER	RR	ZZZZ	USA
CLARA	30	F	W	RR	ZZZZ	USA
JOHANN	6	M	CHILD	RR	ZZZZ	USA
MARGARETHA	4	F	CHILD	RR	ZZZZ	USA
MARGARETHA	2	F	CHILD	RR	ZZZZ	USA
MARTIN	.06	M	INFANT	RR	ZZZZ	USA
SCHAEFER, JOSEF	22	M	FARMER	RR	ZZZZ	USA
CATHARINA	21	F	W	RR	ZZZZ	USA
MARIANNA	.06	F	INFANT	RR	ZZZZ	USA
FRIEDSON, BALTHAR	50	M	FARMER	RR	ZZZZ	USA
SUCKMILLA	42	F	W	RR	ZZZZ	USA
HELENA	16	F	CH	RR	ZZZZ	USA
CATHARINA	15	F	CH	RR	ZZZZ	USA
GENOFEFA	6	F	CHILD	RR	ZZZZ	USA
BALTHASAR	4	M	CHILD	RR	ZZZZ	USA
LUDWIG	3	M	CHILD	RR	ZZZZ	USA
FRANCISKA	.06	F	INFANT	RR	ZZZZ	USA
JOSEPH	28	M	FARMER	RR	ZZZZ	USA
EVA	29	F	W	RR	ZZZZ	USA
PHILIPP	18	M	FARMER	RR	ZZZZ	USA
SALIE, SEBASTIAN	40	M	FARMER	RR	ZZZZ	USA
GERTRUDE	40	F	W	RR	ZZZZ	USA
JOHANN	.01	M	INFANT	RR	ZZZZ	USA
JAEGER, BERNHARD	25	M	FARMER	RR	ZZZZ	USA
CHRISTINA	25	F	W	RR	ZZZZ	USA
CATHARINA	.06	F	INFANT	RR	ZZZZ	USA
FOLIK, CYRIL	46	M	FARMER	RR	ZZZZ	USA
CATHARINA	40	F	W	RR	ZZZZ	USA
JACOB	13	M	CH	RR	ZZZZ	USA
JOSEF	9	M	CHILD	RR	ZZZZ	USA
PETER	5	M	CHILD	RR	ZZZZ	USA
EVA	2	F	CHILD	RR	ZZZZ	USA
PFLIGNER, ANTON	46	M	FARMER	RR	ZZZZ	USA
MAGDALENA	45	F	W	RR	ZZZZ	USA
PAUL	17	M	FARMER	RR	ZZZZ	USA
BARBARA	15	F	CH	RR	ZZZZ	USA
GERTRUDE	8	F	CHILD	RR	ZZZZ	USA
VICTORIA	6	F	CHILD	RR	ZZZZ	USA
ELIDABETH	4	F	CHILD	RR	ZZZZ	USA
ANTON	19	M	FARMER	RR	ZZZZ	USA
WENZ, PETER	51	M	FARMER	RR	ZZZZ	USA
CATHARINA	46	F	W	RR	ZZZZ	USA
PETER	18	M	FARMER	RR	ZZZZ	USA
EVA	16	F	CH	RR	ZZZZ	USA
ANTON	13	M	CH	RR	ZZZZ	USA
MAGDALENA	7	F	CHILD	RR	ZZZZ	USA
JOSEFA	4	F	CHILD	RR	ZZZZ	USA
GOLDADE, JOHANNES	37	M	FARMER	RR	ZZZZ	USA
JOHANNE	31	F	W	RR	ZZZZ	USA
MICHAEL	10	M	CH	RR	ZZZZ	USA
STEFAN	8	M	CHILD	RR	ZZZZ	USA
MAGDALENA	6	F	CHILD	RR	ZZZZ	USA
ROSA	.01	F	INFANT	RR	ZZZZ	USA
WOETSCH, JOHANNES	19	M	FARMER	RR	ZZZZ	USA
ANTON	16	M	FARMER	RR	ZZZZ	USA
JUNG, GEORG	18	M	FARMER	RR	ZZZZ	USA
PHILIPP	15	M	FARMER	RR	ZZZZ	USA
KELLER, JULIAN	23	M	FARMER	RR	ZZZZ	USA
ELISABETH	20	F	W	RR	ZZZZ	USA
JOHANN	.06	M	INFANT	RR	ZZZZ	USA
SATTLER, MICHAEL	71	M	FARMER	RR	ZZZZ	USA
CHRISTINE	50	F	W	RR	ZZZZ	USA
STEPHAN	17	M	FARMER	RR	ZZZZ	USA
WEIGEL, JACOB	30	M	FARMER	RR	ZZZZ	USA
JOHANNES	63	M	FARMER	RR	ZZZZ	USA

PASSENGER	AGE	SEX	OCCUPATION	PRIVL	DES
THERESE	28	F	W	RRZZZZ	USA
ANTON	7	M	CHILD	RRZZZZ	USA
MAGDALENA	4	F	CHILD	RRZZZZ	USA
FRANZ	2	M	CHILD	RRZZZZ	USA
FETT, WENDELIN	73	M	FARMER	RRZZZZ	USA
CATHARINA	73	F	W	RRZZZZ	USA
WELTER, JOHANN	38	M	FARMER	RRZZZZ	USA
BARBARA	34	F	W	RRZZZZ	USA
ANTON	8	M	CHILD	RRZZZZ	USA
ADAM	6	M	CHILD	RRZZZZ	USA
NICOALUS	4	M	CHILD	RRZZZZ	USA
JULIANNE	15	F	CH	RRZZZZ	USA
MARGARETHA	11	F	CH	RRZZZZ	USA
MAGDALENA	2	F	CHILD	RRZZZZ	USA
GICSINGER, ANTON	29	M	FARMER	RRZZZZ	USA
AGNESS	19	F	W	RRZZZZ	USA
SATTLER, PHILOMEN	39	M	FARMER	RRZZZZ	USA
ANTON	11	M	CH	RRZZZZ	USA
FRANZ	10	M	CH	RRZZZZ	USA
ELISABETH	15	F	CH	RRZZZZ	USA
CATHARINA	8	F	CHILD	RRZZZZ	USA
ALOYSA	6	F	CHILD	RRZZZZ	USA
JULIANNE	2	F	CHILD	RRZZZZ	USA
GIMPEL, PHILIPP	29	M	FARMER	RRZZZZ	USA
JOHANNE	26	F	W	RRZZZZ	USA
HEINRICH	2	M	CHILD	RRZZZZ	USA
MAGDALENE	.04	F	INFANT	RRZZZZ	USA
HEINRICH	58	M	FARMER	RRZZZZ	USA
CAROLINE	55	F	W	RRZZZZ	USA
SIMON	20	M	FARMER	RRZZZZ	USA
HEINRICH	11	M	CH	RRZZZZ	USA
WOLSKY, LUDWIG	52	M	LABR	RRZZZZ	USA
DANIEL	27	M	TNM	RRZZZZ	USA
SUSANNE	15	F	CH	RRZZZZ	USA
ANNA	12	F	CH	RRZZZZ	USA
SLISZKEMITZ, JAN	30	M	LABR	RRZZZZ	USA
MAREIN, LYS	30	M	LABR	RRZZZZ	USA
WUSZINSKA, ANTON	20	M	LABR	RRZZZZ	USA
CATHARINA	25	F	W	RRZZZZ	USA
STANISLAUS	.11	M	INFANT	RRZZZZ	USA
ANDRE, MAHIVA	37	M	LABR	RRZZZZ	USA
BAJHAJUS, LAWREN	45	M	LABR	RRZZZZ	USA
BARKSEWICZ, FRANZ	26	M	LABR	RRZZZZ	USA
TOMASCHEK, JOSEF	30	M	LABR	RRZZZZ	USA
SHIRAS, SURGIS	32	M	LABR	RRZZZZ	USA
MOTSHAITE, MARIE	26	F	UNKNOWN	RRZZZZ	USA
ADLER, BENJAMIN	37	M	FARMER	RRZZZZ	USA
SCHUBERT, CARL	44	M	SHMK	RRZZZZ	USA

SHIP: DEVONIA

FROM: GLASGOW
TO: NEW YORK
ARRIVED: 01 MAY 1889

PASSENGER	AGE	SEX	OCCUPATION	PRIVL	DES
FELDMAN, HILLEL	25	M	LABR	RRZZZZ	USA
FEMELEWITZ, JERSE	25	M	LABR	RRZZZZ	USA
GUMINSKI, STEPHAN	28	M	LABR	RRZZZZ	USA
GRUDECKI, PETER	40	M	LABR	RRZZZZ	USA
JONSIK, VINZENTI	23	M	LABR	RRZZZZ	USA
KOWALSKI, UKASECK	30	M	LABR	RRZZZZ	USA
KRAKOWSKI, MAZEI	34	M	LABR	RRZZZZ	USA
KIRMELEWITZ, KAREL	24	M	LABR	RRZZZZ	USA
KASCHILINESCH, PIOTR	18	M	LABR	RRZZZZ	USA
LIPSCHITZ, NOCHEM	35	M	LABR	RRZZZZ	USA
CHANE	40	F	UNKNOWN	RRZZZZ	USA
ESTER	12	F	UNKNOWN	RRZZZZ	USA
RIFKE	8	F	CHILD	RRZZZZ	USA
HINDE	6	F	CHILD	RRZZZZ	USA
SCHEINE	1	F	CHILD	RRZZZZ	USA
MOSELOWSKI, ZINPOLES	30	M	LABR	RRZZZZ	USA
NOWAK, FRANZ	33	M	LABR	RRZZZZ	USA
OSZANOWSKY, JACOB	24	M	LABR	RRZZZZ	USA
PIERTSIAK, JAN	34	M	LABR	RRZZZZ	USA
PRISCHENISCH, MICH.	26	M	LABR	RRZZZZ	USA
RONANOWSKI, LEONARD	30	M	LABR	RRZZZZ	USA
RUNBOWSKY, MICOL	28	M	LABR	RRZZZZ	USA
SAROWSKI, SCHEZEPAN	45	M	LABR	RRZZZZ	USA
WOLANGEWITZ, SOLEUIK	26	M	LABR	RRZZZZ	USA
TOLECKO, TEOFILE	26	M	LABR	RRZZZZ	USA
TASKO, FRANK	19	M	LABR	RRZZZZ	USA
WORNE, WOICECH	29	M	LABR	RRZZZZ	USA
ZIMMER, WM.	25	M	LABR	RRZZZZ	USA

SHIP: STATE OF NEBRASKA

FROM: GLASGOW AND LARNE
TO: NEW YORK
ARRIVED: 02 MAY 1889

PASSENGER	AGE	SEX	OCCUPATION	PRIVL	DES
TAUVENBAUM, RACHEL	00	F	WI	RRZZZZ	USA
MASTY, ELISABETH	30	F	W	RRZZZZ	USA
HORBATZ, MINGE	44	F	W	RRZZZZ	USA
ARON	20	M	LABR	RRZZZZ	USA
SARAH	17	F	SP	RRZZZZ	USA
MEREL	11	F	CH	RRZZZZ	USA
PESCHE	8	F	CHILD	RRZZZZ	USA
ITZIG	6	M	CHILD	RRZZZZ	USA
GOLDE	2	F	CHILD	RRZZZZ	USA
NETZKY, MERE	22	F	W	RRZZZZ	USA
ESTHER	1	F	CHILD	RRZZZZ	USA
LUCZAK, JOSEF	34	M	LABR	RRZZZZ	USA
JOSEFA	28	F	W	RRZZZZ	USA
ANDRYCI	2	M	CHILD	RRZZZZ	USA
SILVESTRE	1	M	CHILD	RRZZZZ	USA
U, U	38	M	UNKNOWN	RRZZZZ	USA
MISCKEWITSCH, JAN	32	M	LABR	RRZZZZ	USA
JOZWIAK, MICHAEL	30	M	LABR	RRZZZZ	USA
KOWALSKY, MARTIN	23	M	LABR	RRZZZZ	USA
JOSLICZ, IWAN	27	M	LABR	RRZZZZ	USA
SYMANIA, BARTOLOMY	54	M	LABR	RRZZZZ	USA
KRZYZANSKI, MICHAEL	45	M	LABR	RRZZZZ	USA
ALEXANDER	16	M	LABR	RRZZZZ	USA
KWIETKOFSKI, MICHAEL	30	M	LABR	RRZZZZ	USA
PIETRAK, FRANZ	24	M	LABR	RRZZZZ	USA
CHOJNACKI, VINCENTY	27	M	LABR	RRZZZZ	USA
CZESLARZYK, JAN	28	M	LABR	RRZZZZ	USA
PATER, PIETR	37	M	LABR	RRZZZZ	USA
HOYJECKY, WAWJEWITZ	30	M	LABR	RRZZZZ	USA
JOZEWIAK, MICHAEL	27	M	LABR	RRZZZZ	USA
PILARSKY, STSNISALW	20	M	LABR	RRZZZZ	USA
ADAM, JOHN	36	M	LABR	RRZZZZ	USA

SHIP: LAHN

FROM: BREMEN AND SOUTHAMPTON
TO: NEW YORK
ARRIVED: 03 MAY 1889

PASSENGER	AGE	SEX	OCCUPATION	PRIVL	DES
HAURU, MATEUS	50	M	LABR	RRAFWJ	USA
LISA	18	F	UNKNOWN	RRAFWJ	USA
JARD, ANTON	30	M	LABR	RRAFWJ	USA

PASSENGER	AGE	SEX	OCCUPATION	PRIVL	DES

SHIP: UMBRIA

FROM: LIVERPOOL
TO: NEW YORK
ARRIVED: 06 MAY 1889

PASSENGER	AGE	SEX	OCCUPATION	PRIVL	DES
ADOMOWICZ, ADOLPH	40	M	TLR	RRACBF	USA
DOBCZINSKA, JOSEPH	36	M	TLR	RRAFWJ	USA
ROSA	33	F	W	RRAFWJ	USA
ANNA	.11	F	INFANT	RRAFWJ	USA
JOSEPH	.11	M	INFANT	RRAFWJ	USA
ESIKSON, BEITHE	18	F	SVNT	RRAFWJ	USA
GTOVIACK, J.	30	M	LABR	RRZZZZ	USA
KAPELA, FELD	25	M	LABR	RRZZZZ	USA
KUSEK, JOSEPH	33	M	LABR	RRZZZZ	USA
KRESEL, SOLOMON	20	M	LABR	RRACBF	USA
MISCOGEIS, JOHAS	27	M	LABR	RRACBF	USA
PLATAKIS, JOHANN	25	M	LABR	RRACBF	USA

SHIP: SORRENTO

FROM: HAMBURG
TO: NEW YORK
ARRIVED: 06 MAY 1889

PASSENGER	AGE	SEX	OCCUPATION	PRIVL	DES
DRZEWSCKI, THEOFIL	23	M	LABR	RRZZZZ	NY
KUMMEL, GOTTLIEB	21	M	LABR	RRZZZZ	NY
MALENOWSKI, MICHAEL	30	M	LABR	RRZZZZ	NY
ZABETZKY, ANTON	24	M	LABR	RRZZZZ	NY
BRUSTECK, JOSEF	36	M	LABR	RRZZZZ	NY
STANISLAUS	7	M	CHILD	RRZZZZ	NY
FRANZ	7	M	CHILD	RRZZZZ	NY
BEREZ, ALBERT	38	M	FARMER	RRZZZZ	CH
MARIE	37	F	W	RRZZZZ	CH
THERESE	16	F	CH	RRZZZZ	CH
NICOLAI	7	M	CHILD	RRZZZZ	CH
BASTIAN	6	M	CHILD	RRZZZZ	CH
STEFAN	4	M	CHILD	RRZZZZ	CH
ROMANDES	.02	M	INFANT	RRZZZZ	CH

SHIP: ALASKA

FROM: LIVERPOOL AND QUEENSTOWN
TO: NEW YORK
ARRIVED: 06 MAY 1889

PASSENGER	AGE	SEX	OCCUPATION	PRIVL	DES
LIND, EWERT.	20	M	PNTR	FNZZZZ	USA

SHIP: ENGLAND

FROM: LIVERPOOL AND QUEENSTOWN
TO: NEW YORK
ARRIVED: 06 MAY 1889

PASSENGER	AGE	SEX	OCCUPATION	PRIVL	DES
NOYOK, HERMAN	30	M	LABR	RRZZZZ	NY
SOODERICK, JACOB	30	M	LABR	RRZZZZ	NY
MISOCHI, TOM	28	M	LABR	RRZZZZ	NY
WAWSEN, ZOEDORECK	40	M	LABR	RRZZZZ	NY
KOSKOWSKY, IGNATZ	37	M	LABR	RRZZZZ	NY
HUSEL, HERZ	20	M	LABR	RRZZZZ	NY
SLAMSKY, MICHE.	30	M	LABR	RRZZZZ	NY
ROZOLISCH, HANEON	28	M	LABR	RRZZZZ	NY
STOLNEICK, JOSEPH	19	M	LABR	RRZZZZ	NY
NASZADKA, STANISLAW	22	M	LABR	RRZZZZ	NY
ZUETOWSKY, ANTON	24	M	LABR	RRZZZZ	NY
GUTMAN, SCHEMAN	30	M	LABR	RRZZZZ	NY
HURKUS, WOLF	26	M	LABR	RRZZZZ	NY
SCHREUS, JACOB	24	M	LABR	RRZZZZ	NY
VANDERHINDEN, JOAB	24	M	LABR	RRZZZZ	NY
KLEMASZENSKY, RUDOLF	30	M	LABR	RRZZZZ	PHI
MARIA	31	F	W	RRZZZZ	PHI
ROSCHACK, MARIA	20	F	SP	RRZZZZ	CH
JANEWIEZ, ELIZABETH	48	F	W	RRZZZZ	BRO
MARY	11	F	CH	RRZZZZ	BRO
ELIZABETH	10	F	CH	RRZZZZ	BRO
ANDREW	8	M	CHILD	RRZZZZ	BRO
ELLEN	6	F	CHILD	RRZZZZ	BRO
GEOGE	1	M	CHILD	RRZZZZ	BRO
RASCHEWSKY, SCHEMEL	55	F	UNKNOWN	RRZZZZ	NY
LEA	19	F	SP	RRZZZZ	NY
GRINDBERG, OLSIE	45	F	W	RRZZZZ	NY
ROSA	15	F	SP	RRZZZZ	NY
FRITZ	1	M	CHILD	RRZZZZ	NY
KHLOWSKI, ANTON	26	M	LABR	RRZZZZ	NY

SHIP: ELBE

FROM: BREMEN AND SOUTHAMPTON
TO: NEW YORK
ARRIVED: 07 MAY 1889

PASSENGER	AGE	SEX	OCCUPATION	PRIVL	DES
LEWANDOWSKI, JAN	30	M	FARMER	RRZZZZ	NY
MOEZYNSKI, ANT.	44	M	FARMER	RRZZZZ	NY
KOCHEL, STANISL.	49	M	FARMER	RRZZZZ	NY
PAMCZYNSKY, JOH.	29	M	FARMER	RRZZZZ	NY
CYBURSKI, JAN	21	M	LABR	RRZZZZ	USA
BURWINSKI, JAN	27	M	LABR	RRZZZZ	USA
NEUMANN, GUST.	23	M	LABR	RRZZZZ	USA
LEH, GUST.	26	M	MCHT	RRZZZZ	NY
GIZEWSKI, JAN	40	M	LABR	RRZZZZ	NY
FEDOROWICZ, MARGAN	27	M	LABR	RRZZZZ	NY
STEFANSKI, VALENT.	18	M	LABR	RRZZZZ	OH
JOS	21	M	LABR	RRZZZZ	NY
DOGONSKI, FRANZ	32	M	LABR	RRZZZZ	OH
OTT, HEINR.	42	M	LABR	RRZZZZ	OH
DONBROWSKY, KONST.	21	M	LABR	RRZZZZ	OH
GORSKY, JOS.	27	M	LABR	RRZZZZ	OH
STAWICKY, STAN	40	M	LABR	RRZZZZ	NY
JOS.	37	M	LABR	RRZZZZ	NY
DOCHNOWSKY, U	44	M	LABR	RRZZZZ	NY
DESENROWICZ, JOS.	21	M	LABR	RRZZZZ	NY
RIOSCHNER, CARL	33	M	LABR	RRZZZZ	OH
DORN, ADOLPH	23	M	LABR	RRZZZZ	OH
RIEMER, JOH.	49	M	LABR	RRZZZZ	OH
JUL.	18	M	LABR	RRZZZZ	OH
DOBER, MIKOLAI	24	M	LABR	RRZZZZ	NY
BULIBYR, MICH.	24	M	LABR	RRZZZZ	NY
PAWLAK, JACUB	24	M	LABR	RRZZZZ	NY
BARTUMESCHAK, STAN.	24	M	LABR	RRZZZZ	NY
NABATZKI, FRANTISEK	24	M	LABR	RRZZZZ	NY
BLASZAK, JAN	22	M	LABR	RRZZZZ	PA
BUDKA, JOS.	26	M	LABR	RRZZZZ	PA
DUBKIEWICZ, JAC.	40	M	LABR	RRZZZZ	NY
FRIEDRICH, CARL	22	M	TLR	RRZZZZ	NY
KLATT, ANDRAS	50	M	SEMN	RRZZZZ	NY
KRUEGER, AUG.	32	M	UNKNOWN	RRZZZZ	NY
MUND, MICHAL	29	M	CL	RRZZZZ	NY
KUESSER, LUD.	26	M	MLR	RRZZZZ	NY
LIEDKE, JOSEF	45	M	SEMN	RRZZZZ	NY

PASSENGER	AGE	SEX	OCCUPATION	PRV VIL DES
LINZ, AUGUST	33	M	GDNR	RRZZZZNY
BERTHOLD, EMIL	24	M	FARMER	RRZZZZNY
RUESSLER, JOH.	28	M	FARMER	RRZZZZNY
RICHHOECZKY, KAZM.	30	M	LABR	RRZZZZNY
ULHOWSKY, U	50	M	LABR	RRZZZZNY
MOSKIWIENSKY, MART.	24	M	LABR	RRZZZZNY
KOMIENSKY, ADAM	22	M	LABR	RRZZZZNY
DERMEJKIS, ANT.	40	M	LABR	RRZZZZUSA
PAROCZKO, FRANZ	38	M	LABR	RRZZZZUSA
LACASCHEWICZ, JOS.	25	M	LABR	RRZZZZUSA
---SON, U	26	F	W	RRZZZZUSA
FEIGE	7	F	CHILD	RRZZZZUSA
DUMANCKY, ALEXANDRINE	21	F	W	RRZZZZNY
AND.	21	M	LABR	RRZZZZNY
KOWIELIZAK, FRANZ	30	M	FARMER	RRZZZZNY
FRANZ.	20	F	UNKNOWN	RRZZZZNY

SHIP: CITY OF PARIS

FROM: LIVERPOOL
TO: NEW YORK
ARRIVED: 08 MAY 1889

PASSENGER	AGE	SEX	OCCUPATION	PRV VIL DES
TUHONPOIKI, ELIAS	20	M	LABR	FNZZZZNY
KIEPONEN, ADI	26	M	LABR	FNZZZZNY
TEWMANPOIKI, JACKO	25	M	LABR	FNZZZZNY
LACKINSKY, STANISL.	28	M	LABR	FNZZZZPA
LIPKA, KARL	25	M	LABR	PLZZZZPA
MAKILA, ISAK	30	M	LABR	PLZZZZNY
MAILANEN, JUKA	40	M	MECH	PLAAYKNY
NOWICKI, J.	24	M	LABR	PLAAYKNY
HUKOTA, JUHS	25	M	LABR	PLAAYKNY
HEITOKANZOS, MALAKIAS	32	M	LABR	PLAAYKNY
JAAKOTA, JOHAN	23	M	LABR	PLACBFNY
PAAKOLOVOOVA, MATTI	25	M	LABR	PLACBFNY
SPULANSKY, MATEUS	21	M	LABR	PLACBFPA
STACHELEK, FRANZ	29	M	LABR	PLACBFPA
SALADIEGA, M.	44	M	LABR	PLACBFNY
SIROWEY, JOSEF	27	M	LABR	PLACBFNY
KIETTO, ELIAS	28	M	LABR	FNZZZZPA
WILLBERG, HEIKI	18	M	LABR	FNZZZZNY
WAHAMAX, ELIAS	20	M	LABR	FNZZZZPA
WAISANEN, MATTI	28	M	LABR	FNZZZZNY

SHIP: EIDER

FROM: BREMEN AND SOUTHAMPTON
TO: NEW YORK
ARRIVED: 10 MAY 1889

PASSENGER	AGE	SEX	OCCUPATION	PRV VIL DES
GLOGOCZEWSKI, ADAM	30	M	LABR	RRZZZZUSA
CIESILSKI, SZ.	23	M	LABR	RRZZZZUSA
PRZESACKI, STAN.	28	M	LABR	RRZZZZUSA
GRABOWSKI, PAW.	29	M	LABR	RRZZZZUSA
STANISZEWSKI, STAN.	21	M	LABR	RRZZZZUSA
WINNICKI, ANTONI	27	F	UNKNOWN	RRZZZZUSA
LUDJIKOWSKI, MACEJ	40	M	LABR	RRZZZZUSA
BORKOWSKI, JOSEF	30	M	LABR	RRZZZZUSA
FRANZKA.	24	F	W	RRZZZZUSA
ANIDA	19	F	UNKNOWN	RRZZZZUSA
JOSEFA	7	F	CHILD	RRZZZZUSA
MARTHA	3	F	CHILD	RRZZZZUSA
MARIANNA	2	F	CHILD	RRZZZZUSA
STANISLAUS	.06	M	INFANT	RRZZZZUSA
CHABEREK, U	23	M	LABR	RRZZZZUSA
SADOWSKI, STANISL.	41	M	LABR	RRZZZZUSA
SZUERJIK, JAN	23	M	LABR	RRZZZZUSA
JANISZESKI, ALEX	25	M	FARMER	RRZZZZUSA
SKOWRONSKI, ANT.	47	M	FARMER	RRZZZZUSA
LEWICKI, JAN	31	M	FARMER	RRZZZZUSA
FREI, JOHANN	26	M	LABR	RRZZZZUSA
CHRISTNE.	24	F	W	RRZZZZUSA
JOHANN	.06	M	INFANT	RRZZZZUSA
MARTEL, HEINR.	52	M	FARMER	RRZZZZUSA
MARIE	46	F	W	RRZZZZUSA
CARL	18	M	FARMER	RRZZZZUSA
DOERR, RUD.	29	M	FARMER	RRZZZZUSA
CAROLINE	29	F	W	RRZZZZUSA
JUSTINE	.06	F	INFANT	RRZZZZUSA
FREI, FRIEDR.	46	M	FARMER	RRZZZZUSA
CAROLINE	45	F	W	RRZZZZUSA
CHRISTINE	21	F	UNKNOWN	RRZZZZUSA
PHILIP	15	M	UNKNOWN	RRZZZZUSA
ALBINE	10	F	CH	RRZZZZUSA
JAKOB	8	M	CHILD	RRZZZZUSA
AUGUST	4	M	CHILD	RRZZZZUSA
CATHA.	18	F	UNKNOWN	RRZZZZUSA
ZILLNER, ADAM	24	M	FARMER	RRZZZZUSA
CATHARINA	24	F	W	RRZZZZUSA
LISBETH	1	F	CHILD	RRZZZZUSA
HANCK, JACOB	33	M	FARMER	RRZZZZUSA
CAROLINE	26	F	W	RRZZZZUSA
PHILIP	3	M	CHILD	RRZZZZUSA
CHRISTINE	.06	F	INFANT	RRZZZZUSA
KRAEMER, JACOB	29	M	FARMER	RRZZZZUSA
PHILIPPINE	27	F	W	RRZZZZUSA
CHRIST.	6	F	CHILD	RRZZZZUSA
MAGDA.	4	F	CHILD	RRZZZZUSA
JACOB	.06	M	INFANT	RRZZZZUSA
REGINA	14	F	UNKNOWN	RRZZZZUSA
GUSTE.	13	F	UNKNOWN	RRZZZZUSA
FREI, DANIEL	41	M	FARMER	RRZZZZUSA
EVA	41	F	W	RRZZZZUSA
CHRISTE.	16	F	UNKNOWN	RRZZZZUSA
ADOLF	8	M	CHILD	RRZZZZUSA
FRIEDR.	.06	M	INFANT	RRZZZZUSA
GOEHRING, JAC.	28	M	FARMER	RRZZZZUSA
MARGARETE	23	F	W	RRZZZZUSA
JOHANN	60	M	FARMER	RRZZZZUSA
SPRENGER, PHILIPP	29	M	FARMER	RRZZZZUSA
CHRISTE.	23	F	W	RRZZZZUSA
JACOB	.06	M	INFANT	RRZZZZUSA
ADAM	22	M	FARMER	RRZZZZUSA
ROSAINE	17	F	UNKNOWN	RRZZZZUSA
FRIEDR.	17	M	FARMER	RRZZZZUSA
PUDWILL, JOH.	47	M	FARMER	RRZZZZUSA
CAROLE.	38	F	W	RRZZZZUSA
DORA	20	F	UNKNOWN	RRZZZZUSA
JOHANN	14	M	UNKNOWN	RRZZZZUSA
JULIE	9	F	CHILD	RRZZZZUSA
LUDIA	7	F	CHILD	RRZZZZUSA
ROBERT	5	M	CHILD	RRZZZZUSA
JOHA.	3	F	CHILD	RRZZZZUSA
OTTO	.06	M	INFANT	RRZZZZUSA
JULIE	56	F	W	RRZZZZUSA
BROKOWSKI, CARL	37	M	FARMER	RRZZZZUSA
ELIDABETH	30	F	W	RRZZZZUSA
EMANUEL	6	M	CHILD	RRZZZZUSA
CARL	4	M	CHILD	RRZZZZUSA
HEINR.	2	M	CHILD	RRZZZZUSA
ALEX	.06	M	INFANT	RRZZZZUSA
BUCHHOLZ, ANDR.	51	M	FARMER	RRZZZZUSA
ANNA	42	F	W	RRZZZZUSA
CATHA.	16	F	UNKNOWN	RRZZZZUSA
LYDIA	10	F	CH	RRZZZZUSA
ANDRES	8	M	CHILD	RRZZZZUSA
JOH.	3	M	CHILD	RRZZZZUSA
MEIDINGER, CHRIST	45	M	FARMER	RRZZZZUSA
CHRISTE.	43	F	W	RRZZZZUSA
ROSINE	9	F	CHILD	RRZZZZUSA

PASSENGER	AGE	SEX	OCCUPATION	PRV VIL DES
GOTTLIEB	7	M	CHILD	RRZZZZUSA
JACOB	5	M	CHILD	RRZZZZUSA
CATHA.	3	F	CHILD	RRZZZZUSA
ADAM	.06	M	INFANT	RRZZZZUSA
KLEIN, SIMON	23	M	FARMER	RRZZZZUSA
CHRIST.	22	F	W	RRZZZZUSA
GEORG	3	M	CHILD	RRZZZZUSA
ELIDABETH	.06	F	INFANT	RRZZZZUSA
FISCHER, HEINR.	32	M	FARMER	RRZZZZUSA
JOH.	28	F	W	RRZZZZUSA
JACOB	2	M	CHILD	RRZZZZUSA
MEIER, GEORG	32	M	FARMER	RRZZZZUSA
CHRISTE.	32	F	W	RRZZZZUSA
CAROLE.	3	F	CHILD	RRZZZZUSA
CARL	.06	M	INFANT	RRZZZZUSA
FREI, PHILIPP	39	M	LABR	RRZZZZUSA
CAROLE.	37	F	W	RRZZZZUSA
CAROLE.	17	F	UNKNOWN	RRZZZZUSA
CATHA.	10	F	CH	RRZZZZUSA
GEORG	8	M	CHILD	RRZZZZUSA
ANDR.	7	M	CHILD	RRZZZZUSA
ALB.	5	F	CHILD	RRZZZZUSA
U	3	M	CHILD	RRZZZZUSA
CHRISTE.	2	F	CHILD	RRZZZZUSA
EVA	.06	F	INFANT	RRZZZZUSA
BECKER, PH.	44	M	FARMER	RRZZZZUSA
SOPHIE	44	F	W	RRZZZZUSA
CATHA.	21	F	UNKNOWN	RRZZZZUSA
MARGA.	19	F	UNKNOWN	RRZZZZUSA
JACOB	10	M	CH	RRZZZZUSA
CAROLE.	7	F	CHILD	RRZZZZUSA
CHRISTE	3	F	CHILD	RRZZZZUSA
MATHIAS	4	M	CHILD	RRZZZZUSA
THERESE	.06	F	INFANT	RRZZZZUSA
JUOSTARI, MARIA	24	F	W	FNZZZZUSA
ANNA	.05	F	INFANT	FNZZZZUSA
HANTAEKANGAS, JOH.	40	M	FARMER	FNZZZZUSA
LINDSTROEM, ERIK	32	M	FARMER	FNZZZZUSA
WUOLLAT, ALEXANDER	29	M	FARMER	FNZZZZUSA
AHO, ANTTI	19	M	FARMER	FNZZZZUSA
JOHANN	18	M	FARMER	FNZZZZUSA
RANTIO, ANDRU	32	M	FARMER	FNZZZZUSA
AHOMAKI, ALFRED	19	M	FARMER	FNZZZZUSA
MUSTIKKAMENNI, DANIEL	29	M	FARMER	FNZZZZUSA
ISOTALA, AUGUST	21	M	FARMER	FNZZZZUSA
BINTALA, INHA	19	M	FARMER	FNZZZZUSA
WAHALUMINIKKA, MATTS	31	M	FARMER	FNZZZZUSA
KELTTA, MATTS	24	M	FARMER	FNZZZZUSA
HELLA, GUST.	19	M	FARMER	FNZZZZUSA
ESTOLA, JOHANN	43	M	FARMER	FNZZZZUSA
RINTEMAEKI, JOHANN	26	M	FARMER	FNZZZZUSA
HORTANNI, SOFIA	21	F	UNKNOWN	FNZZZZUSA
MAENFAA, JOHANN	48	M	FARMER	FNZZZZUSA
RLTARI, JOAHNN	41	M	FARMER	FNZZZZUSA
KATTIKKI, FREDK.	18	M	FARMER	FNZZZZUSA
JAARILA, EM.	20	M	FARMER	FNZZZZUSA
KOIVISTO, JEREMIAS	34	M	FARMER	FNZZZZUSA
HANTALA, JAKOB	28	M	FARMER	FNZZZZUSA
MALAKAMAEKI, GUSTA	20	M	FARMER	FNZZZZUSA
FASNIEN, ADOLF	31	M	FARMER	FNZZZZUSA
FRAN	28	F	W	FNZZZZUSA
ILKA, SALOMON	36	M	LABR	FNZZZZUSA
KRANS, MATTS	21	M	LABR	FNZZZZUSA
ILOLA, ARON	47	M	LABR	FNZZZZUSA
GUSTAFSSON, MITTS	00	M	LABR	FNZZZZUSA
QUNTINEN, MATTI	37	M	LABR	FNZZZZUSA
CHRISTMANN, JACOB	30	M	LABR	RRZZZZUSA
EVA	27	F	W	RRZZZZUSA
JACOB	6	M	CHILD	RRZZZZUSA
WILH.	3	M	CHILD	RRZZZZUSA
JOHANNES	.06	M	INFANT	RRZZZZUSA
SCHROEDER, WILH.	20	M	LABR	RRZZZZUSA
GOLDMANN, KILMANN	26	M	MCHT	RRZZZZUSA
MATTSSON, HEIKKE	29	M	LABR	FNZZZZUSA
FRAN	26	F	W	FNZZZZUSA
KALAIPEN	3	M	CHILD	FNZZZZUSA
GRUENSPALM, INDEL	24	M	MCHT	RRZZZZUSA
GOLDE	20	F	W	RRZZZZUSA
WISKANTUS, KASUS	26	M	FARMER	RRZZZZUSA
SCHMIDT, CHAJE	27	F	UNKNOWN	RRZZZZUSA
HARTANO, ANDERS	28	M	FARMER	FNZZZZUSA

SHIP: GELLERT

FROM: HAMBURG AND HAVRE
TO: NEW YORK
ARRIVED: 11 MAY 1889

PASSENGER	AGE	SEX	OCCUPATION	PRV VIL DES
LAMUKA, JAN	33	M	UNKNOWN	FNAHUIUSA
JAN	33	M	UNKNOWN	FNAHUIUSA
SERACZKI, STANISLAV	29	M	UNKNOWN	FNAHUIUSA
MAZEZTZ, JAN	26	M	UNKNOWN	FNAHUIUSA
SAFRAN, JACOB	23	M	UNKNOWN	FNAHUIUSA
GOLONOWSKY, ANTONI	31	M	UNKNOWN	FNAHUIUSA
PERTA, ANTONI	30	M	UNKNOWN	FNAHUIUSA
KAINSKA, PATHA.	28	F	SGL	RRZZZZUSA
KNIPS, MARIE	19	F	SGL	RRAIECUSA
EMMA	13	F	UNKNOWN	RRAIECUSA
WERNER, DAVID	20	M	LABR	RRZZZZUSA
NETZLER, ROSA	18	F	UNKNOWN	RRZZZZUSA
KERNY, JOSEF	30	M	UNKNOWN	RRZZZZUSA
WALDMANN, JOH.	42	M	UNKNOWN	RRZZZZUSA
KARBINSKI, MICHAEL	42	M	UNKNOWN	RRZZZZUSA
SALEWSKI, ANTONI	58	M	UNKNOWN	RRAHUFUSA
OKCENSKI, JOSEF	22	M	LABR	RRAHUFUSA
BUNETZKI, FRANZ	28	M	LABR	RRAHUFUSA
PABLONSKI, JAN	23	M	LABR	RRAHUFUSA
STASZKOWSKI, JAN	32	M	LABR	RRAHUFUSA
FRANZ	25	M	LABR	RRAHUFUSA
RESCHINSKI, ULIAN	21	M	LABR	RRAHUFUSA
BJESCHINAKI, MATH.	27	M	LABR	RRAHUFUSA
SEPPELA, MATTS	26	M	LABR	FNZZZZUSA
KAASTO, DANIEL	28	M	LABR	FNZZZZUSA
MAHALA, LEANDER	40	M	LABR	FNZZZZUSA
SZCHIONA, JOH.	38	M	LABR	FNZZZZUSA
SCHAWINSKI, ULIAN	27	M	LABR	FNAHUFUSA
GAITKOWSKI, ANTONY	31	M	LABR	FNAHUFUSA
LEWANDOWSKI, JAN	35	M	LABR	FNAHUFUSA
WIEZNEWSKI, PELAGIA	29	F	SGL	FNAHUFUSA
BRUSKI, JAN	37	M	LABR	FNAHUFUSA
WICZNEWSKI, JULIAN	23	M	LABR	FNAHUFUSA
DOMBROWSK, ADAM	30	M	LABR	FNZZZZUSA
KOBSCHINSKI, JAN	21	M	LABR	FNZZZZUSA
FELIX	23	M	LABR	FNZZZZUSA
HAARANAN, ERIK	27	M	LABR	FNZZZZUSA
POSANEN, ANTTI	32	M	LABR	FNZZZZUSA
WAINIONPAA, ISAAC	40	M	LABR	FNZZZZUSA
MANNULA, HENRIK	32	M	LABR	FNZZZZUSA
WUERTOLA, SIMONSON	30	M	LABR	FNZZZZUSA
TONRUNEN, HENDRIK	25	M	LABR	FNZZZZUSA
SARKINIENEN, MATTS	30	M	LABR	FNZZZZUSA
HAARAENS, JOH.	30	M	LABR	FNZZZZUSA
SILLANPIA, THOMAS	25	M	LABR	FNZZZZUSA
KANGATIENI, HENRICHSEN	40	M	LABR	FNZZZZUSA
PALDANI, AXEL	29	M	LABR	FNZZZZUSA
LIKALA, HENRIK	28	M	LABR	FNZZZZUSA
POSPANEN, MATTS	25	M	LABR	FNZZZZUSA
KIRSMINEN, JOH.	25	M	LABR	FNZZZZUSA
PEURALA, JOHANSON	52	M	LABR	FNZZZZUSA
LAPPENEN, MATS	28	M	LABR	FNZZZZUSA
ARGELONELER, EVA	30	F	SGL	FNZZZZUSA
NIEMILI, ENOCH	30	M	LABR	FNZZZZUSA
TURPEISEN, MATTS	23	M	LABR	FNZZZZUSA
MARA, ERIK	17	M	LABR	FNZZZZUSA
SUREDS, JOH.	27	M	LABR	FNZZZZUSA

PASSENGER	AGE	SEX	OCCUPATION	PV RIV L	D E S
HANKILATHS, JOH.	23	M	LABR	FNZZZZ	USA
ANDRUCZIK, JAN	28	M	LABR	FNAHZS	USA
RULOTSCH, JOHN	48	M	LABR	FNAHZS	USA
ANNA	34	F	W	FNAHZS	USA
BAJKOWSKI, JOSEF	33	M	LABR	FNAHUI	USA
STEZNARSKI, STANISLAUS	31	M	LABR	FNAHUI	USA
MACELKOWSKI, JAN	48	M	LABR	FNAHUI	USA
TUSENSKI, JAN	41	M	LABR	FNAHUI	USA
SERENA, IGNATZ	19	M	LABR	FNAHUI	USA
PUTNICZKI, JAN	47	M	LABR	FNAHUI	USA
LUKASEWSKI, JOSEF	38	M	LABR	FNAHUI	USA
BRAVORSKI, ANTON	39	M	LABR	FNAHUI	USA
SWIDNSKI, ANTON	27	M	LABR	FNAHUI	USA
SLOTKI, JUDEL	27	M	LABR	FNAHUI	USA
BUTKEWIEZ, IBNAT	39	M	LABR	RRZZZZ	USA
KORYNKIEWICZ, JOSEF	28	M	LABR	RRZZZZ	USA
KEWCZYNEK, STANISLAUS	28	M	LABR	RRZZZZ	USA
RYBACKI, FRANZ	26	M	LABR	RRZZZZ	USA
SZEPAN	23	M	LABR	RRZZZZ	USA
KONECKY, MORITZ	40	M	UNKNOWN	RRAFWJ	USA
CAECILIE	38	F	W	RRAFWJ	USA
ESTHER	7	F	CHILD	RRAFWJ	USA
PESA	6	F	CHILD	RRAFWJ	USA
HERZ	5	M	CHILD	RRAFWJ	USA
JOSEF	4	M	CHILD	RRAFWJ	USA
STOSZINSKA, EWIA	27	F	WO	RRZZZZ	USA
LUDWIG	3	M	CHILD	RRZZZZ	USA
MILEWSKY, JULIAN	17	M	LABR	RRZZZZ	USA
BURDA, JANOS	60	M	LABR	RRAHUL	USA
SARA	50	F	W	RRAHUL	USA
PIKZELINGER, JERZEJ	22	M	LABR	RRAHZS	USA
WLADESCH, FRANCEK	23	M	LABR	RRZZZZ	USA
ADAMEK, MELCHIOR	25	M	LABR	RRZZZZ	USA
ZIMACHUWITZ, ISRAEL	28	M	DLR	RRAHQU	USA
RATSCHINKOSTI, PETER	17	M	LABR	RRZZZZ	USA
TIKALOWSKI, JAN	40	M	LABR	RRZZZZ	USA
JANKATZKAS, JURGIS	30	M	LABR	RRAHVJ	USA
ELISABETA	28	F	W	RRAHVJ	USA
MOELLER, FRANZ	32	M	LABR	RRZZZZ	USA
ZABORNI, IGNATZ	48	M	LABR	RRZZZZ	USA
ZATORSKI, FRANZ	43	M	LABR	RRZZZZ	USA
SPLIET, ANTONIA	24	F	WO	RRAHUI	USA
JOHA.	.11	F	INFANT	RRAHUI	USA
MARIANNE	.01	F	INFANT	RRAHUI	USA
NOWAKOWSKY, JOSEF	23	M	LABR	RRAHUI	USA
NISCHMISKY, JAN	23	M	LABR	RRAHUI	USA
CZARNEWSKY, ANTON	23	M	LABR	RRAHUI	USA
ERSCHNISKY, JOSEF	25	M	LABR	RRAHUI	USA
TEGNISKY, JOSEF	25	M	LABR	RRAHUI	USA
GORCINSKY, JAN	24	M	LABR	RRAHUI	USA
PSCHEBOROWSKY, ANTON	19	M	LABR	RRAHUI	USA
KRULL, JOSEF	23	M	LABR	RRAHUI	USA
JUCHS, JACOB	33	M	LABR	RRAHUI	USA

SHIP: ALLER

FROM: BREMEN AND SOUTHAMPTON
TO: NEW YORK
ARRIVED: 11 MAY 1889

PASSENGER	AGE	SEX	OCCUPATION	PV RIV L	D E S
BUSKEWIEZ, JOSAPPAT	30	M	LABR	RRZZZZ	USA
ZOLT, ADOLF	18	M	LABR	RRZZZZ	USA
FEUSKE, LUDW.	38	M	LABR	RRZZZZ	USA
MANTHER, HERM.	32	M	LABR	RRZZZZ	USA
BUESKEWISZ, JAN	24	M	FARMER	RRZZZZ	USA
WITHUS, JOSEF	25	M	LABR	RRZZZZ	USA
GLIKNA, PETER	23	M	LABR	RRZZZZ	USA
MIKOTOIS, BUTROIN	30	M	LABR	RRZZZZ	USA
LIEBERMANN, JACOB	17	M	FARMER	RRZZZZ	USA
LISCHENSKI, STEFAN	25	M	FARMER	RRZZZZ	USA
BR---WSKY, FRANZ	34	M	FARMER	RRZZZZ	USA
VI---KY, FRANZ	23	M	FARMER	RRZZZZ	USA
KOBBUSKY, JAN	20	M	FARMER	RRZZZZ	USA
SLIEPIRSKY, FRANZ	26	M	FARMER	RRZZZZ	USA
ZOKRZEWSKI, ANTON	25	M	FARMER	RRZZZZ	USA
KILINSKI, ANT.	26	M	LABR	RRZZZZ	USA
WARSCHEFSKY, TOMAS	40	M	LABR	RRZZZZ	USA
EPPIG, MATHIAS	28	M	LABR	RRZZZZ	USA
WOLFF, LUDWIG	40	M	LABR	RRZZZZ	USA
PFEIFFER, HENRY	17	M	LABR	RRZZZZ	USA
KASELEINSKA, JOSEFA	19	F	UNKNOWN	RRZZZZ	USA
MURAWSKA, MARIANNE	23	F	UNKNOWN	RRZZZZ	USA
WADISL.	2	M	CHILD	RRZZZZ	USA
MAGDALENA	24	F	UNKNOWN	RRZZZZ	USA
MUELLER, JOHANN	37	M	LABR	RRZZZZ	USA
MARGAR.	36	F	W	RRZZZZ	USA
JACOB	7	M	CHILD	RRZZZZ	USA
CATH.	6	F	CHILD	RRZZZZ	USA
JOH.	4	M	CHILD	RRZZZZ	USA
ADAM	.11	M	INFANT	RRZZZZ	USA
REISER, CARL	28	M	LABR	RRZZZZ	USA
SOPHIE	26	F	W	RRZZZZ	USA
ELISABWTH	3	F	CHILD	RRZZZZ	USA
CARL	.06	M	INFANT	RRZZZZ	USA
MULLER, ADAM	29	M	LABR	RRZZZZ	USA
BARB.	24	F	W	RRZZZZ	USA
JACOB	.10	M	INFANT	RRZZZZ	USA
REISER, FRIEDR.	22	M	LABR	RRZZZZ	USA
ELISABETH	20	F	W	RRZZZZ	USA
LAUT, JOH.	33	M	FARMER	RRZZZZ	USA
MAGD.	29	F	W	RRZZZZ	USA
ROSINE	7	F	CHILD	RRZZZZ	USA
U	2	F	CHILD	RRZZZZ	USA
JOHANN	.07	M	INFANT	RRZZZZ	USA
ZIEGLER, CHRIST.	56	M	LABR	RRZZZZ	USA
CHRIST.	56	F	W	RRZZZZ	USA
JACOB	19	M	LABR	RRZZZZ	USA
CHRIST.	21	F	W	RRZZZZ	USA
BACHMEYER, ELI.	42	M	LABR	RRZZZZ	USA
LISBET.	40	F	UNKNOWN	RRZZZZ	USA
EVA	15	F	CH	RRZZZZ	USA
FRANZ	7	M	CHILD	RRZZZZ	USA
CATH.	6	F	CHILD	RRZZZZ	USA
PHILIPP	3	M	CHILD	RRZZZZ	USA
LUCIANNA	2	F	CHILD	RRZZZZ	USA
MICHAL	.09	M	INFANT	RRZZZZ	USA
KLAFF, HEIN.	23	M	JNR	RRZZZZ	USA
MARG.	22	F	W	RRZZZZ	USA
LEIB	2	F	CHILD	RRZZZZ	USA
HEIN.	.07	M	INFANT	RRZZZZ	USA
BECKER, PETER	34	M	GDNR	RRZZZZ	USA
ELISAB.	30	F	W	RRZZZZ	USA
ROSINA	7	F	CHILD	RRZZZZ	USA
PETER	6	M	CHILD	RRZZZZ	USA
CHRIST.	4	F	CHILD	RRZZZZ	USA
JOHANN	3	M	CHILD	RRZZZZ	USA
HEINR.	.08	M	INFANT	RRZZZZ	USA
PFAFF, HEIN.	45	M	LABR	RRZZZZ	USA
OTTILIE	43	F	W	RRZZZZ	USA
SIMON	17	M	LABR	RRZZZZ	USA
BARB.	15	F	UNKNOWN	RRZZZZ	USA
CATH.	7	F	CHILD	RRZZZZ	USA
OTTILIE	6	F	CHILD	RRZZZZ	USA
JOH.	5	M	CHILD	RRZZZZ	USA
MAGD.	4	F	CHILD	RRZZZZ	USA
ROSINE	3	F	CHILD	RRZZZZ	USA
CHRISTIAN	.11	M	INFANT	RRZZZZ	USA
RITZ, DANIEL	27	M	LABR	RRZZZZ	USA
FRIED.	25	F	W	RRZZZZ	USA
ELISAB.	64	F	UNKNOWN	RRZZZZ	USA
MUELLER, PHILIPP	57	M	LABR	RRZZZZ	USA
ROSINE	26	F	W	RRZZZZ	USA
PHILIPP	7	M	CHILD	RRZZZZ	USA
JOSEPH	6	M	CHILD	RRZZZZ	USA
MARTIN	5	M	CHILD	RRZZZZ	USA

PASSENGER	AGE	SEX	OCCUPATION	PV RI VL	DES
ELISAB.	.09	F	INFANT	RRZZZZ	USA
ROSINE	.09	F	INFANT	RRZZZZ	USA
KRAMER, JOS.	28	M	CPTR	RRZZZZ	USA
CHRIST.	26	F	W	RRZZZZ	USA
CHRIST.	2	F	CHILD	RRZZZZ	USA
GOLDNER, DOROTHEA	48	F	UNKNOWN	RRZZZZ	USA
EMIL	7	M	CHILD	RRZZZZ	USA
ESTER	6	M	CHILD	RRZZZZ	USA

SHIP: SERVIA

FROM: LIVERPOOL AND QUEENSTOWN
TO: NEW YORK
ARRIVED: 13 MAY 1889

PASSENGER	AGE	SEX	OCCUPATION	PV RI VL	DES
MAKOLIN, JOH.	36	M	LABR	RRZZZZ	MI
MATTBAK, AND.	30	M	LABR	RRZZZZ	MI
MAKINEN, JOHAN	28	M	LABR	RRZZZZ	NY
MALOMOKI, MATTE	27	M	LABR	RRZZZZ	NY
NUMAN, JOHAN	24	M	LABR	RRZZZZ	MI
HENPI, KARL	27	M	LABR	RRZZZZ	MI
KARTESOJA, JAKOB	57	M	LABR	RRZZZZ	NY
KUKUMENIE, MATH.	30	M	LABR	RRZZZZ	NY
KARE, JOHN	25	M	SLR	RRZZZZ	NY
BLANK, JOHN	21	M	TLR	RRZZZZ	NY
PJILLIP	19	M	TLR	RRZZZZ	NY
ANTINOJA, JERMIAS	35	M	LABR	RRZZZZ	WI
ANDIO, HENNAN	18	M	LABR	RRZZZZ	NY
WARTI, JULIUS	17	M	LABR	RRZZZZ	NY
LARSFOLK, CHAS.	26	M	LABR	RRZZZZ	IL
CARLSON, JOHAN	20	M	LABR	RRZZZZ	MI
OSK.	20	M	LABR	RRZZZZ	MN
ERKILA, ISAK	20	M	LABR	RRZZZZ	OH
MATTE	43	M	LABR	RRZZZZ	OH
ERIKSON, JOHAN	37	M	LABR	RRZZZZ	UNK
FRACSOIK, ERIK	27	M	LABR	RRZZZZ	NY
MANNINEN, KATHE.	20	F	SP	RRZZZZ	NY
SEPPANEN, BRITTA	57	F	MA	RRZZZZ	NY
HENDRICK	11	M	CH	RRZZZZ	NY
PENNIVORA, JOH.	31	M	LABR	RRZZZZ	MI
KAJSA	23	F	W	RRZZZZ	MI
WELLERSTEIN, JOHN	49	M	UNKNOWN	RRZZZZ	USA

SHIP: LYDIAN MONARCH

FROM: LONDON
TO: NEW YORK
ARRIVED: 13 MAY 1889

PASSENGER	AGE	SEX	OCCUPATION	PV RI VL	DES
SEMELMACHER, J.	20	M	PNTR	FNZZZZ	NY
GMELINGER, JACOB	12	M	UNKNOWN	FNZZZZ	NY

SHIP: WYOMING

FROM: LIVERPOOL AND QUEENSTOWN
TO: NEW YORK
ARRIVED: 15 MAY 1889

PASSENGER	AGE	SEX	OCCUPATION	PV RI VL	DES
ANDERSSON, HULD.C.	35	F	W	FNZZZZ	USA
HEROGA, ELIAS	18	M	PMBR	FNZZZZ	USA

PASSENGER	AGE	SEX	OCCUPATION	PV RI VL	DES
IVERSSON, GERIN	52	M	UNKNOWN	PLZZZZ	USA
KORSWSKY, JACOB	25	M	GZR	PLZZZZ	USA
BRALOSTOTZKI, SACHIE	26	M	GZR	PLZZZZ	USA
STAIKUILE, DOMK.	20	M	GZR	PLZZZZ	USA
KOPANKA, KOMCA.	28	M	GZR	PLZZZZ	USA
KILISKI, GABRIEL	28	M	GZR	PLZZZZ	USA
BRANCK, ROSE	31	F	W	PLZZZZ	USA
MILDORF, ANNIE	3	F	CHILD	PLZZZZ	USA
NEUMAN, TOBIAS	24	M	TLR	PLZZZZ	USA
FISCHMANN, HOFFMAN	21	M	TLR	PLZZZZ	USA
BLANTTEIN, RATAN	18	M	TLR	PLZZZZ	USA
LEFKOWITZ, ANNA	18	F	SP	PLZZZZ	USA
BUCHOCHINEWSKI, SORE	18	M	MSN	PLZZZZ	USA
WIRNBLEWSKI, MICHL.	18	M	MSN	PLZZZZ	USA
BEROL	7	M	CHILD	PLZZZZ	USA
PINDAK, ANTOIN	23	M	MSN	FNZZZZ	USA
MACAS, FRANZ	30	M	MSN	FNZZZZ	USA
JACEWIEZ, CAPOLIT	34	M	MSN	PLZZZZ	USA
SCHARF, WELHELM	42	M	MSN	PLZZZZ	USA
FISCHMAN, SCHMON	.02	F	INFANT	PLZZZZ	USA
NADCLAM, JANKEL	24	M	PMBR	PLZZZZ	USA
HIKASKY, JOHAN	38	M	PMBR	PLZZZZ	USA
TWOMIAHO, JOHAN	39	M	PMBR	FNZZZZ	USA
JOKEAHO, JOHAN	20	M	PMBR	FNZZZZ	USA
VELIAHS, JOHN	23	M	PMBR	FNZZZZ	USA
MAYENPAN, ERHKI	25	M	PNTR	FNZZZZ	USA
GMUSA, JOHAN	26	M	PNTR	FNZZZZ	USA
HASTERHOHN, ADOLF	19	M	PNTR	FNZZZZ	USA
WUTEMAKI, JOHAN	23	M	PNTR	FNZZZZ	USA
POKJALA, JOHN	21	M	PNTR	FNZZZZ	USA
ISOSOARI, MATTE	30	M	PNTR	FNZZZZ	USA
HAKALA, MIHKO	18	M	BKR	FNZZZZ	USA
TIPPALES, JOHAN	23	M	BKR	FNZZZZ	USA
WAEPOA, APA	28	M	BKR	FNZZZZ	USA
ANTILLA, WILHELM	31	M	BKR	FNZZZZ	USA
WARTONEN, ELIAS	28	M	BKR	FNZZZZ	USA
HENRIK	30	M	FARMER	FNZZZZ	USA
RINTELAN, DAVID	19	M	FARMER	FNZZZZ	USA
DIKARE, ERIK	28	M	FARMER	FNZZZZ	USA
WARTONEN, OTTO	25	M	FARMER	FNZZZZ	USA
ZITTLAS, GABRIEL	19	M	FARMER	FNZZZZ	USA
GRANFORS, JOSEF	28	M	FARMER	FNZZZZ	USA
GMASA, CARL	32	M	BKR	FNZZZZ	USA
HAGSTROM, ISAK	20	M	BKR	FNZZZZ	USA
PIETALA, HENRIK	34	M	BKR	FNZZZZ	USA
KARJANEN, ELIAS	25	M	MSN	FNZZZZ	USA
SAKKI, MATTS	35	M	MSN	FNZZZZ	USA
TWIE, THOMAS	40	M	MSN	FNZZZZ	USA
KANTOLA, MATTS	26	M	MSN	FNZZZZ	USA
ALLILA, JACOB	30	M	MSN	FNZZZZ	USA
ANNULA, MATTS	30	M	MSN	FNZZZZ	USA
LOASANEN, JACOB	29	M	UNKNOWN	FNZZZZ	USA
OLSEN, JOHAN	33	M	UNKNOWN	FNZZZZ	USA
LEINATAINEN, JOHAN	27	M	UNKNOWN	FNZZZZ	USA
RASI, JOHAN	34	M	UNKNOWN	FNZZZZ	USA
LAURAMAKI, KOSTANTINE	51	M	UNKNOWN	FNZZZZ	USA
MAKILOSKO, ALBERT	51	M	UNKNOWN	FNZZZZ	USA
PONTINEN, GUSTAF	27	M	MNR	FNZZZZ	USA
SIRILA, MATTI	25	M	MNR	FNZZZZ	USA
NIEMANEN, MATTI	31	M	MNR	FNZZZZ	USA
KUHMUNEN, JOHAN	30	M	MNR	FNZZZZ	USA
SILVONEN, TIMS	25	M	MNR	FNZZZZ	USA
PAHJASMAKI, ALPHA	26	M	MNR	FNZZZZ	USA
FEROMAKI, KRISTIAN	34	M	SMH	FNZZZZ	USA
ISAKYYTI, KRISTIAN	28	M	SMH	FNZZZZ	USA
HONKYOKI, JOHAN	26	M	SMH	FNZZZZ	USA
JUSSILO, HENRICK	32	M	SMH	FNZZZZ	USA
NORALA, JOHAN	45	M	SMH	FNZZZZ	USA
DAHMEN, KARL	26	M	SMH	FNZZZZ	USA
ANDERSSON, JAN	24	M	PMBR	FNZZZZ	USA
PERRAS, JOHAN	28	M	PMBR	FNZZZZ	USA
ROPS, JOHANNES	23	M	PMBR	FNZZZZ	USA
SKON, CARL	36	M	PMBR	FNZZZZ	USA
BERG, GABRIEL	20	M	PMBR	FNZZZZ	USA
SKALD, MATTS	23	M	PMBR	FNZZZZ	USA

PASSENGER	AGE	SEX	OCCUPATION	PRV VIL DES
ROHS, JOSEF	20	M	PMBR	FNZZZZUSA
FRONAS, ERIK	31	M	PNTR	FNZZZZUSA
JASKARI, SOLOMON	44	M	PNTR	FNZZZZUSA
HERMANSON, GERARD	19	M	PNTR	FNZZZZUSA
OJALA, HORMAN	30	M	PNTR	FNZZZZUSA
HANTAMAKI, HEIKI	20	M	PNTR	FNZZZZUSA
RAJALA, JOHAN	24	M	PNTR	FNZZZZUSA
ALEX	24	F	W	FNZZZZUSA
JOLKARI, MATTI	20	M	UNKNOWN	FNZZZZUSA
HAPARANDA, ALEX	20	M	UNKNOWN	FNZZZZUSA
UNGARI, JOHAN	20	M	UNKNOWN	FNZZZZUSA
SIVE, JACOB	50	M	UNKNOWN	FNZZZZUSA
JOHAN	19	M	UNKNOWN	FNZZZZUSA
WUSRENMOA, ANTI	23	M	UNKNOWN	FNZZZZUSA
LAPISTO, MALAPIA	28	M	TLR	FNZZZZUSA
KEROLA, JAKOB	19	M	TLR	FNZZZZUSA
GRANAD, THOMAS	23	M	TLR	FNZZZZUSA
AHO, GUSTAF	20	M	TLR	FNZZZZUSA
LEIPKORI, VICKOLAUS	34	M	TLR	FNZZZZUSA
UNTIO, MATTS	20	M	PLSTR	FNZZZZUSA
WALLIMALKI, ELIAS	36	M	PLSTR	FNZZZZUSA
SOAPELTO, KALLE	26	M	PLSTR	FNZZZZUSA
KALTIALA, JOHAN	44	M	PLSTR	FNZZZZUSA
LIENATAINEN, HENDRIK	30	M	BKR	FNZZZZUSA
KAIKELANEN, ANTTI	40	M	BKR	FNZZZZUSA
KARLSOON, NESTA	24	M	MSN	FNZZZZUSA
MAKINEN, ALEX	30	M	MSN	FNZZZZUSA
MATTSON, VISTAR	36	M	MSN	FNZZZZUSA
SWEDS, KARL	49	M	MSN	FNZZZZUSA
MICHILSON, ERIK	42	M	MSN	FNZZZZUSA
ERIK	35	M	MSN	FNZZZZUSA
ANNA	36	F	W	FNZZZZUSA
JAHANSSON, KARL	18	M	MNR	FNZZZZUSA
ENET, MARKUS	17	M	MNR	FNZZZZUSA
ROSENKOF, JOHAN	25	M	MNR	FNZZZZUSA
ENGELGVIST, ALEX	25	M	MNR	FNZZZZUSA
WESKEHOHN, GABRIEL	45	M	MNR	FNZZZZUSA
JOAHNSON, AUGUST	30	M	MNR	FNZZZZUSA
LAPPIETO, ERIK	44	M	UNKNOWN	FNZZZZUSA
ERIK	44	M	UNKNOWN	FNZZZZUSA
KLENANEN, ERIK	36	M	UNKNOWN	FNZZZZUSA
RAWENA, MATTS	21	M	UNKNOWN	FNZZZZUSA
LEPISTO, ABRAM	44	M	UNKNOWN	FNZZZZUSA
RANTALA, ABRAHAM	33	M	UNKNOWN	FNZZZZUSA
ALAKOSKI, ABRAHAM	27	M	TLR	FNZZZZUSA
MATTILA, MATTS	44	M	TLR	FNZZZZUSA
KANALD, ANDERS	26	M	TLR	FNZZZZUSA
BACHMAN, ERIK	27	M	TLR	FNZZZZUSA
RYMAN, JOHAN	30	M	TLR	FNZZZZUSA
HOGLUD, VIKTOR	20	M	TLR	FNZZZZUSA
ENTBACHA, JOHAN	20	M	UNKNOWN	FNZZZZUSA
WITSGO, VIKTOR	18	M	UNKNOWN	FNZZZZUSA
JOHAN	23	M	UNKNOWN	FNZZZZUSA
GASTGIVAS, JOHAN	18	M	UNKNOWN	FNZZZZUSA
KAUPELS, MATTA	20	M	QA	FNZZZZUSA
RIEMILA, ALEX	20	M	QA	FNZZZZUSA
MARTAIS, JOHAN	33	M	QA	FNZZZZUSA
HILLI, HENRIK	20	M	PMBR	FNZZZZUSA
JUSTIN, ANDERS	20	M	PMBR	FNZZZZUSA
WATTALA, KARL	37	M	PMBR	FNZZZZUSA
HELLBERG, ERIK	42	M	PMBR	FNZZZZUSA
ALASTRAA, ERIK	30	M	PMBR	FNZZZZUSA
ALEX	42	M	PMBR	FNZZZZUSA
WAHAMOTTENEN, JACOB	20	M	PNTR	FNZZZZUSA
ROCKI, SERAFIA	21	M	PNTR	FNZZZZUSA
POKOI, SOFIA	19	F	SP	FNZZZZUSA
RORKO, AUGUST	32	M	MLR	FNZZZZUSA
JYLHO, MATTS	23	M	MLR	FNZZZZUSA
PAHKI, MATTS	34	M	MLR	FNZZZZUSA
MAKINEN, ERIK	41	M	MLR	FNZZZZUSA
KOSKI, HERMANN	27	M	MLR	FNZZZZUSA
SANTOGO, BARTH.	22	M	MLR	FNZZZZUSA
MASTOMAKI, JOHAN	23	M	BKR	FNZZZZUSA
LUOMANEN, GUS.	20	M	BKR	FNZZZZUSA
LAUSMAKI, ERIK	23	M	BKR	FNZZZZUSA

PASSENGER	AGE	SEX	OCCUPATION	PRV VIL DES
ISOVILME, MATHIAS	23	M	BKR	FNZZZZUSA
HARGU, NIKOLAI	34	M	BKR	FNZZZZUSA
ERIKSON, JONAS	34	M	BKR	FNZZZZUSA
STUBB, ERIK	26	M	LABR	FNZZZZUSA
NUGARD, MATTS	21	M	LABR	FNZZZZUSA
ROGBY, MATTS	18	M	LABR	FNZZZZUSA
NYBERGER, KARL	33	M	LABR	FNZZZZUSA
CARLSSON, AXEL	33	M	LABR	FNZZZZUSA
PETTERSSON, KNUT	21	M	LABR	FNZZZZUSA
TALVITIA, ALEX	34	M	LABR	FNZZZZUSA
AHOHAS, JACOB	32	M	LABR	FNZZZZUSA
HANKOMAKI, NIKOLAI	31	M	LABR	FNZZZZUSA
LASSILA, HEIKA	53	M	LABR	FNZZZZUSA
HAKOLA, EUS.J.	27	M	LABR	FNZZZZUSA
RAJOLA, JACOB	28	M	LABR	FNZZZZUSA
PATSEMPARA, HERKS	26	M	LABR	FNZZZZUSA
HANDBAKA, JOHAN	36	M	LABR	FNZZZZUSA
TANBACKA, JOHAN	24	M	MNR	FNZZZZUSA
MAKARI, GUS.	32	M	MNR	FNZZZZUSA
WILKI, MATTI	27	M	MNR	FNZZZZUSA
KALKA, CONSTANTIN	28	M	MNR	FNZZZZUSA
PARRALLA, GUS.	34	M	MNR	FNZZZZUSA
PERNA, JOHAN	19	M	CBLR	FNZZZZUSA
ZUANA, FRED.	24	M	CBLR	FNZZZZUSA
NISMI, NICKOLA	18	M	CBLR	FNZZZZUSA
ORAND, VALENTINE	25	M	CBLR	FNZZZZUSA
HARGILL, ELIZ	23	F	SP	FNZZZZUSA
BACKOTROM, PETER	20	M	FARMER	FNZZZZUSA

SHIP: WERRA

FROM: BREMEN AND SOUTHAMPTON
TO: NEW YORK
ARRIVED: 15 MAY 1889

PASSENGER	AGE	SEX	OCCUPATION	PRV VIL DES
JAROWSKY, HIRSCH	17	M	MCHT	RRZZZZUSA
RUBINOWITZ, SELIG	18	M	MCHT	RRZZZZUSA
TOSTAPWITCH, JOSEFA	22	F	UNKNOWN	RRZZZZUSA
IZBRECHT, MICHAELE	25	F	UNKNOWN	RRZZZZUSA
GEISIK, WOLL	52	M	MCHT	RRZZZZUSA
FREITAG, FRIEDRICH	29	M	GDNR	RRZZZZUSA
BERTHA	26	F	UNKNOWN	RRZZZZUSA
MARTHA	.11	F	INFANT	RRZZZZUSA
KIJEWSKY, PAWEL	26	M	LABR	RRZZZZUSA
PASCHUETZKY, PAWEL	22	M	UNKNOWN	RRZZZZUSA
KRAWZIK, ANDRAS	32	M	UNKNOWN	RRZZZZUSA
PALAWEJUS, ZWINKA	26	F	UNKNOWN	RRZZZZUSA
LOGORSKY, U	25	M	LABR	RRZZZZUSA
SCHADON, SAMSON	25	M	LABR	RRZZZZUSA
SCHOMSKY, VICENTY	26	M	LABR	RRZZZZUSA
KOLESA, MARTENS	30	M	LABR	RRZZZZUSA
ORZECKOWSKY, JAN	15	M	LABR	RRZZZZUSA
DOELKER, JACOB	35	M	LABR	RRZZZZUSA
REGINA	34	F	UNKNOWN	RRZZZZUSA
MATHILDE	15	F	UNKNOWN	RRZZZZUSA
EMANUEL	7	M	CHILD	RRZZZZUSA
NATHAN	6	M	CHILD	RRZZZZUSA
CARIE	4	F	CHILD	RRZZZZUSA
GOTTHILF	.09	M	INFANT	RRZZZZUSA
OWCZACAK, ANDREAS	22	M	LABR	RRZZZZUSA
PAWLAC, LEON	31	M	LABR	RRZZZZUSA
JASCHINSKY, FRANZ	37	M	LABR	RRZZZZUSA
STACHOWIAK, MICHAEL	30	M	LABR	RRZZZZUSA
PRZYBOROWSKY, JACOB	30	M	LABR	RRZZZZUSA
STRECKER, GOTTLIEB	35	M	LABR	RRZZZZUSA
SANDLER, SAL.	44	M	LABR	RRZZZZUSA
MAKOWSKY, KAZM.	27	M	FARMER	RRZZZZUSA
WIRANI, MARIE	29	M	FARMER	RRZZZZUSA
BEIGES, BALTR.	22	M	FARMER	RRZZZZUSA
MILUS, MARCIN	17	M	FARMER	RRZZZZUSA

PASSENGER	AGE	SEX	OCCUPATION	PRV VIL DES
SIESNOWITZ, U	18	M	LABR	RRZZZZUSA
LUTZ, LEONHARD	23	M	LABR	RRZZZZUSA
SUCHOSKY, ADAM	30	M	LABR	RRZZZZUSA
RISCHOWSKY, ALAX	28	M	LABR	RRZZZZUSA
KUSESKY, FRERICK	26	M	LABR	RRZZZZUSA
RZEPNICKY, JAN	30	M	LABR	RRZZZZUSA
SCHWETNITZKAS, JOSAS	24	M	LABR	RRZZZZUSA
LAPINSKY, WINSEUS	22	M	LABR	RRZZZZUSA
KUNIGANI, JERSEI	19	M	LABR	RRZZZZUSA
LUBANIRSKY, IGNATZ	29	M	LABR	RRZZZZUSA
PETZKUS, MARCIN	22	M	LABR	RRZZZZUSA
JANOWITZ, MATEUS	23	M	LABR	RRZZZZUSA
MUENZ, CARL	7	M	CHILD	RRZZZZUSA
SEEBECK, JOHANNA	18	F	UNKNOWN	RRZZZZUSA
HOCHHATTER, CHRISTIAN	30	M	FARMER	RRZZZZUSA
MAGDA.	26	F	UNKNOWN	RRZZZZUSA
RUDOLF	.11	M	INFANT	RRZZZZUSA
THURN, JOHANN	18	M	FARMER	RRZZZZUSA
ZIMMERMANN, GOTTLIEB	27	M	FARMER	RRZZZZUSA
FRIEDERIKE	20	M	FARMER	RRZZZZUSA
KERDER, JOHANN	36	M	LABR	RRZZZZUSA
MARGARETHA	6	F	CHILD	RRZZZZUSA
GOTTLIEB	4	M	CHILD	RRZZZZUSA
JOHANN	.11	M	INFANT	RRZZZZUSA
CATHARINE	30	F	UNKNOWN	RRZZZZUSA
BOLLINGER, JACOB	50	M	LABR	RRZZZZUSA
BERTHA	47	F	UNKNOWN	RRZZZZUSA
JOHANN	20	M	TLR	RRZZZZUSA
ELISE	18	F	UNKNOWN	RRZZZZUSA
U	8	M	CHILD	RRZZZZUSA
FRIEDRICH	6	M	CHILD	RRZZZZUSA
ROSINE	4	F	CHILD	RRZZZZUSA
SCHWARZWAELDER, JACOB	30	M	LABR	RRZZZZUSA
CATHARINA	28	F	UNKNOWN	RRZZZZUSA
JACOB	4	M	CHILD	RRZZZZUSA
WITTLEITER, JACOB	32	M	LABR	RRZZZZUSA
ROSINE	30	F	UNKNOWN	RRZZZZUSA
JOHANN	20	M	LABR	RRZZZZUSA
ROSINE	6	F	CHILD	RRZZZZUSA
EVA	4	F	CHILD	RRZZZZUSA
JACOB	3	M	CHILD	RRZZZZUSA
MARTIN	.06	M	INFANT	RRZZZZUSA
MAGDALENE	.06	F	INFANT	RRZZZZUSA
DEINES, JACOB	30	M	FARMER	RRZZZZUSA
MAGDALENE	28	F	UNKNOWN	RRZZZZUSA
MARIE	.04	F	INFANT	RRZZZZUSA
MAGDALENE	.02	F	INFANT	RRZZZZUSA
RETZE-, CHRISTIAN	26	M	FARMER	RRZZZZUSA
ROSINE	27	F	UNKNOWN	RRZZZZUSA
CHRISTIAN	4	M	CHILD	RRZZZZUSA
CHRISTINE	57	F	UNKNOWN	RRZZZZUSA
JACOB	6	M	CHILD	RRZZZZUSA
CHRISTOPH	19	M	FARMER	RRZZZZUSA
SCHANER, CHISTIAN	36	M	FARMER	RRZZZZUSA
CATHARINA	36	F	UNKNOWN	RRZZZZUSA
JOHANN	20	M	FARMER	RRZZZZUSA
LUDWIG	18	M	FARMER	RRZZZZUSA
JACOB	7	M	CHILD	RRZZZZUSA
MARGARETHA	6	F	CHILD	RRZZZZUSA
CATHARINE	4	F	CHILD	RRZZZZUSA
MAGDALENE	.11	F	INFANT	RRZZZZUSA
KRAUSE, JOHANN	23	M	FARMER	RRZZZZUSA
MAGDALENA	21	F	UNKNOWN	RRZZZZUSA
ERBELL, JACOB	26	M	FARMER	RRZZZZUSA
MARIA	25	F	UNKNOWN	RRZZZZUSA
MARIA	.05	F	INFANT	RRZZZZUSA
MAIER, JOHANN	30	M	FARMER	RRZZZZUSA
DOROTHEA	29	F	UNKNOWN	RRZZZZUSA
FRIEDRICH	2	M	CHILD	RRZZZZUSA
MARIE	9	F	CHILD	RRZZZZUSA
KNODEL, JOHANN	32	M	FARMER	RRZZZZUSA
MARIE	22	F	UNKNOWN	RRZZZZUSA
MARIA	5	F	CHILD	RRZZZZUSA
MICHAEL	4	M	CHILD	RRZZZZUSA
BARBARA	3	F	CHILD	RRZZZZUSA

PASSENGER	AGE	SEX	OCCUPATION	PRV VIL DES
GOTTLIEB	2	M	CHILD	RRZZZZUSA
CHRISTINE	.09	F	INFANT	RRZZZZUSA
FRIEDRICH	18	M	FARMER	RRZZZZUSA
SCHULZ, HEINRICH	20	M	FARMER	RRZZZZUSA
HIEB, GEORG	42	M	FARMER	RRZZZZUSA
ROSINE	38	F	UNKNOWN	RRZZZZUSA
GEORG	16	M	FARMER	RRZZZZUSA
FRIEDRICH	4	M	CHILD	RRZZZZUSA
ROSINE	.06	F	INFANT	RRZZZZUSA
KNODEL, HEINRICH	27	M	FARMER	RRZZZZUSA
RANIK, CHRISTOPH	48	M	FARMER	RRZZZZUSA
CATHARINA	47	F	UNKNOWN	RRZZZZUSA
FRIEDRICH	22	M	FARMER	RRZZZZUSA
JACOB	8	M	CHILD	RRZZZZUSA
MARIA	5	F	CHILD	RRZZZZUSA
ANTON	4	M	CHILD	RRZZZZUSA
JOHANN	2	M	CHILD	RRZZZZUSA
CHRISTOPF	.11	M	INFANT	RRZZZZUSA
GOTTLIEB	20	M	FARMER	RRZZZZUSA
CHRISTINE	20	F	UNKNOWN	RRZZZZUSA
CATHARINA	20	F	UNKNOWN	RRZZZZUSA
WILHELM	.06	M	INFANT	RRZZZZUSA
SATTLER, JOHANN	21	M	CL	RRZZZZUSA
PINSKY, FILE	26	F	UNKNOWN	RRZZZZUSA
WEERS	5	M	CHILD	RRZZZZUSA
KNOL	4	M	CHILD	RRZZZZUSA
OBREMSKI, JOSEPH	18	M	FARMER	RRZZZZUSA
GOLDBERG, RACHEL	28	F	UNKNOWN	RRZZZZUSA
SCHEINE	7	F	CHILD	RRZZZZUSA
ABRAHAMS	4	M	CHILD	RRZZZZUSA
FANAIEN	4	M	CHILD	RRZZZZUSA
JAWAREK, VALENTIN	44	M	FARMER	RRZZZZUSA
WLADISLAUS	6	M	CHILD	RRZZZZUSA
SOLINOWSKI, MARTIN	28	M	FARMER	RRZZZZUSA
JONKOLSKI, RAFAEL	30	M	LABR	RRZZZZUSA
LEIKAS, ---S-MATSON	27	M	LABR	RRZZZZUSA
BRUDERI, JOHA.INHAUP	23	M	LABR	RRZZZZUSA
HIPAKKA, HEIKKI	30	M	LABR	RRZZZZUSA
LIPPALA, ERIK	34	M	LABR	RRZZZZUSA
JOHNSON, JOHN	25	M	LABR	RRZZZZUSA
TUMANN, LEANDER	21	M	LABR	RRZZZZUSA
RAHJA, ADAMI	19	M	LABR	RRZZZZUSA
KUJULA, JUHA.	28	M	LABR	RRZZZZUSA
YEKANEN, MARIA-J.	22	F	UNKNOWN	RRZZZZUSA
SAAVOLA, U	21	M	LABR	RRZZZZUSA
TEROAKOSKI, WULPARI	24	M	LABR	RRZZZZUSA
NASI, JOHN	41	M	LABR	RRZZZZUSA
HAUTALA, KURTAA	39	M	LABR	RRZZZZUSA
TOURI, JACOB-J.	28	M	LABR	RRZZZZUSA
RINTASALO, JOHANA	23	M	LABR	RRZZZZUSA
LUMA, JOHANN	33	M	LABR	RRZZZZUSA
WAHARI, KARL-A.	30	M	LABR	RRZZZZUSA
HAWINKSATO, ALBERT-H.	35	M	LABR	RRZZZZUSA
NISKALA, BERTIL-K.	27	M	LABR	RRZZZZUSA
SALO, JOHANN-E.	25	M	LABR	RRZZZZUSA
LUPPIO, EMANUEL-J.	29	M	LABR	RRZZZZUSA
RULLO, MATTS-M.	31	M	LABR	RRZZZZUSA
BURACK, MOSES	33	M	LABR	RRZZZZUSA
SCHULTZ, CHRISTIAN	41	M	LABR	RRZZZZUSA
BRUMMER, HANS	39	M	LABR	RRZZZZUSA
PETERSEN, MARTIN	47	M	LABR	RRZZZZUSA
HANSEN, SVEN	32	M	LABR	RRZZZZUSA
TOULA, JOHANN	37	M	FARMER	RRZZZZUSA
MAKKYLA, MICKEL-J.	34	M	FARMER	RRZZZZUSA
KUNDSEN, MAREN	18	F	UNKNOWN	RRZZZZUSA
LAURITZ	25	M	PRNTR	RRZZZZUSA
PETERSEN, SARA	22	F	UNKNOWN	RRZZZZUSA
WALKER, LUDWIG	30	M	FARMER	RRZZZZUSA
FRIEDERIKE	30	F	FARMER	RRZZZZUSA
CATHARINE	6	F	CHILD	RRZZZZUSA
FRIEDERIKE	4	F	CHILD	RRZZZZUSA
JOHANN	.06	M	INFANT	RRZZZZUSA
TESKA, SAMUEL	29	M	FARMER	RRZZZZUSA
ROSINA	29	F	UNKNOWN	RRZZZZUSA
ELISABETH	7	F	CHILD	RRZZZZUSA

PASSENGER	AGE	SEX	OCCUPATION	PRV	VIL	DES
GOTTLIEB	4	M	CHILD	RR	ZZZZ	USA
JOHANN	3	M	CHILD	RR	ZZZZ	USA
JACOB	.06	M	INFANT	RR	ZZZZ	USA
LANG, GOTTLIEB	23	M	FARMER	RR	ZZZZ	USA
MARIA	20	F	UNKNOWN	RR	ZZZZ	USA
JALUCKO, GOTTLIEB	24	M	FARMER	RR	ZZZZ	USA
U	21	F	UNKNOWN	RR	ZZZZ	USA
AHLT, U	43	M	FARMER	RR	ZZZZ	USA
FRIEDERIKE	39	F	UNKNOWN	RR	ZZZZ	USA
CATHARINE	7	F	CHILD	RR	ZZZZ	USA
LYDIA	5	F	CHILD	RR	ZZZZ	USA
ELISE	3	F	CHILD	RR	ZZZZ	USA
CHRISTINE	4	F	CHILD	RR	ZZZZ	USA
FRIEDERIKE	2	F	CHILD	RR	ZZZZ	USA
BENJAMIN	.02	M	INFANT	RR	ZZZZ	USA
KNODEL, JOHANN	20	M	PNTR	RR	ZZZZ	USA
FEIGERT, WILHELM	18	M	FARMER	RR	ZZZZ	USA
JACOB	17	M	FARMER	RR	ZZZZ	USA
EHRESMANN, PHILIPP	37	M	FARMER	RR	ZZZZ	USA
MAGDALENE	33	F	UNKNOWN	RR	ZZZZ	USA
CONRAD	4	M	CHILD	RR	ZZZZ	USA
JACOB	.06	M	INFANT	RR	ZZZZ	USA
WAGEMANN, JACOB	38	M	FARMER	RR	ZZZZ	USA
BARBARA	37	F	UNKNOWN	RR	ZZZZ	USA
JACOB	16	M	FARMER	RR	ZZZZ	USA
PHILIPP	7	M	CHILD	RR	ZZZZ	USA
U	5	M	CHILD	RR	ZZZZ	USA
U	4	F	CHILD	RR	ZZZZ	USA
LUDWIG	3	M	CHILD	RR	ZZZZ	USA
CAROLINE	2	F	CHILD	RR	ZZZZ	USA
FRIEDRICH	.06	M	INFANT	RR	ZZZZ	USA
FEIGERT, CONRAD	28	M	FARMER	RR	ZZZZ	USA
CATHARINE	26	F	UNKNOWN	RR	ZZZZ	USA
FIRIEDRICH	6	M	CHILD	RR	ZZZZ	USA
CONRAD	4	M	CHILD	RR	ZZZZ	USA
CATRHARINE	3	F	CHILD	RR	ZZZZ	USA
FREIMARK, GOTTLIEB	36	M	FARMER	RR	ZZZZ	USA
ROSINA	32	F	UNKNOWN	RR	ZZZZ	USA
CHRISTINE	6	F	CHILD	RR	ZZZZ	USA
CATHARINE	4	F	CHILD	RR	ZZZZ	USA
MAGDALENE	2	F	CHILD	RR	ZZZZ	USA
GUTMUELLER, GEORG	38	M	FARMER	RR	ZZZZ	USA
CATHARINA	37	F	UNKNOWN	RR	ZZZZ	USA
CATHARINA	7	F	CHILD	RR	ZZZZ	USA
GEORG	6	M	CHILD	RR	ZZZZ	USA
THEOBALD	5	M	CHILD	RR	ZZZZ	USA
CAROLINE	2	F	CHILD	RR	ZZZZ	USA
FRIEDRICH	.02	M	INFANT	RR	ZZZZ	USA
PHILIPP	.04	M	INFANT	RR	ZZZZ	USA
LUDWIG	.06	M	INFANT	RR	ZZZZ	USA
ERBERLE, MARTIN	53	M	FARMER	RR	ZZZZ	USA
ELISE	52	F	UNKNOWN	RR	ZZZZ	USA
HEINRICH	17	M	FARMER	RR	ZZZZ	USA
U, ANTON	26	M	FARMER	RR	ZZZZ	USA
CATHARINE	20	F	UNKNOWN	RR	ZZZZ	USA
WAGEMANN, DANIEL	26	M	FARMER	RR	ZZZZ	USA
U	20	F	UNKNOWN	RR	ZZZZ	USA
CHRESMANN, PHILIPP	60	M	FARMER	RR	ZZZZ	USA
CATRHARINE	60	F	UNKNOWN	RR	ZZZZ	USA
MARGARETHA	18	F	UNKNOWN	RR	ZZZZ	USA
CHRISTINE	16	F	UNKNOWN	RR	ZZZZ	USA
EHRESMANN, GEORG	32	M	FARMER	RR	ZZZZ	USA
MARGARETHA	30	F	UNKNOWN	RR	ZZZZ	USA
JACOB	6	M	CHILD	RR	ZZZZ	USA
KNODEL, SAMUEL	41	M	FARMER	RR	ZZZZ	USA
CHRISTINE	32	F	UNKNOWN	RR	ZZZZ	USA
U	5	M	CHILD	RR	ZZZZ	USA
U	00	F	UNKNOWN	RR	ZZZZ	USA
LUDIA	3	F	CHILD	RR	ZZZZ	USA
JACOB	2	M	CHILD	RR	ZZZZ	USA
GOTTLIEB	.01	M	INFANT	RR	ZZZZ	USA
KERN, GOTTLIEB	23	M	LABR	RR	ZZZZ	USA
CHRISTINE	19	F	LABR	RR	ZZZZ	USA
AICHLE, JACOB	42	M	FARMER	RR	ZZZZ	USA
ELISE	40	F	UNKNOWN	RR	ZZZZ	USA

PASSENGER	AGE	SEX	OCCUPATION	PRV	VIL	DES
DOROTHEA	17	F	UNKNOWN	RR	ZZZZ	USA
CATHARINA	7	F	CHILD	RR	ZZZZ	USA
ELISE	5	F	CHILD	RR	ZZZZ	USA
JOHANN	.03	M	INFANT	RR	ZZZZ	USA
JACOB	2	M	CHILD	RR	ZZZZ	USA
FRIEDRICH	.02	M	INFANT	RR	ZZZZ	USA
WAL-ER, LUDWIG	59	M	FARMER	RR	ZZZZ	USA
CHRISTINE	54	F	UNKNOWN	RR	ZZZZ	USA
CHRISTINE	15	F	UNKNOWN	RR	ZZZZ	USA
MARIE	19	F	UNKNOWN	RR	ZZZZ	USA
ANDREAS	15	M	WTR	RR	ZZZZ	USA
ZELLER, U	44	M	FARMER	RR	ZZZZ	USA
U	44	F	UNKNOWN	RR	ZZZZ	USA
JOHANN	22	M	FARMER	RR	ZZZZ	USA
MARIE	22	F	UNKNOWN	RR	ZZZZ	USA
VALENTIN	4	M	CHILD	RR	ZZZZ	USA
MARGARETHA	5	F	CHILD	RR	ZZZZ	USA
MAGDALENE	7	F	CHILD	RR	ZZZZ	USA
JOHANNE	.06	F	INFANT	RR	ZZZZ	USA
LANG, CAROLINE	40	F	UNKNOWN	RR	ZZZZ	USA
CAROLINE	13	F	UNKNOWN	RR	ZZZZ	USA
MARIA	7	F	CHILD	RR	ZZZZ	USA
JACOB	.06	M	INFANT	RR	ZZZZ	USA
CAROLINE	40	F	UNKNOWN	RR	ZZZZ	USA
CAROLINE	13	F	CH	RR	ZZZZ	USA
MARIA	7	F	CHILD	RR	ZZZZ	USA
JACOB	6	M	CHILD	RR	ZZZZ	USA
POCHER, ANDREAS	35	M	FARMER	RR	ZZZZ	USA
MARIE	34	F	UNKNOWN	RR	ZZZZ	USA
MARIE	7	F	CHILD	RR	ZZZZ	USA
LIDIA	6	F	CHILD	RR	ZZZZ	USA
CHRISTINE	5	F	CHILD	RR	ZZZZ	USA
THERESIA	3	F	CHILD	RR	ZZZZ	USA
MAGDALENA	.06	F	INFANT	RR	ZZZZ	USA
PLOM, CHRISTIAN	58	F	INF	RR	ZZZZ	USA
LIDIA	16	F	INF	RR	ZZZZ	USA
WALKNER, THERESIA	23	F	INF	RR	ZZZZ	USA
OLZEWSKOI, STAN.	29	M	LABR	RR	ZZZZ	USA
GOSEKA, PIOTR.	37	M	LABR	RR	ZZZZ	USA
GRODKIEWICZ, U	39	M	LABR	RR	ZZZZ	USA
NOWAKOWSKY, U	22	M	LABR	RR	ZZZZ	USA
BLOKOWSKY, FRANZ	30	M	LABR	RR	ZZZZ	USA
CZBULSKY, ANTONIE	28	F	UNKNOWN	RR	ZZZZ	USA
JABLAWSKY, MICHAEL	39	M	LABR	RR	ZZZZ	USA
DOMBROWSKY, STANISLAUS	23	M	LABR	RR	ZZZZ	USA
MAKOWSKY, FRANZ	44	M	LABR	RR	ZZZZ	USA
KUROWSKY, JOSEPH	30	M	LABR	RR	ZZZZ	USA
SELENSKY, MAREUS	47	M	LABR	RR	ZZZZ	USA
KOHEN, DAVID	54	M	LABR	RR	ZZZZ	USA
GINIEWSKY, CHASK.	26	M	LABR	RR	ZZZZ	USA
GOLDBERG, SALOMON	58	M	MCHT	RR	ZZZZ	USA
JETTE	45	F	UNKNOWN	RR	ZZZZ	USA
MATULIS, FRANZ	41	M	MCHT	RR	ZZZZ	USA
KRIWICKI, RAGINNIE	23	M	MCHT	RR	ZZZZ	USA
POLPAWSKI, SZADOR	31	M	LABR	RR	ZZZZ	USA
VINCENTZ	6	M	CHILD	RR	ZZZZ	USA
ZALTEWITZ, JOSEF	20	M	LABR	RR	ZZZZ	USA
SCHER, SCHOBSI	19	M	UNKNOWN	RR	ZZZZ	USA
OPENOWSKY, LUDWIKA	13	F	UNKNOWN	RR	ZZZZ	USA
BOSCHIKOWSKI, JOHN	33	M	LABR	RR	ZZZZ	USA
FRED, SALOMON	21	M	MCHT	RR	ZZZZ	USA
LOUIS	15	M	MCHT	RR	ZZZZ	USA
BECKER, AUGUST	23	M	LABR	RR	ZZZZ	USA
GORDON, ABRAHAM	33	M	FARMER	RR	ZZZZ	USA
TANNER	.11	M	INFANT	RR	ZZZZ	USA

PASSENGER	AGE	SEX	OCCUPATION	PRV	VIL	DES

SHIP: CITY OF RICHMOND

FROM: LIVERPOOL AND QUEENSTOWN
TO: NEW YORK
ARRIVED: 15 MAY 1889

PASSENGER	AGE	SEX	OCCUPATION	PRV VIL DES
MALKOE, HERMAN	19	M	FARMER	RRZZZZMI
KERDOLA, HERMAN	42	M	FARMER	RRZZZZMI
MACKIEWICZ, MARIE	31	F	SVNT	RRZZZZMI
KINZALA, THOS.	32	M	FARMER	RRZZZZMI
LUKTALA, JOHN	34	M	FARMER	RRZZZZMI
HERKKALA, HERMAN	41	M	FARMER	RRZZZZMI
GLILNANA, ERICK	44	M	FARMER	RRZZZZMI
HEUPALA, MATIS	30	M	FARMER	RRZZZZMI
JACOB	4	M	CHILD	RRZZZZMI
FERMAN, HERMAN	50	M	CH	RRZZZZMI
BROOI, JOHN	50	M	CH	RRZZZZMI
MIKKELA, JENOB.	44	F	SVNT	RRZZZZMI
LENNEH	17	F	SVNT	RRZZZZMI
SARVOLA, MATTI	28	M	LABR	RRZZZZCAL
JACOB	24	M	LABR	RRZZZZCAL
LESHOR	19	M	LABR	RRZZZZCAL

SHIP: OBDAM

FROM: ROTTERDAM
TO: NEW YORK
ARRIVED: 16 MAY 1889

PASSENGER	AGE	SEX	OCCUPATION	PRV VIL DES
PESKOWSKY, AD.	30	M	LABR	RRZZZZUSA
KLAS, PAWEL	27	M	LABR	RRZZZZUSA
PIECHOWRAT, ING.	52	M	LABR	RRZZZZUSA
MARYAN	20	M	LABR	RRZZZZUSA
STEFANOWITZ, JOH.	26	M	LABR	RRZZZZUSA
GAUZOWSKI, MICH.	24	M	LABR	RRZZZZUSA
SCHIP, ADAM	18	M	LABR	RRZZZZUSA
SCHLINRICH, JOS.	44	M	LABR	RRZZZZUSA
HUSSOH, VENDA	18	M	LABR	RRZZZZUSA
EISMAR, N.	50	M	MUSN	RRZZZZUSA
URBAN-H, JOH.	34	M	LABR	RRZZZZUSA
RUSSINKA, MICH.	50	M	LABR	RRZZZZUSA
CSISELLOH, MART.	23	M	LABR	RRZZZZUSA
TARRA, IGN.	38	M	LABR	RRZZZZUSA
SANDA, HAW.	13	M	LABR	RRZZZZUSA
ZIELINSKI, J.	18	M	LABR	RRZZZZUSA
OSSOWSKY, KOCH.	24	M	LABR	RRZZZZUSA
MARASOS, LEOP.	22	M	LABR	RRZZZZUSA
BUTKOWSKY, ANT.	28	M	LABR	RRZZZZUSA
STANISLAW, MICH.	27	M	LABR	RRZZZZUSA
NIEPERT, JEAN	39	M	LABR	RRZZZZUSA
WEHLINSKI, ANDR.	42	M	LABR	RRZZZZUSA
BEGROWSTAD, LUDW.	32	M	LABR	RRZZZZUSA
JADRAC, THOMAS	23	M	LABR	RRZZZZUSA
ANDERSON, M.	22	F	UNKNOWN	RRZZZZUSA
STRUMAN, IW.	54	M	UNKNOWN	RRZZZZUSA
PALEWSKY, JOH.	30	M	UNKNOWN	RRZZZZUSA
DUBKOWSKY, AD.	36	M	UNKNOWN	RRZZZZUSA
WEISMANN, JACOB	18	M	MCHT	RRZZZZUSA
OMILONOWSKY, PETER	36	M	MCHT	RRZZZZUSA
MEYER, KASAN	20	M	MCHT	RRZZZZUSA
BARUCH, SAM.	28	M	MCHT	RRZZZZUSA
SOVIANSKY, JAC.	46	M	MCHT	RRZZZZUSA
SCHILEWSK, WOJTEH	21	M	MCHT	RRZZZZUSA
SCHILEWSKY, ANDR.	28	M	MCHT	RRZZZZUSA
JASEK, JOH.	26	M	MCHT	RRZZZZUSA
SZUBOTI, JANOS	24	M	MCHT	RRZZZZUSA
BEIGROWITI, VAL.	24	M	MCHT	RRZZZZUSA
RUSEN, DAV.	28	M	MCHT	RRZZZZUSA
PETROWSKY, PETER	32	M	MCHT	RRZZZZUSA
DAPITALSKI, MATH.	32	M	MCHT	RRZZZZUSA
ANDOMATIS, FRANS	26	M	MCHT	RRZZZZUSA
WITKOWSKI, VLAD.	20	M	MCHT	RRZZZZUSA
KUZOWSKI, FR.	21	M	MCHT	RRZZZZUSA
ROISCHIEWSKY, AND.	26	M	MCHT	RRZZZZUSA
TUNENSKI, JAN	22	M	MCHT	RRZZZZUSA
LABENSKI, ADAM	40	M	MCHT	RRZZZZUSA
STASNEWITZ, MOS.	24	M	MCHT	RRZZZZUSA
RUTIN, JOS.	39	M	MCHT	RRZZZZUSA
TOLKOVICZ, SOM.	27	M	LABR	RRZZZZUSA
CHRIRE, CHAJKE	20	M	LABR	RRZZZZUSA
ECHLER, ESZTY	19	M	LABR	RRZZZZUSA
RUSKOWSKY, ANT.	20	M	LABR	RRZZZZUSA
KURTZ, SAM.	00	M	MCHT	RRZZZZUSA
JANUSKIEWITZ, ANT.	26	M	LABR	RRZZZZUSA
MEYER, ARLUK	26	M	LABR	RRZZZZUSA
SPECTOR, SCHEIE	24	M	LABR	RRZZZZUSA
KURPJEWSKI, PETER	30	M	LABR	RRZZZZUSA
NEUMANN, M.	22	M	LABR	RRZZZZUSA
POTTAWSKY, JOH.	29	M	LABR	RRZZZZUSA
WOTOWSKY, M.	20	M	LABR	RRZZZZUSA
PACKOWSKA, JOS.	20	F	LABR	RRZZZZUSA
IGN.	23	M	LABR	RRZZZZUSA
KLUECK, JOS.	33	M	LABR	RRZZZZUSA
JOS.	33	F	LABR	RRZZZZUSA
SUMEIKA, PIETR.	32	M	LABR	RRZZZZUSA
PLASZYNSKI, FR.	18	F	LABR	RRZZZZUSA
REICH, FEIW.	25	M	LABR	RRZZZZUSA
ZIPEKIES, HERM.	19	M	MCHT	RRZZZZUSA

SHIP: POLYNESIA

FROM: STETTIN
TO: NEW YORK
ARRIVED: 17 MAY 1889

PASSENGER	AGE	SEX	OCCUPATION	PRV VIL DES
SEISERING, FRANZ	26	M	SEMN	RRZZZZNY
KOHLHASE, AUGUST	40	M	MCHT	RRZZZZNY
TRAPP, GOTTLIEB	32	M	FARMER	RRZZZZNY
DANKSCHIS, IGNATZ	22	M	LABR	RRZZZZNY
POLLES, FRANZ	22	M	LABR	RRZZZZNY
JANKOWSKY, STANISL.	23	M	LABR	RRZZZZNY
TECHNER, WILH.	33	M	LABR	RRZZZZNY
TOINILA, CONSTANT	28	M	LABR	RRZZZZNY
WAJKOKAITS, JOHAN	25	M	LABR	RRZZZZNY
GATZUNTIS, IGNATS	23	M	LABR	RRZZZZNY
MIKOLIN, ADAM	40	M	UNKNOWN	RRZZZZNY
BUEINSKY, AMBROSI	18	M	UNKNOWN	RRZZZZNY
WARSUCHOWSKY, JESSKY	18	M	UNKNOWN	RRZZZZNY
MUTOLKIEWITZ, ANDZY	30	M	UNKNOWN	RRZZZZNY
DIEL, FRANZEK	33	M	UNKNOWN	RRZZZZNY
CORNEKY, ANDREAS	30	M	LABR	RRZZZZNY
MEYSNER, EVA	23	F	WO	RRZZZZNY
JOSEPHA	1	F	CHILD	RRZZZZNY
WILLEMAITIS, ELSA	32	F	WO	RRZZZZNY
\JURGIS	4	M	CHILD	RRZZZZNY
BALIZUNAS, EVA	25	F	SGL	RRZZZZNY
BUSISKY, MARIE	20	F	SGL	RRZZZZNY
KISELEWSKY, MARIANNE	22	F	SGL	RRZZZZNY
STRUNGOWSKA, FRANZISKA	65	F	WO	RRZZZZNY
KASWURM, CHRISTINE	21	F	SGL	RRZZZZNY
AUGUSTE	14	F	SI	RRZZZZNY
HARTUNG, MINNA	24	F	SGL	RRZZZZNY
SZWEDA, JOSEPH	25	M	LABR	RRZZZZNY
FRANZISKA	19	F	W	RRZZZZNY
MIKOLAJEZEWSKI, FRANZEK	29	M	LABR	RRZZZZNY
STEPHANIE	10	F	CH	RRZZZZNY
RENDEL, OWSIC	18	M	TLR	RRZZZZNY
BENJAMIN	13	M	CH	RRZZZZNY
TAUBE	15	F	CH	RRZZZZNY

PASSENGER	AGE	SEX	OCCUPATION	PRV VIL DES
MAJER, LORENZ	60	M	LABR	RRZZZZNY
EVA	49	F	W	RRZZZZNY
THOMAS	27	M	LABR	RRZZZZNY
WIELEWSKY, EVA	90	F	UNKNOWN	RRZZZZNY
MAJER, JULIANE	16	F	CH	RRZZZZNY
ANNA	11	F	CH	RRZZZZNY
FRANZ	9	M	CHILD	RRZZZZNY
DEVEZYNSKI, ROSALIE	57	F	WO	RRZZZZNY
JOSEPHA	15	F	CH	RRZZZZNY
VINCENT	9	M	CHILD	RRZZZZNY
WLADISLAW	7	M	CHILD	RRZZZZNY
CHAIMSON, CIRLE	16	F	CH	RRZZZZNY
ABRAHAM	12	M	CH	RRZZZZNY
ROSE	49	F	WO	RRZZZZNY

SHIP: SAALE

FROM: BREMEN AND SOUTHAMPTON
TO: NEW YORK
ARRIVED: 18 MAY 1889

PASSENGER	AGE	SEX	OCCUPATION	PRV VIL DES
WIENCZKOWSKI, STANISL.	35	M	SMH	RRZZZZUSA
NUSSBAUM, LEIB	28	M	TLR	RRZZZZUSA
MANNULA, GUSTAVA	38	F	UNKNOWN	RRZZZZUSA
MYLLYKOSKI, INKO	28	M	FARMER	RRZZZZUSA
KIRKUMAR, JOH.	35	M	FARMER	RRZZZZUSA
KETEMSKI, JAC.	26	M	SMH	RRZZZZUSA
MARTINMAKI, ROB.	27	M	SMH	RRZZZZUSA
KURUNPERA, ISAAC	27	M	SMH	RRZZZZUSA
RINTAKANGAS, JUHA	26	F	UNKNOWN	RRZZZZUSA
SCHLUWE, CARL	28	M	PNTR	RRZZZZUSA
HENRIETTE	26	F	W	RRZZZZUSA
LUDOLPH	4	M	CHILD	RRZZZZUSA
LEON	.11	M	INFANT	RRZZZZUSA
DRESENER, JUL.	21	M	FARMER	RRZZZZUSA
STEINBART, HEIN.	21	M	FARMER	RRZZZZUSA
BETZINSKI, RUDOLPH	20	M	FARMER	RRZZZZUSA
WAGENKNECHT, ED.	46	M	FARMER	RRZZZZUSA
WILH.	36	F	W	RRZZZZUSA
EMILIE	8	F	CHILD	RRZZZZUSA
JULIANNA	6	F	CHILD	RRZZZZUSA
THERESIA	4	F	CHILD	RRZZZZUSA
HUGO	.11	M	INFANT	RRZZZZUSA
HELLERSOHN, AJCOB	48	M	FARMER	RRZZZZUSA
ROKOWSKY, ALTER	22	M	FARMER	RRZZZZUSA
ORZCHOVSKY, ALTER	22	M	FARMER	RRZZZZUSA
BILLUK, HIRSCH	17	M	FARMER	RRZZZZUSA
BERGER, U	30	M	FARMER	RRZZZZUSA
SUDEN, U	16	M	FARMER	RRZZZZUSA
HAHL, CHRIST.	16	M	FARMER	RRZZZZUSA
HEINSOHN, PETER	16	M	FARMER	RRZZZZUSA
HAMPKE, HEINR.	23	M	FARMER	RRZZZZUSA
BRANDT, JUERGEN	29	M	FARMER	RRZZZZUSA
SINGER, MARIA	20	F	UNKNOWN	RRZZZZUSA
RAGES, LUCIE	22	F	UNKNOWN	RRZZZZUSA
DEHNER, SIMON	15	F	UNKNOWN	RRZZZZUSA
STAHLHUT, LUDW.	16	M	CL	RRZZZZUSA
HORSTMANN, DIEDR.	29	M	CL	RRZZZZUSA
GOEHRING, RICH.	15	M	CL	RRZZZZUSA
BUECHNER, JOH.	65	F	UNKNOWN	RRZZZZUSA
KLAUS, MARIA	41	F	UNKNOWN	RRZZZZUSA
MARIA	10	F	CH	RRZZZZUSA
BARBARA	7	F	CHILD	RRZZZZUSA
WILH.	3	F	CHILD	RRZZZZUSA
GEORG	.06	M	INFANT	RRZZZZUSA
TENTENMACHER, WILH.	28	M	FARMER	RRZZZZUSA
WEIDLE, MARTHA	24	F	UNKNOWN	RRZZZZUSA
LUTZ, ANNA	22	F	UNKNOWN	RRZZZZUSA
RASQUIN, WILH.	28	M	FARMER	RRZZZZUSA
TRIQUARDT, VAL.	24	M	FARMER	RRZZZZUSA
WAEGELEIN, PHIL.	27	M	FARMER	RRZZZZUSA
PEBLER, WILH.	14	M	FARMER	RRZZZZUSA
GAASVIG, DINS	51	M	FARMER	RRZZZZUSA
JENS	10	M	CH	RRZZZZUSA
SVENDSEN, LARS	59	M	SMH	RRZZZZUSA
KOEHLER, BERNH.	43	M	MCHT	RRZZZZUSA
LINA	22	F	W	RRZZZZUSA
EICHLER, LOUISE	19	F	UNKNOWN	RRZZZZUSA
FELGNER, OSCAR	28	M	PNTR	RRZZZZUSA
GIESBRECHT, HEIN.	33	M	FARMER	RRZZZZUSA
ELEONORE	31	F	W	RRZZZZUSA
EMILIE	9	F	CHILD	RRZZZZUSA
MATH.	8	M	CHILD	RRZZZZUSA
FROEHLKE, EMILIE	24	F	UNKNOWN	RRZZZZUSA
GIESBRECHT, AD.	3	M	CHILD	RRZZZZUSA
MORGENSTERN, RIVE	18	F	UNKNOWN	RRZZZZUSA
BAERWALD, ADELPH.	22	M	FARMER	RRZZZZUSA
MEYER, ERNST	18	M	FARMER	RRZZZZUSA
GRAFF, FRIEDR.	29	M	FARMER	RRZZZZUSA
MAGD.	25	F	W	RRZZZZUSA
LUDW.	6	M	CHILD	RRZZZZUSA
EMIL	.09	M	INFANT	RRZZZZUSA
KLEEBAUM, JOH.	34	M	FARMER	RRZZZZUSA
JULIAN	35	F	W	RRZZZZUSA
EDUARD	10	M	CH	RRZZZZUSA
ALBERTINE	6	M	CHILD	RRZZZZUSA
LUDW.	4	M	CHILD	RRZZZZUSA
ADOELPH.	.01	M	INFANT	RRZZZZUSA
BECKER, LUDW.	38	M	FARMER	RRZZZZUSA
CAROL.	25	F	W	RRZZZZUSA
EDUARD	3	M	CHILD	RRZZZZUSA
IDA	2	F	CHILD	RRZZZZUSA
BLACK, LOUSE	22	F	UNKNOWN	RRZZZZUSA
ARCH, GEORG	27	M	SHMK	RRZZZZUSA
RAUSCH, MAGD.	20	F	UNKNOWN	RRZZZZUSA
WELLER, GOTTL.	45	M	FARMER	RRZZZZUSA
LOUISE	42	F	W	RRZZZZUSA
ELISAB.	21	F	CH	RRZZZZUSA
GEORG	19	M	FARMER	RRZZZZUSA
JOH.	10	M	CH	RRZZZZUSA
PAULINE	9	F	CHILD	RRZZZZUSA
MARIA	6	F	CHILD	RRZZZZUSA
GOTTL.	4	M	CHILD	RRZZZZUSA
ELISAB.	3	F	CHILD	RRZZZZUSA
FRIEDR.	.01	M	INFANT	RRZZZZUSA
ALBRECHT, HEINR.	33	M	FARMER	RRZZZZUSA
MAGD.	33	F	W	RRZZZZUSA
MARG.	11	F	CH	RRZZZZUSA
JACOB	8	M	CHILD	RRZZZZUSA
JOH.	6	M	CHILD	RRZZZZUSA
CATH.	2	F	CHILD	RRZZZZUSA
CHRIST.	.06	M	INFANT	RRZZZZUSA
BANDEL, JACOB	29	M	FARMER	RRZZZZUSA
MARG.	22	F	W	RRZZZZUSA
JOH.	2	M	CHILD	RRZZZZUSA
CHRIST.	.06	M	INFANT	RRZZZZUSA
WILH.	32	M	FARMER	RRZZZZUSA
EVA	28	F	W	RRZZZZUSA
MATHILDE	6	F	CHILD	RRZZZZUSA
CHRISTINE	4	F	CHILD	RRZZZZUSA
WILH.	2	F	CHILD	RRZZZZUSA
KOENIG, HENECH	22	M	FARMER	RRZZZZUSA
PLASSLER, MORITZ	22	M	FARMER	RRZZZZUSA
STOLNITZKI, ABRAH.	31	M	FARMER	RRZZZZUSA
JOHNSEN, PETER	24	M	FARMER	RRZZZZUSA
BRODER, JANKE	27	M	FARMER	RRZZZZUSA
RAPPOST, KUSIL	26	M	FARMER	RRZZZZUSA
KELLER, LEVY	25	M	FARMER	RRZZZZUSA
SWIETZKY, JAN	28	M	FARMER	RRZZZZUSA
KORNITZKY, FRANZ	26	M	FARMER	RRZZZZUSA
GLOWSKY, WIC.	25	M	FARMER	RRZZZZUSA
KRISTAK, JAN	23	M	FARMER	RRZZZZUSA
JOHKA, MATHIAS	17	M	FARMER	RRZZZZUSA
ZARNICKA, MARYANNA	25	F	UNKNOWN	RRZZZZUSA
PAWEL	.11	M	INFANT	RRZZZZUSA

PASSENGER	A G E	S E X	OCCUPATION	P V R I V L	D E S
GUDLEWSKY, CATH.	27	F	UNKNOWN	RRZZZZ	USA
WELLERS, GUST.	14	M	UNKNOWN	RRZZZZ	USA
THIESS, JOH.	21	M	UNKNOWN	RRZZZZ	USA
----TZKY, WEN.	00	M	UNKNOWN	RRZZZZ	USA
ANESCHKA	28	F	W	RRZZZZ	USA
MARIA	4	F	CHILD	RRZZZZ	USA
FRANZ	2	M	CHILD	RRZZZZ	USA
ALOIS	.03	M	INFANT	RRZZZZ	USA
KUDRENA, ALOIS	28	M	FARMER	RRZZZZ	USA
JOSEPHINE	28	F	W	RRZZZZ	USA
HELENE	8	F	CHILD	RRZZZZ	USA
ALOIS	4	M	CHILD	RRZZZZ	USA
FRANZ	1	M	CHILD	RRZZZZ	USA
PIWATZKA, ANNA	51	F	UNKNOWN	RRZZZZ	USA
JOHANN	24	M	SMH	RRZZZZ	USA
U	00	U	UNKNOWN	RRZZZZ	USA
KRUEGER, U	48	M	FARMER	RRZZZZ	USA
CATH.	41	F	W	RRZZZZ	USA
CARL	22	M	FARMER	RRZZZZ	USA
ROSINE	18	F	CH	RRZZZZ	USA
CHRIST.	11	M	CH	RRZZZZ	USA
ELISAB.	9	F	CHILD	RRZZZZ	USA
SCHIFROWITZ, MARK	61	M	FARMER	RRZZZZ	USA
JEDOZASKY, MARK	29	M	FARMER	RRZZZZ	USA
PETERSKY, ZUELL	24	M	FARMER	RRZZZZ	USA

SHIP: BOTHNIA

FROM: BREMEN AND SOUTHAMPTON
TO: NEW YORK
ARRIVED: 18 MAY 1889

PASSENGER	A G E	S E X	OCCUPATION	P V R I V L	D E S
EHRENBERG, ROSE	44	F	W	PLZZZZ	USA
WALLIS, DAVID	22	M	LABR	RRZZZZ	USA
SOPHIE	22	F	W	RRZZZZ	USA
BITSEN, MARIE	20	F	SP	FNZZZZ	USA
JAVVILA, MARIA	23	F	SP	FNZZZZ	USA
OLLI, MATTI	23	M	LABR	FNZZZZ	USA
FRITZA, JOSEF	27	M	LABR	FNZZZZ	USA
HLAUGO, THOMAS	30	M	UNKNOWN	FNZZZZ	USA
WILIAM	8	M	CHILD	FNZZZZ	USA
HYRAUER, JOHAN	35	M	FARMER	FNZZZZ	USA
HAKKARHIEN, JOHAN	27	M	FARMER	FNZZZZ	USA
HOHN, HERMAN	25	M	FARMER	FNZZZZ	USA
HEIMEN, ANDREAS	19	M	FARMER	FNZZZZ	USA
HYGTMEN, LENA	19	F	CNF	FNZZZZ	USA
JAKOB	32	M	LABR	FNZZZZ	USA
JAKOB	26	M	LABR	FNZZZZ	USA
JAKOB	19	M	LABR	FNZZZZ	USA
HEMENING, JAKOB	27	M	LABR	FNZZZZ	USA
HAAPORA, GUSTAF	27	M	CPTR	FNZZZZ	USA
JAKOBSEN, LEANDOR	28	M	LABR	FNZZZZ	USA
FRANSE	24	M	LABR	FNZZZZ	USA
JANKILA, SAKRIAS	40	M	SHMK	FNZZZZ	USA
JUOPORI, JOHAN	21	M	LABR	FNZZZZ	USA
KAUTAUPRA, GUSTAF	29	M	LABR	FNZZZZ	USA
KATENPUSSI, MATTS	27	M	LABR	FNZZZZ	USA
KAROOLA, FRANS	25	M	SEMN	FNZZZZ	USA
KAWANENNI, SAKRIAS	31	M	LABR	FNZZZZ	USA
KUNION, HENRIK	25	M	SEMN	FNZZZZ	USA
MATTS	19	M	LABR	FNZZZZ	USA
KLOSS, SCHOLEM	30	M	LABR	FNZZZZ	USA
KAUSMAN, JAKOB	50	M	FARMER	FNZZZZ	USA
KONOOAN, FRANZ	21	M	LABR	FNZZZZ	USA
KALAPOKKA, JOHAN	23	M	LABR	FNZZZZ	USA
LIGLY, HERMAN	20	M	LABR	FNZZZZ	USA
LAPPUROEN, MATTS	25	M	LABR	FNZZZZ	USA
LAKARILLA, JOHAN	23	M	LABR	FNZZZZ	USA
LUOMALA, ERIK	24	M	LABR	FNZZZZ	USA
LUISTROM, JOHAN	18	M	LABR	FNZZZZ	USA
MATTILA, JAKOB	18	M	LABR	FNZZZZ	USA
MICKELSON, NICKEL	32	M	LABR	FNZZZZ	USA
MARTANA, ISAK	40	M	LABR	FNZZZZ	USA
JOHAN	19	M	LABR	FNZZZZ	USA
NISKANON, MATT	30	M	LABR	FNZZZZ	USA
NIKOLA, GUSTAF	24	M	LABR	FNZZZZ	USA
ANTI	30	M	LABR	FNZZZZ	USA
OTTILA, MATH.	27	M	LABR	FNZZZZ	USA
OJVERMARK, JAKOB	17	M	LABR	FNZZZZ	USA
PEKERMAN, ANTI	43	M	LABR	FNZZZZ	USA
PALLINLA, JAKOB	44	M	LABR	FNZZZZ	USA
RIEKONEN, ERIK	25	M	LABR	FNZZZZ	USA
RAUTIS, JOSEF	30	M	LABR	FNZZZZ	USA
KAUL	30	M	LABR	FNZZZZ	USA
RAULAKAUGAS, JAKOB	20	M	LABR	FNZZZZ	USA
LEANDR	29	M	LABR	FNZZZZ	USA
RAUTANKAYAS, ANDERS	33	M	LABR	FNZZZZ	USA
RAULAKAUGO, JAKOB	28	M	LABR	FNZZZZ	USA
DERVISKI, AUGUST	31	M	LABR	FNZZZZ	USA
SISK, SALOMON	18	M	LABR	FNZZZZ	USA
SEGOR, JOHAN	25	M	BCHR	FNZZZZ	USA
TOKOG, ERIK	18	M	LABR	FNZZZZ	USA
TUNO, ANDERS	29	M	CNF	FNZZZZ	USA
BOYUSCH, KONSTANTIN	25	M	LABR	PLZZZZ	USA
BORAN, TAUCHEN	40	M	TLR	PLZZZZ	USA
CHIMEL, JOSEPH	40	M	TLR	PLZZZZ	USA
FORDRUSKI, ISAAC	34	M	TLR	PLZZZZ	USA
GUMARE, SAMUEL	21	F	LABR	PLZZZZ	USA
GRODECKI, ALEX	30	M	MSN	PLZZZZ	USA
HAKALA, ERIK	30	M	LABR	FNZZZZ	USA
JACUBOWIT, HEYMAN	25	M	LABR	FNZZZZ	USA
KOLERASCH, HIRSCH	34	M	LABR	FNZZZZ	USA
KAMBER, ISAC	19	M	TLR	FNZZZZ	USA
KULYOWSKI, JAN	25	M	LABR	FNZZZZ	USA
KANERISKI, FRANZ	36	M	LABR	FNZZZZ	USA
MASHIC, NICKOLAUS	25	M	LABR	FNZZZZ	USA
MAZULAIT, GOTTLIEF	37	M	LABR	FNZZZZ	USA
MOLINSKI, MICHAEL	32	M	LABR	FNZZZZ	USA
MIESIOWITZ, ISRAEL	22	M	LABR	FNZZZZ	USA
PRNSTEIN, JOSEPH	22	M	LABR	FNZZZZ	USA
PLOK, KAY	21	M	LABR	FNZZZZ	USA
RUOYCUS, WIGDER	40	M	SHMK	FNZZZZ	USA
STZKOWITZ, ABRAHAM	27	M	FARMER	FNZZZZ	USA
SCHINBAUM, ABRAHAM	19	M	LABR	FNZZZZ	USA
TENDOWSKI, ELISA	37	F	W	FNZZZZ	USA
LEIB, DAVID	17	M	LABR	PLZZZZ	USA
WOLF, NANIF	24	M	BKBNDR	PLZZZZ	USA
ZUNAGTIS, PETER	22	M	LABR	PLZZZZ	USA
ZAWARTOWSKY, FRANZ	24	M	LABR	PLZZZZ	USA
MAULANION, REGINA	22	F	SMH	PLZZZZ	USA
DAUWERT, LUDWIG	48	M	LABR	PLZZZZ	USA
MATHILDE	48	F	W	PLZZZZ	USA
OTTILIE	24	F	SP	PLZZZZ	USA
SHAPORS, ABRAHAM	18	M	LABR	PLZZZZ	USA
JAKOB	16	M	LABR	PLZZZZ	USA
MENNCHE	11	M	BY	PLZZZZ	USA
WILLNOR, ANTONIA	18	F	SP	PLZZZZ	USA
OKONSKI, ANTONIA	16	F	SP	PLZZZZ	USA

SHIP: VICTORIA

FROM: HAMBURG
TO: NEW YORK
ARRIVED: 20 MAY 1889

PASSENGER	A G E	S E X	OCCUPATION	P V R I V L	D E S
OPPENHEIM, HIRSCH	19	M	CL	PLAIMR	USA
ANDRUZKIEWICZ, JOSEF	36	M	LABR	PLAHZS	USA
ZBRESNICK, PETER	30	M	LABR	PLAHZS	USA
ROTARSKI, WLADISLAUS	28	M	LABR	PLAHZS	USA
PAWLOWSKI, JOSEF	25	M	LABR	PLAHZS	USA

PASSENGER	AGE	SEX	OCCUPATION	PRV	VIL	DES
WACZKIEWICZ, STANISL.	37	M	LABR	PL	AHZS	USA
MACZIEJEWSKI, JOSEF	32	M	LABR	RR	ZZZZ	USA
POWLATSCHEK, JOSEF	27	M	LABR	RR	ZZZZ	USA
ZIMNAWODA, MICHAEL	38	M	LABR	RR	ZZZZ	USA
RUTKOWSKI, PETER	37	M	LABR	RR	ZZZZ	USA
KEYAWA, JULIAN	27	M	LABR	RR	ZZZZ	USA
OCHOTZKA, FRANZISCA	21	F	SGL	RR	ZZZZ	USA
BUGDANSKI, RADZIMIR	28	M	SGL	RR	ZZZZ	USA
U, U	24	M	SGL	RR	ZZZZ	USA
SWILKA, JAN	27	M	LABR	RR	ZZZZ	USA
KUNKOWSKI, FRANZ	24	M	LABR	RR	ZZZZ	USA
KOBUS, JACOB	39	M	LABR	RR	ZZZZ	USA
CHRISTIAN, STANISLAUS	7	M	CHILD	RR	ZZZZ	USA
BROSTEK, LEON	27	M	LABR	RR	ZZZZ	USA
DRONSK, TEOFIL	19	M	LABR	RR	ZZZZ	USA
BIELKA, FRANZ	28	M	LABR	RR	ZZZZ	USA
CZERWINSKI, VALENTI	39	M	LABR	RR	ZZZZ	USA
MUSCHINSKI, WLADISLAUS	24	M	LABR	RR	ZZZZ	USA
KROSTEK, VALENTY	28	M	LABR	RR	ZZZZ	USA
GLINKA, STANISLAW	24	M	LABR	RR	ZZZZ	USA
NIEWSKI, FRANZ	21	M	LABR	RR	ZZZZ	USA
DRONSECK, TEOFIL	25	M	LABR	RR	ZZZZ	USA
KALISCHEWSKI, FRANZ	25	M	LABR	RR	ZZZZ	USA
BAZUTOWSKI, JAN	41	M	LABR	RR	ZZZZ	USA
VIETI, IGNAZ	22	M	LABR	RR	ZZZZ	USA
POPIOLEK, FRANZ	20	M	LABR	RR	ZZZZ	USA
CHRISTIAN, JOSEF	28	M	LABR	RR	ZZZZ	USA
GSCHASTA, JAN	26	M	LABR	RR	ZZZZ	USA
GWIASTA, PETER	27	M	LABR	RR	ZZZZ	USA
LADUSCH, FRANZ	29	M	LABR	RR	ZZZZ	USA
ZUCHTA, PIETER	45	M	LABR	RR	ZZZZ	USA
KURR, FRANZ	24	M	LABR	RR	ZZZZ	USA
BORRUCH, FRANZ	25	M	LABR	RR	ZZZZ	USA
PHILIPPOWITZ, JOSEF	20	M	LABR	RR	AHZS	USA
TSCHIMMERICH, FRANZ	55	M	UNKNOWN	RR	AHUI	USA
URIENOWICZ, JAN	32	M	UNKNOWN	RR	AHUI	USA
BOBROWSKI, JOSEF	28	M	UNKNOWN	RR	AHZS	USA
DAVID, WOICYECH	30	M	BCHR	RR	ZZZZ	USA
LIPKE, FRANZ	22	M	LABR	RR	ZZZZ	USA
JANKOWSKI, FRANZ	26	M	LABR	RR	ZZZZ	USA
BONASZAK, CONST.	26	M	LABR	RR	AHUI	USA
MAKKALA, LUKAS	40	M	LABR	FN	ZZZZ	USA
MARIE	32	F	W	FN	ZZZZ	USA
SOPHIE	7	F	CHILD	FN	ZZZZ	USA
MARIE	6	F	CHILD	FN	ZZZZ	USA
KURIKOSKI, LEANDER	20	M	UNKNOWN	FN	ZZZZ	USA
PELDEMAR, PETER	30	M	LABR	FN	ZZZZ	USA
LOBINOJA, GUSTAV	20	M	LABR	FN	ZZZZ	USA
RAGUSE, FRANZISCA	20	F	SGL	FN	ZZZZ	USA
HILDEBRANDT, JOHANN	30	M	FARMER	RR	ZZZZ	USA
KATHA.	30	F	W	RR	ZZZZ	USA
JACOB	5	M	CHILD	RR	ZZZZ	USA
JOHA.	4	F	CHILD	RR	ZZZZ	USA
KAROLINE	3	F	CHILD	RR	ZZZZ	USA
MARGA.	.11	F	INFANT	RR	ZZZZ	USA
KOENIG, KAROLINE	25	F	SGL	RR	ZZZZ	USA
HILDEBRANDT, ISRAEL	27	M	FARMER	RR	ZZZZ	USA
SUSANNE	28	F	W	RR	ZZZZ	USA
LISBETH	3	F	CHILD	RR	ZZZZ	USA
BARBA.	.11	F	INFANT	RR	ZZZZ	USA
BITZ, GEORGE	32	M	FARMER	RR	ACNZ	USA
ANNA	28	F	W	RR	ACNZ	USA
WILH.	5	M	CHILD	RR	ACNZ	USA
KATHA.	.11	F	INFANT	RR	ACNZ	USA
FRITSCHLE, HERRM.	20	M	FARMER	RR	AEGT	USA
ELISABETH	17	F	W	RR	AEGT	USA
KATHA.	.11	F	INFANT	RR	AEGT	USA
REMISCH, HEINR.	19	M	FARMER	RR	AEGT	USA
MARGA.	18	F	SGL	RR	AEGT	USA
ACKERMANN, JOHANN	34	M	FARMER	RR	AEGT	USA
CHRISTINE	36	F	W	RR	AEGT	USA
KATHA.	14	F	CH	RR	AEGT	USA
PETER	7	M	CHILD	RR	AEGT	USA
CHRISTINE	6	F	CHILD	RR	AEGT	USA
MARIE	4	F	CHILD	RR	AEGT	USA
LIESE	3	F	CHILD	RR	AEGT	USA
JOHS.	.11	M	INFANT	RR	AEGT	USA
GEORG	26	M	FARMER	RR	AEGT	USA
ELISABETH	24	F	W	RR	AEGT	USA
LIESE	4	F	CHILD	RR	AEGT	USA
HUMMET, JOHANN	22	M	UNKNOWN	RR	ZZZZ	USA
WEISSENBURG, ELISABETH	18	F	CH	RR	AIDG	USA
VALENTIN	16	M	CH	RR	AIDG	USA
CHRISTIAN	7	M	CHILD	RR	AIDG	USA
ANDREAS	6	M	CHILD	RR	AIDG	USA
CHRISTINE	5	F	CHILD	RR	AIDG	USA
HANKKOLA, JOH.	22	M	LABR	FN	ZZZZ	USA
MAKKOLA, HENRIK	18	M	LABR	FN	ZZZZ	USA
BRAUNFORS, JOH.	27	M	LABR	FN	ZZZZ	USA
SIDDBAEGK, JOH.	40	M	LABR	FN	ZZZZ	USA
LAENG, MATTHS.	33	M	LABR	FN	ZZZZ	USA
JOHS.	34	M	LABR	FN	ZZZZ	USA
MALO, JOHS.	55	M	LABR	FN	ZZZZ	USA
ANNA	50	F	LABR	FN	ZZZZ	USA
CATHA.	7	F	CHILD	FN	ZZZZ	USA
ALSDIUS, GEORG	35	M	LABR	RR	ZZZZ	USA
GERTSCH, JOSEF	30	M	LABR	RR	ZZZZ	USA
KRAKOWSKA, ANNA	35	F	SGL	RR	AHZS	USA
SLANAITES, LEONORE	23	F	WO	RR	AHZS	USA
FRANZ	.09	M	INFANT	RR	AHZS	USA
RENISCH, ANNA	35	F	WO	RR	AEFL	USA
HEDWIG	9	F	CHILD	RR	AEFL	USA

SHIP: MARSALA

FROM: HAMBURG
TO: NEW YORK
ARRIVED: 20 MAY 1889

PASSENGER	AGE	SEX	OCCUPATION	PRV	VIL	DES
WEHELEWSKI, JAN	23	M	LABR	RR	AHZS	NY
MICHALOWITZ, SIMON	29	M	LABR	RR	AHZS	PA
BROGEWITZ, JOSEF	28	M	LABR	RR	AHTF	PA
BOWDEW, JOSEF	30	M	LABR	RR	AHTF	NY
DWIECZYNSKI, THOMAS	28	M	LABR	RR	AHTF	PA
JAGIELSKI, CONSTANTIN	33	M	LABR	RR	AHTF	PA
MURAECKI, STANISLAW	38	M	LABR	RR	ZZZZ	PA
GALINSKI, SEZEPAN	00	M	LABR	RR	ZZZZ	PA
SIEDLEKI, SIMON	38	M	LABR	RR	ZZZZ	NY
DEPKOWSKI, THEOD.	20	M	LABR	RR	AHTK	NY
SUXCZAK, FILAR	26	M	LABR	RR	ZZZZ	NY
TROEZECZAK, PETRO	25	M	LABR	RR	ZZZZ	NY
SKOLDYSKO, JOSEPHINE	25	F	WO	RR	AIKB	NY
ANIELA	7	F	CHILD	RR	AIKB	NY
STARIA	5	F	CHILD	RR	AIKB	NY
BOLESLAW	4	M	CHILD	RR	AIKB	NY
WLADZIN	3	M	CHILD	RR	AIKB	NY
JOSEF	.06	M	INFANT	RR	AIKB	NY
GRABOSKI, FELIX	17	M	LABR	RR	AHZS	NY
NIWNARTOWICZ, KAZIMIR	25	M	LABR	RR	ZZZZ	NY
RACZUS, FRANZ	40	M	LABR	RR	ZZZZ	NY
JOSEF	7	M	CHILD	RR	ZZZZ	NY
TOCKKA, ANDREW	23	M	LABR	RR	AHZS	NY
MAMELOWSKI, WOJCIECH	27	M	LABR	RR	ZZZZ	NY
LUKASCHIES, MARTIN	26	M	LABR	RR	AHZS	NY
KRATASZNOS, JOSEF	42	M	LABR	RR	AHTF	IL
MACZAK, JOSEF	23	M	UNKNOWN	RR	AHUI	NY
MAREINKOWSKI, JOSEF	19	M	UNKNOWN	RR	AHTO	NY
BOERDALDKI, JAN	23	M	UNKNOWN	RR	AHTO	MO
DOROTHEA	20	F	UNKNOWN	RR	AHTO	MO
JAZEMBROWSKI, MICHAEL	35	M	UNKNOWN	RR	AHUI	MO
ANNA	35	F	UNKNOWN	RR	AHUI	MO
MARIE	7	F	CHILD	RR	AHUI	MO
ANTONIE	00	F	UNKNOWN	RR	AHUI	MO
FENKE, AUGUST	30	M	UNKNOWN	RR	ZZZZ	NY
STERNE, MICHAEL	23	M	UNKNOWN	RR	ZZZZ	NY

PASSENGER	AGE	SEX	OCCUPATION	PRIVIL	DES
SIEBERT, ANTON	33	M	LABR	RRAHUI	MO
ANIELA	24	F	W	RRAHUI	MO
FRANCISKA	2	F	CHILD	RRAHUI	MO
JOSEFA	.03	F	INFANT	RRAHUI	MO
STEFANOWICZ, VINCENTI	25	M	LABR	RRAHTF	IL
MOTYKUS, VINCENTI	23	M	LABR	RRAHTF	NY
GAITZIS, FRANZ	45	M	LABR	RRAHTF	IL
WITOWSKI, FRANZ	40	M	LABR	RRAHZS	NY
GEGRATIS, SIMON	31	M	LABR	RRAHZS	NY
FEDOROWICZ, FRANZ	82	M	LABR	RRAHZS	NY
CRISEILLA, ANDIE	34	M	LABR	RRAHZS	NY
ZESKO, KASIMIR	24	M	LABR	RRAHZS	NY
RICHELEFSKI, PAUL	29	M	LABR	RRAHZS	NY
LOSCHEFSKI, STANISLAUS	30	M	LABR	RRAHZS	NY
OSTOPOWICZ, JULIAN	22	M	LABR	RRAHZS	NY
BRUSNOWSKI, JACOB	22	M	LABR	RRAHZS	NY
WAWZIK, MICHAEL	23	M	LABR	RRZZZZ	NY
BARK, JOHANN	35	M	LABR	RRZZZZ	NY
PUBIEG, CASPER	33	M	LABR	RRAHTO	NY
SAMBSCHUSKI, FRANZ	23	M	LABR	RRAHTO	NY
NAPIERKOWSKI, JAN	28	M	LABR	RRAHTO	NY
GRATZIK, FRANZ	28	M	LABR	RRAHTO	NY
KIRSTANSKI, JACOB	27	M	LABR	RRAHTO	NY
PRUSZAZEK, JAN	20	M	LABR	RRAHTO	NY
BRUST, FRANZ	28	M	LABR	RRAHTO	NY
OLKOWSKI, JAN	27	M	LABR	RRAHTO	NY
SABIELSKI, EDUARD	33	M	LABR	RRAHTO	NY
WUTKIEWICZ, JOSEF	25	M	LABR	RRAHTO	NY
WEBER, FRIEDR.	28	M	FARMER	RRZZZZ	NY
JOHANN	43	M	FARMER	RRZZZZ	NY
REGINA	44	F	W	RRZZZZ	NY
RATZIS, ANDREY	23	M	LABR	RRZZZZ	NY
SITZKOWSKI, ANDREY	18	M	LABR	RRZZZZ	NY
MURAUSKI, JOSEF	21	M	LABR	RRZZZZ	NY
TILENDA, FRANZ	28	M	LABR	RRZZZZ	NY
RUTKOWSKI, ADAM	27	M	LABR	RRZZZZ	NY
DOMALEWSKI, FRANZ	25	M	LABR	RRZZZZ	NY
SALONOWSKI, FRANZ	24	M	LABR	RRZZZZ	NY
DWIATKOWSKI, JOSEF	25	M	LABR	RRZZZZ	NY
SENTZKAUTZKUS, JOSEF	31	M	LABR	RRZZZZ	NY
STOWICKI, PAUL	22	M	LABR	RRZZZZ	NY
NOWOTKA, LUDWIKA	23	F	SGL	RRZZZZ	NY
MAREINIAK, ANTONINA	33	F	WO	RRZZZZ	NY
VICTORIA	7	F	CHILD	RRZZZZ	NY
FRANZ	4	M	CHILD	RRZZZZ	NY
MARIANNE	00	F	INF	RRZZZZ	NY
MER, SCHOEL	17	M	MCHT	RRAILM	NY
ROZLECKA, AGNES	27	F	WO	RRZZZZ	NY
PELATIA	3	F	CHILD	RRZZZZ	NY
CZESLAW	1	F	CHILD	RRZZZZ	NY
STRUZEWSKI, MARIANNE	21	F	SGL	RRZZZZ	NY
WOJEICHOWSKI, JOSEFA	21	F	SGL	RRZZZZ	NY
ROPOWCHIN, MARIANNE	22	F	SGL	RRZZZZ	NY
SOBECKI, VALT.	44	M	LABR	RRAIKP	NY
MARIAN	34	M	LABR	RRAHUF	NY
RECZETZKI, HINDES	18	F	SGL	RRZZZZ	NY
PAWLAK, SIMON	21	M	LABR	RRZZZZ	NY
PETRSCHEWITZ, JAN	30	M	LABR	RRAHZS	PA
CHMILEWSKI, FRANZ	23	M	LABR	RRAHZS	MI
CSGENSKI, FRANZ	25	M	LABR	RRAHZS	MI
ZNINSKI, FRANZ	27	M	LABR	RRZZZZ	NY
POLITOWSKI, STANISLAUS	23	M	LABR	RRZZZZ	NY
ZIWINSKI, JOSEF	27	M	LABR	RRZZZZ	NY
WITTOWSKI, MAXIMILIA	17	M	LABR	RRZZZZ	NY
MADTANISCH, JOSEFA	29	F	WO	RRAHUI	NY
NASTE	.09	F	INFANT	RRAHUI	NY
REICHHARD, BARTHA	25	F	WO	RRAAKH	NY
FRIEDA	5	F	CHILD	RRAAKH	NY
PAULA	.03	F	INFANT	RRAAKH	NY
KURZEDEM, JOSEF	31	M	SHMK	RRAAKH	NY
GOERKE, GEORG	28	M	LABR	RRZZZZ	NY

SHIP: ARISONA

FROM: LIVERPOOL AND QUEENSTOWN
TO: NEW YORK
ARRIVED: 20 MAY 1889

PASSENGER	AGE	SEX	OCCUPATION	PRIVIL	DES
TOPARRI, JOHAN	29	M	MECH	FNZZZZ	USA
ROCKJOKE, JOHAN	24	M	MSN	FNZZZZ	USA
WALSKY, FRANKEL	34	M	MECH	PLZZZZ	USA
KROSCHINSKY, WOGE	26	M	LABR	RRZZZZ	USA
SAKARSKY, ANGE	30	M	ART	PLZZZZ	USA
MELLOCH, PARISTJE	28	M	ART	PLZZZZ	USA
MARKUS, RUBIN	24	M	MSN	RRZZZZ	USA
WILKOWISCH, LOUIS	30	M	SMH	RRZZZZ	USA
SEFT, BENJAMIN	20	M	LABR	PLZZZZ	USA
KARS, MATTI	30	M	FARMER	FNZZZZ	USA
KARHOLM, ANDERS	18	M	SHPR	FNZZZZ	USA
RUOTA, MATTI	39	M	ART	FNZZZZ	USA
POHRI, SAKRIS	21	M	FLABR	FNZZZZ	USA
RUOTAALA, A.	48	M	SMH	FNZZZZ	USA
ERIK	18	M	LABR	FNZZZZ	USA
LUOSTALA, ERIK	30	M	PMBR	FNZZZZ	USA
REISA	34	F	W	FNZZZZ	USA
HAKKARMANN, KARL	28	M	MSN	FNZZZZ	USA
SEWANEN, JOHAN	19	M	LABR	FNZZZZ	USA
HAKKARMANN, ERIK	38	M	ART	FNZZZZ	USA
MUHANEN, JOHAN	28	M	ART	FNZZZZ	USA
PITKANE, ELIAS	29	M	ART	FNZZZZ	USA
WISANEN, KARL	31	M	FARMER	FNZZZZ	USA
KALAJARIR, GUSTAF	28	M	PNTR	FNZZZZ	USA
AMPIALA, MATTI	28	M	SMH	FNZZZZ	USA
NORBACKAA, ANDERS	21	M	FLABR	FNZZZZ	USA
BACK, WILHELM	43	M	MECH	FNZZZZ	USA
ISOMARTONEN, NESTOR	27	M	SDLR	FNZZZZ	USA
SILVOLA, ANDERS	17	M	SHPR	FNZZZZ	USA
AMASSA, ANDERS-J.	25	M	PRNTR	FNZZZZ	USA
HERMAN-A.	25	M	PRNTR	FNZZZZ	USA
SARREDS, ISAAC	24	M	MSN	FNZZZZ	USA
PROST, JOHAN-E.	34	M	FTR	FNZZZZ	USA
SEPPA, SANNA-J.	25	M	SP	FNZZZZ	USA
AHOLA, ISAK	27	M	PMBR	FNZZZZ	USA
MATTESON, NILS-J.	22	M	LABR	FNZZZZ	USA
BJORKGOIST, WILHELM	30	M	BCHR	FNZZZZ	USA
KARJALNOTE, EWANE.	37	M	ART	FNZZZZ	USA
LANTARI, DANIEL	28	M	PNTR	FNZZZZ	USA
BEXT, MATTE	30	M	PNTR	FNZZZZ	USA
PALKI, JOHAN	35	M	TKR	FNZZZZ	USA
EPPEL, JOSEPH	19	M	FLABR	FNZZZZ	USA
KITALANEN, STINA	23	F	SP	FNZZZZ	USA
JASSO, SAMUEL	42	M	FARMER	FNZZZZ	USA
JAWAMEN, OTTO	28	M	SHPR	FNZZZZ	USA
NIKKOLA, ANTI	25	M	PNTR	FNZZZZ	USA
FOSSE, GABRIEL	19	M	LABR	FNZZZZ	USA
PACKALA, JOHAN	30	M	BKLYR	FNZZZZ	USA
JAKAMMAKKI, MATTS	28	M	JNR	FNZZZZ	USA
OTTAVA, JACOB	42	M	SMH	FNZZZZ	USA
TUAHILOAMA, ANAMIAS	27	M	FLABR	FNZZZZ	USA
JOKI, JOSEF-S.	19	M	FLABR	FNZZZZ	USA
KARPIAJA, NIKOLAS	50	M	MECH	FNZZZZ	USA
RINEMAKI, JOHAN	35	M	CPTR	FNZZZZ	USA
RIBACKA, JOHAN	29	M	MSN	FNZZZZ	USA
JOHANNES	28	M	MSN	FNZZZZ	USA
VESTERBACK, KARL	23	M	FLABR	FNZZZZ	USA
LOLAX, JOHANNES	19	M	FLABR	FNZZZZ	USA
VICTOR	18	M	FLABR	FNZZZZ	USA
STOLPI, SOPHIA	20	F	SP	FNZZZZ	USA
BRANBACKA, JOHAN	36	M	ART	FNZZZZ	USA
HAGBLOM, MATHIAS	20	M	FLABR	FNZZZZ	USA
S--TER, JOHANNES	19	M	FLABR	FNZZZZ	USA
MATTSSON, ANNA-L.	23	F	SP	FNZZZZ	USA
KULP, JOHAN-M.	31	M	PMBR	FNZZZZ	USA
TOBES, ERIK	19	M	LABR	FNZZZZ	USA
OSTMAN, MICHAEL	22	M	BKR	FNZZZZ	USA
ISOMARTAUEN, ANDERS	27	M	JNR	FNZZZZ	USA

PASSENGER	AGE	SEX	OCCUPATION	PRV	VIL	DES
KARL	19	M	JNR	FN	ZZZZ	USA
VONALFVEGREN, JOHAN	21	M	SHPR	FN	ZZZZ	USA
LAUGSJO, JOHAN	23	M	LABR	FN	ZZZZ	USA
TENGSJO, ERIK	31	M	PRNTR	FN	ZZZZ	USA
FORSTI, MATTS-E.	23	M	MSN	FN	ZZZZ	USA
HAUTANEN, JOHAN	28	M	SMH	FN	ZZZZ	USA
ALIN, HENRIK	48	M	ART	FN	ZZZZ	USA
WAHAKANGAS, MATTS	48	M	ART	FN	ZZZZ	USA
LEPISTO, JOHAN	40	M	CPTR	FN	ZZZZ	USA
HOLMESTAPA, MATTS	25	M	SHPR	FN	ZZZZ	USA
ANTILLA, MAGA	19	F	SP	FN	ZZZZ	USA
ANDERS	18	M	LABR	FN	ZZZZ	USA
TOBS, JAN	30	M	ART	RR	ZZZZ	USA
BARENISKY, JOSEF	25	M	ART	RR	ZZZZ	USA
PEPSCHINSKY, MATHIAS	31	M	ART	RR	ZZZZ	USA
SIPNEWSKY, AUGUST	40	M	PNTR	PL	ZZZZ	USA
WEIN, JANKEL	40	M	SMH	RR	ZZZZ	USA
KARPELOWOITZ, ABRAHAM	23	M	LABR	RR	ZZZZ	USA
BJORKOID, JOHANNES	32	M	SMH	FN	ZZZZ	USA
KOURKO, ALEXANDER	20	M	LABR	FN	ZZZZ	USA
LANDSTROM, J.	26	M	TKR	FN	ZZZZ	USA
SAND, JULIUS	43	M	ART	FN	ZZZZ	USA
KAWALA, HENRIK-M.	40	M	CPTR	FN	ZZZZ	USA
JAKOBSSON, JOHAN	36	M	BKLYR	FN	ZZZZ	USA
MARTINSSON, MARTIN	36	M	ART	FN	ZZZZ	USA
JOHANSSON, JAKOB	35	M	ART	FN	ZZZZ	USA
ANDERSSON, WILHELM	40	M	CPTR	FN	ZZZZ	USA
JAKOBSSON, JAKOB	34	M	CPTR	FN	ZZZZ	USA
HERMANSON, HENRIK	37	M	PDLR	FN	ZZZZ	USA
GUSTAFSON, HERMAN	25	M	MSN	FN	ZZZZ	USA
KULLS, HERMAN-F.	24	M	MSN	FN	ZZZZ	USA
LEHRFELD, SIMON	19	M	LABR	PL	ZZZZ	USA
LIBERT, JOHAN	25	M	LABR	PL	ZZZZ	USA
LEHRFELD, RUCHEL	14	F	SP	PL	ZZZZ	USA
HARTSIFZKY, LEON	21	M	LABR	PL	ZZZZ	USA

SHIP: ETRURIA

FROM: LIVERPOOL AND QUEENSTOWN
TO: NEW YORK
ARRIVED: 20 MAY 1889

PASSENGER	AGE	SEX	OCCUPATION	PRV	VIL	DES
HOLM, JOHAN	24	M	LABR	RR	ZZZZ	NY
MALKENVICK, FELIX	20	M	LABR	RR	ACBF	NY
KROPLIN, JOHANNES	23	M	LABR	RR	ACBF	NY
MI--BERGER, MARKUS	31	M	LABR	RR	ACBF	NY
STOLER, KATIRAN	45	M	LABR	RR	ACBF	NY
GLUCKMANN, H	16	M	LABR	RR	ACBF	NY
ST-ZN-S, JOHAN	16	M	LABR	RR	ACBF	NY
KLONI-, --ISTIAN	29	M	SLR	RR	ACBF	NY
PADA, AUG	19	M	LABR	RR	ACBF	NY
MATTSON, KARL	23	M	SLR	RR	ACBF	NY
FREDRICKSON, JOHAN	25	M	SLR	RR	ACBF	NY
MA--S--RUS, KARL	40	M	SLR	RR	ACBF	NY
SODERLA-D, OTTO	24	M	SLR	RR	ACBF	NY
ANDREAS	21	M	SLR	RR	ACBF	NY
--DERMANN, ED	34	M	SLR	RR	ACBF	NY
MA-KO--KA, ANTONIA	20	F	SP	RR	ACBF	NY
MICHOW, JULIA	24	F	SP	RR	ACBF	NY
VICTORIA	20	F	SP	RR	ACBF	NY
GLUCK, RE-I	28	F	MA	RR	ACBF	NY
MA-K-TER, I	45	F	MA	RR	ACBF	NY
J	14	F	SP	RR	ACBF	NY
FORSEN, KRAUS	40	M	LABR	RR	AEWS	NY
EMMA	35	F	W	RR	AEWS	NY
SWARTZ, BERNARD	29	M	LABR	RR	AEWS	BO
KASKA-ARAND, B	39	M	MCHT	RR	ADBQ	BO

INDEX